Roget's Thesaurus

OF ENGLISH WORDS AND PHRASES

New Edition completely Revised and
Modernized by

ROBERT A. DUTCH O.B.E.

Sometime Senior Scholar of Christ's College, Cambridge

LONGMAN

LONGMAN GROUP LIMITED
London

Associated companies, branches and representatives
throughout the world

First Edition by Peter Mark Roget 1852

New and Enlarged Edition by John Lewis Roget 1879

New Edition Revised and Enlarged
by Samuel Romilly Roget 1936

This Edition First Published 1962
Authorized Copyright Edition
in the Berne Convention Countries

Ninth impression with corrections 1975
Thirteenth impression 1980

ISBN 0 582 11771 2

Printed in Great Britain by
Butler & Tanner Ltd,
Frome and London

CONTENTS

CONTENTS

PREFACE

to the Revised Edition 1962

To most people who know it, *Roget's Thesaurus* suggests a collection of synonyms on a grand scale with an index, very useful if you are looking for an alternative expression or are simply at a loss for a word to fit a thought. That the popular idea largely represents Roget's practical aim is clear from his Introduction to the first edition of 1852 (reproduced here on pp. xxiii–xxxvi); and that this aim was not ill-directed is shown by the scores of reprints, new editions (some unauthorized), imitations and adaptations demanded by generations of users, a demand still continuing after more than a hundred years.

Roget laid his foundations well. This new edition, issued by the same publishers as ushered the first into the world, is indeed somewhat altered in appearance, with a text entirely rewritten and greatly expanded, and an index wholly recompiled, but organically identical with Roget's original. It observes the same principles and stands in the true line of descent from the successive editions brought out by Peter Mark Roget himself, and by his son and grandson. For there was nothing haphazard in Roget's design. He set out to make 'a collection of words . . . arranged not in alphabetical order, as they are in a Dictionary, but according to the ideas which they express'. Words express ideas—the ideas we have of tangible objects as well as of abstractions. Words expressing related ideas may be grouped under general heads; these general heads may be sorted into a system, so that we have a comprehensive classification into which, theoretically, any word in the language may be fitted and related to a context. Such an arrangement imposes the collocation of synonymous expressions in categories and thus attains Roget's object: 'The idea being given, to find the word or words by which that idea may be most fitly and aptly expressed.'

This is the opposite of a dictionary's function, which is: 'The word being given, to find its signification or the idea it is intended to convey.' The two functions should not be confused. A thesaurus (in the sense it acquired after Roget used it in the title of his work) does not seek, like a dictionary, to define a word in all its meanings and in one place. Its business is with contexts, not with definitions. It discourses rather than analyses. It starts with a meaning, not with a word, and sets the words which symbolize some aspect of that meaning in a context, rather like sentences in a book. A valid context exhibits the related aspect of the component words, throwing into relief, by a kind of mutual reflection, those elements of meaning which each individual word can contribute

to the governing idea, and suppressing senses which are ambiguous, irrelevant, or incompatible. In itself, the word 'lion' holds a variety of associations. When we find it in a context of cats, leopards and tigers, we realize we are dealing with *Felis Leo*; in a context of fighters, heroes and knights, it suggests courage; associated with 'favourite' and similar words, it presents the idea of a 'catch'— a person much sought after. A thesaurus proceeds to register 'lion' under the distinct heads of 'animal', 'courage' and 'favourite', and within those heads associates it with as unambiguous a context as possible. Probably most of the complaints of occasional pointlessness in the vocabulary entries of a thesaurus arise because certain words do not appear in the right milieu to display their relevance. Certainly a reader should not have to grope for the meaning, but should be enabled, by a right context, to find immediately the application of a given word to the head under which it stands. But the vocabulary listed under a head is there, not for the purpose of defining words, but of using words to illuminate an idea—as we use them in ordinary speech. Hence the unique advantage of the thesaurus arrangement as a help to the employment of words for their natural purpose—the expression of ideas. A thesaurus is operating on the same lines as a speaker or writer in the process of composition. It images in some measure the working of his brain when, having his idea (corresponding to a thesaurus head), he mentally scans his stock of words (corresponding to the vocabulary of a thesaurus) for the right expression.

It might be objected, on the contrary, that a thesaurus *is* a dictionary, and a clumsy one at that, inasmuch as it attempts to define the meanings inherent in the words chosen as titles for particular heads. We have some hundreds of heads (or thousands, if we include the subheads with which this edition is equipped)— existence, motion, death, life, etc.—and all that the listed vocabulary does (so the argument would run) is to provide words to define those other words— existence, motion and so on—without the precision and economy of a dictionary or the convenience of an alphabetical arrangement. This objection mistakes the function of the words employed in the headings. They are not chosen for themselves but as labels for the general idea treated in the article concerned. They can be changed, so long as the idea remains intact. So far from being *defined*, it is obvious that these titles frequently hold possible meanings which have to be ignored as incommensurate with the idea which is the true definition of the head. When Roget chose 'Investment' as a label for the idea of dress, he was not thinking of the investment of money. Some other word might have been selected, and in this edition the same head is labelled 'Dressing'. In so far as these labels are words and are to be treated as part of the vocabulary, their meaning, as that of the other words in the list, is to be gathered from the context. Roget's distinction between dictionary and thesaurus is in fact unassailable.

It is Roget's great merit that he devised a system of categories, logically ordered, that is both workable and comprehensive. As edition followed edition, more and more words have been drawn in without destroying the framework. In the course of a century of testing, modifications have been made only in matters of detail. The present editor's experience confirms that of his predecessors. Very large extensions of vocabulary have been fitted in, easily and

naturally, without slurring the meaning or blunting the point of the inserted words. Details will be more appropriate when the special features of this edition are discussed. How far these categories are 'philosophic' (as Roget would say), is a matter for argument. The existing classification having been found so accommodating, the prolonged research necessary for the construction of a fresh one lay outside the scope of this revision.

To construct such a system at all, with no useful guiding precedent, was no mean achievement. Perhaps Roget's happiest inspiration was to utilize methodically the correlation of positive and negative. By setting categories of synonyms and antonyms over against each other he brought into play a wealth of related contexts which otherwise might easily have been overlooked. Moreover, the opposition of two extremes suggested a place for intermediate terms, whether these were, as regards the extremes, neutral (e.g. *Beginning, Middle, End*); or the simple negative of the two opposite positions (*Desire, Indifference, Aversion*); or representing the common standard with which the two opposites are compared (*Insufficiency, Sufficiency, Redundance*). These examples, and the distinctions on which they are based, are taken from Roget's Introduction at p. xxviii. It is not only the logical neatness which appeals, but also the value of the device as a check on the omission of valid categories of thought for which vocabulary should be supplied. Other arrangements of categories have been tried; notably, in recent years, and most impressively, by the German philologist and classical scholar Franz Dornseiff;[1] others no doubt will be tried in the future. It is difficult to imagine that they will renounce this fruitful expedient, which apparently we owe to Roget himself. Sometimes, perhaps, too fruitful! It would be possible to generate in this way a category which was not only devoid of an exclusive vocabulary of its own (the same could be said of most categories) but which was fully represented, both in idea and verbal content, by some other differently titled category. A few such categories appear to have been noticed in Roget's scheme by successive editors, and have been left to wither away. They have been taken out of this edition.

The point is interesting in its bearing on the validity of categories—a question which goes to the root of the relationship between thought and language. Language behaves like a continuum, coextensive with the thought it symbolizes, and does not easily lend itself to partitioning into self-contained categories. John L. Roget, Peter's son and successor, observes in his preface to the 1879 edition: 'Any attempt at a philosophical arrangement under categories of the words of our language must reveal the fact that it is impossible to separate and circumscribe the several groups by absolutely distinct boundary lines.' The real trouble, one must suspect, is that apparently no meaning can exist in isolation but each one is an aspect of some other meaning. Probably, every single context in this new edition—it may be, every single word—could be equipped with a cross-reference. The whole network of cross-references is a necessary concession to the nature of language which thus exerts itself to restore the unity of what man, with his artificial categories, has put asunder. Practical convenience alone

---

[1] *Der Deutsche Wortschatz nach Sachgruppen* (Walter de Gruyter & Co., Berlin. 5th edition 1959). This work has a valuable introduction.

decides where, in this expanse of words, we erect our dykes and construct our somewhat leaky reservoirs. Since an arbitrary element cannot be excluded from our choice of heads, it would be gratifying if we had an accepted alphabet of ideas under which to list our vocabularies. If, like the Chinese, we had adopted a system of pictograms to write our language, symbolizing words by sense not by sound, we should long ago have been forced to arrange our lexicons by categories of thought, and our dictionaries would, in effect, be thesauruses. What order of words we should have chosen is an interesting speculation. Words, unfortunately, are not like numbers, or we might have found an order of verbal signs as logically compelling as the simple arithmetical series 1, 2, 3. . . . However that may be, a common alphabet of ideas, based on categories equally relevant to the habits of thought and speech of all peoples at all times, would surely show something of the anatomy of language and teach us to differentiate what is conventional in our verbal distinctions from what lies nearer bedrock. We ought to encourage all attempts to build that ultimate, multilingual thesaurus which Roget envisaged with his customary prescience. Equipped at last with a set of truly 'philosophic' categories, a philologist might face the perplexing riddle of language and say 'I of these will wrest an alphabet, and with still practice learn to know thy meaning.'

Such explorations must be left to those more deeply versed in linguistic science. Concerning the present revision of what is purely an English thesaurus, the following account is rendered.

The vocabulary has been enlarged by some 50,000 entries. These are not all new in the sense that none of them has previously appeared anywhere in the text. The majority are old words in new places. They are not idle repetitions. They are the furniture of new contexts; for our ideas outrun our stock of words, and to express them we must turn over our vocabulary again and again. This accretion of fresh material is fairly evenly spread, and most of the lists have undergone a notable expansion. Deletions were, by comparison, very much fewer and were intended only for the clearance of dead wood. The axe fell mainly on the numerous French and Latin expressions which have not become anglicized, and on the 'phrases' (the separate subdivision for which has been suppressed) where these were merely quotations or proverbs and could not with any benefit be transplanted to some other subdivision of the head. Expressions thought to be insipid or unidiomatic have been dropped, along with some archaic and obsolete matter. Archaisms have not been cleared away wholesale. There are multifarious reasons for consulting a thesaurus, and Samuel Roget observed, in his preface to the 1933 edition, that archaic and even obsolete words may be sought by authors. Of some it may be said that though dead they will not lie down. The time for them to go is when they are not only dead, but buried. No resurrections, however, have been attempted by way of importing extinct material.

The sources of new vocabulary were sought only to a limited extent in printed word-lists in any shape or form, though at the beginning of the revision standard dictionaries were combed through. Abundant inspiration was found in the living word, spoken or written. Sometimes, no interlocutor was necessary.

You talked to yourself, and overheard your own idioms. The colloquial idiom was as welcome as the literary, without any censorship of the 'speech level', for living usage was the constant criterion. The prolific vitality of American speech furnished many inspirations. It seemed quite unnecessary to mark or isolate these by way of editorial comment. Usage on both sides of the Atlantic shows at the present day a tendency to coalesce and it is no part of the function of this work to supply certificates of origin for what is all equally native. Outright slang, with its transient and shifting vocabulary, so frequently an esoteric jargon, is not specifically drawn on; but many of its terms gain currency in the colloquial idiom, and then, if apt, are welcome. Technical expressions, of which nowadays the general public is increasingly conscious, play their part in non-specialist writings, and it was from this source, on the whole, that technical terms have been introduced, as embellishments of an educated vocabulary. It was felt to be less requisite to compile detailed lists of specialized and recondite terms which experts seldom use except for mutual communication and for which interested persons would hardly consult a thesaurus. Space is limited and had to be reserved for more generally useful words. In general the aim has been to provide a full and comprehensive vocabulary, employing words met with at all levels of speech, with no conscious bias towards either literary or colloquial style. In fact, the vocabulary here presented is not only far ampler, but is also fresher and more modern and contemporary than in previous editions. Absolute completeness is unattainable, but the co-operation of readers will be welcome towards remedying what is lacking, so that omissions can be repaired when opportunity arises.

Peter Roget digested his vocabulary under exactly 1000 heads. Later, he himself or subsequent editors inserted others. That they are here reduced to 990 does not imply any significant revaluation of the original scheme, which is as serviceable as ever. The reduction is due to a few heads having been left with only a token vocabulary, or none at all: these have been deleted. More frequently heads expressing the idea of the *agent* have in this edition been transferred to the related general head, except where the idea of agent is of primary importance or has a large vocabulary of its own. This adjustment helps to preserve a parity among the heads as a whole by suppressing some that were essentially subsidiary, and by leaving the heads more uniformly equipped with the full complement of nouns, adjectives and verbs. Occasionally, a single head has been split into two. Those interested in such changes should consult the scheme of classification on pp. xxxix–xlviii, where they are tabulated.

A modified order of printing has somewhat altered the appearance of the text. In previous editions, the parallel arrangement of contrasted heads in opposite columns was a conspicuous feature, and to many readers doubtless a helpful one. It was, however, liable to involve a somewhat confusing lay-out of the printed page when, as usually happened, the opposing lists were of unequal length, and when the succession of contrasted heads was interrupted by a correlative head which, having no opposite, was printed the whole width of the page. Moreover, much valuable space was sacrificed in maintaining this pattern. In the present edition, an arrangement in straightforward double column is adopted, numbered sections following in serial order. The contrasted heads are

still in juxtaposition and the rearrangement serves the convenience of the user. There is even a gain in logical propriety by according a uniform treatment to all forms of correlation, of which the antithesis of positive and negative is but a special case. The text is no longer divided into chapters corresponding to the major divisions of Roget's scheme of classification. The numbered sections follow on without interruption.

A conspicuous change will be noticed in the paragraphing of the heads. It was found that with the help of keywords, printed in italics, the vocabulary, within the subdivisions by parts of speech, could be broken up into compact and homogeneous groups to make subheads. This arrangement offers distinct advantages. The keyword, being chosen to denote the tone and general coverage of the subhead, introduces a further element of formal classification. This becomes very useful when the mass of words presented is only very broadly covered by the main heading, and the individual contexts diverge from one another widely in meaning. The subhead, labelled by its keyword, narrows the field of search and within closer limits the enquirer knows what to expect. The same keyword is used in all cross-references and in the index references—occasions when unambiguous information is requisite. With its italic type and prominent position in the text it at once catches the eye. Its part in the referencing apparatus is explained in the Instructions, at p. xlix. It is believed that this feature of the revision will justify itself in greater directness, speed and facility of consultation.

Within the subheads, great care has been given to the ordering of vocabulary in context, and to the provision of a multiplicity of cross-references. It is for this that the whole text has been rewritten. The aim of a thesaurus is to suggest words of synonymous meaning. Granted that synonyms are never identical, some words are nevertheless closer in meaning than others. The suggestiveness of a synonymous arrangement is enhanced by bringing such words together. When they are separated by an arbitrary order—e.g. the alphabetical—or haphazardly disordered, something of their force is lost. The mind is jolted to and fro, concentration is impaired, valid connections are overlooked. Where they are knit in a relevant context and juxtaposed in a series of steps with as few gaps in meaning as possible, the mind is led by easy transitions from one nuance to another without distraction. It begins to run on rails and by its own momentum may even elicit an apt word or expression which has escaped record in that part of the text. In such instances the compiler must confess a particular inadequacy in his lists, but may raise a claim for the general effectiveness of his arrangement. Moreover, if the obvious utility of internal cross-references is conceded, the cross-reference should be placed where it is most relevant and demands a context. On such considerations, every word was weighed and its possible relationships examined before it was assigned to its niche. If on the whole the text reads easily, if the rightness of a word in its place is felt, and the suggestiveness of a context acts as a prompt and stimulus, the intended object will have been attained, despite any drawback inherent in the attempt itself. The drawback consists in that quality of words which endows them with several distinct affinities even within a narrow range of context. A context is a great aid

to definition, but a definition implies a limitation. The choice of one context for a word eliminates other contexts which might prove as useful. Yet it is impossible to repeat, under the same subhead, all items of vocabulary in all their permutations and combinations of context, in the vain effort to exhaust their affinities. Even if time permitted, space would not. In this dilemma we must accept the fact that words, like atoms, have multiple affinities; they must combine in contexts, as atoms in molecules. Where the molecules are very different, they may appear under different heads. Where, though distinct, they have a family likeness and would in any case appear in the same subhead, a single representative is chosen to stand for the whole proliferating family. This also may be borne in mind. Individual words are not smothered in their context. They may be considered, whenever the reader wishes, in isolation from their neighbours.

The internal cross-references are supplied more liberally than ever before. Lest they be thought excessive, it must be stated that despite their multitude they register only a fraction of the innumerable points of contact within the interlocking network of Roget's system. In their respective places, these references focus the ample resources of the thesaurus on the particular problem in hand. One can hardly be too lavish in setting up signposts where roads are so many and it cannot be foreknown on what route the traveller is bent. In this function, the index is complementary, not a substitute. When once engaged with the text, the enquirer, if he uses the cross-references, will probably be spared the occasion to refer back to the index. Even when not followed up, the reference is not superfluous. The verbal element—the keyword—may be treated as part of the vocabulary.

The sequences of figures appearing under the heading **See**: at the foot of each numbered section, are the section numbers of all references quoted in the main head. Most readers will have no occasion for them. They have been consolidated for the benefit of students of language whose theoretical enquiries into the relationships of words may be assisted by such an apparatus. The desirability of an aid of this kind has more than once been expressed.

The subdivision of heads by part of speech has been preserved. Adjectives have been transferred to follow the nouns instead of the verbs. The adverb subdivision sometimes includes expressions which could be called adverbial only by courtesy. Likewise, expressions grammatically adverbial have been admitted among the adjectives, in places where the context seemed propitious. The Phrases (as a separate subdivision) have finally succumbed to the erosion undergone in previous editions.

The Index has been carefully prepared as a necessary aid to finding the right place in the text at which to begin a search. It is by no means a complete alphabetical reference for the whole vocabulary, and it should not be inferred that a word unregistered in the Index is absent from the text. Guidance for its use will be found in the Instructions at p. xlix. All that need be said here is that (i) index entries were extracted from a complete set of all the words in the text, and all omissions are deliberate; (ii) every index reference is set out fully with section number, part of speech, and keyword. The last particular is important. In previous editions, references were frequently given by section number only

and then the enquirer was left with no clue to whether the word was recorded in the sense he had in mind. As now recompiled, the Index is free from this obstacle to speedy reference. The keyword—the same as used to introduce a subhead or to define an internal reference—functions similarly in the Index to label a reference and to explain the sense.

Whom does a thesaurus help? It is of prime importance in philological studies and is complementary to dictionary work. Its structure, arrangement and content hold the greatest interest for those concerned with the fundamental symbolism of language. It is an instrument by which a language, viewed as a whole, may be compared with itself at some earlier stage, and with other languages similar and disparate. More particularly, it provides an excellent means to enable workers in the field of machine translation to match the vocabularies of two or more languages. Wherever the concern is not so much with words themselves as with the things that words describe and the way in which people have regarded them, a thesaurus may be called in aid. Also, it generalizes, where a dictionary particularizes. Both a dictionary and a thesaurus take a census of the word-population. The dictionary counts and records individual particulars. It corresponds to the enumeration. A thesaurus more nearly resembles the final reports, where the population is massed in groups, first in this class, then in that, and general conclusions are drawn regarding the state of the nation. The state of the word-population is perhaps not without its relevance in social enquiries.

It is the same method of arrangement that makes a thesaurus so helpful to speakers and writers—to all persons concerned with the expression of ideas. It is the counterpart of the thesaurus we all carry in our memories in which mentally we track down a word. Surely, this characteristic is implied in those criticisms which impugn the merits of all thesauruses: that it is the lazy man's book; that it saves him the trouble of thinking. It would not do this unless it were patterned on our processes of thought and speech. But it is not only the lazy man who has the sense to avail himself of it and so to enhance his faculty of finding words for things.

In the stress of verbal composition we may use a thesaurus as legitimately as a dictionary. Much of our vocabulary is a 'recognition' vocabulary. We know a word when we see it which without prompting we should fail to call to mind. We often have this experience when reading a book. Here, then, is a special kind of book in which one may renew that experience at will. It tells you where to look. You are following your line of thought until words begin to fail and thought is embarrassed for want of a verbal mould to give it shape. Then some word— probably a word previously rejected as 'not quite near enough'—is turned up in the index, a choice is made from the range of connotations offered in the references under that word, the place is found in the text (the Instructions on pp. xlix–lii explain how this is done), and there, or in some related place to which the internal references point, the right word or expression is met; or a helpful context suggests a better idea—as Dryden observed that the search for a rhyme might sometimes help you to a thought. It may be a problem of changing

a word, or of recasting a sentence. It makes no difference, provided the word you think of to look up in the index impinges, however obliquely, on the notion you are entertaining. It might express the exact opposite of your intention. If so, you will find that opposite ideas are juxtaposed in Roget's scheme and you have only to skip to the following or preceding head; or you may stay where you are, and recast your thought in negative form. If you cannot get beyond a word of the vaguest generality—like 'greatness' or 'motion'—such words are found in the index as freely as the more specific. Indeed, it is the more general words which are most often chosen for the headings of the numbered sections ('Greatness' and 'Motion' are examples); and the most general heads afford plenty of references to the more specific which participate in the generalized meaning. Under 'Greatness' many kinds of greatness are touched upon, directly or by reference; under 'Motion' many kinds of motion. For this reason, the habitual user might do well to acquaint himself with the titles of the headings. Practice will make them familiar, and he will find his facility in using the thesaurus much improved.

Thus every kind of author is served by a thesaurus: original writers struggling with a thought, or simply wanting a word (it is no more heinous to forget a word and to consult a thesaurus, than to forget a meaning and look up a dictionary); translators, groping for an equivalent idiom or a corresponding metaphor; copy-writers, précis writers, paraphrasers; the solver of crosswords (it is not cheating to look up a clue in the index); the setter of crosswords—but here the danger is that the solver may be using the same edition! the orator who tells his secretary: 'Give me a word, not "majesty", suggestive of majesty': the secretary looks up 'majesty' and 'majestic' in the index; the librettist who must provide a good singable vowel for his vocalist. Reporters in a hurry may consult this book with speed and facility. A more deliberate writer may use it for browsing. I have known a poet who read Roget regularly in order to induce a mood—the heads dealing with sensation and emotion are just right for this. It is good for students of English—native or foreign; in conjunction with a dictionary, it provides beneficial exercises for the enrichment of vocabulary and the distinction of meanings.

Without the capacity for making distinctions, the enrichment may prove a snare. This book does not usurp the function of a dictionary. It keeps to Peter Roget's rule that the words are assumed to be known. It furnishes no labels for 'speech level'—for what is scholarly, literary or vulgar, or archaic and obsolete. The occasion and manner of use are left to the reader's tact. It is his responsibility. If he is not sure of a word he should avoid it or make a check in the appropriate work of reference. Otherwise, beware of pitfalls. There was an orator—English was not his native idiom—who on the arrival of a high official had to pronounce an address of welcome expressing the common grief at the death of the reigning monarch and the common joy at the official's condescending visit. He spoke of his two eyes—one dropping tears for the king who had 'gone to that bourne from which no traveller turns up'—the other 'beaming with happy simpering'. 'Hail', he went on, 'august and up to snuff! Gramercy, gramercy! Single-hearted and monocephalous are we. . . .' It cannot be too firmly stressed that a thesaurus does not displace a dictionary. They are complementary.   R. A. DUTCH

Acknowledgments

Particular thanks are due to Heinz Norden for many detailed suggestions relative to this revision; and to Professor Norman Davis for some valuable comments. With gratitude I acknowledge indebtedness to Margaret Masterman, Director of the Cambridge Language Research Unit, who showed me unsuspected ways of thinking about a thesaurus and its problems.

R. A. D.

A NOTE ON PETER MARK ROGET
1779–1869

Peter Mark Roget was born in Broad Street, Soho, on 18 January 1779. His father, John Roget, a native of Geneva, was pastor of the French Protestant church in Threadneedle Street. His mother, Catharine, was the only surviving sister of Sir Samuel Romilly, the legal reformer whose successful efforts to humanize the English criminal law won him fame and honour. The name is recalled in that of Samuel Romilly Roget, Peter's grandson and third editor of Roget's *Thesaurus*. Descended from Genevan Calvinists on his father's side and from French Huguenots on his mother's, the author of the celebrated *Thesaurus of English Words and Phrases* probably had no English blood in his veins. His Genevan connection stood him in good stead in 1803, when, acting as travelling tutor to the sons of a rich Manchester merchant, he was overtaken in Geneva by the rupture of the Peace of Amiens. He was detained on parole, and only secured his release by pleading the Genevan citizenship of his family.

His father died when Peter was still a child. His mother, from whom he is said to have inherited his systematic habits of thinking, took charge of his education. After a few years in the private school of a Mr. Chauvet—another native of Geneva—at Kensington Square, where he rendered himself proficient in mathematics, he was entered (1793) at Edinburgh University. He took up medicine in 1795 and graduated M.D. at the age of nineteen, having survived the testing experience of an attack of typhus contracted on the wards of the Edinburgh Infirmary.

He opened his professional career with a paper on 'The non-prevalence of consumption among butchers, fisherman, etc.', which was published by Dr. Beddoes in his 'Essay on the Causes etc. of Pulmonary Consumption'. At about the same time he began a correspondence with Davy and with Jeremy Bentham. In 1803, after his return from the continent, having passed a short spell as private physician to the Marquess of Lansdowne, he was appointed Physician to the Manchester Infirmary; and before he transferred himself to London in 1808 he had helped to found the Manchester Medical School and had become a popular lecturer on physiology in the Manchester Philosophic and Literary Society, of which he was vice-president. His migration to London initiated half a century of enormous activity in medical work, scientific research, lecturing and writing.

There is no biography of Roget, but the bare details of his *curriculum vitæ*

[xvii]

display the intellectual zest of a scholar and the practical zeal of an active social conscience. No doubt he kept himself by his medical practice; and his election, in 1831, as Fellow *speciali gratia* of the Royal College of Physicians is testimony to his professional competence; but the activities we hear of most are not of the profit-making kind. He projected the North London Dispensary and as its first Physician (1810) performed his duties gratuitously for eighteen years. In 1823 he served as Physician of the Millbank Penitentiary—during a dysentery epidemic. In 1828, at the Government's request, he prepared a report on London's water-supply. He took an active part in founding the University of London, and was examiner in physiology and comparative anatomy in 1839. He remained a member of the Senate until his death. He was the first Fullerian Professor of Physiology at the Royal Institution and gave many public lectures. The same concern for the public is shown by the type of a good deal of his writing—such as his contributions to the *Encyclopædia Britannica* (6th and 7th editions), the *Encyclopædia Metropolitana*, Rees's *Cyclopædia* and the *Cyclopædia of Popular Medicine*; most conspicuously in the treatises on electricity, galvanism, magnetism and electro-magnetism that he wrote for the Society for the Diffusion of Useful Knowledge, of which he was co-founder. There were articles also in the *Edinburgh Review* and the *Quarterly*, among other periodicals; and papers in the *Annals of Philosophy*. His Bridgewater treatise on *Animal and Vegetable Physiology considered with reference to Natural Theology* was a considerable work, re-issued for the third time in 1862.

He was no idle member of the learned societies he supported. He became secretary and vice-president of the Medico-Chirurgical Society, to whose Transactions he contributed many specialist studies. In 1815 the invention of a slide-rule which measured the powers of numbers proved to be his passport to the Fellowship of the Royal Society. Subsequently he became secretary to that Society and for twenty-two years (1827-1849), in addition to his other secretarial duties, edited their Proceedings and prepared for publication the abstracts of the papers.

On retirement from professional practice in 1840, he was much occupied with the construction of a calculating machine, and of a very delicate balance, of which the fulcrum, to avoid friction, was set in a small barrel floating on water. He amused himself—and the readers of the *Illustrated London News*— with the setting of ingenious chess problems; and in 1845 he brought out his 'Economic Chessboard', the forerunner of many pocket chessboards.

It was not till 1849, when he was in his seventy-first year, that he resumed work on what is really his greatest invention. After three or four years of incessant labour, as he tells us in his preface, he gave to the world (through the same publishers as have issued successive editions up to the present day) the celebrated *Thesaurus of English Words and Phrases, classified and arranged so as to facilitate the Expression of Ideas and assist in Literary Composition.* Nearly fifty years earlier he had compiled a proto-thesaurus for his own use (he was then teaching in the Manchester Medical School), which employed much the same system of classification. The finished work exemplifies his qualities of systematic thinking, habits of observation, patient industry and sense of the practical.

These qualities, and especially the last, ensured its success. In his own lifetime 28 editions were published, and the edition of 1879, brought out by his son John Lewis Roget, embodies his final additions. *Roget's Thesaurus* has since become a familiar title, cherished in all countries to which the English language has spread.

Peter Mark Roget died, at West Malvern, in his ninety-first year, on 12 September 1869. He married in 1824. His wife died in 1833 leaving two children, of whom John Lewis Roget (author of *The History of the Old Water Colour Society*) edited the *Thesaurus* after his father's death and bequeathed the same responsibility to his son Samuel Romilly Roget. The edition of 1936 is Samuel Romilly's latest revision.

PREFACE
to The First Edition 1852

It is now nearly fifty years since I first projected a system of verbal classification similar to that on which the present Work is founded. Conceiving that such a compilation might help to supply my own deficiencies, I had, in the year 1805, completed a classed catalogue of words on a small scale, but on the same principle, and nearly in the same form, as the Thesaurus now published. I had often during that long interval found this little collection, scanty and imperfect as it was, of much use to me in literary composition, and often contemplated its extension and improvement; but a sense of the magnitude of the task, amidst a multitude of other avocations, deterred me from the attempt. Since my retirement from the duties of Secretary of the Royal Society, however, finding myself possessed of more leisure, and believing that a repertory of which I had myself experienced the advantage might, when amplified, prove useful to others, I resolved to embark in an undertaking which, for the last three or four years, has given me incessant occupation, and has, indeed, imposed upon me an amount of labour very much greater than I had anticipated. Notwithstanding all the pains I have bestowed on its execution, I am fully aware of its numerous deficiencies and imperfections, and of its falling far short of the degree of excellence that might be attained. But, in a Work of this nature, where perfection is placed at so great a distance, I have thought it best to limit my ambition to that moderate share of merit which it may claim in its present form; trusting to the indulgence of those for whose benefit it is intended, and to the candour of critics who, while they find it easy to detect faults, can at the same time duly appreciate difficulties.

P. M. ROGET

29 April, 1852

INTRODUCTION

to the original edition, 1852

Notes within brackets are by the previous editors. Unbracketed footnotes followed by [Ed.] are by the editor of the 1962 edition.

The present Work is intended to supply, with respect to the English language, a desideratum hitherto unsupplied in any language; namely, a collection of the words it contains and of the idiomatic combinations peculiar to it, arranged, not in alphabetical order as they are in a Dictionary, but according to the *ideas* which they express. The purpose of an ordinary dictionary is simply to explain the meaning of the words; and the problem of which it professes to furnish the solution may be stated thus:—The word being given, to find its signification, or the idea it is intended to convey. The object aimed at in the present undertaking is exactly the converse of this: namely,—The idea being given, to find the word, or words, by which that idea may be most fitly and aptly expressed. For this purpose, the words and phrases of the language are here classed, not according to their sound or their orthography, but strictly according to their *signification*.

The communication of our thoughts by means of language, whether spoken or written, like every other object of mental exertion, constitutes a peculiar art, which, like other arts, cannot be acquired in any perfection but by long and continued practice. Some, indeed, there are more highly gifted than others with a facility of expression, and naturally endowed with the power of eloquence; but to none is it at all times an easy process to embody, in exact and appropriate language, the various trains of ideas that are passing through the mind, or to depict in their true colours and proportions, the diversified and nicer shades of feeling which accompany them. To those who are unpractised in the art of composition, or unused to extempore speaking, these difficulties present themselves in their most formidable aspect. However distinct may be our views, however vivid our conceptions, or however fervent our emotions, we cannot but be often conscious that the phraseology we have at our command is inadequate to do them justice. We seek in vain the words we need, and strive ineffectually to devise forms of expression which shall faithfully portray our thoughts and sentiments. The appropriate terms, notwithstanding our utmost efforts, cannot be conjured up at will. Like 'spirits from the vasty deep,' they come not when we call; and we are driven to the employment of a set of words and phrases either too general or too limited, too strong or too feeble, which suit not the occasion, which hit not the mark we aim at; and the result of our prolonged

exertion is a style at once laboured and obscure, vapid and redundant, or vitiated by the still graver faults of affectation or ambiguity.

It is to those who are thus painfully groping their way and struggling with the difficulties of composition, that this Work professes to hold out a helping hand. The assistance it gives is that of furnishing on every topic a copious store of words and phrases, adapted to express all the recognizable shades and modifications of the general idea under which those words and phrases are arranged. The inquirer can readily select, out of the ample collection spread out before his eyes in the following pages, those expressions which are best suited to his purpose, and which might not have occurred to him without such assistance. In order to make this selection, he scarcely ever need engage in any critical or elaborate study of the subtle distinction existing between synonymous terms; for if the materials set before him be sufficiently abundant, an instinctive tact will rarely fail to lead him to the proper choice. Even while glancing over the columns of this Work, his eye may chance to light upon a particular term, which may save the cost of a clumsy paraphrase, or spare the labour of a tortuous circumlocution. Some felicitous turn of expression thus introduced will frequently open to the mind of the reader a whole vista of collateral ideas, which could not, without an extended and obtrusive episode, have been unfolded to his view; and often will the judicious insertion of a happy epithet, like a beam of sunshine in a landscape, illumine and adorn the subject which it touches, imparting new grace and giving life and spirit to the picture.

Every workman in the exercise of his art should be provided with proper implements. For the fabrication of complicated and curious pieces of mechanism, the artisan requires a corresponding assortment of various tools and instruments. For giving proper effect to the fictions of the drama, the actor should have at his disposal a well-furnished wardrobe, supplying the costumes best suited to the personages he is to represent. For the perfect delineation of the beauties of nature, the painter should have within reach of his pencil every variety and combination of hues and tints. Now, the writer, as well as the orator, employs for the accomplishment of his purposes the instrumentality of words; it is in words that he clothes his thoughts; it is by means of words that he depicts his feelings. It is therefore essential to his success that he be provided with a copious vocabulary, and that he possess an entire command of all the resources and appliances of his language. To the acquisition of this power no procedure appears more directly conducive than the study of a methodized system such as that now offered to his use.

The utility of the present Work will be appreciated more especially by those who are engaged in the arduous process of translating into English a work written in another language. Simple as the operation may appear, on a superficial view, of rendering into English each of its sentences, the task of transfusing, with perfect exactness, the sense of the original, preserving at the same time the style and character of its composition, and reflecting with fidelity the mind and the spirit of the author, is a task of extreme difficulty. The cultivation of this useful department of literature was in ancient times strongly recommended both by Cicero and by Quintilian, as essential to the formation of a good writer and

accomplished orator. Regarded simply as a mental exercise, the practice of translation is the best training for the attainment of that mastery of language and felicity of diction, which are the sources of the highest oratory, and are requisite for the possession of a graceful and persuasive eloquence. By rendering ourselves the faithful interpreters of the thoughts and feelings of others, we are rewarded with the acquisition of greater readiness and facility in correctly expressing our own; as he who has best learned to execute the orders of a commander, becomes himself best qualified to command.

In the earliest periods of civilization, translators have been the agents for propagating knowledge from nation to nation, and the value of their labours has been inestimable; but, in the present age, when so many different languages have become the depositories of the vast treasures of literature and of science which have been accumulating for centuries, the utility of accurate translations has greatly increased, and it has become a more important object to attain perfection in the art.

The use of language is not confined to its being the medium through which we communicate our ideas to one another; it fulfils a no less important function as an *instrument of thought*; not being merely its vehicle, but giving it wings for flight. Metaphysicians are agreed that scarcely any of our intellectual operations could be carried on to any considerable extent, without the agency of words. None but those who are conversant with the philosophy of mental phenomena, can be aware of the immense influence that is exercised by language in promoting the development of our ideas, in fixing them in the mind, and in detaining them for steady contemplation. Into every process of reasoning, language enters as an essential element. Words are the instruments by which we form all our abstractions, by which we fashion and embody our ideas, and by which we are enabled to glide along a series of premises and conclusions with a rapidity so great as to leave in the memory no trace of the successive steps of the process; and we remain unconscious how much we owe to this potent auxiliary of the reasoning faculty. It is on this ground, also, that the present Work founds a claim to utility. The review of a catalogue of words of analogous signification, will often suggest by association other trains of thought, which, presenting the subject under new and varied aspects, will vastly expand the sphere of our mental vision. Amidst the many objects thus brought within the range of our contemplation, some striking similitude or appropriate image, some excursive flight or brilliant conception, may flash on the mind, giving point and force to our arguments, awakening a responsive chord in the imagination or sensibility of the reader, and procuring for our reasonings a more ready access both to his understanding and to his heart.

It is of the utmost consequence that strict accuracy should regulate our use of language, and that every one should acquire the power and the habit of expressing his thoughts with perspicuity and correctness. Few, indeed, can appreciate the real extent and importance of that influence which language has always exercised on human affairs, or can be aware how often these are determined by causes much slighter than are apparent to a superficial observer. False logic, disguised under specious phraseology, too often gains the assent of

the unthinking multitude, disseminating far and wide the seeds of prejudice and error. Truisms pass current, and wear the semblance of profound wisdom, when dressed up in the tinsel garb of antithetical phrases, or set off by an imposing pomp of paradox. By a confused jargon of involved and mystical sentences, the imagination is easily inveigled into a transcendental region of clouds, and the understanding beguiled into the belief that it is acquiring knowledge and approaching truth. A misapplied or misapprehended term is sufficient to give rise to fierce and interminable disputes; a misnomer has turned the tide of popular opinion; a verbal sophism has decided a party question; an artful watchword, thrown among combustible materials, has kindled the flame of deadly warfare, and changed the destiny of an empire.

In constructing the following system of classification of the ideas which are expressible by language, my chief aim has been to obtain the greatest amount of practical utility. I have accordingly adopted such principles of arrangement as appeared to me to be the simplest and most natural, and which would not require, either for their comprehension or application, any disciplined acumen, or depth of metaphysical or antiquarian lore. Eschewing all needless refinements and subtleties, I have taken as my guide the more obvious characters of the ideas for which expressions were to be tabulated, arranging them under such classes and categories as reflection and experience had taught me would conduct the inquirer most readily and quickly to the object of his search. Commencing with the ideas expressing abstract relations, I proceeded to those which relate to space and to the phenomena of the material world, and lastly to those in which the mind is concerned, and which comprehend intellect, volition, and feeling; thus establishing six primary Classes of Categories.

1. The first of these classes comprehends ideas derived from the more general and ABSTRACT RELATIONS among things, such as *Existence, Resemblance, Quantity, Order, Number, Time, Power.*

2. The second class refers to SPACE and its various relations, including *Motion,* or change of place.

3. The third class includes all ideas that relate to the MATERIAL WORLD; namely, the *Properties of Matter,* such as *Solidity, Fluidity, Heat, Sound, Light,* and the *Phenomena* they present, as well as the simple *Perceptions* to which they give rise.

4. The fourth class embraces all ideas of phenomena relating to the INTELLECT and its operations; comprising the *Acquisition,* the *Retention,* and the *Communication of Ideas.*

5. The fifth class includes the ideas derived from the exercise of VOLITION; embracing the phenomena and results of our *Voluntary and Active Powers;* such as *Choice, Intention, Utility, Action, Antagonism, Authority, Compact, Property,* &c.

6. The sixth and last class comprehends all ideas derived from the operation of our SENTIENT AND MORAL POWERS; including our *Feelings, Emotions, Passions,* and *Moral and Religious Sentiments.*[1]

---

[1] It must necessarily happen in every system of classification framed with this view, that ideas and expressions arranged under one class must include also ideas relating to another

The further subdivisions and minuter details will be best understood from an inspection of the Tabular Synopsis of Categories prefixed to the Work, in which are specified the several *topics* or *heads of signification*, under which the words have been arranged. By the aid of this table the reader will, with a little practice, readily discover the place which the particular topic he is in search of occupies in the series; and on turning to the page in the body of the Work which contains it, he will find the group of expressions he requires, out of which he may cull those that are most appropriate to his purpose. For the convenience of reference, I have designated each separate group or heading by a particular number, so that if, during the search, any doubt or difficulty should occur, recourse may be had to the copious alphabetical Index of Words at the end of the volume, which will at once indicate the number of the required group.[1]

The object I have proposed to myself in this Work would have been but imperfectly attained if I had confined myself to a mere catalogue of words, and had omitted the numerous phrases and forms of expression composed of several words, which are of such frequent use as to entitle them to rank among the constituent parts of the language.[2] Very few of these verbal combinations, so essential to the knowledge of our native tongue, and so profusely abounding in its daily use, are to be met with in ordinary dictionaries. These phrases and forms of expression I have endeavoured diligently to collect and to insert in their proper places, under the general ideas that they are designed to convey. Some of these conventional forms, indeed, partake of the nature of proverbial expressions; but actual proverbs, as such, being wholly of a didactic character, do not come within the scope of the present Work; and the reader must therefore not expect to find them here inserted.[3]

For the purpose of exhibiting with greater distinctness the relations between words expressing opposite and correlative ideas, I have, whenever the subject admitted of such an arrangement, placed them in two parallel columns in the same page, so that each group of expressions may be readily contrasted with

class; for the operations of the *Intellect* generally involve also those of the *Will*, and *vice versa*; and our *Affections* and *Emotions*, in like manner, generally imply the agency both of the *Intellect* and of the *Will*. All that can be effected, therefore, is to arrange the words according to the principal or dominant idea they convey. *Teaching*, for example, although a Voluntary act, relates primarily to the Communication of Ideas, and is accordingly placed at No. 537, under Class IV Division (II). On the other hand, *Choice, Conduct, Skill*, &c., although implying the co-operation of Voluntary with Intellectual acts, relate principally to the former, and are therefore arranged under Class V.

[1] It often happens that the same word admits of various applications, or may be used in different senses. In consulting the Index the reader will be guided to the number of the heading under which that word, in each particular acceptation, will be found, by means of *supplementary words* printed in Italics; which words, however, are not to be understood as explaining the meaning of the word to which they are annexed, but only as assisting in the required reference. I have also, for shortness' sake, generally omitted words immediately derived from the primary one inserted, which sufficiently represents the whole group of correlative words referable to the same heading. Thus the number affixed to *Beauty* applies to all its derivatives, such as *Beautiful, Beauteous, Beautifulness, Beautifully*, &c., the insertion of which was therefore needless.

[2] For example:—To take time by the forelock;—to turn over a new leaf;—to show the white feather;—to put a finger in the pie;—to let the cat out of the bag;—to take care of number one;—to kill two birds with one stone, &c., &c.

[3] See Trench, *On the Lessons in Proverbs*.

those which occupy the adjacent column, and constitute their antithesis.[1] By carrying the eye from the one to the other, the inquirer may often discover forms of expression, of which he may avail himself advantageously, to diversify and infuse vigour into his phraseology. Rhetoricians, indeed, are well aware of the power derived from the skilful introduction of antitheses in giving point to an argument, and imparting force and brilliancy to the diction. A too frequent and indiscreet employment of this figure of rhetoric may, it is true, give rise to a vicious and affected style; but it is unreasonable to condemn indiscriminately the occasional and moderate use of a practice on account of its possible abuse.

The study of correlative terms existing in a particular language, may often throw valuable light on the manners and customs of the nations using it. Thus, Hume has drawn important inferences with regard to the state of society among the ancient Romans, from certain deficiencies which he remarked in the Latin language.[2]

In many cases, two ideas which are completely opposed to each other, admit of an intermediate or neutral idea, equidistant from both; all these being expressible by corresponding definite terms. Thus, in the following examples, the words in the first and third columns, which express opposite ideas, admit of the intermediate terms contained in the middle column, having a neutral sense with reference to the former.

Identity	*Difference*	*Contrariety*
Beginning	*Middle*	*End*
Past	*Present*	*Future*

In other cases, the intermediate word is simply the negative to each of two opposite positions; as, for example—

Convexity	*Flatness*	*Concavity*
Desire	*Indifference*	*Aversion*

[1] This arrangement has been modified; see p. xi of the 1962 Preface. [Ed.]

[2] 'It is an universal observation', he remarks, 'which we may form upon language, that where two related parts of a whole bear any proportion to each other, in numbers, rank, or consideration, there are always correlative terms invented which answer to both the parts, and express their mutual relation. If they bear no proportion to each other, the term is only invented for the less, and marks its distinction from the whole. Thus, *man* and *woman*, *master* and *servant*, *father* and *son*, *prince* and *subject*, *stranger* and *citizen*, are correlative terms. But the words *seaman*, *carpenter*, *smith*, *tailor*, &c., have no correspondent terms, which express those who are no seamen, no carpenters, &c. Languages differ very much with regard to the particular words where this distinction obtains; and may thence afford very strong inferences concerning the manners and customs of different nations. The military government of the Roman emperors had exalted the soldiery so high that they balanced all the other orders of the state: hence *miles* and *paganus* became relative terms; a thing, till then, unknown to ancient, and still so to modern languages.'—'The term for a slave, born and bred in the family, was *verna*. As *servus* was the name of the genus, and *verna* of the species without any correlative, this forms a strong presumption that the latter were by far the least numerous: and from the same principles I infer that if the number of slaves brought by the Romans from foreign countries had not extremely exceeded those which were bred at home, *verna* would have had a correlative, which would have expressed the former species of slaves. But these, it would seem, composed the main body of the ancient slaves, and the latter were but a few exceptions.'—HUME, *Essay on the Populousness of Ancient Nations*.

The warlike propensity of the same nation may, in like manner, be inferred from the use of the word *hostis* to denote both a *foreigner* and *an enemy*.

Sometimes the intermediate word is properly the standard with which each of the extremes is compared; as in the case of

Insufficiency	Sufficiency	Redundance

for here the middle term, *Sufficiency*, is equally opposed, on the one hand to *Insufficiency*, and on the other to *Redundance*.[1]

These forms of correlative expressions would suggest the use of triple, instead of double, columns, for tabulating this threefold order of words; but the practical inconvenience attending such an arrangement would probably over-balance its advantages.

It often happens that the same word has several correlative terms, according to the different relations in which it is considered. Thus, to the word *Giving* are opposed both *Receiving* and *Taking*; the former correlation having reference to the *persons* concerned in the transfer, while the latter relates to the *mode* of transfer. *Old* has for opposite both *New* and *Young*, according as it is applied to *things* or to *living things*. *Attack* and *Defence* are correlative terms; as are also *Attack* and *Resistance*. *Resistance*, again, has for its other correlative *Submission*. *Truth in the abstract* is opposed to *Error*; but the opposite of *Truth communicated* is *Falsehood*. *Acquisition* is contrasted both with *Deprivation* and with *Loss*. *Refusal* is the counterpart both of *Offer* and of *Consent*. *Disuse* and *Misuse* may either of them be considered as the correlative of *Use*. *Teaching* with reference to what is taught, is opposed to *Misteaching*; but with reference to the act itself, its proper reciprocal is *Learning*.

Words contrasted in form do not always bear the same contrast in their meaning. The word *Malefactor*, for example, would, from its derivation, appear to be exactly the opposite of *Benefactor*: but the ideas attached to these two words are far from being directly opposed; for while the latter expresses one who confers a benefit, the former denotes one who has violated the laws.

Independently of the immediate practical uses derivable from the arrangement of words in double columns, many considerations, interesting in a philosophical point of view, are presented by the study of correlative expressions. It will be found, on strict examination, that there seldom exists an exact opposition between two words which may at first sight appear to be the counterparts of one another; for in general, the one will be found to possess in reality more force or extent of meaning than the other with which it is contrasted. The correlative term sometimes assumes the form of a mere negative, although it is really endowed with a considerable positive form. Thus *Disrespect* is not merely the absence of *Respect*: its signification trenches on the opposite idea, namely, *Contempt*. In like manner, *Untruth* is not merely the negative of *Truth*; it involves a degree of *Falsehood*. *Irreligion*, which is properly *the want of Religion*, is understood as being nearly synonymous with *Impiety*. For these reasons, the

[1] [In the following cases, the intermediate word signifies an imperfect degree of each of the qualities set in opposition—

Light	Dimness	Darkness
Transparency	Semitransparency	Opacity
Vision	Dimsightedness	Blindness]

reader must not expect that all the words which stand side by side in the two columns shall be the precise correlatives of each other; for the nature of the subject, as well as the imperfections of language, renders it impossible always to preserve such an exactness of correlation.

There exist comparatively few words of a general character to which no correlative term, either of negation or of opposition, can be assigned, and which therefore require no corresponding second column. The correlative idea, especially that which constitutes a sense negative to the primary one, may, indeed, be formed or conceived; but, from its occurring rarely, no word has been framed to represent it; for, in language, as in other matters, the supply fails when there is no probability of a demand. Occasionally we find this deficiency provided for by the contrivance of prefixing the syllable *non*; as, for instance, the negatives of *existence, performance, payment*, &c., are expressed by the compound words, *non-existence, non-performance, non-payment*, &c. Functions of a similar kind are performed by the prefixes *dis-*,[1] *anti-, contra-, mis-, in-*, and *un-*.[2] With respect to all these, and especially the last, great latitude is allowed according to the necessities of the case; a latitude which is limited only by the taste and discretion of the writer.

On the other hand, it is hardly possible to find two words having in all respects the same meaning, and being therefore interchangeable; that is, admitting of being employed indiscriminately, the one or the other, in all their applications. The investigation of the distinctions to be drawn between words apparently synonymous, forms a separate branch of inquiry, which I have not presumed here to enter upon; for the subject has already occupied the attention of much abler critics than myself, and its complete exhaustion would require the devotion of a whole life. The purpose of this Work, it must be borne in mind, is, not to explain the signification of words, but simply to classify and arrange them according to the sense in which they are now used, and which I presume to be already known to the reader. I enter into no inquiry into the changes of meaning they may have undergone in the course of time.[3] I am content to accept them at the value of their present currency, and have no concern with their etymologies, or with the history of their transformations; far less do I venture to thrid the mazes of the vast labyrinth into which I should be led by any attempt at a general discrimination of synonyms. The difficulties I have had to contend with have already been sufficiently great, without this addition to my labours.

[1] The words *disannul* and *dissever*, however, have the same meaning as *annul* and *sever*; *to unloose* is the same as *to loose*, and *inebriety* is synonymous with *ebriety*.

[2] In the case of adjectives, the addition to a substantive of the terminal syllable *less*, gives it a negative meaning: as *taste, tasteless; care, careless; hope, hopeless; friend, friendless; fault, faultless*; &c.

[3] Such changes are innumerable: for instance, the words *tyrant, parasite, sophist, churl, knave, villain*, anciently conveyed no opprobrious meaning. *Impertinent* merely expressed *irrelative*, and implied neither *rudeness* nor *intrusion*, as it does at present. *Indifferent* originally meant *impartial; extravagant* was simply *digressive;* and *to prevent* was properly *to precede* and *assist*. The old translations of the Scriptures furnish many striking examples of the alterations which time has brought in the signification of words. Much curious information on this subject is contained in Trench's *Lectures on the Study of Words.*

The most cursory glance over the pages of a Dictionary will show that a great number of words are used in various senses, sometimes distinguished by slight shades of difference, but often diverging widely from their primary signification, and even, in some cases, bearing to it no perceptible relation. It may even happen that the very same word has two significations quite opposite to one another. This is the case with the verb *to cleave*, which means *to adhere tenaciously*, and also *to separate by a blow*. *To propugn* sometimes expressed *to attack*; at other times *to defend*. *To let* is *to hinder*, as well as *to permit*. *To ravel* means both *to entangle* and *to disentangle*. *Shameful* and *shameless* are nearly synonymous. *Priceless* may either mean *invaluable* or *of no value*. *Nervous* is used sometimes for *strong*, at other times for *weak*. The alphabetical Index at the end of this Work sufficiently shows the multiplicity of uses to which, by the elasticity of language, the meaning of words has been stretched, so as to adapt them to a great variety of modified significations in subservience to the nicer shades of thought, which, under peculiarity of circumstances, require corresponding expression. Words thus admitting of different meanings have therefore to be arranged under each of the respective heads corresponding to these various acceptations. There are many words, again, which express ideas compounded of two elementary ideas belonging to different classes. It is therefore necessary to place these words respectively under each of the generic heads to which they relate. The necessity of these repetitions is increased by the circumstance, that ideas included under one class are often connected by relations of the same kind as the ideas which belong to another class. Thus we find the same relations of *order* and of *quantity* existing among the ideas of *Time* as well as those of *Space*. Sequence in the one is denoted by the same terms as sequence in the other; and the measures of time also express the measures of space. The cause and the effect are often designated by the same word. The word *Sound*, for instance, denotes both the impression made upon the ear by sonorous vibrations, and also the vibrations themselves, which are the cause or source of that impression. *Mixture* is used for the act of mixing, as well as for the product of that operation. *Taste* and *Smell* express both the sensations and the qualities of material bodies giving rise to them. *Thought* is the act of thinking; but the same word denotes also the idea resulting from that act. *Judgment* is the act of deciding, and also the decision come to. *Purchase* is the acquisition of a thing by payment, as well as the thing itself so acquired. *Speech* is both the act of speaking and the words spoken; and so on with regard to an endless multiplicity of words. Mind is essentially distinct from Matter; and yet, in all languages, the attributes of the one are metaphorically transferred to those of the other. Matter, in all its forms, is endowed by the figurative genius of every language with the functions which pertain to intellect; and we perpetually talk of its phenomena and of its powers, as if they resulted from the voluntary influence of one body on another, acting and reacting, impelling and being impelled, controlling and being controlled, as if animated by spontaneous energies and guided by specific intentions. On the other hand, expressions, of which the primary signification refers exclusively to the properties and actions of matter, are metaphorically applied to the phenomena of thought and volition, and even to the feelings and passions of the soul;

and in speaking of a *ray of hope*, a *shade of doubt*, a *flight of fancy*, a *flash of wit*, the *warmth of emotion*, or the *ebullitions of anger*, we are scarcely conscious that we are employing metaphors which have this material origin.

As a general rule, I have deemed it incumbent on me to place words and phrases which appertain more especially to one head, also under the other heads to which they have a relation, whenever it appeared to me that this repetition would suit the convenience of the inquirer, and spare him the trouble of turning to other parts of the work; for I have always preferred to subject myself to the imputation of redundance, rather than incur the reproach of insufficiency.[1] When, however, the divergence of the associated from the primary idea is sufficiently marked, I have contented myself with making a reference to the place where the modified signification will be found.[2] But in order to prevent needless extension, I have, in general, omitted *conjugate words*,[3] which are so obviously derivable from those that are given in the same place, that the reader may safely be left to form them for himself. This is the case with adverbs derived from adjectives by the simple addition of the terminal syllable -*ly*; such as *closely, carefully, safely*, &c., from *close, careful, safe*, &c., and also with adjectives or participles immediately derived from the verbs which are already given. In all such cases, an ' &c.' indicates that reference is understood to be made to these roots. I have observed the same rule in compiling the Index; retaining only the primary or more simple word, and omitting the conjugate words obviously derived from them. Thus I assume the word *short* as the representative of its immediate derivatives *shortness, shorten, shortening, shortened, shorter, shortly*, which would have had the same references, and which the reader can readily supply.

The same verb is frequently used indiscriminately either in the active or transitive, or in the neuter or intransitive sense. In these cases, I have generally not thought it worth while to increase the bulk of the Work by the needless repetition of that word; for the reader, whom I suppose to understand the use of the words, must also be presumed to be competent to apply them correctly.

There are a multitude of words of a specific character which, although they properly occupy places in the columns of a dictionary, yet, having no relation to general ideas, do not come within the scope of this compilation, and are

---

[1] Frequent repetitions of the same series of expressions, accordingly, will be met with under various headings. For example, the word *Relinquishment* with its synonyms, occurs as a heading at No. 624, where it applies to *intention*, and also at No. 782, where it refers to *property*. The word *Chance* has two significations, distinct from one another: the one implying the *absence of an assignable cause*; in which case it comes under the category of the relation of Causation, and occupies the No. 156: the other, the *absence of design*, in which latter sense it ranks under the operations of the Will, and has assigned to it the place No. 621. I have, in like manner, distinguished *Sensibility, Pleasure, Pain, Taste*, &c., according as they relate to *Physical*, or to *Moral Affections*; the former being found at Nos. 375, 377, 378, 390, &c., and the latter at Nos. 822, 827, 828, 850, &c.

[2] See 1962 Preface, p. xiii. [Ed.]

[3] By '*conjugate* or *paronymous* words is meant, correctly speaking, different parts of speech from the same root, which exactly corresponds in point of meaning'.—*A Selection of English Synonyms*, edited by Archbishop Whately.

consequently omitted.[1] The names of objects in Natural History, and technical terms belonging exclusively to Science or to Art, or relating to particular operations, and of which the signification is restricted to those specific objects, come under this category. Exceptions must, however, be made in favour of such words as admit of metaphorical application to general subjects, with which custom has associated them, and of which they may be cited as being typical or illustrative. Thus, the word *Lion* will find a place under the head of *Courage*, of which it is regarded as the type. *Anchor*, being emblematic of *Hope*, is introduced among the words expressing that emotion; and in like manner, *butterfly* and *weathercock*, which are suggestive of fickleness, are included in the category of *Irresolution*.

With regard to the admission of many words and expressions, which the classical reader might be disposed to condemn as vulgarisms, or which he, perhaps, might stigmatize as pertaining rather to the slang than to the legitimate language of the day, I would beg to observe, that, having due regard to the uses to which this Work was to be adapted, I did not feel myself justified in excluding them solely on that ground, if they possessed an acknowledged currency in general intercourse. It is obvious that, with respect to degrees of conventionality, I could not have attempted to draw any strict lines of demarcation; and far less could I have presumed to erect any absolute standard of purity. My object, be it remembered, is not to regulate the use of words, but simply to supply and to suggest such as may be wanted on occasion, leaving the proper selection entirely to the discretion and taste of the employer.[2] If a novelist or a dramatist, for example, proposed to delineate some vulgar personage, he would wish to have the power of putting into the mouth of the speaker expressions that would accord with his character; just as the actor, to revert to a former comparison, who had to personate a peasant, would choose for his attire the most homely garb, and would have just reason to complain if the theatrical wardrobe furnished him with no suitable costume.

Words which have, in process of time, become obsolete, are of course rejected from this collection.[3] On the other hand, I have admitted a considerable number of words and phrases borrowed from other languages, chiefly the French and Latin, some of which may be considered as already naturalized; while others, though avowedly foreign, are frequently employed in English composition, particularly in familiar style, on account of their being peculiarly expressive,

[1] [The author did not in all cases rigidly adhere to this rule; and the editors have thought themselves justified both in retaining and in adding some words of the specific character here mentioned, which may be occasionally in request by general writers, although in categories of this nature no attempt at completeness has been made.]

[2] [It may be added that the Thesaurus is an aid not only in the choice of appropriate forms of expression, but in the rejection of those which are unfit; and that a vulgar phrase may often furnish a convenient clue to the group of classic synonyms among which it is placed. Moreover, the slang expressions admitted into the work bear but a small proportion to those in constant use by English writers and speakers.]

[3] [A few apparently obsolete words have nevertheless found their way into the Thesaurus. In justification of their admission, it may be contended that well-known words, though no longer current, give occasional point by an archaic form of expression, and are of value to the novelist or dramatist who has to depict a bygone age.]

and because we have no corresponding words of equal force in our own language.[1] The rapid advances which are being made in scientific knowledge, and consequent improvement in all the arts of life, and the extension of those arts and sciences to so many new purposes and objects, create a continual demand for the formation of new terms to express new agencies, new wants, and new combinations. Such terms, from being at first merely technical, are rendered, by more general use, familiar to the multitude, and having a well-defined acceptation, are eventually incorporated into the language, which they contribute to enlarge and to enrich. *Neologies* of this kind are perfectly legitimate, and highly advantageous; and they necessarily introduce those gradual and progressive changes which every language is destined to undergo.[2] Some modern writers, however, have indulged in a habit of arbitrarily fabricating new words and a new-fangled phraseology, without any necessity, and with manifest injury to the purity of the language. This vicious practice, the offspring of indolence or conceit, implies an ignorance or neglect of the riches in which the English language already abounds, and which would have supplied them with words of recognized legitimacy, conveying precisely the same meaning as those they so recklessly coin in the illegal mint of their own fancy.

A work constructed on the plan of classification I have proposed might, if ably executed, be of great value, in tending to limit the fluctuations to which language has always been subject, by establishing an authoritative standard for its regulation. Future historians, philologists, and lexicographers, when investigating the period when new words were introduced, or discussing the import given at the present time to the old, might find their labours lightened by being enabled to appeal to such a standard, instead of having to search for data among the scattered writings of the age. Nor would its utility be confined to a single language; for the principles of its construction are universally applicable to all languages, whether living or dead. On the same plan of classification there might be formed a French, a German, a Latin, or a Greek Thesaurus, possessing, in their respective spheres, the same advantages as those of the English model.[3] Still more useful would be a conjunction of these methodized compilations in two languages, the French and English, for instance; the columns of each being placed in parallel juxtaposition. No means yet devised would so greatly facilitate the acquisition of the one language, by those who are acquainted with the other:

---

[1] All these words and phrases are printed in Italics. [A few of these expressions, although widely used by writers of English, are of a form which is really incorrect or unusual in their own language; in some more extreme cases of this kind, the more widely used or incorrect form has been given.]

[2] Thus, in framing the present classification, I have frequently felt the want of substantive terms corresponding to abstract qualities or ideas denoted by certain adjectives, and have been often tempted to invent words that might express these abstractions; but I have yielded to this temptation only in the four following instances, having framed from the adjectives *irrelative, amorphous, sinistral,* and *gaseous,* the abstract nouns *irrelation, amorphism, sinistrality,* and *gaseity.* I have ventured also to introduce the adjective *intersocial* to express the active voluntary relations between man and man.

[3] [This suggestion has been followed, in French, in a '*Dictionnaire Idéologique*' by T. Robertson (Paris, 1859); and, in German, in a '*Deutscher Sprachschatz*' by D. Sanders (Hamburg, 1878), and '*Deutscher Wortschatz oder Der passende Ausdruck*' by A. Schelling (Stuttgart, 1892).]

none would afford such ample assistance to the translator in either language; and none would supply such ready and effectual means of instituting an accurate comparison between them, and of fairly appreciating their respective merits and defects. In a still higher degree would all those advantages be combined and multiplied in a *Polyglot Lexicon* constructed on this system.

Metaphysicians engaged in the more profound investigation of the Philosophy of Language will be materially assisted by having the ground thus prepared for them, in a previous analysis and classification of our ideas; for such classification of ideas is the true basis on which words, which are their symbols, should be classified.[1] It is by such analysis alone that we can arrive at a clear perception of the relation which these symbols bear to their corresponding ideas, or can obtain a correct knowledge of the elements which enter into the formation of compound ideas, and of the exclusions by which we arrive at the abstractions so perpetually resorted to in the process of reasoning, and in the communication of our thoughts.

Lastly, such analysis alone can determine the principles on which a strictly *Philosophical Language* might be constructed. The probable result of the construction of such a language would be its eventual adoption by every civilized nation; thus realizing that splendid aspiration of philanthropists—the establishment of a Universal Language. However utopian such a project may appear to the present generation, and however abortive may have been the former

---

[1] The principle by which I have been guided in framing my verbal classification is the same as that which is employed in the various departments of Natural History. Thus the sectional divisions I have formed, correspond to Natural Families in Botany and Zoology, and the filiation of words presents a network analogous to the natural filiation of plants or animals.

The following are the only publications that have come to my knowledge in which any attempt has been made to construct a systematic arrangement of ideas with a view to their expression. The earliest of these, supposed to be at least nine hundred years old, is the AMERA CÓSHA, or *Vocabulary of the Sanscrit Language*, by Amera Sinha, of which an English translation, by the late Henry T. Colebrooke, was printed at Serampoor, in the year 1808. The classification of words is there, as might be expected, exceedingly imperfect and confused, especially in all that relates to abstract ideas or mental operations. This will be apparent from the very title of the first section, which comprehends '*Heaven, Gods, Demons, Fire, Air, Velocity, Eternity, Much*': while *Sin, Virtue, Happiness, Destiny, Cause, Nature, Intellect, Reasoning, Knowledge, Senses, Tastes, Odours, Colours*, are all included and jumbled together in the fourth section. A more logical order, however, pervades the sections relating to natural objects, such as *Seas, Earth, Towns, Plants*, and *Animals*, which form separate classes; exhibiting a remarkable effort at analysis at so remote a period of Indian literature.

The well-known work of Bishop Wilkins entitled '*An Essay towards a Real Character and a Philosophical Language*', published in 1668, had for its object the formation of a system of symbols which might serve as a universal language. It professed to be founded on a 'scheme of analysis of the things or notions to which names were to be assigned'; but notwithstanding the immense labour and ingenuity expended in the construction of this system, it was soon found to be far too abstruse and recondite for practical application.

In the year 1797, there appeared in Paris an anonymous work, entitled 'PASIGRAPHIE, *ou Premiers Eléments du nouvel Art-Science d'écrire et d'imprimer une langue de manière à être lu et entendu dans toute autre langue sans traduction*', of which an edition in German was also published. It contains a great number of tabular schemes of categories; all of which appear to be excessively arbitrary and artificial, and extremely difficult of application, as well as of apprehension. [Systems of grouping with relation to ideas are also adopted in an '*Analytical Dictionary of the English Language*' by David Booth (London, 1835), a '*Dictionnaire Analogique de la Langue Française*' by P. Boissière (Paris), and a '*Dictionnaire Logique de la Langue Française*' by L'Abbé Elie Blanc (Paris, 1882).]

endeavours of Bishop Wilkins and others to realize it,[1] its accomplishment is surely not beset with greater difficulties than have impeded the progress to many other beneficial objects, which in former times appeared to be no less visionary, and which yet were successfully achieved, in later ages, by the continued and persevering exertions of the human intellect. Is there at the present day, then, any ground for despair, that at some future stage of that higher civilization to which we trust the world is gradually tending, some new and bolder effort of genius towards the solution of this great problem may be crowned with success, and compass an object of such vast and paramount utility? Nothing, indeed, would conduce more directly to bring about a golden age of union and harmony among the several nations and races of mankind than the removal of that barrier to the interchange of thought and mutual good understanding between man and man, which is now interposed by the diversity of their respective languages.

[1] 'The Languages', observes Horne Tooke, 'which are commonly used throughout the world, are much more simple and easy, convenient and philosophical, than Wilkins' scheme for a *real character*; or than any other scheme that has been at any other time imagined or proposed for the purpose.'—Ἔπεα Πτερόεντα, p. 125.

PLAN OF CLASSIFICATION

The numbers in the right-hand column relate to the present edition

TABULAR SYNOPSIS OF CATEGORIES

N.B. In the column for heads, the arabic numeral on the left is the number of the head in this edition: that on the right (in brackets) is the corresponding number in the previous edition. Heads with no number on the left do not appear as separate categories in this edition. Heads with no number on the right are new, and do not appear in the previous edition. Where the title of a head has been changed, only the title adopted in this edition is given.

CLASS I. ABSTRACT RELATIONS

Section		Head		Section		Head	
I Existence				**III Quantity**			
1° ABSTRACT	1	Existence	(1)	1° SIMPLE			
	2	Non-existence	(2)		26	Quantity	(25)
					27	Degree	(26)
2° CONCRETE	3	Substantiality	(3)	2° COMPARATIVE	28	Equality	(27)
	4	Unsubstantiality	(4)		29	Inequality	(28)
					30	Mean	(29)
3° FORMAL					31	Compensation	(30)
internal	5	Intrinsicality	(5)				
external	6	Extrinsicality	(6)	*by comparison*	32	Greatness	(31)
				with a standard	33	Smallness	(32)
4° MODAL				*by comparison*	34	Superiority	(33)
absolute	7	State	(7)	*with an object*	35	Inferiority	(34)
relative	8	Circumstance	(8)	*changes in*	36	Increase	(35)
				quantity	37	Decrease	(36)
				3° CONJUNCTIVE	38	Addition	(37)
II Relation					39	Subduction	(38)
1° ABSOLUTE	9	Relation	(9)		40	Adjunct	(39)
	10	Irrelation	(10)		41	Remainder	(40)
	11	Consanguinity	(11)		42	Decrement	(40a)
	12	Correlation	(12)		43	Mixture	(41)
	13	Identity	(13)		44	Simpleness	(42)
	14	Contrariety	(14)		45	Junction	(43)
	15	Difference	(15)		46	Disjunction	(44)
					47	Bond	(45)
2° CONTINUOUS	16	Uniformity	(16)		48	Coherence	(46)
	17	Non-uniformity	(16a)		49	Non-coherence	(47)
					50	Combination	(48)
3° PARTIAL	18	Similarity	(17)		51	Decomposition	(49)
	19	Dissimilarity	(18)				
	20	Imitation	(19)	4° CONCRETE	52	Whole	(50)
	21	Non-imitation	(20)		53	Part	(51)
		(Variation	20a)		54	Completeness	(52)
	22	Copy	(21)		55	Incompleteness	(53)
	23	Prototype	(22)		56	Composition	(54)
					57	Exclusion	(55)
4° GENERAL	24	Agreement	(23)		58	Component	(56)
	25	Disagreement	(24)		59	Extraneousness	(57)

TABULAR SYNOPSIS OF CATEGORIES

TABULAR SYNOPSIS OF CATEGORIES

Section		Head		Section		Head	
2°	DEGREES OF	277	Velocity (274)			298	Egress (295)
	MOTION	278	Slowness (275)			299	Reception (296)
3°	CONJOINED	279	Impulse (276)			300	Ejection (297)
	WITH FORCE	280	Recoil (277)			301	Food (298)
						302	Excretion (299)
4°	WITH REF. TO	281	Direction (278)			303	Insertion (300)
	DIRECTION	282	Deviation (279)			304	Extraction (301)
		283	Precession (280)			305	Passage (302)
		284	Following (281)			306	Overstepping (303)
		285	Progression (282)			307	Shortcoming (304)
		286	Regression (283)			308	Ascent (305)
		287	Propulsion (284)			309	Descent (306)
		288	Traction (285)			310	Elevation (307)
		289	Approach (286)			311	Depression (308)
		290	Recession (287)			312	Leap (309)
		291	Attraction (288)			313	Plunge (310)
		292	Repulsion (289)			314	Circuition (311)
		293	Convergence (290)			315	Rotator (312)
		294	Divergence (291)			316	Evolution (313)
		295	Arrival (292)			317	Oscillation (314)
		296	Departure (293)			318	Agitation (315)
		297	Ingress (294)				

CLASS III. MATTER

Section		Head		Section		Head	
I	Matter in General				in motion	349	Island (346)
							(Stream 347)
		319	Materiality (316)			350	Stream (348)
		320	Immateriality (317)			351	Conduit (350)
		321	Universe (318)			352	Wind (349)
		322	Gravity (319)			353	Air-pipe (351)
		323	Levity (320)				
				3°	IMPERFECT	354	Semiliquidity (352)
II	Inorganic Matter				FLUIDS	355	Bubble. Cloud (353)
						356	Pulpiness (354)
1°	SOLIDS	324	Density (321)			357	Unctuousness (355)
		325	Rarity (322)				(oil 356)
		326	Hardness (323)				(resin 356a)
		327	Softness (324)				
		328	Elasticity (325)	III	Organic Matter		
			(Inelasticity 326)	1°	VITALITY		
		329	Toughness (327)		general	358	Organization (357)
		330	Brittleness (328)			359	Mineral (358)
		331	Structure (329)			360	Life (359)
		332	Pulverulence (330)			361	Death (360)
		333	Friction (331)			362	Killing (361)
		334	Lubrication (332)			363	Corpse (362)
						364	Interment (363)
2°	FLUIDS				special	365	Animality (364)
	in general	335	Fluidity (333)			366	Vegetability (365)
		336	Gaseity (334)				(Animal 366)
		337	Liquefaction (335)				(Vegetable 367)
		338	Vaporization (336)			367	Zoology (368)
	specific	339	Water (337)			368	Botany (369)
		340	Air (338)			369	Animal
		341	Moisture (339)				husbandry (370)
		342	Dryness (340)			370	Agriculture (371)
		343	Ocean (341)			371	Mankind (372)
		344	Land (342)			372	Male (373)
		345	Gulf (343)			373	Female (374)
		346	Lake				
		347	Marsh (345)	2°	SENSATION		
		348	Plain (344)		general	374	Sensibility (375)

CLASS IV. INTELLECT

DIVISION (I). FORMATION OF IDEAS

TABULAR SYNOPSIS OF CATEGORIES

Division (II). Intersocial Volition

CLASS VI. AFFECTIONS

Section	Head		Section	Head	
	887 Love	(897)	4° PRACTICE	942 Temperance	(953)
	888 Hatred	(898)		943 Intemperance	(954)
	889 Endearment	(902)		944 Sensualism	(954a)
	890 Darling	(899)		945 Asceticism	(955)
	891 Resentment	(900)		946 Fasting	(956)
	892 Irascibility	(901)		947 Gluttony	(957)
	893 Sullenness	(901a)		948 Sobriety	(958)
	894 Marriage	(903)		949 Drunkenness	(959)
	895 Celibacy	(904)		950 Purity	(960)
	896 Divorce	(905)		951 Impurity	(961)
2° DIFFUSIVE	897 Benevolence	(906)		952 Libertine	(962)
	898 Malevolence	(907)	5° INSTITUTIONS	953 Legality	(963)
	899 Malediction	(908)		954 Illegality	(964)
	900 Threat	(909)		955 Jurisdiction	(965)
	901 Philanthropy	(910)		956 Tribunal	(966)
	902 Misanthropy	(911)		957 Judge	(967)
	903 Benefactor	(912)		958 Lawyer	(968)
	904 Evildoer	(913)		959 Litigation	(969)
3° SPECIAL	905 Pity	(914)		960 Acquittal	(970)
	906 Pitilessness	(914a)		961 Condemnation	(971)
	(Condolence 915)			962 Reward	(973)
4° RETROSPECTIVE	907 Gratitude	(916)		963 Punishment	(972)
	908 Ingratitude	(917)		(Penalty 974)	
	909 Forgiveness	(918)		964 Means of	
	910 Revenge	(919)		punishment	(975)
	911 Jealousy	(920)			
	912 Envy	(921)			

V Religious

Section	Head		Section	Head	
IV Moral			1° SUPERHUMAN	965 Divineness	(976)
1° OBLIGATION	913 Right	(922)		966 Gods in general	
	914 Wrong	(923)		967 Pantheon	
	915 Dueness	(924)		968 Angel	(977)
	916 Undueness	(925)		(Satan 978)	
	917 Duty	(926)		(Jupiter 979)	
	918 Dutilessness	(927)		969 Devil	(980)
	919 Non-liability	(927a)		970 Fairy	
2° SENTIMENTS	920 Respect	(928)		971 Heaven	(981)
	921 Disrespect	(929)		972 Hell	(982)
	922 Contempt	(930)	2° DOCTRINES	973 Religion	(983)
	923 Approbation	(931)		974 Irreligion	(989)
	924 Disapprobation	(932)		975 Revelation	(985)
	925 Flattery	(933)		(Pseudo-revelation 986)	
	926 Detraction	(934)		976 Orthodoxy	(983a)
	(Flatterer 935)			977 Heterodoxy	(984)
	(Detractor 936)			978 Sectarianism	
	927 Vindication	(937)	3° SENTIMENTS	979 Piety	(987)
	928 Accusation	(938)		980 Impiety	(988)
3° CONDITIONS	929 Probity	(939)	4° ACTS	981 Worship	(990)
	930 Improbity	(940)		982 Idolatry	(991)
	(Knave 941)			983 Sorcery	(992)
	931 Disinterestedness	(942)		(Spell 993)	
	932 Selfishness	(943)		(Sorcerer 994)	
	933 Virtue	(944)		984 Occultism	
	934 Wickedness	(945)	5° INSTITUTIONS	985 Churchdom	(995)
	935 Innocence	(946)		986 Clergy	(996)
	936 Guilt	(947)		987 Laity	(997)
	937 Good man	(948)		988 Ritual	(998)
	938 Bad Man	(949)		989 Canonicals	(999)
	939 Penitence	(950)		990 Temple	(1000)
	940 Impenitence	(951)			
	941 Atonement	(952)			

INSTRUCTIONS

INDEX. Having read the Preface to this edition, or that part of it beginning 'Whom does a thesaurus help?' (p. xiv), the reader will understand what kind of words he will be looking up. These words—the main entries—are in roman type and are listed in alphabetical order. When the main entry is a phrase of two or more words, hyphenated or not, its place will still be found in the alphabetical order of consecutive letters, as though it were a single word. When the entry is double, being two distinct words separated by a comma, these are to be regarded as alternatives, either of which may be found in the particular text to which the references point; (s) after an entry means that it may appear in the text in its singular or plural form.

In order to avoid the frequent repetition of references, a word once entered as, say, a noun may not be separately indexed in the form it assumes as a verb or adjective, provided (i) its place in the index, if it were entered, would be very close to that form of the word which is actually indexed; (ii) it occurs only *under the same heads* as that form which *is* indexed; (iii) no difference in meaning is involved, apart from its being a different part of speech. Thus, the verb 'admire' is not indexed, while the noun 'admiration' has four references. This means that the verb 'admire' occurs only in the same four heads, and not elsewhere. On the other hand, the verb 'deteriorate' is indexed with four references only; the noun 'deterioration' with fourteen. This means that 'deteriorate' has four references to heads under which the noun 'deterioration' does not occur, and that the other occurrences of the verb 'deteriorate' must be looked for among the fourteen heads referenced for the noun 'deterioration'. The full coverage for the *idea* of deterioration is obtained by combining the references under 'deteriorate' and 'deterioration', making eighteen in all. This is a typical case, and a safe rule when consulting the index is to include in the same purview adjacent entries, if these register different forms of the same word. Adverbs in -ly are not usually indexed; nor are participial forms in -ed and -ing, except where they have acquired idiomatic senses which differentiate them from the corresponding noun and verb.

The subentries are the references. These comprise three elements—a keyword (in italics), a number, and an abbreviation for part of speech (n. = noun; adj. = adjective; vb. = verb; adv. = adverb). The keyword is not a definition, but gives broadly the sense of the main entry for that particular reference and thus

distinguishes it from the other references. It also tells the enquirer that in the head of text corresponding in number, in that subdivision corresponding to the part of speech, there is a subhead denoted by the same italicized keyword. In that subhead he will find the word he has just looked up, associated with words of similar meaning. The number, of course, is the number of the head in which the keyword occurs. The part of speech indicates the particular subdivision of the head to which the subhead appertains. It also removes ambiguity, when the meaning of a word depends upon its part of speech. For instance, to understand the word 'well', we have to know whether it is being used as a noun, as an adjective, as a verb, or as an adverb.

Condensed references will sometimes be met with. Thus 'amputate' occurs with a reference: *cut, sunder* 46 vb. This means that in the head numbered 46, among the verbs, there is a subhead with the keyword *cut*, and another with the keyword *sunder*, and 'amputate' is found in both. Another type is exampled under 'claim' which has a reference: *desire* 859 n., vb. This means that in the head numbered 859, the keyword *desire* occurs both in the subdivision for nouns and in that for verbs; and the word 'claim' (itself both noun and verb) will be found in both places.

To sum up: to find your place in the text, you turn up some suitable word in the index and select the most promising reference, noting the number and the keyword, and the part of speech. You turn to the head bearing the corresponding number. In the subdivision corresponding to the part of speech, you will find the same keyword at the head of a paragraph. In that paragraph you may start your search.

Example (i). Suppose you look up 'besetting'. It is found with three references, of which perhaps you choose, as closest to your meaning, the one with the keyword *habitual*. This reference is *habitual* 610 adj. You turn to the head of text numbered 610 (it is entitled **Habit**), and note that the subdivision for adjectives (beginning **Adj.**) has three subheads beginning respectively with the italicized keywords *habitual, usual, habituated*. The one you want is, of course, the subhead *habitual*. In this paragraph you find 'besetting' in the immediate context of 'haunting, clinging, obsessive'; and it is surrounded with other contexts all bearing on the idea of 'habitual'.

Example (ii). You look up 'bungling'. It is not in the Index. 'Bungle', however, occurs with five references, mainly verbal. You decide that '*be clumsy*' gives the *idea* you have in mind, though you are not wanting a verb. This reference is '*be clumsy* 695 vb.' You turn to the head numbered 695. Under this head, entitled **Unskilfulness**, you have two noun subheads denoted by *unskilfulness* and *bungling*: and three adjectival subheads, viz. *unskilful, unskilled, clumsy*. According as you wish for a noun or an adjective you start looking in the subhead you think most appropriate.

TEXT. The heads are the numbered sections (1–990) which run consecutively through the text and contain the listed vocabulary. The numbers in the top corner of each page are the numbers of those heads whose vocabulary, in whole or in part, is listed on that page. The heads have separate subdivisions (vocabulary permitting) for nouns, adjectives, verbs, adverbs and interjections. Within

these subdivisions (interjections excepted) there are paragraphs beginning with a keyword in italics. These are the subheads.

Having reached his subhead, the reader will find in it the word he has looked up, standing by itself, or as the dominant word in a phrase. It will be in a fairly close context, which may offer him immediately what he wants. If not, as he reads through the subhead he will pass in smooth transitions from context to context. To render transitions more distinct, a word or expression is sometimes inserted which is more a pointer to the context than a part of vocabulary. He will frequently encounter cross-references with the same three elements of number, keyword and part of speech as he has found in the index, pointing to other heads. Before following them up, he may wish to expand his field of choice locally. He may begin by looking at some other subhead within the same numbered section. Occasional directions in the text advise him to do so. They occur in the form See followed by the keyword in italics. He need not confine himself to the same part of speech, for nouns, adjectives and verbs may often, with little or no variation, be interchanged. This is sometimes suggested in the text by 'etc. n.', 'etc. adj.', 'etc. vb.', which means that fresh vocabulary may be generated from the nouns, adjectives or verbs by modifying them according to the example given. Thus, 206 begins 'Narrowness etc. adj.', meaning that more nouns may be made by adding -ness to appropriate adjectives. It will be noticed that among the adjectives listed, 'close', 'tight' and 'strait' may be treated in this way. Many verbal keywords are made by joining the auxiliary verb 'be' with an adjective. When the reader meets such a case as 'Vb. be short,—brief etc. adj.' (under 204), it is a hint that other compound expressions like 'be brief' can be made by utilizing the adjectival vocabulary. It should not be overlooked that keywords themselves may be treated as part of the vocabulary, and are frequently indexed as such.

Neighbouring heads—and not only those that express opposite relationships—frequently have a close bearing on one another. A particular case is when one head expresses a passive or intransitive aspect and another expresses the active aspect of the same idea. 60 Order represents mainly the notion of a state of order, and 62 Arrangement that of reduction to order. Similar is the relationship between 230 Circumjacence (with 233 Outline) and 232 Circumscription (with 235 Inclosure). The enquirer may therefore with good reason first turn to the neighbouring heads before striking further afield in following up the internal references; but of course it is the internal references that will offer him the widest range.

Explanatory comment in the text is kept to a minimum and is reserved for the removal of possible ambiguities. Thus, under Adj. broad, the adj. 'wide-awake' is explained by (hat); under N. knock, the entries 'cut, drive', and 'innings', are both followed by (cricket). In two instances only are these explanatory terms abbreviated: astron. = astronomy; mus. = music.

The titles of the heads are printed in bold type, after the number. A head may have more than one such title: e.g. 132 Young person. Young animal. Young plant. A word or phrase, following a title and printed in roman type, is intended for further definition; e.g. 141 Periodicity: regularity of recurrence.

PUNCTUATION. In the text, commas are used to separate words; semicolons, roughly, to distinguish contexts; but semicolons no less frequently associate words in subgroups without necessarily exhausting the context. Punctuation is omitted in front of the internal references in order to show that they are part of the context and may even help to sum it up.

ABBREVIATIONS. In the vocabulary, an abbreviation consisting of an initial letter and a full stop denotes that a preceding word, or that part of it which begins with the same letter, is to be repeated. Thus the context 'deck, top d., lower d.' is to be read as 'deck, top deck, lower deck'. Abbreviations for parts of speech occur at the beginning of the appropriate subdivisions of the head: **N.** = noun; **Adj.** = adjective; **Vb.** = verb; **Adv.** = adverb; **Int.** = interjection. The first four of these abbreviations also occur in the references.

1 Existence

N. *existence*, esse, being, entity; absolute being, absoluteness, givenness; aseity, self-existence; unit of being, monad, Platonic idea, Platonic form; a being, entity, ens; subsistent being, subsistence 360n. *life*; survival, eternity 115n. *perpetuity*; pre-existence 119n. *priority*; co-existence, this life 121n. *present time*; existence in space, presence, currency, prevalence 189n. *presence*; entelechy, becoming, evolution 147n. *conversion*; creation 164n. *production*; potentiality 469n. *possibility*; ontology, metaphysics, existentialism, realism 449n. *philosophy*.

reality, realness, actuality, actual existence, entelechy; thatness 80n. *speciality*; positiveness; historicity, factuality, factualness 494n. *truth*; fact, matter of f., positive f., brute f., stubborn f., fait accompli, event 154n. *eventuality*; real thing, not a dream, no joke, no mockery, no kidding; realities, basics, fundamentals, bedrock, brass tacks 638n. *important matter*.

essence, finite existence; nature, real n., quiddity, hypostasis, substance 3n. *substantiality*; constitutive principle, inner being, sum and substance 5n. *intrinsicality*; prime constituent, soul, heart, core, centre 224n. *interiority*.

Adj. *existing*, existent, ontal, entitative, outside nothingness, more than potential; existential; essential 5adj. *intrinsic*; absolute, given, self-existing, increate, uncreated; unimagined, unideal; being, in existence, under the sun; pre-existent 119adj. *prior*; co-existent 121adj. *present*; subsistent, living, undying, immortal, eternal 115adj. *perpetual*; standing, surviving, extant, undestroyed, indestructible 360adj. *alive*; current, rife, prevalent, in vogue, afloat, on foot 189adj. *ubiquitous*; ontological, metaphysical.

real, essential, quidditative; subsistential, substantive 3adj. *substantial*; actual, positive, factual, historical, grounded, well-g. 494adj. *true*; natural, of nature, physical, of flesh and blood 319adj. *material*; concrete, solid 324adj. *dense*.

Vb. *be*, exist, have being, share in existence; be so and not otherwise; be the case 494vb *be true*; consist in, inhere in, reside in 5vb. *be intrinsic*; pre-exist 119vb. *be before*; coexist, coincide 123vb. *synchronize*; subsist 121vb. *be now*; abide, continue 146vb. *go on*; endure, stand 113vb. *last*; vegetate, pass the time, live one's life; be alive, draw breath, see the sun 360vb. *live*; exist in space, be found, be met, stand, lie 186vb. *be situate*; be here, be there, meet one 189vb. *be present*; obtain, prevail, reign, spread, be rife 189vb. *pervade*; take place, come about, occur 154vb. *happen*; hold, hold good 494vb. *be true*; represent, stand for, stand as 13vb. *be identical*.

become, come to be, come into existence, first see the light of day, take flesh 360vb. *be born*; arise, spring up 68vb. *begin*; unfold, develop, grow, take form, take shape 316vb. *evolve*; turn out, change into 147vb. *be turned to*.

Adv. *actually*, really, substantively; essentially, substantially, inherently, intrinsically; ipso facto; in essence, virtually to all intents and purposes; potentially 469adv. *possibly*; factually, in fact, in point of f. 494adv. *truly*.

See: 3, 5, 13, 68, 80, 113, 115, 119, 121, 123, 146, 147, 154, 164, 186, 189, 224, 316, 319, 324, 360, 449, 469, 494, 638.

2 Non-existence

N. *non-existence*, non-subsistence, inexistence, non-being, nonentity; non-existence in time 109n. *neverness*; non-existence in space, nullibiety 190n. *absence*; blank, vacuum 190n. *emptiness*; nothing, nil, cipher 103n. *zero*; a nothing, nonentity, thing of naught 4n. *insubstantial thing*; no such thing, no one 190n. *nobody*; nihilism, negativeness 533n. *negation*; negative result 728n. *failure*.

extinction, oblivion, nirvana; no life 361n. *death*; dying out, decay, obsolescence 127n. *oldness*; annihilation, nihilism 165n. *destruction*; abeyance, suspension 752 n. *abrogation*; amnesty 506n. *oblivion*; cancellation, rubbing out, sponge, clean slate, tabula rasa 550n. *obliteration*.

Adj. *non-existent*, non-subsistant, inexistent, unexisting, without being; null, minus; nowhere, lost, missing, omitted 190adj. *absent*; negatived, null and void 752adj. *abrogated*; sponged, cancelled 550adj. *obliterated*.

unreal, non-actual; without reality, baseless, groundless, unfounded, false 495 adj. *erroneous*; visionary, fabulous 513 adj. *imaginary*; without substance, without content 4 adj. *insubstantial*; unrealized, unmaterialized, unevolved, undeveloped, ungrown 670 adj. *immature*; potential, only possible 469 adj. *possible*; only supposed 512 adj. *suppositional*.

unborn, uncreated, unmade; unbegotten, unconceived; undiscovered, uninvented, unimagined; yet to come, in the womb of time 124 adj. *future*.

extinct, died out, vanished, lost and gone for ever; no more, dead and gone, defunct 361 adj. *dead*; obsolescent, vanishing 361 adj. *dying*; obsolete; functus officio, finished, over and done with.

Vb. *not be*, have no existence, have no life; lack reality, exist only in the imagination; be null and void; not happen, never happen, fail to materialize, not come off; be yet unborn.

pass away, cease to exist, become extinct, die out, perish from the earth; be no more 361 vb. *die*; lose one's life 361 vb. *perish*; come to nothing, lapse into nothingness; sink into oblivion 506 vb. *be forgotten*; go, fly away, vanish, leave no trace; dematerialize, melt into thin air, sink into the earth 446 vb. *disappear*; evaporate 338 vb. *vaporize*; melt, dissolve 337 vb. *liquefy*.

nullify, reduce to nothing, annihilate, snuff out, blow o.; render null and void, suspend 752 vb. *abrogate*; negative 533 vb. *negate*; cancel 550 vb. *obliterate*; abolish, wipe out 165 vb. *destroy*.

Adv. *negatively*, in vacuo; not really, by courtesy only.

See: 4, 103, 109, 124, 127, 165, 190, 337, 338, 361, 446, 469, 495, 506, 512, 513, 533, 550, 670, 728, 752.

3 Substantiality

N. *substantiality*, essentiality 1 n. *reality*; substantivity, objectivity; hypostasis, personality, personal existence; corporeity, visibility, tangibility, palpability, concreteness, solidity 319 n. *materiality*; ponderability, weight 322 n. *gravity*; pithiness, meatiness; stuff, world-s., hyle 319 n. *matter*; totality of existence, plenum, world, world of nature 321 n. *universe*.

substance, subsistent entity, hypostasis; substratum; thing, something, somebody 319 n. *object*; person, creature; body, flesh and blood, living matter 360 n. *life*; solid, concretion, corpus 324 n. *solid body*; pith, marrow 224 n. *interiority*; gist 514 n. *meaning*.

Adj. *substantial*, hypostatic, personal 5 adj. *intrinsic*; real, objective, natural, of nature, physical 319 adj. *material*; concrete, solid, tangible, palpable 324 adj. *dense*; considerable 638 adj. *important*; bulky 195 adj. *large*; heavy 322 adj. *weighty*; pithy, meaty, full of substance.

Adv. *substantially*, corporeally, bodily, physically; personally, in person; essentially 5 adj. *intrinsically*; largely, mainly, in the main 32 adv. *greatly*.

See: 1, 5, 32, 195, 224, 319, 321, 322, 324, 360, 514, 638.

4 Unsubstantiality

N. *insubstantiality*, nothingness 2 n. *nonexistence*; naught, nothing, nothing at all, not a whit, not a particle, not a scrap 103 n. *zero*; no one, not a soul 190 n. *nobody*; abstraction, incorporeity, incorporeality 320 n. *immateriality*; lack of substance, imponderability, lightness 323 n. *levity*; meagreness, tenuity 206 n. *thinness*; sparseness 325 n. *rarity*; lack of depth, superficiality 212 adj. *shallowness*; intangibility, invisibility; inanity, vanity, vacuity, vacancy, void, hollowness 190 n. *emptiness*; fatuity 497 n. *absurdity*; pointlessness 10 n. *irrelevance*; hallucination, self-delusion 542 n. *deception*; fantasy 513 n. *imagination*; maya, unreality.

insubstantial thing, emblem, token, symbol 547 n. *indication*; abstraction, shadow without substance, shadow, shade, dream, vision; ghost, spirit, optical illusion, will-o'-the wisp, ignis fatuus 440 n. *visual fallacy*; air, thin a., wind, breath, vapour, mist; bubble, gossamer, snowman 163 n. *weak thing*; wisp, straw 639 n. *trifle*; vain thing, vanity, vanity of vanities, inanity, fatuity, fool's paradise 499 n. *folly*; flight of fancy, figment of the imagination, golden dreams, pipe-dream 413 n. *fantasy*; all talk, moonshine, cock and bull story; idle talk, gossip, gup, rumour 515 n.

empty talk; tall talk 546n. *exaggeration*; thing of naught, mockery, pretence, chimera, figment, courtesy title; nine days' wonder, flash in the pan, damp squib, blank cartridge; empty voice, vox et præterea nihil; cry of 'wolf', 665n. *false alarm*; figurehead, lay figure, dummy, man of straw; fictitious person, invented character, John Doe and Richard Roe; pompous ass, stuffed shirt 639n. *nonentity*.

Adj. *insubstantial*, unsubstantial, abstract; inessential, not intrinsic; non-physical 320adj. *immaterial*; bodiless, bloodless, incorporeal; lightweight 323adj. *light*; light as air, airy, ætherial; thin, tenuous, gauzy, gossamer 422adj. *transparent*; pale 426adj. *colourless*; vaporous, misty 336adj. *gaseous*; fragile 330adj. *brittle*; ghostly, spectral 970adj. *spooky*; fleeting, shadowy vague 419adj. *disappearing*; vacuous, vacant, hollow, void 190adj. *empty*; vain, inane; honorary, nominal, paper, fictitious; emblematic, symbolic, token 547adj. *indicating*; without substance, groundless, unfounded; visionary, dreamy, chimerical, fantastical 513adj. *imaginary*; pointless, senseless, meaningless 515adj. *unmeaning*; blank, characterless, featureless, null; without depth, superficial 212 adj. *shallow*.

Vb. 2vb. *not be*; pass away, nullify.

Adv. *insubstantially*, unreally; nominally, by courtesy; in a vacuum.

See: 2, 10, 103, 163, 190, 206, 320, 323, 325, 330, 336, 413, 422, 426, 440, 446, 497, 499, 513, 515, 542, 546, 547, 639, 664, 970.

5 Intrinsicality

N. *intrinsicality*, inbeing, inexistence, inherence, inhesion, immanence; inwardness, reflexiveness; virtuality, potentiality 160n. *power*; subjectiveness, subjectivity, subjectivism, self-reference; ego, personality 80n. *self*.

essential part, essence, important part, prime ingredient, prime constituent; principle, property, virtue, capacity; quintessence, substance, stuff, quiddity; incarnation, embodiment; life, life-blood, heart's blood, sap; jugular vein, artery; heart, soul, heart and soul; backbone,

marrow, pith, fibre; core, kernel; flower; gist, nub, nucleus 638n. *chief thing*.

character, nature, quality; constitution, diathesis, ethos; type, make, stamp, breed; characteristics, complex; cast, colour, hue; aspects, features; diagnosis, diagnostics; mark, note.

temperament, temper, humour, disposition, mood, spirit 817n. *affections*; crasis, idiosyncrasy; grain, vein, streak, strain, trait 179n. *tendency*; habit, peculiarity 80 n. *speciality*.

heredity, endowment; id, gene, allelomorph, inherited characteristic; inborn capacity; inborn tendency, original sin; ancestry 169n. *genealogy*; telegony, atavism 106n. *recurrence*; traducianism, generationism; Galton's law, Mendelian ratio.

Adj. *intrinsic*, intrinsical, immanent, deep down, deep-seated, deep-rooted; inherent 58adj. *ingredient*; inward, internal 224 adj. *interior*; absorbed, inwrought, inwoven, implicit; derived from within, autistic, subjective, introversive, reflexive, inward-looking, introverted; characteristic, personal, indigenous, native; basic, fundamental, radical; a priori, original, primary, elemental, cardinal, normal; essential, substantive; virtual, potential, capable.

genetic, inherited, hereditary, atavistic, heritable, inborn, ingenerate; native, connate, congenital, connatural; incarnate, ingrained, bred in the bone.

characteristic 80adj. *special*; characterizing, qualitative; diagnostic, idiomorphic, proper; ineradicable, settled, incurable, invariable; constant, unchanging.

Vb. *be intrinsic,*—immanent etc. adj.; inexist, inhere 773n. *belong*; be born like it; inherit, take after, run in the blood; be marked with, be stamped with, be characterized by; involve, mean 523vb. *imply*.

Adv. *intrinsically* etc. adj.; at bottom, fundamentally, essentially, substantially, virtually; in effect, in the main.

See: 58, 80, 106, 160, 169, 179, 224, 523, 638, 773, 817.

6 Extrinsicality

N. *extrinsicality*, objectiveness, objectivity; transcendence 34n. *superiority*;

otherness, the other, non-ego, not-self 59 n. *extraneousness*; externality, outwardness, outer darkness, outer space 223 n. *exteriority*; objectification, externalization; projection, extrapolation, extratensivity, extraversion, extravert; accidence, modality 7 n. *state*; accident, contingency, casuality 159 n. *chance*; accrual, accessory, acquired characteristic 40 n. *adjunct.*
Adj. *extrinsic*, extrinsical 59 adj. *extraneous*; transcendent 34 adj. *superior*; outward, external, extramural 223 adj. *exterior*; outward-looking, extroitive, extraverted; derived from without, acquired, engrafted, inbred, instilled, inculcated; supervenient, accessory, adventitious, adscititious 38 adj. *additional*; incidental, accidental, contingent, fortuitous 159 adj. *casual*; non-essential, inessential; subsidiary, subordinate 35 adj. *inferior.*
Vb. *be extrinsic*, lie without, not belong; transcend 34 vb. *be superior*; come from without, supervene 38 vb. *accrue.*
make extrinsic, objectify, realize, project, extrapolate 223 vb. *externalize*; body forth 551 vb. *represent.*
Adv. *extrinsically*, outwardly; from outside.
See: 7, 34, 35, 38, 40, 59, 159, 223, 551.

7 State: absolute condition

N. *state*, modal existence, suchness; estate, lot, walk, walk of life; case, way, plight, pickle 8 n. *circumstance*; position, category, status, footing, standing, rank; condition, trim, fettle, fig; habitude, habit, diathesis, complexion 5 n. *temperament*; temper, mood 817 n. *affections*; state of health, physical condition.
modality, mode, fashion, style; stamp, set, fit, mould 243 n. *form*; frame, fabric, bone 331 n. *structure*; aspect, phase, light, complexion, guise 445 n. *appearance*; tenor 179 n. *tendency.*
Adj. *conditionate*, conditional, such; modal, formal 243 adj. *formative*; organic 331 adj. *structural*; in a state of; in condition, in form, in good f. 694 adj. *skilful*; in bad form 695 adj. *clumsy.*
Vb. *be in a state of*, be such, be so; be on a footing; stand, lie, labour under; do, fare; possess a state, enjoy a s.
Adv. *conditionally*, it being so, as it is, as

things are, as the matter stands, provisionally.
See: 5, 8, 27, 179, 243, 331, 445, 694, 695, 817.

8 Circumstance

N. *circumstance*, circumstances, factors, situation; total situation, personal world, idioverse, life space; environment, milieu 230 n. *circumjacence*; context 9 n. *relation*; régime, set-up 7 n. *state*; posture, posture of affairs, look of things, appearances 445 n. *appearance*; lay of the land, how the land lies 186 n. *bearings*; footing, standing, status, relative position 27 n. *degree*, 9 n. *relation*; plight, pickle, awkward situation, pass, pinch, corner, hole, jam, dilemma 700 n. *predicament.*
juncture, conjuncture, stage, point 154 n. *eventuality*; crossroads, crossways, turning point, match point, point of no return; moment, hour, right time, opportunity 137 n. *occasion*; critical moment, crucial m., hour of decision, emergency 137 n. *crisis.*
Adj. *circumstantial*, given, modal 7 adj. *conditionate*; surrounding, environmental, contextual 230 adj. *circumjacent*; circumscribing, limiting 232 adj. *circumscribed*; provisional, temporary 114 adj. *transient*; variable 152 adj. *changeful*; dependent on circumstances, contingent, incidental, adventitious 154 adj. *eventful*; emergent, critical, crucial; auspicious, favourable 137 adj. *opportune*; fitting the circumstances, suitable, seemly 24 adj. *agreeing*; appropriate, convenient 642 adj. *expedient.*
Adv. *thus*, so, in such wise; like this, in this way; from that angle.
accordingly, and so, according as, depending on; according to circumstances, as the wind blows, as it turns out, as the case may be.
if, if so be, should it so happen, should it be that; in the event of, in the case of, in case; provisionally, provided that 7 adv. *conditionally*; supposing, assuming, granting, allowing, taking it that; if not, unless, except, without.
See: 7, 9, 24, 27, 114, 137, 152, 154, 186, 230, 232, 445, 642, 700.

9 Relation

N. *relation,* relatedness, connectedness, 'rapport', reference, respect, regard; bearing, direction; concern, concernment, interest, import 638 n. *importance;* involvement, implication 5 n. *intrinsicality;* appetency 859 n. *desire;* relationship, homogeneity, cognation, affinity, affiliation, filiation, kinship 11 n. *consanguinity;* classification, classifiability 62 n. *arrangement;* belongingness, association, alliance, intimacy 880 n. *friendship;* liaison, linkage, connection, link, tie-up, bond of union 47 n. *bond;* something in common, common reference, common source, common denominator 775 n. *joint possession;* syntax 60 n. *order;* context, milieu, environment 8 n. *circumstance;* import, intention 514 n. *meaning.*

relativeness, relativity, functionality, interconnection, mutual relation, function 12 n. *correlation;* same relation, homology, correspondence 13 n. *identity,* 28 n. *equality;* similar relation, analogy 18 n. *similarity;* comparability 462 n. *comparison;* close relation, apposition, approximation 289 n. *approach,* 200 n. *nearness,* 202 n. *contiguity,* 89 n. *accompaniment;* parallel relation, collaterality, registration (printing) 219 n. *parallelism,* 245 n. *symmetry;* proportionality, perspective, proportion, ratio, scale; causal relation, causality, cause and effect 156 n. *cause;* governing relation 178 n. *influence;* dependence 745 n. *subjection,* 157 n. *effect;* subordinate relation 35 n. *inferiority;* logical relation (see *relevance*); relative position, stage, status, rank 27 n. *degree;* serial order 65 n. *sequence;* relativism, relationism 449 n. *philosophy;* relativist, relationist.

relevance, logical relation, logicality, logical argument 475 n. *reasoning;* chain of reasoning, syllogism, sorites 475 n. *argumentation;* fitness, suitability, just relation, due proportion 24 n. *agreement;* point, application, applicability, appositeness, pertinence, propriety, comparability; case in point, good example, crass e., palmary instance 83 n. *example.*

referral, making reference, referment, reference; application, allusion, mention; citation, quotation; frame of reference, object of reference, referent; referendary, referee.

Adj. *relative,* not absolute; relational,

referential, respective; relativist, relativistic; referable, referrible; en rapport, related, connected, linked, entwined; bearing upon, concerning, in aid of; of concern, of interest, of import 638 adj. *important;* belonging, appertaining, appurtenant 773 adj. *possessed;* in common 775 adj. *sharing;* mutual, reciprocal, corresponding, answering to 12 adj. *correlative;* classifiable, in the same category 62 adj. *arranged;* serial, consecutive 65 adj. *sequent;* affinitive, congenial, affiliated, cognate, kindred 11 adj. *akin;* homologous, analogous, like 18 adj. *similar;* comparative, comparable 462 adj. *compared;* approximative, approximating, approaching 200 adj. *near;* collateral 219 adj. *parallel;* proportional, proportionate, varying as, in ratio, to scale; in due proportion, proportionable, commensurate 245 adj. *symmetrical;* perspectival, in perspective; contextual, environmental.

relevant, logical, in context; apposite, pertinent, applicable; pointed, to the point, well-directed 475 adj. *rational;* proper, appropriate, suitable, fitting 24 adj. *apt;* alluding, allusive; quotable, worth mentioning.

Vb. *be related,* have a relation, stand in a r., lie in a perspective; have a reference, refer to, regard, respect, have to do with; bear upon, be a factor 178 vb. *influence;* touch, concern, deal with, interest, affect; own a connection 11 vb. *be akin;* belong, pertain, appertain; approximate to 289 vb. *approach;* answer to, correspond, reciprocate 12 vb. *correlate;* have a connection, tie in with; be congruent, register with (printing) 24 vb. *accord;* be proportionate, vary as; be relevant, have point, support an analogy, serve as an example; come to the point, get down to brass tacks.

relate, bring into relation, put in perspective; connect with, gear to, gear with; apply, bring to, bear upon; link, connect, entwine, tie up with 45 vb. *tie;* frame, provide a background; compare 18 vb. *liken;* proportion, symmetrize, parallel; balance 28 vb. *equalize;* establish a connection, draw a parallel, find an example 475 vb. *reason;* make a reference to, refer to, touch on, allude to, mention; index, supply *or* furnish with references 547 vb. *indicate.*

Adv. *relatively*, not absolutely, in a context; in relation, contextually; in its degree, comparatively, in comparison; proportionally, in ratio, to scale, in perspective; conditionally, circumstantially; appropriately 24 adv. *pertinently*.

concerning, touching, regarding; as to, as regards, with regard to, with respect to; relating to, with reference to, about, anent, on, under; in connection with; in relation to, bearing on; speaking of, à propos, by the way, by the bye, on the subject of; on the point of, as far as concerns; in the matter of, in re; under the head of; on the part of, on the score of; whereas; forasmuch, inasmuch; concerning which, whereto, whereunder; thereto, thereunder; hereto, hereunder; whereof, thereof, hereof.

See: 5, 8, 11, 12, 13, 18, 24, 27, 28, 35, 45, 47, 60, 62, 65, 83, 89, 156, 178, 200, 202, 219, 245, 289, 449, 462, 475, 514, 547, 638, 745, 773, 775, 859, 880.

10 Irrelation: absence of relation

N. *irrelation*, unrelatedness, absoluteness; independence 744 n. *freedom*; arbitrariness, unilaterality; separateness, insularity, isolation 46 n. *separation*; unclassifiability, rootlessness, homelessness; singularity, individuality 80 n. *speciality*; lack of connection, inconnection, unconnectedness, no context; inconsequence (see *irrelevence*); disconnection, dissociation 46 n. *disjunction*, 72 n. *discontinuity*; misconnection, wrong association, misdirection, wrong address 495 n. *error*; disproportion, asymmetry 246 n. *distortion*; incommensurability, disparity 29 n. *inequality*; diversity, heterogeneity, multifariousness 15 n. *difference*, 17 n. *non-uniformity*, 82 n. *multiformity*; incongruence 84 n. *unconformity*; irreconcilability 14 n. *contrariety*; intrusion, intrusiveness, untimeliness 138 n. *intempestivity*; no concern, no interest, no business, nobody's b.; square peg in a round hole 25 n. *misfit*; exotic, alien element, intruder, cuckoo in the nest 59 n. *extraneousness*.

irrelevance, irrelevancy; illogicality, unreason 477 n. *sophistry*; pointlessness, inapplicability, bad example, no e.;

impertinence, ineptitude; inconsequence, non sequitur; parenthesis, obiter dictum 231 n. *interjacence*; diversion, red herring 612 n. *incentive*; episode, incidental 154 n. *eventuality*; inessential, non-essential 639 n. *unimportance*.

Adj. *irrelative*, without relation, unrelated, absolute, self-existing; independent 744 adj. *unconfined*; owing nothing to, original 21 adj. *unimitated*; irrespective, regardless, non-regarding, unilateral, arbitrary; irrelated, unclassified, unidentified; unclassifiable, rootless, homeless, kinless, birthless, from nowhere; adrift, wandering, astray 282 adj. *deviating*; detached, isolated, insular 88 adj. *alone*; unconcerned, uninvolved 860 adj. *indifferent*; unconnected, without context, misconnected, disconnected, unallied 46 adj. *disjoined*; digressive, parenthetic, anecdotal; episodic, incidental 72 adj. *discontinuous*; separate, singular, individual 80 adj. *special*; private, of no concern, without interest, nothing to do with; inessential 639 adj. *trivial*; exotic, foreign, alien, strange, outlandish 59 adj. *extraneous*; uncongenial, ungermane; intrusive, untimely 138 adj. *ill-timed*; inappropriate, inept 25 adj. *unapt*; not comparable, incommensurable, disparate 29 adj. *unequal*; disproportionate, out of proportion, asymmetrical 246 adj. *distorted*; incongruent, discordant 84 adj. *unconformable*; irreconcilable 14 adj. *contrary*; heterogeneous 17 adj. *non-uniform*; multifarious 82 adj. *multiform*.

irrelevant, illogical; inapposite, inapplicable, pointless; impertinent, inept, inappropriate 25 adj. *disagreeing*; out of order, misapplied, misplaced, misdirected, misaimed, to the wrong address 495 adj. *erroneous*; off-target, off the beam, off-centre, peripheral; rambling, wandering 570 adj. *diffuse*; adrift, beside the point, beside the mark, beside the purpose, foreign to the p., neither here nor there; trivial, inessential 639 adj. *unimportant*; inconsequent, inconsequential; parenthetic, obiter; episodic, incidental, ungermane; remote, far-fetched, out-of-the-way, forced, strained; academic, impractical.

Vb. *be unrelated*, have no concern with, have nothing to do w., owe nothing to, disown: have no right to be there, have no place

[8]

in 190vb. *be absent*; not be one's business, be nobody's b.; not concern, not touch, not interest; be irrelevant, be off the point, avoid the issue, cloud the i., draw a red herring; force, strain; lug in by the heels; ramble, wander, lose the thread 570vb. *be diffuse.*

Adv. *unrelatedly*, irrespective, regardless; without regard, without respect, without reference; irrelevantly, illogically, inappropriately; parenthetically, incidentally, obiter; episodically.

See: 14, 15, 17, 21, 25, 29, 46, 59, 72, 80, 82, 84, 88, 138, 154, 190, 231, 246, 282, 477, 495, 570, 612, 639, 744, 860.

11 Consanguinity: relations of kindred

N. *consanguinity*, relationship, kinship, kindred, blood 169n. *parentage*; filiation, affiliation, apparentation, affinity, propinquity, joking relationship; blood-relationship, agnation, cognation; ancestry, lineage, descent; connection, alliance, family, family connection; ties of family, ties of blood, ties of race, nationality 371 n. *nation*; nepotism; atavism.

kinsman, kinswoman, sib; kindred, kith and kin, kinsfolk, relations; near relative, next of kin, distant relation, blood r.; relation by marriage, step-relation; brethren, children, offspring, issue, one's flesh and blood; agnate, cognate, congener, affine; twin, identical t.; brother, sister, uterine brother, blood b., half b., stepbrother; cousin, cousin german, first cousin, second c., cousin once removed; uncle, nunky; aunt, auntie; nephew; niece; father, mother 169n. *parent*; clansman, tribesman, compatriot, fellow.

family, matriarch, patriarch; motherhood, fatherhood, brotherhood, sisterhood, cousinhood; fraternity, sorority, phratry; gens, gotra, one's people; foster son, godson, stepson, adopted s.; godparents, gossip; relations by marriage, in-laws; circle, family c., home c. 882n. *sociality*; hearth and home, household, the old folks at home, homefolks; tribe, horde.

race, stock, stirps, generation, breed, strain, line, side; tribe, phyle, clan, sept; blood group, totem g., ethnic g.; tribalism, nationality, gentility; inbreeding, interbreeding.

Adj. *akin*, sib, kindred, consanguineous, twin-born; matrilinear, out of; patrilinear, by; maternal, paternal; fraternal, brotherly, sisterly, cousinly; avuncular; novercal; related, family, collateral, allied affined; connatural, congenerous; agnate, cognate, german, uterine; near, related, intimately r. 9 adj. *relative*; once removed, twice r.; next-of-kin; step-.

ethnic, racial, tribal, phyletic, clannish, gentile 371 adj. *national*; inter-racial, inter-tribal; interbred, inbred; Aryan, Hamitic, Semitic; Caucasian, Mongolian, Amerindian, Australasian, Negroid, Negrito.

Vb. *be akin*, share the blood of; claim relationship etc. n.; own a connection 9 vb. *be related*; father, sire, dam 164vb. *generate*; be brother to, be sister to, brother, sister; affiliate, adopt, bring into the family.

See: 9, 164, 169, 371, 882.

12 Correlation: double or reciprocal relation

N. *correlation*, correlativity, co-relation, mutual r., functionality 9n. *relation*; proportionment, proportionality, proportion 245n. *symmetry*; texture, design, pattern, choreography 62n. *arrangement*; network, grid 222n. *network*; correspondence, opposite number 18n. *similarity*, 13n. *identity*; mutuality, interrelation, interconnection; interdependence, mutual dependence; mutualism, mutualist; interaction, interplay, mutual influence; alternation, turn and turn about, see-saw 317 n. *oscillation*; reciprocity, reciprocalness, reciprocality, reciprocation 151n. *interchange*; each, each other, one another; give and take 770n. *compromise*; exchange, change, payment in kind 791n. *barter*; lex talionis 714n. *retaliation*.

Adj. *correlative*, reciprocal, commutual, functional 9adj. *relative*; corresponding, correspondent, opposite, answering to, analogous, parallel 18adj. *similar*; proportioned, proportional, proportionate 245adj. *symmetrical*; complementary, complemental, heterosexual; interconnecting, interlocking; mutual, reciprocatory, reciprocating 714adj. *retaliatory*; reacting 280adj. *recoiling*; alternating,

alternate, see-saw 317 adj. *oscillating*; interlocking, geared, interacting; patterned, woven; interchangeable, exchangeable 151 adj. *interchanged*; inter-, intertribal, inter-racial, international, inter-state, inter-world; two-way.

Vb. *correlate*, interrelate, interconnect, interlock, interplay, interact; interdepend, mutualize; vary as, be a function of; proportion, symmetrize; correspond, answer to, reflect 18 vb. *resemble*; react 280 vb. *recoil*; alternate 317 vb. *oscillate*, 151 vb. *interchange*; reciprocate 714 vb. *retaliate*; exchange, counterchange, chop, swop, barter 791 vb. *trade*; balance 28 vb. *equalize*; set off 31 vb. *compensate.*

Adv. *correlatively*, proportionately, as . . . so . . . ; mutually, reciprocally, each to each, each other, one another; compensatively, equivalently 28 adv. *equally*; interchangeably, in mutual exchange 151 adv. *in exchange*; barteringly, in kind 791 adv. *in trade*; alternately, by turns, turn and turn about, first one and then the other; contrariwise, vice versa 14 adv. *contrarily*; inter, between, shuttlewise 317 adv. *to and fro.*

See: 9, 13, 14, 18, 28, 31, 62, 151, 222, 245, 280, 317, 714, 770, 791.

13 Identity

N. *identity*, sameness, oneness, identism 88 n. *unity*; the same, no other, the very same, the very one; genuineness 494 n. *authenticity*; the real thing, it, absolutely it 21 n. *no imitation*; tautology, the very words, ipsissima verba, ditto, quotation 106 n. *repetition*; one's very self, oneself, myself 80 n. *self*; other self, alter ego, ka, ba, genius, double; oneness with, identification, coincidence, congruence 24 n. *agreement*; coalescence, mergence, absorption 299 n. *reception*; convertibility, interchangeability, equivalence 28 n. *equality*; no difference, distinction, without a d., indistinguishability; same meaning, synonymity, synonymy 514 n. *meaning*; same kind, homogeneity, co-substantiality 16 n. *uniformity*; no change, invariability, invariant, constant 153 n. *fixture*; counterpart, duplicate 22 n. *copy*; fellow, pair, match, twin, Tweedledum and Tweedledee 18 n. *analogue*; homonym

homophone, homophene, synonym 559 n. *word.*

Adj. *identical*, same, self, selfsame, of that ilk; one and the same, one and only 88 adj. *one*; coalescent, merging, absorbed; co-substantial, homoousian; identified with, indistinguishable, interchangeable, convertible, equivalent 28 adj. *equal*; homonymous, synonymous, synonymic; coincident, congruent 24 adj. *agreeing*; always the same, invariable, invariant, constant, unchanging, unaltered 153 adj. *unchangeable* ; monotonous 838 adj. *tedious*; homogeneous, monolithic 16 adj. *uniform*; tautologous, repetitive, repetitional 106 adj. *repeated.*

Vb. *be identical*, show no difference, ditto 106 vb. *repeat*; coincide, coalesce, merge, be one with, sink one's identity; be congruent, register, agree in all respects 24 vb. *accord*; phase 123 vb. *synchronize.*

identify, make as one, treat as o., unify; treat as the same, not distinguish, recognize no distinction 464 vb. *not discriminate*; homologate, equate, tar with the same brush 28 vb. *equalize*; assimilate, match, pair 18 vb. *liken*; assert the identity, recognize the i. 561 vb. *name*, 80 vb. *specify.*

Adv. *identically*, interchangeably, without distinction; in phase, on all fours, in register; ibidem; ditto; in like case, same here.

See: 16, 18, 21, 22, 24, 28, 80, 88, 106, 123, 153, 299, 464, 494, 514, 559, 561, 838.

14 Contrariety

N. *contrariety*, non-identity, non-coincidence, absolute difference, world of d. 15 n. *difference*; exclusiveness, mutual e., irreconcilability 10 n. *irrelation*; antipathy, repugnance, hostility 888 n. *hatred*; adverseness, contrariness, antagonism 704 n. *opposition*; antidote 182 n. *counteraction*; conflict, clash 279 n. *collision*; discord 25 n. *disagreement*; contradistinction, contrast, relief, light r., variation, undertone, counterpoint 463 n. *discrimination*; contradiction, flat c. 533 n. *negation*; contraindication, counter - symptom 467 n. *counter-evidence*; counter-meaning, counter-sense, counterterm, antonym 514 n. *meaning*; antinomy, inconsistency, two voices 17 n. *non-uniformity*; paradox,

ambivalence 518n. *equivocalness*; oppositeness, antithesis, direct opposite, antipodes, antipole, counterpole, opposite
pole; other extreme, opposite e., quite the
contrary, quite the reverse; other side,
opposite s., weather s., weatherboard 240
n. *contraposition*; reverse, wrong side 238
n. *rear*; inverse 221 n. *inversion*; converse,
reverse image, mirror, mirror symmetry
417n. *reflection*; opposite direction, headwind, undertow, counter-stream 182n.
counteraction.
polarity, contraries 704n. *opposites*; positive
and negative; north and south; east and
west; day and night; light and darkness;
hot and cold; fire and water; black and
white; good and bad; Hyperion to a
satyr.
Adj. *contrary*, non-identical, as different as
chalk from cheese, anything but 15adj.
different; contrasting, contrasted, clashing, conflicting, discordant 25adj. *disagreeing*; inconsistent, not uniform 17
adj. *non-uniform*; ambivalent, bitter sweet,
sweet and sour; contradictory, antithetic,
adversative 533adj. *negative*; antithetical
diametrically opposite, poles asunder,
antipodal, antipodean 240adj. *opposite*;
reverse, converse, inverse; antipathetic,
repugnant, abhorrent, inimical, hostile
888adj. *hating*; adverse, contrarious,
contrariant, untoward, antagonistic 704
adj. *opposing*; counteractive, antidotal
182adj. *counteracting*; counter-, anti-.
Vb. *be contrary*, have nothing in common
10vb. *be unrelated*, 15vb. *differ*, 57vb.
exclude; contrast, stand out 25vb. *disagree*; clash, discord; run counter 240vb.
be opposite; speak with two voices 518vb.
be equivocal; contravene, fly in the face of
704vb. *oppose*, 738vb. *disobey*; contradict, contra - indicate 533 vb. *negate* ;
counteract 658vb.*remedy*; reverse 752vb.
abrogate; antithesize, turn the tables 221
vb. *invert.*
Adv. *contrarily*, contra, per c., on the other
hand,conversely,contrariwise;vice versa,
topsy-turvy, upside down; invertedly, inversely; on the contrary, nay rather;
otherwise, quite the other way; in contrast, in opposition to; by contraries, by
opposites.

See: 10, 15, 17, 25, 57, 182, 221, 238, 240,
279, 417, 463, 467, 514, 518, 533, 658,
704, 738, 752, 888.

15 Difference
N. *difference*, unlikeness 19n. *dissimilarity*;
disparity, odds 29n. *inequality*; margin,
differential, minus, plus 41n. *remainder*;
wide margin 199n. *distance*; narrow margin, approximation 200n. *nearness*; heterogeneity, variety, diverseness, diversity, all sorts and conditions, mixed bag
17n. *non-uniformity*; divergence, departure from 282n. *deviation*; otherness,
differentia, distinctness, originality 10n.
irrelation, 21n. *non-imitation*; discrepancy, incongruity 25n. *disagreement*;
incompatibility, antipathy 861n. *dislike*;
disharmony, discord, variance 709n.
dissension; contrast 14n. *contrariety*;
opposite, antithesis 240n. *contraposition*;
non-conformity 84n. *unconformity*; variation, modification, alteration 143n.
change, 147n. *conversion.*
differentiation 463n. *discrimination*; specification 80n. *speciality*; contradistinction,
distinction, nice d., delicate d., subtle d.;
nuance, nicety, shade of difference, fine
shade of meaning 514n. *meaning*; distinction without a difference 13n. *identity*;
moods and tenses, declension 564n.
grammar.
variant, differential, different thing, another
t., something else, this, that or the other;
another story, another version, another
pair of shoes, horse of another colour;
special case 80n. *speciality*; new version,
new edition, re-issue 589n. *edition.*
Adj. *different*, differing, unlike 19adj. *dissimilar* ; original 21 adj. *unimitated* ;
various, variform, diverse, diversified,
heterogeneous 17adj. *non-uniform*; multifarious 82adj. *multiform*; assorted, of all
sorts, all manner of, divers 43adj. *mixed*;
distinct, distinguished, differentiated, dis-
criminated, divided, separated 46adj.
disjoined; divergent, departing from 282
adj. *deviating*; discrepant, discordant,
clashing, incongruent, incongruous 25
adj. *disagreeing*; disparate 29adj. *unequal*;
contrasting, contrasted, far from it, wide
apart, poles asunder, anything but 14adj.
contrary; other, another, not the same,
peculiar 80adj. *special*; in a different class
34adj. *superior*, 35adj. *inferior*; somehow
different, the same yet not the same,
changed, altered 147adj. *converted.*
distinctive, diagnostic 5adj. *characteristic*;
differentiating, distinguishing, marking

out, differentiating; elative, comparative, superlative, augmentative.

Vb. *differ*, be different etc. adj.; show variety; vary from, diverge f., depart f. 282 vb. *deviate*; divaricate, ablude; contrast, clash, jar, conflict 25 vb. *disagree*; be at variance 709 vb. *quarrel*; modify, vary, make alterations 143 vb. *change*. *differentiate*, distinguish, mark out, single o., severalize 463 adj. *discriminate*; shade, refine, make a distinction, sharpen a d.; particularize 80 vb. *specify*.

Adv. *differently*, variously, as modified, after alteration; otherwise, not so, some other way, in a different fashion; in different ways, in many w., multifariously.

See: 5, 10, 13, 14, 17, 19, 21, 25, 29, 34, 35, 36, 41, 43, 46, 80, 82, 84, 143, 147, 199, 200, 240, 282, 463, 514, 564, 589, 709, 861.

16 Uniformity

N. *uniformity*, uniformness, consistency, constancy, steadiness 153 n. *stability*; persistence 71 n. *continuity*, 146 n. *continuance*; order, regularity, method, centralization 60 n. *order*; connaturality 18 n. *similarity*; homogeneity, homology, monolithic quality; unity, unison, correspondence, accordance 24 n. *agreement*; levelness, flushness 258 n. *smoothness*; roundness 245 n. *symmetry*; sameness, invariability, monotony, level, dead l., even tenor, mixture as before; even pace, rhythm; round, daily r., routine, drill, treadmill 610 n. *habit*; monotone, greyness; droning, drone, sing-song, monologue; monolith; pattern, same p., type, stereotype; stamp, common s., same stamp, same mint; set, assortment; suit, flush; standard dress 228 n. *uniform*; assimilation, standardization, mass-production 83 n. *conformity*; cliché 106 n. *repetition*; regimentation, intolerance, closed shop 740 n. *compulsion*.

uniformist, drill sergeant; leveller, egalitarian, eraser of all distinctions; uniformitarian, regimenter.

Adj. *uniform*, all of a piece, one-piece; same all through, monolithic; of one kind, connatural, homogenetic, homologous, of a piece, of a pattern 18 adj. *similar*;

same, consistent, self-c., constant, steady, stable 153 adj. *fixed*; undeviating, unchanging, unvarying, invariable 144 adj. *permanent*; rhythmic, measured, even-paced, jog-trot 258 adj. *smooth*; undiversified, undifferentiated, unrelieved, unbroken 573 adj. *plain*; uncontrasting, without contrast, in uniform, uniformed, liveried; characterless, featureless, faceless, blank; monotonous, droning, sing-song; monotone, drab, grey; repetitive, running through 106 adj. *repeated*; standard, normal 83 adj. *typical*; patterned, standardized, stereotyped, mass-produced; sorted, assorted, sized; drilled, dressed, aligned, in line; orderly, regular, square, equilateral, circular 245 adj. *symmetrical*; straight, level, even, flush, flat 258 adj. *smooth*.

Vb. *be uniform*,—homogeneous etc. adj.; follow routine 610 vb. *be wont*; sing in unison, sing the same song, chorus 24 vb. *accord*; typify 83 vb. *conform*; dress, fall in; wear uniform, be in u.

make uniform, stamp, characterize, run through 547 vb. *mark*; assimilate, level, level up, level down, tar with the same brush 18 vb. *liken*; size, assort; drill, dress, align; standardize, stereotype, pattern; put into uniform; normalize, regularize 83 vb. *make conform*.

Adv. *uniformly*, etc. adj.; like clockwork, methodically, habitually, invariably, eternally, endlessly; without exception, in a rut, in a groove.

See: 18, 24, 60, 71, 83, 106, 144, 146, 153, 228, 245, 258, 547, 573, 610, 740.

17 Non-uniformity

N. *non-uniformity*, variability, patchiness 72 n. *discontinuity*; unpredictability 152 n. *changeableness*; inconstancy, inconsistency, capriciousness 604 n. *caprice*; irregularity, no system, no pattern, chaos 61 n. *disorder*; untidiness, dishevelment 63 n. *derangement*; ruggedness, asymmetry 244 n. *amorphism*; raggedness, unevenness, choppiness, jerkiness, 259 n. *roughness*; heterogeneity, heteromorphism 15 n. *difference*; contrast 14 n. *contrariety*, 19 n. *dissimilarity*; divarication, divergence 282 n. *deviation*; diversity, variety, various-

ness, multifariousness 82n. *multiformity*; all sorts and conditions, mixed bag, ragbag, lucky dip, odds and ends 43n. *mixture*; patchwork, motley, crazy paving, mosaic; abnormality, exception, special case, sport, new type 84n. *unconformity*; odd man out, lone wolf, rogue elephant 59n. *extraneousness*; uniqueness, nonce word; lack of uniform, mufti; every man in his humour; quot homines tot sententiæ; decentralization.

Adj. *non-uniform*, variable, unpredictable, changeable, never the same 152adj. *changeful*; inconstant, inconsistent 604 adj. *capricious*; irregular, unsystematic; patternless, unpatterned, shapeless 244 adj. *amorphous*; untidy, dishevelled, haywire, chaotic 61adj. *orderless*; uneven, bumpy, choppy, jerky 259adj. *rough*; erratic, out of step, out of time, fast, slow, gaining, losing, out of order; contrasting, contrasted 14adj. *contrary*; heterogeneous, various, diverse 15adj. *different*, 19adj. *dissimilar*; multifarious, diversified, of many kinds, of all sorts 82 adj. *multiform*; divergent, divaricating 282adj. *deviating*; aberrant, atypical, heterotactous 84adj. *unconformable*; exceptional, unusual, crazy 84adj. *abnormal*; unique, lone 59adj. *extraneous*; out of uniform, in mufti, incorrectly dressed.

Adv. *non-uniformly*, irregularly, erratically, unsystematically; unsmoothly, unevenly bumpily, jerkily; confusedly, chaotically; all anyhow, all haywire; here, there and everywhere.

See: 14, 15, 19, 43, 59, 61, 63, 72, 82, 84, 152, 244, 259, 282, 604.

18 Similarity

N. *similarity*, resemblance, likeness, similitude; semblance, seeming, appearance, look, form, fashion 445n. *appearance*, 243n. *form*; common feature, point in common, point of resemblance 775n. *participation*; congruity 24n. *agreement*; affinity, kinship 11n. *consanguinity*; homogeneity, homomorphism, connaturality; comparability, analogicalness, analogy, correspondence, parallelism 12n. *correlation*; equivalence, parity 28n. *equality*; proportionality 245n. *symmetry*; no difference 13n. *identity*;

general resemblance, family likeness; close resemblance, good likeness, perfect l.; striking likeness, faithful l., photographic l. 553n. *picture*; approximation 200n. *nearness*; partial likeness, distant l., faint resemblance; adumbration, hint; fair comparison, sufficient resemblance, the size of it.

assimilation, likening 462n. *comparison*; reduction to, identification 13n. *identity*; simulation, camouflage, disguise 20n. *imitation*; portrayal 590n. *description*; portraiture 551n. *representation*; alliteration, assonance, homoeoteleuton, rhyme 106n. *repetition*; pun, equivoque paronomasia 518n. *equivocalness*; homonymy, homophony.

analogue congener, the like, such like, likes of; type, good example, perfect e. 83n. *example*; correlate, correlative 12n. *correlative*; simile, parallel; equivalent 150n. *substitute*; brother, sister, twin; match, fellow, mate, companion, pendant; pair, sister-ship; double, ringer; complement, counterpart, other half; alter ego, other self, genius, ka, ba; likeness, reflection, shadow, the very picture 551n. *image*; another edition of, spit of, dead spit, living image, chip off the old block; twins, two peas, couple, two of a kind, Arcades ambo, birds of a feather; reproduction, copy 22n. *duplicate*.

Adj. *similar*, resembling, like, much l.; alike, ridiculously a., twin, matching, like as two peas, cast in the same mould; of a piece 16adj. *uniform*; similative, analogical; analogous, parallel, equivalent 28 adj. *equal*; corresponding, bracketed with; consubstantial, homogeneous, connatural, congeneric, ejusdem generis; cognate 11adj. *akin*; close, approximate 200 adj. *near*; typical, representative 551n. *representing*; reproducing, reflecting; much the same, something like, such like, such as, quasi; rhyming, alliteral, assonant 106adj. *repeated*; punning 518 adj. *equivocal*.

lifelike, realistic, photographic, exact, faithful, natural, typical; good of one, true to life, true to nature, true to type; clearly seen, vivid, eidetic, eidotropic 443adj. *well-seen*.

simulating 20adj. *imitative*; seeming, deceptive, camouflaged 542adj. *deceiving*; mock, pseudo 542adj. *spurious*; making

a show of 875 adj. *showy*; synthetic, artificial, ersatz 150 adj. *substituted.*
Vb. *resemble,* be similar to, pass for; mirror, reflect 20 vb. *imitate*; seem, seem like, sound l., look as if; look like, take after, have the look of; savour of, smack of; compare with, approximate to, come near to 289 vb. *approach*; match, correspond to, answer to 9 vb. *relate*; register, match 24 vb. *agree*; be bracketed; assonate, rhyme; run in pairs; typify 551 vb. *represent.*
liken, assimilate to, approximate, bring near; reduce to 13 vb. *identify*; match, twin, bracket with 28 vb. *equalize*; make a simile of; connaturalize; portray 20 vb. *imitate*; alliterate, rhyme 10 vb. *repeat*; pun 518 vb. *be equivocal.*
Adv. *similarly,* as, like, as if, quasi, so to speak, as it were; just as, in a way; as in a mirror.
See: 10, 14, 15, 17, 18, 21, 25, 29, 34, 35, 59, 82, 84, 126, 143, 147, 199, 246, 525, 527, 541, 552.

19 Dissimilarity

N. *dissimilarity,* dissimilitude, unlikeness; incomparability 10 n. *irrelation*; disparity 29 n. *inequality*; diversity, divergence 15 n. *difference*; variation, variance, variety 17 n. *non-uniformity*, 82 n. *multiformity*; contrast 14 n. *contrariety*; little in common, nothing in c., no match, not a pair 25 n. *disagreement*; novelty, originality, uniqueness 21 n. *non-imitation*; dissemblance, dissimilation, camouflage, make-up 525 n. *concealment,* 527 n. *disguise*; caricature, bad likeness, false copy 552 n. *misrepresentation*; foreign body, alien element 59 n. *intruder.*
Adj. *dissimilar,* unlike, diverse 15 adj. *different*; various 82 adj. *multiform*; disparate 29 adj. *unequal*; unalike, not comparable 10 adj. *irrelative*; far above 34 adj. *superior*; far below 35 adj. *inferior*; unrelated, unmatched, unpaired 25 adj. *mismatched,* 17 adj. *non-uniform*; unique, without a second, one and only, original 21 adj. *unimitated*; incongruent 25 adj. *disagreeing*; untypical, atypical, exotic 84 adj. *unconformable*; unprecedented, new and strange, novel 126 n. *new*; a far cry from 199 adj. *distant*; not true, bad of.

Vb. *be unlike,* etc. adj.; bear no resemblance, have nothing in common 15 vb. *differ*; stand out 34 vb. *be superior,* 35 vb. *be inferior.*
make unlike, discriminate 15 vb. *differentiate*; innovate, modify, modulate 143 vb. *change,* 147 vb. *convert*; caricature 552 vb. *misrepresent,* 246 vb. *distort*; dissemble 542 vb. *deceive*; disguise 525 vb. *conceal*; camouflage 18 vb. *liken,* 541 vb. *fake.*
Adv. *dissimilarly,* discordantly, contrastingly, variously 15 adv. *differently.*

See: 9, 10, 11, 12, 13, 16, 20, 22, 24, 28, 83, 106, 150, 200, 243, 245, 289, 443, 445, 462, 518, 542, 551, 553, 590, 775, 875.

20 Imitation

N. *imitation,* copying etc. vb; sincerest form of flattery; rivalry, emulation, competition 911 n. *jealousy*; conventionality, convention, doing as Rome does, traditionalism 83 n. *conformity*; want of originality, following, literalism, slavishness, slavish imitation; imitativeness, parrotry (see *mimicry*); affectedness 850 n. *affectation*; mimesis 551 n. *representation*; reflection, mirror, echo, shadow 18 n. *assimilation*; quotation, citation, echolalia 106 n. *repetition*; paraphrase, translation 520 n. *interpretation*; borrowing, cribbing, plagiary, plagiarism, literary theft 788 n. *stealing*; forgery, literary f., falsification, counterfeit, fake 541 n. *falsehood*; copying, transcribing, transcription, transliteration, tracing 586 n. *writing*; duplication, reduplication, multiplication 166 n. *reproduction,* 551 n. *photography.*
mimicry, mimesis 551 n. *representation*; noises off 594 n. *dramaturgy*; mime, pantomime, sign language, gesticulation 547 n. *gesture*; ventriloquism 579 n. *speech*; portrayal, portraiture 553 n. *painting,* 590 n. *description*; realism 494 n. *accuracy*; mockery, caricature, parody, burlesque 851 n. *satire*; travesty 552 n. *misrepresentation,* 246 n. *distortion*; imitativeness, apery, apishness, parrotry 106 n. *repetition,* 850 n. *affectation*; conjuring, illusionism; simulation, semblance, disguise, camouflage, dissimulation 18 n. *similarity,* 19 n. *dissimilarity*;

pretence, mockery, simulacrum, shadow 524n. *sham*, 4n. *insubstantiality*.
imitator, copycat, ape, sedulous a., monkey; mocking-bird, parrot, poll-p., echo; sheep 84n. *conformist*, 284n. *follower*; poseur 850n. *affector*; echoer, yes-man 925n. *flatterer*; mocker, burlesquer, travester 839n. *humorist*, 926n. *detractor*; mime, mimic, impersonator, ventriloquist, conjuror, illusionist 594n. *entertainer*; actor, portrayer, portraitist 556n. *artist*; copyist, scribe, printer, compositor, tracer, copy-typist, transliterator; translator, paraphraser 520n. *interpreter*; transcriber of life, realist; simulator, hypocrite, 545n. *impostor*; borrower, plagiarist; counterfeiter, forger, faker; duplicator, multiplier, mimeograph, stencil.

Adj. *imitative*, apish, aping, parroting, parrot-like; following; echoing, flattering; posing 850adj. *affected*; disguised, camouflaged; simulating, shamming 541adj. *hypocritical*; pseudo, sham, phony, counterfeit 541n. *false*; ersatz, synthetic 150 adj. *substituted*; unoriginal, uninventive, unimaginative, derivative, second-hand, conventional 83adj. *conformable*; paraphrastic, modelled, moulded on; copied, slavish, literal, caricatured, parodied, travestied, burlesque; transcribed, transliterated; easy to copy, imitable.

Vb. *imitate*, ape, parrot, flatter, echo, mirror, reflect 18vb. *resemble*; make a show of, pose 850vb. *be affected*; pretend, make-believe, make as if; act, mimic, mime, portray, paint 551vb. *represent*; parody, caricature, burlesque, travesty 851vb. *ridicule*; sham, simulate, put on, play the hypocrite 541vb. *dissemble*; disguise, camouflage 525vb. *conceal*; ventriloquize, conjure 542vb. *deceive*.
copy, draw, counterdraw, trace; copy faithfully, catch, realize; quote, cite, echo, re-echo, chorus 106vb. *repeat*; follow copy, compose 587vb. *print*; reprint, duplicate, mimeograph; make copies, replicate, reduplicate, multiply, reel off 166vb. *reproduce*; copy out, transcribe, transliterate, type, type out; paraphrase, translate 520vb. *interpret*; copy from, crib, plagiarize, borrow 788vb. *steal*; counterfeit, forge 541vb. *fake*.
do likewise, do as the Romans do, mould oneself on, pattern oneself on, take as a model, understudy; follow, follow suit, follow my leader, follow in all things; step in the footprints of, follow in the track of, travel in the wake of 65vb, *come after*; do after, say a., echo, re-echo, chorus 106vb. *repeat*; follow, precedent, follow example, join in the cry, hunt with the hounds, jump on the bandwagon 83 vb. *conform*; emulate, rival, compete 911 vb. *be jealous*; take a leaf out of another's book, dish the Whigs 34vb. *be superior*.

Adv. *imitatively*, emulously, jealously, in rivalry; like master like man; literally, strictly, to the letter, word for word, verbatim, literatim 494 adv. *truly*; sic, as per copy.

See: 4, 18, 19, 34, 65, 83, 106, 150, 166, 246, 284, 494, 520, 525, 541, 542, 545, 574, 551, 552, 553, 556, 579, 586, 587, 590, 594, 788, 839, 850, 851, 911, 925, 926.

21 Non-imitation

N. *non-imitation*, creativeness, inventiveness 513n. *imagination*; creation, all my own work 164n. *production*; originality 119n. *priority*, 10n. *irrelation*; uniqueness, the one and only 88n. *unity*; inimitability, transcendence 34n. *superiority*; independence, defiance of precedent, line of one's own 744n. *freedom*; precedent, example 23n. *prototype*; new departure 68n. *beginning*; something new, novelty, freshness 126n. *newness*; eccentricity, individuality 84n. *unconformity*; unlikeness 19n. *dissimilarity*.
no imitation, genuineness, sincerity 494n. *authenticity*; real thing, the very thing, genuine article; it, absolutely it 13n. *identity*, 80n. *self*; autograph, holograph, one's own hand, usual signature 586n. *writing*.

Adj. *unimitative*, creative, inventive 513adj. *imaginative*; original, underived, not derivative; prototypal, archetypal; primordial, primary; first, first-hand, first in the field 119adj. *prior*; fresh, novel 126 adj. *new*; individual, personal 80adj. *special*; independent 744adj. *free*; eccentric 84adj. *unconformable*.
unimitated, inimitable, transcendent, unmatched, incomparable, out of reach 34 adj. *superior*; uncopied, unhackneyed, unplagiarized; unique, one and only 88

adj. *one*; authentic, true 494 adj. *genuine*; sincere, unadulterated 44 adj. *unmixed*.

See: 10, 13, 19, 23, 34, 44, 68, 80, 84, 88, 119, 126, 164, 494, 513, 586, 744.

22 Copy

N. *copy*, exact c., reproduction, replica, facsimile, tracing; apograph, fair copy, transcript, transcription, counterpart 18 n. *analogue*; cast, death mask; ectype, stamp, seal, impress, impression, squeeze; mechanical copy, stereotype, electrotype, collotype, lithograph, print, printed matter, pull, proof, revise 587 n. *letterpress*, 555 n. *engraving*; photograph, photoprint, photostat, positive, negative, contact print 551 n. *photography*; 'counterfeit presentment', an imitation, dummy, pastiche, pasticcio; forgery, plagiarism, crib 20 n. *imitation*; a likeness, resemblance, semblance 18 n. *similarity*; study, portrait, drawing 553 n. *picture*; icon, image 551 n. *representation*; form, model, effigy, sculpture, statue, bronze 554 n. *sculpture*; faithful copy, servile imitation, reflex, echo, mirror 106 n. *repetition*, 417 n. *reflection*; bad copy, apology for, mockery of 552 n. *misrepresentation*; malicious copy, distorted image, caricature, cartoon, travesty, parody 851 n. *ridicule*; hint, adumbration, shadow; silhouette, outline, sketch, diagram, first copy, draft; metaphrase, paraphrase 520 n. *translation*.

duplicate, counterpart, reproduction, cast; carbon copy, carbon; stencil, jellygraph; transfer, rubbing; photograph, photoprint, print, contact p., enlargement, blow-up 551 n. *photography*; proof, pull, revise; reprint, straight r., second edition, réchauffé 589 n. *book*; model, specimen, show copy 83 n. *example*.

See: 18, 20, 83, 106, 417, 520, 551, 552, 553, 554, 555, 587, 589, 851.

23 Prototype

N. *prototype*, archetype, antitype, countertype; type, biotype, common type, everyman 30 n. *average*; primitive form, protoplasm 358 n. *organism*; original, protoplast, negative; first occurrence, pre-

cedent, test case 119 n. *priority*; guide, rule, maxim 693 n. *precept*; standard, criterion, standard of comparison, frame of reference 12 n. *correlation*; ideal 646 n. *perfection*; cynosure, mirror 646 n. *paragon*; keynote, tuning fork, metronome 465 n. *gauge*; module, unit 465 n. *meter*; specimen, sample, ensample 83 n. *example*; model, subject; exemplar, pattern, paradigm; dummy, mock-up; copybook, copy, printer's c., text, manuscript; blueprint, design, master-plan, scheme 623 n. *plan*; rough plan, outline, draft, scantling, sketch.

living model, model, artist's m., poser, sitter, subject; fashion model, mannequin; fugleman, stroke, band-leader, conductor, drum-major, drill master 690 n. *leader*.

mould, matrix, mint; plate, shell; frame, wax figure, lay-f., tailor's dummy; last; boot-tree; die, stamp, punch, seal, intaglio.

Adj. *prototypal*, exemplary, standard, classic, copybook.

Vb. *be example*, set an e., serve as e., stand as e.; serve as a model, model, sit for, pose.

See: 12, 30, 83, 119, 358, 465, 623, 646, 690, 693.

24 Agreement

N. *agreement*, consentaneity 181 n *concurrence*; consentience, consent 488 n. *assent*; accord, accordance, chorus, unison 16 n. *uniformity*; harmony, syntony, concent 410 n. *melody*; consonance, concinnity, concordance, attunement; concert, understanding, mutual understanding, entente, entente cordiale; convention, pact 765 n. *compact*; unanimity 488 n. *consensus*; consortium 706 n. *co-operation*; union 50 n. *combination*; peace 710 n. *concord*.

conformance 83 n. *conformity*; congruence, coincidence 13 n. *identity*; consistency 16 n. *uniformity*; consequentiality, consequence, logic, logical conclusion 475 n. *reasoning*; correspondence, parallelism 18 n. *similarity*.

fitness, aptness, qualification, capability 694 n. *aptitude*; suitability, sortance, propriety 642 n. *expedience*; the right man in the right place, perfect candidate, the very thing, it, the absolute it 13 n. *identity*;

relevancy, pertinence, admissibility, appositeness, case in point, good example 9n. *relevance*; cognation, commensurability, proportion 9n. *relation*; timeliness, right moment, fit occasion, 137n. *occasion.*

adaptation, conformation, harmonization, synchronization, matching 18n. *assimilation*; reconciliation, reconcilement 719n. *pacification*; coaptation, accommodation, graduation, attunement, adjustment 62n. *arrangement*; compatibility, congeniality, naturalness; fitting, suiting, good fit, perfect f., close f., tight f.; making an agreement, negotiation 770n. *compromise.*

Adj. *agreeing*, right, accordant, in accord, in accordance with; corresponding, correspondent, answering; proportionable, proportional, proportionate, commensurate 12adj. *correlative*; coincident, coinciding, congruent, congruous 28adj. *equal*; squared with, on all fours w., consistent w., conforming 83adj. *conformable*; in conformity, in step, in phase, in tune, synchronized 123adj. *synchronous*; of a piece with, consistent, self-c. 16adj. *uniform*; consonant, concordant, harmonized 410adj. *harmonious*; combining, mixing; suiting, matching 18adj. *similar*; becoming 844adj. *ornamental*; natural, congenial, sympathetic; reconcilable, compatible, co-existent, coexisting, symbiotic; consentaneous, consensual, consentient, agreeable, acquiescent 488adj. *assenting*; concurrent, agreed, all a., at one, in unison, in chorus, unanimous, united; like-minded, of like mind, bi-partisan 706 adj. *co-operative*; treating, treaty-making, in treaty, negotiating 765adj. *contractual.*

apt, applicable, admissible, germane, appropriate, pertinent, in point, to the point, pointed, well-aimed 9adj. *relevant*; to the purpose, bearing upon 178adj. *influential*; in loco, pat, in place, à propos; right, happy, felicitous, idiomatic 575adj. *elegant*; at home, in one's element; seasonable, opportune 137adj. *timely.*

fit, suitable, sortable, fitting, suited, well-adapted, adaptable, idoneous; capable, qualified, cut out for, deft 694adj. *skilful*; meet, up one's street 642adj. *expedient.*

adjusted, well-a. 60adj. *orderly*, 494adj. *accurate*; timed, synchronized; tuned, strung, pitched, attuned 412adj. *musical*; trimmed, balanced 28adj. *equal*; well-cut,

fitting, well-fitting, close-fitting, tight-fitting, tight; made to measure, tailored, snug, comfortable.

Vb. *accord*, be accordant etc.adj.; agree, homologate, concur 488vb. *assent, 758 vb. consent*; respond, echo, chorus, chime in, ditto 106vb. *repeat*; coincide, register, square with, quadrate w., mesh w., gear w., dove-tail 45vb. *join*; fit, fit like a glove, fit to a T.; tally, correspond, match, twin 18vb. *resemble*; go with, tone in w., harmonize; comport with, sort w., fadge w., come natural; fit in, belong, feel at home; answer, meet, suit, do 642vb. *be expedient*; fall pat, come à propos, prove timely, fit the occasion, beseem, befit, keep together, march t., run t., hunt t. 706vb., *co-operate*; be consistent, be logical, hang t., hold t. 475vb. *be reasonable*; seek accord, treat, negotiate, come to terms 766vb. *make terms*; get on with, hit it off, fraternize, make friends 880vb. *befriend*; sing together, choir 413vb. *sing*; be natural, behave naturally, act one's nature.

adjust, make adjustments 654vb. *rectify*; render accordant etc.adj.; readjust, repair 656vb. *restore*; fit, suit, adapt, accommodate, conform; attune, tune, tune up, pitch, string 410vb. *harmonize*; modulate, tune in; regulate 60vb. *order*; graduate, proportion 12vb. *correlate*; dress, align, size 62vb. *arrange*; balance 28vb. *equalize*; cut, trim 31vb. *compensate*; tailor, make to measure; concert; synchronize.

Adv. *pertinently* etc.adj.; à propos of; in register; in the right context.

See: 9, 12, 13, 16, 18, 28, 31, 45, 50, 60, 62, 83, 106, 123, 137, 178, 181, 410, 412, 413, 475, 488, 494, 575, 642, 654, 656, 694, 706, 710, 719, 758, 765, 766, 770, 844, 880.

25 Disagreement

N. *disagreement*, disaccord; non-agreement, failure to agree, agreement to disagree 489n. *dissent*; dissidence 84n. *unconformity*; divergent opinions, conflict of opinion, controversy, argumentation 475n. *argument*; wrangle, wrangling, bickering 709n. *quarrel*; disunion, disunity, faction 709n. *dissension*; jarring, clash 279n. *collision*; challenge 711n. *defiance*,

rupture, breach 718n. *war*; variance, divergence, discrepancy 15n. *difference*; two voices, ambiguity, ambivalence 518n. *equivocalness*; variety 437n. *variegation*; opposition, contradiction, conflict 14n. *contrariety*; dissonance, discordance, disharmony, inharmoniousness, tunelessness 411n. *discord*; non-coincidence, incongruence, incongruity 10n. *irrelation*; disparity 29n. *inequality*; disproportion, asymmetry 246n. *distortion*; unconformability, incompatibility, irreconcilability, hostility 881n. *enmity*; lack of sympathy 861n. *dislike*; interference 702n. *hindrance*. *inaptitude*, unfitness, incapacity, incompetence 695n. *unskilfulness*; unfittingness, impropriety 643n. *inexpedience*; inconcinnity 576n. *inelegance*; inapplicability, inadmissibility, irrelevancy 10n. *irrelevance*; intrusiveness, intrusion, interruption, untimeliness 138n. *intempestivity*; inconsistency 17n. *non-uniformity*; maladjustment, incompatibility, unconformability 84n. *unconformity*.
misfit, maladjustment, bad fit; bad match, misalliance, mésalliance 894n. *marriage*; misjoinder; syncretism; oxymoron; paradox; incongruity, false note, jar 411n. *discord*; fish out of water, square peg in a round hole; outsider, foreigner, foreign body 59n. *intruder*; joker, odd man out, sport 84n. *abnormality*; eccentric, oddity 851n. *laughing stock*; ass in a lion's skin 501n. *fool*.
Adj. *disagreeing*, dissenting, unagreed, not unanimous 489adj. *dissenting*; challenging 711adj. *defiant*; at odds, at cross purposes, at variance; at loggerheads, at war 718adj. *warring*; bickering, snapping 709 adj. *quarrelling*; hostile, antagonistic 881 adj. *inimical*; uncongenial, antipathetic, repulsive, nauseating 861adj. *disliked*; contrarious, conflicting, clashing, contradictory 14adj. *contrary*; unnatural, against one's nature; inconsistent 17adj. *non-uniform*; inconsonant, incompatible, irreducible 84adj. *unconformable*; exceptional, outstanding 84adj. *abnormal*; odd, foreign 59adj. *extraneous*; not combining, not mixing; incommensurable 10adj. *irrelative*; disproportionate, disproportioned, out of proportion, unsymmetrical 246adj. *distorted*; inharmonious, grating 411adj. *discordant*; mismatched, misallied, misjoined; ill-matching, ill-

matched, ill-assorted, ill-combined; discrepant 15adj. *different*; incongruous 497 adj. *absurd*.
unapt, inept, incapable, incompetent 695 adj. *unskilful*; unfitted, unsuited, illadapted, maladjusted 695adj. *clumsy*; wrong, unfit, unfitting, unsuitable, unbecoming, not for one, improper, inappropriate 643adj. *inexpedient*; impracticable 470adj. *impossible*; ineligible 607 adj. *rejected*; intrusive, not wanted, inopportune, unseasonable 138adj. *untimely*; mal-à-propos, inapplicable, inadmissible 10adj. *irrelevant*; unidiomatic 576adj. *inelegant*; out of character, out of keeping; misplaced, out of place, out of joint, out of tune, out of time, out of step, out of phase.
Vb. *disagree* 489vb. *dissent*; differ, dispute 475vb. *argue*; jar, jangle, bicker 709vb. *quarrel*; clash, conflict, collide, contradict 14vb. *be contrary*; be discrepant,—unapt etc. adj.; not play, non-cooperate 702vb. *hinder*; have nothing to do with 10vb. *be unrelated*; come amiss, interfere, intrude, butt in 138vb. *mistime*.
mismatch, mismate, misjoin; misadapt, misfit, misadjust; miscast; mistime.
Adv. *in defiance of*, in contempt of, despite, in spite of; discordantly etc. adj.
See: 10, 14, 15, 17, 29, 59, 84, 138, 246, 279, 411, 437, 470, 475, 489, 497, 501, 518, 576, 607, 643, 695, 702, 709, 711, 718, 851, 861, 881, 894.

26 Quantity

N. *quantity*, amount, sum 38n. *addition*; total 52n. *whole*; magnitude, amplitude, extent 465n. *measurement*; mass, substance, bulk 195n. *size*; dimension, dimensions, longitude 203n. *length*; width, thickness 205n. *breadth*; altitude 209n. *height*; deepness 211n. *depth*; area, volume, extension 183n. *space*; weight 322n. *gravity*, 323n. *levity*; strength, force, flow, potential, pressure, tension, stress, strain, torque 160n. *energy*; numbers 104n. *multitude*; quotient, fraction, multiple, function, quantic, vector 85n. *number*, 86n. *mathematics*, 101n. *plurality*, 102n. *fraction*, 103n. *zero*, 107 n. *infinity*; mean, median 30n. *average*.

finite quantity, limited amount, definite figure; lower limit, upper l., ceiling 236n. *limit*; definite amount, quantum, quotum, quota, quorum; measured quantity, measure, dose, dosage 465n. *measurement*; avoirdupois 322n. *weighment*; ration, whack, take 783n. *portion*; pittance, driblet, cupful, spoonful, thimbleful; capful, bagful, sackful; whole amount, lot, batch, boiling; lock, stock and barrel 52n. *whole*; large amount, masses, heaps 32n. *great quantity*; small amount, bit 33n. *small quantity*; greater amount, more, most, majority 36 n. *increase*, 104n. *greater number*; smaller amount, less, not so much 37n. *decrease*, 39n. *subduction*, 105n. *fewness*; stint, piece, task 682n. *labour*.

Adj. *quantitative*, some, certain, any, more or less; quantified, measured.

Vb. *quantify*, express the quantity, allot, rate, ration 783vb. *apportion*.

Adv. *to the amount of*; to the sum of, to the tune of; to such an extent.

See: 30, 32, 33, 36, 37, 38, 39, 52, 85, 86, 101, 102, 103, 104, 105, 107, 160, 183, 195, 203, 205, 209, 211, 236, 322, 323, 465, 682, 783.

station, status, standing, footing 8n. *circumstance*; gradualism, gradualness 278n. *slowness*.

Adj. *gradational*, hierarchical, graduated, scalar, calibrated, graded, scaled; gradual, shading off, tapering; fading, fading out.

comparative, relative, proportional, in scale 9adj. *relative*; within the bounds of 236 adj. *limited*; measured by.

Vb. *graduate*, rate, class, rank 73vb. *grade*; scale, calibrate; compare, measure.

shade off, taper, die away, pass into, melt into, change gradually, dissolve, fade, fade out; raise by degrees 36vb. *augment*; lower by degrees 37vb. *bate*; whittle down, pare, trim 204vb. *shorten*.

Adv. *by degrees*, gradually, little by little, step by step, drop by drop, bit by bit, inch by inch; by inches, by slow degrees; in some degree, in slight measure; to some extent, just a bit; however little, however much.

See: 8, 9, 12, 15, 26, 36, 37, 73, 77, 86, 183, 187, 204, 209, 211, 236, 265, 278, 308, 410, 452, 462, 465, 547, 725, 733, 783.

27 Degree: relative quantity

N. *degree*, relative quantity, proportion, ratio, scale 12n. *correlation*, 462n. *comparison*; standard, stint 183n. *measure*; amplitude, extent, intensity, frequency, magnitude, size 26n. *quantity*; level, pitch, altitude 209n. *height*, 211n. *depth*; key, register 410n. *musical note*; reach, compass, scope 183n. *range*; rate, tenor, way, speed 265n. *motion*; gradation, graduation, calibration 15n. *differentiation*; differential, shade, nuance; grade, remove, stepping-stone; step, rung, round, tread, stair 308n. *ascent*; point, stage, milestone, turning point, crisis 8n. *juncture*; climax 725n. *completion*; mark, peg, notch, score 547n. *indicator*; bar, line, interval 410n. *notation*; valuation, value 465n. *measurement*; ranking, grading 77n. *classification*; class, kind 77n. *sort*; rank, grade 73n. *serial place*; military rank, lieutenancy, captaincy, majority, colonelcy; hierarchy 733n. *authority*; place, position, situation 187n. *location*; sphere,

28 Equality: sameness of quantity or degree

N. *equality*, same quality, same degree; parity, co-equality, co-extension, coincidence 24n. *agreement*; symmetry, balance, poise; evenness, level 258n. *smoothness*, 216n. *horizontality*; equability, monotony 16n. *uniformity*; roundness 250n. *circularity*; impartiality 913n. *justice*.

equivalence, likeness 18n. *similarity*; sameness 13n. *identity*, 219n. *parallelism*; interchangeability 151n. *interchange*; equipollence, isotropy, isotropism, isotopism; synonymity, synonym; reciprocation, exchange, fair e. 791n. *barter*; par, quits; equivalent, value, fair v., just price, ransom 809n. *price*; not a pin to choose, six of one and half a dozen of the other, distinction without a difference; level bet, even money; equation.

equilibrium, equipoise, equiponderance, stable equilibrium, balance; even keel, steadiness, uprightness; state of equilibrium, balance of forces, balance of

power, balance of trade; deadlock, stalemate 145 n. *cessation*; status quo, stable state, equilibration, homeostasis; roadholding ability 153 n. *stability*; sea-legs, seat; fin, aileron 153 n. *stabilizer*; balance, equilibrant; equilibrist, tight-rope walker, rope-dancer 162 n. *athlete.*

equalization, equation, equiparation, equilibration; weighing 322 n. *weighment*; co-ordination, adjustment, re-a., levelling up, levelling down 656 n. *restoration*, 31 n. *compensation*; going halves, equal division 92 n. *bisection*, 775 n. *participation*; reciprocity 12 n. *correlation*; tit for tat 714 n. *retaliation*, 910 n. *revenge*; equalizer, counterpoise 31 n. *offset*; equator 92 n. *dividing line*; equalization fund; standardizer, bed of Procrustes; return match, second m., second chance.

draw, drawn game, drawn battle, dingdong; level-pegging; tie, dead heat; no decision, stalemate, deadlock; neck and neck race, photo finish; love all, fifteen etc. all, deuce; near thing, narrow margin 200 n. *nearness.*

compeer, peer, equal, coequal, match, mate, twin; fellow, brother 18 n. *analogue*; equivalent, parallel, opposite number, shadow; rival, corrival, competitor 716 n. *contender.*

Adj. *equal,* equi-, iso-, co-; same 13 adj. *identical*; like 18 adj. *similar*; neither more nor less, coequal, co-ordinate, coextensive, coincident, congruent, homologous 24 adj. *agreeing*; equiponderant, equipondious; equipollent; equidistant; isoperimetric; isotropic; balanced, in equilibrium, equipendent; homeostatic, steady, stable 153 adj. *fixed*; even, level, round, square, flush 258 vb. *smooth*; symmetrical, even-sided, equilateral, regular 16 adj. *uniform*; equable, unvarying, monotonous, ding-dong 153 adj. *unchangeable*; competitive, rival 716 adj. *contending*; matched, drawn, tied; parallel, level-pegging, running level, abreast, neck-and-neck; equalized, bracketed; sharing, co-sharing; equally divided, half-and-half, fifty-fifty; impartial, democratic 913 adj. *just*; on equal terms, on the same footing, on a par, on a level; par, quits.

equivalent, comparable, parallel, interchangeable, synonymous, virtual, convertible; corresponding, reciprocal 12 adj. *correlative*; as good as, no better, no

worse; tantamount, virtually the same, indistinguishable; much the same, all the s., all one, as broad as it is long 18 adj. *similar*; worth, valued at, priced at, standing at 809 adj. *priced.*

Vb. *be equal,* equal, countervail, counterpoise, compensate 31 vb. *set off*; add nothing, detract n., make no difference, come to the same thing, coincide with, agree w. 24 vb, *accord*; be equal to, measure up to, reach, touch; cope with 160 vb. *be able*; make the grade, pass muster 635 vb. *suffice*; hold one's own, keep up with, keep pace w., run abreast, be level; parallel 219 vb. *be parallel*; match, twin 18 vb. *resemble*; tie, draw, halve the match; break even; make it all square; leave no remainder; go halves, go shares 775 vb. *participate.*

equalize, equiparate, equate 322 vb. *weigh*; bracket, match; parallel 462 vb. *compare*; balance, strike a b., poise; trim, dress, square, round off, make flush 258 vb. *smooth*, 16 vb. *make uniform*; fit, accommodate, readjust 24 vb. *adjust*; add a makeweight, counterpoise 31 vb. *set off*; give points to, handicap 31 vb. *compensate*; equilibrate, equilibrize, restore to equilibrium 153 vb. *stabilize*; right oneself, ride steady, keep one's balance, hold the road.

Adv. *equally* etc. adj.; pari passu, ceteris paribus; at the same rate; to all intents and purposes, as good as; au pair, on equal terms; in equilibrium; on an even keel.

See: 12, 13, 16, 18, 24, 31, 92, 145, 151, 153, 160, 162, 200, 216, 219, 250, 258, 322, 462, 635, 656, 714, 716, 775, 791, 809, 910, 913.

29 Inequality: difference of degree or quality

N. *inequality,* difference of degree 34 n. *superiority*, 35 n. *inferiority*; irregularity 17 n. *non-uniformity*; variability, patchiness 437 n. *variegation*; disproportion, asymmetry 246 n. *distortion*, 25 n. *disagreement*; oddness, oddity, skewness, lop-sidedness 220 n. *obliquity*; imparity, disparity 15 n. *difference*; unlikeness 19 n. *dissimilarity*; disequilibrium, unstable

equilibrium, imbalance, unbalance; dizziness, staggers; inclination of balance, tilting of the scales, preponderance, overweight, top-hamper 322 n. *gravity*; underweight, short weight, lack of ballast 323 n. *levity*; defect, shortcoming, inadequacy 636 n. *insufficiency*; odds 17 n. *differential*; makeweight, counterpoise 31 n. *offset*; grace marks 40 n. *extra*; casting vote 605 n. *choice*; partiality 481 n. *bias*, 914 n. *injustice*.

Adj. *unequal*, disparate, incongruent 15 adj. *different*, 25 adj. *disagreeing*, 19 adj. *dissimilar*; unique, unequalled 34 adj. *superior*, 644 adj. *excellent*; below par 35 adj. *inferior*; disproportionate, disproportioned, asymmetrical 246 adj. *distorted*; irregular, scalene, lop-sided 17 adj. *nonuniform*; askew, awry 220 adj. *sloping*; odd, uneven 84 adj. *uncomformable*; unequable, variable, patchy 437 adj. *variegated*; deficient, defective, falling short, inadequate 636 adj. *insufficient*; underweight, in ballast 323 adj. *light*; overweight 322 adj. *heavy*; in disequilibrium, unbalanced, swinging, swaying, rocking 217 adj. *pendent*; untrimmed, unballasted, uncounterpoised, uncompensated; overweighted, top-heavy, unwieldy 695 adj. *clumsy*; listing, leaning, canting, heeling 220 adj. *oblique*; overbalanced, losing balance, dizzy, toppling, falling 309 adj. *descending*; capsizing 221 adj. *inverted*; partial, unfair 914 adj. *unjust*, 481 adj. *biased*; undemocratic 871 adj. *proud*.

Vb. *be unequal*, be mismatched 25 vb. *disagree*; not balance, not equate, leave a remainder 15 vb. *differ*; fall short 35 vb. *be inferior*; preponderate, have the advantage, give points to, overtop, outclass, outrank 34 vb. *be superior*; outstrip 306 vb. *outdo*; be deficient 636 vb. *not suffice*; lag 136 vb. *be late*; overcompensate, overweight, tip the scale 322 vb. *weigh*; kick the beam, need a makeweight 323 vb. *be light*; throw the casting vote; overbalance, capsize 221 vb. *be inverted*; list, tilt, lean 220 vb. *be oblique*; rock, swing, sway 317 vb. *fluctuate*; vary 143 vb. *change*.

Adv. *unevenly* etc. adj.

See: 15, 17, 19, 25, 31, 34, 35, 40, 84, 136, 143, 217, 220, 221, 246, 306, 309, 317, 322, 323, 437, 481, 605, 636, 644, 695, 871, 914.

30 Mean

N. *average*, medium, mean, median; intermedium, middle term 73 n. *serial place*; balance; happy medium, golden mean 177 n. *moderation*; standard product 79 n. *generality*; ruck, ordinary run, run of the mill 732 n. *mediocrity*; norm 81 n. *rule*; the normal 610 n. *habit*.

middle point, mediety, half way 70 n. *middle*; middle distance, middle age; middle of the road, mid-way, middle course 625 n. *mid-course*; splitting the difference 770 n. *compromise*; neutrality 606 *no choice*; central position 225 n. *centre*.

middle class, bourgeoisie, bourgeois, black-coat worker, white-collar w., salaried class 732 n. *mediocrity*.

common man 869 n. *commoner*; everywoman, man-in-the-street, little man, ordinary m., plain m. 79 n. *everyman*; typical individual, average specimen 732 n. *mediocrity*.

Adj. *median*, mean, average, medial 70 adj. *middle*, 225 adj. *central*; neither hot nor cold, lukewarm; intermediate, grey; normal, standard, ordinary, commonplace, middling, fifty-fifty, much of a muchness, mediocre; moderate, neutral, middle-of-the-road; middle class, middle-grade, bourgeois.

Vb. *average out*, average, take the mean, keep to the middle; split the difference, go half way 770 vb. *compromise*; strike a balance, pair off 28 vb. *equalize*.

Adv. *on an average*, in the long run 79 adv. *generally*; on the whole, all in all; taking one thing with another, taking all things together; in round numbers.

See: 28, 70, 73, 79, 81, 177, 225, 606, 610, 625, 732, 770, 869.

31 Compensation

N. *compensation*, weighting 28 n. *equalization*; rectification, recovery, break-back, come-b. 654 n. *amendment*; reaction, neutralization, nullification 182 n., *counteraction*; commutation 151 n. *interchange*, 150 n. *substitution*; redemption, recoupment, recovery; retrieval 771 n. *acquisition*; indemnification, reparation 787 n. *restitution*, 656 n. *restoration*; amends, expiation 941 n. *atonement*;

recompense, repayment 962 n. *reward*, 910 n. *revenge*, 714 n. *retaliation*; reciprocity, measure for measure 12 n. *correlation*. *offset*, set-off, allowance, makeweight, balance, casting weight, counterweight, counterpoise, counterbalance, ballast 28 n. *equalization*; indemnity, reparations, costs, damages 787 n. *restitution*; amends 741 n. *atonement*; penance 939 n. *penitence*; equivalent, quid pro quo, cover, collateral 150 n. *substitute*; counterclaim, cross demand 627 n. *requirement*; counter-blow 713 n. *defence*; counterattraction 291 n. *attraction*; concession, cession 770 n. *compromise*; bribe, hush money, tribute 804 n. *payment*, 962 n. *reward*.

Adj. *compensatory*, compensating, countervailing, balancing 28 adj. *equivalent*; self-correcting, self-cancelling; indemnificatory, in damages, restitutory 787 adj. *restoring*; amendatory, expiatory 741 adj. *atoning*; in the opposite scale, weighed against 462 adj. *compared*.

Vb. *compensate*, offer compensation, make amends, make compensation etc. n.; do penance 941 vb. *atone*; indemnify, restore, pay back 787 vb. *restitute*; make good, make up, make up for, do instead 150 vb. *substitute*; add a makeweight, ballast; pay, repay 714 vb. *retaliate*; bribe, square 762 vb. *reward*; overcompensate, lean over backwards.

set off, offset, allow for; counterpoise, countervail, balance 28 vb. *equalize*; neutralize, cancel, nullify 182 vb. *counteract*; cover, hedge 858 vb. *be cautious*; give and take, concede, cede 770 vb. *compromise*.

recoup, recover 656 vb. *retrieve*; make up lee-way, take up the slack; indemnify oneself, take back, get back 786 vb. *take*; make a come-back 656 vb. *be restored*.

Adv. *in return*, in consideration, in compensation, in lieu; though, although; at the same time, on the other hand; nevertheless, regardless of; despite, maugre, for all that, notwithstanding; but, still, even so, be that as it may; after all, allowing for; when all is said and done, taking one thing with another; at least, at all events, at any rate.

See: 12, 28, 150, 151, 182, 291, 462, 627, 654, 656, 713, 714, 741, 762, 770, 771, 786, 787, 804, 858, 910, 939, 941, 962.

32 Greatness

N. *greatness*, largeness, bigness, girth 195 n. *size*: large scale, generous proportions, outsize dimensions, vastness, enormousness, gigantism 195 n. *hugeness*; muchness, abundance 635 n. *plenty*; amplitude, ampleness, fulness, plenitude, maximum 54 n. *completeness*; superabundance, superfluity, more than enough 637 n. *redundance*; immoderation 176 n. *violence*; exorbitance, excessiveness, excess 546 n. *exaggeration*; enormity, immensity, boundlessness 107 n. *infinity*; numerosity, numerousness, countlessness 104 n. *multitude*; dimensions, magnitude 26 n. *quantity*, 27 n. *degree*; extension, extent 203 n. *length*, 205 n. *breadth*, 209 n. *height*, 211 n. *depth*; expanse, area, volume, capacity 183 n. *space*; spaciousness, roominess 183 n. *room*; mightiness, might, strength, intensity 160 n. *power*, 178 n. *influence*; intensification, magnification, multiplication 197 n. *expansion*; aggrandizement 36 n. *increase*; seriousness 638 n. *importance*; eminence 34 n. *superiority*; grandeur, grandness 868 n. *nobility*, 871 n. *pride*; majesty 733 n. *authority*; fame, renown 866 n. *repute*; noise, din 400 n. *loudness*.

great quantity, muchness, galore 635 n. *plenty*; crop, harvest, profusion, abundance, productivity 171 n. *productiveness*; superfluity, superabundance, flood, spring-tide, spate 637 n. *redundance*, 350 n. *stream*; expanse, sheet, sea, ocean, world, universe, sight of, world of, power of; much, lot, whole l., fat l., deal, good d., great d.; not a little, not peanuts; too much, more than one bargained for; stock, mint, mine 632 n. *store*; quantity, peck, bushel, pints, gallons; lump, heap, mass, stack 74 n. *accumulation*; packet, pack, load, full l., cargo, shipload, boatload, trainload, carload, wagonload, truckload, sackload 193 n. *contents*; quantities, lots, lashings, oodles, scads, wads, pots, bags; heaps, loads, masses, stacks; oceans, seas, floods, streams; volumes, reams, pages; numbers, not a few, quite a f., crowds, masses, hosts, swarms, multitudes 104 n. *multitude*; all, entirety, corpus 52 n. *whole*.

main part, almost all, principal part, best p., essential p. 52 n. *chief part*; greater part,

major p., majority 104n. *greater number*; body, bulk, mass 3n. *substance*; soul 1n. *essence*.

Adj. *great*, greater, main, most, major 34 adj. *superior*; maximum, greatest 34 adj. *supreme*; grand, big, mickle 195 adj. *large*; fair-sized, largish, biggish, pretty big; substantial, considerable, respectable; sizeable, of size, large-s., full-s., man-s.; bulky, massy, massive, heavy 322 adj. *weighty*; prolonged, lengthy 203 adj. *long*; wide, thick 205 adj. *broad*; ample, generous, voluminous, capacious 183 adj. *spacious*; profound 211 adj. *deep*; great in stature, tall, lofty, towering, mountainous, alpine 209 adj. *high*; great in strength, Herculean 162 adj. *strong*; mighty 160 adj. *powerful*, 178 adj. *influential*; intense 174 adj. *vigorous*; noisy 400 adj. *loud*; soaring, mounting, climbing 308 adj. *ascending*, 197 adj. *expanded*; culminating, at the maximum, at the peak, at the top, at its height, in the zenith, at the limit, at the summit 213 adj. *topmost*; great in quantity, plentiful, abundant, overflowing 635 adj. *plenteous*; superabundant 637 adj. *redundant*; great in number, many, swarming, teeming 104 adj. *multitudinous*; great in age, antique, ancient, venerable, immemorial 127 adj. *olden*, 131 adj. *aged*; great in honour, imperial, august, goodly, precious, of value 644 adj. *valuable*, 868 adj. *noble*; sublime, exalted 821 adj. *impressive*; glorious, worshipful, famed, famous 866 adj. *renowned*; grave, solemn, serious 638 adj. *important*; excelling, excellent 306 adj. *surpassing*, 644 adj. *best*.

extensive, ranging, far-flying, far-flung, far-reaching, far-stretching 183 adj. *spacious*; wide-spread, prevalent, epidemic; world-wide, universal, cosmic; mass, indiscriminate, wholesale, whole-hogging, all-embracing, comprehensive 78 adj. *inclusive*.

enormous, immense, vast, colossal, giant, gigantic, monumental, massive 195 adj. *huge*; record, record-breaking, record-smashing, excelling 306 adj. *surpassing*.

prodigious, marvellous, astounding, amazing, astonishing 864 adj. *wonderful*; fabulous, incredible, unbelievable, passing belief 486 adj. *unbelieved*, 472 adj. *improbable*, 470 adj. *impossible*; stupendous, terrific, frightful 854 adj. *frightening*;

breath-taking, overwhelming, out of this world 821 adj. *impressive*.

remarkable, signal, noticeable, worth looking at 866 adj. *noteworthy*; outstanding, extraordinary, exceptional, uncommon 84 adj. *unusual*; eminent, distinguished, marked, of mark 648 adj. *notable*.

whopping, whacking, thumping, thundering, rattling, howling, screaming, swingeing; father and mother of; hefty, tall, hulking, strapping, overgrown, clumsy 195 adj. *unwieldy*.

flagrant, flaring, glaring, stark, staring; signal, shocking 867 adj. *disreputable*; red hot, white hot, burning 379 adj. *fiery*.

unspeakable, unutterable, indescribable, indefinable, ineffable; beyond expression, past speaking 517 adj. *inexpressible*.

exorbitant, harsh, stringent, severe 735 adj. *oppressive*; excessive, exceeding, passing, extreme 306 adj. *surpassing*; monstrous, outrageous, swingeing, unconscionable; unbearable 827 adj. *intolerable*; inordinate, preposterous, extravagant 546 adj. *exaggerated*; beyond the limit, going too far, far-going.

consummate 54 adj. *complete*; finished, flawless 646 adj. *perfect*; entire, sound 52 adj. *whole*; thorough, thorough-paced, thorough-going; whole-hogging, utter, out and out, arch, crass, gross, arrant, regular, downright, desperate, unmitigated; far gone.

absolute, the veriest; essential, positive, unequivocal; stark, pure, mere 44 adj. *unmixed*; unlimited, unrestricted 107 adj. *infinite*; undiminished, unabated, unreduced.

Vb. *be great*—large, etc. adj.; bulk, bulk large, loom, loom up; stretch 183 n. *extend*; tower, soar, mount 308 vb. *ascend*; scale, transcend 34 vb. *be superior*; clear, overtop; exceed, know no bounds, run to extremes, go off the deep end 306 vb. *overstep*; enlarge 36 vb. *augment*; 197 vb. *expand*; swamp, overwhelm 727 vb. *defeat*.

Adv. *positively*, verily, veritably, actually, indeed, in fact 494 adv. *truly*; seriously, indubitably, in all conscience 473 adv. *certainly*; decidedly, absolutely, finally, unequivocally, without equivocation; directly, specifically, unreservedly; essentially, fundamentally, radically;

downright, plumb; flagrantly, blatantly, emphatically.

greatly, much, well; passing, very, right; very much, mighty, ever so; fully, quite, entirely, utterly, without reservation 52 adv. *wholly*, 54 adv. *completely*; thoroughly, by wholesale; widely, extensively, universally 79 adv. *generally*; largely, mainly, mostly, to a large extent; considerably, fairly, pretty, pretty well; a deal, a great d., ever so much, never so m.; increasingly, more than ever, doubly, trebly; specially, particularly; exceptionally; on a large scale, in a big way; vastly, hugely, enormously, gigantically, colossally; heavily, strongly, powerfully, mightily 178 adv. *influentially*; actively, strenuously, intensely; closely, narrowly, intensively, zealously, fanatically, hotly, bitterly, fiercely; acutely, sharply, shrewdly, exquisitely; enough, more than e., abundantly, profusely; generously, richly, worthily, magnificently, splendidly, nobly; supremely, pre-eminently, superlatively; rarely, unusually, wonderfully, strangely; indefinitely, immeasurably, incalculably, infinitely, unspeakably, ineffably; awfully, badly.

extremely, ultra, to extremes, to the limit, without a l., no end of; beyond measure, beyond all bounds; beyond comparison, beyond compare; overly, unduly, improperly, to a fault; out of all proportion, out of all whooping; bitterly, harshly, cruelly, unconscionably, with a vengeance 735 adj. *severely*; immoderately, uncontrollably, desperately, madly, frantically, furiously, fanatically, bitterly 176 adv. *violently*; exceedingly, excessively, exorbitantly, inordinately, preposterously; foully, abominably, grossly, beastly, monstrously, horribly; confoundedly, deucedly, devilishly, damnably, hellishly; tremendously, terribly, fearfully; finally, irretrievably; unforgiveably, mortally.

remarkably, noticeably, markedly, pointedly; sensibly, feelingly; notably, strikingly, signally, emphatically, prominently, glaringly, flagrantly, blatantly; publicly 400 adv. *loudly*; eminently, pre-e., egregriously; singularly, peculiarly 80 adv. *specially*; curiously, oddly, queerly, strangely, uncommonly, unusually 84 adv. *unconformably*; surprisingly,

astonishingly, amazingly, incredibly, marvellously, magically 864 adv. *wonderfully*; awfully, tremendously, stupendously, fearfully, frighteningly; excitedly, impressively.

painfully, unsparingly, till it hurts; badly, bitterly, hard; seriously, sorely, grievously; sadly, miserably, wretchedly; distressingly, pitiably, piteously, woefully, lamentably; shrewdly, cruelly; savagely; exquisitely, excruciatingly, shockingly, frightfully, dreadfully, terribly, horribly, frighteningly; banefully, poisonously, balefully, mortally.

See: 3, 26, 27, 34, 36, 52, 54, 74, 78, 79, 84, 104, 107, 127, 131, 160, 162, 171, 174, 176, 178, 183, 193, 195, 197, 203, 205, 209, 211, 213, 306, 308, 322, 350, 379, 400, 470, 472, 473, 486, 494, 517, 546, 632, 635, 637, 638, 644, 646, 727, 733, 735, 821, 827, 854, 864, 866, 867, 868, 871.

33 Smallness

N. *smallness*, exiguousness, exiguity, scantiness, moderateness, moderation; small size, diminutiveness, minuteness 196 n. *littleness*; brevity 204 n. *shortness*; leanness, meagreness 206 n. *thinness*; rarefaction 325 n. *rarity*; briefness, momentariness 114 n. *transientness*; paucity 105 n. *fewness*; rareness, sparseness, sparsity 140 n. *infrequency*; scarceness, scarcity 636 n. *insufficiency*, 307 n. *shortcoming*; small means 801 n. *poverty*; pettiness, insignificance, meanness 639 n. *unimportance*, 35 n. *inferiority*; averageness 30 n. *average*, 732 n. *mediocrity*; no depth 212 n. *shallowness*; tenuity 4 n. *insubstantiality*; compression, abbreviation, abridgment 198 n. *contraction*; diminution 37 n. *decrease*; vanishing point, nothingness 2 n. *nonexistence*, 103 n. *zero*, 444 n. *invisibility*.

small quantity, modicum, minimum 26 n. *finite quantity*; minutiæ, trivia; detail, petty detail 80 n. *particulars*; nutshell 592 n. *compendium*; drop in the bucket, drop in the ocean; homœopathic dose, trifling amount 639 n. *trifle*; thimbleful, spoonful, mouthful, capful; trickle, dribble, sprinkling, sprinkle, dash, splash; tinge, tincture, trace, spice, smack, smell, lick; nuance, soupçon, thought, suggestion, shade,

shadow, touch, cast; spark, scintilla, gleam, flash; pinch, snatch; snack, sip, bite, mite, morsel, sop; scantling, dole, iron ration; fragment 53n. *piece*; whit, bit, mite; iota, jot, tittle; ounce, penny-weight, grain, scruple, minim 322n. *weighment*; inch, millimetre 200n. *short distance*; second, moment 116n. *instant*; vanishing point, next to nothing, hardly anything, just enough to swear by; the shadow of a shade 4n. *insubstantial thing*.

small thing 196n. *miniature*; dot, stop, point, pinpoint; dab, spot, fleck, speck, mote, smut; grain, granule, seed, crumb, groats 332n. *powder*; drop, droplet, driblet, gout; thread, shred, rag, tatter, fritters, fragment 53n. *piece*; cantlet, scrap, flinders, smithereens; flake, snip, snippet, gobbet, small slice, finger; flitters, confetti; chip, clipping, paring, shaving; shiver, sliver, slip; pinprick, snick, prick, nick; hair 208n. *filament*.

small coin, cent, nickel, dime; groat, farthing, half-farthing, nap, mite, widow's m.; sou, centime, doit, stiver, anna, pice, pie, cowrie, bean, cash 797n. *coinage*.

small animal 196n. *animalcule*; grub, tit, whippet; homunculus, atomy, mite, dwarf, midget, Tom Thumb, minimus, minikin, mannikin.

particle, material point, corpuscle; atom, electron, positron, proton, neutron; meson, neutrino, hyperion, mucon; anti-particle, anti-proton, anti-electron; molecule, photon; ion, cation, anion.

Adj. *small*, exiguous, not much, moderate, modest, homeopathic, minimal, infinitesimal; microscopic, ultra-m. 444adj. *invisible*; tiny, weeny, wee, minute, diminutive, miniature 196adj. *little*; smaller 35adj. *lesser*; least, minimum; small-sized, small-framed, small-boned, under-sized 196adj. *dwarfish*; slim, slender, lean, meagre, thin 206adj. *narrow*; slight, feeble, puny 163adj. *weak*; delicate, dainty, minikin, fragile 330adj. *brittle*; not heavy, weightless 323adj. *light*; fine, subtle, rarefied 325adj. *rare*; quiet, not loud, soft, low, faint, hushed 401adj. *muted*; not tall, squat 210adj. *low*; not long, brief, skimpy, abbreviated 204adj. *short*; shortened, abridged, cut, compact, compendious, thumbnail 198adj. *contracted*; scanty, scant, scarce 307adj.

deficient; dribbling, trickling 636adj. *insufficient*; reduced, limited, restricted 747adj. *restrained*; declining, ebbing, at low ebb 37adj. *decreasing*; below par, off peak, below the mark 35adj. *inferior*; less, lesser, least.

inconsiderable, minor, light-weight, trifling, petty, paltry, insignificant 639adj. *unimportant*; not many, soon counted, mighty few 105adj. *few*; inappreciable, unnoticeable 444adj. *invisible*; shadowy, tenuous, evanescent 446adj. *disappearing*, 114adj. *transient*; marginal, negligible 458 adj. *neglected*; slight, superficial, cursory 4adj. *insubstantial*; skin-deep 212adj. *shallow*; average, middling, fair, fairish, so-so 30adj. *median*; moderate, modest, humble, tolerable, passable 732adj. *mediocre*; not much of a, no great shakes, beta minus 35adj. *inferior*; no more than, just, only, mere, bare; plain, simple 44 adj. *unmixed*.

Vb. *be small*, lie in a nutshell; stay small, not grow, have no size 196vb. *be little*; have no height 210vb. *be low*; have no depth; have no weight 323vb. *be light*; make no sound 401vb. *sound faint*; be less 307vb. *fall short*; get less 37vb. *decrease*; shrink 198vb. *become smaller*.

Adv. *slightly*, exiguously, to a small degree, little; lightly, softly, faintly; superficially, cursorily, grazingly; gradually, imperceptibly, insensibly, invisibly; on a small scale, in a small way, modestly, humbly; fairly, moderately, tolerably, quite; comparatively, relatively, rather, enough, well e.; indifferently, poorly, badly, miserably, wretchedly, dismally; hardly, scarcely, barely, only just; hardly at all, no more than; only, merely, purely, simply; at least, at the very least.

partially, to some degree, in some measure, to a certain extent; somehow, after a fashion, in a manner, some, a little, a bit, just a bit, ever so little, as little as maybe; not fully, restrictedly, limitedly, within bounds 55adv. *incompletely*; not wholly, in part 55adv. *partly*; not perfectly 647 adv. *imperfectly*.

almost, all but, within an ace of, within an inch of, on the brink of, on the verge of, within sight of, in a fair way to 200adv. *nigh*; near upon, close u., approximately 200adv. *nearly*; just short of, not quite, hardly, scarcely, barely.

about, somewhere, somewhere about, in the region of, thereabouts; on an average, more or less; near enough, a little more, a little less; at a guess, say.

in no way, no ways, no wise, by no means, not by any manner of means, in no respect, not at all, not in the least, not a bit, not a whit, not a jot, not a shadow, on no account.

See: 2, 4, 26, 30, 35, 37, 44, 53, 55, 80, 103, 105, 114, 116, 140, 163, 196, 198, 200, 204, 206, 208, 210, 212, 307, 322, 323, 325, 330, 332, 401, 444, 446, 458, 592, 636, 639, 647, 732, 747, 797, 801.

34 Superiority

N. *superiority*, superior elevation, higher position; altitude, loftiness, sublimity 209 n. *height*; transcendance 32 n. *greatness*, 306 n. *overstepping*; the tops 213 n. *summit*; quality, excellence 644 n. *goodness*; ne plus ultra 646 n. *perfection*; preferability 605 n. *choice*; primacy, pride of place, seniority 64 n. *precedence*, 119 n. *priority*; eminence, pre-eminence 866 n. *prestige*; higher rank, higher degree 27 n. *degree*, 868 n. *nobility, aristocracy*; overlordship, paramountcy, supremacy, sovereignty, majesty, imperium 733 n. *authority*; domination, predominance, hegemony 178 n. *influence*; directorship, leadership 689 n. *management*; prepollence, preponderance, prevalence 29 n. *inequality*; win, championship 727 n. *victory*; prominence 638 n. *importance*; one-upmanship 698 n. *cunning*, 727 n. *success*; excess, surplus 637 n. *superfluity*; climax, zenith, culmination 725 n. *completion*; maximum, top, peak, crest, crest of the wave; record, high, new h. 213 n. *summit*.

vantage, advantage, privilege, prerogative, favour 615 n. *benefit*; start, flying s., lead, commanding l., winning position; odds, points, bisque, pull, edge, bulge; command, upper hand, whip-h.; one up, something in hand, reserves; majority, the big battalions 104 n. *greater number*; lion's share, Benjamin's mess; leverage, scope 183 n. *room*; vantage ground, coign of vantage.

superior, superior person, superman, wonderman 644 n. *exceller*; better man, first choice 890 n. *favourite*; high-up, top people, best p. 638 n. *bigwig*; one's betters, nobility, aristocracy 868 n. *upper class*; overlord, lord's lord, suzerain 741 n. *master*; commander, chief, boss, prophet, guide 690 n. *leader*; foreman 690 n. *manager*; primate, president, chairman, prime minister, primus inter pares 690 n. *director*; model 646 n. *paragon*; star, top-sawyer 696 n. *proficient*; specialist 696 n. *expert*; world-beater 644 n. *exceller*; winner, prizewinner, prizeman, champion, cup-holder, record-h. 727 n. *victor*; prima donna, first lady, head boy; first-born, elder.

Adj. *superior*, more so; elative, comparative, superlative; major, greater 32 adj. *great*; upper, higher, senior, over, super; supernormal, above the average, in a different class 15 adj. *different*; better, a cut above 644 adj. *excellent*; competitive, more than a match for; one up, ahead, far a., streets a. 64 adj. *preceding*; prior, preferable, preferred, favourite 605 adj. *chosen*; record, a record for, exceeding, overtopping, vaulting, outmatching 306 adj. *surpassing*; on top, winning, victorious 727 adj. *successful*; outstanding, marked, distinguished, rare, not like the rest, not as others are, unusual 84 adj. *unconformable*; top-level, high-l. 689 adj. *directing*, 638 adj. *important*; commanding, in authority 733 adj. *ruling*; revised, reformed, bettered, all the better for 654 adj. *improved*; enlarged, enhanced 197 adj. *expanded*.

supreme, arch-, greatest 32 adj. *great*; highest, uppermost 213 adj. *topmost*; first, chief, foremost 64 adj. *preceding*; main, principal, leading, overruling, overriding, cardinal, capital 638 adj. *important*; excellent, best; superlative, super, champion, tip-top, first-rate, first-class, A1, front-rank, world-beating 644 adj. *best*; facile princeps, on top, top of the class, nulli secundus, second to none, none such; dominant, paramount, pre-eminent, sovereign, royal, every inch a king; incomparable, unrivalled, unparagoned, matchless, peerless, unparalleled, unequalled 29 adj. *unequal*; unapproached, unapproachable, inimitable 21 adj. *unimitated*; unsurpassed 306 adj. *surpassing*; without comparison, beyond compare, beyond criticism 646 adj. *per-*

fect; transcendent, transcendental, out of this world.
crowning, capping, culminating 725 adj. *completive*; climactic, maximal, maximum; record, record-breaking, best ever 644 adj. *best*.
Vb. *be superior*, transcend 10 vb. *be unrelated*; rise above, surmount, overtop, tower over, overlook, command 209 vb. *be high*; go beyond, outrange, outreach, overpass 306 vb. *overstep*; exceed, out-Herod Herod, beat the limit, take the pot, take the cake, take the biscuit; pass, surpass, beat the record, reach a new high; improve on, better, go one b., cap, trump, overtrump; show quality, shine, excel 644 vb. *be good*; assert one's superiority, be too much for; steal the show, outshine, eclipse, overshadow, throw into the shade, cut out; put another's nose out of joint, take the shine out of; score off, have the laugh on 851 n. *ridicule*; best, outrival, outmatch, outclass, outrank 306 vb. *outdo*; outplay, outpoint, outmanoeuvre, outwit 542 vb. *befool*; overtake, leave behind, lap 277 vb. *outstrip*; get the better of, worst, sit on, beat, beat hollow, knock into a cocked hat, beat all comers 727 vb. *defeat*; rise superior to, rise to the occasion.
predominate, 178 vb. *prevail*; preponderate, overbalance, overweigh, tip the scale, turn the s.; change the balance 29 vb. *be unequal*; override, sit on 178 vb. *prevail*; have the advantage, have the start of, have the whip-hand, have the upper h., have the edge on, have the bulge on; lead, hold the l., be up on, be one up.
come first, stand f., head the list 64 vb. *come before*; take precedence, play first fiddle 638 vb. *be important*; take the lead, lead the dance, lead the van 237 vb. *be in front*; lead, play the l., star 689 vb. *direct*.
culminate, come to a head 669 vb. *mature*; cap, crown all 213 vb. *crown*; rise to a peak; set a new record, reach a new high 725 vb. *climax*.
Adv. *beyond*, more, over; over the mark, above the m., above par, over the average; upwards of, in advance of; over and above; at the top of the scale, on the crest, at its height, at the peak, at an advantage.
eminently, egregiously, pre-eminently, sur-

passing, prominently, superlatively, supremely; above all, of all things; the most, to crown all, to cap all; par excellence; principally, especially, particularly, peculiarly; a fortiori, even more, all the m.; even, yea; still more, ever more, far and away.

See: 10, 15, 21, 27, 29, 32, 64, 84, 103, 119, 178, 183, 197, 209, 213, 237, 277, 306, 542, 605, 613, 637, 638, 644, 646, 654, 669, 689, 690, 696, 698, 725, 727, 733, 741, 851, 866, 868, 890.

35 Inferiority

N. *inferiority*, minority, inferior numbers 105 n. *fewness*; littleness 33 n. *smallness*; no record, second best; subordinacy, subordination, dependence 745 n. *subjection*; secondariness, supporting role, second fiddle 639 n. *unimportance*; lowliness, humbleness 872 n. *humility*; second rank, back seat, obscurity 419 n. *dimness*; commonness 869 n. *commonalty*; disadvantage, handicap 702 n. *hindrance*; faultiness, blemish, defect 647 n. *imperfection*; deficiency 307 n. *shortcoming*, 636 n. *insufficiency*; failure 728 n. *defeat*; poor quality 645 n. *badness*, 812 n. *cheapness*; vulgarity 847 n. *bad taste*; beggarliness, shabbiness 801 n. *poverty*; worsening, decline 655 n. *deterioration*; low record, low, minimum, lowest point, nadir, the bottom 214 n. *base*; depression, trough 210 n. *lowness*; flatness, level, plain 216 n. *horizontality*; averageness 732 n. *mediocrity*.
inferior, subordinate, subaltern, sub, underling, understrapper, assistant 703 n. *aider*; subsidiary 707 n. *auxiliary*; agent 755 n. *deputy*, 150 n. *substitute*; tool, pawn 628 n. *instrument*; follower, retainer 742 n. *dependant*; menial 742 n. *servant*; poor relation 639 n. *nonentity*; subject, underdog 742 n. *slave*; backbencher, private, other ranks, lower classes 869 n. *commonalty*; second, second best, second string, second fiddle, second-rater; bad second, poor s., also-ran; failure, reject 607 n. *rejection*; subman, animal; younger, junior.
Adj. *lesser*, less, minor 639 adj. *unimportant*; small 33 adj. *inconsiderable*; smaller, diminished 37 adj. *decreasing*; reduced

198 adj. *contracted*; least, smallest, minimal, minimum; lowest, bottommost 214 adj. *undermost*; minus 307 adj. *deficient. inferior*, lower, junior, under-, sub-; subordinate, subaltern, understrapping 742 adj. *serving*; subject, unfree, dependent, parasitical 745 adj. *subjected*; secondary, subsidiary, auxiliary 703 adj. *aiding*, 639 adj. *unimportant*; second, second-best, second-rate, second-rank 922 adj. *contemptible*; humble, lowly, low-level, menial; low-ranking, unclassified; subnormal, substandard, subgrade, C3 607 adj. *rejected*; slight, under-weight 323 adj. *light*; spoilt, marred, shop-soiled 655 adj. *deteriorated*; unsound, defective, patchy, unequal 647 adj. *imperfect*; failing 636 adj. *insufficient*; shoddy, nasty 645 adj. *bad*, 812 adj. *cheap*, 847 adj. *vulgar*; low, common, low-caste 869 adj. *plebeian*; scratch, makeshift 670 adj. *unprepared*; temporary, provisional 114 adj. *ephemeral*; in a lower class, outclassed, outshone, thrown into the shade, worsted, beat 728 adj. *defeated*; humiliated 872 adj. *humbled*; unworthy, not fit, not fit to hold a candle to, not a patch on.

Vb. *be inferior*, become smaller 37 vb. *decrease*, 198 vb. *become small*; fall short, come short of, not come up to, fall below 307 vb. *fall short*; lag, fall behind; trail 284 vb. *follow*; want, lack 636 vb. *not suffice*; not make the grade, not pass 728 vb. *fail*; bow to 739 vb. *obey*; concede the victory; yield, cede, yield the palm, hand it to, knuckle under 721 vb. *submit*; play second fiddle, play a supporting role 742 vb. *serve*; take a back seat, retire into the shade; hide one's diminished head, sink into obscurity 419 vb. *be dim*; lose face, lose caste, lose izzat 867 vb. *lose repute*; get worse 655 vb. *deteriorate*; slump, sink, sink low, touch depth, reach one's nadir 309 vb. *descend.*

Adv. *less*, minus, short of; beneath 210 adv. *under*; below average, below par, below the mark; at the bottom, in the lowest place, at low ebb; inferiorly, poorly, basely.

See: 33, 37, 105, 114, 150, 198, 210, 214, 216, 284, 307, 309, 323, 419, 607, 628, 636, 639, 645, 647, 655, 670, 702, 703, 707, 721, 728, 729, 732, 739, 742, 745, 755, 801, 812, 847, 867, 869, 872, 922.

36 Increase

N. *increase*, increment, augmentation, waxing, crescendo; advance, progress 285 n. *progression*; growth, build-up, development 164 n. *production*; growing pains 536 n. *learning*; extension, prolongation, protraction 203 n. *lengthening*; widening, broadening; amplification, inflation, dilation 197 n. *expansion*; proliferation, swarming 166 n. *reproduction*; multiplication, squaring, cubing 86 n. *numerical operation*; adding 38 n. *addition*; enlargement, magnification, aggrandizement 32 n. *greatness*; overenlargement, excess 546 n. *exaggeration*; enhancement, heightening, raising 310 n. *elevation*; concentration 324 n. *condensation*; recruitment 162 n. *strengthening*; intensification, stepping up, doubling, redoubling, trebling 91 n. *duplication*, 94 n. *triplication*; acceleration, speeding 277 n. *spurt*; hotting up, calefaction 381 n. *heating*; excitation 174 n. *stimulation*; exacerbation 832 n. *aggravation*; advancement, rise, uprush, upsurge, ebullition, upward curve, upward trend, anabasis 308 n. *ascent*, 654 n. *improvement*; flood, tide, rising t., spring t., swell, surge 350 n. *wave*; progressiveness, cumulativeness, cumulative effect, synergistic e., snowball 74 n. *accumulation*; ascending order 71 n. *series.*

increment, augment, bulge; accretion, access, accession, accrual, addition, contribution 40 n. *adjunct*; supplement 40 n. *extra*; padding, stuffing 303 n. *insertion*; percentage, commission, rake-off; interest, gain, net g., profit 771 n. *acquisition*; plunder, purchase, prey 790 n. *booty*; prize 962 n. *reward*; produce, harvest 164 n. *product*; take, takings, receipts, proceeds 782 n. *receiving.*

Adj. *increasing*, spreading; greater than ever 32 adj. *great*; growing, waxing, filling, crescent, on the increase, anabatic; supplementary 38 adj. *additional*; ever-increasing, snowballing, cumulative 285 adj. *progressive*; augmentative, elative, comparative, intensive; increasable, prolific, fruitful 164 adj. *productive*; increased, stretched, aggrandized, swollen, bloated 197 adj. *expanded.*

Vb. *grow*, increase, gain, earn interest 771 vb. *acquire*; dilate, swell, bulge, wax, fill 197 vb. *expand*; fill out, fatten, thicken

205 vb. *be broad*; put on weight 322 vb. *weigh*; sprout, bud, burgeon, flower, blossom 164 vb. *reproduce itself*; breed, spread, swarm, proliferate, multiply 104 vb. *be many*, 171 vb. *be fruitful*; grow up 669 vb. *mature*, 209 vb. *be high*; start up, shoot up 68 vb. *begin*; run up, climb, mount, rise, gain height 308 vb. *ascend*; flare up, shine out 379 vb. *be hot*, 417 vb. *shine*; gain strength, convalesce, revive, recover 656 vb. *be restored*, 162 vb. *be strong*; improve 654 vb. *get better*; gain ground, advance, get ahead, get on, snowball, accumulate 285 vb. *progress*; gain in value, appreciate, rise in price 811 vb. *be dear*; exceed, overflow 637 vb. *superabound*, 32 vb. *be great*; rise to a maximum 34 vb. *culminate*.

augment, increase, bump up, double, triple 94 vb. *treble*, 97 vb. *quadruple*; redouble, square, cube; duplicate 106 vb. *repeat*; multiply 164 vb. *produce*; grow, breed, raise, rear 369 vb. *breed stock*, 370 vb. *cultivate*, 669 vb. *mature*; enlarge, magnify, distend, inflate, blow up 197 vb. *expand*; amplify, develop, build up, fill out, fill in, pad out 54 vb. *complete*; condense, concentrate 324 vb. *be dense*; implant, infuse 303 vb. *insert*; supplement, superadd, repay with interest; import, read into; bring to, contribute to; increase the numbers, make one of, accrue 38 vb. *add*; increase the dimensions, prolong, stretch, pull out 203 vb. *lengthen*; broaden, widen, thicken, deepen; heighten, enhance, send up 209 vb. *make higher*; raise the score, make runs, convert a try, majorize; raise, exalt 310 vb. *elevate*; advance, aggrandize 285 vb. *promote*; aim higher, raise the sights; speed up 277 vb. *accelerate*; intensify, redouble, step up, screw up, stimulate, energize 174 vb. *invigorate*; recruit, reinforce, revive 685 vb. *refresh*, 656 vb. *restore*, 162 vb. *strengthen*; overenlarge, glorify 546 vb. *exaggerate*, 482 vb. *overestimate*; stoke, add fuel to the flame, exacerbate 832 vb. *aggravate*, 176 vb. *make violent*; maximize, bring to the boil, bring to a head 725 vb. *climax*.

Adv. *crescendo*, increasingly etc. adj.; more so, with a vengeance, with knobs on; on the increase, up and up, more and more, always m., all the m.

See: 32, 34, 38, 40, 54, 68, 71, 74, 86, 91, 94, 97, 104, 106, 162, 164, 166, 171, 174, 176, 197, 203, 205, 209, 277, 285, 303, 308, 310, 322, 324, 350, 369, 370, 379, 381, 417, 482, 536, 546, 637, 654, 656, 669, 685, 725, 771, 782, 790, 811, 832, 962.

37 Decrease: non-increase

N. *decrease*, getting less, lessening, dwindling, falling off; waning, fading; fade-out, dimming, obscuration, 419 n. *dimness*; wane 198 n. *contraction*, 206 n. *narrowing*; ebb, reflux, retreat, withdrawal 286 vb. *regression*; ebb-tide, neap 210 n. *lowness*; descending order 71 n. *series*; subsidence, sinking, decline, declension, catabasis, downward curve, downward trend, fall, drop, plunge 309 n. *descent*, 165 n. *ruin*; deflation, recession, slump 655 n. *deterioration*; loss of value, depreciation 812 n. *cheapness*; loss of reputation 866 n. *disrepute*; weakening, enfeeblement 163 n. *weakness*; impoverishment 801 n. *poverty*; shrinking, diminishing returns; exhaustion 190 n. *emptiness*; shortage, shrinkage, evaporation, deliquescence, erosion, decay, crumbling 655 n. *dilapidation*; attrition 333 n. *friction*; spoilage, leakage, wastage, damage, loss, wear and tear 42 n. *decrement*; using up, consumption 634 n. *waste*; non-increase, anticlimax 14 n. *contrariety*; underproduction 175 n. *inertness*; slackness, slackening 679 n. *inactivity*; limitation, limit, bound, 747 n. *restriction*; forfeit, sacrifice 963 n. *penalty*, 772 n. *loss*.

diminution, making less; subduction, deduction 39 n. *subtraction*; exception 57 n. *exclusion*; abatement, reduction, restriction 747 n. *restraint*; slowing down, deceleration 278 n. *slowness*; retrenchment, cut, economization 814 n. *economy*; cutting back, pruning, paring, shaving, clipping, docking, curtailment, abridgment, abbreviation 204 n. *shortening*; compression, squeeze 198 n. *contraction*; abrasion, erosion 333 vb. *friction*; melting, dissolution 337 vb. *liquefaction*; scattering, dispersal 75 n. *dispersion*; weeding, elimination 62 n. *sorting*, 300 n. *voidance*; extenuation, mitigation, minimization 177 n. *moderation*; belittlement, undervaluation 483 n. *underestimation*, 926 n.

detraction; demotion, degradation 872 n. *humiliation.*
Adj. *decreasing*, dwindling; decrescent, waning, fading, catabatic; deliquescent, melting, evaporating 337 adj. *liquefied*; bated, decreased, diminished etc. vb.; unexpanded, unincreased, unstretched; declining, going down, sinking, ebbing; decaying, ruinous 655 adj. *dilapidated.*
Vb. *bate*, make less, diminish, decrease, lessen, minify, dequantitate; take away, detract from, deduct 39 vb. *subtract*; except 57 vb. *exclude*; reduce, step down, scale d., whittle, pare, scrape 206 vb. *make thin*; shrink, abridge, abbreviate, boil down 204 vb. *shorten*; squeeze, compress, contract 198 vb. *make smaller*; limit, bound 747 vb. *restrain*; cut down, cut back, retrench 814 vb. *economize*; reduce speed, slow down, decelerate 278 vb. *retard*; lower, send down 311 vb. *depress*; minimize, mitigate, extenuate 177 vb. *moderate*; deflate, puncture; belittle, depreciate, undervalue 483 vb. *underestimate*, 812 vb. *cheapen*, 926 vb. *detract*; dwarf, overshadow 34 vb. *be superior*; throw into the shadow, darken, obscure 419 vb. *bedim*; degrade, demote 872 vb. *humiliate*; loosen, ease, relax 701 vb. *disencumber*; remit, pardon 909 vb. *forgive*; unload, throw overboard 323 vb. *lighten*; run down, empty, drain, exhaust 300 vb. *void*; use up, consume, fritter away 634 vb. *waste*; let escape, let evaporate, boil away 338 vb. *vaporize*; melt down 337 vb. *liquefy*; grind, crumble 332 vb. *pulverize*; rub away, abrade, file 333 vb. *rub*; gnaw, nibble at, eat away 301 vb. *eat*; erode, rust 655 vb. *impair*; strip, peel, denude 229 vb. *uncover*; pillage, plunder, dispossess 786 vb. *deprive*, 801 vb. *impoverish*; emasculate, unman 161 vb. *disable*; dilute, water 163 vb. *weaken*, 43 vb. *mix*; thin, thin out, sort o., weed o., depopulate 105 vb. *render few*; eliminate, expel 300 vb. *eject*; decimate, slaughter, kill off, wipe out 165 vb. *destroy*, 361 vb. *kill*; reduce to nothing, annihilate 2 vb. *nullify*; hush, quiet 399 vb. *silence*, 578 vb. *make mute*; damp down, cool, extinguish 382 vb. *refrigerate*; quell 745 vb. *subjugate.*
decrease, grow less, lessen, suffer loss; abate, die down; dwindle, shrink, contract 198 vb. *become small*; wane, waste, decay, wear away, consume a., languish 655 vb.

deteriorate; fade, die away, grow dim 419 vb. *be dim*; set, hide one's diminished head 867 vb. *lose repute*; retreat, withdraw, ebb 286 vb. *regress*, 290 vb. *recede*; run low, run down, ebb away, drain away, dry up, fail 636 vb. *not suffice*; tail off, taper off 206 vb. *be narrow*, 293 vb. *converge*; subside, sink 313 vb. *plunge*; come down, decline, fall, drop, slump, collapse 309 vb. *descend*; not grow, stay down, lag 278 vb. *decelerate*; melt, deliquesce 337 vb. *liquefy*; evaporate 338 vb. *vaporize*; thin, thin out, become scarce 325 vb. *be rare*; lose numbers 105 vb. *be few*, 75 vb. *disperse*; die out, become extinct 2 vb. *pass away*; lose weight, bant, diet, reduce 323 vb. *be light*, 946 vb. *starve*; lose one's voice, stop one's noise, pipe down, dry up 578 vb. *be mute*; lose, shed, rid oneself; cast off 229 vb. *doff*; forfeit, sacrifice 963 vb. *be punished.*
Adv. *diminuendo*, decrescendo, decreasingly; less and less, ever l.; in decline, on the wane, at low ebb.

See: 2, 14, 34, 39, 42, 43, 57, 62, 71, 75, 105, 161, 163, 165, 175, 177, 190, 198, 204, 206, 210, 229, 278, 286, 290, 293, 298, 300, 301, 309, 311, 313, 323, 325, 332, 333, 337, 338, 361, 382, 399, 419, 483, 578, 634, 636, 655, 679, 701, 745, 747, 772, 786, 801, 812, 814, 866, 867, 872, 909, 946, 963.

38 Addition
N. *addition*, adding to, annexation, adjection, adjunction, fixture, agglutination 45 n. *junction*; imposing, imposition 187 n. *location*; superposition, superaddition, superjunction, superfetation; prefixion, anteposition 64 n. *precedence*; suffixion, affixture, affixation 65 n. *sequence*; supplementation, suppletion 725 n. *completion*; contribution, reinforcement 703 n. *aid*; accession, accretion, accrual, supervention; interposition, interjection, epenthesis 303 n. *insertion*, 78 n. *inclusion*; reinforcement 36 n. *increase*; increment, supplement, addendum, appendage, appendix 40 n. *adjunct*; extra time, overtime 113 n. *protraction*; appurtenance 89 n. *accompaniment*; summation, adding up, total, toll 86 n. *numeration.*
Adj. *additional*, additive; added, **included**

etc. vb.; supervenient, adopted, adscititious, occasional 59 adj. *extraneous*; supplementary, supplemental, suppletory 725 adj. *completive*; subjunctive; conjunctive 45 adj. *conjunct*; subsidiary, auxiliary, contributory 703 adj. *aiding*; supernumerary, supererogatory; extra, spare 637 adj. *superfluous*; interjected, interposed, epenthetic 303 adj. *inserted*, 231 adj. *interjacent*; prosthetic 64 adj. *preceding*.

Vb. *add*, add up, sum, total, do the addition 86 vb. *do sums*; carry over 272 vb. *transfer*; add to, annex, append, subjoin; attach, pin to, clip to, tag on, tack on; conjoin; hitch to, yoke to, unite to 45 vb. *join, tie*; stick on, glue on, plaster on 48 vb. *agglutinate*; add on, preface, prefix, affix, suffix, postfix, infix; introduce 231 vb. *intromit*; interpose, interject; read into, import; engraft, let in 303 vb. *insert*; bring to, contribute to, make one's contribution, add one's share 36 vb. *augment*; swell, extend, expand 197 vb. *enlarge*; supplement 54 vb. *complete*; lay on, place on, impose, clap on, saddle with, burden w., load w. 187 vb. *stow*, 702 vb. *hinder*; superadd, superimpose, pile on, heap on; glorify, ornament, add frills, supply the trappings 844 vb. *decorate*; plaster, paint over, smear o., coat 226 vb. *overlay*; mix with, mix in 43 vb. *mix*; take to oneself, annex 786 vb. *take*; absorb, take in, include, receive 299 vb. *admit*.

accrue, be added 78 vb. *be included*; supervene 295 vb. *arrive*, 189 vb. *be present*; accede, adhere, join 708 vb. *join a party*; mix with, combine w. 50 vb. *combine*; make an extra, make an addition to, make one more; reinforce, recruit 162 vb. *strengthen*; swell the ranks, fill the gap.

Adv. *in addition*, additionally, more, plus, extra; with interest, with a vengeance, with knobs on; and, too, also, item, furthermore, further; likewise, and also, and eke, to boot; else, besides; et cetera; and so on, and so forth, moreover, into the bargain, over and above, including, inclusive of, with, as well as, not to mention, let alone, not forgetting; together with, along w., coupled w., in conjunction w.; conjointly, jointly; even with, despite, for all that.

See: 36, 40, 43, 45, 48, 50, 54, 59, 64, 65, 78, 86, 89, 113, 162, 187, 189, 197, 226, 231, 272, 295, 299, 303, 637, 702, 703, 708, 725, 786, 844.

39 Subduction: non-addition

N. *subtraction*, subduction, deduction, ablation, sublation 86 n. *numerical operation*; diminution 37 n. *decrease*; abstraction, removal, withdrawal 786 n. *taking*; elimination 62 n. *sorting*; detrusion, expulsion 300 n. *ejection*; clearance 300 n. *voidance*; unloading, unpacking 188 n. *displacement*, 304 n. *extraction*; precipitation, sedimentation, abrasion, erosion, detrition 333 n. *friction*; retrenchment, curtailment 204 n. *shortening*; severance, detruncation, amputation, excision, abscision, recision, circumcision 46 n. *disjunction*; castration, mutilation 655 n. *impairment*; expurgation, bowdlerization, garbling 648 n. *cleansing*; deletion 550 n. *obliteration*; minuend 85 n. *numerical element*; subtrahend, discount 42 n. *decrement*; non-addition, loss of interest.

Adj. *subtracted*, subtractive; mutilated etc. vb.; curtailed, docked, excaudal, acaudal, tailless; beheaded, headless, decapitated; minus, without.

Vb. *subtract*, take away, subduct, deduct, do subtraction; detract from, diminish, decrease 37 vb. *bate*; cut 810 vb. *discount*; except, take out, keep o., leave o. 57 vb. *exclude*; expel 300 vb. *eject*; abstract 786 vb. *take*, 788 vb. *steal*; withdraw, remove; unload, unpack 188 vb. *displace*; shift 272 vb. *transfer*; empty 300 vb. *void*; abrade, scrape, file away, erode 333 vb. *rub*; eradicate, uproot, pull up, pull out 304 vb. *extract*; pick, pick out, put on one side 605 vb. *select*; cross out, blot o., delete, blue-pencil, censor 550 n. *obliterate*; expurgate, bowdlerize, garble, mutilate 655 vb. *impair*; sever, separate, amputate, excise, abscind; shear, shave off, clip 46 vb. *disjoin*; retrench, cut back, cut down, prune, pare, whittle, pollard, lop; decapitate, behead, dock, curtail, detruncate, abridge, abbreviate 204 vb. *shorten*; geld, castrate, caponize, spay, emasculate 161 vb. *unman*; peel, skin, shuck, strip, divest, denude 229 vb. *uncover*.

Adv. *in deduction*, by subtraction etc. n.; less; short of; minus, without, except,

excepting, with the exception of, barring, bar, save, exclusive of, save and except, with a reservation.

See: 37, 46, 57, 62, 86, 161, 188, 204, 229, 272, 300, 304, 333, 550, 605, 648, 655, 786, 788, 810.

40 Adjunct: thing added

N. *adjunct*, addition, something added, contribution 38n. *addition*; additament, addendum, carry-over; attachment, fixture; annexure; inflection, affix, suffix, prefix, infix, postfix, subscript; preposition, postposition; adjective, adverb 564 n. *part of speech*; label, ticket, tab, tag 547n. *indication*; appendage, tail, train, cortège, following 67n. *sequel*; wake, trail 65n. *sequence*; appendix, postscript, envoi, coda, ending 69n. *extremity*; codicil, rider 468n. *qualification*; corollary, complement 725n. *completion*; appurtenance, concomitant, marginalia, footnotes 89n. *accompaniment*; pendant, companion piece, twin, pair, fellow 18n. *analogue*; extension, supplement, prolongation, continuation, second part; annexe, wing (of a house), offices, outhouse 164n. *edifice*; offshoot 53n. *branch*; arm 53n. *limb*; extremity 267n. *leg*, 214n. *foot*; increment 37n. *increase*; augment, leaf (of a table); patch, darn, reinforcement 656n. *repair*; piece, strip, length 53 n. *part*; padding, stuffing 227n. *lining*; interpolation, interlineation 303n. *insertion*; interlude, intermezzo, episode 231n. *interjacence*; insertion, gusset; flap, fold, lappet, lapel; oddment, accessory, ingredient 58n. *component*; skirt, fringe, border, frill, edging 234n. *edge*; embroidery 844n. *ornamentation*; garnish, garnishing, condiment 389n. *sauce*; frills, trimmings, all that goes with it; trappings 228n. *dress*, 226n. *covering*; equipment, furnishing 633n. *provision*.

extra, additive, addendum, something over and above, by-product; percentage, primage, interest, compound i., simple i. 771 n. *gain*; refresher, bonus, tip, solatium, something on the side 962n. *reward*; free gift, gratuity, grace marks 781n. *gift*; find, lucky f.; acquisition, accession; oddment, item, odd i.; bye (cricket); supernumerary; reserves, spare parts,

spares 633n. *provision*; extra help, reinforcement, ripieno 707n. *auxiliary*; fifth wheel of the coach 641n. *inutility*; luxury, work of supererogation 637n. *superfluity*; extra time, overtime 113n. *protraction*.

See: 18, 37, 38, 53, 58, 65, 67, 69, 89, 113, 164, 214, 226, 227, 228, 231, 234, 267, 303, 389, 468, 547, 564, 633, 637, 641, 656, 707, 725, 771, 781, 844, 962.

41 Remainder: thing remaining

N. *remainder*, residue, residuum; residuals, result, resultant 157n. *effect*, 164n. *product*; margin 15n. *difference*; outstanding, balance, net b. 31n. *offset*; surplus, carry-over 36n. *increment*; overplus, overtrick, excess 637n. *superfluity*; relic, rest, remnant 105n. *fewness*; rump, stump, scrag, end, fag e., butt e. 69n. *extremity*; frustum, torso, trunk 53n. *piece*; fossil, skeleton, bones 363n. *corpse*; husk, empty h.; wreck, wreckage 165n. *ruin*; debris 332n. *powder*; track, trace 548n. *record*; wake, afterglow 65n. *sequence*; all that is left, memories 505n. *remembrance*; remanence, survival 113n. *durability*; vestige, remains.

leavings, left-overs; precipitate, deposit; alluvium, silt 344n. *soil*; sediment; drift, loess, moraine, detritus 272n. *thing transferred*; grounds, lees, heel-taps, dregs; scum, skimmings, dross, scoria, slag, sludge; bilge, dottle; scrapings, shavings, filings, sawdust, crumbs 332n. *powder*; husks, bran, chaff, stubble; peel, peelings; skin, slough, scurf; parings, combings; shorts, trimmings, clippings, cabbage, remnants, strips; scraps, candle-ends, odds and ends, lumber 641n. *rubbish*; rejects 799n. *derelict*; sweepings, scourings, offscourings; refuse, waste, sewage 649n. *dirt*, 302n. *excrement*.

survivor, finisher; inheritor, heir, successor 776n. *beneficiary*; widower, widow, relict 896n. *widowed spouse*; orphan 779n. *derelict*; descendant 170n. *posterity*.

Adj. *remaining*, surviving, left, vestigial resting, resultant; residual; left behind, sedimentary, precipitated 779adj. *not retained*; over, left over, odd; net, surplus; unspent, unexpended, unexpired, unconsumed; outstanding, carried over;

spare, to s., superfluous 637adj. *redundant*; cast-off, pariah, outcast 607adj. *rejected*; orphaned, orphan, widowed.
Vb. *be left*, remain, rest, result, survive. *leave over*, leave out 57vb. *exclude*; leave 607vb. *reject*.

See: 15, 31, 36, 53, 57, 65, 69, 105, 113, 157, 164, 165, 170, 272, 302, 332, 344, 363, 505, 584, 607, 637, 641, 649, 776, 779, 896.

42 Decrement: thing deducted
N. *decrement*, deduction, cut 37n. *diminution*; allowance, free a.; rebate 810n. *discount*; reprise, tare, drawback, shortage, defect 307n. *shortcoming*, 636n. *insufficiency*; loss, sacrifice, forfeit 963n. *penalty*; leak, leakage, primage, escape 298 n. *egress*; shrinkage 204n. *shortening*; spoilage, wastage; off-take, consumption 634n. *waste*; subtrahend, rake-off 786n. *taking*.

See: 37, 204, 298, 307, 634, 636, 786, 810, 963.

43 Mixture
N. *mixture*, mingling, mixing, stirring; blending, harmonization; concord 23n. *agreement*; admixture 38n. *addition*; commixture, commixion 45n. *junction*; immixture 303n. *insertion*; intermixture, interlarding, interpolation 231n. *interjacence*; interweaving, interlacing 222n. *crossing*; amalgamation, integration 50n. *combination*; merger 706n. *association*; syncretism, eclecticism; fusion, interfusion, alloyage; infusion, suffusion, transfusion, instillation, impregnation 341n. *moistening*; adulteration, watering down, sophistication 655n. *deterioration*; contamination, infection 653n. *insalubrity*, 659n. *poison*; infiltration, penetration, pervasion, permeation 297 n. *ingress*; interbreeding, miscegenation, intermarriage 894n. *marriage*; syngamy, allogamy, amphimixis 164n. *propagation*; hybridization, mongrelism, touch of the tar brush; miscibility, solubility 337 n. *liquefaction*; crucible, melting-pot; variety 427n. *variation*.

tincture, something mixed, admixture; in-gredient, 58n. *component*; strain, streak; sprinkling, infusion; tinge, touch, drop, dash, soupçon 33n. *small quantity*; smack 386n. *taste*; seasoning, spice 389n. *condiment*; colour, dye 425n. *hue*; stain, blot 845n. *blemish*.

a mixture, mélange; blend, harmony 710n. *concord*; composition 331n. *texture*; amalgam, fusion, compound, confection 50n. *combination*; cento, pastiche, pasticcio; alloy, bronze, brass, billon, pewter, electrum; magma, paste; culinary compound, sauce, salad, stew, hash, ragout, olla podrida, salmagundi, chowchow, mishmash 301n. *dish*; cocktail, brew, witches' b.; medicinal compound, the mixture, drug 658n. *remedy*.

medley, heterogeneity, complexity 17n. *non-uniformity*, 82n. *multiformity*; motley, patchwork, mosaic 437n. *variegation*; miscellany, miscellanea, old curiosity shop; farrago, gallimaufry, hotchpotch, hash, mash; pot-pourri; jumble, mess; pie, printer's p.; tangle, entanglement, imbroglio 61n. *confusion*; phantasmagoria, kaleidoscope; clatter 411n. *discord*; omnium gatherum, everybody 74n. *crowd*; Noah's ark 369n. *zoo*; multiracial state; all sorts, odds and ends, paraphernalia, oddments.

hybrid, bigener, cross, cross-breed, mongrel; half-blood, half-breed, half-caste; mestizo, mestee; Eurasian, Cape-coloured, mulatto; quadroon, octaroon; sambo, griffe, griffin; mule, hinny.

Adj. *mixed*, in the melting pot, mixed up, stirred, well-s.; mixed up in, deep in; blended, harmonized, syncretic, eclectic; fused, alloyed 50adj. *combined*; tempered, adulterated, sophisticated, qualified, watered, weak 163adj. *weakened*; merged, amalgamated 45adj. *conjunct*; composite, half-and-half, fifty-fifty, linsey-wolsey, chryselephantine; complex, complicated, implex, involved 251adj. *convoluted*; tangled, confused, jumbled 63adj. *deranged*; unclassified, unsorted, out of order; heterogeneous 17adj. *non-uniform*; kaleidoscopic, phantasmagoric 82adj. *multiform*; patched, patchy, dappled, motley 437adj. *variegated*; shot 437 adj. *iridescent*; miscellaneous, hotchpotch, medley, promiscuous 464adj. *indiscriminate*; miscible, soluble 337adj. *liquefied*; pervasive, spreading 653adj.

infectious; hybrid, bigenerous, cross-bred, crossed; half-blooded, mongrel; interbred, Eurasian; intermixed, multiracial.

Vb. *mix*, make a mixture, mix up, stir, shake; shuffle, transfuse 272vb. *transpose*, 63vb. *jumble*; knead, pound together, hash, mash 332vb. *pulverize*; brew, compound 56vb. *compose*; fuse, alloy, merge, amalgamate, conjoin 45vb. *join*; blend, harmonize 24vb. *adjust*; mingle, intermingle, intersperse 437n. *variegate*; lace, immix, intermix, interlard, interleave 303vb. *insert*; intertwine, interlace, interweave 222vb. *weave*; tinge, dye 425 vb. *colour*; imbue, instil, impregnate 303vb. *infuse*; dash, sprinkle, besprinkle 341vb. *moisten*; water, adulterate, sophisticate 163vb. *weaken*; temper, attemper, doctor, medicate 468vb. *qualify*; season, spice 390vb. *appetize*; hybridize, mongrelize, cross, cross-breed 164vb. *generate*.

be mixed, be entangled with, be involved, be mixed up in, be deep in, get into; pervade, permeate, run through, overrun 297vb. *infiltrate*; infect, contaminate; tinge, dye, stain 425vb. *colour*; miscegenate, intermarry, interbreed, cross with 164 vb. *reproduce itself*.

Adv. *among*, amongst, amid, amidst, with; in the midst of, in the crowd; amongst many, inter alia.

See: 17, 24, 33, 38, 45, 50, 56, 58, 61, 63, 74, 82, 163, 164, 222, 231, 251, 272, 297, 301, 303, 331, 332, 337, 341, 369, 386, 389, 390, 411, 425, 437, 464, 468, 653, 655, 658, 659, 706, 710, 845, 894.

44 Simpleness: freedom from mixture

N. *simpleness* etc. adj.; homogeneity 16n. *uniformity*; purity 648n. *cleanness*; oneness 88n. *unity*; absoluteness, sheerness; fundamentality, bedrock; elementarity, atomicity, indivisibility, insolubility, asexuality; lack of complication, simplicity 516n. *intelligibility*, 573n. *plainness*, 699n. *artlessness*; freedom from mixture, not a trace of, not a hint of 190n. *absence*.

simplification, purification 648n. *cleansing*; reduction 51n. *decomposition*; unification, assimilation 13n. *identity*.

elimination, riddance, clearance 300n. *ejec-*

tion; sifting, bolting 62n. *sorting*; expulsion 57n. *exclusion*.

Adj. *simple*, homogeneous, monolithic, of a piece 16adj. *uniform*; absolute, sheer, mere, nothing but; undifferentiated, asexual; single, unified 88adj. *one*; elemental, atomic, indivisible 52adj. *whole*; primary, irreducible, fundamental, basic 5adj. *intrinsic*; elementary, uncomplicated, unravelled, disentangled, simplified 516adj. *intelligible*; direct, unmediated 249adj. *straight*; unsophisticated, homespun 573adj. *plain*, 699adj. *artless*; single-minded, open-hearted, whole-h., sincere, downright, unaffected 540adj. *veracious*, 929n. *honourable*; bare, naked 229adj. *uncovered*.

unmixed, pure and simple, without alloy; clear, pure, clarified, purified, cleansed 648adj. *clean*; whole-blooded, thoroughbred 868adj. *noble*; free from, exempt f., exclusive 57adj. *excluding*; unmingled, unblended, unalloyed, uncompounded, uncombined; undiluted, unadulterated, neat, proof, overproof 162 adj. *strong*; unqualified, unmodified; unmedicated, unfortified, unstrengthened; unflavoured, unspiced, unseasoned 387adj. *tasteless*; untinged, undyed, uncoloured 427adj. *white*.

Vb. *simplify*, unmix, unscramble; render simple 16vv. *make uniform*; narrow down, factorize, reduce, reduce to its element 51 vb. *decompose*; disentangle, unravel 46vb. *disjoin*; unify, make one, unite.

eliminate, sift 62vb. *class*; winnow, bolt, pan; purge 648vb. *purify*; clear; get rid of weed 57vb. *exclude*; rid 304vb. *extract*; expel 300vb. *eject*.

Adv. *simply* etc. adj.; simply and solely; only, merely, exclusively.

See: 5, 13, 16, 46, 51, 52, 57, 62, 88, 162, 190, 229, 249, 300, 304, 387, 427, 516, 540, 573, 648, 699, 868, 929.

45 Junction

N. *junction*, joining etc. vb.; coming together, meeting, concurrence, conjunction 293n. *convergence*; clash 279n. *collision*; contact 202n. *contiguity*, 378n. *touch*; congress, concourse, forgathering, reunion 74n. *assembly*; confluence, meeting-point, meeting-place 76n. *focus*; con-

crescence, coalescence, symphysis, fusion, merger 43 n. *mixture*; unification, synthesis 50 n. *combination*; cohesion, tenacity, inextricability, agglutination 48 n. *coherence*; concretion, consolidation, solidification, coagulation 324 n. *condensation*; closeness, tightness, compactness, impaction; union, coalition, alliance, symbiosis 706 n. *association*; connection, linkage, tie-up, hook-up 47 n. *bond*; syngamy, wedlock 894 n. *marriage*; interconnection, cross-connection, anastomosis, inosculation; interlocking 222 n. *crossing*; communication 305 n. *passage*; intercommunication, intercourse, commerce 882 n. *sociability*; trade, traffic, exchange 151 n. *interchange*, 791 n. *trade*; involvement 9 n. *relation*; arrival, new a., comer, late-c. 297 n. *incomer*; partner, yoke-fellow, sharer 775 n. *participator*; accompanist 89 n. *concomitant*.

joinder, bringing together 74 n. *assemblage*; unification 50 n. *combination*; compagination, articulation 56 n. *composition*, 331 n. *structure*; joining, stringing together, threading t., linking t., concatenation; suture, stitching, knitting, sewing, weaving 222 n. *crossing*; tightening, astriction, drawing together, contraction 198 n. *compression*, 264 n. *closure*; knotting, tying, binding, bandaging, vincture, ligation, alligation; fastening, pinning, infibulation; attaching, attachment, annexing, annexure 38 n. *addition*; connecting, earthing; affixture, affixation, suffixment, suffixion, prefixion; fixture, grafting, planting, inosculation 303 n. *insertion*; sticking on, agglutination 48 n. *coherence*; coupling, accouplement, yoking, pairing, matching 18 n. *assimilation*, 462 n. *comparison*; bracketing 28 n. *equalization*; hyphenization 547 n. *punctuation*; joiner, coupler, riveter, welder; comparer, matcher; go-between 231 n. *intermediary*, 894 n. *matchmaker*.

coition, coitus, copulation, sexual intercourse, intimacy, carnal knowledge; generation 164 n. *propagation*; pairing, mating, coupling, couplement; union 894 n. *marriage*; enjoyment, consummation; violation, ravishment 951 n. *rape*.

joint, joining, juncture, line of j., commissure; crease 261 n. *fold*; inner margin, gutter; suture, seam, stitching, stitch 47 n. *bond*; weld, weld-joint; splice, splice-joint; mitre-joint, mitre; dovetail-joint, dovetail and mortise; ball and socket; hasp; latch, catch, 218 n. *pivot*; hinge-joint, ginglymus, knee, elbow 247 n. *angle*; finger, wrist, ankle, knuckle; node; junction, point of j., inter-section, crossways 222 n. *crossing*; decussation, optic d., chiasm, chiasma, figure X 222 n. *cross*.

Adj. *conjunct*, joined etc. vb.; connected, earthed; coupled, matched, paired 28 adj. *equal*; conjoined, partnered, participant 775 adj. *sharing*; rolled into one, united; joint, allied, incorporated, associated, symbiotic 706 adj. *co-operative*, 708 adj. *corporate*; betrothed, wedded 894 adj. *married*; handfast, holding hands, hand in hand, arm in arm; intimate, involved 5 adj. *intrinsic*; coalescent, symphysian 48 adj. *cohesive*; composite 50 adj. *combined*; put together 74 adj. *assembled*; articulated, jointed 331 adj. *structural, textural*; stitched, patched; stitched up, sutural.

conjunctive, subjunctive, adjunctive, copulative, adhesive 48 adj. *cohesive*; coagulate, astringent 324 adj. *solidifying*; coincident 181 adj. *concurrent*; coital, venereal.

firm-set, firm, close, fast, secure 153 adj. *fixed*; solid, set, solidified 324 adj. *dense*; glued, cemented 48 adj. *cohesive*; put, pat; planted, rooted, ingrown, impacted; close-printed, close-set, crowded 587 adj. *printed*; tight, tight-fitting, wedged, jammed, stuck; inextricable, immovable, unshakable; inseparate, unseverable, insecable; packed, jam-p. 54 adj. *full*.

tied, bound, knotted, roped, lashed, belayed; stitched, sewn, gathered; attached, adhering 48 adj. *cohesive*; well-tied, tight, taut, tense, fast, secure; intricate, intervolved, tangled, inextricable, indissoluble.

Vb. *join*, conjoin, couple, yoke, hyphenate, harness together, partner; pair, match 18 n. *liken*, 462 vb. *compare*, 894 vb. *marry*; bracket 28 vb. *equalize*; put together, lay t., clap t., fit t., piece t., assemble, unite 50 vb. *combine*; collect, gather, mobilize, mass 74 vb. *bring together*; add to, amass, accumulate 38 vb. *add*, 632 vb. *store*; associate, ally; merge 43 vb. *mix*; embody, re-embody, incorporate, consolidate, make one, unify 88 vb. *be one, make uniform*; lump together, roll into one 464 vb. *not discriminate*;

include, embrace 78 vb. *comprise*; grip, grapple 778 vb. *retain*; make a joint, hinge, articulate, dovetail, mortise, rabbet; fit, set, interlock, engage, gear to; wedge, jam 303 vb. *insert*; weld, solder, braze, fuse, cement 48 vb. *agglutinate*; draw together, bring ends t., lace, knit, sew, stitch; pin, infibulate, buckle; do up, button up 264 vb. *close*; lock, latch; close a gap, seal up; darn, patch, mend, heal over, scab over 656 vb. *repair*.

connect, attach, annex (see *affix*); tag, clip; thread together, string to., rope t., link t., concatenate; contact 378 vb. *touch*; make contact, plug in, earth 202 vb. *juxtapose*; interconnect, anastomose, inosculate, open into; link, bridge, span, straddle, bestride 205 vb. *be broad*; communicate, intercommunicate, establish communication, hook up with, tie up w. 9 vb. *relate*; link closely, entwine.

affix, attach, fix, fasten; fix on, yoke, leash, harness, limber, saddle, bridle, bit; tie up, moor, anchor; tie to, tether, picket; pin on, hang on, hook on, screw on, nail on, shoe; stick on, gum on 48 vb. *agglutinate*; suffix, prefix 38 vb. *add*; infix, splice, engraft, implant 303 vb. *insert*; impact, set, enchase, frame 235 vb. *inclose*; drive in, knock in, hammer in 279 vb. *strike*; wedge, jam; screw, nail, treenail, rivet, bolt, clamp, clinch; thread, reeve, pass through, weave t.

tie, knot, hitch, bend; lash, belay; knit, cast on, sew, stitch, suture; tack, baste; braid, plait, crochet, twine, twist, intertwine, lace, interlace, interweave 222 vb. *weave*; truss, string, rope, strap; lace up, frap, lash up, trice up, brail; tether, picket, moor; pinion, manacle, handcuff; hobble, shackle 747 vb. *fetter*; bind, splice, gird, girdle, cinch; bandage, swathe, swaddle, wrap; enfold, embrace, clinch, grip, grapple 235 vb. *inclose*, 778 vb. *retain*.

tighten, jam, impact; constrict, compress, straiten, narrow; fasten, screw up, make firm, make fast, secure; tauten, draw tight, pull t., lace t.; frap, brace, trice up, brail.

unite with, be joined, linked etc. vb.; join, meet 293 vb. *converge*; fit tight, hold t., fit close, adhere, hang together, hold t., stick t. 48 vb. *cohere*; interlock, engage, grip, grapple, embrace, entwine, clinch; link up with, hold hands; associate with,

mix w. 882 vb. *be sociable*; marry 894 vb. *wed*; live with, cohabit, bed; lie with, sleep w., have intercourse, have carnal knowledge; consummate marriage, consummate a union; know, enjoy, have, do; board, tumble; deflower, rape, ravish, violate, force 951 vb. *debauch*; copulate, couple, mate, pair; mount, tup; cross with, breed w.

Adv. *conjointly*, jointly, in conjunction, in partnership; all together, as one; with, to, on, in.

inseparably, inextricably; securely, firmly, fast, tight.

See: 5, 9, 18, 28, 38, 43, 47, 48, 50, 54, 56, 74, 76, 78, 88, 89, 151, 153, 164, 181, 198, 202, 205, 218, 222, 231, 235, 247, 261, 264, 279, 293, 297, 303, 305, 324, 331, 378, 462, 464, 547, 587, 632, 656, 706, 708, 747, 775, 778, 791, 882, 894, 951.

46 Disjunction

N. *disjunction*, being separated; disconnection, disconnectedness, unthreading, break, ladder, run 72 n. *discontinuity*; looseness, incoherence, separability, fissionability 49 n. *non-coherence*, 335 n. *fluidity*; diffusion, dispersal, scattering 75 n. *dispersion*; break-up, disintegration, dissolution, decay 51 n. *decomposition*, 655 n. *dilapidation*; abstraction, absent-mindedness 456 n. *abstractedness*; dissociation, withdrawal, disengagement, retirement 621 n. *relinquishment*, 753 n. *resignation*; surrender, sacrifice 779 n. *non-retention*, 37 n. *decrease*; moving apart, broadening, widening 294 n. *divergence*, 282 n. *deviation*; separation 896 n. *divorce*; detachment, non-attachment 860 n. *indifference*, 606 n. *no choice*; neutrality 625 n. *mid-course*; isolation, loneliness, quarantine, segregation 883 n. *seclusion*; zone, compartment, box, cage 748 n. *prison*; insularity 620 n. *avoidance*; disunion 709 n. *dissension*; dissilience 182 n. *counteraction*, 280 n. *recoil*; immiscibility, separateness, severalness, severalty 80 n. *speciality*; isolationism, separatism 80 n. *particularism*; no connection, asyndeton 10 n. *irrelation*; distance apart 199 n. *farness*; dichotomy 15 n. *difference*; interval, space, opening, hole, breach, break, rent,

rift, split; fissure, crack, cleft, chasm; cleavage, slit, slot, incision 201 n. *gap.*

separation, disjoining, severance, parting, diremption; uncoupling, divorcement 896 n. *divorce*; untying, undoing, unthreading, unravelment, laddering; loosening, loosing, freeing 746 n. *liberation*; setting apart, sejunction, seposition, segregation 883 n. *seclusion*; exception, exemption 57 n. *exclusion*; boycott 620 n. *avoidance*; expulsion, voidance 300 n. *ejection*; picking out, selection 605 n. *choice*; putting aside, keeping a. 632 n. *storage*; conservation 666 n. *preservation*; taking away 39 n. *subtraction*; abstraction, deprivation, expropriation 786 n. *taking*; detaching, detachment, withdrawal, removal, transfer 188 n. *displacement*, 272 n. *transference*; denudation, stripping, peeling, plucking 229 n. *uncovering*; disjointing, dislocation, luxation; scattering, dispersal 75 n. *dispersion*; dissolution, resolution, disintegration 51 n. *decomposition*; dissection, analysis, breakdown; disruption, shattering, fragmentation, pulverization, mastication 165 n. *destruction*; splitting, fission, nuclear f. 160 n. *nucleonics*; breaking, cracking, rupture, fracture 330 n. *brittleness*; dividing line, cæsura; wall, hedge 231 n. *partition*; curtain 421 n. *screen*; boundary 236 n. *limit.*

scission, section, cleavage, cutting, tearing; division, dichotomy 92 n. *bisection*; subdivision, segmentation; partition 783 n. *apportionment*; abscission, cutting off, decapitation, curtailment 304 n. *shortening*, 37 n. *diminution*; elision, syncope 39 n. *subtraction*; cutting away, resection, circumcision; cutting open, incision, opening 658 n. *surgery*; dissection, discerption; rending, clawing, laceration, dilaceration, divulsion; tearing off, avulsion; nipping, pinching, biting etc. vb.

Adj. *disjunct*, disjoined, divorced; separated, disconnected, unplugged, unstuck; dismounted; broken, interrupted 72 adj. *discontinuous*; divided, subdivided, partitioned, bipartite, multipartite; in pieces, quartered, dismembered; severed, cut; torn, rent, riven, cleft, cloven; digitate 201 adj. *spaced*; radiating, divergent 282 adj. *deviating*; scattered, dispersed, fugitive, uncollected 75 adj. *unassembled*; noncohesive, melting, flowing 335 n. *fluid*;

untied, loosened, loose, free 746 adj. *liberated*; unattached, open-ended.

separate, apart, asunder; adrift, lost; unjoined, unfixed, unfastened; unattached, unannexed, unassociated; distinct, discrete, differentiated, separable, distinguishable 15 adj. *different*; exempt, excepted 57 adj. *excluded*; abstract, abstracted 304 adj. *extracted*; immiscible, unassimilable, unassimilated 324 adj. *indissoluble*; alien, foreign 59 adj. *extraneous*, 84 adj. *uncomformable*; external 6 adj. *extrinsic*, 223 adj. *exterior*; insular, self-sufficient, lonely, isolated 88 adj. *alone*, 883 adj. *friendless*; shunned, dropped, avoided, boycotted 620 adj. *avoiding*; cast-off 607 adj. *rejected*; picked out 605 adj. *chosen*; abandoned, left 41 adj. *remaining*; hostile, opposed, antipathetic 881 adj. *inimical*, 14 adj. *contrary*, 240 adj. *opposite*; disjunctive, separative, asyndetic; dichotomous, dividing; selective, diagnostic 15 adj. *distinctive.*

severable, separable, detachable; partible, divisible, fissionable, scissile, tearable; dissoluble, dissolvable; distinguishable, not belonging 10 adj. *irrelative.*

Vb. *be disjoined*, stand apart, not mix 620 vb. *avoid*; go, go away 296 vb. *depart*; go apart, go different ways, radiate 294 vb. *diverge*; go another way 282 vb. *deviate*; separate, part, part company, cut adrift, divorce; split off, hive off; get free, get loose 667 vb. *escape*; disengage, unclinch, break away 746 vb. *achieve liberty*; cast off, unmoor, let go 779 vb. *not retain*; leave, quit, fall away 621 vb. *relinquish*; scatter, break it up 75 vb. *disperse*; spring apart 280 vb. *recoil*; come apart, fall a., break, come to bits, disintegrate 51 vb. *decompose*; come undone, unravel, ladder, run; fall off 49 vb. *come unstuck*; start, split, crack 263 vb. *open*; leak 298 vb. *flow out*; melt, run 337 vb. *liquefy*, 338 vb. *vaporize.*

disjoin, disunite, dissociate, divorce; dispart, part, separate, sunder, sever, dissever; uncouple, dispair; unhitch, disconnect, unplug; cast off (knitting); disengage, ungear, throw out of gear; disjoint, dislocate, wrench; detach, unseat, dismount 49 vb. *unstick*; remove, detract, deduct 39 vb. *subtract*, 272 vb. *transfer*; skin, denude, strip, peel, pluck 229 vb. *uncover*; undo, unbutton, unhook, unclasp,

unlock, unlatch 263 vb. *open*; untie, un-knot, cut the knot, disentangle 62 vb. *un-ravel*; loosen, relax, slacken, unstring 177 vb. *moderate*; unbind, unchain, unfetter, unloose, loose, free, release 746 vb. *liber-ate*; unharness, unsaddle, unbridle 701 vb. *disencumber*; unload, unpack, unbundle 188 vb. *displace*, 323 vb. *lighten*; expel 300 vb. *eject*; dispel, scatter, break up, disband, demobilize 75 vb. *disperse*; melt, melt down, evaporate 337 vb. *liquefy*, 338 vb. *vaporize*; disintegrate 51 vb. *de-compose*, 332 vb. *pulverize*, 165 vb. *des-troy*; unstitch, unpick.

set apart, put aside 632 vb. *store*; con-serve 666 vb. *preserve*; mark out, tick off, distinguish 15 vb. *differentiate*, 463 vb. *discriminate*; single out, pick o. 605 vb. *select*; except, exempt, leave out 57 vb. *exclude*; boycott, send to Coventry 620 vb. *avoid*; taboo, black, black-list 757 vb. *prohibit*; insulate, isolate, cut off 235 vb. *inclose*; zone, compartmentalize, screen off 232 vb. *circumscribe*; segregate, se-quester, quarantine, maroon 883 vb. *seclude*; keep apart, hold a., drive a.; drive a wedge between, estrange, alienate, set against 881 vb. *make enemies*, 888 vb. *excite hate*.

sunder (see *disjoin*); divide, keep apart, flow between, stand b.; subdivide, fragment, chunk, segment, sectionalize, fractionize; reduce, factorize, analyze; dissect, anato-mize 51 vb. *decompose*; dichotomize, halve 92 vb. *bisect*; divide up, split, parti-tion, parcel out 783 vb. *apportion*; dis-member, disbranch, quarter, carve (see *cut*); behead, decapitate, curtail, dock, amputate 204 vb. *shorten*; take apart, take to pieces, cannibalize, dismantle, break up, dismount; force open, force apart, wedge a. 263 vb. *open*; slit, split, rive; cleave 263 vb. *pierce* (see *break*).

cut, hew, hack, hackle, slash, gash 655 vb. *wound*; prick, stab, knife 263 vb. *pierce*; cut through, cleave, rive, saw, chop; cut open, slit 263 vb. *open*; cut into, make an incision, incise 555 vb. *engrave*; cut deep, cut to the bone, carve, slice; cut round, pare, whittle, chip, trim, bevel, skive; clip, snick, snip; cut short, shave 204 vb. *shorten*; cut down, scythe, mow; cut off, abscind, lop, prune, dock, curtail, behead, decapitate, amputate, circumcise (see *sunder*); cut up, chop up, quarter, dis-

member; mince, make mincemeat of 332 vb. *pulverize*; bite, bite into, bite through, masticate 301 vb. *chew*; scratch, scarify, score, plough 262 vb. *groove*; nick 260 vb. *notch*.

rend, rive (see *sunder*); tear, scratch, claw, scarify, score; gnaw, fret, fray, make ragged; strip, flay, skin, peel, pluck 229 vb. *uncover*; rip, slash, slit (see *cut*); lacerate, dilacerate, dislimb, dismember; tear piecemeal, tear to pieces, tear to shreds, tear to tatters 165 vb. *destroy*; pluck to pieces, divellicate, scamble; mince, grind, crunch, scrunch 301 vb. *chew*, 332 vb. *pulverize*; explode, blow up, blow to pieces, burst.

break, fracture, rupture, bust; split, burst, blow up, explode; break in pieces, smash, shatter, splinter, shiver 165 vb. *de-molish*; fragment, comminute, crumble, grind, triturate 332 vb. *pulverize*; disin-tegrate 51 vb. *decompose*; break up, dis-mantle (see *sunder*); chip, crack, damage 655 vb. *impair*; bend, buckle, warp 246 vb. *distort*; break in two, snap, knap; cleave, force apart, wedge a. 263 vb. *open*.

Adv. *separately*, severally, singly, one by one, bit by bit, piecemeal, in bits, in pieces, in halves, in twain; discontinuously, uncon-nectedly, disjointedly, interruptedly.

apart, open, asunder, adrift; off, up, down; to pieces, to bits, to tatters, to shreds; limb from limb.

See: 2, 6, 10, 14, 15, 37, 39, 41, 49, 51, 57, 59, 62, 72, 75, 80, 84, 88, 92, 160, 165, 177, 182, 188, 199, 201, 204, 223, 229, 231, 232, 235, 236, 240, 246, 260, 262, 263, 272, 280, 282, 294, 296, 298, 300, 301, 304, 323, 324, 330, 332, 335, 337, 338, 421, 456, 463, 555, 605, 606, 607, 620, 621, 625, 632, 655, 658, 666, 667, 701, 709, 746, 748, 753, 757, 779, 783, 786, 860, 881, 883, 888, 896.

47 Bond: connecting medium

N. *bond*, connecting medium, vinculum, chain, tie, band, hoop, yoke; bond of union, sympathy, fellow-feeling 905 n. *pity*; nexus, connection, link, liaison 9 n. *relation*; junction, hinge 45 n. *joint*; ramification 53 n. *branch*; connective, copula; hyphen, dash, bracket, hook, crotchet 547 n. *punctuation*; intermedium, cement (see *adhesive*); bondstone,

binder; tie-beam, stretcher, girder 218n.
beam; strut, stay, prop 218n. *supporter*;
interconnection, intercommunication,
channel, passage, corridor 624n. *way*;
stepping-stone 624n. *bridge*; span, arch;
isthmus, neck; col, ridge; stair, ladder
308n. *ascent*; life-line; umbilical cord;
chord (of an arc).

cable, line, hawser, painter, moorings;
guest-rope, guess-warp, tow-line, tow-
rope, ripcord, lanyard, communication
cord; rope, cord, string, strand, thread
208n. *fibre*; tape, inkle; chain, wire,
earth-w.

tackling, tackle, cordage; rigging, running
r., standing r., shroud, ratline; sheets,
guy, stay; clew line, garnet, halliard, bowline, lanyard; harness.

ligature, binding, end-paper; ligament, tendon, muscle; tendril, with, withy, osier,
bast, raffia 208n. *fibre*; lashing, lasher;
string, cord, thread, tape, inkle; band,
fillet, ribbon, ribband; bandage, roller b.,
roller, tourniquet 198n. *compressor*;
draw-string, thong, latchet, lace, boot-l.,
tag; braid, plait 222n. *textile*; tie, stock,
cravat 228n. *neckwear*; knot, hitch, clinch,
bend; Gordian knot, running k., slip k.,
granny k., reef k., sailor's k.; half-hitch,
clove h.; sheepshank, Turk's head.

fastening 45n. *joinder*; fastener, snap f.,
press f., zip f., zip; drawstring, ripcord;
button, buttonhook, buttonhole, frog;
hook and eye; eyelet, eyelet-hole; stud,
cufflink; garter, suspender, braces; tie-
pin, stickpin; brooch, fibula; ouch 844n.
jewellery; clip, grip, slide, curlers; hairpin,
hatpin; skewer, spit, brochette; pin,
drawing p., push-p., safety-p., toggle p.,
cotter p., linch p., king p.; peg, dowel,
treenail, trennel; nail, brad, tack, tintack,
hobnail, blakey 256n. *sharp point*; holdfast, staple, clamp, batten, cramp, rivet;
nut, bolt, screw; buckle, clasp, morse;
hasp, hinge 45n. *joint*; catch, safety-c.,
spring c., pawl, click, detent; latch, bolt;
lock, lock and key 264n. *closure*; combination lock, yale l.; padlock, handcuffs,
bracelets 748n. *fetter*; hank, ring, varvel,
terret; hold, bar, post, pile, pale, stake,
bollard; cleat, bitt, pawl-b.

coupling, yoke; coupler, draw-bar, draw-
head, draw-link, traces; grappling iron,
hook, claw; anchor, sheet-a. 662n. *safeguard*.

girdle, band, strap 228n. *belt*; waist-band,
waist-string, cummerbund, bellyband,
girth, roller, cinch, surcingle; cestus, zone;
sash, shoulder-belt, bandoleer; collar,
neckband 228n. *neckwear*; bandeau,
fillet, taenia, tiara; hatband; banderole;
equator, zodiac.

halter, collar, noose; tether, lead, leash,
jess, trash-cord, reins, ribbons; lasso,
lariat 250n. *loop*; shackle 748n. *fetter*.

adhesive, glue, fish-glue, bee-glue, lime, bird-
lime, gum, seccotine, fixative, hair fixer,
brilliantine, grease; solder; paste, size,
lute, clay, cement, putty, mortar, stucco,
plaster, grout 226n. *facing*; wafer, sealing-
wax; scotch tape; fly-paper 542n. *trap*.

See: 9, 45, 53, 198, 208, 218, 222, 226, 228,
250, 256, 264, 308, 542, 547, 624, 662, 748,
844, 905.

48 Coherence

N. *coherence*, connection, connectedness 71
n. *continuity*; chain 71n. *series*; holding
together, cohesion, cohesiveness; holding
on, tenacity, tenaciousness 778n. *retention*; adherence, adhesion, adhesiveness;
cementation, cementing, sticking, solder-
ing, agglutination, conglutination 45n.
junction; compaction, conglomeration,
agglomeration, consolidation, set 324n.
condensation; inseparability, indivisibility,
union 88n. *unity*; indigestibility 329n.
toughness; phalanx, serried ranks, unbroken front; monolith, agglomerate,
concrete 324n. *solid body*; sticker, burr,
leech, limpet, remora, barnacle, parasite;
gum, plaster, sticking-p., 47n. *adhesive*;
tights, combinations; stickjaw, toffee.

Adj. *cohesive*, coherent, adhesive, adherent;
sessile, clinging, tenacious; indigestible
329adj. *tough*; sticky, gummy, gluey,
viscous 354adj. *viscid*; compact, well-
knit, solid, coagulate, concrete, frozen
324adj. *dense*; shoulder to shoulder,
phalanxed, serried; monolithic 16adj.
uniform; united, infrangible, indivisible,
inseparable, inextricable, inseparable;
close, tight, fitting, skin-tight, moulding.

Vb. *cohere*, hang together, grow together 50
vb. *combine*; hold, stick close, hold fast;
bunch, close the ranks, stand shoulder to
shoulder, rally 74vb. *congregate*; grip,
take hold of 778vb. *retain*; hug, clasp,

embrace, twine round; close with, clinch; fit, fit tight, mould the figure; adhere, cling, stick; stick to, cleave to, come off on, rub off on; stick on to, freeze on to; stick like a leech, stick like wax, stick like a burr, stick like a limpet, cling like a shadow, hold on like a bulldog, cling like the ivy; cake, coagulate, agglomerate, conglomerate, solidify, consolidate, freeze 324 vb. *be dense.*

agglutinate, conglutinate, glue, gum, paste, lute, cement, weld, braze 45 vb. *join;* stick to, affix 38 vb. *add.*

Adv. *cohesively,* indivisibly, unitedly, solidly, compactly.

See: 38, 45, 47, 50, 71, 74, 88, 324, 329, 354, 354, 778.

49 Non-coherence

N. *non-coherence,* incoherence 72 n. *discontinuity;* uncombined state, non-combination, chaos 51 n. *decomposition;* scattering 75 n. *dispersion;* separability, immiscibility; looseness, bagginess; loosening, relaxation, laxity, freedom 46 n. *disjunction;* wateriness, runniness 335 n. *fluidity;* slipperiness 258 n. *smoothness;* frangibility, rope of sand 330 n. *brittleness;* non-adhesion, aloofness; individualist, lone wolf, separatist 84 n. *non-conformist.*

Adj. *non-adhesive,* non-adhering, slippery 258 adj. *smooth;* not sticky, dry; detached, semi-detached 46 adj. *separate;* non-cohesive, incoherent, unconsolidated, loose, like grains of sand; unconfined, unpent, free, at large 746 adj. *liberated;* loose-knit, relaxed, lax, slack, baggy, flopping, floppy, flapping, flying, streaming; watery, liquid, runny 335 adj. *fluid;* open-ended, pendulous, dangling 217 adj. *pendent;* uncombined 51 adj. *decomposed;* immiscible 59 adj. *extraneous;* aloof 620 adj. *avoiding.*

Vb. *unstick,* unglue, peel off; detach, unpin; free, loosen, loose, slacken 46 vb. *disjoin;* shake off, unseat, dismount; shed, slough 229 vb. *doff.*

come unstuck, peel off, melt, thaw, run 337 vb. *liquefy;* sit loose to, waver 601 vb. *be irresolute;* totter, slip 309 vb. *tumble;* dangle, flap 217 vb. *hang.;* rattle, shake.

See: 46, 51, 59, 72, 75, 84, 217, 229, 258, 309, 330, 335, 337, 601, 620, 746.

50 Combination

N. *combination,* composition, joining together 45 n. *joinder;* growing together, coalescence, symphysis 45 n. *junction;* fusion, crasis, blending, conflation, synthesis, syncretism 43 n. *mixture;* amalgamation, merger, assimilation, digestion, absorption, ingestion 299 n. *reception;* uniting, adunation, unification, integration, centralization 88 n. *unity;* union, Enosis, Anschluss; incorporation, embodiment, incarnation; synchronization 123 n. *synchronism,* 706 n. *co-operation;* coagency 181 n. *concurrence;* marriage, league, alliance, federation, confederation 706 n. *association;* conspiracy, cabal 623 n. *plot;* combination of sounds, counterpoint 412 n. *music;* chorus 24 n. *agreement;* harmony, orchestration 710 n. *concord;* aggregation, assembly 74 n. *assemblage;* synopsis, conspectus, bird's-eye view 438 n. *view;* mosaic, jigsaw.

compound, compound resultant; alloy, amalgam, blend; make up 56 n. *composition.*

Adj. *combined* etc. vb.; united, unified 88 adj. *one;* integrated, centralized; incorporate, embodied, incarnate; inbred, ingrained, absorbed 5 adj. *intrinsic;* fused, impregnated 43 adj. *mixed;* blended, harmonized, adapted 24 adj. *adjusted;* connected, yoked, linked, conjugate, conjoint 45 adj. *conjunct;* aggregated, congregated 74 adj. *assembled;* coalescent, symphysical; synchronized 123 vb. *synchronous;* in harmony, in partnership, in league; associated, leagued allied 706 adj. *co-operative;* conspiratorial; coagent 181 adj. *concurrent.*

Vb. *combine,* put together, fit t.; compose, make up, intertwine, interweave 222 vb. *weave;* harmonize, synchronize 24 vb. *accord;* bind, tie 45 vb. *join;* unite, unify, centralize; incorporate, absorb, assimilate; merge, amalgamate; blend, compound 43 vb. *mix;* fuse, conflate; impregnate, imbue, instil, inoculate 303 vb. *infuse;* lump together 38 vb. *add;* embody, group, re-embody, regroup, rally 74 vb.

bring together; band together, brigade, associate; federate, ally, league with; partner, join hands, team up with 706 vb. *cooperate*; fraternize, make friends 880 vb. *be friendly*; cement a union, marry 894 vb. *wed*; mate, pair, couple 90 vb. *pair*; lay heads together, cabal, conspire 623 vb. *plot*; coalesce, grow together, run t.; have an affinity, combine with; combine with water, hydrate 339 vb. *add water*.

See: 5, 24, 38, 43, 45, 56, 74, 88, 90, 123, 181, 222, 299, 303, 339, 412, 438, 623, 706, 710, 880, 894.

51 Decomposition

N. *decomposition* 46 n. *disjunction*; separation, diæresis; division, partition, compartition; dissection, dismemberment; analysis, breakdown; break-up, factorization, syllabification 44 n. *simplification*; parsing 564 n. *grammar*; resolution, electrolysis, hydrolysis, photolysis, catalysis; dissolving, dissolution 337 n. *liquefaction*; decentralization, relaxation; disintegration 165 n. *destruction*; uncombined state, chaos 17 n. *non-uniformity*.

decay 655 n. *dilapidation*; erosion, wear and tear 37 n. *diminution*; disintegration 361 n. *death*; corruption, mouldering, rotting, putrefaction, mortification, necrosis, gangrene, adipocere 649 n. *uncleanness*; rot, rust, mould 659 n. *blight*; carrion 363 n. *corpse*.

Adj. *decomposed* etc. vb.; resolved, reduced, disintegrated, uncombined, chaotic 46 adj. *disjunct*; corrupted, mouldering; rotten, bad, off, high, rancid.

Vb. *decompose*, decompound, unmix, unscramble; resolve, reduce, factorize 44 vb. *simplify*; separate, separate out, parse, dissect; break down, analyse 46 vb. *disjoin*; electrolyse, catalyse; split, fission 46 vb. *sunder*; disband, break up 75 vb. *disperse*; decentralize, relax 746 vb. *liberate*; discompose, disconcert, unsettle, disturb, confuse 63 vb. *derange*; render chaotic 61 vb. *disorder*; dissolve, melt 337 vb. *liquefy*; erode 37 vb. *bate*; rot, rust, moulder, decay, consume, waste, crumble, wear, perish 655 vb. *deteriora'e*; corrupt, putrefy, mortify, gangrene 649 vb. *make unclean*; disintegrate, go to

pieces 165 vb. *be destroyed*; slack, slake 339 vb. *add water*.

Adv. *analytically*, partitively; on analysis, by a.

See: 17, 37, 44, 46, 61, 63, 75, 165, 337, 339, 361, 363, 564, 649, 655, 659, 746.

52 Whole: principal part

N. *whole*, wholeness, integrality, omneity, fullness 54 n. *completeness*; integration, indivisibility, indiscerptibility, integrity, oneness 88 n. *unity*; a whole, whole number, integer, integral 88 n. *unit*; entirety, ensemble, corpus, complex, four corners of; totality, summation, sum 38 n. *addition*; holism, holistic approach, universalization, generalization 79 n. *generality*; comprehensiveness, comprehensivity, inclusiveness 78 n. *inclusion*; collectivity, world, cosmos 321 n. *universe*; idioverse, life space, total situation 7 n. *state*; grand view, bird's eye v., panorama, conspectus, synopsis 438 n. *view*; whole course, round, circuit 314 n. *circuition*.

all, no omissions, one and all, everybody, everyone; the world, all the w. 74 n. *crowd*; the whole, total, aggregate, gross amount, sum, sum total; ensemble, tout e., length and breadth, rough with the smooth; Alpha and Omega, 'be all and and all', lock, stock and barrel, hook, line and sinker; unit, family; set, complete s. 71 n. *series*; outfit, pack; complete list, inventory 87 n. *list*; lot, whole l., the whole caboodle, the whole kit and boodle.

chief part, best part, principal p., major p., essential p. 638 n. *chief thing*; ninety-nine per cent, bulk, mass, substance; heap, lump 32 n. *great quantity*; tissue, staple; body, torso, trunk, bole, stem, stalk; hull, hulk, skeleton; lion's share, Benjamin's mess; gist, sum and substance, the long and the short; almost all, nearly all; all but a few, majority 104 n. *greater number*.

Adj. *whole*, total, universal, holistic; integral, pure, unadulterated 44 adj. *unmixed*; entire, ungelded 646 adj. *perfect*; grand, gross, full 54 adj. *complete*; individual, single, integrated 88 adj. *one*; in one piece, seamless; fully restored 656 adj. *restored*.

intact, untouched, unaffected; undivided, unsevered, undiminished, unclipped,

uncropped, unshorn; undissolved, unabolished, still there; unbroken, undemolished, undestroyed, unbruised, unmangled, unimpaired; uncut, unabridged, unedited, uncensored, unexpurgated 646adj. *undamaged.*
indivisible, impartible 324adj. *indissoluble;* undissolvable, indiscerptible; inseparable 45adj. *conjunct;* monolithic 16adj. *uniform.*
comprehensive, omnibus, all-embracing, full-length 78adj. *inclusive;* holophrastic 557adj. *linguistic;* wholesale, sweeping 32adj. *great;* wide-spread, epidemic 79adj. *general;* international, world, world-wide, cosmic 79adj. *universal,* 189adj. *ubiquitous.*
Adv. *wholly,* integrally, body and soul, as a whole; entirely, totally, fully, every inch 54adv. *completely;* without deduction, one hundred per cent, in extenso.
on the whole, by and large, altogether, all in all, all things considered, in the long run; substantially, essentially, in substance, in essence; virtually, to all intents and purposes, effectually, in effect; as good as; mainly, in the main 32adv. *greatly;* almost, all but 200adv. *nearly.*
collectively, one and all, all together; comprehensively, and all; in bulk, in the lump, in the mass; in sum, in the aggregate; bodily, en masse, en bloc.
See: 7, 16, 32, 38, 44, 45, 54, 71, 74, 78, 79, 87, 88, 104, 189, 200, 314, 321, 324, 438, 557, 638, 646, 656.

53 Part

N. *part,* not the whole, portion; proportion, certain p.; majority 32n. *main part,* 104n. *greater number;* minority 105n. *fewness,* 33n. *small quantity;* fraction, half, moiety, quarter, tithe, percentage; factor, aliquot, aliquant 85n. *number;* balance, surplus, overplus 41n. *remainder;* quota, contingent; dividend, share, whack 783n. *portion;* item, particular, detail 80n. *particulars;* sentence, paragraph 563n. *phrase;* ingredient, member, constituent, integrant, element 58n. *component;* dissident element, schism, faction 708n. *party;* lap, round 110n. *period;* leg, side 239n. *laterality;* group, sub-group, species, sub-species (see *subdivision);*

detachment 42n. *decrement;* attachment, fixture, wing 40n. *adjunct;* part of a book, page, leaf, folio, sheet, signature 589vb. *book;* excerpt, extract, passage, quotation, selection 605n. *choice;* text, pericope; geometric part, frustum 41n. *remainder;* segment, sector, section 46n. *scission;* arc 248n. *curve;* hemisphere 252n. *sphere;* part payment, instalment, advance, earnest money 804n. *payment;* sample, foretaste 83n. *example;* fragment, cantle, torso, trunk (see *piece).*
limb 234n. *edge;* member (see *part);* hinderlimb 267n. *leg;* forelimb 271n. *wing;* flipper, fin 269n. *propeller;* arm, forearm, cubit, ulna, brace, hand 378n. *feeler;* elbow, funny-bone 247n. *angularity.*
subdivision, segment, sector, section 46n. *scisson;* division, compartment; group, sub-g., species, sub-s., family 74n. *group;* classification 62n. *arrangement;* ward, parish, department 184n. *district;* chapter, paragraph, clause, sub-clause, phrase, verse; fascicle, part, number, issue, instalment, book, volume 589n. *edition, reading matter;* canto, fit 593n. *poem.*
branch, sub-b., ramification, offshoot 40n. *adjunct;* bough, limb, spur, twig, tendril, leaf, leaflet; shoot, scion, sucker, slip, sprig, spray 366n. *foliage.*
piece, frustum, torso, trunk 41n. *remainder;* limb, segment, section (see *part);* patch, insertion 40n. *adjunct;* length, roll 222n. *textile;* strip, swatch; fragment, unfinished symphony 55n. *incompleteness;* bit, scrap, shred, wisp, rag 33n. *small thing;* frustulum 33n. *particle;* morsel, bite, crust, crumb 33n. *small quantity;* splinter, sliver, chip, snip; cantle, cut, wedge, finger, slice, rasher; gobbet, collop, cutlet, chop, steak; hunk, chunk, lump, mass 195n. *bulk;* clod, turf, divot, sod 344n. *land;* sherd, shard, potsherd, brickbat; flake, scale 207n. *lamina;* dollop, dose, whack, share 783n. *portion;* bits and pieces, odds and ends, miscellanea, flotsam and jetsam 43n. *medley;* clippings, shavings, parings, brash, rubble, scree, detritus, moraine, debris 41n. *leavings;* refuse 641n. *rubbish;* shreds, rags, tatters 801n. *poverty;* piece of land, parcel.
Adj. *fragmentary,* broken, brashy, crumbly; in bits, in pieces 46adj. *disjunct;* not whole, limbless, armless, legless, in torso 647adj. *imperfect;* partial, bitty, scrappy 636adj.

insufficient; half-finished 55 adj. *unfinished*; fractional, half, semi, hemi, aliquot; sectional, divided, multifid; departmentalized, compartmentalized, in compartments 46 adj. *separate*; shredded, wispy, sliced, minced 33 adj. *small.*

brachial, brachio-cephalic; membered, brachiate, brachiferous, brachigerous; ulnar, cubital; with branches, branchy.

Vb. *part,* divide, partition, segment, chunk; compartmentalize 46 vb. *sunder*; share out 783 vb. *apportion*; fragment 46 vb. *disjoin.*

Adv. *partly,* in part, scrappily, partially; in a sense 55 adv. *incompletely.*

piecemeal, part by part, limb from limb; by instalments, by snatches, by inches, by driblets; bit by bit, inch by inch, foot by foot, drop by drop; in detail, in lots.

See: 32, 33, 40, 41, 42, 43, 55, 58, 61, 74, 80, 83, 85, 104, 105, 110, 184, 195, 207, 222, 234, 239, 247, 248, 252, 267, 269, 271, 344, 366, 378, 563, 589, 593, 605, 636, 641, 647, 708, 783, 801, 804.

54 Completeness

N. *completeness,* nothing lacking, nothing to add, entireness, wholeness 52 n. *whole*; integration, integrality 88 n. *unity*; solidity, solidarity 324 n. *density,* 706 n. *co-operation*; harmony, balance 710 n. *concord*; self-sufficiency 635 n. *sufficiency*; entirety, totality 52 n. *all*; universality, comprehensivity, comprehensiveness 79 n. *generality*; the ideal 646 n. *perfection*; ne plus ultra, the limit 236 n. *limit*; peak, culmination, crown 213 n. *summit*; finish 69 n. *end*; last touch 725 n. *completion*; fulfilment, consummation 69 n. *finality*; whole hog; nothing less than, the utmost 69 n. *extremity.*

plenitude, fullness, amplitude, capacity, maximum, one's fill, saturation 635 n. *sufficiency*; saturation point 863 n. *satiety*; completion, impletion, filling, replenishment, refill; filling up, brimming, over-filling, swamping, drowning; over-fulfilment 637 n. *redundance*; full house, not a seat empty; complement, full c., full crew, full load; full measure, brimmer, bumper; bellyful, sickener; full size, full length, full extent, full volume; complement, supplement, make-weight 31 n. *compensation.*

Adj. *complete,* plenary, full; utter, total; integral, integrated 52 adj. *whole*; entire, with all its parts, with nothing missing, with supplement 52 adj. *intact,* 646 adj. *perfect*; unbroken, undivided, solid 324 n. *dense*; self-contained, self-sufficient, self-sufficing 635 adj. *sufficient*; fully furnished 633 adj. *provisionary*; comprehensive, omnibus 78 adj. *inclusive*; exhaustive, circumstantial, detailed 570 adj. *diffuse*; absolute, extreme, radical; thorough, thoroughgoing, whole-hogging, sweeping, wholesale, regular 32 adj. *consummate*; unmitigated, downright, plumb, plain 44 adj. *unmixed*; crowning, completing, culminating, consummating, supplementary, complementary 725 adj. *completive,* 38 adj. *additional*; unconfined, unqualified 744 adj. *unconditional.*

full, replete 635 adj. *filled*; replenished, refilled, topped up 633 adj. *provisionary*; well-filled, well-lined, bulging; brim-full, top-f., brimming, level with, flush; over-full, overflowing, slopping, swamped, drowned; saturated, oozing, leaking 637 adj. *redundant*; coming out at the ears, bursting at the seams; crop-full, gorged, full as a tick, sickened with 863 adj. *sated*; chock-full, chock-a-block, not an inch to spare; cram-full, crammed, stuffed, packed, full-p., jam-p., packed like sardines, jammed, tight 45 adj. *firm-set*; laden, heavy-l., freighted, fraught, full-f., full-charged, full to the hatches; infested, overrun, crawling, with, lousy w., stiff w.; full of, rolling in; soaked in, dripping with 341 adj. *drenched*; ever-full, inexhaustible 146 adj. *unceasing.*

Vb. *be complete,* be integrated, make a whole; reach *or* touch perfection, have everything; culminate, come to a head 725 vb. *climax*; reach an end, come to a close, be all over 69 vb. *end*; suffice for oneself 635 vb. *have enough*; want nothing, lack n. 828 vb. *be content*; become complete, fill out, attain full growth, reach maturity 669 vb. *mature*; be filled, fill, fill up, brim, hold no more, run over, slop o., overflow 637 vb. *superabound*; gorge, eat *or* drink one's fill 947 vb. *gluttonize,* 949 vb. *get drunk.*

make complete, complete, integrate, make into a whole 45 vb. *join*; make whole 656 vb. *restore*; build up, make up, piece together 56 vb. *compose*; eke out,

supplement, supply, fill a gap 38 vb. *add*; make good 31 vb. *compensate*; do thoroughly, leave nothing to add, carry out 725 vb. *carry through*; overfulfil 637 vb. *be superfluous*; put the finishing touch, tie the last thread, cast off 69 vb. *terminate*.
fill, fill up, brim, top; soak, saturate 341 vb. *drench*; overfill, swamp, drown, overwhelm; top up, replenish 633 vb. *provide*; satisfy 635 vb. *suffice*, 828 vb. *content*, 863 vb. *sate*; fill to capacity, cram, pack, stuff, line, bulge out, pack in, pile in, squeeze in, ram in, jam in 303 vb. *insert*; load, charge, ram down; lade, freight 187 vb. *stow*; fill space, occupy 226 vb. *cover*; reach to, extend to 183 vb. *extend*; spread over, sprawl o., overrun 189 vb. *pervade*; leave no corner, fit tight, be chock-a-block 45 vb. *tighten*; fill in, put in, write in, enter 38 vb. *add*.
Adv. *completely*, fully, wholly, totally, entirely, utterly, extremely 32 adv. *greatly*; all told, in all, in toto; effectually, virtually, as good as; to all intents, to all intents and purposes; on all accounts, in all respects, every way; quite, all of, altogether; outright, downright; to the heart, to the core, to the marrow; thoroughly, clean, stark, hollow; to one's fill, to the top of one's bent, to the utmost, to the end; out and out, all out, heart and soul, through thick and thin; over head and shoulders, head over heels, neck and crop; to the brim, up to the hilt, up to the neck, up to the ears, up to the eyes; hook, line and sinker; root and branch; down to the ground; with a vengeance, with all the trimmings, and then some; to the last man, to the last breath; without remainder, every whit, every inch; at full length, in extenso; as . . . as can be; as far as possible; to capacity, not an inch to spare.
throughout, all the way, all round, from first to last, from beginning to end, from end to end, from one end to the other, from coast to coast, from Dan to Beersheba, from Land's End to John o' Groats, from Maine to California, from north and south and east and west; fore and aft; from top to bottom, de fond en comble; from top to toe, from head to foot, cap-à-pie; to the bitter end, to the end of the chapter, for good and all.
See: 31, 32, 38, 44, 45, 52, 56, 69, 78, 79, 88, 146, 183, 187, 189, 213, 226, 236, 303, 324, 341, 570, 633, 635, 637, 646, 656, 669, 706, 710, 725, 744, 828, 863, 947, 949.

55 Incompleteness

N. *incompleteness*, defectiveness; unfinished state 647 n. *imperfection*; unreadiness 670 n. *non-preparation*; underdevelopment, immaturity 670 n. *undevelopment*; first beginnings 68 n. *début*; sketch, outline, first draft, rough d. 623 n. *plan*; torso, trunk 53 n. *piece*; half-measures, sketchiness, scrappiness, a lick and a promise 726 n. *non-completion*; perfunctoriness, superficiality, hollowness 4 n. *insubstantiality*, 458 n. *negligence*; nonfulfilment, deficiency, falling short 307 n. *shortcoming*, 636 n. *insufficiency*; nonsatisfaction, dissatisfaction 829 n. *discontent*; mutilation, impairment 655 n. *deterioration*; omission, break, gap, missing link 72 n. *discontinuity*, 201 n. *interval*, 108 n. *interim*; semi-, half, quarter; instalment, part payment 53 n. *part*.
deficit, part wanting, screw loose, missing link, omission, caret 190 n. *absence*; defect, shortfall, ullage 42 n. *decrement*, 772 n. *loss*; default, defalcation 930 n. *improbity*; want, lack, need 627 n. *requirement*.
Adj. *incomplete*, defective 307 adj. *deficient*; short, scant 636 adj. *insufficient*; omitting, wanting, lacking, needing, requiring 627 adj. *demanding*; short of, shy of; maimed, lame, limping; mangled, marred, mutilated; without, -less; limbless, armless, legless, one-armed, one-legged, one-eyed 163 adj. *crippled*; garbled, impaired 655 adj. *deteriorated*; cropped, lopped, docked, bobtailed, truncated, shortened 204 adj. *short*; blemished, flawed 647 adj. *imperfect*; half, semi-, partial, 53 adj. *fragmentary*; left unfinished, half-f., neglected 726 adj. *uncompleted*; not ready, unready 670 adj. *unprepared*; undeveloped, underdeveloped, unripe 670 adj. *immature*; raw, crude, rough-hewn 244 adj. *amorphous*; sketchy, scrappy, bitty, hollow, superficial, meagre, thin, poor 4 adj. *insubstantial*; perfunctory, runthrough, half-done, undone 458 adj. *neglected*; left, left in the air, left hanging; omitted, missing, lost 190 adj. *absent*; interrupted 72 adj. *discontinuous*; in default, in arrears, defaulting, defalcating.

unfinished, in progress 285 adj. *progressive*; in hand, going on; in embryo, begun 68 adj. *beginning*; in preparation, on the stocks.

Vb. *be incomplete*, miss, lack, need 627 vb. *require*, 307 vb. *fall short*; be wanting 190 vb. *be absent*; leave undone 458 vb. *neglect*; omit, miss out 57 vb. *exclude*; break off, interrupt 72 vb. *discontinue*; leave in the air, leave hanging; default, defalcate.

Adv. *incompletely*, partially, by halves, in instalments; in arrear, in default.

See: 4, 42, 53, 57, 68, 72, 108, 163, 190, 201, 204, 244, 285, 307, 458, 623, 627, 636, 647, 655, 670, 726, 772, 829, 930.

inclose; involve, imply 5 vb. *be intrinsic*; hide 525 vb. *conceal*.

compose, compound 43 vb. *mix*, 50 vb. *combine*; organize, set in order 62 vb. *arrange*; synthesize, put together 45 vb. *join*; compile, assemble 74 vb. *bring together*; compose, set up 587 vb. *print*; draft, draw up, indite 586 vb. *write*; orchestrate, score 413 vb. *compose music*; draw 553 vb. paint; construct, build, make, fabricate 164 vb. *produce*; knit, interweave 222 vb. *weave*; pattern, design 12 vb. *correlate*.

See: 5, 12, 43, 45, 50, 58, 62, 74, 78, 164, 222, 235, 299, 331, 340, 358, 412, 413, 525, 551, 553, 554, 563, 586, 587, 589, 591, 592, 593, 594, 837.

56 Composition

N. *composition*, constitution, set-up, make-up; make, conformation, formation, construction, build-up, build, organization 331 n. *structure*; temper, crasis, habit, nature, character, condition 5 n. *temperament*; climate, meteorology 340 n. *weather*; embodiment, incorporation 78 n. *inclusion*; compound 43 n. *mixture*, 50 n. *combination*, 358 n. *organism*; syntax, sentence, period 563 n. *phrase*; artistic composition 551 n. *art*, 412 n. *music*, 553 n. *painting*, 554 n. *sculpture*; architecture 164 n. *edifice*; authorship 586 n. *writing*, 593 n. *poetry*; dramatic art 594 n. *drama*; composing, setting-up, printing, typography 587 n. *print*; compilation 74 n. *assemblage*; work, construction 164 n. *production*; choreography 837 n. *dancing*; orchestration, instrumentation, score 412 n. *musical piece*; work of art, picture, sculpture, model; literary work 589 n. *book*, 593 n. *poem*, 591 n. *dissertation*, 592 n. *anthology*; play 594 n. *stage play*; ballet 837 n. *dance*; pattern, design 12 n. *correlation*.

Adj. *composing*, constituting, making; composed of, made of; containing, having 78 adj. *inclusive*.

Vb. *constitute*, compose, be the whole of, form, make; make up, build up to; inhere, belong to, go to the making of, enter into 58 vb. *be one of*.

contain, subsume, include 78 vb. *comprise*; hold, have, take in, absorb 299 vb. *admit*; comprehend, embrace, embody 235 vb.

57 Exclusion

N. *exclusion*, preclusion, preoccupation, pre-emption; anticipation, forestalling 702 n. *hindrance*; possessiveness, monopoly, dog-in-the-manger policy, exclusiveness, closed shop 932 n. *selfishness*; non-inclusion, exception; an exception, special case; exception in favour of, exemption, dispensation 746 n. *liberation*; leaving out, omission, deliberate o. 607 n. *rejection*; non-admission, blackball; no entry, no admission; closed door, lock-out; ban, bar, taboo 757 n. *prohibition*; ostracism, boycott 620 n. *avoidance*; segregation, seposition, quarantine, colour-bar, apartheid, casteism 883 n. *seclusion*; intolerance, repression, suppression 481 n. *prejudice*; extrusion, expulsion, disbarment, dismissal, deportation, exile, expatriation; removal, elimination, eradication 188 n. *displacement*; cancellation, blotting out 550 n. *obliteration*; dam, coffer-d., wall, screen, partition, pale, curtain, iron c., bamboo c. 235 n. *barrier*; great wall of China, Hadrian's wall 713 n. *defence*; customs' barrier, tariff, tariff wall 809 n. *tax*; place of exile, place of segregation, ghetto, outer darkness 223 n. *exteriority*.

Adj. *excluding*, exclusive, exclusory, exemptive; preventive, interdictive, prohibitive 757 n. *prohibiting*; preclusive, pre-emptive; silent about 582 adj. *taciturn*.

excluded, barred, excepted etc. vb.; extra-, not included, not admitted; peripheral, hardly in, half in, half out; included out,

counted o.; not told, unrecounted, suppressed, stifled; not allowed, disallowed, banned 757 adj. *prohibited*; disbarred, struck off 550 adj. *obliterated*; shut out, outcaste 607 adj. *rejected*; inadmissible, beyond the pale 470 adj. *impossible*; foreign 59 adj. *extraneous*, 84 adj. *unconformable*; removable, exemptile.

Vb. *be excluded*, not belong, stay outside, gain no admission; suffer exile, go into e., 296 vb. *depart*, 190 vb. *be absent*.

exclude, preclude 470 vb. *make impossible*; preoccupy, pre-empt, forestall 64 vb. *come before*; keep out, warn off 747 vb. *restrain*; black-ball, deny entry, shut out, shut the door on, spurn 607 vb. *reject*; bar, ban, taboo, black, disallow 757 vb. *prohibit*; ostracise, cold-shoulder, boycott, outcaste, send to Coventry 620 vb. *avoid*; not include, leave out, count o.; exempt, dispense, excuse 746 vb. *liberate*; except, make an exception, treat as a special case 19 vb. *make unlike*; omit, miss out, pass over, disregard 458 vb. *neglect*; lay aside, put a., relegate 46 vb. *set apart*; take out, strike o., cancel 550 vb. *obliterate*; disbar, strike off, remove, disqualify 188 vb. *displace*, 963 vb. *punish*; rule out, draw the line; wall off, curtain off, quarantine 232 vb. *circumscribe*, 235 vb. *inclose*; excommunicate, segregate, sequester 883 vb. *seclude*; thrust out, extrude, dismiss, deport, exile, banish, outlaw, expatriate; weed, sift, winnow, bolt 44 vb. *eliminate*; sort out, declassify; eradicate, uproot 300 vb. *void*; expurgate, garble, censor 648 vb. *purify*; deny 533 vb. *negate*, 760 vb. *refuse*; abandon 621 vb. *relinquish*.

Adv. *exclusive of*, excepting, barring, not counting, except, with the exception of, save; bating, short of; let alone, apart from; outside of, extra-.

See: 19, 44, 46, 59, 64, 84, 188, 190, 223, 232, 235, 296, 300, 458, 470, 481, 533, 550, 582, 607, 620, 621, 648, 702, 713, 746, 747, 757, 760, 809, 883, 932, 963.

58 Component

N. *component*, component part, integral p., integrant p., element; link, stitch; word, letter; constituent, part and parcel 53 n.

part; factor, leaven 178 n. *influence*; additive, appurtenance, feature 40 n. *adjunct*; one of, member, one of us; staff, crew, men, company, complement 686 n. *personnel*; ingredient, content 193 n. *contents*; works, insides, interior 224 n. *interiority*; spare part 40 n. *extra*; components, set, outfit 88 n. *unit*; complete set, complement.

Adj. *ingredient*, entering into, belonging, proper, native, inherent 5 adj. *intrinsic*; component, constituent 56 adj. *composing*; built-in, appurtenant 45 adj. *conjunct*; admitted, entered, made a member, part of, one of, on the staff; involved, implicated, deep in 43 adj. *mixed*.

Vb. *be one of*, make part of, be a member etc. n.; inhere, belong 5 vb. *be intrinsic*; enter into, enter into the composition of, become involved with, be implicated in, share 775 vb. *participate*; merge in, be merged in 43 vb. *be mixed*; belong to, appertain to 9 vb. *be related*.

See: 5, 9, 40, 43, 45, 53, 56, 88, 178, 193, 224, 686, 775.

59 Extraneousness

N. *extraneousness*, extraneity, foreignness 6 n. *extrinsicality*, 223 n. *exteriority*; foreign parts 199 n. *farness*; foreign body, foreign substance, alien element, unassimilated e. 84 n. *unconformity*; alienism.

foreigner, alien, man from foreign parts, stranger, easterling, Sassenach, Southron; continental, tramontane, ultramontanist; non-Greek, barbarian; Celtic fringe; Celestial, Chink; Easterner, Westerner, Southerner, Northerner; Canuck, limejuicer, Afrikander, Aussie, Malagasy, Monegasque, Muscovite; greaser, dago, wog; paleface, squaw-man; gringo; Martian, Venusian, Saturnian; colonial, creole 188 n. *settler*; resident alien, metic, uitlander, expatriate; migrant, emigrant, immigrant, declarant, pommie, hunky, bohunk; refugee, deraciné, displaced person, D.P. 268 n. *wanderer*; foreign population, diaspora, ten lost tribes.

intruder, interloper, cuckoo, squatter; uninvited guest, gate-crasher, stowaway; outsider, novus homo, upstart; not one of us, the stranger in our midst; arrival,

new a., new face, new-comer, tenderfoot 297n. *incomer*; invader 712n. *attacker*.

Adj. *extraneous*, of external origin, ulterior, outside 223adj. *exterior*, 6adj. *extrinsic*; interplanetary, inter-stellar 199adj. *distant*; not indigenous, imported, foreign-made; foreign, alien, peregrine; strange, outlandish, barbarian; oversea, continental, tramontane, ultramontane, Italianate; exotic, hot-house, unacclimatized; gypsy, nomad, wandering 267adj. *travelling*; unassimilated, undigested; indigestible 84adj. *unconformable*; immigrant 297adj. *incoming*; intrusive, interloping, trespassing; infringing, invading 712adj. *attacking*; exceptional 84adj. *unusual*; un-American, un-English 84adj. *abnormal*; not of this world, unnatural, supernatural 983adj. *magical*; inadmissible 57adj. *excluded*.

Adv. *abroad*, in foreign parts, in foreign lands; beyond seas, overseas; from outer space.

See: 6, 57, 84, 188, 199, 223, 267, 268, 297, 712, 983.

60 Order

N. *order*, state of order, orderliness, tidiness, neatness 648n. *cleanness*, 258n. *smoothness*; proportion 245n. *symmetry*; peace, quiet 266n. *quietude*; harmony, music of the spheres 710n. *concord*; good order, economy, system, method, methodicalness, methodology, systematization; fixed order, rule 81n. *regularity*, 16n. *uniformity*; custom, routine 610n. *habit*; strict order, discipline 739n. *obedience*; due order, gradation, subordination, rank, place, position 73n. *serial place*; unbroken order, course, even tenor, progression, series 71n. *continuity*; logical order, serial o., alphabetical o. 65n. *sequence*, 12n. *correlation*; organization, putting in order, disposition, array 62n. *arrangement*, 56n. *composition*.

Adj. *orderly*, harmonious 710adj. *concordant*, 245adj. *symmetrical*; well-behaved, well-drilled, disciplined 739adj. *obedient*; well-regulated, under control, according to rule 81adj. *regular*; ordered, classified, schematic 62adj. *arranged*; methodical, systematic, businesslike; strict, invariable 16adj. *uniform*; routine, steady 610

adj. *habitual*; correct, shipshape, trim, neat, tidy, dinky, neat and tidy, neat as a pin; in good trim, in apple-pie order, in perfect o., in its proper place, unconfused 62adj. *arranged*; unruffled, unrumpled 258adj. *smooth*; direct 249adj. *straight*; clear, lucid 516adj. *intelligible*.

Vb. *order*, take order for; dispose 62vb. *arrange*; schematize, systematize, organize 62vb. *regularize*; harmonize, synchronize, regulate 24vb. *adjust*; normalize, standardize 16vb. *make uniform*; keep order, police, control, govern 733vb. *rule*, 737vb. *command*.

be in order, harmonize, synchronize 24vb. *accord*; fall in, range oneself, draw up, line up; fall into place, find one's level; station oneself, take station; take one's place, take one's rank, take one's position 187vb. *place oneself*; keep one's place; rally, rally round 74vb. *congregate*; follow routine 610vb. *be wont*.

Adv. *in order*, strictly, just so, by the book, by the card, according to Cocker, by order, as directed; in turn, in its t., seriatim; gradatim, step by step, by regular steps, by regular gradations, by regular stages, at regular intervals, at stated periods 141adv. *periodically*; orderly, in orderly fashion, methodically, systematically, schematically; all correct, O.K.

See: 12, 16, 24, 56, 62, 65, 71, 73, 74, 81, 141, 187, 245, 249, 258, 266, 516, 610, 648, 710, 733, 737, 739.

61 Disorder

N. *disorder*, random order, non-arrangement, non-classification; inco-ordination, muddle, no plan, no order, no method, no system (see *confusion*); chaotic state, chaos, anarchy 734n. *laxity*; irregularity, anomalousness, anomaly 17 n. *non-uniformity*; disunion, disaccord, 25n. *disagreement*; irregularity, ectopia; disharmony 411n. *discord*; disorderliness, unruliness, no discipline 738n. *disobedience*; violent behaviour, storm, outbreak 176vb. *violence*; nihilism 738 n. *sedition*; untidiness, littering, sluttishness, slovenliness, slovenry 649n. *uncleanness*; neglect 458n. *negligence*;

discomposure, disarray, dishevelment 63 n. *derangement*; dissolution, scattering 75 n. *dispersion,* 51 n. *decomposition*; upheaval, convulsion 149 n. *revolution*; subversion 221 n. *overturning*; destruction 165 n. *havoc.*

confusion (see *disorder*); welter, jumble, hugger-mugger, mix-up, medley, embroilment, imbroglio 43 n. *mixture*; wilderness, jungle; chaos, fortuitous concourse of atoms; omnium gatherum, huddle, seething mass, scramble, shambles 74 n. *crowd*; muddle, litter, clutter, lumber 641 n. *rubbish*; farrago, mess, mass, mash, mishmash, hash, hotch-potch, stock pot, witch's brew, jumble sale, lucky dip; Babel, bedlam, madhouse, confusion worse confounded (see *turmoil*).

complexity, complication 700 n. *difficulty*, 702 n. *hindrance*; implication, involvement, imbroglio, embroilment; intricacy, interlocking, involution, kink 251 n. *convolution*; maze, labyrinth; web, spider's w. 222 n. *network*; coil, sleave, tangle, twist, tangled skein, ravelment; knot, Gordian k. 47 n. *ligature*; wheels within wheels, clockwork, machinery; puzzle 517 n. *unintelligibility*; situation, pretty kettle of fish, pretty piece of business, a nice b. 700 n. *predicament.*

turmoil, turbulence, tumult, frenzy, ferment, storm, convulsion 176 n. *violence*; pandemonium, inferno; hullabaloo, row, riot, uproar 400 n. *loudness*; affray, fight, fracas, mêlée 718 n. *battle*; to-do, rumpus, ruction, pudder, pother, trouble, disturbance 318 n. *agitation*; whirlwind, tornado, hurricane 352 n. *gale*; beargarden, shambles, madhouse, Bedlam; Saturnalia, Donnybrook Fair; rough house, rough and tumble, free for all, spill and pelt, hell broke loose, bull in a China shop; streetfighting, gang warfare 709 n. *quarrel*; fat in the fire, Devil to pay.

slut, sloven, slattern, draggletail, litterer, litter-lout 649 n. *dirty person*; ragamuffin tatterdemalion 801 n. *poor man.*

anarch, anarchist, nihilist; lord of misrule, mohawk, sons of Belial 738 n. *rioter.*

Adj. *orderless*, in disorder, in disarray, disordered, disarranged, disorganized, jumbled, shuffled 63 adj. *deranged*; unclassified, ungraded, unsorted; out of order, not in working order, not working 641 adj. *useless*; out of joint, out of gear, dislocated 46 adj. *disjunct*; out of sorts 651 adj. *sick*; irregular, ectopic, in the wrong place, misplaced 188 adj. *displaced*; awry, snafu; topsy-turvy, upside down 221 adj. *inverted*; wandering, straggling dispersed 75 adj. *unassembled*; random, unarranged, unorganized, unco-ordinated, unclassified; unschematic, planless; incoherent, skimble-skamble; irregular, anomalous 17 adj. *non-uniform*; unsystematic, unmethodical, desultory, aimless, casual; promiscuous, *indiscriminate* 464 adj. *indiscriminating*; confused, chaotic, in chaos, in a mess, messy, all anyhow, haywire; unkempt, uncombed, dishevelled, tumbled, windswept, windblown, tousled, discomposed; littering, untidy, slovenly, sluttish, slatternly, bedraggled, messy 649 adj. *dirty*; sloppy, slipshod, slack, informal, careless 456 adj. *inattentive.*

complex, intricate, involved, complicated, over-c., over-involved, over-complicated 251 adj. *coiled,* 517 adj. *puzzling*; mazy, winding, inextricable 251 adj. *labyrinthine*; entangled, balled up, snarled 702 adj. *hindered*; knotted 45 adj. *tied.*

disorderly, undisciplined, tumultous, rumbustious 738 adj. *riotous*; frantic 503 adj. *frenzied*; orgiastic, Saturnalian, Bacchic, Dionysiac 949 adj. *drunken*; rough, tempestuous, turbulent 176 adj. *violent,* 318 adj. *agitated*; anarchical, lawless 954 adj. *lawbreaking*; wild, harum-scarum, scatter-brained 456 adj. *light-minded.*

Vb. *be disordered,* lose all order, fall into disarray, scatter, break up 75 vb. *disperse*; get in a mess, fall into confusion, lose cohesion 49 vb. *come unstuck*; get out of hand, throw off discipline, riot 738 vb. *disobey*; not keep one's place, jump the queue 64 vb. *come before*; disorder 63 vb. *derange.*

rampage, storm 176 vb. *be violent*; rush, mob, break the cordon; roister, roil, riot, 738 vb. *revolt*; romp 837 vb. *amuse oneself*; play the fool 497 vb. *be absurd*; fête, maffick 886 vb. *gratulate.*

Adv. *confusedly*, in confusion, in disorder, without order, anyhow; irregularly; by fits and snatches, by fits and starts; chaotically, pell-mell, higgledy-piggledy, helter-skelter, harum-scarum; in turmoil, in a ferment; on the rampage; at sixes and sevens, at cross purposes; topsy-turvy,

upside down 221 adv. *inversely*; inextricably.

See: 17, 25, 43, 45, 46, 47, 49, 51, 63, 64, 74, 75, 149, 165, 176, 188, 221, 222, 251, 318, 352, 400, 411, 456, 458, 463, 497, 503, 517, 641, 649, 651, 700, 702, 709, 718, 734, 738, 801, 837, 886, 949, 954.

62 Arrangement: reduction to order

N. *arrangement*, reduction to order; ordering, disposal, disposition, marshalling, arraying, placing 187 n. *location*; collocation, grouping 45 n. *joinder*, 74 n. *assemblage*; division, distribution, allocation, allotment 783 n. *apportionment*; method, systematization, organization, reorganization; rationalization 44 n. *simplification*; streamlining 654 n. *improvement*; centralization 48 n. *coherence*; decentralization 49 n. *non-coherence*; administration, staff-work 689 n. *management*; planning, making arrangements 623 n. *contrivance*, 669 n. *preparation*; taxonomy, categorization, classification 561 n. *nomenclature*; analysis 51 n. *decomposition*; codification, digestion, consolidation; syntax, conjugation 564 n. *grammar*; grading, gradation, subordination, graduation, calibration 465 n. *measurement*, 71 n. *series*; continuation, serialization 71 n. *continuity*; timing, synchronization 123 n. *synchronism*; formulation, construction 56 n. *composition*; result of arrangement, array, system, form 60 n. *order*; cosmos 321 n. *universe*; organic creature 358 n. *organism*; orchestration, score 412 n. *music*; lay-out, pattern, architecture 331 n. *structure*; weave 222 n. *crossing*; choreography 837 n. *dance*; collection, assortment 74 n. *accumulation*; schematic arrangement, schematism; register, file 548 n. *record*; inventory, catalogue, table 87 n. *list*; syntagma, code, digest, synopsis 592 n. *compendium*; treatise, essay, article 591 n. *dissertation*, 589 n. *book*; atlas 551 n. *map*; scheme 623 n. *plan*; composition 770 n. *compromise*, 765 n. *compact*, 766 n. *conditions*; class, group, sub-g. 77 n. *classification*.

sorting, grading, seeding; reference system, cross-reference 12 n. *correlation*; file, filing system, card index, pigeon-hole;

sieve, strainer 263 n. *porosity*; sorter, sifter.

Adj. *arranged*, disposed, marshalled, arrayed etc. vb.; ordered, schematic, tabulated, tabular; methodical, systematic, organizational; precise, definite, cut and dried; analyzed, classified, assorted; unravelled, disentangled, unscrambled, straightened out; regulated 81 n. *regular*; unconfused 60 adj. *orderly*; sorted, seeded.

Vb. *arrange*, set, dispose, set up, set out; formulate, form, put into shape, orchestrate, score 56 vb. *compose*; form into ranks, rank, range, align, line up, form up; position 187 vb. *place*; marshal, array; bring back to order, rally 74 vb. *bring together*; place *or* put *or* set in order; fix the order, grade, size, group, space; collocate, thread together 45 vb. *connect*; settle, fix, determine, define; allot, allocate, assign, distribute, deal, parcel out 783 vb. *apportion*; allot the parts, decide the role, cast 594 vb. *dramatize*; improve the order, trim, neaten, tidy, tidy up (see *unravel*); arrange for, make arrangements 669 vb. *prepare*, 623 vb. *plan*, 689 vb. *manage*.

regularize, reduce to order, bring order into, straighten out, put to rights 654 vb. *rectify*, 24 vb. *adjust*; adjust the type, justify 587 vb. *print*; regulate, co-ordinate, phase; organize, systematize, methodize, schematize; standardize, normalize, centralize 16 vb. *make uniform*.

class, classify, subsume, group; specify 561 vb. *name*; process, process the data; analyze, anatomize, divide; dissect 51 vb. *decompose*; rate, rank, grade, evaluate 480 vb. *estimate*; sort, sift, seed; sift out, bolt, riddle 44 vb. *eliminate*; file, pigeonhole; index, reference, cross-r.; tabulate, alphabeticize; catalogue, inventory 87 vb. *list*; register 548 vb. *record*; codify, digest.

unravel, untangle, disentangle, disembroil, ravel, card, comb out, unweave, uncoil, untwist, untwine 316 vb. *evolve*; iron, press, uncrease, iron out 258 vb. *smooth*; unscramble, straighten out, tidy up, clean up, neaten 654 vb. *make better*; clear the air, remove misunderstanding, explain 520 vb. *interpret*.

See: 12, 16, 24, 44, 45, 48, 49, 51, 56, 60, 71, 74, 77, 81, 87, 123, 187, 222, 258, 263, 316, 321, 331, 358, 412, 465, 480, 520, 548, 551,

561, 564, 587, 589, 591, 592, 594, 623, 654, 669, 689, 765, 766, 770, 783, 837.

63 Derangement

N. *derangement*, subversion of order; shuffling 151 n. *interchange*; translocation 272 n. *transference*; sabotage, obstruction 702 n. *hindrance*; disarrangement, disorganization, discomposure, dishevelment; dislocation 46 n. *separation*; displacement, evection (astron.), perturbation (astron.); disturbance, interruption 138 n. *intempestivity*; creasing, corrugation 261 n. *fold*; madness 503 n. *insanity*; upsetting 221 n. *inversion*; convulsion 176 n. *violence*, 318 n. *agitation*; state of disorder 61 n. *disorder*.

Adj. *deranged* 61 adj. *orderless*; demented 503 adj. *insane*; sabotaged 702 n. *hindered*.

Vb. *derange*, disarrange, disorder, tumble, put out of gear, throw out of order; disturb, touch 265 vb. *move*; meddle, interfere 702 vb. *hinder*; mislay, lose 188 vb. *misplace*; disorganize, muddle, confound, confuse, convulse, throw into confusion, make havoc, scramble; tamper, spoil, mar, damage, sabotage 655 vb. *impair*; force, strain, bend, twist 176 vb. *be violent*; unhinge, dislocate, sprain, rick 188 vb. *displace*; unseat, dislodge, derail, throw off the rails; unbalance, upset, overturn, capsize 221 vb. *invert*, 149 vb. *revolutionize*; unsettle, declassify, detribalize, denationalize; shake, jiggle, toss 318 vb. *agitate*; trouble, perturb, discompose, disconcert, ruffle, rattle, flurry, fluster 456 vb. *distract*; interrupt, break in on 138 vb. *mistime*; misdirect, disorientate, throw one off his bearings 495 vb. *mislead*, 655 vb. *pervert*; dement, drive mad 503 vb. *make mad*, 891 vb. *enrage*.

jumble, shuffle 151 vb. *interchange*, 272 vb. *transpose*; mix up 43 vb. *mix*; toss, tumble 318 vb. *agitate*; ruffle, dishevel, tousle, fluff; rumple, crumple, crease, crush 261 vb. *fold*; untidy, mess, muck up; muddle, huddle, mess up, litter, clutter; scatter, fling about 75 vb. *disperse*.

bedevil, confuse, make a mess *or* hash of; confound, complicate, perplex, involve, ravel, ball up, entangle, tangle, embroil;

turn topsy-turvy, turn upside down 221 vb. *invert*; send haywire.

See: 43, 46, 61, 75, 138, 149, 151, 176, 188, 221, 261, 265, 272, 318, 456, 495, 503, 655, 702, 891.

64 Precedence

N. *precedence*, antecedence, antecedency, going before, coming b., queue-jumping 283 n. *precession*; anteriority 119 n. *priority*; front position, anteposition, prefixion, prothesis 237 n. *front*; higher position, pride of place 34 n. *superiority*; preference 605 n. *choice*; pre-eminence, excellence 638 n. *importance*; captaincy, leadership, hegemony 733 n. *authority*; the lead, le pas; leading, guiding, pioneering; precedent 66 n. *precursor*; past history 125 n. *preterition*.

Adj. *preceding*, etc. vb.; precedent, prodromous; antecedent, foregoing, outgoing; anterior, former, previous, 119 adj. *prior*; before-mentioned, above-m.; aforesaid, said; precursory, precursive, prevenient; leading, guiding, pioneering; preliminary, prefatory, introductory; prelusive, prelusory; proemial, preparatory, anacrustic; prepositive, prosthetic, prefixed, prepositional 237 adj. *fore*; first come, first served.

Vb. *come before*, be first to arrive 283 vb. *precede*; go first, run ahead, jump the queue; lead, guide, conduct, show the way, point the trail 547 vb. *indicate*; forerun, pioneer, clear the way, blaze the trail 484 vb. *discover*; head, take the lead, have the pas 237 vb. *be in front*; have precedence, take p., outrank 34 vb. *be superior*; lead the dance, set the fashion, set the example 178 vb. *influence*; open, lead off, kick off 68 vb. *begin*; preamble, prelude, preface, prologize; introduce, usher in, ring in 68 vb. *auspicate*; have the start, get ahead 119 vb. *be before*.

prepose, put in front, lead with, head w.; advance, station, station before, throw out a screen 187 vb. *place*; prefix 38 vb. *add*; front, face, tip, top 237 vb. *be in front*; presuppose 512 vb. *suppose*, 475 vb. *premise*; preface, prelude 68 vb. *initiate*.

Adv. *before*, in advance 283 adv. *ahead*; preparatory to, as a preliminary; earlier

[50]

119 adv. *before* (in time); ante, supra, above 237 adv. *in front.*

See: 34, 38, 66, 68, 119, 125, 178, 187, 237, 283, 475, 484, 512, 547, 605, 638, 773.

65 Sequence

N. *sequence, coming after, subsequence,* descent, line, lineage 120 n. *posteriority*; going after 284 n. *following*; logical sequence, inference 475 n. *reasoning*; postposition, suffixion, suffixment 38 n. *addition,* 45 n. *joinder*; sonship 170 n. *posterity*; succession, successorship, Elijah's mantle 780 n. *transfer*; series 71 n. *continuity*; successiveness, alternation, serialization; continuation, prolongation 113 n. *protraction,* 146 n. *continuance*; consecution, pursuance 619 n. *pursuit*; overtaking 306 n. *overstepping,* 727 n. *success*; secondariness, subordinacy, subordination, second place, proxime accessit, honourable mention 35 n. *inferiority*; last place 238 n. *rear*; no priority 639 n. *unimportance*; consequence 67 n. *sequel,* 157 n. *effect*; conclusion 69 n. *end.*

Adj. *sequent,* following, succeeding, incoming; ensuing, sequacious; proximate, next 200 adj. *near*; posterior, latter, later 120 adj. *subsequent*; successive, consecutive 71 adj. *continuous*; alternating, amœbæan, antiphonal 12 adj. *correlative*; alternative, every second, every other; postpositive, postpositional 238 adj. *back*; consequent, resulting 157 adj. *caused.*

Vb. *come after,* have one's turn, come next, ensue 284 vb. *follow*; follow close, tread on the heels 200 vb. *be near*; succeed, inherit, step into the shoes of, supplant 150 vb. *substitute*; alternate, turn and turn about 141 vb. *be periodic*; relieve, take over.

place after, suffix, append; subscribe, subjoin 38 vb. *add.*

Adv. *after,* following; afterwards 120 adv. *subsequently,* 238 adv. *behind*; at the end, in relays, in waves, successively; as follows, consequentially 157 adj. *consequently*; in the end 69 adv. *finally*; next, later; infra, below.

See: 12, 35, 38, 45, 67, 69, 71, 113, 120, 141, 146, 150, 157, 170, 200, 238, 284, 306, 475, 619, 639, 727, 780.

66 Precursor

N. *precursor,* predecessor, ancestor, forbear, patriarch 169 n. *parent*; first man, Adam, antediluvian 125 n. *antiquity*; eldest, firstborn; protomartyr; discoverer, inventor 461 n. *experimenter*; pioneer, voortrekker, pathfinder, explorer 268 n. *traveller*; guide, link-boy, voorlooper, bell-wether 690 n. *leader*; scout, scouter, skirmisher; vanguard, avant-guard, innovator; forerunner, prodrome, van-courier, outrider; herald, harbinger, announcer 531 n. *messenger*; dawn, false d.; anticipation, prefiguration, foretaste, preview, premonition, forewarning 664 n. *warning,* 511 n. *omen*; precedent 83 n. *example*; antecedent, prefix, preposition 40 n. *adjunct*; eve, vigil, day before 119 n. *priority.*

prelude, preliminary, anacrusis, prolusion, preamble, preface, prologue, foreword, avant-propos; headline; proem, opening, exordium, prolegomena, introduction 68 n. *beginning*; lead, heading, frontispiece 237 n. *front*; groundwork, foundation 218 n. *basis,* 669 n. *preparation*; overture, voluntary, ritornello 412 n. *musical piece*; premisses, presupposition 512 n. *supposition.*

Adj. *precursory,* preliminary, exploratory 669 n. *preparatory*; prelusive, prelusory, anacrustic; proemial, introductory, prefatory 68 adj. *beginning*; inaugural, foundational; precedent, prodromous 64 adj. *preceding.*

See: 40, 64, 68, 83, 119, 125, 169, 218, 237, 268, 412, 461, 511, 512, 531, 664, 669, 690.

67 Sequel

N. *sequel,* consequence, result, by-product 157 n. *effect*; conclusion 69 n. *end*; sequela, after-effect; hangover, morning after 949 n. *crapulence*; after-taste; afterglow; aftermath, aftergrowth, after-crop 157 n. *growth*; afterbirth, afterburden, placenta, secundines, afterpain 164 n. *propagation*; inheritance, legacy, testament, will 777 n. *dower*; surprise, afterclap 508 n. *inexpectation*; afterthought, second t., better t., ésprit d'escalier; double-take, second try, aftercast, aftergame; afterpiece, postlude, epilogue, postscript; peroration, envoi, last words, more last w.;

follow-through, follow-up 725 n. *completion*; continuation, sequel, second part, second volume, next chapter 589 n. *book*; tag, tailpiece, heelpiece, colophon, coda 238 n. *rear*; appendage, appendix, codicil, supplement 40 adj. *adjunct*; suffix, affix, subscript, inflection, enclitic, proclitic 564 n. *grammar*; afterpart, tail; queue, ponytail 259 n. *hair*; after-course, afters, dessert 301 n. *dish*; survival, after-life, hereafter 124 n. *future state.*

retinue, following, followers 284 n. *follower*; suite, train, cortège, rout 71 n. *procession*; tail, queue, wake 89 n. *concomitant*; trailer 274 n. *vehicle.*

aftercomer, after-generations, the unborn, descendant 170 n. *posterity*; heir, inheritor 776 n. *beneficiary*; next man in, successor; replacement, supplanter 150 n. *substitute*; relief, reserve 707 n. *auxiliary*; fresh blood, new broom 126 n. *modernist, upstart*; latecomer, new-c., new arrival 297 n. *incomer*; gleaner 370 n. *husbandman*; jackal 742 n. *dependant*; last man in, finalist, finisher 41 n. *survivor.*

See: 40, 69, 71, 89, 124, 126, 150, 157, 164, 170, 238, 259, 274, 284, 297, 301, 370, 508, 564, 589, 707, 725, 742, 776, 777, 949.

68 Beginning

N. *beginning*, birth, rise (see *origin*); infancy, babyhood 130 n. *youth* 126 n. *newness*; primitiveness 127 n. *oldness*; commencement; onset 295 n. *arrival*; incipience, inception, inchoation, foundation, establishment; origination, invention 484 n. *discovery*; initiative, démarche; exordium, introduction 66 n. *prelude*; end of the beginning, curtain-raiser; alpha, first letter, initial; head, heading, headline, caption 547 n. *label*; title-page, prelims; van, front, forefront 237 n. *front*; dawn 128 n. *morning*; handsel, running in, teething troubles; first blush, first glance, first sight, first impression, first lap, first round, first stage; primer, outline; rudiments, elements, principia, first principles, alphabet, ABC; leading up to 289 n. *approach*; outbreak, onset, brunt 712 n. *attack*; débutant, starter 538 n. *beginner*; precedent 66 n. *precursor*; preliminaries 669 n. *preparation.*

début, coming out, inauguration, opening, unveiling; first night, première, first appearance, first offence; premier pas, first step, first move, move, gambit; maiden voyage, maiden speech.

start, outset; starting point, point of departure, zero hour, D-day; send-off, setting out, embarkation 296 n. *departure*; rising of the curtain; kick-off; fresh start, new beginning, resumption, reopening 148 n. *reversion*; new departure, thin end of the wedge, precedent; standing start, flying s.; starter, self-s.

origin, origination, derivation; genesis, birth, nativity; provenance, ancestry 169 n. *parentage*; fount, fons et origo; rise 156 n. *source*; bud, germ, egg, protoplasm; first beginnings, cradle, incunabula 192 n. *home.*

entrance 297 n. *way in*; inlet 345 n. *gulf*; mouth, opening 263 n. *orifice*; threshold, vestibule, porch, portico, propylon, gateway 624 n. *access*; gate, postern 263 n. *doorway*; frontier, border 236 n. *limit*; outskirts, skirts, environs, suburbs 230 n. *circumjacence*; foothills, outlier; pass, ghat, corridor 289 n. *approach*, 305 n. *passage.*

Adj. *beginning*, initiatory, initiative, inceptive, inchoative; introductory, prefatory, proemial 66 adj. *precursory*; inaugural, foundational; elemental, rudimental 156 adj. *fundamental*; aboriginal, primeval, 127 adj. *primal*; rudimentary, elementary, crude 670 adj. *immature*; embryonic, nascent, budding, incipient, inchoate, raw, begun, in preparation 726 adj. *uncompleted*; just begun, newly-opened, launched.

first, initial, maiden, starting, natal; original 21 adj. *unimitated*; unprecedented 126 adj. *new*; foremost, front 237 adj. *fore*; leading, principal, head, chief 34 adj. *supreme.*

Vb. *begin*, make a beginning, commence, inchoate; set in, open, dawn, break out, burst forth, spring up, crop up; arise, rise, take one's r., take one's birth; spring from; come into existence, come into the world 360 vb. *be born*; make one's debut, come out; start, enter upon, embark on 296 vb. *start out*; start work, clock in; handsel, run in; begin at the beginning, start from scratch, begin ab ovo; resume, begin again, begin de novo, make a fresh

start 148 vb. *revert*; start afresh, shuffle the cards, reshuffle, resume, recommence, reopen; set to, set about, set to work; attack, wade into, tackle, face, address oneself; go to it 672 vb. *undertake*.

initiate, found, launch; originate, invent, think of 484 vb. *discover*; usher in, ring in, open the door to, introduce; start, start up, switch on; prompt, promote, set going; raise, set on foot; put to work 622 vb. *employ*; handsel, run in; take the initiative, lead, lead off, lead the way, take the lead, pioneer, open up, break new ground 64 vb. *come before*; broach, open, raise the subject, ventilate, air; open the ball, break the ice, set the ball rolling; throw the first stone, open fire; take the first step, take the plunge, cross the Rubicon, burn one's boats; apply the match, touch off, spark off, set off.

auspicate, inaugurate, open; institute, install, induct 751 vb. *commission*; found, set up, establish 156 vb. *cause*; baptize, christen, launch 561 vb. *name*; initiate, blood, flesh; lay the foundations, lay the foundation stone, cut the first turf 669 vb. *prepare*.

Adv. *initially*, originally, at the beginning, in the b., in the bud, in embryo, in its infancy, from the beginning, from its birth; ab initio, ab ovo; first, firstly, in the first place, imprimis; primarily, first of all, before everything, first and foremost; as a start, for a beginning.

See: 21, 34, 64, 66, 126, 127, 128, 130, 148, 156, 169, 192, 230, 236, 237, 263, 289, 295, 296, 297, 305, 345, 360, 484, 538, 547, 561, 622, 624, 669, 670, 672, 712, 726, 751.

69 End

N. *end*, close, conclusion, consummation, apodosis 725 n. *completion*; pay-off, result, end-r. 157 n. *effect*; termination, determination, closure, guillotine; finishing stroke, death blow, quietus, coup de grâce; knock-out, stopper, finisher 279 n. *knock*; ending, finish, finale, curtain; term, period, stop, halt 145 n. *cessation*; final stage, latter end 129 n. *evening*; beginning of the end, peroration, last words, swansong, envoi, coda 67 n. *sequel*; last stage, last round, last lap, home stretch; last ball, last over; last

breath, last gasp, extremities; final examination, finals 459 n. *exam*. See *finality*.

extremity, final point, omega; ultimate point, extreme, pole; extreme case, ne plus ultra; farthest point, world's end, ultima Thule, where the rainbow ends 199 n. *farness*; fringe, verge, brink 234 n. *edge*; frontier, boundary 236 n. *limit*; terminal point, terminus, terminal 295 n. *goal*, 617 n. *objective*; dregs, last d.; heel, toe, bottom, nadir 214 n. *base*; bottom dollar, last penny 801 n. *poverty*; tip, nib, cusp, point, vertex, peak, top 213 n. *summit*; tail 67 n. *sequel*, 53 n. *limb*; shirt-tail, coat-t. 217 n. *pendant*; end, head, terminal, butt-end, gable-e., fag-e. 238 n. *rear*; tag, epilogue, postscript, appendix 40 n. *adjunct*; desinence, inflection, suffix 564 n. *grammar*.

finality, bitter end; time, time up; conclusion, end of the matter 54 n. *completeness*; drop of the curtain, break-up, wind-up 145 n. *cessation*; dissolution 361 n. *death*; eschatology, last things, doom, destiny 596 n. *fate*; last trump, crack of doom, Götterdämmerung; resurrection day, Day of Judgment, end of the world, end of time, end of all things 124 n. *future state*.

Adj. *ending*, final, terminal, last, ultimate; extreme, polar; definitive, conclusive, crowning, completing 725 adj. *completive*; conterminate, conterminous, conterminable; ended, at an end; settled, terminated, finalized, decided, set at rest; over, over and done with; off, all off, cancelled; played out, finished; penultimate, last but one; antepenultimate, last but two; hindmost, rear 238 n. *back*; caudal.

Vb. *end*, come to an end, expire, run out 111 vb. *elapse*; close, finish, conclude, be all over; become extinct, die out 361 vb. *die*, 2 vb. *pass away*; come to a close, draw to a c., have run its course; fade away, peter out; stop, clock out, go home 145 vb. *cease*.

terminate, conclude, close, determine, decide, settle; apply the closure, bring to an end, put an end to, put a term to, put a stop to, make an end of, put paid to; finish, achieve, consummate, get through, play out, act o., see it o. 725 vb. *carry through*; ring down the curtain, draw stumps, put up the shutters, shut up shop, wind up,

close down; switch off, ring off, hang up; stop 145vb. *halt.*

Adv. *finally,* in conclusion, in fine; at last; once for all; to the bitter end, to the last gasp, to the end of the chapter.

See: 2, 40, 53, 54, 67, 111, 124, 129, 145, 157, 199, 213, 214, 217, 234, 236, 238, 279, 295, 361, 459, 596, 617, 725, 801.

70 Middle

N. *middle,* midst, mediety; mean 30n. *average;* medium, middle term; thick, thick of things; heart, body, kernel; nave, hub, navel, umbilicus, omphalos 225n. *centre;* nucleus, nucleolus 224n. *interiority;* midweek, midwinter, half-tide, slack water 625n. *mid-course;* bisection, midline, equator, the Line 28n. *equalization;* midrib, midriff, diaphragm 231n. *partition;* half distance, middle d., equidistance, halfway house; mixed economy 43n. *mixture.*

Adj. *middle,* medial, mesial, mean, mid; mediate, middlemost, midmost 225adj. *central;* middling 177adj. *moderate,* 625 adj. *neutral;* intermediate, intervocalic 231adj. *interjacent;* equidistant; mediterranean, equatorial.

Adv. *midway,* in the middle, in the thick, midway, halfway; midships.

See: 28, 30, 43, 177, 224, 225, 231, 625.

71 Continuity: uninterrupted sequence

N. *continuity,* continuousness, uninterruptedness, unbrokenness, monotony 16n, *uniformity;* consecution, overlap; immediacy, directness; consecutiveness. successiveness, succession; line, lineage, descent, dynasty; one thing after another, serialization 65n. *sequence;* continuous time, endlessness 115n. *perpetuity;* continuous motion 146n. *continuance;* endless band 315n. *rotation;* repetitiveness, alternation, recurrence 106n. *repetition,* 141n. *periodicity,* 139n. *frequency;* cumulativeness, snowball 36n. *increase;* gradualism, Fabianism 278n. *slowness;* course, run, career, flow, steady f., trend, steady t. 179n. *tendency;* progressiveness 285n. *progression;* circuit, round 314n. *circuition;* daily round, routine, practice,

custom 610n. *habit;* track, locus, trail, wake 67n. *sequel;* catenation, concatenation, catena, chain, chain-reaction, chain-letter; circle 250n. *circularity.*

series, seriation, gradation 27n. *degree;* succession, run, progression, arithmetical p., geometrical p.; ascending order 36n. *increase;* descending order 37n. *decrease;* pedigree, family tree, lineage 169n. *genealogy;* chain, line, string, thread; unbroken line, line of battle, thin red line; rank, file, echelon; array 62n. *arrangement;* row, windrow; colonnade, peristyle, portico; ninepins; ladder, steps, stairs, staircase 308n. *ascent;* range, tier, storey 207n. *layer;* keyboard, manual; set, suite, suit (of cards); assortment 77n. *classification;* team, crew, eight, eleven, fifteen 74n. *group;* gamut, scale 410n. *musical note;* stepping stones 624n. *bridge;* cursus honorum; hierarchy.

procession 267n. *marching;* cavalcade 875n. *pageant;* crocodile, queue, tail, cortège, train, suite 67n. *retinue;* caravan, file, single f.; funeral procession, funeral 364 n. *obsequies;* ovation, triumph, Lord Mayor's Show 876n. *celebration.*

Adj. *continuous,* continued, run-on 45adj. *conjunct;* consecutive, running, successive, sequential 65adj. *sequent;* serial, serialized; seriate, catenary; progressive, gradual 179adj. *tending;* overlapping, unbroken, uninterrupted, circular; direct, immediate, unmediated; continual, incessant, unremitting, unintermitted, nonstop, constant, perennial, evergreen 115 adj. *perpetual;* rhythmic 110adj. *periodic;* repetitive, recurrent, monotonous 106 adj. *repeated,* 16adj. *uniform;* linear, lineal, rectilinear 249adj. *straight.*

Vb. *run on,* continue, following in a series; line up, fall in, queue up; succeed, overlap 65adj. *come after;* file, defile, keep single file; circle 626vb. *circuit.*

continuate, run on, extend, prolong 113vb. *spin out,* 203vb. *lengthen;* serialize, arrange in succession, catenate, thread, string 45vb. *connect;* dress, size, grade 27vb. *graduate;* file, tabulate 87vb. *list;* maintain continuity, keep the succession, provide an heir.

Adv. *continuously* etc. adj.; serially, seriatim; successively, in succession, in turn; one after another; at a stretch, handrunning, running; cumulatively, progressively;

gradually, step by step, hand over hand; in procession, in file, in single f., in Indian f., in column, in line ahead, nose to tail.

See: 16, 27, 36, 37, 45, 62, 65, 67, 74, 77, 87, 106, 110, 113, 115, 139, 141, 146, 169, 179, 203, 207, 249, 250, 267, 278, 285, 308, 314, 315, 364, 410, 610, 624, 626, 875, 876.

72 Discontinuity: interrupted sequence

N. *discontinuity*, solution of continuity, intermittence; discontinuation, discontinuance 145 n. *cessation*; interval, intermission, pause 145 n. *lull*; disconnectedness, randomness 61 n. *disorder*; unevenness, joltiness, jerkiness 17 n. *non-uniformity*, 259 n. *roughness*; dotted line; broken ranks; ladder, run 46 n. *disjunction*; interruption, intervention, interposition; parenthesis, episode 231 n. *interjection*; cæsura, division 46 n. *separation*, 547 n. *punctuation*; break, fracture flaw, fault, split, crack, cut 201 n. *gap*; missing link, lost connection; broken thread, anacoluthon, non sequitur; illogicality, sophism 477 n. *sophistry*; patchwork, crazy quilt, crazy paving 437 n. *variegation*; incoherence, rhapsody, purple patch 568 n. *imperspicuity*, 25 n. *misfit*; alternation 141 n. *periodicity*; irregularity, ragged volley 142 n. *fitfulness*.
Adj. *discontinuous*, unsuccessive, non-recurrent, unrepeated; discontinued; interrupted, broken, stopping; disconnected 46 adj. *disjunct*; discrete 46 adj. *separate*; few and far between 140 adj. *infrequent*; patchy 437 adj. *variegated*, 17 adj. *non-uniform*; desultory, intermittent, intermitting 142 adj. *fitful*; alternate, alternating 141 adj. *periodic*; spasmodic 17 adj. *non-uniform*; jerky, jolty, bumpy, uneven 259 adj. *rough*; incoherent, anacoluthic 477 adj. *illogical*; parenthetic, episodic, not belonging 303 adj. *inserted*, 59 adj. *extraneous*.
Vb. *be discontinuous*, pause, rest 145 vb. *stop*; alternate, intermit.
discontinue, interrupt, intervene, chip in, break, break in upon 231 vb. *interfere*; interpose, interject, punctuate 231 vb. *put between*; disconnect, break the connection, snap the thread 46 vb. *disjoin*.
Adv. *discontinuously*, at intervals, occasionally, infrequently, irregularly, by snatches, by jerks, by skips, by catches, by fits and starts; skippingly, desultorily.

See: 17, 25, 46, 59, 61, 140, 141, 142, 145, 201, 231, 259, 303, 437, 477, 547, 568.

73 Term: serial position

N. *serial place*, term, order, remove 27 n. *degree*; rank, ranking, grade, gradation; station, place, position, pitch; status, standing, footing; point, mark, pitch, level, storey; step, tread, round, rung; stage, milestone, climacteric, climax 213 n. *summit*; bottom rung, nadir 214 n. *base*.
Vb. *grade*, rank, rate, place; put one in his place; bring down a peg; stagger, space out 201 vb. *space*, 27 vb. *graduate*.
have rank, hold r., hold a place, occupy a position, 186 vb. *be situate*; fall into place, drop into p., find a niche 187 vb. *place oneself*.

See: 27, 186, 187, 201, 213, 214.

74 Assemblage

N. *assemblage*, bringing together, collection 50 n. *combination*, 62 n. *arrangement*; collocation, juxtaposition 202 n. *contiguity*; colligation, contesseration 45 n. *joinder*; compilation, corpus, anthology 56 n. *composition*; gathering, ingathering, reaping, harvest, vintage 370 n. *agriculture*, 771 n. *acquisition*; harvest-home 632 n. *storage*, 876 n. *celebration*; consolidation, concentration; centering, focusing; mobilization, muster, levy, call-up 718 n. *war measures*; review, parade, wappenshaw 875 n. *pageant*; rally, whipping in, round-up, line-up; herding, shepherding, stock-breeding, cicuration 369 n. *animal husbandry*; collectivization, collective, kolkhoz 740 n. *compulsion*, 370 n. *farm*; party-making, conspiracy, caucus 708 n. *party*; noun of assembly; portmanteau word; syntax 564 n. *grammar*.
assembly, mutual attraction 291 n. *attraction*; getting together, ganging up; forgathering, congregation, concourse, conflux, concurrence 293 n. *convergence*; gathering, meeting, mass-m., meet, coven; conventicle, business meeting, board m.,

convention; gemote, shire-moot, legislature, conclave 692 n. *council*; eisteddfod, festival 876 n. *celebration*; social gathering, levée, reunion, get-together, conversazione; company, at home, drawing room, salon, party 882 n. *sociality*; circle, knitting-bee, spelling-b.; discussion meeting, symposium 584 n. *conference*.

group, constellation, galaxy, cluster, star 321 n. *star*; bevy, flock, herd; drove, team; pack, kennel; stable, string; nest, eyrie; brood, hatch; gaggle, flight, covey; shoal, school; unit, brigade 722 n. *formation*; batch, lot, clutch; brace, pair, span, pride of lions 90 n. *duality*; leash, four-in-hand 96 n. *quaternity*; set, class, genus, species, sub-s. 77 n. *sort*; breed, tribe, clan, household 11 n. *family*; brotherhood, fellowship, college 706 n. *association*; movement 708 n. *party*; sphere, quarter, circle 524 n. *informant*; charmed circle, coterie 644 n. *élite*; social group, the classes 868 n. *nobility*, 869 n. *commonalty*; we-group, in-group, they-group, out-group, they 80 n. *self*; age-group, stream 123 n. *synchronism*; hand (at cards) set, partially-ordered s. 71 n. *series*.

band, company, circus; troupe, cast 594 n. *actor*; brass band, string b. 413 n. *orchestra*; team, string, eleven, eight; knot, bunch; set, coterie, ring; gang, party, work p., fatigue p.; committee, commission 754 n. *consignee*; ship's company, crew, complement, man-power, staff 686 n. *personnel*; following 67 n. *retinue*; meinie; squadron, troop, platoon; unit, regiment, corps 722 n. *formation*; squad, posse, posse comitatus; force, body, host 722 n. *armed force*, 104 n. *multitude*; brotherhood, band of brothers, merry men; Band of Hope; panel 87 n. *list*; establishment, cadre 331 n. *structure*.

crowd, throng 104 n. *multitude*; huddle, swarm, colony, bee-hive, bike, vespiary; small crowd, knot, bunch; the masses, mass, mob, rout 869 n. *rabble*; sea of faces, full house, houseful 54 n. *completeness*; congestion, press, squash, jam, scrum, rush, crush; rush-hour, crush-h. 680 n. *haste*; flood, spate, deluge, stream, streams of 32 n. *great quantity*, volley, shower, hail, storm, condensation, populousness, over-population 324 n. *density*; infestation, invasion, 297 n. *ingress*; herd

instinct, crowd psychology, mass emotion 818 n. *feeling*.

bunch, assortment, lot, mixed l. 43 n. *medley*; clump, tuft, wisp, handful; pencil of rays; bag 194 n. *receptacle*; clip, bundle, packet, package, parcel, budget; file, dossier 548 n. *record*; bale, roll, bolt, seron; load, pack, fardel 193 n. *contents*; fascine, faggot; fasces; shock, sheaf, stook, truss, heap; swathe, gavel, rick, stack, haycock 632 n. *storage*; forest, copse 366 n. *wood*; bouquet, nosegay, posy; clue, skein, hank.

accumulation, heaping up, acervation, cumulation; agglomeration, conglomeration, conglobation, aggregation; co-acervation, coagmentation; massing, amassment; concentration, collectivization; pile-up 279 n. *collision*; masonry, mass, pile, pyramid 164 n. *edifice*, 209 n. *high structure*; congeries, heap; drift, snowdrift; snowball 36 n. *increment*; debris, detritus 41 n. *leavings*; dustheap, dump, shoot 641 n. *rubbish*; cumulus, storm-cloud 355 n. *cloud*; store, storage 633 n. *provision*, 799 n. *treasury*; magazine, armoury, quiver 723 n. *arsenal*; park, artillery p., car p.; set, lot 71 n. *series*; mixed lot, mixed bag 43 n. *medley*; kit, stock; range, selection, assortment 795 n. *merchandise*; shop-window, display 522 n. *exhibit*; museum 632 n. *collection*; menagerie, Noah's Ark, aquarium 369 n. *zoo*; literary collection 589 n. *library*; miscellanea, miscellany, collectanea, compilation 56 n. *composition*; symposium, festschrift 591 n. *dissertation*.

accumulator, miser 816 n. *niggard*, 798 n. *treasurer*; connoisseur 492 n. *collector*; gatherer, reaper, harvester, picker, gleaner 369 n. *husbandman*; convener, assembler; whip, whipper-in; shepherd, sheep dog 369 n. *herdsman*; battery 632 n. *storage*.

Adj. *assembled*, met, well-met, ill-m.; convened, summoned; mobilized, called-up, banded; collectivized; crowded, packed, huddled, serried 324 adj. *dense*; close-printed, tight; populated, over-p., over crowded, humming with, lousy with, stiff with 54 adj. *full*; populous, teeming, swarming, thick on the ground, thick as flies 104 adj. *multitudinous*; in a crowd, seething, milling; in formation, ranked, in order 62 adj. *arranged*.

Vb. *congregate*, meet, forgather, rendez-

vous; assemble, reassemble, rejoin; associate, come together, get t., join t., flock t., pig t.; make a crowd, gather, collect, troop, rally, roll up, swell the ranks; resort to, centre on, focus on, make for 293 vb. *converge*; band, gang up; mass, concentrate, mobilize; conglomerate, huddle, cluster, bunch, crowd, nest; throng, swarm, seethe, mill around; surge, stream, flood 36 vb. *grow*; swarm in, infest, invade 297 vb. *irrupt.*

bring together, assemble, put together, draw t. 45 vb. *join*; draw 291 vb. *attract*; gather, collect, rally, muster, call up, mobilize; concentrate, consolidate; collocate, lump together, group, brigade, unite; compile 56 vb. *compose*; bring into focus, focus, centre; convene, convoke, convocate, hold a meeting; herd, shepherd, get in, whip in, call in, round up, corral 235 vb. *inclose*; mass, aggregate, acervate, rake up, dredge up; accumulate, conglomerate, heap, pile, amass; catch, take, rake in, net 771 vb. *acquire*; scrape together, save 632 vb. *store*; truss, bundle, parcel, package; bunch, bind, colligate, fasciculate 45 vb. *tie*; pack, cram, stuff 54 vb. *fill*; build up, pile up, pile Pelion on Ossa 310 vb. *elevate.*

Adv. *together*, unitedly, as one; collectively, all together, en masse, in a mass in a body.

See: 11, 32, 36, 41, 43, 45, 50, 54, 56, 62, 67, 71, 77, 80, 87, 90, 96, 104, 123, 164, 193, 194, 202, 209, 235, 279, 291, 293, 297, 310, 321, 324, 331, 355, 366, 369, 370, 413, 492, 522, 524, 548, 564, 584, 589, 591, 594, 632, 633, 641, 644, 680, 686, 692, 706, 708, 718, 722, 723, 740, 754, 771, 795, 798, 799, 816, 818, 868, 869, 875, 876, 882.

75 Non-assemblage. Dispersion

N. *dispersion*, scattering, diffraction, breakup 46 n. *disjunction*; branching out, fanning o., spread, scatter, radiation 294 n. *divergence*; distribution 783 n. *apportionment*; delegation, decentralization; disintegration 51 n. *decomposition*; evaporation, boiling away 338 n. *vaporization*, 337 n. *liquefaction*; dissipation 634 n. *waste*; circulation, diffusion; dissemination, broadcasting; spraying, sprinkling, spargefaction, circumfusion, interspersion 341 n. *moistening*; dispersal, going

home; sprawl, sprawling, trailing; disbandment, demobilization; flotsam and jetsam, sea-drift, driftwood 272 n. *thing transferred*; disjecta membra; waifs and strays, displaced person; dispersed population, diaspora.

Adj. *unassembled*, dispersed, disbanded, demobilized etc. vb.; scattered, strung out, sporadic, sparse, few and far between 140 n. *infrequent*; broadcast, diffused; spreading, widespread, far-flung 183 adj. *spacious*; epidemic 79 adj. *universal*; spread, dispread, separated 46 adj. *separate*; dishevelled, streaming, sprawling 61 adj. *orderless*; decentralized; branching, radiating, centrifugal 294 adj. *divergent*; off-centre, adrift, astray; straggling, wandering 267 adj. *travelling*.

Vb. *be dispersed*, disperse, scatter, spread, spread out, fan o., thin o., rarefy 325 vb. *be rare*; spread fast, spread like wildfire, flood; radiate, branch, branch out, 294 vb. *diverge*; break up, separate, break ranks, fall out, dismiss 46 vb. *be disjointed*; lose coherence, break away 49 vb. *come unstuck*; hive off, go on one's own way, go each his own w. 267 vb. *wander*; drift away, drift apart; straggle, trail, fall behind 282 vb. *stray*; spread over, sprawl over, cover 226 vb. *overlie*; explode, blow up, burst, fly apart, fly in all directions 176 vb. *be violent*; evaporate, melt 338 vb. *vaporize*, 337 vb. *liquefy*; disintegrate, dissolve, decay 51 vb. *decompose*.

disperse, scatter, diffract; dispread, separate 46 vb. *sunder*; thin out, string o.; disseminate, broadcast, sow, strew, strow, bestrew, spread; dissipate, dispel, disintegrate 51 vb. *decompose*; scatter to the winds 634 vb. *waste*; dispense, deal, deal out, allot 783 vb. *apportion*; decentralize; break up, disband, disembody, demobilize send home 46 vb. *disjoin*; draft, draft off, detach 272 vb. *send*; diffuse, sprinkle, besprinkle, splash, spray, spatter, bespatter 341 vb. *moisten*; circulate, put into circulation, utter; retail 793 vb. *sell*; throw into confusion, disorder 63 vb. *derange*; rout 727 vb. *defeat*.

Adv. *sporadically*, here and there, sparsely, in twos and threes; passim, everywhere, in all quarters.

See: 46, 49, 51, 61, 63, 79, 140, 176, 183, 226, 267, 272, 282, 294, 325, 337, 338, 341, 634, 727, 783, 793.

76 Focus: place of meeting

N. *focus*, corradiation; focal point, point of convergence, town centre 293 n. *convergence*, 225 n. *centre*; crossways, crossroads; switchboard, exchange; hub, nub, core, heart, kernel 70 n. *middle*; hall, civic centre, village hall, village green; campus; market place, agora, forum 796 n. *mart*; resort, retreat, haunt, stamping ground, place of resort; club, pub, local 192 n. *tavern*; headquarters, depot; rallying point, standard; venue, rendezvous, trysting place 192 n. *meeting place*; tryst, assignation; nest, fireside, home ground 192 n. *home*; cynosure, centre of attraction, honey-pot 291 n. *magnet*; place of pilgrimage, Mecca, Rome, Zion, promised land 295 n. *goal*, 617 n. *objective*.

Vb. *focus*, centre, corradiate 293 vb. *converge*; centralize, concentrate, focus upon; bring to a point, bring to a focus, bring to an issue.

See: 70, 192, 225, 291, 293, 295, 617, 796.

77 Class

N. *classification*, categorization, generification; diagnosis, specification, designation; category, class, predicament, bracket; cadre; head, heading, sub-head, section, subsection 53 n. *subdivision*; division, branch, department, faculty; pocket, pigeon-hole 194 n. *compartment*; province, sphere, range; sex, gender; blood group, age g., stream 74 n. *group*; coterie, clique 74 n. *band*; persuasion, denomination 978 n. *sect.*

sort, order, type, variety, kind; manner, genre, style; character, quality, grade 5 n. *character*; mark, brand 547 n. *label*; kidney, feather, colour; stamp, mould, shape, make 243 n. *form*; assortment, kit, set, suit, lot.

breed, strain, blood, family, kin, tribe, clan, sept, line 11 n. *race*, 169 n. *genealogy*; caste, subcaste, gotra, phylum, genus, species, sub-species; genotype, monotype.

Adj. *generic*, sexual, masculine, feminine, neuter.

classificatory, classificational, taxonomic; sectional, denominational 978 adj. *sectarian.*

See: 5, 11, 53, 74, 169, 194, 243, 547, 978.

78 Inclusion

N. *inclusion*, comprising, comprisal; incorporation, embodiment, assimilation, incapsulation; comprehension, admission 299 n. *reception*; admissibility, eligibility; membership 775 n. *participation*; inclusiveness, inclusivity, coverage, full c. 79 n. *generality*; all-roundness, versatility 694 n. *skill*; comprehensiveness, no exception, no omission, nothing omitted; set, complete s., complement, package 52 n. *whole*; package deal 765 n. *compact*; constitution 56 n. *composition*; capacity, volume, measure 183 n. *space*, 465 n. *measurement*; accommodation 183 n. *room.*

Adj. *inclusive*, including, comprising, counting, containing, having; holding, consisting of 56 adj. *composing*; incorporative, incorporating; non-exclusive, accommodating; overall, all-embracing 52 adj. *comprehensive*; wholesale, sweeping, without omission, with no exception, total, global, world-wide, universal 52 adj. *whole*; synoptical 79 adj. *general*; broad-based, wide 205 adj. *broad.*

included, admitted, admissible, eligible; component, constituent, making up 56 adj. *composing*; inherent 58 adj. *ingredient*, 5 adj. *intrinsic*; belonging, pertinent 9 adj. *relative*; classified with, of the same class 18 adj. *similar*; congenerous, congeneric 11 adj. *akin*; entered, recorded, on the list 87 adj. *listed*; merged 38 adj. *additional*, 45 adj. *conjunct*; inner 224 adj. *interior.*

Vb. *be included*, be contained, be comprised, make one of 58 vb. *be one of*; enlist, enrol oneself, swell the ranks, join, obtain membership 708 vb. *join a party*; come under, fall u., range u., range with, merge in 43 vb. *be mixed*; appertain to, pertain, refer to 9 vb. *be related*; come in, go in, enter into 297 vb. *enter*; constitute 56 vb. *compose*; overlap, inhere, belong 5 vb. *be intrinsic.*

comprise, include, consist of, hold, have, count, boast 56 vb. *contain*; take, measure 28 vb. *be equal*; receive, take in 299 vb. *admit*; accommodate, find room for; comprehend, incapsulate 226 vb. *cover*; embody, incorporate; embrace, encircle, ensphere, envelop, embox, encase, ensepulchre; enisle, embower 235 vb. *inclose*; have everything, exhaust the possibilities 644 vb. *be good*; involve, imply.

number with, count w., reckon among,

enumerate in; subsume, place under, classify as; put in, arrange in 62vb. *class*; not omit, take into account.

Adv. *including*, inclusively; from A to Z; et cetera.

See: 5, 9, 11, 18, 28, 38, 43, 45, 52, 56, 58, 62, 79, 87, 183, 205, 224, 226, 235, 297, 299, 465, 644, 694, 708, 765, 775.

79 Generality

N. *generality*, universality, general applicability; catholicity, catholicism 976n. *orthodoxy*; ecumenicity, ecumenicalism; generalization, the universals; macrocosm 321n. *universe*, 52n. *whole*; panorama, synopsis, conspectus, bird's eye view 438n. *view*; inclusiveness, comprehensivity, something for everybody, open house, dragnet 78n. *inclusion*; currency, prevalence, custom 610n. *habit*, 848n. *fashion*; pervasiveness, rifeness, ubiquity 189n. *presence*; pandemic, epidemic 651n. *disease*; broadness, looseness, imprecision 495n. *inexactness*, 464n. *indiscrimination*; open letter, circular 528n. *publicity*; commonness, ruck, run, general r., run of the mill 30adj. *average*; ordinariness 732n. *mediocrity*; internationalism, cosmopolitanism 901n. *philanthropy*; impersonality; generification 77n. *classification*.

everyman, everywoman; man in the street, little man; common type 30n. *common man*; everybody, every one, one and all, all and sundry, every mother's son, every man Jack, all hands 52n. *all*; all the world and his wife, Tom, Dick and Harry, the masses 869n. *commonalty*; all sorts, anyone, whosoever, N or M; whatsoever, what have you, what you will, 562n. *no name*.

Adj. *general*, generic, typical, representative, standard; encyclopædic, broadbased; collective, all-embracing, pan-; blanket 52adj. *comprehensive*; broad, sweeping, panoramic, synoptic, current, prevalent 189adj. *ubiquitous*; usual, customary 610adj. *habitual*; vague, loose, indefinite 495adj. *inexact*; undetermined, unspecified, undenominational, unsectarian, impersonal 10adj. *irrelative*; common, ordinary, average 30adj.

median; popular, mass, vulgar 869adj. *plebeian*; for everybody, multipurpose.

universal, catholic, ecumenical, cosmopolitan, international, global, worldwide, nation-w., state-w., widespread 75 adj. *unassembled*; pervasive, penetrating, besetting, prevalent, epidemic, pandemic 189adj. *ubiquitous*; every, each, all, all without exception 52adj. *whole*.

Vb. *be general*, cover all cases 78vb. *comprise*; prevail, obtain, be the rule, have currency 610vb. *be wont*; go about, stalk abroad; penetrate 189vb. *pervade*.

generalize, render general etc. adj.; broaden, widen, universalize; spread, broadcast 75 vb. *disperse*.

Adv. *generally*, without exception, universally etc. adj.; mainly 52adv. *wholly*; to a man, to the last m.; always, for better for worse; generally speaking, in the long run, by and large 30adv. *on an average*; loosely, vaguely.

See: 10, 30, 52, 75, 77, 78, 189, 321, 438, 464, 495, 528, 562, 610, 651, 732, 848, 869, 901, 976.

80 Speciality

N. *speciality*, specific quality, specificity, personality, uniqueness; singularity; originality, individuality, particularity; personality, make-up 5n. *character*; characteristic, personal c., recessive c., dominant c.; speciality, idiosyncrasy, peculiarity, distinctive feature, mannerism; trait, mark, feature, attribute; sine qua non 89n. *accompaniment*; distinction, point of difference, personal equation, differentiæ 15n. *difference*; idiom, peculiar i.; jargon, patter, brogue, patois 560n. *dialect*; technical language, private l. 557 n. *language*; variant reading, version, lection 15n. *variant*; exception, isolated instance, special case 84n. *unconformity*; special skill, special study, specialization 694n. *skill*.

particulars, details, minutiæ, items, counts, special points, specification; circumstances; the ins and outs of.

particularism, chosen race, Peculiar People; exclusiveness, class consciousness, caste; nationality, nationalism, individualism, private enterprise.

self, ego, id-ego, identity, selfhood,

personality; I, myself, number one; we, ourselves; yourself, himself, herself, itself, themselves; we-group, in-g. 74 n. *group*; real self, inner s.; outward s.; the other; the absolute; Atman; a person, a character, individual, being 371 n. *person*.

Adj. *special*, specific, respective, particular; sui generis, peculiar, singular, unique; individual, idiosyncratic, idiomatic, original 21 adj. *unimitated*; native, proper, personal, private, selfish; appropriate 642 adj. *expedient*; typical, diagnostic 5 adj. *characteristic*; distinctive, uncommon, marked, noteworthy, out of the ordinary 84 adj. *unusual*; several 15 adj. *different*.

definite, definitive, defining; determinate, quantified; distinct, concrete, express; clear-cut, clean-c., cut and dried; certain, exact, precise 494 adj. *accurate*; itemized, detailed, circumstantial; bespoke, made to order, made to measure.

private, intimate, esoteric, personal, exclusive; patented; extra-professional; off the record, for one's private ear, secret 523 adj. *latent*.

Vb. *specify*, be specific, express in figures, enumerate, quantify 86 vb. *number*; particularize, itemize, detail, inventorize 87 vb. *list*; descend to particulars, enter into detail 570 vb. *be diffuse*; define, determine 236 vb. *limit*, 463 vb. *discriminate*; pinpoint, locate 187 vb. *place*; come to the point, explain 520 vb. *interpret*; signify, denote 514 vb. *mean*; designate, point out 547 vb. *indicate*; realize, translate into fact, substantiate 156 vb. *cause*; individualize, personalize 15 vb. *differentiate*; specialize 455 vb. *be attentive*, 536 vb. *study*.

Adv. *specially*, especially, in particular, personally, for one's own part; specifically, ad hominem, to order; with respect to.

severally, each, apiece, one by one; respectively, in turn, seriatim; in detail, bit by bit.

namely, that is to say, videlicet, viz., to wit, i.e., e.g.

See: 5, 15, 21, 74, 84, 86, 87, 89, 156, 187, 236, 371, 455, 463, 494, 514, 520, 523, 536, 547, 557, 560, 570, 642, 694.

81 Rule

N. *rule*, norm, formula, canon, code; maxim, principle 693 n. *precept*; law, law of nature; firm principle, hard and fast rule, settled law; strict law, law of the Medes and Persians; incongruous law, Procrustean law, subsidiary law, by-law; regulation, order, standing o., party line; guide, precedent, model, pattern 23 n. *prototype*; form, standard, keynote 83 n. *example*.

regularity, consistency, constancy 16 n. *uniformity*; order, natural o., established o., order of things 60 n. *order*; normality, normalcy, normal state, natural condition; form, set f., routine, drill, practice, custom 610 n. *habit*; fixed ways, rut, groove, tramlines; methodicalness, method, system, 62 n. *arrangement*; convention, parrotry 83 n. *conformity*.

Adj. *regular*, constant, steady 141 adj. *periodical*; even 258 adj. *smooth*; circular, square 646 adj. *perfect*; systematized, standardized 16 adj. *uniform*; regulated, according to rule, methodical, systematic 60 adj. *orderly*; regulative, normative; normal, unexceptional 83 adj. *typical*; customary 610 adj. *usual*; conforming, conventional 83 adj. *conformable*.

Adv. *by rule*, by the book, by the clock; regularly.

See: 16, 23, 60, 62, 83, 141, 258, 610, 646, 693.

82 Multiformity

N. *multiformity*, omniformity; heterogeneity, variety, diversity 17 n. *non-uniformity*; multifariousness, many-sidedness, many-headedness, polymorphism; polypsychism; schizophrenia, split personality 503 n. *psychopathy*; metamorphism, metamorphosis; variability, changeability 152 n. *changeableness*, 437 n. *variegation*; capriciousness 604 n. *caprice*; all-rounder; Proteus, Jekyll and Hyde; kaleidoscope.

Adj. *multiform*, polymorphic; multifold, multifid; multifarious, multigenerous; multiplex, multiplicate, manifold, many-headed, many-sided; omniform, omnigenerous, omnifarious; polygenous, metamorphic; protean, versatile, all-round; variform, heterogeneous, motley, mosaic 17 adj. *non-uniform*; epicene; indiscriminate, irregular, diversified, many-coloured, polychrome 437 adj.

variegated; divers, sundry; all manner of, of every description, of all sorts and kinds 16 adj. *different*; variable, changeable 152 adj. *changeful*; whimsical 604 adj. *capricious*; polypsychical; schizophrenic.
See: 16, 17, 152, 437, 503, 604.

83 Conformity

N. *conformity*, conformation 24 n. *conformance*; faithfulness 768 n. *observance*; accommodation, adjustment, reconcilement, reconciliation 24 adj. *agreement, adaptation*; self-adaptation, pliancy, malleability 327 adj. *softness*; acquiescence 721 n. *submission*; assimilation, acclimatization, naturalization 147 n. *conversion*, 18 n. *similarity*; conventionality 850 n. *affectation*, 848 n. *etiquette*; traditionalism, orthodoxism, orthodoxness 976 n. *orthodoxy*; formalism, strictness 735 n. *severity*; convention, form 848 n. *fashion*, 610 n. *practice*; parrotry, parrot cry 106 n. *repetition*, 925 n. *flattery*, 20 n. *imitation*; ordinariness 79 n. *generality*.
example, exemplar, type, pattern, model 23 n. *prototype*; exemplification, stock example, crass e., locus classicus; case, case in point, instance, palmary i.; illustration, practical demonstration, object lesson; sample, random s., cross section; representative, specimen, specimen page, representative selection; trailer, foretaste 66 n. *precursor*; precedent.
conformist, conformitant, conventionalist, traditionalist; Philistine, Babbitt; formalist, pedant, precisian; copycat 20 n. *imitator*, 925 n. *flatterer*; follower, loyalist, orthodoxist 976 n. *the orthodox*.
Adj. *conformable*, adaptable, adjustable, consistent with; malleable, pliant 327 adj. *flexible*; agreeable, complaisant, accommodating 24 adj. *agreeing*; conforming, following, faithful, loyal, true-blue 768 adj. *observant*; conventional, traditional 976 adj. *orthodox*; slavish, servile 20 adj. *imitative*, 925 adj. *flattering*; adjusted, adapted, acclimatized 610 adj. *habituated*; absorbed, digested, assimilated, naturalized 78 adj. *included*.
typical, normal, natural, of daily occurrence, everyday, ordinary, common, common

or garden; average 30 adj. *median*, 732 adj. *mediocre*; true to type; commonplace, prosaic; conventional; habitual 610 adj. *usual*; representative, stock, standard; normative, exemplary, illustrative; in point 9 adj. *relevant*.
regular, regulated, according to the book, according to rule, technical, shipshape, copybook; correct, sound, proper, canonical 976 adj. *orthodox*; precise, scrupulous, point-device 875 adj. *formal*; rigid, strict, unbending, uncompromising. Procrustean 735 adj. *severe*.
Vb. *conform*, correspond, conform to 24 vb. *accord*; trim, rub off the corners, adapt oneself, accommodate o., adjust o., mould o.; fit in, know one's place; pass, pass muster, pass current 635 vb. *suffice*; bend, yield, take the shape of 327 vb. *soften*; fall into line, toe the l., fall in with 721 vb. *submit*; comply with 768 vb. *observe*; tally with, chime in with 24 vb. *accord*; rubberstamp, say ditto, echo 106 vb. *repeat*; take dictation 30 vb. *copy*; stick to rule, obey regulations, follow precedent 739 vb. *obey*; keep in step, follow the fashion, follow the crowd, do as others do, do as the Romans do; join in the cry, join the majority, jump on the bandwagon, emulate; have no will of one's own, drift with the tide, swim with the stream 601 vb. *be irresolute*; follow in the steps of, keep to the beaten track, run on tramlines, run in a groove, stick in a rut 610 vb. *be wont*; support, keep one in countenance 701 vb. *patronize*, 925 vb. *flatter*.
make conform, conform, assimilate, naturalize 18 vb. *liken*; acclimatize 610 vb. *habituate*; bring under rule, systematize 62 vb. *regularize*; normalize, conventionalize, standardize; put in uniform, dress, drill 16 vb. *make uniform*; shape, form, press 243 vb. *efform*; stamp, imprint 547 vb. *mark*; train, lead 689 vb. *direct*; bend, twist, force 740 vb. *compel*; accommodate, fit, fit in, square, trim 24 vb. *adjust*; rub off the corners 258 vb. *smooth*.
exemplify, illustrate, cite, quote, instance; produce an example, give an instance.
Adv. *conformably* etc. adj.; by rule; by the card; agreeably to, in conformity, in line with, in accordance, in keeping with; according to; according to plan; consistently with; as usual, of course, as a

matter of c.; for form's sake; for the look of it; for example, for instance.

See: 9, 18, 20, 23, 24, 30, 62, 66, 78, 79, 106, 147, 243, 258, 327, 601, 610, 635, 689, 701, 721, 732, 735, 739, 740, 768, 848, 850, 864, 875, 925, 976.

84 Unconformity

N. *unconformity*, disconformity, inconsistency 25 n. *disagreement*, 17 adj. *nonuniformity*; contrast, oasis 14 n. *contrariety*; exceptionality, strangeness 59 n. *extraneousness*; nonconformity, nonconformism, unorthodoxy 977 n. *heterodoxy*; dissidence 489 n. *dissent*, 769 n. *nonobservance*; deviationism, Titoism 744 n. *independence*; anomalousness, eccentricity, irregularity 282 n. *deviation*; informality, unconventionality, angularity, awkwardness 893 n. *sullenness*; bizarrerie, piquancy, freakishness, oddity; rarity 140 n. *infrequency*; infringement, infraction, infraction of rule, violation of law 954 n. *illegality*; breach of practice, defiance of custom, departure from usage; replacement 188 n. *displacement*, 63 n. *derangement*; anomaly, ectopia; monstrosity, wonder, miracle 864 n. *prodigy*; exception 57 n. *exclusion*; exemption, salvo, saving clause 919 n. *non-liability*; special case, isolated instance 80 n. *speciality*; individuality, idiosyncrasy, peculiarity, singularity, mannerism; originality, uniqueness 21 n. *non-imitation*.

abnormality, aberration 282 n. *deviation*; abortion, miscreation, monstrous birth, terata, teratogenesis, monstrosity, monster; sexual abnormality, homosexualism, lesbianism; nymphomania, andromania, necrophilia, sadism, masochism; transvestism; virilism, viraginity, gynandry 372 n. *male*; androgyny 373 n. *female*; hermaphroditism 161 n. *impotence*.

nonconformist, dissident, dissenter 489 n. *dissentient*, 977 n. *heretic*; sectarian 978 n. *sectarist*; deviationist, Titoist 603 n. *tergiversator*; non-striker, blackleg, scab 938 n. *cad*; unconventionalist, Bohemian; rebel, angry young man; handful, recalcitrant 738 n. *revolter*; fanatic 504 n. *crank*; outsider, outlaw, criminal 904 n. *offender*;

pariah 883 n. *outcaste*; hermit 883 n. *solitary*; gypsy, nomad, tramp 268 n. *wanderer*; odd man out, joker, ugly duckling; square peg in a round hole, fish out of water 25 n. *misfit*; odd type, black swan, sport, freak, variety, lusus naturæ; oddity, original, character, card, queer fish 851 n. *laughing stock*; curiosity, rarity, rare example, one in a million; neither fish, flesh, fowl nor good red herring, neither one thing nor the other; hermaphrodite, gynander, androgyn 161 n. *eunuch*; homosexual, lesbian, pansy, fairy, queer, pervert; sadist, masochist; mongrel, half-breed, cross-breed, half-blood, mulatto, mestizo, métis; mule 43 n. *hybrid*.

rara avis, mythical beast, unicorn, phœnix, griffin, simurgh, wyvern, roc, liver; sphinx, hippogriff, manticore, chimera, centaur, sagittary; minotaur, dragon, hydra; cockatrice, basilisk, salamander; kraken, sea-serpent, Loch Ness monster, sea-horse, hippocampus; Cerberus, Gorgon, Snark; Cyclops; merman, mermaid, siren, Lorelei.

Adj. *unconformable*, inadjustable 25 adj. *unapt*; contrarious, antipathetic 14 adj. *contrary*; unmalleable, stiff 326 adj. *rigid*, 602 adj. *obstinate*; recalcitrant 711 adj. *defiant*; crotchety, prickly, awkward, all edges 604 adj. *capricious*, 893 adj. *sullen*; arbitrary, a law to oneself 744 adj. *independent*; freakish, egregious; original, sui generis, unique, 80 adj. *special*; not joining, keeping out, standing o., staying o.; blacklegging 603 adj. *tergiversating*; nonconformist, dissident 489 adj. *dissenting*, 978 adj. *sectarian*; unorthodox, heretical 977 adj. *heterodox*; unconverted, nonpractising 769 adj. *non-observant*; unconventional, Bohemian, informal, unfashionable; irregular, against the rules, off-side, not done 924 adj. *disapproved*; infringing, lawless, criminal 954 adj. *illegal*; aberrant, astray, off the beam, off the rails 282 adj. *deviating*; misplaced, out of one's element, out of place, ectopic, out of order 188 adj. *displaced*, 61 adj. *orderless*; incongruous, out of step, out of line, out of tune, out of keeping 25 adj. *disagreeing*, 411 adj. *discordant*; alien, exotic 59 adj. *extraneous*; unidentifiable, unclassifiable, hard to place, nondescript, nameless 491 adj. *unknown*; eremetical,

solitary, exclusive 883adj. *unsociable*; stray, nomadic, wandering 267adj. *travelling*; amphibious, ambiguous 518adj. *equivocal*; exempted, exempt 919adj. *nonliable*.

unusual, uncustomary, unwonted 611adj. *unaccustomed*; unfamiliar 491adj. *unknown*; new-fangled 126adj. *new*; out of the way, outlandish 59adj. *extraneous*; extraordinary, phenomenal, supernormal; unparalleled, unexampled; singular, unique 80adj. *special*, 140adj. *infrequent*; rare, choice, recherché 644adj. *excellent*; strange, bizarre, curious, odd, queer, rum, rummy; funny, peculiar, fantastic, grotesque 849adj. *ridiculous*; noteworthy, remarkable, surprising, astonishing, miraculous, teratical 864adj. *wonderful*; mysterious, inexplicable, unaccountable 523adj. *occult*; unimaginable, incredible 470adj. *impossible*, 472adj. *improbable*; monstrous, unnatural, preternatural, supernatural; outsize 32adj. *enormous*; outré 546adj. *exaggerated*; shocking, scandalizing 924adj. *disapproved*; unmentionable, indescribable, left undescribed 517adj. *inexpressible*.

abnormal, unnatural, supernatural, preternatural (see *unusual*); aberrant, freakish; untypical, atypical, unrepresentative, exceptional; eccentric, anomalous, anomalistic 17adj. *non-uniform*; homosexual, lesbian, queer; epicene, androgenous, gynandrous; mongrel, hybrid 43 adj. *mixed*; irregular, heteroclite; unidiomatic, solecistic 565adj. *ungrammatical*; non-standard, substandard, subnormal; supernormal 32adj. *great*; ridiculous 497adj. *absurd*; asymmetrical, deformed, amorphous, shapeless 246adj. *distorted*.

Vb. *be unconformable*, have no business there; infringe a law, infringe a habit, infringe usage, infringe custom; break a law, break a habit, break a usage, break custom; violate a law, violate habit, violate usage, violate custom; put the clock back 117vb. *time*; get round, drive a coach and six through; stretch a point; leave the beaten track, baffle all description, beggar all d.

Adv. *unconformably* etc. adj.; except, unless, save, barring, beside, without, save and except, let alone; however, yet, but.

See: 14, 17, 21, 25, 32, 43, 57, 59, 61, 63, 80, 117, 126, 140, 161, 188, 246, 267, 268, 282, 326, 372, 373, 411, 470, 472, 489, 491, 497, 504, 517, 518, 523, 564, 565, 602, 603, 604, 611, 644, 711, 738, 744, 769, 849, 851, 864, 883, 893, 904, 919,924,938, 954,977,978.

85 Number

N. *number*, any n., numeric; cardinal number, ordinal n.; round n., indefinite numeral; prime number, odd n., even n., whole n., integer; figurative numbers, pyramidal n., polygonal n.; numeral, numeral adjective; cipher, digit, figure, recurring f., repetend; numerals, Arabic n., Roman n., algorism; quantity, unknown q., X, symbol; function, variable; surd; expression, algebraism; formula, series.

numerical element, subtrahend; totitive, totient; multiplicand, multiplier, multiplicator; coefficient, multiple, dividend, divisor, aliquant, aliquot part, quotient, factor, sub-multiple, fraction, proper f., improper f.; mixed number; numerator, denominator; decimal system, decimal, circulating d., recurring d., repetend; common measure, common factor, common denominator; reciprocal, complement; power, root, square r., cube r.; exponent, index, logarithm, antilogarithm; modulus, differential, integral, fluxion, fluent; operator, sign.

ratio, proportion; progression, arithmetical progression, geometrical p., harmonical p.; trigonometrical ratio, sine, tangent, secant; cosine, cotangent, cosecant; percentage, per cent, per mil, per hour.

numerical result, answer, product, equation; sum, total, aggregate 52n. *whole*; difference, residual 41n. *remainder*; bill, score, tally 38n. *addition*.

Adj. *numerical*, numerary, numeral; arithmetical; cardinal, ordinal; round, whole; even, odd; prime; figurate; positive, negative, surd, radical; divisible, aliquot; multiple; reciprocal, complementary; fractional, decimal; incommensurable; commensurable, proportional; exponential, logarithmic, logometric, differential, fluxional, integral, rational, irrational; real, imaginary.

See: 38, 41, 52.

86 Numeration

N. *numeration*, numbering, enumeration, census, recension, counting, ciphering, figuring, reckoning, dead r.; sum, tale, tally, score, break, runs, points; count, recount; figure-work, summation, calculation, supputation, computation 465 n. *measurement*; page-numbering, pagination; algorithm, algorism, decimal system; counting on the fingers, dactylonomy; money-counting, accountancy 808 n. *accounts*; counting heads, poll, capitulation; head-count, hand-c.; counting again, recapitulation.

mathematics, arithmetic, algebra, fluxions; differential calculus, integral c., infinitesimal c.; calculus of differences; geometry, trigonometry; graphs, logarithms; rhabdology; Napier's bones.

numerical operation, figure-work, notation; addition, subtraction, multiplication, division, proportion, rule of three, practice, equations, analysis, ancient a., modern a., extraction of roots, reduction, involution, evolution, approximation, interpolation; differentiation, integration, permutation, combination, variation.

statistics, figures, tables, averages; statistical enquiry, poll, Gallup p. 605 n. *vote*; census, capitation; roll-call, muster, muster-roll, account 87 n. *list*; demography, birth rate, death r., vital statistics; price index, cost of living 809 n. *price*.

counting instrument, abacus, swan-pan, quipu; ready reckoner, multiplication table; logometer, scale measure, tape-m., yardstick 465 n. *gauge*; sliding rule, slide r.; tallies, counters, Napier's bones; comptometer, calculating machine, adding m., computing m.; difference engine; cash register, totalizator, tote, calculator; electronic computer, Ernie.

computer, numberer, enumerator, census-taker; abacist; calculator, counter, teller, pollster; mathematician, wrangler; arithmetician, geometrician, algebraist; statistician, statist, bookkeeper 808 n. *accountant*; actuary, geometer, geodesist 465 n. *surveyor*.

Adj. *numerable*, numberable, countable; calculable, computable, measurable, mensurable 465 adj. *metric*; commensurable, commensurate 28 adj. *equal*; proportionable 9 adj. *relative*; incommensurable, incommensurate 29 adj. *unequal*, 10 adj. *irrelative*; eligible, admissible 78 adj. *included*.

statistical, expressed in numbers, ciphered, numbered, figured out; mathematical, arithmetical, algebraical; geometrical, trigonometrical; in ratio, in proportion, percentile.

Vb. *number*, cast, count, tell; score, keep the s., keep the count; tell off, tick off; affix numbers, foliate, paginate; enumerate, census, poll, count heads, count hands, count noses; take the number, take a poll, take a census; muster, call over, call the roll, take roll-call; take stock, inventorize 87 vb. *list*; recount, recapitulate, recite, go over 106 vb. *repeat*; check, audit, balance, book-keep, keep accounts 808 vb. *account*; aggregate, amount to, total, tot up to, come to.

do sums, cast up, carry over, totalize, tot up 38 vb. *add*; take away 39 vb. *subtract*; multiply 36 vb. *augment*; divide 46 vb. *sunder*; algebraize, geometrize, square, cube, extract roots; figure, cipher; work out, reduce; compute, calculate, reckon, reckon up 465 vb. *measure*; estimate 465 vb. *appraise*.

See: 9, 10, 28, 29, 36, 38, 39, 46, 78, 87, 106, 465, 605, 808, 809.

87 List

N. *list*, enumeration, items; list of items, inventory, stock list; table, catalogue; portfolio 767 n. *security*; statement, tabular s., schedule, manifest, bill of lading; check-list; invoice; numerical list, score; price-list, tariff, bill, account, itemized a. 809 n. *price*; registry, cartulary; cadastre, terrier, Domesday Book; file, register, death r., birth r. 548 n. *record*; ticket, docket, tally 547 n. *label*; ledger, books 808 n. *account book*; table of contents, bill of fare, menu, diet-sheet 301 n. *eating*; playbill, programme, prospectus 759 n. *offer*; synopsis, syllabus 592 n. *compendium*; roll, electoral r., voting list 605 n. *electorate*; muster-roll, check-r., payroll; civil list, army l., navy l., active l., retired l. 686 n. *personnel*; statistical list, census l., returns 86 n. *numeration*; book-list, reading list, library l. 589 n. *reading matter*; bibliography, publisher's cata-

logue, catalogue raisonnée 524 n. *guide-book*; list of names, rota, roster, panel; waiting list, short l.; string of names, visitors' book; dramatis personæ, characters in the play; family tree, pedigree 169 n. *genealogy*; scroll, roll of honour, honours' board, martyrology, bead-roll, diptych; black list 928 n. *accused person*, 924 n. *censure*; sick list 651 n. *sick person*; date-list, calendar, engagement book 505 n. *reminder*; question-list, questionnaire; alphabetical list, alphabet 60 n. *order*, 558 n. *letter*; repertory, repertoire.

word list, vocabulary, glossary, lexicon, thesaurus, gradus 559 n. *dictionary*.

directory, gazetteer, atlas; almanac, calendar, timetable 117 n. *chronology*; army list, navy l., Crockford, Burke's Peerage 524 n. *guide-book*; index, card i., thumb i. 547 n. *indication*.

Adj. listed etc. vb.; entered, catalogued, tabulated, indexed; cadastral.

Vb. list, make a l., enumerate; itemize, inventory, catalogue, calendar, index, tabulate; file, docket, schedule, enter, book, post 548 vb. *register*; enlist, matriculate, enrol, empanel, inscribe; score, keep s., keep count 86 vb. *number*.

See: 60, 86, 117, 169, 301, 505, 524, 547, 548, 558, 559, 589, 592, 605, 651, 686, 759, 767, 808, 809, 924, 928.

88 Unity

N. unity, oneness, absoluteness 44 n. *simpleness*; integrality, integration, wholeness 52 n. *whole*; uniqueness, singularity, individuality 80 n. *speciality*; univocity 514 n. *meaning*; singleness, single state 895 n. *celibacy*; isolation, solitude, loneliness 883 n. *seclusion*; isolability 46 n. *separation*; union, undividedness, indivisibility, solidarity 324 n. *density*, 706 n. *association*, unification 50 n. *combination*.

unit, integer, one, ace, item, piece; individual, point, atom, monad, entity, a being, a person 371 n. *person*; single piece, monolith; singleton, monotype, nonce-word; none else, no other, naught beside; single instance, isolated i., only exception; sole survivor 41 n. *survivor*; solo, solo performance; single person, bachelor 895 n. *celibate*; hermit 883 n. *solitary*; monocle;

set, outfit, package 58 n. *component*; package deal.

Adj. one, not plural, singular, sole, single; unique, only, lone, one and only; unrepeated, only-begotten; without a second, first and last; a, an, a certain 562 adj. *anonymous*; individual 80 adj. *special*; absolute, universal 79 adj. *general*; unitary, unific, univocal, unicameral, unilateral; mono-; monocular; monotonous, monolithic 16 adj. *uniform*; unified, rolled into one, compact, solid 45 adj. *conjunct*, 324 n. *dense*, 48 adj. *cohesive*; indivisible, insecable, inseverable, indiscerptible, indissoluble, irresolvable.

alone, lonely, homeless, rootless, orphaned, kithless 883 adj. *friendless*; lonesome, solitary, lone, eremetical 883 adj. *unsociable*; isolable, isolated 46 adj. *disjunct*; insular, enisled 199 adj. *removed*; single-handed, on one's own; unaccompanied, unescorted, unchaperoned; unpaired, fellowless, azygous; monadic, monatomic; celibate, bachelor 895 adj. *unwedded*.

Vb. be one, stand alone, stew in one's own juice; unite 50 vb. *combine*; isolate 46 vb. *set apart*.

Adv. singly, one by one, one at a time; once, once only, for the nonce, for this time only, never again, only, solely, simply; alone, on one's own, by oneself, per se; in the singular.

See: 41, 44, 45, 46, 48, 50, 52, 58, 79, 80, 199, 324, 371, 514, 562, 706, 883, 895.

89 Accompaniment

N. accompaniment, concomitance, togetherness 71 n. *continuity*, 45 n. *junction*, 5 n. *intrinsicality*; inseparability, sine qua non, permanent attribute; society, associating with, companionship, partnership, consortship, association 706 n. *co-operation*; operating with, coefficience, coagency 181 n. *concurrence*; coincidence, contemporaneity, simultaneity 123 n. *synchronism*; bearing company, fellow-travelling, escort, company, attendance; parallel course 219 n. *parallelism*; life with, coexistence.

concomitant, attribute, sine qua non 5 n. *essential part*; coefficient, accessory, appendage, appurtenance, fixture 40 adj.

adjunct; epiphenomenon, symptom 547n. *indication*; coincidence 159n. *chance*; context, circumstance 7n. *state*; background, noises off; accompaniment, musical a., obbligato; accompanist 413n. *musician*; entourage, court 742n. *retainer*; attendant, following, suite, cortège, train, tail 67n. *retinue*; rout 71n. *procession*; convoy, escort, guide, cicerone 690n. *leader*; chaperon, squire 660n. *protector*, 749n. *keeper*; cavalier, wooer 887n. *lover*; tracker, dogger 619n. *hunter*; inseparable, shadow, Mary's little lamb 284n. *follower*; consort 894n. *spouse*; comrade, companion, boon c. 880n. *friend*; stable companion, yoke-fellow, mate, co-worker, partner, associate 707n. *colleague*; fellow-traveller 707n. *collaborator*; twin, fellow, pair 18n. *analogue*; satellite, parasite, hanger on, client, stooge 742n. *dependant*; waiter 742n. *servant*; embroidery, decoration 844n. *ornamentation*; fringe 234n. *edging*.

Adj. *accompanying*, with, concomitant, attendant, background; always with, inseparable, built-in 45adj. *conjunct*; partnering, associated, coupled, paired; hand-in-glove 706adj. *co-operative*, 181n. *concurrent*; obbligato 410adj. *harmonious*; accessory, belonging 78adj. *included*, 58 adj. *ingredient*; satellite, satellitic 745adj. *subject*; epiphenomenal, symptomatic 547 adj. *indicating*; incidental, coincidental 159adj. *casual*; co-existent, contemporaneous, contemporary, simultaneous.

Vb. *accompany*, be found with, be seen w.; coexist, have a life with; cohabit, live with, stable w., walk w., keep company w., consort w., walk out w.; string along with, row in the same boat; attend, wait on, come to heel, dance attendance on 284vb. *follow*; bear one company, squire, chaperon, protect, keep 660vb. *safeguard*; convoy, escort, guide, conduct, lead, usher 64vb. *come before*; track, dog, shadow 619vb. *pursue*; associate, partner 706vb. *co-operate*; gang up with, chum up w. 880vb. *befriend*; coincide, keep time with 123vb. *synchronize*, 181vb. *concur*; imply 5vb. *be intrinsic*; carry with, bring in its train 156vb. *cause*; be inseparable, follow as night follows day 157vb. *depend*; belong, go with, go together 9vb. *be related*.

Adv. *with*, withal; therewith, herewith 38

adv. *in addition*; with others, together with, along w., in company w.; in convoy, hand in hand, arm in arm, side by side; cheek by jowl; jointly, all together, in a body, collectively, inseparably, unitedly.

See: 5, 7, 9, 18, 40, 45, 58, 64, 67, 71, 78, 123, 156, 157, 159, 181, 219, 234, 284, 410, 413, 547, 619, 660, 690, 706, 707, 742, 745, 749, 844, 880, 887, 894.

90 Duality

N. *duality*, dualism; two times, twice; double-sidedness; duplicity; biformity, polarity; dyad, two, deuce, twain, couple, brace, pair, fellows; cheeks, jaws; doublets, twins, Castor and Pollux, Gemini, Siamese twins, identical t., Tweedledum and Tweedledee; yoke, span, conjugation, couplet, distich; double harness, twosome; duel, duet, tandem, bireme, two-seater; Janus; biped; dyarchy.

Adj. *dual*, dualistic; dyadic, binary, binomial; bilateral, bicameral; twin, biparous; conduplicate, duplex 91adj. *double*; paired, coupled etc. vb.; conjugate, both the one and the other; in twos, both; tête-à-tête; double-sided, bipartisan; amphibious; ambidextrous 91 adj. *double*; biform, bifront, bifrontal, two-faced; dihedral; di-, bi-.

Vb. *pair*, unite in pairs, couple, match, bracket, yoke; conduplicate, mate; pair off.

See: 91.

91 Duplication

N. *duplication*; doubling 261n. *fold*; gemination, ingemination; reduplication, encore, repeat, repeat performance; iteration, echo 106n. *repetition*; renewal 656n. *restoration*; copy, carbon c., stencil 22n. *duplicate*; repeater.

Adj. *double*, doubled, twice; duplex, bifarious; bicapital, bi-fold, biform, bivalent; twofold, two-sided, two-headed, two-edged; bifacial, bifrontal, bifronted, double-faced; amphibious, ambidextrous; double-sided; of double meaning 518adj. *equivocal*; of double sex, hermaphrodite; twin, duplicate, ingeminate; second; dual 90adj. *dual*.

Vb. *double*, multiply by two; redouble, square; ingeminate, encore, echo, second 106vb. *repeat*; renew 656vb. *restore*; duplicate, twin; reduplicate, stencil 22vb. *copy*.

Adv. *twice*, once more; over again 106adv. *again*; once and again, as much again, twofold; secondly, in the second place, again; twice as much.

See: 22, 90, 106, 261, 518, 656.

92 Bisection

N. *bisection*, bipartition, dichotomy, subdichotomy; dividing by two, halving etc. vb.; dimidiation; hendiadys; half, moiety, fifty per cent 53n. *part*; hemisphere 252n. *sphere*.

bifurcation, forking, branching, furcation, ramification, divarication 294n. *divergence*; fork, prong 222n. *cross*.

dividing line, diameter, diagonal, equator; parting, suture, seam; date-line; partywall 231n. *partition*.

Adj. *bisected*, halved etc. vb.; dimidiate, bifid; bipartite, biconjugate, bicuspid; bifurcous, bifurcate, bifurcated; dichotomic, dichotomous; semi-, demi-, hemi-; cloven, cleft 46adj. *disjunct*.

Vb. *bisect*, transect; divide, split, cleave 46 vb. *sunder*; cut in two, dimidiate, dichotomize, share, go halves, divide with, go fifty-fifty 783vb. *apportion*; halve, divide by two.

bifurcate, separate, fork; branch off, branch out, ramify, divaricate 294vb. *diverge*.

See: 46, 53, 222, 231, 252, 294, 783.

93 Triality

N. *triality*, trinity, trimurti; triunity; triplicity 94n. *triplication*.

three, triad, trine; threesome, triumvirate, leash; troika; triplet, trey, trio, ternion, trinomial; trimester, triennium; trefoil, shamrock, triangle, trident, tripod; tricorn, triphthong, triptych, trilogy, trireme, triobol; third power, cube; third person; tertium quid.

Adj. *three*, trinal, triform, trinomial; tertiary, trimetric; three in one, triune, tripartite; three-dimensional, tridimen-

sional; three-sided, triangular, trilateral, leg-of-mutton; three-pointed, trinacrian: three-monthly, trimestrial, quarterly; tri-

Adv. *in threes*, three by three; three times, thrice.

See: 94.

94 Triplication

N. *triplication*, triplicity; trebleness; hat-trick.

Adj. *treble*, triple; trine, tern, ternary; triplex, triplicate, threefold, trilogistic; third, trinal; trihedral; trilateral.

Vb. *treble*, triple, triplicate, cube.

Adv. *trebly*, triply, threefold; three times, thrice; twice and again; in the third place, thirdly.

95 Trisection

N. *trisection*, tripartition, trichotomy; third, third part; tierce.

Adj. *trifid*, trisected; tripartite, trichotomous, trisulcate; tierce, tierced.

Vb. *trisect*, divide into three parts, divide by three; trifurcate.

96 Quaternity

N. *quaternity*, four, tetrad, tetractys; square, tetragon, quadrilateral, quadrangle, quad; quadrature, quarter; tetrastich, tetrapod, tetrameter; tetragrammaton; tetramorph; quaternion, quartet, foursome; four-in-hand, quadriga; quatrefoil; quadruplet, quad; quadruped; quadrennium; quadrilateral; four corners of 52n. *whole*.

Adj. *four*, quaternary, quaternal; quartite; quartic, tetractic, quadratic; quadrate, square, quadrilateral, tetrahedral, foursquare; quadrennial, quadrivalent; quadrilateral; quadri-.

See: 52.

97 Quadruplication

N. *quadruplication*, quadruplicity; squaring.

Adj. *fourfold*, quadruplicate, quadruplex; squared; quadrable.

Vb. *quadruple*, quadruplicate, multiply by four; square, biquadrate; quadruplex.

Adv. *four times*; fourthly, in the fourth place.

98 Quadrisection

N. *quadrisection*, quadripartition; quartering etc. vb.; fourth, fourth part; quart, quarter, quartern; farthing, quarto.

Adj. *quartered*; quadrifid, quadripartite.

Vb. *quadrisect*, quarter, divide into four parts, divide by four.

99 Five and over

N. *five*, five, cinque, quint, quintuplet; pentad, fiver; quincunx; pentagon; pentameter; Pentateuch, pentacle; pentapolis; pentarchy.

over five, six, half-a-dozen, sextet, hexad, sixer; hexagon; Hexateuch; hexameter; seven, heptad, week, week of Sundays, sabbatical year; septennium; heptarchy; eight, octave, octet, octad; octagon; nine, three times three; ennead; novena; ten, tenner, decade, decad; tetractys; decury, decemvirate; eleven, hendecasyllable; twelve, dozen; thirteen, baker's dozen, long d.; twenty, a score; double figures.

over twenty, four and twenty, two dozen; twenty-five, pony; forty, two score; fifty, half a hundred, jubilee; sixty, three score; sexagenarian; seventy, three score and ten, septuagenarian; eighty, four score, octogenarian; ninety, nonagenarian.

hundred, century, centenary; hecatomb; hundredweight; centurion; centenarian; centipede; the hundred days; hundred per cent; treble figures.

over one hundred, a gross; thousand, chiliad, grand; millennium; ten thousand, myriad; hundred thousand, plum, lakh; million; ten million, crore, hundred lakhs; thousand million, milliard; billion; million million; trillion, quadrillion, centillion, multimillion; millionaire, billionaire, milliardaire.

Adj. *fifth and over*, five, quinary, quintuple; fifth; senary, sextuple; sixth; seventh; octuple; eighth; ninefold, ninth; tenfold, decimal, denary, decuple, tenth; eleventh; twelfth; duodenary, duodenal; in one's

'teens; vigesimal, twentieth; centesimal, centuple, centuplicate, centennial, centenary, centenarian, centurial; secular, hundredth; thousandth, millenary; millionth, billionth.

Vb. *centuriate*, centesimate.

100 Multisection

N. *multisection*, quinquesection, decimation, centesimation.

Adj. *multifid*, quinquefid, quinquepartite; quinquarticular; octifid; decimal, tenth; tithe, teind; duodecimal, twelfth; sexagesimal, sexagenary; hundredth, centesimal; millesimal.

Vb. *multisect*, decimate, quinquesect.

101 Plurality

N. *plurality*, the plural; multiplicity, many-sidedness 104 n. *multitude*; a number, a certain number; some, one or two, two or three; a few, several; majority 104 n. *greater number*.

Adj. *plural*, in the p., not singular; composite, multiple, many-sided; more than one, some, certain; not alone, accompanied, in company 45 adj. *conjunct*; upwards of, more, in the majority 104 adj. *many*.

Adv. *et cetera*.

See: 45, 104.

102 Fraction: less than one

N. *fraction*, fractional part, fragment 53 n. *part*, 783 n. *portion*; shred 33 n. *small quantity*.

Adj. *fractional*, portional, partial 53 adj. *fragmentary*, 33 adj. *small*.

See: 33, 53, 783.

103 Zero

N. *zero*, nil, nothing, simply n., next to nothing, infinitely little; naught, nought, nix; no score, love, duck's egg, duck; blank; figure nought, cipher; nullity, nothingness 2 n. *non-existence*, 4 n. *in-*

substantiality; none, nobody, not a soul 190 n. *absence*; zero level, nadir.

Adj. *not one*, not any, null, zero; invisible, infinitely little, null 4 adj. *insubstantial*, 2 adj. *non-existent.*

Adv. *at zero*, from scratch.

See: 2, 4, 190.

104 Multitude

N. *multitude*, numerousness, numerosity, multiplicity; large number, round n., enormous n., multimillion 99 n. *over one hundred*; a quantity, clutter, hantle, lots, loads, heaps 32 n. *great quantity*; numbers, scores, myriads, millions, lakhs, crores; a sea of, a world of, a sight of; host, array, squadrons, legion, phalanx, battalions 722 n. *army*; throng, mob, rout, all the world and his wife 74 n. *crowd*; tribe, horde.

certain quantity, peck, bushel, pinch; galaxy, bevy, cloud, flock, flight, covey; shoal, school; flock, herd, drove; swarm, hive, ant-heap, colony 74 n. *group*; nest, clutch, litter, farrow, fry 132 n. *youngling.*

greater number, weight of numbers, majority, great m., mass, bulk, mainstream 32 n. *main part*; multiplication, multiple 101 n. *plurality.*

Adj. *many*, several, sundry, divers, various, a thousand and one; quite a few, not a f., considerable, numerous, very many, ever so m., many more; untold, unnumbered, uncounted 107 adj. *infinite*; multinomial; many-headed 82 adj. *multiform*; ever-recurring 139 adj. *frequent*, 106 adj. *repeated*; much, ample, multiple, multiplied; profuse, in profusion, abundant, superabundant, generous, lavish, overflowing, galore 635 adj. *plenteous*, 32 adj. *great.*

multitudinous, massed, crowded, thronged, studded with 54 adj. *full*; populous, peopled, populated, over-p. 324 adj. *dense*; multiferous, teeming, crawling, humming, alive with 171 adj. *prolific*; thick, thick on the ground, thick as hops, thick as hail; coming thick and fast 139 adj. *frequent*; incalculable, innumerable, inexhaustible, countless, endless 107 adj. *infinite*; countless as the stars, countless as the sands; as the hairs on one's head; heaven knows how many.

Vb. *be many*,—various etc. adj.; swarm with, crawl w., hum w., bristle w., teem w. 54 vb. *fill*; pullulate, multiply 171 vb. *be fruitful*; clutter, crowd, throng, swarm, mass, flock, troop 74 vb. *congregate*; swarm like ants, swarm like locusts; flood, overflow; swamp, overwhelm 341 vb. *drench*; infest, overrun, irrupt 297 vb. *infiltrate*; add to the number, swell the ranks 36 vb. *augment*; overweigh, outnumber, make a majority 32 vb. *be great.*

See : 32, 36, 54, 74, 82, 99, 101, 106, 107, 132, 139, 171, 297, 324, 341, 635, 722.

105 Fewness

N. *fewness*, paucity, underpopulation; exiguity, thinness, sparsity, sparseness, rarity 140 n. *infrequency*; stringency 636 n. *scarcity*; a few, a handful, maniple; thin house, sparse population; small number, trickle, mere t. 33 n. *small quantity*; limited number, too few, no quorum; minority, one or two, two or three, half a dozen, not enough to matter; remnant, sole survivor 41 n. *remainder.*

Adj. *few*, weak in numbers, scant, scanty 636 adj. *scarce*; thin, thin on the ground, sparse, rare, scattered, few and far between 140 adj. *infrequent*; soon counted, to be counted on one's fingers; fewer, reduced, diminished in number, losing n. 37 adj. *decreasing*; too few, in a minority, without a quorum.

Vb. *be few*, be weak in numbers, be underpopulated; seldom occur.

render few, reduce, diminish, pare 198 vb. *make smaller*; scale down, decimate, thin the ranks; eliminate, weed, thin, sort out 300 vb. *eject*; defect, desert; underman, understaff.

Adv. *here and there*, in dribs and drabs, in a trickle; sparsely, rarely, infrequently.

See: 33, 37, 41, 140, 198, 300, 636.

106 Repetition

N. *repetition*, doing again, iteration, reiteration; doubling, ditto, reduplication 20 n. *imitation*, 91 n. *duplication*; going over, recital, recapitulation; practising, rehearsal 610 n. *practice*; beginning again, renewal, resumption, reprise 68 n.

beginning; saying again, palillogy, anadiplosis, anaphora 566n. *style*, 574n. *ornament*; harping, tautology, tautophony 570n. *diffuseness*; stammering, battology 580n. *speech defect*; a repetition, repeat, repeat performance, encore; replay, return match, revenge; chorus, chant, song, refrain, burden, ritornello, ritornel 412n. *vocal music*; echo, repercussion, reverberation, chime 404n. *resonance*; cliché, quotation, citation, plagiarism; sound-echo, alliteration, assonance, rhyme (see *recurrence*); twice-told tale, old story, chestnut 838n. *tedium*; parrot-cry; gramophone record; rehandling, restatement, new edition, reprint, new impression, reissue 589n. *edition*; refacimento, réchauffé, rehash 656n. *restoration*; repeater, cuckoo, parrot; creature of habit.

recurrence, repetitiveness 139n. *frequency*; cycle, round, rebirth, reincarnation 141n. *regular return*; succession, run, series, serial 71n. *continuity*; recurring decimal, repetend; throw-back, atavism 5n. *heredity*; reappearance, curtain call, curtain; return 295n. *arrival*; rhythm, drumming, hammering 141n. *periodicity*; alliteration, assonance, rhyme 18n. *assimilation* 593n. *prosody*; stale repetition, monotony, ding-dong 16n. *uniformity*, 838n. *tedium*; same old round, mixture as before, busman's holiday, routine 610n. *habit*.

Adj. *repeated*, repetitional, repetionary; repeatable, quotable 950adj. *pure*; recurrent, recurring, ever-r. 141adj. *periodical*; haunting 505adj. *remembered*; tautological, repetitive, repetitious, harping, iterative; stale, cliché-ridden 572adj. *feeble*; echoing, rhyming, chiming, alliterative, assonant 18adj. *similar*; monotonous, sing-song, ding-dong 16adj. *uniform*, 838adj. *tedious*; rhythmical, drumming, hammering; incessant, habitual 139adj. *frequent*; retold, twice-told, said before, quoted, cited; above-mentioned, aforesaid 66adj. *precursory*; plagiarized 20adj. *imitative*.

Vb. *repeat*, do again, iterate, cut and come again; duplicate, reduplicate, redouble 91vb. *double*; multiply 166vb. *reproduce*; reiterate, ingeminate, say again, recapitulate, go over; retell, restate, reword, rephrase; always say, trot out; say one's piece, recite, say over, say after; echo, ditto, parrot, plagiarize 20vb. *copy*,

925vb. *flatter*; quote, cite 505vb. *remember*; go over the same ground, practise, rehearse; play back (a record); begin again, restart, resume 68vb. *begin*; replay, give an encore; reprint, reissue, republish; rehash, renew, revive 656vb. *restore*; belch 300vb. *eruct*.

repeat oneself, reverberate, re-echo 404vb. *resound*; drum, beat a tattoo; chant, chorus 16vb. *be uniform*; give an encore; quote onself, tautologize 570vb. *be diffuse*; battologize 580vb. *stammer*; trot out, plug, labour, harp on, harp on the same string; din into one's ears, go on at, hammer at; recur to, revert to, return to 505vb. *remember*; go back, retrace one's steps 286vb. *regress*; go the same round, commute, be a creature of habit 610vb. *be wont*.

reoccur, recur, return, revert, happen again; reappear, pop up, show up again; never hear the last of; turn up like a bad penny; haunt, obsess 505vb. *be remembered*.

Adv. *repeatedly*, recurrently, frequently 139 adv. *often*; again and again, over and over, many times o., times without number, time and again; time after time, day after day, year after year; day by day, year in year out; morning, noon and night.

again, afresh, anew, over again, for the second time, once more; ditto; encore, bis; de novo, da capo; re-.

See: 5, 16, 18, 20, 66, 68, 71, 91, 139, 141, 166, 286, 295, 300, 404, 412, 505, 566, 570, 572, 574, 580, 589, 593, 610, 656, 838, 925, 950.

107 Infinity

N. *infinity*, infinitude, infiniteness, boundlessness, limitlessness, illimitability; eternity 115n. *perpetuity*.

Adj. *infinite*, indefinite; immense, measureless; eternal 115adj. *perpetual*; numberless, countless, sumless, innumerable, immeasurable, illimitable, interminable; incalculable, unfathomable, incomprehensible, unapproachable; inexhaustible, without number, without limit, without end, no end of; without measure, limitless, endless, boundless, termless; untold, unnumbered 104adj. *many*; unmeasured, unbounded, unlimited.

Adv. *infinitely*, to infinity, ad infinitum; without end, indefinitely; boundlessly, illimitably; immeasurably 32 adv. *greatly.*

See: 32, 104, 115.

108 Time

N. *time*, tide; tense 564 n. *grammar*; duration, extent 183 n. *space*; limited time, season, term, semester, tenancy, tenure; spell, stint; span, space 110 n. *period*; a bit, a while; the whole time, the entire period, life, life-time; stream of time, lapse, course 111 n. *course of time*; years, days; whirligig of time, Time's scythe, Time's hour-glass, sands of time, ravages of t., noiseless foot of t.; fourth dimension; aorist, indefinite time; past time, past tense, retrospective time 125 n. *preterition*, 119 n. *priority*; prospective time 124 n. *futurity*; contemporaneity 121 n. *present time*; recent time 126 n. *newness*; antiquity, distant time 127 n. *oldness*.

interim, intermediate time, pendency, while; interval, entr'acte, break, playtime, recess, pause 145 n. *lull*; interval of leisure 681 n. *leisure*; intermission, intermittence, interregnum, interlude, episode 72 n. *discontinuity*; close season 145 n. *halt*; respite, adjournment 136 n. *delay*; midweek 70 n. *middle*.

date, day, age, day and a., reign 110 n. *era*; vintage, year, regnal y., time of life 117 n. *chronology*; birthday, nativity 141 n. *anniversary*; day of the week, kalends, ides, nones; moment 116 n. *instant*; target date, zero hour, D-day; term, fixed day, day of settlement, quarter-day, pay-d.

Adj. *continuing*, permanent 115 adj. *perpetual*, 146 adj. *unceasing*; on foot, in process of; repetitive, recurrent 106 adj. *repeated*; temporal 141 adj. *periodical*.

intermediate, interglacial, interlunar, interwar; midweek; intercalary, intercalated, inter-.

dated, calendared; pre-Christian 119 adj. *prior*; post-Christian, post-war 120 adj. *subsequent*.

Vb. *continue*, endure, drag on 113 vb. *last*; roll on, intervene, pass 111 vb. *elapse*; take time, take up t., fill t., occupy t. 183 vb. *extend*; live through, sustain; stay, remain, abide, outlive, survive 113 vb. *outlast*; take its time, wait 136 vb. *pend*.

pass time, vegetate, breathe, subsist 360 vb. *live*; age, grow old 127 vb. *be old*; spend time, consume t., use t., employ t. 678 vb. *be busy*; while away t., kill t., summer, winter, week-end 681 vb. *have leisure*; waste t. 679 vb. *be inactive*; mark time, tide over 136 vb. *wait*; take the right time, seize an opportunity 137 vb. *profit by*; have one's day, enjoy a spell.

fix the time, calendar, date, put a date to 117 vb. *time*; make an engagement.

Adv. *while*, whilst, during, pending; during the time, during the interval; day by day; in the course of; for the time being, meantime, meanwhile; between whiles, in the meantime, in the interim; from day to day, from hour to hour; hourly 139 adv. *often*; for a time, for a season; till, until, up to, yet; always, the whole time, all the time 139 adv. *perpetually*; all along 54 adv. *throughout*; for good 113 adv. *for long*.

when, what time; one day, once upon a time, one fine morning; in the days of, in the time of, in the year of.

anno domini, A.D.; ante Christum A.C.; before Christ, B.C.; before the Christian era, B.C.E.; anno urbis conditæ, A.U.C.; anno regni, A.R., in the year of his reign.

See: 54, 70, 72, 106, 110, 111, 113, 115, 116, 117, 119, 120, 121, 124, 125, 126, 127, 136, 137, 139, 141, 145, 146, 183, 360, 564, 678, 679, 681.

109 Neverness

N. *neverness*, Greek Kalends; Tib's eve; blue moon; dies non; no time, datelessness, eternity 115 n. *perpetuity*.

Adv. *never*, not ever, at no time, at no period, on no occasion, not in donkey's years; nevermore, never again; over one's dead body; never before, never in one's born days; without date, sine die; before the beginning of time; out of time.

See: 115.

110 Period

N. *period*, matter of time; long period, long run 113 n. *diuturnity*; short period, short run 114 n. *transientness*; season; close season 145 n. *lull*; time of day, morning,

evening; time of year, spring, summer, autumn, winter 128n. *morning*, 129n. *evening*; one's time, fixed t., term; notice, warning, ultimatum 766n. *conditions*; time up 69n. *finality*; measured time, spell, stint, shift, span, stretch, sentence; innings, turn; round, chukker, bout, lap; vigil, watch, nightwatch, dogwatch; length of time, second, minute, hour; particular time, rush-hour, crush-h.; pause, interval 108n. *interim*; day, weekd., working d.; week, sennight, octave, novena; fortnight, month, moon, lunation; quarter, trimester; half year, semester; twelve month, year, sidereal y., light y., sabbatical y.; Olympiad, lustrum, quinquennium; decade, decennium, the Nineties, the Twenties; indiction; silver wedding, golden w., jubilee, diamond j. 141n. *anniversary*; century, millennium; annus mirabilis; time up to now, one's born days; life, lifetime, life-sentence.

era, time, age, days; epoch, samvat; cycle, Sothic c., Metonic c.; Platonic year, Great Year, Annus Magnus, Yuga, Kalpa; geological period, Ice Age, Stone A., Saturnian A.

Adj. *periodic*, seasonal; hourly, horary; annual, biennial, quinquennial, decennial, centennial.

secular, epochal, millennial; archæan, primary, palæozoic; secondary, mesozoic; tertiary, cainozoic; quaternary, recent; eocene, miocene, pliocene, pleistocene, neocene; eolithic, palæolithic, mesolithic, neolithic, chalcolithic.

Adv. *man and boy*, in a lifetime; by periods, periodically, seasonally; for a term, for the term of one's natural life, for a lifetime.

See: 69, 108, 113, 114, 128, 129, 141, 145, 766.

111 Course: indefinite duration

N. *course of time*, matter of t., progress of t., process of t., succession of t., lapse of t., flow of t., flux of t., effluxion, stream of time, tide of t., march of t., step of t., flight of t.; duration 108n. *time*, 146n. *continuance*; continuous tense, imperfect t. 564n. *grammar*; indefinite time, infinite t. 113n. *diuturnity*.

Adj. *elapsing*, wearing, passing, rolling 285

adj. *progressive*, 146n. *unceasing*; consuming 114adj. *transient*; ageing, getting older 131adj. *aged*.

Vb. *elapse*, pass, lapse, flow, run, roll, proceed, advance, press on 285vb. *progress*; wear on, drag on, crawl 278vb. *move slowly*; flit, fly, slip, slide, glide 277vb. *move fast*; run its course, expire 69vb. *end*; go by, pass by, slip by 125vb. *be past*; have one's day, enjoy a spell 108vb. *pass time*.

Adv. *in time*, in due time, in due season; in course of time, in process of t., in the fulness of t., with the years.

See: 69, 108, 113, 114, 125, 131, 146, 277, 278, 285, 564.

112 Contingent Duration

Adv. *during pleasure*, during good behaviour; provisionally, precariously, by favour; for the present; so long as it lasts; as *or* so long as.

113 Diuturnity: long duration

N. *diuturnity*, length of time, a long t., unconscionable t.; a week of Sundays, years, years on end; a lifetime, life sentence; generations, a century, an age, ages, æons 115n. *perpetuity*; length of days, cat's nine lives, longevity 131n. *age*; distance of time, corridor of t., antiquity 125n. *preterition*.

durability, lasting quality, endurance, defiance of time; survival, survivance 146n. *continuance*; permanence 153n. *stability*; inveteracy, long standing, good age 127n. *oldness*; long run, long innings.

protraction, prolongation, extension 203n. *lengthening*; dragging out, spinning o., filibustering, stonewalling 702n. *hindrance*, 715n. *resistance*; interminability, wait, long w. 136n. *delay*, 278n. *slowness*; extra time, overtime 38n. *addition*; long spell, long innings, long run.

Adj. *lasting*, abiding, diuturnal 146adj. *continuing*; secular, agelong, lifelong, livelong; longstanding, inveterate, deepseated, deep-rooted; of long duration, long-term, long-service, marathon 203 adj. *long*; too long, unconscionable; durable, perdurable, enduring 162adj.

strong; longeval, longlived, macrobiotic 131 adj. *aged*; evergreen, sempervirent, unfading, fresh 126 adj. *new*; eternal, perennial 115 adj. *perpetual*; persistent, chronic 602 adj. *obstinate*; intransmutable, intransient, constant, stable, permanent 153 adj. *unchangeable*.

protracted, prolonged, lengthened, extended, stretched, spun out, drawn o. 197 adj. *expanded*; lingering, delayed, tarrying 278 adj. *slow*; long-pending, long-awaited 136 adj. *late*; interminable, long-winded, time-wasting 570 adj. *prolix*.

Vb. *last*, endure, stand, stay, remain, abide, continue 146 vb. *go on*; have roots, brave the years, defy time, never end 115 vb. *be eternal*; carry one's years 131 vb. *grow old*; wear, wear well 162 vb. *be strong*.

outlast, outlive, outwear, outstay, survive; remain 41 vb. *be left*; live to fight another day; have nine lives.

spin out, draw o., drag o.; protract, prolong 203 vb. *lengthen*; temporize, gain time, procrastinate 136 vb. *put off*; talk out, filibuster 702 vb. *obstruct*.

drag on, be interminable, never end; drag its slow length along, inch, creep, linger, dawdle 278 vb. *move slowly*; tarry, delay, waste time, wait 136 vb. *be late*.

Adv. *for long*, long, for a long time, for ages, for years, many a long day; for good, for all time, for better for worse; till blue in the face; till the cows come home.

all along, all day, all day long, the livelong day; all the year round, round the clock, hour by hour, day by day; before and since; ever since.

long ago, long since, in the distant past, long, long ago; in ancient days, in bygone times 125 adv. *formerly*.

at last, in the long run, after many days, not before it was time.

See: 38, 41, 115, 125, 126, 127, 131, 136, 146, 153, 162, 197, 203, 278, 570, 602, 702, 715.

114 Transientness

N. *transientness*, transience, transitoriness 4 n. *insubstantiality*; ephemerality, impermanence; evanescence 446 n. *disappearance*; volatility 338 n. *vaporization*; fugacity 277 n. *velocity*; caducity, fragility 330 n. *brittleness*; mortality, perishability 361 n. *death*; frailty 163 n. *weakness*; mutability 152 n. *changeableness*; capriciousness, fickleness 604 n. *caprice*; suddenness 116 n. *instantaneity*; temporariness, provisionality; temporary arrangement, acting a., makeshift 150 n. *substitute*; interregnum 108 n. *interim*.

brief span, briefness, brevity 204 n. *shortness*; mortal span, short life and a merry one; summer lightning, meteor-flash, flash in the pan, nine days' wonder; bubble reputation 355 n. *bubble*; May-fly, snowman, snows of yesteryear, snow in the sun, smoke in the wind; April shower, summer cloud 4 n. *insubstantial thing*; milk tooth; short run 110 n. *period*, 277 n. *spurt*; spasm, moment 116 n. *instant*.

Adj. *transient*, time-bound, temporal, impermanent, transitory, fading, passing 4 adj. *insubstantial*; fair-weather, summer; cursory, flying, fleeting, fugitive, fugacious 277 adj. *speedy*; shifty, slippery, slipping; precarious, volatile; evanescent 446 adj. *disappearing*; unsettled, rootless; flickering, mutable, changeable 152 adj. *changeful*; fickle, flighty 604 adj. *capricious*.

ephemeral, of a day, short-lived, non-durable; perishable, mortal 361 adj. *dying*; deciduous, frail 163 adj. *weak*, 330 adj. *brittle*; impermanent, temporary, acting, provisional, for the time being; doomed, under sentence.

brief, short-term, short-service 204 adj. *short*; summary, short and sweet 569 adj. *concise*; quick, fleet, brisk 277 adj. *speedy*; sudden, momentary, meteoric, like a flash 116 adj. *instantaneous*; harried, pressed for time, in a hurry 680 adj. *hasty*; at short notice, extemporaneous, off-hand 609 adj. *spontaneous*.

Vb. *be transient*, — transitory etc. adj.; not stay, not last; flit, fleet, fly, gallop 277 vb. *move fast*; fade, flicker, vanish, evanesce, melt, evaporate 446 vb. *disappear*; fade like a dream, flit like a shadow, pass like a summer cloud, burst like a bubble, have no roots 2 vb. *pass away*.

Adv. *transiently*, briefly, temporarily, provisionally; for the present, for the moment, for a time, for the time being; instantly 116 adv. *instantaneously*; easy come, easy go; here today and gone tomorrow; touch and go.

See: 2, 4, 108, 110, 116, 150, 152, 163, 204, 277, 330, 338, 355, 361, 446, 569, 604, 609, 680.

115 Perpetuity: endless duration

N. *perpetuity*, perennity; endless time, infinite duration 107 n. *infinity*; sempiternity, everlastingness; eternity, timelessness; never-endingness, interminability 113 n. *diuturnity*; immortality, athanasia, incorruption 146 n. *continuance*; perpetuation, immortalization; lasting monument 505 n. *reminder*.

Adj. *perpetual*, long-lasting, durable, perdurable 113 adj. *lasting*; æonian, agelong 127 adj. *immemorial*; non-stop, constant, continual, ceaseless, incessant 146 adj. *unceasing*; flowing, ever-flowing, uninterrupted 71 adj. *continuous*; dateless, ageless, unageing, unchanging, immutable 144 adj. *permanent*; evergreen, unfading, amaranthine, incorruptible; imperishable, undying, deathless, immortal; unending, never-ending, interminable; indesinent, endless, without end, timeless, eternal, eterne, co-eternal.

Vb. *perpetuate*, make permanent, establish; immortalize, eternalize, eternize.

be eternal, — perpetual etc. adj.; last for ever, endure for e., live for e.; go on for e., have no end, never stop.

Adv. *forever*, in perpetuity, on and on; ever and always, for aye, evermore, ever and ever, for ever and a day; time without end, world without e.; for keeps, for good and all, for better for worse; to the end of time, till doomsday, to the crack of doom; to infinity; unchangeably, constantly, non-stop, as a matter of habit 610 adv. *habitually*.

See: 71, 107, 113, 127, 144, 146, 505, 610.

116 Instantaneity: point of time

N. *instantaneity*, instantaneousness, immediateness, immediacy; simultaneity 121 n. *present time*; suddenness, abruptness 508 n. *inexpectation*; precise time 135 n. *punctuality*; momentariness 114 n. *transientness*.

instant, moment, point, point of time; second, split s., half a s., tick, trice, jiffy, half a j.; breath; burst, crack; stroke, coup; flash, lightning f.; twinkle, twinkling, the twinkling of an eye; two shakes; the very moment, the very hour, the stroke of.

Adj. *instantaneous*, simultaneous, immediate, instant, sudden, abrupt; flickering, flashing; quick as thought, quick as lightning, with the speed of light, like a flash 277 adj. *speedy*; on time, punctual 135 adj. *early*.

Adv. *instantaneously*, instantly, instanter, immediately; punctually, without delay, in half a mo, soon; promptly, readily, presto, pronto; without warning, without notice, abruptly; overnight, all at once, all of a sudden 135 adj. *suddenly*; plump, slap, slap-bang, in one's tracks; in the same breath, at the same instant, at a stroke, at one jump, at one swoop; in a trice, in a moment, in a tick, in the twinkling of an eye; at the drop of a hat, on the spot, on the dot; extempore, impromptu, on the spur of the moment, slapdash, off-hand, before you could say Jack Robinson, before you could say knife; like a flash, like a shot, like greased lightning 277 adv. *swiftly*; touch and go; no sooner said than done.

See: 114, 121, 135, 277, 508.

117 Chronometry

N. *chronometry*, chronoscopy, horometry, horology; horography, watch-making; calendar-making; timing, dating; timekeeping, watching.

clock time, right time, exact t., correct t., B.B.C. t., true t., astronomer's t., solar t., sidereal t., Greenwich t., mean t., standard t., local t., continental t.; the time now, the hour, time of day, time of night; bedtime; summer time, double summer t., daylight saving.

timekeeper, chronometer, marine c., ship's c.; timepiece, horologe; clock, dial, face; hand, second h., minute h., hour h. 547 n. *indicator*; bob, pendulum 317 n. *oscillation*; electric clock, pendulum c., grandfather c., calendar c., alarm c., alarum; Big Ben; water-clock, clepsydra; watch, ticker; fob-watch, hunter, repeater; wristwatch; sundial, gnomon; hour-glass, sand-glass, egg-glass; chronograph,

chronoscope, chronopher; time-signal, pip, siren, hooter; gong, bell, five-minute b., minute-b., minute-gun, time-ball; timer, stopwatch, parking-meter, traffic light 305 n. *traffic control*; time-fuse, time-switch; metronome, conductor, band-leader 413 n. *musician*; watchmaker, clock-maker, horologer.

chronology, dendrochronology; carbon 14; dating, chronogram; date, age, epoch, style 110 n. *era*; old style, O.S., new style, Gregorian s.; almanac, Old Moore, calendar, perpetual c., fixed c., Gregorian c., Julian c.; ephemeris, Nautical Almanac; menology, chronicle, annals, fasti, diary, journal, log-book 548 n. *record*; date list, time-chart 87 n. *list*; timetable 87 n. *directory*.

chronologist, chronographer, chronologer, calendar-maker, calendarist, datary, chronogrammatist; chronicler, annalist, diarist 549 n. *recorder*.

Adj. *chronological*, chronometrical, horological, timekeeping; chronographic; annalistic, diaristic 548 adj. *recording*; calendarial, chronogrammatical, datal, temporal; isochronous, isochronal 123 adj. *synchronous*; in time 137 adj. *timely*.

Vb. *time*, clock; fix the time, fix the date; match times 123 vb. *synchronize*; phase 24 vb. *adjust*; adjust the hands, put the clock forward 135 vb. *be early*; put the clock back 136 vb. *be late*, 84 vb. *be unconformable*; wind the clock, set the alarm 669 vb. *make ready*; calendar, chronologize, chronicle, diarize, 548 vb. *record*; date, be dated, bear date; measure time, mark t., beat t., keep t; count the minutes, watch the clock; clock in 68 vb. *begin*; clock out 145 vb. *cease*; ring in 68 vb. *initiate*; ring out 69 vb. *terminate*.

Adv. *o'clock*, a.m., p.m.

See: 24, 68, 69, 84, 87, 110, 123, 135, 136, 137, 305, 317, 413, 547, 548, 549, 669.

118 Anachronism

N. *anachronism*, metachronism, parachronism, prochronism; wrong date, wrong day, chronological error, antichronism; mistiming, previousness, prolepsis 135 n. *anticipation*; disregard of time, unpunctuality 136 n. *lateness*; neglect of time, oblivion of t. 506 n. *oblivion*;

untimeliness, wrong moment 138 n. *intempestivity*.

Adj. *anachronistic*, misdated, undated; antedated, foredated, prochronous, previous, before time, too early 135 adj. *early*; metachronous, post-dated 136 adj. *late*; overdue, unpunctual, behind time; slow, losing; fast, gaining; out of due time, out of season, out of date, behind the times, old fashioned 84 adj *unconformable*.

Vb. *misdate*, mistake the date 138 vb. *mistime*; antedate, foredate, anticipate 135 vb. *be early*; be overdue, be behind time, postdate 136 vb. *be late*; be fast, gain; be slow, lose; be unpunctual, take no note of time.

See: 84, 135, 136, 138, 506.

119 Priority

N. *priority*, antecedence, anteriority, previousness, pre-occurrence, pre-existence; primogeniture, birthright; eldest, first, born, son and heir; flying start 64 n. *precedence*; leading 283 n. *precession*; the past, yesteryear, yesterday 125 n. *preterition*; eve, vigil, day before; precedent, antecedent; foretaste, preview, pre-release; aperitif 66 n. *precursor*.

Adj. *prior*, pre-, fore; carliest, first, first in the field, precedent 64 adj. *preceding*; previous, earlier, anterior, antecedent; prewar, prenatal, predeceased; pre-existing, pre-existent; elder, eldest, first-born; former, ci-devant, one-time, whilom, erstwhile, ex-, retired; foregoing, aforementioned, before-mentioned, abovementioned; aforesaid, said; introductory, prefatory, preluding 66 adj. *precursory*; premised, given, presupposed 512 adj. *supposed*.

Vb. *be before* 135 vb. *be early*, come before, go b. 283 vb. *precede*; forerun, antecede; pre-exist.

do before, premise, presuppose 512 vb. *suppose*; predecease, prefabricate, prearrange, precontract, pre-exempt, precondemn, prenotify, preview; be previous, anticipate, forestall, jump the gun, jump the queue; steal a march on, gain the start 277 vb. *outstrip*; lead 283 vb. *precede*, 64 vb. *come before.*

Adv. *before*, pre-, prior to, beforehand; just before, on the eve of; earlier, previously; ultimo, ult.; afore, ere, theretofore, erewhile; aforetime, ere now, before n.; ere then, before t., already, yet; in anticipation, anticipating; precedently, until now.

See: 64, 66, 125, 135, 277, 283, 283, 512.

120 Posteriority

N. *posteriority*, subsequence, supervention; ultimogeniture, succession 65 n. *sequence*, 284 n. *following*; days to come 124 n. *futurity*; line, lineage, descent, successor, descendant 170 n. *posterity*; postnatus, cadet; late-comer, new arrival; remainder, reversion, inheritance, post-obit; aftermath, morning after 67 n. *sequel*.

Adj. *subsequent*, post-, posterior, following, next, after, later; last in date, puisné, junior, cadet, younger, youngest 130 adj. *young*; succeeding, designate, to be 124 adj. *future*; postliminious; postnate; postdiluvial, postdiluvian; posthumous, post-obit; post-war, post-Christian; postprandial, after-dinner 65 adj. *sequent*.

Vb. *ensue*, supervene, follow after 65 vb. *come after*; go after 284 vb. *follow*, 157 vb. *result*; succeed, step into the shoes of 771 vb. *inherit*.

Adv. *subsequently*, later, next time; after, afterwards; at a subsequent period, at a later p.; next, in the sequel, in process of time; thereafter, thereupon, upon which, eftsoons; since, from that time, from that moment; from the start, from the word 'go'; after a while, after a time; soon after, close upon; next month, proximo.

See: 65, 67, 124, 130, 157, 170, 284, 771.

121 The Present Time

N. *present time*, contemporaneity, contemporaneousness, topicality 126 n. *modernism*; time being, the present, the now; present time, present day, present moment; this hour, this moment, this instant 116 n. *instantaneity*; juncture, opportunity, crisis 137 n. *occasion*; this time, nonce; the times, modern t., current

t., these days; today, twentieth century, now-a-days; this date, current d., even d.; one's age, one's present a., mental a., physical a.; present generation, one's contemporaries 123 n. *contemporary*.

Adj. *present*, actual, instant, current, existing, that is; of this date, of today's d., of even d.; topical, contemporary, contemporaneous; present-day, latest, up-to-the-minute, up-to-date 126 adj. *modern*; for the occasion, occasional.

Vb. *be now*, exist 1 vb. *be*; live in the present, live for the day, live from hand to mouth; be modern 126 vb. *modernize*; be one's age, admit one's a., 123 vb. *synchronize*.

Adv. *at present*, now, at this time, at this moment; at the present time, contemporaneously, contemporarily; to-day, now-a-days; at this time of day, even now; already, but now, just now; this time, on the present occasion; for the time being, for the nonce; on the nail, on the spot 116 adv. *instantaneously*; on the spur of the moment 609 adv. *extempore*; now or never; now as always.

until now, to this day, to the present day, up to now; including today, through; from the start, from the word 'go' 113 adv. *all along*.

See: 1, 113, 116, 123, 126, 137, 609.

122 Different Time

N. *different time*, other times, better t.; another time, some other t., not now, not today, any time but this; jam yesterday, and jam tomorrow, but never jam today 124 n. *futurity*; parachronism 118 n. *anachronism*.

Adj. *non-contemporary*, unmodern 84 adj. *unconformable*; behind the times 127 adj. *antiquated*; before the times, futuristic 124 adj. *future*; metachronous 118 adj. *anachronistic*.

Adv. *not now*, ago, earlier, later, then; sometimes, somewhiles; once, once upon a time; one day, one fine morning, one of these days; sometime, somewhen; some time or other, sooner or later; any-time, any old t.; any time now; soon; whenever you will, as soon as you like; otherwhile, otherwhiles.

See: 84, 118, 124, 127.

123 Synchronism

N. *synchronism,* co-existence, coincidence, concomitance 89n. *accompaniment,* 181 n. *concurrence;* simultaneity, same time 116n. *instantaneity;* contemporaneity, contemporaneousness, same date, same day 121n. *present time;* coevality, same age, twin birth 28n. *equality;* level-pegging, level time, dead heat 28n. *draw;* synchronization, phasing, syntony, isochronism.

contemporary, coeval, twin 28n. *compeer;* one's contemporaries, one's own generation, one's age group; age-group, stream, class, year 74n. *group.*

Adj. *synchronous,* synchronal, synchronic; contemporary, contemporaneous 121adj. *present,* 126adj. *modern;* simultaneous, coincident, co-existent, co-eternal, conterminous, concomitant 24adj. *agreeing,* 89adj. *accompanying;* level, neck and neck 28adj. *equal;* matched in age, coeval, twin, born together, of the same age, of the same year, of the same vintage; synchronized, timed, syntonic, phased, isochronous, on the beat, punctual; met, well-m. 74adj. *assembled.*

Vb. *synchronize,* contemporize, coexist 89 vb. *accompany;* encounter, coincide, arrive together 295vb. *meet;* keep time, watch the beat 284vb. *follow;* syntonize, tune, phase 24vb. *adjust;* run neck and neck, run a dead heat, equal another's time, equal the record 28vb. *equal;* pace, keep in step with; take the same time, isochronize; reach the same age, die together.

Adv. *synchronously,* concurrently, at the same time, isochronously, for the same time, along with, pari passu, in time, on the beat, simultaneously, as soon as, just as, at the moment of, in the same breath 116adv. *instantaneously;* while, whilst, concomitantly 89adv. *with.*

See:24,28,74,89,116,121,126,181,284,295.

124 Futurity: prospective time

N. *futurity,* future tense; womb of time, time to come, days and years to come; morrow 120n. *posteriority;* future, time ahead, prospect, outlook 507n. *expectation;* coming events, fate 154n. *eventuality,* 155n. *destiny;* near future, tomorrow,

mañana, next week, next year 121n. *present time,* 200n. *nearness;* advent 289n. *approach;* distant future, remote f., after ages 199n. *distance;* future generations, descendants, heirs, heritage 170n. *posterity;* successorship, shadow cabinet 65n. *sequence,* 669n. *preparation.*

future state, latter end 69n. *finality;* what fate holds in store 155n. *destiny,* 596n. *fate;* doomsday, crack of doom, judgment day, resurrection day 956n. *tribunal;* post-existence, after-life, life to come, hereafter, kingdom come 971n. *heaven;* damnation 972n. *hell;* good time coming, millennium 730n. *prosperity;* rebirth, reincarnation 106n. *repetition.*

looking ahead, anticipation 669n. *preparation;* prospect, prospects, outlook 507n. *expectation;* great expectations, expectances 852n. *hope;* horoscope, foresight 511n. *prediction.*

Adj. *future,* not in the present, to be, to come; about to be, coming, nearing 289n. *approaching;* nigh, near in time, close at hand 200adj. *near;* due, destined, fated, threatening, imminent, overhanging 155 adj. *impending;* in the future, ahead, yet to come, waiting, millennial 154adj. *eventual;* prospective, designate, earmarked 605adj. *chosen;* promised, looked for 507adj. *expected,* 471adj. *probable;* predicted, predictable, foreseeable, sure 473adj. *certain;* ready to, rising, getting on for; potential, on, maturing, ripening 469adj. *possible;* later, ulterior, posterior 120adj. *subsequent.*

Vb. *be to come,* lie ahead, lie in the future, be for tomorrow; be destined, threaten, overhang 155vb. *impend;* near, draw nigh 289vb. *approach;* be imminent, be just round the corner, cast its shadow before, stare one in the face 200vb. *be near;* shall, will.

look ahead, look forward, see it coming, await 507vb. *expect,* 852vb. *hope;* foresee 511vb. *predict;* anticipate, forestall 135 vb. *be early.*

Adv. *prospectively,* eventually, ultimately, later; in fulness of time, in due course, in the long run; tomorrow, soon, sooner or later, some day; hereafter, not today, not yet, on the eve of, on the point of; close upon; about to.

henceforth, in future, from this time forth, from now on; thenceforward.

See: 65, 69, 106, 120, 121, 135, 154, 155, 170, 199, 200, 289, 469, 471, 473, 507, 511, 596, 605, 669, 730, 852, 956, 971, 972.

125 Preterition: retrospective time

N. *preterition* 119 n. *priority*; retrospection, looking back 505 n. *remembrance*; past tense, historic t., narrative t., preterit, perfect, pluperfect 564 n. *grammar*; the past, recent p., only yesterday 126 n. *nearness*; distant past, history, antiquity; old story, matter of history 127 n. *oldness*; past times, times of yore, days of y., olden days, good old d., bygone d.; auld lang syne, yesterday, yesteryear, former times; ancien régime; Victorian Age, Elizabethan A., Renaissance, Cinquecento, part of history.

antiquity, high a., rust of a., eld; creation, when time began, time immemorial, distance of time, distant t.; remote ages; prehistory, ancient h., mediæval h.; geological times, palæolithic age, stone a., prehistoric a., heroic a., mythological a., Vedic a., classical a.; Dark Ages, Middle A. 110 n. *era*; the ancients, ancientry; relic, fossil, eolith, microlith 41 n. *leavings*, 127 n. *archaism*; ruin, ancient monument, megalith, Stonehenge 548 n. *monument*; antiquarium, museum 632 n. *collection*; ancient lineage, old descent 169 n. *genealogy*.

palætiology, palæontology, palæozoology, palæology, palæography, archæography; archæology, digging up the past; antiquarianism; medievalism.

antiquarian, palæontologist, archæologist; palæologist; antiquary, Dryasdust, Oldbuck 492 n. *scholar*; historian, prehistorian; medievalist 549 n. *chronicler*; Egyptologist, Assyriologist, Semiticist, Hebraist, Arabist, Sanskritist, classicist 557 n. *linguist*; revivalist; archaist, Preraphaelite 556 n. *artist*.

Adj. *past*, in the p., historical; ancient, prehistoric, Ogygian 127 adj. *olden*; early, primitive, proto-, dawn 127 adj. *primal*; recently past 126 adj. *new*; wholly past, gone, bygone, lost, irrecoverable, dead and buried 506 adj. *forgotten*; passed away, no more, died out, dead as the Dodo 2 adj. *extinct*, 361 adj. *dead*; passé, has-been, obsolete, exploded 674 adj. *disused*,

127 adj. *antiquated*; over, blown o., done, over and done with, behind one; elapsed, lapsed, expired, run out, ended, finished 69 adj. *ending*; unrenewed, unrevived.

former, late, pristine, quondam, erstwhile; whilom, sometime, one-time, ci-devant, ex-; retired, outgoing 753 adj. *resigning*; ancestral, ancient, prehistoric 127 adj. *immemorial*; not within living memory.

preterite, grammatically past, in the past tense; simple past, past continuous, perfect, imperfect, pluperfect.

foregoing, last, latter, above-mentioned, aforesaid 64 adj. *preceding*; recent, overnight 126 adj. *new*.

retrospective, looking back, backward-looking; archaizing 505 adj. *remembering*; retroactive, going back; with hind-sight 148 vb. *reverted*.

Vb. *be past*, have elapsed, have expired; have run its course, have had its day; pass, elapse, blow over, be o., pass off; be a dead letter.

look back, trace back, cast the eyes b.; antiquarianize, archæologize, dig up the past, exhume; put the clock back, go back to the past, archaize, hark back 505 vb. *retrospect*.

Adv. *formerly*, aforetime, of old, of yore; erst, whilom, erewhile, time was, ago, in olden times; anciently, long ago, long since; a long while, a long time ago; once upon a time; years ago, ages a.; lately, some time ago, some time since, some time back; yesterday, the day before yesterday; yestreen, yestereve, yesternight; yesterweek, yesteryear; last year, last season, last month, ultimo.

retrospectively; retroactively; historically speaking, ere now, before now, hitherto, heretofore; no longer; from time immemorial; in the memory of man; time out of mind; already, yet; till now, up to this time; from the start, from the word 'go' 121 adv. *until now*; ex post facto; supra, above 64 adv. *before*.

See: 2, 41, 64, 69, 110, 119, 121, 126, 127, 148, 169, 361, 492, 505, 506, 548, 549, 556, 557, 564, 632, 674, 753.

126 Newness

N. *newness*, recency, recent date, recent occurrence, recent past 124 n. *preterition*,

121 n. *present time*; neonomianism, innovation, neoterism 560 n. *neology*; originality 21 n. *non-imitation*; novelty, gloss of n.; freshness, dewiness 648 n. *cleanness*; greenness, immaturity, rawness 130 n. *youth*; renovation, renewal, revival 656 n. *restoration*.

modernism, modernity, modernness, modernization; up-to-dateness, topicality, contemporaneity 121 n. *present time*; the latest, the latest thing, latest fashion; the last word, dernier cri; new look, contemporary style 848 n. *fashion*.

modernist, neologist, neoteric, futurist; advanced thinker, avant-garde, neonomian; bright young thing; modern generation.

upstart, novus homo, mushroom, parvenu, nouveau riche 847 n. *vulgarian*.

Adj. *new*, recent, of recent date, of recent occurrence; upstart, mushroom; novel, original, unhackneyed, unprecedented, unheard of 68 adj. *beginning:* brand-new, fire-n., span-n.; like new, in mint condition, new-looking 648 adj. *clean*; green, evergreen, dewy, juicy, sappy 128 adj. *vernal*; fresh, fresh as a rose, fresh as a daisy, fresh as paint; virgin, maiden, fledgling; new-born, born yesterday 130 adj. *young*; raw, unripe, unfledged 670 adj. *immature*; just out, just published, new-made, straight from the factory; untried, untrodden, unbeaten, unexplored 491 adj. *unknown*; untested 461 adj. *experimental*; unhandselled, unbroken, not broken in, not yet run in; unfleshed, new-fleshed, new-fledged; budding, prentice.

modern, late, latter-day; contemporary, topical 121 adj. *present*; up-to-the-minute, up-to-date; à la mode, abreast of the fashion; ultramodern, advanced, avant-garde, futuristic, untraditional, non-traditional; innovating, neoteric, new-fangled, new-fashioned 560 adj. *neological*; revolutionary, neonomian.

modernized, renewed, renovated, redone, repainted 656 n. *restored*; given a new look, brought up to date, re-edited; looking like new, freshened up 648 adj. *clean*.

Vb. *modernize*, bring up to date, adapt to modern needs; have the new look, go modern, go contemporary; move with the times 285 vb. *progress*.

Adv. *newly*, afresh, anew, like new; recently,

just now, only yesterday, the other day; not long ago, a short time a.; lately, latterly, of late.

See: 21, 68, 121, 124, 128, 130, 285, 461, 491, 560, 648, 656, 669, 847, 848.

127 Oldness

N. *oldness*, primitiveness, the prime 68 n. *beginning*; age, eld, hoary e.; cobwebs of antiquity, dust of ages, ruin, ruins 125 n. *antiquity*, 649 n. *dirt*; maturity, ripeness, mellowness 669 n. *maturation*; decline, rust 51 n. *decay*; senility 131 n. *age*; eldership, primogeniture 131 n. *seniority*.

archaism, antiquities 125 n. *antiquity*; thing of the past, relic of the p.; ancien régime; vieux jeu; museum piece, antique, fossil, prehistoric animal; Gothic script, black-letter type; fogy, old timer, has-been, back number, extinct volcano 728 n. *loser*.

tradition, lore, folklore, mythology; inveteracy, custom, prescription, immemorial usage 610 n. *habit*; common law, smriti, sunna, hadis; ancient wisdom, the way of our forefathers; word of mouth 579 n. *speech*.

Adj. *olden*, old, ancient, antique, of historical interest; venerable, patriarchal; archaic, ancient, old-world; time-worn, ruined; prehistoric, mythological, heroic, Vedic, classic, Byzantine, Dark Age, feudal, medieval, Pre-Raphaelite; elder, senior, eldest, first-born 131 adj. *older*; historical 125 adj. *past*, 866 adj. *renowned*.

primal, prime, primitive, primeval, primordial, primogenous, primordinate, aboriginal 68 adj. *beginning*; geological, palaeocrystic, palaeozoic, fossil, preglacial, palaeolithic; early, proto-, dawn-, eo-; antemundane, pre-adamite, antediluvian; diluvian, out of the Ark, patriarchal; Cronian, Saturnian, Ogygian.

immemorial, ancestral, traditional, time-honoured, prescriptive, customary, used 610 adj. *habitual*; venerable 866 adj. *worshipful*; inveterate, rooted, established, long-standing 153 adj. *fixed*; Ogygian, old as the hills, old as Adam, old as Methuselah, old as history, old as time, hoary with age, age-old 131 adj. *aged*.

antiquated, of other times, archaic, black-letter; last-century, Victorian, pre-war

119 adj. *prior*; anachronistic, archaizing 125 adj. *retrospective*; fossilized, ossified, static 144 vb. *permanent*; behind the times, out of date, out of fashion, antediluvian, out of the Ark; conservative, old-fashioned, old-school; passé, outworn, exploded, gone by, gone out, run o. 125 adj. *past*; decayed, perished 655 adj. *dilapidated*; rusty, moth-eaten, crumbling; mildewed, moss-grown, mouldering, rotting, rotten 51 adj. *decomposed*; fusty, stale, second-hand; obsolete, over-age, obsolescent; superseded, superannuated, on the shelf; out of use 674 adj. *disused*; ageing, old, senile 131 adj. *aged*.

Vb. *be old,*—antiquated etc. adj.; go back in time, belong to the past, have had its day, have seen its d. 69 vb. *end*; age 131 vb. *grow old*; fade, wither 655 vb. *deteriorate*; moulder, stale, fust; rot, rust, perish, decay 51 vb. *decompose*.

Adv. *anciently,* since the world was made, since the year one, since the days of Methuselah; Anno Domini.

See: 51, 68, 69, 119, 125, 131, 144, 153, 579, 6 10, 649, 655, 659, 669, 674, 728, 866.

128 Morning. Spring. Summer

N. *morning*, morn, forenoon, a.m.; small hours 135 n. *earliness*; matins, prime, tierce, terce; dawn, false d., dawning, morning twilight, cockcrow 66 n. *precursor*; sunrise, sun-up, daybreak, day-spring 417 n. *light*; peep of day, break of d.; first blush of day, alpenglow; full day, prime of the morning; Aurora, Eos, Usha; day-star, orb of day 321 n. *sun*.

noon, high noon, meridian, midday, noonday, noontide; eight bells, twelve o'clock.

spring, springtime, springtide, vernal season, spring s., seed-time, Primavera, Ver; vernal equinox, first point of Aries.

summer 379 n. *heat*; summertime, summertide, midsummer, midsummer's day, high summer; Indian summer, St. Luke's s., St. Martin's s.

Adj. *matinal*, matutinal, morning; auroral, dawning, fresh, dewy 135 adj. *early*; antemeridian; noon.

vernal, equinoctial, spring; springlike, sappy, juicy, flowering, florescent 130 adj. *young*.

summery, summer, æstival 379 adj. *warm*.

Adv. *at sunrise*, at dawn of day, with the lark; past midnight, in the small hours; a.m.

See: 66, 130, 135, 321, 379, 417.

129 Evening. Autumn. Winter

N. *evening*, eventide, even, eve, dewy e.; evensong, vespers, afternoon, p.m.; matinée (theatre); afternoon tea, five o'clock; dog-watches, sunset, sundown, setting sun, going down of the sun; alpenglow; dusk, crepuscule, twilight, gloaming 419 n. *half-light*; candlelight, cockshut; close of day, nightfall, dark, blind man's holiday, night-time 418 n. *darkness*; bed-time 679 n. *sleep*; curfew, last post 136 n. *lateness*, 69 n. *finality*.

midnight, dead of night, night's high noon; witching time; night-watch, small hours.

autumn, fall, fall of the year, fall of the leaf; harvest, harvest-time; harvest moon, hunter's m.; Indian summer; autumnal equinox; 'season of mists and mellow fruitfulness.'

winter 380 n. *wintriness*; winter-time, winter-tide; midwinter, winter solstice 70 n. *middle*.

Adj. *vespertine*, afternoon, postmeridian; evening; dusky, crepuscular 418 adj. *dark*, 419 n. *dim*; nightly, nocturnal, noctivagant; benighted, late; bed-time.

autumnal, equinoctial.

wintry, winter, brumal, hiemal, winter-bound 380 adj. *cold*.

Adv. *post meridiem*, late, late at night; at night, by n.; all through the night.

See: 69, 70, 136, 380, 418, 419, 679.

130 Youth

N. *youth*, freshness, juiciness, sappiness 126 n. *newness*, 174 n. *vigorousness*; young blood, youthfulness, youngness, juvenility, juvenescence; juniority 35 n. *inferiority*; incunabula, earliest stage, infancy, babyhood, childhood, childish years, tender age 68 n. *beginning*; puppyhood, puppy fat; boyhood, girlhood, youthhood, school-going age; one's teens, teenage, adolescence, pubescence, age of puberty, boyishness, girlishness, awkward age, growing pains; younger generation,

rising g. 132n. *youngster*; growing boy, minor, ward.

nonage, tender age, immaturity, minority, infancy, pupillage, puceiage, wardship, leading strings, status pupillaris, cradle, nursery, kindergarten.

salad days, school d., student d., undergraduate d.; Flegeljahre, heyday, heyday of the blood, springtime of youth; prime of life, flower of l., seed-time of l.; golden season of l., bloom, florescence.

Adj. *young*, youthful, boyish, girlish; virginal, maidenly, teenage, juvenile, adolescent, pubescent; growing, ripening 136 adj. *increasing*; budding, sappy, florescent, flowering 128 adj. *vernal*; beardless, unripe, green, callow, awkward, raw, unfledged 670 adj. *immature*; of school-going age, under-age, minor, infant, in statu pupillari; younger, minor, junior, puisné, cadet; youngest, minimus; childish 132 adj. *infantine*; ever-young, ever-green, unwrinkled, ageless.

See: 35, 68, 126, 128, 132, 136, 174, 670.

131 Age

N. *age*, eld 127 n. *oldness*; one's age, time of life, years; middle age, ripe a., riper a.; pensionable age, retiring a., superannuation 753 n. *resignation*; old age, hoary old a., grey hairs, white h.; three score years and ten, four score and upward; senescence, evening of one's days, decline of life, declining years, vale of y.; the sere and yellow leaf, autumn of life, winter of l.; ricketiness, decrepitude, caducity, senility, anility, second childhood, dotage 51 n. *decay*; longevity, green old age, ripe old a.; change of life, menopause; critical age, climacteric, grand c. 137 n. *occasion*.

seniority, old man's privilege 64 n. *precedence*; primogeniture 119 n. *priority*; higher rank 34 n. *superiority*; eldership, deanship, doyen; elders, presbytery, senate, gerousia 692 n. *council*.

gerontology, nostology, gerontotherapy, geriatrics, care of the aged 658 n. *therapy*.

Adj. *aged*, old, elderly, matronly; middle-aged, ripe, mature, mellow 669 adj. *matured*; overblown, overripe, run to seed; of a certain age, not so young as one was, no chicken; past one's prime, getting old, going grey, greying, white-haired,

grey-h., hoary, hoary-headed; ageing, senescent, waning, declining, decaying, moribund 361 adj. *dying*; wrinkled, lined, marked with crow's feet, rheumy-eyed, toothless, palsied, withered, decrepit, rickety 655 adj. *deteriorated*; drivelling, doddering, doting, doited, crazy 499 adj. *foolish*; senile, anile, failing, with softening of the brain; in years, advanced in y., stricken in y., with one foot in the grave; old as Methuselah, old as Adam; venerable, patriarchal 920 adj. *respected*; so many years old, turned of, rising; too old, past it, past the time for; superannuated, effete, passé 127 adj. *antiquated*; gerontic, senatorial 733 adj. *governmental*.

older, big, major; elder, senior 34 adj. *superior*; first-born, eldest, primogenital 119 adj. *prior*; eldest, maximus.

Vb. *grow old*, age; show one's years, wrinkle, go grey, turn white; pass three-score years and ten, have one foot in the grave.

See: 34, 51, 64, 119, 127, 137, 361, 499, 655, 658, 669, 692, 733, 753, 793, 920.

132 Young person. Young animal. Young plant

N. *child*, childer, children, nursery; young boy, man child, babe, baby; infant, nursling, suckling, weanling, fosterling; bairn, little one, little tot, little chap, mite, tiny, toddler, bantling; brat, kid, kidlet; papoose, bambino, bacha, pickaninny; little darling, little angel, little monkey; cherub, young innocent, gosling; imp, elf, changeling. See *youngling*.

youngster, juvenile, young person, young hopeful; boy, schoolboy, stripling, adolescent; youth, callant, lad, laddie; urchin, nipper, shaver, whipper-snapper; codling, cub, unlicked c.; hobbledehoy, Teddy-boy; minor, master, junior, cadet; midshipman, cabin-boy, powder-monkey; buttons, call-boy, page-b. 742 n. *servant*; girl, schoolgirl, lass, lassie, missie, wench, maid, maiden, virgin; chit, chicken, chick, miss, young m., junior m.; teenager, bobbysoxer, flapper, tomboy, hoyden, romp; giglet, minx, baggage; colleen, mademoiselle, damsel, damozel, nymph, nymphet. See *youngling*.

youngling, young animal, yearling, lamb, lambkin, ewelamb, kid, calf, heifer·

pigling, piglet; fawn, colt, foal, filly; kit, kitten; puppy, pup, whelp, cub; chick, chicken, pullet; duckling, gosling, cygnet 365n. *animal, bird*; fledgling, nestling, eyas, squab; fry, litter, farrow, clutch, spawn, brood; larva, pupa, nymph; chrysalis, cocoon, tadpole; embryo, fœtus 156b. *source.*

young plant, seedling, set; sucker, shoot, sprout, slip; twig, sprig, scion, sapling 366n. *plant.*

Adj. *infantine*, baby, dolly, infantile, babyish, childish, childlike; juvenile, boyish, girlish 130adj. *young*; kittenish, coltish, hoydenish; new-born, new-fledged, fledgy, unfledged, unbreeched 126adj. *new*; in the cradle, in arms, in swaddling bands, in long clothes, in leading strings; small, knee-high 196adj. *little.*

See: 126, 130, 156, 196, 365, 366, 742.

133 Old person

N. *old man*, old gentleman; elder, senior, sir 34n. *superior*; oldster, greybeard, gaffer, pantaloon, antiquity; dotard; veteran, old soldier, Chelsea pensioner, old age p.; old 'un, old hand, dugout; old stager, old timer 696n. *expert*; fossil, old fogy 501n. *fool*; grandfather, grandsire, grandpa, patriarch; elders, ancestors, forefathers 169n. *parent*; sexagenarian, octogenarian, nonagenarian, centenarian; Methuselah, pre-adamite, antediluvian; Nestor, Rip van Winkle, Old Parr.

old woman, old lady, grandmother, granny, grandam, beldam; no chicken, gammer, crone, carline; old dutch 894n. *spouse*; hag, witch 904n. *hell-hag.*

old couple, Darby and Joan, Philemon and Baucis, the old folks.

See: 34, 169, 501, 696, 894, 904.

134 Adultness

N. *adultness*, adulthood, grown-upness, maturescence; riper years, years of discretion 463n. *discrimination*; legal age, voting a., majority, full age, man's estate; manhood, womanhood, virility 372n. *male*, 373n. *female*; badge of manhood, beard, toga virilis, key of the door;

maturity, prime, prime of life, life's high noon; bloom, florescence 669n. *maturation*; meridian of life, floruit.

adult, grown-up, big boy, big girl; man 372n. *male*; woman, matron 373n. *female*; no chicken; youth, jawan, stripling.

Adj. *grown up*, adult, out of one's teens, in long trousers; major, of age, responsible; mature, full grown 669adj. *matured*; nubile 894adj. *marriageable*; virile, manly 372adj. *male*; womanly, matronly 373 adj. *female*; blooming, florescent, full-blown, in full bloom, full-fledged; in one's prime 130adj. *young.*

Vb. *come of age*, be grown up, reach man's estate, attain majority, be twenty-one, have the key of the door; grow a beard, put on long trousers, assume the toga virilis; put one's hair up; have sown one's wild oats, settle down, earn one's living.

See: 130, 372, 373, 463, 669, 894.

135 Earliness

N. *earliness*, early hour, prime 128n. *morning*; beginnings, early stage, primitiveness 68n. *beginning*; early riser, early bird; early comer, first arrival 66n. *precursor*; primitive, aborigine, earliest inhabitant 191n. *native.*

punctuality, timeliness 137n. *occasion*; despatch, promptitude 678n. *activity*; haste 277n. *velocity*; suddenness 113n. *instantaneity.*

anticipation, prevenience, a stitch in time 510n. *foresight*, 669n. *preparation*; prematurity, early maturity, precocity; forestalling 64n. *precedence.*

Adj. *early*, prime, in the small hours; prevenient, previous 119adj. *prior*; timely, in time, on t., in good t., punctual, prompt; forward, advance, in advance; advanced, precocious, rareripe, fresh 126 adj. *new*; summary, sudden, immediate 116adj. *instantaneous*, 508adj. *unexpected*; expected soon, next on the list, forthcoming, ready 669adj. *prepared*; impending, imminent, at hand 200adj. *near*; too early, over-early, premature, abortive, misfired 670adj. *immature.*

Vb. *be early*,—premature etc. adj.; be betimes, be beforehand etc. adv.; anticipate, draw on futurity; forestall, get there first 64vb. *come before*; seize the occasion,

take time by the forelock; gain the start, steal a march on 306vb. *outdo*; engage, book, pre-engage, pre-empt, reserve, pay in advance; secure, order, bespeak; expedite 277vb. *accelerate*; lose no time 680vb. *hasten*; be precocious, ripen early; start too soon, jump the gun; put the clock forward, gain time, gain, go fast.

Adv. *betimes*, early, soon, anon, rathe; eft, eftsoons; ere long, before long; first thing, at the first opportunity; with time enough, punctually, to the minute, in time, in good time, in due time; time enough.

beforehand, in advance, in anticipation; without waiting, precipitately 680adv. *hastily*; precociously, prematurely, too soon, before one's time.

suddenly, without notice 508adv. *unexpectedly*; without delay, without a pause 116 adv. *instantaneously*; at the sight of; before the ink was dry; forthwith, incontinent, shortly, directly; at short notice, off-hand, extempore, at the drop of a hat.

See: 64, 66, 68, 113, 116, 119, 126, 128, 137, 191, 200, 227, 306, 508, 510, 669, 670, 678, 680.

136 Lateness

N. *lateness*, late hour, small hours; high time, eleventh hour, last minute; unreadiness, backwardness, slow development 670n. *non-preparation*, 499n. *unintelligence*; opsimathy 536n. *study*; tardiness, lagging, hysteresis 278n. *slowness*; afterthought, delayed reaction, double take 67n. *sequel*; latecomer, last arrival; opsimath 538n. *learner*; slow starter, late riser 278n. *slowcoach*; lie-abed, laggard 679n. *idler*; Micawber, Fabius Cunctator; waiter on Providence.

delay, cunctation, Fabian policy, 'wait and see' 858n. *caution*; extension, prolongation, gaining time, dragging out, obstruction, filibustering, filibuster 113n. *protraction*, 702n. *hindrance*; deceleration, retardation, check 278n. *slowness*; detention, hold-up 747n. *restraint*; postponement, adjournment, ampliation; prorogation, remand, pause, truce 145n. *lull*; deferment, moratorium, respite, days of grace; suspension, stay, stay of execution; suspension of penalty, re-

prieve 752n. *abrogation*, 909n. *forgiveness*; putting off, procrastination, mañana 679n. *sluggishness*; dilatoriness, redtapeism, red-tape, law's delays, chancery suit; shelving, pigeon-hole, cold storage 679n. *inactivity*; penalty for delay, demurrage, contango 805n. *non-payment*.

Adj. *late*, late in the day, eleventh-hour, last-minute, deathbed; too late, twelfth hour; overdue, delayed, belated, benighted; behindhand, lagging, after time, behind t.; sluggish, hysteresial; backward, long about it 278 adj. *slow*; cunctatious, cunctatory 858adj. *cautious*; unready, unpunctual, never on time; procrastinating, dilatory 679adj. *inactive*; deferred etc. vb.; postliminious; posthumous 120adj. *subsequent*.

Vb. *be late*, sit up late, rise late, keep late hours, burn the midnight oil; lag, lag behind 284vb. *follow*; stay, tarry, take time, be long about it, linger, dawdle, saunter, loiter 278vb. *move slowly*; hang about, hang around, hang back 679vb. *be inactive*; dally, dilly-dally; miss, miss a chance, lose an opportunity, let the moment pass, oversleep 138vb. *lose a chance*; be behindhand, have leeway to make up; put the clock back, not move with the times 125vb. *look back*; be losing, lose, stop (clock).

wait 507vb. *await*; bide, stay, bide one's time, take one's t., wait and see, bide the issue, sleep on it, consult one's pillow 677 vb. *not act*; stand and wait, stand about, sit a.; be kept waiting, wait impatiently, cool one's heels, dangle, dance attendance.

pend, hang, drag 113vb. *drag on*; hang fire, hang in the balance, tremble in the b. 474 vb. *be uncertain*; stand, stand over, lie o., stay put 266vb. *be quiescent*.

put off, defer, prorogue, postpone, adjourn, lay over; keep, reserve, hold over; keep pending, file, pigeonhole; table, lay on the t.; shelve, put in cold storage, keep on ice; remand, send back; suspend, hold in abeyance; respite, reprieve, waive 909vb. *forgive*; procrastinate, protract, delay, retard, hold up, lengthen out, gain time, filibuster 113vb. *spin out*; temporize, tide over; stall, keep one waiting; withhold, deny 760vb. *refuse*.

Adv. *late*; after time, behind t.; late in the day, at sunset, at the eleventh hour, last thing; at length, at last, at long l.,

ultimately; till all hours; too late, too late for 138 adv. *inopportunely.*

tardily, slowly, leisurely, deliberately, at one's leisure.

See: 67, 112, 120, 125, 138, 145, 266, 278, 284, 474, 499, 507, 536, 538, 670, 677, 679, 702, 747, 752, 760, 805, 858, 909.

137 Occasion: timeliness

N. *occasion,* event, welcome e. 154n. *eventuality*; meeting of events, juncture, conjuncture 181n. *concurrence*; timeliness, tempestivity, opportuneness, readiness, ripeness; fittingness 24n. *fitness,* 642 n. *expedience*; just the time, just the moment; right time, proper t., suitable season; auspicious hour, moment, well-chosen m., well-timed initiative; high time, nick of t., eleventh hour 136n. *lateness*; occasionalism 449n. *philosophy.*

opportunity, given time, borrowed t., time's forelock 759n. *offer*; favourable opportunity, fine o., golden o. 469n. *possibility*; one's chance, lucky moment, luck, piece of l. 159n. *chance*; best chance 605n. *choice*; only chance 606n. *no choice*; opening, room, elbow r., field 183n. *space*; liberty, independence, freedom of choice 744n. *freedom*; convenience, spare time 681n. *leisure*; no let, no hindrance, fair field, clear f., clear stage 159n. *fair chance*; handle, lever, instrument 630n. *tool,* 629n. *means*; stepping-stone 624n. *bridge.*

crisis, critical time, key point, key moment; turning point, psychological moment, crucial m., emergency, extremity, pressure, pinch, push 700n. *predicament*; eleventh hour, last minute 136n. *lateness.*

Adj. *timely,* timeous, in time, within the time limit; on time, to the minute, punctual 135adj. *early*; seasonable, welcome, well-timed; just in time, in the nick of t., at the eleventh hour.

opportune, favourable, providential, heaven-sent, auspicious, propitious; fortunate, lucky, happy 730adj *prosperous*; for the occasion, fitting 24adj. *apt,* 642adj. *expedient*; as occasion requires, occasional 140adj. *infrequent.*

crucial, critical, key, momentous, decisive 638adj. *important.*

Vb. *profit by,* improve the occasion; seize the chance, take the opportunity, make an opening, create an o.; take time by the forelock, strike while the iron is hot, make hay while the sun shines; spare the time for; cash in on, capitalize.

Adv. *opportunely,* in proper time, in due time, in proper course, in due c., in the fulness of time; in proper season, in due s.; at the right time, all in good time; in the nick of time, just in time, at the eleventh hour, now or never.

incidentally, by the way, by the by; en passant, à propos; parenthetically, by way of parenthesis; while speaking of, while on this subject; extempore, on the spur of the moment, on the spur of the occasion; for this occasion, for the nonce.

See: 24, 135, 136, 140, 154, 159, 181, 183, 449, 469, 605, 606, 624, 629, 630, 638, 642, 681, 700, 730, 744, 759.

138 Intempestivity

N. *intempestivity,* wrong time, unsuitable t., improper t., untimeliness, unseasonableness 643n. *inexpedience*; inopportunity, contretemps; evil hour 731n. *ill fortune*; intrusion, interruption, disturbance 72n. *discontinuity*; mistiming 118n. *anachronism.*

Adj. *ill-timed,* mistimed, misjudged, ill-judged, ill-advised 481n. *misjudging*; untimely, intempestive, untoward; interrupting, intrusive; mal à propos, inconvenient, unsuited 25adj. *unapt,* 643adj. *inexpedient*; unseasonable, off-season; unpunctual, not in time 136adj. *late*; premature, too soon for 135adj. *early*; wise after the event 118adj. *anachronistic.*

inopportune, untoward, inauspicious, unpropitious, unfavourable, ill-omened, ill-starred, unlucky, unhappy 731adj. *unfortunate.*

Vb. *mistime,* time it badly 481vb. *misjudge*; intrude, disturb, break in upon, find engaged.

be engaged, be too busy, be occupied, be not at home; be otherwise engaged, have other fish to fry 678vb. *be busy.*

lose a chance, waste time, miss the bus, miss the boat, miss the train 728vb. *fail*; drop a sitter, bungle 695vb. *be unskilful*; over-

sleep, lose the opportunity, let the opportunity slip, let the occasion pass 136vb. *be late*; allow to lapse, let slip through one's fingers 458vb. *neglect*; spoil a good chance, stand in one's own light, shut the stable door when the steed is stolen 695 vb. *stultify oneself.*

Adv. *inopportunely*, amiss; as ill luck would have it, in an evil hour; the time having gone by, a day after the fair.

See: 25, 72, 118, 135, 136, 458, 481, 643, 678, 695, 728, 731.

139 Frequency

N. *frequency*, rapid succession, rapid fire 71 n. *continuity*; oftenness, hourliness, unfailing regularity 141n. *periodicity*; doubling, redoubling 106n. *repetition*; frequenting, haunting, regular visits, assiduous attendance.

Adj. *frequent*, recurrent 106adj. *repeated*; common, of common occurrence, not rare 104adj. *many*; thick-coming 104adj. *multitudinous*; incessant, perpetual, continual, non-stop, constant, sustained, steady 146adj. *unceasing*; regular, hourly 141adj. *periodical*; haunting, frequenting, assiduous 610adj. *habitual.*

Vb. *recur* 106vb. *reoccur*; do nothing but; keep, keep on, fire away 146vb. *go on*; frequent, haunt 882vb. *visit*; obsess; plague, pester 827vb. *incommode.*

Adv. *often*, oft, many a time and oft; ofttimes, often-t., a thousand t.; frequently, commonly, often to be met with; not once or twice; not seldom, not infrequently, again and again 106adv. *repeatedly*; in quick succession, in rapid succession; regularly, daily, hourly, every day, every hour, every moment; in innumerable cases, in many instances; as often as you like, ad lib, ad libitum.

perpetually, continually, constantly, incessantly, steadily, without ceasing 71 adv. *continuously*; at all times, daily and hourly, night and day, day and night, day after day, morning, noon and night; ever and anon.

sometimes, occasionally, every so often, at times, now and then, from time to time, there being times when, often enough; and again 106adv. *again.*

See: 71, 104, 106, 141, 146, 610, 827, 882.

140 Infrequency

N. *infrequency*, infrequence, rareness, rarity 105n. *fewness*; seldomness, uncommonness; intermittence 72n. *discontinuity*; phœnix 84n. *rara avis.*

Adj. *infrequent*, uncommon, sporadic, occasional; intermittent 72adj. *discontinuous*; scarce, rare, rare as a blue diamond 105adj. *few*; almost unheard of, unprecedented 84adj. *unusual*; not to be repeated; single 88adj. *one.*

Adv. *seldom*, once in a way; rarely, scarcely, hardly, only sometimes, only occasionally; not often, infrequently, unoften; scarcely ever, hardly e., once in a blue moon; once, once for all, just this once, once only; like angel's visits, few and far between.

See: 72, 84, 88, 105.

141 Periodicity: regularity of recurrence

N. *periodicity*, regularity, punctuality, regularity of recurrence, rhythm, steadiness, evenness 16n. *uniformity*; timing, phasing, serialization 71n. *continuity*; alternation, in and out system (politics); reciprocity 12n. *correlation*; tidal flow, ebb and f., alternating current, wave movement, tidal m. 317n. *fluctuation*; to-and-fro movement, pendulum m., piston m., shuttle m.; shuttle service; pulsation, pulse, beat, rhythm, pendulum, piston, shuttle, swing 317n. *oscillation*; chorus, refrain 106n. *recurrence*; throb 318n. *agitation*; drum-beat 403n. *roll*; tide 350n. *wave*; rate of pulsation, frequency, wave f.; turn, round, circuit, lap, chukker; shift, relay 110n. *period.*

regular return, rota, cycle, circuit, revolution, life cycle, wheel of life 314n. *circuition*, 315n. *rotation*; yearly cycle, seasons 128n. *morning*, 129n. *evening*; synodical period; fixed interval, stated time 110n. *period*; routine, daily round 60n. *order*, 610n. *habit*; catamenia, menses, monthlies, flowers; days of the week, months of the year; week-end, black Monday, quarter-day; leap year; feast, fast, saint's day, red-letter day 876 n. *special day.*

anniversary, birthday, jubilee, silver wedding, golden w.; centenary, bi-centenary, tercentenary, quater-centenary; Lent,

Good Friday, Easter, Christmas, Boxing Day, New Year, Hogmanay; St. George's Day, St. Andrew's D., St. Patrick's D., St. David's D.; King's or Queen's Birthday, Lincoln's B.; Empire Day, Independence D., Republic D.; Fourth of July, 14 Juillet; Durga Poojah, Diwali; Ramadan, Mohurram.

Adj. *periodical,* periodic, cyclic, circling, revolving 315adj. *rotary;* tidal, undulatory, fluctuating 317adj. *oscillating;* measured, rhythmical, steady, even, regular, constant, punctual, methodical, like clockwork 81adj. *regular;* breathing, pulsating, pulsatory, pulsatile; throbbing, beating 318adj. *agitated;* recurrent, recurring, intermittent, remittent 106adj. *repeated;* reciprocal, alternate, alternating 12adj. *correlative;* serial, successive, serialized 65adj. *sequent,* 71adj. *continous.*

seasonal, anniversary; paschal, lenten; at fixed intervals, hourly, daily, nightly, diurnal, semi-diurnal, quotidian, tertian, bi-weekly, weekly, hebdomadal, hebdomadary, fortnightly, monthly; menstrual, catamenial; yearly, annual, biennial, triennial, quadrennial, quinquennial, decennial; bissextile, centennial, secular.

Vb. *be periodic,* recur 106vb. *reoccur;* serialize, recur in regular order, recur in constant succession 60vb. *be in order,* 71 vb. *run on,* 65vb. *come after;* turn, revolve, circle 315vb. *rotate;* return, come round again; take its turn, turn and turn about, alternate; be intermittent, intermit; reciprocate 12vb. *correlate;* fluctuate, undulate 317vb. *oscillate;* beat, pulse, pulsate, throb 318vb. *be agitated;* heave, pant 352vb. *breathe;* swing, sway 217vb. *hang;* ply, go and return, commute 610vb. *be wont.*

Adv. *periodically* etc. adj.; regularly, at regular intervals, at stated times; at fixed periods, at established p. ; punctually etc. adj.; seasonally, hourly, daily, weekly, monthly, yearly; from day to day, day by day; per diem, per annum; at intervals, intermittently, every now and then, every so often, ever and anon.

by turns, in turn, in rotation, turn and turn about, alternately, every other day, off and on, ride and tie; round and round, to and fro, up and down, from side to side.

See: 12, 16, 60, 65, 71, 81, 106, 110, 128, 129, 217, 314, 315, 317, 318, 350, 352, **403,** 610, 876, 998.

142 Fitfulness: irregularity of recurrence

N. *fitfulness,* irregularity, irregularity of recurrence 61n. *disorder;* jerkiness, fits and starts 17n. *non-uniformity,* 318n. *spasm;* remittency 114n. *transience,* 72n. *discontinuity;* unsteadiness, inconstancy, variability 152adj. *changeableness,* 143n. *change;* whimsicality, capriciousness, April weather, unpredictability 604n. *caprice;* eccentricity; wobbling, staggering, lurching 318 n. *oscillation.*

Adj. *fitful,* periodic, remittent, intermittent 72adj. *discontinuous;* irregular 84adj. *unconformable;* uneven 29adj. *unequal;* occasional 140adj. *infrequent;* unrhythmical, unsteady, fluttering 17adj. *non-uniform;* inconstant, uncertain, unpunctual; variable, veering 152adj. *changeful;* spasmodic, jerky 318adj. *agitated;* wobbling, halting, wavering, flickering, guttering, rambling, rhapsodical, desultory, unsystematic 61 adj. *orderless;* erratic, eccentric, moody 604adj. *capricious.*

Adv. *fitfully,* irregularly etc. adj.; unevenly, by fits and starts, now and then 72adv. *discontinuously.*

See: 17, 29, 61, 72, 84, 114, 140, 143, 152, 318, 604.

143 Change: difference at different times

N. *change,* alteration, variation 15n. *difference;* mutation, permutation, modulation, inflexion, declension; frequent change, mutability, variability 152n. *changeableness;* partial change, modification, adjustment, process, treatment 468n. *qualification;* total change 147n. *conversion;* sudden change, violent c. 149n. *revolution;* break, break with the past, innovation 126n. *newness;* change for the better, reformation 654n. *improvement;* change for the worse 655n. *deterioration;* change of direction, diversion, shift, turn 282n. *deviation,* 286n. *regression;* change of position, transition, metastasis 305n. *passage;* translation, transposition,

metathesis 272n. *transference*, 188n. *displacement*, 151n. *interchange*; alternation, metagenesis; everting, eversion, overthrow 221n. *inversion*; contact action, catalysis, leavening; change of opinion, resilement 603n. *tergiversation*.

transformation, transfiguration, transfigurement; unrecognizability, transmogrification; metamorphosis, geological m., metasomatosis; metabolism, constructive m., anabolism; destructive metabolism, katabolism; transmutation, transubstantiation 147n. *conversion*; transanimation, transmigration, metempsychosis; reincarnation, avatar; transcription (mus.), version, adaptation, translation 520n. *interpretation*, 521n. *misinterpretation*.

alterer, alterant, alterative; converter, transformer; catalytic agent, catalyst, enzyme, ferment, leaven; adapter, modifier, reviser, editor; censor, bowdlerizer; alchemist, chemist; dyer; changer; money-changer; quick-change artist 545 n. *conjuror*; magician 983n. *sorcerer*; kaleidoscope 437n. *variegation*; weathercock, renegade 603n. *tergiversator*; improver 654n. *reformer*.

Adj. *changeable*, variable, mutable; fickle 604adj. *capricious*; affected, changed etc. vb.; new-fangled 126adj. *new*; transitional, provisional, modifiable, qualifiable; alternative, transmutative; checkered, kaleidoscopic 437adj. *variegated*.

Vb. *change*, be changed, alter 152vb. *vary*; wax and wane 36vb. *increase*, 37vb. *decrease*; change colour, change countenance 426vb. *lose colour*; change one's tune 603vb. *tergiversate*; vacillate, wobble 474vb. *be uncertain*; blow hot and cold, chop and change 604vb. *be capricious*; turn, shift, veer, back 282vb. *deviate*; change course, tack, gybe 269vb. *navigate*; make a transition, pass to 305vb. *pass*; take a turn, turn the corner 656vb. *revive*; turn over a new leaf, convert 654 vb. *get better*; submit to change, come under the influence 83vb. *conform*; move with the times 126vb. *modernize*.

modify, alter, vary, modulate, diversify, shift the scene 437vb. *variegate*; superinduce, superimpose 38vb. *add*; make a change. introduce changes, innovate, bring in new blood 126vb. *modernize*; turn upside down, subvert, evert 149vb.

revolutionize, 221vb. *invert*; reverse, turn back 148vb. *revert*; make changes, rearrange, reorder, reset 62vb. *arrange*; adapt 24vb. *adjust*; conform 83vb. *make conform*; recast, remould, reshape 243vb. *efform*; process, treat; revise, edit, re-edit, correct 654vb. *rectify*; reform 654vb. *improve*; vamp, revamp, patch, darn 656vb. *restore*; change for the worse, deteriorate 655vb *pervert*; tamper with, fiddle w., mar, spoil 656vb. *impair*; warp, bend, strain, twist, deform 246vb. *distort*; stain, dye, discolour 425vb. *colour*, 426vb. *decolorize*; adulterate, denature, doctor, qualify 43vb. *mix*, 163vb. *weaken*; cover, mask, disguise 525vb. *conceal*; change round, shuffle the cards 151vb. *interchange*, 272 vb. *transpose*; try a change, spin the wheel 461vb. *experiment*; effect a change, work a c., leaven, 156vb. *cause*; affect, turn the scale 178vb. *influence*; transform, transfigure, metamorphose, transmute, transubstantiate, alchemize 147vb. *convert*; metabolize, digest; conjure, juggle 542vb. *deceive*.

Adv. *mutatis mutandis*.

See: 15, 24, 36, 37, 38, 43, 62, 83, 126, 147, 148, 149, 151, 152, 156, 163, 178, 188, 221, 243, 246, 269, 272, 282, 286, 305, 425, 426, 437, 461, 468, 474, 520, 521, 525, 542, 545, 603, 604, 654, 655, 656, 983.

144 Permanence: absence of change

N. *permanence*, permanency, no change, status quo; invariability, unchangeability, immutability 153n. *stability*; lasting quality, persistence 600n. *perseverance*; endurance, duration 113n. *durability*, 115n. *perpetuity*; fixity, fixity of purpose, immobility, immoveableness 602n. *obstinacy*; firmness, rock, bedrock, foundation, solidity 324n. *density*; sustenance, maintenance, conservation 666 n. *preservation*, 146n. *continuance*; law, rule 81n. *regularity*; fixed law, law of the Medes and Persians, written constitution, entrenched clause 153n. *fixture*; standing, long s., inveteracy 127n. *oldness*; tradition, custom, practice 610n. *habit*; fixed attitude, conversatism, Bourbonism, die-hardism; routine, fixed r., standing order, standing dish 60n. *order*;

unprogressiveness, static condition 266n. *quiescence*; traditionalist, Bourbon, conservative, stick-in-the-mud, no-changer, die-hard 602n. *opinionist.*

Adj. **permanent,** enduring, durable 113adj. *lasting*; persisting, persistent, continuing, unfailing, sustained, maintained 146adj. *unceasing,* 115adj. *perpetual*; inveterate, prescriptive, long-standing 127adj. *immemorial*; perpetuated, standing, established, well-e., entrenched, fixed, unchangeable, immutable, unmodifiable, unrepealable 153adj. *vested*; intact, inviolate, undestroyed, unchanged, unsuppressed; living, well-preserved 666 adj. *preserved*; unchanging, conservative, Bourbon, die-hard 602adj. *obstinate*; unprogressive, stationary, static, immobile 266adj. *quiescent*; unaltered, uninfluenced, unaffected, still the same, recognizable 13adj. *identical.*

Vb. **stay,** come to stay, set in 153vb. *be stable*; abide, bide, endure, subsist, outlive, survive, outlast 113vb. *last*; persist, hold, hold good; hold on, hold it, maintain, sustain, keep up, keep on 146vb. *go on*; rest, remain, tarry, live 192vb. *dwell*; stand fast, dig one's toes in 600vb. *persevere*; stand on, stand pat, take one's position, stand one's ground, hold *or* keep one's ground *or* footing 599vb. *stand firm*; stand still, resist change, stick in the mud 266vb. *be quiescent*; grow moss 127 vb. *be old*; remain the same, not change one's spots; allow to stand, let be, let alone, laisser faire, let sleeping dogs lie 756vb. *permit.*

Adv. **as before,** in statu quo, uti possidetis, without a shadow of turning; at a stand, at a standstill; permanently, for good.

See: 13, 60, 81, 113, 115, 127, 146, 153, 192, 266, 324, 599, 600, 602, 610, 666, 756.

145 Cessation: change from action to rest

N. **cessation,** surcease, desinence; desistance, discontinuance, discontinuation 72n. *discontinuity*; arrest 747n. *restraint*; withdrawal 753n. *resignation,* 621n. *relinquishment.*

stop, halt, stand; dead stop, dead stand; standstill, deadlock, stalemate 28n. *draw*; checkmate 728n. *defeat*; breakdown 728 n. *failure*; discontinuance, stoppage,

stall; shut-down, closing d., non-resumption 69n. *end*; hitch, check 702n. *hindrance*; stopping-up, blockage 264n. *closure*; interruption 72n. *discontinuity*; abruption, breaking-off, walk-out 709n. *dissension*; closure of debate, guillotine 399n. *silence*; full stop 547n. *punctuation.*

strike, stopping work 679n. *inactivity*, 715n. *resistance*; general strike, 'national holiday', hartal; slow down, working to rule, meticulosis; stoppage, walk-out, sit-down strike, lightning s.; unofficial strike, mutiny 738n. *disobedience*; lock-out 57n. *exclusion.*

lull, rest, interval (mus.) 410n. *tempo*; pause, remission, recess, break 685n. *refreshment*; holiday, day off, time o. 681n. *leisure*; intermission, interlude, interregnum 108n. *interim*; abeyance, suspense, suspension; close season, respite, moratorium, truce, armistice, cease-fire, standstill 136n. *delay.*

stopping place, port of call, port, harbour 192n. *stable*; stop, halt, pull-up, whistle-stop, station; bus-stop, request s.; terminus, terminal, air t. 271n. *air travel*; dead end, blind alley, cul-de-sac; billet, destination, the grave 295n. *goal*, 69n. *finality.*

Vb. **cease,** stay, desist, refrain, hold, hold one's hand; stop, halt, stand, rest, surcease, rest on one's oars, repose on one's laurels 683vb. *repose*; have done with, see the last of, end, finish 69vb. *terminate*; interrupt, leave off, knock o.; break o., let up 72vb. *discontinue*; ring off, hang up 578vb. *be mute*; withhold one's labour, cease work, stop w., strike w., down tools, strike, come out 715vb. *resist*; lock out 57vb. *exclude*; pipe down 399vb. *be silent*; come to an end, dry up, peter out, run o., run down 634vb. *waste*; fade out, fade away 446vb. *disappear*; come off, end its run, be taken off; fold up, collapse 728vb. *fail*; die away, blow over, clear up 125vb. *be past*; stand down, withdraw, retire 753vb. *resign*; leave, leave off; give up, give over 621 vb. *relinquish*; shut up, shut down, close; shut up shop, put up the shutters, go out of business, wind up; shut off steam, switch off; cease fire 719vb. *make peace*; sound the last post, ring down the curtain, call it a day 266vb. *be quiescent*; go to sleep 679vb. *sleep.*

halt, stop, put a stop to; arrest, check, dam 702vb. *obstruct*; hold up, call off; pull up, cut short, call a halt, interrupt; intervene 747vb. *restrain*; cause a stoppage, call out, stage a strike, bring to a stand, bring to a standstill, freeze 679vb. *make inact-ive*; checkmate, stalemate, thwart 702vb. *hinder*; check oneself, stop short, drop in one's tracks, stand in one's t.; grind to a halt, seize, seize up, stall, jam, stick, catch; brake, put on the b., pull the check cord 278vb. *retard*.

pause, halt for a moment, stop for breath; hold back, hang fire 278vb. *move slowly*; wait awhile, suspend, intermit, remit, allow an interval 136vb. *wait*; recess, sit down, take breath, relax, rest 683vb. *repose*.

Int. halt! hold! stop! enough! avast! have done! a truce to! soft! desist! refrain! forbear! leave off! shut up! give over! chuck it! drop it! come off it! stow it! cheese it! scram! skedaddle!

See: 28, 57, 69, 72, 108, 125, 136, 192, 264, 266, 271, 278, 295, 399, 410, 446, 547, 578, 621, 634, 679, 681, 683, 685, 702, 709, 715, 719, 728, 738, 747, 753.

146 Continuance in action

N. *continuance*, continualness, continua-tion 71n. *continuity*, 144n. *permanence*; 179n. *tendency*; extension, prolongation 113n. *protraction*; maintenance, per-petuation 115n. *perpetuity*; sustained action, persistence 600n. *perseverance*; progress 285n. *progression*; uninter-rupted course, break, run, unbroken r., not-out score, rally 71n. *series*; recurrence 106n. *repetition*.

Adj. *unceasing*, continuing etc. vb.; con-tinual, steady, sustained, unstopped; non-stop, uninterrupted, unintermitting, unremitting 71adj. *continuous*; unvary-ing, unshifting 81adj. *regular*; unrevers-ed, unrevoked, unvaried 153adj. *fixed*; undying, 115n. *perpetual*; unfailing, ever-running, inexhaustible 635adj. *plenteous*; invariable, inconvertible 153 adj. *unchangeable*; batting, not out, still in, in play 113adj. *lasting*; persistent, persisting 600adj. *persevering*; haunting, recurrent 106adj. *repeated*; standing, incessant; obsessive.

Vb. *go on*, keep going, march on, drive on, proceed, advance 285vb. *progress*; run on, never end 115vb. *be eternal*;—and— (e.g. rain and rain, pour and pour); roll on, pursue its course, take its c., trend 179 vb. *tend*; endure, stick, hold, abide, rest, remain, 143vb. *stay*; obsess, haunt, fre-quent 139vb. *recur*; keep at it, persist, hold on, carry on, jog on, plod on, plug on, slog on 600vb. *persevere*; sit it out, wait, wait till the end, see the end of, hang on 725vb. *carry through*; be not out, bat all day, carry one's bat; see one's days out, live out one's time 69vb. *end*.

sustain, maintain, uphold, keep on foot 218 vb. *support*; follow up, follow through 71 vb. *continuate*; keep up, keep alive 666vb. *preserve*; keep on, harp on 106vb. *repeat*; keep it up, prolong, protract 113vb. *spin out*, 114vb. *perpetuate*; keep the pot boiling, keep the ball rolling; prolong the rally, keep the ball in play; not interfere, let be, let alone, let things take their course, laisser faire, let it rip 756vb. *permit*.

Int. carry on! drive on! never say die! not out!

See: 69, 71, 81, 106, 113, 115, 139, 143, 144, 153, 179, 218, 285, 600, 635, 666, 725, 756.

147 Conversion: change to something different

N. *conversion*, converting, turning into, making i.; processing 164n. *production*; reduction, resolution, crystallization; fermentation, ferment, leaven; chemis-try, alchemy; mutation, transmutation, transfiguration 143n. *transformation*; bewitchment, enchantment, bedevil-ment 983n. *sorcery*; progress 285n. *pro-gression*, 157n. *growth*; course, lapse, flux 113n. *course of time*; development 36n. *increase*, 316n. *evolution*; degeneration, perversion 655n. *deterioration*; regenera-tion, reformation 654n. *improvement*; assimilation, naturalization 78n. *in-clusion*; alienization, denaturalization 916n. *loss of right*; brainwashing 178n. *influence*; evangelization, proselytization 534n. *teaching*, 612n. *inducement*; con-vertibility 469n. *possibility*.

transition, transit 305n. *passage*; move-ment, shift, translation, transfer 272n.

transference; transports, ecstasy 818n. *feeling*; life cycle; transmigration; conjugation, declension 564n. *grammar.*

crucible, melting pot, alembic, cauldron, alfet, retort, test tube 461n. *testing agent.*

changed person, new man; convert, neophyte, catechumen, proselyte, disciple 538n. *learner*; renegade, deserter, apostate, turncoat 603n. *tergiversator*; pervert, degenerate 938n. *bad man.*

Adj. *converted,* influenced, affected; turned into, made i. etc. vb.; assimilated, naturalized, reborn, regenerate; proselytized, brainwashed; becoming, transitional; evolving, developing, growing into; transformed, transfigured, bewitched, unrecognizable 15adj. *different*; convertible, impressionable 143adj. *changeable.*

Vb. *be turned to,* be converted into, become, get; come to, turn to, ferment, develop into, evolve i., ripen i. 316vb. *evolve*; fall into, pass i., slide i., shift i., illapse 305vb. *pass*; melt into, merge i. 43vb. *be mixed*; settle into, sink i.; mellow 669vb. *mature*; wax 36vb. *grow*; degenerate 655vb. *deteriorate*; take the impress of, take the shape of, take the nature of, assume the character of; be transformed, not know oneself; suffer a sea-change, undergo a secular change 143vb. *change*; enter a phase, enter a stage.

convert, reduce, ferment, leaven; make into, reduce to, resolve into, turn i., conjure i., enchant 983vb. *bewitch*; transmute, alchemize; render, process, make, mould, form, shapen, shape, hew into shape 244vb. *efform*; brainwash 178vb. *influence*; proselytize, evangelize, missionize 534vb. *teach*; regenerate 656vb. *revive*; paganize, dechristianize 655vb. *pervert.*

transform, transfigure; camouflage, disguise 525vb. *conceal*; render 520vb. *translate*; traduce 521vb. *misinterpret*; reshape, deform 246vb. *distort*; change the face of, change out of recognition 149vb. *revolutionize*; reform, make something of 654vb. *make better*; refound, new-model, reorganize, redress 656vb. *restore*; assimilate, absorb, naturalize, Americanize, Anglicize, Europeanize, Hellenize, Indianize, sinify, orientalize; internationalize; detribalize, denaturalize, alienize 916vb. *disentitle*, 57vb. *exclude.*

Adv. *convertibly,* evolvingly; on the way to, in transit.

See: 15, 36, 43, 57, 78, 113, 143, 149, 157, 164, 178, 244, 246, 272, 285, 305, 316, 461, 469, 520, 521, 525, 534, 538, 564, 603, 612, 654, 655, 656, 669, 818, 916, 938, 983.

148 Reversion

N. *reversion,* reverting, going back, return, regress, retrogression, retrocession, retreat, withdrawal, ebb 286n. *regression*; tracing back, derivation 156n. *source*; return to the past, harking back 126n. *archaism*; atavism, throwback 5n. *heredity*; looking back, retrospection 505n. *remembrance*; retrospective action, retrospectivity, retroaction; reaction 182n. *counteraction,* 31n. *compensation*; repercussion, kick, back-kick, back-fire 280n. *recoil*; revulsion, revulsion of feeling, disenchantment 830n. *regret*; counterrevolution, reversal 149n. *revolution,* 603n. *tergiversation*; volte face, about turn, U-t., right about t. 240n. *contraposition*; backsliding, recidivism 657n. *relapse*; reconversion 656n. *restoration*; retroversion, retroflexion, retortion 248n. *curvature,* 246n. *distortion*; chiasmus, chiastic order 221n. *inversion*; giving back, cession, replacement, reinstatement 787n. *restitution*; getting back, recovery, retrieval 771n. *acquisition*; retort, tu quoque 479n. *confutation*; turn, turning point, turn of the tide, calm before the storm 137n. *crisis*; alternation, swing, swing of the pendulum 141n. *periodicity,* 106n. *recurrence,* 317n. *oscillation*; to-and-fro movement, coming and going, commuting; round trip, there and back, out and home; return journey, return ticket; retroversion, retranslation 520n. *translation*; back where one started, status quo; resumption, recommencement 68vb. *start*; taking back, escheat 786n. *taking.*

Adj. *reverted,* reversed, reversionary, retrogressive, recessive, reflexive 286adj. *regressive*; chiastic 221adj. *inverted*; revulsive 280adj. *recoiling*; reactionary, retroactive 125adj. *retrospective*; atavistic 5adj. *genetic*; recovered, disenchanted 656adj. *restored.*

Vb. *revert,* go back, turn b., turn, return, retrace 286vb. *regress*; reverse, face about,

turn a. 221 vb. *invert*; ebb, retreat, withdraw 290 vb. *recede*; kick back, kick 280 vb. *recoil*; slip back, slide b., backslide 657 vb. *relapse*; hark back, archaize; start again, restart, go back to the beginning, undo, unmake 68 vb. *begin*; restore the status quo, revive 656 vb. *restore*; derestrict, decontrol, deration 746 vb. *liberate*; reconvert, disenchant, remove the spell 656 vb. *cure*; take back, recover 656 vb. *retrieve*; resume, escheat 771 vb. *acquire*; give back, make restitution, reinstate, replace 787 vb. *restitute*.

Adv. *reversibly*, back to the beginning, as you were; invertedly, wrong side out.

See: 5, 31, 68, 106, 125, 126, 137, 141, 149, 156, 182, 221, 240, 246, 248, 280, 286, 290, 317, 479, 505, 520, 603, 656, 657, 746, 771, 786, 787, 830.

149 Revolution: sudden or violent change

N. *revolution*, full circle, circuit 315 n. *rotation*; radical change, organic c.; tabula rasa, clean slate, clean sweep 550 n. *obliteration*; sudden change, catastrophe, peripeteia, surprise, coup d'état 508 n. *inexpectation*; transilience, leap, plunge, jerk, start, throe 318 n. *spasm*; shift, swing, switch, switch over, landslide; violent change, bouleversement, upset, overthrow, subversion, inversion 221 n. *overturning*; convulsion, shake-up, upheaval, eruption, explosion, cataclysm 176 n. *outbreak*; avalanche, landslip, crash, debacle 309 n. *descent*, 165 n. *havoc*; revulsion, counter-revolution 148 n. *reversion*, 738 n. *revolt*; total change, abolition, nullification 752 n. *abrogation*, deposal.

revolutionist, abolitionist, radical, revolutionary, Marxist, Red 738 n. *revolter*; seditionist 738 n. *agitator*; anarchist 168 n. *destroyer*.

Adj. *revolutionary* 126 adj. *new*; innovating, radical, thoroughgoing, root and branch 54 adj. *complete*; cataclysmic, catastrophic, seismic, world-shaking 165 adj. *destructive*; seditious, subversive, Marxist, red 738 adj. *disobedient*; anarchistic 176 adj. *violent*; transilient.

Vb. *revolutionize*, subvert, overturn 221 vb. *invert*; switch over 603 vb. *tergiversate*; uproot, eradicate, make a clean sweep

550 vb. *obliterate*, 165 vb. *demolish*; break with the past, remodel, new-model, refashion 126 vb. *modernize*; change the face of, change beyond recognition 147 vb. *transform*.

See: 54, 126, 147, 148, 165, 168, 176, 221, 309, 315, 318, 508, 550, 603, 738, 752.

150 Substitution: change of one thing for another.

N. *substitution*, subrogation, surrogation; by-election 605 n. *vote*; commutation, exchange, switch, shuffle 151 n. *interchange*; supplanting, supersession, replacement, transfer 272 n. *transference*; metonymy 519 n. *trope*; vicariousness, devotion, self-d., self-sacrifice 931 n. *disinterestedness*; expiation, compensation 941 n. *atonement*; compounding, composition.

substitute, sub, badli, succedaneum; proxy, alternate, agent, representative 759 n. *deputy*; understudy, stand-in 594 n. *actor*; ghost, ghost-writer 589 n. *author*; locum tenens, locum 658 n. *doctor*; reserve, reservist, twelfth man 707 n. *auxiliary*; replacement, remount; relief, successor, supplanter 67 n. *aftercomer*; double, ringer, changeling 545 n. *imposter*; dummy 4 n. *insubstantial thing*; synonym, doublet 559 n. *word*; alternative, second best, pis aller, ersatz 35 n. *inferiority*; whipping-boy, chopping-block, scapegoat, sin-offering, guilt-o., sacrifice 981 n. *oblation*; makeshift, stopgap, jury mast; palimpsest; expedient, temporary e., working arrangement, modus vivendi 770 n. *compromise*, 642 n. *expedience*.

quid pro quo, equivalent 28 n. *compeer*; consideration, purchase money; value, worth 809 n. *price*; payment in lieu, composition, scutage, redemption 804 n. *payment*; something in exchange, new lamps for old, replacement; change 797 n. *money*.

Adj. *substituted*, substitutive, substitutionary, substitutional; vicarious 941 adj. *atoning*; substitutable, interchangeable, commutable 28 adj. *equivalent*; dummy, imitation, mock, ersatz 35 adj. *inferior*; makeshift, stopgap, provisional, temporary 114 adj. *ephemeral*.

Vb. *substitute*, change for, commute; exchange, switch 151 vb. *interchange*; take

or offer in exchange, compound 770 vb.
compromise; make do with, put up w.,
make a shift w.; put in the place of,
replace with; count as, treat as, regard as;
replace, step into the shoes of, succeed
65 vb. *come after*; supersede, supplant,
displace, oust 300 vb. *eject*; take the place
of, be substitute for, do duty f., count f.,
stand in f., act f., understudy f. 755 vb.
deputize; act the part of, ghost for;
shoulder the blame for, take the rap f.,
cover up f., compound f.; rob Peter to pay
Paul; overprint 550 vb. *obliterate*.

Adv. *instead*, in place, in lieu, in the stead,
in the room, in the room of; by proxy;
alternatively, as an alternative; in default
of, for want of better.

See: 4, 28, 35, 65, 67, 114, 151, 272, 300, 519,
545, 550, 559, 589, 594, 605, 642, 658, 707,
755, 759, 770, 797, 804, 809, 931, 941, 981.

151 Interchange: double or mutual change

N. *interchange*, interchangeability, reciprocality; swap, counterchange, exchange
791 n. *barter*; commutation, permutation,
intermutation; transposal, transposition,
mutual transfer; castling (chess), shuffle,
shuffling 272 n. *transference*; reciprocity,
mutuality; interplay, two-way traffic,
reciprocation 12 n. *correlation*; quid pro
quo; rally (tennis), battledore and shuttlecock, give and take; retort, repartee 460 n.
rejoinder; tit for tat, eye for an eye, tooth
for a tooth, a Roland for an Oliver 714 n.
retaliation; log-rolling 706 n. *co-operation*.

Adj. *interchanged*, switched, exchanged,
counter-changed etc. vb.; bartered,
swapped; in exchange, au pair; reciprocating, mutual, two-way 12 adj. *correlative*; in exchange 714 adj. *retaliatory*;
inter-, intercurrent, intercontinental,
interdepartmental; interchangeable, substitutable, convertible, commutable 28
adj. *equivalent*.

Vb. *interchange*, exchange, counterchange;
change money, convert; chop, swap,
barter 791 vb. *trade*; permute, commute;
switch, shuffle, castle (chess) 272 vb.
transpose; give and take 770 vb. *compromise*; reciprocate 12 vb. *correlate*; give
as good as one gets 714 vb. *retaliate*;

bandy words, answer back, return the
compliment, rejoin 460 vb. *answer*; take
in each other's washing, scratch each
other's back 706 vb. *co-operate*.

Adv. *in exchange*, vice versa, mutatis
mutandis; backwards and forwards, to
and fro, by turns, turn and turn about,
turn about; each in his turn, every one in
his turn; in kind; au pair; interchangeably, conversely.

See: 12, 28, 272, 460, 706, 714, 770, 791.

152 Changeableness

N. *changeableness*, changeability, mutability, changefulness 143 n. *change*;
variability, variety 17 n. *non-uniformity*,
437 n. *variegation*; inconsistency, inconstancy, irregularity; instability, imbalance, disequilibrium, unstable equilibrium 29 n. *inequality*; weak foundation, unsteadiness, rockiness, wobbliness, vertigo, staggers; plasticity, pliancy
327 n. *softness*; unfixity, fluidity 335 n.
fluidity; lubricity, slipperiness 258 n.
smoothness; mobility, restlessness, darting, starting, fidgeting, fidget, inquietude,
disquiet 318 n. *agitation*; fluctuation,
alternation 317 n. *oscillation*; turning,
veering, chopping and changing 142 n.
fitfulness; impermanence, transience,
flicker, flash 114 n. *transientness*; vacillation, hesitation, wavering, floating vote
601 n. *irresolution*; yea and nay 603 n.
tergiversation; fickleness, capriciousness
604 n. *caprice*; flightiness, light-mindedness 456 n. *inattention*; versatility 694 n.
aptitude.

changeable thing, moon, Proteus, chameleon; variety show, shifting scene, kaleidoscope; wax, clay; mercury, quicksilver
335 n. *fluid*; wind, weathercock, vane;
eddy; April showers; wheel, whirligig;
fortune, wheel of Fortune; vicissitude,
luck 159 n. *chance*; variable, variable
quantity 85 n. *numerical element*; play of
expression, mobile features 445 n. *appearance*.

Adj. *changeful*, changing, mutable, alterable,
phased 143 adj. *changeable*; varying,
variable 17 adj. *non-uniform*; kaleidoscopic, protean 82 adj. *multiform*; quick-
change, versatile 694 adj. *skilful*; uncer-

tain, unreliable, vacillating, wavering 601 adj. *irresolute*; unpredictable, unaccountable 508 n. *unexpected*; never the same, unstaid, mercurial 15 adj. *different*; wayward, fickle, whimsical 604 adj. *capricious*; giddy, dizzy, flighty, wanton, irresponsible 456 adj. *light-minded*; shifty, inconstant, unfaithful, disloyal 603 adj. *tergiversating*.

unstable, unsteady, unstaid; wavering, wobbling, rocky, tottering, staggery, reeling, rolling; mobile, unquiet, restless, fidgety 318 adj. *agitated*; desultory, spasmodic, flickering 142 adj. *fitful*; touch and go 114 adj. *transient*; shifting, veering, turning, chopping and changing 282 adj. *deviating*; whiffling, gusty 352 adj. *puffing*; unsettled, unfixed, loose, unattached, floating; erratic, mercurial; rootless, homeless 59 adj.*extraneous*; vagrant, rambling, roving, wandering 267 adj. *travelling*; vibrating, vibratory, alternating, fluctuating, tidal 317 adj. *oscillating*; yielding, impressionable, malleable, alterable, plastic 327 adj. *soft*; flowing, running, melting 335 adj. *fluid*.

Vb. *vary*, be changeful, show variety 437 vb. *variegate*; ring the changes, go through phases, show p., have as many phases as the moon 143 vb. *change*; chop and change, change and change about; dodge, double 620 vb. *avoid*; shuffle, be shifty 518 vb. *be equivocal*; writhe 251 vb. *wriggle*; dart, flit, flitter 265 vb. *be in motion*; leap, dance, flicker, gutter 417 vb. *shine*; twinkle, flash; wave, wave in the wind, flutter, flap 217 vb. *hang*; shake, tremble 318 vb. *be agitated*; wobble, stagger, rock, reel, sway, swing, vibrate 317 vb. *oscillate*; alternate, ebb and flow, wax and wane 317 vb. *fluctuate*; veer, tack, yaw 282 vb. *deviate*, 269 vb. *navigate*; whiffle, puff, 352 vb. *blow*; vacillate, waver, hesitate, float, drift, change one's mind 601 vb. *be irresolute*; hover, hover between two extremes, blow hot and cold, play fast and loose 603 vb. *tergiversate*; be inconstant, change one's fancy 604 vb. *be capricious*.

Adv. *changeably*, variably; fitfully, off and on, now this now that.

See: 15, 17, 29, 59, 82, 85, 114, 142, 143, 159, 217, 251, 258, 265, 267, 269, 282, 317, 318, 327, 335, 352, 417, 437, 445, 456, 508, 518, 601, 603, 604, 620, 694.

153 Stability

N. *stability*, immutability; unchangeableness, unchangeability; irreversibility, invariability, constancy 16 n. *uniformity*; firmness, fixity, rootedness; indelibility 144 n. *permanence*; rest, immobility, immovability 266 n. *quiescence*; steadiness, stable equilibrium, stable state, homeostasis, balance 28 n. *equality*; stabilization, stabiliment; nerve, unshaken n., aplomb 601 n. *resolution*; stiffness, inflexibility 326 n. *hardness*, 602 n. *obstinacy*; solidarity, solidity 324 n *density*; stiffening, ankylosis 326 n. *hardening*.

fixture, establishment, firm foundation; foundations, rock, bedrock, pillar, pyramid; invariant, constant; fast dye, fast colour; leopard's spots, Ethiopian's skin; law, law of the Medes and Persians, the twelve tables, the ten commandments, written constitution, entrenched clause, prescriptive right 953 n. *legality*.

stabilizer, fin, centre-board, keel; counterweight, ballast 31 n. *offset*; stabilimeter.

Adj. *unchangeable*, unsusceptible of change; stiff, inflexible 602 adj. *obstinate*; unwavering 599 adj. *resolute*; fiducial, predictable, reliable 473 adj. *certain*; immutable, intransmutable, incommutable; inconvertible; irresoluble, irreducible, indissoluble; changeless, unchanging, unchanged, unaltered, inalterable, irreversible; unshrinkable, shrinkproof; indeclinable; stereotyped, unvarying, invariable, constant 16 adj. *uniform*; steady, undeviating 81 adj. *regular*; durable 113 adj. *lasting*, 144 adj. *permanent*; undying, perennial, indeciduous, evergreen 115 adj. *perpetual*; imperishable, indestructible, inextinguishable 660 adj. *invulnerable*. See *fixed*.

vested, established, well-e., well-founded, entrenched, settled; inveterate, prescriptive; irrevocable, irreversible, reverseless; incontrovertible, indefeasible, of right; valid, confirmed, ratified 473 adj. *undisputed*, 488 adj. *assented*.

fixed, steadfast, firm, immovable, irremovable; steady, stable, balanced, homeostatic; fast, in grain, ingrained, indelible; ineradicable, rooted, well-r., deep-r.; deep-seated, firm-s., well-based, on a rock; standing, pat; tethered, moored, anchored 45 adj. *tied*; at rest, at anchor,

riding at a.; run aground, stuck fast, stranded, grounded, high and dry; pinned down, transfixed; immobile, like a statue, quiet as a stone 266adj. *still*.

Vb. *be stable*,—fixed etc. adj.; stand, stick fast, hold 599 vb. *stand firm*; show aplomb, show self-assurance, not bat an eyelid; weather the storm 113vb. *outlast*; set in, come to stay 144vb. *stay*; settle, settle down 192 vb. *dwell*; strike root, take r., strike deep, have long roots.

stabilize, stabilitate, root, entrench, found, establish, stablish, build on a rock 115vb. *perpetuate*; erect, set up, set on its feet 215vb. *render vertical*; float, set afloat; fix, set, stereotype, grave on granite; make valid, validate, confirm, ratify 488vb. *endorse*; retain, stet; bind, make sure, make fast 45vb. *tie*; keep steady, hold the road, retain equilibrium, balance 28vb. *equalize*.

See: 16, 28, 31, 45, 81, 113, 115, 144, 192, 215, 266, 324, 326, 473, 488, 599, 601, 602, 660, 953.

154 Eventuality: present events

N. *eventuality*, incidence, eventuation, realization; event, phenomenon, incidental; fact, matter of f., naked f. 1n. *reality*; case, circumstance, state of affairs 7n. *state*; occurrence, hap, happening, incident, adventure 137n. *occasion*; fortune, accident, casualty, contingency 159n. *chance*; misadventure, mishap 731 n. *ill-fortune*; emergency, pass 137n. *crisis*; coincidence 181n. *concurrence*; advent 289n. *approach*; encounter, meeting; transaction, proceeding, affairs 676n. *action*; result, product, consequence, issue, outcome, upshot 157n. *effect*; dénouement, solution, unravelling 316n. *evolution*; peripeteia, catastrophe 69n. *end*.

affairs, matters, doings, transactions 676n. *deed*; agenda, order of the day; involvement, concern, concerns, interests, irons in the fire, axes to grind 622n. *business*; world, life, situation 8n. *circumstance*; affairs in general, state of affairs; course of events, march of e., stream of e., tide, of e. 111n, *course of time*; run of affairs, chapter of accidents, ups and downs of life, vicissitudes 730n. *prosperity*, 731n. *adversity*.

Adj. *eventual*, consequential, resulting, resultant, eventuating, issuing in 157adj. *caused*; circumstantial, contingent.

happening, incidental, accidental, occasional; doing, adoing, current, on foot, afloat, in the wind, on the agenda; on the anvil, in preparation.

eventful, stirring, bustling, busy, full of incidents, crowded with i. 678adj. *active*; momentous, critical 638adj. *important*.

Vb. *happen*, become, come into existence 360vb. *be born*; materialize, be realized, come off 727vb. *succeed*; take place, occur, come about, come to pass; befall, betide 159vb. *chance*; turn up, pop up, crop up, start up, spring up, arise 295vb. *arrive*; present itself, announce i. 189vb. *be present*; supervene 284vb. *follow*; eventuate, issue, emanate 157vb. *result*; turn out, fall o., work o., pan o.; be on foot, take its course, hold its c., advance 285vb. *progress*; continue 146vb. *go on*; go off, pass o. 125vb. *be past*; fall to one's lot, be one's great chance; be so, prove, prove to be; bring about, occasion 156vb. *cause*.

meet with, incur, encounter 295vb. *meet*; realize, find 484vb. *discover*; experience, pass through, go t.; have been through 490vb. *know*, 818vb. *feel*; have adventures, endure, undergo 825vb. *suffer*.

Adv. *eventually*, ultimately, in the event of, in case; in the course of things, in the natural course of t., in the ordinary course of t.; as things go, as times go; as the world goes, as the world wags; as the cat jumps; as it may turn out, as it may happen.

See: 1, 7, 8, 69, 111, 125, 137, 146, 156, 157, 159, 181, 189, 284, 285, 289, 295, 316, 360, 484, 490, 622, 638, 676, 678, 727, 730, 731, 818, 825.

155 Destiny: future events

N. *destiny*, what's to come, one's stars 596 n. *fate*; horoscope, forecast 511n. *prediction*; prospect, outlook 507n. *expectation*; coming events, future plans, intentions 124 n. *futurity*, 617 n. *intention*; something in store, rod in pickle 900n. *threat*; imminence, impendence, proximity 200 n. *nearness*, 289n. *approach*; post-existence, future existence, hereafter 124

n. *future state*; next world, after-w.,world to come 971n. *heaven*; foredoom, predestination 596n. *necessity*, 473n. *certainty*; danger 900n. *threat*.

Adj. *impending*, overhanging, hanging over, lowering, hovering, imminent 900adj. *threatening*; preparing, brewing, cooking, stewing 669adj. *preparatory*; destined, predestined, in the stars, on the knees of the gods 596adj. *fated*; predicted, forthcoming, forecast 511adj. *predicting*; inescapable, inevitable, going to be, bound to happen 473adj. *certain*; due, owing 596adj. *necessary*; in the wind, in the cards 471adj. *probable*; on the agenda, intended, decided on 608adj. *predetermined*; in prospect, in view, in the offing, on the horizon, looming on the h., in the distance 443adj. *visible*; in the future, to come, in the womb of time 124adj. *future*; at hand, close 200adj. *near*, 289adj. *approaching*; instant, immediate, about to be, on the point of 116adj. *instantaneous*; pregnant with, heavy w. 511adj. *presageful*; in store, in reserve, in pickle, ready, kept r. 669adj. *prepared*; in embryo 68 adj. *beginning*.

Vb. *impend* 124vb. *be to come*; hang over, lie o., hover, lour, loom 900vb. *threaten*; come on, draw nigh 289vb. *approach*; front, face, stare one in the f. 237vb. *be in front*; breathe down one's neck 200vb. *be near*; ripen 669vb. *mature*.

predestine, destine, doom, foredoom, preordain, fore-ordain 596vb. *necessitate*; foreshadow, adumbrate, presage 511vb. *predict*; have ready, get r., have in store, have in pickle 669vb. *make ready*; plan, intend 608vb. *predetermine*.

Adv. *in the future*, in time, in the long run; all in good time; in the event 154adv. *eventually*; whatever may happen; expectedly 471adv. *probably*; soon, at any moment.

See: 68, 116, 124, 154, 200, 237, 289, 443, 471, 473, 507, 511, 596, 608, 617, 669, 900, 971.

156 Cause: constant antecedent

N. *causation*, causality, cause and effect, ground and consequent; ætiology 158n. *attribution*; authorship; origination, originality 21n. *non-imitation*; invention

484n. *discovery*; inspiration 178n. *influence*; generation, evocation, provocation 164n. *production*; impulsion, stimulation, fomentation, encouragement, motivation 612n. *motive*; planting watering, cultivation 370n. *agriculture*; abetment 706n. *co-operation*; temptation, inciting 612n. *inducement*.

cause, first c., final c., remote c., proximate c., causa causans; vera causa, mover, first m., primum mobile, God 965n. *the Deity*; creator, maker 167n. *producer*; begetter, only b., father 169n. *parent*; causer, effecter, occasioner; author, originator, founder; inventor, agent, leaven; stimulus 174n. *stimulant*; contributor, factor, decisive f., moment, determinant; inspirer, tempter, mainspring 612n. *motivator*; fomentor, aider, abettor; hidden hand, undercurrents 178 n. *influence*; planetary influence, stars 155 n. *destiny*; fate 596n. *necessity*; force 740 n. *compulsion*.

source, fountain, fount, fons et origo 68n. *origin*; head-waters, spring, well-head, fountain-h.,well-spring; mine, quarry 632 n. *store*; birthplace 192n. *home*; genesis, ancestry, lineage, descent 169n. *parentage*; parent, ancestor, progenitor; loins 164n. *genitalia*; rudiment, element, principle, first p., first thing; germen, germ, seed, sperm; egg, fœtus, embryo; chrysalis, cocoon 194n. *receptacle*; bud, stem, stalk, staple, stock, trunk, bole; taproot, root, bulb; radix, radical, etymon, derivation, etymology 557n. *linguistics*; foundation, bedrock 214n. *base*; groundwork, spadework, beginnings 68n. *beginning*; raw material, ore 631n. *materials*.

seedbed, hotbed, nidus 192n. *nest*; cradle, nursery 68n. *origin*; breeding place, incubator, womb 164n. *propagation*; hothouse, conservatory 370n. *garden*.

causal means, appliance 629n. *means*; pivot, hinge, lever, instrument 630n. *tool*; dynamo, generator, battery 160n. *energy*; motor, engine, turbine 630n. *machine*; last straw that breaks the camel's back.

reason why, reason, cause, the why and wherefore; explanation 460n. *answer*, 520n. *interpretation*; excuse 614n. *pretext*; ground, basis, rationale, occasion, causa causans, raison d'être.

Adj. *causal*, causative, formative, factitive,

effective, effectual 727 adj. *successful*; pivotal, determinant, decisive, final 69 adj. *ending*; seminal, germinal 164 adj. *productive*; inceptive, embryonic 68 adj. *beginning*; suggestive, inspiring 178 adj. *influential*; impelling 740 adj. *compelling*; answerable, responsible; at the bottom of, original; ætiological, explanatory; creative, inventive 21 adj. *unimitated*.

fundamental, primary, elemental; foundational, radical, basic; crucial, central 638 adj. *important*; original, aboriginal 68 adj. *first*; primitive, primordial 127 adj. *primal*.

Vb. *cause*, originate, create, make 164 vb. *produce*; beget, be the author of 164 vb. *generate*; invent 484 vb. *discover*; be the reason 158 vb. *account for*; underlie, be *or* lie at the bottom of, be answerable, be responsible; institute, found, lay the foundations, inaugurate 68 vb. *auspicate*; set up, erect 310 vb. *elevate*; launch, set afloat, set afoot, set going, spark off, touch o. 68 vb. *start*; open, open up, broach 68 vb. *initiate*; seed, sow, plant, water 370 vb. *cultivate*; effect, effectuate, bring about, bring off, bring to pass 727 vb. *succeed*; procure, provide the means, engineer 623 vb. *plan*; bring on, superinduce, precipitate 680 vb. *hasten*; bring out, draw o., evoke, elicit 304 vb. *extract*; provoke, arouse, awaken 821 vb. *excite*; stimulate 174 vb. *invigorate*; kindle, inspire, incite, tempt 612 vb. *induce*; occasion, give occasion for 612 vb. *motivate*; have an effect, show its result, make or mar 178 vb. *influence*; be the agent, do the deed 676 vb. *do*; determine, decide, give the decision 480 vb. *judge*; decide the result, turn the scale, give the casting vote 178 vb. *prevail*, 34 vb. *predominate*.

conduce, tend to 179 vb. *tend*; lead to 64 vb. *come before*; contribute to, operate to 703 vb. *minister to*; involve, imply 5 vb. *be intrinsic*; have the effect, entail, draw down, give rise to, open the door to 68 vb. *initiate*; promote, advance, encourage, foster, foment, abet 703 vb. *aid*.

Adv. *casually*, because, by reason of, behind the scenes 178, vb. *influentially*.

See: 5, 21, 34, 64, 68, 69, 127, 155, 158, 160, 164, 167, 169, 174, 178, 179, 192, 194, 214, 304, 310, 370, 460, 480, 520, 557, 596, 612, 614, 623, 629, 630, 631, 632, 638, 676, 680, 703, 706, 727, 740, 821, 965.

157 Effect: constant sequel

N. *effect*, consequent, consequence 65 n. *sequence*; result, resultance; derivation, derivative, precipitate 41 n. *remainder*; upshot, outcome, issue, dénouement 154 n. *eventuality*; final result, termination 69 n. *end*; visible effect, mark, print, impress 548 n. *trace*; after-effect, aftermath, sequela, legacy, backwash, wake, repercussion 67 n. *sequel*; resultant action, response 460 n. *answer*; performance 676 n. *deed*; reaction 182 n. *counteraction*; handiwork 164 n. *product*; karma 596 n. *fate*; moral effect 178 n. *influence*.

growth, outgrowth, development 36 n. *increase*; bud, blossom, florescence, fruit; ear, spica, spike; produce, crop, harvest; woolclip; profit 771 n. *gain*.

Adj. *caused*, owing to, due to, attributed to; consequential, resulting from, consequent upon 65 adj. *sequent*; contingent, depending, dependent on 745 adj. *subject*; resultant, derivable, derivative, descended; unoriginal, secondary 20 adj. *imitative*; arising, emergent, emanating, developed from, evolved f.; born of, out of, by; ending in, issuing in 154 adj. *eventual*; effected, done.

inherited, heritable, hereditary, Mendelian.

Vb. *result*, be the r., come of; follow on, wait on, accrue 284 vb. *follow*; be owing to, be due to; owe everything to, borrow from 785 vb. *borrow*; have a common origin 9 vb. *be related*; take its source, derive from, descend f., originate f., originate in, come from, come out of; issue, proceed, emanate 298 vb. *emerge*; begin from, grow f., spring f., arise f.; develop, unfold 316 vb. *evolve*; bud, sprout, germinate 36 vb. *grow*; show a trace, show an effect, receive an impression, bear the stamp 522 vb. *show*; bear the consequences 154 vb. *meet with*, 963 vb. *be punished*; turn out, pan o., work o., eventuate 154 vb. *happen*.

depend, hang upon, hinge on, pivot on, turn on 12 vb. *correlate*, 745 vb. *be subject*.

Adv. *consequently*, as a consequence, in consequence; because of, as a result, all along of; of course, naturally, necessarily; eventually; it follows that, and so.

See: 9, 12, 20, 36, 41, 65, 67, 69, 154, 164, 178, 182, 284, 298, 316, 460, 522, 548, 596, 676, 745, 771, 785, 963.

158 Attribution: assignment of cause

N. *attribution*, assignment of cause; reference to, imputation, ascription; theory, hypothesis, assumption, conjecture 512n. *supposition*; explanation 520n. *interpretation*; finding reasons, accounting for; ætiology, palætiology 459n. *enquiry*; rationale 156n. *reason why*; apparentation, filiation, affiliation 169n. *parentage*, derivation 130n. *source*, an attribute 89n. *concomitant*; credit, credit title, acknowledgement 915n. *dueness*.

Adj. *attributed* etc. vb.; attributable, assignable, imputable, referable, referrible; assigned to, referred to 9adj. *relative*; credited, imputed, putative 512 adj. *supposed*; inferred, inferable, derivable, traceable; owing to, explained by 157adj. *caused*.

Vb. *attribute*, ascribe, impute; say of, assert of, predicate 532vb. *affirm*; accord, grant, allow 781vb. *give*; put down to, set down to; assign to, refer to, point to, trace to, derive from 9vb. *relate*; lay at the door of, filiate, father upon; charge with, charge on, saddle with, saddle on; found upon, ground u.; make responsible, blame for 928vb. *accuse*; bring home to 478vb. *demonstrate*; credit, credit with, acknowledge 915vb. *grant claims*.

account for, explain, say how it happens 520 vb. *interpret*; theorize, hypothesize, assume 512vb. *suppose*; infer the cause, derive the reason.

Adv. *hence*, thence, therefore; whence, wherefore; for, since, forasmuch as; on account of, because, owing to, thanks to, on that account, from this cause, from that cause, propter hoc, ergo, thus, so; that's why.

why? wherefore? whence? how? how come? cui bono?

somehow, in some way, in some such way; somehow or other.

See: 9, 89, 156, 157, 169, 459, 478, 512, 520, 532, 781, 915, 928.

159 Chance: no assignable cause

N. *chance*, blind c., fortuity, indeterminacy; randomness; indetermination, fortuitousness; uncertainty principle, unpredictability 474n. *uncertainty*; unaccountability, inexplicability 517n. *unin-*telligibility; lot, fortune, wheel of f. 596n. *fate*; whatever comes, potluck; good fortune, luck, good l., run of l. 730n. *prosperity*; bad luck, rotten l. 731n. *ill fortune*; hap, hazard, accident, casualty, contingency, coincidence, chapter of accidents 154n. *eventuality*; non-intention, chance hit, lucky shot, fluke 618n. *non-design*; rare chance, chance in a million 140n. *infrequency*; chance meeting, chance encounter 508n. *inexpectation*; chance discovery, serendipity 484n. *discovery*.

equal chance, even c., fifty-fifty 28n. *equality*; toss-up, spin of the coin, heads or tails, throw of the dice, turn of the card; lucky dip, random sample; lottery, raffle, tombola, sweepstake, premium bond, football pool 618n. *gambling*; sortes Virgilianæ, sortes Biblicæ 511n. *divination*.

fair chance, sporting c., fighting c., gambling c. 469n. *possibility*; good chance, main c., best c., favourable c. 137n. *opportunity*; long odds, odds on, odds 34n. *vantage*; small risk, good bet, the probabilities 471 n. *probability*.

calculation of chance, theory of probabilities, doctrine of chance, actuarial calculation, mathematical probability; risk-taking, assurance, insurance, underwriting 672n. *undertaking*; speculation 461n. *experiment*; bookmaking 618n. *gambling*.

Adj. *casual*, fortuitous, chance, haphazard, random, stray 618n. *designless*; adventitious, adventive, accidental, incidental, contingent 154adj. *happening*; non-causal, epiphenomenal, coincidental 89 n. *accompanying*; chancy, fluky, dicey, incalculable 474adj. *uncertain*.

causeless, groundless, uncaused, unforeseeable, unpredictable, undetermined, indeterminate 474adj. *uncertain*; unmotivated, unintended, undesigned, unplanned, unmeant 618adj. *unintentional*; unaccountable, inexplicable 517 adj. *puzzling*.

Vb. *chance*, hap, turn up, pop up, fall to one's lot, so happen 154vb. *happen*; chance upon, light u., hit u., stumble u., blunder u. 154vb. *meet with*, 484vb. *discover*; risk it, chance it, leave it to chance 618vb. *gamble*; have small chance 472vb. *be unlikely*.

Adv. *by chance*, by accident; accidentally, casually, unintentionally, fortuitously,

randomly 618 adv. *at random*; perchance, perhaps; for aught one knows 469 adv. *possibly*; luckily, as good luck would have it; unluckily, as ill-luck would have it; according to chance, as it may be, as it may chance, as it may turn up, as it may happen, as the case may be, whatever happens, in any event; unpredictably 508 adv. *unexpectedly*; unaccountably, inexplicably.

See: 28, 34, 89, 137, 140, 154, 461, 469, 471, 472, 474, 484, 508, 511, 517, 596, 618, 672, 730, 731.

160 Power

N. *power*, potency, puissance, mightiness 32 n. *greatness*; prepotency, prepollence, prevalence, predominance 34 n. *superiority*; omnipotence, almightiness 733 n. *authority*; control, sway 733 n. *governance*; moral power, ascendancy 178 n. *influence*; spiritual power, mana; witchcraft 983 n. *sorcery*; staying power, endurance 153 n. *stability*; physical power, might, muscle, right arm, right hand 162 n. *strength*; dint, might and main, effort, endeavour 682 n. *exertion*; force 740 n. *compulsion*; stress, strain, shear; weight 322 n. *gravity*; weight of numbers 104 n. *greater number*; manpower 686 n. *personnel*; position of power, vantage ground 34 n. *vantage*; validity 494 n. *truth*; cogency, emphasis 532 n. *affirmation*; extra power, overdrive.

ability, ableness, capability, potentiality, virtuality 469 n. *possibility*; competency, efficiency, efficacy, effectuality 694 n. *skill*; capacity, faculty, virtue, property 5 n. *intrinsicality*; qualification 24 n. *fitness*; attribute 89 n. *concomitant*; endowment, gift 694 n. *aptitude*; compass, reach, grasp 183 n. *range*; susceptibility, affectibility 180 n. *liability*; trend 179 n. *tendency*; empowering, enablement, authorization 756 n. *permission*.

energy, liveliness, vigour, dynamism 174 n. *vigorousness*; physical energy, chemical e., kinetic e., dynamic e., electrical e., atomic e., nuclear e.; mechanical energy, engine power, horse-power; inertia, vis inertiæ 175 n. *inertness*; resistance 333 n. *friction*; force, field of f.; force of gravity 322 n. *gravity*; buoyancy 323 n. *levity*;

compression, spring 328 n. *elasticity*; pressure, head, charge, steam; full pressure, steam up; tension, high t.; motive power, electromotive force; pulling power 288 n. *traction*; pushing power, thrust, jet, jet propulsion 287 n. *propulsion*, 279 n. *impulse*; magnetism 291 n. *attraction*; negative magnetism 292 n. *repulsion*; suction 299 n. *reception*; expulsion 300 n. *ejection*; potential function, potential; unit of work, erg, action; foot-pound, poundal.

electricity, active e., static e.; positive electricity, negative e.; voltaic electricity, galvanic e.; atmospheric electricity, free e., induced e.; animal electricity, organic e.; lightning, spark; electro-dynamics, electrostatics, electromagnetism; electrification, inductance, capacitance, voltaism, galvanism; electric shock, electric pulse; amperage, electric current, direct c., alternating c.; circuit, short c., closed c., open c.; lightning conductor, live wire; cable, pylon, grid, distributor; generator, dynamo; battery, storage b., dry b., wet b., cell, fuel c.; electric unit, volt, watt, kilowatt, megawatt; resistance, ohm; current, ampere, amp, milliamp; potential, voltage.

nucleonics, electronics, nuclear physics; atomic fission, nuclear f., thermonuclear f.; cyclotron, atom-smasher, betatron, bevatron; cosmotron, high-energy accelerator; atomic pile, reactor, chain-reactor, breeder-r.; moderator, Zeta, zero energy thermo-nuclear apparatus; mushroom, fall-out, radioactive cloud 659 n. *poison*, 417 n. *radiation*.

Adj. *powerful*, potent, multipotent 162 adj. *strong*; puissant, mighty, overmighty 32 adj. *great*; ascendant, rising, in the ascendant 36 adj. *increasing*; prepotent, prevalent, prevailing, predominant 178 adj. *influential*; almighty, omnipotent, irresistible 34 adj. *supreme*; with full powers, empowered, plenipotent 733 adj. *authoritative*; competent, capable, able, adequate, equal to, up to 635 adj. *sufficient*; omnicompetent, multicompetent 694 adj. *expert*; efficacious, effectual, effective 727 adj. *successful*; of power, of might, operative, workable, having teeth; in force, valid, unrepealed, unrepealable 153 adj. *vested*; cogent, compulsive 740 adj. *compelling*; forcible 176 adj. *violent*;

armipotent, bellicose 718 adj. *warlike*; with resources 800 adj. *rich*; productive 171 adj. *prolific*; virtual, potential 469 adj. *possible*.

dynamic, energetic 174 adj. *vigorous*; high-potential, high-tension, super-charged; magnetic 291 adj. *attracting*; tractive 288 adj. *drawing*; propelling 287 adj. *propulsive*, 279 adj. *impelling*; locomotive, kinetic 265 adj. *moving*; powered, engined, driven by; live, electric, electro-magnetic, hydroelectric; atomic, electronic, nuclear, thermonuclear; radioactive.

Vb. *be able*, — powerful etc. adj.; can, have it in one's power, have it in one; be capable of, have the virtue, have the property; compass, manage 676 vb. *do*; measure up to 635 vb. *suffice*; have power, exercise p., control 733 vb. *dominate*; force, 740 vb. *compel*; gain power, come to p. 178 vb. *prevail*.

empower, enable, endow, authorize; endow with power, invest with p.; put teeth into, arm 162 vb. *strengthen*; electrify, charge, magnetize; impart engine-power, power, engine.

Adv. *powerfully* etc. adj.; by virtue of, by dint of, with might and main.

See: 5, 24, 32, 34, 36, 89, 104, 153, 162, 171, 174, 176, 178, 179, 180, 183, 265, 279, 287; 288, 291, 292, 299, 300, 322, 323, 328, 333, 417, 469, 494, 532, 635, 659, 676, 682, 686, 694, 718, 727, 733, 740, 756, 800, 983.

161 Impotence

N. *impotence*, lack of power, no authority, power vacuum; invalidity, impuissance 163 n. *weakness*; inability, incapacity; incapability, incompetence, inefficiency 728 n. *failure*, 695 n. *unskilfulness*; ineptitude, unfitness 25 n. *inaptitude*; decrepitude 131 n. *age*; caducity 114 n. *transientness*; invalidation, disqualification 752 n. *abrogation*; sterility, sterilization 172 n. *unproductivity*; disarmament, demilitarization 719 n. *pacification*; demobilization 75 n. *dispersion*.

helplessness, defencelessness 661 n. *vulnerability*; harmlessness 935 n. *innocence*; powerlessness 745 n. *subjection*; impotent fury, gnashing of teeth 830 n. *regret*; prostration, exhaustion, inanition 684 n. *fatigue*; collapse, breakdown 728 n.

failure; unconsciousness, deliquium, faint, swoon, coma; numbness, narcosis 375 n. *insensibility*; stroke, syncope, apoplexy, hemiplegia, paraplegia 651 n. *disease*; sideration 651 n. *paralysis*; cramp, cramps 747 n. *restraint*; torpor 677 n. *inaction*; atrophy, sweeny, mortification 655 n. *deterioration*; palsy, senility, old age 131 n. *age*; ataxia, locomotor a.; loss of control, incontinence; mental decay, softening of the brain 503 n. *insanity*; mental weakness, imbecility 499 n. *unintelligence*; mutism, deaf mutism 578 n. *aphony*; legal incapacity, pupillage, minority 130 n. *nonage*; babyhood, infancy 130 n. *youth*; invalid 651 n. *sick person*, 163 n. *weakling*.

eunuch, castrato; no-man; gelding, capon, bullock, steer, neuter; freemartin, hermaphrodite.

ineffectuality, ineffectiveness, futility 497 n. *absurdity*; vanity 4 n. *insubstantiality*; uselessness 641 n. *inutility*; flash in the pan 114 n. *transientness*; dead letter, waste paper, scrap of p. 752 n. *abrogation*; figurehead, dummy, man of straw 4 n. *insubstantial thing*; blank cartridge, vox et praeterea nihil, empty thunder.

Adj. *powerless*, not able, unable; not enabled, unempowered, unauthorized, without authority; nominal, figurehead, constitutional 4 adj. *insubstantial*; nugatory, invalid, null and void, of none effect; unconstitutional 954 adj. *illegal*; lame and impotent, without a leg to stand on 163 adj. *weak*; inoperative, not working, unexercised, unemployed 679 adj. *inactive*; suspended, in abeyance, cancelled, withdrawn 752 adj. *abrogated*; abolished, swept away, gone by the board 165 adj. *destroyed*; obsolete, laid on the shelf 127 adj. *antiquated*; disabled, disqualified, deposed; unqualified, unfit, unfitted, inept 25 adj. *unapt*; unworkable, dud, good for nothing 641 adj. *useless*; inadequate 636 adj. *insufficient*; ineffective, inefficacious, ineffectual, feeble 728 adj. *unsuccessful*; incapable, incompetent, inefficient 695 adj. *unskilful*; mechanically powerless, unpowered, unengined; unequipped 670 adj. *unprepared*.

defenceless, helpless, without resource; bereaved, bereft 772 adj. *losing*; kithless, kinless, orphan, unfriended 883 adj. *friendless*; seely, harmless 935 adj.

innocent; barehanded, weaponless, armless, unarmed, disarmed 670 adj. *unequipped*; unfortified, exposed, indefensible, untenable, pregnable, vincible 661 adj. *vulnerable.*

impotent, powerless, feeble 163 adj. *weak*; emasculated, castrated, caponized, gelded, unsexed, unmanned 163 adj. *crippled*; sexless, neuter; sterile, barren, infertile 172 adj. *unproductive*; worn out, exhausted, used up, effete; senile, palsied 131 adj. *aged*; paralytic, arthritic, stiff 326 adj. *hard*; unconscious, comatose, numb, benumbed 375 adj. *insensible*; disjointed 61 adj. *orderless*; out of joint 46 adj. *disjunct*; without self-control, incontinent; done up, dead-beat, foundered 684 adj. *fatigued*; prostrated, flat 216 adj. *supine*; nerveless, spineless, invertebrate 601 adj. *irresolute*; shattered, unhinged, unnerved, demoralized 854 adj. *nervous*; hors de combat, out of the running 728 adj. *defeated*; helpless, rudderless, drifting 282 adj. *deviating*; waterlogged, swamped; on one's beam ends, laid on one's back 728 adj. *grounded*; baffled, thwarted, gnashing one's teeth 702 adj. *hindered.*

Vb. *be impotent,*—defenceless etc. adj.; be unable, cannot, not work, not do, not alter things; not help, have no help to offer 641 vb. *be useless*; strive in vain, avail nothing, end in smoke, fade out 728 vb. *fail*; have no power 745 vb. *be subject*; lose power of resistance 721 vb. *submit*; feel helpless, shrug, wring one's hands; gnash one's teeth 830 vb. *regret*; do nothing, look on, stand by 441 vb. *watch*; have a hopeless case, not have a leg to stand on; go by the board 446 vb. *disappear*; lose consciousness, faint, swoon, pass out 375 vb. *be insensible*; drop, collapse 163 vb. *be weak.*

disable, incapacitate, unfit 641 vb. *make useless*; disqualify 916 vb. *disentitle*; deprive of power, invalidate, decontrol 752 vb. *abrogate*; disarm, demilitarize 163 vb. *weaken*; neutralize 182 vb. *counteract*; undermine, sap, burrow 255 vb. *make concave*; exhaust, use up, consume 634 vb. *waste*; wind, prostrate, bowl over, knock out 279 vb. *strike*; double up, cramp, benumb, paralyse 679 vb. *make inactive*; sprain, rick, wrench, twist, dislocate; cripple, lame, maim, hobble,

nobble, hamstring, hock, hough 702 vb. *hinder*, 655 vb. *impair*; stifle, throttle, suffocate, strangle, garrotte 362 vb. *kill*; muzzle, deaden 399 vb. *silence*; spike the guns, draw the teeth, clip the wings, scotch the snake; tie the hands, cramp one's style; sabotage, ratten, put a spoke into one's wheel, throw a spanner *or* monkey-wrench into the works; deflate, take the wind out of one's sails, put out of gear, unhinge, unbrace, unstring 46 vb. *disjoin*; put out of action, put out of commission 674 vb. *disuse.*

unman, unnerve, enervate, palsy, cowardize 854 vb. *frighten*; devitalize 163 vb. *weaken*; emasculate, castrate, spay, geld, caponize, effeminate 172 vb. *sterilize.*

See: 4, 25, 46, 61, 75, 114, 127, 130, 131, 163, 165, 172, 182, 216, 255, 279, 282, 326, 362, 375, 399, 441, 446, 497, 499, 503, 578, 601, 634, 636, 641, 651, 655, 661, 670, 674, 677, 679, 684, 695, 702, 719, 721, 728, 745, 747, 752, 772, 830, 854, 883, 916, 935, 954.

162 Strength

N. *strength*, might, potency, horse-power, engine-p. 160 n. *power*; energy 174 n. *vigorousness*; force, physical f., main f. 735 n. *brute force*; resilience, spring 328 n. *elasticity*; tone, tonicity, tension, temper, capacity to bear, tolerance; iron, steel, adamant 326 n. *hardness*; oak, heart of oak 329 n. *toughness*; staying power, endurance, grit 600 n. *stamina.*

vitality, healthiness 650 n. *health*; vigour, liveliness 360 n. *life*; animal spirits 833 n. *cheerfulness*; virility, red-bloodedness, red blood 855 n. *manliness*, 372 n. *male*; stoutness, sturdiness 599 n. *resolution*; aggressiveness 718 n. *bellicosity*; physique, muscularity, muscle, biceps, sinews, thews and sinews; bone, marrow, pith, pithiness, beef, brawn 195 n. *size*; grip, iron g., vice-like g. 778 n. *retention*; Titanic strength, strength of Hercules.

athletics 837 n. *sport*; athleticism, gymnastics, feats of strength, callisthenics 682 n. *exercise*; acrobatics, aerobatics 875 n. *ostentation*; agonism, agonistics 716 n. *contest*; palæstra 724 n. *arena.*

athlete, gymnast, tumbler, acrobat, contortionist, trapeze artist, circus rider, bare-

back r.; circus animal, performing flea; agonist, Blue, all-rounder, pancratiast 716n. *contender*; wrestler 716n. *wrestling*; heavyweight 722n. *pugilist*; weight-lifter, strong man; champion 644n. *exceller*; he-man 372n. *male*; strong-arm man, bully, bruiser, tough guy 857n. *desperado*; chucker-out, bouncer 300n. *ejector*; amazon, virago 373n. *woman*; matador, picador, toreador 362n. *killer*; Sandow, Milo, Hercules; Samson, Goliath, Antæus, Atlas, Titan; giant refreshed 195n. *giant*; tower of strength 707n. *auxiliary*.

strengthening etc. vb.; reinforcement 703n. *aid*; stiffening, toughening, tempering 326n. *hardening*; invigoration, tonic effect 174n. *stimulation*; reanimation, refocillation 685n. *refreshment*; revival 656 n. *restoration*; emphasis, stress 532n. *affirmation*.

science of forces, dynamics, statics, hydrodynamics, hydrostatics, electrodynamics, electrostatics; thermodynamics; triangle of forces.

Adj. strong, lusty, youthful 130adj. *young*; mighty, puissant, potent, armed 160adj. *powerful*; high-powered, high-geared, high-tension; all-powerful, omnipotent, overpowering, overwhelming 34adj. *superior*; incontestable, irresistible, resistless, more than a match for, victorious 727adj. *unbeaten*; sovereign, supreme 733adj. *ruling*; valid, in full force; in full swing 146adj. *unceasing*; in the plenitude of power, undiminished 32adj. *great*; like a giant refreshed 685adj. *refreshed*; in high feather, in fine f., in fine mettle, sound as a roach 650adj. *healthy*; heavy 322adj. *weighty*; strong as; strong-arm; forceful, forcible 735adj. *severe*; urgent, pressing, compulsive 740adj. *compelling*; emphatic, emphasized 532adj. *assertive*; tempered, iron-hard, hard as iron, steely, adamantine 326adj. *hard*; case-hardened, toughened 329adj. *tough*; deep-rooted 45 adj. *firm-set*; firm, stable 153adj. *fixed*; thick-ribbed, well-built, stout; strong as a horse, strong as a lion, strong as an ox; strong as brandy, heady, alcoholic 949 adj. *intoxicating*; strengthened, reinforced, double-strength; fortified, entrenched, defended, inviolable, unassailable 660adj. *invulnerable*; strong-smelling, odoriferous 394adj. *odorous*. *unyielding*, staunch 599adj. *resolute*; stub-

born 602adj. *obstinate*; persistent 600adj. *persevering*; unstretchable, inelastic 326 adj. *rigid*; shatter-proof, unbreakable, infrangible, solid 324adj. *dense*; impregnable 660adj. *invulnerable*; indomitable, unconquerable, invincible, unbeatable 727adj. *unbeaten*; inextinguishable, unquenchable, unallayed 146adj. *unceasing*; unflagging, tireless, unexhausted 678adj. *industrious*; unweakened, unwithered, unworn, evergreen 113adj. *lasting*; proof, of proof, sound; waterproof, weatherproof, rustproof, damp-proof, impermeable, gas-proof, leak-p. 264adj. *sealed off*; fire-proof, bullet-p., bomb-p.

stalwart, stout, sturdy, hardy, rugged, robust 174adj. *vigorous*; of good physique, ablebodied, muscular, muscly, brawny; sinewy, wiry 678adj. *active*; strapping, well-knit, well set-up, broad-shouldered, thickset, burly, beefy, husky, hefty 195 adj. *large*; gigantic, colossal, titanic, Herculean 195adj. *huge*.

athletic, gymnastic, acrobatic, agonistic, palæstric 716adj. *contending*; exercised, fit, fighting f., in training, in condition 650adj. *healthy*; amazonian.

manly, masculine 372adj. *male*; unwomanly, amazonian; virile, red-blooded, manful 855adj. *courageous*; in the prime of manhood 134adj. *adult*.

Vb. be strong, —mighty etc. adj.; have what it takes; pack a punch; gird up one's loins 669vb. *prepare*; come in force; be stronger, overpower, overmatch, overwhelm 727vb. *overmaster*; get stronger, convalesce, recover, revive 656vb. *be restored*, 685vb. *be refreshed*; get up, freshen (wind), blow hard, blow great guns 352vb. *blow*.

strengthen, confirm, give strength to, lend force to 36vb. *augment*; underline, stress 532vb. *emphasize*; reinforce, fortify, entrench; stuff 227vb. *line*; buttress, prop, sustain 218vb. *support*; nerve, brace, steel 855vb. *give courage*; stiffen, toughen, temper, case-harden 326vb. *harden*; energize, act like a tonic 174vb. *invigorate*; animate, enliven, quicken 821vb. *excite*; vivify, revivify 656vb. *revive*; recruit, refect 685vb. *refresh*; set one on his legs 656vb. *cure*; set up, build up 310vb. *elevate*; screw up, wind up 45vb. *tighten*; power, engine, motor 160vb. *empower*.

Adv. strongly, powerfully etc. adj.; by force

etc. n.; by main force, by compulsion, with might and main; in force.

See: 32, 34, 36, 45, 113, 130, 134, 146, 153, 160, 173, 195, 218, 227, 264, 300, 310, 322, 324, 326, 328, 329, 352, 360, 372, 373, 394, 532, 599, 600, 602, 644, 650, 656, 660, 669, 678, 682, 685, 703, 707, 716, 718, 722, 724, 727, 733, 735, 740, 778, 821, 883, 837, 855, 857, 875, 949.

163 Weakness

N. *weakness*, lack of strength, feebleness; helplessness, imbecility 161n. *impotence*; incapacity to bear, intolerance; flimsiness, slightness, lightness 323n. *levity*; wispiness, sleaziness; lack of temper, fragility, frailness 330n. *brittleness*; delicacy, tenderness 327n. *softness*; effeminacy, womanishness; unfirmness, unsteadiness, shakiness, wobbliness, giddiness, disequilibrium 29n. *inequality*; weak foundation, feet of clay, instability 152n. *changeableness*; moral weakness, frailty, infirmity of purpose 601n. *irresolution*; bodily weakness, weakliness, debility, infirmity, decrepitude, caducity, senility 131n. *age*; invalidism, delicate health 651n. *ill-health*; atony, no tone, no toughness, flaccidity, flabbiness, floppiness 335n. *fluidity*; fleshiness, corpulence 195n. *bulk*; weak state, asthenia, adynamy, cachexia; anæmia, bloodlessness; loss of strength, enervation, inanition, faintness, langour, torpor, inactivity 679n. *sluggishness*; exhaustion, prostration, collapse 684n. *fatigue*; unconsciousness, swoon 375n. *insensibility*; decline, declension 655n. *deterioration*; weakening, softening, mitigation 177n. *moderation*; relaxation 734n. *laxity*; loosening 46n. *disjunction*; adulteration, watering, dilution 43n. *mixture*; emasculation; invalidation 752n. *abrogation*; effect of weakness, crack, fault 201n. *gap*; flaw 845n. *blemish*; strain, sprain, dislocation 63n. *derangement*; inadequacy 636n. *insufficiency*, 647n. *defect*.

weakling, effeminate, pansy; lightweight 639 n. *nonentity*; softling, softy, sissy, milksop, mollycoddle; old woman, invalid, hypochrondriac 651n. *sick person*; lame dog, lame duck 731n. *unlucky person*; infant, babe-in-arms, babe 132n. *child*;

baby, cry-baby 856n. *coward*; mamma's boy, mother's darling, teacher's pet 890n. *favourite*; doormat, jellyfish, victim 825n. *sufferer*; gull 544n. *dupe*.

weak thing, flimsy article, reed, broken r., thread, rope of sand; sandcastle, mud pie, house built on sand, house of cards, house of bricks, cobweb, gossamer 4n. *insubstantial thing*; matchwood, matchstick, egg-shell, paper, tissue-p.; glass, china 330n. *brittleness*; water, dishwater, slops, milk and water, thin gruel.

Adj. *weak*, powerless, strengthless, without force, invalid, unconfirmed 161 adj. *impotent*; under-strength, under-proof; unfortified, unstrengthened, aidless, helpless 161 adj. *defenceless*; harmless, seely 935 adj. *innocent*; baby, babyish 132 adj. *infantine*; effeminate, pansy, womanish 373 adj. *female*; poor, feeble, slight, puny 33 adj. *small*; lightweight 323 adj. *light*; slightly built, of poor physique 196 adj. *little*; thin 206 adj. *lean*; feeble-minded, imbecile 499 adj. *foolish*; sheepish, gutless, weak-willed, half-hearted 601 adj. *irresolute*; nerveless, unnerved 854 adj. *nervous*; spineless, invertebrate, submissive, yielding 721 adj. *submitting*; marrowless, pithless 4 adj. *insubstantial*; sapless 342 adj. *dry*; bloodless, anaemic, pale 426 adj. *colourless*; untempered, unhardened, limp, flaccid, flabby, floppy 327 adj. *soft*; drooping, sagging, giving 217 adj. *pendent*; untaut, unstrung, slack, loose, relaxed 734 adj. *lax*, 46 adj. *disjunct*; watery, washy, wishy-washy, milk-and-water, insipid 387 adj. *tasteless*; low, quiet, faint, hardly heard 401 adj. *muted*; palsied, doddering, tottering, decrepit, old 131 adj. *aged*; too weak, past it, weak as a child, weak as a baby; weak as water 604 adj. *capricious*; rickety, tottery, shaky, wobbly 152 adj. *unstable*; torpid 679 adj. *inactive*, 266 adj. *quiescent*; in its beginnings, only beginning, infant 68 adj. *beginning*, 126 adj. *new*, 130 adj. *young*. See *flimsy*.

weakened, debilitated, diminished, deflated 37 adj. *decreasing*; tapped, drained 190 adj. *empty*; wasted, spent, effete, used up, burnt out 673 adj. *used*; misused, abused; sapped, undermined, disarmed, disabled, laid low 161 adj. *defenceless*; stripped, denuded, exposed, bare 229 adj. *uncovered*; flagging, failing, exhausted,

wearied, weary 684adj. *fatigued*; strained, overstrained 246adj. *distorted*; weather-beaten, worn, broken, crumbling, tumble-down 655adj. *dilapidated*; the worse for wear, not what it was, on its last legs; rotten, rusting, withered, decaying, in decay 51adj. *decomposed*; deactivated, neutralized 175adj. *inert*; diluted, adulterated, watered, watered down 43adj. *mixed*. See *crippled*.

weakly, infirm, debile, asthenic, adynamic, delicate, sickly 651adj. *unhealthy*; groggy, rocky; seedy, poorly; pulled down, reduced 206adj. *lean*; languid, languishing; faint, fainting, faintish; sallow, lacklustre 426adj. *colourless*; listless, lustless.

crippled, halt, lame, game, limping, hobbling; hamstrung, hobbled, hipshot; knock-kneed; stiff in the joints, arthritic, rheumatic, gouty; legless, armless, handless, eyeless 647adj. *imperfect*.

flimsy, delicate, gossamer, sleazy, wispy, tenuous 4adj. *insubstantial*; frail, tearable, fragile, frangible, friable, shattery 330adj. *brittle*; gimcrack, jerry-built, shoddy 641adj. *useless*; rickety, ramshackle, shaky, tottery, teetering, creaky, crazy, tumble-down 655adj. *dilapidated*.

Vb. *be weak*, grow w., weaken; sicken 651 vb. *be ill*; faint, fail, languish, flag 684vb. *be fatigued*; drop, fall 309vb. *tumble*; decline 655vb. *deteriorate*; droop, wilt, fade 131vb. *grow old*; wear thin, crumble; soften 327vb. *soften*; yield, give way, sag, spring, start 263vb. *open*; totter, teeter, sway, reel 317vb. *oscillate*; tremble, shake 318 vb. *be agitated*; halt, limp, hirple, go lame 278vb. *move slowly*; have one foot in the grave 127vb. *be old*.

weaken, enfeeble, debilitate, enervate; unnerve, rattle 854vb. *frighten*; relax, slacken, unbrace, loosen 46vb. *disjoin*; shake, soften up 327vb. *soften*; strain, sprain, cripple, lame 161vb. *disable*; cramp 702vb. *obstruct*; effeminate 161vb. *unman*; disarm, take the edge off, obtund 257vb. *blunt*; impoverish, starve; deprive, rob 786vb. *take away*; reduce, extenuate, thin, lessen 37vb. *bate*; dilute, water, water down, adulterate 43vb. *mix*; denature, devitalize; deactivate, neutralize 182vb. *counteract*; reduce in number, decimate 105vb. *render few*; invalidate 752vb. *abrogate*; damage, spoil 655vb. *impair*; dismantle, slight 165vb. *demolish*;

sap, undermine, burrow; hurt, injure 655vb. *wound*; sicken, distemper.

See: 4, 29, 33, 37, 43, 46, 51, 63 68, 105, 126, 127, 130, 131, 132, 152, 161, 165, 175, 177, 182, 190, 195, 196, 201, 203, 206, 217, 229, 246, 257, 263, 266, 278, 309, 317, 318, 323, 327, 330, 335, 342, 373, 375, 387, 401, 426, 499, 544, 601, 604, 636, 639, 641, 647, 651, 655, 673, 679, 684, 702, 721, 731, 734, 752, 786, 823, 849, 854, 858, 890, 933.

164 Production

N. *production*, producing, creation; mental creation, cerebration 449n. *thought*; origination, invention, original work 21n. *non-imitation*, 484n. *discovery*; creative urge, productivity 171n. *productiveness*; effort, endeavour 671n. *essay*, 672n. *undertaking*; artistic effort, composition, authorship 551n. *art*, 553n. *painting*, 554 n. *sculpture*, 586n. *writing*; musicianship 413n. *musical skill*; doing, performance, output, outturn, through-put 676n. *action*; execution, accomplishment, achievement 725n. *effectuation*; concoction, brewing 669n. *preparation*; formation, shaping, forming, conformation, workmanship, craftsmanship 243n. *efformation*; organization 331n. *structure*, 62n. *arrangement*; tectonics, engineering, building, edification, architecture; construction, establishment, erection 310n. *elevation*; making, fabrication, manufacture, industry 622vb. *business*; processing, process 147n. *conversion*; machining, assembly; assembly-line, production l. 630n. *machine*; industrialization, increased output, mass-production, automation; minting 797n. *coinage*; book production, printing, publication 587n. *print*, 589n. *book*; farming, growing 370n. *agriculture*; breeding 369n. *animal husbandry*; development, ribbon-d. 316n. *evolution*.

product, creature, creation, result 157n. *effect*; output, outturn; end-product, by-p.; extract, essence, confection; work of one's hands, handiwork, artifact; manufacture, article, thing 319n. *object*; ware 795n. *merchandise*; earthenware 381n. *pottery*; stoneware, hardware, ironware; production, work, opus, œuvre, piece 56n.

164

composition; chef d'œuvre, crowning achievement 694 n. *masterpiece*; fruit, flower, blossom, berry; produce, yield, harvest, crop, reaping, mowing, vintage 157 n. *growth*; interest, increase, return 771 n. *gain*; mental product, brain-child, conception 451 n. *idea*; figment, fiction 513 n. *ideality*; offspring, young, egg, spat, seed 132 n. *youngling*.

edifice, piece of architecture, building, structure, fabric, erection, pile, dome, tower, skyscraper 209 n. *high structure*; pyramid 548 n. *monument*; church 990 n. *temple*; mausoleum 364 n. *tomb*; habitation, mansion, hall 192 n. *house*; college 539 n. *school*; fortress 713 n. *fort*; sandcastle, mud pie 163 n. *weak thing*; stonework, brickwork, bricks and mortar.

propagation 166 n. *reproduction*; fertility, fecundity 171 n. *productiveness*; proliferation, multiplication 36 n. *increase*; breeding, hatching, incubation; copulation 45 n. *coition*; generation, procreation, genesis, biogenesis, homogenesis, xenogenesis; parthenogenesis, virgin birth; autogenesis, abiogenesis, spontaneous generation; arrenotoky; thelytoky, gynogenesis, teratogenesis 84 n. *abnormality*; fertilization, fecundation, superfecundation; impregnation, insemination, artificial i., pollination; conception, pregnancy, epigenesis, germination, gestation; birth, nativity 68 vb. *origin*; growth, development, birthrate 157 n. *growth*; fructification, fruition, florescence, efflorescence, flowering 669 n. *maturation*; parenthood, motherhood, fatherhood, paternity 169 n. *parentage*; genesiology.

obstetrics, midwifery, midders, maternity work; parturition, birth, childbirth, childbed, confinement, lying-in; accouchement, twilight sleep; labour, labour pain, travail, throe, birth-t., birth-pang, pains; delivery, forceps d.; cæsar, cæsarian operation; omentum, caul, umbilical cord, placenta, afterbirth; obstetrician, maternity specialist; midwife, dai, accoucheur, accoucheuse 658 n. *nurse*; stork, gooseberry bush.

genitalia, loins, womb 156 n. *source*; organs of generation, parts, private p., privities; parts of shame, pudenda; intromittent organ, male o., member, penis; testicle, scrotum; vulva, vagina, uterus, ovary, Fallopian tubes; seed, pollen; seminal fluid, sperm, spermatozoa; phallus, phallic emblem, lingam; yoni.

Adj. *productive*, creative, inventive; shaping, constructive, architectonic 331 adj. *structural*; manufacturing, industrial 243 adj. *formative*; genesial, genesiological; philoprogenitive, fertile, proliferating, spawning, teeming 171 adj. *prolific*; potent, genial, genetic, germinal, seminal 171 adj. *generative*; polliniferous, pollinigerous; pregnant, enceinte; breeding, broody; expecting, carrying, gravid, heavy with, big w., fraught w.; with child, with young, in the family way; parturient, brought to bed of, in the straw, obstetric, obstetrical 658 adj. *medical*; puerperal, puerperous; thelytokous, arrenotokous; viviparous, oviparous, autogenous, abiogenetic; parthenogenetic; genital, vulvar, vaginal, phallic, priapic.

produced, made, created, creaturely; artificial, cultivated; manufactured, processed; hand-made, done by hand; untouched by hand, machine-made, mass-produced; multiplied; begotten 360 adj. *born*; fathered, sired, dammed; bred, hatched; sown, grown; thought of, invented.

Vb. *produce*, create, originate, make; invent 484 vb. *discover*; think up, conceive 513 vb. *imagine*; operate 676 vb. *do*; frame, form, shape 243 vb. *efform*; loom 222 vb. *weave*; forge, chisel, carve, sculpt, cast; coin 797 vb. *mint*; manufacture, fabricate, prefabricate, process, machine; mass-produce, churn out, multiply; construct, build, upbuild, raise, rear, erect, set up, run up 310 vb. *elevate*; put together, assemble, compose 45 vb. *join*; mine 304 vb. *extract*; establish, found, constitute, institute 68 vb. *initiate*; organize, get up 62 vb. *arrange*; engineer, contrive 623 vb. *plan*; perform, implement, execute, achieve, accomplish 725 vb. *carry out*; bring about, yield results, effect 156 vb. *cause*; unfold, develop 316 vb. *evolve*; breed, hatch, rear 369 vb. *breed stock*; sow, grow, farm 370 vb. *cultivate*; bring up, educate 534 vb. *train*.

reproduce itself, yield, give increase, flower, seed, sprout, blossom, bud, bloom, be out; burgeon 197 vb. *expand*; fruit, bear fruit, fructify 669 vb. *mature*; multiply, breed,

hatch, teem, spawn, spat, pullulate 104 vb. *be many*; carry, bear, bring forth, give birth; ean, yean, farrow, lamb, foal, drop, calve, pup, whelp, kitten, kindle, lay, seed; lie in, be brought to bed of; have offspring, have progeny; come to birth 360 vb. *be born.*

generate, evolve, produce; fecundate, cover, impregnate, inseminate, pollinate; copulate 45 vb. *unite with*; procreate, progenerate, propagate; beget, get, engender; father, sire; bring into being, bring into the world, usher into the w.; give life to, bring into existence, call into being; breed, hatch, incubate, raise, rear 369 vb. *breed stock*; raise from seed, grow 370 vb. *cultivate.*

See: 21, 36, 45, 56, 62, 68, 84, 104, 132, 147, 156, 157, 163, 166, 169, 171, 192, 197, 209, 222, 243, 304, 310, 316, 319, 331, 360, 364, 369, 370, 381, 413, 449, 451, 484, 513, 534, 539, 548, 551, 553, 554, 586, 587, 589, 622, 623, 630, 658, 669, 671, 672, 676, 694, 713, 725, 771, 795, 797, 990.

165 Destruction: non-production

N. *destruction*, unmaking, undoing 148 n. *reversion*; blotting out 550 n. *obliteration*; blowing out, snuffing o., annihilation, nullification 2 n. *extinction*; abolition, suppression, supersession 752 n. *abrogation*; suffocation, stifling, silencing 599 n. *silence*; subversion 221 n. *overturning*, 149 n. *revolution*; prostration, precipitation, overthrow 311 n. *depression*; levelling, razing, flattening 216 n. *horizontality*; dissolving, dissolution 51 n. *decomposition*; breaking up, tearing down, demolition, demolishment, slighting 655 n. *dilapidation*, 46 n. *disjunction*; disruption, diruption 46 n. *scission*; crushing, grinding, pulverization 332 n. *pulverulence*; incineration 381 n. *burning*; liquidation, elimination, extirpation, eradication, deracination, uprooting 300 n. *ejection*; wiping out, mopping up 725 n. *completion*; decimation, mass murder, genocide 362 n. *slaughter*; doing in, spifflication; destructiveness, mischief, persecution, iconoclasm, biblioclasm, vandalism; wrecking activities, sabotage 702 n. *hindrance*; fire-raising 381 n. *incendiarism. havoc*, scene of destruction, chaos 61 n.

confusion, turmoil; desolation, wilderness, scorched earth 172 n. *desert*; carnage, shambles, Belsen 362 n. *slaughter-house*; upheaval, cataclysm, inundation, storm 176 n. *violence*; devastation, laying waste, ravages; depredation, razzia, raid 788 n. *spoliation*; blitz 712 n. *bombardment*; holocaust, hecatomb 981 n. *oblation*; consumption, reckless expense 634 n. *waste.*

ruin, downfall, ruination, perdition, one's undoing; crushing blow, catastrophe 731 n. *adversity*; collapse, débâcle, landslide 149 n. *revolution*; breakdown, break-up, crack-up 728 n. *failure*; wreck, shipwreck, wreckage, wrack; sinking, loss, total l.; Waterloo, Caudine Forks, Sedan 728 n. *defeat*; knock-out blow, K.O. 279 n. *knock*; beginning of the end, road to ruin 655 n. *deterioration*; apocalypse, doom, crack of doom, knell, end 69 n. *finality*, 961 n. *condemnation*; ruins 127 n. *oldness.*

Adj. *destructive*, destroying, internecine, annihilating etc. vb.; root and branch 54 adj. *complete*; consuming, ruinous 634 adj. *wasteful*; sacrificial, costly 811 adj. *dear*; exhausting, crushing 684 adj. *fatiguing*; apocalyptic, cataclysmic, overwhelming 176 adj. *violent*; raging 176 adj. *furious*; merciless 906 adj. *pitiless*; mortal, suicidal, cut-throat 362 adj. *deadly*; subversive, subversionary 149 adj. *revolutionary*; incendiary, mischievous, pernicious 645 adj. *harmful*; poisonous 653 adj. *toxic.*

destroyed, undone, ruined, fallen; wiped out etc. vb.; crushed, ground; pulped, broken up; suppressed, squashed, quashed 752 adj. *abrogated*; lost, foundered, torpedoed, sunk, sunk without trace; done for, kaput, spifflicated; falling, perishing, in ruins 655 adj. *dilapidated*; doomed, marked out for destruction; in course of demolition, in the breaker's hands 69 adj. *ending.*

Vb. *destroy*, undo, unmake 148 vb. *revert*; abolish, annihilate, liquidate, exterminate 2 vb. *nullify*; devour, consume, eat up 301 vb. *eat*; swallow up, engulf 299 vb. *absorb*; swamp, overwhelm, drown 341 vb. *drench*; incinerate, burn up, gut 381 vb. *burn*; wreck, shipwreck, sink, torpedo, scupper 313 vb. *plunge*; end, put an end to 69 vb. *terminate*; do for, do in, put down, put away, do away with, make away w.,

get rid of 362vb. *kill*; poison 362vb. *murder*; decimate 105vb. *render few*; spare none, leave no survivor 362vb. *slaughter*, 906vb. *be pitiless*; remove, extirpate, eradicate, deracinate, uproot, root up 300vb. *eject*; wipe out, wipe off the map, expunge, efface, erase, delete, blot out, strike out, cancel 550vb. *obliterate*; annul, revoke 752vb. *abrogate*; dispel, scatter, dissipate 75vb. *disperse*; dissolve 337vb. *liquefy*; evaporate 338vb. *vaporize*; disrupt 46vb. *disjoin*; disorganize, confuse, confound 63vb. *derange*; destroy form, deface 244vb. *deform*; destroy an argument 479vb. *confute*; knock out, flatten out; spifflicate; put the kibosh on, make short work of, mop up; dish, cook one's goose, sabotage 702vb. *obstruct*; play hell with, play the deuce with 63vb. *bedevil*, 634vb. *waste*; ruin, be the ruin of, be one's undoing.

demolish, damage, slight 655vb. *impair*; dismantle, break down, knock d., pull d., tear d. 46vb. *disjoin*; level, raze, level to the ground, lay in the dust 216vb. *flatten*; throw down, prostrate, steam-roller, bulldoze 311vb. *fell*; blow down, blow away, carry a.; cut down, mow d. 204vb. *shorten*, 362vb. *slaughter*; knock over, kick o.; subvert, overthrow, overturn, overset, upset 221vb. *invert*; sap, sap the very foundations 163vb. *weaken*; undermine, mine, blow up, blow sky-high; bombard, bomb, blitz, blow to pieces 712vb. *fire at*; break up, smash up; smash, shatter, shiver, smash to smithereens 46vb. *break*; pulp, crush, grind 332vb. *pulverize*; crush to pieces, atomize, knock to atoms, grind to bits, make mincemeat of; rend, tear up, rend to pieces, tear to bits, tear to shreds, tear to rags, pull to pieces, pluck to p., pick to p. 46vb. *sunder*; shake to pieces 318vb. *agitate*; beat down, batter, ram 279vb. *strike*; strip, bare, unwall, unroof 229vb. *uncover*.

suppress, quench, blow out, put o., snuff o. 382vb. *extinguish*; nip in the bud, cut short, cut off 72vb. *discontinue*; quell, put down, stamp out, trample out, trample under foot, stamp on, sit on 735vb. *oppress*; squelch, squash 216vb. *flatten*; quash, revoke 752vb. *abrogate*; blanket, stifle, suffocate, burke; keep under, repress, cover 525vb. *conceal*;

drown, submerge, sink, scuttle, scupper, torpedo, sink without trace 313vb. *plunge*, 311vb. *depress*; kill, kill out.

lay waste, desolate, devastate, depopulate 300vb. *void*; despoil, depredate, raid 788vb. *rob*; damage, spoil, mar, ruin, ruinate 655vb. *impair*; ravage, deal destruction, run amok, make havoc, make a shambles, fill with carnage 176vb. *be violent*; scorch the earth, sow with salt 172vb. *sterilize*; lay in ruins 311vb. *abase*; lay in ashes 381vb. *burn*; waste with fire and sword 634vb. *waste*.

consume, devour, eat up, lick up, gobble up; swallow up, engulf 299vb. *absorb*; squander, run through, fling to the winds, play ducks and drakes 634vb. *waste*; throw to the dogs, cast before swine 675vb. *misuse*.

be destroyed, go west, go under, be lost 361vb. *perish*; sink, go down 313vb. *plunge*; be all over with, be all up with 69vb. *end*; fall, fall to the ground, totter to its fall, bite the dust 309vb. *tumble*; go on the rocks, break up, split, go to wreck, go to shivers, go to pieces, crumple up; fall into ruin, go to rack and ruin, crumble, crumble to dust 665vb. *deteriorate*; go to the wall, succumb; go to pot, go to the dogs, go to hell.

Adv. *destructively*, crushingly, with crushing effect, with a sledge hammer.

See: 2, 46, 51, 54, 61, 63, 69, 72, 75, 105, 127, 148, 149, 163, 172, 176, 204, 216, 221, 229, 244, 279, 299, 300, 301, 309, 311, 313, 318, 332, 337, 338, 341, 361, 362, 381, 382, 479, 525, 550, 559, 634, 645, 653, 655, 665, 675, 684, 702, 712, 725, 728, 731, 735, 752, 788, 811, 906, 961, 981.

166 Reproduction

N. *reproduction*, procreation, syngenesis, 164n. *production*; remaking, refashioning, reshaping, reconstruction; rediscovery 484n. *discovery*; redoing 106n. *repetition*; reduplication, mass-production 171n. *productiveness*; multiplication, duplication, printing 587n. *print*; renovation, renewal 656n. *restoration*; regeneration, revivification, resuscitation, reanimation 656n. *revival*; resurrection, resurgence; reappearance 106n. *recurrence*; atavism 5n. *heredity*; rein-

carnation, palingenesis, metempsychosis, transmigration of souls 124n. *future state*; new edition, reprint 589n. *edition*; copy 22n. *duplicate*; Phœnix, Alcestis.

Adj. *reproductive*, progenitive; reproduced, renewed, renewing; resurrectional, re- surrectionary; renascent, resurgent, re- appearing; Hydra-headed, Phœnix-like.

Vb. *reproduce*, remake, refashion, recoin, reconstruct, rebuild, refound, re-estab- lish, rediscover; duplicate 20vb. *copy*, 106 vb. *repeat*; take after, throw back to, inherit 18vb. *resemble*, 148vb. *revert*; renovate, renew 656vb. *restore*; regener- ate, revivify, resuscitate, reanimate 656 vb. *revive*; reappear, resurge 106vb. *reoccur*; resurrect, stir up the embers; mass-produce, multiply; print off, reel o. 587vb. *print*; crop up, spring up like mushrooms, breed 164vb. *reproduce itself*, 104vb. *be many*.

See: 5, 18, 20, 22, 104, 106, 124, 148, 164, 171, 484, 587, 589, 656.

167 Producer

N. *producer*, creator, maker, Nature; originator, inventor, discoverer, mover, instigator 612n. *motivator*; founder, establisher; generator, fertilizer, pollin- ator; inseminator, donor; begetter 169n. *parent*; creative worker, writer 589n. *author*; composer 413n. *musician*; painter, sculptor 556n. *artist*; deviser, designer 623n. *planner*; constructor, builder, architect, engineer; manufacturer, in- dustrialist 686n. *agent*; executive 676n. *doer*; labourer 686n. *worker*; artificer, craftsman 686n. *artisan*; farmer, grower, planter, cultivator, agriculturist, gar- dener 370n. *husbandman*; stock-farmer, raiser, cattle-r., sheep farmer 369n. *breeder*; miner, extractor; stage-pro- ducer 594n. *stage-manager*.

See: 169, 369, 370, 413, 556, 589, 594, 612, 623, 676, 686.

168 Destroyer

N. *destroyer*, remover, leveller, abolition- ist, iconclast, annihilationist, nihilist, anarchist 149n. *revolutionist*; wrecker, destructionist, arsonist, pyromaniac 381

n. *incendiarism*; spoiler, despoiler, rava- ger, raider 712n. *attacker*, 789n. *robber*; saboteur 702n. *hinderer*; defacer, eraser 550n. *obliteration*; killer, assassin 362n. *murderer*; executioner 963n. *punisher*; barbarian, Hun, Tartar, Vandal; time, hand of t., time's scythe 111n. *course of time*; angel of death 361n. *death*; destruc- tive agency, locust 947n. *glutton*; moth, worm, rust, erosion 51n. *decay*; corrosive, acid, cankerworm, mildew, blight, poison 659n. *bane*; earthquake, fire, flood; instrument of destruction, sword 723n. *weapon*; gunpowder, dynamite, blasting powder 723vb. *explosive*; torpedo 723n. *bomb*; fire-extinguisher 382n. *extin- guisher*; sponge, eraser.

See: 51, 111, 149, 361, 362, 381, 382, 550, 659, 702, 712, 723, 789, 947, 963.

169 Parentage

N. *parentage*, paternity, maternity; parent- hood, fatherhood, motherhood; loins, womb 156n. *source*; kinship 11n. *con- sanguinity*.

parent, father, sire, dad, daddy, papa, pop, governor, the old man; head of the family, paterfamilias; genitor, progenitor, pro- creator, begetter, author of one's exist- ence; grandfather, grandsire, grandad, great-grandfather 133n. *old man*; founder of the family, ancestor, forefather, for- bear, patriarch, predecessor 66n. *pre- cursor*; first parents, Adam and Eve 371n. *mankind*; foster-father, stepfather.

genealogy, family tree, lineage 11n. *family*; race history, pedigree, phylogamy, here- dity; line, blood-l., blood, strain; blue blood 868n. *nobility*; stock, stem, tribe, house, race, clan, sept 11n. *race*; descent, extraction, birth, ancestry 68n. *origin*; theogony.

maternity, motherhood; mother, dam, mamma, momma, ma, mummy, mum; grandmother, grandam, grandma, gran, granny; materfamilias, matron, matri- arch; beldam 133n. *old woman*; foster- mother, stepmother, mother-in-law.

Adj. *parental*, paternal; maternal, matron- ly; fatherly, fatherlike; motherly, step- motherly; family, linear, patrilineal, matrilinear; ancestral; hereditary;

patriarchal 127 adj. *immemorial*; racial, phyletic 11 adj. *ethnic*.

See: 11, 66, 68, 127, 133, 156, 371, 868.

170 Posterity

N. *posterity*, progeny, issue, offspring, young, little ones 132 n. *child*; breed 11 n. *race*; brood, seed, litter, farrow, spawn, spat 132 n. *youngling*; fruit of the womb, children, grandchildren 11 n. *family*; aftercomers, succession, heirs, inheritance, heritage; rising generation 130 n. *youth*.

descendant, son, daughter, pledge; child, bantling, chip of the old block, infant 132 n. *child*; scion, shoot, sprout, sprit 132 n. *young plant*; heir, heiress, heir of the body 776 n. *beneficiary*; branch, ramification, daughter-house, daughter-nation, colony; graft, offshoot, offset.

sonship, filiation, line, lineage, descent, straight d., male d.; indirect descent, collaterality, ramification; irregular descent, illegitimacy 954 n. *bastardy*; succession, heredity, heirship; primogeniture 119 n. *priority*.

Adj. *filial*, daughterly; descended, lineal; collateral; primogenital 119 n. *prior*; adopted, adoptive; step-; hereditary, inherited, Mendelian.

See: 11, 119, 130, 132, 776, 954.

171 Productiveness

N. *productiveness*, productivity, mass-production; booming economy 730 n. *prosperity*; overproductivity, superabundance, glut 637 n. *redundance*; high birthrate, fecundity, fertility, luxuriance, lushness, exuberance, richness, uberty 635 n. *plenty*; productive capacity, biotic potential; procreation, multiplication 164 n. *propagation*; fructification 669 n. *maturation*; fecundation, superfetation; fertilization, pollination, insemination, artificial i., A.I.D.; inventiveness, resourcefulness 513 n. *imagination*.

fertilizer, chemical f., manure, artificial m., fish-m., guano, fish-g., dung, mould, silt, compost 370 n. *agriculture*; semen, sperm, seed, roe, soft r., milt, milter; spermatic fluid.

abundance, wealth, riot, foison, harvest 32 n. *great quantity*; teeming womb, mother earth, rich soil; hotbed, nursery 68 n. *origin*; cornucopia, land flowing with milk and honey; second crop, aftergrowth, aftermath 67 n. *sequel*; warren, ant heap 104 n. *multitude*; mother goddess, Earth-mother; milch cow; rabbit.

Adj. *prolific*, fertile, fecund, feracious; teeming, multiparous, spawning 164 adj. *productive*; fruitful, fruitbearing, frugiferous, fructiferous; pregnant, heavy with, parturient; exuberant, lush, luxuriant, rich, fat, uberous 635 adj. *plenteous*; copious, streaming, pouring; paying 640 adj. *profitable*; creative, inventive, resourceful.

generative, procreant, procreative, philoprogenitive, potent; life-giving, spermatic, seminal, germinal; originative, all-creating, omnific; propagable.

Vb. *make fruitful*, make productive etc. adj.; plant, fertilize, water, irrigate, manure, guanize, dung, top-dress 370 vb. *cultivate*; impregnate, fecundate, inseminate, spermatize; procreate, produce 164 vb. *generate*.

be fruitful, — prolific etc. adj.; conceive, germinate, bud, blossom; bear, give birth, have children; teem, proliferate, pullulate, swarm, multiply, propagate 104 vb. *be many*; send up the birthrate; populate.

See: 32, 67, 68, 104, 164, 370, 513, 635, 637, 640, 669, 730.

172 Unproductiveness

N. *unproductivity*, unproductiveness, dearth, famine 636 n. *scarcity*; sterility, barrenness, infertility, infecundity; contraception, sterilization 161 n. *impotence*; dying race, falling birthrate, slow growth 37 vb. *decrease*; virginity 895 n. *celibacy*; change of life, menopause; unprofitableness, poor return, losing business 772 n. *loss*; unprofitability 641 n. *inutility*; stagnation, waste of time, maiden over 641 n. *lost labour*; slack market, idleness 679 n. *inactivity*.

desert, dryness, aridity 342 n. *dryness*; desolation, waste, barren w., unsown w., heath, barren h., wild, wilderness, howling w.; sand, dustbowl; salt flat 347 n. *marsh*;

icy waste 380n. *ice*; Sahara, Gobi; waste of waters 343n. *ocean*; desert island, solitude 883n. *seclusion.*

Adj. *unproductive*, dried up, exhausted, wasted, sparse, scarce 636adj. *insufficient*; waste, desert, desolate; poor, stony, shallow; unprolific, barren, infertile, sterile; unfruitful, acarpous, infecund, teemless; rootless, seedless, ungerminating, arid, unwatered, unirrigated 342adj. *dry*; fallow, stagnating 674adj. *disused*; unsown, unmanured, unploughed, untilled, uncultivated, unharvested; otiose 679adj. *inactive*; childless, issueless, without issue; celibate 895adj. *unwedded*; fruitless, unprofitable 641adj. *profitless*; inoperative, null and void, of no effect 161adj. *impotent*; ineffective 728adj. *unsuccessful*; addled, abortive 670adj. *unprepared.*

Vb. *be unproductive* — unprolific etc. adj.; rust, stagnate, lie fallow 679vb. *be inactive*; cease work 145vb. *cease*; bury one's talent 674vb. *not use*; hang fire, come to nothing, come to naught 728vb. *fail*; flash in the pan, abort 728vb. *miscarry*; have no issue, lower the birthrate. *sterilize*, castrate, geld 161vb. *unman*; sow with salt 165vb. *lay waste*; addle 51vb. *decompose*; disinfect 648vb. *purify.*

See: 37, 51, 145, 161,165,342, 343, 347, 380, 636, 641, 648, 670, 674, 679, 728, 772, 883, 895.

173 Agency

N. *agency*, operation, work, working, doing 676n. *action*; job, office 622n. *function*; exercise 673n. *use*; force, strain, stress, play, swing 160n. *power*; interaction, interworking 178n. *influence*; procuration, procurement 689n. *management*; service 628n. *instrumentality*; effectiveness, efficiency 156n. *causation*; quickening power 174n. *stimulation*; maintenance 218n. *support*; co-agency 706n. *co-operation*; homestroke, execution 725 n. *effectuation*; process, treatment, handling.

Adj. *operative*, effectual, efficient, efficacious 727adj. *successful*; drastic 735adj. *severe*; executive, operational, functional; acting, working, in action, in operation, in force, in play, in exercise, at work 676

adj. *doing*, 673adj. *used*; on foot, on the active list, up and doing 678adj. *active*; live, potent, of power 160adj. *dynamic*, 174adj. *vigorous*; practical, workable, applicable 642adj. *expedient*; serviceable 640adj. *useful*; worked upon, acted u., wrought u.

Vb. *operate*, be in action, be in play, play; act, work, go, run 676vb. *do*; start up, tick over, idle; serve, execute, perform 622vb. *function*; do its job 727vb. *be successful*; take effect 156vb. *cause*; have effect, act upon, bear u., work u., play u. 178vb. *influence*; put forth one's power, strike 678vb. *be active*; maintain, sustain 218vb. *support*; make operate, bring into play, wind up, turn on, switch on, flick *or* flip the switch; actuate, power, drive 265vb. *move*; process, treat; manipulate, handle, wield, brandish 378vb. *touch*, 673vb. *use*; stimulate, excite 174vb. *invigorate.*

See: 156, 160, 174, 178, 218, 265, 378, 622, 628, 640, 642, 673, 676, 678, 689, 706, 725, 727, 735.

174 Vigour: physical energy

N. *vigorousness*, lustiness, energy, vigour, life 678n. *activity*; dynamism, physical energy, dynamic e., pressure, force 160n. *energy*; intensity, high pressure 162n. *strength*, 32n. *greatness*; dash, élan, rush, impetuosity 680n. *haste*; exertion, effort 682n. *labour*; zest, zestfulness 824n. *joy*; liveliness, spirit, vim, fire, mettle, blood 855n. *courage*; ginger, fizz, verve, pep, drive, go; enterprise, initiative 672n. *undertaking*; vehemence 176n. *violence*; aggressiveness, thrust, push, kick, punch 712n. *attack*; grip, bite, teeth, backbone, gristle, spunk 599n. *resolution*; live wire, dynamo, dynamite, quicksilver; rocket, jet; display of energy 277n. *spurt*; show of force, demonstration 854n. *intimidation*. *stimulation*, activation, tonic effect; intensification, boost, stepping up, bumping up 36n. *increase*; excitement 821n. *excitation*; stir, bustle, splutter 678n. *activity*; perturbation 318n. *agitation*; ferment, fermentation, leaven; ebullience, ebullition 318n. *commotion*; froth, foam 355n. *bubble*; steam 381n. *heating.*

keenness, acritude, acridity, acrimony, mordancy, causticity, virulence 388n. *pungency*; poignancy, point, edge 256n. *sharpness*; zeal 597n. *willingness*.

stimulant, energizer, activator, booster; stimulus, fillip, shot, shot in the arm; crack of the whip, spur, prick, prod, goad, lash, 612n. *incentive*; hormone, restorative, tonic; bracer, pick-me-up, apéritif, appetizer 390n. *savouriness*; seasoning, spice 389n. *sauce*; drink, alcohol 301n. *liquor*; aphrodisiac, philtre, love p.; cantharides, Spanish fly; pep talk, rousing cheer 821n. *excitant*.

Adj. *vigorous*, energetic, 678adj. *active*; radio-active 362adj. *deadly*; forcible, forceful 162adj. *strong*; vehement 176 adj. *violent*; vivid, vibrant 160n. *dynamic*; high-pressure, intense, strenuous 678adj. *industrious*; enterprising, go-ahead 285 adj. *progressive*; aggressive, pushful, thrustful 712adj. *attacking*; keen, alacritous 597adj. *willing*; double-edged, double-shotted, double-distilled, potent 160adj. *powerful*; full of beans, full of punch, full of pep, peppy, zestful, lusty, mettlesome, brisk, live 819adj. *lively*; nippy, snappy; fizzy, heady, racy; tonic, bracing, rousing, invigorating, stimulating 821adj. *exciting*; drastic, stringent, harsh, punishing 735adj. *severe*; intensified, stepped up, gingered up, hepped up, souped up 656adj. *restored*; recruited 685 adj. *refreshed*; thriving, lush 171adj. *prolific*; hearty, full-blooded.

keen, acute, sharp, incisive, trenchant 571 adj. *forceful*; mordant, biting, pointed, sarcastic 851adj. *derisive*; virulent, corrosive, caustic, escharotic 388adj. *pungent*; acrid, acid, acidulous 393adj. *sour*.

Vb. *be vigorous*, thrive, have zest, enjoy life 650vb. *be healthy*; burst with energy, overflow with e., feel one's oats 162vb. *be strong*; show energy 678vb. *be active*; be up and doing 682vb. *exert oneself*; exert energy, drive, push 279vb. *impel*; bang, slam, wrench, cut right through 176vb. *force*; raise the pressure, get up steam, turn on the s., spurt 277vb. *accelerate*; be thorough, strike home 725 vb. *carry through*; strike hard, hammer, dint, dent 279vb. *strike*; show one's power, tell upon, make an impression 178 vb. *influence*, 821vb. *impress*; throw one's weight about 678vb. *meddle*; show fight, take the offensive 712vb. *attack*.

invigorate, energize, activate; intensify, double, redouble; wind up, step up, bump up, pep up, ginger up, boost 160vb. *strengthen*; rouse, kindle, enflame, stimulate, enliven, quicken 821 vb. *excite*; act like a tonic, hearten, animate 833vb. *cheer*; go to one's head, intoxicate 949vb. *inebriate*; freshen, recruit 685vb. *refresh*; give an edge to 256vb. *sharpen*; force, dung, manure, fertilize 370vb. *cultivate*.

Adv. *vigorously*, forcibly, with telling effect; zestfully, lustily.

See: 32, 36, 160, 162, 171, 176, 178, 256, 277, 279, 285, 301, 318, 355, 362, 370, 381, 388, 389, 390, 393, 571, 597, 599, 612, 650, 656, 672, 678, 680, 682, 685, 712, 725, 735, 819, 821, 824, 833, 851, 854, 855, 949.

175 Inertness

N. *inertness*, inertia 677n. *inaction*; lifelessness, languor, paralysis, torpor, torpidity 375n. *insensibility*; rest, vegetation, stagnation, passivity 266n. *quiescence*; dormancy 523n. *latency*; mental inertness, dullness, sloth 679n. *sluggishness*; immobility 602n. *obstinacy*; impassiveness, stolidity 823n. *inexcitability*; gutlessness 601n. *irresolution*; spent fires, extinct volcano.

Adj. *inert*, unactivated, unaroused, passive, dead 677adj. *non-acting*; lifeless, languid, torpid, numb 375adj. *insensible*; heavy, lumpish, sluggish 278adj. *slow*, 679adj. *inactive*; quiet, vegetating, stagnant 266 adj. *quiescent*; slack, low-pressure, untensed 734adj. *lax*; apathetic, neutral 860 adj. *indifferent*, 820adj. *impassive*; pacific, unwarlike, unaggressive 717adj. *peaceful*, 823adj. *inexcitable*; uninfluential 161adj. *powerless*; deactivated, unexerted, suspended, in abeyance 752adj. *abrogated*; smouldering, dormant 523adj. *latent*.

Vb. *be inert*, be inactive etc. adj.; slumber 679vb. *sleep*; hang fire, not catch; smoulder 523vb. *lurk*; lie, stagnate, vegetate 266vb. *be quiescent*.

Adv. *inactively* etc. adj.; at rest; in suspense, in abeyance, in reserve.

See: 161, 266, 278, 375, 523, 601, 602, 677, 679, 717, 734, 752, 820, 823, 860.

176 Violence

N. *violence*, vehemence, impetuosity 174n. *vigorousness*; destructiveness, vandalism 165n. *destruction*; boisterousness, turbulence, storminess 318n. *commotion*; bluster, uproar, riot, row, rumpus, furore 61n. *turmoil*; roughness, ungentleness, severe handling, extremities 735n. *severity*; force, hammer blows, high hand, coup de main, strong-arm work, outrage, terrorism 735n. *brute force*; barbarity, brutality, savagery, blood-lust 898n. *inhumanity*; malignity, mercilessness 906 n. *pitilessness*; exacerbation, exasperation 832n. *aggravation*; brainstorm, hysterics 822n. *excitable state*; fit, throes, paroxysm 318n. *spasm*; shock, clash 279 n. *collision*; wrench, twist, dislocation, torture 63n. *derangement*, 246n. *distortion.*

outbreak, outburst, ebullition, effervescence 318n. *agitation*; cataclysm, flood, tidal wave 350n. *wave*; convulsion, earthquake, quake, tremor 149n. *revolution*; eruption, volcano 383n. *furnace*; explosion, blow-up, burst, blast 165n. *destruction*; displosion, dissilience 46n. *disjunction*; detonation 400n. *loudness*; rush, onrush, outrush, sortie 712n. *attack*; gush, spurt, jet 350n. *stream*; torrent, rapids 350n. *current.*

storm, turmoil, ferment, war of the elements; weather, dirty w., rough w., inclement w., inclemency; tempest, hurricane 352n. *gale*; thunder, thunder and lightning, fulguration; rainstorm, cloudburst 350n. *rain*; hailstorm, snowstorm, blizzard 380 n. *wintriness*; sandstorm, duststorm 352 n. *gale*; magnetic storm; gale force.

violent creature, brute, beast, wild b.; dragon, tiger, wolf, she w., mad dog; demon, devil, hell-hound, hell-cat, fury 938n. *monster*; savage, barbarian, Vandal, iconoclast 168vb. *destroyer*; he-man, cave m. 372n. *male*; man of blood, assassin, executioner, butcher, Herod 362 n. *murderer*; berserk, homicidal maniac 504n. *madman*; rough, tough, rowdy; hooligan, bully, terror, holy t. 735n. *tyrant*; thunderer, fire-eater, bravo 877 n. *boaster*; fire-brand, incendiary 738n. *agitator*; revolutionary, anarchist, nihilist, terrorist 149n. *revolutionist*; hotspur, madcap 855n. *brave person*; virago, termagant, Amazon; spitfire,

scold 892n. *shrew*; Erinnys, Tisiphone, Megæra, Alecto 891n. *Fury.*

Adj. *violent*, vehement, forcible 162adj. *strong*; acute 256adj. *sharp*; unmitigated; excessive, outrageous, extravagant 32adj. *exorbitant*; rude, ungentle, abrupt, brusque, bluff 885adj. *discourteous*; extreme, severe, tyrannical, heavy-handed 735adj. *oppressive*; primitive, barbarous, savage, brutal, bloody 898adj. *cruel*; hot-blooded 892adj. *irascible*; aggressive, bellicose 718 adj. *warlike*; rampant, charging 712adj. *attacking*; struggling, kicking, thrashing about 61adj. *disorderly*; rough, boisterous, wild, raging, blustery, blustrous, tempestuous, stormy 352adj. *windy*; drenching, torrential 350adj. *rainy*; uproarious, obstreperous 400adj. *loud*; rowdy, turbulent, tumultuous, tumultuary 738adj. *riotous*; incendiary, anarchistic, nihilistic 149adj. *revolutionary*; intemperate, immoderate, unbridled; ungovernable, unruly, uncontrollable 738adj. *disobedient*; unrepressed, unquelled, irrepressible. 744adj. *independent*; unextinguished, inextinguishable, quenchless, unquenched 174adj. *vigorous*; ebullient, hot, red-hot, inflamed 381adj. *heated*; inflammatory, scorching, flaming 379adj. *fiery*; eruptive, cataclysmic, overwhelming, volcanic, seismic 165adj. *destructive*; detonating, explosive, bursting; convulsive, spasmodic 318adj. *agitated*; full of violence, disturbed, troublous, stirring 61 adj. *orderless.*

furious, boiling, on the boil, towering; infuriate, maddened 891adj. *angry*; impetuous, rampant, gnashing; roaring, howling; headstrong 680adj. *hasty*; desperate 857adj. *rash*; savage, tameless, wild; blustering, threatening, cursing 899adj. *maledicent*; vicious, fierce, ferocious 898adj. *cruel*; blood-thirsty, ravening, berserk 362adj. *murderous*; waspish, tigerish; frantic, hysterical, in hysterics 503adj. *frenzied.*

Vb. *be violent*, break bounds, run wild, run riot, run amuck; tear, rush, rush about, rush headlong, rush head foremost 277 vb. *move fast*; surge forward, mob 712vb. *charge*; break the peace, raise a storm, riot, make a riot, kick up a row, kick up a fuss, kick up a dust 61vb. *rampage*; resort to violence, take to arms 718vb. *go to war*, 738vb. *revolt*; see red, go

berserk 891 vb. *be angry*; storm, rage, roar, bluster, come in like a lion 352 vb. *blow*; ferment, foam, fume, run high, boil over 318 vb. *effervesce*; burst its banks, flood, overwhelm 350 vb. *flow*; explode, go off, blow up, detonate, burst, fly, flash, flare; let fly, let off, fulminate; erupt, break out, fly o., burst o.; struggle, strain, scratch, bite, kick, lash out 715 vb. *resist*; savage, maul 655 vb. *wound*; bear down, bear hard on, ride roughshod, tyrannize, out-Herod Herod 735 vb. *oppress*; spread like wildfire, overrun 297 vb. *irrupt*, 165 vb. *lay waste.*

force, use f., smash 46 vb. *break*; tear, rend 46 vb. *sunder*; bruise, crush 332 vb. *pulverize*; convulse, blow up 165 vb. *demolish*; strain, wrench, pull, dislocate; torture, twist, warp, deform 246 vb. *distort*; force open, prize o., pry o., jimmy 263 vb. *open*; blow open, burst o.; shock, shake 318 vb. *agitate*; do violence to, abuse 675 vb. *misuse*; violate, ravish, rape 951 vb. *debauch.*

make violent, stir, quicken, stimulate 821 vb. *excite*; urge, goad, lash, whip 612 vb. *incite*; poke, stoke, stir up, enflame 381 vb. *kindle*; add fuel to the flame, blow the embers 381 vb. *heat*; foment, exacerbate, exasperate 832 vb. *aggravate*; whet 256 vb. *sharpen*; irritate, infuriate, lash into fury, fan into f. 891 vb. *enrage*; madden 503 vb. *make mad.*

Adv. *violently*, forcibly, by storm, by force, by main force, amain; with might and main; tooth and nail, hammer and tongs, vi et armis, at the sword's point, at the point of the bayonet; tyrannously, with a high hand; at one fell swoop, through thick and thin, in desperation, with a vengeance; precipitately, headlong, head foremost, head first; like a bull at a gate, like Gaderene swine.

See: 32, 46, 61, 63, 149, 162, 165, 168, 174, 246, 256, 263, 277, 279, 297, 318, 332, 350, 352, 362, 372, 379, 380, 381, 383, 400, 503, 504, 612, 655, 675, 680, 712, 715, 718, 735, 738, 744, 821, 822, 832, 855, 857, 877, 885, 891, 892, 898, 899, 906, 938, 951.

177 Moderation

N. *moderation*, non-violence, gentleness 736 n. *lenity*; harmlessness, innocuous-ness 935 n. *innocence*; moderateness, reasonableness, measure, golden mean 732 n. *mediocrity*; temperateness, restraint, self-control 942 n. *temperance*; soberness 948 n. *sobriety*, 874 n. *modesty*; impassivity, mental calmness 823 n. *inexcitability*; impartiality, neutrality 625 vb. *mid-course*; correction, adjustment, modulation; mutual concession 770 n. *compromise*; mitigation 831 n. *relief*; relaxation, remission 734 n. *laxity*; easing, alleviation, mollification; appeasement, assuagement, détente 719 n. *pacification*; tranquillization, sedation; quiet, calm, dead c. 266 n. *quietude*; control, check 747 n. *restraint.*

moderator, palliative, stopgap, solvent 658 n. *remedy*; lenitive, alleviative, demulcent 658 n. *balm*; rose water, soothing syrup, milk, oil on troubled waters; calmative, sedative, tranquillizer, nightcap, bromide, barbiturate 679 n. *soporific*; anodyne, opiate, poppy, opium, laudanum 375 n. *anæsthetic*; wet blanket, damper 613 n. *dissuasion*; cooler, cold water, cold shower 382 n. *extinguisher*; brake 747 n. *restraint*; neutralizer; antaphrodisiac 658 n. *antidote*; cushion, shock-absorber 327 n. *softness*; mollifier, peacemaker, pacificator 720 n. *mediator*; controller, restraining hand, rein.

Adj. *moderate*, unextreme, non-violent, reasonable, judicious 480 n. *judicial*; tame, gentle, gentle as a lamb, harmless, mild, mild as milk 736 adj. *lenient*; milk and water, innocuous 935 adj. *innocent*, 163 adj. *weak*; measured, restricted, limited 747 adj. *restrained*; chastened, subdued, self-controlled, tempered 942 adj. *temperate*, 948 adj. *sober*; cool, calm 823 adj. *inexcitable*; still, quiet, untroubled 266 adj. *tranquil*; peaceful, peaceable, pacific 717 adj. *peaceful*; leftish, pink, non-extreme 625 adj. *neutral*, 860 adj. *indifferent.*

lenitive, unexciting, unirritating, abirritant 658 adj. *remedial*; alleviative, assuaging, pain-killing, anodyne, calmative, sedative, hypnotic, narcotic 679 adj. *somnific*; smooth 327 adj. *soft*; soothing, bland, demulcent; emollient; oily 334 adj. *lubricated*; comforting 685 adj. *refreshing*; disarming 719 adj. *pacificatory.*

Vb. *be moderate,* — gentle etc. adj.; hold a mean 625 vb. *be half-way*, 732 vb. *be*

middling; keep within bounds, keep within compass 942vb. *be temperate*; sober down, settle 266vb. *be quiescent*; disarm, keep the peace 717vb. *be at peace*; remit, relent 905vb. *show mercy*; show consideration, not press 736vb. *be lenient*; not resist, go quietly, go out like a lamb; shorten sail 278vb. *decelerate.*

moderate, mitigate, temper, attemper, contemper; correct 24vb. *adjust*; tame, check, curb, control, govern, limit, keep within limits 747vb. *restrain*; abate, lessen, diminish, slacken 37vb. *bate*; palliate, extenuate, qualify 163vb. *weaken*; obtund, take the edge off, slake, sheathe the sword 257vb. *blunt*; break the fall, cushion 218 vb. *support*; moderate language, tone down, chasten, blue-pencil, euphemize 648vb. *purify*; sober, sober down, dampen, damp, cool, chill, throw cold water on 382vb. *refrigerate*, 613vb. *dissuade*; reduce the temperature, bank down the fires; blanket, smother, subdue, quell 382vb. *extinguish.*

assuage, ease, pour balm, mollify, lenify 327vb. *soften*; alleviate, lighten 831vb. *relieve*; deactivate, take the sting out 182 vb. *counteract*; allay, lay, deaden 375vb. *render insensible*; soothe, calm, compose, tranquillize, still, quiet, hush, lull, rock, cradle, rock to sleep 266vb. *bring to rest*; dulcify 392vb. *sweeten*; disarm, appease, smooth over, pour oil on the troubled waters 719vb. *pacify*; assuage one's thirst, slake 301vb. *drink.*

Adv. *moderately*, within bounds, within limits, within compass, within reason; at half speed, under easy sail; so-so, averagely; gingerly, half-heartedly, nervously.

See: 24, 37, 163, 182, 218, 257, 266, 278, 301, 327, 334, 375, 382, 392, 480, 613, 625, 648, 658, 679, 685, 717, 719, 720, 732, 734, 736, 747, 770, 823, 831, 860, 874, 905, 935, 942, 948.

178 Influence

N. *influence*, capability, power, potentiality 160n. *ability*; prevalence, predominance 34n. *superiority*; mightiness, overmightiness, magnitude 32n. *greatness*, 638n. *importance*; position of influence,

vantage ground, footing, hold, grip; leverage, play 744n. *scope*; purchase, fulcrum 218n. *pivot*; physical influence, weight, heft, pressure, gravitation 322n. *gravity*; pull, drag, magnetism 291n. *attraction*; counter-attraction 292n. *repulsion*, 182n. *counteraction*; thrust, drive 287n. *propulsion*; impact 279n. *impulse*; leaven, contagion, infection; atavism, telegony 5n. *heredity*; occult influence, mana, magic, spell 983n. *sorcery*; stars, heavens, destiny 596n. *fate*; fascination, hypnotism, mesmerism; malign influence, curse, ruin 659n. *bane*; emotion, impulse, impression, feeling 817 n. *affections*; suasion, persuasion, insinuation, suggestion, impulsion, inspiration 612n. *motive*; personality, leadership, credit, repute 866n. *prestige*; hegemony, ascendancy, domination, tyranny 733n. *authority*; sway, control, dominance, reign 733n. *governance*; factor, contributing f., vital role, leading part 156n. *cause*; indirect influence, patronage, interest, favour, pull, friend at court, wire-pulling; strings, wires, lever 630n. *tool*; secret influence, hidden hand, power behind the throne, Grey Eminence 523n. *latency*; manipulator, wire-puller, mover, manœuvrer 612n. *motivator*; man of influence, uncrowned king, big wheel, a host in himself 638n. *bigwig*; powers that be, the Establishment 733n. *government*; atmosphere, climate.

Adj. *influential*, dominant, predominant, prevalent, prevailing 34adj. *supreme*; in power, ruling, regnant, reigning, commanding, listened to, obeyed; recognized, with authority, of a., in a. 733adj. *authoritative*; rising, ascendant, in the ascendant 36adj. *increasing*; strong, potent, mighty, overmighty 32adj. *great*, 160 adj. *powerful*; leading, guiding, hegemonical 689adj. *directing*; activating, inspiring, encouraging; active in, busy, meddling 678adj. *active*; contributing, effective 156adj. *causal*; weighty, key, momentous, decisive, world-shattering, earth-shaking 638adj. *important*; telling, moving, emotional 821adj. *impressive*; appealing, attractive 291adj. *attracting*; gripping, fascinating; irresistible, hypnotic, mesmeric 740adj. *compelling*; persuasive, suggestive, insinuating, tempting 612adj. *inducive*; habit-forming;

educative, instructive 534 adj. *educational*; spreading, catching, contagious 653 adj. *infectious*; pervasive 189 adj. *ubiquitous*.

Vb. *influence*, have i., command i., have a pull, have drag, carry weight, cut ice, have a hold on, have in one's power; have the ear of, be listened to, be recognized, be obeyed 737 vb. *command*; dominate, tower over, bestride; lead by the nose, have under one's thumb, wind round one's little finger, wear the breeches 34 vb. *be superior*; exert influence, make oneself felt, assert oneself; pull one's weight, throw one's weight into the scale, weigh in; put pressure on, lobby, pull strings, pull the s. 612 vb. *motivate*; make one's voice heard, gain a hearing 455 vb. *attract notice*; affect, tell, turn the scale; bear upon, work u., tell u. 821 vb. *impress*; urge, prompt, tempt, incite, inspire, work upon, dispose, persuade, prevail upon, convince, carry with one 612 vb. *induce*; force 740 vb. *compel*; sway, tyrannize; colour, prejudice 481 vb. *bias*; appeal, allure, fascinate, hypnotize, mesmerize 291 vb. *attract*; disgust, put off 292 vb. *repel*; make, be the making of 654 vb. *make better*; make or mar, change 147 vb. *transform*; infect, leaven, colour 143 vb. *modify*; contaminate, mar 655 vb. *impair*; actuate, work 173 vb. *operate*; play a part, play a leading p., guide 689 vb. *direct*; lead the dance, set the fashion, be the model for 23 vb. *be example*.

prevail, establish one's influence, outweigh, overweigh, override, overbear, turn the scale 34 vb. *predominate*; overawe, overcome, subdue, subjugate; gain head, gain the upper hand, gain full play, master 727 vb. *overmaster*; control, rule, lead 733 vb. *dominate*; take a hold on, take a grip on, hold 778 vb. *retain*; gain a footing, take root, take hold, strike root in, settle 144 vb. *stay*; permeate, run through, colour 189 vb. *pervade*; catch on, spread, rage, be rife, spread like wildfire.

Adv. *influentially*, to good effect, with telling e.; within one's orbit.

See: 5, 23, 32, 34, 36, 143, 144, 147, 156, 160, 173, 182, 189, 218, 279, 287, 291, 292, 322, 455, 481, 523, 534, 596, 612, 630, 638, 653, 654, 655, 659, 678, 689, 727, 733, 737, 740, 744, 745, 778, 817, 821, 866, 983.

179 Tendency

N. *tendency*, trend, tenor; tempo, set, drift 281 n. *direction*; course, stream, main current, main stream, zeitgeist, spirit of the times, spirit of the age; conatus, nisus; affinity 291 n. *attraction*; polarity 240 n. *contraposition*; aptness 24 n. *fitness*; gift, instinct for 694 n. *aptitude*; proneness, proclivity, propensity, predisposition, readiness, inclination, penchant, liking, leaning, bias, prejudice; weakness 180 n. *liability*; cast, bent, turn, grain; a strain of 43 n. *tincture*; vein, humour, mood; tone, quality, nature, characteristic 5 n. *temperament*; special gift, idiosyncrasy 80 n. *speciality*.

Adj. *tending*, trending, conducive, leading to, pointing to; tendentious, working towards, aiming at 617 adj. *intending*; in a fair way to, calculated to 471 adj. *probable*; centrifugal 620 adj. *avoiding*; subservient 180 adj. *liable*; ready to, about to 669 adj. *prepared*.

Vb. *tend*, trend, verge, lean, incline; set in, set, set towards, gravitate t. 289 vb. *approach*; affect, dispose, carry, bias, bend to, warp, turn 178 vb. *influence*; point to, lead to 156 vb. *conduce*; bid fair to, be calculated to 471 adj. *be likely*; redound to, contribute to 285 vb. *promote*.

See: 5, 24, 43, 80, 156, 178, 180, 240, 281, 285, 289, 291, 471, 617, 620, 669, 694.

180 Liability

N. *liability*, liableness, weakness 179 n. *trend*; exposure 661 n. *vulnerability*; susceptibility, susceptivity, impressibility 374 n. *sensibility*; potentiality 469 n. *possibility*; likelihood 471 n. *probability*; obligation, responsibility, accountability, amenability 917 n. *duty*.

Adj. *liable*, apt to 179 adj. *tending*; subject to, obnoxious to, the prey of, at the mercy of 745 adj. *subject*; open to, exposed to, in danger of 661 adj. *vulnerable*; dependent on, contingent 157 adj. *caused*; incident to, incidental; possible, on the cards, within the range of 469 adj. *possible*; incurring, unexempt from; susceptible 819 adj. *impressible*; answerable, responsible, amenable, accountable 917 adj. *dutied*.

Vb. *be liable*, — subject to etc. adj.; be responsible, answer for 917 vb. *incur a*

duty; incur, lay oneself open to, run the chance of, stand the chance of; stand to, stand to gain, stand to lose; expose oneself 661 vb. *be in danger*; lie under 745 vb. *be subject*; open a door to 156 vb. *conduce.*

See: 156, 157, 179, 374, 469, 471, 661, 745, 819, 917.

181 Concurrence: combination of causes

N. *concurrence*, combined operation, joint effort, collaboration, coagency, synergy, synergism 706 n. *co-operation*; coincidence, consilience 83 n. *conformity*; concord, harmony 24 n. *agreement*; compliance 758 n. *consent*; concurrent opinion, consensus 488 n. *assent*; acquiescence, non-resistance 721 n. *submission*; concert, joint planning, collusion, conspiracy 623 n. *plot*; league, alliance, partnership 706 n. *association*; conjunction, union, liaison 45 n. *junction.*

Adj. *concurrent*, concurring etc. vb.; coagent, synergic 706 adj. *co-operative*; coincident, concomitant, parallel 89 adj. *accompanying*; in alliance, banded together 708 adj. *corporate*; of one mind, at one with 488 adj. *assenting*; joint, combined 45 adj. *conjunct*; conforming 83 adj. *conformable*; colluding, conniving, abetting, contributing, involved 703 adj. *aiding.*

Vb. *concur*, acquiesce 488 vb. *assent*; collude, connive, conspire 623 vb. *plot*; agree, harmonize 24 vb. *accord*; hang together, pull t. 706 vb. *co-operate*; contribute, help, aid, abet, serve 703 vb. *minister to*; promote, subserve 156 vb. *conduce*; go with, go along w., go hand in hand w., keep pace w., keep abreast of, run parallel to 89 vb. *accompany*; unite, stand together 48 vb. *cohere.*

Adv. *concurrently*, with one consent, with one accord, in harmony, hand in hand, hand in glove.

See: 24, 45, 48, 83, 89, 156, 488, 623, 703, 706, 708, 721, 758.

182 Counteraction

N. *counteraction*, opposing causes, action and reaction; polarity 240 n. *contraposition*; antagonism, antipathy, clash, conflict, mutual c. 14 n. *contrariety*, 279 n. *collision*; return action, reaction, retroaction, repercussion, back-fire, back kick

back-lash 280 n. *recoil*; renitency, recalcitrance, kicking back 715 vb. *resistance*, 704 n. *opposition*; inertia, vis inertiæ, friction, drag, check 702 n. *hindrance*; interference, counterpressure, repression, suppression 747 n. *restraint*; intolerance, persecution 735 n. *severity*; neutralization, deactivation 177 n. *moderation*; nullification, cancellation 165 n. *destruction*; cross-current, counter-sea, head-wind 702 n. *obstacle*; counter-spell, counter-charm, counter-irritant, neutralizer 658 n. *antidote*; counter-balance, counterweight 31 n. *offset*; counterblast, counter-move 688 n. *tactics*; defensive measures, deterrent 713 n. *defence*; prevention, preventive, preventative, inhibitor 757 n. *prohibition.*

Adj. *counteracting*, counter, counteractive; conflicting 14 adj. *contrary*; antipathetic, antagonistic, hostile 881 adj. *inimical*; resistant, recalcitrant, renitent 715 adj. *resisting*; reactionary, retroactionary 280 adj. *recoiling*; frictional, retarding, checking 747 adj. *restraining*; preventive, preventative; antidotal, corrective 658 adj. *remedial*; balancing, off-setting 31 adj. *compensatory.*

Vb. *counteract*, counter, run c., cross, traverse, work against, go a., militate a.; not conduce to 702 vb. *hinder*; react 280 vb. *recoil*; agitate against, persecute 881 vb. *be inimical*; resist, withstand, defend oneself 704 vb. *oppose*; antagonize, conflict with 14 vb. *be contrary*; clash, jostle 279 vb. *collide*; interfere 678 vb. *meddle*; countervail, cancel out, counterpoise, overpoise 31 vb. *set off*; repress 165 vb. *suppress*; undo, cancel 752 vb. *abrogate*; neutralize, deactivate, demagnetize, degauss; find a remedy, cure 658 vb. *remedy*; recover 656 vb. *retrieve*; prevent, inhibit 757 vb. *prohibit.*

Adv. *although*, in spite of, despite, notwithstanding; against, contrary to 704 adv. *in opposition.*

See: 14, 31, 165, 177, 240, 279, 280, 656, 658, 678, 688, 702, 704, 713, 715, 735, 747, 752, 757, 881.

183 Space: indefinite space

N. *space*, expanse, expansion; extension, spatial e., extent, superficial e., surface,

area; volume, cubic content; continuum, stretch 71 n. *continuity*; empty space 190 n. *emptiness*; depth of space, abyss 211 n. *depth*; unlimited space, infinite s. 107 n. *infinity*; sky, outer space, interstellar s. 321 n. *heavens*; world, wide w., length and breadth of the land; geographical space, terrain, open space, open country; lung, green belt, wide horizons, wide open spaces 348 n. *plain*; upland, moorland, campagna, veld, prairie, steppe 348 n. *grassland*; outback, back blocks 184 n. *region*; wild, wilderness, waste 172 n. *desert*; everywhere, ubiquity 189 n. *presence.*

measure, proportions, dimension 203 n. *length*, 205 n. *breadth*, 209 n. *height*, 211 n. *depth*; area, surface a.; square measure, acreage, acres, rods, poles and perches; square inch, square yard, hectare, hide; volume, cubic content 195 n. *size.*

range, reach, carry, compass, coverage; stretch, grasp; radius, latitude, amplitude; sweep, spread, ramification; play, swing 744 n. *scope*; sphere, field, arena 184 n. *region*; purview, prospect 438 n. *view*; perspective, focal distance 199 n. *distance*; telescopic range, light-grasp; magnifying power 417 n. *optics.*

room, space, accommodation; capacity, internal c., roomage, storage, storage space 632 n. *storage*; seating capacity, seating; standing room, breathing r.; margin, free space, clearance, windage; room overhead, headroom, headway; sea room, seaway, leeway; opening, way 263 n. *open space*; living space, Lebensraum, development area; elbow room, room to swing a cat in.

Adj. *spatial*, space; spatio-temporal; volumetric, cubic, three-dimensional; flat, superficial, two-dimensional.

spacious 32 adj. *extensive*; expansive, roomy; ample, vast, capacious, broad, deep, wide; amplitudinous, voluminous, baggy 195 adj. *large*; broad-based 79 adj. *general*; far-reaching, widespread, world-wide, global, world 52 adj. *whole*; uncircumscribed, boundless, spaceless 107 adj. *infinite*; shoreless, trackless, pathless; extending, spreading, branching, ramified.

Vb. *extend*, spread, spread out, range, cover; span, straddle, bestride 226 vb. *overlie*; extend to, reach to 202 vb. *be contiguous*; branch, ramify.

Adv. *widely*, capaciously, voluminously; extensively, everywhere, wherever; far and near, far and wide, all over, all the world over, throughout the world; under the sun, on the face of the earth, in every quarter, in all quarters, in all lands; from end to end, from pole to pole, from coast to coast, from China to Peru, from Dan to Beersheba, from Land's End to John o' Groats, from Maine to California 54 adv. *throughout*; from all the points of the compass; to the four winds, to the uttermost parts of the earth; from here to nowhere, from here to the back of beyond; at every turn, here, there and everywhere, right and left.

See: 32, 52, 54, 71, 79, 107, 172, 184, 189, 190, 195, 199, 203, 205, 209, 211, 226, 263, 321, 348, 417, 438, 632, 744.

184 Region: definite space

N. *region*, locality, parts 185 n. *place*; sphere, orb, hemisphere; zone, belt; latitude, parallel, meridian; clime, climate; tract, terrain, country, ground, soil 344 n. *land*; geographical unit, island, peninsula, continent, land-mass; sea 343 n. *ocean*; compass, circumference, circle, circuit 233 n. *outline*; boundaries, bound, shore, confine, march 236 n. *limit*; pale, precincts, enclosure, close, enclave, exclave, salient 235 n. *inclosure*; corridor 624 n. *access*; area, field, theatre 724 n. *arena*; exclusive area, charmed circle. See *territory.*

territory, sphere, zone; beat, pitch, ground; lot, holding, claim 235 n. *inclosure*; grounds, park, allodium 777 n. *estate*; national boundaries, domain, territorial waters, twelve-mile limit; continental shelf, air-space; possession, dependency, dominion; colony, settlement; motherland, fatherland, homeland 192 n. *abode*; commonwealth, republic, kingdom, realm, state, empire 733 n. *polity*; principality, duchy, arch-d., grand-d., palatinate; debatable territory, no-man's land, Tom Tiddler's ground 774 n. *nonownership.*

district, purlieus, haunt 187 n. *locality*; subregion, quarter, division, 53 n. *subdivision*; state, province, county, shire, bailiwick, riding, lathe, wapentake, hundred, soke,

tithing; diocese, bishopric, archbishopric, parish, ward, constituency; borough, township, urban district, rural d., metropolitan area; village, town, city, conurbation 192 n. *abode*; zilla, taluk, canton, volost, department, arrondissement, commune; deme, nome, nomarchy, toparchy; suburb, suburbia, down town, up t., West End, East End, City; clubland, theatreland, dockland; Highlands, Lowlands, Wild West; outland, back blocks; hinterland, heart-land.

Adj. *regional*, territorial, continental, peninsular, insular; national, state; subdivisional, local, municipal, parochial, provincial, red-brick; suburban, urban, rural, up-country; district, town, country.

See: 53, 185, 187, 192, 233, 235, 236, 343, 344, 624, 724, 733, 774, 777.

185 Place: limited space

N. *place*, emplacement, site, location, position 186 n. *situation*; station, sub-station; quarter, locality 184 n. *district*; assigned place, pitch, beat, billet, socket, groove; centre, meeting-place 76 n. *focus*; birthplace, dwelling p., fireside 192 n. *home*; place of residence, address, habitat 187 n. *location*; premises, building, mansion 192 n. *house*; spot, plot; point, dot, pinpoint; niche, nook, corner, hole, glory h., pigeon-hole, pocket 194 n. *compartment*; confine, bound, baseline, crease (cricket) 236 n. *limit*; confined place, prison, coffin, grave; precinct, bailey, garth, enclosure, paddock, compound, pen, close, quadrangle, square; yard, area, areaway, backyard, courtyard, court, base-c., fore-c., centre c. 235 n. *inclosure*; patio, atrium, hall; farmyard, home farm, field 371 n. *farm*; walk, sheeprun 369 n. *stockfarm*; highways and byways, ins and outs, every nook and corner.

Adv. *somewhere*, some place, wherever it may be, here and there, in various places, passim; locally 200 adv. *nigh*.

See: 76, 184, 186, 187, 192, 194, 200, 235, 236, 369, 371.

186 Situation

N. *situation*, position, setting; time and place, when and where; location, address, whereabouts; point, stage, milestone 27 n. *degree*; site, seat, emplacement, habitat, base 185 n. *place*; post, station; status, standing, ground, footing 7 n. *state*; standpoint, point of view 480 n. *estimate*; side, aspect 445 n. *appearance*; attitude, posture, pose 688 n. *conduct*; one's place, place in a book, reference, chapter and verse; topography, chorography, cosmography 321 n. *geography*; chart 551 n. *map*.

bearings, compass direction, latitude and longitude, declination, right ascension, northing, southing 281 n. *direction*; radio-location 187 n. *location*.

Adj. *situated*, situate, located at, living at, to be found at; settled, set; stationed, posted; occupying 187 adj. *located*; local, topical; topographical, geographical.

Vb. *be situate*, be situated, centre on; be found at, have one's address at, have one's seat in; have its centre in; be, lie, stand; be stationed, be posted; live, live at 192 vb. *dwell*; touch 200 vb. *be near*.

Adv. *in place*, in situ, in loco, here, there; in, on, over, under; hereabout, thereabout; whereabout; here and there, passim; in such and such surroundings, in such and such environs; at the sign of.

See: 7, 27, 185, 187, 192, 200, 281, 321, 445, 480, 551, 688.

187 Location

N. *location*, placing, placement, emplacement, collocation, disposition; posting, stationing; finding the place, locating, pinpointing; centering, localization 200 n. *nearness*; localization, domestication, naturalization, indenization; settling, colonization, population; settlement, lodgment, establishment, fixation, installation; putting down, deposition, putting back, reposition 62 n. *arrangement*; putting in 303 n. *insertion*; packing, stowage, loading, lading 632 n. *storage*.

locality, quarters, purlieus, environs, environment, surroundings, milieu, neighbourhood, parts 184 n. *district*; address, street, place of residence, habitat 192 n. *abode*; seat, site 185 n. *place*; meeting place, venue, haunt 76 n. *focus*.

station, seat, site, emplacement, position 186 n. *situation*; depot, base, military b.,

naval b., air b.; colony, settlement; anchorage, roadstead, mooring, mooring mast 662n. *refuge*; cantonment, lines, police l., civil l.; camp, encampment, bivouac, camp-site, temporary abode; hostel 192n. *abode*; halting place, lay-by, park, parking place 145n. *stopping place*.

Adj. *located*, placed etc.vb.; positioned, stationed, posted 186adj. *situated*; ensconced, embedded, embosomed 232adj. *circumscribed*; rooted, settled, domesticated 153adj. *fixed*; encamped, camping, lodged 192adj. *residing*; moored, anchored, at anchor 266adj. *quiescent*; vested in, in the hands of, in the possession of 773adj. *possessed*; reposed in, transferred to 780adj. *transferred*; well-placed, favourably situated.

Vb. *place*, collocate, assign a place 62vb. *arrange*; situate, position, site, locate; base, centre, localize; narrow down, pinpoint, pin down; find the place, put one's finger on; place right, aim well, hit, hit the mark 281vb. *aim*; put, lay, set, seat; station, post, park; install, ensconce, set up, establish, fix 153vb. *stabilize*; fix in, root, plant, implant, embed, graft 303vb. *insert*; bed, bed down, put to bed, tuck in, tuck up, cradle; accommodate, find a place for, find room for, lodge, house, quarter, billet; quarter upon, billet on; impose, saddle on; moor, tether, picket, anchor 47vb. *tie*; dock, berth 266vb. *bring to rest*; deposit, lay down, put d., set d.; stand, put up, erect 310vb. *elevate*; place with, transfer, bestow, invest 780vb. *convey*; array, deploy.

replace, put back, sheathe, put up (a sword), bring back, reinstate 656vb. *restore*; redeposit, reinvest, replant, reset.

stow, put away, put by; imburse, pocket, pouch, purse; pack, bale, store, lade, freight, put on board 193vb. *load*; fill, squeeze in, cram in 54vb. *make complete*.

place oneself, stand, take one's place, take one's stand, anchor, drop a., cast a., come to a. 266vb. *come to rest*; settle, strike root, take r., gain a footing, entrench, dig in 144vb. *stay*; perch, alight, sit on, sit, squat, park; pitch on, pitch one's tent, encamp, camp, bivouac, stop at, lodge, put up; hive, burrow; ensconce oneself, locate oneself, establish o., find a home; settle, colonize, populate, people 192vb.

dwell; indenizen, get naturalized, become a citizen.

See: 47, 54, 62, 76, 144, 145, 153, 184, 185, 186, 192, 193, 200, 232, 266, 281, 303, 310, 632, 656, 662, 773, 780.

188 Displacement

N. *displacement*, dislocation, derailment 63n. *derangement*; misplacement, wrong place, ectopia 84n. *abnormality*; shift, move 265n. *motion*; light-shift, Doppler effect; aberration, aberration of light, perturbation (astron.) 282n. *deviation*; translocation, transposition, trans-shipment, transfer 272n. *transference*; mutual transfer 151n. *interchange*; relief, supersession 150n. *substitution*; removal, taking away 304n. *extraction*; unloading, unpacking, unshipment, disencumbrance 831n. *relief*; ejectment, expulsion, ablegation 300n. *ejection*; weeding, eradication 300n. *voidance*; exile, banishment 883n. *seclusion*; refugee, displaced person, D.P. 268n. *wanderer*; fish out of water, square peg in a round hole 25n. *misfit*; unloader, remover, removal man.

Adj. *displaced* etc.vb.; removed, transported 272adj. *transferable*; aberrant 282adj. *deviating*; unplaced, unhoused, unharboured; unestablished, rootless, unsettled; roofless, houseless, homeless; out of a job, out of the picture, out of touch, out in the cold 57adj. *excluded*.

misplaced, ectopic 84adj. *abnormal*; out of one's element, like a fish out of water; out of place, inappropriate 10adj. *irrelevant*; mislaid, lost, missing 190adj. *absent*.

Vb. *displace*, disturb, disorientate, derail, dislocate; dislodge, unseat, unfix, unstick 46vb. *disjoin*; dispel, scatter, send flying 75vb. *disperse*; shift, remove, translate 265vb. *move*; cart away, transport 272vb. *transfer*; alter the position, change round; transpose, translocate 151vb. *interchange*; despatch, post 272vb. *send*; ablegate, relegate, banish, exile 300vb. *dismiss*; set aside, supersede 150vb. *substitute*, 752vb. *depose*; displant, disnest, eradicate, uproot 300vb. *eject*; discharge, unload, off-load, unship, tranship; clear away, rake, sweep, sweep up 648vb. *clean*; take away, take off, cart off;

lift, raise, uplift 310 vb. *elevate*; draw, draw out, pull o. 304 vb. *extract*.

misplace, mislay, lose, lose touch with, lose track of.

See: 10, 25, 46, 57, 63, 75, 84, 150, 151, 190, 265, 268, 272, 282, 300, 304, 310, 648, 752, 831, 883.

189 Presence

N. *presence*, being there, existence, whereness; being everywhere, ubiety, ubiquity, ubiquitariness, omnipresence; permeation, pervasion, diffusion; availability, bird in the hand; physical presence, bodily p., personal p.; attendance, personal a.; residence, occupancy, occupation, lodgement 773 n. *possession*; visit, descent, stay; nowness, present moment 121 n. *present time*; man on the spot; spectator, bystander 441 n. *onlookers*.

Adj. *on the spot*, present, existent, in being 1 adj. *existing*; occupying, in occupation; inhabiting, resident, resiant, residentiary, domiciled 192 adj. *residing*; attendant, waiting, still there, not gone, hanging on; ready, on tap, available, on the menu, on 669 vb. *prepared*; at home, at hand, within reach, on call, on sight; under one's nose, before one's eyes 443 adj. *well-seen*; looking on, standing by.

ubiquitous, ubiquitary, omnipresent, permeating, pervading, pervasive, diffused through.

Vb. *be present*, exist, be; take up space, occupy, hold 773 vb. *possess*; stand, lie 186 vb. *be situate*; look on, stand by, witness 441 vb. *watch*; resort to, frequent, haunt, meet one at every turn; stay, sojourn, summer, winter, revisit 882 vb. *visit*; attend, assist at, grace the occasion; make one at, make one of, answer one's name, answer the roll-call; occur 154 vb. *happen*; turn up, present oneself, announce o., send in one's card 295 vb. *arrive*; show one's face, put in an appearance, look in on; face, confront; present, introduce, bring in, produce 522 vb. *show*.

pervade, permeate, fill 54 vb. *make complete*; be diffused through, be disseminated, imbue, impregnate, soak, run through; overrun, swarm over, spread, meet one at every turn 297 vb. *infiltrate*; make one's presence felt 178 vb. *influence*.

Adv. *here*, there, where, everywhere, all over the place; in situ, in place, in front; aboard, on board, at home; on the spot; in presence of, before, under the eyes of, under the nose of, in the face of; personally, in person, in propria persona.

See: 1, 54, 121, 154, 178, 186, 192, 295, 297, 441, 443, 522, 669, 773, 882.

190 Absence: nullibiety

N. *absence*, non-presence, disappearing trick 446 n. *disappearance*; being nowhere, nullibiety, Utopia, inexistence 2 n. *non-existence*; being elsewhere, alibi; non-residence, living away; leave of absence, furlough; non-attendance, truancy, absenteeism 620 n. *avoidance*; absentee, truant 620 n. *avoider*; deprivation 772 vb. *loss*.

emptiness, bareness, empty space, void, vacuity, inanity, vacancy; nothing inside, hollowness, shell; vacuum, air-pocket; empties, dead men (empty bottles); blank cartridge, blank paper, clean sheet; virgin territory, no-man's land; waste, desolation 172 n. *desert*; vacant lot, building site 183 n. *room*.

nobody, no one, nobody present, nobody on earth; not a soul, not a cat, not a living thing; empty house, non-existent audience.

Adj. *absent*, not present, not found, unrepresented; away, not resident; gone from home, on tour, on location; out, not at home; gone, flown, disappeared 446 adj. *disappearing*; lacking, minus, to seek, wanting, missing, wanted; truant, absentee 667 adj. *escaped*; unavailable, unprocurable, off the menu, off 636 adj. *unprovided*; lost, nowhere to be found; inexistent 2 adj. *non-existent*; exempt from, spared, exempted; on leave, on furlough; omitted, left out 57 adj. *excluded*.

empty, vacant, vacuous, inane; void, devoid, bare; blank, clean; characterless, featureless; without content, hollow; vacant, unoccupied, uninhabited, untenanted, tenantless; unstaffed, crewless, unofficered, unmanned; depopulated; desert, deserted 621 adj. *relinquished*; unpeopled, unsettled, uncolonized; godforsaken, lonely; unhabitable, uninhabitable.

Vb. *be absent,* have no place in, take no part in; absent one's self, spare one's presence; stay away, keep away, keep out of the way, play truant 620vb. *avoid;* be missed, leave a gap; leave empty, evacuate, vacate; empty, exhaust 300vb. *void.*

go away, withdraw, leave, relieve of one's presence 296vb. *depart;* make oneself scarce, slip out, slip away, be off, retreat 296vb. *decamp,* 667vb. *escape;* vanish 446vb. *disappear;* move over, make room, vacate.

Adv. *without,* minus, sans; in default of, for want of; in vacuo.

not here, not there; neither here nor there; elsewhere, somewhere else; nowhere, no place; in one's absence, behind one's back.

See: 2, 57, 172, 183, 296, 300, 446, 620, 621, 636, 667, 772.

191 Inhabitant

N. *dweller,* inhabitant, habitant, denizen, indweller; sojourner, commorant, parasite; mainlander, Continental; insular, islander, isthmian; landsman, landlubber; mountaineer, hillman, hill-billy, dalesman, highlander, lowlander, plainsman; forester, woodman, backwoodsman; frontiersman, borderer, marcher; city-dweller, town-d., suburbanite; countryman, rustic, ruralist, villager; peasant 370 *husbandman;* steppedweller, desert-d., tent-d., bedouin; cave-dweller, troglodyte; slum-dweller 801n. *poor man.* See *native.*

resident, householder, goodman, family man; housewife, hausfrau, chatelaine, housekeeper; cottager, cottar, cottier, crofter; addressee, occupier, occupant, incumbent, residentiary 776n. *possession;* locum tenens 150n. *substitute;* tenant, renter, lessee, lease-holder; inmate, in-patient; indoor servant 742n. *domestic;* houseman 658n. *doctor;* garrison, crew 686n. *personnel;* lodger, boarder, roomer, paying guest, p.g.; guest, visitor, someone to stay; uninvited guest, cuckoo, squatter 59n. *intruder.*

native, aboriginal, aborigines, autochthones, earliest inhabitants, first-comers 66n. *precursor;* people, tribe 371n. *nation;* local, local inhabitant, tribal; parishioner, townsman, townee, city man, cit, oppidan,

cockney, suburbanite, yokel; compatriot, fellow-countryman, fellow-citizen; national, citizen, burgess, burgher, voter; Yankee, Yank, Briton, Britisher; Caledonian, Scottie, Taffy, Paddy; Londoner, Mancunian, Liverpudlian, Aberdonian; New Yorker, Virginian; Canuck 59n. *foreigner;* earth-dweller, terrestrial, tellurian; space-dweller, Martian, Venusian.

settler, pioneer; backsettler 66n. *precursor;* immigrant, colonist, colonial, creole; squatter 59n. *intruder;* planter 370n. *husbandman;* inquiline, metic, resident alien 59n. *foreigner;* Ditcher, Pilgrim Fathers; parasite, parasitical organism.

habitancy, population, urban p., rural p., townspeople, country folk; populace, people, people at large, citizenry, tenantry, yeomanry; villagery, villadom, suburbia; city-full, house-full; household, menage 11n. *family;* settlement, stronghold; colony, plantation, community, village c.

Adj. *native,* vernacular, popular, national, swadeshi; indigenous, autochthonous, aboriginal, enchorial, terrigenous; earth-bound, terrestrial, tellurian; home, home-made; domestic, domiciliary, domesticated; settled, domiciliated, naturalized.

occupied, occupied by, indwelt; garrisoned by, manned, staffed.

See: 11, 59, 66, 150, 370, 371, 658, 686, 742, 776, 801.

192 Abode: place of habitation or resort

N. *abode,* abiding place, habitat, haunt, place to live in, place, province, sphere; habitation, local h., street, house, home; address, house-number, number; where one lives, where one's lot is cast; domicile, residence, residency; town, city, capital, metropolis; headquarters, base 76n. *focus;* temporary abode, hang-out, camp; holiday home, seaside resort, watering place, hill-station; spa, sanatorium 658n. *hospital;* outstation, cantonment, lines, civil l. 187n. *station;* bivouac, encampment, castrametation; rus in urbe, home from home.

quarters, accommodation, billet, berth;

barrack, casemate, casern; bunkhouse, lodging, lodgings, rooms, chambers, diggings, digs, chummery; residential hotel, guest house, boarding h., lodging h., pension, boarding, hostel, dormitory, dorm; sorority house, fraternity h.

dwelling, roof over one's head 226 n. *roof*; prehistoric dwelling, lake-d., crannog, broch, brough; tower, keep; cave, hut, kraal, igloo; wigwam, tepee, wicky-up, tent, tabernacle 226 n. *canopy*; lair, den, hole, tree; hive, bee-h., burrow, warren, earth, set 662 n. *shelter*; apiary, aviary 369 n. *zoo*.

nest, nidification, nidus; branch 366 n. *tree*; aerie, eyry, perch, roost; covert, gullery, rookery, swannery, hatchery, aviary, apiary, wasp's nest, ant-heap, ant-hill; chrysalis, cocoon 226 n. *wrapping*; cradle 68 n. *origin*.

home, hearth, fireside, chimney corner, ingle nook, rooftree, roof, paternal r., homestead, toft, household; cradle, birthplace, 'house where I was born' 68 n. *origin*; native land, la patrie, motherland, fatherland, homeland, one's country, God's own country, the Old Country, blighty, Albion; native soil, native ground, native heath, homeground, hometown; haunt, stamping ground; household gods, teraphim, Lares and Penates; Hestia, Vesta.

house, religious house, house of God 990 n. *temple*; home, residence, dwelling-house, country h., town h.; dower-house, semi-detached h., thatched h.; Queen Anne house, Georgian h., Regency h., colonial h.; council house, prefab; bungalow, ranchhouse, villa, chalet; seat, place, mansion, hall; chateau, castle, keep, tower; manor house, manor, grange, lodge, priory, abbey; palace, alcazar; palatial residence, dome; steading, farmstead, croft, messuage, toft and croft, hacienda; official residence, White House, Mansion H.; embassy, consulate; building, skyscraper 164 n. *edifice*; convent 986 n. *monastery*.

small house, bijou residence, flatlet; snuggery, chalet, lodge, cottage, cot; cabin, log c., hut, shebang, adobe; hovel, dump, hole, slum-dwelling; box, shooting b., hunting lodge; shed, shanty, shack, lean-to, penthouse, outhouse; shelter, tent, booth, bothy, stall, sheiling; barn, grange

632 n. *store*; houseboat, budgerow 275 n. *boat*; house on wheels, caravan, trailer, house-t. 274 n. *vehicle*. See *flat*.

housing, bricks and mortar, built-up area; housing estate, hutments; urbanization, conurbation; city, town, burgh, suburb, satellite town; dormitory area, industrial a., development a.; crescent, terrace, circus, square; block, court, row, mansions, villas, buildings; houses, tenements; slum, condemned building; hamlet, ham, village, thorp, dorp, bustee; villadom, suburbia.

street, high s., avenue 624 n. *road*; lane, alley, wynd, by-street, back street, side s., passage, arcade, covered way 624 n. *path*; mall, grove, walk, parade, promenade, boulevard; pier, embankment.

flat, service f., mews f., penthouse; apartment, suite, suite of rooms, chambers 194 n. *chamber*; maisonette, duplex, walkup; apartment house, block of flats, mews, tenements, rents.

stable, byre, cowshed, cowhouse, shippen; kennel, doghouse, dog-hole; sty, pigpen, fold, sheep-f., sheepcote 235 n. *inclosure*; dove-cote, pigeon-c., pigeon-hole; stall, cage, coop, hencoop, hutch; stabling, mews, coach-house, garage, hangar; boathouse; marina, dock, dry d., floating d., graving d.; basin, wharf, roads, roadstead, port, interport 662 n. *shelter*; berth, lay-by, quay, jetty, pier, ghat 266 n. *resting place*.

inn, hotel, hostelry, hospice, motel, bed and breakfast; doss-house, bunk-h., kip, flophouse; auberge, posada, caravanserai, khan; dak bungalow, circuit house, rest-house; rest-room, waiting-room.

tavern, alehouse, pothouse, mughouse; public house, pub, local, roadhouse; gin palace, gin mill, grog-shop, dram-s., toddy-s.; speakeasy, dive, honky-tonk, shebeen; estaminet, bodega; wine cellar, beer c., beer hall, brauhaus; bar, saloon, tap-room.

café, restaurant, self-service r., cafeteria, automat; eating-house, chop-house; beanery, diner, dinette, luncheonette; brasserie, bistro; grill-room, rôtisserie; coffee house, espresso café, milk-bar, soda-fountain; lunch-counter, snack-bar, self-service b.; teahouse, teashop, tea-room, refreshment r., buffet, canteen, Naafi; coffee stall; pull-up, carman's rest.

meeting place, conventicle, meeting house 990n. *church*; assembly rooms, pumproom; club, night-c., holiday camp 837n. *place of amusement*; race-course, dog track 724n. *arena*; theatre, auditorium, stadium, stand 441n. *onlooker*; gymnasium, drill hall, parade ground 539n. *school*; piazza, quadrangle, quad, campus, village green 76n. *focus*; market, market square, forum, supermarket 796n. *mart*.

pleasance, park, grounds, pleasure g., gardens, walk, mall, green, bowling g., game reserve, national park, parkland, chase 837n. *pleasure ground*.

pavilion, kiosk, rotunda, folly, bower, grotto, solar, solarium 194n. *arbour*; stoa, colonnade, arcade, peristyle, cloister; tent, marquee, shamiana 226n. *canopy*.

retreat, sanctuary, refuge, asylum, ark 662 n. *shelter*; den, snuggery, sanctum sanctorum, study 194n. *chamber*; cell, hermitage 883n. *seclusion*; cloister 986n. *monastery*; ashram; almshouse, grace and favour house; workhouse, poorhouse; ghetto 748n. *prison*; cache, hole 527n. *hiding-place*.

Adj. *residing*, abiding, dwelling, keeping, living; at home, in residence; residential, fit for habitation; parasitical, autoecious.

urban, towny, oppidan, metropolitan, cosmopolitan, suburban; built-up, citified, urbanized, suburbanized.

provincial, parochial, regional, local, domestic; up-country, countrified, rural, rustic.

architectural, architectonic, edificial; Gothic, classical; cottage-style, bungalow type; palatial, grand; detached, semid.; single-storey, double-s.; doublefronted.

Vb. *dwell*, dwell in, inhabit, populate, people 189vb. *be present*; settle, colonize 786vb. *appropriate*; frequent, haunt 882 vb. *visit*; take up one's abode, reside, remain, abide, sojourn, live 185vb. *be situate*; take rooms, put up at, stay, keep, lodge, lie, sleep at; have an address, hang out; tenant, occupy, squat 773vb. *possess*; bunk, room, chum with, p.g.; stable, nestle, perch, roost, nest, hive, burrow; camp, encamp, bivouac, pitch, pitch one's tent, make one's quarters 187vb. *place oneself*; tent, tabernacle, shelter 662vb. *seek refuge*; berth, dock, anchor 266vb. *come to rest*.

urbanize, citify, suburbanize, conurbate, town-plan, develop, build up.

See: 68, 76, 164, 185, 187, 189, 194, 226, 235, 266, 274, 275, 366, 369, 441, 527, 539, 624, 636, 658, 662, 724, 748, 773, 786, 796, 837, 882, 883, 986, 990.

193 Contents: things contained

N. *contents*, ingredients, items, components, constituents, parts 58n. *component*; inventory 87n. *list*; furnishings, equipment 633n. *provision*; load, payload, cargo, lading, freight, shipment, cartload, busload, shipload 272n. *thing transferred*; enclosure, inside 224n. *insides*; stuffing, filling, stopping, wadding 227n. *lining*; handful, cupful, quiverful 104n. *certain quantity*.

Vb. *load*, lade, freight, charge, burden 187 vb. *stow*; take in, take on board, ship; overburden, break one's back 322vb. *weigh*; pack, pack in, fit in, tuck in 303 vb. *insert*; pack tight, squeeze in, cram, stuff 54vb. *fill*; pad, wad 227vb. *line*; hide, conceal 56vb. *contain*.

See: 54, 56, 58, 87, 104, 187, 224, 227, 272, 303, 322, 633.

194 Receptacle

N. *receptacle*, container; tray, in-t., out-t.; recipient, holder; frame 218n. *supporter*; cage 748n. *prison*; folder, wrapper, envelope, cover, file 235n. *enclosure*; net, seine, trawl, beam-t. 222n. *network*; hairnet, snood 228n. *headgear*; sheath, chrysalis, cocoon 226n. *wrapping*; capsule, ampoule; pod, calyx, boll; inkwell, ink-horn; socket, mortise 255n. *cavity*; groove, slot 262n. *furrow*; hole, cave, cavity 263n. *opening*; bosom, lap 261n. *fold*; slot-machine; pin-cushion; catchall, trap; well, reservoir, hold 632n. *store*; drain, pool, cess-pool, sump 649n. *sink*; crockery, chinaware, glassware 381 n. *pottery*.

bladder, air-bladder, water-wings; balloon, gas-bag; sac, cyst, vesicle, utricle, blister, bubble 253n. *swelling*; udder, bag, teat 253n. *bosom*.

maw, stomach, tummy, breadbasket, little Mary; abdomen, belly, paunch, venter 253 n. *swelling*; gizzard, gullet, weasand, crop, craw, jaws, mouth, œsophagus 263 n. *orifice*.

compartment, cell, cellule, follicle, ventricle; tray, in-t., out-t.; cage, iron-lung; cubicle, loculus; driving-seat, cab; sentry-box; box 594 n. *theatre*; pew, stall, choir-stall, chancel 990 n. *church interior*; niche, nook, cranny, recess, bay, oriel, mihrab; pigeon-hole, cubby-h., drawer; shelving, rack 218 n. *shelf*; storey, floor, mezzanine f., entresol, deck, between-decks, 'tween-d., lazaret 207 n. *layer*.

cabinet, closet, commode, wardrobe, press, chest of drawers, tallboy, highboy; cupboard, corner c., dresser; buffet, sideboard 218 n. *stand*; chiffonier, cellaret, dumb-waiter; sécretaire, écritoire, davenport, bureau, desk, writing d.; bookcase; china cabinet.

basket, cran, creel; hamper, luncheon basket; breadbasket, canister; pannier, dosser, dorser; trug, maund, punnet, rush basket, frail; crib, cradle, bassinet, whisket; clothes basket, buckbasket; work-basket, waste-paper b.; wicker-work, basket-work, corbeille; framework, crate, kit 218 n. *frame*; gabion 713 n. *fortification*.

box, chest, ark; coffer, locker; case, canteen; safe, till, money-box 799 n. *treasury*; boot, imperial; coffin, sarcophagus, cist 364 n. *tomb*; packing-case, tea-chest; provision box, tuck-box; attaché case, dispatch c., dispatch box; suitcase, expanding s.; trunk, valise, portmanteau, uniform case; sea-chest, ditty-box; bandbox, hat-box; ammunition box, canister, caisson 723 n. *ammunition*; boxes, luggage, baggage, impedimenta; brake-van, luggage v.

small box, pill b., snuff b., tinder b., match-b., cigarette-b., cigar-b., pencil-b.; card-board box, carton, packet, metal box, can, tin, cigarette t., tobacco t., caddy, tea-caddy, canister, casket, pyx, reliquary, shrine; pepper-box, pepper-mill, caster; nest of boxes.

bag, sack; handbag, vanity bag, reticule, tidy; shopping bag, paper b.; cornet, twist; Gladstone bag, carpet b., travelling-bag, overnight b., last-minute b.; sleeping-bag, flea-b.; bedding-roll; hold-all, grip-sack, grip, haversack, knapsack, rucksack, kitbag, ditty-bag, duffle b., saddlebag, nosebag; satchel, sabretache, budget, scrip, bundle, swag.

case, pocket c., étui, housewife, wallet, scrip-case; billfold, note-case, card case, spectacle c., jewel c., compact, vasculum; brief-case, portfolio; scabbard, sheath; pistol case, holster; arrow case, quiver 632 n. *store*; pen-holder; finger-stall.

pocket, waistcoat p., side-p., hip-p., trouser-p., breast pocket; fob, placket; purse, pouch, poke, money-bag; sleeve, sporran.

vat, dye-v., butt, water-b., cask, barrel, tun, tub, keg, breaker; wine-cask, puncheon, pipe, hogshead, tierce, firkin, kilderkin, pottle 465 n. *metrology*; brewer's vat, hopper, cistern, tank 632 n. *store*.

vessel, vase, urn, jar, amphora, ampulla, cruse, crock, pot, water-p.; pipkin, gugglet, pitcher, ewer, jug, toby-jug; goird, calabash 366 n. *plant*; carafe, decanter, bottle, water-b.; leather bottle, blackjack, wineskin; wine bottle, demi-john, magnum, jeroboam; flask, hip-f., flagon, nipperkin, vial, phial; cruet; honeypot, jam-jar; gallipot, carboy, bolt-head, crucible, retort, receiver, alembic, cucurbit, matrass, cupel, test-tube 463 n. *testing agent*; cupping-glass; chamber-pot, potty, jerry, bed-pan, commode, thunder-box 302 n. *excretion*; trough, trug; pail, milk-p., milk-can; bucket, wooden b., piggin, skeel; lota, can, watering c.; flower-pot, jardinière; bin, dust-b., garbage can, trash c., gubbins 649 n. *sink*; scuttle, coal-s., perdonium; kibble, tub; bath, hip-b.

cauldron 383 n. *heater*; alfet; boiler, copper, kettle, posnet, skillet, etna, dixie, pan, sauce-p., stew-p., frying-p., casserole, pyrex dish, mess-tin, mess can; tea urn, teapot, samovar, coffee-pot, percolator, biggin; censer, cassolette; hot-water bottle, warming pan.

cup, egg-c., tea-c., coffee-c.; tea-service, tea-set; chalice, goblet, beaker; drinking-cup, loving c.; quaich; horn, drinking-h., tankard, stoup, can, cannikin, pannikin, mug, stein, toby, noggin, rummer, tyg, tass, tassie; tumbler, glass, wineglass, liqueur g.; cupel.

bowl, basin, hand-b., wash-b., laver, shaving-mug; slop-bowl, mixing-bowl, crater, punchbowl, drinking-b., jorum;

soup-plate, soup-bowl, porringer, pottinger; manger, trough; colander, vegetable dish, tureen, terrine, sauce-boat, gravyboat; spittoon, cuspidor; flower-bowl, jardinière 844n. *ornamentation*; watchglass, crystal.

plate, salver, tray, paten, patera, patella; platter, trencher, charger, dish, centre d., epergne; saucer; pan, scale 322n. *scales*; palette; mortar-board, hod.

ladle, dipper, baler, scoop, cupped hands; spoon, table-s., dessert-s., tea-s., egg-s., soup-s.; spade, trowel, spatula 274n. *shovel*.

chamber, room, apartment 192n. *flat*; cockpit, cubicle, cab; cabin, stateroom; roundhouse, cuddy; audience chamber, presence c., throne-room; cabinet, closet, study, den, sanctum, adytum 192n. *retreat*; library, studio, atelier, workroom, office 687n. *workshop*; playroom, nursery, schoolroom; drawing room, sitting r., reception r.; living room, lounge, parlour, saloon, salon, boudoir; bedroom, sleeping room, dormitory; dressing room; bathroom, bath-house; dining room, salle-à-manger, messroom, mess, hall, refectory, canteen, grill-room 192n. *café*; gunroom, wardroom, smoking room, billiard r.; bar, tap-room, writing room, scriptorium; cook-house, galley, kitchen; scullery, pantry, larder, still-room; dairy, laundry, offices, outhouse; coachhouse, garage 192n. *stable*; store-room, lumber r. glory hole 632n. *storage*; retiring room, cloakroom, lavatory 649n. *latrine*. See *compartment*.

lobby, vestibule, foyer, anteroom, waitingroom 263n. *doorway*; corridor, passage; verandah, piazza, loggia, balcony, portico, porch, stoa, propylæum, atrium.

cellar, cellarage, vault, crypt, basement 214n. *base*; coal-hole, bunker 662n. *storage*; dust-hole, dust-bin 694n. *sink*; hold, dungeon 748n. *prison*.

attic, loft, hayloft, cockloft; penthouse, garret, top storey 213n. *summit*.

arbour, alcove, bower, grotto, grot, summer-house, gazebo, pergola 192n. *pavilion*; conservatory, greenhouse, glasshouse 370n. *garden*.

Adj. *recipient*, receptive, capacious, voluminous 183adj. *spacious*; containing, hiding, framing, enclosing; pouchy, baggy.

cellular, multicellular, camerated, compartmentalized; locular, multilocular, loculated; marsupial, polygastric, ventricular; abdominal, gastral, ventral stomachic, ventricose, bellied 253adj. *convex*.

capsular, saccular, sacculated, cystic, siliquous; vascular, vesicular.

See: 192, 207, 214, 218, 222, 226, 228, 235, 253, 255, 261, 262, 263, 274, 302, 322, 364, 366, 370, 381, 383, 463, 465, 594, 632, 649, 662, 687, 713, 723, 748, 799, 844, 990.

195 Size

N. *size*, magnitude, order of m.; proportions, dimensions, measurements 183n. *measure*; extent, expanse, area 183n. *space*; extension 203n. *length*, 209n. *height*, 211n. *depth*; width, amplitude 205n. *breadth*; volume, cubature; girth, circumference 233n. *outline*; bulk, mass, weight 322n. *gravity*; capacity, intake, tunnage, tonnage; measured size, scantling, calibre 465n. *measurement*; real size, true dimensions 494n. *accuracy*; greatest size, maximum 32n. *greatness*; full size, life size 54n. *plenitude*; large size, king s., magnum; largest portion 52n. *chief part*; excessive size, hypertrophy, giantism, gigantism.

hugeness, largeness, bigness, grandiosity 32n. *greatness*; enormity, enormousness, immensity, vastness, giantship; towering proportions, monstrosity, gigantism 209n. *height*.

bulk, mass, weight, heft 322n. *gravity*; lump, block, clod, nugget 324n. *solid body*; bushel, mound, heap 32n. *great quantity*; mountain, pyramid 209n. *high structure*; massiveness, bulkiness, turgidity, obesity, corpulence, fatness, plumpness, chunkiness, fleshiness, meatiness; flesh and blood, full habit, chunky figure, corporation, gorbelly 253n. *swelling*; fat man, tun, tun of flesh, Falstaff.

giant, colossus 209n. *tall creature*; mountain of a man, young giant, lusty infant; ogre, monster; leviathan, behemoth, whale, porpoise, Triton among the minnows; hippopotamus, elephant; mammoth, megatherium, dinosaur; giantry,

Gargantua, Brobdingnagian, Goliath, Gog and Magog, Typhon, Antaeus, Briareus, Cyclops, Kraken.
whopper, spanker, thumper, strapper; a mountain of a . . .
Adj. *large*, of size, big 32adj. *great*; large size, king s., jumbo; pretty large, fairsized, considerable, sizeable, good-sized; bulky, massive, massy 322adj. *weighty*; ample, capacious, voluminous, baggy; amplitudinous, comprehensive 205adj. *broad*; extensive 183adj. *spacious*; monumental, towering, mountainous 290adj. *tall*; fine, magnificent, spanking, thumping, thundering, whacking 32adj. *whopping*; man-size, life-s., large as life; wellgrown, large-limbed, elephantine; macroscopic, large-scale, megalithic; big for one's age, lusty, healthy 162adj. *strong*; so big, of that order.
huge, immense, enormous, vast, mighty, grandiose, stupendous, monstrous 32adj. *prodigious*; biggest ever, record size; colossal, gigantic, giant, giant-like, mountainous; Brobdingnagian, Titanic, Herculean, Gargantuan; Cyclopean, megalithic; outsize, oversize, overlarge 32adj. *exorbitant*; limitless 107adj. *infinite*.
fleshy, meaty, fat, stout, obese, overweight; plump, plumpish, chubby, podgy, pudgy, fubsy; squat, five by five, square, dumpy, chunky; tubby, portly, corpulent, paunchy, pot-bellied, gorbellied 253adj. *convex*; puffy, pursy, bloated, blowzy, bosomy 197adj. *expanded*; round, full, full-faced, chub-f., chubby-f.; round, full, double-chinned, dimpled, dimply, jolly, chopping, goodly, lusty; in condition, in good c., in good case, well-fed, wellgrown, strapping, beefy, brawny, 162adj. *stalwart*; plump as a dumpling, plump as a partridge, fat as a quail, fat as butter, fat as brawn, fat as bacon, fat as a pig.
unwieldy, hulking, lumbering, gangling, lolloping; hulky, lumpy, lumpish, lubberly; too big, elephantine, overweight; awkward, muscle-bound 695adj. *clumsy*.
Vb. *be large*, — big etc. adj.; become large 197vb. *expand*; have size, loom large, bulk l., bulk, fill space 183vb. *extend*; tower, soar 209vb. *be high*.
See: 32, 52, 54, 107, 162, 183, 197, 203, 205, 206, 209, 211, 233, 253, 322, 324, 332, 465, 494, 695.

196 Littleness
N. *littleness* etc.adj.; small size, miniature quality 33n. *smallness*; lack of height 204 n. *shortness*; diminutiveness, dwarfishness, stuntedness; scantiness, paucity, exiguity 105n. *fewness*; meagreness 206n. *thinness*; — kin, — let.
minuteness, point, mathematical p., vanishing p.; pinpoint, pinhead; crystal; monad, atom, electron, molecule; drop, droplet, dust, grain; seed, mustard s., grass s., millet-s., barleycorn 33n. *small thing*, *particle*; bubble, button, molehill 639n. *trifle*.
miniature 553n. *picture*; microphotograph, reduction 551n. *photography*; Elzevir edition, duodecimo 589n. *edition*; thumbnail sketch, epitome 592n. *compendium*; model, microcosm; bubble car, minicar 274n. *automobile*.
dwarf, midget, pigmy, elf, atomy, Lilliputian, blastie; chit, pigwidgeon, urchin, dapperling, dandiprat, cock-sparrow, pipsqueak; mannikin, doll, puppet; Tom Thumb, Hop-o'-my-thumb, homunculus; shrimp, runt, miserable specimen.
animalcule, micro-organism, microzoon; amoeba, protozoon, bacillus, bacteria, infusoria, anærobe, microbe, germ, virus, entozoon; mite, tick, nit, maggot, grub, worm; insect, ant, pismire, emmet; midge, gnat, fly, tit, tom-tit; fingerling, small fry, shrimp, sprat, minnow; mouse, tit-mouse, shrew-mouse; whippet, bantam, runt.
micrology, microscopy, micrography, microphotography; microscope, microspectroscope, micrometer, Vernier scale.
Adj. *little* 33adj. *small*; petite, dainty, dinky, dolly, elfin; diminutive, pigmy, Lilliputian; wee, titchy, tiny, teeny, teeny-weeny, itsy-witsy; toy, baby, pocket, pocket-size, pint-size, duodecimo; miniature, model; portable, compact, handy; runty, puny 163adj. *weak*; petty 33adj. *inconsiderable*; one-horse 639adj. *unimportant*.
dwarfish, dwarf, dwarfed, pigmy, undersized, stunted, weazen, wizened, shrunk 198adj. *contracted*; squat, dumpy 204 adj. *short*; runty, knee-high, knee-high to a grasshopper.
exiguous, minimal, slight, scant, scanty, homœopathic 33adj. *small*; thin, meagre, scrubby, scraggy 206adj. *lean*; rudimentary,

embryonic 68 adj. *beginning*; bitty 53 adj. *fragmentary*.

minute, micro-, microscopic, ultramicroscopic, infinitesimal; atomic, molecular, corpuscular; granular 322 adj. *powdery*; inappreciable, imperceptible, intangible, impalpable 444 adj. *invisible*.

Vb. *be little,*— petite etc. adj.; contract 198 vb. *became small*; dwindle 37 vb. *decrease*; require small space, take up no room, lie in a nutshell, fit in a small compass, fit on the head of a pin.

Adv. *in small compass*, in a nutshell; on a small scale, in miniature.

See: 33, 37, 53, 68, 105, 163, 198, 204, 206, 274, 332, 444, 551, 553, 589, 592, 639.

197 Expansion

N. *expansion*, increase of size, ascending order, crescendo; enlargement, augmentation, aggrandizement 36 n. *increase*; ampliation, amplification, supplementation, reinforcement 38 n. *addition*; hypertrophy, giantism, gigantism; overenlargement, hyperbole 546 n. *exaggeration*; stretching, stretching oneself, pandiculation; extension, spread, deployment, fanning out 75 n. *dispersion*; increment, accretion 40 n. *adjunct*; upgrowth, overgrowth, germination, pullulation, development 157 n. *growth*, 164 n. *production*; overstaffing, Parkinson's law 637 n. *superfluity*; extensibility, expansibility, dilatability 328 adj. *elasticity*.

dilation, dilatation, distension, diastole; blowing up, inflation, reflation, puffing, puff 352 n. *sufflation*; swelling up, turgescence, turgidity, tumescence, intumescence, tumefaction; tympany; puffiness, dropsy, tumour 253 n. *swelling*.

Adj. *expanded* etc. vb.; larger, bigger, bigger than before, bigger than ever; expanding 36 adj. *increasing*; stuffed, padded out, supplemented; spreading, widespread, deployed; expansive 183 adj. *spacious*; fan-shaped, flabelliform 204 adj. *broad*; wide open, patulous, gaping 263 adj. *open*; tumescent, budding, bursting, florescent, flowering, out 134 adj. *adult*; full-blown, full-grown, full-formed 669 adj. *matured*; overblown, overgrown, hypertrophied 546 adj. *exaggerated*;

obese, pursy, puffy, swag-bellied, pot-b., bloated, fat 195 adj. *fleshy*; swollen, turgescent, turgid; distended, stretched, tight; tumid, dropsical, varicose, bulbous 253 adj. *convex*; bladder-like; ampullaceous, ampullar, pouchy.

Vb. *expand*, greaten, grow larger, increase, wax, grow, snowball, 36 vb. *grow*; widen, broaden 205 vb. *be broad*; spread, fan out, deploy, extend, take open order 75 vb. *be dispersed*; spread over, spread like wild-fire, overrun, mantle, straddle 226 vb. *cover*; incrassate, thicken; rise, prove (e.g. dough); gather, swell, distend, dilate, fill out; balloon, belly 253 vb. *be convex*; get fat, gain flesh, put on weight; split one's breeches, burst at the seams; grow up, spring up, germinate, bud, burgeon, shoot, sprout, open, put forth, burst f., blossom, flower, floresce, blow, bloom, be out 171 vb. *be fruitful*; stretch oneself, pandiculate.

enlarge, greaten, aggrandize; make larger, expand; rarefy (by expansion); leaven 310 vb. *elevate*; bore, ream; widen, broaden, let out; open, pull out; stretch, extend 203 vb. *lengthen*; intensify, heighten, deepen, draw out; amplify, supplement, reinforce 38 vb. *add*; develop, build up 36 vb. *augment*; distend, inflate, reflate, pump up, blow up, puff, puff up, puff out 352 vb. *sufflate*; stuff, pad 227 vb. *line*; cram, fill to bursting 54 n. *fill*; feed up, fatten, plump up, bloat, pinguefy 301 vb. *feed*; enlarge, blow up 551 vb. *photograph*; magnify, over-enlarge, over-develop 546 vb. *exaggerate*; double, redouble.

See: 36, 38, 40, 54, 75, 134, 157, 164, 171, 183, 195, 203, 204, 205, 226, 227, 250, 253, 263, 301, 310, 328, 352, 546, 551, 637, 669.

198 Contraction

N. *contraction*, reduction, abatement, lessening, deflation 37 n. *diminution*; decrease, shrinkage, descending order, diminuendo 42 n. *decrement*; curtailment, abbreviation, sycope, elision 204 n. *shortening*; state of contraction, contracture; consolidation 324 n. *condensation*; freezing 382 n. *refrigeration*; pulling together, drawing t. 45 n. *joinder*, 264 n. *closure*;

attenuation, emaciation, tabefaction, consumption, marasmus, withering, atrophy; decline, retreat, recession, slump 655n. *deterioration*; neck, isthmus, bottleneck, hourglass, wasp-waist 206n. *narrowness*; epitome 592n. *compendium.*

compression, coarctation, pressure, compressure, compaction, squeeze, squeezing, stricture, stenosis, strangulation; constriction, constringency, astriction, astringency; contractility, compressibility.

compressor, squeezer, mangle, roller 258n. *smoother*; tightener, constrictor, astringent; bandage, binder, tourniquet 658n. *surgical dressing*; belt, band, cingle, garter 47n. *girdle*; whalebone, stays, corset 228n. *underwear*; straitjacket, iron boot, bed of Procustes 964n. *instrument of torture*; bear, python, boa-constrictor.

Adj. contracted, shrunk, shrunken, smaller 33 adj. *small*; waning 37 adj. *decreasing*; constricted, strangled, strangulated; unexpanded, deflated, condensed 324 adj. *dense*; compact, compacted, compressed; pinched, nipped, tightened, drawn tight 206 adj. *narrow*, 264 adj. *closed*; compressible, contractile, systaltic; stunted, wizened 196 adj. *dwarfish*; tabid, tabescent, marasmic, wasting, consumptive 655 adj. *deteriorated.*

compressive, contractional, astringent, binding, constipating.

Vb. become small, grow less, lessen, dwindle, wane, ebb, fall away 37 vb. *decrease*; wither, waste, decay 51 vb. *decompose*; lose weight, lose flesh 323 vb. *be light*; contract, shrink, narrow, taper, taper off, draw in 206 vb. *be narrow*; condense 324 vb. *be dense*; evaporate 338 vb. *vaporize*; draw together, close up 264 vb. *close*; pucker, purse, corrugate, wrinkle 261 vb. *fold*; stop expanding, level off.

make smaller, lessen, reduce 37 vb. *bate*; contract, shrink, abridge, take in, cut down to life size, dwarf, bedwarf 204 vb. *shorten*; bant, diet, slim, take off weight 323 vb. *lighten*; taper, narrow, attenuate, thin, emaciate 206 vb. *make thin*; puncture, deflate, de-gas, rarefy, pump out, exhaust, empty, drain 300 vb. *void*; boil down, evaporate 338 vb. *vaporize*; coarctate, constrict, constringe, pinch, nip, squeeze, bind, bandage, garter, corset; draw in, draw tight, strain, tauten 45 vb. *tighten*; draw together 264 vb. *close*, 45

vb. *join*; compress, hug, crush, strangle, strangulate; compact, constipate, condense, nucleate 324 vb. *be dense*; squeeze in, pack tight, cram 193 vb. *load*; cramp, restrict 747 vb. *restrain*; limit 232 vb. *circumscribe*; chip, whittle, share, shear, clip, trim, shingle, poll, pollard 46 vb. *cut*; scrape, file, grind 332 vb. *pulverize*; fold up, crumple 261 vb. *fold*; roll, press, flatten 258 vb. *smooth*; huddle, crowd.

See: 33, 37, 42, 45, 46, 47, 51, 193, 196, 204, 206, 228, 232, 258, 261, 264, 300, 323, 324, 332, 338, 382, 592, 655, 658, 747, 964.

199 Distance

N. distance, astronomical d., depths of space 183n. *space*; measured distance, mileage, footage 203n. *length*; focal distance; parallax; longinquity, elongation, greatest e., aphelion, apogee; far distance, horizon, false h., skyline, offing; background 238n. *rear*; periphery, circumference 233n. *outline*; reach, grasp, compass, span, stride, giant's s. 183n. *range*; far cry, long long trail, long run, marathon; drift, dispersion 282n. *deviation.*

farness, far distance, remoteness, aloofness; removal 46n. *separation*; antipodes, pole 240n. *contraposition*; world's end, ultima Thule, Pillars of Hercules; ne plus ultra, back of beyond; Far West, Far East; foreign parts, outlands 59n. *extraneousness*; outpost, out-station 883n. *seclusion*; outskirts 223n. *exteriority*; outer edge, frontier 236n. *limit*; unavailability 190n. *absence.*

Adj. distant, distal, peripheral, terminal; far, farther; ulterior; ultimate, furthermost, farest; long-distance, long-range; yon, yonder; not local, away; off-shore, on the horizon; remote, aloof; hyperborean, antipodean, enisled; out of range, telescopic; lost to sight, lost to view, out of sight 444 adj. *invisible*; off-centre, wide, wide of the mark.

removed, incontiguous, separated, inaccessible, unapproachable, ungetatable, out of touch, out of the way; beyond, over the horizon; overseas, transmarine, transpontine, transoceanic, transatlantic, trans-Pacific, transpolar, transalpine, transpadane, ultramontane; ultramundane, out of this world.

Vb. *be distant*, stretch to, reach to, extend to, spread to, go to, get to, stretch away to, carry to, carry on to 183 vb. *extend*; carry, range; outdistance, outrange, outreach 306 vb. *outdo*; keep distance, remain at a d., keep off, hold off, stand off, lie off; keep clear of, stand aloof, stand clear of, keep a safe distance, give a wide berth 620 vb. *avoid*.

Adv. *afar*, away, not locally; far, far away, far afield, far off, way o., wide away, way behind, way in front; uptown, downtown; yonder, in the distance, in the offing, on the horizon; at a distance, a great way off, a long way away, a far cry to; at the limit of vision, out of sight; nobody knows where, out of the way; to the ends of the earth, to the back of beyond, to the uttermost end; far and wide 183 adv. *widely*; from pole to pole, asunder, apart, abroad, afield; at arm's length.

beyond, further, farther; further on, ahead, in front; clear of, wide of, wide of the mark; below the horizon, hull down; up over, down under, over the border, over the hills and far away.

too far, out of reach, out of range, out of sight, out of hearing, out of earshot, out of the sphere of, out of bounds.

See: 46, 59, 183, 190, 203, 223, 233, 236, 238, 240, 282, 306, 444, 620, 883.

200 Nearness

N. *nearness*, proximity, propinquity, closeness, near distance, foreground 237 n. *front*; vicinage, neighbourhood 230 n. *circumjacence*; brink, verge 234 n. *edge*; adjacency 202 n. *contiguity*; collision course, 293 n. *convergence*; approximation 289 n. *approach*; centering, localization 187 n. *location*.

short distance, no d., shortest d., bee-line, short cut; step, short s., no distance, walking d.; striking distance, close quarters, close grips; close range, earshot, gun-shot, pistol-shot, bowshot, arrow-shot, stone's throw, biscuit toss, spitting distance; short span, inch, millimetre, finger's breadth, hair's breadth, hairspace 201 n. *gap*; close-up, near approach; nearest approach, perigee, perihelion; close finish, photo f., near thing 716 n. *contest*.

near place, vicinage, neighbourhood, purlieus, environs, banlieu, suburbs, confines 187 n. *locality*; approaches, borderlands; ringside seat, next door 202 n. *contiguity*; second place, proxime accessit 65 n. *sequence*.

Adj. *near*, proximate, proximal; very near, approximate; approximating, getting warm, warm 289 adj. *approaching*; about to meet 293 adj. *convergent*; near-by, wayside, roadside 289 adj. *accessible*; not far, hard by, inshore; near at hand, at hand, handy, present 189 adj. *on the spot*; near the surface 212 adj. *shallow*; home, local, in the neighbourhood; close to, next to, neighbouring, limitrophe, bordering on, verging on, adjacent, adjoining, jostling, rubbing shoulders 202 adj. *contiguous*; fronting, facing 237 adj. *fore*; close, intimate, inseparable 45 adj. *conjunct*; at close quarters, at close grips; close-run, neck-and-neck, with nothing between, level 716 adj. *contending*; near in blood, related 11 adj. *akin*.

Vb. *be near*, be around, be about 189 vb. *be present*; hang around, hang about; approximate, draw near, get warm 289 vb. *approach*; meet 293 vb. *converge*; neighbour, stand by, abut, adjoin, border, verge upon 202 vb. *be contiguous*; trench upon 306 vb. *encroach*; come close, skirt, graze, shave, brush, skim, hedge-hop, hover over; jostle, buzz, get in the way 702 vb. *obstruct*; sit on one's tail, follow close, make a good second; come to heel, tread on the heels of 284 vb. *follow*; fawn on, spaniel; clasp, cling to, hug, cuddle 889 vb. *caress*; huddle, crowd, close up, close the ranks 74 vb. *congregate*.

bring near, approach, approximate; move up, place side by side 202 vb. *juxtapose*.

Adv. *nigh*, not far, locally; near, hard by, fast by, close to, close up to, close upon, in the way, at close range, at close quarters; within call, within hearing, within earshot, within a stone's throw, only a step, at no great distance, not far from; at one's door, at one's feet, at one's elbow, at one's side, under one's nose; in the presence of, face to face; in juxtaposition, next door, side by side, cheek by jowl, tête-à-tête, arm in arm, beside, alongside, yard-arm to yard-arm; on the circumference, on the periphery, on *or* in the confines of, on the skirts of, in the out-

skirts, at the threshold; brinking on, verging on, on the brink of, on the verge of, on the tip of one's tongue.

nearly, practically, almost, all but; more or less, near enough, roughly, around, somewhere around; in the region of; about, much a., hereabouts, thereabouts, nearabouts, circa; closely, approximately, hard on, close on; well-nigh, as good as, on the way to; within an ace of, just about to.

See: 11, 45, 65, 74, 187, 189, 201, 202, 212, 230, 234, 236, 284, 289, 293, 306, 702, 716, 889.

201 Interval

N. *interval*, distance between, space, jump; narrow interval, half-space, hair space 200n. *short distance*; interspace, daylight, head, length; metope, demi-m., semi-m. (architecture); clearance, margin, freeboard 183n. *room*; interval of time, interregnum 107n. *interim*; pause, break, truce 145n. *lull*; interruption, incompleteness, jump, leap; musical interval, tone, semitone, third, fourth, fifth 410n. *musical note*.

gap, interstice, mesh 222n. *network*; cavity, hole 263n. *orifice*; pass, defile, gat, ghat, wind-gap 305n. *passage*; ditch, dyke, nullah, trench 351n. *drain*; water-jump, ha-ha, sunk fence 235n. *barrier*; ravine, gorge, gully, crevasse, canyon, intervale 255n. *valley*; fatiscence, cleft, crevice, chink, crack, rift, rime, scissure, cut, gash, tear, rent, slit 46n. *scission*; flaw, fault, breach, break, split, fracture, rupture, fissure, chap 46n. *separation*; slot, groove 262n. *furrow*; indentation 260n. *notch*; seam, join 45n. *joint*; leak 298n. *outlet*; abyss, abysm, chasm 211n. *depth*; yawning gulf, void 190n. *emptiness*; inlet, creek, gulch 345n. *gulf*.

Adj. *spaced*, spaced out, intervalled, with an interval, leaded; gappy, gapped; fatiscent, split, cloven, cleft, cracked, rimous, rimose 46adj. *disjunct*; dehiscent, gaping 263adj. *open*; far between; latticed, meshed, reticulated.

Vb. *space*, interval, space out, lead (typography) 46vb. *set apart*; seam, crack, split, start, gape, dehisce 263vb. *open*; win by a head, win by a length; clear,

show daylight between; lattice, mesh, reticulate; raft 370vb. *cultivate*.

Adv. *at intervals* 72adv. *discontinuously*; now and then, now and again, every so often, off and on; with an interval, by a head, by a length.

See: 45, 46, 72, 107, 145, 183, 190, 200, 211, 222, 235, 255, 260, 262, 263, 298, 305, 345, 351, 370, 410.

202 Contiguity

N. *contiguity*, juxtaposition, apposition, proximity, close p. 200n. *nearness*; touching 378n. *touch*; no interval 71n. *continuity*; contact, tangency; abuttal, abutment; intercommunication, osculation; meeting, encounter, rencounter 293n. *convergence*; appulse, appulsion, conjunction, syzygy (astron.) 45n. *junction*; close contact, adhesion, cohesion 48n. *coherence*; coexistence, coincidence, concomitance 89n. *accompaniment*; grazing contact, tangent; border, fringe 234n. *edge*; borderland, frontier, 236n. *limit*; buffer state 231n. *interjacence*.

Adj. *contiguous*, touching, in contact; osculatory, intercommunicating; tangential, grazing, brushing, abutting, end to end; conterminous, adjacent, with no interval 71adj. *continuous*; adjoining, close to, jostling, rubbing shoulders 200 adj. *near*.

Vb. *be contiguous*, overlap 378vb. *touch*; make contact, come in c., brush, rub, skim, scrape, graze, kiss; join, meet 293 vb. *converge*; stick, adhere 48vb. *cohere*; lie end to end, abut; abut on, adjoin, reach to, extend to 183vb. *extend*; sit next to, rub shoulders with, crowd, jostle 200 vb. *be near*; border with, march w., skirt 234vb. *hem*; coexist, coincide 89vb. *accompany*; osculate, intercommunicate 45vb. *connect*; get in touch, contact.

juxtapose, set side by side, range together, bring into contact, knock persons' heads together.

Adv. *contiguously*, tangentially; in contact, in close c.; next, close; end to end; cheek by jowl; hand in hand, arm in arm; from hand to hand.

See: 45, 48, 71, 89, 183, 200, 231, 234, 236, 293, 378.

203 Length. Longimetry

N. *length*, longitude; extent, extension; reach, long arm; full length, over-all l.; stretch, span, mileage, footage 199 n. *distance*; perspective 211 n. *depth*.

lengthening etc. vb.; prolongation, extension, production, spinning out 113 n. *protraction*; stretching, tension, tensure; spreading out, stringing o.

line, bar, rule, tape, strip, stripe, streak; spoke, radius; single file, line ahead 65 n. *sequence*; straight line, right l. 249 n. *straightness*; bent line 248 n. *curvature*; cord, thread 208 n. *fibre*; rope 47 n. *cable*.

long measure, linear m., measurement of length, longimetry, micrometry 465 n. *measurement*; unit of length, finger, hand, hand's breadth, palm, span, cubit; arm's length, fathom; head, length; pace, step; inch, nail, foot, yard, ell; rod, pole, perch; chain, furlong, stade; mile, statute m., sea m., nautical m., knot, German mile, league; millimetre, centimetre, metre, kilometre; kos, verst, parasang; degree of latitude, degree of longitude; micro-inch, micron, wavelength; astronomical unit, light-year, parsec.

Adj. *long*, lengthy, extensive, longsome, measured in miles; long-drawn 113 adj. *protracted*; lengthened, elongated, outstretched, extended, strung out 75 adj. *unassembled*; wire-drawn, lank 206 adj. *lean*; lanky, long-legged 209 adj. *tall*; as long as my arm, as long as today and tomorrow, long as a wet week; interminable, no end to 838 adj. *tedious*; polysyllabic; sesquipedalian 570 adj. *prolix*; unshortened, unabridged, full-length 54 adj. *complete*.

longitudinal, oblong, lineal, linear; one-dimensional.

Vb. *be long,*—lengthy etc. adj.; stretch, outstretch, stretch out; make a long arm; reach, stretch to 183 vb. *extend*; drag, trail, drag its slow length along 113 vb. *drag on*.

lengthen, stretch, elongate, draw out, wiredraw 206 vb. *make thin*; pull out, stretch o., spreadeagle; stretch oneself, pandiculate 197 vb. *expand*; spread oneself out, sprawl 216 vb. *be horizontal*; spread out, string o., deploy 75 vb. *disperse*; extend, pay out, uncoil, unfurl, unroll, unfold 316 vb. *evolve*; let out, drop the hem;

produce, continue; prolong, protract 113 vb. *spin out*; drawl 580 vb. *stammer*.

look along, view in perspective; have a clear view, see from end to end 438 vb. *scan*; enfilade.

Adv. *longwise*, longways, lengthwise; along, endlong; longitudinally, radially, in line ahead, in single file; one in front and one behind, tandem; in a line, in perspective; at full length, end to end, overall; fore and aft; head to foot, head to tail, stem to stern, top to toe, head to heels, from the crown of the head to the sole of the foot.

See: 47, 54, 65, 75, 113, 183, 197, 199, 206, 208, 209, 211, 216, 248, 249, 316, 438, 465, 570, 580, 838.

204 Shortness

N. *shortness* etc. adj.; brevity, briefness; transience 114 n. *brief span*; inch, micro-i. 200 n. *short distance*; low stature, dwarfishness, short legs, duck's disease 196 n. *littleness*; no height 210 n. *lowness*; shortage 41 n. *decrement*, 307 n. *shortcoming*; scantiness, exiguity 105 n. *fewness*; scarceness 636 n. *insufficiency*; concision 569 n. *conciseness*; short hair, Eton crop, crew cut.

shortening, abridgement, abbreviation, abbreviature, curtailment, cut-back, decurtation, reduction 37 n. *diminution*; contraction 198 n. *compression*; retrenchment 814 n. *economy*; ellision, ellipsis, aphæresis, apocope, syncope.

shortener, cutter, abridger, abstracter 592 n. *epitomizer*.

Adj. *short*, brief 114 adj. *transient*; not big, dwarfish 196 adj. *little*; not tall, squab, squabby, squat, dumpy, stumpy, stocky, thick-set, stub, stubby 195 adj. *fleshy*; not high, flat 210 n. *low*; flat-nosed, pug, snub, snubby, retroussé, blunt 257 adj. *unsharpened*; not long, inch-long; skimpy, scanty, scrimpy, revealing (of dress) 636 adj. *insufficient*; foreshortened 246 adj. *distorted*; shortened, half-length, abbreviated, abridged, catalectic; cut, curtailed, docked, beheaded, truncated, headless, topless, crownless; shaven, shorn, mown, well-m.; short of speech, sparing of words, terse 569 adj. *concise*; elliptical (of style); half-finished 55 adj.

unfinished; epitomized, potted, compact 592 adj. *compendious*; compacted, compressed 198 adj. *contracted.*

Vb. *be short,*—brief etc. adj.; come short 307 vb. *fall short.*

shorten, abridge, abbreviate; pot, epitomize, boil down 592 vb. *abstract*; sum up, recapitulate 569 vb. *be concise*; compress, contract, telescope 198 vb *make smaller*; reduce, diminish 37 vb. *bate*; foreshorten 246 vb. *distort*; take in, put a tuck in, raise the hem, turn up, tuck up, kilt; behead, obtruncate, guillotine, axe, chop up, hew 46 vb. *cut*; cut short, dock, curtail, truncate; cut back, cut down, pare d., lop, poll, pollard, prune; shear, shave, trim, clip, bob, shingle; taper, narrow down; mow, reap, crop; nip, snub, nip in the bud, frostbite 655 vb. *wound*; stunt, check the growth of 278 vb. *retard*; scrimp, skimp, scant 636 vb. *make insufficient*; retrench 814 vb *economize.*

Adv. *shortly* etc. adj.; in short; compendiously, in brief compass, economically.

See: 37, 41, 46, 55, 105, 114, 195, 196, 198, 200, 210, 246, 257, 278, 307, 569, 592, 636, 655, 814.

205 Breadth. Thickness

N. *breadth*, width, latitude; width across, diameter, radius, semi-diameter; gauge, broad g., bore, calibre; broadness, expanse, superficial extent, amplitude 183 n. *range*; wideness, fullness, bagginess.

thickness, crassitude, stoutness, corpulence 195 n. *size*; dilatation 197 n. *dilation.*

Adj. *broad*, wide, expansive, unspanned, ample 183 adj. *spacious*; wide-cut, full, baggy; discous, fan-like, flabelliform, umbelliferous; outspread, outstretched; broad-bottomed, broad-based; callipygic, wide-hipped; broad in the beam, beamy, wide as a church door; broad-brimmed, wide-awake (hat); wide-mouthed 263 adj. *open*; broad-shouldered, broad-chested 162 adj. *stalwart*; non-specific 79 adj. *general*; indecent 951 adj. *impure.*

thick, stout, dumpy, squat, squab, thickset, tubby, stubby 195 adj. *fleshy*; thick-lipped, blubber-l., full-l.; thick-ribbed, stout-timbered 162 adj. *strong*; thick as a rope; pycnic, solid 324 adj. *dense*; semi-

liquid, ropy, to be cut with a knife 354 adj. *viscid.*

Vb. *be broad,*—thick etc. adj.; get broad, broaden, widen, fatten, thicken; fan out, deploy 197 vb. *expand*; straddle, bestride, span 226 vb. *overlie.*

Adv. *broadwise*, thick end first.

See: 79, 162, 183, 195, 197, 226, 263, 324, 354, 951.

206 Narrowness. Thinness

N. *narrowness* etc. adj.; narrow interval, closeness, tight squeeze, hair's breadth, finger's b. 200 n. *short distance*; lack of breadth, length without b., line, strip, stripe, streak; vein, capillary 208 n. *filament*; knife-edge, razor's edge, tight-rope, wire; narrow gauge; bottleneck, narrows, strait, euripus 345 n. *gulf*; ridge, col, saddle 209 n. *high land*; ravine, gully 255 n. *valley*; pass, ghat 305 n. *passage*; neck, isthmus, land-bridge 624 n. *bridge.*

thinness etc. adj.; lack of thickness, exility, tenuity, macilency, emaciation, consumption; scrag, skin and bone, skeleton, anatomy; scarecrow, rake, shadow, spindle-shanks, barebones; haggardness, lantern jaws, hatchet face, sunken cheeks; thread, paper, tissue 422 vb. *transparency*; shaving, slip, tendril, tapeworm 163 n. *weakling.*

narrowing, angustation, coarctation, compression 198 n. *contraction*; taper, tapering 293 n. *convergence*; neck, isthmus; stricture, constriction, middle c., waistline; middle, waist, wasp-w., hour-glass; wasp.

Adj. *narrow*, not wide, narrow-gauge; strait, tight, close, incapacious; compressed, pinched, unexpanded 198 adj. *contracted*; not thick, fine, thin 422 adj. *transparent*; tight-drawn, spun, fine-s., wire-drawn 203 adj. *long*; extenuated, thread-like, capillary 208 adj. *fibrous*; taper, tapering 293 adj. *convergent*; slight, slight-made, delicate 163 adj. *weak*; gracile, slender, slim, svelte, slinky, sylph-like; willowy, arrowy, rangy; long-legged, lanky, gangling; narrow-waisted, wasp-w.; isthmian; bottlenecked.

lean, thin, spare, meagre, skinny, bony; cadaverous, fleshless, skin-and-bone, skeletal, bare-boned, raw-b.; haggard,

gaunt, lantern-jawed, hatchet-faced; spindly, spindling, spindle-shanked, spidery; undersized, weedy, scrawny, scrub, scraggy, rickety; extenuated, tabid, marcid 51 adj. *decomposed*; consumptive, emaciated, wasted, withered, wizened, pinched, peaky 651 adj. *sick*; sere, shrivelled 131 adj. *aged*; starved, starveling 636 adj. *underfed*; miserable, herringgutted; macilent, jejune; wraith-like, worn to a shadow, thin as a rake, thin as a lath, thin as a wafer, thin as a pencil, thin as a whipping-post, without an ounce of flesh to spare.

Vb. *be narrow,*—thin etc. adj.; straiten, narrow, taper 293 vb. *converge.*

make thin, contract, compress, pinch, nip 198 vb. *make smaller*; make oneself thin, starve, underfeed, bant, reduce, take off weight; improve one's figure, slenderize, slim; draw, wiredraw, spin, spin fine 203 vb. *lengthen*; attenuate 325 vb. *rarefy.*

See: 51, 131, 163, 198, 200, 203, 208, 209, 255, 293, 305, 325, 345, 422, 624, 651, 636.

207 Layer

N. *layer*, stratum, substratum, underlayer, floor 214 n. *base*; outcrop, basset 254 n. *projection*; bed, course, master-c., range, row; zone, vein, seam, lode; thickness, ply; storey, tier, floor, mezzanine f., entresol, landing; stage, planking, platform 218 n. *frame*; deck, top-d., lowerd., upperd., orlop d., quarter d., bridge 275 n. *ship*; film 423 n. *opacity*; bloom, dross, scum; patina, coating, coat, top-layer 226 n. *covering*; scale, scab, membrane, peel, pellicle, sheathe, bark, integument 226 n. *skin*; level, water-l., table, water-t.; atmospheric layer 340 n. *atmosphere.*

lamina, sheet, slab, foil, strip; plate-glass, plate, tin-p., sheet-iron, sheet-steel; latten, white l.; plank, board, clapboard; slat, lath, leaf, trencher, table, table-top; tablet, plaque, panel; slab, flag, flagstone, slate, shale; shingle, tile; brick, domino; slide; wafer, shaving, flake, slice, cut, rasher; cardboard, sheet of paper, page, folio; card, playing-c.; discolith, dish.

stratification, stratigraphy; layering, lamination; laminability, flakiness, schistosity, scaliness, squamation; overlapping, overlap; nest of boxes, Chinese b., sandwich;

coats of an onion, layer on layer, level upon level 231 n. *interjacence.*

Adj. *layered*, lamellar, lamelliform, lamellated; laminated, laminiferous; laminal, laminar, laminary, laminous; laminable, flaky; schistose, schistous, micaceous, slaty, shaly; foliated, foliate, foliaceous, membranous; bedded, stratified, stratiform; zoned, seamed; overlapping, clinker-built; tabular, decked, storied, in stories, in layers; scaly, squamose, squamous, squamiferous; filmy 226 adj. *covered.*

Vb. *laminate*, lay, deck, layer, shingle, overlap 226 vb. *overlay*; zone, stratify, sandwich; plate, veneer, coat 226 vb. *coat*; delaminate, flake off, whittle, skive, pare, peel, strip 229 vb. *uncover*; shave, slice.

See: 214, 218, 226, 229, 231, 254, 275, 340, 423.

208 Filament

N. *filament*, capillament, cilium, lash, eyelash, beard, down 259 n. *hair*; flock, lock, lock of wool, lock of hair, wisp, curl; list, thrum 234 n. *edging*; fibril, funicle, barb, tendril 778 n. *nippers*; whisker, antenna, antennule, funiculus 378 n. *feeler*; gossamer, cobweb, web 222 n. *network*; capillary, vein, venule, veinlet 351 n. *conduit*; ramification, branch; wire, element, wick, spill 420 n. *torch.*

fibre, natural f., animal f., hair, camel-h., rabbit-hair; Angora, goat's hair, mohair, cashmere; llama hair, alpaca, vicuna; wool, merino; mungo, shoddy; silk, real s.; wild silk, tussah, tussore; vegetable fibre, cotton, raw c., cotton wool, silk-cotton; linen, flax; hemp, cannabis; jute, sisal, coir, kapok; harl, hards; tow, oakum; bast, raffia; worsted, sewing-silk; yarn, staple; spun yarn, continuous filament y.; thread, pack t.; twine, twist, strand, cord, whipcord, string, line, rope, ropework 47 n. *cable*; artificial fibre, rayon, nylon 222 n. *textile.*

strip, fascia, band, bandage, linen; tape, strap, ribbon, ribband; fillet 47 n. *girdle*; lath, slat, batten, spline 207 n. *lamina*; shaving, wafer; splinter, shiver 53 n. *piece*; streak, strake 203 n. *line.*

Adj. *fibrous*, fibrillous; woolly, cottony, silky; filamentous, filaceous, filiform;

whiskery, downy, fleecy 259 adj. *hairy*; wiry, threadlike, funicular; capillary, capilliform; fine-spun, wire-drawn 206 adj. *narrow*; stringy, ropy 205 adj. *thick*; anguilliform 248 adj. *convoluted*; flagelliform, lashlike; lingulate, strap-shaped; antenniform, antennary, antennal.

See: 47, 53, 203, 205, 206, 207, 222, 234, 248, 259, 351, 378, 420, 778.

209 Height

N. *height*, perpendicular length, vertical range, long way to fall; altitude, elevation, ceiling, pitch 213 n. *summit*; loftiness, steepness, dizzy height; tallness, stature; eminence, sublimity; sky, stratosphere 340 n. *atmosphere*.

high land, height, highlands, heights, steeps, uplands, wold, moor, moorland, downs, rolling country; rising ground, rise, bank, brae, slope, climb; knap, hill, eminence, mount, mountain; fell, scar, tor, Alp, Everest; mountain range, sierra, massif, Alps, Himalaya, Andes, Rockies; ridge, hog's back, col, saddle 624 n. *bridge*; spur, foothill, ledge 254 n. *projection*; crest, peak, pike, hilltop 213 n. *summit*; steepness, precipice, cliff, chalk c., white walls of Old England; crag, scar, bluff, steep, escarpment; chine, clough, barranca 255 n. *valley*; summit level, mesa; butte, plateau, tableland, Tibet 216 n. *horizontality*.

monticle, knoll, hillock, kopje, hummock, hump, dune, sand-d.; barrow, long b., round b. 364 n. *tomb*; mound, heap, spoilheap 641 n. *rubbish*; tell 548 n. *monument*; molehill, tussock, pimple 253 n. *swelling*.

high structure, column, pillar, turret, tower, 'cloud-capped towers'; dome, pile, noble p., skyscraper 164 n. *edifice*; steeple, spire, belfry, campanile 990 n. *church exterior*; minaret, muezzin's tower; obelisk, Cleopatra's Needle; roof, cupola, dome; colossus 554 n. *sculpture*; mausoleum, pyramid 364 n. *tomb*; pagoda, gopuram 990 n. *temple*; ziggurat, Tower of Babel; Eiffel Tower; mast, topmast, topgallant mast; flagstaff, pikestaff; pole, maypole; lamp-post, standard; pylon, radio-mast; masthead, truck 213 n. *summit*; watch-tower, crow's nest, eyrie 438 n. *view*; column of smoke, mushroom.

tall creature, giraffe, elephant, mammoth, longlegs, lamp-post, beanpole, six-footer, seven-f., grenadier, colossus 195 n. *giant*; pine, cedar, cedar of Lebanon, sequoia, California red-wood 366 n. *tree*.

high water, high tide, flood t., spring t. 350 n. *current*; billow, tidal wave, tsunami 350 n. *wave*; cataract 350 n. *waterfall*; flood, flood level.

altimetry, altimeter, height-finder, hypsometer, barograph 465 n. *meter*.

Adj. *high*, high-up, sky-high; eminent, uplifted, exalted, lofty, sublime, supernal 310 adj. *elevated*; highest 213 adj. *topmost*; perching, hanging (gardens); aerial, air-borne, flying; soaring, aspiring 308 adj. *ascending*; towering, cloud-capp'd, cloud-topped, cloud-touching, heaven-kissing; sky-scraping; steep, dizzy, vertiginous; knee-high, breast-h., shoulder-h., high as one's heart; altitudinal, altimetric.

tall, lanky, rangy, long-legged, long-necked, giraffelike; statuesque, colossal, gigantic, monumental 195 adj. *huge*; tall as a maypole, tall as a poplar, tall as a steeple.

alpine, sub-alpine, alpestrine, Andean, Himalayan; mountainous, hilly, moorland, upland, highland; not flat, rolling; monticolous, hill-dwelling; orogenical.

overhanging, hovering; floating over, supernatant; beetling, superimposed, overlying; overshadowing, dominating; incumbent, superincumbent; over one's head, aloft; projecting, prominent 254 adj. *salient*.

Vb. *be high*, — tall etc. adj.; tower, soar; surmount, clear, overtop, overlook, dominate, command 34 vb. *be superior*; overhang, overshadow 226 vb. *cover*; beetle, impend 254 vb. *jut*; over, hang over 217 vb. *hang*; culminate, north, south, be in the zenith 725 vb. *climax*; mount, bestride, bestraddle; grow taller, add to one's inches; upgrow; rise 380 vb. *ascend*; stand on tiptoe, stand on another's shoulders, mount on stilts 310 vb. *lift oneself*.

make higher, heighten, build up, raise, hold aloft 310 vb. *elevate*.

Adv. *aloft*, up, on high, high up, in the clouds; atop, on top, on the crest; above, overhead, up over; above stairs, upstairs; upwards, skyward, heavenward; straight up, steeply 215 adv. *vertically*; on tiptoe,

on stilts, on the shoulders of; breast high, up to the teeth, over head and ears; from top to bottom 54adv. *throughout*.

See: 34, 54, 164, 195, 213, 215, 216, 217, 226, 253, 254, 255, 308, 310, 340, 350, 394, 366, 438, 465, 548, 554, 624, 641, 725, 990.

210 Lowness

N. *lowness*, debasement 311n. *depression*; prostration, recumbency 216n. *supination*; non-elevation, no height, sea-level, flatness 216n. *horizontality*; levelness, Flatland, steppe 348n. *plain*; low elevation, lowlands, molehill, pimple 196n. *littleness*; gentle slope, slight gradient 220 n. *acclivity*; subjacency, lower level, foothill 35n. *inferiority*; bottomlands, bottom, hollow, depression 255n. *valley*; seabottom, sea-floor, benthos 343n. *ocean*; subterraneity, depths, cellarage, well, mine 211n. *depth*; floor, foot 214n. *base*; underside, undersurface, underbelly 240 n. *contraposition*; nadir, lowest position; low water, low ebb, low tide, ebb t., neap t. 350n. *current*.

Adj. *low*, not high, squat 204adj. *short*; unerect, not upright, crouched, crouching, stooping, bending 220adj. *oblique*; recumbent, laid low, prostrate 216adj. *supine*; low-lying, flat, level with the ground, at sea-level 216adj. *horizontal*; subjacent, lower, under, nether 35adj. *inferior*; lowered, debased 311adj. *depressed*; flattened, rounded, blunt 257 adj. *unsharpened*; subterranean, subterrene, underground, below the surface, submarine 523adj. *latent*, 211adj. *deep*; underfoot 745adj. *subjected*.

Vb. *be low*,—flat etc.adj.; lie low, lie flat 216vb. *be horizontal*; be beneath, underlie 523vb. *lurk*; slouch, stoop, crouch 311 vb. *stoop*; crawl, wallow, grovel 721vb. *knuckle under*; lower, debase, depress 311 vb. *abase*.

Adv. *under*, beneath, underneath, neath; below, at the foot of; downwards; adown, down, face-down; underfoot, underground, downstairs, below stairs; at a low ebb; below par.

See: 35, 196, 204, 211, 214, 216, 220, 240, 255, 257, 311, 343, 348, 350, 523, 721, 745.

211 Depth

N. *depth*, deepness etc.adj.; perspective 203 n. *length*; vertical range, profundity, lowest depth, lowest point, nadir; deeps, deep water 343n. *ocean*; unknown depths 663n. *pitfall*; depression, bottom 255n. *valley*; hollow, pit, shaft, mine, well 255n. *cavity*; abyss, abysm, chasm, yawning depths 345n. *gulf*; subterraneity, cellarage 194n. *cellar*; cave, hypogeum, bowels of the earth 210n. *lowness*; underworld, bottomless pit 972n. *hell*; fathoming, soundings, sounding machine, sounding rod, sounding line, sound, probe, plummet, lead, sounding l.; diving bell, bathysphere, bathyscaph; submarine, submariner, frogman 313n. *diver*; depth required, draught, displacement, sinkage; bathymeter, bathymetry 465n. *measurement*.

Adj. *deep*, steep, plunging, profound; abysmal, yawning, cavernous; abyssal, deep-sea; deep-seated, deep-rooted 152 adj. *fixed*; unplumbed, bottomless, reachless, soundless, fathomless; unsounded, unfathomed, unsoundable, unfathomable; subjacent, subterranean, underground, subterrene, hypogeal; underwater, undersea, subaqueous, submarine; buried, deep in, immersed, submerged 311adj. *depressed*; sunk, foundered, drowned; deepish, navigable; knee-deep, ankle-d.; deep-bosomed, bathycolpic; deep as a well; infernal, deep as hell; depth-haunting, bathyphilous; depth-measuring, bathymetric.

Vb. *be deep*,— profound etc.adj.; deepen, hollow, dig 255vb. *make concave*; fathom, sound, take soundings, plumb, heave the lead; go deep, plumb the depth, touch bottom, reach one's nadir 210vb. *be low*; sink to the bottom, plunge 313vb. *founder*; gape, yawn.

Adv. *deeply*, profoundly; deep down, beyond one's depth, out of one's depth, deep in, over one's head, over head and ears, up to the eyes.

See: 152, 194, 203, 210, 255, 311, 313, 343, 345, 465, 663, 972.

212 Shallowness

N. *shallowness* etc.adj.; no depth, superficiality 4n. *unsubstantiality*; thin surface

223 n. *exteriority*; veneer, thin coat 226 n. *skin*; surface injury, scratch, mere s., pin-prick, graze 639 n. *trifle*; shoal water, shoals, shallows; pond, puddle 346 n. *lake*; ripple, catspaw 350 n. *wave*; light soil, stony ground 344 n. *soil*.

Adj. *shallow*, slight, superficial 4 adj. *insubstantial*; surface, skin-deep; near the surface, not deep; ankle-deep, knee-d.; shoal, shoaly, unnavigable; just enough to wet one's feet; light, thin, thinly spread 206 adj. *narrow*.

See: 4, 206, 223, 226, 344, 346, 350, 639.

213 Summit

N. *summit*, summity; fountain-head, well-head 156 n. *source*; sky, heaven, seventh h.; pole, north p., south p.; highest point, top, peak, crest, apex, pinnacle, crown; maximum height, utmost h., pitch; zenith, meridian, high noon, culmination, apogee; culminating point, crowning p.; acme, ne plus ultra 646 n. *perfection*; crest of the wave, top of the tree 730 n. *prosperity*; top of the curve, highwater mark 236 n. *limit*; climax, turning point, turn of the tide 137 n. *crisis*; dividing line, divide, watershed, water-parting, Great Divide 231 n. *partition*; coping, coping-stone, capstone, keystone; lintel, pediment, entablature, architrave, epistyle; frieze, zoophorus; tympanum, capital, cornice; battlements, parapet 713 n. *fort*.

vertex, apex, crown, cap, brow, head; tip, cusp, spike, nib, end 69 n. *extremity*; spire, finial 990 n. *church exterior*; stairhead, landing 308 n. *ascent*; acropolis 713 n. *fort*; summit level, hilltop, mountaint., plateau, tableland 209 n. *highland*; tree-top, house-t., roof-t.; gable, gable-end; fastigium, leads, ceiling 226 n. *roof*; upper chamber, garret 194 n. *attic*; top storey; topside, upperdeck, quarter-d., hurricane d., boatd., bridge 275 n. *ship*; topmast, topgallant mast; masthead, crow's nest, truck 209 n. *high structure*; upper works, top-hamper.

head, headpiece, pate, poll, sconce; noddle, nob, nut, crumpet, bean; upper storey, belfry; brow, dome, forehead; brain, grey matter 498 n. *intelligence*; epicranium, pericranium; scalp, crown, double

c.; skull, cranium, brainpan 255 n. *cavity*; occiput, sinciput; meninx, pia mater, dura m., arachnoid; fontanelle; craniology, craniognomy, craniognosy, cranioscopy, craniometry.

Adj. *topmost*, top, highest 209 adj. *high*; uppermost, overmost 34 adj. *supreme*; polar, apical, crowning; capital, head; cephalic, cranial, occipital, sincipital; culminating, zenithal, meridian, meridional; tip-top, super 644 adj. *topping*.

Vb. *crown*, cap, head, top, tip, surmount, crest, overtop 34 vb. *be high*; culminate, consummate 725 vb. *climax*; go up top, take top place 34 vb. *be superior*.

Adv. *atop*, on top, at the top, at the top of the tree, at the top of the ladder; on the crest, on the crest of the wave; tip-toe, on tip-toe.

See: 34, 69, 156, 194, 209, 226, 231, 236, 255, 275, 308, 498, 644, 646, 713, 725, 730, 990.

214 Base

N. *base*, foot, toe, skirt 210 n. *lowness*; bottom, fundament; lowest point, rock-bottom, nadir, low water; footing, foundation 218 n. *basis*; root, fundus, fundamental 68 n. *origin*; groundwork, substructure, chassis, 218 n. *frame*; substratum, floor, underlayer, bed, bedrock; ground, earth, foundations; baseline, sill; base-level, basement, ground floor 194 n. *cellar*; flooring, pavement, paving-stone, flag, 226 n. *paving*; carpet, drugget 226 n. *floor-cover*; baseboard, wainscot, plinth, dado; keel, kelson; hold, orlop, bilge; sump, drain 649 n. *sink*.

foot, feet, tootsies, pedal extremities; fore-foot, hindfoot; sole, pad; heel, instep, arch; toe, toe-nail, great toe, hallux; trotter, hoof, cloven h.; paw, pug; claw, talon 778 n. *nippers*; ankle, ankle-bone, fetlock, pastern.

Adj. *undermost*, lowermost, nethermost, bottom, rock-b. 210 adj. *low*; basic, basal, fundamental; fundal; grounded, on the bottom, touching b.; based on, founded on, grounded on, built on, underlying 218 adj. *supporting*.

footed, pedal; hoofed, cloven-h., ungulate, clawed, taloned; soled, heeled, shod,

shoed; toed, five-t.; club-footed, hammer-toed 845 adj. *blemished.*

Adv. *in the trough,* at the bottom; basically, fundamentally.

See: 68, 194, 210, 218, 226, 649, 778, 845.

215 Verticality

N. *verticality,* the vertical, erectness, uprightness, upright carriage; steepness, sheerness, precipitousness 209 n. *height;* perpendicularity, right angle, square; elevation, azimuth circle; vertical line, plumbline, plummet; vertical structure, hoist, upright, pole, wall, palisade; sheer face, precipice, cliff, bluff, steep 209 n. *high land;* perpendicular drop, straight d., vertical height, rise.

Adj. *vertical,* upright, erect, standing; perpendicular, rectangular, orthogonal; sheer, abrupt, steep, precipitous 209 adj. *high;* straight, plumb; straight up, straight down; upstanding, standing up, on one's feet, on one's legs; bolt upright, stiff as a ramrod, unbowed, head-up; rampant, rearing; on end.

Vb. *be vertical,* stick up, cock up, bristle, stand on end; stand erect, stand upright, hold oneself straight; rise, stand, rise to one's feet, ramp, rear; vacate one's seat 920 vb. *show respect;* keep standing, have no seat, sit on one's thumb.

make vertical, erect, rear, raise, pitch 310 vb. *elevate;* raise on its legs, up-end; stand, set up, stick up, raise up, cock up.

Adv. *vertically* etc. adj.; palewise (heraldry); upright, head-up; on end, up on end, endwise, up; on one's legs, standing, all standing; at right angles, perpendicularly; down, straight-d., plumb.

See: 209, 310, 920.

216 Horizontality

N. *horizontality,* horizontal, horizontal angle, azimuth; horizontalism, horizontalization; horizontal line, ruling, rule; horizontal course, strike; flatness 258 n. *smoothness;* level, plane, dead level, dead flat, level plane; sea-level, water l., water table; stratum; slab, tablet, table 207 n. *layer;* level stretch, steppe 348 n. *plain;* flats 347 n. *marsh;* platform, ledge 254 n.

projection; terrace, esplanade, estrade; plateau, tableland 209 n. *high land;* bowling green, cricket ground, court, baseball diamond, hockey rink, tennis court, croquet lawn 728 n. *arena;* billiard table; flatbed; gridiron; pancake; dish, platter 194 n. *plate;* spirit-level, T-square 465 n. *gauge;* horizon, false h., horizon line 236 n. *limit.*

supination, resupination; recumbency, lying down etc. vb.; reclination, decumbence, decumbency, discumbency; prostration; proneness; accumbation.

flattener, iron, flat-i., mangle, press, trouser-p.; rolling-pin, roller, garden-r., road-r., steam-r. 258 n. *smoother.*

Adj. *flat,* horizontal, level, plane, even, flush 258 adj. *smooth;* trodden, trodden flat, beaten f.; flat as a pancake, flat as a board, flat as my hand, flat as a fluke, flat as a flounder, flat as a billiard table, flat as a bowling green; unwrinkled, smooth, smooth as glass, calm, calm as a mill-pond; alluvial.

supine, flat on one's back; prone, face down, prostrate; recumbent, decumbent, procumbent, accumbent; jacent, lying down, couchant; abed, laid out; sprawling, lolling.

Vb. *be horizontal,* lie, lie down, lie flat, lie prostrate, lie on one's back; recline, couch, sprawl, loll 311 vb. *sit down;* grovel 311 vb. *stoop;* become horizontal, straighten out, level out.

flatten, lay out, roll o., lay down, spread; lay flat, beat f., tread f., stamp down, trample d., squash; make flush, align, level, even, plane 28 vb. *equalize;* iron, iron out, roll, mangle 258 vb. *smooth;* smooth down, plaster d.; prostrate, knock down, floor, gravel, ground 311 vb. *fell.*

Adv. *horizontally,* flat, on one's back; fesse-wise, fesse-ways (heraldry).

See: 28, 194, 207, 209, 236, 254, 258, 311, 347, 348, 465, 728.

217 Pendency

N. *pendency,* pensility, pensileness; dependency, dependence; suspension, hanging, danglement, dangle; set, hang.

pendant 18 n. *analogue;* hanging ornament, pendicle, dangler, drop, eardrop, earring 844 n. *jewellery;* tassel, bobble, tag 844 n.

trimming; hangings, draperies, drapes, curtains, arras, tapestry 226 n. *covering*; train, skirt, coat-tail; flap, lappet, tippet 228 n. *dress*; queue, pigtail, tail, brush 67 n. *sequel*, 259 n. *hair*; dewlap, lobe, appendix 40 n. *adjunct*; pendule, pendulum, bob, swing, hammock 317 n. *oscillation*; chandelier, gaselier, electrolier, ceiling light 420 n. *lamp*; icicle, stalactite.

hanger, coat-h. curtain-rod, curtain-ring, runner, ring; hook, tenterhook, staple, peg, knob, nail, yoke, cowlstaff 218 n. *supporter*; suspender, braces, suspender-belt 228 n. *underwear*; clothes-line 47 n. *cable*; clothes-horse 218 n. *frame*; davit, crane, derrick 310 n. *lifter*; spar, mast 218 n. *pillar*; gallows, gibbet, crucifix 964 n. *pillory*; garter 47 n. *halter*.

Adj. *pendent*, hanging, pendulous, pensile; hanging from, dependent, suspended, dangling etc. vb.; hanging the head, nodding, drooping, weeping; lowering, overhanging; beetling 254 adj. *salient*; decumbent, open-ended, loose 46 adj. *disjunct*; baggy, flowing; floating (in the wind), waving, streaming, rippling; pedunculate, tailed, caudate; penduline.

Vb. *hang*, be pendent, drape, set; hang down, depend, trail, flow; hang on to, swing, sway, dangle, bob; hang the head, nod, weep, droop, sag, swag, daggle; hang in the wind, stream, wave, float, ripple, flap; hang over, hover; overhang, lower 226 vb. *overlie*; suspend, hang up, sling, hook up, hitch, fasten to, append 45 n. *join*; curtain 226 vb. *cover*.

See: 18, 40, 45, 46, 47, 67, 218, 226, 228, 254, 259, 310, 317, 420, 844, 964.

218 Support

N. *support*, moral s., encouragement 703 n. *aid*; uplift, sustenance, sustentation, maintenance, upkeep, nurture 633 n. *provision*; subsidy 703 n. *subvention*; point d'appui, locus standi, footing, ground, leg to stand on; hold, foothold, handhold, toe-hold 778 n. *retention*; life-buoy, life-belt 662 n. *safeguard*.

supporter, carriage, carrier; support, mounting, bearing; underframe, chassis; buttress, flying b., arc-boutant; abutment, embankment, wall, retaining w.; under-

pinning, shore, jack, prop, clothes-p.; flagstaff, jackstaff, sprag, stanchion, rod, bar, transom, steadier, brace, strut; stay, mainstay, guy, shrouds, rigging 47 n. *tackling*; sprit, boom, spar, mast, yard, yardarm, fid, cross-tree, outrigger, cat-head 254 n. *projection*; trunk, stem, stalk, caudex, pedicle, pedicel, peduncle 366 n. *plant*; arch, roman a., gothic a., Saracenic a., ogive 248 n. *curve*; keystone, head stone, corner-stone, springer; cantilever; pier (see *pillar*); bandage, jock-strap, truss, splint; stiffener, whalebone; stays 228 n. *underwear*; suspender, garter, braces; yoke, cowlstaff 217 n. *hanger*; rest, headrest, backrest, footrest, stirrup; handrail (see *handle*); skid, chock, sprag, wedge 702 n. *obstacle*; stang, staff, baton, stick, walking s., cane, alpenstock, bourdon, crutch, crook; leg-support, irons; bracket (see *shelf*;) trivet, hob (see *stand*); arm, back, shoulder, broad shoulders; shoulder-blade, clavicle, collar-bone, backbone, spine, neck, cervix; world-bearer, Atlas; helper, patron 707 n. *auxiliary*.

handle, holder, pen-h., cigarette-h. 195 n. *receptacle*; hold, grip, hilt, pommel, haft; knob, door-handle; lug, ear, loop; railing, handrail, rail, poop-r., taffrail, balustrade; shaft, spear-s., oar-s., loom; handlebar, tiller; winder, crank, crank-handle; lever, trigger 630 n. *tool*.

basis, foundation, solid f., concrete f.; sleeper; stereobate, substratum 207 n. *layer*; ground, groundwork, floor, bed, bedrock, rock bottom 214 n. *base*; flooring, pavement 226 n. *paving*; terra firma 344 n. *land*; perch, footing, foothold.

stand, tripod, trivet, hob; wine-stand, coaster; lampstand, lamp-post, standard; anvil, block, bench; table, tea-t., teapoy; dining-table, board; console, console table; sideboard, dresser 194 n. *cabinet*; work-table, desk, counter; pedestal, plinth, socle; stylobate, podium; platform, staddle, gantry; emplacement, banquette; firestep; footplate; foot-pace, landing, half-l.; landing-stage, pier; dais, pulpit, stage 539 n. *rostrum*; doorstep, threshold 263 n. *entrance*; altar-step, predella 990 n. *altar*; step, stair, tread, rung, round 308 n. *ascent*; stilt 310 n. *lifter*; sole, heel 214 n. *foot*; shank 267 n. *leg*; shoe, boot 228 n. *footwear*.

seat, throne, sedes gestatoria, masnad, guddi, woolsack; bank, bench, form, settle, podium; window-seat, rumble s., bucket s., sofa s., box s., box, dickey; pew, choir-stall, miséricorde 990 n. *church interior*; stall, fauteuil 594 n. *theatre*; chair, armchair, easy c., elbow c., rocking c., basket c., high c., chaise longue; dining chair, triclinium; sofa, settee, divan, couch, ottoman, Chesterfield, sociable, loveseat; stool, footstool, campstool, faldstool; tabouret, pouffe, mora; priedieu, kneeler, cushion; riding seat, saddle, side-s., pack s., flat s., stock s., pillion, spring-seat; howdah, pad; stocks, ducking-stool 964 n. *pillory*; electric chair, hot seat 964 n. *means of execution*; lap, knees; carpet 226 n. *floor-cover*.

bed, cot, crib, cradle, bassinet; marriage bed, bridal b., double b., single b., trundle b., day-b.; couch, tester, four-poster; charpoy, truckle bed, camp-b., pallet, shake-down, bunk; hammock 217 n. *pendant*; sick bed, litter, hurdle, stretcher 658 n. *hospital*; bedding 226 n. *coverlet*; bedstead, bedstock, slats; bier 364 n. *funeral*.

cushion, air-c., pillow; bolster, Dutch wife; mattress, spring m.; straw mattress, under-m., palliasse; squab, hassock, kneeler; prayer-mat.

beam, baulk, joist, girder, rafter, raft, tie-beam 47 n. *bond*; summer, breast-s., summer-beam, summer-tree; cross-beam, transom, cross-bar, traverse, travis, trave; architrave, lintel.

pillar, shaft, pier, pile, pendentive, post, kingpost, stock; jamb, door-j.; newel-post, bannister, balustrade, baluster; mullion; pilaster, column, Doric c., Ionic c., Corinthian c., portico, stoa; caryatid, telamon, Atlantes; spinal column, spine, backbone, vertebræ; neck, cervix.

pivot, fulcrum, fulciment, lever, purchase; hinge 45 n. *joint*; pole, axis; axle, axle-tree, spindle, arbor, pintle 315 n. *rotator*; bearing, gudgeon, trunnion; rowlock, thole-pin; centre-board, keel.

shelf, ledge, offset 254 n. *projection*; corbel, bracket, console, ancon; retable, niche 194 n. *compartment*; sill, window-s., mantelpiece, mantelshelf, rack, cupboard, dresser 194 n. *cabinet*; counter, plank, board, table, leaf, slab 207 n. *lamina*.

frame, bony f., skeleton, ribs; framework, scaffolding 331 n. *structure*; chassis, fuse-lage, body (of a car), undercarriage; trestle; easel, clothes-horse; cage, trave 235 n. *inclosure*; tailor's dummy, farthingale, hoop 228 n. *skirt*; picture-frame, window f., sash, window-s. 223 n. *outline*.

Adj. *supporting*, sustentative, sustaining; fundamental, basal; columellar, columnar; cervical, spinal; structural, skeletal; framing, holding.

Vb. *support*, sustain, bear, carry, hold, shoulder; uphold, upbear; hold up, bear up, buoy up; prop, shore up, underprop, underpin, jack up 310 vb. *elevate*; bolster, bolster up, cushion; reinforce, underset 162 vb. *strengthen*; bandage, brace, truss 45 vb. *tighten*; steady, stay; cradle, pillow, cup, cup one's chin; nourish, nurture 301 vb. *feed*; maintain, keep on foot 804 vb. *pay*; back up, give support, lend s., furnish s., afford s., supply s. 703 vb. *aid*; frame, set, mount 235 vb. *enclose*; give foundations, bottom, ground, found, base, embed 153 vb. *stabilize*; stand, endure, stand up to, stand the strain, take the s. 635 vb. *suffice*.

be supported, stand on, recline on, lie on, sit on, loll on, repose on, rest on; bear on, press, press on, step on, lean on, abut on; rely on, ground oneself on, be based on; command support, have at one's back, have behind one.

Adv. *astride*, astraddle, pick-a-back.

See: 45, 57, 153, 162, 194, 195, 207, 214, 217, 223, 226, 228, 235, 248, 254, 263, 267, 301, 308, 310, 315, 331, 344, 364, 366, 539, 594, 630, 633, 635, 658, 662, 702, 703, 707, 778, 804, 964, 990.

219 Parallelism

N. *parallelism*, non-convergence, non-divergence, equidistance, coextension, collimation, concentricity; parallel, correspondence 28 n. *equality*; parallel lines, lines of latitude; tramlines, rails, railroad tracks; parallelogram, parallelepiped.

Adj. *parallel*, coextensive, collateral, concurrent, concentric; equidistant 28 adj. *equal*; corresponding, correspondent 18 adj. *similar*.

Vb. *be parallel*, run together, run abreast, lie parallel; correspond, concur; collimate, parallel, draw a p.

Adv. *in parallel,* alongside, collaterally; side by side, abreast.

See: 18, 28.

220 Obliquity

N. *obliquity,* obliqueness, skewness; oblique line, diagonal; oblique figure, rhomboid 247 n. *angular figure*; oblique angle, inclination 247 n. *angularity*; oblique direction, side-pressure; indirection, indirectness, squint; curvature, camber, bend, springing line, skewback 248 n. *curve*; changing direction, crankiness, crookedness, scoliosis, zigzag, chevron; switchback 251 n. *meandering*; oblique motion, knight's move, divagation, digression, swerve, lurch, stagger, swag 282 n. *deviation*; splay, bias, twist, warp, perversion 246 n. *distortion*; leaning, list, tip, cant; slopeness, slope, slant, tilt, rake, rakish angle; sloping face, batter; sloping edge, bevel, bezel; inclined plane, ramp, chute, slide; Tower of Pisa, leaning tower; measurement of inclination 247 n. *angular measure.*

acclivity, rise, ascent; ramp, incline, gradient; hill, rising ground 209 n. *monticle*; hillside, khud, khudside, bank, 239 n. *laterality*; declivity, fall, dip, downhill, devexity, shelving beach 309 n. *descent*; easy ascent, easy descent, gentle slope, rapid s.; steepness, cliff, precipice 215 n. *verticality*; escarpment, scarp, glacis 713 n. *fortification*; talus, landslide, scree.

Adj. *oblique,* inclined, abaxial, plagihedral; bevel, bezel; tipsy, tilted, rakish; biased, askew, skew, slant, aslant, ajee; out of the perpendicular, battered, clinal, leaning; recumbent, stooping; cater-cornered, rhomboidal 247 adj. *angular*; wry, awry, wonky, skew-whiff, crooked, squinting, cock-eyed, knock-kneed 246 adj. *distorted*; diagonal, transverse, transversal, antiparallel; athwart, thwart, cross 222 adj. *crossed*; indirect, zigzag, herringbone, bent 248 adj. *curved*; stepped, in echelon; divergent, non-parallel 282 adj. *deviating.*

sloping, acclivous, uphill 308 adj. *ascending*, rising, declivous, downhill, falling, declining, devex 309 adj. *descending*; anticlinal, anaclinal, synclinal, cataclinal; steep, abrupt, sheer, precipitous, break-neck 215 adj. *vertical*; easy, gentle, rounded.

Vb. *be oblique,* — tilted etc. adj.; incline, lean; tilt, slope, slant, shelve, decline 309 vb. *descend*; rise, climb 308 vb, *ascend*; cut, cut across, diagonalize, transect 222 vb. *cross*; lean, tip, lean over, bank, heel, careen, cant; bend, sag, swag, give; bend over 311 vb. *stoop*; walk sideways, edge, sidle, sidestep; look sideways, squint; zigzag, jink, swerve; diverge, converge.

render oblique, incline, lean, slant, slope, cant, tilt, tip, rake; splay 282 vb. *deviate*; bend, crook, twist, warp 246 vb. *distort*; chamfer, bevel; sway, bias, divert 282 vb. *deflect*; curve, camber 248 vb. *make curved.*

Adv. *obliquely* etc. adj.; diagonally, crosswise 222 adv. *across*; on the cross, on the bias; askew, rakishly, tipsily; aslant, slantwise, on the slant; askance, asquint; edgewise, sidelong, sideways; aslope, off the vertical, off plumb, at an angle, at a rakish a.; on one side, all on one s.; by a side wind.

See: 209, 215, 222, 239, 246, 247, 248, 251, 282, 308, 309, 311, 713.

221 Inversion

N. *inversion,* turning back to front, palindrome, hysteron proteron; turning inside out, eversion; turning backwards, retroversion, reversal 148 n. *reversion*; turning inward, introversion, invagination; turning over, pronation, capsizal (see *overturning*); turn of the tide, return 286 n. *regression*; oppositeness 14 n. *contrariety*, 240 n. *contraposition*; transposition, transposal, metathesis 151 n. *interchange*; inverted order (linguistic), chiasmus, anastrophe, hyperbaton, hypallage 519 n. *trope*; confused order, synchysis, spoonerism; interrupted order, tmesis, parenthesis 72 n. *discontinuity*, 231 n. *interjacence.*

overturning, capsize, capsizal, upset, spill, overset; somersault, summerset, culbute, cartwheel, hand-spring; subversion, undermining 149 n. *revolution*; pronation 216 n. *supination.*

Adj. *inverted,* inverse, back-to-front; palindromic; upside down, everted, invaginated, inside out, wrong side out; capsized,

upside down, bottom up, keel upwards; capsizing, topheavy; topsy-turvy, head over heels, on one's head; flat, prone 216 n. *supine*; reverse, reversed 14 adj. *contrary*; antipodean, antipodal 240 adj. *opposite*; hyperbatic, chiastic, antithetic.

Vb. *be inverted*, turn round, go r., wheel r., turn about, face a., right about turn 286 vb. *turn back*; turn over, heel o., capsize, turn turtle; tilt over 220 vb. *be oblique*; go over, topple o. 309 vb. *tumble*; stand on one's head; reverse, back, back away, go backwards 286 vb. *regress*.

invert, transpose, put the cart before the horse 151 vb. *interchange*; reverse, turn the tables; retrovert, turn back; turn down 261 vb. *fold*; introvert, invaginate; turn inside out, evaginate; upturn, overturn, tip over, spill, upset, capsize; turn topsy turvy.

Adv. *inversely* etc. adj.; vice versa; contrariwise, other way round; arsy-versy, topsy-turvy, head over heels, heels in the air; face down, face downwards.

See: 14, 72, 148, 149, 151, 216, 220, 231, 240, 261, 286, 309, 519.

222 Crossing: intertexture

N. *crossing*, crossing over and under, plain weaving; criss-cross, transversion, transection, intersection; decussation, X-shape; chiasma, quincunx; intertexture, interlacement; intertwinement, arabesque; interdigitation; anastomosis, inosculation; plexure, plexus, braid, wreath, plait 251 n. *convolution*; entanglement, intricacy, skein, sleave, cat's cradle 61 n. *complexity*; crossway, cross-roads, intersection, road-junction 624 n. *road*; level crossing 624 n. *railroad*; viaduct, fly-over 624 n. *bridge*, 305 n. *traffic control*.

cross, crux, rood, crucifix 988 n. *ritual object*; pectoral 989 n. *vestments*; ansate cross, Lorraine c., Greek c., Maltese c., Celtic c., St. Andrew's C.; saltire 547 n. *heraldry*; crosslet, swastika, fylfot, tau; cross-bar, transom 218 n. *beam*; scissors, pincers, nutcrackers, forceps 778 n. *nippers*.

network, reticulation, meshwork, netting, webbing, matting, wickerwork, mokes, trellis, wattle, raddle; lattice, grating, grid, grill, gridiron; tracery, fretwork, filigree 844 n. *ornamental art*; lace, crochet, knitting; web, cobweb; net, fishnet, seine, drag-net, trawl, beam-t. 235 n. *inclosure*; plexus, mesh, moke, reticle.

textile, weave, web, loom; woven stuff, piecegoods, dry goods; bolt, roll, length, piece, cloth, stuff, material; broadcloth, fabric, tissue, suiting; jute, burlap, hessian, gunny, sacking, sackcloth; hemp, canvas; linen, lawn, cambric; duck; tapestry, blanketing, towelling, crash; mohair, cashmere; alpaca, vicuna, Angora; wool, merino, worsted; frieze, felt; jersey, stockinette, paramatta; homespun, khadi, khaddar, duffle, hodden, kersey, tweed, serge, shalloon, baize; flannel, flannelette, swansdown; swanskin; linenette, cotton, drill, nankeen, muslin, mull, mulmull, nainsook, jaconet; silesia, calico, dowlas, long-cloth, fustian, moleskin, sharkskin, dimity, gingham, voile, madras, percale, rep, seersucker, poplin; chintz, cretonne, holland, silk, foulard, georgette, grosgraine, damask, brocade, samite, satin, sateen, ninon, taffeta, tussah, tussore, sarcenet, shantung, chiffon, surah, pongee; velvet, velveteen, velours; corduroy; tulle, organdie, organza; lace, bullion, chenille, crochet-work, crewel-work; artificial fabric, cellulose f., artificial silk, rayon.

weaving, texture, weftage; web, warp, weft, woof; frame, loom, shuttle; weaver, stockinger, knitter; spinning wheel, distaff, whorl; spinner, spinster; spider.

Adj. *crossed*, crossing, cross, criss-cross; quadrivial; diagonal, transverse, cross-eyed, squinting 220 adj. *oblique*; decussated, X-shaped, chiastic, quincunxial; cross-legged, cruciform, crucial, forked, furcate, furcular 247 adj. *angular*; plexal, plexiform; knotted, matted, balled-up, ravelled 61 adj. *complex*; pleached, plaited, interlaced, interfretted, inter-woven; textile, loomed, woven, hand-woven, tweedy; trellised, latticed, grated, mullioned, barred; streaked, striped.

reticular, reticulated, retiform, webbed, webby; netted, meshed 201 adj. *spaced*.

Vb. *cross*, cross over, cross under 305 vb. *pass*; intersect, cut, diagonalize 220 vb, *be oblique*; decussate, anastomose, inosculate, interdigitate; splice, dovetail. link 45 vb. *join*; reticulate, mesh, net, knot; fork, bifurcate 247 vb. *angulate*.

222-224

weave, loom; pleach, plait, braid; felt, twill, knit, crochet; spin, slub.

enlace, interlace, interlink, interlock, interdigitate, intertwine, intertwist, interweave, enmesh, engage gear; twine, entwine, twist, raddle, wreathe, pleach; mat, ravel, tangle, entangle, dishevel 63 vb. *derange.*

Adv. *across*, thwart, transversely; decussatively, crosswise, saltire-wise; with folded arms, arm in arm.

See: 45, 61, 63, 201, 218, 220, 235, 247, 251, 305, 547, 624, 778, 844, 988, 989.

223 Exteriority

N. *exteriority*, the external; outwardness, externality 230 n. *circumjacence*; periphery, circumference, side-lines 233 n. *outline*; exterior, outward appearance 445 n. *mien*; surface, superficies, superstratum, crust, cortex, shell 226 n. *skin*; outer side, face, facet, façade 237 n. *front*; outside, out of doors, open air; outer space 199 n. *distance*; other side 240 n. *contraposition*; externalism, regard for externals 982 n. *idolatry*; externalization, extraversion, extravert 6 n. *extrinsicality*; extraterritoriality 57 n. *exclusion*; foreignness 59 n. *extraneousness*; eccentricity 84 n. *unconformity*; outsider 84 n. *nonconformist.*

Adj. *exterior*, outward, extra-; external 10 adj. *irrelative*; roundabout, peripheral 230 adj. *circumjacent*; outer, outermost, outlying 199 adj. *distant*; outside, outboard; outdoor, extramural; foreign 59 adj. *extraneous*; extraterritorial 57 adj. *excluding*; extravert, extra-regarding, outward-looking 6 adj. *extrinsic*; centrifugal 620 adj. *avoiding*; exogenous; eccentric 282 adj. *deviating*; outstanding, egregious 34 adj. *superior*; surface, superficial, epidermic, cortical; skin-deep 212 adj. *shallow*; frontal, facial 237 adj. *fore.*

Vb. *be exterior*, lie beyond, lie outside etc. adv.; frame, enclose 230 vb. *surround*; look outward 6 vb. *be extrinsic.*

externalize, body forth, objectify 6 vb. *make extrinsic*; project, extrapolate; extern 300 vb. *eject.*

Adv. *externally*, outwardly, outwards, superficially, on the surface; on the face of it, to the outsider; outside, extra muros;

out, out of doors, in the cold, in the sun, in the open, in the open air, al fresco.

See: 6, 10, 34, 57, 59, 84, 199, 212, 226, 230, 233, 237, 240, 282, 300, 445, 620, 982.

224 Interiority

N. *interiority*, interior, inside, indoors; inner surface, undersurface; endoderm 226 n. *skin*; sap-wood, heart-w. 366 n. *wood*; inmost being, heart's blood, soul; marrow, pith; heart, centre, breast, bosom 225 n. *centrality*; inland, heartland, hinterland, up-country; pith, marrow 3 n. *substance*; subsoil, substratum 214 n. *base*; permeation, pervasion 189 n. *presence*, 231 n. *interjacence*; interspace 201 n. *interval*; deepness, cave, pit, penetralia, recesses, innermost r. 211 n. *depth*; endogamy 894 n. *marriage*; introversion 5 n. *intrinsicality*; self-absorption, egoism, egotism, egocentrism 932 n. *selfishness*; introvert, egoist 932 n. *egotist*; inmate, indweller 191 n. *dweller*; internee 750 n. *prisoner.*

insides 193 n. *contents*; inner man, interior man; internal organs, vitals; heart, ticker; bowels, entrails, guts, pluck, tripe; intestines, colon, rectum; viscera, liver and lights; spleen; milt; abdomen, belly, paunch, underbelly; womb, uterus; stomach, tummy 194 n. *maw*; chest, solar plexus; gland; endocrine; cell 358 n. *organism*; offal, chitterlings, haslet, kidney, liver.

Adj. *interior*, internal, inward 5 adj. *intrinsic*; inside, inner, innermost, midmost 225 adj. *central*; inland, up-country 211 adj. *deep*; domestic, home, vernacular; intimate, familiar 490 adj. *known*; indoor, intramural, shut in, enclosed; inboard, built-in, inwrought; endemic 192 adj. *residing*; deep-seated, ingrown 153 adj. *fixed*; intestinal, visceral, alvine; intravenous, subcutaneous; interstitial, endocardial 231 adj. *interjacent*; inward-looking, intra-regarding, introvert 5 adj. *intrinsic*; endo-, endogamous; endogenous.

Vb. *be inside*, —internal etc. adj.; be within etc. adv.; lie within, lie beneath, be at the bottom of; show through 443 vb. *be visible.*

enclose, hold 78 vb. *comprise*; place within, embed 303 vb. *insert*; keep inside, intern

747 vb. *imprison*; enfold, embay 235 vb. *inclose*.

Adv. *inside*, within, in, deep in, deep down; inly, intimately; deeply, profoundly, at heart; inwardly, herein, therein, wherein; withinside, within doors, indoors, at home, ben, chez, at the sign of.

See: 3, 5, 78, 153, 189, 191, 192, 193, 194, 201, 211, 214, 225, 226, 231, 235, 303, 358, 366, 443, 490, 747, 750, 894, 932.

225 Centrality

N. *centrality*, centricality, centricity; centricalness, middleness 70 n. *middle*; centripetence; centralization, focalization, concentration, nucleation 324 n. *condensation*; central position, mid p. 231 n. *interjacence*; waist-line, centre-line, parting 231 n. *partition*; Ptolemaic system, Copernican s.

centre, dead c.; centroid, centre of mass, centre of gravity, centre of pressure, centre of percussion, centre of buoyancy, metacentre, epicentre; storm-centre, hotbed; heart, core, kernel, nub, hub, nave, nucleus, nucleolus; navel, umbilicus; spine, backbone, chine, midrib; marrow, pith 224 n. *interiority*; pole, axis, fulcrum, centre-board 218 n. *pivot*; centre point, mid p. 70 n. *middle*; fesse-point 547 n. *heraldry*; eye, pupil; bull's-eye, blank, target 617 n. *objective*.

Adj. *central*, centro-, centric, centrical, centroidal; nuclear, nucleal, nucleolar; centremost, midmost 70 adj. *middle*; axial, focal, pivotal; mesogastric, umbilical, umbilicate; homocentric, concentric; geocentric; heliocentric; spinal, vertebral; centripetal; metropolitan, chief, head 34 adj. *supreme*.

Vb. *centralize*, centre, take c.; focus, bring to a f., centre upon, concentrate, nucleate, consolidate 324 vb. *be dense*.

Adv. *centrally*, at heart, at the core, middle, midst, amongst; in the midst, in the middle.

See: 34, 70, 218, 224, 231, 324, 547, 617.

226 Covering

N. *covering*, obduction, superposition, superimposition, overlaying; overlap, overlapping, imbrication; coating, stratification 207 n. *layer*; top-layer, top-dressing, mulch, top-soil 344 n. *soil*; cover, covercle, lid; grave-stone, ledger 364 n. *tomb*; flap, shutter, operculum 421 n. *screen*; glass, glass front, watch-glass, crystal 422 n. *transparency*; cap, top, plug, bung, cork 263 n. *stopper*; pledget, dossil, tampon, tompion 658 n. *surgical dressing*; carapace, shell, tortoise-shell, snail s., oyster s. 326 n. *hardness*; mail, plate, armour p. 713 n. *armour*; shield, cowl, cowling, bonnet, hood (of a car); scab 207 n. *lamina*; crust, fur 649 n. *dirt*; capsule, ferrule, sheath, envelope 194 n. *receptacle*; finger-stall, pillow-case, pillow-slip; chair cover, antimacassar; hangings, curtains, window c., drapes, arras, tapestry, wallpaper 217 n. *pendant*; mask, gas-m., iron m. 527 n. *disguise*; air 340 n. *atmosphere*.

roof, cupola 253 n. *dome*; mansard roof, pitched r., gable r., flat r.; housetop, roof-top, roof-ridge 213 n. *vertex*; leads, slates, slating, tiles, tiling, pantile, shingle, thatch, thatching; eaves 234 n. *edge*; ceiling, rafters; deck.

canopy, ciborium, baldachin; tilt, awning, velarium, sun-blind 421 n. *screen*; marquee, shamiana, pavilion, tent, bell-tent; tent-cloth, canvas, tarpaulin, mosquito net 222 n. *network*.

shade, film 421 n. *screen*; hood, eyelid, eyelash; blind, sun-b., venetian b., persiennes, shutters, slats; curtain, veil; umbrella, gamp, bumbershoot, brolly; parasol, sunshade; sun-bonnet, sun-helmet, sola topee 228 n. *headgear*; visor, sun-screen; peak (of a cap); dark glasses 442 n. *eye-glass*.

wrapping, wrapper, paper, cellophane; bandage, roll 45 n. *girdle*; lint, plaster, cast, dressing 658 n. *surgical dressing*; book-cover, binding, boards, covers, straw-board, mill-b., dust-jacket 589 n. *bookbinding*; jacket, coat 228 n. *tunic*; mantle 228 n. *cloak*; comforter, scarf, chudder 228 n. *shawl*; loincloth 228 n. *shirt*; life-belt, Mae West 662 n. *safeguard*; cocoon, chrysalis; cerement, shroud, winding sheet, mummy-cloth 364 n. *grave clothes*.

skin, outer s., scarf-s., cuticle, epidermis, ecderm; true skin, cutis, derm, corium, enderm; tegument; integument, peel,

bark, crust, rind, coat, cortex; husk, hull, shell, pod, cod, shuck, jacket; pellicle, film; scalp 213 n. *head*; scale 207n. *lamina*; pelt, peltry, fleece, fell, fur; leather, hide, rawhide, imitation leather, leatheroid; shagreen, calf, cowhide, morocco, pigskin, crocodile, alligator, elk, kid, sealskin, deerskin, doeskin; lambskin, sheepskin, woolfell, woolskin; rabbit skin; chinchilla; sable, mink, muskrat; vair, ermine, miniver, marten; feathers, coverts 259 n. *plumage.*

paving, flooring, floor, parquet; deck, floorboards, duck-b.; pavement, pavé; flags, paving-stone; sett, cobble, cobblestone; tarmac 624 n. *road.*

coverlet, bedspread, counterpane, bedding, bed-clothes, bed-sheets; sheet, contours., quilt, eiderdown, blanket, rug; caparison, housings, trappings; saddlecloth, horsecloth, numdah.

floor-cover, carpet, stair-c., pile c., persian c.; mat, doormat; rug, scatter r., hooked r.; drugget, numdah; linoleum, oilcloth; matting; red carpet 875 n. *formality.*

facing, revetment 162n. *strengthening*; veneer, coating, varnish, japan, lacquer, enamel, glaze; incrustation, rough-cast, pebble-dash; stucco, compo, plaster, parget, rendering; wash, whitewash, distemper, stain, polish, smearing, inunction, ointment; impasto, paint 425n. *pigment.*

Adj. *overlying*, overlaying, over-arching; overlapping, tegular, imbricated; cloaking etc. vb.

covered, roofed, roofed in, ceiled, wall-papered, carpeted; tented, garaged, under cover, under canvas; under shelter 660n. *safe*; cloaked, cowled, veiled, hooded 525 adj. *concealed*; loricated, armour-plated, iron-clad; metalled, paved; overbuilt, built over; snow-capped, ice-covered; inundated, flooded; smothered, plastered.

dermal, cutaneous, cortical, cuticular; tegumentary; scaly, squamous; epidermic, epidermoid.

Vb. *cover*, superpose, superimpose; roof, roof in, put the lid on, cap, tip; spread, lay (a table); overlay, smother; lap, wrap, enwrap, enfold 235vb. *inclose*; blanket, mantle, muffle, moble; hood, veil 525vb. *conceal*; case, bind, cover (books); bandage, swathe, wrap round, dress 658

vb. doctor; sheathe, incapsulate, encase 303vb. *insert*; embox; wall in, wall up; keep under cover, lock up, garage.

overlie, overarch, overhang, overlap; overshadow 417vb. *bedim*; span, bestride, straddle, bestraddle 205vb. *be broad*; overflood, inundate, 341vb. *drench*; skin, skin over, crust, scab.

overlay, pave, floor, cement; ceil, roof, dome, overarch, deck; paper, wallpaper 227vb. *line*; overspread, top-dress, mulch; spread, smear, besmear; butter, anoint; powder, dust, sand.

coat, revet, face, do over; grout, rough-cast, incrust, shingle; stucco, plaster, parget, render; veneer, varnish, lacquer, japan, enamel, glaze; paint, whitewash, distemper, stain 425vb. *colour*; tar, pitch, pay; daub, bedaub, scumble, overpaint, grease, lay it on thick; gild, plate, silver, besilver; electroplate, silverplate; waterproof, fire-p. 660vb. *safeguard.*

See: 45, 162, 194, 205, 207, 213, 217, 222, 227, 228, 234, 235, 253, 259, 263, 303, 326, 340, 341, 344, 364, 419, 421, 422, 425, 442, 525, 527, 589, 624, 649, 658, 660, 662, 713, 875.

227 Lining

N. *lining*, interlining 231 n. *interjacence*; coating, inner c.; stuffing, wadding, padding, bombast; interlining, inlay; backing, facing; doublure 589 n. *bookbinding*; upholstery; papering, wallpaper; wainscotting, panelling, wainscot, brattice; metal lining, bushing; brake-lining; packing, pack, dunnage; filling, stopping (dentistry); washer, shim.

Vb. *line*, incrust 226vb. *coat*; interlard, inlay; back, face, paper, wall-p.; upholster, cushion; stuff, pad, wad; fill, pack; bush; fother.

See: 226, 231, 589.

228 Dressing

N. *dressing*, investment, investiture; clothing, covering, dressing up, toilet, toilette; overdressing, foppishness 848 n. *fashion*; vesture, dress, garb, attire, trim; garniture, accoutrement, caparison, harness,

housing, trappings; rigging, rig; rig-out, turn-out; tailoring, millinery, mercery.

clothing, wear; raiment, linen; apparel, wearing a.; clothes, garments, weeds, things, doings; gear, vestments, habiliments; wardrobe, outfit, trousseau; layette, baby clothes, swaddling c., baby linen; togs, toggery, duds, traps; old clothes, slops; reach-me-downs, hand-me-downs, rags, tatters; best, best clothes, clean linen, fine raiment; Sunday best, Sunday-go-to-meeting clothes, best bib and tucker; party dress, glad rags; pearlies, ostrich feathers, frippery 844n. *finery*; fancy dress; theatrical properties; change of raiment, new suit; masquerade; woollens, cottons. See *dress*.

dress, frock, gown, creation; garment, costume, habit, riding h.; suiting, suit, store s., lounge s., office s., ready-made s., tailormade s., bespoke s.; boiler s., siren s., track s.; three-piece s., two-piece s., two-piece; salwar kameez, sari, dhoti, lungi, sarong; civilian dress, civvies, mufti.

formal dress, correct d., coronation d., regalia, court dress, durbar d., full d.; grande toilette, evening dress, tails, white tie and tails; morning dress; academical dress, cap and gown; mourning, black, weepers, widow's weeds.

uniform, regimentals, accoutrement; full dress, undress, mess kit; battle dress, fatigues; khaki, jungle green, field grey, red coat 547n. *livery*; robes, vestments, priestly v., clerical dress 989n. *canonicals*; academicals, cap and gown.

informal dress, undress, mufti, déshabillé, dishabille, négligé, boudoir dress, dressing gown, peignoir, bathrobe, wrapper, pyjamas, bed-jacket; housecoat, kimono, tea-gown, cocktail dress; tuxedo, dinner jacket, smoking j., shooting coat; slippers, slacks.

robe, robes, sweeping r., trailing garments; baby clothes, long clothes, drapery, drapes 217n. *pendant*; sari; himation; pallium, peplum, peplos; stole, pelisse, domino (see *cloak*); sheet, winding s., shroud 364n. *grave clothes*.

tunic, body-coat; coat, cut-away c., swallow-tail c., tail c., frock c.; coatee, jacket, reefer j., single-breasted j., double-breasted j.; dinner jacket, smoking j., tuxedo, monkey jacket, pea-j., pilot j., Eton j.,

mess j., short j., blazer; Norfolk jacket, shooting coat; parka, wind-breaker; leotard; gym dress, drill d.; tabard, dolman, gambeson; jerkin, doublet, jama; paletot, caftan, gaberdine, sanbenito; cassock, soutane; toga, chiton.

vest, waistcoat, bolero; stomacher, jumper, jersey, guernsey, cardigan, spencer, pullover, sweater, banian, singlet, zephyr.

trousers, long t., peg-top t., pants, long p., peg-p., ski-p., frontier p.; trews, breeks, kerseys, overalls, pantaloons, pantalettes; bloomers, bag-trousers, petticoat t., salwar; slacks, bags, Cambridge b., Oxford b.; chaparejos, chaps, dungarees, overalls, denims, jeans, blue j., Levis, pedalpushers, sweat pants; drawers, shorts, Bermuda s., half-pants, short p.

breeches, knee b., riding b., jodhpurs; buckskins, unmentionables, inexpressibles; small-clothes, smalls; knickerbockers, knickers; galligaskins, plus fours; toreador pants; rompers, crawlers.

skirt, outer petticoat, kirtle; grass skirt, Hawaian s., full s., divided s., slit s., hobble s., jupe, crinoline, hoop-skirt, farthingale, pannier, hoop; ballet skirt, tutu; kilt, filibeg; overskirt, peplum; bustle, tournure.

apron, pinafore, pinner, jumper, overall; bib, tucker, front, false shirt, dickey; fichu.

loincloth, breechcloth, breechclout, malkoch; loin-guard; diaper, nappy.

bodywear, linen, lingerie; shirt, punjabi, vest, singlet; banian; smock, shift, chemise, slip, petticoat, princess p., waist-p.; blouse, waist, shirt-waist, basque; stomacher, bodice, choli, camisole, chemisette, corsage; corslet.

underwear, undies, dessous, lingerie, frillies; underclothes, underlinen, undershirt, underbodice, undervest, underskirt, underdrawers, underpants; pants, combinations, woollies; drawers, knickers, bloomers, pettipants; panties, scanties, briefs, step-ins, camiknickers, camibockers; foundation garment, corset, stays, whalebone; two-way stretch, girdle, pantie-girdle; brassière, bra; braces, suspenders; suspender belt, garter, shoulder-straps.

nightwear, sleeping suit, nightgown, nightshirt, nighty; pyjamas, shorties; bed-socks, bed-jacket, nightcap.

beachwear, play-suit, bikini; bathing cos-

tume, swim-suit, bathing drawers, bathing-suit, trunks.

overcoat, coat, fur c., fur-lined c., mink c.; top-coat, long-c., greatcoat, uniform coat; trench-coat, surtout, redingote, riding coat; duffel coat, loden c.; waterproof, mackintosh, raincoat; storm-coat, sou'-wester, oilskins; slicker, pea-jacket, wind-cheater, wrap-rascal; spencer, raglan, burberry, benjamin.

cloak, mantle, mantlet, chlamys; military cloak, sagum; capote, cape, talma, poncho, manteau, mantua, pelisse, roquelaure, cardinal, tippet, pelerine; huke, haik, burnous, yashmak, veil 421 n. *screen*; domino 527 n. *disguise*.

shawl, mantilla, ascot; stole, chudder; scarf, wrapper, choker; comforter, muffler, plaid; prayer-scarf, tallith.

headgear, head-dress, mantilla; plumes, feathers, ostrich f.; ribbons 844 n. *finery*; crown, coronet, tiara 743 n. *regalia*; fillet, snood, coif, wimple 47 n. *girdle*; headband, kerchief; turban, puggree; fez, tarboosh; hood, cowl, calash; helmet, Balaclava h., busby, bearskin, shako, képi, forage cap, side-c., pill-box; casque, morion, steel hat 713 n. *armour*; cap, cloth c., skull-c., smoking c., peaked c., riding c., jockey c.; fast-cap, stocking c.; beret, tam-o'-shanter, tam; Balmoral, glengarry; hat, tile, lid, beany; crown, peak, brim; soft hat, homburg, trilby; pork pie hat, billycock; fedora, felt hat; beaver, castor, coonskin cap; slouch hat, terai h.; stetson, ten-gallon hat, tyrolean h.; broadbrimmed hat, wideawake, petasus; bowler hat, derby, topper, top-hat, tall h., silk h., chimney-pot h.; opera hat, crush h., gibus; straw hat, boater, panama, astrakhan, leghorn; bonnet, sun-bonnet, mobcap, toque, cloche hat, picture h., Dolly Varden h.; three-cornered hat, tricorne; witch's hat, dunce's cap; priest's cap, biretta, cardinal's hat, red h., shovel h. 989 n. *canonicals*.

wig, peruke, periwig, full-bottomed w., bagwig, curled wig, tie-w., barrister's w.; false hair, toupee; coiffure 259 n. *hair*.

footwear, footgear, buskin, sock; bootee, footlet, bootikin; boot, ammunition b.; top-boot, riding b., jack-b., Russian b., Wellington, Hessian; border boots, high-heel b., thigh-boot, gambado; hipboot, waders; shoe, court s.; wooden shoe, clog,

sabot, patten, karam; high heels, peg h., spike h.; brogues, mocassin, sandal, chapli; rope shoe, espadrilles; gumshoe, rubbers, plimsol, sneakers, creepers, loafers; overshoe, galosh; slipper, mule, pump; ballet shoe, toe-slipper; snowshoe, ski-boot; boot-tree, stretcher; skate, roller s., ice-s., ski 274 n. *sled.*

legwear, hosiery; stockings, nylons; tights, fleshings; trunks, hose, gaskins; half-hose, socks, knee-s., golf-s.; leggings, gaiters, cutikins, galligaskins; spatterdashes, spats; puttees, antigropelos; greaves 713 n. *armour*; garter; gambado, waders. See *footwear.*

neckwear, ruff, collar, high c., stiff c., soft c.; dog-collar, white choker 989 n. *canonicals*; neckband, choker, cravat, stock, tie; neckerchief, neckcloth, bandana; boa, fur, scarf, stole, tallith (see *shawl*); necklace 844 n. *finery.*

belt, waistband; cummerbund, sash, obi; armlet, armband; bandolier, bellyband, girth 47 n. *girdle.*

glove, gauntlet, long gloves; mitten, bootikin; muff, muffettee.

sleeve, arm, armhole; leg-of-mutton sleeve, raglan s.; wristband, cuff.

clothier, outfitter, costumier; tailor, snip, cutter, couturier; dressmaker, sempstress, seamstress, modiste; breeches-maker; shoemaker, bootmaker; cobbler, cordwainer, souter, Crispin 686 n. *artisan*; hosier, hatter, milliner, draper, linen-draper, haberdasher, mercer; slopshop; valet, tirewoman 742 n. *domestic*; dresser, mistress of the wardrobe 594 n. *stage hand.*

Adj. *dressed*, clothed, clad, dight; rigged out, invested, garmented, habited, costumed, breeched; uniformed, liveried; shod, gloved, hatted; well-dressed, soigné, en grande toilette, en grande tenue; tailored, tailor-made, ready-made; wearable, sartorial.

Vb. *dress*, clothe, breech; array, apparel, garment, dight, garb, tire, attire, habilitate; robe, enrobe, drape, sheet, mantle; accoutre, uniform, put in u., equip, rig, rig out, fit o., harness, caparison 669 vb. *make ready*; dress up, bedizen, deck, prank, perk, trim 843 vb. *primp*; envelop, wrap, lap, enfold, wrap up, fold up, muffle up, roll up in, swaddle, swathe, shroud, sheathe 226 vb. *cover.*

D

wear, put on, assume, don, slip on, slip into, get i., huddle i.; clothe oneself, attire o., get one's clothes on; have on, dress in, carry, sport; dress up 875 vb. *be ostentacious*; change one's clothes, change, change into.

See: 47, 217, 226, 259, 274, 364, 421, 527, 547, 594, 669, 686, 713, 742, 743, 843, 844, 848, 875, 989.

229 Uncovering

N. *uncovering*, divestment, undressing etc. vb.; exposure, cult of the nude, nudism, naturism; striptease 594 n. *stage show*; undress, dishabille, déshabillé 228 n. *informal dress*; moulting, shedding; decortication, exfoliation, excoriation, peeling, desquamation; depilation, shaving; denudation, devastation 165 n. *havoc*.

bareness, décolleté, décolletage, bare neck, low n., plunging neckline; nudity, nakedness, state of nature, birthday suit, nu intégral, the altogether, the buff, the raw, not a stitch on; baldness, hairlessness, falling hair, alopecia, acomia; tonsure; shaveling, baldpate, baldhead.

stripper, nudist, naturist, ecdysiast, stripteaser; skinner, furrier, flayer, peeler; nude figure, nude.

Adj. *uncovered*, bared; exposed, unveiled, showing 522 adj. *manifest*; divested, forcibly d., debagged; stripped, peeled; without one's clothes, unclad, unclothed, undressed, unapparelled; décolleté, barenecked, low-n., bare-armed, bare-backed, bareback; bare-legged, barefoot, unshod, discalced; hatless, bareheaded, en déshabillé, in one's shirt-sleeves; underclothed, underdressed; bare, naked, nude, raw; in a state of nature, in nature's garb, in nature's buff, au naturel, in one's birthday suit, with nothing on, without a stitch; stark, stark naked, starkers; acomous, leafless; moulting, unfeathered, unfledged; poorly dressed, threadbare, out-at-elbows, ragged 801 adj. *poor*; drawn, unsheathed 304 adj. *extracted*.

hairless, bald, baldheaded, smooth, beardless, shaved, shaven, clean-s., tonsured; bald as a coot, bald as an egg, bald as a billiard ball, bare as the back of one's hand; napless, threadbare; mangy 651 adj. *diseased*; thin, thin on top.

Vb. *uncover*, unveil, undrape, unrobe, undress, unclothe; divest, debag; strip, skin, scalp, flay, tear off; pluck, peel, bark, decorticate, excoriate, exfoliate, desquamate; hull, shuck, shell, stone; bone, fillet 300 vb. *void*; denude, denudate 165 vb. *lay waste*; expose, bare, lay open 526 vb. *disclose*; unsheathe, draw (a sword) 304 vb. *extract*; unwrap, unfold, unpack; unroof, take the lid off 263 vb. *open*; scrape, scrape off, abrade 333 vb. *rub*.

doff, uncap, uncover, raise one's hat; take off, strip off, slip off, slip out of, step out of; change, change one's clothes; shed, cast, cast a clout; moult, mew, cast its skin; divest oneself, undress, disrobe, uncase, uncoif, peel, strip; undo, unbutton, unlace, untie 46 vb. *disjoin*.

See: 46, 165, 228, 263, 300, 304, 333, 522, 526, 594, 651, 801.

230 Circumjacence

N. *circumjacence*, circumambience, ambience, medium, atmosphere, aura; halo 250 n. *loop*; encompassment, containment 235 n. *inclosure*; compass, circuit, circumference, periphery, perimeter 233 n. *outline*; surrounding, milieu, environment, entourage; background, setting, scene 594 n. *stage set*; neighbourhood, vicinity 200 n. *near place*; outskirts, environs, boulevards, suburbs, faubourgs, banlieue; purlieus, precincts 192 n. *street*; outpost, border 236 n. *limit*; wall, fortification 235 n. *fence*; wrap-around 47 n. *girdle*.

Adj. *circumjacent*, circum-; circumambient, circumfluent, ambient, atmospheric; surrounding etc. vb.; framing, circumferential, peripheral; shutting in, claustral; roundabout 314 adj. *circuitous*; suburban 200 adj. *near*.

Vb. *surround*, lie around, compass, encompass, environ, lap; encircle 314 vb. *circle*; girdle, begird, engird, cincture, encincture 235 vb. *inclose*; wreathe around, twine a.; embrace, hug 889 vb. *caress*; contain, keep in, cloister, shut in, hem in, embay 232 vb. *circumscribe*; beset, invest, blockade 712 vb. *besiege*.

Adv. *around*, about, on every side, round about, all round; on all sides, right and

left; without, outside, in the neighbour-hood, in the outskirts.

See: 47, 192, 200, 232, 233, 235, 236, 250, 314, 594, 712, 889.

231 Interjacence

N. *interjacence*, intermediacy, interlocation; intervenience, intervention, intercurrence, penetration, interpenetration, permeation, infiltration 189 n. *presence*; inter-digitation 222 n. *crossing*; dovetailing 45 n. *junction*; middle position 70 n. *middle*.
partition, curtain, iron c., bamboo c. 421 n. *screen*; Great Wall of China 713 n. *defences*; wall, party-w., brattice, bulk-head 235 n. *fence*; divide, watershed, parting 46 n. *separation*; division, cloison, panel 57 n. *subdivision*; interface, septum, diaphragm, midriff; field-boundary, balk, ridge, ail; common frontier 236 n. *limit*.
intermediary, medium, intermedium, link 47 n. *bond*; negotiator, go-between, broker 720 n. *mediator*; ghatak, marriage broker 894 n. *match-maker*; agent 755 n. *deputy*; middleman, retailer 794 n. *merchant*; intercessor, pleader, advocate 707 n. *patron*; buffer, bumper, fender, cushion 662 n. *safeguard*; buffer-state, no man's land, half-way house 70 n. *middle*.
interjection, putting between, interposition, sandwiching; interpolation, intercalation, embolism, interlineation, interspersion, intromission 303 n. *insertion*; interruption, interference, obtrusion, intrusion, butting in 72 n. *discontinuity*; interference, meddling 702 n. *hindrance*; thing inserted, episode, parenthesis, obiter dictum 40 n. *adjunct*; infix, insert, fly-leaf; glide-sound, glide, thematic, vowel; wedge, washer, shim.
interjector, interpolator; intruder, inter-loper 702 n. *hinderer*.
Adj. *interjacent*, interposed, sandwiched; episodic, parenthetical, in brackets; inter-current, intermediary, intervenient, inter-vening etc. vb.; intercessory, mediating 720 n. *mediatory*; intercalary, embolismal 303 adj. *inserted*; intrusive 59 adj. *extraneous*; inter-, interstitial, intercostal, intermural; interplanetary, interstellar; intermediate, thematic 303 adj. *inserted*; median, medium, mean, mediterranean

70 adj. *middle*; embosomed, merged 78 adj. *included*; partitioning, septal.
Vb. *lie between*, come b., stand b.; intervene 625 vb. *be half-way*; slide in, interpenetrate, permeate, soak in 189 vb. *pervade*.
intromit, let in 299 vb. *admit*; introduce, sheathe, invaginate; throw in, foist in, plough in, work in, wedge in, edge in, jam in, force in 303 vb. *insert*; ingrain 303 vb. *infuse*; splice, dovetail, mortise 45 vb. *join*; smuggle in, slide in, worm in, insinuate 297 vb. *infiltrate*.
put between, sandwich; cushion 227 vb. *line*; interpose, interject; interpolate, intercalate, interline; interleave, interlard, intersperse; interweave, interdigitate 222 vb. *enlace*; bracket, put between brackets, parenthesize.
interfere, come between, get b., intercept 702 vb. *hinder*; intervene, intercede 720 vb. *mediate*; interrupt, obtrude, thrust in, thrust one's nose in, butt in 297 vb. *intrude*; invade, trespass 306 vb. *encroach*; put one's oar in, put one's clap in; have a finger in the pie 678 vb. *meddle*.
Adv. *between*, betwixt, 'twixt, betwixt and between; among, amongst, amid, amidst, mid, midst; in the middle of; in the thick of; sandwich-wise, parenthetically; in the meanwhile, in the meantime 108 adv. *while*.

See: 40, 45, 46, 47, 57, 59, 70, 72, 108, 189, 222, 227, 235, 236, 297, 299, 303, 306, 421, 625, 662, 678, 702, 707, 713, 720, 755, 794, 894.

232 Circumscription

N. *circumscription*, enclosing 235 n. *inclosure*; drawing round, circle, balloon; ringing round, hedging r., fencing r.; surrounding, framing, girdling, encincture; circumvallation, investment, siege, blockade 712 n. *attack*; envelopment, encirclement, containment, confinement, limitation 747 n. *restriction*; ring 235 n. *fence*.
Adj. *circumscribed* etc. vb.; encircled, encompassed, enveloped; surrounded, begirt; lapt, embosomed, embayed, land-locked; in a ring fence; framed 233 adj. *outlined*; boxed, boxed up, encysted; walled in, mewed up, cloistered, immured 747 adj. *imprisoned*; invested, beleaguered,

besieged; held in, contained, confined 747adj. *restrained*; limited, restricted, finite.

Vb. *circumscribe*, describe a circle, ring round, encircle, encompass; envelop, close in, cut off, circumvallate, invest, beleaguer, blockade 712vb. *besiege*; hem in, corral; enclose, rail in, hedge in, fence in; box, cage, wall in, immure, cloister 747 vb. *imprison*; frame 230vb. *surround*; encase, enfold, enshrine, embosom, embay; edge, border 236vb. *limit*; clasp, clip, embrace 889vb. *caress*.

See: 230, 233, 235, 236, 712, 747, 889.

233 Outline

N. *outline*, circumference, perimeter, periphery; surround, frame, rim 234n. *edge*; ambit, compass, circuit 250n. *circle*; delineation, lines, lineaments, features 445n. *feature*; profile, relief 239n. *laterality*; silhouette 553n. *picture*; sketch, rough s. 623n. *plan*; skeleton, framework 331n. *structure*; tournure, contour contour line, shape 243n. *form*; isogonic line, coast-l., land l., bounds 236n. *limit*; zone, zodiac, belt, baldric, Sam Brown, girth, girdle, band, cingle, tire, fillet, circlet 250n. *loop*; line drawn round, balloon, circle 232n. *circumscription*; ring, cordon 235n. *barrier*; figure, diagram; trace, tracing.

Adj. *outlined*, framed etc.vb.; in outline, etched; peripheral, perimetric, circumferential.

Vb. *outline*, describe a circle, construct a figure 232vb. *circumscribe*; frame 230vb. *surround*; delineate, draw, silhouette, profile, trace 551vb. *represent*; etch 555 vb. *engrave*; map, block out, sketch o., sketch; diagrammatize, not fill in.

See: 230, 232, 234, 235, 236, 239, 243, 250, 331, 445, 551, 553, 555, 623.

234 Edge

N. *edge*, verge, brim; outer edge, fly (of a flag); tip, brink, skirt, fringe, margin, margent 69n. *extremity*; inner edge, hoist (of a flag); confines, bounds, boundary, frontier, border 236n. *limit*; littoral, coast, land-line, beach, strand,

seaside, seashore, water-line, water's edge, front, water-f. 344n. *shore*; wharf, quay, dock 192n. *stable*; side-line, side, brim, kerb, kerbside, wayside, roadside, riverside, bank 239n. *laterality*; hedge, railing 235n. *fence*; felloe, felly, tire 250n. *wheel*; projecting edge, lip, ledge, eave, rim, welt, flange, gunwale 254n. *projection*; raised edge, coaming; horizon, ends of the earth, skyline 199n. *farness*.

threshold, limen; doorstep, door, portal, porch 263n. *doorway*; mouth, jaws, chops, chaps, fauces 194n. *maw*.

edging, frame 233n. *outline*; thrum, list, selvedge; hem, hemline, border; skirting, purfling, piping; basque, fringe, frill, flounce, furbelow, valance 844n. *trimming*; exergue; crenation, milling 260n. *notch*; wavy edge, scallop 251n. *coil*.

Adj. *marginal*, liminal, border, skirting, marginated; riverine, coastal; riverside, roadside, wayside; labial, labiated; edged, trimmed, bordered.

Vb. *hem*, edge, border, trim, fringe, purfle; mill, crenellate 260vb. *notch*; bound, confine 236vb. *limit*.

See: 69, 192, 194, 199, 233, 235, 236, 239, 250, 251, 254, 260, 263, 344, 844.

235 Inclosure

N. *inclosure*, enclosure, envelope, case 194 n. *receptacle*; wrapper 226n. *wrapping*; girdle, zone, ring, perimeter, circumference, periphery 233n. *outline*; surround, frame, picture-f.; clausure, enceinte, precinct; temenos 990n. *holy place*; reserve 883n. *seclusion*; lot, holding, claim 184n. *territory*; fold, pen, pinfold, infold, sheepfold, shippern, sty 369n. *cattle pen*; stock-yard, croft 370n. *farm*; garth, park 370n. *garden*; compound, yard, pound, paddock, field; parking lot, car-park 192n. *stable*; corral, kraal, stockade, zareba, circumvallation, lines 713n. *defences*; net, fishnet, seine, trawl 222n. *network*; fish-trap 542n. *trap*; cell, box, cage 748n. *prison*.

fence, ring f., wire f., sunk f., ha-ha, hedge, quickset h., hedgerow, espalier; rails, balustrade, banisters, paling, railing, taffrail; pale, wall, Chinese w.; moat, dike, dyke, ditch, fosse, trench, vallum, curtain 713n. *defences*.

barrier, wall, brick w.; barricade, cordon, pale; turnstile 702n. *obstacle*; palisade, stockade, zareba 713n. *fort*; portcullis, gate, door, bolt, bar 264n. *closure*.

Vb. *inclose*, enclose, fence in, cordon, cordon off, surround; pen, hem, ring 232vb. *circumscribe*; cloister, immure, cage 747 vb. *imprison*; wrap, lap, enwrap, enfold, fold up 261vb. *fold*; fold in one's arms, hug, embrace 889vb. *caress*; frame, set, mount, box, embox.

See: 184, 192, 194, 222, 226, 232, 233, 261, 264, 369, 370, 542, 702, 713, 747, 748, 883, 889, 990.

236 Limit

N. *limit*, limitation 747n. *restriction*, 468n. *qualification*; definition, delimitation, demarcation 783n. *apportionment*; limiting factor, upper limit, ceiling, high-water mark 213n. *summit*; lower limit, threshold, low-water mark 214n. *base*; utmost, uttermost, extreme, furthest point, farthest reach, ne plus ultra, pole 69n. *extremity*; ends of the earth, Ultima Thule, Pillars of Hercules, Ocean 199n. *farness*; terminus, terminal, butt 69n. *end*; goal, target, winning-post, touch, touch-line, home, base 617n. *objective*; turning-point 137n. *crisis*; point of no return, Rubicon 599n. *resolution*; limit of endurance, tolerance, capacity, end of one's tether; physical limit, outside edge, perimeter, periphery, circumference 233 n. *outline*; tide-mark, sea-m. 344n. *shore*; landmark, boundary stone, mere s.; milestone 27n. *degree*; kerb, kerbstone 624n. *road*; bourne, boundary, verge, mere, green belt; frontier, border, marches 234 n. *edge*; national frontier, state boundary, three-mile limit; line, demarcation l., date-l., partition-l., isogonic l.; divide, parting 231n. *partition*; horizon, equator, terminator; crease; deadline, time-limit, term 110n. *period*; ultimatum 900n. *threat*; speed limit 278n. *slowness*.

Adj. *limited*, definite, conterminate, conterminable, limitable; finite; limitary, terminal; frontier, border, borderline, bordering, boundary.

Vb. *limit*, bound, border, edge 234vb. *hem*; top 213vb. *crown*; define, confine, condition 468vb. *qualify*; restrict, stint 747vb.

restrain; encompass, beat the bounds 232 vb. *circumscribe*; draw the line, delimit, demarcate, stake out; mere, mark out, chalk o. 547 vb. *mark*.

Adv. *thus far*, so far, thus far and no further; between the tide-marks, on the borderline.

See: 27, 69, 110, 137, 199, 213, 214, 231, 232, 233, 324, 278, 344, 468, 547, 599, 617, 624, 747, 783, 900.

237 Front

N. *front*, fore, front, forefront 64n. *precedence*; forepart, forepiece; prefix, frontispiece; forelock 259n. *hair*; forecourt, anteroom, entrance 263n. *doorway*; foreground, proscenium 200n. *nearness*; anteriority 119n. *priority*; anteposition, front rank, fore r., first line, front l.; forward line, centre forward; avant garde, vanguard, van, advance guard; spearhead, forlorn hope 712n. *attacker*; outpost, scout; forerunner, pioneer 66n. *precursor*.

face, frontage, façade, facia; face of a coin, obverse, head; right side, outer s.; front view, front elevation; brow, forehead, glabella; chin, mentum; physiognomy, metoposcopy, features, visage, countenance, frontispiece, figurehead, phiz, map, mug, pan, kisser, dial, disk, disc 445n. *feature*; prominent feature, nose, snout, conk 254n. *protuberance*.

prow, prore, nose, beak, rostrum, figurehead; bow, bows; bowsprit; jib, foremast, forecastle, fo'c'sle, forestay, forepeak 275n. *ship*.

Adj. *fore*, forward, front, obverse; frontal, head-on, oncoming, facing 240adj. *opposite*; anterior, prepositional, prosthetic, prefixed 64adj. *preceding*.

Vb. *be in front*, stand in front etc.adv.; front, confront, face, face up to 240vb. *be opposite*; breast, stem, brave; bend forwards, lean f. 220vb. *be oblique*; come to the front, come to the fore, forge ahead, take the lead, head 64vb. *come before*.

Adv. *in front*, before, in advance, in the lead, in the van, vanward; ahead, right a., infra, further on 199adv. *beyond*; far ahead, coastward, landward; before one's face, before one's eyes; face to face, vis à vis; in the foreground, in the forefront;

head first, head foremost; feet first, feet foremost.

See: 64, 66, 119, 199, 200, 220, 240, 254, 259, 263, 275, 445, 712.

238 Rear

N. *rear*, rearward, afterpart, back end, tail e., stern 69n. *extremity*; tail-piece, heel, colophon; coda 412n. *musical piece*; tail, brush, scut, pigtail, queue 67n. *sequel*; wake, train 67n. *retinue*; last place, rear rank, back seat 35n. *inferiority*; rearguard 67n. *aftercomer*; subsequence 120 n. *posteriority*; background, hinterland, depths, far corner 199n. *distance*; behind, backstage, back side; reverse side, wrong s., verso 240n. *contraposition*; reverse, other side of the medal; backdoor, back entrance, postern 263n. *doorway*; back (of the body), dorsum, chine; backbone, spine, rachis 218n. *supporter*; back of the neck, scruff of the n., nape, scruff, short hairs; back of the head, occiput 213n. *head*.

buttocks, breech, backside, posterior, posteriors, cheek; bottom, seat, sit-me-down; bum, arse, ass; rear, stern, tail; fanny, hips; hindquarters, croup, crupper, haunches, haunch, ham, hunkers, hunkies; rump, loin; dorsal region, lumbar r., lower back, coccyx; fundament, anus.

poop, stern, stern-sheets, afterpart, quarter, counter, rudderpost, rudder, rear-mast, mizen-mast 275n. *ship*.

Adj. *back*, rear, postern; posterior, after, hind, hinder, hindmost, rearmost; mizen; bent back, backswept 253adj. *convex*; reverse 240adj. *opposite*; placed last 35adj. *inferior*; spinal, rachial, vertebral, retral, dorsal, lumbar, gluteal, popliteal; anal; caudal, caudate, caudiform.

Vb. *be behind*, stand b.; back on; back; back up 703vb. *aid*; follow, bring up the rear 65vb. *come after*; lag, trail, drop behind, fall astern 278vb. *move slowly*; tail, shadow, dog 619vb. *pursue*; follow at heel 284vb. *follow*; bend backwards, lean b. 220vb. *be oblique*.

Adv. *rearward*, behind, back of; in the rear, in the ruck; at the back, in the background; behind one's back; after, aftermost, sternmost; aft, abaft, astern, aback;

to the rear, hindward, backward, retro; supra, above; on the heels of, at the tail of, at the back of, close behind; overpage, overleaf; back to back.

See: 35, 65, 67, 69, 120, 199, 213, 218, 220, 240, 253, 263, 275, 278, 284, 412, 619, 703.

239 Laterality

N. *laterality*, sidedness; side movement 317 n. *oscillation*; sidestep 282n. *deviation*; side-line, side, bank 234n. *edge*; coast 344 n. *shore*; siding, side-entrance, side-door; gable, gable-end; broadside; beam; quarter 236n. *poop*; flank, ribs, pleura; wing, fin, hand; cheek, jowl, chops, chaps, gill; temples, side-face, half-face; profile, side elevation; lee, lee-side, leeward; weatherside, windward 281n. *direction*; orientation, east, orient, Levant; west, occidental 281n. *compass point*; offside, on-s., near s. 241n. *dextrality*, 242n. *sinistrality*.

Adj. *lateral*, laparo-; side 234adj. *marginal*; sidelong, glancing; parietal, buccal, side-face; costal, pleural, winglike, aliform; flanking, skirting; flanked, sided; many-sided, multilateral, bilateral, trilateral, quadrilateral; collateral 219adj. *parallel*; moving sideways, edging, sidling; eastern, eastward, easterly, orient, oriental, auroral, Levantine, Anatolian; west, western, westerly, westward, occidental, Hesperian 281adj. *directed*.

Vb. *flank*, side, edge, skirt, border 234vb. *hem*; coast, move sideways, passage, sidle; sideslip, sidestep 282vb. *deviate*; extend sideways, deploy, outflank 306vb. *overstep*.

Adv. *sideways*, laterally; askance, asquint; sidelong, broadside on; on one side, abreast, abeam, alongside; aside, beside; by the side of, side by side, cheek by jowl 200adv. *nigh*; to windward, to leeward, alee; coastwise; right and left; on her beam ends.

See: 200, 219, 234, 236, 241, 242, 281, 282, 306, 317, 344.

240 Contraposition

N. *contraposition*, antithesis, opposition, antipodes 14n. *contrariety*; opposite side, other s.; reverse, back 238n. *rear*; polarity

polarization; opposite poles, North and South; cross-current, headwind 704n. *opposition*; reversal, inverse 221n. *inversion*.

Adj. *opposite*, contrapositive, reverse, inverse 221adj. *inverted*; contrary, subcontrary 14adj. *contrary*; facing, fronting, confronting, oncoming 239adj. *fore*; diametrically opposite, antipodal, antipodean; polarized, polar; antarctic, arctic, northern, septentrional, Boreal, southern, austral 281adj. *directed*.

Vb. *be opposite* etc. adj.; stand opposite, lie o.; subtend; face, confront 237vb. *be in front*; run counter 182vb. *counteract*; oppose, contrapose.

Adv. *against*, over the way, over against; as poles asunder; facing, face to face, vis à vis; back to back; on the other side, overleaf, overpage, next page; contrariwise, vice versa.

See: 14, 182, 221, 237, 238, 239, 281, 704.

241 Dextrality

N. *dextrality*, right hand, right-handedness; ambidexterity, ambidextrousness 694n. *skill*; right, dexter; offside, starboard; right-hand page, recto; right wing, right-winger.

Adj. *dextral*, right-hand, starboard, offside; right-handed, dexterous, ambidextral, ambidextrous 694adj. *skilful*; dextrorsal, dextrad; dexiotropic, dextro-rotatory; right-wing.

Adv. *dextrally*, on the right; right-handedly, ambidextrously; to the right, dextrad, a-starboard.

See: 694.

242 Sinistrality

N. *sinistrality*, left hand, left-handedness; left, sinister, nearside, on-s.; larboard, port; left wing, left-winger; lævogyration.

Adj. *sinistral*, sinister, sinistrous, left, left-handed, sinistro-manual, gauche, gauchi-pawed 695adj. *clumsy*; offside, nearside, sinistrad, sinistrorse, sinistrorsal; lævogyrate; lævogyrous.

Adv. *sinistrally*, on the left, a-port, offside; leftwards, sinistrad.

See: 695.

243 Form

N. *form*, substantial f., Platonic f., idea; essence 3n. *substance*; significant form, inner f., inscape; art form 551n. *art*, 593 n. *verse form*; word form 557n. *linguistics*; shape, turn, lines, architecture; formation, conformation, configuration, fashion, style, design 331n. *structure*; contour, silhouette, relief, profile, frame, outline; figure, cut, set, trim, build, cut of one's jib, lineament 445n. *feature*; physiognomy 237n. *face*; look, expression, appearance 445n. *mien*; posture, attitude, stance; type, kind, pattern, stamp, cast, mould, blank 23n. *prototype*; format, type-face, typography 587n. *print*; morphology, morphography, isomorphism.

efformation, formation, forming, shaping, creation 164n. *production*; expression, formulation 62n. *arrangement*; designing, patterning; moulding 554n. *sculpture*; turning, joinery; etymology, word-formation 557n. *linguistics*.

Adj. *formed* etc. vb.; receiving form, plastic, fictile; sculptured, carved, moulded, turned, rounded, squared; shaped, fashioned, fully f., styled, stylized; readymade, tailored in advance; matured, ready 669adj. *prepared*; solid, concrete 324adj. *dense*; dimensional, two-d., three-d.; isomorphous.

formative, plasmic, informing, normative; giving form, formal; plastic, glyptic, architectural 331adj. *structural*.

Vb. *efform*, inform, form; create, make 164 vb. *produce*; snape, fashion, figure, pattern; turn, round, square; cut, tailor; cut out, silhouette 233vb. *outline*; sketch, draw 551vb. *represent*; model, carve, chisel 554vb. *sculpt*; hew, rough-h. 46vb. *cut*; mould, cast, rough-c.; stamp, coin, mint; hammer out, blank o., block o., knock o., punch o.; carpenter, mason; forge, smith, smithy; knead, work, work up into; construct, build, frame 310vb. *elevate*; express, formulate, put into shape, pull into s., lick into s., knock into s.

See: 3, 23, 46, 62, 164, 233, 237, 310, 324, 331, 445, 551, 554, 557, 587, 593, 669.

244 Amorphism: absence of form

N. *amorphism*, informity, unformedness, prime matter; confusion, chaos 61n.

disorder; amorphousness, lack of shape, mussiness, shapelessness; lack of definition, vagueness, fuzziness; rawness, uncouthness 670n. *undevelopment*; rough diamond, unlicked cub; disfigurement, defacement, mutilation, deformation, deformity 246n. *distortion*.

Adj. *amorphous*, formless, unformed; liquid 335adj. *fluid*; shapeless, featureless, characterless; messy, chaotic 61adj. *orderless*; undefined, ill-defined, lacking definition, vague, fuzzy, blurred 419adj. *shadowy*; unfashioned, unshapen, unformed, unmade; embryonic 68adj. *beginning*; raw, unlicked 670adj. *immature*; unhewn, in the rough 55adj. *incomplete*; rude, inchoate, uncouth, barbarous, Gothic 699 adj. *artless*; rugged 259adj. *rough*; unshapely 842adj. *unsightly*; malformed, misshapen, gnarled 246adj. *deformed*.

Vb. *deform*, deprive of form, unmake, unshape 165vb. *destroy*; dissolve, melt 337 vb. *liquefy*; knock out of shape, batter 46 vb. *break*; grind, pulp 332vb. *pulverize*; warp, twist 246vb. *distort*; deface, disfigure 842vb. *make ugly*; mutilate, truncate 655vb. *impair*; jumble, disorder 63 vb. *derange*.

See: 46, 55, 61, 63, 68, 165, 246, 259, 332, 335, 337, 419, 655, 670, 699, 842.

245 Symmetry: regularity of form

N. *symmetry*, bilateral s., trilateral s., multilateral s., correspondence, proportion 12 n. *correlation*; balance 28n. *equilibrium*; regularity, evenness 16n. *uniformity*; arborescence, branching, ramification 219n. *parallelism*; shapeliness, regular features, classic f. 841n. *beauty*; harmony; eurhythmy, eurhythmic 24n. *agreement*; rhythm 141n. *periodicity*; finish 646n. *perfection*.

Adj. *symmetrical*, balanced 28adj. *equal*; proportioned, well-p. 12adj. *correlative*; rhythmical, harmonious, congruent 24 adj. *agreeing*; congruent, co-extensive; corresponding 219adj. *parallel*; analogous 18adj. *similar*; smooth, even 16adj. *uniform*; squared, rounded, round, even-sided, isosceles, equilateral 81adj. *regular*; crystalline; arborescent, arboriform, dendriform, branching, ramose; formal, classic, comely 841adj. *shapely*; unde-

formed, well set-up 249adj. *straight*; undistorted, unwarped, unbiased 493adj. *true*; finished, complete in all its parts 54 adj. *complete*.

See: 12, 16, 18, 24, 28, 54, 81, 141, 219, 249, 493, 646, 841.

246 Distortion: irregularity of form

N. *distortion*, asymmetry, disproportion, misproportion, want of symmetry 10n. *irrelation*; imbalance, disequilibrium 29 n. *inequality*; lop-sidedness, crookedness 220n. *obliquity*; anamorphosis, projection, Mercator's p. 551n. *map*; detortion, contortion; thrust, stress, strain, shear, bending moment, twisting m.; bias, warp; buckle, bend, screw, twist 251n. *convolution*; facial distortion, grimace, mop, mow, moue, snarl, rictus 547n. *gesture*; misconstruction 521n. *misinterpretation*; perversion 552n. *misrepresentation*; misdirection 542n. *deception*.

deformity, malformation, malconformation, monstrosity, abortion 84n. *abnormality*; curvature of the spine, kyphosis 248 n. *curvature*; teratogeny; clubfoot, talipes, valgus 845n. *blemish*; ugliness, hideosity 842n. *eyesore*; teratology.

Adj. *distorted* etc.vb.; irregular, asymmetric, unsymmetrical, disproportionate 17 adj. *non-uniform*; weighted, biased; not true, not straight; anamorphous, grotesque; out of shape, warped 244adj. *amorphous*; buckled, twisted, gnarled 251 adj. *convoluted*; wry, awry, askew, crazy, crooked, cock-eyed; on one side 220adj. *oblique*; contortive, grimacing, scowling, snarling.

deformed, ugly 842adj. *unsightly*; misproportioned, ill-proportioned, scalene; defective 647adj. *imperfect*; ill-made, misshapen, misbegotten; rickety, rachitic; crump, hunchbacked, humpbacked, bunchbacked; kyphotic, crook-backed, crooked as a ram's horn; wry-necked; bandy, bandy-legged, bow-legged, bow-kneed; knock-kneed, cow-hocked; pigeon-toed; splay-footed; club-footed, taliped; web-footed; round-shouldered, pigeon-chested; snub-nosed, simous, hare-lipped 845adj. *blemished*; curtailed of one's fair proportions; stumpy 204adj.

short; haggard, gaunt 206adj. *lean*; bloated, 195adj. *fleshy*.
Vb. *distort*, disproportion, weight, bias; contort, screw, twist, knot 251vb. *twine*; bend, warp 251vb. *crinkle*; buckle, crumple; strain, sprain, wrest, torture, rack 63vb. *derange*; misshape, botch 244 vb. *deform*; batter, knock out of shape; pervert 552vb. *misrepresent*; misconstrue 521vb. *misinterpret*; writhe 251vb. *wriggle*; grimace, make faces, mop and mow 547vb. *gesticulate*; snarl, scowl, frown 893vb. *be sullen*.

See: 10, 17, 29, 63, 84, 195, 204, 206, 220, 244, 248, 251, 521, 542, 547, 551, 552, 647, 842, 845, 893.

247 Angularity

N. *angularity*, angulation, aduncity, hookedness, crotchet, bracket, hook; bend, scythe, sickle, scimitar 248n. *curvature*; chevron, zigzag 220n. *obliquity*; V-shape, elbow, knee, knee-joint; shoulder, withers 253n. *camber*; knuckle, ankle, groin 45n. *joint*; crutch, crotch, fluke 222n. *cross*; fork, bifurcation, crossways, branching 222n. *crossing*; corner, nook, niche, recess, oriel 194n. *compartment*; wedge, arrow-head, broad arrow, cusp 254n. *prominence*; flexure 261n. *fold*; indentation 260n. *notch*.
angle, right a., acute a., obtuse a., salient a., re-entrant a., spherical a., trigonometric a., solid a., dihedral a.
angular measure, goniometry, trigonometry, altimetry; angular elevation, angular distance, angular velocity; second, degree, minute; radian; goniometer, altimeter; clinometer, graphometer; level, theodolite; transit circle; sextant, quadrant; protractor.
angular figure, triangle, isosceles t., equilateral t., scalene t., spherical t., trigon; parallelogram, rectangle, square, quadrangle, quadrature; quadrilateral, lozenge, diamond; rhomb, rhombus, rhomboid; tetragon, polygon, pentagon, hexagon, heptagon, octagon, decagon, decahedron, polyhedron; cube, pyramid, wedge; prism, parallelepiped; Platonic bodies.
Adj. *angular*, aduncous, aduncate, hooked, uncinated, hook-nosed, aquiline, ros-

trate; falciform, falcated 248adj. *curved*; angled, sharp-a., cornered; crooked, zigzag 220adj. *oblique*; jagged, serrated, crinkled 260adj. *notched*; jointed, geniculated, elbowed; akimbo; knock-kneed; crotched, forked, bifurcate, furcated, furcular, V-shaped.
angulated, triangular, trigonal, trilateral; wedge-shaped, cuneate, cuneiform, fusiform; rectangular, right angled, orthogonal; square, square-shaped, foursquare, quadrangular, quadrilateral, four-sided, squared; diamond-shaped, lozenge-s.; multilateral, polygonal, decahedral, polyhedral; cubical, rhomboidal, pyramidal.
Vb. *angulate*, angle, make corners, corner; hook, crook, bend 248vb. *make curved*; wrinkle, fold 251vb. *crinkle*; zigzag 220 vb. *be oblique*; fork, bifurcate, divaricate, branch, ramify 294vb. *diverge*; go off at a tangent 282vb. *deviate*.

See: 45, 194, 220, 222, 248, 251, 253, 254, 260, 261, 282, 294.

248 Curvature

N. *curvature*, curvity, curvation; incurvity, incurvation, inward curve 255n. *concavity*; outward curve 253n. *convexity*; flexure, flexion, conflexure, inflexion 261 n. *fold*; arcuation, sweep, bending; bowing, stooping 311n. *obeisance*; bending down, deflexion; turning away, detour 282n. *deviation*; downward bend, devexity 309n. *descent*; recurvature, recurvity, retroflexion 221n. *inversion*; curling, curliness, sinuosity 251n. *convolution*; aduncity 247n. *angularity*; curvature of the spine, kyphosis 246n. *deformity*.
curve, slight c. 253n. *camber*; turn, bend, sharp b., hairpin b., U-turn; bay, bight 345n. *gulf*; figure of eight 250n. *loop*; tracery, curl, festoon 251n. *convolution*; bow, Cupid's b., rainbow 250n. *arc*; arch, spring of an a., arcade, vault 253n. *dome*; crescent, lunule, half-moon, horseshoe, meniscus, lens; catenary, parabola, hyperbola, conic section; caustic line, caustic, diacaustic, catacaustic, cardioid, conchoid; arch (of the foot), instep; crane-neck, swan-n.
Adj. *curved*, cambered etc.vb.; flexed, bent,

re-entrant 220 adj. *oblique*; bowed, stooping 311 adj. *depressed*; curviform, bowlike, curvilineal, curvilinear; rounded, curvaceous, bosomy, wavy, billowy 251 adj. *undulatory*; aquiline, hook-nosed, parrot-beaked 247 adj. *angular*; rostrate, beaked, beaklike, bill-shaped; bent back, recurved, recurvous, recurvative; retroussé, turned-up, tip-tilted 221 adj. *inverted*; circumflex; arched, archiform, vaulted 253 adj. *arcuate*; bow-legged 246 adj. *deformed*; down-curving, devex 309 adj. *descending*; hooked, falciform, falcated; semicircular 250 adj. *circular*; crescentic, luniform, lunular, lunate, semilunar, horned; meniscal, lentiform, lenticular, reniform; cordiform, cordated, cardioidal, heart-shaped, bell-s., pear-s., fig-s.; conchoidal.

Vb. *be curved,* — bent etc. adj.; curve, bend, loop, camber, arch, sweep, sag, swag, give, give in the middle 217 vb. *hang*; re-enter, recurve, recurvate; curvet 312 vb. *leap*.

make curved, bend, crook 247 vb. *angulate*; turn, round 250 vb. *make round*; bend in, incurvate, inflect; bend back, recurve, retroflect 221 vb. *invert*; bend over, bend down, bow, incline 311 vb. *stoop*; turn over 261 vb. *fold*; turn away 282 vb. *deflect*; arcuate, arch, arch over, concamerate; coil 251 vb. *twine*; loop, curl, wave, frizzle 251 vb. *crinkle*; loop the loop, make figures-of-eight.

See: 217, 220, 221, 246, 247, 250, 251, 253, 255, 261, 282, 309, 311, 312, 345.

249 Straightness

N. *straightness,* directness, rectilinearity; perpendicularity 215 n. *verticality*; inflexibility, rigidity 326 n. *hardness*; chord, straight line, right l., direct l., bee-l., air l.; Roman road; straight stretch, straight, reach; short cut 200 n. *short distance*; rectitude 929 n. *probity*.

Adj. *straight,* direct, even, right, true; in a line, linear; straight-lined, rectilinear, rectilineal; perpendicular 215 adj. *vertical*; unbent, unwarped, unturned, undistorted; stiff, inflexible 326 adj. *rigid*; uncurled, out of curl; straightened, unfrizzed, dekinked; dead straight, undeviating, unswerving, undeflected, on the beam, straight as an arrow, like a homing pigeon.

Vb. *be straight,* — direct etc. adj.; go straight, ride the beam; steer straight, follow the great circle; have no turning, not incline, not bend, not turn, not deviate, not deviate to either side, turn neither right nor left.

straighten, make straight, set s., set right, put straight 654 vb. *rectify*; iron out 216 vb. *flatten*; unbend (a bow); dekink, uncurl 258 vb. *smooth*; stretch tight; unwrap 62 vb. *unravel*; uncoil, unroll, unfurl, unfold 316 vb. *evolve*.

Adv. *straight on,* directly, as the crow flies; straight, plumb.

See: 62, 200, 215, 216, 258, 316, 326, 654, 929.

250 Circularity: simple circularity

N. *circularity,* orbicularity, roundness, rondure 252 *rotundity*; annulation, annularity.

circle, full c., circumference 233 n. *outline*; great circle, equator; orb, annulus; rundle, roundel, roundlet; areola; plate, saucer; round, disc, disk, discus; coin, sequin, confetti; hoop, ring, quoit; runner, washer, terret, varvel; eye, iris; eyelet, loophole, keyhole 263 n. *orifice*; circular course, circuit, roundabout; fairy ring; zodiac; ring formation, annulation, smoke-ring.

loop, figure-of-eight 251 n. *convolution*; ringlet, curl 259 n. *hair*; bracelet, armlet, armilla, torque, clasp 844 n. *finery*; crown, coronet 743 n. *regalia*; corona, aureole, halo; wreath, garland, fillet, chaplet, snood, fascia 228 n. *headgear*; collar, necklace, neckband 228 n. *neckwear*; band, cordon, sash, girdle, zone, cestos, cincture, waistband, cummerbund 228 n. *belt*; baldric, bandolier 47 n. *girdle*; lasso, lariat 47 n. *halter*; knot, tie.

wheel, truckle, pulley, caster; truck; hub, nave-plate; felloe, felly, tyre; rubber tyre, tubeless t., inner tube, outer t.; roller 252 n. *rotundity*.

arc, semicircle, half-circle, hemicycle, half-moon, crescent, rainbow 248 n. *curve*; sector, quadrant, sextant; ellipse, oval, ovule; ellipsoid, cycloid, epicycloid.

orbit, cycle, epicycle, circuit, ecliptic; circulation 314n. *circuition*.

Adj. *round*, rounded, circular, cyclic, discoid; orbicular, ringlike, ringed, annular, annulate, annulose, semicircular, hemicyclic; oval, ovate; elliptic, ovoid, egg-shaped, crescent-s.,pear-s.248 adj. *curved*; cycloidal, spherical 252 adj. *rotund*.

Vb. *make round* etc. adj.; round, turn.

go round, girdle, encircle 230 vb. *surround*; describe a circle 233 vb. *outline*; move round, circulate, orbit, go into o. 314 adj. *circle*.

See: 47, 228, 233, 248, 251, 252, 259, 263, 314, 743, 844.

251 Convolution: complex circularity

N. *convolution*, involution, circumvolution; intricacy; flexuosity, anfractuosity, sinuosity, sinuousness; tortility, tortuosity, torsion, intorsion; inosculation; reticulation 222 n. *network*; twine, crape, twist 208 n. *fibre*; ripple 350 n. *wave*; wrinkle, corrugation 261 n. *fold*; indentation, ragged edge 260 n. *notch*; waviness, undulation.

coil, roll, twist; turban, puggree 228 n. *headgear*; spiral, cochlea, helix; screw, screw-thread, worm, corkscrew; spring, wound s., coiled s.; armature; whorl, snailshell, ammonite; verticil, rundle; whirlpool 350 n. *eddy*, 315 n. *vortex*; tendril, creeper, convolvulus 366 n. *plant*; scollop, scallop, scalloped edge 234 n. *edging*; kink, curl; ringlet, lovelock 259 n. *hair*; scroll, volute, fiddlehead, flourish, curlicue, squiggle 844 n. *ornamentation*; Cupid's bow; hairpin.

meandering, meander, winding course, crankiness; winding, windings and turnings, twists and turns, ambages, circumbendibus 282 n. *deviation*; labyrinth, maze 530 n. *enigma*; switchback, crank, zigzag 220 n. *obliquity*.

serpent, snake, eel, worm, wriggler 365 n. *reptile*.

Adj. *convoluted*, twisted, contorted, intorted 246 adj. *distorted*; tortile, tortive, torsile; cranky, ambagious; winding, twining, anfractuous, sinuous, tortuous, flexuous; indented, crumpled, ragged 260 adj. *notched*; crumpled, buckled 261 adj. *folded*.

labyrinthine, mazy, meandering, serpentine; twisting, turning 314 adj. *circuitous*.

snaky, serpentine, serpentiform; eel-like, anguilliform, wormlike, vermiform, vermicular; squirming, wriggling, peristaltic, sigmoidal.

undulatory, undulating, rolling, heaving; up-and-down, switchback; wavy, curly, frizzy, kinky, crinkly, woolly, crimped; scolloped, wrinkled, corrugated, indented, ragged 260 adj. *notched*; flamboyant.

coiled, spiral, helical, turbinated, cochlear; wormed, turbinate, whorled, verticillate; wound, wound up; coiling, spiralling.

intricate, involved, complicated, ravelled, perplexed 61 adj. *complex*.

Vb. *twine*, twist, twirl, roll, coil, corkscrew, spire, spiral 315 vb. *rotate*; wreathe, entwine 222 vb. *enlace*; be convuluted, — twisted etc. adj.; turn and twist, bend 248 vb. *be curved*.

crinkle, crimp, frizz, crape, crisp, curl; wave, undulate, ripple, popple; wrinkle, corrugate 261 vb. *fold*; indent, scallop, scollop 260 vb. *notch*; crumple 246 vb. *distort*.

meander, snake, crank, crankle, twist and turn, zigzag, corkscrew. See *twine*.

wriggle, writhe, squirm, shimmy, shake; move sinuously, worm, serpentine.

Adv. in and out, round about, crankily.

See: 61, 208, 220, 222, 228, 234, 246, 248, 259, 260, 261, 282, 314, 315, 350, 365, 366, 530, 844.

252 Rotundity

N. *rotundity*, rondure, roundness, orbicularity 250 n. *circularity*; sphericity, sphericality, spheroidicity; globularity, globosity, cylindricity, gibbosity, gibbousness 253 n. *convexity*.

sphere, globe, spheroid, oblate s., ellipsoid, globoid, geoid; hollow sphere, bladder; balloon, air-b. 276 n. *airship*; soap-bubble 355 n. *bubble*; ball, football, pelota, wood (bowls), billiard ball, marble, alley, taw; cannon-ball, bullet, shot, pellet; bead, pill, pea, boll, oakapple; spherule, globule, globulite; drop, droplet, dewdrop, ink-drop, blot; vesicle, bulb, onion, knob, pommel 254 n. *protuberance*; thread-ball, clew; boulder, rolling stone; hemisphere, hump, mushroom 253 n. *dome*; round head, bullet h., turnip h.

cylinder, roll, roly-poly; roller, rolling-pin 258 n. *smoother*; rod; round, rung; round tower, column; bole, trunk, stalk 218 n. *supporter*; pipe, drain-pipe 263 n. *tube*; funnel, chimney-pot 263 n. *chimney*; round box, pill-b.; drum 194 n. *vessel.*

cone, conoid; shadow-cone, penumbra 419 n. *half-light*; sugarloaf 253 n. *dome*; cornet, horn, drinking-h. 194 n. *cup*; top, spinning t., peg-t.; pear-shape, bell-s., egg-s.

Adj. *rotund*, orbicular 250 adj. *round*; spherical, sphery, spherular; globular, globy, globulous, global; round-headed, bullet-headed; beady, beadlike, globulitic; hemispheric; spheroidal, ovoid, oviform, egg-shaped; cylindrical, columnar, tubular, lumbriciform; conic, conical; conoid, conoidal; bell-shaped, campaniform, campanulate, napiform, pyriform, pear-shaped, egg-s.; heart-shaped, cardiac; fungiform, moniliform; humped, gibbous; onion-shaped; bulbous 253 adj. *convex*; pot-bellied 195 adj. *fleshy*; sphered, balled.

Vb. *round*, make spherical; form into a sphere, form into a globe etc. n.; sphere, globe, ball; balloon; mushroom; clew, coil up, roll.

See: 194, 195, 218, 250, 253, 254, 258, 263, 276, 355, 419.

253 Convexity

N. *convexity*, convexness; lordosis, arcuation, arching; sphericity 252 n. *rotundity*; gibbosity, bulginess, humpiness, bulge, bilge; projection, protrusion, protuberance 254 n. *prominence*; excrescency, intumescence, tumescence, tumidity, turgidity 197 n. *expansion*; paunchiness 195 n. *bulk*; pimpliness, wartiness, wart-hog; double convexity, lenticular form; lens 442 n. *optical device.*

swelling, growth, excrescence, knot, nodosity, node, nodule; exostosis, apophysis, condyle, knuckle; œdema, emphysema, condylema, sarcoma; bubo, bump, gall, carbuncle, bunion, corn, blain, wart, wen; boil, furuncle, stye, pimple, papula, blister, vesicle; polypus, adenoids, hæmorrhoids, piles; proud flesh, wheal; ink-drop, blot 252 n. *sphere*; bleb, air-bubble, soap-b. 355 n. *bubble*; boss, torus,

knob, bullion, nub, nubble; bulb, button, bud; belly, pot-belly, corporation, paunch 195 n. *bulk*; billow, swell 350 n. *wave*; bulge, bunt.

bosom, bust, breast, breasts, bubs; mamma, mamilla, papilla, nipple, pap, dug, teat, udder; thorax, chest; cuirass, breast-plate.

dome, cupola, vault 226 n. *roof*; beehive 192 n. *nest*; brow, forehead 237 n. *face*; skull, cranium, bald head 213 n. *head*; hemisphere, arch of heaven; mound, round barrow, long b., hummock, hillock, mole-hill, tussock, mamelon, sugarloaf 209 n. *monticle*; mushroom, umbrella.

camber, gentle curve 248 n. *curve*; arch, bow, rainbow; hump, humpback, hunch-back; dorsum, back 238 n. *rear*; shoulder, withers 218 n. *supporter*; calf 267 n. *leg*; elbow 247 n. *angularity.*

Adj. *convex*, out-bowed, protruding 254 adj. *salient*; hemispheric, domelike 252 adj. *rotund*; lentiform, lenticular; gibbous, humpy, lumpy; curvaceous, bosomy, billowy 248 adj. *curved*; billowing, bulging, bellying, ballooning; swelling, swollen 197 adj. *expanded*; bloated, pot-bellied 195 adj. *fleshy*; turgid, tumid, tumescent, tumorous, tuberous; verrucose, warty, papulous, papulose, pimply; wart-shaped, verruciform; blistery, vesicular.

arcuate, cambered, arched, bowed 248 adj. *curved*; rounded; hillocky, hummocky, moutonné, mammiform.

Vb. *be convex*, camber, arch, bow; swell, belly, bulge, balloon, mushroom; bag, bunt, pout; convex, emboss, chase, beat out 254 vb. *jut.*

See: 192, 195, 197, 209, 213, 218, 226, 237, 247, 248, 252, 254, 267, 350, 355, 442.

254 Prominence

N. *prominence*, eminence 209 n. *high land*, 638 n. *importance*; solar prominence, solar flare; tongue, tongue of flame.

projection, salient, salient angle 247 n. *angle*; outstretched arm, forefinger, index f.; sprit, bowsprit; outrigger; tongue of land, spit, point, mull, promontory, foreland, headland 344 n. *land*; peninsula, chersonese 349 n. *island*; spur, foothill; jetty, mole, breakwater, groyne, pier 662 n.

shelter; outwork 713n. *fortification*; pilaster, buttress 218n. *supporter*; shelf, sill, ledge, soffit, balcony; eaves 226n. *roof*; overhang, forerake, sternrake 220n. *obliquity*; flange, lip 234n. *edge*; tang, tongue; tenon 45n. *joint*; snag, stump, outcrop; cartographical projection 551n. *map*.

protuberance, bump 253n. *swelling*; prominent feature; nose, snout, conk; beak, rostrum; muzzle, proboscis, trunk; antenna 378n. *feeler*; chin, mentum, jaw, brow, beetle-brow 237n. *face*; figurehead 237n. *prow*; horn, antler 256n. *sharp point*.

rilievo, relief, basso rilievo, alto r., mezzo r., low relief, bas r., high r.; embossment 844vb. *ornamental art*; cameo 554n. *sculpture*.

Adj. *salient*, bold, jutting, prominent, protuberant; emissile, protruding, popping, popping out; overhung, beetle-browed; underhung, undershot; repoussé, embossed, in relief, in high r., in low r.

Vb. *jut*, project, protrude, pout, pop, pop out, start o.; stand out, stick o., poke o., hang o. 443vb. *be visible*; bristle up, cock up 259vb. *roughen*; shoot up, start up, swell up 197vb. *expand*; overhang, hang over, beetle over, impend 217vb. *hang*.

See: 45, 197, 209, 217, 218, 220, 226, 234, 237, 247, 253, 256, 259, 344, 349, 378, 443, 551, 554, 638, 662, 713, 844.

255 Concavity

N. *concavity*, concaveness, incurvation, incurvity 248n. *curvature*; hollowness 190n. *emptiness*; depression, dint, dent, impression, stamp, imprint, footprint 548n. *trace*; intaglio 555n. *engraving*; ploughing, furrowing 262n. *furrow*; indentation 260n. *notch*; gap, lacuna 201n. *interval*.

cavity, hollow, niche, recess, corner 194n. *compartment*; hole, den, burrow, warren 192n. *dwelling*; pit, chasm, abyss 211n. *depth*; cave, cavern, antre; grot, grotto, alcove 194n. *arbour*; cul-de-sac, blind alley, impasse 702n. *obstacle*; hollow vessel, cup, saucer, bowl, basin, trough 194n. *vessel*; sewer 649n. *sink*; cell, follicle; sentellum, pore 263n. *orifice*; dimple, pockmark; honeycomb, sponge,

263n. *porosity*; funnel, tunnel 263n. *tube*; groove, mortise, socket 262n. *furrow*; tooth-socket, alveolus; antrum, sinus; bay, bight, cove, creek, inlet 345n. *gulf*; channel, alveus, river-bed, wadi, ditch, nullah 351n. *conduit*; hole in the ground, dip, depression, pot-hole, punch-bowl, crater; volcano 383n. *furnace*.

valley, vale, dell, dingle, combe, cwm, U-valley, river valley, strath; glen, glade, dip, depression, slade, dene; ravine, gorge, crevasse, barranca, canyon, gully 201n. *gap*.

excavation, dug-out, grave, grave-pit 364n. *tomb*; vertical excavation, shaft, mine, coal m., pit, coal p., colliery, quarry 632n. *store*; gallery, working g., adit, sap, trench, tunnel, burrow, warren 263n. *tunnel*; underground railway, tube; archælogical excavation, dig; cutting, cut.

excavator, miner, coal-m., quarrier; digger, dredger; sapper, burrower, tunneller; grave-digger, fossor.

Adj. *concave*, hollow, cavernous, speluncar; vaulted, arched 248adj. *curved*; hollowed out, scooped o., dug o.; caved in, stove in; depressed, sunk, sunken; spoonlike, saucer-shaped, cupped; capsular, funnel-shaped, infundibular, infundibuliform; bell-shaped, campaniform; cellular, socketed, alveolate, alveolar; full of holes, honeycombed; spongy, spongious, porous 263adj. *perforated*.

Vb. *be concave*, retreat, retire, cave in; cup, incurve.

make concave, depress, press in, punch in, stamp, impress; buckle, dent, dint, stave in; crush, push in, beat in; excavate, hollow, dig, spade, delve, scrape, scratch, scrabble, trench 262vb. *groove*; mine, sap, undermine, burrow, tunnel, bore; honeycomb, perforate 263vb. *pierce*; scoop out, dig o., gouge o., scratch o. 300vb. *eject*; hole, pit, pockmark; indent 260vb. *notch*; sink a shaft, make a hole.

See: 190, 192, 194, 201, 211, 248, 260, 262, 263, 300, 345, 351, 364, 383, 548, 555, 632, 649, 702.

256 Sharpness

N. *sharpness*, acuity, acuteness, acumination, pointedness, sting; serration, saw-edge 260n. *notch*; spinosity, thorniness,

prickliness; acridity 388n. *pungency*; suddenness 116n. *instantaneity*.

sharp point, sting, prick, point, cusp 213n. *vertex*; nail, tack, staple 47n. *fastening*; nib, tag, pin, needle, bodkin, skewer, skiver, spit, broach, brochette; lancet, fleam, awl, bradawl, drill, borer, auger 263n. *perforator*; arrow, shaft, bolt, quarrel, arrow-head, barb, sword-point, rapier, lance, pike 723n. *spear*; fishing spear, gaff, harpoon; dagger, poniard, stiletto 723n. *weapon*; spike, caltrop, chevaux-de-frise, barbed wire, barbwire 713n. *defences*; spur, rowel; gaffle, cockspur; goad, ox-g., ankus 612n. *incentive*; fork, prong, tine, pick, pickaxes, horn, antler, quill; claw, talon, nails 778n. *nippers*; spire, flèche, steeple; peak, crag, arête 213n. *summit*.

prickle, thorn, brier, bramble, thistle, nettle, cactus; bristle 259n. *hair*; beard, awn, spica, spiculum, spicula; porcupine, hedgehog; spine, needle.

tooth, tusk, tush, fang; brick-tooth, gag-t.; first teeth, milktooth; caninetooth, incisor, grinder, molar, premolar teeth; pearls, ivories; dentition, front teeth, back t., cheek t.; set of teeth, denture, false teeth, artificial t., gold t. plate, bridge; comb, saw, hand-s.; cog, ratchet, sprocket, denticulation 260n. *notch*.

sharp edge, cutting e., edged tool, edge-tool; razor's edge, knife-e., sword-e.; broken glass; cutlery, steel, razor; blade, razor-blade; share, plough-s., coulter 370n. *farm tool*; spade, mattock, trowel 274n. *shovel*; scythe, sickle, hook, reaping-h., rip-h., bill-h., pruning-h.; cutter, grass-c., lawn-mower; scissors, barber's s., pinking s., aesculap; shears, clippers, secateurs, surgical knife, scalpel, bistoury, catling; chisel, plane, spokeshave, scraper, draw-knife 258n. *smoother*; knife, bread-k., carver, carving knife, fish k., slicer; penknife, sheath-k., clasp-k., jack-k., bowie-k., shive-k., gully, whittle; machete, dao, dah, kukri, kris, creese, parang, panger; chopper, cleaver, wedge; hatchet, axe, adze; battle-axe, seax; bill, tomahawk; sword, broadsword, falchion, hanger, cutlass, scimitar 723n. *side arms*.

sharpener, knife-s., pencil-s., oilstone, whetstone, grindstone, rubstone; hone, steel, file, strop; emery, emery-paper, sand-p.

Adj. *sharp*, stinging, keen, acute; edged, cutting; swordlike, ensiform; pointed, unblunted, unbated; sharp-pointed, cusped, cuspidate, mucronate; barbed, spurred; sagittal, arrowy; spiked, spiky, spiny, spinous, thorny, brambly, briery, thistly; needlelike, aciform, acicular, aciculated; aculeiform, prickly, bristly, bristling, bearded 259adj. *hairy*; awned, awning; hastate, spear-like; studded, muricated, snaggy, craggy, jagged 259adj. *rough*; comblike, pectinated 260adj. *notched*; sharp-edged, knife-e., razor-e.; sharp as a razor, keen as a r., sharp as a needle; sharpened, whetted etc.vb.; set, sharp-set, razor-sharp.

toothed, odontoid; toothy, brick-toothed; tusky, fanged, dental, denticulate, dentiform; cogged, serrated, saw-edged, emarginate 260adj. *notched*.

tapering, acuminate, conical, pyramidal 293 adj. *convergent*; horned, cornute, corniculate; spindle-shaped, fusiform, lanceshaped, lanceolate, lanceolar.

Vb. *be sharp*,—stinging etc.adj.; have a point, prick, sting; have an edge, bite 46 vb. *cut*; taper, come to a point, end in a point 293vb. *converge*.

sharpen, edge, put an edge on, whet, hone, oilstone, grind, file, strop, set; barb, spur, point, aculeate, acuminate, spiculate; stud.

See: 46, 47, 116, 213, 258, 259, 260, 263, 274, 293, 370, 388, 612, 713, 723, 778.

257 Bluntness

N. *bluntness*, flatness, bluffness; curves, hard c., flat c.; rustiness, dullness; toothlessness, lack of bite; blunt instrument, foil; blunt edge, blade, flat.

Adj. *unsharpened*, unwhetted; blunt, blunted, unpointed, bated (of a sword); rusty, dull, dull-edged; edgeless, pointless; lacking bite, toothless, edentulous, edentate; obtuse, dull-witted 499adj. *unintelligent*; numb, insensitive 375adj. *unfeeling*; blunt-nosed, stub, stubby, snub, square; round, rounded, curving 248adj. *curved*; flat, flattened, bluff; blunting, obtundent.

Vb. *blunt*, make blunt, turn, turn the edge, disedge; take off the point, bate (a foil); obtund, dull, rust; draw the teeth 161vb.

disable; be blunt, not cut, pull, scrape, tear.

See: 161, 248, 375, 499.

258 Smoothness

N. *smoothness* etc. adj.; glabreity; smooth texture, silkiness; silk, satin, velvet, velure; fleeciness, down, swansdown 327 n. *softness*; smooth hair, sleekness; smooth surface, mahogany, marble, glass, ice; flatness, levelness, lawn, plumb wicket, bowling green, billiard table 216 n. *horizontality*; pavement, tarmac, asphalt, flags 226 n. *paving*; levigation, polish, varnish, gloss, glaze, shine, finish; slipperiness, slip-way, slide; lubricity, oiliness, greasiness 334 n. *lubrication*; smooth water, dead w., calm, dead c. 266 n. *quiescence*.

smoother, roller, garden r., steam-r., road r.; bulldozer; rolling-pin 216 n. *flattener*; iron, flat-i., smoothing-i., tailor's goose; mangle, wringer; press, hot-p., trouser-p.; plane, spokeshave, draw-knife 256 n. *sharp edge*; sand-paper, emery-p., emery-board; file, nail-f.; burnisher, turpentine and beeswax, powder; polish, varnish, enamel 226 n. *facing*; lubricator, grease, oil, grease-gun, oil-can 334 n. *lubricant*.

Adj. *smooth*, non-friction, non-adhesive, stream-lined; slithery, slippery, skiddy; lubricous, lubric, oily, greasy, buttery, soapy; greased, oiled 334 adj. *lubricated*; polished, shiny, varnished, waxed, enamelled, lacquered, glazed; soft, suave, bland, soothing 177 adj. *lenitive*; smooth-textured, silky, silken, satiny, velvety; downy, woolly, lanate 259 adj. *fleecy*; marble, glassy; bald, glabrous; sleek, slick, well-brushed, unruffled; unwrinkled, uncrumpled; plane, rolled, even, unbroken, level, flat, plumb, flush 216 adj. *horizontal*; calm, glassy, quiet, 266 adj. *still*; rounded 248 adj. *curved*; edgeless, blunt 257 adj. *unsharpened*; smooth - skinned, barkless; smooth - haired, leiotrichous; smooth as marble, smooth as glass, smooth as ice, smooth as bark, smooth as velvet, smooth as oil, slippery as an eel.

Vb. *smooth*, remove friction, streamline; oil, grease, butter 334 vb. *lubricate*; smoothen, plane, planish, even, level;

file, rub down 333 vb. *rub*; roll, calender, steam-roll; press, hot-p., uncrease, iron, mangle 216 vb. *flatten*; mow, shave, cut 204 vb. *shorten*; smooth over, smooth down 177 vb. *assuage*; iron out 62 vb. *unravel*; starch, launder 648 vb. *clean*; shine, burnish 417 vb. *make bright*; levigate, buff, polish, glaze, wax, varnish 226 vb. *coat*; pave, macadamize, tarmac 226 vb. *overlay*.

go smoothly, glide, float, roll, bowl along, run on rails; slip, slide, skid 265 vb. *be in motion*; skate, ski; feel no friction, coast, free-wheel.

See: 62, 177, 204, 216, 226, 248, 256, 257, 259, 265, 266, 327, 333, 334, 417, 648.

259 Roughness

N. *roughness*, asperity, harshness 735 n. *severity*; rough treatment 176 n. *violence*; salebrosity, broken ground; broken water, choppiness 350 n. *wave*; rough air, turbulence 352 n. *wind*; shattered surface, brokenness, broken glass; jaggedness, toothiness; serration, saw-edge, deckle-e. 260 n. *notch*; ruggedness, cragginess; sierra 209 n. *high land*; rough course, uneasy progress; unevenness, joltiness, bumpiness; corrugation, rugosity, ripple, ripple mark, corrugated iron 261 n. *fold*; rut 262 n. *furrow*; coarseness, coarse grain, knobbliness, nodosity 253 n. *convexity*; rough surface, washboard, grater, file, sand-paper, emery-p.; rough texture, sackcloth, corduroy; creeping flesh, goose-flesh, horripilation; rough skin, chap, crack; bristliness, hispidity, shagginess; hairiness, villosity; undergrowth, overgrowth 366 n. *wood*; stubble, burr, bristle, scrubbing-brush, awn 256 n. *prickle*.

hair, head of h., shock of h., matted h.; mop, mane, fleece, shag; bristle, stubble; locks, flowing l.; tresses, curls, ringlet, tight curl; kiss-curl; strand, plait; pigtail, pony-tail; topknot, forelock, elflock, lovelock, scalplock, tika; cowlick, quiff; pompadour, roll; fringe, bang, fuzz, ear-phones, bun, chignon; false hair, switch, wig, toupée 228 n. *headgear*; thin hair, wisp; beard, beaver, goatee, imperial, Van Dyke; whiskers, mutton-chops; moustache, moustachio, toothbrush, handlebars; eyebrows, eyelashes, cilia 208 n.

filament; woolliness, fleeciness, downiness, fluffiness; down, pubescence, pappus, wool, fur, budge 226n. *skin*; tuft, flock; goat's hair, mohair, cashmere, llama's hair, alpaca, vicuna 208n. *fibre*; pile, nap; shag; velvet, velour, plush 327 n. *softness*; floss, fluff, fuzz, thistledown 323n. *levity*; horsehair 227n. *lining*.

plumage, pinion 271n. *wing*; plumosity, feathering; feathers, coverts, wing c.; neck feathers, hackle f., hackle; plume, panache, crest; peacock's feathers, ostrich f., osprey f. 844n. *finery*; quill.

Adj. *rough*, unsmooth, uneven, broken; asperous, salebrous; rippling, choppy, storm-tossed; rutty, rutted, pitted, potholed, poached; bumpy, jolting, bonebreaking; chunky, crisp, rough-cast; lumpy, stony, nodular, nubbly, knobby, studded, muricate; knotted, gnarled, cross-grained, coarse-g., coarse; lined, wrinkled, corrugated, ridged 262adj. *furrowed*; rough-edged, deckle-e. 260adj. *notched*; craggy, cragged, jagged; crankling, crinkled 251adj. *convoluted*; horripilant, creeping; scabrous, scabby; blistered, blebby; ruffled, unkempt, unpolished; unbolted, unsifted; roughhewn, sketchy 55adj. *incomplete*.

hairy, pilous, villous, crinose, crinite; woolly, fleecy, furry; hirsute, shaggy, shagged, tufty, matted, shock-headed; hispid, bristly, bristling 256adj. *sharp*; setous, setose, setaceous; wispy, filamentous, fimbriated, ciliated, fringed, befringed; bewhiskered, bearded, moustached; unshaven, unshorn; unplucked; curly, frizzy, fuzzy, tight-curled, woolly.

downy, nappy, shaggy; pubescent, tomentous, pappous; velvety, peachy; fluffy, feathery, plumose, plumigerous, fledged.

fleecy, woolly, fluffy; lanate, lanated, lanuginous.

Vb. *be rough*,—hairy etc. adj.; bristle, bristle up 254vb. *jut*; creep (of flesh), horripilate; go against the grain; scratch, catch; jolt, bump, jerk 278vb. *move slowly*.

roughen, rough-cast, rough-hew; knurl, mill, crenate, serrate, indent, engrail 260vb. *notch*; stud, boss; crinkle, crisp, corrugate, wrinkle, ripple, popple 262vb. *groove*; disorder, ruffle, tousle, shag 63 vb. *derange*; rumple, crumple 261vb. *fold*; rub up the wrong way, set on edge.

Adv. *on edge*, against the grain; in the rough.

See: 55, 63, 176, 208, 209, 226, 227, 228, 251, 253, 254, 256, 260, 261, 262, 271, 278, 323, 327, 350, 352, 366, 735, 844.

260 Notch

N. *notch*, serration, serrulation, saw-edge, ragged e. 256n. *sharpness*; indentation, deckle-edge; machicolation, crenellation 713n. *fortification*; nick, cut, gash, kerf; crenation, crenature 201n. *gap*; indent, dent, dimple 255n. *concavity*; scollop, scallop, Vandyke (lace), dog-tooth 844n. *pattern*; cog, ratchet, cog-wheel, rachet-w.; saw, hacksaw, circular saw 256n. *tooth*; battlement, embrasure, crenelle.

Adj. *notched*, notchy, jagged, jaggy 256adj. *sharp*; crenate, crenated, crenellated; toothed, dentate, dentated, denticulated; serrated, palmate, emarginated; finely serrated, serrulate; serratodentate.

Vb. *notch*, serrate, tooth, cog; nick, score, scratch, scotch, scarify, bite, slice 46vb. *cut*; crenellate, crenulate, machicolate; indent, scallop, Vandyke; jag, pink, slash; dent, mill, knurl; pinch, snip, crimp 198vb. *make smaller*.

See: 46, 198, 201, 255, 256, 713, 844.

261 Fold

N. *fold*, plicature, plication, flexure, flexion, duplicature, doubling; reverse, hem; lapel, cuff, turn-up, dog's ear; plait, ply, pleat, box-p., accordion p.; tuck, gather, pucker, ruche, ruffle; flounce, frounce; crease, crushed fold; wrinkle, rivel, frown, wrinkles, crow's feet 131n. *age*; crinkle, crankle; crumple, rumple; joint, elbow 247n. *angularity*.

Adj. *folded*, doubled; gathered; creasy, wrinkly, puckery; dog-eared; creased, crumpled, crushed 63adj. *deranged*; turn-down, turn-over.

Vb. *fold*, plicate, double, turn over, roll; crease, pleat; corrugate, furrow, wrinkle 262vb. *groove*; rumple, rimple, crumple 63vb. *derange*; curl, frizzle, frizz 251vb. *crinkle*; ruffle, pucker, cockle up, gather, frounce, ruck, shirr, smock, twill; tuck, tuck up, kilt; hem, cuff; turn up, turn down, turn under, double down; enfold,

enwrap, wrap, swathe, 235vb. *inclose*; fold up, roll up, furle, reef.

See: 63, 131, 247, 251, 235, 262.

262 Furrow

N. *furrow*, groove, chase, slot, slit, crack, chink, cranny 201n. *gap*; trough, hollow 255n. *cavity*; engraving, sulcus; glyph, triglyph; fluting, goffering, rifling; chamfer, bezel, incision, gash, scratch, score 46vb. *scission*; streak, striate 437n. *striation*; wake, wheel-mark, rut 548n. *trace*; gutter, runnel, kennel, ditch, dike, dyke, trench, dug-out, moat, fosse, channel 351n. *conduit*; ravine 255n. *valley*; furrowed surface, corduroy, whipcord, corrugated iron, washboard, ploughed field; ripple, catspaw 350n. *wave*.

Adj. *furrowed*, ploughed etc.vb.; fluted, rifled, goffered; striated, sulcated, bisulcous, trisulcate; canalled, canaliculated; channelled, rutty; wrinkled, lined 261 adj. *folded*; rippling, wavy 350 adj. *flowing*.

Vb. *groove*, slot, flute, chamfer, rifle; chase; gash, scratch, score, incise 46vb. *cut*; claw, tear 655vb. *wound*; striate, streak 437vb. *variegate*; grave, carve, enchase, bite in, etch, cross-hatch 555vb. *engrave*; furrow, plough, channel, rut, wrinkle, line; corrugate, goffer 261vb. *fold*.

See: 46, 201, 255, 261, 350, 351, 437, 548, 555, 655.

263 Opening

N. *opening*, patefaction, throwing open, flinging wide; unstopping, uncorking 229 n. *uncovering*; pandiculation, stretching 197n. *expansion*; yawn, yawning, oscitation; oscitancy; dehiscence, hiation, gaping; fatiscence, hiatus, lacuna, space, interval, gat 201n. *gap*; aperture, split, crack, leak 46n. *disjunction*; hole, hollow 255n. *cavity*; placket-hole 194n. *pocket*.

perforation, piercing, tattooing etc.vb.; empalement, puncture, acupuncture, venepuncture; pertusion, appertion, terebration, trephining; boring, borehole, bore, calibre; pin-hole, eyelet.

porosity, porousness, sponge; sieve, sifter, cribble, riddle, screen 62n. *sorting*;

strainer, tea-s., colander; holeyness, honeycomb.

orifice, blind o., aperture, slot; oral cavity, mouth, gob, trap, clap, jaws, muzzle; throat, gullet, weasand, œsophagus 194n. *maw*; sucker; mouthpiece, mouthpipe, flue-pipe 353n. *air-pipe*; nozzle, spout, vent, vent-hole, vomitory, blower, blowhole, air-h., spiracle; nasal cavity, nostril; inlet, outlet; river-mouth, embouchure; small orifice, ostiole; foramen, pore; breathing pores, stomata; hole, crater, pot-hole 255n. *cavity*; touch-hole, pin-h., button-h., arm-h., key-h., punch-h.; manhole, pigeon-hole 194n. *compartment*; eye, eye of a needle, eyelet, deadeye; grommet, ring 250n. *loop*.

window, fenestration; shop-window, glass front; casement, embrasure, loophole 713n. *fortification*; bay-window, sash-w., box-w.; lattice, grill; rose-window, perpendicular w., decorated w., lancet w. 990n. *church exterior*; oriel, dormer; light, light-well, fan-light, skylight, transom, companion, window-frame; cabin window, port, porthole; peep-hole, keyhole; hagioscope, squint 990n. *church interior*; car window, window screen, rear window, side w.; window pane 422n. *transparency*.

doorway, archway; threshold 68n. *entrance*; approach, drive, drive-in, entry 297n. *way in*; exit, vomitory; passage, corridor, gangway, adit, gallery 624n. *access*; gate, city gates; portal, porch, propylæum; door, house-d., church-d.; lychgate; back door, postern 238n. *rear*; small door, wicket; scuttle, hatch, hatchway; trapdoor, companion-way; door-jamb, gatepost, lintel; doorstep; door-keeper, ostiary, durwan 264n. *janitor*.

open space 183n. *space*; yard, court 185n. *place*; opening, clearing, glade; panorama, vista 438n. *view*; landscape, champaign 348n. *plain*; alley, aisle, corridor, thoroughfare 305n. *passage*; estuary 345n. *gulf*.

tunnel, boring; subway, underpass, underground, tube; mine, shaft, pit, gallery, adit 255n. *excavation*; bolt-hole, rabbit-h., fox-hole, mouse-h.; funnel 252n. *cone*; sewer 351n. *drain*.

tube, pipe 351n. *conduit*; main, tap, faucet; efflux tube, adjutage; tubule, pipette, cannula; tubing, piping, pipe-line, hose;

artery, vein, capillary; colon, gut 224n. *insides*; funnel, fistula.

chimney, factory c., smoke-stack, funnel; smoke-duct, flue; volcano, fumarole, smoke-hole 383n. *furnace*.

opener, key, master-k., skeleton-k., passe-partout; corkscrew, tin-opener, can-o., bottle-o. ; aperient, purgative, pull-through; password, open sesame; passport, safe conduct; pass, ticket 756n. *permit*.

perforator, piercer, borer, corer; gimlet, wimble, corkscrew; auger, drill, pneumatic d., road d., dentist's d.; bur, bit, spike b., brace and b.; reamer, rimer; trepan, trephine; probe, lancet, fleam, stylet, trocar; bodkin, needle, hypodermic n.; awl, bradawl 256n. *sharp point*; pin, nail 47n. *fastening*; skewer, spit, broach, stiletto 723n. *weapon*; punch, puncheon, stapler; dibble; digging-stick; pickaxe, pick, ice-p.

Adj. *open*, patent, exposed to view 522adj. *manifest*; unclosed, unstopped, unshut, ajar; unobstructed, admitting 289adj. *accessible*; wide-open, agape, gaping; yawning, oscitant; open-mouthed, slack-jawed; opening, aperient; blooming, out.

perforated etc.vb.; perforate, drilled, bored; honeycombed, riddled; peppered, shot through; cribriform, foraminous; holey, full of holes; windowed, fenestrated, fenestrate.

porous, permeable, pervious, spongy, percolating, leachy, leaky, leaking.

tubular, tubulous, tubulated, canalular, piped; cylindrical 252adj. *rotund*; funnel-shaped, infundibular; fistulous; vascular, capillary.

Vb. *open*, unclose, unfold, ope; unlock, unlatch; open the door, fling wide the gates 299vb. *admit*; pull out (a drawer); uncover, bare 229vb. *doff*; unstop, uncork; unrip, unseam 46vb. *disjoin*; lay open, throw o. 522vb. *show*; force open, steam o. 176vb. *force*; cut open, rip o., tear o., crack o.; enlarge a hole, ream; dehisce, fly open, split, gape, yawn; burst, explode; crack at the seams, start, leak; space out, interval 201vb. *space*; open out, fan o., deploy 75vo. *be dispersed*; separate, part, hold a.; unclench, open one's hand; bloom, be out.

pierce, empierce, transpierce, transfix; gore, run through, stick, pink, lance, bayonet,

spear 655vb. *wound*; spike, skewer, spit; prick, puncture, tattoo; probe, stab, poke; inject; perforate, hole, riddle, pepper, honeycomb; nail, drive, hammer in 279vb. *strike*; knock holes in, punch, punch full of holes; hull (a ship), scuttle, stave in; tap, drain 304vb. *extract*; bore, drill, wimble; trephine, trepan; burrow, tunnel, mine 255vb. *make concave*; cut through, penetrate 297vb. *enter*; impale.

Adv. *openly* etc.adj.; patently, frankly, unguardedly; on the rooftops; out, out in the open.

See: 46, 47, 62, 68, 75, 176, 183, 185, 194, 197, 201, 224, 229, 238, 250, 252, 255, 256, 264, 279, 289, 297, 299, 304, 305, 345, 348, 351, 353, 383, 422, 438, 522, 624, 655, 713, 723, 756, 990.

264 Closure

N. *closure*, closing, shutting etc.vb.; door in one's face; occlusion, stoppage; contraction, strangulation 198n. *compression*; sealing off, blockade 232n. *circumscription*; investment 235n. *inclosure*; embolism, obstruction, obturation; infarction, constipation, obstipation, strangoury; dead-end, cul-de-sac, impasse, blank wall 702n. *obstacle*; blind gut, cæcum; imperforation, imperviousness, impermeability.

stopper, stopple, cork, plug, fid, bung, peg, spill, spigot, spike (of a gun); ramrod, rammer, piston; valve, slide v.; wedge, embolus, wad, dossil, pledget, tampon, tampion, wadding, padding, stuffing, stopping 227n. *lining*; gobstopper, stick-jaw 301n. *sweetmeat*; gag, muzzle, silencer 748n. *fetter*; obturator, shutter 421n. *screen*; tight bandage, tourniquet 198n. *compressor*; damper, choke, cut-out; vent-peg, tap, faucet, stopcock, bib-cock; top, lid, cap, cover 226n. *covering*; lock, key, bolt, bar, staple 47n. *fastening*; cordon 235n. *fence*; stopgap 150n. *substitute*.

janitor, doorkeeper, gatekeeper, porter, durwan, ostiary; commissionaire, concierge; sentry, sentinel, watchman 660n. *protector*; warden, guard 749n. *keeper*; jailer, turnkey, Cerberus, Argus 749n. *gaoler*.

Adj. *closed*, unopened, shut etc.vb.; operculated, shuttered, bolted, barred; stop-

pered, obturated; unpierced, imporous, non-porous; imperforate, unholed; impervious, impermeable 324 adj. *dense*; impenetrable, impassable, unpassable 470 adj. *impracticable*; invious, pathless, wayless, untrodden 883 adj. *secluded*; cæcal, dead-end, blank; infarcted, stuffed up, bunged up; strangulated, strangurious 198 adj. *contracted*; drawn, drawn together, joined 45 adj. *conjoint.*

sealed off, sealed, hermetically s.; cloistered, claustral; close, unventilated, stuffy, muggy; staunch, tight, air-t., gas-t.; proof, water-p., gas-p., air-p., mouse-p. 660 adj. *invulnerable.*

Vb. *close,* shut, occlude, seal; clinch, fix, bind, make tight 45 vb. *tighten*; put the lid on 226 vb. *cover*; batten down the hatches, make all tight; put the door to, clap to, slam, bang (a door); lock, fasten, snap, snap to; fill, stuff, wad, pack, jam 193 vb. *load*; plug, fother; bung, cork, stopper, obturate, spike (a gun); button, do up 45 vb. *join*; knit, draw the ends together; block, dam, staunch, choke, throttle, strangle, smother, asphyxiate 702 vb. *obstruct*; blockade 712 vb. *besiege*; enclose, surround, shut in, seal off 232 vb. *circumscribe*; trap, bolt, bar, lock in 747 vb. *imprison*; shut down, clamp d., batten d., ram d., tamp d., cram d.; put an end to 69 vb. *terminate*; come to an end 69 vb. *end*, 145 vb. *cease.*

See: 45, 47, 69, 145, 150, 193, 198, 226, 227, 232, 235, 301, 324, 421, 470, 660, 702, 712, 747, 748, 749, 883.

265 Motion: successive change of place

N. *motion,* change of position 143 n. *change*; movement, going, move, march; speed-rate, speed, air-s., ground-s.; pace, tempo; power of movement, motility, mobility, moveableness; kinetic energy, motive power, motivity; proper motion, radial m., angular m.; forward motion, advance, progress, headway 285 n. *progression*; backward motion, sternway 286 n. *regression*, 290 n. *recession*; motion towards 289 n. *approach*, 293 n. *convergence*; motion away, driftway, declension 294 n. *divergence*, 282 n. *deviation*; upward motion, rising 308 n. *ascent*; downward motion, sinking 309 n. *descent*, 313 n. *plunge*;

motion round, circumnavigation 314 n. *circuition*; axial motion 315 n. *rotation*; to and fro movement, fluctuation 317 n. *oscillation*; irregular motion 318 n. *agitation*; stir, bustle, unrest, restlessness 678 n. *activity*; rapid motion 277 n. *velocity*; slow motion 278 n. *slowness*; regular motion 16 n. *uniformity*, 71 n. *continuity*; recurring movement, rhythm 141 n. *periodicity*, motion in front 283 n. *precession*; motion after 284 n. *following*, 619 n. *pursuit*; process 316 n. *evolution*; conduction, conductivity 272 n. *transference*; current, flow, flux, drift 350 n. *stream*; course, career, run; locomotion, traffic, traffic movement, flow of traffic 305 n. *passing along*; transit 305 n. *passage*; transportation 272 n. *transport*; running, walking, foot-slogging 267 n. *pedestrianism*; riding 267 n. *equitation*; travel 267 n. *land travel*, 269 n. *water travel*, 271 n. *air travel*; dancing, gliding, sliding, skating, rolling; manœuvre, manœuvring 688 n. *tactics*; bodily movement, exercise 162 n. *athletics*; gesticulation 547 n. *gesture*; bowel movement 302 n. *cacation*; cinematography, motion picture 445 n. *cinema*; laws of motion, kinematics, kinetics, dynamics; kinesiatrics, kinesipathy, kinesitherapy 658 n. *therapy.*

gait, walk, port, carriage 688 n. *conduct*; tread, tramp, footfall, stamp; pace, step, stride; run, lope; jog-trot, dog-t.; dance-step, hop, skip, jump 312 n. *leap*; waddle, shuffle; swagger, proud step, stalk, strut, goose-step 875 n. *formality*; march, slow m., quick m., double; trot, piaffer, amble, canter, gallop, hand-g. 267 n. *equitation.*

Adj. *moving* etc. vb.; in motion; motive, motory, motor; motile, movable, mobile; progressive, regressive; locomotive, automotive; transitional, shifting 305 adj. *passing*; mercurial 152 adj. *changeful*; unquiet, restless 678 adj. *active*; nomadic 267 adj. *travelling*; drifting, erratic, runaway 282 adj. *deviating*; kinematic, kinematical; kinetic, kinesodic; cinematographic.

Vb. *be in motion,* move, go, hie, gang, wend, trail; gather way 269 vb. *navigate*; budge, stir; stir in the wind, flutter, wave, flap 217 vb. *hang*; march, tramp 267 vb. *walk*; place one's feet, tread; trip, dance 312 vb. *leap*; shuffle, waddle 278 vb. *move slowly*; toddle, patter; run 277 vb. *move fast*; run

on wheels, roll, taxi; stream, roll on, drift 350vb. *flow*; paddle 269vb. *row*; skitter, slide, slither, slithe, skate, ski, toboggan, glide 258vb. *go smoothly*; volitate, fly, frisk, flit, flitter, dart, hover; climb 308 vb. *ascend*; sink, plunge 309vb. *descend*; cruise, steam, chug, keep going, proceed 146vb. *go on*; make one's way, pick one's w., fight one's w., elbow one's w. 285vb. *progress*; pass through, wade t., pass by 305vb. *pass*; shift, dodge, duck, shift about, jink, tack, manœuvre 282vb. *deviate*; hover about, hang a. 136vb. *wait*; remove, move house, change one's address, shift one's quarters; change places 151vb. *interchange*; move over, make room 190vb. *go away*; travel, stray 267vb. *wander*; develop 316vb. *evolve*; motion, gesture 547vb. *gesticulate*.

move, impart motion, put in m.; render moveable, set going, power; put on wheels, put skates under; actuate, flick, flip, switch 173vb. *operate*; stir, stir up, jerk, pluck, twitch 318vb. *agitate*; budge, shift, manhandle, trundle, roll, wheel 188vb. *displace*; push, shove 279vb. *impel*; move on, drive, hustle 680vb. *hasten*; tug, pull 288vb. *draw*; fling, throw 287vb. *propel*; convey, transport 272vb. *transfer*; despatch 272vb. *send*; mobilize, set on foot 74vb. *bring together*; scatter 75vb. *disperse*; raise, uplift 310vb. *elevate*; throw down, let fall, drop 311vb. *depress*; make a move, manœuvre; transpose 151vb. *interchange*.

Adv. *on the move*, under way, on one's w., on the go, on the hop, on the run, on the fly; on the march, on the tramp, on the wing.

See: 16, 71, 74, 75, 136, 141, 143, 146, 151, 152, 162, 173, 188, 190, 217, 258, 267, 269, 271, 272, 277, 278, 279, 282, 283, 284, 285, 286, 287, 288, 289, 290, 293, 294, 302, 305, 308, 309, 310, 311, 312, 313, 314, 315, 316, 317, 318, 350, 445, 547, 619, 658, 678, 680, 688, 875.

266 Quiescence

N. *quiescence*, dying down, running down, subsidence 145n. *cessation*; rest, stillness; deathliness, deadness; stagnation, stagnancy 679n. *inactivity*; pause, truce, standstill 145n. *lull*; stand, stoppage,

halt; fix, deadlock, lock; full stop, dead s., dead stand 145n. *stop*; embargo 757n. *prohibition*; immobility, fixity, rigidity, stiffness 326n. *hardness*; steadiness, equilibrium 153n. *stability*; numbness, trance, catalepsy 375n. *insensibility*.

quietude, quiet, quietness, stillness, hush 399 n. *silence*; tranquillity, peacefulness, indisturbance 717n. *peace*; rest 683n. *repose*; eternal rest 361n. *death*; sleepiness, slumber 679n. *sleep*; calm, dead c., flat c. 258n. *smoothness*; windlessness, not a breath of air; dead quiet, not a mouse stirring; home-keeping, domesticity; passivity, quietism; quietist 717n. *pacifist*; tranquillizer 177n. *moderator*.

resting place, bivouac 192n. *quarters*; house of rest, roof 192n. *home*; shelter, haven 662n. *refuge*; place of rest, pillow 218n. *bed*; journey's end 295n. *goal*; last rest, grave 364n. *tomb*.

Adj. *quiescent*, quiet, still; asleep 679adj. *sleepy*; resting, at rest, becalmed; at anchor, anchored, moored, docked; at a stand, at a standstill, stopped, idle 679 adj. *inactive*; unemployed, out of commission 674adj. *unused*; dormant, unaroused, dying 361adj. *dead*; stagnant, vegetating, unprogressive, static, stationary 175adj. *inert*; sitting, sedentary, chair-borne; on one's back 216adj. *supine*; settled, stay-at-home, home-keeping, home-loving, domesticated 828adj. *content*; untravelled, unadventurous 858 adj. *cautious*; unmoved 860adj. *indifferent*.

tranquil, undisturbed, sequestered 883adj. *secluded*; peaceful, restful; unhurried, easy-going 681adj. *leisurely*; unstirring, uneventful, without incident 16adj. *uniform*; calm, windless, airless; unbroken, glassy 258adj. *smooth*; sunny, halcyon 730adj. *palmy*; at ease, easeful, comfortable, relaxed, unstrung, unemphatic 683 adj. *reposeful*; unruffled, unwrinkled, unworried, serene 823adj. *inexcitable*.

still, unmoving, unstirring, unbudging; standing, unbubbly, unfrothy, flat 387 adj. *tasteless*; immobile, moveless, motionless, gestureless; expressionless, deadpan, poker-faced 820adj. *impassive*; steady, unwinking, unblinking 153adj. *unchangeable*; standing still, rooted, rooted to the ground 153adj. *fixed*; immoveable, unable to move, stuck; stiff, frozen 326adj. *rigid*; benumbed, numb,

petrified, paralysed 375 adj. *insensible*; quiet, hushed, soundless 399 adj. *silent*; stock-still, still as a statue, still as a post, still as death; quiet as a stone, quiet as a mouse.

Vb. *be quiescent* etc. adj.; quiesce, subside, die down 37 vb. *decrease*; pipe down 399 vb. *be silent*; stand still, lie s., keep quiet; stagnate, vegetate 175 vb. *be inert*; stand, mark time 136 vb. *wait*; stay put, sit tight, stand pat, remain in situ, not stir, not budge, remain, abide 144 vb. *stay*; stand to, lie to, ride at anchor; tarry 145 vb. *pause*; rest, sit down, take breath, rest on one's laurels, rest on one's oars, rest and be thankful 683 vb. *repose*; retire, go to bed, doss down 679 vb. *sleep*; settle, settle down 187 vb. *place oneself*; keep within doors, stay at home, not go out 883 vb. *be unsocial*; ground, stick fast; catch, jam; stand fast, stand like a post; not stir a step, not stir a peg; be at a stand 145 vb. *cease*.

come to rest, stop, hold, stop short, stop in one's tracks, stop dead in one's tracks 145 vb. *halt*; pull up, draw up; slow down 278 vb. *decelerate*; anchor, cast a., come to an a., alight 295 vb. *land*; relax, calm down, rest, pause 683 vb. *repose*.

bring to rest, quiet, make q., quieten, quell, hush 399 vb. *silence*; lull, soothe, calm down 177 vb. *assuage*; lull to sleep, cradle, rock; let alone, let well alone, let sleeping dogs lie 620 vb. *avoid*; bring to a standstill, bring to, lay to, heave to; brake, put the brake on 278 vb. *retard*; stay, immobilize 679 vb. *make inactive*; put a stop to, lay an embargo on 757 vb. *prohibit*.

Adv. *at a stand*, at a halt; in repose, far from the madding crowd; after life's fitful fever.

Int. stop! stay! halt! whoa! hold! hold hard! hold it! don't move! lay off! avast! basta! bas! pipe down!

See: 16, 37, 136, 144, 145, 153, 175, 177, 187, 192, 216, 218, 258, 278, 295, 326, 361, 364, 375, 387, 399, 620, 662, 674, 679, 681, 683, 717, 730, 757, 820, 823, 828, 858, 860, 883.

267 Land travel

N. *land travel*, travel, travelling, wayfaring; seeing the world, globe-trotting, tourism; ambulation, walking; riding, ride and tie; driving, coaching, motoring, cycling; journey, voyage, trip; course, passage, sweep, reconnaissance, peregrination, pilgrimage, hadj; expedition, safari, trek; hunting expedition, stalk; exploration, gold-rush 484 n. *discovery*; business trip, errand 917 n. *duty*; pleasure trip, tour, continental t., grand t.; circuit, turn, round trip, round tour 314 n. *circuition*; jaunt, hop; ride, joy-r., drive, lift, free l.; excursion, outing, airing, ramble, constitutional, promenade; ambulation, perambulation, walk, heel and toe; stroll, saunter, hike, march, run, jog-trot 265 n. *gait*; paddling, wading.

wandering, errantry, wanderlust, nomadism; vagrancy, vagabondage, vagabondism; no fixed address; roving, rambling, pererration, waltzing Matilda; tramping, trapesing, flitting, gadding, gallivanting; migration, emigration 298 n. *egress*; immigration 297 n. *ingress*; demigration, intermigration; transmigration 305 n. *passage*.

pedestrianism, walking, going on foot, footing it, shanks's mare; foot-slogging, heel and toe; stumping, tramping, marching; ambulation, perambulation; circumambulation 314 n. *circuition*; walk, promenade, constitutional; stroll, saunter, amble, ramble; hike, tramp, march, walking-tour; run, trot, jog-t., lope; amble, canter, gallop, hand g. 265 n. *gait*; paddle, paddling, wading; foot-race, running-r. 716 n. *racing*; stalking, stalk 619 n. *chase*; walking about, peripateticism; prowling, loitering; sleep-walking, noctambulation, noctambulism, somnambulism 375 n. *insensibility*; going on all fours, creeping, crawling, crawl.

marching, campaigning, campaign; manœuvres, marching and countermarching, advance, retreat; march, route-m., night-m.; quick march, slow m., route-m.; cavalcade, procession, parade, march past 875 n. *formality*; column, file, cortège, train, caravan.

equitation, equestrianism, horsemanship, manège, dressage 694 n. *skill*; show-jumping, steeplechasing 716 n. *contest*; horse-racing; riding, bare-back r. 162 n. *athletics*; haute école, caracol, piaffer, curvet 265 n. *gait*.

conveyance, lift; flat feet, legs, shanks's

mare; horseback, mount 273 n. *horse*; bicycle, car, bus, train, tram, caravan, ambulance 274 n. *vehicle*; traffic, wheeled t., motor t., road t. 305 n. *passing along.*

leg, foreleg, hindleg; limb, nether l. 53 n. *limb*; shank, knee, shin, calf; thigh, ham, hock, hough; popliteal tendons, hamstrings; gluteal muscle, gluteus; legs, pegs, pins, underpinnings 218 n. *supporter*; stumps, stilts; stump, wooden leg, artificial l.; bow legs, bandy l. 845 n. *blemish*; long legs, spindle shanks 206 n. *thinness*; thick legs, piano l.; shank bone, shin bone, tibia.

itinerary, route 624 n. *way*; march, course 281 n. *direction*; route-map, road m., plan, chart 551 n. *map*; guide, Baedeker, Murray, road-book, handbook, timetable, Bradshaw 524 n. *guide book*; milestone, finger-post 547 n. *signpost*; halt, stop, stop-over, terminus 145 n. *stopping place.*

Adj. *travelling* etc. vb.; journeying, itinerant, wayfaring, peregrine; travel-stained, dusty 649 adj. *dirty*; travelled, much-t.; touring, globe-trotting, rubbernecking; passing through, stopping over, visiting 305 adj. *passing*; nomadic, nomad, floating, unsettled; mundivagrant, migratory, homeless, rootless, déraciné 59 adj. *extraneous*; footloose, on the road, roving, roaming, rambling, hiking, errant, wandering 282 adj. *deviating*; ambulant, strolling, circumforaneous, peripatetic; tramping, vagabond; walking, pedestrian, ambulatory, perambulatory; marching, foot-slogging; discursive, gadding, flitting, trapesing, gallivanting; automotive, locomotive, self-moving 265 adj. *moving*; self-driving, self-driven, self-drive; noctivagrant, somnambular, sleep-walking.

crural, genual, femoral, popliteal, gluteal; legged, bow-l., bandy-l. 845 adj. *blemished*; thighed, strong-t., round-t.; well-calved, well-hocked; long-legged, leggy, leggity 209 adj. *tall*; spindly, spindle-shanked, calfless 206 adj. *lean*; piano-legged, thick-ankled 205 adj. *thick.*

Vb. *travel*, fare, journey, peregrinate; tour, see the world, visit, explore 484 vb. *discover*; go places, sightsee, rubberneck; pilgrimage, go on a pilgrimage; make a journey, take a j., go on a j.; go on safari, trek, hump bluey; set out, fare forth,

pack, bundle, take wing, flit 296 vb. *depart*; migrate, emigrate, immigrate, settle 187 vb. *place oneself*; go to, hie to, repair to, resort to, betake oneself to 295 vb. *arrive*, 882 vb. *visit*; go, cruise 265 vb.

be in motion; wend, wend one's way, stir one's stumps, bend one's steps, bend one's course, shape one's c., lay a c., tread a path, pursue a p., follow the road; make one's way, pick one's way, thread one's w., plough one's w.; jog on, trudge on, peg on, wag on, shuffle on, pad on, tramp on, march on, chug on 146 vb. *sustain*; course, race, post 277 vb. *move fast*; proceed, advance 285 vb. *progress*; coast, free-wheel, glide, slide, skate, ski, skim, roll along, bowl a., fly a. 258 vb. *go smoothly.*

traverse, cross, range, pass through, range t., peragrate, pererrate, perambulate 305 vb. *pass*; circumambulate, go round, beat the bounds, fetch a circle 314 vb. *circle*; go the rounds, go one's rounds, patrol; scout, reconnoitre 438 vb. *scan*; sweep, sweep through; scour, scour the country 297 vb. *irrupt.*

wander, nomadize, migrate; rove, roam; knock around, bum, ramble, stroll, saunter, dawdle, walk about, walk aimlessly; gad, trapes, gallivant, gad about, hover, flit about, dart a. 265 vb. *be in motion*; prowl, skulk 523 vb. *lurk*; straggle, trail 75 vb. *be dispersed*; lose the way, wander away 282 vb. *stray.*

walk, step, tread, pace, stride; stride out 277 vb. *move fast*; strut, stalk, prance 871 vb. *be proud*; tread lightly, tiptoe, trip, dance, curvet 312 vb. *leap*; tread heavily, stamp, tramp, goose-step; toddle, patter; stagger, lurch; halt, limp; waddle, straddle; shuffle, dawdle 278 vb. *move slowly*; paddle, wade; go on foot, go by shanks's mare, foot it, hoof it, stump, hike, plod, trudge, jog; go, go for a walk, ambulate, perambulate; peripateticize, pace up and down; have a run, take the air, take one's constitutional; march, quick march, double, slow-march; file, file off, defile, march in procession 65 vb. *come after*; walk behind 284 vb. *follow*; walk in front 283 vb. *precede.*

ride, mount, back (horse), take horse; trot amble, tittup, canter, gallop; prance, curvet, piaff, caracol, passage; cycle, bicycle, push-bike, motor-cycle; drive,

motor, taxi, cab; go by car, go by bus, go by tram, go by taxi; go by road, go by tube, go by train; go by air 271 vb. *fly*; take a lift, cadge a l., thumb a l., hitch-hike.

Adv. *on foot*, on hoof, on horseback, on shanks's mare, on shanks's pony, by the marrowbone stage; en route 272 adv. *in transit*; by road, by rail.

Int. come along! get along! get out! git! go away! be off! buzz off! hop it! skedaddle! scram!

See: 53, 59, 75, 145, 146, 162, 187, 205, 206, 209, 218, 258, 265, 271, 273, 274, 277, 278, 281, 282, 283, 284, 285, 295, 296, 297, 298, 305, 312, 314, 375, 438, 484, 523, 524, 547, 551, 619, 624, 649, 694, 716, 845, 871, 875,

268 Traveller

N. *traveller*, itinerant, wayfarer, peregrinator; voyager 270 n. *mariner*; space-traveller, space-man 271 n. *aeronaut*; pilgrim, palmer, haji; walker, hiker, trekker; globe-trotter, tourist, rubberneck, sightseer 441 n. *spectator*; tripper, excursionist; holiday-maker, visitor; pioneer, pathfinder, explorer 66 n. *precursor*; adventurer, forty-niner; alpinist, mountaineer, cragsman 308 n. *climber*; roundsman, hawker 794 n. *pedlar*; travelling salesman, commercial traveller 793 n. *seller*; messenger, errand-boy 531 n. *courier*; pursuivant, process-server 955 n. *law officer*; daily traveller, commuter, season-ticket holder; Ulysses, Gulliver, Wandering Jew.

wanderer, migrant, bird of passage, visitant 365 n. *bird*; floating population, nomad, gypsy, Romany, Bohemian, zigane, Arab, bedouin, rover, ranger, rambler, straggler; stroller; strolling player, wandering minstrel 594 n. *entertainer*; rolling stone, drifter, vagrant, scatterling, vagabond, tramp, swagman, sundowner, hobo, bum, bummer, landloper; loafer, beachcomber 679 n. *idler*; ski-bum 162 n. *athlete*; emigrant, immigrant, emigré 59 n. *foreigner*; refugee, displaced person, D.P., stateless person; runaway, fugitive, escapee 620 n. *avoider*; déraciné, homeless wanderer, solivagant 883 n. *solitary*; waif, stray, street-arab, street-beggar 801 n. *poor man*; Wandering Jew, Flying Dutchman; comet 321 n. *meteor*.

pedestrian, foot-passenger, walker, hoofer, tramper; pacer; runner, foot-racer; wader, paddler; skater, skier; ambulator, peripatetic; hiker, hitch-h.; marcher, foot-slogger; footman 722 n. *infantry*; noctambulist, somnambulist, sleepwalker; prowler, night-walker; footpad 789 n. *robber*; toddler.

rider, horse-rider, camel-r., cameleer; elephant-rider, mahout; horseman, horsewoman, equestrian, equestrienne; postilion, post-boy 531 n. *courier*; man on horseback, cavalier, knight, chivalry 722 n. *cavalry*; hunt, huntsman 619 n. *hunter*; jockey, show-jumper 716 n. *contender*; trainer, breaker 369 n. *breeder*; rough-rider, bronco-buster, cowboy, cow-puncher, gaucho, centaur; cyclist, bicyclist, wheelman, pedal-pusher; circus-rider, trick-rider 162 n. *athlete*; motor-cyclist; back-seat driver; passenger, strap-hanger, commuter.

driver, drover, teamster, muleteer; mahout, elephant-driver, camel-d., cameleer; charioteer, coachman, whip; postilion, post-boy; carter, waggoner, drayman, truckman; cabman, cabdriver, cabby, hackie, jarvey; voiturier, vetturino, gharry wallah; car-driver, chauffeur, motorist, automobilist; scorcher 277 n. *speeder*; joy-rider; L-driver 538 n. *beginner*; taxi-driver, taximan; bus-driver, tram-d; lorry-d., truck-d., van-d., tractor-d.; motorman, engine-driver, engineer, shunter; stoker, footplate man; guard, conductor, brakeman; Jehu, Autolycus.

See: 59, 66, 162, 270, 271, 277, 308, 321, 365, 369, 441, 531, 538, 594, 619, 620, 679, 716, 722, 789, 793, 794, 801, 883, 955.

269 Water travel

N. *water travel*, ocean t., sea t., river t., underwater t.; seafaring, sea service, nautical life, life on the ocean wave; navigation, voyaging, sailing, cruising; coasting, gutter-crawling; boating, yachting, rowing (see *aquatics*); voyage, navigation, cruise, sail, steam; course, run, passage, crossing; circumnavigation, periplus 314 n. *circuition*; marine exploration, submarine e. 484 n. *discovery*; sea adventures, naval exploits; sea trip, river t., breath of sea air 685 n. *refreshment*;

way, headway, steerage way, sternway, seaway 265 n. *motion*; leeway, driftway 282 n. *deviation*; wake, track, wash, backwash 350 n. *eddy*; sea-path, ocean track, steamer route, sea lane, approaches 624 n. *route*; ship 275 n. *ship*; sailor 270 n. *mariner.*

navigation, piloting, steering, pilotage, pilotism 689 n. *directorship*; plane sailing, plain s., spherical s., great-circle s., parallel s.; compass reading, dead reckoning 465 n. *measurement*; pilotship, helmsmanship, seamanship 694 n. *skill*; nautical experience, weather eye, sea legs; naval exercises, naval manœuvres, fleet operations, naval tactics, weather gauge 688 n. *tactics.*

aquatics, water-sports 837 n. *sport*; boating, sailing, yachting, cruising; rowing, sculling, canoeing; boat racing, yacht r., speedboat r. 716 n. *racing*; water-skiing, aquaplaning, surf-riding; natation, swimming, floating; stroke, breast-s., side-s., crawl; diving, plunging 313 n. *plunge*; wading, paddling; bathing costume, swimsuit, bathing trunks, bikini 228 n. *beachwear*; bathing machine.

sailing aid, navigational instrument, sextant, quadrant, backstaff 247 n. *angular measure*; chronometer, ship's c. 117 n. *timekeeper*; log, line, lead, plummet 313 n. *diver*; compass, magnetic c., ship's c.; needle, magnetic n., south-pointing instrument; card, compass c.; binnacle; gyrocompass; radar 689 n. *directorship*; Asdic; helm, wheel, tiller, rudder, steering oar; sea-mark, buoy, lighthouse, pharos, lightship 547 n. *signpost*; chart, Admiralty c., portolano 551 n. *map*; nautical almanac, ephemeris 524 n. *guide-book.*

propeller, screw, twin screw, blade; paddlewheel, stern-w., float-board; oar, sweep, paddle, scull; pole, punt-p. 287 n. *propellant*; fin, flipper, fish's tail 53 n. *limb*; sails, canvas 275 n. *sail.*

Adj. *seafaring*, sea, salty, deep-sea; sailorlike, sailorly 270 adj. *seamanlike*; nautical, naval 275 adj. *marine*; navigational, navigating, sailing, steaming, plying, coasting, ferrying; sea-going, ocean-g.; at sea, on the high seas, afloat, water-borne, on board; pitching, tossing, rolling, wallowing; seasick, green; seaworthy, tight, snug; navigable, boatable; deep, broad, smooth.

swimming, natatory, floating, sailing; launched, afloat, buoyant; natatorial, aquatic, like a duck.

Vb. *go to sea*, follow the s., join the navy; become a sailor, get one's sea legs; be in sail, sail before the mast; live on board, live afloat; go sailing, boat, yacht; launch, launch a ship, christen a s. 68 vb. *auspicate.*

voyage, sail, go by sea, go by ship, take the sea-route; take ship, take a cabin, book one's berth, book a passage; embark, go on board, put to sea, set sail 296 vb. *start out*; cross the ocean, cross the sea 267 vb. *traverse*; disembark, land 295 vb. *arrive*; cruise, visit ports; navigate, steam, ply, run, tramp, ferry; coast, hug the shore; gutter-crawl; roll, pitch, toss, tumble, wallow 317 vb. *oscillate.*

navigate, man a ship, work a s., crew; put to sea, set sail; launch, push off, boom off; unmoor, cast off, weigh anchor; raise steam, get up s.; hoist sail, spread canvas; get under way, gather w., make w., carry sail 265 vb. *be in motion*; drop the pilot; set a course, make for, head for 281 vb. *steer for*; read the chart, go by the card 281 vb. *orientate*; pilot, steer, hold the helm, captain 689 vb. *direct*; stroke, cox, coxswain; trim the sails, square, square away; change course, veer, gybe, yaw 282 vb. *deviate*; put about, wear ship 282 vb. *turn round*; run before the wind, scud 277 vb. *move fast*; put the helm up, fall to leeward, pay off; put the helm down, luff, bring into the wind; beat to windward, tack, weather; round, double a point, circumnavigate 314 vb. *circle*; be taken aback, be caught amidships 700 vb. *be in difficulty*; career, list, heel over 220 vb. *be oblique*; turn turtle, capsize, overturn, overset 221 vb. *invert*; ride out, ride out the storm, weather the s., keep afloat 667 vb. *escape*; run for port 662 vb. *seek refuge*; lie to, lay to, heave to 266 vb. *bring to rest*; take soundings, heave the lead 465 vb. *measure*; tide over 507 vb. *await*; tow, haul, warp, kedge, clubhaul 288 vb. *draw*; ground, run aground, wreck, cast away 165 vb. *destroy*; sight land, raise, make a landfall, take on a pilot 289 vb. *approach*; make port; cast anchor, drop a.; moor, tie up, dock, disembark 296 vb. *land*; cross one's bows, take the wind out of one's sails, outmanœuvre, gain the weather gauge 702 vb. *obstruct*;

foul 279 vb. *collide*; back, go astern 286 vb. *regress*; surface, break water 298 vb. *emerge*; flood the tanks, dive 313 vb. *plunge*; shoot, shoot a bridge, shoot the rapids 305 vb. *pass.*

row, ply the oar, get the sweeps out; pull, stroke, scull; feather; punt; paddle, canoe; boat; shoot the rapids.

swim, float, sail, ride, ride on an even keel; scud, skim, skitter; surf-ride, surf-board, water-ski, aquaplane; strike out, breast the current, stem the stream; tread water; dive 313 vb. *plunge*; bathe, dip, duck; wade, paddle, splash about, get wet 341 vb. *be wet.*

Adv. *under way*, all aboard; under sail, under canvas, under steam; before the mast; on deck, on the bridge, on the quarterdeck; at the helm, at the wheel; swimmingly 701 adv. *easily.*

See: 53, 68, 117, 165, 220, 221, 228, 247, 265, 266, 267, 270, 275, 277, 279, 281, 282, 286, 287, 288, 289, 295, 296, 298, 305, 313, 314, 317, 341, 350, 465, 484, 507, 524, 547, 551, 624, 662, 667, 685, 688, 689, 694, 700, 701, 702, 716, 837.

270 Mariner

N. *mariner*, sailor, sailor-man, seaman, seafarer, seafaring man; salt, old s., sea-dog, shellback; tar, Jack Tar, matelot; no sailor, bad s., landlubber 697 n. *bungler*; shipman, skipper, master mariner, master, ship's m.; mate, boatswain, bo'sun; coxswain; able seaman, A.B. 696 n. *expert*; deckhand, swabbie, lascar; ship's steward, cabin boy 742 n. *servant*; crew, complement, ship's c., men 686 n. *personnel*; trawler, whaler, deep-sea fisherman; sea-rover, privateer, sea-king, Viking, pirate 789 n. *robber*; sea-scout; argonaut, Jason; Ancient Mariner, Flying Dutchman, Captain Ahab, Gulliver, Old Man of the Sea; sea-god, Neptune, Poseidon, Varuna.

navigator, pilot, sailing master, helmsman, steersman, wheelman, man at the wheel, quartermaster; coxswain, cox 690 *leader*; leadsman, look-out man; foretopman, reefer; boatswain, bo'sun's mate; circumnavigator 314 n. *circler*; compass, binnacle, gyrocompass 269 n. *sailing aid.*

naval man 722 n. *navy man*; man-o'-war's man, blue-jacket, gob, rating, petty-officer, midshipman, middy, midshipmite, snotty, lieutenant, sub-l., lieutenant-commander, commander, captain, flag officer, commodore, admiral, vice-a., rear-a.; Sea Lord; submariner; marine, royal m., jolly; coastguardsman, coastguard 749 n. *keeper.*

boatman, waterman, hoveller; rower, rowing man, wet bob; gigsman, gig; galleyman, galley-slave; oar, oarsman, sculler, punter; yachtsman, yachter; canoer, canoeist; ferryman, gondolier; wherryman, bargeman, bargee, lighterman; stevedore, docker, longshoreman.

Adj. *seamanlike*, sailorly, like a sailor 694 adj. *expert*; nautical, naval 275 adj. *marine.*

See: 269, 275, 314, 686, 690, 694, 696, 697, 722, 742, 749, 789.

271 Aeronautics

N. *aeronautics*, aeromechanics, aerodynamics, aerostatics, aerodonetics; aero-station, ballooning, balloonry; rocketry 276 n. *rocket*; volitation, flight, bird-f., natural f.; aerial flight, vertical f., horizontal f., level f.; jet flight, subsonic f., supersonic f. 277 n. *velocity*; stratospheric flight, hypersonic f., space f.; aviation, flying, night f., blind f., instrument f.; formation flying 875 n. *formality*; stunt flying, aerobatics 875 n. *ostentation*; gliding, planing, volplaning, looping the loop; spin, roll, side-slip; volplane, nose-dive, pull-out; crash-dive, crash, prang 309 n. *descent*; pancake, crash-landing, forced l.; touch down 295 n. *arrival*; take off 296 n. *departure.*

air travel, space t.; air transport, airlift 272 n. *transport*; air service, airline, airways; airlane, air course, air route 624 n. *route*; line of flight 281 n. *direction*; air space 184 n. *territory*; take off, touch-down, landing, three-point l.; landing ground, air-strip, runway, tarmac, airfield, aerodrome airport, heliport; terminal, air-t. 295 n. *goal*; hangar 192 n. *stable.*

aeronaut, aerostat, balloonist; glider; parachutist; paratrooper 722 n. *soldier*; aviator, airman, birdman; astronaut, spaceman, space traveller; air traveller, air

passenger 268 n. *rider*; air-hostess 742 n. *servant*; flier, flying-man, pilot, air-p., jet-p.; air-crew, navigator, observer, bombardier; pilot officer, flying o., flight sergeant, flight-lieutenant, squadron leader, wing commander, group captain, air commodore, air marshal; aircraftman 722 n. *air force*; air personnel, ground staff 686 n. *personnel*; Icarus, Dædalus.

wing, pinion, feathers, wing-feather, wingspread 259 n. *plumage*; backswept wing, Delta-w., variable w.; aileron, flaps; talaria, winged heels.

Adj. *flying*, on the wing; volitant, volant; fluttering, flitting, hovering 265 adj. *moving*; winged, alar, pinnate, feathered; aerial 340 adj. *airy*; air-worthy, air-borne, soaring, climbing 308 adj. *ascending*; airsick; losing height 309 adj. *descending*; grounded 311 adj. *depressed*; aeronautical aviational; aerodynamic, aerostatic; aerobatic.

Vb. *fly*, flight, wing, take the w., be on the w.; wing one's way, wing one's flight, be wafted, cross the sky; soar, rise 308 vb. *ascend*; hover, hang over 217 vb. *hang*; flutter, volitate 265 vb. *be in motion*; taxi, take off, clear, leave the ground, climb, circle 296 vb. *depart*; glide, plane 258 vb. *go smoothly*; float, drift, drift like a balloon 282 n. *deviate*; stunt, spin, roll, side-slip, loop the loop, volplane; hedgehop, skim the rooftops, buzz 200 vb. *be near*; stall, dive, nose-d., spiral 313 vb. *plunge*; crash, prang, force-land 309 vb. *tumble*; pull out, flatten o.; touch down 295 vb. *land*; bale out, jump, parachute, hit the silk; keep in flight, stay up, not fall; orbit, go into o. 314 vb. *circle*.

Adv. *in flight*, on the wing, on the beam.

See: 184, 192, 200, 217, 258, 259, 265, 268, 272, 276, 277, 281, 282, 295, 296, 308, 309, 311, 313, 314, 340, 624, 686, 722, 742, 875.

272 Transference

N. *transference*, change of place, translocation, transplantation, transshipment, transfer; shifting, shift, drift, continental d. 282 n. *deviation*; translation (to a post), posting, cross-p. 751 n. *mandate*; transposition, metathesis 151 n. *interchange*; removal, remotion, amotion, relegation, deportation, expulsion 300 n. *ejection*; unpacking, unloading 188 n. *displacement*; exportation, export 791 n. *trade*; mutual transfer 791 n. *barter*; importation, import 299 n. *reception*; transmittal, sending, remittance, despatch; recalling, recall, revocation, revoke 752 n. *abrogation*; extradition 304 n. *extraction*; recovery, retrieval 771 n. *acquisition*; handing over, delivery, hand-over, take-o., conveyance, transfer of property, donation 780 n. *transfer*; committal, trust 751 n. *commission*; gaol delivery, habeas corpus, release 746 n. *liberation*; transition, metastasis; passing over, trajection, ferry, ferriage 305 n. *passage*; transmigration, transmigration of souls, metempsychosis; transmission, throughput; transduction, conduction, convection; transfusion, complete t. (of blood), perfusion; decantation; diffusion, dispersal 75 n. *dispersion*; communication, contact 378 n. *touch*; contagion, infection, contamination 178 n. *influence*; literary conversion, transcription, transumption, copying, transliteration 520 n. *translation*; felonious removal, asportation, helping oneself 788 n. *stealing*.

transport, transportation, vection, vectitation, vecture; conveyance, carriage, water-c., waft, waftage, shipping, shipment; carrying, humping, portage, porterage, haulage, draught 288 n. *traction*; carting, cartage, wagonage, drayage, freightage, air freight, airlift; means of transport, rail, road, sea; air; escalator, moving staircase, travolator, moving pavement, vehicle 274 n. *conveyor*.

thing transferred, carry-over 40 n. *extra*; flotsam, jetsam, driftwood, drift, sea-d.; alluvium, detritus, scree, moraine 53 n. *piece*; sediment, deposit 649 n. *dirt*; pledge, hostage, trust 767 n. *security*; gift, legacy, bequest 781 n. *gift*; lease, 777 n. *property*; cargo, load, payload, freight, consignment, shipment 193 n. *contents*; goods, mails; luggage, baggage, impedimenta; person transferred, passenger, rider, commuter 268 n. *traveller*.

transferrer, transferor, testator, conveyancer 781 n. *giver*; sender, remitter, despatcher, despatch clerk, consignor addresser; shipper, shipping agent, transporter; exporter, importer 794 n. *merchant*; conveyor, ferryman 273 n. *carrier*;

post office, post, express p., mail, postman 531n. *mails*; communicator, transmitter, diffuser; infectious person, vector, carrier (of a disease) 651n. *sick person*; pipe-line, tap 632n. *store*; decanter, siphon.

Adj. *transferable*, conveyable, assignable, negotiable, devisable; transportable, movable, portable, carriageable; roadworthy, airworthy, seaworthy; portative, transmissive, conductive; transmissible, communicable; contagious 653adj. *infectious*.

Vb. *transfer*, hand over, deliver 780vb. *convey*; devise, leave 780vb. *bequeath*; commit, assign, entrust 751vb. *commission*; transmit, hand down, hand on, pass on; make over, turn over, hand to, pass to; pass, pass the buck; export, transport, ship, waft, lift, fly 273vb. *carry*; traject, ferry, set across; put across, put over 524vb. *communicate*; infect, contaminate 178vb. *influence*; conduct, convect; radiate 300vb. *emit*; carry over 38vb. *add*; transfer itself, come off (e.g. wet paint), adhere, stick 48vb. *cohere*.

transpose, shift, move 188vb. *displace*; switch, shunt, shuffle, castle (chess), cross-post 151vb. *interchange*; transfer, post, translate; detach, detail, draft; relegate, deport, expel 300vb. *eject*; drag, pull 288vb. *draw*; push, shove 279vb. *impel*; transfuse, decant, strain off, siphon off, draft off 300vb. *void*; unload, remove 188vb. *displace*; shovel, ladle, spoon out, dip, bail; spade, dig 255vb. *make concave*; transliterate, transdialect 520vb. *translate*; transume, copy, make a c., take a c.

send, have conveyed, remit, transmit, despatch; ship, rail, truck; direct, consign, address; post, mail; redirect, re-address, post on, forward; send by hand, send by post, send through the mail, despatch by mail; send for, order, order in, order up 627vb. *require*; send away, detach, detail; send flying 287vb. *propel*.

Adv. *in transit*, en route, on the way; by hand, per manus; by remittance, by transfer; by gift, by will; from hand to hand, from pillar to post.

See: 38, 40, 48, 53, 75, 151, 178, 188, 193, 255, 268, 273, 274, 279, 282, 287, 288, 299, 300, 304, 305, 378, 520, 524, 531, 627, 632, 649, 651, 653, 746, 751, 572, 767, 771, 777, 780, 781, 788, 791, 794.

273 Carrier

N. *carrier*, common c., haulier, carter, wagoner, tranter; shipper, transporter, exporter, importer 272n. *transferrer*; gondolier, ferryman 270n. *boatman*; lorry-driver, truck-d., taxi-d., bus-d., busman, tram-driver 268n. *driver*; delivery van, lorry, truck, tractor, goods-train 274n. *vehicle*; cargo vessel, freighter, tramp 275n. *ship*; conductor, lightning c., lightning rod; carriage, undercarriage 218n. *supporter*; carrier bag 194n. *bag*; conveyor belt, escalator, moving staircase, travolator, moving pavement 274n. *conveyor*; skate, ski, snowshoe; germ-carrier, vector.

bearer, litter-b., palki-b., stretcher-b.; caddy, golf-c.; shield-bearer, cup-bearer 742n. *retainer*; porter, red-cap, coolie, hammal; coalheaver, bummaree, stevedore; letter-carrier, carrier pigeon, postman, special messenger, express 531n. *courier*.

beast of burden, jument, pack-horse, pack-mule, sumpter-horse, sumpter-mule; ass, she-a., donkey, moke, Neddy, cuddy, burro; ox, oxen, cattle, plough-c., draught-c.; sledge-dog, husky; reindeer, llama; camel, dromedary, elephant 365n. *animal*.

horse, equine species, quadruped, horse-flesh; courser, steed; stallion, gelding, mare, colt, filly, foal; stud-horse, brood-mare, stud, stable; roan, grey, bay, chestnut, sorrel, liver-chestnut, black, piebald, skewbald, pinto, paint, dun, palamino, buckskin; dobbin, Rosinante; winged horse, Pegasus.

thoroughbred, blood-horse, blood-stock; Arab, Waler, Hambletonian; Barbary horse, barb; pacer, stepper, high-s., trotter; courser, race-horse, racer, goer, stayer; sprinter, quarter-horse 277n. *speeder*; steeplechaser, hurdler, fencer, jumper, hunter; Morgan, Tennessee Walker.

drafthorse, draught-horse, cart-h., dray-h.; shaft-horse, trace-h.; carriage-horse, coach-h., post-h.; plough-h., shire-h., Clydesdale, punch, Suffolk P., Percheron, Belgian; pit-pony.

war-horse, cavalry h., remount; charger, courser, steed 722n. *cavalry*; Bucephalus, Bayard, Copenhagen, Marengo, Rosinante.

saddle-horse, riding-h., cow-pony, cow-cutting horse, roping-h.; mount, hack, roadster; jade, tit, screw, nag; pad-nag, pad, ambler; mustang, bronco; palfrey, genet; riding mule, alborak.

pony, cob, tit, galloway, garron, sheltie; Shetland pony, fell p., Welsh mountain p., Dartmoor p., Exmoor p., New Forest p.

Adj. *bearing*, carrier, shouldering, burdened, freighted, loaded, overloaded, hag-ridden; pick-a-back.

equine, horsy, horse-faced; roan, grey (see *horse*); asinine; mulish.

Vb. *carry*, bear 218vb. *support*; hump, heave, tote; caddy; stoop one's back to, shoulder, bear on one's back, carry on one's shoulders; fetch, bring, reach; fetch and carry, trant; transport, cart, vehicle, truck, rail, railroad; ship, waft, raft; lift, fly 272vb. *transfer*; carry through, carry over, pass o., carry across, traject, ferry; convey, conduct, convoy, escort 89vb. *accompany*; have a rider, be ridden, be mounted; be saddled with, be burdened w., endure 825vb. *suffer*; be loaded with, be fraught 54vb. *be complete*.

See: 54, 89, 194, 218, 268, 270, 272, 274, 275, 277, 365, 531, 722, 742, 825.

274 Vehicle

N. *vehicle*, conveyance, public c.; transport, public t., vehicular traffic, wheeled t., road t.; sedan-chair, palanquin, palankeen, palki, dooly, dandy; litter, horse-l.; brancard, stretcher, hurdle, crate; ambulance, fire-engine; Black Maria, paddy-wagon; tumbril, dead-cart, hearse; snowplough; Snocat, weasel; tractor, caterpillar t., tracked vehicle; hobby-horse; roller-coaster, switchback, bumping car.

sled, sledge, sleigh, dog-s., horse-s., deer-s., kibitzka, carriole; bob-sleigh, bob-sled, toboggan, luge, coaster, ice-yacht; skate, ice-skate, roller-s.; snowshoes, skis, runners.

bicycle, velocipede, cycle, pedal-c., bike, push-b., safety-bicycle, safety, lady's bicycle, sit-up-and-beg, tandem; penny-farthing, bone-breaker; monocycle, unicycle, tricycle, quadricycle; motorized bicycle, moped; scooter, motor-s., motor-cycle, motor-bike; motorcycle combina-

tion, side-car; invalid carriage; cycle-rickshaw.

pushcart, perambulator, pram, baby-carriage, kiddy-cart, bassinet; Bath-chair, wheel-c., invalid-c.; jinricksha, rickshaw; barrow, wheel-b., hand-b., coster-b.; hand-cart, go-c., golf-c.; trolley, lawn-mower, garden-m., grass-cutter.

cart, ox-c., bullock-c., bail gharry, hackery; horse-and-cart, horse-cart, dog-c., gig; van, furniture-v., removal-v., moving-v., pantechnicon; horse-van, dray, milkfloat; farm-cart, haywain, hay-wagon; wain, wagon, covered w., prairie-schooner, Cape-cart; caravan, trailer; limber, gun-carriage; tumbril, dead-cart, dust-c.; bathing machine.

carriage, horse-c., equipage, turn-out, rig; chariot, coach, state c., coach and four; riding-carriage, caroche, landau, landaulette, berlin, victoria, brougham, barouche, phæton, clarence, sociable, coupé; surrey, buckboard, buggy, wagonette; travelling carriage, dormeuse, chaise, shay, calèche, calashe, britzka, unicorn; droshky, kibitzka, tarantass, araba; racing chariot, quadriga; four-in-hand, drag, tally-ho, brake, char-à-banc; two-wheeler, cabriolet, curricle, tilbury, whiskey, whitechapel, vis-à-vis, outside car, jaunting-c., beachwagon; ekka, tonga, hackery; trap, gig, pony-cart, dog-c., governess-c.; carriole, sulky, désoblige-ant; shandrydan, rattletrap; house on wheels, caravan, trailer, house-t. 192n. *small house*.

war-chariot, scythed c., weapon carrier; gun-carriage, caisson, limber, ammunition wagon; tank, armoured car, armour 722n. *cavalry*; jeep, staff car.

stage-coach, stage-wagon, stage, tally-ho, mail-c., mail-phæton; diligence, post-chaise, omnibus, horse-bus. **See** *bus*.

cab, hackney-carriage, horse-cab, four-wheeler, growler, hansom, fly; fiacre, droshky, thika-gharry; taxi-cab, taxi, jitney, hack; rickshaw, jinricksha, cycle-rickshaw.

bus, horse-b., steam-b., motor-b.; omnibus, double-decker, single-d.; autobus, trolley-bus, motor-coach, coach.

tram, horse-t., tram-car, trolley-c., trolley, street-car, cable-c.

automobile, horseless carriage, motor-car, motor, auto, car; limousine, landaulette,

sedan, saloon, hard-top, open-car, tourer, sports car, racing c.; convertible; coupé, two-seater, two-door, four-door; jeep; roadster, runabout; station-wagon, beachwagon, estate-car, shooting-brake; motor-van, lorry, truck, bowser, tanker; flivver, model-T, tin Lizzie; rattletrap, old crock, bus, jalopy; hotrod, souped-up car; autocar, tricar; bubblecar, mini-car; motor ambulance; steam-car.

train, railway train, parliamentary t., special t.; boat-t., corridor t.; express train, through t.; stopping train, local t., omnibus t., passenger t., passenger, workmen's t., goods t., freight t., luggage t., milk t., mail t., night t.; Pullman, wagon-lit, sleeping-car, sleeper; club-car, observation c.; restaurant car, dining c., diner; smoker, non-smoker, ladies only; rolling stock coach, car, carriage, compartment, coupé; caboose; brake-van, guard's van, brake, luggage van; truck, goods t., flat-car, freight c.; cattle-truck, horse-box; hand-car, trolley; bogie; electric train, diesel t., underground t., elevated t.; railway, railroad, railway line, line, track, rails, sleepers, fish-plate; electric railway, underground r., underground, tube, metro, subway; elevated, monorail, funicular.

locomotive, steam-engine, pony-e., shunter, tanker; choo-choo, puff-puff, puffer, pufferbelly, Puffing Billy, Rocket; traction engine, steam-roller; steam-car, steam-omnibus; diesel, diesel engine.

conveyor; conveyor belt, escalator, moving staircase, travolator, moving pavement.

shovel, spoon, spatula 194n. *ladle*; spade, spud, spaddle, loy, hoe, trowel, hod; pitchfork, hay-fork; knife and fork, chop-sticks.

Adj. *vehicular*, wheeled, on wheels; on rails, on runners, on sleds, on skates; automobile, automotive, locomotive; non-stop, express, through; stopping, omnibus, local.

See: 192, 194, 722.

275 Ship

N. *ship*, vessel, boat, craft; great ship, tall s.; little ship, cockboat, cockle-shell; bottom, keel, sail; tub, hull; hulk, prison-ship; Argo, Ark, Noah's Ark; steamer,

screw-s. steamship, steamboat, motor-ship, rotor s.; paddle-boat, stern-wheeler, river-boat, showboat; passenger ship, liner, ocean greyhound, floating palace; channel steamer, ferry, train-f.; deck unit; mail-ship, mail-steamer, packet, steam-p.; dredger, hopper, hopper-barge, mud-hopper; transport, hospital ship; store-ship, tender, escort vessel; pilot vessel; tug, launch; lightship, cable-s.; cog, galleon, dromond, carrack, caravel, carvel, gallivat, grab, junk; underwater craft, submarine, U-boat 722n. *warship*; fireship.

galley, war-g., galley-foist, foist, gallias, galleass, galliot, lymphad; catur; pirate-ship, Viking-s., corsair, penteconter, bireme, trireme, quadrireme, quinquereme.

merchant ship, merchantman, merchant, trader; cog, galleon, argosy, levanter, dromond, carrack, polacre, polacca; caraval, galliot; Indiaman, East I., West I.; cargo-boat, freighter, tramp; coaster, coasting-vessel, chasse-marée, hoy, crumster, bilander, hooker; collier, tanker; banana-boat, tea-clipper; slaver, slave-ship.

fishing-boat, whaler, sealer, trawler, dogger, drifter, dory, fishing smack, herring-fisher, trow, buss, coble.

sailing-ship, sailboat, sailing vessel, sailer; wind-jammer, clipper, ship, tall s., full-rigged s., square-rigged s., fore-and-aft-rigged s., schooner-rigged s., lateen-rigged s.; four-masted ship, three-masted s., three-master, bark, barque, barquentine; two-masted ship, brig, hermaphro-dite-b., cutter-b., brigantine, schooner, pinnace, snow, grab; frigate, sloop, corvette 722n. *warship*; cutter, ketch, yawl, dandy, lugger; xebec, felucca, tartane, saic, caique, dhow, gallivat, junk, lorcha, sampan; sailing barge, smack, gabbard, hoy, hooker, nobby, bawley; yacht, skiff.

sail, sail-cloth, canvas; square sail, lug-s., lug, lateen-s., fore-and-aft s., leg-of-mutton s., spanker; course, mainsail, main-course, foresail, fore-course; topsail, topgallant s., royal, skysail; jib, staysail, spinnaker, balloon-s., studding-s., stud-s., boomsail.

boat, skiff, cockle-shell, foldboat, cockboat; lifeboat; ship's boat, long-b., jolly-b.,

fly-b., bumboat; picket boat, pinnace; cutter, gig, cutter-g., whale-g.; barge, trow, lighter; state-barge, bucentaur, dahabiya;wherry, ferry, ferry-boat, canal-b., hooker, bilander; towboat, tug; launch, motorboat, motor launch, cris-craft, speedboat, cabin-cruiser, outboard; yacht, pleasure boat; house boat, budgerow 192 n. *small house.*

rowboat, rowing boat, galley; eight, racing e.; sculler, shell, funny, randan; eight-oar, four-o., pair-o.; gig-pair; dinghy, flat-bottomed d., rubber d.; outrigger, punt, gondola, coracle, currach; canoe, double-c., trow; dug-out; piragua, proa, prahu, kayak, umiak.

raft, balsa r., float, log, catamaran, jangada.

shipping, craft, forest of masts; argosy, fleet, flotilla, squadron 722 n. *navy*; marine, mercantile marine, merchant navy, shipping line.

Adj. *marine*, maritime, naval, nautical, seagoing, ocean-g. 269 adj. *seafaring*; seaworthy, water-w., weatherly; snug, tight, shipshape; rigged, square-r. (see *sailing ship*); clinker-built, cruiser-b., flush-decked.

Adv. *afloat*, aboard, on board ship, on ship-board; under sail, under steam, under canvas.

See: 192, 269, 722.

276 Aircraft

N. *aircraft* 271 n. *aeronautics*; aerodyne, flying machine, heavier-than-air m.; aeroplane, airplane, clipper; plane, monoplane, biplane, triplane; hydroplane, sea-plane, flying-boat; passenger plane, freight-plane, mail-p.; warplane, fighter, bomber 722 n. *air force*; stratocruiser, jet-plane, jet, turbo-j., turbo-prop; helicopter, autogiro, rotodyne; flying bedstead; hovercraft, air car; glider, sail-plane; flying instruments, controls, joystick, rudder, tail, wings, flaps, aileron; prop 269 n. *propeller*; cockpit, cat-walk, under-carriage, landing gear; parachute, ejector-seat 300 n. *ejector*; flight simulator; aerodrome 271 n. *air travel.*

airship, aerostat, balloon, gas-b., fire-b., Montgolfier b.; captive balloon, observation b., weather b., blimp; dirigible, Zeppelin; kite, box-k.; parachute; magic carpet; balloon-basket, nacelle, car, gondola.

rocket, rocketry, sky-rocket; guided missile, intercontinental ballistic m. 723 n. *missile weapon*; doodlebug, V2.

space-ship, flying saucer; satellite, artificial s., sputnik, blip, lunik; communications satellite, radio-mirror, echo balloon; space-station.

Adj. *aviational*, aeronautical, aerodynamic, aerostatic; balloonistic, astronautical, space-flying 271 adj. *flying*; air-worthy; heavier than air, lighter than air.

See: 269, 271, 300, 722, 723.

277 Velocity

N. *velocity*, pernicity, celerity, rapidity, swiftness, quickness, liveliness; instantaneousness, speed of thought 116 n. *instantaneity*; no loss of time, promptness, expedition, despatch;.speed, tempo, rate, pace, bat 265 n. *motion*; speed-rate, miles per hour, knots; speed of light, speed of sound, supersonic speed; great speed, lightning s., telegraphic s.; maximum speed, express s., full s., full steam; utmost speed, press of sail, full s., crowded canvas; precipitation, hurry, flurry 680 n. *haste*; reckless speed, headlong s. 857 n. *rashness*; type of speed, streak, blue s., streak of lightning, flash, lightning f.; flight, swallow f., jet f., supersonic f.; wind, storm, torrent; electricity, telegraph, lightning, greased l.; thought; quicksilver; speed measurement, velocimeter, tachometer, speedometer 465 n. *gauge*; wind gauge 340 n. *pneumatics*; log, log-line; speed-trap 542 n. *trap.*

spurt, acceleration, speed-up, overtaking; burst, burst of speed, burst of energy; thrust, drive, impetus 279 n. *impulse*; jump, spring, bound, leap, pounce 312 n. *leap*; whizz, swoop, swoosh, zip, uprush, zoom; down rush, dive, power-d.; flying start, rush, dash, scamper, run, sprint, gallop.

speeding, driving, hard d., overdriving; no speed limit, scorching, racing; bowling along, rattling a.; course, race, career, full c.; full speed, full lick, full bat; pace, smart p., strapping p., rattling p., spank-

ing rate; quick march, quick step, double, forced march; post-haste 680 n. *haste*; clean pair of heels, quick retreat 667 n. *escape*; race-course, speed-track 716 n. *racing*.

speeder, hustler, speed merchant, scorcher, racing-driver, Jehu 268 n. *driver*; runner, racer; galloper, jockey; courser, race-horse 273 n. *thoroughbred*; greyhound, hunting leopard; hare, deer, doe, antelope; flyer, bird, eagle, swallow; arrow, arrow from the bow, bullet, cannon-ball 287 n. *missile*; jet, rocket; fast sailer, clipper 275 n. *ship*; express, express train; express messenger, Ariel, Mercury 531 n. *courier*; magic carpet, seven-leagued boots.

Adj. *speedy*, swift, fast, quick, rapid; dashing, lively, smart, snappy, zippy 174 adj. *vigorous*; wasting no time, expeditious, hustling 680 adj. *hasty*; prompt 135 adj. *early*; immediate 116 adj. *instantaneous*; high-geared, high-speed, adapted for speed, stream-lined; speeding, racing; running, charging, runaway; flying, whizzing, hurtling, pelting; whirling, tempestuous; breakneck, headlong, precipitate 857 adj. *rash*; fleet, fleet of foot, light-footed, nimble-f., quick-f., light of heel; darting, starting, flashing; swift-moving, agile, nimble, slippery, evasive; mercurial, like quicksilver 152 adj. *changeful*; winged, eagle-w., like a bird; arrowy, like an arrow; like a flash, like greased lightning, like the wind, quick as lightning, quick as thought, quick as the wind, like a bat out of hell; meteoric, electric, telegraphic, transonic, supersonic, hypersonic.

Vb. *move fast*, move, shift, travel, speed; drive, pelt, streak, flash, flare; scorch, burn the ground, scour the plain, tear up the road; scud, careen; skim, nip, cut; bowl along 258 vb. *go smoothly*; sweep along, tear a., rattle a., thunder a., storm a.; tear, rip, zip, rush, dash; fly, wing, whizz, hurtle; zoom, dive; dash off, tear o., dart o., dash on, dash forward; run, lap; trot, double, lope, gallop; bolt, cut and run, scoot, skedaddle, scamper, scurry, skelter, scuttle; show a clean pair of heels 620 vb. *run away*; hare, run like a h., run like a rabbit, run like the wind, run like mad; start, dart, dartle, flit; fisk, frisk, whisk; spring, bound, leap, jump; pounce; ride hard, ride and spur, put one's

best foot forward, stir one's stumps, step out; hie, hurry, post, haste 680 vb. *hasten*; charge, career, go full tilt, go full pelt, go full lick, go full bat, go full steam, go all out; ignore the speed limit.

accelerate, raise the tempo; gather momentum, impart m., spurt, sprint, put on speed, pick up s., whip up s., step on it, step on the gas, open the throttle, open up, crowd canvas; quicken one's speed, mend one's pace, get a move on; set off at a score, get off to a flying start; make up time, make forced marches, make the best of one's way; quicken, step up, give one his head, drive, spur, urge, urge on; clap spurs to, lend wings to, put dynamite under, expedite 680 vb. *hasten*.

outstrip, overtake, overhaul, catch up, catch up with; lap, outpace, outrun, outmarch, outsail, outwalk, outdrive 306 vb. *outdo*; gain on, distance, outdistance, leave behind, leave standing; make the running, have the legs of, have the heels of, romp home, win the race 34 vb. *be superior*.

Adv. *swiftly* etc. adj.; trippingly, apace; post haste, with speed, at express s., at full s., at full tilt; in full career, in full gallop, with whip and spur, all out, flat out, ventre à terre; helter-skelter, headlong, tantivy, presto, pronto; like a shot, like an arrow, before you could say Jack Robinson; in full sail, under press of sail *or* canvas; on eagle's wings, with giant strides, in seven-league boots; in double-quick time, nineteen to the dozen, as fast as one's legs *or* heels would carry one; in high gear, at the top of one's speed; by leaps and bounds, in geometrical progression; immediately 116 adv. *instantaneously*.

See: 34, 116, 135, 152, 174, 258, 265, 268, 273, 275, 279, 287, 306, 312, 340, 465, 531, 542, 620, 667, 680, 716, 857.

278 Slowness

N. *slowness*, slackness, lentor, languor 679 n. *sluggishness*; inertia 175 n. *inertness*; refusal to be hurried, festina lente, deliberation, tentativeness, gradualism, Fabianism; hesitation 858 n. *caution*; reluctance 598 n. *unwillingness*; go-slow, go-slow

strike, slow-down, meticulosis, working to rule 145 n. *strike*; slowing down, deceleration, retardation, drag 333 n. *friction*; brake, curb 747 n. *restraint*; leisureliness, no hurry, time to spare, leisurely progress, easy stages 681 n. *leisure*; slow motion, low gear; slow march, dead m.; slow time, andante; slow pace, foot-p., snail's p., crawl, creep, dawdle; mincing steps, walk, piaffer, amble, jog-trot, dog-t. 265 n. *gait*; limping, claudication; standing start, slow s.; lagging, lag, hysteresis 136 n. *delay*.

slowcoach, snail, slug, tortoise; stopping train, omnibus t., slow t.; funeral procession, cortège; dawdler, loiterer, lingerer, slow starter, non-starter, laggard, sluggard, lie-abed, sleepy-head, Weary Willie; sloucher 598 n. *slacker*; drone 679 n. *idler*.

Adj. *slow*, go-slow; slow-paced, andante, low-geared, slow-motion; oozy, trickling; snail-like, tortoise-l., creeping, crawling, dragging; slow-moving 695 adj. *clumsy*; limping, halting; taking one's time, tardy, tardigrade, dilatory, lagging, hysteresial 136 adj. *late*; long about it, unhurried 681 adj. *leisurely*; deliberate 823 adj. *patient*; Fabian, cunctative 858 adj. *cautious*; groping, tentative 461 adj. *experimental*; languid, slack, sluggish 679 adj. *lazy*; apathetic, phlegmatic 375 adj. *insensible*; gradual, imperceptible, unnoticeable; invisible, stealthy.

Vb. *move slowly*, go slow, amble, crawl, creep, inch, inch along, ease a.; ooze, drip, trickle, dribble 350 vb. *flow*; drift 282 vb. *deviate*; hang over, hover; shamble, slouch, shuffle, scuff; toddle, waddle, take short steps, mince; plod, trudge, tramp, lumber, stump, stump along; wobble, totter, stagger, lurch; struggle, chug, jolt, bump, creak; halt, limp, hobble, hirple, claudicate, go lame; drag one's steps, flag, falter 684 vb. *be fatigued*; trail, lag, fall behind 284 vb. *follow*; not get started, not start, hang fire, drag one's feet, drag oneself 598 vb. *be loth*; tarry, be long about it, not be hurried, take one's time 136 vb. *be late*; laze, slug, idle 679 vb. *be inactive*; take it easy, stroll, saunter, dawdle 267 vb. *walk*; march in slow time, march in funeral procession; barely move, hardly beat, tick over; grope, feel one's way 461 vb. *be tentative*; hesitate 858 vb.

be cautious; speak slowly, drawl 580 vb. *stammer*.

decelerate, slow down, slow up, ease up, lose momentum; reduce speed, slacken s., slacken one's pace; smell the ground (of ships); relax, slacken, ease off 145 vb. *pause*; lose ground, flag, falter 684 vb. *be fatigued*.

retard, check, curb, rein in, throttle down 177 vb. *moderate*; reef, shorten sail, take in s., strike s. 269 vb. *navigate*; brake, put on the b., put on the drag 747 vb. *restrain*; back-pedal, back-water, back-paddle, put the engines astern, reverse 286 vb. *regress*, 221 vb. *invert*; handicap, clip the wings 702 vb. *hinder*; dowse, dim, dip, turn down (a wick) 419 vb. *bedim*.

Adv. *slowly* etc. adj.; leisurely, lazily, sluggishly; creepingly, creakily, joltily; at half speed, at low s., in low gear, in bottom g.; with mincing steps, at a foot's pace, at a snail's p., at a funeral p.; with clipped wings, slower than molasses; in slow time, piano, adagio, largo, larghetto, lente andante.

gradatim, gradually etc. adj.; by degrees, by slow d., by inches, little by little, bit by bit, inch by inch, step by step, by easy stages.

See: 136, 145, 175, 221, 265, 267, 269, 282, 284, 286, 333, 350, 375, 419, 461, 580, 598, 679, 681, 684, 695, 702, 747, 823, 858.

279 Impulse

N. *impulse*, impulsion, pressure; impetus, momentum; boost, stir-up 174 n. *stimulant*; encouragement 612 n. *incentive*; pulsion, drive, thrust, push, shove, heave; batting, on-drive, off-d., straight d. (cricket); throw, fling 287 n. *propulsion*; lunge, riposte, kick 712 n. *attack*; percussion, beating, tapping, drumming; beat, drum-b. 403 n. *roll*; recoilless beat, dead b., thud, douse; arietation, ramming, bulldozing, hammering; butting, butt (see *collision*); concussion, shaking, rattling; shock, impact; slam, bang; flick, clip, tap 378 n. *touch*; shake, rattle, jolt, jerk, yerk, wrench 318 n. *agitation*; pulsation, pulse 318 n. *spasm*; overdrive, transmission (mechanics); science of forces, mechanics, dynamics.

collision, head-on c., frontal c.; grazing collision, scrape 333n. *friction*; clash 14 n. *contrariety*; cannon, carambole; impact, bump, shock, crash, smash, encounter, meeting; brunt, charge, élan 712 n. *attack*; collision course 293n. *convergence*; multiple collision, pile-up 74n. *accumulation.*

hammer, sledge-h., sledge, steam-hammer, trip-h.; hammer-head, peen; hammerstone, pile-driver, punch, puncher; bat, beetle, maul, mall, mallet; flail; tapper, knocker, door-k.; cosh, blackjack, knuckle-duster, brass knuckle, cudgel, mace, bicycle chain, sandbag 723n. *weapon*; boxing glove; pestle, anvil; hammerer, cudgeller, pummeller, beater, carpet-b.

ram, battering-r., bulldozer; pile-driver, monkey; ramrod; rammer, tamper, tamp, tamping-iron, tamping-bar, stemmer; cue billiard c., pusher; shover.

knock, dint, dent 255n. *concavity*; rap, tap, clap; dab, pat, fillip, flip, flick; nudge, dig 547n. *gesture*; smack, slap; cuff, clout, clump, buffet, box on the ears; blow, douse; stroke, hit, crack; cut, drive (cricket); thwack, thump, biff, bang; punch, left, right, straight left, uppercut, jab, hook; body-blow, wild b., haymaker, swipe; knock-out blow, shrewd b.; stamp, kick, calcitration; whap, swat; spanking, paddling, trouncing, dusting, licking, leathering, whipping, flogging, beating, hammering, pummelling, rain of blows; hiding 963n. *corporal punishment*; assault, assault and battery 712n. *attack*; exchange of blows, fisticuffs, cut and thrust, hammer and tongs 61n. *turmoil*; innings (cricket).

Adj. *impelling* etc.vb. impellent, impulsive; dynamic, dynamical, thrustful; impelled etc.vb.

Vb. *impel,* fling, heave, throw 287vb. *propel*; give an impetus, impart momentum; slam, bang 264vb. *close*; press, press in, press up, press down; push, thrust, shove; ram down, tamp; shove off, boom off; boom, punt; hustle, prod, urge, spur 277vb. *accelerate*; fillip, flip, flick; jerk, yerk, shake, rattle, shock, jog, jolt, jostle, justle 318vb. *agitate*; shoulder, elbow, push out of the way, push around 282vb. *deflect*; throw out, run out, expel 300vb. *eject*; frogmarch; drive forward, flog on, whip on; goad 612vb. *incite*;

drive, start, run, set going, set moving 173vb. *operate*; raise 310vb. *elevate*; plunge, dip, douse 311 vb. *depress.*

collide, make impact 378vb. *touch*; appulse 289vb. *approach*; impinge 306vb. *encroach*; come into collision 293vb. *converge*; meet, encounter, clash; cross swords, fence 712vb. *foin*; ram, butt, bunt, batter, dint, dent; batter at, bulldoze; bump into, bump against; graze, graze against 333vb. *rub*; butt against, collide a.; drive into, crash i., run i., run over; clash with, collide w., foul, fall foul of; run one's head against, run into a brick wall, run against, charge a., dash a. 712 vb. *charge*; clash against, grate a., bark one's shins, stub one's toe; trip, trip over 309vb. *tumble*; knock together, knock heads t., clash the cymbals, clap one's hands.

strike, smite, hit, land a blow, plant a b.; aim a blow, hit out at; lunge, lunge at, poke at, strike at; hit wildly, swing, flail, beat the air; strike hard, slam, bang, knock; knock down, floor 311 vb. *fell*; pat, patter; flip, fillip, tickle; tap, rap, clap; slap, smack, skelp; clump, clout, box the ears of; box, spar, fisticuff 716vb. *fight* buffet, punch, thump, thwack, whack, wham, rain blows, pummel, trounce, belabour, beat up; pound, batter 332vb. *pulverize*; biff, bash, slosh, sock, slug, cosh, cudgel, club; blackjack, sandbag, hit over the head, crown; concuss, stun, knock out, leave senseless; spank, paddle, thrash, beat, whip, cane 963vb. *flog*; dust, tan, tress, hide, leather, strap, give a hiding 963vb. *punish*; hammer, peen; thresh, scutch, swingle, shingle, flail; flap, squash, swat 216vb. *flatten*; paw, stroke 889vb. *caress*; scratch, maul 655 vb, *wound*; run through, bayonet, pink 263 vb.*pierce*; tear 46vb. *cut*; throw stones at, stone, pelt, snowball 712,vb. *lapidate*; head (a football); bat, strike a ball, swipe, drive, turn, glance, cut, crack, lift (at cricket); smash, volley (tennis).

kick, spurn, boot, knee, calcitrate; trample, tread on, stamp on, kneel on; ride over, ride roughshod; spur, dig in one's heels; heel, punt, dribble, shoot (a football).

See: 14, 46, 61, 74, 173, 174, 216, 255, 263, 264, 277, 282, 287, 289, 293, 300, 306, 309, 310, 311, 318, 332, 333, 378, 403, 547, 612, 655, 712, 716, 723, 889, 963.

280 Recoil

N. *recoil*, revulsion, revulsion of feeling; reaction, retroaction, reflux 148 vb. *reversion*; repercussion, reverberation, echo 404 n. *resonance*; reflex 417 n. *reflection*; kick, kick-back, back-lash; ricochet, cannon, carom, carambole; rebound, bounce, spring, springboard 328 n. *elasticity*; ducks and drakes; swing-back, swing of the pendulum 317 n. *oscillation*; return (at tennis), boomerang; rebuff, repulse, bloody nose, contrecoup 292 n. *repulsion*; reactionary, reactionist.

Adj. *recoiling*, rebounding etc. vb.; recalcitrant, repercussive, refluent, revulsive; retroactive, reactionary 148 adj. *reverted*.

Vb. *recoil*, react 182 vb. *counteract*; shrink, wince, flinch, jib, shy 620 vb. *avoid*; recalcitrate, kick back, hit b.; ricochet, cannon, cannon off; uncoil, spring back, fly b., bound b., rebound; return, swing back 148 vb. *revert*; repercuss, have repercussions; reverberate, echo 404 vb. *resound*; shine again, reflect 417 vb. *shine*; return on one's head, boomerang 714 vb. *retaliate*.

See: 148, 182, 292, 317, 328, 404, 417, 620, 714.

281 Direction

N. *direction*, bearing, compass reading 186 n. *bearings*; lie of the land 186 n. *situation*; orientation, collimation, alignment; set, drift 350 n. *current*; tenor, trending, bending 179 n. *tendency*; aim; course, beam; bee-line, air-line, straight shot, line of sight, optical axis 249 n. *straightness*; course, tack; line, line of march, track, way, path, road 624 n. *route*; steering, steerage; aim, target 295 n. *goal*; compass, pelorus 269 n. *sailing aid*; collimator, sights 442 n. *optical device*; fingerpost 547 n. *signpost*; direction-finder, range f. 465 n. *gauge*.

compass point, cardinal points, half points, quarter points; quarter, North, East, South, West; magnetic North; rhumb, azimuth, line of collimation.

Adj. *directed* etc. vb.; orientated, directed towards, pointing t., signposted; aimed, well-a., well-directed, well-placed 187 adj. *located*; bound for 617 adj. *intending*; aligned with 219 adj. *parallel*; axial, diagonal 220 adj. *oblique*; cross-country, downtown; upwind, downwind; direct, undeviating, unswerving, straightforward, one-way 249 adj. *straight*; northern, northerly, southerly, meridional; western occidental; eastern, oriental; directive, guiding; directable, under sailing orders.

Vb. *orientate*, orientate oneself, box the compass, take one's bearings, shoot the sun, check one's course, plot one's c. 269 vb. *navigate*; find which way the wind blows, see how the land lies; take a direction, have a d., bear; direct oneself, ask the way, enquire the address; direct, show the way, signpost, point out the way 547 vb. *indicate*; pinpoint, locate 187 vb. *place*; keep on the beam 249 vb. *be straight*; face, front 237 vb. *be in front*.

steer for, steer, shape a course for, set the helm f., be bound f., head f., run f., stand f., make f., aim f.; make towards, bend one's steps to, go to, go towards, go straight for, go direct f., march f.; march on, align one 's march, march on a point; go straight to the point, hold the line, keep on the beam, keep the nose down 249 vb. *be straight*.

point to, point out, point, point towards, signpost 547 vb. *indicate*; trend, trend towards, incline t., verge, dip, bend 179 vb. *tend*.

aim, level, point; take aim, aim at; train one's sights, draw a bead on, level at; collimate, sight, set one's sights; aim well, hit the mark, land, plant 187 vb. *place*.

Adv. *towards*, versus, facing; on the way, on the road to, on the high r. to; through, via, by way of; straight, direct, straight forwards; point blank, straight as an arrow; in a direct line, in a straight line, in a line with, in a line for; directly, full tilt at, as the crow flies; upstream, downstream; upwind, downwind; before the wind, close to the w., near the w.; against the w., in the wind's eye, close hauled; down town; in all directions, in all manner of ways, from *or* to the four winds; hither, thither; clockwise, anti-clockwise, counter-clockwise, widdershins; whither, which way?

See: 179, 186, 187, 219, 220, 237, 249, 269, 295, 350, 442, 465, 547, 617, 624.

282 Deviation

N. *deviation*, disorientation, misdirection, wrong course, wrong turning; aberration, aberrancy, deflection, refraction; diversion, digression; departure, declension 220 n. *obliquity*; flection, flexion, swerve, bend, obliquation 248 n. *curvature*; branching off, divarication 294 n. *divergence*; deviousness, detour, bypath, circumbendibus, long way round, 626 n. *circuit*; exorbitation, short circuit; evagation, vagrancy 267 n. *wandering*; fall, lapse 495 n. *error*; wandering mind 456 n. *abstractedness*; drift, leeway; oblique motion, passaging, crab-walk, sidestep, sideslip; break, leg-b., off-b., googly (cricket); knight's move (chess); zigzag, slalom course; deployment, fanning out 75 n. *dispersion*.

Adj. *deviating*, aberrant, non-conformist, abnormal, deviant 84 adj. *unconformable*; eccentric, off-centre; excursive, out of orbit, exorbitant, extravagant; errant, wandering, rambling, roving, vagrant, loose, foot-l. 267 adj. *travelling*; undirected, unguided, random, without rule, erratic 495 adj. *inexact*; desultory 72 adj. *discontinuous*; abstracted 456 adj. *inattentive*; discursive, off the subject 10 adj. *irrelevant*; disorientated, without bearings, off-course, off-beam, lost, stray, astray; misdirected, misaimed, ill-a., off-target, off the mark, wide of the m., wide; off the fairway, in the rough (golf); devious, winding, roundabout 314 adj. *circuitous*; indirect, crooked, zigzag, zigzagging 220 adj. *oblique*; branching, divaricating, once removed, twice r. 294 adj. *divergent*.

Vb. *deviate*, tralineate, leave the straight, digress; branch out, divaricate 294 vb. *diverge*; turn, filter, turn a corner, swerve; turn out of one's way, go out of one's way, depart from one's course; step aside, make way for; alter course, change direction, yaw, tack; veer, back (wind); trend, bend, curve 248 vb. *be curved*; zigzag, twine, twist 251 vb. *meander*; swing, wobble 317 vb. *oscillate*; steer clear of, sheer off, edge o., ease o., bear o.; sidle, passage; slide, skid, sideslip; break (cricket); glance, fly off at a tangent 220 vb. *be oblique*; shy, jib, sidestep 620 vb. *avoid*.

turn round, turn about, about turn, wheel, wheel about, face a., face the other way; reverse, reverse direction, return 148 vb. *revert*; go back 286 vb. *turn back.*

stray, err, ramble, rove, drift, divagate, straggle 267 vb. *wander*; go astray, go adrift, miss one's way, lose the w., get lost; lose one's bearings, lose one's sense of direction, take the wrong turning, foul the line 495 vb. *blunder*; lose track of, lose the thread 456 vb. *be inattentive*.

deflect, bend, crook 220 vb. *render oblique*; warp, screw; put off the scent, misdirect, misaddress 495 vb. *mislead*; avert 713 vb. *parry*; divert, change the course of, put rudder on; draw aside, push a., pull a.; bias, put screw on (billiards); slice, pull, shank (golf); hook, glance, bowl a break, bowl wide (cricket); shuffle, shift, switch, shunt 151 vb. *interchange*; wear ship 269 vb. *navigate*; put on one side, side-track, sidestep.

Adv. *astray*, adrift; out; wide of the mark, off the mark; right about; round about; erratically, all manner of ways; indirectly, at one remove, at a tangent, sideways, diagonally 220 adv. *obliquely*; sidling, crabwise.

See: 10, 72, 75, 84, 148, 151, 220, 248, 251, 267, 269, 280, 294, 314, 317, 456, 495, 620, 626, 713.

283 Precession: going before

N. *precession* 119 n. *priority*, 64 n. *precedence*; going before, prevention, queue-jumping; leading, heading, flying start; pride of place, head of the table, head of the school, head of the form, head of the river; lead, leading role 34 n. *superiority*; pioneer 66 n. *precursor*; van, vanguard 237 n. *front*.

Adj. *foremost*, first; leading etc. vb.

Vb. *precede*, go before, forerun, herald; usher in, introduce; head, lead, take the van, head the queue; go in front, go in advance, clear the way, lead the w., lead the dance, guide, conduct 689 vb. *direct*; take the lead, get the lead, get the start, have the start; steal a march, get before, get in front, jump the queue; get ahead of, lap 277 vb. *outstrip*; be beforehand 135 vb. *be early*; take precedence over, have right of way 64 vb. *come before*.

Adv. *ahead*, before, in advance, in the van,

in front, foremost, headmost; primarily, first of all; elders first.

See: 34, 64, 66, 119, 135, 237, 277, 689.

284 Following: going after

N. *following* 65n. *sequence*; run, suit, thirteen of a suit 71 n. *series*; one after another, O.D.T.A.A.; subsequence 120 n. *posteriority*; pursuit, pursuance 619n. *chase*; succession, reversion 780n. *transfer*; last place 238 n. *rear*.
follower, attendant, hanger-on, dangler, client 742 n. *dependant*; train, tail, wake, cortège, suite, followers 67 n. *retinue*; following, party, adherent, supporter 703 n. *aider*; satellite, moon, artificial satellite, sputnik, space-station 276 n. *spaceship*; trailer, house-t. 274 n. *carriage*; tender 275 n. *ship*.
Adj. *following*, subsequent 65 adj. *sequent*.
Vb. *follow*, come behind, succeed, follow on, follow after, follow close upon, sit on one's tail, follow in the wake of, tread on the heels of, tread in the steps of, follow the footprints of, come to heel 65 vb. *come after*; stick like a shadow, bedog, spaniel, tag after, hang on the skirts of, beset; attend, wait on, dance attendance on 742 vb. *serve*; dog, shadow, trail, tail, track 619 vb. *pursue*; drop behind, fall b., lag, trail, dawdle 278 vb. *move slowly*; bring up the rear 238 vb. *be behind*.
Adv. *behind*; in the rear 238 adv. *rearward*; in the train of, in the wake of 65 adv. *after*; later 117 adv. *o'clock*.
See: 65, 67, 71, 117, 120, 238, 274, 275, 276, 278, 619, 703, 742, 780.

285 Progression: motion forwards

N. *progression*, arithmetical p., geometrical p. 36 n. *increase*; ongoing, march, way, course, career; march of time 111 n. *course of time*; progress, steady p., forward march 265 n. *motion*; sudden progress, stride, leap, jump, leaps and bounds 277 n. *spurt*; irreversibility, irresistible progress, majestic p., flood, tide 350 n. *current*; gain, ground gained, advance, headway 654 n. *improvement*; getting ahead, overtaking 306 n. *overstepping*; encroachment 712n. *attack*; next step, development, evolution 308 n. *ascent*; mystic progress, purgation, illumination, union 979 n. *piety*, 981 n. *worship*; furtherance, promotion, advancement, preferment; rise, raise, lift, leg-up 310 n. *elevation*; progressiveness, 'onward and upward department' 654 n. *reformism*; enterprise, go-getting 672 n. *undertaking*; achievement 727 n. *success*; economic progress 730 n. *prosperity*; progressive, improver 654 n. *reformer*; go-getter, coming man, upstart 730 n. *made man*.
Adj. *progressive*, progressing, enterprising, go-getting, forward-looking, reformist; advancing etc. vb.; profluent, flowing on 265 adj. *moving*; unbroken, irreversible; advanced, up-to-date, abreast of the times 126 adj. *modern*.
Vb. *progress*, proceed 265 vb. *be in motion*; advance, take a step forward, come on, develop 316 vb. *evolve*; show promise 654 vb. *improve*; get on, do well 730 vb. *prosper*; march on, run on, flow on, pass on, jog on, wag on, rub on, hold on, keep on 146 vb. *go on*; move with the times 126 vb. *modernize*; maintain progress, never look back, hold one's lead; press on, push on, drive on, push forward, press f., press onwards 680 vb. *hasten*; make a good start, make initial progress, make good p., break the back of; gain, gain ground, make headway, make head, make way; make strides, make rapid s., get over the ground, cover g. 277 vb. *move fast*; get forwards, get a move on, get ahead, shoot a., forge a., advance by leaps and bounds; gain on, distance, outdistance, leave behind 277 vb. *outstrip*; gain height, rise, rise higher 308 vb. *climb*; reach towards, reach out to, raise the sights; make up leeway, recover lost ground 31 vb. *recoup*; gain time, make up t.
promote, further, contribute to, advance 703 vb. *aid*; prefer, move up, raise, lift, bounce up, jump up 310 vb. *elevate*; bring forward, push, force, develop, grow 36 vb. *augment*; step up 277 vb. *accelerate*; put ahead, put in front, put forward 64 vb. *prepose*; favour, make for, bring on, conduce 156 vb. *cause*.
Adv. *forward*, onward, forth, on, ahead, forrard; progressively, by leaps and bounds; on the way, on one's way, under w., en route for, on the road to, on the

high r. to 272 adv. *in transit*; in progress, in mid p., in sight of.

Int. Forward! Forrard! Forrard on! Advance! Proceed! March! Excelsior!

See: 31, 36, 64, 111, 126, 146, 156, 265, 272, 277, 306, 308, 310, 316, 350, 654, 672, 680, 703, 712, 727, 730, 979, 981.

286 Regression: motion backwards

N. *regression*, regress, infinite r.; reverse direction, retroflexion, retrocession, retrogression, retrogradation, retroaction, backward step 148 n. *reversion*; motion from, recess, retreat, withdrawal, retirement, disengagement 290 n. *recession*; regurgitation 300 n. *voidance*; crab-like motion 220 n. *obliquity*; reversing, backing, reining back; falling away, decline, drop, fall, slump 655 n. *deterioration*.

return, remigration, homeward journey; home-coming 295 n. *arrival*; re-entrance, re-entry 297 n. *ingress*; going back, turn of the tide, reflux, refluence, ebb, regurgitation 350 n. *current*; veering, backing; relapse, backsliding, recidivation 603 n. *tergiversation*; U-turn, volte-face, about-turn 148 n. *reversion*; counter-march, counter-movement, counter-motion 182 n. *counteraction*; turn, turning point 137 n. *crisis*; resilience 328 n. *elasticity*; reflex 280 n. *recoil*; return to starting point, argument in a circle.

Adj. *regressive*, receding, declining, ebbing; refluent, reflex; retrogressive, retrograde, backward; backward-looking 125 adj. *retrospective*; reactionary 280 adj. *recoiling*; backing, anticlockwise, counterclockwise; reverse, reversible 148 adj. *reverted*; resilient 328 adj. *elastic*; remigrating, returning, homing, homeward-bound.

Vb. *regress*, recede, retrogress, retrograde, retrocede; retreat, sound a r., beat a r.; retire, withdraw, fall back, draw b.; turn away, turn tail 620 vb. *run away*; disengage, back out, back down 753 vb. *resign*; give way, give ground, lose g.; recede into the distance 446 vb. *disappear*; fall behind, fall astern, drop a. 278 vb. *move slowly*; reverse, back, go backwards; crawfish, back-water; run back, flow back, regurgitate; not hold, slip back; ebb, slump,

fall, drop, decline 309 vb. *descend*; bounce back 280 vb. *recoil*.

turn back, put b., retrace one's steps; remigrate, go back, home, return 148 vb. *revert*; look back, look over one's shoulder, hark back 505 vb. *retrospect*; turn one's back, turn on one's heel; veer round, wheel r., about face, execute a volte face 603 vb. *tergiversate*; double, double back, counter-march; start back, jib, shy, shrink 620 vb. *avoid*; go back, come b., come back again, go home, come h.; come back to where one started, box the compass.

Adv. *backwards*, back, astern, in reverse; to the right about; reflexively; back to where one started.

Int. back! hard astern! hands off!

See: 125, 137, 148, 182, 220, 278, 280, 290, 295, 297, 300, 309, 328, 350, 446, 505, 603, 620, 655, 753.

287 Propulsion

N. *propulsion*, jet-p., drive; impulsion, push 279 n. *impulse*; projection, jaculation; throwing, tossing, hurling, pelting, slinging, stone-throwing; precipitation; defenestration 300 n. *ejection*; cast, throw, chuck, toss, pitch and t.; fling, sling, shy, cock-shy; pot-shot, pot, shot, long s.; shooting, firing, discharge, volley 712 n. *bombardment*; bowling, pitching, throw-in, full toss, yorker, lob (cricket); kick, punt, dribble (football); stroke, drive, straight d., on-d., off-d., swipe 279 n. *knock*; pull, slice (golf); service, return, rally, volley, kill, smash (tennis); ballistics, gunnery, musketry, sniping, pea-shooting; archery, toxophily; marksmanship 694 n. *skill*; gun-shot, bow-s., stone's throw 199 n. *distance*.

missile, projectile, shell, rocket, cannon-ball, grape-shot, grape, ball, bullet, shot, small-s.; sling-stone, sling-shot, pellet, brickbat, stone, snowball; arrow, quarrel, bolt, shaft, javelin, dart 723 n. *missile weapon*; ball, tennis-b., golf-b., cricket-b., hockey-b., floater; football, leather; bowl, wood, puck, curling-stone; quoit, discus; hammer, caber.

propellant, thrust, driving force, jet, steam 160 n. *energy*; thruster, pusher, shover;

tail-wind, following w. 352 n. *wind*; lever, pedal, bicycle-p.; oar, sweep, paddle; screw, blade, paddle-wheel 269 n. *propeller*; coal, petrol, gasoline, gas, oil, diesel o. 385 n. *fuel*; gunpowder, guncotton, dynamite, cordite 723 n. *explosive*; blunderbuss, shotgun, rifle, sporting r., double-barrelled r., repeating r., elephant gun 723 n. *firearm*; revolver, six-shooter 723 n. *pistol*; pop-gun, water-pistol 723 n. *toy gun*; blow-pipe, pea-shooter; catapult, mangonel, sling, bow, longbow, crossbow 723 n. *missile weapon*.

shooter, gunman, rifleman, musketeer, pistoleer; gunner, gun-layer; archer, bowman, toxophilite, slinger, catapultier 722 n. *soldier*; marksman, sharpshooter, sniper, shot, good s., crack s. 696 n. *proficient*.

thrower, hurler, caster, pelter, stoner, snowballer; knife-thrower, javelin-t., discus-t., stone-t., slinger; bowler, pitcher, curler; server, striker (tennis); projector.

Adj. *propulsive*, propellant, propelling etc. vb. expulsive, explosive, propelled etc. vb.; projectile, missile.

Vb. *propel*, jaculate, launch, project; flight, throw, cast, heave, pitch, toss, cant, chuck, shy; bowl, lob, york; hurl, fling, sling, catapult; dart, flick; pelt, stone, shower, snowball 712 vb. *lapidate*; precipitate, send flying, send headlong, defenestrate; expel, pitchfork 300 vb. *eject*; blow away, puff a.; blow up, fulminate, put dynamite under; serve, return, volley, smash, kill (tennis); bat, slam, slog; sky, loft; drive, on-d., straight-d.; cut, pull, hook, glance (cricket); shank, slice 279 vb. *strike*; kick, dribble, punt (football); push, shove, shoulder, ease along 279 vb. *impel*; wheel, pedal, roll, bowl, trundle, bowl a hoop 315 vb. *rotate*; move on, drive, hustle 265 vb. *move*; sweep, sweep up, sweep before one, drive like leaves; put to flight 727 vb. *defeat*.

shoot, fire, open fire, fire off; volley, fire a v.; discharge, explode, let off, send off; let fly, shower with arrows, volley and thunder; draw a bead on, pull the trigger; cannonade, bombard 712 vb. *fire at*; snipe, pot, pot at; pepper 263 vb. *pierce*.

See: 160, 199, 263, 265, 269, 279, 300, 315, 352, 385, 694, 696, 712, 722, 723, 725, 727.

288 Traction

N. *traction*, drawing etc. vb. pulling back, retractiveness, retraction; retractility, retractability; magnetism 291 n. *attraction*; towage, haulage; draught, pull, haul; tug, tow; tow-line, tow-rope; rake, dragnet; drawer, puller, tugger, tower, hauler, haulier; retractor; lugsail, square sail 275 n. *sail*; windlass 310 n. *lifter*; tug, tugboat 275 n. *ship*; tractor, traction, engine 274 n. *locomotive*; loadstone 291 n. *magnet*; rowing, a strong pull and a long pull and a pull all together; strain, tug of war 716 n. *contest*; thing drawn, trailer 274 n. *train*.

Adj. *drawing* etc. vb., tractive; pulling back, retractive, retractile, retractable; attractive, magnetic 291 adj. *attracting*; tractile, ductile; drawn, horse-d.

Vb. *draw*, pull, haul, hale, trice, warp, kedge 269 vb. *navigate*; tug, tow, take in tow; lug, drag, draggle, train, trail, trawl; rake, rake in, rake out; wind in, wind up, lift, heave 310 vb. *elevate*; drag down 311 vb. *depress*; pull out 304 vb. *extract*; wrench, yank 63 vb. *derange*; jerk, twitch, pluck, snatch at 318 vb. *agitate*; pull towards 291 vb. *attract*; pull back, draw b., pull in, draw in, retract.

See: 63, 269, 274, 275, 291, 304, 310, 311, 318, 716.

289 Approach: motion towards

N. *approach*, coming towards, advance 285 n. *progression*; near approach, approximation, appulse 200 n. *nearness*; access, accession 38 n. *addition*; flowing towards, afflux, affluxion 350 n. *stream*; meeting, confluence 293 n. *convergence*; attack, onset, advent, coming 295 n. *arrival*, 189 n. *presence*; approach from behind, overtaking, overlapping 619 n. *pursuit*; adient behaviour, adient response (psychology); advances, overture 759 n. *offer*; means of approach, accessibility, approaches 624 n. *access*.

Adj. *approaching*, nearing, getting warm etc. vb.; close, approximative 200 adj. *near*; meeting 293 adj. *convergent*; confluent, affluent, tributary; overhanging, hovering, closing in, imminent 155 adj. *impending*; advancing, coming, oncoming 295 adj. *arriving*.

accessible, approachable, get-at-able; within reach, attainable 469adj. *possible*; available, obtainable 189adj. *on the spot*; wayside, roadside, near-by 200adj. *near*; welcoming, inviting 291adj. *attracting*, 882adj. *sociable*; well-paved, metalled, well-laid, smooth 624adj. *communicating*.

Vb. *approach*, approximate, verge on 18vb. *resemble*; appropinquate 200vb. *be near*; come within range 295adj. *arrive*; feel the attraction of, be drawn; come to close quarters, come closer, meet 293vb. *converge*; run down 279vb. *collide*; near, draw n., get n., go n., come n.; move near, run up to, step up to, sidle up to; roll up 74vb. *congregate*; roll in 297vb. *enter*; accost 884vb. *greet*; make up to, make overtures, make passes 889vb. *caress*; lean towards, incline, trend 179vb. *tend*; move towards, walk t., make t., drift t., set t., fall t.; advance 285vb. *progress*; advance upon, bear down on 712vb. *attack*; close, close in, close in on 232vb. *circumscribe*; hover 155vb. *impend*; gain upon, catch up with, overtake 277vb. *outstrip*; follow hard, narrow the gap, breathe down one's neck, tread on one's heels, run one close; be in sight of, make the land, make a landfall 295vb. *land*; hug the coast, hug the shore, hug the land, coast, gutter-crawl 269vb. *navigate*; accede, adhere, join 38vb. *accrue*.

Int. this way! come closer! roll up!

See: 18, 38, 74, 155, 179, 189, 200, 232, 269, 277, 279, 285, 291, 293, 295, 297, 350, 469, 619, 624, 712, 759, 882, 884, 889.

290 Recession: motion from

N. *recession*, retirement, withdrawal, retreat, retrocession 286n. *regression*; leak 298n. *outflow*; emigration, evacuation 296n. *departure*; resignation 621n. *relinquishment*; flight 667n. *escape*; shrinking, flinching 620n. *avoidance*; abient behaviour, abient response (psychology) 280n. *recoil*.

Adj. *receding* etc.vb.; retreating 286adj. *regressive*.

Vb. *recede*, retire, withdraw, fall back, draw b., retreat 286vb. *regress*; ebb, subside, shrink, decline 37vb. *decrease*; go, go away, leave, evacuate, emigrate 296vb. *depart*; go outside, go out, pour out 298vb. *emerge*; leak, leak out 298 vb. *flow out*; move from, move away, move off, move further, stand off, put space between, widen the gap 199vb. *be distant*; stand aside, make way, veer away, sheer off 282vb. *deviate*; drift away 282vb. *stray*; back away, shrink a., flinch 620vb. *avoid*; flee 620vb. *run away*, get away 667vb. *escape*; go back 286vb. *turn back*; jump back 280vb. *recoil*; come off, come away, come unstuck 46vb. *be disjoined*.

See: 37, 46, 199, 280, 286, 296, 298, 620, 621, 667.

291 Attraction

N. *attraction*, adduction, pull, drag, draw, tug; drawing to, pulling towards; magnetization, magnetism, gravity, force of g.; itch, itch for 859n. *desire*; affinity, sympathy; attractiveness, seductiveness, appeal, allure; allurement, seduction, temptation, lure, bait, decoy, charm, siren song 612n. *inducement*; charmer, temptress, siren, Circe 612n. *motivator*; centre of attraction, cynosure 890n. *favourite*.

magnet, bar m.; coil magnet, solenoid; magnetite, magnetized iron, siderite, loadstone; lodestar 520n. *guide*; magnetizer.

Adj. *attracting* etc.vb., attrahent, adducent, adductive, associative, attractive; magnetic, magnetized; seductive, charming 612adj. *inducive*; centripetal.

Vb. *attract*, magnetize, pull, drag, tug 288 vb. *draw*; adduct, exercise a pull, draw towards, pull t., drag t., tug t.; appeal, charm, move, pluck at one's heartstrings 821vb. *impress*; lure, allure, bait 612vb. *tempt*; decoy 542vb. *ensnare*.

See: 288, 520, 542, 612, 821, 859, 890.

292 Repulsion

N. *repulsion*, repellance, repellancy, repellence, repellency; repulsive force, centrifugal f.; repellent quality, repulsiveness 842n. *ugliness*; reflection 280n. *recoil*; driving off, beating o. 713n. *defence*; repulse, rebuff, snub, refusal 607n. *rejection*; brush off, dismissal 300n. *ejection*.

Adj. *repellent*, repelling etc. vb.; repulsIve 842 adj. *ugly*; off-putting, antipathetic 861 adj. *disliked*; abducent, abductive; centrifugal.

Vb. *repel*, retrude, put away; push away, butt a., butt, head 279 vb. *impel*; drive away, chase a., retund, repulse, beat off, fend off, block, stonewall 713 vb. *parry*; dispel 75 vb. *disperse*; turn away, reflect 282 vb. *deflect*; be deaf to 760 vb. *refuse*; rebuff, snub, brush off, reject one's advances 607 vb. *reject*; give one the bird, give the cold shoulder, keep at arm's length, make one keep his distance 883 vb. *make unwelcome*; show the door to, shut the door in one's face, send one off with a flea in his ear, send packing, send one about his business, give one his walking papers; boot out, sack 300 vb. *dismiss*; prove antipathetic, put off, excite nausea 861 vb. *cause dislike*.

See: 75, 279, 280, 282, 300, 607, 713, 760, 842, 861, 883.

293 Convergence

N. *convergence*, mutual approach 289 n. *approach*; narrowing gap; collision course 279 n. *collision*; concourse, confluence, conflux, meeting 45 n. *junction*; congress, concurrence, concentration, resort, assembly 74 n. *assemblage*; closing in, pincer movement 232 n. *circumscription*; centering, corradiation, focalization 76 n. *focus*; narrowing, coming to a point, tapering, taper 206 n. *narrowness*; converging line, asymptote, tangent; convergent view, perspective, vanishing point, vanishing line, vanishing plane 438 vb. *view*.

Adj. *convergent*, converging etc. vb.; focusing, focused; centripetal, centering; confluent, concurrent 45 adj. *conjunctive*; asymptotical, tangential; pointed, tapering, conical, pyramidal; knock-kneed.

Vb. *converge*, come closer, draw in, close in; narrow the gap; fall in with, come together 295 vb. *meet*; unite, gather together, get t., roll up 74 vb. *congregate*; roll in, pour in, enter in 297 vb. *enter*; close with, intercept, head off, close in upon 232 vb. *circumscribe*; pinch, nip 198 vb. *make smaller*; concentrate, corradiate, focus, bring into f.; align convergently, toe in; centre, centre on, centre in 225 vb.

centralize; taper, come to a point, narrow down 206 vb. *be narrow*.

See: 45, 74, 76, 198, 206, 225, 232, 279, 289, 295, 297, 438.

294 Divergence

N. *divergence*, divergency 15 n. *difference*; complete divergence, contradiction 14 n. *contrariety*; centrifugence, going apart, divarication; moving apart, parting 46 n. *separation*; aberration, declination 282 n. *deviation*; spread, fanning out, deployment 75 n. *dispersion*; parting of the ways, fork, bifurcation, cross-roads 222 n. *crossing*; radiation, ramification, branching out; rays, spokes.

Adj. *divergent*, diverging etc. vb.; divaricate, separated; radiating, radiant; centrifugal, centrifuge; aberrant 282 adj. *deviating*.

Vb. *diverge* 15 vb. *differ*; radiate, star; ramify, branch off, branch out; split off, fork, bifurcate; part, part ways, part company 46 vb. *be disjoined*; file off, go one's own way; change direction, switch; glance off, fly off, fly off at a tangent 282 vb. *deviate*; deploy, fan out, spread, scatter 75 vb. *be dispersed*; divaricate, straddle, step wide; spread-eagle; splay, splay apart.

See: 14, 15, 46, 75, 222, 282.

295 Arrival

N. *arrival*, advent, accession 289 n. *approach*, 189 n. *presence*; onset 68 n. *beginning*; coming, reaching, making; landfall, landing, touch-down, docking, mooring 266 n. *quiescence*; debarkation, disembarkation 298 n. *egress*; rejoining, meeting, rencounter, encounter 154 n. *eventuality*; home-coming, recursion, remigration 286 n. *return*; prodigal's return, reception, welcome, aloha 876 n. *celebration*; visitor, visitant, new arrival, recent a., homing pigeon 297 n. *incomer*; arrival at the winning post, finish, close f., photo f. 716 n. *contest*; last lap, home stretch.

goal 617 n. *objective*; bourne, terra firma 192 n. *home*; journey's end, final point, terminal p. 69 n. *end*; stop, stopover, stage, halt 145 n. *stopping place*; billet,

resting place, landing p.; port, interport, harbour, haven, anchorage, roadstead 662n. *shelter*; dock, dry-d., berth 192n. *stable*; aerodrome, airport, heliport, terminal, air-t. 271n. *air travel*; terminus, railway t., railway station, junction, depot, rendezvous 192n. *meeting-place*.

Adj. *arriving* etc.vb.; homing, homeward-bound; terminal; nearing 289adj. *approaching*, 155adj. *impending*.

Vb. *arrive*, come, reach, fetch up at, get there 189vb. *be present*; reach one's destination, make land, sight, raise; make a landfall, make port; dock, berth, tie up, moor, drop anchor 266vb. *come to rest* (see *land*); unharness, unhitch, outspan; home, come h., get h., return h. 286vb. *regress*; hit, make, win to, gain, attain; finish the race, breast the tape; reach one's goal, be in at the death 725vb. *carry through*; stand at the door, be on the doorstep, be on the threshold, knock at the door, look for a welcome 297vb. *enter*; burst in 297 vb. *irrupt*; make one's appearance, show up, pop up, turn up, roll up, drop in 882 vb. *visit*; put in, pull in, stop at, stop over, stop off, break journey, stop 145vb. *pause*; clock in, time one's arrival 135vb. *be early*; arrive at, find 484vb. *discover*; arrive at the top 727vb. *be successful*, 730 vb. *prosper*; be brought, be delivered, come to hand.

land, unload, discharge 188vb. *displace*; beach, ground, run aground, touch down, make a landing; step ashore, go a., disembark, debouche, pour out 298vb. *emerge*; surrender one's ticket, detrain, debus, get off the plane; get off, get down, alight, light on, perch 309vb. *descend*; dismount, quit the saddle, set foot to ground.

meet, join, rejoin, see again; receive, greet, welcome, shake hands 882vb. *be sociable*; go to meet, come to m., meet the train, meet the plane, meet the bus, be at the station; keep a date, rendezvous; come upon, encounter, come in contact, run into, meet by chance 154vb. *meet with*; hit, bump into, butt i., knock i., collide with 279vb. *collide*; burst upon, light u., pitch u.; gather, assemble 74 vb. *congregate*.

Int. home at last! home again! welcome! greetings! well-met! hullo! pleased to meet you!

See: 68, 69, 74, 135, 145, 154, 155, 188, 189, 192, 266, 271, 279, 286, 289, 297, 298, 309, 484, 617, 662, 716, 725, 727, 730, 876, 882.

296 Departure

N. *departure*, leaving, parting, removal, going away; walk-out, exit 298n. *egress*; pulling out, emigration 290n. *recession*; remigration, going back 286n. *return*; migration, exodus, Hejira; hop, flight, flit, moonlight f., decampment, elopement, get-away 667n. *escape*; embarkation, going on board 297n. *ingress*; mounting, saddling 267n. *equitation*; setting out, starting out, outset 68n. *start*; take-off 308n. *ascent*; zero hour, time of departure, moment of leave-taking; point of departure, place of d., port of embarkation, place of e., departure platform; starting-point, starting-post, stake-boat.

valediction, valedictory, funeral oration, epitaph, obituary 364n. *obsequies*; leave-taking, congé, dismissal; goodbye, good night, farewell, adieu; one's adieus, last handshake, waving goodbye; send-off, farewell address, speeches; farewell song, aloha; last post, last words, parting shot; stirrup-cup, doch-an-doris, one for the road, nightcap.

Adj. *departing* etc.vb.; valedictory, farewell; parting, leaving, taking l.; outward bound; emigrational.

Vb. *depart*, quit, leave, abandon 621vb. *relinquish*; retire, withdraw 286vb. *turn back*; remove, leave the neighbourhood, leave the country, leave home, emigrate, expatriate oneself, absent o. 190vb. *go away*; leave the nest, take wing; take one's leave, take one's departure, take a ticket; be gone, be going, have one for the road; bid farewell, say goodbye, say good night, make one's adieus, tear oneself away, receive one's congé, call for one's passport; leave work, cease w. 145vb. *cease*; clock out, go home 298vb. *emerge*; quit the scene, leave the stage, exit, make one's e. 753vb. *resign*; depart this life 361vb. *die*.

decamp, up sticks, strike tents, fold up one's tent, break camp, break up; march out, pack up, pack off, clear o.; clear out, evacuate; make tracks, walk one's chalks, sling one's hook; be off, beetle o., buzz o.,

slink o., slope o., push o., shove o.; take wing 271vb. *fly*; vamoose, skedaddle, beat it, hop it, scram, bolt, skip, slip away, cut a., cut, cut and run 277vb. *move fast*; flee, take flight 620vb. *run away*; flit, make a moonlight f., leave no trace 446vb. *disappear*; elope, welsh, abscond, give one the slip 667vb. *escape*.

start out, be off, get going, set out 68vb. *begin*; set forth, sally f., issue f., strike out, march out, debouch 298vb. *emerge*; gird oneself, be ready to start, warm up 669 vb. *make ready*; take ship, embark, go on board 297vb. *enter*; hoist the Blue Peter, unmoor, cast off, weigh anchor, push off, get under way, set sail, spread s., spread canvas, drop the pilot, put out to sea, leave the land behind 269vb. *navigate*; mount, set foot in the stirrup, bit, bridle, harness, saddle 267vb. *ride*; hitch up, inspan, pile in, hop on; emplane, entrain; catch a train, catch a plane, catch a bus; pull out of the station, take off, be on one's way, be in flight, be on the first lap; see off, wave goodbye, speed the parting guest.

See: 68, 145, 190, 267, 269, 271, 277, 286, 290, 297, 298, 308, 361, 364, 446, 620, 621, 667, 669, 753.

297 Ingress: motion into

N. *ingress*, introgression, entry, entrance; re-entry, re-entrance 286n. *return*; incoming, income 807n. *receipt*; inflow, influx, flood 350n. *stream*; inpouring, inrush; invasion, forced entry, inroad, raid, irruption, incursion 712n. *attack*; illapse, immersion, diffusion, osmose, osmosis; penetration, interpenetration, infiltration, insinuation 231n. *interjacence*, 303n. *insertion*; immigration, expansionism; indrawal, indraught, intake 299n.*reception*; import, importation 272n. *transference*; right of entry, non-restriction, admission, admittance, access, entrée 756n. *permission*; free trade, free imports, free market, free port, open-door policy 791n. *trade*, 744n. *scope*; ticket, pass 756n. *permit*.

way in, way, path 624n. *access*; entrance, entry, door 263n. *doorway*; mouth, opening 263n. *orifice*; intake, inlet 345n.

gulf; channel 351n. *conduit*; open door, free port 796n. *mart*.

incomer, newcomer, new arrival, new member, new face; new boy 538n. *beginner*; visitant, visitor, caller 882n. *social person*; immigrant, migrant, colonist, settler, uitlander, metic 59n. *foreigner*; stowaway, unwelcome guest 59n. *intruder*; invader, raider 712n. *attacker*; housebreaker, picklock 789n. *thief*; entrant, competitor 716n. *contender*; person admitted, ticket-holder, card-h.; audience, house, gate 441n. *onlookers*.

Adj. *incoming*, ingressive, ingoing, inward, inward bound, homing; intrusive, trespassing; irruptive, invasive 712adj. *attacking*; penetrating, flooding; allowed in, imported.

Vb. *enter*, turn into, go in, come in, move in, drive in, run in, step in, walk in, file in; follow in 65vb. *come after*; set foot in, cross the threshold, darken the doors; let oneself in; unlock the door, turn the key 263vb. *open*; gain admittance, have the entrée, be invited; look in, drop in, blow in, drop in, call 882vb. *visit*; board, get aboard; get in, hop in, jump in, pile in; squeeze into, wedge oneself i., pack oneself i., jam oneself i.; creep in, slip in, edge in, slink in, sneak in, steal in; work one's way into, buy one's way into, work oneself into, insinuate oneself; worm into, bore i. 263vb. *pierce*; bite into, eat i., cut i. 260vb. *notch*; put one's foot in, tread in, fall into, drop i. 309vb. *tumble*; sink into, plunge i., dive i. 313vb. *plunge*; join, enlist in, enroll oneself 58vb. *be one of*; immigrate, settle in 187vb. *place oneself*; let in 299vb. *admit*; put in 303 vb. *insert*; enter oneself, enter for 716vb. *contend*.

infiltrate, percolate, seep, soak through, go t., soak into, leak i., drip i.; sink in, penetrate, mix in, interpenetrate, interfuse 43vb. *mix*; taint, infect 655vb. *impair*; filter in, wriggle into, worm one's way i., insinuate oneself i.; look for an entrance, find one's way in.

irrupt, rush in, burst in, charge in, crash in, smash in, break in, storm in 176vb. *force*; flood, overflow, flow in, pour in, flood in 350vb. *flow*; crowd in, throng in, roll in, swarm in, press in 74vb. *congregate*; invade, raid, break through, board, lay aboard, storm, escalade 712vb. *attack*.

intrude, trespass, gate-crash, outstay one's welcome; horn in, barge in, break in upon, burst in u., interrupt 63 vb. *derange*; break in, burgle, housebreak, pick the lock 788 vb. *steal*.

See: 43, 58, 59, 65, 74, 187, 231, 260, 263, 272, 286, 299, 303, 309, 313, 345, 350, 351, 441, 538, 624, 655, 712, 716, 744, 756, 789, 791, 796, 807, 882.

298 Egress: motion out of

N. *egress*, egression, going out; exit, walk-off; walk-out, exodus, evacuation 296 n. *departure*; emigration, expatriation, exile 883 n. *seclusion*; emergence, emerging, debouchment; emersion, surfacing; emanation, efflux, issue; evaporation, exhalation 338 n. *vaporization*; eruption, proruption, outburst 176 n. *outbreak*; break-out 667 n. *escape*; outcome, issue 157 n. *effect*; off-take, consumption 634 n. *waste*; outgo, outgoings, outlay 806 n. *expenditure*; export, exportation 272 n. *transference*; migrant, emigrant, emigré 59 n. *foreigner*; expatriate, colonist 191 n. *settler*; expellee, exile, remittance man.

outflow, effluence, efflux, effluxion, effusion; issue, outpouring, gushing, streaming; exudation, oozing, dribbling, weeping; extravasation, extravasation of blood, bleeding, hæmophilia 302 n. *hæmorrhage*; transudation, perspiration, diaphoresis, sweating, sweat; percolation, distillation; leak, escape, leakage, seepage 634 n. *waste*; drain, running sore 772 n. *loss*; defluxion, outfall, discharge, disemboguement, drainage, draining 300 n. *voidance*; overflow, spill, flood, inundation 350 n. *waterfall*; jet, fountain, spring 156 n. *source*; gusher, well; streaming eyes, runny nose.

outlet, vent, chute, exhaust; spout, tap; pore, blow-hole, spiracle 263 n. *orifice*, 352 n. *respiration*; sluice, flood-gate 351 n. *conduit*; exhaust, exhaust-pipe, adjutage; spout, drain-pipe, gargoyle; exit, way out, path 624 n. *access*; out-gate, sally-port 263 n. *doorway*; escape, loophole 667 n. *means of escape*.

Adj. *outgoing*, outward bound; egressive, emergent, issuing, emanating; oozy, runny, leaky; running, leaking, bleeding; effusive, effused, extravasated; erupting,

eruptive, explosive, volcanic 300 adj. *expulsive*; spent 806 adj. *expended*.

Vb. *emerge*, pop out, project 254 vb. *jut*; surface, break water 308 vb. *ascend*; emanate, transpire 528 vb. *be published*; egress, issue, debouch, sally; issue forth, sally f., come f., go f.; issue out, go o., come o., pass o., walk o., march o. 267 vb. *walk*; jump out, bale o. 312 vb. *leap*; clear out, evacuate 296 vb. *decamp*; emigrate, demigrate 267 vb. *travel*; exit, walk off 296 vb. *depart*; erupt, break out, break through, burst the bonds 667 vb. *escape*; get the boot, get the bird, get the push.

flow out, flood o., pour o., stream o. 350 vb. *flow*; gush, spirt, spout, jet; drain out, run, drip, dribble, trickle, ooze; rise, surge, well, well up, well over, boil o.; overflow, spill, spill over, slop o.; run off, escape, leak, effuse, find vent, vent itself, discharge i., disembogue, debouch; flood, inundate 341 vb. *drench*; bleed, weep, effuse, extravasate 300 vb. *emit*.

exude, transude, perspire, sweat, steam 379 vb. *be hot*; ooze, seep, seep through, run t., leak t.; transcolate, percolate, strain, strain out, filter, filtrate, distil; run, dribble, drip, drop, drivel, drool, slaver, slabber, slobber, salivate, water at the mouth 341 vb. *be wet*; transpire, exhale 352 vb. *breathe*.

See: 59, 156, 157, 176, 191, 254, 263, 267, 272, 296, 300, 302, 308, 312, 338, 341, 350, 351, 352, 379, 528, 624, 634, 667, 772, 806, 883.

299 Reception

N. *reception*, admission, admittance, entrée, access; calling in, invitation 759 n. *offer*; receptivity, acceptance; open arms, welcome, effusive w. 876 n. *celebration*; taking in, introception, enlistment, enrolment, naturalization 78 n. *inclusion*; initiation, baptism 534 n. *teaching*; asylum, sanctuary, shelter 660 n. *protection*; bringing in, introduction; importation, import 272 n. *transference*; indrawal, indraught; in-breathing, inhalation 352 n. *respiration*; sucking, suction; assimilation, digestion, absorption, resorption, resorbence; engulfing, engulfment, swallowing, ingurgitation; ingestion (of food) 301 n. *eating*; imbibition, fluid intake 301 n. *drinking*;

intake, consumption 634n. *waste*; intromission, immission 303n. *insertion*; interjection 231n. *interjacence*; receptibility, admissibility.

Adj. *admitting*, receptive, introceptive; freely admitting, inviting, welcoming 289 adj. *accessible*; receivable, receptible, admissible, acceptable; absorptive, absorbent; ingestive; digestive, assimilative; introductory, initiatory, baptismal; intromittent.

Vb. *admit*, re-admit; receive, accept, naturalize; grant asylum, afford sanctuary, shelter 660vb. *safeguard*; welcome, fling wide the gates; invite, call in 759vb. *offer*; enlist, enrol, take on 622vb. *employ*; give entrance *or* admittance to, pass in, allow in, allow access; give a ticket to, sell tickets; throw open, open the door, open the hatches 263vb. *open*; bring in, import, land 272vb. *transfer*; let in, show in, usher, usher in, introduce 64vb. *come before*; send in 272vb. *send*; initiate, baptize 534vb. *teach*; intromit, infiltrate 303vb. *insert*; take, be given, get 782vb. *receive*; not deny 488vb. *assent*; avow 526 vb. *confess*.

absorb, incorporate, engross, assimilate, digest; suck, suck in; soak up, sponge, mop up, blot 342vb. *dry*; resorb, re-absorb; take in, ingest, ingurgitate, imbibe; lap up, swallow, swallow up, engulf, engorge, gulp, gobble 301vb. *eat, drink*; breathe in, inhale 352vb. *breathe*; sniff, snuff, snuff up, sniff up 394vb. *smell*; get the smell of, scent, scent out, smell out 484vb. *detect*; get the taste of 386vb. *taste*.

See: 64, 78, 231, 263, 272, 289, 301, 303, 342, 352, 386, 394, 484, 488, 526, 534, 622, 634, 660, 759, 782, 876.

300 Ejection

N. *ejection*, ejaculation, extrusion, expulsion; precipitation, defenestration 287n. *propulsion*; disbarment, striking off, disqualification 57n. *exclusion*; throwing out, chucking o., drumming o., rogue's march; dismissal, discharge, sack, boot, push, bounce 607n. *rejection*; externment, deportation, extradition; relegation, exile, banishment 883n. *seclusion*; eviction, dislodgement 188n. *displace-*

ment; ejectment, dispossession, deprivation, ouster 786n. *expropriation*; jettison, throwing overboard 779n. *non-retention*; total ejection, clean sweep, elimination 165n. *destruction*; emission, effusion, shedding, spilling; libation 981n. *oblation*; secretion 46n. *separation*; salivation 302n. *excretion*; emissivity, radio-activity 417n. *radiation*; expellee, deportee, refugee 883n. *outcaste*.

ejector, evicter, dispossessor, depriver 786n. *taker*; displacer, supplanter, superseder 150n. *substitute*; expeller, chucker-out, bouncer; expellant, emetic, sickener; aperient 658n. *cathartic*; secretory; salivant, sialagogue; propellant 723n. *explosive*; belcher; volcano 383n. *furnace*; emitter, radiator; ejecting mechanism, ejector-seat 276n. *aircraft*; cuckoo 59n. *intruder*.

voidance, clearance, clearage, drainage; eruption, eruptiveness 176n. *outbreak*; egestion, regurgitation, disgorgement; vomition, vomiting, nausea, vomit; ructation, eructation, gas, wind, burp, belch; breaking wind, crepitation, belching, rumbling, grumbling, collywobbles; blood-letting, cupping, bleeding, venesection, phlebotomy, paracentesis, tapping; elimination, evacuation, 302n. *excretion*.

Adj. *expulsive*, expellent, extrusive, explosive; eruptive, effusive; radiating, emitting, emissive; salivant, secretory, salivary; sickening, emetic; cathartic, emetocathartic; sialagogue, emmenagogic.

vomiting, sick, sickened, nauseated; belching, sea-sick, air-s., car-s., train-s.

Vb. *eject*, expel, send down 963vb. *punish*; strike off, strike off the roll, disbar 57vb. *exclude*; export, send away 272vb. *transfer*; deport, extern, expatriate, exile, banish, transport 883vb. *seclude*; extrude, detrude; throw up, cast up, wash up, wash ashore; spit out, spew o.; put out, push o., turf o., throw o., chuck o., fling o., bounce; kick out, boot o.; bundle out, hustle o.; drum out, play the rogue's march; defenestrate, precipitate 287vb. *propel*; pull out 304vb. *extract*; unearth, root out, weed o., uproot, eradicate, deracinate 165vb. *destroy*; rub out, cross o., erase, eliminate 550vb. *obliterate*; exorcise, rid, get rid of, rid oneself, get shot of; shake off, brush o.; dispossess,

expropriate 786 vb. *deprive*; out, oust, evict, dislodge, unhouse, turn out, turn adrift, turn out of house and home 188 vb. *displace*; hunt out, smoke o. 619 vb. *hunt*; jettison, discard, throw away, throw overboard 779 vb. *not retain*; blackball 607 vb. *reject*; ostracize, cut, cut dead, send to Coventry, give the cold shoulder 883 vb. *make unwelcome*; take the place of, supplant, supersede, replace 150 vb. *substitute*.

dismiss, discharge, lay off, turn off, make redundant, drop 674 vb. *disuse*; axe, sack, fire, give the sack, give the boot, give the push; turn away, send one about his business, send to the right about, send one away with a flea in his ear, send packing, send to Jericho; see off, shoo o., shoo away 854 vb. *frighten*; show the door, give the gate, show out, bow o.; bowl out, run o., catch o., take one's wicket; exorcize, tell to go, order off, order away 757 vb. *prohibit*.

void, evacuate, eliminate 302 vb. *excrete*; vent, disgorge, discharge; empty, drain; pour out, decant 272 vb. *transpose*; drink up, drain to the dregs 301 vb. *drink*; drain off, strain off, bail, bail out, pump o., suck o., run o.; run off, siphon o., open the sluices, open the floodgates, turn on the tap 263 vb. *open*; draw off, milk, bleed, tap, broach 263 vb. *pierce*; cup, let blood, draw b., tap one's claret 304 vb. *extract*; clear, sweep away, clear a., sweep off, clear o., clean up, make a clean sweep of 648 vb. *clean*; clean out, clear out, curette; unload, unlade, unship, unpack, break bulk, discargo 188 vb. *displace*; exenterate, disembowel, eviscerate, gut, clean, bone, fillet 229 vb. *uncover*; denazify, disinfest 648 vb. *purify*; desolate, depopulate, dispeople, unpeople 105 vb. *render few*; empty a fire-arm, fire 287 vb. *shoot*.

emit, send out 272 vb. *send*; emit rays 417 vb. *radiate*; emit a smell, give off, exhale, breathe out, perfume, scent 394 vb. *smell*; vapour, fume, smoke, steam, puff 338 vb. *vaporize*; spit, spatter, sputter, splutter; effuse, pour, spend, spill, shed, sprinkle; spirt, spirtle, squirt, jet, gush 341 vb. *moisten*; extravasate, bleed 341 vb. *be wet*; drip, drop, ooze; drivel, dribble, drool, slobber, slaver, salivate 298 vb. *exude*; sweat, perspire 379 vb. *be hot*; secrete 632 vb. *store*; egest, pass 302

vb. *excrete*; drop (a foal), lay (an egg) 164 vb. *generate*; let out, pass o., give an exit to.

vomit, be sick, bring up, throw up, cast up, disgorge, retch, keck; spew, puke, cat; feel nausea, heave.

eruct, eructate, crepitate, rumble inside; belch, burp, gurk; break wind, blow off, fart; hiccup, cough, hawk, clear the throat, expectorate, spit, gob.

See: 46, 57, 59, 105, 150, 164, 165, 176, 187, 188, 229, 263, 272, 276, 287, 298, 301, 302, 304, 338, 341, 379, 383, 394, 417, 550, 607, 619, 632, 648, 658, 674, 723, 757, 779, 786, 854, 883, 963, 981.

301 Food: eating and drinking

N. *eating* etc. vb.; taking food, ingestion; alimentation, nutrition; food instinct, alimentiveness; feeding, forcible f.; consumption, devouring; swallowing, deglutition; biting, chewing, mastication; manducation, carnal m., literal m., spiritual m. (theology); rumination, digestion; animal feeding, grass f., pasture, pasturing, cropping; eating meals, table, diet, dining, lunching; communal feeding, messing; dining out, regalement 882 n. *sociability*; partaking, delicate feeding; tasting, nibbling, pecking, licking, playing with one's food; ingurgitation, guzzling, heavy eating, overeating, overindulgence 944 n. *sensualism*, 947 n. *gluttony*; appetite, voracity, wolfishness 859 n. *hunger*; omnivorousness, pantophagy 464 n. *indiscrimination*; eating habits, table manners 610 n. *practice*; flesh-eating, carnivorousness, creophagy, hippophagy, ichthyophagy; man-eating, cannibalism; herbivorousness, vegetarianism; edibility, digestibility.

feasting, eating and drinking, ingurgitation, guzzling, swilling; banqueting, epulation; lavish entertainment, regalement; orgy, Roman o., Lucullan banquet, Sardanapalian b., feast, banquet, state-b., bump-supper, spree, beanfeast, beano; picnic, barbecue, cookout, clambake; Christmas dinner, blow-out, spread (see *meal*); good table, festal cheer, groaning board; fleshpots, milk and honey 635 n. *plenty*; banquet-hall, hall (of a college), dining room, mess r., refectory 192 n. *café*.

dieting, dietetics 658 n. *therapy*; banting, thinning 206 n. *thinness*; reducing 946 n. *fasting*; diet, balanced d.; glossop lunch, Oslo breakfast; regimen, régime, course, dietary, diet sheet; meagre diet, poor table; vitamins, proteins, carbohydrates, roughage (see *food content*); digestive pill, food tablet, vitamin t.; dietician, nutritionist, nutrition expert.

gastronomy, gastronomics, gastrology, palate-tickling, epicureanism, epicurism 944 n. *sensualism*; gourmandise, gourmandism, good living, high l. 947 n. *gluttony*; dainty palate, refined p. 463 n. *discrimination*; epicure, gourmet, Lucullus (see *eater*).

cookery, cooking, baking, dressing; domestic science, home economics, catering 633 n. *provision*; culinary department, cuisine; baker, cook, chef, cuisinier; cookshop, bakery, rotisserie, restaurant 192 n. *café*; kitchen, cook-house, bake-h.; oven 383 n. *furnace*; cooking medium, butter, grease, dripping lard; barm 323 n. *leaven*; cookery book, cookbook 589 n. *textbook*; recipe, receipt 496 n. *maxim*.

eater, feeder, consumer, partaker, taster, nibbler, picker, pecker; boarder, messer, messmate; breakfaster, luncher, diner; banqueter, feaster, picnicker; diner-out, dining club 882 n. *sociability*; dainty feeder, connoisseur, gourmet, epicure, trencherman, gourmand, bon viveur, epicure, Lucullus, belly-worshipper; smell-feast, parasite 947 n. *glutton*; flesh-eater, meat-e., carnivore; man-eater, cannibal, anthropophage, anthropophaginian, anthropophagist; vegetarian, wheat-eater, rice-e., herbivore; hearty eater, hungry e.; wolf, cormorant, vulture, locust 168 n. *destroyer*; teeth, jaws, mandibles 256 n. *tooth*; mouth, pecker, gullet, stomach, belly, paunch 194 n. *maw*.

provisions, stores, commissariat; provender, contents of the larder, foodstuff, tinned *or* canned food, groceries; provisioning, keep, board, entertainment, sustenance 633 n. *provision*; commons, sizing, provend, ration, helping. 783 n. *portion*; buttery, buttery-hatch, pantry, larder, still-room 632 n. *storage*; hot-box, meat-safe; ice-box, frigidaire, fridge 384 n. *refrigerator*.

provender, animal food, fodder, feed, pasture, pasturage, forage; corn, oats, grain, barley, hay, grass, mast, seed; foodstuffs, dry feed, winter f., cow f., chicken f.; salt-lick.

food, meat, bread, staff of life; aliment, nutriment, liquid n.; alimentation, nutrition; nurture, sustenance, nourishment, food and drink, pabulum, pap; food for the body, food for the mind, food for the spirit; food for the gods, nectar and ambrosia, amrita; one's daily bread, one's bread-and-butter 622 n. *vocation*; bread and dripping, bread and cheese, bread and onions; foodstuffs, comestibles, edibles, eatables, eats, victuals, viands, provender; belly-timber, grub, tuck, prog, scoff, tack, hard t., biscuit, salt pork, dogsbody, pemmican; bad food, carrion, offal; cheer, good c., good food, good table, regular meals, fleshpots, fat of the land; creature comforts, cakes and ale, cates; dainties, titbits, luxuries 637 n. *superfluity*; flavouring, sauce 389 n. *condiment*.

food content, vitamins; calories, roughage; mineral salts; calcium, phosphorus, iron, water; protein; fat, oil; carbohydrates, starch, sugar; monosaccharid, simple sugar; glucose, galactose, fructose; disaccharid, double sugar; maltose, malt sugar; lactose, milk sugar.

mouthful, bite, nibble, morsel 33 n. *small quantity*; sop, sip, swallow; gobbet, slice, titbit, sandwich, snack, crust; chocolate, chow, candy, sweet, gobstopper, toffee, stickjaw, chewing gum (see *sweetmeat*); cud, quid, something to chew; tablet, pill 658 n. *drug*.

meal, refreshment, fare; light meal, snack, sandwich, club-s., grinder, hamburger, hot dog; heavy meal, square m., full m., substantial m.; sit-down meal, repast, collation, regalement, regale, refection, spread, feed, blow, blow-out, bust, bean-feast, beano (see *feasting*); picnic, fête champêtre, barbecue, cookout, clambake, wiener roast; junket 837 n. *festivity*; chance meal, pot-luck; morning tea, chota hazri; breakfast, elevenses, luncheon, lunch, tiffin; tea, five o'clock, high tea; dinner, supper, fork s., buffet s.; ordinary, table d'hôte; ordered meal, à la carte, order; menu, carte, bill of fare, diet-sheet 87 n. *list*; dietary (see *dieting*); cover, table, place; help, helping 783 n. *portion*; serving, serving up, dishing up; self-service.

dish, cover, course; hors d'œuvres, eggs, omelette, salad, Russian s., vegetable s., mayonnaise 389 n. *sauce*; main dish, side-d., dessert, savoury; speciality, specialité de la maison, pièce de résistance, plat du jour; eggs and bacon, liver and b., fish and chips, sausages and mash, bubble and squeak, waffles and creamed chicken, tripe and onions; mixed grill; curry and rice, pilau, pilaff; hotchpotch, haggis, jugged hare, hash, stew, Irish s.; chowder, chop suey, sweet and sour pork; spaghetti, macaroni, risotto, mince, ragout, fricassee salmi, casserole, goulash; made-up dish, réchaufée.

soup, thin s., thick s., clear s.; broth, brew, potage, consommé; stock, bouillon, bisque, purée; mulligatawny, minestrone, borsch, bouillabaisse, gumbo, skilly.

fish food, fish 365 n. *table fish*; freshwater f., saltwater f.; fish cakes, fish pie; fresh fish, smoked f.; fried fish, boiled f., soused f.; kipper, bloater, herring, buckling, sardine, brisling; gurnet; haddock, mackerel, plaice, whitebait, turbot, mullet, carp, salmon, rock s., trout; hilsa, beckti, pomfret, mahseer; shellfish, oyster, bivalve; lobster, langouste, crab, shrimp, prawn, scampi, chingri; scallop; mussel, cockle, whelk, winkle; smoked salmon, caviar, fish roe, cod's r., shad roe, soft r., hard r.

meat, flesh; roast, rôti, roast beef of Old England; red meat, beef, mutton, pork, venison; white meat, game 365 n. *poultry*; kebab; minced meat, sausage m., force-m., meat extract, meatball; cut, joint, leg, half l., fillet end, shank e.; baron of beef, sirloin; saddle, undercut, shoulder, neck, collar, chuck, skirt, knuckle; aitch-bone, scrag end, breast, brisket; shin, loin, flank, ribs, rolled r., topside, silver s.; chop, loin c., chump c., mutton c., lamb c., pork c.; steak, fillet s., rump s., porterhouse s., ham s., hamburger; pork, suckling pig, sucking p., pork pie, ham, bacon, streaky b., boiled b.; gammon; fried bacon, rasher; tongue, ox-tongue, lamb's t.; knuckle, oxtail, cow-heel, calf's head; pig's trotters, pig's knuckles, chitterlings, haslet, pig's fry; offal, tripe, giblets, kidney, liver, heart, brain, sweetbread; sausage, banger, pork sausage, liver s., breakfast s., salami; hot dog, wiener, frankfurter, cocktail sausage; grease,

lard, bard, dripping; bacon fat, bacon rind.

pudding, hasty p., batter p., Yorkshire p., pease p., Christmas p., plum p., suet p.; duff, plum d., spotted dog, roly-poly, dumpling; sweet, rice pudding, semolina p., tapioca p., sago p., bread-and-butter p.; sweet, trifle, jelly, blancmange, custard; ice, vanilla ice, sundae; fritters, fruit salad, compote; soufflé, mousse, crumble.

sweetmeat, sweets, sugar plum, candy, chocolate, liqueur c., caramel; marzipan, Turkish delight, marshmallows, liquorice; toffee, butterscotch, rock, lollipop, lolly, all-day sucker 392 n. *sweet*; preserves, compote, jam, jelly, marmalade, cranberry sauce; crystallized fruit, ginger, stone g., chow-chow; sandesh, rashagula, halwa, barfi, jelapi.

fruit, soft f.; stone-fruit, drupe; orange, Jaffa o., navel o., tangerine, mandarin; apple, pippin, medlar; pear, avocado p., alligator p.; peach, apricot; banana, plantain; pineapple, pomegranate; lichi, mangosteen, mango, passion fruit, grenadilla, guava, pomelo; grape, muscat, raisin; plum, prune, damson, maraschino cherry; cherry, wild-c., gean; currant, red c., white c., black c.; olive, date, fig; berry, gooseberry, cape-g, tipari; bilberry, dewberry, elderberry, blackberry, strawberry, raspberry, redberry, loganberry, blueberry, whortleberry, cranberry, huckleberry; jackfruit, breadfruit; pawpaw, papaya; melon, water-m., cantaloupe, honeydew melon, musk-m., Persian m., casaba m., Spanish m.; nut, coconut, almond, chestnut, walnut; filbert, hazel nut, Brazil n., pea-nut, monkey-nut, ground-nut, cashew n., Barcelona n., pistachio n.

tuber, root, rhizome; ginger; artichoke, Jerusalem a.; underground fungus, truffle; potato, spud, sweet potato, yam, turnip, swede, nalkal, parsnip, beetroot; carrot; fried potatoes, french-fried p., chips, crisps, mashed p., creamed p., baked p.

vegetable 366 n. *plant*; greens, vegetables, garden-stuff; cabbage, red c., pickled c., sauerkraut, slaw, coleslaw, cauliflower, kale, seakale, curly kale, cole, colewort, broccoli, sprouts, Brussels s.; beans, haricot b., string b., runner b., scarlet runner; broad beans, lima b., waxed b., soya b.; lettuce, cabbage l., cos l.; okra,

gumbo, rhubarb, celery, horse radish, spinach, sag, bamboo shoots; egg-plant, aubergine, brinjal; asparagus, sparrow-grass; artichoke, Jerusalem a.; chicory, endive, leek, chive, garlic; onion, spring o., Spanish o., shallot, scallion; squash, summer s., acorn s., zucchini, ladies' fingers; marrow, courgette; cucumber, pumpkin, gourd; tomato, love-apple; pepper, red p., green p., chilli, capsicum, paprika, pimento; pea, green p., petits pois, split peas; pulse, lentil, gram; edible fungus, boletus edilis, bolet, mushroom, truffle.

potherb, herb, culinary h., sweet h., marjoram, rosemary, mint, thyme, bay, dill, mace, sage, sorrel, fennel; laxative herb, senna; parsley, cress, water-c.; clove, caper, chicory, borage, hops.

cereal, gruel, skilly, brewis, brose; porridge, stirabout, oatmeal; cornflakes, cream of wheat; bread, wheat b., rye b., black b., pumpernickel; loaf, cottage l., currant l., teacake; roll, croissant, rusk; crust; toast, buttered t.; roti, chapatti, luchi; batter-cake, pancake; flapjack, waffle, succotash; crumpet, muffin; corn, maize, grain, wheat, rye, oats, barley, millet; meal, flour, atta; barley-meal, pease-m.

pastry, bakemeat, patty, patsy, singara, turnover, crumble; tart, flan, puff, pie, pie-crust; cake, seed c.; birthday cake, wedding c., layer c.; delicatessen, confectionary; patisserie, gateau; shortbread, gingerbread; biscuit, zwieback, snap, cracker, wafer; barley-cake, bannock; oat-cake, scone; crumpet, muffin, English m.; bun, Bath b.; doughnut, jelly-d., cruller.

milk product, cream, curds, junket, yogurt; whey, cheese, goat's c., cream c., cottage c., Dutch c., Edam, Cheddar, Cheshire, Camembert, Roquefort, Gruyère, Brie, Parmesan; ripe cheese, Gorgonzola, Stilton; toasted cheese, Welsh rabbit.

drinking, imbibing, imbibition, fluid intake; potation; sipping, tasting, wine-tasting 463 n. *discrimination*; gulping, swilling, soaking 299 n. *reception*; one's cups, bibbing, wine-b.; drinking to excess 949 n. *drunkenness*; giving to drink, watering, drenching; libation 981 n. *oblation*; drinking time, bever; drinker, bibber, swiller, sipper, quaffer.

potion, something to drink, thirst-quencher; drink, draught, dram, drench; gulp, sop, sup; noggin, stoup, bottle, bowl, glass 194 n. *vessel*; glassful, bumper; swig, nip, tot, peg, double p., wallop, snorter, snifter chaser, long drink, short d.; quick one, short o., short; snort; backhander; nightcap, stirrup-cup, one for the road; health, toast; beverage, posset; mixed drink, concoction, cocktail 43 n. *mixture*; decoction, infusion (see *liquor*).

soft drink, teetotal d., non-alcoholic beverage, thirst-quencher, water, drinking w., filtered w., eau potable, spring water, fountain; soda water, fizzy-w., soda, soda-fountain, siphon; table-water, mineral w., mineral, barley water; milk, milkshake, frappé, float; ginger beer, ginger pop, ginger ale, kola, coca cola, coke; fizz, pop, lemonade, orangeade; cordial, fruit juice, lime j., orange j., lemon j., grapefruit j., tomato j.; cocoanut milk, dab-juice; tea, cha, Pekoe, Bohea, Indian tea, China t., green t., Russian t., maté; coffee, Turkish c.,white c., cappuccino; chocolate, cocoa; shrub, sherbet, syrup. See *milk*.

liquor, liquid 335 n. *fluid*; nectar, soma; booze, stimulant; brew, fermented liquor, intoxicating l. (see *wine*); alcohol, wood-a., alc; malt-liquor, hops, beer, small b., swipes; draught beer; bottled b.; ale, strong a., nog; stout, lager, bitter, porter, home-brew; cider, perry, mead, Athole brose; wheat-wine, rice-beer, saki, pachwai, marua, mhowa; pagla pani, arrack, raki, toddy; distilled liquor, spiritous l., spirits, ardent s., raw s., firewater, hooch; brandy, cognac, eau-de-vie; gin, sloe g., schnapps, mother's ruin, blue r.; whisky, usquebaugh, Scotch whisky, scotch; rye, bourbon; whiskey, Irish w., potheen; rum, grog, hot g., punch, rum p., milk p., eggnog; cordial, spiced wine, negus, posset, hippocras; mulled wine, caudle; flavoured wine, cup, claret-c.; mixed drink, shandy, stingo, highball, brandy and soda, whisky and s.; julep, cocktail; áperitif; liqueur.

wine, the grape, juice of the g., blood of the g.; red wine, tawny w., white w., vin rosé; spumante, sparkling wine, still w., sweet w., dry w., medium w., heavy w., light w., vintage w.; vin ordinaire, vin du pays; sherry, sack, port, madeira; claret, lal shrub; champagne, fizz, bubbly; hock, Rhenish, Burgundy, sparkling B., Bor-

deau, Tokay; chianti, rezina; Falernian, Chian.

milk, top of the m., cream; cow's milk, beestings; goat's milk, camel's m., mare's m.; koumiss; mother's milk, breast m.; dried m., skimmed m., condensed m., predigested m., pasteurized m.; curdled milk, curds, junket. See *milk product.*

Adj. *feeding,* eating, grazing etc. vb.; flesh-eating, meat-e.; carnivorous, creophagous, cannibalistic; omophagic, omophagous; herbivorous, graminivorous, frugivorous, phytovorous; wheat-eating, rice-e., vegetarian; omnivorous 464 adj. *indiscriminating;* greedy, wolfish 947 adj. *gluttonous;* water-drinking, teetotal, tee-totalling, tea-drinking 942 adj. *temperate;* liquorish, swilling, bibulous, tippling, drinking 949 adj. *drunken;* well-fed, well-nourished; nursed, breast-fed; full up, crammed 863 adj. *sated.*

edible, eatable; ritually pure, kosher; esculent, cibarious, comestible; manducable, digestible, predigested; potable, drinkable; milky, lactic; worth eating, palatable, succulent, palate-tickling, dainty, delicious 386 adj. *tasty,* 390 adj. *savoury;* cereal, wheaten; fermented, spirituous, alcoholic, hard 949 adj. *intoxicating;* non-alcoholic, soft.

nourishing, feeding, sustaining; nutricious, nutritive, nutritional; alimentary, cibarious; vitaminous, dietetic; fattening, rich, calorific; wholesome 652 adj. *salubrious;* body-building, bone-b.

culinary, dressed, oven-ready, made-up; underdone, red, rare, raw; done, well-d.; over-cooked, burnt; roasted etc. vb. (see *cook*); gastronomic, epicurean.

mensal, prandial, commensal; messing, dining, lunching; before-dinner, pre-prandial; after-dinner, post-prandial; self-service.

Vb. *eat,* feed, fare, board, mess, keep hall; partake, discuss 386 vb. *taste;* take a meal, have a feed, break one's fast, break bread; breakfast, lunch, have tea, dine, sup; dine out, regale, feast, banquet, carouse 837 vb. *revel;* eat well, feed full, have a good appetite, do justice to, ply a good knife and fork, be a good trencherman, ask for more; water at the mouth, drool, raven 859 vb. *be hungry;* fall to, set to, tuck in, lay in, stuff oneself, fill one's stomach 863 vb. *sate;* guzzle, gormandize 947 vb.

gluttonize; go through a meal, take every course, eat up, make a clean plate; lick the platter, lick the plate 165 vb. *consume;* swallow, gulp down, snap up, devour, dispatch, bolt, wolf, make short work of; play the parasite, feed on, live on, fatten on, batten on, prey on; nibble, peck, lick, play with one's food, have a poor appetite; nibble at, peck at, sniff at; ingest, digest 299 vb. *absorb.*

chew, masticate, manducate, champ, munch, crunch, scrunch; mumble, mouth, worry, gnaw; press with one's teeth, bite; grind 332 vb. *pulverize;* tear, rend, chew up 46 vb. *cut.*

graze, browse, pasture, crop, feed; ruminate, chew the cud.

drink, imbibe, ingest, suck, 299 vb. *absorb;* quaff, drink up, drink one's fill, slake one's thirst, lap, sip, sup; wet one's lips, wet one's whistle; draw the cork, crack a bottle; lap up, soak, sponge up, wash down; swill, swig, tipple, tope 949 vb. *get drunk;* toss off one's glass, drain one's g., empty the g., empty the bottle; raise one's glass, pledge 876 vb. *toast;* take a backhander, have another, wet the other eye, take one for the road; refill one's glass 633 vb. *replenish;* give to drink, wine, water, drench; prepare a drink, medicine, posset, caudle; lay in drink, lay down a cellar 633 vb. *provide.*

feed, nourish, vitaminize; nurture, sustain, board; victual, cater, purvey 633 vb. *provide;* nurse, breast-feed, give suck; pasture, graze, drive to pasture, put out to grass; fatten, fatten up 197 vb. *enlarge;* give to eat, fill one's mouth; dine, wine, feast, banquet, have to dinner 882 vb. *be hospitable.*

cook, prepare a meal, do to a turn; put in the oven, bake, scallop; roast, spit; broil, grill, griddle, devil, curry; sauté, fry; fry sunny side up, double-fry (eggs); scramble, poach; boil, parboil; coddle, seethe, simmer, steam; casserole, stew; baste, lard, bard; whip, whisk, stir; draw, gut, bone, fillet; stuff, dress, garnish; sauce, flavour, spice.

See: 33, 43, 46, 87, 165, 168, 192, 194, 197, 206, 256, 299, 323, 332, 335, 365, 366, 383, 384, 386, 389, 390, 392, 463, 464, 496, 589, 610, 622, 632, 633, 635, 637, 652, 658, 783, 837, 859, 863, 876, 882, 942, 944, 946, 947, 949, 981.

302 Excretion

N. *excretion*, discharge, secretion, extrusion 300 n. *ejection*; effusion, extravasation, ecchymosis; emanation 298 n. *egress*; exhalation, breathing out 352 n. *respiration*; exudation, sudation, perspiration, sweating, induced sweat, diaphoresis 298 n. *outflow*; cold, catarrh, hay fever, pollinosis; salivation, expectoration, spitting; coughing, cough; urination, micturition, passing.

hæmorrhage, bleeding, extravasation of blood, hæmophilia 335 n. *blood*; monthly discharge, menses, catamenia, flowers, leucorrhœa.

cacation, defecation, evacuation, elimination, clearance 300 n. *voidance*; movement, motion; regular motion, one's daily functions; frequency, diarrhœa, dysentery; copremesis.

excrement, fæces, stool, excreta, ordure; hardened fæces, coprolith; dung, horse-dung, cow-pat; droppings, guano; piss, urine, water; spittle, spit, sputum, sputa; saliva, slaver, slabber, slobber, froth, foam; rheum, phlegm; slough, cast, exuviæ, exuvial; feculence, egesta, ejecta 649 n. *dirt*.

Adj. *excretory*, secretory; purgative, eliminant; ejective, diuretic; diaphoretic, sudorific; perspiratory, sudoriparous; fæcal, feculent; rheumy, watery; cast-off, exuvial.

Vb. *excrete*, secrete; pass, move; defecate, ease oneself, stool, go to s.; urinate, piddle, wet; make water, spend a penny; piss, stale; sweat, perspire, steam 379 vb. *be hot*; salivate, slobber 298 vb. *exude*; water at the mouth 859 vb. *be hungry*; foam at the mouth 891 vb. *be angry*; cast, slough, shed one's skin 229 vb. *doff*.

See: 229, 298, 300, 335, 352, 379, 649, 859, 891.

303 Insertion: forcible ingress

N. *insertion*, intercalation, embolism, interpolation, parenthesis 231 n. *interjection*; adding 38 n. *addition*; introduction, insinuation 297 n. *ingress*; importation 299 n. *reception*; infixion, impaction, impactment; planting, transplantation 370 n. *agriculture*; inoculation, injection, shot 263 n. *perforation*; infusion, enema, cly-

ster; thing inserted, insert, inset; stuffing 227 n. *lining*.

immersion, submersion, submergence 311 n. *depression*; dip, bath 313 n. *plunge*; baptism 988 n. *Christian rite*; burial, burial at sea 364 n. *interment*.

Adj. *inserted* etc. vb.; added 38 adj. *additional*; thematic, intermediate 231 adj. *interjacent*; coffined 364 adj. *buried*.

Vb. *insert*, intromit, introduce; import 299 vb. *admit*; put into, thrust i., intrude; poke into, stick i.; empierce 264 vb. *pierce*; ram into, jam i., stuff i., pack i., tuck i., press i., pop i., whip i. 193 vb. *load*; pocket, impocket, purse 782 vb. *receive*; knock into, hammer i., drive i. 279 vb. *impel*; put in, inlay, inset 227 vb. *line*; mount, frame 232 vb. *circumscribe*; subjoin 38 vb. *add*; interject 231 vb. *put between*; drop, drop in, put in the slot 311 vb. *let fall*; putt, hole out; pot, hole; put in the ground, lay to rest, bury 364 vb. *inter*; sheathe, incapsulate, embox, encase 226 vb. *cover*.

infuse, drop in, instil, pour in 43 vb. *mix*; imbue, imbrue, impregnate; transfuse, decant 272 vb. *transpose*; squirt in, inject, poke 263 vb. *pierce*.

implant, plant, transplant, plant out 187 vb. *place*; graft, ingraft, imp, bud; inoculate; embed, bury; infix, wedge in, impact, dovetail 45 vb. *join*.

immerse, immerge, merge, bathe, steep, souse, marinate, soak 341 vb. *drench*; baptize 988 vb. *perform ritual*; duck, dip 313 vb. *plunge*; submerge, flood; immerse oneself, bury oneself in, be deep in, plunge in medias res 455 vb. *be attentive*.

See: 38, 43, 45, 187, 193, 226, 227, 231, 232, 263, 272, 279, 297, 299, 311, 313, 341, 364, 370, 455, 782, 988.

304 Extraction: forcible egress

N. *extraction*, withdrawal, outing, removal 188 n. *displacement*; elimination, eradication 300 n. *ejection*; extermination, extirpation 165 n. *destruction*; extrication, unravelment, disengagement, liberation 668 n. *deliverance*; evulsion, avulsion, tearing out, ripping o.; cutting out, exsection, embryectomy; expression, squeezing out; exsuction, sucking out; drawing out, pull, tug, wrench 288 n.

traction; digging out, excavation; extractive industry, mining, quarrying; fishery; distillation 338 n. *vaporization*; drawing off, tapping, milking; thing extracted, essence, extract.

extractor, gouger; miner, quarrier; wrench, forceps, pincers, pliers, tweezers 778 n. *nippers*; corkscrew, screwdriver 263 n. *opener*; lever 218 n. *pivot*; scoop, spoon 274 n. *shovel*; pick, pickaxe; rake; toothpick 648 n. *cleaner*; excavator, dredge, dredger; syringe, siphon; Persian wheel, shadoof, swipe 341 n. *irrigator*.

Adj. *extracted* etc. vb.; extractive.

Vb. *extract*, pull 288 vb. *draw*; draw out, elicit, educe; unfold 316 vb. *evolve*; pull out, take o., get o., pluck; withdraw, exsect, cut out, rip o., tear o., whip o.; excavate, mine, quarry, dig out; dredge, dredge up; expel, lever out, winkle o., smoke o. 300 vb. *eject*; extort, wring; express, press out, squeeze o., gouge o.; force out, wring o., wrench o., drag o.; draw off, milk, tap; suck, void; wring from, squeeze f., drag f.; pull up, weed up, dig up, grub up, rake up; remove, eliminate, root up, uproot, pluck up by the roots, eradicate, deracinate, unroot, averruncate 165 vb. *destroy*; prune, thin out, deforest 105 vb. *render few*; distil 338 vb. *vaporize*; extricate, unravel, free 746 vb. *liberate*; unwrap, unpack, unload 300 vb. *void*; eviscerate, gut, shuck, shell 229 vb. *uncover*; pick out 605 vb. *select*.

See: 105, 165, 188, 218, 229, 263, 274, 288, 300, 316, 338, 341, 605, 648, 668, 746, 778.

305 Passage: motion through

N. *passage*, transmission 272 n. *transference*; transduction 272 n. *transport*; passing, passing through, traversing; transition, abrupt t., transilience 306 n. *overstepping*; transcursion, transit, traverse, crossing, journey, voyage, perambulation, patrol, 267 n. *land travel*; passage into, penetration, interpenetration, permeation, infiltration; transudation, osmosis, osmose, endosmose 297 n. *ingress*; exosmose 298 n. *egress*; intercurrence, intervention 231 n. *interjacence*; pass, defile, ghat 624 n. *access*; stepping-stone, flyover, underpass 624 n. *bridge*; track, route, orbit 624 n. *path*; intersection,

cross-road 222 n. *crossing*; channel 351 n. *conduit*.

passing along, thoroughfare; traffic, pedestrian t., wheeled t., vehicular t.; road traffic, ocean t., air-t.; traffic movement, flow of traffic, circulation; traffic pattern, walking, crossing, cycling, driving, carrying; loading, unloading; waiting, parking. kerb-side p., off-street p.; traffic load, traffic density; traffic conflict, traffic jam, procession, queue.

traffic control, traffic engineering; traffic rules, highway code, rule of the road 496 n. *maxim*; traffic lane, one-way street, fly-over, underpass; clearway 624 n. *road*; diversion, alternative route 282 n. *deviation*; street furniture, white line, double white l., traffic lights, roundabout; clover leaf, pedestrian crossing, zebra c., Belisha beacon, refuge, island; car-park, parking place, parking area *or* zone; parking meter, lay-by; traffic police, traffic cop, road patrol; traffic engineer; traffic warden, meter maid, Lapp Lizzie.

Adj. *passing* etc. vb.; transitional, transilient; intercurrent, osmotic, endosmotic.

Vb. *pass*, pass by, leave on one side, skirt, coast 200 vb. *be near*; flash by 277 vb. *move fast*, 114 vb. *be transient*; pass along, join the traffic, keep in the t., circulate, weave; pass through, transit, traverse; shoot through, shoot a bridge, shoot the rapids 269 vb. *navigate*; pass out, come out the other side 298 vb. *emerge*; go through, soak t., percolate, permeate 189 vb. *pervade*; pass and repass, patrol, work over, beat, scour, go over the ground; pass into, penetrate, infiltrate 297 vb. *enter*; bore, perforate 263 vb. *pierce*; thread, thrid, thread through 45 vb. *connect*; enfilade 203 vb. *look along*; open a way, force a passage 297 vb. *irrupt*; worm one's way, elbow through, muscle t., clear the ground 285 vb. *progress*; cross, go across, cross over, make a crossing, reach the other side 295 vb. *arrive*; wade across, ford; get through, get past, negotiate; pass in front, cut across, cross one's bows 702 vb. *obstruct*; step over, straddle, bestride 205 vb. *be broad*; bridge, bridge over 226 vb. *cover*; carry over, carry across, traject, transmit 272 vb. *transpose*; pass to, hand, reach, pass from hand to hand, hand over

780 vb. *convey*; let pass, skip 458 vb. *disregard*; pass a test, graduate 727 vb. *succeed*; barely pass, scrape through, struggle t.; repass 286 vb. *turn back*; pass beyond 306 vb. *overstep*.

Adv. *en passant*, by the way.

See: 45, 114, 189, 200, 203, 205, 222, 226, 231, 263, 267, 269, 272, 277, 282, 285, 286, 295, 297, 298, 297, 306, 351, 458, 496, 624, 702, 727, 780.

306 Overstepping: motion beyond

N. *overstepping*, transcursion, transilience, leap-frog 305 n. *passage*; transcendence 34 n. *superiority*; excursion, extravagation 282 n. *deviation*; transgression, trespass 936 n. *guilt*; usurpation, encroachment 916 n. *arrogation*; infringement, infraction, intrusion 916 n. *undueness*; expansionism, greediness 859 n. *desire*; over-extension, ribbon development 197 n. *expansion*; overfulfilment; excessiveness 637 n. *redundance*; overrating 482 n. *overestimation*; overdoing it 546 n. *exaggeration*; over-indulgence 943 n. *intemperance*.

Adj. *surpassing* etc. vb.; one up on 34 adj. *superior*; over-extended, overlong, overhigh; too strong, overpowered; excessive 32 adj. *exorbitant*; out of bounds, out of reach.

Vb. *overstep*, overpass, overgo, leave behind; go beyond, go too far; exceed, exceed the limit; overrun, override, overshoot, overshoot the mark, aim too high; overlap 226 vb. *overlie*; surmount, jump over, leap o., skip o. leap-frog 312 vb. *leap*; step over, cross 305 vb. *pass*; cross the Rubicon, pass the point of no return; overfill, brim over, spill o. 54 vb. *fill*; overfulfil 637 vb. *superabound*; overdo 546 vb. *exaggerate*; strain, stretch, stretch a point; overbid, overcall one's hand, have one's bluff called, overestimate 482 vb. *overrate*; over-indulge 943 vb. *be intemperate*; overstay, oversleep 136 vb. *be late*.

encroach, break bounds, make inroads 712 vb. *attack*; infringe, transgress, trespass 954 vb. *be illegal*; poach 788 vb. *steal*; squat, usurp 786 vb. *appropriate*; barge in, horn in 297 vb. *intrude*; overlap, impinge, trench upon, intrench on; eat away, erode 655 vb. *impair*; infest, over-

run 297 vb. *irrupt*; overflow, flood 341 vb. *drench*.

outdo, exceed, surpass, outclass; transcend, rise above, mount a., soar a., outsoar, outrange, outrival 34 vb. *be superior*; go one better, overcall, overbid, outbid; outwit, overreach 542 vb. *befool*; outmanœuvre, outflank, gain the weather-gauge; steal a march on; make the running 277 vb. *move fast*; outgo, outpace, outwalk, outmarch, outrun, outride, outjump, outsail, outdistance, distance; overhaul, gain upon, overtake, come in front, shoot ahead; lap, leave standing 277 vb. *outstrip*; leave behind, race, beat, beat hollow 727 vb. *defeat*.

See: 32, 34, 54, 136, 197, 226, 277, 282, 297, 305, 312, 341, 482, 542, 546, 637, 655, 712, 727, 786, 788, 859, 916, 936, 943, 954.

307 Shortcoming

N. *shortcoming*, falling short, inadequacy etc. vb. 636 n. *insufficiency*; a minus, deficit, short measure, shortage, shortfall, loss 42 n. *decrement*; leeway, drift 282 n. *deviation*; unfinished state 55 n. *incompleteness*; non-fulfilment, delinquency, default, defalcation 726 n. *non-completion*; labour in vain 641 n. *lost labour*; no go 728 n. *failure*; fault, defect 647 n. *imperfection*, 845 n. *blemish*; something missing want, lack, need 627 n. *requirement*.

Adj. *deficient*, short, short of, minus, wanting, lacking, missing; catalectic; underpowered, substandard; half-done, perfunctory 55 adj. *incomplete*; out of one's depth, not up to scratch, inadequate 636 adj. *insufficient*; failing, running short 636 adj. *scarce*; unattained, unreached, tantalizing.

Vb. *fall short*, come s., run s. 636 vb. *not suffice*; not stretch, not reach to; lack, want, be without 627 vb. *require*; miss, miss the mark; lag 136 vb. *be late*; stop short, fall by the way, not stay the course; break down, stick in the mud, get bogged down; fall behind, lose ground, slip back; slump, collapse 286 vb. *regress*; fall through, fall to the ground, come to nothing, end in smoke, fizzle out, fail 728 vb. *miscarry*; miss stays, lose s.; labour in vain 641 n. *waste effort*; tantalize, not

come up to expectations 509 vb. *disappoint.*

Adv. *behindhand*, in arrears; not enough; below the mark, far from it; to no purpose, in vain.

See: 42, 55, 136, 282, 286, 509, 627, 636, 641, 647, 726, 728, 845.

308 Ascent: motion upwards

N. *ascent*, ascension, upward motion, gaining height; defiance of gravity, levitation; taking off, leaving ground, take-off 296 n. *departure*; flying up, soaring, spiralling, mushrooming; zooming, zoom 271 n. *aeronautics*; culmination 213 n. *summit*; floating up, surfacing, breaking surface; going up, rising, uprising; rise, uprise, upgrowth; uprush, upsurge 36 n. *increase*; updraught, rising air, rising current; sunrise, sun-up, dawn 128 n. *morning*; moonrise, star-rise; mounting, climbing, skylarking; hill-climbing, mountaineering, Alpinism; ladder-climbing, escalade 712 n. *attack*; jump, vault, pole-v., pole-jump 312 n. *leap*; bounce 280 n., *recoil*; rising ground, hill 209 n. *high land*; gradient, slope, ramp 220 n. *acclivity*; rising pitch 410 n. *musical note*; means of ascent, stairs, steps, flight of stairs, staircase, stairway, landing; ladder, step-l., accommodation l., Jacob's l., companion way; rope-ladder, ratlin; stair, step, tread, rung; lift, ski-l., elevator, escalator 310 n. *lifter*; fire escape 667 n. *means of escape.*
climber, mountaineer, alpinist, cragsman, Alpine Club; stegophilist; foretopman, steeple-jack; excelsior-figure; rocket, sky-r.; soarer, lark, skylark, laverock; gusher, spouter, geyser, fountain 350 n. *stream.*

Adj. *ascending*, rising etc. vb., climbing, scansorial, scandent; rearing, rampant; buoyant, floating 323 adj. *light*; supernatant, superfluitant; air-borne, gaining height; excelsior; anabatic, in the ascendant; uphill, steep 215 n. *vertical*; ladder-like, scalar, scalariform; scalable, climbable.

Vb. *ascend*, rise, uprise, leave the ground; defy gravity, levitate; take off, become air-borne, fly up 271 vb. *fly*; gain height, mount, soar, spiral, zoom, climb; reach the top, reach the zenith, culminate; float up, bob up, surface, break water; jump

up, spring; dance, toss 312 vb. *leap*; bounce 280 vb. *recoil*; push up, grow up, upheave; tower, aspire, spire 209 vb. *be high*; gush, spirt, spout, jet, play 298 vb. *flow out*; get up, start up, stand up, rear, rear up, ramp 215 vb. *be vertical*; rise to one's feet, vacate one's seat 920 vb. *show respect*; trend upwards, wind u., slope u., steepen 220 vb. *be oblique*; take an upturn, improve 654 vb. *get better*; go up, blow up, explode.
climb, walk up, struggle up; mount, make or work one's way up; go climbing, mountaineer; skylark; clamber, scramble, swarm up, shin up, monkey up, climb hand over fist; surmount, top, breast, scale, scale the heights 209 vb. *be high*; go over the top, escalade 712 vb. *attack*; go upstairs, mount a ladder; mount (a horse), climb into the saddle.

Adv. *up*, uphill, upstairs; excelsior, ever higher; hand over fist.

See: 36, 128, 209, 213, 215, 220, 271, 280, 296, 298, 310, 312, 323, 350, 410, 654, 667, 712, 920.

309 Descent

N. *descent*, descension, declension; declination 282 n. *deviation*; falling, dropping, landing; downward trend, decline, drop, slump 37 n. *decrease*; come-down, demotion 872 n. *humiliation*; downfall, débâcle, collapse 165 n. *ruin*; trip, stumble; titubation, lurch, capsize 221 n. *overturning*; tumble, cropper, crash, fate of Icarus; downrush, swoop, stoop, pounce; dive, header, belly-flop 313 n. *plunge*; nose-dive, power-d. 271 n. *aeronautics*; sliding down, glissade; subsidence, landslide, avalanche; downdraught 352 n. *wind*; downpour, shower 350 n. *rain*; cascade, nappe 350 n. *waterfall*; downthrow (geology); declivity, hill, slope, tilt, dip 220 n. *acclivity*; precipice, sheer drop 215 n. *verticality*; submergence, sinkage 311 n. *depression*; boring, tunnelling, burrowing, mining, sapping, undermining 263 n. *tunnel*; speleology, pot-holing; descender, faller, tumbler; plunger 313 n. *diver*; burrower, miner, sapper 255 n. *excavator*; parachutist 271 n. *aeronaut*; paratrooper 722 n. *soldier*; speleologist, pot-holer.

Adj. *descending* etc. vb.; descendent, declining, declivitous 220 adj. *sloping*; labent, decurrent, decursive, swooping; deciduous; tumble-down, falling, titubant, tottering; tilting, nodding to its fall; sinking, foundering; burrowing, sapping; demoted, downcast, down at heart, drooping 311 adj. *depressed*; submersible, sinkable.

Vb. *descend* come down, go d., dip d.; decline, abate, ebb 37 vb. *decrease*; go downhill, slump 655 vb. *deteriorate*; reach a lower level, fall, drop, sink; soak in, seep down 297 vb. *infiltrate*; get lower and lower, reach the depths, touch depth, touch bottom 210 vb. *be low*; reach one's nadir 35 vb. *be inferior*; sink to the bottom gravitate, precipitate, settle, set; fall down, fall in, cave in, fall to the ground, collapse; sink in, subside, slip, give way; hang down, prolapse, droop, sag, swag 217 vb. *hang*; go under water, draw, have draught; submerge, fill the tanks, dive 313 vb. *plunge*; drown 313 vb. *founder*; go underground, sink into the earth; dig down, burrow, bore, tunnel, mine, sap, undermine 255 vb. *make concave*; drop from the sky, parachute; swoop, stoop, pounce; fly down, flutter d.; lose height, drop down, swing low; touch down, alight, light, perch 295 vb. *land*; lower oneself, get down, climb d., step d., get off, fall o., dismount; slide down, glissade, luge, toboggan; fall like rain, shower, pour, cascade, drip, drizzle, patter 350 vb. *rain*; take a lower place, come down a peg 872 vb. *be humble*; make an obeisance, bow down, dip, duck 311 vb. *stoop*; flop, plop.

tumble, fall; tumble down, fall d.; topple, nod to its fall; topple over, overbalance, capsize 221 vb. *be inverted*; miss one's footing, slip, slip up, trip, stumble; lose one's balance, titubate, stagger, totter, lurch, tilt 220 vb. *be oblique*; rise and fall, pitch, toss, roll; take a header, dive 313 vb. *plunge*; take a running jump, precipitate oneself 312 vb. *leap*; fall off, take a fall, be thrown, come a cropper, go for a Burton; fall on one's face, fall prostrate, bite the dust, measure one's length; plop, plump, plump down 311 vb. *sit down*; slump, sprawl; fall through the air, spiral, spiral down, nose-dive, crash, prang.

Adv. *down*, downwards, adown; downhill, downstairs, downstream; nose-down.

See: 35, 37, 165, 210, 215, 217, 220, 221, 255, 263, 271, 282, 295, 297, 311, 312, 313, 350, 352, 655, 722, 872.

310 Elevation

N. *elevation*, raising etc. vb.; erection, sublevation, upheaval; picking up, lift; uplift, leg-up 703 vb. *aid*; sublimation, exaltation; assumption, bodily a.; uprising, uptrend, upswing 308 n. *ascent*; defiance of gravity, levitation; an elevation, eminence 209 n. *high land*, 254 n. *prominence*; height above sea level 209 n. *height*.

lifter, erector, builder, steel-erector, spiderman; raiser, lightener, yeast 323 n. *leaven*; lever, jack 218 n. *pivot*; dredger; crane, derrick, hoist, windlass; winch, capstan, jeer-c.; purchase, rope and pulley, block and tackle, luff-tackle, jeers; dumb waiter, lift, ski-l., elevator; escalator, moving staircase 274 n. *conveyor*; hot air, gas, hydrogen, helium; spring, springboard, trampoline.

Adj. *elevated* etc. vb.; exalted, uplifted; erectile, attollent; erected, set up; upright, erect, upstanding, rampant 215 adj. *vertical*; mounted, on high; lofty, sublime 209 adj. *high*.

Vb. *elevate*, heighten 209 vb. *make higher*; puff up, blow up, swell, leaven 197 vb. *enlarge*; raise, erect, set up, put up, run up, rear up, build up, build; lift, lift up, raise up, heave up; uplift, upraise; jack up, prop 218 vb. *support*; prevent from falling, hold up, bear up, upbear; prevent from sinking, buoy, buoy up; raise aloft hold a., hold up, wave; hoist, haul up, brail, trice; furl 261 vb. *fold*; raise from the ground, pick up, take up; pull up, wind up; weigh, trip (anchor); fish up, drag up, dredge up, dredge 304 vb. *extract*; exalt, sublimate; chair, shoulder; put on a pedestal; put on top, mount 313 vb. *crown*; jump up, bounce up 285 vb. *promote*; give a lift, give a leg-up 703 vb. *aid*; throw in the air, throw up, cast up, toss up; sky, loft; send up, shoot up, lob 287 vb. *propel*; perk, perk up (one's head); prick up (one's ears); bristle, bristle up.

lift oneself, arise, rise 308 vb. *ascend*; stand up, get up, jump up, leap up, spring up,

spring to one's feet; pull oneself up; hold oneself up, hold one's head up, draw oneself up to one's full height, stand on tiptoe 215vb., *be vertical.*

Adv. *on*, on stilts, on tiptoe; on one's legs, on one's hind legs; on the shoulders of, on the back of.

See: 197, 209, 215, 218, 254, 261, 274, 285, 287, 304, 308, 313, 323, 703.

311 Depression

N. *depression*, lowering, hauling down etc. vb.; pushing down, detrusion 279 n. *impulse*; ducking, sousing 313 n. *plunge*; debasement 655 n. *deterioration*; demotion, reduction 872 n. *humiliation*; subversion 149 n. *revolution*; overthrow, prostration 216 n. *supination*; overturn, overset, upset 221 n. *overturning*; precipitation, defenestration 287 n. *propulsion*; keeping under, suppression; a depression, dent, dip, hollow 255 n. *cavity*; low pressure 340 n. *weather.*

obeisance, reverence, bow, salaam, kowtow, kissing hands 884 n. *courtesy*; curtsy, court c., bob, duck, nod 884 n. *courteous act*; kneeling, genuflexion 920 n. *respect.*

Adj. *depressed* etc. vb.; at a low ebb 210 adj. *low*; prostrate 216 adj. *supine*; sedentary, sitting, sit-down; depressive, detrusive; submersible.

Vb. *depress*, detrude, push down, thrust d. 279 vb. *impel*; shut down (a lid) 264 vb. *close*; hold down, keep d., hold under 165 vb. *suppress*; lower, let down, take d.; lower a flag, dip, half-mast, haul down, strike; deflate, de-fizz, puncture 198 vb. *make smaller*; let drop (see *let fall*); pitch, precipitate, defenestrate, fling down, send headlong, drop over the side; sink, scuttle, send to the bottom, drown 309 vb. *descend*; duck, souse, douse, dip 313 vb. *plunge*; weigh on, press on 322 vb. *weigh*; capsize, roll over, tip, tilt 221 vb. *invert*; crush, stave in, bash in, dent, hollow 255 vb. *make concave.*

let fall, drop, shed; let go 779 vb. *not retain*; let slip *or* slide through one's fingers; pour, pour out, decant 300 vb. *void*; spill, slop 341 vb. *moisten*; sprinkle, shower, scatter, dust; sow, broadcast 75 vb. *disperse*; lay down, put d., set d., throw down, fling d. (see *fell*); pitch *or* chuck

overboard, drop over the side; precipitate, send headlong, defenestrate 287 vb. *propel.*

fell, trip, topple, tumble, overthrow; prostrate, lay low, lay one on his back 216 vb. *flatten*; knock down, bowl over, floor, drop, down; throw down, cast d., fling d. (see *let fall*); pull down, tear d., dash d., raze, slight, level, raze to the ground, pull about one's ears, trample in the dust 165 vb. *demolish*; hew down, cut d., lumber 46 vb. *cut*; blow down 352 vb. *blow*; bring down, undermine; bring down, shoot d., wing 287 vb. *shoot.*

abase, debase, lower the standard; water, adulterate 655 vb. *deteriorate*; demote, reduce to the ranks, cashier 752 vb. *depose*; humble, deflate, puncture, debunk, bate one's pretensions, take down a peg, cut down to size, take the wind out of one's sails, take a rise out of 872 vb. *humiliate*; crush, squash 165 vb. *suppress*; snub 883 vb. *make unwelcome.*

sit down, sit, be seated, sit on the ground, squat, squat on one's hunkers; kneel, recline, couch, stretch oneself out 216 vb. *be horizontal*; roost, nest 683 vb. *repose*; take a seat, seat oneself, park one's hips; perch, alight 309 vb. *descend.*

stoop, bend, bend down, get d.; bend over, bend forward, bend backward; lean forward, lean over backwards; cringe, crouch, cower 721 vb. *knuckle under*; bow, scrape, arch one's back; duck, bob, curtsy, bob a c. 884 vb. *pay respects*; nod, incline one's head 488 vb. *assent*; bow down, do reverence, make obeisance, kiss hands, salaam, prostrate oneself, kowtow 920 vb. *show respect*; kneel, kneel to, genuflect.

See: 46, 75, 149, 165, 198, 210, 216, 221, 255, 264, 279, 287, 300, 309, 313, 322, 340, 341, 352, 488, 655, 683, 721, 752, 779, 872, 883, 884, 920.

312 Leap

N. *leap*, saltation, skipping, capering, leapfrogging; jump, hop, skip; spring, bound, vault; high jump, long j., running j.; hop, skip and a jump; caper, gambol, frolic; kick, high k.; prance, curvet, caracole, capriole, demivolt, gambade, buck, buckjump; springy step, light tread 265 n.

gait; dance step; dance, reel, jig, Highland fling, cakewalk 837n. *dancing*.

jumper, high-j., pole-vaulter, hurdler, steeplechaser; skipper, hopper, leapfrogger; caperer, prancer; dancer, waltzer, foxtrotter, jiver, hoofer, shuffler; tapdancer, soft-shoe d.; ballerina, corps de ballet; male dancer, dancing man; dancing girl, nautch girl 594n. *entertainer*; kangaroo, stag, goat, chamois, springbok, jumping-mouse; jerboa, grasshopper, cicada, frog, flea; bucking horse, bucker; jumping cracker, jumping bean; jumping jack, Jack-in-the-box 837n. *plaything*.

Adj. *leaping* etc.vb.; saltatory, saltatorial; skittish, frisky, fresh 819adj. *lively*; skipping, hopping; dancing, choric; bobbing, bucking, bouncing; tossing.

Vb. *leap*, jump, take a running j.; spring, bound, vault, pole-v., hurdle, jump over the sticks, steeplechase, take one's fences; skip, hop, leap-frog, bob, bounce, buck, bob up and down, dab; trip, foot it, tread a measure, stamp, hoof it 837vb. *dance*; caper, cut capers, gambol, frisk, gambado; prance, paw the ground, ramp, rear, backjump, plunge; cavort, curvet, caracole; start, startle, give a jump; jump up, leap up, spring up 308vb. *ascend*; jump over, clear, leap over the moon; flounce, flounder, jerk 318vb. *be agitated*; writhe 251vb. *wriggle*.

Adv. *by leaps and bounds*, on the light fantastic toe, trippingly; at a single bound.

See: 251, 265, 308, 318, 594, 819, 837.

313 Plunge

N. *plunge*, swoop, pounce, stoop 309n. *descent*; nose-dive, power dive 271n. *aeronautics*; dive, header, belly-flop; dip, ducking; immersion, submergence; crash-dive; drowning, sinking; gambler's plunge, gamble 618n. *gambling*.

diver, frogman, under-water swimmer; diving bird, merganser 365n. *waterfowl*; submariner; submarine, bathysphere, sinker, diving-bell; plunger, lead, plummet; fathometer 465n. *meter*.

Vb. *plunge*, dip, duck, bathe 341vb. *be wet*; fall in, jump in, plump, plop; dive, make a plunge, take a header; welter, wallow, pitch and toss; souse, douse, immerse, submerse, drown; submerge, flood the

tanks, crash-dive 309vb. *descend*; sink, scuttle, send to the bottom, send to Davy Jones's locker 311vb. *depress*; sound, fathom, plumb the depths, heave the lead 465vb. *measure*; plunge into 857vb. *be rash*.

founder, go down 309vb. *descend*; get out of one's depth; drown, settle down, go to the bottom, go down like a stone; sink, sink like lead, sink like a sack of potatoes.

See: 271, 309, 311, 341, 365, 465, 618, 857.

314 Circuition: curvilinear motion

N. *circuition*, circulation, circumambulation, circumnavigation, circling, wheeling, gyre, spiral 315n. *rotation*; turning, cornering, turn, U-turn 286n. *return*; orbit; ambit, compass, lap; circuit, tour, round trip, full circle; helix 251n. *coil*; unwinding 316n. *evolution*; circuitousness, circumbendibus, roundabout way, north-west passage.

circler, girdler, circumambulator; circumnavigator 270n. *mariner*; circuiter 957n. *judge*; circuitor 690n. *manager*; roundsman 794n. *tradesman*; patrol, patrolman 441n. *spectator*; moon, satellite 321n. *planet*.

Adj. *circuitous*, turning etc.vb.; circumforaneous, peripatetic 267adj. *travelling*; circumfluent, circumambient; circumflex 248adj. *curved*; circumnavigable; devious 626adj. *roundabout*, 282adj. *deviating*; orbital.

Vb. *circle*, circulate, go the round, make the round of; compass, circuit, make a c.; lap; tour, do the round trip; go round, skirt; circumambulate, circumnavigate, circumaviate; go round the world, put a girdle round the earth; turn, round, double a point, weather a p.; round a corner, corner, turn a c.; revolve, orbit; wheel, spiral, come full circle, box the compass, chase one's tail 315vb. *rotate*; turn round, bend r.; put about, wheel a., face a., turn on one's heel 286vb. *turn back*; draw a circle, describe a circle 232vb. *circumscribe*; curve, wind, twist, wind one's way 251vb. *meander*; make a detour 626vb. *circuit*.

See: 232, 248, 251, 267, 270, 282, 286, 315, 316, 321, 441, 626, 690, 794, 957.

315 Rotation: motion in a continued circle

N. *rotation*, orbital motion, revolving, orbiting; revolution, full circle; gyration, circling, spiralling; circulation, circumfluence; spinning motion, spin, circumrotation, circumgyration, circumvolution, turbination; rolling, volutation 285 n. *progression*; spiral, roll, turn, twirl, waltz, pirouette, reel 837 n. *dance*; whirlabout, whirl, whirr; dizzy round, rat race 678 n. *overactivity*; dizziness, vertigo; turning power, turning tendency, verticity; science of rotatory motion, gyrostatics, trochilics.

vortex, whirl; whirlwind, whirlblast, tornado, cyclone 352 n. *gale*; waterspout, whirlpool, swirl, surge, gurge 350 n. *eddy*; Maelstrom, Charybdis; smoke-ring 250 n. *loop*.

rotator, rotor, spinner; whirl, whirligig, teetotum, yo-yo, top, peg t., spinning t., humming t.; roundabout, merry-go-round; churn, whisk; potter's wheel, lathe, mandrel, circular saw; spinning wheel, charka, spinning jenny, whorl; flywheel, prayer-w., roulette-w., wheel of Fortune 250 n. *wheel*; gyroscope, gyrostat; turntable; gramophone record; windmill, fan, sail; propeller, prop, screw, air-s.; winder, capstan 310 n. *lifter*; swivel, hinge, spit, jack; spindle, axle, axis, shaft 218 n. *pivot*; reel, roller, rolling-pin 252 n. *cylinder*; rolling stone, planet 268 n. *wanderer*; Ixion.

Adj. *rotary*, trochilic; rotating, spinning etc. vb.; rotary, rotatory, circumrotatory; gyratory, gyroscopic, gyrostatic; gyral; circling, cyclic; vortical, vorticose, vorticular; cyclonic, turbinated; vertiginous, dizzy.

Vb. *rotate*, revolve, orbit, go into orbit, assume an o. 314 vb. *circle*; turn right round, box the compass, chase one's own tail; spin, spin like a top, spin like a teetotum, twirl, pirouette; circumvolve, gyre, gyrate, waltz, wheel; whirl, whirr, hum 404 vb. *resound*; swirl, eddy 350 vb. *flow*; bowl, trundle, troll, trill; set rolling, roll, roll along; spin with one's fingers, twirl; churn, whisk 43 vb. *mix*; turn, crank, wind, reel, spin, yarn; slew, slew round, swing round; roll up, furl 261 vb. *fold*; roll itself up, scroll; wallow, welter; mill around.

Adv. *round and round*, in a circle, in circles, clockwise, anticlockwise, counter-clockwise, sunwise, widdershins; head over heels.

See: 43, 218, 250, 252, 261, 268, 285, 310, 314, 350, 352, 404, 678, 837.

316 Evolution: motion in a reverse circle

N. *evolution*, unrolling, unfolding, unfurling; explication, dénouement 154 n. *eventuality*; counter-spin, eversion 221 n. *inversion*; development 157 n. *growth*; evolutionism, Darwinism.

Adj. *evolving*, unwinding etc. vb.; evolved etc. vb.; evolutionary, evolutionistic.

Vb. *evolve*, unfold, unfurl, unroll, unwind, uncoil, uncurl, untwist, untwine, explicate, unravel, disentangle 60 vb. *order*; evolute, develop, grow into 147 vb. *be turned to*; roll back 263 vb. *open*.

See: 60, 147, 154, 157, 221, 263.

317 Oscillation: reciprocating motion

N. *oscillation*, libration, nutation, lunar n.; harmonic motion, pendular m., swing of the pendulum; vibration, vibratiuncle, tremor; vibrancy, resonance 141 n. *periodicity*; pulsation, throbbing, drumming, pulse, beat, throb; flutter, palpitation 318 n. *agitation*; breathing 352 n. *respiration*; undulation, wave-motion, frequency, frequency band, wave-length 417 n. *radiation*; heat wave, sound w., radio w., sky-w., tidal w., tsunami 350 n. *wave*; seismic disturbance, earthquake, ground wave, tremor 176 n. *violence*; seismology, seismograph, vibroscope; oscillator, vibrator; pendulum, bob 217 n. *pendant*. **See** *fluctuation*.

fluctuation, wave motion (see *oscillation*); alternation, reciprocation 12 n. *correlation*; to and fro movement, coming and going, shuttle service; ups and downs, boom and bust, ebb and flow, flux and reflux, systole and diastole; night and day 14 n. *contrariety*; reeling, lurching, rolling, pitching; roll, pitch, lurch, stagger, reel; shake, wag, dance; springboard 328 n. *elasticity*; swing, see-saw; rocker, rocking chair, rocking-horse; shuttlecock, shuttle; mental fluctuation, wavering, vacillation 601 n. *irresolution*, 474 n. *dubiety*.

Adj. *oscillating* etc.vb.; oscillatory, undulatory; swaying, libratory; pulsatory, palpitating, vibratory, vibratile; earth-shaking, seismic; pendular, pendulous, dangling; reeling, staggery, groggy; rhythmic, rhythmical 141 adj. *periodical.*

Vb. *oscillate*, emit waves 417vb. *radiate*; undulate; vibrate, pulsate, pulse, beat, drum; tick, throb, palpitate; respire, exhale, inhale, pant, heave 352vb. *breathe*; nutate, librate; play, sway, nod; swing, dangle 217vb. *hang*; see-saw, rock; give, swag; hunt, lurch, reel, stagger, totter, teeter, waddle, wobble, wiggle, waggle, wag; bob, bounce, bob up and down, dance 312vb. *leap*; toss, roll, pitch, tumble, wallow; rattle, chatter, shake; flutter, quiver, shiver 318vb. *be agitated*; flicker 417vb. *shine*; echo 404vb. *resound.* See *fluctuate.*

fluctuate, alternate, reciprocate 12vb. *correlate*; ebb and flow, come and go, pass and repass, leap-frog; wamble, slop about inside one; wallow, flounder 313 vb. *plunge.*

brandish, wave, wag, waggle, shake, flourish; wave to and fro, shake up and down, flutter.

Adv. *to and fro*, backwards and forwards, in and out, up and down, side to side, left to right and right to left; zig-zag, see-saw, wibble-wabble; like buckets in a well; shuttlewise.

See: 12, 14, 141, 176, 217, 312, 313, 318, 328, 350, 352, 404, 417, 474, 601.

318 Agitation: irregular motion

N. *agitation*, irregular motion, jerkiness, fits and starts, unsteadiness 152 n. *changeableness*; joltiness, bumpiness, broken water, choppiness, pitching, rolling 259 n. *roughness*; unsteady beam, flicker, twinkle 417 n. *flash*; sudden motion, start, jump 508 n. *inexpectation*; shaking, succussion, shake, jig, jiggle; toss 287 n. *propulsion*; shock, jar, jolt, jerk, jounce, bounce, bump, rock 279 n. *knock*; nudge, dig 547 n. *gesture*; vibration, thrill, throb, pulse, pit-a-pat, palpitation, flutter 317 n. *oscillation*; shuddering, shudder, shiver, frisson; quiver, quaver, tremor; tremulousness, trembling, palsy (see *spasm*); restlessness, feverishness, fever; tossing,

turning, jactitation, jactitance; jiving, hopping 678 n. *activity*, 837 n. *dancing*; itchiness, itch, vellication 378 n. *formication*; twitchiness, twitch, grimacing, grimace; mental agitation, perturbation, disquiet 825 n. *worry*; trepidation, jumpiness, twitter, flap 854 n. *nervousness*; the shakes, jumps, jitters, shivers, fidgets, 'the channels', aspen, aspen-leaf.

spasm, ague, rigor, chattering; uncontrollable tremor, palsy; twitch, subsultus; tic, nervous t.; chorea, St. Vitus' dance, the jerks; tarantism; lockjaw, tetanus; cramp, the cramps; throe 377 n. *pang*; convulsion, paroxysm, access, orgasm 503 n. *frenzy*; staggers, megrims; fit, epilepsy, falling sickness; pulse, throb 317 n. *oscillation*; attack, seizure, stroke.

commotion, turmoil, turbulence, tumult, tumultuation; hurly-burly, hubbub, bobbery, brouhaha; fever, rush, rout 680 n. *haste*; furore 503 n. *frenzy*; fuss, bother 678 n. *restlessness*; racket, din 400 n. *loudness*; stir, ferment, boiling, fermentation, ebullition, effervescence 355 n. *bubble*; ground swell, heavy sea 350 n. *wave*; tempest, thunderstorm, magnetic s. 176 n. *storm*; whirlpool 315 n. *vortex*; whirlwind 352 n. *gale*; disturbance, atmospherics.

Adj. *agitated*, shaken, fluttering, waving, brandished; shaking, successive; troubled, unquiet 819 adj. *lively*; feverish, fevered, restless; scratchy, jittery, jumpy, all of a twitter, in a flap, in a flutter 854 adj. *nervous*; hopping, leaping, like a cat on hot bricks; breathless, panting; subsultory, twitching, itchy; convulsive, spasmodic, spastic; saltatory, choreic, choreal; giddy-paced 456 adj. *light-minded*; doddering, palsied, aguey; shaky, tremulous, a-tremble; thrilling, vibrating 317 adj. *oscillating.*

Vb. *be agitated*, ripple, popple, boil 355vb. *bubble*; stir, move, dash; shake, tremble, quiver, quaver, shiver; have an ague, throw a fit; writhe, squirm, itch, twitch, 251vb. *wriggle*; jactitate, toss, turn, toss about, thresh a.; kick, plunge 176vb. *be violent*; flounder, flop, wallow, roll, reel, pitch 317vb. *fluctuate*; sway, swag 220 vb. *be oblique*; pulse, beat, thrill, vibrate; wag, waggle, wobble, stagger, lurch, dodder, totter, teeter, dither 317vb. *oscillate*; whirr, whirl 315vb. *rotate*; jump about, hop, bob, bounce, dance 312

vb. *leap*; flicker, twinkle, gutter, sputter, spatter 417vb. *shine*; flap, flutter, twitter, start, jump; throb, pant, palpitate, go pit-a-pat 821vb. *be excited*; bustle, rush, mill around 61vb. *rampage*; ramp, roar 891vb. *be angry*.

agitate, disturb, rumple, ruffle, untidy 63vb. *derange*; discompose, perturb, worry 827 vb. *displease*; ripple, puddle, muddy; stir, stir up 43 vb., *mix*; whisk, whip, beat, churn 315vb. *rotate*; toss, wallop 287 vb. *propel*; shake up, success, shake; wag, waggle, wave, flourish 317vb. *brandish*; flutter, fly (a flag); jog, joggle, jiggle, jolt, jounce, nudge, dig; jerk, pluck, twitch, vellicate.

effervesce, froth, spume, foam, foam at the mouth, bubble, bubble up 355vb. *bubble*; boil, boil over, seethe, simmer, sizzle, spit 379vb. *be hot*; ferment, work.

Adv. *jerkily*, pit-a-pat; subsultorily etc. adj.; by fits and starts, with a hop, skip and a jump; spasmodically, convulsively, in convulsions, in fits, in spasms.

See: 43, 61, 63, 152, 176, 220, 251, 259, 279, 287, 312, 315, 317, 350, 352, 355, 377, 378, 379, 400, 417, 456, 503, 508, 547, 678, 819, 821, 825, 827, 837, 854, 891.

319 Materiality

N. *materiality*, materialness, empirical world, world of experience; corporeity, corporeality, corporality, corporalness, bodiliness; material existence, world of nature 3n. *substantiality*; physical being, physical condition 1n. *existence*; plenum 321n. *world*; concreteness, tangibility, palpability, solidity 324n. *density*; weight 322n. *gravity*, 638 n. *importance*; personality, individuality 80n. *speciality*; embodiment, incarnation, reincarnation, metempsychosis; realization, materialization; hylism, positivism, materialism, dialectical m., Marxism; unspirituality, worldliness, sensuality 944n. *sensualism*; materialist, hylicist; realist, somatist, positivist.

matter, brute m., stuff; plenum; hyle, prime matter, prima materia; mass, material, body, frame 331n. *structure*; substance, solid s., corpus; organic matter, flesh, flesh and blood, plasma, protoplasm 358n.

organism; real world, world of nature, Nature.

object, tangible o., bird in the hand; inanimate object, still life; flesh and blood, real person 371n. *person*; thing, gadget, something, commodity, article, item; stocks and stones 359n. *mineral*; raw material 631n. *materials*.

element, elementary unit, sense datum; principle, first p. 68n. *origin*; the four elements, earth, air, fire, water; unit of being, monad; factor, ingredient 58n. *component*; chemical element, basic substance; physical element, atom, molecule; fundamental particle, sub-atom, electron, beta-particle, negatron, positron, neutron, meson, proton 33n. *particle*; nucleus, nucleon; helium nucleus, alpha-particle; neutrino, hyperion; anti-particle, anti-electron; photon; quantum; ion.

physics, physical science, science of matter; science of bodies, somatics, somatology; nuclear physics; applied physics, technology 694n. *skill*; natural philosophy, experimental p. 490n. *science*.

Adj. *material*, hylic; real, natural; massy, solid, concrete, palpable, tangible, ponderable, sensible; weighty 638adj. *important*; somatoscopic, somatic; physical, spatiotemporal; objective, impersonal, neuter; hypostatic 3adj. *substantial*; incarnate, incorporate; corporeal, bodily, fleshly, of flesh and blood, incorporated, reincarnated, realized, materialized; materialistic, worldly, unspiritual 944n. *sensual*.

Vb. *materialize*, substantialize, hypostatize, corporealize; objectify 223vb. *externalize*; realize, make real, body forth; embody, incorporate; incarnate, personify; substantiate.

See: 1, 3, 33, 58, 68, 80, 223, 321, 322, 324, 331, 358, 359, 371, 490, 631, 638, 694, 944.

320 Immateriality

N. *immateriality*, unreality 4n. *insubstantiality*; incorporeity, incorporeality, dematerialization, disembodiment, inextension, imponderability, intangibility, ghostliness, shadowiness; superficiality 639adj. *unimportance*; immaterialism, idealism, Platonism; spirituality, otherworldliness; animism; spiritualism, psychism 984n.

occultism; other world, world of spirits, astral plane; eternity 115n. *perpetuity*; animist, spiritualist 984n. *occultist*; idealist 449n. *philosopher*; astral body 970n. *ghost*.

subjectivity, personality, selfhood, myself, me, yours truly; ego, id, superego; psyche, higher self, spiritual s. 80n. *self*.

Adj. *immaterial*, immateriate, without mass; incorporeal, incorporal, asomatous; aery, ghostly, shadowy 4adj. *insubstantial*; unextended, imponderable, intangible; superficial 639adj. *unimportant*; bodiless, unembodied, discarnate, disembodied; supernal, extramundane, unearthly, supersensory, psychic, pneumatoscopic, spiritistic, astral 984adj. *psychical*; spiritual, otherwordly 973adj. *religious*; personal, subjective.

Vb. *disembody*, spiritualize, dematerialize, disincarnate.

See: 4, 80, 115, 449, 639, 970, 973, 984.

321 Universe

N. *universe*, omneity 52n. *whole*; world, creation, all c.; sum of things, plenum, matter and anti-matter; cosmos, macrocosm, microcosm; space-time continuum; expanding universe, island u.; anagalactic space, metagalactic s.

world, wide w., four corners of the earth; home of man, sublunary sphere; earth, middle e.; globe, sphere, terrestrial s., terraqueous globe, geoid, terrestrial surface, crust; sub-crust, moho; atlas, world-map 551n. *map*; Old World, New World; earth-shine; geocentric system, Ptolemaic s.; personal world, idioverse; life space, total situation 8n. *circumstance*.

heavens, sky, welkin, empyrean, ether, ethereal sphere; firmament, vault of heaven; night-sky, starlit s., aurora borealis, northern lights, aurora australis; zodiacal light, counterglow, gegenschein.

star, heavenly body, celestial b.; sidereal sphere, starry host, host of heaven; asterism, constellation, Great Bar, Little B., Plough, Dipper, Charles' Wain, Cassiopeia's Chair, Pleiades, Orion, Orion's belt, Southern Cross; starlight, starshine; population I, population II; main sequence, blue star, white s., yellow s., red s.; double star, binary, spectroscopic b., primary, secondary, component, comes; triple star, quadruple s., multiple s.; variable star, long-period variable, Mirid; short-period variable, Cepheid; pseudo-Cepheid; eclipsing variable, Algolid, Lyrid; irregular variable, secular v.; giant, supergiant, Betelgeuse; subgiant, dwarf, red d., white d., Sirius B; new star, nova, super-nova, Tycho's star; pole star, North Star, Polaris, circumpolar star; Star of David, Star of Bethlehem; Milky Way, galactic plane, star cloud; star cluster, globular c., open c., moving c., local c.; galaxy, super-g., island universe; stellar motion, star stream, radial velocity, proper motion.

nebula, galactic n., gaseous n., green n., irregular n., planetary n., invisible n., dark n., interstellar matter; extra-galactic nebula, white n., Magellanic n., spiral n.

zodiac, signs of the z., Aries (the Ram), Taurus (the Bull), Gemini (the Twins), Cancer (the Crab), Leo (the Lion), Virgo (the Virgin), Libra (the Balance), Scorpius *or* Scorpio (the Scorpion), Sagittarius (the Archer), Capricornus (the Goat), Aquarius (the Man with the Watering-pot), Pisces (the Fish); ecliptic; house, mansion, lunar m.

planet, major p., minor p., asteroid, planetoid; Mercury; Venus, morning star, evening s.; Mars, red planet; Earth, Jupiter, Saturn, Uranus, Neptune, Pluto; comet, hairy star, wandering s., Halley's comet; planetary orbit, cometary o., parabolic o., hyperbolic o.; ascending node, descending n.

meteor, falling star, shooting s., fire-ball, meteorite, aerolite, bolide, chondrite; meteoroid; micrometeorite; meteor shower; radiant point.

sun, day-star, orb of day, midnight sun; parhelion, mock sun; sunlight, photosphere, chromosphere; facula, flocculus, sun spot, solar prominence, solar flare, corona; Sol, Helios, Titan, Phœbus; solar system, heliocentric s.

moon, satellite; new moon, old moon in the young moon's arm, waxing moon, waning m., half-m., crescent m., horned m., gibbous m., full m., harvest m., hunter's m.; pareselene, mock moon; man in the moon, lunarian; Luna, Diana, Phœbe, Cynthia, Hecate; moonlight.

satellite, earth s., artificial s., space-ship, space station, sputnik, lunik, arknik; moons of Mars, Phobos, Deimos; moons of Jupiter, Io, Europa, Ganymede, Callisto etc.; moons of Saturn, Mimas, Enceladus, Tethys, Dione, Rhea, Titan, Hyperion, Iapetus, Phœbe; moons of Uranus, Miranda, Ariel, Umbriel,Titania, Oberon; moons of Neptune, Triton, Nereid.

astronomy, star-lore, star-gazing, star-watching, meteor-w; radio-astronomy; astrophysics; stellar photography; selenography, uranography, uranology; astrology, astromancy, horoscope 511 n. *divination*; observatory, planetarium; telescope, astronomical t., radio t., refractor, reflector, Newtonian telescope, Cassegrainian t., Gregorian t.; finder, eyepiece; object-glass, optic g., mirror, flat 442 n. *telescope*; spectroscope, orrery, eidouranion, astrolabe; astronomer, radio a., astrophysicist; star-gazer, star-watcher; astrologer, astromancer.

uranometry, right ascension, declension, hour angle, hour circle, declination c.; reference c., great c.; celestial pole, galactic p., celestial equator, galactic e.; equinoctial colure, solstitial c., true equinox, vernal e., first point of Aries, autumnal equinox; geocentric latitude *or* longitude, heliocentric latitude *or* longitude, galactic latitude *or* longitude; node, ascending n., descending n.; libration, nutation; precession, precession of the equinox; solstice, lunistice.

cosmography, cosmology, cosmogony, cosmogonist, cosmographer.

geography, orography, oceanography, cosmography, physiography, geodesy, geology; geographer, geodesist, geologist; hydrology, hydrography, hydrogeology.

Adj. *cosmic*, universal, cosmical, cosmological, cosmogonic, cosmographical; interstellar, intersidereal; galactic, metagalactic.

celestial, heavenly, empyreal, sphery; starry, star-spangled; sidereal, astral, stellar; solar, heliacal, zodiacal; lunary, lunar, selenic, lunate; lunisolar; nebular, nebulous; heliocentric, geocentric, planetocentric; cometary, meteoric, meteorological; uranological, uranometrical; equinoctial, solstitial.

planetary, planetoidal, asteroidal, satellitic, planetocentric; Mercurian, Venerean, Martian, Jovian, Saturnian, Neptunian, Plutonian.

telluric, tellurian, terrestrial, terrene, terraqueous; sublunary, subastral; Old-World, New-World; polar, equatorial; world-wide, world, global, international, universal 183 adj. *spacious*; worldly, earthly.

astronomic, astronomical, astrophysical, star-gazing, star-watching; astrological, astromantic; telescopic, spectroscopic.

geographic, geographical, oceanographic, orographical; geological; geodesic, geodetic, physiographic; hydrogeological, hydrographic, hydrological.

Adv. *under the sun*, on the face of the globe, here below, on earth.

See: 8, 52, 183, 442, 511, 551.

322 Gravity

N. *gravity*, gravitation, force of gravity, gravitational pull; weight, weightiness, heaviness, ponderosity; specific gravity; incumbency, pressure, displacement, sinkage, draught; incubus, encumbrance, load, lading, freight; burden, burthen; ballast, makeweight, rider, counterpoise 31 n. *offset*; mass, lump 324 n. *solid body*; lump of, weight of, mass of; plummet 313 n. *diver*; weight, bob, sinker, lead, stone, millstone; geostatics, statics.

weighment, weighing, ponderation; balancing, equipoise 28 n. *equalization*; weights, avoirdupois weight, troy w., apothecary's w.; grain, carat, carat-grain, scruple, pennyweight, drachm; ounce, pound, stone, quarter, tod, quintal, hundredweight, ton; gramme, kilogramme; tola, seer, maund; megaton, kiloton; axle-load, laden weight.

scales, weighing-machine; steelyard, beam; balance, spring-b.; pan, scale, weight; platform scale, weigh-bridge.

Adj. *weighty*, heavy, ponderous; leaden, heavy as lead; weighing etc. vb.; cumbersome, cumbrous 195 adj. *unwieldy*; lumpish, massy, massive 324 adj. *dense*; pressing, incumbent, superincumbent 735 n. *oppressive*; having weight, weighing, with a weight of; weighted, loaded, charged, burdened; overweighted, overburdened, overloaded; gravitational, gravitative.

Vb. *weigh*, have weight, exert w., gravitate; wcigh equal, balance 28vb. *be equal*; counterpoise, counterweigh 31vb. *compensate*; outweigh, overweigh, overbalance 34vb. *predominate*; tip the scale, turn the s., depress the s.; wallow, sink, gravitate, settle 313vb. *founder*, 309vb. *descend*; weigh heavy, be h., lie h.; press, weigh on, weigh one down, hang like a millstone 311vb. *depress*; load, cumber 702vb. *hinder*; try the weight of, take the weight of, put on the scales, lay in the scale 465vb. *measure*; weigh oneself, stand on the scales.

make heavy,weight, hang weights on; charge, burden, overweight, overburden, overload 193vb. *load*.

Adv. *weightily*, heavily, leadenly.

See: 28, 31, 34, 193, 195, 309, 311, 313, 324, 465, 702.

323 Levity

N. *levity*, lightness etc.adj.; thinness, air, ether 325n. *rarity*; buoyance, buoyancy; volatility 338n. *vaporization*; weightlessness, imponderability, imponderableness; defiance of gravity, levitation 308n. *ascent*; feather-weight, feather-down, fluff, thistle-down, cobweb, gossamer; dust, mote, straw 4n. *insubstantial thing*; cork, buoy, bubble; gas, hot air, helium, hydrogen 310n. *lifter*.

leaven, lightener; ferment, enzyme, zymogen, barm, yeast, baking-powder, self-raising flour.

Adj. *light*, underweight 307adj. *deficient*; light-weight, feather-w.; portable, handy 196adj. *little*; light-footed, light-fingered, pussy-foot; non-gravitational, weightless, without weight; imponderous, imponderable, unweighable; sublime, ethereal, airy, gaseous, astatic, volatile, sublimated 325 adj. *rare*; uncompressed, doughy, barmy, yeasty, fermenting, zymotic, enzymic; aerated, frothy, foamy, whipped; peptic, digestible 301 adj. *edible*; floating, buoyant, unsinkable; feathery, light as air, light as a feather, light as a fairy; lightening, unloading; raising, self-raising, leavening.

Vb. *be light* etc.adj.; defy gravity, levitate, surface, float to the surface, float 308vb. *ascend*; swim; balloon 197vb. *expand*; be outweighed, kick the beam.

lighten, make light, make lighter, reduce weight; ease 701vb. *disencumber*; lighten ship, throw overboard, jettison 300vb. *void*; volatilize, gasify, vaporize 340vb. *aerify*; leaven, work; raise, levitate 310 vb. *elevate*.

See: 4, 196, 197, 300, 301, 307, 308, 310, 325, 338, 340, 701.

324 Density

N. *density*, solidity; compactness, solidness, concreteness, thickness, concentration; consistence, spissitude; incompressibility 326 n. *hardness*; impenetrability, impermeability, imporosity; indissolubility, indiscerptibility, indivisibility; cohesion, inseparability 48n. *coherence*; relative density, specific gravity; densimeter, hydrometer, aerometer.

condensation, inspissation, constipation; thickening etc.vb.; incrassation, consolidation, concentration; concretion, nucleation; caseation, coagulation; solidation, solidification, consolidation; congealment, gelatination, jellification; glaciation; ossification, petrifaction, fossilization 326n. *hardening*; crystallization; sedimentation, precipitation; condenser, compressor, thickener, gelatine, rennet, pepsin 354n. *thickening*.

solid body, solid; lump, mass 319n. *matter*; knot, block; condensation, nucleus, hard core; conglomerate, concretion; concrete, cement; stone, crystal, hardpan, burl, trap 344n. *rock*; precipitate, deposit, sediment, silt, slag, clay, cake, clod; bone, ossicle; gristle, cartilage 329n. *toughness*; coagulum, curd, clot, blood-c., grume, thrombosis; embolus, tophus, calculus; solid mass, phalanx, serried ranks; wall, blank w. 702n. *obstacle*.

Adj. *dense*, thick, crass; close, heavy, stuffy (air); foggy, murky, to be cut with a knife; lumpy, ropy, grumous, clotted, curdled; caked, caky; matted, knotted, tangled 48 adj. *cohesive*; coherent, consistent, monolithic; firm, close-textured, knotty, gnarled; substantial, massy, massive 322adj. *weighty*; concrete, solid, frozen, solidified etc.vb.; crystallic, crystalline, crystallized; condensed, nuclear, nucleal; costive,

constipated; compact, close-packed, firm-p.; thickset, thick-growing, thick, bushy, luxuriant 635 adj. *plenteous*; serried, massed, densely arrayed; incompressible, inelastic 326 adj. *rigid*; impermeable, impenetrable, impervious, imporous, without holes; indivisible, indiscerptible, infrangible, unbreakable 162 adj. *strong*.

indissoluble, undissolvable, insoluble, infusible; undissolved, unliquefied, unmelted, unthawed, hard-frozen; precipitated, sedimentary.

solidifying, binding, constipating; freezing, congealing; styptic, styptical, astringent, hæmostatic.

Vb. *be dense,*—solid etc. adj.; become solid, solidify, consolidate; conglomerate, cement 48 vb. *cohere*; condense, nucleate, form a core *or* kernel; densen, thicken, inspissate, incrassate; precipitate, deposit; freeze, glaciate 380 vb. *be cold*; set, take a set.; gelatinize, jellify, jell; congeal, coagulate, clot, curdle; cake, crust, candy; crystal, crystallize; fossilize, petrify, ossify 326 vb. *harden*; compact, compress, contract, squeeze 198 vb. *make smaller*; pack, squeeze in, cram, ram down 193 vb. *load*; mass, crowd 74 vb. *bring together*; bind, constipate; sediment, precipitate, deposit.

See: 48, 74, 162, 193, 198, 319, 322, 326, 329, 344, 354, 380, 635, 702.

325 Rarity

N, *rarity,* low pressure, vacuum, near v. 190 n. *emptiness*; subtility, compressibility, sponginess 327 n. *softness*; tenuity, fineness 206 n. *thinness*; insolidity 4 n. *insubstantiality*; lightness 323 n. *levity*; incorporeality, ethereality 320 n. *immateriality*; airiness, windiness, ether, gas 336 n. *gaseity*, 340 n. *air*; rarefaction, expansion, dilatation, pressure-reduction, attenuation; subtilization, etherealization; seldomness 140 n. *infrequency*.

Adj. *rare,* tenuous, thin, fine, subtile, subtle; flimsy, slight, 4 adj. *insubstantial*; low-pressure, uncompact, uncompressed; compressible, spongy 328 adj. *elastic*; rarefied, aerified, aerated 336 adj. *gaseous*; void, hollow 190 adj. *empty*; ethereal,

aery 323 adj. *light*; incorporeal 320 adj. *immaterial*; wispy, straggly.

Vb. *rarefy,* reduce the pressure, expand, dilate; make a vacuum, pump out, exhaust 300 vb. *void*; subtilize, attenuate, refine, thin; dilute, adulterate 163 vb. *weaken*; gasify, volatilize 338 vb. *vaporize*.

See: 4, 140, 163, 190, 206, 300, 320, 323, 327, 328, 336, 338, 340.

326 Hardness

N. *hardness,* durity; unyielding quality, intractability, renitency, resistance; starchiness, stiffness, rigour, rigidity, inflexibility; inextensibility, inelasticity; firmness, temper; grittiness 329 n. *toughness*; callosity, callousness; stoniness, rockiness, cragginess; grit, stone, pebble, boulder, crag; granite, flint, silica, quartz, marble, diamond 344 n. *rock*; adamant, metal, duralumin; steel, hard s., iron, wrought i., cast i.; nails, hardware, stoneware; cement, concrete, ferro-c.; brick, baked b.; block, board, heart-wood, duramen; hardwood, teak, oak, heart of o. 366 n. *wood*; bone, gristle, cartilage; a callosity, callus, corn, kibe; blain, chilblain; shell, hard s.; hard core, hard centre, jaw-breaker; brick wall; stiffener, starch, wax; whalebone, corset, splint 218 n. *supporter*.

hardening, induration; stiffening, backing; starching; steeling, tempering; vulcanization; petrifaction, lapidification, lapidescence; fossilization; crystallization, vitrification, glaciation; ossification, cornification; sclerosis, scleriasis, hardening of the arteries; toughening 682 n. *exercise*.

Adj. *hard,* adamant, adamantine, adamantean; unbreakable, infrangible 162 adj. *strong*; fortified, armoured, steeled, proof; iron, cast-i.; steel, steely; concrete, ferro-c.; hardboiled 329 adj. *tough*; hard as iron, hard as steel, hard as stone, hard as bone, hard as nails; callous, stony, rocky, flinty; gritty, gravelly, pebbly; lithic, granitic; crystalline, vitreous, glassy; horny, corneous; bony, osseous, ossific; cartilaginous, gristly; hardened, indurate, indurated, tempered, case-hardened, calloused; petrified, fossilized, ossified; icy,

frozen, hard-f., frozen over 329 adj. *tough*; sclerotic.

rigid, stubborn, obdurate 602 adj. *obstinate*; intractable, unmalleable, unadaptable; firm, inflexible, unbending 162 adj. *unyielding*; incompressible, inextensible, resistant; inelastic, unsprung, springless; unadaptable; starch, starchy, starched; unlimber, muscle-bound 695 adj. *clumsy*; tense, taut, tight, tight-strung, firm-packed 45 adj. *firm-set*; stiff, stark, stiff as a poker, stiff as a ramrod, stiff as buckram, stiff as a board.

Vb. **harden**, render hard etc. adj.; steel 162 vb. *strengthen*; indurate, temper, vulcanize, toughen; hardboil 301 vb. *cook*; petrify, fossilize, ossify; calcify, vitrify, crystallize; glaciate, freeze 382 vb. *refrigerate*; stiffen, back, starch, wax (a moustache), tauten 45 vb. *tighten*.

See: 45, 162, 218, 301, 329, 344, 366, 382, 602, 682, 695.

327 Softness

N. *softness*, tenderness, gentleness; pliableness etc. adj.; compliance 739 n. *obedience*; pliancy, pliability, flexibility, plasticity, ductility, tractility; malleability, sequacity, adaptability; suppleness, litheness; springiness, turfiness, springing, suspension 328 n. *elasticity*; extendibility, extensibility; impressibility, doughiness 356 n. *pulpiness*; sponginess, flaccidity, flabbiness, floppiness; laxity, looseness 335 n. *fluidity*; sogginess, squelchiness, marshiness 347 n. *marsh*; flocculence, downiness; velvetiness; butter, grease, oil, wax, plasticine, clay, dough, pudding, soap, plastic; padding, wadding, pad 227 n. *lining*; cushion, pillow, armchair, feather-bed 376 n. *euphoria*; velvet, plush, down, eiderdown, fleece 259 n. *hair*; feathers 259 n. *plumage*; snowflake 330 n. *brittleness*; soft handling, light touch, light rein, velvet glove 736 n. *lenity*.

Adj. *soft*, not tough, tender 301 adj. *edible*; melting 335 adj. *fluidal*; giving, yielding, compressible; springy, sprung 328 adj. *elastic*; pneumatic, cushiony, pillowy, padded; impressible, as wax, waxy, doughy, argilaceous; spongy, soggy, mushy, squelchy 347 n. *marshy*; medullary, pithy; pulpy, squashy, juicy, mellow,

overripe 669 n. *matured*; fleecy, flocculent 259 adj. *downy*; turfy, mossy, grassy; plushy, velvety, silky 258 adj. *smooth*; unstiffened, unstarched, limp; flaccid, flabby, floppy; unstrung, relaxed; gentle, light; soft as butter, soft as wax, soft as soap, soft as down, soft as velvet, soft as silk; tender as a chicken; softening, emollient 177 adj. *lenitive*.

flexible, whippy, bendable; pliant, pliable; ductile, tractile, malleable, mouldable, sequacious, adaptable; plastic, thermoplastic; extensile, stretchable 328 adj. *elastic*; lithe, supple, lissom, limber, loose-limbed, double-jointed; acrobatic 162 adj. *athletic*.

Vb. **soften**, mollify 177 vb. *assuage*; render soft, velvet, tenderize; mellow 669 vb. *mature*; oil, grease 334 vb. *lubricate*; knead, massage, mash, pulp, squash 332 vb. *pulverize*; macerate, steep 341 vb. *drench*; cushion, pillow, temper 177 vb. *moderate*; relax, unstring 46 vb. *disjoin*; yield, give, give way, relax, bend; unbend 683 vb. *repose*; relent 736 vb. *be lenient*.

See: 46, 162, 177, 227, 258, 259, 301, 328, 330, 332, 334, 335, 341, 347, 356, 376, 683, 669, 736, 739.

328 Elasticity

N. *elasticity*, give, stretch; spring, springiness; suspension, knee action; stretchability, tensibility, extensibility; resilience, bounce 280 n. *recoil*; renitency, buoyancy, rubber, india-r., elastic, gum e.; caoutchouc, guttapercha; whalebone, baleen; elasticin.

Adj. *elastic*, stretchy, stretchable, tensile, extensile, extensible; springy, bouncy, resilient 280 adj. *recoiling*; renitent, buoyant; sprung, well-s.; ductile 327 adj. *soft*; systaltic, peristaltic.

Vb. *be elastic*—tensile etc. adj.; bounce, spring, spring back 280 vb. *recoil*; stretch, give.

See: 280, 327.

329 Toughness

N. *toughness*, durability, infrangibility 162 n. *strength*; stubbornness 602 n. *obstinacy*; tenacity, holding quality 778 n. *retention*; cohesion 48 n. *coherence*; viscidity 354 n.

semiliquidity; leatheriness, inedibility, indigestibility; leather, gristle, cartilage 326n. *hardness.*

Adj. *tough*, durable, resisting; close-woven, strong-fibred 162adj. *strong*; tenacious, retentive, clinging, adhesive, sticky, gummy 48adj. *cohesive*; viscid 354adj. *semiliquid*; infrangible, unbreakable, untearable, shock-proof; vulcanized, toughened; hardboiled, overdone; stringy, fibrous; gristly, cartilaginous; rubbery, leathery, coriaceous, tough as whit-leather; indigestible, inedible; non-elastic, inelastic, unsprung, springless 326adj. *rigid*; unyielding, stubborn 602adj. *obstinate.*

Vb. *be tough,*—durable, etc.adj.; resist fracture, be unbreakable; toughen, tan, case-harden; mercerise, vulcanize, temper, anneal 162vb. *strengthen.*

See: 48, 162, 326, 326, 354, 602, 778.

330 Brittleness

N. *brittleness* etc.adj.; frangibility; friability, friableness, crumbliness 332n. *pulverulence*; fissility 46n. *scission*; laminability, flakiness 207n. *lamina*; fragility, frailty, flimsiness 163n. *weakness*; bubble, egg-shell, matchwood, rice-paper, pie-crust; shale, slate; glass, china, crockery 381n. *pottery*; pane, window, glasshouse; house of cards, sand-castle, mud pie 163n. *weak thing.*

Adj. *brittle*, breakable, frangible; fragile, glassy, brittle as glass; papery, like parchment; shattery, shivery, splintery; friable, crumbly 332adj. *powdery*; crisp, crimp, short, like shortbread; flaky, laminable; fissile, splitting; scissile, lacerable, tearable 46adj. *severable*; frail, delicate, flimsy, egg-shell 163adj. *weak*; gimcrack, crazy, ill-made 4adj. *insubstantial*; tumble-down 655adj. *dilapidated*; ready to break, ready to burst, explosive.

Vb. *be brittle,*—fragile etc.adj.; fracture 46 vb. *break*; crack, snap; star, craze; split, shatter, shiver, fragment; splinter, break short, snap off; burst, fly, explode; give way, fall in, crash 309vb. *tumble*; fall to pieces 655vb. *deteriorate*; wear thin; crumble 332vb. *pulverize*; crumble to dust 131vb. *grow old*; live in a glass house.

Int. fragile! with care!

See: 4, 46, 131, 163, 207, 332, 309, 381, 655.

331 Structure. Texture

N. *structure*, organization, pattern, plan; complex 52n. *whole*; mould, shape, build 243n. *form*; constitution, set-up, content, substance 56n. *composition*; construction, make, works, workings; compaction, architecture, tectonics, architectonics; fabric, work, brickwork, stonework, woodwork 631n. *materials*; scaffold, framework, chassis, shell 218n. *frame*; lamination, cleavage 207n. *stratification*; body, carcass, person, physique, anatomy 358n. *organism*; bony structure, skeleton, bone, horn; science of structure, organology, physiology, myology, splanchnology, neurology, angiology, adenology, histology, angiography, adenography 358n. *biology.*

texture, intertexture, contexture, network 222n. *crossing*; tissue, fabric, stuff 222n. *textile*; staple, denier 208n. *fibre*; web, weave, warp and woof, warp and weft 222n. *weaving*; nap, pile 259n. *hair*; granular texture, granulation, grain, grit; fineness of grain 258n. *smoothness*; coarseness of grain 259n. *roughness*; surface 223n. *exteriority*; feel 378n. *touch.*

Adj. *structural*, organic; skeletal; anatomic, anatomical; organismal, organological; organizational, constructional; tectonic, architectural.

textural, textile, woven 222adj. *crossed*; fine-woven, close-w.; ribbed, twilled; grained, granular; fine-grained, silky, satiny 258adj. *smooth*; coarse-grained, gritty 259adj. *rough*; fine, fine-spun, delicate, subtile, gossamery, filmy; coarse, homespun, hodden, linsey-woolsey.

See: 52, 56, 207, 208, 218, 222, 223, 243, 258, 259, 358, 378, 631.

332 Pulverulence

N. *pulverulence*, powderiness; efflorescence, 'flowers' (chemistry), dustiness 649n. *dirt*; sandiness, sabulosity; grittiness; granulation; friability, crumbliness 330n. *brittleness*; pulverization, levigation, trituration; attrition, detrition, attenuation,

disintegration, erosion 51 n. *decomposition*; grinding, milling, multure; abrasion, filling, limation 333 n. *friction*; fragmentation, comminution, contusion 46 n. *disjunction*; spreading dust, dusting, powdering, frosting.

powder, face-p. 843 n. *cosmetic*; pollen, spore, microspore, sporule; dust, coal-d., soot, ash 649 n. *dirt*; smeddum, smithan; flour, atta, farina; grist, meal, bran; sawdust, filings, limature, scobs; powdery deposit, efflorescence, flowers; flocculi, magistery; débris, detritus 41 n. *leavings*; sand, grit, gravel; grain, seed, pip, crumb 53 n. *piece*; granule, grain of powder 33 n. *particle*; flake, snow f.; smoke, column of s., smoke-cloud, dust-c.; fog, smog 355 n. *cloud*; dust storm, dust devil 176 n. *storm*.

pulverizer, miller, grinder; roller, crusher, masher, atomizer; mill, millstone, muller, quern, quernstone; pestle, pestle and mortar; hand-mill, coffee-m., pepper-m.; grater, cheese-g., nutmeg-g., grindstone, file; abrasive, sandpaper, emery paper; molar, teeth 256 n. *tooth*; chopper 256 n. *sharp edge*; sledge, sledge-hammer 279 n. *hammer*; bulldozer 279 n. *ram*.

Adj. *powdery*, pulverulent, scobiform; dusty, dust-covered, sooty, smoky 649 adj. *dirty*; sandy, sabulous, arenose, arenarious, arenaceous; farinaceous, branny, floury; granulated, granular; gritty, gravelly; flocculent, furfuraceous, efflorescent; grated, milled, ground, sifted, bolted; crumbling, crumbled; crumbly, friable 330 adj. *brittle*.

Vb. *pulverize*, powder, reduce to p., grind to p.; triturate, levigate, granulate; crush, kibble, kevel, mash, comminute, contuse, contund, shatter, fragment, disintegrate 46 vb. *break*; grind, mill, mince, beat, bruise, pound, bray; knead; crumble, crumb; crunch, scrunch 301 vb. *chew*; chip, flake, grate, scrape, rasp, file, abrade, rub down 333 vb. *rub*; weather, wear down, rust, erode 51 vb. *decompose*.

See: 33, 41, 46, 51, 53, 176, 256, 279, 301, 330, 333, 355, 649, 843.

333 Friction

N. *friction*, frictional force, drag 278 n. *slowness*; frication, confrication, affriction; rubbing etc. vb.; attrition, rubbing against, rubbing together 279 n. *collision*; rubbing out, erasure 550 n. *obliteration*; abrasion, scraping; limature, filing 332 n. *pulverulence*; wearing away, erosion 165 n. *destruction*; scrape, graze, scratch; brushing, rub; polish, levigation, elbow grease; shampoo, massage, facial m., facial 843 n. *beautification*; eraser, rubber, rosin; masseur, masseuse, shampooer 843 n. *beautician*.

Adj. *rubbing*, frictional, fretting, grating; anatriptic, abrasive; fricative.

Vb. *rub*, friction; rub in 303 vb. *insert*; rub against, strike (a match); fret, fray, chafe, gall; graze, scratch, scarify 655 vb. *wound*; rub off, abrade; scrape, scrub, scour; brush, rub down, curry, curry-comb 648 vb. *clean*; polish, buff, levigate 258 vb. *smooth*; rub out, erase 550 vb. *obliterate*; gnaw, erode, wear away 165 vb. *consume*; rasp, file, grind 332 vb. *pulverize*; knead, shampoo, massage; wax, rosin, chalk (one's cue); grate, be rusty, catch, stick; rub gently, stroke 889 vb. *caress*; iron 258 vb. *smooth*.

See: 165, 258, 278, 279, 303, 332, 550, 648, 655, 843, 889

334 Lubrication

N. *lubrication*, lubrification; anointment, unction, oiling etc. vb.; lubricity 357 n. *unctousness*; non-friction 258 n. *smoothness*.

lubricant, graphite, plumbago, black lead; glycerine, wax, grease, cart g. 357 n. *oil*; soap, lather 648 n. *cleanser*; saliva, spit, spittle, synovia; ointment, salve 658 n. *balm*; emollient, lenitive 357 n. *unguent*; lubricator, oil-can, grease-gun.

Adj. *lubricated* etc. vb.; smooth-running, well-oiled, well-greased; not rusty, silent.

Vb. *lubricate*, lubricitate, oil, grease, wax, soap, lather; grease leather, liquor; butter 357 vb. *pinguefy*; anoint, pour balm.

See: 258, 357, 648, 658.

335 Fluidity

N. *fluidity*, fluidness, liquidity, liquidness; fluxure, fluxility; wateriness, rheuminess 339 n. *water*; juiciness, sappiness 356 n. *pulpiness*; non-viscosity, non-coagula-

tion, hæmophilia; solubility, solubleness, fluxibility, liquidescence 337 n. *liquefaction*; gaseous character 336 n. *gaseity*; bloodiness, goriness 354 n. *semiliquidity*; hydrology, hydrometry, hydrostatics, hydrodynamics; hydraulics, hydrokinetics.

fluid, elastic f. 336 n. *gas*; non-elastic fluid, liquid; water, running w. 339 n. *water*; drink 301 n. *liquor*; milk, whey, ghee, buttermilk; juice, sap, latex; humour, chyle, rheum, mucus, saliva 302 n. *excrement*; serum, serosity, lymph, plasma; ichor, pus, sanies; gore (see *blood*); sauce, gravy, meat juice, gippo, gruel 301 n. *soup*; hydrocele, dropsy 651 n. *disease*.

blood, ichor, claret; life-blood 360 n. *life*; blood-stream, circulation; red blood 372 n. *male*; blue blood 868 n. *nobility*; gore, cruor, sanies, grume; clot, blood c., thrombosis 324 n. *solid body*; hæmad, corpuscle, red c., white c., platelet; lymph, plasma, serum, blood s., serosity; serolin; cruorin, hæmoglobin, hæmatoglobulin; hæmatogenesis, hæmatosis, sanguification; blood group; blood-count; hæmatoscopy, hæmatoscope, hæmometer; hæmatics, hæmatology.

Adj. *fluidal*, fluidic, fluid 244 adj. *amorphous*; liquid, liquiform, not solid, not gaseous; not congealing, uncongealed; fluxible, fluxive, apt to flow; unclotted, clear, clarified; soluble, liquescent, melting 337 adj. *liquefied*; fluent, running 350 adj. *flowing*; runny, rheumy, phlegmy 339 adj. *watery*; succulent, juicy, sappy, squashy 327 adj. *soft*; plasmatic, lymphatic, serous; sanious, ichorous, gory; pussy, mattery, suppurating 653 adj. *toxic*; hydrostatic, hydrodynamic.

sanguineous, hæmic, hæmal, hæmogenic; serous, lymphatic, plasmatic; bloody, sanguinary 431 adj. *bloodshot*; gory, sanious, ichorous; bleeding, hæmophilic.

See: 244, 301, 302, 324, 327, 336, 337, 339, 350, 354, 356, 360, 372, 431, 651, 653, 868.

336 Gaseity

N. *gaseity*, gaseousness, vaporousness etc. adj.; windiness, flatulence, flatulency 352 n. *wind*; aeration, gasification; volatility 338 n. *vaporization*; pneumatostatics;

aerostatics, aerodynamics 340 n. *pneumatics*.

gas, vapour, elastic fluid; ether 340 n. *air*; effluvium, exhalation, miasma 298 n. *egress*; flatus 352 n. *wind*; fume, reek, smoke; steam, water vapour 355 n. *cloud*; laughing gas, coal g.; marsh gas, poison g., mustard g. 659 n. *poison*; damp, afterd., black d., choke d., fire d.; heavy hydrogen, deuterium; air-bladder, inner tube 194 n. *bladder*; balloon, gas-b., air-b. 276 n. *airship*; gasworks, gas plant, gasification p. 687 n. *workshop*; gas-holder, gasometer 632 n. *storage*; gaselier 420 n. *lamp*; gas-meter, gasoscope 465 n. *meter*.

Adj. *gaseous*, gasiform; vaporous, steamy, volatile, evaporable 338 adj. *vaporific*; aerial, airy, aeriform, ethereal 340 adj. *airy*; gassy, windy, flatulent; effluvial, miasmic 659 adj. *baneful*; pneumatic, aerostatic, aerodynamic.

Vb. *gasify*, aerate 340 vb. *aerify*; vapour, steam, emit vapour 338 vb. *vaporize*; let off steam, blow off s. 300 vb. *emit*; turn on the gas; combine with gas, oxygenate, hydrogenate, hydrogenize.

See: 194, 276, 298, 300, 338, 340, 352, 355, 420, 465, 632, 659, 687.

337 Liquefaction

N. *liquefaction*, liquidization; liquescence; solubility, deliquation, liquescency, deliquescence, fluxibility; fluidification 335 n. *fluidity*; fusion, colliquation, colliquefaction 43 n. *mixture*; lixiviation, dissolution; thaw, melting, unfreezing 381 n. *heating*; solvent, dissolvent, flux, diluent, menstruum, alkahest, aqua fortis; liquefier, liquefacient; anticoagulant 658 n. *antidote*.

solution, decoction, infusion, apozem; flux, lixivium, lye.

Adj. *liquefied*, molten; runny, liquescent, uncongealed, deliquescent; liquefacient, colliquative, solvent; soluble, dissoluble, liquefiable, fluxible 335 adj. *fluidal*.

Vb. *liquefy*, liquidize, render liquid, unclot, clarify 350 adj. *make flow*; liquate, dissolve, resolve, deliquesce, run 350 n. *flow*; unfreeze, melt, thaw 381 vb. *heat*; melt down, fuse, render, clarify; leach, lixiviate; hold in solution; cast, found.

See: 43, 335, 350, 381, 658.

338 Vaporization

N. *vaporization*, atomization; exhalation 355 n. *cloud*; gasification, aerification; evaporation, volatilization, distillation, cohobation, sublimation; steaming, fumigation, vaporability, volatility.

vaporizer, evaporater; atomizer, spray, fine s.; retort, still, distillery, vaporimeter, atmometer.

Adj. *vaporific*, volatilized etc. vb.; reeking; vapouring, steaming etc. vb.; vaporous, vapoury, vapourish; steamy, gassy, smoky; evaporable, vaporable, vaporizable, volatile.

Vb. *vaporize*, evaporate; render vaporous, render gaseous; aerify 336 adj. *gasify*; volatilize, distil, sublime, sublimate, exhale, transpire, emit vapour, blow off steam 300 vb. *emit*; smoke, fume, reek, steam; fumigate, spray; make a spray, atomize.

See: 300, 336, 355.

339 Water

N. *water*, H_2O; heavy water D_2O; hard water, soft w.; drinking water, tap w., mineral w., soda w. 301 n. *soft drink*; water vapour, steam 355 n. *cloud*; rain water 350 n. *rain*; spring water, running w. 350 n. *stream*; holy water 988 n. *ritual object*; eye-water, tear 836 n. *lamentation*; high water, high tide, spring t., neap t., low water 350 n. *wave*; standing water, still w. 346 n. *lake*; sea water, salt w., brine, briny, blue water 343 n. *ocean*; soap and water, bath water, lotion, douche, splash, ablution, balneation, bath 648 n. *cleansing*; lavender water, scent 843 n. *cosmetic*; diluent, adulteration, dilution 655 n. *impairment*; wateriness, damp, wet; watering, spargefaction 341 n. *moistening*; water-carrier, bheestee; water-cart, watering-cart, water jug, ewer 194 n. *vessel*; tap, standpipe, hydrant 351 n. *conduit*; waterer, hose 341 n. *irrigator*; hydrometry 341 n. *hygrometry*.

Adj. *watery*, aqueous, aquatic, lymphatic; hydro-, hydrated, hydrous; hydrological, hydrographic 321 adj. *geographic*; adulterated, diluted 163 adj. *weak*; still, noneffervescent; fizzy, effervescent; wet, moist, drenching 341 adj. *humid*; balneal

648 adj. *cleansing*; hydrotherapeutic 658 adj. *medical*; sudorific, hydrotic, hydragogue.

Vb. *add water*, water, water down, adulterate, dilute 163 vb. *weaken*; steep, soak, liquor; irrigate, drench 341 vb. *moisten*; combine with water, hydrate; slack, slake 51 vb. *decompose*.

See: 51, 163, 194, 301, 321, 341, 343, 346, 350, 351, 355, 648, 655, 658, 836, 843, 988.

340 Air

N. *air*, 336 n. *gas*; thin air 325 n. *rarity*; cushion of air, air-pocket 190 n. *emptiness*; blast 352 n. *wind*; common air, oxygen, nitrogen, neon, argon, ozone; welkin, blue, blue sky 355 n. *cloud*; open air, open, out-of-doors, exposure 183 n. *space*; airing 342 n. *desiccation*; aeration 338 n. *vaporization*; ventilation, fanning 685 n. *refreshment*; air-conditioning, air-cooling 382 n. *refrigeration*; ventilator, blower, fan, air-conditioner 384 n. *refrigerator*; air-filter 648 n. *cleanser*.

atmosphere, aerosphere; Heaviside Layer, Kennelly-Heaviside L.; radiation layer, Van Allen belt 207 n. *layer*; ionosphere, troposphere, tropopause, stratosphere; isothermal layer.

weather, the elements; fair weather, calm w., halcyon days; windless weather, doldrums; atmospheric pressure, anticyclone, high pressure; cyclone, low pressure; rough weather 176 n. *storm*; bad weather, foul w., wet w.; changeable weather, rise and fall of the barometer; meteorology, aeroscopy, aeromancy, weather forecast 511 n. *prediction*; isobar, decibar, millibar; glass, mercury, barometer; weather-ship; barograph, weather glass, weather gauge; vane, weather-v., weathercock; hygrometer, weather-house; weather-prophet, weather-man; meteorologist; climate, climatology, climatography; climatologist.

pneumatics, aerodynamics, aerography, aeroscopy, aerology, barometry, anemometry 352 n. *anemology*; aerometer, baroscope, barometer, aneroid b., barograph, barogram; vane, weather-vane, weathercock.

Adj. *airy*, ethereal 4 adj. *insubstantial*; skyey; aerial, aeriform; pneumatic, aeriferous, containing air, aerated; inflated, blown up, flatulent 197 adj. *expanded*; effervescent, oxygenated 355 adj. *bubbly*; breezy, 352 adj. *windy*; well-ventilated, fresh, air-conditioned 382 adj. *cooled*; meteorological, weather-wise; atmospheric, baric, barometric; cyclonic, anticyclonic; high-pressure 324 n. *dense*, low-pressure 325 adj. *rare*; climatic, climatological.

Vb. *aerify*, aerate, oxygenate; air, expose 342 vb. *dry*; ventilate, freshen, deodorize 648 vb. *clean*; fan, winnow, make a draught 352 vb. *blow*; take an airing 352 vb. *breathe*.

Adv. *alfresco*, out of doors, in the open air, in the open, under the open sky, in the sun.

See: 4, 176, 183, 190, 197, 207, 324, 325, 336, 338, 342, 352, 355, 382, 384, 511, 648, 685.

341 Moisture

N. *moisture*, humidity, sap, juice 335 n. *fluid*; dampness, wetness, moistness; dewiness; dankishness, dankness; sogginess, swampiness, marshiness; saturation, saturation point 863 n. *satiety*; leakiness 298 n. *outflow*; pluviosity, raininess, showeriness; rainfall, high r., wet weather; damp, dank, wet; spray, spindrift, froth, foam 355 n. *bubble*; mist, fog, fog bank 355 n. *cloud*; scotch mist, drizzle 350 n. *rain*; drip, dew, night-d., morning-d.; drop, rain-d., dew-d., tear-d.; wet eyes, tears 836 n. *lamentation*; saliva, salivation, slabber, slobber, spit, spittle 302 n. *excrement*; ooze, slime, mud, squelch, fen 347 n. *marsh*; soaked object, sop.

moistening, madefaction, humidification; humectation, bedewing, rorification; damping, wetting, drenching, soaking; saturation, deluge 350 n. *rain*; spargefaction, sprinkling, sprinkle, asperge, aspersion, ducking, submersion, total immersion 303 n. *immersion*; overflow, flood, inundation 350 n. *waterfall*; lotion, balneation, wash, bath 648 n. *ablution*; baptism 988 n. *Christian rite*; infiltration, percolation, leaching; irrigation, watering, spraying, hosing; injection; gargle; hydrotherapy 658 n. *therapy*.

irrigator, sprinkler, aspergillum; waterer, watering-cart; watering-pot, watering-can; spray, rose; hose, garden h., syringe, water-pistol, squirt, squirt-gun; pump, fire-engine; Persian wheel, shadoof, swipe; cistern, dam, reservoir 632 n. *store*; sluice, water-pipe 351 n. *conduit*.

hygrometry, hydrography, hydrology; hygrometer, udometer, rain-gauge, pluviometer, nilometer; hygroscope, weather-house.

Adj. *humid*, moistened; moistening, humective, humectant; wet 339 adj. *watery*; pluvious, pluvial; drizzling, drizzly 350 adj. *rainy*; undried, damp, moist, dripping; dank, muggy, foggy, misty 355 adj. *cloudy*; undrained, oozy, muddy, slimy, slushy, squashy, squelchy, fenny 347 adj. *marshy*; dewy, fresh, bedewed, roric, roscid, roriferous; juicy, sappy 335 adj. *fluidal*; dribbling, drip-dropping, seeping, percolating; wetted, steeped, sprinkled; dabbled; gory, bloody 335 adj. *sanguineous*.

drenched, saturated, irriguous, irrigated; soaking, sopping, slopping, streaming, reeking; sodden, soaked, deluged; wet through, wet to the skin, wringing wet; weltering, wallowing, waterlogged, awash, swamped, drowned.

Vb. *be wet*, —moist etc. adj.; be soggy, squelch, suck; slobber, salivate, sweat, perspire 298 vb. *exude*; steam, reek 300 vb. *emit*; percolate, seep 297 vb. *infiltrate*; weep, bleed, stream; ooze, drip, leak 298 vb. *flow out*; trickle, drizzle, rain, pour, come down cats and dogs 350 n. *rain*; get wet, — drenched etc. adj.; not have a dry thread; dip, duck, dive 313 vb. *plunge*; bathe, wash; paddle, wade, ford; wallow, welter.

moisten, humidify, humectate, humect; wet, dampen; dilute, hydrate 339 vb. *add water*; lick, lap, wash; splash, swash; spill, slop 311 vb. *let fall*; flood, spray, syringe, sprinkle, besprinkle; sparge, asperse, asperge; bedew, bedabble, dabble; baste, affuse 303 vb. *infuse*; gargle.

drench, saturate, imbrue, imbue; soak, deluge, wet through, make run with; leach, lixiviate; wash, lave, bathe; sluice, sloosh, rinse 648 vb. *clean*; baptize 988 vb. *perform ritual*; plunge, dip, duck, submerge, drown 303 vb. *immerse*; swamp whelm, flood, inundate, flood out,

waterlog; douse, souse, steep; macerate, steep; pickle, brine 666 vb. *preserve.*

irrigate, water, supply w., hose, pump; inundate, flood, overflow, submerge; percolate 297 vb. *infiltrate*; syringe, gargle; squirt, inject.

See: 297, 298, 300, 302, 303, 311, 313, 335, 339, 347, 350, 351, 355, 632, 648, 658, 666, 836, 863, 988.

342 Dryness

N. *dryness*, siccity, aridity; need for water, thirst 859 n. *hunger*; drought, drouth, low rainfall, rainlessness, desert conditions; sandiness, sands 172 n. *desert*; dry climate, sunny South; sun, sunniness 379 n. *heat.*

desiccation, exsiccation, arefaction; drying, drying up; airing, evaporation 338 n. *vaporization*; draining, drainage; dehydration, dephlegmation; insolation, aprication, sunning 381 n. *heating*; bleaching, fading, withering, searing 426 n. *achromatism*; blotting, mopping 648 n. *cleansing.*

drier, desiccator, evaporator; siccative, sand, blotting paper, blotter, blotting; absorbent, absorbent material; mop, swab, swabber, sponge, towel, towelling 648 n. *cleanser*; dehydrator, drying machine, hair-dryer; wringer, mangle 198 n. *compressor.*

Adj. *dry*, needing water, thirsty, drouthy 859 adj. *hungry*; unirrigated, irrigable; arid, rainless, waterless, riverless; sandy, dusty 332 adj. *powdery*; bare, brown, grassless; desert, Saharan; anhydrous, dehydrated, desiccated; shrivelled, withered, sere, faded 426 adj. *colourless*; dried up, sapless, juiceless, mummified, parchmentlike; sunned, insolated; aired; sundried, wind-d., bleached; burnt, scorched, baked, parched 379 adj. *hot*; free from rain, sunny, fine, cloudless, fair; freed from wet, dried out, drained, evaporated; squeezed dry, mangled; protected from wet, waterproofed, waterproof, rainproof, damp-p., watertight, tight, snug, proof; unwetted, unmoistened, dry-footed, dry-shod; out of water, high and dry; dry as a bone, dry as a stick, dry as a biscuit, dry as a mummy; dry as dust 838

adj. *tedious*; adapted to drought, xerophilous; non-greasy, non-skid, skidproof; unsweetened 393 adj. *sour.*

Vb. *be dry*, — thirsty etc.adj.; keep dry, wear a mackintosh, hold off the wet, keep watertight; dry up, evaporate 338 vb. *vaporize*; become dry, dry off.

dry, dehumidify, desiccate; dehydrate, anhydrate; ditch, drain; wring out, mangle, hang on the clothes line, hang out, peg o., air, evaporate 338 vb. *vaporize*; sun, expose to sunlight, insolate, apricate, sun-dry; smoke, kipper, cure; parch, scorch, bake, burn 381 vb. *heat*; sere, shrivel, bleach; mummify 666 vb. *preserve*; dry up, stop the flow 350 vb. *stanch*; blot, blot up, mop, mop up, soak up, sponge 299 vb. *absorb*; swab, wipe, wipe up, wipe dry 648 vb. *clean.*

See: 172, 198, 299, 332, 338, 350, 379, 381, 393, 426, 648, 666, 838, 859.

343 Ocean

N. *ocean*, sea, blue water, salt w., brine, briny; waters, billows, waves, tide 350 n. *wave*; Davy Jones's locker; main, deep, deep sea; high seas, great waters; trackless deep, watery waste, kala pani; herring pond, big drink; sea-lane, steamer track; sea floor, sea bottom, ooze, benthos; the seven seas; Atlantic, Pacific, Antarctic Ocean, Red Sea, Yellow S., White S., Sargasso S.; prehistoric sea or ocean, Tethys.

sea-god, Oceanus, Neptune, Varuna, Triton, Amphitrite, Tethys; old man of the sea, merman.

sea-nymph, Oceanid, Naiad, Nereid, siren; Calypso, Undine; mermaid; bathingbeauty; water-sprite 970 *fairy.*

oceanography, hydrography, bathymetry; sea-survey, Admiralty chart; bathysphere, bathyscaph, bathymeter; oceanographer, hydrographer.

Adj. *oceanic*, thalassic, pelagic, pelagian; sea, marine, maritime; ocean-going, seag., seaworthy 269 adj. *seafaring*; submarine, undersea, underwater; benthic, benthonic; hydrographic, bathymetric.

Adv. *at sea*, on the sea, on the high seas; afloat.

See: 269, 350, 970.

344 Land

N. *land,* dry l., terra firma; earth, ground, crust, earth's c. 321 n. *world;* continent, mainland; heart-land, hinterland; midland, inland, interior 224 n. *interiority;* peninsular, delta, promontory, tongue of land 254 n. *projection;* isthmus, neck of land, land-bridge; terrain, heights, highlands 209 n. *high land;* lowlands 210 n. *lowness;* steppe, fields 348 n. *plain;* wilderness 172 n. *desert;* oasis, Fertile Crescent; isle 349 n. *island;* zone, clime; country, district, tract 184 n. *region;* territory, possessions, acres, estate, real e. 777 n. *lands;* physical features, stratigraphy, geology 321 n. *geography;* landsman, landlubber, continental, mainlander, islander, isthmian 191 n. *dweller.*

shore, coast-line 233 n. *outline;* coast, rock c., iron-bound c. 234 n. *edge;* strand, beach, sands, shingle; sea-beach, sea-board, seashore, seaside; sea-cliff, sea-bank; plage, lido, riviera; bank, river-bank, river-side, lea, water-meadow; submerged coast, continental shelf.

soil, glebe, farmland, arable land 370 n. *farm;* pasture 348 n. *grassland;* deposit, æolian d., moraine, geest, silt, alluvium, alluvion, loess; topsoil, sand, dust, under-soil, subsoil; mould, leaf m., humus; loam, clay, bole, marl; cledge, Fuller's earth; argil, potter's clay, China clay, kaolin 381 n. *pottery;* flinty soil, gravel, chalk, limestone; stone, pebble, flint; turf, divot, sod, clod 53 n. *piece.*

rock, cliff, scar, crag; stone, boulder; submerged rock, reef, skerry; igneous rock; granite, hypabyssal rock, abyssal r., volcanic r.; lava, lapilli, tuff; volcanic glass, obsidian; sedimentary rock, bedded r., sandstone, shale, limestone, chalk, calcite; metamorphic rock, conglomerate, schist, marble; massive rock; mineral rock.

Adj. *territorial,* landed, predial, farming, agricultural 370 adj. *agrarian;* terrigenous, terrene 321 adj. *telluric;* earthy, alluvial, silty; loamy, humic, clayey, marly, chalky; flinty, pebbly, gravelly, stony, lithic, rocky; granitic, marble, metamorphic; slaty, shaly, skerry.

coastal, coasting; littoral, riparian, ripuarian, riverine, riverside, seaside; shore, on-shore.

inland, continental, midland, highland, interior, central.

Adv. *on land,* on dry l., by l., overland, ashore, on shore; between the tide-marks.

See: 53, 172, 184, 191, 209, 210, 224, 233, 234, 254, 321, 348, 349, 370, 381, 777.

345 Gulf: inlet

N. *gulf,* bay, bight, cove, creek, lagoon; natural harbour, road, roadstead; inlet, outlet, bayou; indraught, arm of the sea, fiord; mouth, estuary 263 n. *orifice;* firth, frith, kyle; sound, strait, belt, gut, euripus, channel.

See: 263.

346 Lake.

N. *lake,* mere, lagoon, land-locked water; loch, lough, linn; fresh-water lake, salt l.; inland sea, Dead Sea; ox-bow lake, bayou; broad, broads; standing water, dead w., sheet of w.; mud flat, wash 347 n. *marsh;* pool, tarn, pond, dew-p.; fish-pond, fish-pool, piscina, aquarium; swimming pool, swimming bath; millpond, millpool, mill-race, milldam; artificial lake, dam, reservoir 632 n. *storage;* well, artesian w.; basin, tank, cistern, sump, cesspool, sewer 649 n. *sink;* ditch, irrigation d., dike 351 n. *drain;* water-hole, puddle, sough, splash, wallow; Irish bridge.

Adj. *lacustrine,* lake-dwelling, land-locked.

See: 347, 351, 632, 649.

347 Marsh

N. *marsh,* marish; marshland, slobland; fen, moorland, moor; everglade, jheel, wash; flat, mud f., salt f., salt-marsh, salt pan, salina; morass, slough, swamp, bog, moss, quagmire, quicksand; bottom, undrained basin, playa; wallow, hog-wallow, sough; thaw, slush, squash, mire, mud, ooze; forest swamp, taiga, Serbonian bog; Slough of Despond.

Adj. *marshy,* paludine, paludial; moorish, moory; swampy, boggy, fenny; oozy, quaggy, poachy; squashy, squelchy, spongy 327 adj. *soft;* slushy 354 adj.

semiliquid; muddy, miry, slabby 649 adj. *dirty*; undrained, waterlogged, uliginous 341 adj. *drenched*; growing in swamps, uliginal.

See: 327, 341, 354, 649.

348 Plain

N. *plain*, peneplane; dene, dale, basin, lowlands 255 n. *valley*; flats 347 n. *marsh*; delta, alluvial plain, landes; sands, desert s., waste, wild 172 n. *desert*; tundra, ling t.; ice-plain, ice-field, ice-floe 380 n. *ice*; grasslands, steppe, prairie, savanna, pampas, llanos, campos; heath, common, wold, weald; moor, moorland, fell; upland, plateau, tableland, mesa, paramo; bush, veld, High V., Middle V., Low V., Bush V.; range, open country, rolling c., champaign, campagna; fields, green belt, lung, parkland, national park 263 n. *open space*; fairway, green 216 n. *horizontality*; lowlands, low countries 210 n. *lowness*.

grassland, pasture, pasturage, grazing 369 n. *animal husbandry*; sheep-run, sheep-walk; field, meadow, water-m., mead, lea; chase, park, grounds; green, greensward, sward, lawn, turf, sod; plot, plat, grass-p. 370 n. *garden*.

Adj. *champaign*, campestrian, campestral; flat, open, steppe-like, rolling.

See: 172, 216, 255, 263, 347, 369, 370, 380.

349 Island

N. *island*, isle, islet; river-island, eyot, ait, holm; lagoon-island, atoll, reef, coral r.; cay, key; sandbank, bar; floating island, iceberg; 'all-but island', peninsula; island continent; island universe, galaxy 321 n. *star*; archipelago; insularity, insulation 883 n. *seclusion*; insular, islander, islesman 191 n. *dweller*.

Adj. *insular*, circumfluous, sea-girt; islanded, isolated, marooned; isleted, archipelagian, archipelagic.

See: 191, 321, 883.

350 Stream: water in motion

N. *stream*, running water, river, subterranean r.; navigable river, waterway; tributary, branch, feeder, affluent, effluent, distributary; reach; watercourse, streamlet, rivulet, creek, brook, brooklet, bourne, burn, gipsy, beck, rill, rillet, gill, runnel, runlet; fresh, freshet, torrent, mountain t., force; sike, arroyo, wadi; spring, fountain, fount, fountain-head 156 n. *source*; jet, spout, gush; gusher, geyser, hot spring, well 632 n. *store*.

current, flow, set; flux, defluxion; profluence 285 n. *progression*; effluence 298 n. *egress*; confluence, corrivation 293 n. *convergence*; indraught, inflow 297 n. *ingress*; outflow, reflux 286 n. *regression*; undercurrent, undertow, cross-current, rip tide 182 n. *counteraction*; tide, spring t., neap t.; tidal flow, tidal current, ebb and flow, tidal rise and fall 317 n. *fluctuation*; tideway, bore, eagre; race, tidal r., mill-r., mill-stream; tap, standpipe, hydrant 351 n. *conduit*; blood-stream, circulation 314 n. *circuition*.

eddy, whirlpool, swirl, maelstrom, charybdis 315 n. *vortex*; surge, gurge, regurgitation, reflux 290 n. *recession*; wash, backwash, wake 67 n. *sequel*.

waterfall, cataract, catadupe, niagara; cascade, force, overfall, rapids, watershoot, weir, nappe; flush, chute, spillway, sluice; overflow, spill; flood, inundation, cataclysm 341 n. *moistening*, 298 n. *outflow*.

wave, bow-w.; wash, backwash; ripple, cat's-paw 262 n. *furrow*; swell, ground s. 197 n. *expansion*; billow, roller, comber, beach-c.; breaker, surf, white horses, white caps; tidal wave, tsunami 176 n. *storm*; bore, eagre; rip, overfall; broken water, choppiness 259 n. *roughness*; sea, choppy s., cross s., long s., short s., heavy s., angry s; waviness, undulation.

rain, rainfall 341 n. *moisture*; precipitation; drizzle, mizzle; shower, downpour, drencher, soaker, cloud-burst; flurry 352 n. *gale*; pouring rain, teaming r., drenching r., drowning r.; raininess, wet spell, foul weather; rainy season, the rains, monsoon; predominance of Aquarius, reign of St. Swithin; plash, patter; dropping, dripping etc. vb.; hyetography; rain-gauge 341 n. *hygrometry*.

Adj. *flowing* etc. vb.; fluxive, fluid, runny 335 adj. *fluidal*; fluent, profluent, affluent, diffluent; streamy, fluvial, fluviatile, tidal; making, running, coursing, racing; streaming; in flood, in spate; flooding,

inundatory, cataclysmic; surging, rolling, rippling, purling, eddying; popply, choppy 259 adj. *rough*; winding, meandering, meandrous 251 adj. *labyrinthine*; oozy, sluggish 278 adj. *slow*; pouring, sheeting, dripping, dropping, stillicidous; gushing, spirting, spouting 298 adj. *outgoing*; inflowing 297 adj. *incoming*.
rainy, showery, drizzly, spitting, spotting; wet 341 adj. *humid*; monsoonish.
Vb. *flow*, run, course; set, make; ebb, regurgitate 286 vb. *regress*; swirl, eddy 315 vb. *rotate*; surge, break, dash, ripple, popple, wrinkle; roll, swell; buck, bounce 312 vb. *leap*; gush, rush, spirt, spout, jet, play, squirt, splutter; well, well up, issue 298 vb. *emerge*; pour, stream; trickle, dribble 298 vb. *exude*; drip, drop 309 vb. *descend*; plash, lap, wash, swash, splash 341 vb. *moisten*; flow softly, purl, trill, murmur, babble, bubble, burble, gurgle, guggle; flow over, overflow, flood, inundate, deluge 341 vb. *drench*; flow into, fall i., drain i., empty i., spill i., leak i., distil i. 297 vb. *enter*; open, disembogue, discharge itself 298 vb. *flow out*; flow through, leak, percolate 305 vb. *pass*; ooze, wind 251 vb. *meander*.
rain, shower, stream, pour, pelt; come down, rain hard, pour with rain, rain in torrents, rain cats and dogs, rain pitchforks; sheet, come down in sheets, come down in buckets; patter, drizzle, mizzle, drip, drop, spit, sprinkle; be wet, rain and rain, set in.
make flow, cause to f., make a current, send out a stream; make *or* pass water 302 vb. *excrete*; pump 300 vb. *eject*; broach, tap, turn on the t., open the cocks, open the sluice gates 263 vb. *open*; pour, pour out, spill 311 vb. *let fall*; transfuse, decant 272 vb. *transpose*; empty, drain out 300 vb. *void*; water 341 vb. *irrigate*; unclot, clear, clarify, melt 337 vb. *liquefy*.
stanch, stop the flow, stem the course 342 vb. *dry*; apply a tourniquet, compress 198 vb. *make smaller*; stop a leak, plug 264 vb. *close*; obstruct the flow, stem, dam, dam up 702 vb. *obstruct*.
See: 67, 156, 176, 182, 197, 198, 251, 259, 262, 263, 264, 272, 278, 285, 286, 290, 293, 297, 298, 300, 302, 305, 309, 311, 312, 314, 315, 317, 335, 337, 341, 342, 351, 352, 632, 702.

351 Conduit

N. *conduit*, water channel, tideway, river-bed, alveus; arroyo, wadi; trough, basin, river-b. 194 n. *receptacle*; canyon, ravine, gorge, barranca, gully 255 n. *valley*; ditch, dyke, nullah; trench, moat, watercourse, canal, channel, gutter, runnel, runner; duct, aqueduct; plumbing, water-pipe, main, water m.; pipe, hose-p., hose; standpipe, hydrant, siphon, tap, spout, waterspout, gargoyle, funnel 263 n. *tube*; valve, penstock; sluice, weir, lock, floodgate, watergate, spillway; oil-pipe, pipeline, Pluto 272 n. *transferrer*; gullet, throat 194 n. *maw*; neck (of a bottle); blood vessel, vein, artery, aorta, jugular vein; veinlet, capillary 208 n. *filament*.
drain, kennel, gutter, pantile; gargoyle, waterspout; scupper, overflow, piscina, waste-pipe, drain-p.; ajutage, efflux-tube; covered drain, culvert; open drain, ditch, sewer, sough 649 n. *sink*; emunctory, intestine, colon, alimentary canal 224 n. *insides*; clyster, catheter, enema-can 302 n. *excretion*.

See: 194, 208, 224, 255, 263, 272, 302, 649.

352 Wind: air in motion

N. *wind* 340 n. *air*; draught, downdraught, updraught; windiness etc. adj.; blowiness, gustiness, breeziness, squalliness, storminess, weather; flatus, afflatus; blast, blow (see *breeze, gale*); current, air-c., cross-c. 350 n. *current*; headwind 182 n. *counteraction*; tailwind, following wind 287 n. *propellant*; air-stream, slip-s.; air pocket; windlessness, calm air 266 n. *quietude*; cold draught, cold wind, icy blast; hot wind, sirocco, leveche, khamsin, haramattan, lu, samun; seasonal wind, monsoon, etesian winds, meltemi; regular wind, prevailing w., trade w., antitrades, Brave West Winds, Roaring Forties; north wind, Boreas, bise, mistral, tramontano; south wind, föhn, chinook; east wind, Eurus, levanter; west wind, Zephyr, Favonius; wind god, Æolus, cave of Æolus.
anemology, aerodynamics, anemography 340 n. *pneumatics*; wind-rose, Beaufort scale; anemometer, wind-gauge, weathercock, weather-vane, wind-sock, windcone; wind-tunnel.

breeze, zephyr, light air; breath, **breath of** air, waft, whiff, puff, gust, capful of wind; light breeze, gentle b., stiff b.; sea-breeze, cooling b., doctor.

gale, half g., fresh wind, strong w., high w., violent w., howling w.; blow, hard b., blast, gust, flurry, flaw; squall, thick s., black s., white s.; storm-wind, buster, northwester, sou'wester, hurricane; whirl-wind, whirlblast; cyclone, tornado, typhoon, simoom 315n. *vortex*; thunder-storm, windstorm, dust-storm, dust-devil, blizzard 176n. *storm*; weather, dirty w., ugly w., stormy w., windy w., stress of w; gale force.

sufflation, insufflation, perflation; inflation 197n. *dilation*; blowing up, pumping, pumping up; pumping out, exhaustion 300n. *voidance*; pump, air-p., stirrup-p., bicycle-p.; bellows, windbag, bagpipe; blow-pipe; exhaust-pipe, exhaust 298n. *outlet*.

ventilation, airing 340n. *air*; cross-ventila-tion, draught; fanning, cooling; venti-duct, ventilator; blower, fan, electric f., punkah, pull-p., chowrie, thermantidote, air-conditioner 384n. *refrigerator*.

respiration, breathing, breathing in, breath-ing out, inhalation, exhalation, expira-tion, inspiration; stomach wind, windi-ness, ventosity, eructation, belch; lungs, bellows, iron lung, oxygen tent; windpipe 353n. *air-pipe*; sneezing, sternutation 406 n. *sibilation*; coughing, cough, whooping c., croup, strangles; sigh, sob, gulp, hiccup, catching of the breath; hard breathing, panting; wheeze, rattle, death r.

Adj. *windy*, airy, exposed, draughty, blowy; ventilated, fresh; blowing, breezy, puffy, gusty, squally; blusterous, blustery, blasty, dirty, foul, stormy, tempestuous, boister-ous 176adj. *violent*; windswept, wind-blown; storm-tossed, storm-bound; flatu-lent, ventose; fizzy, gassy, æolian, favon-ian, boreal, zephyrous; monsoonish, cyclonic.

puffing, huffing; snorting, wheezing; wheezy, asthmatic, stertorous, panting, heaving; breathless 318adj. *agitated*; sniffy, snuffly, sneezy; pulmonic, pulmonary, pulmon-ate; coughy, chesty.

Vb. *blow*, puff, breeze, blast; freshen, blow hard, blow great guns, blow a hurricane, rage, storm 176vb. *be violent*; howl, roar,

bellow 409vb. *ululate*; screech, **scream,** whistle, pipe, sing in the shrouds 407vb. *shrill*; hum, moan, mutter, sough, sigh 401vb. *sound faint*; stream in the air, wave, flap, shake, flutter 318vb. *agitate*; draw, make a draught, ventilate, fan 382 vb. *refrigerate*; blow along, waft 287vb. *propel*; veer, back 282vb. *deviate*.

breathe, respire, breathe in, inhale, draw; breathe out, exhale; aspirate, puff, huff, whiff, whiffle; sniff, sniffle, snuffle, snort; breathe hard, breathe heavily, sough, gasp, pant, heave; wheeze, sneeze, cough 407vb. *rasp*; sigh, sob, gulp, suck one's breath, catch the b., hiccup; belch, burp 300vb. *eruct*.

sufflate, inflate, perflate, dilate; blow up, pump up 197vb. *enlarge*; pump out, exhaust 300vb. *void*.

See: 176, 182, 197, 266, 282, 287, 298, 300, 315, 318, 340, 350, 353, 382, 384, 401, 406, 407, 409.

353 Air-pipe

N. *air-pipe*, air-shaft, air-way; air-passage, wind-way, wind-tunnel; air-tube, blow-pipe; pea-shooter 287n. *shooter*; wind-pipe, trachea, larynx; weasand, bronchia, bronchus; throat, gullet; nose, nostril, spiracle, blow-hole, nozzle, vent, mouth-piece 263 n. *orifice*; mouth-pipe, flue-p. 414n. *organ*; gas-main, gas-pipe; tobacco pipe, pipe, briar, hookah 388n. *tobacco*; funnel, smoke-stack, flue, chimney-pot, chimney-stack 263n. *chimney*; ventiduct, air-duct, ventilator; air-hole, smoke-duct 263n. *window*; jalousie, venetian blind, grating.

See: 263, 287, 388, 414.

354 Semiliquidity

N. *semiliquidity*, stodginess, spissitude, crassitude 324n. *density*; mucosity, vis-cidity; lentor, clamminess, ropiness, colloidality; semiliquid, colloid, emul-sion, emulsoid, albumen, mucus, mucil-age, phlegm, pituita, clot, grume, gore 324 n. *solid body*; pus, matter; juice, sap 356n. *pulpiness*; soup, gumbo, gravy, pudding, cornflour, cream, curds, junket, pap, mush, mash; mud, slush, squash,

thaw, ooze, slime, slob; sullage, silt 347 n, *marsh*; sediment, grounds 649 n. *dirt*; molten lava 381 n. *ash.*

thickening, inspissation, incrassation, co- agulation, curding, clotting 324 n. *con- densation*; gelation, gelefaction; emulsi- fication; thickener, starch, flour, rennet, curdler; gelatin, isinglass, pepsin.

viscidity, glutinosity, glueyness, gummi- ness, gummosity, stickiness, treacliness, slabbiness, adhesiveness 48 n. *coherence*; glue, gluten, gum, mastic, wax, beeswax 47 n. *adhesive*; emulsion, collodion, col- loid; glair, size, paste, glaze, slip; treacle, jam, syrup, honey 392 n. *sweetness.*

Adj. *semiliquid*, semifluid; stodgy, thick, soupy, lumpy, ropy 324 adj. *dense*; un- clarified, curdled, clotted, jellied, gelified, gelatinous, pulpy, juicy, sappy, milky, creamy, lactescent, lacteal, lactiferous; starchy, amylaceous; emulsive; colloidal; thawing, half-frozen, half-melted, slushy, waterlogged, muddy, mushy, slabby, squashy, squelchy 347 adj. *marshy*; slimy, silty, sedimentary. See *viscid.*

viscid, lentous, grumous, gummy, adhesive 48 adj. *cohesive*; clammy, sticky, tacky; jammy, treacly, syrupy, gluey; glairy, glaireous, glarigenous; mucous, mucoid, mucilaginous, muciferous, muciparous, mucigenous; muculent, phlegmatic, pituitous.

Vb. *thicken*, inspissate, incrassate 324 vb. *be dense*; coagulate 48 vb. *cohere*; emul- sify; collodionize; gelatinize, gelatinify, gel, jell; starch 326 n. *harden*; curdle, clot, churn, beat up, mash, pulp 332 vb. *pulverize*; muddy, puddle 649 vb. *make unclean.*

See: 47, 48, 324, 326, 332, 347, 356, 381, 392, 649.

355 Bubble. Cloud: air and water mixed

N. *bubble*, bubbles, suds, lather, foam, froth; head, top; sea-foam, spume, surf, spray, spindrift 341 n. *moisture*; yeast, barm 323 n. *leaven*; scum 649 n. *dirt*; bubbling, boiling, effervescence; ferment- ation, yeastiness, fizziness, fizz.

cloud, cloudlet, scud, rack; rain-cloud, nimbus; woolpack, cumulus, cirrus, cirro- cumulus, stratus, cirrostratus; mackerel sky, mare's tail; dirty sky; vapour, steam

338 n. *vaporization*; haze, mist, fog, smog, London special; overcast; cloudiness, film 419 n. *dimness*; nebulosity 321 n. *nebula*; nephology, nephelognosy.

Adj. *bubbly*, bubbling etc. vb.; effervescent, fizzy, sparkling; foaming, foamy; spumy, spumous, spumose; with a head on, frothy, soapy, lathery; yeasty, up, aer- ated 323 adj. *light*; scummy 649 adj. *dirty.*

cloudy, clouded, overcast, overclouded; nubiferous, nubilous, nebulous; cirrose, cirrostratous, cirrocumular; thick, foggy, hazy, misty, brumous 419 adj. *dim*; vaporous, steamy, steaming 338 adj. *vaporific*; nephological.

Vb. *bubble*, spume, foam, froth, form a head; mantle, scum; ream, cream; boil, fizzle, guggle, gurgle, 318 vb. *effervesce*; ferment, fizz, sparkle; aerate 340 vb. *aerify*; steam 338 vb. *vaporize.*

cloud, cloud over, overcast; be cloudy,— misty etc. adj.; becloud, befog, mist up 419 vb. *be dim.*

See: 318, 321, 323, 338, 340, 341, 419, 649.

356 Pulpiness

N. *pulpiness*, doughiness, sponginess; juici- ness, sappiness 327 n. *softness*; poultice, pulp, pith, paste, porridge; pudding, pap; mush, mash, squash; dough, batter, sponge, fool, mashed potato; rob, jam 354 adj. *viscidity*; mousse, guava cheese; grume, gore 354 n. *semiliquidity*; papier mâché, wood-pulp; dental pulp, pulp- canal, pulp-cavity, pulp-chamber; pulper, pulp-digester; pulping, mastication; steeping, maceration, macerator.

Adj. *pulpy*, pulpous, pulped, mashed 354 adj. *semiliquid*; mushy, pappy 327 adj. *soft*; succulent, juicy, sappy, squashy, ripe, overripe 669 adj. *mature*; flabby, dimply 195 adj. *fleshy*; doughy, pasty; macerated, steeped 341 adj. *drenched*; soggy, spongy 347 adj. *marshy.*

See: 195, 327, 341, 347, 354, 669.

357 Unctuousness

N. *unctuousness* etc. adj.; unctuosity, oili- ness, greasiness, lubricity, soapiness 334

n. *lubrication*; fattiness, pinguescence; anointment, unction.

oil, volatile o., essential o.; lubricating oil, brain o., signal o.; animal oil, whale o., cod-liver o., shark-liver o., halibut-liver o., neat's-foot o.; vegetable oil, olive o., cocoanut o., linseed o., cotton seed o., colza o., castor o., rape o., ground-nut o.; mineral oil, shale o., rock o., crystal o., coal o.; fuel oil, paraffin, kerosene, petroleum, petrol, gasoline, gas 385 n. *fuel.*

fat, animal f., adeps, adipocere, grease; blubber, tallow, spermaceti; sebum, cerin, wax; suet, lard, dripping, bacon-fat; glycerine, stearine, oleogine, olein, elain, butyrin; butter, clarified b., ghee; margarine, butterine; cream, Devon-shire c., Cornish c.; rich milk, top m.; buttermilk; soap, carbolic s.; washing soap, bath s., scented s., soap flakes 648 n. *cleanser.*

unguent, salve, unction, ointment, cerate; liniment, embrocation, lanolin; spike oil, spikenard, nard; hair-oil, macassar o., brilliantine; pomade, pomatum; cream, face-cream, hand-c. 843 n. *cosmetic.*

resin, resinoid, rosin, colophony, resinate, gum, gum arabic, tragacanth, mastic, myrrh, frankincense, camphor, labda-num; lac, amber, ambergris; pitch, tar, bitumen, asphalt; varnish, copal, megilp, shellac, lacquer, japan; synthetic resin, Bakelite.

Adj. *fatty*, pinguid, pinguescent; fat, adipose 195 adj. *fleshy*; sebaceous, cereous, waxy, waxen, cerated; lardaceous, lardy; sapon-aceous, soapy; butyric, butyraceous, buttery, creamy, milky, rich 390 adj. *savoury.*

unctuous, unguentary, greasy, oleic, oily, oleaginous; anointed, dripping with oil, basted; slippery, greased, oiled 334 adj. *lubricated.*

resinous, resiny, resinic, resiniform, resin-aceous, resiniferous; bituminous, pitchy, tarry, asphaltic; myrrhy, masticic, gum-mic, gummiferous, gummous; varnished, japanned.

Vb. *pinguefy*, fatten; oleaginize, grease, oil 334 vb. *lubricate*; baste; butter, butter up; resinify, resin, rosin.

See: 195, 334, 385, 390, 648, 843.

358 Organization

N. *organism*, organic matter, organization; organized world, organized nature, or-ganic n., living n., animized n., living beings; animal and vegetable kingdom, flora and fauna, biota; biotype, living matter, cell, protoplasm, cytoplasm, bio-plasm, bioplast, nucleoplasm; cytoblast; idioplasm, germ plasm; chromosome, chromatin; albumen, protein; organic remains, fossil.

biology, microbiology; biognosy, science of life, natural history, nature study; bio-geny, phylogeny; organic chemistry, bio-chemistry, plasmology; anatomy, phy-siology 331 n. *structure*; zoography 367 n. *zoology*; phytography 368 n. *botany*; animal economy, ecology, bionomics; genetics, biogenetics, eugenics, caco-genics; cytogenetics, cytology; embryo-logy, morphology; evolution, natural selection, survival of the fittest, vitalism; Darwinism, Lamarckism, neo-Darwin-ism; biogenist, naturalist, biologist, zoologist; evolutionist, Darwinist.

Adj. *organic*, organized, organizational; cellular, unicellular, multicellular; plasmic, protoplasmic.

biological, biogenetic; physiological, zoo-logical, palæontological; embryological; vitalistic, evolutionary, Darwinian.

See: 331, 367, 368.

359 Mineral: inorganic matter

N. *mineral*, mineral world, mineral king-dom; inorganic matter, unorganized m., inanimate m., brute m.; metal, noble m., precious m., base m.; mineralogical de-posit, coal measures 632 n. *store.*

mineralogy, geology, geognosy, geoscopy; mineralogy, lithology, petrology; oryctol-ogy, oryctography; metallurgy, metallo-graphy; speleology, glaciology.

Adj. *inorganic*, unorganized; inanimate, azoic; mineral, non-animal, non-vege-table; mineralogical; metallurgical.

See: 632.

360 Life

N. *life*, living, being alive, animate existence, being 1 n. *existence*; the living, living and

breathing world; living being, being, soul, spirit; vegetative soul 366n. *vegetability*; animal soul 365n. *animality*; living soul 371n. *mankind*; gift of life, birth, nativity 68n. *origin*; new birth, revivification 656 n. *revival*; life to come 124n. *future state*; immortal life 971n. *heaven*; imparting life, vivification, vitalization, animation; vitality, vital force, beating heart, strong pulse; hold on life, survival, cat's nine lives, longevity 113n. *diuturnity*; animal spirits, liveliness, animation 819n. *sensibility*; wind, breath, breathing 352n. *respiration*; vital air, breath of life, breath of one's nostrils; life-blood, heart's blood 335n. *blood*; vital spark, vital flame; seat of life, heart, artery, jugular vein; vital necessity, nourishment, staff of life 301n. *food*; biological function, parenthood, motherhood, fatherhood 164n. *propagation*; sex, sexual activity 45n. *coition*; living matter, germinal m., protoplasm, bioplasm, tissue, living t.; macromolecule, bioplast; cell, unicellular organism 358n. *organism*; co-operative living, symbiosis 706n. *association*; lifetime, one's born days; capacity for life, viability, viableness 469n. *possibility*.

Adj. *alive*, living, quick, live; breathing, alive and kicking; animated 819adj. *lively*; in life, incarnate, in the flesh; not dead, surviving, in the land of the living, above ground, on this side of the grave; long-lived, tenacious of life 113adj. *lasting*; capable of life, viable; vital, vivifying, Promethean; vivified, enlivened 656adj. *restored*; biotic, symbiotic, biological; protoplasmatic, protoplasmic, protoplastic, bioplastic.

born, born alive; begotten, fathered, sired; mothered, dammed; foaled, dropped; out of, by 11adj. *akin*; spawned, littered; laid, new-l., hatched 164adj. *produced*.

Vb. *live*, be alive, have life; respire, draw breath 352vb. *breathe*; exist, subsist 1n. *be*; live one's life, walk the earth, strut and fret one's hour upon the stage; come to life, come to, liven, liven up, quicken, revive 656vb. *be restored*; not die, be spared, survive 41vb. *be left*; cheat death, have nine lives; live in 192vb. *dwell*.

be born, come into the world, first see the light 68vb. *begin*; have one's nativity, be incarnated; fetch breath, draw b.; be begotten, be conceived.

vitalize, give birth to, beget, conceive, support life 164vb. *generate*; vivify, vivificate, liven, enliven, breathe life into, bring to life 174vb. *invigorate*; revitalize, put new life into, reanimate 656vb. *revive*; support life, provide a living, keep alive, keep body and soul together, keep the wolf from the door 301vb. *feed*.

See: 1, 11, 41, 45, 68, 113, 124, 164, 174, 191, 301, 335, 352, 358, 365, 366, 371, 469, 656, 706, 819, 971.

361 Death

N. *death*, no life 2n. *extinction*; process of death, dying (see *decease*); mortality, perishability, ephemerality 114n. *transientness*; martyrdom; sentence of death, doom, crack of d., knell, death-k.; death-blow, quietus 362n. *killing*; mortification, putrefaction 51n. *decay*; the beyond, the great divide, the great adventure; deathliness, rest, eternal r., long sleep 266n. *quietude*; Abraham's bosom 971n. *heaven*; the grave, Sheol 364n. *tomb*; hand of death, jaws of d., shadow of d., shades of d.; lower regions, Stygian darkness; Death, the last summoner, Angel of Death, King of D., King of Terrors, Pluto, Hades; post mortem, autopsy, necropsy, necrotomy 364n. *inquest*; mortuary, dead-house, charnel h., morgue 364n. *cemetery*.

decease, end of life, extinction, end, exit, demise; departure, passing, passing away, passing over; natural death, easy d., quiet end, euthanasia 376n. *euphoria*; release, happy r., welcome end; fatality, fatal casualty; sudden death, violent d., untimely end; death by drowning, watery grave; death on the roads; heart failure, suffocation, asphyxia, apnœa; hæmorrhage, bleeding to death; fatal disease, killing d. 651n. *disease*; dying day, last hour; death-bed, death-watch, death scene; last agony, last gasp, last breath, dying b.; swan-song, death-rattle 69n. *finality*; stroke of death, article of d.; extreme unction; passing bell 364n. *obsequies*; knell, death k., death's door.

the dead, forefathers 66n. *precursor*; loved ones, the great majority; the shades, the spirits, ghosts, phantoms 970n. *ghost*;

dead corpses 363 n. *corpse*; next world 124
n. *future state*; world of spirits, underworld, netherworld, halls of death, Hades,
Stygian shore, Styx; Elysium, meads of
asphodel, happy hunting grounds 971 n.
mythic heaven.
death roll, mortality, death-toll, death-rate;
bill of mortality, casualty list; necrology,
death register 87 n. *list*; death certificate
548 n. *record*; martyrology; obituary,
death column, death notice; the dead, the
fallen, the lost; casualties, the dead and
dying.
Adj. *dying* etc.vb.; mortal, ephemeral,
perishable 114 adj. *transient*; moribund,
half-dead, with one foot in the grave,
deathlike, deathly; hippocratic, deathly
pale; given over, given up, despaired of;
slipping, going, going off, slipping away,
sinking; sick unto death 651 adj. *sick*; on
one's death-bed, at death's door; at the
last gasp, struggling for breath; on one's
last legs, in articulo mortis, at the point
of death; sentenced to death, under sentence of death, doomed, fey 961 adj.
condemned.
dead, deceased, demised, no more; passed
over, passed away, released, departed,
gone; long gone, dead and gone, dead
and buried, in the grave, six feet under
364 adj. *buried*; born dead, stillborn; lifeless, breathless, still; extinct, inanimate,
exanimate, bereft of life; stone dead, cold,
stiff; dead as mutton, dead as a doornail,
dead as a herring, dead as nits; departed
this life, out of this world, called to one's
eternal rest, gathered to one's fathers, in
Abraham's bosom, numbered with the
dead; launched into eternity, behind the
veil, on the other side, beyond the grave,
beyond mortal ken; gone to Elysium,
gone to the happy hunting-grounds;
defunct, late, lamented, regretted, sainted;
martyred, slaughtered, massacred, killed.
Vb. *die* (see *perish*); be dead, lie in the grave,
be gone, be no more, cease to be, cease
to live 2 vb. *pass away*; end one's life,
decease, demise; go, succumb, expire, stop
breathing, give up the ghost, resign one's
breath, breathe one's last; drop off, close
one's eyes, fall asleep, sleep one's last
sleep; pass, pass over, be taken; go 296
vb. *depart*; ring down the curtain, shuffle
off this mortal coil, pay the debt of
nature, go the way of all flesh, go to one's

last home, go to one's long account; join
the majority, join the choir invisible, join
the angels, meet one's Maker, go to glory,
reach a better world, awake to life immortal; croak, peg out, go o., snuff o.,
go west, hop the twig, kick the bucket,
turn up one's toes, push up the daisies.
perish, die out, become extinct 2 vb. *pass
away*; go to the wall 165 vb. *be destroyed*;
come to dust, turn to d. 51 vb. *decompose*;
meet one's death, meet one's end, meet
one's fate, die with one's boots on; get
killed, be killed, fall, lose one's life, be
lost; relinquish one's life, lay down one's
l., surrender one's l.; become a martyr,
make the supreme sacrifice; catch one's
death, die untimely, snuff out like a
candle, drop dead; die a violent death,
break one's neck; bleed to death; drown,
go to Davy Jones's locker 313 vb. *founder*;
suffer execution, die the death, walk the
plank, receive one's death warrant;
commit suicide 362 vb. *kill oneself.*
Adv. *post-obit*, post mortem; in the article
of death, in the event of d.
See: 2, 51, 66, 69, 87, 114, 124, 165, 266, 296,
313, 362, 363, 364, 376, 548, 651, 961, 970,
971.

362 Killing: destruction of life

N. *killing* etc.vb., slaying 165 n. *destruction*;
destruction of life, phthisozoics; taking
life, dealing death, trucidation; occision;
blood-sports, hunting, shooting 619 n.
chase; blood-shedding, blood-letting; vivisection; mercy-killing, euthanasia; murder, assassination, bumping off, thuggee
(see *homicide*); poisoning, drowning,
suffocation, strangulation, hanging;
ritual killing, immolation, sacrifice;
martyrization, martyrdom; crucifixion,
execution 963 n. *capital punishment*;
judicial murder, auto da fé, burning
alive; despatch, deathblow, coup de
grâce, final stroke, quietus; violent death,
fatal accident, fatal casualty, death on
the roads, car smash, train s., plane
crash.
homicide, manslaughter; murder, capital m.;
assassination, thuggee, Burkism; crime
passionel 911 n. *jealousy*; regicide,
tyrannicide, parricide, patricide, matri-

cide, fratricide; aborticíde, infanticide, exposure, exposure of infants; genocide (see *slaughter*).

suicide, self-slaughter, self-destruction, felo de se; self-devotion, suttee, hara-kiri; mass-suicide, race-suicide.

slaughter, bloodshed, high casualties, butchery, carnage, shambles; wholesale murder, blood-bath, massacre, noyade, fusillade, battue, holocaust; pogrom, purge, liquidation, decimation, extermination, annihilation 165n. *destruction*; race-murder, genocide; war, battle 718n. *warfare*; Roman holiday, gladiatorial combat 716n. *duel*; Massacre of the Innocents, Sicilian Vespers, massacre of St. Bartholomew's Day.

slaughter-house, abattoir, knacker's yard, shambles; bull-ring 724n. *arena*; field of battle; battlefield 724n. *battleground*; field of blood, Aceldama; Auschwitz, Belsen, gas-chamber.

killer, slayer, man of blood; mercy-killer 905n. *pity*; soldier 722n. *combatant*; slaughterer, butcher, knacker; huntsman 619n. *hunter*; trapper, rat-catcher, exterminator; toreador, picador, matador 162 n. *athlete*; executioner, hangman, headsman 963n. *punisher*; homicide (see *murderer*); homicidal maniac, head-hunter; beast of prey, man-eater; block, gibbet, axe, guillotine, scaffold 964n. *means of execution*; insecticide, poison, hemlock 659n. *bane*.

murderer, homicide, killer; Cain, assassin, poisoner, strangler, garrotter, thug; gangster, gunman; bravo, desperado, cutthroat, high-binder 904n. *ruffian*; parricide, regicide, tyrannicide.

Adj. *deadly*, killing, lethal; fell, mortal, fatal, deathly; involving life, capital; death-bringing, lethiferous, mortiferous, poisonous 653adj. *toxic*; asphyxiant, suffocating, stifling; unhealthy, miasmic 653n. *insalubrious*; inoperable, incurable.

murderous, homicidal, genocidal; suicidal, self-destructive; internecine, slaughterous, death-dealing; sanguinary, sanguinolent, ensanguined, bloody, gory, bloodstained, red-handed; blood-guilty, bloodthirsty, thirsting for blood 898adj. *cruel*; head-hunting, man-eating, cannibalistic.

Vb. *kill*, slay, take life, end l., deprive of l.; do in, do for 165vb. *destroy*; cut off, nip in the bud, shorten one's life; put down, put to sleep; hasten one's end, bring down to the grave; drive to death, work to d.; put to d., hang, gibbet, turn off, send to the scaffold, behead, guillotine, impale 963vb. *execute*; stone, stone to death 712 vb. *lapidate*; make away with, do away w., despatch, send out of the world, get rid of, send one to his long account, launch into eternity; deal a deathblow, give the coup de grâce, put one out of his misery, give one his quietus; shed blood, sabre, spear, put to the sword, lance, bayonet, stab, run through 263vb. *pierce*; shoot down, pistol, blow the brains out 287vb. *shoot*; strangle, wring the neck of, garrotte, bowstring; choke, suffocate, smother, overlay, stifle, drown; smite, brain, spill the brains of, pole-axe, sandbag, blackjack 279vb. *strike*; send to the stake, burn alive, roast a. 381vb. *burn*; immolate, sacrifice, offer up; martyr, martyrize; condemn to death, sign the death warrant, ring the knell 961vb. *condemn*; wither, deaden.

slaughter, butcher, pole-axe, cut the throat of, drain the life-blood of; do execution, massacre, slay en masse, smite hip and thigh, put to the sword; decimate, scupper, wipe out; cut to pieces, cut to ribbons, cut down, shoot d., mow d.; steep one's hands in blood, wade in b., give no quarter, spare none 906vb. *be pitiless*; annihilate, exterminate, liquidate, purge, send to the gas-chamber, commit genocide 165 vb. *destroy*.

murder, commit m., assassinate, do for, settle, bump off, rub out; take for a ride, make to walk the plank; smother, burke, strangle, poison, gas.

kill oneself, do oneself in, commit suicide, suicide, put an end to one's life; commit hara-kiri, commit suttee; hang oneself, shoot oneself, blow out one's brains, cut one's throat; fall on one's sword, die in the high Roman fashion; put one's head in the oven, gas oneself, take poison; jump overboard, drown oneself; get oneself killed, have a fatal accident 361 vb. *perish*.

Adv. *in at the death*, in at the kill.

Int. no quarter! cry havoc!

See: 162, 165, 263, 279, 287, 361, 381, 619, 653, 659, 712, 716, 718, 722, 724, 898, 904, 905, 906, 911, 961, 963, 964.

363 Corpse

N. *corpse,* corse, dead body, body; dead man, murderee, victim; defunct, goner, stiff; cadaver, carcass, skeleton, bones, dry b.; embalmed corpse, mummy; reliquiæ, mortal remains, relics, ashes; clay, dust, earth; tenement of clay, mortal coil; carrion, food for worms, food for fishes; organic remains, fossil 125 n. *palætiology;* shade, manes, zombie 970 n. *ghost.*

Adj. *cadaverous,* corpselike; deathlike, deathly; stiff, carrion.

See: 125, 970.

364 Interment

N. *interment,* burial, sepulture, entombment; encoffinment, urning, urn burial; disposal of the dead, burial customs, inhumation, cremation, incineration, embalming, mummification; embalmment, myrrh, spices; coffin, kist, shell, casket, urn, cinerary u., funerary u.; sarcophagus, mummy-case; pyre, funeral pile, crematorium; mortuary, charnel-house; bone-urn, ossuary; funeral parlour; sexton, grave-digger; mortician, undertaker, funeral director; embalmer, pollinator.

obsequies, exequies, obit; mourning, weeping and wailing, wake 836 n. *lamentation;* last rites, burial service; funeral rites, funeral solemnity, funeral procession, cortège; knell, passing bell; dead march, muffled drum, last post, taps; memorial service, requiem, funeral hymn, Dies Irae, funeral oration, funeral sermon; elegy, dirge 836 n. *lament;* inscription, epitaph, necrologue, obituary, lapidary phrases, R.I.P., hic jacet; sepulchral monument, stele, tombstone, gravestone, headstone, ledger; brass; hatchment; stone cross, war memorial; cenotaph 548 n. *monument;* epitaphist, necrologist, obituary-writer; monumental mason.

funeral, hearse, bier, pall, catafalque, coffin; mourner, weeper, keener; mute, pall-bearer, dom; lych-gate (see *obsequies*).

grave clothes, cerements, cere cloth, shroud, winding sheet, mummy-wrapping.

cemetery, burial place; God's acre, garden of sleep, garden of remembrance; churchyard, graveyard, boneyard; urn cemetery, catacomb, columbarium; tower of silence;

necropolis, city of the dead; valley of dry bones, Golgotha; mortuary, morgue.

tomb, vault, crypt; mummy-chamber; pyramid, mastaba; tower of silence; mausoleum, sepulchre, tope, stupa; grave, narrow house, long home; grave pit, cist, sepulchral c., beehive tomb, shaft t.; barrow, long b., round b., tumulus, cairn, cromlech, dolmen, menhir 548 n. *monument;* memorial, cenotaph.

inquest 459 n. *enquiry;* necropsy, autopsy, post-mortem, post-mortem examination; exhumation, disinterment, disentombment.

Adj. *buried,* interred, coffined, urned etc. vb.; laid to rest, in the grave, below ground, under g., six feet under, pushing up the daisies 361 adj. *dead.*

funereal, funerary, funebral; sombre, sad 428 adj. *black;* mourning; elegiac, mortuary, cinerary, crematory, sepulchral; obsequial, obituary; lapidary, epitaphial, epitaphic; necrological, dirgelike 836 adj. *lamenting.*

Vb. *inter,* inhume, bury; lay out, prepare for burial, close the eyes; embalm, mummify; coffin, encoffin, kist; urn, inurn, entomb, ensepulchre; lay in the grave, consign to earth, lay to rest, put to bed with a shovel, burn on the pyre, cremate, incinerate 381 vb. *burn;* go to a funeral, take the burial service, say prayers for the dead, sing a requiem, sing a dirge; toll the knell, sound the last post, play taps; mourn, keen, hold a wake 836 vb. *lament.*

exhume, disinter, unbury; disentomb, untomb, unsepulchre; unearth, dig up.

Adv. *in memoriam,* post-obit, post-mortem, beneath the sod.

See: 361, 381, 428, 459, 548, 836.

365 Animality. Animal

N. *animality,* animation, animal life, animal spirits; animal kingdom, fauna, brute creation; physique, flesh, flesh and blood; animalization, zoomorphism, Pan; animal behaviour 944 n. *sensualism.*

animal, created being, living thing; birds, beasts and fishes; creature, brute, beast, dumb animal, creeping thing; protozoon, metazoon; zoophyte 196 n. *animalcule;* mammal, marsupial, batrachian, amphibian, fish, mollusc, crustacean, bird,

reptile, worm, insect, arachnid; invertebrate, vertebrate, articulate, biped; quadruped, ass, donkey, moke; mule 273n.

horse, beast of burden; wild horse, kiang, warrigal; zebra, giraffe; carnivore, herbivore, omnivore, man-eater; wild animal, animal feræ naturæ, game, beast of prey, beast of the field; pack, wolf-p.; flock, herd; stock, livestock 369n. *stock farm*; tame animal, domestic a., pet; extinct animal, dodo, auk, moa; prehistoric animal, pterodactyl, coelenterate; saurian, ichthyosaurus, plesiosaurus, dinosaur, brontosaur, megatherium; big animal, bruin, bear, grizzly, brown bear, black b., white b., Polar b.; elephant, rogue e., tusker; mammoth, mastodon; pachyderm, hippopotamus, rhinoceros; keitloa; fabled animal, unicorn, griffin, abominable snowman, yeti 84n. *rara avis*.

bird, winged thing, fowl, fowls of the air, denizens of the day; young bird, fledgling, squab 132n. *youngling*; avi-fauna, birdlife; migrant, winter visitor, summer v.; bird of omen, raven, jackdaw, crow, rook, albatross; cagebird; song-bird, hummingbird, singing-b., songster, warbler, nightingale, bulbul, lark; thrush, mavis; blackbird, merle, linnet, canary, cuckoo, koel; talking bird, parrot, polly, macaw, myna, parakeet, budgerigar, magpie; dove, turtle-d., ring-dove, cushat, culver, pigeon, wood-p., pouter p., homing p., carrier p.; sparrow, wheatear, finch, tit, wren, babbler; woodpecker, yaffle; coloured bird, peacock, bird of paradise, golden oriole, scarlet minivet, scarlet tanager, cardinal, bluebird, blue jay, goldfinch, robin; swift, chimney s., swallow, martin; nightbird, owl, night-o., barn-o., screech-o., hoot-o., nightjar, stone-curlew, bat, flying fox; scavenging bird, carrion crow, king-c., drongo, jungle-crow, adjutant bird, vulture, bird of Mars, King Vulture, Bengal V., White Scavenger; Pharaoh's Chicken, Arctic Skua.

bird of prey, lammergeyer, eagle, eaglet, erne, golden eagle, sea-e., Crested Serpent Eagle, bird of Jove; gled, kite, pariah k.; Brahminy k.; harrier, osprey, buzzard, buzzard-eagle; hawk, sparrow-h., chicken-h., falcon, peregrine f., hobby, merlin, shrike; fishing bird, kingfisher, gannet, cormorant, shag, skua, Arctic S.; gull, herring g., kittiwake, tern, oyster-catcher;

puffin, razorbill, Guillemot; petrel, Stormy P., shearwater, ocean bird; marsh bird, wading b., stork, crane, demoiselle c., avocet, heron, herne, paddy-bird, spoon-bill, ibis, flamingo.

waterfowl, swan, cob, pen, cygnet; duck, drake, duckling; goose, gander, gosling; teal, whistling t.; ousel, mallard, widgeon, moorhen, coot, jaçana, diver, grebe, dabchick; merganser, goosander.

flightless bird, ratite, ostrich, emu, cassowary; apteryx, kiwi; moa, dodo, penguin.

table bird, game bird, woodcock, woodpigeon, squab, peacock, peahen, peafowl, grouse, ptarmigan, capercailzie, pheasant, partridge, duck, snipe, snippet; quail, ortolan; turkey, gobbler; guinea-fowl, guinea-hen, goose, chicken.

poultry, hen, biddy, Dame Partlet, cock, cockerel, dunghill cock, rooster, Chanticleer; barndoor fowl, barnyard fowl; chicken, pullet; spring chicken, boiler, broiler, roaster, capon; Orpington, Rhode Island hen, Wyandotte.

cattle, herd, livestock, neat, kine, beeves; bull, cow, calf, heifer, fatling, yearling; maverick; Brahminy bull, Apis, ox, oxen, steer, stot, stirk, bullock; beef cattle, highland c., Black Angus, Aberdeen A., Hereford, beef Shorthorn, Galloway, Belted G.; dairy cattle, dairy herd, milchcow, Guernsey, Jersey, Alderney, Friesian, Dexter; dual purpose cattle, Red Poll, Shorthorn, Lincoln; buffalo, bison, aurochs, urus, nilgai; yak, musk-ox; goat, billy-g., nanny-g., mountain g., wild g.

sheep, baa-baa, ram, tup, wether, bell-w., ewe, lamb, ewe-l., lambkin; tag, teg; South Down, Hampshire D., Dorset Horn, Cheviot; mountain sheep, Ovis Poli.

pig, swine, boar, wild b., tusker; hog, sow; piglet, pigling, sucking-pig, suckling-p., shoat, porker; Large White, Large Black, Middle White, Wessex Saddleback, Berkshire, Tamworth.

dog, bow-wow, bitch, whelp, puppy-dog, pup, puppy, mutt; cur, hound, tyke; mongrel, pariah dog, pi-d.; coach-dog, Dalmatian; watch-dog, house-d., ban-d., police d., bloodhound, mastiff; sheepdog, collie, Welsh c., Newfoundland, Dobermann pinscher; bulldog, boxer, bull-terrier, wolfhound, Russian wolf-h.,

borzoi, Afghan hound, Alsatian; Great Dane; St. Bernard; greyhound, courser, running-dog, whippet; pack, hunting p.; game dog, elk-hound, deer-h., stag-h., boar-h., fox-h., otter-h., badger-h., basset-h.; badger-dog, dachshund; lurcher; harrier, beagle, whippet; gun-dog, retriever, golden r., Labrador r., pointer, setter, Irish s.; spaniel, water s., terrier, smooth-haired t., short-haired t., wire-haired t., wire-haired fox-t., Jones t., sealyham, black-and-tan terrier, long-haired t., rough-haired t., Scotch t., Skye t., Irish t., Kerry Blue t., Dandy Dinmont, Cairn, Airedale; cocker spaniel, springer s., King Charles s.; show dog, fancy d., toy d., Mexican hairless, Pomeranian; lap-dog, chow, Pekinese, pug-dog; Welsh corgie; poodle, French p., miniature p., toy p.; husky, sledge-dog; wild dog, Dingo; canine, wolf, prairie w., prairie dog; barking wolf, coyote.

cat, grimalkin, puss, pussy, kitten, kit, kitty-cat, pussy c.; tom, tom-c., gib-c.; mouser; Cheshire cat; tabby cat, Persian c., Siamese c., Angora c., Abyssinian c., Manx c., tortoishell c., marmalade c., blue c., black c., cream c.; feline, lion, tiger, leopard, cheetah, panther, puma, jaguar, cougar, red lion, American l.; wildcat, bobcat, catamountain, lynx.

deer, cervidæ, cervine family; stag, hart, hind, buck, fawn, pricket; red deer, fallow d., roe d., roe, roebuck; musk-deer, reindeer, caribou; hog-deer, Babiroussa; gazelle, antelope, springbok, wildebeest, gnu; elk, moose, Cape-elk, eland.

monkey, jacko, rhesus monkey, squirrel m., Midas m., marmoset, tamarin; hanuman, langur; ape, anthropoid a., chimpanzee, Jocko, gorilla, baboon, orang-outang, mandrill; monkeydom, bandarlog; monkey god, Hanuman.

reptile, creeping thing; ophidian, serpent, sea-s.; snake, rattlesnake, water-s., water-mocassin, adder, asp; viper, Russell's v.; copperhead; krait; cobra, king c., hamadryad; cerastes, mamba, anaconda, boa-constrictor, python; amphibian, crocodile, alligator, cayman, mugger, gavial; annelid, worm, earthworm; lizard, slow-worm, chameleon, iguana, gecko, tiktiki, salamander, polywog, amphisbæna; basilisk, cockatrice; chelonian, turtle, tortoise, terrapin; malacostracan, crab.

frog, batrachian, bull-frog, croaker, paddock, toad, horned t.; eft, newt, tadpole.

marsupial, kangaroo, wallaby, opossum, wombat, marmose.

rodent, rat, brown r., black r., sewer r., plague r., pack r., bandicoot; mouse, field-m., shrewmouse; mole, hamster, guinea-pig; gopher, marmot, woodchuck; beaver, squirrel, red s., grey s., black s., striped s., chipmunk, Hackee; mongoose, racoon, ichneumon; porcupine.

fly, winged insect; house-fly, blue-bottle, horsefly, dragonfly, butterfly, moth; caddis-fly, may-f., greenfly, blackfly; ladybird; firefly; gadfly, gnat, midge, mosquito, gallinipper, culex, anopheles; bee, honey-b., queen b., worker b., bumble-b., humble-b., drone; wasp, yellow-jacket, hornet; beetle, stag b., flying b., Japanese b., Colorado b., cockroach.

vermin, parasite; insect, chrysalis, cocoon; perfect insect, imago; bug, bedbug, louse, bed-l., flea, nit; maggot, earwig, mite, cheese-m.; weevil, bull-w., curculio; ant, emmet, pismire; red ant, white a., winged a., soldier a., worker a.; termite; pest, garden p., slug, wireworm, caterpillar; woodworm, death-watch beetle; locust, grasshopper, cicada, cicala; cricket, house-c., field-c.; rabbit, bunny, bunny-rabbit, cony; hare, leveret; Reynard, fox, dog-f., vixen; stoat, ferret, weasel, skunk, polecat.

fish, sea f., river f.; marine animal, cetacean, whale, Leviathan, delphinoid, grampus; sperm whale, baleen w., bottle-nosed w., narwhal; dolphin, porpoise, seal, sea-lion, sea-bear, walrus; shark, sharkray, angel fish, Monk f., Tiddle f.; swordfish, sawfish, starfish, sea-urchin, sea-horse, jelly-fish, ray fish, stingray; torpedo, numb-fish, cramp-f., cramp-ray; flying fish; goldfish; cephalopod, octopus, calamary, cuttle fish, squid, pen-fish, ink-fish, sepia; goby, gudgeon; wrasse, ballan; pike, jack, luce; mollusc, bivalve. See *table fish*.

table fish 301 n. *fish food*; salmon, grilse; pirling; grayling; trout, bream, roach, dace, perch, bass, carp, rui; tunny, tuna, mackerel, sturgeon, mullet, turbot, halibut, brill, cod, hake, haddock, herring,

buckling, shad, dory, plaice, skate, sole, flounder, whiting, smelt, sprat, sardine, whitebait; hilsa, beckti, pomfret; mangofish, mahseer; shell-fish, lobster, langouste, homard, crawfish, crayfish, crab; shrimp, prawn, chingree; oyster, bluepoint o.; clam, quahog, cherry-stone clam, little-neck c.; winkle, mussel, cockle, whelk; eel, sea-e., conger-e., elver, grig.

Adj. *animal*, animalcular, animalculine; beastly, bestial; human, manly, subhuman; therianthropic, theriomorphic, zoomorphic; zoological; mammalian, warm-blooded; primatial, anthropoidal, lemurine; equine, asinine, mulish; cervine; bovine, taurine, ruminant; ovine, sheepish; hircine, goatish; porcine, piggy; ursine; elephantine; rhinocerotic; canine, doggy; lupine, wolfish; feline, catty, tigerish, leonine; tigroid, pantherine; vulpine, vixenish, foxy; avian, birdlike; aquiline, vulturine; passerine, columbine, columbaceous, dovelike; cold-blooded, fishy, piscine, piscatorial, piscatory, molluscous; amphibian, amphibious; batrachian, reptilian, ophidian, snaky, serpentine, viperish, colubrine, colubriform; vermicular, wormy, weevilly; insectile, entomological.

See: 84, 132, 196, 273, 301, 369, 944.

366 Vegetability. Plant

N. *vegetability*, vegetable life, vegetable kingdom; flora, vegetation; flowering, blooming, florescence, frondescence; lushness, rankness, luxuriance 635 n. *plenty*; green belt 348 n. *plain*; vegetation god, Dionysus, Flora, Pan, Silenus; faun, dryad, hamadryad, woodnymph 967 n. *nymph*.

wood, timber, lumber, softwood, hardwood, heart-wood; forest, virgin f., primeval f.; rain-forest; taiga; weald, wold, jungle, bush, heath, scrub, maquis 348 n. *grassland*; greenwood, woodland, bocage, copse, coppice, spinney, spinet; thicket, brake, covert; park, chase, game-preserve; frith, shaw, hurst, holt; plantation, arboretum, pinery; orchard, orangery 370 n. *garden*; grove, clump, tope, clearing; brushwood, underwood, under-

growth; bushiness, shrubbery, bushes, windbreak, hedge, hedgerow.

forestry, dendrology, silviculture, tree-planting, afforestation, conservation; woodman, forester, forest-guard, verderer; wood-cutter, lumberman, lumberjack; dendrologist.

tree, shrub, sapling, scion, stock; pollard; shoot, sucker, trunk, bole; limb, branch, bough, twig; leguminous tree, coniferous t., greenwood tree, evergreen t., deciduous t., softwood t., hardwood t., ironwood t.; fruit tree, nut t., timber t.; oak, holm o., ilex; teak, sal; mahogany, walnut, ebony; ash, mountain a., rowan; beech, copper b.; birch, silver b., chestnut, horse c.; willow, weeping w.; alder; poplar, Lombardy p., white p., black p., trembling p., aspen; lime, linden; elm, sycamore, plane; cornel, dogwood; pine, white p., fir, Scotch f., silver f., Douglas f., redwood, sequoia, Wellingtonia; cedar, deodar, larch, spruce, Norway s.; maple, Japanese m., sugar m., rock m., striped m., moosewood; silver maple, red m.; cypress, yew, box, holly; myrtle, laurel, bay; casuarina, beef-wood; fig-tree, peepul, banyan; palm, date-p., cocoanut-p., fan-p., bottle-p.; acacia, flowering tree, Japanese cherry, purple prunus, magnolia, camellia, rhododendron, azalea, ixora, lilac, laburnum, asoka; gul mor *or* gold mohur; mandara, coral-tree, simmul t., silk-cotton t.; gum-tree, eucalyptus, rubber-tree, aloes, lignaloes, agave; bamboo, cane, sugar c.

foliage, foliation, frondescence; leafiness, leafage, umbrage; ramage, limb, branch, bough, twig; spray, sprig; tree-top; leaf, frond, flag; leaflet, foliole; fir-cone, pine-needle; seed-leaf, cotyledon; leaf-stalk, petiole, stalk, stem, tigella, caulicle, radical.

plant, growing thing; sucker, wort, weed; seed, root, bulb; thallophyte, gametophyte, sporophyte; greenery, herb 301 n. *potherb*, *vegetable*, *tuber*: succulent plant, leguminous p., legume, vetch, pulse, lentil, bean; parasitic plant, ivy, creeper, vine, bine, tendril; cucurbit, calabash, gourd, marrow, melon; thorn, thistle, cactus, euphorbia; spurge; heath, heather, ling; broom, furze, gorse, fern, bracken; moss, bog m., peat m., sphagnum; lichen, fungus, bolet, mushroom,

truffle, toadstool, puffball, spore; mould, mucor, penicillin; osier, sedge, reed, rush, bullrush; algæ, conferva, confervite, seaweed, wrack, sea-w., sargasso, Gulf-weed.

flower, floweret, blossom, bloom, bud, node, burgeon; petal, sepal; calyx, wild flower, garden-f., annual, biennial, triennial, perennial; hot-house plant, exotic; flowerbed, seedbed; gardening, horticulture, floriculture.

grass 348 n. *grassland*; pasture, pasturage, herbage, verdure, turf, sod, divot; bent, Rhode Island b., esparto-grass, Spanish g., spear-g., couch-g., blue-g., Kentucky blue g., Marion blue g., citronella; lawn grass, wild g.; cut grass, hay; graminiferous plant, millet; trefoil, shamrock; clover, four-leaved c.

corn, grain, cereal plant, farinaceous p. 301 n. *cereal*; wheat, oats, barley, rye, buckwheat, spelt, emmer; Indian corn, maize, mealies, rice, paddy; Indian millet, sorghum, Guinea-corn, durra; straw, stubble; chaff, husk; ground corn, hominy, meal, flour.

Adj. *vegetal*, vegetative, vegetable, botanical; evergreen; deciduous; horticultural, floricultural; floral, flowery, blooming, bloomy; rank, lush, overgrown; weedy, weed-ridden; verdant, verdurous, green; grassy, mossy; turfy, cespitose; turfen, cespititious; gramineous, graminiferous, poaceous, herbaceous, herbal; leguminous, vetchy; fungous, fungoid, fungiform; exogenous, endogenous.

arboreal, arborical, arboreous, dendriform, dendritic, treelike, forestal; arborescent, forested, timbered; woodland, woody, wooded, sylvan, beechy; grovy, bosky; wild, jungly, scrubby; bushy, shrubby, copsy; silvicultural, afforested, planted; dendrologous, dendrological.

wooden, wood, xyloid, ligneous, lignous; hard-grained, soft-grained.

Vb. *vegetate*, germinate, sprout, shoot 164 vb. *produce*; plant, grow, garden, botanize 370 vb. *cultivate*; forest, afforest, reforest.

See: 164, 301, 348, 370, 635, 967.

367 Zoology: the science of animals

N. *zoology*, zoonomy, zoography, zootomy; animal physiology, comparative p., mor-

phology 331 n. *structure*; ichthyotomy, anatomy, comparative a.; anthropology, ornithology, bird lore, bird watching, ornithoscopy, ichthyology, herpetology, malacology, helminthology, entomology; oryctology, palæontology; taxidermy.

zoologist, ornithologist, ichthyologist, entomologist, anatomist.

Adj. *zoological* etc. n.

See: 331.

368 Botany: the science of plants

N. *botany*, phytography, phytology, phytonomy; vegetable physiology, plant pathology; herborization, botanization; dendrology 366 n. *forestry*; mycology, fungology, algology; botanical garden 370 n. *garden*; hortus siccus, herbarium, herbal.

botanist, herbist, herbarist, herbalist, herborist, herbarian.

Adj. *botanical* etc. n.

Vb. *botanize* etc. n.

See: 366, 370.

369 Animal husbandry

N. *animal husbandry*, animal management, training, manège; thremmatology, domestication, breeding, stock-b., rearing, cicuration; taming etc. vb.; zoohygiantics, veterinary science; phthisozoics 362 n. *killing*; horse-breeding, cattle-raising, sheep-farming, pig-keeping, chicken-k., bee-k.; stirpiculture, pisciculture, apiculture, sericulture; veterinary surgeon, vet, horse doctor 658 n. *doctor*; ostler, groom, stable boy 742 n. *servant*; farrier, blacksmith; keeper, gamekeeper, gillie.

stock farm, stud f., stud; dairy farm, cattle f.; fish farm, fishery, hatchery; fish pond, fish tank, piscina, vivarium; duck pond; pig farm, piggery; beehive, hive, apiary; pasture, grazing, sheep-run, sheep-walk; chicken farm, chicken-run, hen-r., free range; hen-battery, deep litter.

cattle pen, byre 192 n. *stable*; sheepfold, pinfold 235 n. *inclosure*; coop, hencoop, henhouse, cowhouse, cowshed, pigsty; swannery, goosery; aquarium, bird-cage 748 n. *prison*; bear-pit, cockpit 724 n. *arena*; Noah's Ark.

zoo, zoological gardens, menagerie, circus; aviary, vivarium, terrarium, aquarium.

breeder, stock-b., horse-b.; trainer, animal t., lion-tamer; cattle-farmer, sheep-f., wool-grower, pig-keeper, bee-k., apiarist; fancier, bird-f., pigeon-f.

herdsman, herd, neatherd, cattleherd, cowherd; stockman, cattleman; rancher; cowman, cowkeeper, cowboy, cowpuncher, bronco-buster, gaucho; shepherd, shepherdess; goatherd; goose-girl; milkmaid; fodderer.

Adj. *tamed*, broken, broken in; gentle, docile; domestic, domesticated; reared, raised, bred; pure-bred, thoroughbred, half-bred; stirpicultural.

Vb. *break in*, tame, cicurate; domesticate, acclimatize 610vb. *habituate*; train 534 vb. *teach*; back, mount, whip, spur 267 vb. *ride*; yoke, harness, hitch, bridle, saddle; cage, corral, round up, ride, herd 747vb. *restrain*.

breed stock, breed, grow, hatch, culture, incubate, nurture, fatten; ranch, farm 370vb. *cultivate*; hive, swarm 104vb. *be many*; rear, raise.

groom, currycomb, rub down, stable, bed down; tend, herd, shepherd; shear, fleece; milk; drench, water, fodder 301vb. *feed*.

See: 104, 192, 235, 267, 301, 362, 370, 534, 610, 658, 724, 742, 747, 748.

370 Agriculture

N. *agriculture*, agronomy, agronomics, rural economy; cultivation, sowing, reaping; growth, harvest, crop, vintage 632n. *store*; husbandry, farming, mixed f., intensive f., contour f.; cattle farming, dairy f. 369n. *animal husbandry*; wheat farming, arable f.; geoponics, hydroponics, tray agriculture, tank farming; spade farming, tillage, tilth, spadework; floriculture, flower-growing; horticulture, gardening; fruit-growing, pomiculture, citriculture; olericulture, kitchen gardening; viticulture, viniculture, winegrowing, vine-dressing; arboriculture, silviculture, afforestation 366n. *forestry*; landscape gardening, landscape architecture; water, dung, manure 171n. *fertilizer*; fodder, winter feed 301n. *provender*; silage, ensilage 632n. *storage*.

farm, home f., grange; arable farm, dairy f., stock f., sheep f., cattle f., ranch, hacienda; model farm; state farm, collective f., kolkhoz, kibbutz; farmland, arable land, plough-l., fallow 344n. *soil*; herbage, pasturage, pasture, fields, meadows 348 n. *grassland*; demesne, manor-farm, estate, holding, small-h., croft 777n. *lands*; allotment, kitchen garden; market garden, truck g., hop g.; tea-garden, tea-estate; nursery-garden, nursery; vinery, vineyard; fruit-farm, orchard.

garden, botanical g., flower-g., rose-g., rock g., ornamental g., winter g.; vegetable garden, cabbage patch, kitchen garden, allotment; fruit garden, orchard, orangery; tree garden, arboretum, pinery 366 n. *wood*; patch, plot, plat, grass-p., grass, lawn, park 235n. *inclosure*; border, bed, flower-b., knot, parterre 844n. *ornamental art*; seedbed, frame, cold f., cucumber f. 164n. *propagation*; cloche, conservatory, hot-house, greenhouse, glass-house 383n. *heater*; flowerpot 194n. *vessel*.

husbandman, farmer, farm manager, farm-bailiff, granger; cultivator, planter, tea-p., coffee-p., rubber-p.; agriculturist, tiller of the soil, peasant, rayat, under-r., kulak, moujik, paysan; serf, ascriptus glebæ; share-cropper, metayer, tenant-farmer; gentleman farmer, yeoman; smallholder, crofter, allotment-holder, lambardar, zamindar; fruit-farmer, orchardist; wine-grower, vineyardist; farm hand, plougher, sower, reaper, harvester, mower, gleaner; thresher, barnsman; picker, hop-p., vintager; agricultural folk, farming community, peasantry; good farmer, improving landlord 654n. *reformer*; farming type, Boer, Adam, Triptolemus.

gardener, horticulturist, mali, flower-grower; topiarist, landscape gardener; seedsman, nurseryman; market gardener; hop-grower, fruit-g., citriculturist, vine-grower, vine-dresser; forester 366n. *forestry*; planter, digger, delver.

farm tool, plough, ploughshare, coulter; harrow, chain h., spike h.; spade, hoe, rake, trowel; dibble, digging-stick; hay-rake, hay-fork, pitchfork; scythe, sickle, reaping hook, shears, secateur 256n. *sharp edge*; flail, winnowing fan; wine-press; cutter, reaper, thresher, binder, baler, combine-harvester; tractor; hay-wagon; byre, cowshed; barn, hayloft, silo 632n. *storage*.

Adj. *agrarian*, peasant, farming; agrestic,

georgic, bucolic, pastoral, rustic, Boeotian; agricultural, agronomic, geoponic, predial, manorial, collective; arable, cultivable; ploughed, dug, planted, transplanted.

horticultural, garden, gardening, topiary; cultured, hot-house, exotic, artificial.

Vb. *cultivate,* farm, ranch, garden, grow; till, till the soil, scratch the s.; dig, delve, spade, dibble; seed, sow, broadcast, scatter the seed, set, plant, dibble in, transplant, plant out, bed o.; plough, raft 201 vb. *space;* replough, backset; harrow, rake, hoe; weed, prune, top and lop, thin out 204 vb. *shorten;* graft, ingraft, imp 303 vb. *implant;* force, fertilize, dung, manure 174 vb. *invigorate;* grass over, sod, rotate the crop; leave fallow 674 vb. *not use;* harvest, gather in 632 vb. *store;* glean, reap, mow, cut, scythe, cut a swathe; bind, bale, stook, sheaf; flail 332 vb. *pulverize;* thresh, winnow, sift, bolt 46 vb. *separate;* crop, pluck, pick, gather; tread out the grapes; ensile, ensilate; improve one's land 654 vb. *make better;* enclose, fence 235 vb. *inclose;* ditch, drain 342 vb. *dry;* water 341 vb. *irrigate.*

See: 46, 164, 171, 174, 194, 201, 204, 235, 256, 301, 303, 332, 341, 342, 344, 348, 366, 369, 383, 632, 654, 674, 777, 844.

371 Mankind

N. *mankind,* womankind, humankind; humanity, human nature, creaturehood; flesh, mortality; generations of man, peoples of the earth; the world, everyone, everybody, the living, ourselves; human race, human species, man; tellurian, earthling; human being, Adam, Adamite, lord of creation; civilized man, political animal, civilized world, comity of nations 654 n. *civilization;* uncivilized man, savage, backward peoples; zoological man, hominidæ, hominid, homo sapiens; oreanthropus, early man, Dawn Man, eoanthropus, plesianthropus, sinanthropus; Neanderthal Man, Peking M., Java M., caveman; ape-man, Australopithecus, pithecanthropus; non-Adamical man; nation, ethnic type 11 n. *race.*

anthropology, anthropography, anthroposophy; anthropometry, craniometry, craniology; anthropogenesis, somato-

logy; ethnology, ethnography, folklore, mythology; social anthropology, demography; social science, humanitarianism 901 n. *sociology.*

person, individual, human being, everyman, everywoman; creature, fellow c., mortal, body; a being, soul, living s.; God's image; one, somebody, someone, so and so, such a one; party, customer, character, type, element; chap, guy, bloke, fellow, cove, johnny 372 n. *male;* personage, figure, person of note, V.I.P. 638 n. *bigwig;* star 890 n. *favourite;* dramatis personæ, all those concerned 686 n. *personnel;* unit, head, hand, nose.

social group, society, community 706 n. *association;* human family 11 n. *family;* primitive society, tribalism; organized society, international s., comity of nations 654 n. *civilization;* community at large, people, persons, folk; public, general p., man in the street, you and me; population, populace, citizenry 191 n. *native;* stratified society, the classes; the masses, the million, hoi polloi, the herd, the lower orders, working classes 869 n. *commonalty.*

nation, nationality, statehood, nationalism, national consciousness; ultranationalism, chauvinism, expansionism, imperialism; civil society, body politic, Leviathan, people, demos; state, city-s., welfare s., civil s., nation s., multi-racial s.; realm, commonwealth, commonweal 733 n. *polity;* democracy, aristocracy.

Adj. *human,* creaturely, mortal, fleshly; Adamite, Adamitic, Adamitical; earth-born, tellurian; anthropoid, hominal; anthropological, ethnographical, racial 11 adj. *ethnic;* anthropocentric, personal, individual.

national, state, civic, civil, public, general, communal, tribal, social, societal, societary; cosmopolitan, international.

See: 11, 191, 372, 638, 654, 686, 706, 733, 869, 890, 901.

372 Male

N. *male,* male sex, man, he; manliness, masculinity, manhood; androcentricism, male exclusiveness; mannishness, viraginity, gynandry; he-man, cave-m.; gentleman, sir, esquire, master; lord, my l., his

lordship; Mr., mister, monsieur, Herr, señor, don, dom, senhor, signor; sahib, shri, srijut, babu, mirza; tovarich, comrade, citoyen; yeoman, wight, swain, fellow, guy, blade, bloke, beau, chap, cove, card, chappie, johnny, buffer; gaffer, goodman; father, grandfather 169n. *parent*; uncle, nephew, brother; boy, man-child 132n. *youngster*; son 170n. *sonship*; husband 894n. *spouse*; groom, bridegroom 894n. *bridesman*; bachelor; Adonis, Adam; stag party, menfolk.

male animal, cock, cockerel, rooster; drake, gander; male swan, cob; buck, stag, hart, staggard, spayd, pricket, brocket, fawn; horse, stallion, entire horse, stud h., colt, foal; bull, calf, bull-c., bullock, ox, steer, stot; boar, hog, ram, tup; he-goat, Billy-g.; dog, dog-fox, tom-cat, gib-c.; gelding, capon, neuter cat.

Adj. *male*, masculine, androcentric; manly, he, virile; mannish, unfeminine, unwomanly; viraginous, gynandrous; manlike, trousered, pipe-smoking; arrenotokous.

See: 132, 169, 170, 894.

373 Female

N. *female*, feminine gender, she, her, -ess; femineity, feminality, muliebrity; femininity, the eternal feminine; womanhood 134n. *adultness*; womanliness, girlishness; feminism; womanishness, effeminacy, androgyny 163n. *weakness*; gynecology, gyniatrics, gynics; gynogenesis 164 n. *propagation*.

womankind, the sex, female s., fair s., gentle s., softer s.; the distaff side, womenfolk, women, matronage; hen party; gynæceum, women's quarters, zenana, purdah, seraglio, harem.

woman, Eve, she; petticoat, skirt; girl, girlie; virgin, maiden; nun, unmarried woman, old maid 895n. *spinster*; co-ed, undergraduette; bachelor girl, new woman, career w., suffragette; bride, matron, dowager, married woman, wife, squaw 894n. *spouse*; mother, grandmother 169n. *parent*; wench, lass, nymph; lady, burd; filly 132n. *youngster*; grisette, midinette; blonde, brunette, platinum blonde; sweetheart, bird 887n. *loved one*; moll, doll, bit of fluff, broad, mistress, courtesan 952n. *loose woman*; quean, cotquean; shrew, virago, Amazon; goddess, Venus, Aphrodite; aunt, niece, sister, daughter.

lady, gentlewoman; dame, madam, ma'am, mistress, Mrs., miss, madame, mademoiselle, Fraulein, Frau; signora, signorina, señora, señorita, srijukta, srimati, mem-sahib, mem; milady, ladyship, donna; goody, gammer, goodwife.

female animal, hen, duck, goose; pen (female swan); bitch, she-dog; mare, filly; cow, heifer, sow, gilt; ewe, ewe-lamb, gimmer; nanny-goat, she-g.; hind, doe; vixen, she-fox; tigress, lioness, she-bear.

Adj. *female*, gynecic, gynecian, mammiferous; she, feminine, petticoat; girlish, womanly, ladylike, maidenly, matronal, matronly; feminist, feministic; womanish, effeminate, unmanly; feminized, androgynous; thelytokous 164 adj. *productive*.

See: 132, 134, 163, 164, 169, 887, 894, 895, 952.

374 Physical sensibility

N. *sensibility*, sensitiveness, tenderness, exposed nerve; soreness, sensitivity, touchiness, sore point; perceptivity, awareness, consciousness 819n. *moral sensibility*; physical sensibility, susceptivity, susceptibility, affectibility, soft spot; passibility, hyperæsthesia, allergy; æstheticism, æsthetics; æsthete 846n. *man of taste*; touchy person, sensitive plant, thin skin 892n. *irascibility*.

sense, sensory process, external senses; touch, hearing, taste, smell, sight, sixth sense; sensation, impression 818n. *feeling*; effect, response, reaction, reflex, synæsthesia; auto-suggestion, auto-hypnosis, Couéism; extra-sensory perception, telepathy, thought-transference.

Adj. *sentient*, sensitive, sensitized; sensible, affectible, susceptible, passible; thin-skinned, touchy 892 adj. *irascible*; sensuous 818 adj. *feeling*; perceptive, aware, conscious 490 adj. *knowing*; acute, sharp, keen 377 adj. *painful*; tender, raw, sore, exposed; impressionable, alive, alive to, responsive; suggestible, over-impressionable, over-sensitive, hypersensitive, over-quick, high-strung, over-s. 822 adj. *excitable*; ticklish, itchy.

striking, keen, sharp, acute, vivid, clear, lively; sudden, sensational 821 adj. *impressive*.
Vb. *have feeling*, sense, become aware, awaken, wake up; perceive, realize 490 vb. *know*; be sensible of 818 vb. *feel*; react, tingle 819 vb. *be sensitive*; have one's senses, hear, see, touch, taste; not contain one's feelings, burst, gush, overflow 822 vb. *be excitable*.
cause feeling, stir the senses, stir the blood; stir, disturb 318 vb. *agitate*; arouse, awaken, excite, strike, make *or* produce an impression 821 vb. *impress*; arrest, astonish, cause a sensation 508 vb. *surprise*; make sensible, bring home 534 vb. *teach*; sharpen, cultivate 174 vb. *invigorate*; refine, æstheticize; touch the quick, touch on the raw 377 vb. *give pain*; increase sensitivity, sensitize.
Adv. *to the quick*, to the heart, on the raw.
See: 174, 318, 377, 490, 508, 534, 818, 819, 821, 822, 846, 892.

375 Physical insensibility

N. *insensibility*, physical i., impassibility, insensitiveness; mental insensibility, impercipience, obtuseness 499 n. *unintelligence*; insentience, anæsthesia, hysterical anæsthesia, la belle indifference; analgesia, narcotization, hypnosis, hypnotism, auto-hypnosis, auto-suggestion; paralysis, palsy; numbness, narcosis; catalepsy, stupor, coma, trance, unconsciousness; narcolepsy, narcotism, sleeping-sickness 651 n. *disease*; twilight sleep 679 n. *sleep*; Sleeping Beauty, Rip van Winkle; amorality 820 n. *moral insensibility*.
anæsthetic, dope 658 n. *drug*; anæsthetic agent, local anæsthetic, general a., ether, chloroform, morphia, cocaine, novocaine, chloral; gas, nitrous oxide, laughing gas; narcotic, sleeping tablets, sleeping draught 679 n. *soporific*; opium, laudanum, poppy-seed; pain-killer, analgesic 177 n. *moderator*.
Adj. *insensible*, insensitive, insentient, insensate; obtuse, dull, stupid 499 adj. *unintelligent*; imperceptive, impercipient; unhearing 416 adj. *deaf*; unseeing 439 adj. *blind*; senseless, sense-bereft, uncon-scious; inert 679 adj. *inactive*; stony, stiff, cold, dead 266 adj. *quiescent*; numb, benumbed, frozen; paralysed, paralytic, palsied; doped, dopy, drugged; anæsthetized, hypnotized; punch-drunk, dazed, stupefied; tranced, comatose 679 adj. *sleepy*; anæsthetic, analgesic; hypnotic, mesmeric 679 adj. *somnific*.
unfeeling, callous, inured, indurated, hardened, case-h.; insensitive, tactless; pachydermatous, thick-skinned; impassible, proof, shock-p.; impersonal 820 adj. *impassive*.
Vb. *be insensible*,—insentient etc. adj.; not react 679 vb. *be inactive*; have a thick skin 820 vb. *be insensitive*; become insensible, harden oneself; indurate, cease to feel.
render insensible, make insensible; obtund 257 vb. *blunt*; paralyse, benumb; freeze 382 vb. *refrigerate*; deaden, put to sleep, induce s., hypnotize, mesmerize 679 vb. *make inactive*; anæsthetize, put under gas, chloroform; narcotize, drug, dope; dull, stupefy; stun, concuss, brain, knock out, render unconscious 279 vb. *strike*; pall, cloy 863 vb. *sate*.
See: 177, 257, 266, 279, 382, 416, 439, 499, 651, 658, 679, 820, 863.

376 Physical Pleasure

N. *pleasure*, material p., physical p., sensual p., sensuous p.; gratification, sensuousness, sensuality, self-indulgence, bodily enjoyment, animal gratification, luxuria, luxuriousness, hedonism 944 n. *sensualism*; dissipation, round of pleasure, cup of Circe 943 n. *intemperance*; rest 685 n. *refreshment*; treat, diversion, entertainment, divertissement 837 n. *amusement*; feast, regale 301 n. *feasting*; good feeding, eutrophy, bonne-bouche, titillation, relish 386 n. *taste*; gusto, zest, keen appreciation; enjoyment, delight, happiness 824 n. *joy*.
euphoria, well-being, contentment 828 n. *content*; easeful living, gracious l.; ease, heart's-ease; convenience, comfort, cosiness, snugness, creature comforts; luxury, luxuries 637 n. *superfluity*; lap of luxury, clover, purple and fine linen 800 n. *wealth*; feather-bed, bed of down, bed of roses, velvet, cushion, pillow 327 n. *softness*;

peace, quiet, rest 683n. *repose*; quiet dreams 679n. *sleep*; painlessness, euthanasia.

Adj. *pleasant*, pleasure-giving 826adj. *pleasurable*; pleasing, tickling, titillating; delightful, delightsome; welcome, grateful, gratifying, satisfying 685adj. *refreshing*; genial, congenial, cordial, heartwarming; nice, agreeable, enjoyable 837 adj. *amusing*, palatable, delicious 386adj. *tasty*; sugary 392adj. *sweet*; perfumed 396adj. *fragrant*; tuneful 410adj. *melodious*; lovely 841adj. *beautiful*.

comfortable, affording comfort, comfy, homely, snug, cosy, warm, comforting, restful 683 adj. *reposeful*; peaceful 266 adj. *tranquil*; convenient, easy, painless; easeful, downy 327adj. *soft*; luxurious, de luxe; enjoying comfort, euphoric, in comfort, at one's ease, slippered; happy, gratified 828adj. *content*; relieved 685 adj. *refreshed*.

sensuous, of the senses, appealing to the s.; bodily, physical 319adj. *material*; voluptuous, pleasure-loving, enjoying, epicurean, hedonistic 944adj. *sensual*.

Vb. *enjoy*, relish, like, quite l.; feel pleasure, receive p., experience p. 824vb. *be pleased*; luxuriate in, revel in, riot in, swim in, roll in, wallow in 683vb. *repose*; gloat on, gloat over, get a kick out of; lick one's lips, smack one's l. 386vb. *taste*; aprciate, bask, bask in the sunshine 379vb. *be hot*; live on the fat of the land, live comfortably, live in comfort 730vb. *prosper*; give pleasure 826vb. *please*.

Adv. *in comfort* etc.n.; at one's ease; in clover, on velvet, on a bed of roses.

See: 266, 301, 319, 327, 379, 386, 392, 396, 410, 637, 679, 683, 685, 730, 800, 824, 826, 828, 837, 841, 943, 944.

377 Physical pain

N. *pain*, physical p., bodily p.; discomfort, malaise, inconvenience; distress, thin time, hell 731vb. *adversity*; sufferance 825n. *suffering*; exhaustion, weariness, strain 684n. *fatigue*; hurt, bruise; cut, gash 655n. *wound*; aching, smarting; heart-ache, dolour, anguish, agony, lancination, slow death, death by inches, torment, torture, cruciation; crucifixion, martyrdom, vivisection; rack, wheel, thumbscrew 964n. *instrument of torture*; painfulness, sore, soreness, tenderness; malaise, discomfort; painful aftermath, hangover 949n. *crapulence*; nightmare, ephialtes 854n. *fear*.

pang, smart, twinge, nip, pinch; throe, thrill; stitch, cramp, cramps, convulsion 318n. *spasm*; sting, sharp pain, shooting p., darting p., gnawing p.; ache, headache, splitting head, migraine, megrim, hemicrania; tooth-ache, ear-a., belly-a., gripe, colic, collywobbles; neuritis, neuralgia, angina; arthritis, rheumatoid a., rheumatism, fibrositis; sciatica, lumbago, gout.

Adj. *painful*, paining, aching, agonizing, excruciating, exquisite; harrowing, racking, tormenting; poignant 827adj. *distressing*; burning, biting, stabbing, shooting, tingling, smarting, throbbing; sore, raw, tender, exposed; bitter, bitter-sweet 393adj. *sour*; disagreeable, uncomfortable, inconvenient 827adj. *unpleasant*.

pained, hurt, tortured, martyred, agonized etc.vb.; suffering, aching, flinching, wincing, quivering, writhing.

Vb. *give pain*, ache, hurt, pain, sting; inflict pain, excruciate, put to torture, lacerate, torment, twist the arm of, rack, wring 963 vb. *torture*; flog, crucify, martyr 963vb. *punish*; vivisect, lancinate, tear, harrow, lacerate 46vb. *cut*; prick, stab 263vb. *pierce*; gripe, nip, pinch, tweak, twinge, shoot, throb; devour, bite, gnaw 301vb. *eat*; grind, grate, jar, set on edge; fret, chafe, gall 333vb. *rub*; irritate 832vb. *aggravate*; put on the rack, break on the wheel; kill by inches, prolong the agony; grate on the ear 411vb. *discord*; inconvenience, annoy, distress 827vb. *incommode*.

feel pain, suffer p., feel the pangs 825vb. *suffer*; agonize, ache, smart, chafe; twitch, wince, flinch, writhe, squirm, creep, shiver, quiver, jactitate 318vb. *be agitated*; tingle, get pins and needles; sit on thorns, have a thin time, be a martyr, go through it 731vb. *have trouble*; shriek, yell, scream, howl, groan 408vb. *cry*; weep 836vb. *lament*; lick one's wounds.

See: 46, 263, 301, 318, 333, 393, 408, 411, 655, 684, 731, 825, 827, 832, 836, 854, 949, 963, 964.

378 Touch: sensation of touch

N. *touch*, taction, tactility, palpability; contrectation, handling, feeling, palpation, manipulation; massage, kneading, squeeze, pressure 333n. *friction*; graze, contact 202n. *contiguity*; stroke, pat; flick, flip, tap 279n. *impulse*; tact, feel 463 n. *discrimination*; sense of touch, fine t., precision 494n. *accuracy*; delicacy, artistry 694n. *skill*.

formication, titillation, tickling sensation; creeps, goose-flesh; tingle, tingling, pins-and-needles; scratchiness, itchiness, itch, urtication, urticaria, nettlerash, hives; dhobi's itch, prickly heat 651n. *skin disease*; phthiriasis, pediculosis 649n. *uncleanness*.

feeler, organ of touch, palp, palpus, antenna, whisker; proboscis, tongue; digit, forefinger, thumb (see *finger*); green fingers; hand, paw, palm, flipper.

finger, forefinger, index, middle finger, ring f., little f.; thumb, pollex; hallux, great toe 214n. *foot*; five fingers, bunch of fives, 'pickers and stealers'; hand, fist 778n. *nippers*; finger-nail, talon.

Adj. *tactual*, tactile; palpal, palpiform; touching, lambent, licking, grazing etc. vb.; touchable, tangible, palpable 324adj. *dense*; light of touch, light-fingered; heavy-handed 695adj. *clumsy*.

handed, with hands; right-handed 241adj. *dextral*; left-handed 242adj. *sinistral*; thumbed, fingered; five-finger; manual, digital.

Vb. *touch*, make contact, graze, scrape, brush, glance; kiss, osculate 202vb. *be contiguous*; impinge, overlap; hit, meet 279vb. *collide*; feel, palp, palpate; finger, thumb, take between finger and thumb, pinch, nip, vellicate, massage 333vb. *rub*; palm, run the hand over, pass the fingers o.; stroke, pat down 258vb. *smooth*; wipe, sweep 648vb. *clean*; touch lightly, tap, pat, flick, flip, tickle, scratch; lick, tongue; paw, clip, fondle 889vb. *caress*; handle, twiddle, tweedle, fiddle with; manipulate, wield, manhandle 173 vb. *operate*; touch roughly, bruise, crush 377vb. *give pain*; fumble, grope, grabble, grubble, put out a feeler, throw out a f. 461vb. *be tentative*.

itch, tickle, tingle, creep, have goose-flesh, have the creeps; prick, prickle, titillate, urticate, scratch; thrill, excite, irritate.

See: 173, 202, 214, 241, 242, 258, 279, 324, 333, 377, 461, 463, 494, 648, 649, 651, 694, 695, 778, 889.

379 Heat

N. *heat*, calidity, caloric, phlogiston; radiant heat; convected heat; incalescence, recalescence, decalescence; emission of heat, diathermancy; incandescence, flame, glow, flush, blush; warmth, fervour, ardour; specific heat, blood h., body h.; fever heat, pyrexia, fever, hectic, inflammation 651n. *disease*; high temperature, white heat; ebullition, boiling point, flash p., melting p.; torrid heat, tropical h., sweltering h., swelter, summer heat, high summer, flaming June; dog-days, canicule 128n. *summer*; heat wave, scorcher; hot wind, simoom, sirocco; hot spring, geyser, hot water, steam; insolation 381 n. *heating*; sun, solar heat 420n. *luminary*.

fire, devouring element, flames; bonfire, bale-fire, watch-f., beacon f., St. Elmo's f.; death-fire, pyre 364n. *obsequies*; coal fire, gas f., electric f. 383n. *heater*; empyrosis, deflagration, conflagration; wild-fire, forest f., prairie f.; blaze, flame, sheet of f., wall of f.; spark, scintillation, flash, arc 417n. *light*; eruption, volcano 383n. *furnace*; fireworks, pyrotechnics; arson 381n. *incendiarism*; fire worship 981n. *worship*; smell of burning, empyreuma 381n. *burning*.

thermometry, heat measurement, thermometer, differential t., clinical t., Fahrenheit t., centigrade t., Réaumur t.; diathermometer; thermometrograph, thermoscope, pyroscope, thermopile, thermostat, air-conditioner; pyrometer, radio micrometer, calorimeter; thermal unit, British Thermal Unit, B.T.U., therm, calorie; pyrology, thermology, thermotics, thermodynamics; thermography, thermograph.

Adj. *hot*, heated, superheated, overheated; inflamed, fervent, fervid; flaming, glowing, red-hot, white-h.; diathermic, diathermanous; piping hot, smoking h.; hot as pepper 388adj. *pungent*; calescent, incalescent, recalescent; feverish, febrile, fevered; sweltering, sudorific, sweating, perspiring; on the boil, boiling, ebullient, scalding; tropical, torrid, scorching, gril-

ling, baking, toasting, roasting; scorched, scalded 381adj. *heated*; thirsty, burning, parched 342adj. *dry*; running a temperature, in a fever, in a heat, in a sweat, in a muck s.

fiery, ardent, burning, blazing, flaming, flaring; unquenched, unextinguished; smoking, smouldering; ablaze, afire, on fire, in flames; candescent, incandescent, molten, glowing, aglow; pyrogenic, igneous, pyrogenous; ignited, lit, alight, kindled, enkindled; volcanic, erupting, plutonic.

warm, tepid, lukewarm, unfrozen; temperate, mild, genial, balmy; fair, set f., sunny, sunshiny 417adj. *undimmed*; summery, estival; tropical, equatorial; canicular, torrid, sultry; stuffy, close; overheated, uncooled, unventilated; oppressive, suffocating, stifling 653adj. *insalubrious*; warm as toast; snug 376adj. *comfortable*; at room temperature, at blood heat.

Vb. *be hot*, be warm, get warm etc. adj.; incalesce, recalesce, incandesce; burn, kindle, catch fire, take f., draw; blaze, flare, flame, flame up, burst into flame; glow, flush; smoke, smoulder, reek, fume, let off steam 300vb. *emit*; boil, seethe 318 vb. *effervesce*; toast, grill, roast, sizzle, crackle, frizzle, fry, bake 381vb. *burn*; get burnt, scorch, boil dry; apricate, bask, sun oneself, sun-bathe; get sunburnt, tan; swelter, sweat, perspire; melt, thaw 337vb. *liquefy*; thirst, parch 342vb. *be dry*; stifle, pant, gasp for breath, fight for air; be in a fever, have f., run a temperature; keep warm, wrap up.

See: 128, 300, 318, 337, 342, 364, 376, 381, 383, 388, 417, 420, 651, 653, 981.

380 Cold

N. *coldness*, etc. adj.; low temperature, drop in t.; cool, coolness, freshness; cold, absolute c., zero temperature, zero; frigidity, gelidity; iciness, frostiness; sensation of cold, chilliness, algidity, algor, rigor, shivering, shivers, chattering of the teeth, goose-flesh, goose pimples, gooseskin, frostbite, chilblains; chill, catching cold; cold climate, high latitude, Siberia, Nova Zembla, North Pole, South P.; Arctic, Antarctica.

wintriness, winter, depth of w., hard w.;

cold weather, cold front; inclemency, wintry weather, arctic conditions, polar temperature, degrees of frost; snowstorm, hail-s., blizzard; frost, Jack Frost, rime, hoarfrost, white frost, sharp f., hard f.; sleet, hail, silver thaw, freeze.

snow, snow flake, snow-crystal, snow-fall, avalanche, snow-drift, snow-storm, flurry of snow; snow-line, snowball, snowman; snow-plough, snow-shoe.

ice, dry i., ice-cube; hailstone, icicle; ice-cap, ice-sheet, ice-field, floe, ice-f., ice-hill, ice-foot, ice-belt, ice-ledge; iceberg, berg, ice-island; ice-drift, ice-stream, glacier, ice-fall, sérac; shelf-ice, pack-i.; driven snow, frozen s., névé, frozen sea; ice-work, ice-action, ice-quake; ice-ship, ice-yacht, ice-plough, ice-chamber, ice-box 382n. *refrigeration*; ice-master; ice-craft.

Adj. *cold*, without heat, impervious to heat, adiathermic; cool, temperate; shady, chill, chilly; unheated, unwarmed, unthawed; fresh, raw, keen, bitter, nipping, biting, piercing, aguish; inclement, freezing, frore, ice-cold, bitterly c.; frigid, hiemal, brumal 129adj. *wintry*; winterbound, frosty, frost-bound, snowy, niveous, sleety, icy; glacial, ice-capped, glaciered; boreal, polar, Arctic, Antarctic, Siberian; like ice, cold as charity, cold as Christmas; isocheimal, isocheimenal.

a-cold, feeling cold, chilly, shivering, chattering, shivery, algid, aguish, aguey; blue, blue with cold; starved with cold, chilled to the bone, hypothermal, frozen, frostbitten, frost-nipped; cold as a frog, cold as marble, stone-cold, clay-cold, cold as death.

Vb. *be cold* etc. adj.; grow cold, lose heat, drop in temperature; feel cold, chatter, shiver, tremble, shake, quake, quiver, shudder, didder; freeze, starve, perish with cold; catch cold, get a chill; chill 382vb. *refrigerate*.

Adv. *frostily*, frigidly, bitterly, coldly.

See: 129, 382.

381 Calefaction

N. *heating*, superheating, increase of temperature, tepefaction, calefaction, torrefaction; diathermy, diathermancy, transcalency; calorification, calorific value,

thermal efficiency; inflammation, warming, aprication, insolation, sunning 342 n. *desiccation*; melting, thawing 337 n. *liquefaction*; smelting, scorification, cupellation; boiling, ebullition; coction, digestion, cooking 301 n. *cookery*; decoction, distillation; anti-freeze mixture.

burning, combustion, incension; inflammation, kindling, ignition, accension; flagration, deflagration, conflagration 379 n. *fire*; incineration, calcination, concremation; ustulation, roasting; cremation 364 n. *interment*; suttee, self-burning 362 n. *suicide*; auto-da-fé, holocaust 981 n. *oblation*; cauterization, cautery, branding; scorching, singeing, charring, carbonization; inflammability, combustibility; burner, touch-hole 383 n. *furnace*; cauterant, cauterizer, caustic, moxa, vitriol; hot-iron, branding i., brand; match, touch-paper 385 n. *lighter*; fire-attendant, fueller, stoker, fireman; burn-mark, burn, brand, singe, scald, sunburn, tan, empyreuma.

incendiarism, arson, fire-raising, pyromania; incendiary, arsonist, fire-raiser, fire-bug, petroleur, petroleuse; firebrand, revolutionary 738 n. *agitator*.

warm clothes, furs, woollens, woollies, flannel; parka, wrapper, wrap, muffler, muff; warm 228 n. *overcoat*; blanket 226 n. *coverlet*; padding, wadding 227 n. *lining*.

ash, ashes, volcanic ash, lava, tuff; carbon, soot, smut, lamp-black, smoke; product of combustion, clinker, charcoal, ember, cinder, coke, slag, dross, scoria, sullage, oxide, bone-ash.

pottery, ceramics; earthenware, lustre ware, glazed w.; majolica, faience, chinaware, porcelain; crockery, china, bone c., Wedgwood c., Worcester c., Derby c., Sèvres c., Delft c., Dresden c.; willow-pattern, terracotta, tile, brick, sun-dried b., mud b.; pot, urn 194 n. *vessel*.

Adj. *heated*, superheated 379 adj. *hot*; centrally-heated, winterized; lit, kindled, fired; incendiarized, burnt, burnt out, burnt down, gutted; cooked, roasted, toasted, grilled, baked; réchauffé, hotted up, warmed up; melted, fused, molten; overheated; steamy, smoky; scorched, charred, adust, singed, branded; tanned, sun-t., sunburnt; empyreumatic.

heating, warming etc. vb.; calefactive, calorific, caustic, burning; incendiary, inflammatory; diathermal, diathermanous 385 adj. *combustible*; antifreeze.

Vb. *heat*, raise the temperature, warm; provide heating, winterize; keep the cold out, take off the chill; hot up, warm up, stoke up; thaw, thaw out; inflame, chafe, foment 832 vb. *aggravate*; overheat, stive, stew, stifle, suffocate; insolate, sun, parch, shrivel, sear 342 vb. *dry*; torrefy, toast, bake, grill, fry, roast 301 vb. *cook*; melt, de-frost, de-ice 337 vb. *liquefy*; smelt, cupel, scorify; fuse, weld, vulcanize, cast, found

kindle, enkindle, ignite, light, strike a l.; apply the match, apply the torch, set fire to, touch off 385 vb. *fire*; rekindle, relume; fuel, stoke, feed the flames, fan the fire, add fuel to the f., poke the f., stir the f., blow the f.; make the fire, rub two sticks together.

burn, burn up, burn out, gut; commit to the flames, consign to the f.; make a bonfire of, send to the stake; fire, incendiarize; cremate, incinerate, burn to ashes; boil dry 342 vb. *dry*; carbonize, calcine, oxidize, corrode; coal, char, singe, scorch, tan; cauterize, brand, burn in; scald.

See: 194, 226, 227, 228, 301, 337, 342, 362, 364, 379, 383, 385, 738, 832, 981.

382 Refrigeration

N. *refrigeration*, infrigidation, cooling, reduction of temperature; icing etc. vb.; freezing, freezing up, glaciation, conglaciation, congelation 380 n. *ice*; solidification 324 n. *condensation*; exposure; ventilation, air-conditioning; deep-freeze 384 n. *refrigerator*.

incombustibility, incombustibleness, non-inflammability, fire-resistance; asbestos, amiant, amiantus.

extinguisher, fire-e., fire-annihilator; water, hose, sprinkler, hydrant, standpipe; fire-engine, fire-brigade, fire-station; fireman, fire-fighter.

Adj. *cooled* etc. vb.; ventilated, air-conditioned; frozen, frozen up; ice-capped, glaciered; frosted, iced, glacé; with ice, on the rocks 380 adj. *cold*; cooling etc. vb.; frigorific, refrigerative, deep-freeze.

incombustible, unburnable; uninflammable, non-inflammable; fire-resistant, fire-

proof, flame-p., burn-p.; asbestic, amiantine; damped, wetted 341 adj. *drenched.*

Vb. *refrigerate,* cool, fan, air-condition, freshen up 685 vb. *refresh*; ventilate, air 340 vb. *aerify*; reduce the temperature, turn off the heat; keep the heat out, keep the sun off, shade, shadow 421 vb. *screen*; frost, freeze, congeal, glaciate; make ice, ice, glacify; ice up, ice over; chill, benumb, starve, petrify, nip, pinch, bite, pierce; chill to the marrow, make one's teeth chatter; expose to the cold, frost-nip, frost-bite.

extinguish, quench, snuff, put out, blow o., snuff o.; choke, stifle 165 vb. *suppress*; damp, douse, damp down, bank d.; rake out, stamp o., stub o.; stop burning, go out, burn o., die down.

See: 165, 324, 340, 341, 380, 384, 421, 685.

383 Furnace

N. *furnace,* fiery f.; the stake 964 n. *means of execution*; volcano, solfatara, fumarole; touch-hole, gun-barrel; forge, blast-furnace, reverbatory, kiln, lime-k., brick-k.; oast, oast-house; incinerator, destructor; crematory, crematorium; stove, kitchen s., charcoal s., gas s., electric s., primus s., oil s.; oven, gas-o., electric o., chula; range, kitchen r., kitchener; cooker, oil c., gas c., electric c., fireless c.; gas-ring, burner, alcohol b., bunsen b.; blow-lamp, oxyacetylene l.; fire, kitchen f., coal f., coke f., wood f. 379 n. *fire*; fire-box, fire-place, grate, hearth, ingle; fire-irons, andirons, fire-dog; poker, tongs, shovel; hob, trivet; fireguard, fender; flue 263 vb. *chimney.*

heater, radiator, hypocaust, hot-water pipe, boiler, salamander, copper, cauldron, kettle, electric k. 194 n. *caldron*; brazier, fire-pan, warming p., chafing dish, hot-water bottle; electric blanket, hand-warmer, foot-warmer; hot-case, hot-plate; still, retort, alembic, cucurbit, crucible, athanor 461 n. *testing agent*; blowpipe, bellows, tuyère, damper; hot baths, thermæ, hammam, Turkish bath, calidarium, tepidarium, sudatorium 648 n. *ablution*; hotbed, hot-house, conservatory 370 n. *garden*; sun-trap, solarium; kitchen, galley, cookhouse, caboose; gridiron, grill, frying-pan, stew-pan;

toaster, electric t.; flat-iron, electric i. 258 n. *smoother*; curling-iron; heating agent, flame, sunlight 381 n. *calefaction*; gas, electricity; steam, hot air; wood, coal 385 n. *fuel.*

See: 194, 258, 263, 370, 379, 381, 385, 461, 648, 964.

384 Refrigerator

N. *refrigerator,* cooler; ventilator, fan, punkah, air-conditioner; cooling-room, frigidarium; frigidaire, fridge, refrigeratory, refrigerating plant, refrigerating machine, freezer, wine-cooler, ice-pail; coolant, freezing mixture, snow, ice; icehouse, ice-chest, ice-box, ice-pack, ice-bag; ice-cubes, rocks; cold storage, deep-freeze 382 n. *refrigeration.*

See: 382.

385 Fuel

N. *fuel,* inflammable material, combustible, food for the flames; firing, kindling, briquette, fire-ball; wood, brushwood, firewood, faggot, log, Yule l.; turf, peat, peat-moss, peat-hag, peat bog; lignite, brown coal, wood c., charcoal; chemical fuel, oil, fuel o., petrol, gasoline, gas, high octane, diesel oil, derv, hidyne; paraffin, kerosene, spirit, methylated s., napalm; gas, natural g., coal g., acetylene.

coal, black diamond, sea-coal, steam-c., hard c., anthracite, wallsend, cannel coal, bituminous c.; coal dust, culm, slack, nutty s.; coal seam, coal deposit, coal measure, coalfield 632 n. *store*; cinders, embers 381 n. *ash*; coke, gas-c.; smokeless fuel.

lighter, petrol-l., cigarette l., igniter, light, illuminant, taper, spill, candle 420 n. *torch*; coal, ember, brand, fire-b.; fire-barrel, fire-ship; wick, fuse, touch-paper, match, slow m.; linstock, portfire 723 n. *fire-arm*; cap, detonator; safety-match, friction m., lucifer, vesta, vesuvian, congreve, fusee, locofoco; self-igniting match; flint, steel, tinder, German t., touchwood, punk, spunk, amadou; tinder-box, match-box.

fumigator, incense, joss-stick, sulphur, brimstone.

Adj. *combustible*, burnable, inflammable, explosive; carboniferous, carbonaceous, coal-bearing, coaly.

Vb. *fire*, stoke, feed, fuel, coal, add fuel to the flames; make the fire; rub two sticks together 381 vb. *kindle*.

See: 381, 420, 632, 723.

386 Taste

N. *taste*, sapor, sapidity, savour; flavour, flavouring; smack, smatch, tang, twang, after-taste; relish, gust, gusto, zest, appetite 859 n. *liking*; tasting, gustation, degustation; palate, velum, tongue, gustatory nerve, taste-buds; tooth, stomach; refinement 846 n. *good taste.*

Adj. *tasty*, sapid, saporific, palatable, gustable, well-tasting, appetizing 390 adj. *savoury*; flavoured, doctored, spiced, spicy, racy, rich, strong, full-flavoured, full-bodied, generous, vintage; gustatory, gustative.

Vb. *taste*, degust, find palatable, smack the lips, roll on the tongue, lick one's fingers; savour, sample, try; sip, lick, sup, nibble 301 vb. *eat*; have a taste, taste of, savour of, smack of, relish of 18 vb. *resemble*; taste well, tickle the palate 390 vb. *appetize.*

See: 18, 301, 390, 846, 859.

387 Insipidity

N. *insipidity*, vapidity, jejunity, vapidness, jejuneness, flatness, staleness, tastelessness etc. adj.; water, milk and water, pap, cat-lap.

Adj. *tasteless*, without taste, void of taste; jejune, vapid, insipid, watery, milk-and-water; mild, underproof; with water, diluted, adulterated 163 adj. *weakened*; wishy-washy, deadish, flat, stale; savourless, gustless, flavourless, unflavoured, unspiced; unsavoured, untasted; in bad taste 847 adj. *vulgar.*

See: 163, 847.

388 Pungency

N. *pungency*, piquancy, poignancy, sting, bite, edge; burning taste, causticity; hot taste, spiciness; sharp taste, acridity, sharpness, acerbity, acidity 393 n. *sourness*; roughness, harshness; strong taste, strength, tang, twang, race; bad taste 391 adj. *unsavouriness*; salt, brine, ginger, pepper, mustard, curry, chilli 389 n. *condiment*; nitre, saltpetre, ammonia, sal-ammoniac, smelling salts, hartshorn 656 n. *restoration*; cordial, pick-me-up, bracer 174 n. *stimulant*; dram, nip, tot 301 n. *potion*; hemp, ganja 658 n. *drug.*

tobacco, baccy, nicotine; the weed, fragrant w., Indian w.; tobacco-leaf, Virginia tobacco, Turkish t., Russian t.; snuff, rappee, maccoboy; plug of tobacco, plug, quid, fid, twist; chewing tobacco, pipe-t., shag; cigar, cheroot, Burma c., segar, Havanna; cigarette, fag, gasper, reefer, nail, woodbine; tobacco-pipe, clay-p., dudeen, churchwarden; briar, corncob; meerschaum, hubble-bubble, hookah, narghile; pipe of peace, calumet; bowl, stem; tobacco juice, tobacco stain; snuff-taker; tobacco-chewer; smoker, pipe-s., cigarette-s., cigar-s.; tobacconist, tobacco shop, cigar store, cigar divan; snuff-box, cigarette-case, cigar-c., cigarette-box, cigar-box; pipe-rack; pipe-cleaner, reamer; tobacco-pouch, tobacco-jar; smoking jacket, smoking cap; smoker, smoking carriage.

Adj. *pungent*, penetrating, strong; stinging, mordant, biting 256 adj. *sharp*; caustic, burning; harsh 259 adj. *rough*; bitter, acrid, tart, astringent 393 adj. *sour*; heady, overproof, meracious; full-flavoured, nutty; strong-flavoured, high-tasted, high, gamy, off; high-seasoned, spicy, spiced, curried; hot, peppery, hot as pepper; smoky.

salty, salt, brackish, briny, salsuginous, saline, pickled; salt as brine, salt as a herring, salt as Lot's wife.

Vb. *be pungent*, sting, bite the tongue, set the teeth on edge, make the eyes water.

season, salt, brine, pickle; flavour, sauce; spice, pepper, devil, curry; smoke, smoke-dry, kipper 666 vb. *preserve.*

smoke, use tobacco, indulge, smoke a pipe, draw, suck, inhale; puff, blow smoke-rings; blow smoke, funk; chew, quid; take snuff, take a pinch.

See: 174, 256, 259, 301, 389, 391, 393, 656, 658, 666.

389 Condiment

N. *condiment*, seasoning, flavouring, dressing, relish; caviar; jam, marmalade 392n. *sweet*; pickles, achar; salt, garlic s.; mustard, French m.; pepper, cayenne, chilli, chilli pepper; capsicum, paprika, pimento, red pepper, green p.; black pepper, peppercorn; curry, curry powder; vegetable curry, meat c.; onion, garlic 301 n. *potherb*; spicery, spices, spice, allspice, Jamaica pepper, mace, cinnamon, turmeric, saffron, galingale, ginger, nutmeg, clove, caper, caraway.
sauce, roux; sauce piquante, sauce tartare, tabasco sauce, horseradish s., caper s.; apple sauce, cranberry s., mint s.; tomato sauce, ketchup; pepper-sauce; chutney, sweet c., mango c., strong c.

Vb. See 388 vb. *season.*

See: 301, 388, 392.

390 Savouriness

N. *savouriness*, right taste, tastiness, palatability; raciness, fine flavour, full f., richness; body, bouquet; savoury, relish, appetizer; delicacy, dainty, cate, bakemeat, titbit, bonne-bouche; caviar; cocktail eats, hors d'œuvre; game, venison, turtle; ambrosia, nectar, amrita; epicure's delight.
Adj. *savoury*, nice, good, good to eat, worth eating; flavoured, spicy 386 adj. *tasty*; well-dressed, well-cooked, done to a turn; tempting, appetizing, gustful; well-tasted, to one's taste, palatable, toothsome, sweet; dainty, lickerish, delicate; delectable, delicious, exquisite, epicurean; ambrosial, nectareous, fit for the gods; luscious, juicy, succulent; creamy, rich, greasy; right-flavoured, racy; rare-flavoured, full-f., vintage.
Vb. *appetize*, spice, 388 vb. *season*; be savoury, tickle the appetite, tickle the palate, flatter the p.; taste good, taste sweet 392 vb. *sweeten*; like, relish, savour, lap up, smack the lips, roll on one's tongue, lick one's fingers, water at the mouth 386 vb. *taste.*

See: 386, 388, 392.

391 Unsavouriness

N. *unsavouriness* etc. adj.; unpalatability, nasty taste, wrong t.; rankness, rottenness, unwholesomeness 653 n. *insalubrity*; roughness, coarseness, plain cooking 573 n. *plainness*; amaritude, acerbity, acritude 393 n. *sourness*; austerity, prison fare, bread and water, water of affliction, bread of a.; aloes, quassia, rue; bitter pill, gall and wormwood; asafœtida, emetic, sickener, poison 659 n. *bane.*
Adj. *unsavoury*, flat 387 adj. *tasteless*; ill-flavoured, unpalatable, unappetizing; coarse, raw, undressed, ill-cooked; uneatable, inedible; hard, leathery 329 adj. *tough*; sugarless, unsweetened; rough 388 adj. *pungent*; bitter, bitter as gall, acrid, acid 393 adj. *sour*; undrinkable, corked; rank, rancid, stinking 397 adj. *fetid*; nasty, filthy, offensive, repulsive, disgusting, loathsome 827 adj. *unpleasant*; sickening, emetic, nauseous, nauseating 861 adj. *disliked*; poisonous 653 adj. *toxic.*
Vb. *be unpalatable* etc. adj.; disgust, repel, sicken, nauseate, turn the stomach 861 vb. *cause dislike*; poison; lose its savour, pall.

See: 329, 387, 388, 393, 397, 573, 653, 659, 827, 861.

392 Sweetness

N. *sweetness*, dulcitude; sweetening, dulcification, dulcoration; sugariness, saccharinity; charm 826 n. *pleasurableness*; sweet smell 396 n. *fragrance*; sweet music 410 n. *melody*; saccharometer 465 n. *gauge.*
sweet, sweetening, honey, honeycomb, honeypot, honeydew; honeysuckle 396 n. *fragrance*; saccharine, saccharose, sucrose, glucose, dextrose, fructose, galactose; sugar, cane s., beet s., malt s., milk s.; invert sugar, saccharum; molasses, jaggery; syrup, treacle; sweet drink, julep, nectar, hydromel, mead, metheglin, liqueur, sweet wine; conserve, preserve, condensed milk, jam, marmalade, jelly; candy, sugar-c., sugar-plum; icing; sugar-coating; sweets, marzipan, Turkish delight, chocolate, toffee, toffee-apple, fudge, butterscotch, liquorice, gum; comfit, bonbon, jujube, caramel, lollipop, rock; confectionery, confection, cake, pastry, tart, puff, pie, pudding; crystallized fruits 301 n. *sweetmeat.*
Adj. *sweet*, sweet to the taste, sweetened,

honied, honeyed, candied, crystallized; sugared, sugary, saccharine, sacchariferous; honey-bearing, melliferous; ambrosial, nectareous, luscious, sweet as honey, sweet as sugar, sweet as a nut 390adj. *savoury*; sweet to the ear, mellifluous, dulcet, harmonious 410adj. *melodious*; sweet to the senses 376adj. *pleasant*; sweet to the mind 826adj. *pleasurable*.

Vb. *sweeten*, sugar, candy, crystallize, ice; sugar the pill, coat the p.; dulcify, dulcorate, edulcorate, saccharize; sweeten wine, mull.

See: 301, 376, 390, 396, 410, 465, 826.

393 Sourness

N. *sourness*, acidity, acerbity; tartness, bitterness, vinegariness; sharpness 388n. *pungency*; acetous fermentation, acidosis; acid, argol, tartar; lemon, vinegar; crab, crab-apple; verjuice, alum, bitter aloes, bitters; gall, wormwood, absinth.

Adj. *sour*, sourish, acid, acidulous, acidulated, sub-acid, acescent, acetous, acetose, acid-forming, tartaric; acerb, crabbed, tart, bitter; vinegary, sour as vinegar; unripe, green, hard, rough 670adj. *immature*; astringent, styptic; sugarless, unsugared, dry.

Vb. *be sour* etc. adj.; sour, turn, turn sour; acetify, acidify, acidulate; ferment; tartarize; set one's teeth on edge.

See: 388, 670.

394 Odour

N. *odour*, smell, aroma, bouquet; sweet smell, perfume, essence 396n. *fragrance*; bad smell, stink 397n. *fetor*; exhalation, effluvium, emanation; smoke, fume, reek, nidor; breath, whiff; strong smell, odorousness, redolence, graveolence; scent, trail 548n. *trace*; olfaction, sense of smell, act of smelling; olfactory, nostril, nose 254n. *protuberance*; keen-scentedness, flair.

Adj. *odorous*, endowed with scent, odoriferous, smelling; scented, perfumed 396adj. *fragrant*; graveolent, strong, heady, heavy, full-bodied 388adj. *pungent*; smelly, redolent, nidorous, reeking; malodorous, whiffy, niffy 397adj. *fetid*; smelt,

reaching one's nostrils; olfactory, quick-scented, sharp-nosed.

Vb. *smell*, have an odour, reach one's nostrils; smell of, breathe of, smell strong of, reek of, reek; give out a smell, exhale; smell out, scent, nose, wind, get wind of 484vb. *detect*; snuff, snuff up, sniff, breathe in, inhale 352vb. *breathe*; make to smell, scent, perfume, incense, fumigate, thurify, cruse.

See: 254, 352, 388, 396, 397, 484, 548.

395 Inodorousness

N. *inodorousness*, odourlessness, scentlessness; absence of smell, want of s.; loss of s.; inability to smell, anosmia; noselessness, lack of flair; deodorant, deodorizer, fumes, incense, pastil, pastille; deodorization, fumigation, ventilation, purification 648 n. *cleansing*.

Adj. *odourless*, inodorous, inodorate, scentless, without smell, wanting s.; unscented, unperfumed; deodorized; deodorizing; noseless, without sense of smell, without flair.

Vb. *have no smell*, not smell, want s.; be inodorous, — scentless etc.adj.; deodorize, take away the smell, defumigate; ventilate, clear the air 648vb. *purify*; lose the scent 495vb. *err*.

See: 495, 648.

396 Fragrance

N. *fragrance*, sweet smell, sweet savour, balminess 392n. *sweetness*; odour of sanctity 979n. *piety*; redolence, aroma, bouquet 394n. *odour*; violet, rose; bank of violets, bed of roses; flower-garden, rose-g. 370n. *garden*; buttonhole, boutonnière, nosegay; thurification, fumigation; perfumery, perfumer.

scent, perfume, aromatic p., aromatic gum, balm, myrrh, incense, frankincense; spicery 389 n. *condiment*; breath-sweetener, cloves, pastel, pastille; musk, civet, ambergris, camphor; sandal, sandalwood otto, ottar, attar; lavender, thyme, spearmint, chypre, vanilla, citronella oil; frangipane, bergamot, orris root, woodruff; toilet water, lavender w., rose-w., attar of roses, eau-de-cologne; sandal-

wood paste, patchouli, pomade, hair-oil, face-powder, scented soap 843 n. *cosmetic*; scent-bag, lavender-b., sachet, pouncet box; pomander, pot-pourri, scent-bottle, smelling-b., vinaigrette; joss-stick, censer, thurible, incense-bearer, incense-boat.

Adj. *fragrant*, redolent, aromatic, scented, perfumed; incense-breathing, balmy, ambrosial; sweet-scented, sweet-perfumed; thuriferous, perfumatory, musky, muscadine; spicy, fruity; of roses, fragrant as a rose; laid up in lavender.

Vb. *be fragrant*, smell sweet, smell like a rose, have a perfume, scent, perfume, fumigate, thurify, cense; embalm, lay up in lavender.

See: 370, 389, 392, 394, 843, 979.

397 Fetor

N. *fetor*, fedity, fetidness, offensiveness; offence to the nose, graveolence, bad smell, bad odour, foul o., malodour; body-odour, B.O., armpits; foul breath, halitosis; stink, stench, reek; noxious stench, mephitis; smell of burning, empyreuma; smell of death, taint, corruption, rancidity, putrefaction 51 n. *decay*; foulness 649 n. *dirt*; mustiness, fustiness, staleness, stale air, frowst; fungus, garlic, assafœtida; stoat, skunk, polecat; stinkard, stinker, stink-pot, stink-bomb, bad egg; dung 302 n. *excrement*; latrine, sewer 649 n. *sink*.

Adj. *fetid*, olid, graveolent, strong-smelling, heavy, strong; reeking, nidorous; ill-smelling, ill-scented, malodorous, not of roses; smelly, whiffy, niffy; stinking, rank, hircine; fruity, gamy, high; bad, gone b., tainted, rancid; suppurating, gangrenous 51 adj. *decomposed*; stale, musty, reasty, fusty, frowsty, frowzy, unventilated, stuffy, suffocating; foul, noisome, noxious, sulphurous, mephitic 653 adj. *toxic*; acrid 388 adj. *pungent*; burning, empyreumatic; nasty, disagreeable, fulsome 827 adj. *unpleasant*.

Vb. *stink*, smell, reek; make a smell, funk, fart, blow off; have a bad smell, smell strong, smell offensively; smell bad 51 vb. *decompose*; stink in the nostrils, stink to high heaven, make one hold one's nose; smell like a bad egg, smell like a drain; stink like a fen, stink like a pig, stink like a goat, stink like a polecat; overpower with stink, stink out.

See: 51, 302, 388, 649, 653, 827.

398 Sound

N. *sound*, auditory effect, distinctness; audibility, reception 415 n. *hearing*; sounding, sonance, sound-making; stereophonic sound; radio noise 417 n. *radiation*; sonority, sonorousness 404 n. *resonance*; noise, loud sound 400 n. *loudness*; low sound, softness 401 n. *faintness*; quality of sound, tone, pitch, level, cadence; accent, intonation, twang, timbre 577 n. *voice*; tune, strain 410 n. *melody*, 412 n. *music*; types of sound 402 n. *bang*, 403 n. *roll*, 404 n. *resonance*, 405 n. *non-resonance*, 406 n. *sibilation*, 407 n. *stridor*, 408 n. *cry*, 409 n. *ululation*, 412 n. *discord*; transmission of sound, telephone 531 n. *telecommunication*; phonograph 414 n. *gramophone*; loud-speaker 415 n. *hearing aid*; unit of sound, decibel, sone; sonic barrier, sound b.

acoustics, phonics; catacoustics, cataphonics, diacoustics, diaphonics, phonology, phonography; phonetics; acoustician; phonetician, phoneticist, phonetist, phonographer; audiometer, sonometer.

speech sound, simple sound, phone, syllable, dissyllable, polysyllable; consonant, spirant, liquid, sibilant; dental, nasal, palatal, guttural, velar, labiovelar; fricative; aspirate, rough breathing, smooth b.; stop; click; plosive, semiplosive; sonant; surd; semi-vowel; glide, glide sound; voiced breath, vowel, front v., middle v., back v.; diphthong, triphthong 577 n. *voice*; monophthongization, diphthongization; modified sound, allophone; vowel gradation, ablaut; umlaut; guna, vriddhi; assimilation, dissimulation; samdhi; vocable 559 n. *word*; sound symbol, phonogram 558 n. *spoken letter*, 586 n. *script*.

Adj. *sounding*, soniferous, sonorific; sonic; supersonic; plain, audible, distinct, heard; resounding, sonorous 404 adj. *resonant*; stentorian 400 adj. *loud*; auditory, acoustic; phonic, phonetic; sonantal, vocal, vowelled, voiced, monophthongal, diphthongal; sonant, sonorant; consonantal; spirantal, surd, unvoiced.

Vb. *sound,* produce s., give out s., emit s., make a noise 400vb. *be loud,* 404vb. *resound;* phonetize, phonate.

See: 400, 401, 402, 403, 404, 405, 406, 407, 408, 409, 410, 412, 414, 415, 417, 531, 558, 559, 577, 586.

399 Silence

N. *silence,* soundlessness, inaudibility, not a sound, not a squeak; stillness, hush, lull, rest, peace, quiet 266n. *quiescence;* muteness, speechlessness 578n. *aphony;* solemn silence, awful s., pin-drop s., deathlike s., dead s., perfect s.

Adj. *silent,* still, stilly, hushed, whist; calm, peaceful, quiet 266adj. *quiescent;* soft, faint 401n. *muted;* noiseless, soundless, frictionless, soundproof; aphonic, speechless, tongueless, mute 578n. *voiceless;* unsounded, unuttered, unspoken; solemn, awful, deathlike, silent as the grave.

Vb. *be silent,* not open one's mouth, hold one's tongue 582vb. *be taciturn;* not speak 578vb. *be mute;* be still, make no noise, make not a sound; become silent, relapse into silence, pipe down, lose one's voice. *silence,* still, lull, hush, quiet, quieten, make silent; play down, soft-pedal; stifle, muffle, gag, stop, stop someone's mouth, muzzle, put the lid on, put to silence 578 vb. *make mute;* drown, drown the noise.

Int. hush! sh! silence! quiet! peace! soft! whist! hold your tongue! keep your mouth shut! shut up! keep your trap shut! dry up! cut the cackle! stow it! be still! mum's the word!

See: 266, 401, 578, 582.

400 Loudness

N. *loudness,* distinctness, audibility 398n. *sound;* noise, loud n., ear-splitting n.; broken *or* shattered silence, knock, knocking; burst of sound, report, loud r., slam, clap, thunderclap, burst, shell-b., explosion 402n. *bang;* alarum, alarm, honk, toot, tootle 665n. *danger signal;* prolonged noise, reverberation, plangency, boom, rattle 403n. *roll;* thunder, rattling t., war in heaven 176n. *storm;* dashing, surging, hissing 406n. *sibilation;* fire, gunfire, artillery, blitz 712n. *bombardment;*

stridency, brassiness, shrillness, blast, blare, bray, fanfare, flourish, tucket, flourish of trumpets 407n. *stridor;* trumpet blast, clarion call, view halloo 547n. *call;* sonority, organ notes, clang, clangour 404n. *resonance;* bells, peal, carillon 412n. *campanology;* diapason, swell, crescendo, fortissimo, full blast, full chorus; vociferation, clamour, outcry, roaring, shouting, screaming, shout, howl, scream, roar 408n. *cry,* 409n. *ululation;* loud laughter, cachinnation 835n. *laughter;* loud breathing, stertorousness 352n. *respiration;* noisiness, din, row, deafening r., racket, clatter, hubbub, hullabaloo, ballyhoo, song and dance, slamming, banging, stamping, chanting, hooting, uproar, tumult, rowdiness, fracas, brawl, pandemonium, hell let loose 61n. *turmoil. megaphone,* amplifier, loud pedal; loudhailer, loudspeaker, speaker, microphone, mike; ear-trumpet 415n. *hearing aid;* loud instrument, whistle, siren, hooter, horn, klaxon; buzzer, bell, alarum, doorknocker; trumpet, brass; stentorian voice, lungs, good l., lungs of brass, iron throat; Stentor, town-crier.

Adj. *loud,* distinct, audible, heard; noisy, full of noise, rackety, uproarious, rowdy, rumbustious, riproaring, obstreperous, tumultuous 61 adj. *orderless;* multisonous, many-tongued 411 adj. *discordant;* clamorous, clamant, shouting, screaming, bellowing 408adj. *crying;* bigmouthed, loud-m.; sonorous, booming, deep, full, powerful; lusty, full-throated, stentorian, brazen-mouthed, trumpettongued; deafening, dinning; piercing, ear-splitting, ear-rending; thundering, thunderous, rattling, crashing; pealing, clangorous, plangent, strepitous; shrill, high-sounding 407 adj. *strident;* blatant, blaring, brassy; echoing, resounding 404adj. *resonant;* swelling, crescendo; fortissimo, enough to waken the dead.

Vb. *be loud,*—noisy etc.adj.; break the silence; speak up, give tongue, raise the voice, strain one's v., strain; call, cat-call, caterwaul; skirl, scream, whistle 407vb. *shrill;* vociferate, shout 411vb. *cry;* cachinnate 835vb. *laugh;* roar, bellow, howl 412vb. *ululate;* din, sound, boom, reverberate 404vb. *resound;* rattle, thunder, fulminate, storm; surge, clash 406vb. *hiss;* ring, peal, clang, crash; bray, blare;

slam 402 vb. *bang*; burst, explode, detonate, go off; knock, knock hard, hammer; deafen, stun; split the ears, rend the eardrums, ring in the ear; swell, fill the air; rend the skies, make the welkin ring, rattle the windows, awake the echoes, startle the e., awake the dead; raise Cain, kick up a shindy, stamp 61 vb. *rampage*.

Adv. *loudly* etc. adj.; noisily, dinningly; aloud, at the top of one's voice, lustily; in full cry, full blast, full chorus; fortissimo, crescendo.

See: 61, 176, 352, 398, 402, 403, 404, 406, 407, 408, 409, 411, 412, 415, 547, 665, 712, 835.

401 Faintness

N. *faintness*, softness, indistinctness, inaudibility; less sound, reduction of s., noise abatement; dull sound, thud, thump, bump 405 n. *non-resonance*; whisper, susurration; breath, bated b., under-b., undertone, undersong, undercurrent of sound; murmur, hum, sigh, sough, moan; scratch, squeak, creak, pop; tick, click; tinkle, clink, chink; buzz, whirr; purr, purl, plash, swish; rustle, frou-frou; patter, pitter-p., pit-a-pat; soft footfall, pad; soft voice, quiet tone, conversation level.

silencer, noise-queller, mute, damper, sordine, soft pedal; stopper 414 n. *mute*; rubber heel, rubber soles; grease, oil 334 n. *lubricant*.

Adj. *muted*, distant, faint, inaudible, uncaught; just heard, barely h., half-h.; trembling in the air, dying away; weak, feeble, unemphatic, unstressed, unaccented; soft, low, gentle; purling, rippling; piano, subdued, hushed, stealthy, whispered; dull, dead 405 adj. *non-resonant*; muffled, stifled, bated 407 adj. *hoarse*.

Vb. *sound faint*, drop one's voice, whisper, breathe, murmur, mutter 578 vb. *speak low*; sing low, hum, croon, purr; purl, babble, ripple, plash, lap, gurgle, guggle 350 vb. *flow*; tinkle, chime; moan, sigh, sough 352 vb. *blow*; rustle, swish; tremble, melt; float on the air, steal on the air, melt on the a., die on the ear; squeak, creak; plop, pop; tick, click; clink, chink; thud, thump 405 vb. *sound dead*.

mute, soften, dull, deaden, dampen, soft-pedal; hush, muffle, stifle 399 vb. *silence*.

Adv. *faintly*, in a whisper, with bated breath, between the teeth; sotto voce, aside, in an undertone; piano, pianissimo; à la sourdine; inaudibly, distantly, out of earshot.

See: 334, 350, 352, 399, 405, 407, 414, 578.

402 Bang: sudden and violent noise

N. *bang*, report, explosion, detonation, blast, blow-out, back-fire; crash 400 n. *loudness*; crepitation, crackling, crackle; smack, crack, snap; slap, clap, tap, rap, rat-tat-tat; knock, slam; plop, plunk; burst, burst of fire, firing, crackle of musketry; volley, round, salvo; shot, pistol-s.; cracker, squib, phataka, bomb, grenade; gun, rifle, shot-gun, pop-g. 723 n. *fire-arm*.

Adj. *rapping* etc. vb.

Vb. *crackle*, crepitate; sizzle, fizzle, spit 318 vb. *effervesce*; crack, split; click, rattle; snap, clap, rap, tap, slap, smack; plop, plump, plonk, plunk.

bang, slam, clash, crash, boom; explode, blast, detonate; pop, go p.; back-fire; burst, burst on the ear.

See: 318, 400, 723.

403 Roll: repeated and protracted sounds

N. *roll*, rumbling, grumbling; din, rattle, racket, clatter, chatter, clutter; booming, clang, ping, reverberation 404 n. *resonance*; drumming, tattoo, devil's t., rub-a-dub, rat-a-tat, pit-a-pat; tantara, peal, carillon 412 n. *campanology*; ding-dong, tick-tock, cuckoo 106 n. *repetition*; trill, tremolo, vibrato 410 n. *musical note*; quaver; hum, whirr, buzz; ringing, singing, tinnitus; drumfire, barrage, machine-gun.

Adj. *rolling* etc. vb.; ding-dong, monotonous 106 adj. *repeated*; like a bee in a bottle.

Vb. *roll*, drum, tattoo, beat a t.; drum in the ear; roar, din in the ear; grumble, rumble, drone, hum, whirr; trill, chime, peal, toll; tick, beat; rattle, chatter, clatter, clack; reverberate, clang, ping, ring, sing, sing in the ear; quaver, shake, tremble, vibrate; patter 401 vb. *sound faint*.

See: 106, 401, 404, 410, 412.

404 Resonance

N. *resonance,* vibration 317 n. *oscillation;* reverberation, reflection; lingering note, echo 106 n. *recurrence;* ringing, ringing in the ear, singing, tinnitus; bell-ringing, tintinnabulation 412 n. *campanology;* peal, carillon; sonority, clang, clangour, plangency; brass 400 n. *loudness;* peal, blare, bray, flourish, tucket; sounding brass, tinkling cymbal; tinkle, jingle; chink, clink; ping, ring, chime; low note, deep n., grave n., bass n., pedal n. 410 n. *musical note;* low voice, basso, basso profondo, bass, baritone, bass-b., contralto.

Adj. *resonant,* vibrant, reverberant, resounding etc. vb.; echoing, reboant, reboantic; lingering; sonorous, plangent; ringing, tintinnabulary; basso, deep-toned, deep-sounding, deep-mouthed; booming, hollow, sepulchral.

Vb. *resound,* vibrate, reverberate, echo, re-echo; whirr, buzz; hum, ring in the ear, sing; ping, ring, ding; jingle, jangle, chink, clink, clank, clunk; tink, tinkle; gong, chime, tintinnabulate; tootle, toot, trumpet, blare, bray 400 vb. *be loud;* gurgle, guggle, plash, splash.

See: 106, 317, 400, 410, 412.

405 Non-resonance

N. *non-resonance,* non-vibration, dead sound, dull s.; thud, thump, bump; plump, plop, plonk, plunk; cracked bell 411 n. *discord;* muffled drums 401 n. *faintness;* mute, damper, sordine 401 n. *silencer.*

Adj. *non-resonant,* muffled, damped 401 adj. *muted;* dead, dull, heavy; cracked 407 adj. *hoarse;* soundproof 399 adj. *silent.*

Vb. *sound dead,* be non-resonant, not vibrate, arouse no echoes, fall dead on the ear; tink, click, flap; thump, thud, bump, pound; stop the vibrations, damp the reverberations; soft-pedal, muffle, damp, stop, soften, deaden, stifle, silence 401 vb. *mute.*

See: 399, 401, 407, 411.

406 Sibilation: hissing sound

N. *sibilation,* sibilance, hissing, hiss; assibilation, sigmatism, sigma, sibilant; sneeze, sternutation; sputter, splutter; surge, splash, plash; rustle, frou-frou 407 n. *stridor;* sucking noise, squelch; swish, swoosh, escape of air; hisser, goose, viper, adder, serpent.

Adj. *sibilant,* sibilatory, hissing, sigmatic; wheezy, asthmatic.

Vb. *hiss,* sibilate, sigmate, assibilize, assibilate; sneeze, snort, wheeze, snuffle, whistle; buzz, fizz, fizzle, sizzle, sputter, splutter, spit; seethe, surge, splash, plash, boil, bubble 318 vb. *effervesce;* swish, swoosh, whizz; squelch, suck; rustle 407 vb. *rasp.*

See: 318, 407.

407 Stridor: harsh sound

N. *stridor,* stridency, discordance, cacophony 411 n. *discord;* roughness, raucousness, hoarseness, huskiness; harsh sound, aspirate, guttural; squeakiness, rustiness 333 n. *friction;* scrape, scratch, creak, squeak; stridulation, screechiness; shriek, screech, squawk, yawp, yelp 409 n. *ululation;* high pitch, shrillness, piping, whistling, wolf whistle; piercing note, high n., acute n., sharp n. 410 n. *musical note;* high voice, soprano, falsetto, tenor, counter-tenor; nasality, twang, drone; skirl, brassiness, brass, blare 400 n. *loudness;* pipe, fife, piccolo 414 n. *flute;* penny trumpet, whistle, penny w.; treble.

Adj. *strident,* stridulent, stridulous; unoiled, grating, rusty, creaky, creaking (see *hoarse*); harsh, horrisonous; brassy, brazen, metallic; high, high-pitched, high-toned, acute, shrill, piping; piercing, tinny, ear-splitting 400 adj. *loud;* blaring, braying; dry, reedy, squeaky, squawky, scratchy; cracked 405 adj. *non-resonant;* sharp, flat, inharmonious, cacophonous 411 adj. *discordant.*

hoarse, husky, throaty, guttural, raucous, rough, gruff; rasping, scraping, creaking; grunting, growling; hollow, deep, grum, sepulchral; snoring, stertorous.

Vb. *rasp,* stridulate, grate, crunch, scrunch, grind, saw, scrape, scratch; snore, snort; cough, hawk, clear the throat, choke, gasp, sob, catch the breath; bray, croak, caw, screech 409 vb. *ululate;* grunt, speak in the throat, burr, aspirate, gutturalize; crack, break (of the voice); jar, grate on

the ear, set the teeth on edge, clash, jangle, twang, twangle, clank, clink 411 vb. *discord.*

shrill, stridulate; play the bagpipes, drone, skirl; trumpet, blare 400 vb. *be loud*; pipe, flute, wind the horn 413 vb. *play music*; whistle, cat-call, caterwaul 408 vb. *cry*; scream, squeal, yelp, screech, squawk; buzz, hum, whine 409 vb. *ululate*; split the ears, lift the roof; strain, crack one's voice, strain one's vocal chords.

See: 333, 400, 405, 408, 409, 410, 411, 413, 414.

408 Human Cry

N. *cry,* animal cry 409 n. *ululation*; human cry, exclamation, ejaculation 577 n. *voice*; utterances 579 n. *speech*; talk, chat, conversation 584 n. *interlocution*; raised voice, vociferation, vociferousness, clamorousness, shouting, outcry, clamour, hullabaloo 400 n. *loudness*; yodel, song, chant, chorus, 412 n. *vocal music*; shout, yello, whoop, bawl; howl, scream, shriek 407 n. *stridor,* 377 n. *pain*; halloo, hail 547 n. *call*; view halloo, yoiks, hue and cry 619 n. *chase*: cheer, hurrah, huzza 835 n. *rejoicing*; cachinnation, laugh, giggle, snigger 835 n. *laughter*; hoot, boo 924 n. *disapprobation*; plaint, complaint 762 n. *deprecation*; plaining, plaintiveness, sob, sigh 836 n. *lamentation*; caterwaul, squeal, wail, whine, boo-hoo; grunt, gasp 352 n. *respiration*; shouter, bawler, yeller; rooter, cheerer; crier; barker; town-crier, Stentor.

Adj. *crying,* bawling, clamant, clamorous; loud, vocal, vociferous; stentorian, full-throated, full-lunged, lusty; rousing, cheering; fretful, tearful 836 adj. *lamenting.*

Vb. *cry,* cry out, exclaim, ejaculate, pipe up 579 vb. *speak*; call, call out, hail, halloa 884 vb. *greet*; raise a cry, whoop, yoiks; hoot, boo, whistle 924 vb. *disapprove*; cheer, hurrah, root (see *vociferate*); shout, bawl, holla, yell; scream, screech, howl, groan 377 vb. *feel pain*; cachinnate snigger, giggle 835 vb. *laugh*; caterwaul, squall, boo-hoo, whine, whimper, wail, fret, mewl, pule 836 vb. *weep*; yammer, moan, sob, sigh 836 vb. *lament*; mutter,

grumble 401 vb. *sound faint*, 825 vb. *be discontented*; gasp, grunt, snort, snore 352 vb. *breathe*; squeak, squawk, yap, yaup, bark 409 vb. *ululate.*

vociferate, clamour, start shouting, shout, bawl, yell; chant, chorus 413 vb. *sing*; cheer, give three times three, hurrah, huzza, exult 835 vb. *rejoice*; cheer for, root; hiss, hoot, boo, bawl out, shout down 924 vb. *disapprove*; roar, bellow 409 vb. *ululate*; yell, cry out, sing o., thunder o.; raise the voice, give v., strain one's lungs, crack one's throat, make oneself hoarse, shout at the top of one's voice, shout at the top of one's lungs 400 vb. *be loud.*

See: 352, 377, 400, 401, 407, 409, 412, 413, 547, 577, 579, 584, 619, 762, 825, 835, 836, 884, 924.

409 Ululation: animal sounds

N. *ululation,* animal noise, howling, belling; barking, baying, latration, buzzing, humming, bombilation, drone; twittering, fritiniency; call, cry, note, woodnote, bird-note, bird-call; squeak, cheep, twitter, tweet-tweet; buzz, hum; croak, cronk crunk, caw; coo, hiss; quack, squawk, screech; baa, moo, neigh, whinny, hee-haw; cock-a-doodle-doo, cuckoo, tu-whit tu-whoo; miaow, bark, yelp, yap, snap, snarl, growl (see under vb. *ululate*).

Adj. *ululant,* mugient, remugient, reboant; blatant, latrant; deep-mouthed, full-m.; full-throated 400 adj. *loud*; roaring, lowing, cackling etc. vb.

Vb. *ululate,* cry, call; squawk, screech; caterwaul, yawl, howl, wail; roar, bellow; hum, drone, buzz, bombinate, bombilate; spit 406 vb. *hiss*; latrate, bark, bay, bay at the moon; yelp, yap, yaup; snap, snarl, gnarr, growl, whine; trumpet, bell, troat; bray, neigh, whinny; bleat, baa; low, moo; miaow, mew, mewl, purr; quack, cackle, gaggle, guggle; gobble, gabble, cluck, clack, crow; grunt, gruntle, snort; pipe, pule; blatter, chatter, sing, chirp, chirrup, cheep, tweet, twitter, chuckle, churr, whirr, coo; caw, croak, crunk; hoot, honk, boom; grate, chirk, crick; stridulate, squeak 407 vb.

rasp; sing like a bird, warble, carol, whistle 413 vb. *sing*.

See: 400, 406, 407, 413.

410 Melody: concord

N. *melody*, musicality 412 n. *music*; musicalness, melodiousness, musical quality, tonality, euphony, euphonism; harmoniousness, chime, harmony, concent, concord, concert 24 n. *agreement*; consonance, assonance, attunement; unison, unisonance, homophony; preparation, resolution (of a discord); harmonics, harmonization, counterpoint, polyphony; faux-bourdon, faburden, thorough bass, ground b. Alberti b.; part, second, chorus; orchestration, instrumentation; phrasing 413 n. *musical skill*; phrase, passage, theme, leit-motiv, coda; movement 412 n. *musical piece.*

musical note, note, keys, keyboard, manual, pedal point, organ p.; black notes, white n., sharp, flat, natural, tone, semitone, quartertone; keynote, fundamental n.; leading note, tonic, supertonic, submediant, mediant, subdominant, dominant, subtonic; interval, second, third, fourth, fifth, sixth, seventh, octave; diatesseron, diapason; gamut, scale 410 n. *key*; chord, broken c., primary c., secondary c., tertiary c., tetrachord, perfect fourth, arpeggio; grace note, grace, crush note, appoggiatura, appoggiato, acciaccatura, mordent, shake, tremolo, trill, cadenza; tone, tonality, register, pitch, concert p., high p., low p.; high note 407 n. *stridor*; low note 404 n. *resonance*; undertone, overtone, harmonic, upper partial; sustained note, monotone, drone; sennet, flourish 412 n. *tune*; bugle-call 547 n. *call*.

notation, musical n., tonic solfa, solmization; written music, score; signature, clef, treble c., bass c., tenor c., bar, stave, line, shaft, space, brace; rest, pause, interval; breve, semibreve, minim, crotchet, quaver, semiquaver, demisemiquaver, hemidemisemiquaver.

tempo, time, beat; rhythm 593 n. *prosody*; measure, timing; syncopation, syncope; suspension, prolongation, long note, short n., suspended n.; prolonged n.; tempo rubato; rallentando, andante 412 adv. *adagio*.

key, signature, clef, modulation, major key, minor k.; scale, gamut, major scale, minor s., diatonic s., chromatic s., harmonic s., enharmonic s., twelve-tone s.; mode, Gregorian m., Greek m., Lydian m., Phrygian m., Ionian m., Æolian m., Doric m., mixolydian, hypolydian; oriental mode, Indian m., raga, rag.

Adj. *melodious*, melodic, musical, canorous, tuneful, tuneable, singable, catchy; tinkling, low, soft 401 adj. *muted*; sweet, dulcet, mellifluous; high-fidelity, clear, clear as a bell, ringing, chiming; silvery, silver-toned, silver-tongued; fine-toned, full-t. 404 adj. *resonant*; euphonious, euphonic, true, well-pitched.

harmonious, harmonizing, concordant, consonant 24 adj. *agreeing*; in pitch; in chorus; assonant, rhyming, matching 18 adj. *similar*; symphonic, symphonious, polyphonic; homophonous, unisonant, isotonic, homophonic, monophonic; monotonous, droning.

harmonic, enharmonic, diatonic, chromatic; tonal, atonal, sharp, flat, twelve-toned; keyed, modal, minor, major, Doric, Lydian.

Vb. *harmonize*, concert, have the right pitch, blend, chime 24 vb. *accord*; chorus 413 vb. *sing*; attune, tune, tune up, pitch, string 24 vb. *adjust*; be in key, be in unison, be on the beat; compose, melodize, put to music, symphonize, orchestrate 413 vb. *compose music*; modulate, arpeggio, run, shake, trill; resolve a discord, restore harmony.

See: 18, 24, 401, 404, 407, 410, 412, 413, 547, 593.

411 Discord

N. *discord*, conflict of sounds, discordance, dissonance, disharmony 25 n. *disagreement*; atonality, consecutive fifths; preparation (of a discord); harshness, hoarseness, cacophony 407 n. *stridor*; confused sounds, Babel, Dutch concert, cat's c., sweeper's band, marrowbones and cleavers, caterwauling 400 n. *loudness*; row, din, noise, pandemonium, Bedlam, tumult, racket, atmospherics 61 n. *turmoil*.

Adj. *discordant*, dissonant, absonant, jangling, discording 25 adj. *disagreeing*; conflicting 14 adj. *contrary*; jarring, grating, scraping, rasping, harsh, raucous, caco-

phonous 407 adj. *strident*; inharmonious, unharmonized; unmelodious, unmusical, intuneable, untuneful, musicless; untuned, cracked; off pitch, off key, out of tune, sharp, flat; atonal, toneless, tuneless, droning, sing-song.

Vb. *discord*, lack harmony 25 vb. *disagree*; jangle, jar, grate, clash, crash; saw, scrape, 407 vn. *rasp*; be harsh, be out of tune; play sharp, play flat; drone, whine; prepare, prepare a discord; render discordant, unstring, untune.

See: 14, 25, 61, 400, 407.

412 Music

N. *music*, harmony; sweet music 410 b. *melody*; musicianship 413 n. *musical skill*; music-making, playing; minstrelsy, harping; strumming, vamping; writing music, composing, composition; instrumental music, pipe m., military m.; counterpoint, contrapuntal music; classical music., chamber m., organ m., sacred m., folk m., traditional m.; popular music, light m.; descriptive music, programme m., modern m., electronic m., musique concrète; gramophone music, tinned m., canned m., recorded m.; dance music, hot m., syncopation; ragtime, jazz, jive, swing, bebop, bop, blues, boogie-woogie, rock 'n' roll; written music, the music, score, full s.; performance, concert, orchestral c., choral c., smoking-c., singsong; music festival, eisteddfod; school of music, conservatoire, tin-pan alley.
campanology, bell-ringing, hand-r., mechanical r.; ringing, chiming; peal, full p., muffled p.; touch, chime; method-ringing, change-r., hunting, dodging, making place; hunt, hunt forward, hunt backward, dodge; round, change; method, Grandsire, Plain Bob, Treble Bob, Stedman; set of bells, carillon, doubles, triples, caters, cinques; minor, major, royal; maximus; bell, Great Tom, Great Paul, Tsar Kolokol; treble bell, tenor b. 414 n. *gong*; church-bell 547 n. *call*; bell-ringer, carilloneur, campanologist.
tune, signature t., hymn t.; refrain; melodic line; air, popular a., aria, solo; melody, strain; peal, chime, carillon; flourish, sennet, tucket; phrase, passage, measure; Lydian airs, Siren strains.

musical piece, piece, composition, opus, work, piece of music; record, recording; orchestration, instrumentation; arrangement, adaptation, setting, transcription; voluntary, prelude, overture, intermezzo, finale; accompaniment, incidental music, background m.; romance, rhapsody, extravaganza, impromptu, fantasia, caprice, capriccio, humoresque, divertissement, variations, ricercari; medley, switchback, pasticcio, pot-pourri; étude, study; suite, fugue, canon, toccata, toccatina, ricercata; sonata, sonatina, symphony; symphonic poem, tone p.; pastorale, scherzo, rondo, jig, reel; passacaglia, chaconne, rigadon, sarabande, galliard, gavotte, minuet, tarantella, siciliano, mazurka, polonaise, schottische, waltz, polka 837 n. *dance*; march, bridal m., wedding m., dead m., funeral m., dirge, pibroch, coronach; nocturne, nachtmusik, abend musik, serenade, berceuse; aubade; introductory phrase, anacrusis; statement, exposition, development, variation; theme, motive, leitmotiv, signature tune; movement; passage, phrase; chord, mordent, cadenza, coda; feminine ending.
vocal music, singing, vocalism, lyricism; part, singing p.; opera, operetta, light opera, comic o., opéra bouffe, musical comedy, musical 594 n. *stage play*; choirsinging, oratorio, cantata, chorale; hymnsinging, psalmody, hymnology; descant, chant, plain c., Gregorian c., plainsong; canto fermo, cantus, cantillation, recitative; bel canto, coloratura, bravura; singing practice, solfeggio, solfa, solmization; introit, anthem, canticle, psalm, 981 n. *hymn*; song, lay, carol, lyric; canzonet, cavatina, lieder, lied, ballad; ditty, chanty calypso; part song, glee, madrigal, round, catch; stave, verse; chorus, refrain, burden, undersong; choral hymn, antiphony, dithyramb; boat-song, barcarole; lullaby, cradlesong, berceuse; serenade, aubade; bridal hymn, wedding h., epithalamium, prothalamium; love-song, amorous ditty; song, bird-s., bird-call, dawn chorus; dirge, threnody, coronach 836 n. *lament*; musical declamation, recitative; words to be sung, libretto; song-book, hymnbook, psalter.
duet, duo, trio, quartet, quintet, sextet,

septet, octet; concerto, concerto grosso, solo, monody; ensemble, tutti.

Adj. *musical* 410 adj. *melodious*; philharmonic, symphonic; melodic, arioso, cantabile; vocal, singable; operatic, recitative; lyric, melic; choral, dithyrambic; hymnal, psalmodic; harmonized 410 adj. *harmonious*; contrapuntal; orchestrated, scored; set, set to music, arranged; instrumental, orchestral, for strings; hot, jazzy, syncopated, swing, swung.

Adv. *adagio*, lento, largo, larghetto, andante, andantino, maestoso, moderato; allegro, allegretto; spiritoso, vivace, veloce, accelerando, presto, prestissimo; piano, mezzo-p., pianissimo, forte, mezzo-f., fortissimo, sforzando, con brio, capriccioso, scherzo, scherzando; legato, sostenuto, staccato; crescendo, diminuendo, rallentando; affettuoso, arioso, cantabile, parlante; obbligato, tremolo, pizzicato, vibrato; rubato.

See: 410, 413, 414, 547, 594, 836, 837, 981.

413 Musician

N. *musician*, artiste, virtuoso, soloist; bravura player 696 n. *proficient*; player, executant, performer, concert artist; ripieno 40 n. *extra*; bard, minstrel, jongleur, troubadour, trovatore, minnesinger, gleeman; composer, symphonist, contrapuntist; scorer, arranger, harmonist; syncopator, jazzer, swinger, bebopper, bobster, hepcat; music-writer, librettist, song-writer, lyrist, lieder-writer, hymn-w., hymnographer, psalmist; music teacher, music-master, concert-m., kapellmeister, master of the music, band-leader, conductor (see *orchestra*); Apollo, Pan, Orpheus, Amphion, Marsyas, Pied Piper; music critic, concert-goer, opera-g.

instrumentalist, player, piano-p., pianist, cembalist, accompanist; keyboard performer, organist, accordionist, concertinist; violinist, fiddler, crowder, scraper; violist, violoncellist, cellist; harper, harpist, lyrist, clairschacher, luter, lutanist, theorbist, guitarist, mandolinist., banjoist; strummer, thrummer; piper, fifer, piccolo-player, flautist, flutist, clarinettist, oboist, bassoonist; saxophonist, horn-player, trumpeter, bugler, corneter, cornetist, clarionist; bell-ringer, carilloneur, campanologist; drummer, drummer-boy, drum-major; timpanist; organ-grinder, hurdy-gurdy man.

orchestra, symphony o., string o., quartet, quintet; strings, brass, wood-wind, percussion, drums; band, string b., German b., jazz b., ragtime b., Pandean b., drum and fife b., brass b., military b., pipe-b., percussion b., sweepers' b., skiffle-group; conductor, baton-wielder, maestro, bandmaster; band-leader, leader, first violin; orchestra-player, bandsman; ripieno 40 n. *extra*.

vocalist, singer, songster, warbler, caroller, chanter; chantress, chanteuse, songstress; Siren, mermaid, Lorelei; melodist, troubadour, gleeman, gleesinger, madrigal singer, minstrel, wandering m., nigger m., coon; ballad-singer, street-s., carol-s.; serenader, crooner; opera singer, prima donna, diva; cantatrice, coloratura; aria-singer, lieder s.; castrato, soprano, mezzo-s., contralto, alto, tenor, counter-t., baritone, bass-b., bass, basso, basso profondo; song-bird, nightingale, philomel, lark, thrush, mavis, blackbird 365 n. *bird*.

choir chorus, waits, carol-singers, glee-club; choir-festival, massed choirs, eisteddfod; chorister, choir-boy, choir-man; precentor, cantor, choir-master, choir-leader; the Muses, tuneful Nine.

musical skill, musical ability, musical appreciation; musicianship, bardship, minstrelsy; performance, execution, fingering, touch, expression; virtuosity, bravura 694 n. *skill*.

Adj. *musicianly*, fond of music, knowing music, musical; minstrel, Orphean, bardic; vocal, coloratura, lyric, melic, choral; plain-song, Gregorian, melodic 410 adj. *melodious*; instrumental, orchestral, symphonic, contrapuntal; songful, warbling, carolling etc. vb.; scored, arranged, composed; in music, to m.

Vb. *be musical*, learn music, teach m., like m., read m., sight-read; have a good ear, have a correct e., have perfect pitch.

compose music, compose, write music, put to music, set to m., score, arrange, transpose, orchestrate, arrange in parts, supply the counterpoint, harmonize, melodize, improvise, extemporize.

play music, play, perform, execute, render, interpret; conduct, wield the baton, beat time, mark the time; syncopate; play the

piano, accompany; pedal, vamp, strum; brush the ivories, tickle the i., thump the keyboard; harp, pluck, sweep the strings, strike the lyre, pluck the guitar; thrum, twang, twangle; violin, fiddle, bow, scrape, saw; play the concertina, squeeze the box, grind the organ; wind, wind the horn, blow, bugle, blow the b., sound the horn, sound, trumpet, sound the t., toot, tootle; pipe, flute, whistle; doodle, squeeze the bag; clash the cymbals; drum, tattoo, beat, tap, beat the drum, beat a ruffle 403 vb. *roll*; ring, peal the bells, ring a change; toll, knell; tune, string, fret, set to concert pitch; practise, do scales, improvise, extemporise, play a voluntary, prelude; begin playing, strike up.

sing, vocalize, chant, hymn; intone, cantillate, descant; warble, carol, lilt, trill, quaver, shake; croon, hum, whistle, yodel; solfa, solmizate; harmonize, sing seconds; chorus, choir; sing to, serenade; sing the praises, minstrel; chirp, chirrup, twitter, pipe 409 vb. *ululate* ; purl 401 vb. *sound faint*.

See: 40, 365, 401, 403, 409, 410, 694, 696.

414 Musical instruments

N. *musical instrument*, band, music, concert 413 n. *orchestra*; strings, brass, wind, wood-wind, percussion, batterie; sounding board, diaphragm, sound box; comb.

harp, stringed instrument, monochord, heptachord, Eolian harp, Jew's h.; clairschach; lyre, lute, archlute, theorbo; bandore, bandurria; cithara, cithern, zither, gittern, guitar, electric g., mandoline, mandola, harp-lute; banjo, ukelele, uke, balalaika; psaltery, vina, samisen; plectrum, fret.

viol, rebeck, violin, Cremona, Stradivarius, fiddle, kit-f., kit, crowd; viola, tenor, violin, viola d'amore, viola da gamba, violon-cello, cello, bass-viol, contrabasso, double-bass; polychord; bow, fiddlestick; string, catgut; bridge; resin.

piano, pianoforte, grand piano, concert grand, baby g.; upright piano, cottage p.; virginals, cymbalo, dulcimer, harpsichord, spinet; clavichord, clarichord, manichord; piano-organ, piano-player, player-piano, pianola, electric piano;

xylophone, marimba; clavier, keyboard, manual, keys, ivories; loud pedal, soft p., celeste, damper.

organ, pipe-o., church o., Hammond o., electric o., steam o., calliope; reed organ, seraphina, American o., melodeon, harmonium, harmoniphon; mouth organ, harmonica; accordion, piano-a., concertina; barrel-organ, hurdy-gurdy; humming top; organ-pipe, mouth-p., flue-p., organ-stop, flue-s.; manual, keyboard; organ-loft, organ-blower.

flute, bass f., fife, piccolo, flageolet, recorder; wood-wind, reed instrument, clarinet, tenor c., corno di bassetto, basset horn, bass clarionet; shawm, hautboy, oboe, tenor o., cor Anglais; bassoon, double b., contrafagotto; ocarina, sweet potato; pipe, oaten p., oat, reed, straw; bagpipes, musette, Irish bagpipes, union pipes; pan-pipes, Pandean p., syrinx; whistle, penny w., tin w.; sirene, pitch-pipe; siren; mouthpiece.

horn, bugle-h., post-h., hunting h.; bugle, trumpet, clarion; alpenhorn, French horn, flugelhorn, saxhorn, althorn, helicon horn, bass h.; euphonium, ophicleide, serpent, bombardon; saxophone, sax, saxcornet, cornet, cornet à pistons, cornopean; trombone, sackbut, tuba, sax-t., bass-t.; conch, shell.

gong, bell, tintinnabulum; treble bell, tenor b.; church-bell, dinner-b., telephone-b.; alarm-bell, fire-b., tocsin 665 n. *danger signal*; tintinnabulation, peal, carillon, chimes, bells; knackers, bones, rattle b., clappers, castanets, cymbals; rattle, sistrum; xylophone, marimba; musical glasses, harmonica; tubular bell, glockenspiel; triangle; tuning fork; sounding board; percussion instrument.

drum, big d., bass d., tenor d., side d., kettle d., war d., tom-tom; tabor, tabret, tabouret, tambourine, timbrel; tabla, timpanum, timpani; caisse, grosse c.

gramophone, phonograph, victrola; record-player, radiogram, play-back, pick-up; record, recording, disc, platter, long-playing record, long-player; musical box, juke b., nickel-odeon; needle, fibre-n.; diaphragm; baffle-board; soundbox, speaker.

mute, damper, sordine, pedal, soft p., celeste 401 n. *silencer*.

See: 401, 413, 665.

415 Hearing

N. *hearing*, audition 398 n. *acoustics*; sense of hearing, good h.; good ear, nice e., sharp e., acute e., quick e., sensitive e., correct e., musical e., ear for music; audibility, reception, good r.; earshot, carrying distance, range, reach; something to hear, earful.

listening, hearkening 739 n. *obedience*, 455 n. *attention*; auscultation, aural examination 459 n. *enquiry*; listening-in, tuning-in; lip-reading 520 n. *interpretation*; eavesdropping, overhearing, phone-tapping 523 n. *latency*; sound-recording 548 n. *record*; audition, voice-testing 461 n. *experiment*; interview, audience, hearing 584 n. *conference*; legal hearing 959 n. *legal trial.*

listener, auscultator; stethoscopist; hearer, audience, auditorium, auditory; stalls, pit, gallery 441 n. *spectator*; audient, disciple, lecture-goer 538 n. *learner*; auditor, examiner 459 n. *questioner.*

ear, auditory apparatus, auditory nerve, acoustic organ; lug, lobe, auricle, ear-hole; external ear, pinna; inner ear, internal e.; aural cavity, cochlea, ear-drum, tympanum; malleus, incus, stapes; auditory canal, labyrinth; otology; otoscopy.

hearing aid, stethoscope, otoscope, hearing instrument, ear-trumpet, audiphone, auriphone; loud-speaker, loud-hailer, public address system 528 n. *publication*; microphone, mike, amplifier 400 n. *megaphone*; speaking-tube, blower; telephone, phone, receiver, headphone, earphone, radiophone, walkie-talkie 531 n. *telecommunication*; sound-recorder, Asdic, sound-tape, dictaphone 549 n. *recording instrument*; radiogram, phonograph 414 n. *gramophone.*

Adj. *auditory*, hearing, auricular, aural, otological, otoscopic, stethoscopic; auditive, acoustic, audile, keen-eared, sharp-e., open-e.; listening, prick-eared, all ears 455 adj. *attentive*; within earshot, audible, heard 398 adj. *sounding.*

Vb. *hear*, catch; listen, examine by ear, auscultate, put one's ear to; lip-read 520 vb. *interpret*; listen in, switch on, tune in, adjust the receiver; prepare to hear, lift the receiver; overhear, eavesdrop; intercept, tap, tap the wires; hearken, give ear, lend e., incline one's e.; give audience, interview, grant an interview 459 vb. *interrogate*; hear confession, shrive 526 vb. *confess*; be all ears, hang on the lips of 455 vb. *be attentive*; strain one's ears, prick up one's e.; catch a sound, pick up a message; be told, hear say 524 vb. *be informed.*

be heard, become audible, reach the ear, fill the e., sound in the e., fall on the e. 398 vb. *sound*; ring in the e. 400 vb. *be loud*; gain a hearing, have audience.

Adv. *in earshot*, in one's hearing, with ears agog.

See: 398, 400, 414, 441, 455, 459, 461, 520, 523, 524, 528, 531, 538, 548, 549, 584, 739, 959.

416 Deafness

N. *deafness*, dull hearing, hardness of hearing; deaf ears, surdity, deaf-mutism; deaf-and-dumb speech, dactylogy; deaf-and-dumb person, deaf-mute, the deaf and dumb; inaudibility 399 n. *silence.*

Adj. *deaf*, earless, dull of ear, hard of hearing, stone-deaf, deaf as a post, deaf as an adder, deaf as a beetle; deaf and dumb, deaf-mute; deafened, stunned, unable to hear; deaf to, unhearing, not listening 456 adj. *inattentive*; deaf to music, tone-deaf, unmusical; hard to hear 401 adj. *muted*; inaudible, out of earshot, out of hearing 399 adj. *silent.*

Vb. *be deaf*, not hear, hear nothing, fail to catch; not listen, refuse to hear, shut one's ears, stop one's e., close one's e., plug one's e. 458 vb. *disregard*; turn a deaf ear to 760 vb. *refuse*; be hard of hearing, use a hearing aid; lip-read, use lip-reading 520 vb. *translate*; talk with one's fingers.

deafen, make deaf, stun, split the ear-drum, drown one's hearing 400 vb. *be loud.*

See: 399, 400, 401, 456, 458, 520, 760.

417 Light

N. *light*, day-l., light of day, noonday, noontide, noon, broad day, sunlight, sun 420 n. *luminary*; starlight, moonlight, moonshine, earthshine; half-light, twilight 419 n. *dimness*; artificial light, candle-l., fire-l.

420 n. *lighting*; illumination, irradiation, splendour, effulgence, refulgence, intensity, brightness, vividness, brilliance; albedo, luminosity, candle-power; incandescence, radiance (see *glow*); sheen, shine, gloss, lustre (see *reflection*); blaze, blaze of light, sheet of l., flood of l.; glare, dazzle, dazzlement; flare, prominence, flame 379 n. *fire*; halo, nimbus, glory, gloriole, aura, aureole, corona; variegated light, spectrum, visible s., iridescence, rainbow 437 n. *variegation*; coloration, riot of colour 425 n. *colour*; white 427 n. *whiteness*.

flash, emication, fulguration, coruscation; lightning, lightning flash, levin; beam, ray, green r., green flash; Baily's beads; streak, meteor-flash; scintillation, sparkle, spark; glint, glitter, play, play of light; blink, twinkle, twinkling, flicker, flickering, glimmer, glim, gleam, shimmer, shimmering; spangle, tinsel; flash-light, firefly 420 n. *glow-worm*.

glow, flush, sunset glow, afterglow, dawn, sunset; steady flame, steady beam; lambency, lambent light, soft l.; aurora, aurora borealis, aurora australis; northern lights; Milky Way, galaxy, zodiacal light, gegenschein; radiance, incandescence 379 n. *heat*; luminescence, fluorescence, phosphorescence; ignis fatuus, jack-o'-lantern, friar's lantern, will-o'-the-wisp, St. Elmo's fire 420 n. *glow-worm*.

radiation, visible r., invisible r.; radiant heat, radiant energy; actinism, emission; radioactivity, fall-out, mushroom, radio-active cloud; radiation belt, Van Allen layer 340 n. *atmosphere*; ray, beam, pencil; searchlight, headlight, stream of light; infra-red ray, ultra-violet r., Roentgen rays, X-ray, gamma r., beta r., cosmic r., microwave; light wave, radio w.; long w., sky w., short w.; wavelength, beam width; high frequency; interference; photon; photoelectric cell.

reflection, refractivity, refraction, double r.; dispersion, scattering, interference, polarization; albedo, polish, gloss, sheen, lustre; glare, dazzle, blink, ice-b.; reflecting surface, reflector, mirror 442 n. *mirror*; mirror-image 551 n. *image*.

light contrast, tonality, chiaroscuro, clair-obscur; light and shade, black and white, half-tone, mezzotint; highlights.

optics, photics, photometry, actinometry; dioptrics, catoptrics, spectrology, spectroscopy; heliography 551 n. *photography*; radioscopy, radiometry, radiology; magnification, magnifying power, light-grasp 197 n. *expansion*.

Adj. *luminous*, luminiferous, lucific, lucid, lucent; luculent; light, lit, well-lit, flood-l., flooded with light; bright, gay, shining, resplendent, splendent, splendid, brilliant, vivid; colourful 425 adj. *coloured*; radiant, effulgent, refulgent; dazzling, blinding, glaring, garish; incandescent, flaring, flaming, aflame, aglow, ablaze 379 adj. *fiery*; glowing, blushing, auroral, orient 431 adj. *red*; luminescent, phosphorescent, noctilucous; soft, lambent, playing; beaming, beamy, beamish; glittery, flashing, glinting, rutilant, meteoric; scintillant, scintillating, sparkling; lustrous, shiny, sheeny, glossy; reflecting, catoptric; refractive, dioptric, anaclastic; optical, photometric.

undimmed, clear, bright, fair, set f.; cloudless, shadowless, unclouded, unshaded; sunny, sunshiny; moonlit, starlit, starry; light as day, bright as noonday, bright as silver; burnished, polished, glassy, gleaming; lucid, pellucid, diaphanous, translucent 422 adj. *transparent*.

radiating, radiant, radio-active, reflective, reflecting.

Vb. *shine*, be bright, burn, blaze, flame, flare 379 vb. *be hot*; glow, incandesce, phosphoresce; shine full, glare, dazzle, bedazzle, blind; play, dance; flash, fulgurate, coruscate; glisten, glister, blink; glimmer, flicker, twinkle; glitter, shimmer, glance; scintillate, sparkle, spark, make sparks; shine again, reflect; take a shine, come up, gleam.

radiate, beam, shoot, shoot out rays 300 vb. *emit*; reflect, refract; be radio-active, bombard; X-ray.

make bright, lighten, dispel the darkness, dawn, rise; clear, clear up, lift, brighten; light, strike a l., ignite, enflame 381 vb. *kindle*; light up, switch on; show a light, hang out a l.; shed lustre, throw light on; shine upon, flood with light, illuminate, illume, relume; shine within, shine through 443 vb. *be visible*; transilluminate, pass light through; polish, burnish, rub up 648 vb. *clean*.

See: 197, 300, 340, 379, 381, 419, 420, 422, 425, 431, 437, 442, 443, 452, 551, 648.

418 Darkness

N. *darkness*, dark; black 428 n. *blackness*; night, dark n., nightfall, blind man's holiday; dead of night, witching time 129 n. *midnight*; pitchy darkness, thick d., total d.; Cimmerian darkness, Egyptian d., Stygian d., Erebus; obscurity, murk, gloom, dusk 421 n. *obfuscation*; tenebrosity, umbrageousness, shadiness, shadows 419 n. *dimness*; shade, shadow, umbra, penumbra; silhouette, skiagraph, radiograph; skiagraphy; groping, noctivagation; dark place, dark-room; cavern, mine, dungeon, depths.

obscuration, obfuscation, darkening; black-out, brown-o., dim-o., fade-o.; occultation, eclipse, total e. 446 n. *disappearance*; extinction of light, lights out; tenebrae 988 n. *ritual act*; sunset, sundown 129 n. *evening*; blackening, adumbration, shading, hatching; distribution of shade, chiaroscuro; dark-lantern; dimmer, dipper 382 n. *extinguisher*; obscurantist, darkener of counsel.

Adj. *dark*, subfusc, sombre, dark-coloured, swart, swarthy 428 adj. *black*; darksome, obscure, pitch-dark, pitchy, sooty, black as night; cavernous, dark as a tunnel, black as a pit; Cimmerian, Stygian, Tartarean; caliginous, murky; funereal, gloomy, dismal; dingy, lurid; tenebrous, shady, umbrageous 419 adj. *shadowy*; all black, silhouetted; shaded, darkened 421 adj. *screened*; darkling, benighted; nocturnal, noctivagous, noctivagant; hidden, veiled, secret 523 adj. *occult*.

unlit, unlighted, unilluminated; not shining, aphotic, lightless; beamless, sunless, moonless, starless; eclipsed, overshadowed, overcast 421 adj. *screened*; misted, befogged, clouded, beclouded, cloudy 423 adj. *opaque*; switched off, extinguished; dipped, dimmed, blacked out; obscured, obfuscated.

Vb. *be dark*, grow d., lour, gather; fade out 419 vb. *be dim*; lurk in the shadows 523 vb. *lurk*; look black, gloom.

darken, black, brown; black out, brown o., dim o.; lower the light, turn down, turn down the wick; occult, eclipse, mantle 226 vb. *cover*; curtain, shutter, veil 421 vb. *screen*; obscure, obfuscate, obumbrate; bedarken, begloom, bemist, befog, dim, tone down 419 vb. *bedim*; overcast, overcloud, overshadow, cast in the shade,

spread gloom; spread a shade, cast a shadow; adumbrate, silhouette 551 vb. *represent*; shade, hatch, fill in; paint over 440 vb. *blur*; over-expose, over-develop 428 vb. *blacken*.

snuff out, extinguish, quench, put out the light, pinch out, blow o., switch off, dip, douse.

Adv. *darkling*, in the dark, in the shade, in the shadows; at night, by night.

See: 129, 226, 382, 419, 421, 423, 428, 440, 446, 523, 551, 988.

419 Dimness

N. *dimness*, bad seeing, indistinctness, vagueness, fuzziness, blur; loom; faintness, paleness 426 n. *achromatism*; greyness 429 n. *grey*; dullness, lack of sparkle, rustiness; blue light, red l.; cloudiness, smokiness, fuliginosity 423 n. *opacity*; mistiness, fogginess, nebulosity; murk, gloom 418 n. *darkness*; fog, mist 355 n. *cloud*; shadowiness, shadow, shade, shadow of a shade; spectre 970 n. *ghost*.

half-light, semidarkness, bad light; waning light, gloaming 129 n. *evening*; shades of evening, twilight, dusk, crepuscule, cockshut time; daybreak, break of day, demijour, grey dawn; penumbra, half-shadow, partial eclipse, annular e.

glimmer, flicker 417 n. *flash*; 'ineffectual fire', noctiluca, firefly 420 n. *glow-worm*; candle-light, rush-l., fire-l. 417 n. *light*; ember, coal 381 n. *ash*; smoky light, farthing candle, dip-c., dip; dark-lantern 420 n. *lamp*; moonbeam, moonlight, starlight, earthlight, earthshine.

Adj. *dim*, darkish, darksome; dusky, dusk, twilight, crepuscular; wan, dun, subfusc, grey, pale 426 adj. *colourless*; faint, faded, waning; indistinct, blurred, bleary; glassy, dull, lack-lustre, leaden; filmy, hazy, foggy, fog-bound, misty, obnubilated, nebulous, nebular 355 adj. *cloudy*; thick, smoky, sooty, muddy 423 adj. *opaque*; dingy, grimy, rusty, rusted, mildewed, unpolished, unburnished 649 adj. *dirty*.

shadowy, umbrageous, shady, shaded, overspread, overshadowed, overcast, overclouded 226 vb. *covered*; vague, indistinct, undefined, confused, fuzzy, blurry, looming; deceptive; half-seen, half-glimpsed,

withdrawn, half-hidden 444 adj. *invisible*; half-lit, partially eclipsed 418 adj. *unlit*; dreamlike, ghostly 523 adj. *occult*; coming and going 446 adj. *disappearing*.

Vb. *be dim*, — faint etc. adj.; be indistinct, loom; grow grey, grizzle, fade, wane, fade out, pale, grow p. 426 vb. *lose colour*; lour, lower, gloom, darkle; glimmer, flicker, gutter, sputter; lurk in the shade, be lost in the shadows 523 vb. *lurk*.

bedim, dim, dip; lower the flame, turn down the wick, turn down, fade out 418 vb. *snuff out*; obscure, blur the outline, blear 440 vb. *blur*; smirch, smear, besmirch, besmear, sully; rust, mildew, begrime, muddy, dirty 649 vb. *make unclean*; smoke, fog, mist, befog, bemist, becloud 423 vb. *make opaque*; overshadow, overcast; shade, shadow, veil, veil the brightness 226 vb. *cover;* shade in, hatch 418 vb. *darken*.

Adv. *dimly*, vaguely, indistinctly etc. adj.; at half-lights.

See: 129, 226, 355, 381, 417, 418, 420, 423, 426, 429, 440, 444, 446, 523, 649, 970.

420 Luminary: source of light

N. *luminary*, illuminant 417 n. *light*; naked light, flame 379 n. *fire*; flare, gas-f. (see *lamp*); source of light, orb of day 321 n. *sun*; orb of night 321 n. *moon*; starlight 321 n. *star*; bright star, first magnitude s., Sirius, Vega, Aldebaran, Betelgeuse, Canopus, Alpha Centauri; evening star, Hesperus, Vesper, Venus; morning star, Phosphorus, Lucifer; shooting-star, fireball 321 n. *meteor*; galaxy, Milky Way, zodiacal light, gegenschein, aurora, northern lights 321 n. *heavens;* fulguration, lightning, sheet-l., fork-l., summer l., lightning flash, levin; scintilla, spark, sparkle 417 n. *flash*.

glow-worm 417 n. *glow*; lampyrine, firefly, fire-beetle; noctiluca; fata morgana, ignis fatuus, will-o'-the-wisp, Friar's lantern, Jack-o'-lantern; fire-ball, St. Elmo's fire, corposant; phosphorescent light, corpsecandle, deadlight, death-fire, death-flame, fire-drake, fiery dragon.

torch, brand, coal, ember 381 n. *ash*; torchlight, link, flambeau cresset, match 385 n. *lighter*; candle, bougie, tallow candle, wax c., corpse-c.; taper, wax-t.; spill, wick, dip, farthing d., rush, rush-light, night-l., naked l., flare, gas-f., burner, Bunsen b.; torch-bearer, lampadist, linkboy.

lamp, lamplight; lantern, dark-l., lanthorn, glim, bull's-eye; safetyl amp, Davy l., miner's l.; oil lamp, hurricane l., duplex l., moderator l., moderator, lampion, Argand; gas lamp, incandescent l., gas mantle, mantle; electric lamp, torch, flashlight, searchlight, arc light, headlamp, headlight, side-light; anti-dazzle l., fog-lamp; stoplight, tail-light, reflector; bulb, flashbulb, photoflood, electric bulb, filament; vapour light, neon l., neon tube; magic lantern, projector; chandelier, gaselier, lustre, electrolier, candelabra, girandole; lamp-post, lampstand, sconce, candlestick; link-boy, lamplighter.

lighting, illumination, irradiation; artificial lighting, street-l.; indirect lighting; gaslighting, electric lighting, neon l., daylight l., fluorescent l.; floodlighting, son et lumière, limelight, spotlight, footlight.

signal light, warning l. 665 n. *danger signal*; traffic light, red l., green l., amber l., stoplight, trafficator, blinker; Very light, Bengal l., rocket, star shell, parachute light; flare, beacon, beacon-fire, bale-f.; lighthouse, lightship.

fireworks, illuminations, firework display, pyrotechnics; sky-rocket, Roman candle, Catherine wheel, sparkler, fizgig; thunderflash 723 n. *explosive*; Greek fire, Bengal light.

Adj. *luminescent*, luminous, self-l., incandescent, shining; lampyrine, lampyrid; phosphoric, phosphorescent, fluorescent, neon; radiant 417 adj. *radiating*; colourful 425 adj. *coloured*; illuminated, well-lit; bright, gay.

Vb. *illuminate*, light up, light 417 vb. *shine*, make bright.

See: 321, 379, 381, 385, 417, 425, 665, 723.

421 Screen

N. *screen*, shield 660 n. *protection*; covert 662 n. *shelter*; bower 194 n. *arbour*; glade, umbrage, shady nook 418 n. *darkness*; windshield, windscreen, sunshade, parasol; sun helmet, sola topee 226 n. *shade*; awning, dust-cover 226 n. *canopy*; sunscreen, visor; lamp-shade; eye-shade,

blinkers, blinders; eyelid, eyelashes 438 n. *eye*; dark glasses, blue spectacles, coloured s., sun glasses; frosted lens, smoked glass, frosted g., opaque g., polarized g. 423 n. *opacity*; stained glass 437 n. *variegation*; filter, sieve 62 n. *sorting*; partition, wall, hedge, windbreak 235 n. *fence*; iron curtain, bamboo c. 57 n. *exclusion;* mask 527 n. *disguise*; hood, veil, mantle 228 n. *cloak.*

curtain 226 n. *shade*; window curtain, bead c.; shade, blind, sunblind, khus khus tatti, chick; persienne, venetian blind, roller b.; shutter, window s., deadlight.

obfuscation, smoke-screen; fog, mist 341 n. *moisture*; pall, cloud, dust, film, scale 423 n. *opacity.*

Adj. *screened*, sheltered; sunproof, cool 380 adj. *cold*; shady, umbrageous, bowery 419 adj. *shadowy*; blindfolded, hooded 439 adj. *blind*; screening, impervious, impermeable.

Vb. *screen*, shield, shelter 660 vb. *safeguard*; protect 713 vb. *defend*; be a blind, cover up for; ward off, fend off 713 vb. *parry*; blanket, keep off, keep out 57 vb. *exclude*; cover up, veil, hood 226 vb. *cover*; mask, hide, occult 525 vb. *conceal*; intercept 702 vb. *obstruct*; blinker, blindfold 439 vb. *blind*; keep out the light, shade, shadow, darken; curtain, curtain off, canopy, draw the curtains, pull down the blind, spread the awning; put up the shutters, close the s. 264 vb. *close*; cloud, fog, mist 419 vb. *bedim*; smoke, frost, glaze, film 423 vb. *make opaque*; filter, sieve, bolt, sort, sort out 62 vb. *class.*

See: 57, 62, 194, 226, 228, 235, 264, 341, 380, 418, 419, 423, 437, 438, 439, 525, 527, 660, 662, 702, 713.

422 Transparency

N. *transparency*, transmission of light, transillumination; transparence, translucence, diaphaneity, unobstructed vision; thinness, gauziness; lucidity, pellucidity, limpidity; clearness, clarity; glassiness, vitreosity, hyalescence; transparent medium, hyaline, water, lymph, ice, crystal, mica, glass, sheet-g., plate-g., optical g., magnifying g., lens, eyepiece; pane, window-p., shop-window; watch-glass, crystal; sheer silk, diaphane; gossamer, gauze, lace, chiffon 4 n. *insubstantial thing.*

Adj. *transparent*, seen through, transpicuous, diaphanous, revealing, sheer; thin, fine, gauzy, pellucid, translucid; translucent, tralucent; liquid, limpid; crystal, crystalline, hyaline, vitreous, glassy; clear, serene, lucid; crystal-clear, clear as crystal.

Vb. *be transparent*, —transpicuous etc. adj.; transmit light, show through; shine through, transilluminate, pass light through 417 vb. *make bright*; render transparent, clarify.

See: 4, 417.

423 Opacity

N. *opacity*, opaqueness; thickness, solidity 324 n. *density*; filminess, frost; turbidity, fuliginosity, muddiness, dirtiness 649 n. *dirt*; devitrification; fog, mist, dense fog, smog, pea-souper, London special 355 n. *cloud*; film, scale 421 n. *screen*; smoke-cloud, smoke-screen 421 n. *obfuscation.*

Adj. *opaque*, opacious; impervious, adiactinic, adiathermic; non-transparent, thick, impervious to light, blank, windowless; not clear, clear as mud; unclarified, devitrified; cloudy, filmy, turbid, drumly, muddy, muddied, puddled; foggy, fogbound; hazy, misty, murky, smoky, sooty, fuliginous 419 adj. *dim*; unwashed, uncleaned 649 adj. *dirty*; nubilous, nubiferous; vaporous, fumid; coated, frosted, misted, clouded.

Vb. *make opaque*, devitrify; cloud, cloud over, thicken; frost, film, smoke 419 vb. *bedim*; obfuscate; scumble, overpaint 226 vb. *coat*; be opaque, obstruct the light 421 vb. *screen.*

See: 226, 324, 355, 419, 421, 649.

424 Semitransparency

N. *semitransparency*, milkiness, lactescence; pearliness, opalescence; smoked glass, frosted g., coloured spectacles, dark glasses; gauze, muslin; horn, mica; tissue, tissue paper.

Adj. *semitransparent*, semipellucid, semiopaque, semidiaphanous, gauzy; translucent, opalescent, opaline, milky, lactes-

cent, pearly; frosted, matt, misty, fumé 419 adj. *dim*, 355 adj. *cloudy*.

See: 355, 419.

425 Colour

N. *colour*, natural c., pure c., positive c., neutral c., primitive c., primary c.; three primaries, complementary colour, secondary c., tertiary c.; broken colour, chromatic dispersion, chromatic aberration; range of colour, chromatic scale; prism, spectrum, rainbow 437 n. *variegation*; mixture of colours, harmony, discord; coloration 553 n. *painting*; local colour 590 n. *description*; riot of colour, splash 437 n. *variegation*; heraldic colour, tincture, metal, fur 547 n. *heraldry*.
chromatics, science of colour, chromatoscopy, chromatology, spectrum analysis; chromascope, tintometer; spectroscope, prism.
hue, colour quality, chromatism, tone, value, key; brilliance, intensity, warmth, loudness; softness, deadness, dullness; coloration, livery; pigmentation, colouring, complexion, natural colour; hue of health, flush, blush, glow; ruddiness 431 n. *redness*; sickly hue, pallor 426 n. *achromatism*; faded hue, discoloration; tint, shade, cast, grain, dye; tinge, patina; half-tone, half-light, mezzotint.
pigment, colouring matter, rouge, warpaint, peroxide 843 n. *cosmetic*; dyestuff, dye, fast d., grain; vegetable dye, madder, cochineal 431 n. *red pigment*; indigo 434 n. *purple*; woad 435 n. *blue*; artificial dye, synthetic d., aniline d.; stain, fixative, mordant; wash, colour-wash, whitewash, distemper; paint, medium, oil paints 553 n. *art equipment*; oils, water-colours, tempera, pastel; palette, paint-box, paints.
Adj. *coloured*, in colour, painted, toned, tinged, dyed, double-d., tinted etc. vb.; colorific, tinctorial, tingent; fast, unfading, constant; colourful, chromatic, polychromatic; monochromatic 16 adj. *uniform*; prismatic, spectroscopic; kaleidoscopic, many-coloured, parti-coloured 437 adj. *variegated*.
florid, colourful, high-coloured, full-c., deep-c., bright-hued; ruddy 431 adj. *red*; intense, deep, strong, emphatic; unfaded,

vivid, brilliant; warm, glowing, rich, gorgeous; painted, gay, bright; gaudy, garish, showy, flashy; glaring, flaring, flaunting, spectacular; harsh, stark, raw, crude; lurid, loud, screaming, shrieking; clashing, discordant 25 adj. *disagreeing*.
soft-hued, soft, quiet, tender, delicate, refined; pearly, creamy 427 adj. *whitish*; light, pale, pastel; dull, flat, matt, dead; simple, sober, sad 573 adj. *plain*; sombre, dark 428 adj. *black*; drab, dingy, faded; patinated, weathered, mellow; matching, toning, harmonious 24 adj. *agreeing*.
Vb. *colour*, lay on the c., daub, scumble 553 vb. *paint*; rouge 431 vb. *redden*, 843 vb. *primp*; pigment, tattoo; dye, dip, imbue, imbrue; grain, woad 435 vb. *blue*; tint, touch up; shade, shadow 428 vb. *blacken*; tinct, tinge; wash, colour-wash, distemper, varnish, japan, lacquer 226 vb. *coat*; stain, discolour; come off (e.g. on one's fingers); tan, weather, mellow; illuminate, miniate, emblazon; whitewash, calcimine, silver 427 vb. *whiten*; yellow 433 vb. *gild*; enamel, pie 437 vb. *variegate*.

See: 16, 24, 25, 226, 426, 427, 428, 431, 433, 434, 435, 437, 547, 553, 573, 590, 843.

426 Achromatism: absence of colour

N. *achromatism*, achromaticity, colourlessness; fade, decoloration, discoloration, etiolation, fading, bleaching 427 n. *whiteness*; under-exposure 551 n. *photography*; pallor, pallidity, paleness; no colour, anæmia, bloodlessness; pigment-deficiency, albinism; neutral tint; monochrome; black and white; albino, blond, platinum b.
bleacher, decolorant, peroxide, bleaching powder, lime; bleachery.
Adj. *colourless*, hueless, toneless, lustreless; uncoloured, achromatic, achromatistous; decoloured, discoloured; bleached, etiolated, under-exposed; faded, fading; unpigmented, albino, light-coloured, fair, blond 433 adj. *yellow*; glossless, mousy; bloodless, exsanguine, anæmic; without colour, drained of colour, drained of blood; washed out, off-colour; pale, pallid 427 adj. *white*; ashy, ashen, ashen-hued, livid, tallow-faced, whey-f.; pasty, sallow, sickly 651 adj. *unhealthy*; dingy, dull, leaden 429 adj. *grey*; blank, glassy,

lack-lustre; lurid, ghastly, wan 419 adj. *dim*; deathly, cadaverous, pale as a corpse, pale as death, pale as ashes 361 adj. *dead.*

Vb. *lose colour* 419 vb. *be dim*; pale, fade, bleach, blanch, turn pale, change countenance 427 vb. *whiten*; run, come off.

decolorize, decolour, achromatize, fade, etiolate; blanch, bleach, peroxide 427 vb. *whiten*; deprive of colour, drain of c., drain, wash out; tone down, deaden, weaken; pale, dim 419 vb. *bedim*; dull, tarnish, discolour, stain 649 vb. *make unclean.*

See: 361, 419, 427, 429, 433, 551, 649, 651.

427 Whiteness

N. *whiteness*, albescence, albification, albication; etiolation; lack of pigment, leucosis, albinism, leucoderma; whitishness, lactescence, creaminess, pearliness; hoariness, canescence; white light 417 n. *light*; white heat 379 n. *heat.*

white thing, alabaster, marble; snow, driven s., snow-drift, snowflake; chalk, paper, milk, flour, ivory, lily; silver, white metal, white gold, pewter, platinum; pearl, teeth; white man, paleface, white; albino, albiness.

whiting, white lead, pipeclay; calamine, whitewash, white paint, Chinese white, Spanish w., Paris w., flake w., zinc w.

Adj. *white*, candid, pure, albescent; dazzling, light, bright 417 adj. *luminous*; silvered, silvery, silver, argent, argentine; alabaster, marble; chalky, cretaceous; snowy, niveous, snow-capped, snow-covered; hoar, frosty, frosted; foaming, spumy, foam-flecked; soapy, lathery; white hot 379 adj. *hot*; white as marble, white as alabaster, white like ivory, white as a statue, white as a lily, white as milk, white as paper, white as a sheet; pure white, lily-white, milk-w., snow-w.; white-skinned, Caucasian; lacking pigment, leucous, albinistic, leucodermatous; whitened, whitewashed, bleached 648 adj. *clean.*

whitish, pearly, milky, creamy 424 adj. *semi-transparent*; ivory, eburnean; waxen, sallow, pale; off-white, half-w.; unbleached, ecru; canescent, grizzled 429 adj. *grey*; pepper-and-salt 437 adj. *mottled*; blond, fair, ash-blond, platinum b.,

fair-haired, flaxen-h., tow-neaded; dusty, white with dust.

Vb. *whiten*, white, pipeclay, whitewash, calcimine, wash 648 vb. *clean*; blanch, bleach; etiolate, fade 426 vb. *decolorize*; frost, besnow; silver, grizzle.

See: 379, 417, 424, 426, 429, 437, 648.

428 Blackness

N. *blackness*, nigrescence, nigritude 418 n. *darkness*; inkiness, lividity, black, sable; melanism, swarthiness, swartness, pigmentation, pigment, dark colouring, touch of the tar brush, colour; depth, deep tone; black and white, chiaroscuro 437 n. *chequer*; blackening, nigrification, infuscation 418 n. *obscuration*; denigration 926 n. *detraction.*

negro, negress, mammy; nigger, buck n., black, darky, sambo, coon, piccaninny; blackamoor, Ethiopian, man of colour, coloured man; the coloured; negrito, negrillo.

black thing, coal, charcoal, soot, pitch, tar, tar-barrel; ebony, jet, ink, smudge, black eye; blackberry, blackthorn, sloe; crow, raven, blackbird; black clothes, crape, mourning.

black pigment, blacking, lamp-black, ivory-b., blue-b., nigrosine; ink, writing-i., drawing-i., India i., printer's i., printing i.; japan, niello; burnt cork.

Adj. *black*, atramentous, sable; jetty, ebon, inky, pitchy 418 adj. *dark*; sooty, fuliginous, smoky, smudgy, smutty 649 adj. *dirty*; black-haired, black-locked, raven, raven-haired; black-eyed, sloe-e.; dark, brunette; black-skinned, negroid, Ethiopian; pigmented, coloured; sad, sombre, funereal, mourning 364 adj. *funereal*; atrabilious, gloomy 893 adj. *sullen*; coal-black, collied; jet-black, sloe-b., pitch-b.; deep, of the deepest dye; black as coal, black as jet, black as a shoe, black as my hat, black as a tar-barrel, black as the ace of spades, black as a tinker's pot; nocturnal, black as night, black as midnight 129 adj. *vespertine*; black as November 129 adj. *wintry*; black in the face, black as thunder 891 adj. *angry.*

blackish, rather black, nigrescent; swarthy, swart, black-avised, black-faced, dark, dark-skinned, tanned, sun-t.; coloured,

pigmented; livid, black and blue; over-exposed; low-toned, low in tone 419 adj. *dim.*

Vb. *blacken,* black, nigrify, infuscate, ebonize; ink, ink in; dirty, soot, smoke, blot, smutch, smudge, smirch 649 vb. *make unclean;* deepen, over-develop 418 vb. *darken;* singe, char 381 vb. *burn.*

See: 129, 364, 381, 418, 419, 437, 649, 891, 893, 926.

429 Grey

N. *grey,* greyness, canescence, neutral tint, pepper and salt, chiaroscuro, grisaille; grey hairs, hoary head; Payne's grey, field g., oyster, gunmetal, ashes.

Adj. *grey,* neutral, sad, sombre, dull, leaden, livid; cool, quiet; canescent, greying, grizzled, grizzly, hoary, hoar; glaucous; light-grey, steely, pearly, silvery, silvered, frosted; powder-grey, smoky; ashen, ashy, ash-coloured, cinerary, cinereous; field-grey, steel-g., iron-g.; slate-g., stone-g.; pearl-g., oyster-g.; mouse-g., mousy, mole; dark grey, charcoal-grey; pepper-and-salt, dapple grey, grey-green.

430 Brownness

N. *brownness,* brown, bronze; sun-brown, sun-tan, sun-burn; snuff, tobacco-leaf; autumn colours, dead leaf; coffee, chocolate, walnut, mahogany, amber, copper; khaki; burnt almond; no blond, brunette.

brown paint, bistre, ochre, sepia, Vandyke brown, sienna, burnt s., umber, burnt u.

Adj. *brown,* brownish; browned, adust, singed, charred, toasted; bronzed, tanned, sunburnt; dark, brunette; reddish-brown, bay, bayard, dapple, roan, auburn, chestnut, sorrel; nutbrown, hazel; cinnamon; beige, fawn, bronze, buff, khaki; light-brown, ecru; tawny, fuscous, tan, foxy, russet, maroon; coppery, cupreous, yellowish brown, feuillemort; dark brown, mahogany, puce, chocolate, coffee-coloured; rust-coloured, snuff-c., liver-c.; brown as a berry, brown as mahogany.

Vb. *embrown,* brown, bronze, tan, sunburn; singe, char, toast 381 vb. *burn.*

See: 381.

431 Redness

N. *redness,* flush, hectic f., blush; fire-glow, sunset g. 417 n. *glow;* dawn, Aurora 128 n. *morning;* rubification, reddening, warmth, rubescence, erubescence; rosiness, ruddiness, bloom, red cheeks, apple c., cherry lips; high colour, floridness, full habit, rubicundity; type of red, pink, cyclamen, rose, poppy, geranium, peony, cherry, strawberry, plum, damson, peach; tomato; ruby, garnet, carbuncle, carnelian; coral; rust, iron mould; salmon, lobster; red blood, gore 335 n. *blood;* port wine, claret 301 n. *wine;* flame 379 n. *fire;* cardinal bird, scarlet minivet, redbreast, robin; redskin, Red Indian, redman; redhead, gingernob; redcoat 722 n. *soldier;* rubric, red ink; red planet, Mars.

red colour, red, vermeil, gules; rose-red, poppy-r., coquelicot; Pompeian red, Turkey r., Post Office r., pillar-box r.; scarlet, vermilion; cardinal red, imperial purple, Tyrian red; magenta, crimson, cramoisie, carmine, kermes; cherry, cerise, claret-red, maroon, puce; murrey, damask; pink, salmon p., couleur de rose, rose du Barry, carnation; flesh pink, flesh tint, flesh colour; stammel colour; rust, rust-red; Judas-colour.

red pigment, red dye, grain, scarlet g., murex, cochineal, carmine; kermes; dragon's blood; cinnabar, vermilion; ruddle, madder; crimson lake, Indian l., Venetian red, rosaniline, solferino; corallin, pæonin; red ochre; red lead, minium; red ink; rouge, lipstick 843 n. *cosmetic.*

Adj. *red,* rose-r., rosy, roseate; reddish-pink, rubeous, flesh-coloured; coral, russet; scarlet, vermilion; tomato-red; crimson, imperial purple; murrey, stammel; ruddy, rubicund, sanguine, florid, blowzy; red-cheeked, apple-c.; sandy, carroty, red-haired, ginger-h., rufous; auburn, Titian; rusty, ferrugineous, ferruginous, rubiginous, rust-coloured; lateritious, brick-red; warm, hot, fiery, glowing, flushed, fevered, hectic; flushing, erubescent, rubescent; rose-coloured, ruby-c., cherry-c., plum-c., peach-c., salmon-c.; wine-coloured; wine-dark; tawny, foxy, Judas-coloured; lobster-red; red-hot 379 adj. *hot;* red as fire, red as blood, red as a turkey-cock, red as a lobster; dyed red, reddened, rouged,

carmined, raddled, farded, painted, lip-sticked.

bloodshot, bloodstained, blood-red; san-guinary, bloody, gory, incarnadine, en-sanguined 335 adj. *sanguineous*.

Vb. *redden*, rubify, rubricate, miniate; rouge, raddle 843 vb. *primp*; incarnadine, dye red, stain with blood; flush, blush, glow; mantle, colour, colour up, crimson.

See: 128, 301, 335, 379, 417, 722, 843.

432 Greenness

N. *greenness*, green, verdancy, greenery, greenwood; verdure, viridity, viride-scence; olive, myrtle; lime; grass, moss, turf, green leaf 366 n. *foliage*; jade, emerald, malachite, beryl, chrysoprase, olivenite, verd-antique, green porphyry, aquamarine, verdigris; patina.

green colour, vert, jungle green, leaf-g., grass-g., Lincoln g.; sea-g., channel g., Nile g.; bottle green, forest g., olive g., pea-g., sage g., jade g.; celadon, reseda, mignonette.

green pigment, terre verte, celadonite, viri-dian, verditer, bice, green b., Paris green; chlorophyl, etiolin.

Adj. *green*, viridescent, verdant, emerald; verdurous, grassy, leafy; grass-green, forest-g.; olive, olivaceous, glaucous, virescent, leek-green, porraceous; light green, chlorine; greenish, bilious; lime, chartreuse; dull green, glaucous.

See: 366.

433 Yellowness

N. *yellowness*, yellow colour, canary yellow, mustard y.; yellow metal, gold, old g.; yellow flower, crocus, buttercup, prim-rose, daffodil, saffron, mustard; topaz; light yellow, lemon, honey; biliousness, jaundice, icterus; xanthodermia, xan-thoma, xanthochromism, xanthopsia; yellow fever.

yellow pigment, gamboge, cadmium yellow, chrome y., Indian y., lemon y., orpiment, yellow ochre, Claude tint, massicot, aureolin, luteic acid, lutein; weld, lute-olin, xanthin.

Adj. *yellow*, gold, golden, aureate, gilt, gilded; fulvous, fulvid, flavous, fallow,

sallow, honey-pale; yellowish, icteroid, icteric, bilious, jaundiced, icteritious, xanthic; deep yellow, luteous; light yel-low, sandy, flaxen, fair-haired, blond, platinum b., tawny, buff; creamy, cream-coloured; citrine, lemon-coloured, citron-c., primrose-c., straw-c., sulphur-c., mus-tard-c., saffron-c., butter-c., butter-faced; yellow as parchment, yellow as a quince, yellow as a guinea, yellow as a crow's foot.

Vb. *gild*, gilt, yellow, jaundice.

434 Purple

N. *purple*, blue and red, bishop's purple; heliotrope, lavender, pansy, violet, Parma v.; gridelin, amethyst; purpure, Tyrian purple, gentian violet; dark purple, mul-berry colour, lividness 428 n. *blackness*; bright purple, mauve.

Adj. *purple*, purply, purplish, violet, violace-ous, purple-red; mauve, lavender, lilac, puce, plum-coloured; pansy-coloured, ianthine, hyacinthine, heliotrope; livid, dark purple, mulberry; black and blue 428 adj. *black*.

Vb. *empurple*, purple.

See: 428.

435 Blueness

N. *blueness*, blue, sky, blue s., sea; blue colour, azure, cerulean, celeste, perse, watchet, smalt; robin's egg, peacock, hyacinth, bluebell, cornflower, violet, forget-me-not; sapphire, turquoise, lapis lazuli, beryl, aquamarine; bluishness, cyanosis; lividness, lividity; cyanometer.

blue pigment, blue dye, bice, indigo, woad; cyanin; cyanine; saxony blue, saxe-b., Prussian b., ultramarine, French blue, Persian b., cobalt, cobalt blue, zaffre, smalt; cerulean, azulene; blue-bag.

Adj. *blue*, azure, azurine, cyanic; cerulean, skyey, atmospheric; sky-blue, air-force b., watchet-b.; light blue, Cambridge b., pale b., garter-b., powder b., steel b., robin's egg b.; royal blue, peacock b., pavonian; aquamarine, sea-b., cyan-b., electric b.; ultramarine; deep blue, dark b., Oxford b., midnight b., navy b., navy; hyacinth-ine, blue-black, black and blue, livid; bluish, perse; cold, steely; cyanosed.

Vb. *blue*, azure; dye blue, woad.

436 Orange

N. *orange,* red and yellow, gold, old g.; or 547n. *heraldry;* sunflower, helianthus, apricot, mandarin, tangerine, ginger, copper, flame; ochre, Mars orange, cadmium, henna, helianthin.
Adj. *orange,* ochreous, cupreous, coppery, ginger; orange-coloured, apricot-c., flame-c., copper-c., brass-c; tenné.
Duci 547.

437 Variegation

N. *variegation,* variety, diversification, diversity 15n. *difference;* dancing light, glancing l. 417n. *light;* play of colour, shot colours, iridescence, irisation; pavonine, nacre, mother-of-pearl; shot silk, pigeon's neck, gorge-de-pigeon; dichromatism, trichromatism; dichroism, trichromism, tricolour, polychrome, multi-colour 425n. *colour;* peacock, peacock's tail, butterfly, tortoiseshell, chameleon; Joseph's coat, motley, harlequin, patchwork; mixture of colour, medley of c., riot of c.; stained glass, kaleidoscope; rainbow, rainbow effect, band of colour, spectrum, prism.
chequer, checker, chequerwork, check, pepper-and-salt; plaid, tartan; chessboard pattern, chess-board, draught-b., checker b.; mosaic, tessellation, tesserae, marquetry, parquetry, crazy-paving 82n. *multiformity.*
striation, striae; line, streak, band, bar, stripe, tricolour; zebra, tiger; streakiness, mackerel sky; crack, craze 330n. *brittleness.*
maculation, dappling, stippling, marbling; spottiness, patchiness 17n. *non-uniformity;* patch, speck, speckle, spots, pockmarks, freckle 845n. *blemish;* maculae, sunspot; leopard, spotted dog.
Adj. *variegated* etc. vb., diversified, daedal; embroidered, worked 844adj. *ornamental;* polychromatic, colourful 425adj. *florid;* bicolour, tricolour; dichroic, dichromatic, dichromic; trichromatic, trichroic; many-hued, many-coloured, multi-c., parti-c., motley, patched, crazy, of all colours; kaleidoscopic 82adj. *multiform;* rainbow-coloured, rainbow, iridal, iridian; prismatic, spectral; plaid, mosaic, tessellated, parquet; paned, panelled.

iridescent, irisated, versicolour, chameleon; nacreous, mother-of-pearl; opalescent, opaline, pearly 424adj. *semitransparent;* shot, shot through with, gorge-de-pigeon, pavonian, moiré, watered, chatoyant, cymophanous.
pied, parti-coloured, black-and-white, pepper-and-salt, grizzled, piebald, skewbald, roan, pinto, chequered, check, dappled, patchy.
mottled, marbled, jaspered, veined; studded, maculose, maculous, spotted, spotty, patchy; speckled, speckledy, freckled; streaky, streaked, striated, lined, barred, banded, striped; brinded, brindled, tabby; pocked, pockmarked, fleabitten 845 adj. *blemished;* cloudy, powdered, dusted, dusty.
Vb. *variegate,* diversify, fret; punctuate; chequer, check; patch 656vb. *repair;* embroider, work 844vb. *decorate;* braid, quilt; damascene, inlay, tessellate, tile; stud, mottle, speckle, freckle, spangle, spot; sprinkle, powder, dust; tattoo, stipple, dapple; streak, stripe, striate; marble, jasper, vein, cloud 423vb. *make opaque;* stain, blot, maculate, discolour 649vb. *make unclean;* make iridescent, irisate; interchange colour, play.

See: 15, 17, 82, 330, 417, 423, 424, 425, 649, 656, 844, 845.

438 Vision

N. *vision,* sight, power of s., light-grasp; eyesight; seeing, visualization 513n. *imagination;* perception, recognition; acuity (of vision), good sight, keen s., sharp s., long s., far s., normal s.; defective vision, short sight 440n. *dim sight;* mental sight, perspicacity 498n. *intelligence;* second sight 984n. *occultism;* type of vision, double vision, stereoscopic v., binocular v., radial v., averted v.; aided vision, magnification; tired vision, winking, blinking; eye-testing, sight-t.; oculist, optician, ophthalmologist 417n. *optics;* dream 440n. *visual fallacy.*
eye, visual organ, organ of vision, eyeball, iris, pupil, white, cornea, retina, optic nerve; optics, orbs, lights, peepers, weepers; saucer eyes, goggle e., bugle e., gooseberry e.; eyelashes, eyelid 421n.

screen; lashes, sweeping l.; naked eye, unaided e.; clear eye, sharp e., piercing e., penetrating e., gimlet e., X-ray e.; dull eye, glass e. 439 n. *blindness*; evil eye 983 n. *sorcery*; hawk, eagle, cat, lynx, ferret, Argus; basilisk, cockatrice, Gorgon.

look, regard, glance, side-g., squint; tail *or* corner of the eye; glint, blink; penetrating glance, gaze, steady g.; observation, contemplation, speculation, watch; stare, fixed s.; come-hither look, glad eye, ogle, leer, grimace 889 n. *endearment*; wink 524 n. *hint*; dirty look, scowl, evil eye; peep, peek, glimpse, rapid g., half an eye; mien 445 n. *appearance*.

inspection, ocular i., ocular demonstration; examination, visual e., autopsy 459 n. *enquiry*; view, preview 522 n. *manifestation*; oversight 689 n. *management*; survey, overview; sweep, reconnaissance, reconnoitre, perlustration, tour of inspection; sight-seeing, rubbernecking; look, look-around, look-see, dekko, once-over, coup d'œil, rapid survey, rapid glance; second glance, double take; review, revision; mental inspection, speculation, introspection 449 n. *thought*; conspection, discernment, catching sight, espial, view, first v., first sight; looking round, observation, prying, spying; espionage; peeping, scopophilia, Peeping Tom.

view, full v., eyeful; vista, prospect, outlook, perspective; conspectus, panorama, bird's-eye view, commanding v.; horizon, false h.; line of sight, line of vision; range of view, ken 490 n. *knowledge*; field of view, amphitheatre 724 n. *arena*; scene, setting, stage 594 n. *theatre*; angle of vision, slant, point of view, viewpoint, standpoint 485 n. *opinion*; observation point, look-out, crow's nest, watch-tower; belvedere, gazebo; astrodome, conning tower; observatory, observation balloon; stand, grandstand, stall, ringside seat 441 n. *onlookers*; loophole, peephole, hagioscope 263 n. *window*.

Adj. *seeing* etc. vb., visual, perceptible, specious 443 adj. *visible*; panoramic, perspectual; ocular, ophthalmic; optical; stereoscopic, binocular; orthopic, perspicacious, clear-sighted, sharp-s., sharp-eyed, keen-e., gimlet-e., eagle-e., hawk-e., lynx-e., ferret-e., Argus-e.; far-sighted, sagacious 498 adj. *wise*; second-sighted, visionary 513 adj. *imaginative*.

Vb. *see*, behold, visualize, use one's eyes; see true, keep in perspective; perceive, discern, distinguish, make out, pick o., recognize, ken 490 vb. *know*; take in, see at a glance 498 vb. *be wise*; descry, discover 484 vb. *detect*; sight, espy, spy, spot, observe 455 vb. *notice*; clap eyes on, catch sight of, sight (land), raise; catch a glimpse of, glimpse, have a side-light; view, command a view of, hold in view, have in sight; see with one's own eyes, witness, look on, be a spectator 441 vb. *watch*; dream, see visions, see things 513 vb. *imagine*; see in the dark, have second sight 510 vb. *foresee*; become visible 443 vb. *be visible*.

gaze, regard, quiz, gaze at, look, look at; look full in the face; look intently, eye, stare, peer, squinny; stare at, stare hard, goggle, gape, gawk; focus, rivet one's eyes, fix one's gaze; glare, look black 891 vb. *be angry*; glance, glance at; take a slant, squint, look askance; wink, blink 524 vb. *hint*; give the glad eye, ogle, leer 889 vb. *court*; gloat, gloat over 947 vb. *gluttonize*; steal a glance, peep, peek, take a peep; direct one's gaze, cock one's eye, cast one's eyes on, bend one's looks on, turn one's eyes on; notice, take n., look upon 455 vb. *be attentive*; lift up one's eyes, look up; look down, look round, look in front; look ahead, look before one, look before and after 858 vb. *be cautious*; look away 458 vb. *disregard*; look at each other, exchange glances.

scan, scrutinize, inspect, examine, take stock of; contemplate, pore, pore over 536 vb. *study*; look over, look through; have *or* take a look at, have a dekko; see, go and see, take in, sight-see, rubberneck; pilgrimage, go to see 882 vb. *visit*; view, survey, sweep, reconnoitre; scout, spy out the land; peep, peek 453 vb. *be curious*; spy, speculate, pry, snoop; observe, keep under observation, watch 457 vb. *invigilate*; hold in view, keep in sight; watch out for, look out f. 507 vb. *await*; keep watch, look out, keep looking, keep one's eyes skinned *or* peeled; strain one's eyes, peer; squint at, squinny; crane, crane one's neck, stand on tiptoe.

Adv. *at sight*, at first sight, at the first blush, prima facie; in view 443 adv. *visibly*; in sight of; with one's eyes open.

Int. look! dekko! view halloo!

See: 263, 417, 421, 439, 440, 441, 443, 445, 449, 453, 455, 457, 458, 459, 484, 485, 490, 498, 507, 510, 513, 522, 524, 536, 594, 689, 724, 858, 882, 889, 891, 947, 983, 984.

439 Blindness

N. *blindness*, lack of vision; benightedness, darkness 491 n. *ignorance*; sightlessness, eyelessness, cecity, anopsy, ablepsy; making blind, blinding, excecation; eye-disease, amaurosis, amblyopia, glaucoma, 'drop serene', cataract; night blindness, snow b., colour b.; dim-sightedness 440 n. *dim sight*; blind side, blind spot, blind eye 456 n. *inattention*; glass eye, artificial e.; blind man, the blind; sandman 679 n. *soporific*; aid for the blind, Braille 586 n. *script*; white stick.

Adj. *blind*, sightless, eyeless, visionless, dark; unseeing, undiscerning, unperceiving, unnoticing, unobserving 456 adj. *inattentive*; blinded, excecate; blindfold, blinkered; in the dark, benighted; cataractous, glaucomatic, amaurotic 440 adj. *dim-sighted*; gravel-blind, stone-blind, sand-blind, stark-b.; blind as a mole, blind as a bat, blind as a buzzard, blind as an owl, blind as a beetle.

Vb. *be blind*, not use one's eyes; go blind, lose one's sight, lose one's eyes; not see; lose sight of; grope in the dark, feel one's way 461 vb. *be tentative*; lose one's way, walk in darkness 495 vb. *err*; have the eyes bandaged, wear blinkers; be blind to 491 vb. *not know*; ignore, have a blind spot, not look, shut the eyes to, avert the eyes, turn away the e., look the other way 458 vb. *disregard*; not bear the light, blink, wink, squint 440 vb. *be dim-sighted*.

blind, render b., deprive of sight; excecate, put one's eyes out, gouge one's eyes o.; dazzle, daze; darken, obscure, eclipse 419 vb. *bedim*; screen from sight; blinker, blindfold, bandage 421 vb. *screen*; hoodwink, bluff, throw dust in one's eyes 495 vb. *mislead*.

See: 419, 421, 440, 456, 458, 461, 491, 495, 586, 679.

440 Dim-sightedness: imperfect vision

N. *dim sight*, weak s., failing s., dim-sightedness, dull-sightedness; near-blindness, purblindness 439 n. *blindness*; half-vision, partial v., blurred v., imperfect v., defective v.; weak eyes, eye-strain; amblyopia, half-sight, short s., near s., near-sightedness, myopia; presbyopia, long sight, far s.; double sight, double vision, confusion of v.; astigmatism, teichopsia, cataract, film; glaucoma, iridization; scotoma, dizziness, swimming; colour-blindness, Daltonism, dichromism, red-green blindness; chromato-pseudoblepsis, chromatodysopia; snow-blindness, niphablepsia; day-blindness, hemeralopia; night-blindness, nyctalopy, nyctalopia, moon-blindness, moon-blink; lippitude, bleardness; ophthalmia, ophthalmitis; conjunctivitis, pink eye; obliquity of vision, cast; convergent vision, strabismus, strabism, squint, cross-eye; wall-eye, cock-e., swivel e.; myosis; wink, blink, nictitation, nystagmus; obstructed vision, eye-shade, blinker, blinder, screen, veil, curtain 421 n. *screen*; blind side, blind spot 456 n. *inattention*.

visual fallacy, anamorphosis 246 n. *distortion*; refraction 417 n. *reflection*; aberration of light 282 n. *deviation*; false light 552 n. *misrepresentation*; illusion, optical i., trick of light, trick of the eyesight, phantasmagoria 542 n. *sleight*; mirage 542 n. *deception*; fata morgana, ignis fatuus, will-o'-the-wisp 420 n. *glow-worm*; phantasm, phantasma, phantom, spectre, spectre of the Brocken, wraith, apparition 970 n. *ghost*; vision, dream 513 n. *fantasy*; distorting mirror, magic m., magic lantern 442 n. *optical device*.

Adj. *dim-sighted*, purblind, half-blind gravel-b., dark; weak-eyed, bespectacled; myopic, short-sighted, near-s.; presbyopic, long-sighted, astigmatic; colour-blind, dichromatic; hemeralopic, nyctalopic; dim-eyed, one-e., monocular, monoculous, monoculate; wall-eyed, squinting; strabismal, strabismic, cross-eyed; swivel-eyed, goggle-e., blear-e., moon-e., mope-e., cock-e.; myotic, nystagmic; blinking, dazzled, dazed; blinded, temporarily b. 439 adj. *blind*; swimming, dizzy; amaurotic, cataractous, glaucomatic.

Vb. *be dim-sighted,*—myopic etc. adj.; not see well, need spectacles, change one's glasses; have a mist before the eyes, have a film over the e., get something in one's

e.; grope, peer, screw up the eyes, squint; blink, bat the eyelid; wink, nictitate, nictate; see double, grow dazzled, dazzle, swim; grow blurred, dim, fail; see through a glass darkly.

blur, render indistinct, confuse; glare, dazzle, bedazzle, daze 417 vb. *shine*; darken, dim, mist, fog, smoke, smudge 419 vb. *bedim*; be indistinct, loom 419 vb. *be dim.*

See: 246, 282, 417, 419, 420, 421, 439, 442, 456, 513, 542, 552, 970.

441 Spectator

N. *spectator*, beholder, seer; mystic 513 n. *visionary*; looker, viewer, observer, watcher; inspector, examiner, scrutator, scrutinizer 690 n. *manager*; waiter, attendant 742 n. *servant*; witness, eye-w.; passer-by, bystander, onlooker; looker-on, gazer, starer, gaper, goggler, sidewalk superintendent; eyer, ogler, quizzer; sightseer, rubberneck, tourist, globe-trotter 268 n. *traveller*; star-gazer, astronomer; bird watcher, watchbird; spotter, look-out 484 n. *detector*; watchman, night-w., watch, sentinel, sentry 664 n. *warner*; patrolman, patrol 314 n. *circler*; scout, spy, snoop 459 n. *detective*; movie-goer, cinema-g., theatre-g. 594 n. *playgoer*; televiewer, television fan; art critic 480 n. *estimator*; backseat driver 691 n. *adviser*.

onlookers, audience, auditorium, sea of faces; box-office, gate, house, gallery, peanut g., bleachers, grandstand, pit, stalls; crowd, supporters, followers, aficionados, fans 707 n. *patron*; viewership.

Vb. *watch*, look on, look at, look in, view 438 vb. *see*; witness 189 vb. *be present*; follow, follow with the eyes, observe, attend 455 vb. *be attentive*; eye, ogle, quiz; gape, gawk, stare; spy, spy out, scout, scout out 438 vb. *scan*.

See: 189, 268, 314, 438, 455, 459, 480, 484, 513, 594, 664, 690, 691, 707, 742.

442 Optical Instrument

N. *optical device*, optical instrument; glass, sheet-g., watch-glass, crystal 422 n. *trans-parency*; lens, meniscus, achromatic lens, astigmatic l., bifocal l., telephoto l.; eyepiece, ocular, object-glass; sunglass, burning-glass; optometer, ophthalmoscope, skiascope, retinoscope, amblyoscope; helioscope, coronograph; periscope, teinoscope, omniscope, radar; prism, spectroscope, telespectroscope, diffraction grating, polariscope; multiplying glass, polyscope; kaleidoscope; thaumatrope; stereoscope, stereopticon; photoscope, photometer, lucimeter, actinometer, radiometer, eriometer; projector, megascope, epidiascope, magic lantern 445 n. *cinema*; slide, coloured s.

eyeglass, spectacles, specs, goggles, giglamps, barnacles; glasses, reading g., distance g., horn-rimmed g.; sunglasses, dark glasses; pince-nez, nippers; bifocal glasses, bifocals; thick glasses, pebble g.; contact lens; lorgnette, monocle, quizzing-glass; magnifying glass, reading g.; spectacle-maker, oculist, optician, ophthalmologist; optometrist, optometry.

telescope, astronomical t., terrestrial t., equatorial t., achromatic t., inverting t., refractor, reflector, Newtonian r., Cassegrainian r., Huyghenian r.; finder, view-f., range-f. 321 n. *astronomy*; spy-glass, field-g., night-g.; binoculars, prism b., opera glass.

microscope, photo-m., electron m., ultramicroscope; microscopy, microphotography, microscopist.

mirror, bronze m., steel m., magic m., distorting m., concave m., flat, speculum; rear-view mirror, traffic m.; glass, hand-mirror, hand-glass, looking-g., pier-g., cheval-g., full-length mirror.

camera, camera lucida, camera obscura, pin-hole camera; hand camera, box-c.; stereo-camera, telephoto lens, movie-camera, X-ray c.; microphotography 551 n. *photography*; plate, wet p., dry p.; film, micro-f., fast f., slow f., panchromatic f.

See: 321, 422, 445, 551.

443 Visibility

N. *visibility*, perceptibility, discernibility, observability; visuality, presence to the eyes 445 n. *appearance*; apparency, sight, exposure; distinctness, clearness, clarity,

conspicuity, conspicuousness, prominence; eye-witness, ocular proof, ocular evidence, ocular demonstration, object lesson 522 n. *manifestation*; scene, field of view 438 n. *view*; atmospheric visibility, seeing, good s., bad s., high visibility, low v.; limit of visibility, ceiling, visible distance, eye-range, eye-shot 183 n. *range*.

Adj. *visible*, seeable, viewable; perceptible, perceivable, discernible, observable, detectable; noticeable, remarkable; recognizable, unmistakable, palpable; symptomatic 547 adj. *indicating*; apparent 445 adj. *appearing*; evident, showing 522 adj. *manifest*; exposed, open, naked, outcropping, exposed to view, open to v.; sighted, in view, in full v.; before one's eyes, under one's e. 189 adj. *on the spot*; visible to the naked eye, macroscopic; telescopic, just visible, at the limit of vision; panoramic, stereoscopic, periscopic.

well-seen, obvious, showing, for all to see 522 adj. *shown*; plain, clear, clear-cut, as clear as day; definite, well-defined, well-marked; distinct, unblurred, in focus; unclouded, undisguised, uncovered, unhidden; spectacular, conspicuous, pointed, prominent, cynosural; kenspeckle; eye-catching, striking, shining 417 adj. *luminous*; glaring, staring; pronounced, in bold relief, in strong r., in high r., in high light; visualized, well-visualized, eidetic, eidotropic; under one's nose, in plain sight, plain as plain, plain as a pikestaff, plain as the way to parish church, plain as the nose on your face.

Vb. *be visible*, become visible, be seen, show, show through, shine t. 422 vb. *be transparent*; speak for itself, attract attention, call for notice 455 vb. *attract notice*; meet the eye; hit, strike, catch *or* hit the eye, stand out, act as a landmark; come to light, dawn upon; loom, heave in sight, come into view, show its face 445 vb. *appear*; pop up, crop up, turn up, show up 295 vb. *arrive*; spring up, start up, arise 68 vb. *begin*; surface, break s. 308 vb. *ascend*; emanate, come out, creep out 298 vb. *emerge*; stick out, project 254 vb. *jut*; show, materialize, develop; manifest itself, expose i., betray i. 522 vb. *be plain*; symptomatize 547 vb. *indicate*; come on the stage, make one's entry 297 vb. *enter*;

come forward, come forth, stand f., advance; fill the eyes, dazzle, glare; shine forth, break through the clouds 417 vb. *shine*; have no secrets, live in a glass house; remain visible, stay in sight, float before one's eyes; make visible, expose 522 vb. *manifest*.

Adv. *visibly* etc. adj., in sight of, before one's eyes, within eye-shot; on show, on view.

See: 68, 183, 189, 254, 295, 297, 298, 308, 417, 422, 438, 445, 455, 522, 547.

444 Invisibility

N. *invisibility*, non-appearance 190 n. *absence*; vanishment, thin air 446 n. *disappearance*; imperceptibility, indistinctness, vagueness, indefiniteness; poor visibility, obscurity 419 n. *dimness*; remoteness, distance 199 n. *farness*; littleness, smallness 196 n. *minuteness*; sequestration 883 n. *seclusion*; delitescence, submergence 523 n. *latency*; disguisement, hiding 525 n. *concealment*; mystification, mystery 525 n. *secrecy*; smoke screen, mist, fog, veil, curtain, pall 421 n. *screen*; blind spot, blind eye 439 n. *blindness*; blind corner 663 n. *pitfall*; hidden menace 661 n. *danger*; impermeability, blank wall 423 n. *opacity*.

Adj. *invisible*, imperceptible, unapparent, unnoticeable, indiscernible; indistinguishable, unrecognizable; unseen, unsighted; viewless, sightless, unviewed; unnoticed, unregarded 458 adj. *neglected*; out of sight, out of eye-shot 446 adj. *disappearing*; not in sight, remote 199 adj. *distant*; sequestered 883 adj. *secluded*; hidden, lurking, submerged, delitescent 523 adj. *latent*; disguised, camouflaged 525 adj. *concealed*; shadowy, dark, secret, mysterious 421 adj. *screened*; eclipsed, darkened, dark 418 adj. *unlit*.

ill-seen, part-s., half-s.; unclear, ill-defined, ill-marked, undefined, indefinite, indistinct 419 adj. *dim*; faint, inconspicuous, microscopic 196 adj. *minute*; confused, vague, blurred, blurry, out of focus; fuzzy, misty, hazy 424 adj. *semitransparent*.

Vb. *be unseen*, lie out of sight; hide, couch, ensconce oneself, lie in ambush 523 vb. *lurk*; escape notice, blush unseen 872 vb. *be humble*; become invisible, pale, fade,

die 419vb. *be dim*; hide one's diminished head 872vb. *be humbled*; move out of sight, be lost to view, vanish 446vb. *disappear*; make invisible, hide away, submerge 525vb. *conceal*; blind, veil 421vb. *screen*; darken, eclipse 419vb. *bedim.*

Adv. *invisibly*, silently 525adv. *stealthily*; behind the scenes; in the dark.

See: 190, 196, 199, 418, 419, 421, 423, 424, 439, 446, 458, 523, 525, 661, 663, 872, 883.

445 Appearance

N. *appearance*, phenomenon, epiphenomenon 89n. *concomitant*; event, happening, occurrence 154n. *eventuality*; apparency, apparition 443n. *visibility*; first appearance, rise, arising 68n. *beginning*; becoming, realization, materialization, embodiment, presence 1n. *existence*; showing, exhibition, display, view, demonstration 522n. *manifestation*; preview, premonstration; shadowing forth 511n. *prediction*, 471n. *probability*; revelation 484n. *discovery*; externals, outside 223n. *exteriority*; appearances, look of things; visual impact, face value, first blush; impression, effect; show, seeming, semblance; side, aspect, guise, colour, light, outline, shape, dimension 243n. *form*; set, hang, look; respect, point *or* angle of view 438n. *view*; a manifestation, emanation, theophany; vision 513n. *fantasy*; false appearance, mirage, hallucination, illusion 440n. *visual fallacy*; apparition, phantasm, spectre 970n. *ghost*; reflection, image, mirror i. 18n. *similarity*; mental image, after-image.

spectacle, impressiveness, effectiveness, impression, effect; speciousness, meretriciousness, decoration 844n. *ornamentation*; feast for the eyes, eyeful, vision, sight, scene; panorama, bird's-eye view 438n. *view*; display, lavish d., pageantry, pageant, parade, review 875n. *ostentation*; illuminations, son et lumière; pyrotechnics 420n. *fireworks*; presentation, show, exhibition, exposition 522n. *exhibit*; art exhibition 553n. *picture*; visual entertainment, peep-show, raree-s., gallanty s.; phantasmagoria 440n. *visual fallacy*; kaleidoscope 437n. *variegation*;

diorama, cyclorama, georama, cosmorama; staging, tableau, transformation scene; set, decor, setting, backcloth, background 594n. *stage set*; revue, extravaganza, pantomime, floor show 594n. *stage show*; television, video (see *cinema*); cynosure, landmark, sea-mark 547n. *signpost*.

cinema, cinematograph, bioscope, biograph, cinema - screen, silver s.; photoplay, motion picture, moving p.; movie-show, film s., cinerama; movies, flickers, flicks, films; celluloid, film, stereoscopic f., three-dimensional f., 3D; silent film, sound f., talkie; cartoon, animated c., newsreel, documentary, short, double feature, trailer, blip, preview; film production, montage, continuity, cutting, scenario; cinema studio, Hollywood; cinema house, picture palace, nickelodeon 594n. *theatre*; projector, ciné-camera 442n. *camera.*

mien, look, face; play of feature, expression; countenance, favour; complexion, colour, cast; air, demeanour, carriage, port, presence; gesture, posture, behaviour 688n. *conduct.*

feature, trait, mark, lineament; lines, cut, shape, fashion, figure 243n. *form*; contour, relief, elevation, profile, silhouette; visage, physiognomy, cut of one's jib, phiz 237n *face.*

Adj. *appearing*, apparent, phenomenal; seeming, specious, ostensible; deceptive 542adj. *deceiving*; outward, external 233adj. *exterior*; outcropping, showing, on view 443adj. *visible*; open to view, exhibited 522adj. *shown*; impressive, effective, spectacular 875adj. *showy*; decorative, meretricious 844adj. *ornamental*; showing itself, revealed, theophanic 522adj. *manifest*; visionary, dreamlike 513adj. *imaginary.*

Vb. *appear*, show, show through 443vb. *be visible*; seem, look so 18vb. *resemble*; have the look of, wear the look of, present the appearance of, exhibit the form of, assume the guise of, take the shape of; figure in, display oneself, cut a figure 875vb. *be ostentatious*; be on show, be on exhibit; exhibit 522vb. *manifest*; start, rise, arise; dawn, break 68vb. *begin*; eventuate 154vb. *happen*; materialize, pop up 295vb. *arrive*; haunt, walk 970vb. *goblinize.*

Adv. *apparently*, manifestly, distinctly 443 adv. *visibly*; ostensibly, seemingly, to all appearances, as it seems, to all seeming, to the eye, at first sight, at the first blush; on the face of it; to the view, in the eyes of; on view, on show, on exhibition.

See: 1, 18, 68, 89, 154, 223, 237, 243, 295, 420, 437, 438, 440, 442, 443, 471, 484, 511, 513, 522, 542, 547, 553, 594, 688, 844, 875, 970.

446 Disappearance

N. *disappearance*, vanishment; disappearing trick, vanishing t. 542 n. *sleight*; flight 667 n. *escape;* exit 296 n. *departure*; evanescence, evaporation 338 n. *vaporization*; dematerialization, dissipation, dissolution 51 n. *decomposition*; extinction 2 n. *ron-existence*; occultation, eclipse 418 n. *obscuration*; dissolving views, fade-out; vanishing point, thin air 444 n. *invisibility*.

Adj. *disappearing*, vanishing; evanescent 114 adj. *transient*; dissipated, dispersed; missing, vanished 190 adj. *absent*; lost, lost to sight, lost to view 444 adj. *invisible*; gone 2 adj. *extinct*.

Vb. *disappear*, vanish, do the vanishing trick; dematerialize, melt into thin air; evanesce, evaporate 338 vb. *vaporize*; dissolve, melt, melt away 337 vb. *liquefy*; waste, consume, wear away, wear off, dwindle, dwindle to vanishing point 37 vb. *decrease*; fade, fade out, pale 426 vb. *lose colour*; fade away 114 vb. *be transient*; be occulted, suffer *or* undergo an eclipse 419 vb. *be dim*; disperse, dissipate, diffuse, scatter 75 vb. *be dispersed*; absent oneself, fail to appear, play truant 190 vb. *be absent*; go, be gone, depart 296 vb. *decamp*; run away, get a. 667 vb. *escape*; hide, lie low, be in hiding 523 vb. *lurk*; cover one's tracks, leave no trace 525 vb. *conceal*; be lost to sight 444 vb. *be unseen*; retire from view, seclude oneself 883 vb. *seclude*; become extinct, leave not a rack behind 2 vb. *pass away*; make disappear, erase, dispel 550 vb. *obliterate*.

See: 2, 37, 51, 75, 114, 190, 296, 337, 338, 418, 419, 426, 444, 523, 525, 542, 550, 667, 883.

447 Intellect

N. *intellect*, mind, psyche, psychic organism, mentality; understanding, intellection, conception; thinking principle, intellectual faculty, cogitative f.; rationality, reasoning power; reason, discursive r., association of ideas 475 n. *reasoning*; philosophy 449 n. *thought*; awareness, sense, consciousness, self-c., stream of c. 455 n. *attention*; cognisance, noesis, perception, apperception, percipience, insight; extra-sensory perception, instinct 476 n. *intuition*; flair, judgment 463 n. *discrimination*; noology, intellectualism, intellectuality; mental capacity, brains, parts, wits, senses, sense, grey matter 498 n. *intelligence*; great intellect, genius; mental evolution, psychogenesis; seat of thought, organ of t., brain, anterior b., cerebrum; hinder brain, little b., cerebellum; medulla oblongata; meninx, pia mater, dura m., arachnoid 213 n. *head*; sensorium, sensory 818 n. *feeling*.

psychology, science of mind, psychics, metapsychology, metapsychics; parapsychology, abnormal psychology 503 n. *psychopathy*; psychosomatics, Freudianism, Freudian psychology, Jungian p., Adlerian p.; Gestalt psychology, Gestalt theory, configurationism, behaviourism; empirical psychology; psychography, psychometry, psychoanalysis; psychopathology, psychiatry, psychotherapy 658 n. *therapy*; psychophysiology, psychophysics, psychobiology.

psychologist, psychoanalyst, psychiatrist, psychotherapist, psychopathist, mental specialist, alienist, mad doctor 658 n. *doctor*.

spirit, soul, mind, inner m., inner sense, second s.; heart, heart's core, breast, bosom, inner man 224 n. *interiority*; double, ka, ba, genius 80 n. *self*; psyche, pneuma, id, ego, superego, self, subliminal s., the unconscious, the subconscious; personality, dual p., multiple p., split p. 503 n. *psychopathy*; spiritualism, spiritism, psychomancy, psychical research 984 n. *occultism*; spiritualist, occultist.

Adj. *mental*, thinking, endowed with reason, reasoning 475 adj. *rational*; cerebral, intellectual, conceptive, noological; noetic, conceptual, abstract; theoretical 512 adj. *suppositional*; unconcrete 320 adj. *immaterial*; perceptual, percipient,

perceptive; cognitive, cognizant 490 adj. *knowing*; conscious, self-c., subjective.

psychic, psychical, psychological; subconscious, subliminal; spiritualistic, mediumistic, psychomantic 984 adj. *psychical*; spiritual, otherworldly 320 adj. *immaterial.*

Vb. *cognize*, perceive, apperceive 490 vb. *know*; realize, sense, become aware of, become conscious of; objectify 223 vb. *externalize*; note 438 vb. *see*; advert, mark 455 vb. *notice*; ratiocinate 475 vb. *reason*; understand 498 vb. *be wise*; conceptualize, intellectualize 449 vb. *think*; conceive, invent 484 vb. *discover*; ideate 513 vb. *imagine*; appreciate 480 vb. *estimate.*

See: 80, 213, 223, 224, 320, 438, 449, 455, 463, 475, 476, 480, 484, 490, 498, 503, 512, 513, 658, 818, 984.

448 Non-intellect

N. *non-intellect*, unintellectuality; brute creation 365 n. *animality*; vegetation 366 n. *vegetability*; inanimate nature, stocks and stones; instinct, brute i. 476 n. *intuition*; unreason, vacuity, brainlessness, mindlessness 450 n. *incogitance*; brain injury, brain damage, disordered intellect 503 n. *insanity.*

Adj. *mindless*, non-intellectual, unintellectual; animal, vegetable; mineral, inanimate 359 adj. *inorganic*; unreasoning 450 adj. *unthinking*; instinctive, brute 476 adj. *intuitive*; unoriginal, uninventive, unidea'd 20 adj. *imitative*; brainless, empty-headed 499 adj. *foolish*; moronic, wanting 503 adj. *insane.*

20, 359, 365, 366, 450, 476, 499, 503.

449 Thought

N. *thought*, mental process, thinking; mental act, ideation; intellectual exercise, mental e., mental action, mentation, cogitation; cerebration, lucubration, head-work, thinking-cap; brain-work, brain-fag; hard thinking, hard thought, worry, concentrated thought, concentration 455 n. *attention*; deep thought, profound t., depth of t. profundity 498 n. *wisdom*; abstract thought, imageless t.; thoughts,

ideas 451 n. *idea*; conception, conceit, workings of the mind, inmost thoughts 513 n. *ideality*; flow of thought, current of t., train of t., succession of t.; association of ideas, reason 475 n. *reasoning*; brown study, reverie, musing, wandering thoughts 456 n. *abstractedness*; thinking out, excogitation (see *meditation*); invention, inventiveness 513 n. *imagination*; second thoughts, afterthought, reconsideration, esprit d'escalier 67 n. *sequel*; retrospection, hindsight 505 n. *memory*; mature thought 669 n. *preparation*; forethought, prudence 510 n. *foresight*; thought transference, telepathy 531 n. *telecommunication.*

meditation, thoughtfulness, speculation 459 n. *enquiry*; reflection, deep r., brooding, rumination, consideration, pondering; contemplation 438 n. *inspection*; introspection, self-thought, self-communing 5 n. *intrinsicality*; self-consultation, self-advising, wishful thinking 932 n. *selfishness*; religious contemplation, retreat, mysticism 979 n. *piety*; deliberation, taking counsel 691 n. *advice*; excogitation, thinking out 480 n. *judgment*; examination, close study, concentration, application 536 n. *study.*

philosophy, ontology, metaphysics; speculation, philosophical thought, abstract t., systematic t.; scientific thought, science, natural s., natural philosophy; philosophical doctrine, philosophical system, philosophical theory 512 n. *supposition*; school of philosophy; idealism, subjective i., objective i., conceptualism, transcendentalism; phenomenalism, realism, nominalism, positivism, logical p.; existentialism, voluntarism; holism, holoism; rationalism, humanism, hedonism, eudæmonism; utilitarianism, materialism; probabilism, pragmatism; relativism, relativity; agnosticism, scepticism, Pyrrhonism 486 n. *doubt*; eclecticism; atheism 974 n. *irreligion*; fatalism 596 n. *fate*; Pythagoreanism, Platonism, Aristotelianism; Stoicism, Epicureanism, Cynicism; Neo-Platonism, gnostic philosophy, gnosticism; scholasticism, Thomism, Scotism, Averroism; Cartesianism, Berkeleyanism, Kantianism, Hegelianism, Neo-H., dialectical materialism, Marxism; Bergsonism; Hindu philosophy, Vedanta, Sankhya, Mimansa, Yoga,

Advaita, monism; Dvaita, pluralism; unitarianism 973 n. *deism.*

philosopher, thinker, man of thought 492 n. *intellectual*; metaphysician, Vedantist (see *philosophy*); school of philosophers, Pre-Socratics, Eleatics, Peripatetics, Academy, Stoa; Garden of Epicurus, Diogenes' tub.

Adj. *thoughtful,* conceptive, ideative, speculative (see *philosophic*); cogitative, deliberative; full of thought, pensive, meditative, contemplative, reflective; self-communing, introspective; ruminant, wrapt in thought, lost in t., deep in t.; absorbed 455 adj. *obsessed*; musing, dreaming, dreamy 456 adj. *abstracted*; concentrating, concentrated 455 adj. *attentive*; studying 536 adj. *studious*; thoughtful for others, considerate 901 n. *philanthropic*; prudent 510 adj. *foreseeing.*

philosophic, metaphysical, ontological, speculative, abstract, systematic, rational, logical.

Vb. *think,* ween, trow 512 vb. *suppose*; conceive, form ideas, ideate; fancy 513 vb. *imagine*; devote thought to, bestow thought upon, think about, cogitate (see *meditate*); employ one's mind, use one's brain, put on one's thinking-cap; concentrate, collect one's thoughts, pull one's wits together 455 vb. *be attentive*; bend the mind, apply the m., trouble one's head about, animadvert; lucubrate, cerebrate, mull, work over, hammer at 536 vb. *study*; think hard, beat one's brains, cudgel one's b., rack one's b., worry at; think out, think up, excogitate, invent 484 vb. *discover*; devise 623 vb. *plan*; take into one's head, have an idea, entertain an i., cherish an i., become obsessed, get a bee in one's bonnet 481 vb. *be biased*; bear in mind, be mindful, think on 505 vb. *remember.*

meditate, ruminate, chew the cud, chew over, digest, discuss; enquire into 459 vb. *enquire*; reflect, contemplate, study; speculate, philosophize; intellectualize 447 vb. *cognize*; think about, consider, take into consideration; take stock of, perpend, ponder, weigh 480 vb. *estimate*; think over, turn o., revolve, con over, run over in the mind 505 vb. *memorize*; bethink oneself, reconsider, review, re-examine, have second thoughts; take counsel, advise with, consult one's pillow,

sleep on it 691 vb. *consult*; commune with oneself, introspect; brood, brood upon, muse, fall into a brown study; go into retreat.

dawn upon, occur to, flash on the mind, cross the m., float in the m., rise in the m.; suggest itself, present itself to the mind.

cause thought, provoke *or* challenge t., make one think, impress the mind, strike 821 vb. *impress*; penetrate, sink in, fasten on the mind, become an idée fixe, obsess 481 vb. *bias.*

engross, absorb, preoccupy, monopolize; engross one's thoughts, run in one's head, occupy the mind, fill the m., be uppermost in one's mind, come first in one's thoughts; haunt, obsess 481 vb. *bias*; fascinate 983 vb. *bewitch.*

Adv. *in mind,* in contemplation, under consideration; taking into consideration, bearing in mind, all things considered; on reflection, on consideration, on second thoughts; come to think of it.

See: 5, 67, 438, 447, 451, 455, 456, 459, 475, 480, 481, 484, 486, 492, 498, 505, 510, 512, 513, 531, 536, 596, 623, 669, 691, 821, 901, 932, 973, 974, 979, 983.

450 Absence of thought

N. *incogitance,* inability to think 448 n. *nonintellect*; blank mind, fallow m. 491 n. *ignorance*; vacancy, abstraction 456 n. *abstractedness*; inanity, blankness, fatuity, empty head 499 n. *unintelligence*; want of thought, thoughtlessness 456 n. *inattention*; conditioned reflex, automatism; instinctiveness, instinct 476 n. *intuition*; stocks and stones.

Adj. *unthinking,* incogitant, unreflecting, unphilosophic, unintellectual 448 adj. *mindless*; incapable of thought, unidea'd, unimaginative, uninventive 20 adj. *imitative*; blank, vacant, empty-headed 190 adj. *empty*; incogitant, not thinking 456 adj. *inattentive*; unoccupied, relaxed; thoughtless, inconsiderate 932 adj. *selfish*; irrational 477 adj. *illogical*; beef-witted, stolid, stupid, wanting 499 adj. *unintelligent*; inanimate, inorganic; animal, vegetable, mineral.

unthought, unthought of, inconceivable, incogitable, unconsidered, undreamt, not

to be thought of, not to be dreamt of 470 adj. *impossible.*

Vb. *not think*, not reflect; leave the mind fallow *or* unoccupied, leave one's mind uncultivated 491 vb. *not know*; be blank, be vacant; not think of, put out of one's mind, dismiss from one's thoughts, laugh off 458 vb. *disregard*; dream, indulge in reveries 456 vb. *be inattentive*; go by instinct 476 vb. *intuit*; think wrongly 481 vb. *misjudge.*

See: 20, 190, 448, 456, 458, 470, 476, 477, 481, 491, 499, 932.

451 Idea

N. *idea*, noumenon, notion, a thought; object of thought, abstract idea, concept; mere idea, theory 512 n. *supposition*; percept, image, mental i.; Platonic idea, archetype 23 n. *prototype*; conception, perception, apprehension 447 n. *intellect*; reflection, observation 449 n. *thought*; impression, conceit, fancy, phantasy 513 n. *imagination*; product of imagination, figment, fiction; associated ideas, complex; invention, brain-creation, brain-child; brain wave, happy thought 484 n. *discovery*; wheeze, wrinkle, device 623 n. *contrivance*; what one thinks, view, point of v., slant, attitude 485 n. *opinion*; principle, leading idea, main idea.

Adj. *ideational*, ideative 449 adj. *thoughtful*; notional, ideal 513 adj. *imaginary.*

See: 23, 447, 449, 484, 485, 512, 513, 623.

452 Topic

N. *topic*, subject of thought, food for t., mental pabulum; gossip, rumour 529 n. *news*; subject matter, subject; contents, chapter, section, head, main h. 53 n. *subdivision*; what it is about, argument, plot, theme; text, commonplace, burden, motif; musical topic, statement, leitmotiv 412 n. *musical piece*; concern, interest, human i.; matter, affair, situation 8 n. *circumstance*; shop 622 n. *business*; topic for discussion, business on hand, agenda, order paper 623 n. *policy*; item on the agenda, motion 761 n. *request*; resolution 480 n. *judgment*; problem, headache 459

n. *question*; heart of the question, gist, pith; theorem, proposition 512 n. *supposition*; thesis, case, point 475 n. *argument*; issue, moot point, debatable p.; point at issue; field, field of enquiry, field of study 536 n. *study.*

Adj. *topical*, thematic; challenging, thought-provoking; mooted, debatable 474 adj. *uncertain*; thought about, uppermost in the mind, fit for consideration.

Adv. *in question*, in the mind, on the brain, in one's thoughts; on foot, on the tapis, on the agenda; before the house, under consideration, under discussion, under advisement.

See: 8, 53, 412, 459, 474, 475, 480, 512, 529, 536, 622, 623, 761.

453 Curiosity: desire for knowledge

N. *curiosity*, intellectual c., inquiring mind, thirst *or* itch for knowledge 536 n. *study*; morbid curiosity, ghoulishness; prurience, voyeurism, scopophilia; interest, itch, inquisitiveness, curiousness; zeal, meddlesomeness, officiousness 678 n. *overactivity*; wanting to know; asking questions, quizzing 459 n. *question*; sight-seeing, rubbernecking, thirst for travel 267 n. *land travel.*

inquisitor, censor, examiner, cross-e., interrogator, questioner, quizzer, enfant terrible 459 n. *enquirer*; inquisitive person, pry; busybody, ultracrepidarian 678 n. *meddler*; news-hound, gossip, quidnunc 529 n. *newsmonger*; seeker, searcher, explorer, experimentalist 461 n. *experimenter*; sightseer, globe-trotter, rubber-neck 441 n. *spectator*; window-shopper, snoop, snooper, spy 459 n. *detective*; eavesdropper, interceptor, phone-tapper 415 n. *listener*; 'impertinent pry', Paul Pry, Peeping Tom, Actæon; Nosy Parker, Rosa Dartle.

Adj. *inquisitive*, curious, interested; searching, seeking, avid for knowledge 536 adj. *studious*; morbidly curious, ghoulish, prurient; newsmongering, hungering for news, agog, all ears 415 adj. *auditory*; wanting to know, burning with curiosity, itching, hungry for; over-curious, nosy, snoopy, prying, spying, peeping, peeking; questioning, inquisitorial 459 adj. *enquiring*; busy, overbusy, meddlesome, inter-

fering, officious, ultracrepidarian 678 adj. *meddling*.

Vb. *be curious*, want to know, only want to know; seek, look for 459 vb. *search*; test, research 461 vb. *experiment*; feel a concern, be interested, take an interest; show interest, show curiosity, prick up one's ears 455 vb. *be attentive*; dig up, nose out, pick up news; peep, peek, spy 438 vb. *scan*; snoop, pry 459 vb. *enquire*; eavesdrop, tap the line, intercept, listen, listen in 415 vb. *hear*; stick one's nose in, be nosy, interfere, act the busybody 678 vb. *meddle*; ask questions, quiz, question 459 vb. *interrogate*; look, stare, stand and stare, gape, gawk 438 vb. *gaze*; rubberneck, sight-see, window-shop.

Int. what news! what's new? what next?

See: 267, 415, 438, 441, 455, 459, 461, 529, 536, 678.

454 Incuriosity

N. *incuriosity*, lack of interest, incuriousness, no questions; uninterest, unconcern, no interest, insouciance 860 n. *indifference*; apathy, phlegmatism 820 n. *moral insensibility*; adiaphorism, indifferentism; blunted curiosity 863 n. *satiety*.

Adj. *incurious*, uninquisitive, unreflecting 450 adj. *unthinking*; without interest, uninterested; aloof, distant; unadmiring 865 adj. *unastonished*; wearied 838 adj. *bored*; unconcerned, uninvolved 860 adj. *indifferent*; listless, inert, apathetic 820 adj. *impassive*.

Vb. *be incurious,*—indifferent etc. adj.; have no curiosity, not think about, take no interest 456 vb. *be inattentive*; feel no concern, couldn't care less, not trouble oneself, not bother with 860 vb. *be indifferent*; mind one's own business, go one's own way 820 vb. *be insensitive*; see nothing, hear n., look the other way 458 vb. *disregard*.

See: 450, 456, 458, 820, 838, 860, 863, 865.

455 Attention

N. *attention*, notice, regard 438 n. *look*; perpension, advertence 449 n. *thought*;

heed, alertness, readiness, attentiveness, observance, mindfulness 457 n. *carefulness*; observation, watchfulness, eyes on, watch, guard 457 n. *surveillance*; wariness, circumspection 858 n. *caution*; contemplation, introspection 449 n. *meditation*; intentness, intentiveness, earnestness, seriousness 599 n. *resolution*; undivided attention, whole a.; whole mind, concentration, application, studiousness, close study 536 n. *study*; examination, scrutiny, check-up, review 438 n. *inspection*; close attention, minute a., meticulosity, attention to detail, particularity, minuteness, finicalness, pedantry 494 n. *accuracy*; diligent attention, diligence, pains, trouble 678 n. *assiduity*; exclusive attention, rapt a.; single-mindedness; absorption, pre-occupation, brown study 456 n. *inattention*; interest, inquisitive attention 453 n. *curiosity*; obsession, monomania 503 n. *mania*.

Adj. *attentive*, intent, diligent, assiduous 678 adj. *industrious*; heedful, mindful, regardful 457 adj. *careful*; alert, ready, on one's toes; open-eyed, waking, wakeful, awake, wide-a.; awake to, alive to, sensing 819 adj. *sensitive*; conscious, thinking 449 adj. *thoughtful*; observant, sharp-eyed, observing, watching, watchful 457 adj. *vigilant*; attending, paying attention, missing nothing; all eyes 438 adj. *seeing*; all ears, prick-eared; all attention, undistracted, deep in; serious, earnest; study-bent 536 adj. *studious*; close, minute, nice, meticulous, particular, finical, pedantic 494 n. *accurate*; on the watch, on the look-out, on the stretch 507 adj. *expectant*.

obsessed, interested, over-i., over-curious 453 adj. *curious*; single-minded, possessed, engrossed, preoccupied, rapt, suspended, wrapped up in, taken up with; haunted by 854 adj. *fearing*; monomaniacal 503 adj. *crazed*.

Vb. *be attentive*, attend, give attention, pay a.; look to, heed, pay h., mind 457 vb. *be careful*; trouble oneself, care, take trouble *or* pains, bother 682 vb. *exert oneself*; advert, listen, prick up one's ears, sit up, sit up and take notice; take seriously, fasten on 638 vb. *make important*; give one's attention, give one's mind to, bend the mind to, direct one's thoughts to 449 vb. *think*; strain one's

attention, miss nothing; watch, be all eyes 438vb. *gaze*; be all ears, drink in, hang on the lips of 415vb. *hear*; focus (one's mind on), rivet one's attention to, concentrate on, fix on; examine, inspect, scrutinize, vet, review, pass under review 438vb. *scan*; overhaul, revise 654vb. *make better*; study closely, pore, mull, read, re-read, digest 536vb. *study*; pay some attention, glance at, look into, dip into, skip, flick over the leaves, turn the pages.

be mindful, keep in mind, bear in m., have in m. 505vb. *remember*; not forget, think of, spare a thought for, regard, look on 438vb. *see*; lend an ear to 415vb. *hear*; take care of, see to 689vb. *manage*; have regard to, have an eye to, keep in sight, keep in view 617vb. *intend*; not lose sight of, keep track of 619vb. *pursue*.

notice, note, take n., register; make note of, mark, advert, recognize; take cognizance of, take into consideration, review, reconsider 449vb. *meditate*; take account of, consider, weigh, perpend 480vb. *judge*; animadvert upon, comment u., remark on, talk about, discuss 584vb. *converse*; mention, just m., mention in passing, touch on 524vb. *hint*; recall, revert to, hark back 106vb. *repeat*; think worthy of attention, deign to notice, condescend to; have time for, spare time f., find time f. 681vb. *have leisure*; acknowledge, salute 884vb. *greet*.

attract notice, draw the attention, hold the a., focus the a., rivet the a., be the cynosure of all eyes, cut a figure 875vb. *be ostentatious*; arouse notice, arrest one's n., strike one's n.; interest; excite attention, invite a., solicit a., claim a., demand a., meet with a.; catch the eye, fall under observation 443vb. *be visible*; make one see, bring under notice 522vb. *show*; bring forward, call one's attention to, indigitate, advertise 528vb. *publish*; lay the finger on, point the finger, point out, point to 547vb. *indicate*; stress, underline 532vb. *emphasize*; occupy, keep guessing 612vb. *tempt*; fascinate, haunt, monopolize, obsess 449vb. *engross*; call soldiers to attention 737vb. *command*.

Int. see! mark! lo! ecce! behold! lo and behold! look! look here! see here! look out! look alive! look to it! soho! hark! oyez! mind! halloo! observe! nota bene,

N.B., take notice! warning! take care! watch your step!

See: 106, 415, 438, 443, 449, 453, 456, 457, 480, 494, 503, 505, 507, 522, 524, 528, 532, 536, 547, 584, 599, 612, 617, 619, 638, 654, 678, 681, 682, 689, 737, 819, 854, 858, 875, 884.

456 Inattention

N. *inattention*, inadvertence, inadvertency, forgetfulness 506n. *oblivion*; oversight, aberration; parapraxis 495n. *error*; lack of interest, lack of observation 454n. *incuriosity*; aloofness, detachment, unconcern 860n. *indifference*; non-observance, disregard 458n. *negligence*; inconsideration, heedlessness 857n. *rashness*; want of thought, inconsiderateness 481n. *misjudgment*, 932n. *selfishness*; aimlessness, desultoriness 282n. *deviation*; superficiality, flippancy 212n. *shallowness*; étourderie, dizziness, giddiness, light-mindedness, levity, volatility 604n. *caprice*; deaf ears 416n. *deafness*; blind eyes, blind spot, blind side 439n. *blindness*; absent-mindedness, wandering wits 450n. *incogitance*; Johnny-head-in-air, star-gazer, daydreamer.

abstractedness, abstraction, absent-mindedness, wandering attention, absence of mind; wool-gathering, daydreaming, star-gazing, doodling; fit of abstraction, deep musing, reverie, brown study; distraction, preoccupation, divided attention.

Adj. *inattentive*, careless 458adj. *negligent*; off one's guard 508adj. *inexpectant*; unobservant, unnoticing 454adj. *incurious*; unseeing 439adj. *blind*; unhearing 416adj. *deaf*; undiscerning 464adj. *indiscriminating*; unmindful, unheeding, inadvertent, not thinking, unreflecting 450adj. *unthinking*; not concentrating, half asleep, only half awake; listless 860 adj. *indifferent*; apathetic 820adj. *impassive*; oblivious 506adj. *forgetful*; inconsiderate, without consideration, thoughtless, heedless, regardless 857adj. *rash*; off-hand, cursory, superficial, unthorough 212adj. *shallow*.

abstracted, distrait, absent-minded, absent, far away, not there; lost, lost in thought,

wrapped in t., rapt, absorbed, in the
clouds, star-gazing; bemused, sunk in a
brown study, deep in reverie, pensive,
dreamy, dreaming, day-d., mooning,
wool-gathering; nodding, napping, half-
awake, betwixt sleep and waking 679 adj.
sleepy.
distracted, preoccupied, engrossed; otherwise engaged, with divided attention;
dazed, dazzled, disconcerted, put out,
put out of one's stride, put off, put off
one's stroke; rattled, unnerved 854 adj.
nervous.
light-minded, unfixed, unconcentrated,
wandering, desultory, trifling; frivolous,
flippant, insouciant; airy, volatile, mercurial, bird-witted, flighty, giddy, dizzy,
écervelé; scatter-brained, hare-b.; wild,
romping, harum-scarum, rantipole; addled, brainsick 503 adj. *crazed*; inconstant, to one thing constant never 604 adj.
capricious.
Vb. *be inattentive*, not attend, pay no attention, pay no heed, not listen, hear nothing,
see n.; close one's eyes 439 vb. *be blind*;
stop one's ears 416 vb. *be deaf*; not
register, not notice, not use one's eyes;
not hear the penny drop, not click, not
catch; overlook, commit an oversight
495 vb. *blunder*; be off one's guard,
let slip, be caught out, catch oneself
o., catch oneself doing; not remember
506 vb. *forget*; dream, drowse, nod 679 vb.
sleep; not concentrate, trifle, play at; be
abstracted, moider, moither, wander, let
one's thoughts wander, let one's mind w.,
let one's wits go bird-nesting, go wool-
gathering, indulge in reverie, fall into a
brown study, muse, be lost in thought,
moon, star-gaze; idle, doodle 679 vb. *be
inactive*; be distracted, digress, lose the
thread, fluff one's notes 282 vb. *stray*;
be disconcerted, be rattled 854 vb. *be
nervous*; be put off one's stroke, be put
out of one's stride 702 vb. *hinder* (see
distract); disregard, ignore 458 vb. *neglect*; have no time for, think nothing of,
think little of 922 vb. *hold cheap.*
distract, call away, divert, divert one's attention, draw off one's a.; make forget,
put out of one's head, drive out of one's
mind; entice, throw a sop to Cerberus
612 vb. *tempt*; confuse, muddle 63 vb.
derange; disturb, interrupt 72 vb. *discontinue*; disconcert, upset, perplex, dis-

compose, fluster, bother, flurry, rattle
318 vb. *agitate*; put one off his stroke, put
one out of his stride 702 vb. *obstruct*;
daze, dazzle 439 vb. *blind*; bewilder,
flummox 474 vb. *puzzle*; fuddle, addle
503 vb. *make mad*; play with, amuse.
escape notice, escape attention, blush unseen, be overlooked 523 vb. *lurk*; fall on
deaf ears, meet a blind spot, not click;
not hold the attention, go in at one ear
and out at the other, slip one's memory
506 vb. *be forgotten.*
Adv. *inadvertently*, per incuriam, by oversight; rashly, giddily, gaily, light-
heartedly.

See: 63, 72, 212, 282, 318, 416, 439, 450, 454,
458, 464, 474, 481, 495, 503, 506, 508, 523,
604, 612, 679, 702, 820, 854, 857, 860, 922,
932.

457 Carefulness

N. *carefulness*, mindfulness, attentiveness,
diligence, pains 678 n. *assiduity*; heed,
care, utmost c. 455 n. *attention*; anxiety,
solicitude 825 n. *worry*; loving care 897 n.
benevolence; tidiness, orderliness, neatness 60 n. *order*; attention to detail,
thoroughness, meticulousness, minuteness, circumstantiality, particularity;
nicety, exactness, exactitude 494 n.
accuracy; over-nicety, pedantry, perfectionism 862 n. *fastidiousness*; conscience, scruples, scrupulosity 929 n.
probity; vigilance, wakefulness, watchfulness, alertness, readiness 669 n. *preparedness*; circumspection, prudence, wariness
858 n. *caution*; forethought 510 n. *foresight.*
surveillance, an eye on, eyes on, watching,
guarding, watch and ward 660 n. *protection*; vigilance, invigilation, inspection;
baby-sitting, chaperonage; look-out,
weather-eye; vigil, watch, death-w.;
guard, sentry-go; eyes of Argus, taskmaster's eye, watchful e., lidless e. 438 n.
eye; chaperon, sentry, sentinel 660 n.
protection, 749 n. *keeper.*
Adj. *careful*, thoughtful, considerate, considered, mindful, regardful, heedful 455
adj. *attentive*; taking care, painstaking;
solicitous, anxious; gingerly, afraid to
touch; loving, tender; conscientious,

scrupulous, honest 929 adj. *honourable*; diligent, assiduous 678 adj. *industrious*; thorough, thorough-going; meticulous, minute, particular, circumstantial; exact 494 adj. *accurate*; pedantic, overcareful, perfectionist 862 adj. *fastidious*; nice, tidy, neat, clean 60 adj. *orderly*; minding the pence, thrifty, penurious, miserly 816 adj. *parsimonious*.

vigilant, alert, ready 669 adj. *prepared*; on the alert, on guard, on the qui vive, on one's toes; watching, watchful, wakeful, wide-awake; observant, sharp-eyed; all eyes, open-eyed, lidless-e., Argus-e., lynx-e. 438 adj. *seeing*; prudent, provident, forehanded, far-sighted 510 adj. *foreseeing*; surefooted, picking one's steps; circumspect, circumspective, looking before and after 858 adj. *cautious*.

Vb. *be careful*, reck, mind, heed 455 vb. *be attentive*; take precautions, check, re-check 858 vb. *be cautious*; have one's eyes open, have one's wits about one, keep a look-out, look before and after, look right then left, mind one's step, watch one's s.; pick one's steps, feel one's way 461 vb. *be tentative*; speak by the card, mind one's Ps and Qs; mind one's business, count one's money, look after the pence 814 vb. *economize*; tidy, keep t. 62 vb. *arrange*; take pains, do with care, be meticulous; try, do one's best 682 vb. *exert oneself*.

look after, look to, see to, take care of, see to 689 vb. *manage*; take charge of, accept responsibility for; care for, mind, tend, keep 660 vb. *safeguard*; sit up with, baby-sit; nurse, foster, cherish 889 vb. *pet*; regard, tender 920 vb. *respect*; keep an eye, keep a sharp eye on, keep tabs on, chaperon, play gooseberry; serve 703 vb. *minister to*.

invigilate, stay awake, sit up; keep vigil, watch; stand sentinel; keep watch, keep watch and ward; look out, keep a sharp look-out, watch out for; keep one's weather-eye open, sleep with one eye o., keep one's ear to the ground; mount guard, set watch, post sentries, stand to 660 vb. *safeguard*.

Adv. *carefully*, attentively, diligently; studiously, thoroughly; lovingly, tenderly; painfully, anxiously; with care, gingerly.

See: 60, 62, 438, 455, 461, 494, 510, 660, 669, 678, 682, 689, 703, 749, 814, 816, 825, 858, 862, 889, 897, 920, 929.

458 Negligence

N. *negligence*, carelessness 456 n. *inattention*; neglectfulness, forgetfulness 506 n. *oblivion*; remissness, neglect, oversight, omission; non-observance, default, laches, culpable negligence 918 n. *dutilessness*; unwatchfulness, unwariness, unguarded hour, unguarded minute, unpreparedness 670 n. *non-preparation*; disregard, non-interference, laissez-faire 620 n. *avoidance*; unconcern, insouciance, nonchalance, don't-care attitude 860 n. *indifference*; recklessness 857 n. *rashness*; procrastination 136 n. *delay*; supineness, slackness, laziness 679 n. *inactivity*; slovenliness, sluttishness, untidiness 61 n. *disorder*; inaccuracy, inexactitude 495 n. *inexactness*; off-handedness, casualness, laxness 734 n. *laxity*; superficiality 212 n. *shallowness*; trifling, scamping, skipping, dodging, botching 695 n. *bungling*; scamped work, skimped w., botched job, loose ends 728 n. *failure*; passing over, not mentioning, paraleipsis 582 n. *taciturnity*; trifler, slacker, waster 679 n. *idler*; procrastinator, shirker; waiter on Providence, Micawber; sloven 61 n. *slut*.

Adj. *negligent*, neglectful, careless, unmindful 456 adj. *inattentive*; remiss 918 adj. *dutiless*; thoughtless 450 adj. *unthinking*; oblivious 506 adj. *forgetful*; uncaring, insouciant 860 adj. *indifferent*; regardless, reckless 857 adj. *rash*; heedless 769 adj. *non-observant*; casual, off-hand, unstrict 734 adj. *lax*; slapdash, unthorough, perfunctory, superficial; inaccurate 495 adj. *inexact*; slack, supine 679 adj. *lazy*; procrastinating 136 adj. *late*; sluttish, untidy, slovenly 649 adj. *dirty*; not looking, unwary, unwatchful, off guard 508 adj. *inexpectant*; unguarded, uncircumspect 670 adj. *unprepared*; disregarding, ignoring 620 adj. *avoiding*.

neglected, uncared for, untended; ill-kept, unkempt 649 adj. *dirty*; unprotected, unguarded, unchaperoned; deserted; unattended, left alone 621 adj. *relinquished*; lost sight of, unthought of, unheeded, unmissed, unregarded 860 adj. *unwanted*; disregarded, ignored, in the cold; unconsidered, overlooked, omitted; unnoticed, unmarked, unremarked, unperceived, unobserved 444 adj. *invisible*; shelved, pigeon-holed, put aside 136 adj. *late*;

unstudied, unexamined, unsifted, unscanned, unweighed, unexplored, unconned 670adj. *unprepared*; undone, half-done, perfunctory 726adj. *uncompleted*; buried, wrapped in a napkin, hid under a bushel 674adj. *unused*.

Vb. **neglect**, omit, pretermit; pass over; forbear (see *disregard*); lose sight of, overlook 456vb. *be inattentive*; leave undone, not finish, leave half-done, leave loose ends, do by halves 726vb. *not complete*; botch, bungle 695vb. *be clumsy*; slur, skimp, scamp 204vb. *shorten*; skip over, jump, skim through, not mention, gloss over, slur over 525vb. *conceal*; be unthorough, dabble in, play with, trifle, fribble 837vb. *amuse oneself*.

disregard, ignore, pass over, give the go-by, dodge, shirk, blink, blench 620vb. *avoid*; wink at, connive at, take no notice 734 vb. *be lax*; refuse to see, turn a blind eye to, pay no regard to, dismiss 439vb. *be blind*; forbear, forget it, excuse, overlook 909vb. *forgive*; leave out of one's calculations, discount 483vb. *underestimate*; pass by, pass by on the other side 282vb. *deviate*; turn one's back on, slight, cold shoulder, cut, cut dead 885vb. *be rude*; turn a deaf ear to 416vb. *be deaf*; not trouble oneself with, not trouble one's head about, have no time for, laugh off, pooh-pooh, treat as of no account 922 vb. *hold cheap*; leave unregarded, leave out in the cold 57vb. *exclude*; leave in the lurch, desert, abandon 621vb. *relinquish*.

be neglectful, doze, drowse, nod 678vb. *sleep*; be off one's guard, omit precautions; be caught napping, oversleep; be caught with one's pants down 508vb. *not expect*; drift, laisser faire, procrastinate, let slide, let slip, let the grass grow under one's feet; not bother, take it easy, let things rip 679vb. *be inactive*; shelve, pigeon-hole, lay aside, push aside, put a., lay a. 136vb. *put off*; make neglectful, lull, throw off one's guard, put off one's guard, catch napping, catch bending 508 vb. *surprise*.

Adv. **negligently**, per incuriam; anyhow; cursorily, perfunctorily.

See: 57, 61, 136, 204, 212, 282, 416, 439, 444, 450, 456, 483, 495, 506, 508, 525, 582, 620, 621, 649, 670, 674, 678, 679, 695, 726, 728, 734, 769, 837, 857, 860, 885, 909, 918, 922.

459 Enquiry

N. **enquiry**, asking, questioning (see *interrogation*); challenge (see *question*); asking after, asking about, directing oneself, taking information, getting i. 524n. *information*; close enquiry, searching e., strict e., witch-hunt, spy-mania (see *search*); inquisition, examination, investigation, visitation; inquest, post mortem, autopsy, audit, trial 959n. *legal trial*; public enquiry, secret e.; commission of enquiry, work party (see *enquirer*); statistical enquiry, poll, Gallup p., straw vote 605n. *vote*; probe, test, means t., check-up, check, trial run 461n. *experiment*; review, scrutiny, overview 438n. *inspection*; introspection, self-examination; research, blue-sky r., fundamental r., applied r. 536n. *study*; exploration, reconnaissance, reconnoitre, survey 484n. *discovery*; discussion, ventilation, airing, canvassing, consultation 584n. *conference*; philosophical enquiry, metaphysical e., scientific e. 449n. *philosophy*; prying, nosing 453n. *curiosity*.

interrogation, questioning, interpellation, asking questions, putting q., formulating q.; forensic examination, examination-in-chief; leading question, cross-examination, cross-question; re-examination; quiz, brains trust; interrogatory; catechism; inquisition, third degree, grilling; dialogue, dialectic, question and answer, interlocution; Socratic method, Socratic elenchus, zetetic philosophy; question time, question hour.

question, question mark, interrogation m., note of interrogation 547n. *punctuation*; query, request for information, chad; questions, questionnaire 87n. *list*; question list, question paper, examination p.; interrogatory, interpellation, Parliamentary question; challenge, fair question, plain q.; catch, cross-question; indirect question, feeler, leading question; moot point, knotty p., debating p.; quodlibet, question propounded, point at issue, side-issue, porism; controversy, field of c., contention, bone of c. 475n. *argument*; problem, poser, stumper, headache, unsolved mystery 530n. *enigma*.

exam., examination, oral e., viva voce e., viva; interview, audition 415n. *hearing*; practical examination, written e.; test, mental t., intelligence t.; entrance

examination, common entrance, responsions, little go, matriculation, matric., 11-plus examination, school-leaving e., General Certificate of Education, G.C.E., Intermediate, tripos, moderations, mods., Greats, Modern G., finals; doctorate examination, bar e.; advanced level, scholarship l., degree l., pass l., honours l.; catechumen 460 n. *respondent*; examinee, entrant, sitter 461 n. *testee.*

search, probe, investigation, enquiry; quest, hunt, witch-h., treasure-h. 619 n. *pursuit*; house-search, perquisition, domiciliary visit, house-to-house search; search of one's person, frisking; rummaging, turning over; exploration, excavation, archæological e., digging, dig; speleology, pot-holing; search-party; search-warrant.

police enquiry, investigation, criminal i., detection 484 n. *discovery*; detective work, shadowing, house-watching; grilling, third degree; Criminal Investigation Department, C.I.D., Federal Bureau of Investigation, F.B.I., Intelligence Branch, I.B.; secret police, Gestapo, Cheka, Ogpu, N.K.V.D.

secret service, espionage, counter-e., spying, intelligence, M.I.5; informer, spy, undercover agent, cloak-and-dagger man; spy-ring.

detective, investigator, criminologist; plain-clothes man; enquiry agent, private detective, private eye; hotel detective, shop d.; amateur detective; Federal agent, G-man, C.I.D. man; tec, sleuth, bloodhound, gumshoes, flat-foot, dick, snooper, snoop, nose, spy 524 n. *informer*; Bow-street runner; graphologist, handwriting expert.

enquirer, investigator, prober, indagator; asker (see *questioner*); quidnunc 529 vb. *newsmonger*; seeker, thinker, seeker for truth, Diogenes and his lantern 449 n. *philosopher*; searcher, looker, rummager, search-party; inventor, discoverer; dowser, water-diviner 484 n. *detector*; prospector, gold-digger; talent scout; scout, spy, surveyor, reconnoitrer; inspector, visitor 438 n. *inspection*; checker, scrutineer, censor 480 n. *judge*; examiner, examining board, board of examiners; tester, test-pilot, researcher, research worker, analyst, analyser, dissector, vivisector 461 n. *experimenter*; sampler, pollster,

canvasser; explorer 268 n. *traveller*; bag man, carpet-bagger 794 n. *pedlar.*

questioner, cross-q., cross-examiner; interrogator, querist, interpellator, interlocutor, interviewer; catechizer 453 n. *inquisitor*; quizzer, enfant terrible; riddler, enigmatist; examiner of conscience, confessor 986 n. *clergy.*

Adj. *enquiring*, curious, prying, nosy 453 adj. *inquisitive*; quizzing, quizzical; interrogatory, interrogative; requisitory, requisitive, examining, catechetical, inquisitional, cross-questioning; elenctic, dialectic, maieutic, heuristic, zetetic; probing, poking, digging; testing, searching, fact-finding, exploratory, empirical, tentative 461 adj. *experimental*; analytic, diagnostic.

moot, in question, questionable, debatable, problematic, doubtful 474 adj. *uncertain*, knotty, puzzling 700 adj. *difficult*; fit for enquiry, proposed, propounded; undetermined, undecided, untried, left open.

Vb. *enquire*, ask, want to know 491 vb. *not know*; demand 761 vb. *request*; canvass, agitate, air, ventilate, discuss, bring in question, subject to examination 475 vb. *argue*; ask for, look for, enquire for, seek, search for, hunt for 619 vb. *pursue*; enquire into, probe, delve into, dig i., dig down i., go deep i., sound; investigate, conduct an enquiry, hold an e., institute an e., set up an e., throw open to e., call in Scotland Yard; try, hear 959 vb. *try a case*; review, audit, scrutinize, monitor, analyse, dissect, parse, sift, winnow, thresh out; research, study, consider, examine 449 vb. *meditate*; check, check on; feel the pulse, take the temperature; follow up an enquiry, pursue an e., get to the bottom of, fathom, see into, X-ray 438 vb. *scan*; peer, peep, peek, snoop, spy, pry, peep behind the curtain 453 vb. *be curious*; survey, reconnoitre, explore, feel one's way 461 vb. *be tentative*; test, try, sample, taste 461 vb. *experiment*; introspect, examine oneself, take a look at.

interrogate, ask questions, put q., speer; interpellate, question; cross-question, cross-examine, re-examine; interview, hold a viva; examine, subject to questioning, sound, probe, quiz, catechize, grill, give the third degree; put to the question 963 vb. *torture*; pump, pick the brains,

suck the b.; move the question, put the q., pop the q.; pose, propose a question, propound a q., raise a q., moot a q., moot.

search, seek, look for; conduct a search, rummage, ransack, comb; scrabble, scour, clean out, turn over, rake o., turn out, rake through, go t., search t., look into every nook and corner; pry into, peer i., peep i., peek i.; overhaul, frisk, go over, search one's pockets, feel in one's p., search for, feel for, grope for, hunt for, fish, go fishing, fish for, dig for; cast about, seek a clue, follow the trail 619 vb. *pursue*; probe, explore, go in quest of 461 vb. *be tentative*; dig, excavate, archæologize; prospect, dowse, treasure-hunt, embark on a t.

be questionable,—debatable etc. adj.; be open to question, call for enquiry, challenge an answer, be subject to examination, be open to enquiry, be under investigation.

Adv. *on trial,* under investigation, under enquiry, sub judice; up for enquiry.

in search of, on the track of, cui bono?

enquiringly, interrogatively; why, wherefore? why on earth? why, oh why? how? how come?

See: 87, 268, 415, 438, 449, 453, 460, 461, 474, 475, 480, 484, 491, 524, 529, 530, 536, 547, 584, 605, 619, 700, 794, 959, 963, 986.

460 Answer

N. *answer,* replication, reaction; reply, response, responsion; answer by post, acknowledgment, return 588 n. *correspondence*; official reply, rescript, rescription 496 n. *maxim*; returns, results 548 n. *record*; echo, antiphon, antiphony, responsal, respond 106 n. *repetition*; password, countersign; keyword, open sesame; answering back, back-talk, backchat, repartee; retort, counterblast, riposte 714 n. *retaliation*; give and take, question and answer, dialogue 584 n. *interlocution*; last word, final answer; Parthian shot; clue, key, right answer, explanation, solution 520 n. *interpretation*; enigmatic answer, oracle, Delphic Oracle 530 n. *enigma*.

rejoinder, counter-statement, reply, rebuttal,

plea in rebuttal, rebutter, surrejoinder, surrebutter 479 n. *confutation*; defence, speech for the defence, reply; contradiction 533 n. *negation,* 467 n. *counterevidence*; countercharge, counter-accusation, tu quoque 928 n. *accusation*.

respondent, defendant; answerer, responder, replier, correspondent; examinee 461 n. *testee*; candidate, applicant, entrant, sitter 716 n. *contender*.

Adj. *answering,* replying etc. vb.; respondent, responsive, echoic 106 adj. *repeated*; counter 182 adj. *counteracting*; corresponding 588 adj. *epistolary*; antiphonic, antiphonal; corresponding to 28 adj. *equal*; contradicting 533 adj. *negative*; refuting, rebutting; oracular; conclusive, final, Parthian.

Vb. *answer,* give a., return a.; reply, write back, acknowledge, respond, be responsive, echo, re-echo 106 vb. *repeat*; react, answer back, retort, riposte 714 vb. *retaliate*; say in reply, rejoin, rebut, counter 479 vb. *confute*; contradict 533 vb. *negate*; be respondent, defend, have the right of reply; provide the answer, have the a. 642 vb. *be expedient*; answer the question, solve the riddle 520 vb. *interpret*; set at rest, decide 480 vb. *judge*; satisfy the demand, satisfy 635 vb. *suffice*; suit the requirements 642 vb. *be expedient*; answer to, correspond to 12 vb. *correlate*.

Adv. *in reply,* by way of rejoinder; antiphonally.

See: 12, 28, 106, 182, 461, 467, 479, 480, 496, 520, 530, 533, 548, 584, 588, 635, 642, 714, 716, 928.

461 Experiment

N. *experiment,* practical e., scientific e., controlled e., control e.; experimentalism, experimentation, experimental method, verification, verification by experiment; exploration, probe; analysis, examination 459 n. *enquiry*; object lesson, probation, proof 478 n. *demonstration*; assay, docimasy 480 n. *estimate*; testability; check, test, crucial t., acid t., test case; practical test, trial, trials, try-out, work-out, trial run, practice r., trial canter, trial flight 671 n. *essay*; ranging shot; audition, voice-test; ordeal, ordeal by fire, ordeal by water 959 n. *legal trial*; pilot scheme,

rough sketch, first draft, sketch-book; first steps, teething troubles 68 n. *début*.

empiricism, speculation, guesswork 512 n. *conjecture*; tentativeness, tentative method; experience, practice, rule of thumb, trial, trial and error, hit and miss; random shot, shot in the dark, leap in the d., gamble 618 n. *gambling*; instinct, light of nature 476 n. *intuition*; sampling, random sample, straw vote, Gallup poll; feeler 378 n. *touch*; straw to show which way the wind is blowing, kite-flying, trial balloon, ballon d'essai.

experimenter, experimentalist, empiricist, researcher, research worker, analyst, analyser, vivisector; pollster, assayer, chemist; tester; test-driver, test-pilot; speculator, prospector, sourdough, forty-niner; prober, explorer, adventurer 459 n. *enquirer*; dabbler 493 n. *sciolist*; gamester 618 n. *gambler*.

testing agent, criterion, touchstone; standard, yardstick 465 n. *gauge*; control; reagent, litmus paper, crucible, cupel, retort, test-tube; pyx, pyx-chest; alfet 194 n. *cauldron*; proving ground, wind-tunnel; flight-simulator, road-driving simulator.

testee, examinee 460 n. *respondent*; candidate, entrant, sitter 716 n. *contender*; subject of experiment, subject, patient; guinea-pig, rabbit, mouse, hamster, monkey.

Adj. *experimental*, analytic, analytical, docimastic, verificatory, probatory, probative, probationary; provisional, tentative 618 adj. *speculative*; exploratory 459 adj. *enquiring*; empirical, guided by experience; venturesome 671 adj. *essaying*; testable, verifiable, in the experimental stage 474 adj. *uncertain*.

Vb. *experiment*, experimentalize, make experiments; check, check on, verify; prove, put to the proof, submit to the p., bring to p.; assay, analyse; research; dabble; experiment upon, vivisect, make a guinea-pig of, practise upon; test, put to the t., subject to a t. 459 vb. *enquire*; try, try a thing once; try out, give a trial to 671 vb. *essay*; try one's strength, test one's muscles; give one a try, try with, send *or* put a man in (cricket); sample 386 vb. *taste*; take a random sample, take a straw vote, take a Gallup poll; put to the vote 605 vb. *vote*; rehearse, practise 534

vb. *train*; be tested, undergo a test, come to the t.

be tentative, be empirical, seek experience, feel one's way, proceed by trial and error, proceed by guess and God; feel 378 vb. *touch*; probe, grope, fumble; get the feel of 536 vb. *learn*; throw out a feeler, fly a kite, feel the pulse, consult the barometer, see how the land lies; fish, fish for, angle for, bob for, cast one's net, trawl, put out a t.; wait and see, see what happens; try it on, see how far one can go; try one's fortune, try one's luck, speculate 618 vb. *gamble*; venture; explore, prospect 672 vb. *undertake*; probe, sound 459 vb. *enquire*.

Adv. *experimentally*, on test, on trial, on approval; empirically, by rule of thumb, by trial and error, by light of nature, by guess and God; on spec.

See: 68, 194, 378, 386, 459, 460, 465, 474, 476, 478, 480, 493, 512, 534, 536, 605, 618, 671, 672, 716, 959.

462 Comparison

N. *comparison*, analogical procedure; comparing, likening; confrontation, collation, juxtaposition, setting side by side 202 n. *contiguity*; check 459 n. *enquiry*; comparability, points of comparison, analogy, likeness, similitude 18 n. *similarity*; identification 13 n. *identity*; contrast 15 n. *differentiation*; simile, allegory 519 n. *metaphor*; standard of comparison, criterion, pattern, model, check-list, control 23 n. *prototype*; comparer, collator.

Adj. *compared*, collated; compared with, likened, contrasted; comparative, comparable, analogical; relative, correlative; allegorical, metaphorical 519 adj. *figurative*.

Vb. *compare*, collate, confront; set side by side, bring together 202 vb. *juxtapose*; draw a comparison, similize 18 n. *liken*, 13 vb. *identify*; parallel; contrast 15 n. *differentiate*; compare and contrast 463 vb. *discriminate*; match, pair, balance 28 vb. *equalize*; view together, check with 12 vb. *correlate*; institute a comparison, draw a parallel; compare to, compare with, criticize; compare notes, match ideas, exchange views.

Adv. *comparatively*, analogically; in com-

parison, as compared; relatively 12adj. *correlatively.*

See: 12, 13, 15, 18, 23, 28, 202, 459, 463, 519.

See: 15, 46, 62, 378, 386, 462, 468, 475, 480, 490, 494, 498, 513, 520, 605, 638, 819, 846, 862, 913.

463 Discrimination

N. *discrimination,* distinction, diorism 15n. *differentiation*; discernment, discretion, ability to make distinctions, appreciation of differences, discriminating judgment 480n. *judgment*; insight, perception, nice p., acumen, flair 498n. *intelligence*; appreciation, careful a., critique, critical appraisal 480n. *estimate*; sensitivity 494n. *accuracy*; sensibility 819n. *moral sensibility*; delicacy, refinement 846n. *good taste*; tact, feel 378n. *touch*; timing, sense of t., sense of the occasion; diagnosis, diagnostics 520n. *interpretation*; nicety, particularity 862n. *fastidiousness*; fine palate 386n. *taste*; logical nicety, sublety, hair-splitting, logic-chopping 475n. *reasoning*; sifting, separation, sorting out 62n. *sorting*; selection 605n. *choice*; nice difference, shade of d., nuance, fine shade 15n. *difference.*

Adj. *discriminating,* discriminative, selective, dioristic, judicious, discerning, discreet; accurate, sensitive 494adj. *exact*; fine, delicate, nice, particular 862adj. *fastidious*; thoughtful, tactful 513adj. *imaginative*; tasting, appraising, critical 480adj. *judicial*; diagnostic 15adj. *distinctive.*

Vb. *discriminate,* distinguish, diagnose 15 vb. *differentiate*; compare and contrast 462vb. *compare*; sort, sort out, sieve, bolt, sift, van, winnow; severalize, separate, separate the sheep from the goats, sort the wheat from the chaff 46vb. *set apart*; pick out 605vb. *select*; exercise discretion, see the difference, make a distinction, make an exception, draw the line 468vb. *qualify*; refine, refine upon, split hairs, chop logic 475vb. *reason;* criticize, appraise, taste 480vb. *estimate*; weigh, consider, make a judgment 480vb. *judge*; discern, have insight; know what's what, know one's way about, know one's stuff, know a hawk from a handsaw 490n. *know*; take into account, give weight to 638vb. *make important*; attribute just value to 913vb. *be just.*

464 Indiscrimination

N. *indiscrimination,* lack of discrimination, promiscuousness, promiscuity, universality 79n. *generality*; lack of judgment, uncriticalness, simplicity; obtuseness 499n. *unintelligence*; indiscretion, want of consideration 857n. *rashness*; imperceptivity 439n. *blindness*; unimaginativeness, tactlessness, insensitiveness, insensibility 820n. *moral insensibility*; tastelessness, unrefinement, vulgarity 847n. *bad taste*; coarseness, inaccuracy 495n. *inexactness*; vagueness, loose terms.

Adj. *indiscriminate,* unsorted 61adj. *orderless*; rolled into one, undistinguished, undifferentiated, same for everybody 16adj. *uniform*; random, unaimed, undirected; confused, undefined, unmeasured 474adj. *uncertain*; promiscuous, haphazard, wholesale, blanket 79adj. *general.*

indiscriminating, unselective, undiscerning, uncritical 499adj. *unintelligent*; imperceptive, obtuse; tactless, insensitive, unimaginative 820adj. *impassive*; unrefined 847adj. *vulgar*; indiscreet, ill-judged 857adj. *rash*; tone-deaf 416adj. *deaf*; colour-blind 439adj. *blind*; coarse, inaccurate 495adj. *inexact.*

Vb. *not discriminate,* be indiscriminate, avoid precision, confound opposites, be unselective 606vb. *be neutral*; exercise no discretion 499vb. *be foolish*; make no distinction, see no difference, swallow whole; roll into one, lump everything together, heap t. 74vb. *bring together*; jumble, muddle, confuse, confound 63vb. *derange*; ignore distinctions, obliterate d., average, take an a., smooth out 30vb. *average out.*

See: 16, 30, 61, 63, 74, 79, 416, 439, 474, 495, 499, 606, 820, 847, 857.

465 Measurement

N. *measurement,* admeasurement, quantification; mensuration, surveying, triangulation, cadastral survey; geodetics,

465

geodesy; metage, assize, weighment; posology, dose, dosage 26n. *finite quantity* rating, valuation, evaluation; appraisal, appraisement, assessment, appreciation, estimation 480n. *estimate*; calculation, computation, reckoning 86n. *numeration*; gematria 984n. *occultism*; dead reckoning, gauging; checking, check; reading, reading off; metrics, longimetry, micrometry 203n. *long measure*; trigonometry; second, degree, minute, quadrant 247n. *angular measure*; cubature; mecometry; focimetry; focometry; measurement of rhythm, orthometry.

geometry, plane g., planimetry; solid geometry, stereometry; altimetry, hypsometry; Euclidean geometry, non-Euclidean g.; geometer.

metrology, dimensions, length, breadth, height, depth, thickness; weights and measures, metric system; weights 322n. *weighment*; axle-load; linear measure 203n. *long measure*; measure of capacity, volume, cubature, cubic contents 183n. *space*; liquid measure, gill, pint, imperial p., quart, gallon, imperial g.; barrel, pipe, hogshead 194n. *vessel*; litre; apothecaries' fluid measure, minim, dram; dry measure, peck, bushel, quarter; firlot, boll, chalder, chaldron; ephah, homer; unit of energy, ohm, watt 160n. *electricity*; poundal 160n. *energy*; candlepower 417n. *light*; decibel, sone 398n. *sound*.

co-ordinate, ordinate and abscissa, polar co-ordinates, latitude and longitude, right ascension and declination, altitude and azmiuth.

gauge, measure, scale, graduated s.; time scale 117n. *chronometry*; balance 322n. *scales*; nonius, vernier; footrule, yardstick; pace-stick; yard measure, tape m., steel tape, metre bar; standard, chain, link, pole, rod; lead, log, log-line; fathometer; ruler, slide-rule; straightedge, T-square, set sq.; dividers, callipers, compass, protractor; sextant, quadrant 247n. *angular measure*; backstaff, Jacob's staff 269n. *sailing aid*; theodolite, planisphere, alidad; astrolabe, armillary, sphere 321n. *astronomy*; index, Plimsoll line, Plimsoll mark 547n. *indication*; high-water mark, tide-m., watermark 236n. *limit*; axis, co-ordinate; milestone 547n. *signpost*.

meter, measuring-instrument; goniometer, planimeter; altimeter 209n. *altimetry*; thermometer 379n. *thermometry*; barometer, anemometer 352n. *anemology*; dynamometer; hygrometer 341n. *hygrometry*; fluviometer, nilometer; gas meter; speed gauge, speedometer, cyclometer, pedometer 277n. *velocity*; time-gauge, metronome, time-switch, parking-meter 117n. *timekeeper*; micrometer, ultramicrometer, tasimeter, Geiger counter; seismograph; geophone.

surveyor, land s., quantity s.; topographer, cartographer, oceanographer, hydrographer, geodesist; geometer.

appraiser, valuer, estimator, assessor, measurer, surveyor 480n. *judge*.

Adj. *metric*, metrical, mensural, dimensional, three-d., four-d.; cubic, volumetric, linear, longimetrical, micrometric; cadastral, topographical; geodetical.

measured, surveyed, mapped, plotted, taped; graduated, calibrated; mensurable, measurable, meterable, assessable, computable, calculable.

Vb. *measure*, mete, mensurate, survey; compute, calculate, count, reckon, quantize 86vb. *number*; quantify, take the dimensions, measure the length and breadth; size, calculate the s.; estimate the average 30vb. *average out*; beat the bounds, pace out, count one's steps; measure one's length 309vb. *tumble*; tape, span; calliper, use the dividers; probe, sound, fathom, plumb 313vb. *plunge*; take soundings, heave the lead, heave the log; pace, check the speed 117vb. *time*; balance 322vb. *weigh*.

gauge, meter, take a reading, read, read off; standardize, fix the standard, set a standard 16vb. *make uniform*; grade, mark off, calibrate 27vb. *graduate*; reduce to scale, draw to s., draw a plan, map 551 vb. *represent*.

appraise, gauge, value, cost, rate, set a value on, fix the price of 809vb. *price*; evaluate, estimate, make an e., form an e.; appreciate, assess 480vb. *estimate*; form an opinion 480vb. *judge*; tape, have taped, have the measure of, size up.

mete out, mete, measure out, weigh, weigh out, dole o., divide, share, share out 775 vb. *participate*, 783vb. *apportion*.

See: 16, 26, 27, 30, 86, 117, 160, 183, 194, 203, 209, 236, 247, 269, 277, 309, 313, 321,

322, 341, 352, 379, 398, 417, 480, 547, 551, 775, 783, 809, 984.

466 Evidence

N. *evidence*, facts, data, case-history; grounds 475 n. *reasons*; præcognita, premises 475 n. *premise*; hearsay, what the soldier said, hearsay evidence 524 n. *report*; indirect evidence, collateral e., secondary e.; circumstantial evidence 8 n. *circumstance*; constructive evidence 512 n. *supposition*; prima facie evidence; intrinsic evidence, internal e., presumptive e., direct e., demonstrative e., final e., conclusive e., proof 478 n. *demonstration*; supporting evidence, corroboration; verification, confirmation 473 n. *certainty*; rebutting evidence 467 n. *counter-evidence*; one-sided evidence, ex parte e.; piece of evidence, fact, relevant f.; document, exhibit, finger-prints 548 n. *record*; clue 524 n. *hint*; symptom, sign 547 n. *indication*; reference, quotation, citation, chapter and verse; one's authorities, documentation; line of evidence, chain of authorities; authority, scripturality, canonicity.

testimony, witness; statement, evidence in chief 524 n. *information*; admission, confession 526 n. *disclosure*; one's case, plea 614 n. *pretext*; word, assertion, allegation 532 n. *affirmation*; Bible evidence, evidence on oath; sworn evidence, legal e., deposition, affidavit, attestation 532 n. *oath*; State's evidence, Queen's e.; word of mouth, oral evidence, verbal e.; documentary evidence, written e.; evidence to character, compurgation, wager at law 927 n. *vindication*; copy of the evidence, case record, dossier 548 n. *record*; written contract 765 n. *compact*; deed, testament 767 n. *security*.

credential, compurgation 927 n. *vindication*; testimonial, chit, character, recommendation, references; seal, signature, counters., endorsement, docket; voucher, warranty, warrant, certificate, diploma 767 n. *security*; ticket, passport, visa 756 n. *permit*; authority, scripture.

witness, eye-w. 441 n. *spectator*; ear-witness 415 n. *listener*; indicator, informant, telltale 524 n. *informer*; deponent, testifier, swearer, attester, attestant 765 n. *signa-*

tory; witness to character, compurgator, oath-helper; sponsor 707 n. *patron*.

Adj. *evidential*, evidentiary, offering evidence, testificatory; prima facie 445 adj. *appearing*; suggesting, suggestive, significant 514 adj. *meaningful*; showing, indicative, symptomatic 547 adj. *indicating*; indirect, secondary, circumstantial; firsthand, direct, seen, heard; deducible, verifiable 471 adj. *probable*; constructive 512 adj. *suppositional*; cumulative, supporting, corroborative, confirmatory; telling, damning 928 adj. *accusing*; presumptive, reliable 473 adj. *certain*; probative, proving, demonstrative, conclusive, decisive, final 478 adj. *demonstrating*; based on, grounded on; founded on fact, factual, documentary, documented 473 adj. *positive*; authentic, well-grounded, well-based 494 adj. *true*; weighty, authoritative 178 adj. *influential*; biblical, scriptural, canonical 976 adj. *orthodox*; testified, attested, witnessed; spoken to, sworn to; in evidence, on the record, documented 548 adj. *recorded*.

Vb. *evidence*, show, evince, furnish evidence; show signs of, have the makings of 852 vb. *give hope*; betoken, bespeak 551 vb. *represent*; breathe of, tell of, declare 522 vb. *manifest*; lend colour to 471 vb. *make likely*; tell its own tale, speak for itself, speak volumes; have weight, carry w. 178 vb. *influence*; suggest 547 vb. *indicate*; argue, involve 523 vb. *imply*.

testify, witness; take one's oath, swear, be sworn, speak on oath 532 vb. *affirm*; bear witness, take the stand, give evidence, speak to, depose, depone, swear to, vouch for, give one's word; authenticate, certify 473 vb. *make certain*; attest, subscribe, countersign, endorse, sign; plead, state one's case 475 vb. *argue*; admit, avow, acknowledge 526 vb. *confess*; speak to character, compurgate, testimonialize.

corroborate, support, buttress 162 vb. *strengthen*; sustain, uphold in evidence 927 vb. *vindicate*; bear out, circumstantiate, verify; validate, confirm, ratify, establish, make out, make good 473 vb. *make certain*; lead evidence, adduce e.; bring one's witnesses, produce one's w., confront w.; put the evidence, produce the e., document; collect evidence, assemble the facts; concoct evidence, fabricate e. 541 vb. *fake*; outswear 467 vb. *tell against*;

adduce, cite the evidence, quote the e., quote the leading case, quote one's authorities, give the reference, give chapter and verse.
See: 8, 162, 178, 415, 441, 445, 467, 471, 473, 475, 478, 494, 512, 514, 522, 523, 524, 526, 532, 541, 547, 548, 551, 614, 707, 756, 765, 767, 852, 927, 928, 976.

467 Counter-evidence

N. *counter-evidence*, adverse symptom, contra-indication 14 n. *contrariety*; answering evidence, opposite e., rebutting e.; evidence against, evidence on the other side, defence, rebuttal 460 n. *answer*; refutation, disproof 479 n. *confutation*; denial 533 n. *negation*; justification 927 n. *vindication*; oath against oath, one word against another; counter-oath, counter-protest, tu quoque argument, reverse of the shield; conflicting evidence, contradictory e., negative e.; mitigating evidence 468 n. *qualification*; hostile witness, hostile evidence 603 n. *tergiversation*.
Adj. *countervailing*, rebutting 460 adj. *answering*; cancelling out, counteractive 182 adj. *counteracting*; cutting both ways, ambiguous 518 adj. *equivocal*; converse, opposite, in the opposite scale 14 adj. *contrary*; denying, negatory 533 adj. *negative*; damaging, telling against, contra-indicating; refutatory, refutative; qualificatory 468 adj. *qualifying*.
unattested, unsworn; lacking proof, unproven, not proved 474 adj. *uncertain*; unsupported, uncorroborated; disproved 479 adj. *confuted*; trumped-up, fabricated 541 adj. *false*.
Vb. *tell against*, damage the case; weigh against, countervail; contravene, traverse, run counter, contradict, contra-indicate; rebut 479 vb. *confute*; oppose, point the other way 14 vb. *be contrary*; cancel out 182 vb. *counteract*; cut both ways 518 vb. *be equivocal*; prove a negative 533 vb. *negate*; lead counter-evidence, lead for the other side; tell another story, alter the case; not improve, weaken, damage, spoil; undermine, subvert 165 vb. *destroy*; demolish the case, turn the tables, turn the scale, convict of perjury; contradict oneself, turn hostile 603 vb. *tergiversate.*

Adv. *conversely*, per contra, on the other hand, on the other side, in rebuttal, in rejoinder.
See: 14, 165, 182, 460, 468, 474, 479, 518, 533, 541, 603, 927.

468 Qualification

N. *qualification*, specification 80 n. *speciality*; requisite 627 n. *requirement*; leaven, colouring, tinge; modification 143 n. *change*; mitigation 177 n. *moderation*; condition 766 n. *conditions*; limitation 747 n. *restriction*; proviso, reservation; exception, salvo, saving clause, escape c., escalator c.; exemption 919 n. *non-liability*; demur, objection, but 704 n. *opposition*; consideration, discount, abatement, reduction, allowance, grains of a.; extenuating circumstances; redeeming feature 31 n. *offset.*
Adj. *qualifying*, qualificative, qualificatory; modifying, altering the case; mitigatory 177 adj. *lenitive*; extenuating, palliative, excusing, weakening, colouring, leavening; contingent, provisional 766 adj. *conditional*; discounting, abating; saving, excepting, exempting; circumstanced, qualified, not absolute; exceptional, exempted, exempt 919 adj. *non-liable.*
Vb. *qualify*, condition, limit, restrict 747 vb. *restrain*; colour, shade 419 vb. *bedim*; leaven, alter 143 vb. *modify*; temper, palliate, mitigate 177 vb. *moderate*; adulterate 163 vb. *weaken*; excuse 927 vb. *extenuate*; grant, make allowance for, 810 n. *discount*; abate 37 vb. *bate*; make exceptions 919 vb. *exempt*; introduce new conditions, alter the case; insert a qualifying clause; relax, relax the rigour of 734 vb. *be lax*; take exception, object, demur, raise an objection 762 vb. *deprecate.*
Adv. *provided*, provided always, with the proviso that, according as, subject to, conditionally, with the understanding; granting, admitting, supposing; allowing for, with grains of allowance, cum grano salis; not absolutely, not invariably; if, if not, unless 8 adv. *if*; though, although, even if.
nevertheless, even so, all the same; despite, in spite of; but, yet, still, at all events; whether, whether or no.

See: 8, 31, 37, 80, 143, 163, 177, 419, 627, 704, 734, 747, 762, 766, 810, 919, 927.

469 Possibility

N. *possibility*, potentiality, virtuality; capacity, viability, viableness, workability 160 n. *ability*; what is possible, all that is p. 635 n. *sufficiency*; what may be 124 n. *futurity*; what might be, the might-have-been 125 n. *preterition*; the possible, the feasible; what one can do, best one can do, limit of one's endeavour; contingency, a possibility, chance, off-chance 159 n. *fair chance*; good chance 137 n. *opportunity*; bare possibility, ghost of a chance; likelihood 471 n. *probability*; thinkability, credibility 485 n. *belief*; practicability, operability 642 n. *expedience*; practicableness, feasibility, easiness 701 n. *facility*; superability, negotiability; availability, accessibility, approachability; compatibility 24 n. *agreement*; risk of.

Adj. *possible*, virtual, potential, of power, able, capable, viable; arguable, reasonable; feasible, practicable, negotiable 701 adj. *easy*; workable, performable, achievable; doable, operable; attainable, approachable, accessible, obtainable, realizable; superable, surmountable; not too difficult, not impossible, within the bounds of possibility; available, still open, not excluded; conceivable, thinkable, credible, imaginable; practical, compatible with the circumstances 642 adj. *expedient*; allowable, permissible, legal 756 adj. *permitted*; contingent 124 adj. *future*; on the cards, on the dice 471 adj. *probable*; only possible, not inevitable, evitable, revocable 620 adj. *avoidable*; liable, tending.

Vb. *be possible*,—feasible etc. adj.; may, might, maybe, might be; might have been, could have b., should have b.; admit of, allow 756 vb. *permit*; bear, be open to, offer an opportunity for; be a possibility, depend, be contingent, lie within the bounds of possibility.

make possible, enable 160 vb. *empower*; allow 756 vb. *permit*; clear the path, smoothe the way, remove the obstacles, put in the way of 701 vb. *facilitate*.

Adv. *possibly*, potentially, virtually; perhaps, perchance, within reach, within measurable distance; peradventure, may be, haply, mayhap; if possible, if so be; wind and weather permitting, God willing Deo volente, D.V.

See: 24, 124, 125, 137, 159, 160, 471, 485, 620, 635, 642, 701, 756.

470 Impossibility

N. *impossibility* etc. adj.; unthinkability, no chance, not a chance of, not a Chinaman's chance 853 n. *hopelessness*; what cannot be, what can never be; irrevocability, the might-have-been; impasse, deadlock 702 n. *obstacle*; infeasibility, impracticability 643 n. *inexpedience*; no permission 757 n. *prohibition*; unavailability, inaccessibility, unapproachability, sour grapes; insuperability, impossible task, no go, Sisyphean operation 700 n. *hard task*.

Adj. *impossible*, not possible; not allowed, ruled out, excluded, against the rules 757 adj. *prohibited*; out of the question, hopeless; unnatural, against nature; unreasonable, contrary to reason, self-contradictory, 477 adj. *illogical*; unscientific; untrue, incompatible with the facts, untrue to fact 495 adj. *erroneous*; too improbable, incredible, inconceivable, unthinkable, unimaginable, unheard of 486 adj. *unbelieved*; miraculous 864 adj. *wonderful*; visionary, idealistic, unrealistic, out of this world 513 adj. *imaginary*; irrevocable, beyond recall 830 adj. *regretted*.

impracticable, unfeasible, not to be done; unworkable, unviable; unachievable, unrealizable, unsolvable, insoluble, inextricable, too hard 700 adj. *difficult*; incurable, inoperable; insuperable, insurmountable, impassable, unbridgeable, unbridged; impervious, unnavigable, unmotorable; unapproachable, inaccessible, unobtainable, unavailable, not to be had, out of reach, beyond one's reach, not within one's grasp; elusive 667 adj. *escaped*.

Vb. *be impossible*,—impracticable etc. adj., exceed possibility, defy all possibilities; fly in the face of reason 477 vb. *reason ill*; have no chance whatever.

make impossible, rule out, exclude, disallow 757 vb. *prohibit*; put out of reach, tantalize, set an impossible task; deny the possibility, eat one's hat if 533 vb. *negate*.

try impossibilities, labour in vain 641 vb. *waste effort*; have nothing to go upon, grasp at shadows; be in two places at once, square the circle, discover the secret of perpetual motion, discover the philosopher's stone, find the elixir of life. find a needle in a haystack; build castles in the air, weave a rope of sand, skin a flint, gather grapes from thorns, make bricks without straw, catch a weasel asleep, milk a he-goat into a sieve; make cheese from chalk, make a silk purse out of a sow's ear, wash a blackamoor white, change a leopard's spots; extract sunbeams from cucumbers, set the Thames on fire, write on water.

Adv. *impossibly*, nohow.

See: 477, 486, 495, 513, 533, 641, 643, 667, 700, 702, 757, 830, 853, 864.

471 Probability

N. *probability*, likelihood, likeliness, 159 n. *chance*; good chance, favourable c., reasonable c., fair c., sporting c. 469 n. *possibility*; prospect, excellent p. 511 n. *prediction*; fair expectation 507 n. *expectation*; well-grounded hope 852 n. *hope*; real risk, real danger 661 n. *danger*; liability, natural course 179 n. *tendency*; presumption, natural p.; presumptive evidence, circumstantial e. 466 n. *evidence*; credibility; likely belief 485 n. *belief*; plausibility, reasonability, good reason 475 n. *reasons*; verisimilitude, colour, show of, semblance 445 n. *appearance*; theory of probability; probabilism, probabilist.

Adj. *probable*, likely 180 adj. *liable*; on the cards, in a fair way; natural, to be expected, foreseeable; presumable, presumptive; reliable, to be acted on 473 adj. *certain*; hopeful, promising 507 adj. *expected*; in danger of 661 adj. *vulnerable*; highly possible 469 adj. *possible*.

plausible, specious, colourable; apparent, ostensible 445 adj. *appearing*; logical 475 adj. *rational*; convincing, persuasive, believable, easy of belief 485 adj. *credible*; well-grounded, well-founded 494 adj. *true*; ben trovato 24 adj. *apt*.

Vb. *be likely*, — probable etc. adj., have a chance, be on the cards, stand a chance, run a good c. 469 vb. *be possible*; bid fair,

be in danger of; show signs, have the makings of 852 vb. *give hope*.

make likely, make probable, probabilize, increase the chances; involve 523 vb. *imply*; entail 156 vb. *conduce*; put in the way to, promote 703 vb. *aid*; lend colour to, give a colour to 466 vb. *evidence*.

assume, presume, take for granted, flatter oneself 485 vb. *believe*; conjecture, guess, dare say 512 vb. *suppose*; think likely, look for 507 vb. *expect*; read the future, see ahead 510 vb. *foresee*; rely, count upon 473 vb. *be certain*; deduce, infer 475 vb. *reason*.

Adv. *probably*, in all probability, in all likelihood, as is to be expected; very likely, most l., ten to one, by all odds; seeming, apparently, prima facie; belike, as likely as not.

See: 24, 156, 159, 179, 180, 445, 466, 469, 473, 475, 485, 494, 507, 510, 511, 512, 523, 661, 703, 852.

472 Improbability

N. *improbability*, unlikelihood, doubt, real d. 474 n. *uncertainty*; little chance, chance in a million, off-chance, small c., poor c., bad c., unfavourable c., scarcely a c., scarcely any c., not a ghost of a c., no c. 470 n. *impossibility*; long odds, bare possibility; pious hopes, small h., poor prospect 508 n. *inexpectation*; rare occurrence, rarity 140 n. *infrequency*; implausibility, traveller's tale, fisherman's yarn 541 n. *falsehood*.

Adj. *improbable*, unlikely, more than doubtful, dubious 474 adj. *uncertain*; contrary to all reasonable expectations, unforeseeable 508 adj. *unexpected*; hard to believe, unconvincing, implausible 474 adj. *uncertified*; rare 140 adj. *infrequent*; unheard of, unimaginable, inconceivable 470 adj. *impossible*; incredible, too good to be true 486 adj. *unbelieved*.

Vb. *be unlikely*, — improbable, look impossible etc. adj.; have a bare chance, show little hope, offer small chance; be implausible, be hard to believe, lend no colour to, strain one's belief 486 vb. *cause doubt*; think unlikely, throw doubt on 508 vb. *not expect*.

Int. not likely! no fear!

See: 140, 470, 474, 486, 508, 541.

473 Certainty

N. *certainty*, objective c., certitude, certain knowledge 490n. *knowledge*; certainness, assuredness, sureness; certain issue, inevitability, inexorability, irrevocability, necessity 596n. *fate*; inerrancy, freedom from error, infallibilism, infallibility; indubitability, reliability, utter r., unimpeachability 494n. *truth*; certainty of meaning, unambiguity, univocity; no case to answer, incontrovertibility, irrefutability, indisputability, proof 478n. *demonstration*; authentication, ratification, validation; certification, verification, confirmation; attestation 466n. *testimony*; making sure, check 459n. *enquiry*; ascertainment 484n. *discovery*; dead certainty, cert, dead c., sure thing, safe bet, cinch, open and shut case; fact, ascertained f., indubitable f., positive f. 3n. *substantiality*; matter of fact, accomplished f., fait accompli 154n. *eventuality*; res judicata, settled decision 480n. *judgment*; gospel, Bible 511n. *oracle*; dogma 976n. *orthodoxy*; dictum, ipse dixit, ex cathedra utterance, axiom 496n. *maxim*; court of final appeal, judgment seat 956n. *tribunal*; last word, ultimatum 766n. *conditions.*

positiveness, subjective certainty, moral c.; assurance, confidence, conviction, persuasion 485n. *belief*; unshakable opinion, doctrinaire o. 485n. *opinion*; idée fixe, fixity, obsession 481n. *bias*; dogmatism, orthodoxy, hyperorthodoxy, bigotry 602 n. *opiniatry*; infallibility, air of i., self-confidence; pontification, laying down the law.

doctrinaire, self-opinionated person 602n. *opinionist*; dogmatist, infallibilist; bigot, fanatic, zealot; oracle, Sir Oracle, know-all 500n. *wiseacre.*

Adj. *certain*, sure, reliable, solid, unshakable, well-founded, well-grounded 3 adj. *substantial*; authoritative, official 494adj. *genuine*; factual, historical 494adj. *true*; ascertained, certified, attested, guaranteed, warranted; tested, tried, foolproof 660adj. *safe*; infallible, unerring, inerrant 540adj. *veracious*; axiomatic, dogmatic, taken for granted 485adj. *credal*; self-evident, axiomatic, evident, apparent; unequivocal, unambiguous, univocal; unmistakable, clear, clear as day 443adj. *well-seen*; inevitable, unavoidable, ineluctable, irrevocable, inexorable, necessary 596adj. *fated*; bound, bound to be, in the bag; sure as fate, sure as death and taxes 124adj. *future*; sure as a gun, safe as houses 660adj. *invulnerable*; verifiable, testable, demonstrable 478adj. *demonstrated.*

positive, confident, assured, self-assured, certain in one's mind, undoubting, convinced, persuaded, certified, sure 485adj. *believing*; opinionated, self-o; dogmatizing, pontifical, oracular; dogmatic, doctrinaire 976adj. *orthodox*; obsessed, bigoted, fanatical 481 adj. *biased*; unshaken, set, fixed, fixed in one's opinions 153adj. *unchangeable*; clean-cut, clear-c., definite. defined, unambiguous, unequivocal, univocal 516adj. *intelligible*; convincing 485adj. *credible*; classified, in its place 62adj. *arranged*; affirmative, categorical, absolute, unqualified, final, ultimate, conclusive, settled, without appeal.

undisputed, beyond doubt, axiomatic, uncontroversial; unquestioned, undoubted, uncontested, indubitable, unquestionable, questionless, incontrovertible, incontestable, unchallengeable, unimpeachable, undeniable, irrefutable, irrefragable, indefeasible.

Vb. *be certain*, — sure etc. adj.; leave no doubt, be clear as day, stand to reason, be axiomatic 475vb. *be reasonable*; be positive, be assured, satisfy oneself, convince o., feel sure, be clear in one's mind, make no doubt, hold for true 485vb. *believe*; understand, know for certain 490vb. *know*; hold to one's opinions, dismiss all doubt; depend on it, rely on, trust in, swear by; gamble on, bet on, go Nap on, put one's shirt on.

dogmatize, pontificate, lay down the law, play the oracle, know all the answers.

make certain, certify, authenticate, ratify, seal, sign 488vb. *endorse*; guarantee, warrant, assure; finalize, settle, decide 480vb. *judge*; remove doubt, persuade 485vb. *convince*; classify 62vb. *arrange*; make sure, ascertain, check, verify, confirm, clinch 466vb. *corroborate*; reassure oneself, take a second look, do a double take; make assurance doubly sure 660vb. *safeguard*; reinsure 858vb. *be cautious*; ensure, make inevitable 596vb. *necessitate.*

Adv. *certainly*, definitely, certes, for sure, to

be sure, no doubt, doubtless, of course, as a matter of c., no question; no two ways about it; without fail, sink or swim, rain or shine, come what will.

See: 3, 62, 124, 153, 154, 443, 459, 466, 475, 478, 480, 481, 484, 485, 488, 490, 494, 496, 500, 511, 516, 540, 596, 602, 660, 766, 858, 956, 976.

474 Uncertainty

N. *uncertainty*, unverifiability, incertitude, doubtfulness, dubiousness; ambiguity 518 n. *equivocalness*; vagueness, haziness, obscurity 418 n. *darkness*; mist, haze, fog 355 n. *cloud*; yes and no, indeterminacy, indetermination, borderline case; indefiniteness, roving commission; query, question mark 459 n. *question*; open question, anybody's guess; nothing to go on, guesswork 512 n. *conjecture*; contingency, doubtful c., doubtful event 159 n. *chance*; gamble, toss-up, wager 618 n. *gambling*; leap in the dark, bow at a venture, blind bargain, pig in a poke, blind date; something or other, this or that.

dubiety, dubitancy, dubitation 486 n. *doubt*; state of doubt, open mind, suspended judgment, open verdict; suspense, waiting 507 n. *expectation*; doubt, indecision, hesitancy, vacillation, fluctuation, seesaw, floating vote 601 n. *irresolution*; embarrassment, perplexity, bewilderment, bafflement, nonplus, quandary; dilemma, cleft stick, option of difficulties, Morton's fork 530 n. *enigma*.

unreliability, liability to error, fallibility 495 n. *error*; insecurity, precariousness, touch and go 661 n. *danger*; untrustworthiness, treacherousness; fluidity, unsteadiness, variability, changeability 152 n. *changeableness*; unpredictability, unexpectedness 508 n. *inexpectation*; fickleness, capriciousness, whimsicality 604 n. *caprice*; slipperiness, suppleness 930 n. *improbity*; treachery 930 n. *perfidy*, 603 n. *tergiversation*; lack of security, no guarantee, no collateral, bare word, dicer's oath, scrap of paper, paper guarantee.

Adj. *uncertain*, unsure, doubtful, dubious, not axiomatic; unverifiable (see *uncertified*); insecure, chancy, risky 661 adj. *unsafe*; treacherous (see *unreliable*); subject to chance, casual; occasional, spora-

dic 140 adj. *infrequent*; temporary, provisional 114 adj. *transient*; fluid 152 adj. *unstable*; contingent, depending on, dependent 766 vb. *conditional*; unpredictable, unforeseeable 508 adj. *unexpected*; aoristic, indeterminate, undefined, undetermined, unclassified; random 61 adj. *orderless*; indecisive, undecided, open, in suspense; in question, under enquiry; moot, open to question, questionable, arguable, debatable, disputable, controvertible, controversial; problematical, hypothetical, speculative 512 adj. *suppositional*; undefinable, borderline; ambiguous 518 adj. *equivocal*; paradoxical 477 adj. *illogical*; oracular, enigmatic, cryptic, obscure 517 adj. *puzzling*; vague, hazy, misty, cloudy 419 adj. *shadowy*; mysterious, veiled 523 adj. *occult*; unsolved, unresolved, unexplained 517 adj. *unintelligible*; perplexing, bewildering, embarrassing, confusing.

unreliable, undependable, untrustworthy; slippery 930 adj. *dishonest*; treacherous 930 adj. *perfidious*; ratting 603 adj. *tergiversating*; unsteady, unstable, variable, changeable 152 adj. *changeful*; unpredictable, unforeseeable; fickle, whimsical 604 adj. *capricious*; fallible, open to error 495 adj. *erroneous*; precarious, ticklish, touch and go.

doubting, in doubt, doubtful, dubious, full of doubt; agnostic, sceptical 486 adj. *unbelieving*; sitting on the fence, in two minds; in suspense, open-minded; distrustful, mistrustful 858 adj. *cautious*; uncertain, unassured, unconfident; hesitant, undecided, wavering 601 adj. *irresolute*; unable to say, afraid to say; dazed, baffled, perplexed, bewildered, distracted, distraught 517 adj. *puzzled*; nonplussed, stumped, brought to a stand, at one's wits' end, on the horns of a dilemma; lost, disorientated, guessing, abroad, at sea, adrift, drifting, astray, at a loss, at fault, clueless 491 adj. *ignorant*.

uncertified, unverified, unchecked; awaiting confirmation, unconfirmed, uncorroborated, unauthenticated, unratified, unsigned, unsealed, unwitnessed, unattested; unwarranted, unguaranteed; unauthoritative, unofficial, apocryphal, unauthentic; unproved, undemonstrated; unascertained, untold, uncounted; untried, untested, in the experimental stage.

Vb. *be uncertain*, be contingent, lie in the lap of the gods; hinge on, be dependent on 157 vb. *depend*; be touch and go, tremble in the balance; be open to question, non liquet; be ambiguous 518 vb. *be equivocal*; make doubt, have one's doubts 486 vb. *doubt*; wait and see, wait on events 508 vb. *await*; have a suspicion, suspect, wonder, wonder whether; dither, be in two minds, hover, float, sit on the fence, sway, see-saw, waver, vacillate, falter, pause, hesitate 601 vb. *be irresolute*; avoid a decision, boggle, stickle, demur; moider, be in a maze, flounder, drift, be at sea; have nothing to go on, grope, fumble, cast about, beat a., experiment 461 vb. *be tentative*; lose the clue, lose the thread, miss one's way, get lost 282 vb. *stray*; lose the scent, be at fault, come to a stand; not know which way to turn, be at one's wits' end, have no answer, be in a dilemma, be in a quandary; wouldn't swear, could be wrong.

puzzle, perplex, confuse, daze, bewilder, addle the wits; baffle, nonplus, flummox, stump, gravel 727 vb. *defeat*; mystify, keep one guessing; bamboozle 542 vb. *befool*; fuzz, fog, fox, throw off the scent 495 vb. *mislead*; plunge in doubt, vex with d. 486 vb. *cause doubt*; make one think, ask for thought, demand reflection.

Adv. *in suspense*, in a state of uncertainty, on the horns of a dilemma, in a maze, in a daze.

See: 61, 114, 140, 152, 157, 159, 282, 355, 418, 419, 459, 461, 477, 486, 491, 495, 507, 508, 512, 517, 518, 523, 530, 542, 601, 603, 604, 618, 661, 727, 766, 858, 930.

475 Reasoning

N. *reasoning*, ratiocination, force of argument; reason, discursive r.; intuitive reason 476 n. *intuition*; sweet reason, reasonableness, rationality; dialectics, art of reasoning, logic; logical process, logical sequence, inference, general i., generalization; distinction 15 n. *differentiation*; apriorism, apriority, a priori reasoning, deductive r., deduction; induction, inductive reasoning, a posteriori r., empirical r., Baconian method; rationalism, euhemerism, dialecticism, dialectic

449 n. *philosophy*; arithmetic 86 n. *mathematics*; plain reason, simple arithmetic.

premise, postulate, postulate of reason, basis of reasoning; universals, five predictables; principle, general p., first p.; lemma, starting-point; assumption, stipulation 512 n. *supposition*; axiom, self-evident truth 496 n. *maxim*; datum, data; provisional hypothesis, hypothesis ad hoc, one's position.

argumentation, critical examination, analysis 459 n. *enquiry*; method of argument, rules of pleading; dialectic, Socratic elenchus, dialogue, logical disputation; logical scheme, synthesis; epagoge, syllogization, sorites, syllogism, elench, prosyllogism, enthymeme, major premise, minor p.; philosopheme, proposition, thesis, theorem, problem; predication, lemma, predicate, philosopheme; dilemma, horns of d., Morton's fork 474 n. *uncertainty*; conclusion, logical c., Q.E.D. 478 n. *demonstration*; paradoxical conclusion, paradox 497 n. *absurdity*; reductio ad absurdum.

argument, discussion, symposium, dialogue; swapping opinions, give and take, cut and thrust; opposing arguments, disceptation, disputation, controversy, debate 489 n. *dissent*; appeal to reason, set or formal argument, plea, pleading, special p., thesis, case; reasons, submission; defensive argument, apologetics, defence; aggressive argument, destructive a., polemics, polemic; conciliatory argument 719 n. *irenics*; wordy argument, logomachy, war of words, paper war 709 n. *quarrel*; propaganda, pamphleteering 534 n. *teaching*; controversialism, argumentativeness, ergotism, hair-splitting logic-chopping; contentiousness, wrangling, jangling 709 n. *dissension*; bad argument, sophism 477 n. *sophistry*; legal argument, pleadings 959 n. *litigation*; argumentum ad hominem, play on the feelings; argumentum ad baculum 740 n. *compulsion*; argument by analogy, parity of reasoning; tu quoque argument, same to you.

reasons, basis of argument, grounds; real reasons 156 n. *cause*; alleged reason 614 n. *pretext*; arguments, pros and cons; case, good c., case to answer; sound argument, strong a., cogent a., conclusive a., unanswerable a. 478 n. *demonstration*; point, valid p., point well taken, clincher.

reasoner, theologian 449 n. *philosopher*; logician, dialectician, syllogist, syllogizer; rationalist, euhemerist, sophister 477 n. *sophist*; casuist; polemic, polemicist, apologist, controversalist, eristic, controvertist; arguer, debater, disputant; proponent, mooter, canvasser; pleader 958 n. *lawyer*; wrangler 709 n. *quarreller*; argumentative person, sea-lawyer, barrack-room l., logomachist, quibbler, pedant; scholastic, schoolman 492 n. *intellectual*; mathematician, pure m.

Adj. *rational*, clear-headed, reasoning, reasonable; rationalistic, euhemeristic; ratiocinative, ratiocinatory, logical; cogent, acceptable, admissible, to the point, pointed, well-grounded, well-argued 9 adj. *relevant*; sensible, fair 913 adj. *just*; dianoëtic, discursory, analytic, synthetic; consistent, systematic, methodological; dialectic, discursive, deductive, inductive, epagogic, maieutic, inferential, a posteriori, a priori, universal; axiomatic 473 adj. *certain*; tenable 469 adj. *possible*.

arguing, appealing to reason; polemical, irenic, apologetic; controversial, disputatious, eristic, argumentative, logomachic; quibbling 477 adj. *sophistical*; disputable, controvertible, debatable, arguable 474 adj. *uncertain*.

Vb. *be reasonable* 471 vb. *be likely*; stand to reason, follow, hang together, hold water; appeal to reason; listen to reason, be guided by r., obey r., bow to r.; accept the argument, yield to a.; admit, concede, grant, allow 488 vb. *assent*; have a case, have logic on one's side.

reason, philosophize 449 vb. *think*; syllogize, ratiocinate; rationalize, explain away; apply reason, bring reason to bear, put two and two together; infer, deduce, induct; explain 520 vb. *interpret*; chop logic, logomachize.

argue, argufy, bandy arguments, give and take, cut and thrust; hold an argument, hold a symposium; exchange opinions, discuss, canvass; debate, dispute, discept, logomachize; quibble, split hairs, chop logic; indulge in argument, argue the case, argue the point, take a p., stick to one's p.; stress, strain, work an argument to death 532 vb. *emphasize*; put one's case, plead; propagandize, pamphleteer 534 vb. *teach*; take up the case, defend; attack, polemicize; try conclusion, cross swords,

join issue, demur, cavil 489 vb. *dissent*; analyse, pull to pieces; out-argue, overwhelm with argument, bludgeon 479 vb. *confute*; prove one's case 478 vb. *demonstrate*; have words, wrangle 709 vb. *bicker*; answer back, make a rejoinder 460 vb. *answer*; start an argument, open a discussion; propose, bring up, moot; confer 691 vn. *consult*.

premise, posit, postulate, stipulate, lay down, assume, hypothesize 512 vb. *suppose*; take for granted, regard as axiomatic, refer to first principles.

Adv. *reasonably*, fairly, rationally, logically; polemically; hypothetically; a priori, a posteriori, a fortiori, how much the more, much less; consequently; for reasons given; in argument, in one's submission.

See: 9, 15, 86, 156, 449, 459, 460, 469, 471, 473, 474, 476, 477, 478, 479, 488, 489, 492, 496, 497, 512, 520, 532, 534, 614, 691, 709, 719, 740, 913, 958, 959.

476 Intuition: absence of reason

N. *intuition*, instinct, automatic reaction, association; light of nature, sixth sense, psi, psi faculty; telepathy; insight, clairvoyance; direct apprehension, unmediated perception, a priori knowledge; divination, dowsing, radiesthesia; inspiration, presentiment, impulse, mere feeling 818 n. *feeling*; rule of thumb; hunch, impression, sense, guesswork; untutored intelligence, illogic, feminine reason, feminine logic; self-deception, wishful thinking; unreason 503 n. *insanity*.

Adj. *intuitive*, instinctive, impulsive; nondiscursive; involuntary 609 adj. *spontaneous*; above reason, beyond r., independent of r., unknown to logic, inspirational, inspired, clairvoyant, direct, unmediated.

Vb. *intuit*, know by instinct, have a sixth sense; sense, feel in one's bones, somehow feel; react automatically, react instinctively; go by impressions, rely on intuition, dispense with reason, use feminine logic; guess, have a g., use guesswork, work on a hunch.

Adv. *intuitively*, instinctively, by instinct, by guess and God, by nature's light.

See: 503, 609, 818.

477 Sophistry: false reasoning

N. *sophistry*, affective logic, rationalization; illogicalness, illogic; feminine logic 476 n. *intuition*; sophistical reasoning, false r., fallacious r., specious r., vicious r., evasive r.; mental reservation, arrière pensée 525 n. *concealment*; equivocation, mystification; word fence, tongue f.; casuistry, jesuitry; subtlety, over-s.; special pleading, hair-splitting, logic-chopping; claptrap, mere words; logomachy, quibbling, quibble, quillet; chicanery, chicane, subterfuge, shuffle, dodge; evasion 614 n. *pretext*.

sophism, a sophistry, specious argument, insincere a.; exploded argument, fallacious a.; illogicality, fallacy, paralogism; bad logic, loose thinking; solecism, flaw, logical f., flaw in the argument; begging the question, ignoratio elenchi; circular reasoning, arguing in a circle, petitio principii; unwarranted conclusion, non sequitur, post hoc ergo propter hoc; contradiction in terms, antilogy; ignotum per ignotius; weak case, bad c., false c.; lame and impotent conclusion.

sophist, sophister, sophistical reasoner, casuist, quibbler, equivocator; caviller, devil's advocate; captious critic.

Adj. *sophistical*, specious, plausible, ad captandum; evasive, insincere; hollow, empty; deceptive, illusive, illusory; over-refined, over-subtle, fine-spun; pettifogging, captious, quibbling; sophisticated, tortuous; casuistical, jesuitical.

illogical, contrary to reason, irrational, unreasonable; unreasoned, arbitrary; paralogistic, fallacious, fallible; contradictory, self-c., inconsistent; incongruous, absonant, absonous; unwarranted, invalid, untenable, unsound; unfounded, ungrounded, groundless; inconsequent, inconsequential; incorrect, unscientific, false 495 adj. *erroneous*.

ill-reasoned, unrigorous, inconclusive; unproved, unsustained; weak, feeble; frivolous, airy, flimsy; loose, woolly, muddled, confused; woolly-headed, muddle-h.; wishful, instinctive.

Vb. *reason ill*, paralogize, mistake one's logic, mistake one's conclusion, argue in a circle, beg the question, not see the wood for the trees; not have a leg to stand on; talk at random, babble, burble 515 vb. *mean nothing*.

sophisticate, mislead 535 vb. *misteach*; mystify 542 vb. *befool*; quibble, cavil, split hairs 475 vb. *argue*; equivocate 518 vb. *be equivocal*; dodge, shuffle, fence 713 vb. *parry*; not come to the point, beat about the bush 570 vb. *be diffuse*; evade 667 vb. *elude*; varnish, gloss over, whitewash 541 vb. *cant*; colour 552 vb. *misrepresent*; pervert, misapply 675 vb. *misuse*; pervert reason, twist the argument, torture logic; prove that white is black, make the worse appear the better cause.

See: 475, 476, 495, 515, 518, 525, 535, 541, 542, 552, 570, 614, 667, 675, 713.

478 Demonstration

N. *demonstration*, logic of facts, documentation 466 n. *evidence*; proven fact 494 n. *truth*; proof, rigorous p.; comprobation, establishment, apodeixis; conclusive proof, final p.; conclusiveness, irrefragability 473 n. *certainty*; verification, ascertainment, probation, experimentum crucis 461 n. *experiment*; deduction, inference, argument, triumph of a. 475 n. *reasoning*; exposition, clarification 522 n. *manifestation*; burden of proof, onus.

Adj. *demonstrating*, demonstrative, probative 466 adj. *evidential*; deducible, inferential, consequential, following, consectary 9 adj. *relevant*; apodeictic 532 adj. *affirmative*; convincing, proving; conclusive, categorical, decisive, crucial; heuristic 534 adj. *educational*.

demonstrated, evident, in evidence 466 adj. *evidential*; taken as proved, established, granted, allowed; unconfuted, unrefuted, unanswered; open and shut, unanswerable, undeniable, irrefutable, irrefragable, irresistible, incontrovertible 473 adj. *certain*; capable of proof, demonstrable, testable, discoverable.

Vb. *demonstrate*, prove; show, evince 522 vb. *manifest*; justify 927 vb. *vindicate*; bear out 466 vb. *corroborate*; produce the evidence, document, substantiate, establish, verify 466 vb. *evidence*; infer, deduce, draw, draw a conclusion 475 vb. *reason*; settle the question, set the question at rest, satisfy, reduce to demonstration 473 vb. *make certain*; make out, make out a case, prove one's point, clinch an argument,

have the best of an a. 485 vb. *convince*; avoid confutation, save.

be proved, be demonstrated, prove to be true, emerge, follow, follow of course, stand to reason 475 vb. *be reasonable*; stand, hold water, hold good 494 vb. *be true*.

Adv. *of course*, provedly, undeniably; as already proved; Q.E.D.

See: 9, 461, 466, 473, 475, 485, 494, 522, 532, 534, 927.

479 Confutation

N. *confutation*, refutation, redargution, disproof, invalidation; successful cross-examination, elenchus, exposure; conviction 961 n. *condemnation*; rebuttal, rejoinder, crushing *or* effective r., complete answer 460 n. *answer*; clincher, finisher, knock-down argument, crowning a.; tu quoque argument, retort, repartee 839 n. *witticism*; reductio ad absurdum 851 n. *ridicule*; contradiction, denial, denunciation 533 n. *negation*; exploded argument, proved fallacy 477 n. *sophism*.

Adj. *confuted*, disproved etc. vb.; silenced, exposed, without a leg to stand on; convicted 961 adj. *condemned*; convicted on one's showing, condemned out of one's own mouth; disprovable, refutable, confutable; tending to refutation, refutatory, refutative.

Vb. *confute*, refute, redargue, disprove, invalidate; rebut, retort, have an answer, explain away; negative, deny, contradict 533 vb. *negate*; give the lie to, force to withdraw; prove the contrary, show the fallacy of; cut the ground from under; confound, silence, reduce to s., stop the mouth, shut up, floor, gravel, nonplus; condemn one out of his own mouth; show up, expose; convict 961 vb. *condemn*; convict one of unreason, defeat one's reason; riddle, destroy, explode, demolish; demolish one's arguments; have, have in one's hand, have one on the hip; overthrow, squash, crush, overwhelm 727 vb. *defeat*; riddle the defence, outargue, triumph in argument, have the better of the a., get the better of, score off; parry, avoid the trap; stand, stand up to argument; dismiss, override, sweep

aside, brush a.; brook no denial, affirm the contrary 532 vb. *affirm*.

be confuted,—refuted etc. adj.; fall to the ground, have not a leg to stand on; exhaust one's arguments; have nothing left to say, have no answer.

Adv. *in rebuttal*, in disproof; on the other hand, per contra.

See: 460, 477, 532, 533, 727, 839, 851, 961.

480 Judgment: conclusion

N. *judgment*, judging (see *estimate*); good judgment, discretion 463 n. *discrimination*; bad judgment, indiscretion 464 n. *indiscrimination*; power of judgment, discretionary judgment, arbitrement 733 n. *authority*; arbitration, arbitrage, umpirage; judgment on facts, verdict, finding; penal judgment, sentence 963 n. *punishment*; spoken judgment, pronouncement; act of judgment, decision, adjudication, award; order, ruling; order of the court 737 n. *decree*; interlocutory decree, decree nisi; decree absolute; judgment in appeal, appellate judgment; irrevocable decision; settled decision, res judicata; final judgment, conclusion, conclusion of the matter, result, upshot; moral 496 n. *maxim*; reasoned judgment, ergotism, deduction, inference, corollary, porism 475 n. *reasoning*; vox populi, voting, referendum, plebiscite, poll, casting vote 605 n. *vote*.

estimate, estimation, view 485 n. *opinion*; assessment, valuation, evaluation, calculation 465 n. *measurement*; consideration, ponderation; comparing, contrasting 462 n. *comparison*; transvaluation 147 n. *conversion*; appreciation, appraisal, appraisement; criticism, constructive c. 703 n. *aid*; destructive criticism 702 n. *hindrance*; critique, crit, review, notice, press n., comment, comments, observations, remarks 591 n. *dissertation*; summing up, recapitulation; survey 438 n. *inspection*; inspection report 524 n. *report*; favourable report 923 n. *approbation*; unfavourable report, censure 924 n. *disapprobation*; legal opinion, counsel's o., second o. 691 n. *advice*.

estimator, judge, adjudicator; arbitrator, umpire, referee; surveyor, valuer 465 n. *appraiser*; inspector, inspecting officer,

referendary, reporter, examiner 459 n. *enquirer*; counsellor 691 n. *adviser*; censor, critic, reviewer, commentator 591 n. *dissertator*; commentator, observer 520 n. *interpreter*; juror, juryman, assessor 957 n. *jury*; voter, elector, constituent 605 n. *electorate*.

Adj. *judicial*, judicious, judgmatic 463 adj. *discriminating*; unbiased, dispassionate 913 adj. *just*; juridical, juristic, arbitral; judicatory, decretal; determinative, conclusive; moralizing, moralistic, sententious; expressive of opinion, censorial; censorious 924 adj. *disapproving*; critical, appreciative; advisory 691 adj. *advising*.

Vb. *judge*, sit in judgment, hold the scales; arbitrate, referee; hear, try, hear the case, try the cause 955 vb. *hold court*; uphold an objection, disallow an o.; rule, pronounce; find, find for, find against; decree, award, adjudge, adjudicate; decide, settle, conclude; confirm, make absolute; pass judgment, deliver j.; sentence, pass s., doom 961 vb. *condemn*; agree on a verdict, return a v., bring in a v.; consider one's vote 605 vb. *vote*; judge well, see straight; deduct, infer 475 vb. *reason*; gather, collect; sum up, recapitulate; moralize 534 vb. *teach*.

estimate, form an e., make an e., measure, calculate, make 465 vb. *gauge*; value, evaluate, appraise; rate, rank; sum up, size up; ween, weet, conjecture, guess 512 vb. *suppose*; cast up, take stock 808 vb. *account*; consider, weigh, ponder, perpend 449 vb. *meditate*; examine, investigate, vet 459 vb. *enquire*; express an opinion, pass an o., report on; commentate, comment, criticize, review, do reviewing 591 vb. *dissert*; survey, pass under review 438 vb. *scan*; censor, censure 924 vb. *disapprove*.

Adv. *sub judice*, under trial, under sentence.

See: 147, 438, 449, 459, 462, 463, 464, 465, 475, 485, 496, 512, 520, 524, 534, 591, 605, 691, 702, 703, 733, 737, 808, 913, 923, 924, 955, 957, 961, 963.

481 Misjudgment: prejudice

N. *misjudgment*, miscalculation, misreckoning, miscomputation, misconception, misconjecture, wrong impression 495 n. *error*;

loose thinking 495 n. *inexactness*; bad judgment, poor j. 464 n. *indiscrimination*; fallibility, gullibility 499 n. *unintelligence*; obliquity of judgment, misconstruction 521 n. *misinterpretation*; wrong verdict, bad v., miscarriage of justice 914 n. *injustice*; overvaluation 482 n. *overestimation*; undervaluation 483 n. *underestimation*; autosuggestion, self-deception, wishful thinking 542 n. *deception*; fool's paradise 513 n. *fantasy*; false dawn, false appearance.

prejudgment, prejudication, foregone conclusion 608 n. *predetermination*; preconception, pre-apprehension, prenotion; parti pris, mind made up; presentiment 476 n. *intuition*; something on the brain, preconceived idea; idée fixe, infatuation, obsession, monomania 503 n. *mania*.

prejudice, prepossession, predilection; partiality, favouritism 914 n. *injustice*; bias, biased judgment, warped j., jaundiced eye; blind spot, blind side, mote in the eye, beam in the e. 439 n. *blindness*; onesidedness, partialism, party spirit 708 n. *party*; partisanship, clannishness, cliquism, esprit de corps; sectionalism, parochialism, provincialism, insularity; odium theologicum 978 n. *sectarianism*; chauvinism, xenophobia, my country right or wrong; snobbishness, class war, class prejudice, race p.; racialism, racism, Aryanism; colour-prejudice, negrophobia; apartheid, segregation 883 n. *seclusion*; intolerance, persecution, anti-semitism 888 n. *hatred*.

narrow mind, narrow-mindedness, narrow views, narrow sympathies; cramped ideas, confined i.; insularity, parochialism, provincialism; closed mind, one-track m.; one-sidedness, over-specialization; legalism, pedantry, donnishness, hypercriticism 735 n. *severity*; bigotry, fanaticism, odium theologicum 602 n. *opiniatry*; legalist, pedant, stickler; freak 504 n. *crank*; faddist 862 n. *perfectionist*; zealot, bigot, fanatic 473 n. *doctrinaire*.

bias, unbalance, disequilibrium 29 n. *inequality*; warp, bent, slant, liability 179 n. *tendency*; angle, point of view, private opinion 485 n. *opinion*; parti pris, mind made up (see *prejudgment*); infatuation, obsession 503 n. *mania*; crankiness, whimsicality, fad, craze, whim, hobby, crotchet 604 n. *caprice*.

Adj. *misjudging*, misconceiving, misinterpreting etc. vb.; miscalculating, in error, out 495 adj. *mistaken*; fallible, gullible 499 adj. *foolish*; wrong, wrong-headed; unseeing 439 adj. *blind*; myopic, purblind, short-sighted 440 adj. *dim-sighted*; misguided, superstitious 487 adj. *credulous*; subjective, unrealistic, visionary, impractical; crankish, faddy, faddish, crotchety, whimsical, cracked 503 adj. *crazed*; besotted, infatuated 887 adj. *enamoured*; haunted, obsessed, eaten up with.

narrow-minded, narrow, confined, cramped; parochial, provincial, insular; pedantic, donnish 735 adj. *severe*; legalistic, literal, literal-minded, unimaginative, matter-of-fact; hypercritical, over-scrupulous, fussy 862 adj. *fastidious*; stiff, unbending 602 adj. *obstinate*; dictatorial, dogmatic 473 adj. *positive*; opinionated, opinionative; self-opinioned, self-conceited 871 adj. *proud*.

biased, viewy; warped, twisted, swayed; jaundiced, embittered; prejudiced, closed: snobbish, clannish, cliquish 708 adj. *sectional*; partisan, one-sided, party-minded 978 adj. *sectarian*; nationalistic, chauvinistic, xenophobic; predisposed, prepossessed, preconceived; prejudging 608 adj. *predetermined*; unreasoning, unreasonable 477 adj. *illogical*; illiberal, intolerant, persecuting 735 adj. *oppressive*; bigoted, fanatic 602 adj. *obstinate*; blinded 439 adj. *blind*; class-prejudiced, colour-p.

Vb. *misjudge*, miscalculate, miscompute, miscount, misestimate 495 vb. *blunder*; undervalue, minimize 483 vb. *underestimate*; overestimate, overvalue 482 vb. *overrate*; guess wrong, misconjecture, misconceive 521 vb. *misinterpret*; overreach oneself, overplay one's hand; reckon without one's host, get the wrong sow by the ear 695 vb. *stultify oneself*; over-specialize, not see the wood for the trees; not see beyond one's nose 499 vb. *be foolish*; fly in the face of facts 477 vb. *reason ill*.

prejudge, forejudge, judge beforehand, prejudicate 608 vb. *predetermine*; prejudice the issue, precondemn; preconceive, presuppose, presume 475 vb. *premise*; rush to conclusions, jump to c., run away with a notion 857 vb. *be rash*.

bias, warp, twist, bend; jaundice, prejudice, fill with p.; prepossess, predispose 178 vb.

influence; infatuate, haunt, obsess 449 vb. *engross*.

be biased,—prejudiced etc. adj.; be one-sided, see one side only, show favouritism, favour one side 914 vb. *do wrong*; lean, favour, take sides, have a down on, be unfair 735 vb. *oppress*; pontificate 473 vb. *dogmatize*; blind oneself to, have a blind side, have a blind spot 439 vb. *be blind*.

See: 29, 178, 179, 439, 440, 449, 464, 473, 475, 476, 477, 482, 483, 485, 487, 495, 499, 503, 504, 513, 521, 542, 602, 604, 608, 695, 708, 735, 857, 862, 871, 883, 887, 888, 914, 978.

482 Overestimation

N. *overestimation*, overestimate, over-enthusiasm, overvaluation 481 n. *misjudgment*; over-statement 546 n. *exaggeration*; boasting 877 n. *boast*; ballyhoo, build-up, crying-up 528 n. *advertisement*; over-praise, fine talking, rodomontade, panegyric, bombast, gush, gas, hot air, much cry and little wool 515 n. *empty talk*; storm in a teacup, much ado about nothing; megalomania, vanity 871 n. *pride*; over-confidence 857 n. *rashness*; egotism 932 n. *selfishness*; over-optimism, optimistic forecast, optimism; pessimism, defeatism 853 n. *hopelessness*; optimist, prisoner of hope 852 n. *hope*; pessimist, calamity prophet, Jonah, defeatist; exaggerator, puffer, barker, advertiser 528 n. *publicizer*.

Adj. *optimistic*, sanguine, over-sanguine, over-confident; high-pitched, over-p.; enthusiastic, over-enthusiastic, raving.

overrated, overestimated, overvalued, overpraised; puffed, puffed-up, cracked-up, cried-up, overdone 546 adj. *exaggerated*.

Vb. *overrate*, overreckon, overestimate; overvalue, overprice 811 vb. *overcharge*; rave, idealize, overprize, overpraise, think too much of; make too much of 546 vb. *exaggerate*; strain, over-emphasize, overstress, overdo, play up, over-strain, overpitch, inflate, magnify 197 vb. *enlarge*; boost, cry up, puff, panegyrize; attach too much importance to, make mountains out of molehills, catch at straws; maximize, make the most of; make the best of, whitewash.

See: 197, 481, 515, 528, 546, 811, 852, 853, 857, 871, 877, 932.

483 Underestimation

N. *underestimation*, underestimate, undervaluation, minimization, minimism; conservative estimate, modest calculation 177n. *moderation*; depreciation 926n. *detraction*; understatement, litotes, meiosis; euphemism 950n. *prudery*; self-depreciation, over-modesty 872n. *humility*; false modesty, mock-m., irony 850n. *affectation*; pessimism 853n. *hopelessness*; futilitarian, pessimist, minimizer.

Adj. *depreciating*, depreciative, depreciatory, pejorative, slighting, belittling, pooh-poohing 926adj. *detracting*; underestimating, minimizing, conservative 177 adj. *moderate*; modest 872adj. *humble*; pessimistic, despairing 853adj. *hopeless*; mock-modest 850adj. *affected*; glozing, euphemistic 541adj. *hypocritical*.
undervalued, underrated, underpriced, insufficiently appreciated, underpraised, unprized, unappreciated; slighted, pooh-poohed 458adj. *neglected*.

Vb. *underestimate*, underrate, undervalue, underprice; mark down, discount 812vb. *cheapen*; depreciate, underpraise, run down, cry d., disparage 926vb. *detract*; slight, pooh-pooh 922vb. *hold cheap*; misprize, not do justice to, do less than justice 481vb. *misjudge*; understate, spare one's blushes; euphemize, gloze; play down, soft-pedal, slur over; make the least of, minimize, minimalize; deflate, cut down to size, make light of, belittle, make no account of, set no store by, think too little of 922vb. *despise*; set at naught, scorn 851vb. *ridicule*.

See: 177, 458, 481, 541, 812, 850, 851, 853, 872, 922, 926, 950.

484 Discovery

N. *discovery*, finding, rediscovery; invention; exploration, speleology, pot-holing; detective instinct, nose, flair 619n. *pursuit*; detection, spotting, espial 438n. *inspection*; radio-location 187n. *location*; dowsing, radiesthesia; ascertainment 473 n. *certainty*; exposure, revelation 522n.

manifestation; illumination, realization, disenchantment; accidental discovery, serendipity; a discovery, an invention, an inspiration; strike, find, trover, treasure-trove; eye-opener 508n. *inexpectation*; solution, explanation 520n. *interpretation*; key, open-sesame 263n. *opener*.
detector, lie-d., sound d., Asdic, sonar; radar; finder, telescopic f. 442n. *telescope*; dowser; discoverer, inventor; explorer 268n. *traveller*; archæologist, speleologist, pot-holer 459n. *enquirer*.

Adj. *discovering*, exploratory 461adj. *experimental*; on the scent, on the track, on the trail, warm, getting w.; near discovery, ripe for detection.

Vb. *discover*, rediscover, invent, explore, find a way 461vb. *experiment*; find out, hit it, have it; strike, hit, hit upon; come upon, happen on, stumble on; meet, encounter 154vb. *meet with*; realize, tumble to, see the truth, see the light, see as it really is, see in its true colours 516vb. *understand*; locate 187vb. *place*; recognize, identify 490vb. *know*; verify, check 473vb. *make certain*; fish up, dig up, unearth, disinter, bring to light 522vb. *manifest*; elicit, worm out, ferret o., smell o.; get wind of 524vb. *be informed*.
detect, expose, show up 522vb. *show*; get at the facts, find a clue, be on the track, be near the truth, be getting warm, see daylight; put one's finger on the spot, hit the nail on the head, saddle the right horse; spot, sight, catch sight of, perceive 438 vb. *see*; sense, trace, pick up; see the cloven hoof, smell a rat; nose, scent, wind, scent out; follow, trace, track down 619vb. *hunt*; set a trap for, trap, catch out 542vb. *ensnare*; make an arrest, announce the discovery of.

Int. eureka!

See: 154, 187, 263, 268, 438, 442, 459, 461, 473, 490, 508, 516, 520, 522, 524, 542, 619.

485 Belief

N. *belief*, act of believing, suspension of disbelief; credence, credit; state of belief, assurance, conviction, persuasion; strong feeling, firm impression; confidence, reliance, dependence on, trust, faith; religious belief 973n. *religious faith*; full

belief, full assurance, plerophory; ignorance of doubt 487n. *credulity*; implicit belief, firm b., fixed b. 473n. *certainty*; obsession, blind belief 481n. *prejudice*; instinctive belief 476n. *intuition*; subjective belief, self-persuasion, self-conviction; hope and belief, expectation, sanguine e. 852n. *hope*; public belief, popular b., common b., public opinion; credibility 471n. *probability*; one's credit, one's troth 929n. *probity*; token of credit, pledge.

creed, formulated belief, credo, what one holds, what one believes; dogma, doxy 976n. *orthodoxy*; precepts, principles, tenets, articles; catechism, articles of faith, credenda; rubric, canon, rule 496n. *maxim*; declaration of faith, professed belief, profession, confession, confession of faith 526n. *disclosure*; doctrine, system, school, ism 449n. *philosophy*; study of creeds, symbolics 973n. *theology*.

opinion, one's opinions, one's conviction, one's persuasion; sentiment, mind, view; point of view, viewpoint, stand, position, angle; impression 818n. *feeling*; conception, concept, thought 451n. *idea*; thinking, way of thinking, way of thought, body of opinions, Anschauung 449n. *philosophy*; assumption, presumption, principle 475n. *premise*; theory, hypothesis 512n. *supposition*; surmise, guess 512n. *conjecture*; conclusion 480n. *judgment*.

Adj. *believing*, holding, maintaining, declaring etc. vb.; confident, assured, reliant, unshaken, secure 473adj. *certain*; sure, cocksure 473adj. *positive*; convinced, persuaded, satisfied, converted, sold on; imbued with, penetrated w., obsessed w., possessed; firm in, wedded to; confiding, trustful, trusting, unhesitating, undoubting, unquestioning, unsuspecting, unsuspicious 487adj. *credulous*; conforming, loyal, pious 976adj. *orthodox*; having opinions, viewy, opinionated 481adj. *biased*.

credible, plausible, believable, tenable, reasonable 469adj. *possible*; likely, to be expected 471adj. *probable*; reliable, trustworthy, trusty; fiduciary, fiducial; worthy of credence, deserving belief, commanding b., demanding b., persuasive, convincing, impressive 178adj. *influential*; trusted, believed; held, maintained; accepted, credited, accredited; supposed, putative, hypothetical 512adj. *suppositional*.

credal, taught, doctrinal, dogmatic, confessional; canonical, orthodox, authoritative, accredited, ex cathedra; of faith, accepted on trust; undeniable, absolute, unshakable 473adj. *undisputed*.

Vb. *believe*, be a believer 976vb. *be orthodox*; credit, put faith in, give faith to; hold, hold for true; maintain, declare 532vb. *affirm*; believe religiously, perceive as true, take for gospel, believe for certain, firmly believe; profess, confess, recite the creed; receive, accept, admit, agree 488vb. *assent*; take on trust, take on credit; swallow, swallow whole 487vb. *be credulous*; take for granted, assume 475vb. *premise*; have no doubt, make no d., cast doubt away, know for certain, be sold on, be obsessed with 473vb. *be certain*; rest assured, be easy in one's mind about, be secure in the belief, rest in the b.; have confidence in, confide, trust, rely on, depend on, take one at his word; give one credit for, pin one's faith on, pin one's hopes on; have faith in, believe in, swear by, reckon on, count on, calculate on; be told, understand, know 524vb. *be informed*; come to believe, be converted; realize 484vb. *discover*; take as proven, grant, allow.

opine, think, conceive, fancy, ween, trow; have a hunch, surmise, guess 512vb. *suppose*; suspect, rather s.; be under the impression, have the i. 818vb. *feel*; deem, esteem, apprehend, assume, presume, take it, hold; embrace an opinion, adopt an o., imbibe an o., get hold of an idea, get it into one's head; have views, have a point of view, view as, take as, regard as, account as, consider as, look upon as, set down for, hold for; hold an opinion, cherish an o., foster an o.; express an opinion, hazard an o. 532vb. *affirm*; change one's opinion 603vb. *recant*.

convince, make believe, assure, persuade, satisfy; make realize, bring home to; make confident, restore one's faith; convert, win over, bring o., bring round, wean from; bring to the faith, evangelize, spread the gospel; propagate a belief, propagandize, indoctrinate 534vb. *teach*; cram down one's throat; sell an idea to, put over, put across, possess one's mind

with; gain one's confidence, sway one's belief 178 vb. *influence*; compel belief, extort b.; obsess, haunt, mesmerize, hypnotize; convince oneself, be sold on.
be believed, be widely b., be received; go down, go down well, be swallowed; produce conviction, carry c.; find credence, pass current, pass for truth, capture belief, take hold of the mind, possess the m., dominate the m.
Adv. *credibly*, believably, supposedly, to the best of one's knowledge and belief; faithfully, on faith, on trust, on authority; on the strength of, on the evidence of, as warranted.
See: 178, 449, 451, 469, 471, 473, 475, 476, 480, 481, 484, 487, 488, 496, 512, 524, 526, 532, 534, 603, 818, 852, 929, 973, 976.

486 Unbelief. Doubt

N. *unbelief*, non-belief, disbelief, incredulity, discredit; disagreement 489 n. *dissent*; inability to believe, agnosticism; denial, denial of assent 533 n. *negation*; contrary belief, conviction to the contrary 704 n. *opposition;* blank unbelief, unfaith, want of faith; infidelity, misbelief, miscreance 977 n. *heresy*; atheism, nullifidianism 974 n. *irreligion*; derision, scorn, mockery 851 n. *ridicule*; change of belief, loss of faith, reversal of opinion, retraction 603 n. *recantation*; incredibility, implausibility 472 n. *improbability.*
doubt 474 n. *dubiety*; half-belief, critical attitude, hesitation, wavering, uncertainty; misdoubt, misgiving, gaingiving, distrust, mistrust; suspiciousness, scrupulosity; settled doubt, thorough d., scepticism, pyrrhonism; reserve, reservation 468 n. *qualification*; demur, objection 704 n. *opposition*; scruple, qualm, suspicion 854 n. *fear*; jealousness 911 n. *jealousy.*
unbeliever, no believer, disbeliever; misbeliever, infidel, miscreant 977 n. *heretic*; atheist 974 n. *irreligionist*; sceptic, pyrrhonist, agnostic; doubter, doubting Thomas; dissenter 489 n. *dissentient*; lapsed believer, retractor, recanter 603 n. *tergiversator*; denier 533 n. *negation*; absolute disbeliever, dissenter from all creeds, nullifidian; scoffer, mocker, scorner 926 n. *detractor.*

Adj. *unbelieving*, disbelieving, incredulous, sceptical; misbelieving, miscreant, infidel; unfaithful, lapsed 603 adj. *tergiversating*; doubtful, hesitating, wavering 474 adj. *doubting*; suspicious, shy, shy of 854 adj. *nervous*; over-suspicious 911 adj. *jealous*; slow to believe, distrustful, mistrustful; inconvincible, impervious, hard to convince; nullifidian, creedless.
unbelieved, disbelieved, discredited, exploded; distrusted, mistrusted etc. vb.; incredible, unbelievable 470 adj. *impossible*; inconceivable, unimaginable, staggering 864 adj. *wonderful*; hard to believe, hardly credible; untenable, undeserving of belief, unworthy of credit; open to suspicion, open to doubt, unreliable, suspect, suspicious, questionable, disputable 474 adj. *uncertified*; so-called, pretended.
Vb. *disbelieve*, be incredulous, find hard to believe, explain away, discredit, refuse credit, greet with scepticism, withhold assent, disagree 489 vb. *dissent*; mock, scoff at 851 vb. *ridicule*; deny, deny outright 533 vb. *negate*; refuse to admit, ignore; change one's belief, retract, lapse, relapse 603 vb. *recant*; believe amiss, misbelieve.
doubt, half believe 474 vb. *be uncertain*; demur, object, cavil, question, scruple, boggle, stick at, have reservations 468 vb. *qualify*; pause, stop and consider, hesitate, waver 601 vb. *be irresolute*; treat with reserve, distrust, suspect, have fears 854 vb. *be nervous*; be shy of, shy at; oe sceptical, doubt the truth of, take leave to doubt; have questions, have one's doubts, cherish d., cherish scruples; entertain suspicions, smell a rat, scent a fallacy, see the cloven hoof; hold back, not go all the way 598 vb. *be loth.*
cause doubt, cast d., raise questions; involve in suspicion, render suspect; discredit 926 vb. *defame*; shake, shake one's faith, undermine one's belief; stagger, startle 508 vb. *surprise*; pass belief 472 vb. *be unlikely*; argue against, deter, tempt 613 vb. *dissuade*; impugn, attack 479 vb. *confute*; keep one guessing 517 vb. *be unintelligible.*
Adv. *incredibly*, unbelievably; in utter disbelief.
doubtfully, hesitatingly, cum grano salis, with a pinch of salt.

See: 468, 470, 472, 474, 479, 489, 508, 517, 533, 598, 601, 603, 613, 704, 851, 854, 864, 911, 926, 974, 977.

487 Credulity

N. *credulity*, credulousness; simplicity, gullibility, cullibility; rash belief, uncritical acceptance 485 n. *belief*; will to believe, blind faith, unquestioning belief, gross credulity 612 n. *persuasibility*; infatuation, dotage; self-delusion, self-deception, wishful thinking; superstition, blind reasoning 481 n. *misjudgment*; one's blind side 456 n. *inattention*; bigotry, fanaticism 602 n. *opiniatry*; hyperorthodoxy 83 n. *conformity*; credulous person, simpleton, sucker, gull, pigeon 544 n. *dupe.*

Adj. *credulous*, believing, persuasible, amenable; hoaxable, easily taken in, easily deceived 544 adj. *gullible*; naive, simple, green; childish, silly, stupid 499 adj. *foolish;* over-credulous, over-trustful, over-confident; doting, infatuated; obsessed; superstitious 481 adj. *misjudging*; confiding, trustful, unsuspecting.

Vb. *be credulous*, be easily persuaded; think wishfully 477 vb. *reason ill*; follow implicitly, believe at the first word, take the first suggestion, fall for, take on trust, take for granted, take for gospel 485 vb. *believe*; take the bait, swallow, swallow anything, swallow whole, swallow hook, line and sinker; run away with an idea, run away with a notion, rush to a conclusion; think the moon is made of green cheese, take the shadow for the substance; catch at straws, hope eternally; have no judgment, dote 481 vb. *misjudge.*

See: 83, 456, 477, 481, 485, 499, 544, 602, 612.

488 Assent

N. *assent*, yes, yea, amen; hearty assent; welcome; agreement, concurrence 758 n. *consent*; acceptance, agreement in principle 597 n. *willingness*; acquiescence 721 n. *submission*; acknowledgment, recognition, realization; no denial, admission, clean breast, plea of guilty, self-condemnation 939 n. *penitence*; confession, avowal 526 n. *disclosure*; declaration of faith, profession 532 n. *affirmation*; sanction, nod, O.K., imprimatur, green light 756 n. *permission*; approval 923 n. *approbation*; concurrent testimony, accordance, corroboration 466 n. *evidence*; confirmation, verification 478 n. *demonstration*; validation, ratification; authentication, certification, endorsement, seal, signature, mark, cross; visa, pass 756 n. *permit*; stamp, rubber s. 547 n. *label*; favour, sympathy 706 n. *co-operation*; support 703 n. *aid*; assentation 925 n. *flattery.*

concensus, consentience, same mind 24 n. *agreement*; concordance, harmony 710 n. *concord*; unanimity, solid vote, general consent, common c., universal agreement, universal testimony; consentaneity, popular belief, public opinion, vox populi, general voice; chorus, single voice; likemindedness, thinking alike, mutual sympathy, two minds with but a single thought 18 n. *similarity*; bipartisanship, inter-party agreement; bargain 765 n. *compact.*

assenter, follower 83 n. *conformist*; fellow-traveller, co-operator 707 n. *collaborator*; assentator, yes-man 925 n. *flatterer*; the ayes, consentient voice, willing voter; cheerer, acclaimer 923 n. *commender*; upholder, supporter, active s., abettor 703 n. *aider*; seconder, assentor 707 n. *patron*; ratifier, authenticator; subscriber, endorser 765 n. *signatory*; party, consenting p., covenanter; confessor, professor, declarant.

Adj. *assenting*, assentient 758 adj. *consenting*; consentient, concurrent, party to 24 adj. *agreeing*; fellow-travelling, aiding and abetting, collaborating 706 adj. *co-operative*; inclined to assent, assentaneous; likeminded, sympathetic, welcoming 880 adj. *friendly*; consentaneous 710 adj. *concordant*; unanimous, solid, with one voice, in chorus; acquiescent 597 adj. *willing*; delighted 824 adj. *pleased*; allowing, granting 756 adj. *permitting*; sanctionary, ratificatory; not opposed, conceding.

assented, acquiesced in, voted, carried, carried by acclamation, carried nem. con., agreed on all hands; unopposed, unanimous; uncontradicted, unquestioned, uncontested, unchallenged, uncontroverted 473 adj. *undisputed*; admitted, granted,

conceded 756 adj. *permitted*; ratified, confirmed, signed, sealed; uncontroversial, non-party, bipartisan.

Vb. *assent*, concur, agree with 24 vb. *agree*; welcome, hail, cheer, acclaim 923 vb. *applaud*; agree on all points, accept in toto, go all the way with, have no reservations 473 vb. *be certain*; accept, agree in principle, like the idea; not deny, concede, admit, acknowledge, grant, allow 475 vb. *be reasonable*; admit the charge, plead guilty, avow 526 vb. *confess*; signify assent, nod a., nod, say aye, say yes, agree to, give one's assent, yield a. 758 vb. *consent*; sanction 756 vb. *permit*; ratify (see *endorse*); coincide in opinion, voice the same o., enter into another's o., chime in with, echo, ditto, say amen, say hear hear; say the same, chorus; defer to 920 vb. *respect*; be a yes-man, rubber-stamp 925 vb. *flatter*; reciprocate, sympathize 880 vb. *be friendly*; accede, adhere, side with 708 vb. *join a party*; collaborate, go along with, travel w., strike in w. 706 vb. *co-operate*; tolerate (see *acquiesce*); covenant, agree upon, close with, have a mutual agreement 765 vb. *contract*.

acquiesce, not oppose, accept, abide by 739 vb. *obey*; tolerate, not mind, put up with, suffer, endure; sign on the dotted line, toe the l. 721 vb. *submit*; yield, defer to, withdraw one's objections; let the ayes have it, allow 756 vb. *permit*; let it happen, look on 441 vb. *watch*; go with the stream, swim with the s., float with the current, join in the chorus, follow the fashion, run with the pack 83 vb. *conform*.

endorse, second, support, vote for, give one's vote to 703 vb. *patronize*; subscribe to, attest 547 vb. *sign*; seal, stamp, rubber-stamp, confirm, ratify, sanction 758 vb. *consent*; authenticate 473 vb. *make certain*; countersign.

Adv. *consentingly*, willingly, with all one's heart, agreeably; by consent, in full agreement, all the way, on all points.

unanimously, with one accord, with one voice, with one consent, in chorus, to a man, nem. con.; by show of hands, by acclamation.

Int. amen! amen to that! hear, hear! aye, aye! so be it! good! well! very well! well and good! as you say! you said it! just so! how true! yes indeed! granted! yes.

See: 18, 24, 83, 441, 466, 473, 475, 478, 526, 532, 547, 597, 703, 706, 707, 708, 710, 721, 739, 756, 758, 765, 824, 880, 920, 923, 925, 939.

489 Dissent

N. *dissent*, amicable dissent, agreement to disagree; dissidence, difference, the dissidence of dissent, confirmed opposition 704 n. *opposition*; dissentience, no brief for; difference of opinion, diversity of o., cleavage of o., dissentient voice, contrary vote, disagreement, discordance, controversy 709 n. *dissension*; party feeling, party spirit, faction 708 n. *party*; popular clamour 891 n. *anger*; disaffection 829 n. *discontent*; dissatisfaction, disapproval 924 n. *disapprobation*; repudiation 607 n. *rejection*; protestantism, non-conformism, schism 978 n. *sectarianism*; withdrawal, secession 621 n. *relinquishment*; hartal, walk-out 145 n. *strike*; reluctance 598 n. *unwillingness*; recusancy 738 n. *disobedience*; non-compliance 769 n. *non-observance*; denial, non-consent 760 n. *refusal*; contradiction 533 n. *negation*; recantation, retraction 603 n. *tergiversation*; dubitation 486 n. *doubt*; cavilling, demur, objection, demurrer, reservation 468 n. *qualification*; protest, expostulation, protestation, hostile demonstration 762 n. *deprecation*; challenge 711 n. *defiance*; passive resistance, non-cooperation 738 n. *sedition*.

dissentient, objector, caviller, critic 926 n. *detractor*; interrupter, heckler, obstructor 702 n. *hinderer*; dissident, dissenter, protester, recusant, non-juror, protestant 84 n. *nonconformist*; sectary, sectarian 978 n. *sectarist*; separatist, seceder 978 n. *schismatic*; rebel 738 n. *revolter*; grouser 829 n. *malcontent*; odd man out, minority; splinter-group, cave, faction 708 n. *party*; the noes, the opposition 704 n. *opposition*; non-cooperator, conscientious objector, non-juror, passive resister 705 n. *opponent*; challenger, agitator, firebrand, revolutionary 149 n. *revolutionist*; recanter, apostate 603 n. *tergiversator*.

Adj. *dissenting*, dissentient, differing, dissident 709 adj. *quarrelling*; agnostic, sceptical, unconvinced, unconverted 486 adj. *unbelieving*; separatist, schismatic 978

adj. *sectarian*; non-conformist 84 adj. *unconformable*; malcontent, dissatisfied 829 adj. *discontented*; recanting, apostate 603 adj. *tergiversating*; unassenting, un-consenting, not consenting 760 adj. *refusing*; protesting 762 adj. *deprecatory*; non-juring, recusant, non-compliant 769 adj. *non-observant*; disinclined, loth, reluctant 598 adj. *unwilling*; obstructive 702 adj. *hindering*; challenging 711 adj. *defiant*; resistant 704 adj. *opposing*; in-tolerant, persecuting 735 adj. *oppressive*. *unadmitted*, unacknowledged, negatived, denied 533 adj. *negative*; out of the ques-tion, disallowed 757 adj. *prohibited*.

Vb. *dissent*, differ, agree to d. 25 vb. *disagree*; disagree in opinion, beg to differ, make bold to d., combat an opinion, take one up on 479 vb. *confute*; demur, enter a demurrer, object, raise objections, cavil, boggle, scruple 468 vb. *qualify*; protest, raise one's voice against, demonstrate a. 762 vb. *deprecate*; resist 704 vb. *oppose*; challenge 711 vb. *defy*; be unwilling, show reluctance 598 vb. *be loth*; with-hold assent, will otherwise, say no, shake one's head 760 vb. *refuse*; shrug one's shoulders 860 vb. *be indifferent*; disallow 757 vb. *prohibit*; negative, con-tradict 533 vb. *negate*; repudiate, hold no brief for, not defend; have no notion of, never intend to 607 vb. *reject*; look askance at, not hold with, revolt at the idea 924 vb. *disapprove*; go one's own way, secede, withdraw 621 vb. *relinquish*; recant, retract 603 vb. *apostatize*; argue, wrangle, bicker 709 vb. *quarrel*.

Adv. *no*, on the contrary; at issue with, at variance w.; under protest.

Int. God forbid! not on your life! ask me another! tell that to the marines! never again! not so but far otherwise!

See: 25, 84, 145, 149, 468, 479, 486, 533, 598, 603, 607, 621, 702, 704, 705, 708, 709, 711, 735, 738, 757, 760, 762, 769, 829, 860, 891, 924, 926, 978.

490 Knowledge

N. *knowledge*, ken; knowing, cognition, cognizance, recognition, realization; in-tellection, apprehension, comprehension, perception, understanding, grasp, mastery 447 n. *intellect*; conscience, consciousness, awareness; precognition 510 n. *foresight*; illumination, lights, enlightenment, in-sight 498 n. *wisdom*; acquired knowledge, learning, lore (see *erudition*); experience, practical e., acquaintance, acquaintance-ship, familiarity, intimacy; private know-ledge, privity, being in the know, sharing the secret 524 n. *information*; public knowledge, notoriety, common know-ledge, open secret 528 n. *publicity*; com-plete knowledge, omniscience; partial knowledge, intimation, sidelight, glimpse, glimmering, inkling, suggestion 524 n. *hint*; suspicion, scent; sensory knowledge, impression 818 n. *feeling*; self-knowledge, introspection; detection, clue 484 n. *dis-covery*; specialism, expert knowledge, know-how, expertise 694 n. *skilfulness*; half-knowledge, semi-ignorance, smat-tering 491 n. *sciolism*; knowability, know-ableness, cognizability, recognizability 516 n. *intelligibility*; science of know-ledge, theory of k., epistemology.

erudition, lore, wisdom, scholarship, letters, literature 536 n. *learning*; acquired know-ledge, general k., practical k., empirical k., experimental k.; academic knowledge, professional k., encylopædic k., universal k., pansophy; solid learning, deep l., pro-found learning; small l., superficial l., smattering, dilettantism 491 n. *sciolism*; reading, wide r., desultory r.; book-learning, bookishness, bibliomania; ped-antry, donnishness; information, precise i., varied i., general i.; mine of informa-tion, encyclopædia 589 n. *library*; depart-ment of learning, faculty 539 n. *academy*.

culture, letters 557 n. *literature*; the humani-ties, the arts; education, instruction 534 n. *teaching*; liberal education, scientific e., self-e., self-instruction; civilization, culti-vation, cultivation of the mind; sophisti-cation, acquirements, acquisitions, attain-ments, accomplishments, proficiency, mastery.

science, exact s., natural s., etiology, meta-science; natural philosophy, experimental p.; scientific knowledge, systematic k., progressive k., accurate k., verified k., body of k., organized k., technology; tree of knowledge, circle of the sciences, ologies and isms.

Adj. *knowing*, all-k., encyclopædic, omnis-cient 498 adj. *wise*; apprehensive, cogniz-ant, cognitive 447 adj. *mental*; conscious,

aware 455 adj. *attentive*; alive to, sensible of 819 adj. *sensitive*; experienced, no stranger to, at home with, acquainted, familiar with 610 adj. *habituated*; intimate, privy to, sharing the secret, in the know, behind the scenes 524 adj. *informed*; fly, canny, shrewd 498 adj. *intelligent*; conversant, practised, versed in, proficient 694 adj. *expert.*

instructed, briefed, primed, made acquainted, informed of 524 adj. *informed*; taught, trained, bred to; clerkly, lettered, literate; scribal, literary; schooled, educated, well-e.; learned, book-l., book-wise, bookish; erudite, scholarly; read in, well-read, widely-r., deep-r., well-informed, knowledgable; donnish, scholastic, pedantic; highbrow, intellectual, cultured, cultivated, sophisticated; forward in, strong in, well-qualified; professional, specialized 694 adj. *expert.*

known, cognized, perceived, seen, heard; ascertained, verified 473 adj. *certain*; realized, understood; discovered, explored; noted, celebrated, famous 866 adj. *renowned*; no secret, public, notorious 528 adj. *well-known*; familiar, intimate, dear; too familiar, hackneyed, trite; proverbial, household, commonplace, corny 610 adj. *habitual*; current, prevalent 79 adj. *general*; memorized, known by heart, learnt off, learned by rote, well-conned, well-scanned 505 adj. *remembered*; knowable, cognizable, cognoscible; teachable, discoverable 516 adj. *intelligible.*

Vb. *know*, ken, wot, wot of, ween, wit; have knowledge, be acquainted; apprehend, conceive, catch, grasp, twig, click, have, take 516 vb. *understand*; know entirely, possess, comprehend; come to know, realize; get to know, acquaint oneself, familiarize o.; know again, recognize; know the value, appreciate; be conscious of, be aware, have cognizance, be cognizant 447 vb. *cognize*; discern 463 vb. *discriminate*; perceive 438 vb. *see*; examine, study 438 vb. *scan*; go over, mull, con 455 vb. *be attentive*; know well, know full w., be thoroughly acquainted with, see through, read one like a book, know inside out, know down to the ground; know for a fact 473 vb. *be certain*; know of, have knowledge of, know something; be in the know, be in the secret, have the

low-down 524 vb. *be informed*; know by heart, know by rote 505 vb. *memorize*; know backwards, have it pat, have at one's finger tips, be master of, be expert in 694 vb. *be expert*; have some knowledge of, smatter 491 vb. *not know*; experience, know by e., learn one's lesson 536 vb. *learn*; know all the answers, be omniscient; know what's what, know what to do, see one's way, know one's way about 498 vb. *be wise.*

be known, become k., come to one's knowledge, be brought to one's notice 455 vb. *attract notice*; lie within one's cognizance, be knowable, be public, have no secrets 528 vb. *be published.*

Adv. *knowingly*, with knowledge; learnedly, scientifically.

See: 79, 438, 447, 455, 463, 473, 484, 491, 498, 505, 510, 516, 524, 528, 534, 536, 539, 557, 589, 610, 694, 818, 819, 866.

491 Ignorance

N. *ignorance*, unknowing, nescience; lack of news, no word of; unawareness, unconsciousness 375 n. *insensibility*; incognizance, non-recognition, non-realization; incomprehension, incapacity, backwardness 499 n. *unintelligence*; inappreciation, Philistinism 439 n. *blindness*; obstacle to knowledge, obscurantism; false knowledge, superstition 495 n. *error*; blind ignorance, abysmal i., crass i., pit of i.; lack of knowledge, no science; lack of education, uneducation, no schools; untaught state, blankness, blank mind, tabula rasa; unacquaintance, unfamiliarity, inexperience, lack of experience, greenness, rawness; gaucherie, awkwardness; inexpertness, inexpertise, laymanship 695 n. *unskilfulness*; innocence, simplicity, naïveté 699 n. *artlessness*; nothing to go on, lack of information, general ignorance, anybody's guess, bewilderment 474 n. *uncertainty*; moral ignorance, unwisdom 499 n. *folly*; darkness, benightedness, unenlightenment; savagery, heathenism, paganism 982 n. *idolatry*; Age of Ignorance, jahiliyya; imperfect knowledge, semi-ignorance (see *sciolism*); ignorant person, illiterate 493 n. *ignoramus*; layman, non-expert 697 n. *bungler*; obscurantist; Philistine.

unknown thing, obstacle to knowledge; unknown quantity, matter of ignorance; Dark Ages, prehistory 125 n. *antiquity*; sealed book, Greek; terra incognita, unknown country, unexplored ground, virgin soil; dark horse, enigma, mystery 530 n. *secret*; unidentified body; unknown person, Mr. X., anonymity 562 n. *no name*.

sciolism, smattering, a little learning; glimmering, glimpse, half-glimpse 524 n. *hint*; vagueness, half-knowledge 495 n. *inexactness*; unreal knowledge 495 n. *error*; superficiality 212 n. *shallowness*; affectation of knowledge, shallow profundity, pedantry, quackery, charlatanism, charlatanry 850 n. *affectation*; smatterer 493 n. *sciolist*.

Adj. *ignorant*, nescient, unknowing, blank; incognitive, unrealizing; in ignorance, unweeting, unwitting; unaware, unconscious 375 adj. *insensible*; unhearing, unseeing; unfamiliar with, unacquainted, a stranger to, not at home with; in the dark (see *uninstructed*); reduced to guessing, mystified 474 adj. *uncertain*; bewildered, confused, at one's wits' end; clueless, blindfolded 439 adj. *blind*; groping, tentative 461 adj. *experimental*; lay, amateurish, non-professional, unqualified, inexpert 695 adj. *unskilful*; unversed, not conversant, inexperienced, uninitiated, green, raw; innocent of, guiltless 935 adj. *innocent*; naive, simple 699 adj. *artless*; knowing no better, gauche, awkward; without the light, unenlightened, benighted; savage, uncivilized; pagan, heathenish 982 adj. *idolatrous*; backward, dull, dense, dumb 499 adj. *unintelligent*; foolish 499 adj. *unwise*; obscurantist, unscientific; dark, superstitious, pre-scientific 481 adj. *misjudging*; old-fashioned, behind the age, behind the times 125 adj. *retrospective*; unretentive, forgetting 506 adj. *forgetful*; regardless 456 adj. *inattentive*; wilfully ignorant, indifferent 454 adj. *incurious*.

uninstructed, unbriefed, uninformed, unapprized, not told, no wiser, kept in the dark; not rightly informed, misinformed, mistaught, misled, hoodwinked; not fully informed, ill-i., vague, vague about 474 adj. *uncertain*; unschooled, untaught, untutored, untrained; unlettered, illiterate, uneducated; unlearned, bookless,

without arts, without letters; uncultivated, uncultured, low-brow; inerudite, unscholarly, unbookish, unread, Philistine; simple, dull, dense, dumb (see *ignorant*).

unknown, unbeknown, untold, unheard; unspoken, unsaid, unuttered; unbeheld, unseen, never seen 444 adj. *invisible*; hidden, veiled 525 adj. *concealed*; unrecognized 525 adj. *disguised*; unapprehended, unrealized, unperceived; unexplained 517 adj. *unintelligible*; dark, enigmatic, mysterious 523 adj. *occult*; strange, new, unfamiliar, unprecedented; unnamed 562 adj. *anonymous*; unidentified, unclassified, uninvestigated; undiscovered, unexplored, uncharted, unplumbed, unfathomed; untried, untested; virgin, novel 126 adj. *new*; unknowable, incognizable, undiscoverable; unforeseeable, unpredictable 124 adj. *future*; unknown to fame, inconspicuous, obscure, humble 639 adj. *unimportant*; lost, missing 190 adj. *absent*; out of mind 506 adj. *forgotten*.

smattering, sciolistic; unqualified, quack 850 adj. *affected*; half-educated, half-learned, half-baked, semi-literate, semi-educated; half-instructed, knowing half one's brief; shallow, superficial, dilettante, dabbling, coquetting.

Vb. *not know*, be ignorant, be in the dark, lack information, have nothing to go on; be innocent of, be green, know no better; know not, wist not, cannot say 582 vb. *be taciturn*; have no conception, have no notion, have no clue, have no idea, have not the remotest i., can only guess, be reduced to guessing 512 vb. *suppose*; know nothing of, be in a state of nescience, wallow in ignorance; not hear 416 vb. *be deaf*; have a film over one's eyes, not see 439 vb. *be blind*; not know what to make of 474 vb. *be uncertain*; not know the first thing about, have everything to learn 695 vb. *be unskilful*; not know chalk from cheese 464 vb. *not discriminate*; misunderstand 517 vb. *not understand*; misconstrue 481 vb. *misjudge*; half know, know a little, smatter, dabble in, coquette with; half glimpse, guess, suspect, wonder 486 vb. *doubt*; unlearn 506 vb. *forget*; lack interest 454 vb. *be incurious*; refuse to know, ignore 458 vb. *disregard*; make ignorant, unteach 535 vb. *misteach*; keep in the dark, mystify 525 vb. *keep secret*; profess

ignorance, shrug one's shoulders 860 vb. *be indifferent*; want to know, ask 459 vb. *enquire*; grope, fumble 461 vb. *be tentative*.

Adv. *ignorantly*, in ignorance, unawares; unconsciously; unlearnedly, amateurishly, unscientifically.

See: 124, 125, 126, 190, 212, 375, 416, 439, 444, 454, 456, 458, 459, 461, 464, 474, 481, 486, 493, 495, 499, 506, 512, 517, 523, 524, 525, 530, 535, 562, 582, 639, 695, 697, 699, 850, 860, 935, 982.

492 Scholar

N. *scholar*, savant, philologer, learned man, man of erudition, man of learning, man of education; don, professor, pedagogue 537 n. *teacher*; doctor, clerk, learned c., scribe, pedant, bookworm; philomath, polyhistor, pantologist, encyclopædist; prodigy of learning, mine of information, walking encyclopædia, talking dictionary; student, serious student 538 n. *learner*; degree-holder, qualified person, professional, specialist 696 n. *proficient*; world of learning, academic circles, clerisy, professoriate.

intellectual, scholastic, schoolman, clerk 449 n. *philosopher*; brain-worker; mastermind, wise man, brain, genius, prodigy 500 n. *sage*; publicist; know-all, brains trust; highbrow, egghead, bluestocking, long-hair; intelligentsia, literati, illuminati, philosophe; man of science, scientist; academist, academician, Immortal; patron of learning, Mæcenas.

collector, connoisseur, dilettante 846 n. *man of taste*; bibliophile, book-collector, bibliomaniac; librarian, curator 749 n. *keeper*; antiquary 125 n. *antiquarian*; numismatist, philatelist, stamp-collector; collector of words, compiler, lexicographer, glossographer, philologist, etymologist 557 n. *linguist*.

See: 125, 449, 500, 537, 538, 557, 696, 749, 846.

493 Ignoramus

N. *ignoramus*, know-nothing, illiterate, no scholar, lowbrow; duffer, wooden spoon, pudding head, numskull 501 n. *dunce*;

blockhead, goof, goose, moron 501 n. *fool*; greenhorn, novice, raw recruit, griffin, lubber 538 n. *beginner*; simpleton, babe, innocent 544 n. *dupe*; unteachable person, obscurantist.

sciolist, smatterer, half-scholar, pedant 500 n. *wiseacre*; dabbler, dilettante; quack, charlatan 545 n. *impostor*.

See: 500, 501, 538, 544, 545.

494 Truth

N. *truth*, the very t., verity, sooth, good s.; rightness, intrinsic truth; basic truth, primary premise; consistency, self-c., accordance with fact; honest truth, dinkum, fair d., dinkum oil; plain truth, mere t.; sober truth, stern t.; light of truth, revealed t., gospel t., light, gospel, Bible 975 n. *revelation*; nature 321 n. *world*; facts of life 1 n. *existence*; actuality, historicity 1 n. *reality*; factualness, fact, matter of f. 3 n. *substantiality*; hometruth, candour, frankness 929 n. *probity*; naked truth, unvarnished t., unqualified t., unalloyed t., the t., the whole t. and nothing but the t.; truth-speaking, truthfulness 540 n. *veracity*; appearance of truth, verisimilitude 471 n. *probability*; study of truth, alethiology.

authenticity, validity, realness, genuineness; real Simon Pure, the real thing, the very t., the article, it 13 n. *identity*; no illusion, no fake 21 n. *no imitation*.

accuracy, care for truth, attention to fact; verisimilitude, realism, local colour, 'warts and all'; fine adjustment, sensitivity, fidelity, high f., exactitude, exactness, preciseness, precision, mathematical p., clock-work p.; micrometry 465 n. *measurement*; orthology, mot juste, aptness 24 n. *adaptation*; meticulousness 455 n. *attention*; pedantry, rigidity, rigour, letter of the law 735 n. *severity*; literality, literalness 514 n. *meaning*; true report, ipsissima verba 540 n. *veracity*; chapter and verse, facts, statistics 466 n. *evidence*.

Adj. *true*, veritable; correct, right, so; real, tangible 3 adj. *substantial*; actual, factual, historical; well-grounded, well-founded; well-argued, well-taken 478 adj. *demonstrated*; literal, truthful 540 adj. *veracious*; true to the facts, true to scale, true

to the letter (see *accurate*); categorically true, substantially t.; likely 471 adj. *probable*; ascertained 473 adj. *certain*; unimpeachable 473 adj. *undisputed*; consistent, self-c., logical, reasonable 475 adj. *rational*; very likely 471 adj. *probable*; natural, true to life, true to nature, undistorted, faithful; realistic, objective; unromantic, unideal, down to earth; candid, honest, unflattering.

genuine, no other, as represented; authentic, valid, guaranteed, official, pukka; sound, solid, reliable, honest 929 adj. *trustworthy*; natural, pure, sterling, true as steel, true as touch, Simon Pure; true-bred, legitimate; unadulterated, unsophisticated, unvarnished, uncoloured, undisguised, undistorted, unexaggerated; in one's own name, autonymous.

accurate, exact, precise, definite, defined; well-adjusted, well-pitched, high-fidelity, dead-on 24 adj. *adjusted*; well-aimed, direct, straight, dead-centre 281 adj. *directed*; unerring, undeviating; constant, regular 16 adj. *uniform*; punctual, right, correct, true; never wrong, infallible; close, faithful, representative, photographic; fine, nice, delicate, sensitive; mathematical, scientific, micrometric; micrometer-minded, mathematically exact, scientifically e., religiously e.; scrupulous, punctilious, meticulous, strict, severe 455 adj. *attentive*; word for word, literal; literal-minded, rigid, pedantic, just so 862 adj. *fastidious*.

Vb. *be true*, be so, be just so, happen, exist 1 vb. *be*; hold, hold true, hold good, hold water, stand the test, ring true; conform to fact, prove true, hold together, be consistent; have truth, enshrine a t.; speak truth, omit no detail 540 vb. *be truthful*; look true, seem real, come alive, copy nature 551 vb. *represent*; square, set, trim 24 vb. *adjust*; substantiate 466 vb. *corroborate*; prove 478 vb. *demonstrate*; get at the truth, hit the nail on the head 484 vb. *detect*.

Adv. *truly*, verily, undeniably, really, genuinely, actually, indeed; sic, literally, to the letter, word for word; exactly, accurately, precisely, plumb, right, to an inch, to a hair, to a nicety, to a turn, to a T, just right; in every detail, in all respects.

See: 1, 3, 13, 16, 21, 24, 281, 321, 455, 465, 466, 471, 473, 475, 478, 484, 514, 540, 551, 735, 862, 929, 975.

495 Error

N. *error*, erroneousness, wrongness; silliness 497 n. *absurdity*; untruth, unreality, non-objectivity; falsity, unfactualness, non-historicity 2 n. *non-existence*; errancy, deviation from the truth 282 n. *deviation*; logical error, fallacy, self-contradiction 477 n. *sophism*; credal error, unorthodoxy 977 n. *heterodoxy*; mists of error, wrong ideas, exploded i., superstition; liability to error, fallibility 481 n. *misjudgment*; subjective error, subjectivity, unrealism, wishful thinking, self-deceit, self-deception; misunderstanding, misconception, misconstruction, cross-purposes 521 n. *misinterpretation*; misguidance 535 n. *misteaching*; bad memory, paramnesia, forgetfulness 506 n. *oblivion*; falseness, untruthfulness 541 n. *falsehood*; illusion, hallucination, mirage, trick of sight 440 n. *visual fallacy*; false light, false dawn 509 n. *disappointment*; mental error, delusion 503 n. *insanity*; flattering hope, dream 513 n. *fantasy*; false impression, wrong idea (see *mistake*); wrong tendency, warped notion, prejudice 481 n. *bias*.

inexactness, inexactitude, inaccuracy, imprecision, wildness, non-adjustment; faultiness, systematic error, probable e.; unrigorousness, looseness, laxity, broadness, generalization 79 n. *generality*; loose thinking 477 n. *sophistry*; negligence 456 n. *inattention*; mistiming 118 n. *anachronism*; misstatement, misreport, misinformation, bad reporting 552 n. *misrepresentation*; misquotation (see *mistake*); misuse of language, malapropism 565 n. *solecism*.

mistake, bad idea (see *error*); miscalculation 481 n. *misjudgment*; blunder, botching 695 n. *bungling*; wrong impression, mistaken identity, wrong person, wrong address; glaring error, bloomer, boner, clanger, howler, schoolboy h., screamer, gaffe, bull, Irish b. 497 n. *absurdity*; loose thread, oversight 456 n. *inattention*; mishit, bosh shot, bungle 728 n. *failure*; slip, slip of the pen, lapsus calami, slip of the tongue, lapsus linguæ, malapropism

565 n. *solecism*; clerical error, typist's e.; typographical error, printer's e., misprint, erratum, corrigendum; inadvertency, trip, stumble; bad tactics, wrong step, faux pas; blot, flaw 845 n. *blemish.*

Adj. *erroneous,* erring, wrong; solecistical 565 adj. *ungrammatical*; in error (see *mistaken*); unfactual, unhistorical, mythological 2 adj. *unreal*; aberrant 282 adj. *deviating*; wide of the truth, devoid of t. 543 adj. *untrue*; unsound, unscientific, unreasoned, ill-reasoned, self-contradictory 477 adj. *illogical*; implausible 472 adj. *improbable*; unsubstantiated, uncorroborated, unfounded, ungrounded, disproved 479 adj. *confuted*; exploded 924 adj. *disapproved*; fallacious, misleading 535 adj. *misteaching*; unauthentic, apocryphal, unscriptural, unbiblical; perverted, unorthodox, heretical 977 adj. *heterodox*; untruthful, lying 541 adj. *false*; ungenuine, mock 542 adj. *spurious*; hallucinatory, illusive, delusive, deceptive 542 adj. *deceiving*; subjective, unrealistic, wild, fantastical, visionary 513 adj. *imaginary*; fallible, liable to error, wrongheaded, perverse, prejudiced 481 adj. *biased*; superstitious 491 adj. *ignorant.*

mistaken, wrongly taken, mistook, misunderstood, misconceived, misrepresented, perverted; misread, misprinted; miscalculated, misjudged 481 adj. *misjudging*; in error, misled, misguided; misinformed, ill-informed, deluded 491 adj. *uninstructed*; slipping, blundering 695 adj. *clumsy*; straying, wandering 282 adj. *deviating*; wide, misaimed, misdirected, off-target; at fault, out, off the scent, off the track, off the beam, on the wrong tack, on the wrong scent, off the rails, at sea 474 adj. *uncertain.*

inexact, inaccurate, unstrict; unrigorous, broad, generalized 79 adj. *general*; not factual, incorrect, mis-stated, misreported, garbled; imprecise, erratic, wild, hit or miss; insensitive, clumsy; out, wildly o., maladjusted, ill-adjusted, out of adjustment, out of register; untuned, out of tune, out of gear; unsynchronized, slow, losing, fast, gaining; uncorrected, unrevised, uncompared; faulty, full of faults, flawed, botched, mangled 695 adj. *bungled*; misprinted, misread, misinterpreted, mistranslated 521 adj. *misinterpreted.*

Vb. *err,* commit an error, fall into e., go wrong, mistake, make a m.; be under error, labour under a misapprehension, bark up the wrong tree; be in the wrong, be mistaken; delude oneself, suffer hallucinations 481 vb. *misjudge*; be misled, be misguided; receive a wrong impression, play at cross-purposes, misunderstand, misconceive, misapprehend, get it wrong, get one wrong 517 vb. *not understand*; miscalculate, miscount, misreckon 482 vb. *overrate,* 483 vb. *underestimate*; go astray 282 vb. *stray*; gain, be fast 135 vb. *be early*; lose, be slow, stop 136 vb. *be late.*

blunder, trip, stumble, miss, fault 695 vb. *be clumsy*; slip, slip up, drop a brick, commit a faux pas, put one's foot wrong; betray oneself, give onself away 526 vb. *disclose*; blot one's copy-book, blot, flaw, bungle 728 vb. *fail*; play into one's hands 695 vb. *stultify oneself*; misnumber, miscount 481 vb. *misjudge*; misread, misquote, misprint, mistake the meaning, mistranslate 521 vb. *misinterpret.*

mislead, misdirect, give the wrong address 282 vb. *deflect*; misinform, lead into error, pervert, cause to err, involve in error, steep in e., start a heresy 535 vb. *misteach*; beguile, befool, lead one a dance, lead one up the garden path 542 vb. *deceive*; give a false impression, create a false i., falsify, garble 541 vb. *dissemble*; gloze 925 vb. *flatter.*

See: 2, 79, 118, 135, 136, 282, 440, 456, 472, 474, 477, 479, 481, 482, 483, 491, 497, 503, 506, 509, 513, 517, 521, 526, 535, 541, 542, 543, 552, 565, 695, 728, 845, 924, 925, 977.

496 Maxim

N. *maxim,* apothegm, gnome, adage, saw, proverb, byword, aphorism; dictum, saying, pithy s., stock s., common s., received s., true s., truth; epigram, mot, word, sentence, brocard 839 n. *witticism*; wise maxim, sententious utterance, sage reflection; truism, cliché, commonplace, banality, hackneyed saying, trite remark, glimpse of the obvious, bromide; motto, slogan, catchword; text, sloka, sutra, rule 693 n. *precept*; scholium, comment, note, remark, observation 532 n. *affirmation*; moral, edifying story, pious fiction 979 n.

piety; phylactery, formulary; book of proverbs, collection of sayings.

axiom, self-evident truth, truism; principle, postulate, theorem, formula.

Adj. *aphoristic*, gnomic, sententious, proverbial, moralizing 498 adj. *wise*; epigrammatic, piquant, pithy, packed with sense 839 adj. *witty*; terse, snappy 569 adj. *concise*; enigmatic, oracular 517 adj. *puzzling*; common, banal, trite, hackneyed, commonplace, stock 610 adj. *usual*; axiomatic 693 adj. *preceptive*; phylacteric.

Adv. *proverbially*, as the saying goes, as they say; pithily, in a nutshell; aphoristically, epigrammatically, wittily; by way of moral.

See: 498, 517, 532, 569, 610, 693, 839, 979.

497 Absurdity

N. *absurdity*, height of a., absurdness 849 n. *ridiculousness*; ineptitude, inconsequence 10 n. *irrelevance*; false logic 477 n. *sophistry*; foolishness, silliness, silly season 499 n. *folly*; senselessness, futility, fatuity, skiamachy 641 n. *inutility*; wildness, stultiloquy, stultiloquence; nonsense-verse, amphigory; talking rot, talking through one's hat; rot, rubbish, nonsense, gammon, stuff and nonsense, kibosh, farrago, gibberish, jargon, twaddle 515 n. *silly talk*; rhapsody, romance, romancing, fustian, bombast 546 n. *exaggeration*; Irish bull, Irishism, Hibernicism, malapropism, howler, screamer 495 n. *mistake*; paradox 508 n. *inexpectation*; spoonerism, joke 839 n. *witticism*; pun, equivoque, play upon words 518 n. *equivocalness*; riddle, riddle-me-ree 530 n. *enigma*; quibble, verbal q. 477 n. *sophism*; anticlimax, bathos, descent from the sublime to the ridiculous; sell, swizz, catch 542 n. *trap*.

foolery, antics, fooling about, silliness, asininity, tomfoolery; vagary, whimsey, whimsicality 604 n. *whim*; extravagance, extravaganza, silly symphony, escapade, scrape 700 n. *predicament*; practical joke, monkey trick, piece of nonsense; drollery, comicality 849 n. *ridiculousness*; clowning, buffoonery, burlesque, parody, caricature 851 n. *ridicule*; farce, mummery, pretence

850 n. *affectation*; exhibition 875 n. *ostentation*.

Adj. *absurd*, inept 25 adj. *unapt*; ludicrous, laughable, comical, grotesque 849 adj. *ridiculous*; silly, asinine 499 adj. *foolish*; Pickwickian, nonsensical, senseless 515 adj. *unmeaning*; preposterous, without rhyme or reason 477 adj. *illogical*; wild, egregious, overdone, extravagant 546 adj. *exaggerated*; pretentious 850 adj. *affected*; frantic 503 adj. *frenzied*; fanciful, fantastic 513 adj. *imaginative*; futile, fatuous 641 adj. *useless*; paradoxical 508 adj. *unexpected*; inconsistent 10 adj. *irrelevant*; quibbling 477 adj. *sophistical*; punning 518 adj. *equivocal*; macaronic 43 adj. *mixed*.

Vb. *be absurd*, play the fool, act like a fool, behave like an idiot 499 vb. *be foolish*; fool, fool about, play practical jokes; be a laughing-stock 849 vb. *be ridiculous*; clown, burlesque, parody, caricature, guy 851 vb. *ridicule*; talk like a fool, talk rot, talk through one's hat, jargonize, talk gibberish, gibber 515 vb. *mean nothing*; talk wild, rant, rave 503 vb. *be insane*; rhapsodize, romance 546 vb. *exaggerate*.

See: 10, 25, 43, 477, 495, 499, 503, 508, 513, 515, 518, 530, 542, 546, 604, 641, 700, 839, 849, 850, 851, 875.

498 Intelligence. Wisdom

N. *intelligence*, thinking power, intellectualism 447 n. *intellect*; brains, good b., brain, grey matter, head, headpiece, upper storey; practical headpiece, nous, wit, mother-w., commonsense; lights, understanding, sense, good s., horse s., gumption, know-how; wits, sharp w., ready w., quick thinking, quickness, readiness, esprit; ability, capacity, mental c., mental grasp; mental ratio, calibre, mental c., I.Q.; high I.Q., forwardness, brightness; braininess, cleverness 694 n. *aptitude*; mental gifts, giftedness, attainment, brilliance, talent, genius, highest g.; ideas, inspiration, sheer i. 476 n. *intuition*; brainwave, bright idea 451 n. *idea*.

sagacity, judgment, good j., cool j., discretion, discernment 463 n. *discrimination*; perception, perspicacity, clear thought, clear thinking; acumen, sharpness, acuteness, acuity, penetration; practicality,

practical mind, shrewdness, long-headed-ness; level-headedness, balance 502n. *sanity*; prudence, forethought, far-sighted-ness 510n. *foresight*; subtleness, subtlety, craft, craftiness 698n. *cunning*; vigilance, awareness 457n. *carefulness*; policy, good p., tact, statemanship 688n. *tactics*.

wisdom, ripe w., wise understanding, sapience; grasp of intellect, profundity of thought 449n. *thought*; depth, depth of mind, breadth of m., reach of m., enlargement of m.; experience, life-long e., digested e., ripe e., fund of e., ripe knowledge 490n. *knowledge*; tolerance, enlarged views; right views, soundness; mental poise, mental balance, ballast, sobriety, objectivity, enlightenment.

Adj. *intelligent*, endowed with brains, brainy, clever, forward, bright; brilliant, scintillating, talented, of genius 694adj. *gifted*; capable, able, practical 694adj. *skilful*; apt, ready, quick, quick in the up-take, acute, sharp, sharp-witted, quick-w., nimble-w.; alive, aware 455adj. *attentive*; astute, shrewd, fly, smart, canny, not born yesterday; too clever by half, over-clever, clever-clever; sagacious, provident, prudent, watchful 457n. *careful*; far-sighted, clear-s. 510adj. *foreseeing*; discerning 463adj. *discriminating*; penetrating, perspicacious, penetrating, clear-headed, long-h., hard-h., calculating; subtle, crafty, wily, foxy, artful 698adj. *cunning*; politic, statesmanlike.

wise, sage, sapient; thinking, reflecting 449adj. *thoughtful*; reasoning 475adj. *rational*; highbrow, intellectual, profound, deep, oracular; sound, sensible, reasonable 502adj. *sane*; staid, sober 834adj. *serious*; reliable, responsible 929adj. *trustworthy*; experienced, cool, unflattered, undazzled, unperplexed, unbaffled; balanced, level-headed, realistic, objective; judicious, judgmatical, impartial 913adj. *just*; tolerant, fair-minded, enlightened, unbiased, non-partisan; unfanatical, unbigoted, unprejudiced, unprepossessed, unwarped; broad, broad-minded, latitudinarian; tactful, politic, wise in one's generation 698adj. *cunning*; wise as a serpent, wise as an owl, wise as Solomon, wise as Solon; well-advised, well-considered, well-judged, wisely decided 642adj. *expedient*.

Vb. *be wise,*—intelligent etc. adj.; use one's

wits, use one's head, use one's intelligence; accumulate experience, have a fund of wisdom 490vb. *know*; have brains, show one's metal, scintillate, shine 644vb. *be good*; have a head on one's shoulders, have one's wits about one, see through a brick wall; see with half an eye, see at a glance; know what's what, know how to live, get around; be realistic, be one's age; show foresight 510vb. *foresee*; be prudent, take care 858vb. *be cautious*; grasp, fathom 516vb. *understand*; discern, see through, penetrate 438vb. *see*; distinguish 463vb. *discriminate*; have sense, listen to reason 475vb. *be reasonable*; plan well, be politic 623vb. *plan*; have tact, be wise in one's generation 698vb. *be cunning*; come to one's senses, repent 939vb. *be penitent*.

See: 438, 447, 449, 451, 455, 457, 463, 475, 476, 490, 502, 510, 516, 623, 642, 644, 688, 694, 698, 834, 858, 913, 929, 939.

499 Unintelligence. Folly

N. *unintelligence*, lack of i., want of intellect 448n. *non-intellect*; poverty of intellect, clouded i. 503n. *insanity*; weakness of i., bovine understanding, lack of brains, upper storey to let; feeble-mindedness, low I.Q., low mental age, immaturity, infantilism; mental handicap, retarded brain, backwardness; imbecility, idiocy; stupidity, slowness, dullness, obtuseness, thickheadedness, crassness, denseness; blockishness, sottishness, oafishness, owlishness, stolidity, hebetude 820n. *moral insensibility*; one's weak side, poor head, no brain; incapacity, meanest capacity, incompetence 695n. *unskilfulness*; naivety, simplicity, fallibility, gullibility 481n. *misjudgment*; inanity, vacuity, vacuousness, no depth, superficiality 212 n. *shallowness*; unreadiness, delayed reaction; impercipience, tactlessness, awkwardness, gaucherie 464n. *indiscrimination*.

folly, foolishness, extravagance, eccentricity 849n. *ridiculousness*; fool's idea, fool's trick, act of folly 497n. *foolery*; nugacity, trifling, levity, frivolity, giddiness 456n. *inattention*; lip-wisdom, unreason, illogic 477n. *sophistry*; unwisdom, desipience,

ineptitude; fatuity, fatuousness, pointlessness; silliness, asininity; recklessness, wildness, incaution 857n. *rashness*; blind side, obsession, infatuation 481n. *misjudgment*; puerility, boyishness, childishness 130n. *nonage*; second childhood, senility, anility, dotage 131n. *age*; drivelling, babbling, maundering; conceit, empty-headedness 873n. *vanity*.

Adj. *unintelligent*, unintellectual, lowbrow; ungifted, untalented, no genius; incompetent 695adj. *clumsy*; not bright, dull; handicapped, undeveloped, immature; backward, retarded, feeble-minded, moronic, cretinous, imbecile 503adj. *insane*; deficient, wanting, not there, vacant; limited, borné, weak, weak in the upper storey; impercipient, unperceptive, slow, slow in the uptake; stupid, obtuse, dense, crass, gross, heavy, sottish, stolid, bovine, Bœotian, blockish, oafish, doltish, owlish; dumb, dim, dim-witted, dull-w., slow-w., thick-w., beef-w., fat-w., half-w.; thick-skulled, addle-pated, clod-p., muddle-headed, muddy-h., puzzle-h.; lack-brained, half-b., cracked, barmy 503adj. *crazed*; non-understanding, impenetrable, unteachable, impervious; prosaic, literal, matter-of-fact, unimaginative; muddled, addled, wrong-headed, pig-h. 481adj. *misjudging*.

foolish, silly, idiotic, imbecile, asinine, apish; nonsensical, senseless, insensate, fatuous, futile, inane, insulse 497adj. *absurd*; ludicrous, laughable 849adj. *ridiculous*; like a fool, fallible 544adj. *gullible*; simple, naive 699adj. *artless*; inexperienced 491 adj. *ignorant*; tactless, gauche, awkward; soft, wet, soppy, sawney, goody-goody 935adj. *innocent*; gumptionless, gormless; goofy, gawky, sappy, dopy, dizzy, unconscious; childish, babyish, puerile, infantile 132adj. *infantine*; gaga, senile, anile 131adj. *aged*; besotted, fond, doting; amorous, sentimental, spoony 887adj. *enamoured*; dazed, fuddled, maudlin 949 adj. *drunk*; vapouring, babbling, burbling, drivelling, maundering; mindless, witless, brainless (see *unintelligent*); shallow, shallow-minded, shallow-headed, superficial, frivolous, anserine, bird-witted, feather-brained, crack-b., rattle-b., scatter-b. 456adj. *light-minded*; fooling, playing the fool, acting the f., misbehaving, desipient, boyish; eccentric, unstable,

extravagant, wild; scatty, nutty, dotty, daft 503adj. *crazed*.

unwise, unblessed with wisdom, unenlightened; obscurantist, unscientific 491adj. *ignorant*; unphilosophical, unintellectual; unreasoning, irrational 477adj. *illogical*; indiscreet 464adj. *indiscriminating*; injudicious 481adj. *misjudging*; undiscerning, unseeing, unforeseeing, short-sighted 439adj. *blind*; unteachable, insensate; thoughtless 450adj. *unthinking*; uncalculating, impatient 680adj. *hasty*; incautious, reckless 857adj. *rash*; prejudiced, intolerant 481adj. *narrow-minded*; inconsistent, unbalanced, ill-proportioned, penny-wise, pound-foolish; unreasonable, against reason; inept, incongruous, unseemly, improper 643adj. *inexpedient*; ill-advised, ill-judged, miscalculated 495 adj. *mistaken*.

Vb. *be foolish*, maunder, dote, drivel, babble, burble, talk through one's hat 515vb. *mean nothing*; go hay-wire, lose one's wits, take leave of one's senses, go off one's head 503vb. *be insane*; be unintelligent, have no brains, lack b., lack sense; never learn, stay bottom of the class; invite ridicule, look like a fool, look foolish, sit like a block 849vb. *be ridiculous*; make a fool of oneself, play the fool, act the f., act the giddy goat 497vb. *be absurd*; frivol, sow one's wild oats, misbehave 837vb. *amuse oneself*; burn one's fingers 695vb. *stultify oneself*; plunge into error 495vb. *err*; miscalculate 481vb. *misjudge*.

See: 130, 131, 132, 212, 439, 448, 450, 456, 464, 477, 481, 491, 495, 497, 503, 515, 544, 643, 680, 695, 699, 820, 837, 849, 857, 873, 887, 935, 949.

500 Sage

N. *sage*, nobody's fool; wise man, statesman; oracle, elder statesman, counsellor, consultant, expert 691n. *adviser*; genius, master mind; master, mentor, guide, guru, pundit, acharya 537n. *teacher*; rishi, buddha, seer, prophet 511n. *diviner*; yogi, swami, sannyasi 945n. *ascetic*; leading light, shining l., luminary; master spirit, great soul, mahatma; doctor, thinker 449n. *philosopher*; egghead, long

head, highbrow 492n. *intellectual*; wizard 983n. *sorcerer*; magus, magian, Magi, wise men from the East; Solomon, Daniel, second D., Daniel come to judgment, learned judge; Aesop, Nestor, Solon, Seven Sages; Grand Old Man, G.O.M.

wiseacre, know-all, smart aleck; brains trust; witling, wise fool, wise men of Gotham; wisest fool in Christendom.

See: 449, 492, 511, 537, 691, 945, 983.

501 Fool

N. *fool*, Tom fool, Tom o' Bedlam 504n. *madman*; perfect fool, precious f.; ass, donkey, calf; owl, goose, cuckoo, gowk, daw, gull, woodcock, buzzard; mooncalf, idiot, congenital i., born fool, natural, changeling, cretin, moron, imbecile; half-wit, sot, stupid, silly, silly-billy; butt, clown, zany, jester 851n. *laughing-stock*; addle-head, muddle-h., blunderer, incompetent 697n. *bungler*; dizzy, scatterbrains, rattle-head, giddy-h.; trifler 493n. *sciolist*; witling 500n. *wiseacre*; crackpot, eccentric, odd fellow 504n. *crank*; gaffer, old fogy; babbler, burbler, driveller; dotard 133n. *old man*.

ninny, simpleton, simp, Simple Simon; Tom Noddy, charley; tony, gaby, noodle, noddy, nincompoop, moonraker, juggins, muggins, booby, boob, sap, saphead, stiff, big s., stick, poor s., dizzy, dope, gowk, galoot, goof; lubber, greenhorn 538n. *beginner*; wet, drip, milksop, mollycoddle, softy, goody-goody, sawney, soppy; child, babe 935n. *innocent*; butt, mug, flat 544n. *dupe*; gaper, gawker.

dunce, dullard, no conjuror; blockhead, woodenhead, numskull, duffer, dolt, dumb-bell; fathead, thickhead, bonehead, beetle-head, pin-h., dunderhead, blunderhead, muttonhead, bullhead, cabbage-head, chucklehead, jolter-head, jobbernowl; lackwit, lackbrain, dizzard, numps; chump, clot, clod, clod-poll, clod-pate, clod-hopper, oaf, lout, booby, loon, bumpkin; block, stock, stone; ivory, solid i.

See: 133, 493, 500, 504, 538, 544, 697, 851, 935.

502 Sanity

N. *sanity*, saneness, soundness, soundness of mind; reasonableness; rationality, reasonability, reason; balance, mental b.; mental equilibrium; sobriety, common sense; coherence 516n. *intelligibility*; lucidity, lucid interval, lucid moment; normality, proper mind, senses, sober s.; sound mind, mens sana; mental hygiene, mental health.

Adj. *sane*, normal, not neurotic; of sound mind, sound-minded, mentally sound, all there; in one's senses, compos mentis, in one's right mind, in possession of one's faculties; rational, reasonable 498adj. *intelligent*; common-sensical, sober, sober-minded; fully conscious, in one's sober senses; coherent 516adj. *intelligible*; lucid, not wandering, clear-headed; undisturbed, balanced; cool, calculating 480 adj. *judicial*; sane enough, not certifiable.

Vb. *be sane*, have one's wits, keep one's senses, retain one's reason; be of sound mind, become sane, recover one's mind, come to one's senses, sober down, sober up.

make sane, restore to sanity, bring one to his right mind; sober, bring round.

Adv. *sanely*, soberly, lucidly; reasonably, in a reasonable spirit, like a reasonable man.

See: 480, 498, 516.

503 Insanity

N. *insanity*, brain damage, unsoundness of mind, alienation, lunacy, madness, amentia; mental sickness, mental disease; mental instability, intellectual unbalance; psychopathic condition, abnormal psychology; mental derangement, loss of reason, disorder of r., unsound mind, darkened m., troubled brain, clouded b., disordered reason, reason undermined, deranged intellect, mind overthrown; mental decay, senile d., dotage, softening of the brain 131n. *age*; dementia, senile d., presenile d.; mental deficiency, idiocy, congenital i., imbecility, cretinism, morosis, feeblemindedness 499n. *unintelligence*; derangement, aberration 84n. *abnormality*; obsession, craze, fad 481n. *bias*; fanaticism 481n. *prejudice*; alienism, psychiatry, psychotherapy 658n. *therapy*;

mad doctor, alienist, psychiatrist 658 n. *doctor*.

psychopathy, certifiability; psychopathic condition, psychosis; neuropathy, neurosis, psychoneurosis, anxiety neurosis, compulsion n.; nerves, nervous disorder; hysteria, shell-shock; attack of nerves, nervous breakdown, brainstorm; phobia, claustrophobia, agoraphobia, acrophobia, triskaidekaphobia 854 n. *phobia*; the insanities; delusional insanity, paranoia, delusions, hallucinations, lycanthropy; confusion, paraphrenia, katatonia, schizophrenia, split personality, dual p., multiple p.; obsession; frustration; depression, depressed state; manic depression, elation; mania, hypomania; hypochondriasis, hypochondria, pathoneurosis; hyp, melancholia, blues, blue devils 834 n. *melancholy*. See *mania*.

mania, hypomania, megalomania, persecution mania, religious m.; pathomania, kleptomania; homicidal mania, suicidal m.; nymphomania, gamomania, bibliomania, monomania.

frenzy, furore, corybantiasm; rabies, canine madness, hydrophobia; phrenetic condition, paraphronesis, paraphrosyne; ecstasy, delirium, raving; distraction, wandering of the mind 456 n. *abstractedness*; incoherence 517 n. *unintelligibility*; delirium tremens, D.T.'s, jim-jams 949 n. *alcoholism*; epilepsy, fit, paroxysm 318 n. *spasm*; brain fever, cerebral f., calenture of the brain; siriasis, sunstroke; vertigo, dizziness, swimming.

eccentricity, craziness, crankiness, faddishness; queerness, oddness, strange behaviour; oddity, twist, kink, crank, fad 84 n. *abnormality*; a screw loose, a slate l., a tile l., bats in the belfry, rats in the upper storey; obsession, monomania, ruling passion, fixed idea 481 n. *bias*.

madhouse, mental home, mental hospital, nerve h., hospital for mental diseases; asylum, lunatic a., insane a.; Bedlam, Colney Hatch; booby-hatch, loony-bin, nut-house, bug-h., padded cell 658 n. *hospital*.

Adj. *insane*, mad, lunatic, moon-struck, hazy; of unsound mind, not in one's right m., non compos mentis, alienated, bereft of reason, deprived of one's wits, deranged, demented; certifiable, mental;

abnormal, psychologically a., mentally sick, mentally ill, diseased in mind, brain-damaged; psychopathic; psychotic; neurasthenic, neurotic, hysterical; paranoiac, paraphrenic, schizophrenic, schizoid; manic, maniacal; katatonic, depressive, manic-d., elated; hypochondriac, hipped, hippy, hippish 834 adj. *melancholic*; monomaniac; kleptomaniac; claustrophobic; idiotic, imbecile, moronic, cretinous, defective, subnormal, feeble-minded, weak in the head, wanting 499 adj. *unintelligent*; raving mad, horn-m., stark staring m., mad as a hatter, mad as a March hare (see *frenzied*); in an asylum, declared insane, certified.

crazed, wildered in one's wits, wandering, mazed, moidered 456 adj. *abstracted*; not all there, not right in the head; off one's head, round the bend, up the pole; demented, driven mad, maddened, madded (see *frenzied*); unhinged, unbalanced, off one's rocker; bedevilled, pixilated, pixy-led, deluded; infatuated, obsessed, eaten up with, possessed; fond, doting 887 adj. *enamoured*; drivelling, in one's second childhood; brainsick, touched in the head, touched, wanting; idiotic, mad-brained, scatter-brained, shatter-b., crack-brained 499 adj. *foolish*; crackers, scatty, screwy, nutty, nuts, batty, bats, cuckoo, wacky, fruit-cakey, loco; crazy, daft, daffy, dippy, loony, loopy, potty, dotty; cranky, faddy, eccentric, erratic, funny, queer, odd, peculiar 84 adj. *abnormal*; crotchety, whimsical 604 adj. *capricious*; dizzy, vertiginous, giddy 456 adj. *light-minded*.

frenzied, rabid, maddened, madded; horn-mad, furious, foaming at the mouth 891 adj. *angry*; haggard, wild, distraught 456 adj. *distracted*; possessed, possessed with a devil, bedevilled, bacchic, corybantic; frantic, phrenic, demented, like one possessed, beside onself, uncontrollable; berserk, seeing red, running amok 176 adj. *violent*; mast, temporarily insane; epileptic, having fits; delirious, seeing things, raving, rambling, wandering, incoherent, light-headed, fevered, brainsick 651 adj. *sick*.

Vb. *be insane*, — mad, — crazed etc. adj.; have bats in the belfry, have a screw loose; dote, drivel 499 vb. *be foolish*; ramble, wander; babble, rave; corybantiate;

foam at the mouth; be delirious, see things.

go mad, run m., go off one's head, go off one's rocker, go crackers, become a lunatic, have to be certified; lose one's reason, lose one's wits; go berserk, run amok, see red, foam at the mouth, lose one's head 891 vb. *get angry*.

make mad, drive m., send m., drive insane; mad, madden; craze, derange, dement, dementate; send one off his head, send one out of his mind; overthrow one's reason, undermine one's r., turn one's brain; unhinge, unbalance, send one off his rocker; infuriate, make one see red 891 vb. *enrage*; infatuate, possess, obsess; go to one's head, turn one's h. 542 vb. *befool*.

See: 84, 131, 176, 318, 456, 481, 499, 517, 542, 604, 651, 658, 834, 854, 887, 891, 949.

504 Madman

N. *madman*, lunatic, maddy, mental case; bedlamite, Tom o' Bedlam, candidate for Bedlam; screwball, nut, loon, loony; madcap, mad dog; abnormal character, psychopath, psychopathic personality, unstable p., aggressive p., anti-social p., sociopath; hysteric, neurotic, neuropath; psychotic; paranoiac; schizoid; manic-depressive; mænad, bacchante, corybant; raving lunatic, maniac; kleptomaniac, automaniac, pyromaniac, monomaniac, megalomaniac; dipsomaniac 949 adj. *drunkard*; dope addict, dope fiend; drug addict, drug fiend; hypochondriac, melancholic 834 n. *moper*; idiot, congenital i., natural, cretin, moron, mongol, idiot savant 501 n. *fool*.

crank, crackpot, nut, crackbrain, screwball; eccentric, oddity, odd bird, fogy 851 adj. *laughing-stock*; freak, deviationist 84 n. *nonconformist*; fad, faddist, fanatic, extremist, lunatic fringe; fanatico, fan, afficionado, balletomane; seer, dreamer 513 n. *visionary*; rhapsodist, enthusiast; knight-errant, Don Quixote.

See: 84, 501, 513, 834, 851, 949.

505 Memory

N. *memory*, good m., retentivity, retention; tenacious memory, capacious m., trust-

worthy m., correct m., exact m., ready m., prompt m.; collective memory, race m., atavism; tablets of the memory; Mnemosyne.

remembrance, exercise of memory, recollection, recall; commemoration, rememoration, evocation; rehearsal, recapitulation 106 n. *repetition*; memorization, remembering, learning by heart 536 n. *learning*; reminiscence, thoughts of the past, reminiscent vein, retrospection, review, retrospect, hindsight; flash-back, recurrence; afterthought 67 n. *sequel*; regrets 830 n. *regret*; memorabilia, memoirs, reminiscences, recollections; history, narration 590 n. *narrative*; fame, notoriety, place in history 866 n. *famousness*; memoranda, things to be remembered.

reminder, memento, memorial, testimonial, commemoration 876 n. *celebration*; token of remembrance, souvenir, keepsake, autograph; relic, monument, trophy, bust, statue 548 n. *record*; remembrancer, flapper, keeper of one's conscience, prompter; testifier 466 n. *witness*; memorandum, aide-mémoire, note, memorandum book, notebook, diary, engagement d., address book, album, autograph a., photograph a., scrapbook, commonplace-book, prompt b.; leading question, prompt, prompting, suggestion, cue 524 n. *hint*; mnemonic, aid to memory.

mnemonics, mnemotechnics, mnemotechny, art of memory, Pelmanism; mnemonic device, memoria technica, artificial memory, electronic brain; mnemonician, mnemonist.

Adj. *remembered*, recollected etc. vb.; retained, retained in the memory, not forgotten, unforgotten; fresh, fresh in one's memory, green in the remembrance, of recent memory; present to the mind, uppermost in one's thoughts; of lasting remembrance, of blessed memory, missed, regretted; memorable, unforgettable, not to be forgotten; haunting, persistent, undying; deep-rooted, deep-seated, indelible, inscribed upon the mind, lodged in one's m., stamped on one's memory, impressed on one's recollection; embalmed in the memory, kept alive in one's mind; got by heart, memorized 490 adj. *known*.

remembering, mindful, faithful to the memory, keeping in mind, holding in

remembrance; evocative, memorial, commemorative 876adj. *celebrative*; reminiscent, recollecting, anecdotic, anecdotal; unable to forget, haunted, obsessed, plagued; recalling, reminding, mnemonic, prompting, suggesting.

Vb. *remember*, mind, recognize, know again 490vb. *know*; recollect, bethink oneself; not forget, bottle up 666vb. *preserve*; retain, hold in mind, retain the memory of; embalm *or* keep alive in one's thoughts, treasure in one's t., store in one's memories; never forget, be unable to f.; recall, call to mind, think of; reminisce, write one's memoirs; remind oneself, make a note of, keep a memorandum, write it down. See *memorize*.

retrospect, recollect, recall, recapture; reflect, review, think back, think back upon, trace b., retrace, hark back, carry one's thoughts back, cast one's mind b.; bring back to memory, summon up, conjure u., rake up the past, dig up the p., dwell on the p., live in the p.; archaize 125adj. *look back*; rip up old wounds, renew old days, recapture old times; make an effort to remember, rack one's brains to r., flog one's memory.

remind, put one in mind, jog one's memory, refresh one's m., renew one's m.; pluck one by the sleeve 455vb. *attract notice*; drop a hint, prompt, suggest 524vb. *hint*; not allow one to forget, abide in the memory, haunt, obsess; not let sleeping dogs lie, fan the embers 821vb. *excite*; turn another's mind back, make one think of, evoke the memory o.; commemorate, raise a memorial, redeem from oblivion, keep the memory green, toast 876vb. *celebrate*; relate, recount, recapitulate 106vb. *repeat*; memorialize, petition 761vb. *request*; write history, narrate 590vb. *describe*.

memorize, commit to memory, get to know, con 490vb. *know*; con over, get by heart, learn by rote 536vb. *learn*; repeat, repeat one's lesson 106vb. *repeat*; fix in one's memory, rivet in one's m., stamp in one's m., grave on the mind, hammer into one's head, drive into one's h.; burden the memory with, stuff the mind w., cram the mind w., load the mind w.

be remembered, stay in the memory, stick in the mind, recur, recur to one's thoughts 106vb. *reoccur*; flash across one's mind, ring a bell, set one's memory working; haunt, dwell in one's thoughts, abide in one's memory, run in one's thoughts, haunt one's t., not leave one's t.; lurk in one's mind, rise from the subconscious, emerge into consciousness; make history, live in h., leave a name 866vb. *have repute*.

Adv. *in memory*, in memory of, to the memory of, in memoriam; by heart, by rote, from memory.

See: 67, 106, 125, 455, 466, 490, 524, 536, 548, 590, 666, 761, 821, 830, 866, 876.

506 Oblivion

N. *oblivion*, forgetfulness, absent-mindedness 456n. *abstractedness*; loss of memory, amnesia, fugue, absence, total blank; hysterical amnesia 503n. *insanity*; misremembrance, paramnesia; insensibility, insensibility of the past, no sense of history; benefits forgot 908n. *ingratitude*; dim memory, hazy recollection; defective memory, failing m., loose m., slippery m., treacherous m.; decay of memory, lapse of m., memory like a sieve; effacement 550n. *obliteration*; Lethe, waters of L., waters of oblivion; good riddance.

amnesty, letting bygones be bygones, obliteration of grievances, burial of g., burial of the hatchet; pardon, free p., absolution 909n. *forgiveness*.

Adj. *forgotten*, clean f., beyond recall; well forgotten, not missed; unremembered, left; disremembered, misremembered etc. vb.; almost remembered, on the tip of one's tongue; gone out of one's head, passed out of recollection, bygone, out of mind, buried, dead and b., sunk in oblivion, amnestied 909adj. *forgiven*.

forgetful, forgetting, oblivious; sunk in oblivion, steeped in Lethe; insensible, unconscious of the past; not historically minded; unable to remember, suffering from amnesia, amnesic; marked by loss of memory, amnemonic; causing loss of memory, amnestic, Lethean; unmindful, heedless, mindless 458adj. *negligent*; absent-minded, inclined to forget 456adj. *abstracted*; willing to forget, unresentful 909adj. *forgiving*; unwilling to remember,

conveniently forgetting 918 adj. *dutiless*; unmindful of favours, ingrate 908 adj. *ungrateful*.

Vb. *forget*, clean f., misremember, disremember, have no recollection; drop from one's thoughts, think no more of; wean one's thoughts from, discharge from one's memory, bury in oblivion, consign to o., be oblivious; amnesty, let bygones be bygones, bury the hatchet 909 vb. *forgive*; break with the past, unlearn, efface 550 vb. *obliterate*; suffer from amnesia, remember nothing; be forgetful, need reminding; lose sight of, leave behind; be absent-minded, fluff one's notes 456 vb. *be inattentive*; have a short memory, have a memory like a sieve, let in one ear and out of the other, forget one's own name; almost remember, have on the tip of one's tongue, not call to mind.

be forgotten, slip one's memory, escape one's m., fade from one's mind; sink into oblivion, fall into o., drop out of the news; be overlooked 456 vb. *escape notice*.

See: 456, 458, 503, 550, 908, 909, 918.

507 Expectation

N. *expectation*, state of e., expectancy 455 n. *attention*; contemplation 617 n. *intention*; confident expectation, reliance, confidence, trust 473 n. *certainty*; presumption 475 n. *premise*; foretaste 135 n. *anticipation*; optimism, cheerful expectation 833 n. *cheerfulness*; eager expectation, anxious e., sanguine e. 859 n. *desire*; ardent expectation, breathless e. 852 n. *hope*; waiting, suspense 474 n. *uncertainty*; pessimism, dread, apprehension, apprehensiveness 854 n. *fear*; anxiety 825 n. *worry*; waiting for the end 853 n. *hopelessness*; expectance, one's expectations, one's prospects 471 n. *probability*; reckoning, calculation 480 n. *estimate*; prospect, look-out, outlook, forecast 511 n. *prediction*; contingency 469 n. *possibility*; destiny 596 n. *fate*; defeated expectation, frustrated e., tantalization, torment of Tantalus 509 n. *disappointment*; expected thing, the usual 610 n. *practice*.

Adj. *expectant*, expecting, in expectation, in hourly e.; in suspense, on the waiting list, on the short l.; sure, confident 473 adj. *certain*; anticipatory, anticipant, anticipating, banking on; presuming, taking for granted; predicting 511 adj. *foreseeing*; unsurprised 865 adj. *unastonished*; forewarned, forearmed, ready 669 adj. *prepared*; waiting, waiting for, awaiting; on the look-out, on the watch for, standing by, on call 457 adj. *vigilant*; tense, keyed up 821 adj. *excited*; tantalized, on tenterhooks, on the rack, on the tiptoe of expectation, agape, agog 859 adj. *desiring*; optimistic, hopeful, sanguine 852 adj. *hoping*; apprehensive, dreading, worried, anxious 854 adj. *nervous*; pessimistic, expecting the worst 853 adj. *hopeless*; wondering, open-eyed, open-mouthed, curious 453 adj. *inquisitive*; expecting a baby, expecting, parturient 164 adj. *productive*.

expected, long e.; up to expectation, not surprising 865 adj. *unastonishing*; anticipated, presumed, predicted, foreseen, foreseeable 471 adj. *probable.*; prospective, future, on the horizon 155 adj. *impending*; contemplated, intended, in view, in prospect, in one's eye 617 adj. *intending*; hoped for, longed for 859 adj. *desired*; apprehended, dreaded, feared 854 adj. *frightening*.

Vb. *expect*, look for, have in prospect, face the prospect, face; contemplate, have in mind, hold in view, promise oneself 617 vb. *intend*; reckon, calculate 480 vb. *estimate*; predict, forecast 510 vb. *foresee*; see it coming 865 vb. *not wonder*; think likely, presume 471 vb. *assume*; be confident, rely on, bank on, count upon 473 vb. *be certain*; anticipate, forestall 669 vb. *prepare oneself*; look out for, watch out f., be waiting f., be ready f. 457 vb. *be careful*; stand by, be on call; tarry for (see *await*); apprehend, dread 854 vb. *fear*; look forward to, hope for 852 vb. *hope*, 859 vb. *desire*; hope and believe 485 vb. *believe*.

await, be on the waiting list; stand waiting, stand and wait, dance attendance 136 vb. *wait*; queue up, mark time, bide one's t.; stand to attention, stand by, be on call; hold one's breath, be in suspense, open one's mouth for; keep one waiting; have in store for, be in store for, be expected, 155 vb. *impend*; tantalize, make one's mouth water, lead one to expect 859 vb. *cause desire*.

Adv. *expectantly*, in suspense, with bated breath, on edge, on the anxious seat; on the waiting list.

See: 135, 136, 155, 164, 453, 455, 457, 469, 471, 473, 474, 475, 480, 485, 509, 510, 511, 596, 610, 617, 669, 821, 825, 833, 852, 853, 854, 859, 865.

508 Inexpectation

N. *inexpectation*, non-expectation, no expectation 472n. *improbability*; no hope 853n. *hopelessness*; uninterest, apathy 454n. *incuriosity*; unpreparedness 670n. *non-preparation*; unexpectedness, unforeseen contingency, unusual occurrence; unexpected result, miscalculation 495n. *error*; lack of warning, surprise, surprisal, disconcertment; the unexpected, the unforeseen, surprise packet, Jack-in-the-box, afterclap; shock, nasty s., start, jolt, turn; blow, sudden b., staggering b.; bolt from the blue, thunderclap, bombshell; revelation, eye-opener; paradox, reversal, peripeteia 221n. *inversion*; astonishment, amazement 864n. *wonder*; anticlimax, descent from the sublime to the ridiculous; false expectation 509n. *disappointment*.

Adj. *unexpected*, unanticipated, unprepared for, unlooked for, unhoped for; unguessed, unpredicted, unforeseen; unforeseeable, unpredictable 472adj. *improbable*; unheralded, unannounced; without warning, surprising; arresting, eye-opening, staggering, amazing 864 adj. *wonderful*; shocking, startling 854 adj. *frightening*; sudden 116adj. *instantaneous*; like a bombshell, like a bolt from the blue, dropped from the clouds; uncovenanted, unbargained for, uncatered for 670adj. *unprepared*; contrary to expectation, against e.; paradoxical 518 adj. *equivocal*; out of one's reckoning, out of one's ken, out of one's experience, unprecedented, unexampled 84adj. *unusual*; freakish 84adj. *abnormal*; whimsical 604adj. *capricious*; full of surprises, unaccountable 517adj. *puzzling*.

inexpectant, non-e., unexpecting, unguessing, unsuspecting, off guard, unguarded 456adj. *inattentive*; unaware, uninformed 491adj. *ignorant*; unwarned, unforewarned; surprised, disconcerted, taken by surprise, taken aback, caught napping, caught bending, caught on the hop, on the wrong foot 670adj. *unprepared*; astonished, thunderstruck, dazed, stunned 864adj. *wondering*; startled, jolted, shocked; without expectations, unhopeful 853adj. *hopeless*; apathetic, incurious 860adj. *indifferent*.

Vb. *not expect*, not look for, not contemplate, think unlikely, not foresee 472vb. *be unlikely*; not hope for 853vb. *despair*; be caught out, walk into the trap, fall into the t.; be taken aback, be taken by surprise 670vb. *be unprepared*; get a start, have a jolt, start, jump; have one's eyes opened, receive a revelation; look surprised, stare.

surprise, take by s., spring something on one, spring a mine under; catch, trap, ambush 542vb. *ensnare*; catch unawares, catch napping, catch bending, catch off one's guard; startle, jolt, make one jump, give one a turn; take aback, stagger, stun; take one's breath away, knock one down with a feather, bowl one over, give one an eye-opener; astonish, amaze, astound, dumbfound 864vb. *be wonderful*; shock, electrify 821vb. *impress;* come like a thunderclap; drop from the clouds, pop out of the blue; fall upon, burst u., bounce u., spring u., pounce on; steal upon, creep u.; come up from behind, take one on his blind side.

Adv. *unexpectedly*, suddenly, abruptly 116 adv. *instantaneously*; all of a sudden, without warning, without notice, like a thief in the night.

See: 84, 116, 221, 454, 456, 472, 491, 495, 509, 517, 518, 532, 604, 670, 821, 853, 854, 860, 864.

509 Disappointment

N. *disappointment*, sad d., bitter d., regrets 830n. *regret*; continued disappointment, tantalization, frustration, feeling of f., bafflement; blighted hopes, unsatisfied h., betrayed h., hopes unrealized 853n. *hopelessness*; false expectation, vain e., much cry and little wool 482n. *overestimation*; bad news 529n. *news*; not what one expected, disillusionment 829n. *discontent*; miscalculation 481n. *misjudg-*

ment; mirage, false dawn, fool's paradise; blow, setback, balk 702 n. *hitch*; non-fulfilment, partial success, near failure 726 n. *non-completion*; bad luck, trick of fortune, slip 'twixt the cup and the lip 731 n. *ill fortune*; anticlimax 508 n. *inexpectation*; come-down, let-d. 872 n. *humiliation*; damp squib 728 n. *failure*.

Adj. *disappointed*, expecting otherwise 508 adj. *inexpectant*; frustrated, thwarted 702 adj. *hindered*; baffled, foiled 728 adj. *defeated*; disconcerted, crestfallen, out of countenance, humiliated 872 adj. *humbled*; disgruntled, soured 829 adj. *discontented*; sick with disappointment 853 adj. *hopeless*; heartbroken 834 adj. *dejected*; ill-served, let down, betrayed; refused, turned away 607 adj. *rejected*.

disappointing, unsatisfying, unsatisfactory 636 adj. *insufficient*; not up to expectation, less than one's hopes 829 adj. *discontenting*; miscarried, abortive 728 adj. *unsuccessful*; cheating, deceptive 542 adj. *deceiving*.

Vb. *be disappointed*, —unsuccessful etc. adj.; try in vain 728 vb. *fail*; have hoped for something better, not realize one's expectations 307 vb. *fall short*; expect otherwise, be let down, have hoped better of; find to one's cost 830 vb. *regret*; find one a false prophet, listen too often 544 vb. *be duped*; laugh on the wrong side of one's face, be crestfallen, look blue, look blank 872 vb. *be humbled*; be sick with disappointment, be sick at heart, be hopeless 853 vb. *despair*.

disappoint, not come up to expectations 307 vb. *fall short*; falsify *or* belie one's expectation; defeat one's hopes, break one's h., dash one's h., crush one's h., blight one's h., deceive one's h., betray one's h.; burst the bubble, disillusion; serve ill, fail one, let down, leave one in the lurch, not come up to scratch; balk, foil, thwart, frustrate 702 vb. *hinder*; amaze, dumbfound 508 vb. *surprise*; disconcert, humble 872 vb. *humiliate*; betray, play one false 930 vb. *be dishonest*; play one a trick, jilt, bilk 542 vb. *befool*; dash the cup from one's lips, tantalize, leave unsatisfied, discontent, spoil one's pleasure, dissatisfy, disgruntle, sour, embitter with disappointment 829 vb. *cause discontent*; refuse, deny, turn away 607 vb. *reject*.

Adv. *disappointingly*, tantalizingly, so near and yet so far.

See: 307, 481, 482, 508, 529, 542, 544, 607, 636, 702, 726, 728, 731, 829, 830, 834, 853, 872, 930.

510 Foresight

N. *foresight*, prevision, preview, fore-glimpse; anticipation, foretaste; preno-tion, precognition, foreknowledge, pre-science, second sight, clairvoyancy; pre-monition, presentiment, foreboding, fore-warning 511 n. *omen*; prognosis, prog-nostication 511 n. *prediction;* foregone conclusion 473 n. *certainty*; programme, prospectus 623 n. *plan*; forethought, long-sightedness 498 n. *sagacity*; prede-liberation 608 n. *predetermination*; pru-dence, providence 858 n. *caution*; intelli-gent anticipation, readiness, provision, 669 n. *preparation*.

Adj. *foreseeing*, foresighted, prospective, prognostic, predictive 511 adj. *predicting*; clairvoyant, second-sighted, prophetic; prescient, far-sighted, weather-wise, sa-gacious 498 adj. *wise*; looking ahead, provident, prudent 858 adj. *cautious*; anticipant, anticipatory 507 adj. *ex-pectant*.

Vb. *foresee*, foreglimpse, preview, prophesy, forecast, divine 511 vb. *predict*; forewarn 664 vb. *warn*; foreknow, see *or* peep *or* pry into the future, read the f., have second sight; have prior information, know in advance 524 vb. *be informed*; see ahead, look a., see it coming, scent, scent from afar, feel in one's bones; be before-hand, anticipate, forestall 135 vb. *be early*; make provision 669 vb. *prepare*; surmise, make a good guess 512 vb. *suppose*; forejudge, predeliberate 608 vb. *predeter-mine*; show prudence, plan ahead 623 vb. *plan*; look to the future, have an eye to the f., see how the cat jumps, see how the wind blows 124 vb. *look ahead*; have an eye on the main chance 498 vb. *be wise*; feel one's way, keep a sharp look-out 455 vb. *be attentive*; lay up for a rainy day 633 vb. *provide*; take precautions, provide against 858 vb. *be cautious*.

See: 124, 135, 455, 473, 498, 507, 511, 512, 524, 608, 623, 633, 664, 669, 858.

511 Prediction

N. *prediction*, foretelling, forewarning, prophecy; apocalypse 975 n. *revelation*; forecast, weather f.; prognostication, prognosis; presentiment, foreboding 510 n. *foresight*; presage, prefiguration, prefigurement; programme, prospectus 623 n. *plan*; announcement, notice, advance n. 528 n. *publication*; warning, preliminary w., warning shot 665 n. *danger signal*; prospect 507 n. *expectation*; shape of things to come, horoscope, fortune; type 23 n. *prototype*.

divination, clairvoyancy; augury, auguration, hariolation; mantology, vaticination, soothsaying; astrology, astromancy, horoscopy, casting nativities, genethliacs; fortune-telling, palmistry, cheiromancy; crystal-gazing, crystallomancy; sortilege, casting lots; dowsing, radiesthesia 484 n. *discovery*.

theomancy, bibliomancy, psychomancy, sciomancy, aeromancy, chaomancy, meteoromancy, austromancy; haruspicy, hieroscopy, hieromancy, ichthyomancy, anthropomancy; pyromancy, tephromancy, sideromancy, capnomancy; myomancy, orniscopy, ornithomancy, alectryomancy, ophiomancy; botanomancy, hydromancy, pegomancy; rhabdomancy; crithomancy, aleuromancy, alphitomancy, halomancy; cleromancy, sortilege, belomancy, axinomancy, coscinomancy; dactyliomancy, geomancy, lithomancy, pessomancy, psephomancy; catoptromancy.

omen, portent, presage, writing on the wall; prognostic, symptom, sign 547 n. *indication*; augury, auspice; forewarning, caution 664 n. *warning*; harbinger, herald 531 n. *messenger*; prefigurement, foretoken, type; ominousness, portentousness, gathering clouds, signs of the times 661 n. *danger*; bird of omen, bird of ill omen, owl, raven.

oracle, consultant 500 n. *sage*; meteorologist, weather-prophet; calamity prophet, Cassandra 664 n. *warner*; prophet, prophetess, seer; forecaster, soothsayer; clairvoyant, medium 984 n. *occultist*; Delphic oracle, Pythian o., Python, Pythoness, Pythia; Sibyl, Sibylline leaves, Sibylline books, Old Moore; Tiresias, Witch of Endor, Sphinx; cards, dice, lot; tripod, crystal, mirror, tea leaves, palm; Bible, sortes Vergilianae.

diviner, water-d., dowser 983 n. *sorcerer*; tipster 618 n. *gambler*; astrologer, caster of nativities; fortune-teller, gipsy, palmist, crystal-gazer, geomancer; augur, augurist, haruspex.

Adj. *predicting*, etc. vb.; predictive, foretelling; presentient, clairvoyant 510 adj. *foreseeing*; fortune-telling; weather-wise; prophetic, vaticinal, mantic, fatidical, apocalyptic; oracular, Sibylline; monitory, premonitory, foreboding 664 adj. *cautionary*; heralding, prefiguring 66 adj. *precursory*.

presageful, significant, ominous, portentous, big with fate, pregnant with doom; augurial, auspicial, haruspical, extispicious; auspicious, promising, favourable 730 adj. *prosperous*; sinister 731 adj. *adverse*.

Vb. *predict*, forecast, make a prediction, prognosticate, make a prognosis; foretell, prophesy, vaticinate, forebode, bode, ominate, augur, spell; foretoken, presage, portend; foreshow, premonstrate, foreshadow, prefigure, shadow forth, precurse, forerun, herald, be harbinger, usher in 64 vb. *come before*; point to, betoken, typify, signify 547 vb. *indicate*; announce, give notice, notify 528 vb. *advertise*; forewarn, give warning 664 vb. *warn*; look black, lour, lower, menace 900 vb. *threaten*; promise, augur well, bid fair to, give hopes of, hold out hopes, raise expectations, excite e. 852 vb. *give hope*.

divine, auspicate, augurate, haruspicate; take the auspices, take the omens; soothsay, vaticinate, hariolate; draw a horoscope, cast a nativity; cast lots 618 vb. *gamble*; tell fortunes; read the future, read the signs, read the stars; read the cards, read one's hand.

See: 23, 64, 66, 484, 500, 507, 510, 528, 531, 547, 618, 623, 661, 664, 665, 730, 731, 852, 900, 975, 983, 984.

512 Supposition

N. *supposition*, supposal, notion, the idea of 451 n. *idea*; fancy, conceit 513 n. *ideality*; pretence, pretending 850 n. *affectation*; presumption, assumption, presupposition, postulation, postulate, postulatum 475 n. *premise*; condition, stipu-

lation 766n. *conditions*; proposal, proposition 759vb. *offer*; submission 475n. *argument*; hypothesis, working h., theory, theorem 452n. *topic*; thesis, position, stand, attitude, orientation, standpoint 485n. *opinion*; suggestion, loose s., casual s.; suggestiveness 524n. *hint*; basis of supposition, clue, data, datum 466n. *evidence*; suspicion, hunch, inkling (see *conjecture*); instinct 476n. *intuition*; association of ideas 449n. *thought*; supposability, conjecturability 469n. *possibility*.

conjecture, unverified supposition, conjecturability, guess, surmise, suspicion; mere notion, bare supposition, vague suspicion, rough guess, crude estimate; shrewd idea 476n. *intuition*; construction, reconstruction; guesswork, guessing, speculation; gamble, shot, shot in the dark 618n. *gambling*.

theorist, hypothesist, theorizer, theoretician; supposer, surmiser, guesser; academic person, critic, armchair c., armchair detective; doctrinarian 473n. *doctrinaire*; speculator, thinker 449n. *philosopher*; backroom boy 623n. *planner*; plunger 618n. *gambler*.

Adj. *suppositional*, supposing etc. vb.; suppositive, notional, conjectural, guessing, propositional, hypothetical, theoretical, armchair, speculative, academic, of academic interest; gratuitous, unverified; suggestive, hinting, allusive, stimulating, thought-provoking.

supposed etc. vb.; assumed, presumed, premised, taken, postulated; proposed, mooted 452adj. *topical*; given, granted, granted for the sake of argument 488adj. *assented*; suppositive, putative, presumptive; pretended, so-called, quasi; not real 2adj. *unreal*; alleged, supposititious, fabled, fancied 543adj. *untrue*; supposable, surmisable, imaginable 513adj. *imaginary*.

Vb. *suppose*, just s., pretend 850vb. *be affected*; fancy, dream 513vb. *imagine*; think, conceive, take into one's head 485 vb. *opine*; divine, have a hunch 476vb. *intuit*; surmise, conjecture, hazard a c., guess, give a g., make a g.; suppose so, dare say; persuade oneself 485vb. *believe*; presume, assume, presuppose, presurmise 475vb. *premise*; posit, lay down, assert 532vb. *affirm*; take for granted, take, take it, postulate 475vb. *reason*; speculate,

have a theory, hypothesize, theorize 449 vb. *meditate*; sketch, draft, outline 623 vb. *plan*; rely on supposition 618vb. *gamble*.

propound, propose, mean seriously 759vb. *offer*; put on the agenda, moot, move, propose a motion 761vb. *request*; put a case, submit, make one's submission 475vb. *argue*; put forth, make a suggestion, venture to say, put forward a notion, throw out an idea 691vb. *advise*; suggest, adumbrate, allude 524vb. *hint*; put an idea into one's head, urge 612vb. *motivate*.

Adv. *supposedly*, reputedly, seemingly; on the assumption that, ex hypothesi.

See: 2, 449, 451, 452, 466, 469, 473, 475, 476, 485, 488, 513, 524, 532, 543, 612, 618, 623, 691, 759, 761, 766, 850.

513 Imagination

N. *imagination*, power of i., visual i., vivid i., highly-coloured i., fertile i., bold i., wild i., fervent i.; imaginativeness, creativeness; originality, inventiveness 21n. *non-imitation*; ingenuity, resourcefulness 694n. *skill*; fancifulness, stretch of the imagination (see *ideality*); understanding, insight, empathy, sympathy 819n. *moral sensibility*; poetic imagination, frenzy, poetic f., ecstasy, inspiration, afflatus, divine a.; fancy, the mind's eye, visualization, objectification, image-building, imagery, word-painting; artistry, creative work.

ideality, idealization, excogitation, conception 449n. *thought*; concept, image, conceit, fancy, coinage of the brain, brain-creation, notion 451n. *idea*; whim, whimsey, whim-wham, maggot, crimkumcrankum 497n. *absurdity*; vagary 604n. *caprice*; figment, fiction 541n. *falsehood*; work of fiction, story 590n. *novel*; imaginative exercise, flight of fancy, play of f., uncontrolled imagination, romance, extravaganza, rhapsody 546n. *exaggeration*; poetic licence 593n. *poetry*; quixotry, knight-errantry, shadow boxing.

fantasy, wildest dreams; vision, dream, bad d., nightmare; bugbear, phantom 970n. *ghost*; shadow, vapour 419n. *dimness*; mirage, fata Morgana 440n. *visual fallacy*; delusion, hallucination,

chimera 495n. *error*; reverie, brown study 456n. *abstractedness*; trance, somnambulism 375n. *insensibility*; sick fancy, delirium 503n. *frenzy*; subjectivity, autistic distortion, auto-suggestion; wishful thinking 477n. *sophistry*; window-shopping, castle-building, make-believe, daydream, golden d., pipe-d. 859n. *desire*; romanticism, escapism, idealism, Utopianism; Utopia, Erewhon; promised land, El Dorado; Happy Valley, Fortunate Isles, Isles of the Blest; land of Cockaigne, kingdom of Micomicon, Ruritania, Shangri-la, Atlantis; fairyland, wonderland, land of Prester John; cloud-cuckoo land, dream l., dream world, castles in Spain, castle in the air; pie in the sky, good time coming, millennium 124n. *future state*; man in the moon, Flying Dutchman; idle fancy, myth 543n. *fable.*

visionary, seer 511n. *diviner*; dreamer, dayd., mopus, somnambulist; idealist, Utopian 901n. *philanthropist*; castle-builder, escapist, ostrich, ostrich-head 620n. *avoider*; romantic, romancer, romanticist, rhapsodist, myth-maker; enthusiast, knight-errant, fool-e., Don Quixote 504n. *crank*; creative worker 556n. *artist.*

Adj. *imaginative*, creative, lively, original, idea'd, inventive, fertile, ingenious; resourceful 694adj. *skilful*; fancy-led, romancing, romantic, high-flying; high-flown, rhapsodical 546adj. *exaggerated*; poetic, fictional; Utopian, idealistic; rhapsodic, enthusiastic; dreaming, tranced; extravagant, fantastical, whimsical, preposterous, impractical 497adj. *absurd*; visionary, other-worldly, Quixotic; imaginal, visualizing, eidetic, eidotropic.

imaginary, unreal, unsubstantial 4adj. *insubstantial*; subjective, notional, chimerical, illusory 495adj. *erroneous*; dreamy, visionary, not of this world, ideal; cloudy, vaporous 419adj. *shadowy*; unhistorical, fictitious, fabulous, fabled, legendary, mythic, mythological 543adj. *untrue*; fanciful, fancy-bred, fancied, imagined, fabricated, hatched; dreamed-up, air-drawn, air-built; hypothetical 512adj. *suppositional*; pretended, make-believe.

Vb. *imagine*, ideate 449vb. *think*; fancy, dream; excogitate, think of, think up, dream up; make up, devise, invent, origi-

nate, create, have an inspiration 609vb. *improvise*; coin, hatch, concoct, fabricate 164vb. *produce*; visualize, envisage, see in the mind's eye 438vb. *see*; conceive, form an image; figure to oneself, picture to o., represent to o.; paint, word-p., conjure up a vision, objectify, realize, capture, recapture 551vb. *represent*; use one's imagination, give reins to one's i., run riot in imagination 546vb. *exaggerate*; play with one's thoughts, pretend, make-believe, daydream 456vb. *be inattentive*; build Utopias, build castles in the air; see visions, dream dreams; idealize, romanticize, fictionalize, rhapsodize 546 vb. *exaggerate*; enter into, empathize, sympathize 516vb. *understand.*

Adv. *imaginatively*, in imagination, in thought; with imagination; in the mind's eye.

See: 4, 21, 124, 164, 375, 419, 438, 440, 449, 451, 456, 477, 495, 497, 503, 504, 511, 512, 516, 541, 543, 546, 551, 556, 590, 593, 604, 609, 620, 694, 819, 859, 901, 970.

514 Meaning

N. *meaning*, idea conveyed, substance, essence, sum, sum and substance, essence, gist, pith; contents, text, matter, subject m. 452n. *topic*; semantic content, sense, drift, tenor, purport, import, implication, colouring; force, effect; relevance, bearing, scope; meaningfulness, semantic flow, context, running c. (see *connotation*); expression, mode of e., diction 566n. *style*; semantics, semasiology 557n. *linguistics.*

connotation, denotation, signification, significance, reference, application; context; original meaning, derivation 156n. *source*; range of meaning, semantic field, comprehension; extended meaning, extension; intention, main meaning, leading sense; specialized meaning, peculiar m., idiom 80n. *speciality*; subsidiary sense, submeaning; received meaning, usage, acceptance, accepted meaning 520n. *interpretation*; single meaning, univocity, unambiguity 516n. *intelligibility*; double meaning, ambiguity 518n. *equivocalness*; same meaning, equivalent meaning, convertible terms; synonym, synonymousness, synonymity, equivalence, tauto-

nymity 13 n. *identity*; opposite meaning, antonym, antonymity 14 n. *contrariety*; contradictory meaning, countersense; changed meaning, semantic shift; level of meaning, literal meaning, literality, translationese 573 n. *plainness*; metaphorical meaning 519 n. *metaphor*; hidden meaning, esoteric sense 523 n. *latency*; constructive sense, implied s.; Pickwickian sense, nonsense 497 n. *absurdity*.

Adj. *meaningful*, significant, of moment 638 adj. *important*; substantial, pithy, full of meaning, replete with m., packed with m., pregnant; meaning etc. vb.; importing, purporting, significative, significatory, indicative 547 adj. *indicating*; expressive, suggestive, evocative, allusive, implicit; express, explicit 573 adj. *plain*; declaratory 532 adj. *affirmative*; interpretative 520 adj. *interpretive*.

semantic, semasiological, philological, etymological 557 adj. *linguistic*; connotational, connotative; denotational, denotative; literal, verbal 573 n. *plain*; metaphorical 519 adj. *figurative*; biplanar, on two levels; univocal, unambiguous 516 adj. *intelligible*; ambiguous 518 adj. *equivocal*; synonymous, homonymous 13 adj. *identical*; tantamount, equivalent 18 adj. *similar*; tautologous 106 adj. *repeated*; antonymous 14 adj. *contrary*; idiomatic 80 adj. *special*; paraphrastic 520 adj. *interpretive*; obscure 568 adj. *imperspicuous*; clear 567 adj. *perspicuous*; implied, constructive 523 adj. *latent*; Pickwickian, nonsensical 497 adj. *absurd*; meaningless 515 adj. *unmeaning*.

Vb. *mean*, have a meaning, bear a sense, mean something; convey a meaning, get across 524 vb. *communicate*; typify, symbolize 547 vb. *indicate*; signify, denote, connote, stand for 551 vb. *represent*; import, purport, intend; point to, add up to, boil down to, spell, involve 523 vb. *imply*; convey, express, declare, assert 532 vb. *affirm*; bespeak, tell of, speak of, breathe of, speak volumes 466 vb. *evidence*; mean to say, be trying to s., drive at, really mean, have in mind, allude to, refer to; be synonymous, have the same meaning 13 vb. *be identical*; say it in other words, tautologize 106 vb. *repeat*; mean the same thing, agree in meaning, coincide 24 vb. *agree*; conflict in meaning, be opposed in m. 25 vb.

disagree; draw a meaning, infer, understand by 516 vb. *understand*.

Adv. *significantly*, meaningly, with meaning, to the effect that; in a sense, in some s.; as meant, as intended, as understood; in the sense that *or* of; according to the book, from the context; literally, verbally; metaphorically, constructively.

See: 13, 14, 18, 24, 25, 80, 106, 156, 452, 466, 497, 515, 516, 518, 519, 520, 523, 524, 532, 547, 551, 557, 566, 567, 568, 573, 638.

515 Unmeaningness

N. *unmeaningness*, meaninglessness, lack of meaning, absence of m., no meaning, no context; no bearing 10 adj. *irrelevance*; non-significance 639 n. *unimportance*; amphigouri 497 n. *absurdity*; inanity, emptiness, triteness; truism, platitude 496 n. *maxim*; unreason, illogicality 477 n. *sophistry*; invalidity, dead letter, nullity 161 n. *ineffectuality*; illegibility, scribble, scribbling 586 vb. *script*; daub 552 n. *misrepresentation*; empty sound, meaningless noise, strumming; sounding brass, tinkling cymbal 400 n. *loudness*; jargon, rigmarole, rigmarolery, hocus-pocus, galimatias; gibberish, gabble, High Dutch, double d., Greek, Babel 517 n. *unintelligibility*; incoherence, raving, delirium 503 n. *frenzy*; double-talk, mystification 530 n. *enigma*; insincerity 925 n. *flattery*.

silly talk, senseless t., nonsense 497 n. *absurdity*; stuff, stuff and nonsense, balderdash, gammon, rubbish, rot, tommyrot; drivel, twaddle, fiddle-faddle, fudge; bosh, tosh, tripe, piffle, bilge, hogwash, wish-wash.

empty talk, idle speeches, soft nothings, wind, gas, hot air, vapouring, verbiage 570 n. *diffuseness*; rant, bombast, fustian, rodomontade 877 n. *boasting*; blether, blather, blatherskite, blah-blah, flapdoodle; guff, pi-jaw, claptrap, poppycock; humbug 541 n. *falsehood*; moonshine, bunkum, bunk, boloney, hooey; flummery, blarney, 925 n. *flattery*; talk, chatter, prattle, prate, prating, patter, babble, gabble, palaver, jabber, jabberjabber 581 n. *chatter*; cliché.

Adj. *unmeaning*, meaningless, without meaning, Pickwickian; amphigoric, nonsense,

[315]

nonsensical 497 adj. *absurd*; senseless, null; unexpressive, unidiomatic 25 adj. *unapt*; non-significant, insignificant, inane, empty, trivial, trite 639 adj. *unimportant*; fatuous, piffling, blithering, bilgy, washy; trashy, trumpery, rubbishy; twaddling, waffling, windy, ranting 546 adj. *exaggerated*; incoherent, raving, gibbering 503 adj. *frenzied*.

unmeant, unintentional, involuntary, unintended, unimplied, unalluded to; mistranslated 521 adj. *misinterpreted*; insincere 925 adj. *flattering*.

Vb. *mean nothing*, be unmeaning, have no meaning; scribble, scratch, daub, strum; talk bunkum, talk like an idiot 497 vb. *be absurd*; talk, babble, prattle, prate, palaver, gabble, jabber, clack 584 vb. *converse*; talk double Dutch, talk Greek, talk gibberish, doubletalk 517 vb. *be unintelligible*; rant 546 vb. *exaggerate*; rave, drivel, drool, blether, blat, waffle, twaddle; vapour, talk hot air, gas 499 vb. *be foolish*; not mean what one says, blarney 925 vb. *flatter*; make nonsense of 521 vb. *misinterpret*; have no meaning for, pass over one's head 474 vb. *puzzle*.

See: 10, 25, 161, 400, 474, 477, 496, 497, 499, 503, 517, 521, 530, 541, 546, 552, 570, 581, 584, 586, 639, 877, 925.

516 Intelligibility

N. *intelligibility*, knowability, cognizability; explicability, teachability, penetrability; apprehensibility, comprehensibility, adaptation to the understanding; readability, legibility, decipherability; clearness, clarity, coherence, limpidity, lucidity 567 n. *perspicuity*; precision, unambiguity 473 n. *certainty*; simplicity, straightforwardness, plain speaking, plain speech, downright utterance; plain words, plain English, mother tongue; simple eloquence, unadorned style 573 n. *plainness*; easiness, paraphrase, simplification 701 n. *facility*; amplification, popularization, haute vulgarisation 520 n. *interpretation*.

Adj. *intelligible*, understandable, penetrable, realizable, comprehensible, apprehensible; coherent 502 adj. *sane*; distinguishable, audible, recognizable, unmistakable; discoverable, cognizable, knowable 490 adj. *known*; explicable, teachable; unambiguous, unequivocal 514 adj. *meaningful*; explicit, positive 473 adj. *certain*; unblurred, distinct, clear-cut, precise 80 adj. *definite*; plain-spoken, unevasive, unadorned, downright, forthright 573 adj. *plain*; uninvolved, straightforward, simple 701 adj. *easy*; obvious, easy to understand, easy to grasp, made easy, adapted to the understanding, clear to the meanest capacity; explained, predigested, simplified, popularized, popular, for the million 520 adj. *interpreted*; clear, limpid 422 adj. *transparent*; pellucid, lucid 567 adj. *perspicuous*; readable, legible, decipherable, well-written, printed, in print; luminous, clear as daylight, clear as noonday, plain as a pikestaff 443 adj. *visible*.

expressive, telling, vivid, graphic, highly coloured, emphatic, strong, strongly worded 590 adj. *descriptive*; illustrative, explicatory 520 adj. *interpretive*; amplifying, paraphrasing, popularizing.

Vb. *be intelligible*, — clear, — easy etc. adj.; be realized, come alive, take on depth; be readable, read easily; make sense, add up, speak to the understanding 475 vb. *be reasonable*; tell its own tale, speak for itself 466 vb. *evidence*; have no secrets, be on the surface 443 vb. *be visible*; make understood, clarify, clear up, open one's eyes, elucidate 520 vb. *interpret*; make easy, simplify, popularize 701 vb. *facilitate*; recapitulate 106 vb. *repeat*; labour the obvious 532 vb. *emphasize*.

understand, comprehend, apprehend 490 vb. *know*; master 536 vb. *learn*; have, hold, retain 505 vb. *remember*; have understanding 498 vb. *be wise*; see through, penetrate, fathom, get to the bottom of 484 vb. *detect*; spot, descry, discern, distinguish, make out, see at a glance, see with half an eye 438 vb. *see*; recognize, make no mistake 473 vb. *be certain*; grasp, get hold of, seize, seize the meaning, be on to it, cotton on to; get the hang of, take in, register; be with one, follow, savvy; collect, get, catch on, twig; realize, get wise to, tumble to; begin to understand, come to u., have it dawn on one, have one's eyes opened, see it all; be undeceived, be disillusioned 830 vb. *regret*; get to know, be told 524 vb. *be informed*.

Adv. *intelligibly*, expressively, lucidly, plainly, simply, in plain terms, in clear terms, in simplified vocabulary.

See: 80, 106, 422, 438, 443, 466, 473, 475, 484, 490, 498, 502, 505, 514, 520, 524, 532, 536, 567, 573, 590, 701, 830.

517 Unintelligibility

N. *unintelligibility*, incomprehensibility, inapprehensibility, unaccountability, inconceivability; inexplicability, impenetrability; perplexity, difficulty 474 adj. *uncertainty*; obscurity 568 adj. *imperspicuity*; ambiguity 518 n. *equivocalness*; mystification 515 n. *unmeaningness*; incoherence 503 n. *insanity*; double Dutch, gibberish; private language, slang; idioglossia 580 n. *speech defect*; undecipherability, illegibility, unreadability; scribble, scrawl 586 n. *lettering*; inaudibility 401 n. *faintness*; Greek, sealed book 530 n. *secret*; hard saying, paradox, knotty point, obscure problem, pons asinorum, crux, riddle 530 n. *enigma*; mysterious behaviour, Sphinx-like attitude, baffling demeanour; bad pronunciation 580 n. *speech defect*; foreign language, strange idiom 560 n. *dialect*.

Adj. *unintelligible*, incomprehensible, inapprehensible, inconceivable, not understandable, not to be understood, inexplicable, unaccountable, not to be accounted for; unknowable, unrecognizable, incognizable, undiscoverable, as Greek to one 491 adj. *unknown*; unfathomable, unbridgeable, unsearchable, inscrutable, impenetrable; blank, poker-faced, expressionless 820 adj. *impassive*; inaudible 401 adj. *muted*; unreadable, illegible, undecipherable; undiscernible 444 vb. *invisible*; hidden, arcane 523 adj. *occult*; dark, shrouded in mystery; esoteric 80 adj. *private*; Sphinx-like, enigmatic, oracular (see *puzzling*).

puzzling, hard to understand, difficult, hard, crabbed; beyond one, over one's head, recondite, abstruse, elusive; enigmatic, mysterious 523 adj. *occult*; half-understood, nebulous, misty, hazy, dim, obscure 419 adj. *shadowy*; clear as mud, clear as ditch water 568 adj. *imperspicuous*; ambiguous 518 adj. *equivocal*; of doubtful meaning, oracular; paradoxical 508 adj. *unexpec-*

ted; unexplained, without a solution, insoluble, unsolvable; unsolved, unresolved 474 adj. *uncertain*.

inexpressible, unspeakable, unmentionable, untranslatable; unpronounceable, unutterable, ineffable; incommunicable, indefinable; profound, deep; mystic, mystical, transcendental.

puzzled, mystified, unable to understand, wondering, out of one's depth, flummoxed, baffled, perplexed, nonplussed 474 adj. *uncertain*.

Vb. *be unintelligible*, — puzzling, — inexpressible etc. adj.; be hard, be difficult, present a puzzle, make one's head ache 474 vb. *puzzle*; talk in riddles, speak oracles 518 vn. *be equivocal*; talk double Dutch, talk gibberish 515 vb. *mean nothing*; keep one guessing 486 vb. *cause doubt*; perplex, complicate, entangle, confuse 63 vb. *bedevil*; be too deep, go over one's head, be beyond one's reach; elude one's grasp, escape one; pass comprehension, baffle understanding; require explanation, have no answer, need an interpreter; write badly, scribble, scrawl.

not understand, not penetrate, find unintelligible, not make out, not know what to make of, make nothing of, make neither head nor tail of, be unable to account for; puzzle over, find too difficult, give up; be out of one's depth 491 vb. *not know*; wonder, be at sea 474 vb. *be uncertain*; not know what one is about, have no grasp 695 vb. *be unskilful*; misunderstand one another, play at cross-purposes 495 vb. *blunder*; get one wrong 481 vb. *misjudge*; not register 456 vb. *be inattentive*.

See: 63, 80, 401, 419, 444, 456, 474, 481, 486, 491, 495, 503, 508, 515, 518, 523, 530, 560, 568, 580, 586, 695, 820.

518 Equivocalness

N. *equivocalness*, two voices 14 n. *contrariety*; ambiguity, ambivalence 517 n. *unintelligibility*; indefiniteness, vagueness 474 adj. *uncertainty*; double meaning, amphiboly, amphibology, ambiloquy 514 n. *meaning*; doubletalk 515 n. *unmeaningness*; conundrum, riddle, oracle, oracular utterance 530 n. *enigma*; mental

reservation 525 n. *concealment*; prevarication, balancing act; equivocation, white lie 543 n. *untruth*; quibble, quibbling 477 n. *sophistry*; word-play, play upon words, paronomasia 574 n. *ornament*; pun, calembour, equivoque, double entendre 839 n. *witticism*; anagram, paragram, acrostic; synonymy, homonymy, homophone; tautonym.

Adj. *equivocal*, not univocal, ambiguous, epicene, ambivalent; double, double-tongued, two-edged; equivocating, prevaricating; vague, evasive, oracular; amphibolous, homonymous; anagrammatic.

Vb. *be equivocal*, cut both ways; play upon words, pun; have two meanings, have a second meaning 514 vb. *mean*; speak oracles, equivocate, speak with two voices 14 vb. *be contrary*; prevaricate, make a mental reservation 541 vb. *dissemble*.

See: 14, 474, 477, 514, 515, 517, 525, 530, 541, 543, 574, 839.

519 Metaphor: figure of speech

N. *metaphor*, mixed m.; tralatition, transference; allusion, application; misapplication, catachresis; extended metaphor, allegorization, allegory; mystical interpretation, anagoge 520 n. *interpretation*; apologue, fable, parable 534 n. *teaching*; symbolism, non-literality, figurativeness, imagery 513 n. *imagination*; simile, likeness 462 n. *comparison*; personification, prosopopeia.

trope, figure, figure of speech, turn of s., flourish; manner of speech, façon de parler; irony, sarcasm 851 n. *satire*; rhetorical figure 574 n. *ornament*; metonymy, antonomasia, synecdoche, synecdochism, enallage; anaphora, paraleipsis; aposiopesis; litotes 483 n. *underestimation*; hyperbole 546 n. *exaggeration*; stress, emphasis; euphuism, euphemism 850 n. *affectation*; colloquialism 573 n. *plainness*; contrast, antithesis 462 n. *comparison*; metathesis 221 n. *inversion*; paronomasia, word-play 518 n. *equivocalness*; asyndeton 46 n. *disjunction*.

Adj. *figurative*, metaphorical, tropical, tralatitious, catachrestic; allusive, symbolical, typical, allegorical, anagogic; parabolical; comparative, similitudinous

462 adj. *compared*; euphuistic, tortured, euphemistic 850 adj. *affected*; colloquial 573 adj. *plain*; hyperbolic 546 adj. *exaggerated*; satirical, sarcastic, ironical 851 adj. *derisive*; flowery, florid 574 adj. *ornate*; oratorical 574 adj. *rhetorical*.

Vb. *figure*, image, embody, personify; typify, symbolize 551 vb. *represent*; allegorize, parabolize, fable; prefigure, adumbrate; apply, allude; refer, similitudinize, liken, contrast 462 vb. *compare*; employ metaphor, indulge in tropes 574 vb. *ornament*.

Adv. *metaphorically*, not literally, tropically, figuratively, in a figure, by allusion; in a way, so to say, in a manner of speaking.

See: 46, 221, 462, 483, 513, 518, 520, 534, 546, 551, 573, 574, 850, 851.

520 Interpretation

N. *interpretation*, definition, explanation, explication, exposition, exegesis, epexegesis; elucidation, light, clarification, illumination; illustration, exemplification 83 n. *example*; enucleation, resolution, solution, key, clue, the secret 460 n. *answer*; decipherment, decoding, cracking 484 n. *discovery*; emendation 654 n. *amendment*; application, particular interpretation, twist, turn; construction, construe, reading, lection 514 n. *meaning*; euhemerism, demythologization; allegorization 519 n. *metaphor*; accepted reading, usual text, vulgate; alternative reading, variant r.; criticism, textual c., higher c., literary c., critique, review 480 n. *estimate*; critical power, critic's gift 480 n. *judgment*; insight, feeling, sympathy 819 n. *moral sensibility*.

commentary, comment, editorial c., Targum; scholium, gloss, footnote; inscription, caption, legend 563 n. *phrase*; motto, moral 693 n. *precept*; annotation, glossography, notes, marginalia, adversaria; apparatus criticus, critical edition; glossary, lexicon 559 n. *dictionary*.

translation, version, rendering, free translation, loose rendering; faithful translation, literal t., construe; key, crib, Bohn; rewording, paraphrase, metaphrase; précis, abridgment, epitomy 592 n. *compendium*; adaptation, simplification, ampli-

fication 516n. *intelligibility*; transliteration, decoding, decipherment; lip-reading.
hermeneutics, exegetics, science of interpretation, translator's art; epigraphy, palæography 557n. *linguistics*; diagnostics, symptomatology, semeiology, semeiotics; phrenology, metoposcopy; prophecy 511 n. *divination*.

interpreter, clarifier, explainer, exponent, expounder, expositor, exegete 537n. *teacher*; rationalist, rationalizer, euhemerist, demythologizer; editor 528n. *publicizer*; Massorete, textual critic; emender, emendator; commentator, annotator, note-maker, glossographer, scholiast, glossarist; critic, reviewer 480n. *estimator*; oneirocritic, oneiroscopist, medium 511n. *diviner*; polyglot 557n. *linguist*; translator, paraphraser, paraphrast; solver, cipherer, coder, decoder; lip-reader; epigraphist, palæographer 125n. *antiquarian*; spokesman, prolocutor, mouthpiece, representative 754n. *delegate*; executant, player, performer 413n. *musician*; poet, novelist, painter, sculptor 556n. *artist*.

guide, precedent 83n. *example*; lamp, light, star; dragoman, courier, man from Cook's, cicerone 690n. *leader*; showman, demonstrator 522n. *exhibitor*.

Adj. *interpretive*, interpretative, constructive; explanatory, explicatory, explicative, elucidatory; expositive, expository; exegetical, hermeneutic; defining, definitive; illuminating, illustrative, exemplary; glossarial, annotative, scholiastic, editorial; lip-reading, translative, paraphrastic, metaphrastic; polyglot; mediumistic; co-significative, synonymous, equivalent 28adj. *equal*; literal, strict, word-for-word 494adj. *accurate*; faithful 551adj. *representing*; free 495adj. *inexact*.

interpreted etc.vb.; explained, defined, expounded, elucidated, clarified; annotated, commented, commentated, edited; translated, rendered, Englished; deciphered, decoded, cracked.

Vb. *interpret*, define, clarify, make clear; explain, unfold, expound, elucidate 516 vb. *be intelligible*; illustrate 83vb. *exemplify*; comment; demonstrate 522vb. *show*; act as guide, show round; comment on, edit, write notes for, annotate, compose a commentary, gloss, gloze, gloze upon; read, spell, spell out; adopt a

reading, accept an interpretation, construe, put a construction on, understand by, give a sense to, make sense of, put a meaning on 516vb. *understand*; illuminate, throw light on, enlighten 524vb. *inform*; account for, find the cause, deduce, infer 475vb. *reason*; act as interpreter, be spokesman 551vb. *represent*; typify, symbolize; popularize, simplify 701vb. *facilitate*.

translate, make a version, make a key, make a crib; render, do into, turn i., English; retranslate, rehash, reword, rephrase, paraphrase; abridge, amplify, adapt; transliterate, transcribe; code, put into code; lip-read.

decipher, crack, crack the cipher, decode; find the meaning, read hieroglyphics; read, spell out, puzzle o., make o., work o.; piece together, find the sense of, find the key to; solve, resolve, enucleate, unravel, unriddle, disentangle, read between the lines.

Adv. *in plain words*, plainly, in plain English; by way of explanation, as interpreted; in other words, to wit, namely; to make it plain, to explain.

See: 28, 83, 125, 413, 460, 475, 480, 484, 494, 495, 511, 514, 516, 519, 522, 524, 528, 537, 551, 556, 557, 559, 563, 592, 654, 690, 693, 701, 754, 819.

521 Misinterpretation

N. *misinterpretation*, misunderstanding, misconstruction, misapprehension, wrong end of the stick; cross-purposes 495n. *mistake*; misexposition 535n. *misteaching*; mistranslation, misconstrue, translator's error; wrong interpretation, false construction; twist, turn, misapplication, perversion 246n. *distortion*; strained sense; false reading; false colouring, dark glasses, rose-coloured spectacles; garbling, falsification 552n. *misrepresentation*; over-colouring 546n. *exaggeration*; depreciation 483n. *underestimation*; parody, travesty 851n. *ridicule*; abuse of language, misapplication, catachresis 565n. *solecism*.

Adj. *misinterpreted* etc.vb., misconstrued, mistranslated; glozed, badly edited; misread, misexpressed.

Vb. *misinterpret*, misunderstand, misapprehend, misconceive 481 vb. *misjudge*; get wrong, get one wrong, get hold of the wrong end of the stick; misread, misspell 495 vb. *blunder*; misexplain, set in a false light 535 vb. *misteach*; mistranslate, misconstrue, put a false sense *or* construction on; give a twist *or* turn, pervert, strain the sense, wrest the meaning, wrench, twist, twist the words 246 vb. *distort*; equivocate, play upon words 518 vb. *be equivocal*; add a meaning, read into, write i. 38 vb. *add*; leave out, suppress 39 vb. *subtract*; misexpress, misquote; falsify, garble, gloze 552 vb. *misrepresent*; travesty, parody, caricature, guy 851 vb. *ridicule*; overpraise 482 vb. *overrate*; underpraise 483 vb. *underestimate*; inflate 546 vb. *exaggerate*; traduce 926 vb. *defame*.

See: 38, 39, 246, 481, 482, 483, 495, 518, 535, 546, 552, 565, 851, 926.

522 Manifestation

N. *manifestation*, revelation, unfolding, discovery, daylight, divulgence 526 n. *disclosure*; expression, formulation 532 n. *affirmation*; proof, quotation, citation 466 n. *evidence*; confrontation 462 n. *comparison*; presentation, production, projection, enactment 551 n. *representation*; symbolization, typification 547 n. *indication*; sign 547 n. *signal*; premonstration, preview 438 n. *view*; showing, demonstration, exhibition; display, showing off 875 n. *ostentation*; proclamation 528 n. *publication*; unconcealment, openness, flagrance 528 n. *publicity*; candour, plain speaking, plain speech, home-truth 573 n. *plainness*; prominence, conspicuousness, relief 443 n. *visibility*; apparition, vision, materialization 445 n. *appearance*; séance 984 n. *occultism*; shekinah, glory 965 n. *theophany*; incarnation, avatar.
exhibit, specimen, sample 83 n. *example*; piece of evidence, quotation, citation 466 n. *evidence*; show piece, collector's p., museum p. antique, curio; display, show, dress s., mannequin parade 445 n. *spectacle*; scene 438 n. *view*; showplace, showroom, showcase, show-card, bill, affiché, placard, hoarding 528 n. *advertisement*; sign 547 n. *label*; shop-window,

front w., museum, gallery 632 n. *collection*; exhibition, exposition, fair 796 n. *mart*; projection 551 n. *image*.
exhibitor, advertiser, publicist 528 n. *publicizer*; shower, displayer, demonstrator; showman, pageant-maker; producer, impresario 594 n. *stage manager*; exhibitionist, peacock 873 n. *vain person*; wearer, sporter, flaunter.

Adj. *manifest*, apparent, ostensible 445 adj. *appearing*; plain, clear, defined 80 adj. *definite*; explained, plain as a pike-staff, clear as noonday 516 adj. *intelligible*; unconcealed, showing 443 adj. *visible*; conspicuous, noticeable, notable, prominent, pronounced, striking, salient, in relief, in the foreground, in the limelight 443 adj. *well-seen*; open, patent, evident, obvious; gross, crass, palpable; self-evident, autoptical, written all over one, for all to see, unmistakable, recognizable, identifiable, uncontestable 473 adj. *certain*; public, famous, notorious 528 adj. *well-known*; catching the eye, eye-catching 875 adj. *showy*; arrant, glaring, stark staring, flagrant, loud, on the rooftops.
undisguised, unshaded; spoken, overt, explicit, express, emphatic 532 adj. *affirmative*; in the open, public; exoteric; unreserved, open, candid, heart-to-heart, off the record 540 adj. *veracious*; frank, downright, forthright, straightforward, outspoken, blunt, plain-spoken 573 adj. *plain*; bold, daring 711 adj. *defiant*; brazen, shameless, immodest, barefaced 951 adj. *impure*; bare, naked, naked and unashamed 229 adj. *uncovered*; flaunting, unconcealed, inconcealable (see *manifest*).
shown, manifested etc. vb.; declared, divulged 526 adj. *disclosed*; showing, featured, on show, on display, on 443 adj. *visible*; exhibited, shown off; brought forth, produced; adduced, cited, quoted; confronted, brought face to face; worn, sported; unfurled, flaunted, waved, brandished; advertised, publicized 528 adj. *published*; expressible, producible, showable.

Vb. *manifest*, reveal, divulge 526 vb. *disclose*; evince, give sign, give token, show signs of 466 vb. *evidence*; bring to light 484 vb. *discover*; explain, make plain, make obvious 520 vb. *interpret*; expose, lay bare, unroll, unfurl, unsheathe 229 vb.

uncover; open up, throw open, lay o. 263vb. *open*; elicit, draw forth, drag out 304vb. *extract*; invent, bring forth 164vb. *produce*; bring out, shadow forth, body f.; incorporate, incarnate, personify 223 vb. *externalize*; typify, symbolize, exemplify 547vb. *indicate*; point up, enhance, develop 36vb. *augment*; throw light on, enlighten 420vb. *illuminate*; highlight, spotlight, set in strong relief 532vb. *emphasize*; express, formulate 532vb. *affirm*; bring, bring up, adduce, cite, quote; bring to the fore, place in the foreground 638vb. *make important*; bring to notice, trot out, proclaim, publicize 528 vb. *publish*; show for what it is, show up (see *show*); solve, elucidate 520vb. *decipher*.

show, make a spectacle, exhibit, display; set out, expose to view, offer to the v., set before one's eyes, dangle; wave, flourish 317vb. *brandish*; sport 228vb. *wear*; flaunt, parade 875vb. *be ostentatious*; make a show of, affect 850vb. *be affected*; present, feature, enact 551vb. *represent*; put on, put on show, stage, release 594vb. *dramatize*; show off, set o., model (garments); put one through his paces; demonstrate 534vb. *teach*; show round, show over, point out, draw attention, bring to notice 547vb. *indicate*; confront, bring face to face; reflect, image, mirror, hold up the mirror to 20vb. *imitate*; tear off the mask, show up, expose 526vb. *disclose*.

be plain, — explicit etc.adj.; show one's face, unveil 229vb. *doff*; show one's true colours, fly one's flag, have no secrets, make no mystery, wear one's heart on one's sleeve; show one's mind, speak out, tell to one's face, make no secret of 573vb. *speak plainly*; speak for itself, tell its own story 516vb. *be intelligible*; be obvious, stand to reason, go without saying 478vb. *be proved*; be conspicuous, stand out, stand out a mile 443vb. *be visible*; show up, show up well, hold the stage, hold the limelight, stand in full view 455vb. *attract notice*; loom large, stare one in the face 200vb. *be near*; appear on the horizon, rear its head, transpire, emanate, come to light 445vb. *appear*.

Adv. *manifestly*, plainly, obviously, palpably, grossly crassly, openly, publicly, for all to see, notoriously, flagrantly,

undisguisedly; at first blush, prima facie; externally, on the face of it, superficially; open and above-board, with cards on the table; before all, in public, in open court, under the eye of heaven; in full view, on the stage.

See: 20, 36, 80, 83, 164, 200, 223, 228, 229, 263, 304, 317, 420, 438, 443, 445, 455, 462, 466, 473, 478, 484, 516, 520, 526, 528, 532, 534, 540, 547, 551, 573, 594, 632, 638, 711, 796, 850, 873, 875, 951, 965, 984.

523 Latency

N. *latency*, no signs of, delitescence 525n. *concealment*; insidiousness, treachery 930 n. *perfidy*; dormancy, dormant condition, potentiality 469n. *possibility*; esoterism, esotericism, cabbala 984n. *occultism*; occultness, mysticism; hidden meaning, occult m., veiled m. 517n. *unintelligibility*; ambiguous advice 511n. *oracle*; symbolism, allegory, anagoge 519n. *metaphor*; implication, adumbration, symbolization; mystery 530n. *secret*; penetralia 224n. *interiority*; dark 418n. *darkness*; shadowiness 419n. *dimness*; imperceptibility 444n. *invisibility*; more than meets the eye; deceptive appearance, hidden fires, hidden depths; slumbering volcano, sleeping lion 661n. *danger*; dark horse, mystery man, anonymity 562n. *no name*; nigger in the woodpile, snake in the grass 663n. *pitfall*; hidden hand, wire-puller, strings, friend at court, power behind the throne 178n. *influence*; secret influence, lurking disease; unsoundness, something rotten; innuendo, insinuation, suggestion 524n. *hint*; half-spoken word, inexpression, sealed lips 582n. *taciturnity*; undercurrent, undertone, undersong, aside 401n. *faintness*; clandestinity, secret society, cabal, intrigue 623n. *plot*; ambushment 527n. *ambush*; code, invisible writing, steganography, cryptography.

Adj. *latent*, lurking, skulking, delitescent 525adj. *concealed*; dormant, sleeping 679adj. *inactive*; passive 266adj. *quiescent*; potential, undeveloped 469adj. *possible*; unguessed, unsuspected, crypto-491adj. *unknown*; submerged, underlying, subterranean, below the surface 211adj. *deep*; in the background, behind the scenes, backroom, undercover 421adj.

screened; unmanifested, unseen, unspied, undetected, unexposed 444 adj. *invisible*; arcane, obscure 418 adj. *dark*; impenetrable, undiscoverable 517 adj. *unintelligible*; tucked away, sequestered 883 adj. *secluded*; awaiting discovery, undiscovered, unexplored, untracked, untraced, uninvented, unexplained, unsolved.

tacit, unsaid, unspoken, half-spoken, unpronounced, unexpressed, unvoiced, unbreathed; unmentioned, untold of, unsung; undivulged, unproclaimed, undeclared; unwritten, unpublished, unedited; understood, implied, implicit; implicational, suggestive; inferential, allusive, allusory.

occult, mysterious, mystic; symbolic, allegorical, anagogical 519 adj. *figurative*; cryptic, esoteric 984 adj. *cabbalistic*; veiled, muffled, covert; indirect, crooked 220 adj. *oblique*; clandestine, secret; insidious, treacherous 930 adj. *perfidious*; underhand 525 adj. *stealthy*; undiscovered, hush-hush, top-secret; not public, off the record 80 adj. *private*; coded, steganographic, cryptographic 525 adj. *disguised*.

Vb. *lurk*, hide, be latent, be a stowaway; burrow, stay underground; lie hid, lie in ambush; lie low, lie low and say nothing, lie doggo, make no sign 266 vb. *be quiescent*; avoid notice, escape observation 444 vb. *be unseen*; evade detection, escape, recognition, act behind the scenes, pull the wires, laugh in one's sleeve; creep, slink, tiptoe, walk on tiptoe 525 vb. *be stealthy*; underlie, be at the bottom of 156 vb. *cause*; smoke, smoulder 175 vb. *be inert*; leave one's sting behind.

imply, insinuate, whisper, murmur, suggest 524 vb. *hint*; understand, infer, leave an inference, allude, be allusive; symbolize, connote, carry a suggestion, involve, spell 514 vb. *mean*.

See: 80, 156, 175, 178, 211, 220, 224, 266, 401, 418, 419, 421, 444, 469, 491, 511, 514, 517, 519, 524, 525, 527, 530, 562, 582, 623, 661, 663, 679, 883, 930, 984.

524 Information

N. *information*, communication of knowledge, transmission of k., dissemination, diffusion; mailing list, distribution l. 588 n. *correspondence*; chain of authorities, tradition, hearsay; enlightenment, instruction, briefing 534 n. *teaching*; thought-transference, intercommunication 531 n. *telecommunication*; sharing of information, communication; telling, narration 590 n. *narrative*; notification, announcement, annunciation, intimation, warning, advice, notice, mention, tip, tip-off (see *hint*); advertisement 528 n. *publicity*; common knowledge, general information, gen; factual information, facts, the goods, documentary 494 n. *truth*; inside information, dope, lowdown, private source, confidence 530 n. *secret*; earliest information, scoop; stock of information, acquaintance, the know 490 n. *knowledge*; recorded information, file, dossier 548 n. *record*; piece of information, word, report, intelligence 529 n. *news*; a communication, wire, telegram, cable, cablegram, radiogram 529 n. *message*; flood of information, spate of news, outpouring; communicativeness, talking 581 n. *loquacity*; unauthorized communication, indiscretion.

report, information called for 459 n. *enquiry*; paper, command p., White Paper; account, true a., narrative report 590 n. *narrative*; statement, state, return 86 n. *statistics*; specification, estimates 480 n. *estimate*; progress report, confidential r.; information offered, despatch, bulletin, communiqué, hand-out 529 n. *news*; representation, presentation (of ones' case), case; memorial, petition 761 n. *entreaty*; remonstrance, round-robin 762 n. *deprecation*; letters, despatches 588 n. *correspondence*.

hint, gentle h., whisper, aside, subaudition, subauditur 401 n. *faintness*; indirect hint, intimation; broad hint, signal, nod, wink, look, nudge, kick, by-play, gesticulation 547 n. *gesture*; prompt, cue 505 n. *reminder*; suggestion, lead, leading question 547 n. *indication*; caution, monition 664 n. *warning*; something to go on, tip, tip-off (see *information*); word, passing w., word in the ear, word to the wise, verb. sap. 691 n. *advice*; insinuation, innuendo 926 n. *calumny*; clue, symptom 520 n. *interpretation*; sidelight, glimpse, inkling, adumbration 419 n. *glimmer*; suspicion, inference, guess 512 n. *conjecture*; good

tip, wheeze, dodge, wrinkle 623 n. *contrivance.*

informant, teller 590 n. *narrator*; spokesman 579 n. *speaker*; mouthpiece, representative 754 n. *delegate*; announcer, radio a., notifier, advertiser, annunciator 528 n. *publiciser*; harbinger, herald 531 n. *messenger*; testifier 466 n. *witness*; one in the know, authority, source; quarter, channel, circle, grape-vine; go-between, contact 231 n. *intermediary*; informed circles, information centre; communicator, intelligencer, correspondent, special c., reporter, newshound, commentator, columnist, gossip writer 529 n. *newsmonger*; tipper, tipster 691 n. *adviser*; guide, topographer; blurter, 'big mouth'.

informer, common i., delator 928 n. *accuser*; spy, snoop, sleuth 459 n. *detective*; stool-pigeon, nark, copper's n., snitch, fink, blabber, squealer, squeaker, peacher; approver 603 n. *tergiversator*; peek, eavesdropper, tell-tale, tale-bearer, tattler, tattle-tale, gossip 529 n. *newsmonger.*

guide-book, travelogue, topography; Baedeker, Murray; handbook, manual, vade mecum; timetable, Bradshaw, A.B.C.; itinerary, route map, chart, plan 551 n. *map*; gazetteer; nautical almanac, ephemeris; catalogue 87 n. *directory*; cicerone, courier 520 n. *guide.*

Adj. informative, communicative, newsy, chatty, gossipy; informatory, informational, instructive, instructional, documentary 534 adj. *educational*; expressive 532 adj. *affirmative*; expository 520 adj. *interpretive*; in writing 586 adj. *written*; oral, verbal, spoken, nuncupatory, nuncupative 579 adj. *speaking*; annunciatory 528 adj. *publishing*; advisory 691 adj. *advising*; monitory 664 adj. *cautionary*; explicit, clear 80 adj. *definite*; candid, plain-spoken 573 adj. *plain*; over-communicative, talking, indiscreet 581 adj. *loquacious*; hinting, insinuating, suggesting.

informed, well-i., kept i.; posted, primed, briefed, instructed 490 adj. *knowing*; told, certified, au courant, in the know, in on, in the picture.

Vb. inform, certify, advise, beg to a.; intimate, impart, convey (see *communicate*); apprise, acquaint, have one know, give to understand; possess, possess one with the facts, brief, instruct 534 vb. *teach*; let

one know, put one in the picture; enlighten, open the mind, fill with information 534 vb. *educate*; point out, direct one's attention 547 vb. *indicate*; insinuate (see *hint*); entrust with information, confide, get confidential, mention privately; put one wise, put right, correct, disabuse, unbeguile, undeceive, disillusion; be specific, state, name, signify 80 vb. *specify*; mention, refer to, touch on, speak of 579 vb. *speak*; gossip, spread rumours; be indiscreet, open one's mouth, blurt out, talk 581 vb. *be loquacious*; break the news, reveal 526 vb. *disclose*; tell, blab, split, peach, squeal, blow the gaff 526 vb. *confess*; rat, turn Queen's evidence, turn state's e., involve an accomplice 603 vb. *tergiversate*; tell tales, tell on, report against; inform against, lay an information, delate, denounce 928 vb. *accuse.*

communicate, transmit, pass on, pass on information; despatch news 588 vb. *correspond*; report, cover, make a report, submit a r.; report progress, post, keep posted; get through, get across, put it over; contact, get in touch; convey, bring word, send w., leave w., write 588 vb. *correspond*; flash news, flash; send a message, speak, semaphore 547 vb. *signal*; wire, telegraph, telephone, ring, ring up, call, dial; disseminate, broadcast, telecast, televise; announce, annunciate, notify, give notice, serve n. 528 vb. *advertise*; give out, put out, carry a report, publicize 528 vb. *publish*; retail, recount, narrate 590 vb. *describe*; commune 584 vb. *converse*; swap news, exchange information, pool one's knowledge.

hint, drop a h., adumbrate, suggest, throw out a suggestion, put in one's head; prompt, give the cue 505 vb. *remind*; caution 664 vb. *warn*; tip off 691 vb. *advise*; wink, tip the wink; nudge 547 vb. *gesticulate*; insinuate, breathe, whisper, say in one's ear, touch upon, just mention, mention in passing, say by the way, let fall, imply, allude, leave an inference, leave one to gather, intimate.

be informed, have the facts 490 vb. *know*; be told, receive information, have it from; keep one's ears open, get to hear of, use one's ears, overhear 415 vb. *hear*; get wind of, get scent of 484 vb. *discover*; gather, infer, realize 516 vb. *understand*; come to know, get a report, get the facts

536 vb. *learn*; open one's eyes, awaken to, become alive to 455 vb. *be attentive*; ask for information, call for a report 459 vb. *enquire*; have information, have the dope, have something to tell; claim to know 532 vb. *affirm.*

Adv. *reportedly*, as stated, on information received, by report; in the air, according to rumour, from what one can gather, if one can trust one's ears.

See: 80, 86, 87, 231, 401, 415, 419, 455, 459, 466, 480, 484, 490, 494, 505, 512, 516, 520, 526, 528, 529, 530, 531, 532, 534, 536, 547, 548, 573, 579, 581, 584, 586, 588, 590, 603, 623, 664, 691, 754, 761, 762, 926, 928.

525 Concealment

N. *concealment*, confinement, purdah 883 n. *seclusion*; hiding, latitancy 523 n. *latency*; covering up, burial 364 n. *internment*; occultation 446 n. *disappearance*; cache 527 n. *hiding-place*; crypt 364 n. *tomb*; disguisement, disguise, camouflage 542 n. *deception*; masquerade, bal masqué; anonymity, incognito 562 n. *no name*; smoke screen 421 n. *screen*; reticence, reserve, closeness, discretion, no word of 582 n. *taciturnity*; secret thought, mental reservation, arrière pensée; lack of candour, vagueness, evasion, evasiveness 518 n. *equivocalness*; mystification 421 n. *obfuscation*; misinformation 535 n. *misteaching*; white lie 543 n. *mental dishonesty*; subterfuge 542 n. *trickery*; suppression, suppression of the truth 543 n. *untruth*; deceitfulness, dissimulation, obreption 541 n. *duplicity.*

secrecy, close s. 399 n. *silence*; secretness, mystery 530 n. *secret*; seal of secrecy, hearing in camera, auricular confession; Freemasonry; clandestinity, secretiveness, furtiveness, stealthiness, clandestine behaviour; underhand dealing 930 n. *improbity*; conspiracy 623 n. *plot*; cryptography steganography, cipher, code 517 n. *unintelligibility*; invisible ink, sympathetic i.

Adj. *concealed*, crypto-, hidden; hiding, lost, perdu; esconced, in ambush, lying in wait 523 adj. *latent*; confined, incommunicado 747 adj. *imprisoned*; mysterious, recondite, arcane 517 adj. *unintelligible*; cryptic 523 adj. *occult*; private

883 adj. *secluded*; privy, confidential, off the record; auricular, secret, top-secret, hush-hush, inviolable, inviolate, unrevealed, irrevealable; undisclosed, untold; unsigned, unnamed 562 adj. *anonymous*; covert, covered 364 adj. *buried*; hooded, veiled, eclipsed 421 adj. *screened*; stifled, suppressed, clandestine, undercover, underground, subterranean 211 adj. *deep.*

disguised, camouflaged; incognito 562 adj. *anonymous*; unrecognized, unrecognizable 491 adj. *unknown*; disfigured, deformed 246 adj. *distorted*; masked 421 adj. *screened*; overpainted 226 adj. *covered*; blotted 550 adj. *obliterated*; coded, codified, cryptographic, steganographic 517 adj. *unintelligible.*

stealthy, silent, furtive, like a thief; softly treading, feline, catlike, pussyfoot, on tiptoe; prowling, skulking, loitering, lurking; clandestine, hugger-mugger, conspiratorial, cloak-and-dagger; hole-and-corner, backdoor, underhand, surreptitious, obreptitious 930 adj. *dishonest.*

reticent, reserved, withdrawn; non-committal, incommunicative, cagey, evasive; vague, studiously v.; not talking, discreet, silent 582 adj. *taciturn*; tight-lipped, poker-faced; close, secretive, buttoned-up, close as wax, close as an oyster, clamlike; in one's shell 883 adj. *unsociable.*

Vb. *conceal*, hide, hide away, secrete, ensconce, confine, keep in purdah 883 vb. *seclude*; stow away, lock up, seal up, bottle up 632 vb. *store*; hide underground, bury 364 vb. *inter*; put out of sight, sweep under the mat, cover up 226 vb. *cover*; varnish, gloss over 226 vb. *overlay*; overpaint, blot 550 vb. *obliterate*; slur, slur over, not mention 458 vb. *disregard*; smother, stifle 165 vb. *suppress*; veil, muffle, mask, disguise, camouflage; shroud, becurtain, draw the curtain 421 vb. *screen*; shade, obscure, eclipse 418 vb. *darken*; befog, becloud, obfuscate 419 vb. *bedim*; hide one's identity, assume a mask, masquerade 541 vb. *dissemble*; code, encode, use a cipher 517 vb. *be unintelligible.*

keep secret, keep it dark, keep snug, keep close, keep under one's hat; look blank, look poker-faced, keep a straight face, be mum, keep one's mouth shut, hold one's tongue, breathe not a word, not

atter a syllable, not talk, keep one's counsel, make no sign 582 vb. *be taciturn*; be discreet, neither confirm nor deny; keep back, reserve, withhold, let it go no further; hush up, cover up, suppress, sink; keep in the background, keep in the shade; let not one's right hand know what one's left hand does; blindfold, bamboozle, keep in the dark 542 vb. *deceive.*

be stealthy, — furtive, — evasive etc. adj.; hugger-mugger, conspire 623 vb. *plot*; snoop, sneak, slink, creep; steal along, steal by, steal past; tiptoe, go on t., pussyfoot; prowl, skulk, loiter; be anonymous, stay incognito; wear a mask, assume a disguise 541 vb. *dissemble*; lie doggo 523 vb. *lurk*; evade, shun, hide from, dodge 620 vb. *avoid*; play hide-and-seek, play bo-peep, hide in holes and corners; leave no address, cover one's tracks, take cover; vanish 446 vb. *disappear*; hide from the light, retire from sight, withdraw into seclusion, bury oneself, stay in one's shell 883 vb. *be unsocial*; lay an ambush 527 vb. *ambush.*

Adv. *secretly*, hugger-mugger, conspiratorially; confidentially, sotto voce, with bated breath; entre nous, between ourselves; aside, to oneself, in petto; in one's sleeve; sub rosa, without beat of drum; not for publication, privately, in camera; behind closed doors, anonymously, incognito, with nobody the wiser.

stealthily, furtively, by stealth, like a thief in the night; in the dark 444 adv. *invisibly*; underhand, by the back-door, in a hole-and-corner way; on the sly, by subterfuge.

See: 165, 211, 226, 246, 364, 399, 418, 419, 421, 444, 446, 458, 491, 517, 518, 523, 527, 530, 535, 541, 542, 543, 550, 562, 582, 620, 623, 632, 747, 883, 930.

526 Disclosure

N. *disclosure*, revealment, revelation, apocalypse; daylight, hard d.; discovery, uncovering; unwelcome discovery, disillusionment 509 n. *disappointment*; dénouement, catastrophe, peripeteia 154 n. *eventuality*; lid off, divulgement, divulgence 528 n. *publication*; exposure, showing up 522 n. *manifestation*; explanations, clearing the air, showdown; communica-

tion, leak, indiscretion; bewrayment, betrayal, give-away; cloven hoof, tell-tale sign, blush, self-betrayal; state's evidence, Queen's e. 603 n. *tergiversation*; acknowledgement, admission, avowal, confession; auricular confession, confessional 939 n. *penitence*; clean breast, whole truth, cards on the table 494 n. *truth.*

Adj. *disclosed*, exposed, revealed 522 adj. *shown*; showing 443 adj. *visible*; confessed, avowed, acknowledged; with the lid off 263 adj. *open*; divested 229 adj. *uncovered.*

disclosing, uncovering, unclosing, opening; revelatory, apocalyptic, manifesting; revealing 422 adj. *transparent*; expository, explicatory, explanatory 520 adj. *interpretive*; divulgatory 528 adj. *publishing*; communicative 524 adj. *informative*; leaky, indiscreet, garrulous 581 adj. *loquacious*; tell-tale, indicative 547 adj. *indicating*; bewraying, betraying; confessing, confessional, penitent 939 adj. *repentant.*

Vb. *disclose*, reveal, expose, show up 522 vb. *manifest*; bare, lay b., strip b., denude 229 vb. *doff*; unfold, unroll, unfurl, unpack, unwrap 229 vb. *uncover*; unshroud unscreen, uncurtain, unveil, lift the veil, draw the v., raise the curtain, let in daylight; unseal, break the seal, break the wax, unclose 263 vb. *open*; lay open, open up 484 vb. *discover*; catch out 484 vb. *detect*; bewray, not hide 422 vb. *be transparent*; give away, betray; uncloak, unmask, tear off the mask; expose oneself, betray o., give oneself away 495 vb. *blunder*; declare oneself, lift the mask, drop the m., throw off the m., throw off all disguise; show for what it is, cut down to life size, debunk; disabuse, correct, set right, undeceive, unbeguile, disillusion, open the eyes 524 vn. *inform*; take the lid off, unkennel, let the cat out of the bag (see *divulge*).

divulge, be open about, declare, vent, ventilate, air, canvass, publicize 528 vb. *publish*; let on, blurt out, blow the gaff, talk out of turn, spill the beans, let the cat out of the bag; speak of, talk, must tell; utter, breathe 579 vb. *speak*; let out, leak 524 vb. *communicate*; let drop, let fall 524 vb. *hint*; come out with 573 vb. *speak plainly*; get it off one's chest, unbosom oneself; confide, let one into the secret, open one's

mind, bare one's m.; declare one's intentions, show one's hand, show one's cards, put one's cards on the table; report, tell, tell tales out of school, tell on 928vb. *accuse*; betray the secret, split, peach, squeal, blab 524vb. *inform*; rat 603vb. *tergiversate.*

confess, admit, avow, acknowledge; concede, grant, allow, own 488vb. *assent*; own up, implicate oneself, plead guilty, admit the soft impeachment; come out with, come across with, come clean, tell all, admit everything, speak the truth 540vb. *be truthful*; make a clean breast, unburden one's conscience, go to confession, recount one's sins, be shriven 939vb. *be penitent*; turn Queen's evidence 603vb. *tergiversate.*

be disclosed, come out, blow up 445vb. *appear*; come out in evidence, come to light 478vb. *be proved*; show the cloven hoof, show its face, show its colours, stand revealed 522vb. *be plain*; transpire, become known 490vb. *be known*; leak out, ooze o., creep o. 298vb. *emerge*; peep out, show 443vb. *be visible*; show through 422vb. *be transparent*; come as a revelation, break through the clouds, flash on the mind 449vb. *dawn upon*; give oneself away, there speaks . . . .

See: 154, 229, 263, 298, 422, 443, 445, 449, 478, 484, 488, 490, 494, 495, 509, 520, 522, 524, 528, 540, 547, 573, 579, 581, 603, 928, 939.

527 Hiding. Disguise

N. *hiding-place*, hide, hide-out, hole, hidy-h., funk-h. 662n. *refuge*; lair, den 192n. *retreat*; cache, secret place, abditory, oubliette; crypt, vault 194n. *cellar*; closet, secret drawer, hidden panel, safe place, safe, safe deposit 632n. *storage* recess, corner, nook, cranny, niche, holes and corners, secret passage, underground p.; cover, underground 662n. *shelter*; backstairs, backroom, adytum, penetralia, inmost recesses 224n. *interiority.*

ambush, ambuscade, ambushment 525n. *concealment*; lurking-place, spider's web 542n. *trap*; catch 663n. *pitfall*; stalking horse, Trojan h., decoy, stool-pigeon 545n. *impostor*; agent provocateur 663 n. *trouble-maker.*

disguise, blind, camouflage, protective colouring 542n. *deception*; dummy, lath painted to look like iron 20n. *imitation*; veneer 226n. *covering*; mask, visor, veil 228n. *cloak*; domino, masquerade dress, fancy d.; cloud, smoke-screen, cover 421 n. *screen.*

hider, lurker, skulker, stowaway, nigger in the woodpile; dodger 620n. *avoider*; masker, masquerader; wolf in sheep's clothing 545n. *impostor.*

Vb. *ambush*, set an a., lie in a., lie in wait 523vb. *lurk*; set a trap for 542vb. *ensnare*; assume a disguise, wear a mask; throw out a smoke-screen, obfuscate; waylay.

See: 20, 192, 194, 224, 226, 228, 421, 523, 525, 542, 545, 620, 632, 662, 663.

528 Publication

N. *publication*, spreading abroad, dissemination, divulgation 526n. *disclosure*; promulgation, proclamation; edict, ukase, ban 737vb. *decree*; arrière-ban; call-up, summons; cry, rallying c., call, bugle-c., trumpet-c. 547n. *call*; tucket, sennet, flourish, beat of drum, flourish of trumpets 400n. *loudness*; notification, public notice, official bulletin; announcement, pronouncement, pronunciamento, manifesto, programme, platform; publishing, book-trade, bookselling 589n. *book*; broadcasting 531n. *telecommunication*; broadcast, telecast, newscast 529n. *news*; kite-flying 529n. *rumour*; circulation, circular, encyclical.

publicity, publicness, common knowledge 490n. *knowledge*; open discussion, ventilation, canvassing, canvass; openness, flagrancy, blatancy 522n. *manifestation*; cry, open secret, open scandal; notoriety, fame 866n. *famousness*; currency, wide c.; circulation, wide c., country-wide c.; sale, extensive sales; readership, viewership; public relations, propaganda; display, showmanship, salesmanship, window-dressing 875n. *ostentation*; sensationalism, ballyhoo 546n. *exaggeration*; publicization, advertising, press a., radio a., sky-writing; medium of publicity, radio 531n. *telecommunication*; public address system, loud speaker, loud hailer 415n. *hearing aid*; public comment,

journalism, reporting, rapportage, coverage, report, write-up (see *the press*); newsreel, newscast, newsletter 529 n. *news*; correspondence column, open letter; editorial 591 n. *article*; pulpit, platform, hustings, soap-box 539 n. *rostrum*; printing press 587 n. *print*; letters of fire, letters of gold.

advertisement, public notice, press n., gazette, insertion, ad, small a., want ad, personal column; agony c.; headline, banner, streamer, screamer, spread; puff, blurb, boost, ballyhoo, build-up, limelight, spotlight; bill, affiche, poster, show-card 522 n. *exhibit*; bill board, hoarding, placard, sandwich-board, display b., notice b., bulletin b.

the press, fourth estate, Fleet Street, newspaper world, news business, the papers; newspaper, news-sheet, sheet, paper, rag, tabloid, comic strip; serious press, gutter p., yellow p., tabloid p.; organ, journal, daily paper, daily, morning paper, evening p., Sunday p., illustrated p., picture p.; issue, edition, late e., stop-press e., sports e., extra; magazine section, serial, supplement, trade s.; leaflet, handbill, pamphlet, brochure, broadsheet, squib, open letter, newsletter.

journal, review, magazine, periodical, daily, weekly, monthly, quarterly half-yearly, annual; gazette, trade organ, house o., trade publication 589 n. *reading matter*.

publicizer, canvasser, advertiser, notifier, announcer; herald, trumpet 531 n. *messenger*; proclaimer, crier, town-crier, bellman; barker, booster; bill-sticker, sandwichman; publicist, printer, publisher 589 n. *bookman*; reporter, correspondent, gentleman of the press, press representative, cub, news-hound, pressman, journalist 589 n. *author*; copywriter, blurb-w., commercial artist, publicity agent, press a., advertising a.; public relations officer, P.R.O., propagandist, pamphleteer 537 n. *preacher*.

Adj. *published*, in print 587 adj. *printed*; in circulation, circulating, passing round, current; in the news, public 490 adj. *known*; open, exoteric; distributed, circularized, disseminated, broadcast; ventilated, canvassed.

publishing, promulgatory, declaratory, notificatory, annunciative.

well-known, public, celebrated, famous,

notorious, crying, flagrant, blatant, glaring, sensational 522 adj. *manifest*.

Vb. *publish*, make public, carry a report 524 vb. *communicate*; report, cover, write up; write an open letter, drag into the limelight, bring into the open, reveal 526 vb. *divulge*; highlight, spotlight 532 vb. *emphasize*; radio, broadcast, telecast, televise, relay, diffuse 524 vb. *inform*; spread, circulate, distribute, disseminate, circularize; canvass, ventilate, discuss 475 vb. *argue*; pamphleteer, propagate 534 vb. *teach*; use the press 587 vb. *print*; serialize, edit, issue, get out, put o., give o., send forth, give to the world, lay before the public; spread a rumour, fly a kite; rumour, make news of, bruit, noise abroad, spread a.; talk about, retail, pass round, put about, bandy a., hawk a., buzz a. 581 vb. *be loquacious*; voice, broach, talk of, speak of, utter, emit 579 vb. *speak*.

proclaim, announce, promulgate, notify, gazette; ban, denounce, raise a hue and cry 928 vb. *accuse*; pronounce, declare 532 vb. *affirm*; make a proclamation, issue a pronouncement, publish a manifesto; celebrate, noise, trumpet, blazon, herald, cry, shout, scream, thunder 400 vb. *be loud*; declaim, shout from the housetops, proclaim at the crossroads, warn by beat of drum, announce with a flourish of trumpets, send round the town-crier.

advertise, publicize, canvass, insert a notice, bill, placard, post, stick up a notice, put on the hoardings; tell the world, put on the map, put in headlines, headline, splash; put in lights, spotlight, build up; make much of, feature; sell, boost, puff, cry up, write up, glorify 482 vb. *overrate*; din, din into one's ears, plug 106 vb. *repeat*.

be published, become public, issue, come out; acquire notoriety, hit the headlines; circulate, pass current, pass from mouth to mouth, pass round, go the rounds, get about, spread abroad, spread like wildfire, fly about, buzz a.; find a publisher, see oneself in print, get printed, get into the papers; have a circulation, sell well, go like a best-seller 793 vb. *be sold*.

Adv. *publicly*, openly, in open court, with open windows, with open doors; in the limelight.

See: 106, 400, 415, 475, 482, 490, 522, 524,

526, 529, 531, 532, 534, 537, 539, 546, 547, 579, 581, 587, 589, 591, 737, 793, 866, 875, 928.

529 News

N. *news*, good n.; **bad news** 509 n. *disappointment*; tidings, glad t.; gospel, evangel 973 n. *religion*; budget of news, packet of n., newspacket, despatches, diplomatic bag; intelligence, report, despatch, word, advice; piece of information, something to tell, titbit, flash 524 n. *information*; bulletin, communiqué, hand-out; newspaper report, press notice; fresh news, stirring n., latest n., stop-press n.; sensation, scoop; old news, stale n.; copy, filler; yarn, story, old s., tall s.; broadcast, telecast, newscast, newsreel 528 n. *publicity*; news-value.

rumour, unverified news, unconfirmed report; flying rumour, fame; hearsay, gossip, gup, talk, talk of the town, tittle-tattle 584 n. *chat*; scandal 926 n. *calumny*; noise, cry, buzz, bruit; false report, hoax, canard; grape-vine; kite-flying.

message, oral m., word of mouth, word, advice, tip 524 n. *information*; communication 547 n. *signal*; marconigram, wireless message, radiogram, cablegram, cable, telegram, wire, lettergram 531 n. *telecommunication*; letter, postcard, letters, despatches 588 n. *correspondence*; ring, phone-call; errand, embassy 751 n. *commission*.

newsmonger, quidnunc, gossip, talker 584 n. *interlocutor*; tattler, chatterer; scandalmonger 926 n. *defamer*; retailer of news, news-pedlar; newsman, news-hound, news reporter, reporter, sob-sister, special correspondent 589 n. *author*; newsboy, news-agent, newsvendor.

Adj. *rumoured*, talked about, in the news, in the papers; reported, currently r., going about, passing round; rife, afloat, in circulation, in everyone's mouth, on all tongues; full of news, newsy, gossipy, chatty 524 adj. *informative*.

Vb. *rumour*, fly a kite; send or despatch news 588 vb. *correspond*. See 524 vb. *inform*, 526 vb. *disclose*, 528 vb. *publish*.

See: 509, 524, 526, 528, 531, 547, 584, 588, 589, 751, 926, 973.

530 Secret

N. *secret*, dead s., profound s.; secret lore, esotery, esoterism, arcanum, mystery 984 n. *occultism*; confidential matter, sealed orders, hush-hush subject, top-secret file; confidential communication, confidence; sphinx, man of mystery, enigmatic personality; Mr. X. 562 n. *no name*; dark horse, unknown quantity; unmentionable thing, skeleton in the cupboard; unknown country, terra incognita 491 n. *unknown thing*; sealed book, secrets of the prison house.

enigma, mystery, puzzle, Chinese p.; problem, hyperproblem, poser, brain-twister, teaser; hard nut to crack, hard saying, knotty point, vexed question, crux, crux criticorum 700 n. *difficulty*; cipher, code, cryptogram, hieroglyphics 517 n. *unintelligibility*; word-puzzle, logogriph, anagram, acrostic, crossword; riddle, riddle-me-ree, conundrum, rebus; charade, dumb c.; intricacy, labyrinth, maze, labyrinthine m., Hyrcanian wood 61 n. *complexity*.

See: 61, 491, 517, 562, 700, 984.

531 Messenger

N. *messenger*, forerunner 66 n. *precursor*; harbinger 511 n. *omen*; message-bearer (see *courier*); announcer, crier, town-crier, bellman 528 n. *publicizer*; ambassador, minister, nuncio, legate, spokesman 754 n. *envoy*; apostle, emissary; flag-bearer, parlementaire, herald, trumpet; pursuivant, summoner, process-server 955 n. *law-officer*; go-between, contact, contact-man 231 n. *intermediary*.

courier, runner, King's messenger, express m., express, dispatch-bearer, dispatch-rider, estafette, mounted courier; post-boy, telegraph boy, messenger b., errand b., office-b., corridor girl; call-boy, bell-hop, page, buttons, commissionaire; harkara, peon, chaprassi; carrier pigeon 273 n. *carrier*; Iris, Hermes, Mercury, Ariel.

mails, letters 588 n. *correspondence*; mail, post, pigeon-p.; surface mail, sea-m., air-m.; mail-train, mail-coach, mail car, mail boat, mail packet, mail plane; mail service, delivery, postal d., express d.; sorter, postman, mailman, dakwallah,

letter-carrier; postmaster, postmistress, Postmaster-General; post-office, mail o., G.P.O., poste restante; postbox, letter box, pillar b.; mailbag, letter-bag, diplomatic bag.

telecommunication, long-distance communication; cable, cablegram, telegram, wire 529n. *message*; signalling, flag-s., semaphore, smoke-signal, beacon, beacon fire 547n. *signal*; wireless, wireless communication, radio c., radio, sound r., television; radio signal, morse, morse code; pip; telephone, radio t., walkie-talkie, telegraph, grape-vine t., radio t.; teleprinter; transmitter, radio mast, aerial, antenna; telegraph wire, telegraph pole; receiver, earphone, headphone; microphone, mike, loud-speaker, loud hailer, public address system; broadcasting, broadcast, simulcast, relay; broadcaster, wireless announcer; listener-in; televiewer, looker-in.

See: 66, 231, 273, 511, 528, 529, 547, 588, 754, 955.

532 Affirmation

N. *affirmation*, affirmance; proposition, subject and predicate; saying, dictum 496n. *maxim*; predication, statement, truth-claim 512n. *supposition*; sentence, expressed opinion, conclusion 480n. *judgment*; voice, choice, suffrage, ballot 605n. *vote*; expression, formulation; written statement, prepared text; one's position, one's stand; declaration, profession, jactitation; allegation 928n. *accusation*; assertion, unsupported a., ipse dixit, say-so; asseveration, averment, admission; confession, avowal 526n, *disclosure*; corroboration, confirmation, assurance, avouchment, one's word, warrant 466n. *testimony*; insistence, vehemence, peremptoriness 571n. *vigour*; stress, accent, accent on, emphasis, overstatement; palillogy 106n. *repetition*; challenge, provocation 711n. *defiance*; protest 762n. *deprecation*; appeal, representation, adjurement, adjuration 761n. *entreaty*; observation, remark, interjection 579n. *speech*; comment, criticism, positive c., constructive c. 480n. *estimate*; assertiveness, self-assertion, push, thrust,

drive 174n. *vigorousness*; pontification, dogmatism 473n. *positiveness*.

oath, Bible o., oath-taking, oath-giving, adjurement, swearing, assertory oath, solemn affirmation, statement on oath, deposition, affidavit 466n. *testimony*; promissory oath, word of a gentleman, pledge, promise, warrant, guarantee 764n. *promise*.

Adj. *affirmative*, affirming, professing etc. vb.; not negative 473adj. *positive*; predicatory, predicative; declaratory, declarative 526adj. *disclosing*; pronunciative, enunciative 528adj. *publishing*; valid, in force, unretracted, unretractable 473 adj. *undisputed*; committed, pledged, guaranteed, promised 764adj. *promissory*; earnest, meaning 617adj. *intending*; solemn, sworn, on oath, formal; affirmable, predicable.

assertive, assertorial, saying, telling; assured, dogmatic, confident, self-assured 473adj. *positive*; pushing, thrustful, trenchant, incisive, pointed, decisive, decided 571adj. *forceful*; distinct 80adj. *definite*; express, peremptory, categorical, absolute, brooking no denial, emphatic, insistent; vehement, thundering 176adj. *violent*; making no bones, flat, broad, round, blunt, strong, outspoken, strongly-worded 573adj. *plain*; pontifical, of faith, unquestionable, ex cathedra 485adj. *credal*; challenging, provocative 711adj. *defiant*.

Vb. *affirm*, state, express, formulate, set down; declare, pronounce, enunciate 528vb. *proclaim*; give expression to, voice 579vb. *speak*; remark, comment, observe, say; state with conviction, be bound, dare be sworn 485vb. *opine*; mean what one says, vow, protest; make a statement, make an assertion, assert, predicate; maintain, stand for, hold, contend 475vb. *argue*; make one's point 478vb. *demonstrate*; advance, urge 512vb. *propound*; represent, put one's case, submit; appeal, adjure, claim 761vb. *request*; allege, pretend, asseverate, avouch, aver; bear witness 466vb. *testify*; certify, confirm, warrant, guarantee 466vb. *corroborate*; commit oneself, go as far as; pledge, engage 764vb. *promise*; hold out 759vb. *offer*; profess, avow; admit 526vb. *confess*; abide by, not retreat, not retract 599vb. *stand firm*; challenge 711vb. *defy*;

repudiate 533 vb. *negate*; speak up, speak out, say outright, assert roundly, put it bluntly, make no bones about 573 vb. *speak plainly*; be assertive, brook no denial, shout, shout down; claim to know, say so, lay down, lay down the law, speak ex cathedra, pontificate 473 vb. *dogmatize*; have one's say, have the last word.

swear, be sworn, swear an oath, take o., take one's Bible o.; attest, confirm by oath 466 vb. *corroborate*; swear down, outswear 533 vb. *negate*; cross one's heart, solemnly affirm, make solemn affirmation 466 vb. *testify*; kiss the book, swear on the Bible, swear by all that is holy, take God's name in vain.

emphasize, stress, lay stress on, accent, accentuate, shout; underline, put in italics, italicize, dot the i's and cross the t's; raise one's voice, speak up, roar thunder, fulminate 400 vb. *be loud*; bang *or* thump the table; be urgent, be instant, be earnest; insist, positively i. 737 vb. *command*; say with emphasis, drive home, impress on, rub in; plug, dwell on, say again and again, re-affirm, re-assert, labour 106 vb. *repeat*; single out, highlight, enhance, point up 638 vb. *make important*; urge, enforce.

Adv. *affirmatively*, positively, without fear of contradiction, ex cathedra; seriously, joking apart, in sober earnest; on oath, on the Bible; in all conscience, upon one's word, upon one's honour 543 adv. *truly*.

See: 80, 106, 174, 176, 400, 466, 473, 475, 478, 480, 485, 496, 512, 526, 528, 533, 543, 571, 573, 579, 599, 605, 617, 638, 711, 737, 759, 761, 762, 764, 928.

533 Negation

N. *negation*, negative, nay; denial 760 n. *refusal*; refusal of belief, disbelief 486 n. *unbelief*; disagreement 489 n. *dissent*; contrary assertion, rebuttal, appeal, cross-a. 460 n. *rejoinder*; refutation, disproof 479 n. *confutation*; emphatic denial, contradiction, flat c., gainsaying; the lie, lie direct, démenti; challenge 711 n. *defiance*; demurrer 468 n. *qualification*; protest 762 n. *deprecation*; repudiation, disclaimer, disavowal, disownment, dissociation, non-association 607 n. *rejec-*

tion; abnegation, renunciation 621 n. *relinquishment*; retractation, palinode, abjuration, abjurement, swearing off 603 n. *recantation*; negative attitude, non-corroboration, inability to confirm; refusal of consent, disallowance 757 n. *prohibition*; recusancy 769 n. *non-observance*; contravention 738 n. *disobedience*; cancellation, invalidation, revocation 752 n. *abrogation*.

Adj. *negative*, denying, negating, negatory; adversative, contradictory 14 adj. *contrary*; contravening 738 adj. *disobedient*; protesting, protestant 762 adj. *deprecatory*; recusant, non-juring 769 adj. *non-observant*; abrogative, revocatory; abnegatory, renunciatory 753 adj. *resigning*; denied, disowned, unfathered.

Vb. *negate*, negative; contravene 738 vb. *disobey*; deny, gainsay, give the lie to, belie, contradict, deny flatly, contradict absolutely, issue a démenti; deny the possibility, eat one's hat if 470 vb. *make impossible*; disaffirm, repudiate, disavow, disclaim, disown, leave unfathered 607 vb. *reject*; not confirm, refuse to corroborate; not maintain, hold no brief for 860 vb. *be indifferent*; deny in part, demur, object 468 vb. *qualify*; disagree 489 vb. *dissent*; dissociate oneself 704 vb. *oppose*; affirm the contrary, controvert, traverse, impugn, question, call in q., refute, rebut, disprove 479 vb. *confute*; refuse credence 486 vb. *disbelieve*; protest, appeal against 762 vb. *deprecate*; challenge, stand up to 711 vb. *defy*; thwart 702 vb. *obstruct*; say no, shake one's head 760 vb. *refuse*; disallow 757 vb. *prohibit*; revoke, invalidate 752 vb. *abrogate*; abnegate, renounce 621 vb. *relinquish*; abjure, forswear, swear off 603 vb. *recant*; go back on one's word 603 vb. *tergiversate*.

Adv. *nay* 489 adv. *no*; negatively.

Int. never! a thousand times no! nothing of the kind! quite the contrary!

See: 14, 460, 468, 470, 479, 486, 489, 603, 607, 621, 702, 704, 711, 738, 752, 753, 757, 760, 762, 769, 860.

534 Teaching

N. *teaching*, pedagogy, pædeutics, hypnopedagogics; private teaching, tutoring; education, schooling, upbringing; tute-

lage, leading strings; direction, guidance, instruction, edification; spoon-feeding; dictation; tuition, preparation, coaching, tutorial; initiation, introduction; training, discipline, drill, exercitation 682 n. *exercise*; inculcation, catechization, indoctrination, preaching, pulpitry, homiletics; proselytism, propagandism; persuasion, conversion, conviction; conditioning, brainwashing; pamphleteering, propaganda 528 n. *publicity*; Cominform; information centre.

education, liberal arts, liberal education, classical e., scientific e., technical e., religious e., denominational e., secular e.; moral education, moral tuition, moral training; technical training, sloyd, technological training, vocational t.; co-education, progressive e., Froebel e., Froebelism, kindergarten method, Montessori m.; monitorial system; elementary education, primary e., secondary e., university e., advanced e., advanced studies, postgraduate s.; physical education, gymnastics, physical jerks, callisthenics, eurhythmics.

curriculum, course of study 536 n. *learning*; course, preliminary c.; first lessons, propædeutics, A.B.C., the three R's 68 n. *beginning*; set books, prescribed text 589 n. *textbook*; set task, exercise, homework, prep; trivium, grammar, rhetoric, logic; quadrivium, arithmetic, geometry, astronomy, music; Greats, Modern G. 459 n. *exam*; correspondence course, course of lectures, university extension l., classes, evening c., night c., seminar.

lecture, reading, prelection, discourse, disquisition; sermon, preachment, homily, lesson, apologue, parable; discussion-play 594 n. *stage play*; readership, lectureship, professorship, chair.

Adj. *educational*, pedagogic, pædeutic, tutorial; scholastic, scholarly, academic; instructional, informational; instructive 524 adj. *informative*; educative, didactive, didactic, hortative; doctrinal, normative; edifying, moralizing, homiletic, preachy; primary, secondary etc. n.; cultural, humane, scientific.

Vb. *educate*, edify (see *teach*); breed, rear, nurse, nurture, bring up, develop, form, lick into shape; put to school, send to s., have taught; tutor, teach, school; ground, coach, cram, prime 669 vb. *prepare*;

guide 689 vb. *direct*; instruct 524 vb. *inform*; enlighten, illumine, enlarge the mind, open the m.; sharpen the wits, open the eyes; fill with new ideas, stuff with knowledge, cram with facts, impress on the memory; knock into the head, inculcate, indoctrinate, imbue, impregnate, infuse, instil, infix, implant, engraft, sow the seeds of; remove falsehood, disabuse, unteach; chasten, sober.

teach, be a teacher, profess, give lessons, teach class, hold classes; lecture, deliver lectures; tutor, impart instruction; dictate, read out; preach, harangue, sermonize; discourse, hold forth; moralize, point a moral; elucidate, expound 520 vb. *interpret*; train the mind, indoctrinate, inoculate; pamphleteer, disseminate propaganda, propagandize, proselytize, condition, brainwash 178 vb. *influence*.

train, coach 669 vb. *prepare*; take on, take in hand, initiate, tame 369 vb. *break in*; nurse, foster, inure, put through the mill, put through the grind; drill, exercise, practise, make second nature, familiarize, accustom 610 vb. *habituate*; make fit, qualify; house-train, teach manners, teach how to behave 369 vb. *groom*.

See: 68, 178, 369, 459, 520, 524, 528, 536, 589, 594, 610, 669, 682, 689.

535 Misteaching

N. *misteaching*, misinstruction, misguidance, misleading, misdirection; quackery, a case of the blind leading the blind; misintelligence, misinformation 552 n. *misrepresentation*; mystification 421 n. *obfuscation*; allonym, false name 525 n. *concealment*; wrong attribution, wrong emendation, miscorrection 495 n. *mistake*; obscurantism 490 n. *ignorance*; false teaching, bad t., propaganda 541 n. *falsehood*; perversion 246 n. *distortion*; false logic, illogic 477 n. *sophistry*; college of Laputa.

Adj. *misteaching* etc. vb.; unedifying, propagandist; obscurantist 491 adj. *ignorant*; mistaught, misled, misdirected 495 adj. *mistaken*.

Vb. *misteach*, miseducate, bring up wrong; misinstruct, misinform, miscorrect, misname, misdirect, misguide 495 vb. *mislead*; not edify, corrupt, abuse the mind

934vb. *make wicked*; pervert 246vb. *distort*; misdescribe 552vb. *misrepresent*; cry wolf, put on a false scent 542vb. *deceive*; lie 541vb. *be false*; preach to the wise, teach one's grandmother to suck eggs; leave no wiser, keep in ignorance, take advantage of one's ignorance; suppress knowledge, unteach; propagandize, brainwash; explain away.

See: 246, 421, 477, 490, 491, 495, 525, 541, 542, 552, 934.

536 Learning

N. *learning*, lore, wide reading, scholarship, attainments 490n. *erudition*; acquisition of knowledge, acquisition of skill; thirst for knowledge, intellectual curiosity 453 n. *curiosity*; pupillage, tutelage, apprenticeship, prenticeship, novitiate, tirocinium, initiation 669n. *preparation*; first steps, teething troubles 68n. *beginning*; docility, teachability 694n. *aptitude*, self-instruction, self-education, self-improvement; culture, cultivation, self-c.; late learning, opsimathy.

study, studying; application, studiousness; cramming, grind, cram, mugging, mulling; studies, course of s., lessons, class, class-work, desk-w.; homework, prep, preparation; revision, refresher course, further reading, further study; perusal, reading, close r., attentive r. 455n. *attention*; research, research work, investigation 459n. *enquiry*.

Adj. *studious*, devoted to studies, academic; partial to reading, bookish, well-read, scholarly, erudite, learned, scholastic 490adj. *knowing*; sedulous, diligent, degree-hungry 678adj. *industrious*; receptive, teachable, docile 597adj. *willing*; self-taught, self-instructed, autodidact; immersed in study, deep in 455adj. *attentive*.

Vb. *learn*, pursue one's education, get oneself taught, go to school, attend college, read, take lessons, sit at the feet of, hear lectures, take a course, take a refresher c.; acquire knowledge, gain information, collect i., glean i., assimilate learning, imbibe, drink in, cram oneself with facts, know one's f. 490vb. *know*; apprentice oneself, learn one's trade, serve an apprenticeship, article oneself

669vb. *prepare oneself*; train, practise, exercise 610vb. *be wont*; get the feel of, master; get by heart, learn by rote 505vb. *memorize*; finish one's education, graduate.

study, prosecute one's studies, apply oneself, burn the midnight oil; do, take up; research into 459vb. *enquire*; study particularly, specialize, major in; swot, cram, grind, mug, mull, get up; revise, go over, brush up; read, peruse, spell, pore, wade through; thumb, browse, skip, turn the leaves, dip into; be studious, be a reading man, mind one's book, pore over; devote oneself to reading, bury oneself in one's books, become a polymath.

Adv. *studiously*, at one's books; under training, in articles.

See: 68, 453, 455, 459, 490, 505, 597, 610, 669, 678, 694.

537 Teacher

N. *teacher*, preceptor, mentor 520n. *guide*; minister 986n. *pastor*; guru, acharya 500n. *sage*; instructor, institutor; tutor, private t., private teacher, munshi; crammer, coach; bear-leader, governor, governess, nurse, dry-nurse, duenna 749n. *keeper*; educationist, pedagogue; pedant 500n. *wiseacre*; dominie, beak, abecedarian; master, schoolmaster, classmaster, house master, headmaster, principal; schoolmistress, school-marm, dame, schooldame, lady teacher; underteacher, pupil t., usher, monitor; disciplinarian, proctor, prefect; don, fellow; lecturer, expositor, exponent 520n. *interpreter*; prelector, reader, professor, Regius p., faculty member; catechist, catechizer; initiator, mystagogue, coryphæus; confidant, consultant 691n. *adviser*; teaching staff, faculty, professoriate, senior common room.

trainer, instructor, physical i., gymnastic i., swimming i.; coach, athletic c.; choirmaster; dancing-master; drill-sergeant; disciplinarian, rod, cane-wielder; animal trainer, horse-t., breaker-in, lion-tamer 369n. *breeder*.

preacher, lay p. 986n. *pastor*; pulpiteer, Boanerges, orator 579n. *speaker*; gospeller, evangelist; apostle, missionary,

pioneer 66 n. *precursor*; seer, prophet, major p., minor p. 511 n. *oracle*; pamphleteer, propagandist 528 n. *publicizer*; proverbialist 500 n. *sage*.
Adj. See 534 adj. *educational*.
See: 66, 369, 500, 511, 520, 528, 534, 579, 691, 749, 986.

538 Learner

N. *learner*, disciple, follower, chela; proselyte, convert, catechumen; late learner, opsimath; self-taught person, do-it-yourself fan, autodidact; empiricist 461 n. *experimenter*; swotter, mugger, bookworm 492 n. *scholar*; alumnus, student, pupil, scholar, schoolboy, schoolgirl, school-miss, school-goer, day-scholar, day-boy, boarder; school-fellow, schoolmate, classmate; fellow-student, condisciple.
beginner, young idea, novice, inceptor, débutant; abecedarian, alphabetarian; new boy, fag, tyro, greenhorn, tenderfoot, neophyte; rabbit, amateur 987 n. *layman*; recruit, raw r., buck private; initiate, catechumen; colt, trainee, apprentice, 'prentice, articled clerk; probationer, probationer nurse, pupil teacher; first offender; L-driver, examinee 461 n. *testee*.
college student, colleger, collegian, seminarist; undergraduate, undergraduette; freshman, frosh, first-year man; sophomore, soph, junior, senior; sophister; man student, woman s., girl s.; commoner, pensioner, sizar, exhibitioner; scholarship-holder, state scholar, Rhodes s.; prize boy, prizeman; passman; honours student, advanced s.; graduate, post-g. student, fellow; law student, mootman; art student; research worker, researcher, specialist.
class, standard, form, grade, remove, shell, stream; lower form, upper f., sixth f., scholarship class; art class, life c.; seminar.
Adj. *studentlike*, schoolboyish 130 adj. *young*; undergraduate, collegiate, sophomoric; pupillary, discipular; prentice; scholarly 536 adj. *studious*; rudimentary, raw, abecedarian; probationary; in leading strings, in statu pupillari.
See: 130, 461, 492, 536, 987.

539 School

N. *academy*, institute, institution, teaching i.; college, seminary, lycée, gymnasium; conservatoire, school of music, school of dancing, dancing school, art s., academy of dramatic art; wrestling school, palaestra; school of deportment, finishing school; university, university college; school of philosophy, Academy, Lyceum, Stoa.
school, nursery s., crèche, kindergarten; infant school, dame s.; private school; aided school; preparatory school, prep s., preprep-s., pre-school; primary school, elementary s., middle s., middle English s.; higher grade school, central s., secondary school, high-s., high English s., secondary modern s., grammar s., comprehensive s.; collegiate school, public s., boarding s., day s.; Board school, L.C.C. s., village s., parish s., county s., state s., night s., continuation s.; convent school, denominational s., Church s., Sunday s.; school for the blind, deaf-and-dumb s., school for backward children, school for the educationally subnormal; reformatory, reform school, borstal s., Borstal, remand home; school building, school architecture.
training school, nursery, training ground, gymnasium 724 n. *arena*; crammer; finishing school; training ship, training college, teachers training c., teachers training school, école normale, normal school; law school, medical school, medical college, teaching hospital; military school, military college, staff college; Dartmouth, Sandhurst, Woolwich, Cranwell; West Point, Annapolis.
trade school, vocational s., technical training s.; technical college, technical institute, polytechnic; engineering school, engineering college; research laboratory, research institute; commercial institute, secretarial school, business college.
classroom, schoolroom; study; lecture-room, lecture-hall, auditorium, theatre, amphitheatre; desk, reading d., class d.; schoolbook, reader, crib, hornbook, abecedary, primer 589 n. *textbook*; slate, copybook, exercise book; visual aid.
rostrum, bema, tribune, dais, forum; platform, stage, hustings, soap-box; chair 534 n. *lecture*; pulpit, lectern, ambo; leader page, column 528 n. *publicity*.

Adj. See 534 adj. *educational.*
See: 528, 534, 589, 724.

540 Veracity

N. *veracity,* veraciousness, truthfulness, truth-telling, truth-speaking; nothing but fact, fidelity, fidelity to fact, verisimilitude, realism, exactitude 494 n. *accuracy;* openness, frankness, candour 522 n. *manifestation;* bona fides, honour bright, no kidding; love of truth, honesty, sincerity 929 n. *probity;* simplicity, ingenuousness 699 n. *artlessness;* downrightness, plain speaking, plain dealing 573 n. *plainness;* baldness, plain words, hometruth, unvarnished tale, undisguised meaning, unambiguity, true statement, honest truth, sober t. 494 n. *truth;* clean breast, true confession, unqualified admission 526 vb. *disclosure;* circumstantiality, particularity, full details, nothing omitted 570 n. *diffuseness;* truth-speaker, no liar, prophet.

Adj. *veracious,* truthful 494 adj. *true;* telling the truth, veridical, not lying, unperjured; as good as one's word, reliable 929 adj. *trustworthy;* factual, sticking to fact, ungarbled, undistorted, bald, unembroidered, unvarnished, unexaggerated, scrupulous, exact, just 494 adj. *accurate;* full, particular, circumstantial 570 adj. *diffuse;* simple, ingenious 699 adj. *artless;* bona fide, meant, intended; unaffected, unpretentious, unfeigned, undissembling, open, above-board 522 adj. *undisguised;* candid, unreserved, forthcoming; blunt, free, downright, forthright, plain-speaking, outspoken, straightforward 573 adj. *plain;* unambiguous 516 adj. *intelligible;* honest, sincere, truehearted, true-blue, loyal 929 adj. *honourable;* truly spoken, fulfilled, proved, verified 478 adj. *demonstrated;* infallible, prophetic 511 adj. *presageful.*

Vb. *be truthful,* tell the truth, tell no lie, swear true 532 vb. *swear;* stick to the facts 494 vb. *be true;* speak in earnest, mean it, really mean, honestly m.; not joke, weigh one's words 834 vb. *be serious;* speak one's mind, open one's heart, keep nothing back 522 vb. *show;* make a clean breast, confess the truth 526 vb. *confess;* drop the mask, appear in one's true

colours 526 vb. *disclose;* be prophetic 511 vb. *predict;* verify one's words, say truly 478 vb. *demonstrate.*

Adv. *truthfully,* really and truly, bona fide, sincerely, from the bottom of one's heart 494 adv. *truly;* to tell the truth, frankly, candidly, without fear or favour; factually, exactly, just as it happened.

See: 478, 494, 511, 516, 522, 526, 532, 570, 573, 699, 834, 929.

541 Falsehood

N. *falsehood,* falseness, spuriousness, falsity; treachery, bad faith, Punic f., Judas kiss 930 n. *perfidy;* untruthfulness, unveracity, mendacity, deceitfulness; lying, habitual l., pathological l., mythomania; oath-breaking, perjury, false swearing 543 n. *untruth;* invention of lies, fabrication, fiction; faking, forgery, falsification 542 n. *deception;* imaginativeness, invention 513 n. *imagination;* disingenuousness, prevarication, equivocation, evasion, shuffling, fencing 518 n. *equivocalness;* economy of truth, suppressio veri, suggestio falsi; jesuitry, jesuitism, casuistry; overstatement 546 n. *exaggeration;* perversion 246 n. *distortion;* false colouring, misrepresentation 521 n. *misinterpretation;* meretriciousness 875 n. *ostentation;* humbug, bunkum, boloney, hokum, hooey, gammon, flim-flam, bam 515 n. *empty talk;* cant, eyewash, hogwash (see *duplicity*); euphemism, mealy-mouthedness, blarney, soft soap, taffy 925 n. *flattery.*

duplicity, false conduct, double life, double-dealing 930 n. *improbity;* guile 542 n. *trickery;* hollowness, front, façade, outside, show, window-dressing 875 n. *ostentation;* pretence, hollow p., bluff, act, fake, counterfeit, imposture 542 n. *sham;* hypocrisy, acting, play-a., simulation, dissimulation, dissembling, insincerity, tongue in cheek, cant; lip-homage, mouth-honour, cupboard love; pharisaism, false piety; crocodile tears, show of sympathy; Judas kiss, Cornish hug; fraud, pious f., legal fiction, diplomatic illness; cheat, cheating; put-up job, frame-up 930 n. *foul play;* quackery, charlatanry, charlatanism 850 n. *pretension;* low cunning, artfulness 698 n. *cunning.*

Adj. *false*, not true, truthless, without truth; untruthful, lying, unveracious, imaginative, mendacious 543 adj. *untrue*; perfidious, treacherous, forsworn, perjured; sly, artful 698 adj. *cunning*; disingenuous, dishonest, uncandid, unfair, ambiguous, evasive, shuffling 518 adj. *equivocal*; falsified, garbled; meretricious, embellished, touched up, varnished, painted; overdone 546 adj. *exaggerated*; ungenuine, imitated, counterfeit, fake, phoney, sham, snide, quack, bogus 542 adj. *spurious*; cheating, deceptive, deceitful, fraudulent 542 adj. *deceiving*; covinous, collusive, collusory, engineered, rigged, packed.

hypocritical, hollow, empty, insincere, diplomatic; put on, imitated, pretended, seeming, feigned; make-believe, acting, play-a.; double, two-faced, double-hearted, double-tongued, double-handed, treacherous, double-dealing, Machiavellian 930 adj. *perfidious*; sanctimonious, tartuffish, pharisaical; jesuitical, casuistical; plausible, smooth, smooth-tongued, smooth spoken, oily; mealy-mouthed, euphemistic 850 adj. *affected*; canting, gushing 925 adj. *flattering*.

Vb. *be false*, — perjured, — forsworn etc. adj.; perjure oneself, bear false witness, swear falsely, swear that black is white; forswear 603 vb. *recant*; palter, palter with the truth, economize t.; lie, tell lies, utter a falsehood; tell the tale, swing the lead; strain, strain the truth, tell a tall story 546 vb. *exaggerate*; tell a fib, tell a whopper, lie hard, lie like a trooper; invent, make believe, make up, romance 513 vb. *imagine*; put a false construction on 521 vb. *misinterpret*; garble, falsify, pervert 246 vb. *distort*; overstate, understate 552 vb. *misrepresent*; misreport, misquote, miscite, misinform, cry wolf 535 vb. *misteach*; lull, soothe 925 vb. *flatter*; play false, play a double game 930 vb. *be dishonest*; break faith, betray 769 vb. *not observe*.

dissemble, dissimulate, disguise 525 vb. *conceal*; simulate, counterfeit 20 vb. *imitate*; put on, assume, affect, dress up, play-act, play a part, go through the motions, make a show of 594 vb. *act*; feign, pass off for, sham, pretend, show false colours, sail under false c.; malinger, sham Abraham 542 vb. *deceive*; lack candour, hide the truth, say less than

the t., keep something back; not give a straight answer, prevaricate, palter, beat about the bush, shuffle, dodge, trim 518 vb. *equivocate*.

cant, gloze, euphemize, mince matters, garble; colour, varnish, paint, embroider, varnish right and puzzle wrong; gloss over, put a gloss on, clean the outside of the platter; play the hypocrite, act a part, put on an act; say the grapes are sour 850 vb. *be affected*.

fake, fabricate, coin, forge, plagiarize, counterfeit 20 vb. *imitate*; get up, trump up, frame; manipulate, rig, pack (a jury); spin, weave, cook, cook up, concoct, hatch, invent 623 vb. *plot*.

Adv. *falsely*, slily, deceitfully, under false pretences; hypocritically, à la Tartufe, with a double tongue, mendaciously.

See: 20, 246, 513, 515, 518, 521, 525, 535, 542, 543, 546, 552, 594, 603, 623, 698, 769, 850, 875, 925, 930.

542 Deception

N. *deception*, ingannation, kidding, tongue in cheek; circumvention, outwitting; self-deception, wishful thinking 487 n. *credulity*; infatuation 499 n. *folly*; fallacy 477 n. *sophistry*; illusion, delusion, hallucination, imagination's artful aid 495 n. *error*; deceptiveness 523 n. *latency* (see *trap*); false appearance, mockery, mirage, will-o'-the-wisp 440 n. *visual fallacy*; show, outward s., meretriciousness, paint (see *sham*); false reputation, feet of clay; hollowness, bubble 4 n. *insubstantiality*; falseness, deceit, quackery, imposture, lie 541 n. *falsehood*; deceitfulness, guile, craft, artfulness 698 n. *cunning*; hypocrisy, insincerity 541 n. *duplicity*; treachery, betrayal 930 n. *perfidy*; practice, machination, hanky-panky, collusion, covin 623 n. *plot*; fraudulence, cozenage, cheating, cheat, diddling, diddle; spoofery, hoax (see *trickery*); ventriloquism (see *sleight*).

trickery, coggery, gullery, dupery, swindling, skulduggery, shenanigan; jockeyship, sharp practice, chicane, chicanery, legal c., pettifogging; swindle, chouse, ramp, wangle, fiddle, diddle, swizzle, swiz, sell, bite, fraud, cheat; cardsharping, cogging 930 n. *foul play*; trick, bag of tricks, tricks of the trade, confidence

trick, wile, ruse, shift, dodge, artful d., fetch, reach, blind, dust, feint 698n. *stratagem*; wrinkle 623 n.*contrivance*;bait, diversion, tub to a whale; hocus, hoax, bluff, spoof, leg-pull; game, sport, joke, practical j., rag 839n. *witticism*; April fooling, spoofery.

sleight, pass, sleight of hand, quickness of the h., legerdemain, prestidigitation, conjuring, hocus-pocus, illusion, ventriloquism; juggling, jugglery, juggle, googly; thimblerig, three-card trick; magic 983n. *sorcery.*

trap, deathtrap 527n. *ambush*; catch 530n. *enigma*; plant, frame-up 930n. *foul play*; noose, snare, gin, net, spring-n., spring-gun; springe, springle, hook, sniggle, mine; diversion, blind, decoy, decoy duck, kill, bait, lure; baited trap, rat t., mouse t., fly-paper, lime-twig, bird-lime; booby-trap, trip-wire, deadfall, pit, keddah 663n. *pitfall*; trapdoor, sliding panel, false bottom 530n. *secret*; fatal gift, poisoned chalice, Trojan horse.

sham, false front 541n. *duplicity*; make-believe, pretence 850n. *affectation*; paint, whitewash, varnish, gloss; whited sepulchre, man of straw, wolf in sheep's clothing, lath painted to look like iron; dummy, scarecrow 4n. *insubstantial thing*; imitation, simulacrum, facsimile 22n. *copy*; mockery, hollow m.; counterfeit, forgery, fake; masquerade, mummery, mask, disguise, borrowed plumes, false colours 525n. *concealment*; shoddy, Brummagem, jerry-building 641n. *rubbish*; imitation ware, tinsel, paste; ormolu, ormolu varnish, Mosaic gold; German silver, Britannia metal.

Adj. *deceiving*, deceitful, lying 543adj. *untrue*; deceptive 523adj. *latent*; hallucinatory, illusive, delusive, elusive, illusory; slippery 258adj. *smooth*; fraudulent, humbugging, cheating, cogging, lulling, soothing 925adj. *flattering*; beguiling, treacherous, insidious 930adj. *perfidious*; trumped-up, framed, colourable 541adj. *false*; feigned, pretended 541adj. *hypocritical*; juggling, conjuring, prestigious; sleightful, tricky, crafty, wily, guileful, artful 698adj. *cunning*; collusive, covinous; painted, whited, whitewashed, sugared, coated, plated (see *spurious*).

spurious, base-born, illegitimate, adulterine 954adj. *bastard*; ungenuine, false, faked, fake; sham, counterfeit; make-believe, mock, ersatz, bogus, phoney; pseudo, so-called; not natural, artificial, paste, cultured; shoddy, rubbishy 641adj. *useless*; tinsel, meretricious, flash, catchpenny, pinchbeck, Brummagem 812adj. *cheap*; jerry-built, cardboard 330adj. *brittle*; adulterated, sophisticated 43adj. *mixed*; underweight 323adj. *light.*

Vb. *deceive*, delude, illude, dazzle; beguile, sugar the pill, gild the p.; let down 509vb. *disappoint*; hoodwink, blinker, blindfold 439vb. *blind*; kid, bluff, bamboozle, hoax, humbug, hornswoggle, gammon; snatch a verdict, throw dust in the eyes, lead up the garden path 495vb. *mislead*; spoof, mystify 535vb. *misteach*; play false, leave in the lurch, betray, double-cross 930vb. *be dishonest*; practise, practise upon, intrigue 623vb. *plot*; circumvent, overreach, outreach, outwit, outmanœuvre 306vb. *outdo*; forestall, steal a march on 135vb. *be early*; pull a fast one, be too smart for, outsmart 698vb. *be cunning*; trick, dupe (see *befool*); cheat, cozen, sharp, swindle, swizzle, sell, bite, do, do down; diddle, bubble, do out of, bilk, gyp, chouse, pluck, obtain money by false pretences 788vb. *defraud*; juggle, conjure, make a pass, force a card, palm off, foist o.; fob, fob off with; live on one's wits, try it on, practise chicanery, pettifog; gerrymander, tinker; cog, cog the dice, load the d., mark the cards, pack the c., stack the deck; play the hypocrite, impose upon 541vb. *dissemble*; brazen out, put a good face upon, whitewash 541vb. *cant*; counterfeit 541vb. *fake.*

befool, fool, make a fool of, make an ass of, make one look silly, fool one to the top of his bent; mock, make game of 851vb. *ridicule*; rag, play tricks on, pull one's leg, have one on, make an April fool of, play a joke on 497vb. *be absurd*; sport with, trifle w., throw over, jilt; take in, have, dupe, cully, victimize, gull, outwit; trick, trap, catch, catch out, take advantage of, practise upon, practise on one's credulity, kid, stuff up, dope; spoof, bamboozle, fake out, string, hocus (see *deceive*); cog, cajole, get round, flatter, fawn on, make things pleasant for, lull, soothe 925vb. *flatter*; let down, let in for, leave in the lurch, leave one holding the baby, leave one holding the bag 509vb.

disappoint; send on a fool's errand, send on a wild-goose chase 495 vb. *mislead.*

ensnare, snare, trap, entrap, set a trap for, lay a trap for, lime, lime the twig, entoil, enmesh, entangle, illaqueate, net, benet; trip, trip up, catch, catch out, hook, sniggle; bait, bait the trap, bait the hook, dangle a bait, lure, decoy, entice, inveigle 612 vb. *tempt*; divert, throw a tub to a whale; lie in wait, waylay, forelay 527 vb. *ambush*; nab, nick, kidnap, crimp, trepan, shanghai 788 vb. *steal.*

Adv. *deceptively,* deceitfully; under cover of, in the garb of, disguisedly; over the left.

See: 4, 22, 43, 135, 258, 306, 323, 330, 439, 440, 477, 487, 495, 497, 499, 509, 523, 525, 527, 530, 535, 541, 543, 612, 623, 641, 663, 698, 788, 812, 839, 850, 851, 925, 930, 954, 983.

543 Untruth

N. *untruth,* thing that is not, reverse of the truth 541 n. *falsehood*; less than the truth, understatement 483 n. *underestimation*; more than the truth, overstatement 546 n. *exaggeration*; lie, downright l., shameless l., calm l.; taradiddle, fib, whopper, crammer; false statement, terminological inexactitude; broken word, dicer's oath, lover's o., breach of promise 930 n. *perfidy*; perjury, false oath; false evidence, pack of lies, trumped-up story, frame-up 466 n. *evidence*; concoction, fiction, fabrication, invention 513 n. *ideality* (see *fable*); misstatement, misinformation 535 n. *misteaching*; misrepresentation, perversion 246 n. *distortion*; gloss, varnish, garbling, falsification 521 n. *misinterpretation*; lie factory, propaganda machine. *mental dishonesty,* disingenuousness, economy of truth, half-truth, partial t., near t., half-lie, white l., pious fraud, mental reservation 468 n. *qualification*; suggestio falsi, suppressio veri 525 n. *concealment*; show, make-believe; tongue in cheek, pretence, profession, false plea, excuse 614 n. *pretext*; evasion, subterfuge, shift, shuffle, ambiguity 518 n. *equivocalness*; self-depreciation, irony, backhanded compliment 850 n. *affectation*; artificiality, unnaturalness; sham, empty

words 541 n. *duplicity*; Judas kiss 930 n. *perfidy*; mask 527 n. *disguise.*
fable, invention, fiction, imaginative exercise 513 n. *ideality*; story, tale 590 n. *narrative*; tall story, tall order, shaggy dog story, fishy s., fish s., fisherman's yarn, traveller's tale 546 n. *exaggeration*; Canterbury tale, fairy-t., nursery t., märchen, romance, tale, yarn, story, cock-and-bull s., all my eye and Betty Martin 497 n. *absurdity*; claptrap, gossip, gup, guff, bazaar rumour, canard 529 n. *rumour*; myth, mythology; moonshine, farce, mare's nest, sell, swiz, hum, hoax, humbug, flummery 515 n. *empty talk.*

Adj. *untrue,* lying, mendacious 541 adj. *false*; trumped-up, framed, cooked, hatched, concocted; far from the truth, nothing less true; mythological, fabulous; unfounded, empty; fictitious, imagined, make-believe, well-imagined, ben trovato; faked, artificial, synthetic, factitious; phoney, bogus, soi-disant, so-called; overstated 546 adj. *exaggerated*; boasting 877 adj. *boastful*; perjured, forsworn 930 adj. *perfidious*; evasive, shuffling, surreptitious 518 adj. *equivocal*; ironical 850 adj. *affected*; satirical, mocking 851 adj. *derisive.*

Vb. *be untrue,* sound u., not ring true 472 vb. *be unlikely*; lie, be a liar 541 vb. *be false*; spin a yarn, draw the long bow 546 vb. *exaggerate*; make-believe, draw on one's imagination 513 vb. *imagine*; be phoney, pretend, sham, counterfeit, forge, falsify 541 vb. *dissemble.*

See: 246, 466, 468, 472, 483, 497, 513, 515, 518, 521, 525, 527, 529, 535, 541, 546, 590, 614, 850, 851, 877, 930.

544 Dupe

N. *dupe,* fool, old f., April f. 851 n. *laughing-stock*; Simple Simon 501 n. *ninny*; credulous fool, one easily taken in, easy prey, victim, sucker, gull, pigeon, jay, cull, cully, mug, flat, dude, greenhorn, innocent 538 n. *beginner*; puppet, cat's-paw, pawn 630 n. *tool*; ignorant masses, admass.

Adj. *gullible* 487 adj. *credulous*; duped, taken in, had, done, diddled 542 adj. *deceiving*; innocent, green, silly 499 adj. *foolish.*

Vb. *be duped*, be had, be done, be taken in; fall for, walk into the trap, rise, nibble, swallow the bait, swallow hook line and sinker; take wooden nickels, buy a gold brick; catch a Tartar 508 vb. *not expect.*
See: 487, 499, 501, 508, 538, 542, 630, 851.

545 Deceiver

N. *deceiver*, gay d., seducer 952 n. *libertine*; kidder, ragger, leg-puller; dissembler, actor, shammer, hypocrite, canter, whited sepulchre, Pharisee, Pecksniff, Tartufe, Joseph Surface, Mawworm; false friend, fair-weather f., jilt, jilter, shuffler, turncoat, trimmer, rat 603 n. *tergiversator*; traitor, Judas, four-flusher, double-crosser 938 n. *knave*; serpent, snake in the grass, snake in one's bosom 663 n. *trouble-maker*; plotter, intrigant, conspirator 623 n. *planner*; counterfeiter, forger, faker, plagiariser 20 n. *imitator.*
liar, confirmed l., pathological l. 541 n. *falsehood*; fibster, fibber, story-teller; romancer, fabulist; imaginative person, yarner, yarn-spinner; angler, traveller, mythologist; pseudologist, fabricator, equivocator, palterer; oath-breaker, perjurer, false witness; Ananias, father of lies.
impostor, shammer, malingerer, adventurer, usurper; cuckoo in the nest 59 n. *intruder*; ass in the lion's skin, wolf in sheep's clothing; boaster, bluffer, ringer; pretender, quack, quack-salver, mountebank, saltimbanco, medicaster, empiric 850 n. *affector*; fake, fraud, humbug; masquerader, mummer 525 n. *concealment.*
trickster, hoaxer, spoofer, bamboozler; cheat, cheater, cozener; jockey, horse-coper, carpet-bagger; sharper, card-s., thimblerigger, cogger; shyster, pettifogger; swindler, bilker, diddler, gyp 789 n. *defrauder*; slicker, spieler, twister, chiseller, jobber, rogue 938 n. *knave*; confidence trickster, confidence man, con-man, magsman 477 n. *sophist*; crimp, decoy, stool-pigeon, decoy-duck, agent provocateur; fiddler, manipulator, rigger, fixer; wily bird, fox 698 n. *slyboots.*
conjuror, illusionist, prestidigitator, galigali man, juggler, ventriloquist; quick-change artist; magician, necromancer 983 n. *sorcerer.*
See: 20, 59, 477, 525, 541, 603, 623, 663, 698, 789, 850, 938, 952, 983.

546 Exaggeration

N. *exaggeration*, over-emphasis, inflation, magnification, enlargement 197 n. *expansion*; optimism 482 n. *overestimation*; stretch, strain, straining; extravagance, exaggerated lengths, extremes, immoderation, extremism; excess, excessiveness, violence 943 n. *intemperance*; inordinacy, exorbitance, overdoing it, piling Ossa upon Pelion; overacting, histrionics 875 n. *ostentation*; sensationalism, ballyhoo, puffery 528 n. *publicity*; overstatement, hyperbole, figure of speech 519 n. *trope*; adulation 925 n. *flattery*; colouring, high c. 574 n. *ornament*; embroidery 38 n. *addition*; disproportion 246 n. *distortion*; caricature, burlesque 851 n. *satire*; exacerbation 832 n. *aggravation*; big talk, boast 877 n. *boasting*; rant, ranting, tirade, rodomontade, grandiloquence 574 n. *magniloquence*; overpraise, excessive loyalty, chauvinism 481 n. *prejudice*; tall story, yarn, shaggy dog story, traveller's tale 543 n. *fable*; aretalogy, miracle-mongering; men in buckram, flight of fancy, stretch of the imagination 513 n. *imagination*; fuss, pother, excitement, storm in a teacup, much ado about nothing 318 n. *commotion*; extremist, exaggerator; sensationalist, miracle-monger, aretalogist; Baron Munchausen 545 n. *liar.*
Adj. *exaggerated*, magnified, enlarged 197 adj. *expanded*; added to, embroidered; strained, over-emphasized, overweighted, overdone, overstated, over-coloured, inflated, hyperbolical 574 adj. *rhetorical*; overacted, histrionic; bombastic, swelling 877 adj. *boastful*; tall, fanciful, high-flying, steep, egregious, preposterous, outrageous 497 adj. *absurd*; extravagant, excessive, outré, extremist; violent, immoderate 32 adj. *exorbitant*; inordinate 943 adj. *intemperate.*
Vb. *exaggerate*, maximize, magnify, expand, inflate 197 vb. *enlarge*; over-amplify, over-elaborate; add to, pile up 38 vb. *add*; touch up, enhance, heighten, add a

flourish, embroider 844 vb. *decorate*; lay it on thick, overdo, over-colour, over-draw, overcharge, overload; overweight, overstress, over-emphasize 638 vb. *make important*; overpraise, puff, oversell, cry up 482 vb. *overrate*; make much of, make too much of 925 vb. *flatter*; stretch, strain 246 vb. *distort*; caricature 851 vb. *satirize*; go to all lengths, not know when to stop, protest too much, speak in superlatives, hyperbolize; overact, dramatize, out-Herod Herod; rant, talk big 877 vb. *boast*; run riot, go to extremes, pile Pelion on Ossa; draw the long bow, over-shoot the mark 306 vb. *overstep*; spin a yarn, draw on the imagination, deal in the marvellous, tell travellers' tales 541 vb. *be false*; make mountains out of molehills, make a storm in a tea cup; intensify, exacerbate 832 vb. *aggravate*; overcompensate, lean over backwards.

See: 32, 38, 197, 246, 306, 318, 481, 482, 497, 513, 519, 528, 541, 543, 545, 574, 638, 832, 844, 851, 875, 877, 925, 943.

547 Indication

N. *indication*, pointing out, drawing attention, showing 522 n. *manifestation*; signification, meaning 514 n. *connotation*; notification 524 n. *information*; symbolization, symbolism 551 n. *representation*; symbol, conventional s., x, letter; magic symbol, pentacle 983 n. *talisman*; natural symbol, image, type, figure; token, emblem, figurehead (see *badge*); something to go by, symptom, sign 466 n. *evidence*; tell-tale sign, blush 526 n. *disclosure*; nudge, wink 524 n. *hint* (see *gesture*); straw in the wind, sign of the times 511 n. *omen*; clue, scent, whiff 484 n. *detector*; noise, footfall 398 n. *sound*; interpretation of symptoms, symptomatology, semeiology, semeiotics 520 n. *hermeneutics*; pointer, finger, forefinger, index finger (see *indicator*); indice, exponent 85 n. *number*; guide, index, thumb-i. 87 n. *directory*; key 520 n. *interpretation*; marker, mark, guide-m.; white mark, blaze; nick, scratch 260 n. *notch*; line, score, stroke; note, side-n., under-runner, catchword (see *punctuation*); stamp, print, impression; stigma, stigmata;

prick, tattooing, tattoo-mark 263 n. *perforation*; mole, scar, birth mark, strawberry mark 845 n. *blemish*; legend, caption 590 n. *description*; inscription, epitaph; motto, cipher; love-token, favour (see *badge*).

identification, naming 561 n. *nomenclature*; 77 n *classification*; means of identification, brand, trade-mark, imprint (see *label*); name and address; autograph, signature, hand 586 n. *script*; finger-print, footprint, spoor, track, trail 548 n. *trace*; secret sign, password, open sesame, watchword, countersign; diagnostic, markings, stripes, spots, colour, colouring, cloven hoof; characteristic, trait, lineament, outline, form, shape 445 n. *feature*; personal characteristic, trick, trick of speech, shibboleth; mole, scar, birth-mark, strawberry mark 845 n. *blemish*; divining rod 484 n. *detector*; criterion 461 n. *testing agent*; mark, note.

symbology, symbolization, dactylogy; cipher, code 525 n. *secrecy*; symbolography, picture-writing, hieroglyphics 586 n. *script*; gypsy signs, hobo s., scout s.

gesture, gesticulation, sign-language, semeiology, dactylogy; deaf-and-dumb language; sign 524 n. *hint*; pantomime, by-play, dumb-show, charade, dumb c.; demeanour, look in one's eyes, tone of one's voice 445 n. *mien*; motion, move; tick, twitch 318 n. *spasm*; shrug, shrug of the shoulders; wag of the head, nod, beck, wink, flicker of the eyelash, twinkle, glance, ogle, leer, grimace 438 n. *look*; smile, laugh 835 n. *laughter*; touch, kick, nudge, jog, dig in the ribs 279 n. *knock*; hug, clap on the shoulders; hand-pressure, squeeze of the hand, handshake, grip 778 n. *retention*; push, shove 279 n. *impulse*; pointing, signal, waving, wave, hand-signal, wave of the hand; raising one's hand, wagging one's forefinger; drumming one's fingers, tapping one's foot, stamp of the foot 822 n. *excitable state*; clenching one's teeth, gritting one's t. 599 n. *resolution*; gnashing one's teeth, snap, snapping one's jaws 892 n. *irascibility*; wringing one's hands, tearing one's hair 836 n. *lamentation*; clenched fist 711 n. *defiance*; flag-waving, umbrella w., hat-w. 876 n. *celebration*; clap, clapping, hand-c., cheer 923 n. *applause*; hiss, hissing, hooting, boo, booing, Bronx

cheer 924 n. *disapprobation*; frown, scowl, 893 n. *sulleness*; pout, moue, pursing of the lips 829 n. *discontent*.

signal 529 n. *message*; sign, symptom 522 n. *manifestation*; flash, rocket, Very light; signalling, railway signal, smoke-s., heliograph, semaphore, telegraph, morse 531 n. *telecommunication*; flashlamp, signal l. 420 n. *lamp*; warning light, beacon, beacon fire, bale-f., watch-f. 379 n. *fire*; balize, warning signal, red flag, warning light, red l., green l., traffic l., Belisha beacon 420 n. *signal light*; alarum, alarm, warning signal, distress s., S.O.S. 665 n. *danger signal*; whistle, police w.; siren, hooter; bell, electric b., buzzer, knocker, door-k. 414 n. *gong*; door-bell, alarm-b., Inchcape b., Lutine b.; church bells, angelus, carillon, sacring bell; time-signal, pip, minute-gun, dinner-gong, dinner-bell 117 n. *chronometry*; passing bell, knell, muffled drum 364 n. *obsequies*.

indicator, index, pointer, arrow, needle, compass n., magnetic n.; arm, finger, index-f.; hand, hour-h., minute-h., second-h., clock-h., watch-h. 117 n. *timekeeper*; Plimsoll line 465 n. *gauge*; traffic indicator, trafficator, semaphore; direction-finder, radar; white line 305 n. *traffic control*; weathercock, wind sock, straw in the wind 340 n. *weather*.

signpost, direction post, finger-p., hand-p., milestone, milepost, milliary column, waymark; lighthouse, lightship, buoy 662 n. *safeguard*; compass 269 n. *sailing aid*; lodestar, guiding s., pole s. 690 n. *leader*; North Star, Polaris, Southern Cross 321 n. *star*; cynosure, landmark, sea-mark, Pillars of Hercules; cairn, monument, memorial 505 n. *reminder*; tide-mark 236 n. *limit*; guide-mark, bench mark.

call, proclamation, ban, hue-and-cry 528 n. *publication*; shout, hail; invitation; call to prayer, church-bell, muezzin's cry 981 n. *worship*; summons, word, word of command 737 n. *command*; bugle, trumpet, bugle-call, reveillé, assemble, charge, advance, rally, retreat; lights out, last post; peal, sennet, flourish; drum, drum-beat, drum-roll, tattoo, taps 403 n. *roll*; call to arms, Fiery Cross; battle-cry, war-c., rallying c., slogan, catchword, watchword, shibboleth; challenge, countersign; paying calls, round of calls,

visiting 882 n. *social round*; calling, profession 622 n. *vocation*.

badge, token, emblem, symbol, sign, figurehead (see *indication*); insignia (see *heraldry*); markings, military m., roundel; badge of sovereignty, throne, sceptre, orb, crown 743 n. *regalia*; mark of authority, badge of office, wand of o., Black Rod, mace, keys 743 n. *badge of rule*; baton, stars, pips, spurs, stripes, epaulette 743 n. *badge of rank*; medal, gong, cross, Victoria Cross, George C., Iron C.; order, star, garter, sash, ribbon 729 n. *decoration*; badge of merit, laurels, bays, wreath, fillet, chaplet, garland 729 n. *trophy*; blue, half-b., cap, oar; badge of loyalty, favour, rosette, primrose, love-knot; badge of mourning, black, crape, weepers, widow's weeds 228 n. *dress*.

livery, dress, national d. 228 n. *uniform*; tartan, tie, old school t., blazer; regimental badge, brassard, epaulette, chevron, stripes, pips, wings; flash, hackle, cockade, rosette.

heraldry, armoury, blazonry; heraldic register, Roll of Arms; armorial bearings, coat of arms; achievement, funereal a., hatchment; shield, escutcheon; crest, torse, wreath, helmet, crown, coronet, mantling, lambrequin; supporters, motto; compartment, lozenge; ordinary, honourable ordinaries, chief, base, pale, fess, bend, bend sinister, chevron, pile, saltire, cross; subordinaries, orb, inescutcheon, bordure, lozenge, fusil, pall, gyron, flaunches; marshalling, quartering, impaling, dimidiating; differencing, difference; fess point, honour p., nombril p.; charge, beacon, bugle, garb, water-bouget, fetterlock; animal charge, lion, unicorn, griffin, yale, cockatrice, eagle, alerion, falcon, martlet; floral charge, Tudor rose, cinquefoil, trefoil, planta genista; badge, antelope, bear and ragged staff, portcullis; national emblem, rose, thistle, leek, daffodil, shamrock, lilies, fleur-de-lys; device, national d., charkha, eagle, bear, hammer and sickle; swastika, fylfot; skull and crossbones; heraldic tincture, colour, gules, azure, vert, sable, purpure, tenné, murray; metal, or, gold, yellow, argent, silver, white; fur, ermine, ermines, erminois, pean, vair, potent; heraldic personnel, College of Arms, herald, Earl

Marshal, King of Arms, Garter, Clarenceaux, Norroy and Ulster, Chief Herald of Ireland; Lyon King of Arms; herald, Chester, Somerset, Richmond, York, Windsor, Lancaster; Albany, Marchmont, Rothesay, herald extraordinary, Maltravers, Norfolk, Fitzalan; pursuivant, Bluemantle, Rouge Croix, Rouge Dragon; Carrick, Kintyre, Unicorn.

flag, ensign, white e., blue e.; red ensign, Red Duster; jack, pilot j., merchant j.; colours, ship's c., regimental c., King's Colour, Queen's C.; cavalry colours, guidon; standard, banner, gonfalon; banneret, bannerol, banderole, oriflamme; pennant, swallowtail, triple tail; pendant, broad p., burgee; bunting, Blue Peter, yellow flag; white flag 721 n. *submission*; eagle, Roman e.; crescent; tricolour; Union Jack; Stars and Stripes, Old Glory, star-spangled banner; Red Flag; black flag, pirate f., bloody banner, Jolly Roger, Old R., skull and crossbones; parts of a flag, hoist, fly, canton; flagpole, flag-mast, colour pike.

label, mark of identification, tattoo-mark, caste-m. (see *identification*); ticket, billet, bill, docket, counterfoil, stub, duplicate; tally, tessera, counter, chip; tick, letter, number, check, mark, countermark; tie-label, tab, tag; name-tape, name-plate, name-board, sign-b.; sign, bush, barber's pole, three balls 522 n. *exhibit*; plate, brass p., trade sign, trade-mark, hall-m., cachet; earmark, brand, stigma, broad arrow, mark of Cain; fool's-cap, dunce's c.; seal, signet, sigil, stamp, impress, impression, seal-i.; caption, heading, title, superscription, rubric; imprint, colophon, signation, watermark; bookplate, monomark, name, name and address; card, visiting c., address c.; birth certificate, identification papers; passport, pass 756 n. *permit*; endorsement 466 n. *credential*; witness, signature, sign-manual, autograph, cipher, mark, cross, initials, monogram, paraph; finger-print, thumb-print, footprint 548 n. *trace*.

punctuation, punctuation mark, point, stop, full s., period; comma, virgule, colon, semicolon; inverted commas, quotation marks, apostrophe, quotes; exclamation mark, exclamation point, question mark, note of interrogation, parentheses, brackets, square b., crotchet, crook,

brace; hyphen, hyphenation; dash, dot, caret mark, omission m., blank; asterisk, asterism, star; obelus, dagger, squiggle, marginal finger, hand, index; accent, grave a., acute a., circumflex a.; barytone, oxytone, paroxytone, proparoxytone, perispomenon, properispomenon; diæresis, cedilla, tilde; diacritical mark, vowel point, macron, breve, umlaut; sigla, stroke, mark of abbreviation paragraph; plus sign, minus s., multiplication s., division s., equals s., decimal point; underlining, sublineation; italics, bold type, heavy t. 587 n. *print-type*; capital letter, cap, initial c.

Adj. *indicating*, indicative, indicatory, pointing; significative, connotative, expressive, implicative, suggestive, suggesting 514 adj. *meaningful*; figuring, typical, representative, token, symbolic, emblematic, nominal, diagrammatic 551 adj. *representing*; tell-tale, revealing, betraying, bewraying 526 adj. *disclosing*; signalising, symptomatic 466 adj. *evidential*; diagnostic, semeiological, symptomatological; characteristic, personal, individual 80 adj. *special*; demonstrative, explanatory, exponential 520 adj. *interpretive*; ominous, prophetic 511 adj. *presageful*; gesticulatory, pantomimic; signalling, signing, thumbing.

heraldic, emblematic; crested, armorial, blazoned, emblazoned, marshalled, quartered, impaled, dimidiated, differenced; paly, pily, barry, gyronny; dexter, sinister; gules, azure, vert, purpure, sable, tenné, murray, or, argent, ermine; rampant, guardant, reguardant, forcene, couchant, statant, sejant, genuant, passant.

marked etc. vb.; recognized, characterised, known by; scarred, branded, stigmatized, earmarked; denoted, numbered, lettered; referenced, indexed; denotable; indelible.

Vb. *indicate*, point 281 vb. *point to*; point out, exhibit 522 vb. *show*; describe heraldically, blazon; mark out, blaze; register, read, tell 548 vb. *record*; name, identify, classify 80 vb. *specify*; index, make an i., reference, supply references, refer; point the way, show the w., guide 689 vb. *direct*; signify, denote, connote, suggest, imply, involve, spell, bespeak, argue 514 vb. *mean*; symbolize, typify,

betoken, stand for, be the sign of 551vb. *represent*; declare 532vb. *affirm*; signalize, highlight 532vb. *emphasize*; evince, show signs of, bear the marks of, bear the stamp of, give evidence of, attest, testify, witness 466vb. *evidence*; intimate 524vb. *hint*; betray, reveal 526vb. *disclose*; inform against 524vb. *inform*; prefigure, forebode, presage 511vb. *predict*.

mark, mark off, mark out, chalk o., flag o., lay o., demarcate, delimit 236vb. *limit*; label, ticket, docket, tag, tab, keep tabs on; earmark, designate; note, annotate, put a mark on, trace upon, line, score, underline, underscore; number, letter, page; tick, tick off; nick 260vb. *notch*; chalk, chalk up; scratch, scribble, cover 586vb. *write*; blot, stain, blacken 649vb. *make unclean*; scar, disfigure 842vb. *make ugly*; punctuate, dot, dash, cross, obelize, asterisk; put one's mark on, leave finger-prints, leave footprints; blaze, brand, burn in; stigmatize, prick, tattoo 263vb. *pierce*; stamp, seal, punch, impress, emboss; imprint, overprint 587vb. *print*; etch 555vb. *engrave*; mark heraldically, crest, emblazon; impale, dimidiate, quarter, difference; marshal, charge.

sign, ratify, countersign 488vb. *endorse*; autograph, write one's signature, write one's name; put one's hand to, subscribe, undersign; initial, paraph; put one's mark, put one's cross; make signation; attest, witness 466vb. *testify*.

gesticulate, pantomime, mime, mimic, suit the action to the word 20vb. *imitate*; wave one's hands, talk with one's h., saw the air; wave, wag, waggle; wave to, hold out one's hand 884vb. *greet*; wave one's hat, stamp 923vb. *applaud*; wave one's arms, semaphore; gesture, motion, sign; point, thumb, beckon, raise one's hand 455vb. *attract notice*; nod, beck, wink, shrug; jog, nudge, poke, dig in the ribs, clap on the back; look, look volumes, glance, leer, ogle 438vb. *gaze*; twinkle, smile 835vb. *laugh*; raise one's eyebrows, wag the finger, wag the head 924vb. *disapprove*; wring one's hands, tear one's hair 836vb. *lament*; grit one's teeth, clench one's t. 599vb. *be resolute*; gnash one's teeth 891vb. *be angry*; snap, bite 893vb. *be sullen*; grimace, pout, scowl, frown 829vb. *be discontented*; cock a snook, curl one's lip 922vb. *despise*;

shuffle, scrape one's feet, paw the ground; pat, stroke 889vb. *caress*.

signal, make a s., hang out a s., send a s., exchange signals, speak 524vb. *communicate*; tap out a message, semaphore, heliograph; flag, thumb; wave on, wave by, wave through; unfurl the flag, fly the f., break the f., dip the f., dip, half-mast, salute; alert, alarum, sound the alarm, dial the police 665vb. *raise the alarm*; beat the drum, sound the trumpets; fire a warning shot 664vb. *warn*.

Adv. *symbolically*, heraldically; by this token, in token of; in dumb show, in sign language, in pantomime.

See: 20, 77, 80, 85, 87, 117, 228, 236, 260, 263, 269, 279, 281, 305, 318, 321, 340, 364, 379, 398, 403, 414, 420, 438, 445, 455, 461, 465, 466, 484, 488, 505, 511, 514, 520, 522, 524, 525, 526, 528, 529, 531, 532, 548, 551, 555, 561, 586, 587, 590, 599, 622, 649, 664, 665, 689, 690, 711, 721, 729, 737, 743, 756, 778, 822, 829, 835, 836, 842, 845, 876, 882, 884, 889, 891, 892, 893, 922, 923, 924, 981, 983.

548 Record

N. *record*, recording, documentation; historical record, memoir, chronicle, annals, history 590n. *narrative*; biographical record, case history, psychic profile, histogram, psychogram 590n. *biography*; dossier, rogues gallery; public record, gazette, official journal, Hansard, Congressional Record; official publication, Blue Book, White Paper; recorded material, minutes, transactions, acta; notes, annotations, marginalia, adversaria, jottings, dottings, cuttings, press-c.; memorabilia, memorandum 505n. *reminder*; reports, returns, statements 524n. *report*; tally, score-sheet, scoreboard; evidentiary record, form, document, muniment; voucher, certificate, diploma 466n. *credential*; birth certificate, death c., marriage lines 767n. *title-deed*; copy, spare c., carbon c. 22n. *duplicate*; documentation, records, preserved r., old r., archives, papers, correspondence; record, book, roll, register, registry, cartulary; tablet, table, notebook, minute-b., log-b., log, diary, journal, scrap-book, album; ledger,

cash-book, day-b., cheque-b. 808 n.
account-book; file, index, waiting list 87 n.
list; card, microcard, microfilm; inscription, legend, caption, heading 547 n.
indication; wall-writing, graffito 586 n.
script.

egistration, registry, record-keeping; recording, sound r., tape-r.; inscribing, engraving, epigraphy; enrolment, enlistment; booking, reservation; entering, entry, double-e., book-keeping, accountancy 808 n. *accounts*; filing, indexing, docket, docket-stamp.

nonument, memorial 505 n. *reminder*; mausoleum 364 n. *tomb*; statue, bust 551 n. *image*; brass, tablet, slab, inscription 364 n. *obsequies*; hatchment, funerary achievement 547 n. *heraldry*; pillar, column, memorial arch, obelisk, monolith; ancient monument, archaeological m., cromlech, dolmen, cairn, menhir, gilgal, megalith, barrow, tell 125 n. *antiquity*; testimonial, cup, prize, ribbon, decoration 729 n. *trophy*.

race, vestige, relic, remains 41 n. *leavings*; footstep, footprint, footmark, hoofmark, pug-mark, tread; spoor, slot; scent, smell, piste; wake, wash, trail, smoke-t., track, sound-t.; furrow, swathe, path; finger-mark, thumb-impression 547 n. *indication*; finger-print, dabs 466 n. *evidence*; mark, stain, scar, cicatrix, scratch, weal, wale, welt 845 n. *blemish*.

Adj. *recording* etc. vb., recordative 505 adj. *remembering*; annalistic, record-making; self-recording; recordable; monumental, epigraphic, inscriptional.

ecorded, on record, in the file, documented; filed, indexed, entered, booked, registered; down, put d.; in writing 586 adj. *written*; in print, in black and white 587 adj. *printed*; traceable, vestigial, extant 41 adj. *remaining*.

Vb. *record*, tape-record; document, put on record, place on r.; docket, file, index, catalogue, store in the archives; inscribe, cut, carve, grave, incise 555 vb. *engrave*; take down, set down in black and white, put in a book, commit to writing 586 vb. *write*; have printed 587 vb. *print*; write down, jot d.; note, mark, make a note of; minute, calendar; chronicle, historify 590 vb. *describe*.

egister, mark up, chalk up, tick off, score; tabulate, table, enrol, enlist 87 vb.

list; fill in, fill up, enter, post, book; reserve, put on the list, put on the waiting l.; inscribe, inscroll, blazon; log, diarize, journalize 808 vb. *account*.

Adv. *on record*, in the file, in the index, on the books.

See: 22, 41, 87, 125, 364, 466, 505, 524, 547, 551, 555, 586, 587, 590, 729, 767, 808, 845.

549 Recorder

N. *recorder*, registrar, record-keeper, archivist, remembrancer; Master of the Rolls, Custos Rotulorum; notary, protonotary; amanuensis, stenographer, scriniary, scribe; secretary, referencer, receptionist; writer, penpusher; clerk, babu; record-clerk, tally-c., filing-c., book-keeper 808 n. *accountant*; engraver 555 n. *engraving*; draughtsman 556 n. *artist*; photographer, cameraman, snapshotter 551 n. *photography*; filing cabinet, record room, muniment r., Record Office; Recording Angel.

chronicler, saga-man, annalist, diarist, historian, historiographer, biographer, autobiographer 590 n. *narrator*; archæologist, antiquary 125 n. *antiquarian*; memorialist 763 n. *petitioner*; reporter, pressman, journalist, columnist, gossip-writer, newsman 529 n. *newsmonger*; press photographer, candid camera.

recording instrument, recorder, tape-r.; record, disc, long-player 414 n. *gramophone*; dictaphone, telautograph, printing telegraph, teleprinter, tape-machine, ticker-tape; cash register; turnstile; seismograph, speedometer 465 n. *gauge*; time-recorder, stopwatch 117 n. *timekeeper*; hygrometer 341 n. *hygrometry*; anemometer 340 n. *pneumatics*; camera, photostat; pen, pencil 586 n. *stationery*.

See: 117, 125, 340, 341, 414, 465, 529, 551, 555, 556, 586, 590, 763, 808.

550 Obliteration

N. *obliteration*, erasure, rasure, effacement; overprinting, defacement; deletion, blue pencil, censorship; crossing out, cancellation, cancel; circumduction, annulment, cassation 752 n. *abrogation*; burial, oblivion 506 n. *amnesty*; blot, stain 649 n.

dirt; tabula rasa, clean slate, clean sweep 149n. *revolution*; eraser, duster, sponge, rubber, indiarubber; paint-stripper, abrasive 648n. *cleaning utensil.*

Adj. *obliterated*, wiped out, effaced; out of print, leaving no trace, printless, unrecorded, unregistered, unwritten; intestate.

Vb. *obliterate*, remove the traces, cover, cover up 525vb. *conceal*; overpaint, overprint, deface, make illegible; efface, erase, rase, scratch out, rub o.; abrade 333vb. *rub*; expunge, sponge out, wash o., wipe o.; blot, black out, blot o.; rub off, wipe o., wash o.; take out, cancel, delete, dele; strike out, cross out, ring, score through, draw the pen t., censor, blue-pencil; wipe off the map, bury, cover 364vb. *inter*; sink in oblivion 506 vb. *forget*; submerge 165vb. *suppress*; drown 399vb. *silence*; leave no trace 446vb. *disappear*; be effaced 506vb. *be forgotten.*

See: 149, 165, 333, 364, 399, 446, 506, 525, 648, 649, 752.

551 Representation

N. *representation*, acting for, agentship 751n. *commission*; personification, incarnation, embodiment; typifying, typification, symbolization 547n. *indication*; conventional representation, diagram, picture-writing, hieroglyphics 586n. *writing*; presentment, presentation, projection, realization, evocation 522n. *manifestation*; assuming the part of, personation, impersonation; enactment, performance, doing 594n. *acting*; mimesis, mimicry, noises off, charade, dumbshow 20n. *imitation*; depiction, characterization 590n. *description*; delineation, graphic d., drawing, illustration, graphic treatment, iconography 553n. *painting*; likeness, similitude 18n. *similarity*; exact likeness, double, facsimile 22n. *duplicate*; trace, tracing, diagraph 233n. *outline*; reflection (see *image*); portraiture, portrayal; pictorial equivalent, true picture, striking likeness, speaking l., photographic l., realism 553n. *picture*; bad likeness, indifferent l. 552n. *misrepresentation*; reproduction, lithograph, oleograph, collotype 555n. *printing*;

etching 555n. *engraving*; design, blue print, draft, rough d., cartoon, sketch outline 623n. *plan*; slide 422n. *transparency.*

image, very i., exact i. 22n. *duplicate*; eidetic image, clear i.; mental image, after image 451n. *idea*; projection, reflected image 417n. *reflection*; idol, graven image 982n. *idolatry*; painted image, icon statuary, statue, colossus; statuette, bust torso, head 554n. *sculpture*; effigy, figure figurine; wax figure, waxwork; dummy tailor's d., lay figure; model, working m.; doll, poupée, golliwog; marionette fantoccini; puppet, maumet, manikin snowman, gingerbread man; scarecrow robot, automaton; type, symbol.

art, fine a., graphic a. 553n. *painting*; plastic art 554n. *sculpture*; architecture; modern art, classical a., Renaissance a., Hellenistic a., Greek a., oriental a.; Byzantinism, Romanesque art, Gothic a., baroque a., rococo a.; expressionism, modernism functional art, commercial a., non-functional a., decorative a. 844n. *ornamental art*; the minor arts, illumination, calligraphy, weaving, tapestry, embroidery pottery.

photography, radiography, skiagraphy cinematography 445n. *cinema*; rotograph, photograph, photo, photostat snapshot, snap, shot; colour photo transparency, slide; print, photo-p., still exposure, over-e., under-e.; reduction enlargement, blow-up, close-up; plate film, colour f., panchromatic f., fast f. skiagram, radiograph, X-ray; heliotype calotype, talbotype, daguerreotype; camera obscura 442n. *camera*; cameraman cinematographer, photographer, snap shotter; radiographer.

map, chart, plan, outline, sketch map relief m., political m., survey m., road m. air m., star m.; Admiralty chart, portulan, portolano; ground plan, ichnography; scenograph, elevation, side-e. projection, Mercator's p., Chad's p. atlas, world a.; map-making, cartography

Adj. *representing*, reflecting etc.vb.; representative 590adj. *descriptive*; pictorial graphic, vivid; emblematic, symbolic figurative, illustrative, diagrammatic representational, realistic, naturalistic impressionist, surrealistic; photographic photogenic, paintable.

represented, drawn, delineated etc. vb.; fairly drawn, well represented; reflected, imaged; painted, pictured; being drawn, sitting for.

Vb. *represent*, act for 755 vb. *deputize*; stand for, symbolize 514 vb. *mean*; type, typify, incarnate, embody, personify; act the part of, assume the role of; personate, impersonate, pose as 542 vb. *deceive*; pose, model, sit for 23 vb. *be example*; present, enact, perform, do 594 vb. *dramatize*; project, shadow forth, shadow out, adumbrate, suggest; reflect, image, hold the mirror up to nature; mimic, mime, copy 20 vb. *imitate*; depict, characterize 590 vb. *describe*; delineate, limn, draw, picture, portray, figure; illustrate, emblazon 553 vb. *paint*; hit off, make a likeness, catch a l., catch, realize, register; make an image, carve, cast 554 vb. *sculpt*; cut 555 vb. *engrave*; mould, shape 243 vb. *efform*; take the shape, follow the s., mould upon, fashion u.; design, blueprint, draft, sketch out, chalk o. 623 vb. *plan*; diagrammatize, diagram, make a d., construct a figure, describe a circle 233 vb. *outline*; sketch, dash off 609 vb. *improvise*; map, chart, survey, plot.

photograph, photo, take a p.; snapshot, snap, take a s.; take, shoot, film; X-ray, radiograph, daguerreotype; expose, develop, enlarge, blow up, reduce.

See: 18, 20, 22, 23, 233, 243, 417, 422, 442, 445, 451, 514, 522, 542, 547, 552, 553, 554, 555, 586, 590, 594, 609, 623, 751, 755, 844, 982.

552 Misrepresentation

N. *misrepresentation*, false light, not a true picture 541 n. *falsehood*; unfair picture, bad likeness 914 n. *injustice*; travesty, parody 546 n. *exaggeration*; caricature, burlesque, guy 851 n. *ridicule*; flattering portrait 925 n. *flattery*; non-realism, non-representational art 551 n. *art*; bad art, daubing, sign-painting; daub, botch; twist, turn, misapplication, anamorphosis, deformation, distorted image, false i., distorting mirror 246 n. *distortion*; misreport, misquotation, misinformation 535 n. *misteaching*; misexposition 521 n. *misinterpretation*.

Adj. *misrepresented* etc. vb.

Vb. *misrepresent*, misdescribe 535 vb. *misteach*; deform 246 vb. *distort*; give a twist or turn, miscolour, tone down 925 vb. *flatter*; over-dramatize 546 vb. *exaggerate*; overdraw, caricature, guy, burlesque, parody, travesty; daub, botch, splash; lie about, traduce 926 vb. *detract*; lie 541 vb. *be false*.

See: 246, 521, 535, 541, 546, 551, 851, 914, 925, 926.

553 Painting

N. *painting*, graphic art, colouring, rubrication, illumination; daubing, finger-painting; washing, tinting, touching up; depicting, drawing, sketching 551 n. *representation*; artistry, composition, rectilinear c., design, technique, draughtsmanship, brushwork; treatment, tone, values, atmosphere, ambience, local colour; monotone, monochrome, polychrome 425 n. *colour*; black and white, chiaroscuro, grisaille.

art style, style of painting, grand style, grand manner; intimate style, genre (see *art subject*); pasticcio, pastiche; iconography, portrait-painting, portraiture, historical painting, landscape p., scene-p., scenography, sign-painting, miniature p.; oil-painting, water-colouring, painting in tempera; fresco painting, mural p., encaustic p., impasto.

school of painting, the Primitives, Byzantine school, Renaissance s., Sienese s., Florentine s., Venetian s., Perugian s., Umbrian s., Dutch s., Flemish s., German s., American s.; Proto-Baroque, Mannerism, Baroque, Rococo, Pre-Raphaelitism, Neo-Classicism, Realism, Romanticism, Impressionism, Post-Impressionism, Neo-I., Cubism, Expressionism, Pointillism, Vorticism, Neo-plasticism, Functionalism, Futurism, Surrealism; abstract art; Tachism, action painting; Euston Road, Bloomsbury, Greenwich Village.

art subject, landscape, seascape, skyscape, cloudscape; view, scene, prospect, diorama, panorama, bird's-eye view; interior, still life, nocturne, nude; crucifixion, pietà.

picture, pictorial equivalent 551 n. *representation*; easel-picture, cabinet p.; tableau, mosaic, tapestry; painting, pastiche, icon,

triptych, diptych; fresco, mural, wall-painting; canvas, daub; drawing, line-d.; sketch, outline, cartoon; oil-painting, water-colour, aquarelle, pastel, black-and-white drawing, pen-and-ink d., pencil d., charcoal d.; cartoon, chad, caricature, silhouette; miniature, vignette, thumbnail sketch, illuminated initial; old master, masterpiece; study, nocturne, nude, portrait, full-length p., three-quarter length p., half-l. p., kit-cat, head, profile, full-face portrait; print, photoprint 551 n. *photography*; rotograph, photogravure, reproduction, photographic r., half-tone; aquatint, woodcut 555 n. *engraving*; print, plate; illustration, picture postcard, cigarette card, fag-c., stamp, transfer; picture book, photograph album, illustrated work 589 n. *book*.

art equipment, palette, palette knife, paint-brush, paint-box, paint-tube; paints, oils, oil paint, poster p.; water-colours, tempera, distemper, gouache, gesso, varnish 226 n. *facing*; ink, crayon, pastel, chalk, charcoal; pen, pencil; canvas, easel, picture-frame; studio, atelier, art museum, picture-gallery; model, sitter, poser, subject; drysaltery 633 n. *provision*.

Adj. *painted*, daubed, scumbled, plastered etc. vb.; graphic, pictorial, scenic, picturesque, decorative 844 adj. *ornamental*; pastel, in paint, in oils, in water-colours, in tempera 425 adj. *coloured*; linear, black-and-white, shaded, stippled; chiaroscuro, grisaille 429 adj. *grey*; painterly, paintable 551 adj. *representing*.

Vb. *paint*, colorize 425 vb. *colour*; tint, touch up, daub; dead-colour, scumble, put on, paint on; spread a colour, drive a c., lay on the c., lay it on thick 226 vb. *coat*; splash the colour, slap on the c.; paint a picture, portray, do a portrait, draw, sketch, limn, cartoon 551 vb. *represent*; miniate, rubricate, illuminate; do in oils, do in water-colours, do in tempera, do in black-and-white; ink, chalk, crayon, pencil, stencil, shade, stipple; pinxit, delineavit, fecit.

See: 226, 425, 429, 551, 555, 589, 633, 844.

554 Sculpture

N. *sculpture*, plastic art 551 n. *representation*; modelling, figuring; carving, stone cutting, wood-carving; moulding, ceroplastics; petroglyph, rock-carving, bone-c., shell-c., scrimshaw; statuary; group; statue, colossus; statuette, figurine, bust, torso, head, cast, plaster c., waxwork 551 n. *image*; ceramics 381 n. *pottery*; anaglyph, cameo, intaglio, relief, half-relief, mezzo-relievo 254 n. *relievo*; stone, marble, Parian m.; bronze, clay, wax, plasticine; modelling tool, chisel, burin.

Adj. *glyptic*, sculptured, carved; statuary, statuesque, marmoreal; anaglyptic, in relief 254 adj. *salient*; ceroplastic; toreutic.

Vb. *sculpt*, sculpture, cut, carve, chisel, chip; model, mould, cast; sculpsit.

See: 254, 381, 551.

555 Engraving

N. *engraving*, etching, line engraving, plate e., steel e., copper e., chalcography; zincography, cerography, glyptography, gem-cutting, gem-engraving; mezzotint, aquatint; wood-engraving, xylography, lignography, woodcut; drypoint; steel plate, copper p., graphotype; stone, block, wood-b.; chisel, graver, burin, bur, bur-chisel, needle, dry-point, etching-p., style.

printing, type-p. 587 n. *print*; plate printing, copper-plate p., intaglio p., anastatic p.; lithography, photolithography, photogravure, chromolithography, colour-printing, three-colour p., four-colour p.; stereotype, autotype, graphotype, heliotype; stamping, impression; die, punch, stamp.

Vb. *engrave*, grave, incise, cut; etch, stipple, scrape; bite, bite in; impress, stamp; lithograph 587 vb. *print*; mezzotint, aquatint; incisit, sculpsit, imprimit.

See: 587.

556 Artist

N. *artist*, craftsman 686 n. *artisan*; art-master, designer, draughtsman; fashion-artist, dress-designer, couturier; drawer, sketcher, delineator, limner; copyist; caricaturist, cartoonist; illustrator, commercial artist; painter, colourist, luminist, luminarist; dauber, pavement artist, scene-painter, sign-p.; oil-painter, water-colour p., aquarellist, pastellist; illumi-

nator, miniaturist; portrait-painter, land-scape-p., marine p., genre p., still-life p., fruit-and-flower p.; Academician, R.A., old master, modern m.; Pre-Raphelite, Impressionist, Fauvist, Dadaist, Cubist, Futurist, Vorticist, Surrealist, action painter 553 n. *school of painting.*

sculptor, carver, statuary, monumental mason, modeller, wax-m., moulder, figurist; image-maker, idol-m.

engraver, etcher, aquatinter; lapidary, chaser, gem-engraver, enameller, enamel-list; typographer, type-cutter 587 n. *printer.*

See: 553, 587, 686.

557 Language

N. *language*, tongue, speech, idiom; spoken language, living l.; patter, lingo, bat 560 n. *dialect*; mother tongue, native t., native language; vernacular, common speech, folk s., vulgar dialect; correct speech, idiomatic s., Queen's English; lingua franca, Koine, Hindustani, kitchen H., Swahili, pidgin, pidgin English, Chinook; sign-language, semeiology 547 n. *gesti-culation*; diplomatic language, interna-tional l.; artificial language, Esperanto, Ido, Volapuk; universal language, pasi-laly; private language, invented l., idioglossia, idolalia; official language, Mandarin, Hindi, standard English; written language, officialese, transla-tionese; learned language, dead l., Latin, Greek, Sanskrit, Pali, Pahlevi, Coptic, Ethiopic; confusion of tongues, polyglot medley, Babel, babble 61 n. *confusion.*

language type, inflected language, analyti-cal l., agglutinative l., monosyllabic l., tonal l.; language group, family of languages, Aryan, Indo-European, Indo-Germanic, Indo-Aryan, Hamitic, Semitic, Dravidian; Turanian, Ural-Altaic, Finno-Tartar, Finno-Ugrian; Sino-Tibetan, Tibeto-Chinese; Bantu.

linguistics, language study, glossology, glottology, dialectology, philology, com-parative p.; comparative grammar 564 n. *grammar*; phonetics 577 n. *pronunciation*; Grimm's law, Verner's l.; derivation 559 n. *etymology*; morphology; semasiology, semantics 514 n. *meaning*; onomasiology 561 n. *nomenclature*; palæography 125 n.

palætiology; linguistic distribution, lin-guistic geography, word-g.; genius of a language, feel of a l., sprachgefühl, sense of idiom; polyglottism, bilingualism.

literature, polite l., written language, belles lettres 589 n. *reading matter*; letters, humane scholarship, arts, humanities, litteræ humaniores 654 n. *civilization*; Muses, literary circles, republic of letters, P.E.N. 589 n. *author*; literary history, history of literature; Golden Age, Silver A., Augustan A., Classical A.; compen-dium of literature 592 n. *anthology*; digest, chrestomathy, reader 589 n. *textbook.*

linguist, language student, philologist, glot-tologist; etymologist, lexicographer 559 n. *etymology*; semasiologist, onomasiolo-gist; grammarian 564 n. *grammar*; phone-tician 398 n. *acoustics*; student of litera-ture, man of letters, belletrist 492 n. *scholar*; humanist, humane scholar, clas-sical s., oriental s.; Hellenist, Latinist, Sanskritist, Sinologist, Semiticist, Arab-ist, Hebraist, Hispanist; polyglot, bi-lingual speaker, bilinguist.

Adj. *linguistic*, philological, etymological, grammatical, morphological; lexicogra-phical, onomasiological, semasiological; analytic; agglutinative; monosyllabic; tonal, inflected; holophrastic; correct, pure; written, literary, standard; spoken, living, idiomatic; vulgar, colloquial, ver-nacular, slangy 560 adj. *dialectical*; local, enchorial; current, common, demotic; bilingual, diglot; multilingual, polyglot.

literary, written, polished, polite, human-istic, classical, belletristic; lettered, learned, dead.

See: 61, 125, 398, 492, 514, 547, 559, 560, 561, 564, 577, 589, 592, 654.

558 Letter

N. *letter*, part of the alphabet; sign, charac-ter, written c. 586 n. *script*; alphabetism, alphabetics, alphabet, ABC, abecedary, criss-cross row; syllabic alphabet, sylla-bary; Chinese character, ideogram, ideo-graph; pictogram, cuneiform, hierogly-phic; ogham alphabet, runic a., futhorc; Greek alphabet, Roman a., Cyrillic a.; Devanagari, Nagari, Brahmi; runic letter, wen; lettering, black letter, Gothic, italic; ampersand; big letter, capital l.,

cap, majuscule; small letter, minuscule; block letter, uncial; printed letter, letterpress, type, bold t. 587n. *print-type*.

initials, first letter; monogram, cipher; anagram, acrostic.

spoken letter, phone, phoneme 398n. *speech sound*; consonant, spirant, fricative, aspirate; labial, liquid, dental, palatal, cerebral, guttural, mute, surd; sonant, voiced letter; vowel, semi-v., diphthong, triphthong 577n. *voice*; syllable, monosyllable, disyllable, polysyllable; prefix, affix, suffix.

spelling, orthography, cacography; phonography, lexigraphy; anagrammatism, metagrammatism; spelling game, spelling bee.

Adj. *literal*, in letters, lettered; alphabetical, abecedarian; in syllables, syllabic; Cyrillic; runic, oghamic; cuneiform, hieroglyphic 586adj. *written*; Gothic, italic, roman, uncial; large, majuscule, capital, initial; small, minuscule; lexigraphical, spelt, orthographic; ciphered, monogrammatic; anacrostic, anagrammatic; phonetic, consonantal, vocalic, voiced 577adj. *vocal*.

Vb. *spell*, spell out, read, syllable; use an alphabet, alphabetize; letter, form letters, uncialize 586vb. *write*; initial 547vb. *sign*; cipher, make a monogram; anagrammatize.

Adv. *alphabetically*, by letters; syllabically, in syllables.

See: 398, 547, 577, 586, 587.

559 Word

N. *word*, Verbum, Logos 965n. *the Deity*; expression, locution 563n. *phrase*; term, vocable 561n. *name*; phoneme, syllable 398n. *speech sound*; semanteme 514n. *meaning*; gloss, glossa; isogloss, synonym, tautonym 13n. *identity*; homonym, homophone, homophone, pun 518n. *equivocalness*; antonym 14n. *contrariety*; etymon, root, false r., back-formation; derivation, derivative, paronym, doublet; morphological unit, morpheme, stem, inflexion, affix, suffix, prefix, infix; part of speech 564n. *grammar*; diminutive, pejorative, intensive; cliché, vogue-word; nonce-word, new word, loan-w., loan-translation, calque 560n. *neology*; rhym-

ing word, assonant 18n. *similarity*; bad word, nasty w., swear-word 899n. *malediction*; hard word, jawbreaker, long word, polysyllable; short word, monosyllable; many words, verbiage, wordiness, verbosity 570n. *pleonasm*; lexicography, speedwriting 569n. *conciseness*.

dictionary, rhyming d., polyglot d.; lexicon, wordbook, wordstock, word-list, glossary, vocabulary; thesaurus, gradus; compilation, concordance.

etymology, derivation of words, philology 557n. *linguistics*; morphology; semasiology 514n. *meaning*; phonology, orthoepy 577n. *pronunciation*; onomasiology, terminology 561n. *nomenclature*; lexicology, lexicography; logophile, philologist, etymologist, lexicographer, compiler, dictionarian.

Adj. *verbal*, literal; titular, nominal; etymological, lexical, vocabular; philological, lexicographical, lexigraphical; derivative, conjugate, cognate, paronymous; synonymous, autonymous 514adj. *semantic*; wordy, verbose 570adj. *pleonastic*.

Adv. *verbally*, lexically; verbatim 494adv. *truly*.

See: 13, 14, 18, 398, 494, 514, 518, 557, 560, 561, 563, 564, 569, 570, 577, 899, 965.

560 Neology

N. *neology*, neologism, neolalia, neoterism 126n. *newness*; coinage, new c., new word, nonce-w., vogue-w., cliché; imported w., loan-w., loan translation, calque 559n. *word*; unfamiliar word, jawbreaker, newfangled expression, slang e.; technical language, jargon, technical term, term of art; barbarism, caconym, hybrid, hybrid expression; corruption, monkish Latin, dog L.; novelese, journalese, officialese, newspeak; affected language, archaism, Lallans 850n. *affectation*; abuse of language, abuse of terms, missaying, antiphrasis, malapropism 565n. *solecism*; word-play, spoonerism 839n. *witticism*; paraphrasia, paralalia, idioglossia, idiolalia 580n. *speech defect*.

dialect, idiom, lingo, patois, brogue, vernacular 557n. *language*; cockney, Doric, broad Scots, Lallans; broken English, pidgin E., pidgin, Chinook; Koine, lingua

franca, hybrid language; Briticism, Anglicism, Americanism, Scoticism, Hibernicism, Gallicism, Teutonism, Sinicism; chi-chi, babuism; provincialism, localism, vernacularism; sigmatism, iotacism 580n. *speech defect*; neologist, word-coiner, neoterist; dialectology 557n. *linguistics.*

slang, vulgarism, colloquialism, byword; jargon, argot, cant, patter; gipsy lingo, Romany; flash tongue, thieves' Latin, pedlar's French, St. Giles Greek, rhyming slang; Billingsgate; Wall St. slang; doubletalk, backchat; macaronics, gibberish 515n. *empty talk.*

Adj. *neological*, neoteristic, newfangled, newly coined, not in the dictionary; barbaric, barbarous, unidiomatic, hybrid, corrupt, pidgin; loaned, borrowed, imported, foreign, revived, archaic, obsolete; irregular, solecistic 565adj. *ungrammatical.*

dialectical, vernacular, kailyard; Doric, Cockney, broad; provincial, local; homely, colloquial; unliterary, slangy, argotic, canting, cant; jargonistic, journalistic; technical, special.

Vb. *neologize*, coin words, invent vocabulary; talk slang, jargonize, cant; talk cockney, talk Doric, burr.

See: 126, 515, 557, 559, 565, 580, 839, 850.

561 Nomenclature

N. *nomenclature*, naming etc.vb.; calling, nomination, cognomination; giving one's name, eponymy; onomatology, terminology, orismology; dedication, nuncupation, declaration 532n. *affirmation*; description, designation, appellation, denomination; antonomasia 519n. *trope*; addressing, compellation, apostrophe, roll-call 583n. *allocution*; christening, naming ceremony, baptism 988n. *Christian rite*; study of place-names, toponymy.

name, nomen, first name, fore-n., Christian n., prenomen; surname, patronymic, matronymic, cognomen; maiden name, married n.; appellation, moniker; nickname, pet name, by-name, agnomen, kenning; epithet, description; title, handle, style, signature; heading, head, caption 547n. *indication*; designation,

apellative; name and address 547n. *label*; term, cant t., special t., technical t., term of art 560n. *neology*; name-child, same name, namesake, synonym, eponym, tautonym, counter-term, antonym; pseudonym 562n. *misnomer*; noun, proper n. 564n. *part of speech*; list of names, onomasticon; place name, local n.

nomenclator, roll-caller, announcer, toastmaster; onomatologist; terminologist; namer, namegiver, eponym, christener, baptizer.

Adj. *named*, called etc.vb.; titled, entitled, christened; known as, alias; so-called, soi-disant; hight, yclept; nominal, titular; named after, eponymous, theophoric; fitly named, what one may fairly call; nameable.

naming, nuncupative, nuncupatory 532adj. *affirmative*; appellative, compellative, terminological, orismological.

Vb. *name*, call, give a name, christen, baptize 988vb. *perform ritual*; give one's name to, eponymize; call by the name of, surname, nickname, dub, clepe; give one his title, sir, bemadam; title, entitle, style, term 80vb. *specify*; distinguish 463vb. *discriminate*; define, characterize 547vb. *label*; call by name, call the roll, call out the names, nomenclate, announce; divulge the name 526vb. *divulge*; blacklist 924vb. *exprobate.*

be named, own or bear or go by the name of; answer to; sail under the flag of.

Adv. *by name*; namely; terminologically.

See: 80, 463, 519, 526, 532, 547, 560, 562, 564, 583, 924, 988.

562 Misnomer

N. *misnomer*, misnaming, miscalling; malapropism 565n. *solecism*; wrong name, false n., alias, assumed title; nom de guerre, nom de plume, pen-name; nom de theatre, stage name, pseudonym, allonym; nickname, pet name 561n. *name*; pseudonymity.

no name, anonymity; anonym, certain person, so-and-so, N. or M., sir or madam; Mr. X, Monsieur Tel, A. N. Other; what d'ye call 'em, thingummy bob; this or that; and co.; some, any, what-have-you.

Adj. *misnamed*, miscalled, mistitled etc. vb.; self-christened, self-styled, soi-disant, would-be, so-called, quasi, pseudonymous.

anonymous, unknown, nameless, without a name; incognito, innominate, unnamed, unsigned; a certain, certain, such; some, any, this or that.

Vb. *misname*, mistake the name of, miscall, misterm, mistitle; nickname, dub 561 vb. *name*; misname oneself, assume an alias; conceal one's name, be anonymous; not subscribe, refuse to sign; write under an assumed name, usurp the name.

See: 561, 565.

563 Phrase

N. *phrase*, form of words; clause, sentence, period, paragraph; expression, locution; idiom, idiotism, mannerism 80 n. *speciality*; fixed expression, formula, set phrase, set terms; hackneyed expression, well-worn phrase, cliché, commonplace 610 n. *habit*; saying, motto, moral, epigram 496 n. *maxim*; lapidary phrase, epitaph 364 n. *obsequies*; inscription, legend, caption 548 n. *record*; phrases, empty p., words, compliments 515 n. *empty talk*; terminology 561 n. *nomenclature*; phraseology, phrasing, diction, wording, choice of language, choice of expression, turn of e.; well-turned phrase, rounded p. 575 n. *elegance*; roundabout phrase, periphrasis, circumlocution 570 n. *diffuseness*; paraphrase 520 n. *translation*; written phrase, phraseogram, phraseograph 586 n. *script*; phrase-monger, phrase-maker, epigraphist, epigrammatist, proverbialist 575 n. *stylist*.

Adj. *phraseological*, sentential, periodic, in phrases, in sentences; idiomatic; well-rounded, well-couched.

Vb. *phrase*, word, articulate, syllable; re-word, rephrase 520 vb. *translate*; express, put in words, clothe in w., find words for, state 532 vb. *affirm*; put words together, turn a sentence, round a period 566 vb. *show style*.

Adv. *in terms*, in good set t., in round t., in set phrases.

See: 80, 364, 496, 515, 520, 532, 548, 561, 566, 570, 575, 586, 610.

564 Grammar

N. *grammar*, comparative g., philology 557 n. *linguistics*; grammarianism, grammatical studies, analysis, parsing, construing; praxis, paradigm; accidence, inflection, case; conjugation, mode, voice, tense; number, gender, agreement of g.; accentuation, pointing, vowel p. 547 n. *punctuation*; nunation, mimation; guna, vriddhi; umlaut, ablaut, attraction, assimilation, dissimilation; ablative absolute, genitive a., locative a.; syntax, word order, parataxis, asyndeton, ellipsis, apposition; bad grammar 565 n. *solecism*; good grammar, grammaticalness, correct style, jus et norma loquendi.

part of speech, substantive, noun, undeclined n., asymptote; common noun, proper n.; adjective; adnoun; verb, irregular v.; adverb, preposition, postposition, copula conjunction; particle, augment, syllabic a., temporal a.; augmentative, affix, suffix, postfix, infix; inflexion, case-ending; formative, morpheme, semanteme; denominative, deverbative; diminutive, intensive.

Adj. *grammatical*, correct; syntactical, inflexional; heteroclite, asymptote; irregular, anomalous; masculine, feminine, neuter; singular, dual, plural; substantival, adjectival, adnominal; verbal, adverbial; participial; prepositional; denominative, deverbal; conjunctive, copulative; elative, comparative, superlative.

Vb. *parse*, analyse, inflect, punctuate, conjugate, decline; construe 520 vb. *interpret*; know one's grammar.

See: 520, 547, 557, 565.

565 Solecism

N. *solecism*, bad grammar, false g., faulty syntax, false concord, non-sequence of tenses, misconjugation; missaying, antiphrasis; misapplication, catachresis; irregularity, impropriety, barbarism 560 n. *neology*; malapropism, cacology, bull, slip, faux pas, slip of the pen, lapsus calami, slip of the tongue, lapsus linguæ 495 n. *mistake*; mispronunciation, dropping one's aitches, lisp, lallation, lambdacism 580 n. *speech defect*; misspelling, cacography.

Adj. *ungrammatical,* solecistic, solecistical; irregular, abnormal; faulty, improper, incongruous; misapplied, catachrestic.

Vb. *solecize,* ignore grammar, disdain g., violate g., forget one's syntax; break Priscian's head, murder the Queen's English; mispronounce 580 vb. *stammer;* lisp, drop one's aitches; misspell 495 vb. *blunder.*

See: 495, 560, 580.

566 Style

N. *style,* fashion, mode, tone, manner, vein, strain 688 n. *conduct;* one's own style, personal s., idiosyncrasy, mannerism, trick 80 n. *speciality;* mode of expression, diction, parlance, phrasing, phraseology 563 n. *phrase;* choice of words, vocabulary, choice v.; literary style, command of language, command of idiom, raciness, power 571 n. *vigour;* tact, feeling for words, sprachgefühl, sense of language; literary charm, grace 575 n. *elegance;* word magic, word-spinning 579 n. *oratory;* weak style 572 n. *feebleness;* severe style, vernacular s., kailyard school 573 n. *plainness;* elaborate style 574 n. *ornament;* clumsy style 576 n. *inelegance.*

Adj. *stylistic,* mannered, literary; elegant, ornate, rhetorical, word-spinning; racy, idiomatic; plain, perspicuous, forceful.

Vb. *show style,* conform to idiom, care for words, spin w.; style, express, measure one's words 563 vb. *phrase.*

See: 80, 563, 571, 572, 573, 574, 575, 576, 579, 688.

567 Perspicuity

N. *perspicuity,* perspicuousness, clearness, clarity, lucidity, limpidity 422 n. *transparency;* limpid style 516 n. *intelligibility;* directness 573 n. *plainness;* definition, definiteness, exactness 494 n. *accuracy.*

Adj. *perspicuous,* lucid, limpid 422 adj. *transparent;* clear, unambiguous 516 adj. *intelligible;* explicit, clear-cut 80 adj. *definite;* exact 494 adj. *accurate;* uninvolved, direct 573 adj. *plain.*

See: 80, 422, 494, 516, 573.

568 Imperspicuity

N. *imperspicuity,* imperspicuousness, obscurity 517 n. *unintelligibility;* cloudiness, fogginess 423 n. *opacity;* abstraction, abstruseness; complexity, involved style, cultism, gongorism 574 n. *ornament;* hard words, Johnsonese, Carlylese 700 n. *difficulty;* imprecision, impreciseness, vagueness 474 n. *uncertainty;* inaccuracy 495 n. *inexactness;* ambiguity 518 n. *equivocalness;* mysteriousness, oracular style 530 n. *enigma;* profundity, deepness 211 n. *depth;* over-compression, ellipsis 569 n. *conciseness;* cloud of words, verbiage 570 n. *diffuseness.*

Adj. *imperspicuous,* unclear, untransparent, cloudy 423 adj. *opaque;* obscure 418 adj. *dark;* oracular, mysterious, enigmatic 517 adj. *unintelligible;* abstruse, profound 211 adj. *deep;* allusive, indirect 523 adj. *latent;* vague, imprecise, indefinite 474 adj. *uncertain;* ambiguous 518 adj. *equivocal;* confused, tangled, involved 61 adj. *complex;* harsh, crabbed, stiff 576 adj. *inelegant;* hard, full of long words, Johnsonian 700 adj. *difficult.*

See: 61, 211, 418, 423, 474, 495, 517, 518, 523, 530, 569, 570, 574, 576, 700.

569 Conciseness

N. *conciseness,* concision, succinctness, brevity, soul of wit; pithiness, pithy saying 496 n. *maxim;* aphorism, epigram 839 n. *witticism;* economy of words, verbal economy, no words wasted, few words, terseness, Spartan brevity, laconism; compression, telegraphese; ellipsis, aposiopesis; syncope, abbreviation, contraction 204 n. *shortening;* compendiousness, epitome, outline, brief sketch 592 n. *compendium;* monostich, Japanese poem; compactness, portmanteau word, telescope w.; clipped speech, monosyllabism 582 n. *taciturnity;* nutshell, the long and the short of it 204 n. *shortness.*

Adj. *concise,* brief, not long in telling, short and sweet 204 adj. *short;* laconic, monosyllabic, sparing of words 582 adj. *taciturn;* irreducible, succinct; to the point, trenchant; curt, brusque 885 adj. *ungracious;* compendious, condensed, tight,

close, compact; pithy, pregnant, sententious, neat, exact, pointed, aphoristic,
epigrammatic, Tacitean; elliptic, telegraphic, contracted, compressed; summary, cut short, abbreviated.

Vb. *be concise,* — brief etc.adj.; need few
words, not beat about the bush, come to
the point, cut a long story short; telescope, compress, condense, contract,
abridge, abbreviate 204vb. *shorten*; outline, sketch; summarize, sum up, resume
592vb. *abstract*; allow no words, be short
with, cut short, cut off; laconize, spare
speech, economize words, waste no w.,
clip one's w. 582vb. *be taciturn*; express
pithily, epigrammatize 839vb. *be witty.*

Adv. *concisely*, pithily, summarily, briefly;
without wasting words, in brief, in short,
in a word, in one sentence, in a nutshell;
to cut a long story short; to sum up.

See: 204, 496, 582, 592, 839, 885.

570 Diffuseness

N. *diffuseness* etc.adj.; profuseness, copiousness, amplitude; amplification, dilation
197n. *expansion*; expatiation, circumstantiality, minuteness; fertility, output,
productivity, penny-a-lining, word-spinning 171n. *productiveness*; inspiration,
vein, flow, outpouring; abundance, overflow, overflowing words, exuberance, redundancy 637n. *redundance*; richness,
rich vocabulary, wealth of terms; poly-
logy, verbosity, wordiness, verbiage, flatulence, vapouring, cloud of words; fluency,
non-stop talking, verbal diarrhœa 581n.
loquacity; long-windedness, prolixity,
length, epic l.; repetitiveness, reiteration
106n. *repetition*; twice-told tale 838n.
tedium; gush, rigmarole, drivel 515n.
empty talk; effusion, tirade, harangue,
sermon, speeches 579n. *oration*; descant,
disquisition 591n. *dissertation.*

pleonasm, superfluity, redundancy 637n.
redundance; hypercharacterization; perissology; battology, tautology, palillogy
106n. *repetition*; prolixity, macrology;
circumlocution, periphrasis, roundabout
phrases, periphrasis; ambages, beating
about the bush 518n. *equivocalness*;
padding, expletive, verse-filler 40n. *extra*;
episode, excursus, excursion, digression
10n. *irrelevance.*

Adj. *diffuse*, verbose, non-stop 581adj.
loquacious; profuse, copious, ample,
rich: fertile, abundant 171adj. *prolific*;
inspired, in the vein, flowing, fluent;
exuberant, overflowing 637adj. *redundant*; expatiating, circumstantial, detailed, minute; gushing, effusive; flatulent, windy, vapouring, frothy; polysyllabic, sesquipedalian, magniloquent
574adj. *ornate.*

prolix, of many words, long-winded, wordy,
prosy, prosing; spun out, made to last,
long drawn out, long-drawn 113a.
protracted; longsome, boring 838adj.
tedious; lengthy, epic, never-ending 203
adj. *long;* spreading, diffusive, discursive,
excursive, digressing, episodic; rambling
maundering 282adj. *deviating*; desultory,
pointless 10adj. *irrelevant*; indirect, circumlocutory, periphrastic, ambagious,
roundabout.

pleonastic, hypercharacterized; redundant,
excessive 637adj. *superfluous*; repetitious,
repetitional, repetitive, battological 106
adj. *repeated*; tautologous, tautological;
padded, padded out.

Vb. *be diffuse,* — prolix etc.adj.; dilate,
expatiate, amplify, particularize, detail,
expand, enlarge upon; descant, discourse
at length; repeat, tautologize, battologize
106vb. *repeat oneself*; pad, pad out, swell
o., draw o., spin o., protract 203vb.
lengthen; gush, pour out 350vb. *flow*; let
oneself go, rant, harangue, perorate
579vb. *orate*; be in the vein, launch out
on; spin a long yarn 838vb. *be tedious*;
wander, branch out, digress 282vb.
deviate; ramble, maunder, drivel, yarn,
never end; beat about the bush, not come
to the point 518vb. *equivocate.*

Adv. *diffusely*, at large, in extenso, at full
length, about it and about.

See: 10, 40, 106, 113, 171, 197, 203, 282,
515, 518, 574, 579, 581, 591, 637, 838.

571 Vigour

N. *vigour* 174n. *vigorousness*; power,
strength, vitality, drive, force, forceful-
ness 160n. *energy*; incisiveness, trenchancy, decision; vim, punch, pep, guts;
sparkle, verve, vivacity, liveliness, vividness, raciness; spirit, fire, ardour, glow,
warmth, vehemence, enthusiasm, passion

818n. *feeling*; bite, piquancy, poignancy, sharpness, mordancy 388n. *pungency*; strong language, serious l., stress, underlining, emphasis 532n. *affirmation*; palillogia, iteration, reiteration 106n. *repetition*; seriousness, gravity, weight, sententiousness; impressiveness, loftiness, elevation, sublimity, grandeur, grandiloquence, declamation 574n. *magniloquence*; rhetoric 579n. *eloquence*.

Adj. *forceful*, powerful, nervous 162adj. *strong*; energetic, peppy, with punch 174adj. *vigorous*; racy, idiomatic; bold, dashing, spirited, sparkling, vivacious 819adj. *lively*; warm, glowing, fiery, ardent, enthusiastic, impassioned 818adj. *fervent*; vehement, emphatic, insistent, reiterative, positive 532adj. *affirmative*; slashing, cutting, incisive, trenchant 256 adj. *sharp*; pointed, pungent, mordant, salty 839adj. *witty*; grave, sententious, full of point, strongly-worded 834adj. *serious*; heavy, meaty, solid; weighty, crushing 740adj. *compelling*; vivid, graphic, effective 551adj. *representing*; flowing, inspired, in the vein 579adj. *eloquent*; high-toned, lofty, grand, sublime 821adj. *impressive*.

Adv. *forcefully*, vigorously, energetically, vehemently; in good set terms, in glowing t.

See: 106, 160, 162, 174, 256, 388, 532, 551, 574, 579, 740, 818, 819, 821, 834, 839.

572 Feebleness

N. *feebleness* 163n. *weakness*; weak style, enervated s.; prosiness, frigidity, ineffectiveness, flatness, staleness, vapidity 387n. *insipidity*; jejunity, poverty, thinness; enervation, flaccidity, lack of force, lack of sparkle; lack of style, baldness 573n. *plainness*; anticlimax.

Adj. *feeble*, weak, thin, flat, vapid, insipid 387adj. *tasteless*; wishy-washy, watery; sloppy, sentimental; meagre, jejune, exhausted; colourless, bald 573adj. *plain*; languid, flaccid, nerveless, tame; undramatic, unspirited, uninspired, unelevated, unimpassioned, unemphatic; ineffective, cold, frigid, uninspiring, unexciting; monotonous, prosy, dull, dry, boring 838adj. *tedious*; cliché-ridden, stale, pretentious, flatulent, over-ambi-

tious; forced, over-emphatic, forcible-feeble; inane, empty; juvenile, childish; careless, slovenly, slipshod, limping; limp, loose, lax, inexact, disconnected, disjointed, rambling, vapouring; bad, poor, trashy 847adj. *vulgar*.

See: 163, 387, 573, 838, 847.

573 Plainness

N. *plainness*, naturalness, honesty, simplicity, unadorned s. 699n. *artlessness*; austerity, severity, baldness, bareness, starkness; matter-of-factness, plain prose 593n. *prose*; plain words, plain English 516n. *intelligibility*; homespun, household words; rustic flavour, vernacular, common speech, vulgar parlance; idiom, natural i.; unaffectedness 874n. *modesty*; frankness, coarseness, four-letter word, Anglo-Saxon monosyllable.

Adj. *plain*, simple 699adj. *artless*; austere, severe, disciplined; bald, stark, bare; neat 648adj. *clean*; unadorned, uncoloured, unpainted, unvarnished, unembellished; unemphatic, undramatic, unsensational; unassuming, unpretentious 874adj. *modest*; uninflated, chaste, not meretricious 950adj. *pure*; unaffected, honest, unartificial, natural, idiomatic; homely, homey, homespun, vernacular, Saxon; prosaic, sober 834adj. *serious*; dry, stodgy 838adj. *tedious*; humdrum, workaday, everyday, commonplace 610adj. *usual*; unimaginative, uninspired, unpoetical 593adj. *prosaic*.

Vb. *speak plainly*, call a spade a spade, use the vernacular 516vb. *be intelligible*; chasten one's style, purify one's diction, moderate one's vocabulary; say outright, come to the point, come down to brass tacks.

Adv. *plainly*, simply; prosaically, in prose; in the vernacular, in plain words, in common parlance; directly, point-blank; not to put too fine a point upon it.

See: 516, 593, 610, 648, 699, 834, 838, 874, 950.

574 Ornament

N. *ornament*, embellishment, colour, decoration, embroidery, frills 844n. *ornamentation*; floridness, floweriness, flowers of speech, taffeta phrases, word-arabesque

563 n. *phrase*; prose run mad, Gongorism, cultism, euphuism; preciosity, preciousness, euphemism, rhetoric, flourish of r., purple patch, sillabub; figurativeness, figure of speech 519 n. *trope*; alliteration, assonance, homoeoteleuton; palillogy, anaphora, epistrophe, symploce; anadiplosis; inversion, anastrophe, hyperbaton; chiasmus, chiastic order; parison; enjambement; metaphor, simile, antithesis.

magniloquence, high tone 579 n. *eloquence*; grandiloquence, declamation, orotundity 571 n. *vigour*; overstatement 546 n. *exaggeration*; turgidity, turgescence, flatulence, inflation, swollen diction, swelling utterance; pretentiousness, affectation, pomposity 875 n. *ostentation*; talking big 877 n. *boasting*; highfalutin, high-sounding words, bombast, rant, fustian, rodomontade 515 n. *empty talk*; Johnsonese, long words, sesquipedalian w. 559 n. *word*; teratology, tales of marvel 513 n. *fantasy*.

phrasemonger, fine writer, word-spinner, euphuist, euphemist 575 n. *stylist*; rhetorician, orator 579 n. *speaker*.

Adj. *ornate*, beautified 844 adj. *ornamented*; rich, florid, flowery; precious, gongoresque, euphuistic, euphemistic; pretentious 850 adj. *affected*; meretricious, flashy, flaming, flamboyant, frothing, frothy 875 adj. *showy*; brassy, sonorous, clanging 400 adj. *loud*; tropical, alliterative, antithetical 519 adj. *figurative*; overloaded, stiff, stilted; pedantic, longworded, sesquipedalian, Johnsonian.

rhetorical, declamatory, oratorical 579 adj. *eloquent*; resonant, sonorous 400 adj. *loud*; mouthy, orotund; high-pitched, high-flown, high-flying, highfalutin; grandiose, stately; bombastic, pompous, fustian; grandiloquent, magniloquent, altiloquent; inflated, tumid, turgid, tumescent, swelling, swollen; antithetical, alliterative, metaphorical, tropical 519 adj. *figurative*.

Vb. *ornament*, beautify, grace, adorn, enrich 844 vb. *decorate*; charge, overlay, overload; elaborate, load with ornament, grace with all the flowers of speech; euphuize, euphemize; smell of the lamp, over-elaborate.

See: 400, 513, 515, 519, 546, 559, 563, 571, 575, 579, 844, 850, 875, 877.

575 Elegance

N. *elegance*, style, perfect s.; grace, gracefulness 841 n. *beauty*; refinement, taste 846 n. *good taste*; propriety, restraint, distinction, dignity; clarity 567 n. *perspicuity*; Attic quality, purity, simplicity; idiom, natural i. 573 n. *plainness*; harmony, euphony, concinnity, balance, proportion 245 n. *symmetry*; rhythm, numerosity, ease, flow, smoothness, fluency, readiness, felicity, the right word in the right place; neatness, polish, finish; well-turned period, rounded p.; elaboration, artificiality.

stylist, stylish writer 574 n. *phrasemonger*; classical author, classic, Atticist, purist.

Adj. *elegant*, concinnous, concinnate 841 adj. *beautiful*; graced, well-g., graceful; stylish, polite, refined 846 adj. *tasteful*; uncommon, distinguished, dignified; not meretricious, chaste 950 adj. *pure*; good, correct, idiomatic, sensitive; expressive, clear 567 adj. *perspicuous*; simple, natural, unaffected 573 adj. *plain*; unlaboured, ready, easy, smooth, flowing, fluent, tripping, rhythmic, mellifluous, euphonious; harmonious, balanced, proportioned 245 adj. *symmetrical*; neat, felicitous, happy, right, neatly put, well-turned; artistic, wrought, elaborate, artificial; polished, finished, soigné, manicured, chic; restrained, controlled; flawless 646 adj. *perfect*; classic, classical, Attic, Ciceronian, Augustan.

Vb. *be elegant*, show taste 846 vb. *have taste*; have a good style, write well, have a light touch; elaborate, polish, refine 646 vb. *perfect*; manicure, trim 841 vb. *beautify*; grace one's style, turn a period, point an antithesis 566 vb. *show style*.

See: 245, 567, 573, 646, 841, 846, 950.

576 Inelegance

N. *inelegance*, inconcinnity; clumsiness, roughness, uncouthness 699 n. *artlessness*; coarseness, lack of finish, lack of polish 647 n. *imperfection*; harshness, cacophony 411 n. *discord*; lack of ease, lack of flow, stiffness, stiltedness 326 n. *hardness*; unwieldiness, cumbrousness, cumbrous language, sesquipedalianism, sesquipedality, hard words, jawbreaker; impropriety, barbarism, Gothicism,

Saxonism; incorrectness, catachresis, misapplication 565 n. *solecism*; mispronunciation 580 n. *speech defect*; vulgarism, vulgarity 847 n. *bad taste*; mannerism, unnaturalness, artificiality 850 n. *affectation*; exhibitionism 875 n. *ostentation*; meretriciousness, shoddy, tinsel 542 n. *sham*; unrestraint, excess 637 n. *superfluity*; turgidity, pomposity 574 n. *magniloquence*.

Adj. *inelegant*, *inconcinnous*, ungraceful, graceless 842 adj. *ugly*; faulty, incorrect, unclassical; unfinished, unpolished, unrefined 647 adj. *imperfect*; unclear 568 adj. *imperspicuous*; coarse, crude, rude, doggerel, uncouth, barbarous, Gothic 699 adj. *artless*; impolite, tasteless 847 adj. *vulgar*; unchaste, impure, meretricious; unrestrained, immoderate, excessive; turgid, pompous 574 adj. *rhetorical*; forced, laboured, artificial, unnatural, mannered 850 adj. *affected*; ludicrous, grotesque 849 adj. *ridiculous*; offensive, repulsive, jarring, grating 861 adj. *disliked*; heavy, ponderous, insensitive; rough, harsh, crabbed, uneasy, abrupt; halting, cramped, unready, unfluent; clumsy, awkward, gauche; stiff, stilted 875 adj. *formal*.

See: 326, 411, 542, 565, 568, 574, 580, 637, 647, 699, 842, 847, 849, 850, 861, 875.

577 Voice

N. *voice*, vocal sound 398 n. *sound*; speech signal, speaking voice 579 n. *speech*; singing voice, musical v., fine v. 412 n. *vocal music*; powerful voice, vociferation 400 n. *loudness*; tongue, vocal organs, vocal cords *or* chords, vocal bands, lungs, bellows; larynx; artificial larynx, oral vibrator; vocalization, phoneme, vowel, broad v., pure v., diphthong, triphthong, open vowel, closed v., semi-vowel, voiced consonant, syllable 398 n. *speech sound*; articulation, clear a., distinctness; utterance, enunciation, delivery, attack; articulate sound 408 n. *cry*; exclamation, ejaculation, gasp; mutter, whisper, stage-w. 401 n. *faintness*; tone of voice, accents, timbre, pitch, tone, intonation; ventriloquism, gastriloquism. *pronunciation*, articulation, elocution, enunciation, inflexion, accentuation,

stress, emphasis; ictus, arsis, thesis; accent, tonic a., speech a., sentence a.; pure accent, correct a.; native accent, broad a., foreign a.; burr, brogue, trill, roll; aspiration, rough breathing, glottal stop; iotacism, sigmatism, lisping, lallation 580 n. *speech defect*; mispronunciation 565 n. *solecism*.

Adj. *vocal*, voiced, oral, aloud, out loud; vocalic, vowel-like, sonant; phonetic, enunciative; articulate, distinct, clear; well-spoken, well-sung, in good voice 410 adj. *melodious*; pronounced, uttered, spoken, dictated, read out, read aloud; aspirated 407 adj. *hoarse*; accented, tonal, accentual, accentuated; open, broad-vowelled, closed, close-vowelled; guttural, cerebral, palatal, liquid, lingual, nasal, fricative, labial.

Vb. *voice*, pronounce, syllable 579 vb. *speak*; mouth, give tongue, give voice, express, utter, enunciate, articulate; labialize, palatalize, vocalize, vowelize; breathe, aspirate, sound one's aitches; trill, roll, burr; stress 532 n. *emphasize*; accent, pronounce with stress; raise the voice, lower the v., whisper, stage-w.; exclaim, ejaculate, rap out, blurt o. 408 vb. *cry*; chant, warble, carol, hum 413 vb. *sing*; shout, vociferate, use one's voice 400 vb. *be loud*; mispronounce, lisp, distort one's vowels, swallow one's consonants, speak thick 580 vb. *stammer*.

See: 398, 400, 401, 407, 408, 410, 412, 413, 532, 565, 579, 580.

578 Aphony

N. *aphony*, aphonia, voicelessness, no voice, loss of v.; difficulty in speaking, dysphony, disphonia, inarticulation; thick speech, hoarseness, huskiness, raucity; wilful silence, obmutescence 399 n. *silence*; going dumb, dumbness, mutism, deaf-m.; bad voice, harsh v., unmusical v., tuneless v. 407 n. *stridor*; childish treble, falsetto; changing voice, breaking v., cracked v.; sob, sobbing; undertone, low voice, small v., muffled tones, whisper, bated breath 401 n. *faintness*; surd, unvoiced consonant; mute, deaf-m., dummy; voiceless speech, sign language, deaf and dumb language 547 n. *gesticulation*.

Adj. *voiceless,* aphonic, dysphonic; unvoiced, surd; breathed, whispered, muffled, low-voiced, inaudible 401 adj. *muted*; mute, dumb, deaf and dumb; incapable of utterance, speechless, tongueless, wordless; inarticulate, unvocal, tongue-tied; not speaking, obmutescent, mum, silent 582 adj. *taciturn*; silenced, gagged; dry, hollow, sepulchral, breaking, cracked, croaking, hoarse as a raven 407 adj. *hoarse*; breathless, out of breath.

Vb. *be mute,* be mum 582 vb. *be taciturn*; hold one's tongue 525 vb. *keep secret*; bridle one's tongue, check one's speech, dry up, ring off, hang up; lose one's voice, be struck dumb, lose power of speech; talk with one's hands 547 vb. *gesticulate*; have difficulty in speaking 580 vb. *stammer.*

make mute, strike dumb, dumbfound, take one's breath away, rob one of words; tie one's tongue, stick in one's throat, choke one's utterance; muffle, hush, deaden 401 vb. *mute*; shout down, drown one's voice; muzzle, gag, stifle 165 vb. *suppress*; put a gag on, stop one's mouth, cut out one's tongue; shut one up, cut one short, hang up on; still, hush, put to silence, put to sleep 399 vb. *silence.*

speak low, speak softly, whisper, stage-w. 401 vb. *sound faint*; whisper in one's ear 524 vb. *hint*; lower one's voice, drop one's v., cover one's mouth, put one's hand before one's m.

Adv. *voicelessly,* in hushed tones, in a whisper, with bated breath; in an undertone, sotto voce, under one's breath, in an aside.

See: 165, 399, 401, 407, 524, 525, 547, 580, 582.

579 Speech

N. *speech,* faculty of s., organ of s., tongue, lips 557 n. *language*; oral communication, word of mouth 524 n. *report*; spoken word, accents, tones 559 n. *word*; verbal intercourse, conference, colloquy, conversation, talk, palaver, prattle, chinwag 584 n. *interlocution*; address, apostrophe 583 n. *allocution*; ready speech, fluency, talkativeness, volubility 581 n. *loquacity*; prolixity, effusion 570 n. *diffuseness*; cultivated speech, elocution, voice production; mode of speech, articulation, utterance, delivery, enunciation, prolation, emission 577 n. *pronunciation*; ventriloquism, gastriloquism 542 n. *sleight*; speech without words, sign language, eye l. 547 n. *gesticulation*; thing said, say, speech, dictum, utterance, remark, observation, comment, interjection 532 n. *affirmation*; pretty speeches, compliments 889 n. *endearment*; given word, parole 764 n. *promise.*

oration, speech, effusion; allowed speech, one's say; public speech, formal s., prepared s., discourse, address, talk; salutatory, welcoming address, illuminated a. 876 n. *celebration*; valedictory, farewell address, funeral oration 364 n. *obsequies*; final speech, winding-up s., after-dinner s.; prelection, lection, broadcast, travelogue 534 n. *lecture*; recitation, recital, reading; set speech, declamation, oratorical display (see *eloquence*); pulpit eloquence, pulpitry, sermon, preachment, homily, exhortation; platform eloquence, harangue, tub-thumping, rodomontade, earful, mouthful; hostile eloquence, tirade, diatribe, philippic, invective; monologue 585 n. *soliloquy*; written speech, dictation, paper, screed 591 n. *dissertation*; parts of a speech, rhetorical divisions, proemium, prologue, diegesis, narration, digression, proof, peroration.

oratory, art of speaking, rhetoric, public speaking, forensic oratory, parliamentary o., mob o., tub-thumping; speechmaking, speechifying, speechification; declamation, elocution, vapouring, ranting, rant; vituperation, invective.

eloquence, facundity, eloquent tongue, oratorical gifts, gift of the gab, fluency, command of words, art of w., wordspinning 566 n. *style*; power of speech, power 571 n. *vigour*; grandiloquence, orotundity, sublimity 574 n. *magniloquence*; elocution, good delivery, impressive diction, burst of eloquence, storm of words, peroration, purple patch, sillabub.

speaker, sayer, utterer; talker, spieler, prattler, gossiper 581 n. *chatterer*; conversationalist, colloquist 584 n. *interlocutor*; speechifier, speech-maker, speech-writer, rhetor, rhetorician, elocutionist; orator, Public O., oratress, oratrix, public

speaker, after-dinner s.; improviser, ad-libber; declaimer, ranter, platform orator, stump o., soap-box o., tub-thumper; word-spinner, spellbinder; haranguer, diatribist; lecturer, broadcaster, dissertator, dissertationist; pulpiteer, Boanerges; cushion thumper 534n. *preacher*; spokesman, prolocutor, prologue, presenter, narrator, chorus 594n. *actor*; mouthpiece 754n. *delegate*; advocate, pleader, mediator 231n. *intermediary*; gabber, patterer, salesman 793n. *seller*; Demosthenes, Cicero; monologuist, soliloquizer 585n. *soliloquist*.

Adj. *speaking*, talking; able to speak, with a tongue in one's head, fluent, outspoken, free-speaking, talkative 581n. *loquacious*; oral 577adj. *vocal*; well-spoken, soft-s., loud-s.; audible, spoken, verbal; elocutionary.

eloquent, spellbinding, silver-tongued, trumpet-t.; elocutionary, oratorical 574n. *rhetorical*; grandiloquent, declamatory, tub-thumping, ranting, word-spinning.

Vb. *speak*, mention, say; utter, articulate, syllable 577vb. *voice*; pronounce, declare, say a mouthful 532vb. *affirm*; say out, blurt 526vb. *divulge*; whisper, breathe 524n. *hint*; confabulate, talk, put in a word or two, permit oneself to say 584vb. *converse*; emit, give out, give utterance; break silence, open one's mouth *or* lips, pipe up, speak up, raise one's voice; wag one's tongue, give t., rattle on, spiel, gossip, prattle, chatter 581vb. *be loquacious*; patter, jabber, gabble; have one's say, talk one's fill, expatiate 570vb. *be diffuse*; trot out, reel off, recite; read, read aloud, read out, dictate; speak a language, speak with tongues, sling the bat; have a tongue in one's head, speak for oneself; talk with one's hands 547vb. *gesticulate*.

orate, make speeches, speechify, oratorize; declaim, deliver a speech, read a s.; hold forth, spout, be on one's legs; take the floor, rise to speak, mount the tribune, mount the pulpit; preach, preachify, sermonize, homilize, harangue; lecture, discourse, address 534vb. *teach*; invoke, apostrophize 583vb. *speak to*; flourish, perorate, mouth, rant, stump, tub-thump; speak like an angel, spellbind, be eloquent, have the gift of the gab; talk to oneself, monologize 585vb. *soliloquize*.

See: 231, 364, 524, 526, 532, 534, 542, 547, 557, 559, 566, 570, 571, 574, 577, 581, 583, 584, 585, 591, 594, 754, 764, 793, 876, 889.

580 Speech defect

N. *speech defect*, aphasia, loss of speech, aphonia 578n. *aphony*; paraphemia, paraphasia, paralalia, aboiement; idioglossia, idiolalia 560n. *neology*; stammering, traulism, stammer, stutter, lambdacism, lallation, lisp; dysphony, impediment in one's speech, hesitation, drawl; indistinctness, inarticulateness, thick speech, plum in one's mouth, cleft palate; burr, brogue 560n. *dialect*; accent, twang, nasal t. 577n. *pronunciation*; affectation, Oxford accent, haw-haw 246n. *distortion*.

Adj. *stammering*, stuttering etc.vb.; balbutient; nasal, adenoidal; indistinct, thick, inarticulate; tongue-tied, aphasic, aphasiac; breathless 578adj. *voiceless*.

Vb. *stammer*, stutter, balbutiate, balbucinate; drawl, hesitate, falter, quaver, hum and haw; mammer, mumble, mutter; lisp, lambdacise, lallate; blabber, snuffle, snort, sputter, splutter; nasalize, speak through the nose, drone; clip one's words, swallow one's w., gabble; blubber, sob; mispronounce 565vb. *solecize*.

See: 246, 560, 565, 577, 578.

581 Loquacity

N. *loquacity*, loquaciousness, garrulity, talkativeness, conversableness, communicativeness; volubility, flowing tongue, flow of words, fluency 570n. *diffuseness*; verbosity, wordiness, prolixity; much speaking, multiloquence, running on, spate of words, logorrhœa, verbal diarrhœa, inexhaustible vocabulary; gab, gift of the g. 579n. *eloquence*; garrulous old age, anecdotage 505n. *remembrance*.

chatter, chattering, gossiping, gabble, gibble-gabble, gab, jabber, palaver, much talk, talkee-talkee, clack, clappers, claver, quack, cackle, babble, prattle; small talk, gossip, tittle-tattle; froth, gush, prate, jaw, gas, hot air 515n. *empty talk*.

chatterer, non-stop talker, rapid speaker; chinwag, rattle, chatterbox; gossip, tattler 529n. *newsmonger*; magpie, parrot,

jay; talker, gabber, driveller, haverel, ranter, quacker; preacher, sermonizer; proser, windbag, gas-bag, gasser; conversationalist 584 n. *interlocutor*.

Adj. *loquacious*, talkative, garrulous, tongue-wagging, gossiping, tattling; communicative, chatty, gossipy, newsy 524 adj. *informative*; gabbing, babbling, gabbling, gassy, windy, prosing, verbose, long-winded, long-tongued 570 adj. *prolix*; non-stop, voluble, running on, fluent, glib, ready, effusive, gushing; conversable, conversational 584 adj. *conversing*.

Vb. *be loquacious*, — talkative etc. adj.; have a long tongue, chatter, rattle, run on, reel off; gossip, tattle 584 vb. *converse*; clack, quack, gabble, jabber, patter, twaddle 515 vb. *mean nothing*; talk, jaw, gab, prate, prose, gas, waffle, haver; drone, maunder, drivel; launch out, start talking, shoot; be glib, oil one's tongue; have one's say, talk at length; expatiate, effuse, gush 570 vb. *be diffuse*; outtalk, talk down; talk out time, filibuster 113 vb. *spin out*; talk oneself hoarse, talk oneself out of breath, talk the hind leg off a donkey, din in the ears; talk shop, bore 838 vb. *be tedious*; engage in conversation, buttonhole; must have an audience; not let one get a word in edgeways.

Adv. *loquaciously*, glibly, fluently etc. adj.

See: 113, 505, 515, 524, 529, 570, 579, 584, 838.

582 Taciturnity

N. *taciturnity*, silent habit 399 n. *silence*; incommunicativeness, reserve, reticence, guarded utterance 525 n. *secrecy*; few words, shortness, brusqueness, curtness, gruffness 885 n. *rudeness*; wilful silence, obmutescence 578 n. *aphony*; breaking off, aposiopesis; paucilloquy, economy of words, laconism 569 n. *conciseness*; no speaker, no orator; no talker, not a gossip, man of few words, laconian; clam, oyster, statue.

Adj. *taciturn*, mute 399 adj. *silent*; sparing of words, saying little, monosyllabic, short, curt, laconic, brusque, gruff 569 adj. *concise*; not talking, obmutescent, mum; inconversable, incommunicative; not effusive, withdrawn; reserved, guarded 525 adj. *reticent*; close, close-mouthed, close-tongued, tight-lipped; not to be drawn, discreet 858 adj. *cautious*; inarticulate, tongue-tied 578 adj. *voiceless*; not hearing 416 adj. *deaf*.

Vb. *be taciturn*, — laconic etc. adj.; spare one's words, need few w. 569 vb. *be concise*; not talk, say nothing, have little to say; observe silence, make no answer; not be drawn, refuse comment, neither confirm nor deny; keep one's counsel 525 vb. *keep secret*; recommend silence, put one's finger to one's lips; hold one's peace, hold one's tongue, put a bridle on one's t.; fall silent, relapse into s., pipe down, dry up, run out of words 145 vb. *cease*; be speechless, lose one's tongue 578 vb. *be mute*; waste no words on, save one's breath, not mention, leave out, pass over, omit 458 vb. *disregard*.

Int. hush! shut up! mum! chut! no comment!

See: 145, 399, 416, 458, 525, 569, 578, 858, 885.

583 Allocution

N. *allocution*, alloquy, apostrophe; address, lecture, talk, speech 579 n. *oration*; feigned dialogue, dialogism 584 n. *interlocution*; greeting, salutation, hail; invocation, appeal, interjection, interpellation; buttonholing, word in the ear, aside; hearers, listeners, audience 415 n. *listener*.

Adj. *vocative*, salutatory, invocatory.

Vb. *speak to*, speak at; address, talk to, lecture to; turn to, direct one's words at, apostrophize; appeal to, pray to, invoke; sir, bemadam; approach, accost; hail, call to, salute, say good-morning, 884 vb. *greet*; pass the time of day, parley with 584 vb. *converse*; take aside, buttonhole.

See: 415, 579, 584, 884.

584 Interlocution

N. *interlocution*, parley, colloquy, converse, conversation, causerie, talk; dialogue, question and answer; exchange, repartee; confabulation, verbal intercourse, social i. 882 n. *sociality*; commerce, communion, intercommunion, communication, intercommunication 524 n. *information*; duologue, trialogue, symposium, tête-à-tête.

chat, causerie, chit-chat, talk, small t., table-t., tea-table t.; town talk, village t., gossip 529n. *rumour*; tattle, tittle-tattle 581n. *chatter*; cosy chat, tête-à-tête.

conference, colloquy, conversations, talks, pourparler, parley, pow-wow, palaver; discussion, debate, symposium, seminar; controversy, polemics, logomachy 475n. *argument*; exchange of views, talks across the table, high-level talks, summitry; negotiations, bargaining, treaty-making 765n. *treaty*; conclave, convention, meeting, gathering 74n. *assembly*; reception, conversazione, party, crush 882n. *social gathering*; audience, interview, audition 415n. *hearing*; consultation, putting heads together, huddle, council, war-c., round-table conference, summit 691n. *advice*; conference room, boardroom, council chamber 692n. *council*; debating hall, lecture h. 539n. *classroom*; durbar, audience-chamber, reception-room; auditorium 441n. *onlookers*.

interlocutor, collocutor, colloquist, dialogist, symposiast; examiner, interviewer, cross-examiner, interpellant 459n. *enquirer*; answerer 460n. *respondent*; partner in a conversation, addressee, confabulator, conversationalist, talker 581n. *chatterer*; gossip, tattler, tabby 529n. *newsmonger*.

Adj. *conversing*, interlocutory, confabulatory, collocutory, dialogistic; conversable, conversational; chatty, gossipy 581 adj. *loquacious*; newsy, communicative 524adj. *informative*; conferring, in conference; discursive, conferential; consultatory, consultative, advisory 691adj. *advising*.

Vb. *converse*, parley, talk together (see *confer*); confabulate, collogue, pass the time of day; partake in a symposium, engage in a duologue; lead one on, draw one out; buttonhole, enter into conversation, carry on a c., join in a c., put in a word, bandy words, exchange w., question, answer; shine in conversation, have a good talk; chat, have a c., have a cosy c., let one's hair down ; gossip, tattle 581vb. *be loquacious*; commune with, talk privately, get confidential with, be closeted with; whisper together, talk tête-à-tête, get in a huddle.

confer, talk it over, take counsel, sit in council, hold conclave, meet in the board-room; hold a council of war, pow-wow, palaver; canvass, discuss, debate 475vb. *argue*; parley, negotiate, hold conversations; advise with, consult w., sit w. 691vb. *consult*.

See: 74, 415, 441, 459, 460, 475, 524, 529, 539, 581, 691, 692, 765, 882.

505 Soliloquy

N. *soliloquy*, soliloquium, monologue, monody; apostrophe; aside.
soliloquist, soliloquizer, monologist, monodist.
Adj. *soliloquizing* etc. vb.; monological.
Vb. *soliloquize*, talk to oneself, say to oneself, say aside, think aloud; apostrophize, pray to, pray aloud; answer one's own questions, be one's own interlocutor; talk to the four walls, address an empty house, have onself for audience.

586 Writing

N. *writing*, creative w., composition, literary c., literary activities, authorship, journalism, cacoethes scribendi 590n. *description*; output, literary o. 557n. *literature*; a writing, script, copy, writings, works, books 589n. *reading matter*; ink-slinging, inkshed; quill-driving, scrivenership, writership, clerkship, paper-work 548n. *record*; copying, transcribing, transcription, rewriting, overwriting; autography, holography; ways of writing, handwriting, chirography, stylography, cerography; writing small, micrography; longhand, longhand reporting, logography; shorthand writing, shorthand, lexigraphy, polygraphy, brachygraphy, speedwriting, phonography; contraction, phonogram, phraseogram, phraseography; stenography, typewriting, typing 587n. *print*; braille; secret writing, steganography, ciphering, cipher, code 530n. *secret*; picture-writing, ideography; sign-writing, sky-writing 528n. *advertisement*; inscribing, carving, cutting, graving, epigraphy 555n. *engraving*; writing left to right *or* right to left, boustrophedon; study of handwriting, graphology.
lettering, formation of letters, stroke, stroke of the pen, up-stroke, down-s., pothook, pothooks and hangers; line, dot, point;

flourish, curlicue, squiggle, scroll 251 n. *convolution*; handwriting, hand, fist; calligraphy, pencraft, penmanship; fair hand, clerkly h., copper-plate h., law-h., 'fair Roman hand'; cursive hand, running h., flowing h., round h.; script writing, print-w., beacon-w., italic; bad writing, cacography, clumsy hand; botched writing, overwriting; illegible writing, scribble. scrawl, illegible signature 517 n. *unintelligibility*; script, letters, characters, alphabet, block letter, uncial; capital, majuscule, initial, small letter, minuscule 558 n. *letter*; Ogham, runes, futhorc; pictogram, ideogram; ideograph; cuneiform, arrowhead; Minoan linear B.; embossed writing, braille; letters of fire, letters of gold.

script, written matter, inscribed page, illuminated address; well-written specimen, calligraph; writing, screed, scrawl, scribble; manuscript, palimpsest, codex 589 n. *book*; original, one's own hand, autograph, holograph; signature, sign-manual, initial, cross, mark 547 n. *indication*; copy, transcript, transcription, fair copy 22 n. *duplicate*; typescript, stencil; printed matter 587 n. *letterpress*; letter, epistle, rescript, written reply, rescription 588 n. *correspondence*; tablet, table; inscription, epigraph, graffito 548 n. *record*; superscription, caption, heading; letters of fire, letters of gold.

stationery, writing materials, pen and paper, pen and ink; ink, writing i., printing i., drawing i., copying i., marking i., indelible i., invisible i.; stylus, reed, quill, pen, quill-p., fountain p., ball-point p.; nib, steel n.; stylograph, stylo; pencil, slate-p., lead-p.; crayon, chalk; papyrus, palm leaves, parchment, vellum, rice paper, foolscap 631 n. *paper*; newsprint; writing paper, note-p., wove p., laid p., scented p.; notebook, pad, block, slate, tablet, table; slate, blackboard; stone, brick, rock, wall; inkpot, ink-bottle, ink-horn, inkstand, inkwell; pen-holder, pen-wiper, pen-sharpener, penknife; blotting paper, sand; typewriter, typewriter ribbon, ribbon, stencil; writing room, scriptorium.

penman, calligraphist, calligrapher; cacographer, scribbler, scrawler; inkster, writer, pen-driver, quill-d., scrivener, scribe, clerk 549 n. *recorder*; copyist,

transcriber; sign-writer, sky-w. 528 n. *publicizer*; epigrapher, inscriber; subscriber, signer, initialler, signatory; longhand writer, logographer; creative writer, script-w. 589 n. *author*; letter-writer 588 n. *correspondent*; graphologist, handwriting expert 484 n. *detector*.

stenographer, shorthand writer, tachygraph, typewriter, typist, stenotypist.

Adj. *written*, inscribed, inscriptional, epigraphic; in black and white 548 adj. *recorded*; in writing, in longhand, in shorthand; logographic, stenographic; handwritten, manuscript, autograph, holograph; signed, under one's hand; scriptory, penned, pencilled, scrawled, scribbled etc. vb.; fairly written, copybook copperplate, clerkly, literate; cursive, demotic, hieratic, ideographic, hieroglyphic, cuneiform; lettered, alphabetic, runic, Gothic, uncial, roman, italic; perpendicular, upright, sloping, spidery.

Vb. *write*, be literate, use the pen, scribe; form characters, character, engrave, inscribe; letter, block, print; flourish, scroll; write a good hand, calligraph; write a bad hand, write badly, scribble, scrabble, scrawl, blot, erase, interline, overwrite; reduce to writing, put in w., set down, set down in black and white, write down, jot d., note 548 vb. *record*; transcribe, copy, copy out, fair-copy, write out, write fair, engross; take down, take dictation, take shorthand, stenotype, typewrite, type, type out; take down longhand, logograph; throw on paper, draft, formulate, redact; compose, concoct, indite; pen, pencil, dash off; write letters 588 vb. *correspond*; write one's name, make one's signature, subscribe 547 vb. *sign*; take up the pen, put pen to paper, spill ink, stain paper, cover reams; be an author, write books 590 vb. *describe*, 591 vb. *dissert*; write poetry 593 vb. *poetize*.

See: 22, 251, 484, 517, 528, 530, 547, 548, 549, 555, 557, 558, 587, 588, 589, 590, 591, 593, 631.

587 Print

N. *print*, printing, typing, typewriting 586 n. *writing*; typography, printing from type, block printing, plate p., offset process, lithography, photolithography 555 n. *en-*

graving; photocopying, varitype; type-setting, composing, composition, make-up, setting, hand-setting; monotype, lino-type, stereotype, electrotype; plate, shell; presswork, make-ready, printing off, running off, machining.

letterpress, lettering, linage, printed matter, print, impression, presswork; copy, pull, proof, first p., galley p., page p., revise; sheet, forme, quire, signature; printed page, imposed sheet; caption, heading, colophon, imprint; margin, gutter; dummy, trial copy, proof c.; offprint.

print-type, type, movable t., fixed t., stereotype, plate; type-mould, matrix; type-matter, setting, set type, standing t., broken t., distributed t., pie, printer's p.; upper case, lower c., capitals, caps, initial c.; fount, type-face, body f., bastard type, bold type, heavy t., leaded t., Clarendon; roman, italic, Gothic, black letter 558 n. *letter*; shoulder, shank, beard, ascender, descender, serif, san-serif; lead, rule, swelled r., en. r., em r.; space, hair-space, en space, em s.; type bar, slug.

type size, point s., type measure, type scale; excelsior, brilliant, diamond, pearl, agate, ruby, nonpareil, minion, brevier, bour-geois, long primer, small pica, pica, English, Columbian, great primer.

press, printing p., printing works, press-works, printers; type-foundry; compos-ing room, press r., machining r.; hand-press, flatbed, rotary press, linotype, monotype, offset press; quoin, frame, composing stick, case.

printer, book-p., jobbing p., pressman; setter, type-s., compositor, printer's devil, printer's reader, proof r.; typographer, type-cutter.

Adj. *printed*, in print 528 adj. *published*; set, composed, machined, imposed etc. vb.; in type, in italic, in bold, in roman; typographical; leaded 201 adj. *spaced*; close-printed, tight, crowded.

Vb. *print*, stamp; set, compose; align, justify; set up in type, make ready, im-pose, machine, run off, pull off, strike off, print off; finish printing, distribute the type; lithograph, litho, offset, stereotype; get ready for the press, send to p., see through the p., proof-read, correct; have printed, bring out 528 vb. *publish*.

See: 201, 528, 555, 558, 586.

588 Correspondence

N. *correspondence*, stream of c., exchange of letters; communication, epistolary c., postal c. 524 n. *information*; mailing list, distribution l.; mail, letters, post, postbag, mailbag, budget, diplomatic bag 531 n. *mails*; letter, epistle, missive, billet, dis-patch, bulletin; love-letter, billet doux, Valentine 889 n. *endearment*; postcard, picture postcard, card, letter c.; air letter, airgraph, air mail, sea mail; business letter, favour, enclosure; open letter 528 n. *publicity*; circular letter, circular, chain letter; official correspondence, des-patch, rescript; demi-official letter, note, line, chit; answer, acknowledgement; envelope, cover, stamp, seal; letter-box, pillar box.

correspondent, letter-writer, pen-friend, poison pen; recipient, addressee; foreign correspondent, contributor; contact 524 n. *informant*.

Adj. *epistolary*, postal, by post; under cover of, enclosed.

Vb. *correspond*, correspond with, exchange letters, maintain *or* keep up a corre-spondence, keep in touch with 524 vb. *communicate*; use the post, write to, send a letter to, drop a line, send a chit; com-pose dispatches, report 524 vb. *inform*; finish one's correspondence, do one's mail; acknowledge, reply, write back, reply by return 460 vb. *answer*; circularize 528 vb. *publish*; write again, bombard with letters; post off, forward, mail, air-mail; stamp, seal, frank, address; open a letter, unstick, unseal 263 vb. *open*.

Adv. *by letter*, by mail, through the post.

in correspondence, in touch, in contact; on the phone, on the line.

See: 263, 460, 524, 528, 531, 889.

589 Book

N. *book*, title, volume, tome, roll; codex, manuscript, MS., palimpsest; script, type-script, unpublished work; published work, publication, best-seller, potboiler; unsold book, remainder; work, standard w., classic; major work, monumental w., magnum opus; opuscule, slim volume; chapbook, booklet; illustrated work, picture book 553 n. *picture*; magazine, periodical, rag 528 n. *journal*; brochure,

pamphlet 528 n. *the press*; bound book, cased book, hard-back, paperback (see *edition*).

reading matter, printed word, written w. 586 n. *writing*; script, copy; text, the words, libretto, scenario, 'book of the play'; proof, revise, pull 587 n. *letterpress*; writings, prose literature 593 n. *prose*; poetical literature 593 n. *poetry*; classical literature, standard l., serious l., light l. 557 n. *literature*; literary subject, fiction, history, biography, travel 590 n. *description*; work of fiction 590 n. *novel*; biographical work, memoirs, memorabilia 590 n. *biography*; addresses, speeches 579 n. *oration*; essay, tract, tractate 591 n. *dissertation*; piece, occasional pieces, fugitive p. 591 n. *article*; miscellanea, marginalia, jottings, thoughts, pensées; poetical works, divan 593 n. *poem*; selections, flowers, beauties 592 n. *anthology*; early works, juvenilia; posthumous works, remains; complete works, corpus, omnibus volume; periodical, review, magazine, weekly, monthly, quarterly, annual 528 n. *journal*; issue, number, back n.; part, instalment, serial, sequel, continuation, second part; reader.

textbook, school book, class book, desk b., copybook 539 n. *classroom*; abecedary, hornbook; primer, grammar, gradus; text, plain t., annotated t., prescribed t.; selection, chrestomathy, delectus 592 n. *anthology*; standard text, handbook, manual, enchiridion, breviary; cookery book, cook-book, recipe b. (see *reference book*).

reference book, work of reference, encyclopædia, cyclopædia 490 n. *erudition*; lexicon 559 n. *dictionary*; biographical dictionary, dictionary of quotations, dictionary of place-names, gazetteer, time-table 87 n. *directory*; calendar 548 n. *record*; guide 524 n. *guide-book*; note-book, diary, album 505 n. *reminder*; bibliography, publisher's catalogue, reading list.

edition, series, set, collection, library; bound edition, library e., de luxe e., best e., prize e., school e., popular e., cheap e., standard e., major e., complete e., collected e., complete works; incunabula, old edition, first e., new e., revised e.; reissue, reprint; illustrated edition, special e., limited e., connois-

seur's e., expurgated e.; adaptation, abridgment 592 n. *compendium*; duodecimo, sextodecimo, octodecimo, octavo, quarto, folio; book production, layout, preliminary matter, prelims, preface, prefatory note, publisher's n., author's n., bibliographical n.; dedication, invocation, acknowledgements; title, bastard t., half-t.; fly-leaf, title page, end-p., colophon; table of contents, table of illustrations; errata, corrigenda, addenda; appendix, supplement, index; heading, page h., folio h., chaper h., section h.; headline, running h., footnote; margin, head m., foot m., gutter; folio, page, leaf, recto, verso; sheet, forme, signature, quire; chapter, division, part, section; paragraph, clause, passage, excerpt, inset; plate, print, illustration, half-tone, line-drawing 553 n. *picture*.

bookbinding, binding, casing, rebinding, stripping; folding, gathering, sewing, stitching; case, cover, jacket, dust j. 226 n. *wrapping*; boards, paper b., straw-board, cardboard; cloth, limp c., linen, scrim, buckram, leather, pigskin, morocco, vellum, parchment; tooling, blind-t., gold-t., gilding, marbling; bindery, bookbinder.

library, bibliotheca, book-collection, series; national library, state l., public l., branch l., travelling l., mobile l., lending l., circulating l., book club; bookshelf, bookcase, book-rack, book-ends; bookshop, book store, booksellers.

bookman, man of letters, littérateur, literary gent; reader, bookworm 492 n. *scholar*; bibliophile, book-lover, book-collector, bibliomaniac; bibliographer; librarianship, librarian, library assistant; bookselling, bibliopole, stationer, bookseller, antiquarian b., book-dealer, second-hand b.; publisher, book-p.; editor, redactor; reviewing, book-reviewer, reviewer 480 n. *estimator*.

author, authoress, writer, creative w.; literary man, man of letters; fiction-writer, novelist, historian, biographer 590 n. *narrator*; essayist, editorialist 591 n. *dissertator*; prose-writer; verse-writer 593 n. *poet*; playwright, librettist, script writer 594 n. *dramatist*; freelance; journalist 528 n. *publicizer*; pressman, reporter, reporterette, sob-sister 529 n. *newsmonger*; editor, sub-editor, contri-

butor, correspondent, special c., war c., sports c., columnist, gossip-writer, diarist; scribbler, penpusher, hack, Grub Street h., penny-a-liner; ghost, ghostwriter; reviser, Yahwist, Elohist.

Adj. *bibliographical*, bookways, bookwise, in book form; cloth-bound, paperbacked; tooled, marbled, gilt; bookloving, book-selling, book-publishing.

See: 87, 226, 480, 490, 492, 505, 524, 528, 529, 539, 548, 553, 557, 559, 579, 586, 587, 590, 591, 592, 593, 594.

590 Description

N. *description*, account, full a.; statement, exposé, statement of facts, summary 524 n. *report*; brief, abstract, inscription, caption, legend 592 n. *compendium*; narration, relation, rehearsal, recital (see *narrative*); specification, characterization, details, particulars, catalogue raisonnée 87 n. *list*; portrayal; delineation, depiction; sketch, character s., profile, prosopography 551 n. *representation*; psychography, psychognosis; psychic profile, case history 548 n. *record*; evocation, word-painting, picture, true p., realism, Zolaism; descriptive account, travelogue 524 n. *guide-book*; vignette, thumbnail sketch; idyll, eclogue 593 n. *poem*; eulogy, satire; obituary, epitaph, lapidary inscription 364 n. *obsequies*.

narrative, argument, plot, sub-plot, scenario; historiography, history, annals, chronicle 548 n. *record*; account, imaginary a., fiction; story, tale, fabliau, tradition, legend, legendry, mythology, myth, saga, epic, epos; allegory, parable, apologue, story with a moral; fairy-tale, old wive's t., yarn 543 n. *fable*; anecdote, reminiscence, sayings, logia 505 n. *remembrance*.

biography, real-life story, human interest; life, curriculum vitae, life story, life and death of; experiences, adventures, fortunes; aretalogy, hagiology, hagiography, martyrology; obituary, necrology; rogue's gallery, Newgate calendar; personal account, autobiography, confessions, memoirs, memorabilia, memorials 505 n. *remembrance*; diary, journals 548 n. *record*; personal correspondence, letters 588 n. *correspondence*.

novel, fiction, tale; historical novel, fictional biography; novelette, short story; light reading, bedside r. 589 n. *reading matter*; romance, love-story, fairy-s., adventure s., Western, science fiction; novel of low life, picaresque novel; crimestory, detective s., 'tecker, whodunnit; thriller, shocker, shilling s., penny dreadful, dime novel, horror comic; paperback, pulp magazine; popular novel, best-seller; potboiler, trash 589 n. *book*.

narrator, describer, delineator, descriptive writer; reporter, relater; raconteur, anecdotist; yarner, story-teller, fabler, fabulist, mythologist; fiction writer 589 n. *author*; romancer, novelist, plot-constructor; biographer, Boswell, Plutarch; aretalogist, hagiographer, martyrologist, autobiographer, memoir-writer, diarist; historian, historiographer, chronicler, annalist, saga-man 549 n. *recorder*; Muse of History, Clio.

Adj. *descriptive*, descriptional, graphic, vivid, representational, well-drawn, sharp 551 adj. *representing*; true to nature, natural, realistic, real-life, photographic, convincing; picturesque 821 adj. *impressive*; impressionistic, suggestive; full, detailed, circumstantial, particular 570 adj. *diffuse*; storied, traditional, legendary, mythological; epic, heroic, aretalogical, romantic; picaresque, sordid; narrative, historical, biographical, autobiographical; factual, documentary 494 adj. *accurate*; fictional, imaginative 513 adj. *imaginary*.

Vb. *describe*, delineate, draw, picture, depict, paint 551 vb. *represent*; evoke, bring to life, tell vividly, make one see; characterize, particularize, detail, enter into, descend to 80 vb. *specify*; sketch, adumbrate 233 vb. *outline*; relate, recount, rehearse, recite, report, give an account 524 vb. *communicate*; write, write about 548 vb. *record*; write history, historify; narrate, tell, tell a story, yarn, spin a y.; have a plot, construct a p., make a story out of; put into a novel, fictionalize; romance, fable 513 vb. *imagine*; review, recapitulate 106 vb. *repeat*; reminisce, fight one's battles over again 505 vb. *retrospect*.

See: 80, 87, 106, 233, 364, 494, 505, 513, 524, 543, 548, 549, 551, 570, 588, 589, 592, 593, 821.

591 Dissertation

N. *dissertation,* treatise, pandect, tract, tractate; exposition, summary e., aperçu; theme, thesis 475n. *argument;* disquisition, essay, examination, survey 459n. *enquiry;* discourse, descant, discussion; excursus, memoir, paper, monograph, study; introductory study, prolegomena; screed, harangue, homily, sermon 534n. *lecture;* commentary, textbook, almagest. *article,* signed a., magazine a., syndicated a.; leading article, leader, editorial; essay, causerie; comment, commentary, review, notice, critique, criticism, write-up, write-down.

dissertator, essayist, expositor, tractator, tractarian; pamphleteer, publicist 528n. *publicizer;* editor, leader-writer, editorialist; writer, belletrist, contributor 589n. *author;* reviewer, critic, commentator 520n. *interpreter.*

Adj. *discursive,* discursory, discursive, disquisitional 475adj. *arguing;* expository, critical 520adj. *interpretive.*

Vb. *dissert,* treat, handle, write about, deal with; descant, dissertate, discourse upon 475vb. *argue;* pursue a theme, develop a thesis, descant upon a subject; go into, enquire into, survey; set out, discuss, canvass, ventilate, air one's views; notice, criticize, comment upon, write up, write down; write an essay, produce a treatise, do a paper; annotate, commentate 520 vb. *interpret.*

See: 459, 475, 520, 528, 534, 589.

592 Compendium

N. *compendium,* epitome, resumé, summary, brief; contents, heads, analysis; abstract, sum and substance, docket; consolidation, digest, pandect; breviary, textbook; multum in parvo, précis; aperçu, conspectus, synopsis, bird's-eye view, survey; review, recapitulation; draft, minute, note 548n. *record;* sketch, thumbnail s., outline, skeleton; blueprint 623n. *plan;* syllabus, prospectus 87n. *list;* abridgment, abbreviation 204n. *shortening;* contraction, compression 569 n. *conciseness.*

anthology, spicilegium, treasury, flowers, beauties, best pieces; selections, delectus, chrestomathy 589n. *textbook;* collection, compilation, collectanea, miscellanea, miscellany; collection of poems, divan; analecta, analects, fugitive pieces; gleanings, chapters, leaves, pages, chips; album, scrap-a., scrap-book, note b., sketch-b., commonplace-b.; anthologist.

epitomizer, abridger, abbreviator, cutter; abstractor, summarizer, potter, précis-writer 204n. *shortener.*

Adj. *compendious,* pithy 569adj. *concise;* analytical, synoptic; abstracted, abridged 204adj. *short;* potted, compacted; analectic, collected, excerpted etc.vb.

Vb. *abstract,* sum up, resume, summarize, epitomize, reduce, abbreviate, abridge 204vb. *shorten;* docket 548vb. *record;* condense, pot, give sum and substance 569vb. *be concise;* consolidate, compile 87vb. *list;* collect 74vb. *bring together;* excerpt, glean, select, anthologize; diagrammatize, sketch, sketch out 233vb. *outline.*

Adv. *in sum,* in substance, in brief, at a glance, synoptically.

See: 74, 87, 204, 233, 548, 569, 589, 623.

593 Poetry. Prose

N. *poetry,* poesy, balladry, minstrelsy, song; versification (see *prosody*); poetic art, poetics; verse, rhyme, numbers; poetic fire, poetic vein, poetic inspiration, numen, afflatus, divine a.; Muses, tuneful Nine, Pierides, Calliope; Parnassus, Helicon, Castalian spring, Pierian s., Hippocrene.

poem, poetic composition; versification, lines, verses, stanzas, strains; narrative verse, heroic poem, epic, mock-e.; dramatic poem, lyric drama, verse-play; Greek tragedy, Greek comedy, satyric play, trilogy, tetralogy 594n. *drama;* lyric verse, melic v., gnomic v.; ode, epode, choric ode, Pindaric o., Sapphic o., Horatian o.; palinode; dithyramb; dirge, elegiac poem, elegy; idyll, eclogue; georgic, bucolic poem; occasional poem, prothalamium, epithalamium; song, hymn, chanty, lays 412n. *vocal music;* warsong, marching song; love-song, erotic poem; drinking song, anacreontic; collected poems, divan 592n. *anthology;* canto, fit.

doggerel, lame verse, balladry; jingle, crambo, runes, nursery rhyme; cento,

macaronic verse, macaronics, Leonine verses, Fescennine v., Hudibrastic v., satire, limerick.

verse form, sonnet, sestet, Petrarchan sonnet, Shakespearean s.; ballade, rondeau, virelay, triolet; burden, refrain, envoi; couplet, heroic c., elegiac c.; distich, sloka; triplet, terza rima,quatrain, ghazal; sestina, ottava rima, Spenserian stanza; Sapphic verse, Alcaic v., Anacreontic v.; hendecasyllables; limping iambics, scazon; blank verse, free v., vers libre; verse, versicle, stanza, stave, laisse, strophe, antistrophe; stichomythia; broken line, half l., hemistich. See *prosody*.

prosody, versification, metrics, metre, syllabic m., measure, numbers, scansion; rhyme, rhyme royal, bout rimé; assonance, alliteration, masculine ending, feminine e.; rhythm, sprung r.; prose rhythm; metrical unit, foot, catalectic f., acatalectic f., pada; iambus, trochee, choreus, Bacchius, tribrach, amphibrach, amphimacer, cretic, ionic, glyconic, pherecratian; dactyl, anapaest; logaœdic verse, dactylo-epitrite; dimeter, trimeter, tetrameter; hexameter, pentameter; senarius, iambic line, iambic trimeter, iambic pentameter, blank verse; couplet, sloka; Alexandrine, heroic couplet, elegiac c.; arsis, thesis, ictus, beat, stress, accent, accentuation; elision; enjambement, cæsura, diæresis.

poet, major p., minor p., poet laureate; versemonger, poetaster; prosodist, versifier, metrist, hexametrist, iambist, verslibrist; rhymer, rhymester,rhymist, jingler, bard, minstrel, balladist, skald, troubadour, minnesinger, meistersinger; epic poet, lyric p., lyrist, bucolic poet, dramatic p., dithyrambist, elegist, elegiac poet, sonneteer, ballad-monger; songwriter, librettist; improviser, improvisatore; reciter, rhapsode, rhapsodist, jongleur.

prose, not verse, prose rhythm; prosaicism, prosaism, prosiness, prose-writing, everyday language; prosaist, prose-writer 589 n. *author*.

Adj. *poetic*, poetical, bardic; songful, tuneful; Castalian, Pierian; heroic, Homeric, Dantesque, Miltonic; mock-h., satiric; elegiac, lyrical, dithyrambic, rhapsodic; lyric, Pindaric, Sapphic, Alcaic, Horatian; bucolic, eclogic, Theocritean, Vergilian;

rhyming, jingling, etc. vb.; doggerel, macaronic; Leonine, Fescennine; prosodic, prosodical, metrical, scanning, scanned; iambic, trochaic, spondaic, dactylic, anapæstic; in verse, stanzaic; catelectic; Petrarchan, Chaucerian, Shakespearean, Spenserian.

prosaic, unpoetical, unversified; prosy 570 adj. *diffuse*; in prose, matter-of-fact 573 adj. *plain*; pedestrian.

Vb. *poetize*, sing, tune one's lyre, mount Pegasus; metrify, prosodize, scan; rhyme, jingle; versify, put in verse, put in rhyme; make verses, elegize, compose an epic, write a lyric, write a sonnet, sonneteer; celebrate in verse, berhyme; lampoon, satirize.

write prose, stick to prose, prose.

See: 412, 570, 573, 589, 592, 594.

594 Drama

N. *drama*, traffic of the stage; the drama, the theatre, the stage, the play, the scene, the boards, the footlights; theatre world, stage w., theatreland; cinema world, silver screen, Hollywood 445 n. *cinema*; show business, dramatic entertainment, straight drama, legitimate theatre; stock, summer s., repertory, rep; theatricals, amateur t.; masque, charade, dumb c., tableau 551 n. *representation*; tragic mask, comic m., buskin, sock, cothurnus; Tragic Muse, Melpomene; Comic Muse, Thalia; Thespis.

dramaturgy, play construction, dramatic form; dramatization, theatricals, dramatics; melodramatics, histrionics; theatricality, staginess; good theatre, bad t., good cinema; play-writing, scenario-w., script-w., libretto-w.; play-craft, stage-c., histrionic art, Thespian a.; action, movement, plot, sub-p., under-p. 590 n. *narrative*; characterization 551 n. *representation*; production, choregy, revival; casting; rehearsal; dress rehearsal; direction, stage-production, stage-management, showmanship; staging, stage directions; dialogue, soliloquy, stage-whisper, aside; gagging, business; entrance, parodos; exit, exodos (see *acting*); rising of the curtain, prologue, chorus; opening scene, first act, last a., finale, epilogue, curtain; interval, intermission, break;

594

enactment, performance, command p., first p., première, first night, gala n., matinée, first house, second h.; encore, curtain-call; successful production, sell-out, hit, smash h., long run.

stage play, play, work; piece, show; libretto, scenario, script, text, playbook, prompt book; masque, mystery, miracle play, morality p., Nativity p., Passion p., Oberammergau; drama, Greek d., trilogy, tetralogy; problem play, discussion p.; dramatic representation 551 n. *representation*; five-act play, one-act p.; prologue, induction; curtain-raiser, interlude, entr'acte, divertissement, afterpiece, postlude, exode; monodrama; melodrama; tragedy, high t.; comedy, light c.; tragicomedy, comédie larmoyante; comedy of manners, Restoration comedy, drawing-room c.; low comedy, farce, slapstick, burlesque, extravaganza 849 n. *ridiculousness*; pantomime, harlequinade; musical comedy, musical, light opera, comic o., opera bouffe, grand opera; photoplay, screen-play, Western, horse-opera 445 n. *cinema*; radio play, radio drama, soap opera; ballet, dumb-show, mime, mimodrama, miming; puppetry, puppet-show, Punch and Judy, marionettes, fantoccini.

stage show 445 n. *spectacle*; variety, music hall, vaudeville; review, revue, one-man r., intimate r.; Follies, leg-show, flesh-s., strip-s., non-stop s.; floor-show, cabaret; song and dance, act, turn; star turn, transformation scene, set piece, tableau.

stage set, stagery, set, setting, décor, mise-en-scène, scenery, scene 445 n. *spectacle*; drop-scene, drop, backdrop, back-cloth, side-scene, scrim; screen, tormentor, wings, flat; background, foreground, front stage, upstage, downstage, backstage; stage, boards; apron-stage, revolving s.; proscenium, proscenium arch; curtain, fire c., safety c.; act-drop; trap, star t., grave t. (see *theatre*); properties, props, costume, theatrical c.; make-up, grease-paint.

theatre, amphitheatre, stadium 724 n. *arena*; circus, hippodrome; cinema, drive-in c., passion pit; cinema house, picture h., movie h., picture palace 445 n. *cinema*; Greek theatre, Elizabethan t., open-air t.; showboat, pier, pavilion; theatre-house, playhouse, house, opera h., music

hall, vaudeville theatre, puppet t., variety house; night club, bôite de nuit, cabaret; parts of a theatre (see *stage set*); stage, boards, proscenium, wings, coulisses, flies, tormentor, screen flats; dressing room, green r.; footlights, floats, battens, spotlight, bunch light, limelight; auditorium, orchestra; seating, stalls, orchestra s., fauteuil, front rows; box, stage-b.; pit, parterre; circle, dress c., upper c., mezzanine; gallery, balcony, gods; vestibule, foyer, bar, box-office, stage-door.

acting, personification, mimesis 551 n. *representation*; pantomime, miming, taking off 20 n. *mimicry*; histrionics, play-acting, stage-a., film-a., character-a.; ham-acting, barnstorming; overacting, staginess, theatricality; repertoire; character, role, creating a r.; starring role, lead, second l.; part, good p., fat p.; supporting part, playing opposite; speaking part, walking-on p.; stock part, ingénue, soubrette, confidante, heavy father, injured husband, merry widow, stage villain; chief part, name p.; hero, heroine; stage fright.

actor, play-a., Thespian, Roscius; mimic, mime, pantomimist, 20 n. *imitator*; mummer, guisard; player, stage p., strolling p., trouper; barnstormer, ham actor; old stager, rep player, character actor; star, star actor, star player, matinée idol 890 n. *favourite*; opera singer, prima donna, diva; ballet dancer, ballerina, prima b., danseuse, première coryphée; tragedian, tragedienne; comedian, comedienne, light comedian, low c., comic, (see *entertainer*); protagonist, deuteragonist, lead, second l., leading man, leading lady, juvenile lead, jeune premier; chorus, gentlemen of the chorus; chorus girl, show g., chorine; understudy, stand-in 150 n. *substitute*; mute, figurante, supernumerary, super, extra, general utility; concert-party, pierrot, pierrette; troupe, company, cast, corps de ballet; dramatis personæ, characters, cast of c. persons in the play; member of the cast, one of the company; presenter, narrator; chorus, prologue, compère 579 n. *speaker*.

entertainer, public e., performer; artiste, artist, quick-change a.; street artist, busker, nigger minstrel; diseuse, patterer, monologist; minstrel, jongleur; crooner, pop singer; juggler 545 n. *conjuror*; contortionist, posture artist, equilibrist,

trapezist, tumbler 162 n. *athlete*; gladiator 722 n. *combatant*; mountebank, fool, coxcomb, cap and bells, pantaloon, harlequin, columbine, pierrot, pierrette, Punch, Punchinello, buffoon, clown, merry-andrew, stooge; dancing girl, nautch g., geisha g.

stage-hand, prop-man, stage carpenter, scene-painter, scene-shifter; electrician, machinist; costumier, costume-mistress, wigmaker, make-up man; prompter, call-boy, programme-seller, usher, usherette.

stage-manager, producer, director, compère, manager, actor m., business m., press agent; impresario, showman; backer, angel, choregus.

dramatist, dramaturge, dramaturgist; tragic poet, comic p. 593 n. *poet*; mimographer; playwright, scenario writer, script-w., lyric-w., librettist; gag-man, joke-writer; dramatic critic.

playgoer, theatre-goer, opera-goer, film-g.; theatre fan, film f., movie f.; ballet fan, balletomane; first-nighter, queuer; stage-door Johnny; audience, house, packed h., full h., sell-out; stalls, boxes, pit, circle, gallery, balcony; groundling, pittite, galleryite, gallery gods, gods 441 n. *spectator*; claque, claqueur; deadhead, free seats; dramatic critic, play-reviewer.

Adj. *dramatic*, dramaturgical; scenic, theatrical, stagy 551 adj. *representing*; live, legitimate; Thespian, histrionic, mimetic 20 adj. *imitative*; tragic, buskined; Thalian, comic, tragi-comic; farcical, burlesque, knockabout, slapstick 849 adj. *funny*; operatic; melodramatic, sensational 821 adj. *exciting*; produced, released, showing, running 522 adj. *shown*; dramatized, acted; badly-acted, ham, hammy, barnstorming; on the stage, acting, play-a., trouping; cast, cast for; featured, starred, billed; well-cast, all-star; stage-struck, theatre-minded, film-m., theatre-going.

Vb. *dramatize*, be a dramatist, write plays, write for the stage; make a play of, put in a play; do a play, put on the stage, stage, stagify, produce, direct, stage-manage; rehearse, cut; cast, give a part, assign a role; star, feature, bill; present, put on, release 522 vb. *show*; open, open a season; raise *or* ring up the curtain; be produced, come out.

act, go on the stage, tread the boards,

troupe; perform, enact, play, play-act, do a play 551 n. *represent*; personify, personate, act the role, take the part; mime, pantomime, take off 20 vb. *imitate*; create a role, play a part, play lead; play opposite, support; star, steal the show, take the centre of the stage, upstage, take all the limelight; ham, barnstorm, over-act, overdramatize 546 vb. *exaggerate*; rant, roar, out-Herod Herod; underact, throw away; walk on; understudy, stand in 150 vb. *substitute*; con one's part, rehearse, speak one's lines, patter, gag; dramatize oneself 875 vb. *be ostentatious*.

Adv. *on stage*, off s., up s., down s.; backstage, behind the footlights, in the limelight; dramatically.

See: 20, 150, 162, 441, 445, 522, 545, 546, 551, 579, 590, 593, 722, 724, 821, 849, 875, 890.

595 Will

N. *will*, willing, volition; mere will, non-conative w., velleity; disposition, inclination, mind, preference 597 n. *willingness*; conative will, conation, conatus, act of will, effort of w. 682 n. *exertion*; strength of will, will-power, determination 599 n. *resolution*; controlled will, self-control 942 n. *temperance*; intent, purpose 617 n. *intention*; decision 608 n. *predetermination*; one's will and pleasure 737 n. *command*; appetence, appetency 859 n. *desire*; sweet will 932 n. *selfishness*; self-will, wilfulness 602 n. *obstinacy*; whimsicality 604 n. *caprice*; free will, self-determination 744 n. *independence*; free choice, option, discretion 605 n. *choice*; unprompted will, voluntariness, voluntaryism, spontaneousness, spontaneity 597 n. *voluntary work*; primacy of will, voluntarism.

Adj. *volitional*, willing, volitive, conative, pertaining to will; unprompted, unasked, unbidden, freewill, spontaneous, original 597 adj. *voluntary*; discretional, discretionary, optional 605 adj. *choosing*; minded, so m. 617 adj. *intending*; self-willed, wilful 602 adj. *obstinate*; arbitrary, autocratic, dictatorial 735 adj. *authoritarian*; independent, self-determined 744 adj. *free*; determined 599 adj. *resolute*; de-

cided, prepense, intentional, willed, intended 608 adj. *predetermined.*

Vb. *will,* have volition, exercise the will; impose one's will, have one's w., have one's way, have it all one's own w. 737 vb. *command;* do what one chooses, please oneself 744 vb. *be free;* be so minded, list, see fit, think f. 605 vb. *choose;* purpose, determine 617 vb. *intend;* wish 859 vb. *desire;* have a mind *or* will of one's own, be independent, go one's own way 734 vb. *please oneself;* exercise one's discretion, judge for oneself 480 vb. *judge;* act on one's own authority, take the responsibility; be self-willed, take the law into one's own hands, take the bit between one's teeth 602 vb. *be obstinate;* volunteer, offer, do of one's own accord, do without prompting 597 vb. *be willing;* originate 156 vb. *cause.*

Adv. *at will,* at pleasure, ad libitum, ad lib., as it seems good; voluntarily, of one's own free will, of one's own accord; spontaneously, out of one's own head, for the heck of it.

See: 156, 480, 597, 599, 602, 604, 605, 608, 617, 682, 734, 735, 737, 744, 859, 932, 942.

596 Necessity

N. *necessity,* hard n., stern n., compelling n.; no alternative, no escape, no option, Hobson's choice 606 n. *no choice;* last shift, last resort 700 n. *predicament;* inevitability, inevitableness 155 n. *destiny;* necessitation, dictation, necessitarianism, determinism, fatalism 608 n. *predetermination;* dictation of events, force of circumstances, act of God, fatality 154 n. *eventuality;* no freedom 745 n. *subjection;* physical necessity, law of nature; force, superior f. 740 n. *compulsion;* logical necessity, logic, necessary conclusion, proof 478 n. *demonstration;* legal necessity, force of law 953 n. *law;* moral necessity, obligation, conscience 917 n. *duty;* necessitude, indispensability, a necessity, a necessary, a must 627 n. *requirement;* necessitousness, want, lack 801 n. *poverty;* involuntariness, reflex action, reflex, conditioned r.; instinct, impulse, blind i. 476 n. *intuition.*

fate, inexorable f., lot, inescapable l., karma, kismet; doom, foredoom, pre-

destination, pre-ordination, election 155 n. *destiny;* book of fate, God's will, will of Allah, will of heaven, weird; fortune 159 n. *chance;* stars, planets, astral influence; the Fates, Parcæ, Norns; sisters three, Lachesis, Clotho, Atropos.

fatalist, determinist, predestinarian, necessitarian; pawn, automaton, robot, machine 630 n. *tool.*

Adj. *necessary,* indispensable, requisite, unforgoable 627 adj. *required;* logically necessary, logical, dictated by reason, unanswerable; demonstrable 478 adj. *demonstrated;* necessitating, imperative, compulsive 740 adj. *compelling;* overriding, irresistible, resistless 34 adj. *superior;* binding 917 adj. *obligatory;* with force of law 953 adj. *legal;* necessitated, inevitable, unavoidable, inescapable, inexorable, irrevocable 473 adj. *certain;* leaving no choice, dictated, imposed, necessitarian, deterministic 606 adj. *choiceless.*

involuntary, instinctive 476 adj. *intuitive;* unpremeditated, unwilled, unintended 618 adj. *unintentional;* unconscious, unthinking, unwitting, blind, impulsive 609 adj. *spontaneous;* unassenting 598 adj. *unwilling;* conditioned, reflex, controlled, automatic, machinelike, mechanistic, mechanical.

fated, decided by fate, karmic; appointed, destined, predestined, ordained, preordained 608 adj. *predetermined;* subject to fate, forechosen, elect 605 adj. *chosen;* doomed, foredoomed, prejudged, precondemned 961 adj. *condemned;* bound, obliged 745 adj. *subject.*

Vb. *be forced,* suffer compulsion, incur the necessity, lie under the n.; admit the necessity, submit to the n. 721 vb. *submit;* be fated, bow to fate, dree one's weird; be cornered, be driven into a corner, be pushed to the wall 700 vb. *be in difficulty;* know no alternative, have no choice, have no option; be unable to help it, be so constituted; be subject to impulse, be guided by instinct 745 vb. *be subject.*

necessitate, dictate, impose, oblige 740 vb. *compel;* bind by fate, destine, doom, foredoom, predestinate 155 vb. *predestine;* insist, brook no denial; leave no choice, impose the necessity, drive into a corner; demand 627 vb. *require.*

Adv. *necessarily,* of necessity, of course,

perforce 740 adv. *by force*; willy-nilly, nolens volens, bon gré mal gré, coûte que coûte.

See: 34, 154, 155, 159, 473, 476, 478, 598, 605, 606, 608, 609, 618, 627, 630, 700, 721, 740, 745, 801, 917, 953, 961.

597 Willingness

N. *willingness*, voluntariness, volunteering; spontaneousness 609 n. *spontaneity*; free choice, option 605 n. *choice*; disposition, mind, animus; inclination, leaning, bent, bias, penchant, propensity 179 n. *tendency*; facility 694 n. *aptitude*; predisposition, readiness, right mood, favourable humour, receptive frame of mind; cordiality, good will 897 n. *benevolence*; acquiescence 488 n. *assent*; compliance 758 n. *consent*; ready acquiescence, cheerful consent, alacrity, promptness, zeal, earnestness, eagerness, zealousness, ardour, enthusiasm; initiative, forwardness; impatience, over-eagerness, over-zealousness, ardour of the chase 678 n. *overactivity*; devotion, self-d., dedication, sacrifice 931 n. *disinterestedness*; helpfulness 706 n. *co-operation*; loyalty 739 n. *obedience*; pliancy, docility, tractability 612 n. *persuasibility*; submissiveness 721 n. *submission*; obsequiousness 879 n. *servility*.

voluntary work, voluntary service 901 n. *philanthropy*; honorary employment, unpaid labour, labour of love, self-appointed task; gratuitous effort, work of supererogation 637 n. *superfluity*; freewill offering 781 n. *gift*.

volunteer, unpaid worker, ready w., no shirker, no sloucher 678 n. *busy person*.

Adj. *willing*, acquiescent 488 adj. *assenting*; compliant, agreeable, content 758 adj. *consenting*; in the mood, in the vein, receptive, favourable, favourably minded, inclined, disposed, well-d., predisposed, amenable; gracious, genial, cordial; happy, pleased, glad, charmed, delighted; ready 669 adj. *prepared*; ready and willing, prompt, quick 678 adj. *active*; forward, anticipating; alacritous, zealous, eager, enthusiastic, dedicated; over-eager, impatient, spoiling for, raring to go; dependable, reliable 768 adj. *observant*; earnest, trying, doing one's best 671 adj.

essaying; helpful 706 adj. *co-operative*; docile, teachable, suasible, biddable 24 adj. *apt*; loyal 739 adj. *obedient*; submissive 721 adj. *submitting*; obsequious 879 adj. *servile*; fain, desirous, dying to 859 adj. *desiring*; would-be 852 adj. *hoping*; meaning, meaning to 617 adj. *intending*.

voluntary, offered, unprompted, unforced, unsought, unasked, unbidden 609 adj. *spontaneous*; unsolicited, uncalled for, self-imposed; non-mandatory, discretional, open to choice, optional 605 adj. *chosen*; volunteering 759 adj. *offering*; gratuitous, free, honorary, unpaid 812 adj. *uncharged*.

Vb. *be willing*, — ready etc. adj.; not mind, have half a mind to; feel like, have a great mind to 595 vb. *will*; be fain 859 vb. *desire*; mean 617 vb. *intend*; agree, acquiesce 488 vb. *assent*; comply 758 vb. *consent*; hearken, lend an ear to, give a willing ear, be found willing 739 vb. *obey*; try, do one's best 671 vb. *essay*; show zeal, go out of one's way to, lean over backwards, overcompensate; collaborate 706 vb. *co-operate*; anticipate, meet halfway; swallow, jump at, catch at; can't wait, be thrilled at the idea; stomach, make no bones, have no scruple, not hesitate; choose freely 605 vb. *choose*; volunteer, sacrifice oneself 759 vb. *offer oneself*.

Adv. *willingly*, with a will, readily, cordially, heartily; voluntarily, spontaneously, without asking, before a.; with open arms, with all one's heart, heart and soul, con amore, with a good grace, without demur, nothing loth; gladly, with pleasure.

See: 24, 179, 488, 595, 605, 609, 612, 617, 637, 669, 671, 678, 694, 706, 721, 739, 758, 759, 768, 781, 812, 852, 859, 879, 897, 901, 931.

598 Unwillingness

N. *unwillingness*, disinclination, indisposition, reluctance; disagreement 489 n. *dissent*; demur, objection 468 n. *qualification*; protest 762 n. *deprecation*; renitence 704 n. *opposition*; rejection 760 n. *refusal*; unhelpfuless, non-cooperation 702 n. *hindrance*; dissociation, non-association, abstention 190 n. *absence*; unenthusiasm, lifelessness, want of alacrity, lack of zeal 860 n. *indifference*;

backwardness 278 n. *slowness*; hesitation 858 n. *caution*; scruple, qualm of conscience 486 n. *doubt*; repugnance 861 n. *dislike*; recoil, aversion, averseness, no stomach for, shrinking 620 n. *avoidance*; bashfulness 874 n. *modesty*; nonobservance 738 n. *disobedience*; indocility, refractoriness, fractiousness; sulks, sulkiness 893 n. *sullenness*; perfunctoriness, grudging service; undependability, unreliability 474 n. *uncertainty*; shelving, postponement, procrastination 136 n. *delay*; laziness 679 n. *sluggishness*; neglect, remissness 458 n. *negligence*.

slacker, forced labour, unwilling servant 278 n. *slowcoach*; idle apprentice 679 n. *idler*.

Adj. *unwilling*, indisposed, loth, reluctant, averse; not prepared, not minded, not so m., not in the mood 760 adj. *refusing*; unconsenting, unreconciled 489 adj. *dissenting*; renitent, adverse, opposed, unalterably o., irreconcilable 704 adj. *opposing*; demurring, protesting 762 adj. *deprecatory*; squeamish, with no stomach for 861 adj. *disliking*; full of regrets, regretful, with regret 830 adj *regretting*; hesitant 858 adj. *cautious*; shy, bashful 874 adj. *modest*; shrinking, shirking 620 adj. *avoiding*; unzealous, unenthusiastic, half-hearted; backward, dragging 278 adj. *slow*; unhelpful, uncooperative, go-slow 702 adj. *hindering*; non-cooperating, fractious, restive, recalcitrant, kicking 738 adj. *disobedient*; not trying, perfunctory, unthorough, remiss 458 adj. *negligent*; grudging, sulky 893 adj. *sullen*; unspontaneous, forced, begrudged.

Vb. *be loth*, — unwilling etc. adj.; not have the heart to, not stomach 861 vb. *dislike*; disagree, stickle, stick, boggle 489 vb. *dissent*; object, demur, protest, kick 762 vb. *deprecate*; resist 704 vb. *oppose*; reject 760 vb. *refuse*; recoil, turn away, back a., not face, blench, fight shy, duck, jib, shirk 620 vb. *avoid*; skimp, scamp 458 vb. *neglect*; drag one's feet, look over one's shoulder, hang back, hang fire, go slow, run rusty 278 vb. *move slowly*; slack, not try, not pull one's weight 679 vb. *be inactive*; not play, non-cooperate, dissociate oneself, abstain 702 vb. *obstruct*; grudge, begrudge, make faces, grimace 893 vb. *be sullen*; drag oneself, make o.; do with regret, have regrets

830 vb. *regret*; tear oneself away 296 vb. *depart*.

Adv. *unwillingly*, reluctantly, under protest, under pressure, with a bad grace, in spite of oneself, against one's will, sore against the grain; regretfully, with regret.

See: 136, 190, 278, 296, 458, 468, 474, 486, 489, 620, 679, 702, 704, 738, 760, 762, 830, 858, 860, 861, 874, 893.

599 Resolution

N. *resolution*, sticking point, resoluteness, determination, grim d.; zeal, earnestness, seriousness; resolve, fixed r., mind made up, decision 608 n. *predetermination*; drive, vigour 174 n. *vigorousness*; energy, frantic e., desperate e., desperation 678 n. *activity*; thoroughness 725 n. *completion*; fixity of purpose, concentration, iron will, will-power 595 n. *will*; self-control, self-restraint, self-mastery, self-conquest, self-command, self-possession; tenacity 600 n. *perseverence*; aplomb, mettle, daring, dash, élan 712 n. *attack*; guts, pluck, grit, backbone; heroism, moral courage 855 n. *courage*; single-mindedness, devotedness, devotion, utter d., self-d., dedication; firm principles, reliability, staunchness, steadiness, constancy, firmness 153 n. *stability*; insistence, pressure 740 n. *compulsion*; sternness, relentlessness, ruthlessness, inexorability, implacability 906 n. *pitilessness*; inflexibility, steeliness 326 n. *hardness*; iron, cast i., steel, rock; clenched teeth, hearts of oak, bull-dog breed 600 n. *stamina*.

Adj. *resolute*, resolved, made up, determined 597 adj. *willing*; desperate, stopping at nothing; serious, earnest, concentrated; intent upon, set u., bent u. 617 adj. *intending*; insistent, pressing, urgent, driving, forceful, energetic, heroic 174 adj. *vigorous*; zealous, thorough, whole-hogging 455 adj. *attentive*; steady, firm, staunch, reliable, constant 153 adj. *unchangeable*; iron-willed, strong-w., strong-minded, unbending, immovable, unyielding, inflexible, uncompromising, intransigent 602 adj. *obstinate*; stern, grim, inexorable, implacable, relentless, ruthless, merciless 906 adj. *pitiless*; iron, cast-i., steely, tough as steel, hard as iron

326adj. *hard*; undaunted, nothing daunted 855adj. *unfearing*; unshaken, unshakable, unshrinking, unflinching, game, tenacious 600adj. *persevering*; indomitable 727adj. *unbeaten*; steeled, armoured, proof; self-controlled, self-restrained 942 adj. *temperate*; self-possessed, self-reliant, self-confident; purposeful, serious, earnest, whole-hearted, single-minded, devoted, dedicated.

Vb. *be resolute,* — determined etc. adj.; steel oneself, brace o., set one's face, grit *or* clench one's teeth (see *stand firm*); make up one's mind, take a resolution, will, resolve, determine, purpose 617vb. *intend*; decide, fix, seal, conclude, finish with 69vb. *terminate*; take on oneself, accept responsibility; know one's own mind, insist, press, urge, not take 'no' for an answer 532vb. *emphasize*; cut through, override, put one's foot down, stand no nonsense; stick at nothing, not stop at trifles, go to all lengths, push to extremes; go the whole hog, see it through 725vb. *carry through*; face, face the odds 661vb. *face danger*; outface, dare 711vb. *defy*; endure, go through fire and water 825vb. *suffer*; face the issue, bring to a head, take the bull by the horns; take the plunge, cross the Rubicon, burn one's boats, burn one's bridges, throw away the scabbard, nail one's colours to the mast; be single-hearted, set one's heart on, take up, go in for, take up in earnest, devote *or* dedicate oneself, give oneself to, give up everything for; set to, buckle to, go to it, put one's shoulder to the wheel, put one's heart into, grapple, strain 682vb. *exert oneself.*

stand firm, dig in, dig one's toes in, stand one's ground, stay put, stand pat; not budge, not yield, not compromise; never despair, stand fast, hold f., stick f., hold out 600vb. *persevere*; bear the brunt, have what it takes, fight on, stick it out, grin and bear it, endure 825vb. *suffer*; die hard, die game, die fighting, die with one's boots on; go down with colours flying, nail one's colours to the mast.

Adv. *resolutely,* seriously, earnestly, in good earnest; with firm determination, with fixed resolve; at any price, at all costs, at any hazard; manfully, like a man; come what may, live or die, neck or nothing, once for all.

See: 69, 153, 174, 326, 455, 532, 595, 597, 600, 602, 608, 617, 661, 678, 682, 711, 712, 725, 727, 740, 825, 855, 906, 942.

600 Perseverance

N. *perseverance,* persistence, tenacity, pertinacity, pertinaciousness, stubbornness 602n. *obstinacy*; staunchness, constancy, steadfastness 599n. *resolution*; single-mindedness, singleness of purpose, concentration 455n. *attention*; sedulity, application, tirelessness, indefatigability, assiduousness, industriousness 678n. *assiduity*; doggedness, plodding, hard trying, hard work 682n. *exertion*; endurance, patience 825n. *suffering*; maintenance 146n. *continuance*; ceaselessness 144n. *permanence*; iteration, repeated efforts, unflagging e. 106n. *repetition.*

stamina, staying power, indefatigability 162n. *strength*; grit, backbone, game, pluck, bottom; bulldog courage, diehard c. 855n. *courage*; hard core, diehard, last ditcher, old guard 602n. *opinionist*; trier, hard t., stayer, willing worker 686n. *worker.*

Adj. *persevering,* persistent, tenacious, stubborn 602adj. *obstinate*; game, plucky; hard-trying, patient, plodding, dogged 678adj. *industrious*; strenuous 682adj. *laborious*; steady, unfaltering, unwavering, undrooping, enduring, unflagging, unwearied, untiring, indefatigable; unsleeping, sleepless 457adj. *vigilant*; unfailing, unremitting, unintermittent, constant 146adj. *unceasing*; renewed, iterated, reiterated 106adj. *repeated*; indomitable, unconquerable, unconquered 727 adj. *unbeaten*; undaunted, undiscouraged, game to the last, true to the end 599adj. *resolute.*

Vb. *persevere,* persist, keep at it, not take 'no' for an answer; not despair, never d., never say die, hope on 852vb. *hope*; endure, have what it takes, come up for more 825vb. *suffer*; try, keep on trying, try and try again 671vb. *essay*; maintain, keep up, follow up 146vb. *sustain*; plod, slog, slog away, peg a., peg at, plug at, hammer at, work at 682vb. *work*; continue, go on, keep on, keep the pot boiling,

keep the ball rolling, rally, keep going; not let go, cling, hold fast, maintain one's grip 778vb. *retain*; hang on, stick it out, sit out, see through, wait till the end; be in at the death, stand by the grave of, survive 41vb. *be left*; maintain one's ground, not budge, not stir 602vb. *be obstinate*; stick to one's guns, hold out, hold out to the last, die in the last ditch, die at one's post 599vb. *stand firm*; work till one drops, die in harness; labour unceasingly, spare no pains, move heaven and earth, knock at every door 682vb. *exert oneself*; bring to conclusion, see the end of, complete 725vb. *carry through*.

Adv. *persistently*, perseveringly; through thick and thin, through fire and water, sink or swim 599adv. *resolutely*; repeatedly, unendingly, ceaselessly.

See: 41, 106, 144, 146, 162, 455, 457, 599, 602, 671, 678, 682, 686, 725, 727, 778, 825, 852, 855.

601 Irresolution

N. *irresolution*, infirmity of purpose, faint-heartedness, loss of nerve, no grit 856n. *cowardice*; non-perseverance, broken resolve, broken promise 603n. *tergiversation*; unsettlement, indecision, uncertainty, floating vote 474n. *dubiety*; hesitation, overcaution 858n. *caution*; inconstancy, fluctuation, vacillation, blowing hot and cold 152n. *changeableness*; levity, fickleness, whimsicality, irresponsibility 604n. *caprice*; lack of will-power, lack of drive 175n. *inertness*; good nature, easy-goingness, compromise 734n. *laxity*; lack of thoroughness, half-heartedness, half-measures 726n. *non-completion*; lukewarmness, listlessness, apathy 860n. *indifference*; no will of one's own, aboulia, weak will 163n. *weakness*; impressibility, suggestibility 612n. *persuasibility*; pliancy, over-pliancy 327n. *softness*; obsequiousness 879n. *servility*; submissiveness, slavishness 721n. *submission*.

waverer, wobbler, dodderer, shilly-shallyer; shuttlecock, butterfly, feather 152n. *changeable thing*; ass between two bundles of hay, floating voter; weathercock,

chameleon, turncoat 603n. *tergiversator* faintheart, compromiser.

Adj. *irresolute*, undecided, indecisive, o two minds, vacillating; unable to make up one's mind, undetermined, unresolved uncertain 474adj. *doubting*; squeamish boggling, hesitating 598adj. *unwilling* gutless, timid, tremulous, faint-hearted unheroic, faint, nerveless 856adj *cowardly*; shaken, rattled 854adj. *nervous*; half-hearted, lukewarm 860adj *indifferent*; wobbling, unstaunch, un steadfast, infirm, infirm of purpose 474 adj. *unreliable*; characterless, featureless 175adj. *inert*; compromising, weak-willed, weak-minded, weak-kneed 163 adj. *weak*; suggestible, flexible, pliant 327adj. *soft*; easy-going, good-natured 734adj. *lax*; inconstant, various, variable, temperamental 152adj. *changeful* whimsical, mercurial, not to be pinned down 604adj. *capricious*; emotional restless, unfixed, unballasted, without ballast 152adj. *unstable*; irresponsible giddy, feather-brained, light 456adj. *light-minded*; fidgety, impatient, unpersevering; unthorough, superficial 456adj *inattentive*; unfaithful 603adj. *tergiversating*.

Vb. *be irresolute*, — undecided etc.adj. back away, blink, jib, shy, shirk 620vb *avoid*; palter, shuffle, shilly-shally 518vb *equivocate*; fluctuate, vacillate, see-saw wobble, waver, sway, hover, teeter dodder, dither 317vb. *oscillate*; blow hot and cold, back and fill, hum and haw will and will not, be in two minds, turn round in circles, not know what to do, be at one's wits' end 474vb. *be uncertain* leave in suspense, keep undecided, delay put off a decision 136vb. *put off*; dally dilly-dally 136vb. *wait*; debate, balance 475vb. *argue*; hesitate 858vb. *be cautious* falter, grow weary 684vb. *be fatigued*; no persevere, give up 621vb. *relinquish*; make a compromise, take half-measures 770vb *compromise*; yield, give way 721vb *submit*; change sides, go over 603vb *apostatize*.

Adv. *irresolutely*, faint-heartedly, hesitantly from pillar to post; see-saw; between the devil and the deep blue sea.

See: 136, 152, 163, 175, 317, 327, 456, 474 475, 518, 598, 603, 604, 612, 620, 621, 684 721, 726, 734, 770, 854, 856, 858, 860, 879

602 Obstinacy

N. *obstinacy*, unyielding temper; determination, will 599 n. *resolution*; grimness, doggedness, tenacity 600 n. *perseverance*; stubborness, obduracy, obduration; pervicacity, self-will, pig-headedness; inelasticity, inflexibility, woodenness, toughness 326 n. *hardness*; no compromise, intransigence; constancy, irreversibility, fixity 153 n. *stability*; stiff neck, contumacy 715 n. *resistance*; incorrigibility 940 n. *impenitence*; indocility, intractability, mulishness, dourness, sulkiness 893 n. *sullenness*; perversity, wrongheadedness, bloody mindedness.

opiniatry, self-opinion, opiniativeness, opinionatedness 473 n. *positiveness*; dogmatism, bigotry, zealotry; rigorism, intolerance, fanaticism 735 n. *severity*; ruling passion, infatuation, obsession, monomania, idée fixe 481 n. *bias*; blind side 439 n. *blindness*; illiberality, obscurantism 491 n. *ignorance*; old school, ancien régime.

opinionist, stubborn fellow, mule; stick-in-the-mud, Blimp; fanatic, rigorist, stickler, pedant, dogmatist, zealot, bigot, persecutor 481 n. *narrow mind*; sticker, stayer; chronic; last-ditcher, die-hard, bitter-ender; fogy 504 n. *crank*.

Adj. *obstinate*, stubborn, pervicacious; pig-headed, mulish; unyielding, firm, determined 599 adj. *resolute*; dogged, tenacious 600 adj. *persevering*; stiff, rigid, inelastic, wooden 326 adj. *hard*; inflexible, unbending, stiff-backed; obdurate, hardened, case-h., rock-ribbed; uncompromising, intransigent; unmoved, uninfluenced, immovable 153 adj. *unchangeable*; inexorable, unappeasable, implacable, merciless 906 adj. *pitiless*; set, wedded, set in one's ways, hidebound, ultraconservative, blimpish 610 adj. *habituated*; unteachable, obscurantist, impervious, blind, deaf; opinionated, dogmatic, pedantic 473 adj. *positive*; obsessed, bigoted, fanatic 481 adj. *biased*; dour, grim 893 adj. *sullen*; indocile, hard-mouthed, stiff-necked, contumacious, impenitent (see *wilful*); perverse, incorrigible, bloody-minded; possessive, dog-in-the-manger; irremoveable, irreversible; persistent, incurable, chronic 113 adj. *lasting*.

wilful, self-willed, forward, wayward, arbitrary; entêté, headstrong, perverse; unruly, jibbing, restive, refractory; irrepressible, ungovernable, unmanageable, intractable, uncontrollable 738 adj. *disobedient*; impersuasible, incorrigible, contumacious; cross-grained, crotchety 892 adj. *irascible*.

Vb. *be obstinate*, — stubborn etc. adj.; persist 600 vb. *persevere*; brazen it out 940 vb. *be impenitent*; stick to one's guns, stand out, not budge, stay put, stand pat 599 vb. *stand firm*; insist, brook no denial, not take 'no' for an answer; go one's way, want one's own w., must have one's w. 734 vb. *please oneself*; opinionate 473 vb. *dogmatize*; be wedded to one's own opinions, not change one's mind 473 vb. *be certain*; stay in a rut, cling to custom 610 vb. *be wont*; not listen, take no advice, take the bit between one's teeth, damn the consequences 857 vb. *be rash*; not yield to treatment, become chronic 113 vb. *last*.

Adv. *obstinately*, pigheadedly, mulishly, like a mule.

See: 113, 153, 326, 439, 473, 481, 491, 504, 599, 600, 610, 715, 734, 735, 738, 857, 892, 893, 906, 940.

603 Tergiversation

N. *tergiversation*, change of mind, better thoughts; afterthought, second thought 67 n. *sequel*; change of purpose, alteration of plan, new resolve; good resolution, break with the past, repentance 939 n. *penitence*; revulsion 280 n. *recoil*; backsliding, recidivation, recidivism 657 n. *relapse*; change of direction 282 n. *deviation*; resilement, reversal, about-face, volte-face, looking back 286 n. *return*; versatility, slipperiness, suppleness, unreliability, untrustworthiness 930 n. *improbity*; apostasy, recreancy (see *recantation*); defection, desertion 918 n. *dutilessness*; ratting, going over, treachery 930 n. *perfidy*; secession, withdrawal 978 n. *schism*; abandonment 621 n. *relinquishment*; change of mood, temperament; coquetry 604 n. *caprice*.

recantation, palinode, eating one's words, retractation, retraction; resilement, withdrawal; renunciation, abjuration, abjurement, forswearing, swearing off 532 n. *oath*; disavowal, disclaimer, denial 533 n.

negation; revocation, revokement, recall 752n. *abrogation*.

tergiversator, turncoat, turnabout, rat; weathercock 152n. *changeable thing*; time-server, trimmer, Vicar of Bray 518n. *equivocalness*; double-dealer, Janus, two-faced person, Mr. Facing-both-ways 545n. *deceiver*; jilt, flirt, coquet 604n. *caprice*; recanter, recreant, apostate, renegade, runagate, renegado, forswearer; traitor, betrayer 938n. *knave*; medizer, quisling, fifth columnist, collaborationist 707n. *collaborator*; lost leader, deserter, quitter, ratter; tell-tale, peacher, squealer, approver 524n. *informer*; strike-breaker, blackleg, scab; deviationist, secessionist, seceder, schismatic, mugwump 978n. *schismatic*; runaway, bolter, flincher 620n. *avoider*; recidivist, backslider 904n. *offender*; convert, proselyte 147n. *changed person*.

Adj. *tergiversating*, trimming etc.vb.; shuffling 518adj. *equivocal*; slippery, supple, versatile, treacherous 930adj. *perfidious*; double-dealing 541adj. *hypocritical*; reactionary, going back 286adj. *regressive*; fickle 604adj. *capricious*; time-serving, time-pleasing 925adj. *flattering*; vacillating 601adj. *irresolute*; apostate, recanting, renegade; recidivist, relapsed; false, unfaithful, disloyal 918adj. *dutiless*.

Vb. *tergiversate*, change one's mind, think again, think better of it, change one's tune 601vb. *be irresolute*; back out, scratch, withdraw 753vb. *resign*; back down, crawl 872vb. *be humbled*; apologize (see *recant*); change front, change round, swerve, tack, wheel about 282vb. *turn round*; turn one's back on 286vb. *turn back*; turn over a new leaf, make good resolutions, repent 939vb. *be penitent*; reform, mend one's ways 654vb. *get better*; fall back, backslide 657vb. *relapse*; trim, shuffle, face both ways, run with the hare and hunt with the hounds 518vb. *be equivocal*; ditch, jilt, throw over, desert 918vb. *fail in duty*; forsake, abandon, wash one's hands of 621vb. *relinquish*; turn against, play false.

apostatize, turn one's coat, change sides, medize; let down the side, change one's allegiance; switch, switch over, join the opposition, cross over, cross the floor; blackleg, rat; betray, collaborate 930vb. *be dishonest*; be off with the old love,

jump on the band wagon, follow the rising star.

recant, unsay, eat one's words, eat one's hat; eat humble pie, apologize; take back, go back on, recall one's words, resile, withdraw; retract, disavow, disclaim, repudiate, deny 533vb. *negate*; renounce, renunciate, abjure, forswear, swear off; recall, revoke, rescind 752vb. *abrogate*.

See: 67, 147, 152, 280, 282, 286, 518, 524, 532, 533, 541, 545, 601, 604, 620, 621, 654, 657, 707, 752, 753, 872, 904, 918, 925, 930, 938, 939, 978.

604 Caprice

N. *caprice*, fancy, fantastic notion 513n. *fantasy*; capriciousness, arbitrariness, motivelessness, purposelessness; whimsicality, freakishness, crankiness 497n. *absurdity*; faddishness, faddiness, faddism 481n. *bias*; inconsistency 25n. *disagreement*; fitfulness, changeability, variability, fickleness, unreliability, temperament, levity, giddiness, lightmindedness, irresponsibility 152n. *changeableness*; inconstancy, coquettishness, flirtatiousness; playfulness; temperament, fretfulness, pettishness 892n. *irascibility*.

whim, caprice, whimsey, whimwam, vagary, sweet will, humour, fit, crotchet, bee in the bonnet, maggot, quirk, kink, fad, craze, freak; escapade, prank, boutade, wild-goose chase 497n. *foolery*; coquetry, flirtation.

Adj. *capricious*, motiveless, purposeless; whimsical, fanciful, fantastic; humoursome, temperamental, crotchety, maggoty, fitful; hysterical, mad 503adj. *insane*; freakish, prankish, wanton, wayward, erratic, inconsistent; faddy, faddish, particular 862adj. *fastidious*; captious, arbitrary, unreasonable; fretful, contrary, uncomfortable 892adj. *irascible*; undisciplined, refractory 602adj. *wilful*; uncertain, unpredictable 508adj. *unexpected*; volatile, mercurial, skittish, giddy, frivolous 456adj. *light-minded*; inconsistent, inconstant, variable 152adj. *unstable*; irresponsible, unreliable, fickle 603adj. *tergiversating*; flirtatious, coquettish, playful.

Vb. *be capricious*, — whimsical etc.adj.; show caprice, take it into one's head;

pick and choose 862 vb. *be fastidious*; chop and change, blow hot and cold 152 vb. *vary*; have a bee in one's bonnet, have a maggot in one's brain; be fickle, take up a thing and drop it; vacillate 318 vb. *fluctuate*; play pranks, play tricks 497 vb. *be absurd*; flirt, coquette 837 vb. *amuse oneself.*

Adv. *capriciously*, fitfully, by fits and starts, now this, now that; as the humour takes one, at one's own sweet will.

See: 25, 152, 318, 456, 481, 497, 503, 508, 513, 602, 603, 837, 862, 892.

605 Choice

N. *choice*, act of choosing, election 463 n. *discrimination*; picking and choosing, eclecticism 862 n. *fastidiousness*; picking out, selection; co-option, co-optation, adoption; designation, nomination, appointment 751 n. *commission*; right of choice, option, pre-option; freedom of choice, discretion, pick; deliberate choice, decision 481 n. *judgment*; preference, predilection, inclination, leaning, bias 179 n. *tendency*; taste 859 n. *liking*; availability 759 n. *offer*; range of choice, selection, list, short l.; possible choice, alternative, embarras de choix; difficult choice, option of difficulties, dilemma 474 n. *dubiety*; limited choice, no real alternative; only choice, Hobson's choice, nothing for it but 606 n. *no choice*; blind choice 464 n. *indiscrimination*; better choice, preferability, desirability, greater good, lesser evil 642 n. *expedience*; one's preference, favour, fancy, first choice, top seed; thing chosen, selection, pickings, gleanings, excerpts; literary selection 592 n. *anthology*; unlucky choice, bad bargain; unfair choice, favouritism 914 n. *injustice.*

vote, voice 485 n. *opinion*; representation, proportional r., cumulative vote, transferable v., casting v., ballot, secret b., open vote; card vote; vote-counting, show of hands, division, poll, Gallup p., plebiscite, referendum; suffrage, universal s., adult s., manhood s.; franchise, right of representation, votes for women, women's suffrage, suffragettism; Parliamentary system, electoral s., ballot-box, vox populi; polling, counting heads,

counting noses; election, general e., 'democracy's feast'; by-election; indirect election, primary e., primary; polls, voting, electioneering, canvassing, canvass, hustings, candidature; successful election, return.

electorate, voters, balloter, elector, plumper, straw voter, faggot v.; electoral college; quorum; electoral roll, voting list, voter's l.; constituent, constituency; borough, pocket b., rotten b.; polling booth, ballot-box, voting paper; slate, ticket.

Adj. *choosing*, optional, discretional 595 adj. *volitional*; exercising choice, showing preference, preferential, favouring 923 adj. *approving*; selective, eclectic; co-optative, elective, electoral; voting, present and v.; vote-catching, electioneering, canvassing.

chosen, well-c.; worth choosing, not to be sniffed at; preferable, better 642 adj. *expedient*; select, choice, recherché, picked, hand-p. 644 adj. *excellent*; sorted, assorted, seeded, 62 adj. *arranged*; elect, designate; elected, returned; on approval; preferred, special, favourite, fancy, pet; God's own; by appointment.

Vb. *choose*, have a voice, have free will 595 vb. *will*; eliminate the alternatives, make one's choice, make one's bed; exercise one's discretion, accept, opt, opt for, take up an option; elect, co-opt, adopt, put on the list 923 vb. *approve*; would like, favour, fancy, like best; incline, lean, have a bias 179 vb. *tend*; prefer, have a preference, like better, have rather; might as well, might do worse; go in for, take up; think fit, think it best to, decide, make up one's mind 480 vb. *judge*; come out for, come down f., plump f., come down on one side; take the plunge, cross the Rubicon, burn one's boats 599 vb. *be resolute*; range oneself, take sides, side, back, support, embrace, espouse, cast in one's lot with 703 vb. *patronize*; take for better or worse 894 vb. *wed*.

select, pick, pick out, sort o., seed; pass 923 vb. *approve*; nominate, appoint 751 vb. *commission*; designate, mark out, mark down 547 vb. *mark*; pre-select, earmark, reserve 46 vb. *set apart*; recommend, put up, propose, second 703 vb. *patronize*; excerpt, cull, anthologize 592 vb. *abstract*; glean, winnow, sift,

bolt 463vb. *discriminate*; draw the line, separate; skim, skim off, cream, pick the best; indulge one's fancy, pick and choose 862vb. *be fastidious*.

vote, have a v., have a voice; have the vote, be enfranchised, be on the electoral roll; poll, go to the polls; cast a vote, register one's v., raise one's hand, divide; vote for, elect, return; electioneer, canvass; accept a candidature, stand 759vb. *offer oneself*; put to the vote, present the alternatives, take a poll; count heads, count noses; hold an election, go to the country, appeal to the electorate.

Adv. *optionally*, at pleasure; by ballot; alternatively, either . . . or; preferably, rather, sooner; by choice, à la carte.

See: 46, 62, 179, 463, 464, 474, 480, 481, 485, 547, 592, 595, 599, 606, 642, 644, 703, 751, 759, 859, 862, 894, 914, 923.

606 Absence of Choice

N. *no choice*, choicelessness, no alternative, dictation 596n. *necessity*; dictated choice, Hobson's c. 740n. *compulsion*; any, the first that comes 464n. *indiscrimination*; no favouritism, impartiality, first come first served 913n. *justice*; no preference, non-committal, neutrality, apathy 860n. *indifference*; moral apathy, amoralism, amorality; no difference, six of one and half a dozen of the other, 'a plague on both your houses' 28n. *equality*; indecision, open mind, open-mindedness 474n. *dubiety*; floating vote 601n. *irresolution*; refusal to vote, non-election, abstention 598n. *unwillingness*; no election, spoilt ballot paper; disfranchisement, disqualification, no vote, no voice.

Adj. *choiceless*, without alternative, necessitated 596adj. *necessary*; without a preference, unable to choose, happy either way 625adj. *neutral*; open-minded, open to conviction, unresolved, undecided, undetermined 601adj. *irresolute*; uninterested, apathetic 860adj. *indifferent*; morally neutral, amoral, amoralistic; disinterested, motiveless; without favouritism, impartial 913adj. *just*; not voting, abstaining 598adj. *unwilling*; non-voting, voteless, disfranchised, disqualified; nothing to offer, featureless, characterless 860adj. *unwanted.*

Vb. *be neutral*, take no sides, make no choice, not vote, refuse to v., withhold one's v., abstain; waive, waive one's choice, stand aside 621vb. *relinquish*; stand between 625vb. *be half-way*; sit on the fence 601vb. *be irresolute*; not care 860vb. *be indifferent*.

have no choice, have no alternative, suffer dictation, have Hobson's choice, take it or leave it, make a virtue of necessity 596vb. *be forced*; have no voice, have no vote; lose one's vote, spoil one's ballot paper.

Adv. *neither*, neither. . . . nor.

See: 28, 464, 474, 596, 598, 601, 621, 625, 740, 860, 913.

607 Rejection

N. *rejection*, non-acceptance, declination, waiver, waiving; non-approval, disapproval 924n. *disapprobation*; abnegation, repudiation, denial 533n. *negation*; apostasy 603n. *recantation*; rebuff, repulse 760n. *refusal*; spurn, kick, more kicks than ha'pence; rejection at the polls, electoral defeat, lost election, hostile vote, forfeiture of deposit 728n. *defeat*; elimination, outcasting 300n. *ejection*; non-consideration, counting out, exception, exemption 57n. *exclusion*; disuse, discarding, disemployment 674n. *non-use*; discard, reject, wallflower; unpopular cause, lost c.

Adj. *rejected* etc.vb.; ineligible, unchosen, outvoted 860adj. *unwanted*; unaccepted, returned, sent back, tried and found wanting, declined with thanks 924adj. *disapproved*; kept out, excluded, outcasted 57adj. *excluded*; unfit for consideration, not be thought of, out of the question 643adj. *inexpedient*; discarded 674adj. *disused*.

Vb. *reject*, not accept, decline, say no to, rebuff, repulse, spurn, kick 760vb. *refuse*; not approve, not pass, return, send back, return with thanks 924n. *disapprove*; not consider, pass over, ignore 458vb. *disregard*; vote against, not vote, not choose, outvote 489vb. *dissent*; scrap, discard, ditch, throw away, throw aside, lay a., give up 674vb. *disuse*; disallow, revoke 752vb. *abrogate*; set aside, supersede 752vb. *depose*; expel, out-

caste, thrust out, fling o. 300 vb. *eject*; sort out, draw the line 44 vb. *eliminate*; except, count out, exempt 57 vb. *exclude*; cold-shoulder, turn one's back on 885 vb. *be rude*; not want, not cater for 883 vb. *make unwelcome*; disclaim, disavow, deny 533 vb. *negate*; abnegate, repudiate, apostatize 603 vb. *recant*; scout, scorn, set at naught, disdain, laugh at, mock, deride 851 vb. *ridicule*; sniff at, look a gift horse in the mouth 922 vb. *hold cheap.*

See: 44, 57, 300, 458, 489, 533, 603, 643, 674, 728, 752, 760, 851, 860, 883, 885, 922, 924.

608 Predetermination

N. *predetermination*, predestination 596 n. *necessity*; appointment, fore-ordination, pre-ordination 155 n. *destiny*; decree 595 n. *will*; premeditation, predeliberation, resolve, project 617 n. *intention*; prearrangement 669 n. *preparation*; work on hand, order of the day, orders, order paper, agenda 622 n. *business*; frame-up, put-up job, packed jury 623 n. *plot*; parti pris, closed mind 481 n. *prejudice*; predisposal, foregone conclusion, ready-made verdict, agreed result.

Adj. *predetermined*, decreed, premeditated etc. vb.; appointed, predestined, fore-ordained 596 n. *fated*; deliberate, willed, aforethought, prepense 617 adj. *intending*; with a motive, designed, studied, calculated; weighed, considered, advised; well-devised, devised, controlled, contrived 623 adj. *planned*; put-up, framed, stacked, packed, ready-made, pre-arranged 669 adj. *prepared.*

Vb. *predetermine*, destine, appoint, predispose, foreordain, predestinate 155 vb. *predestine*; premeditate, preconceive, resolve beforehand 617 vb. *intend*; agree beforehand, preconcert; will the end 595 vb. *will*; contrive a result, ensure a r. 156 vb. *cause*; contrive, arrange, prearrange 623 vb. *plan*; frame, put up, pack a jury, stack the cards 541 vb. *fake.*

See: 155, 156, 481, 541, 595, 596, 617, 622, 623, 669.

609 Spontaneity

N. *spontaneity*, unpremeditation; ad hoc measures, improvisation; extemporiza-

tion, ad libbing, impromptu 670 n. *non-preparation*; involuntariness, reflex, automatic r.; impulsiveness, impulse, blind i., spurt 476 n. *intuition*; inconsideration, spur of the moment; inspiration, sudden thought, hunch, flash 451 n. *idea.*

improviser, extemporizer, improvisatore, improvisatrice; creature of impulse.

Adj. *spontaneous*, off-hand, ad hoc, improvised, extemporaneous, sudden, snap; makeshift, catch-as-catch-can 670 adj. *unprepared*; impromptu, unpremeditated, unmeditated, unrehearsed, indeliberate 618 adj. *unintentional*; unprompted, unmotivated, unprovoked; unguarded, incautious 857 adj. *rash*; natural, instinctive, involuntary, automatic 476 adj. *intuitive*; untaught 699 adj. *artless*; impulsive, emotional 818 adj. *feeling.*

Vb. *improvise*, not prepare, extemporize, vamp 670 vb. *be unprepared*; obey an impulse, act on the spur of the moment; blurt, come out with, say what comes uppermost, flash out with an answer; rise to the occasion.

Adv. *extempore*, extemporaneously, impromptu, ad hoc, on the spur of the moment, off-hand, off the cuff.

See: 451, 476, 618, 670, 699, 818, 857.

610 Habit

N. *habit*, native h. 5 n. *character*; habitude, assuetude, force of habit; consuetude, familiarity, second nature; study, occupation; addiction, confirmed habit, daily h., constitutional; knack, trick, instinct, leaning 179 n. *tendency*; bad habit, cacoethes; usage, standard u., long habit, custom, standing c., old c., one's old way; use, wont, user 146 n. *continuance*; inveteracy, prescription 113 n. *diuturnity*; tradition, law, precedent; way, ways, the old w.; beaten track, tram-lines, groove, rut; fixed ways, round, daily r., dailiness, regularity 141 n. *periodicity*; run, routine, system 60 n. *order*; red tape, red-tapism, beadledom, conventionalism, traditionalism, conservatism, old school 83 n. *conformity*; occupational disease.

practice, common p., usual custom, matter of course; conformism, conventionalism, conventionality 83 n. *conformity*; institution, ritual, observance 988 n. *rite*;

religious observance, cultus, 981n. *cult*; mode, vogue, craze 848n. *fashion*; convention, protocol, done thing, the usual; form, good f. 848n. *etiquette*; manners, manners and customs; table manners, eating habits; rules and regulations, standing order, rules of business, routine 688n. *conduct*; spit and polish, pipeclay, bull 60n. *order*.

habituation, assuefaction, training 534n. *teaching*; inurement, seasoning, hardening 669n. *maturation*; naturalization, acclimatization, radication; conditioning, association, reflex, conditioned r., fixation, complex; drill, repetitive job 106n. *repetition*.

habitué, creature of habit, addict, drug a., dope-fiend; routine-monger, traditionalist, conventionalist 83n. *conformist*; customer, regular c., client 792n. *purchaser*; frequenter, devotee, fan.

Adj. habitual, customary, consuetudinal, familiar 490n. *known*; routine, stereotyped 81adj. *regular*; conventional, traditionary, traditional 976adj. *orthodox*; inveterate, prescriptive, time-honoured, permanent 113adj. *lasting*; resulting from habit, occupational; haunting, besetting, clinging, obsessive; habit-forming 612adj. *inducive*; fast, ingrained, dyed in the wool; rooted, deep-r., deep-seated, implanted, ingrafted 153adj. *fixed*; imbued, dyed, soaked, permeated 341adj. *drenched*. See *usual*.

usual, accustomed, wonted, traditional; in character, natural; household, familiar, well-known 490adj. *known*; unoriginal, trite, trodden, beaten, well-worn, hackneyed; banal, commonplace, common, ordinary 79adj. *general*; set, stock 83adj. *typical*; prevalent, widespread, obtaining, current 79adj. *universal*; monthly, daily, everyday, of everyday occurrence 139adj. *frequent*; practised, done; admitted, acknowledged, received, accepted, accredited, recognized, understood; right, settled, established, professional, official 923adj. *approved*; de rigueur 740adj. *compelling*; invariable 153adj. *unchangeable*; modish, in the mode 848adj. *fashionable*.

habituated, in the habit of, accustomed to, known to; given to, addicted to; dedicated, devoted to, wedded to; used to, familiar with, conversant w., at home in

490adj. *knowing*; practised, inured, seasoned, hardened 669adj. *prepared*; broken in, trained, tame 369adj. *tamed*; naturalized, acclimatized.

Vb. be wont, love to, be known to, be used to, use to; have the habit of, be a creature of habit; go daily, haunt, frequent; make a habit of, take up, go in for; never vary, observe routine, move in a rut, stick in a groove, tread the beaten track, go on in the jog-trot way, cling to custom; become a habit, catch on, gain upon one, grow on o., take hold of o.; stick, cling, adhere 48vb. *cohere*; settle, take root, radicate; be the rule, obtain 178vb. *prevail*; come into use, acquire the force of custom, hold good for.

habituate, accustom oneself, get used to, get in the way of, get the knack of, get the feel of, play oneself in, take in one's stride; take to, acquire the habit, learn a h., cultivate a h.; fall into a habit; grow into a habit, catch oneself doing; keep one's hand in, practise 106vb. *repeat*; accustom, inure, season, harden, case-harden 534vb. *train*; domesticate, tame 369vb. *break in*; sanctify by custom, naturalize, acclimatize; implant, ingraft, imbue 534vb. *teach*.

Adv. habitually, regularly, with regularity 141adv. *periodically*; customarily, wontedly, occupationally, in the habit of; of course, as usual, according to one's wont; mechanically, automatically, by force of habit; in one's stride.

See: 5, 48, 60, 79, 81, 83, 106, 113, 139, 141, 146, 153, 178, 179, 341, 369, 490, 534, 612, 669, 688, 740, 792, 848, 923, 976, 981, 988.

611 Desuetude

N. desuetude, disusage, discontinuance, disuse, insuitation 674n. *non-use*; rust, decay 655n. *deterioration*; lost habit, lost skill, rustiness, lack of practice 695n. *unskilfulness*; discarded custom, abolition 752n. *abrogation*; forgotten custom 506n. *oblivion*, 550n. *obliteration*; outgrown custom, outgrowing, weaning, ablactation 134n. *adultness*; new custom, originality 21n. *non-imitation*; unwontedness, no such custom, non-prevalence; not the form, not the thing, not protocol, not etiquette, unconventionality 84n.

unconformity; want of habit, inexperience, unfamiliarity 491 n. *ignorance.*

Adj. *unwonted*, not customary, uncurrent, non-prevalent; unused, unpractised, unobserved, not done; unnecessary, not de rigueur; not in vogue, unfashionable 847 adj. *vulgar*; out of fashion, old-fashioned, defunct 125 adj. *past*; outgrown, discarded 674 adj. *disused*; against custom, unconventional 84 adj. *unconformable*; unsanctified by custom, untraditional, unprecedented, unhackneyed, original 21 adj. *unimitative.*

unhabituated, unaccustomed, not in the habit of 769 adj. *non-observant*; untrained, unbacked, unbroken, not broken in, untamed, undomesticated; uninured, unseasoned, unripe 670 adj. *immature*; unfamiliar, inexperienced, new to, new, raw, fresh, green 491 adj. *uninstructed*; disaccustomed, weaned; out of the habit, rusty 695 adj. *unskilful.*

Vb. *disaccustom*, wean from, cure of 656 vb. *cure*; disaccustom oneself, break a habit, drop a h., lose a h.; wean oneself from, outgrow; throw off, slough, slough off, shed 229 vb. *doff.*

be unused, not catch on; try a thing once, not do it again; not be done, offend custom, infringe protocol; lapse, fall into disuse, wear off, wear away 127 vb. *be old*; rust 655 vb. *deteriorate.*

See: 21, 84, 126, 127, 134, 229, 491, 506, 550, 655, 656, 670, 674, 695, 752, 769, 847.

612 Motive

N. *motive*, cause of action 156 n. *cause*; rationale, reason, ground 156 n. *reason why*; motivation, driving force, impulsion, spring, mainspring 156 n. *causation*; ideal, principle, guiding star, lodestar, direction 689 n. *directorship*; aspiration 852 n. *hope*; ambition 859 n. *desire*; calling, call 622 n. *vocation*; conscience, dictate of c., honour 917 n. *duty*; shame 854 n. *fear*; personal reasons, ulterior motive 932 n. *selfishness*; impulse, spur of the moment, inspiration 609 n. *spontaneity.*

inducement, pressure, instance, urgency, press, insistence; pressure group, lobby, lobbying 178 n. *influence*; indirect influence, side-pressure; provocation, urg-

ing, incitement, encouragement, incitation, instigation, prompting, inspiration, 821 n. *excitation*; countenance, support, abetment 703 n. *aid*; solicitation, invitation 761 n. *request*; temptation, enticement, allurement, seduction, seductiveness, tantalization, witchery, bewitchment, fascination, charm, attractiveness, magnetism 291 n. *attraction*; cajolery, blandishment 925 n. *flattery*; coaxing, wheedling 889 n. *endearment*; persuasion, persuasiveness, salesmanship, sales talk 579 n. *oratory*; pep-talk, trumpet-call, rallying cry 547 n. *call*; exhortation, preachment 534 n. *lecture*; pleading, advocacy 691 n. *advice*; propaganda, advertising 528 n. *advertisement*; bribery, palm-greasing 962 n. *reward*; castigation 963 n. *punishment*; honeyed words, siren song, voice of the tempter, winning ways.

persuasibility, docility, tractability, teachableness 597 adj. *willingness*; pliancy, pliability 327 n. *softness*; susceptibility, susceptivity, attractability, suggestibility, impressibility, sensitivity, emotionalism 819 n. *moral sensibility*; credulousness 487 n. *credulity.*

incentive, inducement; stimulus, fillip, flip, tickle, tickler, prod, spur, goad, ankus, whip, riding w., crop, riding c.; rod, big stick, crack of the whip 900 n. *threat*; energizer, tonic, provocative, carrot, sop, sop to Cerberus, dram 174 n. *stimulant*; charm 983 n. *spell*; attraction, loadstone 291 n. *magnet*; lodestar, gleam; will-o'-the-wisp 440 n. *visual fallacy*; lure, decoy, decoy duck, bait, golden b., fly, cast 542 n. *trap*; profit 771 n. *gain*; cash, gold 797 n. *money*; pay, salary, perks, pay increase, rise, raise, bonus 804 n. *payment*; donation, donative 781 n. *gift*; gratification, tip, backsheesh, bribe 962 n. *reward*; golden apple, forbidden fruit; tempting offer 759 n. *offer.*

motivator, mover, prime m. 156 n. *cause*; manipulator, manager, wire-puller 178 n. *influence*; manoeuvrer, tactician, strategist 623 n. *planner*; instigator, prompter, suggester, hinter; inspirer, counsellor 691 n. *adviser*; abettor, aider and abettor 703 n. *aider*; agent provocateur 545 n. *deceiver*; tantalizer, tempter, seducer; temptress, vamp, siren, Circe; hypnotizer, hypnotist; persuader, orator, rhetorician 579 n. *speaker*; advocate, pleader; coaxer,

wheedler, cozener 925n. *flatterer*; vote-catcher, vote-snatcher; patterer, salesman, advertiser, propagandist 528n. *publicizer*; ringleader 690n. *leader*; firebrand, incendiary, seditionist, sedition-monger 738n. *agitator*; lobbyist, lobby, pressure-group.

Adj. *inducive*, protreptic, directive, motive; motivating, wire-pulling, lobbying 178 adj. *influential*; inductive, incentive, provocative; energizing, stimulating, tonic, peppy; challenging, encouraging, rousing, incendiary 821 adj. *exciting*; prompting, hortatory, insinuating, hinting; teasing, tantalizing; inviting, tempting, alluring, attractive 291 adj. *attracting*; fascinating, bewitching 983 adj. *sorcerous*; irresistible, hypnotic, mesmeric; habit-forming 610 adj. *habitual*.

induced, brought on 157 adj. *caused*; inspired, motivated; incited, egged on, tarred on 821 adj. *excited*; receptive, tractable, docile 597 adj. *willing*; spellbound 983 adj. *bewitched*; smitten 887 adj. *enamoured*; suasible, persuasible 487 adj. *credulous*.

Vb. *motivate*, motive, move, actuate, manipulate 173 vb. *operate*; work upon, play u., act u., operate u. 178 vb. *influence*; weigh, count, be a consideration, sway 178 vb. *prevail*; call the tune, override, overbear 34 vb. *predominate*; work on the feelings, appeal, challenge, shame into (see *incite*); infect, inject with, inoculate, poison; interest, intrigue 821 vb. *impress*; charm, fascinate, captivate, hypnotize, spellbind 983 vb. *bewitch*; enamour, turn one's head 887 vb. *excite love*; pull 291 vb. *attract*; drag 288 vb. *draw*; push 279 vb. *impel*; force, enforce 740 vb. *compel*; bend, incline, dispose; predispose, prejudice 481 vb. *bias*; predestine 608 vb. *predetermine*; lead, direct 689n. *manage*; lead astray 495 vb. *mislead*; give a lead, ringlead; set the fashion, set an example, set the pace, lead the dance 283 vb. *precede*.

incite, energize, lend force to, stimulate 174 vb. *invigorate*; sound the trumpet, encourage, keep in countenance 855 vb. *give courage*; inspirit, inspire, animate, provoke, rouse, rally 821 vb. *excite*; evoke, call forth, challenge; exhort, invite, urge, insist, press, exert pressure, put pressure on, lobby; nag, goad, prod, spur, prick,

tickle; whip, lash, flog; tar on, hound on, set on, egg on; drive, hurry, hurry up 680 vb. *hasten*; instigate, prompt, put up to; abet, aid and a. 703 vb. *aid*; insinuate, suggest 524 vb. *hint*; advocate, recommend, counsel 691 vb. *advise*; start, kindle 68 vb. *initiate*.

induce, bring about 156 vb. *cause*; persuade, overpersuade, carry with one 485 vb. *convince*; carry one's point, prevail upon, talk into, push i., drive i., bully i., browbeat (see *motivate*); bring round, talk round 147 vb. *convert*; bring to one's side, bring over, win o., gain o., procure, enlist, engage; talk over, cajole, coax, blandish 889 vb. *pet*; conciliate, appease 719 vb. *pacify*; entice, seduce (see *tempt*).

tempt, try, lead into temptation; entice, dangle before one's eyes, make one's mouth water; tantalize, tease; allure, lure, bait, inveigle 542 vb. *ensnare*; tickle, coax, wheedle, blandish, cajole, pat, pat on the back, stroke 889 vb. *pet*; pander to, make things easy for, gild the pill, sugar the p. 925 vb. *flatter*.

bribe, offer an inducement 759 vb. *offer*; suborn, seduce, tamper with, doctor, corrupt; square, buy off, buy over; oil, grease the palm, tickle the p., give a sop to Cerberus; tip, gratify 962 vb. *reward*.

be induced, yield, succumb 721 vb. *submit*; concede 758 vb. *consent*; obey one's conscience, act on principle; come *or* fall under the influence; admit the influence, feel the urge, hear the call; be infected, catch, catch the infection.

See: 34, 68, 147, 156, 157, 173, 174, 178, 279, 283, 288, 291, 327, 440, 481, 485, 487, 495, 524, 528, 534, 542, 545, 547, 579, 597, 608, 609, 610, 622, 623, 680, 689, 690, 691, 703, 719, 721, 738, 740, 758, 759, 761, 771, 781, 797, 804, 819, 821, 852, 854, 855, 859, 887, 889, 900, 917, 925, 932, 962, 963, 983.

613 Dissuasion

N. *dissuasion*, dehortation, contrary advice; caution 664n. *warning*; discouragement 702n. *hindrance*; deterrence 854n. *intimidation*; objection, expostulation, remonstrance, reproof, admonition 762n. *deprecation*; no encouragement, disincentive; deterrent 665n. *danger signal*; contra-indication, counter-symptom 14n. *con-*

trariety; cold water, damper, wet blanket; kill-joy, spoilsport 702 n. *hinderer.*
Adj. *dissuasive*, discouraging, chilling, damping; dehortatory, expostulatory 762 adj. *deprecatory*; monitory, warning against 664 adj. *cautionary.*
Vb. *dissuade*, dehort, persuade against, advise a., argue a., convince to the contrary 479 vb. *confute*; caution 664 vb. *warn*; wag a forefinger 924 vb. *reprove*, expostulate, remonstrate, cry out against, protest a. 762 vb. *deprecate*; shake, stagger, give one pause 486 vb. *cause doubt*; intimidate 900 vb. *threaten*; terrorize, deter, frighten away, daunt, cow 854 vb. *frighten*; choke off, head off, steer one away from, turn one aside 282 vb. *deflect*; wean away from 611 vb. *disaccustom*; hold one back, keep back, act as a drag 747 vb. *restrain*; render averse, disenchant, disillusion, disincline, indispose, disaffect; set against, put off, repel, disgust, fill with distaste 861 vb. *cause dislike*; dishearten, discourage, dispirit, depress 834 vb. *deject*; throw cold water on, dampen, quench, cool, chill, damp the ardour; take the edge off 257 vb. *blunt*; calm, quiet 177 vb. *moderate.*
See: 14, 177, 257, 282, 479, 486, 611, 664, 665, 702, 747, 762, 834, 854, 861, 900, 924.

614 Pretext

N. *pretext*, ostensible motive, alleged m.; statement, allegation, profession, claim 532 n. *affirmation*; plea, excuse, defence, apology, apologia, justification 927 n. *vindication*; let-out, loophole, alibi 667 n. *means of escape*; locus standi, leg to stand on, peg to hang something on 218 n. *supporter*; shallow pretext, thin excuse, equivocation 518 n. *equivocalness*; special pleading, quibble 477 n. *sophism*; salvo, proviso 468 n. *qualification*; subterfuge 698 n. *stratagem*; false plea, pretence, previous engagement, diplomatic illness 543 n. *untruth*; blind, dust thrown in the eyes 421 n. *obfuscation*; stalking horse, smoke-screen, cloak, cover 421 n. *screen*; apology for, simulacrum, makeshift 150 n. *substitute*; colour, gloss, guise 445 n. *appearance*; bluff, sour grapes.

Adj. *ostensible*, alleged, pretended; colourable, specious, plausible; seeming.
excusing, self-e., exculpatory, apologetic, vindicatory, justificatory 927 adj. *vindicating.*
Vb. *plead*, allege, claim, profess 532 vb. *affirm*; pretext, make one's pretext, take the plea of 475 vb. *argue*; make excuses, offer an excuse, excuse oneself, defend o. 927 vb. *justify*; gloss over, palliate 927 vb, *extenuate*; express regret, apologize 830 vb. *regret*; shelter under, take shelter u., take hold as a handle for, use as a peg, use as a stalking horse; make capital of 137 vb. *profit by*; find a loophole, wriggle out of, ride off on 667 vb. *escape*; bluff, say the grapes are sour; varnish 425 vb. *colour*; blind, throw dust in the eyes 542 vb. *befool*; pretend, affect 850 vb. *be affected.*
Adv. *ostensibly*, as an excuse, as alleged, as claimed; on the plea of, on the pretext of.
See: 137, 150, 218, 421, 425, 445, 468, 475, 477, 518, 532, 542, 543, 667, 698, 830, 850, 927.

615 Good

N. *good*, one's g., what is good for one; the best, supreme good, summum bonum; public weal, common weal, common good; balance of interest, greater good, lesser evil, the greatest happiness of the greatest number, utilitarianism 642 n. *expedience*; weal, well-being, welfare 730 n. *prosperity*; riches 800 n. *wealth*; luck, good l., fortune, fair *or* good f.; happy days, happy ending 824 n. *happiness*; blessing, benison, world of good (see *benefit*); well-wishing, benediction 897 n. *benevolence.*
benefit, something to one's advantage, advantage, interest, commodity; service, behoof, behalf 640 n. *utility*; crop, harvest, return 771 n. *acquisition*; profit, increment, unearned i. 771 n. *gain*; edification, betterment 654 n. *improvement*; boon 781 n. *gift*; good turn 897 n. *kind act*; favour, blessing, blessing in disguise; godsend, windfall, piece of luck, treasure-trove, find, prize, nuts; good thing, desirable object, the very thing, just the t. 859 n. *desired object.*

Adj. *good,* goodly, fine; blessed, beatific 824 adj. *happy;* gainful 640 adj. *profitable;* advantageous, heaven-sent 644 adj. *beneficial;* worth-while 644 adj. *valuable;* helpful 706 adj. *co-operative;* praiseworthy, commendable, recommended 923 adj. *approved;* edifying, moral 933 adj. *virtuous;* pleasure-giving 826 adj. *pleasurable.*

Vb. *benefit,* favour, bless; do good, help, serve, avail, be of service 640 vb. *be useful;* edify, advantage, profit; pay, repay 771 vb. *be profitable;* turn out well, be all for the best, come right in the end.

flourish, thrive, do well; rise, rise in the world, be on top of the w., ride high on the hog's back 730 vb. *prosper;* arrive 727 vb. *succeed;* benefit by, gain by, be the better for, improve 654 vb. *get better;* turn to good account, make capital of, cash in on 137 vb. *profit by;* make a profit 771 vb. *gain;* make money 800 vb. *get rich.*

Adv. *well,* aright, satisfactorily, favourably, profitably, happily, not amiss; to one's advantage, to one's benefit, for the best; in fine style, on the up and up.

See: 137, 640, 642, 644, 654, 706, 727, 730, 771, 781, 800, 824, 826, 859, 897, 923, 933.

616 Evil

N. *evil,* moral e., fault, wickedness, devilment 934 n. *vice;* evil conduct, mischievousness, injuriousness, disservice, injury, dirty trick 930 n. *foul play;* wrong, injury, outrage 914 n. *injustice;* crying evil, shame, abuse; curse, scourge, poison, pest, plague, sore, running s. 659 n. *bane;* ill, ills that flesh is heir to, Pandora's box; sad world, vale of tears; bale, trouble, troubles 731 n. *adversity;* affliction, bread of a., misery, distress 825 n. *suffering;* grief, woe 825 n. *sorrow;* unease, malaise, discomfort 825 n. *worry;* nuisance 827 n. *annoyance;* hurt, bodily harm, wound, bruise, cut, gash 377 n. *pain;* blow, mortal b., buffet, stroke 279 n. *knock;* outrageous fortune, slings and arrows, misfortune, calamity, bad luck, ill hap 731 n. *ill fortune;* casualty, accident 154 n. *eventuality;* fatality 361 n. *death;* catastrophe 165 n. *ruin;* tragedy, sad ending 655 n. *deterioration;* mischief, harm,

damage 772 n. *loss;* ill effect, bad result damaged interest, prejudice; disadvantage 35 n. *inferiority;* drawback, flaw 647 n. *defect;* setback 702 n. *hitch;* evil plight 700 n. *predicament;* indigence 801 n. *poverty;* sense of injury, grievance, complaint, protest 829 n. *discontent;* vindictiveness 910 n. *revengefulness;* principle of evil 969 n. *Satan.*

Adj. *evil,* wicked 934 adj. *vicious;* black, foul, shameful 914 adj. *wrong;* bad, too bad, sad, plaguy 645 adj. *damnable;* unlucky, inauspicious, sinister 731 adj. *adverse;* insidious, injurious, prejudicial, disadvantageous 645 adj. *harmful;* troublous, troubled 827 adj. *distressing;* fatal, fell, mortal, deathly 362 adj. *deadly;* ruinous, disastrous 165 adj. *destructive;* catastrophic, calamitous, tragic 731 adj. *unfortunate;* all wrong, awry, out of joint; satanic 969 adj. *diabolic.*

Adv. *amiss,* wrong, all wrong, awry; unfortunately, unhappily, unluckily; to one's cost, for one's sins; worse luck!

See: 35, 154, 165, 279, 361, 362, 377, 645, 647, 655, 659, 700, 702, 731, 772, 801, 825, 827, 829, 910, 914, 930, 934, 969.

617 Intention

N. *intention,* intent, intendment; intentionality, deliberateness; calculation, calculated risk 480 n. *estimate;* purpose, set p., settled p., determination, predetermination, resolve 599 n. *resolution;* animus, mind; guilty mind, mens rea 936 n. *guilt;* good intention 897 n. *benevolence;* view, prospect, purview; future intention, contemplation 124 n. *looking ahead;* constant intention, study, pursuit, occupation 622 n. *business;* project, design 623 n. *plan;* enterprise 672 n. *undertaking;* ambition 859 n. *desire;* formulated intention, decision 480 n. *judgment;* final decision, ultimatum 766 n. *conditions;* proposal, bid, final b. 759 n. *offer;* engagement 764 n. *promise;* solemn threat 900 n. *threat;* final intention, destination 69 n. *end;* teleology, final cause 156 n. *causation;* be-all and end-all, raison d'être 156 n. *reason why;* trend 179 n. *tendency;* drift 514 n. *meaning;* tendentiousness 597 n. *willingness.*

objective, destination, object, end, end in view, aim; by-end, by-aim, axe to grind; mark, butt, target; target area, bull's-eye 225n. *centre*; tape, winning-post 295n. *goal*; quarry, game, prey 619n. *chase*; prize, crown, wreath 729n. *trophy*; dream, aspiration, heart's desire, Promised Land, El Dorado 859n. *desired object.*

Adj. *intending,* intent, studying, serious; hell-bent 599n. *resolute*; intentional, deliberate, voluntary 595adj. *volitional*; out to, out for, all out f.; having in view, purposive, teleological; meaning 514adj. *meaningful*; minded, disposed, inclined 597adj. *willing*; prospective, would-be, aspiring, ambitious 859adj. *desiring.*

intended, for a purpose, tendential, tendentious; deliberate, intentional, studied, designed, purposed, purposeful, aforethought 608adj. *predetermined.*

Vb. *intend*, purpose, propose; have in mind, have in view, contemplate; study, meditate; reckon to, calculate, look for 507vb. *expect*; foresee the necessity of 510vb. *foresee*; mean to, really mean, have every intention 599vb. *be resolute*; have a purpose, harbour a design; resolve, determine, premeditate 608vb. *predetermine*; project, design, plan for 623vb. *plan*; take on oneself, shoulder 672vb. *undertake*; engage 764vb. *promise*; threaten to 900vb. *threaten*; intend for, destine f., destine, doom 155vb. *predestine*; mark down for, earmark 547vb. *mark*; hold for, keep f., reserve f.; intend for oneself (see *aim at*); mean by it 514vb. *mean.*

aim at, make one's target, go for, go in for, take up; go after, go all out for, drive at, labour for, study f., strive after 619vb. *pursue*; try for, bid f., make a bid, endeavour 671vb. *essay*; be after, have an eye on, have designs on, promise oneself, propose to oneself, nurse an ambition, aspire to, dream of, think of, talk of 859vb. *desire*; take aim, point at, level at, train one's sights, raise one's s., aim high 281vb. *aim.*

Adv. *purposely*, on purpose, seriously, with one's eyes open, in cold blood, deliberately, pointedly, intentionally; designedly, advisedly, knowingly, wittingly, voluntarily; with malice aforethought; for, for a purpose, in order to; with the intention of, with a view to, with the object of, in pursuance of, pursuant to; as planned, as

designed, according to plan, as arranged; to design, to one's own d.

See: 69, 124, 155, 156, 179, 225, 281, 295, 480, 507, 510, 514, 547, 595, 597, 599, 608, 619, 622, 623, 671, 672, 729, 759, 764, 766, 859, 897, 900, 936.

618 Non-design. Gamble

N. *non-design*, indetermination, indeterminacy, unpredictability 159n. *chance*; involuntariness, instinct 609n. *spontaneity*; coincidence, mere c. 89n. *accompaniment*; accident, casualty, fluke, luck, mere l. 154n. *eventuality*; good luck, windfall; bad luck, mischance 616n. *evil*; lottery, luck of the draw (see *gambling*); sortilegy, sortition, drawing lots, casting l., sortes Vergilianae, sortes Biblicæ 511n. *divination*; lot, wheel of Fortune 596n. *fate*; mascot, amulet, charm, porte-bonheur, swastika 983n. *talisman.*

gambling, taking a chance, risk-taking; plunge, risk, hazard 661n. *danger*; gamble, pot-luck 159n. *chance*; venture, speculation, flutter 461n. *experiment*; shot, random s., shot in the dark, leap in the d., pig in a poke, blind bargain 474n. *uncertainty*; bid, throw; toss of a coin, turn of a card; wager, bet, stake, ante, psychic bid; last throw, desperate bid 857n. *rashness*; dice-box, dice, die, bones, ivories, craps; element of risk, game of chance, play, roulette, rouge et noir 837n. *gambling game*; betting, turf, horse-racing, dog-r. 716n. *racing*; draw, lottery, raffle, tombola, sweepstake, premium bond, football pool; tontine; gambling on the market, futures.

gaming-house, hell, gambling h., betting house, pool room, casino; racecourse, turf; totalisator, tote, pari mutuel.

bourse, exchange, stock e., curb e., bucket shop.

gambler, gamester, player, dicer; better, layer, backer, punter; bookmaker, bookie, tipster; man of enterprise, risk-taker; gentleman of fortune, venturer, adventurer, merchant a., undertaker, entrepreneur 672n. *undertaking*; speculator, piker, plunger, manipulator; bear, bull, stag; experimentalist 461n. *experimenter.*

Adj. *unintentional,* non-intentional, unintended, unmeant, not meant 596 adj. *involuntary*; unpurposed, undesigned, unpremeditated, unrehearsed 609 adj. *spontaneous*; accidental, fortuitous, coincidental 159 adj. *casual.*

designless, aimless, planless, purposeless; motiveless 159 n. *causeless*; promiscuous 464 adj. *indiscriminate*; undirected, unguided, random, haphazard 282 adj. *deviating*; wandering, footloose 267 adj. *travelling*; meaningless, driftless 515 adj. *unmeaning.*

speculative, experimental 474 vb. *uncertain*; hazardous, risky, chancy, dicey, aleatory; risk-taking, venturesome, adventurous, enterprising.

Vb. *gamble,* game, play; throw, dice, bet, stake, wager, lay; call one's hand, overcall; gamble deep, play high, play for high stakes, double the s.; take bets, make a book; back, punt; cover a bet, cover, hedge 660 vb. *seek safety*; play the market, speculate, have a flutter 461 vb. *experiment*; hazard, risk, run a r., take risks, buy blind, buy a pig in a poke 857 vb. *be rash*; venture, chance it, take one's chance, tempt fortune, try one's luck, trust to chance, spin the wheel, shuffle the cards; cut for aces; raffle, draw, draw lots, cast l., stand the hazard.

Adv. *at random,* by the way, incidentally, haphazardly; unintentionally, unwittingly; chancily, riskily; at a venture, by guess and God, on the off-chance.

See: 89, 154, 159, 267, 282, 461, 464, 474, 511, 515, 596, 609, 616, 660, 661, 672, 716, 837, 857, 983.

619 Pursuit

N. *pursuit,* pursuing, pursuance, hunting, seeking, looking for, quest 459 n. *search*; adient behaviour, adient response, approach r. 289 n. *approach*; persecution, witch-hunt; tracking, trailing, dogging 284 n. *following*; trial, prosecution, 959 n. *legal trial*; enterprise, adventure 672 n. *undertaking*; calling 622 n. *vocation*; avocation, profession, hobby, activities, affairs 622 n. *business.*

chase, stern-c., hard c., run, run for one's money; steeplechase, paperchase 716 n. *racing*; hunt, hunting, hounding, hue and cry, tally-ho, hark; beat, drive, battue, beating; shooting, gunning, hunting and shooting 837 n. *sport*; blood sport, foxhunt, deer-h., lion-h., tiger-h.; elephant hunt, keddah; boar-hunt, pigsticking; stalking, deer-s.; hawking, fowling, falconry; fishing, angling, fly-fishing, trawling; beagling, coursing, ratting, trapping; fishing rod, rod and line, bait, fly; fowling-piece 287 n. *shooter*; fish-trap, rat-t. 542 n. *trap*; game, quarry, prey, victim 617 n. *objective*; catch 771 n. *acquisition.*

hunter, quester, seeker, searcher 459 n. *enquirer*; search-party; pursuer, dogger, tracker, trailer, shadow; huntsman, huntress; whip, whipper-in; Nimrod, Diana; sportsman, sportswoman 837 n. *player*; gun, shot, good s., marksman 287 n. *shooter*; head-hunter 362 n. *killer*; foxhunter, stag-h., lion-h., courser, beagler, cony-catcher, rat-c., ratter, trapper, stalker, deer-s.; bird-catcher, fowler, falconer, hawker; fisher, fisherman, piscator, angler, compleat a.; shrimper; trawler, trawlerman, whaler; field, pack, hounds, cry of h.; hound, fox-h., deer-h., boar-h. 365 n. *dog*; hawk 365 n. *bird of prey*; beast of prey, man-eater 365 n. *animal*; mouser 365 n. *cat.*

Adj. *pursuing,* pursuant, seeking, questing 459 adj. *enquiring*; in quest of, sent after; chasing, in pursuit, in hot p., in full cry, on the scent, on the trail 284 adj. *following*; hunting, shooting; fishing, piscatorial.

Vb. *pursue,* seek, look for, cast about; be gunning for, hunt for, fish for, dig for 459 vb. *search*; send after, send for, send out a search party 272 vb. *send*; stalk, prowl after, sneak a.; shadow, dog, track, trail, tail, sit on one's t., follow the scent 284 vb. *follow*; scent out 484 vb. *discover*; witch-hunt, harry, persecute 735 vb. *oppress*; chase, give c., hunt, whoop, halloo, hark, hark on, cry on; raise the hunt, raise the hue and cry; run down, ride d., rush at, tilt at, ride full tilt at, charge at 712 vb. *charge*; leap at, jump at 312 vb. *leap*; snatch at 786 vb. *take*; make one's game, make one's quarry 617 vb. *aim at*; set one's course 281 vb. *steer for*; be after, make it one's business 617 vb. *intend*; pursue one's ends, ride one's hobby 622 vb. *busy oneself*; run after, set one's cap at, woo 889 vb. *court*; press on 680 vb.

hasten; push one's way, elbow one's w., fight one's w. 285 vb. *progress.*

hunt, go hunting, go shooting, go ratting; follow the chase, ride to hounds, pig-stick; fish, angle, fly-fish; trawl; whale; shrimp; net, catch 542 vb. *ensnare*; mouse, play cat and m.; stalk, deer-s., fowl, hawk; course, beagle; start game, flush, start, start up; hunt men, head-hunt.

Adv. *pursuant to*, in pursuance of, in quest of, after; in chase, on the trail, on the track.

See: 272, 281, 284, 285, 287, 289, 300, 312, 362, 365, 459, 484, 542, 617, 622, 672, 680, 712, 716, 735, 771, 786, 837, 889, 959.

620 Avoidance

N. *avoidance*, prevention 702 n. *hindrance*; abstinence, abstention 942 n. *temperance*; forbearance, refraining 177 n. *moderation*; refusal 607 n. *rejection*; inaction 679 n. *inactivity*; passivity 266 n. *quiescence*; non-intervention, non-involvement, neutrality 860 n. *indifference*; evasiveness 518 n. *equivocalness*; evasive action, dodge, jink, sidestep; delaying action, non-cooperation 769 n. *non-observance*; centrifugal force; retreat, withdrawal 286 n. *regression*; evasion, slip, flight, elusion, avolation 667 n. *escape*; start aside, jib, shy, shrinking 854 n. *fear*; shunning, wide berth, safe distance 199 n. *distance*; shyness 598 n. *unwillingness*; shirking 458 n. *negligence*; skulking 523 n. *latency*; abient behaviour 280 n. *recoil*; defence mechanism, defence reaction 713 n. *defence*; repression, suppression 757 n. *prohibition*; escapism.

avoider, non-drinker 942 n. *abstainer*; dodger, sidestepper, evader, levanter, bilker, welsher 545 n. *trickster*; shrinker, quitter 856 n. *coward*; slacker, sloucher, scrimshanker 679 n. *idler*; skulker 527 n. *hider*; truant, deserter 918 n. *dutilessness*; apostate, renegade, runagate 603 n. *tergiversator*; runaway, fugitive, refugee, displaced person, D.P., escapee 667 n. *escaper*; escapist 513 n. *visionary*.

Adj. *avoiding*, shunning; evasive, elusive, slippery, hard to catch; untamed, wild; shy 874 adj. *modest*; blinking, blenching, shrinking, cowering 854 adj. *nervous*;

backward, non-cooperative, reluctant 598 adj. *unwilling*; non-committal, unforthcoming 582 adj. *taciturn*; passive, inert 679 adj. *inactive*; non-involved, non-committed, uncommitted 625 adj. *neutral*; centrifugal; fugitive, hunted, runaway, fly-by-night 667 adj. *escaped*; hiding, skulking 523 adj. *latent*; repressive, suppressive; defensive, abient.

avoidable, evasible, escapable, preventable; unsought, unattempted.

Vb. *avoid*, not go near, keep off, keep away; by-pass, give one the go-by, look the other way, take the other w., turn aside 294 vb. *diverge*; boycott, cold-shoulder 883 vb. *make unwelcome*; hold aloof, stand apart, have no hand in, not soil one's fingers, keep one's hands clean, wash one's hands of, shun, eschew, leave, let alone, have nothing to do with; fight shy, back away, draw back 290 vb. *recede*; hold off, stand aloof, keep one's distance, keep a respectful d., give a wide berth, keep out of the way, keep clear, stand c., get out of the way, make way for; forbear, spare; refrain, abstain, forswear, deny oneself, do without, not touch 942 vb. *be temperate*; avoid hitting, pull one's punches 177 vb. *moderate*; hold back, hang b., not try, not attempt 598 vb. *be loth*; shelve, postpone 136 vb. *put off*; shirk 458 vb. *neglect*; shrink, flinch, start aside, jib, refuse, shy, blink, blench 854 vb. *be nervous*; take evasive action, lead one a dance, throw one off the scent, play hide-and-seek; jink, sidestep, dodge, duck, deflect 713 vb. *parry*; evade, escape, be spared 667 vb. *elude*; skulk, cower, hide 523 vb. *lurk*; disown, deny 533 vb. *negate*; repress, suppress 757 vb. *prohibit*; make excuses, ride off 614 vb. *plead*; prevent, foil 702 vb. *hinder*.

run away, desert, play truant, take French leave 918 vb. *fail in duty*; abscond, welsh, flit, levant, elope 667 vb. *escape*; absent oneself 190 vb. *be absent*; withdraw, retire, retreat, beat a r., turn tail, turn one's back 282 vb. *turn round*, flee; flit, fly, take to flight, run for one's life; be off, make o., slope o., scamper o., bolt, run, cut and run, show a clean pair of heels, take to one's h., make oneself scarce, run for one's life, scoot, scram, skedaddle 277 vb. *move fast*; slip the cable, part

company, break away 296vb. *decamp*; steal away, sneak off, slink o., shuffle o., creep o.; scuttle, bunk, do a b.

Int. *hands off!* keep off! beware! forebear!

See: 136, 177, 190, 199, 266, 277, 280, 282, 286, 290, 294, 296, 458, 513, 518, 523, 527, 533, 545, 582, 598, 603, 607, 614, 625, 667, 679, 702, 713, 757, 769, 854, 860, 874, 883, 918, 942.

the side 603vb. *apostatize*; throw over, ditch, jilt, break it off, go back on one's word 541vb. *be false*; abandon discussion, waste no more time, pass on to the next, shelve, postpone 136vb. *put off*; annul, cancel 752vb. *abrogate*.

See: 136, 145, 190, 229, 296, 506, 541, 603, 611, 620, 674, 721, 752, 753, 772, 779, 780, 860, 872, 883, 918, 978.

621 Relinquishment

N. *relinquishment,* abandonment; going, leaving, evacuation 296n. *departure*; dereliction, desertion, truancy, defection 918n. *dutilessness*; withdrawal, secession 978n. *schism*; walk-out 145n. *strike*; yielding, giving up, handing over, cession 780n. *transfer*; forgoing, waiver, renunciation 779n. *non-retention*; retirement 753n. *resignation*; disuse 674n. *non-use*; disusage, non-continuance 611n. *desuetude*; cancellation, annulment 752n. *abrogation*; world well lost 883n. *seclusion.*

Adj. *relinquished,* forsaken, cast-off, marooned, abandoned etc.vb.; waived, forgone 779n. *not retained.*

Vb. *relinquish,* drop, let go, leave hold of, unclench, quit one's hold, loosen one's grip 779vb. *not retain*; surrender, resign, give up, yield; waive, forgo; bate one's pretensions 872vb. *be humble*; cede, hand over, transfer 780vb. *convey*; forfeit 772vb. *lose*; renounce, swear off, abnegate, recant, change one's mind 603vb. *tergiversate*; not proceed with, drop *or* give up the idea, forget it 506vb. *forget*; wean oneself 611vb. *disaccustom*; forswear, deny oneself, abstain 620vb. *avoid*; shed, slough, cast off, divest 229vb. *doff*; drop, discard, write off 674vb. *disuse*; lose interest 860vb. *be indifferent*; abdicate, back down, scratch, stand down, withdraw, retire 753vb. *resign*; give in, throw up the sponge, throw up the game, throw in one's hand 721vb. *submit*; leave, quit, move out, vacate, tear oneself away 296vb. *depart*; forsake, abandon, quit one's post, desert 918vb. *fail in duty*; play truant 190vb. *be absent*; strike work, strike, come out 145vb. *cease*; walk out, secede 978vb. *schismatize*; go over, rat, let down

622 Business

N. *business,* affairs, business a., interests, iron in the fire; main business, occupation, concern, care; aim, ambition 617n. *intention*; business on hand, case, agenda; enterprise, undertaking, pursuit 678n. *activity*; routine, business r., office r., round, daily r. 610n. *practice*; business life, daily work, journey w., course of w.; business circles, business world, City; art, industry, commerce, commerce and industry; big business; cottage industry, home i.; industrialism, industrialization, industrial arts, manufacture 164n. *production*; trade, craft, handicraft, mystery 694n. *skill*; guild, business association 706n. *association*; employment, work, avocation (see *vocation*); side-interest, hobby, pastime 837n. *amusement*; religious business 981n. *cult.*

vocation, calling, life-work, mission, apostolate 751n. *commission*; life, walk, walk of life, race, career; chosen career, labour of love, self-imposed task 597n. *voluntary work*; livelihood, daily bread, one's bread and butter; profession, métier, craft, trade; line, line of country (see *function*); exacting profession, high calling; religious profession, ministry, cure of souls; cloth, veil, habit 985n. *churchdom*; military profession, arms 718n. *war*; naval profession, sea; legal profession 953n. *law*; teaching profession, education 534n. *teaching*; medical profession, medicine, practice; business profession, industry, commerce 791n. *trade*; government service, service, administration 733n. *government*; public service, public life; social service 901n. *sociology.*

job, ploys, activities 678n. *activity*; chores, odd jobs, work, task, set task, exercise 682n. *labour*; duty, charge, commission,

mission, errand, quest 751 n. *mandate*; employ, service, employment, full e.; hours of work, working day, work-day; occupation, situation, position, berth, incumbency, appointment, post, office; regular employment, full-time job, permanency; temporary job, part-time j.; situation wanted, vacancy; labour office, labour exchange, employment agency, Ministry of Labour.

function, what one has to do; capacity, office, duty; realm, province, sphere; scope, field, terms of reference 183 n. *range*; department, line, line of country; role, part; business, job; concern, care, look-out.

Adj. *businesslike*, efficient 694 adj. *skilful*; industrious, busy 678 adj. *active*; vocational, professional, career; industrial, commercial, financial; occupational, functional; official, governmental; routine, systematic 60 adj. *orderly*; work-a-day 610 adj. *habitual*; earning, in employment, employed, self-e.; in hand, on h., on foot 669 adj. *preparatory*.

Vb. *employ*, busy, occupy, take up one's time, fill one's t., keep one engaged; give employment, engage, recruit, hire, enlist, appoint, post 751 vb. *commission*; entertain, take on the payroll, wage 804 vb. *pay*; give a situation to, offer a job to, fill a vacancy, staff with, staff; industrialize.

busy oneself, work, work for 742 vb. *serve*; have a profession, be employed, do a job, earn, earn one's living; take on a job, apply for a j., take a situation, accept a s.; be doing, be up and d. 678 vb. *be busy*; concern oneself with, make it one's business, touch 678 vb. *meddle*; work at, ply.; engage in, turn to, turn one's hand to, take up, engage in, go in for; have to do, have on one's hands, have one's hands full, take on oneself, bear the burden, bear the brunt, take on one's shoulders 917 vb. *incur a duty*; work with one's hands, work with one's brains, ride one's hobby 837 vb. *amuse oneself*.

function, work, go 173 vb. *operate*; fill a role, play one's part, carry on; officiate, act, do the offices, discharge the functions, exercise the f., serve as, do duty, perform the duties, do the work of; substitute, stand in for 755 vb. *deputize*; hold office, hold a portfolio, hold a place, hold down a job, have a job, serve (see *busy oneself*).

do business, transact, negotiate 766 vb. *make terms*; ply a trade, ply a craft, exercise a profession, follow a calling, work at a job; have a business, engage in, carry on, drive a trade, carry on a t., keep shop; do business with, deal w., enter into trade relations 791 vb. *trade*; transact business, mind one's b., attend to one's b., go about one's b.; labour in one's vocation, earn one's living (see *busy oneself*); be an employer, be an industrialist; set up in business, open a shop, put up one's sign.

Adv. *professionally*, in businesslike fashion; in the course of, all in the day's work.

See: 60, 164, 173, 183, 534, 597, 610, 617, 669, 678, 682, 694, 706, 718, 733, 742, 751, 755, 766, 791, 804, 837, 901, 917, 953, 981, 985.

623 Plan

N. *plan*, scheme, design; planning, contrivance; organization, systematization, rationalization, centralization 60 n. *order*; programme, project, proposal 617 n. *intention*; proposition, suggestion, motion, resolution (see *policy*); master-plan, five-year p., detailed p.; ground-p., blueprint 551 n. *map*; sketch, outline, rough scheme, pilot s., draft, first d., memorandum; skeleton, rough cast; model, dummy 23 n. *prototype*; proof, revise, proof copy, show c. 22 n. *copy*; planning office, back room, headquarters, base of operations.

policy, forethought 510 n. *foresight*; statesmanship 498 n. *wisdom*; course of action, procedure, strategy 688 n. *tactics*; address, approach, attack 624 n. *way*; steps, measures 676 n. *action*; stroke of policy, coup d'état 676 n. *deed*; proposed action, forecast 511 n. *prediction*; programme, prospectus, platform, plank, ticket, slate; schedule, agenda, order of the day 622 n. *business*; line, party l.

contrivance, expedient, resource, recourse, resort, card, trump, card up one's sleeve 629 n. *means*; recipe, receipt, nostrum 658 n. *remedy*; loophole, way out, alternative, answer 667 n. *means of escape*; artifice, device, gimmick, dodge, shift, flag of convenience 698 n. *stratagem*; wangle, fiddle 930 n. *foul play*; knack,

trick 694n. *skill*; stunt, wheeze; inspiration, hit, happy thought, bright idea, right i. 451n. *idea*; notion, invention; tool, weapon, contraption, gadget 628n. *instrument*; ad hoc measure, improvisation 609n. *spontaneity*; makeshift, make-do 150n. *substitute*; feat, tour de force; stroke, master-s., coup 676n. *deed*.

plot, sub-p., under-p.; deep-laid plot, intrigue; web, web of intrigue, practice; cabal, conspiracy, inside job; frame-up, machination; manipulation, wire-pulling 612n. *motive*; secret influence 523n. *latency*; counterplot, countermine 713n. *defence*; argument 590n. *narrative*.

planner, contriver, engineer, framer, inventor, originator, hatcher; proposer, promoter, projector; founder, author, builder; designer, schematist, backroom boy, boffin 696n. *expert*; organizer, systematizer; strategist, tactician, manoeuvrer; statesman, politician, Machiavellian; schemer, axe-grinder; careerist, go-getter 678n. *busy person*; plotter, intriguer, intrigant, spinner, spider; cabal, conspirator; fifth column, fifth columnist.

Adj. *planned*, blueprinted, schematic, worked out, matured 669adj. *prepared*; organized, systematized 60adj. *orderly*; under consideration, in draft, in proof; strategic, tactical; framed, plotted, engineered.

planning, contriving, resourceful, ingenious 698adj. *cunning*; purposeful, scheming, up to something; involved, deep in; intriguing, plotting, conspiratorial; Machiavellian.

Vb. *plan*, resolve 617vb. *intend*; approach, approach a problem, attack; make a plan, draw up, design, draft, blueprint; frame, shape 243vb. *efform*; revise, recast 654vb. *rectify*; project, plan out, work o., cut o., sketch o., chalk o., strike o., map o., lay o.; programme, lay down a plan, lay the foundation; shape a course, mark out a c.; organize, systematize, rationalize, schematize, methodize 60vb. *order*; schedule, phase, adjust; invent, think up hit on, fall on 484vb. *discover*; find a way, tide over ; contrive, devise, engineer; hatch, concoct, mature 669vb. *prepare*; arrange, prearrange 608vb. *predetermine*; calculate, think ahead, look a. 498vb. *be wise*; have a policy, order one's measures, follow a plan, work to a

schedule; do everything with a purpose, have an axe to grind, grind one's axe.

plot, scheme, have designs, be up to something; manipulate, pull wires 178vb. *influence*; cabal, intrigue, practise; conspire, concert, concoct, hatch a plot, lay a p., lay a train, dig a pit, undermine, countermine 542vb. *ensnare*; work against, manoeuvre a.; frame 541vb. *fake*.

See: 22, 23, 60, 87, 150, 178, 243, 451, 484, 498, 510, 511, 523, 541, 542, 551, 590, 608, 609, 612, 617, 622, 624, 628, 629, 654, 658, 667, 669, 676, 678, 688, 694, 696, 698, 713, 930.

624 Way

N. *way*, route 267n. *itinerary*; manner, wise, guise; fashion, style 243n. *form*; method, mode, line, approach, address, attack; procedure, process, way of, way of doing things, modus operandi 688n. *tactics*; operation, treatment; modus vivendi, working arrangement 770n. *compromise*; usual way, routine 610n. *practice*; technique, know-how 694n. *skill*; going, gait 265n. *motion*; forward way, progress 285n. *progression*; way of life, behaviour 688n. *conduct*. See *route*.

access, means of a., right of way, communications; way to, direct approach 289n. *approach*; entrance, door 263n. *doorway*; side-entrance, back-e., tradesman's e.; adit, drive, gangway; porch, hall, hallway, vestibule, lobby, corridor; way through, pass, defile 305n. *passage*; intersection, junction, crossing; zebra crossing, pedestrian c. 305n. *traffic control*; strait, sound, gut 345n. *gulf*; channel, artery, canal, culvert 351n. *conduit*; lock, stile, turnstile, tollgate; way up, stairs, flight of s., stairway, staircase, step, tread, ladder, step-l., fireman's l. 308n. *ascent*.

bridge, way over; footbridge, overbridge, fly-over; suspension bridge, cantilever b., hump-b.; viaduct, span; railway bridge; bridge of boats, pontoon, floating bridge, bascule-b., Bailey b.; drawbridge; stepping-stone, gangway, gangplank, catwalk, duck-boards; ford, ferry 305n. *passage*; way under, underpass 263n. *tunnel*; bridge-way, culvert, Irish bridge; land-bridge, isthmus, neck.

route, direction, way to, way through, way by, way up, way over, way out; line, course, march, tack, track, beaten t., beat; trajectory, orbit; lane, traffic l., air l., sea l., sea-path; short cut, by-pass; détour, circumbendibus, roundabout way 626n. *circuit*; line of communication, line of retreat, line of advance.

path, pathway, footpath, sidewalk, pavement, by-path, tow-p., side-p.; bridlepath, ride, horse-track; by-way, lane, track, sheep-t., trail, mountain t.; glade, walk, run, drive, carriage-d.; promenade, esplanade, parade, front, sea-f., avenue, boulevard, mall 192n. *street*; arcade, colonnade, aisle, cloister, ambulatory; race-track, running t., speed-t. 724n. *arena*; channel, fairway.

road, high-r., highway, Queen's h., highways and by-ways; main road, side-r., approach r., service r., private r., occupation r.; turnpike, pike, national road, route nationale; thoroughfare, through road, trunk r., arterial r., artery, by-pass; motor road, autobahn, autostrada, speedtrack, express-way, throughway, parkway; motorway; slipway, acceleration lane; clearway 305n. *traffic control*; crossroad, crossways, junction, intersection, roundabout, clover leaf; crossing, pedestrian c., zebra c.; roadway, carriageway, dual c., twin-track; paved road, pavement, causeway, chaussée 192n. *street*; high street, one-way s., two-way s., sides.; alley-way, wynd, alley, blind a., cul-de-sac; pavement, sidewalk, trottoir, kerb, kerbstone; paving, pavé, cobbles, paving-stone, flag, flagstones; macadam, tarmac, asphalt; surface, road-s., skidproof s.; road-building, traffic engineering.

railroad, railway, line; permanent way, track, lines, railway l., tram-l.; monorail, funicular, cableway, ropeway, telpher line; overhead railway, elevated r., underground r., subway, tube 274n. *train*; light railway, metre gauge, broad g., standard g.; junction, level crossing, tunnel, cutting; siding, marshalling yard; station, stop, whistle s., platform 145n. *stopping place*; signal, signal box, cabin; rails, points, sleepers, frog, fishplate.

Adj. *communicating*, granting access; through, main, arterial, trunk; bridged, fly-over; paved, metalled, cobbled; well-paved, well-laid, smooth, skid-proof; signposted, lit, well-lit; trafficky, busy; trodden, beaten.

Adv. *via*, by way of, in transit.
how, in what manner? by what means? on what lines?

See: 145, 192, 243, 263, 265, 267, 274, 285, 289, 305, 308, 345, 351, 610, 626, 688, 694, 724, 770.

625 Mid-course

N. *mid-course*, middle course, middle of the road, via media; balance, golden mean, happy m., mediocrity, aurea mediocritas 30n. *average*; central position, half-way, half-way house, mid-stream 30n. *middle point*; slack water, half tide; direct course, non-deviation, straight line, short cut, bee-line, short circuit 249n. *straightness*; great-circle sailing 269n. *navigation*; non-committal, neutrality, correctness 177n. *moderation*; lukewarmness, half-measures 601n. *irresolution*; mutual concession 770n. *compromise*.

moderate, non-extremist, Minimalist, Menshevist; middle-of-the-roader, half-and-halfer; neutral, uncommitted person, uncommitted nation; Laodicean.

Adj. *neutral*, impartial, correct 913 adj. *right*; non-committal, uncommitted, unattached; detached 860 adj. *indifferent*; moderate, non-extreme, unextreme, middle-of-the-road 225 adj. *central*; sitting on the fence, lukewarm, half-and-half 601 adj. *irresolute*; neither one thing nor the other, grey.

undeviating, unswerving, keeping to the middle 225 adj. *central*; looking neither to right nor left, direct 249 adj. *straight*; in between, half-way, intermediate 231 adj. *interjacent*.

Vb. *be mid-stream*, keep to the middle, steer a middle course, hold straight on, not deviate, not swerve, look neither to right not to left.

be half-way, go half-way, meet h. 770 vb. *compromise*; be in between, occupy the centre, hold the scales, balance 28 vb. *equalize*; sit on the fence 474 vb. *be uncertain*; trim, equivocate 518 vb. *be equivocal*.

See: 28, 30, 177, 225, 231, 249, 269, 474, 518, 601, 770, 860, 913.

626 Circuit

N. *circuit*, roundabout way, longest w., circuitous route, by-pass, détour, loop, loop-line, divagation, digression 282n. *deviation*; ambages 251n. *convolution*; circulation, circumambulation, ambit, orbit, gyre, round, lap 314n. *circuition*; circumference 250n. *circle*; full circle, looping the loop.

Adj. *roundabout*, circuitous, indirect, out of the way; circumlocutory 570adj. *diffuse*; circulatory, circumambulating; rounding, skirting; encompassing, surrounding 230adj. *circumjacent*.

Vb. *circuit*, round, lap, beat the bounds, go round, make a circuit, loop the loop 314 vb. *circle*; make a detour, go out of one's way 282vb. *deviate*; turn, by-pass, short-circuit 620vb. *avoid*; lead one a dance, beat about the bush; divagate, zigzag 294 vb. *diverge*; encircle, embrace, encompass 230vb. *surround*; keep to the circumference, skirt, edge round.

Adv. *round about*, round the world, in a roundabout way, circuitously, indirectly, from pillar to post.

See: 230, 250, 251, 282, 294, 314, 570, 620.

627 Requirement

N. *requirement*, requisite, desideratum, want, lack, need 636n. *insufficiency*; defect, shortage 42n. *decrement*; stipulation, prerequisite, first condition, prior conditions 766n. *conditions*; essential, sine qua non, a necessary, a must 596n. *necessity*; needs, necessities, necessaries; indent, order, requisition, shopping list; demand, consumer d., call for, run upon, seller's market 792n. *purchase*; consumption, input, intake 634n. *waste*; balance due, what is owing 803n. *debt*; claim 761n. *request*; ultimatum, imposition, mandate, charge, injunction 737n. *command*.

needfulness, case of need, occasion; necessity for, essentiality, indispensability, desirability; necessitousness, want, pinch, stress 801n. *poverty*; exigence 740n. *compulsion*; urgency, emergency 137n. *crisis*; vitalness, matter of life and death 638n. *important matter*; obligation 917n. *duty*; bare minimum, the least one can do, face-saving measures; possible need, in-casement.

Adj. *required*, requisite, prerequisite, needful, needed; necessary, essential, vital, indispensable, not to be spared; called for, in request, in demand 859adj. *desired*; reserved, earmarked, booked; wanted, lacking, missing, desiderated, to seek 190adj. *absent*.

necessitous, in want, in need, pinched, feeling the pinch; lacking, deprived of; needing badly, craving; destitute 801adj. *poor*; starving 636adj. *underfed*.

demanding, crying, crying out for, calling for, imperative, urgent, instant, exigent, pressing, pinching; compulsory 740adj. *compelling*.

Vb. *require*, need, want, lack 636vb. *be unsatisfied*; not have, be without, stand in need of, feel a need, have occasion for; miss, desiderate; need badly, crave 859vb. *desire*; call for, cry out f., shout f., clamour f.; claim, put in a claim for, apply f. 761vb. *request*; find necessary, find indispensable, be unable to do without, must have; consume, take 634vb. *waste*; create a need, invent a want, render necessary, necessitate, oblige 740vb. *compel*; make demands, raise a demand 737vb. *demand*; stipulate 766vb. *give terms*; order, send an order for, indent, requisition 633vb. *provide*; reserve, book, earmark.

Adv. *in need*, in want; necessarily, sine qua non; of necessity, at a pinch.

See: 42, 137, 190, 596, 633, 634, 636, 638, 737, 740, 761, 766, 792, 801, 803, 859, 917.

628 Instrumentality

N. *instrumentality*, operation 173n. *agency*; occasion 156n. *cause*; result 157n. *effect*; pressure 178n. *influence*; efficacy 160n. *power*; occult power, magic 983n. *sorcery*; services, help, assistance, midwifery 703n. *aid*; support 706n. *co-operation*; intervention, intermediacy, interference 678n. *activity*; subservience 739n. *obedience*; medium 629n. *means*; use, employment, application, serviceability, handiness 640n. *utility*; use of machinery, instrumentation, mechanization, automation 630n. *machine*.

Instrument, hand, organ, sense o.; hand-maid, minister, slave, slave of the lamp 742 n. *servant*; agent, midwife, medium, help, assistant 703 n. *aider*; pawn, piece on the board 837 n. *chessman*; robot 630 n. *machine*; cat's-paw, stooge; weapon, implement, appliance, lever 630 n. *tool*; magic ring, Aladdin's lamp 983 n. *spell*; key, pass-k., skeleton k., latch-k. 263 n. *opener*; open sesame, watchword, pass-word, passport, safeconduct, warrant 756 n. *permit*; stepping-stone 624 n. *bridge*; channel, high road, highway 624 n. *road*; push-button, switch; device, ex-pedient, makeshift, gadget 623 n. *con-trivance*; card, trump.

Adj. *instrumental*, working, automatic, push-button 173 adj. *operative*; effective, efficient, efficacious, effectual 160 adj. *powerful*; telling, weighty 178 adj. *in-fluential*; magic 983 adj. *magical*; con-ducive 156 adj. *causal*; practical, applied; serviceable, general-purpose, employable, handy 640 adj. *useful*; ready, available 597 adj. *willing*; forwarding, promoting, assisting, helpful 703 adj. *aiding*; obstet-ric, maieutic; functional, agential, sub-servient, ministerial; mediational, inter-mediate, intervening; mediated by.

Vb. *be instrumental*, work, act 173 vb. *operate*; perform 676 vb. *do*; minister, serve, work for, subserve, lend oneself (*or* itself) to, pander to 703 vb. *minister to*; help, assist 703 vb. *aid*; advance, promote 703 vb. *patronize*; have a hand in 775 vb. *participate*; be the instrument, be the hand, be a cat's-paw, pull an-other's chestnuts out of the fire 640 vb. *be useful*; intermediate, interpose, inter-vene 720 vb. *mediate*; use one's influence, pull strings 178 vb. *influence*; effect 156 vb. *cause*; tend 156 vb. *conduce*; achieve 725 vb. *carry through*.

Adv. *through*, per, by the hand of, by means of, using the help of.

See: 156, 157, 160, 173, 178, 263, 597, 623, 624, 629, 630, 640, 676, 678, 703, 706, 720, 725, 739, 742, 756, 775, 837, 983.

629 Means

N. *means*, ways and m., wherewithal; power, capacity 160 n. *ability*; good hand, card, right c., trump, aces; conveniences,

facilities; appliances, tools, tools of the trade, bag of tricks 630 n. *tool*; technique, know-how 694 n. *skill*; equipment, sup-plies, stock, munitions, ammunition 633 n. *provision*; resources, economic r., natural r., raw material 631 n. *materials*; labour resources, pool of labour, man-power 686 n. *personnel*; financial re-sources, sinews of war 800 n. *wealth*; liquidity 797 n. *money*; capital, working c. 628 n. *instrument*; assets, stock-in-trade 777 n. *property*; stocks and shares, invest-ments, investment portfolio; revenue, income, receipts, credits 807 n. *receipt*; borrowing capacity, line of credit 802 n. *credit*; reserves, stand-by, shot in one's locker, card up one's sleeve, two strings to one's bow 662 n. *safeguard*; freedom of choice, alternative 605 n. *choice*; method, measures, steps 624 n. *way*; cure, specific 658 n. *remedy*; expedient, device, resort, recourse 623 n. *contrivance*; make-shift, ad hoc measure 150 n. *substitute*; let-out 667 n. *means of escape*; desperate remedy, last resort, last hope, last throw 618 n. *gambling*; method of working, mechanical means 630 n. *mechanics*.

Vb. *find means*, provide the wherewithal, supply, find, furnish 633 vb. *provide*; equip, fit out 669 vb. *make ready*; finance, raise the money, promote, float; have the means, be able, be in a position to 160 vb. *be able*; contrive, be resourceful, not be at a loss, find a way 623 vb. *plan*; beg, borrow or steal, get by hook or by crook 771 vb. *acquire*.

Adv. *by means of*, with, wherewith; by, using, through; with the aid of; by dint of.

See: 150, 160, 605, 618, 623, 624, 628, 630, 631, 633, 658, 662, 667, 669, 686, 694, 771, 777, 797, 800, 802, 807.

630 Tool

N. *tool*, precision t., implement 628 n. *in-strument*; apparatus, appliance, utensil; weapon, arm 723 n. *arms*; device, mechani-cal d., gadget 623 n. *contrivance*; mechani-cal aid, inclined plane; screw, turnscrew, screwdriver 263 n. *perforator*; wrench, spanner; pliers, tweezers 778 n. *nippers*; chisel, wedge, edged tool 256 n. *sharp edge*; rope 47 n. *cable*; peg, nail 217 n. *hanger*, 218 n. *support*; leverage, lever,

jemmy, crow, crowbar, handspike, jack 218n. *pivot*; grip, lug, helve, haft, shaft, thill, tiller, helm, rudder 218n. *handle*; pulley, sheave, parbuckle 250n. *wheel*; switch, cock, stopcock; gunlock, trigger; pedal, pole, punt-p. 287n. *propulsion*; prehistoric tool, flint; tools of the trade, tool-kit, do-it-yourself k., bag of tricks.

machine, mechanical device; machinery, mechanism, works; clockwork, wheel-work, wheels within wheels; spring, mainspring, hairspring; gears, gearing, spur g., bevel g., syncromesh, automatic change; motor, engine, internal combustion e., diesel e., gas e., steam e.; robot, automation; learning machine, self-organizing system.

mechanics, engineering, telemechanics; servo-mechanics, cybernetics; automatic control, automation; mechanical power, mechanical advantage; technicology, technology.

equipment, furniture, appointments; gear, tackle 47n. *tackling*; fittings, fixture 40 adj. *adjunct*; upholstery, furnishing, soft f.; outfit, kit; trappings, accoutrement 228n. *dress*; harness 226n. *covering*; utensils, impedimenta, paraphernalia, chattels 777n. *property*; ware, stock-in-trade 795n. *merchandise*.

machinist, operator, driver, minder, machine-m. 686n. *agent*; engineer, mechanic, fitter; tool-user, craftsman 686n. *artisan*.

Adj. *mechanical*, mechanistic, powered, power-driven; automatic; robot, self-acting 628adj. *instrumental*; machine-minded, tool-using.

See: 40, 47, 217, 218, 226, 228, 250, 256, 263, 287, 623, 628, 686, 723, 777, 778, 795.

631 Materials

N. *materials*, resources 629n. *means*; material, stuff, staple, stock 3n. *substance*; raw material, grist; meat, fodder 301n. *food*; oil 385n. *fuel*; chemical material, fissionable m., uranium, thorium; ore, mineral, metal, pig-iron, ingot; clay, adobe, china clay, potter's c., argil, kaolin, gypsum 344n. *soil*; crockery 381n. *pottery*; plastic, latex, celluloid; rope, cord, fibre glass 208n. *fibre*; leather 226n. *skin*; timber, log, faggot, stick 366n. *wood*; rafter, beam, balk, stretcher,

board, plank, planking, lath, stave 207n. *lamina*; cloth, fabric 222n. *textile*.

building material, brick 381n. *pottery*; bricks and mortar, lath and plaster, slate, tile, shingle, stone, marble, rance, ashlar, masonry; compo, composition, cement, concrete, ferro-concrete; paving material, flag, flagstone, cobble; gravel, macadam, tarmac, asphalt.

paper, rag-p., pulp, wood-p., newsprint; calendered paper, art p., drawing p., carbon p., tissue-p.; papier mâché, cardboard, pasteboard, straw-board, carton; sheet, foolscap, quire, ream; note-paper 586n. *stationery*.

See: 3, 207, 208, 222, 226, 301, 344, 366, 381, 385, 586, 629.

632 Store

N. *store*, mass, heap, load, stack, stock-pile, build-up 74n. *accumulation*; packet, bundle, budget, bagful 26n. *quantity*; harvest, crop, vintage, mow 771n. *acquisition*; haystack, haycock, rick, hay-r.; stock, stock-in-trade 795n. *merchandise*; assets, capital, holding, investment 777n. *property*; fund, reserve f., reserves, something in hand, backlog; unexpended balance, savings, savings account, nest-egg; deposit, hoard, treasure, honey-comb; buried treasure, cache 527n. *hiding place*; bottom drawer, hope chest, trousseau, two of everything 633n. *provision*; pool, kitty; common fund, common stock, community chest 775n. *joint possession*; quarry, mine, gold-m.; natural deposit, mineral d., coal d.; coal-field, gas-f., oil-f.; coal-mine, colliery, working, shaft; coal-face, seam, stringer, lode; pipe, pipe-vein; vein, rich v.; bonanza, strike 484n. *discovery*; well, oil-w., gusher; fountain, fount 156n. *source*; supply, constant s., stream; tap, pipe-line; milch-cow, cornucopia, abundance 635n. *plenty*; repertoire, range (see *collection*).

storage, stowage, gathering, garnering 74n. *accumulation*; conservation, ensilage, bottling 666n. *preservation*; safe deposit 660n. *protection*; stabling, warehousing; storage, storage space, shelf-room, space, accommodation 183n. *room*; hold, bunker 194n. *cellar*; store-town, supply base,

promptuary, storehouse, store-room, stockroom; warehouse, goods-shed, godown; depository, depot, entrepôt; dock, wharf, garage 192n. *stable*; magazine, arsenal, armoury, gun-room; treasurehouse 799n. *treasury*; exchequer, bank, safe, strongroom, vault, coffer, moneybox, money-bag, till, slot-machine; hive, honeycomb; granary, garner, barn, silo, silo pit; reservoir, cistern, tank, gasholder, gasometer; battery, storage b., dry b., wet b.; garage, petrol station, filling s., petrol pump; dump, sump, drain, cesspool, sewage farm 649n. *sink*; panary, pantry, larder, buttery, still-room 194n. *chamber*; spence, cupboard, shelf 194n. *cabinet*; refrigerator, fridge, deepfreeze; portmanteau, hold-all, packing-case 194n. *box*; container, holder, quiver 194n. *receptacle*.

collection, set, complete s.; archives, file 548n. *record*; folder, bundle, portfolio 74n. *accumulation*; museum, antiquarium 125n. *antiquity*; gallery, art g.; book-collection, library, thesaurus 559n. *dictionary*; menagerie, aquarium 369n. *zoo*; waxworks, exhibition 522n. *exhibit*; repertory, repertoire, bag of tricks.

Adj. *stored*, hived etc.vb.; in store, in deposit; in hand, held; in reserve, unexpended; banked, funded, invested; available, in stock; spare, supernumerary.

Vb. *store*, stow, pack, bundle 193vb. *load*; roll up, fold up; lay up, stow away, put a.; dump, garage, stable, warehouse; garner, barn; gather, harvest, reap, mow, pick, glean 370n. *cultivate*; stack, heap, pile, amass, accumulate 74vb. *bring together*; stock up, lay in, stockpile, pile up, build up, build up one's stocks 36vb. *augment*; take on, take in, fuel, coal, bunker 633vb. *provide*; fill, fill up, top up, refill, refuel 633vb. *replenish*; put by, save, keep, hold, file, hang on to, keep by one 778vb. *retain*; bottle, bottle up, pickle 666vb. *preserve*; leave, set aside, keep back, keep in hand, reserve, put to r.; fund, bank, deposit, invest; hoard, treasure, hive; bury, hide 525vb. *conceal*; husband, save up, salt away, make a nest-egg, prepare for a rainy day 814vb. *economize*; equip oneself, put in the bottom drawer 669vb. *prepare oneself*; pool, put in the kitty 775vb. *socialize*.

See: 26, 36, 74, 125, 156, 183, 192, 193, 194, 369, 370, 484, 522, 525, 527, 548, 559, 633, 635, 649, 660, 666, 669, 771, 775, 777, 778, 795, 799, 814.

633 Provision

N. *provision*, providing, furnishing, logistics, equipment 669n. *fitting out*; purveyance, catering; service, delivery; self-service; procuring, pandering; feeding, entertainment, bed and board, board and lodging, maintenance; assistance, lending, lend-lease 703n. *subvention*; supply, food-s., water-s., constant s., feed; commissariat, provisioning, supplies, stores, rations, iron r., emergency r., reserves 632n. *store*; reinforcement, replenishment, refill, filling-up 54n. *plenitude*; food, sizing 301n. *provisions*; provender; help, helping, portion 301n. *meal*; grist, grist to the mill; fuel, fuel to the flame; produce 164n. *product*; increase, return 771n. *gain*; budgeting, budget 808n. *accounts*; possible need, incasement 669n. *preparation*.

provider, donor 781n. *giver*; creditor, money-lender, uncle 784n. *lender*; wetnurse, feeder; purser 798n. *treasurer*; steward, butler, pantler, comprador, commissary, quartermaster, storekeeper; supplier, victualler, sutler; provision merchant, drysalter, grocer, green-g., baker, poulterer, fishmonger, butcher, vintner, wine merchant; retailer, middleman, shopkeeper 794n. *tradesman*; procurer, pander, pimp 952n. *bawd*.

caterer, purveyor, hotelier, hotelkeeper, restaurateur; innkeeper, alewife, landlord, mine host, publican; housekeeper, housewife; cook, chef; pastry-cook, confectioner.

Adj. *provisionary*, commissarial; self-service; sufficing, all-s. 635adj. *sufficient*; supplied, provided, well-found, all found; available, on tap, on the menu, on 189adj. *present*.

Vb. *provide*, afford, offer, lend 781vb. *give*; provision, find, find one in; equip, furnish, arm, man, fit out 669vb. *make ready*; supply, suppeditate; maintain supply, keep fed with; yield 164vb. *produce*; bring in a supply, lead, pump in, pipeline; cater, purvey; procure, pander, pimp; service, service an order, fill an o.

793 vb. *sell*; deliver, make deliveries, deliver the goods; hand out, hand round, serve, serve up, dish up; victual, feed, cook for, board, put up, maintain, keep, clothe; stock, keep a s.; budget, make provision, make due p.; provide for oneself, provision o., take on supplies, stock up, lay in a stock 632 vb. *store*; fuel, coal, bunker; gather food, forage, water; tap, draw, draw on, milk 304 vb. *extract*; export, import 791 vb. *trade*.

replenish, reinforce, recruit, make good, make up; fill up, top up, refill 54 vb. *fill*; revictual, restock, refuel, reload.

See: 54, 164, 189, 301, 304, 632, 635, 669, 703, 771, 781, 784, 791, 793, 794, 798, 808, 952.

634 Waste

N. *waste*, wastage 42 n. *decrement*; leakage, ebb 298 n. *outflow*; inroad, consumption; intake 627 n. *requirement*; spending, outlay, expense 806 n. *expenditure*; using up, depletion, exhaustion, drainage 300 n. *voidance*; dissipation 75 n. *dispersion*; evaporation 338 n. *vaporization*; melting 337 n. *liquefaction*; damage 772 n. *loss*; wear and tear 655 n. *deterioration*; wastefulness, uneconomy, over-lavishness, extravagance, overspending, unnecessary expenditure 815 n. *prodigality*; misapplication, useless expenditure, frittering away 675 n. *misuse*; mischief, wanton destruction, destructiveness, sabotage 165 n. *destruction*; waste product, refuse, exhaust 641 n. *rubbish*.

Adj. *wasteful*, extravagant, unnecessary, uneconomic 815 adj. *prodigal*; mischievous 165 adj. *destructive*.

wasted, exhausted, depleted, consumed; gone to waste, gone down the sink; fruitless, bootless, profitless 641 adj. *useless*; ill-spent, misapplied; of no avail, futile, in vain.

Vb. *waste*, consume, make inroads on, wade into; drink, swallow, devour, eat up 301 vb. *eat*; spend, lay out 806 vb. *expend*; take, use up, exhaust, deplete, drain, suck dry 300 vb. *void*; dissipate, scatter, broadcast 75 vb. *disperse*; abuse, overstrain, overwork, overcrop, impoverish, milk, milk dry 675 vb. *misuse*; wear out, dilapidate, damage 655 vb. *impair*; put to wrong use, misapply, fritter away, cast

before swine; make no use of 674 vb. *not use*; labour in vain 641 vb. *waste effort*; be extravagant, overspend, squander, run through, throw away, pour down the drain, burn the candle at both ends 815 vb. *be prodigal*; be careless, slop, spill; be destructive, ruin, destroy, sabotage, play havoc 165 vb. *lay waste*; be wasted, wane, decay, suffer loss 37 vb. *decrease*; leak, ebb, run low, dry up 298 vb. *flow out*; melt, melt away 337 vb. *liquefy*; evaporate 338 vb. *vaporize*; run out, give o. 636 vb. *not suffice*; burn out, burn away, gutter 381 vb. *burn*; run to seed 655 vb. *deteriorate*; run to waste, go down the drain.

See: 37, 42, 75, 165, 298, 300, 301, 337, 338, 381, 627, 636, 641, 655, 674, 675, 772, 806, 815.

635 Sufficiency

N. *sufficiency*, right amount; right qualities, qualification; right number, quorum; adequacy, enough, pass marks; assets, adequate income, competence, living wage; exact requirement, no surplus; minimum, no less, bare minimum, least one can do; full measure, satisfaction, ample s., contentment, all that could be desired 828 n. *content*; acceptability, the possible, all that is p. 469 n. *possibility*; fulfilment 725 n. *completion*; repletion, one's fill, bellyful 863 n. *satiety*.

plenty, God's p., horn of p., cornucopia 171 n. *abundance*; outpouring, showers of, flood, tide, spate, streams 350 n. *stream*; lots, lashings, galore 32 n. *great quantity*; fullness, copiousness, amplitude 54 n. *plenitude*; affluence, riches 800 n. *wealth*; fat of the land, luxury, full table, feast, banquet 301 n. *feasting*; orgy, riot, profusion 815 n. *prodigality*; richness, fat; fertility, productivity, luxuriance, lushness, rankness 171 n. *productiveness*; foison, harvest, rich h., bumper crop; rich vein, bonanza, ample store, more where it came from 632 n. *store*; more than enough, too much, superabundance 637 n. *redundance*.

Adj. *sufficient*, sufficing, all-s. 633 adj. *provisionary*; self-sufficient 54 adj. *complete*; enough, adequate, competent; equal to, a match for 28 adj. *equal*; satisfactory, satisfying 828 adj. *contenting*;

measured, commensurate, up to the mark; just right, not too much, not too little; barely sufficient, no more than enough; usable 673 adj. *used*; makeshift, provisional 150 adj. *substituted*.

plenteous, plentiful, ample, enough and to spare, more than enough 637 adj. *superfluous*; open-handed, generous, lavish 813 adj. *liberal*; extravagant 815 adj. *prodigal*; wholesale, without stint, unsparing, unmeasured, exhaustless, inexhaustible 32 adj. *great*; luxuriant, luxuriating, riotous, lush, rank, fertile, fat 171 adj. *productive*; profuse, abundant, copious, overflowing 637 adj. *redundant*; rich, opulent, affluent 800 adj. *moneyed*.

filled, well-f., flush 54 adj. *full*; chock-full, replete, satiated 863 adj. *sated*; satisfied, contented 828 adj. *content*; well-provided, well-stocked, well-furnished 633 adj. *provisionary*; rich in, teeming, crawling with 104 adj. *multitudinous*.

Vb. *suffice*, be enough, do, answer 642 vb. *be expedient*; just do, work, serve, serve as a makeshift; qualify, reach, make the grade 727 vb. *be successful*; pass, pass muster, wash; measure up to, meet requirements, fill the bill; do all that is possible, rise to the occasion; stand, stand up to, take the strain 218 vb. *support*; do the needful 725 vb. *carry out*; fill, fill up, saturate 54 vb. *complete*; refill 633 vb. *replenish*; prove acceptable, satisfy 828 vb. *content*; more than satisfy, satiate, give one his bellyful 863 vb. *sate*; provide for, make adequate provision 633 vb. *provide*.

abound, be plentiful, proliferate, teem, swarm, bristle with, crawl w. 104 vb. *be many*; exuberate, riot, luxuriate 171 vb. *be fruitful*; flow, shower, snow, pour, stream, sheet 350 vb. *rain*; brim, overflow 637 vb. *superabound*; roll in, wallow in, swim in 800 vb. *be rich*.

have enough, be satisfied 828 vb. *be content*; eat one's fill 301 vb. *eat*; drink one's fill 301 vb. *drink*; be sated, have one's bellyful, be fed up 829 vb. *be discontented*; have the means 800 vb. *afford*.

Adv. *enough*, sufficiently, amply, to the full, to one's heart's content; ad libitum, ad-lib, on tap, on demand; abundantly, inexhaustibly, interminably.

See: 28, 32, 54, 104, 150, 171, 218, 301, 350, 469, 632, 633, 637, 642, 673, 725, 727, 800, 813, 815, 828, 829, 863.

636 Insufficiency

N. *insufficiency*, not enough; non-satisfaction 829 n. *discontent*; inadequacy, incompetence; minginess, little enough, nothing to spare, less than somewhat 33 n. *small quantity*; too few, no quorum 105 n. *fewness*; deficiency, imperfection 647 n. *defect*; deficit 55 n. *incompleteness*; non-fulfilment 726 n. *non-completion*; half-measures, tinkering, failure, weakness 307 n. *shortcoming*; bankruptcy 805 n. *insolvency*; bare subsistence, subsistence level, pittance, dole, mite; stinginess 816 n. *parsimony*; short allowance, short commons, iron rations, half r.; austerity, Lenten fare, Spartan f., starvation diet, bread and water 945 n. *asceticism*; fast day 946 n. *fasting*.

scarcity, scarceness, paucity 140 n. *infrequency*; dearth, leanness, seven lean years; drought, famine, starvation; infertility 172 n. *unproductiveness*; shortfall 307 n. *shortcoming*; power-cut 37 n. *decrease*; short supply, seller's market; stint, scantiness, meagreness 801 n. *poverty*; lack, want, need 627 n. *needfulness*; ebb, low water 212 n. *shallowness*.

Adj. *insufficient*, not satisfying, unsatisfactory, disappointing 829 adj. *discontenting*; inadequate, not enough, too little; too small, cramping 33 adj. *small*; deficient, lacking 55 adj. *incomplete*; wanting, found w., poor 35 adj. *inferior*; incompetent, unequal to, not up to it 695 adj. *unskilful*; weak, thin, watery, unnourishing 4 adj. *insubstantial*; niggardly, sparing, mingy 816 adj. *parsimonious*.

unprovided; unsupplied, unfurnished, ill-furnished, ill-supplied, unreplenished; vacant, bare 190 adj. *empty*; empty-handed 728 adj. *unsuccessful*; unsatisfied, unfilled, unsated 829 adj. *discontented*; insatiable 859 adj. *greedy*; deficient in, starved of; cramped 702 adj. *hindered*; under-capitalized, understaffed, undermanned, under-officered; stinted, rationed, skimped; not provided, unavailable, off the menu, off 190 adj. *absent*.

underfed, undernourished, under-vitaminized; half-fed, half-starved, on short commons; unfed, famished, starved, famine-stricken, starving 946 adj. *fasting*; starveling, spare, scurvy, thin, meagre, scrimp, stunted, jejune 206 adj. *lean*.

scarce, rare 140 adj. *infrequent*; sparse 105

adj. *few*; short, in short supply, hard to get, hard to come by, not to be had, unavailable, unprocurable, unobtainable, out of season, out of stock.

Vb. *not suffice*, be insufficient, —inadequate etc. adj.; not meet requirements 647 vb. *be imperfect*; want, lack, need, require, leave a gap 627 vb. *require*; fail 509 vb. *disappoint*; fall below 35 vb. *be inferior*; come short, default 307 vb. *fall short*; run out, dry up; take half measures, tinker, paper over the cracks 726 vb. *not complete*.

be unsatisfied, ask for more, beg for m., come again, take a second helping, feel hungry 859 vb. *be hungry*; feel dissatisfied, increase one's demands 829 vb. *be discontented*; spurn an offer, reject with contempt 607 vb. *reject*; desiderate, miss, want, feel the lack, stand in need of, feel something is missing 627 vb. *require*; be a glutton for, be unable to have enough of 947 vb. *gluttonize*.

make insufficient, ask *or* expect too much; overwork, overcrop, impoverish, damage 655 vb. *impair*; exhaust, deplete, run down, squander 634 vb. *waste*; stint, skimp, scant, ration, put on half rations, put on short commons, put on short allowance 816 vb. *be parsimonious*; disinherit, cut off with a shilling 786 vb. *deprive*; cramp 747 vb. *restrain*.

Adv. *insufficiently*, not enough; in default, failing, for want of.

See: 4, 33, 35, 37, 55, 105, 140, 172, 190, 206, 212, 307, 509, 607, 627, 634, 647, 655, 695, 702, 726, 728, 747, 786, 801, 805, 816, 829, 859, 945, 946, 947.

637 Redundance

N. *redundance*, over-brimming, overspill, overflow, inundation, flood 298 n. *outflow*; abundance, superabundance, exuberance, luxuriance, riot, profusion 635 n. *plenty*; richness, bonanza 632 n. *store*; upsurge, uprush 36 n. *increase*; avalanche, spate 32 n. *great quantity*; too many, mob 74 n. *crowd*; saturation, saturation point, over-saturation 54 n. *plenitude*; excessiveness, nimiety, exorbitance, excess, extremes, too much 546 n. *exaggeration*; overdoing it, over-extension, over-expansion, too many irons in the fire 678 n.

overactivity; over-politeness, officiousness; overpraise, over-optimism 482 n. *overestimation*; overmeasure, overpayment, overweight; burden, load, overload, last straw 322 n. *gravity*; more than is fair, lion's share 32 n. *main part*; overindulgence 943 n. *intemperance*; overfeeding 947 n. *gluttony*; overdrinking 949 n. *drunkenness*; overdose, surfeit, engorgement, plethora, congestion 863 n. *satiety*; more than enough, bellyful 635 n. *satisfaction*; glut, drug on the market (see *superfluity*); fat, fattiness.

superfluity, more than is needed, luxury, luxuriousness; luxuries, non-necessaries, luxury article; overfulfilment, duplication, supererogation, work of s.; something over, bonus, spare cash, money to burn 40 n. *extra*; margin, overlap, excess, overplus, surplusage, surplus, balance 41 n. *remainder*; superfluousness, excrescence, accessory, parasite 641 n. *inutility*; useless word, expletive, verse-filler 570 n. *pleonasm*; tautology 570 n. *diffuseness*; redundancy, more men than jobs, under-employment, unemployment 679 n. *inactivity*; more jobs than men, over-employment 678 n. *activity*; too much of a good thing, glut, drug on the market; surfeit, sickener, overdose 863 n. *satiety*.

Adj. *redundant*, too many, one too m. 104 adj. *many*; overmuch, excessive 32 adj. *exorbitant*; overdone 546 adj. *exaggerated*; overflowing, overfull, slopping, running over, brimming, filled to overflowing 54 adj. *full*; flooding, streaming 350 adj. *flowing*; saturated, supersaturated 341 adj. *drenched*; cloying, satiating 838 adj. *tedious*; cloyed, satiated 863 adj. *sated*; replete, gorged, crammed, stuffed, bursting; overcharged, overloaded; congested, plethoric; dropsical, turgid 197 adj. *expanded*.

superfluous, supererogatory, supervacaneous; supernumerary; adscititious, excrescent; needless, unnecessary, unrequired, uncalled for 641 adj. *useless*; excessive, more than one asked for; luxury, luxurious; expletive 570 n. *pleonastic*; surplus, extra, over and above 41 adj. *remaining*; above one's needs, spare, to spare 38 adj. *additional*; de trop, on one's hands, a-begging 860 adj. *unwanted*; dispensable, expendable, replaceable 812 adj. *cheap*.

Vb. *superabound*, riot, luxuriate 635 vb. *abound*; run riot, overproduce, overpopulate 171 vb. *be fruitful*; bristle with, burst w., meet one at every turn, outnumber 104 vb. *be many*; overflow, brim over, well o., ooze at every pore, burst at the seams 54 vb. *be complete*; stream, flood, inundate, burst its banks, deluge, overwhelm 350 vb. *flow*; whelm, engulf 299 vb. *absorb*; know no bounds, spread far and wide 306 vb. *overstep*; overlap 183 vb. *extend*; soak, saturate 341 vb. *drench*; stuff, gorge, cram 54 vb. *fill*; congest, choke, suffocate; overdose, oversatisfy, glut, cloy, satiate, sicken 863 vb. *sate*; overfeed, pamper oneself, overeat, overdrink 943 vb. *be intemperate*; overfulfil, oversubscribe, do more than enough; oversell, drug the market; overstock, pile up, overemploy; overdo, pile it on, lay it on thick, lay it on with a trowel 546 vb. *exaggerate*; overload, overburden; overcharge, surcharge; lavish, lavish upon 813 vb. *be liberal*; be lavish, make a splash 815 vb. *be prodigal*; roll in, crawl with, stink of 800 vb. *be rich.*

be superfluous, — redundant etc. adj.; go a-begging, remain on one's hands 41 vb. *be left*; hang heavy on one's hands 679 vb. *be inactive*; do twice over, duplicate; carry coals to Newcastle, gild refined gold, paint the lily, teach one's grandmother to suck eggs; labour the obvious, kill the slain, flog a dead horse 641 vb. *waste effort*; exceed requirements, have no use 641 vb. *be useless*; go in for luxuries.

Adv. *redundantly*, over and above, too much, overly, excessively, beyond measure; enough and to spare; in excess of requirements.

See: 32, 36, 38, 40, 41, 54, 74, 104, 171, 183, 197, 298, 299, 306, 322, 341, 350, 482, 546, 570, 632, 635, 641, 678, 679, 800, 812, 813, 815, 838, 860, 863, 943, 947, 949.

638 Importance

N. *importance*, first i., primacy, priority, urgency 64 n. *precedence*; paramountcy, supremacy 34 n. *superiority*; essentiality, irreplaceability; import, consequence, significance, weight, weightiness, gravity, seriousness, solemnity; materiality, materialness, substance, pith, moment 3 n. *substantiality*; interest, consideration, concern 622 n. *business*; notability, memorability, mark, prominence, distinction, eminence 866 n. *repute*; influence 866 n. *prestige*; size, magnitude 32 n. *greatness*; rank, optimacy 868 n. *nobility*; value, excellence, merit 644 n. *goodness*; use, usefulness 640 n. *utility*; stress, emphasis, insistence 532 n. *affirmation*.

important matter, vital concern; turning point 137 n. *crisis*; breath of one's nostrils, be-all and end-all; grave affair, not peanuts, no joke, no laughing matter, matter of life and death; notable point, memorandum, memoranda, notandum 505 n. *reminder*; big news, great n. 529 n. *news*; great doings, exploit 676 n. *deed*; red-letter day, great d. 876 n. *special day.*

chief thing, what matters, the thing, great t., main t.; issue, supreme i. 452 n. *topic*; fundamentals, bedrock, fact 1 n. *reality*; essential, sine qua non 627 n. *requirement*; priority, first choice 605 n. *choice*; gist 514 n. *meaning*; substance 5 n. *essential part*; best part, cream, salt, pick 644 n. *élite*; keynote, cornerstone, mainstay; head and front, spearhead; sum and substance, heart of the matter, heart, core, hard c., kernel, nucleus, nub 225 n. *centre*; hub 218 n. *pivot*; cardinal point, main p., salient p., half the battle 32 n. *main part*; chief hope, trump card, main chance.

bigwig, personage, notability, personality, man of mark 866 n. *person of repute*; great man, V.I.P., brass hat; his nibs, big shot, big noise, big bug, big wheel, big man on campus, B.M.O.C.; great card, panjandrum; leading light, master spirit 500 n. *sage*; king pin, key man 696 n. *expert*; first fiddle, prima donna, star, catch, great c. 890 n. *favourite*; lion, big game; uncrowned king, head, chief, Mr. Big 34 n. *superior*; superior person, superman, wonderman, lord of creation; king, lord 868 n. *nobility*; summit, top people, establishment 733 n. *authority.*

Adj. *important*, weighty, grave, solemn, serious; pregnant, big; of weight, of consideration, of importance, of concern; considerable, worth considering; world-shattering, earth-shaking, seismic 178 adj. *influential*; momentous, critical, fateful 137 adj. *timely*; chief, capital, cardinal,

staple, major, main, paramount 34 adj. *supreme*; essential, material, to the point 9 adj. *relevant*; pivotal 225 n. *central*; basic, fundamental, bedrock, radical, going to the root; primary, prime, foremost, leading; overriding, overruling, uppermost 34 adj. *superior*; worth-while, not to be despised, not to be overlooked, not to be sneezed at 644 adj. *valuable*; necessary, indispensable, irreplaceable, key 627 adj. *required*; helpful 640 adj. *useful*; significant, telling, trenchant 514 adj. *meaningful*; pressing, insistent, urgent, high-priority; overdue 136 adj. *late*; high-level, top-l., summital 213 adj. *topmost*; top-secret 523 adj. *latent*; high, grand, noble 32 adj. *great*.

notable, of mark, egregious 32 adj. *remarkable*; memorable, signal, unforgettable 505 adj. *remembered*; first-rate, outstanding, excelling 34 adj. *superior*; ranking, top-rank, top-flight 644 adj. *excellent*; big-time, conspicuous, prominent, eminent, distinguished, exalted, august 866 adj. *noteworthy*; dignified, imposing, commanding 821 adj. *impressive*; newsworthy, front-page; eventful, stirring, breath-taking, shattering, earth-shaking, seismic, epoch-making.

Vb. *be important*, matter, be a consideration, be an object 612 vb. *motivate*; weigh, carry, tell, count 178 vb. *influence*; import, signify 514 vb. *mean*; concern, interest, affect 9 vb. *be related*; have priority, come first 34 vb. *predominate*; take the lead 64 vb. *come before*; be something, be somebody 920 vb. *command respect*; take the limelight, deserve notice, make a stir, create a sensation, cut a figure, cut a dash 455 vb. *attract notice*.

make important, give weight to, attach *or* ascribe importance to; seize on, fasten on; bring to the fore, place in the foreground; enhance, highlight; rub in, stress, underline, labour 532 vb. *emphasize*; put in capital letters, headline, splash, splosh 528 vb. *advertise*; bring to notice, put on the map 528 vb. *proclaim*; write in letters of gold 876 vb. *celebrate*; magnify 197 vb. *enlarge*; overweight 546 vb. *exaggerate*; honour, glorify, exalt 920 vb. *show respect*; take seriously, make a fuss about make a stir, make much ado; value, esteem, make much of, set store by, think

everything of 920 vb. *respect*; overestimate 482 vb. *overrate*.

Adv. *importantly*, primarily, significantly; materially, largely, in the main, above all, to crown all; par excellence.

See: 1, 3, 5, 9, 32, 34, 64, 136, 137, 178, 197, 213, 218, 225, 452, 455, 482, 500, 505, 514, 523, 528, 529, 532, 546, 605, 612, 622, 627, 640, 644, 676, 696, 733, 821, 866, 868, 876, 890, 920.

639 Unimportance

N. *unimportance*, inconsequence; secondariness 35 n. *inferiority*; insignificance 515 n. *unmeaningness*; immateriality, inessentiality 4 n. *insubstantiality*; vanity, vacancy 190 n. *emptiness*; nothingness, nullity 2 n. *non-existence*; pettiness 33 n. *smallness*; paltriness, meanness 922 n. *despisedness*; triviality, nugacity; superficiality 212 n. *shallowness*; flippancy, snap of the fingers, frivolity; nominalness, worthlessness 812 n. *cheapness*; uselessness 641 n. *inutility*; irrelevance, sideshow, red herring 10 n. *irrelation*.

trifle, inessential, triviality, technicality; nothing, mere n., no matter, no great m., parish pump; accessory, secondary matter, side-show; nothing in particular, matter of indifference, neither mass nor matins; no great shakes, nothing to speak of, nothing to boast of; smatter; tithe, fraction 53 n. *part*; fribble, bagatelle, tinker's curse, straw, rush, chaff, pin, button, row of buttons, feather, dust; cobweb, gossamer 330 n. *brittleness*; small item, twopence, small change, small beer, small potatoes; chicken-feed, flea-bite, pap; pinprick, scratch; nothing to it, child's play 701 n. *easy thing*; jest, joke, practical j., farce 837 n. *amusement*; peccadillo, venial sin; trifles, trivia, minutiæ, detail, petty d. 80 n. *particulars*; whit, jot, tittle, the least bit, trickle, drop in the ocean 33 n. *small quantity*; doit, cent, brass farthing, bawbee 33 n. *small coin*; nonsense, fudge, fiddlesticks 497 n. *absurdity*.

bauble, toy, rattle 837 n. *plaything*; gewgaw, knick-knack, kickshaw, bric-à-bac; novelty, trinket, bibelot; tinsel, trumpery, frippery, trash, gimcrack, stuff; froth, foam 355 n. *bubble*.

nonentity, nobody, obscurity; man of straw 4n. *insubstantial thing*; figurehead, cipher, sleeping partner; fribble, trifler, smatterer; mediocrity, light-weight, small beer; tail (of a team) 697n. *bungler*; small fry, small game; other ranks, lower orders 869n. *commonalty*; second fiddle 35n. *inferior*; underling, understrapper 742n. *servant*; pawn, pawn in the game, piece on the board, stooge, puppet 628n. *instrument*; Cinderella 801n. *poor man*; pipsqueak, squit, trash 867n. *object of scorn*.

Adj. *unimportant*, immaterial 4adj. *insubstantial*; ineffectual, uninfluential, inconsequential; insignificant 515adj. *unmeaning*; off the point 10adj. *irrelevant*; inessential, non-essential, not vital; unnecessary, dispensable, expendable; puny 196adj. *little*; small, petty, trifling, nugatory, flimsy, paltry 33adj. *inconsiderable*; negligible, inappreciable, not worth considering, out of the running; weak, powerless 161adj. *impotent*; wretched, miserable, pitiful, pitiable, pathetic; poor, mean, sorry, scurvy, scruffy, shabby, vile 645adj. *bad*; obscure, disregarded, overlooked 458adj. *neglected*; of no account, overrated, beneath notice, beneath contempt 922adj. *contemptible*; low-level, of second rank, secondary, minor, by, subsidiary, peripheral 35adj. *inferior*.

trivial, trifling, piffling, piddling, peddling, fiddling, niggling, whiffling; pettifogging, pinpricking; technical; footling, frivolous, puerile, childish 499adj. *foolish*; windy, airy, frothy 4adj. *insubstantial*; superficial 212adj. *shallow*; slight 33adj. *small*; light-weight 323adj. *light*; not serious, forgivable, venial; twopenny-halfpenny, one-horse, second-rate, third-r.; rubbishy, trumpery, trashy, tawdry, catchpenny, pinchbeck, pot-boiling, shoddy, gimcrack 645adj. *bad*; two-a-penny 812adj. *cheap*; worthless, valueless 641adj. *useless*; not worth while, not worth a thought, not worth a curse 922adj. *contemptible*; toy, token, nominal, symbolic 547adj. *indicating*; commonplace, ordinary, uneventful 610adj. *usual*.

Vb. *be unimportant*, — valueless etc.adj.; not matter, weigh light upon, have no weight, not weigh, not count, count for nothing, cut no ice, signify little; think unimportant, not overrate, shrug off,

snap one's fingers 922vb. *hold cheap*; reduce one's importance, cut down to size 872vb. *humiliate*.

Int. no matter! what matter! never mind! so what!

See: 2, 4, 10, 33, 35, 53, 80, 161, 190, 196, 212, 323, 330, 355, 458, 497, 499, 515, 547, 610, 628, 641, 645, 697, 701, 742, 801, 812, 837, 867, 869, 872, 922.

640 Utility

N. *utility*, use, usefulness; employability, serviceability, handiness 628n. *instrumentality*; efficacy, efficiency 160n. *ability*; adequacy 635n. *sufficiency*; adaptability, applicability, suitability 642n. *expedience*; readiness, availability 189n. *presence*; service, avail, help, great h., stead 703n. *aid*; value, worth, merit 644n. *goodness*; virtue, function, capacity, potency 160n. *power*; advantage, commodity; profitability, earning capacity, productivity 171n. *productiveness*; profit 771n. *gain*; convenience, benefit, general b., public utility, common weal, public good 615n. *good*; utilitarianism, employment, utilization 673n. *use*.

Adj. *useful*, of use, helpful, of service 703adj. *aiding*; sensible, practical, applied, functional; versatile, multipurpose, all-purpose, of all work; practicable, commodious, convenient 642adj. *expedient*; handy, ready, rough and r.; at hand, available, on tap; serviceable, fit for, good for, disposable, adaptable, applicable; fit for use, ready for u., usable, employable; good, valid, current; subsidiary, subservient 628adj. *instrumental*; able, competent, efficacious, effective, effectual, efficient 160adj. *powerful*; conducive 179adj. *tending*; adequate 635adj. *sufficient*; pragmatic, utilitarian.

profitable, paying, remunerative 771adj. *gainful*; prolific, fertile 164adj. *productive*; beneficial, advantageous, to one's advantage, edifying, worth-while 615n. *good*; worth one's salt, worth one's keep, invaluable, priceless 644adj. *valuable*.

Vb. *be useful*, — of use etc.adj.; avail, bestead, stead, stand one in good s.; come in handy, have some use, perform a function; function, work 173vb. *operate*; perform 676vb. *do*; serve, subserve,

serve one's turn, answer one's turn 635 vb.
suffice; suit one's purpose 642 vb. *be
expedient*; favour one's purpose, help,
advance, promote 703 vb. *aid*; do service,
do yeoman s. 742 vb. *serve*; conduce 179
vb. *tend*; benefit, profit, advantage 644 vb.
do good; bear fruit 171 vb. *be fruitful*;
pay, make a profit, bring in a p., remunerate, bring grist to the mill 771 vb. *be
profitable*.
find useful, have a use for, employ, make
use of, utilize 673 vb. *use*; turn to account,
improve on, find one's account in, find
one's advantage in, make capital of 137
vb. *profit by*; count one's winnings, take
one's profit, reap the benefit of 771 vb.
gain; be the better for 654 vb. *get better*;
enjoy, enjoy the possession of 773 vb.
possess.
Adv. *usefully*, serviceably; advantageously;
pro bono publico; cui bono? to whose
advantage?
See: 137, 160, 164, 171, 173, 179, 189, 615,
628, 635, 642, 644, 654, 673, 676, 703, 742,
771, 773.

641 Inutility

N. *inutility*, uselessness; no function, no
purpose, superfluousness 637 n. *superfluity*; nugacity, futility, inanity, vanity,
vanity of vanities 497 n. *absurdity*; worthlessness, unemployability; inadequacy
636 n. *insufficiency*; inefficiency, ineffec-
tualness, inability 161 n. *impotence*; inefficiency, incompetence, ineptitude 695 n.
unskilfulness; unserviceableness, inconvenience, unsuitability, unfitness 643 n.
inexpedience; inapplicability, unadapta-
bility; unprofitability, no benefit 172 n.
unproductivity; disservice, mischief,
damage, detriment 772 n. *loss*; unsubser-
vience, recalcitrance 598 n. *unwillingness*.
lost labour, wasted l. 728 n. *failure*; waste of
breath, waste of time; lost trouble,
labour in vain, wild-goose chase, fool's
errand, sleeveless e.; labour of Sisyphus,
Penelope's web; half-measures, tinkering.
rubbish, good riddance, trash, stuff; waste,
refuse, lumber, junk, old iron, litter;
spoilage, waste paper, mullock; scourings, off-s., sweepings, dregs, lees, dottle,
combings, shavings 41 n. *leavings*; chaff,
husks, bran; scraps, bits, orts, broken
meats, crumbs; offal, carrion; dust, muck,
débris, slag, dross, scum 649 n. *dirt*; peel,
orange-p.; dead wood, stubble, weeds,
tares; odds and ends, bits and pieces,
rags, old clothes, cast-offs; reject, throw-
out; midden, rubbish-heap, dust-h., spoil-
h., spoil bank; dust-hole, dump; picked
bone, sucked orange, empty bottle,
empties, deads; dead letter, caput mor-
tuum; back number 127 n. *archaism*.
Adj. *useless*, functionless, purposeless,
pointless; futile, nugatory 497 adj. *absurd*; unpractical, impracticable, unworkable, effort-wasting; non-functional
844 adj. *ornamental*; otiose, redundant,
excrescent 637 adj. *superfluous*; expendable, dispensable, unnecessary, unneeded,
uncalled for 860 adj. *unwanted*; unfit,
unapt, inapplicable 643 adj. *inexpedient*;
fit for nothing, unuseable, unemployable,
unadaptable; unqualified, inefficient, incompetent 695 adj. *unskilful*; unable,
ineffective, ineffectual, feckless 161 adj.
impotent; non-functioning, inoperative;
uncurrent, invalid 752 adj. *abrogated*;
unserviceable, out of order, not working,
disordered 63 adj. *deranged*; broken down,
effete, worn out, past work, hors de combat, obsolete, outmoded 127 adj. *antiquated*; hopeless, vain, idle (see *profitless*).
profitless, loss-making, unprofitable, not
worth while, wasteful, not paying, ill-
spent 772 adj. *losing*; vain, in vain, abortive 728 adj. *unsuccessful*; unrewarding,
unrewarded, thankless; fruitless, barren,
sterile 172 adj. *unproductive*; idle 679 n.
lazy; worthless, good for nothing, valueless, no earthly use; rubbishy, trashy, no
good, not worth powder and shot, not
worth the paper it is written on 645 adj.
bad; unsaleable, dear at any price 811 adj.
dear.
Vb. *be useless*, have no use, waste one's
time; achieve no purpose, end in futility;
not help 702 vb. *hinder*; not work, not
function 728 vb. *fail*; refuse to work 677
vb. *not act*; fall by the wayside 172 vb.
be unproductive; go a-begging 637 vb. *be
superfluous*.
make useless, disqualify, unfit, disarm, take
the sting out of 161 vb *disable*; castrate
161 vb. *unman*; cripple, lame, clip the
wings 655 vb. *impair*; dismantle, un-
mount, dismast, unrig, put out of commission, lay up 679 vb. *make inactive*;

sabotage, throw a spanner in the works, put a spoke in one's wheel 702 vb. *obstruct*; disassemble, undo, take to pieces, break up 46 vb. *disjoin*; deface, withdraw from currency, render uncurrent 752 adj. *abrogate*; devalue 812 vb. *cheapen*; make barren, sow with salt 172 vb. *sterilize*.

waste effort, labour the obvious; spend one's breath, lose one's labour, labour in vain, sweat for nothing, flog a dead horse, beat the air, lash the waves, cry for the moon; attempt the impossible 470 vb. *try impossibilities*; tinker, paper over the cracks, spoil the ship for a ha'porth of tar 726 vb. *not complete*.

Adv. *uselessly*, to no purpose; helplessly, ineffectually.

See: 41, 46, 63, 127, 161, 172, 470, 497, 598, 636, 637, 643, 645, 649, 655, 677, 679, 695, 702, 726, 728, 752, 772, 811, 812, 844, 860.

642 Expedience

N. *expedience*, expediency, good policy; answer, right a., advisability, desirability, worthwhileness, suitability 640 n. *utility*; fitness, propriety 915 n. *dueness*; high time, due t., right t., proper t., opportunity 137 n. *occasion*; rule of expediency, convenience, pragmatism, utilitarianism, opportunism, time-serving; profit, advantage 615 n. *benefit*; facilities, conveniences 629 n. *means*; an expedient, pis aller 623 n. *contrivance*.

Adj. *expedient*, expediential, advisable, commendable; better to, desirable, worthwhile; acceptable 923 adj. *approved*; up one's street, suitable 24 adj. *fit*; fitting, befitting, seemly, proper 913 adj. *right*; owing 915 adj. *due*; in loco, well-timed, opportune 137 adj. *timely*; politic 498 adj. *wise*; advantageous, profitable 640 adj. *useful*; convenient, workable, practical, pragmatic, practicable, negotiable; qualified, cut out for; to the purpose, adapted to, applicable; handy, effective, effectual.

Vb. *be expedient*, speak to one's condition, come not amiss, serve the time, suit the occasion, beseem, befit; be to the purpose, expedite one's end, help 703 vb. *aid*; forward, advance, promote 640 vb. *be useful*; answer, have the desired effect, produce results 156 vb. *conduce*; wash, work, do, serve, deliver the goods, fill the bill 635 vb.

suffice; achieve one's aim 727 vb. *succeed*; qualify for, fit, be just the thing 24 vb. *accord*; profit, advantage, benefit 644 vb. *do good*.

Adv. *expediently*, conveniently, fittingly, opportunely; in the right place at the right time.

See: 24, 137, 156, 498, 615, 623, 629, 635, 640, 644, 703, 727, 913, 915, 923.

643 Inexpedience

N. *inexpedience*, inexpediency; no answer, not the a., bad policy, counsel of despair 495 n. *error*; inadvisability, undesirability; unsuitability, unfitness 25 n. *inaptitude*; impropriety, unfittingness, unseemliness 916 n. *undueness*; wrongness 914 n. *wrong*; inopportuneness, untimeliness 138 n. *intempestivity*; disqualification, disability, handicap 702 n. *obstacle*; discommodity, inconvenience, disadvantage, detriment; doubtful advantage, mixed blessing, pis aller.

Adj. *inexpedient*, better not, unadvisable, uncommendable, not recommended 924 adj. *disapproved*; ill-advised, impolitic 499 adj. *unwise*; inappropriate, unfitting, out of place, unseemly 916 adj. *undue*; not right, improper, objectionable 914 adj. *wrong*; unfit, ineligible, inadmissible, unsuitable, unhappy, inept 25 adj. *unapt*; unseasonable, inopportune, untimely, wrongly timed 138 adj. *ill-timed*; unsatisfactory 636 adj. *insufficient*; discommodious, inconvenient; detrimental, disadvantageous, hurtful 645 adj. *harmful*; unhealthy, unwholesome 653 adj. *insalubrious*; unprofitable 641 adj. *useless*; unhelpful 702 adj. *hindering*; untoward 731 adj. *adverse*; ill-contrived, awkward 695 adj. *clumsy*; incommodious, cumbersome, lumbering, hulking 195 adj. *unwieldy*.

Vb. *be inexpedient*, — inadvisable etc. adj.; not fit, come amiss, won't do, won't wash, not answer; not help 641 vb. *be useless*; bother, discommode, put to inconvenience 827 vb. *incommode*; disadvantage, penalize, hurt 645 vb. *harm*; work against 702 vb. *obstruct*; embarrass 700 vb. *be difficult*.

See: 25, 138, 195, 495, 499, 636, 641, 645, 653, 695, 700, 702, 731, 827, 914, 916, 924.

644 Goodness

N. *goodness*, soundness 650n. *health*; virtuosity 694n. *skill*; quality, good q., classic q., vintage; good points, redeeming feature; merit, desert, title to fame; nothing like, excellence, eminence, supereminence 34n. *superiority*; virtue, worth, value 809n. *price*; pricelessness, superexcellence 32n. *greatness*; flawlessness 646n. *perfection*; distilled essence, quintessence 1n. *essence*; beneficence 897n. *benevolence*; virtuous character 933n. *virtue*.

élite, chosen few, chosen people, the saints; pick, prime, flower; cream, crême de la crême, salt of the earth, flower of the flock, pick of the bunch, seeded player; crack troops, corps d'élite; top people 638n. *bigwig*; charmed circle, top drawer, upper ten, best people 868n. *nobility*; choice bit, titbit, prime cut, pièce de resistance; plum, prize 729n. *trophy*.

exceller, nonpareil, nonesuch; prodigy, genius; superman, wonderman, wonder, wonder of the world, Stupor Mundi, Admirable Crichton 646n. *paragon*; grand fellow, one of the best 937n. *good man*; one in a thousand, treasure, perfect t. 890n. *darling*; jewel, pearl, ruby, diamond 844n. *gem*; gem of the first water, pearl of price, gold, pure g., refined g.; chef-d'œuvre, pièce de résistance, collector's piece, museum p. 694n. *masterpiece*; record-smasher, record-breaker, best-seller, best ever; the goods, winner, fizzer, whizz-banger, lallapalooza, humdinger, corker, knockout, hit, smash h.; star, idol 890n. *favourite*; best of its kind, the tops, top-notcher, top seed, first-rater; champion, cock of the walk, cock of the roost, title-holder, world-beater, prizewinner 727n. *victor*.

Adj. *excellent*, eximious; well-done, exemplary, worth imitating; good, good as gold 933adj. *virtuous*; above par, preferable, better 34adj. *superior*; very good, first-rate, super-excellent, alpha plus 306adj. *surpassing*; prime, quality, good q., fine, superfine, most desirable; God's own, superlative; all-star, of the first water, rare, vintage, classic 646adj. *perfect*; choice, select, picked, hand-picked, tested, exquisite, recherché 605adj. *chosen*; exclusive, pure 44adj. *unmixed*; worthy, meritorious 915adj. *deserving*; admired, admirable, estimable,

praiseworthy, creditable 923adj. *approvable*; famous, great; couleur de rose, glorious, dazzling, splendid, magnificent, marvellous, wonderful, terrific, superb.

topping, top-notch, top-hole (see *best*); lovely, glorious, heavenly, out of this world; super, wizard, zingy; smashing, stunning, corking, ripping, spiffing; swell, great, grand, famous, dandy, crackajack, hunky-dory; scrumptious, delicious, juicy, plum 826adj. *pleasurable*.

best, very b., optimum, A1, champion, bonzer, tip-top, top-notch, nothing like; first, first-rate, crack; second to none 34adj. *supreme*; unequalled, unmatched, peerless, matchless, unparalleled, unparagoned; best-ever, record, record-smashing, best-selling 34adj. *crowning*; capital, cardinal 638adj. *important*.

valuable, of value, invaluable, inestimable, priceless, above price, costly, rich 811adj. *of price*; irreplaceable, unique, rare, precious, golden, worth its weight in gold, worth a king's ransom; sterling, gilt-edged, sound, solid.

beneficial, wholesome, healthy, salutary, sound 652adj. *salubrious*; refreshing, edifying, worth-while, advantageous, profitable 640adj. *useful*; favourable, kind, propitious 730adj. *prosperous*; harmless, hurtless, inoffensive, unobnoxious, innocuous 935adj. *innocent*.

not bad, tolerable, passable, standard, up to the mark, in good condition, in fair c., fair, satisfactory 635adj. *sufficient*; nice, decent, pretty good, all right; sound, fresh, unspoiled; unexceptionable, unobjectionable; indifferent, middling, mediocre, ordinary, fifty-fifty, average 30adj. *median*.

Vb. *be good*, — sound etc. adj.; have quality; have merit, deserve well 915vb. *deserve*; qualify, stand the test, pass, pass muster, pass with flying colours 635vb. *suffice*; challenge comparison, vie, rival, equal the best 28vb. *equal*; excel, transcend, overtop, bear away the bell, take the prize 34vb. *be superior*.

do good, have a good effect, edify; do a world of good 652vb. *be salubrious*; be the making of, make a man of 654vb. *make better*; help 615vb. *benefit*; favour, smile on 730vb. *prosper*; do a favour, do a good turn, confer an obligation, put

in one's debt 897 vb. *be benevolent*; not hurt, do no harm, break no bones.

Adv. *aright*, well, rightly, properly, admirably, excellently, famously.

See: 1, 28, 30, 32, 34, 44, 306, 615, 635, 638, 640, 646, 650, 652, 654, 694, 727, 729, 730, 809, 811, 826, 844, 868, 890, 897, 915, 923, 933, 935, 937.

645 Badness

N. *badness*, bad qualities, obnoxiousness, nastiness, beastliness, foulness, grossness, rottenness; demerit, unworthiness, worthlessness; low quality, low standard 35 n. *inferiority*; faultiness, flaw 647 n. *imperfection*; poor make, shoddiness 641 n. *inutility*; clumsiness 695 n. *unskilfulness*; rankness, unsoundness, taint, decay, corruption 655 n. *deterioration*; disruption, confusion 61 n. *disorder*; peccancy, morbidity 651 n. *disease*; harmfulness, hurtfulness, balefulness, ill, hurt, harm, injury, detriment, damage, mischief 616 n. *evil*; noxiousness, poisonousness, deadliness, virulence 653 n. *insalubrity*; poison, blight 659 n. *bane*; pestilence 651 n. *plague*; contamination, centre of infection, plague spot, hotbed 651 n. *infection*; affair, scandal 867 n. *slur*; abomination, filth 649 n. *uncleanness*; sewer 649 n. *sink*; bitterness, gall, wormwood 393 n. *sourness*; painfulness, sting, ache, pang, thorn in the flesh 377 n. *pain*; molestation 827 n. *annoyance*; anguish 825 n. *suffering*; harshness, tyranny, maltreatment, oppression, persecution, intolerance 735 n. *severity*; unkindness, cruelty, malignancy, malignity, spitefulness, spite 898 n. *malevolence*; depravity, vice 934 n. *wickedness*; sin 936 n. *guilt*; bad influence, evil genius; evil spirit 970 n. *demon*; ill wind, evil star 731 n. *misfortune*; black magic, evil eye, hoodoo, jinx 983 n. *sorcery*; curse 899 n. *malediction*; snake in the grass 663 n. *trouble-maker*; bad character 904 n. *evildoer*.

Adj. *bad*, arrant, vile, base, ill-conditioned; gross, black; utterly bad, irredeemable, as bad as bad can be; bad of its kind, poor, mean, wretched, measly, low-grade, not good enough, execrable, awful 35 adj. *inferior*; no good, worthless, shoddy, ropy, punk 641 adj. *useless*;

unsatisfactory, faulty, flawed 647 adj. *imperfect*; bad at, incompetent, inefficient, unskilled, skilless 695 adj. *clumsy*; badly done, mangled, spoiled 695 adj. *bungled*; scruffy, filthy 649 adj. *dirty*; foul, fulsome, noisome 397 adj. *fetid* (see *not nice*); gone bad, rank, unfresh, unsound, affected, tainted 655 adj. *deteriorated*; corrupt, decaying, decayed, rotten to the core 51 adj. *decomposed*; peccant, disordered, infected, envenomed, poisoned, septic 651 adj. *diseased*; irremediable, incurable; depraved, vicious, villainous, accursed 934 adj. *wicked*; heinous, sinful 936 adj. *guilty*; wrongful, unjust 914 adj. *wrong*; sinister 616 adj. *evil* (see *harmful*); immeritorious, unworthy; shameful, scandalous 867 adj. *discreditable*; sad, melancholy, lamentable, deplorable, pitiable, pitiful, woeful, grievous, sore 827 adj. *distressing*; unendurable 827 adj. *intolerable*; heavy, onerous, burdensome 684 adj. *fatiguing*; too bad 827 adj. *annoying*.

harmful, hurtful, scatheful; malefic, mischievous, wanton, outrageous 898 adj. *maleficent*; injurious, damaging, detrimental, prejudicial, disadvantageous, disserviceable 643 adj. *inexpedient*; deleterious, corrosive, wasting, consuming 165 adj. *destructive*; pernicious, fatal 362 adj. *deadly*; costly 811 adj. *dear*; disastrous, ruinous, calamitous 731 adj. *adverse*; degenerative, noxious, malign, malignant, unhealthy, unwholesome, noisome, miasmal, infectious 653 adj. *insalubrious*; poisonous, venomous 653 adj. *toxic*; unsafe, risky 661 adj. *dangerous*; sinister, ominous, dire, dreadful, baleful, baneful, accursed 616 adj. *evil*; spiteful, malicious, ill-conditioned, mischief-making, puckish, impish 898 adj. *unkind*; bloody, bloodthirsty, inhuman 898 adj. *cruel*; outrageous, rough, furious 176 adj. *violent*; harsh, intolerant, persecuting 735 adj. *oppressive*.

not nice, unlikeable, obnoxious, poisonous, septic; nasty, beastly, horrid, horrible, ghastly, awful, dreadful, perfectly d.; scruffy 867 adj. *disreputable*; foul, rotten, lousy, putrid, stinking, stinky, sickening, revolting, nauseous, nauseating 861 adj. *disliked*; loathsome, detestable, abominable 888 adj. *hateful*; vulgar, low, indecent, improper, gross, filthy, obscene

951 adj. *impure*; shocking, disgusting, reprehensible, monstrous, horrendous 924 adj. *disapproved*; plaguy, wretched, miserable 827 adj. *annoying*.

damnable, damned, blasted, confounded, blinking, blankety-blank; execrable, accursed, cursed, hellish, infernal, devilish, diabolic, diabolical.

Vb. *harm*, do h., do a hurt, do a mischief, scathe 827 vb. *hurt*; cost one dear 811 vb. *be dear*; injure, damage, damnify 655 vb. *impair*; corrupt 655 vb. *pervert*; do no good 641 vb. *be useless*; do evil, work e. 914 vb. *do wrong*; molest, pain 827 vb. *torment*; plague, vex, trouble 827 vb. *incommode*; land one in trouble, spite, mischief, be unkind 898 vb. *be malevolent*.

ill-treat, maltreat, mishandle, abuse 675 vb. *misuse*; ill-use, burden, overburden, put upon, tyrannize, bear hard on, tread on, trample on, victimize, prey upon; persecute 735 vb. *oppress*; wrong, aggrieve 914 vb. *do wrong*; distress 827 vb. *torment*; outrage, violate, force 176 vb. *be violent*; savage, maul, bite, scratch, tear 655 vb. *wound*; stab 263 vb. *pierce*; bruise, buffet 279 vb. *strike*; agonize, rack, crucify 963 vb. *torture*; spite, use dispitefully, wreak one's malice on 898 vb. *be malevolent*; crush 165 n. *destroy*.

Adv. *badly*, amiss, wrong, ill; to one's cost; where the shoe pinches.

See: 35, 51, 61, 165, 176, 263, 279, 362, 377, 393, 397, 616, 641, 643, 647, 649, 651, 653, 655, 659, 661, 663, 675, 684, 695, 731, 735, 811, 825, 827, 861, 867, 888, 898, 899, 904, 914, 924, 934, 936, 951, 963, 970, 983.

646 Perfection

N. *perfection*, sheer p.; finish, classic quality; perfectness, the ideal; nothing wrong with, immaculacy, faultlessness, flawlessness; correctness, correctitude, irreproachability; impeccancy, impeccability, infallibility, indefectibility; transcendence 34 n. *superiority*; quintessence, essence; peak, top 213 n. *summit*; height *or* pitch of perfection, acme of p., pink of of p., ne plus ultra, extreme, last word; chef d'œuvre, flawless performance, chanceless innings 694 n. *masterpiece*.

paragon, nonesuch, nonpareil, flower, a beauty 644 n. *exceller*; ideal, beau idéal,

prince of; classic, pattern, pattern of perfection, standard, norm, model, mirror 23 n. *prototype*; phœnix, rarity 84 n. *rara avis*; superman, wonderman 864 n. *prodigy*.

Adj. *perfect*, perfected, finished, brought to perfection, ripened; ripe, fully r. 669 adj. *matured*; just right, ideal, flawless, faultless, impeccable, infallible, indefectible; correct, irreproachable; immaculate, unblemished, unflawed, unstained; spotless, unspotted, without blemish, without a stain; uncontaminated, pure 44 adj. *unmixed*; guiltless 935 adj. *innocent*; sound, uncracked, sound as a bell, right as a trivet, in perfect condition; tight, seaworthy; whole, entire, hundred per cent; complete 52 adj. *intact*; dazzling, beyond praise 644 adj. *excellent*; consummate, unsurpassable 34 adj. *supreme*; brilliant, masterly 694 adj. *skilful*; pattern, standard, model, classic, classical, Augustan.

undamaged, safe and sound, with a whole skin, unhurt, unscathed, scatheless; unscarred, unscratched, unmarked; unmarred, unspoilt; unreduced, undiminished, without loss, whole, entire 52 adj. *intact*; in the pink 650 adj. *healthy*.

Vb. *perfect*, consummate, bring to perfection; ripen 669 vb. *mature*; correct 654 vb. *rectify*; put the finishing touch 213 vb. *crown*; complete, leave nothing to be desired 725 vb. *carry through*.

Adv. *perfectly*, flawlessly, impeccably, irreproachably, to perfection, as one would wish.

See: 23, 34, 44, 52, 84, 213, 644, 650, 654, 669, 694, 725, 864, 935.

647 Imperfection

N. *imperfection*, imperfectness, not hundred per cent; room for improvement, not one's best; possibility of perfection, perfectibility 654 n. *improvement*; faultiness, erroneousness, defectibility, fallibility 495 n. *error*; patchiness, unevenness, curate's egg 17 n. *non-uniformity*; immaturity, unripeness, underdevelopment 670 n. *undevelopment*; defectiveness, incompletion, missing link, broken set 55 n. *incompleteness*; lack, want 627 n. *requirement*; deficiency, inadequacy 636 n. *insufficiency*; unsoundness 661 n. *vulnera-*

bility; failure, failing, weakness 307n. *shortcoming*; low standard, pass degree; inferior version, poor relation 35n. *inferiority*; second best, pis aller, consolation prize, makeshift 150n. *substitute*; mediocrity, averageness 30n. *average*; loss of fitness, staleness 684n. *fatigue*; adulteration 43n. *mixture*.

defect, fault 495n. *error*; flaw, rift, leak, loophole, crack 201n. *gap*; deficiency, limitation 307n. *shortcoming*; kink, twist, screw loose 503n. *eccentricity*; weak point, soft spot, vulnerable point, chink in one's armour, Achilles' heel 661n. *vulnerability*; feet of clay, weak link in the chain 163n. *weakness*; scratch, taint, stain, spot, streak, touch of the tar-brush 845n. *blemish*; drawback, snag, fly in the ointment 702n. *obstacle*; half-blood 43n. *hybrid*.

Adj. *imperfect*, not quite right, not ideal, less than perfect, not classic; fallible, peccable; uneven, patchy, good in parts, like the curate's egg 17adj. *non-uniform*; faulty, botched 695adj. *bungled*; flawed, cracked; unstaunch, leaky, not proof; unsound 661adj. *vulnerable*; soiled, shops., tainted, stained, marked, scratched 845adj. *blemished*; not at one's best, below par, off form; stale 684adj. *fatigued*; off-colour, not in the pink 651adj. *unhealthy*; not good enough, inadequate, deficient, wanting, lacking 636adj. *insufficient*; defective, not entire 55adj. *incomplete*; partial, broken 53adj. *fragmentary*; maimed, legless, armless 163adj. *crippled*; unfilled, half-filled, under-manned, short-handed, below strength, under complement 670adj. *unequipped*; half-finished 55adj. *unfinished*; unthorough, perfunctory 456adj. *inattentive*; overwrought, over-elaborated, overdone 546adj. *exaggerated*; warped, twisted, distorted 246adj. *deformed*; mutilated, maimed, lame, halt 163adj. *weakened*; undeveloped, raw, crude, untrained, scratch 670adj. *immature*; makeshift, provisional, substitutionary, substitutional 150adj. *substituted*; secondary 639adj. *unimportant*; second-best, second-rate 35adj. *inferior*; poor, unimpressive, negative 645adj. *bad*; ordinary, much of a muchness, so-so, middling, middle-grade, average 30adj. *median*; moderate, unheroic; only passable, toler-

able, bearable, better than nothing 923adj. *approvable*.

Vb. *be imperfect*, fail of perfection, have a fault; be defective 307vb. *fall short*; lie open to criticism, not bear inspection, not pass muster, fail the test, dissatisfy 636vb. *not suffice*; barely pass, scrape through; fail of approval, not impress, not make the grade 924vb. *incur blame*; have feet of clay 163vb. *be weak*; show a crack, not hold water, leak 298vb. *flow out*.

Adv. *imperfectly*, to a limited extent, barely, almost, not quite, all but; with all its faults.

See: 17, 30, 35, 43, 53, 55, 150, 163, 201, 246, 298, 307, 456, 495, 503, 546, 627, 636, 639, 645, 651, 654, 661, 670, 684, 695, 702, 845, 923, 924.

648 Cleanness

N. *cleanness*, freedom from dirt, absence of dust, immaculateness 950n. *purity*; freshness, dewiness, whiteness; shine, polish, spit and polish; cleanliness, kid gloves, daintiness, dainty habits 862n. *fastidiousness*.

cleansing, clean, spring-c., dry-c.; washing, cleaning up, mopping up, washing up, wiping up; refining, clarification, purification, epuration; sprinkling, asperges, lustration, mundation, purgation; washing out, flushing; purging, defecation 302n. *excretion*; airing, ventilation, fumigation 338n. *vaporization*; deodorization 395n. *inodorousness*; antisepsis, sterilization, disinfection, disinfestation, delousing; sanitation, conservancy, drainage, sewerage, plumbing, water-system 652n. *hygiene*; water-closet, flush 649n. *latrine*.

ablution, washing, detersion; lavage, lavation, douche, flush, wash; balneation, bathing, dipping; soaping, scrubbing, sponging, rinsing, shampoo; dip 313n. *plunge*; bath, tub; bath-tub., wash-t., hip-bath, bidet; wash-basin, wash pot, ewer, lota; hot bath, cold b., steam b., vapour b., blanket b.; shower bath, shower, cold s.; Turkish bath, Russian b., Swedish b.; Finnish bath, sauna; wash-house, lavatory, bath-house, bathroom, washroom, public baths, thermæ,

hammam, sudarium; plunge bath, swimming bath, swimming pool, natatorium; bathing machine; wash, laundry, home-l., washing machine, launderette.

cleanser, purifier; disinfectant, carbolic, quicklime, deodorant; soda, washing s., lye, spirit; fuller's earth, detergent, soap, scented s., soap flakes; water, hot water, soap and w.; wash, hair-w., mouth w., gargle, lotion, hand-l.; cream, hand-c., face-c., glycerine; dentifrice, toothpaste, tooth-powder; pumice stone, hearth-s., holy-s.; polish, furniture p., boot p., blacking; wax, varnish; whitewash, paint 427n. *whiting*; blacklead 428n. *black pigment*; diuretic, pull-through 658n. *cathartic*; sewer, drain-pipe, waste-pipe 351n. *drain*.

cleaning utensil, broom, besom, mop, sponge, swab, swabber; washing board; duster, feather-d., whisk, brush, scrubbing-b., nail-b., toothbrush, toothpick, toothstick; dustpan, dustpan and brush, crumb-tray; dustbin, ashcan; carpet-sweeper, carpet-beater, vacuum cleaner; fulling mill; doormat, foot-scraper; scraper, tongue-s., strigil; squeegee, squilgee; pipe-cleaner, pull-through, reamer; windscreen wiper; screen, sieve, riddle, strainer 263n. *porosity*; filter, air-f., oil-f., water-f.; blotter, eraser 550n. *obliteration*; comb, hair-c., pocket-c.; rake, hoe; snow-plough, water-cart, dust-c.; sprinkler, hose 341n. *irrigator*; washing machine.

cleaning cloth, duster, jharan, dish-cloth, dish-clout, dish-rag; glass-cloth, leather, wash-l.; buff, flannel, face-f., towel, hand-t., face-t., bath-t., peignoir; bib, handkerchief, paper h., tissue; face-cloth, sudary, sweat-rag; napery, napkin, table-n., table-mat, doyley, table-cloth; mat, drugget 226n. *floor-cover*; cover, chair-c., dust-c. 226n. *coverlet*.

cleaner, refiner, distiller; dry-cleaner, launderer, laundryman, laundress, washer-woman, dhobi; fuller; scrub, scrubber; swabber; washer-up, dish-washer, scullion, masalchi; charwoman, char, help; scavenger, dustman, sweeper, road-s., crossing-s.; lavatory attendant, sanitary engineer; chimney-sweep, window-cleaner; shoe-black, shoe-shiner; barber, hairdresser 843n. *beautician*; gleaner, picker; scavenger bird, crow, vulture, kite.

Adj. *clean*, dirt-free; whitened 427adj. *white*; polished, clean, bright, shiny, shining 417adj. *undimmed*; cleanly, dainty, nice 862adj. *fastidious*; dewy, fresh; cleaned, well-c., washed etc.vb.; shaven, shorn, barbered, trimmed; cleaned up, laundered, starched; spruce, natty, spick and span, neat, tidy 60adj. *orderly*; deodorized, disinfected, aseptic, antiseptic, hygienic, sterilized, sterile 652adj. *salubrious*; pure, purified, refined, immaculate, spotless, stainless, unsoiled, unmuddied, untarnished, unsullied 646 adj. *perfect*; untouched, blank; ritually clean, kosher 301adj. *edible*.

cleansing, lustral, purificatory; disinfectant; hygienic; purgative, purgatory; detergent, abstersive; ablutionary, balneal.

Vb. *clean*, spring-clean, clean up; take the dirt off, lay the dust; valet, spruce, neaten, trim 62vb. *arrange*; wash, wipe, wash clean, wipe c., wash up, wipe up, dry, wring, wring out; sponge, mop, mop up, swab, wash down; scrub, scour; flush, flush out; holystone, scrape 333vb. *rub*; do the washing, launder, starch, iron; buck, bleach, dry-clean; soap, lather, shampoo; bathe, dip, rinse, sluice, douche 341vb. *drench*; dust, whisk, sweep, sweep up, broom, beat, vacuum-clean; brush, brush up; comb, rake; buff, polish; shine, black, blacklead 417vb. *make bright*; whitewash 427vb. *whiten*; blot, erase 550vb. *obliterate*; strip, pick, pick clean, clean out, clear, clear out, rake o., make a clean sweep 300vb. *eject*.

purify, purge, clean up; bowdlerize, expurgate; sublimate, elevate 654vb. *make better*; cleanse, lave, lustrate, asperge; purify oneself, wash one's hands of; freshen, ventilate, fan, deodorize, fumigate; edulcorate, desalt 392vb. *sweeten*; disinfect, sterilize, antisepticize, chlorinate, pasteurize 652vb. *sanitate*; free from impurities, depurate, refine, distil, clarify, rack, skim, scum, despumate; decarbonize; elutriate, strain, filter, percolate, lixiviate, leach 341vb. *drench*; sift, winnow, van, bolt, riddle, screen, sieve 44vb. *eliminate*; sort out, weed; flush, clean out, wash o., drain 652vb. *sanitate*.

See: 44, 60, 62, 226, 263, 300, 301, 302, 313, 333, 338, 341, 351, 392, 395, 417, 427, 428, 550, 646, 649, 652, 654, 658, 843, 862, 950.

649 Uncleanness

N. *uncleanness*, immundity, immundicity, uncleanliness, dirty habits, wallowing, beastliness; dirtiness (see *dirt*); muckiness, miriness 347 n. *marsh*; soilure, soiliness; scruffiness, scurfiness, filthiness; lousiness, pediculosis, phthiriasis; squalidity, squalidness, squalor, slumminess 801 n. *poverty*; untidiness, sluttishness, slovenliness 61 n. *disorder*; stink 397 n. *fetor*; pollution, defilement, defedation; corruption, taint, tainting, putrescence, putrefaction 51 n. *decomposition*; contamination 651 n. *infection*; abomination, scatology, obscenity 951 n. *impurity*; unwashed body, dirty linen.

dirt, filth, stain, patch, blot; muck, mud, clay 344 n. *soil*; quagmire, bog 347 *marsh*; night-soil, dung, ordure, faeces, stool 302 n. *excrement*; snot, mucus; dust, mote 332 n. *pulverulence*; cobweb, grime, smut, smudge, soot, smoke; grounds, grouts, dregs, lees, heeltap; sordes, sweepings, rinsings, scourings, off-scourings 41 n. *leavings*; sediment, sedimentation, deposit, precipitate, residuum, fur; scum, off-scum, dross, froth; scoriæ, ashes, cinders, clinker, slag 381 n. *ash*; recrement, waste product; drainage, sewerage; cast-offs, cast skin, exuviæ, slough; scurf, dandruff; furfur, tartar, argol; pus, matter, feculence; raff, refuse, garbage 641 n. *rubbish*; rot, dry-r., wet-r., rust, mildew, mould, fungus 51 n. *decay*; carrion, offal; flea, nit 365 n. *vermin*.

swill, pig-s., hogwash, draff; bilge, bilge-water; ditch-w., dish-w., slops; sewage, drainage; wallow, hog-w., sough.

latrine, privy, jakes, bogs, necessary house, comfort-station; closet, earth-c., water-c., W.C.; indoor sanitation, out-door sanitation, septic tank; cloakroom, lavatory, loo, toilet; urinal, public convenience; close-stool, commode, thunderbox, bed-pan, jerry 302 n. *cacation*.

sink, sink of corruption; kitchen sink, draining board; cesspool, sump, slough; gutter, sewer, main, cloaca 351 n. *drain*; laystall, dunghill, midden, rubbish-heap, dust-h., compost-h.; dustbin, trash-can, garbage-c., gubbins 194 n. *vessel*; dust-hole 194 n. *cellar*; colluvies, Augean stables, sty, pig-s., pigpen 192 n. *stable*; slum, tenement 192 n. *housing*; shambles

362 n. *slaughter-house*; plague-spot 651 n. *infection*; spittoon, cuspidor.

dirty person, sloven, slattern, slammerkin, drab, draggletail, trapes 61 n. *slut*; litterer, litter lout; mudlark, street-arab; dustman, sweep, chimney-s., scavenger 648 n. *cleaner*; beast, pig, wallower, leper.

Adj. *unclean*, unhallowed, unholy 980 adj. *profane*; obscene, corrupt 951 adj. *impure*; coarse, unrefined, unpurified; septic, festering, poisonous 653 adj. *toxic*; unsterilized, non-sterile 653 adj. *infectious*; squalid, slummy 653 adj. *insalubrious*; foul, offensive, nasty, noisome, abominable, disgusting, repulsive, nauseous, nauseating, stinking, malodorous 397 adj. *fetid*; uncleanly, unfastidious, beastly, hoggish; scrofulous, scruffy, scurfy, scorbutic, impetiginous; leprous, scabby; lousy, pediculous, crawling; faecal, dungy, stercoraceous, excrementitious 302 adj. *excretory*; carious, rotting, rotted, tainted, high; flyblown, maggoty, carrion 51 adj. *decomposed*.

dirty, filthy; dusty, grimy, sooty, smoky, snuffy; thick with dust, unswept, ungarnished, Augean; untidy, unkempt, slovenly, sluttish, bedraggled 61 adj. *disordered*; unsoaped, unwashed, unwashen, unscoured, unrinsed, unwiped; black, dingy, uncleaned, unpolished, unburnished; tarnished, stained, soiled; greasy, oily; clotted, caked, matted, begrimed, collied; messy, mucky, muddy, slimy 347 adj. *marshy*; thick, turbid; dreggy, scummy; musty, fusty, cobwebby; moth-eaten, thread-bare, patched 801 adj. *beggarly*.

Vb. *be unclean*, — dirty etc. adj.; get dirty, collect dust, foul up, clog; rust, mildew, moulder, fester, gangrene, mortify, putrify, rot, go bad, addle 51 vb. *decompose*; grow rank, smell 397 vb. *stink*; wallow, roll in the mud.

make unclean, foul, befoul; dirty, dirt, soil; grime, begrime, cover with dust; stain, blot, sully, tarnish; muck, mess, untidy 61 vb. *disorder*; daub, smirch, smut, smutch, smudge, blur, smoke 419 vb. *bedim*; spot, patch, maculate 437 vb. *variegate*; streak, smear, besmear, grease; cake, clog, bemire, beslime, muddy, roil, rile; draggle, drabble, daggle; spatter, bespatter, splash, slobber, slubber, slaver 341 vb. *moisten*; poison, taint, infect,

contaminate 655 vb. *impair*; corrupt 655 vb. *pervert*; pollute, defile, profane, desecrate, unhallow 980 vb. *be impious*.

See: 41, 51, 61, 192, 194, 302, 332, 341, 344, 347, 351, 362, 365, 381, 397, 419, 437, 641, 648, 651, 653, 655, 801, 951, 980.

650 Health

N. *health*, rude h., robust h., good h.; healthiness, good constitution, health and strength 162 n. *vitality*; fitness, condition, good c., pink of condition; bloom, rosiness, rosy cheeks; well-being, physical w.; eupepsia 376 n. *euphoria*; whole skin, soundness; incorruption, incorruptibility 644 n. *goodness*; long life, longevity, ripe old age 131 n. *age*; hygiene, healthy state, clean bill of health; goddess of health, Hygeia.

Adj. *healthy*, healthful, wholesome, hygienic, sanitary 652 adj. *salubrious*; in health, in good h., bursting with h., eupeptic, euphoric; fresh, blooming, ruddy, rosy, rosy-cheeked, florid; hale, hearty, hale and hearty, sound, fit, well, fine, bobbish, full of beans; of good constitution, never ill, robust, hardy, strong, vigorous, robustious, staunch 162 adj. *stalwart*; fighting fit, in condition, in good condition, in the pink, in good case, in good heart, in fine fettle, in fine feather; sound in wind and limb, sound as a bell, sound as a roach, fit as a fiddle; fresh as a daisy, fresh as April; a picture of health, feeling good; getting well, convalescent, on the up-grade, well again, on one's legs 656 adj. *restored*; pretty well, no worse, as well as can be expected; safe and sound, unharmed 646 adj. *undamaged*; fat and well-liking.

Vb. *be healthy*, — well etc. adj.; mind one's health, look after oneself; feel fine, bloom, flourish, enjoy good health; be in the pink, have never felt better; wear well, look young; keep one's health, keep fit, keep well, keep body and soul together, keep on one's legs; have a clean bill of health, have no mortality.

get healthy, — fit etc. adj.; recuperate, be well again, return to health, recover one's health, get the colour back in one's cheeks; mend, convalesce, become con- valescent, take a fresh lease of life, become a new man 656 vb. *revive*.

See: 131, 162, 376, 644, 646, 652, 656.

651 Ill-health. Disease

N. *ill-health*, bad h., delicate h., failing h.; delicacy, weak constitution, unhealthiness, weakliness, infirmity, debility 163 n. *weakness*; seediness, loss of condition, manginess; morbidity, indisposition. cachexia; chronic complaint, allergy, hay-fever, catarrh; chronic ill-health, invalidism, valetudinarianism, hypochondria, medicine habit.

illness, loss of health 655 n. *deterioration*; affliction, disability, handicap, infirmity, inanition 163 n. *weakness*; sickness, ailment, complaint, complication; condition, history of; bout of sickness, visitation, attack, acute a.; spasm, stroke, seizure, apoplexy, fit; shock, shell-s.; sign of illness, headache, migraine 377 n. *pain*; temperature, feverishness, fever, shivers, shakes, rigor 318 n. *spasm*; pyrexia, calenture; delirium 503 n. *frenzy*; breakdown, collapse, prostration; last illness 361 n. *decease*; sick-bed, deathbed.

disease, malady, distemper, disorder; epidemic disease, endemic d.; congenital disease; occupational disease; deficiency disease, malnutrition, avitaminosis, beriberi, pellagra, rickets, scurvy; degenerative disease, wasting d., marasmus, atrophy; traumatic disease, trauma; organic disease, functional d., circulatory d., neurological d., nervous d., epilepsy, falling sickness; musculo-skeletal disease; cardio-vascular d.; endocrine disease, diabetes; urogenital disease; haemopoietic disease; dermatological disease; neoplasmic disease; respiratory disease; gastro-intestinal disease; infectious disease, communicable d.; virus disease, bacillary d., water-borne d., filth d.; brain disease 503 n. *insanity*; febrile disease, sweating sickness; hydrocele, dropsy.

plague, pest, scourge 659 n. *bane*; pestilence, murrain, infection, contagion; epidemic, pandemic; pneumonic plague, bubonic p., Black Death.

infection, contagion, miasma, pollution, taint; infectiousness, contagiousness 653

n. *insalubrity*; toxicity, sepsis, poisoning 659 n. *poison*; plague-spot, hotbed; vector, carrier, germ-c.; virus, bacillus, bacteria, germ, pathogen; blood-poisoning, toxæmia, septicæmia; food-poisoning, ptomaine p., botulism; gastro-enteritis, diarrhœa and vomiting, D. and V.; pyrogenic infection, pyrogenesis, pyæmia, suppuration, festering, purulence; infectious disease, cold, common c., influenza, diphtheria, pneumonia; measles, morbilli; German measles, rubella; whooping-cough, pertussis; mumps, parotitis; scarlet fever, scarlatina; chicken-pox, varicella; smallpox, variola; cholera morbus, cholera, Asiatic c.; blackwater fever, yellow f., kala azar, dengue; typhus, prison fever, trench f.; typhoid, paratyphoid; glandular fever; encephalitis, meningitis; poliomyelitis, polio-encephalitis; tetanus, lockjaw; gangrene.

malaria, ague, malarial fever, remittent f., quotidian f., quartern f., tertian f., benign, tertian, subtertian, malignant s.; enlarged spleen.

dysentery, protozoal d., amœbic d., bacillary d., blood d.; diarrhœa, loose stool 302 n. *cacation*; diarrhœa and vomiting, gastro-enteritis; enteritis; colitis.

indigestion, fat i., steatorrhea; dyspepsia, liverishness, liver spots, dizziness, vertigo; biliousness, nausea, vomiting, retching; flatulence, wind; acidosis, heartburn; colic, gripes; gastralgia, stomach ache, tummy a., belly a.; stomach ulcer, peptic u.; stomach disorder, gastritis, œsophagitis, duodenitis; jaundice, hepatogenous j., hæmatogenous j., toxic j.; cholecystitis, cholelithiasis, gall-stones, biliary calculus; constipation, auto-intoxication.

respiratory disease, cough, cold, sore throat, common cold, infectious catarrh, coryza; rhinitis, rhinorrhœa; sinusitis, frontal s., maxillary s., sphenoidal s., ethmoidal s.; tonsilitis, pharyngitis; laryngitis, laryngo-tracheitis, tracheitis, perichondritis; bronchitis; asthma; pneumonia, broncho-pneumonia; diphtheria; whooping-cough, pertussis.

heart disease, cardiac d., cardio-vascular d.; carditis, pancarditis, endocarditis, myocarditis, pericarditis, angina pectoris; breast-pang, heart-stroke, chest-spasm; brachycardia; tachycardia; gallop rhythm, palpitation, dyspnœa; valvular lesion; enlarged heart, cardiac hypertrophy, athlete's heart; fatty degeneration of the heart; heart condition, bad heart, weak h.

blood pressure, high blood p., hypertension; hypotension, low blood pressure; vascular disease, atheroma, aneurysm; angiospasm; hardened arteries, arteriosclerosis; arteritis, endarteritis, aortitis; phlebitis, thrombophlebitis, varicose veins; thrombosis, coronary t., clot, blood-c.

blood disease, anæmia, aplastic a., hæmolytic a., pernicious a., leukæmia; hæmophilia; hæmorrhage.

phthisis, wasting disease, consumptiveness, decline, graveyard cough, tuberculosis, consumption, galloping c.

carcinosis, epithelioma, cancer; neoplasm, growth; tumour, indolent t., benign t.; malignant tumour, cancerous growth; melanoma, black cancer.

skin disease, cutaneous d.; mange; leucoderma; leprosy; albinism; dermatitis, erythema, flush; erysipelas, St. Anthony's fire, the rose; tetters, impetigo, herpes, herpes zoster, shingles; eczema, serpigo, ringworm, itch, dhobi's i. 378 n. *formication*; hives, urticaria; rash, eruption, breaking out, ecchymosis, acne, spots, macule, pustule, favus, papule, vesicle, pimple, blister, wart, verruca 253 n. *swelling*; miliaria, yaws, frambœsia; athlete's foot, Bengal rot, Singapore ear; mole, freckle, birth-mark, pockmark 845 n. *blemish*; dry skin, xeroma, xeroderma; cowpox, vaccinia; pox, smallpox, chicken-pox.

venereal disease, French disease, pox; syphilis, gonorrhœa, clap; venereal ulcer, chancre, syphilitic sore.

ulcer, ulceration, gathering, festering, purulence; inflammation, -itis; sore, imposthume, abscess, fistula; blain, chilblain, kibe; corn, hard c., soft c. 253 n. *swelling*; gangrene, rot 51 n. *decay*; discharge, pus, matter.

rheumatism, rheumatics; articular rheumatism, rheumatic fever; muscular rheumatism, myalgia; fibrositis; frozen shoulder; arthritis, rheumatoid a.; gout.

paralysis, involuntary movements, palsy, tic, tremor 318 n. *spasm*; general paralysis, atrophy 375 n. *insensibility*; cerebral paralysis, stroke, spasm, seizure, hemiplagia, diplegia, paraplegia; petit mal,

epilepsy, falling sickness; infantile paralysis, poliomyelitis, polio; arthropathy, spasticity; Parkinson's disease; sleeping sickness.

animal disease, veterinary d.; distemper, foot-and-mouth disease; rinderpest, murrain; splenic disease, anthrax, sheep-rot, bloat; pine; megrims, staggers; glanders, farcy, sweeny, spavin, thrush; psittacosis; hard pad; mange.

sick person, sick man, sufferer; patient, in-p., out-p.; case, stretcher-c., hospital-c.; mental case 504n. *madman*; invalid, chronic i., chronic; valetudinarian, hypochondriac, martyr to ill-health; consumptive, asthmatic, bronchitic, dyspeptic, diabetic; hæmophiliac, bleeder; insomniac; neuropath, addict, alcoholic; spastic, arthritic, paralytic; crock, old c., cripple 163 n. *weakling*; sick-list.

pathology, case-making, diagnosis, prognosis; etiology, nosology, epidemiology, bacteriology, parasitology 658n. *therapy*.

Adj. *unhealthy*, healthless, unsound, sickly; infirm, decrepit, weakly 163 adj. *weak*; delicate, of weak constitution, liable to illness, always ill; in bad health, in poor h.; in poor condition, mangy; undernourished, under-vitaminized 636adj. *underfed*; sallow, pale 426adj. *colourless*; bilious 433adj. *yellow*; invalid, valetudinarian, hypochondriac.

sick, ill, unwell, not well, indisposed, out of sorts, under the weather, off-colour; poorly, seedy, squeamish, groggy, queer, ailing; sickening for, showing symptoms of; feverish, headachy; confined, laid up, bedridden, on one's back, in bed, in hospital, on the sick-list, invalided; seized, taken ill, taken bad; prostrate, collapsed; on the danger list, not allowed visitors; chronic, incurable, inoperable; mortally ill, moribund 361adj. *dying*; peaky, drooping, flagging, pining, languishing, wasting away, in a decline.

diseased, pathological, disordered, distempered; affected, infected, plague-stricken; contaminated, tainted, vitiated, tabid, rotten, rotting, gangrenous 51adj. *decomposed*; peccant, morbid, morbose, morbific, pathogenic; infectious, poisonous, festering, purulent 653adj. *toxic*; measly, morbillous; degenerative, consumptive, phthisical, tuberculous, tubercular; diabetic, dropsical, hydrocephalic; anæmic;

bloodless, leukæmic, hæmophilic; arthritic, rheumatic, rheumatoid, rheumaticky; rickety, palsied, paralysed, paralytic, spastic; leprous, leucodermatous; carcinomatous, cancerous, cankered; syphilitic, venereal; swollen, œdematous; gouty; bronchial, throaty, bronchitic, croupy, coughy, coldy; asthmatic; allergic; pyretic, febrile, fevered, shivering, aguish, feverish, delirious; sore, tender; ulcerous, fistular; ulcerated, inflamed; rashy, spotty, erythematous, erysipelatous; spavined, broken-winded; mangy.

Vb. *be ill*,—sick etc. adj.; enjoy ill-health; ail, suffer, labour under, have treatment; have a complaint, have an affliction, be a chronic invalid; not feel well, complain of; feel queer etc.adj.; lose one's health, sicken, fall sick, fall ill; catch, take an infection, contract a disease; break out with, break out in; be seized, be stricken, be taken, be taken bad, not feel so good; have a stroke, collapse; be laid up, take to one's bed, go to hospital, become a patient; languish, pine, peak, droop, waste away, go into a decline, fall into a consumption; fail, flag, lose strength, get worse 655vb. *deteriorate*; grow weak 163 vb. *be weak*; gather, fester, suppurate.

Adv. *morbidly*, unhealthily 653adv. *unwholesomely*; in sickness; in hospital, in the doctor's hands, under treatment.

See: 51, 163, 253, 302, 318, 361, 375, 377, 378, 426, 433, 503, 504, 636, 653, 655, 658, 659, 845.

652 Salubrity

N. *salubrity*, healthiness, state of health; well-being 650n. *health*; salubriousness, healthfulness, wholesomeness; ventilation, fresh air, open a., sea-a., ozone 340 n. *air*; sunshine, out-doors; fine climate, genial c. 340n. *weather*.

hygiene, sanitation, cleanliness 648n. *cleanness*; preventive medicine, prophylaxis 658n. *prophylactic*; quarantine, cordon sanitaire 660n. *protection*; immunity, immunization, inoculation, auto-inoculation, vaccination, pasteurization; antisepsis, sterilization, disinfection, chlorination; sanitarium, sanatorium, spa 658n. *hospital*; hot-springs, thermæ 658n. *ther-*

apy; keeping fit, exercise, out-door e., tonic e.; science of health, hygiology, hygienics.

sanitarian, hygienist, sanitationist, sanitary inspector, public health officer; sanitary engineer; Public Health Department; fresh-air fiend, sun-worshipper, nudist.

Adj. *salubrious*, healthful, healthy, wholesome; pure, fresh 648 adj. *clean*; ventilated 340 adv. *airy*; tonic, bracing, invigorating, refreshing, sanative 656 adj. *restorative*; hygienic, sanitary, disinfected, chlorinated, pasteurized, sterilized, sterile, aseptic, antiseptic; prophylactic, immunizing, protective 658 adj. *remedial*; good for, salutary, what the doctor ordered 644 adj. *beneficial*; nutritious, nourishing, health-preserving; uninjurious, harmless, benign, non-malignant; uninfectious, non-infectious, innoxious, innocuous; immune, immunized, vaccinated, inoculated, protected 660 adj. *invulnerable*.

Vb. *be salubrious,*—bracing etc. adj.; be good for one's health, agree with one, make one fit; have a good climate; prevent disease; keep fit 650 vb. *be healthy*.

sanitate, disinfect, sterilize, antisepticize, chlorinate, pasteurize; immunize, inoculate, vaccinate; quarantine, put in q., isolate, segregate 883 vb. *seclude*; ventilate, freshen 648 vb. *purify*; cleanse 648 vb. *clean*; drain 342 vb. *dry*; conserve 666 vb. *preserve*.

Adv. *healthily*, wholesomely, salubriously, hygienically.

See: 340, 342, 644, 648, 650, 656, 658, 660, 666, 883.

653 Insalubrity

N. *insalubrity*, unhealthiness, unwholesomeness; uncleanliness, lack of hygiene, lack of sanitation; dirty habits, verminousness 649 n. *uncleanness*; unhealthy conditions, unwholesome surroundings; mephitism, bad air, bad climate; infectiousness, contagiousness; bad drains, slum, sewer 649 n. *sink*; infectious person, carrier, germ-c., vector; plague-spot, pesthouse, contagion 651 n. *infection*; pollution, radio-activity, fall-out; deadliness, poisonousness 659 n. *bane*; non-naturals.

Adj. *insalubrious*, unwholesome, unhealthful, unhealthy; bad for one's health, insanitary, unhygienic; ungenial, bad, nasty, noxious, noisome, injurious 645 adj. *harmful*; verminous, infested; undrained 347 adj. *marshy*; foul, polluted, undrinkable, inedible; indigestible, unnutritious, non-vitaminous; unsound, unfresh, stale, gone bad 655 adj. *deteriorated*; unventilated, windowless, airless; stuffy; overheated, underheated.

infectious, morbific, morbiferous, pathogenic; infective, germ-laden; zymotic; contagious, catching, taking, communicable; pestiferous, pestilent, pestful, plaguy, plague-stricken; malarious, malarial, aguish; epidemic, pandemic, endemic; epizootic, enzootic, sporadic; unsterilized, non-sterile, infected 649 adj. *dirty*.

toxic, narcotic, azotic; poisonous, mephitic, pestilential, germ-laden; venomous, envenomed, poisoned, steeped in poison; septic, pussy, mattery, gathering, festering, purulent, suppurating; mortiferous 362 adj. *deadly*.

Adv. *unwholesomely*, insalubriously, poisonously; unhealthily, unhygienically 651 adv. *morbidly*.

See: 347, 362, 645, 649, 651, 655, 659.

654 Improvement

N. *improvement*, betterment, uplift, amelioration, melioration; good influence, the making of 178 n. *influence*; change for the better, transfiguration 143 n. *transformation*; conversion, new leaf 939 n. *penitence*; revival, recovery 656 n. *restoration*; evolution, development, perfectibility; elaboration, enrichment; decoration 844 n. *ornamentation*; advance, onward march, march of time, progress 285 n. *progression*; furtherance, advancement, preferment, promotion, kick upstairs, rise, raise, lift, jump 308 n. *ascent*; uptrend, upswing 310 n. *elevation*; revaluation, enhancement 36 n. *increase*.

amendment, mending etc. vb.; mend 656 n. *repair*; organization, better o. 62 n. *arrangement*; reformation, reform, radical r. (see *reformism*); Borstal, reformatory, house of correction 539 n. *school*;

purification, sublimation 648 n. *cleansing*; refining, rectification, putting right, removal of errors; redaction, castigation, correction, revision, red ink, blue pencil; emendation, happy conjecture; recension, revised edition, new e., improved version 589 n. *edition*; revise, proof, corrected copy; second thoughts, better t., review, reconsideration, re-examination; further reflection 67 n. *sequel*; polish, finishing touch 725 n. *completion*; perfectionism 862 n. *fastidiousness*.

civilization, culture, kultur; civility, refinement 846 n. *good taste*; training 534 n. *education*; cultivation, polish, improvement of the mind, menticulture; improvement of the race, eugenics; physical culture, callisthenics 682 n. *exercise*; telesis, euthenics.

reformism, meliorism, perfectionism, idealism; radicalism; extremism, revolution 738 n. *sedition*; minimalism, maximalism; progressivism, progressism, onward and upward department; gradualism, Fabianism; social adjustment 901 n. *sociology*.

reformer, improver, repairer, restorer 656 n. *mender*; emender, corrector, castigator, editor, reviser, second hand; progressive, progressist, progressionist; minimalist, gradualist, Fabian 625 n. *moderate*; radical, extremist, maximalist, revolutionary 738 n. *agitator*; communist, Marxist, Red; reformist, New Dealer; idealist, Utopian 862 n. *perfectionist*; sociologist, social worker, muckraker, slummer 901 n. *philanthropist*.

Adj. *improved*, bettered, enhanced; touched up 843 adj. *beautified*; reformed, revised 34 adj. *superior*; better, better off, all the better for; better advised, wiser 498 adj. *wise*; improvable, corrigible, curable, reformable, perfectible.

improving, reformative, reformatory, remedial, medicinal 656 adj. *restorative*; reforming, reformist, progressive, radical; civilizing, cultural, accultural; idealistic, perfectionist, Utopian, millenarian, chiliastic; perfectionist 862 n. *fastidious*.

Vb. *get better*, grow b., improve, mend, take a turn for the better, turn the corner; pick up, rally, revive, recover 656 vb. *be restored*; make progress, advance, develop, evolve 285 vb. *progress*; mellow, ripen 669 vb. *mature*; fructify 171 vb. *be*

fruitful; rise 308 vb. *ascend*; graduate 727 vb. *succeed*; rise in the world, better oneself, make one's way 730 vb. *prosper*; mend one's ways, reform, turn a new leaf, go straight 939 n. *be penitent*; improve oneself, learn by experience 536 vb. *learn*; take advantage of, make capital out of, cash in on 137 vb. *profit by.*

make better, better, improve, ameliorate, meliorate, reform; make improvements, improve upon, refine u.; polish, elaborate, enrich, enhance; improve out of recognition, transfigure 147 n. *transform*; make, be the making of, have a good influence, leaven 178 vb. *influence*; refine, uplift, elevate, sublimate 648 vb. *purify*; moralize; civilize, socialize, teach manners; mend 656 vb. *repair*; restore 656 vb. *cure*; recruit, revive, infuse fresh blood into 685 vb. *refresh*; soften, lenify, mitigate, palliate, lessen an evil 177 vb. *moderate*; forward, advance, upgrade 285 vb. *promote*; foster, fatten, mellow 669 vb. *mature*; make the most of, get the best out of 673 vb. *use*; develop, open up, reclaim; plant, till, dress, water 370 vb. *cultivate*; weed 44 vb. *eliminate*; tidy, tidy up, neaten 62 vb. *arrange*; spruce, freshen, valet, freshen up 648 vb. *clean*; do up, vamp up, tone up, tighten up; renovate, refurbish, reface, renew; bring up to date 126 vb. *modernize*; touch up 841 vb. *beautify*; improve on nature, make up, titivate 843 vb. *primp*; embellish, adorn, ornament 844 vb. *decorate*; straighten, straighten out (**see** *rectify*).

rectify, refine 648 vb. *purify*; put right, set right, straighten, straighten out 24 vb. *adjust*; mend, patch 656 vb. *repair*; correct, make corrections, blue-pencil, proof-read, remove errors; revise, redact, edit, amend, emend; rewrite, redraft, retell, recast, remould, refashion, remodel, new-model, recreate, refound, reform; reorganize 62 vb. *regularize*; make improvements, streamline; review, re-examine, reconsider; correct one's mistakes, stop in time, think again, think better of, have second thoughts; appeal from Philip drunk to Philip sober.

See: 24, 34, 36, 44, 62, 67, 126, 137, 143, 147, 171, 177, 178, 285, 308, 310, 370, 498, 534, 536, 539, 589, 625, 648, 656, 669, 673, 682, 685, 725, 727, 730, 738, 841, 843, 844, 846, 862, 901, 939.

655 Deterioration

N. *deterioration,* debasement, coarsening; cheapening, devaluation; retrogradation, retrogression, slipping back, losing ground 286 n. *regression;* reversion to type, throw-back 5 n. *heredity;* decline, declension, declination, ebb 37 n. *decrease;* twilight, obscuration, fading 419 n. *dimness;* falling off, down-trend, slump, depression 290 n. *recession;* impoverishment 801 n. *poverty;* law of diminishing returns; Gresham's law; Malthusianism; exhaustion, consumption 634 n. *waste;* vitiation, corruption, perversion, prostitution, depravation, demoralization, degeneration, loss of morale, degeneracy, degenerateness, decadence, depravity 934 n. *wickedness;* downward course, primrose path 309 n. *descent;* recidivism 603 n. *tergiversation;* set-back 657 n. *relapse;* bad ending, tragedy 731 n. *ill fortune.*

dilapidation, caducity, collapse, ruination 165 n. *destruction;* lack of maintenance, disrepair, neglect 458 n. *negligence;* slum, backstreet 801 n. *poverty;* ravages of time, wear and tear, erosion, corrosion, oxidization, rustiness, rust, moth and rust, canker, corruption, gangrene, rot, dry-r., rottenness 51 n. *decay;* mouldiness, mildew 659 n. *blight;* decrepitude, senility 131 n. *age;* marasmus, atrophy 651 n, *disease;* shadow, shadow of one's former self, ruin, wreck, mere w., perfect w., physical w., shotten herring.

impairment, spoiling 675 n. *misuse;* detriment, damage, inroad, waste 772 n. *loss;* discoloration, weathering, patina; pollution, inquination, defilement, corruption, defedation 649 n. *uncleanness;* ulceration, venenation, poisoning, intoxication, autointoxication, suppuration, contamination, contagion 651 n. *infection;* adulteration, sophistication, watering down, alloy 43 n. *mixture;* assault, insult, outrage 712 n. *attack;* ruination, dilaceration, demolishment 165 n. *destruction;* injuriousness, injury, mischief, ravage, scathe, harm 165 n. *havoc;* disablement, crippling, laming, hobbling, nobbling, disabling, mutilation, weakening 163 n. *weakness;* disorganization, bedevilment, sabotage 63 n. *derangement;* exacerbation 832 n. *aggravation.*

wound, injury, trauma; open wound, fresh w., bloody nose; sore, running s. 651 n.

ulcer; laceration, lesion; cut, gash, incision, abrasion, scratch 46 n. *scission;* stab, prick, jab, puncture 263 n. *perforation;* contusion, bruise, bump, discoloration, black eye, thick ear 253 n. *swelling;* burn, scald; rupture, broken head, broken bones 46 n. *disjunction;* scar, mark, cicatrice 845 n. *blemish.*

Adj. *deteriorated,* not improved, the worse for; exacerbated 832 adj. *aggravated;* spoilt, impaired, damaged, hurt, ruined etc. vb.; worn out, effete, exhausted, shotten, worthless 641 adj. *useless;* stale, gone bad, rotten 645 adj. *bad;* corked, flat 387 adj. *tasteless;* undermined, sapped, honeycombed, shaken 163 adj. *weakened;* tired, over-t., done up 684 adj. *fatigued;* no better, deteriorating, worse, getting w., worse and worse, in a bad way; failing, past one's best, declining, in decline, on the d.; ageing, senile, senescent 131 adj. *aged;* on the way out, on the down grade, on the downward path; falling, slipping, nodding, tottering, deciduous 309 adj. *descending;* faded, withered, sere, decaying 51 adj. *decomposed;* consuming, wasting, wasting away, ebbing, at low ebb; slumping, falling off 37 adj. *decreasing;* degenerative, retrogressive, retrograde, unprogressive, unimproved, backward 286 adj. *regressive;* lapsed, recidivist 603 adj. *tergiversating;* degenerate, depraved, vitiated, corrupt 934 adj. *vicious;* come down in the world, impoverished 801 adj. *poor.*

dilapidated, the worse for wear, in ruins, in shreds; broken, in bits, in pieces; cracked, battered, weather-beaten; decrepit, ruinous, ramshackle, tottery, tumbledown, on its last legs; slummy, condemned; worn, well-w., frayed, shabby, tatty, holey, in holes, in tatters, in rags; worn out, worn to a frazzle, worn to a shadow, done for 641 adj. *useless;* seedy, down at heel, down and out 801 adj. *poor;* rusty, rotten, mildewed, mouldering, mossgrown, moth-eaten, worm-e., dog-eared 51 adj. *decomposed;* dingy, drab.

Vb. *deteriorate,* not improve, get no better; worsen, get worse, go from bad to worse; slip, slide, go downhill, take the downgrade; not maintain 657 vb. *relapse;* fall off, slump, decline, wane, ebb, sink, fail 37 vb. *decrease;* slip back, retrograde 286 vb. *regress;* lapse 603 vb. *tergiversate;*

degenerate, lose morale; tread the primrose path, go to the bad, spoil oneself, ruin o. 934vb. *be wicked*; collapse, break down, fall, totter, droop, stoop 309vb. *tumble*; contract, shrink 198vb. *become small*; wear out, age 131vb. *grow old*; fade, wither, wilt, shrivel, perish, crumble, moulder, mildew, grow moss, grow weeds; bolt, run to seed; weather, rust, rot, decay 51vb. *decompose*; spoil, stale, fust, lose its sap, lose its taste, lose its flavour, grow stale, go flat, cork 391vb. *be unpalatable*; go bad, smell 397vb. *stink*; corrupt, putrefy, rankle, fester, suppurate, gangrene, sicken 651vb. *be ill*; do worse, make things worse, jump from the frying pan into the fire, go farther and fare worse 832vb. *aggravate*.

pervert, deform, warp, twist 246vb. *distort*; abuse, prostitute 675vb. *misuse*; demoralize, deprave, deflower 951vb. *debauch*; vitiate, corrupt 934vb. *make wicked*; lower, degrade, debase, embase 311vb. *abase*; brutalize, dehumanize, barbarize, decivilize; denature, denaturalize 147vb. *transform*; denationalize, detribalize; propagandize, brainwash 535 vb. *misteach*.

impair, damage, damnify, hurt, injure, mischieve, scathe, shend 645vb. *harm*; jumble, mess up, muck up, untidy, crease 63vb. *derange*; disorganize, dismantle, dismast; spoil, maul, mar, botch 695vb. *be clumsy*; touch, tinker, tamper, meddle with, fool w., monkey w. 678vb. *meddle*; not improve, worsen, deteriorate, exacerbate, embitter 832vb. *aggravate*; do no good, kill with kindness 499vb. *be foolish*; stale, degrade, lower, coarsen 847vb. *vulgarize*; devalue, debase 812vb. *cheapen*; blacken, blot, spot, stain, uglify 842vb. *make ugly*; scar, mark, wrinkle 845vb. *blemish*; deface, disfigure, deform, warp 246vb. *distort*; corrupt, vitiate (see *pervert*); mutilate, maim, lame, cripple, hobble, nobble, hock, hough, hamstring 161 vb. *disable*; scotch, clip the wings, cramp, hamper 702vb. *hinder*; castrate, caponize 161vb. *unman*; expurgate, eviscerate, bowdlerize; curtail, dock 204vb. *shorten*; cream, skim, take the heart out of; adulterate, sophisticate, alloy 43vb. *mix*; denature, deactivate 679vb. *make inactive*; subvert, shake, sap, mine undermine, labefy 163vb. *weaken*; honeycomb, bore,

gnaw, gnaw at the roots, eat away, erode, corrode, rust, rot, mildew 51vb. *decompose*; blight, blast; ravage, waste, scorch, overrun 165vb. *lay waste*; wreck, ruin, overthrow 165vb. *destroy*; crumble 332 vb. *pulverize*; dilapidate, fray, wear out, reduce to rags; exhaust, consume, use up 634vb. *waste*; infect, contaminate, poison, envenom, ulcerate; taint, canker, foul, pollute 649vb. *make unclean*; defile, desecrate, profane, unhallow 980vb. *be impious*.

wound, scotch, draw blood, let b.; tear, rend, lacerate, laniate, mangle, rip, rip up 46 vb. *disjoin*; maul, savage 176vb. *be violent*; bite, scratch, claw; hack, incise 46vb. *cut*; scarify, score 262vb. *groove*; nick 260vb. *notch*; sting, prick, pink, stab, run through 263vb. *pierce*; bruise, contuse, buffet 279vb. *strike*; crush, grind 332 vb. *pulverize*; chafe 333vb. *rub*; smash 46 vb. *break*; graze, pepper, wing.

See: 5, 37, 43, 46, 51, 63, 131, 147, 161, 163, 165, 176, 198, 204, 246, 253, 260, 262, 263, 279, 286, 290, 309, 311, 332, 333, 387, 391, 397, 419, 458, 499, 535, 603, 634, 641, 645, 649, 651, 657, 659, 675, 678, 679, 684, 695, 702, 712, 731, 772, 801, 812, 832, 842, 845, 847, 934, 951, 980.

656 Restoration

N. *restoration*, returning, giving back, retrocession 787n. *restitution*; redress, amends, reparation, reparations 941n. *atonement*; finding again, getting back, retrieval, recovery 786n. *taking*; refoundation, re-establishment, reinstallation, reinvestment, restauration, recall, replacement, reinstatement, reinstalment; rehabilitation; replanting, reafforestation, reclamation; rescue, salvage, redemption, ransom, salvation 668n. *deliverance*; reconstitution, re-erection, rebuilding, reformation, reconstruction, reorganization; readjustment; remodelling 654n. *reformism*; reconversion, revalorization; rehash, réchauffé; reaction, counter-reformation 182n. *counteraction*; resumption, return to normal, derestriction; recruitment, reinforcement 162n. *strengthening*; replenishment 633n. *provision*.

repair, reparation, repairs, renovation,

renewal, reconditioning, redintegration, reassembling; rectification, emendation; restoration, making like new 126 n. *newness*; mending, invisible m., darning, patching, patching up; cobbling, soling, heeling, tinkering etc. vb.; clout, patch, darn, insertion, reinforcement; new look, face-lift 843 n. *beautification*.

revival, recruitment, recovery 685 n. *refreshment*; renewal, reawakening, revivescence, resurgence, recurrence, recovery, come-back, break-b.; fresh spurt, new energy; economic recovery, economic miracle, boom 730 n. *prosperity*; reactivation, revivification, reanimation, resuscitation, artificial respiration; rejuvenation, rejuvenescence, second youth, Indian summer; face-lift, new look; rebirth, renaissance, new birth, second b.; regeneration, regeneracy, regenerateness 654 n. *amendment*; new life, resurrection, awaking from the dead, recall from the grave; resurrection-day 124 n. *future state*.

sanation, cure, certain c., perfect c.; recure, healing, mending; cicatrization, closing, scabbing over, healing o.; convalescence, recuperation, recovery, pulling through, restoration to health 658 n. *remedy*; moderation, easing 831 n. *relief*; psychological cure, catharsis, abreaction; curability.

mender, restorer, repairer, renovator, decorator; emendator, rectifier; rebuilder, second founder; refurbisher, face-lifter; patcher, darner, cobbler, boot-repairer, botcher; thatcher; knife-grinder, tinker, plumber, fixer; salvor, salvager; curer, healer, bone-setter, witch-doctor 658 n. *doctor*; faith-healer; psychiatrist; reformist 654 n. *reformer*.

Adj. *restored*, revived, refreshed etc. vb.; remade, reconditioned, redone, rectified; like new, renewed; reborn, redivivus, renascent, Phœnix-like; cured, none the worse, better, convalescent, on the mend, pulling through; in one's right mind, back to normal; retrievable, restorable, recoverable; mendable, amendable; medicable, curable, sanable, operable; found, recovered, salvaged, reclaimed.

restorative, reparative, analeptic, recuperative, curative, sanative, healing, medicated, medicinal 658 adj. *remedial*.

Vb. *be restored*, recover, come round, come to, revive, pick up, rally 685 vb. *be*

refreshed; pull through, get over, get up, get well, convalesce, recuperate; weather the storm, survive, live through; reawake, live again, relive, resurrect, come to life again, arise from the dead, return from the grave; reappear, make a come-back; find one's strength, be oneself again, sleep off; return to normal, get back to n., go on as before; resume, start again 68 vb. *begin*; look like new, undergo repairs.

restore, give back, hand b., retrocede, yield up 787 vb. *restitute*; make amends 941 vb. *atone*; put back, bring b., replace; recall, reappoint, reinstall, refound, re-establish, rehabilitate; reconstitute, reconstruct, reform, reorganize 654 vb. *make better*; renovate, renew, rehash, warm up; rebuild, re-erect, remake, redo; refurbish, make like new 126 vb. *modernize*; make whole, redintegrate; reforest, reafforest, replant, reclaim; revalidate, reinforce, recruit 162 vb. *strengthen*; fill up, fill up the ranks 633 vb. *replenish*; rally, reassemble 74 vb. *bring together*; redeem, ransom, rescue, salvage 668 vb. *deliver*; release, derestrict 746 vb. *liberate*.

revive, revivify, revitalize, resuscitate, regenerate, recall to life, resurrect, reanimate, re-inspire, rekindle; breathe fresh life into, rejuvenate; freshen, recruit 685 vb. *refresh*; service; valet.

cure, recure, heal, make well, cure of, break of; nurse, physic, medicine, medicate 658 vb. *doctor*; bandage, bind up one's wounds; nurse through, work a cure, snatch from the grave, restore to health, set up; set (a bone); cicatrize, heal over, scab o., skin o., close; right itself, put itself right, work its own cure.

repair, do repairs; amend, emend, right, set to rights, put right, make all square, straighten 654 vb. *rectify*; overhaul, mend, fix; tinker, cobble, botch, sole, re-sole, heel, heel-piece; reface, retread, re-cover, thatch 226 vb. *cover*; re-line 227 vb. *line*; darn, patch, repatch, patch up, clout; stop, fill (teeth); make over, do up, touch up, freshen up, retouch, vamp, vamp up, plaster up, fill in the cracks, paper over; stanch, stop a gap, plug a hole 350 vb. *stanch*; caulk, careen 264 vb. *close*; splice, bind, bind up 45 vb. *tie*; pick up the pieces, piece together, refit, reassemble, cannibalize 45 vb. *join*; face-lift,

refurbish, recondition, renovate, renew, remodel, reform.

retrieve, get back, recover, regain, retake, recapture; find again, reclaim, claim back, compensate oneself 31 vb. *recoup*; make up for, make up time, make up leeway, take up the slack.

See: 31, 45, 68, 74, 124, 126, 162, 182, 226, 227, 264, 350, 633, 654, 658, 668, 685, 730, 746, 786, 787, 831, 843, 941.

657 Relapse

N. *relapse*, lapse, falling back; throw-back, return; retrogression, retrogradation 286 n. *regression*; sinking, falling off, fall 655 n. *deterioration*; backsliding, recidivation, recidivism, apostasy 603 n. *tergiversation*; recrudescence, reinfection, recurrence, fresh outbreak.

Vb. *relapse*, slip back, slide b., sink b., fall b.; throw back, return, retrograde 286 vb. *regress*; degenerate 655 vb. *deteriorate*; backslide, recidivate, lapse, fall from grace 603 vb. *apostatize*; fall off again, return to one's vomit; have a relapse, suffer a recurrence, not maintain an improvement.

See: 286, 603, 655.

658 Remedy

N. *remedy*, succour, help, present help in time of trouble 703 n. *aid*; oil on troubled waters 177 n. *moderator*; remedial measure, corrective, correction 654 n. *amendment*; redress, amends 787 n. *restitution*; expiation 941 n. *atonement*; cure, radical c., certain c., perfect c. 656 n. *sanation*; medicinal value, healing gift, healing quality *or* property; sovereign remedy, specific r., specific, answer, right a., solution; prescribed remedy, prescription, recipe, receipt, nostrum; universal remedy, panacea, cure-all, catholicon; elixir, elixer vitæ, philosopher's stone.

medicine, materia medica, pharmacopœia; vegetable remedy, Galenical, herb, simple; medicinal herb, balm, agaric, linseed, camomile, orris root, mandrake; medica-

tion, medicament, patent medicine, drug, proprietary d.; tablet, tabloid, capsule, lozenge; physic, draught, potion, dose, drench, drenching; pill, purge, bolus; preparation, mixture, powder, electuary, linctus; plaster (see *surgical dressing*); medicine chest, medicine bottle.

prophylactic, preventive; sanitation, sanitary precaution, cordon sanitaire, quarantine 652 n. *hygiene*; prophylaxis, immunization, inoculation, vaccination; antisepsis, disinfection, sterilization; antiseptic, disinfectant, iodine, creosote, carbolic, boric acid, boracic a., chloride of lime; mothball, camphor, lavender; bactericide, germicide, insecticide 659 n. *poison*; incense, fumigant; dentifrice, toothpaste, tooth-powder 648 n. *cleanser*; mouthwash gargle; essential oils; quinine.

antidote, abirritant; analgesic, pain-killer; counter-irritant, urtication, bee-sting; counter-poison, antitoxin, mithridate, theriac; anti-dysenteric; antemetic; antaphrodisiac; antifebrile, antifebrific, anticaustic, febrifuge, quinine; cold water; vermifuge, helminthagogue, anthelmintic; antigen, antibody; antibiosis, antibiotic; antispasmodic, mescal; anticoagulant.

cathartic, purge, purgative, laxative, aperient, pull-through; agaric, castor oil, Epsom salts, calomel, senna pods; isaf gul, flea-seed; expectorant, emetic, nauseant, emetine, ipecacuanha, nux vomica; carminative, digestive, pepastic.

tonic, corroborant, restorative, analeptic; cordial, tonic water; bracer, reviver, refresher, pick-me-up 174 n. *stimulant*; spirits, smelling salts, sal volatile, hartshorn; camomile, effusion, tisane, ptisan; vitamin; benzedrine.

drug, dope, opium, cocaine, snow, morphia, morphine, codeine, caffeine, mescalin; synthetic drug, wonder d., miracle d.; antibiotic, sulpha drug; penicillin; aureomycin, streptomycin, insulin, cortisone; tranquillizer, aspirin, narcotic, analgesic 375 n. *anæsthetic*; nepenthe, kef, kief.

balm, balsam, oil, soothing syrup, emollient, lenitive 177 n. *moderator*; salve, cerate, ointment, collyrium, eye-salve, cream, face-c. 843 n. *cosmetic*; lanoline, liniment, embrocation; lotion, wash.

surgical dressing, dressing, lint, gauze; swab; bandage, suspensory, sling, splint, cast, tourniquet; fingerstall; patch; cata-

pasm, vesicant, vesicatory; application, external a., cataplasm, epithem, epithemation; plaster, sticking p., corn p., court p., mustard p., sinapism, fomentation, poultice, compress; tampion, tent, roll, pledget; pessary, suppository; vulnerary, traumatic.

medical art, leechcraft; therapeutics, acology, art of healing, healing touch 656n. *sanation*; medical advice, practice, medical p.; allopathy, homoeopathy, ayurvedic system, unani s.; medicine, clinical m., preventive m., virology; diagnosis, prognosis 651n. *pathology*; healing, faith-h., Christian Science; sexology, gynaecology, midwifery 164n. *obstetrics*; gerontology, geriatrics, pediatrics; psychopædics; iatrochemistry, psychopharmocology; pharmaceutics, pharmacology, posology, dosology; veterinary medicine.

surgery, chirurgery, general surgery, brain s., heart s.; plastic surgery, anaplasty, rhinoplasty; manipulative surgery, chiropraxis, chiropractice; operation, surgical o., op.; phlebotomy, venesection; bleeding, blood-letting, cupping, transfusion, perfusion; amputation, trephination, tonsillectomy, appendectomy, colostomy, laparotomy; dentistry, drawing, extracting, stopping, filling, crowning; massage, shampoo; chiropody, pedicure, manicure.

therapy, therapeutics, medical care; treatment, medical t., clinical t.; nursing, bedside manner; first aid, after-care; course, cure, faith c., nature c., cold-water c., hydrotherapy; regimen, diet, dietary; chiropody, bone-setting, orthopaedy, osteopathy, osteotherapy, orthopraxy; hypnotherapy, hypnopedagogics; physiotherapy, radiotherapy, phototherapy; occupational therapy; electrotherapy, shock treatment; mental treatment, clinical psychology; child psychology, psychopædics; psychotherapy, psychiatry, psychoanalysis; acupuncture, needling; injection, shot, stab, jab; enema, clyster, purge, bowel-wash, douche; cathetic, catheterism, catheterization; fomentation, poulticing.

hospital, infirmary, general hospital, fever h., maternity h., children's h.; mental hospital 503n. *madhouse*; dispensary, clinic, pre-natal c.; nursing home, convalescent h., rest h.; home for the dying, terminal home; lazaret, lazaretto, hospice, pest-house; lazar-house, leper asylum, leper colony; hospital ship, hospital train; stretcher, ambulance; ward, hospital w., casualty w., isolation w., sick bay, sickroom, sick-bed; hospital bed, ripple-b.; tent, oxygen t., iron lung; dressing station, first-aid s., casualty s.; operation room, operating theatre, operating table; consulting room, surgery, clinic; sanatorium, spa, hydro, watering-place; pump-room, baths, hot-springs, thermæ; solarium, sun-deck, sun lamp.

doctor, medical man; leech, quack; veterinary surgeon, vet, horse-doctor; herbalist, herb-doctor; faith-healer, Christian Scientist; allopath, homoeopath, ayurvedist, hakim; witch-doctor, medicine-man 983n. *sorcerer*; medico, medical student; houseman, intern, house physician, resident p., house surgeon, resident s., registrar; medical practitioner, general p., G.P.; locum tenens, locum; physician, clinician, therapeutist, healer; operator, surgeon, general s., plastic s., neuro-s.; chirurgeon, barber, barber-surgeon, sawbones; medical officer, health o., sanitary inspector; medical adviser, consultant, specialist; diagnostician, pathologist; alienist, psychiatrist, psychoanalyst, psychopathist, brain-specialist, neurologist, neuropath; anæsthetist, radiotherapist; pediatrician, geriatrician; obstetrician, accoucheur, midwife; gynaecologist; sexologist; dermatologist; orthopaedist, osteopath, bonesetter, chiropractor, masseur, masseuse; pedicurist, chiropodist, manicurist; ophthalmologist, optician, oculist; aurist; dentist, dental surgeon, tooth-drawer; nutritionist, dietician; medical profession, Harley Street; Red Cross, St. John's Ambulance; Æsculapius, Hippocrates, Galen.

druggist, apothecary, chemist, pharmaceutical c., pharmacopolist, pharmacist; dispenser, posologist, pharmacologist; drug store, pharmacy.

nurse, male n., probationer n., pro.; sister, night s., ward s., theatre s., sister tutor, matron, hospital m.; Nightingale, state-registered nurse, S.R.N., registered sick children's nurse, R.S.C.N.; special nurse, day n., night n.; district nurse, home-n., Sairy Gamp; nursing auxiliary, ward orderly, dresser, medical

attendant, stretcher-bearer, ambulance-driver; probationer officer, court missionary, lady almoner 901 n. *sociology.*

Adj. *remedial*, corrective, analeptic, curative, first-aid 656 adj. *restorative*; helpful 644 adj. *beneficial*; therapeutic, medicinal, sanative, hygienic, salutiferous 652 adj. *salubrious*; specific, sovereign; panacean, all-healing; soothing, paregoric, balsamic, demulcent, emollient, palliative 177 adj. *lenitive*; anodyne, analgesic, narcotic, hypnotic, anæsthetic 375 adj. *insensible*; peptic, digestive; depurative, detersive 648 adj. *cleansing*; cathartic, emetic, vomitory, laxative; antidotal 182 adj. *counteracting*; alexipharmic, theriacal, therial; prophylactic, disinfectant, antiseptic; febrifugal, alexipyretic; tonic, stimulative, corroborant; enlivening; dietetic, alimentary, nutritive, nutritional.

medical, pathological, physicianly, Æsculapian, Hippocratic, Galenic; allopathic, homoeopathic, ayurvedic; surgical, chirurgical, anaplastic, rhinoplastic, orthopaedic, chiropractic; chiropodical, pedicuristic, manicuristic; vulnerary, traumatic; obstetric, obstetrical; medicable, medicinable, operable, curable.

Vb. *remedy*, fix, put right, correct 656 vb. *restore*; succour, help 703 vb. *aid*; apply a remedy, treat, heal, work a cure 656 vb. *cure*; palliate, soothe, neutralize 831 vb. *relieve.*

doctor, be a d., practise, have a practice; treat, prescribe, advise; attend 703 vb. *minister to*; tend, nurse; give first aid, call an ambulance, hospitalize, put on the sick-list; physic, medicine, medicate, drench, dose, purge; inject, poke, stab, jab; dress, bind, swathe, bandage; stop the bleeding, apply a tourniquet 350 vb. *stanch*; poultice, plaster, foment; set, put in splints; drug, dope, anæsthetize; operate, use the knife, cut open, amputate; trepan, trephine; curette; cauterize; bleed, leech, cup, let blood, venesect, phlebotomize; transfuse, perfuse; massage, rub, shampoo; draw, extract, pull, stop, fill, crown; pedicure, manicure; immunize, vaccinate, inoculate; sterilize, pasteurize, antisepticise, disinfect 652 vb. *sanitate.*

See: 164, 174, 177, 182, 350, 375, 503, 644, 648, 651, 652, 654, 656, 659, 703, 787, 831, 843, 901, 941, 983.

659 Bane

N. *bane*, cause of injury, malevolent influence; curse, plague, pest, scourge, ruin 616 n. *evil*; malady 651 n. *disease*; weakness, bad habit, besetting sin 934 n. *vice*; hell, cup, visitation, affliction 731 n. *adversity*; woe, funeral 825 n. *sorrow*; cross, trial; bore 838 n. *tedium*; bugbear, bête noire 827 n. *annoyance*; burden, imposition, tax, white elephant; thorn in the flesh, stone round one's neck; perpetual worry, constant anxiety, torment, nagging pain 825 n. *worry*; running sore 651 n. *ulcer*; bitterness, acid, gall, wormwood 393 n. *sourness*; sickener, emetic 391 n. *unsavouriness*; sword, sting, serpent's tooth, fang, bramble, brier, nettle 256 n. *sharp point*; source of trouble, hornet's nest 663 n. *pitfall*; viper, adder, serpent 365 n. *reptile*; snake, snake in the grass 663 n. *trouble-maker*; parasite, leech, locust 168 n. *destroyer*; oppressor, terror 735 n. *tyrant.*

blight, blast, rust, rubigo, rot, dry-r.; mildew, mould, fungus; moth, moth and rust; worm, canker-w., canker, cancer; visitation 651 n. *plague*; frost, nip, cold 380 n. *coldness*; drought 342 n. *desiccation.*

poison, poisonousness, virulence, venomousness, toxicity; bad food, bad water; bacteria, bacillus, germ, virus 651 n. *infection*; venom, toxicant, toxin; deadly poison, snake p., rat p., ratsbane, germicide, insecticide, pesticide, acaricide, vulpicide, fungicide, weed-killer, D.D.T.; acid, corrosive; hemlock, arsenic, strychnine, cyanide, hyocyamine, Prussic acid, vitriol; nicotine, verdigris; asphyxiant, poison gas, Lewisite, mustard g., tear g., lachrymatory g.; carbon monoxide, carbon dioxide, carbonic acid gas, choke damp, after-d.; foul air, mephitis, miasma, effluvium, sewer gas 653 n. *insalubrity*; smog 355 n. *cloud*; radio-activity, radioactive cloud, mushroom, fall-out, strontium 90 417 n. *radiation*; dope, opium, hashish, bhang, marijuana, morphine, cocaine, snow 658 n. *drug*; intoxicant, depressant 949 n. *alcoholism*; toxicology.

poisonous plant, hemlock, deadly nightshade, belladonna, dhatura, henbane, wolfsbane, monkshood, aconite, hellebore, digitalis, foxglove; opium poppy, Indian hemp, bhang, hashish, upas tree.

poisoning, venenation, venefice 362n. *homicide*; blood poisoning, toxæmia 651n. *infection*; food poisoning, ptomaine p., botulism; poisoner 362n. *murderer*.

Adj. *baneful*, plaguy, pestilent, noisome 645adj. *harmful*; blighting, withering, poisonous, venomous 653adj. *toxic*; cursed, accursed 616adj. *evil*.

See: 168, 256, 342, 355, 362, 365, 380, 391, 393, 417, 610, 643, 631, 653, 658, 663, 731, 735, 825, 827, 838, 934, 949.

660 Safety

N. *safety*, safeness, security, surety; social security, welfare state 901n. *sociology*; invulnerability, impregnability, immunity, charmed life; numbers, safety in n. 104n. *multitude*; secure position, permanent post, safe job; safe distance, wide berth 620n. *avoidance*; all clear, coast c., danger past, danger over, storm blown over; guarantee, warrant 473n. *certainty*; sense of security, assurance, confidence 855n. *courage*; safety-valve 667n. *means of escape*; close shave, narrow escape 667 n. *escape*; rescue 668n. *deliverance*.

protection, self-p., self-preservation 666n. *preservation*; insurance, re-i., self-i. 858n. *caution*; patronage, auspices, fatherly eye; protectorate, guardianship, wardenship, wardship, tutelage, custody, protective c. 747n. *restraint*; custodianship, sake-keeping, keeping, charge, safe hands, grasp, grip, embrace 778n. *retention*; ward, watch and w. 457n. *surveillance*; safeguard, precaution, preventive measure 713n. *defence*; sanitary precaution, sanitation, immunization, prophylaxis, quarantine, cordon sanitaire 652n. *hygiene*; segregation 883n. *seclusion*; cushion, screen; means of protection, deterrent 723n. *weapon*; safe-conduct, passport, pass 756n. *permit*; escort, convoy, guard 722n. *armed force*; defence, sure d., bastion, bulwark, tower of strength 713n. *defences*; ark, palladium, haven, sanctuary, asylum, earth, hole 662n. *refuge*; anchor, sheet-a. 662n. *safeguard*; moat, ditch, palisade, stockade 235n. *fence*; shield, breastplate, panoply, armour plate 713n. *armour*; umbrella, ægis.

protector, protectress, guardian, tutor; guardian angel, tutelary god, liege lord,

feudal l., patroness 707n. *patron*; defender, preserver, shepherd; bodyguard, lifeguard, strong-arm man 742n. *retainer*; conservator, custodian, curator, warden; warder, castellan, guard; chaperon, duenna, governess, nurse, nursemaid, nanny, mammy, ayah, amah 749n. *keeper*; watcher, look-out, watch, watchman, night-w., chaukidar 441n. *spectator*; fire-watcher, fire-fighter, fireman, policeman, police constable, police sergeant, sheriff; bobby, peeler, blue-bottle, copper, cop, traffic c., bull, flat-foot, Charley, Dogberry 955n. *police*; tec., dick, private eye 459n. *detective*; sentry, sentinel, garrison 722n. *soldiery*; watch-dog, ban-d., police d. 365n. *dog*; Cerberus, Argus 457n. *surveillance*.

Adj. *safe*, without risk, unhazardous; assured, secure, sure; safe and sound, spared 666adj. *preserved*; with a whole skin, intact, unharmed 646adj. *undamaged*; garrisoned, well-kept, well-preserved, well-defended; insured, covered; immunized, vaccinated, inoculated; disinfected, hygienic 652adj. *salubrious*; in safety, in security, on the safe side, on sure ground, on terra firma; in harbour, in port, at anchor; above water, high and dry; out of danger, out of harm's way; clear, in the clear, unaccused, unthreatened, unmolested; unexposed, unhazarded; under shelter, sheltered, shielded, screened, protected etc.vb.; patronized, under the wing of; in safe hands, held, in custody, behind bars, under lock and key 747adj. *imprisoned*; reliable, guaranteed, warranted 929adj. *trustworthy*; benign, harmless, unthreatening 615adj. *good*.

invulnerable, immune, impregnable, inexpugnable, unassailable, unattackable, unbreakable, unchallengeable; founded on a rock, defensible, tenable 162adj. *strong*; proof, fool-proof; weatherproof, waterproof, leak-p., gas-p., fire-p., bullet-p., bomb-p., shatter-p.; snug, tight, seaworthy, air-w.; armoured, steel-clad, panoplied.

tutelary, custodial, guardian, protective, shepherdlike; ready to die for 931adj. *disinterested*; watchful 457adj. *vigilant*; keeping, protecting 666adj. *preserving*; antiseptic, disinfectant 652adj. *salubrious*.

Vb. *be safe*, — invulnerable etc.adj.; find safety, reach s., save one's bacon 667vb.

escape; land on one's feet, tide over, keep one's head above water, weather the storm, ride it out; keep a whole skin, bear a charmed life, have nine lives; be snug, nestle, stay at home, be under shelter, have a roof over one's head; be under cover 523 vb. *lurk*; keep a safe distance, give a wide berth 620 vb. *avoid. safeguard*, keep safe, guard, protect; spare 905 vb. *show mercy*; stand up for, go bail for 713 vb. *defend*; shield, grant asylum, afford sanctuary; cover up for 703 vb. *patronize*; keep, bottle, conserve 666 vb. *preserve*; treasure, hoard 632 vb. *store*; keep in custody 747 vb. *imprison*; ward, watch over, nurse, foster, cherish; have charge of, take charge of, keep an eye on, chaperon, play gooseberry 457 vb. *look after*; hide, put in a safe place, earth 525 vb. *conceal*; cushion 218 vb. *support*; cover, shroud, cloak, shade, shadow 421 vb. *screen*; keep under cover, garage, lock up; house, shelter, fold; ensconce, embay, enfold, embrace 235 vb. *inclose*; make safe, secure, fortify 162 vb. *strengthen*; entrench, fence, fence round 232 vb. *circumscribe*; arm, armour, clothe in steel; shepherd, convoy, escort; flank, support; garrison, mount guard; immunize, inoculate, vaccinate; pasteurize, chlorinate, disinfect 652 vb. *sanitate*; give assurances, warrant, guarantee 473 vb. *make certain*; keep order, police, patrol.

seek safety, demand assurances, take precautions, play for safety, hedge, insure, re-insure 858 vb. *be cautious*; make assurance doubly sure 473 vb. *be certain*; dig in 599 vb. *stand firm*; run away 667 vb. *escape*; cut and run 277 vb. *move fast*; live to fight another day, think better of it; shorten sail, take in a reef, run for port, take refuge 662 vb. *seek refuge.*

Adv. *under shelter*, under cover, in the lee of; out of harm's way, safely, with impunity.

See: 104, 162, 218, 232, 235, 277, 365, 421, 441, 457, 459, 473, 523, 525, 599, 615, 620, 632, 646, 652, 662, 666, 667, 668, 703, 707, 713, 722, 723, 742, 747, 749, 756, 778, 855, 858, 883, 901, 905, 929, 931, 955.

661 Danger

N. *danger*, peril; dangerousness, perilousness, shadow of death, jaws of d., dragon's mouth; dangerous situation, unhealthy s., desperate s., parlous state, forlorn hope 700 n. *predicament*; emergency 137 n. *crisis*; insecurity, jeopardy, risk, hazard, ticklishness, precariousness, slipperiness, ticklish business, razor's edge 474 n. *uncertainty*; black spot, snag 663 n. *pitfall*; trap, death-t. 527 n. *ambush*; endangerment, imperilment, hazarding, dangerous course; venturesomeness, daring, overdaring 857 n. *rashness*; venture, risky v. 672 n. *undertaking*; leap in the dark 618 n. *gambling*; slippery slope, road to ruin 655 n. *deterioration*; approach of danger, sword of Damocles, menace 900 n. *threat*; sense of danger, apprehension, fears 854 n. *nervousness*; cause for alarm, rocks ahead, breakers a., storm brewing, gathering clouds, cloud on the horizon 665 n. *danger signal*; narrow escape, hairbreadth e., close shave, near thing, Dunkirk 667 n. *escape.*

vulnerability, non-immunity, susceptibility, danger of 180 n. *liability*; exposure, nakedness, defencelessness 161 n. *helplessness*; instability, insecurity, slipperiness 152 n. *changeableness*; exposed part, vulnerable point, chink in the armour, Achilles' heel 163 n. *weakness*; tender spot, soft s., soft underbelly 327 n. *softness*; unsoundness, feet of clay 647 n. *imperfection.*

Adj. *dangerous*, perilous, fraught with danger, treacherous, snaggy; exposed to risk, beset with perils; risky, hazardous, venturous, venturesome, aleatory, dicey, chancy 618 n. *speculative*; serious, ugly, emergent, critical; at stake, in question; menacing, ominous, foreboding, alarming 900 adj. *threatening*; septic, poisonous 653 n. *toxic*; unhealthy, infectious 653 adj. *insalubrious*; inflammable, explosive.

unsafe, not safe, slippery, treacherous, untrustworthy 474 adj. *unreliable*; insecure, unsecure, precarious; top-heavy, unsteady 152 adj. *unstable*; shaky, tottering, crumbling, nodding to its fall, tumbledown, ramshackle, frail 655 adj. *dilapidated*; jerry-built, gimcrack, crazy 163 adj. *weak*; built on sand, on shaky foundations; leaky, waterlogged; critical, ticklish, touch and go, hanging by a thread, trembling in the balance, on the edge, on the brink, on the verge.

vulnerable, expugnable, in danger of, not immune 180 adj. *liable*; open to, exposed, naked, bare 229 adj. *uncovered*; unarmoured, unfortified, unprotected 161 adj. *defenceless*; unshielded, shelterless, helpless, guideless; unguarded, guardless, unescorted, unshepherded, unconvoyed, unsupported, unflanked; unwarned, unadvised 508 adj. *inexpectant*.

endangered, in danger, in peril etc. n.; facing death, in a bad way; slipping, drifting; on the rocks, in shoal water; on slippery ground, on thin ice; surrounded, trapped, under fire; in the lion's den, on the razor's edge; between two fires, between the hammer and the anvil, between the devil and the deep blue sea, between Scylla and Charybdis; on the run, not out of the wood; at bay, with one's back to the wall, at the last stand, reduced to the last extremity; under sentence, with a halter round one's neck, awaiting execution 961 adj. *condemned*.

Vb. *be in danger*, run the risk of 180 vb. *be liable*; run into danger, enter the lion's den, walk into a trap 527 vb. *ambush*; skate on thin ice, sail too near the wind, sit on a powder-barrel, sleep on a volcano; lean on a broken reed, feel the ground slipping; hang by a thread, tremble in the balance, hover on the brink 474 vb. *be uncertain*; totter, slip, slide, sideslip 309 vb. *tumble*; get lost 282 vb. *stray*.

face danger, face death 855 vb. *be courageous*; expose oneself, lay oneself open, live in a glass house; bare one's breast, stand in the breach 711 vb. *defy*; look danger in the face, look down a gun-barrel; brave all hazards, face heavy odds, have the odds against one; engage in a forlorn hope, spurn the odds; challenge fate, tempt providence, court disaster; put one's head in the lion's mouth 857 vb. *be rash*; run the gauntlet, come under fire; venture, dare, risk it, take a chance, accept the hazard 618 vb. *gamble*; stand condemned, lodge in the condemned cell.

endanger, be dangerous, spell danger, expose to d., put in d., face with, confront w.; imperil, hazard, jeopardize, compromise; risk, stake, venture 618 vb. *gamble*; drive headlong, run on the rocks; drive to the danger of the public, put one in fear of his life; be dangerous, threaten danger, loom, forebode, bode ill, menace 900 vb. *threaten*; run one hard, overtake 306 vb. *outdo*.

See: 137, 152, 161, 163, 180, 229, 282, 306, 309, 327, 474, 508, 527, 618, 647, 653, 655, 663, 665, 667, 672, 700, 711, 854, 855, 857, 900, 961.

662 Refuge. Safeguard

N. *refuge*, sanctuary, asylum, retreat, safe, r., safe place; traffic island, zebra crossing; last resort, funk-hole, bolt-hole, fox-hole, burrow; trench, dug-out, air-raid shelter; earth, hole, den, lair, covert, nest, lap, hearth 192 n. *home*; sanctum 194 n. *room*; cloister, cell, hermitage 192 n. *retreat*; sanctum sanctorum, temple, ark, palladium; acropolis, citadel; wall, rampart, bulwark, bastion; stronghold, fastness, fort 713 n. *fort*; keep, ward; cache 527 n. *hiding place*; dungeon 748 n. *prison*; rock, pillar, tower, tower of strength, mainstay 218 n. *support*.

shelter, roof, cover; covert, earth, hole; fold, sheepfold, pinfold; lee; lee-wall, wind-break, hedge 235 n. *fence*; camp, stockade, zareba; umbrella, wing, shield; fireguard, fender, bumper, life-guard, mudguard, splashboard, windscreen 421 n. *screen*; sola topi, sun-helmet, spine pad, sun-glasses, eye-shade; haven, harbour, port 295 n. *goal*; harbourage, anchorage, roadstead, roads; quay, jetty, ghat, marina, dock, dry-d., bunder 192 n. *stable*; asylum, padded cell 503 n. *madhouse*; almshouse, poor-house, orphanage, cat's home, dog's h., charitable institution, home for the dying, Welfare State.

safeguard, means of safety, protection 660 n. *safety*; mail 713 n. *armour*; arms, deterrent 723 n. *weapon*; respirator, gasmask; safety device, dead man's handle, safety catch, safety match, safety-valve, vent peg, lightning rod, lightning conductor, fuse; crash helmet; ejector-seat, parachute; lifeboat, rubber dinghy, liferaft 275 n. *raft*; life-preserver, life-belt, life-jacket, cork j., Mae West, life-line, breeches buoy; rope, plank 667 n. *means of escape*; anchor, sheet-a., mushroom a., kedge, grapnel, grappling iron, killick, drogue; drag, brake, curb 748 n. *fetter*; bolt, bar, lock, key 264 n. *stopper*; ballast

31 n. *offset*; mole, breakwater, groyne, sea-wall, embankment; lighthouse, lightship 269 n. *sailing aid*; jury mast, spare parts 40 n. *extra*; safety belt, safety harness.

Vb. *seek refuge*, take refuge 660 vb. *seek safety*; take to the woods, take to the hills; turn to, throw oneself in the arms of, shelter under the wing of, put up one's umbrella; claim sanctuary, clasp the knees of, nestle under one's wing, hide behind the skirts of; make port, reach safety, reach home, find shelter; lock oneself in, bolt the door, bar the entrance, let down the portcullis, raise the draw-bridge.

See: 31, 40, 192, 194, 218, 235, 264, 269, 275, 295, 421, 503, 527, 660, 667, 713, 723, 748.

663 Pitfall: source of danger

N. *pitfall*, pit, trapdoor, trap for the unwary, catch; snag, pons asinorum 702 n. *obstacle* booby-trap, death-t. 542 n. *trap*; surprise 508 n. *inexpectation*; lying in wait 527 n. *ambush*; sleeping dog; thin ice; quagmire, quicksands, Goodwin Sands, sandbar, flat 347 n. *marsh*; shoal, shoal water, breakers, shallows 212 n. *shallowness*; reef, sunken r., coral r., rock 344 n. *rock*; iron-bound coast, lee shore 344 n. *shore*; steep, chasm, abyss, crevasse, precipice 209 n. *high land*; rapids, cross-current, under-tow 350 n. *current*; vortex, mael-strom, whirlpool 350 n. *eddy*; tidal wave, tsunami, bore 350 n. *wave*; storm, squall, hurricane 352 n. *gale*; volcano 383 n. *furnace*; dynamite, powder magazine, powder-keg 723 n. *explosive*; trouble-spot, danger-spot 661 n. *danger*; plague-spot, hotbed 651 n. *infection*; source of trouble, hornet's nest, hazard 659 n. *bane*.

trouble-maker, mischief-m., wrecker; ill-wisher 881 n. *enemy*; firebrand 738 n. *agi-tator*; dangerous person, ugly customer, undesirable, delinquent 904 n. *ruffian*; nig-ger in the woodpile, snake in the grass, viper in the bosom; hidden hand 178 n. *influence*; yellow peril, red p.; Nemesis 910 n. *avenger*.

See: 178, 209, 212, 344, 347, 350, 352, 383, 508, 527, 542, 651, 659, 661, 702, 723, 738, 881, 904, 910.

664 Warning

N. *warning*, caution, caveat; example, warning e., lesson, object l.; notice, advance n. 524 n. *information*; word, word in the ear, word to the wise 524 n. *hint*; final warning, final notice, ulti-matum 737 n. *demand*; dun 761 n. *request*; monition, admonition, admonishment 924 n. *reprimand*; dehortation 613 n. *dis-suasion*; protest, expostulation 762 n. *deprecation*; foreboding, premonition 511 n. *prediction*; voice, voice of conscience, warning voice 917 n. *conscience*; alarm, siren, foghorn, fog signal, storm s. 665 n. *danger signal*; Mother Carey's chickens, stormy petrel, bird of ill omen 511 n. *omen*; gathering cloud, cloud on the horizon 661 n. *danger*; signs of the times, writing on the wall, symptom, sign 547 n. *indication*; knell, death-k. 364 n. *obsequies*; beacon, light 547 n. *signal, indicator*; menace 900 n. *threat*.

warner, monitor, admonitor, admonitrix, admonisher 691 n. *adviser*; prophet, Cas-sandra 511 n. *diviner*; flagman, signaller; lighthouse-keeper; watchman, look-out, watch; scout, spy, picket, sentinel, sentry 660 n. *protector*; advanced guard, rear-guard; watch-dog, house-d.; dun 763 n. *petitioner*.

Adj. *cautionary*, hinting, warning, moni-torial, monitory, admonitory; dehorta-tive, dehortatory 762 adj. *deprecatory*; exemplary, instructive 524 adj. *informa-tive*; symptomatic, prognostic 547 n. *indicating*; premonitory, boding, ill-omened, ominous 511 adj. *presageful*; menacing, minatory 900 adj. *threatening*; deterrent 854 adj. *frightening*.

warned, cautioned etc. vb.; once bitten 858 adj. *cautious*; forewarned 507 adj. *expect-ant*; forearmed 669 adj. *prepared*.

Vb. *warn*, caution; give fair warning, give notice, notify 524 vb. *inform*; drop a hint 524 vb. *hint*; counsel 691 vb. *advise*; put one in mind 505 vb. *remind*; admonish 924 vb. *reprove*; spell danger, premonish, forewarn 511 vb. *predict*; forearm, put one on his guard 669 vb. *prepare*; lower, menace 900 vb. *threaten*; contra-indicate 14 vb. *be contrary*; advise against 613 vb. *dissuade*; dehort, protest 762 vb. *depre-cate*; sound the alarm 665 vb. *raise the alarm*.

be warned, receive notice; beware, take heed,

mind what one is about 457 vb. *be careful*;
be taught a good lesson, learn one's l.,
profit by the example.

Int. look out! watch out! mind your step!
look where you are going!

See: 14, 364, 457, 505, 507, 511, 524, 547,
613, 660, 661, 665, 669, 691, 737, 761, 762,
763, 854, 858, 900, 917, 924.

665 Danger signal

N. *danger signal*, note of warning 664 n.
warning; murmur, muttering 829 n. *discontent*; writing on the wall, black cap,
evil omen 511 n. *omen*; warning sound,
alarum, alarm clock, alarm-bell, burglar
alarm, police whistle, watchman's rattle;
fire-alarm, fire-bell, foghorn, fog signal,
motor-horn, klaxon; blast, honk, toot
400 n. *loudness*; curfew, tocsin, siren;
alert, alarm, beat of drum, trumpet-call
528 n. *publication*; war-cry, war-whoop,
rallying cry, Fiery Cross; warning light,
red l., Very l., beacon; red flag, yellow f.;
distress signal, S.O.S. 547 n. *signal*; sign
of alarm, start, tremor, sweat, hair on end
854 n. *fear*.

false alarm, cry of 'wolf', scare, scarecrow,
bugbear, bugaboo, bogy, nightmare, bad
dream 854 n. *intimidation*; blank cartridge,
flash in the pan 4 n. *insubstantiality*;
canard 543 n. *untruth*; scaremonger 854 n.
alarmist.

Vb. *raise the alarm*, beat the a., sound the
a., give the a., alarm, alert, arouse, scare,
startle 854 vb. *frighten*; sound one's horn,
honk, toot; turn out the guard, raise a
hue and cry 528 vb. *proclaim*; give a false
alarm, cry wolf, cry too soon; sound a
warning, toll, knell.

See: 4, 400, 511, 528, 543, 547, 664, 829, 854.

666 Preservation

N. *preservation*, safe-keeping, keeping alive;
safe-conduct 660 n. *protection*; saving,
salvation 668 n. *deliverance*; conservation, conservatism, vis conservatrix 144 n.
permanence; upkeep, maintenance, sustentation, support 633 n. *provision*; service, servicing, valeting 648 n. *cleansing*;
saving up 632 n. *storage*; frugality 814 n.
economy; self-preservation 932 n. *selfishness*; keeping fresh, mummification,

embalmment, embalming 364 n. *interment*; deep-freeze, cold pack 382 n.
refrigeration; boiling, drying, sun-d.,
dehydration 342 n. *desiccation*; ensilage;
canning, tinning, packing; prophylaxis,
preventive medicine, quarantine, cordon
sanitaire 652 n. *hygiene*.

preserver, saviour, rescuer, deliverer 668 n.
deliverance; amulet, charm, mascot 983 n.
talisman; preservative, ice, cold; camphor,
moth-ball, flit; lavender, amber; spice,
pickle, brine 389 n. *condiment*; refrigerator, fridge 382 n. *refrigeration*; thermos
flask; silo; cannery, canning factory,
canned goods, tinned g.; safety device,
life-belt, respirator, gas-mask 662 n. *safeguard*; drugget, chair-cover, dust-c. 226 n.
covering; embalmer, mummifier; canner,
bottler.

Adj. *preserving*, conserving etc. vb.; pre-
servatory, preservative, conservative;
prophylactic, protective, preventive,
hygienic 652 adj. *salubrious*.

preserved, well-p., kept, well-k., fresh,
undecayed, intact, whole 646 adj. *perfect*;
iced, frozen, on ice, in the fridge; pickled,
salted, corned, tinned, canned, potted,
bottled; mummified, embalmed, laid up
in lavender, treasured 632 adj. *stored*.

Vb. *preserve*, conserve, keep alive, keep
fresh, ice, freeze, keep on ice; embalm,
mummify; pickle, salt, corn, spice 388 vb.
season; souse, marinate; cure, smoke,
kipper, dehydrate, sun-dry 342 vb. *dry*;
pot, bottle, tin, can; protect, paint, coat,
whitewash, kyanize, waterproof; maintain, keep up, keep in repair, service, valet
656 vb. *repair*; shore, shore up, embank
218 vb. *support*; keep alive, feed, provision
supply 633 vb. *provide*; keep safe, keep
under cover, garage 660 vb. *safeguard*;
save up, bottle up 632 vb. *store*; spare 814
vb. *economize*; nurse, tend 658 vb. *doctor*;
tender, cherish, treasure 457 vb. *look
after*; not let go, hug, hold 778 vb. *retain*;
save, save alive, rescue 668 vb. *deliver*.

See: 144, 218, 226, 342, 364, 382, 388, 389,
457, 632, 633, 646, 648, 652, 656, 658, 660,
662, 668, 778, 814, 932, 983.

667 Escape

N. *escape*, leak, leakage, short circuit 298 n.
egress; extrication, delivery, rescue 668 n.

deliverance; riddance, good r. 831 n. *relief*; getaway, break-out, prison-breaking; decampment, avolation, flight, flit, French leave 296 n. *departure*; withdrawal, retreat, timely r. 286 n. *regression*; disappearing trick 446 n. *disappearance*; elopement, runaway match; evasion, truancy, tax-dodging 620 n. *avoidance*; narrow escape, hairbreadth e., close shave, narrow squeak, near thing 661 n. *danger*; come-off, discharge, reprieve 960 n. *acquittal*; setting free 746 n. *liberation*; immunity, impunity, exemption 919 n. *non-liability*; escapology, escapism; literature of escape.

means of escape, exit, way out, backdoor, secret passage 298 n. *egress*; ladder, fire-escape, escape hatch; drawbridge 624 n. *bridge*; vent, safety-valve 662 n. *safeguard*; dodge, device, trick 623 n. *contrivance*; loophole, saving clause, escape c. 468 n. *qualification*.

escaper, escapee, runaway; truant, escaped prisoner, prison-breaker; fugitive, refugee; survivor, escapologist.

Adj. *escaped*, fled, flown, stolen away; eloping, truant; fugitive, runaway; slippery, elusive, tip-and-run 620 adj. *avoiding*; free, at large, scot free, acquitted; relieved, rid of, well out of, well rid of; exempt 919 adj. *non-liable*.

Vb. *escape*, find *or* win freedom 746 vb. *achieve liberty*; effect one's escape, make good one's e., make a getaway, break prison; flit, elope, skip 620 vb. *run away*; steal away, sneak off; take it on the lam 296 vb. *decamp*; slip through, break t., break out, break loose, break away, get free, break one's chains, slip the collar; get out, bluff one's way o., sneak o. 298 vb. *emerge*; get away, slip through one's fingers; get off, come off, secure an acquittal, go scot free, go unpunished; scrape through, save one's bacon, weather the storm, survive; get away with it, secure exemption 919 vb. *be exempt*; relieve oneself, rid o., be well rid of, find relief 831 vb. *relieve*; leak, leak away 298 vb. *flow out*.

elude, evade, welsh, abscond, dodge 620 vb. *avoid*; lie low 523 vb. *lurk*; make oneself scarce, give one the slip, baffle one's pursuers, give one a run for one's money; escape notice, be found missing 190 vb. *be absent*.

See: 190, 286, 296, 298, 446, 468, 523, 620, 623, 624, 661, 662, 668, 746, 831, 919, 960.

668 Deliverance

N. *deliverance*, delivery, extrication 304 n. *extraction*; disburdenment, disencumberment, riddance 831 n. *relief*; emancipation 746 n. *liberation*; rescue, life-saving; salvage, retrieval 656 n. *restoration*; salvation, redemption 965 n. *divine function*; ransom, buying off 792 n. *purchase*; release, let-off; discharge, reprieve, reprieval 960 n. *acquittal*; day of grace, respite 136 n. *delay*; truce, standstill 145 n. *cessation*; way out 667 n. *escape*; dispensation, exemption 919 n. *non-liability*.

Adj. *extricable*, rescuable, deliverable, redeemable, fit for release; riddable.

Vb. *deliver*, save, rescue, come to the r., throw a life-line; get one out of 304 vb. *extract*; extricate 62 vb. *unravel*; unloose, untie, unbind 46 vb. *disjoin*; bring to birth, act as a midwife, accouche 164 vb. *generate*; disburden 701 vb. *disencumber*; rid, save from 831 vb. *relieve*; release, unlock, unbar; emancipate, free, set free, set at large 746 *liberate*; bring one off, get one off 960 vb. *acquit*; deliver oneself 667 vb. *escape*; save oneself, rid oneself, get rid of, be rid of, make a good riddance; snatch a brand from the burning, be the salvation of; redeem, ransom, buy off 792 vb. *purchase*; salvage, retrieve, recover, bring back 656 vb. *restore*; spare, excuse, dispense from 919 vb. *exempt*.

Int. to the rescue! all hands to the pump! help!

See: 46, 62, 136, 145, 164, 304, 656, 667, 701, 746, 792, 831, 919, 960, 965.

669 Preparation

N. *preparation*, preparing, making ready, bundobust; clearance, clearing the decks; preliminaries, preliminary step, tuning, priming, loading; mobilization 718 n. *war measures*; preliminary course, trial run, trial, trials 461 n. *experiment*; practice, rehearsal, dress r.; brief, briefing; training, hard t., inurement, novitiate, baptism 534 n. *teaching*; study, prep., homework 536 n. *learning*; spadework 68

n. *beginning*; groundwork, foundation 218 n. *basis*; scaffold, scaffolding, 218 n. *frame*; planning, rough sketch, first draft, outline, blueprint, scheme, pilot s. 623 n. *plan*; shadow cabinet, shadow factory; arrangement, prearrangement, pre-concertation, premeditation 608 n. *predetermination*; consultation, pre-consultation 691 n. *advice*; foretaste, forecast, anticipation, incasement 510 n. *foresight*; bottom drawer, hope chest 632 n. *store*.

fitting out, provisioning, furnishing, furnishment, logistics 633 n. *provision*; appointment, commission, equipment, accoutrement, array, marshalling, armament; promotion, company-promoting; inauguration, flotation, launching 68 n. *début*.

maturation, ripening, seasoning, bringing to a head; concoction, brewing, digestion; gestation, hatching, incubation, sitting 164 n. *propagation*; culinary art 301 n. *cookery*; nursing, nurture; cultivation, tilling, tillage, ploughing, sowing, planting, plantation 370 n. *agriculture*.

preparedness, readiness, ripeness, mellowness, maturity; puberty, nubility 134 n. *adultness*; fitness, shipshape condition, height of training, pitch of perfection 646 n. *perfection*.

preparer, trainer, coach, gymnasiarch, drill-sergeant 537 n. *trainer*; torch-bearer, pioneer, bridge-builder 66 n. *precursor*; sappers and miners 722 n. *soldiery*; paver, paviour; loader, packer, stevedore; fitter, equipper, provisioner 633 n. *provider*; cultivator, agriculturist, ploughman, sower, planter 370 n. *husbandman*; brewer, cook 301 n. *cookery*.

Adj. *preparatory*, preparative; preparing etc. adj.; precautionary, preliminary 64 adj. *preceding*; provisional, stop-gap 150 adj. *substituted*; brewing, cooking, stewing; brooding, hatching, incubating, maturing; brooding, gestatory, in embryo; in preparation, on foot, on the stocks, on the anvil; in store, in the offing, forthcoming 155 adj. *impending*; under consideration, agitated, mooted 623 adj. *planned*; under training, learning 536 adj. *studious*.

prepared, ready, always r., semper paratus, alert 457 adj. *vigilant*; made ready, readied, in readiness, at the ready; mobilized, standing by, on call; teed up,

keyed up, spoiling for; trained, fully-t., qualified, well-prepared, practised, in practice, at concert pitch; primed, briefed, instructed 524 adj. *informed*; forewarned, forearmed 664 adj. *warned*; saddled, ready s., booted and spurred, in the saddle; tight, snug, battened down; groomed, fully dressed, in one's best bib and tucker, in full feather, dressed to kill, got up to k., in full war-paint 228 adj. *dressed*; armed, in armour, in harness, fully armed, armed to the teeth, armed at all points, armed cap-à-pie; rigged, fully r.; equipped, furnished, fully f., well-appointed, provided 633 adj. *provisionary*; in store, in hand 632 adj. *stored*; in reserve, ready to hand, ready for use; fit for use, in working order; running, in gear.

matured, ripened, cooked, digested, hatched etc. vb.; ripe, seasoned, weathered, hardened; tried, experienced, veteran 694 adj. *expert*; adult, grown, full-g., fledged 134 adj. *grown up*; overripe, overmature; well-cooked, well-done; elaborate, over-e., wrought, highly w., over-w., worked up, laboured, smelling of the lamp; deep-laid.

ready-made, cut and dried, ready for wear, reach-me-down, off the peg; ready-formed, ready-furnished; oven-ready; predigested, ready-cooked; instant.

Vb. *prepare*, take steps, take measures; make preparations, make a bundobust, mount; make ready, pave, pave the way, show the w., bridge, build a b., lead up to, pioneer 64 vb. *come before*; choose one's ground, erect the scaffolding, lay *or* dig the foundations, lay the groundwork, provide the basis; predispose, incline; prepare the ground, sow the seed 370 vb. *cultivate*; lay a train, dig a mine; set to work, address oneself to, take one's coat off, limber up 68 vb. *begin*; rough-hew, cut out, block o.; sketch, outline, blueprint 623 vb. *plan*; plot, concert, prearrange 608 vb. *predetermine*; prepare for, forearm, guard against, insure, prepare for a rainy day, feather one's nest 660 vb. *seek safety*; anticipate 507 vb. *expect*.

make ready, ready, have r., finish one's preparations; set in order, put in readiness; stow, stow away, pack 632 vb. *store*; trim, make tight, make all snug; commission, put in c.; put one's house in

order, put in working order, bring up to scratch, wind up, screw up, tune, tune up, adjust 62vb. *arrange*; lay the table, spread the table, dish up, serve up; settle preliminaries, clear the decks, close the ranks, array; mobilize 74vb. *bring together*; whet the knife, trim the foils, shuffle the cards, tee up; set, cock, prime, load; fledge, feather; raise steam, warm up, crank, crank up, put in gear; equip, fit, fit out, furnish, accoutre, harness, rig, dress; arm, provide with arms, provide with teeth 633vb. *provide*; improvise, rustle up; rehearse, drill, groom, exercise 534vb. *train*; inure 610vb. *habituate*; coach, brief 524vb. *inform*.

mature, mellow, ripen, bring to fruition 646vb. *perfect*; force, bring on 174vb. *invigorate*; bring to a head 725vb. *climax*; digest, stew, brew 301vb. *cook*; gestate, hatch, incubate, breed 369vb. *breed stock*; grow, farm 370vb. *cultivate*; fledge, nurse, nurture; elaborate, work out 725vb. *carry through*; season, weather, smoke, dry, cure; temper, anneal 326vb. *harden*.

prepare oneself, brace o.; qualify oneself, serve an apprenticeship; study, train, exercise, rehearse, practise 536vb. *learn*; take one's coat off, gird up one's loins, limber up, warm up, flex one's muscles; put on one's armour, buckle on one's breastplate, take sword in hand; be prepared, stand ready, stand by, hold oneself in readiness, keep one's powder dry; anticipate, forearm, set the alarm.

Adv. *in preparation*, in anticipation, in readiness, acock; on the stocks, on the anvil, under construction.

See: 62, 64, 66, 68, 74, 134, 150, 155, 164, 174, 218, 228, 301, 326, 369, 370, 457, 461, 507, 510, 524, 534, 536, 537, 608, 610, 623, 632, 633, 646, 660, 664, 694, 718, 722, 725.

670 Non-preparation

N. *non-preparation*, lack of preparation; pot-luck; unpreparedness, unreadiness; lack of training, want of practice; disqualification, unfitness; rawness, immaturity, crudity, greenness, unripeness 126 n. *newness*; belatedness 136n. *lateness*; improvidence, non-provision, neglect 458 n. *negligence*; no deliberation 857n. *rashness*; hastiness, precipitance, rush 680n.

haste; improvisation, impromptu, snap answer 609n. *spontaneity*; surprise 508n. *inexpectation*; forwardness, precocity 135 n. *earliness*; imperfection 55n. *incompleteness*.

undevelopment, delayed maturity, slow ripening; native state, undeveloped s., virgin soil; unweeded garden 458n. *negligence*; raw material, unlicked cub, rough diamond; rough copy, unfinished attempt; embryo, abortion.

Adj. *unprepared*, unready, not ready, backward, behindhand 136adj. *late*; unorganized, unarranged, makeshift; without preparation, ad hoc, extemporized, improvised, impromptu, snap, catch-as-catch-can 609adj. *spontaneous*; unstudied 699adj. *artless*; rash, careless 458adj. *negligent*; rush, precipitant, overhasty 680adj. *hasty*; unguarded, exposed 661 adj. *vulnerable*; unwarned, caught unawares, caught napping, on the wrong foot, unexpecting 508adj. *inexpectant*; shiftless, improvident, unthrifty, thoughtless, happy-go-lucky 456adj. *light-minded*; scratch, untrained, untaught, untutored 491adj. *uninstructed*; undrilled, unpractised, unexercised, unrehearsed 611adj. *unhabituated*; unworked, untilled, fallow, unhandselled, virgin 674adj. *unused*.

immature, ungrown, half-grown, unripe, green, underripe, half-ripe, unripened, unmellowed; unblown, half-blown; unfledged, unlicked, callow; non-adult, adolescent, juvenile, boyish, girlish 130 adj. *young*; undeveloped, half-developed, half-baked, raw 647adj. *imperfect*; underdeveloped, backward 136adj. *late*; unhatched, unborn, embryonic, rudimentary 68adj. *beginning*; unformed, unfashioned, unhewn, unwrought, unlaboured, rough-hewn, uncut, unpolished, half-finished, unfinished; undigested, ill-digested; before time, premature, abortive, at half-cock 728adj. *unsuccessful*; untrained, prentice, undergraduate 695 adj. *unskilled*; crude, coarse, rude, savage, uncivilised 699adj. *artless*; early matured, forced, precocious.

uncooked, unbaked, unroasted, unboiled; raw, red, rare, underdone; browned, half-baked, cold, unwarmed; unprepared, undressed, ungarnished; indigestible, inedible 329adj. *tough*; undigested, unconcocted; unseasoned, uncured.

unequipped, untrimmed, unrigged, dismasted, dismantled, undressed 229 adj. *uncovered*; unfound, unfurnished, half-furnished, ill-provided 307 adj. *deficient*; unfitted, unqualified, disqualified.

Vb. *be unprepared*,—unready etc. adj.; lack preparation 55 vb. *be incomplete*; lie fallow, rust 655 vb. *deteriorate*; need exercise, want practice, need training; not plan, make no preparation, offer potluck, extemporize, speak off-hand 609 vb. *improvize*; be premature, go off at halfcock 135 vb. *be early*; take no precautions, drop one's guard 456 vb. *be inattentive*; catch unawares 508 vb. *surprise.*

Adv. *unreadily*, extempore, off the cuff, ad hoc, off-hand.

See: 55, 68, 126, 130, 135, 136, 229, 307, 329, 456, 458, 491, 508, 609, 611, 647, 655, 661, 674, 680, 695, 699, 728, 857.

671 Essay

N. *essay*, attempt, bid; step, move, gambit 676 n. *deed*; endeavour, struggle, effort 682 n. *exertion*; coup d'essai, tackle, try, some attempt; good try, stout *or* brave *or* valiant effort; best effort, best one can do; random effort, catch-as-catch-can; determined effort, set, dead s. 712 n. *attack*; trial, probation 461 n. *experiment*; go of it, go at, shot at, stab at, jab at, dab at, crack at, whack at; first attempt, first go, first shot, first offence 68 n. *début*; final attempt, last bid, last throw; thing attempted, operation, exercise, venture, adventure, quest, speculation 672 n. *undertaking*; aim, goal 617 n. *objective*; strain, high endeavour, perfectionism 862 n. *fastidiousness.*

essayer, bidder, tackler, trier 852 n. *hoper*; assayer, tester 461 n. *experimenter*; searcher, quester 459 n. *enquirer*; struggler, striver, fighter 716 n. *contender*; idealist 862 n. *perfectionist*; activist 654 n. *reformer*; undertaker, contractor, entrepreneur, jobber.

Adj. *essaying*, tackling, trying, striving, doing one's best; game, nothing daunted 599 adj. *resolute*; questing, searching 459 adj. *enquiring*; tentative, catch-as-catch-can; testing, probationary 461 adj. *experimental*; ambitious, venturesome, daring 672 adj. *enterprising.*

Vb. *essay*, quest, seek 459 vb. *search*; seek to, aim, make it one's a. 617 vb. *intend*; offer, bid, make a b.; try, attempt, make an a., make a shift to, make the effort, do something about; endeavour, struggle, strive, try hard, try and try again 599 vb. *be resolute*; try one's best, do one's b., use one's best endeavours 682 vb. *exert oneself*; pull hard, push h., strain, sweat blood 682 vb. *work*; tackle, take on, have a go, give it a try, have a shot at, have a crack at, have a stab at 672 vb. *undertake*; get down to, get to grips with, take the bull by the horns, make a go of; take a chance, chance one's arm, try one's luck, venture, speculate 618 vb. *gamble*; tempt, tempt providence 461 vb. *experiment*; test, make trial of, assay; grope, feel one's way 461 vb. *be tentative*; be ambitious, attempt too much, bite off more than one can chew, die in the attempt 728 vb. *fail.*

See: 68, 459, 461, 599, 617, 618, 654, 672, 676, 682, 712, 716, 728, 852, 862.

672 Undertaking

N. *undertaking*, contract, engagement, pledged word, obligation 764 n. *promise*; job, task; self-imposed task, labour of love, pilgrimage 597 n. *voluntary work*; operation, exercise; programme, project, design 623 n. *plan*; tall order, large assumption, large undertaking 700 n. *hard task*; enterprise, emprise; quest, search, adventure 459 n. *enquiry*; venture, speculation, stake 618 n. *gambling*; occupation, matter in hand 622 n. *business*; struggle, effort, campaign 671 n. *essay.*

Adj. *enterprising*, pioneering, adventurous, venturesome, daring; go-ahead, progressive; opportunist, alive to opportunity; ambitious 859 adj. *desiring*; overambitious 857 adj. *rash*; responsible, owning responsibility.

Vb. *undertake*, engage in, betake oneself, take up, go in for, devote oneself to; venture on, take on, tackle 671 vb. *essay*; go about, take in hand, turn one's hand to, put one's hand to; set forward, set going 285 vb. *promote*; proceed to, broach, embark on, launch into, plunge into, fall to, set to, buckle to, set one's shoulder to the wheel 68 vb. *begin*; assume take charge of 689 vb. *manage*; execute

725 vb. *carry out*; set up shop, have irons in the fire 622 vb. *busy oneself*; take on one's shoulders, take upon oneself, assume responsibility, assume an obligation 917 vb. *incur a duty*; engage to, commit oneself, contract 764 vb. *promise*; volunteer 597 vb. *be willing*; show enterprise, pioneer; venture, dare 661 vb. *face danger*; apprentice oneself 669 vb. *prepare oneself*.

See: 68, 285, 459, 597, 618, 622, 623, 661, 669, 671, 689, 700, 725, 764, 857, 859, 917.

673 Use

N. *use*, usufruct, enjoyment, disposal 773 n. *possession*; conversion to use, conversion, utilization, exploitation; employment, employ, application, appliance; adhibition, administration; exercise, exercitation 610 n. *practice*; resort, recourse; mode of use, treatment, good usage, proper treatment 457 n. *carefulness*; ill-treatment, hard usage, wrong use 675 n. *misuse*; effect of use, wear, wear and tear 655 n. *dilapidation*; exhaustion, consumption 634 n. *waste*; usefulness, benefit, service, avail 640 n. *utility*; serviceability, practicality, convertibility, applicability 642 n. *expedience*; office, purpose, point 622 n. *function*; long use, wont, beaten track 610 n. *custom*.

Adj. *used*, applied, employed, availed of etc. vb.; in service, in use, in constant u., in practice; worn, second-hand, well-used, well-thumbed, dog-eared, well-worn 655 adj. *dilapidated*; beaten, well-trodden 490 adj. *known*; staled, vulgarized; pragmatical, practical, utilitarian 640 adj. *useful*; makeshift, provisional 150 adj. *substituted*; subservient, like wax or putty in one's hands 628 adj. *instrumental*; available, usable, employable, utilizable, convertible 642 adj. *expedient*; at one's service, consumable, disposable.

Vb. *use*, employ, exercise, practise; apply, exert, bring to bear, adhibit, administer; consume, spend on, give to, devote to, consecrate to, dedicate to; assign to, allot (see *dispose of*); utilize, make use of, convert, convert to use 640 vb. *find useful*; exploit, use to the full, get the best out of, make the most of, exhaust the possibilities; turn to use, turn to account, capital-

ize, make hay with 137 vb. *profit by*; make play with, play off, play off against; make a tool or handle of; make a pawn or cat's-paw of; put to use, wear, submit to w., wear out, use up 634 vb. *waste*; handle, thumb 378 vb. *touch*; tread, follow, beat (a path); work, drive, manipulate 173 vb. *operate*; wield, ply, brandish; overwork, tax, task 684 vb. *fatigue*; over-use, stale 847 vb. *vulgarize*; prepare for use, work on, work up, mould 243 vb. *efform*.

avail of, take up, adopt; avail oneself of, try; resort to, run to, betake oneself to, have recourse to, recur to, fall back on; avail of unduly, presume on; press into service, enlist in one's s.; make do with, make shift w., do what one can w., make the most of, make the best of.

dispose of, command; have at one's disposal, control, have at one's command, do what one likes with; allot, assign 783 vb. *apportion*; give to, devote to, spare, have to s.; draw forth, call f., put in requisition, call into play, set in play, set in motion, set in action, set going, deploy 612 vb. *motivate*; enjoy, have the usufruct 773 vb. *possess*; consume, expend, absorb, use up 634 vb. *waste*.

See: 137, 150, 173, 243, 378, 457, 490, 610, 612, 622, 628, 634, 640, 642, 655, 675, 684, 773, 783, 847.

674 Non-use

N. *non-use*, abeyance, suspension 677 n. *inaction*; non-availability 190 n. *absence*; stagnation, unemployment 679 n. *inactivity*; forbearance, abstinence 620 n. *avoidance*; savings, unspent balance 666 n. *preservation*; disuse, obsolescence 611 n. *desuetude*; dismissal 300 n. *ejection*; waiver, giving up, surrender 621 n. *relinquishment*; withdrawal, cancellation 752 n. *abrogation*; uselessness, write-off 641 n. *inutility*; superannuation.

Adj. *unused*, not used; not available 190 adj. *absent*; out of order, not in service, unusable, unemployable 641 adj. *useless*; unutilized, unapplied, unconverted; undisposed of, in hand, saved 632 adj. *stored*; spare, extra; unspent, unconsumed 666 adj. *preserved*; unessayed, untried; unexercised, in abeyance, sus-

pended; untrodden, unbeaten; untouched, unhandled; ungathered, unculled, unplucked; unnecessary, not wanted, not required, unrequired, unengaged 860 adj. *unwanted*; dispensed with, waived; not made use of, resting, unemployed, idle 679 adj. *inactive*; jobless, out of work, out of employment, briefless.

disused, derelict, discarded, cast-off, jettisoned, scrapped, written off; sacked, discharged, laid off etc. vb.; laid up, mothballed, out of commission, rusting; done with, used up, run down; on the shelf, retired; superseded, obsolete, discredited 127 adj. *antiquated*.

Vb. *not use*, not utilize, hold in abeyance; not touch, have no use for; abstain, forbear, hold off 620 vb. *avoid*; dispense with, waive, not proceed with 621 vb. *relinquish*; overlook, disregard 458 vb. *neglect*; spare, save, reserve, keep in hand 632 vb. *store*; not accept, decline 607 vb. *reject*.

disuse, leave off 611 vb. *disaccustom*; stop using, leave to rust, lay up, put in mothballs, put out of commission, dismantle 641 vb. *make useless*; have done with, lay aside, put on the shelf, hang up; pension off, put out to grass; discard, dump, ditch, scrap, write off; jettison, throw away, throw overboard 300 vb. *eject*; slough, cast off 229 vb. *doff*; give up, relinquish, resign 779 vb. *not retain*; suspend, withdraw, cancel 752 vb. *abrogate*; discharge, lay off, pay off 300 vb. *dismiss*; drop, supersede, replace 150 vb. *substitute*; be unused, rust 655 vb. *deteriorate*.

See: 127, 150, 190, 229, 300, 458, 607, 611, 620, 621, 632, 641, 655, 666, 677, 679, 752, 779, 860.

675 Misuse

N. *misuse*, abuse, wrong use; misemployment, misapplication; misdirection, diversion; mismanagement, maladministration 695 n. *unskilfulness*; misappropriation, malversation 788 n. *peculation*; perversion 246 n. *distortion*; prostitution, violation; profanation, desecration 980 n. *impiety*; pollution 649 n. *uncleanness*; extravagance 634 n. *waste*; misusage, mishandling, ill-usage, ill-treatment,

force 176 n. *violence*; outrage, injury 616 n. *evil*.

Vb. *misuse*, abuse; use wrongly, misemploy, misdirect; divert, manipulate, misappropriate 788 vb. *defraud*; violate, desecrate, take in vain 980 vb. *profane*; prostitute 655 vb. *pervert*; pollute 649 vb. *make unclean*; do violence to, strain 176 vb. *force*; maltreat 246 vb. *distort*; outrage, ill-treat 735 vb. *oppress*; misgovern, misrule, mishandle, mismanage 695 vb. *be unskilful*; overwork, overtask, overtax 684 vb. *fatigue*; use hard, wear out 655 vb. *impair*; consume, squander, throw away 634 vb. *waste*; misapply, cut a whetstone with a razor, use a sledge hammer to crack a nut 695 vb. *stultify oneself*.

See: 176, 246, 616, 634, 649, 655, 684, 695, 735, 788, 980.

676 Action

N. *action*, doing, militancy; positive action, commission; negative action, omission; steps, measures, move 623 n. *policy*; transaction, enactment, performance, perpetration; despatch, execution, effectuation, accomplishment 725 n. *completion*; procedure, routine 610 n. *practice*; exercitation, praxis; behaviour 688 n. *conduct*; movement, play, swing 265 n. *motion*; operation, working, interaction, evolution 173 n. *agency*; force, pressure 178 n. *influence*; work, labour 682 n. *exertion*; activism, activeness, drama 678 n. *activity*; occupation 622 n. *business*; manufacture 164 n. *production*; employment 673 n. *use*; effort, endeavour, campaign 671 n. *essay*; implementation, administration, handling 689 n. *management*; plot 594 n. *dramaturgy*.

deed, act, overt a.; action, gest, exploit, feat, achievement 855 n. *prowess*; bad deed, crime 930 n. *foul play*; stunt, tour de force 875 n. *ostentation*; measure, step, move 623 n. *policy*; manœuvre, evolution 688 n. *tactics*; stroke, blow, coup, coup de main, coup d'état 623 n. *contrivance*; job, task, operation, exercise 672 n. *undertaking*; proceeding, transaction, deal, doings, dealings 154 n. *affairs*; work, handiwork, workmanship, craftsmanship 694 n. *skill*; pièce de résistance, chef d'œuvre 694 n.

masterpiece; drama, scene; acts, aretalogy 590 n. *narrative.*

doer, man of deeds, man of action, activist 678 n. *busy person*; practical man, realist; achiever, finisher; hero 855 n. *brave person*; practitioner 696 n. *expert*; stunter, stunt-merchant, executant, performer, player 594 n. *actor*; perpetrator, committer; offender, criminal 904 n. *evildoer*; mover, controller, manipulator 612 n. *motivator*; operator 686 n. *agent*; contractor, undertaker, entrepreneur, campaigner; executor, executive, administrator, manager 690 n. *director*; hand, workman, operative 686 n. *worker*; craftsman 696 n. *artisan*; creative worker 556 n. *artist.*

Adj. doing, acting, operating, performing, in the act, red-handed; of commission, of omission; working, in action, in operation, in harness 173 adj. *operative*; up and doing, industrious, busy 678 adj. *active*; occupational 610 adj. *habitual.*

Vb. do, be in action, come into operation; act, perform, do one's stuff 173 vb. *operate*; militate, act upon 178 vb. *influence*; manipulate 612 vb. *motivate*; use tactics, twist, turn, manœuvre 698 vb. *be cunning*; do something, lift a finger, stretch forth one's hand; proceed, proceed with, get going, move, take action, take steps; attempt, try 671 vb. *essay*; tackle, take on 672 vb. *undertake*; adopt a measure, enact, legislate 953 vb. *make legal*; do the deed, perpetrate, commit, inflict, achieve, accomplish, complete 725 vb. *carry through*; do the needful, take care of, despatch, execute, implement, fulfil, put through 725 vb. *carry out*; solemnize, observe; act greatly, make history, win renown 866 vb. *have repute*; practise, exercise, carry on, prosecute, wage, ply, ply one's task, employ oneself, be at work 622 vb. *busy oneself*; officiate 622 vb. *function*; transact, proceed 622 vb. *do business*; administer, administrate, manage, control 689 vb. *direct*; have to do with 688 vb. *deal with*; sweat, labour, campaign 682 vb. *work*; exploit, make the most of 673 vb. *use*; intervene, strike a blow 703 vb. *aid*; have a hand in, play a part in, pull an oar 775 vb. *participate*; deal in, have a finger in, get mixed up in 678 vb. *meddle*; conduct oneself, indulge in 688 vb. *behave*; play about, act a., fool a. 497 vb.

be absurd; stunt, show off 875 vb. *be ostentatious.*

Adv. in the act, in flagrante delicto, red-handed; in the midst of, in the thick of; while one's hand is in, while one is about it.

See: 154, 164, 173, 178, 265, 497, 556, 590, 594, 610, 612, 622, 623, 671, 672, 673, 678, 682, 868, 688, 689, 690, 694, 696, 698, 703, 725, 775, 855, 866, 875, 904, 930, 953.

677 Inaction

N. inaction, non-action, nothing doing, inertia 175 n. *inertness*; inability to act 161 n. *impotence*; failure to act, neglect 458 n. *negligence*; abstinence from action, abstention, refraining 620 n. *avoidance*; suspension, abeyance, dormancy 674 n. *non-use*; immobility, paralysis, impassivity, insensitivity 375 n. *insensibility*; passivity, stagnation, vegetation, doldrums, stillness, quiet, calm 266 n. *quiescence*; time on one's hands, idle hours, hours of idleness, dolce far niente 681 n. *leisure*; rest 683 n. *repose*; no work, sinecure; non-employment, under-e., unemployment, loafing, idleness, indolence 679 n. *inactivity*; do-nothingness, masterly inactivity, Fabian policy, cunctation 136 n. *delay*; unprogressiveness, rust 654 n. *deterioration*; non-interference, neutrality 860 n. *indifference*; defeatism 856 n. *cowardice.*

Adj. non-active, inoperative, suspended, in abeyance; dull, sluggish 175 adj. *inert*; unoccupied, leisured 681 adj. *leisurely*; do-nothing, unprogressive; Fabian, cunctative, delaying, procrastinating; defeatist 853 adj. *hopeless*; stationary, motionless, immobile 266 adj. *quiescent*; cold, extinct; not stirring, without a sign of life, dead or dying 361 adj. *dead*; idle, unemployed, jobless, briefless, out of work, on the dole, without employment 679 adj. *inactive*; incapable of action 161 adj. *impotent*; benumbed, paralysed 375 adj. *insensible*; apathetic, phlegmatic 820 adj. *impassive*; neutral 860 adj. *indifferent*; unhearing 416 adj. *deaf.*

Vb. not act, fail to a., refuse to a., hang fire 599 vb. *be loth*; refrain, abstain 620 vb. *avoid*; look on, stand by 441 vb. *watch*;

watch and wait, wait and see, tide it over, bide one's time 136 vb. *wait*; procrastinate 136 vb. *put off*; live and let live, let it rip, laisser aller, laisser faire, let sleeping dogs lie, let well alone; hold no brief for, stay neutral, observe neutrality 860 vb. *be indifferent*; do nothing, tolerate, squat, fold one's hands, fold one's arms, not move, not budge, not stir, show no sign, not lift a finger, not even attempt 175 vb. *be inert*; drift, slide, coast; have no hope 853 vb. *despair*; let pass, let go by, leave alone, let a., give it a miss 458 vb. *neglect*; stay still, keep quiet 266 vb. *be quiescent*; relax, rest and be thankful 683 vb. *repose*; have no function 641 vb. *be useless*; have nothing to do, kick one's heels 681 vb. *have leisure*; pause, desist 145 vb. *cease*; rust, lie idle, stay on the shelf, lie fallow 674 *not use*; have no life, lie stiff, lie dead 361 vb. *die*.

Adv. *without action*, nothing doing, without movement; hands in one's pockets, with folded arms; with the job half done.

See: 136, 145, 161, 175, 266, 361, 375, 416, 441, 458, 599, 620, 641, 654, 674, 679, 681, 683, 820, 853, 856, 860.

678 Activity

N. *activity*, activeness, activism, militancy 676 n. *action*; interest, active i. 775 n. *participation*; social activity, group a. 882 n. *sociability*; activation 612 n. *motivation*; excitation 174 n. *stimulation*; agitation, movement, mass m. 738 n. *sedition*; life, stir 265 n. *motion*; nimbleness, briskness, smartness, alacrity, promptitude 597 n. *willingness*; readiness 135 n. *punctuality*; quickness, dispatch, expedition 277 n. *velocity*; spurt, burst, fit 318 n. *spasm*; hurry, flurry, hurry-skurry, hustle, bustle, over-haste, frantic haste 680 n. *haste*; fuss, bother, botheration, ado, to-do, racketing, tumult, frenzy 61 n. *turmoil*; whirl, scramble, mad s., rat-race, maelstrom 315 n. *vortex*; drama, great doings, much ado, thick of things, thick of action; working life, battle of l.; plenty to do, irons in the fire 622 n. *business*; call on one's time, press of business; pressure of work, no sinecure; busy place, busy street, market-place, heavy traffic; press,

madding crowd, seething mob; hum, hive, hive of industry 687 n. *workshop*.

restlessness, pottering, aimless activity, desultoriness, no concentration 456 n. *inattention*; unquiet, fidgets, fidgetiness 318 n. *agitation*; jumpiness, jerkiness 822 n. *excitability*; fever, fret 503 n. *frenzy*; eagerness, enthusiasm, ardour, fervour, abandon, vehemence 818 n. *warm feeling*; vigour, energy, ceaseless e., dynamic e., dynamism, aggressiveness, militancy, enterprise, initiative, push, drive, go, pep 174 n. *vigorousness*; vivacity, spirit, animation, liveliness, vitality 360 n. *life*; watchfulness, wakefulness, vigilance 457 n. *carefulness*; sleeplessness, insomnia; tirelessness, indefatigability.

assiduity, application, concentration, intentness 455 n. *attention*; sedulity, industriousness, industry, laboriousness, drudgery 682 n. *labour*; determination, earnestness, empressement 599 n. *resolution*; tirelessness, indefatigability 600 n. *perseverance*; studiousness, painstaking, diligence, habits of business; whole-heartedness, devotedness; Stakhanovism.

overactivity, over-extension, over-expansion, excess 637 n. *redundance*; futile activity, chasing one's own tail 641 n. *lost labour*; thyrotoxic condition, over-exertion, Stakhanovism; officiousness, ultracrepidarianism, meddlesomeness, interference, intrusiveness, interruption, meddling, intermeddling, interfering, finger in every pie; tampering, intrigue 623 n. *plot*.

busy person, new broom, enthusiast, bustler, hustler, man in a hurry; zealot, fanatic 602 n. *opinionist*; slogger, hard worker, tireless w., high-pressure w., Stakhanovite, demon for work, glutton for w. 686 n. *worker*; factotum, maid-of-all-work, housewife, drudge, fag, nigger, slave, galley-s., Trojan; horse, beaver, ant, busy bee; man of active habits, man of action, activist; participator; sharp fellow, blade, live wire, go-getter, pusher, thruster; careerist.

meddler, dabbler, intermeddler, officious person, spoilsport, nosy parker, ultracrepidarian, busybody, pickthank; tamperer, intriguer 623 n. *planner*; interferer, butter-in; kibitzer, back-seat driver 691 n. *adviser*; fusspot, nuisance.

Adj. *active*, stirring 265 adj. *moving*; going,

working, incessant 146 adj. *unceasing*; full of dispatch 622 vb. *businesslike*; able, able-bodied 162 adj. *strong*; quick, brisk, nippy, spry, smart, gleg 277 adj. *speedy*; nimble, light-footed, featly, tripping; energetic, forceful, thrustful 174 adj. *vigorous*; pushing, go-getting, up-and-coming 672 adj. *enterprising*; frisky, coltish, dashing, sprightly, spirited, mettlesome, live, alive and kicking, full of beans, animated, vivacious 819 adj. *lively*; eager, ardent, perfervid 818 adj. *fervent*; fierce, desperate 599 adj. *resolute*; enthusiastic, zealous, prompt, instant, ready, on one's toes 597 adj. *willing*; expeditious, full of dispatch 622 vb. *businesslike*; awake, alert, watchful, wakeful 457 adj. *vigilant*; sleepless, tireless, restless, feverish, fretful, tossing, dancing, fidegty, jumpy, fussy, nervy, like a cat on hot bricks 318 adj. *agitated*; frantic, demonic 503 adj. *frenzied*; overactive, over-extended; over-exerted, thyrotoxic; aggressive, militant, up in arms 718 adj. *warlike*.

busy, bustling, hustling, humming, coming and going, rushing to and fro; pottering, doing chores; up and doing, stirring, eventful; astir, afoot, a-doing, on the move, on the go, in full swing; slogging, hard at work, hard at it, up to one's eyes, full of business, fully engaged; in harness, at work, at one's desk; occupied, fully o., employed, over-e.; busy as a bee, busy as a hen with chickens.

industrious, studious, sedulous, assiduous 600 adj. *persevering*; labouring, hard-working, plodding, slogging, strenuous 682 adj. *laborious*; unflagging, unwearied, unsleeping, tireless, indefatigable, keeping long hours, never-tiring, never-resting, never-sleeping; efficient, workmanlike 622 adj. *businesslike*.

meddling, over-busy, officious, ultra-crepidarian, interfering, meddlesome, intriguing; dabbling; participating, in the business.

Vb. *be active*, show interest, interest oneself in, trouble oneself, join in 775 vb. *participate*; be stirring, stir, come and go, rush to and fro 265 vb. *move*; run riot, have one's fling 61 vb. *rampage*; not sleep, wake up, rouse oneself, bestir o., be up and doing; hum, thrive 730 vb. *prosper*; make progress 285 vb. *progress*; keep moving, keep on the go, keep the ball

rolling 146 vb. *go on*; push, shove, thrust, drive 279 vb. *impel*; elbow one's way 174 vb. *be vigorous*; rush, surge 350 vb. *flow*; roar, rage, bluster 352 vb. *blow*; explode, burst 176 vb. *be violent*; dash, fly, run 277 vb. *move fast*; make the effort, do one's best 671 vb. *essay*; take pains 455 vb. *be attentive*; be about it, be hard at it 682 vb. *exert oneself*; persist 600 vb. *persevere*; polish off, dispatch, make short work of, not let the grass grow under one's feet; rise to the occasion, work wonders 727 vb. *be successful*; jump to it, show zeal, burn with z., be on fire, anticipate 597 vb. *be willing*; be on one's toes, keep awake, wake, watch 457 vb. *be careful*; seize the opportunity, take one's chance 137 vb. *profit by*; assert oneself, not take it lying down, be up in arms, react, react sharply, show fight 711 vb. *defy*; protest, agitate, kick up a shindy, raise the dust 762 vb. *deprecate*.

be busy, keep b., have irons in the fire 622 vb. *busy oneself*; bustle, hurry, scurry 680 vb. *hasten*; live in a whirl, join the rat-race, go all ways at once, run round in circles; chase one's own tail 641 vb. *waste effort*; not know which way to turn 700 vb. *be in difficulty*; have one's hands full, have not a moment to spare, have no time to lose, rise early, go to bed late; fuss, fret, fume, stamp with impatience 822 vb. *be excitable*; have other things to do, have other fish to fry 138 vb. *be engaged*; slave, slog 682 vb. *work*; overwork, overdo it, make work, make a toil of a pleasure; never stop, improve the shining hour; affect zeal, show work 850 vb. *be affected*.

meddle, intermeddle, interpose, intervene, interfere, be officious, not mind one's own business, have a finger in every pie; poke one's nose in, shove one's oar in, butt in 297 vb. *intrude*; pester, bother, dun, annoy 827 vb. *incommode*; be bossy, boss, boss one around, tyrannize 735 vb. *oppress*; tinker, tamper, touch 655 vb. *impair*.

Adv. *actively*, on the go, on one's toes; full tilt, whole hog; with might and main, with life and spirit, for all one is worth.

See: 61, 135, 137, 138, 146, 162, 174, 176, 265, 277, 279, 285, 297, 315, 318, 350, 352, 360, 455, 456, 457, 503, 597, 599, 600, 602,

612, 622, 623, 637, 641, 655, 671, 672, 676, 680, 682, 686, 687, 691, 700, 711, 718, 727, 730, 735, 738, 762, 775, 818, 819, 822, 827, 850, 882.

679 Inactivity

N. *inactivity*, inactiveness 677 n. *inaction*; inertia, heaviness, torpor 175 n. *inertness*; lull, suspension, suspended animation 145 n. *cessation*; immobility, stillness, quietude, doldrums, grave, morgue 266 n. *quiescence*; no progress, stagnation 654 n. *deterioration*; rust, rustiness 674 n. *non-use*; sag, slump, recession 37 n. *decrease*; unemployed, smokeless chimneys; absenteeism 598 n. *unwillingness*; procrastination 136 n. *delay*; idleness, loafing, killing time, dolce far niente; idle hands, idle hours 681 n. *leisure*.

sluggishness, stiffness, segnity, segnitude; laziness, indolence, sloth; lethargy, acedia, accidie; remissness 458 n. *negligence*; dawdling, slow progress 278 n. *slowness*; inanimation, lifelessness; languor, lentor, dullness, listlessness 819 n. *moral insensibility*; stupor, torpor, torpescence, torpidity, numbness 375 n. *insensibility*; apathy 860 n. *indifference*; phlegm, impassivity 823 n. *inexcitability*; supineness, no resistance, line of least r. 721 n. *submission*.

sleepiness, tiredness, weariness, lassitude 684 n. *fatigue*; somnolence, doziness, drowsiness, heaviness, nodding; oscitation, oscitancy, yawning; stretching, pandiculation; tired head, tired eyes, heavy lids, sand in the eyes; dreaminess 513 n. *fantasy*.

sleep, slumber, bye-byes; deep sleep, sound s., heavy s.; untroubled sleep, sleep of the just; arms of Morpheus, Hypnos, sandman; half-sleep, drowse; first sleep, beauty s.; light sleep, nap, catnap, forty winks, shut-eye, snooze, doze, siesta, afternoon rest 683 n. *repose*; winter sleep, hibernation; unconsciousness, coma, trance, catalepsy, hypnosis, somnipathy 375 n. *insensibility*; sleep-walking, somnambulism; sleepy sickness, encephalitis lethargica 651 n. *disease*; dreams, dreamland, Land of Nod; cradle, pillow, bed, shake-down.

soporific, somnifacient, sleeping draught, nightcap; sleeping pill, sleeping tablet; sedative, barbiturate; opiate, poppy, mandragora, opium, morphia 375 n. *anæsthetic*; lullaby, berceuse, cradle-song.

idler, drone, lazybones, lie-abed, loafer, lounger, flâneur, sloucher, slug, sluggard; moper, mopus, sleepy-head; lubber, lubbard; dawdle, dawdler 278 n. *slowcoach*; hobo, bum, tramp 268 n. *wanderer*; mendicant 763 n. *beggar*; spiv, parasite, cadger, sponger; floater, drifter; opium-eater, lotus-e., waiter on Providence 596 n. *fatalist*; non-worker, sinecurist, rentier; fainéant, dummy, passenger, sleeping partner, absentee landlord, afternoon farmer; dreamer, sleeper, slumberer, dozer, drowser; hibernator, dormouse, marmot; Seven Sleepers, Rip van Winkle, Barbarossa, Sleeping Beauty.

Adj. *inactive*, motionless, stationary, at a standstill, still, hushed, extinct 266 adj. *quiescent*; suspended, discontinued, taken off, not working, not operating, not in use, laid up, out of commission 674 adj. *disused*; inanimate, lifeless, exanimate 175 adj. *inert*; torpid, benumbed, unconscious, dopey, drugged 375 adj. *insensible*; sluggish, stiff, rusty 677 adj. *non-active*; listless, lackadaisical 834 adj. *dejected*; tired, faint, languid, languorous 684 adj. *fatigued*; dull, heavy, leaden 838 adj. *tedious*; soulless, lumpish, stolid 820 adj. *impassive*; unresisting, supine, submissive 721 adj. *submitting*; uninterested 454 adj. *incurious*; apathetic 860 adj. *indifferent*; lethargic, unaroused, unawakened 823 adj. *inexcitable*; non-participating, sleeping 190 adj. *absent*; leisured, idle, empty, otiose, unoccupied, disengaged 681 adj. *leisurely*; on strike, out.

lazy, bone-l., do-nothing, fainéant; slothful, sluggish, work-shy, indolent, idle; dronish, spivvish, parasitical; idling, lolling, loafing 681 adj. *leisurely*; dawdling 278 adj. *slow*; tardy, laggard, dilatory, procrastinating 136 adj. *late*; slack, remiss, careless 458 adj. *negligent*.

sleepy, ready for bed, tired 684 adj. *fatigued*; half-awake, half-asleep; slumbrous, somnolent, heavy-eyed, heavy with sleep, stupid with s.; drowsy, dozy, nodding, yawning; napping, dozing; asleep, dreaming, fast asleep, sound a., dead a., dead,

dead to the world; unconscious, out; dormant, hibernating, comatose; in dreamland, in the arms of Morpheus, in bed.

somnific, soporific, somniferous, somnifacient, sleep-inducing, sedative, hypnotic.

Vb. *be inactive,* do nothing, rust, stagnate, vegetate, smoulder, hang fire 677 vb. *not act;* let the grass grow under one's feet, delay 136 vb. *put off;* not bother, take it easy, let it rip, laisser faire 458 vb. *be neglectful;* hang about, kick one's heels 136 vb. *wait;* take one's time, slouch, lag, loiter, dawdle 278 vb. *move slowly;* dally, tarry, stay 136 vb. *be late;* stand, sit, lie, lollop, loll, lounge, laze, rest, take one's ease 683 vb. *repose;* not work, fold one's arms, sit on one's hands; have nothing to do, loaf, idle, mooch, moon, while away the time, twiddle one's thumbs; waste time, consume the golden hours, trifle, dabble, fribble, fiddle-faddle, fritter away the time, piddle, potter, putter 641 vb. *waste effort;* slow down, come to a standstill 278 vb. *decelerate;* dilly-dally, hesitate 474 vb. *be uncertain;* droop, faint, fail, languish, slacken 266 vb. *come to rest;* sag, slump 37 vb. *decrease;* be still, be hushed 266 vb. *be quiescent;* discontinue, stop, come to an end 145 vb. *cease;* strike, come out.

sleep, slumber, snooze, nap; aestivate, hibernate; sleep sound, sleep well, sleep like a log, sleep like a top, lie in the arms of Morpheus; dream; snore; go to sleep, drop off, fall asleep, take a nap, have forty winks; close one's eyes, feel sleepy, yawn, nod, doze, drowse; go to bed, turn in, doss down, kip d., shake d.; settle down, bed, roost, perch.

make inactive, put to sleep, put to bed, seal up the eyelids; send to sleep, lull, rock, cradle; soothe 177 vb. *assuage;* make lazy, sluggardize; deaden, paralyse, benumb, chill, dope, drug, narcotize, put out 375 vb. *render insensible;* stiffen, cramp, immobilize 747 vb. *fetter;* lay up, put out of commission 674 vb. *disuse;* dismantle 641 vb. *make useless;* pay off, stand o., lay o., 300 vb. *dismiss.*

See: 37, 136, 145, 175, 177, 190, 266, 268, 278, 300, 375, 454, 458, 474, 513, 596, 598, 641, 651, 654, 674, 677, 681, 683, 684, 721, 747, 763, 819, 820, 823, 834, 838, 860.

680 Haste

N. *haste,* hurry, scurry, hurry-scurry, hustle, bustle, scuttle, scramble 678 n. *activity;* splutter, flutter, fidget, fuss 318 n. *agitation;* rush, rush job 670 n. *non-preparation;* race, feverish haste, tearing hurry, no time to lose 136 n. *lateness;* push, drive, expedition, dispatch 277 n. *velocity;* hastening, acceleration, forced march, dash 277 n. *spurt;* overhaste, precipitance, impetuosity 857 n. *rashness;* inability to wait, hastiness, impatience 822 n. *excitability;* cause for haste, immediacy, urgency 638 n. *importance.*

Adj. *hasty,* over-h., impetuous, hot-headed, precipitant 857 adj. *rash;* feverish, impatient, all impatience, ardent 818 adj. *fervent;* pushing, shoving; uncontrolled, boisterous, furious 176 adj. *violent;* precipitate, headlong, breathless, scrambling 277 adj. *speedy;* expeditious, prompt, without delay; hasting, hastening, making speed; in haste, in all h., in hot h., hotfoot, running, racing; in a hurry, unable to wait, pressed for time, hard-pressed, driven; done in haste, hurried, scamped, rough and ready, forced, rushed, rush, last-minute 670 adj. *unprepared;* allowing no time, brooking no delay, urgent, immediate 638 adj. *important.*

Vb. *hasten,* expedite, dispatch; urge, drive, spur, goad, whip, lash, flog 612 vb. *incite;* rush, allow no time, brook no delay; be hasty, be precipitate, rush headlong 857 vb. *be rash;* haste, make haste; post, race, run, dash off, tear off 277 vb. *move fast;* catch up, make up for lost time, overtake 277 vb. *outstrip;* spurt, dash, make a forced march 277 vb. *accelerate;* hurry, scurry, hustle, bustle, fret, fume, fidget, rush to and fro, dart to and fro 678 vb. *be active;* be in a hurry, have no time to spare, have no time to lose, cut short the preliminaries, brush aside; cut corners, rush one's fences; rush through, dash through, make short work of; be pressed for time, work against time, work under pressure; do at the last moment 136 vb. *be late;* lose no time, lose not a moment, make every minute count; hasten away, cut one's cable, cut and run, make oneself scarce, stand not upon the order of one's going 296 vb. *decamp.*

Adv. *hastily,* hurriedly, precipitately, feverishly, post-haste, hot-foot, apace 277 vb.

swiftly; with all haste, at short notice, on the spur of the moment; immediately, urgently, with urgency, under pressure, by forced marches, with not a moment to lose.

See: 136, 176, 277, 296, 318, 612, 638, 670, 678, 818, 822, 857.

681 Leisure

N. *leisure*, spare time, convenience; spare hours, vacant moments; time on one's hands, time to kill; not enough work, sinecure; no work, idleness, dolce far niente; off duty, time off, day off, holiday, half-h., vacation, leave, furlough 679n. *inactivity*; time to spare, no hurry, ample time, all the time in the world; rest, ease, slippered e. 683n. *repose*; no more work, retirement 753n. *resignation*.

Adj. *leisurely*, deliberate, unhurried 278 adj. *slow*; at one's convenience, at one's own time, at any odd moment; leisured, at leisure, disengaged, unoccupied; at a loose end, at ease; off duty, on holiday, on vacation, on leave, on furlough; retired, in retirement; affording leisure, laboursaving.

Vb. *have leisure*, have time enough, have plenty of time, have all the time in the world, have time to spare; be master of one's time, take one's ease, spend, pass, while away; see no cause for haste, take one's time 278vb. *move slowly*; want something to do, find time lie heavy on one's hands 679vb. *be inactive*; take a holiday 683vb. *repose*; give up work, go into retirement, retire 753vb. *resign*; find time for, make leisure, save labour.

See: 278, 679, 683, 753.

682 Exertion

N. *exertion*, effort, struggle, strife 671n. *essay*; straining, strain, stress, might and main; tug, pull, stretch, heave, lift, throw, a strong pull, a long pull and a pull all together; drive, force, pressure, full p., maximum p., applied energy 160n. *energy*; ado, trouble, toil and t., mighty efforts, the hard way; muscle, elbow grease, sweat of one's brow; pains, painstaking, operoseness 678n. *assiduity*;

elaboration, artificiality; overwork, over-exertion, over-expansion 678n. *over-activity*; extra work, overtime, busman's holiday; battle, campaign.

exercise, exercitation; employment 673n. *use*; practice, regular p., training, workout 669n. *preparation*; bodily exercise, physical e., gymnastics 162n. *athletics*; eurhythmics, callisthenics; games, sports, out-door s., races 837n. *sport*.

labour, work, hard w., heavy w., uphill w., warm w., punishing w., long haul; spadework, donkey-work; manual labour, sweat of one's brow; housework, chores, toil, travail, swink, drudgery, slavery, sweat, fag, grind, strain, treadmill, grindstone; penal work, hard labour, picking oakum, breaking stones 963n. *penalty*; forced labour, corvée 740n. *compulsion*; fatigue, fatigue duty, spell of d. 917n. *duty*; piecework, taskwork; task, chore, job, operation, exercise 676n. *deed*; shift, trick, stint, stretch, spell of work 110n. *period*; job of work, stroke of w., stitch of w., hand's turn; working life, working day, man-hours.

Adj. *labouring*, born to toil, horny-handed; working, drudging, sweating, grinding, etc. vb.; on the go, on the stretch, hard at it 678adj. *busy*; hard-working, laborious, operose 678adj. *industrious*; slogging, plodding 600adj. *persevering*; strenuous, energetic 678adj. *active*; painstaking, thorough 455adj. *attentive*; exercising, taking exercise, practising; palestric, gymnastic, athletic.

laborious, full of labour, involving effort; operose, crushing, killing, backbreaking; gruelling, punishing; toilsome, troublesome, weary, wearisome, painful, burdensome; heroic, Herculean; arduous, hard, warm, heavy, uphill 700adj. *difficult*; hard-fought, hard-won; thorough, painstaking, laboured; elaborate, artificial; detailed, fiddling; effort-wasting 641adj. *useless*.

Vb. *exert oneself*, apply oneself, use one's exertions, make an effort, try 671vb. *essay*; struggle, strain, strive, sweat blood; trouble oneself, bestir oneself, put oneself out; spare no effort, turn every stone, do one's utmost, try one's best, use one's best endeavours, do all one can, go to all lengths; put one's heart and soul into it, put out one's whole strength,

put one's back into it, strain every nerve, use every muscle; love one's job, have one's heart in one's work 597vb. *be willing*; force one's way, drive through, wade t.; hammer at, slog at 600vb. *persevere*; battle, campaign.

work, labour, toil, moil, drudge, fag, grind, slog, sweat; sweat blood; pull, haul, tug, heave, ply the oar; dig, spade, lumber; do the work, soil one's hands; spit on one's palms, get down to it, set to, take one's coat off 68vb. *begin*; keep at it, plod 600 vb. *persevere*; work hard, work overtime, work double shift, work double tides, work all hours, work night and day, overwork 678vb. *be busy*; slave, work one's fingers to the bone, work like a nigger, work like a slave *or* like a galley-s., work like a horse, work like a Trojan, work like a steam-engine; overdo it, make work; work for, serve 703vb. *minister to*; put to work, give work to, task, tax 684vb. *fatigue*; handle, ply 173vb. *operate*.

Adv. *laboriously*, the hard way; arduously, strenuously, energetically; lustily, heartily, heart and soul, with might and main, with all one's might, tooth and nail, hammer and tongs, for all one is worth.

See: 68, 110, 160, 162, 173, 455, 597, 600, 641, 669, 671, 673, 676, 678, 684, 700, 703, 740, 837, 917, 963.

683 Repose

N. *repose*, rest, rest from one's labours 679 n. *inactivity*; restfulness, ease, comfort, snugness 376n. *euphoria*; sweet sleep, happy dreams 679n. *sleep*; relaxation, breathing time, breather 685n. *refreshment*; pause, respite, recess, break 145n. *lull*; interval 108n. *interim*; holiday, vacation, leave, furlough, day off, Sabbatical year 681n. *leisure*; day of rest, sabbath, Lord's day.

Adj. *reposeful*, restful, easeful, slippered, unbelted, unbuttoned; cushioned, pillowed, snug 376adj. *comfortable*; peaceful, quiet 266adj. *tranquil*; leisured, sabbatical, vacational, holiday 681adj. *leisurely*; post-prandial, after-dinner.

Vb. *repose*, rest, take r., enjoy peace, take it easy, take one's ease; mop one's brow, stretch one's legs; recline, lie down, loll, sprawl 216vb. *be horizontal*; perch, roost

311vb. *sit down*; couch, go to bed, kip down, go to sleep 679vb. *sleep*; relax, unbend, forget work, put on one's slippers, rest and be thankful; breathe, take a breather 685vb. *be refreshed*; rest on one's oars 266vb. *come to rest*; take a holiday, go on leave 681vb. *have leisure*.

Adv. *at rest*, reposefully, restfully, peacefully, on holiday, on vacation.

See: 108, 145, 216, 266, 311, 376, 679, 681, 685.

684 Fatigue

N. *fatigue*, tiredness, weariness, lassitude, languor; physical fatigue, aching muscles; mental fatigue, brain-fag, staleness; jadedness, distress; limit of endurance, exhaustion, collapse, prostration, done-up feeling; strain, over-tiredness, over-exertion 682n. *exertion*; sign of fatigue, shortness of breath, hard breathing, dyspnœa, panting, palpitations 352n. *respiration*; languishment, faintness, fainting, faint, swoon, black-out, deliquium, lipothymy, coma, syncope 375n. *insensibility*.

Adj. *fatigued*, tired, ready for bed 679adj. *sleepy*; tired out, exhausted, spent, fordone; done, done up, done for, pooped, fagged, fagged out, knocked up, washed up, washed out; stupid with fatigue, dull, stale; strained, overworked, overtired, overdriven, overwearied, overfatigued, overstrained; dog-tired, dog-weary, tired to death, dropping, ready to drop, all in, dead beat, beat, whacked; more dead than alive, swooning, fainting, out; aching, sore, toilworn; way-worn, footsore, footweary, walked off one's legs; overwatched, tired-eyed, heavy-e., hollow-e.; tired-looking, haggard, worn; faint, drooping, flagging, languid, languorous; still tired, unrefreshed; tired of, bored with 838adj. *bored*; jaded, satiated 863adj. *sated*.

panting, anhelous, out of breath, short of b.; breathed, breathless, gasping, puffing and blowing, snorting, winded, blown, broken-winded 352adj. *puffing*.

fatiguing, gruelling, punishing 682adj. *laborious*; tiresome, wearisome; exacting, demanding; irksome, trying 838adj. *tedious*.

Vb. *be fatigued*,—fagged etc.adj.; get weary, ache in every muscle, gasp, pant,

puff, blow, grunt, lose one's wind 352 vb. *breathe*; languish, droop, drop, sink, flag, fail 163 vb. *be weak*; stagger, faint, swoon, get giddy, swim; yawn, nod, drowse 679 vb. *sleep*; succumb, drop, collapse, crack up, crock up, pack up; cry out for rest, have no strength left, be at the end of one's strength; can go *or* do no more, must have a rest, must sit down; overwork, get stale, need a rest, need a break, need a change, need a holiday.

fatigue, tire, tire out, wear, fag, wear out, exhaust, do up, whack, knock up, crock up, prostrate; double up, wind; demand too much, task, tax, strain, work, drive, overdrive, flog, overwork, overtax, overtask, overburden, overstrain; distress, harass, irk, jade 827 vb. *incommode*; tire to death, weary, bore, send to sleep 838 vb. *be tedious*; keep from sleep, deprive of rest, stint of r., allow no r.

See: 163, 352, 375, 679, 682, 827, 838, 863.

685 Refreshment

N. *refreshment*, breather, break, recess 145 n. *lull*; renewal, recreation, recruitment, recuperation 656 n. *restoration*; reanimation, refocillation 656 n. *revival*; easing 831 n. *relief*; stimulation, refresher, reviver, nineteenth hole 174 n. *stimulant*; regalement, refection 301 n. *food*; wash, wash and brush up, tidy-up 648 n. *cleansing*.

Adj. *refreshing*, cooling, cool 380 adj. *cold*; comforting 831 adj. *relieving*; bracing, reviving, recruiting 656 adj. *restorative*; easy on, labour-saving.

refreshed, freshened up, breathed, recovered, revived, enlivened 656 adj. *restored*; like a giant refreshed, twice the man one was; perked up, ready for more.

Vb. *refresh*, freshen, freshen up 648 vb. *clean*; air, fan, ventilate 340 vb. *aerify*; shade, cool, cool off, cool one down 382 vb. *refrigerate*; brace, stimulate 174 vb. *invigorate*; recruit, recreate, revive, reanimate, refocillate, recuperate 656 vb. *restore*; ease 831 vb. *relieve*; allow rest, give a breather; regale 301 vb. *feed*.

be refreshed, breathe, draw breath, get one's breath back, regain *or* recover one's breath, take a deep b., respire, clear one's head; come to, perk up, feel like a giant refreshed; recrudesce, revive 656 vb. *be restored*; mop one's brow, renew oneself, recreate o., take a breather, sleep off; go for a change, have a rest 683 vb. *repose*.

See: 145, 174, 301, 340, 380, 382, 648, 656, 683, 831.

686 Agent

N. *agent*, operator, actor, performer, player, executant, practitioner; perpetrator 676 n. *doer*; minister, tool 628 n. *instrument*; factor 754 n. *consignee*; representative 754 n. *delegate*; deputizer, spokesman 755 n. *deputy*; proxy 150 n. *substitute*; executor, executrix, executive, administrator, dealer; employer, manufacturer, industrialist 167 n. *producer*.

worker, volunatry w. 597 n. *volunteer*; social worker 901 n. *philanthropist*; independent worker, free-lance, self-employed person; toiler, moiler, drudge, fag, erk, hack; menial, factotum, maid-of-all-work, domestic servant 742 n. *servant*; hewer of wood and drawer of water, beast of burden 742 n. *slave*; ant, beaver, Stakhanovite 678 n. *busy person*; professional man, business m., business woman, career w., breadwinner, earner, salary-e., wage-e., wage-slave, employee; brainworker, boffin; clerical worker, desk-w., white-collar w., black-coat w.; pieceworker, manual w.; charwoman, charlady, char, help, daily h., cleaner; labourer, casual l., day-l., agricultural l., farm worker, land-girl, farmer's boy 370 n. *husbandman*; ditcher, thatcher; lumberer, lumberjack, woodcutter; working man, workman, man, hand, operative, factory-worker, factory-hand; navvy, ganger, plate-layer; docker, stevedore, packer; porter, coolie, khalasi, coal-heaver; dustman 648 n. *cleaner*.

artisan, artificer, tradesman, technician; skilled worker, semi-skilled w., pastmaster 696 n. *proficient*; journeyman, apprentice 538 n. *learner*; craftsman, turner, potter, joiner, cabinet-maker, carpenter, carver, woodworker, sawyer, cooper; wright, wheelwright, wainwright, coach-builder; shipwright, ship-builder, boat-builder; builder, architect, master-mason, mason, housebuilder, bricklayer,

hodman, tiler, thatcher, decorator, house-d.; forger, smith, blacksmith, copper-smith, tin-smith, brass-smith, goldsmith, silversmith, gunsmith, lock-smith; iron-worker, steel-w., metal-w.; tinker, knife-grinder; collier, worker at the coal-face, miner, tin-m., gold-m.; mechanic, machinist, rigger, fitter, plumber; engineer, civil e., mining e.; electrician, gas-fitter; tailor, cutter, sempstress, needlewoman, shirtmaker, bootmaker, cordwainer, cobbler 228 n. *clothier*; watchmaker, clockmaker; jeweller, jewel-cutter; glass-blower.

personnel, staff, force, company, gang, squad, crew, complement, cadre 74 n. *band*; dramatis personæ 594 n. *actor*; co-worker, fellow-w., mate, colleague, associate, partner, participator, co-operator 707 n. *colleague*; workpeople, hands, men, pay-roll; labour, casual l.; labour pool, labour force, man-power, working classes.

See: 74, 150, 167, 228, 370, 538, 594, 597, 628, 648, 676, 678, 696, 707, 742, 754, 755, 901.

687 Workshop

N. *workshop*, studio, atelier; workroom, study; laboratory, research l.; workhouse, sweatshop; plant, installation; shop, workshop, yard; mill, cotton-m., loom; sawmill, factory, manufactory; foundry, works, iron-w., brassworks; steelyard, steel-works, smelting-w., tin-w., gas-w., gasification plant; blast-furnace, forge, smithy, stithy, crucible, melting-pot 383 n. *furnace*; powerhouse, power station 160 n. *energy*; quarry, mine 630 n. *store*; coal-mine, colliery, coal-face; tin-mine, stannary; mint; arsenal, armoury; dockyard, shipyard, slips; wharf, dock 192 n. *stable*; refinery, distillery, brewery; salt-works; shop, shop-floor, bench, production line; nursery 370 n. *farm*; dairy, creamery 369 n. *stock farm*; kitchen, cook-house, laundry; office, bureau, business house, firm, company; secretariat, Whitehall, offices, administrative buildings; manufacturing town, hive of industry, hive 678 n. *activity*.

See: 160, 192, 369, 370, 383, 630, 678.

688 Conduct

N. *conduct*, behaviour, deportment; bearing, personal b., comportment, carriage, port; demeanour, attitude, posture 445 n. *mien*; aspect, look, look in one's eyes 445 n. *appearance*; tone, tone of voice, delivery 577 n. *voice*; motion, action, gesticulation 547 n. *gesture*; manner, guise, air; poise, dignity; graciousness 884 n. *courtesy*; ungraciousness, rudeness 885 n. *discourtesy*; pose 850 n. *affectation*; mental attitude, outlook 485 n. *opinion*; psychology, mood 818 n. *feeling*; good behaviour 933 n. *virtue*; misbehaviour, misconduct 934 n. *wickedness*; democratic behaviour, common touch; past behaviour, record, history; reward of conduct, deserts 915 n. *dueness*; way of life, ethos, morals, ideals, customs, manners 610 n. *habit*; course of conduct, line of action, speech from the throne, Queen's speech 623 n. *policy*; career, course, race, walk, walk of life 622 n. *vocation*; observance, routine, rules of business 610 n. *practice*; procedure, process, method, modus operandi 624 n. *way*; treatment, handling, manipulation, direction 689 n. *management*; gentle handling, kid gloves, velvet glove 736 n. *lenity*; rough handling, jackboot, iron hand 735 n. *severity*; dealings, transactions 154 n. *affairs*; deeds 676 n. *deed*.

tactics, strategy, campaign, plan of c., programme 623 n. *plan*; line, party l. 623 n. *policy*; political science, art of the possible, politics, realpolitik, statesmanship 733 n. *governance*; lifemanship, gamesmanship, one-upmanship 698 n. *cunning*; brinkmanship, generalship, seamanship 694 n. *skill*; manœuvres, manœuvring, marching and counter-marching, jockeying, jockeying for position; tactical advantage, vantage ground, weather gauge 34 n. *vantage*; manœuvre, shift 623 n. *contrivance*; move, gambit 676 n. *deed*; game, little g. 698 n. *stratagem*.

Adj. *behaving*, behaviourist; psychological; tactical, strategical; political, statesman-like 622 adj. *businesslike*.

Vb. *behave*, act 676 vb. *do*; behave well, play the game 933 vb. *be virtuous*; behave badly, behave ill, misbehave, carry on 934 vb. *be wicked*; deserve well, deserve ill; gesture 547 vb. *gesticulate*; posture, pose,

affect 850vb. *be affected*; conduct oneself, behave o., carry o., bear o., comport o., demean o.; lead one's life, lead a good l., lead a bad l.; indulge in 678vb. *be active*; play one's part 775n. *participate*; run one's race, follow one's career, conduct one's affairs 622vb. *busy oneself*; follow a course, take a c., shape a c., steer a c. 281vb. *steer for*; paddle one's own canoe, shift for oneself 744vb. *be free*; employ tactics, manœuvre, jockey, twist, turn; behave towards, treat.

deal with, have on one's plate, have to do with 676vb. *do*; handle, manipulate 173 vb. *operate*; conduct, carry on, run 689n. *manage*; take order, see to, cope with, do the needful; transact, enact, execute, despatch, carry through, put t., put into practice 725vb. *carry out*; work out 623 vb. *plan*; work at, work through, wade t. 682vb. *work*; go through, read 536vb. *study*.

See: 34, 154, 173, 281, 445, 485, 536, 547, 577, 610, 622, 623, 624, 676, 678, 682, 689, 694, 698, 725, 733, 735, 736, 744, 775, 818, 850, 884, 885, 915, 933, 934.

689 Management

N. *management*, conduct, conduct of affairs, manipulation, running, handling; managership, stewardship, proctorship, agency 751n. *commission*; care, charge, control 733n. *authority*; superintendence, oversight 457n. *surveillance*; patronage 660n. *protection*; art of management, tact, way with 694n. *skill*; business management, work study, time and motion s.; ménage, regimen, régime, dispensation; housekeeping, housewifery, housework; husbandry, economics, political economy; kingcraft, statecraft, statesmanship; government 733n. *governance*; regulation, law-making 953n. *legislation*; reins, reins of government, ministry, cabinet, inner c.; staff work, administration; bureaucracy, civil service; secretariat, government office, kutcherry 687n. *workshop*.

directorship, direction, responsibility, control, supreme c. 737n. *command*; dictatorship, leadership, premiership, chairmanship, captaincy 34n. *superiority*; guidance,

steering, steerage, pilotage, steersmanship, pilotship, pilotism; sailing instructions 737n. *command*; pole-star, lodestar 520n. *guide*; steering instrument, steering oar, joy-stick, controls, helm, rudder, wheel, tiller; needle, magnetic n., compass, binnacle; gyrocompass, gyropilot, autopilot 269n. *sailing aid*; direction-finding, beam, radar 281n. *direction*; remote control, telearchics.

Adj. *directing*, directorial, leading, hegemonic; directional, guiding, steering, holding the rudder; governing, controlling, gubernatorial, holding the reins, in the chair 733adj. *authoritative*; dictatorial 735adj. *authoritarian*; supervisory, managing, managerial; executive, administrative; legislative, nomothetic; high-level, top-l. 638adj. *important*; economic, political; official, bureaucratic 733adj. *governmental*.

Vb. *manage*, manipulate, manœuvre, pull the strings 178vb. *influence*; have taped, have the measure of 490vb. *know*; handle, conduct, run, carry on; minister, administer, prescribe; supervise, superintend, oversee, caretake 457vb. *invigilate*; nurse 457vb. *look after*; have charge of, have in charge, hold the portfolio, hold the reins, handle the ribbons 612vb. *motivate* (see *direct*); keep order, police, regulate; legislate, pass laws 953vb. *make legal*; control, govern, sway 733vb. *rule*; know how to manage, have a way with.

direct, lead, pioneer, precede 64vb. *come before*; boss, dictate 737vb. *command*; hold office, hold a responsible position, have responsibility; assume responsibility 917vb. *incur a duty*; preside, take the chair, be chairman, be in the chair; head, captain; stroke, pull the stroke oar; pilot, cox, steer, take the helm, hold the tiller, wield the rudder 269vb. *navigate*; point 281vb. *point to*; show the way 547vb. *indicate*; shepherd, guide, conduct, lead on; introduce, compère; escort 89vb. *accompany*; channel, canalize; route, train, lead, lead over, lead through; furnish the address 524vb. *inform*.

Adv. *in control*, in charge, at the wheel, at the head, in the chair; ex officio.

See: 34, 64, 89, 178, 269, 281, 457, 490, 520, 524, 547, 612, 638, 660, 687, 694, 733, 735, 737, 751, 917, 953.

690 Director

N. *director*, governing body 741 n. *governor*; steering committee; cabinet, inner c. 692 n. *council*; board of directors, board, chair; staff, brass, top b., management; manager, controller; legislator, lawgiver, law-maker; employer, capitalist, boss 741 n. *master*; headman, chief 34 n. *superior*; principal, headmaster, head, rector, moderator, vice-chancellor, chancellor; president, vice-p.; chairman, speaker; premier, prime minister; captain, team-c.; stroke, cox, master, ship-m., sailing-m., trierarch 270 n. *mariner*; man on the bridge, steersman, helmsman 270 n. *navigator*; pilot 520 n. *guide*; forerunner, torch-bearer, link-boy 66 n. *precursor*; drill-sergeant 537 n. *trainer*; director of studies 537 n. *teacher*; backseat driver 691 n. *adviser*; king-maker, wire-puller, animator 612 n. *motivator*; traffic cop, traffic warden 305 n. *traffic control*.

leader, charismatic l., judge (Old Testament) 741 n. *governor*; messiah, mahdi; leader of the House, leader of the opposition; spearhead, centre-forward; shepherd, teamster, drover 369 n. *herdsman*; bell-wether; fugleman, file-leader; pacemaker; symposiarch, master of ceremonies, director of the feast; high priest, mystagogue; coryphæus, chorus-leader, choragus, conductor, band-c., orchestra leader, first violin; precentor; Fuehrer, Duce 741 n. *autocrat*; ringleader, demagogue, rabble-rouser, firebrand 738 n. *agitator*; chauffeur, Jehu 268 n. *driver*; captain; condottiere.

manager, person in responsibility, responsible person; man in charge, key man, king pin 638 n. *bigwig*; procurator, administrator, executive, executor 676 n. *doer*; statesman, statist, politician; economist, political e.; housekeeper, husband, housewife; steward, bailiff, landreeve; farm-bailiff, reeve, greeve; agent, factor 754 n. *consignee*; superintendent, supervisor, inspector, overseer, foreman; warden, house master, matron, nurse, tutor 660 n. *protector*; proctor, disciplinarian; party-manager, whip; custodian, caretaker, curator, librarian 749 n. *keeper*; master of hounds, whipper-in, huntsman; circus manager, ring-master; compère.

official, office-holder, office-bearer, Jack-in-office, tin god; shop steward; government servant, state-s., public s., civil s. 742 n. *servant*; officer of state, high official, vizier, grand v., minister, cabinet m., secretary of state, secretary-general, secretary, under-s.; secretariat-wallah, bureaucrat, mandarin, red-tapist 741 n. *officer*; judicial officer, district o., collector, magistrate 733 n. *magistrature*; commissioner, prefect, intendant; consul, proconsul, prætor, quæstor, ædile; first secretary, counsellor 754 n. *envoy*; alderman, mayor 692 n. *councillor*; functionary, party-official, petty o., clerk; school prefect, monitor.

See: 34, 66, 268, 270, 305, 369, 520, 537, 612, 638, 660, 676, 691, 692, 733, 738, 741, 742, 749, 754.

691 Advice

N. *advice*, word of a., piece of a.; words of wisdom, rede 498 n. *wisdom*; counsel, adhortation; criticism, constructive c. 480 n. *estimate*; didacticism, moralizing, moral injunction, prescription 693 n. *precept*; recommendation, proposition, proposal, motion 512 n. *supposition*; suggestion, submonition, submission; tip 524 n. *hint*; guidance, briefing, instruction 524 n. *information*; charge, charge to the jury 955 n. *legal trial*; taking counsel, consultation, mutual c., huddle, pow-wow, parley, pourparler, talks, conversations, talks across the table, summitry 584 n. *conference*; seeking advice, reference, referment 584 n. *conference*; advice against 762 n. *deprecation*.

adviser, counsellor, consultant; professional consultant 696 n. *expert*; referee, arbiter 480 n. *estimator*; prescriber, commender, advocate, recommender, mover, prompter 612 n. *motivator*; medical adviser 658 n. *doctor*; legal adviser, counsel 958 n. *lawyer*; guide, philosopher and friend, mentor, confidant 537 n. *teacher*; monitor, admonisher, remembrancer 505 n. *reminder*; Nestor, Egeria, Grey Eminence, Dutch uncle; oracle, wise man 500 n. *sage*; backseat driver, kibitzer, busybody 678 n. *meddler*; committee of enquiry, consultative body 692 n. *council*.

Adj. *advising*, advisory, consultative, deliberative; hortative, recommendatory

612 adj. *inducive*; dehortatory 613 adj. *dissuasive*; admonitory, warning 664 n. *cautionary*; didactic; moral, moralizing.

Vb. *advise*, give advice, counsel, offer c., press advice on; think best, recommend, prescribe, advocate, commend; propose, move, put to, submit, suggest 512 vb. *propound*; prompt 524 vb. *hint*; press, urge, exhort 612 vb. *incite*; dehort, advise against 613 vb. *dissuade*; admonish 664 vb. *warn*; enjoin, charge, dictate 737 vb. *command*; advise well, speak to one's condition 642 vb.

consult, seek advice, refer, make a reference, call in, call on; confide in, be closeted with, have at one's elbow; take advice, listen to, be advised, accept advice, take one's cue from, submit one's judgment to another's, follow advice; sit in council, sit in conclave, lay heads together, advise with, hold a consultation, hold a council of war, deliberate, parley, sit round a table, compare notes 584 vb. *confer*.

See: 480, 498, 500, 505, 512, 524, 537, 584, 612, 613, 642, 658, 664, 678, 692, 693, 696, 737, 762, 955, 958.

692 Council

N. *council*, council board, round table; council chamber, board room; Star Chamber, court 956 n. *tribunal*; Privy Council, Aulic C., presidium; ecclesiastical council, curia, consistory, Bench of Bishops; vestry; cabinet, board, advisory b., consultative body, Royal Commission; staff college; assembly, conventicle, congregation 74 n. *assemblage*; conclave, convocation 985 n. *synod*; convention, congress, meeting, top-level m., summit; durbar, diet; folkmoot, moot, comitia, ecclesia; federal council, amphictyonic c., amphictyony, League of Nations, U.N.O., parliament of nations; municipal council, county c., borough c., town c., parish c.; local board, union b.; zemstvo, soviet; council of elders, genro, sanhedrim; sitting, session, séance, audience, hearing 584 n. *conference*.

parliament, Mother of Parliaments, Westminster, Upper House, House of Lords, House of Peers, 'another place'; Lower House, House of Commons; senate,

senatus; legislative assembly, deliberative a., consultative a.; States-General, Cortes, witenagemot; Chambre des Députés, Reichstag, Reichsrath, Rigsdag, Storthing, Duma, Dail Eireann; Senate, Congress; Legislative Council, Lok Sabha, Majlis, Sejm, Knesset; quorum, division.

councillor, privy councillor; senator, conscript fathers, Areopagite, sanhedrist; peer, life-peer; representative, deputy, congressman, member of Parliament, M.P. 754 n. *delegate*; back-bencher, lobby-fodder; parliamentarian, legislator; municipal councillor, mayor, alderman 690 n. *official*.

Adj. *parliamentary*, senatorial, congressional; unicameral, bicameral; curule, conciliar; convocational, synodal.

See: 74, 584, 690, 754, 956, 985.

693 Precept

N. *precept*, firm advice 691 n. *advice*; direction, instruction, general i.; injunction, charge 737 n. *command*; commission 751 n. *mandate*; order, written o., writ 737 n. *warrant*; rescript, decretal epistle, authoritative reply 480 n. *judgment*; prescript, prescription, ordinance, regulation 737 n. *decree*; canon, form, norm, formula, formulary, rubric; rule, golden r., moral 496 n. *maxim*; recipe, receipt 658 n. *remedy*; commandment, statute, enactment, act, code, penal c., corpus juris 953 n. *legislation*; tenet, article, set of rules, constitution; ticket, party line; Ten Commandments, Twelve Tables, laws of the Medes and the Persians; canon law, common l., unwritten l. 953 n. *law*; rule of custom, convention 610 n. *practice*; technicality, nice point 530 n. *enigma*; precedent, leading case, text 83 n. *example*.

Adj. *preceptive*, prescriptive, decretal, mandatory, binding; canonical, rubrical, statutory 953 adj. *legal*; moralizing 496 adj. *aphoristic*; customary, conventional 610 adj. *usual*.

See: 83, 480, 496, 530, 658, 737, 751, 610, 691, 953.

694 Skill

N. *skill*, skilfulness, dexterity, dexterousness, handiness, ambidexterity; grace, style 575

n. *elegance*; neatness, deftness, adroitness, address; ease 701 n. *facility*; proficiency, competence, efficiency, faculty, capability, capacity 160 n. *ability*; many-sidedness, all-round capacity, universal c., versatility amphibiousness; adaptability, flexibility, suppleness; touch, grip, control; mastery, mastership, wizardry, virtuosity, excellence, prowess 644 n. *goodness*; strong point, métier, forte, major suit; acquirement, attainment, accomplishment; skills, seamanship, airmanship, horsemanship, marksmanship; experience, expertise, professionalism; specialism; technology, science, know-how, technique, technical knowledge, practical k. 490 n. *knowledge*; practical ability, do-it-yourself habit; craftsmanship, art, artistry, ars celare artem, art that conceals art; finish, execution 646 n. *perfection*; ingenuity, resourcefulness, craft, craftiness, callidity 698 n. *cunning*; cleverness, sharpness, worldly wisdom, sophistication, lifemanship 498 n. *sagacity*; savoir faire, tact, discretion 463 n. *discrimination*; feat of skill, trick, hat-t., gimmick, dodge 623 n. *contrivance*; sleight of hand, conjuring 542 n. *sleight*; funambulism, rope-dancing, tightrope walking, brinkmanship; generalship 688 n. *tactics*; skilful use, exploitation 673 n. *use*.

aptitude, inborn a., innate ability; bent, natural b. 179 n. *tendency*; faculty, endowment, gift, flair, parts, natural p.; turn, knack, green fingers; talent, genius, genius for; aptness, fitness, qualification.

masterpiece, chef-d'œuvre, a beauty; pièce de résistance; finished work, workmanlike job, craftsman's j.; masterstroke, coup-de-maître, feat, exploit, hat-trick 676 n. *deed*; tour de force, bravura, fireworks; ace, trump, clincher 644 n. *exceller*; work of art, objet d'art, curio, collector's piece.

Adj. *skilful*, good, good at 644 adj. *excellent*; skilled, crack; apt, handy, dexterous, ambidexterous, deft, adroit, slick, neat; neat-fingered, green-f., fine-f., sure-footed; cunning, clever, quick, shrewd, callid, ingenious 498 adj. *intelligent*; politic, statesmanlike 498 adj. *wise*; adaptable, flexible, resourceful, ready; many-sided, versatile; ready for anything, panurgic; sound, able, competent, efficient, competitive; wizard, masterly, like a master,

magisterial, accomplished, finished 646 adj. *perfect*.

gifted, taught by nature; of parts, talented, endowed, well-e., born for, just made for.

expert, experienced, veteran, seasoned, tried, versed in, up in, well up in, knowing 490 adj. *instructed*; skilled, trained, practised, well-p. 669 adj. *prepared*; finished, passed, specialized 669 adj. *matured*; proficient, efficient, qualified, competent, up to the mark; professional 622 adj. *businesslike*; sailorly 270 adj. *seamanlike*.

well-made, well-done, craftily contrived, deep-laid; finished, felicitious, happy; artistic, artificial, sophisticated, stylish 575 adj. *elegant*; dædalian, cunning; technical, scientific; shipshape, workmanlike.

Vb. *be skilful*, —deft etc. adj.; be good at, do well 644 n. *be good*; shine, excel 34 vb. *be superior*; have a turn for, have a gift for, be born for, show aptitude, show a talent for; have the knack, have the trick of, have the right touch; be in practise, be on form, be in good f., have one's eye in, have one's hand in; hit the right nail on the head, put the saddle on the right horse; play one's cards well, not put a foot wrong, know just when to stop; use skilfully, exploit, squeeze the last ounce out of 673 vb. *use*; take advantage of, make hay while the sun shines 137 vb. *profit by*; live by one's wits, know how to live, get around, know all the answers, have one's wits about one 498 vb. *be wise*; exercise discretion 463 vb. *discriminate*.

be expert, turn professional; be master of one's profession, know one's job, have the know-how; acquire the technique, qualify oneself 536 vb. *learn*; have experience, know the ropes, know all the ins and outs, know backwards, be up to every trick, take in one's stride 490 vb. *know*; know what's what, know a hawk from a handsaw, have cut one's wisdom teeth; show one's skill, play with, demonstrate, stunt 875 vb. *be ostentatious*.

Adv. *skilfully*, craftily, artfully; well, with skill, like a master; handily, neatly, featly; stylishly, artistically; knowledgeably, expertly, scientifically; faultlessly, like a machine; naturally, as to the manner born, in one's stride.

See: 34, 137, 160, 179, 270, 463, 490, 498, 536, 542, 575, 622, 623, 644, 646, 669, 673, 676, 688, 698, 701, 875.

695 Unskilfulness

N. *unskilfulness*, want of skill, no gift; lack of practice, rustiness 674n. *non-use*; rawness, unripeness, immaturity, crudity 670 n. *undevelopment*; inexperience, inexpertness 491n. *ignorance*; incapacity, inability, incompetence, inefficiency 161n. *ineffectuality*; disqualification, unproficiency; quackery, charlatanism 850n. *pretension*; clumsiness, indexterity, unhandiness, lubberliness, left-handedness, awkwardness, gaucherie, étourderie (see *bungling*); folly, stupidity 499n. *unintelligence*.

bungling, botching, tinkering, half-measures, pale imitation 726n. *non-completion*; bungle, botch, botchery; off day, botched performance, bad job, sad work, flop 728 n. *failure*; missed chance 138n. *intempestivity*; hamhandedness, dropped catch, fumble, foozle, muff, fluff, miss, mishit, slice, pull, bosh shot, overthrow, misthrow, misfire 495n. *mistake*; thoughtlessness 456n. *inattention*; tactlessness, infelicity, indiscretion 464n. *indiscrimination*; mishandling, misapplication 675n. *misuse*; impolicy, mismanagement, misrule, misgovernment, maladministration 481n. *misjudgment*; misdoing, misconduct, antics; much ado about nothing, wild-goose chase 641n. *lost labour*.

Adj. *unskilful*, ungifted, untalented, unendowed, unaccomplished; stick-in-the-mud, unversatile 679adj. *inactive*; undexterous, unadroit; disqualified, unadapted, unadaptable, unfit, inept 25adj. *unapt*; unable, lame 161adj. *impotent*; incompetent, inefficient, ineffectual; unpractical, unbusinesslike, unstatesmanlike; impolitic, ill-considered, stupid, foolish 499adj. *unwise*; thoughtless 456adj. *inattentive*; wild, giddy, happy-go-lucky 456adj. *light-minded*; reckless 857adj. *rash*; backward, unforward, failed 728 adj. *unsuccessful*; inadequate 636adj. *insufficient*; futile, feckless.

unskilled, skill-less, raw, green, unripe, undeveloped 670adj. *immature*; uninitiated, under training, untrained, halfbaked, half-skilled, semi-s. 670adj. *unprepared*; unqualified, inexpert, scratch, inexperienced, ignorant, unversed, unconversant, untaught 491adj. *uninstructed*; non-professional, ham, lay, amateurish, amateur, bumble-puppy; unscientific,

unsound, charlatan, quack, quackish; specious, pretentious 850adj. *affected*.

clumsy, awkward, gauche, gawkish; stuttering 580adj. *stammering*; tactless 464adj. *indiscriminating*; lubberly, unhandy, all thumbs, butter-fingered, thick-f.; lefthanded, one-h., heavy-h., ham-h., heavyfooted; ungainly, lumbering, hulking, gangling, stumbling; stiff, rusty 674adj. *unused*; unaccustomed, unpractised, out of practice, out of training, out of form 611adj. *unhabituated*; losing one's touch, slipping, skidding; slovenly, slatternly, slapdash 458adj. *negligent*; fumbling, groping, tentative 461adj. *experimental*; ungraceful, graceless, clownish 576adj. *inelegant*; top-heavy, ill-balanced, lop-sided 29adj. *unequal*; cumbersome, ponderous, clumsily built, unmanageable, unsteerable 195adj. *unwieldy*; maladjusted, creaking, out of joint 495adj. *inexact*.

bungled, ill-done, botched, foozled, mismanaged, mishandled etc. vb.; misguided, misadvised, ill-advised, ill-considered, ill-judged; unplanned 670adj. *unprepared*; ill-contrived, ill-devised, illprepared, ill-conducted; unhappy, infelicitous, ill-chosen; crude, rough and ready, inartistic, home-made, do-it-yourself 699adj. *artless*; slapdash, superficial, perfunctory 458adj. *neglected*; foolish, wild, giddy, thoughtless 456adj. *lightminded*.

Vb. *be unskilful*, —inept,—unqualified etc. adj.; not know how 491vb. *not know*; show one's ignorance, set the wrong way about it, start at the wrong end, get hold of the wrong end of the stick; do things by halves, tinker, paper over the cracks 726vb. *not complete*; burn one's fingers, catch a Tartar, reckon without one's host 508vb. *not expect*; maladminister, mishandle, mismanage, misconduct, misrule, misgovern; misapply 674vb. *misuse*; misdirect, missend 495vb. *blunder*; oversleep 138vb. *lose a chance*; forget one's piece, miss one's cue 506vb. *forget*; ham, overact, underact; lose one's cunning, lose one's skill, go rusty, get out of practice 611vb. *be unused*; lose one's nerve, lose one's head 854vb. *be nervous*.

stultify oneself, not know what one is about, not know one's own interest *or* business, stand in one's own light, cut one's own throat, make a fool of oneself 497vb. *be*

absurd; become an object lesson, quarrel with one's bread and butter, kill the goose that lays the golden eggs, throw a stone into one's own garden, bring one's house about one's ears, knock one's head against a stone wall, put the cart before the horse, have too many eggs in one basket, have too many irons in the fire; put a square peg in a round hole, put new wine into old bottles 495vb. *blunder*; labour in vain 470vb. *try impossibilities*; go on a fool's errand 641vb. *waste effort*; lean on a broken reed, strain at a gnat and swallow a camel; catch a Tartar, burn one's fingers.

be clumsy, lumber, hulk, get in the way, stand in the light; trip, trip over, stumble, hobble, limp, go lame 161vb. *be impotent*; not look where one is going 456vb. *be inattentive*; stutter 580vb. *stammer*; fumble, grope, flounder 461vb. *be tentative*; muff, fluff, foozle; pull, slice, mishit, misthrow; overthrow, overshoot 306vb. *overstep*; play into the hands of, give a catch, give a chance; drop, drop a catch, drop a sitter 311vb. *let fall*; catch a crab; bungle, drop a brick, put one's foot in it, make a faux pas 495vb. *blunder*; botch, spoil, mar, slubber, blot, vitiate 655vb. *impair*; fool with 678vb. *meddle*; make a mess of it, make a hash of it, mash, hash, bosh 728vb. *miscarry*; perpetrate, do a bad job, make sad work of, make a poor fist of 728vb. *fail*.

See: 25, 29, 138, 161, 195, 306, 311, 456, 458, 461, 464, 470, 481, 491, 495, 497, 499, 506, 508, 576, 580, 611, 636, 641, 655, 670, 674, 675, 678, 679, 699, 726, 728, 850, 854, 857.

696 Proficient

N. *proficient*, sound player, expert, adept, dab, dabster; do-it-yourself type, all-rounder, Jack of all trades, handyman, admirable Crichton 646n. *paragon*; master, past master, graduate, cordon bleu; intellectual, master mind, master spirit 500n. *sage*; genius, wizard 864n. *prodigy*; magician 545n. *conjuror*; man of parts, virtuoso; bravura player 413n. *musician*; prima donna, first fiddle, top-sawyer, protagonist, prizeman, prize-winner, medallist, champion, holder, cup-h. 644n. *exceller*; picked man, seeded player, hope,

white h.; crack, crack shot, dead s., good s., marksman 287n. *shooter*; acrobat, rope-dancer, funambulist 159n. *athlete*.

expert, no novice, practitioner; professional, specialist, professor 537n. *teacher*; connoisseur, savant, pantologist, walking encyclopædia 492n. *scholar*; veteran, old hand, old stager, old file, old soldier, sea-dog, shellback; practised hand, practised eye; sophisticate, knowing person, sharp blade, cunning fellow 698n. *slyboots*; sharp, sharper 545n. *trickster*; man of the world, man of business, tactician, strategist, politician; diplomat, diplomatist; technician, skilled worker 686n. *artisan*; experienced hand, right man for the job, key man; consultant 691n. *adviser*; boffin, backroom boy 623n. *planner*; connoisseur, fancier.

See: 159, 287, 413, 492, 500, 537, 545, 623, 644, 646, 686, 691, 698, 864.

697 Bungler

N. *bungler*, failure 728n. *loser*; bad learner, one's despair; botcher, tinker; blunderer, blunderhead, marplot; mismanager, fumbler, muffer, muff, butterfingers; hulker, lump, lout, clumsy l., clumsy, lubber, looby, swab, awkward squad, jaywalker; duffer, stooge, clown, galoot, clot, clod, stick, hick, oaf, ass, calf; Lord of Misrule 501n. *fool*; slob, sloven, slattern, trapes 61n. *slut*; cacographer, dauber, bad hand, poor h., bad shot, poor s., no marksman, no conjuror; novice, greenhorn, colt, raw recruit, apprentice, sorcerer's a. 538n. *beginner*; tail 35n. *inferior*; quack 545n. *impostor*; fair-weather sailor, fresh-water s., horse marine; ass in a lion's skin, jackdaw in peacock's feathers; fish out of water, square peg in a round hole 25n. *misfit*; spoilsport 678n. *meddler*.

See: 25, 35, 61, 501, 538, 545, 678, 728.

698 Cunning

N. *cunning*, craft 694n. *skill*; lore 490n. *knowledge*; resourcefulness, inventiveness, ingenuity 513n. *imagination*; guile, gamesmanship, cunningness, craftiness, artfulness, subtlety, wiliness, slyness,

foxiness; stealthiness, stealth 523 n. *latency*; cageyness 525 n. *reticence*; suppleness, slipperiness, shiftiness; sharp practice, knavery, chicanery, chicane 930 n. *foul play*; finesse, jugglery 542 n. *sleight*; cheating, circumvention 542 n. *deception*; double-dealing, imposture 541 n. *duplicity*; smoothness 925 n. *flattery*; disguise 525 n. *concealment*; manœuvring, temporizing 688 n. *tactics*; policy, diplomacy, Machiavellism; jobbery, gerrymandering 930 n. *improbity*; underhand dealing, practice; backstairs influence 178 n. *influence*; intrigue 623 n. *plot*.

stratagem, ruse, wile, art, artifice, resource, resort, device, wrinkle, ploy, shift, dodge, artful d. 623 n. *contrivance*; machination, game, little g. 623 n. *plot*; subterfuge, evasion; excuse 614 n. *pretext*; white lie 543 n. *mental dishonesty*; juggle, cheat 541 n. *deception*; trick, old t., box of tricks, tricks of the trade, rules of the game 542 n. *trickery*; feint, catch, net, web, ambush, Trojan horse 542 n. *trap*; ditch, pit 663 n. *pitfall*; side-blow, Parthian shot; web of cunning, web of deceit; blind, dust thrown in the eyes, flag of convenience 542 n. *sham*; thin end of the wedge, manœuvre, move, piece of tactics 688 n. *tactics*.

slyboots, crafty fellow, artful dodger, wily person, serpent, snake, fox, Reynard; lurker 527 n. *hider*; nigger in the woodpile 663 n. *trouble-maker*; fraud, shammer, dissembler, hypocrite 545 n. *deceiver*; cheat, sharper 545 n. *trickster*; juggler 545 n. *conjuror*; smooth citizen, glib tongue 925 n. *flatterer*; diplomatist, Machiavellian, intriguer, plotter, schemer 623 n. *planner*; strategist, tactician, manœuvrer; wire-puller 612 n. *motivator*.

Adj. *cunning*, learned, knowledgeable 498 adj. *wise*; crafty, artful, sly, wily, subtle, snaky, serpentine, foxy, vulpine, feline; rusy, full of ruses, tricky, tricksy; secret 525 adj. *stealthy*; scheming, contriving, practising, plotting, intriguing, Machiavellian 623 adj. *planning*; knowing, fly, canny, sharp, astute, shrewd, acute; too clever for, too clever by half, up to everything, not to be caught with chaff, not born yesterday 498 adj. *intelligent*; not to be drawn, cagey 525 adj. *reticent*; experienced 694 adj. *skilful*; resourceful, in-

genious; deep as water 211 adj. *deep*; tactical, strategical, deep-laid, well-l., well-planned; full of snares, insidious 930 adj. *perfidious*; shifty, slippery, time-serving, temporizing 518 adj. *equivocal*; deceitful, flattering 542 adj. *deceiving*; knavish 930 adj. *rascally*; crooked, devious 930 adj. *dishonest*.

Vb. *be cunning*,—sly etc. adj.; proceed by stratagem, play the fox, have a dodge, try a ruse, finesse, shift, dodge; manœuvre, double cross, twist, turn 251 vb. *wriggle*; lie low 523 vb. *lurk*; intrigue, scheme, practise, play a deep game, spin a web, weave a plot, have an axe to grind 623 vb. *plot*; contrive, devise 623 vb. *plan*; play tricks with, tinker, gerrymander; circumvent, overreach, pull a fast one, steal a march on, trick, cheat 542 vb. *deceive*; blarney 925 vb. *flatter*; be too clever for, outsmart, go one better, know a trick worth two of that 306 vb. *outdo*; be too quick for, snatch from under one's nose; waylay, dig a pit, undermine, bait the trap 527 vb. *ambush*; introduce the thin end of the wedge; match in cunning, see the catch, avoid the trap; have a card up one's sleeve, have a shot in one's locker; know all the answers, live by one's wits.

Adv. *cunningly*, artfully, slily, on the sly, by a side wind.

See: 178, 211, 251, 306, 490, 498, 513, 518, 523, 525, 527, 541, 542, 543, 545, 612, 614, 623, 663, 688, 694, 925, 930.

699 Artlessness

N. *artlessness*, simplicity, simple-mindedness; naïveté, ingenuousness, guilelessness 935 n. *innocence*; unaffectedness, unsophistication, naturalness, freedom from artifice 573 n. *plainness*; single-mindedness, sincerity, candour, frankness; bluntness, matter-of-factness, outspokenness 540 n. *veracity*; truth, honesty 929 n. *probity*; purity 874 n. *modesty*; uncivilized state, savagery; darkness, no science, no art 491 n. *ignorance*; indifference to art, Philistinism; no artistry 647 n. *imperfection*; uncouthness, vulgarity, crudity 847 n. *bad taste*.

ingenue, unsophisticated person, child of nature, savage, noble s.; enfant terrible;

lamb, innocent l. 935 n. *innocent*; green-horn, novice 538 n. *beginner*; rough diamond, plain man, Philistine; simple mind, frank heart; hick, hayseed, rube, hillbilly 869 n. *countryman*.

Adj. *artless*, without art, without artifice, without tricks; uncomplicated 44 adj. *simple*; unadorned, unvarnished 573 adj. *plain*; native, natural, unartificial, home-spun, home-made; do-it-yourself 695 adj. *unskilled*; in a state of nature, uncivilized, wild, savage, unguided, untutored, un-learned, unscientific, backward 491 adj. *ignorant*; Arcadian, unsophisticated, in-genuous, naïve, childlike, born yesterday 935 adj. *innocent*; guileless, free from guile, unsuspicious, confiding; unaffected, unreserved 609 adj. *spontaneous*; candid, frank, open, undissembling, straightfor-ward 540 n. *veracious*; undesigning, single, single-minded, single-hearted, true, honest, sincere 929 adj. *honourable*; blunt, outspoken, free-spoken; transparent 522 adj. *undisguised*; unpoetical, prosaic, mat-ter-of-fact, literal, literal-minded 494 adj. *accurate*; shy, inarticulate, unassuming, unpretending 874 adj. *modest*; inartistic, Philistine; unmusical, tone-deaf 416 adj. *deaf*; unrefined, unpolished, uncultured, uncouth, jungly, bush 847 adj. *vulgar*; hoydenish 847 adj. *ill-bred*.

Vb. *be artless*, — natural etc. adj.; live in a state of nature, know no better; have no guile, have no tricks 935 vb. *be innocent*; have no affectations, eschew artifice; confide, wear one's heart upon one's sleeve, look one in the face, look one straight in the eyes, call a spade a spade, say what is in one's mind 573 vb. *speak plainly*; not gloze, not flatter 540 vb. *be truthful*.

Adv. *artlessly*, without art, without preten-sions, without affectations; frankly, sincerely, openly, with an open heart; inartistically, like a Philistine.

See: 44, 416, 491, 494, 522, 538, 540, 573, 609, 647, 695, 847, 869, 874, 929, 935.

700 Difficulty

N. *difficulty*, hardness, arduousness, labor-iousness, the hard way 682 n. *exertion*; impracticability, one's despair 470 n. *impossibility*; intricacy, perplexity, inextricability, involvement 61 n. *com-plexity*; complication 832 n. *aggravation*; obscurity, impenetrability 517 n. *un-intelligibility*; inconvenience, awkward-ness, embarrassment 643 n. *inexpedience*; drag 333 n. *friction*; rough ground, hard going, bad patch 259 n. *roughness*; quag-mire, slough 347 n. *marsh*; knot, Gordian k. 251 n. *coil*; problem, thorny p., crux, hard nut to crack, poser, teaser, puzzle, headache 530 n. *enigma*; impediment, handicap, obstacle, snag, rub, where the shoe pinches 702 n. *hindrance*; teething troubles 702 n. *hitch*; maze, crooked path 251 n. *convolution*; cul-de-sac, dead end, impasse 264 n. *closure*; deadlock, stand, stoppage 145 n. *stop*; stress, brunt, burden 684 n. *fatigue*; trial, temptation, tribula-tion, vexation 825 n. *suffering*; trouble, sea of troubles 731 n. *adversity*; difficult person, handful, one's despair, kittle cattle.

hard task, test, real t., test of strength; labours of Hercules, Herculean task, Augean stables, Sisyphean labour; task, job, work cut out, hard row to hoe; handful, tall order, tough assignment, stiff job, hard work, uphill work 682 n. *labour*; dead weight, dead lift 322 n. *gravity*.

predicament, embarrassment, false position; nonplus, quandary, dilemma, cleft stick, option of difficulties, delicate point, nice p., borderline case 474 n. *dubiety*; fix, jam, hole, scrape, hot water, trouble, peck of troubles, kettle of fish, pickle, stew, imbroglio, mess, muddle; pinch, strait, straits, pass, pretty p.; slippery slope, sticky wicket, tight corner, situa-tion, ticklish s., 661 n. *danger*; critical situation, exigency, emergency 137 n. *crisis*.

Adj. *difficult*, hard, tough, formidable; steep, arduous, uphill; inconvenient, onerous, burdensome, irksome, toilsome, bothersome, plaguy, operose 682 adj. *laborious*; exacting, demanding 684 adj. *fatiguing*; big, of Herculean *or* Sisyphean proportions; insuperable, impracticable 470 adj. *impossible*; offering a problem, problematic; delicate, ticklish, kittle; sooner said than done, more easily said than done; not to be handled with kid gloves, not made with rose water; embarrassing, awkward, unwieldy,

unmanageable, hard to cope with, not easily tackled; out of hand, intractable, refractory 738 adj. *disobedient*; stubborn, unyielding, perverse 602 adj. *obstinate*; ill-behaved, naughty 934 adj. *wicked*; perplexing, clueless, obscure 517 adj. *unintelligible*; knotty, complex, complicated, inextricable, labyrinthine 251 adj. *intricate*; impenetrable, impassable, trackless, pathless, invious, unnavigable; thorny, rugged, craggy 259 adj. *rough*; sticky, critical, emergent 661 adj. *dangerous*.

in difficulties, bested, ill-b.; hampered 702 adj. *hindered*; labouring, labouring under difficulties; in a quandary, in a dilemma, in a cleft stick, between two stools, between Scylla and Charybdis 474 adj. *doubting*; baffled, clueless, nonplussed, at a stand 517 adj. *puzzled*; in a jam, in a fix, up a gum tree, in a spot, in a hole, in a scrape, in hot water, in the soup, in a pickle; in deep water, out of one's depth, under cross fire, not out of the wood, in danger 661 adj. *endangered*; worried, beset with difficulties, harassed with problems, tormented with anxiety 825 adj. *suffering*; up against it, hard pressed, sore p., hard run, hard set, hard put to it, put to it, put to one's shifts, driven to extremities; in straits, reduced to s., straitened, pinched; at one's wits end, at the end of one's tether, cornered, at bay, up a tree; stuck, gravelled, aground 728 adj. *grounded*.

Vb. *be difficult*, — hard etc. adj.; make things difficult, make difficulties for; complicate, complicate matters 63 vb. *bedevil*; trouble, inconvenience, put to i., bother, irk, plague, try one's patience, lead one a dance, be a thorn in one's flesh, go against the grain 827 vb. *incommode*; present difficulties, set one a problem, pose, perplex, baffle, nonplus, ground, stump, gravel, bring one to a stand 474 vb. *puzzle*; encumber, clog, hamper, obstruct 702 vb. *hinder*; make things worse 832 vb. *aggravate*; lead to an impasse, create a deadlock 470 vb. *make impossible*; go hard with, run one hard, put one to his shifts, drive to the wall 661 vb. *endanger*.

be in difficulty, have a problem; walk among eggs, pick one's way 461 vb. *be tentative*; have one's hands full, have all one can do 678 vb. *be busy*; not know which way to turn, be at a loss 474 vb. *be uncertain*; have difficulties, have one's work cut out, be put to it, be put to trouble, have trouble with; run into trouble, fall into difficulties, strike a bad patch, let oneself in for, embarrass oneself, catch a packet, catch a Tartar, rouse a hornet's nest; have a hard time of it, have the wolf by the ears 731 vb. *have trouble*; bear the brunt, feel the wind, feel the pinch 825 vb. *suffer*; have more than enough, sink under the burden 684 vb. *be fatigued*; invite difficulty, make it hard for oneself, make a problem of, make heavy weather, flounder; stick, come unstuck 728 vb. *miscarry*; try it the hard way, swim upstream, breast the current, struggle, fight 716 vb. *contend*; have to face it, live dangerously 661 vb. *face danger*; labour under difficulties, labour under a disadvantage, be handicapped 35 vb. *be inferior*.

Adv. *with difficulty*, with much ado, hardly; the hard way, uphill, against the stream, against the wind, against the grain; despite, in spite of, in the teeth of; at a pinch; in difficulty.

See: 35, 61, 63, 137, 145, 251, 259, 264, 322, 333, 347, 461, 470, 474, 517, 530, 602, 643, 661, 678, 682, 684, 702, 716, 728, 731, 738, 825, 827, 832, 934.

701 Facility

N. *facility*, easiness, ease, convenience, comfort; wieldiness, ease of handling; flexibility, pliancy 327 n. *softness*; capability, capacity, feasibility 469 n. *possibility*; comprehensibility 516 n. *intelligibility*; facilitation 703 n. *aid*; easing, making easy, simplification, making smooth, disencumbrance, disentanglement, disengagement, deoppilation, removal of difficulties 746 n. *liberation*; full play, full scope, clean slate, tabula rasa 744 n. *scope*; facilities, provision of f. 703 n. *aid*; leave 760 n. *permission*; simplicity, no complication 44 n. *simpleness*; straightforwardness, no difficulty, no competition; no friction, easy going, smooth water 258 n. *smoothness*; fair wind, clear coast, clear road 137 n. *opportunity*; straight road, royal r., highway, primrose path 624 n. *road*; downhill 309 n. *descent*.

easy thing, no effort, child's play; short work, holiday task, light work, sinecure 679 n. *inactivity*; picnic, play 837 n. *amusement*; pie, piece of cake, money for jam; smooth sailing, plain s., joy-ride; nothing to it, sitter, easy target, sitting shot; walk-over 727 n. *victory*; cinch, sure thing 473 n. *certainty*; no trouble, pleasure.

Adj. *easy*, facile, undemanding; effortless, painless; light, short; frictionless 258 adj. *smooth*; uncomplicated 44 adj. *simple*; not hard, not difficult, foolproof; easy as pie, easily done, easily managed, no sooner said than done; feasible 469 adj. *possible*; easing, facilitating, deoppilant, helpful 703 adj. *aiding*; downhill, downstream 309 adj. *descending*; with the stream, with the current, with the tide; convenient 376 adj. *comfortable*; approachable, within reach 289 adj. *accessible*; open to all 263 adj. *open*; within comprehension, for the million 516 adj. *intelligible*.

wieldy, manageable, tractable, towardly, easy-going, facile 597 adj. *willing*; submissive 721 adj. *submitting*; yielding, soft, ductile, pliant 327 adj. *flexible*; smooth-running, well-oiled, frictionless, on friction wheels; handy, manœuvrable, labour-saving.

facilitated, simplified, made easy; disembarrassed, disencumbered, disburdened, untrammelled, unloaded, light; disengaged, unimpeded, unobstructed, untrammelled, unfettered, unrestrained 744 vb. *unconfined*; aided, given a chance, helped on one's way; in one's element, at home, quite at home, at ease, on velvet 376 adj. *comfortable*.

Vb. *be easy*, — simple etc. adj.; require no effort, present no difficulties, give no trouble, make no demands; lie open to all, be had for the asking; come out, come out easily, be easily solved, have a simple answer 516 vb. *be intelligible*; run well, go w., work w., work like a machine, go like clockwork, run on smoothly 258 vb. *go smoothly*.

do easily, have no trouble, see one's way; make nothing of, make light of, make no bones about, make short work of, do it on one's head, do it with one hand behind one's back, do it with both eyes shut; have it all one's own way, carry all before one, have the game in one's hands, hold

all the trumps, win hands down, win at a canter, walk over the course, have a walk-over 727 vb. *win*; be at ease, be at home, be in one's element, take in one's stride; take it easy 685 vb. *be refreshed*; not strain oneself, drift with the tide, swim with the stream 721 vb. *submit*; spare effort, save oneself, take the easy way out, take the easiest way, look for a short cut.

facilitate, ease, make easy; iron out 258 vb. *smooth*; grease, oil 334 vb. *lubricate*; explain, simplify, vulgarize, popularize 520 vb. *interpret*; provide the means, enable 160 vb. *empower*; make way for, not stand in the way, leave it open, allow 756 vb. *permit*; give a chance to, put one in the way of 469 vb. *make possible*; help, help on, speed 703 vb. *aid*; pioneer, open up, clear the way, make a path for 64 vb. *precede*; pave the way, bridge over; give full play to, make an opening for, leave open, leave a loophole, leave a hole to creep out of 744 vb. *give scope*.

disencumber, free, liberate, unshackle, unfetter 668 vb. *deliver*; clear, clear the ground, weed, clear away 648 vb. *clean*; derestrict, deobstruct; deoppilate disengage, disembarrass; disentangle, extricate 62 vb. *unravel*; unknot, untie 46 vb. *disjoin*; cut the knot, cut the Gordian k. 46 vb. *cut*; unclog, take the brake off; ease, lighten, take off one's shoulders, unload, unburden, disburden, ease the burden, alleviate 831 vb. *relieve*.

Adv. *easily*, readily, smoothly, without friction; on wheels, swimmingly; effortlessly, with no effort, without difficulty, by the flick of a switch; without a hitch, without let or hindrance, freely, without obstruction; on easy terms.

See: 44, 46, 62, 64, 137, 160, 258, 263, 309, 327, 334, 376, 469, 473, 516, 520, 597, 624, 648, 668, 679, 685, 703, 721, 727, 744, 746, 756, 831, 837.

702 Hindrance

N. *hindrance*, let or h., impedition, impediment, rub; psychological impediment, inhibition, fixation; stalling, thwarting, obstruction, frustration; hampering, shackling, clogging etc. vb.; occlusion, obturation, oppilation, stopping, stopping up, blockage, blocking, shutting 264

n. *closure*; blockade, siege 712n. *attack*; limitation, restriction, control 747n. *restraint*; squeezing, coarctation, stricture 198n. *compression*; arrest 747n. *detention*; check, retardation, retardment, deceleration 278n. *slowness*; drag 333n. *friction*; cramp 651n. *paralysis*; interference, meddling 678n. *overactivity*; interruption, interception, interclusion, interposition, intervention 231n. *interjacence*; obtrusion 303n. *insertion*; objection 762n. *deprecation*; obstructiveness, picketing, sabotage 704n. *opposition*; counter-measure, strikebreaking 182n. *counteraction*; defence 715n. *resistance*; discouragement, active d., disincentive 613n. *dissuasion*; disapproval, frown 924n. *disapprobation*; boycott, 'angry silence' 57n. *exclusion*; forestalling, prevention; prophylaxis, sanitation 652n. *hygiene*; sterilization, birth-control, contraception, contraceptive 172n. *unproductivity*; inability, disability 161n. *impotence*; ban, embargo, estoppal 757n. *prohibition*; capacity for hindrance, nuisance value.

obstacle, impediment, drawback, inconvenience, handicap 700n. *difficulty*; bunker, hazard; bottleneck, blockage, road block, jam, traffic j., log-j.; a hindrance, hamper, let, stay; tie, tether 47n. *bond*; preoccupation, previous engagement 138 n. *intempestivity*; snag, block, stop, stymie; stumbling-block, trip-wire, hurdle, hedge, ditch, moat; jump, water-j.; something in the way, lion in the path (see *hinderer*); barrier, bulkhead, wall, brick w., sea-w., groyne, boom, dam, weir, burrock, dyke, embankment 662n. *safeguard*; bulwark, breastplate, buffer, parapet, portcullis, barbed wire 713n. *defences*; fence, ring, blockade 235n. *inclosure*; curtain, iron curtain, bamboo c. 231n. *partition*; stile, five-barred gate, turnstile, turnpike; check, brake, clog, shoe, skid, trammel, shackle, gag, curb 748n. *fetter*; ill wind, cross-w., headwind, cross-current; impasse, deadlock, stalemate, vicious circle; cul-de-sac, blind alley, dead end.

hitch, unexpected obstacle, snag, catch, lightning strike 145n. *strike*; repulse, rebuff 760n. *refusal*; contretemps, spot of trouble; teething troubles; technical hitch, breakdown, failure, engine f.,

engine trouble; puncture, flat; leak, burst pipe; fuse, short circuit; stoppage, stop, dead s., hold-up, traffic block, traffic jam 145n. *stop*; something wrong, screw loose, spanner in the works, grit in the oil, fly in the ointment.

encumbrance, handicap, remora; drag, clog, shackle, chain 748n. *fetter*; trammels, meshes; impedimenta, baggage, lumber, weight, dead-weight, millstone, millstone round one's neck, weight on one's shoulders, load on one's back 322n. *gravity*; pack, fardel, burden, load, overload, last straw; onus, incubus, Old Man of the Sea, white elephant; women and children, passenger; mortgage, debts 803n. *debt*.

hinderer, hindrance; tripper, tripper-up; red herring 10n. *irrelevance*; wet blanket, damper, spoilsport, kill-joy, pussyfoot; marplot 697n. *bungler*; dog in the manger, thwarter, frustrator; obstructor, staller; obstructionist, filibuster, saboteur; botherer, heckler, interrupter, interjector, barracker; intervener, interferer 678n. *meddler*; interloper, intruder, gatecrasher, uninvited guest 59n. *intruder*; mischief-maker, spoiler, poltergeist, gremlin 663n. *trouble-maker*; lion in the path, challenger 705n. *opponent*; rival, competitor 716n. *contender*.

interceptor, tertius gaudens; fieldsman, fielder, wicket-keeper, keeper, stumper, catcher; stop, longstop, back-stop; goalkeeper, goalie, custodian, back.

Adj. *hindering*, impeditive, impedient, obstructive, strike-happy; stalling, delaying, dragging; frustrating, thwarting etc.vb.; cross, contrary, unfavourable 731adj. *adverse*; restrictive, cramping, clogging 747adj. *restraining*; prohibitive, preventive 757adj. *prohibiting*; prophylactic, counteractive 182adj. *counteracting*; upsetting, disconcerting, confusing; foreign, intrusive, obtrusive, not wanted 59adj. *extraneous*; interloping, intercipient, interfering 678adj. *meddling*; blocking, in the way, in the light; inconvenient, incommodious 643adj. *inexpedient*; hard, rough, snaggy 700adj. *difficult*; onerous, crushing, burdensome, cumbrous 322adj. *weighty*; tripping, entangling; choking, strangling, stifling; disincentive, discouraging; disheartening, damping 613adj. *dissuasive*; unhelpful, unco-operative, unaccommodating 598

adj. *unwilling*; defensive, oppositional 704adj. *opposing*.

hindered, clogged, cramped, waterlogged; handicapped, encumbered, burdened with, saddled w., stuck w.; frustrated, thwarted, stymied etc.vb.; held up, delayed, held back, stuck, wind-bound, fog-b. 747adj. *restrained*; stopped, prevented 757adj. *prohibited*; in check, hard-pressed, cornered, treed, checkmated, stalemated 700adj. *in difficulties*; heavy-laden, overburdened 684adj. *fatigued*; left in the lurch, unaided, single-handed.

Vb. *hinder*, let, obstruct, impede; bother, annoy, inconvenience 827vb. *incommode*; embarrass, disconcert, upset, disorder 63 vb. *derange*; trip, trip up, give one a fall; tangle, entangle, enmesh 542vb. *ensnare*; get in the way, stand in the w., cross one's path; come between, intervene, interpose 678vb. *meddle*; intercept, cut off, head off, undermine, cut the ground from under one's feet, nip, nip in the bud, stifle, choke, overgrow; gag, muzzle 578vb. *make mute*; suffocate, repress 165vb. *suppress*; quell, kill dead 362vb. *kill*; hamper, burden, cumber, encumber; press, press down, hang like a millstone round one's neck 322vb. *weigh*; lade, load with, saddle w. 193vb. *load*; cramp, handicap; shackle, trammel, clog, tie one's hands 747vb. *fetter*; restrict, circumscribe 236 vb. *limit*; check, brake, drag, be a drag on, hold back 747vb. *restrain*; hold up, slow down, set one back 278vb. *retard*; lame, cripple, hobble, hamstring, paralyse 161 vb. *disable*; scotch, wing 655vb. *wound*; clip the wings, cramp the style of, take the wind out of one's sails; discountenance, put out of countenance 867vb. *shame*; intimidate, deter 854vb. *frighten*; discourage, dishearten 613vb. *dissuade*; be the spectre at the feast, mar, spoil, spoil the sport 655vb. *impair*; damp, damp down, throw cold water on 341vb. *moisten*; snub, rebuff 760vb. *refuse*.

obstruct, intervene, interpose, interfere 678 vb. *meddle*; obtrude, interlope 297vb. *intrude*; stymie, stand in the way 231vb. *lie between*; buzz, jostle, crowd, squeeze; sit on one's tail 284vb. *follow*; stop, intercept, occlude, interclude, obturate, stop up, block, block up, wall up 264vb. *close*; jam, jam tight, make a bottleneck, create a stoppage; bandage, bind, stop the flow 350vb. *stanch*; dam, dam up, earth up, embank; divert, avert, draw off 495vb. *mislead*; fend off, stave off, stall off 713 vb. *parry*; barricade 235vb. *inclose*; encompass, fence, hedge in, blockade 232 vb. *circumscribe*; deny access, keep out 57vb. *exclude*; prevent, not allow, cohibit, inhibit, ban, bar, debar, estop 757 vb. *prohibit*.

be obstructive, make it hard for, give trouble 700vb. *be difficult*; stall, keep one in play, occupy; not play, non-cooperate 598vb. *be loth*; thwart, frustrate, stultify, baffle, foil, stymie, balk, be a dog in the manger; counter 182vb. *counteract*; check, countercheck, put in check, checkmate; traverse, contravene 533vb. *negate*; object, raise objections 704vb. *oppose*; interrupt, interject, heckle, barrack; refuse a hearing, shout down 400vb. *be loud*; take evasive action 620vb. *avoid*; talk out time, filibuster 581vb. *be loquacious*; protract, drag out 113vb. *spin out*; strike, strike work 145vb. *halt*; picket, molest; sabotage, throw a spanner in the works, put grit in the machine, draw the teeth, spike the guns; cross one's bows, take the wind out of one's sails 269vb. *navigate*.

See: 10, 47, 57, 59, 63, 113, 138, 145, 161, 165, 172, 182, 193, 198, 231, 232, 235, 236, 264, 269, 278, 284, 297, 303, 322, 333, 341, 350, 362, 400, 495, 533, 542, 578, 581, 598, 613, 620, 643, 651, 652, 655, 662, 663, 678, 684, 697, 700, 704, 705, 712, 713, 715, 716, 731, 747, 748, 757, 760, 762, 803, 827, 854, 867, 924.

703 Aid

N. *aid*, assistance, help, helping hand, leg-up, lift; succour, rescue 668n. *deliverance*; comfort, support, stead, backing, seconding, abetment, encouragement; reinforcement 162n. *strengthening*; helpfulness, willing help, cordial assistance 706n. *co-operation*; service, ministry, ministration, subministration 897n. *kind act*; interest, friendly i., kindly i., good offices; custom 792n. *purchase*; patronage, auspices, sponsorship, countenance, suffrage, favour 660n. *protection*; good will, charity, sympathy 897n. *benevolence*; intercession 981n. *prayers*; advocacy,

championship; good advice, constructive criticism 691 n. *advice*; promotion, furtherance, advancement 654 n. *improvement*; nursing, spoonfeeding; first aid, medical assistance 658 n. *medical art*; relief, recruitment 685 n. *refreshment*; preferential treatment, most favoured nation t.; favourable conditions, favourable circumstances 730 n. *prosperity*; fair wind, following w., tail w. 287 n. *propulsion*; facilitation, facilities, magic carpet, Aladdin's lamp 701 n. *facility*; self-help, do-it-yourself habit 744 n. *independence*.

subvention, economic aid, monetary help, pecuniary assistance; state assistance, poor relief 901 n. *philanthropy*; benefit, sick b.; loan, accommodation, temporary a., benevolence 802 n. *credit*; subsidy, bounty, grant, allowance, expense account; stipend, scholarship, sizarship 962 n. *reward*; supplies, maintenance, support, keep, upkeep, free board and lodging, alimentation, nutrition 633 n. *provision*; manna, manna in the wilderness 301 n. *food*.

aider, help, helper, assister, assistant, lieutenant, right-hand man; stand-by, support; tower of strength, someone to hold one's hand; nurse, spoonfeeder; abettor, instigator 612 n. *motivator*; factor, useful ingredient 58 n. *component*; coadjutor, adjunct, ally, brother-in-arms 707 n. *collaborator*; succours, contingents, supports, relieving force, reinforcements, recruits 707 n. *auxiliary*; deus ex machina, genie of the lamp; promoter 707 n. *patron*; booster, friendly critic 923 n. *commender*; fairy godmother 903 n. *benefactor*; springboard, jump-off 628 n. *instrument*.

Adj. aiding, co-operative, helpful, obliging 706 adj. *co-operative*; kind, well-disposed, well-intentioned 897 adj. *benevolent*; amicable, neighbourly 880 adj. *friendly*; favourable, propitious; supporting, seconding, abetting; encouraging 612 adj. *inducive*; of service, of help, of great assistance 640 adj. *useful*; constructive, well-meant; adjuvant, assistant, auxiliary, subsidiary, ancillary, accessory; in aid of, contributory, promoting; at one's beck and call, subservient 768 adj. *observant*; ministrant 628 adj. *instrumental*.

Vb. aid, help, assist, lend a hand, bear a h., lend one's aid, render assistance; hold out a hand to, take by the hand, take in tow, give a lift to; hold one's hand, spoonfeed; be kind to, give a leg-up to, help a lame dog over a stile 897 vb. *be benevolent*; oblige, accommodate, lend money to 784 vb. *lend*; find the money, help with m., subsidize, subvention, subventionize; facilitate, speed, lend wings to, feather the shaft, further, advance, boost 285 vb. *promote*; abet, instigate, foment, nourish, feed the flame, fan the f. 612 vb. *induce*; make for, contribute to, conduce to, be accessory to, be a factor in 156 vb. *conduce*; lend support to, second, back, back up, stand by, bolster, prop up, stead 218 vb. *support*; comfort, sustain, hearten, give heart to, encourage, rally, embolden 855 vb. *give courage*; succour, come to the help of, send help to, furnish assistance to, relieve 668 vb. *deliver*; reinforce, fortify 162 vb. *strengthen*; recruit 685 vb. *refresh*; set one on his legs 656 vb. *restore*.

patronize, favour, smile on, shine on 730 vb. *be auspicious*; sponsor, back, guarantee; recommend, put up for; propose, second; countenance, give countenance to, connive at, protect 660 vb. *safeguard*; join, enlist under 78 vb. *be included*; contribute to, subscribe to, lend one's name 488 vb. *endorse*; take an interest in, have a kindness for 880 vb. *befriend*; espouse the cause of, take the side of, side with, champion, take up the cudgels for, stick up for, stand up f., stand by 713 vb. *defend*; make interest for, canvass f., vote f. 605 vb. *vote*; give moral support to, pray for, intercede; pay for, pay the piper 804 vb. *defray*; entertain, keep, cherish, foster, nurse, wet-nurse, mother 889 vb. *pet*; force, manure 370 vb. *cultivate*; bestow one's custom, buy from 792 vb. *purchase*.

minister to, wait on, do for, help, oblige 742 vb. *serve*; give first aid to, nurse 658 vb. *doctor*; squire, valet, mother; subserve, be of service to, make oneself useful to 640 vb. *be useful*; anticipate the wishes of, consult the wishes of 597 vb. *be willing*; pander to, toady, humour, suck up to 925 vb. *flatter*; slave, make oneself the slave of, do all one can for, do everything for 682 vb. *work*; be assistant to, be one's lieutenant, make oneself the tool of 628 vb. *be instrumental*.

Adv. in aid of, in the cause of, for the sake

of, on behalf of; by the aid of, thanks to; in the service of, in the name of.

See: 58, 78, 156, 162, 218, 285, 287, 301, 370, 488, 597, 605, 612, 628, 633, 640, 654, 656, 658, 660, 668, 682, 685, 691, 701, 706, 707, 713, 730, 742, 744, 768, 784, 792, 802, 804, 855, 880, 889, 897, 901, 903, 923, 925, 962. 981.

704 Opposition

N. *opposition*, oppositeness, polarity 240n. *contraposition*; contrast 14n. *contrariety*; repugnance 861n. *dislike*; antagonism, hostility 881n. *enmity*; clashing, conflict, friction, lack of harmony 709n. *dissension*; dissociation, non-association, non-co-operation, unhelpful attitude 598n. *unwillingness*; contrariness, cussedness, recalcitrance 602n. *obstinacy*; impugnation, counter-argument 479n. *confutation*; contradiction, denial 533n. *negation*; challenge 711n. *defiance*; oppugnancy, oppugnation, firm opposition, stout o., stand 715n. *resistance*; contravention, infringement 738n. *revolt*; going against, siding a., voting a. 924n. *disapprobation*; withdrawal, walk-out 489 n. *dissent*; physical opposition, headwind, cross-current 702n. *obstacle*; mutual opposition, cross purposes, tug of war; faction, rivalry, corrivalry, emulation, competition, race 716n. *contention*; political opposition, the Opposition, Her Majesty's O., the other party, the party in opposition; the other side, wrong s., ranks of Tuscany.

opposites, contraries, extremes, opposite poles 14n. *contrariety*; rivals, duellists, competitors 716n. *contender*; opposite parties, factions 709n. *quarreller*; town and gown, the right and the left, light and darkness, capital and labour, Democrat and Republican.

Adj. *opposing*, oppositional, opposed; in opposition, on the other side, on the wrong s.; anti, against, agin; antagonistic, hostile, unfriendly, antipathetic, unsympathetic 881adj. *inimical*; unfavourable, unpropitious 731adj. *adverse*; cross, thwarting 702adj. *hindering*; contrarious 14adj. *contrary*; cussed 602adj. *obstinate*; refractory, recalcitrant 738adj. *disobedient*; resistant, frictional 182adj. *counteracting*; clashing, conflicting, at variance

709adj. *quarrelling*; militant, at daggers drawn, with crossed bayonets 716adj. *contending*; facing, face to face, fronting 237adj. *fore*; polarized, at opposite extremes 240adj. *opposite*; mutually opposed, rival, emulous, competitive 911 adj. *jealous*.

Vb. *oppose*, go against, militate a. 14vb. *be contrary*; side against, stand a., hold out a., fight a. 715vb. *resist*; set one's face against, make a dead set a. 607vb. *reject*; object, kick, protest, protest against 762 vb. *deprecate*; run one's head against, beat a. 279vb. *collide*; vote against, vote down 924vb. *disapprove*; not support, dissociate oneself; contradict, belie 533 vb. *negate*; traverse, counter 479vb. *confute*; work against 182vb. *counteract*; countermine, thwart, baffle, foil 702vb. *be obstructive*; be at cross purposes, play at c.; stand up to, challenge, dare 711vb. *defy*; set at naught 922vb. *hold cheap*; fly in the face of 738vb. *disobey*; rebuff, spurn, slap in the face, slam the door in one's f. 760vb. *refuse*; emulate, rival, match oneself with, compete with, play against, bid a. 716vb. *contend*; set against, pit a., match a.

withstand, confront, face, look in the f., stand up to 661vb. *face danger*; rise against 738vb. *revolt*; meet, encounter, cross swords with 716vb. *fight*; struggle against, make head a., breast, stem, breast the tide, stem the t., swim against the stream; cope with, grapple w., wrestle w. 671vb. *essay*; not be beaten 599vb. *stand firm*; hold one's own, bear the brunt 715vb. *resist*.

Adv. *in opposition*, against, versus, agin; in conflict with, against the tide, against the stream, against the wind, with the wind in one's teeth, against the grain, in the teeth of, in the face of, in spite of, despite.

See: 14, 182, 237, 240, 279, 479, 489, 533, 598, 599, 602, 607, 661, 671, 702, 709, 711, 715, 716, 731, 738, 760, 762, 861, 881, 911, 922, 924.

705 Opponent

N. *opponent*, opposer, lion in the path; adversary, antagonist, foe, foeman, 881 n. *enemy*; assailant 712n. *attacker*; opposing party, opposition p., the opposition, ranks

of Tuscany, opposite camp; opposition-
ist, radical; obstructionist, filibuster
702 n. *hinderer*; independent party, cross-
benches; die-hard, bitter-ender, last-
ditcher, irreconcilable; radical of the
right, reactionist, reactionary, counter-
revolutionary, obscurantist; objector,
conscientious o. 489 n. *dissentient*; resister, passive r.; non-cooperator 829 n.
malcontent; agitator, incendiary, terrorist,
extremist, ultraist, Jacobin, Fenian 738 n.
revolter; challenger, other candidate,
rival, emulator, corrival, competitor, runner-up; battler, fighter, contestant, duellist; entrant, the field, all comers 716 n.
contender; factionary, factioneer, brawler, wrangler 709 n. *quarreller*; common
enemy, public e., universal foe, outlaw
904 n. *offender*.

See: 489, 702, 709, 712, 716, 738, 829, 881,
904.

706 Co-operation

N. *co-operation*, helpfulness 597 n. *willingness*; contribution, co-adjuvancy, co-
agency, coefficiency, synergy, symbiosis;
duet, double harness, collaboration, joint
effort, combined operation; team work,
working together, 'a long pull, a strong
pull and a pull all together'; relay, relay-
race, team-r.; team spirit, esprit de corps;
lack of friction, unanimity, agreement,
concurrence, bi-partisanship 710 n. *concord*; clanship, clannishness, party spirit,
cliquishness, partisanship; connivance,
collusion, abetment 612 n. *motivation*;
conspiracy, complot 623 n. *plot*; complicity, participation; sympathy, fraternity, solidarity, fellowship, freemasonry,
fellow-feeling, comradeship, fellow-travelling; common cause, mutual assistance,
helping one another, back-scratching, log-
rolling; reciprocity, give and take, mutual
concession 770 n. *compromise*; mutual
advice, consultation 584 n. *conference*.
association, coming together; colleagueship, co-partnership, partnership 775 n.
participation; nationalization, inter-
nationalization 775 n. *joint possession*;
pooling, pool; membership, affiliation
78 n. *inclusion*; connection, hook-up, tie-
up 9 n. *relation*; combination, consolidation, centralization 45 n. *junction*; inte-

gration, solidarity 52 n. *whole*; unification,
union, synoecism 88 n. *unity*; amalgamation, fusion, merger, Anschluss; voluntary association, coalition, alliance,
league, federation, confederation, confederacy; axis, united front, common f.,
popular f. 708 n. *political party*; an
association, fellowship, college, club,
sodality, fraternity 708 n. *society*; set,
clique, cell 708 n. *party*; workers' association, trade union, chapel; business
association, company, joint-stock c.,
interlocking directorship, combine,
consortium, trust, cartel, ring 708 n.
corporation; Zollverein, common
market, Benelux 708 n. *community*.

Adj. *co-operative*, helpful 703 adj. *aiding*;
frictionless 710 adj. *concordant*; co-adju-
tant, co-adjuvant; symbiotic, synergic;
collaborating, in double harness; married,
associating, associated, leagued, in league,
hand in glove with; bi-partisan; federal
708 adj. *corporate*.

Vb. *co-operate*, collaborate, work together,
pull t., work in t., work as a team; go hand
in hand, hunt in pairs, run in double harness; team up, partner, go into partnership 775 vb. *participate*; play ball, reciprocate, respond; lend oneself to, espouse 703
vb. *patronize*; join in, take part, enter into,
take a hand in, strike in with; hang
together, hold t., sail *or* row in the same
boat, stand shoulder to shoulder, stand
by each other, sink or swim together; be
in league with, make common cause with,
take in each other's washing; band, gang
up, associate, league, confederate, federate, ally; coalesce, merge, unite 43 vb. *be
mixed*; combine, make common cause,
club together; understand one another,
think alike; conspire 623 vb. *plot*; lay
heads together, get into a huddle 691 vb.
consult; collude, connive, play another's
game; work for an understanding, treat
with, negotiate 766 vb. *make terms*.

Adv. *co-operatively*, hand in hand, jointly,
unanimously, as one man, as one.

See: 9, 43, 45, 52, 78, 88, 584, 597, 612, 623,
691, 703, 708, 710, 766, 770, 775.

707 Auxiliary

N. *auxiliary*, relay, recruit, fresh troops,
reinforcement; second line, para-military

formation 722 n. *soldiery*; ally, brother-in-arms, confederate (see *colleague*); co-adjutor, adjuvant, assistant, helper, help-mate, helping hand 703 n. *aider*; right hand, right-hand man, stand-by, support, tower of strength; candle-holder, bottle-h.; gag-man, prompter; adjutant, lieutenant, aide-de-camp; secretary, clerk; mid-wife, handmaid 742 n. *servant*; acolyte, server; paranymph, best man; friend in need 880 n. *friend*; hanger-on, satellite, henchman, follower 742 n. *dependant*; disciple, adherent, votary, sectary 978 n. *sectarist*; loyalist, legitimist; stooge, cat's-paw, puppet 628 n. *instrument*; jackal, running dog, creature, âme damnée.

collaborator, co-operator, co-worker, fellow-w.; team-mate, yoke-fellow, work-f.; sympathizer, fellow-traveller, fifth column, fifth columnist.

colleague, associate, confrère, brother; co-director, partner, co-mate, fellow; sharer 775 n. *participator*; comrade, companion, playmate; confidant, alter ego, second self, faithful companion, fidus Achates, Man Friday; mate, chum, pal, buddy, amigo 880 n. *friend*; stand-by, stalwart; ally, confederate; accomplice, accessory, abettor, aider and abettor, fellow-conspirator, particeps criminis; co-religionist; one's fellows, one's own side.

patron, defender, guardian angel, tutelary genius, special providence 660 n. *protector*; well-wisher, sympathizer; champion advocate, friend at court; supporter, backer, guarantor; proposer, seconder, voter; favourer, sider, partisan, votary, aficionado, fan 887 n. *lover*; good friend, Jack at a pinch, friend in need, deus ex machina; fairy godmother, rich uncle 903 n. *benefactor*; promoter, founder, re-founder; patron of art, Maecenas 492 n. *collector*; customer, client 792 n. *purchaser*.

See: 492, 628, 660, 703, 722, 742, 775, 792, 880, 887, 903, 978.

708 Party

N. *party*, movement; group, class 77 n. *classification*; sub-sect, confession, communion, denomination, church 978 n. *sect*; faction, cave, splinter group 489 n.

dissentient; circle, inner c., closed c., charmed c.; set, clique, coterie; caucus, junto, junta, camarilla, committee, club, cell, ring, closed shop; team, eight, eleven, fifteen; crew, complement, dramatis personæ 686 n. *personnel*; troupe, concert-party 594 n. *actor*; gang, knot, bunch, outfit, push 74 n. *band*; phalanx, horde 74 n. *crowd*; side, camp.

political party, right, left, centre; Conservative, Tories, Unionists; Liberals, Radicals, Whigs; Socialists, Labour, National Liberal, Liblab; Democrats, Republicans; Marxists, Communists, Reds, Bolsheviks, Mensheviks, Maximalists, Minimalists; Fascists, Nazis, Falangists; Blue-shirts, Black-shirts, Red-shirts, Brown-shirts; Jacobins, Girondists; coalition, popular front, bloc, political b.; citoyen, comrade, tovarich, Red, commie; socialist, labourite, Fabian, syndicalist, anarchist; right-winger, rightist; left-winger, leftist; moderate, centrist; party man, party member, politician.

society, partnership, coalition, combination, combine 706 n. *association*; league, alliance, axis; federation, confederation, confederacy; economic association, co-operative, Bund, union, customs u., sodality, Zollverein, Benelux, common market, free trade area; private society, club 76 n. *focus;* secret society, Ku Klux Klan, Freemasonry, lodge, cell, club; trades union; chapel; group, division, branch, local b. 53 n. *subdivision*; movement, Boy Scouts, Brownies, Cubs, Rovers, Rangers, Sea-scouts; Girl Guides, Blue Birds; Mother's Union, Church Army, Church Lads' Brigade; Band of Hope; Colonial Dames, Daughters of the American Revolution, D.A.R.; fellow, honorary f., associate, member; party member, comrade; corresponding member, branch m., affiliate 58 n. *component*.

community, fellowship, brotherhood, body, band of brothers, fraternity, confraternity, sorority, sisterhood; guild, sodality; race, tribe, clan, sect 11 n. *family*; order 77 n. *classification*; social class 371 n. *social group*; state, nation-s., multi-racial s. 371 n. *nation*.

corporation, body; incorporated society, body corporate, mayor and corporation 692 n. *council*; company, livery c., joint-

stock c., limited liability c., holding c.; firm, concern, joint c., partnership; house, business h.; establishment, organization, institute; trust, combine, monopoly, cartel, syndicate 706 n. *association*; trade association, chamber of commerce, guild, consumers g., housewives union, co-operative society.

Adj. *corporate*, incorporate, corporative, joint-stock; joint, partnered, bonded, banded, leagued, federal, federative; allied, federate, confederate; social, clubby, clubbish, clubbable 882 adj. *sociable*; fraternal, comradely 880 adj. *friendly*; co-operative, syndicalist.

sectional, denominational, Masonic 978 adj. *sectarian*; partisan, communal, clannish, cliquish, cliquey, exclusive; class-conscious; rightist, leftist, left-wing, pink, red; Whiggish, Tory; radical, conservative.

Vb. *join a party*, put one's name down, subscribe; join, swell the ranks, become a member, take out membership; sign on, enlist, enrol oneself, get elected; cut in, creep in 297 vb. *enter*; belong to, fit in, make one of 78 vb. *be included*; align oneself, side, take sides, range oneself with, team up w. 706 vb. *co-operate*; club together, associate, ally, league, federate; cement a union, merge; make a party, found a p., lead a p.

Adv. *in league*, in partnership, in the same boat, in cahoots with; hand in hand, side by side, shoulder to shoulder, back to back; all together, en masse, jointly, collectively; unitedly, as one; with all the rest, in the swim.

See: 11, 53, 58, 74, 76, 77, 78, 297, 371, 489, 594, 686, 692, 706, 880, 882, 978.

709 Dissension

N. *dissension*, dissentience 489 n. *dissent*; non-cooperation 704 n. *opposition*; disharmony, dissonance, disaccord, jar, jangle, jarring note, discordant n., rift, rift within the lute 411 n. *discord*; recrimination 714 n. *retaliation*; bickering, cat-and-dog life; differences, odds, variance, friction, unpleasantness; soreness 891 n. *resentment*; no love lost, hostility, mutual h., class war 888 n. *hatred*; disunity, disunion, internal dissension, division in the

camp, house divided against itself 25 n. *disagreement*; cleavage, cleavage of opinion, parting of the ways, separation 294 n. *divergence*; split, faction 978 n. *schism*; misunderstanding, cross purposes 481 n. *misjudgment*; imbroglio, embroilment, embranglement 61 n. *confusion*; breach, rupture, open r., severance of relations, recall of ambassadors; challenge 711 n. *defiance*; ultimatum, declaration of war 718 n. *war*.

quarrelsomeness, factiousness, litigiousness; aggressiveness, combativeness, pugnacity, warlike behaviour 718 n. *bellicosity*; provocativeness, trailing one's coat 711 n. *defiance*; cantankerousness, awkwardness, prickliness, fieriness 892 n. *irascibility*; shrewishness, sharp tongue 899 n. *scurrility*; contentiousness 716 n. *contention*; rivalry, emulation 911 n. *jealousy*; thirst for revenge 910 n. *revengefulness*; mischievousness, mischief, spite 898 n. *malevolence*; apple of discord, spirit of mischief; Ate, Mars.

quarrel, open q.; feud, blood-f., vendetta 910 n. *revenge*; war 718 n. *warfare*; strife 716 n. *contention*; conflict, clash 279 n. *collision*; legal battle 959 n. *litigation*; controversy, dispute, wrangle, polemic, battle of arguments, paper war 475 n. *argument*; wordy warfare, words, war of w., high w., stormy exchange, altercation, rixation, abuse, slanging 899 n. *scurrility*; spat, tiff, squabble, jangle, brabble, breeze, squall, storm in a tea-cup; rumpus, hubbub, racket, row, shindy, commotion, scrimmage, fracas, brawl, fisticuffs, breach of the peace, Donnybrook fair 61 n. *turmoil*; gang warfare, street fighting, riot 716 n. *fight*; domestic difficulties, family jars, cat-and-dog life 411 n. *discord*.

casus belli, ground of quarrel, root of dissension, breaking point; tender spot, sore point; apple of discord, bone of contention, bone to pick; disputed point, point at issue, area of disagreement 724 n. *battle-ground*.

quarreller, disputer, eristic, wrangler 475 n. *reasoner*; duellist, rival, emulator 716 n. *contender*; strange bedfellows, Kilkenny cats, Montagues and Capulets; quarrelmonger, mischief-maker 663 n. *troublemaker*; scold, bitter tongue 892 n. *shrew*; aggressor 712 n. *attacker*.

Adj. *quarrelling*, discordant, discrepant, clashing, conflicting, ill-mated, ill-matched 14 adj. *contrary*; on bad terms, at feud, at odds, at sixes and sevens, at loggerheads, at variance, at daggers drawn, up in arms 881 adj. *inimical*; divided, factious, schismatic 489 adj. *dissentient*; mutinous, rebellious 738 adj. *disobedient*; unco-operative, non-co-operating 704 adj. *opposing*; sore 891 adj. *resentful*; awkward, cantankerous 892 adj. *irascible*; sulky 893 adj. *sullen*; implacable 910 vb. *revengeful*; litigant, litigious 959 adj. *litigating*; quarrelsome, non-pacific, unpacific, bellicose 718 adj. *warlike*; pugnacious, combative, spoiling for a fight, trailing one's coat, aggressive, militant 712 adj. *attacking*; abusive, shrewish, scolding, scurrilous 899 adj. *maledicent*; contentious, disputatious, eristic, wrangling, polemical, controversial 475 adj. *arguing*.

Vb. *quarrel*, disagree 489 vb. *dissent*; clash, conflict 279 vb. *collide*; misunderstand, be at cross purposes, pull different ways, be at variance, have differences, have a bone to pick 15 vb. *differ*; recriminate 714 vb. *retaliate*; fall out, part company, split, break, break with, break squares with; break away 978 vb. *schismatize*; break off relations, declare war 718 vb. *go to war*; go to law, take it to court 959 vb. *litigate*; dispute, try conclusions with, controvert 479 vb. *confute*; have a feud with, cherish a vendetta 910 vb. *be revengeful*; turn sulky, sulk 893 vb. *be sullen*; non-cooperate 704 vb. *oppose*.

make quarrels, pick q., fasten a quarrel on; look for trouble, be spoiling for a fight, trail one's coat, challenge 711 vb. *defy*; irritate, rub the wrong way, tread on one's toes, provoke 891 vb. *enrage*; have a bone to pick, have a crow to pluck; cherish a feud, enjoy a quarrel 881 vb. *make enemies*; embroil, entangle, bedevil relations, estrange, set at odds, set at variance, set by the ears 888 vb. *excite hate*; create discord, sound a discordant note 411 vb. *discord*; sow dissension, stir up strife, be a quarrel-monger, make mischief, make trouble; divide, draw apart, disunite, drive a wedge between 46 vb. *sunder*; widen the breach, fan the flame 832 vb. *aggravate*; set against, pit a., match with; egg on, incite 612 vb. *motivate*.

bicker, spat, tiff, squabble, nag; peck, hen-peck, jar, spar, spar with, live a cat-and-dog life; jangle, brangle, wrangle, dispute with 475 vb. *argue*; scold 899 vb. *cuss*; have words with, altercate, pick a bone w., pluck a crow w., row, row with, have a row, brawl, kick up a shindy, break the peace, make the fur fly, raise the dust, raise a breeze 61 vb. *rampage*.

See: 14, 15, 25, 46, 61, 279, 294, 411, 475, 479, 481, 489, 612, 663, 704, 711, 712, 714, 716, 718, 724, 738, 832, 881, 888, 891, 892, 893, 898, 899, 910, 911, 959, 978.

710 Concord

N. *concord*, harmony 410 n. *melody*; unison, unity, duet 24 n. *agreement*; unanimity, bi-partisanship 488 n. *consensus*; lack of friction, understanding, good u., mutual u., rapport; solidarity, team-spirit 706 n. *co-operation*; reciprocity 12 n. *correlation*; sympathy, fellow-feeling 887 n. *love*; compatibility, coexistence, league, amity 880 n. *friendship*; rapprochement, reunion, reconciliation, conciliation, peace-making 719 n. *pacification*; good offices, arbitration 720 n. *mediation*; entente cordiale, happy family, peace and quiet, 'married calm' 717 n. *peace*; good will, goodwill amongst men, honeymoon.

Adj. *concordant*, blended 410 adj. *harmonious*; en rapport, eye to eye, unanimous, of one mind, bi-partisan 24 adj. *agreeing*; coexistent, compatible, united, cemented, bonded, allied, leagued; fraternal, loving, amicable, on good terms 880 adj. *friendly*; frictionless, happy, peaceable, pacific, at peace 717 adj. *peaceful*; conciliatory 719 adj. *pacificatory*; agreeable, congenial 826 vb. *pleasurable*.

Vb. *concord* 410 vb. *harmonize*; bring into concord 719 vb. *pacify*; agree 24 vb. *accord*; see eye to eye, play a duet, chime in with, pull together 706 vb. *co-operate*; reciprocate, respond, run parallel 181 vb. *concur*; fraternize 880 vb. *be friendly*; keep the peace, remain at peace 717 vb. *be at peace*.

See: 12, 24, 181, 410, 488, 706, 717, 719, 720, 826, 880, 887.

711 Defiance

N. *defiance*, dare, daring, challenge, cartel, gage, gauntlet, hat in the ring; bold front, brave face 855n. *courage*; war-cry, warwhoop, war-song, battle-cry 900n. *threat*; high tone 878n. *insolence*; demonstration, display, bravura 875n. *ostentation.*

Adj. *defiant*, defying, challenging, proud, provocative, bellicose, militant 718adj. *warlike*, saucy, insulting 878adj. *insolent*, greatly daring 855adj. *courageous*; hightoned 871adj. *proud*; reckless, triggerhappy 857adj. *rash.*

Vb. *defy*, challenge, take one up on, demur 489vb. *dissent*; stand up to 704vb. *oppose*; caution 664vb. *warn*; throw in one's teeth, throw down the gauntlet, throw one's hat in the ring; demand satisfaction, call out, send one's seconds, offer choice of weapons; dare, outdare, beard, singe Philip's b.; brave, run the gauntlet 661vb. *face danger*; laugh to scorn, laugh in one's face, laugh in one's beard, set at naught, snap one's fingers at 922vb. *hold cheap*; bid defiance, set at d., hurl d.; call one's bluff, double the bid; show fight, bare one's teeth, show one's fangs, double one's fist, clench one's f., shake one's f. 900vb. *threaten*; take a high tone 871vb. *be proud*; look big, throw out one's chest, slap one's c., show a bold front; wave 317vb. *brandish*; demonstrate, make a demonstration; crow, bluster, brag 877 vb. *boast*; cock a snook 878vb. *be insolent*; trail one's coat 709vb. *make quarrels*; crow over, shout 727vb. *triumph.*

Adv. *defiantly*, challengingly, in defiance of, in spite of one's teeth; under the very nose of.

Int. do your worst! come if you dare!

See: 317, 489, 661, 664, 704, 709, 718, 727, 855, 857, 871, 875, 877, 878, 900, 922.

712 Attack

N. *attack*, hostile a., best method of defence; pugnacity, combativeness, aggressiveness 718n. *bellicosity*; aggression, unprovoked a. 914n. *injustice*; stab in the back 930n. *foul play*; assault, assault and battery 176n. *violence*; armed attack, offensive, drive, push, thrust, pincer movement 688n. *tactics*; run at, dead set at; onslaught, onset, rush, shock, charge; sally, sortie, break-out, breakthrough; counter-attack 714n. *retaliation*; shock tactics, blitzkrieg, coup de main, surprise; encroachment, infringement 306n. *overstepping*; invasion, inroad, incursion, irruption, over-running 297n. *ingress*; raid, razzia, chappow, foray 788n. *brigandage*; blitz, air-raid, air-attack, sea-a., land-a.; night-attack, camisade; storm, taking by s., escalade; boarding, cutting-out expedition; investment, obsession, siege, leaguer, blockade, encirclement 230n. *circumjacence*; challenge, tilt.

terror tactics, intimidation, schrecklichkeit, frightfulness 854n. *intimidation*; war to the knife 735n. *severity*; whiff of grapeshot, battue, dragonnade, noyade, Jacquerie, blood-bath 362n. *slaughter*; devastation, laying waste 165n. *havoc.*

bombardment, cannonade, barrage, strafe, blitz; broadside, volley, salvo; bombdropping, laying eggs, bombing, saturation b.; firing, shooting, fire, gun-f., machine-gun f., rifle f., fusillade, burst of fire, rapid f., cross-f., plunging f.; raking f., enfilade; platoon fire, file f.; anti-aircraft fire, flak; sharp-shooting, sniping, Parthian shot; gunnery, musketry, practice.

foin, thrust, home-t., lunge, pass, passado, carte and tierce; cut, cut and thrust, stoccado, stab, jab; bayonet, cold steel; estrapade; punch, swipe, kick 279n. *knock.*

attacker, assailant, aggressor; militant, war party; spearhead, storm troops, shock t.; fighter pilot, air-ace, bomber 722n. *armed force*; sharp-shooter, sniper, guerrilla; invader, raider, tip-and-run r.; besieger, blockader, stormer, escalader.

Adj. *attacking*, assailing, assaulting etc.vb.; pugnacious, combative, aggressive, offensive 718adj. *warlike*; militant, spoiling for a fight, hostile 881adj. *inimical*; up in arms, on the warpath 718adj. *warring*; storming, charging, cutting-out, boarding, over the top; besieging, obsidional, besetting, obsidious.

Vb. *attack*, aggress, be spoiling for a fight; start a war, start a fight, declare war 718 vb. *go to war*; strike the first blow, fire the first shot; assault, assail, make a dead set at, go for, set on, pounce upon, fall u., pitch into, sail i., have at; attack tooth and

nail, savage, maul, draw blood 655 vb. *wound*; launch out at, let fly at, round on; surprise, blitz, overwhelm; move in, invade 306 vb. *encroach*; raid, foray, overrun, infest 297 vb. *irrupt*; show fight, take the offensive, assume the o., go over to the o., go over to the attack; counterattack 714 vb. *retaliate*; thrust, push, make a drive 279 vb. *impel*; erupt, sally, make a sortie, break out, break through 298 vb. *emerge*; board, lay aboard, grapple; escalade, storm, take by storm, carry, capture 727 vb. *overmaster*; ravage, make havoc, scorch, burn 165 vb. *lay waste*; harry, drive, beat, beat up, corner, bring to bay 619 vb. *hunt*; challenge, enter the lists 711 vb. *defy*; take on 704 vb. *oppose*; take up the cudgels, draw the sword, couch one's lance, break a lance 716 vb. *fight.*

besiege, lay siege, beleaguer, sit down before, invest, surround, beset, blockade 235 vb. *inclose*; engage in siege operations, open the trenches, plant a battery; sap, mine, undermine, spring a mine.

strike at, raise one's hand against; lay about one, swipe, flail, hammer 279 vb. *strike*, *kick*; go beserk, run amok 176 vb. *be violent*; have at, have a fling at, fetch a blow, have a cut at, have a shot at; clash, ram 279 vb. *collide*; make a pass at, lunge; close with, grapple w., come to close quarters, fight hand to hand, cut and thrust; push, butt, thrust, poke at, thrust at; stab, spear, lance, bayonet, run through, cut down 263 vb. *pierce*; strike home, lay low, bring down 311 vb. *abase*; torpedo, sink 313 vb. *plunge*; stab in the back 930 vb. *be dishonest.*

charge, sound the c., advance against, march a., run a., drive a., sail a., fly a.; bear down on, come on, sail in; rush, mob 61 vb. *rampage*; make a rush, rush at, run at, dash at, tilt at, ride full tilt at; ride down, run down, ram, shock 279 vb. *collide*; go over the top.

fire at, shoot at, fire upon; fire a shot at, take a pot-shot, pop at, snipe, pick off 287 vb. *shoot*; shoot down, bring d.; torpedo, sink; soften up, strafe, bombard, blitz, cannonade, shell, fusillade, pepper; bomb, throw bombs, drop b., lay eggs, plaster, prang; open fire, let fly, volley; spend powder and shot, volley and thunder, rattle, blast, pour a broadside into,

rake, straddle, enfilade; take aim, level, draw a bead on 281 vb. *aim.*

lapidate, stone, throw a stone, heave a brick; shy, sling, pelt; hurl at, hurl at the head of 287 vb. *propel.*

Adv. *aggressively*, offensively, on the offensive, on the attack.

See: 61, 165, 176, 230, 235, 263, 279, 281, 287, 297, 298, 306, 311, 313, 362, 619, 655, 688, 704, 711, 714, 716, 718, 722, 727, 735, 788, 854, 881, 914, 930.

713 Defence

N. *defence*, the defensive, self-defence 715 n. *resistance*; art of self-defence, boxing 716 n. *pugilism*; judo, ju-jitsu 716 n. *wrestling*; counter, counterstroke, parry, warding off 182 n. *counteraction*; repression, suppression, insulation; defensiveness 854 n. *nervousness*; posture of defence, guard, ward; defensive arrangement, balance of power; safe-keeping 666 n. *preservation*; self-protection 660 n. *protection*; a defence, rampart, bulwark, ward, screen, buffer, fender, bumper 662 n. *safeguard*; deterrent 723 n. *weapon*; sinews of war, munitions 723 n. *ammunition.*

defences, muniment; lines, entrenchment, fieldwork, redan, lunette; breastwork, parados, contravallation; outwork, circumvallation; earthwork, embankment, mound; mole, boom; wall, barricade, fence 235 n. *barrier*; abatis, palisade, paling, stockade, zareba, laager, sangar; moat, ditch, dyke, fosse; trench, dug-out; traverse, parallel; trip-wire, booby-trap 542 n. *trap*; barbed wire, barbed wire entanglements; spike, caltrop, chevaux de frise; Maginot Line, Siegfried L., Hadrian's Wall, Wall of Antonine, Great Wall of China; air-raid shelter, underground s. 662 n. *shelter*; barrage, antiaircraft fire, flak; barrage-balloon; wooden walls; minefield, mine, countermine; smoke-screen 421 n. *screen.*

fortification (see *fort*); circumvallation, bulwark, rampart, wall; parapet, battlement, machicolation, embrasure, casemate, merlon, loophole; banquette, barbette, emplacement, gun-e.; vallum, scarp, counterscarp, glacis; curtain, bastion; ravelin, demilune, outwork,

hornwork, demibastion; buttress, abutment; gabionage, gabion, gabionade.
fort, fortress, fortalice, stronghold, fastness; citadel, capitol, acropolis 662n. *refuge*; air-raid shelter, underground s. 662n. *shelter*; castle, keep, ward, barbican, tower, turret, bartizan, donjon; portcullis, drawbridge; gate, postern, sally-port; turret, peel-house, pill-h., Martello tower, pill-box, cassine; blockhouse, strong point, redan, lunette; laager, zareba, sangar, enclosure, encampment, camp 235n. *inclosure*; Roman camp, castrum; British camp, Maiden Castle; seafort, military type s., naval type s.
armour, body a., harness; full armour, panoply; mail, chain m.; plate armour, armour-plate; breastplate, poitrel; cuirass lorica, plastron; hauberk, habergeon, brigandine, coat of mail, corslet; cheekpiece, head-p.; helmet, helm, casque, basinet, sallet, morion; visor, beaver; siege cap, steel helmet, tin hat; shako, bearskin, busby, pickelhaube 228n. *headgear*; greaves, gauntlet, vambrace, rerebrace; aegis, shield, buckler; scutum, targe, target; mantlet, testudo, tortoise; carapace, shell; thimble, finger-stall; protective clothing, gas-mask.
defender, champion 927n. *vindicator*; patron 703n. *aider*; knight-errant, paladin; loyalist, legitimist, patriot; house-carl, bodyguard, life-guard, Prætorian, National Guard; watch, sentry, sentinel; patrol, patrolman; garrison, picket, guard, escort, rear-guard; Home Guard, militia, fencible 722n. *soldiery*; fireman, firefighter, fire-watcher; guardian, General Winter 660n. *protector*; warder 749n. *keeper*; wicket-keeper, goal-k., custodian 702n. *interceptor*; deliverer, rescuer, ready help in time of trouble 668n. *deliverance*; challengee, title-defender, title-holder.
Adj. *defending*, challenged, on the defensive 715adj. *resisting*; propugnant, defensive, protective, patriotic 660adj. *tutelary*; exculpatory, self-excusing 927adj. *vindicating*.
defended, armoured, plated, panoplied; heavy-armed, mailed, mail-clad, armour-c., iron-c.; accoutred, harnessed, armed to the teeth, armed cap-à-pie, armed at all points 669adj. *prepared*; moated, palisaded, barricaded, walled, fortified, machicolated, castellated, battlemented, loopholed; entrenched, dug in; defensible, proof, bomb-p., bullet-p. 660adj. *invulnerable*.
Vb. *defend*, guard, protect, keep, watch, ward 660vb. *safeguard*; fence, hedge, moat 232vb. *circumscribe*; palisade, barricade 235vb. *inclose*; block 702vb. *obstruct*; cushion, pad, shield, curtain, shroud, shade, cover 421vb. *screen*; cloak 525vb. *conceal*; provide with arms, munition, arm, accoutre 669vb. *make ready*; harness, armour, clothe in a., plate, panoply; reinforce, fortify, wall, crenellate, machicolate, loophole 162vb. *strengthen*; entrench, dig in 599vb. *stand firm*; stand in front, stand by; garrison, man, man the defences, man the breach, stop the gap; champion 927vb. *vindicate*; fight for, unsheathe one's sword for, take up arms for, break a lance for, take up the cudgels for, cover up f. 703vb. *patronize*; rescue, come to the r. 668vb. *deliver*.
parry, counter, riposte, fend, forfend, fend off, ward off, hold off, keep off, fight off, hold *or* keep at bay, keep at arm's length 620vb. *avoid*; turn, avert 282vb. *deflect*; fence, foin; play, play with, keep in play; stall, stonewall, block 702vb. *obstruct*; act on the defensive, fight a defensive battle, play for a draw, stalemate; fight back, show fight, give a warm reception to 715vb. *resist*; butt away, repulse 292vb. *repel*; bear the brunt, hold one's own 704vb. *withstand*; fall back on 673vb. *avail of*; beat a strategic retreat 286vb. *turn back*; survive, scrape through, live to fight another day 667vb. *escape*.
Adv. *defensively*, on the defensive, at bay; in defence, pro patria, in self-defence.
See: 162, 182, 228, 232, 235, 282, 286, 292, 421, 525, 542, 599, 620, 660, 662, 666, 667, 668, 669, 673, 702, 703, 704, 715, 716, 722, 723, 749, 854, 927.

714 Retaliation

N. *retaliation*, reprisal, lex talionis 910n. *revenge*; requital, recompense 962n. *reward*; desert, deserts 915n. *dueness*; punitive action, poetic justice, retribution, Nemesis 963n. *punishment*; repayment 787n. *restitution*; indemnification

31 n. *compensation*; reaction, boomerang 280 n. *recoil*; counter, counter-stroke, counterblast, counterplot, countermine 182 n. *counteraction*; counter-attack, sally, sortie 712 n. *attack*; recrimination, answering back, riposte, retort, retort courteous 460 n. *rejoinder*; returning good for evil, heaping coals of fire; reciprocation, give and take, like for like, tit for tat, quid pro quo, measure for measure, blow for blow, an eye for an eye and a tooth for a tooth, a Roland for an Oliver, diamond cut diamond, biter bit, a game at which two can play; potential retaliation, deterrent 854 n. *intimidation*.

Adj. *retaliatory*, in retaliation, in reprisal, in self-defence; retaliative, retributive, punitive, recriminatory; like for like, reciprocal; rightly served.

Vb. *retaliate*, return, retort upon; serve rightly, teach one a lesson, exact compensation, take reprisals; make a requital, pay one out, pay off old scores, wipe out a score, square the account, be quits, get even with, get one's own back 910 vb. *avenge*; requite, recompense, compensate 962 vb. *reward*; counter, riposte 713 vb. *parry*; do unto others as you would be done by, return good for evil; heap coals of fire on one's head; reciprocate, give and take, return like for like; return the compliment, give as good as one got, pay in the same coin, give a quid pro quo; retort, cap, answer back 460 vb. *answer*; recriminate 928 vb. *accuse*; react, boomerang 280 vb. *recoil*; round on, kick back, hit b., not take it lying down 715 vb. *resist*; turn the tables on, hoist one with his own petard.

be rightly served, have had one's lesson; pay compensation, have to pay c. 787 n. *restitute*; find one's match, catch a Tartar; get one's deserts, get a dose of one's own medicine 963 vb. *be punished*; it serves one right.

Adv. *en revanche*, by way of return, in requital.

See: 31, 182, 280, 460, 712, 713, 715, 787, 854, 910, 915, 928, 962, 963.

715 Resistance

N. *resistance*, oppugnation, front, stand, firm s. 704 n. *opposition*; contumacy 602 n. *obstinacy*; reluctance, renitence 598 n. *unwillingness*; repugnance 861 n. *dislike*; objection, demur 468 n. *qualification*; recalcitrance, kicking, protest 762 n. *deprecation*; non-cooperation, passive resistance, satyagraha; rising, insurrection, resistance movement 738 n. *revolt*; repulsion, repulse, rebuff, bloody nose 760 n. *refusal*; refusal to work 145 n. *strike*.

Adj. *resisting* etc. vb.; firm against 704 adj. *opposing*; protesting, unconsenting, reluctant 598 adj. *unwilling*; recalcitrant, renitent, unsubmissive, mutinous, insurrectional 738 adj. *disobedient*; contumacious 602 adj. *obstinate*; holding out, unyielding, unconquerable, indomitable, unsubdued, undefeated 727 adj. *unbeaten*; resistant, proof, proofed, grease-p., bullet-p., bomb-p., waterproof; repugnant, repelling 292 adj. *repellent*.

Vb. *resist*, offer resistance, give a warm reception, stand against 704 vb. *withstand*; obstruct 702 vb. *hinder*; challenge, try a fall 711 vb. *defy*; stand out, front, confront, outface 661 vb. *face danger*; struggle against, contend with, stem the tide, breast the current 704 vb. *oppose*; reluctate, recalcitrate, kick, kick against the pricks, protest 762 vb. *deprecate*; demur, object 468 vb. *qualify*; strike work, strike, come out 145 vb. *cease*; engineer a strike, call out 145 vb. *halt*; mutiny, rise, not take it lying down 738 vb. *revolt*; make a stand, fight off, keep at arm's length, keep at bay, hold off 713 vb. *parry*; hold out, not submit, die hard, sell one's life dearly 599 vb. *stand firm*; bear up, bear the brunt, endure 825 vb. *suffer*; be proof against, not admit, repel, rebuff 760 vb. *refuse*; resist temptation, not be tempted; last 113 vb. *outlast*.

See: 113, 145, 292, 468, 598, 599, 602, 661, 702, 704, 711, 713, 727, 738, 760, 762, 825, 861.

716 Contention

N. *contention*, strife, tussle, conflict, clash 709 n. *dissension*; combat, fighting, war 718 n. *warfare*; debate, dispute, controversy, polemics, paper war, ink-slinging 475 n. *argument*; altercation, words, war of w. 709 n. *quarrel*; a word and a

blow 892 n. *irascibility*; stakes, bone of contention 709 n. *casus belli*; competition, rivalry, corrivalry, emulation, prestige-chasing 911 n. *jealousy*; competitiveness, gamesmanship, survival of the fittest; cut-throat competition, war to the knife, no holds barred; sporting, athletics 837 n. *sport*.

contest, trial, trial of strength 461 n. *experiment*; test of endurance, marathon, pentathlon, decathlon, tug-of-war 682 n. *exertion*; tussle, struggle 671 *essay*; equal contest, ding-dong fight; close finish, photo f. 200 n. *short distance*; competition, open c., free-for-all; knock-out competition, tournament; tourney, jousting, joust, tilting, tilt; prize-competition, stakes, Ashes; match, test m.; concourse, rally; event, handicap, run-off; heat, final, semi-f., quarter f., Cup f., Cup tie; set, game, rubber; sporting event, wager, bet 837 n. *sport*; field day 837 n. *amusement*; Derby day (see *racing*); agonism, athletics, gymnastics; gymkhana, horse-show, rodeo; games, Highland Games, Olympics, Olympic g., Pythian g., Isthmian g.; Olympia, Delphi, Isthmus; Wimbledon, Forest Hills; Oval, Lords; Henley 724 n. *arena*.

racing, speed contest 277 n. *speeding*; races, race, foot r., flat r., sprint, dash, quarter-mile, half-m., mile, marathon; long-distance race, cross-country r.; relay race, team-r., torch r., lampadedromy, lampadophoria; the Turf, horse-racing, sport of kings; horse-race, point-to-point, steeplechase, paperchase, hurdles, sticks 312 n. *leap*; chariot-race, trotting-r.; motor race, motor-rally, dirt-track racing, bicycle r.; dog-racing; boat-race, yacht-r., America's Cup competition; regatta, eights, torpids, Lent races, May r., Henley; Epsom, race-course, track, stadium 724 n. *arena*.

pugilism, noble art of self-defence, boxing, shadow-b., sparring, milling, fisticuffs; prize-fighting, boxing match, prize-fight; mill, spar, clinch, in-fighting; round, bout; the ring, the fancy 837 n. *sport*.

wrestling, ju-jitsu, judo, all-in-wrestling, catch-as-catch-can, no holds barred; catch, hold; wrestle, grapple, wrestling match.

duel, triangular d.; affair of honour, pistols for two and coffee for one; match, mono-machy, single combat, gladiatorial c.; jousting, joust, tilting, tilt, tourney, tournament; fencing, fence, digladiation, sword-play, lathi-p., single-stick, quarter-s.; hand-to-hand fighting, close grips; bull-fight, tauromachy, dog-fight, cock-fight; bull-ring, cockpit, lists 724 n. *arena*.

fight, hostilities, appeal to arms 718 n. *warfare*; battle royal, free fight, free-for-all, rough and tumble, rough house, horse-play, shindy, scuffle, scrum, scrimmage, scramble, dog-fight, mêlée, fracas, uproar, rumpus, ruction 61 n. *turmoil*; gang-warfare, street-fight, riot, rumble; brawl, broil, brabble 709 n. *quarrel*; fisticuffs, blows, hard knocks; give and take, cut and thrust; affray, set-to, tussle; running fight, ding-dong f., in-fighting, close f., hand-to-hand f.; close grips, close quarters; combat, fray, clash, conflict 279 n. *collision*; encounter, rencounter, scrap, brush; skirmish, skirmishing, velitation; engagement, action, affair, pitched battle, stand-up fight, set-to, grapple 718 n. *battle*; deed of arms, feat of a., passage of a. 676 n. *deed*; campaign, struggle; death struggle, death grapple, death grips, war to the knife, war to the death; Armageddon, theomachy, gigantomachy; field of battle, battlefield 724 *battleground*.

contender, struggler, trier, striver; tussler, fighter, battler, gamecock; gladiator, bull-fighter 722 n. *combatant*; prize-fighter 722 n. *pugilist*; duellist 709 n. *quarreller*; fencer, swordsman; candidate, entrant, examinee; competitor, rival, corrival, emulator; challenger, runner-up, finalist, semi-f.; starter, also-ran, the field, all comers; contester, pot-hunter; racer, runner, sprinter, miler, team-racer, relay-r., lampadist 277 n. *speeder*; agonist 162 n. *athlete*.

Adj. *contending*, struggling, grappling etc. vb.; rival, rivalling, racing, outdoing 306 adj. *surpassing*; competing, in the business, in the same b.; agonistic, sporting, pot-hunting; starting, running, in the running; agonistic, athletic, palæstric, pugilistic, gladiatorial; contentious, quarrelsome 709 adj. *quarrelling*; aggressive, combative, fight-hungry, spoiling for a fight, pugnacious, bellicose, war-mongering, non-pacific, militant, unpeaceful 718

adj. *warlike*; at loggerheads, at odds, at issue, at war, belligerent 718 adj. *warring*; competitive, keen, cut-throat; hand to hand, close, at close grips; keenly contested, ding-dong; close run; well-fought, fought to a finish.

Vb. *contend*, combat, strive, struggle, battle, fight, tussle, wrestle, grapple 671 vb. *essay*; oppose 715 vb. *resist*; argue for, stick out for, make a point of, insist 532 vb. *emphasize*; contest, compete, challenge, stake, wager, bet; play, play against, match oneself, vie with, race, run a race; emulate, rival 911 vb. *be jealous*; outrival 306 vb. *outdo*; enter, enter for, take on, enter the lists, descend into the arena, take up the challenge, pick up the glove; couch one's lance, tilt with, joust w., break a lance w.; take on, try a fall, try conclusions with, close w., grapple w., engage w. 712 vb. *strike at*; have a hard fight, fight to a finish.

fight, break the peace, have a fight, scuffle, row, scrimmage, scrap, set to 176 vb. *be violent*; pitch into, sail i. 712 vb. *attack*; lay on, lay about one 712 vb. *strike at*; mix it, join in the mêlée; square up to, come to blows, exchange b., exchange fisticuffs, give hard knocks, give and take; box, spar, fib, pummel, jostle, kick, scratch, bite 279 vb. *strike*; fall foul of, join issue with 709 vb. *quarrel*; duel, call out, meet, give satisfaction; encounter, have a brush with, scrap w., exchange shots, skirmish; take on, engage, fight a pitched battle 718 vb. *give battle*; come to grips, come to close quarters, close with, grapple, lock horns; fence, cross swords, measure s.; fight hand to hand, use cold steel; appeal to arms, appeal to the arbitrament of war 718 vb. *go to war*; combat, campaign, fight the good fight 718 vb. *wage war*; fight hard, fight like devils, fight it out 599 vb. *be resolute*.

See: 61, 162, 176, 200, 277, 279, 306, 312, 461, 475, 532, 599, 671, 676, 682, 709, 712, 715, 718, 722, 724, 837, 892, 911.

717 Peace

N. *peace*, state of p., peacefulness, peace and quiet 266 n. *quiescence*; piping times of peace 730 n. *palmy days*; universal peace, Pax Romana, Pax Britannica; end of hostilities, demobilization 145 n. *cessation*; truce, uneasy t., armistice 145 n. *lull*; freedom from war, cold w., co-existence, armed neutrality; neutrality; non-involvement 860 n. *indifference*; non-intervention 620 n. *avoidance*; peaceability, non-aggression 177 n. *moderation*; cordial relations 880 n. *friendship*; pacifism, peace at any price, non-violence, ahimsa; disarmament, peace-making, irenics 719 n. *pacification*; pipe of peace, calumet; league of peace, peace treaty, non-aggression pact 765 n. *treaty*; burial of the hatchet 506 n. *amnesty*.

pacifist, man of peace, peace-lover, peace-monger; peace-party 177 n. *moderator*; neutral, non-combatant, non-belligerent; civilian, women and children; passive resister, conscientious objector, conchy; peacemaker 720 n. *mediator*.

Adj. *peaceful*, quiet, halcyon 266 adj. *tranquil*; piping 730 adj. *palmy*; without war, without bloodshed, bloodless; harmless, dovelike 935 adj. *innocent*; peaceable, law-abiding, peace-loving, pacific, unmilitary, unwarlike, unmilitant, unaggressive, war-weary; pacifist, non-violent; unarmed, non-combatant, civilian; unresisting, passive, submissive 721 adj. *submitting*; peace-making, conciliatory, irenic 720 adj. *mediatory*; without enemies, at peace; not at war, neutral; post-war, pre-war.

Vb. *be at peace*, enjoy p., stay at p., observe neutrality, keep out of war, keep out of trouble; mean no harm, be pacific 935 vb. *be innocent*; keep the peace, avoid bloodshed; work for peace, make p. 720 vb. *mediate*; beat one's sword into a ploughshare, make the lion lie down with the lamb, smoke the pipe of peace.

Adv. *peacefully*, peaceably, pacifically; without violence, bloodlessly; quietly, tranquilly, happily.

See: 145, 177, 266, 506, 620, 719, 720, 721, 730, 765, 860, 880, 935.

718 War

N. *war*, arms, the sword; grim-visaged war, horrida bella, ultima ratio regum; appeal

to arms, arbitrament of war, fortune of w., wager of battle, ordeal of b.; undeclared war, cold w.; paper war, polemic 709n. *quarrel*; war of nerves 854n. *intimidation*; half-war, doubtful w., armed neutrality; disguised war, intervention, armed i., police action; real war, hot w.; internecine war, civil w., war of revolution, war of independence; wars of religion, religious war, holy w., crusade, jehad; aggressive war, war of expansion; colonial war, gunboat w., limited w., localized w.; major war, general w., world w., global w.; total war, blitzkrieg, atomic war; war of attrition, truceless war, war to the knife, war to the death, no holds barred; pomp and circumstance of war, chivalry, nodding plumes, gorgeous uniforms; martial music, bugle, trumpet, tucket, pibroch; call to arms, bugle-call 547n. *call*; battle-cry, war-whoop, war-song 711n. *defiance*; god of war, god of battles, war-god, Ares, Mars, Bellona. See *warfare*.

belligerency, state of war, state of siege; resort to arms, declaration of war, outbreak of w., militancy, hostilities; wartime, war-time conditions, time of war, duration of w.

bellicosity, war fever; love of war, warlike habits, military spirit, pugnacity, combativeness, aggressiveness, militancy 709 n. *quarrelsomeness*; militarism, Prussianism, expansionism, war policy; jingoism, chauvinism 481n. *prejudice*.

art of war, warcraft, siegecraft, strategy, grand s. 688n. *tactics*; castrametation 713n. *fortification*; generalship, soldiership, seamanship, airmanship 694n. *skill*; ballistics, gunnery, musketry practice; drill, training 534n. *teaching*; staff-work, logistics, planning 623n. *plan*; military evolutions, manœuvres; military experience, skill in arms 490n. *knowledge*.

war measures, war footing, war preparations, martial p., arming 669n. *preparation*; call to arms, clarion call, Fiery Cross 547n. *call*; war effort, call-up, mobilization, recruitment, conscription, national service, military duty; volunteering, join-up; rationing; black-out; censorship; internment.

warfare, war, warring, warpath, making war, waging w.; warlike operations, ops.; deeds of blood, bloodshed, battles,

sieges 176n. *violence*; fighting, campaigning, soldiering, active service; military service, naval s., air s.; bombing, saturation b. 712n. *bombardment*; raiding, sea-r.; besieging, blockading, investment 235 n. *inclosure*; aerial warfare, air-w., naval w., submarine w., undersea w., chemical w., gas w., germ w., bacteriological w., atomic w., nuclear w.; economic warfare, blockade, attrition, scorched earth, denial policy; psychological warfare, propaganda; offensive warfare 712n. *attack*; defensive warfare 713n. *defence*; mobile warfare, static w., trench w., desert w., jungle w.; bush-fighting, guerilla warfare; campaign, expedition; operations, land o., sea o., naval o., air o., combined o., joint o., amphibious o.; incursion, invasion, raid; order, word of command, orders 737n. *command*; password, watch-word; battle-cry, slogan 547n. *call*; plan of campaign, battle-orders 623n. *plan*.

battle, ordeal of b., pitched b., battle royal 716n. *fight*; line of battle, order of b., array; line, firing l., first l., front l., front, battle f.; armed conflict, action, scrap, skirmish, brush, collision, clash; offensive, blitz 712n. *attack*; defensive battle, stand 713n. *defence*; engagement, naval e., sea-e., air-e.; sea-fight, air-f.; arena, battlefield, field of battle, area of hostilities 724n. *battleground*.

Adj. *warring*, on the warpath; campaigning, battling etc.vb.; at war, in a state of w.; belligerent, militant, engaged in war, mobilized, uniformed, under arms, in the army, at the front, on active service; militant, up in arms; armed, sword in hand 669adj. *prepared*; arrayed, embattled; engaged, at grips, at loggerheads 709adj. *quarrelling*; on the offensive 712 adj. *attacking*.

warlike, militaristic, bellicose, unpacific; militant, aggressive, pugnacious, combative; war-loving, peace-hating, fierce, untamed 898adj. *cruel*; bloodthirsty, battle-hungry, war-fevered; military, martial, exercised in arms, bearing a.; veteran, battle-scarred; armigerent, knightly, chivalrous; soldierly, soldier-like; Napoleonic; military, naval; operational, strategical, tactical.

Vb. *go to war*, resort to arms; declare war, dig up the hatchet; acknowledge belligerency, commit hostilities; appeal to arms,

unsheathe the sword, throw away the scabbard, whet the sword, take up the cudgels 716vb. *fight*; take to arms, fly to a., rise, rebel 738vb. *revolt*; raise one's banner, set up one's standard, call to arms, send round the Fiery Cross; arm, militarize, mobilize, put on a war footing; call up, call to the colours, recruit, conscript; join the army, join up, enlist, enrol, take the shilling, don a uniform, take a commission.

wage war, make w., warray; go on the warpath, march to war, engage in hostilities, war, war against, war upon; campaign, open a c., open a front, take the field; go on active service, shoulder a musket, smell powder, flesh one's sword; soldier, be at the front; take the offensive, invade 712vb. *attack*; keep the field, hold one's ground 599vb. *stand firm*; act on the defensive 713vb. *defend*; manœuvre, march, counter-march; blockade, beleaguer, besiege, invest 230vb. *surround*; shed blood, put to the sword 362vb. *slaughter*; ravage, burn, scorch 165vb. *lay waste*.

give battle, battle, offer b., accept b.; join battle, meet on the battlefield; engage, provoke an engagement; combat, fight the good fight, fight it out 716vb. *fight*; take a position, choose one's ground, dig in; rally, close the ranks, stand, make a s. 715vb. *resist*; sound the charge, go over the top 712vb. *charge*; open fire, cannonade, spend powder and shot 712vb. *fire at*; skirmish, brush.

Adv. *at war*, at the sword's point, at the point of the bayonet, in the thick of the fray, at the cannon's mouth.

See: 165, 176, 230, 235, 362, 481, 490, 534, 547, 599, 623, 669, 688, 694, 709, 711, 712, 713, 715, 716, 724, 737, 738, 854, 898.

719 Pacification

N. *pacification*, pacifying, peace-making; conciliation, appeasement, mollification 177n. *moderation*; reconciliation, reconcilement, détente, improved relations, rapprochement; accommodation, adjustment 24n. *agreement*; composition 770n. *compromise*; good offices 720n.

mediation; convention, entente, understanding, peace-treaty, peace pact, nonaggression p., league of peace 765vb. *treaty*; suspension of hostilities, truce, armistice, cease-fire, standstill 145n. *lull*; disarmament, demobilization, disbanding; imposed peace, forced reconciliation, shot-gun wedding 740n. *compulsion*.

irenics, irenicon, peace-offering 177n. *moderator*; propitiation, appeasement 736n. *lenity*; olive-branch, overture, peaceful approach, friendly a., hand of friendship, outstretched hand 880n. *friendliness*; flag of truce, white flag, parlementaire, cartel, pipe of peace, calumet 717n. *peace*; weregild, blood-money, compensation 787n. *restitution*; fair offer, easy terms 177n. *moderation*; plea for peace, peace speech 506n. *amnesty*; mercy 909n. *forgiveness*.

Adj. *pacificatory*, conciliatory, placatory, propitiatory; irenic 880adj. *friendly*; disarming, emollient 177adj. *lenitive*; peacemaking, mediatory, trucial; pacified, happy 828adj. *content*.

Vb. *pacify*, make peace, impose p., give peace to; allay, tranquillize, mollify, take the sting out of 177vb. *assuage*; heal 656vb. *cure*; hold out the olive-branch, hold out one's hand, return a soft answer, coo like a dove 880vb. *be friendly*; conciliate, propitiate, disarm, reconcile, placate, appease, satisfy 828vb. *content*; restore harmony 410vb. *harmonize*; win over, bring to terms, meet half-way 770vb. *compromise*; compose differences, settle d., accommodate 24vb. *adjust*; bridge over, bring together 720vb. *mediate*; show mercy 736vb. *be lenient*; grant a truce, grant an armistice, grant peace 766vb. *give terms*; keep the peace 717vb. *be at peace*.

make peace, stop fighting; bury the hatchet, let bygones be bygones, forgive and forget 506vb. *forget*; shake hands, make it up, make friends, patch up a quarrel; lay down one's arms, sheathe the sword, beat swords into ploughshares; make a truce, suspend hostilities, demilitarize, disarm, demobilize; close the gates of Janus, smoke the pipe of peace.

See: 24, 145, 177, 410, 506, 656, 717, 720, 736, 740, 765, 766, 770, 787, 828, 880, 909.

720 Mediation

N. *mediation,* good offices, mediatorship, intercession; umpirage, arbitrage, arbitration; intervention, interposition 231 n. *interjacence;* intermeddling 678 n. *over-activity;* diplomatics, diplomacy; parley, negotiation 584 n. *conference.*
mediator, common friend, middleman, intermedium, match-maker, go-between, negotiator 231 n. *intermediary;* arbitrator, umpire, referee 480 n. *estimator;* diplomat, diplomatist, representative, attorney, agent 754 n. *delegate;* intercessor, pleader, propitiator; moderating influence, peace party 177 n. *moderator;* pacifier, pacificator, trouble-shooter; marriage adviser; peacemaker, make-peace, dove.
Adj. *mediatory,* mediatorial, intercessory, intercessorial, propitiatory 719 adj. *pacificatory.*
Vb. *mediate,* intervene, intermeddle 678 vb. *meddle;* step in, put oneself between, interpose 231 vb. *put between;* proffer one's good offices, offer one's intercession, intercede for, beg off, propitiate; run messages for, be a go-between; bring together, negotiate, act as agent; arbitrate, umpire 480 vb. *judge;* compose differences 719 vb. *pacify.*
See: 177, 231, 480, 584, 678, 719, 754.

721 Submission

N. *submission,* submissiveness 739 n. *obedience;* subservience, slavishness 745 n. *servitude;* acquiescence, compliance, consent 488 n. *assent;* supineness, peace at any price, line of least resistance, non-resistance, passiveness, resignation, fatalism 679 n. *inactivity;* yielding, giving way, white flag, capitulation, surrender, unconditional s., rendition, cession, abandonment 621 n. *relinquishment;* deference, humble submission 872 n. *humility;* act of submission, homage 739 n. *loyalty;* kneeling, genuflexion, kowtow, prostration 311 n. *obeisance.*
Adj. *submitting,* surrendering etc. vb.; quiet, meek, unresisting, non-resisting, law-abiding 717 adj. *peaceful;* submissive 739 adj. *obedient;* fatalistic, resigned, acquiescent 488 adj. *assenting;* pliant 327 adj. *soft;* weak-kneed, bending;

crouching, crawling, lying down, supine, prostrate; kneeling, on bended knees, down on one's marrow-bones 872 adj. *humble.*
Vb. *submit,* yield, give in; not resist, not insist, defer to; bow to, make a virtue of necessity, yield with a good grace, admit defeat, yield the palm 728 vb. *be defeated;* resign oneself, be resigned 488 vb. *acquiesce;* accept 488 vb. *assent;* shrug one's shoulders 860 vb. *be indifferent;* withdraw, make way for, draw in one's horns 286 vb. *turn back;* not contest, let judgment go by default 679 vb. *be inactive;* cease resistance, stop fighting, have no fight left, give up, cry quits, have had enough, throw up the sponge, surrender, hold up one's hands, show the white flag, ask for terms; surrender on terms, capitulate; surrender at discretion, throw oneself on another's mercy; give oneself up, yield oneself, throw down one's arms, hand over one's sword, give one's parole; haul down the flag, strike one's colours; renounce authority, deliver the keys.
knuckle under, succumb, take the count, cave in, collapse; sag, wilt, faint, drop 684 vb. *be fatigued;* show no fight, take the line of least resistance, bow before the storm; be submissive, learn obedience, bow one's neck to the yoke, homage, do h. 745 vb. *be subject;* take one's medicine, swallow the pill 963 vb. *be punished;* apologize, eat humble pie, eat dirt 872 vb. *be humbled;* take it, take it from one, take it lying down, pocket the insult, grin and bear it, suffer in patience, digest, stomach, put up with 825 vb. *suffer;* bend, bow, kneel, kowtow, crouch, cringe, crawl 311 vb. *stoop;* grovel, lick the dust, lick the boots of, kiss the rod; fall on one's knees, throw oneself at the feet of, beg for mercy, cry *or* howl for m. 905 vb. *ask mercy;* yield to temptation, indulge.
Int. Kamerad! aman! hands up!
See: 286, 311, 327, 488, 621, 679, 684, 717, 728, 739, 745, 825, 860, 872, 905, 963.

722 Combatant. Army. Navy

N. *combatant,* fighter, battler, tussler, struggler 716 n. *contender;* aggressor, assailant, assaulter 712 n. *attacker;* besieger, stormer, escalader; stormtroops,

shock t., forlorn hope; belligerent, fighting man, warrior, brave; bodyguard 713 n. *defender*; gunman, bludgeon man, strong-arm m. 362n. *killer*; bully, bravo, rough, rowdy 904n. *ruffian*; fire-eater, swashbuckler, swaggerer, miles gloriosus, Pistol 877n. *boaster*; duellist 709n. *quarreller*; swordsman, sabreur, foilsman, fencer, sword, good s., blade; agonist 162n. *athlete*; gladiator, retiarius; fighting cock, gamecock; bull-fighter, toreador, matador, picador; grappler, wrestler, ju-jitsuist, judoist 716n. *wrestling*; competitor 716n. *contender*; champion, champ 644n. *exceller*; jouster, tilter; knight, knight-errant, paladin 707 n. *patron*; wrangler, disputer, controversialist 475n. *reasoner*; barrister, advocate 959n. *litigant*.

pugilist, pug, boxer, bruiser, sparring partner; prize-fighter, flyweight, bantam-w., feather-w., welter-w., middle-w., cruiser-w., heavy-w.; knuckle-fighter, glove-f. 716n. *pugilism*.

militarist, jingoist, chauvinist, expansionist, militant, crusader, ghazi; Rajput, Kshattriya, Samurai, Mameluke; professional soldier, free-lance, mercenary, free companion, soldier of fortune, adventurer, condottiere, war-lord; freebooter, night-rider, marauder, pirate, land p. 789 n. *robber*; war-monger.

soldier, army man, pongo; military man, soldier man, long-term soldier, regular; armed man, soldiery, troops (see *armed force*); campaigner, old c., conquistador; old soldier, veteran, Chelsea pensioner; fighting man, warrior, brave, myrmidon; man-at-arms, gendarme, redcoat, legionary, legionnaire, centurion; vexillary, standard-bearer, colour escort, colour sergeant, ensign, cornet; heavy-armed soldier, hoplite, phalangist; light-armed soldier, peltast; velites, skirmisher; sharpshooter, sniper, franc-tireur 287n. *shooter*; auxiliary, territorial, Home Guard, militiaman, fencible; yeomanry, yeoman; irregular, irregular troops, guerrilla, moss-trooper, cateran, kern, gallowglass, comitadji, bashi-bazouk; raider, tip-and-run r., fedayeen; underground fighter, Maquis; picked troops 644n. *élite*; guards, Swiss Guard, Switzer, Prætorian, Immortal, janissary, house-carl; Varangian Guard (see *armed force*);

effective, enlisted man; reservist; volunteer; pressed man; conscript, recruit, rookie; serviceman, Tommy, Tommy Atkins, G.I., doughboy, bingboy, Aussie, Anzac, poilu, sepoy, sowar, Gurkha, Sikh, Askari; woman soldier, female warrior, Amazon; battle-maid, valkyrie; Wren, W.A.S.P., W.A.A.C. (see *women's army*).

soldiery, cannon fodder, food for powder; gallant company, merry men, heroes; private, private soldier, common s., man-at-arms; targeteer, slinger, archer, bowyer, bowman, cross-b., arbalester; spearman, pikeman, pike, halberdier, hoplite, phalangist, lancer; arquebusier, matchlockman, musketeer, fusilier, rifleman, rifles, pistoleer, carabineer, bazookaman, grenadier, bombardier, gunner, matross, cannoneer, artilleryman; pioneer, sapper, miner, engineer; signalman; aircraftman; corporal, sergeant, top-s., ensign, cornet, lieutenant, shavetail 741 n. *army officer*.

army, host, camp; phalanx, legion; cohorts, big battalions; horde, mass 104n. *multitude*; warlike people, martial race; nation in arms, levée en masse, general levy, arrière-ban; National Guard, Home G.; militia, yeomanry; landsturm, landwehr; regular army, standing a., professional a., mercenary a., volunteer a., territorial a., conscript a., draft, class; the services, armed forces, all arms, air arm, naval a.

armed force, forces, troops, contingents, effectives, men, personnel; armament. armada; corps d'élite, ceremonial troops, guards, household troops; Household Cavalry, Royal Horse Guards, The Blues; Life Guards, The Tins; Old Guard, Young G., Swiss G., Prætorian G., Varangian G., Immortals, janissaries; picked troops, crack t., shock t., storm t., forlorn hope; spearhead, expeditionary force, striking f., flying column; parachute troops, para-troops, commando, Commandoes, task force, raiding party, guerrilla force; combat troops, field army, line, thin red l., front l., front-line troops, first échelon; wing, van, vanguard, rear, rearguard, centre, main body; second échelon, base troops, reserves, recruits, reinforcements, draft, levy; base, staff; detachment, picket, party, detail; patrol, night patrol, night-watch, sentry, sentinel,

vedette 660 n. *protector*; garrison, occupying force, occupation troops, army of occupation.

formation, array, line; square, British s., schiltron, phalanx; legion, cohort, century, decury, maniple; column, file, rank; unit, group, army g., corps, army c., division, armoured d., panzer d.; brigade, rifle b., light b., heavy b.; artillery brigade, battery; regiment, cavalry r., squadron, troop; battalion, company, platoon, section, squad, detail, party 74 n. *band*.

infantry, bayonets, foot-regiment, infantryman, foot-soldier, foot, peon; footslogger, P.B.I.; mountain infantry, light i.; chasseur, Jäger, Zouave.

cavalry, yeomanry; heavy cavalry, light c., sabres, horse, light h., cavalry regiment; horseman, cameleer, rider; mounted troops, mounted rifles, mounted police, mounted infantry, horse artillery; horse soldier, cavalryman, yeoman; trooper, sowar; chivalry, knight; man-at-arms, lancer, Uhlan, Hussar, cuirassier, dragoon, light d., heavy d., 'big men on big horses'; Ironsides, Cossack, Spahi, Croat, Pandour, rough-rider; armour, armoured car, tank, Panzer; charger, destrier 273 n. *war-horse*.

navy, sea-power, admiralty; sail, wooden walls; fleet arm, naval armament, armada; fleet, moth-ball f., flotilla, squadron; 'little ships'.

navy man, naval service, navy, senior service, silent s.; admiral, sea-lord 741 n. *naval officer*; naval architect, Seabee; sailor boy, sailor, sailor man 270 n. *mariner*; blue-jacket, man-o'-war man, able seaman, rating, pressed man; fore-topman; powder-monkey; coastguardsman; gobbie, gob, swab, swabbie; marine, jolly, leatherneck, Marine Corps; submariner, naval airman 270 n. *naval man*; privateer; naval reserve, R.N.R., Royal Naval Reserve; R.N.V.R., Royal Naval Volunteer Reserve, Wavy Navy.

warship, war vessel, war junk, war-galley, trireme, quinquereme, galleon, galleass 275 n. *ship*; man-o'-war, ship of the line, first-rater, seventy-four; armoured vessel, capital ship, battleship, dreadnought; turret ship, monitor, ironclad; cruiser, light c., armoured c.; raider, surface r., privateer, pirate ship; frigate, sloop, corvette, scout; patrol-boat, despatch-b.,

gunboat, torpedo-boat, mosquito b.; destroyer, torpedo-boat d., catamaran; fire-ship, hell-burner, bomb-vessel; block ship, mine-layer, mine-sweeper; submarine, atomic-powered s., U-boat; submarine chaser, eagle-boat, E-b.; Q-boat, mystery b.; aircraft carrier, flat-top; floating battery; landing-craft, duck, amphibian; transport, troopship, trooper; tender, store ship, supply s., ammunition s., fuel s., depôt s., parent s., guard-s., hospital s.; flagship, flotilla-leader.

air force, R.A.F., U.S. Air Force; Royal Air Force Volunteer Reserve; air arm, flying corps, air service, fleet air arm; squadron, flight, group, wing; warplane 276 n. *aircraft*; battle-plane, bomber, heavy b., light b., pilotless b., fighter, night f.; flying boat, Catalina, patrol plane, scout; transport plane, troop-carrier; Zeppelin, captive balloon, observation b., barrage-b. 276 n. *airship*; air-troops, air-borne division; parachute troops, para-troopers; aircraftman, ground staff; fighter pilot, bomber-p., air crew, bomb-aimer, weaponeer; air-force reserve.

women's army, Q.A.R.N.S. (Queen Alexandra's Royal Nursing Service); F.A.N.Y. (First Aid Nursing Yeomanry); A.F.S. (Auxiliary Fire Service); V.A.D. (Voluntary Aid Detachment); W.V.S. (Women's Voluntary Service); W.A.V.E.S., Waves, (Women Accepted for Voluntary Emergency Service); W.A.C. (Women's Army Corps); W.A.A.C. (Women's Auxiliary Army Corps); W.R.A.C. (Women's Royal Army Corps); W.R.A.F. (Women's Royal Air Force); W.A.F. (Women in the Air Force); W.A.S.P. (Women's Air Force Service Pilots); W.A.F.S. (Women's Auxiliary Ferrying Squadron); W.R.N.S., Wrens (Women's Royal Naval Service.)

See: 74, 104, 162, 270, 273, 275, 276, 287, 362, 475, 644, 660, 707, 709, 712, 713, 716, 741, 789, 877, 904, 959.

723 Arms

N. *arm* (see *weapon*); fleet arm, air a. 722 n. *combatant*; arming, armament, munitioning, munitions, manufacture of m.;

armaments, armaments race; arms traffic, gun-running; ballistics, rocketry, gunnery, musketry, archery, bowmanship.

arsenal, armoury, gun-room, gun-rack, arms chest, stand of arms; arms depôt 632n. *storage*; magazine, powder-m., powder-barrel, powder-keg, powder-flask, powder-horn; caisson, limber-box, magazine-chamber; bullet-pouch, cartridge-belt, bandolier, cartridge-clip; arrow-case, quiver; scabbard, sheath; holster, pistol-case 194n. *receptacle*.

weapon, arm, deterrent; deadly weapon, defensive w.; armour, plate, mail 713b. *defence*; offensive weapon 712n. *attack*; conventional weapon, A.B.C. weapons (atomic w., bacteriological w., chemical w.), T.N.W. (Tactical Nuclear Weapon); anti-missile weapon; weapon of reprisal, Vergeltungswaffe, V.1, V.2; secret weapon, death ray; gas, poison g., mustard g., lachrymatory g., tear g. 659n. *poison*; natural weapon, teeth, claws, nails, horn, antler.

missile weapon, javelin, knobkerrie, harpoon, dart, discus; bolas, lasso; boomerang, woomerang, woomera, throwstick; arrow, reed-a., cloth-yard a., barbed a., shaft, bolt, quarrel; arrowhead, barb; stone, brick, brickbat; slingstone, shot, ball, bullet, pellet, shell, star s., gas s., shrapnel, whizz-bang, rocket (see *ammunition*); bow, long-b., cross-b., arbalest, balister, catapult, mangonel, sling; blow-pipe; bazooka, rocket-thrower (see *gun*); ballistic missile, I.C.B.M., Inter-Continental Ballistic Missile; thunderbolt.

club, mace, knobkerrie, knobstick, war-hammer 279n. *hammer*; battering-ram 279n. *ram*; bat, staff, stave, stick, cane, ferule, ruler, switch, rattan, lathi, quarter-staff, hand-s.; life-preserver, bludgeon, cudgel, shillelagh, blackjack, sandbag, knuckle-duster, brass knuckle, cosh, bicycle-chain, truncheon.

spear, hunting s., fishing s., eel-s., harpoon, gaff; lance, javelin, jerid, pike, sarissa; partisan, bill, halberd 256n. *sharp point*.

axe, battle-axe, tomahawk, hatchet, war-h., halberd, bill, gisarme; pole-axe, chopper 256n. *sharp edge*.

side-arms, sword; heraldic sword, seax; dagger, bayonet, sword-b.; cold steel, naked s.; broadsword, glaive, claymore,

two-edged sword, two-handed s.; cutlass, hanger, whinyard, short sword, swordstick; sabre, scimitar, yataghan, falchion, snickersnee; blade, fine b., bilbo, Toledo, Ferrara; rapier, tuck; fencing sword, épée, foil; dirk, skean, poniard, dudgeon, miséricorde, stylet, stiletto 256n. *sharp point*; matchet, machete, kukri, creese, kris, parang, knife, bowie-k., flick-k., gravity-blade k., pigsticker 256n. *sharp edge*.

fire-arm, small arms, portable gun, hand g., caliver, arquebus, hackbut, hackbush; matchlock, wheel-lock, flint-l., fusil, musket, Brown Bess; blunderbuss, muzzle-loader, smooth-bore, escopette, carbine; breechloader, chassepot, needle-gun; rifle, magazine r., repeating-r., Winchester; fowling-piece, sporting gun, shot-g., single-barrelled g., double-barrelled g., elephant g.; Enfield rifle, Lee-Enfield, Lee-Metford, Martini-Henry, Mauser, Snider, Hotchkiss; bore, calibre; muzzle; trigger, lock; magazine; breech, butt, gunstock; sight, backsight; ramrod.

pistol, duelling p., horse-p.; petronel, pistolet; six-shooter, colt, revolver, repeater, zipgun, rod, gat, shooting-iron; automatic pistol; Beretta, Luger, Webley-Scott.

toy gun, pop-g., air-g., wind-g., water pistol, pea-shooter, blow-pipe 287n. *propellant*.

gun, guns, ordnance, cannonry, artillery, light a., heavy a., mountain a.; horse artillery, galloping guns; battery, broadside; park, artillery p., gun-p.; cannon, brass c., bombard, falconet, swivel, gingal, basilisk, petard, pederero, patararo, carronade, culverin, demi-c.; serpentine, sling; demi-cannon, saker, drake, rabonet, base, murderer, perier, mortar; stern-chaser, bow-c.; piece, field-piece, field-gun, siege-g.; great gun, heavy g., cannon-royal, seventy-four, heavy metal, Big Bertha; howitzer, trench-mortar, mine-thrower, minenwerfer, Minnie, trench gun; anti-aircraft gun, anti-tank g., bazooka; gun, quick-firing g., Gatling g., mitrailleuse, pom-pom, Maxim, Maxim-Nordenfelt g., Lewis g., machine-g., light machine-g., Bren g., Sten g., sub-machine g., Thompson submachine-g., Tommy g.; flammenwerfer, flame-thrower; gun-lock, gun-carriage, limber, caisson; gun-emplacement, rocket site.

ammunition, live a., live shot, sharp s.; round of ammunition, round; powder and shot, powder and ball; shot, round s., case s., langrage, langrel, canister shot, grape s., chain s., small s., mitraille, buckshot; ball, cannon b., bullet, expanding b., soft-nosed b., dum-dum b.; projectile 287n. *missile*; slug, stone, sling-shot, pellet; shell, shrapnel-s.; charge, priming, warhead; wad, cartouche, cartridge, ball-c., live c.; spent cartridge, dud; cartridge-belt, cartridge-clip; cartridge-case, shell-c.; cap, detonator, fuse.

explosive, propellant; powder, blasting p., gunpowder; saltpetre, 'villainous s.'; high explosive, lyddite, cordite, melinite, gun-cotton, dynamite, gelignite, T.N.T., trinitro-toluene, nitro-glycerine, fulgurite; Greek fire; cap, detonator; priming, charge, warhead, atomic w.; fissionable material.

bomb, explosive device; bombshell, egg; grenade, hand-g., Mills bomb; megaton bomb, atomic b., nuclear b., hydrogen b.; mushroom, fall-out; blockbuster, Molotov cocktail; stink-bomb, gas-b., incendiary b., napalm b.; carcass, Greek fire; mine, land-m., magnetic m., acoustic m.; booby-trap; depth-charge, ash-can, torpedo, submarine t., aerial t.; flying bomb, P-plane, V.1, doodlebug, V.2; rocket bomb; time-bomb, infernal machine.

See: 194, 256, 279, 287, 632, 659, 712, 713, 722.

724 Arena

N. *arena*, field, field of action; ground, terrain; centre, scene, stage, theatre; hustings, platform, floor; airfield, flying ground, landing g.; flight deck 276n. *aircraft*; amphitheatre, Flavian a., Colosseum; stadium, stand, grandstand; campus, Campus Martius, Champs de Mars, parade ground, training g. 539n. *training school*; forum, market-place 76n. *focus*; hippodrome, circus, course, race-c., turf; track, running-t., cinder-t., dog-t.; ring, bull-r., boxing r., ropes; rink, skating r., ice-r.; palæstra, callisthenium, gymnasium, gym; range, shooting r., rifle-r., butts, Bisley; riding-school; hunting field; playground, gutter, beach, lido,

pier, fair-ground 837n. *pleasure ground*; playing ground, playing field, football f., gridiron, diamond, pitch, cricket p.; court, tennis c., fives c., squash c.; bowling-green, bowling-alley, skittle a.; lists, tilt-yard, tilting-ground; cockpit, beargarden; chess-board, checker-board; bridge-table; auction room; examination hall; court-room 956n. *law-court*.

battle-ground, battlefield, field of battle, tented field; field of blood, Aceldama; theatre of war, war theatre, front, front line, firing l., trenches, no-man's-land; sector, salient, bulge, pocket; beach-head, bridge-h.; camp, enemy's c.

See: 76, 276, 539, 837, 956.

725 Completion

N. *completion*, finish, termination, conclusion, end of the matter 69n. *end*; terminus 295n. *goal*; issue, upshot 154n. *eventuality*; result, end r., final r., end product 157n. *effect*; fullness 54n. *completeness*; fulfilment 635n. *sufficiency*; maturity, readiness, perfect r. 669n. *maturation*; consummation, culmination, climax, ne plus ultra 646n. *perfection*; exhaustiveness, thoroughness 455n. *attention*; elaboration, rounding off, finishing off, mopping up, winding up; roofing, topping out; top, crown, superstructure, keystone, coping-stone 213n. *summit*; missing link 627n. *requirement*; last touch, last stroke, crowning s., final s., finishing s., coup de grâce; achievement, fait accompli, work done, finished product (see *effectuation*); boiling point, danger p., breaking p., last straw 236n. *limit*; dénouement, catastrophe, last act, final scene 69n. *finality*.

effectuation, carrying through, follow t.; execution, discharge, implementation; despatch, performance 676n. *action*; accomplishment, achievement 727n. *success*; elaboration, working out; holing out.

Adj. *completive*, completory, completing, perfective; crowning, culminating 213 adj. *topmost*; finishing, conclusive, final, last 69adj. *ending*; unanswerable, crushing; thorough, thorough-going, whole-hogging 599adj. *resolute*.

completed, well-c., full 54adj. *complete*;

done, well-d., achieved, accomplished etc. vb.; wrought out, highly wrought, elaborate 646 adj. *perfect*; sped, well-s. 727 adj. *successful*.

Vb. *carry through*, follow t., follow up, hole out; drive home, clinch, seal, set the seal on, put the seal to, seal up; clear up, mop up, wipe up, finish off, polish off; dispose of, despatch, give the coup de grâce; complete, consummate, put the finishing touch, cast off (knitting), nail the roof on, top out 54 vb. *make complete*; elaborate, hammer out, work o. 646 vb. *perfect*; ripen, bring to a head, bring to the boil, bring to boiling point 669 vb. *mature*; sit out, see out, see it through (see *carry out*); get through, get shot of, dispose of, bring to its close 69 vb. *terminate*; set at rest 266 vb. *bring to rest*.

carry out, see through, effect, enact 676 vb. *do*; despatch, execute, discharge, implement, effectuate, realize, compass, bring about, accomplish, consummate, achieve 727 vb. *succeed*; make short work of, make no bones of; do thoroughly, leave no ends hanging, not do by halves, go the whole hog, be in at the death; deliver the goods, bring home the bacon, be as good as one's word, fill the bill.

climax, cap, crown all 213 vb. *crown*; culminate, stand at its peak; scale the heights, conquer Everest; reach boiling point, come to a crisis; reach the limit, touch bottom; put the lid on, add the last straw; come to its end, attain one's e., touch the goal 295 vb. *arrive*; die a natural death, die in one's bed; have enough of, be through with 635 vb. *have enough*.

See: 54, 69, 154, 157, 213, 236, 266, 295, 455, 599, 627, 635, 646, 669, 676, 727.

726 Non-completion

N. *non-completion*, non-success 728 n. *failure*; non-performance, inexecution, neglect 458 n. *negligence*; non-fulfilment 636 n. *insufficiency*; deficiency, deficit 307 n. *shortcoming*; lack 55 n. *incompleteness*; unripeness, immaturity 670 n. *undevelopment*; never-ending task, Penelope's web, Sisyphean labour, argument in a circle, recurring decimal 71 n. *continuity*; perfunctoriness, superficiality a lick and a promise 456 n. *inattention*;

tinkering, work undone, job half-done, ends left hanging, points uncleared; no finality, no result, drawn battle, drawn game; stalemate, deadlock; semi-completion, launching stage.

Adj. *uncompleted*, partial, fragmentary 55 adj. *incomplete*; unfinalized, unbegun 55 adj. *unfinished*; undone, unperformed, unexecuted, unachieved, unaccomplished; unrealized, half-done, half-finished, half-begun, hardly b. 458 adj. *neglected*; half-baked, underdone, unripe 670 adj. *immature*; unthorough, perfunctory, superficial; not cleared up, left hanging, left in the air; lacking finish, unelaborated, not worked out, inchoate, sketchy, in outline 647 adj. *imperfect*; unbleached, unprocessed, semi-processed; never-ending 71 adj. *continuous*.

Vb. *not complete*, hardly begin, leave undone, leave in the air, leave hanging 458 vb. *neglect*; skip, scamp, do by halves, tinker, paper over the cracks 636 vb. *not suffice*; scotch the snake not kill it 655 vb. *wound*; give up, not follow up, not follow through; fall out, drop o., not stay the course; fail of one's goal, fail of one's end, fall down on 728 vb. *fail*; defer, postpone, put off to tomorrow 136 vb. *put off*.

Adv. *on the stocks*, under construction, on the anvil, in preparation, in process of; before the finish.

See: 55, 71, 136, 307, 456, 458, 636, 647, 655, 670, 728.

727 Success

N. *success*, glory 866 n. *famousness*; success all round, happy outcome, happy ending, favourable issue; prowess, success story, progress, steady advance, God-speed, good s., time well spent 285 n. *progression*; fresh advance, breakthrough; one's day, continued success, run of luck, good fortune 730 n. *prosperity*; advantage, lead, temporary l., first blood 34 n. *vantage*; momentary success, flash in the pan; exploit, feat, achievement 676 n. *deed*; accomplishment, goal 725 n. *completion*; a success, feather in one's cap, triumph, hit, smash h., triumphant success, howling s., knock-out, kill; good hit, winning h., good shot 694 n. *skill*; lucky stroke, fluke

618 n. *non-design*; hat-trick, stroke of genius, master-stroke, happy s., scoring s. 694 n. *masterpiece*; trump, trump card, winning c., card up one's sleeve 623 n. *contrivance*; success in examination, pass, qualification; match-winning 34 n. *superiority.*

victory, infliction of defeat, beating, whipping, licking, trouncing 728 n. *defeat*; conquest, subdual 745 n. *subjection*; successful attack, expugnation, storm, escalade 712 n. *attack*; honours of battle, the best of it, triumph; win, game and match; outright win, complete victory, checkmate; narrow win, Pyrrhic victory, well-fought field; easy win, runaway victory, love game, walk-over, push-o., picnic; crushing victory, quelling v., slam, grand s.; kill, knock-out, K.O.; mastery, ascendancy, upper hand, whip-h., advantage, edge, winning position, certain victory 34 n. *vantage*; no defeat, stalemate 28 n. *draw*; celebration of victory, triumph, ovation, epinician ode 876 n. *celebration.*

victor, winner, match-winner, champion, world-beater, medallist, prizeman, first, double f. 644 n. *exceller*; winning side, the winners; conqueror, conquistador, thunderbolt of war; defeater, beater, vanquisher, overcomer, subjugator, subduer, queller; master, master of the field, master of the situation; a success, successful rival, successful man, self-made m., rising m. 730 n. *made man*; triumpher, triumphator, conquering hero.

Adj. *successful*, effective, efficacious; crushing, quelling; efficient; sovereign 658 n. *remedial*; well-spent, fruitful 640 adj. *profitable*; happy, lucky; felicitous, masterly 694 adj. *skilful*; ever-victorious, unbeatable (see *unbeaten*); match-winning, never-failing, surefire, foolproof; unerring, infallible, sure-footed 473 adj. *certain*; prize-winning, victorious, world-beating 644 adj. *excellent*; winning, leading, up, one up 34 adj. *superior*; on top, in the ascendant, rising, on the up and up, sitting pretty 730 adj. *prosperous*; triumphant, crowning; triumphal, epinician; crowned with success, flushed with victory; glorious 866 adj. *renowned.*

unbeaten, undefeated, unsubdued, unquelled, unvanquished, unovercome 599 adj. *resolute*; unbeatable, unconquerable, ever-victorious, invincible.

Vb. *succeed*, succeed in, effect, accomplish, achieve, compass 725 vb. *carry through*; be successful, make out, win one's spurs; make a success of, make a go of, make short work of, rise to the occasion; make good, rise, do well, get promotion, work one's way up the ladder, work one's way up, come to the top 730 vb. *prosper*; pass, make the grade, qualify, graduate, come off well, come well out of it, come off with flying colours, come out on top, have the best of it 34 vb. *be superior*; advance, break through, make a breakthrough 285 vb. *progress*; speed well, strive to some purpose, gain one's end, reach one's goal, secure one's object, obtain one's objective, attain one's purpose; pull it off, be as good as one's word, bring home the bacon; have a success, score a s., make a hit, make a kill; hit the jackpot, break the bank; score a point, win a p., carry a p.; arrive, be a success, get around, make one's mark, click.

be successful, be efficacious, be effective, come off, come right in the end; answer, answer the purpose, do the trick, ring the bell, show results, turn out well; turn up trumps, rise to the occasion; do the job, do wonders, do marvels; compass, manage 676 vb. *do*; work, act, work like magic, act like a charm 173 vb. *operate*; take effect, tell, pull its weight 178 vb. *influence*; bear fruit 171 vb. *be fruitful*; get it, hit it, hit the nail on the head; play one's hand well, not put a foot wrong, never go w.; be sure-footed, keep on the right side of; have the ball at one's feet, hold all the trumps; be irresistible, not know the meaning of failure, brush obstacles aside 701 vb. *do easily*; not know when one is beaten, come up smiling 599 vb. *be resolute*; avoid defeat, hold one's own, maintain one's position 599 vb. *stand firm.*

triumph, have one's day, be crowned with success, wear the laurels of victory, erect a trophy 876 vb. *celebrate*; crow, crow over 877 vb. *boast*; score, score off, be one up on; triumph over difficulties, contrive a success, manage, surmount, overcome obstacles, get over a snag, sweep difficulties out of the way; find a loophole, find a way out, tide over 667 vb. *escape*; make head against, stem the current, weather the storm 715 vb. *resist*;

reap the fruits, reap the harvest 771 vb. *gain.*

overmaster, be too much for, be more than a match for 34 vb. *be superior*; master, overcome, overpower, overmatch, overthrow, overturn, override, overtrump 306 vb. *outdo*; have the advantage, take the a., seize the a., hold the a., keep the a., prevail 34 vb. *predominate*; have one on the hip, checkmate, mate, euchre, trump, ruff; conquer, vanquish, quell, subdue, subject, suppress, put down, crush, reduce 745 vb. *subjugate*; capture, carry, take, storm, take by s., escalade 712 vb. *attack.*

defeat (see *overmaster*); discomfit, dash, put another's nose out of joint, cook one's goose; repulse, rebuff 292 vb. *repel*; confound, dismay 854 vb. *frighten*; best, be too good for, get the better of, get the upper hand, get the whip-h. 34 vb. *be superior*; worst, outplay, outpoint, outflank, outmanœuvre, outgeneral, outclass, outshine 306 vb. *outdo*; disconcert, cut the ground from under one's feet, trip, lay by the heels, baffle, bring to a stand 702 vb. *obstruct*; gravel, nonplus 474 vb. *puzzle*; beat, lick, thrash, whip, trounce, swamp, overwhelm, crush, drub, give a drubbing, roll in the dust, trample underfoot, trample upon; beat hollow, rout, put to flight, scatter 75 vb. *disperse*; silence, put the lid on, put hors de combat, put out of court 165 vb. *suppress*; down one's opponent, flatten, crush, put out for the count, knock out; knock for six, hit for s.; bowl out, skittle o.; run hard, corner, bay, drive to the wall, check, put in check 661 vb. *endanger*; put an end to, wipe out, do for, dish 165 vb. *destroy*; sink, send to the bottom 313 vb. *founder*; break, bankrupt 801 vb. *impoverish.*

win, win the battle, gain the day, achieve victory, defeat the enemy, down one's opponent (see *defeat*); be victorious, remain in possession of the field, erect a trophy, claim the victory; come off best, come off with flying colours; win hands down, carry all before one, have it all one's own way, romp home, have a walk-over 701 vb. *do easily*; win on points, scrape home, survive; win the last battle, win the last round, succeed in the final; win the match, take the prize, take the cup, walk off with the pot, gain the palm, wear the crown, wear the laurel-wreath; be-

come champion, beat all comers 34 vb. *be superior.*

Adv. *successfully,* swimmingly, marvellously well; to some purpose, to good p., with good result, with good effect, with magical e.; to one's heart's content, beyond one's fondest dreams, beyond all expectation; with flying colours, in triumph.

See: 28, 34, 75, 165, 171, 173, 178, 285, 292, 306, 313, 473, 474, 599, 618, 623, 640, 644, 658, 661, 667, 676, 694, 701, 702, 712, 715, 725, 728, 730, 745, 771, 801, 854, 866, 876, 877.

728 Failure

N. *failure,* non-success, successlessness, negative result; no luck, off day 731 n. *ill fortune*; non-fulfilment 726 n. *non-completion*; frustration, slip 'twixt the cup and the lip 702 n. *hindrance*; inefficacy, ineffectiveness 161 n. *ineffectuality*; vain attempt, abortive a., wild-goose chase, futile effort, no result 641 n. *lost labour*; mess, muddle, bungle, foozle 695 n. *bungling*; abortion, miscarriage 172 n. *unproductivity*; hopeless failure, dead f., dud show, wash-out, fiasco, flop, frost; flunk, no ball, bosh shot, misaim, misfire, slip, omission, faux pas 495 n. *mistake*; no go, dead stop, halt 145 n. *stop*; engine failure, seizing up, breakdown 702 n. *hitch*; collapse, fall, stumble, trip 309 n. *descent*; claudication, titubation 161 n. *impotence*; anticlimax, lame and impotent conclusion 509 n. *disappointment*; losses 772 n. *loss*; bankruptcy 805 n. *insolvency.*

defeat, bafflement, bewilderment, puzzlement 474 n. *uncertainty*; nonplus, deadlock, stalemate, stand 145 n. *stop*; lost battle, repulse, rebuff, bloody nose, check, reverse; no move left, checkmate, mate, fool's m.; the worst of it, discomfiture, beating, drubbing, hiding, licking, thrashing, trouncing; retreat; flight 290 n. *recession*; dispersal 75 n. *dispersion*; stampede, panic 854 n. *fear*; rout, landslide; fall, downfall, collapse, débâcle; wreck, perdition, graveyard 165 n. *ruin*; lost cause, losing game, lost g., non-suit; deathblow, quietus; utter defeat, total d., final d., Waterloo; conquest, subjugation 745 n. *subjection.*

loser, unsuccessful competitor, baffled enemy, defeated rival; also-ran, non-starter; has-been, extinct volcano; defeatist, pessimist, misery 834 n. *moper*; foozler, sorcerer's apprentice 697 n. *bungler*; dud, failure, plucked examinee; sacrifice, victim, prey 544 n. *dupe*; underdog 35 n. *inferior*; beat generation, beatnik 25 n. *misfit*; bankrupt, insolvent 805 n. *non-payer*; the losers, losing side, the defeated, the conquered, the vanquished, the fallen.

Adj. *unsuccessful*, ineffective, pale; inglorious, successless, empty-handed; unlucky 731 adj. *unfortunate*; vain, bootless, negative, profitless; dud, misfired, hanging fire; miscarried, stillborn, aborted, abortive, premature; stultified; jilted, ditched, left holding the baby; feckless, manqué, failed, plucked, ploughed, flunked; unplaced, losing, failing; stumbling, tripping, groping, wandering, out of one's depth 474 adj. *uncertain*.

defeated, beaten, bested, worsted, pipped; non-suited, cast; baffled, thwarted, foiled 702 adj. *hindered*; disconcerted, dashed, discomfited, hoist with one's own petard; outmanœuvred, outmatched, outplayed, outvoted; outclassed, outshone 35 adj. *inferior*; thrashed, licked, whacked; on the losing side, among the also-rans, unplaced; in retreat, in flight 290 adj. *receding*; routed, scattered, put to flight; swamped, overwhelmed, sunk; overborne, overthrown, struck down, borne down, knocked out, kaput, brought low, fallen; captured, made a prey, victimized, sacrificed.

grounded, stranded, wrecked, on the rocks, on one's beam-ends 165 adj. *destroyed*; unhorsed, dismounted, thrown, thrown on one's back, brought low; ruined, bankrupt, insolvent 805 adj. *non-paying*.

Vb. *fail*, not succeed, have no success, have no result; be unsuccessful, — ploughed, — plucked etc.adj.; fall down on, flunk, foozle, muddle, botch, bungle 495 vb. *blunder*; not make the grade, be found wanting 636 vb. *not suffice*; fail one, let one down 509 vb. *disappoint*; misaim, misdirect, miss one's aim, go wide, make a bosh shot, miss, hit the wrong target 282 vb. *deviate*; get nothing out of it, get no change out of it, draw a blank, return empty-handed, lose one's pains, labour in vain, have shot one's bolt 641 vb. *waste*

effort; fall, collapse, slide, tumble off one's perch 309 vb. *tumble*; break down, come to pieces, come unstuck; seize, seize up, conk out; stop, come to a dead stop, come up against a blank wall, come to a dead end; stick, stick in the mud, bog down, get bogged d. 145 vb. *cease*; come to a sticky end, come to a bad e. 655 vb. *deteriorate*; go on the rocks, run aground, ground, sink 313 vb. *founder*; make a loss, make losses, crash, bust, break, go bankrupt 805 vb. *not pay*.

miscarry, fall still-born, abort; misfire, hang fire, flash in the pan, fizzle out; fall, fall to the ground, crash 309 vb. *tumble*; come to naught, come to nothing, end in futility 641 vb. *be useless*; fail of success, come to grief, burst, bust, explode, blow up; flop, prove a fiasco, turn out a frost; not go well, go wrong, go amiss, go awry, gang agley, take a wrong turn, take an ugly turn; do no good, make things worse 832 vb. *aggravate*; dash one's hopes, frustrate one's expectations 509 vb. *disappoint*; falter, limp, hobble 278 vb. *move slowly*.

be defeated, lose, lose out, suffer defeat, take a beating, lose the day, lose the battle, lose the match; lose the election, lose one's seat, lose the vote, be outvoted; just lose, just miss, get pipped on the post; get the worst of it, come off second best, go off with one's tail between one's legs, lick one's wounds; lose hands down, come in last, not win a point; take the count, bite the dust; fall, succumb 745 vb. *be subject*; be captured, fall a prey to, be victimized; retreat, lose ground 290 vb. *recede*; take to flight 620 vb. *run away*; admit defeat, give one best, have enough, cry quits 721 vb. *submit*; have not a leg to stand on, have the ground cut from under one's feet; go downhill 655 vb. *deteriorate*; go to the wall, go to the dogs 165 vb. *be destroyed*.

Adv. *unsuccessfully*, like a loser, to no purpose, to little or no p., in vain.

See: 25, 35, 75, 145, 161, 165, 172, 278, 282, 290, 309, 313, 474, 495, 509, 544, 620, 636, 641, 655, 695, 697, 702, 721, 726, 731, 745, 772, 805, 832, 834, 854.

729 Trophy

N. *trophy*, sign of success; war-trophy, spoils, capture, captives 790 n. *booty*;

spolia opima, scalp, head; scars, wounds 655n. *wound*; memorial, war-m., memento 505n. *reminder*; triumphal arch 548n. *monument*; triumph, ovation 876n. *celebration*; plum, benefit, benefit match; prize, first p., booby p., consolation p. 962n. *reward*; sports trophy, Ashes, cup, pot, plate; award, Oscar a.; bays, laurels, crown, laurel c., bay c., coronal, chaplet, garland, wreath, palm, palm of victory; epinician ode, pat on the back; favour, feather in one's cap, sleeve, love-knot 547 n. *badge*; flying colours 875n. *ostentation*; glory 866n. *repute*.

decoration, honour 870n. *title*; blushing honours, battle h., spurs 866n. *honours*; citation, mention in despatches; ribbon, blue r., cordon bleu; athletic honour, blue, oar; medal, gong, star, cross, garter, order, khilat; service stripe, long-service medal, war-m., campaign m.; Victoria Cross, Military C., Croix de Guerre, Iron Cross, Pour le Mérite; Distinguished Service Order; Distinguished Service Cross, Distinguished Flying C., Air Force C., Congressional Medal, Medal of Honour; George Cross, Medal for Merit, civic crown.

See: 505, 547, 548, 655, 790, 866, 870, 875, 876, 962.

730 Prosperity

N. *prosperity,* well-being; economic prosperity, welfare, weal 824n. *happiness*; thriving, health and wealth, having it good 727n. *success*; booming economy, boom; roaring trade, seller's market, favourable trade balance, no unemployment; crest of the wave, high tide, flood, affluence 635n. *plenty*; luxury 800n. *wealth*; golden touch, Midas t.; flesh-pots, fat of the land, milk and honey, loaves and fishes, flesh-pots of Egypt, chicken in every pot, full dinner-pail; auspiciousness, favour, smiles of fortune, good f., blessings, godsend, crowning mercy, goodness and mercy 615n. *good*; luck, run of l., good l., break, lucky b., luck of the draw 159n. *chance*; glory, honour and g., renown 866n. *prestige*.

palmy days, heyday, floruit; halcyon days, bright d., summer, sunshine, fair weather, fair wind, break in the clouds, blue streak;

piping times, easy t.; clover, velvet, bed of roses 376n. *euphoria*; bonanza, golden times, Golden Age, Saturnia Regna, Saturnian Age, Ram Raj 824n. *happiness*; spacious times, Periclean Age, Augustan A., Pax Romana, Elizabethan Age.

made man, man of substance, man of property 800n. *rich man*; rising man, prosperous m., successful m.; favourite of the gods, child of fortune, lucky fellow, lucky dog; arriviste, upstart, parvenu, nouveau riche, profiteer; celebrity, hero 866n. *person of repute*; lion 890n. *favourite*.

Adj. *prosperous,* thriving, flourishing, booming 727adj. *successful*; rising, doing well, up and coming, on the up and up; on the make, profiteering; set-up, established, well-to-do, well-off, warm, comfortable, comfortably off 800adj. *moneyed*; riding high on the hog's back, riding on the crest of a wave, buoyant; fortunate, lucky, born with a silver spoon in one's mouth, born under a lucky star; in clover, on velvet; at ease, in bliss; looking prosperous, fat, sleek, euphoric.

palmy, balmy, halcyon, golden, couleur de rose, rosy; piping, blissful, blessed; providential, favourable, promising, auspicious, propitious, cloudless, clear, fine, fair, set f.; glorious, spacious, ample; euphoric, agreeable, cosy 376adj. *comfortable*.

Vb. *prosper,* thrive, flourish, have one's day; do well, fare w., have a good time of it 376vb. *enjoy*; bask in sunshine, make hay, live in clover, lie on velvet, have it easy, live on milk and honey, live on the fat of the land, 'never have had it so good'; batten on, grow fat, feed well 301vb. *eat*; blossom, bloom, flower 171vb. *be fruitful*; win glory 866vb. *have repute*; boom, drive a roaring trade, enjoy a seller's market; profiteer 771vb. *gain*; get on, rise in the world, make one's way, work one's way up, arrive 727vb. *succeed*; make money, make a fortune, make one's pile, feather one's nest 800vb. *get rich*; go on well, run smoothly, run on oiled wheels 258vb. *go smoothly*; go on swimmingly, swim with the tide, sail before the wind; keep afloat, keep one's head above water, do well enough.

have luck, have all the l., have a stroke of l., have a good break, have a run of luck; strike lucky, strike oil, strike a rich vein,

be on to a good thing; fall on one's feet, enjoy the smiles of fortune, bear a charmed life, be born under a lucky star, be born with a silver spoon in one's mouth, have the ball at one's feet.

be auspicious,—propitious etc.adj.; promise, promise well, set fair; favour, prosper, profit; look kindly on, look benignly on, smile on, shine on, bless, shed blessings on; water, fertilize, make blossom like the rose; turn out well, take a good turn, take a favourable t., turn up trumps 644 vb. *do good*; glorify 866vb. *honour.*

Adv. *prosperously,* swimmingly 727adv. *successfully,* beyond one's wildest dreams, beyond the dreams of avarice; in the swim, in clover, on velvet.

See: 159, 171, 258, 301, 376, 615, 635, 644, 727, 771, 800, 824, 866, 890.

731 Adversity

N. *adversity,* adverse circumstances, misfortune, frowns of fortune, mixed blessing (see *ill fortune*); continual struggle, weary way 700n. *difficulty*; hardship, hard life, no bed of roses 825n. *suffering*; groaning, travail 377n. *pain*; bad times, hard t., ill t., iron age, ice a., dark a., hell upon earth, vale of sorrows 616n. *evil*; burden, load, pressure, pressure of the times; ups and downs of life, vicissitude 154n. *eventuality*; troubles, sea of t., peck of t., trials, cares, worries 825n. *worry*; wretchedness, misery, despondency, Slough of Despond 834n. *dejection*; bitter cup, bitter pill 872 n. *humiliation*; cup, cup of sorrows 825n. *sorrow*; curse, blight, blast, plague, scourge, infliction, visitation 659n. *bane*; bleakness, cold wind, draught, chill, cold, winter 380n. *coldness*; gloom 418n. *darkness*; ill wind, cross w.; blow, hard b., blow between the eyes 704n. *opposition*; setback, check, rebuff, reverse 728n. *defeat*; rub, pinch, plight, funeral 700n. *predicament*; bad patch, rainy day 655n. *deterioration*; slump, recession, depression 679n. *inactivity*; dark clouds, gathering c. 900n. *threat*; decline, fall, downfall 165n. *ruin*; broken fortune, want, need, distress, extremity 801n. *poverty.*

ill fortune, misfortune, bad fortune, outrageous f.; bad luck, bad cess, ill luck; no luck, no luck this time, ill success 728n.

failure; evil dispensation, evil star, malign influence 645n. *badness*; hard case, raw deal, rotten hand, chicane, Yarborough; ill lot, hard l., hard fate, hard lines; ill hap, mishap, mischance, misadventure, contretemps, accident, casualty 159n. *chance*; disaster, calamity, catastrophe, the worst.

unlucky person, constant loser, poor risk; sport of fortune, plaything of fate, Jonah; star-crossed lover 728n. *loser*; underdog 35n. *inferior*; new poor 801n. *poor man*; lame dog, lame duck 163n. *weakling*; scapegoat, victim, anvil, chopping-block, wretch, poor w. 825n. *sufferer*; prey 544n. *dupe.*

Adj. *adverse,* hostile, frowning, ominous, sinister, inauspicious, unfavourable; bleak, cold; opposed, cross, thwart, contrary, untoward 704adj. *opposing*; malign 645adj. *harmful*; dire, dreadful, ruinous 165adj. *destructive*; disastrous, calamitous, catastrophic; too bad 645adj. *bad.*

unprosperous, unblest, inglorious 728adj. *unsuccessful*; not doing well, badly off, not well off 801adj. *poor*; in trouble, up against it, under adverse circumstances, clouded, under a cloud 700adj. *in difficulties*; declining, on the wane, on the down grade, on one's last legs, on the road to ruin 655adj. *deteriorated*; in the wars, in hard case, in an ill plight, in extremities, in utmost need.

unfortunate, ill-fated, unlucky, ill-starred, star-crossed, planet-struck, blasted; unblest, luckless, hapless, poor, wretched, miserable, undone, unhappy; stricken, doomed, devoted, accursed; not lucky, out of luck, down on one's luck; out of favour, under a cloud, out of the sun 924 adj. *disapproved*; born to evil, born under an evil star; liable to accident, accident-prone.

Vb. *have trouble,* be in t., be born to t., be one's own worst enemy; stew in one's own juice; be fortune's sport, be the victim of fate, have no luck; be in for it, go through it, be hard pressed, be up against it, fall foul of 700vb. *be in difficulty*; strike a bad patch, meet adversity 825vb. *suffer*; suffer humiliation 872vb. *be humbled*; come to grief 728vb. *miscarry*; be in low water, feel the pinch, feel the draught, fall on evil days, have seen better d. 801 vb. *be poor*; go downhill, go down in the

world, fall from one's high estate, decline 655vb. *deteriorate*; sink 313vb. *founder*; come to a bad end 728vb. *fail*; go to rack and ruin, go to the dogs 165vb. *be destroyed*; go hard with, be difficult for 700vb. *be difficult.*

Adv. *in adversity*, from bad to worse, from the frying pan into the fire; as ill luck would have it, by mischance, by misadventure.

See: 35, 154, 159, 163, 165, 313, 377, 380, 418, 544, 616, 645, 655, 659, 679, 700, 704, 728, 801, 825, 834, 872, 900, 924.

732 Mediocrity

N. *mediocrity*, mediety, averageness 30n. *average*; golden mean, neither too much nor too little; common lot, ups and downs, mixed blessing; average circumstances, moderate c., a modest competence, enough to get by; modesty, plain living, no excess 177n. *moderation*; respectability, middle classes, bourgeoisie 30n. *middle class*; suburbia, subtopia, villadom; new poor, common man, everyman, man in the street 869n. *commoner.*

Adj. *mediocre*, average, middling; neither good nor bad, betwixt and between, ordinary, commonplace 30adj. *median*; common, representative 83adj. *typical*; non-extreme 177adj. *moderate*; decent, quiet 874adj. *modest*; not striking, undistinguished, inglorious, nothing to boast of; minor, second-rate, second best 35adj. *inferior*; fair, fair to middling; unobjectionable, tolerable, passable, fifty-fifty, much of a muchness; medium, middle, colourless, grey 625adj. *neutral.*

Vb. *be middling*,—mediocre etc. adj.; follow the mean 30vb. *average out*; pass muster 635vb. *suffice*; jog on, manage well enough, go on quietly, avoid excess, keep to the middle 625vb. *be half-way*; live in a suburb; leave something to be desired 647vb. *be imperfect.*

See: 30, 35, 83, 177, 625, 635, 647, 869, 874.

733 Authority

N. *authority*, power; powers that be, 'them', the establishment, ruling classes 741n. *master*; right, divine r., prerogative, royal p.; dynasticism, legitimacy; law, rightful power, legal p., lawful authority 953n. *legality*; delegated authority, regency, committee 751n. *commission*; office of authority, office, place (see *magistrature*); portfolio 955n. *jurisdiction*; vicarious authority, power behind the throne 178n. *influence*; indirect authority, patronage, prestige, credit; leadership, hegemony 689n. *directorship*; ascendance, preponderance, prepollence, predominance, supremacy 34n. *superiority*; pride of place, seniority, priority 64n. *precedence*; majesty, royalty, kingliness, crown, kingly c. 868n. *nobility*; lordliness, authoritativeness, dignity; power of the purse, financial control; sea-power, admiralty, trident, Britannia; acquisition of power, succession, legitimate s., accession; seizure of power, usurpation.

governance, rule, sway, iron s., reins of government, direction, command 689n. *directorship*; control, supreme c.; hold, grip, gripe, clutches, talon, fangs 778n. *retention*; domination, mastery, whiphand, effective control, reach, long arm; dominion, joint d., condominium, sovereignty, suzerainty, overlordship, supremacy 34n. *superiority*; reign, regnancy, regency, dynasty; foreign rule, heterarchy, heteronomy, empery, empire, rod of e. 745n. *subjection*; imperialism, colonialism, expansionism; régime, regiment, regimen; state control, statism, dirigisme, paternalism; bureaucracy, civil service, officialism, red-tapism, beadledom, bumbledom; droit administratif; Parkinson's law 197n. *expansion.*

gynocracy, gynarchy, regiment of women, petticoat government, women's rule; matriarchy, matriarchate; feminism, suffragettism, suffragism, votes for women.

despotism, benevolent d., paternalism; one-man rule, monocracy, tyranny; dictatorship, Cæsarism, kaiserism, tsarism, Stalinism; absolutism, autocracy, absolute monarchy; statism, étatism, omnicompetent state, dictatorship of the proletariat; guided democracy, totalitarianism; police state, dinarchy, rule of terror 735n. *brute force.*

government, direction 689n. *management*; form of government, state system, polity; constitutional government, constitutionalism, rule of law 953n. *legality*; mis-

government 734 n. *anarchy*; theocracy, thearchy, priestly government, hierocracy, clericalism 985 n. *ecclesiasticism*; monarchy, constitutional m., monarchical government, kingship; republicanism, federalism; tribal system, tribalism; feudalism, feudality; aristocracy, meritocracy, oligarchy, minority rule; gerontocracy, senatorial government; duumvirate, triumvirate; rule of wealth, plutocracy; representative government, parliamentary g., government by the ballot box, party system; democracy, people's rule, government of the people, by the people, for the people; democracy unlimited, demagogy, popular will, vox populi; isocracy, pantisocracy, collectivism, proletarianism, ergatocracy; communism, Leninism; party rule, Bolshevism, Fascism; committee rule, sovietism; imperium in imperio, stratocracy, army rule, military government, martial law; ochlocracy, mobocracy, mob rule, mob law; syndicalism, socialism, guild s., fabianism, statism; bureaucracy, technocracy; self-government, autonomy, home rule, Dominion status, autarchy 744 n. *independence*; caretaker government, regency, interregnum; sphere of influence, mandate, mandated territory.

magistrature, magistracy, office, place, office of power, office of dignity; kingship, kinghood, Tsardom, royalty, regality; regency, regentship, protectorship; rulership, burgraviate, chieftainship, sheikhdom, emirate, principate, lordship, seigniory; sultanate, caliphate, wazirate, pashalic, governorship, viceroyalty; satrapy, exarchate, nomarchy, ethnarchy; consulate, consulship, proconsulate, prefecture, tribunate, ædileship; mayoralty, aldermanship; headship, presidentship, presidency, premiership, chairmanship 689 n. *directorship*; overlordship, superintendency, inspectorship; mastery, mastership; seat of government, capital, metropolis, palace, White House, Kremlin, Chequers, Whitehall; secretariat 687 n. *workshop*.

polity, state, commonwealth, commonweal; country, realm, kingdom, sultanate; republic, city state, city, free c., polis; temple state; federation, confederation; principality, duchy, arch-d., dukedom,

palatinate; empire, dominion, colony, dependency, protectorate, mandate, mandated territory 184 n. *territory*; province, county 184 n. *district*; body politic, corporative state, social s., welfare s.; laws, constitution.

Adj. *authoritative*, empowered, competent; in office, in authority, clothed with a., magisterial, official, ex officio; mandatory, binding, compulsory 740 adj. *compelling*; masterful, domineering; commanding, lordly, dignified, majestic; overruling, imperious, bossy; peremptory, arbitrary, absolute, autocratic, tyrannical, dictatorial, totalitarian 735 adj. *authoritarian*; powerful, puissant 162 adj. *strong*; hegemonic, leading 178 adj. *influential*; pre-eminent, preponderant, predominant, prepollent, dominant, paramount 34 adj. *supreme*.

ruling, reigning, regnant, regnal; sovereign, holding the sceptre, on the throne; royal, regal, majestic, kinglike, kingly, queenly, princely, lordly; dynastic; imperial; magisterial; governing, controlling, dictating etc. vb.

governmental, gubernatorial, political, constitutional; administrative, ministerial, official, bureaucratic, centralized; technocratic; matriarchal, patriarchal; monanarchic, feudal, aristocratic, oligarchic, plutocratic, democratic, popular, classless, republican; self-governing, autonomous, autarchic 744 adj. *independent*.

Vb. *rule*, bear r., sway, reign, reign supreme, sit on the throne, wear the crown, wield the sceptre; govern, control 737 vb. *command*; manage, hold the reins, hold office 689 vb. *direct*; hold place, occupy a post, fill a p.; be in power, have authority wield a., exercise a., exert a., use one's a.; rule absolutely, tyrannize 735 vb. *oppress*; dictate, lay down the law; plan, give laws to, legislate for; divide and rule; keep order, police.

take authority, mount the throne, ascend the t., accede to the t., succeed to the t., take command, assume c., take over; assume authority, form a government; get hold of, get a hold on, get the whip hand control; seize power, get the power into one's hands, usurp, usurp the throne.

dominate, have the power, have the prestige; preponderate, turn the scale 34 vb. *predominate*; lord it over, boss, rule the

roost, wear the breeches 737 vb. *command*; have the mastery, have the upper hand, hold the whip-h. 727 vb. *overmaster*; lead by the nose, turn round one's little finger, hold in the hollow of one's hand 178 vb. *influence*; regiment, discipline, drill, drive 735 vb. *be severe*; dictate, coerce 740 vb. *compel*; subject to one's influence, hold by the short hairs, hold down, hold under 745 vb. *subjugate*; override, overrule, overawe; overshadow, bestride 226 vb. *overlie*; have it all one's own way, do as one will 744 vb. *be free*.

be governed, have laws, have a constitution; be ruled, be swayed by, be dictated to; be under authority, owe obedience, owe fealty, owe loyalty 745 vb. *be subject*.

Adv. *by authority*, in the name of, de par le Roi; by warrant of, in virtue of one's authority.

See: 34, 64, 162, 178, 184, 197, 226, 687, 689, 727, 734, 735, 737, 740, 741, 744, 745, 751, 778, 868, 953, 955, 985.

734 Laxity

N. *laxity*, slackness, remissness, indifference 458 n. *negligence*; informality 769 n. *non-observance*; looseness, loosening, relaxation, unbinding 46 n. *disjunction*; loose organization, decentralization; connivance 756 n. *permission*; indulgence, toleration, gentleness, licence, over-indulgence, over-kindness, softness 736 n. *lenity*; line of least resistance 721 n. *submission*; weak will, feeble grasp, weak administration, disordered routine, crumbling power 163 n. *weakness*; no grip, no drive, no push, inertia 175 n. *inertness*; no control, abdication of authority, surrender of control 753 n. *resignation*; renunciation 621 n. *relinquishment*; concession 770 n. *compromise*.

anarchy, breakdown of administration, no authority, writ not running; disorder, disorganization, chaos 61 n. *turmoil*; licence, licentiousness, insubordination, indiscipline 738 n. *disobedience*; anarchism, nihilism, antinomianism 769 n. *non-observance*; interregnum, power vacuum, powerlessness 161 n. *impotence*; misrule, misgovernment; mob law, lynch l., club l., reign of terror 954 n. *lawlessness*; defiance of authority, unauthorized power, usur-

pation 916 n. *arrogation*; dethronement, deposition, uncrowning 752 n. *deposal*.

Adj. *lax*, loose, slack, decentralized, disorganized, unorganized 61 adj. *orderless*; feeble, infirm 163 adj. *weak*; crippled 163 adj. *weakened*; remiss 458 adj. *negligent*; uncaring 860 adj. *indifferent*; relaxed, unstrict, informal, slipshod; tolerant, undemanding, easy, gentle, indulgent, over-i. 736 adj. *lenient*; weak-willed, weak-kneed, infirm of purpose 601 adj. *irresolute*; unmasterful, lacking authority, uninfluential.

anarchic, anarchical; ungoverned, uncontrolled, unbridled, unsubmissive; licentious 878 adj. *insolent*; rebellious 738 adj. *disobedient*; disorderly, unruly 738 adj. *riotous*; unauthorized, without a writ 954 adj. *illegal*; lawless, nihilistic, anarchistic, antinomian 769 adj. *non-observant*.

Vb. *be lax*, not enforce; hold a loose rein, give the reins to, give one his head, give rope enough 744 vb. *give scope*; stretch a point, connive at; tolerate, put up with, suffer; laisser faire, laisser aller 756 vb. *permit*; let one get away with, not say Bo to a goose; spoonfeed, indulge 736 vb. *be lenient*; make concessions 770 vb. *compromise*; relax, unbind 46 vb. *disjoin*; lose control 161 vb. *be impotent*; renounce authority 621 vb. *relinquish*; stand down, abdicate 753 vb. *resign*; misrule, misgovern, mismanage, reduce to chaos 63 vb. *derange*.

please oneself, let oneself go, indulge oneself 943 vb. *be intemperate*; be a law to oneself, stand in no awe of, defy authority, defy control 738 vb. *disobey*; take on oneself, act without authority, act without instructions, act on one's own responsibility; arrogate, usurp authority 916 vb. *be undue*.

unthrone, disthrone, uncrown, unseat, force to resign 752 vb. *depose*; usurp, snatch the sceptre, seize the crown.

See: 46, 61, 63, 161, 163, 175, 458, 601, 621, 721, 736, 738, 744, 752, 753, 756, 769, 770, 860, 878, 916, 943, 954.

735 Severity

N. *severity*, no weakness, rigorousness, strictness, stringency; formalism, pedantry; high standards 862 n.

fastidiousness; rigidity, inflexibility 326 n. *hardness*; discipline, firm control, strong hand, tight h., tight grasp 733 n. *authority*; rod of iron, heavy hand, Draconian laws; harshness, rigor, extremity, extremes; no concession, no compromise, letter of the law, pound of flesh; intolerance, fanaticism, bigotry 602 n. *opiniatry*; press laws, censorship, suppression 747 n. *restraint*; blue laws, puritanism 950 n. *prudery*; infliction, visitation, inquisition, persecution, harassment, oppression; spite, victimization 910 n. *revenge*; lack of feeling, lack of mercy, inclemency, inexorability, no appeal 906 n. *pitilessness*; hard measure, harsh treatment, the hard way, tender mercies, cruelty 898 n. *inhumanity*; self-mortification, self-denial, austerity 945 n. *asceticism*.

brute force, naked f.; rule of might, big battalions 160 n. *power*; coercion, bludgeoning 740 n. *compulsion*; bloodiness 176 n. *violence*; subjugation 745 n. *subjection*; arbitrary power, absolutism, Hobbism, tsarism; autocracy, dictatorship 733 n. *despotism*; tyranny, liberticide; Fascism, Nazism, Hitlerism, Stalinism, totalitarianism; Prussianism, militarism; martial law, iron rule, iron sway, iron hand, iron heel, jackboot, bludgeon.

tyrant, rigorist, pedant, precisian, formalist, stickler, red-tapist; petty tyrant, Jack-in-office; disciplinarian, martinet, drill-sergeant; militarist, Prussian, jackboot; hanging judge, Draco; heavy father, Dutch uncle; Big Brother, authoritarian, despot, dictator, bashaw, shogun 741 n. *autocrat*; boss, commissar, gauleiter; inquisitor, persecutor; oppressor, bully, hard master, taskmaster, slave-driver, slaver; extortioner, blood-sucker, tax-gatherer, publican, predator, harpy, vulture, octopus; brute 938 n. *monster*.

Adj. *severe*, austere, Spartan 945 adj. *ascetic*; strict, rigorous, extreme; strait-laced, puritanical, prudish; donnish, pedagogic, formalistic, pedantic; bigoted, fanatical; hypercritical 862 adj. *fastidious*; intolerant, censorious 924 adj. *disapproving*; rigid 326 adj. *hard*; hard-headed, hard-boiled, dour; inflexible, obdurate, uncompromising 602 adj. *obstinate*; inexorable, relentless, merciless, unsparing, inclement, unforgiving 906 adj. *piti-*

less; heavy, stern, stiff; exemplary, stringent, Draconian, drastic, savage.

authoritarian, masterful, domineering, lordly, arrogant, haughty 878 adj. *insolent*; despotic, absolute, unfettered, arbitrary; totalitarian, Fascist, communistic; anti-democratic, undemocratic; coercive, imperative, compulsive 740 adj. *compelling*; fussy, bossy, governessy.

oppressive, hard on 914 adj. *unjust*; tyrannical, despotic, arbitrary; tyrannous, harsh, over-h.; grinding, withering; exigent, exacting, grasping, griping, extortionate, vulturine, predatory; persecuting, inquisitorial, scarching, unsparing; high-handed, overbearing, overmighty, domineering; heavy-handed, iron-h., iron-heeled; ungentle, rough, bloody 176 adj. *violent*; brutal 898 adj. *cruel*; totalitarian, Hitlerite, Stalinist.

Vb. *be severe*, — harsh, — strict etc. adj.; exert authority, put one's foot down, discipline; bear hard on, deal hard measure, deal hardly with, lay a heavy hand on; permit no liberties, keep a tight rein on 747 vb. *restrain*; be down on, have a down on (see *oppress*); come down on, crack down on, stamp on 165 vb. *suppress*; not tolerate, persecute, hunt down 619 vb. *pursue*; ill-treat, mishandle, use hard, strain 675 vb. *misuse*; treat rough, get tough with, pull no punches; inflict, visit, visit on, visit with, chastise, chastise with scorpions 963 vb. *punish*; mete stern punishment, wreak vengeance 910 vb. *avenge*; exact reprisals 714 vb. *retaliate*; strain one's authority 954 vb. *be illegal*; be extreme, proceed to extremities, have one's pound of flesh; harden one's heart, show no mercy 906 vb. *be pitiless*; give no quarter, put to the sword 362 vb. *slaughter*.

oppress, tyrannize, play the tyrant, play the despot; take liberties, strain one's authority 734 vb. *please oneself*; assume, arrogate 916 vb. *be undue*; domineer, lord it; overawe, intimidate, terrorize 854 vb. *frighten*; bludgeon 740 vb. *compel*; shove around, put upon; bully, haze, harass, plague, annoy 827 vb. *torment*; persecute, spite, victimize 898 vb. *be malevolent*; break, break the spirit, tame 369 vb. *break in*; task, tax, drive 684 vb. *fatigue*; overtax, extort, suck, squeeze, grind 809 vb. *tax*; trample, tread down,

tread underfoot, stamp on, hold down 165 vb. *suppress*; kill liberty, enthral, enslave, rivet the yoke 745 vb. *subjugate*; ride roughshod, injure, inflict injustice 914 vb. *do wrong*; misgovern, misrule; rule with a rod of iron, whip, scourge, rack, put the screw on 963 vb. *torture*; shed blood, dye with b. 362 vb. *murder*; be heavy, weigh on, burden, crush 322 vb. *weigh*.

Adv. *severely*, sternly, strictly etc.adj.; tyrannically, despotically, arbitrarily; the hard way, with a high hand, heavy-handedly; cruelly, mercilessly.

See: 160, 165, 176, 322, 326, 362, 369, 602, 619, 675, 684, 714, 733, 734, 740, 741, 745, 747, 809, 827, 854, 862, 878, 898, 910, 914, 916, 924, 938, 945, 950, 954, 963.

736 Lenity

N. *lenity*, softness 734 n. *laxity*; lenience, leniency, mildness, gentleness, tenderness; forbearance 823 n. *patience*; pardon 909 n. *forgiveness*; quarter, mercy, clemency, mercifulness, compassion 905 n. *pity*; humanity, kindness 897 n. *benevolence*; favour, sop, concession; indulgence, toleration; sufferance, allowance, leave 756 n. *permission*; connivance, complaisance; justice with mercy 177 n. *moderation*; light rein, light hand, velvet glove, kid gloves.

Adj. *lenient*, soft, gentle, mild, mild as milk; indulgent, tolerant; conniving, complaisant; unstrict, easy, easy-going, undemanding 734 adj. *lax*; forbearing, long-suffering 823 adj. *patient*; clement, merciful 909 adj. *forgiving*; tender 905 adj. *pitying*; too soft, over-merciful; tender towards, afraid to touch, velvet-gloved.

Vb. *be lenient*, show consideration, make no demands, make few d.; deal gently, handle tenderly, go easy, pull one's punches, temper the wind to the shorn lamb 177 vb. *moderate*; stroke, pat, featherbed, spoonfeed, spoil, indulge, humour 889 vb. *pet*; gratify, favour 925 vb. *flatter*; tolerate, allow, connive 756 vb. *permit*; stretch a point 734 vb. *be lax*; concede 758 vb. *consent*; not press, refrain, forbear 823 vb. *be patient*; pity, spare, give quarter 905 vb. *show mercy*; pardon 909 vb. *forgive*; amnesty 506 vb. *forget*;

relax, relax the rigor, humanize 897 vb. *be benevolent*.

See: 177, 506, 734, 756, 758, 823, 889, 897, 905, 909, 925.

737 Command

N. *command*, royal c., invitation, summons; commandment, ordinance; injunction, imposition; dictation, bidding, behest, hest, hookum, will and pleasure; dictum, say-so 532 n. *affirmation*; charge, commission, appointment 751 n. *mandate*; instructions, rules, regulations; brief 524 n. *information*; directive, order, order of the day; word of command, word; beck, nod, sign 547 n. *gesture*; signal, bugle-call, trumpet-c. 547 n. *call*; summons, imperative summons; whip, three-line w.; categorical imperative, dictate 740 n. *compulsion*; negative command, taboo, ban, embargo, inhibition, proscription 757 vb. *prohibition*; countermand, counter-order 752 n. *abrogation*.

decree, edict, fiat, ukase, firman, ipse dixit; law, canon, rescript, prescript, prescription 693 n. *precept*; bull, papal decree, decretal; circular, encyclical; decree having the force of law, ordinance, order in council; decree nisi, decree absolute; decision, placet, senatus consultum, placitum 480 n. *judgment*; enactment, act 953 n. *legislation*; plebiscite, electoral mandate 605 n. *vote*; dictate, diktat, dictation.

demand, demand as of right, claim, revendication 915 n. *dueness*; requisition 761 n. *request*; notice, warning n., final n., final demand, peremptory d., ultimatum; foreclosure; blackmail 900 n. *threat*; imposition, exaction, levy, tax demand 809 n. *tax*.

warrant, commission, brevet, authorization, written authority, letters patent, passport 756 n. *permit*; writ, summons, subpœna, citation, mandamus, habeas corpus 959 n. *legal process*.

Adj. *commanding*, imperative, imperatival, categorical, dictatorial; jussive, mandative, mandatory, obligatory, peremptory, compulsive 740 adj. *compelling*; decretory, decretal; exacting obedience 733 adj. *authoritative*; decisive, con-

clusive, final, non-appealable; demanding, clamant, vocal.

Vb. *command*, bid, invite; order, tell, issue a command, pass orders, give an order, send an o.; signal, call, nod, beck, motion, sign, make a s. 547 vb. *gesticulate*; wink, tip the wink 524 vb. *hint*; direct, give a directive, instruct, brief, circularize, send round instructions; rule, lay down, enjoin; give a mandate, charge, call upon 751 vb. *commission*; impose, lay upon, set, set a task, make obligatory 917 vb. *impose a duty*; detail, tell off; call together, convene 74 vb. *bring together*; send for, summon; cite, subpoena, issue a writ 959 vb. *litigate*; send back, remand; dictate, enforce obedience, put one's foot down 740 vb. *compel*; countermand 752 vb. *abrogate*; lay an embargo, ban, taboo, proscribe 757 vb. *prohibit*.

decree, pass a d., sign a d., pass an order in council, issue a ukase, issue a firman, issue one's fiat; promulgate 528 vb. *proclaim*; declare, say, say so, lay down the law 532 vb. *affirm*; signify one's will and pleasure, prescribe, ordain, appoint 608 vb. *predetermine*; enact, make law, pass a l., legislate 953 vb. *make legal*; pass judgment, give j., decide, rule, give a ruling 480 vb. *judge*.

demand, require, requisition 627 vb. *require*; order, order up, indent 761 vb. *request*; make demands on, send a final demand, give final notice, present an ultimatum, demand with threats, blackmail 900 vb. *threaten*; present one's claim, make claims upon, revendicate, reclaim 915 vb. *claim*; demand payment, dun, bill, invoice, foreclose; charge 809 vb. *price*; exact, levy 809 vb. *tax*.

Adv. *commandingly*, imperatively, categorically, authoritatively; at the word of command.

See: 74, 480, 524, 528, 532, 547, 605, 608, 627, 693, 733, 740, 751, 752, 756, 757, 761, 809, 900, 915, 917, 953, 959.

738 Disobedience

N. *disobedience*, indiscipline, unbiddableness, naughtiness, refractoriness 598 n. *unwillingness*; insubordination, mutinousness, mutineering; refusal to obey orders, defiance of o. 711 n. *defiance*;

disregard of orders, non-compliance 769 n. *non-observance*; disloyalty, defection, desertion 918 n. *dutilessness*; violation of orders, violation of the law, infraction, infringement, criminality, crime, sin 936 n. *guilty act*; non-cooperation, non-violent non-c., satyagraha, passive resistance 715 n. *resistance*; conscientious objection 704 n. *opposition*; obstructionism 702 n. *hindrance*; murmuring, restlessness 829 n. *discontent*; seditiousness, kulakism, chartism, sanculottism, sansculotterie (see *sedition*); wildness 954 n. *lawlessness*; banditry, maffia 788 n. *brigandage*.

revolt, mutiny; direct action 145 n. *strike*; faction 709 n. *dissension*; breakaway, secession 978 n. *schism*; defection, Titoism 603 n. *tergiversation*; explosive situation, restlessness, restiveness 318 n. *agitation*; sabotage, wrecking activities 165 n. *destruction*; breach of the peace, disturbance, disorder, riot, street-r., bread-r., rioting, gang warfare, street-fighting, émeute, tumult, barricades 61 n. *turmoil*; rebellion, insurrection, rising, uprising 176 n. *outbreak*; putsch, coup d'état; resistance movement, insurgency, insurgence 715 n. *resistance*; subversion 149 n. *revolution*; terrorism 954 n. *lawlessness*; civil war 718 n. *war*; regicide, tyrannicide 362 n. *homicide*.

sedition, seditiousness, Chartism, kulakism; agitation, cabal, intrigue 623 n. *plot*; subversion, infiltration, fifth-columnism; underground activities 523 n. *latency*; terrorism, anarchism, nihilism; treasonable activities, disloyalty, treason, petty t., high t., misprision of t., lese-majesty 930 n. *perfidy*.

revolter, awkward person, difficult character, handful, naughty boy, kittle cattle; mutineer, rebel; striker 705 n. *opponent*; secessionist, seceder, splinter group, cave 978 n. *schismatic*; Titoist, deviationist; blackleg, scab, non-striker 84 n. *nonconformist*; independant, maverick, lone wolf; seditionary, seditionist; traitor, Quisling, fifth-columnist 603 n. *tergiversator*; insurrectionist, insurgent; guerrilla, partisan; resistance, underground, Maquis; Frondeur, Roundhead; tyrannicide, regicide; extremist, Fenian, Jacobin, sansculotte, carbonaro, Decembrist, Bolshevist, Bolshevik, red,

red republican, maximalist 149n. *revolutionist*; counter-revolutionary, reactionary, monarchist, White Russian, chouan, cagoulard; terrorist, anarchist, nihilist; maffia, bandit 789n. *robber*; rebel against all laws, antinomian.

agitator, factionary, factioneer, protester, demonstrator, marcher; tub-thumper, ranter, rabble-rouser, demagogue; firebrand, stormy-petrel, mischief-maker 663n. *trouble-maker*; seditionist, sedition-monger; red, communist, commie; ringleader, 'leader of revolt', Spartacus, Wat Tyler, Jack Cade, John Brown, Jameson, Young Turk.

rioter, street-r., brawler, corner-boy 904n. *ruffian*; demonstrator, suffragette, chartist, sansculotte; saboteur, wrecker, Luddite; secret society, Klu Klux Klan.

Adj. *disobedient*, undisciplined, ill-disciplined; disobeying, naughty; unfilial, undaughterly; unbiddable, awkward, difficult, self-willed, wayward, restive, impatient of control, vicious, unruly, intractable, ungovernable 598adj. *unwilling*; insubordinate, mutinous, rebellious, bolshie; nonconformist 84 adj. *unconformable*; unsubmissive, recusant, uncomplying, uncompliant 769 adj. *non-observant*; recalcitrant 715adj. *resisting*; challenging 711adj. *defiant*; contumacious 602adj. *obstinate*; subversive, revolutionary, reactionary; seditious, trouble-making; traitorous, disloyal 918adj. *dutiless*; antinomian 734 adj. *anarchic*; gate-crashing, intrusive, uninvited, unbidden; wild, untamed, ferine, savage.

riotous, rioting; anarchic, tumultuary, rumbustious, sansculottic, unruly, wild, rackety 61adj. *disorderly*; law-breaking 954adj. *lawless*; mutinous, mutine; insurrectionary, uprisen, rebellious, in rebellion, up in arms 715adj. *resisting*.

Vb. *disobey*, not obey, not listen, not hearken; not conform 769vb. *not observe*; not do as one is told, disobey orders, show insubordination 711vb. *defy*; defy the whip, cross-vote; snap one's fingers, fly in the face of 704vb. *oppose*; set the law at defiance, break the law, commit a crime 954vb. *be illegal*; violate, infringe, transgress, trespass 306vb. *encroach*; not obey the helm, turn restive, kick, chafe, fret, champ at the bit, play up; kick over the traces, take the bit between one's teeth, bolt, take French leave, take the law into one's own hands, be a law to oneself 734vb. *please oneself*; come uninvited, gate-crash.

revolt, rebel, mutiny; down tools, strike work, come out 145vb. *cease*; sabotage 702vb. *obstruct*; undermine, work underground; secede, break away 978vb. *schismatize*; betray 603vb. *tergiversate*; agitate, demonstrate, protest 762vb. *deprecate*; start a riot, raise Cain, raise a revolt, lead a rebellion; rise, rise up, rise in arms, throw off the yoke, renounce allegiance, fight for independence 746vb. *achieve liberty*; overthrow, upset 149vb. *revolutionize*.

See: 61, 84, 145, 149, 165, 176, 306, 318, 362, 523, 598, 602, 603, 623, 663, 702, 704, 705, 709, 711, 715, 718, 734, 746, 762, 769, 788, 789, 829, 904, 918, 930, 936, 954, 978.

739 Obedience

N. *obedience*, compliance 768n. *observance*; goodness, meekness, biddability, discipline; ductibility, pliancy, malleability 327n. *softness*; readiness 597n. *willingness*; non-resistance, submissiveness, acquiescence 721n. *submission*; passiveness, passivity 679n. *inactivity*; dutifulness, morale, discipline, good d., service d. 917n. *duty*; deference, obsequiousness, slavishness 879n. *servility*; command performance; dumb driven cattle 742n. *slave*.

loyalty, constancy, devotion, fidelity, faithfulness, faith 929n. *probity*; allegiance, fealty, homage, service, deference, submission; vote of confidence.

Adj. *obedient*, complying, compliant, conforming 768adj. *observant*; loyal, leal, faithful, true-blue, steadfast, constant; devoted, dedicated, sworn; offering homage, homageable, submissive 721adj. *submitting*; law-abiding 717adj. *peaceful*; complaisant, docile; good, well-behaved; filial, daughterly; ready 597 adj. *willing*; acquiescent, resigned, unresisting, non-resisting, passive 679 adj. *inactive*; meek, biddable, dutiful, disciplined, under discipline; at one's beck and call, at one's orders, on a string, on leading strings, under control; disciplined,

regimented 917 adj. *dutied*; deferential, obsequious, slavish 879 adj. *servile*.

Vb. *obey*, comply, do to order, act upon 768 vb. *observe*; sign on the dotted line, toe the l., come to heel 83 vb. *conform*; assent 758 vb. *consent*; listen, hearken, obey orders, attend to instructions, do as one is told; observe discipline, wait for the word of command; hold oneself ready, put oneself at one's service 598 vb. *be willing*; answer the helm, obey the rein, obey the spur; obey the whip, vote to order; do one's bidding, come at one's call, wait upon, follow, follow to the world's end 742 vb. *serve*; be loyal, owe loyalty, bear allegiance, do suit and service, homage, pay h., offer h. 768 vb. *observe faith*; be under, pay tribute 745 vb. *be subject*; know one's duty 917 vb. *do one's duty*; make oneself useful, do Trojan service 703 vb. *minister to*; yield, bow, bend, stoop, be submissive 721 vb. *submit*; grovel, cringe 879 vb. *be servile*; play second fiddle 35 vb. *be inferior*.

Adv. *obediently*, complaisantly, submissively etc. adj.; under orders, to order, as ordered, in obedience to.

See: 35, 83, 327, 597, 598, 679, 703, 717, 721, 742, 745, 758, 768, 879, 917, 929.

740 Compulsion

N. *compulsion*, spur of necessity 596 n. *necessity*; law of nature 953 n. *law*; moral compulsion 917 n. *conscience*; Hobson's choice 606 n. *no choice*; dictation, coercion, regimentation; blackmail 900 n. *threat*; negative compulsion 747 n. *restraint*; sanction, sanctions 963 n. *penalty*; enforcement, constraint, duress, force, main force, physical f.; right of the stronger, force majeure, mailed fist, big stick, bludgeon, strong arm, strong arm tactics 735 n. *brute force*; droit administratif; forcible feeding; impressment, press, press-gang, conscription, call-up, draft 718 n. *war measures*; exaction, extortion, 786 n. *taking*; slavery, corvée, forced labour, labour camp 745 n. *servitude*; command performance 737 n. *command*.

Adj. *compelling*, compulsive, involuntary, of necessity, unavoidable, inevitable 596 adj. *necessary*; imperative, dictatorial,

peremptory 737 adj. *commanding*; compulsory, mandatory, binding 917 adj. *obligatory*; urgent, pressing; overriding, constraining, coercive; omnipotent, irresistible, not to be trifled with 160 adj. *powerful*; forcible, forceful, cogent; high-pressure, strong-arm, bludgeoning 735 adj. *oppressive*.

Vb. *compel*, constrain, coerce 176 vb. *force*; enforce, put into force, dictate, necessitate, oblige, bind; order 737 vb. *command*; impose 917 vb. *impose a duty*; make, leave no option; leave no escape, pin down, tie d.; press, impress, draft, conscript; drive, dragoon, regiment, discipline; force one's hand; bludgeon 735 vb. *oppress*; take by force, requisition, commandeer, extort, exact, wring from, drag f. 786 vb. *take*; apply pressure, squeeze, turn the screw, put the screw on, twist one's arm 963 vb. *torture*; blackmail 900 vb. *threaten*; be peremptory, insist, make a point of, press, urge 532 vb. *emphasize*; say it must be done, take no denial, not take no for an answer 532 vb. *affirm*; compel to accept, force upon, cram down one's throat, ram down one's t., inflict, foist, fob off on; hold back 747 vb. *restrain*.

Adv. *by force*, perforce, compulsorily, of necessity, on compulsion, under pressure, under protest, in spite of one's teeth, nolens volens; forcibly, by force majeure, by the strong arm, at the sword's point, at the point of the bayonet.

See: 160, 176, 532, 596, 606, 718, 735, 737, 745, 747, 786, 900, 917, 953, 963.

741 Master

N. *master*, mistress; master of, captor, possessor 776 n. *owner*; sire, lord, lady, dame; liege, lord, lord paramount, overlord, lord's lord, suzerain; protector 707 n. *patron*; seigneur, lord of the manor, squire, laird 868 n. *aristocrat*; senator, signior, oligarch, plutocrat; mister, sir, don, mirza, sahib, thakur 372 n. *male*; madam 373 n. *lady*; master of the house, husband, goodman; patriarch, matriarch 169 n. *parent*; senior, head, principal, provost 34 n. *superior*; schoolmaster, dominie 537 n. *teacher*; president, chairman, speaker 690 n. *director*; employer, capitalist, boss; leader, duce, fuehrer (see

autocrat); commissar, gauleiter (see *officer*); lord of the ascendant, cock of the walk, lord of creation 638 n. *bigwig*; ruling class, ruling party, dominant interest, the Establishment; the authorities, principalities and powers, the powers that be, 'them', Government, Sarkar, Delhi, Whitehall, Pentagon 733 n. *government*; staff, état-major, High Command 689 n. *directorship*.

autocrat, autarch, absolute ruler, absolute master, despot, tyrant, dictator, duce, fuehrer; tycoon, boss, shogun; petty tyrant, gauleiter, commissar, Jack-in-office, tin god 690 n. *official*.

sovereign, suzerain, crowned head, anointed king; Majesty, Highness, Royal H., Excellence; dynasty, house, royal h., royal line, royal blood; royalty, monarch, king, queen; divine king, Pharaoh, Inca; imperator, emperor, empress, King Emperor, Holy Roman E.; Caesar, Kaiser, Kaiserin, Tsar, Tsarina, Tsarevitch; prince, raj kumar, princess, Infante, Infanta, Dauphin, Prince of Wales; Great King, King of Kings, Shahanshah, Padishah, Shah, Sophy; khan, khan khanan, Great Khan, Grand Cham; Celestial Emperor; Mikado; Mogul, Great Mogul; Sultan, Sultana, Grand Turk, Sublime Porte, Sick Man of Europe; mpret, Negus, Prester John; pope, Dalai Lama, Teshu L.; caliph, Commander of the Faithful.

potentate, dynast, ruler; zamorin, chief, chieftain, Highland chief, sheik, cacique, sachem, sagamore; prince, ruling p., princeling, tetrarch; rajah, rani, rao, rawal, thakur, thakurani, maharajah, maharani; emir, sirdar, mehtar, sherif; nawab, begum; Nizam, Peshwa, Gaekwar, Holkar, Scindia, Jam Sahib; archduke, duke, duchess, burgrave, margrave, margravine, Palatine, Elector, Prince Bishop; regent, interrex.

governor, military g., lieutenant-g., High Commissioner, Governor - General, Crown Representative, viceroy, vicereine, khedive; corregidor, adelantado; proconsul, satrap, kshatrapa, vali, wali, hospodar, hetman, vaivode, stadholder, ethnarch, exarch, eparch, nomarch; grand vizier, beglerbeg, beg, bey, pasha, three-tailed p.; ecclesiastical governor, Prince Bishop; ethnarch, eparch, patri-arch, metropolitan, archbishop, cardinal 986 n. *ecclesiarch*; judge, charismatic leader (Old Testament).

officer, man in office, functionary, mandarin, bureaucrat 690 n. *official*; civil servant, public s. 742 n. *servant*; gauleiter, commissar; chief officer, aga, prime minister, grand vizier, vizier, wazir, diwan, chancellor, vice-c., Great Seal; constable, marshal, seneschal, warden; burgomaster, mayor, lord m., lady m., mayoress, alderman, bailie, city father, councillor, syndic, sheriff, bailiff, portreeve, reeve; justice, justice of the peace, alcalde, caid, kazi, munsiff, hakim 957 n. *judge*; archon, archon eponymous, probulus, ephor; magistrate, chief m., city m., podestà; president, doge; consul, proconsul, prætor, quæstor, ædile; prefect, intendant, district officer, landamman; district magistrate, deputy m., subdivisional officer; commissioner, deputy c.; revenue officer, collector, subcollector, talukdar, patel, headman; lictor, apparitor, mace-bearer, beadle, bedel; process-server, pursuivant, bumbaliff, catchpole, tipstaff 955 n. *law officer*; sexton, verger, bell-ringer, 986 n. *church officer*; office-boy 531 n. *messenger*; party official, whip.

naval officer, sea-lord, first s.; senior naval officer, S.N.O., naval attaché; admiral of the fleet, admiral, vice-a., rear-a., port-a.; commodore, captain, post c., flag-c., commander, lieutenant-c., lieutenant, flag-l., sub-l., midshipman, middy, petty officer, warrant o., leading seaman 270 n. *naval man*; trierarch, nauarch.

army officer, staff, High Command, staff officer, brass hat, red-tab; commissioned officer, brevet o.; marshal, field m., commander-in-chief, seraskier, generalissimo, general, captain-g., lieutenant-g., major-g., colonel-g., commandant-general; brigadier, colonel, lieutenant-c., major, captain, lieutenant, second l., subaltern, shavetail, company-commander, platoon-c.; ensign, cornet, cadet; warrant officer, non-commissioned o., N.C.O., brigade-major, drum-m., sergeant-m., sergeant, troop-s., top-s., colour-s., corporal, corporal-major, lance-corporal; adjutant, aide-de-camp, quartermaster, orderly officer; imperator, military tribune, legate, centurion, decurion, vexillary; chiliarch, hipparch; subahdar,

jemadar, havildar, naik, lance-n. 722 n. *soldiery*; war-lord, war minister, commanding officer, commander, commandant.

air officer, marshal of the air-force, air marshal, air commodore, group-captain, wing - commander, squadron - leader, flight-lieutenant, pilot-officer, flight-sergeant 722 n. *air force*.

See: 34, 169, 270, 372, 373, 531, 537, 638, 689, 690, 707, 722, 733, 742, 776, 868, 955, 957, 986.

742 Servant

N. *servant*, public s., civil s. 690 n. *official*; unpaid servant, fag, slave; general servant, factotum 678 n. *busy person*; humble servant, menial; orderly, peon; temple servant, hierodule; verger, sexton, bell-ringer 986 n. *church officer*; subordinate, underling, understrapper 35 n. *inferior*; subaltern, helper, assistant, confidential a., secretary, right-hand man 703 n. *aider*; paid servant, mercenary, hireling, creature, employee, hand, hired man; odd-job man, chore boy, labourer 686 n. *worker*; hewer of wood and drawer of water, hack, drudge, erk; farm-hand 370 n. *husbandman*; shepherd, cowherd, milkmaid 369 n. *herdsman*; shop-assistant, counter-jumper, shop-walker, floor-w. 793 n. *seller*; steward, stewardess, cabin-boy; table servant, waiter, waitress, nippy, table-boy, khidmatgar; head-waiter, wine-w.; bar-tender, barman, barmaid, pot-boy, tapster, drawer, skinker 192 n. *tavern*; stableman, ostler, groom, syce, stable-boy, postilion, post-boy; messenger, runner 531 n. *courier*; doorman, doorkeeper, commissionaire, durwan, concierge, caretaker, housekeeper 264 n. *janitor*; porter, night-p.; caddie 273 n. *bearer*; buttons, call-boy, page-boy, bell-hop, bell-captain; boots, sweeper, mehtar, jamadar, chambermaid 648 n. *cleaner*; occasional servant, help, daily, char, charwoman; universal aunt; baby-sitter; nurse, nursemaid, governess, tutor 749 n. *keeper*; companion, confidante; mistress of the robes, dresser.

domestic, servantry, staff; servant's hall 686 n. *personnel*; servitor, domestic servant, general s., man-servant, man, serving m.; livery servant, footman, flunkey, lackey, houseman; servant girl, abigail, maid, parlour-m., house-m., chambermaid, femme de chambre, camarista; domestic drudge, maid-of-all-work, tweeny, skivvy, slavey; kitchen-maid, scullery m., dairy m., laundry m.; kitchen boy, turn-spit, scullion, cook's mate, masalchi, dish-washer; bheestie; sweeper, jamadar, mehtar, mehtarani; upper servant, house-keeper, steward, chaplain, governess, tutor, nurse, nanny; butler, cook, khansamah, cook-general, cook-bearer; personal servant, page, squire, valet, gentlemen's gentleman, batman; bearer, sirdar; lady's maid, waiting woman; nursemaid, ayah, amah, bonne; gyp, scout, bed-maker, bedder; outdoor staff, gardener, under-g., groom, syce, grass-cutter; coachman, tiger, chauffeur 268 n. *driver*.

retainer, follower, following, suite, train, cortège 67 n. *retinue*; court, courtier; bodyguard, housecarl, henchman, squire, page, page of honour, donzel, armour-bearer, shield-b., train-b.; household staff, major domo, chamberlain, equerry, steward, bailiff, castellan, chatelain, seneschal; chatelaine, housekeeper; cellarer, butler, cup-bearer; taster, sewer; groom of the chamber, eunuch; chaplain, beadsman, bedeman; lady-in-waiting, companion, confidante; governess, nurse, nanny 749 n. *keeper*.

dependant, clientèle, client; hanger-on, led-captain, parasite, satellite, camp-follower, creature, jackal 284 n. *follower*; stooge, puppet 628 n. *instrument*; subordinate 35 n. *inferior*; minion, lackey, flunkey (see *domestic*); man, henchman, liegeman, homager, vassal; feudary, feudatory; pensioner, pensionary, beadsman; protégé, ward, charge, nursling, foster-child.

subject, state s., national, citizen 191 n. *native*; liege, lieger, vassal, feudatory, homager, man; people, citizenry 869 n. *commonalty*; subject population, dependency, colony, provincial, colonial, helot; satellite; helotry (see *slave*).

slave, thrall, bondman, bondwoman, broad-wife, bondmaid, slave-girl; helot, helotry, hewer of wood and drawer of water, doormat; serf, ascriptus glebæ, villein; galley-slave, wage-s., sweated labour 686

n. *worker*; hierodule, temple prostitute; odalisque, eunuch; chattel, puppet, chessman, pawn; machine, robot 628 n. *instrument*; captive, chaingang 750 n. *prisoner*.

Adj. *serving*, ministering, fagging 703 adj. *aiding*; in service, in domestic s., menial; working, in employment, on the payroll; on the staff, in the train of; at one's beck and call 739 adj. *obedient*; unfree, unfranchised, unprivileged; in servitude, in slavery, in captivity, in bonds 745 adj. *subject*.

Vb. *serve*, be in service, wait upon, wait on hand and foot 703 vb. *minister to*; attend upon, follow, do suit and service 739 vb. *obey*; tend, squire, valet, dress; char, chore, do chores, do for, oblige; fag for, do service, make oneself useful 640 vb. *be useful*; work for 622 vb. *function*.

See: 35, 67, 191, 192, 264, 268, 273, 284, 369, 370, 531, 622, 628, 640, 648, 678, 686, 690, 703, 739, 745, 749, 750, 793, 869, 986.

743 Badge of rule

N. *regalia*, royal trappings, emblem of royalty, insignia of r.; crown, kingly c., orb, sceptre; coronet, tiara, diadem; rod of empire, sword of state 733 n. *authority*; robe of state, coronation robes, royal robe, pall; ermine, royal purple; throne, Peacock t., royal seat, seat of kings, guddi, musnud; ensign 547 n. *flag*; royal standard, royal arms 547 n. *heraldry*; lion eagle; Prince of Wales's feathers; uræus.

badge of rule, emblem of authority, staff, wand, wand of office, rod, Black Rod, baton, truncheon, gavel; herald's wand, caduceus; wand of Dionysus, thyrsus; signet, seal, privy s., keys, ring; sword of state, sword of justice, mace, fasces, axes; pastoral staff, crosier; ankh, ansate cross; woolsack, chair, bench; sartorial insignia, triple crown, mitre, bishop's hat, cardinal's hat., shovel h., biretta; bishop's apron, gaiters, lawn sleeves 989 n. *canonicals*; judge's cap, black c. 961 n. *condemnation*; peer's cap, cap of maintenance, cap of dignity; robe, mantle, toga; royal robe, pall; robe of honour, khilat 547 n. *livery*.

badge of rank, sword, belt, sash, spurs, cocked hat, epaulette, tab 547 n. *badge*;

uniform 547 n. *livery*; brass, star, pips, crown, crossed batons; chevron, stripe, anchor, curl, brassard, armlet; garter, order 729 n. *decoration*.

See: 547, 729, 733, 961, 989.

744 Freedom

N. *freedom*, liberty, being at large; freedom of action, initiative; free will, free thought, free speech, freedom of the press, the four freedoms; rights, privilege, prerogative, exemption, immunity, diplomatic i. 919 n. *non-liability*; liberalism, libertarianism, latitudinarianism 913 n. *right*; licence, excess of freedom, indiscipline 738 n. *disobedience*; free love 951 n. *illicit love*; laisser faire, non-interference; non-involvement, non-attachment, detachment, neutralism 860 n. *indifference*; non-alignment, cross benches; isolationism, isolation, splendid i. 883 n. *seclusion*; emancipation, setting free 746 n. *liberation*; enfranchisement, denization, naturalization, citizenship; franchise, secret ballot 605 n. *vote*.

independence, freedom of action, unilaterality; freedom of choice 605 n. *choice*; floating vote 606 n. *no choice*; freedom of thought, emancipation, bohemianism 84 n. *unconformity*; singleness, bachelorhood 895 n. *celibacy*; individualism, self-expression, individuality 80 n. *particularism*; self-determination, statehood, nationhood, national status 371 n. *nation*; autonomy, autarchy, self-rule, home-r., dominion status; autarky, self-support, self-sufficiency 635 n. *sufficiency*; freehold 777 n. *property*; independent means competence 800 n. *wealth*.

scope, free s., full s., play, free p., full p. 183 n. *range*; swing, rope, long r.; manœuvrability, leverage; field, room, living r., lebensraum, living space, elbow-room, sea-r., wide berth, leeway, margin, clearance 183 n. *room*; unstrictness, latitude, liberty, Liberty Hall; the run of; fling, licence, excess 734 n. *laxity*; one's head, one's own way, one's own devices; ball at one's feet 137 n. *opportunity*; facilities, free hand, blank cheque, carte blanche; free field, free trade, free port, open market, free-trade area, non-tariff zone; 'open skies', high seas.

free man, freeman, liveryman, citizen, free c., voter; no slave, freedman, ex-slave; ex-convict, released prisoner; escapee 667 n. *escaper*; free agent, free-lance; independent, cross-bencher; isolationist, neutral 625 n. *moderate*; interloper, free-trader 59 n. *intruder*; antimonopolist, smuggler; free-thinker, latitudinarian, liberal; libertarian, bohemian 84 n. *nonconformist*; lone wolf 883 n. *solitary*.

Adj. *free*, free-born, free-bred, enfranchised, admitted to citizenship; heart-whole, fancy-free; scot-free 960 adj. *acquitted*; uncaught 667 adj. *escaped*; released, freed 746 adj. *liberated*; at large, free as air, free as the wind; footloose, go-as-you-please, ranging 267 adj. *travelling*; ranging freely, having full play (see *unconfined*); licenced, chartered, privileged 756 adj. *permitted*; exempt, immune 919 adj. *non-liable*; free-speaking, plain-spoken 573 adj. *plain*; free-thinking, emancipated, broad, broadminded, latitudinarian (see *independent*); unbiased, unprejudiced, independent, uninfluenced 913 adj. *just*; free and easy, all things to all men 882 adj. *sociable*; loose, licentious, unbridled, incontinent, wanton 951 adj. *impure*; leisured, out of harness; relaxed, unbuttoned, at home, at rest 681 adj. *leisurely*; free of cost, gratis, unpaid for 812 adj. *uncharged*; unclaimed, going begging 860 adj. *unwanted*; free for all, unreserved 289 adj. *accessible*.

unconfined, uncribbed, uncabined, untrammelled, unshackled, unfettered, unreined, unbridled, uncurbed, unchained, unbound, unmuzzled, unkennelled; unchecked, unrestrained; unprevented, unhindered, unimpeded, unobstructed; wandering, random; left to one's choice, at one's own devices.

independent, unnecessitated, uncontrolled; uninduced, unilateral 609 adj. *spontaneous*; unforced, uncompelled, uninfluenced; unattached, detached 860 adj. *indifferent*; free to choose, uncommitted, uninvolved; non-partisan 625 adj. *neutral*; isolationist 883 adj. *unsociable*; unvanquished, unconquered, unconquerable, irrepressible 727 adj. *unbeaten*; enjoying liberty, unsubjected, unenthralled, unenslaved; autonomous, autarchic, self-governing, self-ruling; autarkic, self-sufficient, self-supporting, self-contained; ungoverned, masterless, owning no master, ungovernable 734 adj. *anarchic*; free-lance, unofficial, wildcat; free-minded, free-spirited, free-souled; single, bachelor 895 adj. *unwedded*; breakaway 978 adj. *schismatical*.

unconditional, unconditioned, without strings; unrestricted, unlimited, absolute; discretionary, arbitrary; freehold, allodial.

Vb. *be free*, enjoy liberty, breathe l.; go free, get f., save oneself 667 vb. *escape*; take French leave 738 vb. *disobey*; have the run of, be free of, have the freedom of, feel at home, make oneself at h.; range, have scope, have play, have elbow-room; have rope enough, have one's head, have one's fling, have one's way, have it one's own w., do as one likes *or* chooses 734 vb. *please oneself*; follow one's bent 179 vb. *tend*; go as you please, drift, wander, roam 282 vb. *stray*; go one's own way, go it alone, shift for oneself, paddle one's own canoe, stand alone 88 vb. *be one*; have a will of one's own 595 vb. *will*; have a free mind, worship freedom; be independent, call no man master; stand up for one's rights, defy the whip, cross-vote 711 vb. *defy*; stand on one's own feet, suffice for oneself, ask no favours 635 vb. *suffice*; take liberties, make free with, presume, presume on 878 vb. *be insolent*; dare, venture, make bold to, permit oneself.

give scope, allow initiative, give one his head, allow enough rope 734 vb. *be lax*; allow full play 469 vb. *make possible*; release, set free, enfranchise 746 vb. *liberate*; let, license, charter 756 vb. *permit*; let alone, allow to drift, not interfere, live and let live, laisser aller, laisser faire; leave one to his own devices; leave it open, leave to one's own choice; keep the door open.

Adv. *freely*, liberally, ad libitum.

See: 59, 80, 84, 88, 137, 179, 183, 267, 282, 289, 371, 469, 573, 595, 605, 606, 609, 625, 635, 667, 681, 711, 727, 734, 738, 746, 756, 777, 800, 812, 860, 878, 882, 883, 895, 913, 919, 951, 960, 978.

745 Subjection

N. *subjection*, subordination, subordinate position, inferior rank, cadetship, juniority, inferior status, satellite s. 35 n.

inferiority; creaturehood, creatureliness; dependence, clientship, tutelage, guardianship, wardship, chancery, apron strings, leading s.; mutual dependence, symbiosis 12 n. *correlation*; subjecthood, allegiance, vassalage, nationality, citizenship; subjugation, conquest, colonialism; loss of freedom, disfranchisement, enslavement 721 n. *submission*; constraint, discipline 747 n. *restraint*; oppression 735 n. *severity*; yoke 748 n. *fetter*; slavishness 879 n. *servility*.

service, domestic s., government s., employ, employment; servantship, servitorship, flunkeydom, flunkeyism 739 n. *obedience*; tribute, suit and service; vassalage, vassalship, feudality, feudalism 739 n. *loyalty*; compulsory service, corvée, forced labour 740 n. *compulsion*; conscription 718 n. *war measures*.

servitude, involuntary s., slavery, abject s.; enslavement, captivity, thraldom, bondage, yoke; helotry, helotage, helotism, serfdom, villenage.

Adj. *subjected* etc. vb.; subjugated, overborne, overwhelmed 728 vb. *defeated*; reduced, pacified; captived, taken prisoner, deprived of freedom, robbed of f., disfranchised; colonized, enthralled, enslaved, reduced to slavery, sold into s.; under the lash, under the heel, tyrannized over, oppressed, down-trodden, underfoot; treated like dirt, henpecked; regimented, planned; quelled, tame, domesticated 369 adj. *tamed*; eating out of one's hand, submissive 721 adj. *submitting*; subservient, slavish 879 adj. *servile*.

subject, unfree, not independent, unfranchised, unprivileged; satellite, satellitic 879 adj. *servile*; bond, bound, bounden, tributary, colonial; owing service, owing fealty, vassal, feudal, feudatory 739 adj. *obedient*; under, subordinate, of lower rank, junior, cadet 35 adj. *inferior*; dependent, in chancery, in statu pupillari, in leading strings, tied to the apron s.; subject to, liable to, exposed to 180 adj. *liable*; a slave to 610 adj. *habituated*; in the hands of, in the clutches of, under the control of, in the power of, at the mercy of; parasitical, hanging on; paid, in the pay of, stipendiary; encumbranced, mortgaged, pawned, in pawn 780 adj. *transferred*.

Vb. *be subject*, live under, own the sway of,

homage, pay tribute, be under 739 vb. *obey*; obey the whip, vote to order; depend on, lean on, hang on 35 vb. *be inferior*; be a doormat, let oneself be trampled on; serve, live in subjection, be a slave, drag a chain, grace the triumph of; lose one's independence 721 vb. *submit*; pawn, mortgage 780 vb. *convey*; sacrifice one's freedom, have no will of one's own, be a passive instrument 628 vb. *be instrumental*; cringe, fawn 879 vb. *be servile*.

subjugate, subdue, reduce, subject 727 vb. *overmaster*; colonize, make tributary, vassalize, mediatize; captive, lead in triumph, drag at one's chariot wheels 727 vb. *triumph*; take, capture, lead captive, lay one's yoke upon, reduce to servitude, enslave, helotize, sell into slavery; fetter, bind, hold in bondage 747 vb. *imprison*; rob of freedom, disfranchise; trample on, tread on, wipe one's feet on, treat like dirt 735 vb. *oppress*; keep under, keep down, hold d., repress, sit on, stamp out 165 vb. *suppress*; enthral, captivate 821 vb. *impress*; enchant 983 vb. *bewitch*; dominate, lead by the nose, keep in leading strings, tie to one's apron 178 vb. *influence*; discipline, regiment, plan; tame, quell 369 vb. *break in*; have eating out of one's hand, bring to heel, have at one's beck and call; make one's plaything, do what one likes with 673 vb. *dispose of*.

See: 12, 35, 165, 178, 180, 369, 610, 628, 673, 718, 721, 727, 728, 735, 739, 740, 747, 748, 780, 821, 879, 983.

746 Liberation

N. *liberation*, setting free, unshackling, unbinding, release, discharge, enlargement 960 n. *acquittal*; unravelling, extrication, disinvolvement 46 n. *separation*; riddance, good r. 831 n. *relief*; rescue, redemption, salvation, mukti 668 n. *deliverance*; manumission, emancipation, enfranchisement; parole; liberalization, relaxation (of control) 734 n. *laxity*; decontrol, derationing 752 n. *abrogation*; demobilization, disbandment 75 n. *dispersion*; forgiveness of sins, absolution 909 n. *forgiveness*; justification 927 n. *vindication*; acquittance, deed of release, quittance, receipt, quitclaim.

Adj. *liberated*, rescued, delivered, saved 668 adj. *extricable*; rid of, relieved; paroled, set free, freed, manumitted, unbound 744 vb. *unconfined*; released, enlarged, discharged, acquitted; emancipated, enfranchised etc. vb.

Vb. *liberate*, rescue, save 668 vb. *deliver*; excuse, justify 927 vb. *vindicate*; dispense 919 vb. *exempt*; pardon 909 vb. *forgive*; discharge, absolve 960 vb. *acquit*; make free, emancipate, manumit; enfranchise, give the vote; release, set free, set at liberty, enlarge, let out; release conditionally, parole 766 vb. *give terms*; strike off the fetters, unfetter, unshackle, unchain; unbar, unbolt, unlock 263 vb. *open*; loosen, unloose, loose, unbind, extricate, disengage, clear 62 vb. *unravel*; unstop, uncork, unclog; ungag, unmuzzle; uncoop, uncage, unkennel; unleash, let slip; let loose, leave to wander, turn adrift; license, charter; give play to 744 vb. *give scope*; let out, vent, give vent to 300 vb. *void*; leave hold, unhand, unclinch 779 vb. *not retain*; relax, liberalize, 734 vb. *be lax*; lift, lift off 831 vb. *relieve*; rid, dispel 300 vb. *eject*; lift controls, decontrol, deration 752 vb. *abrogate*; demobilize, disband, send home 75 vb. *disperse*; unyoke, unharness, unload 701 vb. *disencumber*; disentail, pay off the mortgage, clear the debt.

achieve liberty, gain one's freedom, breathe freely; assert oneself, claim freedom of action; free oneself, shake oneself free; break loose, throw off the yoke, cast off one's shackles, slip the collar, kick over the traces, get away 667 vb. *escape*.

See: 46, 62, 75, 263, 300, 667, 668, 701, 734, 744, 752, 766, 779, 831, 909, 919, 927, 960.

747 Restraint

N. *restraint*, self-r., self-control 942 n. *temperance*; suppression, repression, coercion, constraint 740 n. *compulsion*; cramp, check 702 n. *hindrance*; curb, drag, brake, snaffle, bridle 748 n. *fetter*; arrest, retardation, deceleration 278 n. *slowness*; prevention, birth-control; cohibition, inhibition, veto, ban, bar, embargo 757 n. *prohibition*; legal restraint 953 n. *law*; control, strict c., discipline 733 n. *authority*; censorship

550 n. *obliteration*; press laws 735 n. *severity*; binding over 963 n. *penalty*.

restriction, limitation, limiting factor 236 n. *limit*; localization, keeping within limits 232 n. *circumscription*; restriction on movement, curfew; coarctation, constriction, squeeze 198 n. *compression*; duress, pressure 740 n. *compulsion*; control, food-c., rationing; restrictive practice, restraint of trade, exclusive rights, exclusivity 57 n. *exclusion*; monopoly, price ring, closed shop; ring, circle, charmed c.; protection, protectionism, mercantilism, mercantile system, protective s., tariff, protective t., tariff wall; most favoured nation treatment, preference, imperial p.; retrenchment 814 n. *economy*; economic pressure, credit squeeze; blockade, starving out; monopolist, protectionist, restrictionist, mercantilist.

detention, preventive d., custody, protective c. 660 n. *protection*; arrest, house a., open a., restriction on movement; custodianship, keeping, guarding, keep, care, charge, ward; quarantine, internment; lettre de cachet; captivity, durance, durance vile; thraldom, slavery 745 n. *servitude*; entombment, burial 364 *interment*; immurement, walling up; herding, impoundment, confinement, incarceration, imprisonment; remand, refusal of bail.

Adj. *restraining* etc. vb.; restrictive, conditioned, with strings; restringent, limiting, limitary; custodial, keeping; cramping, hidebound; strait-laced, unbending, unyielding, strict 735 adj. *severe*; stiff 326 adj. *rigid*; strait 206 adj. *narrow*; straitening, confining, close 198 adj. *compressive*; confined, poky; coercive, coactive 740 adj. *compelling*; repressive, inhibiting 757 adj. *prohibiting*; monopolistic, protectionist, protective, mercantilist.

restrained, self-r., self-controlled 942 adj. *temperate*; disciplined, controlled, under discipline, under control 739 adj. *obedient*; on a lead, kept on a leash, kept under restraint 232 adj. *circumscribed*; pinned, pinned down; on parole 917 adj. *dutied*; protected, rationed; restricted, scant, tight; cramped, hampered, trammelled, shackled 702 adj. *hindered*; tied, bound; held up, weather-bound, wind-b., snow-b., ice-b.

imprisoned, detained, kept in; confined, earth-bound, land-locked 232 adj. *circumscribed*; entombed, confined 364 adj. *buried*; quarantined, in quarantine; interned, in internment; under detention, kept close, incommunicado; under arrest, laid by the heels, in custody; refused bail, in the lock-up, in hazat; behind bars, incarcerated, locked up; inside, in jug, in quod, in a cell; under hatches, confined to barracks; herded, corralled, impounded, in the pound; in irons, fettered, shackled; pilloried, in the stocks; serving sentence, doing time; mewed, caged, in captivity 750 adj. *captive*; trapped.

Vb. *restrain*, hold back, pull b., call b.; arrest, check, curb, rein in, brake, put a brake on, put a drag on, act as a brake 278 vb. *retard*; cramp, clog, hamper 702 vb. *hinder*; swathe, swaddle 45 vb. *tie*; call off, call a halt, stop, put a stop to 145 vb. *halt*; cohibit, inhibit, veto, ban, bar 757 vb. *prohibit*; bit, bridle, discipline, control 735 vb. *be severe*; subdue 745 vb. *subjugate*; grip, hold, pin, keep a tight hold *or* rein on, hold in leading strings, hold in leash, trash 778 vb. *retain*; hold in, keep in, bottle up; restrict, tighten, limit, keep within bounds, stop from spreading, localize, put a ring round, draw the line 232 vb. *circumscribe*; stanch, damp down, pour water on, assuage 177 vb. *moderate*; hold down, clamp down on, crack down on, keep under, sit on, jump on, repress 165 vb. *suppress*; muzzle, gag, silence 578 vb. *make mute*; censor, black out 550 vb. *obliterate*; restrict access, debar from, rope off, keep out 57 vb. *exclude*; restrict imports, put on a tariff, introduce protection; restrict supplies, withhold, keep back; restrict consumption, ration, dole out, be sparing, retrench 814 vb. *economize*; try to stop, resist 704 vb. *oppose*; police, patrol, keep order.

arrest, make an a., apprehend, lay by the heels, catch, cop, nab, collar, pinch, pick up; handcuff, put the handcuffs on (see *fetter*); take, make a prisoner, take prisoner, capture, lead captive; accept the surrender of, put on parole; put under arrest, take into custody, take charge of, clap in the lock-up, hold.

fetter, manacle, bind, pinion, tie up, handcuff, put in irons, put into bilboes; pillory, put in the stocks; tether, picket

45 vb. *tie*; shackle, trammel, hobble; enchain, chain, load with chains; condition, attach strings.

imprison, confine, quarantine, intern; hold, detain, keep in, gate; keep in detention, keep under arrest, keep close, hold incommunicado; cloister 883 vb. *seclude*; entomb, bury 364 vb. *inter*; wall up, seal up, immure; cage, kennel, impound, corral, herd, pen, mew, crib, cabin, box up, shut up, shut in, trap 235 *inclose*; put under restraint, straiten, put in a straitjacket; incarcerate, throw into prison, send to p., commit to p., remand, give in charge; jug, lock up; turn the key on, keep under lock and key, put in a cell, keep behind bars, lay under hatches, clap in irons; keep prisoner, keep in captivity, keep in custody, refuse bail.

See: 45, 57, 145, 165, 177, 198, 206, 232, 235, 236, 278, 326, 364, 550, 578, 660, 702, 704, 733, 735, 739, 740, 745, 748, 750, 757, 778, 814, 883, 917, 942, 953, 963.

748 Prison

N. *prison*, state p., common p., calaboose; prison-house, panopticon, prison without bars; house of detention, house of correction, penitentiary, federal p., reformatory, approved home, Borstal; prison ship, hulks; dungeon, oubliette, limbo; Bastille, Tower; debtor's prison, sponging house; Fleet, Marshalsea, Newgate, Wormwood Scrubs, Holloway, Sing Sing, Dannemora, Alcatraz; criminal lunatic asylum, Broadmoor.

gaol, jail, quod, clink, tronk, jug, can, stir, cooler, big house, glasshouse, booby hatch.

lock-up, hazat, chauki, choky, thana, police-station; guard-room, roundhouse; cell, prison c., condemned c., dungeon c., dungeon, oubliette, torture-chamber; prison van, Black Maria; dock, bar; hold, hatches, hulks; pound, cattle-p., pen, cage, coop, kennel, den, barracoon, barrack, keddah 235 n. *inclosure*; ghetto, reserve; stocks, pillory; lock, padlock, bolt, bar, barred window.

prison camp, detention c., internment c., prisoner of war c., stalag, oflag; concentration camp, slave c.; Belsen, Auschwitz, Buchenwald; deathhouse, gas chamber,

execution c.; penal settlement, convict s., Botany Bay, Andaman Islands, Devil's Island.

fetter, shackle, trammel, bond, chain, ball and c., ring-bolt, irons, gyve, bilboes, hobble; manacle, pinion, handcuff, bracelet, darbies; strait waistcoat, strait jacket, whalebone, corset; muzzle, gag, bit, bridle, snaffle, headstall, halter; rein, bearing r., martingale; reins, ribbons, traces; yoke, collar, harness; curb, brake, skid, shoe, clog, drag, hobble 702n. *hindrance*; tether, rope, leading string 47n. *halter*.

See: 47, 235, 702.

749 Keeper

N. *keeper*, custodian, curator, custos; archivist, record keeper 549n. *recorder*; charge officer, officer in charge; caretaker, concierge, housekeeper; castellan, seneschal, chatelaine, warden; ranger, gamekeeper; guard, escort, convoy; watchdog, sentry, sentinel, look-out, watchman, night-w., watch, coastguard, garrison 660n. *protector*; invigilator, tutor, chaperon, duenna, governess, nurse, foster-n., wet-n., mammy, nanny, nursemaid, bonne, ayah, amah, baby-sitter 742n. *domestic*; foster-parent, adoptive p.; guardian, legal g.

gaoler, jailer, turnkey, warder, head w., wardress, prison guard, prison governor; Argus.

See: 549, 660, 742.

750 Prisoner

N. *prisoner*, captive, capture, prisoner of war; parolee, ticket-of-leave man; close prisoner, person under arrest, charge; detenue, detainee, state prisoner, prisoner of state; prisoner at the bar, defendant, accused 928n. *accused person*; first offender, Borstal boy, gaol-bird 904n. *offender*; gaol inmate, prisoner behind bars, condemned prisoner, convict; chain-gang, galley-slave 742n. *slave*; hostage 767n *security*.

Adj. *captive*, imprisoned, chained, fettered, shackled in irons, behind bars, under lock and key, under hatches, cooling one's heels; jailed, in prison, in Dartmoor, in

Borstal; in the pillory, in the stocks, in the galleys; in custody, under arrest, without bail, remanded; detained, under detention, detained at her Majesty's pleasure.

See: 742, 904, 928.

751 Commission: vicarious authority

N. *commission*, vicarious authority; committal, delegation; devolution, decentralization; deputation, ablegation; legation, mission, embassy, embassage, High Commission 754n. *envoy*; regency, regentship, vice-regentship, vice-royalty 733n. *authority*; representation, procuracy, procuration, proxy; card vote; agency, agentship, factorship, trusteeship, executorship 689n. *management*; clerkship, public service, civil s., bureaucracy 733n. *government*.

mandate, doctor's m., trust, charge 737n. *command*; commission, assignment, appointment, office, task, errand, mission; enterprise 672n. *undertaking*; nomination, return, election 605n. *vote*; posting, translation, transfer, mutual transfer, cross-posting 272n. *transference*; investment, investiture, installation, inauguration, ordination, enthronement, coronation; power, attorney, power of a., letter of a., written authority, charter, writ 737n. *warrant*; brevet, diploma 756 n. *permit*; terms of reference 766n. *conditions*; responsibility, care, cure (of souls); baby, ward, charge.

Adj. *commissioned*, empowered, entrusted etc.vb.; deputed, delegated, accredited; vicarious, representational, agential, procuratory.

Vb. *commission*, put in c.; empower, authorize, charge, sanction, charter, license 756vb. *permit*; post, accredit, appoint, assign, name, nominate; engage, hire, staff 622vb. *employ*; invest, induct, install, collate, ordain; raise to the throne, enthrone, crown, anoint; commit, put in one's hands, turn over to, leave it to; consign, entrust, trust with, grant powers of attorney; delegate, depute, send on a mission, send on an errand, send out, ablegate; return, elect, give a mandate 605vb. *vote*.

Adv. *by proxy*, by procuration, per procurationem, by delegated authority.

See: 272, 605, 622, 672, 689, 733, 737, 754, 756, 766.

752 Abrogation

N. *abrogation*, annulment, invalidation; voidance, nullification, vacation, defeasance; cancelling, cancellation, cassation, suppression; recall, repeal, revocation, revokement, rescission; abolition, abolishment, dissolution; neonomianism 126 n. *newness*; repudiation 533 n. *negation*; retractation 603 n. *recantation*; suspension, discontinuance, disuse, dead letter 674 n. *non-use*; reversal, undoing 148 n. *reversion*; counter-order, countermand, nolle prosequi; cancel, cancel-page.

deposal, deposition, dethronement; demotion, degradation; disestablishment, disendowment; deconsecration, secularization; discharge, congé, dismissal, sack, removal 300 n. *ejection*; unfrocking 963 n. *punishment*; ousting, deprivation 786 n. *expropriation*; replacement, supersession 150 n. *substitution*; recall, transfer, relief 272 n. *transference*.

Adj. *abrogated*, voided, vacated, set aside, quashed, cancelled etc. vb.; void, null and void; functus officio, dead; dormant, sleeping 674 adj. *unused*; recalled, revoked.

Vb. *abrogate*, annul, disannul, cancel; scrub, scrub out, rub o., wipe o. 550 vb. *obliterate*; invalidate, abolish, dissolve, nullify, void, vacate, render null and void; quash, set aside, reverse, overrule; repeal, revoke, recall; rescind, tear up; unmake, undo 148 vb. *revert*; countermand, counter-order; disclaim, disown, deny 533 vb. *negate*; repudiate, retract 603 vb. *recant*; ignore 458 vb. *disregard*; call off, call a halt 747 vb. *restrain*; suspend, discontinue, make a dead letter of 674 vb. *disuse*; unwish, wish undone 830 vb. *regret*; not proceed with 621 vb. *relinquish*.

depose, discrown, uncrown, dethrone; unseat, unsaddle; divest 786 vb. *deprive*; unfrock, disordain; disbench, disbar, strike off the roll 57 vb. *exclude*; disaffiliate, disestablish, disendow; deconsecrate, secularize; suspend, cashier, break 300 vb. *dismiss*; ease out, oust 300

vb. *eject*; demote, degrade, reduce to the ranks; recall, relieve, supersede, replace, remove 272 vb. *transfer*.

See: 57, 126, 148, 150, 272, 300, 458, 533, 550, 603, 621, 674, 747, 786, 830, 963.

753 Resignation

N. *resignation*, demission, good-bye to office; retirement, retiral; leaving, withdrawal, handshake 296 n. *departure*; pension, compensation, golden handshake 962 n. *reward*; waiver, surrender, abandonment, abdication, renunciation 621 n. *relinquishment*; declaration (of innings at cricket); abjuration, disclaimer 533 n. *negation*; state of retirement 681 vb. *leisure*; feeling of resignation, acquiescence 721 n. *submission*; resigner, quitter; man in retirement, pensioner, Cincinnatus.

Adj. *resigning*, abdicatory, abdicant, renunciatory; outgoing, former, retired, quondam, one-time, ci-devant, passé; stickit, discouraged from.

Vb. *resign*, tender one's resignation, send in one's papers, demit, lay down one's office, break one's staff; be relieved, hand over, vacate, vacate office; vacate one's seat, apply for the Chiltern Hundreds; stand down, stand aside, make way for, leave it to; sign off, declare, declare one's innings closed; scratch, withdraw, back out, retire from the contest, throw in one's hand, surrender, give up 721 vb. *submit*; quit, throw up, chuck it; sign away, give a. 780 vb. *convey*; abdicate, abandon, renounce 621 vb. *relinquish*; retire, go into retirement, take one's pension, find one's occupation gone, lie on the shelf; retire in rotation, finish one's term, conclude one's term of office; decline to stand again, not renew the fight, refuse battle; waive, disclaim, abjure 533 vb. *negate*; retract 603 vb. *recant*.

See: 296, 533, 603, 621, 681, 721, 780, 962.

754 Consignee

N. *consignee*, committee, panel 692 n. *council*; counsellor, wise man, team of experts, working party 691 n. *adviser*; bailee, resignee, stakeholder; nominee,

appointee, licensee; trustee, executor 686 n. *agent*; factor, one's man of business, bailiff, steward 690 n. *manager*; caretaker, curator 749 n. *keeper*; representative (see *delegate*); legal representative, attorney, vakil, muktar, counsel, advocate 958 n. *law agent*; procurator, proctor, proxy 755 n. *deputy*; negotiator, middleman, broker, stockbroker 231 n. *intermediary*; underwriter, insurer; purser, bursar 798 n. *treasurer*; bill-collector, tax-c., revenue-c., tahsildar, income-tax officer; holder of an office of trust, office-bearer, secretary of state 741 n. *officer*; functionary, placeman 690 n. *official.*

delegate, walking d., shop steward; nominee, representative, elected r., member; official representative, commissary, commissioner; man on the spot, correspondent, war c., one's own c., special c. 588 n. *correspondent*; emissary, special messenger 531 n. *messenger*; plenipotentiary (see *envoy*); delegation, trade d., mission.

envoy, emissary, legate, ablegate, nuncio, papal n., internuncio, permanent representative, resident, resident minister, ambassador, ambassadress, High Commissioner, chargé d'affaires; corps diplomatique, diplomatic corps; minister, diplomat, doyen of the diplomatic corps; consul, vice-c.; first secretary, attaché; embassy, legation, mission, consulate, High Commission; diplomatist, negotiator, plenipotentiary.

See: 231, 531, 588, 686, 690, 691, 692, 741, 749, 755, 798, 958.

755 Deputy

N. *deputy,* surrogate, alternate, proxy; scapegoat, chopping block, substitute, locum tenens, understudy, stand-in 150 n. *substitution*; pro, vice, vice-gerent, vice-regent, viceroy, vice-president, vice-chairman, vice-chancellor, vice-admiral, vice-captain, vice-consul; proconsul, proprætor; vicar, vicar-general; second-in-command, deputy prime-minister; right-hand man, lieutenant, secretary 703 n. *aider*; alter ego, Grey Eminence, power behind the throne 612 n. *motivator*; heir, heir apparent, successor designate 776 n. *beneficiary*; spokesman, mouthpiece,

herald 531 n. *messenger*; next friend; advocate, champion 707 n. *patron*; agent, factor, attorney 754 n. *consignee.*

Adj. *deputizing,* representing, acting for, agential; vice, pro; diplomatic, ambassadorial, plenipotentiary; standing-in for 150 adj. *substituted*; negotiatory, intermediary 231 adj. *interjacent.*

Vb. *deputize,* act for 622 vb. *function*; attorney, act on behalf of, represent, hold a mandate for, hold a proxy f., appear for, speak f., answer f., hold a brief f., state the case f.; hold in trust, manage the business of, be executor 689 vb. *manage*; negotiate, broke for; replace, stand for, stand in the stead of, do duty for, stand in another's shoes 150 vb. *substitute*; be the chopping block for, act as scapegoat, hold the baby.

Adv. *on behalf,* for, pro; by proxy.

See: 150, 231, 531, 612, 622, 689, 703, 707, 754, 776.

756 Permission

N. *permission,* general p., liberty 744 n. *freedom*; leave, sanction, clearance; vouchsafement, accordance, grant; licence, authorization, warrant, warranty; allowance, sufferance, tolerance, toleration, indulgence 736 n. *lenity*; acquiescence, passive consent, implied c. 758 n. *consent*; connivance 703 n. *aid*; blessing, approval 923 n. *approbation*; grace, grace and favour 897 n. *benevolence*; concession, dispensation, exemption 919 n. *non-liability*; release 746 n. *liberation.*

permit, express permission, written p.; authority, law 737 n. *warrant*; commission 751 n. *mandate*; brevet, grant, charter, patent, letters p.; pass, password, passport, visa, safe-conduct; ticket, rain check; licence, driving l.; universal licence, free hand, carte blanche, blank cheque 744 n. *scope*; leave, compassionate l., leave of absence, furlough, holiday; parole, ticket of leave; all clear, green light, clearance; nihil obstat, imprimatur.

Adj. *permitting,* permissive, indulgent, complaisant, tolerant 736 adj. *lenient*; conniving 704 adj. *aiding.*

permitted, allowed etc. vb.; licit, legalized 953 adj. *legal*; licensed, chartered, patent; unforbidden, unprohibited, open, optional, discretional, without strings 744

adj. *unconditional*; permissible, allowable; printable, sayable; not strictly necessary, dispensable.

Vb. *permit*, let 469vb. *make possible*; give permission, grant leave, grant, accord, vouchsafe 781vb. *give*; nod, say yes 758 vb. *consent*; bless, give one's blessing; go out of one's way to 759vb. *offer*; sanction, pass 923vb. *approve*; entitle, authorize, warrant, charter, patent, license, enable 160vb. *empower*; ratify, legalize 953vb. *make legal*; restore permission, decontrol; lift, lift a ban, dispense, release 919vb. *exempt*; clear, give clearance 746vb. *liberate*; give the all clear, give the green light, tip the wink; recognize, concede, allow 488vb. *assent*; provide for, make provision for 633vb. *provide*; make it easy for, favour, privilege, indulge 701vb. *facilitate*; leave the way open, open the door to, open the floodgates 263vb. *open*; foster, encourage 156vb. *conduce*; suffer, tolerate, put up with 736vb. *be lenient*; connive, shut one's eyes to, wink at 734vb. *be lax*; laisser faire, laisser aller, allow a free hand, give carte blanche, issue a blank cheque 744 vb. *give scope*; permit oneself, allow o., take the liberty 734vb. *please oneself*.

ask leave, beg l., beg permission, ask if one may, ask one's blessing; apply for leave, request sanction; seek a favour, petition 761vb. *request*; get leave, have permission; receive a charter, take out a patent.

Adv. *by leave*, with permission, by favour of, under favour, under licence; permissibly, allowably, legally, legitimately, licitly.

See: 156, 160, 263, 469, 488, 633, 701, 703, 704, 734, 736, 737, 744, 746, 751, 758, 759, 761, 781, 897, 919, 923, 953.

757 Prohibition

N. *prohibition*, inhibition, interdiction, disallowance, injunction; countermand, counter-order; intervention, interference; interdict, veto, ban, embargo, outlawry; cohibition, restriction, curfew 747 n. *restraint*; proscription, taboo, index expurgatorius; disfavour, rejection 760 n. *refusal*; non-recognition, intolerance 924n. *disapprobation*; prohibition of drink, pussyfootism, licensing laws 942n. *temperance*; sumptuary law 814n. *econo-*

my; repressive legislation, censorship, press laws, repression, suppression 735n. *severity*; abolition, cancellation, suspension 752n. *abrogation*; black-out 550n. *obliteration*; forbidden fruit, contraband article 859n. *desired object*.

Adj. *prohibiting*, prohibitory, forbidding, prohibitive, excessive 470adj. *impossible*; penal 963adj. *punitive*; hostile 881adj. *inimical*; exclusive 57adj. *excluding*.

prohibited, forbidden, barred, banned, under ban; censored, blue-pencilled, blacked-out; contraband, illicit, unlawful, outlawed, against the law 954adj. *illegal*; verboten, taboo, untouchable, black; frowned on, not to be thought of, not done; not to be spoken, unmentionable, unsayable, unprintable; out of bounds 57adj. *excluded*.

Vb. *prohibit*, forbid, forfend; disallow, veto, refuse permission, withhold p., refuse leave, forbid the banns 760vb. *refuse*; withdraw permission, cancel leave; countermand, counter-order, revoke, suspend 752vb. *abrogate*; inhibit, prevent, paralyse 702vb. *hinder*; cohibit, restrict, stop 747vb. *restrain*; ban, interdict, taboo, proscribe, outlaw; black, declare b.; impose a ban, lay under interdict, place out of bounds; bar, debar, warn off 57vb. *exclude*; excommunicate 300vb. *eject*; repress, stifle, kill 165vb. *suppress*; censor, blue-pencil, black-out 550vb. *obliterate*; frown on, discountenance, disfavour 924 vb. *disapprove*; discourage 613vb. *dissuade*; clip, narrow, pinch, cramp 232vb. *circumscribe*; draw the line, block; intervene, interpose, interfere, dash the cup from one's lips.

See: 57, 165, 232, 300, 470, 550, 613, 702, 735, 747, 752, 760, 814, 859, 881, 924, 942, 954, 963.

758 Consent

N. *consent*, free c., full c., willing c. 597n. *willingness*; implied consent, implicit c.; agreement 488n. *assent*; compliance 768 n. *observance*; concession, grant, accord; acquiescence, acceptance, entertainment, allowance 756n. *permission*; sanction, endorsement, ratification, confirmation; partial consent 770n. *compromise*.

Adj. *consenting*, agreeable, compliant, ready,

ready enough 597 adj. *willing*; winking at, conniving 703 adj. *aiding*; yielding 721 adj. *submitting*.

Vb. *consent*, entertain; entertain the idea, say yes, nod; give consent, ratify, confirm 488 vb. *endorse*; sanction, pass 756 vb. *permit*; accord one's approval 923 vb. *approve*; agree, fall in with, accede 488 vb. *assent*; have no objection 488 vb. *acquiesce*; be persuaded, come over, come round 612 vb. *be induced*; yield, give way 721 vb. *submit*; comply, grant a request, do as asked; grant, accord, concede, vouchsafe 781 vb. *give*; deign, condescend 884 vb. *be courteous*; listen, hearken 415 vb. *hear*; turn a willing ear, go half-way to meet 597 vb. *be willing*; meet one's wishes, do all one is asked 828 vb. *content*; satisfy, come up to scratch 635 vb. *suffice*; accept, take one at one's word, embrace an offer, jump at; clinch a deal, close with, settle 766 vb. *make terms*; tolerate, recognize, allow, connive 736 vb. *be lenient*; consent unwillingly, drag oneself, make o.

See: 415, 488, 597, 612, 635, 703, 721, 736, 756, 766, 768, 770, 781, 828, 884, 923.

759 Offer

N. *offer*, fair o., proffer; improper offer, bribery, bribe 612 n. *inducement*; tender, bid, take-over b.; declaration, motion, proposition, proposal; approach, overture, advance, invitation; tentative approach, feeler; present, presentation, offering, gratuity, sacrifice 781 n. *gift*; dedication, consecration; candidature, application, solicitation 761 n. *request*.

Adj. *offering*, inviting; offered, advertised; open, available; on offer, on the market, in the m.; on hire, to let, for sale; on bid, on auction.

Vb. *offer*, proffer, hold out, make an offer, bid, tender; come with, bring, fetch; present, lay at one's feet, place in one's hands 781 vb. *give*; dedicate, consecrate; sacrifice to; introduce, broach, move, propose, make a proposition, put forward, suggest 512 vb. *propound*; not wait to be asked, approach, approach with, make overtures, make advances, hold out one's hand; keep the door ajar, keep one's offer open; induce 612 vb. *bribe*; press,

invite, send an invitation, ask one in 882 vb. *be hospitable*; hawk, hawk about, invite tenders, offer for sale 793 vb. *sell*; auction, declare the bidding open; cater, cater for 633 vb. *provide*; make available, place at one's disposal, place in one's way, make a present of 469 vb. *make possible*; pose, confront with.

offer oneself, sacrifice o.; stand, make one's candidature, compete, run for, enter 716 vb. *contend*; volunteer, come forward 597 vb. *be willing*; apply, put in for 761 vb. *request*; be on offer, look for takers, go begging.

See: 469, 512, 597, 612, 633, 716, 761, 781, 793, 882.

760 Refusal

N. *refusal*, non-acceptance, declining, declension, turning down 607 n. *rejection*; denial, negative answer, no, nay 533 n. *negation*; uncompromising answer, flat refusal, point blank r., peremptory r. 711 n. *defiance*; repulse, rebuff, slap in the face 292 n. *repulsion*; no facilities, denial policy 715 n. *resistance*; withholding 778 n. *retention*; recalcitrance 738 n. *disobedience*; non-compliance 769 n. *non-observance*; recusancy 598 n. *unwillingness*; objection, protest 762 n. *deprecation*; self-denial 945 n. *asceticism*; restraint 942 n. *temperance*; renunciation, abnegation 621 n. *relinquishment*.

Adj. *refusing*, denying, withholding, rejecting etc. vb.; uncomplaisant, recusant, non-compliant, uncompliant 769 adj. *non-observant*; jibbing, objecting 762 adj. *deprecatory*; deaf to, unhearing 598 adj. *unwilling*.

refused, not granted, turned down, ungratified, rebuffed etc. vb.; inadmissible, out of the question 470 adj. *impossible*; unoffered, withheld 778 adj. *retained*.

Vb. *refuse*, say no, shake one's head; disagree 489 vb. *dissent*; deny, negative, repudiate, disclaim 533 vb. *negate*; decline, turn down 607 vb. *reject*; deny firmly, repulse, rebuff 292 vb. *repel*; turn away 300 vb. *dismiss*; resist persuasion, be unmoved, harden one's heart 602 vb. *be obstinate*; not hear, not listen, turn a deaf ear 416 vb. *be deaf*; not give, close one's hand, close one's purse; not consent,

will otherwise, have other fish to fry; be slow to, hang fire, can't drag *or* make oneself 598vb. *be loth*; turn from, have nothing to do with, shy at, jib at 620vb. *avoid*; debar, keep out, shut the door 57 vb. *exclude*; not want, not cater for; look askance at, dislike, disfavour, discountenance, not hear of 924vb. *disapprove*; frown on, disallow 757vb. *prohibit*; set one's face against 715vb. *resist*; oppose 704vb. *withstand*; kick, protest 762vb. *deprecate*; not comply 769vb. *not observe*; grudge, begrudge, withhold, keep from 778vb. *retain*; deny oneself, waive, renounce, give up 621vb. *relinquish*; deprive oneself, go without, do w. 945vb. *be ascetic*.

Adv. *denyingly*, with a refusal, without acceptance; no, never, over one's dead body, not for all the tea in China.

See: 57, 292, 300, 416, 470, 489, 533, 598, 602, 607, 620, 621, 704, 711, 715, 738, 757, 762, 769, 778, 924, 942, 945.

761 Request

N. *request*, simple r., modest r., humble petition; negative request 762n. *deprecation*; asking, first time of a.; canvass, canvassing, hawking 793n. *sale*; strong request, forcible demand, requisition; last demand, final d., last time of asking, ultimatum 737n. *demand*; demand with threats, blackmail 900n. *threat*; postulation, assertion 532n. *affirmation*; assertion of one's rights, claim, counter-c. 915 n. *dueness*; consumer demand, firm d., steady d., strong d., seller's market 627n. *requirement*; postulate 475n. *premise*; proposition, proposal, motion, rogation, prompting, suggestion; overture, approach 759vb. *offer*; bid, application, suit; petition, memorial, round robin; prayer, appeal, plea (see *entreaty*); pressure, instance, insistence, urgency 740n. *compulsion*; clamour, cry, cri de cœur 836n. *lamentation*; dunning, importunity; soliciting, accosting, solicitation, invitation, temptation; mendicancy, begging, street-b., panhandling; appeal for funds, begging letter, subscription list, flag day, bazaar, charity performance; advertising 528n. *advertisement*; want ad., want column; want 859n. *desire*.

entreaty, imploration, imploring, beseeching; submission, humble s., folded hands, bended knees, one's k.; supplication, prayer, hard p., orison 981n. *prayers*; appeal, invocation, apostrophe 583n. *allocution*; solemn entreaty, adjuration, adjurement, conjuration, conjurement, obtestation, obsecration, imprecation; successful entreaty, impetration.

Adj. *requesting*, asking, inviting, begging etc.vb.; mendicant, alms-hunting; invitatory 759adj. *offering*; claiming 627 adj. *demanding*; insisting, insistent; importunate, pressing, urgent, instant; clamorous, dunning.

supplicatory, entreating, suppliant, praying, prayerful; on bended knees, with folded hands, cap in hand; precatory, imploratory, beseeching, with tears in one's eyes; invocatory, adjuratory, imprecatory; precative.

Vb. *request*, ask, invite, solicit; make overtures, approach, accost 759vb. *offer*; sue, sigh, woo, pop the question, put up the banns 889vb. *court*; seek, look for 459 vb. *search*; need, have in request, call for, clamour f. 627vb. *require*; crave, make a request, prefer an appeal, beg a favour, ask a boon, have a request to make, make bold to ask, trouble one for 859vb. *desire*; apply, make application, put in for, bid, bid for, make a bid f.; apply to, call on, appeal to, run to, address oneself to, go cap in hand to; tout, hawk, canvass, solicit orders 793vb. *sell*; petition, memorialize; make interest for, press a claim, expect 915vb. *claim*; make demands 737vb. *demand*; blackmail 900vb. *threaten*; be instant, insist 532vb. *emphasize*; urge, persuade 612vb. *induce*; importune, ply, press, dun, besiege, beset; knock at the door, demand entrance; impetrate; touch, touch for 785vb. *borrow*; requisition 786vb. *take*; raise money, tax 786vb. *levy*; formulate one's demands, state one's terms, send an ultimatum 766vb. *give terms*.

beg, cadge, crave, sponge, play the parasite; mump, scrounge, sorn; thumb, hitch-hike; panhandle, mendicate, beg one's bread, beg from door to door, knock at every d.; appeal for funds, pass the hat, make a collection, raise subscriptions, open a subscription-list 786vb. *levy*; beg in vain, whistle for 627vb. *require*.

entreat, make entreaty, beg hard; supplicate, be a suppliant; pray, implore, beseech, appeal, conjure, adjure, obtest, obsecrate, imprecate; invoke, apostrophize, appeal to, address 583 vb. *speak to*; address one's prayers to, pray to 981 vb. *offer worship*; kneel to, go down on one's knees, go down on one's marrow bones; sue, sigh, sigh at one's feet, fall at one's f.; gain by entreaty, impetrate 771 vb. *acquire.*

See: 459, 475, 528, 532, 583, 612, 627, 737, 740, 759, 762, 766, 771, 785, 786, 793, 836, 859, 889, 900, 915, 981.

762 Deprecation: negative request

N. *deprecation*, negative request, contrary advice, dehortation 613 n. *dissuasion*; begging off, plea for mercy, crossed fingers; intercession, mediation 981 n. *prayers*; counter-petition, counter-claim 761 n. *request*; murmur, cheep, squeak, complaint 829 n. *discontent*; exception, demur, expostulation, remonstrance, protest 704 n. *opposition*; reaction, kick 182 n. *counteraction*; gesture of protest, tut-tut, raised eyebrows, groans, jeers 924 n. *disapprobation*; open letter, round robin; demonstration, indignation meeting, march, hunger-m.; non-compliance 760 n. *refusal*; refusal to work 145 n. *strike.*

Adj. *deprecatory*, dehortative 613 adj. *dissuasive*; protesting, protestant, expostulatory; clamant, vocal; intercessory, mediatorial; averting, apotropaic.

Vb. *deprecate*, ask one not to, dehort, advise against, have a better idea, make a counter-proposal 613 vb. *dissuade*; avert the omen, touch wood, knock on w., cross one's fingers, keep one's fingers crossed 983 vb. *practise sorcery*; beg off, plead for, intercede 720 vb. *mediate*; pray, appeal 761 vb. *entreat*; cry for mercy 905 vb. *ask mercy*; show embarrassment, tut-tut, shake one's head, raise one's eyebrows 924 vb. *disapprove*; remonstrate, expostulate 924 vb. *reprove*; jeer, groan, stamp 926 vb. *detract*; murmur, beef, complain 829 vb. *be discontented*; demur, jib, kick, squeak, protest against, appeal a., petition a., raise one's voice a., cry out a., cry blue murder 704 vb. *oppose*; demonstrate, hold an indignation meeting;

strike, strike work, call out, come out, walk o. 145 vb. *cease.*

See: 145, 182, 613, 704, 720, 760, 761, 829, 905, 924, 926, 981, 983.

763 Petitioner

N. *petitioner*, humble p., suppliant, supplicant; appealer, appellant; claimant, pretender; postulant, aspirant, expectant; solicitor, asker, seeker, enquirer, advertiser; customer, bidder, tenderer; suitor, courter, wooer; canvasser, hawker, touter, tout, ambulance-chaser, barker, spieler; dun, dunner; pressure group, lobby, lobbyist; applicant, candidate, entrant; competitor, runner 716 n. *contender*; complainer, grouser, man with a grievance, irredentist 829 n. *malcontent.*

beggar, street-b., sturdy b., professional b., schnorrer, panhandler; mendicant, almshunter; mendicant friar, beghard, bhikshu, bhikkhu; tramp, bum 268 n. *wanderer*; cadger, borrower, scrounger, sorner, mumper, hitch-hiker; sponger, parasite 879 n. *toady.*

See: 268, 716, 829, 879.

764 Promise

N. *promise*, promise-making, pollicitation 759 n. *offer*; undertaking, engagement, commitment; espousal, betrothal, affiance, unofficial engagement 894 n. *marriage*; troth, plight, plighted word, word, one's bare w., parole, word of honour, sacred pledge, vow, marriage v. 532 n. *oath*; declaration, solemn d. 532 n. *affirmation*; declared intention 617 n. *intention*; profession, professions, fair words; assurance, pledge, credit, honour, warrant, warranty, guarantee, insurance 767 n. *security*; voluntary commitment, gentlemen's agreement, mutual a. 765 n. *compact*; covenant, bond, promise to pay 803 n. *debt*; obligation, debt of honour 917 n. *duty*; pre-engagement, firm date, delivery d. 672 n. *undertaking*; promiser, promise-maker, votary; engager, party 765 n. *signatory.*

Adj. *promissory*, promising, votive; on oath, under o., under hand and seal; on credit, on parole.

promised, covenanted, guaranteed, secured 767 adj. *pledged*; engaged, bespoke, reserved; betrothed, affianced; committed, in for it; bound, obliged, obligated 917 adj. *dutied*.

Vb. *promise*, say one will 532 vb. *affirm*; hold out, proffer 759 vb. *offer*; make a promise, give one's word, pledge one's w.; vow, vow and protest, take oath upon it 532 vb. *swear*; vouch for, go bail for, warrant, guarantee, assure, confirm, secure, insure, underwrite 767 vb. *give security*; pledge, stake; parole oneself, pledge one's honour, plight one's word, stake one's credit; engage, engage for, enter into an engagement, give a firm date 672 vb. *undertake*; make a gentleman's agreement, commit oneself, bind oneself, be bound, covenant 765 vb. *contract*; accept an obligation, take on oneself, answer for, accept responsibility 917 vb. *incur a duty*; accept a liability, promise to pay, incur a debt of honour 785 vb. *borrow*; bespeak, pre-engage, reserve 617 vb. *intend*; plight one's faith, exchange vows 894 vb. *wed*.

take a pledge, demand security 473 vb. *make certain*; put on oath, administer an o., adjure, swear, make one s. 466 vb. *testify*; make one promise, exact a p.; take on credit, take one's word, accept one's parole, parole 485 vb. *believe*; rely on, expect 473 vb. *be certain*.

Adv. *as promised*, according to contract, duly; professedly, upon one's word, upon one's honour, upon one's guarantee, truly 540 adv. *truthfully*.

See: 466, 473, 485, 532, 540, 617, 672, 759, 765, 767, 785, 803, 894, 917.

765 Compact

N. *compact*, contract, bargain, agreement, mutual a., mutual undertaking 672 n. *undertaking*; gentleman's agreement, debt of honour 764 n. *promise*; mutual pledge, exchange of vows; espousal, betrothal 894 n. *marriage*; covenant, indenture, bond 767 n. *security*; league, alliance, cartel 706 n. *co-operation*; pact, paction, convention, understanding 24 n. *agreement*; private understanding, something between them; secret pact, conspiracy 623 n. *plot*; negotiation 766 n.

conditions; deal, give and take 770 n. *compromise*; adjustment, composition, arrangement, settlement; completion, signature, ratification, confirmation 488 n. *assent*; seal, sigil, signet, signature, counter-s.; deed of agreement, indenture 767 n. *title-deed*.

treaty, international agreement; peace treaty, non-aggression pact; convention, concordat, protocol; Zollverein, Sonderbund; Pragmatic Sanction, Berne Convention.

signatory, signer, counter-signer, subscriber, the undersigned; swearer, attester, attestant 466 n. *witness*; endorser, ratifier; adherent, party, consenting p. 488 n. *assenter*; contractor, contracting party, high contracting p.; treaty-maker, negotiator.

Adj. *contractual*, conventional, consensual 488 adj. *assenting*; bilateral, multilateral; agreed to, negotiated, signed, undersigned, sworn, ratified; signed, sealed and delivered; under one's hand and seal.

Vb. *contract*, enter into a contract, engage 672 vb. *undertake*; pre-contract 764 vb. *promise*; covenant, make a compact, strike a bargain, sign a pact, strike hands, do a deal, clinch a d.; join in a compact, adhere; league, ally 706 vb. *co-operate*; treat, negotiate 791 vb. *bargain*; give and take 770 vb. *compromise*; stipulate 766 vb. *give terms*; agree, arrive at a formula, come to terms 766 vb. *make terms*; conclude, set at rest, settle; indent, execute, sign, subscribe, ratify, attest, confirm 488 vb. *endorse*; insure, underwrite 767 vb. *give security*.

See: 24, 466, 488, 623, 672, 706, 764, 766, 767, 770, 791, 894.

766 Conditions

N. *conditions*, making terms, treaty-making, negotiation, bargaining, collective b.; hard bargaining, horse-dealing 791 n. *barter*; formula, terms, set t., written t., stated t., terms for agreement; final terms, ultimatum, time limit 900 n. *threat*; dictated terms 740 n. *compulsion*; part of the bargain, condition, set of terms, frame of reference; articles, articles of agreement; provision, clause, entrench-

ed c., escape c., saving c., proviso, limitation, strings, reservation, exception 468 n. *qualification*; stipulation, sine qua non, essential clause 627 n. *requirement*; rule 693 n. *precept*; contractual terms, casus foederis, the letter of the treaty; embodied terms 765 n. *treaty*; terms of reference 751 n. *mandate.*

Adj. *conditional*, with strings attached, binding 917 adj. *obligatory*; provisional, stipulatory, qualificatory, provisory 468 adj. *qualifying*; limiting, subject to terms, conditioned, contingent; guarded, safeguarded, fenced, entrenched.

Vb. *give terms*, read out the t., propose conditions; condition, bind, tie down, attach strings; hold out for, insist on one's terms, make demands 737 vb. *demand*; stipulate, make it a sine qua non 627 vb. *require*; allow no exception 735 vb. *be severe*; insert a proviso, allow an exception 468 vb. *qualify*; fix the terms, impose the conditions, write the articles, draft the clauses; add a clause, write in.

make terms, negotiate, treat, be in treaty, parley, hold conversations 584 vb. *confer*; deal with, treat w., negotiate w.; make overtures, throw out a feeler 461 vb. *be tentative*; haggle, higgle 791 vb. *bargain*; proffer, make proposals, make a counter-proposal 759 vb. *offer*; give and take, yield a point, stretch a p. 770 vb. *compromise*; negotiate a treaty, do a deal 765 vb. *contract.*

Adv. *on terms*, on one's own t.; conditionally, provisionally, subject to, with a reservation; strictly, to the letter; necessarily, sine qua non; peremptorily, for the last time.

See: 461, 468, 584, 627, 693, 735, 737, 740, 751, 759, 765, 770, 791, 900, 917.

767 Security

N. *security*, precaution 858 n. *caution*; guarantee, warranty, authorization, writ 737 n. *warrant*; sponsorship, sponsion, patronage 660 n. *protection*; suretyship, cautionary, mainprize; surety, bail, caution, replevin, recognizance, personal r., parole; bailor, cautioner, mainpernor; gage, pledge, pawn, pignus, pignoration, hostage; stake, stake money, deposit, earnest, handsel, token, instalment; col-

our of one's money, earnest m., caution m.; token payment 804 n. *payment*; insurance, underwriting 660 n. *safety*; transfer of security, hypothecation, mortgage, bottomry 780 n. *transfer*; collateral, collateral security, real s.

title-deed, deed, instrument; unilateral deed, deed-poll; bilateral deed, indenture; charter, covenant, bond 765 n. *compact*; receipt, I.O.U., voucher, acquittance, quittance; certificate, authentication, marriage lines; verification, seal, stamp, signature, endorsement, acceptance 466 n. *credential*; valuable security, banknote, treasury n., promissory n., note of hand, hundi, bill, bill of exchange; paper, Government p., gilt-edged security; portfolio, scrip, share, debenture; mortgage deed, policy, insurance p.; will, testament, codicil, certificate of probate; matter of record, muniment, archive 548 n. *record.*

Adj. *pledged*, pawned, popped, deposited; in pawn, on deposit; on lease, on mortgage; on bail, on recognizance.

secured, covered, hedged, insured, mortgaged; gilt-edged; guaranteed, covenanted 764 adj. *promised.*

Vb. *give bail*, go b., bail one out, go surety, give s.; take bail, take recognisance, release on bail; hold in pledge, keep in pawn 764 vb. *take a pledge.*

give security, offer collateral, hypothecate, bottomry, mortgage; pledge, impignorate, pawn, pop, hock, spout 785 vb. *borrow*; guarantee, warrant 473 vb. *make certain*; authenticate, verify 466 vb. *corroborate*; execute, endorse, seal, stamp, sign, counter-s., subscribe, give one's signature 488 vb. *endorse*; accept, grant a receipt, write an I.O.U. 782 vb. *receive*; secure, insure, assure, underwrite 660 vb. *safeguard.*

See: 466, 473, 488, 548, 660, 737, 764, 765, 780, 782, 785, 804, 858.

768 Observance

N. *observance*, close o. 610 n. *practice*; full observance, fulfilment, satisfaction 635 n. *sufficiency*; adherence to, attention to; paying respect to, acknowledgment; performance, discharge, acquittance, acquittal 676 n. *action*; compliance 739 n. *obedience*; conformance 83 n. *conformity*;

attachment, fidelity, faith, good f. 739 n. *loyalty*; sense of responsibility, dependability, reliability 929 n. *probity*.

Adj. *observant*, practising 676 adj. *doing*; heedful, watchful, careful of, attentive to 455 adj. *attentive*; conscientious, punctual, diligent, earnest, religious, punctilious; over-conscientious, perfectionist 862 adj. *fastidious*; literal, pedantic, exact 494 adj. *accurate*; responsible, reliable, dependable 929 adj. *trustworthy*; loyal, true, compliant 739 adj. *obedient*; adherent to, adhering to 83 adj. *conformable*; faithful 929 adj. *honourable*.

Vb. *observe*, heed, respect, regard, have regard to, pay respect to, acknowledge, pay attention to, attend to 455 vb. *be attentive*; keep, practise, adhere to, cling to, follow, hold by, abide by, be loyal to 83 vb. *conform*; comply 739 vb. *obey*; fulfil, discharge, perform, execute, carry out, carry out to the letter 676 vb. *do*; satisfy 635 vb. *suffice*.

observe faith, keep f., be faithful to, have loyalty; discharge one's functions 917 vb. *do one's duty*; act up to one's obligations, meet one's o., be as good as one's word, make good one's promise, fulfil one's engagement, be true to the spirit of, stand by 929 vb. *be honourable*; come up to scratch, redeem one's pledge, pay one's debt, pay up 805 vb. *pay*; give one his due, deny no just claim 915 vb. *grant claims*.

Adv. *with observance*, faithfully, religiously, loyally; literally, meticulously, according to the spirit of.

See: 83, 455, 494, 610, 635, 676, 739, 805, 862, 915, 917, 929.

769 Non-observance

N. *non-observance*, no such practice; inobservance, informality, indifference 734 n. *laxity*; inattention, omission, laches 458 n. *negligence*; non-conformity, nonadherence 84 n. *unconformity*; abhorrence 607 n. *rejection*; antinomianism, anarchism 734 n. *anarchy*; non-performance, non-feasance 679 n. *inactivity*; nonfulfilment, shortcoming 726 n. *noncompletion*; infringement, violation, transgression 306 n. *overstepping*; noncompliance, disloyalty 738 n. *disobedience*; protest 762 n. *deprecation*; disregard,

discourtesy 921 n. *disrespect*; bad faith, breach of f., breach of promise 930 n. *perfidy*; retractation 603 n. *tergiversation*; repudiation, denial 533 n. *negation*; failure, bankruptcy 805 n. *insolvency*; forfeiture 963 n. *penalty*.

Adj. *non-observant*, non-practising; nonconforming, standing out, blacklegging, non-adhering, nonconformist 84 adj. *unconformable*; inattentive to, disregarding, neglectful 458 adj. *negligent*; unprofessional, uncanonical, misbehaving; indifferent, informal 734 adj. *lax*; non-compliant 738 adj. *disobedient*; transgressive, infringing, unlawful 954 adj. *lawbreaking*; disloyal 918 adj. *dutiless*; unfaithful 930 adj. *perfidious*; antinomian, anarchical 734 adj. *anarchic*.

Vb. *not observe*, not practise, abhor 607 vb. *reject*; not conform, not adhere, not follow, stand out 84 vb. *be uncomformable*; discard 674 vb. *disuse*; set aside 752 vb. *abrogate*; omit, ignore 458 vb. *neglect*; disregard, slight, show no respect for, snap one's fingers at 921 vb. *not respect*; stretch a point 734 vb. *be lax*; violate, do violence to 176 vb. *force*; transgress 306 vb. *overstep*; not comply with 738 vb. *disobey*; desert 918 vb. *fail in duty*; fail, not come up to scratch 636 vb. *not suffice*; perform less than one promised 726 vb. *not complete*; break faith, break one's promise, break one's word, neglect one's vow, repudiate one's obligations, dishonour 533 vb. *negate*; not stand by one's engagement, go back on, back out 603 vb. *tergiversate*; prove unreliable 930 vb. *be dishonest*; give the go-by, cut, shirk, dodge, evade, elude 620 vb. *avoid*; shuffle, palter, quibble, resort to shifts, equivocate 518 vb. *be equivocal*; forfeit, incur a penalty 963 vb. *be punished*.

See: 84, 176, 306, 458, 518, 533, 603, 607, 620, 636, 674, 679, 726, 734, 738, 752, 762, 805, 918, 921, 930, 954, 963.

770 Compromise

N. *compromise*, non-insistence, concession; mutual concession, give and take, adjustment, formula 765 n. *compact*; composition, commutation; second best, pis aller 35 n. *inferiority*; modus vivendi, working arrangement 624 n. *way*; middle term,

splitting the difference 30n. *average*; half-way 625n. *mid-course*; balancing act.

Vb. *compromise*, make a c., find a formula, find a basis; make mutual concessions, give and take, meet one half-way 625vb. *be half-way*; live and let live, not insist, stretch a point 734vb. *be lax*; strike an average, take the mean, go half and half, split the difference 30vb. *average out*; compound, commute; compose differences, adjust d., arbitrate, go to arbitration; patch up, bridge over 719vb. *pacify*; take the good with the bad, take what is offered, make a virtue of necessity, take the will for the deed; make the best of a bad job.

See: 30, 35, 624, 625, 719, 734, 765.

771 Acquisition

N. *acquisition*, getting, winning; bread-winning, earning; acquirement, obtainment, procurement, milking; collection 74n. *assemblage*; realization, profit-taking 793n. *sale*; conversion, encashment 780n. *transfer*; money-getting, money-grubbing 816n. *avarice*; heap, stack, pile, pool, scoop, jackpot 74n. *accumulation*; trover, finding, picking up 484n. *discovery*; finding again, recovery, retrieval, revendication, recoupment, re-entrance, replevin 656n. *restoration*; redemption 792n. *purchase*; getting hold of 786n. *taking*; subreption, theft 788n. *stealing*; coming into, inheritance, heir-ship, patrimony; thing acquired, acquest, find, trouvaille, windfall, treasure, treasure-trove; something for nothing, free gift 781n. *gift*; gratuity, baksheesh 962n. *reward*; benefit, benefit match, prize, plum 729n. *trophy*; pelf, lucre 797n. *money*; plunder 790n. *booty*.

earnings, income, earned i., wage, salary, screw, pay-packet 804n. *pay*; rate for the job, pay-scale, differential; pension, compensation, 'golden handshake'; reward of office, remuneration, emolument 962n. *reward*; allowance, expense account; pickings, perquisite, perks; cabbage, totting; commission, rake-off 810n. *discount*; return, net r., gross r., receipts, proceeds, sale p., turnover, takings, innings, revenue, taxes 807n. *receipt*; reaping, harvest, vintage, crop,

second c., aftermath, gleanings; output, produce 164n. *product*.

gain, thrift, savings 814n. *economy*; no loss, credit side, profit, net p., winnings; dividend, share-out 775n. *participation*; interest, high i., compound i., simple i. 36n. *increment*; paying transaction, profitable t., lucrative deal, successful speculation, main chance; increase of pay, enhanced salary, rise, raise 36n. *increase*; advantage, benefit; selfish advantage, personal benefit 932n. *selfishness*.

Adj. *acquiring*, acquisitive, accumulative; on the make, getting, winning; hoarding, saving.

gainful, paying, profitable, lucrative, remunerative 962adj. *rewarding*; advantageous 644adj. *beneficial*; fruitful, fertile 164adj. *productive*; not honorary, attended with pay, paid, remunerated, breadwinning.

acquired, had, got, gotten, ill-gotten; inherited, patrimonial; on the credit side.

Vb. *acquire*, get, come by; get by effort, earn, gain, obtain, procure, get at; find, strike, come across, pick up, pitch upon, light u. 484vb. *discover*; get hold of, get possession of, get in one's hand, get between finger and thumb; make one's own, annex 786vb. *appropriate*; win, capture, catch, land, net, bag 786vb. *take*; pick, tot, glean; gather, reap, crop, harvest; derive, draw, tap, milk, mine 304vb. *extract*; collect, accumulate, heap, pile up 74vb. *bring together*; collect funds, raise, levy, raise the wind; save, save up, hoard 632vb. *store*; get by purchase, buy, pre-empt 792vb. *purchase*; get in advance, reserve, book, engage, pre-engage 135vb. *be early*; get somehow, beg, borrow or steal; get a living, earn a l., win one's bread; get money, draw a salary, draw a pension, receive one's wages, be paid one's hire; have an income, be in receipt of, have a turnover, gross, take 782vb. *receive*; turn into money, convert, cash, encash, realize; get back, come by one's own, recover, regain, redeem, recapture, reconquer 656vb. *retrieve*; take back, resume, reassume, reclaim, re-enter; compensate oneself, recover one's losses 31vb. *recoup*; recover one's costs, break even, balance accounts 28vb. *equalize*; attain, reach; come in for, catch, incur, contract.

inherit, come into, be left, receive a legacy, enjoy an inheritance, take one's patrimony; succeed, succeed to, step into the shoes of, be the heir of.

gain, profit, make a p., draw a p., reap a p., earn a dividend; make, win; make money, coin m., make a fortune, make one's pile, rake in the shekels, turn a pretty penny 800vb. *get rich*; scoop, make a s., win, win the jackpot, break the bank; see one's advantage, sell at a profit; draw one's interest, collect one's profit, credit to one's account.

be profitable, profit, repay, be worth while 640vb. *be useful*; pay, pay well; bring in, gross, yield 164vb. *produce*; bring in a return, pay a dividend, show a profit 730 vb. *prosper*; accrue, roll in, come into the till, bring grist to the mill, stick to one's fingers.

See: 28, 31, 36, 74, 135, 164, 304, 484, 632, 640, 644, 656, 729, 730, 775, 780, 781, 782, 786, 788, 790, 792, 793, 797, 800, 804, 807, 810, 814, 816, 932, 962.

772 Loss

N. *loss*, deprivation, privation, bereavement, funeral; dispossession, eviction 786n. *expropriation*; sacrifice, forfeiture, forfeit, lapse; hopeless loss, dead l., total l., utter l., irretrievable l., perdition, deperdition 165n. *ruin*; depreciation 655 n. *deterioration*; diminishing returns 42n. *decrement*; set-back, check, reverse; loss of profit, lack of p.; overdraft, failure, bankruptcy 805n. *insolvency*; consumption 806n. *expenditure*; non-recovery, spilt milk, wastage, leakage 634 n. *waste*; dissipation, evaporation, drain, running sore 37n. *decrease*; riddance, good r. 746n. *liberation*; losing battle 728 n. *defeat*.

Adj. *losing*, unprofitable 641adj. *profitless*; squandering 815adj. *prodigal*; the worse for 655adj. *deteriorated*; forfeiting, sacrificing, sacrificial; deprived, dispossessed, robbed 774adj. *unpossessed*; denuded, stripped of, shorn of, reft of, bereft, bereaved; minus, without, lacking; rid of, quit of; set back, out of pocket, down, in the red, overdrawn, bankrupt, insolvent 805adj. *non-paying*; non-profitmaking 931adj. *disinterested*.

lost, long l., gone, gone for ever; missing, mislaid 188adj. *misplaced*; untraced, untraceable, lost, stolen or strayed 190 adj. *absent*; rid, off one's hands; wanting, lacking, short 307adj. *deficient*; irrecoverable, irretrievable, irredeemable, spent, wasted, gone down the drain, squandered 806adj. *expended*; forfeit, forfeited, sacrificed.

Vb. *lose*, not find, be unable to f., look in vain for; mislay 188vb. *misplace*; miss, let slip, let slip through one's fingers, say good-bye to 138vb. *lose a chance*; have nothing to show for, squander, throw away 634vb. *waste*; deserve to lose, forfeit, sacrifice; spill the milk, allow to leak, let go down the drain; not improve matters, be the worse for 832vb. *aggravate*; be a loser 728vb. *be defeated*; lose one's stake, lose one's bet, pay out, pay the table; make no profit, be down, be out of pocket; be set back, incur losses, meet with l., sell at a loss; be unable to pay, break, go bankrupt 805vb. *not pay*; overdraw, be overdrawn, be in the red, be minus.

be lost, be missing, be declared m., lose one's way 282vb. *stray*; lapse, go down the drain, go down the spout, go to pot 165 vb. *be destroyed*; melt away, never return 446vb. *disappear*; be a good riddance 831 vb. *relieve*.

See: 37, 42, 138, 165, 188, 190, 282, 307, 446, 634, 641, 655, 728, 746, 774, 786, 805, 806, 815, 831, 832, 931.

773 Possession

N. *possession*, right of p., de jure p., ownership, proprietorship, rightful possession, lawful p., peaceful p., enjoyment, uti possidetis; seisin, occupancy, nine points of the law, bird in the hand; mastery, hold, grasp, grip, de facto possession 778 n. *retention*; a possession 777n. *property*; tenancy, holding 777n. *estate*; tenure, fee, fief, feud, feodality, seigniory, knight service, chivalry, socage, villenage; long possession, prescription 610n. *habit*; exclusive possession, sole p., monopoly, corner, ring; prepossession, pre-occupancy, pre-emption, forestalment, squatting; future possession, expectations, heirship, heirdom, inheritance, heritage,

patrimony, reversion, remaindership; taking possession, impropriation, engrossment, making one's own, claiming, hoisting one's flag over 786n. *taking*.

Adj. *possessing*, seized of, having, holding, owning, enjoying etc. vb.; having possessions, propertied; possessed of, in possession, occupying, squatting; endowed with, blest w., fraught w., instinct w.; exclusive, monopolistic, possessive.

possessed, enjoyed, had, held; in the possession of, in the ownership of, in one's hand, in one's grasp, in one's hold; in the bank, in one's account, to one's credit; at one's disposal, on hand, in store; proper, personal 80adj. *special*; belonging, one's own, one's very o., unshared, private, personal; monopolized by, engrossed by, devoured by; booked, reserved, engaged, occupied; included in, inherent, appertaining, attaching; unsold, undisposed of, on one's hands.

Vb. *possess*, be possessed of, own, have; die possessed of, cut up well 780vb. *bequeath*; hold, have and hold, have a firm grip on, hold in one's grasp, grip 778vb. *retain*; have at one's command, have absolute disposal of, command 673 vb. *dispose of*; call oneself owner, boast of 915vb. *claim*; contain, include 78vb. *comprise*; fill, occupy; squat, sit on, settle upon, inhabit; enjoy, have for one's own 673vb. *use*; have all to oneself, be a dog in the manger, monopolize, engross, corner; get, take possession, make one's own, impropriate 786vb. *take*; recover, re-occupy, re-enter 656vb. *retrieve*; pre-occupy, forestall, pre-empt, reserve, book, engage 135vb. *be early*; inherit, come into, come in for, step into, succeed 771vb. *acquire*.

belong, vest, vest in, belong to; be included in, inhere, attach, pertain, appertain, apply; be subject to, owe service to 745vb. *be subject*.

Adv. *possessively*, monopolistically; in one's own right, in full ownership, by right of possession, by prescription.

See: 78, 80, 135, 610, 656, 673, 745, 771, 777, 778, 780, 786, 915.

774 Non-ownership

N. *non-ownership*, non-possession, non-occupancy; tenancy at will, temporary lease; dependence 745n. *subjection*; pauperism 801n. *poverty*; loss of possession 57n. *exclusion*; deprivation, disentitlement 772n. *loss*; exemption, dispensation 919n. *non-liability*; no man's land, debatable territory, Tom Tiddler's ground 184n. *territory*.

Adj. *not owning*, not possessing, dependent 745adj. *subject*; owning nothing, destitute, penniless, propertyless 801adj. *poor*; unblest with, barren; lacking, minus, without 627adj. *required*; dispossessed, disentitled 57adj. *excluded*.

unpossessed, unattached, not belonging; masterless, ownerless, nobody's, no man's; international; not owned, unowned, unappropriated; unclaimed, disowned; unheld, unoccupied, untenanted, unleased; vacant 190adj. *empty*; derelict, abandoned 779adj. *not retained*; ungot, unhad, unobtained, unacquired, untaken, going begging 860adj. *unwanted*.

See: 57, 184, 190, 627, 745, 772, 779, 801, 860, 919.

775 Joint Possession

N. *joint possession*, jointness, possession in common; joint tenancy, tenancy in common; gavel-kind; joint ownership, common o.; public property, public domain 777n. *property*; joint government, condominium 733n. *polity*; joint stock, common stock, pool, kitty 632n. *store*; co-operative system, mutualization, mutualism 706n. *co-operation*; public ownership, state o., socialism, communism, collectivism; community of possessions, community of women; collective farm, collective, kolkhoz, kibbutz 370n. *farm*; share-cropping, métayage.

participation, membership, affiliation 78n. *inclusion*; sharing, co-sharing, partnership, co-p., profit-sharing 706n. *association*; joint mess, syssitia; Dutch party, picnic; dividend, share-out; share, fair s., co-portion, lot, whack 783n. *portion*; complicity, involvement, sympathy; fellow-feeling, sympathetic strike, joint action.

participator, member, co-sharer, partner, co-p., sharer, co-parcener, co-heir, joint h.; shareholder, stock-h. 776n. *possessor*; co-tenant, joint t., tenants in common;

share-cropper, métayer 370n. *husbandman*; co-operator, mutualist; collectivist, socialist, communist; sympathizer 707n. *patron*.

Adj. *sharing*, co-sharing, joint, profit-sharing, co-operative; common, communal, international; collective, socialistic, communistic; partaking, participating, participatory, in on, involved, in the same boat; in the swim, in the thick of things; sympathetic, condoling.

Vb. *participate*, have a hand in, join in, be in on 706vb. *co-operate*; partake of, share in, take a share, come in for a s.; snack, share, go shares, go snacks, go halves, go fifty-fifty, share and share alike 783vb. *apportion*; share expenses, go Dutch 804vb. *defray*.

socialize, mutualize, nationalize, internationalize, communize; have in common, put in the kitty, pool, throw in to the common p., hold in common, have all in c., live in joint mess.

Adv. *in common*, by shares, share and share alike; jointly, collectively, unitedly.

See: 78, 370, 632, 706, 707, 733, 776, 777, 783, 804.

776 Possessor

N. *possessor*, holder, person in possession, impropriator; taker, captor, conqueror; trespasser, squatter; monopolizer, dog in the manger; occupant, lodger, occupier, incumbent; mortgagee, bailee, trustee; renter, hirer, lessee, lease-holder, copyholder, rent-payer; tenantry, tenant, tenant-at-will, tenant for life; householder, freeholder, franklin, yeoman; feudatory, feoffee, tenant in fee, vassal 742n. *dependant*; peasant, actual cultivator of the soil, serf, villein, kulak, moujik, rayat, zamindar 370n. *husbandman*; sublessee, under-tenant, korfa rayat.

owner, monarch, monarch of all one surveys; master, mistress, proprietor, proprietress; purchaser, vendee, buyer 792n. *purchaser*; lord, lord paramount, lord of the manor, mesne lord, feoffer; landed gentry, landed interest 868n. *aristocracy*; man of property, property-owner, property-holder, shareholder, stock-holder, landholder, zamindar, landowner, landlord, land-

lady; mortgagor; testator, testatrix, bequeather, devisor 781n. *giver*.

beneficiary, cestui que trust, cestui que vie; feoffee, releasee, grantee, patentee; impropriator, lay i. 782n. *recipient*; incumbent 986n. *cleric*; devisee, legatee, legatary; inheritor, heritor, successor, successor apparent, tanist; next of kin 11n. *kinsman*; heir, expectant, expectant heir, heiress, 'lady richly left'; heir of the body, heir-at-law, heir general, heir male, heir apparent, heir presumptive; crown prince 741n. *sovereign*; reversioner, remainderman; tertius gaudens; co-heir, joint h., co-sharer 775n. *participator*.

See: 11, 370, 741, 742, 775, 781, 782, 792, 868, 986.

777 Property

N. *property*, meum et tuum, suum cuique; possession, possessions, one's all; stake, venture; personalty, personal property, public p., common p.; church property, temporalities; chose in possession, chattel, real property, moveables, immoveables; goods and chattels, parcels, appurtenances, belongings, paraphernalia, effects, personal e., impedimenta, baggage, luggage, traps, things; cargo, lading 193n. *contents*; goods, wares, stock, stock-in-trade 795n. *merchandise*; plant, fixtures, furniture.

estate, estate and effects, assets, frozen a., liquid a., assets and liabilities; circumstances, what one is worth, what one will cut up for; resources 629n. *means*; substance, one's money, one's gold 800n. *wealth*; revenue, income, rent-roll 807n. *receipt*; valuables, securities, stocks and shares, portfolio; stake, holding, investment; copyright, patent; chose in action, claim, demand, good debts, bad d.; right, title, easement, interest, vested i., contingent i., beneficial i., equitable i., life i.; absolute i., paramount estate; lease, tenure, freehold, copyhold, fee, fee simple, fee tail, estate in tail male, estate in tail female; tenement, hereditament, corporeal h., incorporeal h.

lands, land, acres, broad a.; estate, landed e., property, landed p., zemindari, khas mahall; real estate, real property, realty; hereditament, tenement, holding, tenure,

allodium, freehold, copyhold, fief, feud, manor, honour, seigniory, lordship, domain, demesne; messuage, capital m.; farm, home f., ranch, hacienda; crown lands, folk l., common land, common; dependency, dominion, state 184n. *territory.*

dower, dowry, dot, portion, marriage p., jointure, settlement, peculium; allotment, allowance, pin-money; alimony, patrimony, birthright 915n. *dueness;* appanage, heritage; inheritance, legacy, bequest; expectations, remainder, reversion; limitation, strict settlement, estate for life, estate for years; heirloom.

Adj. *proprietary,* branded, patented; moveable, immoveable, real, personal; propertied, landed, predial, manorial, seignorial, feudal, feodal, allodial, freehold, leasehold, copyhold; patrimonial, hereditary, heritable, testamentary; entailed, limited; dowered, endowed, established.

Vb. *dower,* endow, possess with, bless w. 781 vb. *give;* devise 780 vb. *bequeath;* grant, assign, allot 780 vb. *convey;* possess, put in possession, instal 751 vb. *commission;* establish, found.

Adv. *at credit,* in one's account; to one's heirs and successors.

See: 184, 193, 629, 751, 780, 795, 800, 807, 915.

778 Retention

N. *retention,* prehensility, tenacity; stickiness 354n. *viscidity;* holding on, hanging on, clinging to, prehension; handhold, foothold, toe-hold 218n. *support;* bridgehead, beach-head 34n. *vantage;* clutches, grip, iron g., gripe, grasp, hold, firm h., stranglehold, half-nelson; squeeze 198n. *compression;* clinch, lock; clip, hug, embrace 889n. *endearment;* keep, ward, keeping in 747n. *detention;* containment, holding action, pincer movement 235n. *inclosure;* plug, stop 264n. *stopper;* ligament 47n. *bond.*

nippers, pincers, tweezers, pliers, wrench, tongs, forceps, vice, clamp 47n. *fastening;* talon, claw, nails 256n. *sharp point;* tentacle, tenaculum 378n. *feeler;* teeth, fangs 256n. *tooth;* paw, hand, fingers 378n. *finger;* fist, clenched f., nieve.

Adj. *retentive,* retaining 747 adj. *restraining;* clinging, adhesive, sticky, gummy, gooey 48 adj. *cohesive;* firm, unshakable, indissoluble 45 adj. *tied;* tight, strangling, throttling; costive, bound; fast shut 264 adj. *closed.*

retained, in the grip of, gripped, pinned, clutched, strangled; fast, held; kept in, detained 747 adj. *imprisoned;* penned, held in, contained 232 adj. *circumscribed;* saved, kept 666 adj. *preserved;* booked, reserved, engaged; undisposed of, unsold, not for sale; unforfeited, undeprived; kept back, withheld 760 adj. *refused;* uncommunicated, esoteric, incommunicable 523 adj. *occult;* non-transferable, inalienable; entailed, in mortmain, in strict settlement.

Vb. *retain,* hold; hold up, catch, steady 218 vb. *support;* hold on, hold fast, hold tight, keep a firm hold of, maintain one's hold; cling to, hang on to, freeze on to, stick to, adhere 48 vb. *agglutinate;* fasten on, grip, gripe, grasp, clench, clinch, lock; hug, clip, embrace; pin, pin down, hold d.; have by the throat, throttle, strangle, keep a stranglehold on, put the half-nelson on, tighten one's grip 747 vb. *restrain;* fix one's teeth in, dig one's nails in, dig one's toes in; keep in, detain 747 vb. *imprison;* contain, keep within limits, draw the line 235 vb. *inclose;* keep to oneself, keep in one's own hands, keep back, withhold 525 vb. *keep secret;* keep in one's hand, have in hand, not dispose of 632 vb. *store;* save, keep 666 vb. *preserve;* not part with, keep back, withhold 760 vb. *refuse.*

See: 34, 45, 47, 48, 198, 218, 232, 235, 256, 264, 354, 378, 523, 525, 632, 666, 747, 760, 889.

779 Non-retention

N. *non-retention,* parting with, disposal, alienation 780n. *transfer;* selling off 793 n. *sale;* letting go, leaving hold of, release 746n. *liberation;* unfreezing, decontrol; dispensation, exemption 919n. *nonliability;* dissolution (of a marriage) 896n. *divorce;* cession, abandonment, renunciation 621n. *relinquishment;* cancellation 752n. *abrogation;* disuse 611n. *desuetude;* availability, saleability, disposability;

unsoundness, leaking, leak 298 n. *outflow.*

derelict, deserted village, abandoned position; jetsam, flotsam 641 n. *rubbish*; cast-off, slough; waif, stray, foundling, orphan, maroon; outcaste, untouchable.

Adj. *not retained,* not kept, under notice to quit; alienated, disposed of, sold off; dispensed with, abandoned 621 adj. *relinquished*; released 746 adj. *liberated*; derelict, unclaimed, unappropriated; unowned 774 adj. *unpossessed*; disowned, divorced, disinherited; heritable, inheritable, transferable; available, for sale 793 n. *saleable*; giveable, bestowable.

Vb. *not retain,* part with, alienate, transfer 780 vb. *convey*; sell off, dispose of 793 vb. *sell*; let go, let slip, unhand, leave hold of, relax one's grip, release one's hold; unlock, unclinch, unclench 263 vb. *open*; unbind, untie, disentangle 46 vb. *disjoin*; forego, dispense with, do without, spare, give up, waive, abandon, cede, yield 621 vb. *relinquish*; renounce, abjure 603 vb. *recant*; cancel, revoke 752 vb. *abrogate*; lift, lift restrictions, derestrict, decontrol, deration 746 vb. *liberate*; supersede, replace 150 vb. *substitute*; wash one's hands of, disown, disclaim 533 vb. *negate*; dissolve (a marriage) 896 vb. *divorce*; disinherit, cut off with a shilling 801 vb. *impoverish*; marry off 894 vb. *marry*; get rid of, cast off, ditch, jettison 300 vb. *eject*; cast away, maroon; pension off, invalid out, retire; discharge, give notice to quit, ease out, kick o. 300 vb. *dismiss*; lay off, stand o.; drop, discard 674 vb. *disuse*; withdraw, abandon, one's position 753 vb. *resign*; lose friends, estrange 881 vb. *make enemies*; sit loose to 860 vb. *be indifferent*; let out, leak 300 vb. *emit.*

See: 46, 150, 263, 298, 300, 533, 603, 611, 621, 641, 674, 746, 752, 753, 774, 780, 793, 801, 860, 881, 894, 896, 919.

780 Transfer (of property)

N. *transfer,* transmission, consignment, delivery, livery, hand-over 272 n. *transference*; enfeoffment, feoffment, livery of seisin; impropriation; settlement, limitation; conveyancing, conveyance; bequeathal, testamentary disposition; assignment; alienation, abalienation 779 n.

non-retention; demise, devise, bequest 781 n. *gift*; lease, let, lease and release; bargain and sale 793 n. *sale*; trade 791 n. *barter*; conversion, exchange 151 n. *interchange*; change of hands, change-over 150 n. *substitution*; shifting use, shifting trust; devolution, delegation 751 n. *commission*; heritability, succession, reversion, inheritance; pledge, pawn, hostage.

Adj. *transferred,* made over, impropriated, feoffed; borrowed, lent, pawned, leased; transferable, conveyable, alienable, exchangeable, negotiable; heritable, reversional, reversionary; giveable, bestowable.

Vb. *convey,* transfer by deed; transfer by will (see *bequeath*); grant, assign, sign away, give a. 781 vb. *give*; demise, let, rent, hire 784 vb. *lease*; alienate, abalienate 793 vb. *sell*; negotiate, barter 791 vb. *trade*; change over 150 vb. *substitute*; exchange, convert 151 vb. *interchange*; confer, confer ownership, put in possession, impropriate, invest with, enfeoff; confer citizenship, naturalize; commit, devolve, delegate, entrust 751 vb. *commission*; give away, marry off 894 vb. *marry*; deliver, give delivery, transmit, hand over, make o., pass to, pass the buck 272 vb. *transfer*; pledge, pawn 784 vb. *lend*; leave to 756 vb. *permit*; transfer ownership, withdraw a gift, give to another; disinherit, cut off, cut off with a shilling 801 vb. *impoverish*; dispossess, expropriate, relieve of 786 vb. *deprive*; transfer to the state, nationalize, municipalize 775 vb. *socialize.*

bequeath, will, will and bequeath, devise, demise; grant, assign; leave, leave by will, make a bequest, leave a legacy; make a will, make one's last will and testament, put in one's will, make testamentary dispositions, add a codicil; leave a fortune, cut up well 800 vb. *be rich*; have something to leave.

change hands, pass to another, come into the hands of; change places 151 vb. *interchange*; be transferred, pass, shift; revert to, devolve upon; pass from one to another, pass from hand to hand, circulate, go the rounds 314 vb. *circle*; succeed, inherit 771 n. *acquire.*

See: 150, 151, 272, 314, 751, 756, 771, 775, 779, 781, 784, 786, 791, 793, 800, 801, 894.

781 Giving

N. *giving*, bestowal, donation; alms-giving, charity 901n. *philanthropy*; generosity, generous giving, habit of g. 813n. *liberality*; contribution, subscription to 703n. *subvention*; prize-giving, presentation, award, 962n. *reward*; delivery, commitment, consignment, conveyance 780 n. *transfer*; endowment, dotation, settlement 777n. *dower*; grant, accordance, presentment, conferment; investment, investiture, enfeoffment, infeudation; bequeathal, leaving, will-making.

gift, fairing, cadeau, present, birthday p., Christmas p.; good-luck present, handsel; Christmas box, tip, vail, bribe, fee, honorarium, baksheesh, gratuity, sweetener, douceur, pourboire, trinkgeld, drink money 962n. *reward*; token, consideration; prize, award, presentation 729n. *trophy*; benefit, benefit match, benefit performance; alms, maundy money, dole, benefaction, charity 901n. *philanthropy*; sportule, food parcel, free meal; bounty, manna; largesse, donation, donative, hand-out; bonus, bonus shares, bonanza; something extra, extras, gracemarks; perks, perquisites, expense account; grant, allowance, compassionate a.; subsidy 703n. *subvention*; boon, grace, favour, grace and f.; unremunerated service, labour of love 597n. *voluntary work*; free gift, outright g., ex gratia payment; piece of luck, windfall; repayment, unsolicited r., conscience-money 804n. *payment*; forced loan, benevolence, tribute 809n. *tax*; bequest, legacy 780n. *transfer*.

offering, dedication, consecration; votive-offering, vow 979n. *piety*; peace-offering, thank-o., offertory, collection, sacrifice, self-s. 981n. *oblation*; Easter-offering, widow's mite; contribution, subscription, flag-day; tribute, free t., Peter's pence; offering of land, bhoodan; ante, stake.

giver, donor, bestower; rewarder, tipper; grantor, feoffer, investor; presenter, awarder, prize-giver; settlor, testator, devisor, bequeather; donator, subscriber, contributor; sacrificer, oblationer 981n. *worshipper*; tributary, tribute-payer 742n. *subject*; almoner, lady a., almsgiver, blood-donor 903n. *benefactor*; generous giver, distributor of largesse, Lady Bountiful, rich uncle, Santa Claus, Father Christmas 813n. *good giver*.

Adj. *giving*, granting etc.vb.; tributary 745 adj. *subject*; subscribing, contributory 703adj. *aiding*; alms-giving, charitable, eleemosynary, compassionate 897adj. *benevolent*; sacrificial, votive, sacrificing, oblatory 981adj. *worshipping*; generous, bountiful 813adj. *liberal*.

given, bestowed, gifted; given away, gratuitous, gratis, for nothing, free 812adj. *uncharged*; giveable, bestowable, allowed, allowable, concessional 756adj. *permitted*.

Vb. *give*, bestow, lend, render; afford, provide; vouchsafe, favour with, honour w., indulge w., show favour, grant a boon 736vb. *be lenient*; grant, accord 756vb. *permit*; gift, donate, make a present of; give by will, leave, devise, make legacies 780vb. *bequeath*; dower, endow, enrich; give a prize, present, award 962vb. *reward*; confer, bestow upon, vest, invest with; dedicate, consecrate, vow to 759vb. *offer*; devote, offer up, immolate, sacrifice 981vb. *offer worship*; spare for, have time for; give a present, gratify, tip, consider, remember; grease the palm 612vb. *bribe*; bestow alms, make a benefaction, put in the collection 897vb. *philanthropize*; give freely, open one's hand, open one's purse, put one's hand in one's pocket, lavish, pour out, shower upon 813vb. *be liberal*; spare, give free, give away, not charge; stand, treat, entertain 882vb. *be hospitable*; give out, dispense, dole out, mete o., share o., allot, deal, deal to 783vb. *apportion*; contribute, subscribe, pay towards, subsidize, help, help with money 703vb. *aid*; pay one's share or whack, ante up, divvy up 775vb. *participate*; part with, fork out 804vb. *pay*; share, share with, impart 524vb. *communicate*; render one's due, furnish one's quota 917vb. *do one's duty*; give one his due 915vb. *grant claims*; pay tribute 923vb. *praise*; give up, cede, yield 621vb. *relinquish*; hand over, give o., make o., deliver 780vb. *convey*; commit, consign, entrust 751vb. *commission*; despatch 272vb. *send*.

See: 272, 524, 597, 612, 621, 703, 729, 736, 742, 745, 751, 756, 759, 775, 777, 780, 783, 804, 809, 812, 813, 882, 897, 901, 903, 915, 917, 923, 962, 979, 981.

782 Receiving

N. *receiving*, admittance 299n. *reception*; getting 771n. *acquisition*; acceptance, recipience, suscipience, assumption; inheritance, succession, heirship; collection, collectorship, receivership, receipt of custom; a receipt, windfall 781n. *gift*; toll, tribute, dues, receipts, proceeds, winnings, gettings, takings 771n. *earnings*; receiving end.

recipient, acceptor, taker, biter; trustee 754 n. *consignee*; addressee 588n. *correspondent*; buyer, vendee 792n. *purchaser*; transferee, donee, grantee, feoffee, assignee, allottee, licensee, patentee, concessionnaire, lessee, releasee; devisee, legatee, legatary, inheritor, heir, successor 776n. *beneficiary*; payee, earner, stipendiary, wage-earner; pensioner, oldage p., pensionary, annuitant; remittance-man 742n. *dependant*; winner, prize-w., scholarship-holder, exhibitioner, sizar 644n. *exceller*; free ticket-holder, deadhead; object of charity, sportulary 763n. *beggar*; almsman, bedesman; one at the receiving end, receiver, striker (tennis), batter, batsman (cricket).

receiver, official r., liquidator 798n. *treasurer*; payee, collector, bill-c., rent-c., tax-c., tax-farmer, publican, income-tax officer, excise o., excisemen, customs officer, douanier; booking-clerk; shareholder, bond-holder, rentier; oblationary.

Adj. *receiving*, recipient, suscipient; receptive, welcoming; impressionable 819adj. *sensitive*; receiving pay, paid, stipendiary, wage-earning; pensionary, pensioned; awarded, given, favoured.

Vb. *receive*, be given, have from; get 771vb. *acquire*; collect, take up, levy, toll, take its t. 786vb. *take*; gross, net, pocket, pouch; be in receipt of, have received; get one's share; be dealt a hand; accept, take in 299 vb. *admit*; accept from, take f., draw, encash, be paid; have an income, draw a pension; inherit, succeed, come into, come in for; receipt, give a r., acknowledge.

be received, be drawn, be receipted; be credited, be added unto 38vb. *accrue*; come to hand, come in, roll in, fill the till; pass into one's hands, stick to one's fingers, fall to one's share, fall to one's lot.

See: 38, 299, 588, 644, 742, 754, 763, 771, 776, 781, 786, 792, 798, 819.

783 Apportionment

N. *apportionment*, appointment, assignment, allotment, allocation, appropriation; division, partition, repartition, sharing out; shares, fair s., distribution, deal, new d.; dispensing, dispensation, administration; demarcation, delimitation 236n. *limit*; place, assigned p., allotted sphere, seat, station 27n. *degree*; public sector, private s.

portion, share, share-out, cut, split; dividend, interim d., final d.; allocation, allotment, budget a., block a., blanket a.; lot, contingent; proportion, ratio; quantum, quota; halves, bigger half, moiety 53n. *part*; deal, hand (at cards); dole, mess, meed, modicum, pittance, allowance; ration, iron rations, ration book, coupon; dose, dosage, measure, dollop, whack, helping, melon-cutting, slice 53n. *piece*; rake-off, commission 810n. *discount*; stake, ante; allotted task, taskwork, task, stint 682n. *labour*.

Vb. *apportion*, allot, allocate, appropriate; appoint, assign; assign a part, cast, cast for a rôle; assign a place, detail, billet; partition, zone; demarcate, delimit 236 vb. *limit*; divide, divvy, carve, carve up, split, cut; halve 92vb. *bisect*; share, share out, distribute; dispense, administer, serve, deal, deal out, portion out, dole out, parcel out; mete, measure, ration, dose; divide proportionately, pro-rate; get a share, take one's whack.

Adv. *pro rata*, to each according to his share; proportionately, respectively, each to each, per head, per capita; as dealt.

See: 27, 53, 92, 236, 682, 810.

784 Lending

N. *lending*, hiring, leasing, farming out; letting, subletting, subinfeudation; lending at interest, loan transaction, feneration, usury, giving credit 802n. *credit*; investment; mortgage; advance, imprest, loan, accommodation, temporary a.; lending on security, pawnbroking; lease, long l.; let, sublet.

pawnshop, mont-de-piéte, pop-shop, hock s.; house of credit, finance corporation, International Monetary Fund.

lender, creditor; harsh creditor, extortioner; investor, financier, banker, bania; money-lender, usurer, shark, Shylock; pawn-broker, uncle; mortgagee, lessor, hirer, renter; backer, angel; seller on credit, tallyman; hire-purchase dealer.

Adj. *lending*, investing, laying out; usurious, extortionate; lent, loaned, on credit.

Vb. *lend*, loan, put out at interest; advance, accommodate, allow credit, give one an imprest account 802 vb. *credit*; lend on security, do pawnbroking; put up the money, back, finance; invest, sink; risk one's money 791 vb. *speculate*.

lease, let, demise, let out, hire out, let out on hire, farm out; sublet, subinfeudate.

Adv. *on loan*, on credit, on advance; on security.

See: 791, 802.

785 Borrowing

N. *borrowing*, touching; request for credit, loan application; loan transaction, mortgage 803 n. *debt*; hire purchase, H.P., never-never system; pledging, pawning; temporary misappropriation, joy-ride 788 n. *stealing*; something borrowed, loan, repayable amount 784 n. *lending*; forced loan, benevolence 809 n. *tax*; unauthorized borrowing, infringement, plagiarism, copying 20 n. *imitation*; borrowed plumes 542 n. *deception*; loan-word.

Vb. *borrow*, borrow short, borrow long; touch, touch for; mortgage, pawn, pledge, pop, hock; take a loan, exact a benevolence; get credit, get accommodation, take on loan, take on credit, take on tick; buy in instalments, hire-purchase 792 vb. *purchase*; incur liabilities, run into debt 803 vb. *be in debt*; promise to pay, ask for credit, apply for a loan, raise a loan, raise the wind, float a loan; invite investment, issue debentures, accept deposits; beg, borrow, or steal; cheat, crib, plagiarize, infringe 20 vb. *copy*.

hire, rent, farm, lease, take on lease, take on let, charter.

See: 20, 542, 784, 788, 792, 803, 809.

786 Taking

N. *taking*, snatching; seizure, capture, rape; taking hold, grasp, prehension, apprehension 778 n. *retention*; taking possession, assuming ownership, impropriation, appropriation, assumption 916 n. *arrogation*; requisition, commandeering, nationalization, municipalization, compulsory acquisition 771 n. *acquisition*; compulsory saving, post-war credit, compulsory loan, benevolence 785 n. *borrowing*; exaction, taxation, raising taxes, impost, levy, capital l. 809 n. *tax*; taking back, recovery, retrieval, recoupment; resumption, reprise, re-entry; ablation, taking away; taking in advance, prolepsis 135 n. *anticipation*; removal 188 n. *displacement*; furtive removal, conveyance 788 n. *stealing*; snatching away, abreption; scrounging, totting; bodily removal, abduction, kidnapping, slave-raiding, androlepsy, body-snatching; raid, slave-r. 788 n. *spoliation*; thing taken, take, haul, catch, capture, prize, plum 790 n. *booty*; receipts, takings, winnings, pickings, gleanings 771 n. *earnings*.

expropriation, dispossession, extortion, angary; forcible seizure, attachment, distraint, distress, foreclosure; eviction, expulsion 300 n. *ejection*; take-over, deprivation, divestment 752 n. *abrogation*; disinheritance, disherison 780 n. *transfer*; taking without compensation, confiscation, capital levy; diversion, sequestration.

rapacity, rapaciousness, predacity, thirst for loot; avidity, thirst 859 n. *hunger*; greed, insatiable g., insatiability 816 n. *avarice*; vampirism, blood-sucking; extortion, blackmail.

taker, appropriator, impropriator, impropriatrix; remover, conveyor; seizer, snatcher, grabber; lifter, spoiler, raider, ransacker, sacker, looter, despoiler, depredator 789 n. *robber*; slave-raider, kidnapper, abductor, crimp, press-gang; slave-raider, slaver; captor, capturer 741 n. *master*; usurper, arrogator; extortioner, blackmailer; locust, devourer 168 n. *destroyer*; bloodsucker, leech, parasite, vampire, harpy, vulture, wolf, shark; beast of prey, predator; confiscator, sequestrator 782 n. *receiver*; expropriator, disseisor.

Adj. *taking*, prehensile, clinging 778 adj. *retentive*; abstractive, ablatitious; grasping, extortionate, rapacious, wolfish, lupine, vulturine; harpyian, harpy-ish; devouring, all-d., all-engulfing, voracious, ravening, ravenous 859 adj. *hungry*; raptorial, predatory 788 adj. *thieving*; privative, expropriatory, confiscatory; commandeering, requisitory; acquisitive, possessive 771 adj. *acquiring*; anticipative, proleptic.

Vb. *take*, accept, be given 782 vb. *receive*; take over, take back (see *appropriate*); take in, let in 299 vb. *admit*; take to, bring, fetch 273 vb. *carry*; take up, snatch up, lift, raise 310 vb. *elevate*; take in advance, anticipate 135 vb. *be early*; take hold, fasten on, clutch, grip, cling 778 vb. *retain*; lay hands upon, seize, snatch, grab, pounce, pounce on, spring; snatch at, reach, reach out for, make a long arm; grasp at, clutch at, grab at, make a grab, scramble for, rush f.; capture, rape, storm, take by s. 727 vb. *overmaster*; conquer, captive, lead c. 745 vb. *subjugate*; catch, overtake, intercept 277 vb. *outstrip*; apprehend, take into custody, make an arrest, nab, nobble, collar, lay by the heels 747 vb. *arrest*; make sure of, fasten, pinion 747 vb. *fetter*; hook, fish, angle, trap, snare, lime 542 vb. *ensnare*; net, land, bag, pocket, pouch; gross, have a turnover 771 vb. *acquire*; gather, accumulate, collect 74 vb. *bring together*; cull, pick, pluck; reap, crop, harvest, glean 370 vb. *cultivate*; scrounge, tot, scrabble, pick over, rummage, ransack 459 vb. *search*; pick up, snap up, snaffle; knock off 788 vb. *steal*; pick clean, strip 229 vb. *uncover*; remove (see *take away*); take out, unload, unlade 188 vb. *displace*; draw, draw out, draw off, milk, tap, mine 304 vb. *extract*; withdraw (see *take away*).

appropriate, take to or for oneself, make one's own, spheterize, annex; take possession, stake one's claim; take over, assume, assume ownership, impropriate 773 vb. *possess*; enter, enter into, come i., succeed 771 vb. *inherit*; instal oneself, seat o. 187 vb. *place oneself*; overrun, swarm over, people, populate, occupy, settle, colonize; win, conquer; take back, get back one's own, recover, resume, re-possess, re-enter, recapture, reconquer 656 vb. *retrieve*; reclaim 915 vb. *claim*;

commandeer, requisition 737 vb. *demand*; nationalize, secularize 775 vb. *socialize*; usurp, arrogate, jump a claim, trespass, squat 916 vb. *be undue*; dispossess (see *deprive*); treat as one's own, make free with; monopolize, engross, hog, be a dog in the manger; engulf, suck in, suck up, swallow 299 vb. *absorb*; devour, eat up (see *fleece*).

levy, raise, extort, exact, wrest from, force f. 304 vb. *extract*; exact a benevolence, compel to lend 785 vb. *borrow*; exact tribute, make pay, lay under contribution, toll, take one's t.; raise taxes 809 vb. *tax*; overtax, rack-rent, suck, suck like a leech (see *fleece*); draw off, exhaust, drain, empty 300 vb. *void*; wring, squeeze, squeeze to the last drop, squeeze till the pips squeak 735 vb. *oppress*; divert resources, sequestrate, make a raid on, raid a fund.

take away, remove, shift, unload 188 vb. *displace*; send away 272 vb. *send*; lighten 701 vb. *disencumber*; convey, abstract, relieve, relieve of 788 vb. *steal*; remove bodily, escort 89 vb. *accompany*; kidnap, crimp, shanghai, press, impress, abduct, ravish, carry off, bear off, bear away; hurry off with, run away w., run off w., elope w., clear off w. 296 vb. *decamp*; raid, loot, plunder 788 vb. *rob*.

deprive, bereave, orphan, widow; divest, denude, strip 229 vb. *uncover*; unfrock, unthrone 752 vb. *depose*; dispossess, usurp 916 vb. *disentitle*; disseise, oust, evict, expel 300 vb. *eject*; expropriate, compulsorily acquire, impose a capital levy; confiscate, forfeit, sequester, sequestrate, distrain, attach, foreclose; disinherit, cut out of one's will, cut off, cut off with a shilling.

fleece, pluck, skin, shear, gut; strip, strip bare 229 vb. *uncover*; blackmail, bleed, bleed white, sponge, suck, suck like a leech, suck dry; devour, eat up, eat out of house and home 301 vb. *eat*; take one's all, bankrupt, leave one without a penny or cent 801 vb. *impoverish*.

See: 74, 89, 135, 168, 187, 188, 229, 272, 273, 277, 296, 299, 300, 301, 304, 310, 370, 459, 542, 656, 701, 727, 735, 737, 741, 745, 747, 752, 771, 773, 775, 778, 780, 782, 785, 788, 789, 790, 801, 809, 816, 859, 915, 916.

787 Restitution

N. *restitution*, giving back, return, reversion, rendition; bringing back, repatriation; re-instatement, re-enthronement, re-investment; rehabilitation 656 n. *restoration*; redemption, ransom, rescue 668 n. *deliverance*; recuperation, replevin, recovery; compensation, indemnification; repayment, recoupment; refund, reimbursement, disgorgement; indemnity, damages 963 n. *penalty*; conscience money 941 n. *atonement*.

Adj. *restoring*, restitutory, rendering, refunding; indemnificatory, compensatory 941 adj. *atoning*.

Vb. *restitute*, make restitution, return, render, give back 656 vb. *restore*; pay up, cough up, disgorge 804 vb. *pay*; refund, repay, recoup, reimburse; indemnify, pay an indemnity, pay damages, compensate, make it up to; pay compensation, pay reparations, make reparation, pay conscience-money 941 vb. *atone*; bring back, repatriate; ransom, redeem 668 vb. *deliver*; re-instate, re-invest, rehabilitate, set up again, raise one to his feet, restore one to favour; recover 656 vb. *retrieve*.

See: 656, 668, 804, 941, 963.

788 Stealing

N. *stealing*, thieving, lifting, robbing; theft, larceny, petty l., grand l., compound l.; pilfering, filching, robbing the till, pick-pocketing, shop-lifting; scrounging, totting; burglary, house-breaking; robbery, highway r., gang r., dacoity, thuggee, latrociny; robbery with violence, stick-up, hold-up, smash and grab raid; cattle-lifting, rustling; rape, abduction, kidnapping, androlepsy, man-stealing, plagium, slave-raiding; body-snatching; conveyance, abstraction, removal 786 n. *taking*; literary theft, cribbing, plagiary, plagiarism, copyright infringement 20 n. *imitation*; temporary misappropriation, joy-ride 785 n. *borrowing*; thievery, act of theft; job, fiddle.

brigandage, banditry, outlawry, predacity, piracy, buccaneering, filibustering, filibusterism; privateering, letters of marque 718 n. *warfare*; raiding, raid, razzia, foray 712 n. *attack*.

spoliation, plundering, looting; plundering expedition, chappow (see *brigandage*); direption, sack, sacking; depredation, rapine, ravaging 165 n. *havoc*.

peculation, embezzlement, misappropriation, malversation, breach of trust, fraudulent conversion; illegal evasion, fraud, fiddle, swindle, cheating 542 n. *deception*.

thievishness, thievery, pickery, light-fingeredness, light fingers, kleptomania; predacity 786 n. *rapacity*; dishonesty, unreliability in money matters 930 n. *improbity*; burglarious intent, intention to steal; den of thieves, thieves' kitchen, Alsatia.

Adj. *thieving*, in the act of theft; with intent to steal; thievish, light-fingered; kleptomaniac; furacious, furative, larcenous, burglarious; predatory, predacious, raptorial; piratical, buccaneering, filibustering, privateering, raiding, marauding; scrounging, foraging; dishonest, fraudulent, unreliable in money matters 930 adj. *dishonest*.

Vb. *steal*, lift, thieve, pilfer, shop-lift; cabbage, mooch, tot; be light-fingered, sneak, pick pockets, rob the till; pick locks, blow a safe; burgle, burglarize, house-break; rob, relieve of; rifle, sack, clean out; swipe, nobble, nick, pinch, bone, nim, prig, snaffle, snitch, knock off, annex 786 vb. *take*; forage, scrounge; lift cattle, rustle, drive off, make off with; abduct, kidnap, crimp, shanghai, press, impress; abstract, convey, purloin, filch; make away with, spirit away; crib, copy, plagiarize, infringe copyright, pirate 20 vb. *copy*; smuggle, run, poach, hijack.

defraud, embezzle, peculate, purloin, let stick to one's fingers; fiddle, cook the accounts, commit breach of trust, obtain money on false pretences; swindle, cheat, diddle, chisel, do out of, bilk 542 vb. *deceive*; rook, pigeon, gull, dupe; pluck, skin 786 vb. *fleece*; welsh, levant.

rob, rob with violence, commit highway robbery, hold up, stick up, make stand and deliver; raid, smash and grab; rob in gangs, dacoit; pirate, sail under the skull and cross-bones, buccaneer, filibuster, pickeer, maraud, reave, reive, go freebooting; foray, forage, scrounge; raid; sweep, ransack; plunder, pillage, loot, sack, put to the s., despoil, ravage,

depredate, spoil 165 vb. *lay waste*; make a prey of, victimize, blackmail, levy b., extort, screw, squeeze 735 vb. *oppress*.

See: 20, 165, 542, 712, 718, 735, 785, 786, 930.

789 Thief

N. *thief*, thieving fraternity, swell mob, light-fingered gentry, den of thieves, Alsatia; crook; branded thief, homo trium litterarum; pickers and stealers, light fingers; stealer, lifter, filcher, purloiner, pilferer, snapper-up of unconsidered trifles; sneaker, sneak thief, shoplifter; pickpocket, swell mobsman, cutpurse, purse-snatcher, bag-s.; cattle-lifter, cattle-thief, rustler; burglar, cat-b., house-breaker, safe-b., safe-blower, cracksman, picklock, yegg, yeggman, peteman; free-trader, fair-t., poacher, smuggler, runner, night-r., gun-r., blockade-r.; abductor, kidnapper, crimp 786 n. *taker*; slaver, slave-raider; body-snatcher, resurrectionist; fence, receiver of stolen property; plagiarist, infringer.

robber, robber band, forty thieves; brigand, klepht; ranger, rover, bush-ranger, bandit, outlaw, Robin Hood; footpad, highwayman, knight of the road, land-pirate, road agent, hold-up man, stick-up m.; Dick Turpin, Jack Sheppard, Jonathan Wild; thug, dacoit, gang-robber; gangster, gunman, hijacker; sea-robber, sea-rover, Viking, pirate, buccaneer, picaroon corsair, filibuster, privateer; reaver, marauder, pindarree, fedayeen, raider, night-rider, freebooter, moss-trooper, cateran, rapparee; plunderer, pillager, sacker, ravager, spoiler, despoiler, depredator; wrecker; beast of prey, predator.

defrauder, embezzler, peculator, fiddler; defaulter, levanter, welsher, bilker; swindler, sharper, cheat, shark, magsman, chevalier d'industrie 545 n. *deceiver*; forger, counterfeiter, coin-clipper.

See: 545, 786.

790 Booty

N. *booty*, spoil, spoils; spoils of war, spolia opima 729 n. *trophy*; plunder, loot, pillage; prey, victim, quarry; find, strike,

prize, purchase, haul, catch, winnings, takings 771 n. *gain*; cabbage, pickings, tottings; stolen article, stolen goods, swag, boodle; moonshine, hooch, contraband; illicit gains, graft, blackmail; dole, grant, pork barrel 703 n. *subvention*.

See: 703, 729, 771.

791 Barter

N. *barter*, exchange, chop, swap 151 n. *interchange*; exchange of goods, silent trade, truck, truck system, scorse; traffic, trading, dealing, buying and selling, bargain and sale, nundination, mercature; factorage, factorship, brokerage, agiotage, arbitrage, jobbing, stock-jobbing, share-pushing; negotiation, bargaining, hard b., higgling, haggling, horse dealing.

trade, commercial intercourse; free trade, black market; open market, free m. 796 n. *mart*; trading, traffic, drug t., white slave t., slaving, slave-trade, slave dealing; mercantilism, merchantry; capitalism, free economy, laisser faire 744 n. *freedom*; market economy, boom and bust 317 n. *fluctuation*; profit-making, mutual profit; commerce, business affairs 622 n. *business*; private enterprise, state e., state trading; private sector, public s.; venture, business v. 672 n. *undertaking*; speculation 618 n. *gambling*; transaction, commercial t., deal, business d., bargain, negotiation 765 n. *compact*; clientèle, custom 792 n. *purchase*.

Adj. *trading*, trafficking, exchanging; commercial, commercialistic, mercantile; mercantilist; wholesale, retail; exchangeable, marketable, merchantable 793 adj. *saleable*; for profit 618 adj. *speculative*.

Vb. *trade*, exchange 151 vb. *interchange*; barter, chop, swap, truck, scorse; nundinate, traffic, merchandise; buy and sell, buy cheap and sell dear, export and import; open a trade, drive a t., merchant 622 vb. *do business*; traffic in, deal in, handle; turn over, turn over one's stock 793 vb. *sell*; commercialize, put on a business footing; trade with, do business w., deal w., have dealings w., open an account w.; finance, back, promote; look to one's profit, have an eye to business, go out for trade; be a thorough business

man, know the price of everything and the value of nothing.

speculate, venture, risk 618vb. *gamble*; invest, sink one's capital in, employ one's capital; give a sprat to catch a whale, rig the market, racketeer, profiteer; black-market, deal in the b., sell under the counter; deal in futures, dabble in shares, play the market, go a bust; go on the Stock Exchange, operate, bull, bear, stag.

bargain, negotiate, chaffer, cheap, cheapen; beat up, beat down; merchant, huckster, haggle, higgle, dicker 766vb. *make terms*; bid for, make a bid, make a take-over bid, pre-empt; raise the bid, outbid 759 vb. *offer*; overbid 482vb. *overrate*; underbid 483vb. *underestimate*; stickle, stickle for, hold out for, state one's terms, ask for, charge 766vb. *give terms*; drive a bargain, do a deal, shake hands on 765 vb. *contract*; settle for, take.

Adv. *in trade*, commerce, in business, on 'change; across the counter, under the counter.

See: 151, 317, 482, 483, 618, 622, 672, 744, 759, 765, 766, 792, 793, 796.

792 Purchase

N. *purchase*, emption; buying up, co-emption, cornering, forestalling, pre-emption; redemption, ransom 668n. *deliverance*; purchase on account, purchase on credit 785n. *borrowing*; hire purchase, never-never system; buying, shopping, window-s., spending on, shopping spree 806n. *expenditure*; regular buying, custom, patronage, demand 627n. *requirement*; buying over, bribery 612n. *inducement*; bid, take-over b. 759n. *offer*; first refusal, right of purchase; a purchase, buy, good b., bargain, real b., something worth buying; purchases, shopping list, requirements.

purchaser, buyer, emptor, co-emptor, pre-emptor; vendee, transferee, consignee; hire purchaser, hirer, renter, leaser, lessee; buyer of labour, employer; marketer, shopper, window-s.; customer, patron, client, clientèle, consumer; offerer, bidder, by-b., highest b.; taker, acceptor; bargainer, higgler, haggler; ransomer, redeemer; share-buyer, bull, stag.

Adj. *bought*, paid for, ransomed, redeemed; purchased, bribed; emptional, purchasable, bribable; worth buying 644adj. *valuable*.

buying, purchasing, shopping, marketing; co-emptive, pre-emptive, redemptive; bidding, bargaining, haggling; bullish.

Vb. *purchase*, make a p., complete a p.; buy, acquire by purchase 771vb. *acquire*; shop, window-s., market, go shopping; have a shopping list 627vb. *require*; make a good buy, get one's money's worth; buy outright, buy over the counter, pay cash for, offer cash for; buy on credit, hire-purchase; buy on account, buy on credit, pay by cheque; buy in 632vb. *store*; buy up, pre-empt, regrate, corner, make a corner in; monopolize, engross; buy out, make a take-over bid; buy over, suborn 612vb. *bribe*; buy back, redeem, repurchase, ransom 668vb. *deliver*; pay for, bear the cost of 804vb. *defray*; buy oneself in, invest in, sink one's money in 791vb. *speculate*; buy service, rent 785 vb. *hire*; bid, bid for, bid up 759vb. *offer*; buy shares, bull, stag.

See: 612, 627, 632, 644, 668, 759, 771, 785, 791, 804, 806.

793 Sale

N. *sale*, selling, putting on sale, marketing; vent; disposal, alienation 779n. *non-retention*; clearance, sell-out; clearance sale, summer s., winter s., spring s., white s., jumble s., charity s., bazaar; sale of office, simony 930n. *improbity*; exclusive sale, monopoly 747n. *restraint*; public sale, auctioneering, auction, sale by a., roup, Dutch auction, American a.; good market, market for; sales, good s., boom 730n. *prosperity*; bad sales 731n. *adversity*; salesmanship, service, sales talk; competition, customer-snatching; saleability, vendibility, marketability; vendible, thing sold, seller, good s., best s., selling line 795n. *merchandise*.

seller, vendor, consignor, transferor; share-seller, bear; auctioneer, crier, rouper; huckster, hawker, monger, chapman, colporteur, smouse, smouch, barrow-boy, coster, costermonger 794n. *pedlar*; shopman, dealer 633n. *caterer*; whole-saler, retailer 794n. *tradesman*; salesman,

travelling s., traveller, commercial t., commission agent, canvasser, tout; shop-walker, floor-w., counter-jumper; shop-assistant, shop girl, shopman, shop-woman, saleswoman; clerk, booking c., ticket-agent; roundsman, milkman.

Adj. *saleable*, vendible, marketable, on sale; sold, sold out; in demand, commanding a sale; available, in the market, up for sale; bearish; on auction, under the hammer.

Vb. *sell*, vend, make a sale; flog, alienate, dispose of; market, put on sale, offer for s., have for s.; bring to market, unload, unload on the market, dump; hawk, smouse, peddle, monger; canvass, tout; cater, cater for the market 633 vb. *provide*; put up for sale, auction, put to a., sell by a., bring under the hammer, sell to the highest bidder, knock down to; regrate, wholesale; retail, sell over the counter; turn over, turn over one's stock 791 vb. *trade*; realize one's capital, encash; sell at a profit 771 vb. *gain*; sell at a loss, sacrifice 772 vb. *lose*; undercut 812 vb. *cheapen*; sell off, remainder; sell up, sell out, wind up 145 vb. *cease*; clear stock, hold a sale; sell again, re-sell; sell forward.

be sold, be on sale, pass by sale, come under the hammer 780 vb. *change hands*; sell, have a sale, have a market, meet a demand, be in d., sell well, sell out, boom; be a selling line, be a best-seller; sell badly, stay on the shelf.

See: 145, 633, 730, 731, 747, 771, 772, 779, 780, 791, 794, 795, 812, 930.

794 Merchant

N. *merchant*, merchant prince, merchant adventurer; liveryman, livery company, guild, chamber of commerce, concern, firm 708 n. *corporation*; business man, man of business; trader, trafficker; slaver, slave-trader; importer, exporter; wholesale merchant, wholesaler, re-grater; merchandiser, dealer, chandler, corn-c., ship-c.; middleman, broker, stock-b.; stock-jobber, share-pusher; estate agent, realtor; financier, company promoter; banker, sowkar, banian 784 n. *lender*; moneyer, money-changer, cambist, shroff; gold merchant, bullioner.

tradesman, tradespeople, tradesfolk; re-tailer, middleman, regrater, tallyman; shopkeeper, storekeeper, shopman, storesman 793 n. *seller*; monger, iron-monger, mercer, haberdasher, grocer, provision merchant 633 n. *caterer*.

pedlar, peddler 793 n. *seller*; stall-keeper, booth-k.; huckster, travelling hawker, itinerant tradesman, street-seller, cadger, higgler, smouse, hawker, colporteur, bagman, chapman, cheapjack; rag-and-bone man, coster, costerman, coster-monger, barrow-boy; market woman; sutler, vivandière 633 n. *caterer*.

See: 633, 708, 784, 793.

795 Merchandise

N. *merchandise*, article of commerce, line; article, commodity, saleable c., vendible, stock, stock-in-trade, range, repertoire 632 n. *store*; freight, cargo 193 n. *contents*; stuff, things for sale, supplies, ware, wares, goods, capital g., durables; shop goods, consumer g., consumer durables; perishable goods, canned g., dry g., white g.

See: 193, 632.

796 Mart

N. *mart*, market, daily m., weekly m.; open market, European open m.; market overt, free market; black market, grey m.; seller's market, buyer's m.; market-place, staple, forum, agora; auction room, Tattersalls, Christie's, Sotheby's; fair, world f., international f., trade f., industries f., horse f., goose f., motor show; exhibition, exposition, shop-window 522 n. *manifestation*; corn-market, wheat pit, corn-exchange; exchange, stock e., 'Change, bourse, kerb-market, Wall Street; Rialto, guildhall; tolbooth, custom-house.

emporium, free port, entrepôt, depot, ban-dar, warehouse 632 n. *storage*; wharf; trading centre, trading post; general market, bazaar, arcade, covered market, supermarket, shopping centre.

shop, retailer's; store, multiple s., depart-ment s., chain s.; emporium, bazaar, supermarket; concern, establishment,

house, **trading** h.; corner shop, stall, booth, stand, newstand, kiosk, barrow; shopboard, counter, bargain c.; shop-floor, shop-window; office, bureau, chambers, counting-house, counting-room; premises, place of business 687n. *workshop.*

See: 522, 632, 687.

797 Money

N. *money,* numismatics, chrysology; pelf, Mammon 800n. *wealth;* lucre, filthy l., root of all evil; medium of exchange, circulating medium; currency, decimal c., managed c., fluctuating c., hard c., soft c., falling c.; sound currency, honest money; money of account, sterling, pound s., £. s. d., pounds, shillings and pence; rupees, annas and pies; precious metal, gold, ochre, ringing gold, clinking g.; silver, siller (see *bullion*); ready money, the ready, the best, blunt, cash, spot c., hard c.; change, small c., coppers 33n. *small coin;* pocket money, pin m.

dibs, shekels, spondulics, blunt, brass, tin, rhino, jack, dough, lolly, sugar, salt; dosh, 'ackers, oof, mopus, boodle; soap, palm oil, palm grease.

funds, temporary f., hot money; liquidity, account, bank a., money in the bank, bank annuities; wherewithal, the needful 629n. *means;* sinews of war, ready money, the ready, the actual, financial provision, cash supplies, treasure 633n. *provision;* remittance 804n. *payment;* funds for investment, capital; funds in hand, reserves, balances, sterling b.; sum of money, amount, figure, sum, round s., lump s.; fiver, tenner, pony, monkey, grand; mint of money, wads, scads, pile, packet, millions, billions, crores, lakhs 32 n. *great quantity;* moneybags, purse, bottomless p. 632n. *store.*

finance, high f., financial world; financial control, money power, purse-strings, power of the purse, almighty dollar; money dealings, cash transaction; money market, exchange 796n. *mart;* exchange rate, valuta, parity, par 28n. *equality;* devaluation, depreciation, falling exchange 655n. *deterioration;* rising exchange 654n. *improvement;* bimetallism; gold standard; managed currency, equal-

ization, fund, sinking fund., revolving f.; deficit finance, inflation, inflationary spiral; disinflation, deflation.

coinage, minting, issue; metallic currency, stamped coinage, gold c., silver c., electrum c., copper c., nickel c., billon c., iron c.; specie, minted coinage, coin, coin of the realm; monetary unit, monetary denomination, guinea, sovereign, pound, quid, shiner, chip, half-sovereign, ten bob; crown, cartwheel; half-crown, two-and-six; florin, shilling, bob; sixpence, tanner; threepenny bit, penny, copper, halfpenny, farthing; mohur, gold m., rupee, sicca r., Burmese r., kyen; anna, pice, pie; decimal coinage, dollar, simoleon, buck, half dollar, quarter, dime, nickel, cent; silver dollar; ten-dollar piece, eagle; twenty-dollar piece, double-eagle; napoleon, louis d'or; franc, heavy f., new f.; mark, Reichsmark; gulden, guilder, kroner, lira, scudo, peseta, peso, bolivar, balboa, colon, milreis, reis; drachma, piastre, rouble, kopeck, zloty, yen, sen; talent, mina, obol; daric, dinar, dirhem, shekel; solidus, gold s., bezant, ducat, angel, noble, moidore, piece of eight, pistole; change, small c., centime, sou, naya paisa, cash 33n. *small coin;* shell money, cowrie, wampum.

paper money, fiat m., fiduciary currency, assignat, shinplaster; note, banknote, bank paper, treasury note, ten shilling note, pound note, five pound note, smacker; bill, dollar b., greenback, buck, ten-dollar bill, sawbuck; bill of exchange, exchequer bill, negotiable instrument; draft, sight d., order, money o., postal o., check, cheque, traveller's c., letter of credit; certificate, gold c., silver c.; promissory note, note of hand, hundi; coupon, warrant, scrip, debenture, bond, premium b. 767n. *security.*

false money, bad m., counterfeit m., base coin, snide, rap; forged note, flash n., forgery, slip, kite; dud cheque; clipped coinage, depreciated currency, devalued c.; demonetized coinage, withdrawn c., obsolete c.

bullion, bar, gold b., ingot, nugget; solid gold, solid silver; precious metal, yellow m., platinum, gold, white g., electrum, silver, billon.

moneyer, minter, mint master; coiner, forger, penman; bullionist; bullioner,

money-dealer, money-changer, cambist 794n. *merchant*; cashier 798n. *treasurer*; drawer, drawee, obligor, obligee; financier, capitalist; moneyed man, moneybags, money-spinner 800n. *rich man*.

Adj. **monetary**, numismatical, chrysological; pecuniary, financial, fiscal, budgetary, sumptuary; coined, stamped, minted, issued; nummary, fiduciary; gold-based, sterling, sound, solvent 800 adj. *rich*; inflationary, deflationary; clipped, devalued, depreciated; withdrawn, demonetized; touching the pocket, crumenal.

Vb. **mint**, coin, stamp; monetize, issue, circulate; pass, utter; forge, counterfeit.

demonetize, withdraw, withdraw from circulation, call in an issue; clip, debase, debase the coinage; devalue, depreciate, inflate 812vb. *cheapen*.

draw money, cash, encash, realize, turn into cash, draw upon, cash a cheque, endorse a c., write a c. 804vb. *pay*.

See: 28, 32, 33, 629, 632, 633, 654, 655, 767, 794, 796, 798, 800, 804, 812.

798 Treasurer

N. **treasurer**, honorary t.; purse-bearer, bursar, purser, quæstor; cash-keeper, cashier, teller, croupier; depositary, stakeholder, pawnee, pledgee, trustee, steward 754n. *consignee*; liquidator 782n. *receiver*; bookkeeper 808n. *accountant*; banker, financier; keeper of the purse, paymaster, almoner, budgeteer, Chancellor of the Exchequer, Secretary of the Treasury, Controller of Currency; mint master 797n. *moneyer*; bank 799n. *treasury*.

See: 754, 782, 797, 799, 808.

799 Treasury

N. **treasury**, treasure-house, thesaurus; exchequer, fisc, public purse, pork barrel; hanaper, counting-house, custom-house; bursary, almonry; bank, Bank of England, savings bank, Post Office savings b., penny b.; coffer, chest 194n. *box*; treasure chest, depository 632n. *store*; strong room, strong box, safe, safe

deposit, cash box, money-box, stocking; till, cash register, cash desk, slot-machine; receipt of custom, box office, gate, turnstile; money-bag, purse, purse-strings 194n. *pocket*; wallet, bill-fold, portemonnaie, wad, rouleau 194n. *case*.

See: 194, 632.

800 Wealth

N. **wealth**, Mammon, lucre, pelf, tin, moneybags 797n. *money*; money-making, golden touch, Midas t.; riches, flesh-pots, fat 635n. *plenty*; luxury 637n. *superfluity*; opulence, affluence, well-being 730n. *prosperity*; ease, comfort, easy circumstances, good c., comfortable c. 376n. *euphoria*; solvency, soundness, creditworthiness 802n. *credit*; solidity, substance 3n. *substantiality*; independence, competence, self-sufficiency 635n. *sufficiency*; high income, super-tax bracket 782n. *receiving*; gains 771n. *gain*; resources, large r., long purse, capital, substantial c. 629n. *means*; liquid assets, bank account; limitless resources, bottomless purse, purse of Fortunatus, kamadhuk, golden eggs; nest-egg 633n. *provision*; tidy sum, pile, scads, wad, packet 32n. *great quantity*; fortune, great f., handsome f., large inheritance, ample endowment; broad acres, great possessions 777n. *property*; bonanza, mine, gold m. 632n. *store*; Pactolus, Potosi, Golconda, El Dorado, riches of Solomon; plutocracy, capitalism.

rich man, wealthy man, well-to-do man, warm m., man of means; money-baron, nabob, moneybags, millionaire, multim., milliardaire, billiardaire; Crœsus, Midas, Dives, Plutus; money-maker, money-spinner, capitalist, plutocrat; heiress, 'lady richly left' 776n. *beneficiary*; the haves, moneyed class, propertied c., leisured c., jeunesse dorée; new rich, nouveau riche, parvenu 730n. *made man*; plutocracy, timocracy.

Adj. **rich**, richly endowed, flowing with milk and honey, fat, fertile 164adj. *productive*; abundant 635adj. *plenteous*; richly furnished, luxurious, upholstered, plush, plushy, ritzy, slap-up; diamond-studded 875adj. *ostentatious*; wealthy,

blest with this world's goods, well-endowed, well-provided for, born in the purple, born with a silver spoon in one's mouth; opulent, affluent 730 adj. *prosperous*; well-off, well-to-do, warm, well-feathered, in easy circumstances, overpaid 376 adj. *comfortable*.

moneyed, monied, propertied, worth a lot, worth a packet, worth millions, made of money, lousy with m. rolling in m., rolling dripping; rich as Crœsus, rich as Solomon; high-income, millionaire; in funds, in cash, in credit, on the right side; pecunious, tinny, well-heeled, flush, flush of cash, in the dough; credit-worthy, solvent, sound, able to pay 929 adj. *trustworthy*; out of debt, all straight 804 adj. *paying*; keeping up with the Joneses.

Vb. *be rich*, flow with milk and honey, turn to gold 635 vb. *abound*; have money, have a power of m., have means, draw a large income; roll in money, stink of m., wallow in riches; be born in the purple, be born with a silver spoon in one's mouth; be flush, be in funds etc. adj.; have credit, command capital, have money to burn; die rich, cut up well 780 vb. *bequeath*.

afford, have the means, have the wherewithal, be able to pay, be solvent, make both ends meet, keep one's head above water, keep the wolf from the door, keep up with the Joneses 635 vb. *have enough*.

get rich, come into money 771 vb. *inherit*; enrich oneself, make money, mint m., coin m., spin m., make a packet, make a pile, make a fortune, feather one's nest, line one's pocket, strike oil 771 vb. *gain*; seek riches, worship the golden calf, pay tribute to Mammon.

make rich, enrich, make one's fortune, put money in one's pocket, line one's p.; leave one a fortune 780 vb. *bequeath*; enhance 36 vb. *augment*; improve 654 vb. *make better*.

See: 3, 32, 36, 164, 376, 629, 632, 633, 635, 637, 654, 730, 771, 776, 777, 780, 782, 797, 802, 804, 875, 929.

801 Poverty

N. *poverty*, Lady Poverty 945 n. *asceticism*; renunciation of wealth, voluntary poverty 931 n. *disinterestedness*; poorness, mea-

greness 645 n. *badness*; impecuniosity, hardupness, embarrassment, difficulties, Queer Street 805 n. *insolvency*; impoverishment, loss of fortune, broken f., beggary, mendicancy; utter poverty, penury, pennilessness, pauperism, destitution; privation, indigence, neediness, necessitousness, necessity, need, want, pinch, lack 627 n. *requirement*; bare cupboard, empty larder 636 n. *scarcity*; wolf at the door, famine 946 n. *fasting*; light pocket, empty purse, insufficient income, slender means, narrow m., reduced circumstances, straitened c., low water 636 n. *insufficiency*; straits, distress 825 n. *suffering*; grinding poverty, subsistence level, hand-to-mouth existence, mere e., bare e.; seediness, beggarliness, raggedness, shreds and tatters, 'looped and windowed raggedness'; general poverty, slump, depression 655 n. *deterioration*; squalor, slum, back street 655 n. *dilapidation*.

poor man, broken man, bankrupt, insolvent 805 adj. *non-payer*; pauper, indigent, mendicant, beggar, poor b., rag-picker, starveling, down-and-out 763 n. *beggar*; slum-dweller, sansculotte 869 n. *rabble*; the poor, new poor, the have-nots, the under-privileged; Cinderella 867 n. *object of scorn*; poor relation 35 n. *inferior*.

Adj. *poor*, not well-off, badly o., poorly o., ill-o., not blest with this world's goods, hard up, impecunious, short, short of funds, short of cash, in the red; broke, stony b., bankrupt, insolvent 805 adj. *non-paying*; reduced to poverty or beggary, impoverished, pauperized, broken, beggared; dispossessed, deprived, stripped, fleeced, robbed; penurious, poverty-stricken; needy, indigent, in want, in need 627 adj. *necessitous*; in distress, straitened, pinched, hard put to it, put to one's shifts, on one's beam ends 700 adj. *in difficulties*; unable to make both ends meet, unable to raise the wind, unable to keep the wolf from the door; unprovided, dowerless, portionless; penniless, moneyless, destitute; down to one's last penny, without a bean, without a cent, without a sou, without prospects; poor in, lacking, wanting; poor in quality 645 adj. *bad*; meagre, sterile 172 adj. *unproductive*.

beggarly, starveling, shabby, seedy, down at heel, down and out, in rags, tattered, patched, barefoot, threadbare, tatty 655

adj. *dilapidated*; scruffy, squalid, slummy, back-street 649 adj. *dirty*; poverty-stricken, pinched with poverty, poor as a rat, poor as a church mouse, poor as Job's turkey.

Vb. *be poor*, earn nothing, live on a pittance, eke out a livelihood, scrape an existence, live from hand to mouth; not keep the wolf from the door, starve 859 vb. *be hungry*; want, lack 627 vb. *require*; have not a penny, not have a shot in one's locker; become poor, break, go broke 805 vb. *not pay*; decline in fortune, lose one's money, come down in the world 655 vb. *deteriorate*; take National Assistance, come on the parish, go on relief, go on the dole, go on the rates, go to the workhouse.

impoverish, reduce to poverty, leave destitute, beggar, pauperize; ruin 165 vb. *destroy*; rob, strip 786 vb. *fleece*; dispossess, disinherit, disendow, cut off, cut off with a shilling 786 vb. *deprive*.

See: 35, 165, 172, 627, 636, 645, 649, 655, 700, 763, 786, 805, 825, 859, 867, 869, 931, 945, 946.

802 Credit

N. *credit*, repute, reputation 866 n. *prestige*; credit-worthiness, sound credit, trust, confidence, reliability 929 n. *probity*; borrowing capacity, limit of credit; line of credit, tick; banker's credit, letter of c., paper c., credit note, sum to one's account, credit a., right side; credits, balances, credit balance 807 n. *receipt*; postponed payment, unpaid bill, account, score, tally, bill 808 n. *accounts*; national credit, floating debt 803 n. *debt*; loan, mortgage 784 n. *lending*; sum entrusted, sum voted, vote.

creditor, mortgagee, pledgee, pawnee 784 n. *lender*; depositor, bank d., investor.

Vb. *credit*, give *or* furnish c., extend c., forgo repayment, grant a loan 784 vb. *lend*; place to one's credit, credit one's account, place to one's a.; grant, vote; await payment, charge to one's account, sell on credit; take credit, open an account, keep an account with, run up an account, run up a bill 785 vb. *borrow*.

See: 784, 785, 803, 807, 808, 866, 929.

803 Debt

N. *debt*, indebtedness, state of i. 785 n. *borrowing*; liability, obligation, commitment; encumbrance, mortgage 767 n. *security*; something owing, indebtment, debit, charge; what one owes, debts, bills, hire-purchase debt; national debt, floating d., funded d.; promise to pay, debt of honour, unsecured debt 764 n. *promise*; bad debt, write-off 772 n. *loss*; good debt 771 n. *gain*; tally, account, account owing; deficit, overdraft, unfavourable balance, balance to pay 307 n. *shortcoming*; inability to pay 805 n. *insolvency*; payment refused, frozen balance, blocked b., blocked account, frozen assets 805 n. *non-payment*; deferred payment 802 n. *credit*; overdue payment, arrears, accumulated a., back pay, back rent; no more credit, foreclosure.

interest, simple i., compound i., high i., excessive i., usury, pound of flesh 784 n. *lending*; premium, rate of interest, bank rate.

debtor, debitor; loanee, borrower, loan applicant; obligor, drawee; mortgagor, pledgor; bad debtor, defaulter, insolvent 805 n. *non-payer*.

Adj. *indebted*, in debt, borrowing, indebted; pledged, liable, obliged, committed, responsible, answerable, bound 917 adj. *dutied*; owing, overdrawn, in the red, minus; encumbered, mortgaged; deep in debt, plunged in d., burdened with d., over head and ears in d. 700 adj. *in difficulties*; defaulting, unable to pay, insolvent 805 adj. *non-paying*; at the mercy of one's creditors, in the hands of the receiver.

owed, unpaid, still u.; owing, due, overdue, in arrear; outstanding, unbalanced; on the debit side, chargeable, payable, debited, on credit, on deposit, repayable, returnable, bearing, payable on delivery, C.O.D.

Vb. *be in debt*, owe, have to repay; owe money, pay interest; accept a charge, be debited with, be liable; get credit, overdraw (one's account); go on tick 785 vb. *borrow*; live on credit, buy on c., keep an account with, have charged to one's a.; run up an account, run into debt, have bills to pay; be in the red, be overdrawn; leave one's bills unpaid, cheat one's creditors, bilk, do a moonlight flit, out-

run the constable, welsh, levant 805 vb.
not pay; back another's credit, make oneself responsible, go bail for, be obliged,
be bound 917 vb. *incur a duty*.

See: 307, 700, 764, 767, 771, 772, 784, 785,
802, 805, 917.

804 Payment

N. *payment*, paying for, bearing the cost,
defrayment; paying off, discharge, quittance, acquittance, release, satisfaction,
full s., liquidation, clearance, settlement, settlement on account; receipted
payment, receipt for payment, receipt in
full 807 n. *receipt*; cash payment, down
p.; first payment, earnest, earnest money,
deposit; instalment, kist; deferred
payment, hire purchase 785 n. *borrowing*;
due payment, subscription, tribute 809 n.
tax; voluntary payment, contribution,
collection 781 n. *offering*; payment in lieu,
composition, scutage 150 n. *substitution*;
repayment, compensation, indemnity 787
n. *restitution*; disbursement, remittance
806 n. *expenditure*.

pay, pay-out, pay-off, pay packet; pay day
108 n. *date*; wages bill, wages, salary 771 n.
earnings; grant, grant-in-aid, subsidy 703
n. *subvention*; salary, pension, annuity,
remuneration, emolument, fee, garnish,
bribe 962 n. *reward*; brokerage, factorage
810 n. *discount*; something paid, contribution, subscription, collection, mass-
money, tribute 809 n. *tax*; damages,
indemnity 963 n. *penalty*; compensation,
golden handshake; payer, liquidator,
paymaster, purser, cashier 789 n. *treasurer*.

Adj. *paying*, disbursing 806 adj. *expending*;
paying in full, paying cash, never indebted, unindebted; out of debt, owing
nothing.

Vb. *pay*, disburse 806 vb. *expend*; contribute
781 vb. *give*; pay in kind, barter 791 vb.
trade; make payment, pay out, shell o.,
fork o., stump up, cough up; come across,
do the needful, unloose the purse-strings,
open one's purse; pay back, disgorge,
repay, reimburse, compensate 787 vb.
restitute; tickle the palm, grease the palm,
gratify, tip 612 vb. *bribe*; pay wages,
remunerate, wage 962 vb. *reward*; pay in
advance, pay on sight, pay on call, pay

on demand; pay on the nail, pay on the
dot, pay cash, pay cash down, pay down,
put d.; honour (a bill), pay up, pay in full,
satisfy, redeem, discharge, get a receipt;
discount, take up, meet; clear, liquidate,
settle, settle an account, clear accounts
with, balance accounts w., account w.,
reckon w., square accounts w., strike a
balance 808 vb. *account*; settle accounts
with, settle a score, quit scores; pay off
old scores, wipe off old s., pay one out
714 vb. *retaliate*.

defray, pay for, defray the cost, bear the c.,
stand the c.; pay one's way, pay one's
footing, pay one's shot; foot the bill,
meet the b., pay the piper; pay sauce for
all; stand treat 781 vb. *give*; share
expenses, go Dutch 775 vb. *participate*.

Adv. *cash down*, money d.; cash on delivery,
C.O.D.; with ready money, on the nail,
on the dot, on demand, on sight; without
credit, slap-bang; costing, to the tune of.

See: 108, 150, 612, 703, 714, 771, 775, 781,
785, 787, 789, 791, 806, 807, 808, 809, 810,
962, 963.

805 Non-payment

N. *non-payment*, default; defalcation 930 n.
improbity; reduced payment, stoppage,
deduction 963 n. *penalty*; moratorium,
embargo, freeze; dishonouring, refusal to
pay, protest, repudiation 760 n. *refusal*;
deferred payment, hire purchase 785 n.
borrowing; application of the sponge,
forgiveness of debts, cancellation of d.,
seisachtheia 752 n. *abrogation*; waste
paper bonds, protested bill, dishonoured
cheque, bogus c., dud c.; depreciation,
devaluation, devalued currency 797 n.
false money.

insolvency, inability to pay, failure to meet
one's obligations; crash, failure; failure
of credit, run upon a bank; bankruptcy,
bankruptcy court, proceedings in bankruptcy, whitewash; nothing to pay with,
nothing in the kitty, overdrawn account,
overdraft 636 n. *insufficiency*; hopeless
indebtedness, unpayable debt 803 n. *debt*.

non-payer, defaulter, defalcator, embezzler
789 n. *defrauder*; bilker, welsher, absconder, levanter; failure, lame duck,
man of straw; bankrupt, discharged b.,
undischarged b., insolvent debtor.

Adj. *non-paying*, defaulting, behindhand, in arrear; unable to pay, insolvent, bankrupt, gazetted; overwhelmed with debt, always owing 803 adj. *indebted*; beggared, ruined 801 adj. *poor*.

Vb. *not pay*, default, embezzle, swindle 788 vb. *defraud*; fall into arrears, get behindhand, forget an instalment; stop payment, withhold p., freeze, block; refuse payment, protest a bill; disallow payment, hold an item under objection; divert, sequester 786 vb. *deprive*; bounce one's cheque, dishonour, repudiate; become insolvent, go bankrupt, go through the bankruptcy court, be gazetted, get whitewashed; sink, fail, break, go bust, crash, wind up, go into liquidation; evade one's creditors, outrun the constable, welsh, bilk 542 vb. *deceive*; levant, abscond 296 vb. *decamp*; have no money to pay with 801 vb. *be poor*; go off the gold standard, devalue *or* depreciate the currency 797 vb. *demonetize*; draw the purse-strings, button up one's pocket, sit on the money-bags 816 vb. *be parsimonious*; relieve of payment, cancel a debt, wipe the slate clean, discharge a bankrupt 752 vb. *abrogate*.

See: 296, 542, 636, 752, 760, 785, 786, 788, 789, 797, 801, 803, 816, 930, 963.

806 Expenditure

N. *expenditure*, spending, disbursement 804 n. *payment*; spendings, outgoings, costs, cost incurred, expenses, out-of-pocket e., expense account; expense, outlay, investment; dissaving, disinvestment, run on savings; fee, garnish, tribute 804 n. *pay*; extravagance, spending spree 815 n. *prodigality*.

Adj. *expending*, spending, sumptuary; generous 813 adj. *liberal*; extravagant, splashing one's money 815 adj. *prodigal*; out of pocket, lighter in one's purse.

expended, spent, disbursed, paid, paid out; laid out, invested; costing, at one's expense.

Vb. *expend*, make expenditure, spend; buy 792 vb. *purchase*; lay out, outlay, invest, sink money; be out of pocket, incur costs, incur expenses; meet charges, disburse, pay out 804 vb. *pay*; run down one's account, draw on one's savings, unsave,

dissave, disinvest; unhoard, unbelt, untie the purse-strings, open one's purse, empty one's pocket; give money, donate 781 vb. *give*; spare no expense, go a bust, do it proud, lavish 813 vb. *be liberal*; fling money around, splash one's money, bust, blow, blow one's cash 815 vb. *be prodigal*; use up, spend up, consume, run through, get t. 634 vb. *waste*.

See: 634, 781, 792, 804, 813, 815.

807 Receipt

N. *receipt*, accountable r., voucher, acknowledgment of payment, value received; money received, credits, innings, revenue, royalty, rents, rent-roll, dues; customs, taxes 809 n. *tax*; money coming in, turnover, takings, proceeds, returns, receipts, gross r., net r., box office r., gate-money, gate; income, national i., private i., privy purse; emolument, regular income, pay, half p., salary, wages 771 n. *earnings*; remuneration 962 n. *reward*; pension, annuity, tontine; allowance, personal a.; pocket-money, pin-m.; inadequate allowance, pittance; alimony, maintenance; exhibition, sizarship, perquisite 771 n. *acquisition*; rake-off 810 n. *discount*; interest, return; winnings, profits, gross p., net p., mesne p. 771 n. *gain*; bonus, premium 40 n. *extra*; prize 729 n. *trophy*; draw, lucky d.; legacy, inheritance 777 n. *dower*.

Adj. *received*, paid, receipted, acknowledged, acknowledged with thanks.

Vb. see 781 vb. *acquire*, 782 vb. *receive, be received*, 786 vb. *take*.

See: 40, 729, 771, 777, 781, 782, 786, 809, 810, 962.

808 Accounts

N. *accounts*, accompts; accountancy, accounting, commercial arithmetic; book-keeping, entry, double e., single e.; audit, inspection of accounts; account, profit and loss a., balance sheet, debit and credit, debtor and creditor account, receipts and expenditures; budgeting, budget, budget estimates 633 n. *provision*; running account, current a., cash a.,

suspense a., expense a.; statement of account, account rendered, compte rendu, statement, bill, waybill, invoice, manifest 87n. *list*; college accounts, battels; account paid, account settled 804n. *payment*; reckoning, computation, score, tally, facts and figures 86n. *numeration*.

account book, pass b., cheque b.; cash b., day-b., cost-b., journal, ledger, register, books 548 n. *record*.

accountant, chartered a., certified public a.; bookkeeper, storekeeper; accounting party, cashier 798n. *treasurer*; inspector of accounts, examiner of a., auditor; actuary, statistician.

Adj. *accounting*, book-keeping, in charge of accounts; actuarial, reckoning, computing, inventorial, budgetary; accountable.

Vb. *account*, keep the books, keep accounts, keep the cash; make up an account, cast an a.; budget, prepare a b.; cost, value, write up, write down 480vb. *estimate*; book, bring to book, enter, journalize, post, carry over, debit, credit 548vb. *register*; prepare a balance sheet, balance accounts; settle accounts, square a., finalize a., wind up a.; prepare a statement, present an account, charge, bill, invoice; overcharge, surcharge, undercharge 809vb. *price*; cook the accounts, falsify the a., fiddle, garble, doctor 788vb. *defraud*; audit, inspect accounts, examine the a., go through the books; take stock, check s., inventory, catalogue 87vb. *list*.

See: 86, 87, 480, 548, 633, 788, 798, 804, 809.

809 Price

price, selling p., world p., market p., standard p., list p., price current; rate, rate for the job; rate, piece r., flat r.; high rate 811n. *dearness*; low rate 812n. *cheapness*; price control, fixed price, prix fixe 747n. *restraint*; value, face v., par v., fair v., worth, money's w., what it will fetch; scarcity value, famine price; price list, tariff; quoted price, quotation, price charged; amount, figure, sum asked for; ransom, fine 963n. *penalty*; demand, dues, charge; surcharge, supplement 40n. *extra*; overcharge, excessive charge, extortion, ransom; fare, hire, rental, rent, ground r., house r., quit r., rate of r.; fee, refresher,

salami, commission, rake-off; charges, freightage, wharfage, lighterage; salvage; postage; cover charge, corkage; bill, invoice, reckoning, shot.

cost, buying price, purchase p.; damage, costs, expenses 806n. *expenditure*; business costs, running c., overheads; wages, wage bill, wage-packet; legal costs, damages 963n. *penalty*; cost of living, cost of living index.

tax, taxes, dues; taxation, tax demand 737n. *demand*; rating, assessment, appraisement, valorization 480n. *estimate*; cess, rate, general r., water r.; levy, toll, duty; imposition, impost; tallage; ship-money; charge, scot, scot and lot (see *price*); exaction, forced loan, aid, benevolence 740n. *compulsion*; forced savings 785n. *borrowing*; punitive tax, collective t. 963 n. *penalty*; tribute, danegeld, blackmail, ransom 804n. *payment*; ecclesiastical tax, Peter's pence, tithe, tenths; poll tax, capitation t.; property tax, schedule A, death duty; direct taxation, income tax, surtax, super-tax, company tax, profits t., excess profits t.; capital levy, capital gains tax 786n. *expropriation*; indirect taxation, excise, customs, tariff, tonnage and poundage; local tax, octroi; purchase tax, sales t., multipoint sales t.; salt tax, gabelle; feudal tax, scutage.

Adj. *priced*, charged, fixed; chargeable, leviable, taxable, assessable, rateable, customable, dutiable, excisable; ad valorem; to the tune of, for the price of; taxed, rated, assessed; paid, stipendiary.

Vb. *price*, cost, assess, value, rate 480vb. *estimate*; put a price on, set a price on; place a value on, fix a price for; raise a price, lower a p.; control the p., fix the p.; ask a price, charge, require 737 vb. *demand*; bill, invoice.

cost, be worth, fetch, bring in; amount to, come to, mount up to; be priced at, be valued at; bear a price, have a p., have its p.; sell for, go f., be going f.

tax, lay a tax on, impose a tax; fix a tariff, levy a rate, assess for tax, value, valorize; toll, excise, subject to duty, make dutiable; raise taxes, collect t., take one's toll 786vb. *levy*; take a collection, pass round the hat 761 vb. *beg*; exact a penalty, fine, punish by f., mulct 963vb. *punish*.

See: 40, 480, 737, 740, 747, 761, 785, 786, 804, 806, 811, 812, 963.

810 Discount

N. *discount*, something off, reduction, rebate, cut 42 n. *decrement*; stoppage, deduction; concession, allowance, margin, special price; tare, rate and tret; drawback, rebatement, backwardation, contango, deferment; cut price, bargain p., cut rate, bargain sale 812 n. *cheapness*; poundage, percentage; agio, brokerage; something for oneself, rake-off, dastur.

Vb. *discount*, deduct 39 vb. *subtract*; allow a margin, tare; reduce, depreciate, abate, rebate 37 vb. *bate*; offer a discount, allow a d.; mark down, take off, cut, slash 812 vb. *cheapen*; let stick to one's fingers, rake off, get one's rake-off; take a discount, take one's percentage.

Adv. *at a discount*, below par, less than the market rate.

See: 37, 39, 42, 812.

811 Dearness

N. *dearness*, costliness, expensiveness; value, high v., high worth, pricelessness; famine price, scarcity value, rarity, dearth 636 n. *scarcity*; exorbitance, extortion, overcharge, excessive charge, unfair price, bad value, poor v.; high price, fancy p., luxury p.; cost, high c., heavy c., pretty penny; extravagant price, Pyrrhic victory, white elephant; tax on one's pocket, ruinous charge; rising costs, rising prices, sellers' market, bull m., climbing prices, soaring p.; cheap money, inflation, inflationary pressure, bullish tendency.

Adj. *dear*, high-priced, expensive, ritzy; costly, multimillion; extravagant, dear-bought, Pyrrhic; dear at the price, over-rated, overcharged, overpriced, over-paid; exorbitant, excessive, extortionate; beyond one's means, not affordable, prohibitive, unpayable, more than one can afford, more than one's pocket can stand; rising in price, hardening, rising, soaring, climbing, mounting, inflationary; bullish, at a premium, odds on.

of price, of value, of worth 644 adj. *valuable*; priceless, beyond price, above p.; unpayable; invaluable 640 adj. *useful*; inestimable, worth a king's ransom, worth a Jew's eye; precious, rare, scarce 140 adj. *infrequent*; at a premium, not to be had for love or money.

Vb. *be dear*, cost much, cost a lot, cost a packet, cost a pretty penny, be high-priced; gain in value, rise in price, harden; go up, appreciate, soar, mount, climb; get too dear, price itself out of the market; prove expensive, cost one dear, be a white elephant.

overcharge, overprice, sell dear, oversell, ask too much; profiteer, soak, sting, bleed, skin, extort, rack-rent, hold to ransom 786 vb. *fleece*; bull, raise the price, raise the bid, bid up, auction 793 vb. *sell*.

pay too much, pay through the nose, pay the devil, be stung, be had; pay high, pay dear, buy a white elephant, achieve a Pyrrhic victory; pay beyond one's means, ruin oneself.

Adv. *dearly*, dear, at a price, at great cost, at heavy c., at huge expense; exorbitantly, extravagantly.

See: 140, 636, 640, 644, 786, 793.

812 Cheapness

N. *cheapness*, inexpensiveness, affordability; good value, value for money, bargain, good b., good penny, bon marché; low price, reasonable charge, reasonableness; cheap rate, off-season r., concessional r., excursion fare 810 n. *discount*; nominal price, reduced p., knock-down p., cut p., sale p., sacrificial p.; peppercorn rent, easy terms; buyers' market, sluggish m.; cheapening, Dutch auction; falling prices, declining p., bearishness, bearish tendency, easiness; depreciation, fall, slump, deflation; glut, drug on the market 635 n. *plenty*; superfluity 637 n. *redundance*.

no charge, absence of c., nominal c. 781 n. *gift*; gratuitousness, labour of love 597 n. *voluntary work*; free trade, free port; free entry, free admission, free seats, free pass, free ticket; free quarters, grace and favour; free board, run of one's teeth; free service, free delivery; everything for nothing.

Adj. *cheap*, inexpensive, uncostly, moderate, reasonable, fair; affordable, within one's means; economical, economy, economy size; not dear, worth its price, worth the money; low, low-priced, cheap-p., dirt-cheap, for a song, for peanuts; bargain-rate, cut-price, concessional, marked

down, half-price; tourist-class, off-season; easy to buy, two-a-penny; worth nothing, cheap and nasty, Brummagem 641 adj. *useless*; cheapening, bearish, falling, declining, slumping; unsaleable, unmarketable; unchargeable, valueless 860 adj. *unwanted*; underpaid, underpriced.

uncharged, not charged for, gratuitous, complimentary; gratis, for nothing, for love, for kicks, for nix, for the asking; costing nothing, free, scot-f., free of cost; untaxed, tax-free, rent-f., post-f., post-paid, carriage-p., F.O.B., including extras; unpaid, unsalaried, honorary 597 adj. *voluntary*; given away, unbought, as a gift 781 adj. *given*; costless, free, gratis and for nothing; had for the asking.

Vb. *be cheap*,—inexpensive etc. adj.; cost little, be economical, be easily afforded; be worth the money, be cheap at the price; be bought for an old song, be picked up for nothing, go dirt-cheap; cost nothing, be without charge, be free, be had for the asking; cheapen, get cheaper, fall in price, depreciate, come down, decline, sag, fall, slump, plunge.

cheapen, lower, lower the price, reduce the p.; put a low price on, price low, keep cheap, bate one's charges, trim one's prices, shave one's p., mark down, cut, slash; undercharge, underrate, let go for a song, sacrifice, give away, make a present of 781 vb. *give*; beat down, undercut, undersell, engage in cut-throat competition; dump, unload; spoil the market, glut 637 vb. *superabound*; depress the market, bear; stale, lower, vulgarize 655 vb. *impair*.

Adv. *cheaply*, on the cheap; at cost price, at prime cost, at half-price, for a song, for nothing.

See: 597, 635, 637, 641, 655, 781, 810, 860.

813 Liberality

N. *liberality*, liberalness, bounteousness, bountifulness, munificence, generosity 931 n. *disinterestedness*; open-handedness, open heart, open hand, open purse, hospitality, open house 882 n. *sociability*; free hand, blank cheque, carte blanche 744 n. *scope*; cornucopia 635 n. *plenty*; lavishness 815 n. *prodigality*; bounty,

largesse 781 n. *gift*; handsome offer, sporting o. 759 n. *offer*; benefaction, charity 897 n. *kind act*.

good giver, free g., princely g., generous g., cheerful g., liberal donor, unselfish d., blood d.; good spender, good tipper; Lady Bountiful, Father Christmas, Santa Claus, rich uncle 903 n. *benefactor*.

Adj. *liberal*, free, freely spending, free-handed, open-h., lavish 815 adj. *prodigal*; large-hearted, free-h. 931 adj. *disinterested*; bountiful, charitable 897 adj. *benevolent*; hospitable 882 adj. *sociable*; handsome, generous, munificent, splendid, slap-up; lordly, princely, royal 868 adj. *noble*; ungrudging, unstinting, unsparing, unfailing; in liberal quantities, ample, bounteous, profuse, full, pressed down and running over 635 adj. *plenteous*; overflowing 637 adj. *redundant*.

Vb. *be liberal*,—generous etc. adj.; lavish, shower largesse, shower upon 781 vb. *give*; unbelt, open the purse-strings, head the subscription list; give largely, give with both hands, give till it hurts 897 vb. *philanthropize*; give more than asked, overpay, pay well, tip w.; keep open house 882 vb. *be hospitable*; do it proud, not count the cost, spare no expense; give carte blanche, give a blank cheque 744 vb. *give scope*; spend freely, not ask for the change, throw one's money around 815 vb. *be prodigal*.

Adv. *liberally*, ungrudgingly, with open hand, with both hands.

See: 635, 637, 744, 759, 781, 815, 868, 882, 897, 903, 931.

814 Economy

N. *economy*, thrift, thriftiness, frugality; prudence, care, carefulness; husbandry, good h., good housekeeping, good housewifery; sound stewardship, good management, careful m.; watchful eye on expense, avoidance of waste, sumptuary law, credit squeeze 747 n. *restriction*; economy drive, economy slip; time-saving, labour-s., time and motion study; husbanding of resources, economizing, saving, sparing, pinching, paring, cheese-p.; retrenchment, economies; savings, hoarded s. 632 n. *store*; economizer,

save-all 816 n. *niggard*; economist, physiocrat; good housewife, careful steward.

Adj. *economical*, time-saving, labour-s., money-s., cost-reducing; money-conscious, chary of expense, counting the pence 816 adj. *parsimonious*; thrifty, frugal saving, sparing; unlavish, meagre; marginal, with nothing to spare.

Vb. *economize*, be economical,—sparing etc. adj.; avoid extravagance, keep costs down, waste nothing, find a use for everything; keep within one's budget, keep within compass, cut one's coat according to one's cloth, make both ends meet; watch expenses, pare e., cut down expenditure, trim e., make economies, retrench; pinch, scrape 816 vb. *be parsimonious*; save, spare, hoard 632 vb. *store*; plough back, re-invest, get interest on one's money, not leave money idle, make every penny work 800 vb. *get rich*.

Adv. *sparingly*, economically, frugally, nothing in excess.

See: 632, 747, 800, 816.

815 Prodigality

N. *prodigality*, lavishness, profusion, profuseness 637 n. *redundance*; idle display, idle expenditure 875 n. *ostentation*; extravagance, wasteful expenditure, spendthrift e., reckless e.; wastefulness, dissipation, squandering, squandermania, orgy of spending, spending spree 634 n. *waste*; unthriftiness, indifference to economy, uneconomy, uncontrolled expenditure, unregulated e., deficit finance; misapplication, misuse of funds 675 n. *misuse*; malversation 788 n. *peculation*.

prodigal, prodigal son, spender, reckless s., waster, spend-all, spendthrift, wastethrift, scattergood, squanderer, squandermaniac.

Adj. *prodigal*, lavish 813 n. *liberal*; profuse, overlavish, over-liberal; extravagant, regardless of cost, wasteful, squandering; uneconomic, uneconomical, unthrifty, thriftless, spendthrift, improvident, reckless, dissipated; ill-balanced, penny wise and pound foolish.

Vb. *be prodigal*, prodigalize, go the pace, go a bust, blow; overspend, pour money out, splash money around, flash pound notes; spill, spend money like water, pour

one's money through a sieve; spill one's money, burn one's m., run through one's savings, exhaust one's resources, spend to the last farthing, spend up to the hilt, blow everything, waste one's inheritance, consume one's substance, squander 634 vb. *waste*; play ducks and drakes, burn the candle at both ends, fritter away, throw a., fling a., gamble a., dissipate, pour down the drain; not count the cost, keep no check on expenditure; misspend, fool one's money away, throw good money after bad, throw the helve after the hatchet; have no thought for the morrow, anticipate one's income, spend more than one has, overdraw, outrun the constable; eat up one's capital, kill the goose that lays the golden eggs; save nothing, put nothing by, keep nothing for a rainy day.

Adv. *prodigally*, profusely; like a prodigal, like a spendthrift.

Int. hang the expense! a short life and a merry one! easy come, easy go!

See: 634, 637, 675, 788, 813, 875.

816 Parsimony

N. *parsimony*, parsimoniousness; credit squeeze 814 n. *economy*; false economy, misplaced e., cheese-paring e., policy of penny wise and pound foolish; cheeseparing, scrimping, pinching, scraping; niggardliness, meanness, minginess, stinginess, miserliness; illiberality, ungenerosity, uncharity, grudging hand, closed purse 932 n. *selfishness*.

avarice, cupidity, acquisitiveness, possessiveness, monopoly; money-grubbing, itch for pelf, itching palm; rapacity, avidity, greed 859 n. *desire*; mercenariness, venality, hireling character.

niggard, skinflint, screw, scrimp, scraper, pinchfist, tightwad, no tipper; miser, money-grubber, lickpenny, muckworm; cadger; save-all, hoarder, magpie; hunks, churl, codger, curmudgeon; usurer 784 n. *lender*; Harpagon, Scrooge.

Adj. *parsimonious*, penurious 814 adj. *economical*; over-economical, over-frugal, frugal to excess; money-conscious, pennywise, miserly, mean, mingy, stingy, near, close, tight; tight-fisted, close-f., hard f., close-handed 778 adj. *retentive*; grudging,

curmudgeonly, churlish, illiberal, ungenerous, uncharitable, empty-handed, giftless; chary, sparing, pinching, scraping, scrimping; shabby, peddling.

avaricious, grasping, griping, monopolistic 932 adj. *selfish*; possessive, acquisitive 771 adj. *acquiring*; hoarding, saving; pinching; miserly; cadging; money-grubbing, money-conscious, money-mad, covetous 859 adj. *greedy*; usurious, rapacious, extortionate; mercenary, venal, sordid.

Vb. *be parsimonious*,—niggardly etc. adj.; keep one's fist closed, keep one's purse shut 778 vb. *retain*; grudge, begrudge, withhold, keep back 760 vb. *refuse*; dole out, stint, skimp, starve, famish 636 vb. *make insufficient*; scrape, pinch, gripe, screw, rack-rent, skin a flint 786 vb. *fleece*; be penny-wise, spoil the ship for a ha'porth of tar, stop one hole in a sieve; starve oneself, live like a pauper; hoard wealth, never spend a penny; grudge every farthing, beat down, haggle 791 vb. *bargain*; cadge, beg, borrow; hoard, sit on.

Adv. *parsimoniously*, niggardly, sparingly, on a shoe-string.

See: 636, 760, 771, 778, 784, 786, 791, 814, 859, 932.

817 Affections

N. *affections*, qualities, instincts; passions, emotional life; nature, disposition 5 n. *character*; spirit, temper, tone, grain, mettle 5 n. *temperament*; cast of soul, cast of mind, habit of m., trait, touch 7 n. *state*; personality, psychology, psychological endowment, psychological complex, mental and spiritual make-up, inherited characteristics 5 n. *heredity*; being, innermost b., breast, bosom, heart, soul, core, inmost soul, inner man, cockles of the heart, heart of hearts 5 n. *essential part*; animus, attitude, frame of mind, state of m., vein, strain, humour, mood; predilection, predisposition, turn, bent, bias 179 n. *tendency*; passion, ruling p., master p. 481 n. *prejudice*; fullness of heart, flow of soul, heyday of the blood; force of character; fettle, form, shape 7 n. *state*.

Adj. *with affections*, affected, characterized,

formed, moulded, cast, tempered, framed; instinct with, imbued w., tinctured w., penetrated w., eaten up w., possessed w., obsessed w., devoured w.; inborn, inbred, congenital 5 adj. *genetic*; deep-rooted, ineffaceable 5 adj. *intrinsic*; emotional, demonstrative 818 adj. *feeling*.

See: 5, 7, 179, 481, 818.

818 Feeling

N. *feeling*, experience, emotional life; sentience, sensation, sense of 374 n. *sense*; sensory perception, sense p. 378 n. *touch*; relish, gusto 386 n. *taste*; emotion, crystallized e., sentiment; true feeling, sincerity 540 n. *veracity*; impulse 609 n. *spontaneity*; responsiveness, response, reaction, fellow-feeling, sympathy, involvement, personal i. 880 n. *friendliness*; appreciation, realization, understanding 490 n. *knowledge*; impression, deep feeling, deep sense of 819 n. *moral sensibility*; religious feeling, unction 979 n. *piety*; finer feelings 897 n. *benevolence*; hard feelings 891 n. *resentment*; stirred feeling, thrill, kick 318 n. *spasm*; shock, turn 508 n. *inexpectation*; pathos 825 n. *suffering*; actuating feeling, animus, emotionality, emotionalism, affectivity 822 n. *excitability*; manifestation of feeling, demonstration, demonstrativeness; expression, facial e., play of feature 547 n. *gesture*; blush, flush, hectic f., suffusion; tingling, goose-flesh, tremor, trembling, quiver, flutter, flurry, palpitation, pulsation, heaving, panting, throbbing 318 n. *agitation*; stew, ferment 318 n. *commotion*; control of feeling, stoicism, endurance, sufferance, supportance, toleration 823 n. *patience*.

warm feeling, cordiality, empressement, effusiveness, heartiness, full heart, overflowing h.; hot head, impatience; unction, earnestness 834 n. *seriousness*; eagerness, keenness, fervour, ardour, vehemence, enthusiasm, dash, fire 174 n. *vigorousness*; vigour, zeal 678 n. *activity*; fanaticism, mania 481 n. *prejudice*; emotion, passion, ecstasy, inspiration, elevation, transports 822 n. *excitable state*.

Adj. *feeling*, affective, sensible, sensorial, sensory 374 adj. *sentient*; spirited, vivacious, lively 819 adj. *sensitive*; sensuous

944adj. *sensual*; experiencing, living; enduring, bearing 825adj. *suffering*; responsive, reacting; involved, sympathetic, condoling 775adj. *sharing*; emotional, passionate, full of feeling; unctuous, soulful; intense, tense 821adj. *excited*; cordial, hearty; gushing, effusive; sentimental, romantic; mawkish, treacly, sloppy; thrilling, tingling, throbbing; blushing, flushing.

impressed, affected, influenced; stirred, aroused, moved, touched 821adj. *excited*; struck, awed, awe-struck, overwhelmed; penetrated, imbued with, aflame w., consumed w., devoured by, inspired by; rapt, enraptured, enthralled, ecstatic; lyrical, raving 822adj. *excitable*.

fervent, fervid, perfervid, passionate, tense, intense; eager, breathless, panting, throbbing; impassioned, earnest, zealous, enthusiastic; hot-headed, impetuous, impatient 822adj. *excitable*; warm, fiery, glowing, burning, red-hot, flaming, boiling 379n. *hot*; hysterical, delirious, overwrought, feverish, hectic 503adj. *frenzied*; strong, uncontrollable, furious 176adj. *violent*.

felt, experienced, lived; heartfelt, cordial, hearty, warm, sincerely felt, sincere 540 adj. *veracious*; deeply-felt, profound 211 adj. *deep*; stirring, soul-s., heart-warming, heart-expanding; emotive, impressive, strong, overwhelming 821adj. *impressive*; smart, acute, keen, poignant, piercing, trenchant 256adj. *sharp*; caustic, burning, smarting 388adj. *pungent*; penetrating, absorbing; thrilling, tingling, rapturous, ecstatic 826adj. *pleasurable*; pathetic, affecting 827adj. *distressing*.

Vb. *feel*, sense, receive an impression; entertain, entertain feelings, have f., cherish f., harbour f., feel deeply, take to heart 374adj. *have feelings*; know the feeling, experience, live, live through, go t., pass t., taste, prove; bear, endure, undergo, smart, smart under 825vb. *suffer*; suffer with, feel w., sympathise, condole, share 775vb. *participate*; respond, react, tingle, warm to, fire, kindle, catch, catch the flame, catch the infection, be inspired 821vb. *be excited*; cause feeling 821vb. *impress*.

show feeling, exhibit f., show signs of emotion; demonstrate, not hide one's feelings 522vb. *manifest*; go into ecstasies 824vb. *be pleased*; fly into a passion 891 vb. *get angry*; turn colour, change c., look blue, look black; go livid, go black in the face, go purple 428vb. *blacken*; look pale, blench, turn pale, go white 427vb. *whiten*; colour, blush, flush, glow, mantle, turn red, turn crimson, warm up, go red in the face 431vb. *redden*; quiver, tremble, wince; flutter, shake, quake 318 vb. *be agitated*; tingle, thrill, throb, beat 317vb. *oscillate*; palpitate, pant, heave, draw a deep breath 352vb. *breathe*; reel, lurch, stagger 317vb. *fluctuate*; stutter 580vb. *stammer*.

Adv. *feelingly*, unctuously, earnestly, con amore, heart and soul; with a full heart, with a swelling h., with a bursting h., with a melting h., sympathetically; cordially, heartily, devoutly, sincerely, from the bottom of one's heart.

See: 174, 176, 211, 256, 317, 318, 352, 374, 378, 379, 386, 388, 427, 428, 431, 481, 490, 503, 508, 522, 540, 547, 580, 609, 678, 775, 819, 821, 822, 823, 824, 825, 826, 827, 834, 880, 891, 897, 944, 979.

819 Sensibility

N. *moral sensibility*, sensitivity, sensitiveness; touchiness, prickliness, irritability 892n. *irascibility*; raw feelings, tender f., soft spot, tender spot, quick; sore point, where the shoe pinches 891n. *resentment*; impressibility, affectibility, susceptibility; plasticity, malleability 327n. *softness*; finer feelings, sentimentality, sentimentalism; tenderness, affection 887n. *love*; spirit, spiritedness, vivacity, vivaciousness, liveliness, verve 571n. *vigour*; emotionalism, ebullience, effervescence 822n. *excitability*; fastidiousness, finickiness, æstheticism 463n. *discrimination*; temperament, mobility, changeability 152 n. *changeableness*; physical sensitivity, allergy 374n. *sensibility*; touchy person, sensitive plant, mass of nerves.

Adj. *impressible*, malleable, plastic 327adj. *soft*; sensible, aware, conscious of, awake to, alive to, responsive 374adj. *sentient*; impressed with, touched, moved, touched to the quick 818adj. *impressed*; persuasible 612adj. *induced*; impressionable, impassionable 822adj. *excitable*; susceptible, susceptive; romantic, sentimental;

sentimentalizing, gushing; emotional, warm-hearted; soft, tender, tender as a chicken, tender-hearted, soft-h., compassionate 905 adj. *pitying*.

sensitive, sensitized; tingling, physically sensitive, sore, raw, tender, allergic; æsthetic, fastidious, particular 463 adj. *discriminating*; oversensitive, all feeling 822 adj. *excitable*; touchy, irritable, impatient, thin-skinned, easily stung, easily aroused 892 adj. *irascible*.

lively, alive, tremblingly a.; vital, vivacious, animated; gamesome, skittish; irrepressible, ebullient, effervescent; mettlesome, spirited, high-s., high-flying; alert, aware, on one's toes 455 adj. *attentive*; overquick, impatient; nervous, highly-strung, overstrung, temperamental; mobile, changeable; enthusiastic, impassioned; overenthusiastic, over-zealous, fanatic; lively in style, expressive, racy 571 adj. *forceful*.

Vb. *be sensitive*,—sentimental etc. adj.; have a soft heart; be all feeling, 'die of a rose in aromatic pain'; soften one's heart, let one's heart be touched, weep for 905 vb. *pity*; scratch, tingle 378 vb. *itch*.

Adv. *on the raw*, to the quick, where the shoe pinches, where it hurts most.

See: 152, 327, 374, 378, 455, 463, 571, 612, 818, 822, 887, 891, 892, 905.

820 Insensibility

N. *moral insensibility*, insentience, no sensation, numbness, stupor 375 n. *insensibility*; inertia 175 n. *inertness*; lethargy 679 n. *inactivity*; quietism, stagnation, vegetation 266 n. *quiescence*; woodenness, blockishness, obtuseness, stupidity, dullness, no imagination 499 n. *unintelligence*; slowness, delayed reaction 456 n. *inattention*; uninterest 454 n. *incuriosity*; nonchalance, insouciance, unconcern, detachment, apathy 860 n. *indifference*; no nerves, imperturbation, phlegm, calmness, steadiness, coolness, sang froid 823 n. *inexcitability*; no feelings, aloofness, impassibility, impassivity, impassiveness; repression, repression of feeling, stoicism 823 n. *patience*; inscrutability, poker-face, dead pan 834 n. *seriousness*; insensitivity, coarseness, Philistinism 699 n. *artlessness*; imperception, thick skin, rhinoceros hide; no pride, no

honour; cold heart, frigidity; unsusceptibility, unimpressibility, dourness; unsentimentality, cynicism; callousness 326 n. *hardness*; lack of feeling, dry eyes, no heart, heart of stone, heart of marble, brutishness, brutality, brutalization 898 n. *inhumanity*; no joy, no humour, no life, no animation 838 n. *tedium*; no admiration for 865 n. *non-wonder*.

unfeeling person, iceberg, icicle, cold fish, cold heart, cold-blooded animal; stoic, ascetic; stock, stone, block, marble.

Adj. *impassive*, unconscious 375 adj. *insensible*; unsusceptible, insensitive, unimaginative; unresponsive, unimpressionable, unimpressible 823 adj. *inexcitable*; phlegmatic, stolid; wooden, blockish; dull, slow 499 adj. *unintelligent*; unemotional, passionless, impassible; proof, proof against, steeled a.; stoical, ascetic, controlled, undemonstrative; unconcerned, aloof, distant, detached, disengaged, dégagé 860 adj. *indifferent*; unaffected, calm 266 adj. *tranquil*; steady, unruffled, unshaken, unshocked; imperturbable, without nerves, cool, sang froid; inscrutable, blank, expressionless, deadpan, poker-faced; unseeing 439 adj. *blind*; unhearing 416 adj. *deaf*; unsentimental, cynical; impersonal, dispassionate, without warmth, unforthcoming, frigid, icy, cold, cold-blooded, cold-hearted, cold as charity; unfeeling, heartless, soulless, inhuman; unsmitten, heart-free, fancy-f., heart-whole; unloving, unaffectionate, undemonstrative.

apathetic, unenthusiastic, unambitious; unimpassioned, uninspired, unexcited, unwarmed, unmoved, unstirred, untouched, unsmitten, unstruck, unaroused, unstung; half-hearted, lukewarm, Laodicean 860 adj. *indifferent*; uninterested 454 adj. *incurious*; nonchalant, insouciant, pococurante, careless, regardless, neglectful 458 adj. *negligent*; unspirited, spiritless, lackadaisical; lotus-eating, vegetative, stagnant 266 adj. *quiescent*; sluggish, supine 679 adj. *inactive*; blunted 257 adj. *unsharpened*; cloyed 863 adj. *sated*; torpid, numb, benumbed, palsied, comatose 375 adj. *insensible*.

thick-skinned, pachydermatous; impenetrable, impervious; blind to, deaf to, dead to, closed to; obtuse, unimaginative, insensitive; callous, insensate, tough,

toughened, hardened, case-h. 326 adj. *hard*; hard-bitten, hard-boiled, inured 669 adj. *matured*; shameless, unblushing, unmoral, amoral.

Vb. *be insensitive,*—impassive etc. adj.; have no sensation, have no feelings 375 vb. *be insensible*; not see, miss the point of, be blind to 439 vb. *be blind*; lack animation, lack spirit, lack verve; harden oneself, steel o., harden one's heart against, own no pity 906 vb. *be pitiless*; feel indifference 860 vb. *be indifferent*; feel no emotion, despise e., have no finer feelings, be a Philistine, nil admirari 865 vb. *not wonder*; show no regard for 922 vb. *despise*; take no interest 454 vb. *be incurious*; ignore 458 vb. *disregard*; control one's feelings, quell one's desires 942 vb. *be temperate*; stagnate, vegetate 679 vb. *be inactive*; not stir, not turn a hair, not bat an eyelid 599 vb. *be resolute.*

make insensitive, benumb 375 vb. *render insensible*; render callous, steel, toughen 326 vb. *harden*; sear, dry up 342 vb. *dry*; deafen, stop the ears 399 vb. *silence*; shut the eyes of 439 vb. *blind*; brutalize 655 vb. *pervert*; stale, coarsen 847 vb. *vulgarize*; satiate, cloy 863 vb. *sate*; deaden, obtund, take the edge off 257 vb. *blunt.*

Adv. *in cold blood,* with dry eyes, without emotion, with steady pulse; without enthusiasm.

See: 175, 257, 266, 326, 342, 375, 399, 416, 439, 454, 456, 458, 499, 599, 655, 669, 679, 699, 823, 834, 838, 847, 860, 863, 865, 898, 906, 922, 942.

821 Excitation

N. *excitation,* rousing, arousing, stirring up, working up, whipping up; galvanization, galvanism, electrification 174 n. *stimulation*; possession, inspiration, afflatus, exhilaration, intoxication, headiness; evocation, calling forth; encouragement, animation, incitement, invitation, appeal 612 n. *inducement*; provocation, irritation, casus belli; impression, image, impact 178 n. *influence*; fascination, bewitchment, enchantment 983 n. *sorcery*; rapture, ravishment 824 n. *joy*; emotional appeal, human interest, sentiment, sentimalism, sob-stuff, pathos; sensationalism,

thrill-seeking, melodrama; scandal-mongering, muck-raking 926 n. *detraction*; excitement, high pressure, tension 160 n. *energy*; state of excitement, perturbation, effervescence, ebullience 318 n. *agitation*; shock, thrill 318 n. *spasm*; stew, ferment, flurry, furore, breeze 318 n. *commotion*; pitch of excitement 503 n. *frenzy*; climax 137 n. *crisis*; excited feeling, passion, emotion, enthusiasm, lyricism 818 n. *feeling*; fuss, drama; temper, fury, rage 891 n. *anger*; interest 453 n. *curiosity*; amazement 864 n. *wonder*; awe 854 n. *fear.*

excitant, stimulator, agent-provocateur, rabble-rouser, tub-thumper 738 n. *agitator*; sensationalist, sob-sister, scandal-monger; headline, banner-h. 528 n. *publicity*; fillip, ginger, tonic, pick-me-up 174 n. *stimulant*; sting, prick, goad, spur, whip, lash 612 n. *incentive*; fan; irritant, gadfly, breeze.

Adj. *excited,* activated, stimulated, stung etc. vb.; busy, astir, bustling, rushing 678 adj. *active*; ebullient, effervescent, boiling, seething 355 adj. *bubbly*; tense, wrought up, strung up; overheated, feverish, hectic; delirious, frantic 503 adj. *frenzied*; glowing 818 adj. *fervent*; heated, flushed 379 adj. *hot*; red-hot with excitement, violent 176 adj. *furious*; seeing red, wild, mad, foaming at the mouth, frothing, ramping, stamping, roaring, raging 891 n. *angry*; avid, eager, itching, agog, thrill-seeking, watering at the mouth 859 adj. *desiring*; tingling, a-tremble, a-quiver, 818 adj. *feeling*; flurried, a-twitter, all of a flutter 318 adj. *agitated*; restless, restive, over-excited, over-wrought, distraught, distracted; beside oneself, hysterical, out of control, uncontrollable, running amok, carried away, a prey to passion; inspired, possessed, impassioned, enthusiastic, lyrical, raving 822 adj. *excitable.*

exciting, stimulating, sparkling, intoxicating, heady, exhilarating; provocative, piquant, tantalizing; salty, spicy, appetizing; evocative, suggestive; thrilling, agitating; inspiring, possessing; heating, kindling, rousing, stirring, soul-s., heart-swelling, heart-thrilling; cheering, rousing, rabble-r.; sensational, dramatic, melodramatic, stunning; interesting, gripping, absorbing.

impressive, imposing, grand, stately; digni-

fied, majestic, regal, royal, kingly, queenly 868 adj. *noble*; high-wrought, awe-inspiring, soul-subduing, sublime, humbling; overwhelming, overpowering; picturesque, scenic; striking, arresting, dramatic; telling, forceful 178 adj. *influential*.

Vb. *excite*, affect, infect 178 vb. *influence*; touch, move, draw tears 834 vb. *sadden*; impassion, touch the heart-strings, arouse the emotions, stir the feelings, play on one's f.; quicken the pulse, startle, electrify, galvanize; warm, warm the blood, raise the temperature, raise to fever-pitch, bring to the boil, make one's blood boil 381 vb. *heat*; enflame, enkindle, kindle, draw a spark, set on fire 381 vb. *burn*; sting, pique, irritate 891 vb. *enrage*; tantalize, tease 827 vb. *torment*; touch on the raw, cut to the quick; rip up, open the wound 827 vb. *hurt*; work on, work up, breathe on 612 vb. *incite*; breathe into, enthuse, inspire, possess; stir, rouse, arouse, wake, awaken (see *animate*); evoke, summon up, call forth; thrill, exhilarate, intoxicate; transport, send, send into ecstasies 826 vb. *delight*.

animate, vivify, enliven, quicken 360 vb. *vitalize*; revive, rekindle, resuscitate, breathe fresh life into, bring in new blood 656 vb. *restore*; inspire, inspirit, put one on his mettle; infuse courage into, encourage, hearten 855 vb. *give courage*; give an edge, put teeth into, whet 256 vb. *sharpen*; urge, nag, spur, goad, lash 277 vb. *accelerate*; fillip, give a fillip to, stimulate, ginger 174 vb. *invigorate*; cherish, foster, foment 162 vb. *strengthen*; intensify, fan, fan the flame, blow the coals, stir the embers, poke the fire.

impress, sink in, leave an impression; project *or* present an image; interest, hold, grip, absorb; intrigue, rouse curiosity; strike, claim attention 455 vb. *attract notice*; affect 178 vb. *influence*; let sink in, bring home to, drive home 532 vb. *emphasize*; come home to, make one realize, penetrate, pierce 516 vb. *be intelligible*; arrest, shake, smite, stun, amaze, astound, stagger 508 vb. *surprise*; sensationalize, stupefy, gorgonize, petrify 864 vb. *be wonderful*; dazzle, fill with admiration; inspire with awe, humble; take one's breath away, overwhelm 727 vb. *overmaster*; oppress, perturb, disquiet, upset, worry 827 vb. *incommode*.

be excited, flare, flare up, flame, burn 379 vb. *be hot*; seethe, boil, explode 318 vb. *effervesce*; catch the infection, catch the flame, thrill to 818 vb. *feel*; tingle, tremble, quiver, flutter, palpitate 318 vb. *be agitated*; mantle, flush 818 vb. *show feeling*; squirm, writhe 251 vb. *wriggle*; dance, stamp, ramp; jump 312 vb. *leap*; seek a thrill, capture a t.

Adv. *excitedly*, uncontrollably, frenziedly; all agog, with one's heart in one's mouth, with one's heart beating, with hair on end; a-quiver, a-tremble.

See: 137, 160, 162, 174, 176, 178, 251, 256, 277, 312, 318, 355, 360, 379, 381, 453, 455, 503, 508, 516, 528, 532, 612, 656, 678, 727, 738, 818, 822, 824, 826, 827, 834, 854, 855, 859, 864, 868, 891, 926, 983.

822 Excitability

N. *excitability*, excitableness, explosiveness, inflammability; instability, temperament, emotionalism; hot blood, hot temper, irritability, scratchiness, touchiness 892 n. *irascibility*; impatience, nonendurance; incontinence; intolerance, fanaticism 481 n. *bias*; passionateness, vehemence, impetuosity, recklessness, headstrong behaviour 857 n. *rashness*; hastiness 680 n. *haste*; effervescence, ebullition; turbulence, boisterousness; restlessness, fidgetiness, fidgets, nerves, flap 318 n. *agitation*.

excitable state, exhilaration, elevation, intoxication, abandon, abandonment; thrill, transport, ecstasy, inspiration, lyricism; fever, fever of excitement, fret, fume, perturbation, trepidation, bother, fuss, flurry, whirl 318 n. *agitation*; warmth 379 n. *heat*; ferment, pother, stew; gust, whiff, storm, tempest 352 n. *gale*; effervescence, ebullition, outburst, outbreak, explosion, scene, song and dance 318 n. *commotion*; brainstorm, hysterics, delirium, fit, agony 503 n. *frenzy*; distraction, madness 503 n. *insanity*; mania, passion, master p., ruling p. 817 n. *affections*; rage, fury 176 n. *violence*; temper, tantrums, rampage 891 n. *anger*.

Adj. *excitable*, sensitized, over-sensitive, raw 819 adj. *sensitive*; passionate, emotional; susceptible, romantic; out for

thrills, thrill-loving, thrill-seeking; suggestible, inflammable, like tinder; unstable, easily exhilarated, easily depressed; easily impressed, impressionable; variable, unstaid; temperamental, mercurial, volatile 152 adj. *changeful*; fitful 604 adj. *capricious*; restless, unquiet, nervy, fidgety, edgy, on edge, ruffled 318 adj. *agitated*; highly-strung, nervous, startlish, skittish, mettlesome 819 adj. *lively*; easily provoked, irritable, fiery, hot-tempered, hot-headed 892 adj. *irascible*; impatient 680 adj. *hasty*; impetuous, impulsive, madcap 857 adj. *rash*; savage, fierce; vehement, boisterous, rumbustious, tempestuous, turbulent, stormy, uproarious, clamorous 176 adj. *violent*; restive, uncontrollable 738 adj. *riotous*; effervescent, simmering, seething, boiling; volcanic, explosive, ready to burst; fanatical, intolerant; rabid 176 adj. *furious*; feverish, febrile, frantic, hysterical, delirious 503 adj. *frenzied*; dancing, stamping; like a cat on hot bricks, like a cat on a hot tin roof; tense, electric, atmospheric; inspired, raving, lyrical 821 adj. *excited*.

Vb. *be excitable,*—impatient etc. adj.; show impatience, fret, fume, stamp; dance, shuffle; show excitement, show temperament 818 vb. *show feeling*; be on edge, have nerves, be in a stew, be in a fuss, flap 318 vb. *be agitated*; startle, start, jump 854 vb. *be nervous*; be under strain, break down, be on the verge of a breakdown; have a temper 892 vb. *be irascible*; foam, froth, throw fits, have hysterics 503 vb. *go mad*; abandon oneself, let oneself go, go wild, run riot, run amok, get out of control, see red; storm, rush about 61 vb. *rampage*; ramp, rage, roar 176 vb. *be violent*; fly into a temper, fly off the handle, burst out, break o., explode, create 891 vb. *get angry*; kindle, burn, catch fire, flare up 821 vb. *be excited*; scratch, tingle 378 vb. *itch*.

See: 61, 152, 176, 318, 352, 378, 379, 481, 503, 604, 680, 738, 817, 818, 819, 821, 854, 857, 891, 892.

823 Inexcitability

N. *inexcitability*, inirritability, imperturbability, goodtemper; calmness, steadiness, composure; coolness, sang froid, non-chalance; frigidity, coldness, impassibility 820 n. *moral insensibility*; unruffled state, tranquillity 266 n. *quietude*; serenity, placidity, peace of mind, calm of m. 828 n. *content*; equanimity, balance, poise, even temper, level t., philosophic t., philosophy, balanced mind 28 n. *equilibrium*; self-possession, self-command, self-control, self-restraint 942 n. *temperance*; repression, self-r., stoicism 945 n. *asceticism*; detachment, non-attachment, dispassion, dispassionateness 860 n. *indifference*; gravity, staidness, demureness, sobriety 834 n. *seriousness*; quietism, Quakerism 679 n. *inactivity*; sweetness, gentleness 884 n. *courtesy*; tameness, meekness, lack of spirit, lack of mettle 734 n. *laxity*; tranquillization, soothing 177 n. *moderation*.

patience, patience of Job, patience on a monument; forbearance, endurance, long-suffering, longanimity; tolerance, toleration, refusal to be provoked; sufferance, supportance, stoicism; resignation, acquiescence 721 n. *submission*.

Adj. *inexcitable*, impassible, cold, frigid, heavy, dull, immune to stimulation; stable 153 adj. *unchangeable*; not given to worry, unworrying, unworried, cool, imperturbable, unflappable; steady, composed, controlled; self-controlled, moderate 942 adj. *temperate*; inscrutable, dead-pan 820 adj. *impassive*; deliberate, unhurried, unhasty 278 adj. *slow*; even, level, equable 16 adj. *uniform*; unirritable, good-tempered, sunny; staid, sedate, sober, sober-minded, demure, reserved, grave 834 adj. *serious*; quiet, unemphatic 266 adj. *quiescent*; placid, unruffled, calm, serene 266 adj. *tranquil*; sweet, gentle, mild, lamblike, meek 935 adj. *innocent*; unwarlike 717 adj. *peaceful*; easy, easy-going, undemanding 736 adj. *lenient*; comfortable, gemütlich 828 adj. *content*; philosophic, unambitious 860 adj. *indifferent*; acquiescent, resigned, submissive 739 adj. *obedient*; unlively, unspirited, spiritless, lackadaisical, torpid, passive 175 adj. *inert*; calmed down, in a reasonable frame of mind, tame 369 adj. *tamed*; unenthusiastic, unsentimental, unromantic, unpoetic 593 adj. *prosaic*.

patient, meek, patient as Job, like patience on a monument, armed with patience;

tolerant, long-suffering, longanimous, forbearing, enduring; stoic, stoical, philosophic, philosophical, uncomplaining.

Vb. *keep calm*, be composed, be collected; compose oneself, collect o., **keep cool**; master one's feelings, swallow one's resentment, control one's temper, keep one's hair on; not turn a hair, not bat an eyelid 820 vb. *be insensitive*; relax, not excite oneself, not worry, stop worrying, take things easy 683 vb. *repose*; resign oneself, take in good part, take philosophically, have patience, be resigned 721 vb. *submit.*

be patient, show patience, show restraint, forbear; put up with, stand, tolerate, bear, endure, support, sustain, suffer, thole, aby, abide; resign oneself, grin and bear it; brook, take, take it from, swallow, digest, stomach, pocket 721 vb. *knuckle under*; turn the other cheek 909 vb. *forgive*; be tolerant, condone 736 vb. *be lenient*; turn a blind eye, overlook 734 vb. *be lax*; allow 756 vb. *permit*; ignore provocation, keep the peace 717 vb. *be at peace*; find a modus vivendi, coexist 770 vb. *compromise.*

tranquillize, steady, moderate, moderate one's transports 177 vb. *assuage*; calm, rock, lull 266 vb. *bring to rest*; cool down, compose 719 vb. *pacify*; make one's mind easy, set one's mind at rest 831 vb. *relieve*; control, repress 747 vb. *restrain.*

See: 16, 28, 153, 175, 177, 266, 278, 369, 593, 679, 683, 717, 719, 721, 734, 736, 739, 747, 756, 770, 820, 828, 831, 834, 860, 884, 909, 935, 942, 945.

824 Joy

N. *joy* 376 n. *pleasure*; great pleasure, keen p.; sensation of pleasure, enjoyment, thrill, kick, tickle, piquancy 826 n. *pleasurableness*; joyfulness, joyousness 835 n. *rejoicing*; delight, gladness, rapture, exaltation, exhilaration, transport, abandonment, ecstasy, enchantment, bewitchment, ravishment; unholy joy, gloating, schadenfreude, malice 898 n. *malevolence*; life of pleasure, joys of life, pleasant time, halcyon days, holidays, honeymoon 730 n. *palmy days.*

happiness, felicity, good fortune, well-being, snugness, comfort, ease 376 n. *euphoria*;

flourishing time, palmy days, Saturnia Regna, Ram Raj, golden age 730 n. *prosperity*; blessedness, bliss, beatitude, summum bonum; seventh heaven, paradise, happy home, Fortunate Isles, Isles of the Blessed, Hesperides, Eden, Arcadia, Cockaigne; happy valley, Bower of Bliss.

enjoyment, fruition, gratification, satisfaction, fulfilment 725 n. *completion*, usufruct 773 n. *possession*; delectation, oblectation, relish, zest, gusto 386 n. *taste*; indulgence, luxuriation, wallowing, hedonism 943 n. *intemperance*; full life, eudæmonism, Epicureanism 944 n. *sensualism*; glee, merry-making, lark, frolic, gambol 833 n. *merriment*; fun, treat, excursion, outing 837 n. *amusement*; refreshment, good cheer, cakes and ale, beer and skittles, panem et circenses 301 n. *eating.*

Adj. *pleased*, glad, not sorry; welcoming, receiving with open arms; satisfied, happy 828 adj. *content*; gratified, flattered, pleased as Punch; enjoying, loving it, tickled, tickled to death, tickled pink 837 adj. *amused*; exhilarated 833 adj. *gay*; exalted, elated, elate, overjoyed 833 adj. *jubilant*; cheering, shouting 835 adj. *rejoicing*; delighted, transported, enraptured, ravished, rapturous, ecstatic, raving 923 adj. *approving*; in raptures, in ecstasies, in transports, in the seventh heaven; captivated, charmed, enchanted, fascinated 818 adj. *impressed*; maliciously pleased, gloating.

happy, happy as a king, happy as a sandboy; blithe, joyful, joyous, gladsome, merry 833 adj. *gay*; beaming, smiling 835 adj. *laughing*; radiant, radiating joy, sparkling, starry-eyed; felicitous, lucky, fortunate, to be congratulated 730 adj. *prosperous*; blissful, blest, blessed, beatified; in felicity, in bliss, in paradise; at ease, made comfortable 376 adj. *comfortable.*

Vb. *be pleased* etc. adj.; have the pleasure; feel *or* experience pleasure, hug oneself, congratulate o., purr, purr with pleasure, dance with p., jubilate 833 vb. *be cheerful*; laugh, smile 835 vb. *rejoice*; get pleasure from, get a kick out of, take pleasure in, delight in, rejoice in; go into ecstasies, rave, rave about 821 vb. *show feeling*; indulge in, have time for, luxuriate in, solace oneself with, refresh oneself w.,

bask in, wallow 376 vb. *enjoy*; have fun 837 vb. *amuse oneself*; gloat, gloat over; appreciate, relish, smack one's lips 386 vb. *taste*; take a fancy to, like 887 vb. *love*; think well of 923 vb. *approve*; take in good part, take no offence.

See: 301, 376, 386, 725, 730, 773, 818, 821, 826, 828, 833, 835, 837, 887, 898, 923, 943, 944.

825 Suffering

N. *suffering*, suffering felt, inconvenience, discomfort, disagreeableness, malaise; sufferance, endurance; heart-ache, weltschmerz, lacrimæ rerum 834 n. *dejection*; longing, homesickness, nostalgia 859 n. *desire*; unsatisfied desire 829 n. *discontent*; weariness 684 n. *fatigue*; weight on the spirit, nightmare, ephialtes, incubus; affliction, teen, tine, dolour, anguish, angst, agony, passion, torture, torment, mental t. 377 n. *pain*; twinge, stab, smart, sting, thorn 377 n. *pang*; suffering imposed, crucifixion, cup, Calvary, martyrdom; rack, the stake 963 n. *punishment*; purgatory, hell, pains of h., damnation, eternal d. 961 n. *condemnation*; unpleasantness, mauvais quart d'heure; the hard way, trial, ordeal, fiery o.; shock, blow, infliction, visitation, tribulation 659 n. *bane*; extremity, death's door 651 n. *illness*; living death, death in life, fate worse than death 616 n. *evil*; evil days, unhappy times, iron age 731 n. *adversity*.
sorrow, grief, sadness, mournfulness, gloom 834 n. *melancholy*; dole, woe, wretchedness, misery, depths of m.; prostration, despair, desolation 853 n. *hopelessness*; unhappiness, infelicity, tale of woe 731 n. *adversity*; vexation of spirit, weariness of s., aching heart, bleeding h., broken h.; displeasure, dissatisfaction 829 n. *discontent*; vexation, bitterness, mortification, chagrin, heart-burning, fretting, repining, remorse 830 n. *regret*.
worry, worrying, worriedness, uneasiness, discomfort, disquiet, unquiet, inquietude, fret, fretting 318 n. *agitation*; discomposure, dismay 63 n. *derangement*; something on one's mind, weight on one's m., anxiety, concern, solicitude, thought, care, carking c.; responsibility, weight of r., load, burden, strain, tension; a worry,

worries, cares, cares of the world; trouble, troubles 616 n. *evil*; bother, botheration, annoyance, irritation, pest, thorn in the flesh, death of 659 n. *bane*; bothersome task 838 n. *bore*; something to worry about, look-out, funeral; headache, teaser, puzzle, problem 530 n. *enigma*.
sufferer, victim, scapegoat, sacrifice; prey, shorn lamb, plucked pigeon 544 n. *dupe*; willing sacrifice, martyr; object of compassion, wretch, poor w., misery 731 n. *unlucky person*; patient, chronic 651 n. *sick person*.

Adj. *suffering*, ill 651 adj. *sick*; agonizing, writhing, aching, griped, in pain, on a bed of p., ravaged with p., bleeding, harrowed, on the rack, in torment, in hell 377 adj. *pained*; inconvenienced, uncomfortable, ill at ease; anguished, anguishous; anxious, unhappy about, worried, troubled, disquieted, apprehensive, dismayed 854 adj. *nervous*; discomposed, disconcerted 63 adj. *deranged*; ill-used, maltreated, severely handled; downtrodden 745 adj. *subjected*; victimized, made a prey, sacrificed; stricken, wounded; heavy-laden, crushed 684 adj. *fatigued*; care-worn, sad-looking, worried-l., harassed-l.; woeful, woebegone, haggard, wild-eyed.
unhappy, infelicitous, unlucky, accursed 731 adj. *unfortunate*; despairing 853 adj. *hopeless*; doomed 961 adj. *condemned*; to be pitied, pitiable, poor, wretched, miserable; sad, melancholy, despondent; cut up, heart-broken, heart-scalded, broken-hearted, heavy-h., sick at heart; sorrowful, sorrowing, grieved, grieving, grief-stricken, woebegone 834 adj. *dejected*; plunged in grief, weeping, weepy, wet-eyed, tearful, in tears, in a taking 836 adj. *lamenting*; nostalgic, longing 859 adj. *desiring*; discontent, displeased, dissatisfied, disappointed 829 adj. *discontented*; offended, vexed, annoyed, pained 924 adj. *disapproving*; piqued, chagrined, mortified, humiliated 891 adj. *resentful*; sickened, disgusted, nauseated 861 adj. *disliking*; sorry, remorseful, compunctious, regretful 830 adj. *regretting*.
Vb. *suffer*, undergo, endure, go through, experience 818 vb. *feel*; bear, put up with; bear pain, suffer p., suffer torment, bleed; hurt oneself, be hurt, smart, chafe, ache 377 vb. *feel pain*; wince, flinch, agonize, writhe, squirm 251 vb. *wriggle*; take up

one's cross, become a martyr, sacrifice
oneself; quaff the bitter cup, have a thin
time, have a bad t., go through it, have
trouble enough, sup full of horrors 731 vb.
have trouble; trouble oneself, distress o.,
worry, worry to death, fret, sit on thorns,
be on pins and needles 318 vb. *be agitated*;
mind, let weigh upon one, take it badly;
sorrow, passion, teen, grieve, weep, sigh
836 vb. *lament*; pity oneself, despond 834
vb. *be dejected*; have regrets, kick oneself
830 vb. *regret*.

See: 63, 251, 318, 377, 530, 544, 616, 651,
659, 684, 731, 745, 818, 829, 830, 834, 836,
838, 853, 854, 859, 861, 891, 924, 961, 963.

826 Pleasurableness

N. *pleasurableness*, pleasures of, pleasant-
ness, niceness, delectableness, delectabil-
ity, delightfulness, amenity, sunny side,
bright s.; invitingness, attractiveness, appeal, sex a., come-hither look 291 n. *attraction*; winning ways 925 n. *flattery*; amiability, winsomeness, charm, fascination, enchantment, witchery, loveliness, sight for
sore eyes 841 n. *beauty*; joyfulness,
honeymoon 824 n. *joy*; something nice, a
delight, a treat, a joy; pastime, fun 837 n.
amusement; interest, human i.; melody,
harmony 412 n. *music*; tastiness, delicious-
ness 390 n. *savouriness*; spice, sauce
piquante, relish 389 n. *condiment*; dainty,
titbit, sweet 392 n. *sweetness*; manna in
the wilderness, grateful refreshment, balm
685 n. *refreshment*; land flowing with milk
and honey 635 n. *plenty*; peace, perfect p.,
peace and quiet, tranquillity 266 n.
quietude; pipe-dream 513 n. *fantasy*.

Adj. *pleasurable*, pleasant, nice, good;
pleasure-giving 837 adj. *amusing*; pleasing,
agreeable, grateful, gratifying, flattering;
acceptable, welcome, welcome as flowers
in May; well-liked, to one's taste, to one's
liking; wonderful, marvellous, splendid
644 adj. *excellent*; frictionless, painless
376 adj. *comfortable*; cushy, easeful, refreshing 685 adj. *reposeful*; peaceful, quiet
266 adj. *tranquil*; bowery, luxurious,
voluptuous 376 adj. *sensuous*; genial,
warm, sunny 833 adj. *cheering*; delightful,
delectable, delicious, exquisite, choice;
luscious, juicy 356 adj. *pulpy*; delicate,
tasty 390 adj. *savoury*; sugary 392 adj.

sweet; dulcet, musical, harmonious 410
adj. *melodious*; picturesque, scenic, lovely
841 adj. *beautiful*; amiable, dear, winning,
endearing 887 adj. *lovable*; attractive,
fetching, appealing, interesting 291 adj.
attracting; seductive, enticing, inviting,
captivating; charming, enchanting, bewitching, ravishing; haunting, thrilling,
heart-melting, heart-warming 821 adj.
exciting; homely, cosy; pastoral, idyllic,
elysian, paradisical, heavenly, out of this
world; beatific, blessed, blissful 824 adj.
happy.

Vb. *please*, give pleasure, afford p., yield p.,
agree with; make things pleasant 925 vb.
flatter; lull, soothe 177 vb. *assuage*; comfort 833 vb. *cheer*; put at ease, make comfortable 831 vb. *relieve*; sugar, gild the
pill 392 vb. *sweeten*; stroke, pat, pet, baby,
coddle, nurse 889 vb. *caress*; indulge,
pander 734 vb. *be lax*; charm, interest
837 vb. *amuse*; rejoice, gladden, make
happy; gratify, satisfy, crown one's
wishes, leave nothing more to desire 828
vb. *content*; bless, crown one's bliss, raise
to the seventh heaven, beatify.

delight, surprise with joy; rejoice, exhilarate,
elate, elevate, uplift; rejoice one's heart,
warm the cockles of one's h., do one's
heart good; thrill, intoxicate, ravish;
transport, fetch, send, send one into
raptures *or* ecstasies 821 vb. *excite*; make
music in one's ears 925 vb. *flatter*; take
one's fancy, tickle one's f., hit one's f.
887 vb. *excite love*; tickle one's palate 390
vb. *appetize*; regale, refresh; tickle,
titillate, tease, tantalize; invite, prove
inviting, entrance, enrapture; enchant,
take, charm, becharm 983 vb. *bewitch*;
take one's breath away 821 vb. *impress*;
allure, seduce 291 vb. *attract*.

See: 177, 266, 291, 356, 376, 389, 390, 392,
410, 412, 635, 644, 685, 734, 821, 824, 828,
831, 833, 837, 841, 887, 889, 925, 983.

827 Painfulness

N. *painfulness*, painful treatment, harshness,
roughness, harassment, persecution 735 n.
severity; hurtfulness, harmfulness 645 n.
badness; disagreeableness, unpleasantness; loathsomeness, hatefulness, beastliness 616 n. *evil*; grimness 842 n. *ugliness*;

hideosity 842 n. *eyesore*; friction, irritation, ulceration, inflammation, exacerbation 832 n. *aggravation*; soreness, tenderness 377 n. *pain*; irritability, inflammability 822 n. *excitability*; sore subject, sore point, rub, soft spot, tender s. 819 n. *sensibility*; sore, running s., ulcer, thorn in the flesh, pin-prick, where the shoe pinches 659 n. *bane*; shock 508 n. *inexpectation*; unpalatability, disgust, nausea, sickener 391 n. *unsavouriness*; sharpness, bitterness, waters of bitterness, bitter cup, bitter draught, bitter pill, gall and wormwood, vinegar 393 n. *sourness*; bread of affliction 731 n. *adversity*; tribulation, ordeal, cross, cup, Calvary 825 n. *suffering*; trouble, care 825 n. *worry*; dreariness, cheerlessness; pitifulness, pathos; sorry sight, pathetic s., painful s., sad spectacle, object of pity 731 n. *unlucky person*; heavy news 825 n. *sorrow*; disenchantment, disillusionment 509 n. *disappointment*; horr.et's nest, hot water 700 n. *predicament*.

annoyance, vexation, pain and grief, death of, pest, curse, plague, botheration, embarrassment 825 n. *worry*; cause for annoyance, nuisance, pin-prick; grievance, complaint; hardship, troubles 616 n. *evil*; last straw, limit, outside edge; offence, affront, insult, provocation 921 n. *indignity*; molestation, infestation, persecution, malignity 898 n. *malevolence*; feeling of annoyance, displeasure, mortification 891 n. *resentment*.

Adj. *paining*, hurting, aching, sore, tender; dolorific, dolorous, agonizing, racking, purgatorial 377 adj. *painful*; scathing, searing, scalding, burning, sharp, biting, nipping, gnawing; burning, caustic, corrosive, vitriolic; harsh, hard, rough, cruel 735 adj. *severe*; grinding, gruelling, punishing, searching, exquisite, extreme; hurtful, harmful poisonous, 659 adj. *baneful*.

unpleasant, unpleasing, disagreeable; uncomfortable, comfortless, joyless, dreary, dismal, depressing 834 adj. *cheerless*; unattractive, uninviting; hideous 842 adj. *ugly*; unwelcome, undesired, unacceptable 860 adj. *unwanted*; thankless, unpopular, displeasing 924 adj. *disapproved*; disappointing, unsatisfactory 829 adj. *discontenting*; distasteful, unpalatable, off 391 adj. *unsavoury*; foul, nasty, beastly, horrible 645 adj. *not nice*; fulsome, malodorous, stinking 397 adj. *fetid*; bitter, sharp 393 adj. *sour*; invidious, obnoxious, offensive, objectionable, undesirable, odious, hateful, loathsome, nauseous, disgusting, revolting, repellent 861 adj *disliked*; execrable, accursed 645 adj. *damnable*.

annoying, too bad; troublesome, embarrassing, worrying; bothersome, bothering, wearisome, irksome, tiresome, boring 838 adj. *tedious*; burdensome, onerous, oppressive 322 adj. *weighty*; disappointing, unlucky, unfortunate, untoward 731 adj. *adverse*; awkward, unaccommodating, impossible, pesky, plaguy, harassing 702 adj. *hindering*; importunate, pestering; teasing, trying, irritating, vexatious, aggravating, provoking, maddening; galling, stinging, biting, mortifying.

distressing, afflicting, crushing, grievous; moving, affecting, touching, grieving; harrowing, heartbreaking, heart-rending, tear-jerking; pathetic, tragic, tragical, sad, woeful, rueful, mournful, pitiful, lamentable, deplorable 905 adj. *pitiable*; ghastly, grim, dreadful, shocking, appalling, horrifying, horrific, nerve-racking 854 adj. *frightening*.

intolerable, insufferable, impossible, insupportable, unendurable, unbearable, past bearing, past enduring, not to be borne, not to be endured, not to be put up with; extreme, beyond the limits of tolerance, more than flesh and blood can stand, enough to make one mad, enough to make a parson swear, enough to try the patience of Job, enough to provoke a saint.

Vb. *hurt*, do h., disagree with, injure 645 vb. *harm*; pain, cause p. 377 vb. *give pain*; knock out, wind, double up 279 vb. *strike*; bite, cut, tear, rend 655 vb. *wound*; wound the feelings, hurt the f., gall, pique, nettle, mortify 891 vb. *huff*; rub the wrong way, tread on one's corns; touch a soft spot, cut to the quick, pierce the heart, rend the heart-strings, draw tears, grieve, afflict, distress, cut up 834 vb. *sadden*; plunge into sorrow, bring grief to one's heart, plant an arrow in one's breast, plant a thorn in one's side; corrode, embitter, exacerbate, keep the wound green, gnaw, chafe, rankle, fester 832 vb. *aggravate*; offend, aggrieve (see *displease*); insult, affront 921 vb. *not respect*.

torment, excruciate, martyr; harrow, rack, put to the r., break on the wheel 963 vb. *torture*; put to the question, give the third degree, give one the works; put through the hoop, give one a bad time, maltreat, bait, bully, rag, bullyrag, haze, persecute, assail 735 vb. *oppress*; be offensive, snap at, bark at 885 vb. *be rude*; importune, dun, beset, besiege 737 vb. *demand*; haunt, obsess; annoy, do it to a., pin-prick; tease, pester, plague, nag, badger, wherret, worry, try, chivvy, harass, harry, heckle; molest, bother, vex, provoke, ruffle, irritate, needle, sting, chafe, fret, gall, irk, roil, rile 891 vb. *enrage*.

incommode, discomfort, disquiet, disturb, distemper, discompose, disconcert, throw one out, upset 63 vb. *derange*; worry, embarrass, trouble, perplex 474 vb. *puzzle*; exercise, tire 684 vb. *fatigue*; weary, bore 838 vb. *be tedious*; obsess, haunt, bedevil; weigh upon one, prey on the mind, weigh on the spirits, press on the heart, depress 834 vb. *deject*; infest, get in one's hair, get in one's way, thwart 702 vb. *obstruct*.

displease, not please, not appeal, find no favour 924 vb. *incur blame*; grate, jar, grate on, jar on, set the teeth on edge, go against the grain; disenchant, disillusion, undeceive 509 vb. *disappoint*; dissatisfy, give cause for complaint, aggrieve 829 vb. *discontent*; offend, shock, horrify, scandalize, disgust, revolt, repel, sicken, nauseate, fill one with loathing, stink in the nostrils, stick in the throat, stick in the gizzard, make one's gorge rise, turn one's stomach, make one sick, make one vomit, make one throw up 861 vb. *cause dislike*; make one's flesh creep, make one's blood run cold, curdle the blood, appal 854 vb. *frighten*.

See: 63, 279, 322, 377, 391, 393, 397, 474, 508, 509, 616, 645, 655, 659, 684, 700, 702, 731, 735, 737, 819, 822, 825, 829, 832, 834, 838, 842, 854, 860, 861, 885, 891, 898, 905, 921, 924, 963.

828 Content

N. *content*, contentment, contentedness, satisfaction, entire s., complacence, complacency; self-complacence, self-satisfac-

tion, smugness 873 n. *vanity*; partial content, half-smile, ray of comfort; serenity, quietism, tranquillity, resignation 266 n. *quietude*; ease of mind, trouble-free m., easy m., peace of m., heart's ease, nothing left to worry about 376 n. *euphoria*; conciliation, reconciliation 719 n. *pacification*; snugness, comfort, sitting pretty; wish-fulfilment, desires fulfilled, ambition achieved, port after stormy seas 730 n. *prosperity*; acquiescence 758 n. *consent*; resignation 721 n. *submission*.

Adj. *content*, contented, satisfied, well-s., sweet 824 adj. *happy*; appeased, pacified 717 adj. *peaceful*; cushy, feeling just right 376 adj. *comfortable*; at ease 683 adj. *reposeful*; easy in mind, smiling 833 adj. *cheerful*; flattered 824 adj. *pleased*; with nothing left to wish for, having no desire unfulfilled, having nothing to grumble at 863 adj. *sated*; unrepining, uncomplaining, with no regrets, without complaints; unenvious, unjealous 931 adj. *disinterested*; philosophic, without desire, without passion 823 adj. *inexcitable*; resigned, acquiescent 721 adj. *submitting*; fairly content, better satisfied; easily pleased, easy-going 736 adj. *lenient*; secure 660 adj. *safe*; unmolested, untroubled, unworried, unafflicted, unvexed, unplagued; blessed with contentment, thankful, gratified 907 adj. *grateful*.

contenting, satisfying, satisfactory 635 adj. *sufficient*; lulling, pacifying, appeasing 719 adj. *pacificatory*; tolerable, bearable, endurable, liveable; unobjectionable, passable 923 adj. *approvable*; desirable, wished for, all that is wished for 859 adj. *desired*.

Vb. *be content*, — satisfied etc. adj.; purr, purr with content 824 vb. *be pleased*; rest and be thankful, rest satisfied, take the good that the gods provide; thank, be thankful, be grateful, have much to be thankful for 907 vb. *be grateful*; have all one asks for, have one's wish, attain one's desire, reach the goal of one's ambition 730 vb. *prosper*; congratulate oneself, hug o., lay the flattering unction to one's soul 835 vb. *rejoice*; be at ease, be at home, sit pat, sit pretty 376 vb. *enjoy*; be reconciled 719 vb. *make peace*; get over it, take comfort, take heart of grace 831 vb. *be relieved*; rest content, take in good part; complain of nothing, have no complaints,

have nothing to grouse about, have no regrets, not repine; put up with, acquiesce 721 vb. *submit.*

content, make contented, satisfy, gratify, make one's day 826 vb. *please;* meet with approval, go down well 923 vb. *be praised;* make happy, bless with contentment; grant a boon 781 vb. *give;* crown one's wishes, leave no desire unfulfilled, appease one's desires, quench one's thirst 863 vb. *sate;* comfort 833 vb. *cheer;* bring comfort to, speak peace to 831 vb. *relieve;* be kind to 897 vb. *philanthropize;* lull, set at ease, set at rest; propitiate, disarm, reconcile, conciliate, appease 719 vb. *pacify.*

Adv. *contentedly,* complacently, with satisfaction, to one's heart's content, as one would wish.

See: 266, 376, 635, 660, 683, 717, 719, 721, 730, 736, 758, 781, 823, 824, 826, 831, 833, 835, 859, 863, 873, 897, 907, 923, 931.

829 Discontent

N. *discontent,* discontentment, disgruntlement, slow burn; displeasure, pain, dissatisfaction, acute d. 924 n. *disapprobation;* cold comfort, not what one expected 509 n. *disappointment;* soreness, chagrin, pique, mortification, heart-burning, bitterness, bile, spleen 891 n. *resentment;* uneasiness, disquiet 825 n. *worry;* grief, vexation of spirit 825 n. *sorrow;* maladjustment, strain, tension; restlessness, 'winter of our discontent'; unrest, state of u., restiveness 738 n. *disobedience;* agitation 318 n. *commotion;* finickiness, faddiness, hypercriticism, perfectionism 862 n. *fastidiousness;* querulousness 709 n. *quarrelsomeness;* ill-will 912 n. *envy;* competition 911 n. *jealousy;* objection, kick; chip on one's shoulder, grievance, grudge, complaint, plaint 709 n. *quarrel;* melancholy 834 n. *dejection;* sulkiness, sulks, dirty look, grimace, scowl, frown 893 n. *sullenness;* groan, curse 899 n. *malediction;* cheep, squeak, murmur, murmuring, whispering campaign, 'curses not loud but deep'.

malcontent, grumbler, grouch, grouser, growler, mutterer, croaker, complainer, whiner, bleater, bellyacher, Jonah; plaintiff 763 n. *petitioner;* faultfinder, critic, censurer, crabber, envier 709 n. *quarreller* sorehead, man with a grievance, man with a chip on his shoulder, angry young man laudator temporis acti; irredentist; mur murer, seditionist 738 n. *agitator;* indigna tion meeting, protest m. 762 n. *depreca tion;* the Opposition, Her Majesty's O. leader of the opposition; irreconcilable bitter-ender, last-ditcher, die-hard 705 n *opponent;* hard taskmaster, exacting criti 735 n. *tyrant.*

Adj. *discontented,* displeased, not bes pleased; dissatisfied 924 adj. *disapproving* unsatisfied, ungratified 509 adj. *disap pointed;* defeated 728 adj. *unsuccessful* malcontent, dissident 489 adj. *dissenting* non-cooperative, obstructive 702 adj *hindering;* restless, restive 738 adj. *dis obedient;* disgruntled, ill content, browne off, cheesed o., upset 825 adj. *unhappy* repining 830 adj. *regretting;* sad, uncom forted, unconsoled, unrelieved 834 adj *dejected;* ill-disposed, grudging, jealous envious; bileful, spleenful, bitter, em bittered, soured 393 adj. *sour;* cross, sulky sulking 893 adj. *sullen;* grouchy, grumb ling, grousing, whining, murmuring cursing, swearing 899 adj. *maledicent* protesting 762 adj. *deprecatory;* unflat tered, smarting, sore, mortified, insulted affronted 891 adj. *resentful;* hard t please, hard to satisfy, never satisfied exigent, exacting 862 adj. *fastidious;* faul finding, critical, hypercritical, censoriou 926 adj. *detracting;* irreconcilable, hostil 881 adj. *inimical;* resisting 704 adj. *oppos ing.*

discontenting, unsatisfactory 636 adj. *in sufficient;* leaving unsatisfied, unfilling sickening, nauseating 861 adj. *disliked* upsetting, mortifying 827 adj. *annoying* frustrating 509 adj. *disappointing;* baffling obstructive 702 adj. *hindering;* discourag ing, disheartening 613 adj. *dissuasive.*

Vb. *be discontented,*— dissatisfied etc. adj. be critical, crab, criticise, find fault 862 vb. *be fastidious;* lack, miss, feel some thing is missing 627 vb. *require;* sneer groan, jeer 924 vb. *disapprove;* mind, tak offence, take amiss, take ill, take to heart take on, be offended, smart under 891 vb *resent;* get the hump, sulk 893 vb. *b sullen;* look blue, look glum, make a wr face, pull a long f. 834 vb. *be dejected* moan, mutter, murmur, whine, bleat

beef, protest, complain, object, cry blue murder 762 vb. *deprecate*; bellyache, grumble, grouse, croak, snap, girn; wail 836 vb. *lament*; be aggrieved, have a grievance, cherish a g., have a chip on one's shoulder; join the opposition 704 vb. *oppose*; rise up 738 vb. *revolt*; grudge 912 vb. *envy*; quarrel with one's bread and butter 709 vb. *quarrel*; not know when one is well off, refuse God's gifts, look a gift horse in the mouth; be unwilling, make a piece of work of it 598 vb. *be loth*; refuse to be satisfied, ask for one's money back, return 607 vb. *reject*; remain irreconcilable, be an irredentist; repine 830 vb. *regret*.

cause discontent, dissatisfy 636 vb. *not suffice*; leave dissatisfied, leave room for complaint 509 vb. *disappoint*; spoil for one, spoil one's pleasure, get one down 834 vb. *deject*; dishearten, discourage 613 vb. *dissuade*; sour, embitter, disgruntle; upset, chafe, fret, bite, put on edge, put out of humour, irritate 891 vb. *huff*; put out of countenance, mortify 872 vb. *humiliate*; offend, cause resentment 827 vb. *displease*; shock, scandalize 924 vb. *incur blame*; nauseate, sicken, disgust 861 vb. *cause dislike*; arouse discontent, sow the seeds of d., make trouble, stir up t., agitate 738 vb. *revolt*.

See: 318, 393, 489, 509, 598, 607, 613, 627, 636, 702, 704, 705, 709, 728, 735, 738, 762, 763, 825, 827, 830, 834, 836, 861, 862, 872, 881, 891, 893, 899, 911, 912, 924, 926.

830 Regret

N. *regret*, regretfulness, regretting, repining; mortification, heart-burning 891 n. *resentment*; futile regret, vain r., crying over spilt milk; soul-searching, self-reproach, remorse, contrition, repentance, compunction, regrets, apologies 939 n. *penitence*; disillusion, second thoughts, better t. 67 n. *sequel*; longing, desiderium, homesickness, maladie du pays, nostalgia, nostalgie de la boue 859 n. *desire*; sense of loss, irredentism 737 n. *demand*; laudator temporis acti, irredentist 859 n. *desirer*; matter of regret, pity of it.

Adj. *regretting*, missing, homesick, nostalgic; irredentist; harking back, looking over one's shoulder 125 adj. *retrospective*; mortified, repining, bitter 891 adj. *resentful*; irreconcilable, inconsolable, crying over spilt milk 836 adj. *lamenting*; compunctious, regretful, remorseful, rueful, sorry, full of regrets, apologetic, soul-searching, penitent 939 adj. *repentant*; undeceived, disillusioned, sadder and wiser.

regretted, much r., sadly missed, badly wanted; regrettable, deplorable, much to be deplored, too bad.

Vb. *regret*, rue, deplore, rue the day; curse one's folly, blame oneself, accuse o., reproach o., kick o.; unwish, wish undone, repine, wring one's hands, cry over spilt milk, spend time in vain regrets 836 vb. *lament*; want one's time over again, sigh for the good old days, fight one's battles over again, reopen old wounds, hark back, evoke the past 505 vb. *retrospect*; look back, look over one's shoulder, cast a longing, lingering look behind; miss, sadly m., miss badly, regret the loss, want back; long for, be homesick 859 vb. *desire*; express regrets, apologize, feel compunction, feel remorse, be sorry 939 vb. *be penitent*; ask for another chance 905 vb. *ask mercy*; deplore, deprecate, lament 924 vb. *disapprove*; feel mortified, gnash one's teeth 891 vb. *resent*; have cause for regret, have had one's lesson, regret it, smart for it 963 vb. *be punished*.

See: 67, 125, 505, 737, 836, 859, 891, 905, 924, 939, 963.

831 Relief

N. *relief*, recruitment 685 n. *refreshment*; easing, alleviation, mitigation, palliation, abatement 177 n. *moderation*; good riddance; exemption 668 n. *deliverance*; solace, consolation, comfort, ray of c., crumb of c.; blue streak, rift in the clouds; feeling better, load off one's mind, sigh of relief 656 n. *revival*; lulling, lullaby, cradle-song, berceuse; soothing, soothing syrup, lenitive 177 n. *moderator*; painkiller, analgesic 375 n. *anaesthetic*; sleeping draught, sleeping pill 679 n. *soporific*; pillow 218 n. *cushion*; comforter, consoler, ray of sunshine.

Adj. *relieving*, soothing, smoothing, balsamic 685 adj. *refreshing*; lulling, assuaging, pain-killing, analgesic, anodyne 177 adj. *lenitive*; curative, restorative 658 adj. *remedial*; consoling, consolatory, comforting.

Vb. *relieve*, ease, soften, cushion; relax, lessen the strain; temper, temper the wind to the shorn lamb 177 vb. *moderate*; lift, raise, take off, lighten, unburden, disburden, take the load off one's mind 701 vb. *disencumber*; spare, exempt from 919 vb. *exempt*; save 668 vb. *deliver*; console, dry the eyes, wipe the e., wipe away the tears, solace, comfort, bring c., offer a crumb of c.; cheer up, buck up, encourage, hearten, pat on the back 833 vb. *cheer*; recruit, shade, cool, fan, ventilate 685 vb. *refresh*; restore, repair 656 vb. *cure*; bandage, bind up, poultice, plaster 658 vb. *doctor*; calm, soothe, pour balm, pour oil, palliate, mitigate, moderate, alleviate, deaden 177 vb. *assuage*; smooth the brow, take out the wrinkles 258 vb. *smooth*; stroke, pat 889 vb. *caress*; cradle, lull, put to sleep 679 vb. *sleep*; anaesthetize, kill the pain 375 vb. *render insensible*; take pity on, put one out of one's misery, give the coup de grâce 905 vb. *pity*.

be relieved, relieve oneself, ease o., obtain relief; feel relief, heave a sigh of r., draw breath again; console oneself, solace o.; take comfort, feel better, dry one's eyes, smile again 833 vb. *be cheerful*; recover from the blow, get over it, come to, be oneself again, pull oneself together, snap out of it, buck up, perk up, sleep off 656 vb. *be restored*; rest content 828 vb. *be content*.

See: 177, 218, 258, 375, 656, 658, 668, 679, 685, 701, 828, 833, 889, 905, 919.

832 Aggravation

N. *aggravation*, exacerbation, exasperation, irritation, embittering, embitterment; enhancement, augmentation 36 n. *increase*; intensification 162 n. *strengthening*; heightening, deepening, adding to 482 n. *overestimation*; making worse 655 n. *deterioration*; complication 700 n. *difficulty*; irritant 821 n. *excitant*; previous offence 936 n. *guilt*.

Adj. *aggravated*, intensified; exacerbated, complicated; unrelieved, made worse,

not improved 655 adj. *deteriorated*; aggravable.

Vb. *aggravate*, intensify 162 vb. *strengthen*; enhance, heighten, deepen; increase 36 vb. *augment*; worsen, make worse, render w., make things w., not improve matters 655 vb. *deteriorate*; exacerbate, embitter, further embitter, sour, envenom, inflame 821 vb. *excite*; exasperate, irritate 891 vb. *enrage*; add fuel to the flame, blow the coals; complicate, make bad worse, go from bad to worse, jump from the frying pan into the fire.

Adv. *aggravatedly*, worse and worse, from bad to worse, out of the frying pan into the fire.

Int. so much the worse! tant pis!

See: 36, 162, 482, 655, 700, 821, 891, 936.

833 Cheerfulness

N. *cheerfulness*, alacrity 597 n. *willingness*; optimism, hopefulness 852 n. *hope*; cheeriness, happiness, blitheness 824 n. *joy*; geniality, sunniness, breeziness, smiles, good humour, bon naturel; vitality, spirits, animal s., flow of s., joie de vivre 360 n. *life*; light-heartedness, sunshine in the breast, light heart, optimistic soul, carefree mind; liveliness, sparkle, vivacity, animation, exhilaration, elevation, abandon; life and soul of the party, party spirit 882 n. *sociality*; optimist, perennial o., Pollyanna.

merriment, laughter and joy; cheer, good c.; exhilaration, high spirits, abandon; jollity, joviality, jocularity, gaiety, glee, mirth, hilarity 835 n. *laughter*; levity, frivolity 499 n. *folly*; merry-making, fun, fun and games, sport, good s. 837 n. *amusement*; marriage bells, jubilee 876 n. *celebration*.

Adj. *cheerful*, cheery, cheerly, blithe, blithesome 824 adj. *happy*; hearty, genial 882 adj. *sociable*; smiling, sunny, bright, beaming, radiant 835 adj. *laughing*; breezy, of good cheer, in spirits, in good s., in a good humour; in good heart, unrepining, optimistic, hopeful, buoyant, resilient, irrepressible; carefree, light-hearted; debonair, bonny, buxom, bouncing; pert, jaunty, perky, chirpy, canty, spry, spirited, sprightly, vivacious, animated, vital, sparkling, on the top of one's form 819 adj. *lively*; alacritous 597 adj. *willing*.

gay, light, frivolous 456 adj. *light-minded*; joyous, joyful, merry as a cricket, merry as a thrush, happy as a sandboy, happy as a king, gay as a lark, happy as the day is long; sparkling, mirth-loving, laughter-l., waggish, jocular 839 adj. *witty*; playful, sportive, frisky, frolic, gamesome, frolic-some, kittenish 837 adj. *amusing*; roguish, arch, sly, tricksy; merry, merry-making, mirthful, jocund, jovial, jolly, joking, dancing, laughing, singing, drinking, Anacreontic; wild, rackety, shouting, roaring with laughter, hilarious, uproar-ious, rip-roaring, rollicking, rattling, split-ting one's sides, tickled pink 837 adj. *amused.*

jubilant, jubilous, jubilating, gleeful, glee-some, delighted 824 adj. *pleased*; elate, erect, flushed, exulting, exultant, triumph-ant, cock-a-hoop 727 adj. *successful*; triumphing, celebrating, riotous, rioting 876 adj. *celebrative.*

cheering, exhilarating, enlivening, en-couraging etc.vb.; warming, heart-w., raising the spirits, exhilarating, animat-ing, intoxicating 821 adj. *exciting*; opti-mistic, tonic, comforting, like a ray of sunshine, just what the doctor ordered; balmy, palmy, bracing, invigorating 652 adj. *salubrious.*

Vb. *be cheerful*, be in good spirits, be in good humour, be in good heart; keep cheerful, look on the bright side, keep one's spirits up 852 vb. *hope*; keep one's pecker up, grin and bear it, put a good face upon it 599 vb. *be resolute*; take heart, take heart of grace, cheer up, perk up, buck up 831 vb. *be relieved*; brighten, liven up, grow animated, let oneself go, abandon oneself, drive dull care away; radiate good humour, smile, beam, sparkle; dance, sing, carol, lilt, chirrup, chirp, whistle, laugh 835 vb. *rejoice*; whoop, cheer 876 vb. *celebrate*; have fun, frisk, frolic, rollick, romp, sport, disport oneself, enjoy o., have a good time 837 vb. *amuse oneself*; go gay, have a party, 882 vb. *be sociable.*

cheer, gladden, warm, warm the heart 828 vb. *content*; comfort, console 831 vb. *relieve*; rejoice the heart, put in a good humour 826 vb. *please*; inspire, enliven 821 vb. *animate*; exhilarate, elate 826 vb. *delight*; encourage, inspirit, raise the spirits, buck up, jolly along, bolster,

bolster up 855 vb. *give courage*; act like a tonic, energize 174 vb. *invigorate.*

Adv. *cheerfully*, willingly, joyfully, gaily, joyously, light-heartedly, optimistically, carelessly; airily, breezily.

See: 174, 360, 456, 499, 597, 599, 652, 727, 819, 821, 824, 826, 828, 831, 835, 837, 839, 852, 855, 876, 882.

834 Dejection. Seriousness

N. *dejection*, joylessness, unhappiness, cheerlessness, dreariness, dejectedness, low spirits, dumps, doldrums; droopi-ness, dispiritedness, heart-sinking; dis-illusion 509 n. *disappointment*; defeatism, pessimism, cynicism, despair, death-wish, suicidal tendency 853 n. *hopelessness*; weariness, oppression, exhaustion 684 n. *fatigue*; oppression of spirit, heart-ache, heaviness, sadness, misery, wretchedness, disconsolateness, dolefulness 825 n. *sor-row*; despondency, prostration, pros-tration, languishment; Slough of Des-pond, grey dawn; gloominess, gloom, settled g.; glumness, dejected look, hag-gardness, funereal aspect, long face, downcast countenance, lack-lustre eye; cause of dejection, sorry sight, memento mori, depressant 838 n. *bore*; care, thought, trouble 825 n. *worry.*

melancholy, melancholia, hypochondria, hypochondriasis; black mood, blue devils, blues, horrors, mumps, mopes, moping, mopiness, sighing, sigh; dismals, lachry-mals, vapours, megrims, spleen, bile 829 n. *discontent*; disgust of life, tædium vitæ, weltschmerz, angst, nostalgia, mal du pays, homesickness 825 n. *suffering.*

seriousness, earnestness; gravity, solemnity, sobriety, demureness, staidness, grimness 893 n. *sullenness*; primness, humourless-ness, heaviness, dullness; straight face, dead pan; sternness, heavy stuff; earnest, dead e.; no laughing matter, chastening thought.

moper, croaker, complainer, Jonah 829 n. *malcontent*; pessimist, damper, wet blan-ket, Job's comforter, misery, agelast, sobersides; death's-head, skeleton at the feast; hypochondriac, malade imaginaire, seek-sorrow, self-tormentor.

Adj. *dejected*, joyless, dreary, cheerless, un-happy, sad (see *melancholic*); gloomy, despondent, desponding, unhopeful,

pessimistic, defeatist, despairing 853 adj. *hopeless*; beaten, overcome 728 adj. *defeated*; dispirited, unnerved, unmanned 854 adj. *nervous*; troubled, worried 825 adj. *suffering*; downcast, droopy, low, down, down in the mouth, low-spirited, depressed; unlively, out of sorts, not oneself, out of spirits; sluggish, listless, lackadaisical 679 adj. *inactive*; lack-lustre 419 adj. *dim*; out of countenance, discountenanced, humbled, crushed, chapfallen, chop-f., crestfallen, ready to cry 509 adj. *disappointed*; in the doldrums, in low water, out of luck 731 adj. *unprosperous*; chastened, sobered, sadder and wiser 830 adj. *regretting*; subdued, piano; cynical disillusioned 509 adj. *disappointed*.

melancholic, in the blues, bilious, atrabilious, vapourish, hypochondriacal; jaundiced, sour, hipped, hippish; thoughtful, pensive, penseroso full of thought; melancholy, sad, triste, tristful; saddened, cut up, heavy, heavy-hearted, full of heaviness, sick at heart, heart-sick, soul-s. 825 adj. *unhappy*; sorry, rueful 830 adj. *regretting*; mournful doleful, woeful, tearful, lachrymose 836 adj. *lamenting*; uncheerful, cheerless, joyless, dreary, spiritless, comfortless; miserable, wretched, unrelieved, refusing comfort, disconsolate; moody, sulky, sulking 893 adj. *sullen*; mumpish, mopish, dumpish, dull, dismal, gloomy, glum; long-faced, long in the face, woebegone; wan, haggard, care-worn.

serious, sober, sober as a judge, solemn, sedate, staid, demure, muted, grave, grave as an undertaker, stern 735 adj. *severe*; sour, Puritan, grim, grim-visaged, dark, frowning, scowling, forbidding, saturnine 893 adj. *sullen*; unlaughing, unsmiling; inscrutable, straight-faced, poker f., dead-pan; prim, unlively, humourless; unfunny, unwitty, without a laugh in it, heavy, dull 838 adj. *tedious*; chastening, sobering.

cheerless, comfortless, uncomforting, unconsoling, out of comfort; uncongenial, uninviting; depressing, unrelieved, dreary, dull, flat 838 adj. *tedious*; dismal, lugubrious, funereal, gloomy, dark, forbidding; drab, grey, sombre, overcast clouded, murky, lowering; ungenial, cold.

Vb. *be dejected*, despond, admit defeat 853 vb. *despair*; succumb, lie down 728 vb. *be*

defeated; languish, sink, droop, sag, wilt, flag, give up 684 vb. *be fatigued*; look downcast, look blue, hang the head, pull a long face, laugh on the wrong side of one's mouth; mope, brood 449 vb. *think*; lay to heart, take to h., sulk 893 vb. *be sullen*; eat one's heart out, yearn, long 859 vb. *desire*; sigh, grieve 829 vb. *be discontent*; groan 825 adj. *suffer*; weep 836 vb. *lament*; repine 830 vb. *regret*.

be serious, not smile, repress a s.; not laugh, keep a straight face, keep countenance, maintain one's gravity, recover one's g., sober up; look grave, look glum; lack sparkle, lack humour, not see the joke, take oneself seriously, be a bore 838 vb. *be tedious*; sober, chasten.

sadden, grieve, grieve to the heart, bring grief, bring sorrow, cut up; turn one's hair grey, break one's heart, crack one's heartstrings; draw tears, touch the heart, melt the h., leave not a dry eye 821 vb. *impress*; annoy, pain, spoil one's pleasure 829 vb. *discontent*; deny comfort, render disconsolate, drive to despair 853 vb. *leave no hope*; crush, overcome, overwhelm, prostrate; orphan, bereave 786 vb. *deprive*.

deject, depress, down, get one down; cause alarm and despondency, dishearten, discourage, dispirit, take the heart out of, unman, unnerve 854 vb. *frighten*; spoil the fun, take the joy out of, cast a shade, cast a shadow, cast a gloom over 418 vb. *darken*; damp, dampen, damp the spirits, throw cold water, frown upon 613 vb. *dissuade*; dull the spirits, lie on the mind, weigh heavy on one's heart, oppress the breast; make the heart sick, disgust 827 vb. *displease*; strain, weary 684 vb. *fatigue*; bore 838 vb. *be tedious*; chasten, sober 534 vb. *teach*.

See: 418, 419, 449, 509, 534, 613, 679, 684 728, 731, 735, 786, 821, 825, 827, 829, 830, 836, 838, 853, 854, 859, 893.

835 Rejoicing

N. *rejoicing*, manifestation of joy 837 n. *festivity*; jubilation, jubilee, triumph, exultation 876 n. *celebration*; congratulations, felicitation, self-congratulation, mutual c., self-applause 886 n. *congratulation*; plaudits, clapping, shout, yell 923 n.

applause; cheers, rousing c., three c., huzza, hurrah, hosanna, hallelujah 923 n. *praise*; thanksgiving 907 n. *thanks*; paean, psalm, Te Deum 981 n. *hymn*; revelling, revels 837 n. *revel*; merrymaking, abandon, abandonment 833 n. *merriment*.

laughter, faculty of l., risibility; loud laughter, hearty l., rollicking l. Homeric l.; roar of laughter, shout of l., burst of l., peal of l., immoderate l., cachinnation; mocking laughter, derision 851 n. *ridicule*; laugh, horse l., guffaw; chuckle, throaty c., chortle, gurgle, cackle, crow, coo; giggle, snigger, snicker, titter, tee-hee; fit of laughing, the giggles; smile, sweet s., simper, smirk, grin, broad g., sardonic g.; laughingness, inclination to laughter, twinkle, half-smile; humour, sense of h. 839 n. *wit*; laughableness, laughing matter, comedy, farce 497 n. *absurdity*.

laugher, chuckler, giggler, cackler, sniggerer, titterer; smiler, grinner, smirker, simperer, Cheshire cat; mocker, derider 926 n. *detractor*; rejoicer, rollicker 837 n. *reveller*; god of laughter, Momus; comic muse, Thalia.

Adj. *rejoicing*, revelling, rollicking, cheering, shouting, yelling etc. vb.; exultant, flushed, elated 833 adj. *jubilant*; lyrical, ecstatic 923 adj. *approving*.

laughing, guffawing etc. vb.; splitting one's sides, convulsed with laughter, dying with l.; inclined to laughter, risible; humorous; mocking 851 adj. *derisive*; laughable, derisory 849 adj. *ridiculous*; comic, farcical 497 adj. *absurd*.

Vb. *rejoice*, be joyful, sing for joy, shout for j., leap for j., dance for j., dance, skip 312 vb. *leap*; clap, clap one's hands, throw one's cap in the air, whoop, cheer, huzza, hurrah 923 vb. *applaud*; shout 408 vb. *vociferate*; carol 413 vb. *sing*; sing paeans, shout hosannahs, sing the Te Deum 923 vb. *praise*; exult, triumph, jubilate 876 vb. *celebrate*; felicitate, congratulate 886 vb. *gratulate*; bless, give thanks 907 vb. *thank*; abandon oneself, let oneself go, riot, go mad for joy, run in the streets, maffick 61 vb. *rampage*; make merry 833 vb. *be cheerful*; have a good time, frolic, frisk, rollick 837 vb. *revel*; have a party, celebrate 882 vb. *be sociable*; feel pleased, congratulate oneself, hug o., rub one's hands, smack one's lips, gloat 824 vb. *be pleased*; sigh for pleasure, cry for joy 408

vb. *cry*; purr, coo, gurgle, crow, chirrup, chirp 409 vb. *ululate*.

laugh, laugh outright, start laughing, burst out l., get the giggles; hoot, chuckle, chortle, crow, cackle; giggle, snigger, snicker, titter, tee-hee; make merry over, laugh at, laugh in one's sleeve, mock, deride 851 vb. *ridicule*; shake, hold one's sides, shake one's s., split one's s., burst with laughter, split with l., rock with l., roll with l., hoot with l., roar with l., stifle with l., die with l.

smile, grin, show one's teeth; grimace, curl one's lips, grin like a Cheshire cat; smirk, simper; twinkle, beam, flash a smile.

Int. cheers! three c.! huzza! hurrah! hooray! hosannah! hallelujah! hail the conquering hero! io triumphe!

See: 61, 312, 408, 409, 413, 497, 824, 833, 837, 839, 849, 851, 876, 882, 886, 907, 923, 926, 981.

836 Lamentation

N. *lamentation*, lamenting, ululation, wail, wail of woe, groaning, weeping, wailing; plangency, weeping and wailing, weeping and gnashing of teeth, beating the breast, tearing one's hair; mourning, deep m. 364 n. *obsequies*; rending one's garments, sackcloth and ashes; widow's weeds, weepers, crape, black, mourning ring; cypress, willow; Wailing Wall; crying, sobbing, sighing, blubbering, whimpering, whining, greeting, grizzling, snivelling; tears, tearfulness, dolefulness; tenderness, melting mood, starting tears, tears of pity 905 n. *pity*; wet eyes, red e.; falling tears, fit of t., flood of t., burst of t.; breakdown, hysterics; cry, good c.; tear, tear-drop; sob, sigh, whimper, whine, grizzle, boo-hoo.

lament, plaint, complaint, jeremiad, dirge, knell, requiem, threnody, elegy, nenia, epicedium, Hari bol, death song, swan-song, funeral oration 364 n. *obsequies*; keen, coronach, wake 905 n. *condolence*; howl, shriek, scream, outcry 409 n. *ululation*; tears of grief, tears of rage; sobstuff, sob-story, hard-luck s., tale of woe, jeremiad; cri de coeur; show of grief, crocodile tears 542 n. *sham*.

weeper, wailer, keener, lamenter, threnodist, elegist; mourner, professional m.,

mute 364n. *funeral*; sobber, sigher, grizzler, sniveller, whimperer, whiner, blubberer, cry-baby; complainer, grouser 829n. *malcontent*; Jeremiah, Heraclitus, Niobe; dying duck, dying swan.

Adj. *lamenting*, crying etc.vb.; lachrymatory, tear-shedding, tear-dropping; in tears, bathed in t., dissolved in t.; tearful, lachrymose, in melting mood; wet-eyed, red-e., with moistened eyes; mourning, mournful, doleful 825adj. *unhappy*; woeful, woebegone, haggard, wild-eyed, wringing one's hands 834adj. *dejected*; complaining, plaining, plangent, plaintive, plaintful; elegiac, epecedial, threnodic, threnodial, dirgelike 364adj. *funereal*; condoling, in mourning, in black, in funeral garments, in sackcloth and ashes; half-masted, at half-mast; whining, canting, querulous, querimonious, with a hard-luck story, with a tale of woe; pathetic, pitiful, lamentable, fit for tears, tear-jerking 905adj. *pitiable*; lamented, deplorable 830adj. *regretted*.

Vb. *lament*, grieve, sorrow, sigh 825vb. *suffer*; deplore 830vb. *regret*; condole, grieve for, sigh for, plain, weep over, cry o., bewail, bemoan, elegize, threnodize; bury with lamentation, sing the dirge, sing a requiem, toll the knell 364vb. *inter*; mourn, wail, keen, sit at the wake; express grief, put on black, go into mourning, wear m., wear the willow, put on sackcloth and ashes, wring one's hands, beat the breast, tear one's hair, roll in the dust; take on, carry on, take it badly; complain, bellyache, grouse, tell one's tale of woe 829vb. *be discontented*.

weep, wail, greet, pipe one's eye; shed tears, drop t., burst into t., melt in t., dissolve in t., melt, fall into the melting mood; hold back one's tears, be ready to cry; cry, break down, cry like a child, cry like a baby, boo-hoo, cry one's eyes out; howl, cry out, squall, yell, yammer, clamour, scream, shriek 409vb. *ululate*; sob, sigh, moan, groan 825vb. *suffer*; snivel, grizzle, blubber, pule, whine, whimper; get ready to cry, weep without cause, cry for nothing, cry out before one is hurt.

Adv. *tearfully*, painfully, de profundis.
See: 364, 409, 542, 825, 829, 830, 834, 905.

837 Amusement

N. *amusement*, pleasure, interest, delight 826n. *pleasurableness*; diversion, divertissement, entertainment, light e., popular e.; dramatic entertainment 594n. *drama*; pastime, hobby, labour of love 597n. *voluntary work*; solace, recreation, recruitment 685n. *refreshment*; relaxation 683n. *repose*; holiday, Bank h. 681n. *leisure*; April Fool's Day, gala day, red-letter d., banner d. 876n. *special day*; play, sport, fun, good clean f., good cheer, joviality, jocundity 833n. *merriment*; occasion, do, show, tamasha, rout, commemoration, Gaudy night 876n. *celebration*; outing, excursion, cheap e., jaunt, pleasure trip; treat, Dutch t., wayzgoose, fête champêtre, picnic (see *festivity*); garden party, bun-fight, fête, jamboree, conversazione 74n. *assembly*; game, game of chance, game of skill; whist drive, bridge d. (see *card game*); round games, party g., knitting bee, spelling b. (see *indoor game*).

festivity, playtime, holiday-making, holidaying; visiting 882n. *social round*; fun 835n. *laughter*; whirl, round of pleasure, round of gaiety; seeing life, high life, night l.; good time, hot t.; beating it up, burning the candle at both ends, a short life and a merry one 943n. *intemperance*; festival, high f., fair, fun-f., fun of the fair, kermesse, carnival, fiesta, mi-carême, gala; masque, masqueing, mummery; festivities, fun and games, merry-making, revels, Saturnalia, Yule-tide, poojahs, Durga Poojah 833n. *merriment*; highday, feast d. 876n. *special day*; carouse, carousal, wassail, wake 301n. *feasting*; conviviality, symposium, party, Dutch p., bottle p. 882n. *social gathering*; drinking party, drinking bout 301n. *drinking*; orgy, debauch, carouse 949n. *drunkenness*; bust, binge, beano; barbecue, cookout, clambake, wiener roast, bumpsupper, harvest s., kirn, dinner, grand d., banquet, 301n. *meal*.

revel, rout, jollification, whoopee, fun; fun fast and furious, high jinks, spree, junket, junketing; night out, night on the tiles; bonfire, pyrotechnics, Fifth of November 420n. *fire-works*; play, game, romp, rollick, frolic, lark, skylarking, escapade, prank, rag, trick, monkey-t. 497n. *foolery*.

pleasure-ground, park, deer-p.; green, village

g.; arbour, gardens, pleasure-g., Vauxhall 192n. *pleasance*; seaside, Riviera, lido, bathing-beach, holiday camp; playground, recreation ground, cricket g.; field, flying f., playing-f., football f., hunting-f., links, golf l., golf course; rink, skating r., ice r.; squash-court, fives-c., tennis c., croquet lawn 724n. *arena*; circus, fair, funfair, carousel, wonderland; peep-show, raree show 522n. *exhibit*; swing, roundabout, merry-go-round, scenic railway, tunnel of love, switchback, big wheel, big dipper; see-saw, slide, chute.

place of amusement, amusement park, funfair, shooting-gallery, skittle-alley, bowling a., covered court, billiard room, card-r., assembly r., pump-r., concert r.; concert hall, music h., vaudeville, hippodrome; picture-house 445n. *cinema*; playhouse 594n. *theatre*; dance-room, ballroom, dance-floor; dance-hall, palais de danse; cabaret, night club, boite de nuit; casino, kursaal, gambling hell 618n. *gaming house*.

sport, outdoor life; sportsmanship, gamesmanship 694n. *skill*; sports, field s.; agonism, games, gymnastics 162n. *athletics*, 716n. *contest, racing, pugilism, wrestling*; outdoor sports, camping, picnicking; riding, hacking, archery, shooting, clay-pigeon s.; hunting, shooting, fishing; water sports, swimming, bathing, surf-b., surf-riding, skindiving, aquaplaning, water-polo, boating, rowing, yachting, sailing 269n. *aquatics*; climbing, mountaineering, Alpinism 308 n. *ascent*; exploring, cave-e., speleology; winter sports, ski-ing, ski-jumping, bobsleighing, Cresta-running, tobogganning, luging, skating, ice-s., sliding; ice-hockey; curling; flying, gliding 271n. *aeronautics*; tourism, touring, travelling, exploration 267n. *land travel*.

ball game, pat-ball, bat and ball game; King Willow, cricket, Test c., league c., single-wicket; baseball, soft-b., rounders; trapball, knurr and spell; tennis, real t., Royal t.; deck tennis; table tennis, ping-pong; badminton, battledore and shuttlecock; squash, rackets; hand-ball, hurling; fives, pelota; lacrosse, pallone; wall-game, net-ball, volley-b., basket-b.; football, Association f., soccer; Rugby football, rugger; hockey, ice-h., polo, Kopkarri, water-polo; croquet, table-c., pall mall, golf, clock-g.; skittles, nine-pins, bowls, curling; marbles, dibs; quoits, deck q., hoop-la, discus-throwing; billiards, French b., Carolina, snooker, pyramids, pool, bagatelle; karom, shove ha'penny, shovelboard.

indoor game, nursery g., parlour g., round g., party g.; musical bumps, musical chairs, hunt the thimble, hunt the slipper, postman's knock, kiss in the ring, nuts and May; sardines, rabbits, murders; forfeits, guessing game, Kim's g.; crosswords and crooked answers, twenty questions, what's my line; charades, dumb c., crambo, dumb c., parson's cat; word game, spelling-bee, scrabble, lexicon, word making and word taking; riddles, crosswords, acrostics; paper game, consequences, noughts and crosses; dominoes, mah jong, tiddly-winks, jigsaw puzzle.

board game, chess, three-dimensional c.; draughts, checkers, Chinese c., fox and geese; pachisi; backgammon; race-game, ludo, snakes and ladders, crown and anchor, monopoly, totopoly.

children's games, skipping, swinging, jumping, leap-frog, hop-scotch 312n. *leap*; he, chain he, hide-and-seek, cache-cache, blind man's buff, hares and hounds, French and English, prisoner's base, Tom Tiddler's ground.

card game, cards, game of cards, rubber of whist, rubber of bridge; boston, whist, solo w., auction w., auction bridge, contract b.; nap, Napoleon; euchre, écarté, loo, picquet, cribbage, quadrille, ombre, bezique, pinocle, quinze; rummy, gin r., canasta, option, hearts, black Maria, casino, Parliament, Newmarket, commerce, speculation, Red Dog; solo, solitaire, patience; snap, snip snap snorum, beggar-my-neighbour, old maid, ragged robin, racing demon, slap Jack, Happy Families, animal grab, cheating; lotto, keno, housey-housey, bingo, skat; vingt-et-un, pontoon, black jack; drag, poker, strip p., stud p., seven card stud p., five card stud p.; Russian bank, Polish b., banker, baccarat, faro, fantan, chemin de fer, chemmy; monte, three-card m., rivers, high low, race the ace, cutting for aces (see *gambling game*).

gambling game, dice g., craps, dice, lie d.,

dicing; roulette, rouge et noir; coin-spinning, king-bee game; numbers, sweep-stake, football pool 618 n. *gambling*.

dancing, dance, ball, nautch; bal masqué, masquerade; bal costumé, fancy dress dance, pagal nautch; thé dansant, tea dance; hop, jam session; ballet, Imperial b., Indian b.; ballet dancing, classical d., Brahmanatya; ball-room dancing; dance competition; choreography; eurhyth-mics; muse of dancing, Terpsichore.

dance, war-dance, sword-d., corroboree; shuffle, double-s., cakewalk, shag, break-down; solo dance, pas seul; clog-dance, step-d., tap-d.; fan dance, skirt-d., hula-hula; high kicks, cancan; belly-roll, danse du ventre; gipsy dance, flamenco; coun-try dance, morris d., morisco; barn dance, lindy hop, Sir Roger de Coverley; sailor's dance, hornpipe, keel row; folk-dance, Russian d., Cossack d., polonaise, ma-zurka; jig, Irish j., Walls of Limerick, Waves of Torres; fling, Highland f.; square dance, reel, Virginia r., Scotch r., eightsome, foursome, Strathspey, Gay Gordons, Petronella, Hamilton House, Duke of Perth, strip the willow, Dashing White Sergeant; rigadoon, tarantella, sarabande, bolero, fandango, pavan, gavotte, quadrille, cotillion, minuet, allemande, galop, polka; valse, waltz, Viennese w., hesitation w., St. Bernard; fox-trot, turkey-t., bunny-hug, valeta, Lancers; Charleston, black bottom, blues, one-step, quick-s., two-s., paso-doble, tango, rumba, samba, mambo, conga, conga line, bongo, la raspa, cha cha cha; Big Apple, Boomps-a-Daisy, hokey-cokey, Lambeth Walk, Palais Glide; jazz, shimmy, jive, jitterbug, rock 'n' roll, creep; excuse-me dance, Paul Jones; dancer, tap-d., clog-d., ballet d., ballerina, corps de ballet; nautch-girl; high-kicker, cancanière; waltzer, foxtrotter, shuffler, hoofer, jiver 312 n. *jumper*.

plaything, bauble, knick-knack, souvenir, trinket, toy 639 n. *bauble*; children's toy, bricks, building b., Jack-in-the-box, teddy bear, doll, rag d., doll's house, doll's furniture, doll's pram; top, whipping t., teetotum, yo-yo, diabolo; jacks, jack-stones, fivestones, marbles; ball, bowl, wood 252 n. *sphere*; hoop, skipping-rope, stilts, pogo-stick, rocking-horse; popgun, air-gun, water pistol, toy p., toy cannon

723 vb. *toy gun*; toy soldier, tin s., lead s.; model, model yacht, model aeroplane; magic lantern, raree show, peep-show 522 n. *exhibit*; puppet-show, marionettes, Punch and Judy 551 n. *image*; space suit; pin-table, billiard table; card, cards, pack, stack, deck; domino, tile; draught, draughtsman; counter, chip; tiddly-wink.

chessman, man, piece, red p., white p., black p.; pawn, knight, bishop; castle, rook; queen, king.

player, sportsman, sporting man; pot-hunter 716 n. *contender*; gamesman, games-player, all-rounder; ball-player, cricketer, footballer, baseballer, bowler, hockey-player, tennis-p.; toxophilite 287 n. *shooter*; dicer, gamester 618 n. *gambler*; card-player, chess-p.; fellow-sportsman, playmate 707 n. *colleague*.

reveller, merry-maker, rioter, roisterer, gamboller, rollicker, frolicker; skylarker, ragger; drinker, drunk 949 n. *drunkard*; feaster, diner-out 301 n. *eater*; pleasure-seeker, thrill-s.; playboy, good-time girl; debauchee 952 n. *libertine*; holiday-maker, excursionist, tripper, tourist 268 n. *traveller*; King of Misrule, master of the revels, master of ceremonies, toast-master, symposiarch, arbiter elegantiarum; quizmaster.

Adj. *amusing*, entertaining, diverting etc. vb.; lusory, fun-making, sportive, full of fun 833 adj. *gay*; laying oneself out to please, pleasant 826 adj. *pleasurable*; laughable, ridiculous, clownish 849 adj. *funny*; recreative, recreational 685 adj. *refreshing*; festal, festive, holiday.

amused, entertained, tickled 824 adj. *pleased*; having fun, festive, sportive, rompish, rollicking, roisterous, prankish, playful, kittenish, roguish, waggish, jolly, jovial; out to enjoy oneself, in festal mood, in holiday spirit 835 adj. *rejoicing*; horsy, sporty, sporting, gamesome, games-play-ing 162 adj. *athletic*; disporting, playing, at play; working for pleasure, following one's hobby; entertainable, easy to please, ready to be amused.

Vb. *amuse*, interest, entertain, divert, tickle, make one laugh, take one out of oneself; tickle the fancy, titillate, please 826 vb. *delight*; recreate 685 vb. *refresh*; solace, enliven 833 vb. *cheer*; treat, regale, take out, take for an outing; raise a smile, wake laughter, stir l., convulse with l.,

set the table in a roar, lay them in the aisles, be the death of one 849 vb. *be ridiculous*; humour, keep amused, put in good humour; provide fun, give a party, play the host 882 vb. *be hospitable*; be a sport, be a good s., be great fun.

amuse oneself, kill time, while away the t., pass the t. 681 vb. *have leisure*; ride one's hobby, dabble, trifle, fribble; play, have fun, enjoy oneself, drown care 833 vb. *be cheerful*; make holiday, go a-Maying, have an outing, have a field-day; sport, disport oneself; take one's pleasure, dally, toy, wanton; frisk, frolic, rollick, romp, gambol, caper; cut capers, play tricks, play pranks, fool about, play the fool 497 vb. *be absurd*; jest, jape 839 vb. *be witty*; play cards, take a hand; game, dice 618 vb. *gamble*; play games, be devoted to sport; live the outdoor life, camp, picnic; sail, yacht, fly; hunt, shoot, fish; golf; ride, hack; run, race, jump; bathe, swim; skate, ski, toboggan.

dance, nautch; join the dance, go dancing, attend a jam session; tap-dance, waltz, foxtrot, Charleston, tango, rumba, jive, jitterbug, rock 'n' roll; cavort, caper, shuffle, hoof, trip, tread a measure, trip the light fantastic toe 312 vb. *leap*.

revel, make merry, make whoopee, celebrate 835 vb. *rejoice*; drive dull care away, make it a party, have a good time; go on the razzle, have a night out, have a night on the tiles, beat it up, paint the town red; junket, roister, drown care; feast, banquet, quaff, carouse, wassail, make the rafters ring; commit a debauch, go on a binge, go on a bust 301 vb. *drink*; drown one's sorrows 949 vb. *get drunk*; wanton, run a rig, sow one's wild oats, never go to sleep, burn the candle at both ends.

Int. carpe diem! eat, drink and be merry! vogue la galère! vive la bagatelle!

See: 74, 162, 192, 252, 267, 268, 269, 271, 287, 301, 308, 312, 420, 445, 497, 522, 551, 594, 597, 618, 639, 681, 683, 685, 694, 707, 716, 723, 724, 824, 826, 833, 835, 839, 849, 876, 882, 943, 949, 952.

838 Tedium

N. *tedium*, taedium vitæ, world-weariness 834 n. *melancholy*; lack of interest, un-interest 860 n. *indifference*; weariness 684 n. *fatigue*; wearisomeness, tediousness, irksomeness; dryness, stodginess, heaviness; too much of a good thing, satiation 863 n. *satiety*; disgust, loathing, nausea 861 n. *dislike*; flatness, staleness 387 n. *insipidity*; stuffiness 840 n. *dullness*; prolixity 570 n. *diffuseness*; sameness 16 n. *uniformity*; monotony, dull m. 106 n. *repetition*; leaden hours, time to kill, time the enemy 679 n. *inactivity*.

bore, utter b., no fun; boring thing, twice-told tale, crambe repetita; irk, bind; dull work, boring w.; beaten track, daily round 610 n. *habit*; grindstone, treadmill 682 n. *labour*; boring man, pain in the neck, dry-as-dust, proser, buttonholer; club bore; drip, wet blanket, misery; too much of a good thing.

Adj. *tedious*, uninteresting, devoid of interest; unenjoyable, unexciting, un-entertaining, unamusing, unfunny; slow, dragging, leaden, heavy; dry, dry-as-dust, arid; flat, stale, insipid 387 adj. *tasteless*; bald 573 adj. *plain*; humdrum, suburban, depressing, dreary, stuffy 840 adj. *dull*; stodgy, prosaic, uninspired, unreadable, unread; prosy, long, overlong 570 adj. *prolix*; drowsy, soporific 679 adj. *somnific*; boring, binding, wearisome, tiresome, irksome; wearing, chronic, mortal 684 adj. *fatiguing*; repetitive, repetitious 106 adj. *repeated*; same, unvarying, invariable, monotonous 16 adj. *uniform*; too much, cloying, satiating; disgusting, nauseating, nauseous.

bored, unentertained, unamused, unexcited; afflicted with boredom, counting sheep 679 adj. *inactive*; stale, weary, jaded 684 adj. *fatigued*; blue, world-weary, life-w., weary of life 834 adj. *melancholic*; blasé, uninterested 860 adj. *indifferent*; satiated, cloyed 863 adj. *sated*; nauseated, sick of, fed up, loathing 861 adj. *disliking*.

Vb. *be tedious*, pall, cloy, glut, jade, satiate 863 vb. *sate*; nauseate, sicken, disgust 861 vb. *cause dislike*; bore, irk, try, weary 684 vb. *fatigue*; bore to death, weary to d., tire out, wear o.; get one down, try one's patience, outstay one's welcome, stay too long; fail to interest, make one yawn, send one to sleep; drag 278 vb. *move slowly*; drag its slow length along, go on and on, never end; harp on, prove monotonous 106 vb. *repeat oneself*; buttonhole, be prolix 570 vb. *be diffuse*.

Adv. *boringly*, ad nauseam.

See: 16, 106, 278, 387, 570, 573, 610, 679, 682, 684, 834, 840, 860, 861, 863.

839 Wit

N. *wit*, wittiness, pointedness, point, smartness, epigrammatism; esprit, ready wit, verbal readiness; esprit d'escalier 67 n. *sequel*; saltiness, salt, Attic s. 575 n. *elegance*; sparkle, scintillation, brightness 498 n. *intelligence*; humour, sense of h., pleasant h.; wry humour, pawkiness, dryness, slyness; drollery, pleasantry, waggishness, waggery, facetiousness; jocularity, jocosity, jocoseness 833 n. *merriment*; comicality, vis comica 849 n. *ridiculousness*; lack of seriousness, trifling, flippancy 456 adj. *inattention*; joking, practical j., jesting, tomfoolery, buffoonery 497 n. *foolery*; broad humour, low h., vulgarity 847 n. *bad taste*; farce, broad f., slapstick, ham, harlequinade 594 n. *dramaturgy*; whimsicality, fancy 604 n. *whim*; biting wit, cruel humour, satire, sarcasm 851 n. *ridicule*; irony 850 n. *affectation*; word-fence 477 n. *sophistry*; word-play, play upon words, punning, equivocation 518 n. *equivocalness*.

witticism, piece of humour, stroke of wit, jeu d'esprit, sally, mot, bon mot; Wellerism, Spoonerism; epigram, smart saying, conceit; pun, play upon words, equivoque, calembour 518 n. *equivocalness*; point of the joke, cream of the jest; banter, badinage, persiflage; quiz, retort, repartee, quid pro quo, backchat, back-talk 460 n. *rejoinder*; sarcasm 851 n. *satire*; joke, practical j., standing j., private j., jest, family j., dry j.; quip, jape, quirk, crank, quips and cranks, gag, crack, wisecrack; old joke, stale jest, salt that has lost its savour, chestnut, Joe Miller, bromide; broad jest, low joke, smoking room story, limerick; story, funny s.; jest-book, jokebook.

humorist, wit, bel esprit, epigrammatist, reparteeist; conversationalist; joker, japer; life of the party, wag, witcracker, witsnapper; witworm, witling; joker, Joe Miller, Sam Weller; jokesmith, funnyman, gagsman, gagster, punster; banterer, persifleur, quizzer, leg-puller, ragger, teaser; ironist 850 n. *affector*; mocker, scoffer, satirist, lampooner 926 n. *detractor*; comedian, comic 594 n. *entertainer*; comic writer, comic author, cartoonist, caricaturist; burlesquer, parodist 20 n. *imitator*; jester, court j., wearer of the cap and bells, motley fool, clown, farceur, buffoon 501 n. *fool*.

Adj. *witty*, spirituel, nimble-witted, quick; Attic, salty 575 adj. *elegant*; pointed, full of point, ben trovato, epigrammatic; brilliant, sparkling, smart, clever, too clever by half 498 adj. *intelligent*; snappy, biting, pungent, keen, sharp, sarcastic; dry, sly, pawky; unserious, facetious, flippant 456 adj. *light-minded*; jocular, jocose, joking, joshing, waggish, roguish; lively, pleasant, merry, merry and wise 833 adj. *gay*; comic, funny, rib-tickling 849 adj. *funny*; humorous, droll; whimsical 604 adj. *capricious*; playful, sportive, fooling 497 adj. *absurd*.

Vb. *be witty*, scintillate, sparkle, flash; jest, joke, crack a j., cut a j., gag, wisecrack; tell a good story, set the table in a roar, lay them in the aisles 837 vb. *amuse*; pun, make a p., play upon words, equivocate 518 *be equivocal*; fool, jape 497 vb. *be absurd*; play with, tease, chaff, rag, banter, quip, quiz, twit, pull one's leg, make merry with, make fun of, poke fun at, exercise one's wit upon 851 vb. *ridicule*; mock, caricature, burlesque 851 vb. *satirize*; retort, flash back, come back at 460 vb. *answer*; have a sense of humour, enjoy a joke, see the point.

Adv. *in jest*, in joke, in fun, in sport, in play.

See: 20, 67, 456, 460, 477, 497, 498, 501, 518, 575, 594, 604, 833, 837, 847, 849, 850, 851, 926.

840 Dullness

N. *dullness*, heaviness, infestivity, mopiness 834 *dejection*; stuffiness, dreariness, deadliness; monotony, boringness 838 n. *tedium*; colourlessness, drabness; lack of sparkle, lack of inspiration, want of originality; stodginess, unreadability, prosiness; staleness, flatness 387 n. *insipidity*; banality, triteness, superficiality; lack of humour, no sense of h., inability to see a joke, primness, impenetrable gravity, grimness 834 n. *seriousness*; prose, matter of fact 573 n. *plainness*.

Adj. *dull,* unamusing, uninteresting, unentertaining; unfunny, uncomical, straight; uncharming, uncaptivating; deadly dull, dull as ditchwater; stuffy, dreary, deadly; pointless, meaningless 838 adj. *tedious;* unvivid, unlively, colourless, drab; flat, insipid 387 adj. *tasteless;* unimaginative, uninventive, unoriginal, derivative, superficial; stupid 499 adj. *unintelligent;* without laughter, humourless, grave, prim 834 adj. *serious;* unwitty, unsparkling, unscintillating; graceless, insulse, lacking salt 576 adj. *inelegant;* heavy, heavy-gaited, clod-hopping, ponderous, sluggish 278 adj. *slow;* stodgy, prosaic, pedestrian, unreadable; stale, banal, commonplace, trite, platitudinous 610 adj. *usual.*

Vb. *be dull,* bore 838 adj. *be tedious;* platitudinize, prose, outwrite oneself; hate fun, have no humour in one's composition, never see a joke, not see the point, miss the cream of the jest.

See: 278, 387, 499, 573, 576, 610, 834, 838.

841 Beauty

N. *beauty,* pulchritude, the beautiful; ripe perfection, highest p. 646 n. *perfection;* the sublime, sublimity, grandeur, magnificence 868 n. *nobility;* splendour, gorgeousness, brilliance, brightness, radiance 417 n. *light;* transfiguration 843 n. *beautification;* polish, gloss, ornament 844 n. *ornamentation;* scenic beauty, scenery, view, landscape, seascape, cloudscape 445 n. *spectacle;* form, fair proportions, regular features, classic f. 245 n. *symmetry;* physical beauty, loveliness, comeliness, fairness, handsomeness, bonniness, prettiness; attraction, attractiveness, agreeableness, charm, appeal, glamour, sex appeal, cuteness, kissability; attractions, charms, graces, perfections, ripe p.; good looks, handsome features, pretty face, beaux yeux; shapeliness, belle tournure, trim figure, curves, curvaceousness, vital statistics; gracefulness, grace, concinnity 575 n. *elegance;* chic, style 848 n. *fashion;* delicacy, refinement 846 n. *good taste;* appreciation of beauty, aesthetics, callæsthetics, aestheticism; landscape architecture.

a beauty, thing of beauty, work of art,

masterpiece 644 n. *exceller;* bijou, jewel, pearl, treasure 646 n. *paragon;* fair, fair one, lady bright; belle, raving beauty, reigning b., toast, idol 890 n. *favourite;* beau idéal, dream girl; beauty queen, Miss Universe; bathing belle, pin-up girl, cover g., chocolate-box type; pretty, brighteyes; dream, vision, picture, perfect p., sight for sore eyes; angel, charmer, dazzler; enchantress, femme fatale, witch 983 n. *sorceress;* smasher, scorcher, lovely, cutie, bird, beaut, peach, dish, lulu; flower, rose, lily; fairy, peri, houri; Grace, the Graces, Hebe, Venus, Aphrodite, Helen of Troy; Apollo, Hyperion, Cupid, Endymion, Adonis, Narcissus, Ganymede, Hylas, Antinous; peacock, swan.

Adj. *beautiful,* pulchritudinous, beauteous, of beauty; lovely, fair, bright, radiant; comely, goodly, bonny, pretty; sweet, sweetly pretty, pretty-pretty, nice, good enough to eat; pretty as a picture, paintable, photogenic; handsome, good-looking, well-favoured; graced, well-g.; gracious, stately, statuesque, majestic; leonine, manly; adorable, godlike, goddess-like, divine, 'divinely tall and most divinely fair'; picturesque, scenic, ornamental; artistic, well-grouped, well-composed, cunning, curious, quaint 694 adj. *well-made;* æsthetic 846 adj. *tasteful;* exquisite, choice 605 adj. *chosen;* unspotted, unblemished 646 adj. *perfect.*

splendid, sublime, superb, fine 644 adj. *excellent;* grand 868 adj. *noble;* coloured, in colour, rich, gorgeous, highly-coloured 425 adj. *florid;* bright, resplendent, dazzling, beaming, radiant, sparkling, glowing 417 adj. *radiating;* glossy, polished, magnificent, specious 875 adj. *showy;* ornate, loaded 844 adj. *ornamented.*

shapely, well-proportioned, regular, classic 245 adj. *symmetrical;* formed, well-f., well-turned; rounded, buxom, curved, curvaceous, callipygian, callipygic; clean-limbed, straight-l., straight, slender, slim, svelte, willowy 206 adj. *lean;* petite, dainty, delicate; undeformed, undefaced, unwarped, untwisted.

personable, prepossessing, agreeable, comfortable, buxom, sonsy; attractive, fetching, appealing; snappy, cute, kissable; charming, enchanting, glamorous; lovesome, winsome 887 adj. *lovable;* of good appearance, with a fair outside; blooming,

in bloom, ruddy 431 adj. *red*; rosy, rosy-cheeked, apple-c., cherry-lipped, peachy; bright, bright-eyed; sightly, becoming, fit to be seen, passable, not amiss; presentable, proper, decent, neat, natty, tidy, trim; tight, spruce, jimp, dapper, glossy, sleek; well-dressed, well turned out, smart, stylish 848 adj. *fashionable*; elegant, dainty, delicate, refined 846 adj. *tasteful*.

Vb. *be beautiful*, grow b., be photogenic, photograph well; have good looks, have bright eyes; bloom, glow, beam, dazzle 417 vb. *shine*; be dressed to kill; do one credit, win a beauty contest.

beautify, trim, neaten, improve; brighten 417 vb. *make bright*; prettify, bejewel, tattoo 844 vb. *decorate*; set (a jewel); set off, grace, suit, fit, become, go well, show one off, flatter; bring out the high lights, enhance one's looks, glamorize, transfigure, face-lift; prink, prank, titivate, powder, rouge 843 vb. *primp*.

See: 206, 245, 417, 425, 431, 445, 575, 605, 644, 646, 694, 843, 844, 846, 848, 868, 875, 887, 890, 983.

842 Ugliness

N. *ugliness*, unsightliness, hideousness, repulsiveness; lack of beauty, inconcinnity, gracelessness, clumsiness 576 n. *inelegance*; want of symmetry, asymmetry 246 n. *distortion*; unshapeliness, lack of form 246 n. *deformity*; mutilation, disfigurement 845 a. *blemish*; uglification, disfiguration, defacement, blackening; squalor, filth, beastliness 649 n. *uncleanness*; homeliness, plainness, plain features, ugly face; no beauty, no oil painting, a face to stop a clock; wry face, snarl, forbidding countenance, vinegar aspect, grim look, sour l., hanging l. 893 n. *sullenness*; haggardness, haggard look; fading beauty, dim eyes, wrinkles, hand of time 131 n. *age*.

eyesore, hideosity, botch, blot, patch 845 n. *blemish*; aesthetic crime; blot on the landscape, slum; ugly person, fright, sight, figure, object, not one's type; scarecrow, horror, death's-head, gargoyle, grotesque; monster, abortion; harridan, witch; toad, gorilla, baboon, crow; plain Jane, ugly duckling; satyr, Caliban; Æsop; Beast.

Adj. *ugly*, lacking beauty, beautiless, unbeautiful, unlovely, uncomely, unhandsome; not fair, black; ugly as sin, hideous, foul 649 adj. *unclean*; frightful, shocking, monstrous; repulsive, repellent, odious, loathsome 861 adj. *disliked*; beastly, nasty 645 adj. *not nice*; unpretty, homely, plain, plain-featured, with no looks, without any looks; forbidding, unprepossessing, ill-favoured, ill-featured, hard-f., villainous, grim-visaged, grim, saturnine 893 adj. *sullen*.

unsightly, faded, withered, worn, ravaged, wrinkled 131 adj. *aged*; not worth looking at, not fit to be seen, unseemly; unshapely, shapeless, formless, irregular, asymmetrical 244 adj. *amorphous*; twisted, deformed, disfigured, defaced 246 adj. *distorted*; ill-made, ill-shaped, ill-formed, ill-proportioned, disproportioned, misproportioned, misshapen, misbegotten, curtailed of its fair proportions; dumpy, squat 196 adj. *dwarfish*; stained, discoloured 426 adj. *colourless*; ghastly, wan, grisly, gruesome; tousled, in disarray 61 adj. *orderless*.

graceless, ungraced, ungraceful 576 adj. *inelegant*; inartistic, unæsthetic; unbecoming, unornamental, unpicturesque; squalid, dingy, poky, dreary, drab; garish, gaudy, gross, indelicate, coarse 847 adj. *vulgar*; dowdy, ill-dressed; rude, crude, rough, rugged, uncouth 699 adj. *artless*; clumsy, awkward, ungainly, cumbersome, hulky, hulking, slouching, clod-hopping 195 adj. *unwieldy*.

Vb. *be ugly*, lack beauty, have no looks, lose one's l.; fade, wither, age, show one's a. 131 vb. *grow old*; look ill, look a wreck, look a mess, look a fright.

make ugly, uglify; fade, wither, discolour 426 vb. *decolorize*; darken, shadow 428 vb. *blacken*; spoil 655 vb. *deteriorate*; soil 649 vb. *make unclean*; deface, disfigure, blemish, blot; misshape 244 vb. *deform*; torture, twist 246 vb. *distort*; mutilate 655 vb. *impair*.

See: 61, 131, 195, 196, 244, 246, 426, 428, 576, 645, 649, 655, 699, 845, 847, 861, 893.

843 Beautification

N. *beautification*, beautifying 844 n. *ornamentation*; transfiguration 143 n. *transformation*; scenic improvement, land-

scape gardening, landscape architecture; plastic surgery, rhinoplasty, nose-straightening, skin-grafting, face-lift 658 n. *surgery*; beauty treatment, skin t., scalp t., face-lifting, mole-removing, depilation, eye-brow plucking, eye-brow pencilling; pack, face p., mud p., oatmeal p., facial; massage, face m., skin m., manicure, nail-filing, nail-varnishing, nail-polishing, buffing; pedicure, chiropody; tattooing 844 n. *ornamental art*; ear-piercing, nose-p.; sun-tanning, browning, sun lamp, ultra-violet rays; toilet, make-up, art of m., cosmetology; creaming, farding, larding, rouging, painting, shadowing, dyeing, powdering, patching, scenting, soaping, shampooing; wash and brush up 648 n. *ablution.*

hair-dressing, trichology, hair-treatment, scalp massage; barbering, shaving, shampooing, clipping, trimming, thinning, singeing; depilation, plucking; cutting, hair-c., bobbing, shingling; shave, hair-cut, cut, clip, trim, singe, tidy-up; hair-style, coiffure, crop, Eton c., bob, shingle; crew-cut, cut en brosse, urchin cut, baby-doll c., Italian c., chrysanthemum c., bouffant c.; styling, hair-s., curling, frizzing, tonging, waving, setting, hair-straightening, de-frizzing; hair-do, shape, set, wave, permanent w., home permanent w., Marcel w., finger w., pin w., hot w., cold w.; curl 251 n. *coil*; bang, fringe, pony-tail, chignon, bun, Pompadour, cowlick, quiff 259 n. *hair*; false hair, switch 228 n. *wig*; curling-iron, tongs, curlers, pin-c., rollers, crackers, rags; slide, hair-s., barette, grip, kirby g.; bandeau, Alice band; comb, hair-pin, bobby p., hat-p., hair-net, snood 228 n. *headgear.*

hairwash, shampoo, dry s., wet s., liquid s., cream s., powder s., egg s., beer s., vinegar s., medicinal s., antiseptic s.; rinse, tinting, colour tone, high lights, lightening, bleach, dye, hair-d., peroxide; hair-spray, lacquer, hair-oil, hair-cream, grease, brilliantine, macassar oil, hair-restorer.

cosmetic, beautifier, glamourizer, aid to beauty, patch, beauty spot; make-up, liquid m., stick m.; paint, greasepaint, warpaint, rouge, liquid r., fard, pomade, cream, face-c., cold c., cleansing c., vanishing c., foundation c., night c.,

hormone c., healing c., skin-ointment, lanolin 357 n. *unguent*; lipstick, lipsalve; burnt cork; nail polish, nail varnish, varnish remover; powder, face-p., compressed p., silk p., talcum p.; kohl, collyrium, mascara, eye-shadow; eye-salve, eye lotion; hand lotion, astringent l., sun-tan l.; scented soap, bath salts, bath oil, bath essence 648 n. *cleanser*; scent, perfume, essence, eau-de-cologne, toilet water, cologne stick; eyebrow pencil, eyelash curler; hare's foot, rabbit's f.; powder puff, compact, flapjack; make-up set, manicure s., nail-file, nail scissors, clippers; nail polisher, buffer; styptic pencil; dental floss; toiletry, toiletries.

beauty parlour, beauty shop, beauty salon, reducing s.; parfumerie; boudoir, make-up room, dressing r., powder r., powder closet.

beautician, beauty specialist, beauty doctor; face-lifter, plastic surgeon; make-up artist, glamorizer, tattooer; cosmetician, cosmetologist; barber, hairdresser, hair-stylist; trichologist; manicurist, pedicurist, chiropodist.

Adj. *beautified*, transfigured, transformed; prettified, glamourized, bedizened, made-up, rouged, painted, powdered, raddled, patched, scented, curled; primped, dressed up, dolled up 841 adj. *beautiful.*

Vb. *primp*, prettify, doll up, dress up, bedizen, bejewel; prink, prank, trick out; preen; titivate, make up, put on make-up, apply cosmetics, rouge, paint, shadow; powder; scent oneself; oil, shave, pluck one's eyebrows, varnish one's nails, dye one's hair; curl, wave; have a hair-do, have a facial, have a manicure 841 vb. *beautify.*

See: 143, 228, 251, 259, 357, 648, 658, 841, 844.

844 Ornamentation

N. *ornamentation*, ornature, decoration, adornment, garnish; ornate style, ornateness 574 n. *ornament*; prettyism, pretty-pretty; gaudiness, richness, gilt 875 n. *ostentation*; enhancement, enrichment, embellishment; setting, background; table decoration, centre piece, epergne, silver, china, glass; floral decoration,

flower arrangement, wreath, coronal, crown, bouquet, nosegay, posy, buttonhole; objet d'art, article of virtue, bric-à-brac, curio, medal, medallion.

ornamental art, gardening, landscape g., topiarism; architecture, landscape a., building; interior decoration, furnishing, draping, house-painting 553 n. *painting*; statuary 554 n. *sculpture*; cartouche, metope, triglyph; capital, acanthus; pilaster, caryatid; boss, cornice, gargoyle; moulding, astragal, beading, fluting, fretting, tracery; varnishing 226 n. *facing*; pargeting, veneering, panelling, graining; ormolu, gilding, gilt, gold leaf; lettering, illumination, illustration, illustrating 551 n. *art*; heraldic art 547 n. *heraldry*; tattooing; reeding, strap-work, coquillage; etching 555 n. *engraving*; work, fancy-w., woodwork, fretwork; pokerwork, pyrography; open-work, filigree; relief, embossing, chasing, intaglio 254 n. *rilievo*; inlay, inset, enamelling, smalto, mosaic 437 n. *variegation*; wrought-work, toreutics; gem-cutting, setting; cut glass, wrought iron, figurehead.

pattern, key-p., motif, print, design, composition 331 n. *structure*; detail, elaborate d.; geometrical style, decorated s., rose-window, cyma, ogee, spandrel, fleur-de-lis; alpana, tracery, scrollwork, fiddle-head, arabesque, flourish, curlicue 251 n. *coil*; weave, diaper, Fair Isle 331 n. *texture*; check 437 n. *chequer*; stripe, pin-s. 437 n. *striation*; spot, coin s., dot, polka d. 437 n. *maculation*; herring-bone, zigzag, dog's tooth, hound's t. 220 n. *obliquity*; water-pattern, watermark 547 n. *identification*.

needlework, stitchery, tapestry, arras; embossed needlework, sampler; laid-work, patchwork, appliqué work, open w., drawn-thread w.; embroidery, broidery, brocade, brocatelle; crochet, lace, broderie anglaise; smocking, tatting, knitting; stitch, purl, plain, gros point, petit p., needle p.; cross stitch, chain s., cable s., moss s., garter s., hem s., stem s., blanket s., feather s., back s., satin s., herring-bone s., lace s., French knotting, lazy-daisy.

trimming, passementerie, piping, valance, border, fringe, frieze, frill, galloon, gimp 234 n. *edging*; binding 589 n. *bookbinding*; trapping, frog, lapel, epaulette, shoulder knot, rosette, cockade 547 n. *badge*; bow

knot 47 n. *ligature*; bobble, pom-pom; tassel, danglums, bead, bugle 217 n. *pendant*; ermine, fur 259 n. *hair*; feather, ostrich f., osprey, plume, panache 259 n. *plumage*; streamer, ribbon.

finery, togs, braws, Sunday best 228 n. *clothing*; fal-de-lal, frippery, frills and furbelows, ribbons, chiffon; gaudery, gaud, trinket, knick-knack, gewgaw, bric-à-brac, tinsel, spangle, sequin, clinquant, costume jewellery, glass, paste, paste diamond, rhinestone 639 a. *bauble*.

jewellery, bijouterie, jewel-work; crown jewels, diadem, tiara 743 n. *regalia*; drop, locket 217 n. *pendant*; crucifix 222 n. *cross*; amulet, charm 983 n. *talisman*; rope, string, necklet, necklace, chain, watch-c., albert, chatelaine, carcanet 250 n. *loop*; torque, armlet, anklet, bracelet; wristlet, bangle, ring, earring, nose-ring, signet r., wedding r., eternity r., engagement r., Russian wedding r., mourning r., dress r. 250 n. *circle*; ouch, brooch, fibula, badge, crest; stud, pin, gold p., tie p., sorority p., fraternity p. 47 n. *fastening*; medal, medallion.

gem, jewel, bijou; stone, precious s., semi-precious s.; uncut gem, cut g.; brilliant, sparkler, diamond, rock, ice; solitaire; carbuncle, ruby, oriental r., spinel r., balas r., balas; pearl, Orient p., cultivated p., seed p., pink p.; opal, black o., fire o., girasol; sapphire, white s., yellow s., water s.; turquoise, emerald, beryl, aquamarine, chrysoberyl, chrysoprase, alexandrite; garnet, amethyst, oriental a., topaz, oriental t., occidental t., chalcedony, cornelian, carnelian, sard, jasper, agate, onyx, sardonyx, heliotrope; bloodstone, moonstone, sarkstone, cat's-eye, zircon, jacinth, hyacinth, tourmaline, apatite, chrysolite, olivine, peridot; coral, jade, lapis lazuli.

Adj. *ornamental*, decorative, non-functional, fancy; glamorous, picturesque, pretty-pretty; scenic, landscape, topiary; geometric; Doric, Ionic, Corinthian, Romanesque, Decorated; baroque, rococo; Sheraton, Chippendale; daedal, quaint.

ornamented, decorated, embellished, polished 574 adj. *ornate*; picked out 437 adj. *variegated*; mosaic, inlaid, enamelled; worked, embroidered, trimmed; wreathed, festooned, crowned; overdecorated, overloaded 847 adj. *vulgar*; overcoloured

425 adj. *florid*; luscious, plush, gilt, begilt, gilded 800 adj. *rich*; gorgeous, garish, glittering, flashy, gaudy, meretricious 875 adj. *showy*.

bedecked, groomed, got up, togged up, wearing, sporting; decked, bedight; looking one's best, in one's b., in one's Sunday b., en grande toilette 228 adj. *dressed*; beribboned, festooned, studded, bemedalled; bedizened, bejewelled 843 adj. *beautified*.

Vb. *decorate*, embellish, enhance, enrich; adorn, load; grace, set, set off 574 vb. *ornament*; paint, bedizen, bejewel; adonize, glamorize, prettify 841 vb. *beautify*; garnish, trim; shape, topiarize; array, deck, bedeck, dight, bedight 228 vb. *dress*; deck out, trick o., prank, preen, titivate 843 vb. *primp*; freshen, smarten, spruce up, furbish, burnish 648 vb. *clean*; bemedal, beribbon, garland, crown 866 vb. *dignify*; stud, spangle, bespangle 437 vb. *variegate*; colour-wash, whitewash, varnish, grain, japan, lacquer 226 vb. *coat*; enamel, gold, silver; blazon 590 vb. *describe*; emblazon, illuminate, illustrate 553 vb. *paint*; colourize 425 vb. *colour*; border, trim 234 vb. *hem*; work, pick out, broider, embroider, tapestry; lace 222 vb. *enlace*; chase, tool 555 vb. *engrave*; emboss 254 vb. *jut*; bead, mould; fret, carve; wreathe, festoon, trace, scroll 251 vb. *twine*.

See: 47, 217, 220, 222, 226, 228, 234, 250, 251, 254, 259, 331, 425, 437, 547, 551, 553, 554, 555, 574, 589, 590, 639, 648, 743, 800, 841, 843, 847, 866, 875, 983.

845 Blemish

N. *blemish*, no ornament; scar, cicatrice, weal, welt, mark, pock-m.; injury, flaw, crack, defect 647 n. *imperfection*; disfigurement, deformity 246 n. *distortion*; stigma, blot, blot on the landscape, blot on the scutcheon 843 n. *eyesore*; blur, blotch, splotch, smudge 550 n. *obliteration*; smut, patch, smear, stain, tarnish, rust, patina 649 n. *dirt*; spot, speck, speckle, sun-spot, macula, spottiness 437 n. *maculation*; mole, birthmark, strawberry m.; excrescence, pimpliness, pimple, blackhead, wen, wart 253 n. *swelling*; blotchiness, lentigo, freckle, leucoderma,

albinism 651 n. *skin disease*; hare-lip, cleft palate; cut, scratch, sear, bruise, black eye, shiner, cauliflower ear, broken nose 655 n. *wound*.

Adj. *blemished*, defective, flawed, cracked, damaged 647 adj. *imperfect*; stained, soiled 649 adj. *dirty*; shop-soiled, spoilt 655 adj. *deteriorated*; marked, scarred; spotted, pitted, pock-marked, maculate; spotty, lentiginous, freckled; club-footed, web-f., web-toed, pigeon-t., hammer-t.; knock-kneed, bandy, bandy-legged; hunch-backed, crooked 246 adj. *distorted*.

Vb. *blemish*, flaw, crack, injure, damage 655 vb. *impair*; blot, smudge, stain, smear, soil, cast a slur on 649 vb. *make unclean*; stigmatize, brand 547 vb. *mark*; scar, pit, pock; spoil, spoil the look of 842 vb. *make ugly*; disfigure, deface 244 vb. *deform*.

See: 244, 246, 253, 437, 547, 550, 647, 649, 651, 655, 842, 843.

846 Good Taste

N. *good taste*, tastefulness, taste, refined t., cultivated t.; simple taste, simplicity 573 n. *plainness*; best of taste, choiceness, excellence 644 n. *goodness*; refinement, delicacy, euphemism 950 n. *purity*; fine feeling, nicety, nice appreciation, palate 463 n. *discrimination*; daintiness, finickiness, kid gloves 862 n. *fastidiousness*; decency, seemliness; tact, consideration, natural courtesy, dignity, manners, polished m., breeding, civility, urbanity 884 n. *courtesy*; correctness, propriety, decorum; grace, polish, sophistication, gracious living 575 n. *elegance*; cultivation, culture, connoisseurship, amateurship, dilettantism; epicureanism, gourmandise; aestheticism, aesthetics, criticism, art c. 480 n. *judgment*; artistry, virtuosity, virtu 694 n. *skill*.

man of taste, sophisticate, connoisseur, cognescente, amateur, dilettante; gourmet, epicure; aesthete, critic, art c. 480 n. *estimator*; arbiter of taste, arbiter elegantiarum, Beau Nash 848 n. *fop*; purist, precisian 602 n. *opinionist*; euphemist 950 n. *prude*.

Adj. *tasteful*, gracious, dignified; in good taste, in the best of t.; choice, exquisite 644 adj. *excellent*; simple, unmeretricious

573 adj. *plain*; graceful, Attic, classical 575 adj. *elegant*; chaste, refined, delicate, euphemistic 950 n. *pure*; aesthetic, artistic 819 n. *sensitive*; discriminatory, epicurean 463 adj. *discriminating*; nice, dainty, choosy, finicky 862 adj. *fastidious*; critical, appreciative 480 adj. *judicial*; decent, seemly; proper, correct, comme il faut 848 adj. *fashionable*; house-trained, sophisticated 848 adj. *well-bred*.

Vb. *have taste*, show good t., reveal fine feelings 463 vb. *discriminate*; appreciate, value, criticise 480 vb. *judge*; go in for the best, take only the best 862 vb. *be fastidious*.

Adv. *tastefully*, elegantly, in taste, in the right *or* best t.; becomingly, fittingly, properly, agreeably 24 adj. *pertinently*.

See: 24, 463, 480, 573, 575, 602, 644, 694, 819, 848, 862, 884, 950.

847 Bad Taste

N. *bad taste*, tastelessness, ill taste, poor t., excruciating t. 645 n. *badness*; no taste, lack of t.; bad art, commercial a.; commercialism, commercialization, yellow press, gutter p.; unrefinement, coarseness, barbarism, vulgarism, vandalism, Philistinism, Babbittry 699 n. *artlessness*; vulgarity, gaudiness, loudness, blatancy, flagrancy; tawdriness, shoddiness; shoddy, frippery, tinsel, false ornament, glass, paste, ersatz, imitation 639 n. *bauble*; lack of feeling, insensitivity, crassness, grossness; tactlessness, indelicacy, impropriety, unseemliness; bad joke, untimely jest, misplaced wit; nastiness, obscenity 951 n. *impurity*; unfashionableness, dowdiness, frumpishness; frump, dowdy.

ill-breeding, vulgarity, commonness; loudness, heartiness; rusticity, jungliness; inurbanity, incivility, unfashionableness; bad form, incorrectness; no manners, gaucherie, boorishness, rudeness, impoliteness 885 n. *discourtesy*; ungentlemanliness, caddishness; brutishness, savagery; misbehaviour, indecorum, ribaldry; rowdyism, ruffianism 61 n. *disorder*.

vulgarian, snob, social climber, cad, bounder, low person; rough diamond, unlicked cub; arriviste, parvenu, nouveau riche; man of the people, proletarian, prole

869 n. *commoner*; Goth, Vandal, Philistine, Babbitt; barbarian, savage.

Adj. *vulgar*, undignified; unrefined, unpolished 576 adj. *inelegant*; tasteless, in bad taste, out of t., in the worst t.; gross, crass, coarse, coarse-grained; unfastidious, not particular; knowing no better, Philistine, barbarian 699 adj. *artless*; commercial, commercialized; tawdry, cheap, catchpenny, ginger-bread, tinhorn, ersatz; flashy, meretricious, bedizened 875 adj. *showy*; obtrusive, blatant, loud, screaming, gaudy, garish; flaunting, shameless; overdressed, underdressed; suburban, shabby genteel 850 adj. *affected*; not respectable, ungenteel; common, low, gutter, sordid 867 adj. *disreputable*; improper, indelicate, indecorous; indecent, low-minded, ribald, obscene, risqué.

ill-bred, underbred, unhousetrained; unpresentable; ungentlemanly, unladylike; unfeminine, hoydenish; ungenteel, non-U., not U. 869 adj. *plebeian*; loud, hearty; tactless, insensitive, blunt; uncourtly, uncivil, impolite, mannerless, unmannered, ill-mannered 885 adj. *discourteous*; unfashionable, unsmart, dowdy, rustic, provincial, countrified; rude, boorish, clownish, loutish, clod-hopping, uncouth, uncultured, uncultivated, unpolished, unrefined 491 adj. *ignorant*; unsophisticated, knowing no better 699 adj. *artless*; uncivilized, barbaric; awkward, gauche, lubberly 695 adj. *clumsy*; misbehaving, rowdy, ruffianly, riotous 61 adj. *disorderly*; snobbish, uppish, superior 850 adj. *affected*.

Vb. *vulgarize*, cheapen, coarsen, lower; commercialize, popularize; show bad taste, know no better 491 adj. *not know*; be unfashionable, dress in last year's fashions.

See: 61, 491, 576, 639, 645, 695, 699, 850, 867, 869, 875, 885, 951.

848 Fashion

N. *fashion*, style, mode, cut 243 n. *form*; method 624 n. *way*; vogue, cult 610 n. *habit*; prevailing taste, current fashion 126 n. *modernism*; rage, fad, craze, cry, furore; new look, the latest, latest fashion, newest out 126 n. *newness*; dernier cri,

last word, ne plus ultra; extreme of fashion, height of f., pink of f.; dash 875n. *ostentation*; fashionableness, ton, bon t.; fashion show, mannequin parade 522n. *exhibit*; haute couture, elegance, foppishness, dressiness; foppery 850n. *affectation*; world of fashion, Vanity Fair, passing show, way of the world.

etiquette, point of e., punctilio, pundonor 875n. *formality*; protocol, convention, custom, conventionality 610n. *practice*; snobbery, conventions of society, sanctions of s., done thing, good form; proprieties, appearances, Mrs. Grundy; bienséance, decency, decorum, propriety, right note, correctness 846n. *good taste*; civilized behaviour, comity 884n. *courtesy*; breeding, good b., polish; gentility, gentlemanliness; manners, good m., refined m., polished m., drawing-room m., court m., best behaviour; grand air, poise, dignity, savoir faire, savvy 688n. *conduct*.

beau monde, society, good s., high s., civilized s., civilization; town, West End; court, drawing-room, salon; high circles, right people, best p., right set, upper ten 868n. *nobility*; cream, upper crust, cream of society 644n. *élite*; café society, jeunesse dorée; fashionable person, glass of fashion, mould of form; man about town, man of fashion, woman of f., high stepper, classy dame; slave to fashion, leader of f., star of f., Beau Nash, arbiter elegantiarum; man of the world, woman of the w., mondain, mondaine, socialite, clubman, clubwoman, cosmopolitan 882n. *social person*.

fop, fine gentleman, macaroni, buck, pearly king; fine lady, belle, pearly queen; debutante, deb; dandy, beau, Beau Brummel, exquisite, curled darling, scented d., fribble; popinjay, peacock, clothes-horse, fashion plate, tailor's dummy, man milliner; coxcomb, puppy, dandiprat, jackanapes, petit maitre; jemmy, Johnnie, swell, toff, dude, masher, filbert, knut, nob; Teddy-boy, Teddy-girl; Corinthian, spark, blood, blade, buckeen, bahadur, lad, bhoy, gay dog; carpet knight; squire of dames.

Adj. fashionable, modish, stylish, bon ton; correct, comme il faut; in fashion, in the latest f., à la mode, chi-chi; recherché, exquisite, chic, well-dressed, well-groomed 846adj. *tasteful*; clothes-conscious, foppish, dressy; high-stepping, dashing, doggish, rakish; dandy, smart, classy, toney, swanky, swank, swish, posh; up-to-the-minute, ultra-fashionable, newfangled 126adj. *modern*; groomed, dandified, braw, dressed to the nines, in full dress, en grande tenue 228adj. *dressed*; in society, in the best s., in the right set, moving in the best circles, knowing the right people, belonging to the best clubs; in the swim 83adj. *conformable*; snobbish 850adj. *affected*; conventional, done 610 adj. *usual*.

well-bred, thoroughbred, blue-blooded 875 adj. *noble*; cosmopolitan, sophisticated, civilized, citified, urbane; polished, polite, house-trained; U, gentlemanlike, ladylike 868adj. *genteel*; civil, well-mannered, easy-m., good m., well-spoken 884adj. *courteous*; courtly, stately, distingué, dignified 875adj. *formal*; poised, dégagé, easy, unembarrassed, smooth; correct, decorous, proper, convenable, decent; considerate 884adj. *amiable*; punctilious 929adj. *honourable*.

Vb. be in fashion, have a run, be done, pass current 610vb. *be wont*; be the rage, be the latest 126vb. *modernize*; follow the fashion, jump on the band wagon, change with the times 83vb. *conform*; have the entrée, move in the best circles, be seen in the right places; savoir faire, savoir vivre 882vb. *be sociable*; entertain 882vb. *be hospitable*; keep up with the Jones's, keep up appearances; observe decorum, do the right thing; cut a figure, lead the fashion, set the f., set the tone, give a tone; look right, pass; have an air, have style; dress well, have the right clothes, dandify 843vb. *primp*.

Adv. fashionably, in style, à la mode; for appearances, for fashion's sake.

See: 83, 126, 228, 243, 522, 610, 624, 644, 688, 843, 846, 850, 868, 875, 882, 884, 929.

849 Ridiculousness

N. ridiculousness, ludicrousness, risibility, laughability, height of absurdity 497n. *absurdity*; funniness, pricelessness, comicality, drollery, waggishness 839n. *wit*; quaintness, oddness, queerness, eccen-

tricity 84 n. *abnormality*; bathos, anti-climax 509 n. *disappointment*; boasting 877 n. *boast*; bombast 546 n. *extravagance*; comic interlude, light relief; light verse, comic v., doggerel, limerick, spoonerism, malapropism, Hibernicism, Irish bull 839 n. *witticism*; comedy, farce, burlesque, slapstick, knock-about, clowning, buffoonery 594 n. *stage play*; unexpectedness, paradox, paradoxicality, Gilbertian situation 508 n. *inexpectation.*

Adj. *ridiculous*, ludicrous, preposterous, monstrous, grotesque, fantastic 497 adj. *absurd*; awkward, clownish 695 n. *clumsy*; derisory, contemptible 639 adj. *unimportant*; laughable, risible; bizarre, rum, quaint, odd, queer 84 adj. *unusual*; strange, outlandish 59 adj. *extraneous*; mannered, stilted 850 adj. *affected*; inflated, bombastic, extravagant, outré 546 adj. *exaggerated*; fanciful 513 adj. *imaginary*; whimsical 604 adj. *capricious*; paradoxical.

funny, funny-peculiar 84 adj. *abnormal*; funny-ha-ha, laughter-making 837 adj. *amusing*; comical, droll, drollish, humorous, waggish 839 adj. *witty*; rich, priceless, side-splitting; light, comic, serio-c., tragic-c.; mocking, ironical, satirical 851 adj. *derisive*; burlesque, mock-heroic; doggerel; farcical, slapstick, clownish, knock-about; Aristophanic, Shavian, Gilbertian, Pickwickian.

Vb. *be ridiculous*, make one laugh, excite laughter, raise a laugh; tickle, shake *or* disturb one's gravity, give one the giggles; entertain 837 vb. *amuse*; look silly, be a figure of fun, cut a ridiculous figure, be a laughing-stock, fool, play the fool 497 vb. *be absurd*; come down with a bump, descend to bathos, pass from the sublime to the ridiculous; put oneself out of court 695 vb. *stultify oneself*; poke fun at, make one a laughing-stock 851 vb. *ridicule.*

See: 59, 84, 497, 508, 509, 513, 546, 604, 639, 695, 837, 839, 841, 850, 851, 877, 954.

850 Affectation

N. *affectation*, cult, fad 848 n. *fashion*; affectedness, pretentiousness 875 n. *ostentation*; assumption of airs, affected a., grand a. 873 n. *airs*; striking attitude, high moral tone; artificiality, mannerism,

trick; literary affectation, esoteric vocabulary, prestige terms, grandiloquence 574 n. *magniloquence*; preciosity, euphuism, cultism, Gongorism 574 n. *ornament*; mim, moue, grimace 547 n. *gesture*; coquetry, minauderie 604 n. *caprice*; conceit, conceitedness, foppery, foppishness, dandyism, puppyism, coxcombry 873 n. *vanity*; euphemism, mock modesty, false shame, mauvaise honte 874 n. *modesty*; irony, Socratic i., back-handed compliment 851 n. *ridicule*; insincerity, play-acting, tongue in cheek 541 n. *duplicity*; theatricality, histrionics.

pretension, assumption, pretensions, false p., false claim 916 n. *arrogation*; artifice, pretence 614 n. *pretext*; humbug, quackery, charlatanism, charlatanry 542 n. *deception*; superficiality, shallowness, shallow profundity 4 n. *insubstantiality*; stiffness, starchiness, buckram 875 n. *formality*; pedantry, purism, precisianism 735 n. *severity*; demureness, prunes and prisms 950 n. *prudery*; sanctimony, sanctimoniousness 979 n. *pietism.*

affector, affecter; pretender, false claimant; humbug, quack, charlatan 545 n. *impostor*; play-actor 594 n. *actor*; hypocrite, flatterer 545 n. *deceiver*; bluffer 877 n. *boaster*; coquette, flirt; affectationist, mass of affectation, attitudinizer, poser, poseur; ironist 839 n. *humorist*; coxcomb dandy 848 n. *fop*; grimacer, simperer; formalist, precisian, purist, pedant; prig, puritan, pietist 950 n. *prude*; mannerist, euphuist, cultist, gongorist 575 n. *stylist.*

Adj. *affected*, full of affectations, self-conscious, over-wrought, overdone 546 adj. *exaggerated*; mannered, euphuistic, precious, chi-chi 574 adj. *ornate*; artificial, unnatural, stilted, stiff, starchy 875 adj. *formal*; prim, priggish, prudish, euphemistic, sanctimonious, smug, demure 979 adj. *pietistic*; arch, sly 833 adj. *gay*; coquettish, coy, mock-modest, mincing, simpering, grimacing, languishing; humbugging, canting, hypocritical, tongue-in-cheek, ironical 542 adj. *deceiving*; bluffing 877 adj. *boasting*; shallow, specious, pretentious, big, big-sounding, high-s., big-mouthed, stagy, theatrical, over-dramatized 875 adj. *ostentatious*; coxcombical, foppish, conceited, giving oneself airs, showing off, swanking, posturing, posing, striking poses, striking an attitude,

attitudinizing 873 adj. *vain*; snobbish, climbing, saving appearances 847 adj. *ill-bred*; bogus 541 adj. *false*; for effect, sought, put on.

Vb. *be affected*, affect, put on, wear, assume; pretend, feign, go through the motions, make a show of, bluff 541 vb. *dissemble*; make as if 20 vb. *imitate*; affect zeal, show work 678 vb. *be busy*; perform, act a part, play-act 594 vb. *act*; overact, ham, barnstorm 546 vb. *exaggerate*; try for effect, seek an e., play to the gallery; dramatize oneself, attitudinize, strike attitudes, posture, pose, strike a p. 875 vb. *be ostentatious*; have pretensions, put on airs, give oneself a., swank, show off, make a show 873 vb. *be vain*; air one's knowledge 490 vb. *know*; air one's style, euphuize 566 vb. *show style*; brag, vaunt, talk big 877 vb. *boast*; grimace, moue, simper, smirk 835 vb. *smile*; coquette, flirt, languish 887 vb. *excite love*; play the hypocrite 541 vb. *cant*; save appearances, euphemize; make pretexts, pretext 614 vb. *plead*.

See: 4, 20, 490, 541, 542, 545, 546, 547, 566, 574, 575, 594, 604, 614, 678, 735, 833, 835, 839, 847, 848, 851, 873, 874, 875, 877, 887, 916, 950, 979.

851 Ridicule

N. *ridicule*, derision, derisiveness, poking fun; mockery, scoffing, flippancy 921 n. *disrespect*; sniggering, grinning 835 n. *laughter*; raillery, quizzing, banter, persiflage, badinage, leg-pulling, chaff, quiz, leg-pull; buffoonery, horseplay, clowning, practical joke 497 n. *foolery*; grin, snigger, laugh; scoff, mock, fleer 926 n. *detraction*; irony, tongue in cheek, sarcasm, barbed shaft, backhanded compliment; catcall, hoot, hiss 924 n. *censure*; personality, insult 921 n. *indignity*; ribaldry, fescennine verses 839 n. *witticism*.

satire, denunciation 928 n. *accusation*; parody, burlesque, travesty, caricature, cartoon 552 n. *misrepresentation*; skit, take-off 20 n. *mimicry*; squib, lampoon 926 n. *detraction*.

laughing-stock, gazing-s., object of ridicule, figure of fun, butt, universal b., common jest, by-word; mock, sport, game, fair g.; cock-shy, Aunt Sally; April fool, silly f.,

buffoon, clown, stooge, zany 501 n. *fool*; guy, caricature, travesty, mockery of, apology for; eccentric 504 n. *crank*; original, card, queer fish, odd f.; fogy, old f., geezer, mumpsimus, museum piece, mossback, back number; gink, screwball; victim 728 n. *loser*.

Adj. *derisive*, ridiculing, mocking, chaffing, joshing etc. vb.; flippant 456 adj. *lightminded*; sardonic, sarcastic; ironical, quizzical; satirical, Hudibrastic 833 adj. *witty*; ribald, fescennine 847 adj. *vulgar*; burlesque, mock-heroic.

Vb. *ridicule*, deride, laugh at, grin at, smile at, smirk at; snigger, sniff, laugh in one's sleeve; banter, chaff, rally, twit, josh, roast, rag, pull one's leg, poke fun, make merry with, play w., exercise one's wit on, make fun of, make game of, take the micky out of, have one on, fool, make a fool of, make an April fool of, fool to the top of one's bent 542 vb. *befool*; mock, scoff, fleer, jeer 926 vb. *detract*; turn to a jest, make a joke of, turn to ridicule 922 vb. *hold cheap*; take down, deflate, debunk, make one look silly, make one laugh on the other side of his face 872 vb. *humiliate*.

satirize, lampoon 921 vb. *not respect*; mock, fleer, jibe, scold 899 vb. *curse*; mimic, take off 20 vb. *imitate*; parody, travesty, burlesque, caricature, guy 552 vb. *misrepresent*; expose, show up, denounce, pillory 928 vb. *accuse*.

See: 20, 456, 497, 501, 504, 542, 552, 728, 833, 835, 839, 847, 872, 899, 921, 922, 924, 926, 928.

852 Hope

N. *hope*, hopes, expectations, something to bank on, assumption, presumption 507 n. *expectation*; good hope, certain h., high h., sanguine expectation, hope and belief, conviction 485 n. *belief*; reliance, trust, confidence, faith, assurance 473 n. *certainty*; eager hope 135 n. *anticipation*; hope recovered, heart of grace, reassurance 831 n. *relief*; safe hope, security, anchor, sheet a., mainstay, staff 218 n. *support*; final hope, last h., last throw 618 n. *gambling*; ray of hope, beam of h., gleam of h., glimmer of h. 469 n. *possibility*; good omen, happy o., favourable

auspices, promise, fair prospect, bright p. 511n. *omen*; blue sky, blue streak, silver lining 831n. *relief*; hopefulness, no cause for despair; buoyancy, airiness, breeziness, optimism, enthusiasm 833n. *cheerfulness*; wishful thinking, self-hypnotism, Couéism 477n. *sophistry*; rosy picture; star of hope; Pandora's box.

aspiration, ambition, purpose 617n. *intention*; pious hope, fervent h., fond h., airy h.; vision, pipe-dream, golden d., utopianism, millenarianism, Messianism; castles in Spain, El Dorado, fool's paradise 513n. *fantasy*; promised land, land of promise, utopia, millennium, the day, Der Tag 617n. *objective*.

hoper, aspirant, candidate, waiting list; hopeful, young h.; expectant, heir apparent 776n. *beneficiary*; optimist, prisoner of hope; utopian, millenarian, chiliast 513n. *visionary*; waiter on Providence, Micawber.

Adj. *hoping*, aspiring, soaring, starry-eyed; ambitious, would-be 617adj. *intending*; dreaming, dreaming of 513adj. *imaginative*; hopeful, in hopes 507adj. *expectant*; happy in the hope, next in succession, in sight of, on the verge of; in high hopes, sanguine, confident 473adj. *certain*; buoyant, optimistic, airy, uncritical; elated, enthusiastic, flushed 833adj. *jubilant*; hoping for the best, ever-hoping, undespairing, undiscouraged 855adj. *unfearing*; waiting on Providence, Micawberish; not unhopeful, reasonably confident.

promising, full of promise, favourable, auspicious, propitious 730adj. *prosperous*; bright, fair, golden, roseate, rosy, rose-coloured, couleur de rose; affording hope, hopeful, encouraging, inspiriting; plausible, likely 471adj. *probable*; utopian, millennial, chiliastic; wishful, self-deluding 477adj. *illogical*; visionary 513adj. *imaginary*.

Vb. *hope*, trust, confide; hope in, put one's trust in, rely, lean on, bank on, count on, pin one's hopes on, hope and believe 485 vb. *believe*; presume 471vb. *assume*; speculate, look forward 507vb. *expect*; dream of, aspire, promise oneself, soar, aim high 617vb. *intend*; have a hope, be in hopes, have hopes, have expectations, live in hopes; feel hope, cherish h., nourish h., nurse h.; buck up, take heart

of grace, take hope, pluck up h., recover h., renew h. 831vb. *be relieved*; remain hopeful, not despair, see no cause for d., not despond 599vb. *stand firm*; hope on, hope against hope, cling to h., keep hope alive, never say die; catch at a straw, keep one's spirits up, look on the bright side, hope for the best 833vb. *be cheerful*; flatter oneself, delude o. 477vb. *reason ill*; anticipate, make draughts on the future, count one's chickens before they are hatched; indulge in wishful thinking, dream 513vb. *imagine*.

give hope, afford h., foster h., inspire h., inspirit, encourage, comfort 833vb. *cheer*; show signs of, have the makings of, promise, show p., promise well, shape w., augur w., bid fair 471vb. *be likely*; raise expectations, paint a rosy picture 511vb. *predict*.

Adv. *hopefully*, expectantly, in all hopefulness, in all confidence; without discouragement, without despair; optimistically, airily, lightly, gaily, uncritically.

See: 135, 218, 469, 471, 473, 477, 485, 507, 511, 513, 599, 617, 618, 730, 776, 831, 833, 855.

853 Hopelessness

N. *hopelessness*, no hope, loss of hope, discouragement, defeatism, despondency 834n. *dejection*; pessimism, cynicism, despair, desperation, no way out, last hope gone; overthrow of hope, dashed hopes, hope deferred, hope extinguished, cheated hope, deluded h. 509n. *disappointment*; chimera, vain hope, forlorn h., futile h., impossible h. 513n. *fantasy*; message of despair, wan smile; hopeless situation, bad job, bad business 700n. *predicament*; counsel of despair, Job's comforter, misery, pessimist, defeatist 834n. *moper*.

Adj. *hopeless*, without hope, desponding, despairing, in despair, desperate; unhopeful, pessimistic, cynical; defeatist, expecting the worst, fearing the w.; sunk in despair, inconsolable, disconsolate, comfortless 834adj. *dejected*; wringing one's hands 836adj. *lamenting*; cheated of one's last hope 509adj. *disappointed*; desolate, forlorn; ruined, undone, without resource 731adj. *unfortunate*.

unpromising, holding no hope, offering no h., hopeless, comfortless, without comfort 834 adj. *cheerless*; desperate 661 adj. *dangerous*; unpropitious, inauspicious 731 adj. *adverse*; ill-omened, boding, threatening, ominous 511 adj. *presageful*; inassuageable, immitigable, irremediable, remediless, incurable, cureless, immedicable, inoperable; past cure, past hope, past recall; incorrigible, irreparable, irrecoverable, irrevocable, irredeemable, irreclaimable; irreversible, inevitable; impracticable, out of the question 470 adj. *impossible*.

Vb. *despair*, lose hope, have no h., hope no more; despond, give way to despair, wring one's hands 834 vb. *be dejected*; have shot one's last bolt, give up hope, reject h., abandon h., relinquish h.; hope for nothing more from, write off 674 vb. *disuse*.

leave no hope, offer no h., deny h.; drive to despair, bring to d.; shatter one's last hope 509 vb. *disappoint*; be incurable,—inoperable etc. adj.

See: 470, 509, 511, 513, 661, 674, 700, 731, 834, 836.

854 Fear

N. *fear*, healthy f., dread, awe 920 n. *respect*; abject fear 856 n. *cowardice*; fright, stage-f.; affright, funk, wind up; terror, mortal t., panic t.; state of terror, intimidation, trepidation, alarm, false a.; shock, flutter, flap, flat spin 318 n. *agitation*; fit, fit of terror, scare, stampede, panic 318 n. *spasm*; flight, sauve qui peut; horror, horripilation, hair on end, cold sweat, blood turning to water; consternation, dismay 853 n. *despair*; defence reaction, repression, escapism 620 n. *avoidance*.

nervousness, want of courage, lack of confidence, cowardliness 856 n. *cowardice*; self-distrust, shyness 874 n. *modesty*; defensiveness, blustering, bluster 877 n. *boasting*; timidity, fearfulness, hesitation, fighting shy, backing out 620 n. *avoidance*; loss of nerve, cold feet, fears, suspicions, misgiving, mistrust, apprehension, apprehensiveness, uneasiness, disquiet, disquietude, solicitude, anxiety, care 825 n. *worry*; depression, despondency 834 n. *dejection*; defeatism, pessimism 853 n.

despair; perturbation, trepidation, flutter, tremor, palpitation, blushing, trembling, quaking, shaking, shuddering, shivering, stuttering; nerves, willies, butterflies, qualms, needles, creeps, shivers, jumps, jitters, heebie-jeebies 318 n. *agitation*; gooseflesh, hair on end, knees knocking.

phobia, claustrophobia, agoraphobia, acrophobia, pyrophobia; fear of death; anti semitism, negrophobia, xenophobia 888 n. *hatred*; spy-mania, witch-hunting.

intimidation, deterrence, war of nerves, sabre-rattling, rocket-r., fee, faw, fum; threatening 900 n. *threat*; caution 664 n. *warning*; terror, terrorization, terrorism, reign of terror 735 n. *severity*; alarmism, scaremongering; sword of Damocles, suspended sentence 963 n. *punishment*; deterrent, weapon of retaliation 723 n. *weapon*; object of terror, goblin, hobgoblin 970 n. *demon*; spook, spectre 970 n. *ghost*; Gorgon, Medusa, scarecrow, nightmare, daymare; bugbear, bugaboo, mormo, ogre 938 n. *monster*; death's head, skull and crossbones, raw-head, bloodybones.

alarmist, scaremonger, causer of alarm and despondency; defeatist, pessimist; terrorist, terrorizer, intimidator, horrifier, frightener, nerve-shaker, sabre-rattler.

Adj. *fearing*, afeard, afraid, frightened, funky, panicky; overawed 920 adj. *respectful*; intimidated, terrorized; in fear, in trepidation, in a fright, in a cold sweat, in a flap, in a panic; terror-crazed, panic-stricken, panic-struck; stampeding, in a scare, scared, alarmed, startled; flapping, hysterical, having fits, in hysterics; dismayed, in consternation, consternated, flabbergasted; frozen, petrified, stunned; appalled, shocked, horrified, aghast, horror-struck, awe-s.; unmanned, scared out of one's wits, numbed with fear, palsied with f., frightened to death, fainting with fright, white as a sheet, pale as death, pale as a ghost, pale as ashes; frightened for nothing, more frightened than hurt, suffering from shock.

nervous, defensive, on the d.; defeatist, pessimistic, despairing 853 adj. *hopeless*; timid, timorous, shy, diffident, self-conscious, self-distrustful 874 adj. *modest*; coy, wary, hesitating, shrinking, treading warily 858 adj. *cautious*; doubtful, distrustful, misdoubting, suspicious 474 adj.

doubting; windy, faint-hearted, cold-footed 601 adj. *irresolute*; disturbed, disquieted, dismayed; apprehensive, uneasy, fearful, dreading, anxious, worried 825 adj. *unhappy*; haunted, haunted by fears, a prey to f., terror-ridden, highly-strung, starting at a sound, afraid of one's own shadow, jittery, jumpy, nervy; tremulous, shaky, shaking, trembling, quaking, cowering, cringing 856 adj. *cowardly*; on pins and needles, palpitating, breathless 318 adj. *agitated*.

frightening, shocking, startling, alarming etc. vb.; formidable, redoubtable 661 adj. *dangerous*; tremendous, dreadful, fear-inspiring, awe-i., numinous, fearsome, awesome 821 adj. *impressive*; grim, grisly, hideous, ghastly, revolting, horrifying, horrific, horrible, terrible, awful, appalling; horripilant, hair-raising; weird, eerie, creepy, ghoulish, nightmarish, gruesome, macabre, sinister; portentous, ominous, direful 511 adj. *presageful*; intimidating, terroristic, sabre-rattling, bullying, hectoring 735 adj. *oppressive*; minatory, menacing 900 adj. *threatening*; horrisonous, roaring 400 adj. *loud*; nerve-racking 827 adj. *distressing*.

Vb. *fear*, funk, be afraid,—frightened etc. adj.; stand in fear *or* awe, dread 920 vb. *respect*; flap, be in a f., have the wind up, have the willies; get the wind up, take fright, take alarm; panic, fall into p., stampede, take to flight, fly 620 vb. *run away*; start, jump, flutter 318 vb. *be agitated*; faint, collapse, break down.

quake, shake, tremble, quiver, shiver, shudder, stutter, quaver; quake in one's shoes, shake like a jelly, fear for one's life, be frightened to death, be scared out of one's wits, faint for fear; change colour, blench, pale, go white as a sheet; wince, flinch, shrink, shy, quail, jib, blink 620 vb. *avoid*; quail, cower, crouch, skulk, come to heel 721 vb. *knuckle under*; stand aghast, be horrified, be chilled with fear, freeze, freeze with horror, feel one's blood run cold, feel one's blood turn to water, feel one's hair stand on end.

be nervous,—apprehensive etc. adj.; feel shy 874 vb. *be modest*; have misgivings, suspect, distrust, mistrust 486 vb. *doubt*; shrink, shy, quail, funk it, not face it, put off the evil day; be anxious, dread, feel solicitude, consult one's fears, have f.,

have qualms; hesitate, think twice, have second thoughts, think better of it, not dare 858 vb. *be cautious*; get the wind up, start at one's own shadow, be on edge, sit on thorns 318 vb. *be agitated*.

frighten, fright, affright, play the bogyman, make faces, grimace; scare, panic, stampede; intimidate, put in fear, menace 900 vb. *threaten*; stand over, hang o. 155 vb. *impend*; alarm, cause a., raise the a., cry wolf; make one jump, give one a fright, give one a turn, startle, flutter, flurry 318 vb. *agitate*; start, flush 619 vb. *hunt*; disquiet, disturb, perturb, prey on the mind, haunt, obsess, beset 827 vb. *incommode*; raise apprehensions, make nervous, rattle, shake, unnerve; play on one's nerves, wring one's n., unstring one's n.; unman, make a coward of, cowardize; strike with fear, put the fear of God into, awe, overawe 821 vb. *impress*; quell, subdue, cow 727 vb. *overmaster*; amate, amaze, flabbergast, stun 508 vb. *surprise*; dismay, confound, abash, disconcert 63 vb. *derange*; frighten off, daunt, deter, discourage 613 vb. *dissuade*; terrorize, institute a reign of terror 735 vb. *oppress*; browbeat, bully 827 vb. *torment*; terrify, horrify, harrow, make aghast; chill, freeze, benumb, palsy, petrify, Gorgonize, mesmerize 375 vb. *render insensible*; appal, chill the spine, freeze the blood, make one's blood run cold, turn one's blood to water; make one's flesh creep, make one's hair stand on end, make one's knees knock, make one's teeth chatter, frighten one out of his wits.

See: 63, 155, 318, 375, 400, 474, 486, 508, 511, 601, 613, 619, 620, 661, 664, 721, 727, 723, 735, 821, 825, 827, 834, 853, 856, 858, 874, 877, 888, 900, 920, 938, 963, 970.

855 Courage

N. *courage*, bravery, valiance, valour; moral courage, courage of one's convictions 929 n. *probity*; V.C. courage, heroism, gallantry, chivalry; self-confidence, self-reliance, fearlessness, ignorance of fear, intrepidity, daring, nerve; defiance of danger, boldness, hardihood, audacity 857 n. *rashness*; spirit, mettle, dash, go, élan 174 n. *vigorousness*; enterprise 672 n. *under-*

taking; tenacity, bulldog courage 600 n. *perseverance*; undauntedness, high morale, stoutness of heart, firmness, fortitude, determination, resoluteness 599 n. *resolution*; gameness, pluck, spunk, guts, heart, great h., stout h., heart of oak, backbone, bottom, grit 600 n. *stamina*; sham courage, Dutch c., pot-valiance; desperate courage, courage of despair; brave face, bold front 711 n. *defiance*; fresh courage, encouragement, animation 612 n. *inducement*.

manliness, manhood, feelings of a man; virtue, chivalry; manly spirit, martial s., heroic qualities, soldierly q., morale, devotion to duty; militancy, aggressiveness, fierceness 718 n. *bellicosity*; endurance, stiff upper lip 599 n. *resolution*.

prowess, derring-do, deeds of d., chivalry, knightliness, knightlihood, heroism, heroic achievement, knightly deed, gallant act, act of courage, soldierly conduct; feat, feat of arms, emprise, exploit, stroke, bold s. 676 n. *deed*; desperate venture 857 n. *rashness*; aristeia, heroics.

brave person, hero, heroine, V.C., G.C.; knight, paladin, bahadur; good soldier, stout s., stout fellow, beau sabreur, brave, fighting man 722 n. *soldier*; man, true m., he-man, man of mettle, man of spirit, plucky chap, well-plucked 'un, game dog, bulldog; stranger to fear, daredevil, risk-taker; fire-eater, bully, bravo 857 n. *desperado*; Hector, Achilles, Hotspur, Galahad, Greatheart; Joan of Arc, Amazon; Hercules, Don Quixote, Bayard, knight-errant; the brave, the bravest of the brave; band of heroes, gallant company; forlorn hope, picked troops 644 n. *élite*; lion, tiger, game-cock, fighting c., bulldog.

Adj. *courageous*, brave, valorous, valiant, gallant, heroic; chivalrous, knightly, knight-like; yeomanly, soldierly, soldierlike, martial, Amazonian 718 adj. *warlike*; stout, doughty, tall, bonny, manful, manly, tough, two-fisted, red-blooded; militant, bellicose, aggressive, fire-eating; fierce, bloody, savage 898 adj. *cruel*; bold 711 adj. *defiant*; dashing, hardy, audacious, daring, venturesome 857 adj. *rash*; adventurous 672 adj. *enterprising*; mettlesome, spirited, high-s., high-hearted, stout-h., lion-hearted, bold as a lion, bold as brass; firm-minded, strong-m., full of courage, full of fight, full of spirit, full of spunk, spunky; full of Dutch courage, pot-valiant; firm, steady, dogged, indomitable 600 adj. *persevering*; desperate, determined 599 adj. *resolute*; of high morale, game, plucky, sporting; ready for danger, ready for the fray, ready for anything, unflinching, unshrinking, first in the breach 597 adj. *willing*.

unfearing, unafraid, intrepid, despising danger, danger-loving; sure of oneself, confident, self-c., self-reliant; fearless, dauntless, dreadless, aweless; unshrinking, untrembling, unblenching; undismayed, undaunted, undashed, unabashed, unawed, unalarmed, unconcerned, unapprehensive, unappalled, unshaken, unshakable.

Vb. *be courageous*, —bold etc. adj.; fight with the best 716 vb. *fight*; venture, adventure, bell the cat, take the plunge, take the bull by the horns 672 vb. *undertake*; dare 661 vb. *face danger*; show fight, brave, face, outface, outdare, beard, affront 711 vb. *defy*; confront, look in the face, look in the eyes; speak out, speak up 532 vb. *affirm*; face the music, show a dauntless front, stick to one's guns 599 vb. *stand firm*; go over the top 712 vb. *charge*; laugh at danger, mock at d. 857 vb. *be rash*; show prowess, show valour, win one's spurs; keep one's head 823 vb. *keep calm*; bear up, endure, grin and bear it 825 vb. *suffer*.

take courage, pluck up c., muster c., take heart of grace, nerve oneself, drink courage from, put a bold face on it, show fight, cast away fear, screw one's courage to the sticking place 599 vb. *be resolute*; rally, stand 599 vb. *stand firm*.

give courage, infuse c.; animate, put heart into, hearten, nerve, make a man of; embolden, encourage, inspirit, inspire 612 vb. *incite*; rally 833 vb. *cheer*; pat on the back, keep in countenance, keep in spirits, preserve morale, raise m., keep one's blood up; bolster up, reassure, take away fear, give confidence, increase one's self-reliance.

Adv. *bravely*, courageously, stoutly, doughtily; with one's blood up, as bold as brass.

See: 174, 532, 597, 599, 600, 612, 644, 661, 672, 676, 711, 712, 716, 718, 722, 823, 825, 833, 898, 857, 929.

856 Cowardice

N. *cowardice*, abject fear, funk, sheer f. 854 n. *fear*; cowardliness, craven spirit, no grit, no guts 601 n. *irresolution*; pusill-animity, timidity, want of courage, lack of daring; absence of morale, faint-heartedness, chicken-heartedness; un-manliness, poltroonery, dastardy, dastardliness; defeatism 853 n. *hopeless-ness*; desertion, quitting, shirking 918 n. *dutilessness*; white feather, yellow streak, low morale, faint heart, chicken liver; pot-valiance, Dutch courage, bragga-docio 877 n. *boasting*; cowering, skulking, leading from behind; discretion, better part of valour; safety first, overcaution 858 n. *caution*; moral cowardice, recanta-tion 603 n. *tergiversation*.

coward, utter c., no hero; funk, poltroon, craven; niddering, nidget, white-liver, dastard; sneak, rat, tell-tale 524 n. *in-former*; runaway, runagate 603 n. *tergiver-sator*; coward at heart, dunghill cock, braggart 877 n. *boaster*; sissy, milksop, baby, cry-b. 163 n. *weakling*; skulker, quitter, shirker, flincher, deserter, scut-tler; cur, skunk, chicken, rabbit, hare, mouse, deer, jellyfish, doormat; scare-monger, defeatist 854 n. *alarmist*.

Adj. *cowardly*, coward, craven, poltroonish; not so brave, pusillanimous, timid, timorous, fearful, niddering, unable to say bo to a goose 854 adj. *nervous*; soft, effeminate, womanish, babyish, unmanly, sissy 163 adj. *weak*; spiritless, spunkless, without grit, without guts, poor-spirited, weak-minded, faint-hearted, chicken-h., pigeon-h., white-livered, yellow-l., milk-l., lily-l.; sneaking, skulking, cowering, quailing; dastardly, yellow, abject, base, vile, mean-spirited, currish, recreant, caitiff; unsoldierly, unmilitary, unmartial, unwarlike, unaggressive 717 adj. *peaceful*; cowed, without morale, without fight 721 adj. *submitting*; defeatist 853 adj. *hopeless*; unheroic, unvaliant, uncourageous, pru-dent, discreet, more discreet than valiant 858 adj. *cautious*; bashful, shy, coy 874 adj. *modest*; easily frightened, funky, shakable, unstable, unsteady, infirm of purpose 601 adj. *irresolute*.

Vb. *be cowardly*, lack courage, have no fight, have no pluck, have no grit, have no guts, have no heart *or* stomach for 601 vb. *be irresolute*; have cold feet 854 vb. *be*

nervous; shrink, funk, shy 620 vb. *avoid*; hide, slink, skulk, sneak; quail, cower, cringe 721 vb. *knuckle under*; show a yellow streak, show the white feather, show fear, turn tail, panic, stampede, scuttle, desert 620 vb. *run away*; show discretion, live to fight another day, lead from behind, keep well to the rear, march bravely in the r. 858 vb. *be cautious*.

Adv. *unbravely*, uncourageously, unheroic-ally, pusillanimously, faintheartedly, funkily, in a blue funk.

See: 163, 524, 601, 603, 620, 717, 721, 853, 854, 858, 874, 877, 918.

857 Rashness

N. *rashness*, lack of caution, incaution, incautiousness, incircumspection, un-wariness, heedlessness 456 n. *inattention*; carelessness, neglect 458 n. *negligence*; imprudence, improvidence, indiscretion 499 n. *folly*; lack of consideration, incon-sideration, irresponsibility, frivolity, flip-pancy, levity, light-mindedness; wildness, indiscipline, haughtiness 738 n. *disobedi-ence*; scorn of the consequences, reckless-ness, foolhardiness, temerity, audacity, presumption, over-confidence, over-dar-ing; hot-headedness, fieriness, impatience 822 n. *excitability*; rushing into things, impetuosity, precipitance, hastiness, over-haste 680 n. *haste*; over-enthusiasm, Quixotry, Quixotism, knight-errantry; dangerous game, playing with fire, brink-manship; desperation, courage of despair 855 n. *courage*; needless risk, blind bar-gain, leap in the dark 661 n. *danger*; too many eggs in one basket, under-insurance. 661 n. *vulnerability*; reckless gamble, last throw 618 n. *gambling*; reckless expendi-ture 815 n. *prodigality*.

desperado, dare-devil, madcap, hothead, Hotspur, fire-eater; brinkman, adventurer, plunger, inveterate gambler 618 n. *gam-bler*; enfant perdu, harum-scarum, scape-grace, ne'er-do-well; one who sticks at nothing, dynamitard; bully, bravo 904 n. *ruffian*.

Adj. *rash*, ill-considered, ill-advised, wild-cat, injudicious, indiscreet, imprudent 499 adj. *unwise*; careless, hit-and-miss, slapdash, free-and-easy, accident-prone 458 adj. *negligent*; unforeseeing, not look-ing, uncircumspect, incautious, unwary,

heedless, thoughtless, inconsiderate, un-calculating 456 adj. *inattentive*; light, frivolous, airy, breezy, flippant, giddy, devil-may-care, harum-scarum, trigger-happy, slap-h. 456 adj. *light-minded*; irresponsible, reckless, regardless, couldn't-care-less, don't-care, damning the consequences, wanton, wild, cavalier; bold, daring, temerarious, audacious; over-daring, over-bold, madcap, daredevil, breakneck, suicidal; overambitious, over-sanguine, over-sure, over-confident 852 adj. *hoping*; overweening, presumptuous, arrogant 878 adj. *insolent*; precipitate, headlong, hell-bent, desperate 680 adj. *hasty*; headstrong 602 adj. *wilful*; un-taught by experience 491 adj. *ignorant*; impatient, hot-blooded, hot-headed, hot-brained, fire-eating, furious 822 adj. *excitable*; danger-loving 855 adj. *unfearing*; venturesome 618 adj. *speculative*; adventurous, risk-taking 672 adj. *enterprising*; thriftless 815 adj. *prodigal*.

Vv. *be rash*,—reckless etc. adj.; lack caution, want judgment, lean on a broken reed; expose oneself, drop one's guard, stick one's neck out; not look round, go bull-headed, charge at, rush at, rush into 680 vb. *hasten*; take a leap in the dark, make a blind bargain, buy a pig in a poke; ignore the consequences, damn the c.; plunge 618 vb. *gamble*; put all one's eggs into one basket, not insure, under-insure; not care 456 vb. *be inattentive*; play fast and loose 634 vb. *waste*; spend to the hilt 815 vb. *be prodigal*; play the fool, play with edged tools, play with fire, burn one's fingers; venture to the brink, stand on the edge of a volcano 661 vb. *face danger*; court disaster, ask for trouble, tempt providence; anticipate, reckon without one's host, count one's chickens before they are hatched, aim too high 695 vb. *stultify oneself*.

Adv. *rashly*, inconsiderately, carelessly, incautiously, lightly, gaily, cheerfully; recklessly, like Gadarene swine.

See: 456, 458, 491, 499, 602, 618, 634, 661, 672, 680, 695, 738, 815, 822, 852, 855, 878, 904.

858 Caution

N. *caution*, cautiousness, wariness, heedfulness, care, heed 457 n. *carefulness*; hesita-tion, doubt, second thoughts 854 n. *nervousness*; instinct of self-preservation 932 n. *selfishness*; looking before one leaps, looking twice, looking round, circumspection; guardedness, 'Deutsche Blick'; secretiveness, reticence 525 n. *secrecy*; calculation, careful reckoning, counting the risk, safety first; nothing left to chance 669 n. *preparation*; delibera-tion, mature consideration 480 n. *judgment*; sobriety, balance, level-headedness 834 n. *seriousness*; prudence, discretion, worldly wisdom 498 n. *wisdom*; insurance, re-i., self-i. 662 n. *safeguard*; foresight 511 n. *prediction*; Fabianism, Fabian policy 823 n. *patience*; going slow, watching one's step, festina lente 278 n. *slowness*; wait-and-see policy 136 n. *delay*.

Adj. *cautious*, cautelous, wary, watchful 455 adj. *attentive*; heedful 457 adj. *careful*; hesitating, doubtful, suspicious 854 n. *nervous*; taking no risks, insured, hedging; guarded, secret, secretive, incommunica-tive 525 adj. *reticent*; experienced, taught by experience, once bitten, twice shy 669 adj. *prepared*; on one's guard, circum-spect, looking round, looking all ways, gingerly, stealthy, feeling one's way, watching one's step, tentative 461 adj. *experimental*; conservative 660 adj. *safe*; responsible 929 adj. *trustworthy*; prudent, prudential, discreet 498 adj. *wise*; non-committal 625 adj. *neutral*; frugal, count-ing the cost 814 adj. *economical*; canny, counting the risk; timid, overcautious, unenterprising, unadventurous, over-insured; slow, unhasty, deliberate, Fabian 823 adj. *patient*; sober, cool-headed, level-h., cool; cold-blooded, calm, self-possessed 823 adj. *inexcitable*.

Vb. *be cautious*, take good care 457 vb. *be careful*; take no risks, play safe, play for safety, play for a draw; ca' canny, go slow 278 vb. *move slowly*; bury, cover up 525 vb. *conceal*; not talk 525 vb. *keep secret*; keep under cover, keep on the safe side, keep in the rear, keep in the back-ground, hide 523 vb. *lurk*; look, look out, see how the land lies 438 vb. *scan*; feel ones way 461 vb. *be tentative*; tread warily, watch one's step, walk Spanish, pussyfoot 525 vb. *be stealthy*; look twice, think t. 455 vb. *be mindful*; calculate, reckon 480 vb. *judge*; count the cost, cut one's coat according to one's cloth 814 vb. *economize*;

know when to stop, take one's time, reculer pour mieux sauter; let well alone, let sleeping dogs lie, keep aloof, keep well out of 620vb. *avoid*; consider the consequences, take heed of the results 511vb. *predict*; take precautions 124vb. *look ahead*; look a gift horse in the mouth 480 vb. *estimate*; assure oneself, make sure, make assurance doubly sure 473vb. *make certain*; cover oneself, insure, take out a policy, re-insure, hedge, over-insure 660 vb. *seek safety*; leave nothing to chance 669vb. *prepare*.

Adv. *cautiously*, with caution, gingerly, conservatively; on prudential considerations.

See: 124, 136, 278, 438, 455, 457, 461, 473, 480, 498, 511, 523, 525, 620, 625, 660, 662, 669, 814, 823, 834, 854, 929, 932.

859 Desire

N. *desire*, wish, will and pleasure 595n. *will*; summons, call, cry 737n. *command*; dun 737n. *demand*; desideration, wanting, want, need, exigency 627n. *requirement*; claim 915n. *dueness*; desiderium, nostalgia, homesickness 830n. *regret*; wistfulness, longing, hankering, yearning, sheep's eyes; wishing, thinking, daydreaming, daydream 513n. *fantasy*; ambition, aspiration 852n. *hope*; horme, appetence, appetition; yen, urge 279n. *impulse*; itch, itching, prurience, cacoethes 378n. *formication*; curiousness, thirst for knowledge, intellectual curiosity 453n. *curiosity*; avidity, eagerness, zeal 597n. *willingness*; passion, ardour, warmth, impetuosity, impatience 822n. *excitability*; rage, fury 503n. *frenzy*; craving, appetite, hunger, thirst, hungry look (see *hunger*); land-hunger, expansionism, irredentism; covetise, covetousness, cupidity, itching palm 816n. *avarice*; graspingness, greediness, greed 786n. *rapacity*; voracity, wolfishness, insatiability 947n. *gluttony*; concupiscence, lust (see *libido*); inordinate desire, incontinence 943n. *intemperance*.

hunger, famine, famished condition, empty stomach 946n. *fasting*; appetite, good a., sharp a., keen a., edge of a.; thirst, thirstiness, drought, drouth 342n. *dryness*; burning thirst, unquenchable t.; dipsomania 949n. *alcoholism*.

liking, fancy, fondness, infatuation 887n. *love*; stomach, appetite, zest; relish, tooth, sweet t. 386n. *taste*; leaning, propensity, trend 179n. *tendency*; weakness, partiality; affinity, mutual a.; sympathy, involvement 775n. *participation*; inclination, mind 617n. *intention*; predilection, favour 605n. *choice*; whim, whimsy 604n. *caprice*; hobby, craze, fad, mania 481n. *bias*; fascination, allurement, attraction, temptation, titillation, seduction 612n. *inducement*.

libido, Eros, life instinct; concupiscence, sexual desire, carnal d., passion, rage, rut, heat, œstrus; ruttishness, mating season; libidinousness, lickerishness, prurience, lust 951n. *impurity*; nymphomania, priapism, satyriasis 84n. *abnormality*; monomania 503n. *mania*.

desired object, one's desire, wish, desire, desirable thing, desideratum 627n. *requirement*; catch, prize, plum 729n. *trophy*; lion, idol, cynosure 890n. *favourite*; forbidden fruit, contraband article, envy, temptation; magnet, lure, draw 291n. *attraction*; aim, goal, star, ambition, aspiration, dream 617n. *objective*; ideal 646n. *perfection*; height of one's ambition, consummation devoutly to be wished.

desirer, coveter, envier; wooer, suer, courter 887n. *lover*; glutton, sucker for; fancier, amateur, dilettante 492n. *collector*; devotee, votary, votarist, votaress, idolater 981n. *worshipper*; well-wisher, favourer, sympathizer 707n. *patron*; wisher, aspirant 852n. *hoper*; claimant, irredentist; candidate, solicitant, parasite 763n. *petitioner*; ambitious person, careerist; wanton 952n. *libertine*.

Adj. *desiring*, desirous, wishing, wishful, tempted, unable to resist; lustful, libidinous, concupiscent, rutting, on heat, ruttish, must, œstrous 951adj. *lecherous*; covetous (see *greedy*); craving, needing, wanting 627adj. *demanding*; missing, nostalgic 830adj. *regretting*; fain, inclined, minded, set upon, bent upon 617 adj. *intending*; ambitious, vaulting 852 adj. *hoping*; aspiring, would-be, wistful, longing, yearning, hankering; unsatisfied, irredentist; curious, solicitous, sedulous, anxious; eager, keen, mad k., burning, ardent, agog, breathless, impatient, dying for; itching, spoiling for; clamant, vocal;

avid, over-eager, over-inclined, mad for, mad after; liking, fond, partial to, with a weakness for.

greedy, acquisitive, possessive 932 adj. *selfish*; ambitious, place-hunting; voracious, omnivorous, open-mouthed 947 adj. *gluttonous*; unsated, unsatisfied, unslaked, quenchless, unquenchable, inappeasable, insatiable, insatiate; rapacious, grasping, griping, retentive 816 adj. *avaracious*; exacting, extortionate 735 adj. *oppressive*.

hungry, esurient, hungering, a-hungered; unfilled, empty, foodless, supperless, dinnerless 946 adj. *fasting*; starving, famished 636 adj. *underfed*; with appetite, ravenous, peckish, sharp-set, hungry as a hunter, pinched with hunger; thirsty, thirsting, athirst, dry, drouthy, parched, parched with thirst.

desired, wanted, liked; likable, desirable, worth having, appetible, enviable; acceptable, welcome; appetizing 826 adj. *pleasurable*; fetching, catchy, attractive, appealing 291 adj. *attracting*; wished, self-sought, invited 597 adj. *voluntary*.

Vb. **desire**, want, desiderate, miss, feel the lack of 627 vb. *require*; ask for, cry out f., clamour f. 737 vb. *demand*; desire the presence of, call, summon, ring for 737 vb. *command*; invite 882 vb. *be hospitable*; wish, make a w., pray; wish otherwise, unwish 830 vb. *regret*; wish for oneself, covet 912 vb. *envy*; promise oneself, have a mind to, ambition, set one's heart on, set one's mind on, have designs on, aim at, have at heart 617 vb. *intend*; plan for, angle f., fish f. 623 vb. *plan*; aspire, raise one's eyes to, dream of, dream, daydream 852 vb. *hope*; want a lot, aim high; look for, expect, think one deserves 915 vb. *claim*; wish in vain, whistle for, cry for the moon 695 vb. *stultify oneself*; wish for another, pray for, intercede, invoke, wish on, call down on; wish ill 889 vb. *curse*; wish one well 897 vb. *be benevolent*; welcome, be glad of, jump at, catch at, grasp at, clutch at 786 vb. *take*; lean 179 vb. *tend*; favour, prefer, select 603 vb. *choose*; crave, itch for, hanker after, long for; long, yearn, pine, languish; pant for, gasp f., burn f., die f., be dying f. 636 vb. *be unsatisfied*; thirst for, hunger f., raven f. (see *be hungry*); can't wait, must have; like, have a liking, affect, have a taste for, care for, care 887 vb. *love*; take to, warm

to, fall in love with, dote, dote on, sigh, burn 887 vb. *be in love*; ogle, make eyes at, make passes, solicit, woo 889 vb. *court*; set one's cap at, make a dead set at, run after, chase 619 vb. *pursue*; lust, lust for, lust after, run mad a. 951 vb. *be impure*; rut, be in rut, be on heat.

be hungry, hunger, famish, starve, have an empty stomach 636 vb. *be unsatisfied*; have a good appetite, gape for, open one's mouth for, water at the mouth, raven 301 vb. *eat*; thirst, be athirst, be dry, be dying for a drink.

cause desire, incline 612 vb. *motivate*; arouse desire, provoke d., fill with longing 887 vb. *excite love*; stimulate 821 vb. *excite*; smell good, whet the appetite, parch, raise a thirst 390 vb. *appetize*; dangle, tease, titillate, tantalize 612 vb. *tempt*; allure, draw, catch, fetch 291 vb. *attract*; hold out hope 852 vb. *give hope*.

Adv. **desirously**, wishfully, wistfully, eagerly, with appetite, hungrily, thirstily, greedily; by request, as desired.

See: 84, 179, 279, 291, 301, 342, 378, 386, 390, 453, 481, 492, 503, 513, 595, 597, 603, 604, 605, 612, 617, 619, 623, 627, 636, 646, 695, 707, 729, 735, 737, 763, 775, 786, 816, 821, 822, 826, 830, 852, 882, 887, 889, 890, 897, 912, 915, 932, 943, 946, 947, 949, 951, 952, 981.

860 Indifference

N. **indifference**, unconcern, uninterest 454 n. *incuriosity*; lack of interest, half-heartedness, want of zeal, lukewarmness, Laodiceanism 598 n. *unwillingness*; coolness, coldness, faint praise, two cheers 823 n. *inexcitability*; unsurprise 865 n. *non-wonder*; desirelessness, lovelessness; mutual indifference, nothing between them; anorexy, inappetency, no appetite, loss of a. 375 n. *insensibility*; inertia, apathy 679 n. *inactivity*; nonchalance, insouciance 458 n. *negligence*; perfunctoriness, carelessness 456 n. *inattention*; don't-care attitude 734 n. *laxity*; recklessness, heedlessness 857 n. *rashness*; promiscuity 464 n. *indiscrimination*; amorality, indifferentism; open mind, impartiality, equity 913 n. *justice*; neutrality 625 n. *mid-course*; nil admirari; six of one and half a dozen of the other; indifferentist, neutralist, neutral 625 n. *moderate*; Laodicean 598 n.

slacker; object of indifference, wall-flower.

Adj. *indifferent*, uncaring, unconcerned, insolicitous; uninterested 454 adj. *incurious*; lukewarm, Laodicean, half-hearted 598 adj. *unwilling*; impersonal, passionless, insensible, phlegmatic 820 adj. *impassive*; unimpressed, unwondering, unsurprised 865 adj. *unastonished*; calm, cool, cold 823 adj. *inexcitable*; nonchalant, insouciant, careless, poco-curante, perfunctory 458 adj. *negligent*; supine, lackadaisical, listless 679 adj. *inactive*; undesirous, unambitious, unaspiring; don't-care, easy-going 734 adj. *lax*; unresponsive, unmoved, unallured, unattracted, untempted; loveless, heart-whole, fancy-free, uninvolved; disenchanted, disillusioned, out of love, cooling off, sitting loose; unswerving 625 adj. *undeviating*; impartial, inflexible 913 adj. *just*; non-committal, moderate 625 adj. *neutral*; promiscuous 464 adj. *indiscriminating*; amoral, cynical.

unwanted, undesired, unwished, uninvited, unbidden, unprovoked; loveless, unvalued, uncared for, unmissed 458 adj. *neglected*; all one to 606 adj. *choiceless*; insipid, tasteless 391 adj. *unsavoury*; unattractive, unalluring, untempting, undesirable; unwelcome 861 adj. *disliked*.

Vb. *be indifferent,*— unconcerned etc. adj.; see nothing wonderful 865 n. *not wonder*; take no interest 456 vb. *be inattentive*; not mind, care little for, damn with faint praise; care nothing for, not care a straw about, have no taste for, have no relish f. 861 vb. *dislike*; couldn't care less, take it or leave it; not think twice about, not care, shrug, shrug off, dismiss, let go, make light of 922 vb. *hold cheap*; not defend, hold no brief for, stand neuter, take neither side 606 vb. *be neutral*; grow indifferent, fall out of love, cool off, sit loose to; not repine, have no regrets; fail to move, leave one cold 820 vb. *make insensitive*.

See: 375, 391, 454, 456, 458, 464, 598, 606, 625, 679, 734, 820, 823, 857, 861, 865, 913, 922.

861 Dislike

N. *dislike*, disinclination, no fancy for, no stomach for; reluctance, backwardness 598 n. *unwillingness*; displeasure 891 n. *resentment*; dissatisfaction 829 n. *discontent*; disagreement 489 n. *dissent*; shyness, aversion 620 n. *avoidance*; instinctive dislike, sudden *or* instant d., antipathy, dyspathy, allergy; distaste, disrelish; repugnance, repulsion, disgust, abomination, abhorrence, detestation, loathing; shuddering, horror, mortal h., rooted h. 854 n. *fear*; xenophobia 854 n. *phobia*; prejudice, sectarian p., odium theologicum 481 n. *bias*; animosity, bad blood, ill-feeling, mutual hatred, common h. 888 n. *hatred*; nausea, queasiness, turn, heaving stomach, vomit 300 n. *voidance*; sickener, one's fill 863 n. *satiety*; gall and wormwood, bitterness 393 adj. *sourness*; object of dislike, not one's type, bête noire, pet aversion, Dr. Fell.

Adj. *disliking*, not liking, displeased 829 adj. *discontented*; undesirous, disinclined, loth 598 adj. *unwilling*; squeamish, qualmish, queasy; allergic, antipathetic, feeling Dr. Fellish; disagreeing 489 adj. *dissenting*; averse, hostile 881 adj. *inimical*; averse, shy 620 adj. *avoiding*; repelled, abhorring, loathing 888 adj. *hating*; unfriendly, un-loverlike, loveless, unsympathetic, out of sympathy; disenchanted, disillusioned, out of love, out of conceit with 860 adj. *indifferent*; sick of 863 adj. *sated*; nauseated, dog-sick 300 adj. *vomiting*.

disliked, unwished, undesired, undesirable 860 adj. *unwanted*; unchosen 607 adj. *rejected*; unpopular, out of favour, avoided; disagreeing, not to one's taste, grating, jarring, unrelished, bitter, uncomforting, unconsoling; repugnant, antipathetic, rebarbative, repulsive 292 adj. *repellent*; revolting, abhorrent, loathsome 888 adj. *hateful*; abominable, disgusting 924 adj. *disapproved*; nauseous, nauseating, sickening, fulsome, foul, stinking 391 adj. *unsavoury*; disagreeable, insufferable 827 adj. *intolerable*; loveless, unloveable, unsympathetic; unlovely 842 adj. *ugly*.

Vb. *dislike*, mislike, disrelish, distaste, find not to one's taste; not care for, have no liking f.; have no stomach for, have no heart for 598 vb. *be loth*; not choose, prefer not to 607 vb. *reject*; object 762 vb. *deprecate*; mind 891 vb. *resent*; take a dislike to, feel an aversion for, have a down on 481 vb. *be biased*; react against

280 vb. *recoil*; feel sick at, want to heave
300 vb. *vomit*; shun, turn away, shrink
from, have no time for 620 vb. *avoid*; look
askance at 924 vb. *disapprove*; turn up
the nose at, sniff at, sneer at 922 vb.
despise; make a face, grimace 893 vb. *be
sullen*; be unable to abide, not endure,
can't stand, detest, loathe, abominate,
abhor 888 vb. *hate*; not like the look of,
shudder at 854 vb. *fear*; unwish, wish
undone 830 vb. *regret*.

cause dislike, disincline, deter 854 vb.
frighten; go against the grain, rub the
wrong way, antagonize, put one's back
up 891 vb. *enrage*; set against, set at odds,
make bad blood 888 vb. *excite hate*;
satiate, pall, pall on, jade 863 vb. *sate*;
disagree with, upset 25 vb. *disagree*; put
off, revolt 292 vb. *repel*; offend, grate, jar
827 vb. *displease*; disgust, stick in one's
gizzard, nauseate, sicken, make one's
gorge rise, turn one's stomach, make one
sick; shock, scandalize, make a scandal
924 vb. *incur blame*.

Adv. *ad nauseam*, disgustingly.

Int. ugh! horrible!

See: 25, 280, 292, 300, 391, 393, 481, 489,
598, 607, 620, 762, 827, 829, 830, 842, 854,
860, 863, 881, 888, 891, 893, 922, 924.

862 Fastidiousness

N. *fastidiousness*, niceness, nicety, daintiness, finicalness, finicality, delicacy; discernment, perspicacity, subtlety 463 n.
discrimination; refinement 846 n. *good
taste*; dilettantism, connoisseurship, epicurism; meticulosity, particularity 457 n.
carefulness; idealism, artistic conscience,
over-developed c. 917 n. *conscience*; perfectionism, fussiness, over-nicety, over-
refinement, hypercriticism, pedantry;
primness, prudishness, Puritanism 950 n.
prudery.

perfectionist, idealist, purist, precisian, fusspot, pedant, hard taskmaster; picker and
chooser, gourmet, epicure.

Adj. *fastidious*, concerned with quality,
quality-minded; nice, mincing, dainty,
delicate, epicurean; perspicacious, discerning 463 n. *discriminating*; particular,
choosy, picksome, finicky, finical; over-
nice, over-particular, scrupulous, meticulous, squeamish, qualmish 455 adj. *atten-

tive; punctilious, conscientious, over-c.;
critical, hypercritical, over-critical, fussy,
pernickety, hard to please, fault-finding,
censorious 924 adj. *disapproving*; pedantic, donnish, precise, rigorous, exacting,
difficult 735 adj. *severe*; prim, prudish,
puritanical 950 adj. *pure*.

Vb. *be fastidious*,—choosy etc. adj.; have
only the best; pick and choose 605 vb.
choose; refine, over-refine, split hairs,
mince matters 475 vb. *argue*; draw distinctions 463 vb. *discriminate*; find fault 924
vb. *dispraise*; fuss, turn up one's nose,
wrinkle one's n., say ugh!; look a gift
horse in the mouth, see spots in the sun;
feel superior, disdain 922 vb. *despise*; keep
oneself to oneself 883 vb. *be unsocial*.

See: 455, 457, 463, 475, 605, 735, 846, 883,
917, 922, 924, 950.

863 Satiety

N. *satiety*, jadedness, fullness, repletion 54 n.
plenitude; over-fulness, plethora, stuffing,
engorgement, saturation, saturation
point 637 n. *redundance*; glut, surfeit, too
much of a good thing 838 n. *tedium*; overdose, excess 637 n. *superfluity*; spoiled
child, enfant gaté.

Adj. *sated*, satiated, satisfied, replete,
saturated, brimming 635 adj. *filled*; sur-
feited, gorged, over-gorged, glutted,
cloyed, sick of; jaded, blasé.

Vb. *sate*, satiate; satisfy, quench, slake 635
vb. *suffice*; fill up, overfill, saturate 54 vb.
fill; soak 341 vb. *drench*; stuff, gorge,
glut, surfeit, cloy, jade, pall; overdose,
overfeed; spoil, kill with kindness, bore,
weary 838 vb. *be tedious*.

See: 54, 341, 635, 637, 838.

864 Wonder

N. *wonder*, state of wonder, wonderment,
marvel, stound; admiration, hero-worship
887 n. *love*; awe, fascination; cry of wonder, gasp of admiration, whistle, wolf-w.,
exclamation, note of e.; shocked silence
399 n. *silence*; open mouth, popping eyes;
shock, surprise, surprisal 508 n. *inexpectation*; astonishment, astoundment, amazement; stupor, stupefaction; bewilderment, bafflement 474 n. *uncertainty*;
consternation 854 n. *fear*.

thaumaturgy, wonder-working, miracle-making, spellbinding, magic 983 n. *sorcery*; wonderful works, thaumatology, teratology, aretalogy; stroke of genius, feat, exploit 676 n. *deed*; transformation scene, coup de théatre 594 n. *dramaturgy*. *prodigy*, portent, sign, eye-opener 511 n. *omen*; something incredible, prodigiosity, phenomenon, miracle, marvel, wonder; drama, sensation, cause célèbre, nine-days' wonder, annus mirabilis; object of wonder *or* admiration, wonderland, fairyland 513 n. *fantasy*; seven wonders of the world; sight, breathtaker 445 n. *spectacle*; gazing-stock 851 n. *laughing-stock*; infant prodigy, calculating boy, genius, man of genius; miracle-worker, thaumaturge, aretalogist 983 n. *sorcerer*; cynosure, lion, hero, wonder man, dream man, Admirable Crichton 646 n. *paragon*; freak, sport, curiosity, oddity, monster, monstrosity 84 n. *rara avis*; puzzle 530 n. *enigma*.

Adj. *wondering*, marvelling, admiring etc. vb.; awed, awe-struck, fascinated, spellbound 818 adj. *impressed*; surprised 508 adj. *inexpectant*; astonished, amazed, astounded; in wonderment, lost in wonder, lost in amazement, unable to believe one's eyes *or* senses; wide-eyed, round-e., pop-e.; open-mouthed, agape, gaping; spellbound, dumb, dumb-struck, inarticulate, speechless, breathless, wordless, left without words, silenced 399 adj. *silent*; bowled over, struck all of a heap, thunderstruck; stupent, stupefied, bewildered 517 adj. *puzzled*; aghast, flabbergasted; shocked, scandalized 924 adj. *disapproving*.

wonderful, to wonder at, wondrous, marvellous, miraculous, monstrous, prodigious, phenomenal; stupendous, fearful 854 adj. *frightening*; admirable 644 adj. *excellent*; record-breaking 644 adj. *best*; striking, overwhelming, awesome, awe-inspiring, breath-taking 821 adj. *impressive*; dramatic, sensational; shocking, scandalizing; rare, exceptional, extraordinary, unprecedented 84 adj. *unusual*; remarkable, noteworthy; strange, passing s., odd, very odd, weird, weird and wonderful, unaccountable, mysterious, enigmatic 517 adj. *puzzling*; outlandish, unheard of 59 adj. *extraneous*; fantastic 513 adj. *imaginary*; impossible, hardly possible, too good *or* bad to be true 472 adj. *improbable*; unbelievable, incredible, inconceivable, unimaginable, indescribable; unutterable, unspeakable, ineffable 517 adj. *inexpressible*; surprising 508 adj. *unexpected*; astounding, amazing, shattering, bewildering etc. vb.; wonder-working, thaumaturgic, aretalogical; magic, like m. 983 adj. *magical*.

Vb. *wonder*, marvel, admire, whistle; hold one's breath, gasp, gasp with admiration; hero-worship 887 vb. *love*; stare, gaze and gaze, goggle at, gawk, open one's eyes, rub one's e., not believe one's e.; gape, open one's mouth, stand in amaze 508 vb. *not expect*; be struck, be overwhelmed, stand in awe 854 vb. *fear*; have no words to express, not know what to say 399 vb. *be silent*.

be wonderful, — marvellous etc. adj.; do wonders, work miracles, achieve marvels; surpass belief, stagger b. 486 vb. *cause doubt*; beggar all description, baffle d., beat everything; spellbind, enchant 983 vb. *bewitch*; dazzle, strike with admiration, turn one's head 887 vb. *excite love*; strike dumb, awe, electrify 821 vb. *impress*; make one's eyes open, take away one's breath, bowl over, stagger; stun, daze, stupefy, petrify, dumbfound, confound, astound, astonish, amaze, flabbergast 508 vb. *surprise*; baffle, bewilder 474 vb. *puzzle*; startle 854 vb. *frighten*; shock, scandalize 924 vb. *incur blame*.

Adv. *wonderfully*, marvellously, remarkably, splendidly, fearfully; strange to say, wonderful to relate, to all men's wonder.

See: 59, 84, 399, 445, 472, 474, 486, 508, 511, 513, 517, 530, 594, 644, 646, 676, 818, 821, 851, 854, 887, 924, 983.

865 Non-wonder

N. *non-wonder*, non-astonishment, un-astonishment, unamazement, unsurprise; awelessness, irreverence, refusal to be impressed, nil admirari; blankness, stony indifference 860 n. *indifference*; quietism, composure, calmness, serenity, tranquillity 266 n. *quietude*; imperturbability, equability, impassiveness, cold blood 820 n. *moral insensibility*; taking for granted 610 n. *habituation*; lack of imagination,

unimaginativeness; disbelief 486 n. *unbelief*; matter of course, just what one thought, nothing to wonder at, nothing in it.

Adj. *unastonished*, unamazed, unsurprised; unawed 855 adj. *unfearing*; accustomed 610 adj. *habituated*; calm, collected, composed; unimpressionable, phlegmatic, impassive 820 adj. *apathetic*; undazzled, undazed, unimpressed, unadmiring, unmoved, unstirred, unaroused 860 adj. *indifferent*; cold-blooded, unimaginative; blind to 439 adj. *blind*; disbelieving 486 adj. *unbelieving*; taking for granted, expecting 507 adj. *expectant*.

unastonishing, unsurprising, foreseen 507 adj. *expected*; customary, common, ordinary, all in the day's work, nothing wonderful 610 adj. *usual*.

Vb. *not wonder*, see nothing remarkable 820 vb. *be insensitive*; be blind and deaf to; not believe 486 vb. *disbelieve*; see through 516 vb. *understand*; treat as a matter of course, take for granted, take as one's due; see it coming 507 vb. *expect*; keep one's head 823 vb. *keep calm*.

Int. no wonder; nothing to it; of course; why not? as expected; quite so.

See: 266, 439, 486, 507, 516, 610, 820, 823, 855, 860.

866 Repute

N. *repute*, good r., high r.; reputation, good r., special r.; report, good r.; title to fame, name, honoured n., great n., good n., fair n., character, known c., good c., high c., reputability, respectability 802 n. *credit*; regard, esteem 920 n. *respect*; opinion, good o., good odour, favour, high f., popular f.; popularity, vogue 848 n. *fashion*; acclaim, applause, approval, stamp of a., cachet 923 n. *approbation*.

prestige, aura, mystique, magic; glamour, dazzle, éclat, lustre, splendour; brilliance, prowess; illustriousness, glory, honour, honour and glory, succès d'estime (see *famousness*); esteem, estimation, account, high a., worship 638 n. *importance*; face, izzat, caste; degree, rank, ranking, standing, footing, status, honorary s., brevet rank 73 n. *serial place*; condition, position, position in society; stardom, pre-cedence 34 n. *superiority*; conspicuousness, prominence, eminence, super-e. 443 n. *visibility*; distinction, greatness, high rank, exaltedness, high mightiness, majesty 868 n. *nobility*; impressiveness, dignity, stateliness, solemnity, grandeur, sublimity, awesomeness; name to conjure with 178 n. *influence*; paramountcy, ascendancy, hegemony, primacy 733 n. *authority*; leadership, acknowledged l. 689 n. *directorship*; prestige consideration, snob value.

famousness, title to fame, celebrity, notability, remarkability; illustriousness, renown, fame, name, note; glory 727 n. *success*; notoriety 687 n. *disrepute*; talk of the town 528 n. *publicity*; place in history, posthumous fame 505 n. *memory*; undying name, immortal n., immortality, deathlessness; remembrance, commemoration, temple of fame, niche in fame's temple.

honours, honour, blaze of glory, cloud of g., crown of g.; crown, martyr's c.; halo, aureole, nimbus, glory; blushing honours, battle h.; laurels, bays, wreath, garland, favour; feather, feather in one's cap 729 n. *trophy*; order, star, garter, ribbon, medal 729 n. *decoration*; spurs, sword, shield, arms 547 n. *heraldry*; an honour, distinction, accolade, award 962 n. *reward*; compliment, praise, flattery, incense; memorial, statue, bust, picture, portrait, niche, plaque, temple, monument 505 n. *reminder*; title of honour, dignity, handle 870 n. *title*; patent of nobility, knighthood, baronetcy, peerage 868 n. *nobility*; academic honour, baccalaureate, doctorate, degree, academic d., honours d., pass d., honorary d., diploma, certificate 870 n. *academic title*; source of honour, fount of h., College of Arms; honours list, birthday honours, roll of honour 87 n. *list*.

dignification, glorification, honorification, lionization; honouring, complimenting; crowning, commemoration, coronation, 876 n. *celebration*; sanctification, dedication, consecration, canonization, beatification; deification, apotheosis; enshrinement, enthronement; promotion, advancement, enhancement, aggrandizement 285 n. *progression*; exaltation 310 n. *elevation*; ennoblement, knighting; rehabilitation 656 n. *restoration*.

person of repute, honoured sir, gentle reader, candid r.; worthy, sound man,

good citizen, loyal subject, pillar, pillar of society, pillar of the church, pillar of the state; man of honour 929n. *gentleman*; knight, peer 868n. *nobleman*; somebody 371n. *person*; great man, big pot, big noise, big wheel, V.I.P. 638n. *bigwig*; man of mark, notable, celebrity, notability, figure, public f.; champion 644 n. *exceller*; lion, star, rising star, rising sun; man of the hour, hero of the day, hero, popular h., pop singer, idol, boast, 890n. *favourite*; cynosure, model, mirror 646n. *paragon*; cream, cream of society 644n. *élite*; choice spirit, master s., leading light 690n. *leader*; grand old man, G.O.M. 500n. *sage*; noble army, great company, bevy, galaxy, constellation 74n. *band.*

Adj. *reputable*, of repute, of reputation, of credit; creditworthy 929adj. *trustworthy*; gentlemanly 929adj. *honourable*; worthy, creditable, meritorious 644adj. *excellent*; respectable, regarded, well-r., well thought of 920adj. *respected*; edifying, moral 933 adj. *virtuous*; in good odour, in favour, in high f. 923adj. *approved*; popular, modish 848adj. *fashionable*; sanctioned, allowed, admitted 756adj. *permitted.*

worshipful, reverend, honourable; admirable 864adj. *wonderful*; heroic 855adj. *courageous*; imposing, dignified, august, stately, grand, sublime 821adj. *impressive*; lofty, high 310adj. *elevated*; high and mighty, mighty 32adj. *great*; lordly, princely, kingly, queenly, majestic, royal, regal 868adj. *noble*; aristocratic, well-born, high-caste, heaven-born; glorious, in glory, full of g., full of honours, honoured, titled, ennobled; time-honoured, ancient, age-old 127adj. *immemorial*; sacrosanct, sacred, holy 979adj. *sanctified*; proud, honorific, dignifying.

noteworthy, notable, remarkable, extraordinary 84adj. *unusual*; fabulous 864 adj. *wonderful*; of mark, of distinction, distinguished, distingué 638adj. *important*; conspicuous, prominent, public, in the eye of 443adj. *well-seen*; eminent, pre-e., super-e., peerless, foremost, in the forefront 34adj. *superior*; ranking, starring, leading, commanding; brilliant, bright, lustrous 417adj. *luminous*; illustrious, splendid, glorious 875adj. *ostentatious.*

renowned, celebrated, sung; of renown, of name, of fame; famous, fabled, famed far-f.; historic, illustrious, great, noble glorious 644adj. *excellent*; notorious 86 adj. *disreputable*; known as, well-known 490adj. *known*; of note, noted (see *noteworthy*); talked of, resounding, in al mouths, on every tongue, in the news 52: adj. *published*; unfading, never-f., ever green, imperishable, deathless, immortal eternal 115adj. *perpetual.*

Vb. *have repute*, be reputed, have a reputa tion, enjoy a r., wear a halo; have a name have a name to lose; rank, stand high have status *or* standing, have a position enjoy consideration, be looked up to have a name for, be praised f. 920vb *command respect*; stand well with, ear golden opinions, do oneself credit, wir honour, win renown, gain prestige, gair a reputation, build a r., earn a name acquire a character, improve one's credi 923vb. *be praised*; win one's spurs, gair the laurels, take one's degree, graduate 727vb. *succeed*; cut a figure, cut a dash, cover oneself with glory 875vb. *be ostentatious*; shine, excel 644vb. *be good*; steal the show, throw into the shade, over-shadow 34vb. *be superior*; have precedence, play first fiddle, take the lead, play the l., star 64vb. *come before*; live in glory, have fame, have a great name, bequeath a n.; make history, live in h., be sure of immortality 505vb. *be remembered.*

seek repute, seek the bubble reputation, thirst for honour, strive for glory, nurse one's ambition; be conscious of one's reputation, consider one's position, mind one's prestige 871vb. *be proud*; wear one's honours, show off, flaunt 871vb. *feel pride*; lord it, queen it, prance, strut 875 vb. *be ostentatious*; brag 877vb. *boast.*

honour, revere, regard, look up to, hold in respect, hold in honour 920vb. *respect*; stand in awe of 854vb. *fear*; bow down to 981vb. *worship*; know how to value, appreciate, prize, value, tender, treasure 887vb. *love*; show honour, pay respect, pay regard, pay one's respects to 920vb. *show respect*; be polite to 884vb. *be courteous*; compliment 925vb. *flatter*; grace with, honour w., dedicate to, inscribe to; praise, sing the praises, glorify, shout for glory, acclaim 923vb. *applaud*; make much of, lionize, chair; credit, give

c., honour for 907vb. *thank*; glorify, immortalize, eternize, commemorate 505 vb. *remember*; celebrate, renown, blazon 528vb. *proclaim*; reflect honour, shed lustre, do credit to, be a credit to.

dignify, glorify, exalt; canonize, beatify, deify, consecrate, dedicate 979vb. *sanctify*; install, enthrone, crown 751vb. *commission*; signalize, mark out, distinguish 547vb. *indicate*; aggrandize, advance, upgrade 285vb. *promote*; honour, delight to h., confer an h.; bemedal, beribbon 844vb. *decorate*; bestow a title, create, elevate, raise to the peerage, ennoble, nobilitate; dub, knight, give the accolade; give one his title, sir, bemadam 561vb. *name*; take a title, take a handle to one's name, accept a knighthood.

See: 32, 34, 73, 74, 84, 87, 115, 127, 178, 285, 310, 371, 417, 443, 490, 500, 505, 528, 547, 561, 638, 644, 646, 656, 678, 689, 690, 727, 729, 733, 751, 756, 802, 821, 844, 848, 854, 855, 864, 867, 868, 870, 871, 875, 876, 877, 884, 887, 890, 907, 920, 923, 925, 929, 933, 962, 979, 981.

867 Disrepute

N. *disrepute*, disreputability, no repute, no reputation, bad r., bad name, bad character, shady reputation, past; disesteem 921n. *disrespect*; notoriety, infamy, ill repute, ill fame; no standing, ingloriousness, obscurity; bad odour, ill favour, bad f., disfavour, discredit, black books, bad light 888n. *odium*; derogation, dishonour, disgrace, shame (see *slur*); ignominy, loss of honour, loss of reputation, faded r., withered laurels, tarnished honour; departed glory, Ichabod; dedecoration, demotion, degradation; debasement, abasement, a long farewell to all one's greatness 872n. *humiliation*; abjectness, baseness, vileness, turpitude 934n. *wickedness*; sense of shame, argumentum ad verecundiam.

slur, reproach 924n. *censure*; imputation, aspersion, reflection, slander, obloquy, opprobrium, abuse 926n. *calumny*; insult 921n. *indignity*; scandal, shocking s., disgrace, shame, burning s., crying s.; defilement, pollution 649n. *uncleanness*; stain, smear 649n. *dirt*; stigma, brand, mark, spot, blot, tarnish, taint 845n. *blemish*; dirty linen; blot on one's scutcheon, badge of infamy, mark of Cain.

object of scorn, scandalous person, reproach, a hissing and a reproach, by-word, by-word of reproach, contempt, discredit 938n. *bad man*; reject, the bottom 645n. *badness*; Cinderella, poor relation 639n. *nonentity*; failure 728n. *loser*.

Adj. *disreputable*, of no repute, of no reputation; characterless, without references; not respectable, disrespectable, shady 930 adj. *rascally*; notorious, infamous, of ill fame, nefarious; arrant 645 adj. *bad*; doubtful, questionable, objectionable 645adj. *not nice*; risqué, ribald, improper, indecent, obscene 951adj. *impure*; not thought much of, held in contempt, despised 922adj. *contemptible*; beggarly, pitiful 639adj. *unimportant*; outcast 607adj. *rejected*; degraded, base, abject, despicable, odious 888adj. *hateful*; mean, cheap, low 847adj. *vulgar*; shabby, squalid, dirty, scruffy 649adj. *unclean*; poor, down at heel, out at elbows 655adj. *dilapidated*; in a bad light, under a cloud, discredited, disgraced, in disgrace (see *inglorious*); reproached, blown upon 924 adj. *disapproved*; unpopular 861adj. *disliked*.

discreditable, no credit to, bringing discredit, reflecting upon one, damaging, compromising; ignoble, unworthy; improper, unbecoming 643adj. *inexpedient*; dishonourable 930adj. *dishonest*; despicable 922adj. *contemptible*; censurable 924adj. *blameworthy*; shameful, shame-making, disgraceful, infamous, unedifying, scandalous, shocking, outrageous, unmentionable, disgusting; too bad 645adj. *not nice*.

degrading, lowering, demeaning, ignominious, opprobrious, humiliating; dedecorous, derogatory, wounding one's honour; beneath one, beneath one's dignity, infra dignitatem, infra dig.

inglorious, without repute, without prestige, without note; without a name, nameless 562adj. *anonymous*; grovelling, unheroic 879adj. *servile*; unaspiring, unambitious 874adj. *modest*; unnoted, unremarked, unnoticed, unmentioned 458adj. *neglected*; renownless, unrenowned, unknown to fame, obscure 491 adj. *unknown*;

unseen, unheard 444 adj. *invisible*; unhymned, unsung, unglorified, unhonoured, undecorated; titleless 869 adj. *plebeian*; deflated, cut down to size, debunked, humiliated 872 adj. *humbled*; sunk low, shorn of glory, faded, withered, tarnished; stripped of reputation, discredited, creditless, disgraced, dishonoured, in eclipse; degraded, demoted, reduced to the ranks.

Vb. *have no repute*, have no reputation, have no character, have no name to lose, have a past; have no credit, rank low, stand low in estimation, have no standing, cut no ice 639 vb. *be unimportant*; be out of favour, be in bad odour, be unpopular, be discredited, be in disgrace, lie under reproach, stink in the nostrils; play second fiddle, take a back seat, stay in the background 35 vb. *be inferior*; blush unseen 444 vb. *be unseen*.

lose repute, fall *or* go out of fashion; fall, sink 309 vb. *descend*; fade, wither; fall into disrepute, incur discredit, incur dishonour, incur disgrace, achieve notoriety 924 vb. *incur blame*; spoil one's record, disgrace oneself, compromise one's name, risk one's reputation, lose one's r., outlive one's r.; tarnish one's glory, forfeit one's honour, lose one's halo; earn no credit, earn no honour, win no glory 728 vb. *fail*; come down in the eyes of, sink in estimation, suffer in reputation, lose prestige, lose face, lose caste; admit defeat, slink away, crawl, crouch 721 vb. *knuckle under*; look silly, look foolish, cut a sorry figure, blush for shame, laugh on the wrong side of one's mouth 497 vb. *be absurd*; be exposed, be brought to book 963 vb. *be punished*.

demean oneself, lower o., degrade o.; derogate, condescend, stoop, marry beneath one; compromise one's dignity, make oneself cheap, cheapen oneself, disgrace o., behave unworthily; sacrifice one's pride, disregard prestige, forfeit self-respect; apologize, excuse oneself 614 *plead*; have no class-feeling, affront one's class; have no pride, feel no shame, think no s.

shame, put to s., hold up to s.; pillory, expose, show up, post; scorn, mock 851 vb. *ridicule*; snub, take down a peg or two 872 vb. *humiliate*; discompose, disconcert, put out of countenance, put one's nose out of joint, deflate, cut down to size, debunk; degrade, downgrade, demote, disrate, reduce to the ranks, disbar, defrock, deprive, strip 963 vb. *punish*; blackball 57 vb. *exclude*; vilify, malign, disparage 926 vb. *defame*; blast one's reputation, take away one's name, ruin one's credit; put in a bad light, reflect upon, breathe u., blow u., taint; sully, blacken, tarnish, stain, blot, besmear, smear, bespatter 649 vb. *make unclean*; debase, defile, desecrate, profane 980 vb. *be impious*; stigmatize, brand, cast a slur upon, fix a stain, tar 547 vb. *mark*; dishonour, disgrace, discredit, involve in shame, bring to s., bring shame upon, scandalize, be a public scandal 924 vb. *incur blame*; heap shame upon, heap dirt u., drag through the mire; trample, tread underfoot, outrage 735 vb. *oppress*; contemn, disdain 922 vb. *despise*; make one blush, outrage one's modesty 951 vb. *debauch*; not spare one's blushes, overpraise.

See: 35, 57, 309, 444, 458, 491, 497, 547, 562, 607, 614, 639, 643, 645, 649, 655, 721, 728, 735, 845, 847, 851, 861, 869, 872, 874, 879, 888, 921, 922, 924, 926, 930, 934, 938, 951, 963, 980.

868 Nobility

N. *nobility*, nobleness, high character 933 n. *virtue*; distinction, quality 644 n. *goodness*; rank, high r., titled r., station, order 27 n. *degree*; royalty, kingliness, queenliness, princeliness, majesty, prerogative 733 n. *authority*; birth, high b., gentle b., gentility, noblesse; descent, high d., noble d., ancestry, long a., line, unbroken l., lineage, pedigree, ancient p. 169 n. *genealogy*; noble family, noble house, ancient h., royal h., dynasty, royal d. 11 n. *family*; blood, blue b., best b.; bloodstock, caste, high c.; badge of rank, patent of nobility, coat of arms, crest, 'boast of heraldry' 547 n. *heraldry*.

aristocracy, patriciate, grandeeship, optimacy; nobility, hereditary n., lesser n., noblesse, ancien régime; lordship, lords, peerage, House of Lords, House of Peers, lords spiritual and temporal; dukedom, earldom, viscounty, baronage, baronetcy; knightage, chivalry; landed interest, squirearchy, squiredom; county

family, gentry, landed g., gentlefolk; the great, great folk, the high and the mighty, notables; noblesse de robe; life peerage.

upper class, the classes, upper classes, upper ten, upper crust, top layer; first families, best people, better sort, chosen few 644 n. *élite*; high society, social register, high life, fashionable world 848 n. *beau monde*; ruling class, the twice-born, the Establishment 733 n. *authority*; high-ups, Olympians; the haves 800 n. *rich man*; salaried class, salariat.

aristocrat, patrician, Olympian; man of caste, Brahmin, Rajput; descendant of the Prophet, sayyid; bloodstock, thoroughbred; optimate, senator, magnifico, magnate, dignitary; don, grandee, caballero, hidalgo; gentleman, gentlewoman, armiger; squire, squireen, buckeen, laird, boglord; Junker; cadet; emperor, king, prince 741 n. *sovereign*; nob, swell, gent, panjandrum, superior person 638 n. *bigwig*.

nobleman, man of rank, titled person, noble, noblewoman, noble lord, lady, atheling, seigneur, signior; lording, lordship, milord; peer, life p.; peer of the realm, peeress; Prince of Wales, duke, grand d., archduke, duchess; marquis, marquess, marquise, marchioness, margrave, margravine, count, countess, contessa; earl, belted e.; viscount, baron, thane, baronet, knight, carpet k., banneret, knight-bachelor, knight-banneret; bashaw, three-tailed b., beg, bey, nawab, begum, emir, khan, sheikh 741 n. *potentate, governor.*

Adj. *noble*, of high character 933 adj. *virtuous*; chivalrous, knightly; gentlemanly, gentlemanlike, ladylike (see *genteel*); majestic, royal, regal, every inch a king; kingly, queenly, princely; ducal, baronial, seigneurial; generous, gentle, of birth, of gentle blood, of family, pedigreed, well-born, high-b., born in the purple; thoroughbred, pur sang, blue-blooded; of rank, ennobled, titled; haughty, high, exalted, high-up, grand 32 adj. *great.*

genteel, patrician, senatorial; aristocratic, Olympian; superior, top-drawer, high-class, upper-c., cabin-c., classy, U, highly respectable, comme il faut; of good breeding 848 adj. *well-bred.*

See: 11, 27, 32, 169, 547, 638, 644, 733, 741, 800, 848, 933.

869 Commonalty

N. *commonalty*, commons, third estate, bourgeoisie; plebs, plebeians; citizenry, demos, democracy, King Mob; people at large, populace, the people, the common p., plain p., common sort; vulgar herd, great unwashed; the many, the many-headed, the multitude, the million, hoi polloi; the masses, mass of society, mass of the people, admass, proletariat, proles; the general, rank and file, rag, tag and bobtail, hoc genus omne, Tom, Dick and Harry, Brown, Jones and Robinson.

rabble, rabblement, mob, mobile vulgus, mobility, horde 74 n. *crowd*; clamjamphrie, rout, rabble r., rascal multitude, varletry; riff-raff, scum, off-scourings, fæx populi, dregs of society, canaille, doggery, cattle, vermin.

lower classes, lower orders, one's inferiors 35 n. *inferior*; common sort, small fry, humble folk; lesser breed, great unwashed; working class, servant c.; steerage, steerage class, lower deck; second-class citizens, the have-nots, the underprivileged; proletariat, proles; sans-culottes, submerged tenth, slum population; down-and-outs, depressed class, outcasts, outcasts of society, poor whites, white trash; beatniks, beat generation; demi-monde, underworld, low company, low life; dunghill, slum 649 n. *sink.*

commoner, bourgeois, plebeian; untitled person, plain Mr.; plain man, mere citizen; one of the people, man of the p., democrat, republican; proletarian, prole; workman; little man, small m., man in the street, everyman, everywoman, common type, average t. 30 n. *common man*; common person, cockney, groundling, galleryite 35 n. *inferior*; back-bencher, private; underling 742 n. *servant*; ranker, upstart, parvenu, mushroom, social climber, arriviste, nouveau riche, Philistine 847 n. *vulgarian*; nobody, nobody one knows, nobody knows who 639 n. *nonentity*; low-caste person, Sudra, outcaste; villein, serf 742 n. *slave.*

countryman, yeoman, rustic, Hodge, swain, gaffer, peasant, tiller of the soil, cultivator 370 n. *husbandman*; serf, villein 742 n. *slave*; boor, chuff, churl, carle, kern, bog-trotter; yokel, hind, chawbacon, cider-squeezer, pot-walloper, clod, clod-hopper, ploughman, hobnail, hob,

clay-eater, rube, hay-seed, hick; bumpkin, country b., put, country p., joskin, Tony Lumpkin, country cousin, provincial, hillbilly; clown, lout, loon, looby 501 n. *fool.*

low fellow, fellow, varlet 938 n. *cad*; guttersnipe, slum-dweller 801 n. *poor man*; mudlark, street-arab, gamin, ragamuffin, tatterdermalion, sansculotte; down-and-out, poor white; tramp, bum, weary Willie, vagabond 268 n. *wanderer*; gaberlunzie, panhandler 763 n. *beggar*; low type, rough t., bully, ugly customer, plug ugly, ruffian, rough, roughneck 904 n. *ruffian*; rascal 938 n. *knave*; Teddy-boy, Teddy-girl, zoot-suiter, hood; criminal, delinquent, juvenile d., felon 904 n. *offender*; barbarian, savage, bushman, Goth, Vandal, Yahoo, primitive 371 n. *mankind.*

Adj. *plebeian*, common, simple, untitled, unennobled, without rank, titleless; ignoble, below the salt; below-stairs, servant-class; lower-deck, rank and file; mean, low, low-down, street-corner 867 adj. *disreputable*; base-born, low-born, low-caste, of low origin, of mean parentage, of mean extraction; slave-born, servile; humble, of low estate, of humble condition 35 adj. *inferior*; second-class, low-class, working-c., non-U, proletarian; homely, homespun 573 adj. *plain*; obscure 867 adj. *inglorious*; coarse, brutish, uncouth, unpolished 847 adj. *ill-bred*; unfashionable, cockney, suburban, provincial; parvenu, risen from the ranks 847 adj. *vulgar*; boorish, churlish, loutish 885 adj. *ungracious.*

barbaric, barbarous, barbarian, wild, savage, brutish; uncivilized, uncultured, without arts, primitive, neolithic 699 adj. *artless.*

See: 30, 35, 74, 268, 370, 371, 501, 573, 639, 649, 699, 742, 763, 801, 847, 867, 885, 904, 938.

870 Title

N. *title*, title to fame, entitlement, claim 915 n. *dueness*; title of honour, courtesy title, honorific, handle, handle to one's name; honour, distinction, order, knighthood 866 n. *honours*; dignified style, plural of dignity, royal we, editorial we 875 n. *formality*; mode of address, Royal Highness, Serene H., Excellency, Grace, Lordship, Ladyship, noble, most n., my lord, my lady, dame; the Honourable, Right Honourable; Reverend, Very R., Right R., Most R., Monsignor; dom, padre, father, mother, brother; your reverence, your honour, your worship; sire, esquire, sir, dear s., madam, ma'am, master, mister, mistress, miss; monsieur, madame, mademoiselle; don, señor, señora, señorita; signore, signora, signorina; Herr, mynheer; huzur, sahib, babu; mem-sahib, mem; shri, sri, srijukta, srimati, musammat; effendi, mirza; citoyen, comrade, tovarich.

academic title, doctor, doctor honoris causa; doctor of philosophy, Ph.D.; doctor of literature, D.Litt.; doctor of divinity, D.D.; doctor of laws, LL.D.; doctor of medicine, M.D.; bachelor of arts, B.A.; bachelor of science, B.Sc., B.S.; master of arts, M.A.; master of science, M.Sc.; bachelor of law, B.L.; bachelor of music, Mus.B., Mus.Doc.; Professor, Professor Emeritus; reader, lecturer; doctorate, baccalaureate.

See: 866, 875, 915.

871 Pride

N. *pride*, proudness, proud heart; just pride, modest p., natural p., innocent p.; respect, self-r., self-confidence; self-admiration, conceit, self-c., swelled head, swank, side, chest 873 n. *vanity*; snobbery 850 n. *affectation*; false pride, touchiness, prickliness 819 n. *moral sensibility*; dignity, reputation 866 n. *prestige*; stateliness, loftiness, high mightiness; condescension, hauteur, haughtiness, unapproachability, disdain 922 n. *contempt*; overweening pride, arrogance, hubris 878 n. *insolence*; swelling pride, pomp, pomposity, grandiosity, show, display 875 n. *ostentation*; self-praise, vainglory 877 n. *boasting*; class-consciousness, race-prejudice 481 n. *prejudice*; object of pride, source of p., boast, joy, pride and j. 890 n. *favourite*; cynosure, pick, flower 646 n. *paragon.*

proud man, vain person, snob, parvenu;

mass of pride, pride incarnate; swelled head, swank, swanker; high-flier, high muckamuck, lord of creation 638n. *bigwig*; fine gentleman, grande dame 848 n. *fop*; turkey cock, cock of the walk, swaggerer, bragger 877n. *boaster*; purseproud plutocrat 800n. *rich man*; classconscious person 868n. *aristocrat.*

Adj. *proud*, elevated, haughty, lofty, sublime 209adj. *high*; plumed, crested 875adj. *showy*; fine, grand 848adj. *fashionable*; grandiose, dignified, stately, statuesque 821adj. *impressive*; majestic, royal, kingly, queenly, lordly, 868adj. *noble*; selfrespecting, self-confident, proud-hearted, high-souled 855adj. *courageous*; highstepping, high-spirited, high-mettled 819 adj. *lively*; stiff-necked 602adj. *obstinate*; mighty, overmighty 32adj. *great*; imperious, commanding 733adj. *authoritative*; high-handed 735adj. *oppressive*; overweening, overbearing, hubristical, arrogant 878adj. *insolent*; brazen, unblushing, unabashed, flaunting, hardened 522adj. *undisguised.*

prideful, full of pride, blown with p., flushed with p., puffed-up, inflated, swelling, swollen; overproud, high and mighty, stuck-up, high-hatted, snobbish; upstage, uppish; on one's dignity, on one's high horse, on stilts; haughty, disdainful, superior, holier than thou, supercilious, patronizing, condescending 922adj. *despising*; stand-offish, distant, unapproachable, stiff, starchy, unbending, undemocratic 885adj. *ungracious*; taking pride, purse-proud, house-p; feeling pride, proud of, bursting with pride, inches taller; strutting, swaggering, vainglorious 877adj. *boastful*; cocky, bumptious, conceited 873adj. *vain*; pretentious 850adj. *affected*; swanky, swanking, pompous 875adj. *showy*; proud as Lucifer, proud as a peacock.

Vb. *be proud*, have one's pride, have one's self-respect, be jealous of one's honour, guard one's reputation, hold one's head high, stand erect, refuse to stoop, not bow, stand on one's dignity, mount one's high horse; rear one's head, toss one's h., hold one's nose in the air, hold it beneath one, be too proud to, be too grand to; be stuck-up, swank, show off, swagger, strut 875vb. *be ostentatious*; condescend, patronize; look down on, disdain 922vb.

despise; display hauteur878vb. *be insolent*; lord it, queen it, come it over, throw one's weight about, overween 735vb. *oppress.*

feel pride, swell with p., take pride in, glory in, boast of, not blush for 877vb. *boast*; hug oneself, congratulate o. 824vb. *be pleased*; be flattered, flatter oneself, pride o., plume o., preen o., think a lot of oneself, think too much of o. 873vb. *be vain.*

See: 32, 209, 481, 522, 602, 638, 646, 733, 735, 800, 819, 821, 824, 848, 850, 855, 866, 868, 873, 875, 877, 878, 885, 890, 922.

872 Humility. Humiliation

N. *humility*, humbleness, humble spirit 874 n. *modesty*; abasement, lowness, lowliness, lowlihood; unpretentiousness, quietness; harmlessness, inoffensiveness 935n. *innocence*; meekness, resignation, submissiveness 721n. *submission*; selfknowledge, self-depreciation, self-abnegation, self-effacement, self-abasement, tapinosis, kenosis 931n. *disinterestedness*; condescension, stooping 884n. *courtesy*; humble person, no boaster, mouse, violet.

humiliation, abasement, humbling, let-down, set-d., climb-d., come-d.; crushing retort; shame, disgrace 867n. *disrepute*; sense of shame, sense of disgrace, blush, suffusion, confusion; chastening thought, mortification, hurt pride, injured p., offended dignity 891n. *resentment.*

Adj. *humble*, unproud, humble-minded, self-depreciatory, poor in spirit, lowly; meek, submissive, resigned, unprotesting 721adj. *submitting*; self-effacing, selfabnegating 931adj. *disinterested*; selfabasing, stooping, condescending 884 adj. *courteous*; mouselike, harmless, inoffensive, unoffending, deprecatory 935 adj. *innocent*; unassuming, unpretentious, without airs 874adj. *modest*; mean, low 639adj. *unimportant*; ignoble 869adj. *plebeian.*

humbled, broken-spirited, bowed down; chastened, crushed, dashed, abashed, crestfallen, chap-fallen, disconcerted, out of countenance 834adj. *dejected*; humiliated, let down, set d., taken d., cut down

to size, squashed, deflated, debunked; not proud of, shamed, blushing 867 adj. *inglorious*; scorned, rebuked 924 adj. *disapproved*; brought low 728 adj. *defeated*.

Vb. *be humble*,—lowly etc. adj.; have no pride, humble oneself 867 vb. *demean oneself*; empty oneself 931 vb. *be disinterested*; condescend, unbend 884 vb. *be courteous*; stoop, bow down, crawl, sing small, eat humble pie 721 vb. *knuckle under*; put up with insolence, turn the other cheek, stomach, pocket 909 vb. *forgive*.

be humbled,—humiliated etc. adj.; receive a snub, be taken down a peg; be ashamed, be ashamed of oneself, feel shame, blush, redden, colour up; feel small, hide one's face, hang one's head, avert one's eyes; stop swanking, come off it.

humiliate, humble, chasten, abash, disconcert; lower, take down a peg, debunk, deflate; make one feel small, make one sing small, teach one his place, make one crawl, rub one's nose in the dirt; snub, crush, squash, sit on 885 vb. *be rude*; mortify, hurt one's pride, offend one's dignity, lower in all men's eyes, put to shame 867 vb. *shame*; score off, make a fool of, make one look silly 542 vb. *befool*; throw in the shade 306 vb. *outdo*; get the better of, triumph over, crow o. 727 vb. *overmaster*; outstare, outfrown, frown down, daunt 854 vb. *frighten*.

See: 306, 542, 639, 721, 727, 728, 834, 854, 867, 869, 874, 884, 885, 891, 909, 924, 931, 935.

873 Vanity

N. *vanity*, emptiness 4 n. *insubstantiality*; vain pride, empty p., idle p. 871 n. *pride*; immodesty, conceit, conceitedness, self-importance; swank, side, chest, swelled head; cockiness, bumptiousness, assurance, self-a.; good opinion of oneself, self-conceit, self-esteem, amour-propre, self-love, self-admiration, narcissism; self-complacency, self-approbation, self-praise, self-applause, self-flattery, self-congratulation, self-glorification, vainglory 877 n. *boasting*; self-sufficiency, self-centredness, egotism 932 n. *selfishness*; blatancy, exhibitionism, showing off,

self-display 875 n. *ostentation*; Vanity Fair 848 n. *beau monde*.

airs, fine a., airs and graces, mannerisms, pretensions, absurd p. 850 n. *affectation*; swank, gaudery 875 n. *ostentation*; coxcombry, priggishness, foppery.

vain person, self-admirer, Narcissus; egotist, only pebble on the beach; self-made man in love with his maker; coxcomb 848 n. *fop*; exhibitionist, peacock, show-off; know-all, pantologist; smarty-boots, cleverstick, Sir Oracle; stuffed shirt, vox et praeterea nihil 4 n. *insubstantial thing*.

Adj. *vain*, conceited, stuck-up, proud 871 n. *prideful*; egotistic, egoistic, self-centred, self-satisfied, self-complacent, full of oneself, self-important 932 adj. *selfish*; self-loving, narcissistic; wise in one's own conceit, dogmatic, opinionated, over-subtle, over-clever, too clever by half 498 adj. *intelligent*; swelled-headed, puffed-up, too big for one's boots, overweening, bumptious, cocky, perky; immodest, blatant; showing off, swaggering, vainglorious, self-glorious 877 adj. *boastful*; pompous 875 adj. *ostentatious*; pretentious, soi-disant, so-called; coxcombical, fantastical 850 adj. *affected*.

Vb. *be vain*,— conceited etc. adj.; have a swelled head, have one's head turned; have a high opinion of oneself, set a high value on o., think well of o., think too much of o., exaggerate one's own merits, blow one's own trumpet 877 vb. *boast*; admire oneself, hug o., flatter o., lay the flattering unction to one's soul; plume oneself, preen o., pride o. 871 vb. *feel pride*; swank, stunt, show off, put on airs, show one's paces, display one's talents, talk for effect, talk big, not hide one's light under a bushel, push oneself forward 875 vb. *be ostentatious*; lap up flattery, fish for compliments; get above oneself, have pretentions, give oneself airs 850 vb. *be affected*; play the fop, dress, dress up, dandify 843 vb. *primp*.

make conceited, fill with conceit, puff up, inflate, give a swelled head to, go to one's head, turn one's h. 925 vb. *flatter*; tempt with vanity, accept one's pretentions, take one at his own valuation.

Adv. *conceitedly*, vainly, vaingloriously, swankily.

See: 4, 498, 843, 848, 850, 871, 875, 877, 925, 932.

874 Modesty

N. *modesty*, lack of ostentation, unboastfulness, shyness, retiring disposition; diffidence, constraint, self-distrust, timidity, timidity 854 n. *nervousness*; mauvaise honte, over-modesty, prudishness 950 n. *prudery*; bashfulness, blushfulness, blushing, blush; pudency, shamefastness, verecundity, shockability; chastity, virtue 950 n. *purity*; deprecation, self-depreciation, self-effacement 872 n. *humility*; unobtrusiveness, unpretentiousness, unassuming nature; demureness, reserve; hidden merit; modest person, shy thing, violet.

Adj. *modest*, unvain, without vanity; self-effacing, unobtrusive, unseen, unheard 872 adj. *humble*; deprecating, deprecatory, unboastful; unpushing, unthrustful, unambitious; quiet, unassuming, unpretentious, unpretending; unimposing, unimpressive, moderate, mediocre 639 adj. *unimportant*; shy, retiring, shrinking, timid, diffident, unselfconfident, unsure of oneself 854 adj. *nervous*; overshy, awkward, constrained, embarrassed, shamefast, inarticulate; bashful, blushful, blushing, rosy; shamefaced, sheepish; reserved, demure, coy; shockable, over-modest, prudish 850 adj. *affected*; chaste 950 adj. *pure*.

Vb. *be modest*, show moderation, ration oneself 942 vb. *be temperate*; not blow one's trumpet, have no ambition, shrink from notoriety; efface oneself, yield precedence 872 vb. *be humble*; play second fiddle, keep in the background, take a back seat, know one's place; blush unseen, shun the limelight, hide one's light under a bushel 456 vb. *escape notice*; not look for praise, do good by stealth and blush to find it fame; retire, shrink, hang back, be coy 620 vb. *avoid*; show bashfulness, feel shame, stand blushing, blush, colour, crimson, mantle 431 vb. *redden*; preserve one's modesty, keep oneself pure, guard one's virtue 933 vb. *be virtuous*.

Adv. *modestly*, quietly, soberly, demurely; unpretentiously, without ceremony, privately, without beat of drum.

See: 431, 456, 620, 639, 850, 854, 872, 933, 942, 950.

875 Ostentation

N. *ostentation*, demonstration, display, parade, show 522 n. *manifestation*; unconcealment, blatancy, flagrancy, shamelessness, brazenness 528 n. *publicity*; ostentatiousness, showiness, magnificence, ideas of m., grandiosity; splendour, brilliance; self-consequence, self-importance 873 n. *vanity*; pomposity, fuss, swagger, showing off, pretension, pretensions, airs and graces 873 n. *airs*; swank, side, chest, strut; bravado, heroics 877 n. *boast*; theatricality, histrionics, dramatization, dramatics, sensationalism 546 n. *exaggeration*; demonstrativeness, back-slapping, bonhomie 882 n. *sociability*; showmanship, effect, window-dressing; solemnity (see *formality*); grandeur, dignity, stateliness, impressiveness; declamation, rhetoric 574 n. *magniloquence*; flourish, flourish of trumpets, fanfaronade, big drum 528 n. *publication*; pageantry, pomp, circumstance, pomp and c., bravery, pride, panache, flying colours, dash, splash, splurge; equipage 844 n. *finery*; frippery, gaudiness, glitter, tinsel 844 n. *ornamentation*; idle pomp, idle show, false glitter, unsubstantial pageant, mummery, mockery, idle m., hollow m., solemn m. 4 n. *insubstantiality*; tomfoolery 497 n. *foolery*; travesty 20 n. *mimicry*; exterior, gloss, veneer, polish, varnish 223 n. *exteriority*; pretence, profession 614 n. *pretext*; insincerity 542 n. *deception*; lip honour, mouth h. 925 n. *flattery*.

formality, state, stateliness, dignity; ceremoniousness, stiffness, starchiness; plural of dignity, royal we, editorial we 870 n. *title*; ceremony, ceremonial 988 n. *ritual*; drill, smartness, spit and polish, bull; correctness, correctitude, protocol, form, good f., right f. 848 n. *etiquette*; punctilio, punctiliousness, preciseness 455 n. *attention*; routine, fixed r. 610 n. *practice*; solemnity, formal occasion, ceremonial o., state o., function, grand f., official f. 876 n. *celebration*; full dress, court d., robes, regalia, finery 228 n. *formal dress*; correct dress 228 n. *uniform*.

pageant, show 522 n. *exhibit*; fête, gala, gala performance, tournament, tattoo; field day, great doings 876 n. *celebration*; son et lumière, mis-en-scène, décor, scenery 445 n. *spectacle*; set piece, tableau, scene, transformation s., stage effect, stage trick

594n. *stage set*; display, bravura, stunt; pyrotechnics 420n. *fireworks*; carnival, Lord Mayor's Show 837n. *festivity*, *revel*; procession, promenade, march past, fly-past; changing the guard, trooping the colour; turn-out, review, grand r., parade, array, muster, wappenshaw 74n. *assembly*.

Adj. *ostentatious*, showy, pompous; aiming at effect, striving for e., done for e.; window-dressing, for show; prestige, for p., for the look of the thing; specious, seeming, hollow 542adj. *spurious*; consequential, self-important; pretentious, would-be 850adj. *affected*; showing off, swanking, swanky 873adj. *vain*; inflated, turgid, orotund, windy, magniloquent, declamatory, high-sounding 574adj. *rhetorical*; grand, highfalutin, splendiferous, splendid, brilliant, magnificent, grandiose; superb, royal 813adj. *liberal*; sumptuous, diamond-studded, luxurious, de luxe, plushy, ritzy, costly, expensive 811adj. *dear*; painted, glorified.

showy, dressy, dressed to kill, foppish 848 adj. *fashionable*; colourful, gaudy, gorgeous 425adj. *florid*; tinsel, garish 847 adj. *vulgar*; flaming, flaring, flaunting, flagrant, blatant, public; brave, dashing, gallant, gay, jaunty; spectacular, scenic, dramatic, histrionic, theatrical, stagy; sensational, daring; exhibitionist, stunting.

formal, dignified, solemn, stately, majestic, grand, fine; ceremonious, standing on ceremony, punctilious, stickling, correct, precise, stiff, starchy; of state, public, official; ceremonial, ritual 988adj. *ritualistic*; for a special occasion 876adj. *celebrative*.

Vb. *be ostentatious*,— showy etc.adj.; keep state, stand on ceremony; cut a dash, make a splash, make a figure; glitter, dazzle 417vb. *shine*; flaunt, sport 228vb. *wear*; dress up 843vb. *primp*; wave, flourish 317vb. *brandish*; blazon, trumpet, beat the big drum 528vb. *proclaim*; make a demonstration, trail one's coat 711vb. *defy*; demonstrate, exhibit 522vb. *show*; act the showman, make a display, put up (*or* on) a show; make the most of, put on a front, window-dress; see to the outside, paper the cracks, polish, veneer 226vb. *coat*; intend for effect, strive for e., sensationalize; talk for effect, shoot a

line 877vb. *boast*; take the centre of the stage, stand in the limelight 455vb. *attract notice*; put oneself forward, advertise oneself, dramatize o.; play to the gallery, fish for compliments; show off, stunt, show one's paces, prance, promenade; parade, march, march past, fly past; strut, swank, put on side 873vb. *be vain*; become a spectacle, make people stare.

See: 4, 20, 74, 223, 226, 228, 317, 417, 420, 425, 445, 455, 497, 522, 528, 542, 546, 574, 594, 610, 614, 711, 811, 813, 837, 843, 844, 847, 848, 850, 870, 873, 876, 877, 882, 925, 988.

876 Celebration

N. *celebration*, performance, solemnization 676n. *action*; commemoration 505n. *remembrance*; observance, solemn o. 988 n. *ritual*; ceremony, function, occasion, do; formal occasion, coronation, enthronement, inauguration, installation, presentation 751n. *commission*; début, coming out 68n. *beginning*; reception, welcome, hero's w., official reception 923 n. *applause*; festive occasion, fête, jubilee, diamond j. 837n. *festivity*; jubilation, cheering, ovation, triumph, salute, salvo, tattoo, roll, roll of drums, fanfare, fanfaronade, flourish of trumpets, flying colours, flag waving, mafficking 835n. *rejoicing*; illuminations 420n. *fireworks*; bonfire 379n. *fire*; triumphal arch 729n. *trophy*; harvest home, thanksgiving, Te Deum 907n. *thanks*; pæan, hosannah, hallelujah 886n. *congratulation*; health, toast.

special day, day to remember, great day, red-letter d., banner d., gala d., flag d., field d.; Saint's day, feast d., fast d. 988n. *holy-day*; Armistice Day, VJ d., VE d., D-Day; Fourth of July, Independence Day, Republic D.; birthday, name-day 141n. *anniversary*; wedding anniversary, silver wedding, golden w., diamond w., ruby w.; centenary, bicentenary, tercentenary, quatercentenary, sesquicentenary.

Adj. *celebrative*, celebrating, signalizing, observing, commemorative 505adj. *remembering*; occasional, anniversary, centennial, bicentennial, millennial 141 adj. *seasonal*; festive, jubilant, mafficking

835 adj. *rejoicing*; triumphant, triumphal; welcoming, honorific 886 adj. *gratulatory*.

Vb. *celebrate*, solemnize, perform 676 vb. *do*; hallow, keep holy, keep sacred 979 vb. *sanctify*; commemorate 505 vb. *remember*; honour, observe, keep, keep up, maintain; signalize, make an occasion, mark the o., mark with a red letter 547 vb. *mark*; make much of, welcome, kill the fatted calf, roast an ox whole 882 vb. *be hospitable*; do honour to, fête; chair, carry shoulder-high 310 vb. *elevate*; mob, rush 61 vb. *rampage*; garland, wreathe, crown 962 vb. *reward*; lionize, give a hero's welcome, fling wide the gates, roll out the red carpet, hang out the flags, beat a tattoo, blow the trumpets, clash the cymbals, fire a salute, fire a salvo, fire a feu de joie 884 vb. *pay respects*; cheer, jubilate, triumph, maffick 835 n. *rejoice*; make holiday 837 vb. *revel*; instate, present, inaugurate, install, induct 751 vb. *commission*; make one's début, come out 68 vb. *begin*.

toast, pledge, clink glasses; drink to, raise one's glass to, fill one's glass to, drain a bumper, drink a health 301 vb. *drink*.

Adv. *in honour of*, in memory of, in celebration of, on the occasion of; for the honour of, as an occasion, to make the o.

See: 61, 68, 141, 301, 310, 379, 420, 505, 547, 676, 729, 751, 835, 837, 882, 884, 886, 907, 923, 962, 979, 988.

877 Boasting

N. *boasting*, bragging, braggery, boastfulness, vainglory, gasconism, braggadocio, braggartism; jactitation, jactation, venditation 875 n. *ostentation*; self-glorification, self-glory, self-advertisement, swagger, swank, bounce 873 n. *vanity*; advertisement 528 n. *publicity*; puffery 482 n. *overestimation*; grandiloquence, teratology, rodomontade, vapouring, gassing 515 n. *empty talk*; heroics, bravado; chauvinism, jingoism, spread-eagleism 481 n. *bias*; defensiveness, blustering, bluster 854 n. *nervousness*; sabre-rattling, intimidation 900 n. *threat*.

boast, brag, vaunt, crack; puff 528 n. *advertisement*; shout, gasconade, flourish, fanfaronade, bravado, bombast, rant, rodomontade, highfalutin, tall talk 546

n. *exaggeration*; gab, hot air, gas, bunkum, much cry and little wool 515 n. *empty talk*; bluff, bounce 542 n. *deception*; vain defiance, presumptuous challenge 711 n. *defiance*; big talk, big drum, bluster, idle threat 900 n. *threat*.

boaster, vaunter, braggart, braggadocio; brag, big mouth, shouter, prater; blusterer, charlatan, pretencer 545 n. *impostor* bouncer, bluffer 545 n. *liar*; swank 873 n. *vain person*; gasconader, Gascon, Thraso, miles gloriosus, Pistol, Hector; advertiser, puffer 528 n. *publicizer*; flourisher, fanfaron, trumpeter; ranter, hot air merchant; jingoist, chauvinist; sabre-rattler, intimidator.

Adj. *boastful*, boasting, bragging, vaunting, big-mouthed; braggart, swaggering, vainglorious, self-glorious 873 adj. *vain*; bellicose, sabre-rattling, jingo, jingoistic, chauvinistic 718 adj. *warlike*; bluffing, hollow, pretentious, empty 542 adj. *spurious*; bombastic, magniloquent, grandiloquent 546 adj. *exaggerated*; flushed, exultant, triumphant, cock-a-hoop 727 adj. *successful*.

Vb. *boast*, brag, vaunt, gab, talk big, shoot one's mouth, shoot a line, bluff, bluster, shout; bid defiance 711 vb. *defy*; vapour, prate, gas 515 vb. *mean nothing*; enlarge, magnify 546 vb. *exaggerate*; trumpet, jactitate, venditate, show off 528 vb. *publish*; puff, crack up, cry one's wares 528 vb. *advertise*; sell oneself, advertise o., blow one's trumpet, bang the big drum 875 vb. *be ostentatious*; flourish, wave 317 vb. *brandish*; play the jingo, make the eagle scream, rattle the sabre 900 vb. *threaten*; show off, strut, swagger, prance, swank, throw out one's chest 873 vb. *be vain*; gloat, pat oneself on the back, hug oneself 824 vb. *be pleased*; boast of, plume oneself 871 vb. *be proud*; glory, crow over 727 vb. *triumph*; jubilate, exult 835 vb. *rejoice*.

See: 317, 481, 482, 515, 528, 542, 545, 546, 711, 718, 727, 824, 835, 854, 871, 873, 875, 900.

878 Insolence

N. *insolence*, hubris, arrogance, haughtiness, loftiness, overbearing 871 n. *pride*; domineering, tyranny 735 n. *severity*; high tone

711 n. *defiance*; bluster 900 n. *threat*; disdain 922 n. *contempt*; sneer, sneering 926 n. *detraction*; contumely, contumelious behaviour 899 n. *scurrility*; assurance, self-a., self-assertion, bumptiousness, cockiness, brashness; presumption 916 n. *arrogation*; audacity, hardihood, boldness, effrontery; shamelessness, brazenness, blatancy, flagrancy; face, front, hardened f., face of brass.

sauciness, disrespect, impertinence, impudence; pertness, malapertness; flippancy, nerve, brass, cheek, cool c., calm c.; lip, sauce, snook, snooks; taunt, personality, insult, affront 921 n. *indignity*; rudeness, incivility 885 n. *discourtesy*; petulance, defiance, answer, provocation, answering back, backtalk, backchat 460 n. *rejoinder*; raillery, banter 851 n. *ridicule*.

insolent person, sauce-box, malapert, impertinent, jackanapes; minx, hussy; pup, puppy; upstart, beggar on horseback, Jack-in-office, tin god; blusterer, swaggerer, braggart 877 n. *boaster*; bantam-cock, cockalorum; bully, Mohawk, Mohock, sons of Belial, hoodlum, roisterer, swashbuckler, fire-eater, desperado 904 n. *ruffian*; brazen-face, monument of brass.

Adj. *insolent*, bellicose 718 adj. *warlike*; high-toned 711 adj. *defiant*; sneering 926 adj. *detracting*; insulting, contumelious 921 adj. *disrespectful*; injurious, scurrilous 899 adj. *maledicent*; lofty, supercilious, disdainful, contemptuous 922 adj. *despising*; undemocratic, snobbish, haughty, snorty, snotty, up-stage, high-hat, high and mighty 871 n. *proud*; hubristic, arrogant, presumptuous, assuming; brash, bumptious, bouncing 873 adj. *vain*; flagrant, blatant; shameless, dead to shame, unblushing, unabashed, brazen, brazen-faced; bold, hardy, audacious 857 adj. *rash*; overweening, domineering, imperious, magisterial, lordly, dictatorial, arbitrary, high-handed, harsh, outrageous, tyrannical 735 adj. *oppressive*; blustering, bullying, fire-eating, ruffianly 877 adj. *boastful*.

impertinent, pert, malapert, forward; impudent, saucy, cheeky, brassy, cool, jaunty, cocky, flippant; cavalier, off-hand, familiar, over-f., free-and-easy, breezy, airy 921 adj. *disrespectful*; impolite, rude, uncivil, ill-mannered 885 adj. *discourteous*;

defiant, answering back, provocative, deliberately p., offensive; personal, ridiculing 851 adj. *derisive*.

Vb. *be insolent*, — arrogant etc. adj.; forget one's manners 885 vb. *be rude*; have a nerve, cheek, sauce, give lip, taunt, provoke 891 vb. *enrage*; retort, answer back 460 vb. *answer*; shout down 479 vb. *confute*; not know one's place, presume, arrogate, assume, take on oneself, make bold, make free with; put on airs, hold one's nose in the air, look one up and down 871 vb. *be proud*; look down on, sneer at 922 vb. *despise*; banter, rally 851 vb. *ridicule*; express contempt, snort; cock a snook, put one's tongue out, send to blazes 711 vb. *defy*; outstare, outlook, outface, brazen it out, brave it o.; take a high tone, lord it, queen it, lord it over; hector, bully, browbeat, trample on, ride rough-shod over, treat with a high hand, outrage 735 vb. *oppress*; swank, swagger, swell, look big 873 vb. *be vain*; brag, talk big 877 vb. *boast*; brook no control, own no law, be a law to oneself 738 vb. *disobey*; defy the lightning, exhibit hubris, tempt providence.

Adv. *insolently*, impertinently, pertly; arrogantly, hubristically, outrageously.

See: 460, 479, 711, 718, 735, 738, 851, 857, 871, 873, 877, 885, 891, 899, 900, 904, 916, 921, 922, 926.

879 Servility

N. *servility*, slavishness, abject spirit, no pride, lack of self-respect 856 n. *cowardice*; subservience 721 n. *submission*; submissiveness, obsequiousness, compliance, pliancy 739 n. *obedience*; time-serving 603 n. *tergiversation*; abasement 872 n. *humility*; prostration, prosternation, genuflexion, stooping, stoop, bent back, bow, scrape, duck, bob 311 n. *obeisance*; truckling, cringing, crawling, fawning, toadyism, sycophancy, ingratiation 925 n. *flattery*; flunkeyism 745 n. *service*; servile condition, slavery 745 n. *servitude*.

toady, toad, toad-eater, pickthank, yes-man 488 n. *assenter*; lickspittle, bootlicker, backscratcher, groveller, spaniel, fawner, courtier, fortune-hunter, tuft-h., lion-h. 925 n. *flatterer*; sycophant, parasite, leech, sponger, sponge, smell-feast, beggar;

jackal, hanger-on, led-captain, cavaliere servente, gigolo 742 n. *dependant*; flunkey 742 n. *retainer*; born slave, slave; tool, cat's-paw 628 n. *instrument*.

Adj. *servile*, not free, dependent 745 adj. *subject*; slavish 856 adj. *cowardly*; mean-spirited, mean, abject, base, tame 745 adj. *subjected*; subservient, submissive 721 adj. *submitting*; pliant, compliant, supple 739 adj. *obedient*; time-serving 603 adj. *tergiversating*; bowed, stooping, prostrate, grovelling, truckling, bowing, scraping, cringing, crawling, sneaking, fawning; begging, whining; toadying, sycophantic, parasitical; obsequious, soapy, oily, slimy, over-civil, over-attentive, ingratiating 925 adj. *flattering*.

Vb. *be servile*, forfeit one's self-respect, stoop to anything 867 vb. *demean oneself*; squirm, roll, sneak, cringe, crouch, creep, crawl, grovel, truckle, kiss the hands of, kiss the hem of one's garment, lick the boots of 721 vb. *knuckle under*; bow, scrape, bend, bob, duck, kowtow, make obeisance, kneel 311 vb. *stoop*; make up to, toady, spaniel, fawn, ingratiate oneself, pay court to, curry favour, worm oneself into f. 925 vb. *flatter*; squire, attend, dance attendance on, fetch and carry for, jackal for 742 vb. *serve*; comply 739 vb. *obey*; be the tool of, do one's dirty work, pander to, stooge for 628 vb. *be instrumental*; whine, beg for favours, beg for crumbs 761 vb. *beg*; play the parasite, batten on, sponge, sponge on, hang on; jump on the band wagon, run with the hare and hunt with the hounds 83 vb. *conform*; serve the times 603 vb. *tergiversate*.

Adv. *servilely*, slavishly, with servility, with a bow and a scrape, cap in hand, touching one's forelock.

See: 83, 311, 488, 603, 628, 721, 739, 742, 745, 761, 856, 867, 872, 925.

880 Friendship

N. *friendship*, bonds of f., amity 710 n. *concord*; compatibility, mateyness, chuminess; friendly relations, relations of friendship, intercourse, friendly i., social i., hobnobbing 882 n. *sociality*; alignment, fellowship, comradeship, sodality, freemasonry, brotherhood, sisterhood 706 n. *association*; solidarity, support, mutual s. 706 n. *co-operation*; acquaintanceship, acquaintance, mutual a., familiarity, intimacy 490 n. *knowledge*; fast friendship, close f., warm f., cordial f., passionate f., honeymoon 887 n. *love*; making friends, getting acquainted, introduction, recommendation, commendation; overture, rapprochement 289 n. *approach*; renewal of friendship, reconciliation 719 n. *pacification*.

friendliness, amicability, kindliness, kindness 884 n. *courtesy*; heartiness, cordiality, warmth 897 n. *benevolence*; fraternization, camaraderie, mateyness; hospitality 882 n. *sociability*; greeting, welcome, open arms, handclasp, handshake, hug, rubbing noses 884 n. *courteous act*; regard, mutual r. 920 n. *respect*; goodwill, mutual g.; fellow-feeling, sympathy, response 775 n. *participation*; understanding, friendly u., good u., entente, entente cordiale, honeymoon 710 n. *concord*; partiality 481 n. *prejudice*; favouritism, partisanship 914 n. *injustice*; support, loyal s. 703 n. *aid*.

friend, girl-f., boy-f. 887 n. *loved one*; one's friends and acquaintance, acquaintance, intimate a.; lifelong friend, common f., friend's f.; gossip, crony, old c. (see *chum*); neighbour, good n., fellow-townsman, fellow-countryman; cater-cousin, clansman 11 n. *kinsman*; well-wisher, favourer, partisan, backer 707 n. *patron*; proxenus 660 n. *protector*; fellow, brother, confrère, partner, associate 707 n. *colleague*; ally, brother-in-arms 707 n. *auxiliary*; collaborator, helper, friend in need 703 n. *aider*; invitee, guest, welcome g., frequent visitor, persona grata; guest-friend, protegé; host, kind h. 882 n. *social person*; former friend, fair-weather f. 603 n. *tergiversator*.

close friend, best f., next f., near f.; best man, groomsman 894 n. *bridesman*; dear friend, good f., warm f., close f., fast f., firm f., loyal f.; intimate, bosom friend, friend of one's bosom, confidant, fidus Achates; alter ego, other self, shadow; comrade, companion, boon c., pot c.; good friends all, happy family; mutual friends, inseparables, band of brothers, Three Musketeers, David and Jonathan, Pylades and Orestes, Damon and Pythias, Nisus and Euryalus, Castor and Pollux, Heavenly Twins, par nobile fratrum;

two minds with but a single thought, Arcades ambo, birds of a feather.

chum, gossip, crony; pal, mate, amigo, bully, bully-boy, buddy, bunkie, butty, sidekick; fellow, comrade, shipmate, messmate, room-mate, stable-companion 707 n. *colleague*; playmate, classmate, schoolmate, schoolfellow; pen-friend, pen-pal; hearties, my h.

xenophile, Anglophile, Francophile, Russophile, Sinophile, friend of all the world 901 n. *philanthropist*.

Adj. *friendly*, non-hostile, amicable, well-affected, devoted 887 adj. *loving*; loyal, faithful, staunch, fast, firm, tested, tried 929 adj. *trustworthy*; fraternal, brotherly, sisterly, cousinly; natural, unstrained, easy, harmonious 710 adj. *concordant*; compatible, sympathetic, understanding; well-wishing, well-meaning, well-intentioned, philanthropic 897 adj. *benevolent*; hearty, cordial, warm, welcoming, hospitable 882 adj. *sociable*; effusive, demonstrative, back-slapping, hail-fellow-well-met; comradely, chummy, pally, matey; friendly with, well w., good friends w., at home w.; acquainted 490 adj. *knowing*; free and easy, on familiar terms, on visiting t., on intimate t., on the best of t.; intimate, inseparable, thick, thick as thieves, hand in glove.

Vb. *be friendly*, be friends with, pull on with, get on well w., enjoy friendship w., live on terms of amity w.; have neighbourly relations, hold communication with, have dealings w.; fraternize, hobnob, keep company with, keep up w., keep in w., go about together, be inseparable 882 vb. *be sociable*; have friends, have a wide circle of friends, have many friendships, have a large acquaintance; shake hands, clasp h., strike h., throw oneself into the arms of, embrace 884 vb. *greet*; welcome, entertain 882 vb. *be hospitable*; sympathize 516 vb. *understand*; like, warm to, cotton on to 887 vb. *love*; mean well, have the best intentions, have the friendliest feelings 897 vb. *be benevolent*.

befriend, acknowledge, know, accept one's friendship; take up, favour, protect 703 vb. *patronize*; overcome hostility, gain one's friendship; strike an acquaintance, scrape an a., knit friendship; break the ice, make overtures 289 vb. *approach*; seek one's friendship, pay one's addresses to 889 n. *court*; take to, warm to, cotton on to, fraternize with, frat, hobnob, get pally with, get chummy w., chum up w.; make acquainted, make known to each other, introduce, commend, recommend; renew friendship, become reconciled, shake hands 719 vb. *make peace*.

Adv. *amicably*, friendly-like; as friends, arm in arm; heartily, cordially.

See: 11, 289, 481, 490, 516, 603, 660, 703, 706, 707, 710, 719, 775, 882, 884, 887, 889, 894, 897, 901, 914, 920, 929.

881 Enmity

N. *enmity*, inimicality, hostility, antagonism 704 n. *opposition*; no love lost, unfriendliness, incompatibility, antipathy 861 n. *dislike*; loathing 888 n. *hatred*; animosity, animus, spite, grudge, ill-feeling, ill-will, intolerance, persecution 898 n. *malevolence*; jealousy 912 n. *envy*; coolness, coldness 380 n. *ice*; estrangement, alienation, strain, tension, no honeymoon 709 n. *dissension*; bitterness, bitter feelings, hard f., rancour, soreness 891 n. *resentment*; unfaithfulness, disloyalty 738 n. *disobedience*; breach, open b., breach of friendship 709 n. *quarrel*; hostile act 709 n. *casus belli*; conflict, hostilities, state of war 718 n. *belligerency*; vendetta, feud.

enemy, no friend, bad f., unfriend; ex-friend 603 n. *tergiversator*; back friend, traitor, viper in one's bosom 663 n. *troublemaker*; unquiet neighbour, ill-wisher; antagonist, opposite side, other s. 705 n. *opponent*; competitor, rival 716 n. *contender*; open enemy, foe, foeman, hostile, armed enemy 722 n. *combatant*; national enemy, Amalekite; general enemy, public e., outlaw, pirate 789 n. *robber*; particular enemy, declared e., sworn e., bitter e., confirmed e., irreconcilable e., archenemy; misanthropist, misogynist, misogamist 902 n. *misanthrope*; xenophobe, Anglophobe, Francophobe, negrophobe, anti-semite 481 n. *narrow mind*; persona non grata, pet aversion, bête noire, Dr. Fell 888 n. *hateful object*; aggressor 712 n. *attacker*; secret enemy, Trojan Horse.

Adj. *inimical*, unfriendly, not well-inclined, disaffected; disloyal, unfaithful 738 adj. *disobedient*; distant 883 adj. *unsociable*;

cool, chilly, frigid, icy 380 adj. *cold*; antipathetic, incompatible, unsympathetic 861 n. *disliking*; loathing 888 adj. *hating*; hostile, conflicting, actively opposed 704 adj. *opposing*; antagonized, estranged, alienated, unreconciled, irreconcilable; bitter, embittered, rancorous 891 adj. *resentful*; jealous, grudging 912 adj. *envious*; spiteful 898 adj. *malevolent*; bad friends with, on bad terms, not on speaking t.; at feud, at enmity, at variance, at daggers drawn 709 adj. *quarrelling*; aggressive, militant, at war with, belligerent 718 adj. *warring*; intolerant, persecuting 735 adj. *oppressive*; dangerous, venomous, deadly, fell 659 adj. *baneful*.

Vb. *be inimical*,—unfriendly etc. adj.; show hostility, harden one's heart, bear ill-will, bear malice 898 vb. *be malevolent*; grudge 912 vb. *envy*; hound, persecute 735 vb. *oppress*; chase, hunt down 619 vb. *hunt*; battle 916 vb. *fight*; war, make w. 718 vb. *wage war*; take offence, take umbrage 891 vb. *resent*; fall out, come to blows 709 vb. *quarrel*; be incompatible, conflict, collide, clash 14 vb. *be contrary*; withstand 704 vb. *oppose*.

make enemies, be unpopular, have no friends 883 vb. *be unsocial*; get across, cause offence, antagonize, irritate 891 vb. *enrage*; estrange, alienate, make bad blood, set at odds 709 vb. *make quarrels*; exacerbate 832 vb. *aggravate*.

See: 14, 380, 481, 603, 619, 659, 663, 704, 705, 709, 712, 716, 718, 722, 735, 738, 789, 832, 861, 883, 888, 891, 898, 902, 912, 916.

882 Sociality

N. *sociality*, membership, membership of society, intercommunity, consociation 706 n. *association*; making one of, being one of; clubbism, esprit de corps; fellowship, consortship, comradeship, companionship, society; camaraderie, fraternization, fratting, hobnobbing; intercourse, social i., familiarity, intimacy 880 n. *friendship*; social circle, home c., family c., one's friends and acquaintance 880 n. *friend*; social ambition, social climbing; society, claims of society, social demands, the world.

sociability, social activity, group a.; social adjustment, compatibility 83 n. *conform-*

ity; sociableness, gregariousness, sociable disposition, sociable inclination, fondness for company 880 n. *friendliness*; social success, popularity; social tact, common touch; social graces, savoir vivre, good manners, easy m. 884 n. *courtesy*; urbanity 846 n. *good taste*; ability to mix, clubbability; affability, conversability 584 n. *interlocution*; acceptability, welcome, kind w., hearty w., warm w., reception, fair r., smiling r.; greeting, glad hand, handshake, handclasp, embrace 884 n. *courteous act*; hospitality, home from home, open house, Liberty Hall, pot luck 813 n. *liberality*; good company, good fellowship, geniality, cordiality, heartiness, back-slapping, bonhomie; conviviality, joviality, jollity, merrymaking 824 n. *enjoyment*; gaiety 837 n. *revel*; cheer, good c. 301 n. *food*; eating and drinking, social board, festive b., groaning b., loving cup 301 n. *feasting*.

social gathering, forgathering, meeting 74 n. *assembly*; reunion, social r., get-together, conversazione, social, squash, reception, salon, drawing-room; at home, soirée, levee; entertainment 837 n. *amusement*; sing-song, smoking concert; symposium, party, hen-p., stag-p., mixed p., partie carrée, tête-a-tête; housewarming, house party, week-end p., birthday p., coming out p.; social meal, feast, banquet 301 n. *feasting*; communion, love-feast, agape 988 n. *ritual act*; elevenses, tea-party, dish of tea, five-o'clock, drinks, cocktail party, dinner p., supper p., bump supper, barbecue, bottle party, Dutch p. 837 n. *festivity*; dance, ball, hop, thé dansant 837 n. *dancing*.

social round, social activities, social whirl, season, social s., social entertainment; calling list, round of visits; leaving one's card, seeing one's friends, visiting, calling, dropping in; week-ending, stay, visit, formal v., call, courtesy c.; visiting terms, frequentation, haunting 880 n. *friendship*; social demand, engagement, dating, dating up, trysting, rendezvous, assignation, date, blind d.; meeting place, trysting place, club 76 n. *focus*.

social person, active member, keen m.; caller, visitor, dropper-in, frequenter, habitué; convivial person, bon vivant, good fellow, charming f.; good mixer, good company, life and soul of the party;

social success, catch, lion 890 n. *favourite*; jolly fellow, boon companion, hobnobber, clubman, club woman; Rotarian, good neighbour 880 n. *friend*; hostess, host, good h.; guest, welcome g., one of the family; diner-out, parasite, gate-crasher; socialite, ornament of society, social climber 848 n. *beau monde*.

Adj. *sociable*, gregarious, social, sociably disposed, fond of company, party-minded, good at a party; companionable, fraternizable, affable, conversable, chatty, gossipy, fond of talk, ready for a chat; clubbable, clubby; cosy, folksy; neighbourly, matey, pally 880 adj. *friendly*; hospitable, welcoming, smiling, cordial, warm, hearty, back-slapping, hail-fellow-well-met; convivial, festive, Christmassy, jolly, jovial 833 adj. *gay*; lively, witty 837 adj. *amusing*; urbane 884 adj. *courteous*; easy, free-and-easy, easy-mannered; unbuttoned, post-prandial, after-dinner 683 adj. *reposeful*.

welcomed, fêted, entertained; welcome, ever-w., quite one of the family; popular, liked, sought-after, socially successful, invited, getting around, first on the invitation list.

Vb. *be sociable*,—gregarious etc. adj.; enjoy society, like company, love a party; have friends, like one's f., make friends easily, hobnob, fraternize, mix with, glad-hand, back-slap 880 vb. *be friendly*; mix well, be a good mixer, get around, know how to live, mix in society, go out, dine o., go to parties, accept invitations, cadge i., gate-crash; have fun, beat it up 837 vb. *amuse oneself*; join in, get together, make it a party, club together, go Dutch, share, go shares 775 vb. *participate*; take pot luck, eat off the same platter 301 vb. *eat*; join in a bottle, crack a b. 301 vb. *drink*; pledge 876 vb. *toast*; carouse 837 vb. *revel*; make oneself welcome, make oneself at home, make one of the family; relax, unbend 683 vb. *repose*; make engagements, date, date up; make friends, seek acquaintance, scrape a. 880 vb. *befriend*; introduce oneself, exchange cards; extend one's friendships, enlarge one's acquaintance; keep up with, keep in w., write to 588 n. *correspond*.

visit, see people, go visiting, go for a visit, pay a v., guest with, sojourn, stay, weekend; keep up with, keep in w., see one's friends; go and see, look one up, call, wait on, drop a card, leave a c.; call at, look in, drop in; exchange visits, be on visiting terms; winter, summer.

be hospitable, keep open house 813 vb. *be liberal*; invite, have, be at home, receive; welcome, make w., bid one w., welcome with open arms, hug, embrace 884 vb. *greet*; act the host, do the honours, preside; do proud, kill the fatted calf 876 vb. *celebrate*; send invitations, have company, entertain, regale 301 vb. *feed*; give a party, throw a p. 837 vb. *revel*; accept, cater for, provide entertainment 633 vb. *provide*.

Adv. *sociably*, hospitably, in friendly fashion, like friends, en famille; arm in arm, hand in hand.

See: 74, 76, 83, 301, 584, 588, 633, 683, 706, 775, 813, 824, 833, 837, 846, 848, 876, 880, 884, 890, 988.

883 Unsociability. Seclusion

N. *unsociability*, unsociableness, unsocial habits, shyness 620 n. *avoidance*; refusal to mix, keeping one's own company, keeping oneself to oneself; home-life, domesticity; singleness 895 n. *celibacy*; inhospitality 816 n. *parsimony*; stand-offishness, unapproachability, distance, aloofness, lonely pride 871 n. *pride*; unfriendliness, coolness, coldness, moroseness, savageness 893 n. *sullenness*; cut, dead c., cut direct 885 n. *discourtesy*; silence, inconversability 582 n. *taciturnity*; ostracism, boycott 57 n. *exclusion*; blacklist, blackball 607 n. *rejection*.

seclusion, privacy, private world, world on its own; island universe 321 n. *star*; peace and quiet 266 n. *quietude*; home life, domesticity; loneliness, solitariness, solitude; retirement, withdrawal; hiddenness, delitescence 523 n. *latency*; confinement, purdah 525 n. *concealment*; isolation, splendid i. 744 n. *independence*; division, estrangement 46 n. *separation*; renunciation 621 n. *relinquishment*; renunciation of the world 985 n. *monasticism*; anchoritism, stylitism; self-exile, expatriation; sequestration, segregation, rustication, excommunication, quarantine, deportation, banishment, exile 57 n. *exclusion*; reserve, reservation, ghetto,

native quarter; gaol 748 n. *prison*; sequestered nook, god-forsaken hole, back of beyond; island, desert; hide-out 527 n. *hiding-place*; den, study, sanctum, cloister, cell, hermitage, pillar 192 n. *retreat*; ivory tower, private quarters, shell; backwater.

solitary, unsocial person, iceberg; lone wolf, rogue elephant; isolationist, island; recluse, stay-at-home; ruralist, troglodyte, cave-dweller, cenobite, anchorite, hermit, eremite, desert-dweller; stylite, pillar-monk, Simeon Stylites, Diogenes and his tub; maroon, castaway 779 n. *derelict*; Robinson Crusoe, Alexander Selkirk.

outcaste, outcast, pariah, leper, outsider; expatriate, alien 59 n. *foreigner*; exile, expellee, deportee, evacuee, refugee, displaced person, homeless p., stateless p.; proscribed person, outlaw, bandit; Ishmael, vagabond 268 n. *wanderer*; waif, stray, orphan 779 n. *derelict*; reject, flotsam and jetsam 641 n. *rubbish*.

Adj. *unsociable*, unsocial, antisocial, morose, not fit to live with; unassimilated, foreign 59 adj. *extraneous*; unclubbable, stay-at-home, home-keeping, quiet, domestic; inhospitable, unwelcoming, forbidding, hostile, savage; distant, aloof, unbending, stiff; stand-offish, offish, haughty 871 adj. *prideful*; unwelcoming, frosty, icy, cold 893 adj. *sullen*; unforthcoming, in one's shell; unaffable, inconversable, silent 582 adj. *taciturn*; cool, impersonal 860 adj. *indifferent*; solitary, lonely, lone 88 adj. *alone*; shy, afraid of company, avoiding society 620 adj. *avoiding*; wild, ferine; celibate, unmarried 895 adj. *unwedded*; anchoretic, eremetic, retiring, the world forgetting, by the world forgot.

friendless, unfriended, lorn, forlorn, desolate, god-forsaken; lonely, lonesome, solitary; on one's own, without company 88 adj. *alone*; cold-shouldered, uninvited, without introductions; unpopular, avoided 860 adj. *unwanted*; blacklisted, blackballed, ostracized, boycotted, sent to Coventry 57 adj. *excluded*; expelled, disbarred, deported, exiled; under embargo, banned 757 adj. *prohibited*.

secluded, private, sequestered, retired, hidden, buried, tucked away 523 adj. *latent*; veiled, behind the veil, behind the purdah 421 adj. *screened*; quiet, lonely, isolated, enisled; avoided, god-forsaken, unvisited, unexplored, unseen, unfamiliar, off the beaten track 491 adj. *unknown*; uninhabited, deserted, desert, desolate, vacant 190 adj. *empty*.

Vb. *be unsocial*, keep one's own company, keep oneself to oneself, shun company, see no one, talk to nobody; go it alone, play a lone hand; keep out, stay o., stew in one's own juice; stay in one's shell, shut oneself up, remain private, maintain one's privacy, stand aloof 620 vb. *avoid*; stay at home, cultivate one's garden, bury oneself, vegetate 266 vb. *be quiescent*; retire, go into retirement, give up one's friends, leave the world, take the veil; live secluded, live in purdah.

make unwelcome, frown on 924 vb. *disapprove*; repel, keep at arm's length, make one keep his distance, look cool; not acknowledge, ignore, cut, cut dead 885 vb. *be rude*; cold-shoulder, turn one's back on, shut the door on; turn out, turf o., cast o., expel 300 vb. *eject*; ostracize, boycott, send to Coventry, blacklist, blackball 57 vb. *exclude*; have no time for, refuse to meet, refuse to mix with, refuse to associate w., have nothing to do with, treat as a leper, treat as an outsider 620 vb. *avoid*; excommunicate, banish, outlaw, ban 963 vb. *punish*.

seclude, sequester, island, isolate, quarantine; keep in private, keep in purdah; confine, shut up 747 vb. *imprison*.

See: 46, 57, 59, 88, 190, 192, 266, 268, 300, 321, 421, 491, 523, 525, 527, 582, 607, 620, 621, 641, 744, 747, 748, 757, 779, 816, 860, 871, 885, 893, 895, 924, 963, 985.

884 Courtesy

N. *courtesy*, chivalry, knightliness, gallantry; deference 920 n. *respect*; consideration, condescension 872 n. *humility*; graciousness, politeness, civility, manners, good m., noble m., good behaviour, best b.; good breeding, gentle b., gentlemanliness, gentility 846 n. *good taste*; courtliness, correctness, correctitude 875 n. *formality*; comity, amenity, amiability, sweetness, niceness, obligingness, kindness, kindliness 897 n. *benevolence*; gentleness, mansuetude, mildness 736 n. *lenity*; easy temper, good humour, complacency 734 n. *laxity*; agreeableness, affability, suavity, blandness, common touch,

social tact 882n. *sociability*; soft tongue, smooth address 925n. *flattery*.

courteous act, act of courtesy, polite act, graceful gesture, courtesy, civility, favour, charity, kindness, complaisance 897n. *kind act*; compliment 886n. *congratulation*; kind words, fair w., sweet w. 889n. *endearment*; introduction, presentation 880n. *friendliness*; welcome, polite w., reception, invitation; acknowledgment, recognition, mark of r., salutation, salute, greeting, affectionate g., welcoming gesture, smile, kiss, hug, squeeze, handclasp, handshake 920n. *respects*; capping, salaam, namaskar, kowtow, bow, nod 311n. *obeisance*; terms of courtesy, respects, regards, kind r., best r., duty, devoir, remembrances, love, best l.; love and kisses, farewell 296n. *valediction*.

Adj. *courteous*, chivalrous, knightly, generous 868adj. *noble*; courtly, gallant, old-world, correct 875adj. *formal*; polite, civil, urbane, gentlemanlike, dignified, well-mannered, fine-m. 848adj. *well-bred*; gracious, condescending 872adj. *humble*; deferential, mannerly 920adj. *respectful*; on one's best behaviour, anxious to please 455adj. *attentive*; obliging, complaisant, kind 897adj. *benevolent*; conciliatory, sweet 719adj. *pacificatory*; agreeable, suave, bland, smooth, ingratiating, well-spoken, fair-s., honey-tongued 925adj. *flattering*; obsequious 879adj. *servile*.

amiable, nice, sweet, winning 887adj. *lovable*; affable, conversable, friendly 882adj. *sociable*; considerate, kind 897adj. *benevolent*; inoffensive, harmless 935adj. *innocent*; gentle, easy, mild 736adj. *lenient*; good-tempered, sweet-t., unruffled 823adj. *inexcitable*; well-behaved, good 739adj. *obedient*; pacific, peaceable 717adj. *peaceful*.

Vb. *be courteous*, be on one's best behaviour, mind one's manners, display good m.; show courtesy, treat with politeness, treat with deference 920vb. *respect*; give one his title, sir, bemadam; oblige, put oneself out 703vb. *aid*; condescend 872vb. *be humble*; notice, have time for 455vb. *be attentive*; conciliate, speak fair 719vb. *pacify*; preserve one's manners, be all things to all men; take no offence, take in good part 823vb. *be patient*; become courteous, mend one's manners, express regrets 941vb. *atone*.

pay respects, give one's regards, send one's r., pay one's devoirs, offer one's duty; send one's compliments, do one the honour; pay compliments 925vb. *flatter*; drink to, pledge 876vb. *toast*; homage, pay h., show one's respect, kneel, kiss hands 920vb. *show respect*; honour, crown, wreathe, garland, chair, give a hero's welcome 876n. *celebrate*.

greet, send greetings (see *pay respects*); flag, speak 547vb. *signal*; accost, sidle up 289vb. *approach*; acknowledge, recognize, hold out one's hand 455vb. *notice*; shout one's greeting, hail 408vb. *vociferate*; wave, smile, kiss one's fingers, blow a kiss; say hallo, bid good morning 583vb. *speak to*; salute, make salutation, raise one's hat, uncap, uncover; cap, touch one's hat, tip *or* tilt one's h., pull one's forelock; bend, bow, bob, duck, curtsy, salaam, make obeisance, kiss hands, prostrate oneself, kowtow 311vb. *stoop*; shake hands, clasp h., shake the hand, press *or* squeeze *or* wring *or* pump the hand; advance to meet 920vb. *show respect*; escort 89vb. *accompany*; make a salute, fire a s., present arms, parade, turn out; welcome, welcome in, welcome home 882vb. *be sociable*; welcome with open arms 824vb. *be pleased*; open one's arms, embrace, hug, kiss 889vb. *caress*; usher, usher in, present, introduce 299vb. *admit*.

Adv. *courteously*, politely, with respect, with all due deference; condescendingly, graciously.

See: 89, 289, 296, 299, 311, 408, 455, 547, 583, 703, 717, 719, 734, 736, 739, 823, 824, 846, 848, 868, 872, 875, 876, 879, 880, 882, 886, 887, 889, 897, 920, 925, 935, 941.

885 Discourtesy

N. *discourtesy*, impoliteness, bad manners, ill m., beastly m., sheer bad m., shocking bad m.; no manners, mannerlessness, failure of courtesy, want of chivalry, lack of politeness, lack of manners, scant courtesy, incivility, inurbanity; uncouthness, boorishness 847n. *ill-breeding*; unpleasantness, nastiness, beastliness; misbehaviour, misconduct, unbecoming conduct; tactlessness, inconsiderateness, want of consideration.

rudeness, ungraciousness, gruffness, bluntness, bluffness; sharpness, tartness, acerbity, acrimony, asperity; ungentleness, roughness, harshness 735 n. *severity*; offhandedness 456 n. *inattention*; brusquerie, shortness, short answer, plain a. 569 n. *conciseness*; sarcasm 851 n. *ridicule*; excessive frankness, disregard of circumlocution, unparliamentary language, bad l., bad words, rude w., virulence 899 n. *scurrility*; rebuff, insult 921 n. *indignity*; personality, impertinence, procacity, pertness, sauce, lip, cheek, truculence 878 n. *insolence*; impatience, interruption, shouting 822 n. *excitability*; black look, sour l., scowl, frown 893 n. *sullenness*; a discourtesy, act of d., piece of bad manners.

rude person, no true knight, no gentleman; savage, barbarian, brute, lout, boor; mannerless imp, unlicked cub 878 n. *insolent person*; curmudgeon, crabstick, bear; crosspatch, groucher, grouser, sulker 829 n. *malcontent*.

Adj. *discourteous*, unknightly, ungallant, unchivalrous; uncourtly, unceremonious, ungentlemanly, inurbane, impolite, uncivil, rude; mannerless, unmannerly, illmannered, bad-m., boorish, loutish, uncouth, brutish, beastly, savage, barbarian 847 adj. *ill-bred*; insolent, impudent; cheeky, saucy, pert, forward 878 adj. *impertinent*; unpleasant, disagreeable; cool, not anxious to please, unaccommodating, uncomplaisant 860 adj. *indifferent*; off-handed, cavalier, airy, breezy, tactless, inconsiderate 456 adj. *inattentive*.

ungracious, unsmiling, grim 834 adj. *serious*; gruff, grunting, growling, bearish 893 adj. *sullen*; peevish, testy 892 adj. *irascible*; difficult, surly, churlish, unfriendly, unneighbourly 883 adj. *unsociable*; grousing, grumbling, swearing 829 adj. *discontented*; ungentle, rough, rugged, harsh, brutal 735 adj. *severe*; bluff, free, frank, over-f., blunt, over-b., scant of courtesy; brusque, short 569 adj. *concise*; tart, sharp, biting, acrimonious 388 adj. *pungent*; sarcastic, uncomplimentary, unflattering 926 adj. *detracting*; foul-mouthed, foul-spoken, abusive, vituperative, cursing 899 adj. *maledicent*; contumelious, offensive, injurious, insulting, truculent 921 adj. *disrespectful*.

Vb. *be rude*,—mannerless etc. adj.; want manners, have no m., flout etiquette; know no better 699 vb. *be artless*; scant one's courtesy, display bad manners, show discourtesy 878 vb. *be insolent*; have no time for 456 vb. *be inattentive*; treat rudely, be beastly to, snub, turn one's back on, cold-shoulder, cut, ignore, cut dead 883 vb. *make unwelcome*; show one the door 300 vb. *eject*; cause offence, ruffle one's feelings 891 vb. *huff*; treat with contumely, insult 921 vb. *not respect*; take liberties, make free with, make bold; stare, ogle 438 vb. *gaze*; make one blush 867 vb. *shame*; lose one's temper, shout, interrupt 891 vb. *get angry*; curse, swear, damn 899 vb. *cuss*; snarl, growl, frown, scowl, lower, pout, sulk, refuse to say 'thank you' 893 vb. *be sullen*.

Adv. *impolitely*, discourteously, like a boor, like an ill-mannered fellow.

See: 300, 388, 438, 456, 569, 699, 735, 822, 829, 834, 847, 851, 860, 867, 878, 883, 891, 892, 893, 899, 921, 926.

886 Congratulation

N. *congratulation*, felicitation, gratulation, congratulations, felicitations, compliments, best c., compliments of the season; good wishes, best w., happy returns; salute, toast; welcome, hero's w., official reception 876 n. *celebration*; thanks 907 n. *gratitude*.

Adj. *gratulatory*, congratulatory, complimentary; honorific, triumphal, welcoming 876 adj. *celebrative*.

Vb. *gratulate*, give Heaven thanks for 907 vb. *thank*; congratulate, felicitate, compliment; offer one's congratulations, wish one joy, give one joy, wish many happy returns, wish a merry Christmas; send one's congratulations, send one's compliments 884 vb. *pay respects*; sanction a triumph, vote an ovation, accord an o., give one a hero's welcome, give three cheers, clap 923 vb. *applaud*; fête, mob, rush, lionize 876 vb. *celebrate*; congratulate oneself, hug o., thank one's stars 824 vb. *be pleased*.

See: 824, 876, 884, 907, 923.

887 Love

N. *love*, affection, friendship, charity, Eros; agapism; true love, real thing; natural

affection, parental a., maternal a., mother-love, protective l., protectiveness 931 n. *disinterestedness*; possessive love, possessiveness 911 n. *jealousy*; conjugal love, uxoriousness; sentiment 818 n. *feeling*; kindness, tenderness 897 n. *benevolence*; mutual love, mutual affection, mutual attraction, compatibility, sympathy, fellow-feeling, understanding; fondness, liking, predilection, inclination 179 n. *tendency*; dilection 605 n. *choice*; fancy 604 n. *caprice*; attachment, sentimental a., firm a.; devotion, loyal d., patriotism 739 n. *loyalty*; sentimentality, susceptibility, amorousness 819 n. *moral sensibility*; power of love, fascination, enchantment, bewitchment 983 n. *sorcery*; lovesickness, Cupid's sting, yearning, longing 859 n. *desire*; amativeness, amorism, eroticism, prurience, lust 859 n. *libido*; regard 920 n. *respect*; admiration, hero-worship 864 n. *wonder*; dawn of love, first l., calf l., puppy l., young l.; crush, pash, infatuation; madness 503 n. *insanity*; worship 982 n. *idolatry*; passion, tender p., fire of love, flames of l., enthusiasm, rapture, ecstasy, transport, transports of love 822 n. *excitable state*; erotomania, abnormal affection 84 n. *abnormality*; love psychology, narcissism, Oedipus complex, Electra c.; love-hate, odi et amo.

lovableness, amiability, attractiveness, popularity, gift of pleasing; winsomeness, charm, fascination, appeal, sex-a., attractions, charms, beauties; winning ways, pleasing qualities, endearing q.; coquetry, flirtatiousness; sentimental value.

love affair, romantic a., affair of the heart, affaire de cœur; romance, love and the world well lost; flirtation, amour, amourette, entanglement; loves, amours; liaison intrigue, seduction, adultery 951 n. *illicit love*; falling in love, soft impeachment, something between them; course of love, the old old story; betrothal, engagement, espousal, wedding bells 894 n. *marriage*; broken engagement, broken romance, broken heart.

love-making, flirting, coquetting, honeying, spooning, poodlefaking, billing and cooing 889 n. *endearment*; courtship, courting, walking out, sighing, suing, pressing one's suit, laying siege 889 n. *wooing*; pursuit of love, hoping for conquests, flirting, coquetry, philandering; gallantry,

dalliance, dallying, toying, chambering, chambering and wantonness, libertinage 951 n. *unchastity*; bestowal of love, favours.

love-nest, abode of love, bower, Bower of Bliss; honeymoon cottage, bridal suite, nuptial chamber, bridal bed; women's quarters, gynæceum, zenana, harem, seraglio.

lover, love, true l., sweetheart; young man, boy, boy-friend, Romeo; swain, beau, gallant, spark, squire, escort, date; steady, fiancé; wooer, courter, suitor, follower, captive, admirer, hero-worshipper, adorer, votary, worshipper; aficionado, fan, devoted following, fan-mail; sugar-daddy, dotard; cicisbeo, cavaliere servente, squire of dames, ladies' man, lady-killer, gay seducer, Lothario, Don Juan; paramour, amorist 952 n. *libertine*; flirt, coquette, philanderer; gold-digger, vampire, vamp.

loved one, beloved object, beloved, love 890 n. *darling*; friend, dear head; favoured suitor, lucky man, intended, betrothed, affianced, fiancé, fiancée, bride-to-be 894 n. *spouse*; conquest, inamorata, lady-love, flame, girl-friend, girl, best g., sweetheart, darling, goddess; bird, babe, dear; idol, hero; heart-throb, dream man, dream girl; Amorette, Dulcinea, Amaryllis, Dowsabel; favourite, mistress, leman, concubine 952 n. *kept woman*; dangerous woman, femme fatale.

lovers, pair of lovers, loving couple, engaged c., turtle-doves, love-birds; Daphnis and Chloe, Strephon and Chloe; Benedick and Beatrice, Aucassin and Nicolette, Pierrot and Pierrette, Harlequin and Columbine; star-crossed lovers, tragic l., Pyramus and Thisbe, Romeo and Juliet, Hero and Leander, Leila and Majnun, Tristan and Isolde, Lancelot and Guinevere, Paris and Helen, Troilus and Cressida; historic lovers, Héloïse and Abélard, Dante and Beatrice, Petrarch and Laura, Antony and Cleopatra.

love god, goddess of love, Venus, Aphrodite, Astarte, Freya; Amor, Eros, Kama, Cupid, blind boy; cupidon, amoretto.

love emblem, myrtle, turtle-dove; Cupid's bow, Cupid's arrow, Cupid's dart; pierced heart, bleeding h., broken h. 889 n. *love-token*.

Adj. *loving*, agapistic; attached, loyal, patriotic 931 adj. *disinterested*; wooing,

courting, making love, honeying 889 adj. *caressing*; affectionate, cuddlesome, demonstrative; tender, motherly, wifely, conjugal; loverlike, gallant, sentimental, lovesick; mooning, moping, love-lorn, languishing 834 adj. *dejected*; fond, uxorious, doting; possessive 911 adj. *jealous*; admiring, adoring, devoted, enslaved (see *enamoured*); flirtatious, coquettish 604 adj. *capricious*; amatory, amorous, amative, ardent, passionate 818 adj. *fervent*; liking, desirous 859 adj. *desiring*; lustful, concupiscent, priapic, libidinous 951 adj. *lecherous*.

enamoured, in love, fallen in l., falling in l., inclined to, sweet on, keen on, set on, stuck on, gone on, sold on; struck with, taken w., smitten, bitten, caught, hooked; charmed, enchanted, fascinated 983 adj. *bewitched*; mad on, infatuated, besotted, dippy, crazy, crazy about, wild a. 503 adj. *crazed*; happily in love, blissfully in l. 824 adj. *happy*; rapturous, ecstatic 821 adj. *excited*.

lovable, desirable, likeable, congenial, sympathetic, to one's mind, to one's taste, to one's fancy, after one's heart 859 adj. *desired*; lovesome, winsome, loveworthy 884 adj. *amiable*; sweet, angelic, divine, adorable; lovely, graceful 841 adj. *beautiful*; interesting, intriguing, attractive, seductive, alluring 291 adj. *attracting*; prepossessing, appealing, engaging, winning, endearing, captivating, irresistible; charming, enchanting, bewitching 983 adj. *sorcerous*; liked, beloved, endeared to, dear, darling, pet, fancy, favourite.

erotic, aphrodisiac, erotogenic; amatory, amatorious, amatorial.

Vb. *love*, like, care, rather care for, quite love, take pleasure in, affect, be partial to, take an interest in; sympathize with, feel w., have a kindness for, be fond of; be susceptible, have a heart, have a warm h.; bear love, hold in affection, hold dear, care for, tender, cherish, cling to, embrace; appreciate, value, prize, treasure, think the world of, regard, admire, revere 920 vb. *respect*; adore, worship, idolize, make the god of one's idolatry 982 vb. *idolatrize*; live for, live only f.; burn with love, be on fire with passion (see *be in love*); make love, poodlefake, honey, bestow one's favours; make much of, spoil, pet, fondle, drool over, slobber o. 889 vb. *caress*.

be in love, burn, sweat, faint, die of *or* for love 361 vb. *die*; burn with love, glow with ardour, flame with passion, love to distraction, dote 503 vb. *be insane*; take a fancy to, cotton on to, take to, warm to, look sweet on, look with passion on 859 vb. *desire*; form an attachment, fall for, fall in love, get infatuated, get stuck on; go mad about 503 vb. *go mad*; set one's heart on, lose one's heart, bestow one's affections; declare one's love, admit the soft impeachment; offer one's heart to, woo, sue, sigh, press one's suit, make one's addresses 889 vb. *court*; set one's cap at, chase 619 vb. *pursue*; enjoy one's favours; honeymoon 894 vb. *wed*.

excite love, arouse desire 859 vb. *cause desire*; warm, inflame 381 vb. *heat*; rouse, stir, flutter, enrapture, enthral 821 vb. *excite*; dazzle, bedazzle, charm, enchant, fascinate 983 vb. *bewitch*; allure, draw 291 vb. *attract*; make oneself attractive 843 vb. *primp*; lure, bait, tantalize, seduce 612 vb. *tempt*; lead on, flirt, coquette, philander, break hearts; toy, vamp 889 vb. *caress*; smile, leer, make eyes, ogle, wink 889 vb. *court*; catch one's eye 455 vb. *attract notice*; enamour, take one's fancy, steal one's heart, gain one's affections, engage the a.; make a hit, bowl over, sweep off one's feet, turn one's head, infatuate, craze, madden 503 vb. *make mad*; make a conquest, captivate 745 vb. *subjugate*; catch, lead to the altar 894 vb. *wed*; endear, endear oneself, ingratiate o., insinuate o., wind oneself into the affections; be loved, be amiable, be lovable, make oneself a favourite, become a f., be the rage; steal every heart, set all hearts on fire, have a place in every heart; curry favour 925 vb. *flatter*.

Adv. *affectionately*, kindly, lovingly, tenderly 457 vb. *carefully*; fondly, dotingly, madly.

See: 84, 179, 291, 361, 381, 455, 457, 503, 604, 605, 612, 619, 739, 745, 818, 819, 821, 822, 824, 834, 841, 843, 859, 864, 884, 889, 890, 894, 897, 911, 920, 925, 931, 951, 952, 982, 983.

888 Hatred

N. *hatred*, hate, no love lost; love-hate, odi et amo; revulsion of feeling, disillusion;

aversion, dyspathy, antipathy, allergy, nausea 861n. *dislike*; intense dislike, repugnance, detestation, loathing, abhorrence, abomination; disfavour, displeasure (see *odium*); disaffection, estrangement, alienation 709n. *dissension*; hostility, antagonism 881n. *enmity*; animosity, ill-feeling, bad blood, bitterness, acrimony, rancour 891n. *resentment*; malice, ill-will, evil eye, spite, grudge, ancient g. 898n. *malevolence*; jealousy 912n. *envy*; wrath, vials of w. 891n. *anger*; execration, hymn of hate 899n. *malediction*; scowl, snap, snarl, baring one's fangs 893n. *sullenness*; phobia, xenophobia, Anglophobia, anti-semitism, racialism, racism, Aryanism, colour prejudice 481n. *prejudice*.

odium, disfavour, unpopularity 924n. *disapprobation*; discredit, black books 867n. *disrepute*; bad odour, malodour; odiousness, hatefulness, loathsomeness, beastliness, obnoxiousness; despicability, contemptibility 922n. *despisedness*.

hateful object, unwelcome necessity, bitter pill; abomination, filth; one's hate 881n. *enemy*; not one's type, one's aversion, pet a., bête noire, Dr. Fell, nobody's darling; pest, menace, good riddance 659 n. *bane*; outsider 938n. *cad*; heretic, blackleg, scab 603n. *tergiversator*.

Adj. *hating*, loathing, envying etc.vb.; loveless; antipathetic, revolted, disgusted 861adj. *disliking*; set against 704adj. *opposing*; averse, abhorrent, antagonistic, hostile, antagonized, snarling 881adj. *inimical*; envious, spiteful, spleenful, malicious, full of malice, malignant, fell 898adj. *malevolent*; bitter, rancorous 891 adj. *resentful*; full of hate, implacable; vindictive 910adj. *revengeful*; virulent, execrative 899n. *maledicent*; out of love, disillusioned 509adj. *disappointed*.

hateful, odious, unlovable, unloved; invidious, antagonizing, obnoxious, pestilential 659adj. *baneful*; beastly, nasty, horrid 645adj. *not nice*; abhorrent, loathsome, abominable; accursed, execrable, execrated 899adj. *cursed*; offensive, repulsive, repellent, nauseous, nauseating, revolting, disgusting 861adj. *disliked*; bitter, sharp 393adj. *sour*; unwelcome 860adj. *unwanted*.

hated, loathed etc.vb.; uncared for 458adj. *neglected*; out of favour, unpopular 861

adj. *disliked*; in one's bad books, discredited 924adj. *disapproved*; loveless, unloved, Dr. Fellish; unvalued, unmissed, unregretted, unlamented, unmourned, undeplored, unwept; unchosen, refused, spurned, condemned, jilted, love-lorn, crossed in love 607adj. *rejected*.

Vb. *hate*, bear hatred, have no love for, loathe, abominate, detest, abhor, hold in horror; turn away from, shrink f. 620vb. *avoid*; revolt from, recoil at 280vb. *recoil*; disrelish 861vb. *dislike*; find loathsome, find obnoxious; not choose, refuse 607vb. *reject*; spurn, contemn 922vb. *despise*; execrate, hold accursed, denounce 899vb. *curse*; bear malice 898vb. *be malevolent*; feel envy 912vb. *envy*; bear a grudge, owe a g. 910vb. *be revengeful*; show spleen 891vb. *resent*; scowl, growl, snap, snarl, bare one's fangs 893vb. *be sullen*; insult 878vb. *be insolent*; conceive a hatred for, fall out of love, turn to hate.

excite hate, grate, jar 292vb. *repel*; cause loathing, disgust, nauseate, stink in the nostrils 861vb. *cause dislike*; shock, horrify 924vb. *incur blame*; antagonize, destroy goodwill, estrange, alienate, sow dissension, create bad blood, snap friendship, turn all to hate 881vb. *make enemies*; poison, envenom, embitter, exacerbate 832vb. *aggravate*; exasperate, incense 891vb. *enrage*.

See: 280, 292, 393, 458, 481, 509, 603, 607, 620, 645, 659, 704, 709, 832, 860, 861, 867, 878, 881, 891, 893, 898, 899, 910, 912, 922, 924, 938.

889 Endearment

N. *endearment*, blandishment, compliment 925n. *flattery*; loving words, affectionate speeches, pretty s., pretty names, pet name; soft nothings, lovers' vows; affectionate behaviour, dalliance, billing and cooing, holding hands, slap and tickle; fondling, cuddling, petting, necking, kissing, osculation; caress, embracement, embrace, clip, cuddle, squeeze, pressure, fond p.; salute, kiss, butterfly k., buss, smacker; nibble, bite; stroke, tickle, slap, tap, pat, pinch, nip 378n. *touch*; familiarity, over-f., advances, pass.

wooing, courting, spooning, flirting; play, love-p., love-making; side-glance, glad

eye, come hither look, ogle, amorous glance, sheep's eyes, fond look, languishing l., sigh; flirtation, philandering, coquetry, gallantry, amorous intentions, honourable i.; courtship, suit, love s., addresses, advances; tale of love, serenade, aubade, love-song, love lyric, amorous ditty, caterwauling; love-letter, billet-doux; love-poem, sonnet; love-plight, engagement, betrothal 894n. *marriage.*

love-token, true lover's knot, favour, glove; ring, engagement r., wedding r., eternity r.; valentine, love-letter, billet-doux; language of flowers, posy; arrow, heart, bleeding h.; tattoo-mark.

Adj. *caressing*, clinging, toying, fondling etc. vb.; demonstrative, affectionate 887 adj. *loving*; spoony, cuddlesome, flirtatious, coquettish; wooing, sighing, suing.

Vb. *pet*, pamper, spoil, spoonfeed, mother, smother, kill with kindness; cosset, cocker, coddle; make much of, be all over one; treasure, tender 887vb. *love*; cherish, foster, tender 660vb. *safeguard*; nurse, lap, rock, cradle, baby; sing to, croon over; coax, wheedle 925vb. *flatter.*

caress, love, fondle, dandle, take in one's lap; play with, stroke, smooth, pat, tap, pinch one's cheek, pat one on the head, chuck under the chin; osculate, kiss, buss, brush one's cheek; embrace, enlace, enfold, inarm, lap, fold in one's arms, press to one's bosom, hang on one's neck, fly into the arms of; open one's arms, clip, hug, hold one tight, cling, not let go 778 vb. *retain*; clasp, squeeze, press, cuddle; snuggle, nestle, nuzzle; play, romp, wanton, toy, trifle, dally, spark; make dalliance, make love, poodlefake, carry on, spoon, bill and coo, hold hands, slap and tickle, pet, neck; vamp 887vb. *excite love*; (of animals) lick, fawn, rub oneself against; (of a crowd) mob, rush, snatch at, swarm over.

court, make advances, give the glad eye, accept a pass; make eyes, make sheep's e., ogle, leer, eye 438vb. *gaze*; get off, try to get off, become familiar, make a pass, make passes; gallivant, philander, flirt, coquette 887vb. *excite love*; look sweet on 887vb. *be in love*; set one's cap at, run after, chase 619vb. *pursue*; squire, escort 89vb. *accompany*; hang about, wait on 284vb. *follow*; walk out with, have a steady; sue, woo, go a-wooing, go court-

ing, pay court to, pay one's addresses to, pay attentions to, pay suit to, press one's suit; serenade, caterwaul; sigh, sigh at the feet of, pine, languish 887vb. *love*; offer one's heart, offer one's hand, offer one's fortune; ask for the hand of, propose, propose marriage, pop the question, plight one's troth, become engaged, announce one's engagement, publish the banns, make a match 894vb. *wed.*

Adv. *caressingly*, endearingly, wooingly, suingly.

See: 89, 284, 378, 438, 619, 660, 778, 887, 894, 925.

890 Darling. Favourite

N. *darling*, dear, my dear; dear friend; dearest, dear one, only one; love, beloved 887n. *loved one*; heart, dear h.; sweetheart, fancy, Dowsabel; sweeting, sweetling, sweetie, sugar, honey, honeybunch; precious, jewel, treasure, tesoro; chéri, chou, mavourneen, babe; angel, angel child, cherub; pippin, poppet, popsy, moppet, mopsy, chuck; pet, petkins, lamb, precious l., chick, chicken, duck, ducks, ducky, dearie, lovey; laddie, sonny.

favourite, darling, mignon; spoiled darling, spoiled child, enfant gâté, fondling, cosset, mother's darling, teacher's pet; nursling, fosterchild; jewel, heart's-blood, apple of one's eye, blue-eyed boy; persona grata, man after one's own heart, one of the best, good chap, fine fellow, the tops; sport, good s., real s.; first choice, top seed, only possible choice 644n. *exceller*; someone to be proud of, boast; national figure, Grand Old Man 500n. *sage*; hero, popular h., idol, popular i., matinee i.; star, movie s., film s., top-liner, hit, smash h., knock-out; general favourite, universal f., cynosure, toast; world's sweetheart, Queen of Hearts, pin-up girl 841n. *a beauty*; centre of attraction, cynosure, honey-pot 291n. *attraction*; catch, lion 859n. *desired object.*

See: 291, 500, 644, 841, 859, 887.

891 Resentment. Anger

N. *resentment*, displeasure, dissatisfaction 829n. *discontent*; huffiness, ill-humour,

sulks 893 n. *sullenness*; sternness 735 n. *severity*; heart-burning, heart-swelling, rankling, rancour, soreness, painful feelings; slow burn, growing impatience; indignation (see *anger*); umbrage, offence, taking o., huff, tiff, pique; bile, spleen, gall; acerbity, acrimony, bitterness, bitter resentment, hard feelings; virulence, hate 888 n. *hatred*; animosity, grudge, ancient g., bone to pick, crow to pluck 881 n. *enmity*; vindictiveness, revengefulness, spite 910 n. *revenge*; malice 898 n. *malevolence*; impatience, fierceness, hot blood 892 n. *irascibility*; cause of offence, red rag to a bull, sore point, dangerous subject; pin-prick, irritation 827 n. *annoyance*; provocation, aggravation, insult, affront, last straw 921 n. *indignity*; wrong, injury 914 n. *injustice*.

anger, wrathfulness, irritation, exasperation, vexation, indignation; dudgeon, high d., wrath, ire, choler, dander, wax; rage, tearing r., berserker r., fury, raging f., passion, towering p. 822 n. *excitable state*; crossness, temper, tantrum, paddy, paddywhack, fume, fret, pet, fit of temper, ebullition of t., burst of anger, burst, explosion, storm, stew, ferment, taking, paroxysm, tears of rage 318 n. *agitation*; rampage, fire and fury, gnashing the teeth, stamping the foot; shout, roar 400 n. *loudness*; fierceness, angry look, glare, frown, scowl; growl, snarl, bark, bite, snap, snappishness, asperity 893 n. *sullenness*; warmth, heat, high words, angry w., rixation 709 n. *quarrel*; box on the ear, rap on the knuckles, slap in the face 921 n. *indignity*; blows, fisticuffs 716 n. *fight*.

Fury, Erinys, Alecto, Megaera, Tisiphone, Furies, Eumenides.

Adj. *resentful*, piqued, stung, galled, huffed; stung, hurt, sore, smarting 829 adj. *discontented*; surprised, pained, hurt, offended; warm, indignant; unresigned, reproachful 924 adj. *disapproving*; bitter, embittered, acrimonious, full of hate, rancorous, virulent 888 adj. *hating*; full of spleen, spleenful, bileful, bilious, spiteful 898 adj. *malevolent*; full of revenge, vindictive 910 adj. *revengeful*; jealous, green with envy 912 adj. *envious*; grudging 598 adj. *unwilling*.

angry, displeased, not amused, stern, frowning 834 adj. *serious*; impatient, cross, waxy, ratty, wild, mad; wroth, wrathy, ireful, irate; peeved, annoyed, irritated, vexed, provoked, stung; worked up, wrought up, het up, hot, hot under the collar; indignant, angered, incensed, infuriated; shirty, in a temper, in a paddy, in a wax, in a huff, in a rage, in a boiling r., in a fury, in a taking, in a passion; warm, fuming, boiling, burning; speechless, stuttering, gnashing, spitting with fury, crying with rage; raging, foaming, savage, violent 176 adj. *furious*; apoplectic, rabid, foaming at the mouth, mad, hopping m., dancing, rampaging, rampageous 503 adj. *frenzied*; seeing red, berserk; roaring, ramping, rearing; snarling, snapping, glaring, glowering 893 adj. *sullen*; red with anger, flushed with rage, red-eyed, bloodshot 431 adj. *red*; livid, pale with anger; sulphurous, dangerous, fierce 892 adj. *irascible*.

Vb. *resent*, be piqued, —offended etc. adj.; find intolerable, not bear, be unable to stomach 825 vb. *suffer*; feel, mind, feel resentment, smart under 829 vb. *be discontented*; take amiss, take ill, feel insulted, take offence, take umbrage, take exception 709 vb. *quarrel*; jib, take in ill part, take in bad p., get sore, cut up rough; burn, smoulder, sizzle, simmer, boil with indignation; express resentment, vent one's spleen, indulge one's spite 898 vb. *be malevolent*; take to heart, let it rankle, remember an injury, cherish a grudge, bear malice 910 vb. *be revengeful*; go green with envy 912 vb. *envy*.

get angry, get cross, get wild, get mad; get peeved, get sore, get in a pet; kindle, grow warm, grow heated, colour, redden, flush with anger; take fire, flare up, start up, rear up, ramp; bridle up, bristle up, raise one's hackles, arch one's back; lose patience, lose one's temper, lose control of one's t., forget oneself; get one's dander up, fall into a passion, fly into a temper, fly off the handle; let fly, burst out, let off steam, boil over, blow up, blow one's top, explode; see red, go berserk, go mad, foam at the mouth.

be angry, —impatient etc. adj.; show impatience, interrupt, chafe, fret, fume, fuss, flounce, dance, ramp, stamp, champ, champ the bit, paw the ground; carry on, create, perform, make a scene, make a row 61 vb. *rampage*; turn nasty, cut up

rough, raise Cain; rage, rant, roar, bellow, bluster, storm, thunder, fulminate 400 *be loud*; look like thunder, look black, look daggers, glare, glower, frown, scowl, growl, snarl 893 vb. *be sullen*; spit, snap; gnash one's teeth, grind one's t., weep with rage, boil with r., quiver with r., shake with passion, swell with fury, burst with indignation, stamp with rage, dance with fury, lash one's tail; breathe fire and fury, out-Lear Lear; let fly, express one's feelings, vent one's spleen, open the vials of one's wrath; tiff 709 vb. *quarrel*; fight it out 716 vb. *fight*.

huff, pique, sting, nettle, rankle; ruffle the dignity, wound, wound the feelings 827 vb. *hurt*; antagonize, put one's back up, get across, give umbrage, offend, cause offence, cause lasting o., embitter 888 vb. *excite hate*; stick in the gizzard, raise one's gorge 861 vb. *cause dislike*; affront, insult, outrage 921 vb. *not respect*.

enrage, upset, discompose, ruffle, disturb one's equanimity, ruffle one's temper, irritate, rile, peeve; annoy, vex, pester, bother 827 vb. *incommode*; do it to annoy, tease, bait, pinprick, needle 827 vb. *torment*; bite, fret, nag; put out of patience, put in an ill-humour, try one's patience; push too far, make one lose one's temper, put into a temper, work into a passion; anger, incense, infuriate, madden, drive mad; goad, sting, taunt, trail one's coat, invite a quarrel; drive into a fury, lash into f., fan one's f., rouse one's ire, rouse one's choler, kindle one's wrath, excite indignation, stir the blood, stir one's bile, make one's gorge rise, get one's dander up, get one's monkey up; make one's blood boil, make one see red; cause resentment, embitter, ulcerate, envenom, poison; exasperate, add fuel to the flame 832 vb. *aggravate*; embroil, set at loggerheads, set by the ears 709 vb. *make quarrels*.

Adv. *angrily*, resentfully, bitterly; warmly, heatedly, sulphurously; in anger, in fury, in the heat of the moment, in the height of passion, with one's monkey up, with one's dander up.

See: 61, 176, 318, 400, 431, 503, 598, 709, 716, 735, 822, 825, 827, 829, 832, 834, 861, 881, 888, 892, 893, 898, 910, 912, 914, 921, 924.

892 Irascibility

N. *irascibility*, quick passions, irritability, impatience 822 n. *excitability*; grumpiness, gruffness 883 n. *unsociability*; sharpness, tartness, asperity, gall, bile, vinegar 393 n. *sourness*; sensitivity 819 n. *moral sensibility*; huffiness, touchiness, prickliness, readiness to take offence, pugnacity, bellicosity 709 n. *quarrelsomeness*; temperament, testiness, pepperiness, peevishness, petulance; bad liver, uncertain temper, doubtful t., sharp t., short t.; hot temper, fierce t., fiery t.; limited patience, snappishness, a word and a blow; fierceness, dangerousness, hot blood, fieriness, inflammable nature; bad temper, dangerous t., foul t., nasty t., evil t.

shrew, scold, fishwife, callet; spitfire, termagant, virago, vixen, battle-axe, fury, Xanthippe; Tartar, hornet; bear 902 n. *misanthrope*; crosspatch, mad dog; fiery person, redhead.

Adj. *irascible*, impatient, choleric, irritable, peppery, testy, crusty, peevish, crossgrained; short-tempered, hot-t., sharp-t., uncertain-t.; prickly, touchy, tetchy, huffy, thin-skinned 819 adj. *sensitive*; inflammable, like tinder; hot-blooded, fierce, fiery, passionate 822 adj. *excitable*; quick, warm, hasty, over-h., over-lively, trigger-happy 857 adj. *rash*; dangerous, 'sudden and quick in quarrel' 709 adj. *quarrelling*; scolding, shrewish, vixenish, curst; sharp-tongued 899 adj. *maledicent*; petulant, cantankerous, snarling, querulous; exceptious, captious, bitter, vinegary 393 adj. *sour*; splenetic, spleenful, bilious, liverish, gouty; scratchy, snappish, waspish; tart, sharp, short; fractious, fretful, moody, moodish, temperamental, changeable; gruff, grumpy, pettish, ratty, like a bear with a sore head 829 adj. *discontented*; ill-humoured, currish 893 adj. *sullen*.

Vb. *be irascible*, have a temper, have an uncontrollable t.; have a devil in one; have a bad liver; snort, bark, snap, bite 893 vb. *be sullen*.

See: 393, 709, 819, 822, 829, 857, 883, 893, 899, 902.

893 Sullenness

N. *sullenness*, sternness, grimness 834 adj. *seriousness*; sulkiness, ill-humour, ill

condition, pettishness; morosity, churlishness, crabbedness, crustiness, unsociableness 883 n. *unsociability*; vinegar 393 n. *sourness*; grumpiness, grouchiness, pout, grimace 829 n. *discontent*; gruffness 885 n. *discourtesy*; crossness, peevishness, ill-temper, bad t., savage t., shocking t. 892 n. *irascibility*; spleen, bile, liver; sulks, fit of the s., the pouts, mulligrubs, bouderie, moodiness, temperament; the blues, blue devils 834 n. *melancholy*; black look, hangdog l., torvosity; glare, glower, frown, scowl; snort, growl, snarl, snap, bite; 'curses not loud but deep'.

Adj. *sullen*, forbidding, ugly; black, gloomy, overcast, cloudy, sunless 418 adj. *dark*; glowering, scowling; stern, frowning, unsmiling, grim 834 adj. *serious*; sulky, sulking, cross, out of temper, out of humour, misanthropic 883 adj. *unsociable*; morose, crabbed, crusty, cross-grained, ill-conditioned, difficult; snarling, snapping, snappish, shrewish, vixenish, cantankerous, quarrelsome 709 adj. *quarrelling*; refractory, jibbing 738 adj. *disobedient*; grouchy, grumbling, grumpy 829 adj. *discontented*; acid, tart, vinegary 393 adj. *sour*; gruff, rough 885 adj. *discourteous*; temperamental, moody, humoursome, up and down 152 adj. *changeful*; bilious, jaundiced, blue, down, depressed, melancholy 834 adj. *melancholic*; petulant, peevish, currish, curst, shirty, ill-tempered, bad-t. 892 adj. *irascible*; smouldering, sultry.

Vb. *be sullen*, gloom, glower, glare; look black, scowl, frown, knit one's brows; bare one's teeth, show one's fangs, spit; snap, snarl, growl, snort; make a face, grimace, pout, sulk 883 vb. *be unsocial*; mope, have the pip, have the blues 834 vb. *be dejected*; get out of bed on the wrong side; grout, grouch, grouse, crab, complain, grumble, mutter 829 vb. *be discontented*.

Adv. *sullenly*, sulkily, gloomily, ill-humouredly.

See: 152, 393, 418, 709, 738, 829, 834, 883, 885, 892.

894 Marriage

N. *marriage*, matrimony, holy m., sacrament of m., one flesh; wedlock, wedded state, married s., state of matrimony, conjugal bliss; match, union, alliance; conjugality, nuptial bond, marriage tie, marriage bed, bed and board, cohabitation, living as man and wife, life together; wifedom, wifehood, wifeliness; coverture, matronage, matronhood; banns, marriage certificate, marriage lines; marriage god, Hymen, Juno Pronuba.

type of marriage, matrimonial arrangement, monogamy, monandry, polygamy, Mormonism, polygyny, polyandry; bigamy, gamomania; digamy, deuterogamy, second marriage, remarriage, widow r.; leviration, levirate; arranged match, mariage de convenance, marriage of convenience; love-match, swayamvara, Gandharva marriage; mixed marriage, intermarriage, inter-caste m., miscegenation 43 n. *mixture*; mismarriage, mésalliance, misalliance, morganatic marriage, left-handed m.; spiritual marriage, syneisaktism; companionate marriage, temporary m., probationary m.; free union, free love, concubinage; compulsory marriage, forcible wedlock, shotgun wedding; abduction, Sabine rape.

wedding, getting married, match, matchmaking; nuptial vows, marriage v., ring, wedding r., betrothal, spousal, espousal, bridal, nuptials, spousals; leading to the altar, tying the knot; marriage rites, marriage ceremony; wedding service, nuptial mass, nuptial benediction 988 n. *Christian rite*; church wedding, white w., civil marriage, registry office m.; Gretna Green marriage, run-away match, elopement; solemn wedding, quiet w.; nuptial torch, torch of Hymen, nuptial song, Hymeneal, prothalamium, epithalamium; wedding day, wedding morning; wedding bells, wedding hymn, wedding march, marriage procession, bridelope; marriage feast, wedding breakfast, reception; honeymoon; silver wedding, golden w., wedding anniversary 876 n. *special day*.

bridesman, brideman, groomsman, best man, paranymph, bridal party; matron of honour, bridesmaid, page, train-bearer; attendant, usher.

spouse, espouser, espoused; one's promised, one's betrothed 887 n. *loved one*; marriage partner, man, wife; spouses, man and wife, Mr. and Mrs., Darby and Joan,

Philemon and Baucis; married couple, bridal pair, newlyweds, honeymooners; newlywed, bride, blushing b., young matron, bridegroom, Benedick; consort, partner, mate, yoke-mate, soulmate, affinity; married man, husband, goodman, old man, lord and master; much-married man, henpecked husband; injured husband 952n. *cuckold*; married woman, wedded wife, lady, matron, femme couverte, partner of one's bed and board; wife of one's bosom, helpmate, better half, woman, old w., missus, rib, grey mare; squaw, broadwife; faithful spouse, monogamist; digamist, second husband, second wife, bigamous w.; wife in all but name.

polygamist, polygynist, much-married man, owner of a harem, Turk, Mormon, Solomon; Bluebeard; bigamist.

matchmaker, matrimonial agent, marriage-broker, go-between, ghatak; marriage adviser 720n. *mediator*.

nubility, marriageable age, fitness for marriage, marriageability; eligibility, suitability, good match, proper m., suitable m.; suitable party, eligible p., welcome suitor 887n. *lover*.

Adj. *married*, partnered, paired, mated, matched; wived, husbanded; handfast, tied, spliced, hitched, in double harness; espoused, wedded, united, made man and wife, made one, bone of one's bone and flesh of one's flesh; monogamous; polygynous, polygamous, polyandrous; much-married, polygamistic, Mormonistic; re-married, digamous, bigamous; just married, newly m., newly-wed, honeymooning; mismarried, ill-matched.

marriageable, nubile, concubitant, concubitous; fit for marriage, ripe for m., of age, of marriageable a.; eligible, suitable; handfast, betrothed, promised, engaged, affianced, plighted, bespoke.

matrimonial, marital, connubial, concubinal, concubinary; nuptial, bridal, spousal, hymeneal, epithalamic, epithalamial; conjugal, wifely, matronly, husbandly; digamous, bigamous; polygamous, polygynous, polyandrous; morganatic; gamomaniac; syneisaktical.

Vb. *marry*, marry off, find a husband *or* wife for, match, mate; matchmake, make a match, arrange a m.; betroth, affiance, espouse, publish the banns, bid the b.; bestow in marriage, give in marriage, give away; ring the wedding bells, celebrate a marriage, conduct a wedding, read the wedding service, join in marriage, make fast in wedlock, declare man and wife; join, couple, handfast, splice, hitch, tie the knot.

wed, marry, espouse; wive, take to oneself a wife, find a husband; quit the single state, get married, get hitched, get spliced, mate with, marry oneself to, unite oneself, espouse o., give oneself in marriage, bestow one's hand, accept a proposal, become engaged, put up the banns; lead to the altar, take for better or worse, be made one; pair off, mate, couple; honeymoon, cohabit, set up house together, share bed and board, live as man and wife; marry well, make a good match; mismarry, make a bad match, repent at leisure; make a love match 887vb. *be in love*; marry in haste, run away, elope; contract matrimony, make one an honest woman, go through a form of marriage, receive one's marriage lines; marry again, remarry, commit bigamy; intermarry, miscegenate.

Adv. *matrimonially*, in the way of marriage; bigamously, polygamously, morganatically.

See: 43, 720, 876, 887, 952, 988.

895 Celibacy

N. *celibacy*, singleness, single state, single blessedness 744n. *independence*; bachelorhood, bachelorship, bachelorism, bachelordom; misogamy, misogyny 883n. *unsociability*; spinsterhood, spinsterdom; monkhood, the veil 985n. *monasticism*; encratism, spiritual marriage, syneisaktism 894n. *type of marriage*; maidenhood, virginity, pucelage, pudicity 950n. *purity*.

celibate, unmarried man, single m., bachelor, Benedick, Coelebs; confirmed bachelor, old b., gay b., not the marrying kind; enemy of marriage, agamist, misogamist, misogynist 902n. *misanthrope*; celibatarian, encratite, monastic 986n. *monk*; hermit 883n. *solitary*; monastic order, celibate o. 985n. *holy orders*; bachelry, bachelordom.

spinster, unmarried woman, femme sole, bachelor girl; maid unwed, débutante;

L

maid, maiden, virgo intacta; maiden aunt, old maid; Vestal, Vestal Virgin 986n. *nun*; Amazon, Diana, Artemis.

Adj. *unwedded*, unwed, unmarried; unpartnered, single, mateless, unmated; spouseless, unwived, wifeless; unhusbanded, husbandless; unwooed, unasked; free, uncaught, heart-whole, fancy-free 744n. *independent*; maidenly, virgin, virginal, vestal 950adj. *pure*; spinster, spinsterlike, spinsterish, old-maidish; bachelor, bachelor-like, bachelorly; celibate, celibatarian, monkish, nunnish 986 adj. *monastic*.

Vb. *live single*, stay unmarried, live in single blessedness, keep bachelor hall; refuse marriage, keep heart-whole 744vb. *be free*; have no offers, receive no proposals; live like a hermit 883vb. *be unsocial*; take the veil, get oneself to a nunnery 986vb. *take orders*; enforce celibacy, celibate.

See: 744, 883, 894, 902, 950, 985, 986.

896 Divorce. Widowhood

N. *divorce*, dissolution of marriage, divorcement, putting away, repudiation; bill of divorcement, divorce decree, decree nisi, decree absolute; separation, legal s., judicial s., separatio a mensa et thoro, separatio a vinculo matrimonii; annulment, decree of nullity; no marriage, nonconsummation; nullity, impediment, diriment i., prohibited degree, consanguinity, affinity; desertion, living apart, separate maintenance, alimony; marriage on the rocks, broken marriage, broken engagement, forbidding the banns; divorce court, divorce case, matrimonial cause; divorced person, divorcé, divorcée, nor wife nor maid; co-respondent.

widowhood, widowerhood, viduage, viduity, dowagerism; grass widowhood; widows' weeds 228n. *formal dress*.

widowed spouse, widower, widow, widow woman, relict; dowager, doweress, queen dowager, princess d., dowager duchess; grass widow, grass widower, Merry Widow.

Adj. *divorced*, separated, living apart; dissolved.

widowed, husbandless, wifeless; vidual.

Vb. *divorce*, separate, live separately, live apart, desert 621vb. *relinquish*; dis-

espouse, unmarry, untie the knot; put away, banish from bed and board; sue for divorce, file a divorce suit; wear the horns, be cuckolded; get a divorce, revert to bachelorhood, regain one's freedom; put asunder, dissolve marriage, annul a m., grant a decree of nullity, grant a divorce, pronounce a decree absolute.

be widowed, outlive one's spouse, lose one's wife, mourn one's husband, put on widow's weeds, become a relict.

widow, make a widow, leave one's wife a widow.

See: 228, 621.

897 Benevolence

N. *benevolence*, good will, helpfulness 880n. *friendliness*; ahimsa, harmlessness 935n. *innocence*; benignity, kindly disposition, heart of gold; amiability, bonhomie 882n. *sociability*; milk of human kindness, goodness of nature, warmth of heart, warmheartedness, kind-heartedness, kindliness, kindness, loving-k., goodness and mercy, charity, Christian c. 887n. *love*; godly love, brotherly l., brotherliness, fraternal feeling 880n. *friendship*; squeamishness, tenderness, consideration 736n. *lenity*; understanding, responsiveness, fellow-feeling, sympathy, overflowing s. 818n. *feeling*; condolence 905n. *pity*; decent feeling, humanity, humaneness, humanitarianism 901n. *philanthropy*; utilitarianism 901n. *sociology*; charitableness, hospitality, beneficence, unselfishness, generosity 813n. *liberality*; gentleness, softness, tolerance, toleration 734n. *laxity*; placability, mercy 909n. *forgiveness*; God's love, grace of God.

kind act, kindness, favour, service; good deed, charitable d.; charity, deed of c., relief, alms, almsgiving 781n. *giving*; prayers, good offices, kind o., good turn, helpful act 703n. *aid*; labour of love 597n. *voluntary work*.

kind person, bon enfant, Christian; good neighbour, good Samaritan, well-wisher 880n. *friend*; sympathizer 707n. *patron*; altruist, idealist, do-gooder 901n. *philanthropist*.

Adj. *benevolent*, well meant, well-intentioned, with the best intentions, for the best 880adj. *friendly*; out of kindness, to

oblige; out of charity, eleemosynary; good of one, so good of; sympathetic, wishing well, well-wishing, favouring, praying for; kindly disposed, benign, benignant, kindly, kind-hearted, over-flowing with kindness, full of the milk of human k., warm-hearted, large-h., golden-h.; kind, good, human, decent, Christian; affectionate 887 adj. *loving*; fatherly, paternal; motherly, maternal; brotherly, fraternal; sisterly, cousinly; good-humoured, good-natured, easy, sweet, gentle 884 adj. *amiable*; spleenless, bileless, placable, merciful 909 adj. *forgiving*; tolerant, indulgent 734 adj. *lax*; humane, considerate 736 adj. *lenient*; soft-hearted, tender, squeamish; pitiful, sympathizing, condolent 905 adj. *pitying*; genial, hospitable 882 adj. *sociable*; bounteous, bountiful 813 adj. *liberal*; generous, unselfish, unenvious, unjealous, altruistic 931 adj. *disinterested*; beneficent, charitable, humanitarian, doing good 901 adj. *philanthropic*; obliging, accommodating, helpful 703 adj. *aiding*; complacent, complaisant, gracious, gallant, chivalrous, chivalric 884 adj. *courteous*.

Vb. **be benevolent,**—kind etc. adj.; feel the springs of charity, have one's heart in the right place; sympathize, understand, feel as for oneself, enter into another's feelings, put oneself in another's place, do as one would be done by, practise the golden rule; return good for evil, heap coals of fire 909 vb. *forgive*; wish well, pray for, bless, give one's blessing, bestow a benediction; bear good will, wish the best for, have the right intentions, have the best i., mean well; look with a favourable eye, favour 703 vb. *patronize*; benefit 644 vb. *do good*; be a good Samaritan, do a good turn, render a service, oblige, put one under an obligation 703 vb. *aid*; lenify, humanize, reform 654 vb. *make better*.

philanthropize, do good, go about doing good, do good works, have a social conscience, show public spirit; reform, improve; relieve the poor, go slumming; visit, nurse 703 vb. *minister to*; mother 889 vb. *pet*.

Adv. *benevolently*, kindly, tenderly, lovingly, charitably, generously; in kindness, in charity; out of kindness, to oblige; mercifully, by the grace of God.

See: 597, 644, 654, 703, 707, 734, 736, 781, 813, 818, 880, 882, 884, 887, 889, 901, 905, 909, 931, 935.

898 Malevolence

N. *malevolence*, ill nature, ill will, ill disposition 881 n. *enmity*; truculency, cussedness, bitchiness, beastliness, ill intent, bad intention, worst intentions, cloven hoof; spite, gall, spitefulness, viciousness, malignity, malignancy, malice, deliberate m., malice prepense, malice aforethought; bad blood, hate 888 n. *hatred*; venom, virulence, deadliness, balefulness 659 n. *bane*; bitterness, acrimony, acerbity 393 n. *sourness*; mordacity 388 n. *pungency*; rancour 891 n. *resentment*; gloating, schadenfreude, unholy joy 912 n. *envy*; evil eye 983 n. *spell*.

inhumanity, lack of humanity, lack of charity, uncharitableness; intolerance, persecution 735 n. *severity*; harshness, mercilessness, implacability, hardness of heart, obduracy, heart of stone 906 n. *pitilessness*; cold feelings, unkindness, stepmotherly treatment; callousness 326 n. *hardness*; cruelty, barbarity, bloodthirstiness, bloodiness, bloodlust; barbarism, savagery, ferocity, barbarousness, savageness, ferociousness; atrociousness, outrageousness, immanity; ghoulishness, sadism, devilishness 934 n. *wickedness*; truculency, brutality, ruffianism; destructiveness, Vandalism 165 n. *destruction*.

cruel act, cruel conduct, truculence, brutality; ill-treatment, bad t., ill usage 675 n. *misuse*; victimization, 'tender mercies' 735 n. *severity*; blood, bloodshed 176 n. *violence*; excess, extremes, extremity; act of inhumanity, inhuman deed, atrocity, outrage, devilry; cruelty, cruelties, torture, tortures, barbarity, barbarities; cannibalism, murder 362 n. *homicide*; mass murder, genocide, unlimited war 362 n. *slaughter*.

Adj. *malevolent*, ill-wishing, ill-willed, ill-intentioned, ill-disposed, meaning harm 661 adj. *dangerous*; ill-natured, ill-conditioned 893 adj. *sullen*; nasty, vicious, bitchy, cussed 602 adj. *wilful*; malicious, catty, spiteful 926 adj. *detracting*; mischievous, mischief-making (see *maleficent*); baleful, malign, malignant 645

adj. *harmful*; venomous 362 adj. *deadly*; full of spite, spleenful 888 adj. *hating*; jealous 912 adj. *envious*; disloyal, treacherous 930 adj. *perfidious*; bitter, rancorous 891 adj. *resentful*; implacable, unforgiving, merciless 906 adj. *pitiless*; vindictive, gloating 910 adj. *revengeful*; hostile, fell 881 adj. *inimical*; intolerant, persecuting 735 adj. *oppressive*.

maleficent, hurtful, damaging 645 adj. *harmful*; poisonous, venomous, virulent, caustic, mordacious 659 adj. *baneful*; working ill, spreading evil, mischief-making, spreading mischief 645 adj. *bad*.

unkind, unamiable, ill-natured 893 adj. *sullen*; unkindly, unbenevolent, unbenign, unloving, unaffectionate, untender, stepmotherly, unmaternal, unbrotherly, unfraternal, undaughterly, unfilial; cold, unfriendly, hostile 881 adj. *inimical*; unforthcoming, uncordial, inhospitable 883 adj. *unsociable*; unco-operative, unhelpful, disobliging, inofficious; ungenerous, uncharitable, unforgiving; harsh, gruff, beastly 885 adj. *ungracious*; unsympathetic, unununderstanding, unresponsive, unfeeling, insensible, unmoved 820 adj. *impassive*; stern 735 adj. *severe*; unsqueamish, tough, hardboiled, hardbitten 326 adj. *hard*; inhumane, unnatural.

cruel, grim, fell; steely, grim-faced, cold-eyed, steely-e., hard-hearted, flint-h., stony-h.; ruthless, merciless 906 adj. *pitiless*; tyrannical 735 adj. *oppressive*; gloating, sadistic; bloodthirsty, cannibalistic 362 adj. *murderous*; bloody 176 adj. *violent*; excessive, extreme; atrocious, outrageous; feline, tigerish, wolfish; unnatural, sub-human, dehumanized, brutalized, brutish; brutal, rough, truculent, fierce, ferocious; savage, barbarous, wild, untamed, untameable, tameless; inhuman, ghoulish, fiendish, devilish, diabolical, demoniacal, satanic, hellish, infernal, Tartarean.

Vb. *be malevolent*, bear malice, cherish a grudge, harbour spleen 888 vb. *hate*; show ill-will, betray the cloven hoof; show envy 912 vb. *envy*; disoblige, spite, do one a bad turn; go to extremes, do one's worst, wreak one's spite, break a butterfly on a wheel, have no mercy 906 vb. *be pitiless*; take one's revenge, victimize, gloat 910 vb. *be revengeful*; take it out of one, bully, maltreat 645 vb. *ill-treat*;

molest, hurt, injure, annoy 645 vb. *harm*; malign, run down, throw stones at 926 vb. *detract*; tease, harry, hound, persecute, tyrannize, torture 735 vb. *oppress*; raven, thirst for blood 362 vb. *slaughter*; rankle, fester, poison, be a thorn in the flesh; create havoc, blight, blast 165 vb. *lay waste*; cast the evil eye 983 vb. *bewitch*.

Adv. *malevolently*, with bad intent, with the worst intentions; spitefully, out of spite.

See: 165, 176, 326, 362, 388, 393, 602, 645, 659, 661, 675, 735, 820, 881, 883, 885, 888, 891, 893, 906, 910, 912, 926, 930, 934, 983.

899 Malediction

N. *malediction*, malison, curse, imprecation, anathema; evil eye 983 n. *spell*; no blessing, ill wishes, bad wishes, 'curses not loud but deep' 898 n. *malevolence*; execration, denunciation, commination 900 n. *threat*; onslaught 712 n. *attack*; fulmination, thunder, thunders of the Vatican; ban, proscription, excommunication; exorcism, bell, book and candle.

scurrility, ribaldry, vulgarity; profanity, swearing, profane s., cursing and swearing, blasting; evil speaking, maledicence, bad language, foul l., filthy l., blue l., shocking l., strong l., unparliamentary l., Limehouse, Billingsgate; naughty word, expletive, swear-word, oath, swear, damn, curse, cuss, tinker's c.; invective, vituperation, abuse, volley of a.; mutual abuse, slanging match, stormy exchange; vain abuse, empty curse, more bark than bite 900 n. *threat*; no compliment, aspersion, reflection, vilification, slander 926 n. *calumny*; cheek, sauce 878 n. *sauciness*; personality, affront, insult 921 n. *indignity*; contumely, scorn 922 n. *contempt*; scolding, rough edge of one's tongue, basting, tongue-lashing 924 n. *reproach*.

Adj. *maledictory*, cursing, imprecative, imprecatory, anathematizing, comminatory, fulminatory, denunciatory, damnatory.

maledicent, evil-speaking, cursing, swearing, damning, blasting; profane, foul-mouthed, foul-tongued, foul-spoken, unparliamentary, scurrilous, scurrile, ribald 847 n. *vulgar*; sulphurous, blue; vituperative, abusive, vitriolic, injurious, vilipendious, reproachful 924 adj. *dis-*

approving; unflattering, candid 573 adj. *plain*; contumelious, scornful 922 adj. *despising*.

cursed, wished, wished on one; maledict, accursed, unblest, execrable; anathematized, under a ban, excommunicated, damned 961 adj. *condemned*; under a spell 983 adj. *bewitched*.

Vb. curse, cast the evil eye 983 vb. *bewitch*; accurse, wish, wish on, call down on; wish one joy of; curse with bell, book and candle, curse up hill and down dale; anathematize, imprecate, invoke curses on, execrate, hold up to execration; fulminate, thunder against, inveigh 924 vb. *reprove*; denounce 928 vb. *accuse*; excommunicate, damn, devote to destruction 961 vb. *condemn*; round upon, confound, send to the devil, send to blazes; abuse, vituperate, revile, shend, outscorn, rail, chide, flyte, heap abuse, pour vitriol 924 vb. *exprobate*; bespatter, throw mud 926 vb. *detract*.

cuss, curse, swear, damn, blast; swear like a trooper, use expletives, use Billingsgate, curse and swear; slang, slangwhang, abuse, blackguard 924 vb. *exprobate*; rail, scold, beshrew, give the rough edge of one's tongue.

Int. curse! a curse on! woe to! woe betide! ill betide! confusion seize! devil take it! blast! damn! dang! hang!

See: 573, 712, 847, 878, 898, 900, 921, 922, 924, 926, 928, 961, 983.

ing, hectoring 877 adj. *boastful*; muttering, grumbling 893 adj. *sullen*; bodeful, portentous, ominous, foreboding 511 adj. *presageful*; hovering, lowering, hanging over 155 adj. *impending*; ready to spring, growling, snarling 891 adj. *angry*; abusive 899 adj. *maledicent*; comminatory 899 adj. *maledictory*; in terrorem, deterrent 854 adj. *frightening*; nasty, unpleasant 661 adj. *dangerous*.

Vb. threaten, threat, menace, use threats, hold out t., utter t.; demand with menaces, blackmail 737 vb. *demand*; frighten, deter, intimidate, bully 854 vb. *frighten*; roar, bellow 408 vb. *vociferate*; fulminate, thunder 899 vb. *curse*; bark, talk big, bluster, hector 877 vb. *boast*; shake, wave, flaunt 317 vb. *brandish*; rattle the sabre, clench the fist, draw one's sword, make a pass 711 vb. *defy*; bare the fangs, snarl, growl, mutter 893 vb. *be sullen*; bristle, spit, look daggers, grow nasty 891 vb. *get angry*; draw a bead on, cover, have one covered, keep one c. 281 vb. *aim*; gather, mass, lower, hang over, hover, stand in terrorem 155 vb. *impend*; bode, presage, promise ill, spell danger 511 vb. *predict*; serve notice, forewarn 664 vb. *warn*; breathe revenge, promise r., threaten reprisals 910 vb. *be revengeful*.

Adv. threateningly, menacingly, in terrorem, on pain of death.

See: 155, 281, 317, 408, 511, 661, 663, 664, 711, 723, 737, 854, 877, 891, 893, 899, 910.

900 Threat

N. threat, menace; commination, fulmination 899 n. *malediction*; minacity, threatfulness, ominousness; challenge, dare, 711 n. *defiance*; blackmail 737 n. *demand*; battle-cry, war-whoop, sabre-rattling, war of nerves 854 n. *intimidation*; deterrent 723 n. *weapon*; black cloud, threatening c. 511 n. *omen*; hidden fires, secret weapon 663 n. *pitfall*; impending danger, sword of Damocles 661 n. *danger*; danger signal, fair warning, writing on the wall 664 n. *warning*; bluster, idle threat, hollow t. 877 n. *boast*; bark, growl, snarl 893 n. *sullenness*.

Adj. threatening, menacing, minatory, minatorial, minacious, threatful; sabre-rattling 711 adj. *defiant*; blustering, bully-

901 Philanthropy

N. philanthropy, humanitarianism, humanity, humaneness, the golden rule 897 n. *benevolence*; humanism, cosmopolitanism, internationalism; altruism 931 n. *disinterestedness*; idealism, ideals 933 n. *virtue*; universal benevolence, the greatest happiness of the greatest number, utilitarianism, Benthamism; passion for improvement, 'onward and upward department' 654 n. *reformism*; dedication, crusading spirit, missionary s., nonconformist conscience, social c.; good works, mission, civilizing m., 'white man's burden'; Holy War, crusade, campaign; cause, Messianism, Messiahship 689 n. *directorship*.

sociology, social science, social engineering,

social planning, socialism; Poplarism, poor relief, poor rate; social services, Welfare State; social service, welfare work, slumming, good works.

patriotism, civism, civic ideals, good citizenship, public spirit, concern for the public, zeal for the common good, devotion to the common weal, love of country; local patriotism, parochialism; nationalism, chauvinism, my country right or wrong; irredentism, Zionism.

philanthropist, friend of all the world 903 n. *benefactor*; humanitarian, do-gooder, social worker, slummer 897 n. *kind person*; paladin, champion, crusader, knight, knight errant; Messiah 690 n. *leader*; missionary, man with a mission, dedicated soul; visionary, ideologist; idealist, altruist; reformist 654 n. *reformer*; utilitarian, Benthamite; Utopian, millenarian, chiliast; humanist, cosmopolite, cosmopolitan, citizen of the world, internationalist.

patriot, lover of his country, fighter for his c.; pater patriæ, father of his people; nationalist, irredentist, chauvinist, Zionist.

Adj. *philanthropic*, humanitarian, humane, human 897 adj. *benevolent*; enlightened, humanistic, liberal; cosmopolitan, internationally minded; idealistic, altruistic 931 adj. *disinterested*; visionary, dedicated; sociological, socialistic; utilitarian.

patriotic, civically minded, public spirited; irredentist, nationalistic, chauvinistic; loyal, true, true-blue.

Vb. See 897 vb. *philanthropize*.

See: 654, 689, 690, 897, 903, 931, 933.

902 Misanthropy

N. *misanthropy*, hatred of mankind, distrust of one's fellow man, disillusionment with society, cynicism, unsociality 883 n. *unsociability*; moroseness 893 n. *sullenness*; inhumanity, non-humanism, incivism; egotism.

misanthrope, hater of the human race, man-hater, woman-h., misogynist, misogamist; cynic, Diogenes, Timon; egotist; no patriot, defeatist; world-hater, unsocial animal 883 n. *solitary*; bear, cross-patch, sulker 829 n. *malcontent*.

Adj. *misanthropic*, inhuman, antisocial 883 adj. *unsociable*; cynical, Diogenic, Diogenical; uncivic, unpatriotic, defeatist.

Vb. *misanthropize*, become a misanthrope, lose faith in human kind.

Adv. *misanthropically*, cynically.

See: 829, 883, 893.

903 Benefactor

N. *benefactor*, benefactress 901 n. *philanthropist*; Lady Bountiful, donor, fairy godmother 781 n. *giver*; guardian angel, tutelary saint, good genius 660 n. *protector*; founder, foundress, supporter 707 n. *patron*; tyrannicide, pater patriæ, father of his people 901 n. *patriot*; saviour, ransomer, redeemer, deliverer, rescuer 668 n. *deliverance*; champion 713 n. *defender*; Lady Godiva, Good Samaritan 897 n. *kind person*; good neighbour 880 n. *friend*; helper, present help in time of trouble 703 n. *aider*; salt of the earth, saint 937 n. *good man*.

See: 660, 668, 703, 707, 713, 781, 880, 897, 901, 937.

904 Evildoer

N. *evildoer*, worker of evil, worker of iniquity, wrongdoer, sinner 934 n. *wickedness*; villain, blackguard, bad lot; one up to no good, monkey, little devil, mischiefmaker 663 n. *trouble-maker*; gossip, slanderer, calumniator 926 n. *detractor*; snake, in the grass, viper in the bosom, traitor 545 n. *deceiver*; marplot 702 n. *hinderer*; spoiler, despoiler, wrecker, defacer, Vandal, Hun, iconoclast 168 n. *destroyer*; nihilist, anarchist 738 n. *revolter*; incendiary, pyromaniac 381 n. *incendiarism*; disturber of the peace, bull in a china shop 738 n. *rioter*.

ruffian, blackguard, rogue 938 n. *knave*; lout, hooligan, hoodlum, larrikin, sansculotte, badmash 869 n. *low fellow*; Teddy-boy, gunboy, terror, holy t., terror of the neighbourhood; rough, tough, rowdy, ugly customer, plug-ugly, desperado, Apaehe, Mohawk; bully, bravo, assassin, hired a.; cut-throat, hangman, gunman, bludgeon man, cosh-m., sandbagger; thug, killer, butcher 362 n.

murderer; genocide, mass murderer, plague, scourge, scourge of the human race, Attila 659n. *bane*; petty tyrant, gauleiter 735n. *tyrant*; brute, savage b., beast, savage barbarian, ape-man, cave-m.; cannibal, anthropophagist; homicidal maniac 504n. *madman*.

offender, sinner, black sheep 938n. *bad man*; suspect; culprit, guilty man, law-breaker; wrongdoer, tortfeasor; criminal, misdemeanant, felon; delinquent, juvenile d., first offender; recidivist, backslider, old offender, hardened o., lag, old l., convict, ex-c., gaol-bird; lifer, gallowsbird, 'quare fellow'; parolee, probationer, ticket-of-leave man; malefactor, gangster, racketeer, barrator, housebreaker 789n. *thief*, *robber*; forger 789n. *defrauder*; blackmailer, blood-sucker, vampire; poisoner 362n. *murderer*; outlaw, public enemy 881n. *enemy*; intruder, trespasser; criminal world, underworld, sink of iniquity 934n. *wickedness*.

hell-hag, hell-hound, hell-kite; cat, hell-c., wild c., bitch, virago 892n. *shrew*; she-devil, fury, harpy, siren; ogress, witch, beldam, horror 938n. *monster*.

noxious animal, brute, beast, wild b.; beast of prey, predator; tiger, man-eater, wolf, werewolf, hyena, jackal, fox; kite, vulture, vampire, blood-sucker 365n. *bird of prey*; snake, serpent, viper, adder, asp, rattlesnake, cobra 365n. *reptile*; cockatrice, basilisk, salamander 84n. *rara avis*; scorpion, wasp, hornet; pest, locust, Colorado beetle, worm, wire-w., canker-w. 365n. *vermin*; rat 365n. *rodent*; wild cat, mad dog, rogue elephant.

See: 84, 168, 362, 365, 381, 504, 545, 659, 663, 702, 735, 738, 789, 869, 881, 892, 926, 934, 938.

905 Pity

N. *pity*, springs of p., ruth; remorse, compunction 830n. *regret*; compassion, bowels of c., compassionateness, humanity 897n. *benevolence*; soft heart, tender h.; gentleness, softness, squeamishness 736n. *lenity*; commiseration, touched feelings, melting mood, tears of sympathy 825n. *sorrow*; weltschmerz, lacrimæ rerum 834n. *dejection*; sympathy, understanding, deep u., fellow-feeling (see *condolence*); self-pity, self-compassion, self-commiseration, tears for oneself; plea for pity, argumentum ad misericordiam.

condolence, sympathy and c.; consolation, comfort 831n. *relief*; commiseration, sympathetic grief, sympathy, fellow-feeling, fellowship in sorrow 775n. *participation*; professional condolence, keen, coronach, wake 836n. *lament*.

mercy, tender mercies, clemency, quarter, grace; locus pænitentiæ, second chance; mercifulness, exorability, placability, forbearance, long-suffering 909n. *forgiveness*; light sentence 963n. *penalty*; let-off 960n. *acquittal*.

Adj. *pitying*, compassionate, sympathetic, understanding, condolent, commiserating; pitiful, ruthful, merciful, clement, full of mercy 736adj. *lenient*; melting, tender, tender-hearted, soft, soft-hearted; weak 734adj. *lax*; unhardened, squeamish, easily touched, easily moved; exorable, placable, disposed to mercy 909adj. *forgiving*; remorseful, compunctious; humane, charitable 897adj. *benevolent*; forbearing 823adj. *patient*.

pitiable, compassionable, commiserable, pitiful, piteous, deserving pity, demanding p., claiming p., challenging sympathy.

Vb. *pity*, feel p., weep for p., bleed; compassionate, show compassion, show pity, take p., take compassion; sympathize, sympathize with, enter into one's feelings, feel for, feel with, share the grief of 775vb. *participate*; sorrow, grieve, feel sorry for, weep f., lament f., commiserate, condole, condole with, express one's condolences, send one's c., testify one's pity, yearn over 836vb. *lament*; console, comfort, offer consolation, afford c. 833vb. *cheer*; have pity, have compassion, melt, thaw, relent 909vb. *forgive*.

show mercy, have m., offer m., spare, spare the life of, give quarter; forget one's anger 909vb. *forgive*; be slow to anger, forbear; allow time for repentance, indulge 736vb. *be lenient*; relax, relent, unbend, not proceed to extremes, relax one's rigour, show consideration, not be too hard upon, let one down gently; put one out of his misery, give the coup de grâce, be cruel to be kind.

ask mercy, plead for m., appeal for m., pray for m., beg for m., throw oneself

upon another's mercy, ask for quarter, beg one's life; find mercy, find compassion, propitiate, disarm, melt, thaw, soften 719 vb. *pacify.*

Int. alas! how sad! too bad! for pity's sake! for mercy's s.! for the love of God!

See: 719, 734, 736, 775, 823, 825, 830, 831, 833, 834, 836, 897, 909, 960, 963.

906 Pitilessness

N. *pitilessness,* lack of pity, ruthlessness, mercilessness, unmercifulness; inclemency, intolerance, rigour 735 n. *severity*; callousness, hardness of heart 898 n. *malevolence*; inflexibility 326 n. *hardness*; inexorability, relentlessness, remorselessness, unforgivingness 910 adj. *revengefulness*; letter of the law, pound of flesh; no pity, no bowels, short shrift, no quarter.

Adj. *pitiless,* unpitying, uncompassionate, uncondoling, uncomforting, unconsoling unfeeling, unresponsive 820 adj. *impassive*; unsympathising, unsympathetic; unmelting, unmoved, tearless, dry-eyed; unsqueamish, callous, tough, hardened 326 adj. *hard*; harsh, rigorous, intolerant, persecuting 735 adj. *severe*; brutal, sadistic 898 adj. *cruel*; merciless, ruthless, bowelless; indisposed to mercy, inclement, unmerciful, unrelenting, relentless, remorseless, inflexible, inexorable, implacable; unforgiving, unpardoning, vindictive 910 adj. *revengeful.*

Vb. *be pitiless,* — ruthless etc. adj.; have no bowels, have no compassion, have no pity, know no p.; show no p., show no mercy, give no quarter, spare none; shut the gates of mercy, harden one's heart, be deaf to appeal, admit no excuse; not tolerate, persecute 735 vb. *be severe*; stand on the letter of the law, insist on one's pound of flesh 735 vb. *be severe*; take one's revenge 910 vb. *avenge.*

See: 326, 735, 820, 898, 910.

907 Gratitude

N. *gratitude,* gratefulness, thankfulness, grateful heart, feeling of obligation, sense of o.; grateful acceptance, appreciativeness, appreciation, lively sense of favours to come.

thanks, hearty t.; giving thanks, thanksgiving, eucharist, benediction, blessing; praises, pæan, Te Deum 876 n. *celebration*; grace, bismillah; grace before meat, grace after m., bread-and-butter letter, Collins; credit, credit title, acknowledgment, grateful a., recognition, grateful r., ungrudging r., full praise; tribute 923 n. *praise*; thank-offering, parting present, tip 962 n. *reward*; requital, return, favour returned 714 n. *retaliation.*

Adj. *grateful,* thankful, appreciative; showing appreciation, thanking, blessing, praising; acknowledging favours, crediting, giving credit; obliged, much o., under obligation, beholden, indebted.

Vb. *be grateful,* have a grateful heart, overflow with gratitude; thank one's stars, praise Heaven; feel an obligation, cherish a favour, never forget; accept gratefully, pocket thankfully, not look a gift-horse in the mouth; be privileged, have the honour to.

thank, give thanks, render t., return t., express t., pour out one's t., praise, bless; acknowledge, express acknowledgments, credit, give c., give full c. 158 vb. *attribute*; appreciate, show appreciation, tip 962 vb. *reward*; return a favour, requite, repay, repay with interest 714 vb. *retaliate*; return with thanks 787 vb. *restitute.*

Adv. *gratefully,* thankfully, with gratitude, with thanks, with interest.

Int. thanks! many t.! much obliged! thank Heaven! Heaven be praised!

See: 158, 714, 787, 876, 923, 962.

908 Ingratitude

N. *ingratitude,* ungratefulness, unthankfulness, thanklessness; grudging thanks, cold t., more kicks than ha'pence; no sense of obligation, indifference to favours, oblivion of benefits, 'benefits forgot' 506 n. *oblivion*; no reward, unrewardingness, thankless task, thankless office; thankless person, ingrate, ungrateful wretch.

Adj. *ungrateful,* unthankful, ingrate; unobliged, not obliged, unbeholden; unmindful 506 adj. *forgetful*; unmindful of favours, insensible of benefits, incapable of gratitude 820 adj. *apathetic.*

unthanked, thankless, without credit, unacknowledged, forgotten; rewardless, bootless, unrewarding, unrewarded, unrequited, ill-r., untipped.

Vb. *be ungrateful*, show ingratitude, admit no obligation, acknowledge no favour; take for granted, take as one's due; not thank, omit to t., forget to t.; see no reason to thank, grudge thanks, look a gift-horse in the mouth; forget benefits, return evil for good.

Int. thank you for nothing! no thanks to.

See: 506, 820.

909 Forgiveness

N. *forgiveness*, pardon, free p., full p., reprievement, reprieval, reprieve 506n. *amnesty*; indemnity, act of i., covenant of i., deed of i.; grace, indulgence, plenary i.; cancellation, remission, absolution, shrift 960n. *acquittal*; one-sided forgiveness, condonation; justification, exculpation, exoneration, excuse 927n. *vindication*; mutual forgiveness, reconciliation, renewal of love 719n. *pacification*; forgiving nature, placability, exorability 905n. *pity*; long-suffering, longanimity, forbearance 823n. *patience*; forgiver, pardoner, author of forgiveness.

Adj. *forgiving*, placable, exorable, condoning, admitting excuses, conciliatory; unresentful, forbearing, longanimous, long-suffering 823adj. *patient*; reluctant to punish, more in sorrow than in anger.

forgiven, pardoned, forgiven and forgotten, amnestied, reprieved; remitted, cancelled, blotted out, extinguished; condoned, excused, exonerated, let off 960 adj. *acquitted*; absolved, shriven; unresented, unavenged, unrevenged, unpunished, unchastened; pardonable, forgivable, venial, excusable.

Vb. *forgive*, pardon, reprieve, forgive and forget, amnesty 506n. *forget*; remit, absolve, assoil, shrive; cancel, blot out, blot out one's transgressions 550vb. *obliterate*; relent, unbend, accept an apology 736vb. *be lenient*; be merciful, not be too hard upon, let one down gently 905vb. *show mercy*; bear with, put up w., forbear, tolerate 823vb. *be patient*; take no offence, take in good part, pocket, stomach; forget an injury, ignore a wrong,

overlook, pass over, not punish, leave unavenged, turn the other cheek; return good for evil, heap coals of fire 897vb. *be benevolent*; connive, wink at, condone 458vb. *disregard*; excuse, find excuses for 927vb. *justify*; recommend to pardon, intercede 720vb. *mediate*; exculpate, exonerate 960vb. *acquit*; bury the hatchet, let bygones be bygones, make it up, shake hands, kiss and be friends, be reconciled 880vb. *be friendly*; restore to favour, kill the fatted calf 876vb. *celebrate*.

beg pardon, plead for forgiveness, offer apologies, ask for absolution 905vb. *ask mercy*; propitiate, placate 941vb. *atone*.

Adv. *forgivingly*, without resentment, more in sorrow than in anger.

See: 458, 506, 550, 719, 720, 736, 823, 876, 880, 897, 905, 927, 941, 960.

910 Revenge

N. *revengefulness*, thirst for revenge, revanchism; vindictiveness, spitefulness, spite 898n. *malevolence*; ruthlessness 906 n. *pitilessness*; remorselessness, relentlessness, implacability, irreconcilability, unappeasability; unappeasable resentment, deadly rancour 891n. *resentment*.

revenge, sweet r., 'wild justice'; crime passionel 911n. *jealousy*; vengeance, avengement, day of reckoning 963n. *punishment*; victimization, reprisal, reprisals, punitive expedition 714n. *retaliation*; lex talionis, eye for an eye, tooth for a tooth, blood for blood; vendetta, feud, blood-f., death-f. 881n. *enmity*.

avenger, vindicator, punisher, revanchist; Nemesis, Eumenides, avenging furies.

Adj. *revengeful*, vengeful, breathing vengeance, thirsting for revenge; avenging, taking vengeance, retaliative 714adj. *retaliatory*; at feud 881adj. *inimical*; unforgiving, unforgetting, implacable, unappeasable, unrelenting, relentless, remorseless 906adj. *pitiless*; grudgeful, vindictive, spiteful 898adj. *malevolent*; rancorous 891adj. *resentful*; enjoying revenge, gloating.

Vb. *avenge*, avenge oneself, revenge o., take one's revenge, take vengeance, wreak v., victimize; exact retribution, get one's own back, repay, pay out, pay off *or* settle old scores, put paid to the account; get back

on, give tit for tat 714vb. *retaliate*; sate one's vengeance, glut one's revenge, enjoy one's r., gloat.

be revengeful, — vindictive etc. adj.; cry revenge, breathe r., promise vengeance 888vb. *hate*; nurse one's revenge, cherish a grudge, have a feud, have a rod in pickle, have a crow to pluck, have accounts to settle 881vb. *be inimical*; let it rankle, keep a wound green, remember an injury, brood on one's wrongs 891vb. *resent*.

See: 714, 881, 888, 891, 898, 906, 911, 963.

911 Jealousy

N. *jealousy*, pangs of j., jealousness; jaundiced eye, green-eyed monster; distrust, mistrust 486n. *doubt*; heart-burning 891n. *resentment*; enviousness 912n. *envy*; hate 888n. *hatred*; inferiority complex, prestige-chasing, emulation, competitiveness, competition, rivalry, jealous r. 716n. *contention*; possessiveness 887n. *love*; sexual jealousy, crime passionel 910n. *revenge*; object of jealousy, competitor, rival, hated r., the other man, the other woman; sour grapes.

Adj. *jealous*, green-eyed, yellow-e., jaundiced, envying 912adj. *envious*; devoured with jealousy, horn-mad; possessive 887 adj. *loving*; suspicious, mistrusting, distrustful 474adj. *doubting*; emulative, competitive, rival, competing, in the business, in the same b.

Vb. *be jealous*, scent a rival, suspect, mistrust, distrust 486vb. *doubt*; view with jealousy, view with a jaundiced eye 912 vb. *envy*; resent another's superiority, nurse an inferiority complex; brook no rival, resent competition; strive to keep for oneself.

See: 474, 486, 716, 887, 888, 891, 910, 912.

912 Envy

N. *envy*, envious eye, enviousness, covetousness 859n. *desire*; rivalry 716n. *contention*; envious rivalry, jalousie de métier 911n. *jealousy*; ill-will, spite, spleen, bile 898n. *malevolence*; mortification, unwilling admiration, grudging praise.

Adj. *envious*, envying, envious-eyed, squinte., green with envy, fain to change places with 911adj. *jealous*; greedy, unsated, unsatisfied 829adj. *discontented*; covetous, longing 859adj. *desiring*; grudging; mortified 891adj. *resentful*.

Vb. *envy*, view with e., cast envious looks, turn green with e.; covet, crave, lust after, must have for oneself, long to change places with 859vb. *desire*.

See: 716, 829, 859, 891, 898, 911.

913 Right

N. *right*, rightfulness, rightness, good case for; right lines 642n. *expedience*; freedom from error, correctness, correctitude, exactness 494n. *accuracy*; fittingness, seemliness, propriety, decency 24n. *fitness*; normality 83n. *conformity*; rules, rules and regulations 693n. *precept*; what ought to be, what should be 917n. *duty*; morality, good morals 917n. *morals*; righteousness 933n. *virtue*; uprightness, honour 929n. *probity*; suum cuique, one's right, one's due, deserts, merits, claim; from each according to his ability, to each according to his need 915n. *dueness*; prerogative, privilege, rights and privileges 919n. *non-liability*; rights, interest, vested i., birthright 777n. *property*.

justice, freedom from wrong, justifiability; righting wrong., redress; reform 654n. *reformism*; tardy justice, overdue reform; even-handed justice, impartial j., indifferent j.; scales of justice, justice under the law, process under the l. 953n. *legality*; retribution, retributive justice 962n. *reward*; lex talionis 714n. *retaliation*; fair-mindedness, objectivity, indifference, detachment, impartiality, equalness 28n. *equality*; equity, equitableness, reasonableness, fairness; fair deal, square d., fair break, fair treatment, fair play, fair field and no favour, equal opportunity; good law, Queensberry rules; Astræa, Themis, Nemesis.

Adj. *right*, rightful, proper, right and p., meet and right; on the right lines, fitting, suitable 24adj. *fit*; better, even b. 642adj. *expedient*; good, just right 646adj. *perfect*; quite right, exact, just so, true, correct 494adj. *accurate*; adjusted, put right, redressed, reformed 654adj. *improved*;

normal, standard, classical 83 adj. *conformable.*

just, upright, righteous, right-minded, on the side of the angels 933 adj. *virtuous;* fair-minded, disinterested, unprejudiced, unbiased, unswerving, undeflected 625 adj. *neutral;* detached, impersonal, dispassionate, objective; equal, indifferent, impartial, even-handed; fair, square, fair and s., equitable, reasonable, fair enough; in the right, justifiable, justified, unchallengeable, unchallenged, unimpeachable; legitimate, according to law 953 adj. *legal;* sporting, sportsmanlike 929 adj. *honourable;* deserved, well-d., earned, merited, well-m. 915 adj. *due;* overdue, demanded, claimed, rightly c., claimable 627 adj. *required.*

Vb. be right, stand to reason 494 vb. *be true;* have justice, have cause, be in the right, have right on one's side.

be just,—impartial etc. adj.; play the game 929 vb. *be honourable;* do justice, give the devil his due, give full marks to, hand it to 915 vb. *grant claims;* see justice done, see fair play, hold the scales even, hear both sides, go by merit, consider on the merits 480 vb. *judge;* temper justice with mercy 905 vb. *show mercy;* see one righted, right a wrong, right wrongs, redress, remedy, cure, mend, reform, put right 654 vb. *rectify;* serve one right 714 vb. *retaliate;* try to be fair, lean over backwards, over-compensate; hide nothing, declare one's interest.

Adv. rightly, justly, justifiably, with justice; in the right, within one's rights; like a judge, impartially, indifferently, equally, without distinction, without respect of persons; fairly, without favouritism; naturally, by nature's laws.

See: 24, 28, 83, 480, 494, 625, 627, 642, 646, 654, 693, 714, 777, 905, 915, 917, 919, 929, 933, 953, 962.

914 Wrong

N. wrong, wrongness, something wrong, oddness, queerness 84 n. *abnormality;* something rotten, curse, bane, scandal 645 n. *badness;* disgrace, shame, crying s., dishonour 867 n. *slur;* impropriety, unfittingness, unsuitability 643 n. *inexpedi-*

ence; incorrectness, wrong lines, mistake 495 n. *error;* wrongheadedness, unreasonableness 481 n. *misjudgment;* unreason 477 n. *sophistry;* unjustifiability, what ought not to be, what must not be 916 n. *undueness;* inexcusability, culpability, guiltiness 936 n. *guilt;* immorality, vice, sin 934 n. *wickedness;* dishonesty, unrighteousness 930 n. *improbity;* irregularity, illegitimacy, criminality, crime, lawlessness 954 n. *illegality;* wrongfulness, misdoing, tortiousness, misfeasance, transgression, trespass, encroachment; a wrong, injustice, tort, mischief, outrage, foul 930 n. *foul play;* sense of wrong, complaint, charge 928 n. *accusation;* grievance, just g. 891 n. *resentment;* wrong 'un, immoralist, unjust judge 938 n. *bad man.*

injustice, no justice; miscarriage of justice, wrong verdict 481 n. *misjudgment;* corrupt justice, uneven scales, warped judgment, packed jury 481 n. *bias;* one-sidedness, inequity, unfairness; partiality, leaning, favouritism, favour, nepotism; preferential treatment, discrimination; partisanship, party spirit 481 n. *prejudice;* unlawfulness, no law 954 n. *illegality;* justice denied, right withheld, privilege curtailed 916 n. *undueness;* party capital, mean advantage, 'heads I win, tails you lose'; no equality, wolf and the lamb 29 n. *inequality;* not cricket 930 n. *foul play;* imposition, robbing Peter to pay Paul.

Adj. wrong, not right 645 adj. *bad;* odd, queer, suspect 84 adj. *abnormal;* unfitting, ill-fitting, ill-seeming, unseemly, unfit, improper, inappropriate 643 adj. *inexpedient;* false, incorrect, untrue 495 adj. *erroneous;* off the mark, inaccurate 495 adj. *inexact;* on the wrong lines, misjudged, ill-advised, wrongheaded, unreasonable 481 adj. *misjudging;* wrong from the start, out of court, inadmissible; irregular, against the rules, foul, unauthorized, unwarranted 757 adj. *prohibited;* bad in law, illegitimate, illicit, tortious, criminous, criminal, felonious, nefarious 954 adj. *illegal;* condemnable, culpable, in the wrong, offside 936 adj. *guilty;* unwarrantable, inexcusable, unpardonable, unforgivable, unjustifiable (see *unjust*); open to objection, objectionable, scandalous 861 n. *disliked;* wrongous, wrongful, unrightful, injurious, mischievous 645 adj. *harmful;* unrighteous

930 adj. *dishonest*; iniquitous, sinful, vicious, immoral 934 adj. *wicked*.

unjust, unjustifiable; uneven, weighted 29 adj. *unequal*; inequitable, iniquitous, unfair; hard, hard on 735 adj. *severe*; foul, not playing the game, below the belt, unsportsmanlike; discriminatory, favouring, one-sided, leaning to one side, partial, partisan, prejudiced 481 adj. *biased*; selling justice 930 adj. *venal*; wresting the law 954 adj. *illegal*.

Vb. *be wrong*, — unjust etc. adj.; be in the wrong, go wrong 495 vb. *err*.

do wrong, wrong, hurt, injure, do an injury 645 vb. *harm*; be hard on, have a down on 735 vb. *be severe*; not play the game, not play cricket, hit below the belt; break the rules, commit a foul; commit a tort, commit a crime, break the law, wrest the l., pervert the l. 954 vb. *be illegal*; transgress, infringe, trespass 306 vb. *encroach*; reap where one has not sown, giv̱ an inch and take an ell; leave unrighted, leave unremedied; do less than justice, withhold justice, deny j., load, weight, load the scales, pack *or* rig the jury; lean, lean to one side, discriminate against, show partiality, show favouritism, discriminate 481 vb. *be biased*; favour 703 vb. *patronize*; go too far, overcompensate, lean over backwards; commit, perpetrate.

Adv. *wrongly*, unrightfully, untruly; unjustly, wrongously, tortiously, illegally, criminally, feloniously.

See: 29, 84, 306, 477, 481, 495, 643, 645, 703, 735, 757, 861, 867, 891, 916, 928, 930, 934, 936, 938, 954.

915 Dueness

N. *dueness*, what is due, what is owing; accountability, responsibility, obligation 917 n. *duty*; the least one can do, bare minimum; what one looks for, expectations; payability, dues 804 n. *payment*; something owed, indebtedness 803 n. *debt*; tribute, credit 158 n. *attribution*; recognition, acknowledgment 907 n. *thanks*; something to be said for, case for; qualification, deserts, merits; justification 927 n. *vindication*; entitlement, claim, title 913 n. *right*; birthright, patrimony 777 n. *dower*; interest, vested i., vested right, prescriptive r., absolute r., infeasible r., inalienable r.; legal right, easement, prescription, ancient lights; constitutional right, civil rights, bill of r.; privilege, exemption, immunity 919 n. *non-liability*; prerogative, privilege; charter, warrant, licence 756 n. *permit*; liberty, franchise 744 n. *freedom*; bond, security 767 n. *title-deed*; patent, copyright; recovery of rights, restoration, compensation 787 n. *restitution*; owner, title-holder 776 n. *possessor*; heir 776 n. *beneficiary*; claimant, plaintiff, appellant; man with a grievance, agitator 763 n. *petitioner*.

Adj. *due*, owing, payable 803 adj. *owed*; ascribable, attributable, assignable; merited, well-m., deserved, well-d., richlyd., condign, earned, well-e., coming to one; admitted, allowed, sanctioned, warranted, licit, lawful 756 adj. *permitted*; constitutional, entrenched, untouchable, uninfringeable, unchallengable, unimpeachable, inviolable; privileged, sacrosanct; confirmed, vested, prescriptive, inalienable, imprescriptible; secured by law, legalized, legitimate, rightful, of right, de jure 953 adj. *legal*; claimable, heritable, inheritable, earmarked, reserved; expected, fit, fitting, befitting; proper, en règle 642 adj. *expedient*.

deserving, meriting, worthy of, worthy, meritorious, emeritus; grant-worthy, credit-w.; justifiable, justified; entitled, having the right, having the title, claiming the right, asserting one's privilege, standing up for one's rights.

Vb. *be due*, — owing etc. adj.; ought, ought to be, should be, should have been; be one's due, be due to, have it coming; be the least one can offer, be the least one can do, be the bare minimum; behove, befit, beseem 917 vb. *be one's duty*.

claim, claim as a right, lay a claim, stake a c., take possession 786 vb. *appropriate*; arrogate, demand one's rights, assert one's r., stand up for one's r., vindicate one's r. 927 vb. *vindicate*; draw on, come down on for, lay under contribution, take one's toll 786 vb. *levy*; call in (debts), reclaim, revendicate 656 vb. *retrieve*; publish one's claims, declare one's right, clarigate; sue, demand redress 761 vb. *request*; enforce a claim, exercise a right; establish a right, patent, copyright.

have a right, expect, have a right to e., claim; be entitled, be privileged, have the right

to, have a claim to, make out one's case 478vb. *demonstrate*; have the law on one's side, have the court in one's favour, get a verdict.

deserve, merit, be worthy, be found w., have a claim on; earn, receive one's dues, meet with one's deserts, get one's d.; have it coming to one, have only oneself to thank.

grant claims, give every man his due 913vb. *be just*; ascribe, assign, credit 158vb. *attribute*; hand it to, acknowledge, recognize 907vb. *thank*; allow a claim, sanction a c., warrant, authorize 756vb. *permit*; admit a right, acknowledge a claim, satisfy a c., pay one's dues, honour, meet an obligation, honour a bill 804vb. *pay*; privilege, give a right, confer a r., entitle, vest with a title; allot, prescribe 783vb. *apportion*; legalize, legitimize 953 vb. *make legal*; confirm, validate 488vb. *endorse*.

Adv. *duly*, by right, in one's own right, by law, de jure, ex officio, by divine right, jure divino; as expected of one, as required of one.

See: 158, 478, 488, 642, 656, 744, 756, 761, 763, 767, 776, 777, 783, 786, 787, 803, 804, 907, 913, 917, 919, 927, 953.

916 Undueness

N. *undueness*, not what one expects *or* would expect 508n. *inexpectation*; impropriety, unseemliness 847n. *bad taste*; unfittingness 643n. *inexpedience*; unworthiness, demerit 934n. *vice*; illicitness, illegitimacy, bastardy 954n. *illegality*; no thanks to 908n. *ingratitude*; absence of right, want of title, failure of t., non-entitlement; no claim, no right, no title, false t., weak t., empty t., courtesy t.; gratuitousness, gratuity, bonus, grace marks, baker's dozen, unearned increment; inordinacy, excessiveness, too much, overpayment 637n. *redundance*; imposition, exaction 735n. *severity*; unfair share, lion's s. 32n. *main part*; violation, breach, infraction, infringement, encroachment 306n. *overstepping*; profanation, desecration 980n. *impiety*.

arrogation, assumption, unjustified a., presumption, unwarranted p., swollen claims; pretendership, usurpation, tyran-

ny; misappropriation 786n. *expropriation*; encroachment, inroad, trespass 306 n. *overstepping*.

loss of right, disentitlement, disfranchisement, disqualification; alienization, denaturalization, detribalization 147n. *conversion*; forfeiture 772n. *loss*; dismissal, deprivation, dethronement 752n. *deposal*; ouster, dispossession 786n. *expropriation*; seizure, forcible e., robbery 788n. *stealing*; cancellation 752n. *abrogation*; waiver, abdication 621n. *relinquishment*.

usurper, arrogator 735n. *tyrant*; pretender 545n. *impostor*; desecrator; violator, infringer, encroacher, trespasser, squatter.

Adj. *undue*, not owing, unattributable; unowed, gratuitous, by favour; not expected, unlooked for, uncalled for 508 adj. *unexpected*; improper, unmeet, unseemly, unfitting, unbefitting, inappropriate 643adj. *inexpedient*; preposterous, not to be thought of, out of the question 497adj. *absurd*.

unwarranted, unwarrantable; unauthorized, unsanctioned, unallowed, unlicensed, unchartered, unconstitutional; unlegalized, illicit, illegitimate, ultra vires 954 adj. *illegal*; arrogated, usurped, stolen, borrowed; excessive, presumptuous, assuming 878adj. *insolent*; unjustified, unjustifiable 914adj. *wrong*; unclaimable, undeserved, unmerited, unearned; overpaid, underpaid; invalid, weak; false, spurious 954adj. *bastard*; fictitious, would-be 850adj. *affected*.

unentitled, without title, uncrowned; unqualified, without qualifications, unempowered, incompetent; unworthy, undeserving, meritless, unmeritorious; underprivileged, unprivileged, without rights; unchartered, unfranchised, voteless; disentitled, discrowned; dethroned, deposed; disqualified, invalidated, disfranchised, defrocked; deprived, bereft, dispossessed, expropriated; forfeited, forfeit.

Vb. *be undue*, — undeserved etc.adj.; not be due, be unclaimed, be unclaimable; show ill-taste, misbecome, misbeseem 847vb. *vulgarize*; presume, arrogate 878 vb. *be insolent*; usurp, borrow 788vb. *steal*; trespass, squat 306vb. *encroach*; infringe, break, violate 954vb. *be illegal*; desecrate, profane 980vb. *be impious*; underpay, overpay.

disentitle, uncrown, unthrone 752vb. *depose*; disqualify, unfrock, disfranchise, alienize, denaturalize, detribalize, denationalize; invalidate 752vb. *abrogate*; disallow 757 vb. *prohibit*; dispossess, expropriate 786 vb. *deprive*; forfeit, declare f.; defeat a claim, mock the claims of; make illegitimate, illegalize 954vb. *make illegal*; bastardize, debase 655vb. *impair.*

Adv. *unduly*, improperly; undeservedly, without desert, no thanks to.

See: 32, 147, 306, 497, 508, 545, 621, 637, 643, 655, 735, 752, 757, 772, 786, 788, 847, 850, 878, 908, 914, 934, 954, 980.

917 Duty

N. *duty*, what ought to be done, what is up to one, the right thing, the proper t., the decent t.; one's duty, bounden d., imperative d., inescapable d.; obligation, liability, onus, responsibility, accountability 915n. *dueness*; fealty, allegiance, loyalty 739n. *obedience*; sense of duty, dutifulness, duteousness 597n. *willingness*; discharge of duty, performance, acquittal, discharge 768n. *observance*; call of duty, claims of conscience, case of c., matter of duty; bond, tie, engagement, commitment, word, pledge 764n. *promise*; task, office, charge 751n. *commission*; walk of life, profession 622n. *vocation.*

conscience, professional c., tender c., nonconformist c., exacting c., peremptory c.; categorical imperative, inward monitor, inner voice, 'still, small voice,' 'stern, daughter of the voice of God'.

code of duty, code of honour, unwritten code, professional c., Bushido; decalogue, ten commandments, Twelve Tables, Hippocratic oath 693n. *precept.*

morals, morality 933n. *virtue*; honour 929n. *probity*; moral principles, ideals, high i., standards, high s., professional s.; ethics, Christian e., professional e.; ethology, deontology, casuistry, ethical philosophy, moral p., moral science, idealism, utilitarianism, behaviourism 449n. *philosophy.*

Adj. *dutied*, on duty, duty-bound, bounden, bound by duty, pressed by d., called by d.; under duty, in duty bound; obliged, obligated, beholden, under obligation; tied, bound, sworn, pledged, committed, engaged; unexempted, liable, amenable, chargeable, answerable, responsible, accountable; in honour bound, bound in conscience, answerable to God; warned by conscience, plagued by c., conscience-struck 939adj. *repentant*; conscientious, observant, duteous, dutiful 739adj. *obedient*; vowed, under a vow.

obligatory, incumbent, imposed, behoving, up to one; binding, de rigueur, compulsive, peremptory, operative 740adj. *compelling*; inescapable, unavoidable; strict, unconditional, categorical.

ethical, moral 933adj. *virtuous*; honest, decent 929adj. *honourable*; moralistic, ethological, casuistical; moralizing; idealistic; utilitarian.

Vb. *be one's duty*, be incumbent, behove, become, befit, beseem 915vb. *be due*; devolve on, belong to; pertain to, fall to, be involved in one's office, arise from one's functions; lie, rest, rest on one's shoulders.

incur a duty, make it one's d., take on oneself, accept responsibility, shoulder one's r.; make oneself liable, commit oneself, pledge o., engage for 764vb. *promise*; assume one's functions, enter upon one's office, receive a posting; have the office, have the function, have the charge, have the duty; owe it to oneself, feel it up to one; feel duty's call, accept the c., answer the c., submit to one's vocation.

do one's duty, fulfil one's d. 739vb. *obey*; discharge, acquit, perform 676vb. *do*; do one's office, discharge one's functions 768vb. *observe*; be on duty, stay at one's post, go down with one's ship; come up to what is expected of one, not be found wanting; keep faith with one's conscience, face one's obligations, discharge an obligation, acquit oneself of an o., redeem a pledge; honour, meet, pay up 804vb. *pay.*

impose a duty, require, oblige, look to, call upon; devolve, call to office, swear one in, offer a post, post 751vb. *commission*; assign a duty, saddle with, detail, order, enjoin, decree 737vb. *command*; tax, task, overtask, o'er-labour 684vb. *fatigue*; exact 735vb. *be severe*; demand obedience, expect it of one 507vb. *expect*; bind, condition 766vb. *give terms*; bind over, take security 764vb. *take a pledge.*

Adv. *on duty*, under d., in the line of d., as in duty bound; at one's post; in foro conscientiæ; with a safe conscience.

See: 449, 507, 597, 622, 676, 684, 693, 735, 737, 739, 740, 751, 764, 766, 768, 804, 915, 929, 933, 939.

918 Dutilessness

N. *dutilessness*, default, want of duty, failure of d., dereliction of d.; neglect, laches, culpable negligence 458 n. *negligence*; undutifulness, unduteousness 921 n. *disrespect*; malingering, evasion of duty 620 n. *avoidance*; non-practice, non-performance 769 n. *non-observance*; idleness, laziness 679 n. *sluggishness*; forgetfulness 506 n. *oblivion*; non-cooperation, want of alacrity 598 n. *unwillingness*; truancy, absenteeism 190 n. *absence*; abscondence 667 n. *escape*; infraction, violation, breach of orders, indiscipline, mutiny, rebellion 738 n. *disobedience*; incompetence, mismanagement 695 n. *bungling*; obstruction, sabotage 702 n. *hindrance*; desertion, defection 603 n. *tergiversation*; disloyalty, prodition, treachery 930 n. *perfidy*; secession, break-away 978 n. *schism*; irresponsibility, escapism; truant, absentee, malingerer, defaulter 620 n. *avoider*; deserter, absconder 667 n. *escaper*; betrayer, traitor 603 n. *tergiversator*; saboteur 702 n. *hinderer*; mutineer, rebel 738 n. *revolter*; seceder 978 n. *schismatic*; escapist 620 n. *avoider*.

Adj. *dutiless*, wanting in duty, uncooperative 598 adj. *unwilling*; undutiful, unduteous, unfilial, undaughterly 921 adj. *disrespectful*; mutinous, rebellious 738 adj. *disobedient*; disloyal, treacherous 930 adj. *perfidious*; irresponsible, unreliable; truant, absentee 190 adj. *absent*; absconding 667 adj. *escaped*.

Vb. *fail in duty*, neglect one's d., commit laches 458 vb. *neglect*; ignore one's obligations 458 vb. *disregard*; oversleep 679 vb. *sleep*; default, let one down, leave one in the lurch 728 vb. *fail*; mismanage, bungle 495 vb. *blunder*; not remember 506 vb. *forget*; shirk, evade, wriggle out of, malinger, dodge the column 620 vb. *avoid*; play truant, overstay leave 190 vb. *be absent*; abscond 667 vb. *escape*; quit, scuttle, abandon, abandon one's post,

desert, desert the colours 621 vb. *relinquish*; break orders, disobey o., violate o., exceed one's instructions 738 vb. *disobey*; mutiny, rebel 738 vb. *revolt*; be disloyal, prove treacherous, betray 603 vb. *tergiversate*; strike, strike work, come out 145 vb. *cease*; sabotage 702 vb. *obstruct*; non-cooperate, withdraw, walk out, break away, secede 978 vb. *schismatize*.

See: 145, 190, 458, 495, 506, 598, 603, 620, 621, 667, 679, 695, 702, 728, 738, 769, 921, 930, 978.

919 Non-liability

N. *non-liability*, non-responsibility, exemption, dispensation; conscience-clause, escape-c. 468 n. *qualification*; immunity, impunity, privilege, special p., clergiability, benefit of clergy; extra-territoriality, capitulations; franchise, charter 915 n. *ducness*; independence, liberty, the four freedoms 744 n. *freedom*; licence, leave 756 n. *permission*; congé, ægrotat, certificate of exemption 756 n. *permit*; excuse, exoneration, exculpation 960 n. *acquittal*; absolution, pardon, amnesty 909 n. *forgiveness*; discharge, release 746 n. *liberation*; renunciation 621 n. *relinquishment*; evasion of responsibility, escapism, self-exemption, washing one's hands, passing the buck 753 n. *resignation*.

Adj. *non-liable*, not responsible, not answerable, unaccountable, unpunishable; unbound, unencumbered, unentailed; excused, exonerated 960 adj. *acquitted*; dispensed, exempted, privileged, prerogatived; clergiable; shielded, protected; untouched, exempt, immune; unaffected, well out of; independent, unconfined, scot-free 744 adj. *free*; tax-free, post-f., duty-f. 812 adj. *uncharged*.

Vb. *exempt*, set apart, segregate 883 vb. *seclude*; eliminate, count out, rule o. 57 vb. *exclude*; excuse, exonerate, exculpate 960 vb. *acquit*; grant absolution, absolve, shrive; pardon 909 vb. *forgive*; spare 905 vb. *show mercy*; grant immunity, privilege, charter 756 vb. *permit*; license, dispense, give dispensation, grant impunity; amnesty 506 vb. *forget*; enfranchise, manumit, set at liberty, release 746 vb. *liberate*; pass over, stretch a point 736 vb. *be lenient*.

be exempt, — exempted etc. adj.; have one's

withers unwrung, owe no responsibility, have no liability, not come within the scope of, not within the mischief of; enjoy immunity, enjoy impunity, enjoy a privileged position, enjoy independence 744 vb. *be free*; spare oneself the necessity, exempt oneself, excuse oneself, absent oneself, take leave, go on leave 190 vb. *go away*; transfer the responsibility, pass the buck, shift the blame 272 vb. *transfer*; evade *or* escape liability, get away with 667 vb. *escape*; own *or* admit no responsibility, wash one's hands.

See: 57, 190, 272, 468, 506, 621, 667, 736, 744, 746, 753, 756, 812, 883, 905, 909, 915, 960.

920 Respect

N. *respect*, regard, consideration, esteem, estimation, honour, favour 866 n. *repute*; polite regard, attention, attentions, flattering a. 884 n. *courtesy*; due respect, respectfulness, deference, humbleness 872 n. *humility*; obsequiousness 879 n. *servility*; humble service, fealty, devotion 739 n. *loyalty*; admiration, awe 864 n. *wonder*; terror 854 n. *fear*; reverence, veneration, adoration 981 n. *worship*.

respects, regards, duty, devoirs, kind remembrances, greetings 884 n. *courteous act*; due respect, address of welcome, illuminated address, salutation, salaam, namaskar; nod, bob, duck, bow, scrape, curtsy, genuflexion, one's knees, prostration, kowtow 311 n. *obeisance*; reverence, homage; salute, presenting arms; honours of war, flags flying.

Adj. *respectful*, deferential, knowing one's place 872 adj. *humble*; obsequious, bootlicking 879 adj. *servile*; submissive 721 adj. *submitting*; reverent, reverential 981 adj. *worshipping*; admiring, awe-struck 864 adj. *wondering*; polite 884 adj. *courteous*; ceremonious, with hand at the salute, cap in hand, bare-headed; kneeling on one's knees, prostrate; bobbing, ducking, bowing, scraping, bending, stooping; obeisant, showing respect, rising, standing, on one's feet, all standing.

respected, admired, honoured, esteemed, revered 866 adj. *reputable*; respectable, reverend, venerable; time-honoured 866 adj. *worshipful*; imposing 821 adj. *impres-*

sive; received with respect, received all standing, saluted.

Vb. *respect*, entertain r., hold in r., hold in estimation, hold in honour, think well of, rank high, place h., look up to, esteem, regard, tender, value; admire 864 vb. *wonder*; reverence, venerate, exalt, magnify 866 vb. *honour*; adore 981 vb. *worship*; idolize 982 vb. *idolatrize*; revere, stand in awe, have a wholesome respect for 854 vb. *fear*; know one's place, defer to 721 vb. *submit*; pay tribute to 923 vb. *praise*; do homage to, chair, lionize 876 vb. *celebrate*.

show respect, render honour, homage, pay h., do the honours 884 vb. *pay respects*; make way for, leave room for, keep one's distance, know one's place; go to meet, welcome, hail, meet with flags flying, salute, present arms, turn out the guard 884 vb. *greet*; cheer, drink to 876 vb. *toast*; bob, duck, bow, scrape, make a leg, curtsy, kneel, kowtow, prostrate oneself 311 vb. *stoop*; observe decorum, stand on ceremony, stand, rise, rise to one's feet, rise from one's seat, stand bareheaded; humble oneself, condescend 872 vb. *be humble*.

command respect, inspire r., awe, strike with a., overawe, impose 821 vb. *impress*; enjoy a reputation, rank high, stand h., stand well in all men's eyes 866 vb. *have repute*; compel respect, demand r., extort admiration 864 vb. *be wonderful*; dazzle, bedazzle 875 vb. *be ostentatious*; receive respect, gain honour, gain a reputation, win golden opinions 923 vb. *be praised*.

Adv. *respectfully*, humbly, with all respect, with due deference; obsequiously, reverentially, reverently; saving your grace, saving your presence.

See: 311, 721, 739, 821, 854, 864, 866, 872, 875, 876, 879, 884, 923, 981, 982.

921 Disrespect

N. *disrespect*, want of respect, scant r., disrespectfulness, irreverence, impoliteness, discourtesy 885 n. *rudeness*; disesteem, dishonour, disfavour 924 n. *disapprobation*; neglect, undervaluation 483 n. *underestimation*; low estimation 867 n. *disrepute*; depreciation, disparagement 926 n. *detraction*; vilipendency, contumely

899 n. *scurrility*; scorn 922 n. *contempt*; mockery 851 n. *ridicule*; desecration 980 n. *impiety.*

indignity, humiliation, affront, insult, slight, snub, slap in the face, outrage 878 n. *insolence*; snook, snooks 878 n. *sauciness*; gibe, taunt, jeer, fling 922 n. *contempt*; quip, sarcasm, mock, flout 851 n. *ridicule*; hiss, hoot, boo, catcall, brickbat, brick 924 n. *disapprobation.*

Adj. *disrespectful*, wanting in respect, slighting, neglectful 458 adj. *negligent*; irreverent, irreverential, aweless 865 adj. *unastonished*; sacrilegious 980 adj. *profane*; outspoken, overcandid 573 adj. *plain*; rude, impolite 885 adj. *discourteous*; airy, breezy, off-handed, cavalier, familiar, cheeky, saucy 878 adj. *impertinent*; insulting, outrageous 878 adj. *insolent*; flouting, jeering, gibing, scoffing, mocking, satirical, cynical, sarcastic 851 adj. *derisive*; injurious, contumelious, scurrilous, scurrile 899 adj. *maledicent*; depreciative, pejorative 483 adj. *depreciating*; snobbish, supercilious, disdainful, scornful 922 adj. *despising*; unflattering, uncomplimentary 924 adj. *disapproving.*

unrespected, disrespected, held in low esteem, of no account 867 adj. *disreputable*; ignored, unregarded, disregarded, unsaluted, ungreeted 458 adj. *neglected*; unenvied, unadmired, unflattered, unreverenced, unrevered, unworshipped; underrated, disparaged 483 adj. *undervalued*; looked down on, spat on 922 adj. *contemptible.*

Vb. *not respect*, deny r., disrespect; be unable to respect, have no respect for, have no regard f., have no use f. 924 vb. *disapprove*; misprize, undervalue, underrate 483 vb. *underestimate*; look down on, disdain, scorn 922 vb. *despise*; run down, disparage 926 vb. *defame*; spit on, toss aside 607 vb. *reject*; show disrespect, want respect, fail in courtesy, remain seated, remain covered, keep one's hat on, push aside, shove a., crowd, jostle 885 vb. *be rude*; ignore, turn one's back 458 vb. *disregard*; snub, slight, put a slight upon, insult, affront, outrage 872 vb. *humiliate*; dishonour, disgrace, put to shame, drag in the mud 867 vb. *shame*; trifle with, treat lightly 922 vb. *hold cheap*; cheapen, lower, degrade 847 vb. *vulgarize*; have no awe, not reverence, desecrate, profane

980 vb. *be impious*; call names, vilipend, abuse, indulge in scurrilities 899 vb. *curse*; taunt, twit, cock a snook 878 vb. *be insolent*; laugh at, scoff, mock, flout, deride 851 vb. *ridicule*; make mouths at, jeer, hiss, hoot, boo, point at, spit at 924 vb. *exprobate*; mob, hound, chase 619 vb. *pursue*; pelt, stone, throw stones, heave a brick 712 vb. *lapidate.*

Adv. *disrespectfully*, irreverently, profanely, sacrilegiously, contumeliously, injuriously; mockingly, derisively.

See: 458, 483, 573, 607, 619, 712, 847, 851, 865, 867, 872, 878, 885, 899, 922, 924, 926, 980.

922 Contempt

N. *contempt*, sovereign c., supreme c., utter c., unutterable c.; misprision, scorn, disdain, disdainfulness, superiority, loftiness 871 n. *pride*; contemptuousness, sniffiness; superciliousness, snobbishness 850 n. *affectation*; superior airs, scornful eye, smile of contempt, curl of the lip, snort; slight, humiliation 921 n. *disrespect*; sneer 926 n. *detraction*; scoff, flout, mock 851 n. *ridicule*; snub, rebuff, cut, cut direct 885 n. *discourtesy.*

despisedness, unworthiness, contemptibility, insignificance, puerility, pitiability, futility 639 n. *unimportance*; pettiness, meanness, littleness, paltriness 33 n. *smallness*; reproach, a hissing and a reproach, byword of reproach 867 n. *object of scorn.*

Adj. *despising*, full of contempt, contemptuous, disdainful, holier than thou, snooty, sniffy, snobbish; haughty, lofty, airy, supercilious 871 adj. *proud*; scornful, contumelious, withering, jeering, sneering, booing 924 adj. *disapproving*; disrespectful, impertinent 878 adj. *insolent*; slighting, pooh-poohing 483 adj. *depreciating.*

contemptible, despicable, beneath contempt; abject, worthless 645 adj. *bad*; petty, paltry, little, mean 33 adj. *small*; spurned, spat on 607 adj. *rejected*; scorned, despised, contemned, of no account 921 adj. *unrespected*; trifling, pitiable, futile 639 adj. *unimportant.*

Vb. *despise*, contemn, hold in despite, hold in contempt, feel utter contempt for, have no use for 921 vb. *not respect*; look down on, hold beneath one, be too high

for, be too grand for 871 vb. *be proud*; disdain, spurn, sniff at, snort at 607 vb. *reject*; come it over, turn up one's nose, wrinkle the n., curl one's lips, toss one's head, snort; snub, turn one's back on 885 vb. *be rude*; scorn, whistle, hiss, boo, point, point the finger of scorn 924 vb. *exprobate*; laugh at, turn to scorn, laugh to s., scoff, scout, flout, gibe, jeer, mock, deride 851 vb. *ridicule*; trample on, ride rough-shod over 735 vb. *oppress*; disgrace, roll in the mire 867 vb. *shame*.

hold cheap, disesteem, misprize 921 vb. *not respect*; ignore, dismiss, not mind 458 vb. *disregard*; belittle, disparage, fail to appreciate, underrate, undervalue 483 vb. *underestimate*; disprize, decry 926 vb. *detract*; set no value on, set no store by, think nothing of, think small beer of, not care a rap for, not care a straw; laugh at, treat as a laughing matter, snap one's fingers at, set at naught, shrug away, pooh-pooh, say bah! slight, trifle with, treat lightly, treat like dirt, lower, degrade 872 vb. *humiliate*.

Adv. *contemptuously*, disdainfully, scornfully, with contempt, with disdain.

contemptibly, pitiably, miserably; to one's utter contempt, to all men's contempt.

See: 33, 458, 483, 607, 639, 645, 735, 850, 851, 867, 871, 872, 878, 885, 921, 924, 926.

923 Approbation

N. *approbation*, approval, sober a., modified rapture; satisfaction 828 n. *content*; appreciation, recognition 907 n. *gratitude*; good opinion, golden opinions, kudos, credit 866 n. *prestige*; regard, admiration, esteem 920 n. *respect*; good books, good graces, grace, favour, popularity, affection 887 n. *love*; adoption, acceptance, welcome, favourable reception 299 n. *reception*; sanction 756 n. *permission*; nod of approval, seal of a., blessing; nod, wink, thumbs up, consent 488 n. *assent*; countenance, patronage, championship, advocacy 703 n. *aid*; good word, kind w., testimonial, reference, commendation, recommendation 466 n. *credential*.

praise, loud p., lyrical p., praise and glory, laud, laudation, invocation, benediction, blessing, benison; compliment, high c., encomium, eulogy, panegyric, glorification, adulation, idolatry 925 n. *flattery*; hero-worship 864 n. *wonder*; overpraise 482 n. *overestimation*; faint praise, two cheers; shout of praise, hosannah; praises, song of praise, hymn of p., pæan of p., dithyramb, doxology; tribute, credit, meed of praise, tribute of p. 907 n. *thanks*; complimentary reference, bouquet, citation, commendation, official biography, hagiography; self-praise, self-glorification 877 n. *boasting*; letters of gold; puffing, blurb 528 n. *advertisement*.

applause, clamorous a., acclaim, universal a.; enthusiasm, excitement 821 adj. *excitation*; warm reception, hero's welcome 876 n. *celebration*; acclamation, plaudits, clapping, claque, whistling, cheering; clap, three cheers, pæan, hosannah; thunderous applause, peal of a., shout of a., chorus of a., round of a., storm of a., ovation; encore, curtain call; bouquet, pat on the back.

commender, praiser, laudator, encomiast, eulogist, panegyrist; clapper, shouter, claqueur, claque; approver, friendly critic, admirer, devoted a., hero-worshipper; advocate, recommender, supporter, speaker for the motion 707 n. *patron*; inscriber, dedicator; advertiser, blurb-writer, puffer, booster; agent, tout, touter, barker 528 n. *publicizer*; canvasser, electioneerer, election agent.

Adj. *approving*, uncensorious, uncomplaining, satisfied 828 adj. *content*; favouring, supporting, advocating 703 adj. *aiding*; benedictory 907 adj. *grateful*; approbatory, favourable, well-inclined; appreciative, complimentary, commendatory, laudatory, eulogistic, encomiastic, panegyrical, lyrical; admiring, hero-worshipping, idolatrous; lavish, generous; fulsome, over-praising, uncritical, undiscriminating; acclamatory, plausive, clapping, thundering, thunderous, clamorous 400 adj. *loud*; dithyrambic, ecstatic 821 adj. *excited*.

approvable, admissible, permissible, acceptable; worth-while 640 adj. *useful*; deserving, meritorious, commendable, laudable, estimable, worthy, praiseworthy, creditable, admirable, uncensurable, unimpeachable, beyond all praise 646 adj. *perfect*; enviable, desirable 859 adj. *desired*.

approved, passed, tested, tried; uncensured, free from blame, stamped with approval, blessed; popular, in favour, in high f., in the good graces of, in good odour, in high esteem, thought well of 866 adj. *reputable*; favoured, backed, odds on 605 adj. *chosen*.

Vb. *approve*, see nothing wrong with, sound pleased, have no fault to find, have nothing but praise for; like well 887 vb. *love*; think well of, admire, esteem, tender, value, prize, treasure, cherish, set store by 866 vb. *honour*; appreciate, give credit, salute, take one's hat off to, hand it to, give full marks; think no worse of, think the better of; count it for merit, see the good points, see the good in one, think good, think perfect; think desirable 912 vb. *envy*; think the best, award the palm; see to be good, find g., pronounce g., mark with approbation, seal *or* stamp with approval; accept, pass, tick off, give marks; nod, wink, nod one's approval, give one's assent 488 vb. *assent*; sanction, bless, give one's blessing 756 vb. *permit*; ratify 488 vb. *endorse*; commend, recommend, advocate, support, back, favour, countenance, stand up for, speak up f., put in a word for, give one a reference, give one a testimonial 703 vb. *patronize*.

praise, compliment, pay compliments 925 vb. *flatter*; speak well of, speak highly, swear by; bless 907 vb. *thank*; salute, pay tribute to, hand it to, take one's hat off to; commend, give praise, bepraise, laud, belaud, eulogize, panegyrize, laud to the skies, hymn, sound the praises, sing the p., hymn the p., swell the p., doxologize, exalt, extol, glorify, magnify; not spare one's blushes 546 vb. *exaggerate*; puff, inflate, overpraise, overestimate 482 vb. *overrate*; lionize, hero-worship, idolize 982 vb. *idolatrize*; trumpet, write up, cry up, crack up, boost 528 vb. *advertise*; praise oneself, glorify o. 877 vb. *boast*.

applaud, receive with applause, welcome, hail, hail with satisfaction; acclaim, receive with acclamation, clap, clap one's hands, give a hand, stamp, whistle, thunder one's plaudits; cheer, raise a c., give three cheers, give three times three; cheer to the echo, shout for, root; clap on the back, pat on the back; welcome, garland, chair 876 vb. *celebrate*; drink to 876 vb. *toast*.

be praised, — praiseworthy etc. adj.; get a citation, be mentioned in despatches; recommend oneself 866 vb. *seek repute*; find favour, win praise, gain credit, earn golden opinions 866 vb. *have repute*; get a compliment, receive a tribute, get a hand, get a clap, get a cheer; receive an ovation, take the house by storm 727 vb. *triumph*; deserve praise, be to one's credit, redound to the honour; pass, do, pass muster, pass the test.

Adv. *approvingly*, admiringly, with admiration, with praises, with compliments; ungrudgingly, without demur; enviously.

commendably, admirably, wonderfully, unimpeachably; acceptably, satisfactorily, to satisfaction, to approval.

Int. bravo! well done! hear hear! encore! bis! three cheers! hurrah! hosannah.

See: 299, 400, 466, 482, 488, 528, 546, 605, 640, 646, 703, 707, 727, 756, 821, 828, 859, 864, 866, 876, 877, 887, 907, 912, 920, 925, 982.

924 Disapprobation

N. *disapprobation*, disapproval, dissatisfaction 829 n. *discontent*; non-approval, return 607 n. *rejection*; no permission 760 n. *refusal*; disfavour, displeasure, unpopularity 861 n. *dislike*; disesteem 921 n. *disrespect*; poor opinion, low o. 867 n. *disrepute*; disparagement, decrial, crabbing, carping, niggling 926 n. *detraction*; censoriousness, fault-finding 862 n. *fastidiousness*; hostility 881 n. *enmity*; objection, exception, cavil 468 n. *qualification*; impugnation, improbation 479 n. *confutation*; complaint, clamour, outcry, protest, tut-tut 762 n. *deprecation*; indignation, explosion 891 n. *anger*; sibilation, hissing, hiss, boo, countercheer, whistle, catcall, brick, brickbat 851 n. *ridicule*; ostracism, boycott, bar, colour-b., ban, non-admission 57 n. *exclusion*; blackball, blacklist, bad books; index, index expurgatorius.

censure, dispraise, discommendation, blame, reprehension, impeachment, inculpation 928 n. *accusation*; home-truth, no compliment, poor c., left-handed c., back-handed c.; criticism, hostile c., stricture; hypercriticism, fault-finding; hostile attack, slashing a., onslaught 712 n. *attack*; bad

press, critical review, hostile r., slashing r., slating; open letter, tirade, jeremiad, philippic, diatribe, speech for the opposition 704n. *opposition*; conviction 961n. *condemnation*; false accusation 928n. *false charge*; slur, slander, insinuation, innuendo 926n. *calumny*; brand, stigma.

reproach, reproaches, exprobation; objurgation, rixation, wordy quarrel 709n. *quarrel*; home-truths, invective, vituperation, calling names, bawling out, shouting down 899n. *scurrility*; execration 899n. *malediction*; personalities, personal remarks, aspersion, reflection 921n. *indignity*; taunt, sneer 878n. *insolence*; sarcasm, irony, satire, biting wit, biting tongue, cut, hit, home-thrust 851n. *ridicule*; rough side of one's tongue, tongue-lashing, hard words, cutting w., bitter w. (see *reprimand*); silent reproach, disapproving look, dirty l., black l. 893n. *sullenness*.

reprimand, remonstrance 762n. *deprecation*; stricture, animadversion, reprehension, reprobation; censure, rebuke, reproof, snub; rocket, raspberry; piece of one's mind, expression of displeasure, mark of d., black mark; castigation, correction, rap over the knuckles, box on the ears 963n. *punishment*; inculpation, admonition, admonishment, increpation, tongue-lashing, chiding, upbraiding, scolding, rating, slating, strafing trouncing, dressing down, blowing up, wigging, trimming, carpeting, mauvais quart d'heure; talking to, lecture, curtain l., jobation.

disapprover, no friend, no admirer; non-favourer, non-supporter, non-voter; damper, death's head, spoilsport, misery 834n. *moper*; pussyfoot, puritan, rigorist 950n. *prude*; attacker, opposer 705n. *opponent*; critic, hard c., hostile c., captious c., knocker, fault-finder; reprover, castigator, censurer, censor; satirist, lampooner, mocker 926n. *detractor*; brander, stigmatizer; misogynist 902n. *misanthrope*; grouser, groucher, man with a grievance 829n. *malcontent*.

Adj. *disapproving*, unapproving, unable to approve, not amused, unamused; shocked scandalized; unadmiring, unimpressed; disillusioned 509adj. *disappointed*; sparing of praise, grudging; silent 582adj. *taciturn*; disapprobatory, unfavourable,

spitting, expectoratory; hostile 881adj. *inimical*; objecting, protesting, clamorous 762adj. *deprecatory*; reproachful, chiding, scolding, upbraiding, vituperative, objurgatory, personal, scurrilous 899adj. *maledictory*; critical, unflattering, uncomplimentary; withering, hard-hitting, strongly worded; over-critical, hypercritical, captious, fault-finding, niggling, carping; disparaging, defamatory, damaging 926adj. *detracting*; caustic, sharp, bitter, venomous, trenchant, mordant; sarcastic, sardonic, cynical 851adj. *derisive*; censorious, holier than thou; blaming, faulting, censuring, reprimanding, recriminative, denunciatory, accusatory, condemning, damning, damnatory 928adj. *accusing*.

disapproved, unapproved, blacklisted, blackballed 607adj. *rejected*; unsatisfactory, found wanting 636adj. *insufficient*; ploughed, plucked, failed 728adj. *unsuccessful*; cancelled 752adj. *abrogated*; deleted, censored 550adj. *obliterated*; out of favour, under a cloud; unpraised, dispraised, criticized, shot at, decried, run down, slandered, calumniated; lectured, henpecked, nagged, reprimanded, scolded, chidden; on the mat, on the carpet; unregretted, unlamented, unbewailed, unpitied 861adj. *disliked*; hooted, hissed, hissed off the stage, exploded, discredited, disowned, out; in bad odour, in one's bad books 867adj. *disreputable*.

blameworthy, not good enough, too bad; blamable, exceptionable, open to criticism, censurable, condemnable 645adj. *damnable*; reprehensible, dishonourable, unjustifiable 867adj. *discreditable*; unpraiseworthy, uncommendable, not to be recommended, not to be thought of; reprobate, culpable, to blame 928adj. *accusable*.

Vb. *disapprove*, not admire, hold no brief for, fail to appreciate, have no praise for, not think much of, think little of; think the worse of, think ill of, disprize 922vb. *despise*; not pass, fail, plough, pluck; return 607vb. *reject*; disallow 757vb. *prohibit*; cancel 752vb. *abrogate*; censor 550vb. *obliterate*; withhold approval, look grave, shake one's head, not hold with 489vb. *dissent*; disfavour, reprehend, lament, deplore 830vb. *regret*; abhor, reprobate 861vb. *dislike*; wash one's

hands, disown, look askance, avoid, ignore; keep at a distance, draw the line, ostracize, ban, bar, blacklist 57 vb. *exclude*; protest, tut-tut, remonstrate, object, except, demur 762 vb. *deprecate*; discountenance, show disapproval, exclaim, shout down, bawl d., hoot, boo, counter-cheer, hiss, whistle, explode, drive off the stage; throw mud, throw bad eggs, throw bricks, stone, throw stones 712 vb. *lapidate*; hound, chase, mob, lynch; make a face, make a moue, make mouths at, spit; look black 893 vb. *be sullen*; look daggers 891 vb. *be angry*.

dispraise, discommend, not recommend, give no marks to, damn with faint praise, damn 961 vb. *condemn*; criticize, fault, pick holes, cut up, crab, cavil, depreciate, run down, belittle 926 vb. *detract*; oppose, tilt at, shoot at 712 vb. *attack*; weigh in, hit hard, savage, maul, slash, slate, scourge, flay; inveigh, thunder, fulminate, storm against, rage a. 61 vb. *rampage*; shout down, cry shame, slang, call names, gird, rail, revile, abuse, heap a., pour vitriol, vilipend, objurgate, anathematize, execrate 899 vb. *curse*; vilify, blacken, bespatter 926 vb. *defame*; exprobate, stigmatize, brand, pillory, gibbet, expose: reproach, denounce, recriminate 928 vb. *accuse*; sneer, twit, taunt, jibe 921 vb. *not respect*.

reprove, reprehend, rebuke, administer a r., snub; call to order, caution, wag one's finger 664 vb. *warn*; animadvert, reflect on, notice, take severe n., book, give one a black mark; censure, reprimand, take to task, rap over the knuckles, box the ears; tick off, tell off, have one's head for, carpet, have on the carpet, have on the mat, haul over the coals; remonstrate, expostulate, admonish, castigate, correct; lecture, read one a lecture, read one a lesson, give one a talking to, chide, dress down, trounce, trim, wig, give one a wigging, browbeat, blow up, tear strips off (see *exprobate*); chastise 963 vb. *punish*.

blame, find fault, carp, pick holes in; hit at, peck at, henpeck 709 vb. *bicker*; reprehend, hold to blame, pick on, put the blame on, hold responsible; throw the first stone, inculpate, incriminate, complain against, impute, impeach, charge, criminate 928 vb. *accuse*; round on, return the charge, retort the c., recrimin-

ate 714 vb. *retaliate*; think the worst of 961 vb. *condemn*.

exprobate, exprobate, fall foul of, reproach, heap reproaches, load with r.; reprobate, increpate, upbraid, slate, rate, berate, rail, strafe, shend, revile, abuse, blackguard 899 vb. *curse*; go for, inveigh, scold, tongue, tongue-lash, lash, lick with the rough edge of one's tongue, give one a piece of one's mind, give one what for, not pull one's punches.

incur blame, take the blame, take the rap, stand the racket, be held responsible, have to answer for; be open to criticism, blot one's copy book, get a bad name 867 vb. *lose repute*; be up on a charge, stand accused; stand corrected; be a caution, be an example, be a scandal, scandalize, shock, revolt 861 vb. *cause dislike*.

Adv. *disapprovingly*, reluctantly, against one's better judgment, under protest; reproachfully, complainingly.

See: 57, 61, 468, 479, 489, 509, 550, 582, 607, 636, 645, 664, 704, 705, 709, 712, 714, 728, 752, 757, 760, 762, 829, 830, 834, 851, 861, 862, 867, 878, 881, 891, 893, 899, 902, 921, 922, 926, 928, 950, 961, 963.

925 Flattery

N. *flattery*, cajolery, wheedling, taffy, blarney, blandiloquence, blandishment; butter, soft soap, soft-sawder, salve, lipsalve, rose-water, incense, adulation; voice of the charmer, honeyed words, soft nothings 889 n. *endearment*; compliment, pretty speeches; unctuousness, euphemism, glozing, gloze; captation, coquetry, fawning, backscratching; assentation, obsequiousness, flunkeyism, sycophancy, toadying, tuft-hunting 879 n. *servility*; insincerity, hypocrisy, tongue in cheek, lip-homage, mouth-honour, claque 542 n. *sham*.

flatterer, adulator, blarneyman, cajoler, wheedler; tout, puffer, booster, claqueur 923 n. *commender*; courtier, assentator, yes-man 488 n. *assenter*; pickthank, placebo, fawner, sycophant, parasite, minion, hanger-on 879 n. *toady*; fairweather friend, hypocrite 545 n. *deceiver*.

Adj. *flattering*, overpraising, overdone 546 adj. *exaggerated*; boosting, puffing; complimentary, over-complimentary, full

of compliments; fulsome, adulatory, incense-breathing; cajoling, wheedling, coaxing, blarneying, blandiloquent, smooth-tongued; mealy-mouthed, glozing, canting; smooth, oily, unctuous, soapy, slimy, smarmy; obsequious, all over one, courtierly, courtier-like, fawning, crawling, back-scratching, sycophantic 879 adj. *servile*; specious, plausible, beguiling, ingratiating, insinuating; lulling, soothing; vote-catching, vote-snatching; false, insincere, tongue-in-cheek, unreliable 541 adj. *hypocritical*.

Vb. *flatter*, deal in flattery, have kissed the Blarney Stone; compliment, overpraise, overdo it, lay it on thick, lay it on with a trowel, not spare one's blushes; puff, boost, cry up 482 vb. *overrate*; adulate, burn incense to, assail with flattery, turn one's head 873 vb. *make conceited*; butter up, sawder, soap; coo, blarney, flannel; wheedle, coax, cajole, glaver, cog; lull, soothe, beguile 542 vb. *deceive*; humour, gild the pill, make things pleasant, tell a flattering tale, gloze, collogue; blandish, smooth, smarm; make much of, be all over one 889 vb. *caress*; fawn, fawn on, cultivate, court, pay court to, play the courtier; smirk 835 vb. *smile*; scratch one's back, curry favour, make up to, suck up to; truckle, toady to, pander to 879 vb. *be servile*; insinuate oneself, earwig, creep into one's good graces; flatter oneself, lay the flattering unction to one's soul, have a swelled head 873 vb. *be vain*.

Adv. *flatteringly*, speciously; ad captandum.

See: 482, 488, 541, 542, 545, 546, 835, 873, 879, 889, 923.

926 Detraction

N. *detraction*, faint praise, two cheers, understatement 483 n. *underestimation*; criticism, hostile c., destructive c., Zoilism, unfavourable appreciation, bad review, bad press 924 n. *disapprobation*; onslaught 712 n. *attack*; impeachment 928 n. *accusation*; exposure, bad light 867 n. *disrepute*; decrial, disparagement, depreciation, running down; lowering, derogation; slighting language, scorn 922 n. *contempt*; obtrectation, evil speaking, obloquy 899 n. *malediction*; contumely,

vilification, abuse, invective 899 n. *scurrility*; calumniation, defamation, traducement 543 n. *untruth*; backbiting, cattiness, spite 898 n. *malevolence*; aspersion, reflection (see *calumny*); whisper, innuendo, insinuation, whispering campaign; smear campaign, mud-slinging, smirching, denigration; brand, stigma; muck-raking, scandal-mongering, chronique scandaleuse; gutter 649 n. *sink*; nil admirari, disillusionment, cynicism 865 n. *non-wonder*.

calumny, slander, libel, false report, roorback 543 n. *untruth*; a defamation, defamatory remark, damaging report; smear, smear-word, dirty word 867 n. *slur*; offensive remark, personal r., personality, insult, taunt 921 n. *indignity*; scoff, sarcasm 851 n. *ridicule*; sneer, sniff; caricature 552 n. *misrepresentation*; skit, lampoon, pasquinade, squib 851 n. *satire*; scandal, scandalous talk, gossip.

detractor, decrier, disparager, depreciator, slighter, despiser; non-admirer, laudator temporis acti; debunker, deflater, cynic; mocker, scoffer, satirizer, satirist, lampooner; castigator, denouncer, reprover, censurer, censor 924 n. *disapprover*; no respecter of persons, no flatterer, candid friend, candid critic; critic, hostile c., destructive c., attacker; arch-critic, chief accuser, impeacher 928 n. *accuser*; captious critic, knocker, Zoilus; fault-finder, carper, caviller, niggler, word-catcher; barracker 702 n. *hinderer*; Vandal, Philistine 847 n. *vulgarian*.

defamer, calumniator, traducer, destroyer of reputations; smircher, smearer, slanderer, libeller; backbiter, gossiper, scandal-monger, muck-raker; denigrator, mud-slinger; brander, stigmatizer; vituperator, reviler, abusive person, railer, scold, Thersites 892 n. *shrew*; poison pen.

Adj. *detracting*, derogative, derogatory, pejorative; disparaging, depreciatory, decrying, crying down, slighting, contemptuous 922 adj. *despising*; whispering, insinuating, blackening, denigratory, mud-slinging, smearing; compromising, damaging; scandalous, obloquious, calumnious, calumniatory, defamatory, slanderous, libellous; insulting 921 adj. *disrespectful*; contumelious, injurious, abusive, scurrilous, foul-spoken, evil-speaking 899 adj. *maledicent*; shrewish,

scolding, caustic, bitter, venomous, denunciatory, castigatory, accusatory, blaming 924 adj. *disapproving*; sarcastic, mocking, scoffing, sneering, cynical 851 adj. *derisive*; catty, spiteful 898 adj. *malevolent*; unflattering, candid 573 n. *plain*.

Vb. *detract*, derogate, depreciate, disparage, run down; debunk, deflate, cut down to life size 921 vb. *not respect*; minimize 483 vb. *underestimate*; belittle, slight 922 vb. *hold cheap*; sneer at, sniff at 922 vb. *despise*; decry, cry down, damn with faint praise, fail to appreciate 924 vb. *disapprove*; find nothing to praise, criticize, crab, gird, fault, find f., pick holes in, slash, slate, pull to pieces, tear to p., rend 924 vb. *dispraise*; caricature, guy 552 vb. *misrepresent*; lampoon, berhyme, dip one's pen in gall, pour vitriol 851 vb. *satirize*; scoff, mock 851 vb. *ridicule*; make catty remarks; whisper, insinuate.

defame, dishonour, damage, compromise, scandalize, degrade, lower, put to shame 867 vb. *shame*; give a dog a bad name, lower *or* lessen *or* destroy one's reputation; denounce, expose, gibbet, pillory, stigmatize, brand 928 vb. *accuse*; calumniate, libel, slander, traduce, malign; vilify, denigrate, blacken, tarnish, sully, breathe upon, blow u.; asperse, cast aspersions, reflect upon, put in a bad light; speak ill of, speak evil, gossip, make scandal, talk about, backbite, talk behind one's back; smear, besmear, smirch, besmirch, spatter, bespatter, throw mud, fling dirt, drag in the gutter; hound, witch-hunt 619 vb. *hunt*; look for scandal, smell evil, muckrake, rake in the gutter.

See: 483, 543, 552, 573, 619, 649, 702, 712, 847, 851, 865, 867, 892, 898, 899, 921, 922, 924, 928.

927 Vindication

N. *vindication*, restoration, rehabilitation 787 n. *restitution*; triumph of justice, right triumphant, wrong righted, right asserted, truth established; exoneration, exculpation, clearance 960 n. *acquitted*; justification, good grounds, just cause, every excuse; compurgation, apologetics, self-defence, apologia, defence, legal d., good d., successful d.; alibi, plea, excuse,

whitewash, gloss 614 n. *pretext*; fair excuse, good e., just e. 494 n. *truth*; partial excuse, extenuation, palliation, mitigation, mitigating circumstance, extenuating c., palliative 468 n. *qualification*; counter-argument 479 n. *confutation*; reply, reply for the defence, rebuttal 460 n. *rejoinder*; recrimination, tu quoque, counter-charge, charge retorted; justifiable charge, true bill 928 n. *accusation*; bringing to book, meed of one's deserts, just punishment 963 n. *punishment*.

vindicator, vindicatrix, punisher 910 n. *avenger*; apologist, advocate, defender, champion; justifier, excuser, whitewasher, varnisher; compurgator, oath-helper 466 n. *witness*; self-defender, defendant 928 n. *accused person*.

Adj. *vindicating*, vindicatory, vindicative, avenging; apologetic, exculpatory, justifying, defending; extenuatory, mitigating, palliative.

vindicable, justifiable, maintainable, defensible, arguable; specious, plausible; allowable, warrantable, unobjectionable 756 adj. *permitted*; excusable, having some excuse, pardonable, forgivable, venial, expiable; vindicated, justified, within one's rights, not guilty 935 adj. *innocent*; justified by the event 494 vb. *true*.

Vb. *vindicate*, revenge 910 vb. *avenge*; rescue, deliver 746 vb. *liberate*; do justice to, give the devil his due 915 vb. *grant claims*; set right, restore, rehabilitate 787 vb. *restitute*; maintain, speak up for, argue f., contend f., advocate 475 vb. *argue*; undertake to prove, bear out, confirm, make good, prove the truth of, prove 478 vb. *demonstrate*; champion, stand up for, stick up for 713 vb. *defend*; support, keep one in countenance 703 vb. *patronize*.

justify, warrant, justify by the event, give grounds for, provide justification, furnish an excuse, give a handle, give one cause; put one in the right, put one in the clear, clear, exonerate, exculpate 960 vb. *acquit*; give colour to, colour, whitewash, varnish, gloss; salve one's conscience, justify oneself, defend o. 614 vb. *plead*; plead one's own cause, take a plea, say in defence, rebut the charge, plead ignorance, confess and avoid.

extenuate, excuse, make excuses for, make

allowance for; palliate, mitigate, soften, mince, soft-pedal, slur, slur over, gloss, gloss over, varnish, whitewash; take the will for the deed 736 vb. *be lenient*.

See: 460, 466, 468, 475, 478, 479, 494, 614, 703, 713, 736, 746, 756, 787, 910, 915, 928, 935, 960, 963.

928 Accusation

N. *accusation*, complaint, charge, true c., home-truth; censure, blame, stricture 924 n. *reproach*; challenge 711 n. *defiance*; inculpation, crimination; counter-charge, recrimination, tu quoque argument 460 n. *rejoinder*; twit, taunt 921 n. *indignity*; imputation, allegation, information, delation, denunciation; plaint, suit, action 959 n. *litigation*; prosecution, impeachment, attainder, arraignment, indictment, citation, summons; bill of indictment, bill of attainder, true bill; gravamen, substance of a charge, main c., head and front of one's offending; case, case to answer, case for the prosecution 475 n. *reasons*; items in the indictment, particular charge, count 466 n. *evidence*; no excuses 961 n. *condemnation*.

false charge, faked c., cooked-up c., trumped-up c., put-up job, frame-up; false information, designing i., perjured testimony, hostile evidence, suspect e., false e.; counterfeit evidence, plant; illegal prosecution, vexatious p., sycophancy; lie, libel, slander, scandal, stigma 926 n. *calumny*.

accuser, complainant, plaintiff, petitioner, appellant, libellant, litigant; challenger, denouncer, charger; approver, peacher, nark, copper's n. 524 n. *informer*; common informer, delator, relator; impeacher, indicter, prosecutrix, prosecutor, public p., habitual p., sycophant; libeller, slanderer, calumniator, stigmatizer 926 n. *detractor*; hostile witness 881 n. *enemy*; critic, arch-c.

accused person, the accused, prisoner, prisoner at the bar; defendant, respondent, co-r.; culprit; suspect, victim of suspicion; slandered person, libellee, victim.

Adj. *accusing*, alleging, accusatory, denunciatory, criminatory, recriminatory; incriminating, pointing to, imputative,

stigmatizing, damnatory, condemnatory; delatory, sycophantic, calumnious, defamatory 926 adj. *detracting*; suspicious 924 adj. *disapproving*.

accused, informed against, reported a., complained a., suspect; delated, denounced, impeached etc. vb.; charged, up on a charge, prosecuted, hauled up, booked, summoned; awaiting trial, on bail, remanded; slandered, libelled, calumniated 924 adj. *disapproved*.

accusable, imputable; actionable, suable, chargeable, justiciable, liable to prosecution; inexcusable, unpardonable, unforgivable, indefensible, unjustifiable 924 adj. *blameworthy*; without excuse, without defence, condemnable 934 adj. *heinous*; undefended 661 adj. *vulnerable*.

Vb. *accuse*, challenge 711 vb. *defy*; taunt, twit 878 vb. *be insolent*; point, point a finger at, throw in one's teeth, cast the first stone, reproach 924 vb. *reprove*; stigmatize, brand, pillor, gibbet, cast a slur on, calumniate 926 vb. *defame*; impute, charge with, saddle w., tax w., hold against, lay to one's charge, lay at one's door, hold responsible, make r.; pick on, fix on, hold on blame, put the blame on, pin on, bring home to 924 vb. *blame*; point at, expose, show up, name 526 vb. *divulge*; denounce, delate, inform against, tell, tell on, peach, blab, split, turn Queen's evidence 524 vb. *inform*; involve, implicate, inculpate, incriminate; recriminate, counter-charge, rebut the charge, turn the tables upon 479 vb. *confute*; shift the blame, pass the buck; return to the charge 712 vb. *attack*; accuse oneself, admit the charge, plead guilty 526 vb. *confess*; involve oneself, implicate o., lay oneself open, put oneself out of court.

indict, impeach, attaint, arraign, inform against, complain a., lodge a complaint, lay an information; complain, charge, bring a charge, swear an indictment 959 vb. *litigate*; book, cite, summon, prosecute, sue; bring an action, bring a suit, bring a case; haul up, pull up, put on trial, put in the dock, ask for a verdict against; charge falsely, lie against 541 vb. *be false*; frame, trump up, cook the evidence, use false e., fake the e., plant the e. 541 vb. *fake*.

Adv. *accusingly*, censoriously.

See: 460, 466, 475, 479, 524, 526, 541, 661, 711, 712, 878, 881, 921, 924, 926, 934, 959, 961.

929 Probity

N. *probity*, rectitude, uprightness, goodness, sanctity 933n. *virtue*; stainlessness 950n. *purity*; character, honesty, soundness, incorruptibility, integrity; high character, nobleness 868n. *nobility*; honourableness, decent feelings, tender conscience, squeamishness; honour, personal h., sense of h., principles; conscientiousness, punctuality 768n. *observance*; scrupulousness, scrupulosity, punctiliousness, meticulosity 457n. *carefulness*; ingenuousness, single-heartedness; trustworthiness, reliability, sense of responsibility; truthfulness 540n. *veracity*; candour, plain-speaking, home-truth 573n. *plainness*; sincerity, good faith, bona fides 494n. *truth*; fidelity, faith, troth, faithfulness, trustiness, constancy 739n. *loyalty*; clean hands 935n. *innocence*; impartiality, fairness, sportsmanship 913n. *justice*; respectability 866 n. *repute*; gentlemanliness 846n. *good taste*; principle, point of honour, punctilio, code, code of honour, Bushido 913n. *right*; court of justice, court of honour, field of h.; argumentum ad verecundiam.
gentleman, man of probity, man of honour, man of his word, sound character, true man; squarepusher, square-shooter, knight, true k., chevalier, galantuomo, caballero; Galahad, Bayard; fair fighter, clean f., fair player, good loser, sportsman, white man, Briton; trump, brick, sport, good s., true-penny.
Adj. *honourable*, upright, erect, of integrity, of honour 933adj. *virtuous*; correct, strict; law-abiding, honest, strictly h.; principled, scrupulous, squeamish, soul-searching; incorruptible, unbribable; incorrupt, inviolate, immaculate 935adj. *innocent*; stainless, unstained, untarnished, unsullied 648adj. *clean*; undepraved, undebauched 950adj. *pure*; ingenuous, unsuspicious, guileless, unworldly 699 adj. *artless*; good, white, straight, square, on the square, one hundred per cent; fair, fair-dealing, equitable, impartial 913adj. *just*; manly, sporting, sportsmanlike,

playing the game; high-minded, gentlemanly, chivalrous, knightly 868adj. *noble*; jealous of honour, careful of one's h., respectable 866adj. *reputable*; religious 979adj. *pious*.
trustworthy, creditworthy, reliable, dependable, tried, tested, proven; trusty, true-hearted, true-blue, true to the core, sure, staunch, single-hearted, constant, unchanging, faithful, loyal 739adj. *obedient*; responsible, duteous, dutiful 768adj. *observant*; conscientious, religious, scrupulous, meticulous, punctilious 457adj. *careful*; candid, frank, open, open and above board, open-hearted, transparent, without guile 494adj. *true*; ingenuous, straightforward, truthful, truth-speaking, as good as one's word 540adj. *veracious*; unperjured, unperfidious, untreacherous.
Vb. *be honourable*,—chivalrous etc.adj.; behave like a gentleman 933vb. *be virtuous*; be on the square, deal honourably, play fair, play the game, shoot straight 913vb. *be just*; be a sport, be a brick, turn up trumps; preserve one's honour, fear God 979 vb. *be pious*; keep faith, keep one's promise, be as good as one's word, be loyal to one's engagements; hate a lie, stick to the truth, speak the truth and shame the devil 540 vb. *be truthful*; go straight, reform, turn over a new leaf 654 vb. *get better*.
See: 457, 494, 540, 573, 648, 654, 699, 739, 768, 846, 866, 868, 913, 933, 935, 950, 979.

930 Improbity

N. *improbity*, dishonesty; lack of probity, lack of conscience, lack of principle; suppleness, flexibility, laxity; unconscientiousness 456 n. *inattention*; unscrupulousness, opportunism; insincerity, disingenuousness, unstraightforwardness, untrustworthiness, unreliability, undependability, untruthfulness 541n. *falsehood*; unfairness, partiality 914 n. *injustice*; shuffling, slipperiness, snakiness, artfulness; fishiness, suspiciousness, shadiness, obliquity, twistiness, deviousness, crookedness, crooked ways, bypaths of dishonour; corruption, corruptibility, venality, bribability, graft, jobbery, nepotism, simony, barratry; Tammany;

baseness, shabbiness, abjectness, abjection, debasement, shamefulness, disgrace, dishonour, shame 867 n. *disrepute*; worthlessness, good-for-nothingness, scoundrelism, villainousness, villainy, knavery, roguery, rascality, spivvery, skulduggery, racketeering; criminality, crime, complicity 954 n. *lawbreaking*; turpitude, moral t. 934 n. *wickedness*.

perfidy, perfidiousness, faithlessness, unfaithfulness, infidelity, unfaith 543 n. *untruth*; bad faith, Punic f., questionable f.; divided allegiance, wavering loyalty, disloyalty 738 n. *disobedience*; practice, double-dealing, double-crossing, Judas kiss 541 n. *duplicity*; volte face 603 n. *tergiversation*; defection, desertion 918 n. *dutilessness*; betrayal, prodition, treachery, stab in the back; treason, high t. 738 n. *sedition*; fifth column, Trojan horse; mala fides, breach of faith, broken word, broken faith, broken promise, breach of p., oath forsworn, scrap of paper; cry of treason, Perfide Albion!

foul play, dirty trick, stab in the back; not playing the game, foul 914 n. *wrong*; trick, shuffle, chicane, chicanery 542 n. *trickery*; practice, sharp p., heads I win, tails you lose; misdealing, fishy transaction, dirty work, job, deal, ramp, racket; fiddle, wangle, manipulation, gerrymandering, hanky-panky; false balance-sheet, malversation 788 n. *peculation*; crime, felony 954 n. *lawbreaking*.

Adj. *dishonest*, misdealing 914 adj. *wrong*; not particular, unfastidious, unsqueamish; unprincipled, unscrupulous, conscienceless; shameless, dead to honour, lost to shame; unethical, immoral 934 adj. *wicked*; shaky, untrustworthy, unreliable, undependable; supple, versatile 603 adj. *tergiversating*; disingenuous, unstraightforward, untruthful, uncandid 543 adj. *untrue*; double-tongued, double-faced, insincere 541 adj. *hypocritical*; unerect, creeping, crawling; tricky, artful, dodging, opportunist, slippery, snaky, foxy 698 adj. *cunning*; shifty, shuffling, prevaricating 518 adj. *equivocal*; designing, scheming; sneaking, underhand, subterranean 523 adj. *latent*; not straight, unstraight, indirect, crooked, devious, oblique, tortuous, winding 251 adj. *labyrinthine*; insidious, dark, sinister; shady, suspicious, doubtful, questionable; fishy,

malodorous 397 adj. *fetid*; fraudulent 542 adj. *spurious*; illicit 954 adj. *illegal*; foul 645 adj. *bad*; unclean 649 adj. *dirty*; dishonourable, infamous 867 adj. *disreputable*; derogatory, unworthy, undignified; inglorious, ignominious 867 adj. *degrading*; ignoble, unchivalrous, unknightly, ungentlemanly, unmanly, unhandsome.

rascally, criminal, criminous, felonious 954 adj. *lawless*; knavish, picaresque, spivvish, scampish; infamous, blackguard, villainous; scurvy, scabby, arrant, low, low-down, yellow, base, vile, mongrel, currish; mean, scrubby, shabby, paltry, little, pettifogging, abject, wretched, contemptible 639 adj. *unimportant*; time-serving, crawling 925 adj. *flattering*.

venal, corruptible, purchasable, bribable, for hire, hireling, mercenary 792 adj. *bought*; corrupt, jobbing, grafting, simoniacal, nepotistic; barratrous, selling justice.

perfidious, treacherous, unfaithful, inconstant, trothless, faithless 541 adj. *false*; double-dealing, double-crossing, time-serving 541 adj. *hypocritical*; apostatizing 603 adj. *tergiversating*; false-hearted, guileful, traitorous, treasonous, treasonable, disloyal, untrue 738 adj. *disobedient*; plotting, scheming, intriguing 623 adj. *planning*; insidious, dark, Machiavellian; cheating, cozening 542 adj. *deceiving*; fraudulent 542 adj. *spurious*.

Vb. *be dishonest*, —dishonourable etc. adj.; ignore ethics, forget one's principles, yield to temptation, be lost to shame; lack honesty, live dishonestly, live by one's wits, lead a life of crime 954 vb. *be illegal*; fiddle, wangle, gerrymander, start a racket, racketeer; defalcate, peculate 788 vb. *defraud*; cheat, swindle, chisel 542 vb. *deceive*; betray, play false, stab in the back; play double, double-cross, gloze 541 vb. *dissemble*; fawn 925 vb. *flatter*; break faith, break one's word, forswear, jilt, disregard one's promises, lie 541 vb. *be false*; shuffle, dodge, prevaricate 518 vb. *be equivocal*; sell out, sell down the river, go over 603 vb. *apostatize*; sink into crime, sell one's honour, seal one's infamy 867 vb. *lose repute*.

Adv. *dishonestly*; shamelessly, by fair means or foul; treacherously, mala fide; knavishly, villainously, without regard for honesty.

See: 251, 397, 456, 518, 523, 541, 542, 543, 603, 623, 639, 645, 649, 698, 738, 788, 792, 867, 914, 918, 925, 934, 954.

rise above oneself, surrender personal considerations.

See: 625, 781, 855, 868, 872, 884, 887, 897, 901, 905, 913, 929, 942.

931 Disinterestedness

N. *disinterestedness*, impartiality, indifference 913 n. *justice*; detachment, non-involvement, neutrality 625 n. *mid-course*; unselfishness, unpossessiveness, selflessness, no thought for self, self-effacement 872 n. *humility*; self-control, self-abnegation, self-denial, self-surrender, self-sacrifice, self-immolation, self-devotion, martyrdom, suttee; rising above oneself, heroism, stoicism 855 n. *courage*; loftiness of purpose, elevation of soul, idealism, ideals, high i.; sublimity, elevation, loftiness, nobility, magnanimity; knightliness, chivalry, knight-errantry; generosity, liberality, liberalism 897 n. *benevolence*; purity of motive, dedication, consecration; loyalty, faith, faithfulness 929 n. *probity*; patriotism 901 n. *philanthropy*; altruism, thought for others, consideration, considerateness, kindness 884 n. *courtesy*; compassion 905 n. *pity*; charity 887 n. *love*.

Adj. *disinterested*, dispassionate, impersonal, uninvolved, detached, disengaged, neutral, impartial, indifferent 913 adj. *just*; self-controlled, stoical 942 adj. *temperate*; uncorrupted, unbought, unbribed, honest 929 adj. *honourable*; self-effacing, modest 872 adj. *humble*; unjealous, unpossessive, unenvious, ungrudging; unselfish, selfless, self-forgetful; self-denying, self-sacrificing, ready to die for, martyr-like; devoted, self-d., dedicated, consecrated; loyal, faithful; heroic 855 adj. *courageous*; thoughtful, considerate, kind 884 adj. *courteous*; altruistic, philanthropic, patriotic 897 adj. *benevolent*; pure, unmixed; undesigning; sacrificial, unmercenary, for love, non-profitmaking; idealistic, high-minded, lofty, elevated, sublime, magnanimous, chivalrous, knightly 868 adj. *noble*; generous, liberal, unsparing 781 adj. *giving*.

Vb. *be disinterested*,—unselfish etc. adj.; sacrifice, make a s., sacrifice oneself, devote o., live for, die f.; think of others, put oneself last, take a back seat 872 vb. *be humble*; rise above petty considerations,

932 Selfishness

N. *selfishness*, self-consideration, self-love, self-admiration, narcissism, self-worship, self-approbation, self-praise 873 n. *vanity*; self-pity, self-indulgence 943 n. *intemperance*; self-absorption, ego-centrism, autism; egoism, egotism, individualism, particularism; self-preservation, each man for himself; axe to grind, personal considerations, personal motives, private ends, personal advantage, selfish benefit, self-interest, concern for number one; charity that begins at home, cupboard love; illiberality, no magnanimity, mean-mindedness, pettiness, paltriness; illiberality, meanness, niggardliness 816 n. *parsimony*; greed, acquisitiveness 816 n. *avarice*; possessiveness 911 n. *jealousy*; worldliness, worldly wisdom; 'heads I win tails you lose' 914 n. *injustice*; careerism, selfish ambition, naked a., ruthless a.; power politics.

egotist, egoist, self-centred person, narcissist 873 n. *vain person*; particularist, individualist, mass of selfishness; self-seeker; careerist, arriviste, go-getter, adventurer, gold-digger, fortune-hunter; money-grubber 816 n. *niggard*; monopolist, dog in the manger, hog, road-h.; opportunist, time-server, worldling.

Adj. *selfish*, egocentric, autistic, self-absorbed, wrapped up in oneself; egoistic, egotistic, egotistical; personal, individualistic, concerned with number one; self-interested, self-regarding, self-considering; self-indulgent 944 adj. *sensual*; self-loving, self-admiring, narcissistic 873 adj. *vain*; non-altruistic, interested; unphilanthropic; unpatriotic; uncharitable, unsympathetic, cold-hearted 898 adj. *unkind*; mean, mean-minded, petty, paltry; illiberal, ungenerous, niggardly 816 adj. *parsimonious*; acquisitive, money-grubbing, mercenary 816 adj. *avaricious*; venal 930 adj. *dishonest*; covetous 912 adj. *envious*; hoggish, hogging, monopolistic 859 adj. *greedy*; possessive, dog-in-the-manger; competitive 911 adj. *jealous*;

self-seeking, designing, axe-grinding; go-getting, on the make, gold-digging, opportunist, time-serving, careerist; un-idealistic, materialistic, mundane, worldly, earthly, earthy, worldly-minded, worldly-wise.

Vb. *be selfish,*—egoistic etc. adj.; put oneself first, think only of oneself, take care of number one; love oneself, indulge o., look after o., coddle o., have only oneself to please; feather one's nest, look out for oneself, have an eye to the main chance, know on which side one's bread is buttered, give an inch and take an ell; keep for oneself, hang onto, hog, monopolize, be a dog in the manger 778 vb. *retain;* have personal motives, have private ends, have an axe to grind, have one's own game to play; grind one's axe, pursue one's interests, advance one's own i., sacrifice the interests of others, be a bad neighbour.

Adv. *selfishly,* self-regardingly, only for oneself; on the make, for profit; ungenerously, illiberally; for one's own sake, from personal motives, for private ends; jealously, possessively.

See: 778, 816, 859, 873, 898, 911, 912, 914, 930, 943, 944.

933 Virtue

N. *virtue,* virtuousness, moral strength, moral tone, morale; goodness, sheer g.; saintliness, holiness, spirituality, odour of sanctity 979 n. *sanctity;* righteousness 913 n. *justice;* uprightness, rectitude, moral r., character, integrity, honour, personal h. 929 n. *probity;* perfect honour, stainlessness, irreproachability; avoidance of guilt, guiltlessness 935 n. *innocence;* morality, ethics 917 n. *morals;* sexual morality, chastity 950 n. *purity;* straight and narrow path, virtuous conduct, christian c., good behaviour, well-spent life, duty done; good conscience, conscious rectitude; self-improvement, moral rearmament; quality, efficacy, power 160 n. *ability.*

virtues, moral v., moral laws; theological virtues, faith, hope, charity; cardinal virtues, prudence, justice, temperance, fortitude; qualities, fine q., saving quality, saving grace; a virtue, good fault, fault

on the right side; worth, merit, desert; excellence, perfections 646 n. *perfection;* nobleness 868 n. *nobility;* altruism, unselfishness 931 n. *disinterestedness;* idealism, ideals; self-control 942 n. *temperance.*

Adj. *virtuous,* moral 917 adj. *ethical;* good 644 adj. *excellent;* stainless, white 950 adj. *pure;* guiltless 935 adj. *innocent;* irreproachable, impeccable, above temptation 646 adj. *perfect;* saint-like, seraphic, angelic, saintly, holy 979 adj. *sanctified;* principled, well-p., right-minded, on the side of the angels 913 adj. *right;* righteous 913 adj. *just;* upright, sterling, honest 929 adj. *honourable;* duteous, dutiful 739 adj. *obedient;* unselfish 931 adj. *disinterested;* generous, magnanimous 868 adj. *noble;* idealistic, well-intentioned, philanthropic 897 adj. *benevolent;* chaste, virginal; proper, edifying, improving; elevated, sublimated; meritorious, worthy, praiseworthy, commendable 923 adj. *approved.*

Vb. *be virtuous,*—good etc. adj.; have all the virtues, qualify for sainthood 644 vb. *be good;* behave, be on one's good *or* best behaviour; practise virtue, resist temptation, command one's passions 942 vb. *be temperate;* rise superior to, have a soul above; keep to the straight and narrow path, follow one's conscience, walk humbly with one's God, fight the good fight; discharge one's obligations 917 vb. *do one's duty;* go straight, keep s. 929 vb. *be honourable;* love good, hate wrong 913 vb. *be just;* edify, set a good example, shame the devil 644 vb. *do good.*

Adv. *virtuously,* well, meritoriously; righteously, purely, innocently; holily.

See: 160, 644, 646, 739, 868, 897, 913, 917, 923, 929, 931, 935, 942, 950, 979.

934 Wickedness

N. *wickedness,* principle of evil 616 n. *evil;* Devil, cloven hoof 969 n. *Satan;* fallen nature, Old Adam; unrighteousness, iniquity, sinfulness, sin 914 n. *wrong;* peccability, loss of innocence 936 n. *guilt;* ignorance of good, moral illiteracy; amorality, amoralism 860 n. *indifference;* hardness of heart 898 n. *malevolence;* wilfulness, stubbornness 602 adj. *obstinacy;* naughtiness 738 n. *disobedience;*

immorality, turpitude, moral t.; loose morals, carnality, profligacy 951 n. *impurity*; demoralization, degeneration, degeneracy, vitiation, degradation 655 n. *deterioration*; recidivism, backsliding 603 n. *tergiversation*; corruption, depravity 645 n. *badness*; flagitiousness, heinousness, shamelessness, flagrancy; bad character, viciousness, unworthiness; vice, villainy, knavery, roguery 930 n. *foul play*; obliquity, laxity, want of principle, dishonesty 930 n. *improbity*; crime, criminality 954 n. *lawbreaking*; devilry, hellishness 898 n. *inhumanity*; devil worship, diabolism 982 n. *idolatry*; shame, scandal, abomination, enormity, infamy 867 n. *disrepute*; infamous conduct, misbehaviour, delinquency, wrongdoing, evildoing, transgression, evil courses, wicked ways, career of crime; primrose path, slippery slope; low life 847 n. *ill-breeding*; den of vice, sink of iniquity, hell-broth, Alsatian den, criminal world, underworld, demi-monde 649 n. *sink*.

vice, fault, demerit, unworthiness; human weakness, infirmity, frailty, foible 163 n. *weakness*; imperfection, shortcoming, defect, deficiency, failing, weak side, weakness of the flesh; trespass, injury, outrage, enormity 914 n. *wrong*; sin, capital s., deadly s.; seven deadly sins, pride, covetousness, lust, anger, gluttony, envy, sloth; venial sin, small fault, slight transgression, peccadillo, scrape; impropriety, indecorum 847 n. *bad taste*; crime, felony, deadly crime, capital c. 954 n. *illegality*.

Adj. wicked, virtueless, unvirtuous, immoral; amoral, amoralistic 860 adj. *indifferent*; lax, unprincipled, unscrupulous, conscienceless 930 adj. *dishonest*; unblushing, hardened, callous, shameless, brazen, flaunting; irreligious, profane 980 adj. *impious*; iniquitous, unrighteous 914 adj. *unjust*; evil 645 adj. *bad*; evil-minded, bad-hearted 898 adj. *malevolent*; evildoing 898 adj. *maleficent*; misbehaving, bad, naughty 738 adj. *disobedient*; weak (see *frail*); peccant, erring, sinning, transgressing; sinful, sin-laden, full of sin 936 adj. *guilty*; unworthy, undeserving, unmeritorious; graceless, not in a state of grace, reprobate; hopeless, incorrigible, irreclaimable, unredeemed, irredeemable; accursed, god-forsaken; hellish,

infernal, devilish, fiendish, mephistophelian, satanic 969 adj. *diabolic*.

vicious, steeped in vice, sunk in iniquity; good-for-nothing, ne'er-do-well; hopeless, past praying for; worthless, unworthy, meritless, graceless 924 adj. *disapproved*; villainous, knavish, double-dyed 930 adj. *rascally*; improper, unseemly, indecent, unedifying 847 adj. *vulgar*; moralless, immoral; unvirtuous 951 adj. *unchaste*; profligate, abandoned, characterless, lost to virtue, lost to shame 867 adj. *disreputable*; vitiated, corrupt, degraded, demoralized, debauched, ruined, depraved, perverted, degenerate, rotten, rotten to the core 655 adj. *deteriorated*; brutalized, brutal 898 adj. *cruel*.

frail, infirm, feeble 163 adj. *weak*; having a weaker side, having one's foibles, human, only h., too h. 734 adj. *lax*; suggestible, easily tempted 661 adj. *vulnerable*; not above temptation, not impeccable, not perfect 647 adj. *imperfect*; slipping, sliding, recidivous 603 adj. *tergiversating*.

heinous, heavy, grave, serious, deadly; black, scarlet, of deepest dye; abysmal, hellish, infernal 211 adj. *deep*; sinful, immoral 914 adj. *wrong*; demoralizing, unedifying, contra bonos mores; criminal, nefarious, felonious 954 adj. *lawbreaking*; flagitious, monstrous, flagrant, scandalous, scandalizing, infamous, shameful, disgraceful, shocking, outrageous; gross, foul, rank; base, vile, abominable, accursed; blameworthy, culpable 928 adj. *accusable*; reprehensible, indefensible, unjustifiable 916 adj. *unwarranted*; atrocious, brutal 898 adj. *cruel*; unforgivable, unpardonable, inexcusable, irremissible, inexpiable, unatonable.

Vb. be wicked, — vicious, — sinful etc. adj.; not be in a state of grace, scoff at virtue; fall from grace, spoil one's record, lapse, relapse, backslide 603 vb. *tergiversate*; fall into sin, go to the bad 655 vb. *deteriorate*; do amiss, transgress, misbehave, misdemean oneself, carry on, be naughty, sow one's wild oats; trespass, offend, sin, commit s., err, stray, slip, trip, stumble, fall; have one's foibles, have one's weak side 163 vb. *be weak*.

make wicked, render evil, corrupt, demoralize, deform one's character, brutalize 655 vb. *pervert*; mislead, lead astray, seduce 612 vb. *tempt*; set a bad example.

teach wickedness, dehumanize, brutalize, diabolize.

Adv. *wickedly,* wrongly, sinfully; viciously, vilely, depravedly, devilishly; unforgivably, unpardonably, irredeemably, inexpiably.

See: 163, 211, 602, 603, 612, 616, 645, 647, 649, 655, 661, 734, 738, 847, 860, 867, 898, 914, 916, 924, 928, 930, 936, 951, 954, 969, 980, 982.

935 Innocence

N. *innocence,* blessed i., freedom from guilt, guiltlessness, clean hands; conscious innocence, clear conscience, irreproachability; nothing to declare, nothing to confess; inculpability, blamelessness, freedom from blame, every excuse; declared innocence 960 n. *acquittal;* ignorance of evil 491 n. *ignorance;* inexperience, unworldliness 699 n. *artlessness;* playfulness, harmlessness, inoffensiveness, innocent intentions, pure motives; freedom from sin, unfallen state, state of grace 933 n. *virtue;* undefilement, stainlessness 950 n. *purity;* incorruption, incorruptibility 929 n. *probity;* impeccability 646 n. *perfection;* days of innocence, golden age, Saturnia regna 730 n. *palmy days.*

innocent, Holy Innocents, babe, new-born babe, babe unborn, babes and sucklings: child, ingénue; lamb, dove; angel, white soul; milksop, goody-goody; one in the right, innocent party, injured p., not the culprit.

Adj. *innocent,* pure, unspotted, stainless, unblemished, spotless, immaculate, white 648 adj. *clean;* incorrupt, uncorrupted, undefiled; unfallen, sinless, free from sin, unerring, impeccable 646 adj. *perfect;* green, inexperienced, knowing no better, unhardened, unversed in crime 491 adj. *ignorant;* unworldly, guileless 699 adj. *artless;* well-meaning, well-intentioned, well-intended, well-motived 897 n. *benevolent;* innocuous, harmless, inoffensive, playful, gentle, lamb-like, dove-like, angelic; innocent as a lamb, innocent as a dove, innocent as a babe unborn, innocent as a child; shockable, goody-goody; Saturnian, Arcadian.

guiltless, free from guilt, not responsible,

not guilty 960 adj. *acquitted;* falsely accused, misunderstood; clean-handed, bloodless; blameless, faultless, unblameworthy, unculpable, unblamable; irreproachable, above suspicion; irreprovable, irreprehensible, unobjectionable, unexceptionable, unimpeachable, entirely defensible, with every excuse 923 adj. *approvable;* pardonable, forgivable, excusable, venial, exculpable, expiable.

Vb. *be innocent,* know no wrong, do no man w., have no guile 929 vb. *be honourable;* live in a state of grace, not fall from g. 933 vb. *be virtuous;* have every excuse, have no need to blush, have clean hands, have a clear conscience, have nothing to confess, have nothing to declare; have the best intentions, mean no harm, mean no guile; know no better 699 vb. *be artless;* stand free of blame, stand above suspicion; acquit oneself, salve one's conscience, wash one's hands.

Adv. *innocently,* blamelessly, harmlessly, well-meaningly; with clean hands, with a clear conscience, with a safe c., with an easy c.

See: 491, 646, 648, 699, 730, 897, 923, 929, 933, 950, 960.

936 Guilt

N. *guilt,* guiltiness, blood g., red-handedness; culpability, chargeability; criminality, criminousness, delinquency 954 n. *illegality;* sinfulness, original sin 934 n. *wickedness;* involvement, complicity; charge, onus, burden, responsibility 180 n. *liability;* blame, censure 924 n. *reproach;* guilty feeling, guilt-f., conscious guilt, guilty conscience, bad c.; guilty behaviour, suspicious conduct, blush, stammer; admitted guilt, confessed g., confession 526 n. *disclosure;* twinge of conscience, biting c. 939 n. *penitence.*

guilty act, sin, deadly s., venial s. 934 n. *vice;* misdeed, wicked deed, misdoing, sinning, transgression, trespass, offence, crime, corpus delicti 954 n. *illegality;* misdemeanour, felony; misconduct, misbehaviour, malpractice, malversation; infamous conduct, unprofessional c.; indiscretion, impropriety, peccadillo; naughtiness, scrape; lapse, slip, faux pas,

blunder 495n. *mistake*; omission 458n. *negligence*; culpable omission, laches; sin of commission, fault, failure, dereliction 918n. *dutilessness*; injustice, tort, injury 914n. *wrong*; enormity, atrocity, outrage 898n. *cruel act*.

Adj. *guilty*, found g., convicted 961adj. *condemned*; thought guilty, suspected, blamed, censured, made responsible 924 adj. *disapproved*; responsible 180adj. *liable*; in the wrong, at fault, to blame, culpable, chargeable 928adj. *accusable*; blameful, reprehensible, censurable 924 adj. *blameworthy*; unjustifiable, without excuse, inexcusable, unpardonable, unforgivable; inexpiable, mortal, deadly 934 adj. *heinous*; trespassing, transgressing, peccant, sinful 934adj. *wicked*; criminal, criminous 954adj. *illegal*; blood-guilty 362adj. *murderous*; red-handed, caught in the act, surprised in the attempt; shamefast, shame-faced, blushing.

Vb. *be guilty*, have sins upon one's conscience, have crimes to answer for, have blood upon one's hands; be caught in the act, be caught red-handed; acknowledge one's guilt, plead guilty 526vb. *confess*; have no excuse, stand condemned; trespass, transgress, sin 934vb. *be wicked*.

Adv. *guiltily*, criminally, criminously; inexcusably, without excuse; red-handed, in the very act, flagrante delicto.

See: 180, 362, 458, 495, 526, 898, 914, 918, 924, 928, 934, 939, 954, 961.

937 Good man

N. *good man*, perfect gentleman, fine character 929n. *gentleman*; good example, model of virtue, salt of the earth, perfection 646n. *paragon*; Christian, true C.; saint 979n. *pietist*; mahatma, great saint; seraph, angel 935n. *innocent*; benefactor 897n. *kind person*; idealist 901n. *philanthropist*; the best, one of the b., the tops 890n. *favourite*; hero 855n. *brave person*; good sort, stout fellow, white man, brick, trump, sport; rough diamond, ugly duckling; demigod, god of one's idolatry 982n. *idol*.

See: 646, 855, 890, 897, 901, 929, 935, 979, 982.

938 Bad Man

N. *bad man*, evil m., no saint, sinner, hardened s., limb of Satan, Antichrist 904n. *evildoer*; fallen angel, backslider, recidivist, lost sheep, lost soul, âme damnée, man of no morals, immoralist; reprobate, scapegrace, good-for-nothing, ne'er-do-well, black sheep, the despair of; scalawag, scamp, spalpeen; rake, roué, profligate 952n. *libertine*; wastrel, waster, prodigal son 815n. *prodigal*; scandalous person, reproach, outcast, dregs 867n. *object of scorn*; tramp, vagabond; nasty type, ugly customer, undesirable, bad 'un, wrong 'un, badmash, thug, bully, roughneck 904n. *ruffian*; bad lot, bad egg, bad hat, bad character, scaramouch 869n. *low fellow*; bad influence, bad example; bad boy, naughty b., terror, whelp, monkey, little m., little devil; bad girl, naughty g., jade, wench, slut, Jezebel 952n. *loose woman*.

knave, scurvy k., varlet, vagabond, cullion, caitiff, wretch, dog, rascal, rapscallion, rogue, first-class r., prince of rogues; criminal 904n. *offender*; thief, pirate, freebooter 789n. *robber*; villain, blackguard, scoundrel; cheat, liar, crook; chiseler, impostor, twister, shyster 545n. *trickster*; sneak, squealer, rat 524n. *informer*; renegade, recreant 603n. *tergiversator*; betrayer, traitor, archtraitor, treachour, Quisling, Judas; animal, dog, hound, swine, snake, serpent, viper, reptile, vermin 904n. *noxious animal*.

cad, nasty bit of work, scoundrel, blackguard; rotter, blighter, heel, scab; stinker, bad smell, skunk, dirty dog, filthy hound; bastard, twerp, pimp, pandar, pervert, degenerate; cur, hound, swine, worm, the bottom; louse, insect 365n. *vermin*; pig, beast, horrid b., cat, bitch.

monster, shocker, horror, unspeakable villain; monster of cruelty, brute, savage, sadist; ogre 735n. *tyrant*; monster of wickedness, monster of iniquity, fiend, demon, ghoul 969n. *devil*; hell-hound 904n. *hell-hag*; devil in human shape, devil incarnate, fiend i.; ape-man, gorilla 842n. *eyesore*; King Kong, Frankenstein's monster, bogy, terror, raw-head, bloody-bones.

See: 365, 524, 545, 603, 735, 789, 815, 842, 867, 869, 904, 952, 969.

939 Penitence

N. *penitence*, repentance, contrition, compunction, remorse, self-reproach 830n. *regret*; self-accusation, self-condemnation, humble confession 526n. *disclosure*; public confession, exomologesis 988n. *Christian rite*; self-humiliation 872n. *humility*; guilt-feeling, voice of conscience, uneasy c., unquiet c., bad c., twinge of c., qualms of c., stings of c., pricks of c., 'compunctious visitings of nature' 936n. *guilt*; awakened conscience, resipiscence 603n. *recantation*; last-minute repentance, death-bed r.; room for repentance, locus pænitentiæ; penance, white sheet, sackcloth and ashes, stool of repentance, cutty stool 964n. *pillory*; apology 941n. *atonement*; half-repentance, grudging apology. *penitent*, penitential, flagellant 945n. *ascetic*; magdalen, prodigal son, returned prodigal, a sadder and a wiser man; reformed character, brand plucked from the burning.

Adj. *repentant*, contrite, remorseful, regretful, sorry, apologetic, full of regrets 830 adj. *regretting*; unhardened, softened, melted, weeping 836adj. *lamenting*; compunctious, relenting, conscience-stricken, conscience-smitten, pricked by conscience, plagued by c.; self-reproachful, self-accusing, self-convicted, self-condemned; confessing, in the confessional; penitent, penitential, penitentiary, doing penance 941adj. *atoning*; chastened, sobered, awakened, resipiscent; reclaimed, reformed, converted, regenerate.

Vb. *be penitent*, repent, have compunction, feel shame, blush for s., feel sorry, say one is s., express regrets, apologize; reproach oneself, blame o., reprove o., accuse o., convict o., condemn o.; go to confession, shrive oneself 526n. *confess*; do penance, wear a white sheet, repent in sackcloth and ashes, 941vb. *atone*; bewail one's sins, cry peccavi; sing Miserere, sing De Profundis 836vb. *lament*; beat one's breast, scourge oneself; rue, have regrets, wish undone 830vb. *regret*; think again, think better of, stop in time; learn one's lesson, learn from experience 536vb. *learn*; reform, amend, be reformed, be reclaimed, turn over a new leaf 654vb. *get better*; see the light, convert, put on the new man, turn from sin 147vb. *be turned to*; recant one's error 603vb. *recant*.

Adv. *penitently*, like a penitent, on the stool of repentance, in sackcloth and ashes; repentantly, regretfully.

Int. sorry! mea culpa! repent! for pity!

See: 147, 526, 536, 603, 654, 830, 836, 872, 936, 941, 945, 964, 988.

940 Impenitence

N. *impenitence*, irrepentance, non-contrition; contumacy, recusance, refusal to recant, obduracy, stubbornness 602n. *obstinacy*; hardness of heart, induration 326n. *hardness*; no apologies, no regrets, no compunction 906n. *pitilessness*; incorrigibility, seared conscience, unawakened c.; hardened sinner, despair of 938n. *bad man*.

Adj. *impenitent*, unregretting, unapologizing, unrecanting, recusant; contumacious, obdurate, stubborn 602adj. *obstinate*; unconfessing, unrepentant, uncontrite; unregretful, without regrets; unrelenting, relentless 600adj. *persevering*; uncompunctious, without compunction, without a pang, heartless 898adj. *cruel*; hard, hardened, case-h.; unawakened, sleeping 679adj. *sleepy*; conscienceless, unashamed, unblushing, brazen; incorrigible, irreclaimable, irredeemable, hopeless, despaired of, lost 934adj. *wicked*; graceless, shiftless, unconfessed, unshriven; unchastened, unreformed, unreconciled; unreclaimed, unconverted. *unrepented*, unregretted, unapologized for, unatoned.

Vb. *be impenitent*, make no excuses, offer no apologies, have no regrets, would do it again; abide in one's error, not see the light, refuse to recant 602vb. *be obstinate*; make no confession, die and make no sign, die in one's sins, die in contumacy; stay unreconciled, want no forgiveness; feel no compunction, harden one's heart, steel one's h. 906vb. *be pitiless*.

Adv. *impenitently*, unregretfully, unashamedly, unblushingly.

See: 326, 600, 602, 679, 898, 906, 934, 938.

941 Atonement

N. *atonement*, making amends, amends, amende honorable, apology, full a.,

satisfaction; reparation, compensation, indemnity, indemnification, blood-money, wergild, conscience money 787 n. *restitution*; repayment, quittance, quits 714 n. *retaliation*; composition 770 n. *compromise.*

propitiation, expiation, satisfaction, reconciliation, conciliation 719 n. *pacification*; reclamation, redemption 965 n. *divine function*; sacrifice, offering, burnt-o., peace o., sin o. 981 n. *oblation*; scapegoat, whipping-boy, chopping-block 150 n. *substitute.*

penance, shrift, confession, acknowledgment 939 n. *penitence*; sacrament of penance, penitential exercise, austerities, fasting, maceration, flagellation 945 n. *asceticism*; lustration, purgation 648 n. *cleansing*; purgatorial torments, purgatory; penitent form, anxious seat, stool of repentance, cutty stool, corner, white sheet 964 n. *pillory*; sackcloth and ashes 836 n. *lamentation.*

Adj. *atoning,* making amends 939 adj. *repentant*; reparatory, compensatory, indemnificatory 787 adj. *restoring*; conciliatory, apologetic; propiatory, expiatory, piacular, purgatorial, lustrative, lustral, lustratory 648 adj. *cleansing*; sacrificial, sacrificatory, sacrific 759 adj. *offering*; penitential, penitentiary, doing penance, undergoing p. 963 adj. *punitive.*

Vb. *atone,* salve one's conscience, make amends, make reparation, offer r., indemnify, compensate, pay compensation, make it up to; apologize, make apologies, offer one's a. 909 vb. *beg pardon*; propitiate, conciliate 719 vb. *pacify*; give satisfaction, offer s., make the amende honorable 787 vb. *restitute*; redeem one's error, repair one's fault, wipe out one's offences, be restored to favour; sacrifice to, offer sacrifice; expiate, pay the penalty, pay the forfeit, pay the cost, smart for it 963 vb. *be punished*; be the chopping block, become the whipping boy, make oneself the scapegoat 931 vb. *be disinterested.*

do penance, undergo p., perform penitential exercises, perform austerities; pray, fast, flagellate oneself, scourge o.; purge one's contempt, purge one's offences, suffer purgatory; put on sackcloth and ashes, stand in a white sheet, stand in the corner, sit on the stool of repentance, sit on the anxious seat; take one's

punishment, swallow one's medicine 963 vb. *be punished*; salve one's conscience, shrive oneself, go to confession 526 vb. *confess.*

See: 150, 526, 648, 714, 719, 759, 770, 787, 836, 909, 931, 939, 945, 963, 964, 965, 981.

942 Temperance

N. *temperance,* nothing in excess 177 n. *moderation*; self-denial 931 n. *disinterestedness*; self-restraint, self-control, self-discipline, stoicism 747 n. *restraint*; chastity 950 n. *purity*; continence, encratism; soberness 948 n. *sobriety*; forbearance 620 n. *avoidance*; renunciation 621 n. *relinquishment*; abstemiousness, abstinence, abstention, total abstinence, teetotalism; enforced abstention, prohibition, prohibitionism, pussyfootism 747 n. *restriction*; vegetarianism, Pythagoreanism; dieting, banting 946 n. *fasting*; frugality 814 n. *economy*; plain living, frugal diet, Spartan fare 945 n. *asceticism.*

abstainer, total a., teetotaller 948 n. *sober person*; prohibitionist, pussyfoot; vegetarian, fruitarian, Pythagorean; Encratite; dieter, banter, faster; enemy of excess, Spartan 945 n. *ascetic.*

Adj. *temperate,* unexcessive, within bounds, within compass; measured, tempered 177 adj. *moderate*; plain, Spartan, sparing 814 adj. *economical*; frugal 816 adj. *parsimonious*; forbearing, abstemious, abstinent 620 adj. *avoiding*; dry, teetotal 948 adj. *sober*; fruitarian, vegetarian, Pythagorean; ungreedy, self-controlled, self-disciplined, continent 747 adj. *restrained*; chaste 950 adj. *pure*; self-denying 945 adj. *ascetic*; hardy, unpampered.

Vb. *be temperate,*—moderate etc. adj.; moderate, temper, keep within bounds, observe a limit, avoid excess, know when one has had enough 177 vb. *be moderate*; keep sober 948 vb. *be sober*; forbear, spare, refrain, abstain 620 vb. *avoid*; control oneself, contain o. 747 vb. *restrain*; deny oneself 945 vb. *be ascetic*; go dry, take the pledge, sign the p., join the Band of Hope; ration oneself, tighten one's belt 946 vb. *fast*; diet, bant, reduce 206 vb. *make thin.*

See: 177, 206, 620, 621, 747, 814, 816, 931, 945, 946, 948, 950.

943 Intemperance

N. *intemperance*, want of moderation, immoderation, unrestraint; excess, excessiveness, luxury 637 n. *redundance*; too much 637 n. *superfluity*; wastefulness, waste 815 n. *prodigality*; want of self-control, indiscipline, incontinence 734 n. *laxity*; inabstinence, indulgence, self-i., over i.; addiction, bad habit, drug h. 610 n. *habit*; full life, high living, dissipation, orgy, debauch 944 n. *sensualism*; intoxication, crapulence, hangover 949 n. *drunkenness*.

Adj. *intemperate*, immoderate, exceeding, excessive 637 adj. *redundant*; untempered, unmeasured, unlimited 635 adj. *plenteous*; unforbearing, unsparing, unfrugal, uneconomical, wasteful, spendthrift 815 adj. *prodigal*; luxurious 637 adj. *superfluous*; unascetic, unspartan, indulgent, over-i., self-i., inabstinent, denying oneself nothing; unrestrained, uncontrolled, unselfcontrolled, undisciplined 738 adj. *riotous*; incontinent 951 adj. *unchaste*; unsober, non-teetotal, wet 949 adj. *drunk*; animal 944 adj. *sensual*.

Vb. *be intemperate*,—immoderate etc. adj.; roll in, luxuriate, plunge, wallow; lack self-control, want discipline, lose control 734 vb. *be lax*; deny oneself nothing, indulge oneself 734 vb. *please oneself*; have one's fling, sow one's wild oats 815 vb. *be prodigal*; run to excess, run riot, exceed, have no measure 637 vb. *superabound*; observe no limits, go to all lengths, go the limit, stick at nothing, not know when to stop, over-indulge, burn the candle at both ends 634 vb. *waste*; beat it up, carouse 837 vb. *revel*; overdrink, drink to excess 949 vb. *get drunk*; eat to excess, gorge, overeat, make oneself sick 947 vb. *gluttonize*; be incontinent, grow dissipated 951 vb. *be impure*; addict oneself, become a slave to habit 610 vb. *be wont*.

Adv. *intemperately*, immoderately, excessively; without moderation, without control; incontinently, licentiously; not wisely but too well.

See: 610, 634, 635, 637, 734, 738, 815, 837, 944, 947, 949, 951.

944 Sensualism

N. *sensualism*, life of the senses, unspirituality, leanness of soul, earthiness, materialism 319 n. *materiality*; cultivation of the senses, sensuality, carnality, the flesh; grossness, beastliness, bestiality, animalism, hoggishness, wallowing, Circean cup; craze for excitement 822 n. *excitability*; love of pleasure, search for p., hedonism, epicurism, epicureanism, eudæmonism 376 n. *pleasure*; sybaritism, voluptuousness, voluptuosity, effeminacy, softness, luxuriousness; luxury, lap of l. 637 n. *superfluity*; full life, wine of l., life of pleasure, high living, fast l. 824 n. *enjoyment*; swollen desires, incontinence, dissipation 943 n. *intemperance*; licentiousness, dissoluteness, debauchery 951 n. *impurity*; indulgence, self-i., overindulgence, greediness 947 n. *gluttony*; eating and drinking, Lucullan banquet 301 n. *feasting*; orgy, debauch, saturnalia, Bacchanalia 837 n. *revel*.

sensualist, animal, pig, swine, hog, wallower; no ascetic, hedonist, man of pleasure, pleasure-lover, thrill-seeker; luxury-lover, sybarite, voluptuary; eudæmonist, epicurean, votary of Epicurus, swine of E.; epicure, gourmand, Sardanapalus, Lucullus 947 n. *glutton*; hard drinker 949 n. *drunkard*; loose liver, fast man, rake, debauchee 952 *libertine*; degenerate, Heliogabalus, Nero.

Adj. *sensual*, earthy, gross, unspiritual 319 adj. *material*; fleshly, carnal, bodily; animal, bestial, beastly, brutish, swinish, hoggish, wallowing; Circean, pleasure-giving 826 adj. *pleasurable*; sybaritic, voluptuous, pleasure-loving, thrill-seeking; hedonistic, eudæmonistic, epicurean, Lucullan, luxury-loving, luxurious; pampered, indulged, over-i., self-i.; overfed, full-f. 947 adj. *gluttonous*; high-living, fast-l., incontinent 943 adj. *intemperate*; licentious, dissipated, debauched 951 adj. *impure*; riotous, orgiastic, Bacchanalian 949 adj. *drunken*.

Vb. *be sensual*,—voluptuous etc. adj.; cultivate one's senses, be the slave of one's desires, live for pleasure, wallow in luxury, live well, indulge oneself, pamper o.; run riot, go the pace, burn the candle at both ends 943 vb. *be intemperate*.

Adv. *sensually*, bestially, hoggishly, swinishly.

See: 301, 319, 376, 637, 822, 824, 826, 837, 943, 947, 949, 951, 952.

945 Asceticism

N. *asceticism*, austerity, mortification, self-m., self-torture, self-mutilation; maceration, flagellation 941 n. *penance*; ascetic practice, encratism, yoga, tapas; anchoritism, eremitism 883 n. *seclusion*; cynicism, Diogenes and his tub 883 n. *unsociability*; Lady Poverty 801 n. *poverty*; plain living, Spartan fare, Lenten f. 946 n. *fasting*; fast-day 946 n. *fast*; self-denial 942 n. *temperance*; frugality 814 n. *economy*; Puritanism, Sabbatarianism, Christian Science; sackcloth, hair-shirt, cilice.

ascetic, spiritual athlete, yogi, sannyasi, fakir, dervish, fire-walker; hermit, cremite, anchoret, anchorite, recluse 883 n. *solitary*; cynic, Diogenes; flagellant 939 n. *penitent*; water-drinker 948 n. *sober person*; faster, vegetarian, fruitarian, Encratite 942 n. *abstainer*; Puritan, Plymouth Brother, sabbatarian; spoilsport, kill-joy, pussyfoot 702 n. *hinderer*.

Adj. *ascetic*, yogic, self-mortifying, fasting, flagellating; hermit-like, eremitical, anchoretic; puritanical; sabbatarian; austere, rigorous 735 adj. *severe*; Spartan, unpampered 942 adj. *temperate*; water-drinking 948 adj. *sober*; plain, wholesome 652 adj. *salubrious*.

Vb. *be ascetic*, live like a Spartan; fast, live on nothing, live on air 946 vb. *starve*; live like a hermit, wear a hair-shirt, put on sackcloth; control one's senses, do tapas, lie on nails, walk through fire.

Adv. *ascetically*, austerely, abstinently, plainly, frugally, painfully.

See: 652, 702, 735, 801, 814, 883, 939, 941, 942, 946, 948.

946 Fasting

N. *fasting*, abstinence from food; no appetite 860 n. *indifference*; keeping fast, xerophagy; dieting, banting; lenten entertainment, Barmecide feast; lenten fare, bread and water, spare diet, meagre d., starvation d., soupe maigre; iron rations, short commons 636 n. *scarcity*; no food, starvation, utter s., famishment 859 n. *hunger*.

fast, fast-day, Friday, Good Friday, Lent, Ramadan; day of abstinence, meatless day, fish d., jour maigre, banyan day 945 n. *ascetism*; hunger-strike 145 n. *strike*.

Adj. *fasting*, not eating, off one's food; abstinent 942 adj. *temperate*; keeping fast, keeping Lent, xerophagous; without food, unfed, empty, foodless, dinnerless, supperless; poorly fed, half-starved 636 adj. *underfed*; starved, starving, famished, famishing, dying for food 206 adj. *lean*; wanting food, a-hungered 859 adj. *hungry*; sparing, frugal 814 adj. *economical*; scanty 636 adj. *scarce*; meagre, thin, poor, Spartan; Lenten, quadragesimal.

Vb. *starve*, famish, clem 859 vb. *be hungry*; waste with hunger, show one's bones 206 vb. *be narrow*; have no food, have nothing to eat, live on water, live on air, dine with Duke Humphrey, have a Barmecide feast 801 vb. *be poor*; fast, go without food, abstain from f., eat no meat; keep fast, keep Lent, keep Ramadan; lay off food, give up eating, eat nothing, refuse one's food, go on hunger-strike; reduce one's food, diet, go on a d., bant, reduce, take off weight 37 vb. *bate*; tighten one's belt, go on short commons, live on iron rations; eat sparingly, make two bites of a cherry, control one's appetite 942 vb. *be temperate*; keep a poor table 816 vb. *be parsimonious*.

See: 37, 145, 206, 636, 801, 814, 816, 859, 860, 942, 945.

947 Gluttony

N. *gluttony*, gluttonishness, greediness, greed, rapacity, insatiability, gulosity, voracity, voraciousness, wolfishness; edacity, polyphagia, insatiable appetite 859 n. *hunger*; good living, high l., full-feeding, indulgence, over-i., over-eating, over-feeding 943 n. *intemperance*; guzzling, gorging, gormandizing, gluttonizing, pampered appetite, belly-worship, gourmandise, epicureanism, epicurism, pleasures of the table 301 n. *gastronomy*; bust, blow-out, masses of food 301 n. *feasting*.

glutton, glutton for food, guzzler, gormandizer, bolter, gorger, crammer, stuffer; locust, wolf, vulture, cormorant, pig, hog; vampire, blood-sucker; trencherman, good eater, hearty e. 301 n. *eater*; coarse feeder, pantophagist; greedy-guts, greedy pig; belly-god, gourmand, gastronome, gourmet, epicure, Lucullus.

Adj. *gluttonous*, gluttonish, rapacious 859

adj. *greedy*; devouring, voracious, edacious, wolfish; omnivorous, pantophagous, all-swallowing, all-engulfing 464adj. *indiscriminating*; starving, insatiable, never full 859adj. *hungry*; pampered, full-fed, overfed, feeding full 301adj. *feeding*; guzzling, gormandizing, gorging, stuffing, cramming, belly-worshipping, licking one's lips, licking one's chops, watering at the mouth; gastronomic, epicurean.

Vb. *gluttonize*, glutton, gormandize; guzzle, bolt, wolf, gobble, gobble up, engulf; fill oneself, gorge, over-g., cram, stuff; glut oneself, overeat 301vb. *eat*; have the run of one's teeth, eat one's head off; eat like a trooper, eat like a horse, eat like a pig, make a beast of oneself, make oneself sick; indulge one's appetite, pamper one's a., tickle one's palate; savour one's food, lick one's lips, lick one's chops, water at the mouth; keep a good table, have the best cook; like one's food, worship one's belly, live only for eating.

Adv. *gluttonously*, ravenously, wolfishly, hungrily; at a gulp, with one bite; gastronomically.

See: 301, 464, 859, 943.

948 Sobriety

N. *sobriety*, soberness 942n. *temperance*; water-drinking, tea-d., teetotalism, nephalism, pussyfootism; state of sobriety, unintoxicated state, clear head, unfuddled brain, no hangover; prohibition zone.

sober person, moderate drinker, poor d., no toper; non-addict, non-alcoholic; water-drinker, tea-d., teetotaller, nephalist, total abstainer 942n. *abstainer*; Good Templar, Rechabite, blue-ribboner, Band of Hope, Blue Ribbon Army, Temperance League; prohibitionist, pussyfoot; sobersides 834n. *moper*.

Adj. *sober*, abstinent, abstemious 620adj. *avoiding*; water-drinking, tea-d. 942adj. *temperate*; not drinking, off drink, on the water-wagon; teetotal, pussyfoot, prohibitionist, dry; unintoxicated, unfuddled, clear-headed, with a clear head, sober as a judge, stone-cold sober; sobered, come to one's senses, sobered up, without a

hangover; unfermented, non-alcoholic, soft.

Vb. *be sober*,—abstemious, etc. adj.; drink water, prefer soft drinks; not drink, not imbibe, keep off liquor, never touch drink, drink moderately 942vb. *be temperate*; go on the water-wagon, give up alcohol, become teetotal, sign the pledge, join the Band of Hope; go dry, turn prohibitionist; carry one's liquor, hold one's l., keep a clear head, be sober as a judge; sober up, clear one's head, get the fumes out of one's brain, get rid of a hangover, sleep off.

Adv. *soberly*, with sobriety, abstemiously.

See: 620, 843, 942.

949 Drunkenness

N. *drunkenness*, excessive drinking 943n. *intemperance*; ebriosity, insobriety, inebriety, temulence; bibacity, wine-bibbing, weakness for liquor, fondness for the bottle, worship of Bacchus; sottishness, beeriness, vinousness; influence of liquor, inspiration, exhilaration 821n. *excitation*; Dutch courage 855n. *courage*; intoxication, inebriation, befuddlement, fuddledness, blackout; hiccoughing, hiccup, stammering, stammer, thick speech 580n. *speech defect*; tipsiness, staggering, titubancy 317n. *oscillation*; getting drunk, one over the eight, drop too much, hard drinking, swilling, soaking 301n. *drinking*; compotation, potation, deep potations, libations, libation to Bacchus; one's cups, flowing bowl, booze 301n. *liquor, wine*; drinking bout, spree, jag, lush, blind, debauch, pub-crawl, orgy of drinking, Bacchanalia 837n. *revel*.

crapulence, crapula, crapulousness; next-morning feeling, hangover, head, sick headache.

alcoholism, alcoholic addiction, dipsomania, oinomania 503n. *mania*; delirium tremens, D.T.s, the horrors, heebiejeebies, jim-jams, pink elephants; grog-blossom, red nose, blue n., bottle n., cirrhosis of the liver.

drunkard, habitual d., inebriate, drunk, regular d., tight; slave to drink, addict, drink a., alcoholic, dipsomaniac, pathological drunk; drinker, hard d., gin-d., dram-d.; bibber, wine-b.; toper, boozer,

soaker, soak, souse, sponge, wineskin, tun; sot, love-pot, toss-pot; frothblower, thirsty soul, Pantagruel; intoxicated person, one under the influence of liquor, drunk; devotee of Bacchus, Bacchanal, Bacchante, mænad; carouser, pub-crawler 837 n. *reveller.*

Adj. *drunk,* inebriated, intoxicated, under the influence of liquor; under the influence, having drink taken, having had a drop too much, in one's cups, in liquor, the worse for l.; half-seas over, three sheets in the wind, one over the eight; gilded, boozed up, ginned up, lit up, flushed, merry, gay, happy, nappy, high, elevated, exhilarated 821 adj. *excited;* comfortably drunk, nicely thank you, mellow, ripe, full, fou, primed; gloriously drunk, fighting d., drunk and disorderly 61 adj. *disorderly;* pot-valiant, 'flown with insolence and wine'.

tipsy, squiffy, matty, tight, fresh, flush, lushy, faced, foxed, lushed; sozzled, soused, soaked; pickled, oiled, boiled, fried, frazzled, raddled, corned, potted, canned, housed, whittled, screwed, honked, ploughed, smashed; overtaken, overcome, disguised, blasted, plastered; maudlin, fuddled, muddled, flustered, muzzy, woozy, obfuscated, clouded, stupefied; bottled, glazed, glassy-eyed, pie-e., gravy-e., seeing double; dizzy, giddy, reeling, staggering 317 adj. *oscillating;* hiccupping 580 adj. *stammering.*

dead drunk, stinking d., stinko, blind drunk, blind, blotto; gone, shot, stiff, out; under the table, dead to the world; drunk as a lord, drunk as a piper, drunk as a fiddler; drunk as an owl, drunk as David's sow.

crapulous, crapulent, with a hangover, with a head; bilious, dizzy, giddy, sick.

drunken, inebriate 943 adj. *intemperate;* habitually drunk, always tight, never sober; sottish, sodden, boozy, beery, vinous, smelling of drink, stinking of liquor; thirsty, bibacious, bibulous, bibbing, wine-b., toping, tippling, swilling, swigging, hard-drinking, bottle-cracking, cork-drawing; pub-crawling, carousing, wassailing; red-nosed, blue-n., bottle-n.; bloodshot, gouty, liverish; given to drink, enslaved to d., addicted to d., alcoholic, dipsomaniac.

intoxicating, poisonous, inebriating, enebriative, temulent; exhilarating, going to the head, heady, winy, like wine 821 adj. *exciting;* alcoholic, spirituous, vinous, beery; not soft, hard, potent, double-strength, over-proof 162 adj. *strong;* neat 44 adj. *unmixed.*

Vb. *be drunk,*—tipsy etc. adj.; be under the influence of liquor, have had too much; have a weak head, not hold one's liquor, succumb, be overcome, pass out, see double; hiccup, stutter 580 vb. *stammer;* not walk straight, lurch, stagger, reel, swim, trip up 317 vb. *oscillate.*

get drunk, have too much, drink deep, drink hard, drink like a fish, drink to get tight; liquor up, gin oneself up, lush, bib, tipple, booze, tope, sot, guzzle, swig, swill, soak, souse, hit the bottle 301 vb. *drink;* go on the spree, go on a blind, have a buzz on, go pub-crawling, pub-crawl; drown one's sorrows, commit a debauch, quaff, carouse, wassail, sacrifice to Bacchus 837 n. *revel.*

inebriate, be intoxicating,—heady etc. adj.; exhilarate, elevate 821 vb. *excite;* go to one's head, make one's head swim, be too much, overcome, disguise, fuddle, befuddle, fuzzle, stupefy; make drunk, tipsify, pickle, stew; drink one under the table, put one under.

Adv. *drunkenly,* sottishly, crapulously, boozily, beerily, vinously; intoxicatingly, headily, winily.

See: 44, 61, 162, 301, 317, 503, 580, 821, 837, 855, 943.

950 Purity

N. *purity,* non-mixture, simplicity, nakedness 44 n. *simpleness;* faultlessness 646 n. *perfection;* sinlessness, immaculacy 935 n. *innocence;* moral purity, morals, good m., morality 933 n. *virtue;* decency, propriety, delicacy 846 n. *good taste;* pudicity, pudency, shame, blushfulness 874 n. *modesty;* chastity, continence, encratism 942 n. *temperance;* coldness, frigidity 820 n. *moral insensibility;* honour, one's h., woman's h., honesty; virginity, maidenhood, maidenhead 895 n. *celibacy.*

prudery, prudishness, squeamishness, shockability, Victorianism; overmodesty, false modesty, false shame, mauvaise honte 874 n. *modesty;* demureness, gravity 834 n. *seriousness;* priggishness,

primness, coyness 850 n. *affectation*; sanctimony, sanctimoniousness 979 n. *pietism*; Puritanism, blue laws 735 n. *severity*; euphemism, genteelism, mealy-mouthedness; censorship, expurgation, bowdlerization 550 n. *obliteration.*

virgin, maiden, vestal, vestal virgin, virgo intacta 895 n. *celibate*; encratite, religious celibate 986 n. *monk, nun*; Joseph, Hippolytus, Galahad; pure woman, Diana, Lucretia; maid, old m.

prude, prig, Victorian, euphemist 850 n. *affector*; Puritan, guardian of morality, Watch Committee, Mrs. Grundy; censor, Bowdler.

Adj. *pure*, unadulterated 44 adj. *unmixed*; faultless 646 adj. *perfect*; undefiled, unfallen, sinless 935 adj. *innocent*; maidenly, virginal, vestal, untouched, unhandselled 895 adj. *unwedded*; blushful, blushing, rosy 874 adj. *modest*; coy, shy 620 adj. *avoiding*; chaste, continent 942 adj. *temperate*; unmovable, unassailable, impregnable, incorruptible 660 adj. *invulnerable*; unfeeling 820 adj. *impassive*; frigid 380 adj. *cold*; immaculate, spotless, snowy 427 adj. *white*; good 929 adj. *honourable*; moral 933 adj. *virtuous*; Platonic, sublimated, elevated, purified; decent, decorous, delicate, refined 846 adj. *tasteful*; edifying, printable, quotable, repeatable, mentionable, virginibus puerisque 648 adj. *clean*; censored, bowdlerized, expurgated, edited.

prudish, squeamish, shockable, Victorian; overdelicate, overmodest; old-maidish, straitlaced, puritan, priggish; holy, sanctimonious 979 adj. *pietistic.*

See: 44, 380, 427, 550, 620, 646, 648, 660, 735, 820, 834, 846, 850, 874, 895, 929, 933, 935, 942, 979, 986.

951 Impurity

N. *impurity*, impure thoughts, filthiness, defilement 649 n. *uncleanness*; indelicacy 847 n. *bad taste*; indecency, immodesty, impudicity, shamelessness, exhibitionism; coarseness, grossness, nastiness; ribaldry, bawdry, bawdiness, salaciousness; loose talk, filthy t., blue story, smoking-room s., Milesian s., limerick, double entendre, equivoque; sex, smut, dirt, filth, obscenity, obscene literature, curious l., porno-graphic l., pornography; pornogram; banned book; blue cinema; prurience, voyeurism, scopophilia, skeptophilia.

unchastity, lightness, folly, wantonness; incontinence, easy virtue, no morals; immorality, sexual delinquency; sex consciousness, roving eye; lickerishness, prurience, concupiscence, lust 859 n. *libido*; carnality, sexuality, fleshliness, the flesh 944 n. *sensualism*; sex-indulgence, lasciviousness, lewdness, salacity, lubricity; dissoluteness, dissipation, debauchery, licentiousness, licence, libertinism, libertinage, gallantry; seduction, stupration, defloration; venery, lechery, priapism, fornication, wenching, womanizing, whoring; promiscuity, harlotry, whorishness, whoredom.

illicit love, guilty l., unlawful desires; extramarital relations, criminal conversation, unlawful carnal knowledge; incestuous affection, Caunian love; incest, sodomy, homosexualism, Lesbianism, bestiality 84 n. *abnormality*; satyriasis, priapism, nymphomania; adultery, unfaithfulness, infidelity, marital i., cuckolding, cuckoldry; eternal triangle, liaison, intrigue, amour, amourette, seduction 887 n. *love affair*; free love, unwedded cohabitation, irregular union, concubinage, companionate marriage 894 n. *type of marriage.*

rape, ravishment, violation, forcing, stupration; indecent assault; sex crime, sex murder.

social evil, harlot's trade, harlotry, whoredom; streetwalking, prostitution, open p.; public indecency, indecent exposure; pimping, pandering, panderism, bawd's trade, brothel-keeping, living on immoral earnings, white slave traffic.

brothel, bordel, bagnio, seraglio, stew, lupanar; bawdy-house, house, tolerated h., disorderly h., house of ill-fame, house of ill-repute; kip, dive, knocking shop; red-light district.

Adj. *impure*, defiling, defiled, unclean, nasty 649 adj. *dirty*; unwholesome 653 adj. *insalubrious*; indelicate, unsqueamish, not for the squeamish; vulgar, coarse, gross; ribald, bald, broad, free, loose; strong, racy, bawdy, Fescennine, Rabelaisian; uncensored, unexpurgated, unbowdlerized; suggestive, provocative, piquant, titillating; spicy, juicy; immoral, risqué,

risky, equivocal, naughty, wicked, blue, lurid; unmentionable, unquotable, unprintable; smutty, filthy, scrofulous, scabrous, scatogological, stinking, rank, fulsome, offensive; indecent, obscene, lewd, salacious, lubricious; licentious, Milesian, pornographic, porny; prurient, erotic, phallic, priapic; sexual, sexy, hot.

unchaste, unvirtuous 934 adj. *vicious*; frail, not impregnable, fallen, seduced, prostituted; of easy virtue, of loose morals, moralless, immoral; incontinent, light, wanton, loose, fast, free, gay, skittish, riggish, naughty; wild, rackety; immodest, daring, revealing; unblushing, shameless, flaunting, scarlet, meretricious, whorish, tarty; promiscuous, pandemic, streetwalking; Paphian, Aphrodisian; brothel-keeping, pimping, procuring.

lecherous, carnal, fleshly, carnal-minded, voluptuous 944 n. *sensual*; libidinous, lustful, lickerish, goatish; prurient, concupiscent 859 n. *desiring*; rampant, on heat, rutting, ruttish, must; hot, sexed-up, skittish, randy, riggish; sex-conscious, man-c., woman-c.; priapic, mad for women, woman-mad, woman-crazy; sex-mad, sex-crazy, nymphomaniac; lewd, licentious, libertine, free, loose, rakish, gallant; debauched, dissolute, dissipated, profligate, whoremongering, brothel-haunting.

extramarital, irregular, concubinary; unlawful, incestuous, homosexual, Lesbian, bestial 84 n. *abnormal*; adulterous, unfaithful; committing adultery, anticipating marriage; bed-hopping.

Vb. *be impure*, —unchaste etc. adj.; have no morals, go in for sex; talk sex, swap limericks; be unfaithful, deceive one's spouse, break the marriage vow, commit adultery, cuckold; dissipate 943 vb. *be intemperate*; fornicate, womanize, whore, wench, haunt brothels; keep women, keep a mistress, concubinize; lech, lust, rut, be on heat, be hot 859 vb. *desire*; wanton, rig, be promiscuous, sleep with any one; become a prostitute, street-walk, be on the streets; pimp, pander, procure, keep a brothel.

debauch, defile, smirch 649 vb. *make unclean*; abuse, dishonour, seduce, lead astray, deflower, wreck, ruin; concubinize, strumpet, prostitute, whore, make a whore of; lay, tumble, copulate, lie with,

sleep w. 45 vb. *unite with*; rape, commit r., ravish, violate, force; outrage, assault, indecently a.

Adv. *impurely*, immodestly, shamelessly; loosely, bawdily, sexily, erotically; lewdly, salaciously, suggestively; carnally, sexually 944 adv. *sensually*; lustfully, pruriently, concupiscently.

See: 45, 84, 649, 653, 847, 859, 887, 894, 934, 943, 944.

952 Libertine

N. *libertine*, no Joseph; gay bachelor, not the marrying kind; philanderer, flirt; free-lover, loose liver, loose fellow, fast man, rip, rake, rakehell, roué, debauchee, profligate; lady-killer, gallant, squire of dames; fancy-man, gigolo, mignon; intrigant, intriguer, seducer, deceiver, gay d., false lover, Lothario 887 n. *lover*; co-respondent, adulterer, cuckolder, bed-hopper; immoralist, amorist, Don Juan, Casanova; woman-hunter, woman-chaser, skirt-c., chaser, kerb-crawler; womanizer, fornicator, whore-monger, whoremaster; voyeur, lecher, satyr, goat, one mad for women; raper, rapist, ravisher, Tarquin; homosexual, homo, pæderast, sodomite, pansy, fairy, pervert; protector, ponce, bully.

cuckold, deceived husband, injured h., complaisant h.; wittol, wearer of horns.

loose woman, light w., light o' love, wanton, rig, hot stuff; woman of easy virtue, demirep, one no better than she should be; flirt, piece, bit, bint, wench, quean, jade, hussy, minx, miss, nymphet; baggage, trash, trollop, trull, drab, slut, 'daughter of the game'; adventuress, temptress, seductress, scarlet woman, painted w., Jezebel; adultress, false wife, fornicatress, fornicatrix; nymphomaniac, Messalina.

kept woman, mistress, paramour, leman, hetæra, concubine, unofficial wife; favourite, sweetheart, girl-friend 887 n. *loved one*; petite dame, petite amie, bit of fluff, floosie, moll, mopsy, doxy.

prostitute, common p., white slave, fallen woman, erring sister; frail sisterhood, demi-monde; harlot, trollop, whore, strumpet, laced mutton; street-walker, woman of the streets, woman of the town;

woman of the stews, brothel-inmate; tart, punk, chippy, broad, hustler; pick-up, casual conquest, call-girl; fille de joie, poule, lorette, cocotte, courtesan; demi-mondaine, demi-rep, hetæra, Aspasia, Lais, Thais, Phryne; Cyprian, Paphian; temple-prostitute, hierodule 742 n. *slave.*

bawd, go-between, conciliatrix, pimp, pandar, procurer, procuress, mackerel, brothel-keeper, madam; white slaver, ponce.

See: 742, 887.

953 Legality

N. *legality,* formality, form, formula, rite, due process 959 n. *litigation;* form of law, letter of the l., pale of the l., four corners of the l. (see *law*); respect for law, constitutionality, constitutionalism; good law, judgment according to the l. 480 n. *judgment;* justice under the law 913 n. *justice;* keeping within the law, lawfulness, legitimateness, legitimacy, validity.

legislation, legislature, legislatorship, law-giving, law-making, constitution-m.; codification; legalization, legitimization, validation, ratification, confirmation 532 n. *affirmation;* passing into law, enacting, enactment, regulation, regulation by law, regulation by statute; plebiscite 605 n. *vote;* plebiscitum, psephism, popular decree; law, statute, ordinance, order, standing o., by-law 737 n. *decree;* canon, rule, edict, rescript 693 n. *precept;* legislator, law-giver, law-maker.

law, law and equity, the law; body of law, corpus juris, constitution, written c., unwritten c.; charter, institution; codification, codified law, statute book, legal code, pandect, Twelve Tables, Ten Commandments, Pentateuch, Laws of Manu; penal code, civil c., Napoleonic c.; written law, statute l., common l., unwritten l., natural l.; personal law, private l., canon l., ecclesiastical l.; international law, jus gentium, law of nations, law of the sea, law of the air; law of commerce, commercial law, lex mercatoria, law of contract, law of crime, criminal law, civil l., constitutional l.; arm of the law, legal process 955 n. *jurisdiction;* writ, summons, lawsuit 959 n. *legal trial.*

jurisprudence, nomology, science of law,

knowledge of l., legal learning; law-book, legal textbook, legal journal; law consultancy, legal advice.

Adj. *legal,* lawful 913 adj. *just;* law-abiding 739 adj. *obedient;* legitimate, competent; licit, permissible, allowable 756 adj. *permitted;* within the law, sanctioned by law, according to l., de jure, legally sound, good in law; statutable, statutory, constitutional; nomothetic, law-giving, legislatorial, legislational, legislative, decretal; legislated, enacted, passed, voted, made law, ordained, decreed, ordered, by order; legalized, legitimized, brought within the law; liable *or* amenable to law, actionable, justiciable, triable, cognizable 928 adj. *accusable;* fit for legislation, suitable for enactment; pertaining to law, jurisprudential, nomological, learned in the law.

Vb. *be legal,*—legitimate etc. adj.; come within the law, respect the l., abide by the l., keep within the l.

make legal, legalize, legitimize, validate, confirm, ratify 488 vb. *endorse;* vest, establish 153 vb. *stabilize;* legislate, make laws, give l.; pass, enact, ordain, enforce 737 vb. *decree.*

Adv. *legally,* by law, by order; legitimately, de jure, in the eye of the law.

See: 153, 480, 488, 532, 605, 693, 737, 739, 756, 913, 928, 955, 959.

954 Illegality

N. *illegality,* bad law, legal flaw, irregularity, informality, error of law, mistake of l.; wrong verdict, bad judgment 481 vb. *misjudgment;* contradictory law, antinomy; miscarriage of justice 914 n. *injustice;* wrong side of the law, unlawfulness; unauthorization, incompetence, illicitness, illegitimacy, impermissibility 757 n. *prohibition.*

lawbreaking, breach of law, violation of l., transgression, contravention, infringement, encroachment 306 n. *overstepping;* trespass, offence, offence against the law, tort, civil wrong; champerty, malpractice 930 n. *foul play;* shadiness, dishonesty 930 n. *improbity;* criminality, criminousness 936 n. *guilt;* criminal activity, criminal offence, indictable o., crime, capital c., misdemeanour, felony; misprision, mis-

feasance, malfeasance, wrongdoing 914n. *wrong*; criminology, criminal statistics.

lawlessness, antinomianism; outlawry, disfranchisement; no law, absence of l., paralysis of authority, breakdown of law and order, crime wave 734n. *anarchy*; kangaroo court, gang rule, mob law, lynch l., Lydford l.; riot, race-r., rioting, hooliganism, ruffianism, rebellion 738n. *revolt*; coup d'état, usurpation 916n. *arrogation*; arbitrary rule, arbitrariness, negation of law, abolition of l.; mailed fist, force majeure, droit de plus fort 735n. *brute force.*

bastardy, bastardism, baseness; bastardization, illegitimacy; bastard, illegitimate child, natural c., love c., by-blow, one born out of wedlock; spurious offspring, offspring of adultery, fruit of a.

Adj. *illegal*, illegitimate, illicit, contraband, black-market; impermissible 757adj. *prohibited*; unauthorized, incompetent, without authority, unwarrantable, informal, unofficial; unlawful, wrongous, wrongful 914adj. *wrong*; unlegislated, not covered by law, exceeding the l., bad in law; uncharted, unconstitutional, unstatutory; no longer law, superseded, suspended, null and void, annulled 752 adj. *abrogated*; irregular, contrary to law, not according to l., unknown to l.; injudicial, extrajudicial; on the wrong side of the law, against the l.; outside the law, outlawed, out of bounds, offside; tortious, actionable, cognizable, justiciable, triable, punishable 928adj. *accusable.*

lawbreaking, trespassing, transgressing, infringing, encroaching; sinning 934adj. *wicked*; offending 936adj. *guilty*; criminal, criminous, misdemeanant, felonious; fraudulent, shady 930adj. *dishonest.*

lawless, antinomian, without law, chaotic 734adj. *anarchic*; ungovernable, licentious 738adj. *riotous*; violent, summary; arbitrary, irresponsible, unanswerable, unaccountable; above the law, overmighty; despotic, tyrannical 735adj. *oppressive.*

bastard, illegitimate, spurious, base; misbegotten, misbegot, adulterine, baseborn; without a father, without a name; bastardized.

Vb. *be illegal*, be bad in law, break the law, violate the l., offend against the l.,

circumvent the l., disregard the statute; wrest the law, twist *or* strain the l., torture the l.; be lawless, defy the law, drive a coach and horses through the l. 914vb. *do wrong*; take the law into one's own hands, strain one's authority, encroach 734vb. *please oneself*; have no law, know no l., stand above the law; stand outside the law, suffer outlawry.

make illegal, —unlawful etc. adj.; put outside the law, outlaw; illegalize 757vb. *prohibit*; forbid by law, penalize 963vb. *punish*; bastardize, illegitimize; suspend, annul, cancel, make the law a dead letter 752vb. *abrogate.*

Adv. *illegally*, illicitly, illegitimately, unlawfully, criminally, criminously, feloniously, tortiously, with malice prepense.

See: 306, 481, 734, 735, 738, 752, 757, 914, 916, 928, 930, 934, 936, 963.

955 Jurisdiction

N. *jurisdiction*, portfolio 622vb. *function*; judicature, magistracy, commission of the peace; mayoralty, shrievalty, bumbledom; competence, legal c., legal authority, arm of the law 733n. *authority*; administration of justice, legal administration, Ministry of Justice; local jurisdiction, local authority, corporation, municipality, borough council, town c., parish c., bailiwick 692n. *council*; vigilance committee 956n. *tribunal*; office, bureau, secretariat 687n. *workshop*; legal authority, competence.

law officer, legal administrator, Minister of Justice, Lord Chancellor, Attorney-General, Advocate-General, Solicitor-General, Legal Remembrancer, Queen's Proctor; Crown Counsel, public prosecutor; Judge Advocate, Procurator Fiscal, district attorney 957n. *judge*; mayor, lord m., sheriff 733n. *magistrature*; court officer, clerk of the court, huissier, tipstaff, bailiff, bum-bailiff; summoner, process-server, catchpoll, Bow-street runner; paritor, apparitor, beadle, macebearer 690n. *official.*

police, forces of law and order; police force, the force, Scotland Yard; constabulary, gendarmerie, military police; peace officer,

civil o., police officer, limb of the law, policeman, constable, special c., copper, cop, traffic c., motor police; bluebottle, Peeler, bobby, flatfoot, dick; police-sergeant, police inspector, police super-intendent, commissioner of police, chief constable, provost marshal; sub-inspec-tor, daroga; gendarme, sbirro, alguazil, kavass; watch, posse comitatus; press-gang; plain clothes man 459 n. *detective.*

Adj. *jurisdictional,* jurisdictive, competent; executive, administrative, administra-tional, directive 689 adj. *directing*; justici-ary, judiciary, juridical, causidical; orig-inal, appellate; justiciable, subject to jurisdiction, liable to the law.

Vb. *hold court,* administer justice, sit on the bench, sit in judgment 480 vb. *judge*; hear complaints, hear causes 959 vb. *try a case*; be seized of, cognize, take cognisance, take judicial notice.

See: 459, 480, 622, 687, 689, 690, 692, 733, 956, 957, 959.

956 Tribunal

N. *tribunal,* seat of justice, woolsack, throne; judgment seat, bar, bar of justice; court of conscience, tribunal of penance, con-fessional, judgment-day; forum, ecclesia, wardmote, burghmote 692 n. *council*; public opinion, vox populi, electorate; judicatory, bench, board, bench of judges, panel of j., judge and jury; judicial assembly, Areopagus; judicial committee, judicial committee of the Privy Council, King's Council; Justices in Eyre, com-mission of the peace; Congregation of the Holy Office; original side, appellate s.

lawcourt, court, open c.; court of law, court of justice, criminal court, civil c.; Federal Court, High Court, District Court, County Court; Supreme Court, appellate court, Court of Appeal; court of inferior jurisdiction, subordinate court, small cause c., Court of Requests; court of record, Rolls Court; Court-royal, Board of Green Cloth; King's Court, Court of Exchequer, Exchequer of Pleas, Star Chamber; High Court of Parliament 692 n. *parliament*; High Court of Judica-ture, Queen's Bench, Queen's Bench Divi-sion, Court of Common Pleas, Court of Claims; Court of Admiralty, Probate and Divorce; Court of Chancery, court of equity, court of arbitration; Eyre of Justice, court of oyer and terminer, circuit court; assize; sessions, court of session, quarter sessions, petty s.; Central Crim-inal Court, Old Bailey; magistrate's court, police c.; coroner's court; court of piepowder, court of pie poudre; feudal court, manorial c., Stannary Court, court-baron, court-leet; guild-court, hust-ings; Vice-Chancellor's court; court-martial, drum-head c., summary court; durbar, divan 692 n. *council*.

ecclesiastical court, court of audience, Court of Arches; papal court, curia; Inquisition, Holy Office.

courtroom, court-house, law-courts, cut-cherry; bench, woolsack, jury-box; dock; witness-box, chair.

Adj. *curial,* judicatory, judicial, justiciary, inquisitional, Rhadamanthine; original, appellate 955 adj. *jurisdictional*.

See: 692, 955.

957 Judge

N. *judge,* justice, his justiceship, his Lord-ship; bencher, justicer, justiciar, justici-ary, podestà; deemster, doomster, dooms-man; dicast, Areopagite; prætor urbanus, prætor pergrinus; verderer; Lord Chan-cellor, Lord Chief Justice, Master of the Rolls, Exchequer judge, baron; military judge, Judge Advocate; chief justice, puisné judge, county court j., recorder, common serjeant; sessions judge, assize j., judge on circuit, circuiteer; district judge, subordinate j.; civil judge, munsiff, mufti, cadi, kazi; criminal judge, magis-trate, district m., Presidency m., city m., police m.; stipendiary magistrate; coroner; honorary magistrate, justice of the peace, the great unpaid; bench, judiciary.

magistracy, beak, his Worship, his nibs; arbiter, umpire, referee, assessor, arbi-trator 480 n. *estimator*; revising barrister 549 n. *recorder*; Daniel come to judgment, Solomon, Minos, Rhadamanthus, Re-cording Angel.

jury, twelve good men and true, twelve men in a box; grand jury, special j., petty j., trial j., coroner's j.; juror's panel, jury

list, jurors' book; juror, juryman, jurat, recognitor, assessor; foreman of the jury, chancellor; dicast, judex, dicastery.

See: 480, 549.

958 Lawyer

N. *lawyer*, practising l., legal practitioner, member of the legal profession, man of law; common lawyer, canon l., civil l., criminal l.; one called to the bar, barrister, barrister-at-law, advocate, counsel, learned c., counsel learned in the law; junior barrister, stuff gown, junior counsel; senior barrister, bencher, bencher of the Inns of Court; silk gown, leading counsel, King's C., Queen's C.; serjeant, serjeant at law, King's serjeant, prime s., postman, tubman; circuit barrister, circuiteer; shyster, pettifogger, crook lawyer.

law agent, attorney, public a., attorney at law, proctor, procurator; writer to the signet, solicitor before the Supreme Court; solicitor, legal adviser; legal representative, legal agent, vakil, muktar, pleader, advocate; equity draftsman; conveyancer.

notary, common n., notary public, commissioner for oaths; scrivener, petition-writer; clerk of the court, cursitor, articler 955 n. *law officer*; solicitor's clerk, barrister's c., barrister's devil.

jurist, jurisconsult, legal adviser, legal expert, legal light, master of jurisprudence, pundit, legist, legalist, civilian, canonist; student of law, law student, legal apprentice, devil.

bar, civil b., criminal b., English bar, Scottish b., junior b., senior b.; Inns of Chancery, Inns of Court, Serjeants' Inn, Gray's I., Lincoln's I., Inner Temple, Middle T.; profession of law, legal profession, the Robe, the long robe; barristership, advocacy, pleading; solicitorship, attorneyship, attorneydom, attorneyism, vakilship; legal consultancy.

Adj. *jurisprudential*, learned in the law, called to the bar, at the b., practising at the b., barristerial, forensic; solicitorial, notarial.

Vb. *do law*, study l., go in for l., take up l.; eat one's dinners, be called to the bar; take silk, be called within the bar;

practise at the bar, accept a brief, take a case, advocate, plead; practice law, write to the signet, solicit; attorney.

See: 955.

959 Litigation

N. *litigation*, going to law, litigiousness 709 n. *quarrelsomeness*; legal dispute 709 n. *quarrel*; issue, legal i., matter for judgment, case for decision; lawsuit, suit at law, suit, case, cause, action; prosecution, arraignment, impeachment, charge 928 n. *accusation*; test case 461 n. *experiment*; claim, counter c. 915 n. *dueness*; plea, petition 761 n. *request*; affidavit, written statement, averment, pleading, demurrer 532 n. *affirmation*.

legal process, proceedings, legal procedure, course of law, arm of the l. 955 n. *jurisdiction*; citation, subpœna, summons, search warrant 737 n. *warrant*; arrest, apprehension, detention, committal 747 n. *restraint*; habeas corpus, bail, surety, security, recognisance, personal r.; injunction, stay order, order to show cause; writ, certiorari, latitat, nisi prius.

legal trial, trial, trial by law, trial by jury, trial at the bar, trial in court, assize, sessions 956 n. *lawcourt*; inquest, inquisition, examination 459 n. *enquiry*; hearing, prosecution, defence; hearing of evidence, taking of e., recording of e. 466 n. *evidence*; examination, cross e., re-e., objection sustained, objection overruled 466 n. *testimony*; pleadings, arguments 475 n. *reasoning*; counter argument, rebutter, rebuttal 460 n. *rejoinder*; proof 478 n. *demonstration*; disproof 479 n. *confutation*; summing up, charge to the jury; ruling, finding, decision, verdict 480 n. *judgment*; favourable verdict 960 n. *acquittal*; unfavourable verdict 961 n. *condemnation*; execution of judgment 963 n. *punishment*; appeal, motion of a., writ of error; successful appeal, reversal of judgment, retrial; precedent, case-law, decided case, reported c.; law reports, Newgate Calendar; cause-list; case-record, dossier 548 n. *record*.

litigant, libellant, party, party to a suit, suitor 763 n. *petitioner*; claimant, plaintiff, defendant, appellant, respondent, objector, intervener; accused, prisoner at

the bar 928 n. *accused person*; litigious person, sycophant, common informer 524 n. *informer*; prosecutor 928 n. *accuser*.

Adj. *litigating*, at law with, litigant, suing 928 adj. *accusing*; going to law, appearing in court; contesting, objecting, disputing 475 adj. *arguing*; litigious 709 adj. *quarrelling*; vexatious, sycophantic.

litigated, on trial, coram judice; argued, disputed, contested; up for trial, brought before the court, submitted for judgment, offered for arbitration; sub judice, on the cause-list, down for hearing, ready for h.; litigable, disputable, arguable, suable, actionable, justiciable 928 adj. *accusable*.

Vb. *litigate*, go to law, appeal to l., set the law in motion, start an action, bring a suit, file a s., petition 761 vb. *request*; prepare a case, prepare a brief, brief counsel; file a claim 915 vb. *claim*; have the law on one, make one a party, sue, implead, arraign, impeach, accuse, charge 928 vb. *indict*; cite, summon, serve notice on; prosecute, bring to justice, bring to trial, bring to the bar; challenge the jurors; argue one's case, advocate, plead, call evidence 475 vb. *argue*.

try a case, take cognizance, put down for hearing, empanel a jury, hear a cause; examine the witnesses, take statements; sit in judgment, rule, find, decide, adjudicate 480 vb. *judge*; close the pleadings, sum up, charge the jury; bring in a verdict, pronounce sentence; commit for trial.

stand trial, come before, come up for trial, be put on t., stand in the dock; plead to the charge, ask to be tried, submit to judgment, hear sentence; defend an action, put in one's defence, make one's d.

Adv. *in litigation*, at law, in court, before the judge; coram judice, sub judice, pendente lite; litigiously, sycophantically.

See: 459, 460, 461, 466, 475, 478, 479, 480, 524, 532, 548, 709, 737, 747, 761, 763, 915, 928, 955, 956, 960, 961, 963.

960 Acquittal

N. *acquittal*, favourable verdict, verdict of not guilty, verdict of not proven, benefit of doubt; clearance, exculpation, exoneration 935 n. *innocence*; absolution, dis-

charge; let-off, thumbs up 746 n. *liberation*; whitewashing, justification, compurgation 927 n. *vindication*; successful defence, defeat of the prosecution; no case, withdrawal of the charge, quashing, quietus; reprieve, pardon 909 n. *forgiveness*; non-prosecution, exemption, impunity 919 n. *non-liability*.

Adj. *acquitted*, not guilty 935 adj. *guiltless*; clear, cleared, in the clear, exonerated, exculpated, vindicated; uncondemned, unpunished, unchastised, immune, exempted, exempt 919 adj. *non-liable*; let off, discharged, without a stain on one's character 746 adj. *liberated*; reprieved 909 adj. *forgiven*; recommended to mercy.

Vb. *acquit*, find *or* pronounce not guilty, prove innocent, justify, compurgate, whitewash, get one off 927 vb. *vindicate*; clear, absolve, exonerate, exculpate; find there is no case to answer, not prosecute 919 vb. *exempt*; discharge, let go, let off 746 vb. *liberate*; reprieve, respite, pardon, remit the penalty 909 vb. *forgive*; quash, quash the conviction, set aside the sentence, allow an appeal 752 vb. *abrogate*.

See: 746, 752, 909, 919, 927, 935.

961 Condemnation

N. *condemnation*, unfavourable verdict, hostile v.; finding of guilty, conviction; successful prosecution, unsuccessful defence; final condemnation, damnation; black-list, Index 924 n. *disapprobation*; excommunication 899 n. *malediction*; doom, judgment, sentence 963 n. *punishment*; writing on the wall 511 n. *omen*; outlawry, price on one's head, proscription, attainder; death-warrant, condemned cell, execution chamber, Death Row; thumbs down; black cap; knell.

Adj. *condemned*, found guilty, made liable; convicted, sentenced; proscribed, outlawed, with a price on one's head; self-convicted, confessing; without a case, having no case, without a leg to stand on; cast in one's suit, non-suited, damned 924 adj. *disapproved*; lost, in hell, burning, frying.

Vb. *condemn*, prove guilty, bring home the charge; find liable, find against, non-suit, cast one in his suit; find guilty, pronounce g., convict, sentence; sentence to death,

put on the black cap, sign one's death warrant; reject one's defence, reject one's appeal 607 vb. *reject*; proscribe, attaint, outlaw, bar, put a price on one's head 954 vb. *make illegal*; blacklist, put on the index 924 vb. *disapprove*; damn, excommunicate 899 vb. *curse*; convict oneself, plead guilty 526 vb. *confess*.

See: 511, 526, 607, 899, 924, 954, 963.

962 Reward

N. *reward*, guerdon, remuneration, recompense; meed, deserts, just d. 913 n. *justice*; recognition, acknowledgment, thanks 907 n. *gratitude*; tribute, deserved t., proof of regard 923 n. *praise*; prizegiving, award, presentation, prize, crown, cup, pot, certificate, medal 729 n. *trophy*; honour 729 n. *decoration*; honours 870 n. *title*; prize-money, talent m., money prize, cash p., prize-fellowship, scholarship, bursary, stipend, exhibition, demyship; assistance, alimony, grant, allowance 703 n. *subvention*; reward for service, fee, retainer, honorarium, payment, remuneration, emolument, pension, salary, wage, wages, screw, differential, rate of pay, wage scale, Burnham s. 804 n. *pay*; overtime pay 612 n. *incentive*; perquisite, perks, expense account, dearness allowance; income, turnover 771 n. *earnings*; return, profitable r., profit, margin of p. 771 n. *gain*; compensation, indemnification, satisfaction; consideration, quid pro quo, requital 714 n. *retaliation*; avengement 910 n. *revenge*; reparation 787 n. *restitution*; bounty, honorarium, gratuity, golden handshake, tip, solatium, gratification, douceur, pourboire, trinkgeld, baksheesh, dustoor 781 n. *gift*; tempting offer 759 n. *offer*; bait, lure, bribe 612 n. *inducement*; hush money, smart m., protection m., blackmail.

Adj. *rewarding*, prize-giving, munerary; generous, open-handed 813 adj. *liberal*; paying, profitable, remunerative 771 adj. *gainful*; promising 759 adj. *offering*; compensatory, indemnificatory 714 adj. *retaliatory*; reparatory 787 adj. *restoring*; retributive 910 adj. *revengeful*.

Vb. *reward*, guerdon, recompense; award, present, give a prize, offer a p., offer a reward; bestow a medal, title 866 vb.

honour; recognize, acknowledge, pay tribute, thank, show one's gratitude 907 vb. *be grateful*; remunerate, fee 804 vb. *pay*; satisfy, gratify, tip 781 vb. *give*; tip well 813 vb. *be liberal*; repay, requite 714 vb. *retaliate*; compensate, indemnify, make reparation 787 vb. *restitute*; make amends 941 vb. *atone*; offer a bribe, gain over 612 vb. *bribe*.

be rewarded, gain a reward, get a prize, get a medal, receive a title; get paid, draw a salary, earn an income, have a gainful occupation 771 vb. *acquire*; accept payment, accept a gratification 782 vb. *receive*; take a bribe, have one's palm greased; have one's reward, get one's deserts, receive one's due 915 vb. *deserve*; reap, reap a profit, seize one's advantage 771 vb. *gain*; reap the fruits, reap the whirlwind.

Adv. *rewardingly*, profitably; for a consideration, as a reward, in compensation.

See: 612, 703, 714, 729, 759, 771, 781, 782, 787, 804, 813, 866, 870, 907, 910, 913, 915, 923, 941.

963 Punishment

N. *punishment*, sentence 961 n. *condemnation*; execution of sentence, exaction of penalty, penalization, victimization; punition, chastisement, heads rolling; chastening, castigation, strafing, strafe 924 n. *reprimand*; disciplinary action, discipline; dose, pill, bitter p., hard lines, infliction, trial, visitation, punishing experience 731 n. *adversity*; just deserts, meet reward 915 n. *dueness*; doom, judgment, day of j., day of reckoning, divine justice 913 n. *justice*; poetic justice, retributive j., retribution, Nemesis; reckoning, repayment 787 n. *restitution*; requital, reprisal 714 n. *retaliation*; avengement 910 n. *revenge*; penance, self-punishment 941 n. *atonement*; self-mortification, self-discipline 945 n. *asceticism*; hara-kiri 362 n. *suicide*; penology, penologist.

corporal punishment, bodily chastisement, smacking, slapping, trouncing, hiding, dusting, beating, fustigation, stick law, argumentum ad baculum; caning, whipping, flogging, scourging, flagellation, bastinado, running the gauntlet; defenestration; ducking, keel-hauling; picket,

picketing; slap, smack, rap, rap over the knuckles, box on the ear; drubbing, blow, buffet, cuff, clout, stroke, stripe 279 n. *knock*; third degree, torture, peine forte et dure, racking, strappado, breaking on the wheel, death by a thousand cuts 377 n. *pain.*

capital punishment, extreme penalty 361 n. *death*; death sentence, death warrant; execution 362 n. *killing*; decapitation, beheading, heading, guillotining, decollation; traitor's death, hanging, drawing and quartering; strangulation, garrotte, bow-stringing; hanging, high jump, long drop, 'Tyburn ague'; electrocution; stoning, lapidation; crucifixion, impalement, flaying alive; burning, death by burning, auto da fé; drowning, noyade; massacre, mass murder, mass execution, purge, genocide 362 n. *slaughter*; martyrdom, martyrization, persecution to the death; illegal execution, lynching, lynch law; judicial murder.

penalty, penal character, penality; injury, damage 772 n. *loss*; infliction, imposition, task, lines; prescribed punishment, sentence, penalization, pains and penalties, penal code, penology; devil to pay, liability, legal l. 915 n. *dueness*; damages, costs, compensation, restoration 787 n. *restitution*; amercement, fining, mulct, fine, sconce, deodand, compulsory payment 804 n. *payment*; ransom 809 n. *price*; forfeit, forfeiture, sequestration, escheat, confiscation, deprivation 786 n. *expropriation*; keeping in, gating, imprisonment 747 n. *detention*; binding over 747 n. *restraint*; penal servitude, hard labour, galley service, galleys; transportation; expulsion, deportation, externment 300 n. *ejection*; ostracism, banishment, exile, proscription, ban, outlawing 57 n. *exclusion*; reprisal 714 n. *retaliation.*

punisher, vindicator, retaliator 910 n. *avenger*; inflicter, chastiser, castigator, corrector, chastener, discipliner, persecutor; sentencer, justiciary, magistrate, court, law 957 n. *judge*; spanker, whipper, caner, trouncer, flogger, scourger, flagellator; torturer, inquisitor; executioner, headsman, hangman, Jack Ketch; garrotter, bow-stringer; fire-party; lyncher 362 n. *murderer.*

Adj. *punitive*, penological, penal, punitery; castigatory, disciplinary, corrective; re-

tributive 910 adj. *revengeful*; in reprisal 714 adj. *retaliatory*; penalizing, inflictive, fining, mulctuary, amercing; confiscatory, expropriatory 786 adj. *taking*; scourging, flagellatory, torturing, racking 377 adj. *painful.*

punishable, liable, amerceable, mulctable; inflictable.

Vb. *punish*, visit, afflict; persecute, victimize, make an example of 735 vb. *be severe*, inflict, impose, inflict punishment, administer correction; give one a lesson, chasten, discipline, correct, chastise, castigate; reprimand, strafe, rebuke, have one's head for 924 vb. *reprove*; penalize, impose a penalty, sentence 961 vb. *condemn*; execute justice, execute judgment, execute a sentence, carry out a s.; exact a penalty, exact retribution, settle with, get even w., pay one out 714 vb. *retaliate*; revenge oneself 714 vb. *avenge*; amerce, mulct, fine, forfeit, deprive, sequestrate, confiscate 786 vb. *take away*; unfrock, demote, degrade, downgrade, reduce to the ranks, suspend, supersede; tar and feather, toss in a blanket; pillory, set in the stocks, stand one in a corner; masthead; duck, keelhaul; picket, spreadeagle; lock up 747 vb. *imprison*; transport; condemn to the galleys.

spank, paddle, slap, smack, slipper; cuff, clout, box on the ears, rap over the knuckles; drub, trounce, beat, belt, strap, leather, larrup, wallop, welt, tan, cane, birch, switch, whack, dust, dust one's jacket 279 vb. *strike.*

flog, whip, horsewhip, thrash, hide, belabour, cudgel, fustigate 279 vb. *strike*; scourge, give stripes, give strokes, give one the cat; lash, lay on the l., flay, flay one's back, lay one's back open; flail, flagellate, bastinado.

torture, give the third degree; give one the works 377 vb. *give pain*; put one to torture, thumbscrew, rack, put on the r., break on the wheel; mutilate, trim one's ears; persecute, martyrize 827 vb. *torment.*

execute, punish with death, put to death 362 vb. *kill*; lynch 362 vb. *murder*; dismember, tear limb from limb; decimate; crucify, impale; flay, flay alive; stone, stone to death 712 vb. *lapidate*; shoot, fusillade, stand against a wall; drown, noyade, burn, burn alive, burn at the stake, send to the s.; bow-string, garrotte,

strangle; gibbet, hang, hang by the neck, string up, stretch, turn off, bring to the gallows; hang, draw and quarter; send to the scaffold, bring to the block, strike off one's head, behead, head, decapitate, decollate, guillotine; electrocute; gas, put in the gas-chamber; commit genocide, hold mass executions, purge, massacre 362 vb. *slaughter.*

be punished, suffer punishment, take the consequences, catch it; take the rap, stand the racket, face the music; take one's medicine, take one's gruel, hold one's hand out; get what is coming, get one's deserts; regret it, smart for it; come to execution, lay one's head on the block, ride in a tumbril; come to the gallows, stretch a rope, swing, take the high jump, dance upon nothing, kick the air; pay for it with one's head, die the death, drink the hemlock.

See: 57, 279, 300, 361, 362, 377, 710, 712, 714, 731, 735, 747, 772, 786, 787, 804, 809, 827, 910, 913, 915, 924, 941, 945, 957, 961.

964 Means of Punishment

N. *scourge,* birch, birch-rod, cat, cat-o'-nine-tails, rope's end, knout, cowhide, sjambok, chabouk, kurbash; whip, horse-whip, switch, quirt; lash, strap, thong, belt; cane, lithe and limber c., ratan; stick, big s., rod, ferule, cudgel, ruler 723 n. *club;* rubber hose, bicycle chain, sandbag.

pillory, stocks, whipping post, ducking stool, cucking stool, trebuchet, scold's bridle, branks; stool of repentance, cutty stool, penitent form, white sheet; chain, irons, bilboes 748 n. *fetter;* prison house, prison 748 n. *gaol;* corner.

instrument of torture, rack, thumbscrew, iron boot, pilliwinks; maiden, wooden horse, triangle, wheel, treadmill; torture chamber.

means of execution, scaffold, block, gallows, gibbet, Tyburn tree, tumbril; cross; stake; Tarpeian rock; hemlock 659 n. *poison;* bullet, wall; axe, headsman's a., guillotine; halter, rope, noose, drop; garrotte, bow-string; electric chair, hot seat; death chamber, lethal c., gas c.; condemned cell, Death Row 961 n. *condemnation.*

See: 659, 723, 748, 961.

965 Divineness

N. *divineness,* divinity, deity; godhood, godhead, godship; divine principle, Brahma; numen, numinousness, mana; being of God, divine essence, perfection, the Good, the True and the Beautiful; love, Fatherhood; Brahmahood, nirvana; impersonal God, Atman, Paramatman, oversoul, supreme soul, world s.; Ens Entium, First Cause, Primum Mobile; divine nature, God's ways, Providence.

divine attribute, being 1 n. *existence;* perfect being 646 n. *perfection;* oneness 88 n. *unity;* infinitude 107 n. *infinity;* immanence, omnipresence 189 n. *presence;* omniscience, wisdom 490 n. *knowledge;* omnipotence, almightiness 160 n. *power;* timelessness, eternity 115 n. *perpetuity;* immutability, changelessness 153 n. *stability;* truth, sanctity, holiness, goodness, justice, mercy; transcendence, sublimity, supremacy, sovereignty, majesty, glory, light; glory of the Lord, Shekinah.

the Deity, God, personal god, Supreme Being, Divine B.; the Infinite, the Eternal, the All-wise, the Almighty, the All-holy, the All-merciful; Maker of all things, Creator, Preserver; Allah; Elohim, Jahweh, Jehovah, Adonai, ineffable name, I AM; name of God, Tetragrammaton; God of Abraham, God of Moses, Lord of Hosts, God of our fathers; our Father; Demiurge; All-Father, great spirit; Ahura Mazda, Ormuzd; Baal; Krishna.

Trinity, triad, Hindu Triad, Brahma, Shiva, Vishnu; Holy Trinity, Hypostatic Union; Triune God, Three Persons in one God, Three in One and One in Three; God the Father, God the Son, God the Holy Ghost.

Holy Ghost, third person of the Trinity; Holy Spirit, Spirit of Truth; Paraclete, Comforter, Consoler; Dove.

God the Son, second person of the Trinity, Word, Logos, Son of God, the Only Begotten, Word made flesh, Incarnate Son; Messiah, Son of David, the Anointed, Christ; Immanuel; Lamb of God, Son of Man; Son of Mary, Jesus, Jesus of Nazareth, the Nazarene, the Galilean; the Good Shepherd, Saviour, Redeemer, Atoner, Mediator, Intercessor, Judge; Bread of Life, the Way, the Truth, the Life; Light of the World, Sun of Righteousness; King of Kings,

King of Heaven, King of Glory, Prince of Peace.

divine function, creation, preservation, judgment; mercy, uncovenanted mercies, forgiveness; inspiration, unction, regeneration, comfort, strengthening, consolation, grace, prevenient g.; propitiation, atonement, redemption, justification, salvation, mediation, intercession.

theophany, divine manifestation, divine emanation, descent, descent to earth, divine intervention, irruption into history, incarnation, full incarnation; transfiguration; Shekinah, Glory of the Lord; avatar, avatars of Vishnu, Matsya, Karma, Varah, Narsinha, Vamara, Kalki, Parashurama, Rama, Krishna.

theocracy, divine government, divine dispensation, God's law, Kingdom of God; God's ways, God's dealings, providence, special p., deus ex machina.

Adj. *divine*, holy, hallowed, sanctified, sacred, sacrosanct, heavenly, celestial; transcendental, sublime, ineffable; numinous, mystical, religious, ghostly, spiritual, superhuman, supraphysical, supernatural; unearthly, supramundane, extramundane, not of this world; providential; theophanic; theocratic.

godlike, divine, superhuman; transcendent, immanent; omnipresent 189adj. *ubiquitous*; immeasurable 107adj. *infinite*; absolute, undefined, self-existent, living 1adj. *existing*; timeless, eternal, everlasting, immortal 115adj. *perpetual*; immutable, unchanging, changeless 144 adj. *permanent*; almighty, all-powerful, omnipotent 160adj. *powerful*; creative 160adj. *dynamic*; prescient, providential 510adj. *foreseeing*; all-wise, all-seeing, omniscient, all-knowing 490adj. *knowing*; oracular 511adj. *predicting*; all-merciful, merciful 909adj. *forgiving*; compassionate, pitiful 905adj. *pitying*; fatherly 887 adj. *loving*; holy, all-h., worshipped 979 adj. *sanctified*; sovereign 34adj. *supreme*; majestic 733adj. *authoritative*; transfigured, glorious, all-g. 866adj. *worshipful*; theomorphic, incarnate, in the image of God, deified; messianic, anointed.

deistic, theistic, Jahwistic, Elohistic, Brahmic, Sivaic, Brahmoistic.

redemptive, intercessional, mediatory, propitiatory; incarnational, avatarik; soteriological, messianic.

Adv. *divinely*, as God; under God, by God's will, deo volente, D.V.; by divine right, jure divino; redemptively, soteriologically.

See: 1, 34, 88, 107, 115, 144, 153, 160, 189, 490, 510, 511, 646, 733, 866, 887, 905, 909, 979.

966 Gods in general

N. *god*, goddess, deva, devi; the gods, the immortals; Olympian 967n. *Olympian god*; the unknown god, pagan g., false g., idol; godling, petty god, inferior g., subordinate g. 967n. *lesser god*; demigod, half-god, divine hero, deified person, divine king; object of worship, fetish, totem; numinous presence, mumbo jumbo; theogony; theotechny; pantheon.

mythic god, nature g., Pan, Flora, Faunus; vegetation god, corn g., tree g., fertility g.; Adonis, Thammuz, Atys; earth goddess, mother earth, mother goddess, earth mother, Great Mother, Magna Mater, Cybele; chthonian deity, god of the underworld, Pluto, Hades, Dis, Persephone, Yama, Yami 967n. *Chthonian god*; sky god, Dyaus, Zeus, Jupiter; storm god, Indra, rain g., Jupiter Pluvius; wind god, Aeolus, Maruts; sun god, Apollo, Hyperion, Helios, Surya; river god, sea g., Poseidon, Neptune, Triton, Varuna; war god, Mars, Bellona; god of love, Cupid, Eros, Venus, Aphrodite; household god, Teraphim, Lares, Penates, Hermæ, Hestia, Vesta; tutelary god, genius, good g., good angel, ba, ka; the Fates, Parcæ, Clotho, Lachesis, Atropos, the Norns 596n. *fate*.

Adj. *theotechnic*, theogonic, mythological, mythical; deiform, theomorphic, deific, deified.

See: 596, 967.

967 Pantheon: classical and non-classical gods

N. *classical gods*, gods of Greece and Rome, Græco-Roman pantheon; Homeric gods, Hesiodic theogony; primeval gods, Chaos, Erebus, Nox; Ge, Gaia, Tellus, Terra; Uranus, Coelus, Kronos, Saturn, Rhea, Ops; Oceanus, Tethys, Nereus; Helios,

Sol, Hyperion, Phæthon; Titan, Prometheus, Epimetheus, Typho, Enceladus; the Fates, Parcæ, Clotho, Lachesis, Atropos.

Olympian god, Olympian, Zeus, Jupiter, Jove, president of the immortals; Pluto, Hades, Dis; Poseidon, Neptune; Apollo; Hermes, Mercury; Ares, Enyalios, Mars; Hephæstus, Vulcan; Dionysus, Bacchus; Hera, Juno; Demeter, Ceres; Persephone, Proserpina; Athena, Minerva; Aphrodite, Venus; Artemis, Diana; Eros, Cupid; Iris; Hebe.

Chthonian god, Chthonians, Ge, Gaia, Hades, Pluto, Persephone; Osiris; Cerberus, Charon, Styx; Erectheus, Trophonius, Pytho; Eumenides, Furies; Manes, Shades, spirits of the dead.

lesser god, Pan, Sylvanus, Flora, Faunus, Silenus, Satyr, Faun; Aurora, Eos; Luna, Selene; Aeolus, Boreas, Orithyia 352n. *wind*; Nereus, Triton, Proteus, Glaucus, Melicerte; Ate, Eris, Bellona, Nike; Astræa; Muses, tuneful Nine, Erato, Euterpe, Terpsichore, Polymnia, Clio, Calliope, Melpomene, Thalia, Urania; Asclepius, Aesculapius; Hypnos, Somnus; Hymen; Hestia, Vesta; Teraphim, Lares, Penates, Hermæ; Kabiri; genius.

nymph, wood n., tree n., dryad, oread; water nymph, naiad; sea nymph, nereid, Oceanid; Thetis, Circe, Calypso; siren, Parthenope, Scylla, Charybdis 970n. *mythical being*; Leto, Maia.

demigod, divine offspring, divine hero; Heracles, Hercules; Dioscouroi, Castor and Pollux, Castor and Polydeuces; Amphion, Zethes; Epaphus, Perseus, Achilles, Aeneas, Memnon.

Hindu god, Brahmanic g., Vedic g.; Dyaus, Prithivi, Indra, Mitra, Varuna, Nasatya; Agni, Apam Napat, Brihaspati; Surya, Savitri, Pushan, Asvin, Ushas; Ratri; Vata, Maruts, Rudra; Parjanya, Apas; Soma; Hindu triad, trimurti, Brahma, Siva, Vishnu; Brahmadeva; Rama, Krishna, Narayan, Bhagava; Jagannath; Kumara, Karttikeya, Mahasena; Kama, Kamadeva, Madana; Hanuman; Ganesha, Ganpat; Hindu goddess, Lakshmi, Sarasvati, Indrani, Rati; Sati, Devi, Uma, Parvati, Durga, Gauri, Kali; Manasa, Sitala.

Egyptian gods; theriomorphic deity, theriocephalous d.; Selk (scorpion); Uazit, Nekhebt, Mert-seger, seker (serpent); Hept (frog); Horakhti, Mentu (hawk); Tahuti (ibis); Sebek (crocodile); Taurt (hippopotamus); Hapi, Apis (bull); Khnum (ram); Apuat, Anpu, Anubis (jackal); Sekhet, Bast (lion); anthropomorphic god, Egyptian triad, Isis, Osiris, Horus, elder Horus, younger H.; Set, Nebhat; Amen, Ammon, Jupiter A., Mut, Khonsu, Anher; Net, Neith; cosmic god, Ra, Amen-Ra, Atmu, Nefer-atmu; Khepra, Harakhti (rising sun); Aten; Nut (heaven), Seb (earth), Shu, Tefnut (space); abstract god, Min (all-father), Hathor (all-mother); Ptah (creator), Maat (truth), Imhotep (peace), Khrumu (Modeller), Thoth (writing), Bes (dancing); Serapis.

Semitic gods, El, Baal, Bel, Belus; Ashur; Melkarth, Marduk, Merodach; Adad, Dagon, Rimmon, Moloch, Patekh; Shamash, Astarte; Al-lat, Al-Uzza, Manat.

Nordic gods, Áss, Aesir, Vanir; Odin, Wotan, Woden; brothers of Odin, Frigg, Frija, Frea; sons of Odin, Heimdall, 'white God', Vidarr, 'silent god'; Balder, son of B., Forseti, Foseti; wife of Balder, Nanna; Thunor, Donar, Thor, wife of T., Sif, son of S., Ullr; Tyr, Tyw, Tin, Zio; Loki, Lothur, Hödr, Hotherus, 'blind god'; Hoenir, Bragi, wife of B., Idunn; Nerthus, Njörd, wife of N., Skadi; son of Njörd, Frey; daughter of Njörd, Freys; Mimri, Aegir; Asynjur, Nordic goddesses; Frigg, Freya, Gefrun, Idunn, Gerd, Eri, Sigyn, Fulla, Saga, Sjofn, Lofn, Var, Vor, Syn, Snotra, Gna, Sol, Bil, Hlin, Jörd, Rind.

Celtic gods, Dadga, Oengus, Ogma, Lug, Belenos, Grannos, Esos, Tentates, Totatis, Taranis, Maponus, Borvo, Bormo, Mogounos; Nodons, Nuada, Nudd; Ler, Lhyr, Manannan, Manawyddan; Taliesin; Celtic goddess, Morrigan, Andrasta, Sul, Brigit, Belisuma, Epona, Cerridwen, Danu.

Mexican gods, Nahuan g., Aztec g.; Cipactli, earth-dragon; Tezcatlipoca, Red T., Black T.; Uitzilopochtli; creative god, Tonacatecutli; creative goddess, Tonicaciuatl; Xipi Totec, Itzpapalotl, Ilamatecutli; gods of growth, maize-god, Tlazolteotl, Cinteotl, Chicomecoatl, Ciuacoatl, Xochiquetzal, Xochipilli;

drink-god, octli-g., Mayauel, Totochtin;
rain-god, water-g., Tlaloc, Chalchihuit-
licue, Quetzalcoatl; gods of fire, Xiuhte-
cutli, Chantico, Quaxolotl; sun-god,
Tonatiuh, Piltzintecutli; moon-god, Met-
ztli, Tecciztecutli; sky-god, Mixcoatl,
Camaxtli; planet-god, Tlauizcalpante-
cutli; demons of the air, Tzitzimime;
god of medicine, Patecatl; god of death,
Mictlantecutli, Mictecaciuatl, Tepeyol-
lotl.
See: 352, 970.

968 Angel

N. *angel*, archangel, little angel, angelet;
heavenly host, angelic h., choir invisible;
heavenly hierarchy, thrones, principalities and powers; seraph, seraphim, cherub,
cherubim; ministering spirit, Michael,
Gabriel, Raphael, Uriel, Abdiel, Zadkiel;
angel of death, Azrael; saint, patron s.,
glorified soul; angelhood, archangelship;
angelophany; angelolatry; angelology.
Madonna, Our Lady, Blessed Virgin Mary,
Mother of God, Theotokos; Queen of
Heaven, Queen of Angels, Stella Maris;
Mariolatry.
Adj. *angelic*, angelical, archangelical, seraphic, cherubic, cherubical, cherubinic;
saintly, glorified, celestial.
Vb. *angelize*, angelify, angelogize.

969 Devil

N. *Satan*, Lucifer, Son of the Morning,
archangel ruined; arch-fiend, Prince of
Darkness, Prince of this world; serpent,
Old S., Tempter, Adversary, Antichrist,
Common Enemy, Enemy of mankind;
Diabolus, Father of Lies; the Devil,
Shaitan, Eblis; Apollyon, Abaddon,
angel of the bottomless pit; the Evil
One, Wicked O.; spirit of evil, principle
of e., Ahriman.
Mephisto, Mephistopheles, His Satanic
Majesty, the Old Gentleman, Old Nick,
Old Harry, Old Scratch, Old Gooseberry,
Old Horny, Old Clootie, cloven hoof.
devil, fiend; deviling, devilet, familiar,
imp, imp of Satan, devil's spawn 938 n.

bad man; demon, Asmodeus, Azazel 970
n. *demon*; unclean spirit, dibbuk; powers
of darkness, diabolic hierarchy; damned
spirit, fallen angel, dweller in Pandemonium, denizen of Hell; Mammon, Belial,
Beelzebub; devildom, devilship, devil-
hood, demonship, demonry; cloven hoof.
diabolism, devilry, diablerie 898 n. *inhumanity*; Satanism, devilism, devility; devil-
worship, demonism, demonolatry, de-
monomy; demonomanie, demonomania,
demonopathy, demoniac possession; de-
monomagy, demonomancy, black magic,
Black Mass 983 n. *sorcery*; demonology;
demonization.
diabolist, Satanist, devil-worshipper, demonolater, demonomist; demonologist,
demonologer.
Adj. *diabolic*, diabolical, devil-like, satanic,
fiendish, demoniacal, devilish 898 adj.
malevolent; abysmal, infernal, hellish,
hell-born; devil-worshipping, demono-
latrous; demonomanic, possessed;
dæmonic, demonological.
Vb. *diabolize*, demonize; possess, bedevil
983 vb. *bewitch*; demonologize.
See: 898, 938, 970, 983.

970 Fairy

N. *fairy*, fairy world, magic w., fairyland,
færie; fairy folk, good f., little people;
fairy being, fay, peri; good fairy, fairy
godmother, Santa Claus, Father Christmas 903 n. *benefactor*; bad fairy, witch,
weird sister 983 n. *sorceress*; fairy queen,
Mab, Queen M., Titania; fairy king,
Oberon, Erl King; Puck, Robin Goodfellow; spirit of air, Ariel; elemental
spirit, sylph, sylphide; genius; fairy-ring,
pixie r.; fairyism, fairy-lore, fairy tales,
folk-lore.
elf, elves, elfin folk, alfar, hidden folk,
Huldu, Light Elves, Dark E.; pixie,
brownie; dwarf, dvergar; troll, trow;
gnome, goblin, hobgoblin, kobold, flibbertigibbet; imp, sprite, urchin, hob, oaf,
changeling; leprechaun, clurichaun; pigwidgeon; poltergeist, gremlin; Puck,
Robin Goodfellow; elvishness, goblinry.
ghost, spirit, departed s.; shades, souls of
the dead, Manes, Lemures; revived
corpse, zombie, duffy; revenant, haunter,

walker, poltergeist; spook, spectre, apparition, phantom, phantasm, shape, shade, wraith, presence, doppelganger, fetch 440 n. *visual fallacy*; control 984 n. *spiritualism*.

*d*emon, cacodemon, flibbertigibbet, Friar Rush; imp, familiar, familiar spirit 969 n. *devil*; Afrit, Jinn, genie; deev, asura; bhut, rakshasa; she-demon, lamia, rakshasi; kelpie, banshee; troll, trollwoman, ividjur, wood-women; ogre, ogress, giant, giantess, Rime-giant, Hillg., Sea-g.; bugbear, bugaboo, bogy, bogyman, raw-head, bloody-bones, Frankenstein's monster 938 n. *monster*; ghoul, vampire, lycanthrope, werewolf, werefolk; incubus, succubus, succuba, nightmare; fury, harpy; Gorgon; ogreism, ogreishness, demonry.

mythical being 968 n. *angel*, 969 n. *devil*; asura, deev; Pitri, Siddha, Yaksha, Gandharva, Vidyadhara, Kinnara, Asvamukha; Yakshini 967 n. *nymph*; Apsaras, houri, Valkyrie, battle-maid, wish-m.; sea-nymph, river-n., water-n., Oceanid, Naiad, nix, nixie; merfolk, merman, mermaid, merewife, Lady of the Lake, Lorelei, Siren; water-spirit, Undine; water-kelpie, water-elf; Old Man of the Sea; Yeti, Abominable Snowman, Phœnix 84 n. *rara avis*.

Adj. *fairy-like*, fairy, nymphean; sylph-like 206 adj. *lean*; dwarf-like 196 adj. *dwarfish*; gigantic 195 adj. *huge*; ogreish, devilish, demonic 969 adj. *diabolic*; vampirish, lycanthropic; gorgonian, Scyllan; elf-like, elfin, elvish, impish, Puckish 898 adj. *maleficent*; magic 983 adj. *magical*; mythical, mythic, folklorish 513 adj. *imaginary*.

*s*pooky, spookish, ghostly, ghostish; haunted, ghosted, gnomed, hagridden; nightmarish, macabre 854 adj. *frightening*; weird, uncanny, unearthly, eldritch 84 adj. *abnormal*; eerie, numinous, supernatural, supernormal; spectral, apparitional, wraith-like, mopping and mowing; disembodied, discarnate 320 adj. *immaterial*; ectoplasmic, astral, spiritualistic, mediumistic 984 adj. *psychical*.

Vb. goblinize, haunt, visit, walk; gibber, mop and mow.

Adv. *spookishly*, spectrally, uncannily, nightmarishly; elfishly, puckishly.

See: 84, 195, 196, 206, 320, 440, 513, 854, 898, 903, 938, 967, 968, 969, 983, 984.

971 Heaven

N. *heaven*, presence of God, abode of G., throne of G., kingdom of G., kingdom of heaven, heavenly kingdom, kingdom come; Paradise, abode of the blest, abode of the saints, inheritance of the saints in light; Abraham's bosom, eternal home, happy h.; eternal rest, celestial bliss, blessed state; nirvana, seventh heaven; the Millennium, earthly Paradise, Zion, Land of Beulah, New Jerusalem, Holy City, Celestial C.; afterlife, eternal life, eternity 124 n. *future state*; resurrection; assumption, translation, glorification; deification, apotheosis.

mythic heaven, Olympus; Odin's hall, Idavoll, Valaskjolf, Gladsheim, Valhalla, abode of warriors; Asgard, Troy, Gimle, abode of the righteous; Thor's place, Thrutheim, Bilskirnir; Heimdall's hall, Himinbjorg; Balder's abode, Breithablik; Forseti's abode, Glitnir; Frey's place, Alfheim; house for goddesses, Vingolf; Indraloka, devaloka, pitriloka; Elysium, Elysian fields, happy hunting grounds; Yima's vara, Earthly Paradise, Eden, Garden of E., garden of the Hesperides, Islands of the Blest, Isle of Avalon 513 n. *fantasy*.

Adj. *paradisiac*, paradisiacal, paradisal; heavenly, celestial, supernal, eternal; beatific, blessed, blissful 824 adj. *happy*; resurrectional, glorified; Elysian, Olympian; millennial.

See: 124, 513, 824.

972 Hell

N. *hell*, place of the dead, lower world, nether w., nether regions, underworld; grave, limbo, Sheol, Hades; place of the damned, inferno, Satan's palace, Pandemonium; abyss, bottomless pit, Abaddon; place of torment, Tophet, Gehenna, Jahannum, lake of fire and brimstone; hellfire, everlasting fire, unquenchable f., worm that never dies.

mythic hell, Hel, Niflheim; Narak; Aralu, land of no return; realm of Pluto, Hades, Tartarus, Avernus, Erebus; river of hell, Acheron, Styx, Cocytus, Phlegethon, Lethe; Stygian Ferryman, Charon; infernal watchdog, Cerberus; infernal judge, Minos, Rhadamanthus; nether

gods, Chthonians, Pluto, Yama, Yima, Osiris 967n. *Chthonian god.*
Adj. *infernal,* bottomless 211adj. *deep;* chthonian, subterranean 210adj. *low;* hellish, Plutonian, Avernal, Avernian, Tartarean, Tartareous; Acherontic, Stygian, Lethean; Cerberean, Cerberic; Rhadamanthine; damned, devilish 969 adj. *diabolic.*

See: 210, 211, 967, 969.

973 Religion

N. *religion,* religious instinct, religious bias, religious feeling 979n. *piety;* search for truth, religious quest; natural religion, deism; primitive religion, early faith; paganism 982n. *idolatry;* nature religion, orgiastic r., mystery r., mysteries, Eleusinian m., Orphism, Eleusinianism; dharma, revealed religion, historical r., incarnational r., sacramental r.; religion of the spirit, mysticism, sufism; yoga, dharmayoga, jnanayoga, karmayoga, bhaktiyoga; Eightfold Path; theosophy; theolatry 981n. *worship;* religious cult, state religion, official r. 981n. *cult;* untheological religion, creedless r., personal r.; no religion, atheism 974n. *irreligion.*
deism, belief in a god, theism; animism, pantheism, polytheism, henotheism, monotheism, dualism; gnosticism.
religious faith, faith 485n. *belief;* Christianism, Christianity, Cross; Judaism; Islam, Crescent; Zoroastrianism, Mazdaism, Zarathustrianism; Vedic religion, Dharma, Arya D.; Brahmanism, Hinduism, Vedantism; Vaishnavism 978n. *sectarianism;* Jainism; Buddhism, Dhamma, Hinayana, Lesser Vehicle, Mahayana, Greater Vehicle; Brahmoism; Sikhism; Shintoism; Taoism, Confucianism; Theosophy.
theology, science of religion, Queen of the sciences; natural theology, revealed t.; religious knowledge, religious learning, divinity; scholastic theology, scholasticism, Thomism; Rabbinism; isagogics, theological exegesis; typology; demythologization; soteriology, theodicy; hagiology, hagiography, iconology; dogmatics, dogmatic theology; symbolics, credal theology; tradition, deposit of faith; teaching, doctrine, religious d., received

d., defined d.; definition, canon; doxy, dogma, tenet; articles of faith, credenda, credo 485n. *creed;* confession, Thirty-nine Articles; Islamic exposition, fatwa; fundamentalism 976n. *orthodoxism;* Bibliology, higher criticism.
theologian, theologer, theologaster, theologue; divinity student, divine; doctor, doctor of the Church; doctor of the Law, rabbi, scribe, mufti; schoolman, scholastic, scholastic theologian, Thomist, Talmudist, canonist; theogonist, hagiologist, hagiographer, iconologist; psalmist, hymnwriter; textualist, Masorete; Bible critic, higher c.; scripturalist, fundamentalist.
religious teacher, prophet, rishi, inspired writer; evangelist, apostle, missionary; reformer, religious r.; founder of religion, Messiah, founder of Christianity, Christ; Muhammad, Prophet of God; Zoroaster; Buddha, Gautama B.; Confucius; founder of Mormonism, Joseph Smith; founder of Christian Science, Mary Baker Eddy; expounder, hierophant, gospeller. catechist 520n. *interpreter.*
religionist, deist, theist; monotheist, henotheist, polytheist, pantheist; animist, fetishist 982n. *idolator;* star-worshipper, Sabaist; pagan, gentile 974n. *heathen;* people of the book; believer, true b., orthodoxist 976n. *the orthodox;* Christian, Nazarene; Jew; Muslim, Islamite, Musulman, Mohamedan; Parsee, Zoroastrian, guebre; Hindu, gymnosophist, Brahmanist; Jain; Buddhist, Zen B.; Taoist; Confucianist; Shintoist; Mormon 978n. *sect;* theosophist 984n. *occultist;* gnostic 977n. *heretic.*
Adj. *religious,* divine, holy, sacred, spiritual, sacramental; deistic, theistic, animistic, pantheistic, henotheistic, monotheistic, dualistic; Christian, Islamic, Judaistic, Mosaic; Zoroastrian, Avestan; Confucian, Taoistic; Buddhistic, Hinduistic, Vedic, Brahminical, Upanashadic, Vedantic; yogic, mystic; devotional, devout, practising 981 adj. *worshipping.*
theological, theosophical, scholastic, rabbinic, rabbinical; doctrinal, dogmatic, credal, canonical; Christological, soteriological; doxological 988 adj. *ritualistic;* hagiological, iconological.
See: 485, 520, 974, 976, 977, 978, 979, 981, 982, 984, 988.

974 Irreligion

N. *irreligion*, indevotion, unspirituality, leanness of soul; nothing sacred, profaneness, ungodliness, godlessness 980 n. *impiety*; false religion, heathenism 982 n. *idolatry*; no religion, atheism, nullifidianism, dissent from all creeds, disbelief 486 n. *unbelief*; agnosticism, scepticism, Pyrrhonism 486 n. *doubt*; probabilism, euhemerism 449 n. *philosophy*; lack of faith, want of f., infidelity; lapse, lapse from faith, recidivism, backsliding 603 n. *tergiversation*; paganization, de-Christianization, post-Christian state; amoralism, apathy, indifferentism 860 n. *Indifference*.

antichristianity, antichristianism 704 n. *opposition*; paganism, heathenism, heathendom, gentilism; Satanism 969 n. *diabolism*; free thinking, free thought, rationalism, positivism 449 n. *philosophy*; hylotheism, materialism, dialectical m., Marxism, nihilism; secularism, worldliness, fleshliness 944 n. *sensualism*; Mammonism 816 n. *avarice*.

irreligionist, Antichrist; nullifidian, dissenter, dissenter from all creeds, no believer, atheist 486 n. *unbeliever*; rationalist, euhemerist, free thinker; agnostic, sceptic, Pyrrhonist; Marxist, nihilist, materialist, positivist; secularist, worldling, amoralist, indifferentist.

heathen, non-Christian, pagan, paynim; misbeliever, infidel, kafir, giaour, outcast; gentile, the uncircumcised, the unbaptized, the unconverted; backslider, lapsed Christian 603 n. *tergiversator*.

Adj. *irreligious*, having no religion, without r., without a god, godless, altarless, profane 980 adj. *impious*; nihilistic, atheistic, atheistical; creedless, nullifidian, agnostic, sceptical, Pyrrhonian, Pyrrhonic 486 adj. *unbelieving*; free-thinking, rationalizing, rationalistic, euhemeristic; non-religious, non-worshipping, non-practising, non-theological, non-credal 769 adj. *non-observant*; undevout, devoutless, unspiritual, ungodly 934 adj. *wicked*; amoral, morally neutral 860 adj. *indifferent*; secular, mundane, of this world, worldly, Mammonistic 944 adj. *sensual*; materialistic, Marxist; lacking faith, faithless; backsliding, recidivous, lapsed, paganized, post-Christian 603 adj. *tergiversating*; anti-religious, anti-Christian, anti-Church, anti-clerical.

heathenish, unholy, unhallowed, unsanctified, unblest, unconsecrated 980 adj. *profane*; unchristian, unbaptized, unconfirmed; gentile, gentilic, uncircumcised; heathen, pagan, infidel; pre-Christian, unconverted, in darkness 491 adj. *uninstructed*.

Vb. *be irreligious*, — atheistic etc. adj.; have no religion, lack faith; remain unconverted 486 vb. *disbelieve*; shut one's eyes to the light, love darkness, serve Mammon; lose one's faith, give up the Church 603 vb. *apostatize*; have no use for religion, scoff at r.; euhemerize, rationalize; persecute the faith, deny God, blaspheme 980 vb. *be impious*.

paganize, heathenize, de-Christianize, corrupt one's religion; de-sanctify, deconsecrate, undedicate, secularize.

See: 449, 486, 491, 603, 704, 769, 816, 860, 934, 944, 969, 980, 982.

975 Revelation

N. *revelation*, divine r., apocalypse 526 n. *disclosure*; illumination 417 n. *light*; afflatus, divine a., sruti, inspiration, divine i., theopneustia; prophecy, prophetic inspiration; intuition, mystical i., mysticism; direct communication, the Law, Mosaic L., Ten Commandments; divine message, God's word, gospel, gospel message; God revealed, theophany, burning bush; epiphany, incarnation, Word made flesh; avatar, emanation, divine e.

scripture, word of God, inspired text, sacred t., sacred writings; Holy Scripture, Bible, Holy B., the Book; King James's Bible, Authorized Version, Revised V.; Vulgate, Douai Version, Greek version, Septuagint; canonical writings, canonical books, canon; Old Testament, Pentateuch, Hexateuch, Octateuch, Major Prophets, Minor P.; Torah, the Law and the Prophets, Hagiographa; New Testament, Gospels, Synoptic G., Epistles, Pastoral E., Pauline E., Johannine E., Petrine E.; Acts of the Apostles, Revelation, Apocalypse; non-canonical writings, Apocrypha, Agrapha, Logia, sayings, non-canonical gospel; patristic writings; psalter, psalm-book, breviary, missal; prayer-book, Book of Common Prayer 981 n. *prayers*; hymn-book, hymnal 981 n.

hymn; post-Biblical writings (Hebrew), Targum, Talmud, Mishna, Gemara; textual commentary, Masora; Higher Criticism; fundamentalism, scripturalism.

non-Biblical scripture, Koran, Alcoran, the Glorious Koran; Hadith, Sunna; Hindu scripture, Veda, the Four Vedas, Rigveda, Yajurveda, Samaveda, Atharvaveda; Brahmana, Upanishad, Purana; Bhagavad Gita; sruti, smriti, shastra, sutra; Buddhist scripture, Pitaka, Tripitaka, Digha-Nikaya, Majjhima-N., Dhammapada; Iranian and Zoroastrian scripture, Zend-Avesta, Gatha, Vendidad; Book of the Dead (Egyptian); Book of Mormon.

Adj. *revelational*, inspirational, theopneustic, mystic; inspired, prophetic, revealed; apocalyptic; prophetic, evangelical, evangelic; mystagogic.

scriptural, sacred, holy; hierographic, hieratic; revealed, inspired, prophetic; canonical 733 adj. *authoritative*; biblical, Mosaic, pre-exilic, exilic, post-e.; gospel, evangelistic, apostolic; sub-apostolic, patristic, homiletic; Talmudic, Mishnaic; Koranic, uncreated; Vedic, Upanishadic, Puranic; textuary, textual, Masoretic.

See: 417, 526, 733, 981.

976 Orthodoxy

N. *orthodoxy*, orthodoxness, correct opinion, right belief; sound theology, Trinitarianism; religious truth, gospel t., pure Gospel 494n. *truth*; scripturality, canonicity; the Faith, the true faith, the whole f., deposit of f., 'the faith once delivered unto the saints'; primitive faith, early Church, Apostolic age; ecumenicalism, catholicity, Catholicism, 'quod semper, quod ubique, quod ab omnibus'; formulated faith, credo 485n. *creed*; Apostles' Creed, Nicene C., Athanasian C.; Confession of Augsberg, Thirty-nine Articles, Tridentine decrees; textuary, catechism, Church Catechism.

orthodoxism, strictness, strict interpretation; scripturalism, bibliodulia, fundamentalism, literalism, precisianism; Karaism, Karaitism (Jewish); traditionalism, institutionalism, ecclesiasticism, church-ianity 985n. *churchdom*; sound churchmanship 83n. *conformity*; Christian practice 768n. *observance*; intolerance, heresy-

hunting, persecution; suppression of heresy, extermination of error, Counter-Reformation; religious censorship, Holy Office 956n. *tribunal*; Inquisition 459n. *interrogation*; Index, Expurgatory I., Index Expurgatorius, Index Librorum Prohibitorum 924n. *disapprobation*; guaranteed orthodoxy, imprimatur 923n. *approbation*.

the Church, Christian world, Christendom, undivided Church; Christian fellowship, communion of saints; Holy Church, Mother C.; Body of Christ, universal Church; Church Militant, Church on earth, visible Church; invisible Church, Church Triumphant; established Church, recognized C., denominational C.; Orthodox C., Eastern Orthodox Church, autocephalous c.; Armenian Church; Roman Church, Roman Catholic and Apostolic C.; Church of England, Episcopalian C.; Church of Scotland; Reformed Church, Protestant C., Lutheran C., Calvinist C.

Catholicism, Orthodoxy, Eastern O.; Roman Catholicism, Romanism, popery, papalism, papistry, ultramontanism, Scarlet Woman; Counter-Reformation; Old Catholicism; Anglicanism, Episcopalianism, prelacy; Anglo-Catholicism, High Church, High-Churchmanship, spikiness; Laudianism, Tractarianism, Oxford Movement.

Protestantism, the Reformation, Anglicanism, Lutheranism, Zwinglianism, Calvinism; Presbyterianism, Congregationalism, Baptism; Quakerism, Quakery, Society of Friends; Wesleyanism, Methodism, Wesleyan M., Primitive M.

Catholic, Orthodox, Eastern O.; Roman Catholic, Romanist, papist, papalist, ultramontanist; Old Catholic, Anglo-C., Anglican, Episcopalian, Laudian, High-Churchman, Tractarian.

Protestant, reformer, Anglican, Lutheran, Zwinglian, Calvinist, Huguenot; Presbyterian, Congregationalist, Baptist, Wesleyan, Methodist, Wesleyan M., Primitive M.; Quaker, Friend; Plymouth Brother.

church member, pillar of the church; Christian, the baptized, the confirmed; practising Christian, communicant 981n. *worshipper*; the saints, the faithful, the body of the f., church people, chapel p.;

congregation, co-religionist, fellow-worshipper, pew-fellow.

the orthodox, the believing, the faithful, the converted; believer, true b.; pillar of orthodoxy, conformer 83 n. *conformist*; traditionalist, scripturalist, literalist, fundamentalist; Karaite; rabbinist 973 n. *theologian*.

Adj. *orthodox*, orthodoxical, rightly believing, holding the faith, reciting the creed 485 adj. *believing*; right-minded, sound, balanced 480 adj. *judicial*; non-heretical, unschismatical 488 adj. *assenting*; undivided, seamless 52 adj. *whole*; unswerving, undeviating, loyal, devout 739 adj. *obedient*; practising, conforming, conventional 83 adj. *conformable*; precise, strict, pedantic; hyper-orthodox, over-religious, holier than thou; intolerant, witch-hunting, heresy-h., inquisitional 459 adj. *enquiring*; correct 494 adj. *accurate*; of faith, to be believed, doctrinal 485 adj. *credal*; authoritative, defined, canonical, biblical, scriptural, evangelical, gospel 494 adj. *genuine*; textual, literal, fundamentalist, fundamentalistic; Trinitarian; Athanasian; catholic, ecumenical, universal; accepted, held, widely h., believed, generally b. 485 adj. *credible*; traditional, customary 610 adj. *usual*.

popish, papistical, Roman, Romish, Romanizing, ultramontanist; Catholic, Roman Catholic.

Anglican, episcopalian, prelatical, Laudian; tractarian, Anglo-Catholic, High-Church, high, spiky.

Protestant, reformed; denominational 978 adj. *sectarian*; Lutheran, Zwinglian, Calvinist, Calvinistic; Presbyterian, Congregational, Methodist, Wesleyan, Quakerish; bishopless, non-episcopal.

Vb. *be orthodox*,—catholic etc. adj.; hold the faith, recite the creeds 485 vb. *believe*; support the church, go to c. 83 vb. *conform*; catholicize, Romanize; Protestantize; Anglicanize; Lutheranize; Calvinize; Presbyterianize.

Adv. *orthodoxly*, orthodoxically, catholicly.

See: 52, 83, 459, 480, 485, 488, 494, 610, 739, 768, 923, 924, 956, 973, 978, 981, 983, 985.

977 Heterodoxy

N. *heterodoxy*, other men's doxy; unorthodoxy, unauthorized belief, unauthorized doubts, personal judgment; erroneous opinion, wrong belief, misbelief, false creed, superstition 495 n. *error*; strange doctrine, queer tenets, new teaching, bad t.; perversion of the truth 535 n. *misteaching*; doubtful orthodoxy, heretical tendency, latitudinarianism, modernism, Higher Criticism; unscripturality, non-catholicity, partial truth; heresy, rank h.

heresy, fabrication of h., heresiarchy; heathen theology, gnosticism; monarchianism, modal m., patripassianism, Sabellianism, dynamic monarchianism, adoptionist m.; Arianism, Arian syllogism, Arian creed, 'blasphemy of Sirmium', Socinianism; Unitarianism; Apollinarianism, Nestorianism, Eutychianism; Monophysitism, Monothelitism; Pelagianism, semi-P.; Montanism, Donatism, Manichæism, Albigensianism, Antinomianism; Wycliffism, Lollardism, Lollardy; Erastianism, anti-papalism.

heretic, arch-h., heresiarch; Gnostic, Manichee; Monarchian, Unitarian; Arius, Arian; Nestorius, Nestorian; Eutyches, Eutychian; Apollinaris, Apollinarian; Monophysite, Monothelite; Montanus, millenarian, Montanist; Novatian; Donatist; Catherist, Catheran, Paulician, Albigensian, Antinomian; Wycliffist, Lollard, Hussite.

Adj. *heterodox*, differing, unconventional 15 n. *different*; dissentient 489 adj. *dissenting*; non-doctrinaire, non-conformist 84 adj. *unconformable*; uncatholic, anti-papal; less than orthodox, erroneous 495 adj. *mistaken*; unorthodox, unbiblical, unscriptural, unauthorized, unsanctioned, proscribed 757 adj. *prohibited*; heretical, anathematized, damnable 961 adj. *condemned*.

heretical, heretic; heathen, Gnostic, Manichean, monarchian, patripassian, unitarian, Socinian; Arian, Eutychian, Apollinarian, Nestorian, monophysite, monothelite; Pelagian; Antinomian, Albigensian; Wycliffite, Lollard, Hussite.

Vb. *hereticate*, declare heretical, anathematize 961 vb. *condemn*.

be heretical,—unorthodox etc. adj.; Arianize, Pelagianize, Socianize, Erastianize.

Adv. *heretically*, unorthodoxly.

See: 15, 84, 489, 495, 535, 757, 961.

978 Sectarianism

N. *sectarianism*, sectarism, sectism; particularism, exclusiveness, clannishness, sectionalism 481 n. *prejudice*; bigotry 481 n. *bias*; party-mindedness, party-spirit, factiousness 709 n. *quarrelsomeness*; independence, separatism, schismaticalness, schismatical tendency 738 n. *disobedience*; denominationalism, nonconformism, nonconformity, dissent, 'the dissidence of dissent' 489 n. *dissent*; Lutheranism, Calvinism, Presbyterianism, Puritanism 976 n. *Protestantism*; Puseyism, Tractarianism 976 n. *Catholicism*.

schism, division, divisions, differences 709 n. *quarrel*; dissociation, breakaway, secession, withdrawal 46 n. *separation*; non-recognition, mutual excommunication 883 n. *seclusion*; non-jury, recusancy 769 n. *non-observance*; religious schism, Donatism, Great Schism, Great Western S.

church party, Judaizers, Ebionites; ultramontanists, papalists; Gallicans; Erastians; High-Church party, Laudians, Episcopalians, Puseyites, Tractarians 976 n. *Catholic*; Low-Church party, Evangelicals, Puritans 976 n. *Protestant*; Broad Church party, Latitudinarians, Modernists.

sect, division, off-shoot, branch, group, faction 708 n. *party*; order, religious o., brotherhood, sisterhood 708 n. *community*; nonconformist sect, chapel, conventicle 976 n. *Protestantism*; Society of Friends, Friends, Quakers; Unitarians; Plymouth Brethren; Sabbatarians, Seventh-day Adventists; Fifth Monarchy Men; Church of Christ Scientist; Church of Jesus Christ of the Latter-day Saints, Mormons; Peculiar People, British Israelites; Jehovah's Witnesses; Salvation Army, Salvationists; Oxford Movement, Buchmanism.

non-Christian sect, Jewish s., Nazarites; Pharisees, Sadducees, Herodians; Rabbinists; Karaites; Essenes; Sephardim, Ashkenazim; pagano-christian sect, Gnostics, Mandæans, Euchites; Islamic sect, Sunnis, Shiites, Sufis, Wahhabis; Hindu sect, Vedantists, Vaishnavas, Saivites, Tantrikas; Brahmo Samaj, Brahmoists, Adi Samaj, Nava Vidhan; Arya Samaj 973 n. *religious faith*.

sectarist, sectist, sectarian, particularist; follower, party-man; sectary, Independant; Puritan, wowser; Presbyterian, Covenanter 976 n. *Protestant*; Quaker, Friend 977 n. *heretic*; Salvationist; Buchmanite, grouper; Sunnite, Shiite, Sufi, Wahhabi; Saivite, Vaishnavite, Vedantist; Arya Samajist; Brahmo, Brahmoist.

schismatic, separated brother; schismatics, separated brethren; separatist, separationist; seceder, secessionist; factioneer, factionist 709 n. *quarreller*; rebel, mutineer 738 n. *revolter*; recusant, non-juror; dissident, dissenter, nonconformist 489 n. *dissentient*; wrong believer 977 n. *heretic*; apostate 603 n. *tergiversator*.

Adj. *sectarian*, particularist; party-minded, partisan 481 adj. *biased*; clannish, exclusive 708 adj. *sectional*; Judaizing, Ebionite; Gallican; Erastian; sectarial, High-Church, Laudian, Episcopalian 976 adj. *Anglican*; Low-Church, Evangelical 976 adj. *Protestant*; Puritan, Independant, Presbyterian, Covenanting; Vaishnavite, Saivite, Tantriki, Brahmo, Brahmoistic; Sunni, Shiite, Sufee; Essene, Pharisaic, Pharisæan, Sadducean, Herodian; Sephardi, Ashkenazi.

schismatical, schismatic, secessionist, seceding, breakaway; divided, separated 46 adj. *separate*; excommunicated, excommunicable 977 n. *heretical*; dissentient, nonconformist 489 adj. *dissenting*; non-juring, recusant 769 adj. *non-observant*; rebellious, rebel, contumacious 738 adj. *disobedient*; apostate 603 adj. *tergiversating*.

Vb. *sectarianize*, follow a sect 708 vb. *join a party*; Lutheranize, Calvinize.

schismatize, commit schism, separate, divide, withdraw, secede, break away, hive off 603 vb. *apostatize*; be in a state of schism, be contumacious 738 vb. *disobey*.

See: 46, 481, 489, 603, 708, 709, 738, 769, 883, 973, 976, 977.

979 Piety

N. *piety*, piousness, goodness 933 n. *virtue*; reverence, veneration, honour, decent respect 920 n. *respect*; affection, kind feeling, friendly f. 897 n. *benevolence*; dutifulness, loyalty, conformity, attendance at worship 968 n. *observance*;

churchmanship, sound c. 976 n. *orthodoxy*; religiousness, religion, theism 973 n. *deism*; religious feeling, pious sentiment, theopathy; fear of God, godly fear 854 n. *fear*; submissiveness, humbleness 872 n. *humility*; pious belief, faith, trust, trust in God 485 n. *belief*; devotion, dedication, self-surrender 931 n. *disinterestedness*; devoutness, sincerity, earnestness, unction; inspiration, enthusiasm, fervour, exaltation 821 n. *excitation*; adoration, prostration 981 n. *worship*; prayerfulness, meditation, retreat 981 n. *worship*; contemplation, mysticism, communion with God, mystic communion 973 n. *religion*; act of piety, pious duty, charity 901 n. *philanthropy*; pious fiction, edifying story, moral 496 n. *maxim*; Christian behaviour, Christian life; pilgrimage, hajj.

sanctity, holiness, hallowedness, sacredness, sacrosanctity; goodness, cardinal virtues, theological v. 933 n. *virtue*; co-operation with grace, synergism; state of grace, odour of sanctity 950 n. *purity*; godliness, sanctimony, saintliness, holy character; spirituality, otherworldliness; spiritual life, life in God; sainthood, blessedness, blessed state; conversion, regeneration, rebirth, new birth 656 n. *revival*; edification, sanctification, justification, adoption 965 n. *divine function*; canonization, beatification, consecration, dedication 866 n. *dignification*.

pietism, show of piety, sanctimony; sanctimoniousness, unction, cant 542 n. *sham*; religionism, religiosity, religious mania; over-piety, over-orthodoxy 976 n. *orthodoxism*; scrupulosity, tender conscience; austerity 945 n. *asceticism*; formalism, precisianism, Puritanism 481 n. *narrow mind*; literalness, fundamentalism, Bible-worship, bibliolatry, bibliodulia 494 n. *accuracy*; sabbatarianism 978 n. *sectarianism*; churchianity, churchiness, sacerdotalism, ritualism, spikiness; calendar-worship 985 n. *ecclesiasticism*; preachiness, unctuousness; odium theologicum 888 n. *hatred*; bigotry, fanaticism 481 n. *prejudice*; persecution, witch-hunting, heresy-h. 735 n. *severity*; crusading spirit, missionary s., salvationism 901 n. *philanthropy*.

pietist, pious person, real saint 937 *good man*; the good, the righteous, the just; conformist 488 n. *assenter*; professing Christian, practising C., communicant 981 n. *worshipper*; confessor, martyr; beatified person, saint; man of prayer, contemplative, mystic, sufi; holy man, sadhu, sannyasi, bhikshu, fakir, dervish 945 n. *ascetic*; hermit, anchorite 883 n. *solitary*; monk, nun, religious 986 n. *clergy*; devotee, dedicated soul; convert, neophyte, catechumen, ordinand 538 n. *learner*, believer, true b., the faithful, the elect 976 n. *church member*; the chosen people, children of delight; pilgrim, palmer, hajji; votary.

religionist, euchite; enthusiast, wowser, fanatic, bigot, zealot, image-breaker, iconoclast 678 n. *busy person*; formalist, precisian, Puritan; Pharisee, scribe, scribes and Pharisees; fundamentalist, Bible-worshipper, bibliolater, bibliodule, Sabbatarian 978 n. *sectarist*; sermonizer, pulpiteer 537 n. *preacher*; salvationist, hot-gospeller; missionary 901 n. *philanthropist*; champion of the faith, crusader, militant Christian; militant Islamite, ghazi; persecutor 735 n. *tyrant*.

Adj. *pious*, good, kind 897 adj. *benevolent*; decent, reverent 920 adj. *respectful*; faithful, true, loyal, devoted 739 adj. *obedient*; conforming, traditional 768 adj. *observant*; believing, holding the faith 976 adj. *orthodox*; sincere, practising, professing, confessing 540 adj. *veracious*; pure, pure in heart, holy-minded, heavenly-m.; unworldly, otherworldly, spiritual; godly, religious, devout; praying, prayerful, psalm-singing 981 adj. *worshipping*; in retreat, meditative, contemplative, mystic; saintly, saintlike, sainted; Christian, Christ-like, full of grace.

pietistic, ardent, fervent, seraphic; enthusiastic, inspired; austere 945 adj. *ascetic*; hermit-like, anchoretic 883 adj. *unsociable*; pi, religiose, over-religious, overpious, over-devout, over-righteous, holier than thou; over-strict, precise, Puritan 678 adj. *meddling*; formalistic, Pharisaic, ritualistic 978 adj. *sectarian*; priest-ridden, churchy, spiky; psalm-singing, hymn-s.; preachy, sanctimonious, canting 850 adj. *affected*; goody-goody 933 adj. *virtuous*; crusading, missionary-minded.

sanctified, made holy, consecrated, dedicated, enshrined; reverend, holy, sacred, solemn, sacrosanct 866 adj. *worshipful*;

haloed, sainted, canonized, beatified; saved, redeemed, ransomed 746 adj. *liberated*; regenerate, renewed, reborn 656 adj. *restored*; adopted, justified.

Vb. *be pious,* — religious etc. adj.; be holy, wear a halo; mind heavenly things, think of God; fear God 854 n. *fear*; have one's religion 485 vb. *believe*; keep the faith, fight the good fight 162 vb. *be strong*; walk humbly with one's God, humble oneself 872 vb. *be humble*; go to church, attend divine worship; pray, say one's prayers 981 vb. *worship*; kneel, genuflect, bow 311 vb. *stoop*; cross oneself, make the sign of the cross 547 vb. *gesticulate*; make offering, sacrifice, devote 759 vb. *offer*; give alms and oblations, lend to God 781 vb. *give*; give to the poor 897 vb. *be benevolent*; glorify God 923 vb. *praise*; give God the glory 907 vb. *thank*; revere, show reverence 920 vb. *show respect*; hearken, listen 739 vb. *obey*; sermonize, preachify, preach at 534 vb. *teach*; let one's light shine, set a good example.

become pious, be converted, get religion; change one's religion, go over 603 vb. *tergiversate*; see the light, see the error of one's ways 603 vb. *recant*; mend one's ways, reform, repent 939 vb. *be penitent*; enter the church, become ordained, take holy orders, take vows, take the veil 986 vb. *take orders*; pilgrimize, go on a pilgrimage, do the hajj 267 vb. *travel*.

make pious, bring religion to, bring to God, convert 485 vb. *convince*; christianize, win for Christ, baptize, receive into the church 299 vb. *admit*; depaganize, spiritualize 648 vb. *purify*; edify, confirm, strengthen one's faith, confirm in the f. 162 vb. *strengthen*; inspire, fill with grace, uplift 654 vb. *make better*; redeem, regenerate 656 vb. *restore*.

sanctify, hallow, make holy, keep h. 866 vb. *honour*; spiritualize, consecrate, dedicate, enshrine 866 vb. *dignify*; make a saint of, saint, canonize, beatify, pronounce blessed, invest with a halo; sain, make the sign of the cross.

See: 162, 267, 299, 311, 481, 485, 488, 494, 496, 534, 537, 538, 540, 542, 547, 603, 648, 654, 656, 678, 735, 739, 746, 759, 768, 781, 821, 850, 854, 866, 872, 883, 888, 897, 901, 907, 920, 923, 931, 933, 937, 939, 945, 950, 965, 968, 973, 976, 978, 981, 985, 986.

980 Impiety

N. *impiety,* impiousness; irreverence, disregard 921 n. *disrespect*; non-worship, lack of piety, lack of reverence; undutifulness 918 n. *dutilessness*; godlessness 974 n. *irreligion*; scoffing, mockery, derision 851 n. *ridicule*; scorn, pride 922 n. *contempt*; sacrilegiousness, profanity; blasphemy, evil-speaking, cursing, swearing 899 n. *malediction*; sacrilege, desecration, violation, profanation, perversion, abuse 675 n. *misuse*; sin, pervertedness, immoralism 934 n. *wickedness*; hardening, stubbornness 940 n. *impenitence*; declension, regression 655 n. *deterioration*; backsliding, recidivism, apostasy, recreancy 603 n. *tergiversation*; profaneness, unholiness, worldliness, materialism 319 n. *materiality*; amoralism, indifferentism 464 n. *indiscrimination*; misdevotion 982 n. *idolatry*; paganism, heathenism; rejection, reprobation 924 n. *disapprobation*.

false piety, pious fraud 541 n. *falsehood*; solemn mockery, mummery, imposture 542 n. *sham*; sham piety, sanctimony, sanctimoniousness, Pharisaism 979 n. *pietism*; hypocrisy, religious h., lip-service, lip-reverence 541 n. *duplicity*; cant, snuffling, holy horror 850 n. *affectation*.

impious person, blasphemer, curser, swearer 899 n. *malediction*; mocker, scorner, contemner, despiser, defamer, calumniator 926 n. *detractor*; sacrilegist, desecrator, violator, profaner, law-breaker 904 n. *offender*; profane person, non-worshipper, gentile, pagan, infidel, unbeliever 974 n. *heathen*; misbeliever 982 n. *idolater*; disbeliever, atheist 974 n. *irreligionist*; indifferentist, amoralist; worldling, materialist, immoralist 944 n. *sensualist*; sinner, reprobate, the wicked, the unrighteous, sons of Belial, children of darkness 938 n. *bad man*; recidivist, backslider, apostate, adulterous generation 603 n. *tergiversator*; fallen angel, Tempter, Wicked One 969 n. *Satan*; hypocrite, religious h., Tartuffe 545 n. *imposter*; canter, snuffler, lip-worshipper 850 n. *affector*.

Adj. *impious,* anti-religious, anti-Christian, anti-church 704 adj. *opposing*; recusant, dissenting 977 adj. *heretical*; unbelieving, non-believing, atheistical, godless 974 adj.

irreligious; non-worshipping, undevout, non-practising 769 adj. *non-observant*; misbelieving 982 adj. *idolatrous*; scoffing, mocking, deriding 851 adj. *derisive*; blaspheming, blasphemous, cursing, swearing, evil-speaking 899 adj. *maledicent*; irreverent, without reverence 921 adj. *disrespectful*; sacrilegious, profaning, desecrating, violating, criminal 954 adj. *lawless*; unawed, brazen, bold 855 adj. *unfearing*; hard, unmoved, unfeeling 898 adj. *cruel*; sinning, sinful, hardened, perverted, reprobate, unregenerate 934 adj. *wicked*; backsliding, recidivous, apostate 603 adj. *tergiversating*; canting, snuffling, sanctimonious 850 adj. *affected*; Pharisaical 541 adj. *hypocritical*.

profane, unholy, unhallowed, unsanctified, unblest, sacrilegious; god-forsaken, accursed; undedicated, unconsecrated, deconsecrated; infidel, pagan, gentile; paganized, de-christianized 974 adj. *heathenish*.

Vb. *be impious*, — sacrilegious etc. adj.; rebel against God 871 vb. *be proud*; sin 934 vb. *be wicked*; swear, blaspheme, revile 899 vb. *curse*; have no reverence, show no respect 921 vb. *not respect*; profane, desecrate, violate 675 vb. *misuse*; commit sacrilege, lay profane hands on, sully 649 vb. *make unclean*; misbelieve, worship false gods; cant, snuffle 850 vb. *be affected*; play the hypocrite, play false 541 vb. *dissemble*; backslide 603 vb. *apostatize*; sin against the light, grow hardened, harden one's heart 655 vb. *deteriorate*.

See: 319, 464, 541, 542, 545, 603, 649, 655, 675, 704, 769, 850, 851, 855, 871, 898, 899, 904, 918, 921, 922, 924, 926, 934, 938, 940, 944, 954, 969, 974, 977, 979, 982.

981 Worship

N. *worship*, honour, reverence, homage 920 n. *respect*; holy fear 854 n. *fear*; veneration, adoration, prostration of the soul; humbling oneself, humbleness 872 n. *humility*; devotion, devotedness 979 n. *piety*; prayer, one's devotions, one's prayers; retreat, quiet time, meditation, contemplation, communion.

cult, mystique; type of worship, service 917 n. *duty*; service of God, supreme worship,

latria; inferior worship, dulia, hyperdulia; iconolatry, image-worship; false worship 982 n. *idolatry*.

act of worship, rites, mysteries 988 n. *rite*; laud, laudation, praises, doxology 923 n. *praise*; glorification, giving glory, extolment 866 n. *dignification*; hymning, hymn-singing, psalm-s., psalmody, chanting 412 n. *vocal music*; thanksgiving, blessing, benediction 907 n. *thanks*; offering, oblation, almsgiving, sacrifice, making s., sacrificing, offering (see *oblation*); praying, saying one's prayers, reciting the rosary; self-examination 939 n. *penitence*; self-denial, self-discipline 945 *asceticism*; keeping fast 946 n. *fasting*; hajj, pilgrimage 267 n. *wandering*.

prayers, orisons, devotions; private devotion, retreat, contemplation 449 n. *meditation*; prayer, orison, bidding prayer; petition, petitionary prayer 761 n. *request*; invocation, invocatory prayer 583 n. *allocution*; intercession, intercessory prayer 762 n. *deprecation*; suffrage, prayers for the dead, vigils; special prayer, intention; rogation, supplication, solemn s., litany, solemn l.; comminatory prayer, commination, denunciation 900 n. *threat*; imprecation, imprecatory prayer 899 n. *malediction*; excommunication, ban 883 n. *seclusion*; exorcism 300 n. *ejection*; benediction, benedicite, benison, grace, grace before meat 907 n. *thanks*; prayer for the day, collect; liturgical prayer, the Lord's Prayer, Paternoster, Our Father; Ave, Ave Maria, Hail Mary; Kyrie Eleison, Sursum Corda, Sanctus; Nunc Dimittis; dismissal, blessing; rosary, beads, beadroll; prayer-wheel; prayer-book, missal, breviary, book of hours; call to prayer, muezzin's cry 547 n. *call*.

hymn, song, religious lyric, psalm, metrical p.; processional hymn, recessional; chant, chaunt, descant 412 n. *vocal music*; anthem, cantata, motet; antiphon, response; canticle, Te Deum, Benedicite; song of praise, Magnificat; doxology, Gloria; greater doxology, Gloria in Excelsis; lesser doxology, Gloria Patri; paean, Hallelujah, Hosanna; Homeric hymn; Vedic hymn; hymn-singing, hymnody; psalm-singing, psalmody; hymn-book, hymnal, psalter; Vedic hymns, Rigveda, Samaveda; hymnology, hymnography.

oblation, tribute, Peter's pence, mass money, offertory, collection, alms and oblations 781 n. *offering*; pew-rent, pewage; libation, incense, censing 988 n. *rite*; dedication, consecration 866 n. *dignification*; votive offering, de voto o.; thank-offering 907 n. *gratitude*; sin-offering, victim, scapegoat 150 n. *substitute*; burnt-offering, holocaust; sacrifice, devotion; immolation, hecatomb 362 n. *slaughter*; human sacrifice 362 n. *homicide*; self-sacrifice, self-devotion 931 n. *disinterestedness*; self-immolation, suttee, sutteeism 362 n. *suicide*; expiation, propitiation 941 n. *atonement*; a humble and a contrite heart 939 n. *penitence*.

public worship, common prayer, intercommunion; agape, love-feast; service, divine service, mass, matins, evensong, benediction 988 n. *rite*; psalm-singing, psalmody, hymn-singing 412 n. *vocal music*; church, church-going, chapel-g., attendance at church 979 n. *piety*; meeting for prayer, gathering for worship 74 n. *assembly*; prayer-meeting, revivalist m.; open-air service, street evangelism, revivalism; temple worship, state religion 973 n. *religion*.

worshipper, fellow-w., co-religionist, pew-fellow 976 n. *church member*; adorer, venerator; euchite; votary, devotee, oblate 979 n. *pietist*; glorifier, hymner, praiser, idolizer, admirer, ardent a., humble a. 923 n. *commender*; homager, follower, server 742 n. *servant*; image-worshipper, iconolater 982 n. *idolater*; sacrificer, sacrificator, offerer 781 n. *giver*; invocator, invoker, caller 583 n. *allocution*; supplicator, supplicant, suppliant 763 n. *petitioner*; pray-er, man of prayer, bedesman, intercessor; contemplative, mystic, sufi, visionary; dervish, marabout, enthusiast, revivalist, prophet 973 n. *religious teacher*; celebrant, officiant 986 n. *clergy*; communicant, church-goer, chapel-g., temple-worshipper; worshipping church, congregation, the faithful 976 n. *church member*; psalm-singer, hymn-s., psalmodist 413 n. *vocalist*; psalmist, hymn-writer, hymnologist 988 n. *ritualist*; pilgrim, palmer, hajji 268 n. *traveller*.

Adj. *worshipping*,—adoring etc. vb.; worshipping falsely 982 adj. *idolatrous*; devout, devoted 979 adj. *pious*; reverent, reverential 920 adj. *respectful*; prayerful, fervent, instant in prayer 761 adj. *supplicatory*; meditating, praying, interceding; in act of worship, communicating; kneeling, on one's knees; at one's prayers, at one's devotions, in retreat; regular in worship, church-going, chapel-g., communicant 976 adj. *orthodox*; participating in worship, hymn-singing, psalm-s.; celebrating, officiating, ministering 988 adj. *ritualistic*; mystic, mystical.

devotional, appertaining to worship, latreutic 988 adj. *ritualistic*; worshipful, solemn, sacred, holy 979 adj. *sanctified*; revered, worshipped 920 adj. *respected*; sacramental, mystic, mystical; invocatory 583 adj. *vocative*; precatory, intercessory, petitionary 761 adj. *supplicatory*; imprecatory 899 adj. *maledictory*; sacrificatory, sacrificial; oblationary, votive, ex voto 759 adj. *offering*; doxological, giving glory, praising 923 adj. *approving*.

Vb. *worship*, honour, revere, venerate, adore 920 vb. *respect*; honour and obey 854 vb. *fear*; do worship to, pay homage to, homage, acknowledge 917 vb. *do one's duty*; pay divine honours to, make a god of one, deify, apotheosize 982 vb. *idolatrize*; bow, kneel, genuflect, humble oneself, prostrate o. 872 vb. *be humbled*; lift up the heart, bless, give thanks 907 vb. *thank*; extol, laud, magnify, glorify, give glory to, doxologize 923 vb. *praise*; hymn, anthem, celebrate 413 vb. *sing*; call on, invoke, name, address 583 vb. *speak to*; petition, beseech, supplicate, intercede, make intercession 761 vb. *entreat*; pray, say a prayer, say one's prayers, recite the rosary, tell one's beads; meditate, contemplate, commune with God 979 vb. *be pious*.

offer worship, celebrate, officiate, minister, administer the sacraments 988 vb. *perform ritual*; lead the congregation, lead in prayer; sacrifice, make s., offer up 781 vb. *give*; sacrifice to, propitiate, appease 719 vb. *pacify*; vow, make vows 764 vb. *promise*; dedicate, consecrate 979 vb. *sanctify*; take vows, enter holy orders 986 vb. *take orders*; pilgrimize, go on a pilgrimage 267 vb. *travel*; go to church, go to chapel, go to meeting, meet for prayer, engage in common prayer 979 vb. *be pious*; go to service, hear Mass, take the sacraments, communicate, take Holy

Communion, eat the Lord's Supper; fast, undertake a f. 946vb. *starve*; deny oneself, practise asceticism 945vb. *be ascetic*; go into retreat 449vb. *meditate*; sing hymns, sing psalms, hymnodize, psalmodize, anthem, chant 413vb. *sing*; doxologize 923vb. *praise*.

Int. Alleluia! Hallelujah! Hosanna! Glory be to God! Holy, Holy, Holy! Lift up your hearts, Sursum Corda! Lord, have mercy, Kyrie Eleison! Our Father; Lord, bless us! God save!

See: 74, 150, 267, 268, 300, 362, 412, 413, 449, 547, 583, 719, 742, 759, 761, 762, 763, 764, 781, 854, 866, 872, 883, 899, 900, 907, 917, 920, 923, 931, 939, 941, 945, 946, 973, 976, 979, 982, 986, 988.

982 Idolatry

N. *idolatry*, idolatrousness, false worship, superstition 981n. *worship*; heathenishness, heathenism, paganism 973n. *religion*; fetishism, anthropomorphism, zoomorphism; iconolatry, image-worship; idolism, idol-worship, idolodulia, idolomania; idolomancy, mumbo-jumbo, hocus-pocus 983n. *sorcery*; heliolatry, sun-worship; star-worship, Sabaism; pyrolatry, fire-worship; zoolatry, animal-worship; ophiolatry, snake-worship; demonolatry, devil-worship 969n. *diabolism*; mammonism, money-worship; bibliolatry, ecclesiolatry; idol-offering, idolothyte.

deification, god-making, apotheosis, apocolocyntosis; idolization 920n. *respect*; king-worship, emperor-w. 981n. *worship*.

idol, statue 554n. *sculpture*; image, graven i., molten i.; cult image, fetish, totem-pole; lingam, yoni; golden calf 966n. *god*; godling, thakur, joss; teraphim, lares et penates, totem, kobong, Mumbo-Jumbo.

idolater, idolatress; idol-worshipper, idolatrizer, idolist; anthropomorphite; fetishist, fetisheer, fetish-man, fetish-woman; totemist; iconolater, image-worshipper 981n. *worshipper*; heliolater, sun-worshipper; star-worshipper, sabaist; pyrolater, fire-worshipper, guebre; bibliolater, ecclesiolater 979n. *pietist*; mammonist, mammon-worshipper; de-

monolater, demonist, devil-worshipper 969n. *diabolist*; pagan, heathendom 974 n. *heathen*; idolizer, deifier 923n. *commender*; idol-maker, image-m., maker of graven images.

Adj. *idolatrous*, pagan, heathen 974n. *heathenish*; idolatric, serving images; fetishistic; anthropomorphic, theriomorphic, anthropomorphitic; fire-worshipping, sun w., star w., Sabaist; devil-worshipping 969adj. *diabolic*; offered to an idol, idolothyte.

Vb. *idolatrize*, worship idols, worship the golden calf, bow down to a graven image; anthropomorphize, make God in one's own image, deify, apotheosize 979vb. *sanctify*; idolize, put on a pedestal 923vb. *praise*; heathenize 974vb. *paganize*.

Adv. *idolatrously*, heathenishly.

See: 554, 920, 923, 966, 969, 973, 974, 979, 981, 983.

983 Sorcery

N. *sorcery*, spellbinding, witchery, magic arts, enchantments; witchcraft, sortilege; magianism, gramarye, magic lore 490n. *knowledge*; wizardry, magic skill 694n. *skill*; thaumaturgics, wonder-working, miracle-mongering 864n. *thaumaturgy*; magic, jadu, jugglery, illusionism 542n. *sleight*; sympathetic magic, influence 612 n. *inducement*; white magic, theurgy; black magic, goety, black art, necromancy, diablerie, demonry 969n. *diabolism*; priestcraft, superstition, witch-doctoring, shamanism, obeahism, obeah, voodooism, voodoo, hoodoo; psychomancy, spirit-raising 511n. *divination*; spirit-laying, ghost-l., exorcism, exsufflation 988n. *rite*; magic rite, conjuration, invocation, incantation; ghost dance; coven, witches' sabbath, witches' coven; Walpurgisnacht; witching hour.

spell, charm, glamour, enchantment, cantrip, hoodoo, curse; evil eye, jinx, influence; bewitchment, fascination 291n. *attraction*; obsession, possession, demoniacal p., bedevilment, nympholepsy; Dionysiac frenzy 503n. *frenzy*; incantation, rune; magic sign, pass; magic word, magic formula, open sesame, abracadabra; hocus pocus, mumbo jumbo, fee faw

fum 515n. *unmeaningness*; philtre, love-potion (see *magic instrument*).

talisman, telesm, charm, counter-c.; cross, phylactery, demonifuge 662n. *safeguard*; obeah, fetish 982n. *idol*; periapt, amulet, mascot, luck-bringer, lucky charm; swastika, fylot, gammadion, pentacle; scarab; birth-stone; emblem, flag, national f. 547 n. *flag*; relic, holy r.; palladium 662n. *refuge*.

magic instrument, bell, book and candle, wizard's cap, witches' broomstick; magic recipe, witch-broth, hell-b., witches' cauldron; philtre, potion, moly; magic wheel, rhomb; wand, fairy w.; magic ring, Solomon's seal, Aladdin's lamp, Alf's button; purse of Fortunatus; magic mirror, magic sword, flying carpet; seven-league boots; Excalibur; cloak of darkness, cloak of invisibility; wish-fulfiller, wishing well, kamadhuk, wish-bone, merry-thought; divining rod 484n. *detector*.

sorcerer, wise man, seer, soothsayer, Chaldean, sortileger 511n. *diviner*; astrologer, alchemist 984n. *occultist*; mage, magian, the Magi; thaumaturgist, wonder-worker, miracle-w. 864n. *thaumaturgy*; shaman, witch-doctor, medicine-man, figure-flinger, fetisheer, fetish-man 982n. *idolater*; obi-man, voodooist, hoodooist, spirit-raiser 984n. *occultist*; conjuror, exorcist; charmer, snake-c.; juggler, illusionist 545n. *conjuror*; spellbinder, enchanter, wizard, warlock; magician, theurgist; goetic, necromancer 969n. *diabolist*; familiar, imp, devil, evil spirit 969n. *devil*; sorcerer's apprentice; Merlin, Faust, Pied Piper, Comus.

sorceress, wise woman, Sibyl 511n. *diviner*; enchantress, witch, weird sister; hag, hell-cat; night-hag; succubus, succuba; lamia; vampire; fairy godmother, wicked fairy 970n. *fairy*; Witch of Endor, Hecate, Circe, Medea.

Adj. *sorcerous*, sortilegious; wizardly, witch-like; succubine; Circean; magicianly, magician, Chaldean; thaumaturgic 864adj. *wonderful*; theurgic, theurgical; goetic, necromantic 969adj. *diabolic*; shamanist, shamanistic, voodooistic; spell-like, incantatory, runic; conjuring, spirit-raising; witching, spellbinding, enchanting, fascinating 291adj. *attracting*; malignant, blighting, blasting withering, casting the evil eye, overlook-ing 898adj. *maleficent*; occult, esoteric 984adj. *cabbalistic*.

magical, witching; otherworldly, supernatural, uncanny, eldritch, weird 970adj. *fairy-like*; amuletic, talismanic, telesmatic, phylacteric 660adj. *tutelary*; having magic power, charmed, enchanted 178adj. *influential*.

bewitched, witched, ensorcelled, tranced, enchanted, charmed, becharmed, fey; hypnotized, fascinated, spellbound, under a spell, under a charm; overlooked, under the evil eye; under a curse, cursed; blighted, blasted, withered; hag-ridden, haunted, beghosted.

Vb. *practise sorcery*, — witchcraft etc.n.; cast horoscopes 511vb. *divine*; do magic, weave spells; speak mystically, cabbalize; recite a spell, recite an incantation, say the magic word, make passes; conjure, invoke, call up; raise spirits, command s., shamanize; exorcize, lay ghosts; wave a wand, rub the magic ring, spin the magic wheel; put on one's seven-league boots; ride a broomstick.

bewitch, witch, charm, becharm, enchant, fascinate, take 291vb. *attract*; hypnotize; ensorcell, spellbind, cast a spell on, lay under a spell; hoodoo, voodoo, obi, obeah; overlook, cast the evil eye, blight, blast 898vb. *be malevolent*; put a curse on, lay under a curse 899vb. *curse*; lay under a ban, taboo, make t. 757vb. *prohibit*; hag-ride, haunt, walk, ghost, beghost 970vb. *goblinize*.

Adv. *sorcerously*, by means of enchantment; as under a spell.

See: 178, 291, 484, 490, 503, 511, 515, 542, 545, 547, 612, 660, 662, 694, 757, 864, 898, 899, 969, 970, 982, 984, 988.

984 Occultism

N. *occultism*, esoterism, esotericism, mysticism, transcendentalism 973n. *religion*; mystical interpretation, cabbalism, cabbala, gematria; theosophy, reincarnationism; yogism, yogeeism; sciosophy, hyperphysics, metapsychics; supernaturalism, psychism, pseudo-psychology; secret art, esoteric science, odylism, alchemy, astrology, psychomancy, spiritualism, magic 983n. *sorcery*;

mantology, sortilege 511n. *divination*; fortune-telling, crystal-gazing, palmistry, chiromancy 511n. *prediction*; clairvoyance, second sight 438n. *vision*; sixth sense 476n. *intuition*; animal magnetism, mesmerism, hypnotism; hypnosis, hypnotic trance 375n. *insensibility*; odyl, od, biod, thermod.

psychics, parapsychology, psychism 447n. *psychology*; psychic science, psychical research; paranormal perception, extrasensory p.; telegnosis, telesthesia, cryptesthesia, clairaudience, clairvoyance, second sight 476n. *intuition*; telepathy, telergy; thought-reading, mind-r. thought transference; precognition, psi faculty.

theosophy, esoteric Buddhism, theosophic pantheism, reincarnationism 973n. *religion*; Essence, First Cause, the One; polarization of the One; devas, hierarchies; the Inner Government of the World, the Hierarchy, Great White Lodge; head of the Hierarchy, Lord of the World; Master, Elder Brother, guide.

spiritualism, spiritism; spirit communication, psychomancy 983n. *sorcery*; mediumism, mediumship; séance, sitting; astral body, spirit b., ethereal b. 320n. *immateriality*; spirit manifestation, materialization, ectoplasm, teleplasm 319n. *materiality*; apport, telekinesis; poltergeistery; spirit-rapping, table-tapping, table-turning; automatism, automatic writing, spirit w., psychography 586n. *writing*; spirit message, psychogram; spiritualistic apparatus, psychograph, planchette, ouija board, dark room; control; guide; psychical research.

occultist, mystic, transcendentalist, supernaturalist; esoteric, cabbalist; reincarnationist; theosophist, seer of the real; spiritualist, believer in spiritualism; Rosicrucian; alchemist 983n. *sorcerer*; astrologer, mantologist, sortileger, fortune-teller, crystal-gazer, palmist 511n. *diviner*; Rosenkrantz, Cagliostro, Katafeltro, Mesmer.

psychic, clairvoyant, clairaudient; telepath, telepathist; mind-reader, thought-r.; mesmerist, hypnotist; medium, spirit-rapper, automatist, psychographer, spirit-writer; seer, prophet 511 n. *oracle*; dowser, water-diviner 511n. *diviner*.

psychist, parapsychologist, metapsychologist, psychophysicist, psychical researcher.

Adj. *cabbalistic*, esoteric, cryptic, hidden 523 adj. *occult*; dark, mysterious 491adj. *unknown*; mystic, transcendental, supernatural 973adj. *religious*; theosophic, theosophical, reincarnational; Rosicrucian; odylic; astrological, alchemistic, necromantic 983adj. *sorcerous*; ghosty, poltergeistish 970adj. *spooky*.

psychical, psychic, fey, second-sighted; mantological, prophetic 511adj. *predicting*; telepathic, clairvoyant, clairaudient; thought-reading, mind-r.; spiritualistic, mediumistic; ectoplasmic, telekinetic, spirit-rapping; mesmeric, hypnotic.

paranormal, parapsychological, metapsychological, hyperpsychological, supernatural, hyperphysical.

Vb. *practise occultism*, mysterize, mysticise, esoterize; theosophize; cabbalize; odize, odylize; alchemize 147vb. *transform*; astrologize, mantologize 511 vb. *divine*; hypnotize, mesmerize; practise spiritualism, dabble in s.; hold a séance, attend séances; practise mediumship, have a control, go into a trance, rap tables, write spirit messages; materialize, dematerialize; study spiritualism, engage in psychical research.

See: 147, 319, 320, 375, 438, 447, 476, 491, 511, 523, 586, 970, 973, 983.

985 Churchdom

N. *churchdom*, the church, pale of the c., Christendom 976n. *the Church*; priestly government, hierocracy, theocracy; obedience, Roman o.; rule of the saints 733n. *authority*; the elect, priestly nation, kingdom of priests; church government 733n. *government*; ecclesiastical order, hierarchy 60n. *order*; paparchy, papality, papacy, popedom; popishness, ultramontanism; cardinalism; bishopdom, prelatehood, prelatry, prelacy; archiepiscopacy, episcopacy, lordly e., episcopalianism; presbytery, presbyterianism, congregationalism, independence 978n. *sectarianism*; ecclesiology, ecclesiologist.

ecclesiasticism, clericalism, sacerdotalism; priestliness, priesthood, brahminhood;

priestdom, priestcraft; brahminism; ecclesiastical privilege, benefit of clergy, clergiability 919n. *non-liability*; ecclesiastical censorship, inquisition, Holy Office, Index Expurgatorious 757n. *prohibition.*

monasticism, monastic life, monachism, monachy 895n. *celibacy*; cenobitism 883 n. *seclusion*; monkhood, monkishness, friarhood 945n. *asceticism.*

church ministry, ecclesiastical vocation, call, call to the ministry 622n. *vocation*; apostleship, apostolate, mission, mission to the heathen, conversion of the h. 147n. *conversion*; pastorate, pastorship, cure, cure of souls; spiritual comfort, spiritual leadership 901n. *philanthropy*; spiritual guidance, confession, absolution, shrift 988n. *ministration*; preaching office, predication, preaching, homiletics 534n. *teaching.*

holy orders, orders, minor o. 986n. *cleric*; apostolic succession, ordering, ordination, consecration; induction, reading in; installation, enthronement; nomination, presentation, appointment 751n. *commission*; preferment, translation, elevation 285n. *progression*; episcopal election, congé d'élire.

church office 689n. *management*; ecclesiastical rank 27n. *degree*; priesthood, priestliness; apostolate, apostleship; pontificate, papacy, popeship, Holy See, Vatican; cardinalate, cardinalship; patriarchate, patriarchship; exarchate, metropolitanate; primacy, primateship; archiepiscopate, archbishopric; see, bishopric, episcopate, episcopacy, prelacy; abbotcy, abbotship, abbacy, abbotric; priorate, priorship; archdeaconry, archdeaconate, archdeaconship; deanery, deanship; canonry, canonicate; prebendaryship; deaconship; diaconate, subdiaconate; presbyterate, presbytership, eldership, moderatorship, ministership, pastorship, pastorate; rectorship, vicarship, vicariate; curacy, cure, cure of souls; chaplainship, chaplaincy, chaplainry; incumbency, tenure, benefice 773n. *possession*; preferment, appointment, translation.

parish, deanery; presbytery; diocese, bishopric, see, archbishopric; metropolitanate, patriarchate, province 184n. *district.*

benefice, incumbency, tenure; living, ecclesiastical l., spiritual l., rectorship, parsonage; glebe, tithe; prebend, prebendal stall, canonry; temporalities, church lands, church endowments 777n. *property*; patronage, advowson, right of presentation.

synod, provincial s., convocation, general council, ecumenical c. 692n. *council*; conciliar movement; college of cardinals, consistory, conclave; bench of bishops, episcopal bench; chapter, vestry; kirk session, presbytery, synod, sanhedrim 956n. *tribunal*; consistorial court, Court of Arches 956n. *ecclesiastical court.*

Adj. ecclesiastical, ecclestiastic, churchly, ecclesiological, theocratic; obediential, infallible 733adj. *authoritative*; hierocratic, priest-ridden, ultramontane 976 adj. *orthodox*; apostolic; hierarchical, pontifical, papal 976adj. *popish*; patriarchal, metropolitan; archiepiscopal, episcopal, prelatic, prelatical 986adj. *clerical*; episcopalian, presbyterian 978adj. *sectarian*; prioral, abbatical, abbatial; conciliar, synodic, presbyteral, capitular; sanhedral, consistorial; provincial, diocesan, parochial.

priestly, sacerdotal, hieratic, Aaronic, Levitical; brahminic; sacramental, spiritual; ministering, apostolic, pastoral.

Vb. ecclesiasticize, be churchly, — priestly etc.adj.; episcopize, prelatize; frock, ordain, order, consecrate, enthrone; cowl, tonsure, make a monk of; call, confer, nominate, present; benefice, prefer, bestow a living 781vb. *give*; translate 272vb. *transfer*; elevate 285vb. *promote*; beatify, canonize, saint 979vb. *sanctify*; enter the church 986vb. *take orders*; sanctuarize 660vb. *safeguard.*

Adv. ecclesiastically, church-wise.

See: 27, 60, 147, 184, 272, 285, 534, 622, 660, 689, 962, 733, 751, 757, 773, 777, 781, 883, 895, 901, 919, 945, 956, 976, 978, 979, 986, 988.

986 Clergy

N. clergy, hierarchy; clerical order, parsondom, the cloth, the ministry; sacerdotal order, priesthood, secular clergy, regular clergy, religious.

cleric, clerical; clerk in holy orders, priest, deacon, subdeacon, acolyte, exorcist,

lector, ostiarius; churchman, ecclesiastic, divine; clergyman, black coat, reverend, reverend gentleman; father, father in God; padre, sky-pilot, Holy Joe; beneficed clergyman, beneficiary, pluralist, parson, rector, incumbent, residentiary, resident, residenter 776n. *possessor*; hedgepriest, priestling 639n. *nonentity*; ordinand, seminarist 538n. *learner*.

pastor, shepherd, father in God, minister, parish priest, rector, vicar, perpetual curate, curate, abbé; chaplain; confessor, father c., penitentiary, penitencer; spiritual director, spiritual adviser; pardoner; friar; preaching order, predicant; preacher, pulpiteer, lecturer, lay-preacher, woman p. 537n. *preacher*; field preacher, missioner, missionary 901n. *philanthropist*; evangelist, revivalist, salvationist, hot-gospeller.

ecclesiarch, ecclesiastical potentate, hierarch 741n. *potentate*; pope, Supreme Pontiff, Holy Father, Vicar of Christ; cardinal, prince of the church; patriarch, exarch, metropolitan, primate, archbishop; prelate, diocesan, bishop, bishop in partibus; suffragan, assistant bishop, 'episcopal curate'; bench of bishops, episcopate, Lords Spiritual; archpriest, archpresbyter; archdeacon, dean, subdean, rural dean; canon, canon regular, canon secular, residentiary; prebendary, capitular; archimandrite; superior, mother s.; abbot, abbess; prior, prioress, Grand Prior; elder, presbyter, moderator; bishopess, she-bishop, Pope Joan 545n. *impostor*.

monk, monastic, cloisterer 895n. *celibate*; hermit, cenobite, Desert Father 883n. *solitary*; vagabond monk, circumcellion; Greek monk, caloyer; Islamic monk, santon, marabout; sufi 979n. *pietist*; dervish, faqir 945n. *ascetic*; Buddhist monk, pongye, bonze; brother, regular, conventual; superior, archimandrite, abbot, prior; novice, lay brother; cowl, shaveling; friar, begging f., mendicant; discalced friar, discalceate; monks, religious; fraternity, brotherhood, lay b., friarhood, friary; order, religious o. 708n. *community*; Black Monk, Benedictine, Cistercian, Bernardine, Trappist; Carthusian; Cluniac; Gilbertine; Premonstratensian, Maturine; Dominicans,

Friars Preachers, Black Friars; Franciscans, Poverelli, Grey Friars, Friars Minors, Minorites, Friars Observant, Recollects, Friars Conventual, Capuchins; Augustines, Austin Friars; Carmelites, White Friars; Crutched Friars, Crossed F.; Bonhommes; teaching order, missionary o., Society of Jesus, Jesuits; crusading order, Templars, Knights Templars, Poor Soldiers of the Temple; Hospitallers, Knights Hospitallers, Knights of the Hospital of St. John of Jerusalem, Knights of Malta; Grand Prior; mendicant order, beghard.

nun, cloistress, clergywoman; sister, mother; novice, postulant; lay sister; superioress, mother superior, abbess, prioress, canoness, deaconess; sisterhood, lay s., beguinage, beguine.

church officer, elder, presbyter, moderator 741n. *officer*; priest, chantry p., chaplain, altarist; curate in charge, minister; lay preacher, lay reader, bible-reader, biblewoman; acolyte, server, altar-boy; crucifer, thurifer, boat-boy 988n. *ritualist*; chorister, choirboy, choirman, precentor, succentor, cantor 413n. *choir*; sidesman; churchwarden, vestryman, capitular; clerk, vestry c., parish c.; beadle, verger, pew-opener; sacristan, sexton; grave-digger, bell-ringer; sumner 955n. *law officer*.

priest, chief p., high p., archpriest; priestess, Vestal, Pythia, Pythoness, Pythonissa, prophetess, prophet 511n. *oracle*; Levite; rabbi; imam, mufti, mahdi; brahmin, purohit, pujari; talapoin, pongye, bonze; lama, Dalai L., Grand L., Teshu L.; pontiff, flamen, archflamen; Druid, Druidess; shaman, witch-doctor.

church title, Holy Father; Eminence; Monsignor, Monseigneur; Lordship, Lord Spiritual; Most Reverend, Right R., Very R.; the Reverend; parson, rector, vicar; father, brother, Dom; mother, sister.

monastery, monkery, bonzery, lamasery; friary; priory, abbey; convent, nunnery, beguinage; ashram, hermitage 192n. *retreat*; community house 192n. *abode*; theological college, seminary 539n. *training school*; cell 194n. *chamber*.

parsonage, parson's house, presbytery, rectory, vicarage; glebe-house, pastorage, manse; deanery, archdeaconry 192

n. *abode*; palace, bishop's p., patriarchate; Lambeth, Vatican; church-house, church-hall; close, cathedral c., papal precincts 235 n. *inclosure*.

Adj. *clerical*, in orders, in holy o.; with benefit of clergy, clergiable; regular; secular; ordained, consecrated; gaitered, aproned, mitred 989 adj. *vestured*; prebendal, beneficed, pluralistic; unbeneficed, glebeless, lay; parsonical, rectorial, vicarial; pastoral, ministerial, presbyteral, sacerdotal 985 adj. *priestly*; diaconal, subdiaconal, archidiaconal, prelatical, episcopal 985 adj. *ecclesiastical*.

monastic, monasterial, cloistral, cloisterly; cloistered, conventual, enclosed 232 adj. *circumscribed*; monkish, monachic, celibate 895 adj. *unwedded*; cowled, capuched 989 adj. *vestured*; tonsured, shaven and shorn; bonze-like.

Vb. *take orders*, be ordained, enter the church, enter the ministry, wear the cloth; take vows, take the tonsure, take the cowl; take the veil, become a nun.

Adv. *clerically*, parsonically.

See: 192, 194, 232, 235, 413, 511, 537, 538, 539, 545, 639, 708, 741, 776, 883, 895, 901, 945, 955, 979, 985, 988, 989.

987 Laity

N. *laity*, temporalty, lay people, people, civilians 869 n. *commonalty*; cure, charge, parish; flock, sheep, fold; diocesans, parishioners; brethren, congregation, society 976 n. *church member*; lay brethren, lay sisterhood, lay community 708 n. *community*; the profane, the worldly.

laicality, temporality, secularity; laicization, secularization, deconsecration.

layman, lay woman, laic; lay rector, lay deacon; lay brother, lay sister; catechumen, ordinand, seminarist, novice, postulant 538 n. *learner*; lay preacher, lay reader; parishioner, diocesan, member of the flock 976 n. *church member*; non-professional, amateur 695 n. *unskilfulness*; civilian 869 n. *commoner*; profane person; laicizer, secularizer.

Adj. *laical*, parishional, congregational; laic, lay, non-clerical, non-priestly, unordained, not in orders, non-clergiable; non-ecclesiastical, unclerical, unpriestly, secular; temporal, in the world, of the w.,

non-religious 974 adj. *irreligious*; profane, unholy, unconsecrated; laicized, secularized, deconsecrated; non-professional, amateur, do-it-yourself; amateurish 695 adj. *unskilled*; civilian, popular 869 adj. *plebeian*.

Vb. *laicize*, secularize, undedicate, deconsecrate, dishallow.

Adv. *laically*, as a layman.

See: 538, 695, 708, 869, 974, 976.

988 Ritual

N. *ritual*, procedure, way of doing things, method 624 n. *way*; prescribed procedure, due order, routine, drill, system 60 n. *order*; form, order, liturgy 610 n. *practice*; symbolization, symbolism 519 n. *metaphor*; rituality, ceremonial, ceremony 875 n. *formality*.

ritualism, ceremonialism, ceremony, formalism, spikiness; liturgics.

rite, mode of worship 981 n. *cult*; institution, observance, ritual practice 610 n. *practice*; form, order, ordinance, rubric, formula, formulary 693 n. *precept*; ceremony, solemnity, sacrament, mystery 876 n. *celebration*; rites, mysteries 551 n. *representation*; initiatory rite, circumcision, initiation, baptism 299 n. *reception*; christening (see *Christian rite*).

ministration, functioning, officiation, performance 676 n. *action*; administration, celebration, solemnization; pulpitry, predication, preaching 534 n. *teaching*; preachment, homily 534 n. *lecture*; sacred rhetoric, homiletics 579 n. *oratory*; pastorship, pastoral epistle, pastoral letter; confession, auricular c.; shrift, absolution, penance.

Christian rite, rites of the Church; sacrament, the seven sacraments; baptism, infant b., christening 299 n. *reception*; immersion, total i. 303 n. *immersion*; affusion 341 n. *moistening*; confirmation, bishoping; Holy Communion, Eucharist, reservation of the sacraments; pænitentia prima, pænitentia secunda, exomologesis 941 n. *penance*; absolution 960 n. *acquittal*; Holy Matrimony 894 n. *marriage*; Holy Orders 985 n. *churchdom*; Holy Unction, chrismation, chrism; visitation of the sick, extreme unction, last rites, viaticum; burial of the

dead; requiem mass; liturgy, order of service, order of baptism, marriage service, solemnization of matrimony, nuptial mass; churching of women; ordination, ordering of deacons, ordering of priests; consecration, consecration of bishops; exorcism 300n. *ejection*; excommunication, ban, bell, book and candle 883n. *seclusion*; canonization, beatification 866n. *dignification*, dedication, undedication.

Holy Communion, Eucharist, Eucharistic sacrifice; mass, high m., solemn m., great m., sung m., missa cantata; low mass, little m., dry m., missa sicca; public mass, private m.; communion, the Lord's Supper; celebration, service, order of s., liturgy; preparation, confession, asperges; service of the book, introit, the Kyries, the Gloria, the Lesson, the Gradual, the Collects, the Gospel, the creed; service of the Altar, the offertory, offertory sentence, offertory prayers, the biddings; the blessing, the thanksgiving, Sursum Corda, Preface, Sanctus, Great Amen; the breaking of the bread, the commixture; the Pax; consecration; elevation of the Host; Agnus Dei; the Communion; kiss of peace; prayers of thanksgiving, the dismissal; the blessing.

the sacrament, the Holy Sacrament; Corpus Christi, body and blood of Christ; real presence, transubstantiation, consubstantiation, impanation; the elements, bread and wine, wafer, altar bread; consecrated bread, host; reserved sacrament; viaticum.

church service, office, duty, service; liturgy, celebration, concelebration; canonical hours, mattins, lauds, prime, terce, sext, none, vespers, compline; the little hours; morning prayer, matins; evening prayer, evensong, benediction; tenebræ; vigil, midnight mass, watchnight service; devotional service, three-hour s.; novena.

ritual act, symbolical act, sacramental, symbolism 551n. *representation*; lustration, purification 648n. *cleansing*; thurification 338n. *vaporization*; sprinkling, aspersion, asperges 341n. *moistening*; circumambulation 314n. *circuition*; procession 285n. *progression*; stations of the cross 981n. *act of worship*; obeisance, bowing, kneeling, genuflexion, prostration, homage 920n. *respects*;

crossing oneself, signation, sign of the cross 547n. *gesture*; eucharistic rite, breaking the bread, commixture; intinction 341n. *moistening*; elevating of the Host; kiss of peace.

ritual object, cross, rood, Holy Rood, crucifix; altar, Lord's table, communion t.; altar furniture, altar cloth, rowel c.; candle, candlestick; communion wine, communion bread, cup, chalice, grail, Holy Grail, Sangrail; cruet; paten, ciborium, pyx, pyx-chest, tabernacle; monstrance; chrism, chrismatory; collection-plate, salver; incense, incensory, censer, thurible; holy water; aspergillum; asperger; piscina; sacring-bell, Sanctus bell; font, baptismal f., baptistery; baptismal garment, chrisom; wedding garment, bridal veil, wedding-ring; devotional object, relics, sacred relics; reliquary, shrine, casket 194n. *box*; icon, Pietà, Holy Sepulchre, stations of the cross 551n. *image*; osculatory, pax; Agnus Dei, rosary, beads, beadroll 981n. *prayers*; non-Christian objects, Ark of the Covenant, Mercy-seat; seven-branched candlestick; shewbread; laver; hyssop; sackcloth and ashes; libation dish, patina; joss-stick; sacred thread; prayer-wheel; altar of incense; urim, thummim; temple veil.

ritualist, ceremonialist, sabbatarian, formalist; liturgist, liturgiologist, litanist, euchologist; sacramentarian, sacramentalist; celebrant, masser, minister 986n. *priest*; server, acolyte; thurifer, boat-boy; crucifer, processionist, processioner.

office-book, service-b., ordinal, lectionary; liturgy, litany, euchologion; formulary, farse, rubric, canon 693n. *precept*; book of hours, breviary; missal, mass-book; euchology, prayer-book, book of common prayer 981n. *prayers*; beads, beadroll, rosary.

hymnal, hymnology, hymn-book, choir-b.; psalter, psalm-book, book of psalms 981n. *hymn*.

holy-day, feast, feast-day, festival 837n. *festivity*; fast-day, meatless d. 946n. *fast*; high day, day of observance, day of obligation 876n. *celebration*; sabbath, sabbath-day, day of rest 681n. *leisure*; Lord's Day, Sunday; proper day 876n. *special day*; saint's day 141n. *anniversary*;

All Hallows, All Saints, All Souls, Lady Day, Feast of the Annunciation; Candlemas, Feast of the Purification; Feast of the Assumption; Lammas, Martinmas, Michaelmas; Holy-tide, sacred season; Advent; Christmas, Christmas-tide, Yule-tide, Noel, Nativity, Epiphany, Twelfth Night; Lent, Shrove Tuesday, Ash Wednesday, Maundy Thursday, Good Friday; Holy Week, Passion Week; Easter, Eastertide, Easter Sunday; Ascension Day; Whitsuntide, Whitsun, Whitsunday, Pentecost; Corpus Christi; Trinity Sunday; Passover; Feast of Weeks, Pentecost; Feast of Tabernacles, Feast of Ingathering; Day of Atonement, Sabbath of Sabbaths; Ramadan, lesser Bairam, Greater B.; Mohurram; Poojahs.

Adj. *ritual,* procedural; formal, solemn, ceremonial, liturgical; processional, recessional; symbolic, symbolical, representational 551 adj. *representing*; sacramental, eucharistic; chrismal; baptismal; sacrificial, paschal; festal, pentecostal; fasting, lenten; prescribed, ordained; unleavened; kosher; consecrated, blessed.

ritualistic, ceremonious, ceremonial, formular, formulistic; sabbatarian; sacramentarian; observant of ritual, addicted to r.; lavish of r.; liturgiological, euchological.

Vb. *perform ritual,* do the rites, say office, celebrate, concelebrate, officiate, function; baptize, christen, confirm, ordain, lay on hands; minister, administer the sacraments, give communion, housel; sacrifice, offer s., make s.; offer prayers, bless, give benediction; anathematize, ban, ban with bell, book and candle; excommunicate, unchurch, unfrock; dedicate, consecrate, deconsecrate; purify, lustrate, asperge; thurify, cense; anoint, anele, give extreme unction; confess, absolve, pronounce absolution, shrive; take communion, receive the sacraments, housel oneself; bow, kneel, genuflect, prostrate oneself; sign oneself, make the sign of the cross, sain; take holy water; tell one's beads, say one's rosary; go one's stations, make one's s.; process, go in procession; circumambulate; fast, flagellate, do penance, stand in a white sheet.

ritualize, ceremonialize, institute a rite, organize a cult; sabbatize, sacramentalize, observe, keep, keep holy.

Adv. *ritually,* ceremonially; symbolically, sacramentally; liturgically.

See: 60, 141, 194, 285, 299, 300, 303, 314, 338, 341, 519, 534, 547, 551, 579, 610, 624, 648, 676, 681, 693, 837, 866, 875, 876, 883, 894, 920, 941, 946, 960, 981, 985, 986.

989 Canonicals

N. *canonicals,* clerical dress, cloth, clerical black 228 n. *dress*; frock, soutane, cassock, scapular; cloak, gown, Geneva g. 228 n. *cloak*; robe, cowl, hood, capouch, capuche; lappet, bands; chimer, simar, lawn sleeves; apron, gaiters, shovel hat; cardinal's hat; priests' cap, biretta, black b., purple b., red b.; skull-cap, calotte, zucchetto; Salvation Army bonnet 228 n. *headgear*; tonsure, shaven crown 229 n. *bareness*; prayer-cap; tallith; white sheet, white sheet of repentance; sanbenito, simarra.

vestments, ephod, priestly vesture, canonical robes 228 n. *dress*; pontificalia, pontificals; cassock, surplice, rochet; cappa magna; cope, tunicle, dalmatic, alb 228 n. *robe*; amice, chasuble, stole, deacon's s., orarion; scarf, tippet, pallium; cingulum 47 n. *girdle*; maniple, fanon, fannel; biretta 228 n. *headgear*; mitre, tiara, triple crown 743 n. *regalia*; papal vestment, orale, fanon; crosier, crose, staff, pastoral s. 743 n. *badge of rank*; pectoral 222 n. *cross*; episcopal ring; altar-cloth, frontlet, pall; pyx-cloth, orphrey, orfray, ecclesiastical embroidery 844 n. *ornamentation*.

Adj. *vestimental,* vestimentary, vestiary; canonical, pontifical.

vestured, robed 228 adj. *dressed*; surpliced, stoled etc. n.; cowled, hooded, capuched 986 adj. *monastic*; gaitered, aproned 986 adj. *clerical*; mitred, crosiered; wearing the triple crown, tiara'd.

See: 47, 222, 228, 229, 743, 844, 986.

990 Temple

N. *temple,* fane, pantheon; shrine, sacellum; idol house, joss-h., teocalli 982 n. *idolatry*; house of God, tabernacle, the Temple,

House of the Lord; place of worship 981 n. *worship*; masjid, mosque, Friday m.; mandir, mandap; house of prayer, oratory, oratorium; sacred edifice, pagoda, stupa, tope, dagoba, ziggurat, Tower of Babel 164n. *edifice*; propylæum; pronaos, portico, cella, naos.

holy place, holy ground, sacred precinct, temenos; sacrarium, sanctuary, adytum, cella, naos; Ark of the Covenant, Mercy-seat, Sanctum, Holy of Holies, oracle; martyry, sacred tomb, murabit, marabout, sepulchre, Holy Sepulchre; graveyard, golgotha, God's acre 364n. *cemetery*; place of pilgrimage; Holy City, Zion, New Jerusalem; Mecca, Benares, Banaras.

church, God's house; parish church, daughter c., chapel of ease; chapelry, chapelstead; cathedral, minster, procathedral; basilica; abbey; kirk, chapel, tabernacle, temple, bethel, ebenezer; steeple-house, conventicle, meeting-house, prayer-h.; house of prayer, oratory, chantry, chantry-chapel; synagogue, mosque.

altar, sacrarium, sanctuary; altar-stone, altar-slab, mensa; altar-table, Lord's t., communion t.; altar-bread 988n. *the sacrament*; altar pyx; prothesis, credence, credence-table 988n. *ritual object*; canopy, baldachin, altar-piece, altar-screen, reredos; altar-cloth, altar-frontal, altar-facing, antependium; altar-stair, predella, altar-rails; altar of incense; shewbread.

church utensil, font, baptistry; aumbry, stoup, piscina; chalice, paten 988n.

ritual object; pulpit, lectern; reading-bible, hymnal, prayer-book 981 n. *prayers*; hassock, kneeler; salver, collection-plate, collection-bag; organ, harmonium; bell, church-b., carillon 412n. *campanology*.

church interior, nave, cella, body of the kirk; aisle, apse, ambulatory, transept; rood-steeple, rood-tower; chancel, choir, sanctuary; hagioscope, priest's window, squint; chancel screen, rood-s., jube, rood loft, gallery, organ-loft; stall, choir-s., sedile, sedilia, misericorde; pew; minister's pew, reading-p.; pulpit, ambo; reader's pew, lectern; chapel, Lady c.; confessional; clerestory, triforium, spandrel; stained glass, stained-glass window, rose-w., jesse-w., jesse; cavalry, stations of the cross, Easter sepulchre; baptistry, font; sacristy, vestry; crypt, vault; rood, cross, crucifix.

church exterior, church-door, porch, galilee, tympanum 263n. *doorway*; tower, steeple, spire 209n. *high structure*; bell-tower, belfry, campanile; buttress, flying b. 218n. *supporter*; cloister, ambulatory; chapter-house, presbytery 692 n. *council*; churchyard, kirkyard, lych-gate; close 235n. *inclosure*; gopuram; torii.

Adj. *churchlike*, basilican, cathedralic; cruciform 222adj. *crossed*; apsidal 248 adj. *curved*; Gothic, Romanesque, Norman, Early English, decorated, perpendicular.

See: 164, 209, 218, 222, 235, 248, 263, 364, 412, 692, 981, 982, 988.

INDEX

*For instructions on how to use this Index
see pages xlix–l.*

A

Aaronic *priestly* 985 adj.
A1 *supreme* 34 adj.
  best 644 adj.
abacist *computer* 86 n.
aback *rearward* 238 adv.
abacus
  counting instrument 86 n.
abaft *rearward* 238 adv.
abalienate *convey* 780 vb.
abandon *exclude* 57 vb.
  depart 296 vb.
  disregard 458 vb.
  tergiversate 603 vb.
  relinquish 621 vb.
  assiduity 678 n.
  restlessness 678 n.
  resign 753 vb.
  not retain 779 vb.
  excitable state 822 n.
  cheerfulness 833 n.
  rejoicing 835 n.
abandoned *separate* 46 adj.
  unpossessed 774 adj.
  vicious 934 adj.
abandonment
  tergiversation 603 n.
  relinquishment 621 n.
  submission 721 n.
  resignation 753 n.
  non-retention 779 n.
  excitable state 822 n.
  rejoicing 835 n.
abandon one's post
  fail in duty 918 vb.
abase *be low* 210 vb.
  abase 311 vb.
  pervert 655 vb.
abasement *disrepute* 867 n.
  humility 872 n.
  humiliation 872 n.
  servility 879 n.
abash *abase* 311 vb.
  frighten 854 vb.
  humiliate 872 vb.
abate *decrease* 37 vb.
  moderate 177 vb.
  qualify 468 vb.
  discount 810 vb.
abatement
  contraction 198 n.
  relief 831 n.
abatis *defences* 713 n.
abattoir
  slaughter-house 362 n.
abaxial *oblique* 220 adj.
abbacy *church office* 985 n.
abbatical
  ecclesiastical 985 adj.
abbé *pastor* 986 n.

abbess *ecclesiarch* 986 n.
  nun 986 n.
abbcy *house* 192 n.
  monastery 986 n.
  church 990 n.
abbot *ecclesiarch* 986 n.
  monk 986 n.
abbotship
  church office 985 n.
abbreviate *bate* 37 vb.
  subtract 39 vb.
  shorten 204 vb.
  be concise 569 vb.
  abstract 592 vb.
abbreviation *smallness* 33 n.
  contraction 198 n.
  compendium 592 n.
A.B.C. *beginning* 68 n.
  guide-book 524 n.
  curriculum 534 n.
  letter 558 n.
abdicate *relinquish* 621 vb.
  be lax 734 vb.
  resign 753 vb.
abdication *laxity* 734 n.
  loss of right 916 n.
abdomen *maw* 194 n.
  insides 224 n.
abduct *take away* 786 vb.
  steal 788 vb.
abduction
  type of marriage 894 n.
abeam *sideways* 239 adv.
abed *supine* 216 adj.
aberrant *non-uniform* 17 adj.
  erroneous 495 adj.
aberration
  abnormality 84 n.
  displacement 188 n.
  deviation 282 n.
  divergence 294 n.
  inattention 456 n.
  insanity 503 n.
abet *concur* 181 vb.
  incite 612 vb.
  aid 703 vb.
abetment *causation* 156 n.
  co-operation 706 n.
abettor *cause* 156 n.
  assenter 488 n.
  motivator 612 n.
  colleague 707 n.
abeyance *extinction* 2 n.
  lull 145 n.
  non-use 674 n.
  inaction 677 n.
abeyance, in
  inert 175 adj.
abhor *not observe* 769 vb.
  dislike 861 vb.
  hate 888 vb.

  disapprove 924 vb.
abhorrent *contrary* 14 adj.
abide *be* 1 vb.
  continue 108 vb.
  last 113 vb.
  stay 144 vb.
  go on 146 vb.
  dwell 192 vb.
  be quiescent 266 vb.
  be patient 823 vb.
abide by *acquiesce* 488 vb.
  observe 768 vb.
abiding place *abode* 192 n.
abient *avoiding* 620 adj.
abient behaviour
  recession 290 n.
abient response
  recession 290 n.
ability *ability* 160 n.
  influence 178 n.
  intelligence 498 n.
  utility 640 n.
  skill 694 n.
ab initio *initially* 68 adv.
abiogenesis
  propagation 164 n.
abirritant *lenitive* 177 adj.
  antidote 658 n.
abject *servile* 879 adj.
  disreputable 867 adj.
  cowardly 856 adj.
  contemptible 922 adj.
  rascally 930 adj.
abjure *negate* 533 vb.
  recant 603 vb.
  resign 753 vb.
  not retain 779 vb.
ablative absolute
  grammar 564 n.
ablaze *fiery* 379 adj.
  luminous 417 adj.
able *powerful* 160 adj.
  possible 469 adj.
  intelligent 498 adj.
  useful 640 adj.
  active 678 adj.
  skilful 694 adj.
able-bodied
  stalwart 162 adj.
  active 678 adj.
ablegate *displace* 188 vb.
  commission 751 vb.
  envoy 754 n.
able seaman *mariner* 270 n.
  navy man 722 n.
ablution *water* 339 n.
  moistening 341 n.
  ablution 648 n.
abnegate *negate* 533 vb.
  reject 607 vb.
  relinquish 621 vb.

abnegation *refusal* 760 n.
  temperance 942 n.
abnormal
  non-uniform 17 adj.
  disagreeing 25 adj.
  extraneous 59 adj.
  abnormal 84 adj.
  deviating 282 adj.
  insane 503 adj.
  unexpected 508 adj.
  ungrammatical 565 adj.
  funny 849 adj.
  wrong 914 adj.
  spooky 970 adj.
abnormality
  illicit love 951 n.
abnormal psychology
  psychology 447 n.
  insanity 503 n.
aboard *here* 189 adv.
  afloat 275 adv.
abode *territory* 184 n.
  station 187 n.
  abode 192 n.
aboiement
  speech defect 580 n.
abolish *nullify* 2 vb.
  destroy 165 vb.
  abrogate 752 vb.
abolition *revolution* 149 n.
  desuetude 611 n.
  abrogation 752 n.
  prohibition 757 n.
abolitionist
  revolutionist 149 n.
  destroyer 168 n.
abominable *not nice* 645 adj.
  unclean 649 adj.
  disliked 861 adj.
  hateful 888 adj.
  heinous 934 adj.
abominable snowman
  animal 365 n.
  mythical being 970 n.
abominably
  extremely 32 adv.
abomination *badness* 645 n.
  uncleanness 649 n.
  dislike 861 n.
  hatred 888 n.
  hateful object 888 n.
  wickedness 934 n.
aboriginal
  beginning 68 adj.
  primal 127 adj.
  fundamental 156 adj.
  native 191 n., adj.
aborigine *earliness* 135 n.
abort
  be unproductive 172 vb.
  miscarry 728 vb.

abortion *abnormality* 84 n.
  deformity 246 n.
  undevelopment 670 n.
  failure 728 n.
  eyesore 842 n.
abortive *early* 135 adj.
  unproductive 172 adj.
  disappointing 509 adj.
  profitless 641 adj.
  immature 670 adj.
  unsuccessful 728 adj.
abound *abound* 635 vb.
  superabound 637 vb.
  be rich 800 vb.
about *concerning* 9 adv.
  about 33 adv.
  nearly 200 adv.
  around 230 adv.
about face *turn back* 286 vb.
about it, be
  be active 678 vb.
about to
  prospectively 124 adv.
  tending 179 adj.
about to be
  impending 155 adj.
about turn *reversion* 148 n.
  turn round 282 vb.
  return 286 n.
above *before* 64 adv.
  restrospectively 125 adv.
  aloft 209 adv.
  prideful 871 adj.
above all *eminently* 34 adv.
  importantly 638 adv.
above-board
  veracious 540 adj.
above-mentioned
  preceding 64 adj.
  repeated 106 adj.
  prior 119 adj.
  foregoing 125 adj.
above par *beyond* 34 adv.
  excellent 644 adj.
above price
  valuable 644 adj.
  of price 811 adj.
ab ovo *initially* 68 adv.
abracadabra *spell* 983 n.
abrade *bate* 37 vb.
  subtract 39 vb.
  uncover 229 vb.
  pulverize 332 vb.
  rub 333 vb.
  obliterate 550 vb.
abrasion *wound* 655 n.
abrasive *pulverizer* 332 n.
  rubbing 333 adj.
  obliteration 550 n.
abreaction *sanation* 656 n.
abreast *equal* 28 adj.

  in parallel 219 adv.
  sideways 239 adj.
abridge *bate* 37 vb.
  subtract 39 vb.
  make smaller 198 vb.
  shorten 204 vb.
  translate 520 vb.
  be concise 569 vb.
  abstract 592 vb.
abridgment *edition* 589 n.
  compendium 592 n.
abroad *abroad* 59 adv.
  afar 199 adv.
  doubting 474 adj.
abrogate *nullify* 2 vb.
  disable 161 vb.
  suppress 165 vb.
  negate 533 vb.
  recant 603 vb.
  reject 607 vb.
  relinquish 621 vb.
  disuse 674 vb.
  liberate 746 vb.
  abrogate 752 vb.
  prohibit 757 vb.
  not observe 769 vb.
  not retain 779 vb.
  make illegal 954 vb.
abrogation
  revolution 149 n.
  destruction 165 n.
  desuetude 611 n.
  abrogation 752 n.
abrupt
  instantaneous 116 adj.
  violent 176 adj.
  vertical 215 adj.
  sloping 220 adj.
  inelegant 576 adj.
  hasty 680 adj.
abscess *ulcer* 651 n.
abscission *subtraction* 39 n.
  scission 46 n.
abscond *decamp* 296 vb.
  run away 620 vb.
  elude 667 vb.
  not pay 805 vb.
  fail in duty 918 vb.
absence *non-existence* 2 n.
  deficit 55 n.
  absence 190 n.
  farness 199 n.
  invisibility 444 n.
  oblivion 506 n.
  non-use 674 n.
  dutilessness 918 n.
absent *abstracted* 456 adj.
  unprovided 636 adj.
  inactive 679 adj.
absentee *absence* 190 n.
  dutilessness 918 n.

absenteeism *absence* 190 n.
  inactivity 679 n.
  dutilessness 918 n.
absent-minded
  abstracted 456 adj.
  forgetful 506 adj.
absent oneself
  be absent 190 vb.
  disappear 446 vb.
  run away 620 vb.
  be exempt 919 vb.
absinth
  sourness 393 n.
absolute *existing* 1 adj.
  irrelative 10 adj.
  absolute 32 adj.
  simple 44 adj.
  complete 54 adj.
  self 80 n.
  one 88 adj.
  positive 473 adj.
  credal 485 adj.
  assertive 532 adj.
  authoritative 733 adj.
  authoritarian 735 adj.
  unconditional 744 adj.
  godlike 965 adj.
absolutely *positively* 32 adv.
absolution *amnesty* 506 n.
  liberation 746 n.
  forgiveness 909 n.
  non-liability 919 n.
  acquittal 960 n.
  church ministry 985 n.
  Christian rite 988 n.
  ministration 988 n.
absolutism
  despotism 733 n.
absolve *liberate* 746 vb.
  forgive 909 vb.
  exempt 919 vb.
  acquit 960 vb.
  perform ritual 988 vb.
absonant *discordant* 411 adj.
  illogical 477 adj.
absorb *add* 38 vb.
  combine 50 vb.
  contain 56 vb.
  consume 165 vb.
  absorb 299 vb.
  eat 301 vb.
  be attentive 455 vb.
  dispose of 673 vb.
  appropriate 786 vb.
  impress 821 vb.
absorbed
  thoughtful 449 adj.
  abstracted 456 adj.
absorbent *admitting* 299 adj.
  drier 342 n.
absorbing *felt* 818 adj.

  exciting 821 adj.
absorption *identity* 13 n.
  combination 50 n.
  reception 299 n.
  attention 455 n.
abstain *be loth* 598 vb.
  be neutral 606 vb.
  avoid 620 vb.
  relinquish 621 vb.
  not use 674 vb.
  be temperate 942 vb.
abstainer *abstainer* 942 n.
  ascetic 945 n.
abstemious
  temperate 942 adj.
  sober 948 adj.
abstention
  unwillingness 598 n.
  no choice 606 n.
  avoidance 620 n.
  inaction 677 n.
  temperance 942 n.
abstinence
  avoidance 620 n.
  non-use 674 n.
  temperance 942 n.
abstinent *fasting* 946 adj.
  sober 948 adj.
abstract *insubstantial* 4 adj.
  shorten 204 vb.
  mental 447 adj.
  philosophic 449 adj.
  be concise 569 vb.
  description 590 n.
  compendium 592 n.
  abstract 592 vb.
  take away 786 vb.
  steal 788 vb.
abstracted *separate* 46 adj.
  deviating 282 adj.
  abstracted 456 adj.
  crazed 503 adj.
  forgetful 506 adj.
  compendious 592 adj.
abstractedness
  abstractedness 456 n.
  fantasy 513 n.
abstraction
  insubstantiality 4 n.
  insubstantial thing 4 n.
  subtraction 39 n.
  disjunction 46 n.
  separation 46 n.
  incogitance 450 n.
  abstractedness 456 n.
  imperspicuity 568 n.
  stealing 788 n.
abstractive *taking* 786 adj.
abstruse *puzzling* 517 adj.
  imperspicuous 568 adj.
absurd *disagreeing* 25 adj.

  abnormal 84 adj.
  absurd 497 adj.
  foolish 499 adj.
  imaginative 513 adj.
  unmeaning 515 adj.
  useless 641 adj.
absurdity
  insubstantiality 4 n.
  ineffectuality 161 n.
  argumentation 475 n.
  error 495 n.
  absurdity 497 n.
  ideality 513 n.
  unmeaningness 515 n.
  silly talk 515 n.
  fable 543 n.
  caprice 604 n.
  pretext 614 n.
  trifle 639 n.
  inutility 641 n.
abundance *greatness* 32 n.
  great quantity 32 n.
  abundance 171 n.
  store 632 n.
  plenty 635 n.
  redundance 637 n.
abundant *many* 104 adj.
  diffuse 570 adj.
  rich 800 adj.
abuse *force* 176 vb.
  evil 616 n.
  waste 634 vb.
  ill-treat 645 vb.
  pervert 655 vb.
  misuse 675 n.,vb.
  quarrel 709 n.
  slur 867 n.
  scurrility 899 n.
  curse 899 vb.
  not respect 921 vb.
  dispraise 924 vb.
  exprobate 924 vb.
  detraction 926 n.
  debauch 951 vb.
  impiety 980 n.
abuse of language
  neology 560 n.
abuse the mind
  misteach 535 vb.
abusive *quarrelling* 709 adj.
  ungracious 885 adj.
  maledicent 899 adj.
  threatening 900 adj.
  detracting 926 adj.
abut *be near* 200 vb.
  be contiguous 202 vb.
abutment *supporter* 218 n.
  fortification 713 n.
abut on
  be supported 218 vb.
abysmal *deep* 211 adj.

heinous 934 adj.
diabolic 969 adj.
abyss *space* 183 n.
gap 201 n.
depth 211 n.
cavity 255 n.
pitfall 663 n.
hell 972 n.
acacia *tree* 366 n.
academic *irrelevant* 10 adj.
suppositional 512 adj.
educational 534 adj.
studious 536 adj.
academicals *uniform* 228 n.
academician
intellectual 492 n.
artist 556 n.
academic title
academic title 870 n.
academy *philosopher* 449 n.
academy 539 n.
acarpous
unproductive 172 adj.
accede *accrue* 39 vb.
approach 289 vb.
assent 488 vb.
consent 758 vb.
accede to the throne
take authority 733 vb.
accelerando *adagio* 412 adv.
accelerate *augment* 36 vb.
be early 135 vb.
be vigorous 174 vb.
make violent 176 vb.
accelerate 277 vb.
promote 285 vb.
hasten 680 vb.
animate 821 vb.
accent *sound* 398 n.
prosody 593 n.
affirmation 532 n.
emphasize 532 vb.
punctuation 547 n.
pronunciation 577 n.
voice 577 vb.
speech defect 580 n.
accents *voice* 577 n.
speech 579 n.
accentual *vocal* 577 adj.
accentuate
emphasize 532 vb.
accentuation
grammar 564 n.
pronunciation 577 n.
prosody 593 n.
accept *admit* 299 vb.
believe 485 vb.
acquiesce 488 vb.
choose 605 vb.
undertake 672 vb.
submit 721 vb.

consent 758 vb.
give security 767 vb.
receive 782 vb.
take 786 vb.
be hospitable 882 vb.
approve 923 vb.
acceptability
sufficiency 635 n.
sociability 882 n.
acceptable
admitting 299 adj.
rational 475 adj.
expedient 642 adj.
pleasurable 826 adj.
desired 859 adj.
approvable 923 adj.
acceptance
connotation 514 n.
title-deed 767 n.
(*see* accept)
accept deposits
borrow 785 vb.
accepted *credible* 485 adj.
usual 610 adj.
orthodox 976 adj.
acceptor *recipient* 782 n.
purchaser 792 n.
accept responsibility
look after 457 vb.
promise 764 vb.
incur a duty 917 vb.
access *increment* 36 n.
entrance 68 n.
doorway 263 n.
approach 289 n.
ingress 297 n.
way in 297 n.
reception 299 n.
spasm 318 n.
access 624 n.
accessible *near* 200 adj.
open 263 adj.
accessible 289 adj.
admitting 299 adj.
possible 469 adj.
easy 701 adj.
free 744 adj.
accession *increment* 36 n.
addition 38 n.
extra 40 n.
approach 289 n.
arrival 295 n.
authority 733 n.
accessory
extrinsicality 6 n.
extrinsic 6 adj.
adjunct 40 n.
concomitant 89 n.
accompanying 89 adj.
superfluity 637 n.
trifle 639 n.

aiding 703 adj.
colleague 707 n.
accidence *grammar* 564 n.
accident *extrinsicality* 6 n.
chance 159 n.
evil 616 n.
non-design 618 n.
ill fortune 731 n.
accidental *extrinsic* 6 adj.
happening 154 adj.
casual 159 adj.
unintentional 618 adj.
accident-prone
unfortunate 731 adj.
accidie *sluggishness* 679 n.
acclaim *assent* 488 vb.
repute 866 n.
honour 866 vb.
applause 923 n.
applaud 923 vb.
acclamation *applause* 923 n.
acclimatize
make conform 83 vb.
break in 369 vb.
habituate 610 vb.
acclivity *acclivity* 220 n.
ascent 308 n.
accolade *honours* 866 n.
accommodate *adjust* 24 vb.
equalize 28 vb.
comprise 78 vb.
make conform 83 vb.
place 187 vb.
aid 703 vb.
pacify 719 vb.
lend 784 vb.
accommodating
benevolent 897 adj.
accommodation
room 183 n.
storage 632 n.
subvention 703 n.
accompaniment
relativeness 9 n.
adjunct 40 n.
accompaniment 89 n.
concomitant 89 n.
synchronism 123 n.
musical piece 412 n.
accompanist
instrumentalist 413 n.
accompany
accompany 89 vb.
synchronize 123 vb.
be contiguous 202 vb.
play music 413 vb.
direct 689 vb.
accomplice *colleague* 707 n.
accomplish *produce* 164 vb.
do 676 vb.
carry out 725 vb.

succeed 727 vb.
accomplished
  skilful 694 adj.
accomplished fact
  certainty 473 n.
accomplishment
  culture 490 n.
  skill 694 n.
  (see accomplish)
accord be uniform 16 vb.
  agreement 24 n.
  be equal 28 vb.
  combine 50 vb.
  conform 83 vb.
  concur 181 vb.
  harmonize 410 vb.
  assent 488 vb.
  be expedient 642 vb.
  concord 710 vb.
  permit 756 vb.
  consent 758 n.
  give 781 vb.
according as thus 8 adv.
  provided 468 adv.
according to
  conformably 83 adv.
accordion organ 414 n.
accordionist
  instrumentalist 413 n.
accord, with one
  unanimously 488 adv.
accost approach 289 n.
  speak to 583 vb.
  request 761 vb.
  greet 884 vb.
accouche deliver 668 vb.
accouchement
  obstetrics 164 n.
accoucheur obstetrics 164 n.
  doctor 658 n.
account statistics 86 n.
  list 87 n.
  estimate 480 vb.
  opine 485 vb.
  report 524 n.
  description 590 n.
  narration 590 n.
  funds 797 n.
  credit 802 n.
  debt 803 n.
  accounts 808 n.
  account 808 vb.
  prestige 866 n.
accountability
  liability 180 n.
  dueness 915 n.
  duty 917 n.
accountable
  accounting 808 adj.
accountancy
  numeration 86 n.

registration 548 n.
  accounts 808 n.
accountant computer 86 n.
  recorder 549 n.
  treasurer 798 n.
  accountant 808 n.
account book list 87 n.
  record 548 n.
  account book 808 n.
account for cause 156 vb.
  account for 158 vb.
  interpret 520 vb.
account, in one's
  at credit 777 adv.
account of, take
  notice 455 vb.
account, on no
  in no way 33 adv.
account owing debt 803 n.
accounts accounts 809 n.
account with pay 804 vb.
accouplement joinder 45 n.
accoutre dress 228 vb.
  make ready 669 vb.
  defend 713 vb.
accoutrement
  dressing 228 n.
  uniform 228 n.
  equipment 630 n.
  fitting out 669 n.
accredit commission 751 vb.
accredited credible 485 adj.
  credal 485 adj.
  usual 610 adj.
accretion increment 36 n.
  addition 38 n.
  expansion 197 n.
accrue be extrinsic 6 vb.
  augment 36 vb.
  accrue 38 vb.
  result 157 vb.
  approach 289 vb.
  be profitable 771 vb.
  be received 782 vb.
accumbent supine 216 adj.
accumulate grow 36 vb.
  join 45 vb.
  bring together 74 vb.
  store 632 vb.
  acquire 771 vb.
  take 786 vb.
accumulation
  great quantity 32 n.
accumulative
  acquiring 771 adj.
accumulator
  accumulator 74 n.
accuracy mimicry 20 n.
  attention 455 n.
  carefulness 457 n.
  discrimination 463 n.

accuracy 494 n.
  veracity 540 n.
accurate careful 457 adj.
  descriptive 590 adj.
  orthodox 976 adj.
accursed damnable 645 adj.
  bad 645 adj.
  harmful 645 adj.
  baneful 659 adj.
  unfortunate 731 adj.
  unhappy 825 adj.
  unpleasant 827 adj.
  hateful 888 adj.
  cursed 899 adj.
  heinous 934 adj.
  wicked 934 adj.
  profane 980 adj.
accusable accusable 928 adj.
  illegal 954 adj.
accusation
  affirmation 532 n.
  wrong 914 n.
  detraction 926 n.
  accusation 928 n.
  litigation 959 n.
accusatory
  disapproving 924 adj.
  detracting 926 adj.
accuse attribute 158 vb.
  inform 524 vb.
  oppose 704 vb.
  satirize 851 vb.
  defame 926 vb.
  accuse 928 vb.
  litigate 959 vb.
accuse oneself
  be penitent 939 vb.
accused, the prisoner 750 n.
  accused person 928 n.
  litigant 959 n.
accuser informer 524 n.
  detractor 926 n.
  accuser 928 n.
  litigant 959 n.
accusing evidential 466 adj.
accustom train 534 vb.
  habituate 610 vb.
accustomed usual 610 adj.
  unastonished 865 adj.
ace unit 88 n.
  means 629 n.
  masterpiece 694 n.
acedia sluggishness 679 n.
acerbity pungency 388 n.
  unsavouriness 390 n.
  sourness 393 n.
  rudeness 885 n.
  resentment 891 n.
  malevolence 898 n.
acetify be sour 393 vb.
acetose sour 393 adj.

acetylene *fuel* 385 n.
ache *pang* 377 n.
  feel pain 377 vb.
  give pain 377 vb.
  suffer 825 vb.
achievable *possible* 469 adj.
achieve *terminate* 69 vb.
  produce 164 vb.
  be instrumental 628 vb.
  do 676 vb.
  carry out 725 vb.
  succeed 727 vb.
achievement
  progression 285 n.
  heraldry 547 n.
  monument 548 n.
  (*see* achieve)
Achilles' heel *defect* 647 n.
  vulnerability 661 n.
achromatic
  colourless 426 adj.
achromatism
  desiccation 342 n.
  dimness 419 n.
  achromatism 426 n.
acid *destroyer* 168 n.
  keen 174 adj.
  unsavoury 391 adj.
  sourness 393 n.
  bane 659 n.
  poison 659 n.
acidify *be sour* 393 vb.
acidity *pungency* 388 n.
  sourness 393 n.
acidosis *sourness* 393 n.
  indigestion 651 n.
acid test *experiment* 461 n.
acidulated *sour* 393 adj.
acidulous *keen* 174 adj.
  sour 393 adj.
aciform *sharp* 256 adj.
acknowledge
  attribute 158 vb.
  notice 455 vb.
  answer 460 vb.
  testify 466 vb.
  assent 488 vb.
  confess 526 vb.
  correspond 588 vb.
  observe 768 vb.
  befriend 880 vb.
  greet 884 vb.
  thank 907 vb.
  grant claims 915 vb.
  reward 962 vb.
  worship 981 vb.
acknowledged
  usual 610 adj.
  received 807 adj.
acknowledgment
  (*see* acknowledge)

acme *summit* 213 n.
acne *skin disease* 651 n.
a-cold *a-cold* 380 adj.
acology *medical art* 658 n.
acolyte *auxiliary* 707 n.
  cleric 986 n.
  church officer 986 n.
  ritualist 988 n.
acomia *bareness* 229 n.
aconite
  poisonous plant 659 n.
acoustic *sounding* 398 adj.
  auditory 415 adj.
acoustics *acoustics* 398 n.
  hearing 415 n.
acquaint *inform* 524 vb.
acquaintance
  knowledge 490 n.
  information 524 n.
  friendship 880 n.
  friend 880 n.
acquaint oneself
  know 490 vb.
acquiesce *concur* 181 vb.
  acquiesce 488 vb.
  be willing 597 vb.
  submit 721 vb.
  consent 758 vb.
  be content 828 vb.
acquiescence
  conformity 83 n.
  obedience 739 n.
  permission 756 n.
  patience 823 n.
acquiescent
  agreeing 24 adj.
  inexcitable 823 adj.
acquire *acquire* 771 vb.
  possess 773 vb.
  receive 782 vb.
  take 786 vb.
  be rewarded 962 vb.
acquired *extrinsic* 6 adj.
acquired characteristic
  extrinsicality 6 n.
acquirement *skill* 694 n.
  acquisition 771 n.
acquirements *culture* 490 n.
acquisition *increment* 36 n.
  extra 40 n.
  assemblage 74 n.
  benefit 615 n.
  store 632 n.
  acquisition 771 n.
  receiving 782 n.
  taking 786 n.
acquisitions *culture* 490 n.
acquisitive
  acquiring 771 adj.
  taking 786 adj.
  avaricious 816 adj.

  greedy 859 adj.
  selfish 932 adj.
acquit *deliver* 668 n.
  liberate 746 vb.
  forgive 909 vb.
  do one's duty 917 vb.
  exempt 919 vb.
  justify 927 vb.
  acquit 960 vb.
acquittal *escape* 667 n.
  observance 768 n.
  non-liability 919 n.
  vindication 927 n.
  innocence 935 n.
  legal trial 959 n.
  acquittal 960 n.
acquittance *liberation* 746 n.
  title-deed 767 n.
  observance 768 n.
  payment 804 n.
acre *measure* 183 n.
acreage *measure* 183 n.
acres *land* 344 n.
  lands 777 n.
acrid *keen* 174 adj.
  pungent 388 adj.
  unsavoury 391 adj.
acrimonious
  ungracious 885 adj.
  resentful 891 adj.
acrimony *keenness* 174 n.
  sharpness 256 n.
  rudeness 885 n.
  hatred 888 n.
  resentment 891 n.
  malevolence 898 n.
acrobat *athlete* 162 n.
  proficient 696 n.
acrobatic *athletic* 162 adj.
  flexible 327 adj.
acrobatics *athletics* 162 n.
acrophobia
  psychopathy 503 n.
  phobia 854 n.
acropolis *vertex* 213 n.
  refuge 662 n.
  fort 713 n.
across *obliquely* 220 adv.
  across 222 adv.
acrostic
  equivocalness 518 n.
  enigma 530 n.
  initials 558 n.
act *operate* 173 vb.
  duplicity 541 n.
  dissemble 541 vb.
  represent 551 vb.
  stage show 594 n.
  act 594 vb.
  function 622 vb.
  be instrumental 628 vb.

deed 676 n.
do 676 vb.
behave 688 vb.
precept 693 n.
be successful 727 vb.
decree 737 n.
be affected 850 vb.
acta *record* 548 n.
act a part *cant* 541 vb.
be affected 850 vb.
act-drop *stage-set* 594 n.
acted upon
operative 173 adj.
act for *substitute* 150 vb.
deputize 755 vb.
acting *ephemeral* 114 adj.
operative 173 adj.
representation 551 n.
acting arrangement
transientness 114 n.
actinism *radiation* 417 n.
actinometer
optical device 442 n.
actinometry *optics* 417 n.
act, in the
in the act 676 adv.
action *eventuality* 154 n.
energy 160 n.
production 164 n.
agency 173 n.
dramaturgy 594 n.
policy 623 n.
action 676 n.
activity 678 n.
conduct 688 n.
fight 716 n.
battle 718 n.
effectuation 725 n.
litigation 959 n.
actionable
accusable 928 adj.
legal 953 adj.
illegal 954 adj.
litigated 959 adj.
activate *operate* 173 vb.
invigorate 174 vb.
influence 178 vb.
activation
stimulation 174 n.
activity 678 n.
activator *stimulant* 174 n.
active *stalwart* 162 adj.
operative 173 adj.
vigorous 174 adj.
moving 265 adj.
willing 597 adj.
businesslike 622 adj.
doing 676 adj.
active 678 adj.
labouring 682 adj.
excited 821 adj.

active in *influential* 178 adj.
active list, on the
operative 173 adj.
actively *greatly* 32 adv.
active service *warfare* 718 n.
activism *action* 676 n.
activity 678 n.
activist *essayer* 671 n.
doer 676 n.
busy person 678 n.
activity *vigorousness* 174 n.
stimulation 174 n.
agitation 318 n.
business, job 622 n.
instrumentality 628 n.
action 676 n.
activity 678 n.
actor *imitator* 20 n.
deceiver 545 n.
actor 594 n.
doer 676 n.
agent 686 n.
personnel 686 n.
affector 850 n.
actor manager
stage-manager 594 n.
act out *terminate* 69 vb.
actual *real* 1 adj.
present 121 adj.
true 494 adj.
actuarial *accounting* 808 adj.
actuarial calculation
calculation of chance
159 n.
actuary *computer* 86 n.
accountant 808 n.
actuate *influence* 178 vb.
move 265 vb.
motivate 612 vb.
act upon *operate* 173 vb.
motivate 612 vb.
acuity *sharpness* 256 n.
vision 438 n.
sagacity 498 n.
acumen
discrimination 463 n.
sagacity 498 n.
acuminate *tapering* 256 adj.
sharpen 256 vb.
acupuncture
perforation 263 n.
therapy 658 n.
acute *keen* 174 adj.
violent 176 adj.
sharp 256 adj.
sentient 374 adj.
strident 407 adj.
intelligent 498 adj.
cunning 698 adj.
felt 818 adj.
acute accent

punctuation 547 n.
acuteness *sharpness* 256 n.
sagacity 498 n.
adage *maxim* 496 n.
adagio *slowly* 278 adv.
adagio 412 adv.
Adam *precursor* 66 n.
husbandman 370 n.
mankind 371 n.
male 372 n.
Adam and Eve *parent* 169 n.
adamant *strength* 162 n.
hardness 326 n.
Adamite *mankind* 371 n.
Adamitic *human* 371 adj.
adapt *adjust* 24 vb.
translate 520 vb.
adaptable *fit* 24 adj.
conformable 83 adj.
flexible 327 adj.
useful 640 adj.
skilful 694 adj.
adaptation
adaptation 24 n.
conformity 83 n.
transformation 143 n.
musical piece 412 n.
translation 520 n.
edition 589 n.
adapted *fit* 24 adj.
combined 50 adj.
conformable 83 adj.
adapted to
expedient 642 adj.
adapter *alterer* 143 n.
ad captandum
sophistical 477 adj.
flatteringly 925 adv.
add *add* 38 vb.
join, affix 45 vb.
agglutinate 48 vb.
combine 50 vb.
prepose 64 vb.
modify 143 vb.
enlarge 197 vb.
insert 303 vb.
misinterpret 521 vb.
exaggerate 546 vb.
addenda *edition* 589 n.
addendum *addition* 38 n.
extra, adjunct 40 n.
adder *reptile* 365 n.
sibilation 406 n.
bane 659 n.
noxious animal 904 n.
add fuel to the flame
augment 36 vb.
make violent 176 vb.
aggravate 832 vb.
enrage 891 vb.
addict *habitué* 610 n.

sick person 651 n.
drunkard 949 n.
addiction *habit* 610 n.
intemperance 943 n.
adding machine
counting instrument 86 n.
addition *quantity* 26 n.
increment 36 n.
increase 36 n.
addition 38 n.
adjunct 40 n.
mixture 43 n.
joinder 45 n.
whole 52 n.
sequence 65 n.
numerical result 85 n.
numerical operation 86 n.
expansion 197 n.
insertion 303 n.
exaggeration 546 n.
additional *extrinsic* 6 adj.
additional 38 adj.
included 78 adj.
superfluous 637 adj.
additive *additional* 38 adj.
extra 40 n.
component 58 n.
addle *sterilize* 172 vb.
be unclean 649 vb.
addled
unproductive 172 adj.
light-minded 456 adj.
unintelligent 499 adj.
addle-head *fool* 501 n.
address *place* 185 n.
situation 186 n.
locality 187 n.
abode 192 n.
send 272 vb.
oration 579 n.
orate 579 vb.
allocution 583 n.
speak to 583 vb.
correspond 587 vb.
skill 694 n.
entreat 761 vb.
address book
reminder 505 n.
address card *label* 547 n.
addressee *resident* 191 n.
interlocutor 584 n.
correspondent 588 n.
recipient 782 n.
addresses
reading matter 589 n.
wooing 889 n.
address oneself *begin* 68 vb.
prepare 669 vb.
adduce
corroborate 466 vb.
manifest 522 vb.

adduction *attraction* 291 n.
add up *add* 38 vb.
be intelligible 516 vb.
add up to *mean* 514 vb.
adelantado *governor* 741 n.
adenography
structure 331 n.
adenoidal
stammering 580 adj.
adenoids *swelling* 253 n.
adenology *structure* 331 n.
adeps *fat* 357 n.
adept *proficient* 696 n.
adequacy *sufficiency* 635 n.
utility 640 n.
adhere *accrue* 38 vb.
unite with 45 vb.
cohere 48 vb.
be contiguous 202 vb.
transfer 272 vb.
approach 289 vb.
assent 488 vb.
be wont 610 vb.
contract 765 vb.
retain 778 vb.
adherence *coherence* 48 n.
observance 768 n.
adherent *cohesive* 48 adj.
follower 284 n.
auxiliary 707 n.
signatory 765 n.
adhere to *observe* 768 vb.
adhesion *coherence* 48 n.
contiguity 202 n.
adhesive *conjunctive* 45 adj.
adhesive 47 n.
cohesive 48 adj.
tough 329 adj.
viscid 354 adj.
retentive 778 adj.
adhesiveness
viscidity 354 n.
adhibit *use* 673 vb.
ad hoc *spontaneous* 609 adj.
extempore 609 adv.
unprepared 670 adj.
unreadily 670 vb.
ad hominem
specially 80 adv.
adiactinic *opaque* 423 adj.
adiathermic *cold* 380 adj.
opaque 423 adj.
adieu *valediction* 296 n.
ad infinitum
infinitely 107 adj.
adipocere *decay* 51 n.
fat 357 n.
adipose *fatty* 357 adj.
adit *doorway* 263 n.
tunnel 263 n.
access 624 n.

adjacent *near* 200 adj.
contiguous 202 adj.
adjective *adjunct* 40 n.
part of speech 564 n.
adjoin *be near* 200 vb.
be contiguous 202 vb.
adjourn *put off* 136 vb.
adjournment *interim* 108 n.
delay 136 n.
adjudge *judge* 480 vb.
adjudicate *judge* 480 vb.
try a case 959 vb.
adjudication
judgment 480 n.
adjudicator *estimator* 480 n.
adjunct *increment* 36 n.
adjunct 40 n.
part 53 n.
component 58 n.
extremity 69 n.
concomitant 89 n.
aider 703 n.
adjure *affirm* 532 vb.
entreat 761 vb.
take a pledge 764 vb.
adjurement *oath* 532 n.
adjust *graduate* 27 vb.
equalize 28 vb.
mix 43 vb.
regularize 62 vb.
make conform 83 vb.
synchronize 123 vb.
moderate 177 vb.
harmonize 410 vb.
be true 494 vb.
plan 623 vb.
rectify 654 vb.
make ready 669 vb.
pacify 719 vb.
adjustable
conformable 83 adj.
adjusted *conformable* 83 adj.
accurate 494 adj.
right 913 adj.
adjustment *adaptation* 24 n.
change 143 n.
compact 765 n.
compromise 770 n.
(see adjust)
adjutage *tube* 263 n.
outlet 298 n.
adjutant *auxiliary* 707 n.
army officer 741 n.
adjuvant *aiding* 703 adj.
auxiliary 707 n.
ad-libber *speaker* 579 n.
ad-libbing
spontaneity 609 n.
ad libitum, ad lib.
often 139 adv.
at will 595 adv.

enough 635 adv.
freely 744 adv.
admass *dupe* 544 n.
commonalty 869 n.
administer *use* 673 vb.
do 676 vb.
manage 689 vb.
apportion 783 vb.
administration
arrangement 62 n.
use 673 n.
action 676 n.
management 689 n.
apportionment 783 n.
ministration 988 n.
administrative
directing 689 adj.
governmental 733 adj.
jurisdictional 955 adj.
administrator *doer* 676 n.
agent 686 n.
manager 690 n.
admirable *excellent* 644 adj.
wonderful 864 adj.
worshipful 866 adj.
approvable 923 adj.
Admirable Crichton
exceller 644 n.
proficient 696 n.
prodigy 864 n.
admiral *navy man* 722 n.
naval officer 741 n.
admiralty *navy* 722 n.
authority 733 n.
admiration *wonder* 864 n.
love 887 n.
respect 920 n.
approbation 923 n.
admired *excellent* 644 adj.
respected 920 adj.
admire oneself
be vain 873 vb.
admirer *lover* 887 n.
commender 923 n.
worshipper 981 n.
admissibility *fitness* 24 n.
admissible
numerable 86 adj.
rational 475 adj.
approvable 923 adj.
admission *inclusion* 78 n.
ingress 297 n.
reception 299 n.
testimony 466 n.
assent 488 n.
disclosure 526 n.
affirmation 532 n.
admit *add* 38 vb.
admit 299 vb.
testify 466 vb.
be reasonable 475 vb.

believe 485 vb.
assent 488 vb.
confess 526 vb.
affirm 532 vb.
receive 782 vb.
admit of *be possible* 469 vb.
admitting *provided* 468 adv.
open 263 adj.
admixture *mixture* 43 n.
tincture 43 n.
admonish *warn* 664 vb.
advise 691 vb.
reprove 924 vb.
admonition
dissuasion 613 n.
warning 664 n.
reprimand 924 n.
ad nauseam
ad nauseam 861 adv.
boringly 838 adv.
adnoun
part of speech 564 n.
ado *activity* 678 n.
exertion 682 n.
adobe *small house* 192 n.
materials 631 n.
a-doing *happening* 154 adj.
busy 678 adj.
adolescence *youth* 130 n.
adolescent *young* 130 adj.
youngster 132 n.
immature 670 adj.
Adonis *male* 372 n.
a beauty 841 n.
mythic god 966 n.
adopt *be akin* 11 vb.
choose 605 vb.
avail of 673 vb.
adopted *additional* 38 adj.
filial 170 adj.
sanctified 979 adj.
adoption *choice* 605 n.
approbation 923 n.
sanctity 979 n.
adoptive *filial* 170 adj.
adorable *beautiful* 841 adj.
lovable 887 adj.
adoration *respect* 920 n.
piety 979 n.
worship 981 n.
adore *love* 887 vb.
respect 920 vb.
worship 981 vb.
adorn *ornament* 574 vb.
make better 654 vb.
decorate 844 vb.
adornment
ornamentation 844 n.
adrift *irrelative* 10 adj.
irrelevant 10 adj.
separate 46 adj.

apart 46 adv.
unassembled 75 adj.
astray 282 adv.
doubting 474 adj.
adroit *skilful* 694 adj.
adscititious
extrinsic 6 adj.
additional 38 adj.
superfluous 637 adj.
adulation
exaggeration 546 n.
praise 923 n.
flattery 925 n.
adult *adult* 134 n.
grown up 134 adj.
manly 162 adj.
matured 669 adj.
adulterate *mix* 43 vb.
modify 143 vb.
weaken 163 vb.
abase 311 vb.
rarefy 325 vb.
add water 339 vb.
impair 655 vb.
adulterated *spurious* 542 adj.
adulterer *libertine* 952 n.
adulterine *spurious* 542 adj.
bastard 954 adj.
adulterous
extramarital 951 adj.
adultery *love affair* 887 n.
illicit love 951 n.
adultness
adultness 134 n.
preparedness 669 n.
adultress
loose woman 952 n.
adumbrate
predestine 155 vb.
darken 418 vb.
propound 512 vb.
figure 519 vb.
hint 524 vb.
represent 551 vb.
describe 590 vb.
adumbration *similarity* 18 n.
copy 22 n.
latency 523 n.
adunation *combination* 50 n.
aduncity *angularity* 247 n.
curvature 248 n.
adust *heated* 381 adj.
brown 430 adj.
Advaita *philosophy* 449 n.
ad valorem *priced* 809 adj.
advance *increase* 36 n.
augment 36 vb.
part 53 n.
prepose 64 vb.
elapse 111 vb.
early 135 adj.

go on 146 vb.
motion 265 n.
marching 267 n.
travel 267 vb.
progression 285 n.
progress 285 vb.
promote 285 vb.
approach 289 n., vb.
be visible 443 vb.
affirm 532 vb.
be instrumental 628 vb.
be useful 640 vb.
be expedient 642 vb.
improvement 654 n.
get better 654 vb.
make better 654 vb.
aid 703 vb.
succeed 727 vb.
offer 759 n.
lend 784 vb.
dignify 866 vb.
advance against
    charge 712 vb.
advanced modern 126 adj.
    early 135 adj.
    progressive 285 adj.
advance guard front 237 n.
advance, in early 135 adj.
    in front 237 adv.
    ahead 283 adv.
advancement
    (see advance)
advance notice
    prediction 511 n.
    warning 664 n.
advance of, in
    beyond 34 adv.
advances approach 289 n.
    endearment 889 n.
    wooing 889 n.
advantage vantage 34 n.
    benefit 615 n., vb.
    utility 640 n.
    be useful 640 vb.
    expedience 642 n.
    be expedient 642 vb.
    success, victory 727 n.
    gain 771 n.
advantage, have the
    be unequal 29 vb.
    predominate 34 vb.
advantage of, take
    befool 542 vb.
advantageous
    (see advantage)
advent futurity 124 n.
    eventuality 154 n.
    approach 289 n.
    arrival 295 n.
    holy-day 988 n.
adventitious extrinsic 6 adj.

circumstantial 8 adj.
casual 159 adj.
adventure eventuality 154 n.
    pursuit 619 n.
    essay 671 n.
    undertaking 672 n.
    be courageous 855 vb.
adventurer traveller 268 n.
    experimenter 461 n.
    imposter 545 n.
    gambler 618 n.
    militarist 722 n.
    desperado 857 n.
    egotist 932 n.
adventures biography 590 n.
adventuress
    loose woman 952 n.
adventurous
    speculative 618 adj.
    enterprising 672 adj.
    courageous 855 adj.
    rash 857 adj.
adverb adjunct 40 n.
    part of speech 564 n.
adversaria
    commentary 520 n.
    record 548 n.
adversary opponent 705 n.
    Satan 969 n.
adversative contrary 14 adj.
    negative 533 adj.
adverse contrary 14 adj.
    presageful 511 adj.
    unwilling 598 adj.
    evil 616 adj.
    inexpedient 643 adj.
    harmful 645 adj.
    hindering 702 adj.
    opposing 704 adj.
    adverse 731 adj.
    annoying 827 adj.
    unpromising 853 adj.
    disliking 861 adj.
adversity ruin 165 n.
    evil 616 n.
    difficulty 700 n.
    adversity 731 n.
    suffering 825 n.
    painfulness 827 n.
    punishment 963 n.
advert cognize 447 vb.
    be attentive 455 vb.
    notice 455 vb.
advertence attention 455 n.
advertise
    attract notice 455 vb.
    predict 511 vb.
    communicate 524 vb.
    advertise 528 vb.
    make important 638 vb.
    boast 877 vb.

praise 923 vb.
advertisement exhibit 522 n.
    information 524 n.
    advertisement 528 n.
    inducement 612 n.
    request 761 n.
    boasting 877 n.
advertise oneself
    be ostentatious 875 vb.
    boast 877 vb.
advertiser
    overestimation 482 n.
    exhibitor 522 n.
    informant 524 n.
    publicizer 528 n.
    motivator 612 n.
    petitioner 763 n.
    boaster 877 n.
    commender 923 n.
advice meditation 449 n.
    estimate 480 n.
    information 524 n.
    hint 524 n.
    message 529 n.
    news 529 n.
    inducement 612 n.
    preparation 669 n.
    advice 691 n.
    precept 693 n.
    aid 703 n.
advisable expedient 642 adj.
advise propound 512 vb.
    hint 524 vb.
    inform 524 vb.
    doctor 658 vb.
    warn 664 vb.
    advise 691 vb.
advise against
    dissuade 613 vb.
    warn 664 vb.
advised
    predetermined 608 adj.
advisedly purposely 617 adv.
adviser estimator 480 n.
    sage 500 n.
    teacher 537 n.
    director 690 n.
    adviser 691 n.
    expert 696 n.
    consignee 754 n.
advise with confer 584 vb.
    consult 691 vb.
advisory judicial 480 adj.
    advising 691 adj.
advocacy aid 703 n.
    approbation 923 n.
    bar 958 n.
advocate
    intermediary 231 n.
    speaker 579 n.
    motivator 612 n.

adviser 691 n.
advise 691 vb.
patron 707 n.
combatant 722 n.
consignee 754 n.
deputy 755 n.
approve 923 vb.
vindicator 927 n.
vindicate 927 vb.
lawyer 958 n.
litigate 959 vb.
advowson benefice 985 n.
adynamic weak 163 adj.
adytum chamber 194 n.
hiding-place 527 n.
holy place 990 n.
adze sharp edge 256 n.
ædile official 690 n.
officer 741 n.
ædileship
magistrature 733 n.
ægis protection 660 n.
armour 713 n.
ægrotat non-liability 919 n.
æolian windy 352 adj.
Æolus wind 352 n.
mythic god 966 n.
lesser god 967 n.
æonian perpetual 115 adj.
æons diuturnity 113 n.
aerate gasify 336 vb.
bubble 355 vb.
aerify 340 vb.
aerated light 323 adj.
rare 325 adj.
airy 340 adj.
bubbly 355 adj.
aerial high 209 adj.
flying 271 adj.
gaseous 336 adj.
airy 340 adj.
telecommunication 531 n.
aerie nest 192 n.
aeriform gaseous 336 adj.
airy 340 adj.
aerify lighten 323 vb.
gasify 336 vb.
vaporize 338 vb.
aerify 340 vb.
refrigerate 382 vb.
refresh 685 vb.
aerobatics
aeronautics 271 n.
aerodonetics
aeronautics 271 n.
aerodrome air travel 271 n.
aircraft 267 n.
goal 295 n.
aerodynamic flying 271 adj.
aviational 276 adj.
aerodynamics

aeronautics 271 n.
pneumatics 340 n.
anemology 352 n.
gaseity 336 n.
aerodyne aircraft 276 n.
aerography
pneumatics 340 n.
aerolite meteor 321 n.
aerology pneumatics 340 n.
aeromancy weather 340 n.
theomancy 511 n.
aeromechanics
aeronautics 271 n.
aerometer density 324 n.
pneumatics 340 n.
aeronaut aeronaut 271 n.
aeronautics
aeronautics 271 n.
sport 837 n.
aeroplane aircraft 276 n.
aeroscopy pneumatics 340 n.
weather 340 n.
aerosphere
atmosphere 340 n.
aerostat aeronaut 271 n.
airship 276 n.
aerostatics
aeronautics 271 n.
gaseity 336 n.
aesculap sharp edge 256 n.
Æsculapian medical 658 adj.
Æsop sage 500 n.
eyesore 842 n.
æsthete sensibility 374 n.
man of taste 846 n.
æsthetic sensitive 819 adj.
beautiful 841 adj.
tasteful 846 adj.
æstheticism sensibility 374 n.
moral sensibility 819 n.
beauty 841 n.
æsthetics sensibility 374 n.
beauty 841 n.
good taste 846 n.
æstival summery 128 adj.
æstivate sleep 679 vb.
æthereal
insubstantial 4 adj.
ætiology causation 156 n.
afar afar 199 adv.
affability sociability 882 n.
affable sociable 882 adj.
amiable 884 adj.
affair eventuality 154 n.
topic 452 n.
badness 645 n.
fight 716 n.
affairs affairs 154 n.
pursuit 619 n.
business 622 n.
deed 676 n.

affect be related 9 vb.
modify 143 vb.
influence 178 vb.
tend 179 vb.
show 522 vb.
dissemble 541 vb.
be important 638 vb.
behave 688 vb.
excite 821 vb.
impress 821 vb.
be affected 850 vb.
desire 859 vb.
love 887 vb.
affectation imitation 20 n.
mimicry 20 n.
underestimation 483 n.
sciolism 491 n.
foolery 497 n.
magniloquence 574 n.
inelegance 576 n.
speech defect 580 n.
fashion 848 n.
affectation 850 n.
prudery 950 n.
false piety 980 n.
affected hypocritical 541 adj.
diseased 651 adj.
vain 873 adj.
(see affect, affectation)
affectibility sensibility 374 n.
moral sensibility 819 n.
affection
moral sensibility 819 n.
love 887 n.
approbation 923 n.
piety 979 n.
affectionate loving 887 adj.
caressing 889 adj.
benevolent 897 adj.
affections temperament 5 n.
influence 178 n.
affections 817 n.
affectivity feeling 818 n.
affiance promise 764 n.
marry 894 vb.
affianced promised 764 adj.
marriageable 894 adj.
loved one 887 n.
affiche exhibit 522 n.
advertisement 528 n.
affidavit testimony 466 n.
oath 532 n.
litigation 959 n.
affiliate be akin 11 vb.
society 708 n.
affiliation relation 9 n.
consanguinity 11 n.
association 706 n.
participation 775 n.
affinity relation 9 n.
consanguinity 11 n.

similarity 18 n.
tendency 179 n.
attraction 291 n.
liking 859 n.
spouse 894 n.
affinity, have an
  combine 50 vb.
affirm *believe* 485 vb.
  opine 485 vb.
  suppose 512 vb.
  mean 514 vb.
  affirm 532 vb.
  speak 579 vb.
  plead 614 vb.
  decree 737 vb.
  promise 764 vb.
affirmation *testimony* 466 n.
  assent 488 n.
  affirmation 532 n.
  promise 764 n.
affirmative *positive* 473 adj.
  meaningful 514 adj.
  forceful 571 adj.
affix *add* 38 vb.
  adjunct 40 n.
  affix 45 vb.
  agglutinate 48 vb.
  sequel 67 n.
  spoken letter 558 n.
  word 559 n.
  part of speech 564 n.
afflatus *wind* 352 n.
  imagination 513 n.
  poetry 593 n.
  excitation 821 n.
  revelation 975 n.
afflict *hurt* 827 vb.
  punish 963 vb.
affliction *evil* 616 n.
  illness 651 n.
  bane 659 n.
affluence *plenty* 635 n.
  superfluity 637 n.
  prosperity 730 n.
  wealth 800 n.
affluent *approaching* 289 adj.
  stream 350 adj.
  flowing 350 adj.
  (*see* affluence)
afflux *approach* 289 n.
afford *provide* 633 vb.
  have enough 635 vb.
  give 781 vb.
  afford 800 vb.
affordable *cheap* 812 adj.
afforest *vegetate* 366 vb.
afforestation *forestry* 366 n.
  agriculture 370 n.
affray *turmoil* 61 n.
  fight 716 n.
affright *fear* 854 n.

frighten 854 vb.
affront *annoyance* 827 n.
  hurt 827 vb.
  be courageous 855 vb.
  sauciness 878 n.
  resentment 891 n.
  huff 891 vb.
  scurrility 899 n.
  indignity 921 n.
  not respect 921 vb.
affuse *moisten* 341 vb.
aficionado *patron* 707 n.
afire *fiery* 379 adj.
aflame *luminous* 417 adj.
aflame with
  impressed 818 adj.
afloat *existing* 1 adj.
  happening 154 adj.
  seafaring 269 adj.
  afloat 275 adv.
  at sea 343 adv.
  rumoured 529 adj.
afore *before* 119 adv.
aforesaid *preceding* 64 adj.
  repeated 106 adj.
  prior 119 adj.
  foregoing 125 adj.
aforethought
  predetermined 608 adj.
  intended 617 adj.
aforetime
  before 119 adv.
  formerly 125 adv.
a fortiori
  eminently 34 adv.
  reasonably 475 adv.
afraid *fearing* 854 adj.
afresh *again* 106 adv.
  newly 126 adv.
afrit *demon* 970 n.
aft *rearward* 238 adv.
after *after* 65 adv.
  subsequently 120 adv.
  back 238 adv.
  rearward 238 adv.
  behind 284 adv.
  pursuant to 619 adv.
after, be *pursue* 619 vb.
afterbirth *sequel* 67 n.
  obstetrics 164 n.
after-care *therapy* 658 n.
afterclap *sequel* 67 n.
  inexpectation 508 n.
aftercomer *aftercomer* 67 n.
  substitute 150 n.
after-course *sequel* 67 n.
aftercrop *sequel* 67 n.
after-damp *gas* 336 n.
  poison 569 n.
after-dinner
  subsequent 120 adj.

reposeful 683 adj.
  sociable 882 adj.
after-effect *sequel* 67 n.
  effect 157 n.
afterglow *remainder* 41 n.
  sequel 67 n.
  glow 417 n.
aftergrowth *sequel* 67 n.
  abundance 171 n.
afterlife *sequel* 67 n.
  future state 124 n.
  Heaven 971 n.
aftermath *sequel* 67 n.
  posteriority 120 n.
  effect 157 n.
  abundance 171 n.
  earnings 771 n.
aftermost *rearward* 238 adv.
afternoon *evening* 129 n.
  vespertine 129 adj.
afterpain *sequel* 67 n.
afterpart *sequel* 67 n.
  rear 238 n.
  poop 238 n.
afterpiece *sequel* 67 n.
  stage play 594 n.
after-taste *sequel* 67 n.
  taste 386 n.
afterthought *sequel* 67 n.
  lateness 136 n.
  thought 449 n.
  remembrance 505 n.
  tergiversation 603 n.
afterwards *after* 65 adv.
  subsequently 120 adv.
afterworld *destiny* 155 n.
again *again* 106 adv.
again and again
  repeatedly 106 adv.
  often 139 adv.
against *although* 182 adv.
  against 240 adv.
  opposing 704 adj.
  in opposition 704 adv.
against the grain
  with difficulty 700 adv.
  in opposition 704 adv.
agamist *celibate* 895 n.
agape *open* 263 adj.
  expectant 507 adj.
  wondering 864 adj.
Agape
  social gathering 882 n.
  public worship 981 n.
agapism *love* 887 n.
agaric *medicine* 658 n.
  cathartic 658 n.
agate *type size* 587 n.
  gem 844 n.
age *date* 108 n.
  pass time 108 vb.

era 110 n.
diuturnity 113 n.
chronology 117 n.
oldness 127 n.
grow old 131 vb.
weakness 163 n.
dilapidation 655 n.
deteriorate 655 vb.
ugliness 842 n.
aged *aged* 131 adj.
age, full *adultness* 134 n.
age-group *group* 74 n.
classification 77 n.
contemporary 123 n.
agelast *moper* 834 n.
ageless *perpetual* 115 adj.
young 130 adj.
agelong *lasting* 113 adj.
perpetual 115 adj.
agency *agency* 173 n.
instrumentality 628 n.
action 676 n.
management 689 n.
commission 751 n.
agenda *affairs* 154 n.
topic 452 n.
predetermination 608 n.
business 622 n.
policy 623 n.
agent *inferior* 35 n.
substitute 150 n.
cause 156 n.
producer 167 n.
intermediary 231 n.
instrument 628 n.
doer 676 n.
agent 686 n.
manager 690 n.
mediator 720 n.
consignee 754 n.
deputy 755 n.
agential
instrumental 628 adj.
commissioned 751 adj.
deputizing 755 adj.
agent provocateur
ambush 527 n.
trickster 545 n.
motivator 612 n.
excitant 821 n.
agentship *commission* 751 n.
age, of *grown up* 134 adj.
marriageable 894 adj.
age-old *immemorial* 127 adj.
worshipful 866 adj.
agglomerate *coherence* 48 n.
cohere 48 vb.
agglomeration
coherence 48 n.
accumulation 74 n.
agglutinate

join, affix 45 vb.
agglutinate 48 vb.
retain 778 vb.
agglutinative
linguistic 557 adj.
aggrandize *augment* 36 vb.
enlarge 197 vb.
dignify 866 vb.
aggrandizement
greatness 32 n.
aggravate *augment* 36 vb.
make violent 176 vb.
exaggerate 546 vb.
impair 655 vb.
be difficult 700 vb.
miscarry 728 vb.
hurt 827 vb.
aggravate 832 vb.
enrage 891 vb.
aggregate *all* 52 n.
bring together 74 vb.
numerical result 85 n.
number 86 vb.
aggregation
combination 50 n.
accumulation 74 n.
aggression *attack* 712 n.
aggressive *vigorous* 174 adj.
violent 176 adj.
active 678 adj.
quarrelling 709 adj.
attacking 712 adj.
contending 716 adj.
warlike 718 adj.
courageous 855 adj.
aggressiveness *vitality* 162 n.
bellicosity 718 n.
manliness 855 n.
aggressor *quarreller* 709 n.
attacker 712 n.
combatant 722 n.
aggrieve *ill-treat* 645 vb.
displease 827 vb.
aghast *fearing* 854 adj.
agile *speedy* 277 adj.
agio *discount* 810 n.
agiotage *barter* 791 n.
agitate *derange* 63 vb.
jumble 63 vb.
move 265 vb.
agitate 318 vb.
cause feeling 374 vb.
distract 456 vb.
enquire 459 vb.
be active 678 vb.
revolt 738 vb.
cause discontent 829 vb.
frighten 854 vb.
agitated *fitful* 142 adj.
unstable 152 adj.
agitation

derangement 63 n.
changeableness 152 n.
stimulation 174 n.
motion 265 n.
agitation 318 n.
activity 678 n.
restlessness 678 n.
haste 680 n.
revolt, sedition 738 n.
feeling 818 n.
exhaustion 821 n.
worry 825 n.
discontent 829 n.
fear 854 n.
agitator *dissentient* 489 n.
motivator 612 n.
reformer 654 n.
trouble-maker 663 n.
leader 690 n.
opponent 705 n.
agitator 738 n.
excitant 821 n.
malcontent 829 n.
aglow *fiery* 379 adj.
luminous 417 adj.
agnate *kinsman* 11 n.
akin 11 adj.
agnomen *name* 561 n.
agnostic *doubting* 474 adj.
unbeliever 486 n.
dissenting 489 adj.
irreligionist 974 n.
irreligious 974 adj.
agnosticism
philosophy 449 n.
ago *not now* 122 adv.
formerly 125 adv.
agog *inquisitive* 453 adj.
expectant 507 adj.
desiring 859 adj.
excited 821 adj.
agonism *athletics* 162 n.
contention 716 n.
sport 837 n.
agonize *feel pain* 377 vb.
ill-treat 645 vb.
suffer 825 vb.
agony *pain* 377 n.
excitable state 822 n.
suffering 825 n.
agony column
advertisement 528 n.
agora *focus* 76 n.
mart 796 n.
agoraphobia
psychopathy 503 n.
phobia 854 n.
agrarian *agrarian* 370 adj.
agree *resemble* 18 vb.
accord 24 vb.
conform 83 vb.

concur 181 vb.
believe 485 vb.
assent 488 vb.
be willing 597 vb.
concord 710 vb.
consent 758 vb.
contract 765 vb.
agreeable *agreeing* 24 adj.
conformable 83 adj.
pleasant 376 adj.
willing 597 adj.
concordant 710 adj.
palmy 730 adj.
consenting 758 adj.
pleasurable 826 adj.
personable 841 adj.
agreement *relevance* 9 n.
uniformity 16 n.
symmetry 245 n.
(*see* agree)
agrestic *agrarian* 370 adj.
agriculture
agriculture 370 n.
maturation 669 n.
agronomics
agriculture 370 n.
aground
in difficulties 700 adj.
ague *spasm* 318 n.
malaria 651 n.
aguish *a-cold* 380 adj.
diseased 651 adj.
infectious 653 adj.
ahead *superior* 34 adj.
future 124 adj.
beyond 199 adv.
in front 237 adv.
ahead 283 adv.
forward 285 adv.
ahimsa *peace* 717 n.
benevolence 897 n.
aid *support* 218 n., vb.
instrumentality 628 n.
utility 640 n.
be useful 640 vb.
remedy 658 vb.
facility 701 n.
facilitate 701 vb.
aid 703 n., vb.
tax 809 n.
be benevolent 897 vb.
aid and abet *incite* 612 vb.
aide-de-camp
auxiliary 707 n.
army officer 741 n.
aide-mémoire
reminder 505 n.
aider *aider* 703 n.
(*see* auxiliary)
aidless *weak* 163 adj.
aid of, in *relative* 9 adj.

in aid of 703 adv.
ail *be ill* 651 vb.
aileron *equilibrium* 28 n.
aircraft 276 n.
wing 271 n.
ailment *illness* 651 n.
aim *direction* 281 n.
aim 281 vb.
objective 617 n.
aim at 617 vb.
business 622 n.
essay 671 n., vb.
fire at 712 vb.
desired object 859 n.
aim at *aim at* 617 vb.
pursue 619 vb.
desire 859 vb.
aimless *orderless* 61 adj.
designless 618 adj.
aimlessness
inattention 456 n.
air *insubstantial thing* 4 n.
initiate 68 vb.
transport 272 n.
element 319 n.
levity 323 n.
rarity 325 n.
gas 336 n.
air 340 n.
aerify 340 vb.
dry 342 vb.
tune 412 n.
mien 445 n.
enquire 459 vb.
divulge 526 vb.
salubrity 652 n.
refresh 685 vb.
conduct 688 n.
air-borne *high* 209 adj.
flying 271 adj.
ascending 308 adj.
air-condition
refrigerate 382 vb.
air-conditioner
air 340 n.
ventilation 352 n.
thermometry 379 n.
refrigerator 384 n.
aircraft *aircraft* 276 n.
aircraftman *aeronaut* 271 n.
soldiery 722 n.
air force 722 n.
aircrew *aeronaut* 271 n.
air force 722 n.
air-current *wind* 352 n.
air-duct *air-pipe* 353 n.
airfield *air travel* 271 n.
arena 724 n.
air force *air force* 722 n.
air-gun *toy gun* 723 n.
plaything 837 n.

air-hole *orifice* 263 n.
air-pipe 353 n.
air-hostess *aeronaut* 271 n.
airiness *rarity* 325 n.
airing *land travel* 267 n.
air 340 n.
dryness 342 n.
ventilation 352 n.
enquiry 459 n.
cleansing 648 n.
air, in the
reportedly 524 adv.
airlane *air travel* 271 n.
route 624 n.
airless *tranquil* 266 adj.
insalubrious 653 adj.
air-lift *air travel* 271 n.
transport 272 n.
airline *straightness* 249 n.
air travel 271 n.
direction 281 n.
airmail *mails* 531 n.
correspond 588 vb.
airman *aeronaut* 271 n.
air-pipe *air-pipe* 353 n.
air-pocket *emptiness* 190 n.
air 340 n.
wind 352 n.
airport *air travel* 271 n.
goal 295 n.
air-proof *sealed off* 264 adj.
air-raid *attack* 712 n.
air-raid shelter
refuge 662 n.
defences, fort 713 n.
airs *affectation* 850 n.
airs 873 n.
airscrew *rotator* 315 n.
airship *airship* 276 n.
air-sick *flying* 271 adj.
vomiting 300 adj.
air space *air travel* 271 n.
territory 184 n.
air-stream *wind* 352 n.
airstrip *air travel* 271 n.
air-terminal *goal* 295 n.
stopping place 145 n.
air-tight *sealed off* 264 adj.
air travel *air travel* 271 n.
airworthy *flying* 271 adj.
transferable 272 adj.
aviational 276 adj.
invulnerable 660 adj.
airy *insubstantial* 4 adj.
light 323 adj.
airy 340 adj.
windy 352 adj.
light-minded 456 adj.
trivial 639 adj.
salubrious 652 adj.
rash 857 adj.

impertinent 878 adj.
discourteous 884 adj.
disrespectful 921 adj.
aisle *open space* 263 n.
path 624 n.
church interior 990 n.
ajar *open* 263 adj.
ajutage (*see* adjutage)
akimbo *angular* 247 adj.
akin *akin* 11 adj.
similar 18 adj.
alabaster *white thing* 427 n.
à la carte
optionally 605 adv.
alacrity *willingness* 597 n.
activity 678 n.
cheerfulness 833 n.
Aladdin's lamp
instrument 628 n.
aid 703 n.
magic instrument 983 n.
à la mode *modern* 126 adj.
fashionable 848 adj.
alar *flying* 271 adj.
alarm *loudness* 400 n.
signal 547 n.
warning 664 n.
danger signal 665 n.
raise the alarm 665 vb.
fear 854 n.
frighten 854 vb.
alarmism
intimidation 854 n.
alarmist *false alarm* 665 n.
alarmist 854 n.
coward 856 n.
alarum *timekeeper* 117 n.
loudness 400 n.
megaphone 400 n.
signal 547 n.
danger signal 665 n.
alb *vestments* 989 n.
albedo *light* 417 n.
reflection 417 n.
albert *jewellery* 844 n.
albescence *whiteness* 427 n.
Albigensian
heretic 977 n.
heretical 977 adj.
albinism
achromatism 426 n.
whiteness 427 n.
skin disease 651 n.
blemish 845 n.
albino *achromatism* 426 n.
colourless 426 adj.
white thing 427 n.
album *reminder* 505 n.
record 548 n.
reference book 589 n.
anthology 592 n.

albumen
semiliquidity 354 n.
organism 358 n.
alchemist *alterer* 143 n.
sorcerer 983 n.
occultist 984 n.
occultism 984 n.
alchemy *conversion* 147 n.
alcohol *stimulant* 174 n.
liquor 301 n.
alcoholic *strong* 162 adj.
sick person 651 n.
drunkard 949 n.
drunken 949 adj.
intoxicating 949 adj.
Alcoran
non-Biblical scripture
975 n.
alcove *arbour* 194 n.
cavity 255 n.
alderman *official* 690 n.
councillor 692 n.
officer 741 n.
aldermanship
magistrature 733 n.
ale *liquor* 301 n.
aleatory *speculative* 618 adj.
dangerous 661 adj.
alee *sideways* 239 adv.
alehouse *tavern* 192 n.
alembic *crucible* 147 n.
vessel 194 n.
heater 383 n.
alert *attentive* 455 adj.
vigilant 457 adj.
signal 547 vb.
danger signal 665 n.
raise the alarm 665 vb.
prepared 669 adj.
active 678 adj.
lively 819 adj.
Alexandrine *prosody* 593 n.
alexipharmic
remedial 658 adj.
alfresco *externally* 223 adv.
alfresco 340 adv.
algae *plant* 366 n.
algebra *mathematics* 86 n.
algology *botany* 368 n.
algor *coldness* 380 n.
algorism *number* 85 n.
alias *named* 561 adj.
misnomer 562 n.
alibi *absence* 190 n.
pretext 614 n.
vindication 927 n.
alidad *gauge* 465 n.
alien *irrelative* 10 adj.
foreigner 59 n.
extraneous 59 adj.
unconformable 84 adj.

settler 191 n.
outcaste 883 n.
alienable
transferred 780 adj.
alienate *set apart* 46 vb.
not retain 779 vb.
convey 780 vb.
sell 793 n.
make enemies 881 vb.
excite hate 888 vb.
alienation *insanity* 503 n.
non-retention 779 n.
transfer 780 n.
sale 793 n.
enmity 881 n.
hatred 888 n.
alienism
extraneousness 59 n.
insanity 503 n.
alienist *psychologist* 447 n.
insanity 503 n.
doctor 658 n.
alienization
conversion 147 n.
loss of right 916 n.
aliform *lateral* 239 adj.
alight *place oneself* 187 vb.
come to rest 266 vb.
land 295 vb.
descend 309 vb.
sit down 311 vb.
fiery 379 adj.
align *make uniform* 16 vb.
adjust 24 vb.
arrange 62 vb.
flatten 216 vb.
print 587 vb.
alignment *direction* 281 n.
friendship 880 n.
align oneself
join a party 708 vb.
alike *similar* 18 adj.
aliment *food* 301 n.
alimentary
nourishing 301 adj.
remedial 658 adj.
alimony *dower* 777 n.
receipt 807 n.
divorce 896 n.
aliquant, aliquot
numerical element 85 n.
part 53 n.
alive *alive* 360 adj.
sentient 374 adj.
intelligent 498 adj.
alive to *attentive* 455 adj.
knowing 490 adj.
impressible 819 adj.
alive with
multitudinous 104 adj.
alkahest *liquefaction* 337 n.

all *all* 52n.
  completeness 54n.
  everyman 79n.
  universal 79adj.
all along *while* 108adv.
  all along 113adv.
all and sundry
  everyman 79n.
all attention
  attentive 455adj.
allay *assuage* 177vb.
  pacify 719vb.
all but *almost* 33adv.
  wholly 52adv.
all clear *safety* 660n.
  permit 756n.
all comers *contender* 716n.
all costs, at
  resolutely 599adv.
all ears *auditory* 415adj.
  inquisitive 453adj.
  attentive 455adj.
all edges
  unconformable 84adj.
allegation *testimony* 466n.
  affirmation 532n.
  pretext 614n.
  accusation 928n.
allegiance *loyalty* 739n.
  subjection 745n.
  duty 917n.
allegory *comparison* 462n.
  metaphor 519n.
  latency 523n.
  narrative 590n.
allegro *adagio* 412adv.
allelomorph *heredity* 5n.
all-embracing
  extensive 32adj.
  comprehensive 52adj.
  inclusive 78adj.
  general 79adj.
allergy *dislike* 861n.
  sensibility 374n.
  ill-health 651n.
  moral sensibility 819n.
  hatred 888n.
alleviate *assuage* 177vb.
  disencumber 701vb.
  relieve 831vb.
alley *street* 192n.
  sphere 252n.
  open space 263n.
  road 624n.
all eyes *attentive* 455adj.
  vigilant 457adj.
all found
  provisionary 633adj.
all fours, on
  identically 13adv.
  agreeing 24adj.

alliance *relation* 9n.
  consanguinity 11n.
  junction 45n.
  combination 50n.
  concurrence 181n.
  association 706n.
  society 708n.
  compact 765n.
  marriage 894n.
allied *corporate* 708adj.
  concordant 710adj.
alligator *skin* 226n.
  reptile 365n.
all in *fatigued* 684adj.
all in all
  on an average 30adv.
  wholly 52adv.
alliteration
  assimilation 18n.
  repetition 106n.
  ornament 574n.
  prosody 593n.
all manner of
  different 15adj.
  multiform 82adj.
allocate *arrange* 62vb.
  apportion 783vb.
allocution *speech* 579n.
  allocution 583n.
allodial
  unconditional 744adj.
  proprietary 777adj.
allodium *territory* 184n.
  lands 777n.
all of *completely* 54adv.
all of a piece *uniform* 16adj.
all off *ending* 69adj.
allogamy *mixture* 43n.
all one *equivalent* 28adj.
all, one's *property* 777n.
allonym *misteaching* 535n.
  misnomer 562n.
allopath *doctor* 658n.
allopathy *medical art* 658n.
allophone
  speech sound 398n.
allot *quantify* 26vb.
  arrange 62vb.
  dispose of 673vb.
  dower 777vb.
  apportion 783vb.
  grant claims 915vb.
allotment *farm* 370n.
allottee *recipient* 782n.
  (*see* allot)
all out *completely* 54adv.
  swiftly 277adv.
allow *make possible* 469vb.
  be reasonable 475vb.
  believe 485vb.
  assent, acquiesce 488vb.

  confess 526vb.
  facilitate 701vb.
  be lenient 736vb.
  permit 756vb.
  consent 758vb.
  be patient 823vb.
allowable *possible* 469adj.
  permitted 756adj.
  given 781adj.
  vindicable 727adj.
  legal 953adj.
allowance *offset* 31n.
  decrement 42n.
  qualification 468n.
  subvention 703n.
  lenity 736n.
  permission 756n.
  consent 758n.
  earnings 771n.
  dower 777n.
  gift 781n.
  portion 783n.
  receipt 807n.
  discount 810n.
  reward 962n.
allow for *set off* 31vb.
alloy *a mixture* 43n.
  mix 43vb.
  compound 50n.
  impairment 655n.
all-purpose *useful* 640adj.
all quarters, in
  widely 183adv.
all right *not bad* 644adj.
all-round
  multiform 82adj.
all-rounder *athlete* 162n.
  proficient 696n.
  player 837n.
all sorts
  non-uniform 17adj.
  medley 43n.
  everyman 79n.
allspice *condiment* 389n.
all-star *dramatic* 594adj.
  excellent 644adj.
all the same
  nevertheless 468adv.
all thumbs *clumsy* 695adj.
all told *completely* 54adv.
allude *relate* 9vb.
  propound 512vb.
  mean 514vb.
  figure 519vb.
  imply 523vb.
  hint 524vb.
allure *influence* 178vb.
  attraction 291n.
  attract 291vb.
  tempt 612vb.
  delight 826vb.

cause desire 859 vb.
excite love 887 vb.
allusion *referral* 9 n.
metaphor 519 n.
allusive *relevant* 9 adj.
suppositional 512 adj.
meaningful 514 adj.
figurative 519 adj.
tacit 523 adj.
imperspicuous 568 adj.
alluvial *flat* 216 adj.
territorial 344 adj.
alluvium *leavings* 41 n.
thing transferred 272 n.
soil 344 n.
all work, of *useful* 640 adj.
ally *join* 45 vb.
combine 50 vb.
aider 703 n.
co-operate 706 vb.
colleague 707 n.
join a party 708 vb.
contract 765 vb.
friend 880 n.
almagest *dissertation* 591 n.
almanac *directory* 87 n.
chronology 117 n.
almighty *powerful* 160 adj.
godlike 965
Almighty, the
the Deity 965 n.
almond *fruit* 301 n.
almoner *giver* 781 n.
treasurer 798 n.
almonry *treasury* 799 n.
almost *almost* 33 adv.
nearly 200 adv.
imperfectly 647 adv.
almost all *main part* 52 n.
alms *gift* 781 n.
kind act 897 n.
almshouse *retreat* 192 n.
shelter 662 n.
aloft *aloft* 209 adv.
aloha *valediction* 296 n.
arrival 295 n.
alone *separate* 46 adj.
alone 88 adj.
unsociable 883 adj.
friendless 883 adj.
along *longwise* 203 adv.
alongside *nigh* 200 adv.
in parallel 219 adv.
sideways 239 adv.
along with
in addition 38 adv.
with 89 adv.
synchronously 123 adv.
aloof
non-adhesive 49 adj.
distant 199 adj.

incurious 454 adj.
impassive 820 adj.
unsociable 883 adj.
alopecia *bareness* 229 n.
aloud *loudly* 400 adv.
vocal 577 adj.
Alp *high land* 209 n.
alpaca *fibre* 208 n.
textile 222 n.
alpana *pattern* 844 n.
alpenglow *morning* 128 n.
evening 129 n.
alpenstock *supporter* 218 n.
alpestrine *alpine* 209 adj.
alpha *beginning* 68 n.
Alpha and Omega *all* 52 n.
alphabet *beginning* 68 n.
letter 558 n.
alphabetarian
beginner 538 n.
alphabeticize *class* 62 vb.
alphabetize *spell* 558 vb.
alpha particle *element* 319 n.
alpha plus
excellent 644 adj.
alpine *alpine* 209 adj.
Alpinism *ascent* 308 n.
sport 837 n.
alpinist *traveller* 268 n.
climber 308 n.
already *before* 119 adv.
at present 121 adv.
retrospectively 125 adv.
Alsatia *thievishness* 788 n.
thief 789 n.
also *in addition* 38 adv.
also-ran *inferior* 35 n.
loser 728 n.
altar *stand* 218 n.
ritual object 988 n.
altar 990 n.
altar-boy
church officer 986 n.
altarless *irreligious* 974 adj.
alter *change* 143 vb.
qualify 468 vb.
alterable *unstable* 152 adj.
changeful 152 adj.
alterant *alterer* 143 n.
alteration *difference* 15 n.
change 143 n.
altercate *bicker* 709 vb.
alter course *deviate* 282 vb.
alter ego *identity* 13 n.
analogue 18 n.
colleague 707 n.
deputy 755 n.
close friend 880 n.
alternate *correlative* 12 adj.
correlate 12 vb.
sequent 65 adj.

come after 65 vb.
discontinuous 72 adj.
periodical 141 adj.
be periodic 141 vb.
substitute 150 n.
vary 152 vb.
fluctuate 317 vb.
deputy 755 n.
alternating current
periodicity 141 n.
electricity 160 n.
alternative *substitute* 150 n.
choice 605 n.
means 629 n.
contrivance 623 n.
alternatively
instead 150 adv.
alter the case
tell against 467 vb.
qualify 468 vb.
although *although* 182 adv.
altimeter *altimetry* 209 n.
angular measure 247 n.
meter 465 n.
altimetry *altimetry* 209 n.
angular measure 247 n.
geometry 465 n.
altitude *degree* 27 n.
superiority 34 n.
height 209 n.
alto *vocalist* 413 n.
altogether *wholly* 52 adv.
completely 54 adv.
altogether, the
bareness 229 n.
altruism
philanthropy 901 n.
disinterestedness 931 n.
virtues 933 n.
altruist *kind person* 897 n.
altruistic
disinterested 931 adj.
alum *sourness* 393 n.
alumnus *learner* 538 n.
alveolar, alveolate
concave 255 adj.
alveus *cavity* 255 n.
conduit 351 n.
always *generally* 79 adv.
while 108 adv.
amadou *lighter* 385 n.
amain *violently* 176 adv.
Amalekite *enemy* 881 n.
amalgam *a mixture* 43 n.
compound 50 n.
amalgamate *combine* 50 vb.
amalgamation
association 706 n.
amanuensis *recorder* 549 n.
amaranthine
perpetual 115 adj.

amass
  bring together 74 vb.
  store 632 vb.
amateur beginner 538 n.
  unskilled 695 adj.
  bungler 697 n.
  man of taste 846 n.
  desirer 859 n.
  layman 987 n.
amateurish ignorant 491 adj.
  unskilled 695 adj.
  laical 987 adj.
amateurship
  good taste 846 n.
amativeness love 887 n.
amatory erotic 887 adj.
amaurosis blindness 439 n.
amaurotic
  dim-sighted 440 adj.
amaze surprise 508 vb.
  disappoint 509 vb.
  impress 821 vb.
  frighten 854 vb.
  be wonderful 864 vb.
amazement
  inexpectation 508 n.
  excitation 821 n.
  wonder 864 n.
amazing prodigious 32 adj.
Amazon athlete 162 n.
  woman 373 n.
  soldier 722 n.
  brave person 855 n.
  spinster 895 n.
amazonian manly 162 adj.
ambages meanderings 251 n.
  pleonasm 570 n.
  circuit 626 n.
ambassador
  messenger 531 n.
  envoy 754 n.
ambassadorial
  deputizing 755 adj.
amber resin 357 n.
  brownness 430 n.
  preserver 666 n.
ambergris resin 357 n.
  scent 396 n.
ambidexterity
  dextrality 241 n.
  skill 694 n.
ambience
  circumjacence 230 n.
  painting 553 n.
ambiguity
  disagreement 25 n.
  uncertainty 474 n.
  connotation 514 n.
  unintelligibility 517 n.
  equivocalness 518 n.
  mental dishonesty 543 n.

imperspicuity 568 n.
ambit outline 233 n.
  circuition 314 n.
  circuit 626 n.
ambition motive 612 n.
  intention 617 n.
  business 622 n.
  aspiration 852 n.
  desire 859 n.
  desired object 859 n.
ambitious essaying 671 adj.
  enterprising 672 adj.
  greedy 859 adj.
ambivalence
  contrariety 14 n.
  disagreement 25 n.
  equivocalness 518 n.
amble gait 265 n.
  pedestrianism 267 n.
  ride 267 vb.
  slowness 278 n.
  move slowly 278 vb.
ambo rostrum 539 n.
  church interior 990 n.
ambrosia food 301 n.
  savouriness 390 n.
ambulance vehicle 274 n.
  hospital 658 n.
ambulance-chaser
  petitioner 763 n.
ambulation
  pedestrianism 267 n.
ambulatory
  travelling 267 adj.
  path 624 n.
  church interior 990 n.
  church exterior 990 n.
ambush surprise 508 vb.
  latency 523 n.
  ambush 527 n., vb.
  trap 542 n.
  danger 661 n.
  pitfall 663 n.
  stratagem 698 n.
  be cunning 698 vb.
ambush, in
  disguised 525 adj.
amelioration
  improvement 654 n.
amen assent 488 n.
amenable liable 180 adj.
  credulous 487 adj.
  willing 597 adj.
  dutied 917 adj.
amend rectify 654 vb.
  repair 656 vb.
  be penitent 939 vb.
amendable restored 656 adj.
amende honorable
  atonement 941 n.
amendment

interpretation 520 n.
amends compensation 31 n.
  restoration 656 n.
  remedy 658 n.
  atonement 941 n.
amenity
  pleasurableness 826 n.
  courtesy 884 n.
amentia insanity 503 n.
amerce punish 963 vb.
amerceable
  punishable 963 adj.
amercement penalty 963 n.
Americanize
  transform 147 vb.
amethyst purple 434 n.
  gem 844 n.
amiable well-bred 848 adj.
amiability
  pleasurableness 826 n.
  courtesy 884 n.
  lovableness 887 n.
  benevolence 897 n.
amicable aiding 703 adj.
  concordant 710 adj.
  friendly 880 adj.
amice vestments 989 n.
amid, amidst
  between 231 adv.
amiss inopportunely 138 adv.
  amiss 616 adv.
  badly 645 adv.
amity concord 710 n.
  friendship 880 n.
ammonia pungency 388 n.
ammonite coil 251 n.
ammunition means 629 n.
  defence 713 n.
  ammunition 723 n.
amnesia oblivion 506 n.
amnesty extinction 2 n.
  amnesty 506 n.
  forget 506 vb.
  obliteration 550 n.
  peace 717 n.
  irenics 719 n.
  be lenient 736 vb.
  forgive 909 vb.
  non-liability 919 n.
  exempt 919 vb.
amoeba animalcule 196 n.
amœbæan sequent 65 adj.
among centrally 225 adv.
  between 231 adv.
amoral
  thick-skinned 820 adj.
  indifferent 860 adj.
  wicked 934 adj.
  irreligious 974 adj.
amoralism no choice 606 n.
  wickedness 934 n.

irreligion 974n.
impiety 980n.
amoralist
  indifference 860n.
amorist *lover* 887n.
  libertine 952n.
amorous *foolish* 499adj.
  loving 887adj.
amorphism
  non-uniformity 17n.
  amorphism 244n.
amorphous
  incomplete 55adj.
  amorphous 244adj.
  fluidal 335adj.
  unsightly 842adj.
amount *quantity* 26n.
  degree 27n.
  funds 797n.
  price 809n.
amount to *number* 86vb.
  cost 809vb.
amour *love affair* 887n.
  illicit love 951n.
amour-propre *vanity* 873n.
amperage *electricity* 160n.
ampere, amp
  electricity 160n.
ampersand *letter* 558n.
amphibian *animal* 365n.
  reptile 365n.
amphibious
  unconformable 84adj.
  double 91adj.
amphibology
  equivocalness 518n.
amphibrach *prosody* 593n.
amphictyony *council* 692n.
amphigory
  absurdity 497n.
  unmeaningness 515n.
amphimacer *prosody* 593n.
amphimixis *mixture* 43n.
amphisbæna *reptile* 365n.
amphitheatre *view* 438n.
  classroom 539n.
  theatre 594n.
  arena 724n.
amphora *vessel* 194n.
ample *great* 32adj.
  many 104adj.
  spacious 183adj.
  large 195adj.
  broad 205adj.
  diffuse 570adj.
  plenteous 635adj.
  palmy 730adj.
  liberal 813adj.
amplifier
  megaphone 400n.
  hearing aid 415n.

amplify *augment* 36vb.
  enlarge 197vb.
  translate 520vb.
  be diffuse 570vb.
amplitude *quantity* 26n.
  degree 27n.
  greatness 32n.
  plenitude 54n.
  range 183n.
  size 195n.
  breadth 205n.
  diffuseness 570n.
  plenty 635n.
ampoule *receptacle* 194n.
ampulla *vessel* 194n.
ampullar, ampullaceous
  expanded 197adj.
amputate *subtract* 39vb.
  cut, sunder 46vb.
  doctor 658vb.
amulet *non-design* 618n.
  preserver 666n.
  jewellery 844n.
  talisman 983n.
amuse *distract* 456vb.
  amuse 837vb.
  be witty 839vb.
amusement
  enjoyment 824n.
  pleasurableness 826n.
  amusement 837n.
amusing *pleasant* 376adj.
  gay 833adj.
  amusing 837adj.
  sociable 882adj.
anabatic *increasing* 36adj.
  ascending 308adj.
anabolism
  transformation 143n.
anachronism
  anachronism 118n.
  different time 122n.
  intempestivity 138n.
  inexactness 495n.
anachronistic
  anachronistic 118adj.
  non-contemporary 122adj.
  antiquated 127adj.
  ill-timed 138adj.
anaclastic
  luminous 417adj.
anaclinal *sloping* 220adj.
anacoluthon
  discontinuity 72n.
anaconda *reptile* 365n.
Anacreontic *poem* 593n.
  gay 833adj.
anadiplosis *repetition* 106n.
  ornament 574n.

anæmia *weakness* 163n.
  achromatism 426n.
  blood disease 651n.
anaerobe *animalcule* 196n.
anæsthesia
  insensibility 375n.
anæsthetic *moderator* 177n.
  anæsthetic 375n.
  insensible 375adj.
  drug 658n.
  remedial 658adj.
  soporific 679n.
  relief 831n.
anæsthetist *doctor* 658n.
anaglyph *sculpture* 554n.
anaglyptic *glyptic* 554adj.
anagoge *metaphor* 519n.
  latency 523n.
anagram
  equivocalness 518n.
  enigma 530n.
  initials 558n.
anal *back* 238adj.
analects *anthology* 592n.
analeptic
  restorative 656adj.
  tonic 658n.
  remedial 658adj.
analgesia
  insensibility 375n.
analgesic *antidote* 658n.
  drug 658n.
  remedial 658adj.
  relieving 831adj.
analogical *similar* 18adj.
  compared 462adj.
analogous
  correlative 12adj.
  symmetrical 245adj.
analogue *identity* 13n.
  analogue 18n.
  copy 22n.
analogy *relativeness* 9n.
  similarity 18n.
  comparison 462n.
analyse *sunder* 46vb.
  decompose 51vb.
  class 62vb.
  enquire 459vb.
  experiment 461vb.
  parse 564vb.
analysis
  numerical operation 86n.
  experiment 461n.
  argumentation 475n.
  grammar 564n.
  compendium 592n.
analyst *enquirer* 459n.
  experimenter 461n.
analytic *enquiring* 459adj.
  experimental 461adj.

rational 475 adj.
linguistic 557 adj.
anamorphosis
distortion 246 n.
visual fallacy 440 n.
misrepresentation 552 n.
anapæst *prosody* 593 n.
anaphora *repetition* 106 n.
trope 519 n.
ornament 574 n.
anaplasty *surgery* 658 n.
anarch *anarch* 61 n.
anarchic *disorderly* 61 adj.
anarchic 734 adj.
riotous 738 adj.
disobedient 738 adj.
independent 744 adj.
non-observant 769 adj.
lawless 954 adj.
anarchism *sedition* 738 n.
anarchist
revolutionist 149 n.
destroyer 168 n.
violent creature 176 n.
revolter 738 n.
evildoer 904 n.
anarchy *anarchy* 734 n.
anastomosis *junction* 45 n.
crossing 222 n.
anastrophe *inversion* 221 n.
ornament 574 n.
anathema
malediction 899 n.
anathematize
curse 899 vb.
dispraise 924 vb.
hereticate 977 vb.
perform ritual 988 vb.
anatomic *structural* 331 adj.
anatomist *zoologist* 367 n.
anatomize *sunder* 46 vb.
class 62 vb.
anatomy *thinness* 206 n.
structure 331 n.
biology 358 n.
zoology 367 n.
anatriptic *rubbing* 333 adj.
ancestor *precursor* 66 n.
old man 133 n.
source 156 n.
parent 169 n.
ancestral
immemorial 127 adj.
former 125 adj.
parental 169 adj.
ancestry *heredity* 5 n.
consanguinity 11 n.
origin 68 n.
source 156 n.
genealogy 169 n.
nobility 868 n.

anchor *affix* 45 vb.
coupling 47 n.
place oneself 187 vb.
dwell 192 vb.
come to rest 266 vb.
navigate 269 vb.
protection 660 n.
safeguard 662 n.
badge of rank 743 n.
hope 852 n.
anchorage *station* 187 n.
goal 295 n.
shelter 662 n.
anchoretic *ascetic* 945 adj.
unsociable 883 adj.
anchorite *solitary* 883 n.
ascetic 945 n.
pietist 979 n.
ancien régime
preterition 125 n.
archaism 127 n.
aristocracy 868 n.
ancient *past* 125 adj.
former 125 adj.
olden 127 adj.
worshipful 866 adj.
ancient history
antiquity 125 n.
ancients, the *antiquity* 125 n.
ancillary *aiding* 703 adj.
and, and also
in addition 38 adv.
andante *slowness* 278 n.
slow 278 adj.
tempo 410 n.
adagio 412 adv.
and co. *no name* 562 n.
andirons *furnace* 383 n.
androcentric *male* 372 adj.
androgenous
abnormal 84 adj.
androgyn
nonconformist 84 n.
androgynous
female 373 adj.
androgyny
abnormality 84 n.
female 373 n.
androlepsy *taking* 786 n.
stealing 788 n.
andromania
abnormality 84 n.
and so *thus* 8 adv.
consequently 157 adv.
and then some
completely 54 adv.
anecdotage *loquacity* 581 n.
anecdotal, anecdotic
remembering 505 adj.
anecdote *narrative* 590 n.
anele *perform ritual* 988 vb.

anemography
anemology 352 n.
anemology
pneumatics 340 n.
anemology 352 n.
anemometer
anemology 352 n.
meter 465 n.
recording instrument 549 n.
anemometry
pneumatics 340 n.
aneroid barometer
pneumatics 340 n.
aneurysm
blood pressure 651 n.
anew *again* 106 adv.
newly 126 adv.
anfractuosity
convolution 251 n.
angary
expropriation 786 n.
angel *stage manager* 594 n.
lender 784 n.
coinage 797 n.
a beauty 841 n.
darling 890 n.
angel 968 n.
mythical being 970 n.
angelic *virtuous* 933 adj.
lovable 887 adj.
angelic 968 adj.
angelus *signal* 547 n.
anger *excitation* 821 n.
anger 891 n.
enrage 891 vb.
disapprobation 924 n.
vice 934 n.
angina *pang* 377 n.
angiography
structure 331 n.
angiology *structure* 331 n.
angle *joint* 45 n.
angle 247 n.
angulate 247 vb.
bias 481 n.
opinion 485 n.
hunt 619 vb.
take 786 vb.
Anglican *Anglican* 976 adj.
Protestant 976 n.
Catholic 976 n.
sectarian 978 adj.
Anglicanism
Catholicism 976 n.
Protestantism 976 n.
Anglicism *dialect* 560 n.
Anglicize *transform* 147 vb.
Anglo-Catholic
Catholic 976 n.
Anglican 976 adj.

Anglophile
  xenophile 880 n.
Anglophobe *enemy* 881 n.
Anglophobia *hatred* 888 n.
Angora *fibre* 208 n.
  textile 222 n.
angry *angry* 891 adj.
angry young man
  nonconformist 84 n.
  malcontent 829 n.
angst *suffering* 825 n.
  melancholy 834 n.
anguilliform *fibrous* 208 adj.
  labyrinthine 251 adj.
anguish *pain* 377 n.
  badness 645 n.
  suffering 825 n.
angular *angular* 247 adj.
angularity
  unconformity 84 n.
  obliquity 220 n.
  angularity 247 n.
angular measure
  angular measure 247 n.
angustation
  narrowing 206 n.
anhelous *panting* 684 adj.
anhydrous *dry* 342 n.
anile *aged* 131 adj.
  foolish 499 adj.
aniline dye *pigment* 425 n.
anility *age* 131 n.
  folly 499 n.
animadversion
  reprimand 924 n.
animadvert *think* 449 vb.
  notice 455 vb.
  reprove 924 vb.
animal *inferior* 35 n.
  animal 365 n., adj.
  mindless 448 adj.
  unthinking 450 adj.
  intemperate 943 adj.
  sensualist 944 n.
animal and vegetable king-
    dom
  organism 358 n.
animalcular *animal* 365 adj.
animalcule
  small animal 33 n.
  animalcule 196 n.
animalism *animality* 365 n.
  sensualism 944 n.
animality *life* 360 n.
  animality 365 n.
  non-intellect 448 n.
animal management
  animal husbandry 369 n.
animal spirits *vitality* 162 n.
  life 360 n.
  animality 365 n.

cheerfulness 833 n.
animate *strengthen* 162 vb.
  invigorate 174 vb.
  incite 612 vb.
  animate 821 vb.
  cheer 833 vb.
  give courage 855 vb.
animated cartoon
  cinema 445 n.
animation *life* 360 n.
  animality 365 n.
  restlessness 678 n.
  excitation 821 n.
  cheerfulness 833 n.
  courage 855 n.
animator *director* 690 n.
animism
  immateriality 320 n.
  deism 973 n.
animist
  immateriality 320 n.
  religionist 973 adj.
animosity *dislike* 861 n.
  enmity 881 n.
  hatred 888 n.
  resentment 891 n.
animus *willingness* 597 n.
  intention 617 n.
  affections 817 n.
  feeling 818 n.
ankle *joint* 45 n.
  angularity 247 n.
anklet *jewellery* 844 n.
ankus *sharp point* 256 n.
  incentive 612 n.
anna *small coin* 33 n.
  coinage 797 n.
annalist *chronologist* 117 n.
  chronicler 549 n.
  narrator 590 n.
annals *chronology* 117 n.
  record 548 n.
  narrative 590 n.
anneal *mature* 669 vb.
  be tough 329 vb.
annelid *reptile* 365 n.
annex *add* 38 vb.
  connect 45 vb.
  require 771 vb.
  appropriate 786 vb.
  steal 788 vb.
annexe *adjunct* 40 n.
annexure *adjunct* 40 n.
  joinder 45 n.
annihilate *nullify* 2 vb.
  destroy 165 vb.
  slaughter 362 vb.
anniversary *date* 108 n.
  anniversary 141 n.
  seasonal 141 adj.
  special day 876 n.

celebrative 876 adj.
  holy-day 988 n.
anno domini
  anno domini 108 adv.
  anciently 127 adv.
annotate *interpret* 520 vb.
  mark 547 vb.
annotation
  commentary 520 n.
  record 548 n.
annotator *interpreter* 520 n.
announce *happen* 154 vb.
  predict 511 vb.
  communicate 524 vb.
  proclaim 528 vb.
  name 561 vb.
announcer *precursor* 66 n.
  informant 524 n.
  publicizer 528 n.
  messenger 531 n.
  nomenclator 561 n.
annoy *give pain* 377 vb.
  meddle 678 vb.
  hinder 702 vb.
  oppress 735 vb.
  torment 827 vb.
  sadden 834 vb.
  enrage 891 vb.
  be malevolent 898 vb.
annoyance *bane* 659 n.
  worry 825 n.
  annoyance 827 n.
  resentment 891 n.
annual *periodic* 110 adj.
  seasonal 141 adj.
  flower 366 n.
  journal 528 n.
annuitant *recipient* 782 n.
annuity *pay* 804 n.
  receipt 807 n.
annul *destroy* 165 vb.
  relinquish 621 vb.
  abrogate 752 vb.
  divorce 896 vb.
  make illegal 954 vb.
annular *round* 250 adj.
annularity *circularity* 250 n.
annulment
  obliteration 550 n.
  relinquishment 621 n.
  abrogation 752 n.
  divorce 896 n.
annulus *circle* 250 n.
annunciate
  communicate 524 vb.
annus mirabilis
  period 110 n.
  prodigy 864 n.
anodyne *moderator* 177 n.
  lenitive 177 adj.
  remedial 658 adj.

relieving 831 adj.
anoint *overlay* 226 vb.
  lubricate 334 vb.
  commission 751 vb.
  perform ritual 988 vb.
anointment
  lubrication 334 n.
  unctuousness 357 n.
anomalous *orderless* 61 adj.
  abnormal 84 adj.
  grammatical 564 adj.
anon *betimes* 135 adv.
anonymity
  unknown thing 490 n.
  latency 523 n.
  concealment 525 n.
  no name 562 n.
anonymous
  anonymous 562 adj.
  inglorious 867 adj.
anopheles *fly* 365 n.
anorexy *indifference* 860 n.
anosmia
  inodorousness 395 n.
another *different* 15 adj.
another edition of
  analogue 18 n.
another story *variant* 15 n.
another time
  different time 122 n.
Anschauung *opinion* 485 n.
Anschluss *combination* 50 n.
  association 706 n.
anserine *foolish* 499 adj.
answer *accord* 24 vb.
  numerical result 85 n.
  reason why 156 n.
  answer 460 n., vb.
  counter-evidence 467 n.
  argue 475 vb.
  confutation 479 n.
  confute 479 vb.
  interpretation 520 n.
  converse 584 vb.
  correspondence 588 n.
  contrivance 623 n.
  suffice 635 vb.
  expedience 642 n.
  be expedient 642 vb.
  remedy 658 n.
  retaliate 714 vb.
  be successful 727 vb.
  sauciness 878 n.
answerable *causal* 156 adj.
  liable 180 adj.
  indebted 803 adj.
  dutied 917 adj.
answer back
  interchange 151 vb.
  answer 460 vb.
  argue 475 vb.

retaliate 714 vb.
  be insolent 878 vb.
answer for *be liable* 180 vb.
  deputize 755 vb.
  promise 764 vb.
answer one's name
  be present 189 vb.
answer one's turn
  be useful 640 vb.
answer to *be related* 9 vb.
  correlate 12 vb.
  resemble 18 vb.
  be named 561 vb.
ant *animalcule* 196 n.
  vermin 365 n.
  busy person 678 n.
  worker 686 n.
antagonism
  contrariety 14 n.
  counteraction 182 n.
  opposition 704 n.
  enmity 881 n.
  hatred 888 n.
antagonist *opponent* 705 n.
  enemy 881 n.
antagonize
  counteract 182 vb.
  cause dislike 861 vb.
  make enemies 881 vb.
  excite hate 888 vb.
  huff 891 vb.
antaphrodisiac
  moderator 177 n.
  antidote 658 n.
Antarctic *opposite* 240 adj.
  cold 380 adj.
ante *fore* 64 adv.
  gambling 618 n.
  give 781 vb.
  portion 783 n.
antecedence
  precedence 64 n.
  priority 119 n.
antecedent *precursor* 66 n.
antedate *misdate* 118 vb.
antediluvian *precursor* 66 n.
  primal 127 adj.
  old man 133 n.
antelope *speeder* 277 n.
  deer 365 n.
antemeridian
  matinal 128 adj.
antemetic *antidote* 658 n.
antenna *filament* 208 n.
  projection 254 n.
  feeler 378 n.
  telecommunication 531 n.
antepenultimate
  ending 69 adj.
anteposition
  precedence 64 n.

front 237 n.
anterior *preceding* 64 adj.
  prior 119 adj.
  fore 237 adj.
anteroom *lobby* 194 n.
  front 237 n.
ant-heap *abundance* 171 n.
  nest 192 n.
anthem *vocal music* 412 n.
  hymn 981 n.
  offer worship 981 vb.
ant-hill *nest* 192 n.
anthologize *abstract* 592 vb.
  select 605 vb.
anthology *assemblage* 74 n.
  reading matter 589 n.
  anthology 592 n.
  choice 605 n.
anthracite *coal* 385 n.
anthrax
  animal disease 651 n.
anthropocentric
  human 371 adj.
anthropogenesis
  anthropology 371 n.
anthropography
  anthropology 371 n.
anthropoid *animal* 365 adj.
  human 371 adj.
anthropology
  zoology 367 n.
  anthropology 371 n.
anthropometry
  anthropology 371 n.
anthropomorphic
  idolatrous 982 adj.
anthropomorphize
  idolatrize 982 vb.
anti *contrary* 14 adj.
  opposing 704 adj.
antibiosis *antidote* 658 n.
antibiotic *drug* 658 n.
  antidote 658 n.
antibody *antidote* 658 n.
Antichrist *bad man* 938 n.
  Satan 969 n.
  irreligionist 974 n.
anticipate *misdate* 118 vb.
  do before 119 vb.
  look ahead 124 vb.
  be early 135 vb.
  expect 507 vb.
  foresee 510 vb.
  be willing 597 vb.
  prepare oneself 669 vb.
  be active 678 vb.
  take 786 vb.
  hope 852 vb.
  be rash 857 vb.
anticipation *exclusion* 57 n.
  (*see* anticipate)

anti-clerical
  irreligious 974 adj.
anticlimax *decrease* 37 n.
  absurdity 497 n.
  inexpectation 508 n.
  disappointment 509 n.
  feebleness 572 n.
  failure 728 n.
  ridiculousness 849 n.
anticlinal *sloping* 220 adj.
anticlockwise
  towards 281 adv.
  round and round 315 adv.
  regressive 286 adj.
anticoagulant
  antidote 658 n.
antics *foolery* 497 n.
  bungling 695 n.
anticyclone *weather* 340 n.
antidemocratic
  authoritarian 735 adj.
antidotal
  counteracting 182 adj.
  remedial 658 adj.
antidote *contrariety* 14 n.
  counteraction 182 n.
  antidote 658 n.
anti-freeze *heating* 381 adj.
antigen *antidote* 658 n.
antigropelos *legwear* 228 n.
antilogarithm
  numerical element 85 n.
antilogy *sophism* 477 n.
antimacassar
  covering 226 n.
antimonopolist
  free man 744 n.
antinomian
  anarchic 734 adj.
  revolter 738 n.
  resisting 738 adj.
  non-observant 769 adj.
  lawless 954 adj.
  heretic 977 n.
antinomy
  contrariety 14 n.
  illegality 954 n.
antiparallel *oblique* 220 adj.
anti-particle *particle* 33 n.
antipathetic
  unconformable 84 adj.
antipathy *contrariety* 14 n.
  difference 15 n.
  dislike 861 n.
  enmity 881 n.
  hatred 888 n.
antiphon *answer* 460 n.
  hymn 981 n.
antiphony
  vocal music 412 n.
  answer 460 n.

antiphrasis *neology* 560 n.
  solecism 565 n.
antipodean *inverted* 221 adj.
antipodes *contrariety* 14 n.
  farness 199 n.
  contraposition 240 n.
antipole *contrariety* 14 n.
antiquarianism
  palætiology 125 n.
antiquarium *antiquity* 125 n.
  collection 632 n.
antiquary
  antiquarian 125 n.
  collector 492 n.
  chronicler 549 n.
antiquated *past* 125 adj.
  antiquated 127 adj.
  aged 131 adj.
  powerless 161 adj.
  disused 674 adj.
antique *archaism* 127 n.
  olden 127 adj.
  exhibit 522 n.
antiquities *archaism* 127 n.
antiquity *time* 108 n.
  diuturnity 113 n.
  antiquity 125 n.
  oldness 127 n.
  old man 133 n.
antisemitism
  prejudice 481 n.
  phobia 854 n.
  hatred 888 n.
antiseptic *clean* 648 adj.
  salubrious 652 adj.
  prophylactic 658 n.
  remedial 658 adj.
  tutelary 660 adj.
antisepticize *purify* 648 vb.
  sanitate 652 vb.
  doctor 658 vb.
antisocial
  unsociable 883 adj.
  misanthropic 902 adj.
antispasmodic
  antidote 658 n.
antistrophe
  verse form 593 n.
antithesis *contrariety* 14 n.
  difference 15 n.
  contraposition 240 n.
  trope 519 n.
  ornament 574 n.
antithetic *inverted* 221 adj.
antitoxin *antidote* 658 n.
antitrades *wind* 352 n.
antitype *prototype* 23 n.
antler
  protuberance 254 n.
  sharp point 256 n.
  weapon 723 n.

antonomasia
  trope 519 n.
  nomenclature 561 n.
antonym *contrariety* 14 n.
  connotation 514 n.
  word 559 n.
  name 561 n.
antrum *cavity* 255 n.
anus *buttocks* 238 n.
anvil *stand* 218 n.
  unlucky person 731 n.
anvil, on the
  in preparation 669 adv.
  on the stocks 726 adv.
anxiety (*see* anxious)
anxiety neurosis
  psychopathy 503 n.
anxious *careful* 457 adj.
  expectant 507 adj.
  suffering 825 adj.
  nervous 854 adj.
  desiring 859 adj.
anxious seat *penance* 941 n.
anxious to please
  courteous 884 adj.
any *quantitative* 26 adj.
  no name 562 n.
  anonymous 562 adj.
  no choice 606 n.
anybody's guess
  uncertainty 474 n.
anyhow *confusedly* 61 adv.
  negligently 458 adv.
anyone *everyman* 79 n.
anything but
  contrary 14 adj.
  different 15 adj.
aorist *time* 108 n.
aoristic *elapsing* 111 adj.
  uncertain 474 adj.
aorta *conduit* 351 n.
aortitis *blood pressure* 651 n.
apace *swiftly* 277 adv.
  hastily 680 adv.
apache *ruffian* 904 n.
apart *separate* 46 adj.
  afar 199 adv.
apart from
  exclusive of 57 adv.
apartheid *exclusion* 57 n.
  prejudice 481 n.
apartment *flat* 192 n.
  chamber 194 n.
apathetic *inert* 175 adj.
  slow 278 adj.
  incurious 454 adj.
  inattentive 456 adj.
  inexpectant 508 adj.
  choiceless 606 adj.
  non-active 677 adj.
  inactive 679 adj.

apathetic 820 adj.
  unastonished 865 adj.
apathy (*see* apathetic)
ape *imitator* 20 n.
  imitate 20 vb.
  monkey 365 n.
ape-man *mankind* 371 n.
  ruffian 904 n.
  monster 938 n.
aperçu *dissertation* 591 n.
  compendium 592 n.
aperient *opener* 263 n.
  ejector 300 n.
  cathartic 658 n.
apéritif *stimulant* 174 n.
  liquor 301 n.
aperture *opening* 263 n.
  orifice 263 n.
apex *summit* 213 n.
aphæresis *shortening* 204 n.
aphasia *speech defect* 580 n.
aphelion *distance* 199 n.
aphonic *silent* 399 adj.
  voiceless 578 adj.
aphony, aphonia
  silence 399 n.
  aphony 578 n.
  speech defect 580 n.
aphorism *maxim* 496 n.
  conciseness 569 n.
aphotic *unlit* 418 adj.
aphrodisiac
  stimulant 174 n.
  erotic 887 adj.
Aphrodite *woman* 373 n.
  a beauty 841 n.
  love god 887 n.
  mythic god 966 n.
  Olympian god 967 n.
apiarist *breeder* 369 n.
apiary *dwelling* 192 n.
  nest 192 n.
  stock farm 369 n.
apical *topmost* 213 adj.
apiculture
  animal husbandry 369 n.
apiece *severally* 80 adv.
apish *imitative* 20 adj.
  foolish 499 adj.
aplomb *stability* 153 n.
  resolution 399 n.
apnœa *decease* 361 n.
apocalypse *ruin* 165 n.
  prediction 511 n.
  disclosure 526 n.
  scripture 975 n.
  revelation 975 n.
apocope *shortening* 204 n.
apocrypha *scripture* 975 n.
apocryphal
  uncertified 474 adj.

erroneous 495 adj.
apodeixis
  demonstration 478 n.
apodosis *end* 69 n.
apogee *distance* 199 n.
  summit 213 n.
apograph *copy* 22 n.
Apollinarian
  heretic 977 n.
Apollo *musician* 413 n.
  a beauty 841 n.
  Olympian god 967 n.
Apollyon *Satan* 969 n.
apologetic
  arguing 475 adj.
  excusing 614 adj.
  vindicating 927 adj.
  atoning 941 adj.
  repentant 939 adj.
  regretting 830 adj.
apologetics, apologia
  argument 475 n.
  vindication 927 n.
apologies *regret* 830 n.
apologist *reasoner* 475 n.
  vindicator 927 n.
apologize *recant* 603 vb.
  tergiversate 603 vb.
  plead 614 vb.
  knuckle under 721 vb.
  regret 830 vb.
  demean oneself 867 vb.
  be penitent 939 vb.
  atone 941 vb.
apologue *metaphor* 519 n.
  lecture 534 n.
  narrative 590 n.
apology *penitence* 939 n.
  atonement 941 n.
apology for *copy* 22 n.
  pretext 614 n.
  laughing stock 851 n.
apophthegm *maxim* 496 n.
apophysis *swelling* 253 n.
apoplexy
  helplessness 161 n.
  illness 651 n.
aport *sinistral* 242 adj.
aposiopesis *trope* 519 n.
  conciseness 569 n.
  ornament 574 n.
  taciturnity 582 n.
apostasy (*see* apostatize)
apostate
  changed person 147 n.
  dissentient 489 n.
  (*see* apostatize)
apostatize *dissent* 489 vb.
  be irresolute 601 vb.
  apostatize 603 vb.
  reject 607 vb.

relinquish 621 vb.
  relapse 675 vb.
  be dishonest 930 vb.
  be irreligious 974 vb.
  schismatize 978 vb.
  be impious 980 vb.
apostle *messenger* 531 n.
  preacher 537 n.
  religious teacher 973 n.
Apostles' Creed
  orthodoxy 976 n.
apostolate *vocation* 622 n.
  church office 985 n.
  church ministry 985 n.
apostolic *scriptural* 975 adj.
  ecclesiastical 985 adj.
  priestly 985 adj.
apostolic succession
  holy orders 985 n.
apostrophe
  punctuation 547 n.
  nomenclature 561 n.
apostrophize *orate* 579 vb.
  speak to 583 vb.
  soliloquize 585 vb.
  entreat 761 vb.
apothecary *druggist* 658 n.
apotheosis
  dignification 866 n.
  Heaven 971 n.
  deification 982 n.
apotropaic
  deprecatory 762 adj.
apozem *solution* 337 n.
appal *displease* 827 vb.
  frighten 854 vb.
appanage *dower* 777 n.
apparatus *tool* 630 n.
apparatus criticus
  commentary 520 n.
apparel *clothing* 228 n.
  dress 228 vb.
apparent *visible* 443 adj.
  appearing 445 adj.
  plausible 471 adj.
  certain 473 adj.
  manifest 522 adj.
apparentation
  consanguinity 11 n.
  attribution 158 n.
apparently
  apparently 445 adv.
  probably 471 adv.
apparition
  visual fallacy 440 n.
  appearance 445 n.
  manifestation 522 n.
  ghost 970 n.
apparitor *officer* 741 n.
  law officer 955 n.
appeal *influence* 178 vb.

attraction 291 n.
attract 291 vb.
affirmation 532 n.
affirm 532 vb.
allocution 583 n.
motivate 612 vb.
entreaty 761 n.
request 761 n.
deprecate 762 vb.
excitation 821 n.
pleasurableness 826 n.
beauty 841 n.
lovableness 887 n.
legal trial 959 n.
appeal against
negate 533 vb.
deprecate 762 vb.
appeal to speak to 583 vb.
request 761 vb.
appear be visible 443 vb.
appear 445 vb.
be disclosed 526 vb.
appearance
circumstance 8 n.
similarity 18 n.
situation 186 n.
form 243 n.
visibility 443 n.
appearance 445 n.
probability 471 n.
manifestation 522 n.
appearances etiquette 848 n.
appear for deputize 755 vb.
appease assuage 177 vb.
induce 612 vb.
pacify 719 vb.
content 828 vb.
offer worship 981 vb.
appeasement irenics 719 n.
appellant dueness 915 n.
accuser 928 n.
petitioner 763 n.
litigant 959 n.
appellate curial 956 adj.
appellation
nomenclature 561 n.
appellative name 561 n.
naming 561 adj.
append add 38 vb.
place after 65 vb.
hang 217 vb.
appendage adjunct 40 n.
sequel 67 n.
concomitant 89 n.
appendectomy
surgery 658 n.
appendix addition 38 n.
adjunct 40 n.
sequel 67 n.
extremity 69 n.
pendant 217 n.

edition 589 n.
apperception
intellect 447 n.
appertain be related 9 vb.
be one of 58 vb.
be included 78 vb.
belong 773 vb.
appetence relation 9 n.
will 595 n.
desire 859 n.
appetible desired 859 adj.
appetite eating 301 n.
desire, hunger 859 n.
liking 859 n.
appetize taste 386 vb.
appetize 390 vb.
delight 826 vb.
cause desire 859 vb.
appetizer stimulant 174 n.
savouriness 390 n.
applaud assent 488 vb.
rejoice 835 vb.
honour 866 vb.
gratulate 886 vb.
applaud 923 vb.
apple fruit 301 n.
apple of discord
quarrelsomeness 709 n.
casus belli 709 n.
apple of one's eye
favourite 890 n.
appliance
causal means 156 n.
instrument 628 n.
means 629 n.
tool 630 n.
use 673 n.
applicable relevant 9 adj.
apt 24 adj.
useful 640 adj.
expedient 642 adj.
applicant
respondent 460 n.
petitioner 763 n.
application referral 9 n.
relevance 9 n.
meditation 449 n.
attention 455 n.
connotation 514 n.
metaphor 519 n.
interpretation 520 n.
perseverance 600 n.
instrumentality 628 n.
surgical dressing 658 n.
use 673 n.
assiduity 678 n.
offer 759 n.
request 761 n.
applied instrumental 628 adj.
useful 640 adj.
appliqué work

needlework 844 n.
apply relate 9 vb.
figure 519 vb.
use 673 vb.
request 761 vb.
belong 773 vb.
apply oneself study 536 vb.
appoggiatura
musical note 410 n.
appoint select 605 vb.
predetermine 608 vb.
employ 622 vb.
decree 737 vb.
commission 751 vb.
apportion 783 vb.
appointed fated 596 adj.
appointee consignee 754 n.
appointment job 622 n.
fitting out 669 n.
(see appoint)
appointment, by
chosen 605 adj.
appointments
equipment 630 n.
apport spiritualism 984 n.
apportion arrange 62 vb.
dispose of 673 vb.
apportion 783 vb.
apposite relevant 9 adj.
appositeness fitness 24 n.
apposition relativeness 9 n.
contiguity 202 n.
grammar 564 n.
appraise
discriminate 463 vb.
appraise 465 vb.
estimate 480 vb.
appraiser appraiser 465 n.
estimator 480 n.
appreciate grow 36 vb.
cognize 447 vb.
appraise 465 vb.
know 490 vb.
be dear 811 vb.
be pleased 824 vb.
have taste 846 vb.
honour 866 vb.
love 887 vb.
thank 907 vb.
approve 923 vb.
appreciation
discrimination 463 n.
measurement 465 n.
estimate 480 n.
feeling 818 n.
gratitude 907 n.
approbation 923 n.
appreciative judicial 480 adj.
tasteful 846 adj.
grateful 907 adj.
approving 923 adj.

apprehend *opine* 485 vb.
　know 490 vb.
　expect 507 vb.
　understand 516 vb.
　arrest 747 vb.
　take 786 vb.
apprehensible
　intelligible 516 adj.
apprehension *idea* 451 n.
　knowledge 490 n.
　expectation 507 n.
　danger 661 n.
　taking 786 n.
　nervousness 854 n.
apprehensive
　expectant 507 adj.
　suffering 825 adj.
　nervous 854 adj.
apprentice *beginner* 538 n.
　artisan 686 n.
　bungler 697 n.
apprenticeship
　learning 536 n.
apprise *inform* 524 vb.
approach *resemble* 18 vb.
　entrance 68 n.
　beginning 68 n.
　futurity 124 n.
　be to come 124 n.
　impend 155 vb.
　tend 179 vb.
　nearness 200 n.
　doorway 263 n.
　motion 265 n.
　approach 289 vb.
　arrival 294 n.
　speak to 583 vb.
　pursuit 619 n.
　policy 623 n.
　way 624 n.
　offer 759 n., vb.
　request 761 n., vb.
　greet 884 vb.
approachable
　accessible 289 adj.
　possible 469 adj.
　easy 701 adj.
approaches
　near place 200 n.
approbation
　permission 488 n.
　approbation 923 n.
appropinquate
　approach 289 vb.
appropriate
　circumstantial 8 adj.
　relevant 9 adj.
　apt 24 adj.
　special 80 adj.
　acquire 771 vb.
　apportion 783 vb.

appropriate 786 vb.
　claim 915 vb.
appropriation
　apportionment 783 n.
　taking 786 n.
approvable
　approvable 923 adj.
approval *assent* 488 n.
　permission 756 n.
　repute 866 n.
　approbation 923 n.
approval, on
　experimentally 461 adv.
　chosen 605 adj.
approve *choose* 605 vb.
　select 605 vb.
　permit 756 vb.
　consent 758 vb.
　be pleased 824 vb.
　approve 923 vb.
approved *usual* 610 adj.
approver *informer* 524 n.
　tergiversator 603 n.
　commender 923 n.
　accuser 928 n.
approximate
　be related 9 vb.
　similar 18 adj.
　liken 18 vb.
　resemble 18 vb.
　near 200 adj.
　approach 289 vb.
approximately
　almost 33 adv.
approximation
　numerical operation 86 n.
appulse *contiguity* 202 n.
　collide 279 vb.
　approach 289 n.
appurtenance *adjunct* 40 n.
　component 58 n.
　concomitant 89 n.
　property 777 n.
appurtenant *relative* 9 adj.
　ingredient 58 adj.
apricate *dry* 342 vb.
　enjoy 376 vb.
aprication *heating* 381 n.
apricot *fruit* 301 n.
　orange 436 n.
April fool *dupe* 544 n.
　laughing stock 851 n.
April Fool's Day
　amusement 837 n.
April shower
　brief span 114 n.
　changeable thing 152 n.
a priori *intrinsic* 5 adj.
　rational 475 adj.
　reasonably 475 adj.
a priori knowledge

intuition 476 n.
apriorism *reasoning* 475 n.
apron *apron* 228 n.
　canonicals 989 n.
apron strings
　subjection 745 n.
à propos
　concerning 9 adj.
　apt 24 adj.
　incidentally 137 adv.
apse *church interior* 990 n.
apt *relevant* 9 adj.
　apt 24 adj.
　opportune 137 adj.
　plausible 471 adj.
　skilful 494 adj.
　intelligent 498 adj.
　willing 597 adj.
apteryx *flightless bird* 365 n.
aptitude *fitness* 24 n.
　ability 160 n.
　tendency 179 n.
　intelligence 498 n.
　learning 536 n.
　willingness 597 n.
　aptitude 694 n.
aquamarine *blueness* 435 n.
　greenness 432 n.
　blue 435 adj.
　gem 844 n.
aquaplane *swim* 269 vb.
aquaplaning *aquatics* 269 n.
　sport 837 n.
aquarelle *picture* 553 n.
aquarellist *artist* 556 n.
aquarium
　accumulation 74 n.
　lake 346 n.
　cattle pen 369 n.
　zoo 369 n.
　collection 632 n.
Aquarius *zodiac* 321 n.
aquatic *seafaring* 269 adj.
　watery 339 adj.
aquatics *aquatics* 269 n.
　sport 837 n.
aquatint *picture* 553 n.
　engraving 555 n.
aqueduct *conduit* 351 n.
aqueous *watery* 339 adj.
aquiline *curved* 248 adj.
　animal 365 adj.
Arab *wanderer* 268 n.
　thoroughbred 273 n.
arabesque *crossing* 222 n.
　pattern 844 n.
Arabist *linguist* 557 n.
arable *soil* 344 n.
　farm 370 n.
　agrarian 370 n.
arachnid *animal* 365 n.

arbalest
  missile weapon 723 n.
arbiter *adviser* 691 n.
  magistracy 957 n.
arbiter elegantiarum
  reveller 837 n.
  man of taste 846 n.
  beau monde 848 n.
arbitrage *judgment* 480 n.
  mediation 720 n.
  barter 791 n.
arbitral *judicial* 480 adj.
arbitrament *judgment* 480 n.
arbitrariness
  irrelation 10 n.
  caprice 604 n.
  lawlessness 957 n.
arbitrary
  unconformable 84 adj.
  illogical 477 adj.
  volitional 595 adj.
  wilful 602 adj.
  capricious 604 adj.
  authoritative 733 adj.
  authoritarian 735 adj.
  oppressive 735 adj.
  unconditional 744 adj.
  insolent 878 adj.
  lawless 954 adj.
arbitrary power
  brute force 735 n.
arbitrate *judge* 480 vb.
  mediate 720 vb.
  compromise 770 vb.
arbor *pivot* 218 n.
arboreal *arboreal* 366 adj.
arborescent
  symmetrical 245 adj.
  arboreal 366 adj.
arboretum *garden* 370 n.
arboriculture
  agriculture 370 n.
arbour *pavilion* 192 n.
  arbour 194 n.
  pleasure-ground 837 n.
arc *arc* 250 n.
  fire 379 n.
arcade *pavilion* 192 n.
  street 192 n.
  curve 248 n.
  path 624 n.
  emporium 796 n.
Arcadia *happiness* 824 n.
Arcadian *artless* 699 adj.
  innocent 935 adj.
arcane
  unintelligible 517 adj.
  latent 523 adj.
  concealed 525 adj.
arcanum *secret* 530 n.
arc-boutant *supporter* 218 n.

arch *consummate* 32 adj.
  supreme 34 adj.
  bond 47 n.
  foot 214 n.
  supporter 218 n.
  curve 248 n.
  make *curved* 248 vb.
  be convex 253 vb.
  gay 833 adj.
  affected 850 adj.
archæography
  palætiology 125 n.
archæologist
  antiquarian 125 n.
  enquirer 459 n.
  detector 484 n.
archæology
  palætiology 125 n.
archaic *olden* 127 adj.
  neological 562 adj.
archaism *antiquity* 125 n.
  archaism 127 n.
  reversion 148 n.
  neology 560 n.
archaize *look back* 125 vb.
  retrospect 505 vb.
archangel *angel* 968 n.
archbishop *governor* 741 n.
  ecclesiarch 986 n.
archbishopric *district* 184 n.
  church office 985 n.
  parish 985 n.
archdeacon
  ecclesiarch 986 n.
archdeaconry
  church office 985 n.
  parsonage 986 n.
archduke *potentate* 741 n.
  nobleman 868 n.
archer *shooter* 287 n.
  soldiery 722 n.
archery
  propulsion 287 n.
  arm 723 n.
  sport 837 n.
archetypal
  unimitative 21 adj.
archetype *prototype* 23 n.
  idea 451 n.
archiepiscopacy
  churchdom 985 n.
archiform *curved* 248 adj.
archimandrite
  ecclesiarch 986 n.
  monk 986 n.
archipelago *island* 349 n.
architect *producer* 167 n.
  artisan 686 n.
architectonic
  productive 164 adj.
  architectural 192 adj.

architectonics
  structure 331 n.
architectural
  architectural 192 adj.
  formative 243 adj.
  structural 331 adj.
architecture
  composition 56 n.
  arrangement 62 n.
  production 164 n.
  form 243 n.
  structure 331 n.
  art 551 n.
  ornamental art 844 n.
architrave *summit* 213 n.
  beam 218 n.
archive(s) *title-deed* 767 n.
archivist *recorder* 549 n.
  keeper 749 n.
archpriest
  ecclesiarch 986 n.
  priest 986 n.
archway *doorway* 263 n.
arc light *lamp* 420 n.
Arctic *opposite* 240 adj.
  coldness 380 n.
arcuate *make curved* 248 vb.
  arcuate 253 adj.
ardent (*see* ardour)
ardent spirits *liquor* 301 n.
ardour *heat* 379 n.
  vigour 571 n.
  restlessness 678 n.
  warm feeling 818 n.
  desire 859 n.
arduous *laborious* 682 adj.
  difficult 700 adj.
area *quantity* 26 n.
  space 183 n.
  measure 183 n.
  region 184 n.
  place 185 n.
  size 195 n.
arefaction *desiccation* 342 n.
arena *meeting place* 192 n.
  view 438 n.
  theatre 594 n.
  contest 716 n.
  battle 718 n.
  arena 724 n.
  pleasure-ground 837 n.
arenaceous *powdery* 332 adj.
areola *circle* 250 n.
Areopagite *councillor* 692 n.
  judge 957 n.
Areopagus *tribunal* 956 n.
  law court 956 n.
Ares *war* 718 n.
  Olympian god 967 n.
aretalogical
  descriptive 590 adj.

wonderful 864 adj.
aretalogist
  exaggeration 546 n.
  narrator 590 n.
  prodigy 864 n.
aretalogy
  exaggeration 546 n.
  biography 590 n.
  deed 676 n.
  thaumaturgy 864 n.
arête *sharp point* 256 n.
argent *white* 427 adj.
  heraldry 547 n.
argil *soil* 344 n.
  materials 631 n.
argilaceous *soft* 327 adj.
Argo *ship* 275 n.
argon *air* 340 n.
argonaut *mariner* 270 n.
argosy *shipping* 275 n.
  merchant ship 275 n.
argot *slang* 560 n.
arguable *possible* 469 adj.
  uncertain 474 adj.
  arguing 475 adj.
  vindicable 927 adj.
  litigated 959 adj.
argue *evidence* 466 vb.
  argue 475 vb.
  dissent 489 vb.
  propound 512 vb.
  affirm 532 vb.
  indicate 547 vb.
  confer 584 vb.
  plead 614 vb.
argue against
  dissuade 613 vb.
argue for *contend* 716 vb.
argue in a circle
  reason ill 477 vb.
argument
  disagreement 25 n.
  topic 452 n.
  argument 475 n.
  demonstration 478 n.
  supposition 512 n.
  conference 584 n.
  narrative 590 n.
  quarrel 709 n.
  contention 716 n.
argumentation
  argumentation 475 n.
argumentative
  arguing 475 adj.
argumentum ad baculum
  corporal punishment 963 n.
argumentum ad miseri-
  cordiam
  pity 905 n.
argumentum ad verecun-
  diam

disrepute 867 n.
  probity 929 n.
Argus *janitor* 264 n.
  eye 438 n.
  protector 660 n.
  gaoler 749 n.
aria *tune* 412 n.
Arian *heretic* 977 n.
  heretical 977 adj.
arid *unproductive* 172 adj.
  dry 342 adj.
  tedious 838 adj.
Ariel *speeder* 277 n.
  satellite 321 n.
  courier 531 n.
  fairy 970 n.
Aries *zodiac* 321 n.
arietation *impulse* 279 n.
aright *well* 615 adv.
  aright 644 adv.
arise *become* 1 vb.
  begin 68 vb.
  happen 154 vb.
  lift oneself 310 vb.
  ascend 308 vb.
  be visible 443 vb.
  appear 445 vb.
arise from *result* 157 vb.
aristeia *prowess* 855 n.
aristocracy *superiority* 34 n.
  nation 371 n.
  government 733 n.
  aristocracy 868 n.
aristocrat *aristocrat* 868 n.
  proud man 871 n.
aristocratic
  governmental 753 adj.
  worshipful 866 adj.
  genteel 868 adj.
Aristophanic *funny* 849 adj.
Aristotelianism
  philosophy 449 n.
arithmetic
  mathematics 86 n.
arithmetical
  numerical 85 adj.
  statistical 86 adj.
arithmetical progression
  series 71 n.
  ratio 85 n.
  progression 285 n.
ark *retreat* 192 n.
  box 194 n.
  ship 275 n.
  protection 660 n.
  refuge 662 n.
Ark of the Covenant
  ritual object 988 n.
  holy place 990 n.
arm *adjunct* 40 n.
  limb 53 n.

empower 160 vb.
  supporter 218 n.
  sleeve 228 n.
  indicator 547 n.
  tool 630 n.
  provide 633 vb.
  safeguard 660 vb.
  make ready 669 vb.
  defend 713 vb.
  go to war 718 vb.
  arm 723 n.
  weapon 723 n.
armada *armed force* 722 n.
  navy 722 n.
Armageddon *fight* 716 n.
armament *fitting out* 669 n.
  armed force 722 n.
  arm 723 n.
armature *coil* 251 n.
armband *belt* 228 n.
armchair *seat* 218 n.
  softness 327 n.
armchair critic
  theorist 512 n.
armed force(s)
  armed force 722 n.
  army 722 n.
armed intervention
  war 718 n.
armful
  finite quantity 26 n.
armhole *sleeve* 228 n.
  orifice 263 n.
armiger *aristocrat* 868 n.
armillary *gauge* 465 n.
arm in arm
  conjunct 45 adj.
  with 89 adv.
  nigh 200 adv.
  contiguously 202 adv.
  across 222 adv.
  sociably 882 adv.
armipotent
  powerful 160 adj.
armistice *lull* 145 n.
  peace 717 n.
  pacification 719 n.
armless *fragmentary* 53 adj.
  incomplete 55 adj.
  defenceless 161 adj.
  crippled 163 adj.
  imperfect 647 adj.
armlet *belt* 228 n.
  loop 250 n.
  badge of rank 743 n.
armorial *heraldic* 547 adj.
armorial bearings
  heraldry 547 n.
armour *covering* 226 n.
  war-chariot 274 n.
  protection 660 n.

safeguard 662n.
armour 713n.
defend 713vb.
cavalry 722n.
weapon 723n.
armour-bearer
retainer 742n.
armoured
invulnerable 660adj.
defended 713adj.
armoured car
war-chariot 274n.
cavalry 722n.
armoury
accumulation 74n.
heraldry 547n.
storage 632n.
workshop 687n.
arsenal 723n.
armpits *fetor* 397n.
arms *heraldry* 547n.
vocation 622n.
safeguard 662n.
war 718n.
honours 866n.
arms chest *arsenal* 723n.
arms, in *infantine* 132adj.
warring 718adj.
arm's length, at
afar 199adv.
army *multitude* 104n.
army 722n.
army officer
army officer 741n.
aroma *fragrance* 396n.
around *nearly* 200 adv.
around 230adv.
arouse *cause feeling* 374vb.
incite 612vb.
raise the alarm 665vb.
excite 821vb.
arpeggio *musical note* 410n.
harmonize 410vb.
arquebus *fire-arm* 723n.
arquebusier *soldiery* 722n.
arrack *liquor* 301n.
arraign *indict* 928vb.
arraignment
accusation 928n.
litigation 959n.
arrange *arrange* 62vb.
modify 143vb.
compose music 413vb.
predetermine 608vb.
plan 623vb.
make ready 669vb.
arrangement
adaptation 24n.
regularity 81n.
musical piece 412n.
preparation 669n.

compact 765n.
arrant *consummate* 32adj.
manifest 522adj.
bad 645adj.
disreputable 867adj.
rascally 930adj.
arras *covering* 226n.
needlework 844n.
array *order* 60n.
arrangement 62n.
arrange 62vb.
series 71n.
multitude 104n.
place 187vb.
dress 228vb.
make ready 669vb.
battle 718n.
formation 722n.
decorate 844vb.
pageant 875n.
arrear, in
behindhand 307adv.
owed 803adj.
non-paying 805adj.
arrears *debt* 803n.
arrest *cessation* 145n.
halt 145vb.
cause feeling 374vb.
hindrance 702n.
restraint 747n.
detention 747n.
arrest 747vb.
take 786vb.
impress 821vb.
legal process 959n.
arresting
unexpected 508adj.
impressive 821adj.
arrière-ban
publication 528n.
army 722n.
arrière pensée
sophistry 477n.
concealment 525n.
arrival *junction* 45n.
intruder 59n.
beginning 68n.
arrival 295n.
arrive *accrue* 38vb.
happen 154vb.
be present 189vb.
approach 289vb.
arrive 295vb.
flourish 615vb.
climax 725vb.
succeed 727vb.
prosper 730vb.
arriviste *made man* 730n.
commoner 869n.
egotist 932n.
arrogance *pride* 871n.

insolence 878n.
arrogant
authoritarian 735adj.
rash 857adj.
arrogate
please oneself 734vb.
appropriate 786vb.
be insolent 788vb.
claim 915vb.
be undue 916vb.
arrogation *taking* 786n.
pretension 850n.
insolence 878n.
arrogation 916n.
arrondissement
district 184n.
arrow *sharp point* 256n.
speeder 277n.
missile 287n.
indicator 547n.
missile weapon 723n.
love token 889n.
arroyo *stream* 350n.
conduit 351n.
arsenal *accumulation* 74n.
storage 632n.
workshop 687n.
arsenal 723n.
arsenic *poison* 659n.
arsis *pronunciation* 577n.
prosody 593n.
arson *fire* 379n.
incendiarism 381n.
art *composition* 56n.
production 164n.
art 551n.
business 622n.
skill 694n.
stratagem 698n.
art-critic *spectator* 441n.
man of taste 846n.
artefact *product* 164n.
art equipment
art equipment 553n.
arterial
communicating 624adj.
arteritis
blood pressure 651n.
artery *essential part* 5n.
tube 263n.
conduit 351n.
life 360n.
road 624n.
artesian well *outflow* 298n.
lake 346n.
artful *intelligent* 498adj.
false 541adj.
deceiving 542adj.
cunning 698adj.
dishonest 930adj.
art gallery *collection* 632n.

arthritic *impotent* 161 adj.
  crippled 163 adj.
  sick person 651 n.
  diseased 651 adj.
arthritis *pang* 377 n.
  rheumatism 651 n.
arthropathy *paralysis* 651 n.
artichoke *tuber* 301 n.
  vegetables 301 n.
article *product* 164 n.
  object 319 n.
  publicity 528 n.
  reading matter 589 n.
  article 591 n.
  precept 693 n.
  merchandise 795 n.
article oneself *learn* 536 vb.
articles *creed* 485 n.
  conditions 766 n.
articulate *join* 45 vb.
  phrase 563 vb.
  vocal 577 adj.
  voice 577 vb.
  speak 579 vb.
artifice *contrivance* 623 n.
  stratagem 698 n.
  pretension 850 n.
artificer *producer* 167 n.
  artisan 686 n.
artificial
  simulating 18 adj.
  produced 164 adj.
  horticultural 370 adj.
  spurious 542 adj.
  untrue 543 adj.
  elegant 575 adj.
  inelegant 576 adj.
  laborious 682 adj.
  well-made 694 adj.
  affected 850 adj.
artificial respiration
  revival 656 n.
artificial satellite
  space-ship 276 n.
  satellite 321 n.
artillery *loudness* 400 n.
  gun 723 n.
artilleryman *soldiery* 722 n.
artisan *artist* 556 n.
  machinist 630 n.
  doer 676 n.
  artisan 686 n.
artist *producer* 167 n.
  visionary 513 n.
  artist 556 n.
  entertainer 594 n.
  doer 676 n.
artistic *elegant* 575 adj.
  well-made 694 adj.
  beautiful 841 adj.
  tasteful 846 adj.

artistry *touch* 378 n.
  imagination 513 n.
  painting 533 n.
  skill 694 n.
  good taste 846 n.
artless *simple* 44 adj.
  amorphous 244 adj.
  ignorant 491 adj.
  foolish 499 adj.
  veracious 540 adj.
  plain 573 adj.
  inelegant 576 adj.
  spontaneous 609 adj.
  unprepared 670 adj.
  bungled 695 adj.
  artless 699 adj.
  graceless 842 adj.
  vulgar 847 adj.
  barbaric 869 adj.
  innocent 935 adj.
art master *artist* 556 n.
arts *culture* 490 n.
  literature 557 n.
art, work of
  masterpiece 694 n.
Aryan *ethnic* 11 adj.
  language type 557 n.
Aryanism *prejudice* 481 n.
asafœtida
  unsavouriness 391 n.
  fetor 397 n.
asbestos
  incombustibility 382 n.
ascend *be high* 209 vb.
  be oblique 220 vb.
  fly 271 vb.
  ascend 308 vb.
ascendancy *power* 160 n.
  influence 178 n.
  victory 727 n.
  authority 733 n.
  prestige 866 n.
ascendant, in the
  successful 727 adj.
ascender *print-type* 587 n.
ascending order
  increase 36 n.
  series 71 n.
  expansion 197 n.
ascent *series* 71 n.
  acclivity 220 n.
  motion 265 n.
  progression 285 n.
  ascent 308 n.
  improvement 654 n.
ascertain
  make certain 473 vb.
ascertainment
  certainty 473 n.
  demonstration 478 n.
  discovery 484 n.

ascetic *severe* 735 adj.
  impassive 820 adj.
  unfeeling person 820 n.
  abstainer 942 n.
  temperate 942 adj.
  ascetic 945 n., adj.
  pietist 979 n.
  pietistic 979 adj.
  monk 986 n.
asceticism *temperance* 942 n.
  asceticism 945 n.
  punishment 963 n.
  pietism 979 n.
  act of worship 981 n.
  monasticism 985 n.
ascribable *due* 915 adj.
ascribe *attribute* 158 vb.
  grant claims 915 vb.
ascription *attribution* 158 n.
ascriptus glebæ
  husbandman 370 n.
  slave 742 n.
Asdic *hearing aid* 415 n.
  detector 484 n.
aseity *existence* 1 n.
aseptic *clean* 648 adj.
  salubrious 652 adj.
asexual *simple* 44 adj.
Asgard *mythic heaven* 971 n.
as good as *equivalent* 28 adj.
  equally 28 adv.
  on the whole 52 adv.
  completely 54 adv.
ash *pulverulence* 332 n.
  tree 366 n.
  ash 381 n.
  dirt 649 n.
ash can
  cleaning utensil 648 n.
  bomb 723 n.
ashen *colourless* 426 adj.
  grey 429 adj.
Ashes *trophy* 729 n.
ashes *corpse* 363 n.
ashlar
  building material 631 n.
ashore *on land* 344 adv.
ashram *retreat* 192 n.
  monastery 986 n.
Ash Wednesday
  holy-day 988 n.
ashy *grey* 429 adj.
  colourless 426 adj.
aside *sideways* 239 adv.
  faintly 401 adv.
  latency 523 n.
  hint 524 n.
  secretely 525 adv.
  soliloquy 585 n.
  aside 585 adv.
  dramaturgy 594 n.

as if *similarly* 18 adv.
asinine *equine* 273 adj.
  animal 365 adj.
  absurd 497 adj.
  foolish 499 adj.
as it were *similarly* 18 adv.
ask *enquire* 459 vb.
  not know 491 vb.
  request 761 vb.
askance *obliquely* 220 adv.
  sideways 239 adv.
askew *unequal* 29 adj.
  oblique 220 adj.
  distorted 246 adj.
ask for *enquire* 459 vb.
  bargain 791 vb.
  desire 859 vb.
ask for trouble
  be rash 857 vb.
aslant *oblique* 220 adj.
asleep *quiescent* 266 adj.
  sleepy 679 adj.
as long as
  during pleasure 112 adv.
aslope *obliquely* 220 adv.
asomatous
  immaterial 320 adj.
asp *reptile* 365 n.
  noxious animal 904 n.
asparagus *vegetable* 301 n.
aspect *character* 5 n.
  modality 7 n.
  situation 186 n.
  appearance 445 n.
  conduct 688 n.
aspen *agitation* 318 n.
  tree 366 n.
asperge *moistening* 341 n.
  moisten 341 vb.
  purify 648 vb.
  perform ritual 988 vb.
asperity *roughness* 259 n.
  rudeness 885 n.
  anger 891 n.
  irascibility 892 n.
asperse *moisten* 341 vb.
  defame 926 vb.
aspersion
  moistening 341 n.
  slur 866 n.
  scurrility 899 n.
  reproach 924 n.
  detraction 926 n.
  ritual act 988 n.
asphalt *smoothness* 258 n.
  resin 357 n.
  road 624 n.
  building material 631 n.
asphyxia *decease* 361 n.
asphyxiant *deadly* 362 adj.
  poison 659 n.

asphyxiate *close* 264 vb.
aspirant *petitioner* 763 n.
  hoper 852 n.
  desirer 859 n.
aspirate *breathe* 352 vb.
  speech sound 398 n.
  rasp 407 vb.
  spoken letter 558 n.
  voice 577 vb.
aspiration
  pronunciation 577 n.
  motive 612 n.
  objective 617 n.
  aspiration 852 n.
  desire 859 n.
  desired object 859 n.
aspire *ascend* 308 vb.
  hope 852 vb.
  desire 859 vb.
aspirin *drug* 658 n.
asquint *obliquely* 220 adv.
  sideways 239 adv.
as regards *concerning* 9 adv.
ass
  beast of burden 273 n.
  animal 365 n.
  fool 501 n.
  bungler 697 n.
assail *attack* 712 vb.
  torment 827 vb.
assailant *opponent* 705 n.
  attacker 712 n.
  combatant 722 n.
assassin *destroyer* 168 n.
  violent creature 176 n.
  murderer 362 n.
  ruffian 904 n.
assassinate *murder* 362 vb.
assault *knock* 279 n.
  impairment 655 n.
  attack 712 n., vb.
  debauch 951 vb.
assay *experiment* 461 n., vb.
  essay 671 vb.
assemblage (see assemble)
assemble *join* 45 vb.
  compose 56 vb.
  congregate 74 vb.
  bring together 74 vb.
  produce 164 vb.
  meet 295 vb.
  call 547 n.
assembly *convergence* 293 n.
  conference 584 n.
  council 692 n.
  sociability 882 n.
  (see assemble)
assembly-line
  production 164 n.
assembly room
  place of amusement 837 n.

assent *agreement* 24 n.
  assent 488 n., vb.
  willingness 597 n.
  obey 739 vb.
  permit 756 vb.
  consent 758 n., vb.
assentaneous
  assenting 488 adj.
assentation *flattery* 925 n.
assentient *assenting* 488 adj.
assert *suppose* 512 vb.
  mean 514 vb.
  affirm 532 vb.
assertion *testimony* 466 n.
assertive *assertive* 532 adj.
assert oneself
  influence 178 vb.
  be active 678 vb.
assess *appraise* 465 vb.
  price, tax 809 vb.
assessable *measured* 465 adj.
  priced 809 adj.
assessment
  measurement 465 n.
  estimate 480 n.
  tax 809 n.
assessor *appraiser* 465 n.
  estimator 480 n.
  jury 957 n.
assets *sufficiency* 635 n.
  means 629 n.
  store 632 n.
  estate 777 n.
asseverate *affirm* 532 vb.
assibilate *hiss* 406 vb.
assiduity *attention* 455 n.
  carefulness 457 n.
  perseverance 600 n.
  assiduity 678 n.
  exertion 682 n.
assiduous *frequent* 139 adj.
  (see assiduity)
assign *arrange* 63 vb.
  attribute 158 vb.
  transfer 672 vb.
  dispose of 673 vb.
  commission 751 vb.
  dower 777 vb.
  convey 780 vb.
  bequeath 780 vb.
  apportion 783 vb.
  grant claims 915 vb.
assignable
  attributed 158 adj.
  transferable 272 adj.
  due 915 adj.
assignat *paper money* 797 n.
assignation *focus* 76 n.
  social round 882 n.
assignee *recipient* 782 n.
assignment *mandate* 751 n.

transfer 780n.
apportionment 783n.
assimilate
identify 13vb.
make uniform 16vb.
liken 18vb.
combine 50vb.
make conform 83vb.
transform 147vb.
absorb 299vb.
learn 536vb.
assimilation *inclusion* 78n.
speech sound 398n.
(*see* assimilate)
assimilative
admitting 299adj.
ass in a lion's skin
misfit 25n.
impostor 545n.
bungler 697n.
assist *aid* 703vb.
assistance
instrumentality 628n.
provision 633n.
aid 703n.
assistant *inferior* 35n.
instrument 628n.
auxiliary 707n.
servant 742n.
assist at *be present* 189vb.
assister *aider* 703n.
assize *measurement* 465n.
law-court 956n.
legal trial 959n.
associate *join* 45vb.
combine 50vb.
congregate 74vb.
concomitant 89n.
accompany 89vb.
personnel 686n.
co-operate 706vb.
colleague 707n.
society 708n.
join a party 708vb.
friend 880n.
associate with
unite with 45vb.
association *relation* 9n.
junction 45n.
group 74n.
accompaniment 89n.
concurrence 181n.
intuition 476n.
habituation 610n.
association 706n.
corporation 708n.
participation 775n.
sociality 882n.
association of ideas
intellect 447n.
thought 449n.

supposition 512n.
associative
attracting 291adj.
assonance
assimilation 18n.
recurrence 106n.
melody 410n.
prosody 593n.
ornament 574n.
assonant *word* 559n.
as soon as
synchronously 123adv.
assort *make uniform* 16vb.
assortment
uniformity 16n.
arrangement 62n.
series 71n.
bunch 74n.
accumulation 74n.
sort 77n.
assuage *assuage* 177vb.
soften 327vb.
pacify 719vb.
restrain 747vb.
please 826vb.
relieve 831vb.
assuefaction
habituation 610n.
assuetude *habit* 610n.
assume *account for* 158vb.
wear 228vb.
assume 471vb.
premise 475vb.
believe, opine 485vb.
expect 507vb.
suppose 512vb.
dissemble 541vb.
undertake 672vb.
appropriate 786vb.
be affected 850vb.
hope 852vb.
be insolent 878vb.
assuming *if* 8adv.
supposedly 512adv.
insolent 878adj.
unwarranted 916adj.
assumption
attribution 158n.
elevation 310n.
premise 475n.
opinion 485n.
supposition 512n.
receiving 782n.
taking 786n.
pretension 850n.
hope 852n.
arrogation 916n.
Heaven 971n.
assurance
calculation of chance 159n.
positiveness 473n.

belief 485n.
affirmation 532n.
safety 660n.
promise 764n.
hope 852n.
vanity 873n.
insolence 878n.
assure *make certain* 473vb.
convince 485vb.
promise 764vb.
give security 767vb.
assured *positive* 473adj.
believing 485adj.
assertive 532adj.
safe 660adj.
astatic *light* 323adj.
asterisk *punctuation* 547n.
mark 547vb.
asterism *star* 321n.
punctuation 547n.
astern *rearward* 238adv.
asteroid *planet* 321n.
asthenia *weakness* 163n.
asthma
respiratory disease 651n.
asthmatic *puffing* 352adj.
sibilant 406adj.
sick person 651n.
diseased 651adj.
astigmatism *dim sight* 440n
astir *busy* 678adj.
excited 821adj.
as to *concerning* 9adv.
astonish
cause feeling 374vb.
surprise 508vb.
be wonderful 864vb.
astonishing
prodigious 32adj.
unusual 84adj.
astonishment
inexpectation 508n.
wonder 864n.
astound *surprise* 508vb.
impress 821vb.
be wonderful 864vb.
astraddle *astride* 218adv.
astrakhan *headgear* 228n.
astral *immaterial* 320adj.
celestial 321adj.
spooky 970adj.
astral body
immateriality 320n.
spiritualism 984n.
astray *irrelative* 10adj.
unassembled 75adj.
unconformable 84adj.
deviating 282adj.
astriction *joinder* 45n.
contraction 198n.
astride *astride* 218adv.

astringent *compressor* 198 n.
  compressive 198 adj.
  pungent 388 adj.
astrodome *view* 438 n.
astrolabe *astronomy* 321 n.
  gauge 465 n.
astrologer *astronomy* 321 n.
  diviner 511 n.
  sorcerer 983 n.
  occultist 984 n.
astromancy
  astronomy 321 n.
  divination 511 n.
astronaut *aeronaut* 271 n.
astronautical
  aviational 276 adj.
astronomer
  astronomy 321 n.
astronomical unit
  long measure 203 n.
astrophysics
  astronomy 321 n.
astute *intelligent* 498 adj.
  cunning 698 adj.
asunder *apart* 46 adv.
  afar 199 adv.
asura
  mythical being 970 n.
  demon 970 n.
as usual
  conformably 83 adv.
as well as
  in addition 38 adv.
asylum *retreat* 192 n.
  reception 299 n.
  madhouse 503 n.
  protection 660 n.
  refuge, shelter 662 n.
asymmetry *irrelation* 10 n.
  non-uniformity 17 n.
  disagreement 25 n.
  inequality 29 n.
  distortion 246 n.
  ugliness 842 n.
asymptote
  convergence 293 n.
  part of speech 564 n.
  grammatical 564 adj.
asyndeton *disjunction* 46 n.
  trope 519 n.
  grammar 564 n.
as you were
  reversibly 148 adv.
at all events
  nevertheless 468 adv.
at any moment
  in the future 155 adv.
at a stretch
  continuously 71 adv.
atavism *heredity* 5 n.
  consanguinity 11 n.

recurrence 106 n.
reversion 148 n.
reproduction 166 n.
influence 178 n.
memory 505 n.
ataxia *helplessness* 161 n.
at bottom *intrinsically* 5 adv.
Ate *quarrelsomeness* 709 n.
  lesser god 967 n.
atelier *chamber* 194 n.
  art equipment 553 n.
  workshop 687 n.
athanasia *perpetuity* 115 n.
athanor *heater* 383 n.
at heart *inside* 224 adv.
  centrally 225 adv.
atheism *philosophy* 449 n.
  unbelief 486 n.
  irreligion 974 n.
atheroma
  blood pressure 651 n.
athirst *hungry* 859 adj.
athlete *athlete* 162 n.
  proficient 696 n.
  contender 716 n.
athletics *athletics* 162 n.
  exercise 682 n.
  contention 716 n.
  contest 716 n.
  sport 837 n.
at home *apt* 24 adj.
  assembly 74 n.
  on the spot 189 adj.
  residing 192 adj.
  social gathering 882 n.
at home with
  friendly 880 adj.
athwart *oblique* 220 adj.
  across 222 adv.
at intervals
  discontinuously 72 adv.
Atlantis *fantasy* 513 n.
atlas *arrangement* 62 n.
  directory 87 n.
  world 321 n.
  map 551 n.
Atlas *athlete* 162 n.
  supporter 218 n.
at last *finally* 69 adv.
  late 136 adv.
at least *slightly* 33 adv.
at length *late* 136 adv.
  diffusely 570 adv.
Atman *self* 80 n.
  divineness 965 n.
atmometer *vaporizer* 338 n.
atmosphere
  influence 178 n.
  covering 226 n.
  circumjacence 230 n.
  atmosphere 340 n.

painting 553 n.
atmospheric *blue* 435 adj.
  excitable 822 adj.
atmospherics
  commotion 318 n.
  discord 411 n.
atoll *island* 349 n.
atom *particle* 33 n.
  unit 88 n.
  minuteness 196 n.
  element 319 n.
atomic *simple* 44 adj.
  dynamic 160 adj.
  minute 196 adj.
atomize *demolish* 165 vb.
  vaporize 338 vb.
atomizer
  pulverizer 332 n.
  vaporizer 338 n.
atom-smasher
  nucleonics 160 n.
atomy *small animal* 33 n.
  dwarf 196 n.
atonality *discord* 411 n.
at one *agreeing* 24 adj.
atone *restitute* 787 vb.
  be penitent 939 vb.
  atone 941 vb.
atonement
  substitution 150 n.
  atonement 941 n.
  divine function 965 n.
atony *weakness* 163 n.
atop *aloft* 209 adv.
  atop 213 adv.
atrabilious *black* 428 adj.
  melancholic 834 adj.
at random
  by chance 159 adv.
atrocious *cruel* 898 adj.
  heinous 934 adj.
atrocity *cruel act* 898 n.
  guilty act 936 n.
atrophy *helplessness* 161 n.
  contraction 198 n.
  paralysis 651 n.
  dilapidation 655 n.
attach *add* 38 vb.
  affix, connect 45 vb.
  belong 773 vb.
attaché *envoy* 754 n.
attaché case *box* 194 n.
attached *loving* 887 adj.
attachment
  adjunct 40 n.
  part 53 n.
  observance 768 n.
  expropriation 786 n.
  love 887 n.
attack *beginning* 68 n.
  begin 68 vb.

vigorousness 174 n.
be vigorous 174 vb.
outbreak 176 n.
irrupt 297 vb.
encroach 306 vb.
spasm 318 n.
argue 475 vb.
cause doubt 486 vb.
voice 577 n.
resolution 599 n.
policy 623 n.
plan 623 vb.
way 624 n.
illness 651 n.
essay 671 n.
attack 712 n., vb.
fight 716 vb.
battle 718 n.
wage war 718 vb.
dispraise 924 vb.
detraction 926 n.
attacker *opponent* 705 n.
attacker 712 n.
combatant 722 n.
attain *arrive* 295 vb.
acquire 771 vb.
attainable
accessible 289 adj.
possible 469 adj.
attainder (*see* attaint)
attainment(s) *culture* 490 n.
intelligence 498 n.
learning 536 n.
skill 694 n.
attaint *indict* 928 vb.
condemn 961 vb.
attar *scent* 396 n.
attemper *mix* 43 vb.
moderate 177 vb.
attempt *essay* 671 n., vb.
do 676 vb.
attend *accompany* 89 vb.
be present 189 vb.
follow 284 vb.
watch 441 vb.
be attentive 455 vb.
doctor 658 vb.
be servile 879 vb.
attendance *retinue* 67 n.
(*see* attend)
attendant
accompanying 89 adj.
on the spot 189 adj.
follower 284 n.
spectator 441 n.
bridesman 894 n.
attention *listening* 415 n.
attention 455 n.
carefulness 457 n.
accuracy 494 n.
study 536 n.

assiduity 678 n.
respect 920 n.
attenuate
make smaller 198 vb.
make thin 206 vb.
rarefy 325 vb.
attest *testify* 466 vb.
endorse 488 vb.
swear 532 vb.
sign 547 vb.
contract 765 vb.
attestant *witness* 466 n.
signatory 765 n.
attestation *testimony* 466 n.
certainty 473 n.
attested *evidential* 466 adj.
certain 473 adj.
attic *attic* 194 n.
Attic *elegant* 575 adj.
witty 839 adj.
tasteful 846 adj.
attire *dressing* 228 n.
dress 228 vb.
attitude *situation* 186 n.
form 243 n.
idea 451 n.
supposition 512 n.
affections 817 n.
attitudinize
be affected 850 vb.
attorney *mediator* 720 n.
mandate 751 n.
consignee 754 n.
deputy 755 n.
deputize 755 vb.
law agent 958 n.
attract
bring together 74 vb.
influence 178 vb.
attract 291 vb.
motivate 612 vb.
delight 826 vb.
excite love 887 vb.
attraction *energy* 160 n.
influence 178 n.
tendency 179 n.
traction 288 n.
attraction 291 n.
grammar 564 n.
inducement 612 n.
incentive 612 n.
pleasurableness 826 n.
liking 859 n.
favourite 890 n.
attractions *beauty* 841 n.
lovableness 887 n.
attractive, -ness
(*see* attraction)
attract notice
attract notice 455 vb.
attribute *speciality* 80 n.

concomitant 89 n.
attribute 158 vb.
ability 160 n.
grant claims 915 vb.
attrition *decrease* 37 n.
pulverulence 332 n.
friction 333 n.
warfare 718 n.
attune *adjust* 24 vb.
harmonize 410 vb.
atypical
non-uniform 17 adj.
dissimilar 19 adj.
abnormal 84 adj.
aubade *vocal music* 412 n.
musical piece 412 n.
wooing 889 n.
aubergine *vegetable* 301 n.
auburn *brown* 430 adj.
red 431 adj.
auction *sale* 793 n.
sell 793 vb.
overcharge 811 vb.
auction room *mart* 796 n.
audacity *courage* 855 n.
rashness 857 n.
insolence 878 n.
audible *sounding* 398 adj.
loud 400 adj.
auditory 415 adj.
intelligible 516 adj.
speaking 579 n.
audience *listener* 415 n.
listening 415 n.
onlookers 441 n.
allocution 583 n.
conference 584 n.
playgoer 594 n.
audiometer *acoustics* 398 n.
audiophone
hearing aid 415 n.
audit *enquiry* 459 n.
enquire 459 vb.
accounts 808 n.
account 808 vb.
audition *hearing* 415 n.
listening 415 n.
exam 459 n.
experiment 461 n.
conference 584 n.
auditor *listener* 415 n.
accountant 808 n.
auditorium
meeting place 192 n.
listener 415 n.
onlookers 441 n.
classroom 539 n.
conference 584 n.
theatre 594 n.
Augean stables *sink* 649 n.
auger *sharp point* 256 n.

perforator 263 n.
augment *increment* 36 n.
  augment 36 vb.
  add 38 vb.
  adjunct 40 n.
  strengthen 162 vb.
  part of speech 564 n.
  aggravate 832 vb.
augur *diviner* 511 n.
  predict 511 vb.
augury *divination* 511 n.
  omen 511 n.
august *great* 32 adj.
  notable 638 adj.
  worshipful 866 adj.
Augustan *elegant* 575 adj.
  perfect 646 adj.
Augustan Age
  literature 557 n.
  palmy days 730 n.
auk *animal* 365 n.
aumbry *church utensil* 990 n.
aunt *kinsman* 11 n.
  woman 373 n.
Aunt Sally
  laughing-stock 851 n.
au pair
  in exchange 151 adv.
aura *circumjacence* 230 n.
  light 417 n.
  prestige 866 n.
aural *auditory* 415 adj.
aureate *yellow* 433 adj.
aureole *loop* 250 n.
  light 417 n.
  honours 866 n.
aureomycin *drug* 658 n.
auricle *ear* 415 n.
auricular confession
  secrecy 525 n.
  ministration 988 n.
aurist *doctor* 658 n.
aurochs *cattle* 365 n.
Aurora *morning* 128 n.
  glow 417 n.
  luminary 420 n.
  redness 431 n.
  lesser god 967 n.
Auschwitz
  prison camp 748 n.
auscultation *listening* 415 n.
auspicate *auspicate* 68 vb.
  divine 511 vb.
auspice(s) *omen* 511 n.
  protection 660 n.
  aid 703 n.
auspicious
  circumstantial 8 adj.
  opportune 137 adj.
  presageful 511 adj.
  palmy 730 adj.

promising 852 adj.
austere *plain* 573 adj.
  severe 735 adj.
  ascetic 945 adj.
  pietistic 979 adj.
austerities *penance* 941 n.
austerity
  unsavouriness 391 n.
  plainness 573 n.
  insufficiency 636 n.
  severity 735 n.
  asceticism 945 n.
  pietism 979 n.
Australasian *ethnic* 11 adj.
Australopithecus
  mankind 371 n.
autarch *autocrat* 741 n.
autarchic
  governmental 733 adj.
  independent 744 adj.
autarchy *government* 733 n.
  independence 744 n.
autarkic
  independent 744 adj.
autarky *independence* 744 n.
authentic *unimitated* 21 adj.
  evidential 466 adj.
  genuine 494 adj.
authenticate *testify* 466 vb.
  make certain 473 vb.
  endorse 488 vb.
  give security 767 vb.
authenticity *identity* 13 n.
  authenticity 494 n.
author *cause* 156 n.
  producer 167 n.
  publicizer 528 n.
  penman 586 n.
  author 589 n.
  narrator 590 n.
  dissertator 591 n.
  planner 623 n.
authoritarian *tyrant* 735 n.
  authoritarian 735 adj.
authoritative
  powerful 160 adj.
  influential 178 n.
  evidential 466 adj.
  certain 473 adj.
  credal 485 adj.
  directing 689 adj.
  authoritative 733 adj.
  commanding 737 adj.
  scriptural 975 adj.
  orthodox 976 adj.
authorities *evidence* 466 n.
authorities, the
  master 741 n.
authority *greatness* 32 n.
  superiority 34 n.
  power 160 n.

influence 178 n.
  evidence 466 n.
  credential 466 n.
  informant 524 n.
  authority 733 n.
  commission 751 n.
  permit 756 n.
  jurisdiction 955 n.
authorize *empower* 160 vb.
  commission 751 vb.
  permit 756 vb.
  grant claims 915 vb.
authorship
  composition 56 n.
  causation 156 n.
  production 164 n.
  writing 586 n.
autism *selfishness* 932 n.
auto *automobile* 274 n.
autobahn *road* 624 n.
autobiographer
  chronicler 549 n.
  narrator 590 n.
autobiography
  biography 590 n.
autochthonous
  native 191 adj.
autocracy *despotism* 733 n.
  brute force 735 n.
autocrat *tyrant* 735 n.
  autocrat 741 n.
autocratic
  volitional 595 adj.
  authoritative 733 adj.
auto da fé *killing* 362 n.
  burning 381 n.
  capital punishment 963 n.
autogenesis
  propagation 164 n.
autogiro *aircraft* 276 n.
autograph
  no imitation 21 n.
  identification 457 n.
  label 547 n.
  sign 547 vb.
  script 586 n.
  written 586 adj.
autograph album
  reminder 505 n.
autohypnosis
  insensibility 375 n.
auto-intoxication
  indigestion 651 n.
  impairment 655 n.
automat *café* 192 n.
automatic
  involuntary 596 adj.
  spontaneous 609 adj.
  instrumental 628 adj.
  mechanical 630 adj.
  pistol 723 n.

automatic writing
  spiritualism 984 n.
automation
  production 164 n.
  instrumentality 628 n.
  mechanics 630 n.
automatism
  incogitance 450 n.
  spiritualism 984 n.
automaton *image* 551 n.
  fatalist 596 n.
  machine 630 n.
automobile
  automobile 274 n.
  vehicular 274 adj.
automotive *moving* 265 adj.
  travelling 267 adj.
autonomy
  government 733 n.
  independence 744 n.
autonomous
  genuine 494 adj.
  semantic 514 adj.
autopilot
  directorship 689 n.
autopsy *death* 361 n.
  inquest 364 n.
  inspection 438 n.
  enquiry 459 n.
autoptical *manifest* 522 adj.
autostrada *road* 624 n.
auto-suggestion *sense* 374 n.
  fantasy 513 n.
autumn *autumn* 129 n.
auxiliary *inferior* 35 n., adj.
  additional 38 n.
  extra 40 n.
  supporter 218 n.
  aider 703 n.
  aiding 703 adj.
  auxiliary 707 n.
  soldier 722 n.
avail *benefit* 615 vb.
  utility 640 n.
  be useful 640 vb.
  use 673 n.
availability *possibility* 469 n.
available
  on the spot 189 adj.
  accessible 289 adj.
  possible 469 adj.
  instrumental 628 adj.
  stored 632 adj.
  provisionary 633 adj.
  useful 640 adj.
  used 673 adj.
  offering 759 adj.
  not retained 779 adj.
  saleable 793 adj.
avail of *avail of* 673 vb.
avalanche *revolution* 149 n.

descent 309 n.
  snow 380 n.
  redundance 637 n.
avant-garde *precursor* 66 n.
  modernist 126 n.
  modern 126 adj.
  front 237 n.
avant-propos *prelude* 66 n.
avarice *avarice* 816 n.
  desire 859 n.
  selfishness 932 n.
avaricious *acquiring* 771 adj.
  (*see* avarice)
avatar
  transformation 143 n.
  theophany 965 n.
  revelation 975 n.
avenge *retaliate* 714 vb.
  avenge 910 vb.
  punish 963 vb.
avenger *vindicator* 927 n.
avenue *street* 192 n.
  path 624 n.
aver *affirm* 532 vb.
average *average* 30 n.
  median 30 adj.
  average out 30 vb.
  inconsiderable 33 adj.
  middle 70 n.
  generality 79 n.
  general 79 adj.
  typical 83 adj.
  not discriminate 464 vb.
  mid-course 625 n.
  not bad 644 adj.
  imperfection 647 n.
  imperfect 647 adj.
  mediocre 732 n.
averages *statistics* 86 n.
averment *affirmation* 532 n.
  litigation 959 n.
Avernus
  mythic hell 972 n.
aversion
  unwillingness 598 n.
  dislike 861 n.
  hatred 888 n.
  hateful object 888 n.
avert *deflect* 282 vb.
  obstruct 702 vb.
  parry 713 vb.
avian *animal* 365 adj.
aviary *dwelling* 192 n.
  nest 192 n.
  zoo 369 n.
aviation *aeronautics* 271 n.
aviator *aeronaut* 271 n.
avidity *rapacity* 786 n.
  avarice 816 n.
  desire 859 n.
avifauna *bird* 365 n.

avitaminosis *disease* 651 n.
avocation *pursuit* 619 n.
  avoidance 620 n.
  business 622 n.
avoid
  exclude 57 vb.
  be absent 190 vb.
  be distant 199 vb.
  be loth 598 vb.
  avoid 620 vb.
  circuit 626 vb.
  not use 674 vb.
  parry 713 vb.
  not observe 769 vb.
  dislike 861 vb.
  be unsocial 883 vb.
  make unwelcome 883 vb.
  hate 888 vb.
  disapprove 924 vb.
avoidable *avoidable* 620 adj.
avoidance *escape* 667 n.
  dutilessness 918 n.
  temperance 942 n.
  (*see* avoid)
avoirdupois
  finite quantity 26 n.
  weighment 322 n.
avouch *affirm* 532 vb.
avow *testify* 466 vb.
  assent 488 vb.
  affirm 532 vb.
  confess 526 vb.
avulsion *scission* 46 n.
  extraction 304 n.
avuncular *akin* 11 adj.
await *look ahead* 124 vb.
  wait 136 vb.
  expect, await 507 vb.
awake *attentive* 455 adj.
  active 678 adj.
  impressible 819 adj.
awaken
  have feeling 374 vb.
  cause feeling 374 vb.
  be informed 524 vb.
  excite 821 vb.
  (*see* wake)
award *judgment* 480 n.
  judge 480 vb.
  trophy 729 n.
  gift 781 n.
  give 781 vb.
  reward 962 n., vb.
aware *sentient* 374 adj.
  knowing 490 adj.
  intelligent 498 adj.
  lively 819 adj.
  impressible 819 adj.
awareness *intellect* 447 n.
awash *drenched* 341 adj.
away *absent* 190 adj.

afar 199 adv.
awe *excitation* 821 n.
  fear 854 n.
  frighten 854 vb.
  wonder 864 n.
  be wonderful 864 vb.
  respect 920 n.
  command respect 920 vb.
aweless *unfearing* 855 adj.
  disrespectful 921 adj.
awesome (*see* awe)
awesomeness *prestige* 866 n.
awful *silent* 399 adj.
  not nice 645 adj.
  bad 645 adj.
  frightening 854 adj.
awfully *greatly* 32 adv.
awkward
  unconformable 84 adj.
  young 130 adj.
  unwieldy 195 adj.
  ignorant 491 adj.
  foolish 499 adj.
  inelegant 576 adj.
  inexpedient 643 adj.
  clumsy 695 adj.
  difficult 700 adj.
  quarrelling 709 adj.
  annoying 827 adj.
  ill-bred 847 adj.
  graceless 842 adj.
  ridiculous 849 adj.
  modest 874 adj.
awkward age *youth* 130 n.
awkward squad
  bungler 697 n.
awl *sharp point* 256 n.
  perforator 263 n.
awn *prickle* 256 n.
  roughness 259 n.
awning *canopy* 226 n.
  screen 421 n.
awry *orderless* 61 adj.
  oblique 220 adj.
  distorted 246 adj.
  evil 616 adj.
  amiss 616 adj.
axe *shorten* 204 vb.
  sharp edge 256 n.
  dismiss 300 vb.
  killer 362 n.
  axe 723 n.
  means of execution 964 n.
axe-grinder *planner* 623 n.
  egotist 932 n.
axial *central* 225 adj.
  directed 281 adj.
axiom *certainty* 473 n.
  premise 475 n.
  axiom 496 n.
axis *pivot* 218 n.

  centre 225 n.
  rotator 315 n.
  gauge 465 n.
  association 706 n.
  society 708 n.
axle *rotator* 315 n.
axle-load *weighment* 322 n.
  metrology 465 n.
ayah *protector* 660 n.
  domestic 742 n.
  keeper 749 n.
aye *perpetuity* 115 n.
ayes, the *assenter* 488 n.
ayurvedic *medical* 658 adj.
azalea *tree* 366 n.
azimuth *horizontality* 216 n.
  compass point 281 n.
azoic *inorganic* 359 adj.
azotic *toxic* 653 adj.
azure *blueness* 435 n.
  heraldry 547 n.
azygous *alone* 88 adj.

B

ba *analogue* 18 n.
  spirit 447 n.
  mythic god 966 n.
baa *ululation* 409 n.
  ululate 409 vb.
babble *flow* 350 vb.
  sound faint 401 vb.
  reason ill 477 vb.
  be foolish 499 vb.
  be insane 503 vb.
  empty talk 515 vb.
  mean nothing 515 vb.
  language 557 n.
  chatter 581 n.
babbler *bird* 365 n.
  fool 501 n.
babe *ignoramus* 493 n.
  ninny 501 n.
  darling 890 n.
  innocent 935 n.
  (*see* baby)
Babel *confusion* 61 n.
  discord 411 n.
  unmeaningness 515 n.
  language 557 n.
baboon *monkey* 365 n.
  eyesore 842 n.
babu *male* 372 n.
  recorder 549 n.
baby *child* 132 n.
  infantine 132 adj.
  weakling 163 n.
  weak 163 adj.
  little 196 adj.
  mandate 751 n.
  please 826 vb.

  coward 856 n.
  (*see* babe)
baby-clothes *clothing* 228 n.
  robe 228 n.
babyhood *beginning* 68 n.
  youth 130 n.
  helplessness 161 n.
babyish *infantine* 132 adj.
  weak 163 adj.
  foolish 499 adj.
  cowardly 856 adj.
baby-sit *look after* 457 vb.
baby-sitter *servant* 742 n.
  keeper 749 n.
baccalaureate
  academic title 870 n.
baccarat *card game* 837 n.
Bacchanal *drunkard* 949 n.
Bacchanalia
  sensualism 944 n.
  drunkenness 949 n.
bacchante *madman* 504 n.
  drunkard 949 n.
Bacchic *disorderly* 61 adj.
  frenzied 503 adj.
bacchius *prosody* 593 n.
Bacchus *Olympian god* 967 n.
bachelor *male* 372 n.
  independent 744 adj.
  celibate 895 n.
bachelor girl
  woman 373 n.
  spinster 895 n.
bacillus *animalcule* 196 n.
  infection 651 n.
  poison 659 n.
back *change* 143 vb.
  supporter 218 n.
  be inverted 221 vb.
  line 227 vb.
  rear 238 n.
  back 238 adj.
  contraposition 240 n.
  camber 253 n.
  ride 267 vb.
  navigate 269 vb.
  deviate 282 vb.
  regress 286 vb.
  backwards 286 adv.
  harden 326 vb.
  blow 352 vb.
  break in 369 vb.
  choose 605 vb.
  gamble 618 vb.
  interceptor 702 n.
  aid, patronize 703 vb.
  approve 923 vb.
back and fill
  be irresolute 601 vb.
back-bencher *inferior* 35 n.
  councillor 692 n.

commoner 869 n.
backbite *defame* 926 vb.
backbone *essential part* 5 n.
  vigorousness 174 n.
  supporter 218 n.
  pillar 218 n.
  centrality 225 n.
  rear 238 n.
  resolution 599 n.
  stamina 600 n.
  courage 855 n.
backbreaking
  laborious 682 adj.
backchat *answer* 460 n.
  slang 560 n.
  witticism 839 n.
  sauciness 878 n.
backcloth *spectacle* 445 n.
  stage-set 594 n.
backdoor *rear* 238 n.
  doorway 263 n.
  means of escape 667 n.
  stealthy 525 adj.
back down *regress* 286 vb.
  tergiversate 603 vb.
  relinquish 621 vb.
backdrop *spectacle* 445 n.
  stage-set 594 n.
backer *stage manager* 594 n.
  gambler 618 n.
  patron 707 n.
  lender 784 n.
  friend 880 n.
back-fire *reversion* 148 n.
  counteraction 182 n.
  bang 402 n., vb.
backgammon
  board game 837 n.
background
  concomitant 89 n.
  accompanying 89 adj.
  distance 199 n.
  circumjacence 230 n.
  rear 238 n.
  spectacle 445 n.
  stage-set 594 n.
  ornamentation 844 n.
background, in the
  rearwards 238 adv.
  latent 523 adj.
backing *lining* 227 n.
  (*see* back)
back-lash
  counteraction 182 n.
  recoil 280 n.
backlog *store* 632 n.
back number
  archaism 127 n.
back out *regress* 286 vb.
  tergiversate 603 vb.
  resign 753 vb.

not observe 769 vb.
back-pedal *retard* 278 vb.
backrest *supporter* 218 n.
backroom *latent* 523 adj.
  hiding-place 527 n.
back-scratcher *toady* 879 n.
back-scratching
  co-operation 706 n.
  flattery 925 n.
back seat *inferiority* 35 n.
backseat driver
  spectator 441 n.
  director 690 n.
  adviser 691 n.
backset *cultivate* 370 vb.
backside *rear* 238 n.
  buttocks 238 n.
back-slapping
  ostentation 875 n.
  friendly 880 adj.
  sociability 882 n.
  sociable 882 adj.
backslide *revert* 148 vb.
  tergiversate 603 vb.
  relapse 657 vb.
  be wicked 934 vb.
  be impious 980 vb.
backslider
  tergiversator 605 n.
  offender 904 n.
  bad man 938 n.
backstaff *gauge* 465 n.
backstage *rear* 238 n.
  stage-set 594 n.
  on stage 594 adv.
backstairs
  hiding-place 527 n.
back street
  dilapidation 655 n.
backswept *back* 238 adj.
back-talk *answer* 460 n.
  witticism 839 n.
  sauciness 878 n.
back to back
  rearward 238 adv.
  in league 708 adv.
back-to-front
  inverted 221 adj.
back to the wall, with one's
  endangered 661 adj.
backward *late* 136 adj.
  rearward 238 adv.
  regressive 286 adj.
  ignorant 491 adj.
  unintelligent 499 adj.
  unwilling 598 adj.
  avoiding 620 adj.
  deteriorated 655 adj.
  immature 670 adj.
  unskilful 695 adj.

artless 699 adj.
backwardation
  discount 810 n.
backward-looking
  retrospective 125 adj.
  regressive 286 adj.
backwards
  backwards 286 adv.
backwards and forwards
  in exchange 151 adv.
  to and fro 317 adv.
backwash *effect* 157 n.
  water travel 269 n.
  eddy, wave 350 n.
back-water *retard* 278 vb.
  regress 286 vb.
  seclusion 883 n.
backwoodsman
  dweller 191 n.
backyard *place* 185 n.
bacon *meat* 301 n.
bacteria *animalcule* 196 n.
  infection 651 n.
  poison 659 n.
bactericide
  prophylactic 658 n.
bacteriology
  pathology 651 n.
bad *inferior* 35 adj.
  decomposed 51 adj.
  fetid 397 adj.
  feeble 572 adj.
  evil 616 adj.
  unimportant 639 adj.
  bad 645 adj.
  imperfect 647 adj.
  insalubrious 653 adj.
  deteriorated 655 adj.
  adverse 731 adj.
  disreputable 867 adj.
  wrong 914 adj.
  dishonest 930 adj.
  wicked 934 adj.
bad blood *dislike* 861 n.
  hatred 888 n.
  malevolence 898 n.
bad business
  hopelessness 853 n.
bad cess *ill fortune* 731 n.
bad character
  bad man 938 n.
bad conscience *guilt* 936 n.
  penitence 939 n.
bad egg *fetor* 397 n.
  bad man 938 n.
bad faith *falsehood* 541 n.
  non-observance 769 n.
  perfidy 930 n.
badge *heraldry* 547 n.
  badge 547 n.
  badge of rank 743 n.

jewellery 844 n.
badger *torment* 827 vb.
bad hand *bungler* 697 n.
bad hat *bad man* 938 n.
badinage *witticism* 839 n.
   ridicule 851 n.
bad job *bungling* 695 n.
   hopelessness 853 n.
bad language
   rudeness 885 n.
   scurrility 899 n.
bad light *detraction* 926 n.
bad lot *bad man* 938 n.
bad luck *chance* 159 n.
   disappointment 509 n.
   non-design 618 n.
   ill fortune 731 n.
badly off
   unprosperous 731 adj.
   poor 801 adj.
badminton *ball game* 837 n.
bad name *disrepute* 867 n.
badness (*see* bad)
bad odour *fetor* 397 n.
   disrepute 867 n.
bad patch *difficulty* 700 n.
   adversity 731 n.
bad taste *inelegance* 576 n.
   bad taste 847 n.
bad-tempered *sullen* 893 adj.
bad terms, on
   quarrelling 709 adj.
   inimical 881 adj.
bad to worse, from
   in adversity 731 adv.
   (*see* aggravation)
bad way, in a
   deteriorated 655 adj.
   endangered 661 adj.
bad wishes
   malediction 899 n.
Baedeker *itinerary* 267 n.
   guide-book 524 n.
baffle *be difficult* 700 vb.
   be obstructive 702 vb.
   oppose 704 vb.
   defeat 728 vb.
   be wonderful 864 vb.
baffled *impotent* 161 adj.
   puzzled 517 adj.
bag *bunch* 74 n.
   stow 187 vb.
   bag 194 n.
   bladder 194 n.
   be convex 253 vb.
   carrier 273 n.
   take 786 vb.
bagatelle *trifle* 639 n.
   ball game 837 n.
bagful *finite quantity* 26 n.
   store 632 n.

baggage *youngster* 132 n.
   box 194 n.
   thing transferred 272 n.
   encumbrance 702 n.
   property 777 n.
   loose woman 952 n.
baggy
   non-adhesive 49 adj.
   spacious 183 adj.
   recipient 194 adj.
   large 195 adj.
   broad 205 adj.
   pendent 217 adj.
bagman *enquirer* 459 n.
   pedlar 794 n.
bagnio *brothel* 951 n.
bagpipes *flute* 414 n.
bags *great quantity* 32
   trousers 228 n.
bail *transpose* 272 vb.
   void 300 vb.
   security 767 n.
   legal process 959 n.
bailee *consignee* 754 n.
   possessor 776 n.
bailie *officer* 741 n.
bailiff *manager* 690 n.
   officer 741 n.
   retainer 742 n.
   consignee 754 n.
   law officer 955 n.
bailiwick *district* 184 n.
   jurisdiction 955 n.
bail, on *pledged* 767 adj.
   accused 928 adj.
bailor *security* 767 n.
bairn *child* 132 n.
bait *attraction* 291 n.
   attract 291 vb.
   trickery 524 n.
   trap 542 n.
   ensnare 542 vb.
   incentive 612 n.
   tempt 612 vb.
   chase 619 n.
   torment 827 vb.
   excite love 887 vb.
   enrage 891 vb.
   reward 962 n.
baize *textile* 222 n.
bake *cook* 301 vb.
   be hot 379 vb.
   heat 381 vb.
bakehouse *cookery* 301 n.
baker *cookery* 301 n.
   provider 633 n.
bakers' dozen *over five* 99 n.
   undueness 916 n.
bakery *cookery* 301 n.
baking-powder *leaven* 323 n.
baksheesh *incentive* 612 n.

acquisition 771 n.
   gift 781 n.
   reward 962 n.
balalaika *harp* 414 n.
balance *relate* 9 vb.
   correlate 12 vb.
   adjust 24 vb.
   equilibrium 28 n.
   average 30 n.
   offset 31 n.
   set off 31 vb.
   remainder 41 n.
   part 53 n.
   completeness 54 n.
   stability 153 n.
   stabilize 153 vb.
   symmetry 245 n.
   scales 322 n.
   weigh 322 vb.
   compare 462 vb.
   gauge 465 n.
   measure 465 vb.
   sagacity 498 n.
   elegance 575 n.
   be irresolute 601 vb.
   mid-course 625 n.
   be half-way 625 vb.
   superfluity 637 n.
   account 808 vb.
   inexcitability 823 n.
   caution 858 n.
balance of power
   defence 713 n.
balances *funds* 797 n.
   credit 802 n.
balance sheet
   accounts 808 n.
balancing act
   equivocalness 518 n.
   compromise 770 n.
balas *gem* 844 n.
balbutiate *stammer* 580 vb.
balcony *lobby* 194 n.
   projection 254 n.
   theatre 594 n.
bald *hairless* 229 adj.
   smooth 258 adj.
   veracious 540 adj.
   feeble 572 adj.
   plain 573 adj.
   tedious 838 adj.
   impure 951 adj.
baldachin *canopy* 226 n.
   altar 990 n.
balderdash *silly talk* 515 n.
baldness *bareness* 229 n.
   veracity 540 n.
   feebleness 572 n.
   plainness 573 n.
baldric *outline* 233 n.
   loop 250 n.

bale *bunch* 74 n.
  stow 187 vb.
  cultivate 370 vb.
  evil 616 n.
bale-fire *fire* 379 n.
  signal light 420 n.
  signal 547 n.
baleful *harmful* 645
  adj.
  malevolent 898 adj.
bale out *fly* 271 vb.
  emerge 298 vb.
baler *ladle* 194 n.
  irrigator 341 n.
  farm tool 370 n.
balize *signal* 547 n.
balk, baulk
  partition 231 n.
  disappointment 509 n.
  disappoint 509 vb.
  materials 631 n.
  be obstructive 702 vb.
ball *sphere* 252 n.
  round 252 vb.
  missile 287 n.
  missile weapon 723 n.
  ammunition 723 n.
  dancing 837 n.
  plaything 837 n.
  social gathering 882 n.
ballad *vocal music* 412 n.
ballade *verse form* 593 n.
balladry *poetry* 593 n.
  doggerel 593 n.
ballast *offset* 31 n.
  compensate 31 vb.
  gravity 322 n.
  wisdom 498 n.
  safeguard 662 n.
ballerina *jumper* 312 n.
  actor 594 n.
  dancing 837 n.
ballet *composition* 56 n.
  stage play 594 n.
  dancing 837 n.
balletomane *crank* 504 n.
  playgoer 594 n.
ball game *ball game* 837 n.
ballistics *propulsion* 287 n.
  art of war 718 n.
  arm 723 n.
ballon d'essai
  empiricism 461 n.
balloon *bladder* 194 n.
  expand 197 vb.
  sphere 252 n.
  round 252 vb.
  be convex 253 vb.
  airship 276 n.
  be light 323 vb.
balloonist *aeronaut* 271 n.

ballot *affirmation* 532 n.
  vote 605 n.
ball-player *player* 837 n.
ballroom
  place of amusement 837 n.
ball up *bedevil* 63 vb.
ballyhoo *loudness* 400 n.
  overestimation 482 n.
  advertisement 528 n.
  exaggeration 546 n.
balm *moderator* 177 n.
  lubricant 334 n.
  scent 396 n.
  balm, medicine 658 n.
  pleasurableness 826 n.
balmoral *headgear* 228 n.
balmy *warm* 379 adj.
  fragrant 396 adj.
  palmy 730 adj.
  cheering 833 adj.
balneal *watery* 339 adj.
  cleansing 648 adj.
balneation *water* 339 n.
  moistening 341 n.
  ablution 648 n.
balsam *balm* 658 n.
balsamic *remedial* 658 adj.
  relieving 831 adj.
balustrade *handle* 218 n.
  pillar 218 n.
  fence 235 n.
bambino *child* 132 n.
bamboo *tree* 366 n.
bamboozle *puzzle* 474 vb.
  keep secret 525 vb.
  befool 542 vb.
  deceive 542 vb.
bamboozler *trickster* 545 n.
ban *exclusion* 57 n.
  exclude 57 vb.
  publication 528 n.
  proclaim 528 vb.
  hindrance 702 n.
  obstruct 702 vb.
  command 737 n., vb.
  restraint 747 n.
  restrain 747 vb.
  prohibition 757 n.
  prohibit 757 vb.
  make unwelcome 823 vb.
  malediction 899 n.
  disapprobation 924 n.
  disapprove 924 vb.
  condemn 961 vb.
  penalty 963 n.
banal *usual* 610 adj.
  dull 840 adj.
banality *maxim* 496 n.
banana *fruit* 301 n.
band *ligature* 47 n.
  bond, girdle 47 n.

band 74 n.
  congregate 74 vb.
  compressor 198 n.
  strip 208 n.
  outline 233 n.
  loop 250 n.
  orchestra 413 n.
  striation 437 n.
  personnel 686 n.
  co-operate 607 vb.
  party 708 n.
  formation 722 n.
bandage *tie* 45 vb.
  ligature 47 n.
  compressor 198 n.
  make smaller 198 vb.
  strip 208 n.
  supporter 218 n.
  support 218 vb.
  wrapping 226 n.
  cover 226 vb.
  cure 656 vb.
  surgical dressing 658 n.
  doctor 658 vb.
  obstruct 702 vb.
  relieve 831 vb.
bandanna *neckwear* 228 n.
bandbox *box* 194 n.
band-conductor
  orchestra 413 n.
  leader 690 n.
bandeau
  hairdressing 843 n.
banderole *girdle* 47 n.
  flag 547 n.
bandicoot *rodent* 365 n.
bandit *revolter* 738 n.
  robber 789 n.
  outcaste 883 n.
banditry *brigandage* 788 n.
band-leader
  timekeeper 117 n.
  orchestra 413 n.
band-master
  orchestra 413 n.
band of brothers
  community 708 n.
  close friend 880 n.
bandolier *girdle* 47 n.
  belt 228 n.
  loop 250 n.
  arsenal 723 n.
bands *canonicals* 989 n.
bandsman *orchestra* 413 n.
bandy *deformed* 246 adj.
bandy about *publish* 528 vb.
bandy arguments
  argue 475 vb.
bandy words
  interchange 151 vb.
  converse 584 vb.

bane *evil* 616n.
  badness 645n.
  plague 651n.
  bane 659n.
  pitfall 663n.
  adversity 731n.
  painfulness 827n.
  hateful object 888n.
  wrong 914n.
baneful (*see* bane)
bang *be vigorous* 174vb.
  hair 259n.
  close 264vb.
  impulse, knock 279n.
  impel, strike 279vb.
  loudness 400n.
  be loud 400vb.
  bang 402n.,vb.
  hair-dressing 843n.
banger *meat* 301n.
bangle *jewellery* 844n.
banian *vest* 228n.
  bodywear 228n.
  lender 784n.
  merchant 794n.
banish *exclude* 57vb.
  displace 188vb.
  eject 300vb.
  make unwelcome 883vb.
banishment *seclusion* 883n.
  penalty 963n.
banjo *harp* 414n.
banjoist
  instrumentalist 413n.
bank *high land* 209n.
  seat 218n.
  acclivity 220n.
  be oblique 220vb.
  edge 234n.
  laterality 239n.
  shore 344n.
  storage 632n.
  store 632vb.
  treasurer 798n.
  treasury 799n.
bank account
  wealth 800n.
bank down
  extinguish 382vb.
banker *lender* 784n.
  merchant 794n.
  treasurer 798n.
  card game 837n.
banknote *title-deed* 767n.
  paper money 797n.
bank on *hope* 852vb.
bankrupt *losing* 772adj.
  fleece 786vb.
  poor man 801n.
  poor 801adj.
  non-payer 805n.

non-paying 805adj.
bankruptcy
  insufficiency 636n.
  failure 728n.
  non-observance 769n.
  loss 772n.
  insolvency 805n.
banlieu *near place* 200n.
  circumjacence 230n.
banner
  advertisement 528n.
  flag 547n.
banneret *flag* 547n.
  nobleman 868n.
bannister(s) *pillar* 218n.
  fence 235n.
bannock *pastry* 301n.
banns *marriage* 894n.
banquet *feasting* 301n.
  eat, feed 301vb.
  plenty 635n.
  revel 837vb.
  festivity 837n.
  social gathering 882n.
banquette *stand* 218n.
  fortification 713n.
banshee *demon* 970n.
bant *decrease* 37vb.
  make smaller 198vb.
  make thin 206vb.
  be temperate 942vb.
  starve 946vb.
bantam *animalcule* 196n.
bantam-weight
  pugilist 722n.
banter *witticism* 839n.
  be witty 839vb.
  ridicule 851n.,vb.
  sauciness 878n.
  abstainer 942n.
banterer *humorist* 839n.
banting *dieting* 301n.
  fasting 946n.
bantling *child* 132n.
  descendant 170n.
banyan *tree* 366n.
baptism *reception* 299n.
  immersion 303n.
  moistening 341n.
  nomenclature 561n.
  preparation 669n.
  Christian rite 988n.
baptismal *admitting* 299adj.
  ritual 988adj.
Baptist *Protestant* 976n.
baptistery
  ritual object 988n.
  church interior 990n.
  church utensil 990n.
baptize *auspicate* 68vb.
  admit 299vb.

immerse 303vb.
  drench 341vb.
  name 561vb.
  make pious 979vb.
  perform ritual 988vb.
bar *in deduction* 39adv.
  fastening 47n.
  exclusion 57n.
  exclude 57vb.
  tavern 192n.
  chamber 194n.
  line 203n.
  barrier 235n.
  stopper 264n.
  close 264vb.
  island 349n.
  notation 410n.
  safeguard 662n.
  obstruct 702vb.
  restraint 747n.
  restrain 747vb.
  lock-up 748n.
  bullion 797n.
  disapprobation 924n.
  disapprove 924vb.
  tribunal 956n.
  bar 958n.
barb *filament* 208n.
  sharp point 256n.
  sharpen 256vb.
  thoroughbred 273n.
  missile weapon 723n.
barbarian
  foreigner 59n.
  extraneous 59adj.
  destroyer 168n.
  violent creature 176n.
  vulgarian 847n.
  vulgar 847adj.
  low fellow 869n.
  plebeian 869adj.
  rude person 885n.
  ruffian 904n.
barbarism *neology* 560n.
  solecism 565n.
  bad taste 847n.
  inhumanity 898n.
barbarity *violence* 176n.
  cruel act 898n.
  inhumanity 898n.
barbarize *pervert* 655vb.
barbarous (*see* barbarian, barbarism)
barbecue
  meal, feasting 301n.
  festivity 837n.
  social gathering 882n.
barbed shaft *ridicule* 851n.
barbed wire
  sharp point 256n.
  obstacle 702n.

defences 713 n.
barber *cleaner* 648 n.
  doctor 658 n.
  beautician 843 n.
barbette *fortification* 713 n.
barbican *fort* 713 n.
barbiturate
  moderator 177 n.
  soporific 679 n.
barcarole *vocal music* 712 n.
bard *meat* 301 n.
  cook 301 vb.
  musician 413 n.
  poet 593 n.
bare *inconsiderable* 33 adj.
  simple 44 adj.
  weakened 163 adj.
  demolish 165 vb.
  empty 190 adj.
  uncovered 229 adj.
  uncover 229 vb.
  open 263 vb.
  dry 342 adj.
  undisguised 522 adj.
  disclose 526 vb.
  plain 573 adj.
  unprovided 636 adj.
  vulnerable 661 adj.
barefaced
  undisguised 522 adj.
  false 541 adj.
barefoot *uncovered* 229 adj.
  beggarly 801 adj.
barehanded
  defenceless 161 adj.
bare-headed
  uncovered 229 adj.
  respectful 920 adj.
barely *almost* 33 adv.
  slightly 33 adv.
  imperfectly 647 adv.
bare minimum
  needfulness 627 n.
  dueness 915 n.
bareness *emptiness* 190 n.
  bareness 229 n.
  plainness 573 n.
bargain *consensus* 488 n.
  compact 765 n.
  contract 765 vb.
  make terms 766 vb.
  trade 791 n.
  bargain 791 vb.
  purchase 792 n.
  cheapness 812 n.
  be parsimonious 816 vb.
barge *boat* 275 n.
bargee *boatman* 270 n.
barge in *intrude* 297 vb.
  encroach 306 vb.
baritone *resonance* 404 n.

vocalist 413 n.
bark *layer* 207 n.
  skin 226 n.
  uncover 229 vb.
  sailing-ship 275 n.
  cry 408 vb.
  ululation 409 n.
  anger 891 n.
  be irascible 892 vb.
  sullenness 893 n.
  threat 900 n.
  threaten 900 vb.
barker *overestimation* 482 n.
  publicizer 528 n.
  petitioner 763 n.
  commender 923 n.
barkless *smooth* 258 adj.
barley *cereal* 301 n.
  provender 301 n.
  corn 366 n.
barm *cookery* 301 n.
  leaven 323 n.
  bubble 355 n.
barman *servant* 742 n.
Barmecide feast
  fasting 946 n.
barmy *light* 323 adj.
  unintelligent 499 adj.
barn *small house* 192 n.
  farm tool 370 n.
  storage 632 n.
  store 632 vb.
barnacle *coherence* 48 n.
barnstorm *act* 594 vb.
  be affected 850 vb.
barogram *pneumatics* 340 n.
barograph *altimetry* 209 n.
  pneumatics 340 n.
  weather 340 n.
barometer
  pneumatics 340 n.
  weather 340 n.
  meter 465 n.
baron *nobleman* 868 n.
  judge 957 n.
baronet *nobleman* 868 n.
baronetcy *honours* 866 n.
  aristocracy 868 n.
baronial *noble* 868 adj.
Baroque
  school of painting 553 n.
  ornamental 844 adj.
baroscope *pneumatics* 340 n.
barouche *carriage* 274 n.
barque *sailing-ship* 275 n.
barrack *quarters* 192 n.
  be obstructive 702 vb.
  lock-up 748 n.
barracker *hinderer* 702 n.
  detractor 926 n.
barrage *roll* 403 n.

bombardment 712 n.
  defences 713 n.
barrage-balloon
  defences 713 n.
  air force 722 n.
barranca *high land* 209 n.
  valley 255 n.
  conduit 351 n.
barrator *offender* 904 n.
barratry *improbity* 930 n.
barrel *vat* 194 n.
  cylinder 252 n.
barrel organ *organ* 414 n.
barren *impotent* 161 adj.
  unproductive 172 adj.
  profitless 641 adj.
barricade *barrier* 235 n.
  obstruct 702 vb.
  defences 713 n.
  defend 713 vb.
barricades *revolt* 738 n.
barrier *exclusion* 57 n.
  barrier 235 n.
  obstacle 702 n.
  defences 713 n.
barrister *lawyer* 958 n.
barrow *monticle* 209 n.
  pushcart 274 n.
  tomb 364 n.
  monument 548 n.
  shop 796 n.
barrow-boy *seller* 793 n.
  pedlar 794 n.
bar-tender *servant* 742 n.
barter *equivalence* 28 n.
  interchange 151 n., vb.
  transference 272 n.
  conditions 766 n.
  transfer 780 n.
  convey 780 vb.
  barter 791 n.
  trade 791 vb.
bartizan *fort* 713 n.
barytone *punctuation* 547 n.
basal *undermost* 214 adj.
  supporting 218 adj.
base *inferiority* 35 n.
  serial place 73 n.
  situation 186 n.
  station 187 n.
  place 187 vb.
  abode 192 n.
  layer 207 n.
  lowness 210 n.
  base 214 n.
  basis 218 n.
  limit 236 n.
  heraldry 547 n.
  bad 645 adj.
  cowardly 856 adj.
  disreputable 867 adj.

rascally 930 adj.
heinous 934 adj.
baseball *ball game* 837 n.
base-born *plebeian* 869 adj.
baseless *unreal* 2 adj.
baseline *place* 185 n.
base 214 n.
basement *cellar* 194 n.
base 214 n.
baseness *disrepute* 867 n.
improbity 930 n.
bash *strike* 279 vb.
bashaw *tyrant* 735 n.
nobleman 868 n.
bashful *unwilling* 598 adj.
cowardly 856 adj.
modest 874 adj.
bashi-bazouk *soldier* 722 n.
basic *intrinsic* 5 adj.
simple 44 adj.
fundamental 156 adj.
undermost 214 adj.
important 639 adj.
basics *reality* 1 n.
basilica *church* 990 n.
basilisk *rara avis* 84 n.
reptile 365 n.
eye 438 n.
gun 723 n.
noxious animal 904 n.
basin *stable* 192 n.
bowl 194 n.
cavity 255 n.
lake 346 n.
plain 348 n.
conduit 351 n.
basinet *armour* 713 n.
basis *basis* 218 n.
base 214 n.
bask *enjoy* 376 vb.
be hot 379 vb.
be pleased 824 vb.
basket *basket* 194 n.
basque *bodywear* 228 n.
edging 234 n.
bas relief *riliievo* 254 n.
bass *table fish* 365 n.
resonance 404 n.
vocalist 413 n.
basset *layer* 207 n.
bassinet *basket* 194 n.
bed 218 n.
pushcart 274 n.
bassoon *flute* 414 n.
bassoonist
instrumentalist 413 n.
bast *ligature* 47 n.
fibre 208 n.
bastard *spurious* 542 adj.
unwarranted 916 adj.
cad 938 n.

bastard 954 adj.
bastardize *disentitle* 916 vb.
make illegal 954 vb.
bastardy *sonship* 170 n.
bastardy 954 n.
undueness 916 n.
baste *tie* 45 vb.
strike 279 vb.
cook 301 vb.
moisten 341 vb.
pinguefy 357 vb.
Bastille *prison* 748 n.
bastinado
corporal punishment 963 n.
flog 963 vb.
bastion *protection* 660 n.
fortification 713 n.
bat *velocity* 277 n.
hammer 279 n.
strike 279 vb.
propel 287 vb.
bird 365 n.
language 557 n.
club 723 n.
batch *finite quantity* 26 n.
group 74 n.
bate *bate* 37 vb.
moderate 177 vb.
blunt 257 vb.
discount 810 vb.
bated breath *aphony* 578 n.
make smaller 198 vb.
bated breath, with
faintly 401 adv.
expectantly 507 adv.
voicelessly 578 adv.
bath *vessel* 194 n.
immersion 303 n.
moistening 341 n.
water 339 n.
ablution 648 n.
bath-chair *pushcart* 274 n.
bathe *swim* 269 vb.
immerse 303 vb.
plunge 313 vb.
be wet, drench 341 vb.
clean 648 vb.
amuse oneself 837 vb.
bath-house *chamber* 194 n.
ablution 648 n.
bathing beach
pleasure-ground 837 n.
bathing beauty
sea nymph 343 n.
bathing costume
beachwear 228 n.
bathos *absurdity* 497 n.
ridiculousness 849 n.
bathrobe
informal dress 228 n.
bathroom *chamber* 194 n.

ablution 648 n.
baths *hospital* 658 n.
bath salts *cosmetic* 843 n.
bathymeter *depth* 211 n.
oceanography 343 n.
bathyphilous *deep* 211 adj.
bathyscaph *depth* 211 n.
oceanography 343 n.
bathysphere *depth* 211 n.
diver 313 n.
oceanography 343 n.
batman *domestic* 742 n.
baton *supporter* 218 n.
badge 547 n.
badge of rule 743 n.
batrachian *frog* 365 n.
animal 365 n., adj.
bats *crazed* 503 adj.
battalion *formation* 722 n.
battalions *multitude* 104 n.
battels *accounts* 808 adj.
batten *fastening* 47 n.
batten down *close* 264 vb.
batten on *eat* 301 vb.
prosper 730 vb.
be servile 879 vb.
battens *theatre* 594 n.
batter *demolish* 165 vb.
obliquity 220 n.
deform 244 vb.
distort 246 vb.
strike, collide 279 vb.
pulpiness 356 n.
batterie
musical instrument 414 n.
battering-ram *ram* 279 n.
club 723 n.
battery *electricity* 160 n.
storage 632 n.
formation 722 n.
gun 723 n.
battle *slaughter* 362 n.
exertion 862 n.
exert oneself 682 vb.
fight 716 n.
contend 716 vb.
battle 718 n.
give battle 718 vb.
battle-axe *sharp edge* 256 n.
axe 723 n.
shrew 892 n.
battle-cry *call* 547 n.
defiance 711 n.
war, warfare 718 n.
threat 900 n.
battledore and shuttlecock
interchange 151 n.
ball game 837 n.
battle dress *uniform* 228 n.
battlefield
slaughter-house 362 n.

battle 718 n.
battleground 724 n.
battleground
  casus belli 709 n.
  fight 716 n.
  battle 718 n.
  battleground 724 n.
battlement *summit* 213 n.
  notch 260 n.
  fortification 713 n.
battler *opponent* 705 n.
  contender 716 n.
  combatant 722 n.
battleship *warship* 722 n.
battology *repetition* 106 n.
battue *slaughter* 362 n.
  chase 619 n.
  terror tactics 712 n.
batty *crazed* 503 adj.
bauble *trifle* 639 n.
  bauble 639 n.
  plaything 837 n.
  finery 844 n.
baulk *beam* 218 n.
  (see balk)
bawd *provider* 633 n.
  bawd 952 n.
bawdry *impurity* 951 n.
bawdy-house *brothel* 951 n.
bawl *cry* 408 n., vb.
  vociferate 408 vb.
bawling out *reproach* 924 n.
bay *compartment* 194 n.
  curve 248 n.
  cavity 255 n.
  horse 273 n.
  potherb 301 n.
  gulf 345 n.
  tree 366 n.
  ululate 409 vb.
  brown 430 adj.
  defeat 727 vb.
Bayard *brave person* 855 n.
  gentleman 929 n.
bay, at *endangered* 661 adj.
  in difficulties 700 adj.
  defensively 713 adv.
bayonet *strike* 279 vb.
  kill 362 vb.
  foin 712 n.
  strike at 712 vb.
  side-arms 723 n.
bayou *gulf* 345 n.
  lake 346 n.
bays *badge* 547 n.
  trophy 729 n.
  honours 866 n.
bazaar *sale* 793 n.
  shop 796 n.
  emporium 796 n.
bazooka *gun* 723 n.

missile weapon 723 n.
be *be* 1 vb.
  be situate 186 vb.
  be true 494 vb.
beach *edge* 234 n.
  land 295 vb.
  shore 344 n.
  arena 724 n.
beachcomber
  wanderer 268 n.
  wave 350 n.
beachhead
  battleground 724 n.
  retention 778 n.
beachwear *beachwear* 228 n.
  aquatics 269 n.
beacon *signal light* 420 n.
  telecommunication 531 n.
  heraldry 547 n.
  signal 547 n.
  warning 664 n.
  danger signal 665 n.
bead *sphere* 252 n.
  trimming 844 n.
  decorate 844 vb.
beading
  ornamental art 844 n.
beadle *officer* 741 n.
  law officer 955 n.
  church officer 986 n.
beadledom *habit* 610 n.
  governance 733 n.
beadroll *list* 87 n.
  prayers 981 n.
  ritual object 988 n.
  office-book 988 n.
beadsman *retainer* 742 n.
  dependant 742 n.
beady *rotund* 252 adj.
beagle *dog* 365 n.
  hunt 619 vb.
beak *prow* 237 n.
  projection 254 n.
  teacher 537 n.
  magistracy 957 n.
beaked *curved* 248 adj.
beaker *cup* 194 n.
be-all and end-all *all* 52 n.
  intention 617 n.
  important matter 638 n.
beam *beam* 218 n.
  laterality 239 n.
  direction 281 n.
  scales 322 n.
  radiation 417 n.
  flash 417 n.
  radiate 417 vb.
  materials 631 n.
  directorship 689 n.
  be cheerful 833 vb.
  smile 835 vb.

  be beautiful 841 vb.
beam-ends, on one's
  grounded 728 adj.
beam, off the
  irrelevant 10 adj.
  deviating 282 adj.
  mistaken 495 adj.
beam, on the
  straight 249 adv.
  in flight 271 adv.
beamy *broad* 205 adj.
  luminous 417 adj.
bean *small coin* 33 n.
  head 213 n.
  plant 366 n.
beanery *café* 192 n.
beanfeast *feasting* 301 n.
  meal 301 n.
beany *headgear* 228 n.
bear *reproduce itself* 164 vb.
  be fruitful 171 vb.
  compressor 198 n.
  support 218 vb.
  carry 273 vb.
  orientate 281 vb.
  animal 365 n.
  gambler 618 n.
  speculate 791 vb.
  seller 793 n.
  cheapen 812 vb.
  feel 818 vb.
  be patient 823 vb.
  suffer 825 vb.
  rude person 885 n.
  shrew 892 n.
bearable *imperfect* 647 adj.
  contenting 828 adj.
bear a hand *aid* 703 vb.
beard *filament* 208 n.
  prickle 256 n.
  hair 259 n.
  print-type 587 n.
  defy 711 vb.
  be courageous 855 vb.
beardless *young* 130 adj.
  hairless 229 adj.
bear down *approach* 289 vb.
  charge 712 vb.
bearer *bearer* 273 n.
  domestic 742 n.
bear fruit
  reproduce itself 164 vb.
  be useful 640 vb.
  be successful 727 vb.
beargarden *turmoil* 61 n.
  arena 724 n.
bear hard *be violent* 176 vb.
  ill-treat 645 vb.
  be severe 735 vb.
bearing *relation* 9 n.
  supporter 218 n.

pivot 218 n.
bearing 273 adj.
direction 281 n.
meaning 514 n.
conduct 688 n.
owed 803 adj.
feeling 818 adj.
bearings *circumstance* 8 n.
bearings 186 n.
bearish *saleable* 793 adj.
cheap 812 adj.
ungracious 885 adj.
bear-leader *teacher* 537 n.
bear off *deviate* 282 vb.
take away 786 vb.
bear oneself *behave* 688 vb.
bear out *corroborate* 466 vb.
demonstrate 478 vb.
vindicate 927 vb.
bear-pit *cattle pen* 369 n.
bearskin *headgear* 228 n.
armour 713 n.
bear up *support* 218 vb.
elevate 310 vb.
resist 715 vb.
bear upon *be related* 9 vb.
operate 173 vb.
influence 178 vb.
bear with *be patient* 823 vb.
forgive 909 vb.
beast *violent creature* 176 n.
animal 365 n.
dirty person 649 n.
eyesore 842 n.
ruffian 904 n.
noxious animal 904 n.
cad 938 n.
beastly *extremely* 32 adv.
animal 365 adj.
not nice 645 adj.
unpleasant 827 adj.
ugly 842 adj.
discourteous 885 adj.
hateful 888 adj.
sensual 944 adj.
beast of burden
beast of burden 273 n.
worker 686 n.
beast of prey *killer* 362 n.
animal 365 n.
taker 786 n.
noxious animal 904 n.
beat *be superior* 34 vb.
inferior 35 adj.
periodicity 141 n.
be periodic 141 vb.
territory 184 n.
place 185 n.
impulse 279 n.
strike 279 vb.
pass 305 vb.

outdo 306 vb.
oscillation 317 n.
oscillate 317 vb.
agitate 318 vb.
pulverize 332 vb.
roll 403 vb.
tempo 410 n.
play music 413 vb.
prosody 593 n.
route 624 n.
clean 648 vb.
use 673 vb.
attack 712 vb.
defeat 727 vb.
reprove 924 vb.
spank 963 vb.
beat about the bush
sophisticate 477 vb.
dissemble 541 vb.
be diffuse 570 vb.
circuit 626 vb.
beat down *cheapen* 812 vb.
beaten track *habit* 610 n.
route 624 n.
use 673 n.
beatific *good* 615 adj.
pleasurable 826 adj.
paradisiac 971 adj.
beatify *please* 826 vb.
dignify 866 vb.
sanctify 979 vb.
ecclesiasticize 985 vb.
beating *knock* 279 n.
chase 619 n.
victory 727 n.
defeat 728 n.
corporal punishment 963 n.
beat it *decamp* 296 vb.
beatitude *happiness* 824 n.
beat it up *revel* 837 vb.
beatnik *loser* 728 n.
lower classes 869 n.
beat of drum
publication 528 n.
danger signal 665 n.
beat off *repel* 292 vb.
beat one's brains
think 449 vb.
beat, on the
synchronous 123 adj.
synchronously 123 adj.
beat the air
waste effort 641 vb.
beat the bounds
limit 236 vb.
traverse 267 vb.
measure 465 vb.
beat the record
be superior 34 vb.
beat time *time* 117 vb.
play music 413 vb.

beat up *strike* 279 vb.
thicken 354 vb.
attack 712 vb.
beau *male* 372 n.
fop 848 n.
lover 887 n.
Beaufort scale
anemology 352 n.
beau ideal *paragon* 646 n.
a beauty 841 n.
beau monde
beau monde 848 n.
beautician *beautician* 843 n.
beautification
beautification 843 n.
beautiful *elegant* 575 adj.
pleasurable 826 adj.
beautiful 841 adj.
beautified 843 adj.
lovable 887 adj.
beautify *ornament* 574 vb.
make better 654 vb.
beautify 841 vb.
primp 843 vb.
decorate 844 vb.
beautiless *ugly* 842 adj.
beauty *symmetry* 245 n.
masterpiece 694 n.
beauty 841 n.
a beauty 841 n.
(*see* beautiful)
beauty parlour
beauty parlour 843 n.
beauty specialist
beautician 843 n.
beauty treatment
beautification 843 n.
beaux yeux *beauty* 841 n.
beaver *headgear* 228 n.
hair 259 n.
rodent 365 n.
busy person 678 n.
worker 686 n.
armour 713 n.
bebop *music* 412 n.
because *causally* 156 adv.
hence 158 adv.
beck *stream* 350 n.
gesture 547 n.
gesticulate 547 vb.
command 737 n.
beck and call, at one's
aiding 703 adj.
obedient 739 adj.
serving 742 adj.
beckon *gesticulate* 547 vb.
become *become* 1 vb.
be turned to 147 vb.
beautify 841 vb.
be one's duty 917 vb.
becoming *existence* 1 n.

appearance 445 n.
personable 841 adj.
bed *unite with* 45 vb.
place 187 vb.
layer 207 n.
base 214 n.
basis 218 n.
bed 218 n.
resting place 266 n.
garden 370 n.
sleep 679 n., vb.
bed and board
provision 633 n.
marriage 894 n.
bedbug *vermin* 365 n.
bed-clothes *coverlet* 226 n.
bedel *officer* 741 n.
bedesman *retainer* 742 n.
recipient 782 n.
worshipper 981 n.
bedevil *bedevil* 63 vb.
incommode 827 vb.
diabolize 969 vb.
bedevilment *spell* 983 n.
bedew *moisten* 341 vb.
bed-hopper *libertine* 952 n.
bedim *darken* 418 vb.
bedim 419 vb.
make unclean 649 vb.
bedizen *dress* 228 vb.
decorate 844 vb.
bedizened *bedecked* 844 adj.
vulgar 847 adj.
bedlam *confusion* 61 n.
turmoil 61 n.
discord 411 n.
madhouse 503 n.
bedlamite *madman* 504 n.
bed of roses *euphoria* 376 n.
fragrance 396 n.
bedouin *dweller* 191 n.
wanderer 268 n.
bed out *cultivate* 370 vb.
bed-pan *vessel* 194 n.
latrine 649 n.
bedraggled *orderless* 61 adj.
dirty 649 adj.
bedridden *sick* 651 adj.
bedrock *reality* 1 n.
simpleness 44 n.
permanence 144 n.
source 156 n.
base 214 n.
basis 218 n.
chief thing 638 n.
important 638 adj.
bedroom *chamber* 194 n.
bedside manner
therapy 658 n.
bed-time *clock time* 117 n.
evening 129 n.

vespertine 129 adj.
bee *fly* 365 n.
beech *tree* 366 n.
beechy *arboreal* 366 adj.
beef *vitality* 162 n.
meat 301 n.
be discontented 829 vb.
beef-witted
unthinking 450 adj.
unintelligent 499 adj.
beefy *stalwart* 162 adj.
fleshy 195 adj.
beehive *crowd* 74 n.
dome 253 n.
stock farm 369 n.
bee in the bonnet
whim 604 n.
bee-keeper *breeder* 369 n.
bee-line
short distance 200 n.
straightness 249 n.
direction 281 n.
mid-course 625 n.
Beelzebub *devil* 969 n.
beer *liquor* 301 n.
beer and skittles
enjoyment 824 n.
beery *intoxicating* 949 adj.
drunken 949 adj.
bee-sting *antidote* 658 n.
beestings *milk* 301 n.
beeswax *viscidity* 354 n.
beetle *be high* 209 vb.
hammer 279 n.
fly 365 n.
beetlebrow *projection* 254 n.
beetling
overhanging 209 adj.
pendent 217 adj.
beetroot *tuber* 301 n.
befall *happen* 154 vb.
befit *accord* 24 vb.
be expedient 642 vb.
be due 915 vb.
be one's duty 917 vb.
befool *puzzle* 474 vb.
sophisticate 477 vb.
mislead 495 vb.
disappoint 509 vb.
befool 542 vb.
humiliate 872 vb.
before *fore* 64 adv.
before 119 adv.
retrospectively 125 adv.
here 189 adv.
in front 237 adv.
ahead 283 adv.
beforehand *before* 119 adv.
beforehand 135 adv.
befoul *make unclean* 649 vb.
befriend *patronize* 703 vb.

befriend 880 vb.
be sociable 882 vb.
befuddlement
drunkenness 949 n.
beg *governor* 741 n.
beg 761 vb.
be parsimonious 816 vb.
nobleman 868 n.
be servile 879 vb.
beg, borrow or steal
find means 629 vb.
beget *cause* 156 vb.
generate 164 vb.
vitalize 360 vb.
begetter *cause* 156 n.
producer 167 n.
parent 169 n.
beggar *wanderer* 268 n.
idler 679 n.
beggar 763 n.
recipient 782 n.
poor man 801 n.
impoverish 801 vb.
low fellow 869 n.
toady 879 n.
beggarly *dirty* 649 adj.
beggarly 801 adj.
disreputable 867 adj.
beggary *poverty* 801 n.
beghard *monk* 986 n.
begin *become* 1 vb.
grow 36 vb.
begin 68 vb.
be born 360 vb.
prepare 669 vb.
undertake 672 n.
begin again *repeat* 106 vb.
revert 148 vb.
begin from *result* 157 vb.
beginner *beginner* 538 n.
bungler 697 n.
beginning *new* 126 adj.
earliness 135 n.
source 156 n.
beg off *mediate* 720 vb.
deprecate 762 vb.
begotten *born* 360 adj.
beg pardon
beg pardon 909 vb.
begrime *bedim* 419 vb.
make unclean 649 vb.
begrudge *be loth* 598 vb.
refuse 760 vb.
beg the question
reason ill 477 vb.
beguile *mislead* 495 vb.
deceive 542 vb.
flatter 925 vb.
béguine *nun* 986 n.
begum *potentate* 741 n.
nobleman 868 n.

behalf *benefit* 615 n.
behalf, on
  on behalf 755 adv.
behave *do* 676 vb.
  behave 688 vb.
  be virtuous 933 vb.
behaviour *mien* 445 n.
  way 624 n.
  action 676 n.
  conduct 688 n.
behaviourism
  psychology 447 n.
  morals 917 n.
behead *subtract* 39 vb.
  sunder 46 vb.
  shorten 204 vb.
  kill 362 vb.
  execute 963 vb.
behest *command* 737 n.
behind *rear* 238 n.
  rearward 238 adv.
  behind 284 adv.
behind bars *captive* 750 adj.
behindhand *late* 136 adj.
  behindhand 307 adv.
  unprepared 670 adj.
  non-paying 805 adj.
behind the scenes
  causally 156 adv.
  invisibly 444 adv.
  knowing 490 adv.
  latent 523 adj.
behind the times
  anachronistic 118 adj.
  not now 122 adv.
  antiquated 127 adj.
  ignorant 491 adj.
behind time
  anachronistic 118 adj.
  late 136 adj.
behold *see* 438 vb.
beholden *grateful* 907 adj.
  dutied 917 adj.
beholder *spectator* 441 n.
behove *be due* 915 vb.
  be one's duty 917 vb.
beige *brown* 430 adj.
being *existence* 1 n.
  self 80 n.
  life 360 n.
  affections 817 n.
bejewel *beautify* 841 vb.
  primp 843 vb.
  decorate 844 vb.
belabour *strike* 279 vb.
  flog 963 vb.
belated *late* 136 adj.
belay *tie* 45 vb.
bel canto *vocal music* 412 n.
belch *repeat* 106 vb.
  vomit 300 vb.

respiration 352 n.
  breathe 352 vb.
beldam *old woman* 133 n.
  maternity 169 n.
  hell-hag 904 n.
beleaguer
  circumscribe 232 adj.
  besiege 712 vb.
  wage war 718 vb.
belfry *high structure* 209 n.
  head 213 n.
  church exterior 990 n.
Belial *devil* 969 n.
belie *negate* 533 vb.
  oppose 704 vb.
belief *belief* 485 n.
  religious faith 973 n.
  piety 979 n.
believable *plausible* 471 adj.
  credible 485 adj.
believe *assume* 471 vb.
  believe 485 vb.
  expect 507 vb.
believer *religionist* 973 n.
  pietist 979 n.
belike *probably* 471 adv.
Belisha beacon
  traffic control 305 n.
  signal 547 n.
belittle
  underestimate 483 vb.
  hold cheap 922 vb.
  dispraise 924 vb.
  detract 926 vb.
bell *timekeeper* 117 n.
  megaphone 400 n.
  ululate 409 vb.
  campanology 412 n.
  gong 414 n.
  signal 547 n.
  church utensil 990 n.
belladonna
  poisonous plant 659 n.
bell, book and candle
  malediction 899 n.
  Christian rite 988 n.
belle *a beauty* 841 n.
  fop 848 n.
belles lettres
  literature 557 n.
belletrist *dissertator* 591 n.
bell-hop *courier* 531 n.
  servant 742 n.
bellicose *violent* 176 adj.
  quarrelling 709 adj.
  defiant 711 adj.
  contending 716 adj.
  warring 718 adj.
  courageous 855 adj.
  boastful 877 adj.
  insolent 878 adj.

bellicosity *irascibility* 892 n.
  (*see* bellicose)
belligerency
  belligerency 718 n.
  enmity 881 n.
belligerent
  contending 716 adj.
  warring 718 adj.
  combatant 722 n.
  inimical 881 adj.
bellman *publicizer* 528 n.
  messenger 531 n.
bellow *blow* 352 vb.
  be loud 400 vb.
  vociferate 408 vb.
  ululate 409 vb.
  be angry 891 vb.
  threaten 900 vb.
bellows *sufflation* 352 n.
  respiration 352 n.
  heater 383 n.
  voice 577 n.
bell-ringer
  campanology 412 n.
  instrumentalist 413 n.
  officer 741 n.
  servant 742 n.
  church officer 986 n.
bell the cat
  be courageous 855 vb.
bell-tower
  church exterior 990 n.
bell-wether *precursor* 66 n.
  sheep 365 n.
  leader 690 n.
belly *maw* 194 n.
  expand 197 vb.
  insides 224 n.
  swelling 253 n.
  be convex 253 vb.
  eater 301 n.
belly-ache *pang* 377 n.
  indigestion 651 n.
  be discontented 829 vb.
  lament 836 vb.
belly-band *girdle* 47 n.
  belt 228 n.
belly-flop *plunge* 313 n.
  descent 309 n.
bellyful *plenitude* 54 n.
  sufficiency 635 n.
  redundance 637 n.
belly-worship
  gluttony 947 n.
belong *be intrinsic* 5 vb.
  be related 9 vb.
  accord 24 vb.
  constitute 56 vb.
  be one of 58 vb.
  be included 78 vb.
  accompany 89 vb.

join a party 708 vb.
  belong 773 vb.
belongings *property* 777 n.
beloved *loved one* 887 n.
  lovable 887 adj.
  darling 890 n.
below *after* 65 adv.
  under 210 adv.
below par *under* 210 adv.
  imperfect 647 adj.
  at a discount 810 adv.
below stairs *under* 210 adv.
  plebeian 869 adj.
below the belt
  unjust 914 adj.
below the salt
  plebeian 869 adj.
below the surface
  latent 523 adj.
Belsen
  slaughter-house 362 n.
  prison camp 748 n.
belt *girdle* 47 n.
  region 184 n.
  compressor 198 n.
  belt 228 n.
  outline 233 n.
  loop 250 n.
  badge of rank 743 n.
  spank 963 vb.
  scourge 964 n.
belvedere *view* 438 n.
bema *rostrum* 539 n.
bemedal *decorate* 844 vb.
  dignify 866 vb.
bemire
  make unclean 649 vb.
bemoan *lament* 836 vb.
bemused *abstracted* 456 adj.
bench *stand* 218 n.
  seat 218 n.
  workshop 687 n.
  badge of rule 743 n.
  tribunal 956 n.
bencher *judge* 957 n.
  lawyer 958 n.
bench-mark *limit* 236 n.
  signpost 547 n.
bench of bishops
  synod 985 n.
  ecclesiarch 986 n.
bend *tie* 45 vb.
  break 46 vb.
  ligature 47 n.
  derange 63 vb.
  conform 83 vb.
  modify 143 vb.
  force 176 vb.
  obliquity 220 n.
  be oblique 220 vb.
  distortion 246 n.

distort 246 vb.
  angularity 247 n.
  angulate 247 vb.
  curve 248 n.
  make curved 248 vb.
  twine 251 vb.
  point to 281 vb.
  deviation 282 n.
  deflect 282 vb.
  stoop 311 vb.
  soften 327 vb.
  heraldry 547 n.
  motivate 612 vb.
  knuckle under 721 vb.
  obey 739 vb.
  be servile 879 vb.
  greet 884 vb.
beneath *less* 35 adv.
  under 210 adv.
beneath one
  degrading 867 adj.
Benedick *spouse* 894 n.
  celibate 895 n.
Benedictine *monk* 986 n.
benediction *good* 615 n.
  thanks 907 n.
  praise 923 n.
  prayers 981 n.
  act of worship 981 n.
  church service 988 n.
benefaction *gift* 781 n.
  liberality 813 n.
benefactor *patron* 707 n.
  giver 781 n.
  good giver 813 n.
  philanthropist 901 n.
  benefactor 903 n.
  good man 937 n.
benefice *benefice* 985 n.
  ecclesiasticize 985 vb.
beneficence *goodness* 644 n.
  benevolence 897 n.
beneficial *good* 615 adj.
  profitable 640 adj.
  beneficial 644 adj.
  salubrious 652 adj.
  remedial 658 adj.
  gainful 771 adj.
beneficiary
  beneficiary 776 n.
  recipient 782 n.
benefit *benefit* 615 n.,vb.
  utility 640 n.
  be useful 640 vb.
  be expedient 642 vb.
  do good 644 vb.
  use 673 n.
  subvention 703 n.
  trophy 729 n.
  acquisition 771 n.
  gain 771 n.

gift 781 n.
  be benevolent 897 vb.
benefit of clergy
  non-liability 919 n.
  ecclesiasticism 985 n.
benefit of doubt
  acquittal 960 n.
benefit performance
  gift 781 n.
benevolence *goodness* 644 n.
  aid 703 n.
  subvention 703 n.
  lenity 736 n.
  gift 781 n.
  borrowing 785 n.
  taking 786 n.
  tax 809 n.
  friendliness 880 n.
  love 887 n.
  benevolence 897 n.
  disinterestedness 931 n.
  piety 979 n.
benevolent *liberal* 813 adj.
  friendly 880 adj.
  benevolent 897 adj.
  (*see* benevolence)
benighted
  vespertine 129 adj.
  late 136 adj.
  dark 418 adj.
  blind 439 adj.
  ignorant 491 adj.
benign, benignant
  salubrious 652 adj.
  safe 660 adj.
  benevolent 897 adj.
benison *good* 615 n.
  praise 923 n.
  prayers 981 n.
bent *tendency* 179 n.
  oblique 220 adj.
  angular 247 adj.
  curved 248 adj.
  grass 366 n.
  bias 481 n.
  willingness 597 n.
  aptitude 694 n.
  affections 817 n.
Benthamism
  philanthropy 901 n.
benthonic *oceanic* 343 adj.
benthos *lowness* 210 n.
  ocean 343 n.
ben trovato
  plausible 471 adj.
  witty 839 adj.
bent upon *resolute* 599 adj.
  desiring 859 adj.
benumb *disable* 161 vb.
  render insensible 375 vb.
  refrigerate 382 vb.

make inactive 679 vb.
make insensitive 820 vb.
frighten 854 vb.
benzedrine *tonic* 658 n.
be off *go away* 190 vb.
start out 296 vb.
run away 620 vb.
bequeath *transfer* 272 vb.
dower 777 vb.
bequeath 780 vb.
give 781 vb.
bequest (*see* bequeath)
berate *exprobate* 924 vb.
berceuse
musical piece 412 n.
vocal music 412 n.
soporific 679 n.
relief 831 n.
bereave *deprive* 786 vb.
sadden 834 vb.
bereavement *loss* 772 n.
bereft *defenceless* 161 adj.
unentitled 916 adj.
beret *headgear* 228 n.
berg *ice* 380 n.
berhyme *poetize* 593 vb.
detract 926 vb.
beribbon *decorate* 844 vb.
dignify 866 vb.
berlin *carriage* 274 n.
berm *edge* 234 n.
berry *fruit* 301 n.
berserk *furious* 176 adj.
violent creature 176 n.
frenzied 503 adj.
angry 891 adj.
berth *place* 187 vb.
quarters 192 n.
stable 192 n.
dwell 192 vb.
goal 295 n.
arrive 295 vb.
job 622 n.
beryl *greenness* 432 n.
blueness 435 n.
gem 844 n.
beseech *entreat* 761 vb.
worship 981 vb.
beseem *be due* 915 vb.
be one's duty 917 vb.
beset *surround* 230 vb.
follow 284 vb.
besiege 712 vb.
request 761 vb.
torment 827 vb.
frighten 854 vb.
besetting *universal* 79 adj.
habitual 610 adj.
attacking 712 adj.
beshrew *cuss* 899 vb.
beside *in addition* 38 adv.

unconformably 84 adv.
nigh 200 adv.
sideways 239 adv.
beside oneself
frenzied 503 adj.
besiege *surround* 230 vb.
besiege 712 vb.
wage war 718 vb.
request 761 vb.
besilver *coat* 226 vb.
beslime
make unclean 649 vb.
besmear *overlay* 226 vb.
bedim 419 vb.
make unclean 649 vb.
shame 867 vb.
defame 926 vb.
besmirch *bedim* 419 vb.
defame 926 vb.
besnow *whiten* 427 vb.
besom
cleaning utensil 648 n.
besotted *misjudging* 481 adj.
foolish 499 adj.
enamoured 887 adj.
bespangle *decorate* 844 vb.
bespatter
make unclean 649 vb.
shame 867 vb.
dispraise 924 vb.
defame 926 vb.
bespeak *be early* 135 vb.
evidence 466 vb.
mean 514 vb.
indicate 547 vb.
promise 764 vb.
bespoke *definite* 80 adj.
promised 764 adj.
best *superior* 34 n.
supreme 34 adj.
be superior 34 vb.
best 644 adj.
defeat 727 vb.
money 797 n.
best blood *nobility* 868 n.
bestead *be useful* 640 vb.
bested *in difficulties* 700 adj.
best, for the *well* 615 adv.
bestial *animal* 365 adj.
sensual 944 adj.
bestiality *sensualism* 944 n.
illicit love 951 n.
best, in one's
bedecked 844 adj.
bestir oneself
be active 678 vb.
exert oneself 682 vb.
best man *auxiliary* 707 n.
close friend 880 n.
bridesman 894 n.
best of, make the

avail of 673 vb.
best of terms, on the
friendly 880 adj.
bestow *place* 187 vb.
give 781 vb.
best part *main part* 52 n.
best people *élite* 644 n.
beau monde 848 n.
upper class 868 n.
bestraddle *overlie* 266 vb.
bestride *connect* 45 vb.
influence 178 vb.
extend 183 vb.
be broad 205 vb.
be high 209 vb.
overlie 266 vb.
dominate 733 vb.
best-seller *book* 589 n.
reading matter 589 n.
novel 590 n.
exceller 644 n.
best wishes
congratulation 886 n.
bet *gambling* 618 n.
gamble 618 vb.
contest 716 n.
contend 716 vb.
betake oneself to
travel 267 vb.
avail of 673 vb.
beta minus
inconsiderable 33 adj.
betatron *nucleonics* 160 n.
bête noire *bane* 659 n.
hateful object 888 n.
bethel *church* 990 n.
bethink oneself
meditate 449 vb.
remember 505 vb.
betide *happen* 154 vb.
betimes *betimes* 135 adv.
betoken *evidence* 466 vb.
predict 511 vb.
indicate 547 vb.
bet on *be certain* 473 vb.
betray *disappoint* 509 vb.
disclose 526 vb.
be false 541 vb.
deceive 542 vb.
indicate 547 vb.
apostatize 603 vb.
revolt 738 vb.
fail in duty 918 vb.
be dishonest 930 vb.
betray itself
be visible 443 vb.
betroth *promise* 764 vb.
marry 894 vb.
betrothal *love affair* 887 n.
wooing 889 n.
wedding 894 n.

betrothed *promised* 764 adj.
  loved one 887 n.
  marriageable 894 adj.
better *superior* 34 adj.
  be superior 34 vb.
  gambler 618 n.
  excellent 644 adj.
  improved 654 adj.
  make better 654 vb.
  restored 656 adj.
betterment *benefit* 615 n.
  improvement 654 n.
better sort *upper class* 868 n.
betting *gambling* 618 n.
between *between* 231 adv.
between-decks
  compartment 194 n.
between ourselves
  secretly 525 adv.
between two stools
  in difficulties 700 adj.
betwixt and between
  between 231 adv.
  mediocre 732 adj.
bevel *cut* 46 vb.
  obliquity 220 n.
beverage *potion* 301 n.
bevy *group* 74 n.
bewail *lament* 836 vb.
beware *be warned* 664 vb.
bewilder *distract* 456 vb.
  puzzle 474 vb.
  be wonderful 864 vb.
bewitch *engross* 449 vb.
  motivate 612 vb.
  delight 826 vb.
  be wonderful 864 vb.
  excite love 887 vb.
  be malevolent 898 vb.
  curse 899 vb.
  diabolize 969 vb.
  bewitch 983 vb.
bewitchment
  conversion 147 n.
  (*see* bewitch)
bewray *disclose* 526 vb.
bey *governor* 741 n.
  nobleman 868 n.
beyond *beyond* 199 adv.
beyond one's means
  dear 811 adj.
beyond one's reach
  impracticable 470 adj.
beyond praise
  perfect 646 adj.
beyond price
  of price 811 adj.
beyond the pale
  excluded 57 adj.
bezel *obliquity* 220 n.
  furrow 262 n.

bezique *card game* 837 n.
Bhagavad Gita
  non-Biblical scripture
    975 n.
bhaktiyoga *religion* 973 n.
bhang *poison* 659 n.
  poisonous plant 659 n.
bias *inequality* 29 n.
  influence 178 vb.
  tendency 179 n.
  obliquity 220 n.
  render oblique 220 vb.
  deflect 282 vb.
  prejudice 481 n.
  bias 481 n., vb.
  eccentricity 503 n.
  willingness 597 n.
  opiniatry 602 n.
  choice 605 n.
  motivate 612 vb.
  affections 817 n.
  liking 859 n.
  dislike 861 n.
  injustice 914 n.
bib *apron* 228 n.
  cleaning cloth 648 n.
  get drunk 949 vb.
bibber *drunkard* 949 n.
bibelot *bauble* 639 n.
Bible *certainty* 473 n.
  truth 494 n.
  oracle 511 n.
  scripture 975 n.
Bible critic
  theologian 973 n.
bibliodule *religionist* 979 n.
bibliographer
  bookman 589 n.
bibliography *list* 87 n.
  reference book 589 n.
bibliolatry *pietism* 979 n.
  idolatry 982 n.
bibliomania *erudition* 490 n.
  mania 503 n.
bibliophile *collector* 492 n.
  bookman 589 n.
bibliotheca *library* 589 n.
bibulous *feeding* 301 adj.
  drunken 949 adj.
bicameral
  parliamentary 692 adj.
bice *green pigment* 432 n.
  blue pigment 435 n.
biceps *vitality* 162 n.
bicker *disagree* 25 vb.
  argue 475 vb.
  bicker 709 n.
bicolour *variegated* 437 adj.
bicuspid *bisected* 92 adj.
bicycle *conveyance* 267 n.
  ride 267 vb.

bicycle 274 n.
bicycle chain *club* 723 n.
  scourge 964 n.
bid *intention* 617 n.
  aim at 617 vb.
  gambling 618 n.
  essay 671 n., vb.
  command 737 vb.
  offer 759 n., vb.
  request 761 n., vb.
  purchase 792 n.
bid against *oppose* 704 vb.
biddable *willing* 597 adj.
  obedient 739 adj.
bid defiance *defy* 711 vb.
  boast 877 vb.
bidder *petitioner* 763 n.
  purchaser 792 n.
biddy *poultry* 365 n.
bide *stay* 144 vb.
bide one's time *wait* 136 vb.
  await 507 vb.
  not act 677 vb.
bidet *ablution* 648 n.
bid fair *tend* 179 vb.
  be likely 471 vb.
  give hope 852 vb.
bid up *overcharge* 811 vb.
biennial *periodic* 110 adj.
  seasonal 141 adj.
  flower 366 n.
bier *bed* 218 n.
  funeral 364 n.
bifacial *double* 91 adj.
bifarious *double* 91 adj.
biff *knock* 279 n.
  strike 279 vb.
biform *dual* 90 adj.
  double 91 adj.
bifurcate *bisected* 92 n.
  bifurcate 92 vb.
  cross 222 vb.
  angular 247 adj.
  angulate 247 vb.
  diverge 294 vb.
big *great* 32 adj.
  older 131 adj.
  large 195 adj.
  important 638 adj.
  affected 850 adj.
bigamist *polygamist* 894 n.
bigamy
  type of marriage 894 n.
big bug *bigwig* 638 n.
big drum *boast* 877 n.
bigener *hybrid* 43 n.
biggin *cauldron* 194 n.
bight *curve* 248 n.
  cavity 255 n.
  gulf 345 n.
bigness *greatness* 32 n.

strength 162 n.
hugeness 195 n.
big noise *bigwig* 638 n.
  person of repute 866 n.
bigot *doctrinaire* 473 n.
  opinionist 602 n.
  religionist 979 n.
bigotry *positiveness* 473 n.
  narrow mind 481 n.
  credulity 487 n.
  opiniatry 602 n.
  severity 735 n.
  sectarianism 978 n.
  pietism 979 n.
big shot *bigwig* 638 n.
big stick *incentive* 612 n.
  compulsion 740 n.
big-time *notable* 638 adj.
big way, in a *greatly* 32 adv.
bigwig *superior* 34 n.
  bigwig 638 n.
  master 741 n.
  person of repute 866 n.
  aristocrat 868 n.
  proud man 871 n.
big with
  productive 164 adj.
bijou *a beauty* 841 n.
  gem 844 n.
bike *crowd* 74 n.
  bicycle 274 n.
bikini *beachwear* 228 n.
  aquatics 269 n.
bilateral *dual* 90 adj.
  lateral 239 adj.
  contractual 765 adj.
bilberry *fruit* 301 n.
bilbo *side-arms* 723 n.
bilboes *fetter* 748 n.
  pillory 964 n.
bile *discontent* 829 n.
  melancholy 834 n.
  resentment 891 n.
  irascibility 892 n.
  sullenness 893 n.
  envy 912 n.
bileless *benevolent* 897 adj.
bilge *leavings* 41 n.
  base 214 n.
  convexity 253 n.
  silly talk 515 n.
  swill 649 n.
bilingual *linguistic* 557 adj.
bilious *green* 432 adj.
  yellow 433 adj.
  unhealthy 651 adj.
  melancholic 834 adj.
  resentful 891 adj.
  irascible 892 adj.
  crapulous 949 adj.
biliousness *indigestion* 651 n.

bilk *disappoint* 509 vb.
  deceive 542 vb.
  defraud 788 vb.
  be in debt 803 vb.
  not pay 805 vb.
bilker *trickster* 545 n.
  avoider 620 n.
  defrauder 789 n.
  non-payer 805 n.
bill *numerical result* 85 n.
  list 87 n.
  sharp edge 256 n.
  exhibit 522 n.
  advertisement 528 n.
  advertise 528 vb.
  label 547 n.
  dramatize 594 vb.
  spear, axe 723 n.
  demand 737 vb.
  title-deed 767 n.
  paper money 797 n.
  credit 802 n.
  debt 803 n.
  accounts 808 n.
  account 808 vb.
  price 809 n., vb.
bill and coo *caress* 889 vb.
bill-collector
  consignee 754 n.
  receiver 782 n.
billet *place* 185 n.
  place 187 vb.
  quarters 192 n.
  goal 295 n.
  label 547 n.
  correspondence 588 n.
  apportion 783 vb.
billet doux
  correspondence 588 n.
  love-token 889 n.
billfold *case* 194 n.
  treasury 799 n.
bill-hook *sharp edge* 256 n.
billiards *ball game* 837 n.
billingsgate *slang* 560 n.
  scurrility 899 n.
billion
  over one hundred 99 n.
bill of exchange
  title-deed 767 n.
  paper money 797 n.
bill of fare *list* 87 n.
  meal 301 n.
billon *a mixture* 43 n.
billow *swelling* 253 n.
  wave 350 n.
billowy *curved* 248 adj.
  convex 253 adj.
bill-sticker *publicizer* 528 n.
billycock *headgear* 228 n.
bimetallism *finance* 797 n.

binary *dual* 90 adj.
  star 321 n.
bind *tie* 45 vb.
  combine 50 vb.
  bring together 74 vb.
  stabilize 153 vb.
  make smaller 198 vb.
  cover 226 vb.
  close 264 vb.
  be dense 324 vb.
  cultivate 370 vb.
  repair 656 vb.
  doctor 658 vb.
  obstruct 702 vb.
  compel 740 vb.
  subjugate 745 vb.
  fetter 747 vb.
  give terms 766 vb.
  tedium 838 n.
  impose a duty 917 vb.
binder *bond* 47 n.
  compressor 198 n.
  farm tool 370 n.
bindery *bookbinding* 589 n.
binding *ligature* 47 n.
  compressive 198 adj.
  wrapping 226 n.
  solidifying 324 adj.
  book-binding 589 n.
  necessary 596 adj.
  preceptive 693 adj.
  authoritative 733 adj.
  compelling 740 adj.
  conditional 766 adj.
  tedious 838 adj.
  trimming 844 n.
  obligatory 917 adj.
bind oneself
  promise 764 vb.
bind over
  impose a duty 917 vb.
bind up *repair* 656 vb.
  relieve 831 vb.
bine *plant* 366 n.
binge *festivity* 837 n.
binnacle *sailing aid* 269 n.
binocular *seeing* 438 adj.
binoculars *telescope* 442 n.
biochemistry *biology* 358 n.
biod *occultism* 984 n.
biogenesis
  propagation 164 n.
biogenetic
  biological 358 adj.
biograph *cinema* 445 n.
biographer *chronicler* 549 n.
  author 589 n.
  narrator 590 n.
biography *record* 548 n.
  reading matter 589 n.
  biography 590 n.

biology *structure* 331 n.
 biology 358 n.
 life 360 n.
bionomics *biology* 358 n.
bioplasm *organism* 358 n.
 life 360 n.
bioplast *organism* 358 n.
 life 360 n.
bioscope *cinema* 445 n.
biotic *alive* 360 adj.
biotic potential
 productiveness 171 n.
biotype *prototype* 23 n.
 organism 358 n.
biparous *dual* 90 adj.
bipartisan *agreeing* 24 adj.
 dual 90 adj.
 concurrent 181 adj.
 assented 488 adj.
 co-operative 706 adj.
 concordant 710 adj.
bipartite *disjunct* 46 adj.
 bisected 92 adj.
biped *animal* 365 n.
biplanar *semantic* 514 adj.
biplane *aircraft* 276 n.
birch *tree* 366 n.
 spank 963 vb.
 scourge 964 n.
bird *aeronaut* 271 n.
 speeder 277 n.
 bird 365 n.
 animal 365 n.
 woman 373 n.
 vocalist 413 n.
bird-cage *cattle pen* 369 n.
bird-call *ululation* 409 n.
 vocal music 412 n.
bird in the hand
 object 319 n.
 possession 773 n.
bird-lime *adhesive* 47 n.
 trap 542 n.
bird's-eye view *whole* 52 n.
 generality 79 n.
 view 438 n.
 spectacle 445 n.
 art subject 553 n.
 compendium 592 n.
bird-watching
 zoology 367 n.
bird-witted
 light-minded 456 adj.
 foolish 499 adj.
bireme *galley* 275 n.
biretta *headgear* 228 n.
 badge of rule 743 n.
 canonicals 989 n.
 vestments 989 n.
birth *origin* 68 n.
 beginning 68 n.

propagation 164 n.
 obstetrics 164 n.
 genealogy 169 n.
 life 360 n.
 nobility 868 n.
birth certificate
 label 547 n.
 record 548 n.
birth-control *restraint* 747 n.
birthday *date* 108 n.
 anniversary 141 n.
 special day 876 n.
birthday suit
 bareness 229 n.
birthmark
 identification 547 n.
 skin disease 651 n.
 blemish 845 n.
birth-pang *obstetrics* 164 n.
birthplace *source* 156 n.
 home 192 n.
birthrate *statistics* 86 n.
 propagation 164 n.
birthright *priority* 119 n.
 dower 777 n.
 right 913 n.
 dueness 915 n.
birth-stone *talisman* 983 n.
bis *again* 106 adv.
biscuit *food* 301 n.
 pastry 301 n.
bisect *sunder* 46 vb.
 bisect 92 vb.
 apportion 783 vb.
bisection
 equalization 28 n.
 middle 70 n.
 bisection 92 n.
bishop *chessman* 837 n.
 ecclesiarch 986 n.
bishopless
 Protestant 976 adj.
bishopric *district* 184 n.
 parish 985 n.
 church office 985 n.
bison *cattle* 365 n.
bisque *vantage* 34 n.
 soup 301 n.
bistoury *sharp edge* 256 n.
bistre *brown paint* 430 n.
bistro *café* 192 n.
bit *small quantity* 33 n.
 piece 53 n.
 perforator 263 n.
 woman 373 n.
 restrain 747 vb.
 fetter 748 n.
 loose woman 952 n.
bit by bit
 by degrees 27 adv.
 separately 46 adv.

piecemeal 53 adv.
 severally 80 adv.
 gradatim 278 adv.
bitch *dog* 365 n.
 female animal 373 n.
 hell-hag 904 n.
 cad 938 n.
bitchy *malevolent* 898 adj.
bite *small quantity* 33 n.
 cut 46 vb.
 piece 53 n.
 vigorousness 174 n.
 be violent 176 vb.
 be sharp 256 vb.
 notch 260 vb.
 mouthful 301 n.
 chew 301 vb.
 give pain 377 vb.
 refrigerate 382 vb.
 pungency 388 n.
 trickery 542 n.
 deceive 542 vb.
 engrave 555 vb.
 vigour 571 n.
 ill-treat 645 vb.
 wound 655 vb.
 fight 716 vb.
 hurt 827 vb.
 cause discontent 829 vb.
 endearment 889 n.
 anger 891 n.
 enrage 891 vb.
 be irascible 892 vb.
 sullenness 893 n.
biter bit *retaliation* 714 n.
bite the dust
 be destroyed 165 vb.
 tumble 309 vb.
 be defeated 728 vb.
biting tongue
 reproach 924 n.
bits *rubbish* 641 n.
bitt *fastening* 47 n.
bitter *liquor* 301 n.
 painful 377 adj.
 cold 380 adj.
 pungent 388 adj.
 unsavoury 391 adj.
 sour 393 adj.
 unpleasant 827 adj.
 discontented 829 adj.
 regretting 830 adj.
 disliked 861 adj.
 inimical 881 adj.
 hating, hateful 888 adj.
 resentful 891 adj.
 irascible 892 adj.
 malevolent 898 adj.
 disapproving 924 adj.
 detracting 926 adj.
bitter end *finality* 69 n.

bitter-ender
opinionist 602 n.
opponent 705 n.
malcontent 829 n.
bitterness (*see* bitter)
bitter pill
unsavouriness 391 n.
adversity 731 n.
painfulness 827 n.
hateful object 888 n.
punishment 963 n.
bitters *sourness* 393 n.
bitter-sweet *contrary* 14 adj.
painful 377 adj.
bitty *fragmentary* 53 adj.
incomplete 55 adj.
bitumen *resin* 357 n.
bivalent *double* 91 adj.
bivalve *fish food* 301 n.
fish 365 n.
bivouac *station* 187 n.
place oneself 187 vb.
abode 192 n.
dwell 192 vb.
resting place 266 n.
bizarre *unusual* 84 adj.
ridiculous 849 adj.
blab *inform* 524 vb.
divulge 526 vb.
accuse 928 vb.
blabber *informer* 524 n.
stammer 580 vb.
black *exclude* 57 vb.
funereal 364 adj.
dark 418 adj.
darken 418 vb.
blackness 428 n.
negro 428 n.
black 428 adj.
blacken 428 vb.
evil 616 adj.
bad 645 adj.
clean 648 vb.
dirty 649 adj.
prohibited 757 adj.
lamentation 836 n.
ugly 842 adj.
sullen 893 adj.
heinous 934 adj.
black and white
polarity 14 n.
light contrast 417 n.
achromatism 426 n.
blackness 428 n.
pied 437 adj.
painting 553 n.
black and white, in
written 586 adj.
black art *sorcery* 983 n.
blackball *exclusion* 57 n.
exclude 57 vb.

eject 300 vb.
shame 867 vb.
unsociability 883 n.
make unwelcome 883 vb.
disapprobation 924 n.
blackberry *fruit* 301 n.
black thing 428 n.
blackbird *bird* 365 n.
vocalist 413 n.
black thing 428 n.
black books *odium* 888 n.
black cap
danger signal 665 n.
condemnation 961 n.
black cloud *threat* 900 n.
black coat *cleric* 986 n.
blacken *darken* 418 vb.
colour 425 vb.
blacken 428 vb.
impair 655 vb.
make ugly 842 vb.
shame 867 vb.
dispraise 924 vb.
defame 926 vb.
blackguard *cuss* 889 vb.
ruffian 904 n.
evildoer 904 n.
exprobate 924 vb.
rascally 930 adj.
knave 938 n.
blackhead *blemish* 845 n.
blacking
black pigment 428 n.
cleanser 648 n.
blackjack *vessel* 194 n.
hammer 279 n.
strike 279 vb.
kill 362 vb.
club 723 n.
blacklead *lubricant* 334 n.
cleanser 648 n.
clean 648 vb.
blackleg
nonconformist 84 n.
tergiversator 603 n.
hateful object 888 n.
black-letter
antiquated 127 adj.
letter 558 n.
print-type 587 n.
black-list *set apart* 46 vb.
name 561 n.
unsociability 883 n.
make unwelcome 883 vb.
disapprobation 924 n.
disapprove 924 vb.
condemnation 961 n.
condemn 961 vb.
black magic
diabolism 969 n.
sorcery 983 n.

blackmail *demand* 737 n., vb.
compulsion 740 n.
compel 740 vb.
rapacity 786 n.
fleece 786 vb.
booty 790 n.
tax 809 n.
threat 900 n.
threaten 900 vb.
reward 962 n.
Black Maria *vehicle* 274 n.
lock-up 748 n.
card game 837 n.
black mark *reprimand* 924 n.
black market *trade* 791 n.
speculate 791 vb.
mart 796 n.
illegal 954 adj.
Black Mass
diabolism 969 n.
blackness *darkness* 418 n.
blackness 428 n.
black out *darken* 418 vb.
obliterate 550 vb.
restrain 747 vb.
prohibit 757 vb.
black-out
obscuration 418 n.
fatigue 684 n.
war measures 718 n.
prohibition 757 n.
drunkenness 949 n.
black sheep *offender* 904 n.
Blackshirts
political party 708 n.
blacksmith
animal husbandry 369 n.
artisan 686 n.
black spot *danger* 661 n.
bladder *bladder* 194 n.
blade *sharp edge* 256 n.
propeller 269 n.
male 372 n.
combatant 722 n.
side-arms 723 n.
fop 848 n.
blah-blah
empty talk 515 n.
blain *swelling* 253 n.
hardness 326 n.
ulcer 651 n.
blame *attribute* 158 vb.
censure 924 n.
blame 924 vb.
accusation 928 n.
guilt 936 n.
blameless *guiltless* 935 adj.
blame oneself
be penitent 939 vb.
blameworthy
discreditable 867 adj.

blameworthy 924 adj.
accusable 928 adj.
heinous 934 adj.
guilty 936 adj.
blanch *lose colour* 426 vb.
decolorize 426 vb.
whiten 427 vb.
bland *lenitive* 177 adj.
smooth 258 adj.
courteous 884 adj.
blandiloquence
flattery 925 n.
blandish *induce* 612 vb.
tempt 612 vb.
flatter 925 vb.
blandishment
endearment 889 n.
blank *non-existence* 2 n.
insubstantial 4 adj.
uniform 16 adj.
zero 103 n.
empty 190 adj.
centrality 225 n.
form 243 n.
opaque 423 adj.
colourless 426 adj.
unthinking 450 adj.
ignorant 491 adj.
unintelligible 517 adj.
punctuation 547 n.
clean 648 adj.
impassive 820 adj.
blank cartridge
insubstantial thing 4 n.
ineffectuality 161 n.
emptiness 190 n.
false alarm 665 n.
blank cheque *scope* 744 n.
liberality 813 n.
blanket *general* 79 adj.
suppress 165 vb.
moderate 177 vb.
coverlet 226 v.
cover 226 vb.
warm clothes 381 n.
screen 421 vb.
indiscriminate 464 adj.
blankety-blank
damnable 645 adj.
blank verse
verse form 593 n.
prosody 593 n.
blare *loudness* 400 n.
be loud 400 vb.
resonance 404 n.
resound 404 vb.
stridor 407 n.
blarney *empty talk* 515 n.
mean nothing 515 vb.
falsehood 541 n.
be cunning 698 vb.

flattery 925 n.
blasé *bored* 838 adj.
sated 863 adj.
blaspheme
be irreligious 974 vb.
be impious 980 vb.
blast *outbreak* 176 n.
air 340 n.
wind, gale 352 n.
blow 352 vb.
loudness 400 n.
bang 402 n.
crackle 402 vb.
impair 655 vb.
blight 659 n.
danger signal 665 n.
fire at 712 vb.
adversity 731 n.
be malevolent 898 vb.
bewitch 983 vb.
blat *mean nothing* 515 vb.
blatancy *bad taste* 847 n.
vanity 873 n.
ostentation 875 n.
insolence 878 n.
blatant *loud* 400 adj.
ululant 409 adj.
well-known 528 adj.
(*see* blatancy)
blather *empty talk* 515 n.
blatter *ululate* 409 vb.
blaze *fire* 379 n.
be hot 379 vb.
light 417 n.
shine 417 vb.
mark 547 vb.
blazer *tunic* 228 n.
livery 547 n.
blaze the trail
come before 64 vb.
blazon *proclaim* 528 vb.
heraldry 547 n.
register 548 vb.
decorate 844 vb.
honour 866 vb.
be ostentatious 875 vb.
blazonry *heraldry* 547 n.
bleach *dry* 342 vb.
decolorize 426 vb.
whiten 427 vb.
clean 648 vb.
hairwash 843 n.
bleachers *onlookers* 441 n.
bleak *adverse* 731 adj.
blear *bedim* 419 vb.
blear-eyed
dim-sighted 440 adj.
bleary *dim* 419 adj.
bleat *ululate* 409 vb.
be discontented 829 vb.
bleb *swelling* 253 n.

bleed *flow out* 298 vb.
void, emit 300 vb.
be wet 341 vb.
doctor 658 vb.
fleece 786 vb.
overcharge 811 vb.
suffer 825 vb.
pity 905 vb.
blemish *weakness* 163 n.
deformity 246 n.
impair 655 vb.
eyesore 842 n.
make ugly 842 vb.
blemish 845 n., vb.
slur 867 n.
blench *be loth* 598 vb.
avoid 620 vb.
show feeling 818 vb.
quake 854 vb.
blend *a mixture* 43 n.
mix 43 vb.
compound 50 n.
combine 50 vb.
harmonize 410 vb.
bless *benefit* 615 vb.
be auspicious 730 vb.
permit 756 vb.
rejoice 835 vb.
be benevolent 897 vb.
thank 907 vb.
approve, praise 923 vb.
worship 981 vb.
perform ritual 988 vb.
blessed *good* 615 adj.
palmy 730 adj.
happy 824 adj.
pleasurable 826 adj.
paradisiac 971 adj.
ritual 988 adj.
blessing *benefit* 615 n.
good 615 n.
permission 756 n.
(*see* bless)
blessings *prosperity* 730 n.
blest with *possessing* 773 adj.
blether *empty talk* 515 n.
mean nothing 515 vb.
blight *decay* 51 n.
destroyer 168 n.
badness 645 n.
dilapidation 655 n.
impair 655 vb.
blight 659 n.
adversity 731 n.
be malevolent 898 vb.
bewitch 983 vb.
blighter *cad* 938 n.
Blighty *home* 192 n.
blimp *airship* 276 n.
opinionist 602 n.
blind *shade* 226 n.

shine 417 vb.
curtain 421 n.
screened 421 adj.
blind 439 adj., vb.
be unseen 444 vb.
inattentive 456 adj.
distract 456 vb.
indiscriminating 464 adj.
misjudging 481 adj.
disguise 527 n.
trickery 542 n.
deceive 542 vb.
involuntary 596 adj.
pretext 614 n.
stratagem 698 n.
impassive 820 adj.
unastonished 865 adj.
drunkenness 949 n.
dead drunk 949 adj.
blind alley *cavity* 255 n.
road 624 n.
obstacle 702 n.
blind bargain
uncertainty 474 n.
gambling 618 n.
rashness 857 n.
blind corner
invisibility 444 n.
blindfold *screen* 421 vb.
blind 439 adj., vb.
keep secret 525 vb.
deceive 542 vb.
blinding *luminous* 417 adj.
blindness *blindness* 439 n.
invisibility 444 n.
indiscrimination 464 n.
ignorance 491 n.
opiniatry 602 n.
blind side *blindness* 439 n.
inattention 456 n.
prejudice 481 n.
folly 499 n.
opiniatry 602 n.
blind spot *blindness* 439 n.
invisibility 444 n.
inattention 456 n.
prejudice 481 n.
blink *flash* 417 n.
reflection 417 n.
shine 417 vb.
look 438 n.
gaze 438 vb.
be blind 439 vb.
dim sight 440 n.
be dim-sighted 440 vb.
be irresolute 601 vb.
avoid 620 vb.
blinker *signal light* 420 n.
screen 421 vb.
blind 439 vb.
dim sight 440 n.

deceive 542 vb.
bliss *happiness* 824 n.
blissful *palmy* 730 adj.
happy 824 adj.
pleasurable 826 adj.
paradisiac 971 adj.
blister *bladder* 194 n.
swelling 253 n.
skin disease 651 n.
blithe *happy* 824 adj.
cheerful 833 adj.
blitz *havoc* 165 n.
loudness 400 n.
attack 712 n.
bombardment 712 n.
attack 712 vb.
fire at 712 vb.
battle 718 n.
blizzard *storm* 176 n.
gale 352 n.
wintriness 380 n.
bloat *enlarge* 197 vb.
animal disease 651 n.
bloated *fleshy* 195 adj.
bloater *fish food* 301 n.
bloc *political party* 708 n.
block *housing* 192 n.
bulk 195 n.
stand 218 n.
close 264 vb.
repel 292 vb.
solid body 324 n.
hardness 326 n.
dunce 501 n.
engraving 555 n.
stationery 586 n.
obstacle 702 n.
obstruct 702 vb.
defend 713 vb.
parry 713 vb.
prohibit 757 vb.
not pay 805 vb.
unfeeling person 820 n.
means of execution 964 n.
blockade *surround* 230 vb.
circumscription 232 n.
circumscribe 232 vb.
closure 264 n.
close 264 vb.
hindrance 702 n.
obstruct 702 vb.
attack 712 n.
besiege 712 vb.
warfare 718 n.
wage war 718 vb.
restriction 747 n.
blockage *stop* 145 n.
hindrance 702 n.
obstacle 702 n.
blockhead *ignoramus* 493 n.
dunce 501 n.

blockhouse *fort* 713 n.
blockish
unintelligent 499 adj.
block out *efform* 243 vb.
outline 233 vb.
bloke *male* 372 n.
person 371 n.
blond *achromatism* 426 n.
colourless 426 adj.
whitish 427 adj.
yellow 433 adj.
blood *consanguinity* 11 n.
auspicate 68 vb.
breed 77 n.
genealogy 169 n.
vigorousness 174 n.
fluid, blood 335 n.
life 360 n.
redness 431 n.
fop 848 n.
nobility 868 n.
cruel act 898 n.
blood bath *slaughter* 362 n.
terror tactics 712 n.
blood feud *quarrel* 709 n.
revenge 910 n.
blood-group *race* 11 n.
classification 77 n.
blood 335 n.
blood-guilty
murderous 362 adj.
guilty 936 adj.
blood-horse
thoroughbred 273 n.
bloodhound *dog* 365 n.
detective 459 n.
bloodiness
inhumanity 898 n.
bloodless
insubstantial 4 adj.
weak 163 adj.
colourless 426 adj.
diseased 651 adj.
peaceful 717 adj.
guiltless 935 adj.
blood-letting
voidance 300 n.
killing 362 n.
surgery 658 n.
blood-line *genealogy* 169 n.
blood-lust *violence* 176 n.
inhumanity 898 n.
blood-money *irenics* 719 n.
atonement 941 n.
blood pressure
blood pressure 651 n.
bloodshed *slaughter* 362 n.
warfare 718 n.
cruel act 898 n.
bloodshot
sanguineous 335 adj.

bloodshot 431 adj.
angry 891 adj.
drunken 949 adj.
blood-sport *killing* 363 n.
chase 619 n.
bloodstained
murderous 362 adj.
bloodshot 431 adj.
bloodstock
thoroughbred 273 n.
nobility 868 n.
bloodsucker *tyrant* 733 n.
taker 786 n.
noxious animal 904 n.
blood-sucking
rapacity 786 n.
blood-thirsty *furious* 176 adj.
murderous 362 adj.
harmful 645 adj.
warlike 718 adj.
cruel 898 adj.
blood up, with one's
bravely 855 adv.
blood vessel
conduit 351 n.
bloody *violent* 176 adj.
sanguineous 335 adj.
humid 341 adj.
murderous 362 adj.
bloodshot 431 adj.
oppressive 735 adj.
cruel 898 adj.
bloody-mindedness
obstinacy 602 n.
bloody nose *recoil* 280 n.
defeat 728 n.
bloom *salad days* 130 n.
adultness 134 n.
reproduce 164 vb.
expand 197 vb.
layer 207 n.
open 263 vb.
flower 366 n.
redness 431 n.
health 650 n.
be healthy 650 vb.
prosper 730 vb.
be beautiful 841 vb.
bloomer *mistake* 495 n.
bloomers *trousers* 228 n.
underwear 228 n.
bloomy *vegetal* 366 adj.
blossom *growth* 157 n.
product 164 n.
reproduce itself 164 vb.
be fruitful 171 vb.
(*see* bloom)
blot *tincture* 43 n.
absorb 299 vb.
dry 342 vb.
blacken 428 vb.

variegate 437 vb.
mistake 495 n.
blunder 495 vb.
conceal 525 vb.
mark 547 vb.
obliteration 550 n.
obliterate 550 vb.
write 586 vb.
clean 648 vb.
dirt 649 n.
make unclean 649 vb.
impair 655 vb.
be clumsy 695 vb.
eyesore 842 n.
make ugly 842 vb.
blemish 845 n., vb.
slur 867 n.
shame 867 vb.
blotch *blemish* 845 n.
blot out *subtract* 39 vb.
destroy 165 vb.
obliterate 550 vb.
forgive 909 vb.
(*see* blot)
blotter
cleaning utensil 648 n.
blotto *dead drunk* 949 adj.
blouse *bodywear* 228 n.
blow *be violent* 176 vb.
expand 197 vb.
knock 279 n.
meal 301 n.
aerify 340 vb.
wind, gale 352 n.
blow 352 vb.
inexpectation 508 n.
evil 616 n.
deed 676 n.
be fatigued 684 vb.
expend 806 vb.
be prodigal 815 vb.
suffering 825 n.
corporal punishment 963 n.
blow away *propel* 287 vb.
blow down *demolish* 165 vb.
blower *orifice* 263 n.
air 340 n.
ventilation 352 n.
hearing aid 415 n.
blow-hole *orifice* 263 n.
outlet 298 n.
air-pipe 353 n.
blow hot and cold
vary 152 vb.
be irresolute 601 vb.
be capricious 604 vb.
blow in *enter* 297 vb.
blowiness *wind* 352 n.
blow-lamp *furnace* 383 n.
blown *panting* 684 adj.
blow one's own trumpet

boast 877 vb.
blow one's top
get angry 891 vb.
blow open *force* 176 vb.
blow-out *feasting* 301 n.
meal 301 n.
bang 402 n.
gluttony 947 n.
blow out *nullify* 2 vb.
suppress 165 vb.
enlarge 197 vb.
snuff out 418 vb.
extinguish 382 vb.
blow over *be past* 125 vb.
cease 145 vb.
blow-pipe *propellant* 287 n.
sufflation 352 n.
air-pipe 353 n.
heater 383 n.
missile weapon 723 n.
toy gun 723 n.
blows *fight* 716 n.
anger 891 n.
blow the gaff *inform* 524 vb.
divulge 526 vb.
blow-up *duplicate* 22 vb.
outbreak 176 n.
photography 551 n.
blow up *augment* 36 vb.
break 46 vb.
demolish 165 vb.
be violent 176 vb.
force 176 vb.
enlarge 197 vb.
sufflate 352 vb.
be disclosed 526 vb.
photograph 551 vb.
miscarry 728 vb.
get angry 891 vb.
blow upon *defame* 926 vb.
blowy *windy* 352 adj.
blowzy *fleshy* 195 adj.
expanded 197 adj.
red 431 adj.
blubber *fat* 357 n.
stammer 580 vb.
weep 836 vb.
bludgeon *club* 723 n.
brute force 735 n.
oppress 735 vb.
compulsion 740 n.
compel 740 vb.
blue *athlete* 162 n.
air 340 n.
a-cold 380 adj.
blueness 435 n.
blue 435 adj., vb.
badge 547 n.
decoration 729 n.
bored 838 adj.
impure 591 adj.

Bluebeard
  polygamist 894 n.
blue blood *blood* 335 n.
  nobility 868 n.
blue devils
  psychopathy 503 n.
  melancholy 834 n.
blue-eyed boy
  favourite 890 n.
blue moon *neverness* 109 n.
blue-pencil *subtract* 39 vb.
  obliterate 550 vb.
  rectify 654 vb.
  prohibit 757 vb.
blueprint *prototype* 23 n.
  representation 551 n.
  compendium 592 n.
  plan 623 n., vb.
  preparation 669 n.
blue ribbon
  decoration 729 n.
blues *music* 412 n.
  psychopathy 503 n.
  melancholy 834 n.
  dance 837 n.
  sullenness 893 n.
blue stocking
  intellectual 492 n.
bluff *violent* 176 adj.
  high land 209 n.
  verticality 215 n.
  unsharpened 257 adj.
  blind 439 vb.
  duplicity 541 n.
  trickery 542 n.
  deceive 542 vb.
  plead 614 vb.
  be affected 850 vb.
  boast 877 n.
  ungracious 885 adj.
bluffer *impostor* 545 n.
  affector 850 n.
  boaster 877 n.
blunder *misjudge* 481 adj.
  mistake 495 n.
  blunder 495 vb.
  solecize 565 vb.
  be unskilful 695 vb.
  fail 728 vb.
blunderbuss
  propellant 287 n.
  fire-arm 723 n.
blunderer *fool* 501 n.
  bungler 697 n.
blunt *weaken* 163 vb.
  inert 175 adj.
  moderate 177 vb.
  low 210 adj.
  unsharpened 257 adj.
  blunt 257 vb.
  smooth 258 adj.

render insensible 375 vb.
  undisguised 522 adj.
  assertive 532 adj.
  veracious 540 adj.
  artless 699 adj.
  dibs 797 n.
  make insensitive 820 vb.
  ill-bred 847 adj.
  ungracious 885 adj.
blur *darken* 418 vb.
  dimness 419 n.
  blur 440 vb.
  make unclean 649 vb.
  blemish 845 n.
blurb *advertisement* 528 n.
  praise 923 n.
blurb-writer
  publicizer 528 n.
  commender 923 n.
blurred *amorphous* 244 adj.
  dim 419 adj.
  ill-seen 444 adj.
blurry *shadowy* 419 adj.
  ill-seen 444 adj.
blurt *improvise* 609 vb.
blurt out *inform* 524 vb.
  divulge 526 vb.
  voice 577 vb.
  speak 579 vb.
blush *heat* 379 n.
  hue 425 n.
  redness 431 n.
  redden 431 vb.
  disclosure 526 n.
  indication 547 n.
  feeling 818 n.
  show feeling 818 vb.
  guilt 836 n.
  humiliation 872 n.
  be humbled 872 vb.
  modesty 874 n.
  be modest 874 vb.
blushful *modest* 874 adj.
  pure 950 adj.
bluster *violence* 176 n.
  be violent 176 vb.
  be active 678 vb.
  defy 711 vb.
  nervousness 854 n.
  boast 877 n., vb.
  insolence 878 n.
  be angry 891 vb.
  threaten 900 vb.
  threat 900 n.
blusterer *boaster* 877 n.
  insolent person 878 n.
blustery *violent* 176 adj.
  windy 352 adj.
boa *neckwear* 228 n.
boa-constrictor
  compressor 198 n.

reptile 365 n.
boar *pig* 365 n.
  male animal 372 n.
board *lamina* 207 n.
  stand, shelf 218 n.
  irrupt 297 vb.
  provisions 301 n.
  feed 301 vb.
  hardness 326 n.
  materials 631 n.
  provide 633 vb.
  director 690 n.
  council 692 n.
  attack 712 vb.
  tribunal 956 n.
boarder *resident* 191 n.
  eater 301 n.
  learner 538 n.
boarding house
  quarters 192 n.
board, on *here* 189 adv.
  under way 269 adv.
boardroom
  conference 584 n.
boards *wrapping* 226 n.
  bookbinding 589 n.
  theatre 594 n.
boast *comprise* 78 vb.
  exaggerate 546 vb.
  triumph 727 vb.
  possess 773 vb.
  ridiculousness 849 n.
  be affected 850 vb.
  person of repute 866 n.
  pride 871 n.
  feel pride 871 vb.
  be vain 873 vb.
  be ostentatious 875 vb.
  boast 877 n., vb.
  be insolent 878 vb.
  favourite 890 n.
boaster *impostor* 545 n.
  combatant 722 n.
  (*see* boast)
boasting
  overestimation 482 n.
  empty talk 515 n.
  magniloquence 574 n.
  (*see* boast)
boat *voyage, row* 269 vb.
  ship, boat 275 n.
boatable *seafaring* 269 adj.
boat-boy
  church officer 986 n.
  ritualist 988 n.
boater *headgear* 228 n.
boathouse *stable* 192 n.
boating *aquatics* 269 n.
  sport 837 n.
boatman *boatman* 270 n.
boatswain *mariner* 270 n.

navigator 270 n.
bob *timekeeper* 117 n.
shorten 204 vb.
pendant 217 n.
obeisance 311 n.
stoop 311 vb.
leap 312 vb.
oscillation 317 n.
be agitated 318 vb.
gravity 322 n.
coinage 797 n.
hair-dressing 843 n.
greet 884 n.
show respect 920 vb.
bobbish *healthy* 650 adj.
bobble *pendant* 217 n.
trimming 844 n.
bobby *protector* 660 n.
police 955 n.
bobbysoxer *youngster* 132 n.
bode *predict* 511 vb.
threaten 900 vb.
bodice *bodywear* 228 n.
bodiless *insubstantial* 4 adj.
immaterial 320 adj.
bodily *substantially* 3 adv.
collectively 52 adv.
material 319 adj.
sensual 944 adj.
boding *cautionary* 664 adj.
unpromising 853 adj.
bodkin *sharp point* 256 n.
perforator 263 n.
body *substance* 3 n.
main part 32 n.
middle 70 n.
band 74 n.
frame 218 n.
matter 319 n.
structure 331 n.
corpse 363 n.
person 371 n.
savouriness 390 n.
community 708 n.
corporation 708 n.
body-building
nourishing 301 adj.
body forth
make extrinsic 6 vb.
externalize 223 vb.
materialize 319 vb.
bodyguard *protector* 660 n.
defender 713 n.
combatant 722 n.
retainer 742 n.
body politic *nation* 371 n.
polity 733 n.
body-snatcher *thief* 789 n.
boffin *worker* 686 n.
expert 696 n.
bog *marsh* 347 n.

dirt 649 n.
bog down *fail* 728 vb.
bogey (*see* bogy)
boggle *be uncertain* 474 vb.
doubt 486 vb.
dissent 489 n.
be loth 598 vb.
bogie *train* 274 n.
bogs *latrine* 649 n.
bog-trotter
countryman 869 n.
bogus *false* 541 adj.
spurious 542 adj.
untrue 543 adj.
affected 850 adj.
bogy *false alarm* 665 n.
demon 970 n.
Bohemian
nonconformist 84 n.
wanderer 268 n.
free man 744 n.
bohunk *foreigner* 59 n.
boil *swelling* 253 n.
cook 301 vb.
effervesce 318 vb.
bubble 355 vb.
be hot 379 vb.
hiss 406 vb.
be excited 821 vb.
boil down *bate* 37 vb.
make smaller 198 vb.
shorten 204 vb.
boil down to *mean* 514 vb.
boiler *cauldron* 194 n.
poultry 365 n.
heater 383 n.
boiling
finite quantity 26 n.
boiling point *heat* 379 n.
completion 725 n.
boil over
be violent 176 vb.
effervesce 318 vb.
get angry 891 vb.
boisterous *violent* 176 adj.
windy 352 adj.
hasty 680 adj.
excitable 822 adj.
bolas *missile weapon* 723 n.
bold *salient* 254 adj.
undisguised 522 adj.
forceful 571 adj.
courageous 855 adj.
rash 857 adj.
insolent 878 adj.
bole *origin* 156 n.
cylinder 252 n.
soil 344 n.
tree 366 n.
bolero *vest* 228 n.
dance 837 n.

bolet *vegetable* 301 n.
plant 366 n.
bolide *meteor* 321 n.
boll *sphere* 252 n.
metrology 465 n.
bollard *fastening* 47 n.
boloney *empty talk* 515 n.
falsehood 541 n.
Bolshevik(s)
political party 708 n.
revolter 738 n.
Bolshevism
government 733 n.
bolshie *disobedient* 738 adj.
bolster *cushion* 218 n.
support 218 vb.
aid 703 vb.
cheer 833 vb.
bolt *eliminate* 44 vb.
affix 45 vb.
fastening 47 n.
bunch 74 n.
barrier 235 n.
sharp point 256 n.
stopper 264 n.
close 264 vb.
move fast 277 vb.
missile 287 n.
decamp 296 vb.
discriminate 463 vb.
select 605 vb.
run away 620 vb.
purify 648 vb.
deteriorate 655 vb.
safeguard 662 n.
missile weapon 723 n.
disobey 738 vb.
lock-up 748 n.
gluttonize 947 vb.
bolter *tergiversator* 603 n.
bolt from the blue
inexpectation 508 n.
bolt-hole *tunnel* 263 n.
refuge 662 n.
bolus *medicine* 658 n.
bomb *destroyer* 168 n.
bang 402 n.
fire at 712 vb.
bomb 723 n.
bombard *radiate* 417 vb.
fire at 712 vb.
gun 723 n.
bombardier *aeronaut* 271 n.
soldiery 722 n.
bombardment *havoc* 165 n.
loudness 400 n.
bombardment 712 n.
bombardon *horn* 414 n.
bombast *lining* 227 n.
overestimation 482 n.
absurdity 497 n.

empty talk 515 n.
magniloquence 574 n.
ridiculousness 849 n.
boast 877 n.
bomber *aircraft* 276 n.
  air force 722 n.
bombination
  ululation 409 n.
bomb-proof
  unyielding 162 adj.
  invulnerable 660 adj.
  defended 713 adj.
  resisting 715 adj.
bombshell
  inexpectation 508 n.
  bomb 723 n.
bona fide *veracious* 540 adj.
  truthfully 540 adv.
bona fides *probity* 929 n.
bonanza *plenty* 635 n.
  palmy days 730 n.
bonbon *sweet* 392 n.
bond *relation* 9 n.
  junction 45 n.
  bond 47 n.
  subject 745 adj.
  fetter 748 n.
  promise 764 n.
  compact 765 n.
  title-deed 767 n.
  paper money 797 n.
  dueness 915 n.
  duty 917 n.
bondage *servitude* 745 n.
bond-holder *receiver* 782 n.
bondman *slave* 742 n.
bone *modality* 7 n.
  vitality 162 n.
  uncover 229 vb.
  void 300 vb.
  cook 301 vb.
  solid body 324 n.
  hardness 326 n.
  structure 331 n.
  steal 788 vb.
bonehead *dunce* 501 n.
bon enfant
  kind person 897 n.
bone of contention
  question 459 n.
  casus belli 709 n.
  contention 716 n.
boner *mistake* 495 n.
bones *gong* 414 n.
  corpse 363 n.
  gambling 618 n.
bone-setter *mender* 656 n.
bone-setting *therapy* 658 n.
bone to pick
  casus belli 709 n.
  resentment 891 n.

boneyard *cemetery* 364 n.
bonfire *fire* 379 n.
  revel 837 n.
  celebration 876 n.
bonhomie *sociability* 882 n.
  ostentation 875 n.
  benevolence 897 n.
bon mot *witticism* 839 n.
bonne *domestic* 742 n.
  keeper 749 n.
bonnet *covering* 226 n.
  headgear 228 n.
bonny *cheerful* 833 adj.
  beautiful 841 adj.
  courageous 855 adj.
bon ton *fashion* 848 n.
  fashionable 848 adj.
bonus *extra* 40 n.
  incentive 612 n.
  superfluity 637 n.
  gift 781 n.
  receipt 807 n.
  undueness 916 n.
bon vivant,— viveur
  social person 882 n.
bony *lean* 206 adj.
  hard 326 adj.
bonze *monk* 986 n.
  priest 986 n.
bonzery *monastery* 986 n.
boo *cry* 408 n., vb.
  vociferate 408 vb.
  gesture 547 n.
  not respect 921 vb.
  despise 922 vb.
  disapprove 924 vb.
boob, booby *dunce* 501 n.
  ninny 501 n.
booby hatch *gaol* 748 n.
booby-trap *trap* 542 n.
  defences 713 n.
  bomb 723 n.
boodle *booty* 790 n.
  dibs 797 n.
boo-hoo *cry* 408 n., vb.
  weep 836 vb.
book *subdivision* 53 n.
  register 548 vb.
  book 589 n.
  require 627 vb.
  acquire 771 vb.
  possess 773 vb.
  account 808 vb.
  reprove 924 vb.
  indict 928 vb.
bookbinder
  bookbinding 589 n.
book-case *cabinet* 194 n.
  library 589 n.
book-club *library* 589 n.
book-collector

  collector 492 n.
  bookman 589 n.
book-dealer
  bookman 589 n.
bookie *gambler* 618 n.
booking-clerk
  receiver 782 n.
  seller 793 n.
bookish *instructed* 490 adj.
  studious 536 adj.
book-keep *number* 86 vb.
book-keeper
  computer 86 n.
  recorder 549 n.
  treasurer 798 n.
  accountant 808 n.
book-keeping
  registration 548 n.
  accounts 808 n.
  accounting 808 adj.
book-learning
  erudition 490 n.
bookless
  uninstructed 491 adj.
booklet *book* 589 n.
book-lover *bookman* 589 n.
bookmaker *gambler* 618 n.
book-making
  calculation of chance 159 n.
bookman *bookman* 589 n.
books *account book* 808 n.
bookselling
  publication 528 n.
  bookman 589 n.
  bibliographical 589 adj.
book-shop *library* 589 n.
book-trade
  publication 528 n.
bookworm *scholar* 492 n.
  learner 538 n.
  bookman 589 n.
boom *supporter* 218 n.
  impel 279 vb.
  be loud 400 vb.
  bang 402 vb.
  ululate 409 vb.
  revival 656 n.
  obstacle 702 n.
  defences 713 n.
  prosperity 730 n.
  sale 793 n.
boomerang *recoil* 280 n.
  retaliation 714 n.
  missile weapon 723 n.
boon *benefit* 615 n.
  gift 781 n.
boon companion
  close friend 880 n.
  social person 882 n.
boor *countryman* 869 n.
  rude person 885 n.

boorish *ill-bred* 847 adj.
  plebeian 869 adj.
boorishness
  discourtesy 885 n.
boost *stimulant* 174 n.
  invigorate 174 vb.
  impulse 279 n.
  overrate 482 vb.
  advertise 528 vb.
  aider 703 n.
  praise 923 vb.
booster *publicizer* 528 n.
  commender 923 n.
boot *box* 194 n.
  stand 218 n.
  footwear 228 n.
  kick 279 vb.
  ejection 300 n.
booth *small house* 192 n.
  shop 796 n.
bootikin *footwear* 228 n.
  glove 228 n.
boot-lace *ligature* 47 n.
bootless *wasted* 634 adj.
  unsuccessful 728 adj.
  unthanked 908 adj.
bootlicker *toady* 879 n.
bootmaker *clothier* 228 n.
  artisan 686 n.
boots *servant* 742 n.
boot-tree *mould* 23 n.
booty *trophy* 729 n.
  acquisition 771 n.
  booty 790 n.
booze *liquor* 301 n.
  get drunk 949 vb.
boozer *drunkard* 949 n.
bopster *musician* 413 n.
borage *potherb* 301 n.
border *adjunct* 40 n.
  be near 200 vb.
  contiguity 202 n.
  circumjacence 230 n.
  circumscribe 232 vb.
  edge, edging 234 n.
  hem 234 vb.
  limit 236 vb.
  flank 239 vb.
  garden 370 n.
  trimming 844 n.
  decorate 844 vb.
borderer *dweller* 191 n.
borderland(s)
  contiguity 202 n.
borderline *limited* 236 adj.
borderline case
  predicament 700 n.
bore *breadth* 205 n.
  make concave 255 vb.
  perforation 263 n.
  pierce 263 vb.

pass 305 vb.
descend 309 vb.
current 350 n.
wave 350 n.
impair 655 vb.
bane 659 n.
fatigue 684 vb.
fire-arm 723 n.
worry 825 n.
tedium, bore 838 n.
be dull 840 vb.
sate 863 vb.
boreal *windy* 352 adj.
  cold 380 adj.
boredom *tedium* 838 n.
borer *sharp point* 256 n.
  perforator 863 n.
boring *tunnel* 263 n.
  descent 309 n.
born *born* 360 adj.
born for *gifted* 694 adj.
born in the purple
  rich 800 adj.
  noble 868 adj.
born of *caused* 157 adj.
born yesterday
  artless 699 adj.
borough *district* 184 n.
  electorate 605 n.
borrow *copy* 20 vb.
  request 761 vb.
  borrow 785 vb.
  be undue 916 vb.
borrowed plumes
  sham 542 n.
borrowed time
  opportunity 137 n.
borrower *beggar* 763 n.
  debtor 803 n.
Borstal *school* 539 n.
  amendment 654 n.
  prison 748 n.
bosh *silly talk* 515 n.
bosh shot *mistake* 495 n.
bosky *arboreal* 366 adj.
bosom *receptacle* 194 n.
  interiority 224 n.
  bosom 253 n.
  spirit 447 n.
  affections 817 n.
bosomy *fleshy* 195 adj.
  convex 253 adj.
boss *superior* 34 n.
  swelling 253 n.
  roughen 259 vb.
  meddle 678 vb.
  direct 689 vb.
  director 690 n.
  dominate 733 vb.
  tyrant 735 n.
  master, autocrat 741 n.

ornamental art 844 n.
bossy *authoritative* 733 adj.
  authoritarian 735 adj.
bo'sun *mariner* 270 n.
Boswell *narrator* 590 n.
botanical *vegetal* 366 adj.
  botanical 368 adj.
botanical garden
  botany 368 n.
  garden 370 n.
botanist *botanist* 368 n.
botany *biology* 358 n.
  botany 368 n.
Botany Bay
  prison camp 748 n.
botch *neglect* 458 vb.
  misrepresent 552 vb.
  impair 655 vb.
  repair 656 vb.
  be clumsy 695 vb.
  fail 728 vb.
  eyesore 842 n.
botcher *mender* 656 n.
  bungler 697 n.
both *dual* 90 adj.
bother *commotion* 318 n.
  be attentive 455 vb.
  distract 456 vb.
  activity 678 n.
  meddle 678 vb.
  be difficult 700 vb.
  hinder 702 vb.
  excitable state 822 n.
  worry 825 n.
  torment 827 vb.
  enrage 891 vb.
bottle *vessel* 194 n.
  potion 301 n.
  preserve 666 vb.
bottleneck
  contraction 198 n.
  narrowness 206 n.
  obstacle 702 n.
bottle party *festivity* 837 n.
  social gathering 882 n.
bottle up *conceal* 525 vb.
  preserve 666 vb.
bottom *inferiority* 35 n.
  extremity 69 n.
  lowness 210 n.
  depth 211 n.
  base 214 n.
  undermost 214 adj.
  support 218 vb.
  rear 238 n.
  buttocks 238 n.
  ship 275 n.
  marsh 347 n.
  stamina 600 n.
  courage 855 n.
bottom drawer *store* 632 n.

preparation 669 n.
bottomless *deep* 211 adj.
  infernal 972 adj.
bottommost *lesser* 35 adj.
bottomry *security* 767 n.
bottom, the
  object of scorn 867 n.
  cad 938 n.
bottom up *inverted* 221 adj.
botulism *infection* 651 n.
  poisoning 659 n.
boudoir *chamber* 194 n.
  beauty parlour 843 n.
bough *branch* 53 n.
  foliage 366 n.
boulder *sphere* 252 n.
  hardness 326 n.
  rock 344 n.
boulevard *street* 192 n.
  path 624 n.
bounce *recoil* 280 n.
  eject 300 vb.
  ascend 308 vb.
  leap 312 vb.
  oscillate 317 vb.
  agitation 318 n.
  elasticity 328 n.
  boasting 877 n.
bouncer *ejector* 300 n.
bouncing *cheerful* 833 adj.
bound *bate* 37 vb.
  tied 45 adj.
  hem 234 vb.
  limit 236 vb.
  spurt 277 n.
  move fast 277 vb.
  leap 312 n., vb.
  certain 473 adj.
  fated 596 adj.
  subject 745 adj.
  restrained 747 adj.
  retentive 778 adj.
  indebted 803 adj.
  dutied 917 adj.
boundary *separation* 46 n.
  extremity 69 n.
  edge 234 n.
  limit 236 n.
bounden *subject* 745 adj.
  dutied 917 adj.
bounder *vulgarian* 847 n.
bound for *directed* 281 adj.
boundless *infinite* 107 adj.
  spacious 183 adj.
bounds *region* 184 n.
  outline 233 n.
bounteous *liberal* 813 adj.
  benevolent 897 adj.
bountiful *giving* 781 adj.
bounty *subvention* 703 n.
  gift 781 n.

liberality 813 n.
  reward 962 n.
bouquet *bunch* 74 n.
  savouriness 390 n.
  odour 394 n.
  fragrance 396 n.
  ornamentation 844 n.
  applause, praise 923 n.
bourgeois *median* 30 adj.
  type size 587 n.
  commoner 869 n.
bourgeoisie
  mediocrity 732 n.
  commonalty 869 n.
bourne *limit* 236 n.
  goal 295 n.
  stream 350 n.
bourse *bourse* 618 n.
  mart 796 n.
boustrophedon
  writing 586 n.
bout *period* 110 n.
  periodicity 141 n.
  pugilism 716 n.
bout rimé *prosody* 593 n.
bovine *animal* 365 adj.
  unintelligent 499 adj.
bow *prow* 237 n.
  curve 248 n.
  camber 253 n.
  propellant 287 n.
  obeisance 311 n.
  stoop 311 vb.
  play music 413 vb.
  viol 414 n.
  knuckle under 721 vb.
  missile weapon 723 n.
  obey 739 vb.
  trimming 844 n.
  courteous act 884 n.
  greet 884 vb.
  show respect 920 vb.
  worship 981 vb.
  perform ritual 988 vb.
bow-chaser *gun* 723 n.
Bowdler *prude* 950 n.
bowdlerize *impair* 655 vb.
bow down,— to
  stoop 311 vb.
  honour 866 vb.
  be humble 872 vb.
boweless *pitiless* 906 adj.
bowels *insides* 224 n.
bowel wash *therapy* 658 n.
bower *pavilion* 192 n.
  arbour 194 n.
  screen 421 n.
  love-nest 887 n.
bowery *screened* 421 adj.
  pleasurable 826 adj.
bowl *bowl* 194 n.

cavity 255 n.
  missile 287 n.
  propel 287 vb.
  potion 301 n.
  rotate 315 vb.
bowl along
  go smoothly 258 vb.
  move fast 277 vb.
bow-legged
  deformed 246 adj.
  curved 248 adj.
bowler *thrower* 287 n.
  player 837 n.
bowline *tackling* 47 n.
bowling-alley *arena* 724 n.
bowling-green
  pleasance 192 n.
  horizontality 216 n.
  smoothness 258 n.
  arena 724 n.
bowl out *dismiss* 300 vb.
  defeat 727 vb.
bowl over *disable* 161 vb.
  fell 311 vb.
  surprise 508 vb.
  be wonderful 864 vb.
bowls *ball game* 837 n.
bowman *shooter* 287 n.
  soldiery 722 n.
bow out *dismiss* 300 vb.
bowshot
  short distance 200 n.
bowsprit *prow* 237 n.
  projection 254 n.
Bow-street runner
  detective 459 n.
  law officer 955 n.
bowstring *kill* 362 vb.
  means of execution 964 n.
bow to *be inferior* 35 vb.
bowyer *soldiery* 722 n.
box *disjunction* 46 n.
  small house 192 n.
  compartment 194 n.
  box 194 n.
  seat 218 n.
  circumscribe 232 vb.
  inclosure 235 n.
  strike 279 vb.
  tree 366 n.
  theatre 594 n.
  fight 716 vb.
boxer *dog* 365 n.
  pugilist 722 n.
boxing *pugilism* 716 n.
box-office
  onlookers 441 n.
  theatre 594 n.
  treasury 799 n.
box on the ears
  reprimand 924 n.

box the compass
  orientate 281 vb.
  rotate 315 vb.
box up *imprison* 747 vb.
boy *youngster* 132 n.
  male 372 n.
  lover 887 n.
boycott *set apart* 46 vb.
  exclusion 57 n.
  avoid 620 n.
  hindrance 702 n.
  make unwelcome 883 vb.
  disapprobation 924 n.
boy-friend *friend* 880 n.
  lover 887 n.
boyhood *youth* 130 n.
boyish *young* 130 adj.
  infantine 132 adj.
  foolish 499 adj.
  immature 670 adj.
brabble *quarrel* 709 n.
  fight 716 n.
brace *tighten* 45 vb.
  group 74 n.
  duality 90 n.
  strengthen 162 vb.
  supporter 218 n.
  support 218 vb.
  notation 410 n.
  punctuation 547 n.
  refresh 685 vb.
brace and bit
  perforator 263 n.
bracelet(s) *fastening* 47 n.
  loop 250 n.
  fetter 748 n.
  jewellery 844 n.
brace oneself
  prepare oneself 669 vb.
bracer *stimulant* 174 n.
  pungency 388 n.
  tonic 658 n.
braces *fastening* 47 n.
  hanger 217 n.
  supporter 218 n.
  underwear 228 n.
brachial *brachial* 53 adj.
bracing *salubrious* 652 adj.
  refreshing 685 adj.
  cheering 833 adj.
bracken *plant* 366 n.
bracket *equalize* 28 vb.
  join 45 vb.
  bond 47 n.
  classification 77 n.
  pair 90 vb.
  supporter 218 n.
  shelf 218 n.
  put between 231 vb.
  angularity 247 n.
  punctuation 547 n.

bracket with *liken* 18 vb.
brackish *salty* 388 adj.
brad *fastening* 47 n.
bradawl *sharp point* 256 n.
  perforator 263 n.
Bradshaw *itinerary* 267 n.
  guide-book 524 n.
brae *high land* 209 n.
brag *be affected* 850 vb.
  seek repute 866 vb.
  boast 877 vb.
  be insolent 878 vb.
braggadocio
  cowardice 856 n.
  (see brag)
braggart (see brag)
Brahma *Trinity* 965 n.
  divineness 965 n.
  Hindu god 967 n.
Brahmana
  non-Biblical scripture
  975 n.
Brahmanism
  religious faith 973 n.
Brahmi *letter* 558 n.
brahmin *aristocrat* 868 n.
  priest 986 n.
Brahminic
  religious 973 adj.
  priestly 985 adj.
brahminism
  ecclesiasticism 985 n.
Brahmo *sectarist* 978 n.
  sectarian 978 adj.
Brahmo Samaj
  non-Christian sect 978 n.
braid *tie* 45 vb.
  ligature 47 n.
  crossing 222 n.
  weave 222 vb.
  variegate 437 vb.
brail *tie* 45 vb.
  elevate 310 vb.
braille *lettering* 586 n.
  writing 586 n.
brain *head* 213 n.
  kill 362 vb.
  render insensible 375 vb.
  intellect 447 n.
  intellectual 492 n.
  intelligence 498 n.
brain-child *idea* 451 n.
brain-fag *thought* 449 n.
  fatigue 684 n.
brainless *mindless* 448 adj.
  foolish 499 adj.
brainlessness
  non-intellect 447 vb.
brainpan *head* 213 n.
brainsick
  light-minded 456 adj.

  crazed 503 adj.
  frenzied 503 adj.
brain specialist
  doctor 658 n.
brainstorm *violence* 176 n.
  psychopathy 503 n.
  excitable state 822 n.
brains trust
  interrogation 459 n.
  intellectual 492 n.
brainwash *teach* 534 vb.
  misteach 535 vb.
  pervert 655 vb.
brainwashing
  conversion 147 n.
  teaching 534 n.
brain-wave *idea* 451 n.
brain-work *thought* 449 n.
brain-worker
  intellectual 492 adj.
brainy *intelligent* 498 adj.
brake *halt* 145 vb.
  moderator 177 n.
  bring to rest 266 vb.
  train 274 n.
  retard 278 vb.
  wood 366 n.
  safeguard 662 n.
  obstacle 702 n.
  hinder 702 vb.
  restraint 747 n.
  fetter 748 n.
brakeman *driver* 268 n.
brake-van *train* 274 n.
bramble *prickle* 256 n.
  bane 659 n.
brambly *sharp* 256 adj.
bran *leavings* 41 n.
  powder 332 n.
  rubbish 641 n.
branch *adjunct* 40 n.
  branch 53 n.
  be dispersed 75 vb.
  classification 77 n.
  bifurcate 92 vb.
  descendant 170 n.
  extend 183 vb.
  nest 192 n.
  filament 208 n.
  angulate 247 vb.
  diverge 294 vb.
  tree, foliage 366 n.
  society 708 n.
  sect 978 n.
branching *spacious* 183 adj.
  symmetrical 245 adj.
branch out *be diffuse* 570 vb.
branchy *brachial* 53 adj.
brand *sort* 77 n.
  burn 381 vb.
  lighter 385 n.

torch 420 n.
identification 547 n.
label 547 n.
mark 547 vb.
blemish 845 vb.
slur 867 n.
shame 867 vb.
censure 924 n.
defame 926 vb.
accuse 928 vb.
branding-iron
burning 381 n.
brandish *operate* 173 vb.
brandish 317 vb.
agitate 318 vb.
show 522 vb.
be ostentatious 875 vb.
threaten 900 vb.
brangle *bicker* 709 vb.
brash *piece* 53 n.
insolent 878 adj.
brass *a mixture* 43 n.
obsequies 364 n.
megaphone 400 n.
resonance 404 n.
stridor 407 n.
orchestra 413 n.
musical instrument 414 n.
monument 548 n.
director 690 n.
badge of rank 743 n.
dibs 797 n.
sauciness 878 n.
brassard *livery* 547 n.
badge of rank 743 n.
brasserie *café* 192 n.
brass hat *army officer* 741 n.
brassière *underwear* 228 n.
brass tacks *reality* 1 n.
brassy *loud* 400 adj.
strident 407 adj.
ornate 574 adj.
impertinent 878 adj.
brat *child* 132 n.
brattice *partition* 231 n.
lining 227 n.
bravado *boast* 877 n.
boasting 877 n.
brave *defy* 711 vb.
combatant 722 n.
soldier 722 n.
brave person 855 n.
courageous 855 adj.
be courageous 855 vb.
showy 875 adj.
bravery *courage* 855 n.
ostentation 875 n.
bravo *violent creature* 176 n.
desperado 857 n.
ruffian 904 n.
bravura *musical skill* 413 n.

masterpiece 694 n.
braw *fashionable* 848 adj.
brawl *loudness* 400 n.
quarrel 709 n.
bicker 709 vb.
fight 716 n.
brawler *opponent* 705 n.
rioter 738 n.
brawn *vitality* 162 n.
brawny *stalwart* 162 adj.
fleshy 195 adj.
braws *finery* 844 n.
bray *pulverize* 332 vb.
be loud 400 vb.
resound 404 vb.
rasp 407 vb.
ululate 409 vb.
braze *join* 45 vb.
agglutinate 48 vb.
brazen *strident* 407 adj.
undisguised 522 adj.
false 541 adj.
proud 871 adj.
insolent 878 adj.
impenitent 940 adj.
brazier *heater* 383 n.
breach *disjunction* 46 n.
gap 201 n.
dissension 709 n.
enmity 881 n.
undueness 916 n.
breach of faith
non-observance 769 n.
perfidy 930 n.
breach of the peace
quarrel 709 n.
breach of trust
peculation 788 n.
bread *food* 301 n.
cereal 301 n.
bread and butter *food* 301 n.
vocation 622 n.
bread-and-butter letter
thanks 907 n.
bread and water
unsavouriness 391 n.
insufficiency 636 n.
fasting 946 n.
bread-riot *revolt* 738 n.
breadth *greatness* 32 n.
measure 183 n.
size 195 n.
breadth 205 n.
breadth of mind
wisdom 498 n.
breadwinner *worker* 686 n.
breadwinning
acquisition 771 n.
gainful 771 adj.
break *disjunction* 46 n.
break 46 vb.

be disjoined 46 vb.
incompleteness 55 n.
discontinuity 72 n.
numeration 86 n.
interim 108 n.
change 143 n.
lull 145 n.
continuance 146 n.
demolish 165 vb.
interval 201 n.
be brittle 330 vb.
flow 350 vb.
rasp 407 vb.
wound 655 vb.
repose 683 n.
quarrel 709 vb.
defeat 727 vb.
fail 728 vb.
prosperity 730 n.
oppress 735 vb.
depose 752 vb.
lose 772 vb.
not pay 805 vb.
breakable *brittle* 330 adj.
breakaway *revolt* 738 n.
independent 744 adj.
break away
be dispersed 75 vb.
run away 620 vb.
escape 667 vb.
revolt 738 vb.
schismatize 978 vb.
break-back
compensation 31 n.
break bulk *void* 300 vb.
break camp
decamp 296 vb.
breakdown
decomposition 51 n.
stop 145 n.
helplessness 161 n.
ruin 165 n.
illness 651 n.
hitch 702 n.
failure 728 n.
lamentation 836 n.
dance 837 n.
breaker *vat* 194 n.
wave 350 n.
breaker-in *trainer* 537 n.
break even *be equal* 28 vb.
breakfast *meal* 301 n.
eat 301 vb.
break in *irrupt* 297 vb.
intrude 297 vb.
break in 369 vb.
train 534 vb.
habituate 610 vb.
subjugate 745 vb.
breaking point
casus belli 709 n.

completion 725 n.
breaking voice
  aphony 578 n.
break in on
  derange 63 vb.
  mistime 138 vb.
  intrude 297 vb.
break it up
  be disjoined 46 vb.
breakneck *sloping* 220 adj.
  speedy 277 adj.
  rash 857 adj.
break of *cure* 656 vb.
break of day *morning* 128 n.
  half-light 419 n.
break off
  be incomplete 55 adj.
  cease 145 vb.
break open *force* 176 vb.
break out *begin* 68 vb.
  be violent 176 vb.
  emerge 298 vb.
  escape 667 vb.
  attack 712 vb.
  be excitable 822 vb.
break ranks
  be dispersed 75 vb.
break the news
  inform 524 vb.
breakthrough
  attack 712 n.
  success 727 n.
break-up *disjunction* 46 n.
  decomposition 51 n.
  finality 69 n.
  dispersion 75 n.
  revolution 149 n.
  ruin 165 n.
breakwater
  projection 254 n.
  safeguard 662 n.
break wind *eruct* 300 vb.
break with *quarrel* 709 vb.
bream *table fish* 365 n.
breast *interiority* 224 n.
  be in front 237 vb.
  bosom 253 n.
  climb 308 vb.
  spirit 447 n.
  withstand 704 vb.
  affections 817 n.
breast-feed *feed* 301 vb.
breastplate *bosom* 253 n.
  protection 660 n.
  obstacle 702 n.
  armour 713 n.
breastwork *defences* 713 n.
breath
  insubstantial thing 4 n.
  instant 116 n.
  breeze 352 n.

life 360 n.
  odour 394 n.
  faintness 401 n.
breathe *exude* 298 vb.
  breathe 352 vb.
  live 360 vb.
  sound faint 401 vb.
  hint 524 vb.
  divulge 526 vb.
  voice 577 vb.
  speak 579 vb.
  repose 683 vb.
  be refreshed 685 vb.
breathe down one's neck
  impend 155 vb.
  approach 289 vb.
breathe in *breathe* 352 vb.
  smell 394 vb.
breathe life into
  vitalize 360 vb.
breathe of *evidence* 466 vb.
  mean 514 vb.
breathe out *breathe* 352 vb.
  emit 300 vb.
breather *repose* 683 n.
breathe upon *shame* 867 vb.
  defame 926 vb.
breathing *oscillation* 317 n.
  respiration 352 n.
  life 360 n.
  alive 360 adj.
breathless *agitated* 318 adj.
  puffing 352 adj.
  dead 361 adj.
  voiceless 578 adj.
  stammering 580 adj.
  hasty 680 adj.
  panting 684 adj.
  fervent 818 adj.
  nervous 854 adj.
  wondering 864 adj.
breath-taker *prodigy* 864 n.
breath-taking
  prodigious 32 adj.
  notable 638 adj.
  wonderful 864 adj.
bred (*see* breed)
breech *dress* 228 vb.
  rear, buttocks 238 n.
  fire-arm 723 n.
breech-cloth *loincloth* 228 n.
breeches *breeches* 228 n.
breechloader *fire-arm* 723 n.
breed *character* 5 n.
  race 11 n.
  grow 36 vb.
  breed 77 n.
  generate 164 vb.
  posterity 170 n.
  breed stock 369 n.
  educate 534 vb.

mature 669 vb.
breeder *producer* 167 n.
  breeder 369 n.
breeder-reactor
  nucleonics 160 n.
breeding *good taste* 846 n.
  etiquette 848 n.
breeding-place
  seedbed 156 n.
breed with *unite with* 45 vb.
breeze *breeze* 352 n.
  blow 352 vb.
  quarrel 709 n.
  excitation 821 n.
breezy *airy* 340 adj.
  windy 352 adj.
  cheerful 833 adj.
  disrespectful 921 adj.
brethren *laity* 987 n.
breve *notation* 410 n.
  punctuation 547 n.
brevet *warrant* 737 n.
  mandate 751 n.
  permit 756 n.
breviary *textbook* 589 n.
  compendium 592 n.
  office-book 988 n.
brevier *type size* 587 n.
brevity *smallness* 33 n.
  brief space 114 n.
  shortness 204 n.
  conciseness 569 n.
brew *a mixture* 43 n.
  mix 43 vb.
  soup 301 n.
  liquor 301 n.
  mature 669 vb.
brewer *preparer* 669 n.
brewis *cereal* 301 n.
briar (*see* brier)
bribable *bought* 792 adj.
  venal 930 adj.
bribe *incentive* 612 n.
  bribe 612 vb.
  offer 759 vb.
  reward 962 n.
bribery (*see* bribe)
bric-à-brac *bauble* 639 n.
  ornamentation 844 n.
  finery 844 n.
brick *component* 58 n.
  lamina 207 n.
  hardness 326 n.
  pottery 381 n.
  building material 631 n.
  missile weapon 723 n.
  indignity 921 n.
  disapprobation 924 n.
  gentleman 929 n.
  good man 937 n.
brickbat *piece* 53 n.

missile weapon 723 n.
bricklayer *artisan* 686 n.
bricks *plaything* 837 n.
bricks and mortar
  building material 631 n.
brick wall *hardness* 326 n.
  obstacle 702 n.
brickwork *edifice* 164 n.
  structure 331 n.
bridal *wedding* 894 n.
  matrimonial 894 adj.
bride *woman* 373 n.
  spouse 894 n.
bridegroom *spouse* 894 n.
bridesmaid *bridesman* 894 n.
bridge *connect* 45 vb.
  vertex 213 n.
  tooth 256 n.
  passage 305 n.
  viol 414 n.
  bridge 624 n.
  facilitate 701 vb.
  compromise 770 vb.
  card game 837 vb.
bridgehead
  battleground 724 n.
bridge-table *arena* 724 n.
bridle *break in* 369 vb.
  restrain 747 vb.
  fetter 748 n.
bridle up *get angry* 891 vb.
brief *small* 33 adj.
  brief 114 adj.
  short 204 adj.
  inform 524 vb.
  concise 569 adj.
  be concise 569 vb.
  description 590 n.
  compendium 592 n.
  preparation 669 n.
  make ready 669 vb.
  command 737 n., vb.
brief-case *case* 194 n.
briefing *information* 524 n.
  preparation 669 n.
  advice 691 n.
briefless *unused* 674 adj.
  non-active 677 adj.
briefs *underwear* 228 n.
brier, briar *prickle* 256 n.
  air-pipe 353 n.
  tobacco 388 n.
  bane 659 n.
briery *sharp* 256 adj.
brig *sailing-ship* 275 n.
brigade *combine* 50 vb.
  group 74 n.
  bring together 74 vb.
  formation 722 n.
brigadier *army officer* 741 n.
brigand *robber* 789 n.

brigandage
  brigandage 788 n.
brigantine *sailing-ship* 275 n.
bright *undimmed* 417 adj.
  luminous 417 adj.
  luminescent 420 adj.
  florid 425 adj.
  white 427 adj.
  intelligent 498 adj.
  clean 648 adj.
  cheerful 833 adj.
  beautiful 841 adj.
  promising 852 adj.
brighten
  make bright 417 vb.
  be cheerful 833 vb.
  beautify 841 vb.
bright eyes *a beauty* 841 n.
brightness *light* 417 n.
  wit 839 n.
  beauty 841 n.
bright side
  pleasurableness 826 n.
bright young thing
  modernist 126 n.
brilliance *light* 417 n.
  hue 425 n.
  intelligence 498 n.
  beauty 841 n.
  ostentation 875 n.
brilliant *witty* 839 adj.
  gem 844 n.
  noteworthy 866 adj.
  (*see* brilliance)
brilliantine *adhesive* 47 n.
  unguent 357 n.
  hairwash 843 n.
brim *fill* 54 vb.
  headgear 228 n.
  edge 234 n.
  abound 635 vb.
brimstone *fumigator* 385 n.
brinded *mottled* 437 adj.
brine *water* 339 n.
  drench 341 vb.
  ocean 343 n.
  pungency 388 n.
  season 388 vb.
  preserver 666 n.
bring *carry* 273 vb.
  offer 759 vb.
bring about *cause* 156 vb.
  produce 164 vb.
  induce 612 vb.
  carry out 725 vb.
bring back *replace* 187 vb.
  deliver 668 vb.
  restitute 787 vb.
bring down *fell* 311 vb.
  strike at 712 vb.
bring forth

reproduce *itself* 164 vb.
  manifest 522 vb.
bring forward
  attract notice 455 vb.
bring home to
  attribute 158 vb.
  convince 485 vb.
  impress 821 vb.
bring in *admit* 299 vb.
  be profitable 271 vb.
bring on *cause* 156 vb.
  promote 285 vb.
bring out *manifest* 522 vb.
bring over *convince* 485 vb.
  induce 612 vb.
bring round
  convince 485 vb.
  make sane 302 vb.
  induce 612 vb.
bring to *add* 38 vb.
  bring to rest 266 vb.
bring to a head
  mature 669 vb.
bring to bear *relate* 9 vb.
  use 673 vb.
bring to book
  account 808 vb.
bring together *pacify* 719 vb.
  mediate 720 vb.
bring to heel
  subjugate 745 vb.
bring to life *vitalize* 360 vb.
bring to light
  discover 484 vb.
  manifest 522 vb.
bring to pass *cause* 156 vb.
bring up *produce* 164 vb.
  vomit 300 vb.
  argue 475 vb.
  manifest 522 vb.
  educate 534 vb.
brink *extremity* 69 n.
  nearness 200 n.
  edge 234 n.
brinkman *desperado* 857 n.
brinkmanship *tactics* 688 n.
  skill 694 n.
  rashness 857 n.
brisk *vigorous* 174 adj.
  active 678 adj.
brisling *fish food* 301 n.
bristle with
  be many 104 vb.
  abound 635 vb.
  superabound 637 vb.
bristly *sharp* 256 adj.
  hairy 259 adj.
Briticism *dialect* 560 n.
British Israelites *sect* 978 n.
British square
  formation 722 n.

Briton *native* 191 n.
  gentleman 929 n.
brittle *ephemeral* 114 adj.
  flimsy 163 adj.
  brittle 330 adj.
broach *initiate* 68 vb.
  cause 156 vb.
  sharp point 256 n.
  perforator 263 n.
  void 300 vb.
  make flow 350 vb.
  publish 528 vb.
  undertake 672 vb.
  offer 759 vb.
broad *great* 32 adj.
  general 79 adj.
  spacious 183 adj.
  large 195 adj.
  broad 205 adj.
  lake 346 n.
  woman 373 n.
  inexact 495 adj.
  wise 498 adj.
  dialectical 560 adj.
  free 744 adj.
  impure 951 adj.
  prostitute 952 n.
broad arrow *label* 547 n.
broad-based
  inclusive 78 adj.
  general 79 adj.
broadcast *disperse* 75 vb.
  generalize 79 vb.
  let fall 311 vb.
  cultivate 370 vb.
  communicate 524 vb.
  publish 528 vb.
  telecommunication 531 n.
  oration 579 n.
  waste 634 vb.
broadcloth *textile* 222 n.
broaden *augment* 36 vb.
  generalize 79 vb.
  enlarge 197 vb.
  expand 197 vb.
  be broad 205 vb.
broad-minded *wise* 498 adj.
  free 744 adj.
broadness *generality* 79 n.
  breadth 205 n.
  inexactness 495 n.
  (*see* broad)
broadsheet *the press* 528 n.
broadside *laterality* 239 n.
  bombardment 712 n.
  gun 723 n.
broadwife *slave* 742 n.
  spouse 894 n.
Brobdingnagian
  huge 195 adj.
  giant 195 n.

brocade *textile* 222 n.
  needlework 844 n.
brocatelle
  needlework 844 n.
broccoli *vegetable* 301 n.
brochette *fastening* 47 n.
  sharp point 256 n.
brochure *the press* 528 n.
  book 589 n.
brocket *male animal* 372 n.
brogue *speciality* 80 n.
  dialect 560 n.
  pronunciation 577 n.
  speech defect 580 n.
brogues *footwear* 228 n.
broidery *needlework* 844 n.
broil *cook* 301 vb.
  fight 716 n.
broiler *poultry* 365 n.
broke *poor* 801 adj.
broke for *deputize* 755 vb.
broken *rough* 259 adj.
  imperfect 647 adj.
  tamed 369 adj.
  (*see* break)
broken reed
  weak thing 163 n.
broken thread
  discontinuity 72 n.
broken-winded
  diseased 651 adj.
  panting 684 adj.
broker *intermediary* 231 n.
  consignee 754 n.
  merchant 794 n.
brokerage *pay* 804 n.
  discount 810 n.
bromide *moderator* 177 n.
  maxim 496 n.
  witticism 839 n.
bronchia *air-pipe* 353 n.
bronchitis
  respiratory disease 651 n.
bronchus *air-pipe* 353 n.
bronco *saddle-horse* 273 n.
bronco buster *rider* 268 n.
  herdsman 369 n.
brontosaur *animal* 365 n.
bronze *a mixture* 43 n.
  brownness 430 n.
  sculpture 554 n.
Bronze Age *era* 110 n.
brooch *fastening* 47 n.
  jewellery 844 n.
brood *group* 74 n.
  youngling 132 n.
  posterity 170 n.
  meditate 449 vb.
  be dejected 834 vb.
brooding
  preparatory 669 adj.

brood-mare *horse* 273 n.
broody *productive* 164 adj.
brook *stream* 350 n.
  be patient 823 vb.
brook no denial
  affirm 532 vb.
  necessitate 596 vb.
  be obstinate 602 vb.
broom *plant* 366 n.
  cleaning utensil 648 n.
brose *cereal* 310 n.
broth *soup* 301 n.
brothel *brothel* 951 n.
brothel-keeper *bawd* 952 n.
brother *kinsman* 11 n.
  analogue 18 n.
  compeer 28 n.
  male 372 n.
  colleague 707 n.
  title 870 n.
  friend 880 n.
  monk 986 n.
  church title 986 n.
brotherhood *family* 11 n.
  band 74 n.
  community 708 n.
  friendship 880 n.
  sect 978 n.
  monk 986 n.
brotherly *akin* 11 adj.
  friendly 880 adj.
  benevolent 897 adj.
brougham *carriage* 274 n.
brow *head* 213 n.
  face 237 n.
  dome 253 n.
  projection 254 n.
browbeat *induce* 612 vb.
  frighten 854 vb.
  be insolent 878 vb.
  reprove 924 vb.
brown *dry* 342 adj.
  darken 418 vb.
  brownness 430 n.
browned off
  discontented 829 adj.
brownie *elf* 970 n.
brown study
  thought 449 n.
  abstractedness 456 n.
  fantasy 513 n.
browse *graze* 301 vb.
  study 536 vb.
bruise *pulverize* 332 adj.
  pain 377 n.
  touch 378 vb.
  ill-treat 645 vb.
  wound 655 n., vb.
  blemish 845 n.
bruiser *pugilist* 722 n.
bruit *publish* 528 vb.

rumour 529 n.
brumal *wintry* 129 adj.
cold 380 adj.
Brummagem *sham* 542 n.
spurious 542 adj.
cheap 812 adj.
brunette *woman* 373 n.
black 428 adj.
brown 430 adj.
brunt *collision* 279 n.
difficulty 700 n.
brunt, bear the
be in difficulty 700 vb.
parry 713 vb.
resist 715 vb.
brush *be near* 200 vb.
be contiguous 202 vb.
pendant 217 n.
rear 238 n.
rub 333 vb.
cleaning utensil 648 n.
fight 716 n.
give battle 718 vb.
brush off *repel* 292 vb.
eject 300 vb.
brush up *study* 536 vb.
clean 648 vb.
brushwood *wood* 366 n.
fuel 385 n.
brushwork *painting* 553 n.
brusque *violent* 176 adj.
concise 569 adj.
taciturn 582 adj.
hasty 680 adj.
ungracious 885 adj.
brutal *violent* 176 adj.
oppressive 735 adj.
ungracious 885 adj.
cruel 898 adj.
vicious 934 adj.
heinous 934 adj.
brutality
moral insensibility 820 n.
(*see* brutal)
brutalize *pervert* 655 vb.
make insensitive 820 vb.
make wicked 934 vb.
brute *violent creature* 176 n.
animal 365 n.
mindless 448 adj.
tyrant 735 n.
rude person 885 n.
ruffian 904 n.
noxious animal 904 n.
monster 938 n.
brute creation
animality 365 n.
non-intellect 448 n.
brute fact *reality* 1 n.
brute force *strength* 162 n.
violence 176 n.

brute force 735 n.
brutish *plebeian* 869 adj.
discourteous 885 adj.
cruel 898 adj.
sensual 944 adj.
bubble
insubstantial thing 4 n.
brief span 114 n.
stimulation 174 n.
bladder 194 n.
minuteness 196 n.
sphere 252 n.
effervesce 318 vb.
levity 323 n.
brittleness 330 n.
flow 350 vb.
bubble 355 n., vb.
hiss 406 vb.
deceive 542 vb.
bauble 639 n.
bubbly *wine* 301 n.
bubbly 355 adj.
bubo *swelling* 253 n.
buccal *lateral* 239 adj.
buccaneer *rob* 788 vb.
robber 789 n.
Buchenwald
prison camp 748 n.
Buchmanism *sect* 978 n.
buck *leap* 312 n., vb.
flow 350 vb.
deer 365 n.
male animal 372 n.
clean 648 vb.
paper money 797 n.
fop 848 n.
buck-basket *basket* 194 n.
buckboard *carriage* 274 n.
bucket *vessel* 194 n.
bucket shop *bourse* 618 n.
buckle *join* 45 vb.
break 46 vb.
fastening 47 n.
distort 246 vb.
make concave 255 vb.
buckled *convoluted* 251 adj.
buckler *armour* 713 n.
buckle to *be resolute* 599 vb.
buckling *table fish* 365 n.
buckram *bookbinding* 589 n.
pretension 850 n.
buckshot
ammunition 723 n.
buckskins *breeches* 228 n.
buck up *relieve* 831 vb.
cheer, be cheerful 833 vb.
hope 852 vb.
bucolic *agrarian* 370 adj.
poetic 593 adj.
bud *grow* 36 vb.
origin 68 n.

source 156 n.
growth 157 n.
result 157 vb.
reproduce itself 164 vb.
be fruitful 171 vb.
expand 197 vb.
swelling 253 n.
implant 303 vb.
flower 366 n.
buddha *sage* 500 n.
religious teacher 973 n.
Buddhism
religious faith 973 n.
Buddhist *religionist* 973 n.
budding *young* 130 adj.
new 126 adj.
buddy *colleague* 707 n.
chum 880 n.
budge *hair* 259 n.
move 265 vb.
budgerigar *bird* 365 n.
budgerow
small house 192 n.
boat 275 n.
budget *bunch* 74 n.
bag 174 n.
correspondence 588 n.
store 632 n.
provide 633 vb.
accounts 808 n.
budgetary *monetary* 797 adj.
accounting 808 adj.
budgeteer *treasurer* 798 n.
buff *bareness* 229 n.
smooth 258 vb.
rub 333 vb.
brown 430 adj.
yellow 433 adj.
cleaning cloth 648 n.
buffalo *cattle* 365 n.
buffer *intermediary* 231 n.
male 372 n.
obstacle 702 n.
defence 713 n.
cosmetic 843 n.
buffer state
intermediary 231 n.
buffet *cabinet* 194 n.
knock 279 n.
strike 279 vb.
ill-treat 645 vb.
wound 655 vb.
buffoon
entertainer 594 n.
humorist 839 n.
laughing-stock 851 n.
buffoonery *foolery* 497 n.
ridiculousness 849 n.
bug *vermin* 365 n.
bugaboo *false alarm* 665 n.
intimidation 854 n.

demon 970 n.
bugbear *fantasy* 513 n.
  false alarm 665 n.
  bane 659 n.
  intimidation 854 n.
  demon 970 n.
buggy *carriage* 274 n.
bug-house *madhouse* 503 n.
bugle *play music* 413 vb.
  horn 414 n.
  call 547 n.
  heraldry 547 n.
  war 718 n.
  trimming 844 n.
bugler *instrumentalist* 413 n.
build *compose* 56 vb.
  produce 164 vb.
  form 243 n.
  efform 243 vb.
  elevate 310 vb.
  structure 331 n.
builder *producer* 167 n.
  elevation 310 n.
  planner 623 n.
  artisan 686 n.
building *edifice* 164 n.
  production 164 n.
  house, housing 192 n.
  ornamental art 844 n.
build-up *increase* 36 n.
  composition 56 n.
  overestimation 482 n.
  advertisement 528 n.
build up *strengthen* 162 vb.
built-in *ingredient* 58 adj.
  accompanying 89 adj.
  interior 224 adj.
built-up *urban* 192 adj.
bulb *swelling* 253 n.
  plant 366 n.
  lamp 420 n.
bulbous *expanded* 197 adj.
  rotund 252 adj.
  convex 253 adj.
bulbul *bird* 365 n.
bulge *vantage* 34 n.
  increment 36 n.
  fill 54 vb.
  swelling 253 n.
  be convex 253 vb.
bulk *quantity* 26 n.
  main part 32 n.
  be great 32 vb.
  greater number 104 n.
  bulk 195 n.
bulkhead *partition* 231 n.
  obstacle 702 n.
bulky *substantial* 3 adj.
  great 32 adj.
  large 195 adj.
bull *cattle* 365 n.

male animal 372 n.
  mistake 495 n.
  solecism 565 n.
  practice 601 n.
  gambler 618 n.
  decree 737 n.
  speculate 791 vb.
  purchaser 792 n.
  formality 875 n.
bulldog *dog* 368 n.
  brave person 855 n.
bulldoze *demolish* 165 vb.
  collide 279 vb.
bulldozer *smoother* 258 n.
  ram 279 n.
bull in a china shop
  turmoil 61 n.
bullet *sphere* 252 n.
  speeder 277 n.
  missile weapon 723 n.
  ammunition 723 n.
bulletin *report* 524 n.
  news 529 n.
  correspondence 588 n.
bullet-proof
  unyielding 162 adj.
  invulnerable 660 adj.
bull-fight *duel* 716 n.
bull-fighter
  combatant 722 n.
bullion *textile* 222 n.
  bullion 797 n.
bullionist *moneyer* 797 n.
bullish *buying* 792 adj.
  dear 811 adj.
bull market *dearness* 811 n.
bullock *eunuch* 161 n.
  cattle 365 n.
  male animal 372 n.
bull-ring *arena* 724 n.
bull's-eye *centrality* 225 n.
  lamp 420 n.
  objective 617 n.
bully *athlete* 162 n.
  violent creature 176 n.
  combatant 722 n.
  tyrant 735 n.
  oppress 735 vb.
  torment 827 vb.
  frighten 854 vb.
  brave person 855 n.
  desperado 857 n.
  low fellow 869 n.
  insolent person 878 n.
  be insolent 878 vb.
  chum 880 n.
  be malevolent 898 vb.
  threaten 900 vb.
  ruffian 904 n.
  libertine 952 n.
bulrush *plant* 366 n.

bulwark *protection* 660 n.
  obstacle 702 n.
  defence 713 n.
  fortification 713 n.
bum *wander* 267 vb.
  wanderer 268 n.
  beggar 763 n.
bum-bailiff *law officer* 955 n.
  officer 741 n.
bumbledom
  governance 733 n.
  jurisdiction 955 n.
bumble-puppy
  unskilled 695 adj.
bumboat *boat* 275 n.
bummaree *bearer* 273 n.
bump *swelling* 253 n.
  protuberance 254 n.
  move slowly 278 vb.
  collision 279 n.
  faintness 401 n.
  sound dead 405 vb.
  wound 655 n.
bumper *plenitude* 54 n.
  intermediary 231 n.
  potion 301 n.
  shelter 662 n.
  defence 713 n.
bumper crop *plenty* 635 n.
bumpiness *roughness* 259 n.
bump into *collide* 217 vb.
  meet 295 vb.
bumpkin *dunce* 501 n.
  countryman 869 n.
bump off *murder* 362 vb.
bump-supper
  feasting 301 n.
  festivity 837 n.
  social gathering 882 n.
bumptious *prideful* 871 adj.
  vain 873 adj.
  insolent 878 adj.
bump up *augment* 36 vb.
bumpy *non-uniform* 17 adj.
  discontinuous 72 adj.
  rough 259 adj.
bun *hair* 259 n.
  pastry 301 n.
  hair-dressing 843 n.
bunch *cohere* 48 vb.
  bunch, crowd 74 n.
  congregate 74 vb.
  party 708 n.
bundle *bunch* 74 n.
  bag 194 n.
  collection 632 n.
  store 632 n., vb
bundle out *eject* 300 vb.
bun-fight *amusement* 837 n.
bung *covering* 226 n.
  stopper 264 n.

close 264 vb.
bungalow *house* 192 n.
bungle *lose a chance* 138 vb.
 neglect 458 vb.
 mistake 495 n.
 be clumsy 695 vb.
 fail 728 vb.
bungler *fool* 501 n.
 nonentity 639 n.
 bungler 697 n.
 hinderer 702 n.
 loser 728 n.
bunion *swelling* 253 n.
bunk *dwell* 192 vb.
 bed 218 n.
 empty talk 515 n.
 run away 620 vb.
bunker *cellar* 194 n.
 storage 632 n.
 provide 633 vb.
 obstacle 702 n.
bunkum *falsehood* 141 n.
 empty talk 515 n.
 boast 877 n.
bunt *be convex* 253 vb.
 collide 279 vb.
bunting *flag* 547 n.
buoy *sailing aid* 269 n.
 elevate 310 vb.
 levity 323 n.
 signpost 547 n.
buoyancy *energy* 160 n.
 levity 323 n.
 elasticity 328 n.
 hope 852 n.
buoyant *swimming* 269 adj.
 cheerful 833 adj.
 hoping 852 adj.
buoy up *support* 218 vb.
bur *perforator* 263 n.
 engraving 555 n.
burble *flow* 350 vb.
 reason ill 477 vb.
 be foolish 499 vb.
burbler *fool* 501 n.
burden *repetition* 106 n.
 load 193 vb.
 gravity 322 n.
 make heavy 322 vb.
 vocal music 412 n.
 topic 452 n.
 verse form 593 n.
 ill-treat 645 vb.
 bane 659 n.
 difficulty 700 n.
 encumbrance 702 n.
 adversity 731 n.
 oppress 735 vb.
burdened *bearing* 273 adj.
burdensome
 weighty 322 adj.

bad 645 adj.
 laborious 682 adj.
 difficult 700 adj.
 hindering 702 adj.
 annoying 827 adj.
bureau *cabinet* 194 n.
 workshop 687 n.
 jurisdiction 955 n.
bureaucracy
 management 689 n.
 commission 751 n.
 governance 733 n.
bureaucrat *official* 690 n.
 officer 741 n.
burgee *flag* 547 n.
burgeon *grow* 36 vb.
 reproduce itself 164 vb.
 expand 197 vb.
 flower 366 n.
burgess *native* 191 n.
burgh *housing* 192 n.
burgher *native* 191 n.
burglar *thief* 789 n.
burglar-alarm
 danger signal 665 n.
burglarious *thieving* 788 adj.
burglary *stealing* 788 n.
burgle *steal* 788 vb.
burgomaster *officer* 741 n.
burial *immersion* 303 n.
 interment 364 n.
 concealment 525 n.
 obliteration 550 n.
 detention 747 n.
buried *deep* 211 adj.
 dead 361 adj.
 buried 364 adj.
 neglected 458 adj.
 forgotten 506 adj.
 concealed 525 adj.
 secluded 883 adj.
burin *sculpture* 554 n.
 engraving 555 n.
burke *suppress* 165 vb.
 murder 362 vb.
burl *solid body* 324 n.
burlap *textile* 222 n.
burlesque *mimicry* 20 n.
 foolery 497 n.
 exaggeration 546 n.
 misrepresent 552 vb.
 stage play 594 n.
 ridiculousness 849 n.
 funny 849 adj.
 satirize 851 vb.
burly *stalwart* 162 adj.
burn *dry* 342 vb.
 stream 350 n.
 be hot 379 vb.
 burn 381 vb.
 shine 417 vb.

embrown 430 vb.
 waste 634 vb.
 excite 821 vb.
 desire 859 vb.
 be in love 887 vb.
 resent 891 vb.
 execute 963 vb.
burnable
 combustible 385 adj.
burner *furnace* 383 n.
 burning 381 n.
 torch 420 n.
burn in *mark* 547 vb.
burning *pungent* 388 adj.
 fervent 818 adj.
 angry 891 adj.
burning-glass
 optical device 442 n.
burnish *smooth* 258 vb.
 make bright 417 n.
 decorate 844 vb.
burn one's boats
 be resolute 599 vb.
burn one's fingers
 stultify oneself 695 vb.
 be rash 875 vb.
burnous *cloak* 228 n.
burn-proof
 incombustible 382 adj.
burn the candle at both ends
 waste 634 vb.
 be prodigal 815 vb.
 be intemperate 943 vb.
 be sensual 944 vb.
burn the ground
 move fast 277 vb.
burn the midnight oil
 be late 136 vb.
 study 536 vb.
burnt offering
 propitiation 941 n.
 oblation 981 n.
burp *eruct* 300 vb.
 breathe 352 vb.
burr *coherence* 48 n.
 roughness 259 n.
 rasp 407 vb.
 neologize 560 vb.
 pronunciation 577 n.
 voice 577 vb.
 speech defect 580 n.
burrow *weaken* 163 vb.
 dwelling 192 n.
 excavation 255 n.
 make concave 255 vb.
 pierce 263 vb.
 descend 309 vb.
 lurk 523 vb.
 refuge 662 n.
bursar *treasurer* 798 n.
bursary *treasury* 799 n.

reward 962n.
burst *break, rend* 46vb.
  be dispersed 75vb.
  instant 116n.
  outbreak 176n.
  be violent 175vb.
  open 263vb.
  spurt 277n.
  be brittle 330vb.
  have feeling 374vb.
  be loud 400vb.
  bang 402n.,vb.
  activity 678n.
  miscarry 728vb.
burst forth *begin* 68vb.
  expand 197vb.
burst in
  irrupt, intrude 297vb.
burst open *force* 176vb.
burst out
  be excitable 822vb.
  get angry 891vb.
burst with
  superabound 637vb.
bury *insert* 303vb.
  implant 303vb.
  inter 364vb.
  conceal 525vb.
  obliterate 550vb.
  store 632vb.
  imprison 747vb.
bury the hatchet
  forget 506vb.
  make peace 719vb.
  forgive 909vb.
bus *conveyance* 267n.
  bus 274n.
busby *headgear* 228n.
bush *line* 227vb.
  plain 348n.
  wood 366n.
  artless 699adj.
bushel
  great quantity 32n.
  certain quantity 104n.
  metrology 465n.
Bushido *code of duty* 917n.
  probity 929n.
bushing *lining* 227n.
bushman *low fellow* 869n.
bush-ranger *robber* 789n.
bushy *arboreal* 366adj.
  dense 325adj.
business *affairs* 154n.
  production 164n.
  topic 452n.
  dramaturgy 594n.
  intention 617n.
  business 622n.
  function 622n.
  undertaking 672n.

action 676n.
activity 678n.
trade 791n.
business house
  workshop 687n.
  corporation 708n.
businesslike *orderly* 60adj.
  businesslike 622adj.
  industrious 678adj.
  expert 694adj.
busker *entertainer* 594n.
buskin *footwear* 228n.
  drama 594n.
busman *carrier* 273n.
busman's holiday
  exertion 682n.
buss *fishing-boat* 275n.
  caress 889vb.
bust *bosom* 253n.
  meal 301n.
  monument 548n.
  image 551n.
  sculpture 554n.
  gluttony 947n.
bustle *skirt* 228n.
  be agitated 318vb.
  activity 678n.
bustling *eventful* 154adj.
  excited 821adj.
busy *eventful* 154adj.
  inquisitive 453adj.
  employ 622vb.
  doing 676adj.
busy bee *busy person* 678n.
busybody *inquisitor* 453n.
  meddler 678n.
  adviser 691n.
but *qualification* 468n.
  nevertheless 468adv.
butcher
  violent creature 176n.
  killer 362n.
  slaughter 362vb.
  provider 633n.
  ruffian 904n.
butler *domestic* 742n.
  retainer 742n.
butt *vat* 194n.
  limit 236n.
  collide 279vb.
  repel 292vb.
  fool, ninny 501n.
  objective 617n.
  strike at 712vb.
  laughing-stock 851n.
butte *high land* 209n.
butt-end *remainder* 41n.
  extremity 69n.
butter *overlay* 226vb.
  smooth 258vb.
  lubricate 334vb.

fat 357n.
flatter 925vb.
butter-fingered
  clumsy 695adj.
butterfingers
  bungler 697n.
butterflies
  nervousness 854n.
butterfly *fly* 365n.
  variegation 437n.
  waverer 601n.
butter-in *meddler* 678n.
butterscotch
  sweetmeat 301n.
  sweet 392n.
buttery *provisions* 301n.
  fatty 357adj.
  storage 632n.
butt in *interfere* 231vb.
  meet 295vb.
  meddle 678vb.
buttocks *rear* 238n.
button *fastening* 47n.
  close 264vb.
  trifle 639n.
buttoned-up
  reticent 525adj.
buttonhole
  fastening 47n.
  orifice 263n.
  fragrance 396n.
  be loquacious 581vb.
  speak to 583vb.
  be tedious 838vb.
  ornamentation 844n.
buttonhook
  fastening 47n.
buttons *youngster* 132n.
  courier 531n.
  servant 742n.
buttress *strengthen* 162vb.
  supporter 218n.
  projection 254n.
  corroborate 466vb.
  fortification 713n.
  church exterior 990n.
butts *arena* 724n.
butyraceous *fatty* 357adj.
buxom *cheerful* 833adj.
  shapely 841adj.
buy *acquire* 771vb.
  purchase 792vb.
  expend 806vb.
buy and sell *trade* 791vb.
buyer *owner* 776n.
  recipient 782n.
  purchaser 792n.
buyer's market *mart* 796n.
  cheapness 812n.
buy off *bribe* 612vb.
  deliver 668vb.

buzz *be near* 200 vb.
  fly 271 vb.
  roll 403 n.
  resound 404 vb.
  hiss 406 vb.
  ululation 409 n.
  rumour 529 n.
  obstruct 702 vb.
buzz about *publish* 528 vb.
  be published 528 vb.
buzzard
  bird of prey 365 n.
  fool 501 n.
buzzer *megaphone* 400 n.
  signal 547 n.
buzz off *decamp* 296 vb.
by *akin* 11 adj.
  born 360 adj.
  by means of 629 adv.
by and large
  generally 79 adv.
by-blow *bastardy* 954 n.
bye *extra* 40 n.
by favour
  during pleasure 112 adv.
bygone *past* 125 adj.
  forgotten 506 adj.
by halves
  incompletely 55 adv.
by inches
  by degrees 27 adv.
  piecemeal 53 adv.
by-law *rule* 81 n.
by-pass *avoid* 620 vb.
  road 624 n.
  circuit 626 n., vb.
bypath *deviation* 282 n.
  path 624 n.
by-play *hint* 524 n.
  gesture 547 n.
by-product *sequel* 67 n.
  product 164 n.
byre *stable* 192 n.
  cattle pen 369 n.
  farm tool 370 n.
bystander
  spectator 441 n.
by the book *by rule* 81 adv.
by the way
  concerning 9 adv.
  incidentally 137 adv.
  at random 618 adv.
by turns
  correlatively 12 adv.
by-way *path* 624 n.
byword *maxim* 496 n.
  slang 560 n.
  laughing-stock 851 n.
  object of scorn 867 n.
Byzantine *olden* 127 adj.
Byzantinism *art* 551 n.

C

cab *compartment* 194 n.
  cab 274 n.
cabal *latency* 523 n.
  planner 623 n.
  plot 623 n., vb.
  sedition 738 n.
cabaret *theatre* 594 n.
  stage show 594 n.
  place of amusement 837 n.
cabbage *leavings* 41 n.
  vegetable 301 n.
  earnings 771 n.
  steal 788 vb.
  booty 790 n.
cabbalism *occultism* 984 n.
cabby *driver* 268 n.
caber *missile* 287 n.
cabin *small house* 192 n.
  chamber 194 n.
  railroad 624 n.
  imprison 747 vb.
cabin-boy *youngster* 132 n.
  mariner 270 n.
  servant 742 n.
cabin-class *genteel* 868 adj.
cabinet *chamber* 194 n.
  cabinet 194 n.
  storage 632 n.
  management 689 n.
  director 690 n.
  council 692 n.
cable *cable* 47 n.
  electricity 160 n.
  information 524 n.
  message 529 n.
  telecommunication 531 n.
cabman *driver* 268 n.
caboose *train* 274 n.
  heater 383 n.
cabriolet *carriage* 274 n.
ca' canny *be cautious* 858 vb.
cacation *cacation* 302 n.
cache *retreat* 192 n.
  concealment 525 n.
  hiding-place 527 n.
  store 632 n.
  refuge 662 n.
cachet *label* 547 n.
  repute 866 n.
cachexia *weakness* 163 n.
  ill-health 651 n.
cachinnation
  loudness 400 n.
  cry 408 n.
  laughter 835 n.
cacique *potentate* 741 n.
cackle *ululate* 409 vb.
  chatter 581 n.
  laughter 835 n.

cacoethes *habit* 610 n.
  desire 859 n.
cacogenics *biology* 358 n.
cacography *spelling* 558 n.
cacology *solecism* 565 n.
caconym *neology* 560 n.
cacophony *stridor* 407 n.
  discord 411 n.
  inelegance 576 n.
cactus *prickle* 256 n.
  plant 366 n.
cad *nonconformist* 84 n.
  vulgarian 847 n.
  low fellow 869 n.
  hateful object 888 n.
  cad 938 n.
cadastral *listed* 87 adj.
  metric 465 adj.
cadastre *list* 87 n.
cadaver *corpse* 363 n.
cadaverous *lean* 206 adj.
  cadaverous 363 adj.
  colourless 426 adj.
caddie, caddy
  bearer 273 n.
  carry 273 vb.
  servant 742 n.
caddishness
  ill-breeding 847 n.
caddy *small box* 194 n.
cadence *descent* 309 n.
  sound 398 n.
cadenza *musical note* 410 n.
  musical piece 412 n.
cadet *posteriority* 120 n.
  subsequent 120 adj.
  young 130 adj.
  youngster 132 n.
  army officer 741 n.
cadetship *subjection* 745 n.
cadge *beg* 761 vb.
  be parsimonious 816 vb.
cadger *idler* 679 n.
  beggar 763 n.
  pedlar 794 n.
  niggard 816 n.
cadi *judge* 957 n.
cadre *band* 74 n.
  classification 77 n.
  personnel 686 n.
caduceus
  badge of rule 743 n.
caducity *transientness* 114 n.
  age 131 n.
  impotence 161 n.
  weakness 163 n.
  dilapidation 655 n.
cæcal *closed* 264 adj.
Cæsar *sovereign* 741 n.
cæsarian operation
  obstetrics 164 n.

Cæsarism *despotism* 733 n.
cæsura *separation* 46 n.
  discontinuity 72 n.
  interval 201 n.
  prosody 593 n.
café *café* 192 n.
café society
  beau monde 848 n.
caffeine *drug* 658 n.
caftan *tunic* 228 n.
cage *stable* 192 n.
  receptacle 194 n.
  compartment 194 n.
  frame 218 n.
  circumscribe 232 vb.
  inclosure 235 n.
  break in 369 vb.
  imprison 747 vb.
  lock-up 748 n.
cagebird *bird* 365 n.
cagey *reticent* 525 adj.
  cunning 698 adj.
cahoots with, in
  in league 708 adv.
caid *officer* 741 n.
Cain *murderer* 362 n.
Cainozoic *secular* 110 adj.
caique *sailing-ship* 275 n.
cairn *tomb* 364 n.
  dog 365 n.
  signpost 547 n.
  monument 548 n.
caisse *drum* 414 n.
caisson *box* 194 n.
  war-chariot 274 n.
  arsenal 723 n.
  gun 723 n.
cajole *befool* 542 vb.
  tempt 612 vb.
  flatter 925 vb.
cake *cohere* 48 vb.
  pastry 301 n.
  be dense 324 vb.
  sweet 392 n.
  make unclean 649 vb.
cakes and ale
  food 301 n.
  prosperity 770 n.
  enjoyment 824 n.
cake, take the
  be superior 34 vb.
calabash *vessel* 194 n.
calaboose *prison* 748 n.
calamity *evil* 616 n.
  ill fortune 731 n.
calamity prophet
  overestimation 482 n.
  oracle 511 n.
calashe *carriage* 274 n.
calcify *harden* 326 vb.
calcimine *colour* 425 vb.

whiting 427 n.
calcine *burn* 381 vb.
calcite *rock* 344 n.
calcium *food content* 301 n.
calculate *do sums* 86 vb.
  measure 465 vb.
  estimate 480 vb.
  believe 485 vb.
  expect 507 vb.
  intend 617 vb.
  plan 623 vb.
  be cautious 858 vb.
calculated *tending* 179 adj.
  predetermined 608 adj.
calculating
  intelligent 498 adj.
calculating machine
  counting instrument 86 n.
calculation
  numeration 86 n.
  caution 858 n.
  (*see* calculate)
calculator *computer* 86 n.
calculus *mathematics* 86 n.
  solid body 324 n.
caldron *crucible* 147 n.
  cauldron 194 n.
calefaction *heating* 381 n.
calendar *directory* 87 n.
  fix the time 108 vb.
  timekeeper 117 n.
  chronology 117 n.
  time 117 vb.
  record 548 vb.
  reference book 589 n.
calender *smooth* 258 vb.
calenture *illness* 651 n.
calf *youngling* 132 n.
  skin 226 n.
  leg 267 n.
  cattle 365 n.
  male animal 372 n.
  fool 501 n.
  bungler 697 n.
calibrate *graduate* 27 vb.
  gauge 465 vb.
calibre *size* 195 n.
  breadth 205 n.
  perforation 263 n.
  intelligence 498 n.
  fire-arm 723 n.
calico *textile* 222 n.
calidarium *heater* 383 n.
caliph *sovereign* 741 n.
caliphate
  magistrature 733 n.
caliver *fire-arm* 723 n.
call *enter* 297 vb.
  be loud 400 vb.
  cry 408 n.
  ululation 409 n.

musical note 410 n.
  communicate 524 vb.
  publication 528 n.
  call 547 n.
  name 561 vb.
  motive 612 n.
  command 737 n., vb.
  desire 859 n., vb.
  social round 882 n.
  visit 882 vb.
  prayers 981 n.
call a spade a spade
  speak plainly 573 vb.
  be artless 699 vb.
call at *visit* 882 vb.
call away *distract* 456 vb.
call-boy *courier* 531 n.
  stage-hand 594 n.
caller *incomer* 297 n.
  social person 882 n.
call for *require* 627 vb.
  request 761 vb.
call-girl *prostitute* 952 n.
calligraphist *penman* 586 n.
calligraphy *art* 551 n.
  lettering 586 n.
call in *bring together* 74 vb.
  admit 299 vb.
  consult 691 vb.
  claim 915 vb.
calling *vocation* 622 n.
call in question
  negate 533 vb.
calliper *gauge* 465 n.
  measure 465 vb.
callipygian *broad* 205 adj.
  shapely 841 adj.
callisthenics *athletics* 162 n.
  education 534 n.
  civilization 654 n.
  exercise 682 n.
call it a day *cease* 145 vb.
call names
  not respect 921 vb.
  dispraise 924 vb.
call, on *on the spot* 189 adj.
call on *consult* 691 vb.
  visit 882 vb.
  worship 981 vb.
callosity *hardness* 326 n.
callous *hard* 326 adj.
  unfeeling 375 adj.
  thick-skinned 820 adj.
  pitiless 906 adj.
  wicked 934 adj.
call out *halt* 145 vb.
  defy 711 vb.
  fight 716 vb.
call over *number* 86 vb.
callow *young* 130 adj.
  immature 670 adj.

call to order *reprove* 924vb.
call-up
 war measures 718n.
call up *go to war* 718vb.
 practice sorcery 983vb.
calm *assuage* 177vb.
 flat 216adj.
 smoothness 258n.
 quietude 266n.
 tranquil 266adj.
 silent 399adj.
 inaction 677n.
 impassive 820adj.
 inexcitable 823adj.
 tranquillize 823vb.
 relieve 831vb.
 cautious 858adj.
 indifferent 860adj.
 unastonished 865adj.
calmative *moderator* 177n.
 lenitive 177adj.
calomel *cathartic* 658n.
caloric *heat* 379n.
calories *food content* 301n.
 thermometry 379n.
calorimeter
 thermometry 379n.
calotte *canonicals* 989n.
calotype *photography* 551n.
caloyer *monk* 986n.
calque *word* 599n.
 neology 560n.
caltrop *sharp point* 256n.
 defences 713n.
calumet *tobacco* 388n.
 peace 717n.
 irenics 719n.
calumniate *defame* 926vb.
calumny *slur* 867n.
 scurrility 899n.
 censure 924n.
 calumny 926n.
 false charge 928n.
calvary *suffering* 825n.
 painfulness 827n.
 church interior 990n.
calve *reproduce itself* 164vb.
Calvinism
 Protestantism 976n.
 sectarianism 978n.
calypso *vocal music* 412n.
calyx *receptacle* 194n.
 flower 366n.
camaraderie
 friendliness 880n.
 sociality 882n.
camarilla *party* 708n.
camber *obliquity* 220n.
 be curved 248vb.
 camber 253n.
 be convex 253vb.

cambist *merchant* 794n.
 moneyer 797n.
cambric *textile* 222n.
camel *beast of burden* 273n.
cameleer *driver* 268n.
 cavalry 722n.
camellia *tree* 366n.
cameo *rilievo* 254n.
camera *camera* 442n.
 recording instrument
  549n.
 photography 551n.
camera, in *secretly* 525adv.
cameraman *recorder* 549n.
camiknickers
 underwear 228n.
camisade *attack* 712n.
camisole *bodywear* 228n.
camomile *medicine* 658n.
camouflage
 assimilation 18n.
 make unlike 19vb.
 mimicry 20n.
 transform 147vb.
 conceal 525vb.
 disguise 527n.
camp *place oneself* 187vb.
 station 187n.
 abode 192n.
 dwell 192vb.
 shelter 662n.
 party 708n.
 fort 713n.
 army 722n.
campagna *space* 183n.
 plain 348n.
campaign *marching* 267n.
 undertaking 672n.
 action 676n.
 exert oneself 682vb.
 tactics 688n.
 fight 716n.,vb.
 warfare 718n.
campaigner *soldier* 722n.
campaniform
 rotund 252adj.
 concave 255adj.
campanile
 high structure 209n.
 church exterior 990n.
campanologist
 campanology 412n.
 instrumentalist 413n.
campestral
 champaign 348adj.
camp-follower
 dependant 742n.
camphor *resin* 357n.
 scent 396n.
 prophylactic 658n.
 preserver 666n.

campus
 focus 76n.
 meeting place 192n.
 arena 724n.
can *cup* 194n.
 small box 194n.
 vessel 194n.
 be able 160vb.
 preserve 666vb.
 gaol 748n.
canaille *rabble* 869n.
canal *conduit* 351n.
 access 624n.
canalize *direct* 689vb.
canalular *tubular* 263adj.
canard *rumour* 529n.
 fable 543n.
 false alarm 665n.
canary *bird* 365n.
 yellowness 433n.
canasta *card game* 837n.
cancan *dance* 837n.
cancel *nullify* 2vb.
 set off 31vb.
 destroy 165vb.
 counteract 182vb.
 obliterate 550vb.
 disuse 674vb.
 abrogate 752vb.
cancel out
 counteract 182vb.
 tell against 467vb.
cancel page
 abrogation 752n.
Cancer *zodiac* 321n.
cancer *carcinosis* 651n.
 blight 659n.
candid *true* 494adj.
 undisguised 522adj.
 informative 524adj.
 veracious 540adj.
 artless 699adj.
 maledicent 899adj.
 detracting 926adj.
 trustworthy 929adj.
candidate *testee* 461n.
 contender 716n.
 petitioner 763n.
 hoper 852n.
 desirer 859n.
candidature *vote* 605n.
 offer 759n.
candied *sweet* 392adj.
candle *lighter* 385n.
 torch 420n.
 ritual object 988n.
candle-holder
 auxiliary 707n.
candlelight *evening* 129n.
 light 417n.
 glimmer 419n.

Candlemas *holy-day* 988n.
candle-power *light* 417n.
metrology 465n.
candour (*see* candid)
candy *sweetmeat* 301n.
be dense 324vb.
sweeten 392vb.
cane *supporter* 218n.
strike 279vb.
tree 366n.
club 723n.
spank 963vb.
scourge 964n.
canescence *whiteness* 427n.
grey 429n.
canicule *heat* 379n.
canine *dog* 365n.
animal 365adj.
caning
corporal punishment
963n.
canister *box* 194n.
small box 194n.
basket 194n.
canister shot
ammunition 723n.
canker *dilapidation* 655n.
impair 655vb.
blight 659n.
cankerworm
destroyer 168n.
blight 659n.
noxious animal 904n.
cannabis *fibre* 208n.
cannery *preserver* 666n.
cannibal *eater* 301n.
ruffian 904n.
cannibalistic
murderous 362adj.
cruel 898adj.
cannibalize *sunder* 46vb.
repair 656vb.
cannikin *cup* 194n.
cannonade *shoot* 287vb.
bombardment 712n.
cannon-ball *sphere* 252n.
speeder 277n.
missile 287n.
ammunition 723n.
cannon fodder
soldiery 722n.
cannot
be impotent 161vb.
cannula *tube* 263n.
canny *knowing* 490adj.
intelligent 498adj.
cunning 698adj.
cautious 858adj.
canoe *row* 269vb.
rowboat 275n.
canoeing *aquatics* 269n.

canoeist *boatman* 270n.
canon *rule* 81n.
musical piece 412n.
creed 485n.
precept 693n.
decree 737n.
legislation 953n.
theology 973n.
scripture 975n.
ecclesiarch 986n.
office-book 988n.
canonical *regular* 83adj.
evidential 466adj.
credal 485adj.
preceptive 693adj.
theological 973adj.
scriptural 975adj.
orthodox 976adj.
vestimental 989adj.
canonical books
scripture 975n.
canonical hours
church service 988n.
canonicals
uniform 228n.
badge of rule 743n.
canonicals 989n.
canonicity *orthodoxy* 976n.
canonist *jurist* 958n.
theologian 973n.
canonization
dignification 866n.
sanctity 979n.
Christian rite 988n.
canon law *precept* 693n.
law 953n.
canonry *benefice* 985n.
church office 985n.
can-opener *opener* 263n.
canopy *canopy* 226n.
screen 421n.
altar 990n.
canorous *melodious* 410adj.
cant *obliquity* 220n.
propel 287vb.
sophisticate 477vb.
falsehood 541n.
duplicity 541n.
cant 541vb.
slang 560n.
dialectical 560adj.
be affected 850vb.
false piety 890n.
cantabile *musical* 412adj.
cantaloupe *fruit* 301n.
cantankerous
quarrelling 709adj.
irascible 892adj.
sullen 893adj.
cantata *vocal music* 412n.
hymn 981n.

canteen *café* 192n.
box 194n.
chamber 194n.
canter *gait* 265n.
ride 267vb.
deceiver 545n.
cantharides *stimulant* 174n.
canticle *vocal music* 412n.
hymn 981n.
cantilever *supporter* 218n.
cantillate *sing* 413vb.
cantle *piece* 53n.
canto *subdivision* 53n.
poem 593n.
canton *district* 184n.
flag 547n.
cantor *choir* 413n.
church officer 986n.
cantrip *spell* 983n.
can't stand *dislike* 861vb.
cant term *name* 561n.
canty *cheerful* 833 adj.
Canuck *foreigner* 59n.
native 191n.
canvas *textile* 222n.
canopy 226n.
sail 269n.
picture 553n.
art equipment 553n.
canvass *enquire* 459vb.
argue 475vb.
divulge 526vb.
publish 528vb.
advertise 528vb.
confer 584vb.
dissert 591vb.
vote 605n.,vb.
request 761vb.
sell 793vb.
canvasser *commender* 923n.
(*see* canvass)
canvass for *patronize* 703vb.
canyon *gap* 201n.
valley 255n.
caoutchouc *elasticity* 328n.
cap *be superior* 34vb.
vertex 213n.
crown 213vb.
covering 226n.
headgear 228n.
stopper 264n.
punctuation 547n.
badge 547n.
letter 558n.
retaliate 714vb.
explosive 723n.
climax 725vb.
greet 884vb.
capability *fitness* 24n.
ability 160n.
influence 178n.

skill 694 n.
facility 701 n.
capable *possible* 469 adj.
intelligent 498 adj.
capacious *great* 32 adj.
spacious 183 adj.
recipient 194 adj.
large 195 adj.
capacitance *electricity* 160 n.
capacity *greatness* 32 n.
plenitude 54 n.
inclusion 78 n.
ability 160 n.
room 183 n.
size 195 n.
limit 236 n.
intelligence 498 n.
function 622 n.
utility 640 n.
means 629 n.
skill 694 n.
facility 701 n.
cap and bells
entertainer 594 n.
cap and gown
formal dress 228 n.
uniform 228 n.
caparison *coverlet* 226 n.
dress 228 vb.
cape *cloak* 228 n.
Cape-coloured *hybrid* 43 n.
caper *potherb* 301 n.
leap 312 n., vb.
condiment 389 n.
amuse oneself 837 vb.
dance 837 vb.
capful *finite quantity* 26 n.
small quantity 33 n.
capillament *filament* 208 n.
capillary *narrow* 206 adj.
filament 208 n.
fibrous 208 adj.
tubular 263 adj.
conduit 351 n.
capilliform *fibrous* 208 adj.
cap in hand
respectful 920 adj.
capital *supreme* 34 adj.
abode 192 n.
summit 213 n.
deadly 362 adj.
literal 558 adj.
means 629 n.
store 632 n.
important 638 adj.
best 644 adj.
magistrature 733 n.
funds 797 n.
wealth 800 n.
ornamental art 844 n.
capitalism *barter* 791 n.

wealth 800 n.
capitalist *director* 690 n.
master 741 n.
moneyer 797 n.
rich man 800 n.
capitalize *use* 673 vb.
profit by 137 vb.
capital letter
punctuation 547 n.
letter 558 n.
capital levy *taking* 786 n.
expropriation 786 n.
tax 809 n.
capital punishment
capital punishment 963 n.
capitals *print-type* 587 n.
capitation *numeration* 86 n.
capitol *fort* 713 n.
capitular
ecclesiastical 985 adj.
ecclesiarch 986 n.
church officer 986 n.
capitulate *submit* 721 vb.
capitulation
submission 721 n.
capitulations
non-liability 919 n.
capon *eunuch* 161 n.
poultry 365 n.
male animal 372 n.
caponize *unman* 161 vb.
capriccio
musical piece 412 n.
caprice
non-uniformity 17 n.
fitfulness 142 n.
changeableness 152 n.
musical piece 412 n.
bias 481 n.
will 595 n.
tergiversation 603 n.
caprice 604 n.
liking 859 n.
capricious *multiform* 82 adj.
transient 114 adj.
light-minded 456 adj.
uncertain 474 adj.
(*see* caprice)
Capricorn *zodiac* 321 n.
capriole *leap* 312 n.
capsicum *vegetable* 301 n.
condiment 389 n.
capsize *be unequal* 29 vb.
derange 63 vb.
invert 221 vb.
capstan *lifter* 310 n.
rotator 315 n.
capstone *summit* 213 n.
capsular *capsular* 194 adj.
concave 255 adj.
capsule *receptacle* 194 n.

covering 226 n.
medicine 658 n.
captain *navigate* 269 vb.
naval man 270 n.
direct 689 vb.
leader 690 n.
army officer 741 n.
naval officer 741 n.
captaincy *degree* 27 n.
precedence 64 n.
captation *flattery* 925 n.
caption *commentary* 520 n.
label 547 n.
record 548 n.
name 561 n.
phrase 563 n.
script 586 n.
letterpress 587 n.
description 590 n.
captious *sophistical* 477 adj.
capricious 604 adj.
irascible 892 adj.
disapproving 927 adj.
captivate *motivate* 612 vb.
subjugate 745 vb.
excite love 887 vb.
captive *slave* 742 n.
subjugate 745 vb.
imprisoned 747 adj.
prisoner 750 n.
take 786 vb.
captivity *servitude* 745 n.
detention 747 n.
captor *master* 741 n.
possessor 776 n.
taker 786 n.
capture *imagine* 513 vb.
attack 712 vb.
overmaster 727 vb.
trophy 729 n.
subjugate 745 vb.
arrest 747 vb.
prisoner 750 n.
acquire 771 vb.
take 786 vb.
capuccino *soft drink* 301 n.
capuche *canonicals* 989 n.
car *convenance* 267 n.
train 274 n.
automobile 274 n.
airship 276 n.
carabineer *soldiery* 722 n.
caracole *equitation* 267 n.
ride 267 vb.
leap 312 n., vb.
carafe *vessel* 194 n.
caramel *sweetmeat* 301 n.
sweet 392 n.
carapace *covering* 226 n.
armour 713 n.
carat *weighment* 322 n.

caravan *procession* 71 n.
　small house 192 n.
　land travel 267 n.
　marching 267 n.
　conveyance 267 n.
　carriage 274 n.
caravanserai *inn* 192 n.
caravel *merchant ship* 275 n.
caraway *condiment* 389 n.
carbine *fire-arm* 723 n.
carbohydrate
　food content 301 n.
carbolic *cleanser* 648 n.
　prophylactic 658 n.
carbon *duplicate* 22 n.
　ash 381 n.
carbonaceous
　combustible 385 adj.
carbon copy
　duplication 91 n.
　record 548 n.
carbonize *burn* 381 vb.
carbuncle *swelling* 253 n.
　redness 431 n.
　gem 844 n.
carcanet *jewellery* 844 n.
carcass *structure* 331 n.
　corpse 363 n.
　bomb 723 n.
carcinoma *carcinosis* 651 n.
card *unravel* 62 vb.
　nonconformist 84 n.
　lamina 207 n.
　sailing aid 269 n.
　label 547 n.
　record 548 n.
　correspondence 588 n.
　contrivance 623 n.
　instrument 628 n.
　means 629 n.
　laughing-stock 851 n.
cardboard *lamina* 207 n.
　spurious 542 adj.
　bookbinding 589 n.
　paper 631 n.
card game *card game* 837 n.
cardigan *vest* 228 n.
cardinal *intrinsic* 5 adj.
　supreme 34 adj.
　numerical 85 adj.
　cloak 228 n.
　bird 365 n.
　red colour 431 n.
　important 638 adj.
　best 644 adj.
　ecclesiarch 986 n.
cardinalate
　church office 985 n.
cardinal points
　compass point 281 n.
card index *sorting* 62 n.

directory 87 n.
cardioid *curve* 248 n.
card-sharper *trickster* 545 n.
cardsharping *trickery* 542 n.
cards, on the *liable* 180 adj.
　possible 469 adj.
　probable 471 adj.
cards on the table
　disclosure 526 n.
care *carefulness* 457 n.
　business 622 n.
　management 689 n.
　detention 747 n.
　mandate 751 n.
　economy 814 n.
　worry 825 n.
　painfulness 827 n.
　dejection 834 n.
　nervousness 854 n.
　caution 858 n.
　desire 859 vb.
　love 887 vb.
careen *be oblique* 220 vb.
　navigate 269 vb.
　move fast 277 vb.
　repair 656 vb.
career *continuity* 71 n.
　speeding 277 n.
　move fast 277 vb.
　progression 285 n.
　vocation 622 n.
　conduct 688 n.
careerism
　selfishness 932 n.
careerist *planner* 623 n.
　busy person 678 n.
carefree *cheerful* 833 adj.
careful (*see* care)
careful of *observant* 768 adj.
careless *orderless* 61 adj.
　inattentive 456 adj.
　negligent 458 adj.
　feeble 572 adj.
　unprepared 670 adj.
　lazy 679 adj.
　apathetic 820 adj.
　rash 857 adj.
　indifferent 860 adj.
cares *adversity* 731 n.
　worry 825 n.
caress *touch* 378 vb.
　please 826 vb.
　love 887 vb.
　endearment 889 n.
　caress 889 vb.
　flatter 925 vb.
caret *deficit* 55 n.
　punctuation 547 n.
caretake *manage* 689 vb.
caretaker *manager* 690 n.
　servant 742 n.

keeper 749 n.
　consignee 754 n.
care-worn *suffering* 825 adj.
　melancholic 834 adj.
cargo *contents* 193 n.
　thing transferred 272 n.
　property 777 n.
　merchandise 795 n.
caribou *deer* 365 n.
caricature
　dissimilarity 19 n.
　imitate 20 vb.
　foolery 497 n.
　be absurd 497 vb.
　misinterpret 521 vb.
　exaggeration 546 n.
　misrepresent 552 vb.
　picture 553 n.
　be witty 839 vb.
　laughing-stock 851 n.
　satire 851 n.
　calumny 926 n.
　detract 926 vb.
caricaturist *artist* 556 n.
　humorist 839 n.
caries *decay* 51 n.
carillon *loudness* 400 n.
　roll 403 n.
　resonance 404 n.
　campanology 412 n.
　tune 412 n.
　gong 414 n.
　signal 547 n.
Carlylese
　imperspicuity 568 n.
Carmelites *monk* 986 n.
carminative *cathartic* 658 n.
carmine *red colour* 431 n.
carnage *havoc* 165 n.
　slaughter 362 n.
carnal *sensual* 944 adj.
　lecherous 951 adj.
carnal knowledge
　coition 45 n.
carnation *red colour* 431 n.
carnelian *redness* 431 n.
　gem 844 n.
carnival *festivity* 837 n.
　pageant 875 n.
carnivore *eater* 301 n.
　animal 365 n.
carol *vocal music* 412 n.
　sing 413 vb.
　voice 577 vb.
　be cheerful 833 vb.
　rejoice 835 vb.
carol-singers *choir* 413 n.
carom *recoil* 280 n.
carouse *eat* 301 vb.
　festivity 837 n.
　revel 837 vb.

be sociable 882 vb.
be intemperate 943 vb.
get drunk 949 vb.
carousel
pleasure-ground 837 n.
carp fish food 301 n.
table fish 365 n.
blame 924 vb.
car park inclosure 235 n.
carpenter artisan 686 n.
carper detractor 926 n.
carpet floor-cover 226 n.
reprove 924 vb.
carpet-bagger
trickster 545 n.
carrack ship 275 n.
merchant ship 275 n.
carriage supporter 218 n.
transport 272 n.
carrier 273 n.
gait 265 n.
train 274 n.
carriage 274 n.
mien 445 n.
conduct 688 n.
carriage-paid
uncharged 812 adj.
carriageway road 624 n.
carried assented 488 n.
carried away excited 821 adj.
carrier supporter 218 n.
carrier 273 n.
courier 531 n.
infection 651 n.
insalubrity 653 n.
carrier pigeon
bearer 273 n.
bird 365 n.
courier 531 n.
carriole sled 274 n.
carriage 274 n.
carrion decay 51 n.
food 301 n.
corpse 363 n.
rubbish 641 n.
dirt 649 n.
carronade gun 723 n.
carrot tuber 301 n.
incentive 612 n.
carroty red 431 adj.
carry reproduce itself 64 vb.
tend 179 vb.
be distant 199 vb.
support 218 vb.
wear 228 vb.
carry 273 vb.
overmaster 727 vb.
carry off take away 786 vb.
carry on go on 146 vb.
do 676 vb.
behave 688 vb.

deal with 688 vb.
manage 689 vb.
lament 836 vb.
be angry 891 vb.
carry out deal with 688 vb.
carry out 725 vb.
observe 768 vb.
carry-over remainder 44 n.
thing transferred 272 n.
carry over add 38 vb.
transfer 272 vb.
account 808 vb.
carry through
make complete 54 vb.
terminate 69 vb.
carry through 725 vb.
carry weight
influence 178 vb.
evidence 466 vb.
be important 638 vb.
cart carry 273 vb.
cart 274 n.
cartage transport 272 n.
carte blanche scope 744 n.
permit 756 n.
liberality 813 n.
cartel association 706 n.
corporation 708 n.
defiance 711 n.
compact 765 n.
carter driver 268 n.
carrier 273 n.
Carthusian monk 986 n.
cartilage hardness 326 n.
toughness 329 n.
solid body 324 n.
cartload contents 193 n.
cartographer surveyor 465 n.
cartography map 551 n.
carton small box 194 n.
paper 631 n.
cartoon copy 22 n.
cinema 445 n.
representation 551 n.
picture 553 n.
satire 851 n.
cartoonist artist 556 n.
humorist 839 n.
cartouche script 586 n.
ammunition 723 n.
ornamental art 844 n.
cartridge ammunition 723 n.
cartulary record 548 n.
cartwheel
overturning 221 n.
carve cut, sunder 46 vb.
produce 164 vb.
efform 243 vb.
groove 262 vb.
record 548 vb.
sculpt 554 vb.

apportion 783 vb.
decorate 844 vb.
carvel ship 275 n.
carver sharp edge 256 n.
sculptor 556 n.
artisan 686 n.
carve up apportion 783 vb.
carving sculpture 554 n.
writing 586 n.
caryatid pillar 218 n.
ornamental art 844 n.
cascade descend 309 vb.
waterfall 350 n.
case state 7 n.
example 83 n.
eventuality 154 n.
box 194 n.
case 194 n.
cover 226 vb.
inclosure 235 n.
topic 452 n.
argument 475 n.
report 524 n.
grammar 564 n.
press 587 n.
bookbinding 589 n.
business 622 n.
sick person 651 n.
accusation 928 n.
litigation 959 n.
caseation
condensation 324 n.
case-ending
part of speech 564 n.
case-harden
strengthen 162 vb.
be tough 329 vb.
habituate 610 vb.
case-hardened
strong 162 adj.
unfeeling 375 adj.
obstinate 602 adj.
thick-skinned 820 adj.
impenitent 940 adj.
case-history evidence 466 n.
record 548 n.
case, in if 8 adv.
case in point relevance 9 n.
fitness 24 n.
example 83 n.
case-law legal trial 959 n.
casemate quarters 192 n.
fortification 713 n.
casement window 263 n.
case of need
needfulness 627 n.
case-record
documentary evidence
465 n.
legal trial 959 n.
casern quarters 192 n.

cash *small coin* 33 n.
  acquire 771 vb.
  money 797 n.
  draw money 797 vb.
cash book *record* 548 n.
  account book 808 n.
cash box *treasury* 799 n.
cash desk *treasury* 799 n.
cash down
  cash down 804 adv.
cashier *depose* 752 vb.
  moneyer 797 n.
  treasurer 798 n.
  pay 804 n.
  accountant 808 n.
cash in on
  profit by 137 vb.
cashmere *fibre* 208 n.
  textile 222 n.
cash register
  counting instrument 86 n.
  recording instrument
    549 n.
  treasury 799 n.
casino *gaming-house* 618 n.
  place of amusement 837 n.
  card game 837 n.
cask *vat* 194 n.
casket *small box* 194 n.
  interment 364 n.
  ritual object 988 n.
casque *headgear* 228 n.
  armour 713 n.
Cassandra *oracle* 511 n.
  warner 664 n.
cassation *obliteration* 550 n.
  abrogation 752 n.
casserole *cauldron* 194 n.
  dish 301 n.
  cook 301 vb.
cassock *tunic* 228 n.
  vestments 989 n.
cassolette *cauldron* 194 n.
cassowary
  flightless bird 365 n.
cast *copy* 22 n.
  number 86 vb.
  produce 164 vb.
  tendency 179 n.
  wrapping 226 n.
  doff 229 vb.
  form 243 n.
  efform 243 vb.
  propel 287 vb.
  excrement 302 n.
  liquefy 337 vb.
  heat 381 vb.
  hue 425 n.
  dim sight 440 n.
  mien 445 n.
  sculpture 554 n.

actor 594 n.
  dramatize 594 vb.
  incentive 612 n.
  surgical dressing 658 n.
  defeated 728 adj.
  apportion 783 vb.
castanets *gong* 414 n.
castaway *solitary* 883 n.
  (*see* derelict)
cast before swine
  consume 165 vb.
  waste 634 vb.
caste *breed* 77 n.
  prestige 866 n.
  nobility 868 n.
caste consciousness
  particularism 80 n.
casteism *exclusion* 57 n.
castellan *protector* 660 n.
  retainer 742 n.
  keeper 749 n.
caster *small box* 194 n.
  wheel 250 n.
  thrower 287 n.
castigate (*see* castigation)
castigation
  amendment 654 n.
  reprimand 924 n.
  punishment 963 n.
castigator *reformer* 654 n.
  disapprover 924 n.
  detractor 926 n.
  punisher 963 n.
casting *dramaturgy* 594 n.
casting vote *inequality* 29 n.
  judgment 480 n.
  vote 605 n.
casting weight *offset* 31 n.
cast-iron *hard* 326 adj.
  resolute 599 adj.
castle *interchange* 151 vb.
  house 192 n.
  fort 713 n.
  chessman 837 n.
castle-builder
  visionary 513 n.
castles in Spain
  fantasy 513 n.
  aspiration 852 n.
cast lots *divine* 511 vb.
  gamble 618 vb.
cast-off *excretory* 302 adj.
  relinquished 621 adj.
  derelict 779 n.
cast off *disjoin* 46 vb.
  navigate 269 vb.
  start out 296 vb.
  relinquish 621 vb.
  disuse 674 vb.
  carry through 725 vb.
  not retain 779 vb.

cast of mind
  affections 817 n.
cast on *tie* 45 vb.
castor *headgear* 228 n.
castor oil *cathartic* 658 n.
castrametation
  art of war 718 n.
castrate *subtract* 39 vb.
  unman 161 vb.
  sterilize 172 vb.
  make useless 641 vb.
  impair 655 vb.
castrato *eunuch* 161 n.
  vocalist 413 n.
cast up *do sums* 86 vb.
  estimate 480 vb.
casual *extrinsic* 6 adj.
  orderless 61 adj.
  casual 159 adj.
  negligent 458 adj.
  uncertain 474 adj.
  unintentional 618 adj.
casualties *death roll* 361 n.
casualty *extrinsicality* 6 n.
  eventuality 154 n.
  chance 159 n.
  evil 616 n.
  non-design 618 n.
  ill fortune 731 n.
casualty station
  hospital 658 n.
casuist *reasoner* 475 n.
  sophist 477 n.
casuistry *sophistry* 477 n.
  falsehood 541 n.
  morals 917 n.
casus belli *casus belli* 709 n.
  excitation 821 n.
casus foederis
  conditions 766 n.
cat *vomit* 300 vb.
  cat 365 n.
  hell-hag 904 n.
  cad 938 n.
  scourge 964 n.
catabasis *decrease* 37 n.
catacaustic *curve* 248 n.
catachresis *metaphor* 519 n.
  misinterpretation 521 n.
  solecism 564 n.
cataclinal *sloping* 220 adj.
cataclysm *revolution* 149 n.
  havoc 165 n.
  outbreak 176 n.
cataclysmic *flowing* 350 adj.
  (*see* cataclysm)
catacomb *cemetery* 364 n.
catacoustics *acoustics* 398 n.
catadupe *waterfall* 350 n.
catafalque *funeral* 364 n.
catalectic *short* 204 adj.

poetic 593 adj.
catalepsy *quiescence* 266 n.
  insensibility 375 n.
  sleep 679 n.
catalogue
  arrangement 62 n.
  class 62 vb.
  list 87 n., vb.
  guide-book 524 n.
  record 548 n.
catalysis
  decomposition 51 n.
catalyst *alterer* 143 n.
catamaran *raft* 275 n.
  warship 722 n.
catamenia
  regular return 141 n.
  haemorrhage 302 n.
catamountain *cat* 365 n.
cat and dog life
  dissension 709 n.
cataphonics *acoustics* 398 n.
cataplasm
  surgical dressing 658 n.
catapult *propellant* 287 n.
  missile weapon 723 n.
cataract *high water* 209 n.
  waterfall 350 n.
  blindness 439 n.
  dim sight 440 n.
catarrh *excretion* 302 n.
  ill-health 651 n.
catastrophe
  revolution 149 n.
  eventuality 154 n.
  ruin 165 n.
  disclosure 526 n.
  evil 616 n.
  completion 725 n.
  ill fortune 731 n.
catcall *be loud* 400 vb.
  shrill 407 vb.
  ridicule 851 n.
  disapprobation 924 n.
catch *copy* 20 vb.
  fastening 47 n.
  bring together 74 vb.
  halt 145 vb.
  rub 333 vb.
  vocal music 412 n.
  hear 415 vb.
  question 459 n.
  know 490 vb.
  absurdity 497 n.
  surprise 508 vb.
  understand 516 vb.
  ambush 527 n.
  trap 542 n.
  befool 542 vb.
  ensnare 542 vb.
  represent 551 vb.

  be induced 612 vb.
  hunt 619 vb.
  bigwig 638 n.
  be ill 651 vb.
  pitfall 663 n.
  stratagem 698 n.
  hitch 702 n.
  wrestling 716 n.
  arrest 747 vb.
  acquire 771 vb.
  take 786 vb.
  booty 790 n.
  feel 818 vb.
  desired object 859 n.
  social person 882 n.
  favourite 890 n.
catch a likeness
  represent 551 vb.
catch-all *receptacle* 194 n.
catch as catch can
  spontaneous 609 adj.
  essaying 671 adj.
  wrestling 716 n.
catch at *be willing* 597 vb.
  desire 859 vb.
catch at straws
  overrate 482 vb.
  be credulous 487 vb.
catch a Tartar
  be duped 544 vb.
  stultify oneself 695 vb.
  be in difficulty 700 vb.
  be rightly served 714 vb.
catch bending
  be neglectful 458 vb.
  surprise 508 vb.
catcher *interceptor* 702 n.
catch fire *be hot* 379 vb.
  be excitable 822 vb.
catching *infectious* 653 adj.
catch on *prevail* 178 vb.
  be wont 610 adj.
catch out *dismiss* 300 vb.
  detect 484 vb.
  discover 526 vb.
  ensnare 542 vb.
catchpenny
  spurious 542 adj.
  trivial 639 adj.
  vulgar 847 adj.
catchpoll
  law officer 955 n.
catch the breath
  breathe 352 vb.
  rasp 407 vb.
catch the eye
  attract notice 455 vb.
  be visible 443 vb.
catch up *outstrip* 277 vb.
  approach 289 vb.
  hasten 680 vb.

catchword *maxim* 496 n.
  indication 547 n.
  call 547 n.
catchy *melodious* 410 adj.
  desired 859 adj.
catechism
  interrogation 459 n.
  creed 485 n.
  orthodoxy 976 n.
catechist *teacher* 537 n.
  religious teacher 973 n.
catechize *interrogate* 459 vb.
catechumen
  changed person 147 n.
  learner 538 n.
  beginner 538 n.
  pietist 979 n.
  layman 987 n.
categorical *positive* 473 adj.
  demonstrating 478 adj.
  assertive 532 adj.
  commanding 737 adj.
categorical imperative
  command 737 n.
  conscience 917 n.
categorization
  arrangement 62 n.
category *state* 7 n.
  classification 77 n.
catena *continuity* 71 n.
catenary *curve* 248 n.
catenate *continuate* 71 vb.
cater *feed* 301 vb.
  provide 633 vb.
  offer 759 vb.
  sell 793 vb.
cateran *soldier* 722 n.
  robber 789 n.
cater-cornered
  oblique 220 adj.
caterer *caterer* 633 n.
cater for
  be hospitable 882 vb.
caterpillar *vermin* 365 n.
caters *campanology* 412 n.
caterwaul *be loud* 400 vb.
  shrill 407 vb.
  cry 408 n., vb.
  ululate 409 vb.
  court 889 vb.
catgut *viol* 414 n.
catharsis *sanation* 656 n.
cathartic *ejector* 300 n.
  expulsive 300 adj.
  cleanser 648 n.
  cathartic 658 n.
  remedial 658 adj.
cathead *supporter* 218 n.
cathedral *church* 990 n.
Catheran, Catherist
  heretic 977 n.

catheter *drain* 351 n.
catheterism *therapy* 658 n.
catholic *universal* 79 adj.
　orthodox 976 adj.
Catholic *popish* 976 adj.
　Catholic 976 n.
Catholicism
　orthodoxy 976 n.
　Catholicism 976 n.
catholicity *generality* 79 n.
catholicon *remedy* 658 n.
catlap *insipidity* 387 n.
cat-like *stealthy* 525 adj.
catling *sharp edge* 256 n.
catnap *sleep* 679 n.
cat-o'-nine-tails
　scourge 964 n.
catoptrics *optics* 417 n.
cat's cradle *crossing* 222 n.
cat's-eye *gem* 844 n.
cat's nine lives
　diuturnity 113 n.
　life 360 n.
cat's-paw *shallowness* 212 n.
　furrow 262 n.
　wave 350 n.
　dupe 544 n.
　instrument 628 n.
　auxiliary 707 n.
　toady 879 n.
cattiness *detraction* 926 n.
cattle *beast of burden* 273 n.
　cattle 365 n.
　rabble 869 n.
cattle farm
　stock farm 369 n.
cattle-lifter *thief* 789 n.
cattleman *herdsman* 369 n.
catty *malevolent* 898 adj.
　detracting 926 adj.
catur *galley* 275 n.
catwalk *aircraft* 276 n.
　bridge 624 n.
Caucasian *ethnic* 11 adj.
caucus *assemblage* 74 n.
　party 708 n.
caudal *ending* 69 adj.
　back 238 adj.
caudate *pendent* 217 adj.
　back 238 adj.
caudex *supporter* 218 n.
caudiform *back* 238 adj.
caudle *potion* 301 n.
　liquor 301 n.
　drink 301 vb.
caul *obstetrics* 164 n.
cauldron *cauldron* 194 n.
　heater 383 n.
caulicle *foliage* 366 n.
cauliflower *vegetable* 301 n.
caulk *repair* 656 vb.

causal *causal* 156 adj.
　instrumental 628 adj.
causality *relativeness* 9 n.
　causation 156 n.
causation *causation* 156 n.
　agency 173 n.
cause *cause* 156 n., vb.
　reason why 156 n.
　produce 164 vb.
　influence 178 n.
　promote 285 vb.
　reasons 475 n.
　predetermine 608 vb.
　motive 612 n.
　induce 612 vb.
　philanthropy 901 n.
　litigation 959 n.
cause and effect
　relativeness 9 n.
cause célèbre
　prodigy 864 n.
causeless *causeless* 159 adj.
　designless 618 adj.
cause-list *legal trial* 959 n.
causerie *chat* 584 n.
　interlocution 584 n.
　article 591 n.
causeway *road* 624 n.
causidical
　jurisdictional 955 adj.
caustic *keen* 174 adj.
　curve 248 n.
　burning 381 n.
　heating 381 adj.
　pungent 388 adj.
　felt 818 adj.
　paining 827 adj.
　maleficent 898 adj.
　disapproving 924 adj.
　detracting 926 adj.
caustic line *curve* 248 n.
cauterant *burning* 381 n.
cauterize *burn* 381 vb.
　doctor 658 vb.
cautery *burning* 381 n.
caution *delay* 136 n.
　slowness 278 n.
　carefulness 457 n.
　foresight 510 n.
　omen 511 n.
　hint 524 n.
　unwillingness 598 n.
　irresolution 601 n.
　dissuasion 613 n.
　warn 664 vb.
　intimidation 854 n.
　frighten 854 vb.
　cowardice 856 n.
　caution 858 n.
　reprove 924 vb.
cautionary

cautionary 664 adj.
　advising 691 adj.
cautious *doubting* 474 adj.
　taciturn 582 adj.
　(see caution)
cavalcade *procession* 71 n.
　marching 267 n.
cavalier *rider* 268 n.
　rash 857 adj.
　impertinent 878 adj.
　discourteous 885 adj.
　disrespectful 921 adj.
cavaliere servente
　toady 879 n.
　lover 887 n.
cavalry *rider* 268 n.
　cavalry 722 n.
cavatina *vocal music* 412 n.
cave *dwelling* 192 n.
　receptacle 194 n.
　interiority 224 n.
　cavity 255 n.
　dissentient 489 n.
　party 708 n.
caveat *warning* 664 n.
cave-dweller *dweller* 191 n.
　solitary 883 n.
cave in *be concave* 255 vb.
　descend 309 vb.
cave man
　violent creature 176 n.
　male 372 n.
　mankind 371 n.
　ruffian 904 n.
cavern *cavity* 255 n.
　darkness 418 n.
cavernous *deep* 211 adj.
caviar *fish food* 301 n.
　condiment 389 n.
　savouriness 390 n.
cavil *argue* 475 vb.
　sophisticate 477 vb.
　doubt 486 vb.
　dissent 489 vb.
　disapprobation 924 n.
　dispraise 924 vb.
　disapprove 924 vb.
caviller *(see* cavil)
cavity *receptacle* 194 n.
　gap 201 n.
　cavity 255 n.
cavort *leap* 312 vb.
　dance 837 vb.
caw *rasp* 407 vb.
　ululate 409 vb.
cay *island* 349 n.
cayenne *condiment* 389 n.
cayman *reptile* 365 n.
cease *end* 69 vb.
　cease 145 vb.
　be quiescent 266 vb.

relinquish 621 vb.
 be inactive 679 vb.
 fail 728 vb.
cease-fire lull 145 n.
 pacification 719 n.
ceaseless perpetual 115 adj.
ceaselessly
 persistently 600 adv.
ceaselessness
 perseverance 600 n.
cedar tree 366 n.
cede relinquish 621 vb.
 not retain 779 vb.
 give 781 vb.
cedilla punctuation 547 n.
ceil overlay 226 vb.
ceiling finite quantity 26 n.
 height 209 n.
 vertex 213 n.
 roof 226 n.
 limit 236 n.
 visibility 443 n.
celadon green colour 432 n.
celebrant worshipper 981 n.
 ritualist 988 n.
celebrate remind 505 vb.
 proclaim 528 vb.
 make important 638 vb.
 be cheerful 833 vb.
 rejoice 835 vb.
 revel 837 vb.
 honour 866 vb.
 celebrate 876 vb.
 applaud 923 vb.
 offer worship 981 vb.
 perform ritual 988 vb.
celebrated known 490 adj.
 well-known 528 adj.
 renowned 866 adj.
celebration (see celebrate)
celebrative
 celebrative 876 adj.
celebrity made man 730 n.
 famousness 866 n.
 person of repute 866 n.
celerity velocity 277 n.
celery vegetable 301 n.
celeste mute 414 n.
 piano 414 n.
 blueness 435 n.
celestial foreigner 59 n.
 celestial 321 adj.
 divine 965 adj.
 angelic 968 adj.
 paradisiac 971 adj.
celibacy
 unproductivity 172 n.
 unsociability 883 n.
 celibacy 895 n.
 monasticism 985 n.
celibate alone 88 adj.

celibate 895 n.
 virgin 950 n.
 (see celibacy)
cell electricity 160 n.
 retreat 192 n.
 compartment 194 n.
 insides 224 n.
 inclosure 235 n.
 cavity 255 n.
 organism 358 n.
 life 360 n.
 refuge 662 n.
 party, society 708 n.
 lock-up 748 n.
 seclusion 883 n.
 monastery 986 n.
cella temple 990 n.
 holy place 990 n.
 church interior 990 n.
cellar cellar 194 n.
 depth 211 n.
 sink 649 n.
cellarage cellar 194 n.
 lowness 210 n.
 depth 211 n.
cellarer retainer 742 n.
cellaret cabinet 194 n.
cellist instrumentalist 413 n.
cello viol 414 n.
cellophane
 wrapping 226 n.
cellular cellular 194 adj.
 concave 255 adj.
cellule compartment 194 n.
celluloid cinema 445 n.
 materials 631 n.
Celtic fringe foreigner 59 n.
cembalist
 instrumentalist 413 n.
cement join 45 vb.
 bond 47 n.
 adhesive 47 n.
 agglutinate 48 vb.
 overlay 226 vb.
 solid body 324 n.
 hardness 326 n.
 building material 631 n.
cemented firm-set 45 adj.
 concordant 710 adj.
cemetery cemetery 364 n.
 holy place 990 n.
cenobite solitary 883 n.
 monk 986 n.
cenobitism
 monasticism 985 n.
cenotaph obsequies 364 n.
 tomb 364 n.
cense perform ritual 988 vb.
censer cauldron 194 n.
 scent 396 n.
 ritual object 988 n.

censor exclude 57 vb.
 inquisitor 543 n.
 enquirer 459 n.
 estimator 480 n.
 obliterate 550 vb.
 restrain 747 vb.
 prohibit 757 vb.
 disapprove 924 vb.
 detractor 926 n.
 prude 950 n.
censorial judicial 480 adj.
censorious judicial 480 adj.
 severe 735 adj.
 discontented 829 adj.
 fastidious 862 adj.
 disapproving 924 adj.
censorship estimate 480 n.
 war measures 718 n.
 severity 735 n.
 prohibition 757 n.
 prudery 950 n.
censurable
 discreditable 867 adj.
 blameworthy 924 adj.
 guilty 936 adj.
censure estimate 480 n., vb.
 slur 867 n.
 censure 924 n.
 reprimand 924 n.
 reprove 924 vb.
 accusation 928 n.
 guilt 936 n.
censurer malcontent 829 n.
 (see censure)
census numeration 86 n.
 statistics 86 n.
cent small coin 33 n.
 trifle 639 n.
 coinage 797 n.
centaur rara avis 84 n.
 rider 268 n.
centenarian old man 133 n.
centenary hundred 99 n.
 anniversary 141 n.
 special day 876 n.
centennial
 fifth and over 99 adj.
centering location 187 n.
 convergent 293 adj.
centesimal
 fifth and over 99 adj.
 multifid 100 adj.
centillion
 over one hundred 99 n.
centime small coin 33 n.
centimetre
 long measure 203 n.
cento a mixture 43 n.
 doggerel 593 n.
central median 30 adj.
 fundamental 156 adj.

interior 224 adj.
central 225 adj.
inland 344 adj.
undeviating 625 adj.
important 638 adj.
centrality *centrality* 225 n.
symmetry 245 n.
centralization
uniformity 16 n.
centrality 225 n.
centralize *combine* 50 vb.
regularize 62 vb.
focus 76 vb.
centralize 225 vb.
centre *essence* 1 n.
middle point 30 n.
bring together 74 vb.
focus 76 n., vb.
place 185 n., vb.
arena 224 n.
interiority 224 n.
centre 225 n.
converge 293 vb.
chief thing 638 n.
political party 708 n.
armed force 722 n.
centreboard *stabilizer* 153 n.
centre forward *leader* 690 n.
centre-line *centrality* 225 n.
centremost *central* 225 adj.
centre of gravity
centrality 225 n.
centre on *congregate* 74 vb.
converge 293 vb.
centre piece
ornamentation 844 n.
centrifugal
unassembled 75 adj.
exterior 223 adj.
receding 290 adj.
repellant 292 adj.
divergent 294 adj.
avoiding 620 adj.
centrifugence
divergence 294 n.
centripetal
attracting 291 adj.
convergent 293 adj.
centripetence
centrality 225 n.
centrist
political party 708 n.
centuplicate
fifth and over 99 adj.
centurial
fifth and over 99 adj.
centurion *soldier* 722 n.
army officer 741 n.
century *hundred* 99 n.
period 110 n.
diuturnity 113 n.

formation 722 n.
cephalic *topmost* 213 adj.
cephalopod *fish* 365 n.
ceramics *pottery* 381 n.
sculpture 554 n.
cerastes *reptile* 365 n.
cerate *unguent* 357 n.
balm 658 n.
Cerberus *rara avis* 84 n.
janitor 264 n.
protector 660 n.
Chthonian god 967 n.
mythic hell 972 n.
cereal *cereal* 301 n.
corn 366 n.
cerebral *mental* 447 adj.
spoken letter 558 n.
vocal 577 adj.
cerebrate *think* 449 vb.
cerebration
production 164 n.
thought 449 n.
cerebrum *intellect* 447 n.
cerecloth
grave clothes 364 n.
cerelein *blue pigment* 435 n.
cerement(s) *wrapping* 226 n.
grave clothes 364 n.
ceremonial *formality* 875 n.
formal 875 adj.
ritual 988 n., adj.
ceremonialist *ritualist* 988 n.
ceremonious *formal* 875 adj.
respectful 920 adj.
ritualistic 988 adj.
ceremony *formality* 875 n.
celebration 876 n.
ritual, rite 988 n.
cereous *fatty* 357 adj.
cerin *fat* 357 n.
cerise *red colour* 431 n.
cerography
engraving 555 n.
writing 586 n.
ceroplastics *sculpture* 554 n.
certain *quantitative* 26 adj.
definite 80 adj.
unchangeable 153 adj.
certain 473 adj.
demonstrated 478 adj.
believing 485 adj.
known 490 adj.
true 494 adj.
expectant 507 adj.
anonymous 562 adj.
successful 727 adj.
certain, a *one* 88 adj.
certainty *certainty* 473 n.
positiveness 473 n.
demonstration 478 n.
discovery 484 n.

belief 485 n.
expectation 507 n.
foresight 510 n.
intelligibility 516 n.
certifiable *insane* 503 adj.
certificate *credential* 466 n.
record 548 n.
title-deed 767 n.
paper money 797 n.
honours 866 n.
reward 962 n.
certification
certainty 473 n.
assent 488 n.
certified *positive* 473 adj.
insane 503 adj.
certify *testify* 466 vb.
make certain 473 vb.
inform 524 vb.
affirm 532 vb.
certiorari
legal process 959 n.
certitude *certainty* 473 n.
cerulean *blue* 435 adj.
cervical *supporting* 218 adj.
cervidæ *deer* 365 n.
cervine *animal* 365 adj.
cervix *supporter* 218 n.
pillar 218 n.
cespitose *vegetal* 366 adj.
cess *tax* 809 n.
cessation *end* 69 n.
finality 69 n.
cessation 145 n.
quiescence 266 n.
deliverance 668 n.
peace 717 n.
cession *offset* 31 n.
reversion 148 n.
relinquishment 621 n.
submission 721 n.
non-retention 779 n.
cesspool *receptacle* 194 n.
lake 346 n.
storage 632 n.
sink 649 n.
cestui que trust
beneficiary 776 n.
cestui que vie
beneficiary 776 n.
cestus *girdle* 47 n.
loop 250 n.
cetacean *fish* 365 n.
ceteris paribus
equally 28 adv.
chabouk *scourge* 964 n.
chad *question* 459 n.
picture 553 n.
chafe *rub* 333 vb.
give pain 377 vb.
heat 381 vb.

wound 655 vb.
disobey 738 vb.
suffer 825 vb.
hurt 827 vb.
cause discontent 829 vb.
be angry 891 vb.
chaff *leavings* 41 n.
corn 366 n.
trifle 639 n.
rubbish 641 n.
be witty 839 vb.
ridicule 851 n., vb.
chaffer *bargain* 791 vb.
chafing dish *heater* 383 n.
chagrin *sorrow* 825 n.
discontent 829 n.
chain *cable* 47 n.
bond 47 n.
coherence 48 n.
continuity 71 n.
series 71 n.
long measure 203 n.
gauge 465 n.
encumbrance 702 n.
fetter 748 n.
jewellery 844 n.
chain-gang *slave* 742 n.
prisoner 750 n.
chain-reaction
continuity 71 n.
chain-reactor
nucleonics 160 n.
chain stitch
needlework 844 n.
chain together
connect 45 vb.
chair *seat* 218 n.
elevate 310 vb.
rostrum 539 n.
director 690 n.
badge of rule 743 n.
honour 866 vb.
celebrate 876 vb.
pay respects 884 vb.
respect 920 vb.
applaud 923 vb.
courtroom 956 n.
chairborne
quiescent 266 adj.
chairman *superior* 34 n.
director 690 n.
master 741 n.
chairmanship
directorship 689 n.
magistrature 733 n.
chaise *carriage* 274 n.
chaise longue *seat* 218 n.
chalcedony *gem* 844 n.
chalcography
engraving 555 n.
chalcolithic *secular* 110 adj.

Chaldean *sorcerer* 983 n.
sorcerous 983 adj.
chalet *house* 192 n.
chalice *cup* 194 n.
ritual object 988 n.
church utensil 990 n.
chalk *soil* 344 n.
white thing 427 n.
mark 547 vb.
art equipment 553 n.
chalk out *plan* 623 vb.
chalk up *mark* 547 vb.
register 548 vb.
chalky *territorial* 344 adj.
white 427 adj.
challenge *question* 459 n.
dissent 489 n., vb.
negation 533 n.
call 547 n.
motivate 612 vb.
opposition 704 n.
dissension 709 n.
defiance 711 n.
attack 712 n., vb.
resist 715 vb.
threat 900 vb.
challengee *defender* 713 n.
challenger *dissentient* 489 n.
hinderer 702 n.
opponent 705 n.
contender 716 n.
accuser 928 n.
chamber *chamber* 194 n.
chambering
love-making 887 n.
chamberlain *retainer* 742 n.
chambermaid *servant* 742 n.
domestic 742 n.
chamber of commerce
corporation 708 n.
merchant 794 n.
chamber-pot *vessel* 194 n.
chameleon
changeable thing 152 n.
reptile 365 n.
variegation 437 n.
iridescent 437 adj.
waverer 601 n.
chamfer *furrow* 262 n.
groove 262 vb.
champ *be angry* 891 vb.
champagne *wine* 301 n.
champaign *open space* 263 n.
plain 348 n.
champerty
lawbreaking 954 n.
champion *superior* 34 n.
supreme 34 adj.
athlete 162 n.
exceller 644 n.
proficient 696 n.

patron 707 n.
patronize 703 vb.
defender 713 n.
combatant 722 n.
victor 727 n.
deputy 755 n.
philanthropist 901 n.
benefactor 903 n.
vindicator 927 n.
championship
superiority 34 n.
(*see* champion)
chance *opportunity* 137 n.
eventuality 154 n.
happen 154 vb.
chance 159 n.
possibility 469 n.
gambling 618 n.
chance, have a
be likely 471 vb.
chance it *gamble* 618 vb.
chancel *compartment* 194 n.
church interior 990 n.
chancellor *director* 690 n.
officer 741 n.
chancery *subjection* 745 n.
chancery, in *subject* 745 adj.
chancre
venereal disease 651 n.
chancy *casual* 159 adj.
uncertain 474 adj.
speculative 618 adj.
dangerous 661 adj.
chandelier *pendant* 217 n.
lamp 420 n.
chandler *merchant* 794 n.
change *difference* 15 n.
make unlike 19 vb.
fitfulness 142 n.
change 143 n., vb.
be turned to 147 adj.
substitute 150 n.
changeableness 152 n.
vary 152 vb.
influence 178 vb.
dress 228 vb.
doff 229 vb.
campanology 412 n.
money, coinage 797 n.
changeability *caprice* 604 n.
(*see* changeable)
changeable
non-uniform 17 adj.
multiform 82 adj.
transient 114 adj.
changeable 143 adj.
converted 147 adj.
changeful 152 adj.
uncertain 474 adj.
irresolute 601 adj.
lively 819 adj.

irascible 892 adj.
change course
  deviate 286 vb.
change front
  tergiversate 603 vb.
changeful (*see* changeable)
change hands
  change hands 780 vb.
change into *become* 1 vb.
  (*see* convert)
changeless
  unchangeable 153 adj.
  godlike 965 adj.
changeling *child* 132 n.
  substitute 150 n.
  fool 501 n.
  elf 970 n.
change money
  interchange 151 vb.
change of hands
  transfer 780 n.
change of life *age* 131 n.
  unproductivity 172 n.
change of mind
  tergiversation 603 n.
change over
  transfer 780 n.
  convey 780 vb.
change places
  be in motion 265 vb.
  change hands 780 vb.
change-ringing
  campanology 412 n.
change round
  modify 143 vb.
change sides
  be irresolute 601 vb.
  apostatize 603 vb.
channel *bond* 47 n.
  cavity 255 n.
  furrow 262 n.
  groove 262 vb.
  way in 297 n.
  passage 305 n.
  gulf 345 n.
  conduit 351 n.
  informant 524 n.
  access, path 624 n.
  instrument 628 n.
  direct 689 vb.
chant *repetition* 106 n.
  vociferate 408 vb.
  vocal music 412 n.
  sing 413 vb.
  voice 577 vb.
  hymn 981 n.
chantry *church* 990 n.
chanty *vocal music* 412 n.
  poem 593 n.
chaos *non-uniformity* 17 n.
  non-coherence 49 n.

decomposition 51 n.
  confusion 61 n.
  havoc 165 n.
  amorphism 244 n.
  anarchy 734 n.
chaotic *lawless* 954 adj.
  (*see* chaos)
chap *gap* 201 n.
  roughness 259 n.
  person 371 n.
  male 372 n.
chapel *association* 706 n.
  sect 978 n.
  church 990 n.
  church interior 990 n.
chapel-goer
  worshipper 981 n.
chaperon
  accompany 89 vb.
  look after 457 vb.
  protector 660 n.
  keeper 749 n.
chaperonage
  carefulness 457 n.
chap-fallen
  dejected 834 adj.
  humbled 872 adj.
chaplain *retainer* 742 n.
  pastor 986 n.
  church officer 986 n.
chaplaincy
  church office 985 n.
chaplet *loop* 250 n.
  badge 547 n.
  trophy 729 n.
chapman *seller* 793 n.
  pedlar 794 n.
chaps *trousers* 288 n.
  laterality 239 n.
chapter *subdivision* 53 n.
  topic 452 n.
  edition 589 n.
  synod 985 n.
chapter and verse
  situation 186 n.
  evidence 466 n.
  accuracy 494 n.
chapter-house
  church exterior 990 n.
char *burn* 381 vb.
  blacken 428 vb.
  embrown 430 vb.
  cleaner 648 n.
  servant 742 n.
char-à-banc *carriage* 274 n.
character *character* 5 n.
  composition 56 n.
  sort 77 n.
  nonconformist 84 n.
  person 371 n.
  credential 466 n.

letter 558 n.
  acting 594 n.
  habit 610 n.
  affections 817 n.
  repute 866 n.
  probity 929 n.
  virtue 933 n.
characteristic
  intrinsic 5 adj.
  characteristic 5 adj.
  speciality 80 n.
  special 80 adj.
  tendency 179 n.
  indicating 547 adj.
characterization
  representation 551 n.
  description 590 n.
  dramaturgy 594 n.
characterize
  represent 551 vb.
  name 561 vb.
  describe 590 vb.
characterless
  insubstantial 4 adj.
  uniform 16 adj.
  empty 190 adj.
  amorphous 244 adj.
  disreputable 867 adj.
  vicious 934 adj.
character-sketch
  description 590 n.
charade *enigma* 530 n.
  gesture 547 n.
  representation 551 n.
  drama 594 n.
charcoal *ash* 381 n.
  fuel 385 n.
  black thing 428 n.
  art equipment 553 n.
charge *fill* 54 vb.
  energy 160 n.
  empower 160 vb.
  load 193 vb.
  move fast 277 vb.
  collide 279 vb.
  make heavy 322 vb.
  heraldry 547 n.
  call 547 n.
  mark 547 vb.
  ornament 574 vb.
  pursue 619 vb.
  job 622 n.
  requirement 627 n.
  protection 660 n.
  management 689 n.
  advise 691 vb.
  precept 693 n.
  attack 712 n.
  charge 712 vb.
  give battle 718 vb.
  ammunition 723 n.

explosive 723 n.
demand 737 vb.
command 737 n., vb.
dependant 742 n.
detention 747 n.
prisoner 750 n.
mandate 751 n.
commission 751 vb.
debt 803 n.
account 808 vb.
price 809 n., vb.
duty 917 n.
blame 924 vb.
accusation 928 n.
guilt 936 n.
chargeable *owed* 803 adj.
priced 809 adj.
dutied 917 adj.
accusable 928 adj.
guilty 936 adj.
charge at *be rash* 857 vb.
chargé d'affaires
envoy 754 n.
charge of, take
safeguard 660 vb.
undertake 672 vb.
charge on,— to,— with
attribute 158 vb.
accuse 928 vb.
charger *plate* 194 n.
war-horse 273 n.
cavalry 722 n.
chariot *carriage* 274 n.
charioteer *driver* 268 n.
charitable *liberal* 813 adj.
(*see* charity)
charity *aid* 703 n.
giving, gift 781 n.
liberality 813 n.
courteous act 884 n.
love 887 n.
kind act 897 n.
benevolence 897 n.
disinterestedness 931 n.
piety 979 n.
charivari *discord* 411 n.
charlady *worker* 686 n.
charlatan *sciolist* 493 n.
affector 850 n.
boaster 877 n.
charlatanism *sciolism* 491 n.
duplicity 541 n.
unskilfulness 695 n.
pretension 850 n.
Charley *ninny* 501 n.
protector 660 n.
charm *attraction* 291 n.
sweetness 392 n.
motivate 612 vb.
preserver 666 n.
pleasurableness 826 n.

delight 826 vb.
please 826 vb.
beauty 841 n.
jewellery 844 n.
lovableness 887 n.
spell 983 n.
talisman 983 n.
bewitch 983 vb.
charmed *willing* 597 adj.
charmed circle *élite* 644 n.
charmed life *safety* 660 n.
charmer *attraction* 291 n.
a beauty 841 n.
sorcerer 983 n.
charms *beauty* 841 n.
lovableness 887 n.
charnel house *death* 361 n.
interment 364 n.
chart *situation* 186 n.
itinerary 267 n.
sailing aid 269 n.
guide-book 524 n.
map 551 n.
represent 551 vb.
charter *give scope* 744 vb.
liberate 746 vb.
commission 751 vb.
permit 756 n., vb.
title-deed 767 n.
hire 785 vb.
chartism *disobedience* 738 n.
sedition 738 n.
charwoman
(*see* char, charlady)
chary *parsimonious* 816 adj.
Charybdis *vortex* 315 n.
eddy 350 n.
nymph 967 n.
chase *pleasance* 192 n.
groove 262 n.
grassland 348 n.
wood 366 n.
objective 617 n.
chase 619 n.
pursue 619 vb.
decorate 844 vb.
desire 859 vb.
be inimical 881 vb.
be in love 887 vb.
court 889 vb.
disapprove 924 vb.
chaser *potion* 301 n.
engraver 556 n.
libertine 952 n.
chasm *gap* 201 n.
depth 211 n.
cavity 255 n.
pitfall 663 n.
chasseur *infantry* 722 n.
chassis *base* 214 n.
supporter 218 n.

frame 218 n.
structure 331 n.
chaste *plain* 573 adj.
elegant 575 adj.
tasteful 846 adj.
modest 874 adj.
virtuous 933 adj.
temperate 942 adj.
pure 950 adj.
chasten *moderate* 177 vb.
educate 534 vb.
deject 834 vb.
humiliate 872 vb.
punish 963 vb.
chastened *repentant* 939 adj.
chastise *reprove* 924 vb.
punish 963 vb.
chastity (*see* chaste)
chasuble *vestments* 989 n.
chat *empty talk* 515 n.
rumour 529 n.
converse 584 vb.
chateau *house* 192 n.
chatelaine *resident* 191 n.
retainer 742 n.
keeper 749 n.
jewellery 844 n.
chatoyant *iridescent* 437 adj.
chattel *equipment* 630 n.
slave 742 n.
property 777 n.
chatter *roll* 403 vb.
ululate 409 vb.
empty talk 515 n.
speak 579 vb.
chatter 581 n.
be loquacious 581 vb.
chatterbox *chatterer* 581 n.
chatterer
newsmonger 529 n.
speaker 579 n.
chatterer 581 n.
chattering *spasm* 318 n.
a-cold 380 adj.
chatty *informative* 524 adj.
loquacious 581 adj.
conversing 584 adj.
sociable 882 adj.
chauffeur *driver* 268 n.
domestic 742 n.
chaukidar *protector* 660 n.
chauvinism *nation* 371 n.
prejudice 481 n.
exaggeration 546 n.
bellicosity 718 n.
boasting 877 n.
patriotism 901 n.
chauvinist *militarist* 722 n.
(*see* chauvinism)
cheap *inferior* 35 adj.
spurious 542 adj.

trivial 639 adj.
bargain 791 vb.
cheap 812 adj.
vulgar 847 adj.
disreputable 867 adj.
cheapen
  make useless 641 vb.
  impair 655 vb.
  bargain 791 vb.
  discount 812 vb.
  vulgarize 847 vb.
  not respect 921 vb.
cheapen oneself
  demean oneself 867 vb.
cheapjack *pedlar* 794 n.
cheapness *cheapness* 812 n.
  (*see* cheap)
cheat *duplicity* 541 n.
  trickery 542 n.
  deceive 542 vb.
  stratagem 698 n.
  defrauder 789 n.
  defraud 788 vb.
  be dishonest 930 vb.
  knave 938 n.
check *delay* 136 n.
  stop 145 n.
  halt 145 vb.
  moderate 177 vb.
  counteraction 182 n.
  retard 278 vb.
  chequer 437 n.
  variegate 437 vb.
  be careful 457 vb.
  enquiry 459 n.
  experiment 461 n., vb.
  comparison 462 n.
  measurement 465 n.
  make certain 473 vb.
  obstacle 702 n.
  hinder 702 vb.
  defeat 728 n.
  adversity 731 n.
  restraint 747 n.
  paper money 797 n.
  pattern 844 n.
checkerboard
  chequer 437 n.
  arena 724 n.
checkered
  changeable 143 adj.
checkers *board game* 837 n.
checkmate *stop* 145 n.
  halt 145 vb.
  be obstructive 702 vb.
  victory 727 n.
  overmaster 727 vb.
  defeat 728 n.
check-up *attention* 455 n.
cheek *buttocks* 238 n.
  laterality 239 n.

sauciness 878 n.
be insolent 878 vb.
rudeness 885 n.
scurrility 899 n.
cheek by jowl
  contiguously 202 adv.
  sideways 239 adv.
cheek-piece *armour* 713 n.
cheeky *impertinent* 878 adj.
  disrespectful 921 adj.
cheep *ululate* 409 vb.
  deprecation 762 n.
  discontent 829 n.
cheer *invigorate* 174 vb.
  food 301 n.
  vociferate 408 vb.
  assent 488 vb.
  refresh 685 vb.
  please 826 vb.
  content 828 vb.
  relieve 831 vb.
  merriment 833 n.
  cheer 833 vb.
  rejoice 835 vb.
  amuse 837 vb.
  give hope 852 vb.
  give courage 855 vb.
  celebrate 876 vb.
  show respect 920 vb.
  applaud 923 vb.
cheerful *cheerful* 833 adj.
cheerfulness *vitality* 162 n.
  willingness 597 n.
  cheerfulness 833 n.
  hope 852 n.
cheerless *unhappy* 825 adj.
  cheerless 834 adj.
  dejected 834 adj.
cheers *rejoicing* 835 n.
cheer up *relieve* 831 vb.
  be cheerful 833 vb.
cheery *cheerful* 833 adj.
cheese *milk product* 301 n.
cheesed off
  discontented 829 adj.
cheese-paring
  economy 814 n.
  parsimony 816 n.
cheetah *cat* 365 n.
chef *cookery* 301 n.
  caterer 633 n.
chef d'œuvre *product* 164 n.
  exceller 644 n.
  deed 676 n.
  masterpiece 694 n.
cheiromancy
  divination 511 n.
Cheka *police enquiry* 459 n.
chela *learner* 538 n.
chelonian *reptile* 365 n.
chemise *bodywear* 228 n.

chemist *experimenter* 461 n.
  druggist 658 n.
chemistry *conversion* 147 n.
chenille *textile* 222 n.
cheque *paper money* 797 n.
cheque-book *record* 548 n.
chequer *blackness* 428 n.
  chequer 437 n.
  variegate 437 vb.
cherish *look after* 457 vb.
  safeguard 660 vb.
  preserve 666 vb.
  patronize 703 vb.
  animate 821 vb.
  love 887 vb.
  pet 889 vb.
  approve 923 vb.
cheroot *tobacco* 388 n.
cherry *fruit* 301 n.
  redness 431 n.
chersonese *projection* 254 n.
cherub *child* 132 n.
  darling 890 n.
  angel 968 n.
cherubim *angel* 968 n.
Cheshire cat *laughter* 835 n.
chess *board game* 837 n.
chess-board *chequer* 437 n.
  arena 724 n.
chessman *chessman* 837 n.
chest *box* 194 n.
  insides 224 n.
  bosom 253 n.
  store 632 n.
  treasury 799 n.
  pride 871 n.
  vanity 873 n.
  ostentation 875 n.
Chesterfield *seat* 218 n.
chestnut *repetition* 106 n.
  horse 273 n.
  fruit 301 n.
  tree 366 n.
  brown 430 adj.
  witticism 839 n.
chest of drawers
  cabinet 194 n.
chesty
  puffing 352 adj.
cheval-glass *mirror* 442 n.
chevaux-de-frise
  sharp point 256 n.
  defences 713 n.
chevron *obliquity* 220 n.
  livery 547 n.
  heraldry 547 n.
  badge of rank 743 n.
chew *rend* 46 vb.
  chew 301 vb.
  pulverize 332 vb.
  smoke 388 vb.

chew over *meditate* 449 vb.
chew the cud *graze* 301 vb.
  meditate 449 vb.
chiaroscuro *blackness* 428 n.
  grey 429 n.
  light contrast 417 n.
  obscuration 418 n.
  painting 553 n.
chiasma, chiasmus
  reversion 148 n.
  inversion 221 n.
  crossing 222 n.
  ornament 574 n.
chiastic *reverted* 148 adj.
  inverted 221 adj.
  crossed 222 adj.
chic *elegant* 575 adj.
  beauty 841 n.
  fashionable 848 adj.
chicanery, chicane
  sophistry 477 n.
  trickery 542 n.
  cunning 698 n.
  foul play 930 n.
chi-chi *dialect* 560 n.
  fashionable 848 adj.
  affected 850 adj.
chick *youngling* 132 n.
  youngster 132 n.
  curtain 421 n.
  darling 890 n.
chicken *youngling* 132 n.
  table bird 365 n.
  poultry 365 n.
  coward 856 n.
  darling 890 n.
chicken-feed
  small quantity 33 n.
  provender 301 n.
  trifle 639 n.
chicken-hearted
  cowardly 856 adj.
chicken liver
  cowardice 856 n.
chickenpox *infection* 651 n.
  skin disease 651 n.
chicken run
  stock farm 369 n.
chicory *potherb* 301 n.
chidden *disapproved* 924 adj.
chide *curse* 899 vb.
  reprove 924 vb.
chief *superior* 34 n.
  supreme 34 adj.
  first 68 adj.
  central 225 adj.
  heraldry 547 n.
  bigwig 638 n.
  important 638 adj.
  director 690 n.
  potentate 741 n.

chieftain *potentate* 741 n.
chieftainship
  magistrature 733 n.
chiffon *textile* 222 n.
  finery 844 n.
chiffonier *cabinet* 194 n.
chignon *hair* 259 n.
  hair-dressing 843 n.
chilblain *hardness* 326 n.
  ulcer 651 n.
child *child* 132 n.
  descendant 170 n.
  posterity 170 n.
  ninny 501 n.
  innocent 935 n.
childbed, childbirth
  obstetrics 164 n.
childhood *youth* 130 n.
childish *young* 130 adj.
  infantine 132 adj.
  credulous 487 adj.
  foolish 499 adj.
  feeble 572 adj.
  trivial 639 adj.
childless
  unproductive 172 adj.
childlike *infantine* 132 adj.
  artless 699 adj.
child of fortune
  made man 730 n.
child of nature
  ingenue 699 n.
chiliad *over one hundred* 99 n.
chill *moderate* 177 vb.
  coldness 380 n.
  refrigerate 382 vb.
  dissuade 613 vb.
  make inactive 679 vb.
  adversity 731 n.
  frighten 854 vb.
chilli *vegetable* 301 n.
  pungency 388 n.
  condiment 389 n.
chilly *cold* 380 adj.
  a-cold 380 adj.
  inimical 881 adj.
chime *repetition* 106 n.
  sound faint 401 vb.
  roll 403 vb.
  resonance 404 n.
  melody 410 n.
  harmonize 410 vb.
  tune 412 n.
  campanology 412 n.
chime in (with)
  accord 24 vb.
  conform 83 vb.
  assent 488 vb.
chimer *canonicals* 989 n.
chimera
  insubstantial thing 4 n.

  rara avis 84 n.
  fantasy 513 n.
  hopelessness 853 n.
chimerical (*see* chimera)
chimes *gong* 414 n.
chiming
  campanology 412 n.
chimney *chimney* 263 n.
  air-pipe 353 n.
  furnace 383 n.
chimney corner *home* 192 n.
chimney-stack
  air-pipe 353 n.
chimney-sweep
  cleaner 648 n.
  dirty person 649 n.
chimpanzee *monkey* 365 n.
chin *face* 237 n.
  projection 254 n.
china *brittleness* 330 n.
  pottery 381 n.
  ornamentation 844 n.
China, great wall of
  exclusion 57 n.
chinaware *receptacle* 194 n.
  pottery 381 n.
chinchilla *skin* 226 n.
chine *high land* 209 n.
  centrality 225 n.
  rear 238 n.
Chinese boxes
  small box 194 n.
  stratification 207 n.
chink *gap* 201 n.
  furrow 262 n.
  sound faint 401 vb.
  defect 647 n.
  vulnerability 661 n.
chinook *wind* 352 n.
  dialect 560 n.
chintz *textile* 222 n.
chinwag *speech* 579 n.
  chatterer 581 n.
chip *small thing* 33 n.
  cut 46 vb.
  piece 53 n.
  make smaller 198 vb.
  pulverize 332 vb.
  label 547 n.
  sculpt 554 vb.
  coinage 797 n.
  plaything 837 n.
chipmunk *rodent* 365 n.
chip off the old block
  analogue 18 n.
  descendant 170 n.
chip on one's shoulder,
  have a
  be discontented 829 vb.
Chippendale
  ornamental 844 adj.

chippy *prostitute* 952n.
chirk *ululate* 409vb.
chirography *writing* 586n.
chiromancy
  occultism 984n.
chiropodist *doctor* 658n.
  beautician 843n.
chiropody *therapy* 658n.
  surgery 658n.
  beautification 843n.
chiropractice *surgery* 658n.
chiropractor *doctor* 658n.
chiropraxis *surgery* 658n.
chirp *ululate* 409vb.
  sing 413vb.
  be cheerful 833vb.
  rejoice 835vb.
chirpy *cheerful* 833adj.
chirrup (*see* chirp)
chisel *produce* 164vb.
  efform 243vb.
  sharp edge 256n.
  sculpt 554vb.
  engraving 555n.
  tool 630n.
  defraud 788vb.
  be dishonest 930vb.
chiseller *trickster* 545n.
  knave 938n.
chit *youngster* 132n.
  dwarf 196n.
  credential 466n.
  correspondence 588n.
chit-chat *chat* 584n.
chiton *tunic* 228n.
chitterlings *insides* 224n.
  meat 301n.
chivalrous *warlike* 718adj.
  courageous 855adj.
  noble 868adj.
  courteous 884adj.
  benevolent 897adj.
  honourable 929adj.
  disinterested 931adj.
chivalry *rider* 268n.
  war 718n.
  cavalry 722n.
  courage 855n.
  aristocracy 868n.
  courtesy 884n.
  disinterestedness 931n.
chive *vegetable* 301n.
chivvy *torment* 827vb.
chlamys *cloak* 228n.
chloral *anæsthetic* 375n.
chlorinate *purify* 648vb.
  sanitate 652vb.
  safeguard 660vb.
chlorine *green* 432adj.
chloroform
  anæsthetic 375n.

render insensible 375vb.
chlorophyl
  green pigment 432n.
chock *supporter* 218n.
chock-a-block *full* 54adj.
chocolate *sweetmeat* 301n.
  soft drink 301n.
  sweet 392n.
  brownness 430n.
choice *precedence* 64n.
  unusual 84adj.
  discrimination 463n.
  choice 605n.
  chosen 605adj.
  excellent 644adj.
  independence 744n.
  pleasurable 826adj.
  beautiful 841adj.
  tasteful 846adj.
  liking 859n.
choiceless
  choiceless 606adj.
choicelessness
  no choice 606n.
choiceness *good taste* 846n.
choice spirit
  person of repute 866n.
choir *accord* 24vb.
  choir 413n.
  church officer 986n.
  church interior 990n.
choke *close* 264vb.
  stopper 264n.
  kill 362vb.
  extinguish 382vb.
  rasp 407vb.
  superabound 637vb.
  hinder 702vb.
choke-damp *gas* 336n.
  poison 659n.
choke off *dissuade* 613vb.
choker *shawl* 228n.
  neckwear 228n.
choky *lock-up* 748n.
cholecystitis
  indigestion 651n.
cholelithiasis
  indigestion 651n.
choler *anger* 891n.
cholera *disease* 651n.
choleric *irascible* 892adj.
choli *bodywear* 228n.
chondrite *meteor* 321n.
choose *will* 595vb.
  be willing 597vb.
  choose 605vb.
  desire 859vb.
choosy *tasteful* 846adj.
  fastidious 862adj.
chop *cut* 46vb.
  piece 53n.

interchange 151vb.
  shorten 204vb.
  meat 301n.
  trade 791vb.
chop and change
  change 143vb.
  vary 152vb.
chop-fallen *dejected* 834adj.
chop-house *café* 192n.
chop logic
  discriminate 463vb.
  reason 475vb.
chopper *sharp edge* 256n.
  pulverizer 332n.
  axe 723n.
choppiness
  roughness 259n.
  agitation 318n.
  wave 350n.
chopping-block
  substitute 150n.
  unlucky person 731n.
  propitiation 941n.
choppy *non-uniform* 17adj.
  rough 259adj.
chops *laterality* 239n.
chop-sticks *shovel* 274n.
choragus *leader* 690n.
choral *musical* 412adj.
  musicianly 413adj.
chorale *vocal music* 412n.
chord *bond* 47n.
  straightness 249n.
  musical note 410n.
  musical piece 412n.
chords, vocal *voice* 577n.
chore *job* 622n.
  labour 682n.
  serve 742vb.
chorea *spasm* 318n.
chore boy *servant* 742n.
choregus
  stage-manager 594n.
  leader 690n.
choregy *dramaturgy* 594n.
choreography
  composition 56n.
  arrangement 62n.
  dancing 837n.
choreus *prosody* 593n.
chorine *actor* 594n.
chorister *choir* 413n.
  church officer 986n.
chorography *situation* 186n.
chortle *laugh* 835vb.
chorus *do likewise* 20vb.
  copy 20vb.
  agreement 24n.
  accord 24vb.
  combination 50n.
  repeat oneself 106vb.

periodicity 141 n.
cry 408 n.
vociferate 402 vb.
melody 410 n.
harmonize 410 vb.
vocal music 412 n.
choir 413 n.
sing 413 vb.
consensus 488 n.
speaker 579 n.
dramaturgy 594 n.
actor 594 n.
chorus girl actor 594 n.
chosen voluntary 597 adj.
approved 923 adj.
chosen few élite 644 n.
chosen people pietist 979 n.
chosen race
particularism 80 n.
chouse deceive 542 vb.
chow mouthful 301 n.
dog 365 n.
chowchow a mixture 43 n.
sweetmeat 301 n.
chowder dish 301 n.
chowrie ventilation 352 n.
chrestomathy
literature 557 n.
textbook 589 n.
anthology 592 n.
chrism
Christian rite 988 n.
chrismal ritual 988 adj.
chrismation
Christian rite 988 n.
chrisom
ritual object 988 n.
Christ God the Son 965 n.
religious teacher 973 n.
christen auspicate 68 vb.
name 561 vb.
perform ritual 988 vb.
Christendom
the Church 976 n.
churchdom 985 n.
christening
nomenclature 561 n.
Christian rite 988 n.
Christian
kind person 897 n.
religious 973 adj.
church member 976 n.
pious 979 adj.
Christianity
religious faith 973 n.
christianize
make pious 979 vb.
Christian Science
medical art 658 n.
asceticism 945 n.
Christian Scientist

doctor 658 n.
Christmas anniversary 141 n.
holy-day 988 n.
Christmas box gift 781 n.
Christmassy
sociable 882 adj.
Christological
theological 973 adj.
chromascope
chromatics 425 n.
chromatic harmonic 410 adj.
coloured 425 adj.
chromatics
chromatics 425 n.
chromatic scale
musical note 410 n.
colour 425 n.
chromatin organism 358 n.
chromatism hue 425 n.
chromatodysopia
dim sight 440 n.
chromatology
chromatics 425 n.
chromolithography
printing 555 n.
chromosome
organism 358 n.
chromosphere sun 321 n.
chronic lasting 113 adj.
obstinate 602 adj.
sick person 651 n.
sick 651 adj.
sufferer 825 n.
tedious 838 adj.
chronicle record 548 n., vb.
narrative 590 n.
chronicler
chronologist 117 n.
chronicler 549 n.
narrator 590 n.
chronique scandaleuse
detraction 926 n.
chronogram
chronology 117 n.
chronograph
timekeeper 117 n.
chronological
chronological 117 adj.
chronological error
anachronism 118 n.
chronologist
chronologist 117 n.
chronology date 108 n.
chronology 117 n.
chronometer
timekeeper 117 n.
sailing aid 269 n.
chronometry
chronometry 117 n.
chrysalis youngling 132 n.
source 156 n.

nest 192 n.
receptacle 194 n.
wrapping 226 n.
vermin 365 n.
chryselephantine
mixed 43 adj.
chrysolite gem 844 n.
chrysoprase greenness 432 n.
gem 844 n.
chthonian infernal 972 adj.
chubby fleshy 195 adj.
chuck propel 287 vb.
meat 301 n.
darling 890 n.
chucker-out athlete 162 n.
ejector 300 n.
chuck it resign 753 vb.
chuckle ululate 409 vb.
laughter 835 n.
chuck out eject 300 vb.
chuck under the chin
caress 889 vb.
chudder wrapping 226 n.
shawl 228 n.
chug be in motion 265 vb.
move slowly 278 vb.
chug on travel 267 vb.
chukker period 110 n.
periodicity 141 n.
chum colleague 707 n.
chum 880 n.
chummery quarters 192 n.
chummy friendly 880 adj.
chump dunce 501 n.
chum up with
befriend 880 vb.
chum with dwell 192 vb.
chunk sunder 46 vb.
piece 53 n.
chunkiness bulk 195 n.
chunky fleshy 195 adj.
rough 259 adj.
church the Church 976 n.
churchdom 985 n.
church 990 n.
church bell(s) signal 547 n.
call 547 n.
church utensil 990 n.
churchdom
orthodoxism 976 n.
churchdom 985 n.
church-goer
worshipper 981 n.
church government
churchdom 985 n.
churchianity
orthodoxism 976 n.
pietism 979 n.
churchiness pietism 979 n.
churching of women
Christian rite 988 n.

churchlike
  churchlike 990 adj.
churchly
  ecclesiastical 985 adj.
churchman *cleric* 986 n.
churchmanship *piety* 979 n.
church service
  church service 988 n.
churchwarden
  tobacco 388 n.
  church officer 986 n.
churchy *pietistic* 979 adj.
churchyard *cemetery* 364 n.
  church exterior 990 n.
churl *niggard* 816 n.
  countryman 869 n.
churlish
  parsimonious 816 adj.
  plebeian 869 adj.
  ungracious 885 adj.
churlishness
  sullenness 893 n.
churn *rotator* 315 n.
  rotate 315 vb.
  agitate 318 vb.
  thicken 354 vb.
churn out
  produce 164 vb.
churr *ululate* 409 vb.
chute *obliquity* 220 n.
  outlet 298 n.
  waterfall 350 n.
  pleasure-ground 837 n.
chutney *sauce* 389 n.
chyle *fluid* 335 n.
chypre *scent* 396 n.
cibarious *edible* 301 adj.
  nourishing 301 adj.
ciborium *canopy* 226 n.
  ritual object 988 n.
cicada, cicala *jumper* 312 n.
  vermin 365 n.
cicatrice *wound* 655 n.
  blemish 845 n.
cicatrize *cure* 656 vb.
Cicero *speaker* 579 n.
cicerone *guide* 520 n.
cicuration
  animal husbandry 369 n.
cider *liquor* 301 n.
ci-devant *prior* 119 adj.
  former 125 adj.
  resigning 753 adj.
cigar, cigarette
  tobacco 388 n.
cilia *hair* 259 n.
cilice *asceticism* 945 n.
cilium *filament* 208 n.
Cimmerian *dark* 418 adj.
cinch *tie* 45 vb.
  girdle 47 n.

certainty 473 n.
  easy thing 701 n.
Cincinnatus
  resignation 753 n.
cincture *belt* 228 n.
  loop 250 n.
cinder(s) *ash* 381 n.
  coal 385 n.
  dirt 649 n.
Cinderella *nonentity* 639 n.
  poor man 801 n.
  object of scorn 867 n.
ciné-camera *cinema* 445 n.
cinema *cinema* 445 n.
  photography 551 n.
  theatre 594 n.
  place of amusement 837 n.
cinema-goer *spectator* 441 n.
cinematograph
  cinema 445 n.
cinematographer
  photography 551 n.
cinematographic
  moving 265 adj.
cinematography
  photography 551 n.
cinerama *cinema* 445 n.
cinerary *funereal* 364 adj.
  grey 429 adj.
cinerary urn
  interment 364 n.
cinereous *grey* 429 adj.
cingle *compressor* 198 n.
cingulum *vestments* 989 n.
cinnabar
  red pigment 431 n.
cinnamon *condiment* 389 n.
  brown 430 adj.
cinques *campanology* 412 n.
cipher *non-existence* 2 n.
  number 85 n.
  do sums 86 vb.
  zero 103 n.
  secrecy 525 n.
  enigma 530 n.
  symbology 547 n.
  indication 547 n.
  label 547 n.
  initials 558 n.
  spell 558 vb.
  writing 586 n.
  nonentity 639 n.
cipherer *interpreter* 520 n.
circa *nearly* 200 adv.
Circe *motivator* 612 n.
  nymph 967 n.
  sorceress 983 n.
Circean *sensual* 944 adj.
  sorcerous 983 adj.
circle *family* 11 n.
  continuity 71 n.

run on 71 vb.
  group 74 n.
  be periodic 141 vb.
  region 184 n.
  surround 230 vb.
  outline 233 n.
  circle 250 n.
  circle 314 vb.
  theatre 594 n.
  circuit 626 n.
  party 708 n.
  restriction 747 n.
  change hands 780 vb.
circlet *outline* 233 n.
circuit *whole* 52 n.
  continuity 71 n.
  periodicity 141 n.
  revolution 149 n.
  electricity 160 n.
  region 184 n.
  circumjacence 230 n.
  outline 233 n.
  orbit 250 n.
  circle 250 n.
  land travel 267 n.
  deviation 282 n.
  circuition 314 n.
  route 624 n.
  circuit 626 n., vb.
circuit court
  law-court 956 n.
circuit house *inn* 192 n.
circuition (*see* circuit)
circuitous *deviating* 282 adj.
  labyrinthine 251 adj.
  circuitous 314 adj.
  roundabout 626 adj.
circular *uniform* 16 adj.
  continuous 71 adj.
  generality 79 n.
  regular 81 adj.
  curved 248 adj.
  round 250 adj.
  publication 528 n.
  correspondence 588 n.
  decree 737 n.
circularity
  continuity 71 n.
  circularity 250 n.
circularize *publish* 528 vb.
  correspond 588 vb.
  command 737 vb.
circular reasoning
  sophism 477 n.
circulate *disperse* 75 vb.
  go round 250 vb.
  pass 350 vb.
  circle 314 vb.
  be published 528 vb.
  change hands 780 vb.
  mint 797 vb.

circulation *blood* 335 n.
(*see* circulate)
circulatory
circuitous 626 adj.
circumambience
circumjacence 230 n.
circumambient
circumjacent 230 adj.
circuitous 314 adj.
roundabout 626 adj.
circumambulate
traverse 267 vb.
circle 314 vb.
perform *ritual* 988 vb.
circumambulation
circuition 314 n.
circuit 626 n.
ritual act 988 n.
circumbendibus
meanderings 251 n.
deviation 282 n.
route 624 n.
circumcellion *monk* 986 n.
circumcise *cut* 46 vb.
circumcision *scission* 46 n.
rite 988 n.
circumduction
obliteration 550 n.
circumference *region* 184 n.
size 195 n.
distance 199 vb.
exteriority 223 n.
circumjacence 230 n.
outline 233 n.
inclosure 235 n.
limit 236 n.
circuit 626 n.
circumflex *curved* 248 adj.
circumflex accent
punctuation 547 n.
circumfluence
rotation 315 n.
circumfluent
circumjacent 230 adj.
circuitous 314 adj.
circumfluous *insular* 349 adj.
circumforaneous
travelling 267 adj.
circuitous 314 adj.
circumfusion
dispersion 75 n.
circumgyration
rotation 315 n.
circumjacence
exteriority 223 n.
circumjacence 230 n.
circumlocution
phrase 563 n.
pleonasm 570 n.
circumlocutory
prolix 570 adj.

roundabout 626 adj.
circumnavigate
navigate 269 vb.
circle 314 vb.
circumrotation
rotation 315 n.
circumscribe
set apart 46 vb.
exclude 57 vb.
make smaller 198 vb.
surround 230 vb.
circumscribe 232 vb.
outline 233 vb.
inclose 235 vb.
limit 236 vb.
hinder, obstruct 702 vb.
restrain 747 vb.
prohibit 757 vb.
circumspection
attention 455 n.
carefulness 457 n.
caution 858 n.
circumstance
circumstance 8 n.
degree 27 n.
concomitant 89 n.
eventuality 154 n.
affairs 154 n.
ostentation 875 n.
circumstances
circumstance 8 n.
particulars 80 n.
estate 777 n.
circumstantial
circumstantial 8 adj.
complete 54 adj.
definite 80 adj.
careful 457 adj.
veracious 540 adj.
diffuse 570 adj.
descriptive 590 adj.
circumstantiate
corroborate 466 vb.
circumvallation
circumscription 232 n.
inclosure 235 n.
fortification 713 n.
defences 713 n.
circumvent *deceive* 542 vb.
be cunning 698 vb.
circumvolution
convolution 251 n.
rotation 315 n.
circus *band* 74 n.
housing 192 n.
zoo 369 n.
theatre 594 n.
arena 724 n.
pleasure-ground 837 n.
cirrhosis *hardening* 326 n.
cirrhosis of the liver

alcoholism 949 n.
cirrus *cloud* 355 n.
cist *box* 194 n.
tomb 364 n.
Cistercian *monk* 986 n.
cistern *vat* 194 n.
moistening 341 n.
storage 632 n.
citadel *refuge* 662 n.
fort 713 n.
citation *referral* 9 n.
repetition 106 n.
evidence 466 n.
decoration 729 n.
warrant 737 n.
praise 923 n.
cite *copy* 20 vb.
exemplify 83 vb.
repeat 106 vb.
manifest 522 vb.
command 737 vb.
indict 928 vb.
litigate 959 vb.
cithara, cithern *harp* 414 n.
citified *urban* 192 adj.
well-bred 848 adj.
citizen *native* 191 n.
subject 742 n
free man 744 n.
citizen of the world
philanthropist 901 n.
citizenry *habitancy* 191 n.
social group 371 n.
subject 742 n.
commonalty 869 n.
citizenship
subjection 745 n.
citriculture
agriculture 370 n.
citrine *yellow* 433 adj.
citronella oil *scent* 396 n.
city *district* 184 n.
abode 192 n.
housing 192 n.
business 622 n.
polity 733 n.
city father *officer* 741 n.
city state *nation* 371 n.
polity 733 n.
civet *scent* 396 n.
civic *national* 371 adj.
civic centre *focus* 76 n.
civic crown
decoration 729 n.
civil *national* 371 adj.
well-bred 848 adj.
courteous 884 adj.
civil code *law* 953 n.
civilian *pacifist* 717 n.
peaceful 717 adj.
jurist 958 n.

layman 987n.
laical 987adj.
civility *civilization* 654n.
  good taste 846n.
  courtesy 884n.
  courteous act 884n.
civilization *culture* 490n.
  civilization 654n.
  beau monde 848n.
civilize *make better* 654vb.
civilized *well-bred* 848adj.
civil law *law* 953n.
civil lines *station* 187n.
civil war *war* 718n.
  revolt 738n.
civism *patriotism* 901n.
civvies *dress* 228n.
clack *roll* 403vb.
  ululate 409vb.
  mean nothing 515vb.
  chatter 581n.
  be loquacious 581vb.
clad *dressed* 228adj.
claim *territory* 184n.
  inclosure 235n.
  affirm 532vb.
  plead 614vb.
  requirement 627n.
  require 627vb.
  demand 737n.,vb.
  request 761n.,vb.
  possess 773vb.
  estate 777n.
  appropriate 786vb.
  desire 859n.,vb.
  right 913n.
  have a right 915vb.
  claim 915vb.
  litigation 959n.
claimable *just* 913adj.
  due 915adj.
claimant *petitioner* 763n.
  desirer 859n.
  dueness 915n.
  litigant 959n.
claim relationship
  be akin 11vb.
clairaudience *psychics* 984n.
clair-obscur
  light contrast 417n.
clairschach *harp* 414n.
clairvoyance *intuition* 476n.
  foresight 510n.
  divination 511n.
  psychics 984n.
clairvoyant *oracle* 511n.
  (*see* clairvoyance)
clam *table fish* 365n.
  taciturnity 582n.
clamant *loud* 400adj.
  crying 408adj.

commanding 737adj.
deprecatory 762adj.
desiring 859adj.
clambake *feasting* 301n.
  meal 301n.
  festivity 837n.
clamber *climb* 308vb.
clamjamphrie *rabble* 869n.
clam-like *reticent* 525adj.
clammy *viscid* 354adj.
clamorous (*see* clamour)
clamour *loudness* 400n.
  cry 408n.
  vociferate 408vb.
  request 761n.
  weep 836vb.
  disapprobation 924n.
clamp *affix* 45vb.
  fastening 47n.
  nippers 778n.
clamp down *close* 264vb.
  restrain 747vb.
clan *group* 74n.
  breed 77n.
  genealogy 169n.
  community 708n.
clandestine *occult* 523adj.
  stealthy 525adj.
  concealed 525adj.
clang *loudness* 400n.
  be loud 400vb.
  roll 403n.,vb.
  resonance 404n.
clanger *mistake* 495n.
clangour *loudness* 400n.
  resonance 404n.
clank *resound* 404vb.
  rasp 407vb.
clannish *ethnic* 11adj.
  biased 481adj.
  sectional 708adj.
  sectarian 978adj.
clannishness
  co-operation 706n.
  (*see* clannish)
clanship *co-operation* 706n.
clansman *kinsman* 11n.
  friend 880n.
clap *orifice* 263n.
  strike 279vb.
  loudness 400n.
  bang 402n.
  crackle 402vb.
  gesticulate 547vb.
  venereal disease 651n.
  rejoice 835vb.
  gratulate 886vb.
  applause 923n.
clap on *add* 38vb.
clapper *commender* 923n.
clappers *gong* 414n.

chatter 581n.
clap together *join* 45vb.
claptrap *sophistry* 477n.
  empty talk 515n.
  fable 543n.
claque *playgoer* 594n.
  applause 923n.
  commender 923n.
  flattery 925n.
claqueur *playgoer* 594n.
  commender 923n.
  flatterer 925n.
claret *blood* 335n.
  wine 361n.
  redness 431n.
clarification
  demonstration 478n.
  (*see* clarify)
clarified *unmixed* 44adj.
clarify *eliminate* 44vb.
  liquefy 337vb.
  make flow 350vb.
  be transparent 422vb.
  be intelligible 516vb.
  interpret 520vb.
  purify 648vb.
clarigate *claim* 915vb.
clarinet *flute* 414n.
clarinettist
  instrumentalist 413n.
clarion *horn* 414n.
clarion call *loudness* 400n.
  war measures 718n.
clarity *transparency* 422n.
  visibility 443n.
  intelligibility 516n.
  perspicuity 567n.
  elegance 575n.
clash *contrariety* 14n.
  differ 15vb.
  disagreement 25n.
  violence 176n.
  counteract 182vb.
  collide 279vb.
  bang 402vb.
  rasp 407vb.
  discord 411vb.
  quarrel 709n.,vb.
  strike at 712vb.
  contention 716n.
  battle 718n.
  be inimical 881vb.
clasp *fastening* 47n.
  cohere 48vb.
  circumscribe 232vb.
  loop 250n.
  caress 889vb.
class *degree* 27n.
  graduate 27vb.
  class 62vb.
  group 74n.

classification 77 n.
contemporary 123 n.
study 536 n.
party 708 n.
army 722 n.
class-conscious
sectional 708 adj.
class consciousness
particularism 80 n.
pride 871 n.
classes *curriculum* 536 n.
classes, the
social group 371 n.
upper class 868 n.
classic *prototypal* 23 adj.
olden 127 adj.
symmetrical 245 adj.
stylist 575 n.
elegant 575 adj.
book 589 n.
excellent 644 adj.
perfect 646 adj.
classical *literary* 557 adj.
tasteful 846 adj.
right 913 adj.
classicist *antiquarian* 125 n.
classifiability *relation* 9 n.
classifiable *relative* 9 adj.
classification *relation* 9 n.
degree 27 n.
subdivision 53 n.
arrangement 62 n.
classification 77 n.
identification 547 n.
classificatory
classificatory 77 adj.
classify *class* 62 vb.
make certain 473 vb.
indicate 547 vb.
classify as
number with 78 vb.
classless
governmental 753 adj.
classmate *learner* 538 n.
chum 880 n.
class prejudice
prejudice 481 n.
classroom *classroom* 539 n.
class war *prejudice* 481 n.
dissension 709 n.
class-work *study* 536 n.
classy *fashionable* 848 adj.
genteel 868 adj.
clatter *medley* 43 n.
loudness 400 n.
roll 403 n., vb.
claudicate
move slowly 278 vb.
clause *subdivision* 53 n.
phrase 563 n.
conditions 766 n.

claustral
circumjacent 230 adj.
sealed off 264 adj.
claustrophobia
psychopathy 503 n.
phobia 854 n.
claver *chatter* 581 n.
clavichord *piano* 414 n.
clavicle *supporter* 218 n.
clavier *piano* 414 n.
claw *rend* 46 vb.
coupling 47 n.
foot 214 n.
sharp point 256 n.
wound 655 vb.
nippers 778 n.
clay *adhesive* 47 n.
solid body 324 n.
softness 327 n.
soil 344 n.
corpse 363 n.
sculpture 554 n.
materials 631 n.
dirt 649 n.
claymore *side-arms* 723 n.
clean *unmixed* 44 adj.
completely 54 adv.
empty 190 adj.
make bright 417 vb.
whiten 427 vb.
clean 648 adj., vb.
sanitate 652 adj.
make better 654 vb.
disencumber 701 vb.
pure 950 adj.
clean-cut *definite* 80 adj.
positive 473 adj.
cleaner *cleaner* 648 n.
clean hands *probity* 929 n.
innocence 935 n.
clean-limbed
shapely 841 adj.
cleanliness *cleanness* 648 n.
hygiene 652 n.
clean out *void* 300 vb.
search 459 vb.
clean 648 vb.
steal 788 vb.
cleanse *purify* 648 vb.
sanitate 652 vb.
cleanser *cleanser* 648 n.
clean-shaven
hairless 229 adj.
clean slate
revolution 149 n.
obliteration 550 n.
clean sweep *ejection* 300 n.
clean up *unravel* 62 vb.
purify 648 vb.
clear *unmixed* 44 adj.
eliminate 44 vb.

orderly 60 adj.
displace 188 vb.
space 201 vb.
be high 209 vb.
fly 271 vb.
leap 312 vb.
fluidal 335 adj.
make flow 350 vb.
melodious 410 adj.
undimmed 417 adj.
make bright 417 vb.
transparent 422 adj.
well-seen 443 adj.
certain 473 adj.
semantic 514 adj.
intelligible 516 adj.
manifest 522 adj.
informative 524 adj.
perspicuous 567 adj.
elegant 575 adj.
vocal 577 adj.
clean 648 vb.
safe 660 adj.
disencumber 701 vb.
liberate 746 vb.
permit 756 vb.
pay 804 vb.
justify 927 vb.
acquit 960 vb.
clearance
elimination 44 n.
room 183 n.
interval 201 n.
voidance 300 n.
cacation 302 n.
preparation 669 n.
scope 744 n.
permission 756 n.
sale 793 n.
payment 804 n.
vindication 927 n.
acquittal 960 n.
clear coast *facility* 701 n.
clear conscience
innocence 935 n.
clear-cut *definite* 80 adj.
well-seen 443 adj.
positive 473 adj.
(*see* clear)
clear field *opportunity* 137 n.
clear-headed
intelligent 498 adj.
sane 502 adj.
sober 948 adj.
clearing *open space* 263 n.
wood 366 n.
clearness
transparency 422 n.
(*see* clear)
clear of *beyond* 199 adv.
clear off *decamp* 296 vb.

void 300vb.
clear out *emerge* 298vb.
  decamp 296vb.
  void 300vb.
  clean 648vb.
clear-sighted *seeing* 438adj.
  intelligent 498adj.
clear the air *unravel* 62vb.
clear the decks
  make ready 669vb.
clear the ground *pass* 305vb.
  disencumber 701vb.
clear the path
  make possible 469vb.
clear the throat *eruct* 300vb.
  rasp 407vb.
clear the way
  come before 64vb.
clear up *cease* 145vb.
  make bright 417vb.
  be intelligible 516vb.
  carry through 725vb.
clearway
  traffic control 305n.
  road 624n.
cleat *fastening* 47n.
cleavage *disjunction* 46n.
  scission 46n.
  structure 331n.
  dissension 709n.
cleave *cut, sunder* 46vb.
  bisect 92vb.
cleaver *sharp edge* 256n.
cleave to *cohere* 48vb.
cledge *soil* 344n.
clef *key* 410n.
  notation 410n.
cleft *disjunction* 46n.
  disjunct 46adj.
  bisected 92adj.
  gap 201n.
  spaced 201adj.
cleft stick *dubiety* 474n.
clemency *lenity* 736n.
  mercy 905n.
clench *retain* 778vb.
clench one's fist *defy* 711vb.
  threaten 900vb.
clepsydra *timekeeper* 117n.
clerestory
  church interior 990n.
clergiability
  non-liability 919n.
  ecclesiasticism 985n.
clergy *clergy* 986n.
clergyman *cleric* 986n.
clergywoman *nun* 986n.
cleric *holy orders* 985n.
  cleric 986n.
clerical
  ecclesiastical 985adj.

cleric 986n.
clerical 986adj.
  vestured 989adj.
clericalism
  government 733n.
  ecclesiasticism 985n.
clerisy scholar 492n.
clerk scholar 492n.
  intellectual 492n.
  recorder 549n.
  penman 586n.
  official 690n.
  auxiliary 707n.
  cleric 986n.
clerkly instructed 490adj.
  written 586adj.
clever intelligent 498adj.
  skilful 694adj.
  witty 839adj.
cleverstick
  vain person 873n.
clew sphere 252n.
  round 252vb.
clew line tackling 47n.
cliché uniformity 16n.
  repetition 106n.
  maxim 496n.
  empty talk 515n.
  word 559n.
  neology 560n.
  phrase 563n.
cliché-ridden
  repeated 106adj.
  feeble 572adj.
click fastening 47n.
  speech sound 398n.
  sound faint 401vb.
  crackle 402vb.
  sound dead 405vb.
  know 490vb.
  understand 516vb.
  succeed 727vb.
client concomitant 89n.
  follower 284n.
  habitué 610n.
  patron 707n.
  dependant 742n.
  purchaser 792n.
clientèle dependant 742n.
  purchaser 792n.
clientship subjection 745n.
cliff high land 209n.
  acclivity 220n.
  verticality 215n.
  rock 344n.
climacteric serial place 73n.
  age 131n.
climactic crowning 34adj.
climate influence 178n.
  region 184n.
  weather 340n.

climatology *weather* 340n.
climax *degree* 27n.
  superiority 34n.
  augment 36vb.
  serial place 73n.
  summit 213n.
  crown 213vb.
  mature 669vb.
  completion 725n.
  climax 725vb.
  excitation 821n.
climb *grow* 36vb.
  be oblique 220vb.
  high land 209n.
  fly 271vb.
  ascent 308n.
  climb 308vb.
  be dear 811vb.
climb-down
  humiliation 872n.
climber *traveller* 268n.
  climber 308n.
climbing *great* 32adj.
  sport 837n.
clime *region* 184n.
  land 344n.
clinal *oblique* 220adj.
clinch *tie* 45vb.
  unite with 45vb.
  ligature 47n.
  cohere 48vb.
  close 264vb.
  make certain 473vb.
  pugilism 716n.
  carry through 725vb.
  retention 778n.
clinch an argument
  demonstrate 478vb.
clincher *reasons* 475n.
  confutation 479n.
  masterpiece 694n.
cling *cohere* 48vb.
  persevere 600vb.
  be wont 610vb.
  take 786vb.
  caress 889vb.
clinging *cohesive* 48adj.
  tough 329adj.
  habitual 610adj.
  retentive 778adj.
cling to *be near* 200vb.
  observe 768vb.
  retain 778vb.
clinic *hospital* 658n.
clinician *doctor* 658n.
clink *faintness* 401n.
  resonance 404n.
  rasp 407vb.
  gaol 748n.
clinker *ash* 381n.
  dirt 649n.

clinker-built *layered* 207 adj.
  marine 275 adj.
clinometer
  angular measure 247 n.
clinquant *finery* 844 n.
clip *subtract* 39 vb.
  connect 45 vb.
  cut 46 vb.
  fastening 47 n.
  bunch 74 n.
  make smaller 198 vb.
  shorten 204 vb.
  circumscribe 232 vb.
  touch 378 vb.
  prohibit 757 vb.
  demonetize 797 vb.
  hair-dressing 843 n.
  caress 889 vb.
clip one's words
  be concise 569 vb.
  stammer 580 vb.
clipper *sailing-ship* 275 n.
  aircraft 276 n.
  speeder 277 n.
clippers *sharp edge* 256 n.
  cosmetic 843 n.
clippings *leavings* 41 n.
  piece 53 n.
clip the wings
  disable 161 vb.
  retard 278 vb.
  make useless 641 vb.
  hinder 702 vb.
clique *party* 708 n.
cliquish, cliquey
  biased 481 adj.
  sectional 708 adj.
cliquism *prejudice* 481 n.
cloaca *sink* 649 n.
cloak *wrapping* 226 n.
  cloak 228 n.
  screen 421 n.
  pretext 614 n.
  safeguard 660 vb.
  defend 713 vb.
  canonicals 989 n.
cloak-and-dagger
  stealthy 525 adj.
cloakroom *chamber* 194 n.
  latrine 649 n.
cloche *garden* 370 n.
clock *timekeeper* 117 n.
  time 117 vb.
clock-hand *indicator* 547 n.
clock in *begin* 68 vb.
  arrive 295 vb.
clockmaker
  timekeeper 117 n.
  artisan 686 n.
clock out *end* 69 vb.
  depart 296 vb.

clockwise *towards* 281 adv.
  round and round 315 adv.
clockwork *complexity* 61 n.
  accuracy 494 n.
  machine 630 n.
clod *piece* 53 n.
  bulk 195 n.
  solid body 324 n.
  soil 344 n.
  dunce 501 n.
  bungler 697 n.
  countryman 869 n.
clod-hopping *dull* 840 adj.
  graceless 842 adj.
  ill-bred 847 adj.
clog *footwear* 228 n.
  make unclean 649 vb.
  be difficult 700 vb.
  encumbrance 702 n.
  hinder 702 vb.
  restrain 747 vb.
  fetter 748 n.
cloison *partition* 231 n.
cloister *retreat* 192 n.
  pavilion 192 n.
  surround 230 vb.
  circumscribe 232 vb.
  inclose 235 vb.
  path 624 n.
  refuge 662 n.
  imprison 747 vb.
  seclusion 883 n.
  church exterior 990 n.
cloistered *monastic* 986 adj.
cloistress *nun* 986 n.
close *similar* 18 adj.
  firm-set 45 adj.
  join 45 vb.
  cohesive 48 adj.
  end 69 n., vb.
  cease 145 vb.
  impending 155 adj.
  place 185 n.
  make smaller 198 vb.
  near 200 adj.
  narrow 206 adj.
  close 264 vb.
  approach 289 vb.
  dense 324 adj.
  warm 379 adj.
  attentive 455 adj.
  accurate 494 adj.
  reticent 525 adj.
  concise 569 adj.
  taciturn 582 adj.
  repair 656 vb.
  cure 656 vb.
  restraining 747 adj.
  parsimonious 816 adj.
  parsonage 986 n.
  church exterior 990 n.

closed door *exclusion* 57 n.
closed mind
  narrow mind 481 n.
  predetermination 608 n.
closed shop
  uniformity 16 n.
  exclusion 57 n.
  restriction 747 n.
close finish
  short distance 200 n.
  contest 716 n.
close-fisted
  parsimonious 816 adj.
close fit *adaptation* 24 n.
close grips *duel* 716 n.
close in *circumscribe* 232 vb.
  converge 293 vb.
closeness (*see* close)
close quarters
  short distance 200 n.
close season *interim* 108 n.
  period 110 n.
close-set *conjunct* 45 adj.
close shave *danger* 661 n.
  escape 667 n.
close-stool *latrine* 649 n.
closet *cabinet* 194 n.
  chamber 194 n.
  hiding-place 527 n.
  latrine 649 n.
close the ranks *cohere* 48 vb.
  make ready 669 vb.
  give battle 718 vb.
close to *nigh* 200 adv.
  contiguous 202 adj.
close up
  become small 198 n.
close-up
  short distance 200 n.
  photography 551 n.
close upon *almost* 33 adv.
  subsequently 120 adv.
  prospectively 124 adv.
  nigh 200 adv.
close with *converge* 293 vb.
  assent 488 vb.
  strike at 712 vb.
  fight 716 vb.
  consent 758 vb.
closure *joinder* 45 n.
  end 69 n.
  stop 145 n.
  contraction 198 n.
  closure 264 n.
clot *be dense* 324 vb.
  solid body 324 n.
  blood 335 n.
  semiliquidity 354 n.
  thicken 354 vb.
  dunce 501 n.
  blood pressure 651 n.

bungler 697n.
cloth *textile* 222n.
　bookbinding 589n.
　materials 631n.
　clergy 986n.
　canonicals 989n.
clothe *dress* 228vb.
　provide 633vb.
clothes *clothing* 228n.
clothes-horse *hanger* 217n.
　frame 218n.
　fop 848n.
clothier *clothier* 228n.
　artisan 686n.
clothing *dressing* 228n.
　clothing 228n.
Clotho *fate* 596n.
clotted *dense* 324adj.
　semiliquid 354adj.
　dirty 649adj.
cloud *accumulation* 74n.
　certain quantity 104n.
　gas 336n.
　air 340n.
　moisture 341n.
　cloud 355n.,vb.
　obfuscation 421n.
　screen 421vb.
　opacity 423n.
　variegate 437vb.
　uncertainty 474n.
　disguise 527n.
cloud-burst *storm* 176n.
　rain 350n.
cloud-cuckoo land
　fantasy 513n.
clouded *cheerless* 834adj.
　tipsy 949adj.
　(*see* cloudy)
cloudiness *cloud* 355n.
　dimness 419n.
　imperspicuity 568n.
cloudless *dry* 342adj.
　undimmed 417adj.
　palmy 730adj.
cloud on the horizon
　danger 661n.
　warning 664n.
cloudscape
　art subject 553n.
clouds, in the
　abstracted 456adj.
cloud the issue
　be unrelated 10vb.
cloudy *humid* 341adj.
　cloudy 355adj.
　unlit 418adj.
　dim 419adj.
　opaque 423adj.
　semitransparent 424adj.
　mottled 437adj.

uncertain 474adj.
imaginary 513adj.
imperspicuous 568adj.
sullen 893adj.
clout *strike* 279vb.
　repair 656n.,vb.
　corporal punishment 963n.
　spank 963vb.
clove *potherb* 301n.
　condiment 389n.
　scent 396n.
clove-hitch *ligature* 47n.
cloven (*see* cleft)
cloven hoof
　malevolence 898n.
　wickedness 934n.
　Mephisto 969n.
clover *grass* 366n.
　euphoria 376n.
　palmy days 730n.
clover leaf
　traffic control 305n.
　access 624n.
clown *be absurd* 497vb.
　fool 501n.
　entertainer 594n.
　bungler 697n.
　humorist 839n.
　laughing-stock 851n.
　countryman 869n.
clownish *clumsy* 695adj.
　amusing 837adj.
　ill-bred 847adj.
　ridiculous 849adj.
cloy
　render insensible 375vb.
　superabound 637vb.
　make insensitive 820vb.
　be tedious 838vb.
　sate 863vb.
club *focus* 76n.
　meeting place 192n.
　strike 279vb.
　association 706n.
　party, society 708n.
　club 723n.
　social round 882n.
　scourge 964n.
clubbable *corporate* 708adj.
　sociable 882adj.
clubbism *sociality* 882n.
clubfoot *deformity* 246n.
club-haul *navigate* 269vb.
clubland *district* 184n.
club law *anarchy* 734n.
clubman
　beau monde 848n.
　social person 882n.
club together
　co-operate 706vb.
　join a party 708vb.

be sociable 882vb.
cluck *ululate* 409vb.
clue *bunch* 74n.
　answer 460n.
　evidence 466n.
　knowledge 490n.
　interpretation 520n.
　hint 524n.
　indication 547n.
clueless *doubting* 474adj.
　ignorant 491adj.
　in difficulties 700adj.
clump *bunch* 74n.
　strike 279vb.
　wood 366n.
clumsy *unapt* 25adj.
　unwieldy 195adj.
　slow 278adj.
　inexact 495adj.
　unintelligent 499adj.
　inelegant 576adj.
　inexpedient 643adj.
　bad 645adj.
　clumsy 695adj.
　bungler 697n.
　graceless 842adj.
　ill-bred 847adj.
　ridiculous 849adj.
clunk *resound* 404vb.
cluster *group* 74n.
　congregate 74vb.
clutch *group* 74n.
　certain quantity 104n.
　youngling 132n.
　take 786vb.
clutch at *desire* 859vb.
clutches *governance* 733n.
　retention 778n.
clutches of, in the
　subject 745adj.
clutter *multitude* 104n.
clyster *insertion* 303n.
　drain 351n.
　therapy 658n.
coach *train, carriage* 274n.
　train, educate 534vb.
　trainer, teacher 537n.
　make ready 669vb.
coach-house *stable* 192n.
　chamber 194n.
coachman *driver* 268n.
　domestic 742n.
coadjutant
　co-operative 706adj.
coadjutor *aider* 703n.
　auxiliary 707n.
co-agency
　accompaniment 89n.
　agency 173n.
　concurrence 181n.
　co-operation 706n.

coagulate *cohere* 48 vb.
  be dense 324 vb.
  thicken 354 vb.
coagulum *solid body* 324 n.
coal *propellant* 287 n.
  burn 381 vb.
  heater 383 n.
  coal, lighter 385 n.
  fire 385 vb.
  glimmer 419 n.
  torch 420 n.
  black thing 428 n.
coalesce *be identical* 13 vb.
  combine 50 vb.
coalescence *junction* 45 n.
coal-face *workshop* 687 n.
coal-field *coal* 385 n.
coal-heaver *bearer* 273 n.
  worker 686 n.
coal-hole *cellar* 194 n.
coalition *junction* 45 n.
  political party 708 n.
  society 708 n.
coal measure(s)
  mineral 359 n.
  coal 385 n.
coal-mine, coal-pit
  excavation 255 n.
  workshop 687 n.
coal-scuttle *vessel* 194 n.
coaly *combustible* 385 adj.
coaming *edge* 234 n.
coaptation
  adaptation 24 n.
coarctation
  compression 198 n.
  narrowing 206 n.
  hindrance 702 n.
  restriction 747 n.
coarse *rough* 259 adj.
  textural 331 adj.
  unsavoury 391 adj.
  indiscriminating 464 adj.
  inelegant 576 adj.
  unclean 649 adj.
  immature 670 adj.
  graceless 842 adj.
  vulgar 847 adj.
  plebeian 869 adj.
  impure 951 adj.
coarsen *impair* 655 vb.
  make insensitive 820 vb.
  vulgarize 847 vb.
coarseness
  moral insensibility 820 n.
  plainness 573 n.
coast *edge* 234 n.
  laterality 239 n.
  flank 239 vb.
  go smoothly 258 vb.
  travel 267 vb.

  voyage 269 vb.
  approach 289 vb.
  pass 305 vb.
  shore 344 n.
  not act 677 vb.
coastal *marginal* 234 adj.
  coastal 344 adj.
coaster *stand* 218 n.
  sled 274 n.
  merchant ship 275 n.
coastguard
  naval man 270 n.
  keeper 749 n.
coast-line *outline* 233 n.
  shore 344 n.
coat *add* 38 vb.
  layer 207 n.
  laminate 207 vb.
  skin, wrapping 226 n.
  coat 226 n.
  line 227 vb.
  tunic, overcoat 228 n.
  make opaque 423 vb.
  preserve 666 vb.
coatee *tunic* 228 n.
coating *layer* 207 n.
  covering 226 n.
  facing 226 n.
  lining 227 n.
coat of arms
  heraldry 547 n.
coat-tail *extremity* 69 n.
  pendant 217 n.
coax *induce, tempt* 612 vb.
  pet 889 vb.
  flatter 925 vb.
cob *pony* 273 n.
  waterfowl 365 n.
  male animal 372 n.
cobalt *blue pigment* 435 n.
cobble *paving* 226 n.
  building material 631 n.
cobbler *clothier* 228 n.
  mender 656 n.
  artisan 686 n.
cobbles *road* 624 n.
cobblestone *paving* 226 n.
coble *fishing-boat* 275 n.
cobra *reptile* 365 n.
  noxious animal 904 n.
cobweb *weak thing* 163 n.
  filament 208 n.
  network 222 n.
  levity 323 n.
  trifle 639 n.
  dirt 649 n.
cocaine *anæsthetic* 375 n.
  drug 658 n.
  poison 659 n.
coccyx *buttocks* 238 n.
cochineal *pigment* 425 n.

  red pigment 431 n.
cochlea *ear* 415 n.
  coil 251 n.
cock
  poultry 365 n.
  male animal 372 n.
  tool 630 n.
  make ready 669 vb.
cockade *livery* 547 n.
  trimming 844 n.
cock-a-doodle-doo
  ululation 409 n.
cock-a-hoop
  jubilant 833 adj.
  boastful 877 adj.
cockalorum
  insolent person 878 n.
cock-and-bull story
  insubstantial thing 4 n.
  fable 543 n.
cock a snook at
  be insolent 878 vb.
  not respect 921 vb.
cockatrice *rara avis* 84 n.
  reptile 365 n.
  eye 438 n.
  heraldry 547 n.
  noxious animal 904 n.
cockboat *boat* 275 n.
cock-crow *morning* 128 n.
cocker *pet* 889 vb.
cockerel *poultry* 365 n.
  male animal 372 n.
cock-eyed *oblique* 220 adj.
  distorted 246 adj.
  dim-sighted 440 adj.
cock fight *duel* 716 n.
cockle *fold* 261 vb.
  fish food 301 n.
  table fish 365 n.
cockles of the heart
  affections 817 n.
cockloft *attic* 194 n.
cockney *native* 191 n.
  dialectical 560 adj.
  commoner 869 n.
  plebeian 869 adj.
cock of the walk
  exceller 644 n.
  master 741 n.
  proud man 871 n.
cockpit *chamber* 914 n.
  aircraft 276 n.
  cattle pen 369 n.
  duel 716 n.
  arena 724 n.
cockroach *fly* 365 n.
cockshut *evening* 129 n.
cock-shy *propulsion* 287 n.
  laughing-stock 851 n.
cocksparrow *dwarf* 196 n.

cocksure *believing* 485 adj.
cocktail *a mixture* 43 n.
 potion 301 n.
 liquor 301 n.
cock up *be vertical* 215 vb.
 jut 254 vb.
cocky *prideful* 871 adj.
 vain 873 adj.
 impertinent 878 adj.
cocoa *soft drink* 301 n.
coconut *fruit* 301 n.
cocoon *youngling* 132 n.
 source 156 n.
 nest 192 n.
 receptacle 194 n.
 wrapping 226 n.
 vermin 365 n.
cocotte *prostitute* 952 n.
coction *heating* 381 n.
cod *skin* 226 n.
 table fish 365 n.
coda *adjunct* 40 n.
 sequel 67 n.
 end 69 n.
 rear 238 n.
 melody 410 n.
 musical piece 412 n.
coddle *cook* 301 vb.
 please 826 vb.
 pet 889 vb.
code *arrangement* 62 n.
 rule 81 n.
 translate 520 vb.
 secrecy 525 n.
 conceal 525 vb.
 enigma 530 n.
 symbology 547 n.
 writing 586 n.
 precept 693 n.
 probity 929 n.
codeine *drug* 658 n.
code of honour
 code of duty 917 n.
 probity 929 n.
coder *interpreter* 520 n.
codex *script* 586 n.
 book 589 n.
codger *niggard* 816 n.
codicil *adjunct* 40 n.
 sequel 67 n.
 title-deed 767 n.
codification *law* 953 n.
 legislation 953 n.
codify *class* 62 vb.
co-director *colleague* 707 n.
codling *youngster* 132 n.
co-education
 education 534 n.
coefficience
 accompaniment 89 n.
 co-operation 706 n.

coefficient
 numerical element 85 n.
 concomitant 89 n.
coelenterate *animal* 365 n.
co-emption *purchase* 792 n.
coequal *equal* 28 adj.
 compeer 28 n.
coerce *dominate* 733 vb.
 compel 740 vb.
coercion *brute force* 735 n.
 compulsion 740 n.
 restraint 747 n.
co-eternal *perpetual* 115 adj.
 synchronous 123 adj.
coeval *contemporary* 123 n.
 synchronous 123 adj.
coexist *be* 1 vb.
 accompany 89 vb.
 be contiguous 202 vb.
 be patient 823 vb.
coexistence *existence* 1 n.
 accompaniment 89 n.
 synchronism 123 n.
 contiguity 202 n.
 concord 710 n.
 peace 717 n.
coextension *equality* 28 n.
 parallelism 219 n.
coextensive
 symmetrical 245 adj.
 (*see* coextension)
coffee *soft drink* 301 n.
 brownness 430 n.
coffee house *café* 192 n.
coffee-pot *cauldron* 194 n.
coffee stall *café* 192 n.
coffer *box* 194 n.
 storage 632 n.
 treasury 799 n.
coffin *box* 194 n.
 interment 364 n.
 funeral 364 n.
cog *tooth* 256 n.
 notch 260 n.
 merchant ship 275 n.
 deceive, befool 542 vb.
 flatter 925 vb.
cogent *powerful* 160 adj.
 rational 475 adj.
 compelling 740 adj.
cogged *toothed* 256 adj.
cogger *trickster* 545 n.
coggery *trickery* 542 n.
cogitate *think* 449 vb.
cogitation, cogitative
 (*see* cogitate)
cognac *liquor* 301 n.
cognate *relative* 9 adj.
 kinsman 11 n.
 akin 11 adj.
 similar 18 adj.

 verbal 559 adj.
cognisance (*see* cognizance)
cognition *knowledge* 490 n.
cognitive *mental* 447 adj.
 knowing 490 adj.
cognizable *known* 490 adj.
 intelligible 516 adj.
 legal 953 adj.
 illegal 954 adj.
cognizance
 knowledge 490 n.
 intellect 447 n.
cognizance of, take
 notice 455 vb.
cognizant *mental* 447 adj.
 knowing 490 adj.
cognize *cognize* 447 vb.
 know 490 vb.
 hold court 955 vb.
cognomen *name* 561 n.
cognoscente
 man of taste 846 n.
cog-wheel *notch* 260 n.
cohabit *unite with* 45 vb.
 accompany 89 vb.
 wed 894 vb.
co-heir *participator* 775 n.
 beneficiary 776 n.
cohere *cohere* 48 vb.
 be dense 324 vb.
 thicken 354 vb.
coherence *junction* 45 n.
 coherence 48 n.
 sanity 501 n.
 intelligibility 516 n.
coherent (*see* coherence)
cohesion *coherence* 48 n.
 density 324 n.
 viscidity 354 n.
cohesive *firm-set* 45 adj.
 cohesive 48 adj.
 retentive 778 adj.
cohibit *obstruct* 702 vb.
 restrain 747 vb.
 prohibit 757 vb.
cohort(s) *formation* 722 n.
 army 722 n.
coif *headgear* 228 n.
coiffure *wig* 228 n.
 hair-dressing 843 n.
coign of vantage
 vantage 34 n.
coil *complexity* 61 n.
 twine 251 vb.
 round 252 vb.
 difficulty 700 n.
 hair-dressing 843 n.
coin *produce* 164 vb.
 efform 243 vb.
 imagine 513 vb.
 fake 541 vb.

mint 797vb.
coinage *production* 164n.
  coinage 797n.
coincide *be identical* 13vb.
  accord 24vb.
  accompany 89vb.
coincidence
  synchronism 123n.
  eventuality 154n.
  chance 159n.
  concurrence 181n.
  contiguity 202n.
  (*see* coincide)
coincident
  conjunctive 45adj.
  (*see* coincidence)
coincidental
  accompanying 89adj.
  casual 159adj.
  unintentional 618adj.
coin-clipper *defrauder* 789n.
coiner *moneyer* 797n.
coin words
  neologize 560vb.
coir *fibre* 208n.
coital *conjunctive* 45adj.
coition, coitus *coition* 45n.
  propagation 164n.
coke *soft drink* 301n.
  ash 381n.
  coal 385n.
col *bond* 47n.
  narrowness 206n.
  high land 209n.
colander *bowl* 194n.
  porosity 263n.
cold *wintry* 129adj.
  dead 361adj.
  insensible 375adj.
  coldness 380n.
  feeble 572adj.
  infection 651n.
  respiratory disease 651n.
  blight 659n.
  preserver 666n.
  uncooked 670adj.
  non-active 677adj.
  adversity 731n.
  impassive 820adj.
  inexcitable 823adj.
  cheerless 834adj.
  indifferent 860adj.
  inimical 881adj.
  unsociable 883adj.
  unkind 898adj.
  pure 950adj.
cold-blooded
  animal 365adj.
  impassive 820adj.
  cautious 858adj.
  unastonished 865adj.

cold comfort
  discontent 829n.
cold feet *nervousness* 854n.
cold fish
  unfeeling person 820n.
cold frame *garden* 370n.
cold front *wintriness* 380n.
coldness *coldness* 380n.
  (*see* cold)
cold pack
  preservation 666n.
cold-shoulder
  exclude 57vb.
  disregard 458vb.
  reject 607vb.
  avoid 620vb.
  make unwelcome 833vb.
cold storage *delay* 136n.
  refrigerator 384n.
cold sweat *fear* 854n.
cold war *war* 718n.
cold water *moderator* 177n.
  dissuasion 613n.
  antidote 658n.
cole, coleslaw, colewort
  vegetable 301n.
colic *pang* 377n.
  indigestion 651n.
collaborate
  be willing 597vb.
  apostatize 603vb.
  co-operate 706vb.
collaboration
  concurrence 181n.
  co-operation 706n.
collaborator
  tergiversator 603n.
  personnel 686n.
  collaborator 707n.
  friend 880n.
collapse *decrease* 37vb.
  cease 145vb.
  helplessness 161n.
  weakness 163n.
  ruin 165n.
  fall short 307vb.
  descent 309n.
  illness 651n.
  dilapidation 655n.
  fatigue 684n.
  knuckle under 721vb.
  defeat 728n.
  fail 728vb.
collar *halter* 47n.
  girdle 47n.
  neckwear 228n.
  loop 250n.
  meat 301n.
  arrest 747vb.
  fetter 748n.
  take 786vb.

collate *compare* 462vb.
  commission 751vb.
collateral *relative* 9adj.
  akin 11adj.
  offset 31n.
  parallel 219adj.
  lateral 239adj.
  security 767n.
collaterality *relation* 9n.
  sonship 170n.
collation *meal* 301n.
  comparison 462n.
colleague *personnel* 686n.
  colleague 707n.
  friend 880n.
colleagueship
  association 706n.
collect *join* 45vb.
  bring together 74vb.
  understand 516vb.
  abstract 592vb.
  acquire 771vb.
  receive 782vb.
  take 786vb.
  prayers 981n.
collectanea
  accumulation 74n.
  anthology 592n.
collected
  compendious 592adj.
  unastonished 865adj.
collection
  arrangement 62n.
  accumulation 74n.
  exhibit 522n.
  collection 632n.
  offering 781n.
  payment 804n.
  oblation 981n.
collection bag,— plate
  church utensil 990n.
collective *assemblage* 74n.
  general 79adj.
  agrarian 370adj.
  joint possession 775n.
  sharing 775adj.
collective farm *farm* 370n.
  joint possession 775n.
collectively
  collectively 52adv.
  together 74adv.
  with 89adv.
  in common 755adv.
collectivism
  government 733n.
  joint possession 775n.
collectivity *whole* 52n.
collectivization
  assemblage 74n.
collect oneself
  keep calm 823vb.

collector
  accumulator 74 n.
  collector 492 n.
  official 690 n.
  receiver 782 n.
collectorship
  receiving 782 n.
collector's piece
  exhibit 522 n.
  exceller 644 n.
  masterpiece 694 n.
colleen youngster 132 n.
college group 74 n.
  academy 539 n.
collegian, colleger
  college student 538 n.
collegiate
  student-like 538 adj.
collide disagree 25 vb.
  collide 279 vb.
  approach 289 vb.
  meet 295 vb.
  touch 378 vb.
  strike at 712 vb.
  be inimical 881 vb.
collie dog 365 n.
collied black 428 adj.
  dirty 649 adj.
collier merchant ship 275 n.
  artisan 686 n.
colliery excavation 255 n.
  store 632 n.
  workshop 687 n.
collimation
  parallelism 219 n.
  direction 281 n.
collimator direction 281 n.
colliquation
  liquefaction 337 n.
collision violence 176 n.
  counteraction 182 n.
  collision 279 n.
  convergence 293 n.
  quarrel 709 n.
  fight 716 n.
  battle 718 n.
collision course
  convergence 293 n.
collocate arrange 62 vb.
  bring together 74 vb.
  place 187 vb.
collocation (see collocate)
collocutor
  interlocutor 584 n.
collodion viscidity 354 n.
collogue converse 584 vb.
  flatter 925 vb.
colloid viscidity 354 n.
  semiliquidity 354 n.
collop piece 53 n.
colloquial

figurative 519 adj.
  linguistic 557 adj.
  dialectical 560 adj.
colloquialism trope 519 n.
  slang 560 n.
colloquy speech 579 n.
  interlocution 584 n.
  conference 584 n.
collotype copy 22 n.
  representation 551 n.
collusion
  concurrence 181 n.
  deception 542 n.
  co-operation 706 n.
collusive, collusory
  false 541 adj.
  deceiving 542 adj.
colluvies sink 649 n.
collyrium balm 658 n.
  cosmetic 843 n.
collywobbles
  voidance 300 n.
  pang 377 n.
colon insides 224 n.
  tube 263 n.
  drain 351 n.
  punctuation 547 n.
colonel army officer 741 n.
colonelcy degree 27 n.
colonial foreigner 59 n.
  settler 191 n.
  subject 742 n.
  subject 745 adj.
colonialism
  governance 733 n.
  subjection 745 n.
colonist settler 191 n.
  incomer 297 n.
  egress 298 n.
colonization location 187 n.
colonize
  place oneself 187 vb.
  dwell 192 vb.
  subjugate 745 vb.
  appropriate 786 vb.
colonnade series 71 n.
  pavilion 192 n.
  path 624 n.
colony crowd 74 n.
  certain quantity 104 n.
  descendant 170 n.
  territory 184 n.
  station 187 n.
  habitancy 191 n.
  polity 733 n.
  subject 742 n.
colophon sequel 67 n.
  rear 238 n.
  label 547 n.
  letterpress 587 n.
  edition 589 n.

colophony resin 357 n.
Colorado beetle
  noxious animal 904 n.
coloration light 417 n.
  colour, hue 425 n.
coloratura
  vocal music 412 n.
  vocalist 413 n.
colossal enormous 32 adj.
  stalwart 162 adj.
  huge 195 adj.
  tall 209 adj.
Colosseum arena 724 n.
colossus giant 195 n.
  tall creature 209 n.
  high structure 209 n.
  sculpture 554 n.
colour character 5 n.
  tincture 43 n.
  mix 43 vb.
  sort 77 n.
  modify 143 vb.
  influence 178 vb.
  light 417 n.
  colour 425 n., vb.
  blackness 428 n.
  redden 431 vb.
  mien 445 n.
  qualify 468 vb.
  probability 471 n.
  sophisticate 477 vb.
  cant 541 vb.
  paint 553 vb.
  ornament 574 n.
  pretext 614 n.
  show feeling 818 vb.
  decorate 844 vb.
  be modest 874 vb.
  get angry 891 vb.
  justify 927 vb.
colourable
  plausible 471 adj.
  deceiving 542 adj.
  ostensible 614 adj.
colour-bar exclusion 57 n.
  disapprobation 924 n.
colour-blind
  dim-sighted 440 adj.
  indiscriminating 464 adj.
coloured coloured 425 adj.
  blackish 428 adj.
colourful luminous 417 adj.
  luminescent 420 adj.
  coloured, florid 425 adj.
  variegated 437 adj.
  showy 875 adj.
colouring hue 425 n.
  qualification 468 n.
  meaning 514 n.
  exaggeration 546 n.
  identification 547 n.

painting 553 n.
colouring matter
pigment 425 n.
colourist *artist* 556 n.
colourless *weak* 163 adj.
dim 419 adj.
colourless 426 adj.
feeble 572 adj.
unhealthy 651 adj.
mediocre 732 adj.
dull 840 adj.
colour, man of *negro* 428 n.
colours *flag* 547 n.
colour up *redden* 431 vb.
be humbled 872 vb.
colour-wash *pigment* 425 n.
decorate 844 vb.
colporteur *seller* 793 n.
pedlar 794 n.
colt *youngling* 132 n.
horse 273 n.
male animal 372 n.
beginner 538 n.
bungler 697 n.
coltish *infantine* 132 adj.
active 678 adj.
colubriform *animal* 365 adj.
columbaceous
animal 365 adj.
columbarium
cemetery 364 n.
columbine
entertainer 594 n.
columellar
supporting 218 adj.
column
high structure 209 n.
pillar 218 n.
cylinder 252 n.
marching 267 n.
rostrum 539 n.
monument 548 n.
formation 722 n.
columnar
supporting 218 adj.
rotund 252 adj.
columnist *informant* 524 n.
chronicler 549 n.
author 589 n.
coma *helplessness* 161 n.
insensibility 375 n.
sleep 679 n.
fatigue 684 n.
co-mate *colleague* 707 n.
comatose *impotent* 161 adj.
apathetic 820 adj.
(*see* coma)
comb *tooth* 256 n.
musical instrument 414 n.
cleaning utensil 648 n.
clean 648 vb.

hair-dressing 843 n.
combat
contention, fight 716 n.
give battle 718 vb.
combatant *contender* 716 n.
combatant 722 n.
combative
quarrelling 709 adj.
contending 716 adj.
warlike 718 adj.
combativeness
bellicosity 718 n.
combe *valley* 255 n.
comber *wave* 350 n.
combination *mixture* 43 n.
junction 45 n.
coherence 48 n.
combination 50 n.
composition 56 n.
assemblage 74 n.
numerical operation 86 n.
association 706 n.
society 708 n.
combinations
underwear 228 n.
combine *be one* 88 vb.
association 706 n.
(*see* combination)
combine-harvester
farm tool 370 n.
combings *leavings* 41 n.
rubbish 641 n.
comb out *unravel* 62 vb.
combustibility
burning 381 n.
combustible *fuel* 385 n.
combustible 385 adj.
combustion *burning* 381 n.
come *arrive* 295 vb.
come about *be* 1 vb.
happen 154 vb.
come a cropper
tumble 309 vb.
come across *acquire* 771 vb.
pay 804 vb.
come again
be unsatisfied 636 vb.
come alive
be intelligible 516 vb.
come amiss *disagree* 25 vb.
be inexpedient 643 vb.
come and go
fluctuate 317 vb.
be active 678 vb.
come apart
be disjoined 46 vb.
come-back
compensation 31 n.
revival 656 n.
come by *acquire* 771 vb.
comedian *actor* 594 n.

humorist 839 n.
come-down *descent* 309 n.
disappointment 509 n.
humiliation 872 n.
come down *decrease* 37 vb.
descend 309 vb.
be poor 301 vb.
be cheap 812 vb.
come down on
be severe 735 vb.
restrain 747 vb.
come down on for
claim 915 vb.
comedy *stage play* 594 n.
laughter 835 n.
ridiculousness 849 n.
come forth *emerge* 298 vb.
be visible 443 vb.
come forward
be visible 443 vb.
offer oneself 759 vb.
come from *result* 157 vb.
come-hither look
look 438 n.
pleasurableness 826 n.
wooing 889 n.
come in *be included* 78 vb.
enter 297 vb.
be received 782 vb.
come in for *receive* 782 vb.
come into *inherit* 771 vb.
possess 773 vb.
receive 782 vb.
come into existence
become 1 vb.
happen 154 vb.
come into use
be wont 610 vb.
comely *symmetrical* 245 adj.
beautiful 841 adj.
come natural *accord* 24 vb.
come near *resemble* 18 vb.
approach 289 vb.
come of *result* 157 vb.
come of age
come of age 134 vb.
come off *cease* 145 vb.
happen 154 vb.
transfer 272 vb.
escape 667 vb.
be successful 727 vb.
come off it
be humbled 872 vb.
come off on *cohere* 48 vb.
come on *impend* 155 vb.
progress 285 vb.
charge 712 vb.
come out *begin* 68 vb.
emerge 298 vb.
be visible 443 vb.
be disclosed 526 vb.

dramatize 594 vb.
relinquish 621 vb.
be inactive 679 vb.
be easy 701 vb.
revolt 738 vb.
come out of result 157 vb.
come out with
divulge 526 vb.
come over consent 758 vb.
come round
be periodic 141 vb.
be restored 656 vb.
consent 758 vb.
comes star 321 n.
come short
be inferior 35 vb.
be incomplete 55 vb.
fall short 307 vb.
not suffice 636 vb.
comestible food 301 n.
edible 301 adj.
comet wanderer 268 n.
planet 321 n.
cometary celestial 321 adj.
come to number 86 vb.
be turned to 147 vb.
be restored 656 vb.
be refreshed 685 vb.
cost 809 vb.
come to a head
culminate 34 vb.
be complete 54 vb.
come to be become 1 vb.
come to bits
be disjoined 46 vb.
come to blows fight 716 vb.
be inimical 881 vb.
come together
congregate 74 n.
converge 293 vb.
come to grief
miscarry 728 vb.
have trouble 731 vb.
come to hand
arrive 295 vb.
be received 782 vb.
come to heel
accompany 89 vb.
follow 284 vb.
obey 739 vb.
come to know
be informed 524 vb.
come to life live 360 vb.
be restored 656 vb.
come to light
be visible 443 vb.
be plain 522 vb.
be disclosed 526 vb.
come to nothing
not be 2 vb.
be unproductive 172 vb.

fall short 307 vb.
miscarry 728 vb.
come to pass
happen 154 vb.
come to stay stay 144 vb.
come to terms
accord 24 vb.
contract 765 vb.
come to the point
be related 9 vb.
specify 80 vb.
be concise 569 vb.
speak plainly 573 vb.
come under
be included 78 vb.
come unstuck
be disjoined 46 vb.
come unstuck 49 vb.
be dispersed 75 vb.
be in difficulty 700 vb.
fail 728 vb.
come upon meet 295 vb.
discover 484 vb.
comfit sweet 392 n.
comfort euphoria 376 n.
repose 682 n.
refresh 685 vb.
aid 703 n., vb.
wealth 800 n.
happiness 824 n.
please 826 vb.
content 828 n., vb.
relief 831 n.
cheer 833 vb.
give hope 852 vb.
condolence 905 n.
pity 905 vb.
comfortable adjusted 24 adj.
tranquil 266 adj.
comfortable 376 adj.
reposeful 683 adj.
easy 701 adj.
prosperous, palmy 730 adj.
rich 800 adj.
inexcitable 823 adj.
happy 824 adj.
pleasurable 826 adj.
content 828 adj.
comforter wrapping 226 n.
shawl 228 n.
relief 831 n.
Comforter
Holy Ghost 965 n.
comfortless
unpleasant 827 adj.
cheerless 834 adj.
unpromising 853 adj.
comfort station
latrine 649 n.
comic actor 594 n.
dramatic 594 adj.

laughing 835 adj.
humorist 839 n.
witty 839 adj.
funny 849 adj.
coming future 124 adj.
coming events
futurity 124 n.
destiny 155 n.
coming out début 68 n.
celebration 876 n.
comitia council 692 n.
comity etiquette 848 n.
courtesy 884 n.
comity of nations
mankind 371 n.
comma punctuation 347 n.
command vantage 34 n.
be superior 34 vb.
influence 178 vb.
be high 209 vb.
will 595 n., vb.
requirement 627 n.
dispose of 673 vb.
direct 689 vb.
precept 693 n.
dominate 733 vb.
command 737 n., vb.
compel 740 vb.
mandate 751 n.
possess 773 vb.
commandant
army officer 741 n.
commandeer
appropriate 786 vb.
commander superior 34 n.
naval man 270 n.
army officer 741 n.
naval officer 741 n.
commanding
authoritative 733 adj.
noteworthy 866 adj.
proud 871 adj.
(see command)
commandment
(see command)
commando
armed force 722 n.
comme il faut
tasteful 846 adj.
fashionable 848 adj.
genteel 868 adj.
commemorate
remind 505 vb.
honour 866 vb.
celebrate 876 vb.
commemoration
remembrance 505 n.
amusement 837 n.
(see commemorate)
commence begin 68 vb.
commend advise 691 vb.

befriend 880 vb.
approve 923 vb.
praise 923 vb.
commendable *good* 615 adj.
  expedient 642 adj.
  approvable 923 adj.
  virtuous 933 adj.
commender *adviser* 691 n.
  commender 923 n.
commensal *mensal* 301 adj.
commensurability
  fitness 24 n.
commensurable
  numerical 85 adj.
  numerable 86 adj.
commensurate
  relative 9 adj.
  agreeing 24 adj.
  numerical 85 adj.
  numerable 86 adj.
  sufficient 635 adj.
comment
  notice 455 vb.
  estimate 480 n., vb.
  maxim 496 n.
  interpret 520 vb.
  commentary 520 n.
  affirmation 532 n.
  speech 579 n.
  article 591 n.
  dissert 591 vb.
commentary
  commentary 520 n.
  article 591 n.
commentator
  estimator 480 n.
  intellectual 492 n.
  interpreter 520 n.
  informant 524 n.
  dissertator 591 n.
commerce
  interlocution 584 n.
  business 622 n.
  trade 791 n.
  card game 837 n.
commercial
  businesslike 622 adj.
  trading 791 adj.
  vulgar 847 adj.
commercialism *trade* 791 n.
  bad taste 847 n.
commercialize *trade* 791 vb.
  vulgarize 847 vb.
commercial traveller
  traveller 268 n.
  seller 793 n.
commination
  malediction 899 n.
  threat 900 n.
  prayers 981 n.
comminute *break* 46 vb.

pulverize 332 vb.
commiseration *pity* 905 n.
  condolence 905 n.
commissar *tyrant* 735 n.
  master, officer 741 n.
  autocrat 741 n.
commissarial
  provisionary 633 adj.
commissariat
  provisions 301 n.
  provision 633 n.
commissary *provider* 633 n.
  delegate 754 n.
commission
  increment 36 n.
  band 74 n.
  job 622 n.
  employ 622 vb.
  fitting out 669 n.
  make ready 669 vb.
  action 676 n.
  warrant 737 n., vb.
  commission 751 n., vb.
  permit 756 n.
  earnings 771 n.
  impose a duty 917 vb.
commissionaire
  janitor 264 n.
  courier 531 n.
  servant 742 n.
commissioner *official* 690 n.
  officer 741 n.
  delegate 754 n.
commissioner for oaths
  notary 958 n.
commission of the peace
  jurisdiction 955 n.
  tribunal 956 n.
commissure *joint* 45 n.
commit *transfer* 272 vb.
  do 676 vb.
  commission 751 vb.
  convey 780 vb.
  do wrong 914 vb.
commitment *promise* 764 n.
  giving 781 n.
  debt 803 n.
  duty 917 n.
commit oneself
  affirm 532 vb.
  undertake 762 vb.
  promise 764 vb.
  incur a duty 917 vb.
committal
  transference 272 n.
  commission 751 n.
  legal process 959 n.
committed
  affirmative 532 adj.
  promised 764 adj.
  indebted 803 adj.

dutied 917 adj.
committee *band* 74 n.
  party 708 n.
  authority 733 n.
  consignee 754 n.
commixture *mixture* 43 n.
  ritual act 988 n.
commode *vessel* 194 n.
  cabinet 194 n.
  latrine 649 n.
commodious *useful* 640 adj.
commodity *object* 319 n.
  benefit 615 n.
  utility 640 n.
  merchandise 795 n.
commodore
  naval man 270 n.
  naval officer 741 n.
common *inferior* 35 adj.
  general 79 adj.
  typical 83 adj.
  frequent 139 adj.
  plain 348 n.
  mediocre 732 adj.
  sharing 775 adj.
  lands 777 n.
  vulgar 847 adj.
  unastonishing 865 adj.
  plebeian 869 adj.
commonalty
  social group 371 n.
  commonalty 869 n.
common cause
  co-operation 706 n.
common denominator
  relation 9 n.
  numerical element 85 n.
commoner
  college student 538 n.
  mediocrity 732 n.
  vulgarian 847 n.
  commoner 869 n.
common feature
  similarity 18 n.
common front
  association 706 n.
common knowledge
  knowledge 490 n.
  publicity 528 n.
common lot
  mediocrity 732 n.
commonly *often* 139 adv.
common man
  common man 30 n.
  everyman 79 n.
  mediocrity 732 n.
commonness (*see* common)
common or garden
  typical 83 adj.
commonplace
  median 30 adj.

typical 83 adj.
topic 452 n.
known 490 adj.
maxim 496 n.
aphoristic 496 adj.
phrase 563 n.
plain 573 adj.
usual 610 adj.
trivial 639 adj.
mediocre 732 adj.
dull 840 adj.
commonplace book
reminder 505 n.
anthology 592 n.
common prayer
public worship 981 n.
common run *habit* 610 n.
commons *provisions* 301 n.
commonalty 869 n.
common sense
intelligence 498 n.
sanity 502 n.
common speech
language 557 n.
plainness 573 n.
common stamp
uniformity 16 n.
common stock
joint possession 775 n.
common touch
sociability 882 n.
courtesy 884 n.
commonweal
nation 371 n.
good 615 n.
utility 640 n.
polity 733 n.
commonwealth
territory 184 n.
nation 371 n.
polity 733 n.
commorant *dweller* 191 n.
commotion *violence* 176 n.
commotion 318 n.
exaggeration 546 n.
excitable state 822 vb.
communal *national* 371 adj.
sectional 708 adj.
sharing 775 adj.
commune *district* 184 n.
meditate 449 vb.
communicate 524 vb.
converse 584 vb.
communicable
transferable 272 adj.
infectious 653 adj.
communicant
church member 976 n.
pietist 979 n.
worshipper 981 n.
communicate *connect* 45 vb.

transfer 272 vb.
mean 514 vb.
communicate 524 vb.
give 781 vb.
offer worship 981 vb.
communicating
accessible 289 adj.
communication
information 524 n.
disclosure 526 n.
message 529 n.
interlocution 584 n.
correspondence 588 n.
(*see* communicate)
communications
access 624 n.
communicative
loquacious 581 adj.
communicator
informant 524 n.
communion
interlocution 584 n.
party 708 n.
social gathering 882 n.
worship 981 n.
Holy Communion 988 n.
communiqué
report 524 n.
news 529 n.
communist *reformer* 654 n.
agitator 738 n.
participator 775 n.
communistic
authoritarian 735 adj.
sharing 775 adj.
community
habitancy 191 n.
social group 371 n.
association 706 n.
community 708 n.
sect 978 n.
monk 986 n.
laity 987 n.
community-chest
store 632 n.
community house
monastery 986 n.
communize *socialize* 775 vb.
commutable
substituted 150 adj.
interchanged 151 adj.
commutation
compensation 31 n.
substitution 150 n.
interchange 151 n.
compromise 770 n.
commute
be periodic 141 vb.
substitute 150 vb.
interchange 151 vb.
compromise 770 vb.

commuter *traveller* 268 n.
rider 268 n.
thing transferred 272 n.
compact *small* 33 adj.
cohesive 48 adj.
case 194 n.
little 196 adj.
contracted 198 adj.
short 204 adj.
dense 324 adj.
concise 569 adj.
compact 765 n.
cosmetic 843 n.
compaction *coherence* 48 n.
contraction 198 n.
structure 331 n.
companion *analogue* 18 n.
concomitant 89 n.
window 263 n.
colleague 707 n.
servant, retainer 742 n.
close friend 880 n.
companionable
sociable 882 adj.
companionate marriage
type of marriage 894 n.
illicit love 951 n.
companionship
accompaniment 89 n.
sociality 882 n.
companion-way
entrance 263 n.
ascent 308 n.
company *assembly* 74 n.
band 74 n.
accompaniment 89 n.
actor 594 n.
personnel 686 n.
workshop 687 n.
association 706 n.
corporation 708 n.
formation 722 n.
comparability
relevance 9 n.
relativeness 9 n.
similarity 18 n.
comparable *relative* 9 adj.
equivalent 28 adj.
compared 462 adj.
comparative
figurative 519 adj.
grammatical 564 adj.
comparatively
slightly 33 adv.
comparatively 462 adv.
compare *relate* 9 vb.
graduate 27 vb.
compare 462 vb.
discriminate 463 vb.
compare notes
consult 691 vb.

compare with
  resemble 18 vb.
comparison
  relativeness 9 n.
  assimilation 18 n.
  joinder 45 n.
  comparison 462 n.
  metaphor 519 n.
compartition
  decomposition 51 n.
compartment
  subdivision 53 n.
  place 185 n.
  compartment 194 n.
  train 274 n.
  heraldry 547 n.
compartmentalize
  set apart 46 vb.
compartmentalized
  cellular 194 adj.
compass ability 160 n.
  range 183 n.
  region 184 n.
  distance 199 n.
  circumjacence 230 n.
  surround 230 vb.
  outline 233 n.
  sailing aid 269 n.
  direction 281 n.
  circle 314 vb.
  gauge 465 n.
  signpost 547 n.
  succeed 727 vb.
compassion lenity 736 n.
  pity 905 n.
  disinterestedness 931 n.
compassionable
  pitiable 905 adj.
compassionate
  giving 781 adj.
  impressible 819 adj.
  pitying 905 adj.
  pity 905 vb.
compass point
  compass point 281 n.
compatibility
  adaptation 24 n.
  possibility 469 n.
  concord 710 n.
  friendship 880 n.
  sociability 882 n.
  love 887 n.
compatriot
  kinsman 11 n.
  native 191 n.
compeer compeer 28 n.
  contemporary 123 n.
compel be able 160 vb.
  influence 178 vb.
  motivate 612 vb.
  command 737 vb.

compel 740 vb.
compellation
  nomenclature 561 n.
compelling causal 156 adj.
  powerful 160 adj.
  strong 162 adj.
  influential 178 adj.
  forceful 571 adj.
  necessary 596 adj.
  compelling 740 adj.
compendious small 33 adj.
  short 204 adj.
  concise 569 adj.
  compendious 592 adj.
compendium
  accumulation 74 n.
  miniature 196 n.
  contraction 198 n.
  compendium 592 n.
compensate correlate 12 vb.
  equalize 28 vb.
  compensate 31 vb.
  retaliate 714 vb.
  restitute 787 vb.
  pay 804 vb.
  atone 941 vb.
  reward 962 vb.
compensation
  (see compensate)
compère actor 594 n.
  stage-manager 594 n.
  direct 690 vb.
compete do likewise 20 vb.
  contend 716 vb.
  offer oneself 759 vb.
competence ability 160 n.
  sufficiency 635 n.
  skill 694 n.
  independence 744 n.
  wealth 800 n.
  jurisdiction 955 n.
competent
  legal 953 adj.
  jurisdictional 955 adj.
  (see competence)
compete with oppose 704 vb.
competition imitation 20 n.
  opposition 704 n.
  contention 716 n.
  sale 793 n.
  jealousy 911 n.
competitive equal 28 adj.
  skilful 694 adj.
  selfish 932 adj.
competitor compeer 28 n.
  incomer 297 n.
  hinderer 702 n.
  opponent 705 n.
  contender 716 n.
  petitioner 763 n.
  enemy 881 n.

competitors opposites 704 n.
compilation
  composition 56 n.
  assemblage 74 n.
  accumulation 74 n.
  dictionary 559 n.
  anthology 592 n.
compile compose 56 vb.
  (see compilation)
compiler collector 492 n.
  etymology 559 n.
  anthology 592 n.
complacence content 828 n.
  courtesy 884 n.
complacent
  benevolent 897 adj.
complain deprecate 762 vb.
  be discontented 829 vb.
  lament 836 vb.
  be sullen 893 vb.
  blame 924 vb.
  indict 928 vb.
complainant accuser 928 n.
complainer
  malcontent 829 n.
  moper 834 n.
  weeper 836 n.
complain of be ill 651 vb.
complaint cry 408 n.
  evil 616 n.
  illness 651 n.
  deprecation 762 n.
  annoyance 827 n.
  discontent 829 n.
  lament 836 n.
  wrong 914 n.
  disapprobation 924 n.
  accusation 928 n.
complaisance
  permission 756 n.
  courteous act 884 n.
complaisant
  conformable 83 adj.
  lenient 736 adj.
  obedient 739 adj.
  courteous 884 adj.
  benevolent 897 adj.
complement analogue 18 n.
  adjunct 40 n.
  plenitude 54 n.
  component 58 n.
  band 74 n.
  inclusion 78 n.
  numerical element 85 n.
  personnel 686 n.
complementary
  correlative 12 adj.
complete
  consummate 32 adj.
  make complete 54 vb.
  persevere 600 vb.

sufficient 635 adj.
perfect 646 adj.
do 676 vb.
carry through 725 vb.
completely *wholly* 52 adv.
completeness *whole* 52 n.
  completeness 54 n.
  completion 725 n.
completion *sequel* 67 n.
  sufficiency 635 n.
  completion 725 n.
  (*see* completeness)
complex *character* 5 n.
  mixed 43 adj.
  whole 52 n.
  complex 61 adj.
  intricate 251 adj.
  structure 331 n.
  imperspicuous 568 adj.
  habituation 610 n.
  difficult 700 adj.
complexion *modality* 7 n.
  state 7 n.
  hue 425 n.
  mien 445 n.
complexity *medley* 43 n.
  complexity 61 n.
  enigma 530 n.
  imperspicuity 568 n.
  (*see* complex)
compliance
  concurrence 181 n.
  softness 327 n.
  willingness 597 n.
  submission 721 n.
  obedience 739 n.
  consent 758 n.
  observance 768 n.
  servility 879 n.
compliant (*see* compliance)
complicate *bedevil* 63 vb.
  be unintelligible 517 vb.
  aggravate 832 vb.
complication
  complexity 61 n.
  illness 651 n.
  (*see* complexity)
complicity
  co-operation 707 n.
  participation 775 n.
  improbity 930 n.
  guilt 936 n.
compliment *honours* 866 n.
  courteous act 884 n.
  gratulate 886 vb.
  endearment 889 n.
  praise 923 n., vb.
  flatter 925 vb.
complimentary
  uncharged 812 adj.
compline

church *service* 988 n.
comply (*see* compliance)
compo *facing* 226 n.
  building material 631 n.
component *adjunct* 40 n.
  part 53 n.
  component 58 n.
  included 78 adj.
  unit 88 n.
  contents 193 n.
  element 319 n.
comportment
  conduct 688 n.
comport with *accord* 24 vb.
compose *mix* 43 vb.
  combine 50 vb.
  compose, constitute 56 vb.
  arrange 62 vb.
  be included 78 vb.
  produce 164 vb.
  assuage 177 vb.
  harmonize 410 vb.
  compose music 413 vb.
  write 586 vb.
  print 587 vb.
  tranquillize 823 vb.
composed
  inexcitable 823 adj.
  unastonished 865 adj.
compose differences
  pacify 719 vb.
  mediate 720 vb.
  compromise 770 vb.
compose oneself
  keep calm 823 vb.
composer *producer* 167 n.
  musician 413 n.
composite *mixed* 43 adj.
  conjunct 45 adj.
  plural 101 adj.
composition *a mixture* 43 n.
  combination 50 n.
  composition 56 n.
  arrangement 62 n.
  substitution 150 n.
  quid pro quo 150 n.
  production 164 n.
  structure 331 n.
  musical piece 412 n.
  painting 553 n.
  writing 586 n.
  print 587 n.
  building material 631 n.
  pacification 719 n.
  compact 765 n.
  compromise 770 n.
  payment 804 n.
  pattern 844 n.
compositor *printer* 587 n.
compos mentis *sane* 502 adj.
compost *fertilizer* 171 n.

composure
  inexcitability 823 n.
  non-wonder 865 n.
compote *pudding* 301 n.
  sweetmeat 301 n.
compound *a mixture* 43 n.
  compound 50 n.
  compose 56 vb.
  substitute 150 vb.
  inclosure 235 n.
  compromise 770 vb.
comprador *provider* 633 n.
comprehend *contain* 56 vb.
  comprise 78 vb.
  know 490 vb.
  understand 516 vb.
comprehensible
  intelligible 516 adj.
comprehension
  connotation 514 n.
  (*see* comprehend)
comprehensive
  extensive 32 adj.
  comprehensive 52 adj.
  complete 54 adj.
  inclusive 78 adj.
  general 79 adj.
  large 195 adj.
comprehensivity
  whole 52 n.
  (*see* comprehensive)
compress *tighten* 45 vb.
  make smaller 198 vb.
  shorten 204 vb.
  make thin 206 vb.
  be dense 324 vb.
  stanch 350 vb.
  be concise 569 vb.
  surgical dressing 658 n.
compressible
  contracted 198 adj.
  rare 325 adj.
  soft 327 adj.
compression *smallness* 33 n.
  diminution 37 n.
  energy 160 n.
  compression 198 n.
  narrowing 206 n.
  closure 264 n.
  conciseness 569 n.
  compendium 592 n.
  restriction 747 n.
compressor
  compressor 198 n.
  stopper 264 n.
  condensation 324 n.
comprise *comprise* 78 vb.
comprobation
  demonstration 478 n.
compromise
  adaptation 24 n.

middle point 30 n.
moderation 177 n.
irresolution 601 n.
mid-course 625 n.
endanger 661 vb.
pacification 719 n.
laxity 734 n.
compact 765 n.
make terms 766 vb.
compromise 770 n., vb.
defame 926 vb.
compromising
discreditable 867 adj.
comptometer
counting instrument 86 n.
compulsion
necessity 596 n.
no choice 606 n.
needfulness 627 n.
compulsion 740 n.
restraint 747 n.
compulsive
powerful 160 adj.
strong 162 adj.
necessary 596 adj.
authoritarian 735 adj.
commanding 737 adj.
compelling 740 adj.
obligatory 917 adj.
compulsory
compelling 740 adj.
compulsory acquisition
taking 786 n.
compunction *regret* 830 n.
pity 905 n.
penitence 939 n.
compunctious
unhappy 825 adj.
compurgation
credential 466 n.
vindication 927 n.
acquittal 960 n.
compurgator
witness 466 n.
vindicator 927 n.
computable
numerable 86 adj.
measured 465 adj.
computation
numeration 86 n.
measurement 465 n.
accounts 808 n.
compute *do sums* 86 vb.
measure 465 vb.
computer *computer* 86 n.
comrade *concomitant* 89 n.
male 372 n.
colleague 707 n.
society 708 n.
political party 708 n.
title 870 n.

chum 880 n.
comradely
corporate 708 adj.
friendly 880 adj.
comradeship
co-operation 706 n.
friendship 880 n.
sociality 882 n.
con *meditate* 449 vb.
know 490 vb.
memorize 505 vb.
con amore *willingly* 597 adj.
feelingly 818 adv.
conation *will* 595 n.
concamerate
make curved 248 vb.
concatenate *connect* 45 vb.
concatenation *joinder* 45 n.
continuity 71 n.
concave *concave* 255 adj.
conceal *contain* 56 vb.
cover 226 vb.
screen 421 vb.
conceal 525 vb.
safeguard 660 vb.
concealed *unknown* 491 adj.
latent 523 adj.
cabbalistic 984 adj.
concealment
invisibility 444 n.
equivocalness 518 n.
concealment 525 n.
seclusion 883 n.
concede
be reasonable 475 vb.
assent 488 vb.
confess 526 vb.
be induced 612 vb.
be lenient 736 vb.
permit 756 vb.
consent 758 vb.
conceit *thought* 449 n.
idea 451 n.
folly 499 n.
supposition 512 n.
ideality 513 n.
witticism 839 n.
affectation 850 n.
pride 871 n.
vanity 873 n.
conceivable *possible* 469 adj.
conceive *produce* 164 vb.
be fruitful 171 vb.
vitalize 360 vb.
cognize 447 vb.
opine 485 vb.
know 490 vb.
suppose 512 vb.
imagine 513 vb.
concent *agreement* 24 adj.
melody 410 n.

concentrate *augment* 36 vb.
congregate 74 vb.
focus 76 vb.
centralize 225 vb.
converge 293 vb.
think 449 vb.
be attentive 455 vb.
concentration
centrality 225 n.
convergence 293 n.
condensation 324 n.
resolution 599 n.
perseverence 600 n.
assiduity 678 n.
(see concentrate)
concentration camp
prison camp 748 n.
concentric *parallel* 219 adj.
central 225 adj.
concept *idea* 451 n.
opinion 485 n.
ideality 513 n.
conception *product* 164 n.
propagation 164 n.
intellect 447 n.
thought 449 n.
idea 451 n.
opinion 485 n.
ideality 513 n.
conceptual *mental* 447 adj.
conceptualism
philosophy 449 n.
conceptualize
cognize 447 vb.
concern *relation* 9 n.
be related 9 vb.
affairs 154 n.
topic 452 n.
function, business 622 n.
importance 638 n.
corporation 708 n.
merchant 794 n.
shop 796 n.
worry 825 n.
concern, of no
irrelative 10 adj.
concert *agreement* 24 n.
adjust 24 vb.
concurrence 181 n.
melody 410 n.
harmonize 410 vb.
music 412 n.
musical instrument 414 n.
plot 623 vb.
prepare 669 vb.
concertina *organ* 414 n.
concerto *duet* 412 n.
concert-party *actor* 594 n.
party 708 n.
concert pitch
musical note 410 n.

concert-room
  place of amusement 837 n.
concession *offset* 31 n.
  laxity 734 n.
  lenity 736 n.
  consent 758 n.
  compromise 770 n.
  discount 810 n.
concessional
  given 781 adj.
  cheap 812 adj.
concessionnaire
  recipient 782 n.
conch *horn* 414 n.
conchoid *curve* 248 n.
conchy *pacifist* 717 n.
concierge *janitor* 264 n.
  servant 742 n.
  keeper 749 n.
conciliar
  parliamentary 692 adj.
  ecclesiastical 985 adj.
conciliate *induce* 612 vb.
  pacify 719 vb.
  content 828 vb.
  be courteous 884 vb.
  atone 941 vb.
conciliation *concord* 710 n.
  (*see* conciliate)
conciliatory
  pacificatory 719 adj.
concinnity *elegance* 575 n.
  beauty 841 n.
concise *short* 204 adj.
  compendious 592 adj.
conciseness
  imperspicuity 568 n.
  conciseness 569 n.
conclave *assembly* 74 n.
  conference 584 n.
  council 692 n.
  synod 985 n.
conclude *terminate* 69 vb.
  judge 480 vb.
  be resolute 599 vb.
  contract 765 vb.
conclusion *sequel* 67 n.
  finality 69 n.
  argumentation 475 n.
  judgment 480 n.
  opinion 485 n.
  affirmation 532 n.
  completion 725 n.
conclusions, try
  argue 475 vb.
conclusive *positive* 473 adj.
  demonstrating 478 adj.
  judicial 480 adj.
  completive 725 adj.
  commanding 737 adj.
concoct *imagine* 513 vb.

fake 541 vb.
  write 586 vb.
  plan 623 vb.
concoction
  production 164 n.
  potion 301 n.
  untruth 543 n.
  maturation 669 n.
concomitance
  accompaniment 89 adv.
  synchronism 123 n.
  contiguity 202 n.
concomitant *adjunct* 40 n.
  concomitant 89 n.
  synchronous 123 adj.
  concurrent 181 adj.
concord *agreement* 24 n.
  mixture 43 n.
  order 60 n.
  concurrence 181 n.
  melody 410 n.
  consensus 488 n.
  co-operation 706 n.
  concord 710 vb.
  friendliness 880 n.
concordance
  agreement 24 n.
  dictionary 559 n.
concordat *treaty* 765 n.
concourse *junction* 45 n.
  assembly 74 n.
  convergence 293 n.
  contest 716 n.
concrescence *junction* 45 n.
concrete *real* 1 adj.
  substantial 3 adj.
  coherence 48 n.
  cohesive 48 adj.
  definite 80 adj.
  formed 243 adj.
  material 319 adj.
  solid body 324 n.
  dense 324 adj.
  hard 326 adj.
  building material 631 n.
concreteness
  substantiality 3 n.
  materiality 319 n.
  density 324 n.
concretion *substance* 3 n.
  junction 45 n.
  condensation 324 n.
  solid body 324 n.
concubinage
  type of marriage 894 n.
  illicit love 951 n.
concubinary
  matrimonial 894 adj.
  extramarital 951 adj.
concubine *loved one* 887 n.
  kept woman 952 n.

concubitous
  marriageable 894 adj.
concupiscence *libido* 859 n.
  unchastity 951 n.
concupiscent
  desiring 859 adj.
  loving 887 adj.
  lecherous 951 adj.
concur *accord* 24 vb.
  accompany 89 vb.
  concur 181 vb.
  be parallel 219 vb.
  assent 488 vb.
concurrence *junction* 45 n.
  combination 50 n.
  assembly 74 n.
  accompaniment 89 n.
  synchronism 123 n.
  eventuality 154 n.
  concurrence 181 n.
  convergence 293 n.
  assent 488 n.
  co-operation 706 n.
concurrent
  concurrent 181 adj.
  (*see* concurrence)
concurrently
  synchronously 123 adv.
  concurrently 181 adv.
concuss *strike* 279 vb.
  render insensible 375 vb.
concussion *impulse* 279 n.
condemn *curse* 899 vb.
  condemn 961 vb.
  punish 963 vb.
  hereticate 977 vb.
condemnable
  wrong 914 adj.
  blameworthy 924 adj.
  accusable 928 adj.
condemned
  dilapidated 655 adj.
  hated 888 adj.
  condemned 961 adj.
  heterodox 977 adj.
condemned cell
  lock-up 748 n.
condemn oneself
  be penitent 939 vb.
condensation
  coherence 48 n.
  crowd 74 n.
  contraction 198 n.
  condensation 324 n.
  solid body 324 n.
condense
  make smaller 198 vb.
  be dense 324 vb.
  be concise 569 vb.
  abstract 592 vb.
condescend *consent* 758 vb.

demean oneself 867 vb.
be proud 871 vb.
be humble 872 vb.
be courteous 884 vb.
show respect 920 vb.
condescend to
notice 455 vb.
condescension pride 871 n.
humility 872 n.
courtesy 884 n.
condign due 915 adj.
condiment adjunct 40 n.
food 301 n.
condiment 389 n.
pleasurableness 826 n.
condition state 7 n.
composition 56 n.
limit 236 vb.
qualification 468 n.
supposition 512 n.
teach 534 vb.
health 650 n.
fetter 747 vb.
give terms 766 vb.
conditional
qualifying 468 adj.
uncertain 474 adj.
conditional 766 adj.
conditionally
conditionally 7 adv.
relatively 9 adv.
provided 468 adv.
conditioned
involuntary 596 adj.
conditioned reflex
incogitance 450 n.
necessity 596 n.
habituation 610 n.
condition, in
athletic 162 adj.
fleshy 195 adj.
healthy 650 adj.
conditioning teaching 534 n.
habituation 610 n.
conditions conditions 766 n.
condole feel 818 vb.
lament 836 vb.
pity 905 vb.
condolence (see condole)
condominium
governance 733 n.
joint possession 775 n.
condone be patient 823 vb.
forgive 909 vb.
condottiere
leader 690 n.
militarist 722 n.
conduce conduce 156 vb.
tend 179 vb.
concur 181 vb.
promote 285 vb.

make likely 471 vb.
be useful 640 vb.
be expedient 642 vb.
aid 703 vb.
permit 756 vb.
conduct come before 64 vb.
accompany 89 vb.
transfer 272 vb.
carry 273 vb.
precede 283 vb.
play music 413 vb.
mien 445 n.
practice 610 n.
action 676 n.
conduct 688 n.
manage 689 vb.
conduction
transference 272 n.
motion 265 n.
conductive
transferable 272 adj.
conductivity motion 265 n.
conduct oneself
behave 688 vb.
conductor
timekeeper 117 n.
driver 268 n.
carrier 273 n.
musician 413 n.
orchestra 413 n.
leader 690 n.
conduit outlet 298 n.
passage 305 n.
irrigator 341 n.
conduit 351 n.
condyle, condylema
swelling 253 n.
cone cone 252 n.
confabulate speak 579 vb.
converse 584 vb.
confection
a mixture 43 n.
product 164 n.
sweet 392 n.
confectioner caterer 633 n.
confectionery pastry 301 n.
sweet 392 n.
confederate
co-operate 706 vb.
colleague 707 n.
corporate 708 adj.
confederation
combination 50 n.
association 706 n.
society 708 n.
polity 733 n.
confer argue 475 vb.
confer 584 vb.
consult 691 vb.
give 781 vb.
conference enquiry 459 n.

speech 579 n.
conference 584 n.
advice 691 n.
confess testify 466 vb.
believe 485 vb.
assent 488 vb.
confess 526 vb.
affirm 532 vb.
be guilty 936 vb.
be penitent 939 vb.
perform ritual 988 vb.
confession creed 485 n.
party 708 n.
penance 941 n.
(see confess)
confessional credal 485 adj.
disclosure 526 n.
tribunal 956 n.
church interior 990 n.
confessions biography 590 n.
confessor questioner 459 n.
pietist 979 n.
pastor 986 n.
confidant teacher 537 n.
adviser 691 n.
colleague 707 n.
retainer 742 n.
close friend 880 n.
confide believe 485 vb.
inform 524 vb.
divulge 526 vb.
be artless 699 vb.
hope 852 vb.
confide in consult 691 vb.
confidence
positiveness 473 n.
belief 485 n.
expectation 507 n.
information 524 n.
secret 530 n.
safety 660 n.
credit 802 n.
hope 852 n.
confidence trick
trickery 542 n.
confident positive 473 adj.
believing 485 adj.
expectant 507 adj.
assertive 532 adj.
hoping 852 adj.
unfearing 855 adj.
confidential
concealed 525 adj.
confiding believing 485 adj.
credulous 487 adj.
artless 699 adj.
configuration form 243 n.
configurationism
psychology 447 n.
confine region 184 n.
place 185 n.

circumscribe 232vb.
hem 234vb.
limit 236vb.
conceal 525vb.
make insufficient 636vb.
imprison 747vb.
seclude 883vb.
confined
narrow-minded 481adj.
sick 651adj.
(*see* confine)
confinement
obstetrics 164n.
detention 747n.
seclusion 883n.
confines *near place* 200n.
edge 234n.
confirm *stabilize* 153vb.
strengthen 162vb.
corroborate 466vb.
make certain 473vb.
judge 480vb.
endorse 488vb.
affirm 532vb.
consent 758vb.
promise 764vb.
contract 765vb.
grant claims 915vb.
vindicate 927vb.
make legal 953vb.
make pious 979vb.
perform ritual 988vb.
confirmation
Christian rite 988n.
(*see* confirm)
confirmatory
evidential 466adj.
confiscate *deprive* 786vb.
punish 963vb.
confiscatory *taking* 786adj.
punitive 963adj.
conflagration *fire* 379n.
conflation
combination 50n.
conflict *contrariety* 14n.
differ 15vb.
disagreement 25n.
counteraction 182n.
opposition 704n.
quarrel 709n., vb.
contention 716n.
enmity 881n.
confluence *junction* 45n.
convergence 293n.
current 350n.
conflux *assembly* 74n.
convergence 293n.
conform *be uniform* 16vb.
do likewise 20vb.
adjust 24vb.
conform 83vb.

acquiesce 488vb.
obey 739vb.
observe 768vb.
be servile 879vb.
be orthodox 976vb.
conformable
agreeing 24adj.
regular 81adj.
conformable 83adj.
conformance
(*see* conformity)
conformation
composition 56n.
form 243n.
conforming
orthodox 976adj.
pious 979adj.
conformist
conformist 83n.
assenter 488n.
the orthodox 976n.
pietist 979n.
conformity
uniformity 16n.
regularity 81n.
conformity 83n.
concurrence 181n.
observance 768n.
orthodoxism 976n.
piety 979n.
confound *derange* 63vb.
destroy 165vb.
not discriminate 464vb.
confute 479vb.
defeat 727vb.
frighten 854vb.
be wonderful 864vb.
curse 899vb.
confounded
damnable 645adj.
confoundedly
extremely 32adv.
confraternity
community 708n.
confrère *colleague* 707n.
friend 880n.
confront *be present* 189vb.
be in front 237vb.
be opposite 240vb.
compare 462vb.
show 522vb.
withstand 704vb.
resist 715vb.
confrontation
comparison 462n.
confronting
opposite 240adj.
Confucianism
religious faith 973n.
Confucius
religious teacher 973n.

confuse *bedevil* 63vb.
blur 440vb.
distract 456vb.
not discriminate 464vb.
puzzle 474vb.
be unintelligible 517vb.
confused *mixed* 43adj.
orderless 61adj.
shadowy 419adj.
ill-seen 444adj.
indiscriminate 464adj.
ill-reasoned 477adj.
ignorant 491adj.
imperspicuous 568adj.
confusion *medley* 43n.
confusion 61n.
havoc 165n.
amorphism 244n.
commotion 318n.
psychopathy 503n.
humiliation 872n.
confutation
rejoinder 460n.
counter-evidence 467n.
argumentation 475n.
confutation 479n.
negation 533n.
conga *dance* 837n.
congé *valediction* 296n.
deposal 752n.
non-liability 919n.
congeal *be dense* 324vb.
refrigerate 382vb.
congener *kinsman* 11n.
analogue 18n.
congenerous *akin* 11adj.
congenial *genetic* 5adj.
relative 9adj.
agreeing 24adj.
pleasant 376adj.
concordant 710adj.
lovable 887adj.
congenital *genetic* 5adj.
with affections 817adj.
congeries
accumulation 74n.
congest *superabound* 637vb.
congestion *crowd* 74n.
redundance 637n.
conglaciation
refrigeration 382n.
conglomerate *cohere* 48vb.
bring together 74vb.
solid body 324n.
rock 344n.
conglutination
coherence 48n.
congratulate
gratulate 886vb.
congratulate oneself
be content 828vb.

rejoice 835 vb.
feel pride 871 vb.
congratulation
rejoicing 835 n.
celebration 876 n.
courteous act 884 n.
congratulation 886 n.
congregate
congregate 74 vb.
meet 295 vb.
congregation
assembly 74 n.
council 692 n.
church member 976 n.
worshipper 981 n.
laity 987 n.
congregational
laical 987 adj.
Congregational
Protestant 976 adj.
Congregationalism
Protestantism 976 n.
congress *junction* 45 n.
convergence 293 n.
council 692 n.
parliament 692 n.
congressional
parliamentary 692 adj.
congressman
councillor 692 n.
congruence, congruity
identity 13 n.
similarity 18 n.
conformance 24 n.
congruent *agreeing* 24 adj.
equal 28 adj.
symmetrical 245 adj.
congruity (*see* congruence)
conical *rotund* 252 adj.
tapering 256 adj.
convergent 293 adj.
conic section *curve* 248 n.
conjectural
suppositional 512 adj.
conjecture
attribution 158 n.
assume 471 vb.
uncertainty 474 n.
estimate 480 vb.
conjecture 512 n.
suppose 512 vb.
conjoin *add* 3 vb.
mix 43 vb.
join 45 vb.
conjugal *loving* 887 adj.
matrimonial 894 adj.
conjugate
combined 50 adj.
dual 90 adj.
verbal 559 adj.
parse 564 vb.

conjugation
arrangement 62 n.
(*see* conjugate)
conjunct *conjunct* 45 adj.
combined 50 adj.
indivisible 52 adj.
accompanying 89 adj.
conjunction *junction* 45 n.
concurrence 181 n.
contiguity 202 n.
part of speech 564 n.
conjunctive
grammatical 564 adj.
conjuration *entreaty* 761 n.
sorcery 983 n.
conjure *deceive* 542 vb.
entreat 761 vb.
practise sorcery 983 vb.
conjure into
convert 147 vb.
conjure up *imagine* 513 vb.
conjuror *imitator* 20 n.
conjuror 545 n.
entertainer 594 n.
slyboots 698 n.
sorcerer 983 n.
conk *face* 237 n.
projection 254 n.
conk out *fail* 728 vb.
con-man *trickster* 545 n.
connatural *genetic* 5 adj.
akin 11 adj.
connect *relate* 9 vb.
connect 45 vb.
continuate 71 vb.
be contiguous 202 vb.
connectedness
coherence 48 n.
connection *relation* 9 n.
consanguinity 11 n.
bond 47 n.
(*see* connect)
conning tower *view* 438 n.
connivance
concurrence 181 n.
co-operation 706 n.
laxity 734 n.
lenity 736 n.
permission 756 n.
connive *disregard* 458 vb.
patronize 703 vb.
connoisseur *eater* 301 n.
collector 492 n.
expert 696 n.
man of taste 846 n.
connoisseurship
good taste 846 n.
fastidiousness 862 n.
connotation
connotation 514 n.
meaning 514 n.

indication 547 n.
connotative
semantic 514 adj.
indicating 547 adj.
connote *mean* 514 vb.
imply 523 vb.
connubial
matrimonial 894 adj.
conoid *cone* 252 n.
conoidal, conoid
rotund 252 adj.
conquer *overmaster* 727 vb.
take 786 vb.
conquered, the *loser* 728 n.
conqueror *victor* 727 n.
possessor 776 n.
conquest *victory* 727 n.
defeat 728 n.
subjection 745 n.
loved one 887 n.
consanguinity *relation* 9 n.
consanguinity 11 n.
parentage 169 n.
conscience *knowledge* 490 n.
motive 612 n.
warning 664 n.
conscience 917 n.
conscience-clause
non-liability 919 n.
conscienceless
dishonest 930 adj.
wicked 934 adj.
impenitent 940 adj.
conscience-money
gift 781 n.
restitution 787 n.
atonement 941 n.
conscientious
careful 457 adj.
observant 768 adj.
fastidious 862 adj.
dutied 917 adj.
trustworthy 929 adj.
conscientious objector
dissentient 489 n.
opponent 705 n.
pacifist 717 n.
conscious *sentient* 374 adj.
mental 447 adj.
attentive 455 adj.
knowing 490 adj.
conscript *go to war* 718 vb.
soldier 722 n.
compel 740 vb.
conscription
war measures 718 n.
compulsion 740 n.
consecrate *offer* 759 vb.
give 781 vb.
dignify 866 vb.
sanctify 979 vb.

offer worship 981vb.
ecclesiasticize 985vb.
perform ritual 988vb.
consecrated
disinterested 931adj.
consecrate to *use* 673vb.
consecration *offering* 781n.
Holy Communion 988n.
Christian rite 988n.
consecution *sequence* 65n.
continuity 71n.
consecutive *sequent* 65adj.
continuous 71adj.
consensus *agreement* 24n.
concurrence 181n.
consensus 488n.
consent *agreement* 24n.
accord 24vb.
assent 488n.,vb.
endorse 488vb.
willingness 597n.
be induced 612vb.
obey 739vb.
permission 756n.
consent 758n.,vb.
approbation 923n.
consentaneous
agreeing 24adj.
assenting 488adj.
consentient *agreeing* 24adj.
assenting 488adj.
consequence *sequel* 67n.
eventuality 154n.
effect 157n.
importance 638n.
consequential
eventual 154adj.
caused 157adj.
demonstrating 478adj.
ostentatious 875adj.
consequently
consequently 157adv.
reasonably 475adv.
conservancy *cleansing* 648n.
conservation
permanence 144n.
forestry 366n.
storage 632n.
preservation 666n.
conservatism
permanence 144n.
habit 610n.
preservation 666n.
conservative
permanent 144adj.
depreciating 483adj.
preserving 666adj.
political party 708n.
sectional 708adj.
cautious 858adj.
conservatoire *music* 412n.

academy 539n.
conservator *protector* 660n.
conservatory
seedbed 156n.
arbour 194n.
garden 370n.
heater 383n.
conserve *sweet* 392n.
sanitate 652vb.
safeguard 660vb.
preserve 666vb.
consider *meditate* 449vb.
notice 455vb.
enquire 459vb.
estimate 480vb.
opine 485vb.
give 781vb.
considerable
substantial 3adj.
great 32adj.
many 104adj.
large 195adj.
important 638adj.
considerate
thoughtful 449adj.
careful 457adj.
well-bred 848adj.
amiable 884adj.
benevolent 897adj.
disinterested 931adj.
consideration
quid pro quo 150n.
meditation 449n.
qualification 468n.
importance 638n.
gift 781n.
courtesy 884n.
benevolence 897n.
respect 920n.
disinterestedness 931n.
consideration, be a
motivate 612vb.
consideration, of
important 688adj.
consideration, under
preparatory 669adj.
consign *send* 272vb.
commission 751vb.
consignee *agent* 686n.
consignee 754n.
deputy 755n.
recipient 782n.
purchaser 972n.
consignment
thing transferred 272n.
transfer 780n.
giving 781n.
consignor *seller* 793n.
transferrer 272n.
consistence *density* 324n.
consistency

uniformity 16n.
regularity 81n.
truth 494n.
consistent *rational* 475adj.
(*see* consistency)
consist in *be* 1vb.
consist of *comprise* 78vb.
consistory *council* 692n.
synod 985n.
consolation *relief* 831n.
condolence 905n.
consolatory
relieving 831adj.
console *stand* 218n.
shelf 218n.
relieve 831vb.
cheer 833vb.
pity 905vb.
consolidate *join* 45vb.
cohere 48vb.
bring together 74vb.
centralize 225vb.
be dense 324vb.
abstract 592vb.
consolidation
contraction 198n.
association 706n.
(*see* consolidate)
consommé *soup* 301n.
consonance *agreement* 24n.
melody 410n.
consonant
speech sound 398n.
consonantal
sounding 398adj.
literal 558adj.
consort *concomitant* 89n.
spouse 894n.
consortium
agreement 24n.
association 706n.
consortship
accompaniment 89n.
conspection
inspection 438n.
conspectus *whole* 52n.
generality 79n.
view 438n.
compendium 592n.
conspicuous
well-seen 443adj.
manifest 522adj.
notable 638adj.
noteworthy 866adj.
conspiracy
combination 50n.
concurrence 181n.
secrecy 525n.
plot 623n.
co-operation 706n.
compact 765n.

conspirator *deceiver* 545n.
  planner 623n.
conspiratorial
  stealthy 525adj.
  planning 623adj.
conspire *combine* 50vb.
  (*see* conspiracy)
constable *police* 955n.
constabulary *police* 955n.
constancy *uniformity* 16n.
  stability 153n.
  resolution 599n.
  perseverance 600n.
  obstinacy 602n.
  loyalty 739n.
  probity 929n.
constant
  characteristic 5adj.
  identity 13n.
  identical 13adj.
  uniform 16adj.
  continuous 71adj.
  regular 81adj.
  lasting 113adj.
  perpetual 115adj.
  frequent 139adj.
  periodical 141adj.
  unchangeable 153adj.
  coloured 425adj.
  accurate 494adj.
  resolute 599adj.
  persevering 600adj.
  obedient 739n.
  trustworthy 929adj.
constellation *group* 74n.
  star 321n.
  person of repute 866n.
consternation *fear* 854n.
  wonder 864n.
constipate *be dense* 324vb.
constipation *closure* 264n.
  condensation 324n.
  indigestion 651n.
constituency *district* 184n.
  electorate 605n.
constituent *part* 53n.
  component 58n.
  included 78adj.
  electorate 605n.
constituents
  contents 193n.
constitute *constitute* 56vb.
  be included 78vb.
  produce 164vb.
constitution *character* 5n.
  composition 56n.
  inclusion 78n.
  structure 331n.
  precept 693n.
  polity 733n.
  law 953n.

constitutional
  pedestrianism 267n.
  habit 610n.
  governmental 733adj.
  due 915adj.
  legal 953adj.
constitutionalism
  government 733n.
  legality 953n.
constraint
  compulsion 740n.
  subjection 745n.
  restraint 747n.
  modesty 874n.
constrict *tighten* 45vb.
  make smaller 198vb.
constriction
  narrowing 206n.
constrictor
  compressor 198n.
construction
  composition 56n.
  arrangement 62n.
  production 164n.
  structure 331n.
  conjecture 512n.
  interpretation 520n.
constructional
  structural 331adj.
constructive
  productive 164adj.
  evidential 466adj.
  interpretive 520adj.
  aiding 703adj.
constructor
  producer 167n.
  doer 676n.
construe *translation* 520n.
  interpret 520vb.
  parse 564vb.
consubstantial
  similar 18adj.
consubstantiation
  the sacrament 988n.
consuetude *habit* 610n.
consul *official* 690n.
  envoy 754n.
consulate
  magistrature 733n.
  envoy 754n.
consult *confer* 584vb.
  consult 691vb.
  co-operate 706vb.
consultant *sage* 500n.
  oracle 511n.
  teacher 537n.
  doctor 658n.
  adviser 691n.
  expert 696n.
consultation
  preparation 669n.

  advice 691n.
consultative
  advising 691adj.
consulting room
  hospital 658n.
consumable *used* 673adj.
consume *bate* 37vb.
  decompose 51vb.
  disable 161vb.
  destroy 165vb.
  consume 165vb.
  eat 301vb.
  require 627vb.
  waste 634vb.
  impair 655vb.
  use, dispose of 673vb.
  misuse 675vb.
  expend 806vb.
consumer *eater* 301n.
  purchaser 792n.
consumer goods
  merchandise 795n.
consummate
  consummate 32adj.
  unite with 45vb.
  complete 54adj.
  crown 213vb.
  perfect 646adj.,vb.
  carry through 725vb.
consummation
  coition 45n.
  completeness 54n.
  (*see* consummate)
consumption
  decrement 42n.
  thinness 206n.
  phthisis 651n.
  loss 772n.
  (*see* consume)
consumptive
  sick person 651n.
  diseased 651adj.
contact *junction* 45n.
  connect 45vb.
  be contiguous 202vb.
  informant 524n.
  communicate 524vb.
  messenger 531n.
contact lens
  eyeglass 442n.
contact man
  messenger 531n.
contact print
  copy, duplicate 22n.
contagion *influence* 178n.
  transference 272n.
  infection 651n.
  plague 651n.
  insalubrity 653n.
  impairment 655n.
contagious (*see* contagion)

contain *contain* 56 vb.
 comprise 78 vb.
 circumscribe 232 vb.
 possess 773 vb.
container *receptacle* 194 n.
 storage 632 n.
containment
 circumjacence 230 n.
 circumscription 232 n.
 retention 778 n.
contain oneself
 be temperate 942 vb.
contaminate
 be mixed 43 vb.
 influence 178 vb.
 transfer 272 vb.
 make unclean 649 vb.
 impair 655 vb.
contamination
 badness 645 n.
 (*see* contaminate)
contango *delay* 136 n.
 discount 810 n.
contemn *shame* 867 vb.
 hate 888 vb.
 despise 922 vb.
 detract 926 vb.
contemplate
 meditate 449 vb.
 expect 507 vb.
 intend 617 vb.
 worship 981 vb.
contemplation *look* 438 n.
 attention 455 n.
 (*see* contemplate)
contemplative *pietist* 979 n.
 worshipper 981 n.
contemporaneity
 accompaniment 89 n.
 time 108 n.
 present time 121 n.
 synchronism 123 n.
 modernism 126 n.
contemporary
 present 121 adj.
 contemporary 123 n.
 synchronous 123 adj.
contempt
 object of scorn 867 n.
 pride 871 n.
 contempt 922 n.
 detraction 926 n.
contemptibility
 odium 888 n.
 despisedness 922 n.
contemptible *inferior* 35 adj.
 unimportant 639 adj.
 trivial 639 adj.
 ridiculous 849 adj.
 discreditable 867 adj.
 disreputable 867 adj.

contemptible 922 adj.
 rascally 930 adj.
contempt of, in
 in defiance of 25 adv.
contemptuous
 insolent 878 adj.
 despising 922 adj.
 detracting 926 adj.
contend *affirm* 532 vb.
 oppose 704 vb.
 contend 716 vb.
contender *athlete* 162 n.
 essayer 671 n.
 opponent 705 n.
 contender 716 n.
 combatant 722 n.
contend for
 vindicate 927 vb.
content *component* 58 n.
 structure 331 n.
 euphoria 376 n.
 comfortable 376 adj.
 willing 597 adj.
 suffice 635 vb.
 pacify 719 vb.
 inexcitability 823 n.
 content 828 n., adj., vb.
 cheer 833 vb.
 approving 923 adj.
contented *content* 828 adj.
contenting
 contenting 828 adj.
contention *question* 459 n.
 opposition 704 n.
 quarrel 709 n.
 contention 716 n.
contentious
 quarrelling 709 adj.
 contending 716 adj.
contentment *euphoria* 376 n.
 sufficiency 635 n.
 content 828 n.
contents *contents* 193 n.
 topic 452 n.
 meaning 514 n.
 compendium 592 n.
 property 777 n.
conterminous
 ending 69 adj.
 synchronous 123 adj.
 contiguous 202 adj.
contesseration
 assemblage 74 n.
contest *athletics* 162 n.
 contend 716 vb.
 sport 837 n.
contestant *opponent* 705 n.
contester *contender* 716 n.
context *circumstance* 8 n.
 relation 9 n.
 concomitant 89 n.

meaning 514 n.
 connotation 514 n.
contextual
 circumstantial 8 adj.
 relative 9 adj.
contexture *texture* 331 n.
contiguity *junction* 45 n.
 nearness 200 n.
 contiguity 202 n.
contiguous (*see* contiguity)
continence
 temperance 942 n.
 purity 950 n.
continent *region* 184 n.
 land 344 n.
 temperate 942 adj.
 pure 950 adj.
continental *foreigner* 59 n.
 extraneous 59 adj.
 regional 184 adj.
 dweller 191 n.
 inland 344 adj.
continental shelf
 territory 184 n.
 shore 344 n.
contingency
 extrinsicality 6 n.
 eventuality 154 n.
 chance 159 n.
 liability 180 n.
 possibility 469 n.
 uncertainty 474 n.
 expectation 507 n.
contingent *extrinsic* 6 adj.
 circumstantial 8 adj.
 part 53 n.
 eventual 154 adj.
 caused 157 adj.
 casual 159 adj.
 liable 180 adj.
 qualifying 468 adj.
 possible 469 adj.
 uncertain 474 adj.
 conditional 766 adj.
 portion 783 n.
contingents *aider* 703 n.
 armed force 722 n.
continual *continuous* 71 adj.
 perpetual 115 adj.
 frequent 139 adj.
 unceasing 146 adj.
continuance
 uniformity 16 n.
 sequence 65 n.
 course of time 111 n.
 durability 113 n.
 perpetuity 115 n.
 permanence 144 n.
 continuance 146 n.
 perseverance 600 n.
 habit 610 n.

continuate *continuate* 71 vb.
  sustain 146 vb.
continuation *adjunct* 40 n.
  arrangement 62 n.
  sequence 65 n.
  sequel 67 n.
  continuance 146 n.
  reading matter 589 n.
continue *be* 1 vb.
  run on 71 vb.
  lengthen 203 vb.
  (*see* continuance)
continuity *coherence* 48 n.
  order 60 n.
  continuity 71 n.
  recurrence 106 n.
  frequency 139 n.
  periodicity 141 n.
  continuance 146 n.
  contiguity 202 n.
continuous
  (*see* continuity)
continuum *space* 183 n.
contort *distort* 246 vb.
contorted
  convoluted 251 adj.
contortionist
  entertainer 594 n.
contour *outline* 233 n.
  form 243 n.
  feature 445 n.
contra *contrarily* 14 adv.
contraband
  prohibited 757 adj.
  booty 790 n.
  illegal 954 adj.
contraception
  unproductivity 172 n.
  hindrance 702 n.
contraceptive
  hindrance 702 n.
contract
  bate, decrease 37 vb.
  become small 198 vb.
  shorten 204 vb.
  make thin 206 vb.
  be dense 324 vb.
  be concise 569 vb.
  undertaking 672 n.
  compact 765 n.
  make terms 766 vb.
  acquire 771 vb.
  bargain 791 vb.
contract bridge
  card game 837 n.
contractile
  contracted 198 adj.
contraction
  diminution 37 n.
  contraction 198 n.
  closure 264 n.

writing 568 n.
conciseness 569 n.
compendium 592 n.
contractor *essayer* 671 n.
  signatory 765 n.
contractual *agreeing* 24 adj.
  contractual 765 adj.
contradict
  be contrary 14 vb.
  disagree 25 vb.
  answer 460 vb.
  tell against 467 vb.
  confute 479 vb.
  dissent 489 vb.
  negate 533 vb.
  oppose 704 vb.
contradiction
  (*see* contradict)
contradictory
  illogical 477 adj.
  negative 533 adj.
contradistinction
  contrariety 14 n.
  differentiation 15 n.
contra-indicate
  be contrary 14 vb.
  tell against 467 vb.
  warn 664 n.
contra-indication
  counter-evidence 467 n.
contralto *resonance* 404 n.
  vocalist 413 n.
contraposition
  contrariety 14 n.
  difference 15 n.
  reversion 148 n.
  inversion 221 n.
  contraposition 240 n.
contraption
  contrivance 623 n.
contrapuntal
  musical 412 adj.
  musicianly 413 adj.
contrapuntist
  musician 413 n.
contraries *polarity* 14 n.
  opposites 704 n.
contrariety *irrelation* 10 n.
  contrariety 14 n.
  non-uniformity 17 n.
  disagreement 25 n.
  counteraction 182 n.
  inversion 221 n.
  contraposition 240 n.
  counter-evidence 467 n.
  connotation 514 n.
  opposition 704 n.
contrarious
  unconformable 84 adj.
  opposing 704 adj.
contrariwise

against 240 adv.
contrary *contrary* 14 adj.
  different 15 adj.
  disagreeing 25 adj.
  separate 46 adj.
  counteracting 182 adj.
  opposite 240 adj.
  countervailing 467 adj.
  negative 533 adj.
  capricious 604 adj.
  hindering 702 adj.
  opposing 704 adj.
  adverse 731 adj.
contrary, on the
  no 489 adv.
contrast *contrariety* 14 n.
  difference 15 n.
  differ 15 vb.
  non-uniformity 17 n.
  dissimilarity 19 n.
  compare 462 vb.
  trope 519 n.
  opposition 704 n.
contravallation
  defences 713 n.
contravene
  be contrary 14 vb.
  tell against 467 vb.
  negate 533 vb.
  be obstructive 702 vb.
contravention
  lawbreaking 954 n.
  (*see* contravene)
contrecoup *recoil* 280 n.
contrectation *touch* 378 n.
contretemps
  intempestivity 138 n.
  hitch 702 n.
  ill fortune 731 n.
contribute *concur* 181 vb.
  give 781 vb.
  pay 804 vb.
contribute to
  augment 36 vb.
  add 38 vb.
  conduce 156 vb.
  tend 179 vb.
  aid, patronize 703 vb.
contributing
  influential 178 adj.
  concurrent 181 adj.
contribution
  increment 36 n.
  co-operation 706 n.
  giving, offering 781 n.
  payment 804 n.
contributor *cause* 156 n.
  correspondent 588 n.
  author 589 n.
  dissertator 591 n.
  giver 781 n.

contributory
  additional 38 n.
contrition *regret* 830 n.
  penitence 939 n.
contrivance
  arrangement 62 n.
  idea 451 n.
  contrivance 623 n.
  plan 623 n.
  instrument 628 n.
  means 629 n.
  tool 630 n.
  tactics 688 n.
  skill 694 n.
  stratagem 698 n.
contrive *produce* 164 vb.
  predetermine 608 vb.
  find means 629 vb.
contrived
  predetermined 608 adj.
contriver *planner* 623 n.
control *order* 60 vb.
  be able 160 n.
  moderate 177 vb.
  influence 178 n.
  comparison 462 n.
  do 676 vb.
  management 689 n.
  skill 694 n.
  hindrance 702 n.
  governance 733 n.
  rule 733 vb.
  take authority 733 vb.
  restrain 747 vb.
  tranquillize 823 vb.
  ghost 970 n.
  spiritualism 984 n.
controlled
  involuntary 596 adj.
  predetermined 608 adj.
  restrained 747 adj.
  impassive 820 adj.
  inexcitable 823 adj.
controller *doer* 676 n.
  director 690 n.
control oneself
  be temperate 942 vb.
controls *aircraft* 276 n.
  directorship 689 n.
controversial
  uncertain 474 adj.
  arguing 475 adj.
  quarrelling 709 adj.
controversialist
  reasoner 475 n.
  combatant 722 n.
controversy
  disagreement 25 n.
  question 459 n.
  argument 475 n.
  dissent 489 n.

conference 584 n.
  quarrel 709 n.
  contention 716 n.
controvert *argue* 475 vb.
  negate 533 vb.
controvertible
  uncertain 474 adj.
  arguing 475 adj.
contumacious
  disobedient 738 adj.
  schismatical 978 adj.
  (*see* contumacy)
contumacy
  obstinacy 602 n.
  resistance 715 n.
  impenitence 940 n.
contumelious
  insolent 878 adj.
  ungracious 885 adj.
  maledicent 899 adj.
  disrespectful 921 adj.
  despising 922 adj.
  detracting 926 adj.
contumely *insolence* 878 n.
  scurrility 899 n.
  disrespect 921 n.
  detraction 926 n.
contuse *pulverize* 332 vb.
contusion
  pulverulence 332 n.
  wound 655 n.
conundrum
  equivocalness 518 n.
  enigma 530 n.
conurbate *urbanize* 192 vb.
conurbation *district* 184 n.
  housing 192 n.
convalesce *grow* 36 vb.
  be strong 162 vb.
  get healthy 650 vb.
  be restored 656 vb.
convalescent home
  hospital 658 n.
convection
  transference 272 n.
convene
  bring together 74 vb.
  command 737 vb.
convenience
  opportunity 137 n.
  euphoria 376 n.
  means 629 n.
  utility 640 n.
  expedience 642 n.
  leisure 681 n.
  facility 701 n.
convenient
  (*see* convenience)
convent *house* 192 n.
  monastery 986 n.
conventicle *assembly* 74 n.

meeting place 192 n.
  council 692 n.
  sect 978 n.
  church 990 n.
convention *regularity* 81 n.
  conformity 83 n.
  conference 584 n.
  practice 610 n.
  council 692 n.
  precept 693 n.
  pacification 719 n.
  compact 765 n.
  treaty 765 n.
  etiquette 848 n.
conventional
  orthodox 976 adj.
  (*see* convention)
conventionalist
  conformist 83 n.
  habitué 610 n.
conventionality
  conformity 83 n.
  (*see* convention)
conventionalize
  make conform 83 vb.
conventual *monk* 986 n.
  monastic 986 adj.
converge *congregate* 74 vb.
  focus 76 vb.
  be near 200 vb.
  be narrow 206 vb.
  be oblique 220 vb.
  centralize 225 vb.
  converge 293 vb.
convergence
  junction 45 n.
  (*see* converge)
conversable
  loquacious 581 adj.
  conversing 584 adj.
  well-bred 848 adj.
  sociable 882 adj.
  amiable 884 adj.
conversant *knowing* 490 adj.
conversation *speech* 579 n.
  interlocution 584 n.
conversational
  loquacious 581 adj.
  conversing 584 adj.
conversationalist
  speaker 579 n.
  chatterer 581 n.
  interlocutor 584 n.
  humorist 839 n.
conversation level
  faintness 401 n.
conversations
  conference 584 n.
  advice 691 n.
conversazione
  assembly 74 n.

conference 584n.
amusement 837n.
social gathering 882n.
converse *contrariety* 14n.
countervailing 467adj.
communicate 524vb.
speak 579vb.
be loquacious 581vb.
interlocution 584n.
converse 584vb.
conversely
conversely 467adv.
conversion *change* 143n.
conversion 147n.
production 164n.
teaching 534n.
improvement 654n.
use 673n.
acquisition 771n.
transfer 780n.
convert
make unlike 19vb.
modify 143vb.
changed person 147n.
convert 147vb.
interchange 151vb.
convince 485vb.
learner 538n.
tergiversator 603n.
induce 612vb.
use 673vb.
acquire 771vb.
be penitent 939vb.
make pious 979vb.
convertibility
conversion 147n.
use 673n.
convertible
equivalent 28adj.
interchanged 151adj.
automobile 274n.
convexity *curvature* 248n.
convexity 253n.
convey *move* 265vb.
transfer 272vb.
carry 273vb.
pass 305vb.
mean 514vb.
communicate 524vb.
inform 524vb.
dower 777vb.
not retain 779vb.
convey 780vb.
take away 786vb.
steal 788vb.
conveyance
conveyance 267n.
transport 272n.
transference 272n.
vehicle 274n.
transfer 780n.

taking 786n.
conveyancer
transferrer 272n.
law agent 958n.
conveyor belt *carrier* 273n.
conveyor 274n.
convict *confute* 479vb.
prisoner 750n.
offender 904n.
condemn 961vb.
conviction
positiveness 473n.
confutation 479n.
belief 485n.
teaching 534n.
hope 852n.
condemnation 961n.
convict settlement
prison camp 748n.
convince *influence* 178vb.
make certain 473vb.
demonstrate 478vb.
convince 485vb.
convinced *positive* 473adj.
believing 485adj.
convincing *plausible* 471adj.
demonstrating 478adj.
credible 485adj.
descriptive 590adj.
conviviality *festivity* 837n.
sociability 882n.
convocation *council* 692n.
synod 985n.
convocational
parliamentary 692adj.
convoke
bring together 74vb.
convolution *crossing* 222n.
curvature 248n.
convolution 251n.
convolvulus *coil* 251n.
convoy *concomitant* 89n.
accompany 89vb.
carry 273vb.
protection 660n.
keeper 749n.
convoy, in *with* 89adv.
convulsion
disorder, turmoil 61n.
derangement 63n.
revolution 149n.
outbreak 176n.
spasm 318n.
pang 377n.
convulsive *violent* 176adj.
agitated 318adj.
cony *vermin* 365n.
cony-catcher *hunter* 619n.
coo *ululate* 409vb.
rejoice 835vb.
caress 889vb.

flatter 925vb.
cook *cook* 301vb.
heat 381vb.
fake 541vb.
caterer 633n.
preparer 669n.
mature 669vb.
domestic 742n.
cook-book *cookery* 301n.
cooker *furnace* 383n.
cookery *cookery* 301n.
maturation 669n.
cook-house *chamber* 194n.
heater 383n.
workshop 687n.
cook one's goose
destroy 165vb.
defeat 727vb.
overmaster 727vb.
cookout *meal* 301n.
feasting 301n.
festivity 837n.
cool *moderate* 177vb.
coldness 380n.
refrigerate 382vb.
sane 502adj.
dissuade 613vb.
refresh 685vb.
impassive 820adj.
inexcitable 823adj.
relieve 831vb.
cautious 858adj.
indifferent 860adj.
impertinent 878adj.
inimical 881adj.
unsociable 883adj.
discourteous 885adj.
coolant *refrigerator* 384n.
cooler *moderator* 177n.
refrigerator 384n.
gaol 748n.
coolie *bearer* 273n.
worker 686n.
coolness *coldness* 380n.
(*see* cool)
cool one's heels *wait* 136vb.
coon *vocalist* 413n.
negro 428n.
coop *stable* 192n.
lock-up 748n.
cooper *artisan* 686n.
co-operate *concur* 181vb.
co-operation
combination 50n.
causation 156n.
agency 173n.
concurrence 181n.
assent 488n.
willingness 597n.
instrumentality 628n.
aid 703n.

co-operation 706 n.
concord 710 n.
co-operative
co-operative 706 adj.
society 708 n.
corporate 708 adj.
co-operative society
corporation 708 n.
co-operative system
joint possession 775 n.
co-operator assenter 488 n.
personnel 686 n.
collaborator 707 n.
participator 775 n.
co-opt choose 605 vb.
co-ordinate equal 28 adj.
regularize 62 vb.
gauge 465 n.
metrology 465 n.
coot waterfowl 365 n.
cop protector 660 n.
arrest 747 vb.
police 955 n.
copal resin 357 n.
co-parcener
participator 775 n.
cope vestments 989 n.
cope with be equal 28 vb.
deal with 688 vb.
withstand 704 vb.
coping summit 213 n.
coping stone
summit 213 n.
completion 725 n.
copious prolific 171 adj.
diffuse 570 adj.
plenteous 635 adj.
copper cauldron 194 n.
heater 383 n.
brownness 430 n.
orange 436 n.
protector 660 n.
coinage 797 n.
police 955 n.
copper-coloured
orange 436 adj.
copperhead reptile 365 n.
copperplate engraving 555 n.
written 586 adj.
coppers money 797 n.
coppice wood 366 n.
coprolith excrement 302 n.
copse bunch 74 n.
wood 366 n.
copula bond 47 n.
copulation coition 45 n.
propagation 164 n.
copulative
conjunctive 45 adj.
grammatical 564 adj.
copy analogue 18 n.

copy 20 vb.
copy 22 n.
prototype 23 n.
conform 83 vb.
duplication 91 n.
repeat 106 vb.
reproduce 166 vb.
transpose 272 vb.
news 529 n.
sham 542 n.
represent 551 vb.
write 586 vb.
letterpress 587 n.
reading matter 589 n.
borrow 785 vb.
steal 788 vb.
copybook prototype 23 n.
regular 83 adj.
copycat imitator 20 n.
conformist 83 n.
copyhold
lands, estate 777 n.
proprietary 777 adj.
copy-holder possessor 776 n.
copyist imitator 20 n.
artist 556 n.
penman 586 n.
copyright estate 777 n.
dueness 915 n.
claim 915 vb.
copy-typist imitator 20 n.
copy-writer publicizer 528 n.
coquetry
tergiversation 603 n.
whim 604 n.
affectation 850 n.
love-making 887 n.
wooing 889 n.
flattery 925 n.
coquette
be capricious 604 vb.
affector 850 n.
lover 887 n.
excite love 887 vb.
court 889 vb.
coquillage
ornamental art 844 n.
coracle rowboat 275 n.
coral redness 431 n.
gem 844 n.
corallin
red pigment 431 n.
coral reef island 349 n.
coram judice
litigated 959 adj.
in litigation 959 adv.
cor Anglais flute 414 n.
corbel shelf 218 n.
cord cable, ligature 47 n.
line 203 n.
fibre 208 n.

cordage tackling 47 n.
cordated curved 248 adj.
cordial soft drink 301 n.
pleasant 376 adj.
pungency 388 n.
willing 597 adj.
tonic 658 n.
feeling 818 adj.
felt 818 adj.
friendly 880 adj.
sociable 882 adj.
cordiality (see cordial)
cordite propellant 287 n.
explosive 723 n.
cordon outline 233 n.
barrier 235 n.
inclose 235 vb.
loop 250 n.
stopper 264 n.
cordon bleu proficient 696 n.
decoration 729 n.
cordon sanitaire
hygiene 652 n.
prophylactic 658 n.
protection 660 n.
preservation 666 n.
corduroy textile 222 n.
roughness 259 n.
furrow 262 n.
cordwainer clothier 228 n.
artisan 686 n.
core essence 1 n.
essential part 5 n.
focus 76 n.
centrality 225 n.
chief thing 638 n.
affections 817 n.
co-relation correlation 12 n.
co-religionist
colleague 707 n.
church member 976 n.
worshipper 981 n.
corer perforator 263 n.
co-respondent
divorce 896 n.
libertine 952 n.
coriaceous tough 329 adj.
Corinthian
ornamental 844 adj.
fop 848 n.
cork covering 226 n.
stopper 264 n.
levity 323 n.
deteriorate 655 vb.
corkage price 809 n.
corked unsavoury 391 adj.
deteriorated 655 adj.
corker exceller 644 n.
corkscrew coil 251 n.
meander 251 vb.
opener 263 n.

perforator 263 n.
  extractor 304 n.
cormorant *eater* 301 n.
  bird of prey 365 n.
  glutton 947 n.
corn *swelling* 253 n.
  provender 301 n.
  hardness 326 n.
  corn 366 n.
  ulcer 651 n.
  preserve 666 vb.
corn-chandler
  merchant 794 n.
corncob *tobacco* 388 n.
cornea *eye* 438 n.
cornel *tree* 366 n.
cornelian *gem* 844 n.
corneous *hard* 326 adj.
corner *circumstance* 84 n.
  place 185 n.
  angularity 247 n.
  cavity 255 n.
  circle 314 vb.
  hiding-place 527 n.
  attack 712 vb.
  defeat 727 vb.
  possession 773 n.
  purchase 792 vb.
  pillory 964 n.
corner-boy *rioter* 738 n.
cornered *angular* 247 adj.
  in difficulties 700 adj.
  hindered 702 adj.
cornering *circuition* 314 n.
  purchase 792 n.
corner-stone
  supporter 218 n.
  chief thing 638 n.
cornet *bag* 194 n.
  cone 252 n.
  horn 414 n.
  army officer 741 n.
cornetist
  instrumentalist 413 n.
cornflour
  semiliquidity 354 n.
cornflower *blueness* 435 n.
cornice *summit* 213 n.
cornification
  hardening 326 n.
cornucopia *abundance* 171 n.
  store 632 n.
  plenty 635 n.
  liberality 813 n.
cornute *tapering* 256 adj.
corny *known* 490 adj.
corollary *adjunct* 40 n.
  judgment 480 n.
corona *loop* 250 n.
  sun 321 n.
  light 417 n.

coronach
  musical piece 412 n.
  vocal music 412 n.
  lament 836 n.
  condolence 905 n.
coronal
  ornamentation 844 n.
coronary thrombosis
  blood pressure 651 n.
coronation *mandate* 751 n.
  dignification 866 n.
  celebration 876 n.
coroner *judge* 957 n.
coronet *headgear* 228 n.
  loop 250 n.
  heraldry 547 n.
  trophy 729 n.
  regalia 743 n.
corporal *army officer* 741 n.
corporality
  materiality 319 n.
corporal punishment
  corporal punishment
  963 n.
corporate *conjunct* 45 adj.
  co-operative 706 adj.
  corporate 708 adj.
corporation *bulk* 195 n.
  swelling 253 n.
  association 706 n.
  corporation 708 n.
  jurisdiction 955 n.
corporative state
  polity 733 n.
corporeality
  materiality 319 n.
corporeity
  substantiality 3 n.
  materiality 319 n.
corposant *glow-worm* 420 n.
corps *band* 74 n.
  formation 722 n.
corps de ballet
  jumper 312 n.
  actor 594 n.
corps d'élite *élite* 644 n.
  armed force 722 n.
corps diplomatique
  envoy 754 n.
corpse *corpse* 363 n.
corpse-candle
  glow-worm 420 n.
  torch 420 n.
corpulence *bulk* 195 n.
  thickness 205 n.
corpus *substance* 3 n.
  whole 52 n.
  assemblage 74 n.
  matter 319 n.
  reading matter 589 n.
Corpus Christi

  the Sacrament 988 n.
  holy-day 988 n.
corpuscle *particle* 33 n.
  blood 335 n.
corpuscular *minute* 196 adj.
corpus delicti
  guilty act 936 n.
corradiation *focus* 76 n.
  convergence 293 n.
corral
  bring together 74 vb.
  circumscribe 232 vb.
  inclosure 235 n.
  break in 369 vb.
  imprison 747 vb.
correct *orderly* 60 adj.
  moderate 177 vb.
  true, accurate 494 adj.
  grammatical 564 adj.
  elegant 575 adj.
  print 587 vb.
  neutral 625 adj.
  perfect 646 adj.
  rectify 654 vb.
  remedy 658 vb.
  tasteful 846 adj.
  fashionable 848 adj.
  well-bred 848 adj.
  formal 875 adj.
  right 913 adj.
  reprove 924 vb.
  honourable 929 adj.
  punish 963 vb.
  orthodox 976 adj.
correction
  moderation 177 n.
  amendment 654 n.
  remedy 658 n.
  reprimand 924 n.
correctitude *formality* 875 n.
  (*see* correctness)
corrective
  counteracting 182 adj.
  remedial 658 adj.
  punitive 963 adj.
correctness
  mid-course 625 n.
  perfection 646 n.
  good taste 846 n.
  etiquette 848 n.
  formality 875 n.
  courtesy 884 n.
  right 913 n.
corrector *reformer* 654 n.
  punisher 963 n.
correlate *compare* 462 vb.
  (*see* correlation)
correlation
  relativeness 9 n.
  correlation 12 n.
  similarity 18 n.

equalization 28 n.
symmetry 245 n.
correlative
interchanged 151 adj.
correspondence
relativeness 9 n.
correlation 12 n.
uniformity 16 n.
similarity 18 n.
conformance 24 n.
parallelism 219 n.
symmetry 245 n.
information 524 n.
report 524 n.
record 548 n.
correspondence 588 n.
correspondent
respondent 460 n.
informant 524 n.
publicizer 528 n.
correspondent 588 n.
author 589 n.
delegate 754 n.
recipient 782 n.
correspond to
resemble 18 vb.
corridor bond 47 n.
entrance 68 n.
region 184 n.
lobby 194 n.
doorway 263 n.
open space 263 n.
access 624 n.
corrigendum
mistake 495 n.
corrigible
improved 564 adj.
corrival compeer 28 n.
opponent 705 n.
contender 716 n.
corrivalry opposition 704 n.
contention 716 n.
corrivation current 350 n.
corroborant tonic 658 n.
remedial 658 adj.
corroborate
corroborate 466 vb.
demonstrate 478 vb.
affirm 532 vb.
corroboration
evidence 466 n.
assent 488 n.
corroborative
evidential 466 adj.
corroboree dance 837 n.
corrode burn 381 vb.
impair 655 vb.
hurt 827 vb.
corrosion dilapidation 655 n.
corrosive destroyer 168 n.
keen 174 adj.

harmful 645 adj.
poison 659 n.
paining 827 adj.
corrugate crinkle 251 vb.
roughen 259 vb.
fold 261 vb.
groove 262 vb.
corrugated
undulatory 251 adj.
rough 259 adj.
corrugation (see corrugate)
corrupt decompose 51 vb.
misteach 535 vb.
neological 560 adj.
bribe 612 vb.
bad 645 adj.
harm 645 vb.
unclean 649 adj.
make unclean 649 vb.
deteriorated 655 adj.
deteriorate 655 vb.
impair, pervert 655 vb.
venal 930 adj.
vicious 934 adj.
make wicked 934 vb.
corruptibility
improbity 930 n.
corruptible venal 930 adj.
corruption fetor 397 n.
neology 560 n.
badness 645 n.
uncleanness 649 n.
improbity 930 n.
(see corrupt)
corsage bodywear 228 n.
corsair galley 275 n.
robber 789 n.
corselet bodywear 228 n.
armour 713 n.
corset compressor 198 n.
supporter 218 n.
underwear 228 n.
hardness 326 n.
fetter 748 n.
cortège adjunct 40 n.
retinue 67 n.
procession 71 n.
concomitant 89 n.
marching 267 n.
slowcoach 278 n.
follower 284 n.
obsequies 364 n.
retainer 742 n.
cortes parliament 692 n.
cortex exteriority 223 n.
skin 226 n.
cortical exterior 223 adj.
dermal 226 adj.
cortisone drug 658 n.
coruscation flash 417 n.
corvée labour 682 n.

compulsion 740 n.
corvette
sailing-ship 275 n.
warship 722 n.
corybant madman 504 n.
corybantiasm frenzy 503 n.
coryphæus teacher 537 n.
leader 690 n.
coryphée actor 594 n.
cosecant ratio 85 n.
cosh strike 279 vb.
hammer 279 n.
club 723 n.
co-sharer participator 775 n.
cosh-man ruffian 904 n.
cosine ratio 85 n.
cosiness euphoria 376 n.
cosmetic unguent 357 n.
scent 396 n.
balm 658 n.
cosmetic 843 n.
cosmetician
beautician 843 n.
cosmetology
beautification 843 n.
cosmic extensive 32 adj.
comprehensive 52 adj.
cosmic 321 adj.
cosmogony
uranometry 321 n.
cosmography 321 n.
cosmography
situation 186 n.
uranometry 321 n.
cosmography 321 n.
geography 321 n.
cosmology
uranometry 321 n.
cosmography 321 n.
cosmopolitan
universal 79 adj.
urban 192 adj.
national 371 adj.
beau monde 848 n.
well-bred 848 adj.
philanthropic 901 adj.
cosmopolite
philanthropist 901 n.
cosmorama spectacle 445 n.
cosmos whole 52 n.
universe 321 n.
cosmotron
nucleonics 160 n.
Cossack cavalry 722 n.
cosset pet 889 vb.
favourite 890 n.
cost appraise 465 vb.
account 808 vb.
cost 809 n., vb.
dearness 811 n.
costal lateral 239 adj.

coster,— monger
  seller 793 n.
  pedlar 794 n.
coster-barrow
  pushcart 274 n.
costive *dense* 324 adj.
  retentive 778 adj.
costless *uncharged* 812 adj.
costly *destructive* 165 adj.
  valuable 644 adj.
  harmful 645 adj.
  dear 811 adj.
  ostentatious 875 adj.
cost-reducing
  economical 814 adj.
costs *expenditure* 806 n.
  cost 809 n.
  penalty 963 n.
cost, to one's
  amiss 616 adv.
  badly 645 adv.
costume *dress* 228 n.
  stage-set 594 n.
costumier *clothier* 228 n.
  stage-hand 594 n.
co-substantial
  identical 13 adj.
cosy *comfortable* 376 adj.
  palmy 730 adj.
  pleasurable 826 adj.
  sociable 882 adj.
cot *small house* 192 n.
  bed 218 n.
cotangent *ratio* 85 n.
cote *stable* 192 n.
coterie *group, band* 74 n.
  party 708 n.
cothurnus *drama* 594 n.
cotillion *dance* 837 n.
cottage *small house* 192 n.
cottager, cottar
  resident 191 n.
cotter pin *fastening* 47 n.
cotton *textile* 222 n.
  fibre 208 n.
cotton on to
  be friendly 880 vb.
cottons *clothing* 228 n.
cotton wool *fibre* 208 n.
cotyledon *foliage* 366 n.
couch *be horizontal* 216 vb.
  bed, seat 218 n.
  sit down 311 vb.
  repose 683 vb.
couchant *supine* 216 adj.
  heraldic 547 adj.
Couéism *sense* 374 n.
  hope 852 n.
cougar *cat* 365 n.
cough *eruct* 300 vb.
  excretion 302 n.

breathe 352 vb.
  rasp 407 vb.
  respiratory disease 651 n.
cough up *restitute* 787 vb.
  pay 804 vb.
coughy *puffing* 352 adj.
couldn't care less
  be incurious 454 vb.
  be indifferent 860 adv.
couldn't-care-less
  rash 857 adj.
couleur de rose
  excellent 644 adj.
  palmy 730 adj.
  promising 852 adj.
coulisses *theatre* 594 n.
coulter *sharp edge* 256 n.
  farm tool 370 n.
council *assembly* 74 n.
  director 690 n.
  adviser 691 n.
  council 692 n.
  consignee 754 n.
  conference 884 n.
  jurisdiction 955 n.
  tribunal 956 n.
  synod 985 n.
councillor *official* 690 n.
  councillor 692 n.
  officer 741 n.
counsel *incite* 612 vb.
  warning 664 n.
  advise 691 vb.
  consignee 754 n.
  lawyer 958 n.
counsellor *sage* 500 n.
  official 690 n.
  adviser 691 n.
counsel of despair
  inexpedience 643 n.
  hopelessness 853 n.
count *quantify* 26 vb.
  comprise 78 vb.
  numeration 86 n.
  measure 465 vb.
  motivate 612 vb.
  be important 638 vb.
  nobleman 868 n.
  accusation 928 n.
countable *numerable* 86 adj.
count as
  substitute 150 vb.
countenance *face* 237 n.
  mien 445 n.
  inducement 612 n.
  aid 703 n.
  patronize 703 vb.
  approve 923 vb.
counter *contrary* 14 adj.
  computer 86 n.
  counteract 182 vb.

stand, shelf 118 n.
  poop 238 n.
  answer 460 vb.
  label 547 n.
  be obstructive 702 vb.
  oppose 704 vb.
  parry 713 vb.
  retaliate 714 vb.
  shop 796 n.
  plaything 837 n.
counteract
  be contrary 14 vb.
  weaken 163 vb.
  counteract 182 vb.
  tell against 467 vb.
  oppose 704 vb.
counteraction
  (*see* counteract)
counteractive
  contrary 14 adj.
counter-argument
  opposition 704 n.
  vindication 927 n.
  legal trial 959 n.
counter-attack
  attack 712 vb.
  retaliation 714 n.
counter-attraction
  offset 31 n.
  influence 178 n.
counterbalance *offset* 31 n.
  counteract 182 vb.
counterblast
  counteraction 182 n.
  answer 460 n.
  retaliation 714 n.
counter-caster
  computer 86 n.
counterchange
  correlate 12 vb.
  interchange 151 n., vb.
counter-charge
  rejoinder 460 n.
  vindication 927 n.
  accusation 928 n.
counter-charm
  counteraction 182 n.
  talisman 983 n.
countercheck
  be obstructive 702 vb.
countercheer
  disapprobation 924 n.
counter-claim *offset* 31 n.
  request 761 n.
  deprecation 762 n.
  litigation 959 n.
counterdraw *copy* 20 vb.
counter-espionage
  secret service 459 n.
counter-evidence
  counter-evidence 467 n.

o

counterfeit *imitation* 20n.
duplicity 541n.
fake 541vb.
sham 542n.
spurious 542adj.
deceive 542vb.
be untrue 543vb.
mint 797vb.
counterfeiter
deceiver 545n.
defrauder 789n.
counterfoil *label* 547n.
counterglow *heavens* 321n.
counter-irritant
counteraction 182n.
antidote 658n.
counter-jumper *seller* 793n.
countermand
command 737vb.
abrogate 752vb.
prohibition 757n.
countermarch
turn back 286vb.
wage war 718vb.
countermark *label* 547n.
counter-meaning
contrariety 14n.
connotation 514n.
countermine
plot 623n., vb.
oppose 704vb.
defences 713n.
retaliation 714n.
countermovement
return 286n.
counter-order
abrogation 752n.
prohibition 757n.
counterpane *coverlet* 226n.
counterpart *identity* 13n.
analogue 18n.
copy, duplicate 22n.
counterplot *plot* 623n.
retaliation 714n.
counterpoint
contrariety 14n.
combination 50n.
symmetry 245n.
melody 410n.
music 412n.
counterpoise *equalize* 28vb.
offset 31n.
counteract 182vb.
gravity 322n.
weigh 322n.
counterpole *contrariety* 14n.
Counter Reformation
restoration 656n.
orthodoxism 976n.
Catholicism 976n.
counter-revolution

reversion 148n.
revolution 149n.
counters
counting instrument 86n.
counterscarp
fortification 713n.
countersense
contrariety 14n.
connotation 514n.
countersign *answer* 460n.
testify 466vb.
endorse 488vb.
call 547n.
sign 547vb.
give security 767vb.
counter-signature
credential 466n.
compact 765n.
counterspin *evolution* 316n.
counter statement
rejoinder 460n.
counter-stream
contrariety 14n.
counter-stroke
defence 713n.
retaliation 714n.
counter-symptom
contrariety 14n.
counter-tenor *stridor* 407n.
vocalist 413n.
counter-term *name* 561n.
countertype *prototype* 23n.
countervail *be equal* 28vb.
set off 31vb.
counteract 182vb.
tell against 467vb.
counterweight *offset* 31n.
stabilizer 153n.
counteract 182vb.
weigh 322vb.
countess *nobleman* 868n.
count for nothing
be unimportant 639vb.
counting *inclusive* 78adj.
numeration 86n.
counting heads *vote* 605n.
counting-house *shop* 796n.
treasury 799n.
countless
multitudinous 104adj.
infinite 107adj.
count on *believe* 485vb.
assume 471vb.
expect 507vb.
count out *exclude* 57vb.
reject 607vb.
exempt 919vb.
countrified
provincial 192adj.
ill-bred 847adj.
country *region* 184n.

home 192n.
land 344n.
polity 733n.
countryman *dweller* 191n.
countryman 869n.
counts *particulars* 80n.
count the cost
be cautious 858vb.
count upon (*see* count on)
count with
number with 78vb.
county *district* 184n.
polity 733n.
county family
aristocracy 868n.
coup *instant* 116n.
contrivance 623n.
deed 676n.
coup de grâce *end* 69n.
killing 362n.
completion 725n.
coup de main
violence 176n.
deed 676n.
attack 712n.
coup-de-maître
masterpiece 694n.
coup d'état
revolution 149n.
policy 623n.
deed 676n.
revolt 738n.
lawlessness 954n.
coup de théâtre
thaumaturgy 864n.
coup d'œil *inspection* 438n.
coupé train 274n.
automobile 274n.
carriage 274n.
couple *analogue* 18n.
join 45vb.
unite with 45vb.
combine 50vb.
duality 90n.
marry 894vb.
coupled
accompanying 89adj.
couplet *duality* 90n.
prosody 593n.
verse form 593n.
coupling *joinder* 45n.
coition 45n.
coupling 47n.
coupon *portion* 783n.
paper money 797n.
courage *resolution* 599n.
courage 855n.
courgette *vegetable* 301n.
courier *guide* 520n.
courier 531n.
course *order* 60n.

continuity 71 n.
time 108 n.
tendency 179 n.
layer 207 n.
motion 265 n.
itinerary 267 n.
water travel 269 n.
sail 275 n.
speeding 277 n.
direction 281 n.
dish 301 n.
flow 350 vb.
curriculum 534 n.
hunt 619 vb.
route 624 n.
therapy 658 n.
arena 724 n.
conduct 688 n.
course, of
  necessarily 596 adv.
course of events
  affairs 154 n.
course of, in the
  while 108 adv.
course of law
  legal process 959 n.
course of study
  curriculum 534 n.
  study 536 n.
course of time
  course of time 111 n.
courser horse 273 n.
  war-horse 273 n.
  speeder 277 n.
  dog 365 n.
  hunter 619 n.
coursing chase 619 n.
court place 185 n.
  housing 192 n.
  horizontality 216 n.
  open space 263 n.
  council 692 n.
  arena 724 n.
  retainer 742 n.
  request 761 vb.
  beau monde 848 n.
  desire 859 vb.
  befriend 880 vb.
  be in love 887 vb.
  court 889 vb.
  flatter 925 vb.
  law-court 956 n.
court dress
  formal dress 228 n.
  formality 875 n.
courteous well-bred 848 adj.
  benevolent 897 adj.
  (see courtesy)
courtesan prostitute 952 n.
courtesy obeisance 311 n.
  humility 872 n.

sociability 882 n.
courtesy 884 n.
courteous act 884 n.
disinterestedness 931 n.
courtesy, by
  insubstantially 4 adv.
courtesy call
  social round 882 n.
courtesy title
  insubstantial thing 4 n.
  title 870 n.
  undueness 916 n.
court-house
  courtroom 956 n.
courtier retainer 742 n.
  toady 879 n.
  flatterer 925 n.
court-leet law-court 956 n.
courtly well-bred 848 adj.
  courteous 884 adj.
court manners
  etiquette 848 n.
court-martial
  law-court 956 n.
Court of Appeal
  law-court 956 n.
Court of Arches
  ecclesiastical court 956 n.
  synod 985 n.
court of audience
  ecclesiastical court 956 n.
court of law law-court 956 n.
court plaster
  surgical dressing 658 n.
courtroom
  courtroom 956 n.
courtship
  love-making 887 n.
  wooing 889 n.
courtyard place 185 n.
cousin kinsman 11 n.
couturier clothier 228 n.
  artist 556 n.
cove cavity 255 n.
  gulf 345 n.
  person 371 n.
  male 372 n.
coven assembly 74 n.
  sorcery 983 n.
covenant promise 764 n., vb.
  compact 765 n.
  contract 765 vb.
  title-deed 767 n.
covenanted secured 767 adj.
covenanter assenter 488 n.
  sectarist 978 n.
covenanting
  sectarian 978 adj.
Coventry, send to
  exclude 57 vb.
cover offset 31 n.

fill 54 vb.
generate 164 vb.
extend 183 vb.
receptacle 194 n.
be high 209 vb.
wrapping 226 n.
cover 226 vb.
stopper 264 n.
meal, dish 301 n.
darken 418 vb.
screen 421 vb.
communicate 524 vb.
conceal 525 vb.
hiding-place 527 n.
disguise 527 n.
publish 528 vb.
deception 542 n.
mark 547 vb.
obliterate 550 vb.
correspondence 588 n.
bookbinding 589 n.
pretext 614 n.
gamble 618 vb.
cleaning cloth 648 n.
safeguard 660 vb.
shelter 662 n.
defend 713 vb.
threaten 900 vb.
coverage inclusion 78 n.
  range 183 n.
  publicity 528 n.
cover all cases
  be general 79 vb.
cover girl a beauty 841 n.
cover ground
  progress 285 vb.
coverlet coverlet 226 n.
  warm clothes 381 n.
covert nest 192 n.
  wood 366 n.
  screen 421 n.
  occult 523 adj.
  concealed 525 adj.
  refuge, shelter 662 n.
coverts plumage 259 n.
coverture marriage 894 n.
cover up screen 421 vb.
  keep secret 525 vb.
covet desire 859 vb.
  envy 912 vb.
covetous avaricious 816 adj.
  desiring 859 adj.
  envious 912 adj.
  selfish 932 adj.
covey group 74 n.
  certain quantity 104 n.
covinous false 541 adj.
  deceiving 542 adj.
cow cattle 365 n.
  female animal 373 n.
  dissuade 613 vb.

frighten 854 vb.
coward *weakling* 163 n.
  avoider 620 n.
  coward 856 n.
cowardice
  irresolution 601 n.
  cowardice 856 n.
cowardize *unman* 161 vb.
  frighten 854 vb.
cowardly (*see* cowardice)
cowboy *rider* 268 n.
  herdsman 369 n.
cower *stoop* 311 vb.
  avoid 620 vb.
  quake 854 vb.
  be cowardly 856 vb.
cowherd, cowman
  herdsman 369 n.
  servant 742 n.
cowhide *skin* 226 n.
  scourge 964 n.
cowhouse, cowshed
  stable 192 n.
  cattle pen 369 n.
cowl *covering* 226 n.
  headgear 228 n.
  ecclesiasticize 985 vb.
  monk 986 vb.
  canonicals 989 n.
cowlick *hair* 259 n.
  hair-dressing 843 n.
cowling *covering* 226 n.
cowlstaff *supporter* 218 n.
co-worker *personnel* 686 n.
  collaborator 707 n.
cow-pat *excrement* 302 n.
cowpox
  skin disease 651 n.
cowpuncher *rider* 268 n.
  herdsman 369 n.
cowrie *small coin* 33 n.
  coinage 797 n.
cox *navigator* 270 n.
  direct 689 vb.
coxcomb *entertainer* 594 n.
  fop 848 n.
  affector 850 n.
  vain person 783 n.
coxcombry
  affectation 850 n.
  airs 873 n.
coxswain *navigate* 269 vb.
  (*see* cox)
coy *affected* 850 adj.
  nervous 854 adj.
  cowardly 856 adj.
  modest 874 adj.
  pure 950 adj.
coyote *dog* 365 n.
cozen *deceive* 542 vb.
cozener *trickster* 545 n.

motivator 612 n.
cozening *perfidious* 930 adj.
crab *fish food* 301 n.
  reptile 365 n.
  table fish 365 n.
  sourness 393 n.
  be discontented 829 vb.
  be sullen 893 vb.
  dispraise 924 vb.
  detract 926 vb.
crabbed *sour* 393 adj.
  puzzling 517 adj.
  imperspicuous 568 adj.
  inelegant 576 adj.
  sullen 893 adj.
crabstick
  rude person 885 n.
crab-walk *deviation* 282 n.
crack *disjunction* 46 n.
  break 46 vb.
  discontinuity 72 n.
  instant 116 n.
  weakness 163 n.
  gap 201 n.
  space 201 vb.
  roughness 259 n.
  furrow 262 n.
  opening 263 n.
  knock 279 n.
  be brittle 330 vb.
  bang 402 n.
  crackle 402 vb.
  rasp 407 vb.
  striation 437 n.
  decipher 520 vb.
  best 644 adj.
  defect 647 n.
  skilful 694 adj.
  witticism 839 n.
  blemish 845 n., vb.
crack a bottle *drink* 301 vb.
  be sociable 882 vb.
crack a cipher
  decipher 520 vb.
crackajack *topping* 644 adj.
crack at *essay* 671 n.
crack-brain *crank* 504 n.
crack-brained
  foolish 499 adj.
  crazed 503 adj.
crack down on
  be severe 735 vb.
  restrain 747 vb.
cracked *spaced* 201 adj.
  non-resonant 405 adj.
  strident 407 adj.
  discordant 411 adj.
  misjudging 481 adj.
  unintelligent 499 adj.
  interpreted 520 adj.
  voiceless 578 adj.

imperfect 647 adj.
  dilapidated 655 adj.
  blemished 845 adj.
cracked-up
  overrated 482 adj.
cracker *pastry* 301 n.
  bang 402 n.
crackers *crazed* 503 adj.
  hair-dressing 843 n.
crackle *bang* 402 n.
  crackle 402 vb.
crack of doom
  finality 69 n.
  future state 124 n.
  ruin 165 n.
  death 361 n.
crackpot *fool* 501 n.
  crank 504 n.
cracksman *thief* 789 n.
crack up
  be fatigued 684 vb.
  boast 877 vb.
  praise 923 vb.
cradle *origin* 68 n.
  nonage 130 n.
  seedbed 156 n.
  assuage 177 vb.
  nest, home 192 n.
  basket 194 n.
  support, bed 218 n.
  bring to rest 266 vb.
  make inactive 679 vb.
  relieve 831 vb.
  pet 889 vb.
cradle-song
  vocal music 412 n.
  soporific 679 n.
  relief 831 n.
craft *ship, shipping* 275 n.
  sagacity 498 n.
  deception 542 n.
  vocation 622 n.
  skill 694 n.
  cunning 698 n.
craftiness (*see* crafty)
craftsman *producer* 167 n.
  artist 556 n.
  machinist 630 n.
  doer 676 n.
  artisan 686 n.
craftsmanship *skill* 694 n.
crafty *intelligent* 498 adj.
  deceiving 542 adj.
  cunning 698 adj.
crag *high land* 209 n.
  sharp point 256 n.
  hardness 326 n.
  rock 344 n.
craggy *sharp* 256 adj.
  rough 259 adj.
  difficult 700 adj.

cragsman *traveller* 268 n.
  climber 308 n.
cram *fill* 54 vb.
  bring together 74 vb.
  load 193 vb.
  enlarge 197 vb.
  be dense 324 vb.
  educate 534 vb.
  study 536 n., vb.
  superabound 637 vb.
  gluttonize 947 vb.
crambo *doggerel* 593 n.
  indoor game 837 n.
cram-full *full* 54 adj.
cram in *stow* 187 vb.
crammer *teacher* 537 n.
  training school 539 n.
  untruth 543 n.
  glutton 947 n.
cramoisie *red colour* 431 n.
cramp *fastening* 47 n.
  disable 161 vb.
  weaken 163 vb.
  make smaller 198 vb.
  spasm 318 n.
  pang 377 n.
  make insufficient 636 vb.
  impair 655 vb.
  hinder 702 vb.
  restraint 747 n.
cramped
  narrow-minded 481 adj.
  inelegant 576 adj.
cran *basket* 194 n.
crane *hanger* 217 n.
  lifter 310 n.
  bird of prey 365 n.
crane one's neck
  scan 438 adj.
cranial *topmost* 213 adj.
craniology *head* 213 n.
  anthropology 371 n.
craniometry *head* 213 n.
  anthropology 371 n.
cranium *head* 213 n.
  dome 253 n.
crank *handle* 218 n.
  meandering 251 n.
  rotate 315 vb.
  narrow mind 481 n.
  fool 501 n.
  eccentricity 503 n.
  crank 504 n.
  visionary 513 n.
  make ready 669 vb.
  witticism 839 n.
  laughing-stock 851 n.
crank-handle *handle* 218 n.
crankiness
  (*see* crank, cranky)
crankish

  misjudging 481 adj.
crankle *meander* 251 vb.
  fold 261 n.
cranky *convoluted* 251 adj.
  crazed 503 adj.
crannog *dwelling* 192 n.
cranny *compartment* 194 n.
  furrow 261 n.
  hiding-place 527 n.
crape *convolution* 251 n.
  crinkle 251 vb.
  black thing 428 n.
  badge 547 n.
  lamentation 836 n.
craps *gambling* 618 n.
  gambling game 837 n.
crapulence *sequel* 67 n.
  pain 377 n.
  intemperance 943 n.
  crapulence 949 n.
crash *revolution* 149 n.
  textile 222 n.
  aeronautics 271 n.
  fly 271 vb.
  collision 279 n.
  descent 309 n.
  be brittle 330 vb.
  be loud 400 vb.
  bang 402 n., vb.
  discord 411 vb.
  miscarry, fail 728 vb.
  insolvency 805 n.
crash-dive
  aeronautics 271 n.
  plunge 313 vb.
crash-landing
  aeronautics 271 n.
crasis *temperament* 5 n.
  combination 50 n.
  composition 56 n.
crass *consummate* 32 adj.
  dense 324 adj.
  unintelligent 499 adj.
  manifest 522 adj.
  vulgar 847 adj.
crate *basket* 194 n.
  vehicle 274 n.
crater *bowl* 194 n.
  cavity 255 n.
  orifice 263 n.
cravat *neckwear* 228 n.
crave *require* 627 vb.
  request 761 vb.
  desire 859 vb.
  envy 912 vb.
craven *coward* 856 n.
crawfish *regress* 286 vb.
  table fish 365 n.
crawl *pedestrianism* 267 n.
  aquatics 269 n.
  slowness 278 n.

  move slowly 278 vb.
  tergiversate 603 vb.
  knuckle under 721 vb.
  lose repute 867 vb.
  be humble 872 vb.
  be servile 879 vb.
crawlers *breeches* 228 n.
crawling
  multitudinous 104 adj.
  unclean 649 adj.
crawl with *be many* 104 vb.
  superabound 637 vb.
crayfish *table fish* 365 n.
crayon *paint* 553 vb.
  art equipment 553 n.
craze *be brittle* 330 vb.
  striation 437 n.
  bias 481 n.
  make mad 503 vb.
  whim 604 n.
  practice 610 n.
  fashion 848 n.
  liking 859 n.
  excite love 887 vb.
crazed *foolish* 499 adj.
craziness *eccentricity* 503 n.
crazy *non-uniform* 17 adj.
  aged 131 adj.
  flimsy 163 adj.
  distorted 246 adj.
  brittle 330 adj.
  variegated 437 adj.
  crazed 503 adj.
  unsafe 661 adj.
  enamoured 887 adj.
crazy paving
  discontinuity 72 n.
  chequer 437 n.
creak *move slowly* 278 vb.
  sound faint 401 vb.
  stridor 407 n.
creaking, creaky
  strident 407 adj.
  hoarse 407 adj.
  clumsy 695 adj.
cream *milk* 301 n.
  semiliquidity 354 n.
  bubble 355 vb.
  fat 357 n.
  unguent 357 n.
  select 605 vb.
  chief thing 638 n.
  élite 644 n.
  cleanser 648 n.
  balm 658 n.
  cosmetic 845 n.
  beau monde 848 n.
  person of repute 866 n.
cream-coloured
  yellow 433 adj.
creamery *workshop* 687 n.

creamy *semiliquid* 354 adj.
  fatty 357 adj.
  savoury 390 adj.
  soft-hued 425 adj.
  whitish 427 adj.
  yellow 433 adj.
crease *joint* 45 n.
  jumble 63 vb.
  limit 236 n.
  fold 261 n., vb.
  impair 655 vb.
create *cause* 156 vb.
  produce 164 vb.
  efform 243 vb.
  imagine 513 vb.
  be excitable 822 vb.
  dignify 866 vb.
  be angry 891 vb.
creation *existence* 1 n.
  non-imitation 21 n.
  antiquity 125 n.
  production 164 n.
  dress 228 n.
  efformation 243 n.
  universe 321 n.
  divine function 965 n.
creative
  unimitative 21 adj.
  causal 156 adj.
  productive 164 adj.
  prolific 171 adj.
  imaginative 513 adj.
  godlike 965 adj.
creator *cause* 156 n.
  producer 167 n.
  the Deity 965 n.
creature *substance* 3 n.
  product 164 n.
  animal 365 n.
  person 371 n.
  auxiliary 707 n.
  dependant 742 n.
creature comforts
  food 301 n.
  euphoria 376 n.
creaturehood
  subjection 745 n.
creaturely
  produced 164 adj.
  human 371 adj.
creature of habit
  repetition 106 n.
  habitué 610 n.
crèche *school* 539 n.
credal *credal* 485 adj.
  theological 973 adj.
  orthodox 976 adj.
credence *belief* 485 n.
  altar 990 n.
credenda *creed* 485 n.
  theology 973 n.

credential *credential* 466 n.
  title-deed 767 n.
credible *possible* 469 adj.
  plausible 471 adj.
  credible 485 adj.
credit *attribute* 158 vb.
  influence 178 n.
  believe 485 vb.
  means 629 n.
  subvention 703 n.
  authority 733 n.
  promise 764 n.
  lend 784 vb.
  credit 802 n., vb.
  account 808 vb.
  repute 866 n.
  honour 866 vb.
  thank 907 vb.
  dueness 915 n.
  approbation 923 n.
  praise 923 n.
creditable *excellent* 644 adj.
  reputable 866 adj.
  approvable 923 adj.
creditless *inglorious* 867 adj.
credit, on
  promissory 764 adj.
  lending 784 adj.
  owed 803 adj.
creditor *provider* 633 n.
  lender 784 n.
  creditor 802 n.
credit side *gain* 771 n.
credit title *thanks* 907 n.
credit-worthiness
  wealth 800 n.
  credit 802 n.
credit-worthy
  reputable 866 adj.
  deserving 915 adj.
credo (*see* creed)
credulity *credulity* 487 n.
  deception 542 n.
  persuasibility 612 n.
credulous
  misjudging 481 adj.
  credulous 487 adj.
  gullible 544 adj.
creed *creed* 485 n.
  theology 973 n.
  orthodoxy 976 n.
creedless
  unbelieving 486 adj.
  irreligious 974 adj.
creek *gap* 201 n.
  cavity 255 n.
  gulf 345 n.
  stream 350 n.
creel *basket* 194 n.
creep *drag on* 113 vb.
  be rough 259 vb.

  move slowly 278 vb.
  feel pain 377 vb.
  itch 378 vb.
  lurk 523 adj.
  be stealthy 525 vb.
  dance 837 n.
  be servile 879 vb.
creeper *coil* 251 n.
  plant 366 n.
creepers *footwear* 228 n.
creeping thing *animal* 365 n.
creeps *formication* 378 n.
  nervousness 854 n.
creep upon *surprise* 508 vb.
creepy *frightening* 854 adj.
creese *sharp edge* 256 n.
  side arms 723 n.
cremation *interment* 364 n.
  burning 381 n.
crematorium
  interment 364 n.
  furnace 383 n.
crenation *edging* 234 n.
  notch 260 n.
crenellate *hem* 234 vb.
  notch 260 vb.
  defend 713 vb.
creole *foreigner* 59 n.
  settler 191 n.
creosote *prophylactic* 658 n.
crêpe (*see* crape)
crepitate *eruct* 300 vb.
  crackle 402 vb.
crepuscule *evening* 129 n.
  half-light 419 n.
crescendo *increase* 36 n.
  expansion 197 n.
  loudness 400 n.
crescent *housing* 192 n.
  curve 248 n.
  arc 250 n.
  flag 547 n.
  religious faith 973 n.
cress *potherb* 301 n.
cresset *torch* 420 n.
crest *superiority* 34 n.
  high land 209 n.
  crown 213 vb.
  summit 213 n.
  plumage 259 n.
  heraldry 547 n.
  mark 547 vb.
  jewellery 844 n.
  nobility 868 n.
crestfallen
  disappointed 509 adj.
  dejected 834 adj.
  humbled 872 adj.
cretaceous *white* 427 adj.
cretic *prosody* 593 n.
cretin *fool* 501 n.

madman 504 n.
cretinous
  unintelligent 499 adj.
  insane 503 adj.
cretonne *textile* 222 n.
crevasse *gap* 201 n.
  cavity 255 n.
  pitfall 633 n.
crevice *gap* 201 n.
crew *component* 58 n.
  band 74 n.
  resident 191 n.
  navigate 269 vb.
  mariner 270 n.
  personnel 686 n.
  party 708 n.
crew-cut *shortness* 204 n.
  hair-dressing 843 n.
crewel-work *textile* 222 n.
crewless *empty* 190 adj.
crib *copy* 22 n.
  bed 218 n.

  translation 520 n.
  classroom 538 n.
  imprison 747 vb.
  borrow 785 vb.
  steal 788 vb.
cribbage *card game* 837 n.
cribble *porosity* 263 n.
cribriform
  perforated 263 adj.
crick *pang* 377 n.
  ululate 409 vb.
cricket *ball game* 837 n.
cricket pitch *arena* 724 n.
cri de cœur *request* 761 n.
  lament 836 n.

cried-up *overrated* 482 adj.
crier *cry* 408 n.
  publicizer 528 n.
  seller 793 n.
crime *disobedience* 738 n.
  improbity 930 n.
  foul play 930 n.
  wickedness 934 n.
  vice 934 n.
  guilty act 936 n.
  lawbreaking 954 n.
crime passionel
  homicide 362 n.
  revenge 910 n.
  jealousy 911 n.
crime story *novel* 590 n.
crime wave
  lawlessness 954 n.
criminal
  unconformable 84 adj.
  offender 904 n.
  wrong 914 adj.
  rascally 930 adj.

heinous 934 adj.
  guilty 936 adj.
  knave 938 n.
  lawbreaking 954 adj.
criminal conversation
  illicit love 951 n.
criminal offence
  lawbreaking 954 n.
crimination
  accusation 928 n.
criminologist
  detective 459 n.
criminology
  lawbreaking 954 n.
criminous (*see* criminal)
crimp *crinkle* 251 vb.
  notch 260 vb.
  brittle 330 adj.
  ensnare 542 vb.
  trickster 545 n.
  taker 786 n.
  steal 788 vb.
  thief 789 n.
crimson *red colour* 431 n.
  be modest 874 vb.
cringe *stoop* 311 vb.
  obey 739 vb.
  be subject 745 vb.
  be cowardly 856 vb.
  be servile 879 vb.
crinite, crinose
  hairy 259 adj.
crinkle *distort* 246 vb.
  angulate 247 vb.
  make curved 248 vb.
  crinkle 251 vb.
  roughen 259 vb.
  fold 261 n., vb.
crinkum-crankum
  ideality 513 n.
crinoline *skirt* 228 n.
cripple *disable* 161 vb.
  weaken 163 vb.
  make useless 641 vb.
  sick person 651 n.
  impair 655 vb.
  hinder 702 vb.
crippled *incomplete* 55 adj.
  imperfect 647 adj.
crisis *juncture* 8 n.
  degree 27 n.
  crisis 137 n.
  eventuality 154 n.
  limit 236 n.
  important matter 638 n.
  danger 661 n.
  predicament 700 n.
  excitation 821 n.
crisp *crinkle* 251 vb.
  rough 259 adj.
  roughen 259 vb.

brittle 330 adj.
criss-cross *crossed* 222 adj.
criterion *prototype* 23 n.
  testing agent 461 n.
  comparison 462 n.
  identification 547 n.
critic *estimator* 480 n.
  dissentient 489 n.
  theorist 512 n.
  interpreter 520 n.
  dissertator 591 n.
  malcontent 829 n.
  man of taste 846 n.
  disapprover 924 n.
  accuser 928 n.
critical *circumstantial* 8 adj.
  crucial 137 adj.
  timely 137 adj.
  eventful 154 adj.
  discriminating 463 adj.
  judicial 480 adj.
  discursive 591 adj.
  important 638 adj.
  dangerous 661 adj.
  difficult 700 adj.
  discontented 829 adj.
  tasteful 846 adj.
  fastidious 862 adj.
  disapproving 924 adj.
criticism *estimate* 480 n.
  interpretation 520 n.
  affirmation 532 n.
  article 591 n.
  advice 691 n.
  good taste 846 n.
  censure 924 n.
  detraction 926 n.
criticize *compare* 462 vb.
  discriminate 463 vb.
  be discontented 829 vb.
critique (*see* criticism)
croak *die* 361 vb.
  rasp 407 vb.
  ululation 409 n.
  ululate 409 vb.
  be discontented 829 vb.
croaker *frog* 365 n.
  malcontent 829 n.
  moper 834 n.
croaking *voiceless* 578 adj.
crochet *tie* 45 vb.
  network 222 n.
  needlework 844 n.
crock *vessel* 194 n.
  sick person 651 n.
crockery *receptacle* 194 n.
  brittleness 330 n.
  pottery 381 n.
  materials 631 n.
crock up
  be fatigued 684 vb.

crocodile *procession* 71n.
  skin 226n.
  reptile 365n.
crocodile tears
  duplicity 541n.
crocus *yellowness* 433n.
Crœsus *rich man* 800n.
croft *house* 192n.
  inclosure 235n.
  farm 370n.
crofter *resident* 191n.
  husbandman 370n.
croissant *cereal* 301n.
Croix de Guerre
  decoration 729n.
cromlech *tomb* 364n.
  monument 548n.
crone *old woman* 133n.
Cronian *primal* 127adj.
cronk *ululation* 409n.
crony *chum* 880n.
  friend 880n.
crook *supporter* 218n.
  render oblique 220vb.
  angulate 247vb.
  make curved 248vb.
  deflect 282vb.
  punctuation 547n.
  thief 789n.
  knave 938n.
crook-backed
  deformed 246adj.
crooked *oblique* 220adj.
  distorted 246adj.
  angular 247adj.
  deviating 282adj.
  occult 523adj.
  cunning 698adj.
  blemished 845adj.
  dishonest 930adj.
croon *sing* 413vb.
  sound faint 401vb.
crooner *vocalist* 413n.
  entertainer 594n.
croon over *pet* 889vb.
crop *great quantity* 32n.
  multitude 104n.
  growth 157n.
  producer 164n.
  maw 194n.
  shorten 204vb.
  graze 301vb.
  agriculture 370n.
  cultivate 370vb.
  store 632n.
  earnings 771n.
  acquire 771vb.
  take 786vb.
  hair-dressing 843n.
crop-full *full* 54adj.
cropper *descent* 309n.

crop up *happen* 154vb.
  reproduce 166vb.
  be visible 443vb.
croquet *ball game* 837n.
croquet lawn
  horizontality 216n.
  pleasure-ground 837n.
crose *vestments* 989n.
crosier *badge of rule* 743n.
  vestments 989n.
cross *hybrid* 43n.
  counteract 182vb.
  be oblique 220vb.
  cross 222n.,vb.
  angularity 247n.
  traverse 267vb.
  pass 305vb.
  assent 488n.
  label, badge 547n.
  mark 547vb.
  script 586n.
  bane 659n.
  hindering 702adj.
  opposing 704adj.
  decoration 729n.
  adverse 731adj.
  painfulness 827n.
  jewellery 844n.
  angry 891adj.
  sullen 893adj.
  means of execution 964n.
  religious faith 973n.
  talisman 983n.
  ritual object 988n.
  vestments 989n.
  church interior 990n.
cross-bencher
  free man 744n.
crossbow *propellant* 287n.
  missile weapon 723n.
cross-breed *hybrid* 43n.
  mix 43vb.
  nonconformist 84n.
cross-connection
  junction 45n.
cross-country
  directed 281adj.
cross-current
  counteraction 182n.
  contraposition 240n.
  current 350n.
  wind 352n.
  pitfall 633n.
  obstacle 702n.
  opposition 704n.
cross-examination
  interrogation 459n.
  legal trial 959n.
cross-examiner
  inquisitor 453n.
  questioner 459n.

cross-eyed
  dim-sighted 440adj.
cross-fire
  bombardment 712n.
cross-grained *rough* 259adj.
  wilful 602adj.
  irascible 892adj.
  sullen 893adj.
cross-hatch *groove* 262vb.
crossing *crossing* 222n.
  passage 305n.
  access, road 624n.
crossing-sweeper
  cleaner 648n.
cross oneself
  be pious 979vb.
cross one's heart
  swear 532vb.
cross one's path
  hinder 702vb.
cross, on the
  obliquely 220adv.
cross out *subtract* 39vb.
  eject 300vb.
  obliterate 550vb.
cross over *apostatize* 603vb.
crosspatch
  rude person 885n.
  shrew 892n.
cross-purposes *error* 495n.
  misinterpretation 521n.
  opposition 704n.
  dissension 709n.
cross-question
  question 459n.
  interrogate 459vb.
cross-reference *sorting* 62n.
  class 62vb.
crossroad *juncture* 8n.
  focus 76n.
  crossing 222n.
  divergence 294n.
  road 624n.
cross section *example* 83n.
cross stitch
  needlework 844n.
cross swords *argue* 475vb.
  withstand 704vb.
  fight 716vb.
cross the floor
  apostatize 603vb.
cross the mind
  dawn upon 449vb.
cross the Rubicon
  initiate 68vb.
  overstep 306vb.
  be resolute 599vb.
  choose 605vb.
cross-tree *supporter* 218n.
cross-vote *disobey* 738vb.
  be free 744vb.

crossways *juncture* 8 n.
 joint 45 n.
 focus 76 n.
 angularity 247 n.
 road 624 n.
crosswise *obliquely* 220 adv.
 across 222 adv.
cross with
 unite with 45 vb.
crossword *enigma* 530 n.
 indoor game 837 n.
crotch *angularity* 247 n.
crotchet *angularity* 247 n.
 notation 410 n.
 bias 481 n.
 punctuation 547 n.
 whim 604 n.
crotchety
 unconformable 84 adj.
 misjudging 481 adj.
 crazed 503 adj.
 wilful 602 adj.
 capricious 604 adj.
crouch *be low* 210 vb.
 stoop 311 vb.
 knuckle under 721 vb.
 quake 854 vb.
 be servile 879 vb.
croup *buttocks* 238 n.
 rear 238 n.
 respiration 352 n.
croupier *treasurer* 798 n.
croupy *diseased* 651 adj.
crow *bird* 365 n.
 ululate 409 vb.
 black thing 428 n.
 tool 630 n.
 cleaner 648 n.
 defy 711 vb.
 triumph 727 vb.
 rejoice, laugh 835 vb.
 eyesore 842 n.
 boast 877 vb.
crowbar *tool* 630 n.
crowd *great quantity* 32 n.
 medley 43 n.
 crowd 74 n.
 multitude 104 n.
 be near 200 vb.
 be contiguous 202 vb.
 be dense 324 vb.
 viol 414 n.
 redundance 637 n.
 obstruct 702 vb.
 party 708 n.
crown *completeness* 54 n.
 vertex 213 n.
 summit, head 213 n.
 crown 213 vb.
 headgear 228 n.
 limit 236 vb.

 loop 250 n.
 strike 279 vb.
 badge, heraldry 547 n.
 objective 617 n.
 perfect 646 vb.
 doctor 658 vb.
 completion 725 n.
 climax 725 vb.
 trophy 729 n.
 authority 733 n.
 regalia 743 n.
 badge of rank 743 n.
 commission 751 vb.
 coinage 797 n.
 ornamentation 844 n.
 decorate 844 vb.
 honours 866 n.
 pay respects 884 vb.
 reward 962 n.
crown all *culminate* 34 vb.
 climax 725 vb.
crowned head
 sovereign 741 n.
crowning *topmost* 213 adj.
crowning point
 summit 213 n.
crow over *defy* 711 vb.
 triumph 727 vb.
 boast 877 vb.
crow's feet *fold* 261 n.
crow's nest *vertex* 213 n.
 view 438 n.
crow to pluck
 resentment 891 n.
crozier (*see* crosier)
crucial *circumstantial* 8 adj.
 crucial 137 adj.
 fundamental 156 adj.
 crossed 222 adj.
 demonstrating 478 adj.
crucial moment
 juncture 8 n.
 crisis 137 n.
crucial test
 experiment 461 n.
crucible *mixture* 43 n.
 crucible 147 n.
 vessel 194 n.
 heater 383 n.
 testing agent 461 n.
 workshop 687 n.
crucifer *church officer* 986 n.
 ritualist 988 n.
crucifix *hanger* 217 n.
 cross 222 n.
 ritual object 988 n.
 church interior 990 n.
crucifixion *killing* 362 n.
 pain 377 n.
 art subject 553 n.
 suffering 825 n.

 capital punishment 963 n.
cruciform *crossed* 222 adj.
 churchlike 990 adj.
crucify (*see* crucifixion)
crude *incomplete* 55 adj.
 beginning 68 adj.
 inelegant 576 adj.
 imperfect 647 adj.
 immature 670 adj.
 bungled 695 adj.
 graceless 842 adj.
cruel *violent* 176 adj.
 harmful 645 adj.
 warlike 718 adj.
 oppressive 735 adj.
 paining 827 adj.
 cruel 898 adj.
 pitiless 906 adj.
cruelly *painfully* 32 adv.
cruelty (*see* cruel)
cruet *vessel* 194 n.
 ritual object 988 n.
cruise *be in motion* 265 vb.
 travel 267 vb.
 water travel 269 vb.
cruiser *warship* 722 n.
cruiser-weight
 pugilist 722 n.
crumb *small thing* 33 n.
 piece 53 n.
 powder 332 n.
crumble *break* 46 vb.
 decompose 51 vb.
 be weak 163 vb.
 be destroyed 165 vb.
 pastry 301 n.
 be brittle 330 vb.
 pulverize 332 vb.
 impair 655 vb.
 deteriorate 655 vb.
crumbling
 antiquated 127 adj.
 weakened 163 adj.
 powdery 332 adj.
 unsafe 661 adj.
crumbly
 fragmentary 53 adj.
 brittle 330 adj.
 powdery 332 adj.
crumbs *rubbish* 641 n.
crumenal
 monetary 797 adj.
crumpet *head* 213 n.
 pastry 301 n.
crumple *jumble* 63 vb.
 distort 246 vb.
 crinkle 251 vb.
 fold 261 n., vb.
 impair 655 vb.
crumster
 merchant ship 275 n.

crunch *rend* 46vb.
  chew 301vb.
  pulverize 332vb.
  rasp 407vb.
crunk *ululate* 409vb.
cruor *blood* 335n.
crupper *buttocks* 238n.
  rear 238n.
crusade *war* 718n.
  philanthropy 901n.
crusader *militarist* 722n.
  philanthropist 901n.
  religionist 979n.
crusading spirit
  philanthropy 901n.
  pietism 979n.
cruse *vessel* 194n.
crush *jumble* 63vb.
  crowd 74n.
  demolish 165vb.
  force 176vb.
  make smaller 198vb.
  abase 311vb.
  pulverize 332vb.
  touch 378vb.
  confute 479vb.
  ill-treat 645vb.
  wound 655vb.
  overmaster 727vb.
  oppress 735vb.
  sadden 834vb.
  humiliate 872vb.
  love 887n.
crusher *pulverizer* 332n.
crushing *destructive* 165adj.
  forceful 571adj.
  laborious 682adj.
  hindering 702adj.
  completive 725adj.
  successful 727adj.
  distressing 827adj.
crust *piece* 53n.
  exteriority 223n.
  covering 226n.
  skin 226n.
  mouthful 301n.
  cereal 301n.
  be dense 324vb.
  land 344n.
crustacean *animal* 365n.
crusty *irascible* 892adj.
  sullen 893adj.
crutch *supporter* 218n.
  angularity 247n.
crux *cross* 222n.
  unintelligibility 517n.
  enigma 530n.
  difficulty 700n.
cry *feel pain* 377vb.
  loudness 400n.
  cry 408n., vb.

ululation 409n.
  proclaim 528vb.
  rumour 529n.
  lamentation 836n.
  weep 836vb.
  fashion 848n.
cry-baby *weakling* 163n.
  weeper 836n.
  coward 856n.
cry down *deprecate* 762vb.
  detract 926vb.
cry of 'wolf'
  insubstantial thing 4n.
  false alarm 665n.
cry out against
  dissuade 613vb.
  deprecate 762vb.
cry out for *require* 627vb.
cry over spilt milk
  regret 830vb.
crypt *cellar* 194n.
  tomb 364n.
  concealment 525n.
  hiding-place 527n.
  church interior 990n.
cryptesthesia *psychics* 984n.
cryptic *uncertain* 474adj.
  occult 523adj.
  concealed 525adj.
  cabbalistic 984adj.
crypto *latent* 523adj.
cryptogram *enigma* 530n.
cryptography *latency* 523n.
  secrecy 525n.
cry quits *submit* 721vb.
  be defeated 728vb.
cry shame *dispraise* 924vb.
crystal *minuteness* 196n.
  covering 226n.
  solid body 324n.
  transparency 422n.
  optical device 442n.
  oracle 511n.
crystal-gazer *diviner* 511n.
  occultist 984n.
crystalline
  symmetrical 245adj.
  dense 324adj.
  hard 326adj.
  transparent 422adj.
crystallization
  conversion 147n.
  condensation 324n.
  hardening 326n.
crystallize *efform* 243vb.
  be dense 324vb.
  harden 326vb.
  sweeten 392vb.
cry up *overrate* 482vb.
  praise 923vb.
  flatter 925vb.

cry wolf *misteach* 535vb.
  be false 541vb.
  raise the alarm 665vb.
  frighten 854vb.
cub *youngster* 132n.
  youngling 132n.
cubature *size* 195n.
  measurement 465n.
cubby-hole
  compartment 194n.
cube *do sums* 86vb.
  treble 94vb.
  angular figure 247n.
cube root
  numerical element 85n.
cubic *spatial* 183adj.
  angulated 247adj.
  metric 465adj.
cubic content *space* 183n.
  measure 183n.
  metrology 465n.
cubicle *compartment* 194n.
  chamber 194n.
Cubism
  school of painting 553n.
cubit *limb* 53n.
  long measure 203n.
cubital *brachial* 53adj.
cuckold *spouse* 894n.
  be impure 951vb.
  cuckold 952n.
cuckoldry
  illicit love 951n.
cuckoo *intruder* 59n.
  repetition 106n.
  ejector 300n.
  bird 365n.
  ululation 409n.
  fool 501n.
  crazed 503adj.
cucumber *vegetable* 301n.
cucurbit *vessel* 194n.
  plant 366n.
  heater 383n.
cud *mouthful* 301n.
cuddle *be near* 200vb.
  caress 889vb.
cuddlesome *loving* 878adj.
  caressing 878adj.
cuddy *chamber* 194n.
  beast of burden 273n.
cudgel *strike* 279vb.
  club 723n.
  flog 963vb.
  scourge 964n.
cudgel one's brains
  think 449vb.
cue *ram* 279n.
  reminder 505n.
  hint 524n.
cuff *sleeve* 228n.

fold 261 n.
knock 279 n.
corporal punishment
  963 n.
spank 963 vb.
cuff-link *fastening* 47 n.
cuirass *armour* 713 n.
cuirassier *cavalry* 722 n.
cuisine *cookery* 301 n.
cul-de-sac
  stopping place 145 n.
  cavity 255 n.
  closure 264 n.
  road 624 n.
  difficulty 700 n.
  obstacle 702 n.
culex *fly* 365 n.
culinary *culinary* 301 adj.
cull *dupe* 544 n.
  select 605 vb.
  take 786 vb.
cully *befool* 542 vb.
  dupe 544 n.
culminate *culminate* 34 vb.
  grow 36 vb.
  be complete 54 vb.
  be high 209 vb.
  crown 213 vb.
  ascend 308 vb.
  climax 725 vb.
culpable *wrong* 914 adj.
  blameworthy 924 adj.
  heinous 934 adj.
  guilty 936 adj.
culprit *offender* 904 n.
  accused person 928 n.
cult *practice* 610 n.
  business 622 n.
  fashion 848 n.
  affectation 850 n.
  religion 973 n.
  cult 981 n.
  rite 988 n.
cult image *idol* 982 n.
cultism *ornament* 574 n.
  affectation 850 n.
cultivable *agrarian* 370 adj.
cultivate *produce* 164 vb.
  make fruitful 171 vb.
  cultivate 370 vb.
  make better 654 vb.
  prepare 669 vb.
  patronize 703 vb.
  flatter 925 vb.
cultivated
  instructed 490 adj.
cultivation
  agriculture 370 n.
  culture 490 n.
  learning 536 n.
  civilization 654 n.

maturation 669 n.
good taste 846 n.
cultivator
  husbandman 370 n.
  countryman 869 n.
cultural *educational* 534 adj.
  improving 654 adj.
culture *breed stock* 369 vb.
  culture 490 n.
  learning 536 n.
  civilization 654 n.
  good taste 846 n.
cultured
  horticultural 370 adj.
  instructed 490 adj.
  spurious 542 adj.
cultus *practice* 610 n.
culver *bird* 365 n.
culverin *gun* 723 n.
culvert *drain* 351 n.
  access 624 n.
cumber *weigh* 322 vb.
  hinder 702 vb.
cumbersome, cumbrous
  weighty 322 adj.
  clumsy 695 adj.
  graceless 842 adj.
cummerbund *girdle* 47 n.
  belt 228 n.
  loop 250 n.
cumulative
  increasing 36 adj.
cumulativeness
  increase 36 n.
  continuity 71 n.
cumulus *cloud* 355 n.
cunctation *delay* 136 n.
  slowness 278 n.
  inaction 677 n.
cuneate
  angulated 247 adj.
cuneiform
  angulated 247 adj.
  letter 558 n.
  written 586 adj.
cunning *sagacity* 498 n.
  skill 694 n.
  cunning 698 n., adj.
  dishonest 930 adj.
cup *cup* 194 n.
  support 218 vb.
  cavity 255 n.
  void 300 vb.
  liquor 301 n.
  monument 548 n.
  doctor 658 vb.
  bane 659 n.
  trophy 729 n.
  adversity 731 n.
  suffering 825 n.
  painfulness 827 n.

reward 962 n.
ritual object 988 n.
cup-bearer *retainer* 742 n.
cupboard *cabinet* 194 n.
  shelf 218 n.
  storage 632 n.
cupel *vessel* 194 n.
  cup 194 n.
  heat 381 vb.
  testing agent 461 n.
cupful *finite quantity* 26 n.
cup-holder *superior* 34 n.
  proficient 696 n.
Cupid *a beauty* 841 n.
  love god 887 n.
cupidity *avarice* 816 n.
  desire 859 n.
Cupid's bow *curve* 248 n.
  coil 251 n.
  love emblem 887 n.
cupola *high structure* 209 n.
  roof 226 n.
  dome 253 n.
cupping-glass
  vessel 194 n.
cupreous *orange* 436 adj.
  brown 430 adj.
cups *drunkenness* 949 n.
cur *dog* 365 n.
  coward 856 n.
  cad 938 n.
curable *improved* 654 adj.
  restored 656 adj.
  medical 658 adj.
curacy *church office* 985 n.
curate *pastor* 986 n.
curative *restorative* 656 adj.
  remedial 658 adj.
  relieving 831 adj.
curator *collector* 492 n.
  protector 660 n.
  manager 690 n.
  keeper 749 n.
curb *moderate* 177 vb.
  slowness 278 n.
  retard 278 vb.
  safeguard 662 n.
  obstacle 702 n.
  restrain 747 vb.
  fetter 748 n.
curculio *vermin* 365 n.
curd *solid body* 324 n.
curdle *be dense* 324 vb.
  thicken 354 vb.
curds *milk* 301 n.
  milk product 301 n.
  semiliquidity 354 n.
cure *counteract* 182 vb.
  make better 654 vb.
  sanation 656 n.
  cure 656 vb.

remedy, therapy 658 n.
preserve 666 vb.
mature 669 vb.
relieve 831 vb.
church ministry 985 n.
laity 987 n.
cure-all remedy 658 n.
cureless unpromising 853 adj.
cure of disaccustom 611 vb.
cure of souls
  vocation 622 n.
  mandate 751 n.
  church ministry 985 n.
curette doctor 658 vb.
curfew evening 129 n.
  danger signal 665 n.
  restriction 747 n.
  prohibition 757 n.
curia council 692 n.
  ecclesiastical court 956 n.
curio exhibit 522 n.
  masterpiece 694 n.
  ornamentation 844 n.
curiosity
  nonconformist 84 n.
  curiosity 453 n.
  excitation 821 n.
  desire 859 n.
  prodigy 864 n.
curious beautiful 841 adj.
  (see curiosity)
curious literature
  impurity 951 n.
curl filament 208 n.
  curve 248 n.
  loop 250 n.
  coil 251 n.
  hair 259 n.
  fold 261 vb.
  badge of rank 743 n.
  hair-dressing 843 n.
  primp 843 vb.
curler thrower 287 n.
curlers fastening 47 n.
  hair-dressing 843 n.
curlicue coil 251 n.
  lettering 586 n.
  pattern 844 n.
curling sport 837 n.
curling-iron heater 383 n.
  hair-dressing 843 n.
curly undulatory 251 adj.
  hairy 259 adj.
curmudgeon niggard 816 n.
  rude person 885 n.
currach rowboat 275 n.
currant fruit 301 n.
currency existence 1 n.
  generality 79 n.
  publicity 528 n.
  money 797 n.

current existing 1 adj.
  general 79 adj.
  present 121 adj.
  happening 154 adj.
  electricity 160 n.
  motion 265 n.
  direction 281 n.
  progression 285 n.
  current 350 n.
  wind 352 n.
  known 490 adj.
  published 528 adj.
  usual 610 adj.
curricle carriage 274 n.
curriculum
  curriculum 534 n.
curried pungent 388 adj.
currish cowardly 856 adj.
  irascible 892 adj.
  sullen 893 adj.
  rascally 930 adj.
curry cook 301 vb.
  rub 333 vb.
  pungency 388 n.
  season 388 vb.
  condiment 389 n.
curry-comb rub 333 vb.
  groom 369 vb.
curry favour
  be servile 879 vb.
  flatter 925 vb.
curse influence 178 n.
  badness 645 n.
  bane 659 n.
  adversity 731 n.
  annoyance 827 n.
  discontent 829 n.
  malediction 899 n.
  condemn 961 vb.
  be impious 980 vb.
  spell 983 n.
cursed damnable 645 adj.
  sullen 893 adj.
cursitor notary 958 n.
cursive written 586 adj.
cursory
  inconsiderable 33 adj.
  transient 114 adj.
  inattentive 456 adj.
  hasty 680 adj.
curst irascible 892 adj.
  sullen 893 adj.
curt short 204 adj.
  concise 569 adj.
  taciturn 582 adj.
curtail subtract 39 vb.
  cut, sunder 46 vb.
  shorten 204 vb.
curtain separation 46 n.
  exclusion 57 n.
  end 69 n.

recurrence 106 n.
hang 217 vb.
surround 230 vb.
partition 321 n.
fence 235 n.
darken 418 vb.
screen 421 vb.
invisibility 444 n.
dramaturgy 594 n.
stage-set 594 n.
obstacle 702 n.
fortification 713 n.
curtain-call
  recurrence 106 n.
  dramaturgy 594 n.
  applause 923 n.
curtain lecture
  reprimand 924 n.
curtain-raiser
  beginning 68 n.
  stage play 594 n.
curtsy stoop 311 vb.
  obeisance 311 n.
  greet 884 vb.
  show respect 920 vb.
curule
  parliamentary 692 adj.
curvaceous curved 248 adj.
  convex 253 adj.
  shapely 841 adj.
curvation curvature 248 n.
curvature obliquity 220 n.
  curvature 248 n.
curve obliquity 220 n.
  curve 248 n.
  deviate 282 vb.
  circle 314 vb.
curves bluntness 257 n.
  beauty 841 n.
curvet equitation 267 n.
  leap 312 n., vb.
curvilinear curved 248 adj.
curving
  unsharpened 257 adj.
cushat bird 365 n.
cushion moderate 177 vb.
  seat, cushion 218 n.
  support 218 vb.
  line 227 vb.
  intermediary 231 n.
  put between 231 vb.
  soften 327 vb.
  euphoria 376 n.
  protection 660 n.
  defend 713 vb.
  relieve 831 vb.
cushy pleasurable 826 adj.
  content 828 adj.
cusp extremity 69 n.
  vertex 213 n.
  angularity 247 n.

sharp point 256 n.
cuspidate *sharp* 256 adj.
cuspidor *bowl* 194 n.
cuss *scurrility* 899 n.
   cuss 899 vb.
cussedness *opposition* 704 n.
   malevolence 898 n.
custard *pudding* 301 n.
custodial *tutelary* 660 adj.
   restraining 747 adj.
custodian *protector* 660 n.
   manager 690 n.
   interceptor 702 n.
   defender 713 n.
   keeper 749 n.
custody *protection* 660 n.
   detention 747 n.
custody, in *safe* 660 adj.
   imprisoned 747 adj.
   captive 750 adj.
custom *order* 60 n.
   continuity 71 n.
   generality 79 n.
   regularity 81 n.
   tradition 127 n.
   permanence 144 n.
   habit 610 n.
   barter 791 n.
   purchase 792 n.
   etiquette 848 n.
customable *priced* 809 adj.
customary
   preceptive 693 adj.
   unastonishing 865 adj.
   orthodox 976 adj.
   (*see* custom)
customer *person* 371 n.
   habitué 610 n.
   patron 707 n.
   purchaser 792 n.
customs *conduct* 688 n.
   receipt 807 n.
   tax 809 n.
customs house *mart* 796 n.
   treasury 799 n.
cut *adjust* 24 vb.
   diminution 37 n.
   subtract 39 vb.
   decrement 42 n.
   cut 46 vb.
   piece 53 n.
   discontinuity 72 n.
   gap 201 n.
   shorten 204 vb.
   lamina 207 n.
   form 243 n.
   excavation 255 n.
   be sharp 256 vb.
   smooth 258 vb.
   notch 260 n.
   groove 262 vb.

move fast 277 vb.
   knock 279 n.
   eject 300 vb.
   meat 301 n.
   give pain 377 vb.
   feature 445 n.
   disregard 458 vb.
   sculpt 554 vb.
   engrave 555 vb.
   wound 655 n., vb.
   not observe 769 vb.
   portion 783 n.
   discount 810 n., vb.
   cheapen 812 vb.
   hurt 827 vb.
   hair-dressing 843 n.
   fashion 848 n.
   make unwelcome 883 vb.
   be rude 885 vb.
cut above, a
   superior 34 adj.
cut a dash
   be important 638 vb.
   have repute 866 vb.
   be ostentatious 875 vb.
cut a figure *appear* 445 vb.
   be in fashion 848 vb.
   (*see* cut a dash)
cut and come again
   repeat 106 vb.
cut and dried *definite* 80 adj.
   ready-made 669 adj.
cut and thrust *foin* 712 n.
   fight 716 n.
cutaneous *dermal* 226 adj.
cut back *bate* 37 vb.
   subtract 39 vb.
   shorten 204 vb.
cut both ways
   tell against 467 vb.
   be equivocal 518 vb.
cut down *demolish* 165 vb.
   fell 311 vb.
   slaughter 362 vb.
   strike at 712 vb.
   (*see* cut back)
cute *personable* 841 adj.
cut glass
   ornamental art 844 n.
cut ice *influence* 178 vb.
cuticle *skin* 226 n.
cuticular *dermal* 226 adj.
cutie *a beauty* 841 n.
cut in *join a party* 708 vb.
cutis *skin* 226 n.
cutlass *sharp edge* 256 n.
   side arms 723 n.
cutlery *sharp edge* 256 n.
cutlet *piece* 53 n.
   (*see* meat)
cut off *set apart* 46 vb.

suppress 165 vb.
   circumscribe 232 vb.
   kill 362 vb.
   be concise 569 vb.
   hinder 702 vb.
   impoverish 801 vb.
cut of one's jib *form* 243 n.
   feature 445 n.
cut out *be superior* 34 vb.
   substitute 150 vb.
   efform 243 vb.
   plan 623 vb.
cut out for *fit* 24 adj.
   expedient 642 adj.
cut price *discount* 810 n.
   cheap 812 adj.
cutpurse *thief* 798 n.
cut short *halt* 145 vb.
   suppress 165 vb.
   shorten 204 vb.
   be concise 569 vb.
cutter *clothier* 228 n.
   sharp edge 256 n.
   boat 275 n.
   farm tool 370 n.
   epitomizer 592 n.
   artisan 686 n.
cut the Gordian knot
   disencumber 701 vb.
cut-throat
   destructive 165 adj.
   murderer 362 n.
   contending 716 adj.
   ruffian 904 n.
cut through *pierce* 263 vb.
cutting *scission* 46 n.
   excavation 255 n.
   sharp 256 adj.
   cinema 445 n.
   forceful 571 adj.
   railroad 624 n.
cuttings *record* 548 n.
   anthology 592 n.
cut to the quick *hurt* 827 vb.
cutty stool *penitence* 939 n.
   penance 941 n.
   pillory 964 n.
cut up *unhappy* 825 adj.
   hurt 827 vb.
   sadden 834 vb.
cut up rough
   be angry 891 vb.
   resent 891 vb.
cwm *valley* 255 n.
cyanic *blue* 435 adj.
cyanide *poison* 659 n.
cyanin, cyanine
   blue pigment 435 n.
cyanosis *blueness* 435 n.
cybernetics
   mechanics 630 n.

cyclamen *redness* 431 n.
cycle *recurrence* 106 n.
  era 110 n.
  regular return 141 n.
  orbit 250 n.
  ride 267 vb.
  bicycle 274 n.
cycle-rickshaw *cab* 274 n.
  bicycle 274 n.
cycling *land travel* 267 adj.
cyclist *rider* 268 n.
cycloid *arc* 250 n.
cyclometer *meter* 465 n.
cyclone *vortex* 315 n.
  weather 340 n.
  gale 352 n.
cyclopædia
  reference book 589 n.
Cyclopean *huge* 195 adj.
Cyclops *rara avis* 84 n.
  giant 195 n.
cyclorama *spectacle* 445 n.
cyclotron *nucleonics* 160 n.
cygnet *youngling* 132 n.
  waterfowl 365 n.
cylinder *cylinder* 252 n.
cylindrical *rotund* 252 adj.
  tubular 263 adj.
cymbalo *piano* 414 n.
  gong 414 n.
cynic *misanthrope* 902 n.
  detractor 926 n.
  ascetic 945 n.
cynical *indifferent* 860 adj.
  disrespectful 921 adj.
  disapproving 924 adj.
  detracting 926 adj.
  (*see* cynicism)
cynicism *philosophy* 449 n.
  moral insensibility 820 n.
  dejection 834 n.
  hopelessness 853 n.
  misanthropy 902 n.
  asceticism 945 n.
cynosural *well-seen* 443 adj.
cynosure *prototype* 23 n.
  focus 76 n.
  attraction 291 n.
  spectacle 445 n.
  signpost 547 n.
  desired object 859 n.
  prodigy 864 n.
  person of repute 866 n.
  pride 871 n.
  favourite 890 n.
cypress *tree* 366 n.
  lamentation 836 n.
cyst *bladder* 194 n.
cystic *capsular* 194 adj.
cytoblast, cytoplasm
  organism 358 n.

cytogenetics *biology* 358 n.
cytology *biology* 358 n.

D

dab *knock* 279 n.
  leap 312 vb.
  proficient 696 n.
dabble *moisten* 341 vb.
  make unclean 649 vb.
  be inactive 679 vb.
  amuse oneself 837 vb.
dabbler *experimenter* 461 n.
  sciolist 493 n.
  meddler 678 n.
dabbling *smattering* 491 adj.
dabchick *waterfowl* 365 n.
dabs *trace* 548 n.
dabster *proficient* 696 n.
da capo *again* 106 adv.
dace *table fish* 365 n.
dachshund *dog* 365 n.
dacoit *robber* 789 n.
dacoity *stealing* 788 n.
dactyl *prosody* 593 n.
dactylogy *deafness* 416 n.
  symbology 547 n.
  gesture 547 n.
dactylonomy
  numeration 86 n.
dad, daddy *parent* 169 n.
Dadaist *artist* 556 n.
dado *base* 214 n.
dædal, dædalian
  variegated 437 adj.
  well-made 694 adj.
  ornamental 844 adj.
dæmonic, demonic
  active 678 adj.
  diabolic 969 adj.
daffodil *yellowness* 433 n.
daft, daffy *foolish* 499 adj.
  crazed 503 adj.
dagger *sharp point* 256 n.
  punctuation 547 n.
  side-arms 723 n.
daggers drawn, at
  opposing 704 adj.
  quarrelling 709 adj.
  inimical 881 adj.
daggle *hang* 217 vb.
  make unclean 649 vb.
dago *foreigner* 59 n.
dagoba *temple* 990 n.
daguerreotype
  photograph 551 n.
dah *sharp edge* 256 n.
dai *obstetrics* 164 n.
Dail Eireann
  parliament 692 n.
daily *often* 139 adv.

  seasonal 141 adj.
  periodically 141 adv.
  the press, journal 528 n.
  usual 610 adj.
  servant 742 n.
daily bread *food* 301 n.
  vocation 622 n.
daily round
  uniformity 16 n.
  continuity 71 n.
  regular return 141 n.
  habit 610 n.
  business 622 n.
dainty *small* 33 adj.
  little 196 adj.
  food 301 n.
  savoury 390 adj.
  clean 648 adj.
  pleasurableness 826 n.
  shapely 841 adj.
  personable 841 adj.
  tasteful 846 adj.
  fastidious 862 adj.
dairy *chamber* 194 n.
  workshop 687 n.
dairy farm
  stock farm 369 n.
  farm 370 n.
dairymaid *domestic* 742 n.
dais *stand* 218 n.
  rostrum 539 n.
dak bungalow *inn* 192 n.
Dalai Lama
  sovereign 741 n.
  priest 986 n.
dale *plain* 348 n.
dalesman *dweller* 191 n.
dalliance *love-making* 887 n.
  endearment 889 n.
dally *be late* 136 vb.
  be irresolute 601 vb.
  be inactive 679 vb.
  amuse oneself 837 vb.
  caress 889 vb.
dalmatic *vestments* 989 n.
Daltonism *dim sight* 440 n.
dam *be akin* 11 vb.
  exclusion 57 n.
  halt 145 vb.
  maternity 169 n.
  close 264 vb.
  irrigator 341 n.
  lake 346 n.
  stanch 350 vb.
  obstruct 702 vb.
damage *break* 46 vb.
  derange 63 vb.
  weaken 163 vb.
  lay waste 165 vb.
  tell against 467 vb.
  evil 616 n.

waste 634n.
make insufficient 636vb.
inutility 641n.
harm 645vb.
impairment 655n.
cost 809n.
blemish 845vb.
defame 926vb.
damages offset 31n.
restitution 787n.
cost 809n.
penalty 963n.
damaging harmful 645adj.
discreditable 867adj.
maleficent 898adj.
damascene
variegate 437vb.
damask textile 222n.
red colour 431n.
dame lady 373n.
teacher 537n.
master 741n.
title 870n.
dammed born 360adj.
damn scurrility 899n.
curse, cuss 899vb.
dispraise 924vb.
condemn 961vb.
damnable evil 616adj.
damnable 645adj.
unpleasant 827adj.
heterodox 977adj.
damnably extremely 32adv.
damnation
future state 124n.
suffering 825n.
condemnation 961n.
damnatory
maledictory 899adj.
disapproving 924adj.
accusing 928adj.
damnify harm 645vb.
impair 655vb.
damn the consequences
be obstinate 602vb.
be rash 857vb.
damp moderate 177vb.
gas 336n.
water 339n.
moisture 341n.
extinguish 382vb.
mute 401vb.
sound dead 405vb.
hinder 702vb.
deject 834vb.
damped
incombustible 382adj.
non-resonant 405adj.
dampen dissuade 613vb.
(see damp)
damper moderator 177n.

stopper 264n.
heater 383n.
silencer 401n.
non-resonance 405n.
piano, mute 414n.
dissuasion 613n.
hinderer 702n.
moper 834n.
disapprover 924n.
damp-proof
unyielding 162adj.
dry 342adj.
damp squib
insubstantial thing 4n.
disappointment 509n.
damsel youngster 132n.
damson fruit 301n.
redness 431n.
dance vary 152vb.
be in motion 265vb.
walk 267vb.
ascend 308vb.
leap 312n.,vb.
fluctuation 317n.
oscillate 317vb.
be agitated 318vb.
shine 417vb.
be excited 821vb.
be excitable 822vb.
be cheerful 833vb.
rejoice 835vb.
dance 837n.,vb.
dancing 837n.
social gathering 882n.
be angry 891vb.
dance attendance
accompany 89vb.
wait 136vb.
follow 284vb.
be servile 789vb.
dance-floor, dance-hall
place of amusement 837n.
dancer jumper 312n.
dance 837n.
dance-step gait 265n.
leap 312n.
dancing gay 833adj.
dancing 837n.
dancing girl
entertainer 594n.
dancing-master
trainer 537n.
dancing school
academy 539n.
dander anger 891n.
dandified
fashionable 848adj.
dandiprat dwarf 196n.
fop 848n.
dandle caress 889vb.
dandruff dirt 649n.

dandy vehicle 274n.
sailing-ship 275n.
topping 644adj.
fop 848n.
fashionable 848adj.
affector 850n.
dandyism affectation 850n.
danegeld tax 809n.
danger probability 471n.
unreliability 474n.
omen 511n.
latency 523n.
danger 661n.
pitfall 663n.
danger, in liable 180adj.
endangered 661adj.
in difficulties 700adj.
danger list, on the
sick 651adj.
dangerous harmful 645adj.
dangerous 661adj.
difficult 700adj.
frightening 854adj.
inimical 881adj.
angry 891adj.
irascible 892adj.
malevolent 898adj.
threatening 900adj.
danger signal signal 547n.
dissuasion 613n.
danger signal 665n.
threat 900n.
danger-spot pitfall 663n.
dangle come unstuck 49vb.
wait 136vb.
pendant 217n.
hang 217vb.
oscillate 317vb.
show 522vb.
cause desire 859vb.
dangler follower 284n.
Daniel sage 500n.
dank humid 341adj.
cheerless 834adj.
danseuse actor 594n.
dao sharp edge 256n.
dapper personable 841adj.
dapple brown 430adj.
variegate 437vb.
dappled pied 437adj.
darbies fetter 748n.
dare be resolute 599vb.
face danger 661vb.
undertake 672vb.
oppose 704vb.
defy 711vb.
be free 744vb.
be courageous 855vb.
threat 900n.
dare-devil
brave person 855n.

desperado 857n.
rash 857adj.
dare say *assume* 471vb.
daric *coinage* 797n.
daring *undisguised* 522adj.
  showy 875adj.
  unchaste 951adj.
  (*see* dare)
dark *vespertine* 129adj.
  dark 418adj.
  black 428adj.
  brown 430adj.
  blind 439adj.
  invisible 444adj.
  unknown 491adj.
  ignorant 491adj.
  unintelligible 517adj.
  latent 523adj.
  imperspicuous 568adj.
  sullen 893adj.
  dishonest 930adj.
  cabbalistic 984adj.
Dark Ages *antiquity* 125n.
  unknown thing 491n.
darken *darken* 418vb.
  blind 439vb.
  blur 440vb.
  be unseen 444vb.
  conceal 525vb.
  deject 834vb.
  make ugly 842vb.
dark glasses *screen* 421n.
  eyeglass 442n.
dark horse
  unknown thing 491n.
  latency 523n.
  secret 530n.
dark, in the
  darkling 418adv.
  invisibly 444adv.
  ignorant 491adj.
dark-lantern
  glimmer 419n.
  lamp 420n.
darkness
  uncertainty 474n.
  ignorance 491n.
  (*see* dark)
darkness, in
  heathenish 974adj.
dark-room *darkness* 418n.
dark-skinned
  blackish 428adj.
darky *negro* 428n.
darling *loved one* 887n.
  lovable 887adj.
  darling 890n.
  favourite 890n.
darn *join* 45vb.
  repair 656n.,vb.
dart *vary* 152vb.

move fast 277vb.
missile 287n.
propel 287vb.
missile weapon 723n.
darting *pain pang* 377n.
Darwinism *biology* 358n.
dash *small quantity* 33n.
  tincture 43n.
  bond 47n.
  vigorousness 174n.
  spurt 277n.
  move fast 277vb.
  be agitated 318vb.
  flow 350vb.
  punctuation 547n.
  mark 547vb.
  resolution 599n.
  be active 678vb.
  hasten 680vb.
  racing 716n.
  defeat 727vb.
  warm feeling 818n.
  fashion 848n.
  courage 855n.
  ostentation 875n.
dash against *collide* 279vb.
dash at *charge* 712vb.
dash down *fell* 311vb.
dashed *humbled* 872adj.
dashing (*see* dash)
dash one's hopes
  disappoint 509vb.
  miscarry 728vb.
dastard *coward* 856n.
data, datum
  evidence 466n.
  premise 475n.
  supposition 512n.
datal *chronological* 117n.
datary *chronologist* 117n.
date *date* 108n.
  chronology 117n.
  fruit 301n.
  social round 882n.
  lover 887n.
dateless *perpetual* 115adj.
datelessness *neverness* 109n.
date-line *dividing line* 92n.
  limit 236n.
date-list *chronology* 117n.
date-palm *tree* 366n.
date up *be sociable* 882vb.
datum (*see* data)
daub *coat* 226vb.
  colour 425vb.
  unmeaningness 515n.
  misrepresentation 552n.
  picture 553n.
  paint 553vb.
  make unclean 649vb.
dauber *artist* 556n.

bungler 697n.
daughter *descendant* 170n.
  woman 373n.
daughterly *filial* 170adj.
  obedient 739adj.
daunt *dissuade* 613vb.
  frighten 854vb.
  humiliate 872vb.
dauntless *unfearing* 855adj.
dauphin *sovereign* 741n.
davenport *cabinet* 194n.
davit *hanger* 217n.
daw *fool* 501n.
dawdle *drag on* 113vb.
  be late 136vb.
  wander 267vb.
  walk 267vb.
  move slowly 278vb.
  be inactive 679vb.
dawdler *slowcoach* 278n.
  idler 679n.
dawn *precursor* 66n.
  beginning 68n.
  morning 128n.
  make bright 417vb.
  redness 431n.
  appear 445vb.
Dawn Man *mankind* 371n.
dawn upon
  be visible 443vb.
  dawn upon 449vb.
day *date* 108n.
  period 110n.
day after day
  repeatedly 106adv.
  perpetually 139adv.
day and night
  perpetually 139adv.
day-book *record* 548n.
  account book 808n.
daybreak *morning* 128n.
  half-light 419n.
day by day
  repeatedly 106adv.
  while 108adv.
  all along 113adv.
  periodically 141adv.
daydream *fantasy* 513n.
  desire 959n.,vb.
daydreaming
  abstractedness 456n.
  fantasy 513n.
daylight *interval* 201n.
  light 417n.
  manifestation 522n.
  disclosure 526n.
daylight saving
  clock time 117n.
day of abstinence
  fast 946n.
day off *lull* 145n.

leisure 681 n.
repose 683 n.
day of judgment
  finality 69 n.
  punishment 963 n.
day of obligation
  holy-day 988 n.
day of reckoning
  revenge 910 n.
  punishment 963 n.
day of rest *repose* 683 n.
  holy-day 988 n.
day of the week *date* 108 n.
days *time* 108 n.
  era 110 n.
days of grace *delay* 136 n.
day-star *morning* 128 n.
  sun 321 n.
daze *blur* 440 vb.
  distract 456 vb.
  puzzle 474 vb.
  be wonderful 864 vb.
dazed *insensible* 375 adj.
  dim-sighted 440 adj.
  distracted 456 adj.
  doubting 474 adj.
  foolish 499 adj.
dazzle *light* 417 n.
  shine 417 vb.
  blind 439 vb.
  blur 440 vb.
  be visible 443 vb.
  distract 456 vb.
  deceive 542 vb.
  impress 821 vb.
  be beautiful 841 vb.
  be wonderful 864 vb.
  prestige 866 n.
  be ostentatious 875 vb.
  excite love 887 vb.
  command respect 920 vb.
dazzler *a beauty* 841 n.
dazzling *excellent* 644 adj.
  (*see* dazzle)
D-day *start* 68 n.
  date 108 n.
  special day 876 n.
deacon *cleric* 986 n.
deaconess *nun* 986 n.
deaconship
  church office 985 n.
deactivate *weaken* 163 vb.
  assuage 177 vb.
  impair 655 vb.
deactivated *inert* 175 adj.
dead *unborn* 2 adj.
  past 125 adj.
  inert 175 adj.
  quiescent 266 adj.
  dead 361 adj.
  insensible 375 adj.

muted 401 adj.
non-resonant 405 adj.
soft-hued 425 adj.
colourless 426 adj.
non-active 677 adj.
abrogated 752 adj.
dead against
  in opposition 704 adv.
dead and buried
  forgotten 506 adj.
dead-beat *impotent* 161 adj.
  impulse 279 n.
  fatigued 684 adj.
dead body *corpse* 363 n.
dead centre *centrality* 225 n.
dead-centre
  accurate 494 adj.
dead earnest
  seriousness 834 n.
deaden *disable* 161 vb.
  assuage 177 vb.
  kill 362 vb.
  render insensible 375 vb.
  mute 401 vb.
  sound dead 405 vb.
  decolorize 426 vb.
  make mute 578 vb.
  make insensitive 820 vb.
  relieve 831 vb.
  make inactive 879 vb.
dead end
  stopping place 145 n.
  closure 264 n.
  obstacle 702 n.
dead-eye *orifice* 263 n.
deadfall *trap* 542 n.
deadhead *playgoer* 594 n.
  recipient 782 n.
dead heat *draw* 28 n.
  synchronism 123 n.
dead-house *death* 361 n.
deadish *tasteless* 387 adj.
dead letter
  ineffectuality 161 n.
  unmeaningness 515 n.
  rubbish 641 n.
  abrogation 752 n.
dead level *uniformity* 16 n.
  horizontality 216 n.
deadlight *glow-worm* 420 n.
  curtain 421 n.
deadline *limit* 236 n.
deadliness (*see* deadly)
deadlock *draw* 28 n.
  equilibrium 28 n.
  stop 145 n.
  quiescence 266 n.
  impossibility 470 n.
  difficulty 700 n.
  obstacle 702 n.
  non-completion 726 n.

defeat 728 n.
deadly *destructive* 165 adj.
  vigorous 174 adj.
  deadly 362 adj.
  evil 616 adj.
  harmful 645 adj.
  toxic 653 adj.
  dull 840 adj.
  malevolent 898 adj.
  heinous 934 adj.
dead man's handle
  safeguard 662 n.
dead march *obsequies* 364 n.
  musical piece 412 n.
deadness (*see* dead)
dead of night
  midnight 129 n.
  darkness 418 n.
dead-on *accurate* 494 adj.
dead-pan *still* 266 adj.
  impassive 820 adj.
  inexcitable 823 adj.
  serious 834 adj.
dead reckoning
  navigation 269 n.
  measurement 465 n.
dead set at *attack* 712 n.
dead shot *proficient* 696 n.
dead spit *analogue* 18 n.
dead stop *stop* 145 n.
  quiescence 266 n.
  hitch 702 n.
  failure 728 n.
dead to
  thick-skinned 820 adj.
dead-weight
  encumbrance 702 n.
dead wood *rubbish* 641 n.
deaf *deaf* 416 adj.
  inattentive 456 adj.
  indiscriminating 464 adj.
  obstinate 602 adj.
  non-active 677 adj.
deaf and dumb
  deaf 416 adj.
  voiceless 578 adj.
deaf and dumb language
  gesture 547 n.
deafen *be loud* 400 vb.
  deafen 416 vb.
  make insensitive 820 vb.
deaf-mute *deafness* 416 n.
  aphony 578 n.
deafness *deafness* 416 n.
deal *great quantity* 32 n.
  arrange 62 vb.
  disperse 75 vb.
  compact 765 n.
  deed 676 n.
  give 781 vb.
  portion 783 n.

apportion 783 vb.
trade 791 n.
dealer *agent* 686 n.
seller 793 n.
merchant 794 n.
deal in *do* 676 vb.
trade 791 vb.
dealings *deed* 676 n.
deal with *be related* 9 vb.
dissert 591 vb.
deal with 688 vb.
make terms 766 vb.
trade 791 vb.
dean *ecclesiarch* 986 n.
deanery *church office* 985 n.
parish 985 n.
parsonage 986 n.
deanship *seniority* 131 n.
church office 985 n.
dear *known* 490 adj.
profitless 641 adj.
dear 811 adj.
pleasurable 826 adj.
loved one 887 n.
lovable 887 adj.
darling 890 n.
dearth
unproductivity 172 n.
scarcity 636 n.
dearness 811 n.
death *extinction* 2 n.
decay 51 n.
destroyer 168 n.
quietude 266 n.
death 361 n.
death-bed *decease* 361 n.
illness 651 n.
death, be in at the
arrive 295 vb.
carry out 725 vb.
deathblow *end* 69 n.
death 361 n.
killing 362 n.
defeat 728 n.
death column
death roll 361 n.
death-dealing
murderous 362 adj.
death-duty *tax* 809 n.
deathhouse
prison camp 748 n.
death-knell *decease* 361 n.
death 361 n.
deathless *perpetual* 115 adj.
renowned 866 adj.
deathlessness
famousness 866 n.
deathlike *dying* 361 adj.
cadaverous 363 adj.
silent 399 adj.
deathliness *quiescence* 266 n.

deathly *dying* 361 adj.
deadly 362 adj.
cadaverous 363 adj.
colourless 426 adj.
death mask *copy* 22 n.
death of *worry* 825 n.
annoyance 827 n.
death rate *statistics* 86 n.
death roll 361 n.
death-rattle *decease* 361 n.
death scene *decease* 361 n.
death sentence
capital punishment 963 n.
death's head *moper* 834 n.
eyesore 842 n.
disapprover 924 n.
death-trap *danger* 661 adj.
pitfall 663 n.
death-warrant
condemnation 961 n.
capital punishment 963 n.
death-watch *decease* 361 n.
death-wish *dejection* 834 n.
débâcle *revolution* 149 n.
ruin 165 n.
descent 309 n.
defeat 728 n.
debag *uncover* 229 vb.
debar *obstruct* 702 vb.
restrain 747 vb.
prohibit 757 vb.
refuse 760 vb.
debase *abase* 311 vb.
pervert 655 vb.
impair 655 vb.
demonetize 797 vb.
shame 867 vb.
disentitle 916 vb.
debasement *lowness* 210 n.
improbity 930 n.
(*see* debase)
debatable *topical* 452 adj.
moot 459 adj.
uncertain 474 adj.
arguing 475 adj.
debate *argument* 475 n.
conference 584 n.
be irresolute 601 vb.
contention 716 n.
debater *reasoner* 475 n.
debauch *pervert* 655 vb.
festivity 837 n.
sensualism 944 n.
drunkenness 949 n.
debauch 951 vb.
debauched *vicious* 934 adj.
debauchee *reveller* 837 n.
sensualist 944 n.
libertine 952 n.
debauchery
sensualism 944 n.

unchastity 951 n.
debenture *title-deed* 767 n.
paper money 797 n.
debility *weakness* 163 n.
ill-health 651 n.
debit *debt* 803 n.
account 808 vb.
debonair *cheerful* 833 adj.
debouch *start out* 296 vb.
emerge, flow out 298 vb.
débris *remainder* 41 n.
piece 53 n.
accumulation 74 n.
powder 332 n.
rubbish 641 n.
debt *encumbrance* 702 n.
debt 803 n.
dueness 915 n.
debt of honour
promise 764 n.
compact 765 n.
debtor *debtor* 803 n.
debunk *abase* 311 vb.
ridicule 851 vb.
shame 867 vb.
humiliate 872 vb.
detract 926 vb.
début *début* 68 n.
celebration 876 n.
débutant, -e
beginner 538 n.
fop 848 n.
spinster 895 n.
decad *over five* 99 n.
decade *over five* 99 n.
period 110 n.
decadence
deterioration 655 n.
decagon
angular figure 247 n.
decalogue
code of duty 917 n.
decamp *decamp* 296 vb.
disappear 446 vb.
run away 620 vb.
decant *transpose* 272 vb.
void 300 vb.
let fall 311 vb.
infuse 303 vb.
decanter *vessel* 194 n.
transferrer 272 n.
decapitate *subtract* 39 vb.
cut, sunder 46 vb.
execute 963 vb.
decarbonize *purify* 648 vb.
decathlon *contest* 716 n.
decay *extinction* 2 n.
decrease 37 vb.
decay 51 n.
be old 127 vb.
age 131 n.

destroyer 168 n.
become small 198 vb.
death 361 n.
desuetude 611 n.
waste 634 vb.
badness 645 n.
dirt 649 n.
dilapidation 655 n.
decease *decease* 361 n.
die 361 vb.
deceit *deception* 542 n.
deceitful *false* 541 adj.
deceiving 542 adj.
cunning 698 adj.
deceive *mislead* 495 vb.
dissemble 541 vb.
deceive 542 vb.
be cunning 698 vb.
be affected 850 vb.
flatter 925 vb.
be dishonest 930 vb.
be impure 951 vb.
deceived husband
cuckold 952 n.
deceiver *deceiver* 545 n.
tergiversator 603 n.
slyboots 698 n.
affector 850 n.
libertine 952 n.
deceiving *simulating* 18 adj.
disappointing 509 adj.
deceleration
diminution 37 n.
delay 136 n.
slowness 278 n.
hindrance 702 n.
restraint 747 n.
Decembrist
revolter 738 n.
decency *good taste* 846 n.
etiquette 848 n.
right 913 n.
purity 950 n.
decennial *seasonal* 141 adj.
decennium *period* 110 n.
decent *not bad* 644 adj.
mediocre 732 adj.
personable 841 adj.
tasteful 846 adj.
well-bred 848 adj.
ethical 917 adj.
pure 950 adj.
decentralization
non-uniformity 17 n.
decomposition 51 n.
arrangement 62 n.
dispersion 75 n.
laxity 734 n.
commission 751 n.
deception
insubstantiality 4 n.

concealment 525 n.
(*see* deceptive)
deceptive *simulating* 18 adj.
appearing 445 adj.
sophistical 477 adj.
erroneous 495 adj.
disappointing 509 adj.
false 541 adj.
deceiving 542 adj.
de-christianize
paganize 974 vb.
de-christianized
profane 980 adj.
decibar *weather* 340 n.
decibel *sound* 398 n.
metrology 465 n.
decide *terminate* 69 vb.
cause 156 vb.
answer 460 vb.
make certain 473 vb.
judge 480 vb.
be resolute 599 vb.
choose 605 vb.
decree 737 vb.
try a case 959 vb.
decided *assertive* 532 adj.
volitional 595 adj.
decidedly *positively* 32 adv.
deciduous
ephemeral 114 adj.
descending 309 adj.
vegetal 366 adj.
deteriorated 655 adj.
decimal
numerical element 85 n.
decimal point
punctuation 547 n.
decimal system
numeration 86 n.
decimate *bate* 37 vb.
multisect 100 vb.
render few 105 vb.
weaken 163 vb.
destroy 165 vb.
slaughter 362 vb.
execute 963 vb.
decipher *decipher* 520 vb.
decipherable
intelligible 516 adj.
decipherment
interpretation 520 n.
translation 520 n.
decision *vigour* 571 n.
will 595 n.
(*see* decide)
decisive *timely* 137 adj.
crucial 137 adj.
causal 156 adj.
influential 178 adj.
evidential 466 adj.
demonstrating 478 adj.

assertive 532 adj.
commanding 737 adj.
decivilize *pervert* 655 vb.
deck *compartment* 194 n.
layer 207 n.
roof 226 n.
overlay 226 vb.
dress 228 vb.
plaything 837 n.
decorate 844 vb.
deckhand *mariner* 270 n.
deckle-edge
roughness 259 n.
declaim *proclaim* 528 vb.
orate 579 vb.
declaimer *speaker* 579 n.
declamation *vigour* 571 n.
magniloquence 574 n.
oratory 579 n.
ostentation 875 n.
declarant *foreigner* 59 n.
declaration (*see* declare)
declaration of faith
creed 485 n.
declaratory
meaningful 514 adj.
publishing 528 adj.
affirming 532 adj.
declare *evidence* 466 vb.
believe 485 vb.
mean 514 vb.
divulge 526 vb.
proclaim 528 vb.
affirm 532 vb.
indicate 547 vb.
speak 579 vb.
decree 737 vb.
resign 753 vb.
declare war *quarrel* 709 vb.
attack 712 vb.
go to war 718 vb.
declassify *exclude* 57 vb.
derange 63 vb.
declension
differentiation 15 n.
change 143 n.
transition 147 n.
grammar 564 n.
(*see* decline)
declination *bearings* 186 n.
divergence 294 n.
descent 309 n.
decline *inferiority* 35 n.
decrease 37 n., vb.
oldness 127 n.
weakness 163 n.
be weak 163 vb.
contraction 198 n.
be oblique 220 vb.
regression 286 n.
recede 290 vb.

descent 309 n.
parse 564 vb.
reject 607 vb.
phthisis 651 n.
deterioration 655 n.
not use 674 vb.
adversity 731 n.
declivity *acclivity* 220 n.
descent 309 n.
decoction *potion* 301 n.
solution 337 n.
heating 381 n.
decode *decipher* 520 vb.
decollation
capital punishment 963 n.
décolleté *uncovering* 229 n.
decoloration
achromatism 426 n.
decolorize *decolorize* 426 vb.
make ugly 842 vb.
decompose *disjoin* 46 vb.
decompose 51 vb.
disperse 75 vb.
perish 361 vb.
be unclean 649 vb.
deteriorate 655 vb.
decompound
decompose 51 vb.
deconsecrate *depose* 752 vb.
paganize 974 vb.
laicize 987 vb.
deconsecrated
profane 980 adj.
decontrol *liberation* 746 n.
permit 756 vb.
non-retention 779 n.
décor *spectacle* 445 n.
stage-set 594 n.
pageant 875 n.
decorate *beautify* 841 vb.
(*see* decoration)
decoration
concomitant 89 n.
spectacle 445 n.
badge 547 n.
monument 548 n.
ornament 574 n.
improvement 654 n.
decoration 729 n.
badge of rank 743 n.
ornamentation 844 n.
honours 866 n.
reward 962 n.
decorative *painted* 553 adj.
ornamental 844 adj.
decorator *mender* 656 n.
artisan 686 n.
decorous *well-bred* 848 adj.
pure 950 adj.
decortication
uncovering 229 n.

decorum *good taste* 846 n.
etiquette 848 n.
decoy *attraction* 291 n.
ambush 527 n.
trap 542 n.
trickster 545 n.
incentive 612 n.
decrease *decrease* 37 n., vb.
subtract 39 vb.
unproductivity 172 n.
become small 198 vb.
disappear 446 vb.
waste 634 vb.
scarcity 636 n.
deterioration 655 n.
loss 772 n.
decreasing *lesser* 35 adj.
decreasingly
diminuendo 37 adv.
decree *judgment* 480 n.
publication 528 n.
predetermination 608 n.
precept 693 n.
decree 737 n., vb.
impose a duty 917 vb.
legislation 953 n.
decree absolute
divorce 896 n.
decree nisi *divorce* 896 n.
decrement *decrease* 37 n.
subtraction 39 n.
decrement 42 n.
deficit 55 n.
contraction 198 n.
shortcoming 307 n.
loss 772 n.
discount 810 n.
decrepit *aged* 131 adj.
weak 163 adj.
unhealthy 651 adj.
dilapidated 655 adj.
decretal *judicial* 480 adj.
preceptive 693 adj.
decree 737 n.
commanding 737 adj.
legal 983 adj.
decrial
disapprobation 924 n.
detraction 926 n.
decry *hold cheap* 922 vb.
detract 926 vb.
decuple
fifth and over 99 adj.
decurion
army officer 741 n.
decury *over five* 99 n.
formation 722 n.
decussation *joint* 45 n.
crossing 222 n.
dedecoration
disrepute 867 n.

dedicate *offer* 759 vb.
give 781 vb.
dignify 866 vb.
sanctify 979 vb.
offer worship 981 vb.
perform ritual 988 vb.
dedicated
habituated 610 adj.
obedient 739 adj.
philanthropic 901 adj.
disinterested 931 adj.
dedicate to *use* 673 vb.
honour 866 vb.
dedication
nomenclature 561 n.
edition 589 n.
willingness 597 n.
resolution 599 n.
(*see* dedicated)
dedicator
commender 923 n.
deduce *assume* 471 vb.
reason 475 n.
demonstrate 478 vb.
interpret 520 vb.
deducible *evidential* 466 adj.
demonstrating 478 adj.
deduct *disjoin* 46 vb.
(*see* deduction)
deduction *diminution* 37 n.
subtraction 39 n.
decrement 42 n.
reasoning 475 n.
demonstration 478 n.
judgment 480 n.
non-payment 805 n.
discount 810 n.
deed *deed* 676 n.
conduct 688 n.
title-deed 767 n.
prowess 855 n.
deed of arms *fight* 716 n.
deed-poll *title-deed* 767 n.
deem *opine* 485 vb.
deemster *judge* 957 n.
deep *great* 32 adj.
spacious 183 adj.
deep 211 adj.
interior 224 adj.
ocean 343 n.
loud 400 adj.
hoarse 407 adj.
florid 425 adj.
black 428 adj.
wise 498 adj.
inexpressible 517 adj.
concealed 525 adj.
imperspicuous 568 adj.
cunning 698 adj.
felt 818 adj.
heinous 934 adj.

infernal 972 adj.
deep down *intrinsic* 5 adj.
deepen *augment* 36 vb.
  enlarge 197 vb.
  be deep 211 vb.
  blacken 428 vb.
  aggravate 832 vb.
deep-freeze
  refrigeration 382 n.
  cooled 382 adj.
  refrigerator 384 n.
  storage 632 n.
  preservation 666 n.
deep in *ingredient* 58 adj.
  attentive 455 adj.
  studious 536 adj.
deep-laid *matured* 669 adj.
  well-made 694 adj.
  cunning 698 adj.
deepness *depth* 211 n.
deep-rooted *intrinsic* 5 adj.
  lasting 113 adj.
  fixed 153 adj.
  strong 162 adj.
  deep 211 adj.
  habitual 610 adj.
  with affections 817 adj.
deep-sea *seafaring* 269 n.
deep-seated *intrinsic* 5 adj.
  lasting 113 adj.
  fixed 153 adj.
  deep 211 adj.
  interior 224 adj.
  habitual 610 adj.
deep water, in
  in difficulties 700 adj.
deer *speeder* 277 n.
  deer 365 n.
  coward 856 n.
deer-stalker *hunter* 619 n.
deev *mythical being* 970 n.
  demon 970 n.
deface *destroy* 165 vb.
  deform 244 vb.
  obliterate 550 vb.
  make useless 641 vb.
  impair 655 vb.
  make ugly 842 vb.
  blemish 845 vb.
defacer *destroyer* 168 n.
defæcate (*see* defecation)
defalcate
  be dishonest 930 vb.
defalcation *deficit* 55 n.
  shortcoming 307 n.
  non-payment 805 n.
defamation
  detraction 926 n.
defamatory
  disapproving 924 adj.
  detracting 926 adj.

accusing 928 adj.
defame *shame* 867 vb.
  not respect 921 vb.
  defame 926 vb.
  accuse 928 vb.
default *deficit* 55 n.
  shortcoming 307 n.
  negligence 458 n.
  not suffice 636 vb.
  non-payment 805 n.
  not pay 805 vb.
  fail in duty 918 vb.
defaulter *defrauder* 789 n.
  debtor 803 n.
  non-payer 805 n.
defeasance *abrogation* 752 n.
defeat *ruin* 165 n.
  puzzle 474 vb.
  confute 479 vb.
  defeat 728 n., 727 vb.
defeated, the *loser* 728 n.
defeatism *inaction* 677 n.
  dejection 834 n.
  hopelessness 853 n.
  nervousness 854 n.
  cowardice 856 n.
defeatist
  alarmist 854 n.
  misanthrope 902 n.
  (*see* defeatism)
defecation *cacation* 302 n.
  cleansing 648 n.
defect *inequality* 29 n.
  inferiority 35 n.
  decrement 42 n.
  deficit 55 n.
  shortcoming 307 n.
  requirement 627 n.
  insufficiency 636 n.
  defect 647 n.
  blemish 845 n.
  vice 934 n.
defectibility
  imperfection 647 n.
defection
  tergiversation 603 n.
  relinquishment 621 n.
  disobedience 738 n.
  revolt 738 n.
  dutilessness 918 n.
  perfidy 930 n.
defective *deformed* 246 adj.
  insane 503 adj.
  (*see* defect)
defedation
  uncleanness 649 n.
  impairment 655 n.
defence
  counteraction 182 n.
  rejoinder 460 n.
  counter-evidence 467 n.

argument 475 n.
  avoidance 620 n.
  protection 660 n.
  hindrance 702 n.
  defence 713 n.
  warfare 718 n.
  vindication 927 n.
  legal trial 959 n.
defenceless
  defenceless 161 adj.
  weak 163 adj.
  vulnerable 661 adj.
defences *protection* 660 n.
  defences 713 n.
defend *patronize* 703 vb.
  defend 713 vb.
  resist 715 vb.
defendant *prisoner* 750 n.
  accused person 928 n.
  litigant 959 n.
defended *strong* 162 adj.
defender *protector* 660 n.
  patron 707 n.
  defender 713 n.
  combatant 722 n.
  vindicator 927 n.
defenestrate *propel* 287 vb.
defenestration
  propulsion 287 n.
  corporal punishment 963 n.
defensible
  invulnerable 660 adj.
  defended 713 adj.
  vindicable 927 adj.
defensive *avoiding* 620 adj.
  hindering 702 adj.
  defending 713 adj.
  nervous 854 adj.
defer *put off* 136 vb.
  not complete 726 vb.
deference *submission* 721 n.
  obedience 739 n.
  loyalty 739 n.
  courtesy 884 n.
  respect 920 n.
deferential (*see* deference)
deferment *delay* 136 n.
  discount 810 n.
defer to *assent* 488 vb.
defiance *dissent* 489 n.
  affirmation 532 n.
  negation 533 n.
  opposition 704 n.
  dissension 709 n.
  defiance 711 n.
  disobedience 738 n.
  courage 855 n.
  boast 877 n.
  sauciness 878 n.
defiant
  uncomfortable 84 adj.

undisguised 522 adj.
deficiency *inferiority* 35 n.
 incompleteness 55 n.
 insufficiency 636 n.
 imperfection 647 n.
 defect 647 n.
 non-completion 726 n.
 vice 934 n.
deficient *small* 33 adj.
 deficient 307 adj.
 unintelligent 499 adj.
 unprovided 636 adj.
 unequipped 670 adj.
deficit *deficit* 55 n.
 shortcoming 307 n.
 insufficiency 636 n.
 non-completion 726 n.
 debt 803 n.
deficit finance *finance* 797 n.
 prodigality 815 n.
defile *gap* 201 n.
 walk 267 vb.
 passage 305 n.
 access 624 n.
 make unclean 649 vb.
 impair, pervert 655 vb.
 shame 867 vb.
 debauch 951 vb.
defilement
 uncleanness 649 n.
 impairment 655 n.
 slur 867 n.
 impurity 951 n.
define *specify* 80 vb.
 limit 236 vb.
 interpret 520 vb.
 name 561 vb.
definite *definite* 80 adj.
 limited 236 adj.
 well-seen 443 adj.
 positive 473 adj.
 accurate 494 adj.
 intelligible 516 adj.
 manifest 522 adj.
 informative 524 adj.
 assertive 532 adj.
 perspicuous 567 adj.
definition *limit* 236 n.
 interpretation 520 n.
 perspicuity 567 n.
 theology 973 n.
definitive *ending* 69 adj.
 definite 80 adj.
 interpretive 520 adj.
deflate *bate* 37 vb.
 disable 161 vb.
 make smaller 198 vb.
 abase, depress 311 vb.
 underestimate 483 vb.
 ridicule 851 vb.
 shame 867 vb.

humiliate 872 vb.
 detract 926 vb.
deflation *finance* 797 n.
 cheapness 812 n.
deflationary
 monetary 797 adj.
deflect
 render oblique 220 vb.
 make curved 248 vb.
 impel 279 n.
 deflect 282 vb.
 repel 292 vb.
 dissuade 613 vb.
 avoid 620 vb.
 parry 713 vb.
deflection *deviation* 282 n.
deflexion *curvature* 248 n.
defloration (*see* deflower)
deflower *unite with* 45 vb.
 pervert 655 vb.
 debauch 951 vb.
deforest *extract* 304 vb.
deform *force* 176 vb.
 deform 244 vb.
 distort 246 vb.
 misrepresent 552 vb.
 impair, pervert 655 vb.
 make ugly 842 vb.
 blemish 845 vb.
deformed *abnormal* 84 adj.
 disguised 525 adj.
deformity
 amorphism 244 n.
 deformity 246 n.
 ugliness 842 n.
 blemish 845 n.
defraud *deceive* 542 vb.
 defraud 788 vb.
 not pay 804 vb.
 be dishonest 930 vb.
defrauder
 trickster 545 n.
defrayment *payment* 804 n.
defrock *shame* 867 vb.
 depose 752 vb.
de-frost *heat* 381 vb.
deft *skilful* 694 adj.
defumigate
 have no smell 395 vb.
defunct *extinct* 2 adj.
 dead 361 adj.
 corpse 363 n.
 unwonted 611 adj.
defy *counteract* 182 vb.
 dissent 489 vb.
 negate 533 vb.
 be resolute 599 vb.
 face danger 661 vb.
 oppose 704 vb.
 defy 711 vb.
 resist 715 vb.

disobey 738 vb.
 be free 744 vb.
 be insolent 878 vb.
degauss *counteract* 182 vb.
degeneracy
 deterioration 655 n.
 wickedness 934 n.
degenerate
 changed person 147 n.
 be turned to 147 vb.
 deteriorated 655 adj.
 deteriorate 655 vb.
 relapse 657 vb.
 vicious 934 adj.
 cad 938 n.
 sensualist 944 n.
degenerative
 harmful 645 adj.
 diseased 651 adj.
deglutition *eating* 301 n.
degrade *bate* 37 vb.
 impair, pervert 655 vb.
 depose 752 vb.
 shame 867 vb.
 not respect 921 vb.
 hold cheap 922 vb.
 defame 926 vb.
 punish 963 vb.
degree *relativeness* 9 n.
 degree 27 n.
 series 71 n.
 angular measure 247 n.
 measurement 465 n.
 prestige 866 n.
 nobility 868 n.
degree-holder
 scholar 492 n.
degree-hungry
 studious 536 adj.
degree of latitude
 long measure 203 n.
degree of longitude
 long measure 203 n.
degrees, by
 gradatim 278 adv.
degree, to some
 partially 33 adv.
degustation *taste* 386 n.
dehortation
 dissuasion 613 n.
 warning 664 n.
 deprecation 762 n.
dehumanize *pervert* 655 vb.
 make wicked 934 vb.
dehumanized *cruel* 898 adj.
dehumidify *dry* 342 vb.
dehydration
 desiccation 342 n.
 preservation 666 n.
de-ice *heat* 381 vb.
deific *theotechnic* 966 adj.

deification
  dignification 866n.
  deification 982n.
deify *dignify* 866vb.
  worship 891vb.
  idolatrize 982vb.
deign *consent* 758vb.
deism *philosophy* 449n.
  religion, deism 973n.
deist *religionist* 973n.
deity *divineness* 965n.
Deity, the *cause* 156n.
  the Deity 965n.
dejected *unhappy* 825adj.
dejection *discontent* 829n.
  dejection 834n.
  hopelessness 853n.
de jure *due* 915adj.
  duly 915adv.
  legal 953adj.
  legally 953adv.
dekink *straighten* 249vb.
dekko *inspection* 438n.
delaminate *laminate* 207vb.
delation *accusation* 928n.
delator *informer* 524n.
  accuser 928n.
delay *protraction* 113n.
  delay 136n.
  lull 145n.
  slowness 278n.
  be irresolute 601vb.
  inaction 677n.
  be inactive 679vb.
  caution 858n.
delaying *hindering* 702adj.
delaying action
  avoidance 620n.
dele *obliterate* 550vb.
delectable *savoury* 390adj.
  pleasurable 826adj.
delectation *enjoyment* 824n.
delectus *textbook* 589n.
  reading matter 589n.
  anthology 592n.
delegate *agent* 686n.
  councillor 692n.
  mediator 720n.
  commission 751vb.
  delegate 754n.
delegation
  commission 751n.
  delegate 754n.
  transfer 780n.
deleted *disapproved* 924adj.
deleterious *harmful* 645adj.
deletion *subtraction* 39n.
  obliteration 550n.
deliberate *slow* 278adj.
  predetermined 608adj.
  intended 617adj.

leisurely 681adj.
  consult 691vb.
  cautious 858adj.
deliberation
  meditation 449n.
  slowness 278n.
  caution 858n.
deliberative
  thoughtful 449adj.
  advising 691adj.
deliberative assembly
  parliament 692n.
delicacy *weakness* 163n.
  savouriness 390n.
  discrimination 463n.
  ill-health 651n.
  beauty 841n.
  good taste 846n.
  fastidiousness 862n.
  purity 950n.
delicate *brittle* 330adj.
  textural 331adj.
  soft-hued 425adj.
  accurate 494adj.
  difficult 700adj.
  pleasurable 826adj.
  (*see delicacy*)
delicatessen *pastry* 301n.
delicious *edible* 301adj.
  pleasant 376adj.
  savoury 390adj.
  topping 644adj.
  pleasurable 826adj.
delight *pleasure* 376n.
  excite 821vb.
  joy 824n.
  pleasurableness 826n.
  delight 826vb.
  amusement 837n.
  amuse 837vb.
delighted *willing* 597adj.
  jubilant 833adj.
delightful *pleasant* 376adj.
  pleasurable 826adj.
delight in *be pleased* 824vb.
delimit *limit* 236vb.
  mark 547vb.
  apportion 783vb.
delineation *outline* 233n.
  representation 551n.
  description 590n.
delinquency
  shortcoming 307n.
  wickedness 934n.
  guilt 936n.
delinquent
  trouble-maker 663n.
  low fellow 869n.
  offender 904n.
deliquescence
  decrease 37n.

liquefaction 337n.
deliquium
  helplessness 161n.
  fatigue 684n.
delirium *frenzy* 503n.
  fantasy 513n.
  unmeaningness 515n.
  illness 651n.
  excitable state 822n.
delirium tremens
  frenzy 503n.
  alcoholism 949n.
delitescence
  invisibility 444n.
  latency 523n.
  seclusion 883n.
deliver *transfer* 272vb.
  provide 633vb.
  restore 656vb.
  preserve 666vb.
  deliver 668vb.
  disencumber 701vb.
  aid 703vb.
  liberate 746vb.
  convey 780vb.
  give 781vb.
  restitute 787vb.
  relieve 831vb.
  vindicate 927vb.
deliverance *safety* 660n.
  escape 667n.
  (*see deliver*)
deliverer *preserver* 666n.
  defender 713n.
  benefactor 903n.
deliver the goods
  be expedient 642vb.
  carry out 725vb.
delivery *obstetrics* 164n.
  transference 272n.
  voice 577n.
  speech 579n.
  provision 633n.
  deliverance 668n.
  transfer 780n.
dell *valley* 255n.
delousing *cleansing* 648n.
delta *land* 344n.
  gulf 345n.
  plain 348n.
delude *deceive* 542vb.
  (*see delusion*)
deluge *crowd* 74n.
  drench 341vb.
  flow 350vb.
  superabound 637vb.
delusion *error* 495n.
  fantasy 513n.
  deception 542n.
delusions
  psychopathy 503n.

delusive *erroneous* 495 adj.
  deceiving 542 adj.
de luxe *comfortable* 376 adj.
  ostentatious 875 adj.
delve *make concave* 255 vb.
  cultivate 370 vb.
delve into *enquire* 459 vb.
demagogue *leader* 690 n.
  agitator 738 n.
demagogy
  government 733 n.
demand *enquire* 459 vb.
  require 627 vb.
  warning 664 n.
  demand 737 n., vb.
  request 761 n., vb.
  give terms 766 vb.
  desire 859 n., vb.
  purchase 792 n.
  claim 915 vb.
demanding
  fatiguing 684 adj.
demarcate *limit* 236 vb.
  mark 547 vb.
  apportion 783 vb.
démarche *beginning* 68 n.
dematerialize *not be* 2 vb.
  disembody 320 vb.
  disappear 446 vb.
  practise occultism 984 vb.
demeaning
  degrading 867 adj.
demean oneself
  behave 688 vb.
  demean oneself 867 vb.
demeanour *mien* 445 n.
  gesture 547 n.
  conduct 688 n.
dement *make mad* 503 vb.
démenti *negation* 533 n.
dementia *insanity* 503 n.
demerit *undueness* 916 n.
  vice 934 n.
demesne *farm* 370 n.
  lands 777 n.
demi- *bisected* 92 adj.
demibastion
  fortification 713 n.
demigod *god* 966 n.
  demigod 967 n.
demigration
  wandering 267 n.
demijohn *vessel* 194 n.
demilitarize
  disable 161 vb.
  make peace 719 vb.
demilune *fortification* 713 n.
demi-monde
  lower classes 869 n.
  wickedness 934 n.
  prostitute 952 n.

demi-rep *prostitute* 952 n.
  loose woman 952 n.
demise *decease* 361 n.
  die 361 vb.
  bequeath 780 vb.
  lease 784 vb.
demission *resignation* 753 n.
Demiurge *the Deity* 965 n.
demivolt *leap* 312 n.
demobilization
  dispersion 75 n.
  impotence 161 n.
  peace 717 n.
  pacification 719 n.
  liberation 746 n.
democracy *nation* 371 n.
  government 733 n.
  commonalty 869 n.
democrat *commoner* 869 n.
democratic *equal* 28 adj.
  governmental 733 adj.
demography
  statistics 86 n.
  anthropology 371 n.
demolish *break* 46 vb.
  revolutionize 149 vb.
  demolish 165 vb.
  fell 311 vb.
  confute 479 vb.
demolition
  destruction 165 n.
demon
  violent creature 176 n.
  monster 938 n.
  devil 969 n.
  demon 970 n.
demonetize
  demonetize 797 vb.
  not pay 805 vb.
demoniacal *cruel* 898 adj.
  diabolic 969 adj.
demoniacal possession
  spell 983 n.
demonic *fairylike* 970 adj.
demonifuge *talisman* 983 n.
demonism
  diabolism 969 n.
demonist *idolater* 982 n.
demonolater
  diabolist 969 n.
  idolater 982 n.
demonology
  diabolism 969 n.
demonstrable
  certain 473 adj.
demonstrate
  demonstrate 478 vb.
  interpret 520 vb.
  show 522 vb.
  be expert 694 vb.
  defy 711 vb.

  revolt 738 vb.
  deprecate 762 vb.
  show feeling 818 vb.
demonstrated *true* 494 adj.
demonstration
  ostentation 875 n.
  (*see* demonstrate)
demonstrative
  evidential 466 adj.
  indicating 547 adj.
  with affections 817 adj.
  friendly 880 adj.
  loving 887 adj.
  caressing 889 adj.
demonstrator *guide* 520 n.
  exhibitor 522 n.
  agitator 738 n.
  rioter 738 n.
demoralization
  deterioration 655 n.
  wickedness 934 n.
demos *nation* 371 n.
  commonalty 869 n.
demote *punish* 963 vb.
  (*see* demotion)
demotic *linguistic* 557 adj.
  written 586 adj.
demotion *diminution* 37 n.
  descent 309 n.
  depression 311 n.
  deposal 752 n.
  disrepute 867 n.
demur *qualification* 468 n.
  argue 475 vb.
  doubt 486 n., vb.
  dissent 489 n., vb.
  negate 533 vb.
  be loth 598 vb.
  defy 711 vb.
  resistance 715 n.
  deprecate 762 vb.
  disapprove 924 vb.
demure *inexcitable* 823 adj.
  affected 850 adj.
  serious 834 adj.
  modest 874 adj.
demurrage *delay* 136 n.
demurrer *litigation* 959 n.
  (*see* demur)
demyship *reward* 962 n.
demythologization
  interpretation 520 n.
  theology 973 n.
den
  dwelling, retreat 192 n.
  chamber 194 n.
  cavity 255 n.
  hiding-place 527 n.
  refuge 662 n.
  lock-up 748 n.
  seclusion 883 n.

denary *fifth and over* 99 adj.
denationalize
  derange 63 vb.
  pervert 655 vb.
  disentitle 916 vb.
denaturalization
  conversion 147 n.
  loss of right 916 n.
denaturalize *pervert* 655 vb.
  disentitle 916 vb.
denature *modify* 143 vb.
  weaken 163 vb.
  impair, pervert 655 vb.
denazify *void* 300 vb.
dendrific *arboreal* 366 adj.
dendriform
  symmetrical 245 adj.
  arboreal 366 adj.
dendrological
  arboreal 366 adj.
dendrology *forestry* 366 n.
  botany 368 n.
dene *valley* 255 n.
  plain 348 n.
dengue *infection* 651 n.
denial *confutation* 479 n.
  unbelief 486 n.
  dissent 489 n.
  negation 533 n.
  recantation 603 n.
  rejection 607 n.
  opposition 704 n.
  refusal 760 n.
denier *texture* 331 n.
  unbeliever 486 n.
denigration
  blackness 428 n.
  detraction 926 n.
denims *trousers* 228 n.
denization *freedom* 744 n.
denizen *dweller* 191 n.
denomination
  classification 77 n.
  nomenclature 561 n.
  party 708 n.
denominational
  sectional 708 adj.
  Protestant 976 adj.
  sectarianism 978 n.
denominative
  part of speech 564 n.
denominator
  numerical element 85 n.
denotable *marked* 547 adj.
denotation
  connotation 514 n.
denotative *semantic* 514 adj.
denote *specify* 80 vb.
  mean 514 vb.
  indicate 547 vb.
dénouement

eventuality 154 n.
  effect 157 n.
  evolution 316 n.
  disclosure 526 n.
  completion 725 n.
denounce *inform* 524 vb.
  proclaim 528 vb.
  satirize 851 vb.
  hate 888 vb.
  curse 899 vb.
  dispraise 924 vb.
  defame 926 vb.
  accuse 928 vb.
de novo *again* 106 adv.
dense *firm-set* 45 adj.
  multitudinous 104 adj.
  unyielding 162 adj.
  thick 205 adj.
  closed 264 n.
  dense 324 adj.
  tactual 378 adj.
  ignorant 491 adj.
  unintelligent 499 adj.
densen *be dense* 324 vb.
densimeter *density* 324 n.
density *materiality* 319 n.
  density 324 n.
  semiliquidity 354 n.
  opacity 423 n.
  (*see* dense)
dent *concavity* 255 n.
  notch 260 n., vb.
  depression 311 n.
dental *toothed* 256 adj.
  speech sound 398 n.
  spoken letter 558 n.
dentate *notched* 260 adj.
denticulation *tooth* 256 n.
dentifrice *cleanser* 648 n.
  prophylactic 658 n.
dentist *doctor* 658 n.
dentistry *surgery* 658 n.
dentition, denture
  tooth 256 n.
denudation
  separation 46 n.
  uncovering 229 n.
denude *subtract* 39 vb.
  uncover 229 vb.
  disclose 526 vb.
  deprive 786 vb.
denunciation
  (*see* denounce)
denunciatory
  maledictory 899 adj.
  disapproving 924 adj.
  detracting 926 adj.
  accusing 928 adj.
deny *exclude* 57 vb.
  put off 136 vb.
  confute 479 vb.

disbelieve 486 vb.
  disappoint 509 vb.
  negate 533 vb.
  recant 603 vb.
  reject 607 vb.
  avoid 620 vb.
  abrogate 752 vb.
  refuse 760 vb.
deny oneself
  relinquish 621 vb.
  be temperate 942 vb.
deodand *penalty* 963 n.
deodorant
  inodorousness 395 n.
  cleanser 648 n.
deodorize *aerify* 340 vb.
  have no smell 395 vb.
  purify 648 vb.
deontology *morals* 917 n.
deoppilation *facility* 701 n.
Deo volente, D. V.
  possibly 469 adv.
  divinely 965 adv.
depaganize
  make pious 979 vb.
depart *be disjoined* 46 vb.
  recede 290 vb.
  depart 296 vb.
  emerge 298 vb.
  disappear 446 vb.
  relinquish 621 vb.
departed *dead* 361 adj.
depart from *differ* 15 vb.
  deviate 282 vb.
department
  subdivision 53 n.
  classification 77 n.
  district 184 n.
  function 622 n.
departmentalized
  fragmentary 53 adj.
departure *start* 68 n.
  deviation 282 n.
  recession 290 n.
  departure 296 n.
  decease 361 n.
  (*see* depart)
depend *depend* 157 vb.
  hang 217 vb.
  be possible 469 vb.
  be uncertain 474 vb.
dependability
  observance 768 n.
dependable
  willing 597 adj.
  observant 768 adj.
  trustworthy 929 adj.
dependant *inferior* 35 n.
  auxiliary 707 n.
  dependant 742 n.
  recipient 782 n.

dependence
 relativeness 9 n.
 inferiority 35 n.
 pendency 217 n.
 subjection 745 n.
 non-ownership 774 n.
dependency
 territory 184 n.
 polity 733 n.
 subject 742 n.
 lands 777 n.
dependent *inferior* 35 adj.
 pendent 217 adj.
 uncertain 474 adj.
 subject 745 adj.
 not owning 774 adj.
 servile 879 adj.
dependent on
 caused 157 adj.
 liable 180 adj.
depend on *believe* 485 vb.
 be subject 745 vb.
depict *represent* 551 vb.
 describe 590 vb.
depilation *uncovering* 229 n.
 beautification 843 n.
 hair-dressing 843 n.
deplete *waste* 634 vb.
 make insufficient 636 vb.
deplorable *bad* 645 adj.
 distressing 827 adj.
 regretted 830 adj.
deplore *regret* 830 vb.
 lament 836 vb.
 disapprove 924 vb.
deploy *place* 187 vb.
 expand 197 vb.
 lengthen 203 vb.
 be broad 205 vb.
 flank 239 vb.
 open 263 vb.
 diverge 294 vb.
 dispose of 673 vb.
deponent *witness* 466 n.
depopulate *bate* 37 vb.
 lay waste 165 vb.
 void 300 vb.
deport *exclude* 57 vb.
deportation *exclusion* 57 n.
 transference 272 n.
 ejection 300 n.
 seclusion 883 n.
 penalty 963 n.
deportee *ejection* 300 n.
 outcaste 883 n.
deportment *conduct* 688 n.
deposal *deposal* 752 n.
depose *displace* 188 vb.
 abase 311 vb.
 testify 466 vb.
 unthrone 734 vb.

depose 752 vb.
 deprive 786 vb.
deposed *powerless* 161 adj.
 unentitled 916 adj.
deposit *leavings* 41 n.
 place 187 vb.
 thing transferred 272 n.
 solid body 324 n.
 soil 344 n.
 store 632 n., vb.
 security 767 n.
 payment 804 n.
depositary *treasurer* 798 n.
deposition *location* 187 n.
 testimony 466 n.
 oath 532 n.
 deposal 752 n.
deposit of faith
 theology 973 n.
 orthodoxy 976 n.
depositor *creditor* 802 n.
depository *storage* 632 n.
 treasury 799 n.
depot *station* 187 n.
 storage 632 n.
 emporium 796 n.
deprave *pervert* 655 vb.
depraved *bad* 645 adj.
 deteriorated 655 adj.
 vicious 934 adj.
depravity *badness* 645 n.
 deterioration 655 n.
 wickedness 934 n.
deprecate *dissent* 489 vb.
 dissuade 613 vb.
 warn 664 vb.
 oppose 704 vb.
 resist 715 vb.
 deprecate 762 vb.
 regret 830 vb.
deprecation
 disapprobation 924 n.
 (see deprecate)
deprecatory
 humble 872 adj.
 modest 874 adj.
depreciation *decrease* 37 n.
 underestimation 483 n.
 misinterpretation 521 n.
 loss 772 n.
 finance 797 n.
 non-payment 805 n.
 cheapness 812 n.
 disrespect 921 n.
 detraction 926 n.
depredation *havoc* 165 n.
 spoliation 788 n.
depredator *taker* 786 n.
 robber 789 n.
depress
 make concave 255 vb.

depress 311 vb.
 incommode 827 vb.
 deject 834 vb.
depressant *poison* 659 n.
 dejection 834 n.
depressed *sullen* 893 adj.
depressed class
 lower classes 869 n.
depressed state
 psychopathy 503 n.
depressing
 unpleasant 827 adj.
 cheerless 834 adj.
 tedious 838 adj.
depression *lowness* 210 n.
 depth 211 n.
 valley 255 n.
 descent 309 n.
 depression 311 n.
 psychopathy 503 n.
 deterioration 655 n.
 adversity 731 n.
 poverty 801 n.
 nervousness 854 n.
deprivation
 separation 46 n.
 absence 190 n.
 ejection 300 n.
 deposal 752 n.
 loss 772 n.
 non-ownership 774 n.
 expropriation 786 n.
 loss of right 916 n.
 penalty 963 n.
deprive
 make insufficient 636 vb.
 impoverish 801 vb.
 not pay 805 vb.
 (see deprivation)
de profundis
 tearfully 836 adv.
depth *greatness* 32 n.
 space 183 n.
 size 195 n.
 depth 211 n.
 interiority 224 n.
 wisdom 498 n.
 imperspicuity 568 n.
depth-charge *bomb* 723 n.
depths *rear* 238 n.
depurate *purify* 648 vb.
depurative *remedial* 65 adj.
deputation
 commission 751 n.
depute *commission* 751 vb.
deputize *substitute* 150 vb.
 represent 551 vb.
 function 622 vb.
 deputize 755 vb.
deputy *inferior* 35 n.
 substitute 150 n.

agent 686n.
councillor 692n.
consignee 754n.
deputy 755n.
deracinate *destroy* 165vb.
eject 300vb.
extract 304vb.
déraciné *foreigner* 59n.
wanderer 268n.
derail *derange* 63vb.
displace 188vb.
derange *derange* 63vb.
deform 244vb.
agitate 318vb.
distract 456vb.
make mad 503vb.
impair 655vb.
hinder 702vb.
incommode 827vb.
deranged *insane* 503adj.
derangement
non-uniformity 17n.
disorder 61n.
unconformity 84n.
displacement 188n.
(*see* derange)
deration *liberate* 746vb.
not retain 779vb.
derby *headgear* 228n.
derelict *survivor* 41n.
disused 674adj.
unpossessed 774adj.
derelict 779n.
not retained 779adj.
solitary, outcaste 883n.
dereliction
relinquishment 621n.
dutilessness 918n.
guilty act 936n.
derestrict *revert* 148vb.
restore 656vb.
not retain 779vb.
deride *reject* 607vb.
laugh 835vb.
ridicule 851vb.
not respect 921vb.
despise 922vb.
de rigueur *usual* 610adj.
obligatory 917adj.
derision *unbelief* 486n.
laughter 835n.
ridicule 851n.
impiety 980n.
derisive *derisive* 851adj.
derisory *ridiculous* 849adj.
derivable *caused* 157adj.
attributed 158adj.
derivation *origin* 68n.
reversion 148n.
source 156n.
effect 157n.

attribution 158n.
connotation 514n.
etymology 559n.
derivative *imitative* 20adj.
effect 157n.
word 559n.
dull 840adj.
derive *result* 158vb.
attribute 158vb.
acquire 771vb.
derm *skin* 226n.
dermal *dermal* 226adj.
dermatitis
skin disease 651n.
dermatologist
doctor 658n.
dernier cri
modernism 126n.
fashion 848n.
derogation *disrepute* 867n.
detraction 926n.
derogatory
degrading 867adj.
detracting 926adj.
dishonest 930adj.
derrick *hanger* 217n.
lifter 310n.
dervish *ascetic* 945n.
pietist 979n.
worshipper 981n.
monk 986n.
desanctify *paganize* 974vb.
descant *vocal music* 412n.
sing 413vb.
be diffuse 570vb.
dissertation 591n.
hymn 981n.
descend *decrease* 37vb.
be oblique 220vb.
descend 309vb.
descendant *survivor* 41n.
aftercomer 67n.
posteriority 120n.
descendant 170n.
descendants *futurity* 124n.
descender *print-type* 587n.
descend from *result* 157vb.
descending order
decrease 37n.
series 71n.
contraction 198n.
descent *consanguinity* 11n.
decrease 37n.
sequence 65n.
continuity 71n.
posteriority 120n.
revolution 149n.
source 156n.
genealogy 169n.
sonship 170n.
presence 189n.

acclivity 220n.
motion 265n.
descent 309n.
plunge 313n.
deterioration 655n.
nobility 868n.
theophany 965n.
describe
communicate 524vb.
represent 551vb.
describe 590vb.
description *sort* 77n.
indication 547n.
nomenclature 561n.
writing 586n.
description 590n.
descriptive
expressive 516adj.
descriptive 590adj.
descry *see* 438vb.
understand 516vb.
desecrate
make unclean 649vb.
impair 655vb.
misuse 675vb.
shame 867vb.
be undue 916vb.
not respect 921vb.
be impious 980vb.
desecrator *usurper* 916n.
impious person 980n.
desert *havoc* 165n.
desert 172n.
unproductive 172adj.
emptiness 190n.
dryness 342n.
dry 342n.
land 344n.
tergiversate 603vb.
run away 620vb.
relinquish 621n.
goodness 644n.
retaliation 714n.
not observe 769vb.
be cowardly 856vb.
seclusion 883n.
fail in duty 918vb.
virtues 933n.
(*see* deserts)
deserter *tergiversator* 603n.
avoider 620n.
coward 856n.
dutilessness 918n.
desertion *disobedience* 738n.
divorce 896n.
perfidy 930n.
desert-dweller *dweller* 191n.
solitary 883n.
deserts *conduct* 688n.
retaliation 714n.
right 913n.

dueness 915 n.
  reward 962 n.
deserve *be good* 644 vb.
  deserve 915 vb.
  be rewarded 962 vb.
deserved *just* 913 adj.
  due 915 adj.
deserving *excellent* 644 adj.
  approvable 923 adj.
déshabillé
  informal dress 228 n.
  uncovering 229 n.
desiccation
  desiccation 342 n.
  blight 659 n.
  preservation 666 n.
desiderate *require* 627 vb.
  be unsatisfied 636 vb.
  desire 859 vb.
desideration, desideratum
  requirement 627 n.
  desire 859 n.
  desired object 859 n.
desiderium *regret* 830 n.
  desire 859 n.
design *prototype* 23 n.
  composition 56 n.
  form 243 n.
  representation 551 n.
  painting 553 n.
  intention 617 n.
  plan 623 n.
  undertaking 672 n.
  pattern 844 n.
designate *specify* 80 vb.
  future 124 adj.
  mark 547 vb.
  chosen 605 adj.
  select 605 vb.
designation
  classification 77 n.
  nomenclature 561 n.
  name 561 n.
designer *producer* 167 n.
  artist 556 n.
  planner 623 n.
designing *dishonest* 930 adj.
  selfish 932 adj.
designless
  designless 618 adj.
desinence *extremity* 69 n.
  cessation 145 n.
desipience *folly* 499 n.
desirability
  needfulness 627 n.
  expedience 642 n.
desirable *expedient* 642 adj.
  contenting 828 adj.
  desired 859 adj.
  lovable 887 adj.
  approvable 923 adj.

desire *attraction* 291 n.
  will 595 n., vb.
  motive 612 n.
  intention 617 n.
  require 627 vb.
  request 761 n., vb.
  desire 859 n., vb.
  desired object 859 n.
  love 887 n.
desirous *willing* 597 adj.
desist *cease* 145 vb.
  not act 677 vb.
desk *cabinet* 194 n.
  stand 218 n.
  classroom 539 n.
deskbook
  reading matter 589 n.
desk-work *study* 536 n.
desolate *lay waste* 165 vb.
  unproductive 172 adj.
  void 300 vb.
  hopeless 853 adj.
  friendless 883 adj.
  secluded 883 adj.
desolation *havoc* 165 n.
  desert 172 n.
  emptiness 190 n.
  sorrow 825 n.
despair *not expect* 508 vb.
  be disappointed 509 vb.
  sorrow 825 n.
  dejection 834 n.
  hopelessness 853 n.
despair, counsel of
  inexpedience 643 n.
  hopelessness 853 n.
despair of
  impenitence 940 n.
despair, one's
  bungler 697 n.
  difficulty 700 n.
despatch *punctuality* 135 n.
  move 265 vb.
  send 272 vb.
  kill 362 vb.
  report 523 n.
  correspondence 588 n.
  do 676 vb.
  activity 678 n.
  haste 680 n.
  deal with 688 vb.
  effectuation 725 n.
despatcher *transferrer* 272 n.
despatches *report* 524 n.
  message 529 n.
despatch-rider *courier* 531 n.
desperado *murderer* 362 n.
  brave person 855 n.
  desperado 857 n.
  insolent person 878 n.
  ruffian 904 n.

desperate
  consummate 32 adj.
  furious 176 adj.
  resolute 599 adj.
  active 678 adj.
  hopeless 853 adj.
  courageous 855 adj.
  rash 857 adj.
desperately
  extremely 32 adv.
desperation (*see* desperate)
despicable
  discreditable 867 adj.
  disreputable 867 adj.
  contemptible 922 adj.
despicability *odium* 888 n.
despise
  underestimate 483 vb.
  be proud 871 vb.
  hate 888 vb.
  not respect 921 vb.
  despise 922 vb.
despised
  contemptible 922 adj.
despisedness
  unimportance 639 n.
  despisedness 922 n.
despite
  in defiance of 25 adv.
  although 182 adv.
  nevertheless 468 adj.
  with difficulty 700 adv.
  in opposition 704 adv.
despoil *lay waste* 165 vb.
  impair 655 vb.
  rob 788 vb.
despoiler *taker* 786 n.
  robber 789 n.
  evildoer 904 n.
despondency
  adversity 731 n.
  dejection 834 n.
  hopelessness 853 n.
  nervousness 854 n.
despot *tyrant* 735 n.
  autocrat 741 n.
despotic *oppressive* 735 adj.
  authoritarian 735 adj.
  lawless 954 adj.
despotism *despotism* 733 n.
  brute force 735 n.
desquamation
  uncovering 229 n.
dessert *sequel* 67 n.
  dish 301 n.
dessous *underwear* 228 n.
destination
  stopping place 145 n.
  objective 617 n.
destine *predestine* 155 vb.
  necessitate 596 vb.

predetermine 608 vb.
intend 617 vb.
destined *future* 124 adj.
impending 155 adj.
fated 596 adj.
destiny *finality* 69 n.
futurity 124 n.
destiny 155 n.
cause 156 n.
influence 178 n.
expectation 507 n.
necessity 596 n.
predetermination 608 n.
destitute *necessitous* 627 adj.
not owning 774 adj.
poor 801 adj.
destitution *poverty* 801 n.
destroy *nullify* 2 vb.
destroy 165 vb.
slaughter 362 vb.
confute 479 vb.
waste 634 vb.
defeat 727 vb.
impoverish 801 vb.
destroyer
revolutionist 149 n.
destroyer 168 n.
violent creature 176 n.
bane 659 n.
warship 722 n.
destruction
extinction 2 n.
disorder 61 n.
revolution 149 n.
destruction 165 n.
killing 362 n.
destructive
destructive 165 adj.
wasteful 634 adj.
harmful 645 adj.
adverse 731 adj.
destructiveness
waste 634 n.
destructor *furnace* 383 n.
desuetude *desuetude* 611 n.
non-retention 779 n.
desultoriness
inattention 456 n.
desultory *orderless* 61 adj.
discontinuous 72 adj.
fitful 142 adj.
unstable 152 adj.
deviating 282 adj.
light-minded 456 adj.
prolix 570 adj.
detach *disjoin* 46 vb.
unstick 49 vb.
disperse 75 vb.
send 272 vb.
detachable
severable 46 adj.

detached *irrelative* 10 adj.
non-adhesive 49 adj.
neutral 625 adj.
independent 744 adj.
impassive 820 adj.
just 913 adj.
disinterested 931 adj.
detachment
separation 46 n.
part 53 n.
inattention 456 n.
armed force 722 n.
moral insensibility 820 n.
inexcitability 823 n.
justice 913 n.
disinterestedness 931 n.
detail *small quantity* 33 n.
part 53 n.
specify 80 vb.
send 272 vb.
be diffuse 570 vb.
describe 590 vb.
trifle 639 n.
armed force 722 n.
command 737 vb.
apportion 783 vb.
pattern 844 n.
detailed *complete* 54 adj.
definite 80 adj.
diffuse 570 adj.
descriptive 590 adj.
laborious 682 adj.
details *particulars* 80 n.
detain *imprison* 747 vb.
retain 778 vb.
detainee *prisoner* 750 n.
detect *see* 438 vb.
detect 484 vb.
understand 516 vb.
disclose 526 vb.
detectable *visible* 443 adj.
detection
police enquiry 459 n.
discovery 484 n.
knowledge 490 n.
detective *inquisitor* 453 n.
detective 459 n.
detector *detector* 484 n.
detent *fastening* 47 n.
détente *moderation* 177 n.
pacification 719 n.
detention *delay* 136 n.
hindrance 702 n.
detention 747 n.
retention 778 n.
detention camp
prison camp 748 n.
détenue *prisoner* 750 n.
deter *cause doubt* 486 vb.
dissuade 613 vb.
hinder 702 vb.

frighten 854 vb.
cause dislike 861 vb.
threaten 900 vb.
detergent *cleanser* 648 n.
deteriorate *decompose* 51 vb.
be old 127 vb.
be weak 163 vb.
disuse 674 vb.
deterioration
inferiority 35 n.
decrease 37 n.
mixture 43 n.
change 143 n.
ruin 165 n.
regression 286 n.
desuetude 611 n.
waste 634 n.
badness 645 n.
illness 651 n.
deterioration 655 n.
relapse 657 n.
loss 772 n.
wickedness 934 n.
determinant *cause* 156 n.
determinate *definite* 80 adj.
determination *will* 595 n.
resolution 599 n.
obstinacy 602 n.
intention 617 n.
assiduity 678 n.
courage 855 n.
determinative
judicial 480 adj.
determine *arrange* 62 vb.
terminate 69 vb.
specify 80 vb.
cause 156 vb.
will 595 vb.
be resolute 599 vb.
determinism
necessity 596 n.
determinist *fatalist* 596 n.
deterrence *dissuasion* 613 n.
intimidation 854 n.
deterrent
counteraction 182 n.
dissuasion 613 n.
protection 660 n.
safeguard 662 n.
cautionary 664 adj.
defence 713 n.
retaliation 714 n.
weapon 723 n.
threat 900 n.
detersion *ablution* 648 n.
detersive *remedial* 658 adj.
detest (*see* detestation)
detestable *not nice* 645 adj.
detestation *dislike* 861 n.
hatred 888 n.
dethrone *depose* 752 vb.

dethroned
  unentitled 916 adj.
dethronement
  anarchy 734 n.
  deposal 752 n.
  loss of right 916 n.
detonation *outbreak* 176 n.
  bang 402 n.
detonator *lighter* 385 n.
  ammunition 723 n.
  explosive 723 n.
détour *curvature* 248 n.
  deviation 282 n.
  route 624 n.
  circuit 626 n.
detract *subtract* 39 vb.
detraction *diminution* 37 n.
  underestimation 483 n.
  contempt 922 n.
  detraction 926 n.
detrain *land* 295 vb.
detribalize *derange* 63 vb.
  pervert 655 vb.
  disentitle 916 vb.
detriment *inutility* 641 n.
  inexpedience 643 n.
  badness 645 n.
  impairment 655 n.
detrition *subtraction* 39 n.
  pulverulence 332 n.
detritus *leavings* 41 n.
  piece 53 n.
  accumulation 74 n.
  thing transferred 272 n.
  powder 332 n.
de trop *superfluous* 637 adj.
detrusion *depression* 311 n.
deuce *draw* 28 n.
  duality 90 n.
deucedly *extremely* 32 adv.
deus ex machina
  aider 703 n.
  patron 707 n.
deuteragonist *actor* 594 n.
deuterium *gas* 336 n.
deuterogamy
  type of marriage 894 n.
deva *god* 966 n.
devaloka
  mythic heaven 971 n.
devalue *make useless* 641 vb.
  impair 655 vb.
  demonetize 797 vb.
Devanagari *letter* 558 n.
devastate *lay waste* 165 vb.
devastation *havoc* 165 n.
  terror tactics 712 n.
develop *become* 1 vb.
  augment 36 vb.
  result 157 vb.
  be visible 443 vb.

manifest 522 vb.
educate 534 vb.
photograph 551 vb.
  (*see* development)
development *increase* 36 n.
  conversion 147 n.
  production 164 n.
  propagation 164 n.
  growth 157 n.
  expansion 197 n.
  progression 285 n.
  evolution 316 n.
  musical piece 412 n.
  improvement 654 n.
development area
  room 183 n.
deverbal
  grammatical 564 adj.
deverbative
  part of speech 564 n.
devexity *acclivity* 220 n.
  curvature 248 n.
deviate *be oblique* 220 vb.
  (*see* deviation)
deviation *difference* 15 n.
  non-uniformity 17 n.
  unconformity 84 n.
  change 143 n.
  displacement 188 n.
  distance 199 n.
  curvature 248 n.
  deviation 282 n.
  divergence 294 n.
  error 495 n.
  tergiversation 603 n.
deviationism
  unconformity 84 n.
deviationist
  nonconformist 84 n.
  crank 504 n.
  tergiversator 603 n.
  revolter 738 n.
device *idea* 451 n.
  heraldry 547 n.
  contrivance 623 n.
  instrument 628 n.
  means 629 n.
  tool 630 n.
  means of escape 667 n.
  stratagem 698 n.
devil *violent creature* 176 n.
  cook 301 vb.
  season 388 vb.
  wickedness 934 n.
  monster 938 n.
  jurist 958 n.
  devil 969 n.
  mythical being 970 n.
  demon 970 n.
  sorcerer 983 n.
devilish *cruel* 898 adj.

wicked 934 adj.
diabolic 969 adj.
fairylike 970 adj.
infernal 972 adj.
devil-may-care *rash* 857 adj.
devilment *evil* 616 n.
devilry *cruel act* 898 n.
  wickedness 934 n.
  diabolism 969 n.
devil's advocate
  sophist 477 n.
Devil's Island
  prison camp 748 n.
devil's tattoo *roll* 403 n.
Devil, the *Satan* 969 n.
devil to pay *turmoil* 61 n.
devil-worship
  wickedness 934 n.
  diabolism 969 n.
  idolatry 982 n.
devious *deviating* 282 adj.
  circuitous 314 adj.
  cunning 698 adj.
  dishonest 930 adj.
devisable
  transferable 272 adj.
devise *transfer* 272 vb.
  think 449 vb.
  imagine 513 vb.
  plan 623 vb.
  be cunning 698 vb.
  dower 777 vb.
  bequeath 780 vb.
  give 781 vb.
devisee *beneficiary* 776 n.
  recipient 782 n.
deviser *producer* 167 n.
devisor *owner* 776 n.
  giver 781 n.
devitalize *unman* 161 vb.
  weaken 163 vb.
devitrify
  make opaque 423 vb.
devoid *empty* 190 adj.
devoir *courteous act* 884 n.
  respects 920 n.
devolution
  commission 751 n.
  transfer 780 n.
devolve *convey* 780 vb.
  impose a duty 917 vb.
devolve on
  be one's duty 917 vb.
devote *use* 673 vb.
  give 781 vb.
  be pious 979 vb.
devoted *resolute* 599 adj.
  unfortunate 731 adj.
  obedient 739 adj.
  friendly 880 adj.
  loving 887 adj.

disinterested 931 adj.
pious 979 adj.
worshipping 981 adj.
devotedness
assiduity 678 n.
devoted to
habituated 610 adj.
devotee *habitué* 610 n.
desirer 859 n.
pietist 979 n.
worshipper 981 n.
devote to destruction
curse 899 vb.
devotion *resolution* 599 n.
loyalty 739 n.
love 887 n.
respect 920 n.
piety 979 n.
oblation 981 n.
worship 981 n.
devotional *religious* 973 adj.
devotional 981 adj.
devotions *prayers* 981 n.
devour *destroy* 165 vb.
eat 301 vb.
give pain 377 vb.
waste 634 n.
appropriate, fleece 786 vb.
devoured by
possessed 773 adj.
devouring
gluttonous 947 adj.
devout *religious* 973 adj.
orthodox 976 adj.
pious 979 adj.
worshipping 981 adj.
devoutly *feelingly* 818 adv.
devoutness *piety* 979 n.
dew *moisture* 341 n.
dewiness *newness* 126 n.
moisture 341 n.
cleanness 648 n.
(*see* dewy)
dewlap *pendant* 217 n.
dewy *matinal* 128 adj.
humid 341 adj.
clean 648 adj.
dexiotropic *dextral* 241 n.
dexter *dextrality* 241 n.
dexterity *skill* 694 n.
dexterous *dextral* 241 adj.
skilful 694 adj.
dextral, dextrad
dextral 241 adj.
dextrose *sweet* 392 n.
Dhamma
religious faith 973 n.
Dharma
religion 973 n.
religious faith 973 n.
dhatura

poisonous plant 659 n.
dhobi *cleaner* 648 n.
dhobi's itch
formication 378 n.
skin disease 651 n.
dhoti *dress* 228 n.
dhow *sailing-ship* 275 n.
diabetes *disease* 651 n.
diabetic *sick person* 651 n.
diablerie *diabolism* 969 n.
sorcery 983 n.
diabolic *evil* 616 adj.
damnable 645 adj.
cruel 898 adj.
wicked 934 adj.
diabolic 969 adj.
fairylike 970 adj.
infernal 972 adj.
idolatrous 982 adj.
sorcerous 983 adj.
diabolist *diabolist* 969 n.
idolater 982 n.
sorcerer 983 n.
diabolo *plaything* 837 n.
diacaustic *curve* 248 n.
diaconal *clerical* 986 adj.
diaconate
church office 985 n.
diacritical
indicating 547 adj.
diacritical mark
punctuation 547 n.
diadem *regalia* 743 n.
jewellery 844 n.
diæresis
decomposition 51 n.
punctuation 547 n.
prosody 593 n.
diagnose
discriminate 463 vb.
diagnosis *character* 5 n.
classification 77 n.
discrimination 463 n.
pathology 651 n.
medical art 658 n.
diagnostic
characteristic 5 adj.
distinctive 15 adj.
special 80 adj.
identification 547 n.
diagnostician *doctor* 658 n.
diagnostics
discrimination 463 n.
diagonal
dividing line 92 n.
obliquity 220 n.
crossed 222 adj.
directed 281 adj.
diagram *copy* 22 n.
outline 233 n.
representation 551 n.

diagrammatize
abstract 592 vb.
diagraph
representation 551 n.
dial *timekeeper* 117 n.
face 237 n.
communicate 524 vb.
dialect *speciality* 80 n.
unintelligibility 517 n.
language 557 n.
dialect 560 n.
speech defect 580 n.
dialectic *enquiring* 459 adj.
interrogation 459 n.
reasoning 475 n.
rational 475 adj.
dialectical *linguistic* 557 adj.
dialectical 560 adj.
dialectical materialism
materiality 319 n.
philosophy 449 n.
dialectics *reasoning* 475 n.
dialectology
linguistics 557 n.
dialogism *allocution* 583 n.
dialogue
interrogation 459 n.
answer 460 n.
argument 475 n.
interlocution 584 n.
dramaturgy 594 n.
diameter *dividing line* 92 n.
breadth 205 n.
diamond
angular figure 247 n.
hardness 326 n.
type size 587 n.
exceller 644 n.
arena 724 n.
gem 844 n.
diamond cut diamond
retaliation 714 n.
diamond jubilee
celebration 876 n.
Diana *moon* 321 n.
hunter 619 n.
spinster 895 n.
virgin 950 n.
Olympian god 967 n.
dianoetic *rational* 475 adj.
diapason *loudness* 400 n.
musical note 410 n.
diaper *loincloth* 228 n.
pattern 844 n.
diaphane
transparency 422 n.
diaphanous
transparent 422 adj.
diaphonics *acoustics* 398 n.
diaphoresis *outflow* 298 n.
excretion 302 n.

diaphragm *middle* 70 n.
  partition 231 n.
  musical instrument 414 n.
  gramophone 414 n.
diarist *chronologist* 117 n.
  chronicler 549 n.
  author 589 n.
  narrator 590 n.
diarize *time* 117 vb.
  register 548 vb.
diarrhœa *cacation* 302 n.
  dysentery 651 n.
diary *chronology* 117 n.
  reminder 505 n.
  record 548 n.
  reference book 589 n.
  biography 590 n.
diaspora *foreigner* 59 n.
  dispersion 75 n.
diastole *dilation* 197 n.
diatessaron
  musical note 410 n.
diathermancy *heat* 379 n.
  heating 381 n.
diathermometer
  thermometry 379 n.
diathesis *character* 5 n.
  state 7 n.
diatonic *harmonic* 410 adj.
diatribe *oration* 579 n.
  censure 924 n.
dibble *perforator* 263 n.
  farm tool 370 n.
  cultivate 370 vb.
dibs *dibs* 797 n.
  ball game 837 n.
dicast, dicastery
  judge, jury 957 n.
dice *oracle* 511 n.
  gambling 618 n.
  gambling game 837 n.
dice, on the
  possible 469 adj.
dicer *gambler* 618 n.
  player 837 n.
dicer's oath
  unreliability 474 n.
  untruth 543 n.
dicey *casual* 159 adj.
  speculative 618 adj.
  dangerous 661 adj.
dichotomize *sunder* 46 vb.
  bisect 92 vb.
dichotomy
  disjunction 46 n.
  bisection 92 n.
dichroism
  variegation 437 n.
  dim sight 440 n.
dick *detective* 459 n.
  protector 660 n.

police 955 n.
dicker *bargain* 791 vb.
dickey *seat* 218 n.
  apron 228 n.
dictaphone
  hearing aid 415 n.
  recording instrument 549 n.
dictate *teach* 534 vb.
  speak 579 vb.
  direct 689 vb.
  advise 691 vb.
  rule, dominate 733 vb.
  decree 737 n.
  compel 740 vb.
dictated *vocal* 577 adj.
  necessary 596 adj.
dictation *necessity* 596 n.
  no choice 606 n.
  (*see* dictate)
dictator *tyrant* 735 n.
  autocrat 741 n.
dictatorial
  narrow-minded 481 adj.
  volitional 595 adj.
  directing 689 adj.
  authoritative 733 adj.
  commanding 737 adj.
  compelling 740 adj.
  insolent 878 adj.
dictatorship
  directorship 689 n.
  despotism 733 n.
  brute force 735 n.
diction *meaning* 514 n.
  phrase 563 n.
  style 566 n.
dictionary
  commentary 520 n.
  dictionary 559 n.
  collection 632 n.
dictum *maxim* 496 n.
  affirmation 532 n.
  command 737 n.
didactic *educational* 534 adj.
  advising 691 adj.
diddle *deceive* 542 vb.
  defraud 788 vb.
diddler *trickster* 545 n.
die *mould* 23 n.
  end 69 vb.
  die 361 vb.
  printing 555 n.
  gambling 618 n.
die away *shade off* 27 vb.
  decrease 37 vb.
  cease 145 vb.
died out *extinct* 2 adj.
die down *decrease* 37 vb.
  be quiescent 266 vb.
  extinguish 382 vb.

die for *desire* 859 vb.
  be disinterested 931 vb.
die hard *stand firm* 599 vb.
  resist 715 vb.
die-hard
  unchangeable 153 adj.
  opinionist 602 n.
  opponent 705 n.
  malcontent 829 n.
die in harness
  persevere 600 vb.
die on the ear
  sound faint 401 vb.
die out *pass away* 2 vb.
diesel *locomotive* 274 n.
Dies Irae *obsequies* 364 n.
dies non *neverness* 109 n.
diet *make smaller* 198 vb.
  dieting 301 n.
  therapy 658 n.
  council 692 n.
  be temperate 942 vb.
  starve 946 vb.
dietary *dieting* 301 n.
  meal 301 n.
  therapy 658 n.
dietetic *nourishing* 301 adj.
  remedial 658 adj.
dietetics *dieting* 301 n.
die the death
  be punished 963 vb.
dietician *dieting* 301 n.
  doctor 658 n.
difference *irrelation* 10 n.
  contrariety 14 n.
  difference 15 n.
  dissimilarity 19 n.
  disagreement 25 n.
  inequality 29 n.
  remainder 41 n.
  numerical result 85 n.
  divergence 294 n.
  discrimination 463 n.
  dissent 489 n.
  heraldry 547 n.
  dissension 709 n.
  schism 978 n.
difference, see the
  discriminate 463 vb.
different *contrary* 14 adj.
  non-uniform 17 adj.
  superior 34 adj.
  changeful 152 adj.
differentiæ *speciality* 80 n.
differential *variant* 15 n.
  degree 27 n.
  inequality 29 n.
  numerical element 85 n.
  earnings 771 n.
  reward 962 n.
differentiate *set apart* 46 vb.

diluent *liquefaction* 337n.
　water 339n.
dilute *bate* 37vb.
　weaken 163vb.
　rarefy 325vb.
　add water 339vb.
　moisten 341vb.
diluvian *primal* 127adj.
dim *darken* 418vb.
　bedim 419vb.
　dim 419adj.
　decolorize 426vb.
　blackish 428adj.
　blur 440vb.
　ill-seen 444adj.
　unintelligent 499adj.
　puzzling 517adj.
dime *small coin* 33n.
　coinage 797n.
dimension *quantity* 26n.
　measure 183n.
　appearance 445n.
dimensional *metric* 465adj.
dimensions *size* 195n.
dimeter *prosody* 593n.
dim-eyed
　dim-sighted 440adj.
dimidiate *bisect* 92vb.
　mark 547vb.
diminish *bate* 37vb.
　subtract 39vb.
　render few 105vb.
　moderate 177vb.
diminished *lesser* 35adj.
diminishing returns
　loss 772n.
diminuendo
　diminuendo 37adv.
diminution *smallness* 33n.
　diminution 37n.
　subtraction 39n.
　decrement 42n.
　contraction 198n.
diminutive *small* 33adj.
　little 196adj.
　word 559n.
　part of speech 564n.
dimity *textile* 222n.
dimmer *obscuration* 418n.
dimness *darkness* 418n.
　dimness 419n.
　invisibility 444n.
　latency 523n.
dimple *cavity* 255n.
　notch 260n.
dimpled *fleshy* 195adj.
dim sight *dim sight* 440n.
dim-witted
　unintelligent 499adj.
din *commotion* 318n.
　loudness 400n.

be loud 400vb.
　roll 403n.
　advertise 528vb.
dinar *coinage* 797n.
dinarchy *despotism* 733n.
dine *eat* 301vb.
　feed 301vb.
dine out *be sociable* 882vb.
diner *café* 192n.
　train 274n.
　eater 301n.
diner-out *reveller* 837n.
　social person 882n.
dinette *café* 192n.
ding *resound* 404vb.
ding-dong *draw* 28n.
　equal 28adj.
　repeated 106adj.
　roll 403n.
　contending 716adj.
dinghy *rowboat* 275n.
dingle *valley* 255n.
dingy *dark* 418adj.
　dim 419adj.
　soft-hued 425adj.
　colourless 426adj.
　dirty 649adj.
　graceless 842adj.
dining car *train* 274n.
dining room
　chamber 194n.
　feasting 301n.
din in the ears
　repeat oneself 106vb.
　advertise 528vb.
　be loquacious 581vb.
dinkum *truth* 494n.
dinky *orderly* 60adj.
　little 196adj.
dinner *meal* 301n.
　festivity 837n.
dinner jacket
　informal dress 228n.
　tunic 228n.
dinnerless *hungry* 859adj.
　fasting 946adj.
dinosaur *giant* 195n.
　animal 365n.
dint *power* 160n.
　be vigorous 174vb.
　concavity 255n.
　make concave 255vb.
　knock 279n.
　collide 279vb.
diocesan
　ecclesiastical 985adj.
　ecclesiarch 986n.
　layman 987n.
diocese *district* 184n.
　parish 985n.
Diogenes *solitary* 883n.

misanthrope 902n.
　ascetic 945n.
Dionysiac
　disorderly 61adj.
Dionysiac frenzy *spell* 983n.
Dionysus
　vegetability 366n.
　Olympian god 967n.
dioptrics *optics* 417n.
diorama *spectacle* 445n.
　art subject 553n.
diorism
　discrimination 463n.
dip *acclivity* 220n.
　cavity, valley 255n.
　swim 269vb.
　transpose 272vb.
　retard 278vb.
　impel 279vb.
　point to 281vb.
　immerse 303vb.
　descent 309n.
　depression 311n.
　plunge 313n., vb.
　be wet 341vb.
　drench 341vb.
　snuff out 418vb.
　glimmer 419n.
　bedim 419vb.
　torch 420n.
　colour 425vb.
　signal 547vb.
　ablution 648n.
diphtheria *infection* 651n.
　respiratory disease 651n.
diphthong
　speech sound 398n.
　spoken letter 558n.
　voice 577n.
dip into *be attentive* 455vb.
diplegia *paralysis* 651n.
diploma *credential* 466n.
　record 548n.
　mandate 751n.
　honours 866n.
diplomacy *duplicity* 541n.
　cunning 698n.
　mediation 720n.
diplomat *mediator* 720n.
　envoy 754n.
diplomatic
　hypocritical 541adj.
diplomatics
　mediation 720n.
diplomatist *expert* 696n.
　slyboots 698n.
　mediator 720n.
　envoy 754n.
dipper *ladle* 194n.
　star 321n.
　irrigator 341n.

obscuration 418n.
dippy *crazed* 503adj.
  enamoured 887adj.
dipsomania
  alcoholism 949n.
dipsomaniac *madman* 504n.
  drunkard 949n.
diptych *picture* 553n.
dire *harmful* 645adj.
  adverse 731adj.
direct *simple* 44adj.
  orderly 60adj.
  continuous 71adj.
  straight 249adj.
  send 272vb.
  orientate 281vb.
  towards 281adv.
  intuitive 476adj.
  accurate 494adj.
  educate 534vb.
  indicate 547vb.
  perspicuous 567adj.
  dramatize 594vb.
  motivate 612vb.
  undeviating 625adj.
  direct 689vb.
  rule 733vb.
  command 737vb.
direct action *revolt* 738n.
direction *relation* 9n.
  laterality 239n.
  direction 281n.
  teaching 534n.
  dramaturgy 594n.
  route 624n.
  directorship 689n.
  precept 693n.
  governance 733n.
direction-finder
  direction 281n.
  indicator 547n.
directive *command* 737n.
  jurisdictional 955adj.
direct line
  straightness 249n.
directly *suddenly* 135adv.
  straight on 249adv.
  towards 281adv.
  plainly 573adv.
directness *continuity* 71n.
  straightness 249n.
  perspicuity 567n.
director
  stage-manager 594n.
  director 690n.
  master 741n.
directorial *directing* 689adj.
directorship
  directorship 689n.
directory *directory* 87n.
  guide-book 524n.

direful *frightening* 854adj.
diremption
  separation 46n.
direption *spoliation* 788n.
dirge *obsequies* 364n.
  musical piece 412n.
  poem 593n.
  lament 836n.
dirigible *airship* 276n.
dirigism *governance* 733n.
dirk *side-arms* 723n.
dirt *excrement* 302n.
  opacity 423n.
  rubbish 641n.
  dirt 649n.
  slur 867n.
  impurity 951n.
dirty *windy* 352adj.
  bedim 419vb.
  opaque 423adj.
  black 428adj.
  dirty 649adj.
  make unclean 649vb.
  infectious 653adj.
  disreputable 867adj.
  dishonest 930adj.
  impure 951adj.
dirty dog *cad* 938n.
dirty linen
  uncleanness 649n.
  slur 867n.
dirty look *look* 438n.
  reproach 924n.
dirty trick *foul play* 930n.
dirty weather *storm* 176n.
  gale 352n.
dirty work *foul play* 930n.
disability *impotence* 161n.
  inexpedience 643n.
  illness 651n.
  hindrance 702n.
disable *disable* 161vb.
  weaken 163vb.
  impair 655vb.
  hinder 702vb.
disabuse *inform* 524vb.
  disclose 526vb.
  educate 534vb.
disaccharid
  food content 301n.
disaccord *disagreement* 25n.
  disorder 61n.
  dissension 709n.
disaccustom
  disaccustom 611vb.
  relinquish 621vb.
  disuse 674vb.
disadvantage
  inferiority 35n.
  evil 616n.
  inexpedience 643n.

disadvantageous
  harmful 645adj.
disaffect *dissuade* 613vb.
disaffection *dissent* 489n.
  hatred 888n.
disaffiliate *depose* 752vb.
disaffirm *negate* 533vb.
disagree
  cause dislike 861vb.
  (*see* disagreement)
disagreeable *painful* 377adj.
  fetid 397adj.
  unpleasant 827adj.
  disliked 861adj.
  discourteous 885adj.
disagreement
  contrariety 14n.
  difference 15n.
  dissimilarity 19n.
  disagreement 25n.
  inequality 29n.
  unconformity 84n.
  unbelief 486n.
  dissent 489n.
  negation 533n.
  unwillingness 598n.
  dissension 709n.
disallow *exclude* 57vb.
  make impossible 470vb.
  dissent 489vb.
  negate 533vb.
  reject 607vb.
  refuse 760vb.
  disentitle 916vb.
  disapprove 924vb.
disappear *pass away* 2vb.
  cease 145vb.
  decamp 296vb.
  be unseen 444vb.
  disappear 446vb.
  be stealthy 525vb.
  be lost 772vb.
disappearance
  transientness 114n.
  absence 190n.
  obscuration 418n.
  disappearance 446n.
  escape 667n.
disappoint
  disappoint 509vb.
  deceive 542n.
  miscarry 728vb.
  displease 827vb.
  cause discontent 829vb.
  leave no hope 853vb.
disappointment
  inexpectation 508n.
  (*see* disappoint)
disapprobation
  dissent 489n.
  rejection 607n.

disrespect 921 n.
disapprobation 924 n.
detraction 926 n.
condemnation 961 n.
disapproval
   (*see* disapprobation)
disapprove *oppose* 704 vb.
   deprecate 762 vb.
   prohibit 757 vb.
   dislike 861 vb.
   make unwelcome 883 vb.
   (*see* disapprobation)
disarm *disable* 161 vb.
   weaken 163 vb.
   be moderate 177 vb.
   assuage 177 vb.
   make useless 641 vb.
   pacify 719 vb.
disarmament
   impotence 161 n.
   peace 717 n.
   pacification 719 n.
disarming
   pacificatory 719 adj.
disarrangement
   derangement 63 n.
disarray *disorder* 61 n.
disassemble
   make useless 641 vb.
disaster *ill fortune* 731 n.
disastrous *evil* 616 adj.
   harmful 645 adj.
disavow *negate* 533 vb.
   recant 603 vb.
   reject 607 vb.
disband *disjoin* 46 vb.
   disperse 75 vb.
   liberate 746 vb.
disbar *exclude* 57 vb.
   eject 300 vb.
   depose 752 vb.
   shame 867 vb.
disbelief *unbelief* 486 n.
   negation 533 n.
   non-wonder 865 n.
   irreligion 974 n.
disbeliever
   unbeliever 486 n.
   impious person 980 n.
disburden *deliver* 668 vb.
   disencumber 701 vb.
   relieve 831 vb.
disbursement
   payment 804 n.
   expenditure 806 n.
disc *face* 237 n.
   circle 250 n.
   gramophone 414 n.
   recording instrument
      549 n.
discalceate *monk* 986 n.

discard *eject* 300 vb.
   rejection 607 n.
   reject 607 vb.
   relinquish 621 vb.
   rubbish 641 n.
   disuse 674 vb.
   not observe 769 vb.
   not retain 779 vb.
discarded
   unwonted 611 adj.
discargo *void* 300 vb.
discarnate
   immaterial 320 adj.
   spooky 970 adj.
disceptation
   argument 475 n.
discern *see* 438 vb.
   discriminate 463 vb.
   know 490 vb.
   understand 516 vb.
discernible *visible* 443 adj.
discernment
   inspection 438 n.
   discrimination 463 n.
   sagacity 498 n.
   fastidiousness 862 n.
discerption *scission* 46 n.
discharge *displace* 188 vb.
   propulsion 287 n.
   land 295 vb.
   outflow 298 n.
   ejection 300 n.
   dismiss, void 300 vb.
   excretion 302 n.
   ulcer 651 n.
   deliverance 668 n.
   disuse 674 vb.
   carry out 725 vb.
   liberation 746 n.
   not retain 779 vb.
   deposal 752 n.
   observance 768 n.
   pay 804 vb.
   do one's duty 917 vb.
   non-liability 919 n.
   acquittal 960 n.
disciple
   changed person 147 n.
   listener 415 n.
   learner 538 n.
   auxiliary 707 n.
disciplinarian
   teacher, trainer 537 n.
   tyrant 735 n.
disciplinary *punitive* 963 adj.
discipline *order* 60 n.
   teaching 534 n.
   dominate 733 vb.
   severity 735 n.
   obedience 739 n.
   subjugate 745 vb.

restraint 747 n.
   punishment 963 n.
disciplined *orderly* 60 adj.
   obedient 739 adj.
discipular
   student-like 538 adj.
disclaim *negate* 533 vb.
   recant 603 vb.
   reject 607 vb.
   resign 753 vb.
   refuse 760 vb.
   not retain 779 vb.
disclaimer *negation* 533 n.
   recantation 603 n.
   resignation 753 n.
disclose *inform* 524 vb.
   disclose 526 vb.
   indicate 547 vb.
disclosure
   manifestation 522 n.
   disclosure 526 n.
discoid *round* 250 adj.
discoloration *hue* 425 n.
   achromatism 426 n.
   impairment 655 n.
   wound 655 n.
discolour *variegate* 437 vb.
   make ugly 842 vb.
   (*see* discoloration)
discomfiture *defeat* 728 n.
discomfort *pain* 377 n.
   evil 616 n.
   suffering, worry 825 n.
   incommode 827 vb.
discommendation
   censure 924 n.
discompose
   derange 63 vb.
   agitate 318 vb.
   distract 456 vb.
   incommode 827 vb.
   enrage 891 vb.
discomposure *disorder* 61 n.
   worry 825 n.
disconcert *derange* 63 vb.
   distract 456 vb.
   disappoint 509 vb.
   hinder 702 vb.
   defeat 727 vb.
   incommode 827 vb.
   frighten 854 vb.
   shame 867 vb.
   humiliate 972 vb.
disconcerted
   inexpectant 508 adj.
   disappointed 509 adj.
   (*see* disconcert)
disconformity
   unconformity 84 n.
disconnect *disjoin* 46 vb.
   discontinue 72 vb.

[818]

disconnectedness
discontinuity 72 n.
disconnection
irrelation 10 n.
disjunction 46 n.
disconsolate
melancholic 834 adj.
hopeless 853 adj.
discontent *dissent* 489 n.
disappointment 509 n.
sorrow 825 n.
displease 827 vb.
discontent 829 n.
sadden 834 vb.
resentment 891 n.
sullenness 893 n.
disapprobation 924 n.
discontinuance
discontinuity 72 n.
cessation 145 n.
desuetude 611 n.
abrogation 752 n.
discontinuation
discontinuity 72 n.
discontinuity
irrelation 10 n.
non-uniformity 17 n.
disjunction 46 n.
non-coherence 49 n.
incompleteness 55 n.
discontinuity 72 n.
intempestivity 138 n.
stop 145 n.
interval 201 n.
discord *contrariety* 14 n.
difference 15 n.
disagreement 25 n.
medley 43 n.
disorder 61 n.
rasp 407 vb.
discord 411 n., vb.
dissension 709 n.
discount *subtraction* 39 n.
decrement 42 n.
disregard 458 vb.
qualification 468 n.
underestimate 483 vb.
pay 804 n., vb.
discount 810 n., vb.
discountenance
hinder 702 vb.
prohibit 757 vb.
refuse 760 vb.
disapprove 924 vb.
discourage
dissuade 613 vb.
hinder 702 vb.
prohibit 757 vb.
cause discontent 829 vb.
deject 834 vb.
frighten 854 vb.

discouragement
hopelessness 853 n.
discourse *lecture* 534 n.
teach 534 vb.
oration 579 n.
dissertation 591 n.
discourteous
impertinent 878 adj.
discourtesy
ill-breeding 847 n.
unsociability 883 n.
discourtesy 885 n.
disrespect 921 n.
discous *broad* 205 adj.
discover
come before 64 vb.
meet with 154 vb.
cause 156 vb.
produce 164 vb.
see 438 vb.
think 449 vb.
discover 484 vb.
manifest 522 vb.
be informed 524 vb.
discoverable
intelligible 516 adj.
discoverer *precursor* 66 n.
producer 167 n.
enquirer 459 n.
detector 484 n.
discovery *beginning* 68 n.
appearance 445 n.
discovery 484 n.
knowledge 490 n.
manifestation 522 n.
disclosure 526 n.
discredit *unbelief* 486 n.
disbelieve 486 vb.
cause doubt 486 vb.
disrepute 867 n.
odium 888 n.
discreditable *bad* 645 adj.
discreditable 867 adj.
discredited
disused 674 adj.
disreputable 867 adj.
disapproved 924 adj.
discreet
discriminating 463 adj.
reticent 525 adj.
cowardly 856 adj.
cautious 858 adj.
discrepancy
difference 15 n.
disagreement 25 n.
discrepant
quarrelling 709 adj.
discrete *separate* 46 adj.
discontinuous 72 adj.
discretion
discrimination 463 n.

judgment 480 n.
sagacity 498 n.
will 595 n.
choice 605 n.
skill 694 n.
cowardice 856 n.
caution 858 n.
discretional
volitional 595 adj.
voluntary 597 adj.
choosing 605 adj.
unconditional 744 adj.
discriminate
make unlike 19 vb.
set apart 46 vb.
specify 80 vb.
discrlmlnate 463 vb.
know 490 vb.
be wise 498 vb.
select 605 vb.
be skilful 694 vb.
have taste 846 vb.
be fastidious 862 vb.
discriminate against
do wrong 914 vb.
discrimination
contrariety 14 n.
discrimination 463 n.
judgment 480 n.
moral sensibility 819 n.
fastidiousness 862 n.
injustice 914 n.
(*see* discriminate)
discriminatory
tasteful 846 adj.
unjust 914 adj.
discursive *travelling* 267 adj.
deviating 282 adj.
rational 475 adj.
prolix 570 adj.
conversing 584 adj.
discursive 591 adj.
discursory *rational* 475 adj.
discursive 591 adj.
discus *circle* 250 n.
missile 287 n.
missile weapon 723 n.
discuss *eat* 301 vb.
meditate 449 vb.
argue 475 vb.
publish 528 vb.
confer 584 vb.
dissert 591 vb.
discussion *enquiry* 459 n.
dissertation 591 n.
discussion play
lecture 534 n.
disdain *reject* 607 vb.
be fastidious 862 vb.
pride 871 n.
insolence 878 n.

contempt 922 n.
disease *disease* 651 n.
  bane 659 n.
disembark *land* 295 vb.
disembarkation
  arrival 295 n.
disembarrass
  disencumber 701 vb.
disembodied
  immaterial 320 adj.
  spooky 970 adj.
disembody *disperse* 75 vb.
  disembody 320 vb.
disemboguement
  outflow 298 n.
disembowel *void* 300 vb.
disenchant *dissuade* 613 vb.
  displease 827 vb.
disenchanted
  indifferent 860 adj.
disenchantment
  reversion 148 n.
  discovery 484 n.
  painfulness 827 n.
disencumber *lighten* 323 vb.
  deliver 668 vb.
  disencumber 701 vb.
  liberate 746 vb.
  take away 786 vb.
disencumbrance
  displacement 188 n.
  facility 701 n.
disendow *depose* 752 vb.
  impoverish 801 vb.
disengage
  disencumber 701 vb.
  liberate 746 vb.
disengaged *inactive* 679 adj.
  leisurely 681 adj.
  impassive 820 adj.
  disinterested 931 adj.
disengagement
  disjunction 46 n.
  regression 286 n.
  extraction 304 n.
  facility 701 n.
disentail *liberate* 746 vb.
disentangle *simplify* 44 vb.
  disjoin 46 vb.
  unravel 62 vb.
  evolve 316 vb.
  decipher 520 vb.
  disencumber 701 vb.
  not retain 779 vb.
disentitle *deprive* 786 vb.
disentitlement
  non-ownership 774 n.
  loss of right 916 n.
disentomb *exhume* 364 vb.
disequilibrium
  inequality 29 n.

disestablishment
  deposal 752 n.
disesteem *disrepute* 867 n.
  disrespect 921 n.
  hold cheap 922 vb.
  disapprobation 924 n.
diseuse *entertainer* 594 n.
disfavour *prohibition* 757 n.
  refuse 760 vb.
  disrepute 867 n.
  odium 888 n.
  not respect 921 vb.
  disapprobation 924 n.
disfigure *deform* 244 vb.
  mark 547 vb.
  impair 655 vb.
  make ugly 842 vb.
  blemish 845 vb.
disfranchisement
  subjection 745 n.
  loss of right 916 n.
  lawlessness 954 n.
disgorge *void, vomit* 300 vb.
  restitute 787 vb.
  pay 804 vb.
disgrace
  disrepute, slur 867 n.
  shame 867 vb.
  humiliation 872 n.
  not respect 921 vb.
disgraceful
  discreditable 867 adj.
  heinous 934 adj.
disgruntle *disappoint* 509 vb.
  cause discontent 829 vb.
disguise *assimilation* 18 n.
  dissimilarity 19 n.
  mimicry 20 n.
  modify 143 vb.
  transform 147 vb.
  screen 421 n.
  conceal 525 vb.
  disguise 527 n.
  dissemble 541 vb.
  cunning 698 n.
disguised *unknown* 491 adj.
disgust
  be unpalatable 391 n.
  dissuade 613 vb.
  displease 827 vb.
  cause discontent 829 vb.
  tedium 838 n.
  dislike 861 n.
  excite hate 888 vb.
disgusting
  unsavoury 391 adj.
  unclean 649 adj.
  not nice 645 adj.
dish *destroy* 165 vb.
  plate 194 n.
  horizontality 216 n.

dish 301 n.
  defeat 727 vb.
dishabille
  informal dress 228 n.
  uncovering 229 n.
disharmony
  disagreement 25 n.
  disorder 61 n.
  discord 411 n.
  dissension 709 n.
dish-cloth
  cleaning cloth 648 n.
dishearten *dissuade* 613 vb.
  hinder 702 vb.
  cause discontent 829 vb.
  deject 834 vb.
disherison
  expropriation 876 n.
dishevelment
  non-uniformity 17 n.
  disorder 61 n.
  derangement 63 n.
dishonest *false* 541 adj.
  discreditable 867 adj.
  dishonest 930 adj.
dishonesty
  thievishness 788 n.
  wrong 914 n.
  improbity 930 n.
  wickedness 934 n.
  lawbreaking 954 n.
dishonour
  not observe 769 vb.
  not pay 805 vb.
  disrepute 867 n.
  wrong 914 n.
  disrespect 921 n.
  defame 926 vb.
  improbity 930 n.
  debauch 951 vb.
dishonourable
  discreditable 867 adj.
  blameworthy 924 adj.
  dishonest 930 adj.
dish-rag
  cleaning cloth 648 n.
dish up *make ready* 669 vb.
dish-washer *cleaner* 648 n.
  domestic 742 n.
dish-water
  weak thing 163 n.
  swill 649 n.
disillusion *disappoint* 509 vb.
  disclose 526 vb.
  dissuade 613 vb.
  displease 827 vb.
  regret 830 n.
  dejection 834 n.
  hatred 888 n.
disillusioned
  impassive 820 adj.

indifferent 860 adj.
disincarnate
  disembody 320 vb.
disincentive
  dissuasion 613 n.
  hindrance 702 n.
disinclination
  unwillingness 598 n.
  dislike 861 n.
disincline *dissuade* 613 vb.
  cause dislike 861 vb.
disinfect *sterilize* 172 vb.
  purify 648 vb.
  sanitate 652 vb.
  doctor 658 vb.
  safeguard 660 vb.
disinfectant
  cleanser 648 n.
  prophylactic 658 n.
  remedial 658 adj.
  tutelary 660 adj.
disinfected *clean* 648 adj.
  salubrious 652 adj.
  safe 660 adj.
disinfection
  hygiene 652 n.
disinfest *void* 300 vb.
disinfestation
  cleansing 648 n.
disinflation *finance* 797 n.
disingenuous
  false 541 adj.
  dishonest 930 adj.
disinherit *not retain* 779 vb.
  convey 780 vb.
  deprive 786 vb.
  impoverish 801 vb.
disintegrate
  be disjoined 46 vb.
  break, disjoin 46 vb.
  decompose 51 vb.
  disperse 75 vb.
  pulverize 332 vb.
disinter *exhume* 364 vb.
  discover 484 vb.
disinterested
  choiceless 606 adj.
  benevolent 897 adj.
  philanthropic 901 adj.
  just 913 adj.
  disinterested 931 adj.
  virtuous 933 adj.
disinterment *inquest* 364 n.
disinvestment
  expenditure 806 n.
disjoin *simplify* 44 vb.
  disjoin 46 vb.
  unstick 49 vb.
  decompose 51 vb.
  disperse 75 vb.
  displace 188 vb.

disjunct *disjunct* 46 adj.
  fragmentary 53 adj.
  orderless 61 adj.
  discontinuous 72 adj.
disjunction *irrelation* 10 n.
  subtraction 39 n.
  discontinuity 72 n.
  laxity 734 n.
  (see disjoin)
disjunctive *separate* 46 adj.
disk *face* 237 n.
  circle 250 n.
  (see disc)
dislike
  unwillingness 598 n.
  be loth 598 vb.
  refuse 760 vb.
  dislike 861 n., vb.
  enmity 881 n.
  hatred 888 n.
dislimb *rend* 46 vb.
dislocate *disjoin* 46 vb.
  derange 63 vb.
  disable 161 vb.
  force 176 vb.
  displace 188 vb.
  distort 246 vb.
dislodge *derange* 63 vb.
  displace 188 vb.
  eject 300 vb.
disloyal *changeful* 152 adj.
disloyalty
  disobedience 738 n.
  sedition 738 n.
  non-observance 769 n.
  enmity 881 n.
  dutilessness 918 n.
  perfidy 930 n.
dismal *dark* 418 adj.
  unpleasant 827 adj.
  melancholic 834 adj.
  cheerless 834 adj.
dismals *melancholy* 834 n.
dismantle
  break, sunder 46 vb.
  weaken 163 vb.
  demolish 165 vb.
  uncover 229 vb.
  make useless 641 vb.
  impair 655 vb.
  disuse 674 vb.
  make inactive 679 vb.
dismantled
  unequipped 670 adj.
dismay *defeat* 727 vb.
  worry 825 n.
  fear 854 n.
dismember
  sunder, rend 46 vb.
  execute 963 vb.
dismemberment

decomposition 51 n.
dismiss
  be dispersed 75 vb.
  displace 188 vb.
  dismiss 300 vb.
  disregard 458 vb.
dismissal *exclusion* 57 n.
  valediction 296 n.
  ejection 300 n.
  non-use 674 n.
  deposal 752 n.
  loss of right 916 n.
dismount *disjoin* 46 vb.
  unstick 49 vb.
  land 295 vb.
  descend 309 vb.
disobedience
  unwillingness 598 n.
  disobedience 738 n.
  refusal 760 n.
  non-observance 769 n.
disobedient *wilful* 602 adj.
  difficult 700 adj.
  sullen 893 adj.
  schismatical 978 adj.
  (see disobedience)
disobey *fail in duty* 918 vb.
disoblige
  be malevolent 898 vb.
disordain *depose* 752 vb.
disorder
  non-uniformity 17 n.
  decompose 51 vb.
  disorder 61 n.
  derangement 63 n.
  discontinuity 72 n.
  disperse 75 vb.
  deform 244 vb.
  negligence 458 n.
  badness 645 n.
  disease 651 n.
  hinder 702 vb.
  anarchy 734 n.
  revolt 738 n.
disorderly *violent* 176 adj.
  anarchic 734 adj.
  riotous 738 adj.
  ill-bred 847 adj.
disorderly house
  brothel 951 n.
disorganization
  derangement 63 n.
  destruction 165 n.
  impairment 655 n.
  anarchy 734 n.
disorganized *lax* 734 adj.
disorientate *derange* 63 vb.
  displace 188 vb.
disorientation
  deviation 282 n.
disown *be unrelated* 10 vb.

negate 533 vb.
avoid 620 vb.
abrogate 752 vb.
not retain 779 vb.
disapprove 924 vb.
disparage
underestimate 483 vb.
shame 867 vb.
not respect 921 vb.
hold cheap 922 vb.
detract 926 vb.
disparagement
disrespect 921 n.
disapprobation 924 n.
detraction 926 n.
disparity irrelation 10 n.
difference 15 n.
dissimilarity 19 n.
disagreement 25 n.
inequality 29 n.
dispart disjoin 46 vb.
dispassion
inexcitability 823 n.
justice 913 n.
dispassionate
impassive 820 adj.
just 913 adj.
disinterested 931 adj.
dispatch (see despatch)
dispel disjoin 46 vb.
disperse 75 vb.
destroy 165 vb.
displace 188 vb.
repel 292 vb.
disappear 446 vb.
liberate 746 vb.
dispensable
superfluous 637 adj.
useless 641 adj.
permitted 756 adj.
dispensary hospital 658 n.
dispensation
exclusion 57 n.
deliverance 668 n.
management 689 n.
permission 756 n.
non-retention 779 n.
apportionment 783 n.
non-liability 919 n.
dispense give 781 vb.
exempt 919 vb.
(see dispensation)
dispenser druggist 658 n.
dispense with
not use 674 vb.
not retain 779 vb.
dispeople void 300 vb.
dispersal diminution 37 n.
disjunction 46 n.
dispersion 75 n.
transference 272 n.

disperse disappear 446 vb.
defeat 727 vb.
dispersion separation 46 n.
non-coherence 49 n.
disorder 61 n.
dispersion 75 n.
expansion 197 n.
distance 199 n.
transference 272 n.
divergence 294 n.
reflection 417 n.
waste 634 n.
dispirit dissuade 613 vb.
deject 834 vb.
displace disjoin 46 vb.
exclude 57 vb.
derange 63 vb.
substitute 150 vb.
displace 188 vb.
move 265 vb.
transpose 272 vb.
eject 300 vb.
displaced person
foreigner 59 n.
displacement 188 n.
wanderer 268 n.
outcaste 883 n.
displacement
displacement 188 n.
depth 211 n.
gravity 322 n.
(see displace)
displant displace 188 vb.
display
accumulation 74 n.
spectacle 445 n.
exhibit 522 n.
show 522 vb.
publicity 528 n.
pride 871 n.
ostentation 875 n.
pageant 875 n.
displease displease 827 vb.
cause discontent 829 vb.
cause dislike 861 vb.
displeasure sorrow 825 n.
annoyance 827 n.
discontent 829 n.
dislike 861 n.
hatred 888 n.
resentment 891 n.
disapprobation 924 n.
disport oneself
be cheerful 833 vb.
amuse oneself 837 vb.
disposability
non-retention 779 n.
disposable useful 640 adj.
used 673 adj.
disposal arrangement 62 n.
use 673 n.

non-retention 779 n.
sale 793 n.
disposal, at one's
possessed 773 adj.
dispose order 60 vb.
arrange 62 vb.
influence 178 vb.
tend 179 vb.
motivate 612 vb.
disposed willing 597 adj.
intending 617 adj.
dispose of dispose of 673 vb.
carry through 725 vb.
possess 773 vb.
sell 793 vb.
disposition
temperament 5 n.
order 60 n.
arrangement 62 n.
location 187 n.
will 595 n.
willingness 597 n.
affections 817 n.
dispossess eject 300 vb.
convey 780 vb.
deprive 786 vb.
appropriate 786 vb.
impoverish 801 vb.
disentitle 916 vb.
dispossessed losing 772 adj.
not owning 774 adj.
poor 801 adj.
unentitled 916 adj.
dispossession
ejection 300 n.
loss 772 n.
loss of right 916 n.
dispraise censure 924 n.
dispraise 924 vb.
dispread
unassembled 75 adj.
disperse 75 vb.
disprize hold cheap 922 vb.
disapprove 924 vb.
disproof
counter-evidence 467 n.
confutation 479 n.
negation 533 n.
disproportion
irrelation 10 n.
disagreement 25 n.
inequality 29 n.
distortion 246 n.
exaggeration 546 n.
disproportioned
unsightly 842 adj.
disprovable
confuted 479 adj.
disprove (see disproof)
disproved erroneous 495 adj.
disputable uncertain 474 adj.

arguing 475 adj.
unbelieved 486 adj.
litigated 959 adj.
disputant *reasoner* 475 n.
disputation *argument* 475 n.
disputatious
arguing 475 adj.
quarrelling 709 adj.
dispute *disagree* 25 vb.
argue 475 vb.
quarrel 709 n., vb.
contention 716 n.
disputer
combatant 722 n.
dispute with *bicker* 709 vb.
disqualification
impotence 161 n.
ejection 300 n.
inexpedience 643 n.
non-preparation 670 n.
unskilfulness 695 n.
loss of right 916 n.
disqualify *exclude* 57 vb.
disable 161 vb.
make useless 641 vb.
disentitle 916 vb.
disquiet
changeableness 152 n.
agitation 318 n.
impress 821 vb.
worry 825 n.
incommode 827 vb.
discontent 829 n.
nervousness 854 n.
disquisition *lecture* 534 n.
diffuseness 570 n.
dissertation 591 n.
disquisitional
discursive 591 adj.
disrate *shame* 867 vb.
disregard *exclude* 57 vb.
be deaf 416 vb.
not think 450 vb.
be incurious 454 vb.
inattention 456 n.
disregard 458 vb.
not know 491 vb.
reject 607 vb.
not use 674 vb.
abrogate 752 vb.
non-observance 769 n.
fail in duty 918 vb.
not respect 921 vb.
impiety 980 n.
disregarded
unimportant 639 adj.
(see disregard)
disrelish *dislike* 861 n., vb.
hate 888 vb.
disremember *forget* 506 vb.
disrepair *dilapidation* 655 n.

disreputable
not nice 645 adj.
vulgar 847 adj.
disreputable 867 adj.
plebeian 869 adj.
dishonest 930 adj.
disrepute *disrepute* 867 n.
humiliation 872 n.
odium 888 n.
disrespect
non-observance 769 n.
ridicule 851 n.
disrepute 867 n.
dutilessness 918 n.
disrespect 921 n.
not respect 921 vb.
disapprobation 924 n.
disrespectful
non-observant 769 adj.
insolent 878 adj.
impertinent 878 adj.
dutiless 918 adj.
disrespectful 921 adj.
despising 922 adj.
detracting 926 adj.
disrobe *doff* 229 vb.
disruption *separation* 46 n.
destruction 165 n.
dissatisfaction
dissent 489 n.
sorrow 825 n.
discontent 829 n.
dislike 861 n.
resentment 891 n.
disapprobation 924 n.
dissatisfy *disappoint* 509 vb.
be imperfect 647 vb.
displease 827 vb.
cause discontent 829 vb.
dissaving *expenditure* 806 n.
dissect *sunder* 46 vb.
decompose 51 vb.
class 62 vb.
enquire 459 vb.
disseisin
expropriation 786 n.
disseisor *taker* 786 n.
dissemblance
dissimilarity 19 n.
dissemble
make unlike 19 vb.
mislead 495 vb.
be equivocal 518 vb.
conceal 525 vb.
dissemble 541 vb.
deceive 542 vb.
be affected 850 vb.
dissembler *deceiver* 545 n.
slyboots 698 n.
dissemination
dispersion 75 n.

information 524 n.
publication 528 n.
dissension *difference* 15 n.
disagreement 25 n.
dissent 489 n.
opposition 704 n.
dissension 709 n.
contention 716 n.
enmity 881 n.
dissent *disagreement* 25 n.
unbelief 486 n.
dissent 489 n., vb.
negation 533 n.
reject 607 vb.
opposition 704 n.
dissension 709 n.
refuse 760 vb.
sectarianism 978 n.
dissenter
nonconformist 84 n.
unbeliever 486 n.
dissentient 489 n.
schismatic 978 n.
dissentience *dissent* 489 n.
dissentient
nonconformist 84 n.
unbeliever 486 n.
dissentient 489 n.
opponent 705 n.
heterodox 977 adj.
schismatical 978 adj.
dissenting
unconformable 84 adj.
heterodox 977 adj.
schismatical 978 adj.
dissert *write* 586 vb.
dissert 591 vb.
dissertation
diffuseness 570 n.
oration 579 n.
dissertation 591 n.
disserve *harm* 645 vb.
disservice *evil* 616 n.
inutility 641 n.
dissever *disjoin* 46 vb.
dissidence
disagreement 25 n.
unconformity 84 n.
dissent 489 n.
sectarianism 978 n.
dissident
nonconformist 84 n.
dissentient 489 n.
discontented 829 adj.
schismatic 978 n.
dissilience
disjunction 46 n.
outbreak 176 n.
dissimilar *different* 15 adj.
non-uniform 17 adj.
dissimilar 19 adj.

unequal 29 adj.
dissimilation
　dissimilarity 19 n.
　speech sound 398 n.
　grammar 654 n.
dissimilitude
　dissimilarity 19 n.
dissimulate
　dissemble 541 vb.
dissimulation
　mimicry 20 n.
　concealment 525 n.
　duplicity 541 n.
dissipated *prodigal* 815 adj.
　lecherous 951 adj.
dissipation
　dispersion 75 n.
　pleasure 376 n.
　disappearance 446 n.
　waste 634 n.
　loss 772 n.
　prodigality 815 n.
　intemperance 943 n.
　sensualism 944 n.
　unchastity 951 n.
dissociation
　irrelation 10 n.
　disjunction 46 n.
　unwillingness 598 n.
　opposition 704 n.
　schism 978 n.
dissoluble
　severable 46 adj.
　liquefied 337 adj.
dissoluteness
　sensualism 944 n.
　unchastity 951 n.
dissolution *diminution* 37 n.
　separation 46 n.
　decomposition 51 n.
　disorder 61 n.
　finality 69 n.
　destruction 165 n.
　liquefaction 337 n.
　disappearance 446 n.
　abrogation 752 n.
　non-retention 779 n.
dissolvable
　severable 46 adj.
dissolve *not be* 2 vb.
　shade off 27 vb.
　decompose 51 vb.
　be dispersed 75 vb.
　destroy 165 vb.
　deform 244 vb.
　(*see* dissolution)
dissolvent
　liquefaction 337 n.
dissonance
　disagreement 25 n.
　discord 411 n.

dissension 709 n.
dissuade
　cause doubt 486 vb.
　dissuade 613 vb.
　advise 691 vb.
　hinder 702 vb.
　deprecate 762 vb.
　cause discontent 829 vb.
　frighten 854 vb.
dissuasive
　dissuasive 613 adj.
　advising 691 adj.
　deprecatory 762 adj.
distaff *weaving* 222 n.
distaff side
　womankind 373 n.
distance *difference* 15 n.
　range 183 n.
　distance 199 n.
　length 203 n.
　outstrip 277 vb.
　progress 285 vb.
　outdo 306 vb.
　invisibility 444 n.
　unsociability 883 n.
distance apart
　disjunction 46 n.
distance of time
　diuturnity 113 n.
　antiquity 125 n.
distant *extraneous* 59 adj.
　distant 199 adj.
　exterior 223 adj.
　incurious 454 adj.
　impassive 820 adj.
　prideful 871 adj.
　inimical 881 adj.
　unsociable 883 adj.
distant past
　preterition 125 n.
distaste *dislike* 861 n., vb.
distasteful
　unpleasant 827 adj.
distemper *weaken* 163 vb.
　facing 226 n.
　colour, pigment 425 n.
　art equipment 553 n.
　disease 651 n.
　animal disease 651 n.
　incommode 827 vb.
distend *augment* 36 vb.
　expand 197 vb.
distension *dilation* 197 n.
disthrone *unthrone* 734 vb.
distich *verse form* 593 n.
distil *exude* 298 vb.
　extract 304 vb.
　vaporize 338 vb.
　purify 648 vb.
distillation *outflow* 298 n.
　heating 381 n.

distillery *vaporizer* 338 n.
　workshop 687 n.
distinct *different* 15 adj.
　separate 46 adj.
　definite 80 adj.
　sounding 398 adj.
　loud 400 adj.
　well-seen 443 adj.
　intelligible 516 adj.
　assertive 532 adj.
　vocal 577 adj.
distinction
　differentiation 15 n.
　speciality 80 n.
　discrimination 463 n.
　reasoning 475 n.
　elegance 575 n.
　importance 638 n.
　prestige, honours 866 n.
　nobility 868 n.
　title 870 n.
distinctive *distinctive* 15 adj.
　special 80 adj.
distinctness *sound* 398 n.
　loudness 400 n.
　voice 577 n.
　(*see* distinct)
distinguish
　differentiate 15 vb.
　set apart 46 vb.
　see 438 vb.
　distinguish 463 vb.
　be wise 498 vb.
　understand 516 vb.
　name 561 vb.
　dignify 866 vb.
distinguishable
　separate 46 adj.
distinguished
　superior 34 adj.
　elegant 575 adj.
　notable 638 adj.
　noteworthy 866 adj.
distort
　make unlike 19 vb.
　transform 147 vb.
　render oblique 220 vb.
　distort 246 vb.
　be false 541 vb.
　misinterpret 521 vb.
　misteach 535 vb.
　exaggerate 546 vb.
　misrepresent 552 vb.
　pervert 655 vb.
　misuse 675 vb.
　make ugly 842 vb.
distorted *abnormal* 84 adj.
　imperfect 647 adj.
distorting mirror
　visual fallacy 440 n.
　mirror 442 n.

misrepresentation 552n.
distortion *irrelation* 10n.
  mimicry 20n.
  violence 176n.
  visual fallacy 440n.
  falsehood 541n.
  untruth 543n.
  blemish 845n.
  (*see* distort)
distract *distract* 456vb.
distraction
  abstractedness 456n.
  frenzy 503n.
  excitable state 822n.
distraint
  expropriation 786n.
distrait *abstracted* 456adj.
distraught *doubting* 474adj.
  frenzied 503adj.
  excited 821adj.
distress *pain* 377n.
  give pain 377vb.
  evil 616n.
  ill-treat 645vb.
  fatigue 684n.,vb.
  adversity 731n.
  expropriation 786n.
  poverty 801n.
  hurt 827vb.
distressing *felt* 818adj.
  distressing 827adj.
distress signal
  danger signal 665n.
distributary *stream* 350n.
distribution
  arrangement 62n.
  dispersion 75n.
  apportionment 783n.
district *subdivision* 53n.
  district 184n.
  regional 184adj.
  place 185n.
  locality 187n.
  land 344n.
  parish 985n.
distrust *doubt* 486n.,vb.
  be nervous 854vb.
  jealousy 911n.
disturb *decompose* 51vb.
  derange 63vb.
  mistime 138vb.
  modify 143vb.
  displace 188vb.
  agitate 318vb.
  cause feeling 374vb.
  distract 456vb.
  incommode 827vb.
  frighten 854vb.
disturbance *turmoil* 61n.
  derangement 63n.
  intempestivity 138n.

commotion 318n.
  revolt 738n.
disturbed
  violent 176adj.
  nervous 854adj.
disunion, disunity
  disjunction 46n.
  disorder 61n.
  dissension 709n.
disunite *disjoin* 46vb.
disuse *rejection* 607n.
  desuetude 611n.
  relinquishment 621n.
  non-use 674n.
  make inactive 679vb.
  abrogation 752n.
  non-retention 779n.
disused *past* 125adj.
  antiquated 127adj.
disyllable
  spoken letter 558n.
ditch *gap* 201n.
  fence 235n.
  cavity 255n.
  furrow 262n.
  dry 342vb.
  lake 346n.
  conduit 351n.
  drain 351n.
  cultivate 370vb.
  tergiversate 603vb.
  reject 607vb.
  relinquish 621vb.
  protection 660n.
  disuse 674vb.
  stratagem 698n.
  obstacle 702n.
  defences 713n.
  not retain 779vb.
ditch-water *swill* 649n.
dither *be agitated* 318vb.
  be uncertain 474vb.
  be irresolute 601vb.
dithyramb
  vocal music 412n.
  poem 593n.
  praise 923n.
dithyrambic
  approving 923adj.
dithyrambist *poet* 593n.
ditto *identity* 13n.
  accord 24vb.
  repetition 106n.
  again 106adv.
  assent 488vb.
ditty *vocal music* 412n.
ditty-bag *bag* 194n.
diuretic *excretory* 302adj.
  cleanser 648n.
diurnal *seasonal* 141adj.
diuturnity *diuturnity* 113n.

perpetuity 115n.
diva *vocalist* 413n.
  actor 594n.
divagate *stray* 282vb.
  circuit 626vb.
divan *seat* 218n.
  reading matter 589n.
  anthology 592n.
  poem 593n.
  law court 956n.
divaricate *differ* 15vb.
  bifurcate 92vb.
  angulate 247vb.
  deviate 282vb.
  diverge 294vb.
dive *tavern* 192n.
  swim 269vb.
  navigate 269vb.
  fly 271vb.
  spurt 277n.
  descent 309n.
  plunge 313n.,vb.
  be wet 341vb.
divellicate *rend* 46vb.
diver *depth* 211n.
  diver 313n.
  waterfowl 365n.
diverge
  be oblique 220vb.
  (*see* divergence)
divergence *difference* 15n.
  non-uniformity 17n.
  dissimilarity 19n.
  disagreement 25n.
  disjunction 46n.
  dispersion 75n.
  bifurcation 92n.
  deviation 282n.
  divergence 294n.
  dissension 709n.
divers *different* 15adj.
  multiform 82adj.
  many 104adj.
diverse (*see* diversity)
diversification
  variegation 437n.
diversify *modify* 143vb.
  variegate 437vb.
diversion *change* 143n.
  deviation 282n.
  pleasure 367n.
  trickery, trap 542n.
  misuse 675n.
  expropriation 786n.
  amusement 837n.
diversity *irrelation* 10n.
  difference 15n.
  non-uniformity 17n.
  dissimilarity 19n.
  multiformity 82n.
  variegation 437n.

divert *render oblique* 220vb.
deflect 282vb.
distract 456vb.
ensnare 542vb.
misuse 675vb.
obstruct 702vb.
not pay 805vb.
amuse 837vb.
divertissement
pleasure 376n.
musical piece 412n.
stage play 594n.
amusement 837n.
divest *subtract* 39vb.
uncover 229vb.
relinquish 621vb.
depose 752vb.
deprive 786vb.
divide *sunder* 46vb.
part 53vb.
class 62vb.
do sums 86vb.
bisect 92vb.
summit 213n.
partition 231n.
limit 236n.
mete out 465vb.
vote 605vb.
make quarrels 709vb.
apportion 783vb.
schismatize 978vb.
dividend *part* 53n.
numerical element 85n.
gain 771n.
participation 775n.
portion 783n.
dividers *gauge* 465n.
dividing line
dividing line 92n.
divination *intuition* 476n.
divination 511n.
hermeneutics 520n.
sorcery 983n.
occultism 984n.
divine *foresee* 510vb.
divine 511vb.
suppose 512vb.
beautiful 841adj.
lovable 887adj.
divine 965adj.
godlike 965adj.
theologian 973n.
religious 973adj.
cleric 986n.
divineness *divineness* 965n.
diviner *diviner* 511n.
interpreter 520n.
sorcerer 983n.
sorceress 983n.
occultist, psychic 984n.
divine right *authority* 733n.

divine service
public worship 981n.
diving *aquatics* 269n.
diving-bell *diver* 313n.
divining rod
magic instrument 983n.
divinity *divineness* 965n.
theology 973n.
divisible *severable* 46adj.
numerical 85adj.
division *scission* 46n.
decomposition 51n.
subdivision 53n.
arrangement 62n.
discontinuity 72n.
classification 77n.
numerical operation 86n.
district 184n.
partition 231n.
vote 605n.
parliament 692n.
dissension 709n.
formation 722n.
apportionment 783n.
seclusion 883n.
schism, sect 978n.
divisor
numerical element 85n.
divorce *separation* 46n.
non-retention 779n.
divorce 896n.,vb.
divot *piece* 53n.
soil 344n.
grass 366n.
divulgation
publication 528n.
divulgatory
disclosing 526adj.
divulge *manifest* 522vb.
divulge 526vb.
publish 528vb.
divulsion *scission* 46n.
divvy *apportion* 783vb.
diwan *officer* 741n.
dizzy *unequal* 29adj.
changeful 152adj.
high 209adj.
rotary 315adj.
dim-sighted 440adj.
light-minded 456adj.
foolish 499adj.
ninny 501n.
fool 501n.
crazed 503adj.
crapulous 949adj.
tipsy 949adj.
do *be in a state* 7vb.
accord 24vb.
cause 156vb.
produce 164vb.
operate 173vb.

deceive 542vb.
represent 551vb.
be instrumental 628vb.
suffice 635vb.
be useful 640vb.
be expedient 642vb.
do 676vb.
deal with 688vb.
amusement 837n.
celebration 876n.
doable *possible* 469adj.
do after *do likewise* 20vb.
do again *repeat* 106vb.
do all one can
exert oneself 682vb.
do as others do
conform 83vb.
do away with
destroy 165vb.
kill 362vb.
dobbin *horse* 273n.
doch-an-doris
valediction 296n.
docile *tamed* 369adj.
studious 536adj.
willing 597adj.
induced 612adj.
obedient 739adj.
docility *learning* 536n.
willingness 597n.
persuasibility 612n.
docimasy *experiment* 461n.
dock *subtract* 39vb.
cut 46vb.
stable 192n.
shorten 204vb.
navigate 269vb.
goal 295n.
arrive 295n.
storage 632n.
impair 655vb.
shelter 662n.
workshop 687n.
lock-up 748n.
courtroom 956n.
docker *boatman* 270n.
worker 686n.
docket *list* 87n.,vb.
credential 466n.
label 547n.
mark 547vb.
registration 548n.
compendium 592n.
abstract 592vb.
dockland *district* 184n.
dockyard *workshop* 687n.
doctor *mix* 43vb.
modify 143vb.
scholar 492n.
sage 500n.
bribe 612vb.

cure 656 vb.
doctor 658 n., vb.
relieve 831 vb.
academic title 870 n.
theologian 973 n.
doctorate
academic title 870 n.
doctrinaire
doctrinaire 473 n.
positive 473 adj.
narrow mind 481 n.
theorist 512 n.
doctrinal credal 485 adj.
educational 534 adj.
theological 973 adj.
orthodox 976 adj.
doctrine creed 485 n.
theology 973 n.
document evidence 466 n.
corroborate 466 vb.
demonstrate 478 vb.
record 548 n.
documentary cinema 445 n.
evidential 466 adj.
informative 524 adj.
descriptive 590 adj.
documentation
(see document)
dodder be agitated 318 vb.
be irresolute 601 vb.
dodderer waverer 601 n.
dodge vary 152 vb.
be in motion 265 vb.
deviate 282 vb.
campanology 412 n.
disregard 458 vb.
sophisticate 477 vb.
be stealthy 525 vb.
dissemble 541 vb.
trickery 542 n.
pretext 614 n.
avoid 620 vb.
contrivance 623 n.
means of escape 667 n.
elude 667 vb.
skill 694 n.
stratagem 698 n.
not observe 769 vb.
be dishonest 930 vb.
dodger hider 527 n.
avoider 620 n.
dodo flightless bird 365 n.
do duty function 622 vb.
deputize 755 vb.
doe speeder 277 n.
female animal 373 n.
doer producer 167 n.
doer 676 n.
doeskin skin 226 n.
doff doff 229 vb.
do for destroy 165 vb.

murder 362 vb.
kill 362 vb.
minister to 703 vb.
defeat 727 vb.
serve 742 vb.
dog accompany 89 vb.
be behind 238 vb.
follow 284 vb.
dog 365 n.
male animal 372 n.
pursue 619 vb.
knave 938 n.
dog-cart
carriage, cart 274 n.
dog-collar neckwear 228 n.
canonicals 989 n.
dog-days heat 379 n.
doge officer 741 n.
dog-eared folded 261 adj.
dilapidated 655 adj.
used 673 adj.
dog-fight duel 716 n.
fight 716 n.
dogged obstinate 602 adj.
courageous 855 adj.
doggedness
perseverance 600 n.
obstinacy 602 n.
dogger fishing-boat 275 n.
hunter 619 n.
doggerel inelegant 576 adj.
doggerel 593 n.
poetic 593 adj.
ridiculousness 849 n.
funny 849 adj.
doggish fashionable 848 adj.
dog in the manger
hinderer 702 n.
egotist 932 n.
dogma certainty 473 n.
creed 485 n.
theology 973 n.
dogmatic
certain, positive 473 adj.
narrow-minded 481 adj.
credal 485 adj.
assertive 532 adj.
obstinate 602 adj.
vain 873 adj.
dogmatics theology 973 n.
dogmatism
positiveness 473 n.
affirmation 532 n.
opiniatry 602 n.
dogmatist doctrinaire 473 n.
opinionist 602 n.
dogmatize
dogmatize 473 vb.
be biased 481 vb.
affirm 532 vb.
do good benefit 615 vb.

be useful 640 vb.
do good 644 vb.
philanthropize 897 vb.
do-gooder
kind person 897 n.
philanthropist 901 n.
dogsbody food 301 n.
dog's tooth notch 260 n.
pattern 844 n.
dog-tired fatigued 684 adj.
dog-track
meeting place 192 n.
arena 724 n.
dog-trot gait 265 n.
slowness 278 n.
dog-watch period 110 n.
evening 129 n.
do in destroy 165 vb.
kill 362 vb.
doing happening 154 adj.
production 164 n.
agency 173 n.
operative 173 adj.
representation 551 n.
action 676 n.
doing 676 adj.
doing, be
busy oneself 622 vb.
doings affairs 154 n.
clothing 228 n.
deed 676 n.
doing time
imprisoned 747 adj.
doing well
prosperous 730 adj.
do instead
compensate 31 vb.
do into translate 520 vb.
doit small coin 33 n.
trifle 639 n.
doited aged 131 adj.
do-it-yourself
bungled 695 adj.
artless 699 adj.
laical 987 adj.
do justice to be just 913 vb.
vindicate 927 vb.
doldrums weather 340 n.
inaction 677 n.
inactivity 769 n.
dejection 834 n.
dole small quantity 33 n.
insufficiency 636 n.
gift 781 n.
portion 783 n.
booty 790 n.
sorrow 825 n.
doleful melancholic 834 adj.
lamenting 836 adj.
dole out mete out 465 vb.
give 781 vb.

apportion 783 vb.
be parsimonious 816 vb.
doll *dwarf* 196 n.
woman 373 n.
image 551 n.
plaything 837 n.
dollar *coinage* 797 n.
dollop *piece* 53 n.
portion 783 n.
doll's house
plaything 837 n.
doll up *primp* 843 vb.
dolly *infantine* 132 adj.
little 196 adj.
dolman *tunic* 228 n.
dolmen *tomb* 364 n.
monument 548 n.
dolorific *paining* 827 adj.
dolour *pain* 377 n.
suffering 825 n.
dolphin *fish* 365 n.
dolt *dunce* 501 n.
doltish *unintelligent* 499 adj.
Dom *church title* 986 n.
domain *territory* 184 n.
lands 777 n.
dome *edifice* 164 n.
house 192 n.
high structure 209 n.
head 213 n.
roof 226 n.
sphere 252 n.
dome 253 n.
Domesday Book *list* 87 n.
domestic *native* 191 adj.
provincial 192 adj.
interior 224 adj.
tamed 369 adj.
domestic 742 n.
unsociable 883 adj.
domesticate
break in 369 vb.
habituate 610 vb.
domesticated
native 191 adj.
quiescent 266 adj.
tamed 369 adj.
subjected 745 adj.
domestication
location 187 n.
animal husbandry 369 n.
domesticity *quietude* 266 n.
unsociability 883 n.
domestic science
cookery 301 n.
domicile *abode* 192 n.
domiciled *native* 191 adj.
domiciliary visit
search 459 n.
dominance *influence* 178 n.
dominant *supreme* 34 adj.

influential 178 adj.
musical note 410 n.
authoritative 733 adj.
dominate *be able* 160 vb.
influence 178 vb.
prevail 178 vb.
dominate 733 vb.
subjugate 745 vb.
dominating
overhanging 209 adj.
domination
superiority 34 n.
influence 178 n.
governance 733 n.
domineer *oppress* 735 vb.
domineering
authoritative 733 adj.
oppressive 735 adj.
insolent 878 adj.
Domini, Anno *time* 108 adv.
dominie *teacher* 537 n.
master 741 n.
dominion *territory* 184 n.
governance 733 n.
polity 733 n.
lands 777 n.
dominion status
government 733 n.
independence 744 n.
domino *lamina* 207 n.
robe, cloak 228 n.
disguise 527 n.
plaything 837 n.
don *wear* 228 vb.
male 372 n.
scholar 492 n.
teacher 537 n.
master 741 n.
aristocrat 868 n.
title 870 n.
donation *incentive* 612 n.
giving 781 n.
Donatism *heresy* 977 n.
schism 978 n.
donative *incentive* 612 n.
gift 781 n.
done *culinary* 301 adj.
usual 610 adj.
fashionable 848 adj.
donee *recipient* 782 n.
done for *fatigued* 684 adj.
done thing *practice* 610 n.
etiquette 848 n.
done up *fatigued* 684 adj.
done with *disused* 674 adj.
donjon *fort* 713 n.
Don Juan *libertine* 952 n.
donkey
beast of burden 273 n.
animal 365 n.
fool 501 n.

donna *lady* 373 n.
donnish
narrow-minded 481 adj.
instructed 490 adj.
severe 735 adj.
fastidious 862 adj.
donor *provider* 633 n.
giver 781 n.
benefactor 903 n.
do-nothing
non-active 677 adj.
idler 679 n.
lazy 679 adj.
do nothing but *recur* 139 vb.
Don Quixote *crank* 504 n.
visionary 513 n.
brave person 835 n.
don't-care *rash* 857 adj.
indifferent 860 adj.
donzel *retainer* 742 n.
doodle *play music* 413 vb.
be inattentive 456 vb.
doodlebug *rocket* 276 n.
bomb 723 n.
dooly *vehicle* 274 n.
doom *finality* 69 n.
predestine 155 vb.
ruin 165 n.
death 361 n.
judge 480 vb.
fate 596 n.
necessitate 596 vb.
intend 617 vb.
condemnation 961 n.
punishment 963 n.
doomed *ephemeral* 114 adj.
unfortunate 731 adj.
unhappy 825 adj.
doomsday
future state 124 n.
doomsman *judge* 957 n.
door *entrance* 68 n.
threshold 234 n.
barrier 235 n.
doorway 263 n.
access 624 n.
door-bell *signal* 547 n.
door-keeper, doorman
janitor 264 n.
servant 742 n.
door-knocker
hammer 279 n.
signal 547 n.
doormat *weakling* 163 n.
floor-cover 226 n.
cleaning utensil 648 n.
slave 742 n.
coward 856 n.
doorstep *stand* 218 n.
threshold 234 n.
doorway 263 n.

doubting *irresolute* 601 adj.
  nervous 854 adj.
doubtless *certainly* 473 adv.
douceur *gift* 781 n.
  reward 962 n.
douche *water* 339 n.
  ablution 648 n.
  therapy 658 n.
dough *softness* 327 n.
  pulpiness 356 n.
  dibs 797 n.
doughboy *soldier* 722 n.
doughnut *pastry* 301 n.
doughty *courageous* 855 adj.
do up *join* 45 vb.
  make better 654 vb.
  repair 656 vb.
  fatigue 684 vb.
dour *obstinate* 602 adj.
  severe 735 adj.
douse *retard* 278 vb.
  plunge 313 vb.
  drench 341 vb.
  extinguish 382 vb.
  snuff out 418 vb.
dove *bird* 365 n.
  mediator 720 n.
  innocent 935 n.
  Holy Ghost 965 n.
dovecote *stable* 192 n.
dovelike *peaceful* 717 adj.
dovetail *accord* 24 vb.
  join 45 vb.
  cross 222 vb.
  intromit 231 vb.
  implant 303 vb.
dowager *woman* 373 n.
  widowed spouse 896 n.
dowdy *graceless* 842 adj.
  bad taste 847 n.
  ill-bred 847 adj.
dower *dower* 777 n., vb.
  giving 781 n.
dowerless *poor* 801 adj.
do with, have to
  be related 9 vb.
do without
  not retain 779 vb.
dowlas *textile* 222 n.
down *filament* 208 n.
  under 210 adv.
  smoothness 258 n.
  hair 259 n.
  down 309 adv.
  levity 323 n.
  softness 327 n.
  recorded 548 adj.
  dejected 834 adj.
  sullen 893 adj.
down-and-out
  powerless 161 adj.

dilapidated 655 adj.
  poor man 801 n.
  low fellow 869 n.
down-at-heel
  dilapidated 655 adj.
  beggarly 801 adj.
  disreputable 867 adj.
downcast *dejected* 834 adj.
downdraught *descent* 309 n.
  wind 352 n.
downfall *descent* 309 n.
  ruin 165 n.
  defeat 728 n.
  adversity 731 n.
downgrade *shame* 867 vb.
  punish 963 vb.
downhill *acclivity* 220 n.
  sloping 220 adj.
  down 309 adv.
  facility 701 n.
  easy 701 adj.
downiness (*see* downy)
down in the mouth
  dejected 834 adj.
down on one's luck
  unfortunate 731 adj.
downpour *descent* 309 n.
  rain 350 n.
downright
  consummate 32 adj.
  positively 32 adv.
  simple 44 adj.
  complete 54 adj.
  intelligible 516 adj.
  undisguised 522 adj.
  veracious 540 adj.
downrush *spurt* 277 n.
  descent 309 n.
downs *high land* 209 n.
down stage
  stage-set 594 n.
  on stage 594 adv.
downstairs *under* 210 adv.
  down 309 adv.
downstream
  towards 281 adv.
  down 309 adv.
  easy 701 adj.
down to earth *true* 494 adj.
down to the ground
  completely 54 adv.
down tools *cease* 154 vb.
  revolt 738 vb.
downtown *afar* 199 adv.
  directed 281 adj.
downtrend
  deterioration 655 n.
downtrodden
  subjected 745 adj.
  suffering 825 adj.
down under *beyond* 199 adv.

downwards *under* 210 adv.
  down 309 adv.
downwind *directed* 281 adj.
  towards 281 adv.
downy *fibrous* 208 adj.
  smooth 258 adj.
  downy 259 adj.
  soft 327 adj.
  comfortable 376 adj.
dowry *store* 632 n.
  dower 777 n.
dowse *depress* 311 vb.
  search 459 vb.
dowser *enquirer* 459 n.
  detector 484 n.
  diviner 511 n.
  psychic 984 n.
dowsing *intuition* 476 n.
  divination 511 n.
doxological
  theological 973 adj.
  devotional 981 adj.
doxology *praise* 923 n.
  act of worship 981 n.
  hymn 981 n.
doxy *creed* 485 n.
  kept woman 952 n.
  theology 973 n.
doyen *seniority* 131 n.
doyley, doily
  cleaning cloth 648 n.
doze *be neglectful* 458 vb.
  sleep 679 n., vb.
dozen *over five* 99 n.
drab *uniform* 16 adj.
  soft-hued 425 adj.
  dirty person 649 n.
  dilapidated 655 adj.
  cheerless 834 adj.
  dull 840 adj.
  graceless 842 n.
  loose woman 952 n.
drachm *weighment* 322 n.
drachma *coinage* 797 n.
Draconian *severe* 735 adj.
draff *swill* 649 n.
draft *copy* 22 n.
  prototype 23 n.
  compose 56 vb.
  representation 551 n.
  write 586 vb.
  compendium 592 n.
  plan 623 n., vb.
  army 722 n.
  armed force 722 n.
  compel 740 vb.
  paper money 797 n.
drafthorse *drafthorse* 273 n.
draft off *disperse* 75 vb.
  displace 188 vb.
  transpose 272 vb.

drag *pend* 136vb.
  influence 178n.
  counteraction 182n.
  be long 203vb.
  transpose 272vb.
  carriage 274n.
  slowness 278n.
  draw 288vb.
  attract 291vb.
  friction 333vb.
  motivate 612vb.
  safeguard 662n.
  difficulty 700n.
  encumbrance 702n.
  restraint 747n.
  fetter 748n.
  card game 837n.
  be tedious 838vb.
drag from *extract* 304vb.
  compel 740vb.
dragging *unwilling* 598adj.
  slow 278adj.
dragging out
  protraction 113n.
draggle
  make unclean 649vb.
draggletail *slut* 61n.
  dirty person 649n.
drag-net *generality* 79n.
  network 222n.
  traction 288n.
dragoman *guide* 520n.
drag on *continue* 108vb.
  elapse 111vb.
  drag on 113vb.
  pend 136vb.
  be long 203vb.
dragon *rara avis* 84n.
  violent creature 176n.
drag oneself *consent* 758vb.
drag one's feet
  move slowly 278vb.
  be loth 598vb.
dragonfly *fly* 365n.
dragonnade
  terror tactics 712n.
  penalty 963n.
dragon's blood
  red pigment 431n.
dragon's mouth
  danger 661n.
dragoon *cavalry* 722n.
  compel 740vb.
drag out *spin out* 113vb.
  extract 304vb.
  manifest 522vb.
drain *bate* 37vb.
  receptacle 194n.
  outflow 298n.
  void 300vb.
  drink 301vb.

dry 342vb.
  drain 351n.
  cultivate 370vb.
  storage 632n.
  waste 634vb.
  purify 648vb.
  sink 649n.
  sanitate 652vb.
  loss 772n.
  levy 786vb.
drainage *outflow* 298n.
  voidance 300n.
  desiccation 342n.
  waste 634n.
  cleansing 648n.
  dirt, swill 649n.
drain of colour
  decolorize 426vb.
drain-pipe *cylinder* 252n.
  outlet 298n.
  drain 351n.
  cleanser 648n.
drake *waterfowl* 365n.
  male animal 372n.
  gun 723n.
dram *potion* 301n.
  pungency 388n.
  metrology 465n.
  incentive 612n.
drama, dramatics
  drama, stage play 594n.
  action 676n.
  activity 678n.
  excitation 821n.
  ostentation 875n.
dramatic *dramatic* 594adj.
  impressive 821adj.
  wonderful 864adj.
  showy 875adj.
dramatis personæ *list* 87n.
  person 371n.
  actor 594n.
  personnel 686n.
  party 708n.
dramatist *dramatist* 594n.
dramatize
  exaggerate 546vb.
  represent 551vb.
  dramatize 594vb.
dramatize oneself
  be affected 850vb.
dramaturgy *mimicry* 20n.
  dramaturgy 594n.
drape *hang* 217vb.
  dress 228vb.
draper *clothier* 228n.
drapery *pendant* 217n.
  robe 228n.
drapes *covering* 226n.
  robe 228n.
drastic *vigorous* 174adj.

severe 735adj.
draught *depth* 211n.
  transport 272n.
  traction 288n.
  potion 301n.
  gravity 322n.
  wind 352n.
  medicine 658n.
  adversity 731n.
  plaything 837n.
draught-board
  chequer 437n.
draughts *board game* 837n.
draughtsman
  recorder 549n.
  artist 556n.
draughtsmanship
  painting 553n.
draw *copy* 20vb.
  draw 28n.
  be equal 28vb.
  compose 56vb.
  bring together 74vb.
  displace 188vb.
  make thin 206vb.
  uncover 229vb.
  outline 233vb.
  efform 243vb.
  draw 288vb.
  attraction 291n.
  attract 291vb.
  cook 301vb.
  extract 304vb.
  blow, breathe 352vb.
  be hot 379vb.
  smoke 388vb.
  represent 551vb.
  paint 553vb.
  describe 590vb.
  motivate 612vb.
  gambling 618n.
  provide 633vb.
  acquire 771vb.
  receive 782vb.
  take 786vb.
  receipt 807n.
  desired object 859n.
  excite love 887vb.
draw a bead on
  aim 281vb.
  shoot 287vb.
  fire at 712vb.
  threaten 900vb.
draw a blank *fail* 728vb.
draw aside *deflect* 282vb.
draw attention
  attract notice 455vb.
  show 522vb.
draw back *regress* 286vb.
  recede 290vb.
  avoid 620vb.

drawback *decrement* 42 n.
  evil 616 n.
  obstacle 702 n.
  discount 810 n.
draw-bar *coupling* 47 n.
draw blood *void* 300 vb.
  attack 712 vb.
draw breath *be* 1 vb.
  live 360 vb.
  be born 360 vb.
  be refreshed 685 vb.
drawbridge *bridge* 624 n.
  means of escape 667 n.
  fort 713 n.
drawee *debtor* 803 n.
drawer *compartment* 194 n.
  traction 288 n.
  artist 556 n.
  servant 742 n.
drawers *trousers* 228 n.
  underwear 228 n.
draw in
  make smaller 198 vb.
drawing
  representation 551 n.
  picture 553 n.
drawing and quartering
  capital punishment 963 n.
drawing-room
  assembly 74 n.
  chamber 194 n.
  beau monde 848 n.
  social gathering 882 n.
draw in one's horns
  submit 721 vb.
drawl *move slowly* 278 vb.
  speech defect 580 n.
draw lots *gamble* 618 vb.
drawn *equal* 28 adj.
  closed 264 adj.
drawn game *draw* 28 n.
  non-completion 726 n.
drawn-thread work
  needlework 844 n.
draw off *extract* 304 vb.
  obstruct 702 vb.
  levy 786 vb.
draw out *spin out* 113 vb.
  enlarge 197 vb.
  extract 304 vb.
  be diffuse 570 vb.
drawstring
  fastening 47 n.
  ligature 47 n.
draw stumps
  terminate 69 vb.
draw the curtain
  screen 421 vb.
  conceal 525 vb.
draw the line *exclude* 57 vb.
  discriminate 463 vb.

reject 607 vb.
  restrain 747 vb.
  prohibit 757 vb.
draw the teeth
  disable 161 vb.
  counteract 182 vb.
  be obstructive 702 vb.
draw together *join* 45 vb.
  bring together 74 vb.
draw up *compose* 56 vb.
  be in order 60 vb.
  come to rest 266 vb.
  write 586 vb.
draw upon
  draw money 797 vb.
dray *cart* 274 n.
drayage *transport* 272 n.
drayman *driver* 268 n.
dread *expectation* 507 n.
  fear 854 n.,vb.
dreadful *harmful* 645 adj.
  not nice 645 adj.
  adverse 731 adj.
  distressing 827 adj.
  frightening 854 adj.
dreadfully *painfully* 32 adv.
dreadnought *warship* 722 n.
dream
  insubstantial thing 4 n.
  vision 438 n.
  visual fallacy 440 n.
  not think 450 vb.
  be inattentive 456 vb.
  error 495 n.
  suppose 512 vb.
  fantasy 513 n.
  objective 617 n.
  sleep 679 vb.
  a beauty 841 n.
  hope 852 vb.
  desired object 859 n.
dreamer *crank* 504 n.
  visionary 513 n.
  idler 679 n.
dreamland *fantasy* 513 n.
  sleep 679 n.
dreamlike *shadowy* 419 adj.
dream, not a *reality* 1 n.
dream up *imagine* 513 vb.
dream world *fantasy* 513 n.
dreamy *insubstantial* 4 adj.
  thoughtful 449 adj.
  abstracted 456 adj.
  imaginary 513 adj.
dreary *unpleasant* 827 adj.
  cheerless 834 adj.
  dejected 834 adj.
  melancholic 834 adj.
  tedious 838 adj.
  dull 840 adj.
  graceless 842 adj.

dredge *extract* 304 vb.
  elevate 310 vb.
dredger *excavator* 255 n.
  ship 275 n.
  extractor 304 n.
  lifter 310 n.
dree one's weird
  be forced 596 vb.
dreggy *dirty* 649 adj.
dregs *leavings* 41 n.
  extremity 69 n.
  rubbish 641 n.
  dirt 649 n.
  bad man 938 n.
  rabble 869 n.
drench *potion* 301 n.
  soften 327 vb.
  add water 339 vb.
  drench 341 vb.
  groom 369 vb.
  clean 648 vb.
  medicine 658 n.
  sate 863 vb.
drencher *rain* 350 n.
dress *be uniform* 16 vb.
  adjust 24 vb.
  equalize 28 vb.
  cover 226 vb.
  dress 228 n.,vb.
  cook 301 vb.
  livery 547 n.
  doctor 658 vb.
  make ready 669 vb.
dressage *equitation* 267 n.
dress down *reprove* 924 vb.
dresser *cabinet* 194 n.
  stand, shelf 218 n.
  clothier 228 n.
  nurse 658 n.
  servant 742 n.
dressiness *fashion* 848 n.
dressing *wrapping* 226 n.
  dressing 228 n.
  cookery 301 n.
  condiment 389 n.
  surgical dressing 658 n.
dressing down
  reprimand 924 n.
dressing gown
  informal dress 228 n.
dressing room
  chamber 194 n.
  theatre 594 n.
  beauty parlour 843 n.
dressing station
  hospital 658 n.
dressmaker *clothier* 228 n.
dress rehearsal
  dramaturgy 594 n.
  preparation 669 n.
dress show *exhibit* 522 n.

dress up *dress* 228 vb.
  dissemble 541 vb.
  primp 843 vb.
dressy *fashionable* 848 adj.
  showy 875 adj.
dribble *small quantity* 33 n.
  move slowly 278 vb.
  kick 279 vb.
  propel 287 vb.
  exude 298 vb.
  emit 300 vb.
  flow 350 vb.
driblet *finite quantity* 26 n.
  small thing 33 n.
drier *drier* 342 n.
drift *leavings* 41 n.
  accumulation 74 n.
  vary 152 vb.
  tendency 179 n.
  distance 199 n.
  fly 271 vb.
  thing transferred 272 n.
  move slowly 278 vb.
  direction 281 n.
  deviation 282 n.
  shortcoming 307 n.
  be neglectful 458 vb.
  be uncertain 474 vb.
  meaning 514 n.
  intention 617 n.
  not act 677 vb.
  be free 744 vb.
drifter *wanderer* 268 n.
  fishing-boat 275 n.
  idler 679 n.
drifting *impotent* 161 adj.
driftway *water travel* 269 n.
drift with the tide
  conform 83 vb.
driftwood
  thing transferred 272 n.
drill *make uniform* 16 vb.
  regularity 81 n.
  make conform 83 vb.
  textile 222 n.
  sharp point 256 n.
  perforator 263 n.
  train 534 vb.
  habituation 610 n.
  make ready 669 vb.
  art of war 718 n.
  dominate 733 vb.
  formality 875 n.
  ritual 988 n.
drill dress *tunic* 228 n.
drill-sergeant
  uniformist 16 n.
  trainer 537 n.
  preparer 669 n.
  director 690 n.
  tyrant 735 n.

drink *stimulant* 174 n.
  absorb 297 vb.
  potion 301 n.
  drink 301 vb
  waste 634 vb.
  revel 837 vb.
  get drunk 949 vb.
drinkable *edible* 301 adj.
drink a health *toast* 876 vb.
drinker *drinking* 301 n.
  reveller 837 n.
  drunkard 949 n.
drink in
  be attentive 455 vb.
  learn 536 vb.
drinking bout
  festivity 837 n.
  drunkenness 949 n.
drinking-water
  soft drink 301 n.
  water 339 n.
drinks
  social gathering 882 n.
drink to *toast* 876 vb.
  pay respects 884 vb.
drip *move slowly* 278 vb.
  exude 298 vb.
  emit 300 vb.
  descend 309 vb.
  be wet 341 vb.
  flow, rain 350 vb.
  ninny 501 n.
  bore 838 n.
dripping *meat* 301 n.
  fat 357 n.
dripping with *full* 54 adj.
drive *operate* 173 vb.
  vigorousness 174 n.
  influence 178 n.
  doorway 263 n.
  move 265 vb.
  ride 267 vb.
  spurt 277 n.
  accelerate 277 vb.
  impel 279 vb.
  propulsion 287 n.
  vigour 571 n.
  resolution 599 n.
  incite 612 vb.
  chase 619 n.
  access, path 624 n.
  be active 678 vb.
  haste 680 n.
  exertion 682 n.
  fatigue 684 vb.
  attack 712 n., vb.
  oppress 735 vb.
  compel 740 vb.
drive at *mean* 514 vb.
  aim at 617 vb.
drive away *repel* 292 vb.

drive home
  carry through 725 vb.
drive in *affix* 45 vb.
  insert 303 vb.
drive-in *doorway* 263 n.
  approachable 289 adj.
drive into a corner
  necessitate 596 vb.
drivel *exude* 298 vb.
  be foolish 499 vb.
  be insane 503 vb.
  silly talk 515 n.
  diffuseness 570 n.
  be loquacious 581 vb.
driveller *fool* 501 n.
  chatterer 581 n.
driven *hasty* 680 adj.
driven snow *ice* 380 n.
  white thing 427 n.
driver *driver* 268 n.
  carrier 273 n.
  machinist 630 adj.
  leader 690 n.
drive off *rob* 788 vb.
drive on *progress* 285 vb.
drive out *eject* 300 vb.
drive to the wall
  be difficult 700 vb.
  defeat 727 vb.
drizzle *moisture* 341 n.
  rain 350 n., vb.
drogue *safeguard* 662 n.
droit administratif
  governance 733 n.
  compulsion 740 n.
droll *witty* 839 adj.
  funny 849 adj.
drollery *foolery* 497 n.
  wit 839 n.
  ridiculousness 849 n.
dromedary
  beast of burden 273 n.
dromond *ship* 275 n.
drone *uniformity* 16 n.
  fly 265 n.
  slowcoach 278 n.
  roll 403 vb.
  stridor 407 n.
  ululation 409 n.
  musical note 410 n.
  discord 411 vb.
  be loquacious 581 vb.
  idler 679 n.
drool *exude* 298 vb.
  emit 300 vb.
  mean nothing 515 vb.
droop *be weak* 163 vb.
  hang 217 vb.
  descend 309 vb.
  be ill 651 vb.
  deteriorate 655 vb.

be *inactive* 679 vb.
be *fatigued* 684 vb.
be *dejected* 834 vb.
droopy *dejected* 834 adj.
drop *small thing* 33 n.
decrease 37 n., vb.
tincture 43 n.
be *weak* 163 vb.
reproduce itself 164 vb.
minuteness 196 n.
pendant 217 n.
exude 298 vb.
dismiss 300 vb.
insert 303 vb.
descent 309 n.
let fall 311 vb.
moisture 341 n.
flow, rain 350 vb.
stage-set 594 n.
relinquish 621 vb.
disuse 674 vb.
be *clumsy* 695 vb.
not retain 779 vb.
jewellery 844 n.
means of execution 964 n.
drop a line
correspond 588 vb.
drop anchor
place oneself 187 vb.
navigate 269 vb.
arrive 295 vb.
drop a sitter
lose a chance 138 vb.
be *clumsy* 695 vb.
drop behind
be *behind* 238 vb.
follow 284 vb.
drop by drop
by degrees 27 adv.
piecemeal 53 adv.
drop from the clouds
surprise 508 vb.
drop in *arrive* 295 vb.
enter 297 vb.
visit 882 vb.
drop in the ocean
trifle 639 n.
drop into place *grade* 73 vb.
droplet *small thing* 33 n.
minuteness 196 n.
drop off *die* 361 vb.
sleep 679 vb.
drop of the curtain
finality 69 n.
drop one's voice
speak low 578 vb.
drop out
not complete 726 vb.
dropping *fatigued* 684 adj.
droppings *excrement* 302 n.
drop-scene *stage-set* 594 n.

dropsy *dilation* 197 n.
fluid 335 n.
disease 651 n.
drop the mask
disclose 526 vb.
be *truthful* 540 vb.
drop the pilot
start out 296 vb.
drop too much
drunkenness 949 n.
droshky *cab* 274 n.
carriage 274 n.
dross *leavings* 41 n.
layer 207 n.
ash 381 n.
rubbish 641 n.
dirt 649 n.
drought *dryness* 342 n.
scarcity 636 n.
blight 659 n.
hunger 859 n.
drove *group* 74 n.
drover *driver* 268 n.
leader 690 n.
drown *fill* 54 vb.
destroy, suppress 165 vb.
descend 309 vb.
depress 311 vb.
founder 313 vb.
drench 341 vb.
perish 361 vb.
kill 362 vb.
silence 399 vb.
obliterate 550 vb.
drowned *deep* 211 adj.
drowse
be *inattentive* 456 vb.
be *neglectful* 458 vb.
sleep 679 n.
be *fatigued* 684 vb.
drowser *idler* 679 n.
drowsy *sleepy* 679 adj.
tedious 838 adj.
drub *defeat* 727 vb.
spank 963 vb.
drudge *busy person* 678 n.
work 682 vb.
worker 686 n.
servant 742 n.
drudgery *assiduity* 678 n.
labour 682 n.
drug *anæsthetic* 375 n.
drug 658 n.
doctor 658 vb.
poison 659 n.
make inactive 679 vb.
drugget *floor-cover* 226 n.
cleaning cloth 648 n.
preserver 666 n.
druggist *druggist* 658 n.
drug habit

intemperance 943 n.
drug on the market
superfluity 637 n.
cheapness 812 n.
drug-store *hospital* 658 n.
Druid *priest* 986 n.
drum *repeat oneself* 106 vb.
cylinder 252 n.
oscillate 317 vb.
roll 403 vb.
play music 413 vb.
drum 414 n.
call 547 n.
drum-beat *periodicity* 141 n.
call 547 n.
drumfire *roll* 403 n.
drumly *opaque* 423 adj.
drummer
instrumentalist 413 n.
drum out *eject* 300 vb.
drunk *reveller* 837 n.
intemperate 943 adj.
drunkard 949 n.
drunk 949 adj.
drunkard *reveller* 837 n.
drunkard 949 n.
drunken *sensual* 944 adj.
drunken 949 adj.
drunkenness
intemperance 943 n.
drunkenness 949 n.
drupe *fruit* 301 n.
dry *non-adhesive* 49 adj.
unproductive 172 adj.
dry 342 adj., vb.
stanch 350 vb.
hot 379 adj.
sour 393 adj.
strident 407 adj.
feeble 572 adj.
plain 573 adj.
voiceless 578 adj.
clean 648 vb.
sanitate 652 vb.
preserve 666 vb.
mature 669 vb.
tedious 838 adj.
witty 839 adj.
hungry 859 adj.
temperate 942 adj.
sober 948 adj.
dryad *vegetability* 366 n.
nymph 967 n.
dry-as-dust
antiquarian 125 n.
bore 838 n.
tedious 838 adj.
dry-cleaner *cleaner* 648 n.
dry-dock *goal* 295 n.
shelter 662 n.
dryer (*see* drier)

dry-eyed *pitiless* 906 adj.
dry eyes
  moral insensibility 820 n.
dry goods
  merchandise 795 n.
dry measure
  metrology 465 n.
dryness *desert* 172 n.
  dryness 342 n.
  tedium 838 n.
  wit 839 n.
  hunger 859 n.
dry-nurse *teacher* 537 n.
dry-point *engraving* 555 n.
dry rot *dirt* 649 n.
  dilapidation 655 n.
  blight 659 n.
drysaltery
  art equipment 553 n.
dry up *decrease* 37 vb.
  cease 145 vb.
  dry 342 vb.
  be mute 578 vb.
  waste 634 vb.
  not suffice 636 vb.
dual *dual* 90 adj.
  double 91 adj.
  grammatical 564 adj.
dualism *duality* 90 n.
  deism 973 n.
duality *duality* 90 n.
dual personality
  spirit 447 n.
  psychopathy 503 n.
dub *name* 561 vb.
  misname 562 vb.
  dignify 866 vb.
dubiety *dubiety* 474 n.
  irresolution 601 n.
  no choice 606 n.
  predicament 700 n.
dubious *improbable* 472 adj.
  uncertain 474 adj.
  doubting 474 adj.
ducal *noble* 868 adj.
ducat *coinage* 797 n.
duce *leader* 690 n.
  master 741 n.
  autocrat 741 n.
duchess *potentate* 741 n.
  nobleman 868 n.
duchy *territory* 184 n.
  polity 733 n.
duck *zero* 103 n.
  textile 222 n.
  swim 269 vb.
  immerse 303 vb.
  descend 309 vb.
  stoop 311 vb.
  plunge 313 vb.
  drench 341 vb.

table bird 365 n.
  waterfowl 365 n.
  be loth 598 vb.
  avoid 620 vb.
  darling 890 n.
  show respect 920 vb.
  punish 963 vb.
duck-boards *paving* 226 n.
  bridge 624 n.
ducking *plunge* 313 n.
  moistening 341 n.
  corporal punishment 963 n.
ducking-stool *pillory* 964 n.
duckling *youngling* 132 n.
  waterfowl 365 n.
duck-pond
  stock farm 369 n.
duck's egg *zero* 103 n.
ducky *darling* 890 n.
duct *conduit* 351 n.
ductile *drawing* 288 adj.
  flexible 327 adj.
  elastic 328 adj.
  wieldy 701 adj.
dud *powerless* 161 adj.
  ammunition 723 n.
  loser 728 n.
  unsuccessful 728 adj.
dud cheque
  false money 797 n.
dude *dupe* 544 n.
  fop 848 n.
dudeen *tobacco* 388 n.
dudgeon *anger* 891 n.
duds *clothing* 228 n.
due *future* 124 n.
  expedient 642 adj.
  owed 803 adj.
  due 915 adj.
due course, in
  prospectively 124 adv.
  opportunely 137 adv.
duel *duality* 90 n.
  duel 716 n.
duellist *opponent* 705 n.
  quarreller 709 n.
  contender 716 n.
  combatant 722 n.
dueness *attribution* 158 n.
  expedience 642 n.
  right 913 n.
  dueness 915 n.
  (*see* duty)
duenna *teacher* 537 n.
  protector 660 n.
  keeper 749 n.
due order *ritual* 988 n.
due process *legality* 953 n.
dues *receipt* 807 n.
  tax 809 n.
  dueness 915 n.

duet *duality* 90 n.
  duet 412 n.
  co-operation 706 n.
  concord 710 n.
due to *caused* 157 adj.
duff *pudding* 301 n.
duffel *textile* 222 n.
duffer *ignoramus* 493 n.
  dunce 501 n.
  bungler 697 n.
duffy *ghost* 970 n.
dug *bosom* 253 n.
dug-in *defended* 713 adj.
dug-out *old man* 133 n.
  excavation 255 n.
  furrow 261 n.
  rowboat 275 n.
  refuge 662 n.
  defences 713 n.
duke *potentate* 741 n.
  nobleman 868 n.
dukedom *polity* 733 n.
  aristocracy 868 n.
dulcet *sweet* 392 adj.
  melodious 410 adj.
  pleasurable 826 adj.
dulcify *assuage* 177 vb.
  sweeten 392 vb.
dulcimer *piano* 414 n.
Dulcinea *loved one* 887 n.
dulia *cult* 981 n.
dull *assuage* 177 vb.
  inert 175 adj.
  blunt 257 vb.
  render insensible 375 vb.
  mute 401 vb.
  non-resonant 405 adj.
  dim 419 adj.
  soft-hued 425 adj.
  colourless 426 adj.
  grey 429 adj.
  ignorant 491 adj.
  unintelligent 499 adj.
  feeble 572 adj.
  inactive 679 adj.
  fatigued 684 adj.
  impassive 820 adj.
  cheerless 834 adj.
  melancholic 834 adj.
  tedious 838 adj.
  dull 840 adj.
dullard *dunce* 501 n.
dullness *seriousness* 834 n.
  dullness 840 n.
  (*see* dull)
duly *as promised* 764 adv.
  duly 915 adv.
Duma *parliament* 692 n.
dumb *ignorant* 491 adj.
  unintelligent 499 adj.
  voiceless 578 adj.

wondering 864 adj.
dumb-bell *dunce* 501 n.
dumb charade
  enigma 530 n.
  gesture 547 n.
  drama 594 n.
  indoor game 837 n.
dumbfound *surprise* 508 vb.
  disappoint 509 vb.
  make mute 578 vb.
  be wonderful 864 vb.
dumbness *aphony* 578 n.
dumb show *gesture* 547 n.
  representation 551 n.
  stage play 594 n.
dumb show, in
  symbolically 547 adv.
dumb-struck
  wondering 864 adj.
dumb waiter *cabinet* 194 n.
  lifter 310 n.
dummy
  insubstantial thing 4 n.
  prototype 23 n.
  substitute 150 n.
  ineffectuality 161 n.
  disguise 527 n.
  sham 542 n.
  image 551 n.
  aphony 578 n.
  letterpress 587 n.
  plan 623 n.
  idler 679 n.
dump *accumulation* 74 n.
  storage 632 n.
  rubbish 641 n.
  disuse 674 vb.
  sell 793 vb.
  cheapen 812 vb.
dumpling *pudding* 301 n.
dumps *dejection* 834 n.
dumpy *fleshy* 195 adj.
  dwarfish 196 adj.
  short 204 adj.
  thick 205 adj.
  unsightly 842 adj.
dun *horse* 273 n.
  dim 419 adj.
  warner 664 n.
  demand 737 vb.
  request 761 vb.
  petitioner 763 n.
  torment 827 vb.
dunce *ignoramus* 493 n.
  dunce 501 n.
dunderhead *dunce* 501 n.
dune *monticle* 209 n.
dung *fertilizer* 171 n.
  invigorate 174 vb.
  excrement 302 n.
  agriculture 370 n.

fetor 397 n.
dirt 649 n.
dungarees *trousers* 228 n.
dungeon *cellar* 194 n.
  darkness 418 n.
  refuge 662 n.
  prison 748 n.
dunghill *sink* 649 n.
  lower classes 869 n.
dunghill cock
  coward 856 n.
dunnage *lining* 227 n.
duo *duet* 412 n.
duodecimo *miniature* 196 n.
  little 196 adj.
  edition 589 n.
duodenitis *indigestion* 651 n.
duologue
  interlocution 584 n.
dupe *weakling* 163 n.
  ignoramus 493 n.
  befool 542 vb.
  dupe 544 n.
  loser 728 n.
  defraud 788 vb.
  sufferer 825 n.
duplex *dual* 90 adj.
  double 91 adj.
  flat 192 n.
duplicate *identity* 13 n.
  copy 20 vb.
  duplicate 22 n.
  augment 36 vb.
  double 91 adj., vb.
  repeat 106 vb.
  reproduce 166 vb.
  label 547 n.
  record 548 n.
  representation 551 n.
  be superfluous 637 vb.
duplicity
  equivocalness 518 n.
  duplicity 541 n.
  deception 542 n.
  mental dishonesty 543 n.
  cunning 698 n.
  affectation 850 n.
  perfidy 930 n.
durability *toughness* 329 n.
durable *lasting* 113 adj.
  perpetual 115 adj.
  permanent 144 adj.
  unchangeable 153 adj.
  tough 329 adj.
durables
  merchandise 795 n.
duralumin *hardness* 326 n.
dura mater *head* 213 n.
  intellect 447 n.
duramen *hardness* 326 n.
durance *detention* 747 n.

duration *time* 108 n.
  course of time 111 n.
  permanence 144 n.
durbar *conference* 584 n.
  council 692 n.
  law-court 956 n.
duress *compulsion* 740 n.
  restriction 747 n.
during *while* 108 adv.
durra *corn* 366 n.
durwan *janitor* 264 n.
  servant 742 n.
dusk *evening* 129 n.
  darkness 418 n.
  half-light 419 n.
dusky *vespertine* 129 adj.
  dim 419 adj.
dust *oldness* 127 n.
  minuteness 196 n.
  overlay 226 vb.
  strike 279 vb.
  let fall 311 vb.
  levity 323 n.
  powder 332 n.
  soil 344 n.
  corpse 363 n.
  obfuscation 421 n.
  variegate 437 vb.
  trickery 542 n.
  rubbish 641 n.
  clean 648 vb.
  dirt 649 n.
  spank 963 vb.
dustbin *cellar* 194 n.
  vessel 194 n.
  cleaning utensil 648 n.
  sink 649 n.
dust-bowl *desert* 172 n.
dust-cover *screen* 421 n.
  cleaning cloth 648 n.
  preserver 666 n.
dusted *mottled* 437 adj.
duster *obliteration* 550 n.
  cleaning cloth 648 n.
dust-heap
  accumulation 74 n.
  rubbish 641 n.
  sink 649 n.
dust-hole *cellar* 194 n.
  rubbish 641 n.
  sink 649 n.
dustiness
  pulverulence 332 n.
dusting
  corporal punishment 963 n.
dust in the eyes
  pretext 614 n.
  stratagem 698 n.
dust-jacket *wrapping* 226 n.
dustman *cleaner* 648 n.
  dirty person 649 n.

worker 686n.
dustoor *reward* 962n.
dustpan
  cleaning utensil 648n.
dusty *travelling* 267adj.
  powdery 332adj.
  dry 342adj.
  soft-hued 425adj.
  mottled 437adj.
  dirty 649adj.
Dutch auction *sale* 793n.
  cheapness 812n.
Dutch courage
  courage 855n.
  cowardice 856n.
Dutch party
  participation 775n.
  festivity 837n.
  social gathering 882n.
Dutch uncle *adviser* 691n.
  tyrant 735n.
Dutch wife *cushion* 218n.
duteous (*see* dutiful)
dutiable *priced* 809adj.
dutiful *obedient* 739adj.
  dutied 917adj.
  trustworthy 929adj.
  virtuous 933adj.
dutiless *negligent* 458adj.
  disobedient 738n.
  non-observant 769adj.
  dutiless 918adj.
duty *necessity* 596n.
  motive 612n.
  function 622n.
  needfulness 627n.
  labour 682n.
  tax 809n.
  courteous act 884n.
  right 913n.
  dueness 915n.
  duty 917n.
duty-bound *dutied* 917adj.
duty-free
  non-liable 919adj.
duty, on *dutied* 917adj.
duumvirate
  government 733n.
D.V. *possibly* 469adv.
Dvaita *philosophy* 449n.
dwarf *small animal* 33n.
  bate 37vb.
  dwarf 196n.
  make smaller 198vb.
  star 321n.
  elf 970n.
dwarfish *small* 33adj.
  dwarfish 196adj.
  short 204adj.
  unsightly 842adj.
  fairylike 970adj.

dwell *stay* 144vb.
  be situate 186vb.
  place oneself 187vb.
  dwell 192vb.
  be quiescent 266vb.
dweller *dweller* 191n.
dwelling *dwelling* 192n.
dwell on *emphasize* 532vb.
dwell on the past
  retrospect 505vb.
dwindle *decrease* 37vb.
  be little 196vb.
  become small 198vb.
  disappear 446vb.
dyad *duality* 90n.
dyarchy *duality* 90n.
dye *tincture* 43n.
  modify 143vb.
  hue, pigment 425n.
  colour 425vb.
  hairwash 843n.
dyed *habitual* 610adj.
dyeing
  beautification 843n.
dyer *alterer* 143n.
dyestuff *pigment* 425n.
dying *ephemeral* 114adj.
  quiescent 266adj.
  sick 651adj.
dying breath *decease* 361n.
dying day *decease* 361n.
dying duck *weeper* 836n.
dying to *willing* 597adj.
dyke *fence* 235n.
  furrow 262n.
  conduit 351n.
  obstacle 702n.
  defences 713n.
dynamic *powerful* 160adj.
  operative 173adj.
  vigorous 174adj.
  impelling 279adj.
dynamics
  science of forces 162n.
  motion 265n.
  impulse 279n.
dynamism *energy* 160n.
  vigorousness 174n.
  restlessness 678n.
dynamitard
  desperado 857n.
dynamite *destroyer* 168n.
  vigorousness 174n.
  propellant 287n.
  pitfall 663n.
  explosive 723n.
dynamo *causal means* 156n.
  electricity 160n.
  vigorousness 174n.
dynamometer *meter* 465n.
dynast *potentate* 741n.

dynastic *ruling* 733adj.
dynasticism *authority* 733n.
dynasty *continuity* 71n.
  governance 733n.
  sovereign 741n.
  nobility 868n.
dysentery *cacation* 302n.
  dysentery 651n.
dyspathy *dislike* 861n.
  hatred 888n.
dyspepsia *indigestion* 651n.
dysphony *aphony* 578n.
  speech defect 580n.
dyspnœa *fatigue* 684n.

E

each *universal* 79adj.
  severally 80adv.
each man for himself
  selfishness 932n.
each other *correlation* 12n.
  correlatively 12adv.
eager *willing* 597adj.
  active 678adj.
  fervent 818adj.
  excited 821adj.
  desiring 859adj.
eagle *speeder* 277n.
  bird of prey 365n.
  eye 438n.
  flag, heraldry 547n.
  regalia 743n.
  coinage 797n.
eagle-eyed *seeing* 438adj.
eaglet *bird of prey* 365n.
eagre *current, wave* 350n.
ear *growth* 157n.
  reproduce itself 164vb.
  handle 218n.
  ear 415n.
eardrop *pendant* 217n.
ear-drum, ear-hole
  ear 415n.
earful *hearing* 415n.
  oration 579n.
earl *nobleman* 868n.
earless *deaf* 416adj.
earlier *before* 64adv.
  prior 119adj.
  before 119adv.
  not now 122adv.
earliest *prior* 119adj.
earliness *earliness* 134n.
early *past* 125adj.
  matinal 128adj.
  early 135adj.
  betimes 135adv.
  ill-timed 138adj.
  immature 670adj.

earmark *label* 547n.
 mark 547vb.
 select 605vb.
 intend 617vb.
 require 627vb.
earmarked *future* 124adj.
 due 915adj.
earn *acquire* 771vb.
 deserve 915vb.
earned *just* 913adj.
 due 915adj.
earned income
 earnings 771n.
earner *worker* 686n.
 recipient 782n.
earnest *attentive* 455adj.
 affirmative 532adj.
 willing 597adj.
 resolute 599adj.
 security 767n.
 observant 768adj.
 fervent 818adj.
 seriousness 834n.
earnest money *part* 53n.
 security 767n.
earnestness *assiduity* 678n.
 piety 979n.
 (*see* earnest)
earning capacity
 utility 640n.
earnings *earnings* 771n.
 receiving 782n.
 reward 962n.
earn interest *grow* 36vb.
earn one's living
 do business 622vb.
earphone
 hearing aid 415n.
 telecommunication 531n.
earphones *hair* 259n.
ear-piercing
 strident 407adj.
 beautification 843n.
ear-ring *pendant* 217n.
 jewellery 844n.
earshot *short distance* 200n.
 hearing 415n.
earth *connect* 45vb.
 dwelling 192n.
 base 214n.
 implant 303vb.
 element 319n.
 world 321n.
 planet 231n.
 land 344n.
 corpse 363n.
 refuge 662n.
earthborn *human* 371adj.
earth-bound *native* 191adj.
 imprisoned 747adj.
earth-closet *latrine* 649n.

earth-dweller *native* 191n.
earthenware *pottery* 381n.
earthlight *glimmer* 419n.
earthling *mankind* 371n.
 person 371n.
earthly *telluric* 321adj.
 selfish 932adj.
Earthly Paradise
 mythic heaven 971n.
 Heaven 971n.
Earth-mother
 abundance 171n.
earth, on
 under the sun 321adv.
earthquake
 revolution 149n.
 destroyer 168n.
 oscillation 317n.
earth satellite
 satellite 321n.
earth-shaking
 influential 178adj.
 important 638adj.
earth up *obstruct* 702vb.
earth-wire *cable* 47n.
earthwork *defences* 713n.
earthworm *reptile* 365n.
earthy *territorial* 344adj.
 selfish 932adj.
 sensual 944adj.
ear-trumpet
 megaphone 400n.
 hearing aid 415n.
earwig *vermin* 365n.
 flatter 925vb.
ear-witness *witness* 466n.
ease *bate* 37vb.
 assuage 177vb.
 lighten 323vb.
 euphoria 376n.
 elegance 575n.
 leisure 681n.
 repose 683n.
 refresh 685vb.
 skill 694n.
 facility 701n.
 disencumber 701vb.
 facilitate 701vb.
 wealth 800n.
 happiness 824n.
 relieve 831vb.
ease along
 move slowly 278vb.
 propel 287vb.
ease, at *in comfort* 376adv.
 leisurely 681adj.
 content 828adj.
easeful *tranquil* 266adj.
 comfortable 376adj.
 reposeful 683adj.
 pleasurable 826adj.

easel *frame* 218n.
 art equipment 553n.
easement *estate* 777n.
 dueness 915n.
ease off *deviate* 282vb.
ease of mind *content* 828n.
ease oneself *excrete* 302vb.
ease out *depose* 752vb.
ease up *decelerate* 278vb.
easiness *cheapness* 812n.
 (*see* easy)
easing (*see* ease)
east *laterality* 239n.
 compass point 281n.
 wind 352n.
east and west *polarity* 14n.
easter *anniversary* 141n.
 holy-day 988n.
easterly, eastern
 lateral 239adj.
Easterner *foreigner* 59n.
Eastertide *holy-day* 988n.
East Indiaman
 merchant ship 275n.
eastward *lateral* 239adj.
easy *comfortable* 376adj.
 possible 469adj.
 intelligible 516adj.
 elegant 575adj.
 easy 701adj.
 lax 734n.
 lenient 736adj.
 inexcitable 823adj.
 well-bred 848adj.
 friendly 880adj.
 sociable 882adj.
 amiable 884adj.
easy circumstances
 wealth 800n.
easy going *facility* 701n.
easy-going *tranquil* 266adj.
 irresolute 601adj.
 wieldy 701adj.
 lenient 736adj.
 inexcitable 823adj.
 content 828adj.
 indifferent 860adj.
easy-mannered
 well-bred 848adj.
 sociable 882adj.
easy prey *dupe* 544n.
easy terms *irenics* 719n.
 cheapness 812n.
easy virtue *unchastity* 951n.
eat *absorb* 299vb.
 eat 301vb.
 give pain 377vb.
 waste 634vb.
 gluttonize 947vb.
eatable *food* 301n.
 edible 301adj.

eat away *bate* 37 vb.
　impair 655 vb.
eat dirt
　knuckle under 721 vb.
eater *eater* 301 n.
　glutton 947 n.
eat humble pie
　recant 603 vb.
　knuckle under 721 vb.
　be humble 872 vb.
eating and drinking
　sociability 882 n.
eating house *café* 192 n.
eat one's dinners
　do law 958 vb.
eat one's heart out
　be dejected 834 vb.
eat one's words
　recant 603 vb.
eats *food* 301 n.
eat up *destroy* 165 vb.
　consume 165 vb.
　eat 301 vb.
　appropriate 786 vb.
eau-de-cologne *scent* 396 n.
　cosmetic 843 n.
eau-de-vie *liquor* 301 n.
eave *roof* 226 n.
　edge 234 n.
　projection 254 n.
eavesdrop *hear* 415 vb.
　be curious 453 vb.
eavesdropper
　inquisitor 453 n.
　informer 524 n.
ebb *decrease* 37 n.
　reversion 148 n.
　revert 148 vb.
　become small 198 vb.
　regress 286 vb.
　recede 290 vb.
　flow 350 vb.
　waste 634 n., vb.
　scarcity 636 n.
　deterioration 655 n.
ebb and flow
　periodicity 141 n.
　fluctuation 317 n.
　current 350 n.
ebb-tide *lowness* 210 n.
ebenezer *church* 990 n.
Ebionite *sectarian* 978 adj.
Eblis *Satan* 969 n.
ebony *tree* 366 n.
　black thing 428 n.
ebriosity
　drunkenness 949 n.
ebullience
　stimulation 174 n.
　moral sensibility 819 n.
　excitation 821 n.

ebullient *violent* 176 adj.
　hot 379 adj.
　lively 819 adj.
　excited 821 adj.
ebullition
　stimulation 174 n.
　outbreak 176 n.
　commotion 318 n.
　heat 379 n.
　excitability 822 n.
　excitable state 822 n.
eburnean *whitish* 427 adj.
écarté *card game* 837 n.
eccentric
　unimitative 21 adj.
　misfit 25 n.
　fitful 142 adj.
　exterior 223 adj.
　deviating 282 adj.
　foolish 499 adj.
　fool 501 n.
　crazed 503 adj.
　crank 504 n.
　laughing-stock 851 n.
eccentricity
　unconformity 84 n.
　(*see* eccentric)
ecchymosis *excretion* 302 n.
　skin disease 651 n.
ecclesia *council* 692 n.
　tribunal 956 n.
ecclesiarch *governor* 741 n.
　ecclesiarch 986 n.
ecclesiastic
　ecclesiastical 985 adj.
　cleric 986 n.
ecclesiasticism
　orthodoxism 976 n.
　ecclesiasticism 985 n.
ecclesiolatry *idolatry* 982 n.
ecclesiology
　churchdom 985 n.
ecdysiast *stripper* 229 n.
echelon *series* 71 n.
echo *imitation* 20 n.
　do likewise 20 vb.
　accord 24 vb.
　conform 83 vb.
　duplication 91 n.
　repetition 106 n.
　recoil 280 n.
　resonance 404 n.
　answer 460 n., vb.
　assent 488 vb.
echo balloon
　space-ship 276 n.
echoing *loud* 400 adj.
　resonant 404 adj.
echolalia *imitation* 20 n.
éclat *prestige* 866 n.
eclecticism *mixture* 43 n.

　philosophy 449 n.
　choice 605 n.
eclipse *be superior* 34 vb.
　obscuration 418 n.
　blind 439 vb.
　be invisible 444 vb.
　disappearance 446 n.
　conceal 525 vb.
ecliptic *zodiac* 321 n.
eclogue *description* 590 n.
　poem 593 n.
école normale
　training school 539 n.
ecology *biology* 358 n.
economic *directing* 689 adj.
economical *cheap* 812 adj.
　economical 814 adj.
　cautious 858 adj.
　temperate 942 adj.
economics
　management 689 n.
economist *manager* 690 n.
　economy 814 n.
economize *bate* 37 vb.
　shorten 204 vb.
　preserve 666 vb.
　restrain 747 vb.
　economize 814 vb.
　be cautious 858 vb.
economy *order* 60 n.
　restriction 747 n.
　economy 814 n.
écru *brown* 430 adj.
ecstasy *transition* 147 n.
　frenzy 503 n.
　imagination 513 n.
　warm feeling 818 n.
　excitable state 822 n.
　joy 824 n.
　love 887 n.
ecstatic *approving* 923 adj.
　(*see* ecstasy)
ectopia *disorder* 61 n.
　unconformity 84 n.
　displacement 188 n.
ectoplasm
　spiritualism 984 n.
ectoplasmic *spooky* 970 adj.
　psychical 984 adj.
ectype *copy* 22 n.
ecumenical
　universal 79 adj.
　orthodox 976 adj.
ecumenicalism
　generality 79 n.
　orthodoxy 976 n.
eczema *skin disease* 651 n.
edacity *gluttony* 947 n.
eddy *coil* 251 n.
　vortex 315 n.
　eddy 350 n.

Eden *happiness* 824n.
  mythic heaven 971n.
edentate
  unsharpened 257adj.
edge *vantage* 34n.
  extremity 69n.
  keenness 174n.
  nearness 200n.
  contiguity 202n.
  circumscribe 232vb.
  outline 233n.
  edge 234n.
  limit 236n., vb.
  laterality 239n.
  sharpen 256vb.
  pungency 383n.
edge, have the
  predominate 34vb.
edge in *intromit* 231vb.
edge off *deviate* 282vb.
edge, on *on edge* 259adv.
  expectantly 507adv.
  excitable 822adj.
edge-tool
  sharp edge 256n.
edgewise *obliquely* 220adv.
edging *adjunct* 40n.
  edging 234n.
  trimming 844n.
edgy *excitable* 822adj.
edible *food* 301n.
  edible 301adj.
  clean 648adj.
edict *publication* 528n.
  decree 737n.
  legislation 953n.
edification
  production 164n.
  teaching 543n.
  sanctity 979n.
edifice *edifice* 164n.
edificial
  architectural 192adj.
edify *educate* 534vb.
  benefit 615vb.
  do good 644vb.
  be virtuous 933vb.
  make pious 979vb.
edifying *reputable* 866adj.
  pure 950adj.
edit *interpret* 520vb.
  publish 528vb.
  rectify 654vb.
edited *pure* 950adj.
edition *the press* 528n.
  edition 589n.
editor *interpreter* 520n.
  author 589n.
  bookman 589n.
  dissertator 591n.
  reformer 654n.

editorial *interpretive* 520adj.
  publicity 528n.
  article 591n.
educate *inform* 524vb.
educated *instructed* 490adj.
education *culture* 490n.
  education 534n.
  teaching 534n.
  vocation 622n.
  civilization 654n.
educational
  influential 178adj.
  informative 524adj.
  educational 534adj.
educe *extract* 304vb.
educt *remainder* 41n.
edulcorate *sweeten* 392vb.
  purify 648vb.
eel *serpent* 251n.
  table fish 365n.
eerie *frightening* 854adj.
  spooky 970adj.
efface *destroy* 165vb.
  forget 506vb.
  obliterate 550vb.
efface oneself
  be modest 874vb.
effect *sequel* 67n.
  end 69n.
  eventuality 154n.
  cause 156vb.
  effect 157n.
  product 164n.
  sense 374n.
  spectacle 445n.
  meaning 514n.
  be instrumental 628vb.
  completion 725n.
effective *causal* 156adj.
  powerful 160adj.
  influential 178adj.
  forceful 571adj.
  instrumental 628adj.
  useful 640adj.
  expedient 642adj.
  soldier 722n.
  successful 727adj.
effectiveness *agency* 173n.
effects *property* 777n.
effectual *operative* 173adj.
  (*see* effective)
effectuation *agency* 173n.
  action 676n.
  effectuation 725n.
effeminacy *weakness* 163n.
  female 373n.
  sensualism 944n.
effeminate *unman* 161vb.
  weak 163adj.
  female 373adj.
  cowardly 856adj.

effendi *title* 870n.
effervesce *hiss* 406vb.
  (*see* effervescence)
effervescence
  outbreak 176n.
  commotion 318n.
  bubble 355n.
  moral sensibility 819n.
  excitation 821n.
  excitable state 822n.
effervescent *bubbly* 355adj.
effete *aged* 131adj.
  impotent 161adj.
  weakened 163adj.
  useless 641adj.
  deteriorated 655adj.
efficacious
  successful 727adj.
efficacy *ability* 160n.
  agency 173n.
  instrumentality 628n.
  utility 640n.
  skill 694n.
  virtue 933n.
efficient
  powerful 160adj.
  operative 173adj.
  businesslike 622adj.
  instrumental 628adj.
  useful 640adj.
  industrious 678adj.
  skilful 694adj.
effigy *copy* 22n.
  image 551n.
efflorescence
  propagation 164n.
  pulverulence 332n.
  powder 332n.
effluence *outflow* 298n.
  current 350n.
effluvium *gas* 336n.
  odour 394n.
  poison 659n.
efflux *egress* 298n.
  outflow 298n.
efflux-tube *drain* 351n.
efformation
  production 164n.
  efformation 243n.
effort *power* 160n.
  production 164n.
  vigorousness 174n.
  essay 671n.
  undertaking 672n.
  action 676n.
  exertion 682n.
effortless *easy* 701adj.
effort-wasting
  useless 641adj.
effrontery
  insolence 878n.

effulgence *light* 417 n.
effuse
  be loquacious 581 vb.
effusion *outflow* 298 n.
  ejection 300 n.
  excretion 302 n.
  diffuseness 570 n.
  speech 579 n.
  tonic 658 n.
effusive *diffuse* 570 adj.
  loquacious 581 adj.
  friendly 880 adj.
effusiveness
  warm feeling 818 n.
egalitarian
  uniformist 16 n.
Egeria *adviser* 691 n.
egesta *excrement* 302 n.
egestion *voidance* 300 n.
egg *origin* 68 n.
  source 156 n.
  product 164 n.
egg-cup *cup* 194 n.
egg-glass *timekeeper* 117 n.
egghead *intellectual* 492 n.
  sage 500 n.
egg nog *liquor* 301 n.
egg on *incite* 612 vb.
  make quarrels 709 vb.
egg-shaped *round* 250 adj.
  rotund 252 adj.
egg-shell *weak thing* 163 n.
  brittleness 330 n.
ego *intrinsicality* 5 n.
  subjectivity 320 n.
  spirit 447 n.
egocentric *selfish* 932 adj.
egocentrism
  interiority 224 n.
  selfishness 932 n.
egoism *interiority* 224 n.
  selfishness 932 n.
egoistic *vain* 873 adj.
  selfish 932 adj.
egotism *interiority* 224 n.
  overestimation 482 n.
  vanity 873 n.
  misanthropy 902 n.
  selfishness 932 n.
egregious
  unconformable 84 adj.
  exterior 223 adj.
  absurd 497 adj.
  exaggerated 546 adj.
  notable 638 adj.
egregiously
  eminently 34 adv.
egress *departure* 296 n.
  egress 298 n.
  passage 305 n.
  means of escape 667 n.

Egyptologist
  antiquarian 125 n.
eiderdown *coverlet* 226 n.
  softness 327 n.
eidetic *lifelike* 18 adj.
  well-seen 443 adj.
  imaginative 513 adj.
eidotropic (*see* eidetic)
Eiffel Tower
  high structure 209 n.
eight *band* 74 n.
  rowboat 275 n.
  party 708 n.
eight bells *noon* 128 n.
Eightfold Path
  religion 973 n.
eights *racing* 716 n.
eightsome *dance* 837 n.
eisteddfod *assembly* 74 n.
  music 412 n.
  choir 413 n.
either . . . or
  optionally 605 adv.
ejaculation *ejection* 300 n.
  cry 408 n.
  voice 577 n.
eject *propel* 287 vb.
  reject 607 vb.
  make unwelcome 883 vb.
  (*see* ejection)
ejecta *excrement* 302 n.
ejection *displacement* 188 n.
  ejection 300 n.
  extraction 304 n.
  deposal 752 n.
  expropriation 786 n.
  penalty 963 n.
ejective *excretory* 302 adj.
ejector-seat *ejector* 300 n.
  safeguard 662 n.
eke out
  make complete 54 vb.
elaborate
  ornament 574 vb.
  mature 669 vb.
elaboration *elegance* 575 n.
  improvement 654 n.
  exertion 682 n.
  completion 725 n.
  effectuation 725 n.
élan *vigorousness* 174 n.
  collision 279 n.
  resolution 599 n.
  courage 855 n.
eland *deer* 365 n.
elapse *end* 69 vb.
  continue 108 vb.
  elapse 111 vb.
  be past 125 vb.
elasticity *energy* 160 n.
  strength 162 n.

  expansion 197 n.
  recoil 280 n.
  elasticity 328 n.
elate *pleased* 824 adj.
  delight 826 vb.
  cheer 833 vb.
elation *psychopathy* 503 n.
elative *superior* 34 adj.
  grammatical 564 adj.
elbow *joint* 45 n.
  limb 53 n.
  angularity 247 n.
  camber 253 n.
  fold 261 n.
  impel 279 vb.
elbow-grease *friction* 333 n.
  exertion 682 n.
elbow-room
  opportunity 137 n.
  room 183 n.
  scope 744 n.
eld *antiquity* 125 n.
  oldness 127 n.
  age 131 n.
elder *superior* 34 n.
  prior 119 adj.
  olden 127 adj.
  older 131 adj.
  old man 133 n.
  ecclesiarch 986 n.
  church officer 986 n.
elderberry *fruit* 301 n.
Elder Brother
  theosophy 984 n.
elderly *aged* 131 adj.
eldership *oldness* 127 n.
  seniority 131 n.
  church office 985 n.
El Dorado *fantasy* 513 n.
  objective 617 n.
  wealth 800 n.
  aspiration 852 n.
eldritch *spooky* 970 adj.
Eleatics *philosopher* 449 n.
elect *pietist* 979 n.
  churchdom 985 n.
election *fate* 596 n.
  vote 605 n.
  choice 605 n.
  mandate 751 n.
electioneer *vote* 605 vb.
elective, electoral
  choosing 605 adj.
elector *electorate* 605 n.
  potentate 741 n.
electoral college
  electorate 605 n.
electoral roll *list* 87 n.
  electorate 605 n.
electoral system *vote* 605 n.
electorate *electorate* 605 n.

tribunal 956 n.
electric *dynamic* 160 adj.
  speedy 277 adj.
  excitable 822 adj.
electric chair
  means of execution 964 n.
electrician
  stage-hand 594 n.
  artisan 686 n.
electricity *electricity* 160 n.
  velocity 277 n.
  heater 383 n.
electrify *empower* 160 vb.
  surprise 508 vb.
  excite 821 vb.
  be wonderful 866 vb.
electrocution
  capital punishment 963 n.
electro-dynamics
  electricity 160 n.
  science of forces 162 n.
electrolier *pendant* 217 n.
electrolysis
  decomposition 51 n.
electromagnetism
  electricity 160 n.
electron *particle* 33 n.
  minuteness 196 n.
  element 319 n.
electronic brain
  mnemonics 505 n.
electronics *nucleonics* 160 n.
electroplate *coat* 226 vb.
electrostatics
  electricity 160 n.
  science of forces 162 n.
electrotherapy
  therapy 658 n.
electrotype *copy* 22 n.
  print 587 n.
electrum *a mixture* 43 n.
  bullion 797 n.
electuary *medicine* 658 n.
eleemosynary *giving* 781 adj.
  benevolent 897 adj.
elegance *elegance* 575 n.
  skill 694 n.
  beauty 841 n.
  good taste 846 n.
  fashion 848 n.
elegiac *funereal* 364 adj.
  poetic 593 adj.
  lamenting 836 adj.
elegist *poet* 593 n.
  weeper 836 n.
elegy *obsequies* 364 n.
  poem 593 n.
  lament 836 n.
element *part* 53 n.
  component 58 n.
  source 156 n.

filament 208 n.
element 319 n.
  person 371 n.
elemental *intrinsic* 5 adj.
  simple 44 adj.
  beginning 68 adj.
elementary *simple* 44 adj.
  beginning 68 adj.
  immature 670 adj.
element, in one's
  apt 24 adj.
  facilitated 701 adj.
elements *beginning* 68 n.
  weather 340 n.
  the sacrament 988 n.
elench *argumentation* 475 n.
elenchus *confutation* 479 n.
elenctic *enquiring* 459 adj.
elephant *giant* 195 n.
  beast of burden 273 n.
  animal 365 n.
elephantine
  unwieldy 195 adj.
Eleusinianism
  religion 973 n.
elevate (*see* elevation)
elevated *train* 274 n.
  worshipful 866 adj.
  proud 871 adj.
  drunk 949 adj.
elevated railway
  railroad 624 n.
elevation *height* 209 n.
  verticality 215 n.
  progression 285 n.
  elevation 310 n.
  feature 445 n.
  map 551 n.
  vigour 571 n.
  improvement 654 n.
  warm feeling 818 n.
  excitable state 822 n.
  cheerfulness 833 n.
  dignification 866 n.
  disinterestedness 931 n.
elevation of the Host
  ritual act 988 n.
  Holy Communion 988 n.
elevator *lifter* 310 n.
eleven *band* 74 n.
  party 708 n.
elevenses *meal* 301 n.
  social gathering 882 n.
eleventh hour *lateness* 135 n.
  occasion, crisis 137 n.
elf *child* 132 n.
  dwarf 196 n.
  elf 970 n.
elfin *little* 196 adj.
  fairylike 970 adj.
elf-lock *hair* 259 n.

elicit *cause* 156 vb.
  extract 304 vb.
  discover 484 vb.
  manifest 522 vb.
elide (*see* elision)
eligibility *inclusion* 78 n.
  nubility 894 n.
eligible *numerable* 86 adj.
  expedient 642 adj.
  marriageable 894 adj.
Elijah's mantle
  sequence 65 n.
eliminate *bate* 37 vb.
  eliminate 44 vb.
  exclude 57 vb.
  render few 105 vb.
  eject, void 300 vb.
  extract 304 vb.
  reject 607 vb.
  purify 648 vb.
  exempt 919 vb.
elimination
  destruction 165 n.
  (*see* eliminate)
elision *scission* 46 n.
  contraction 198 n.
  shortening 204 n.
  prosody 593 n.
élite *chief thing* 638 n.
  élite 644 n.
  beau monde 848 n.
  person of repute 866 n.
  upper class 868 n.
elixir *remedy* 658 n.
elk *skin* 226 n.
  deer 365 n.
ell *long measure* 203 n.
ellipse *arc* 250 n.
ellipsis *shortening* 204 n.
  grammar 564 n.
  imperspicuity 568 n.
  conciseness 569 n.
ellipsoid *arc* 250 n.
  sphere 252 n.
elliptic *round* 250 adj.
  concise 569 adj.
elliptical *short* 204 adj.
elm *tree* 366 n.
elocution
  pronunciation 577 n.
  speech, oratory 579 n.
elocutionary *speaking* 579 n.
Elohim *the Deity* 965 n.
elongate *lengthen* 203 vb.
elongation *distance* 199 n.
elope *decamp* 296 vb.
  run away 620 vb.
  escape 667 vb.
  wed 894 vb.
elope with
  take away 786 vb.

eloquence *vigour* 571 n.
  magniloquence 574 n.
  eloquence 579 n.
  loquacity 581 n.
eloquent *inducive* 612 adj.
else *in addition* 38 adv.
elsewhere *not here* 190 adv.
elucidate
  be intelligible 516 vb.
  interpret 520 vb.
  manifest 522 vb.
  teach 534 vb.
elude *sophisticate* 477 vb.
  avoid 620 vb.
  elude 667 vb.
  not observe 769 vb.
elusive *puzzling* 517 adj.
  deceiving 542 adj.
  avoiding 620 adj.
  escaped 667 adj.
elutriate *purify* 648 vb.
elver *table fish* 365 n.
elvish *fairylike* 970 adj.
elysian *pleasurable* 826 adj.
  paradisiac 971 adj.
Elysium *the dead* 361 n.
  mythic heaven 971 n.
emaciation
  contraction 198 n.
  thinness 206 n.
emanate *happen* 154 vb.
  result 157 vb.
  emerge 298 vb.
  be plain 522 vb.
emanation *egress* 298 n.
  excretion 302 n.
  odour 394 n.
  appearance 445 n.
  revelation 975 n.
emancipation
  deliverance 668 n.
  freedom 744 n.
  independence 744 n.
  liberation 746 n.
emarginate *toothed* 256 adj.
  notched 260 adj.
emasculate *subtract* 39 vb.
  unman 161 vb.
emasculation
  weakness 163 n.
embalm *inter* 364 vb.
  be fragrant 396 vb.
  preserve 666 vb.
embalmer *interment* 364 n.
  preserver 666 n.
embalmment
  preservation 666 n.
embank *preserve* 666 vb.
  obstruct 702 vb.
embankment *street* 192 n.
  supporter 218 n.

safeguard 662 n.
  obstacle 702 n.
  defences 713 n.
embarcation
  (*see* embarkation)
embargo *quiescence* 266 n.
  hindrance 702 n.
  command 737 n.
  restraint 747 n.
  prohibition 757 n.
  non-payment 805 n.
embark *voyage* 269 vb.
embarkation *start* 68 n.
  departure 296 n.
embark on *begin* 68 vb.
  undertake 672 vb.
embarras de choix
  choice 605 n.
embarrass
  be inexpedient 643 vb.
  hinder 702 vb.
  incommode 827 vb.
embarrassed
  modest 874 adj.
embarrassment
  dubiety 474 n.
  predicament 700 n.
  poverty 801 n.
  annoyance 827 n.
embassy *house* 192 n.
  message 529 n.
  commission 751 n.
  envoy 754 n.
embattled *warring* 718 adj.
embay *surround* 230 vb.
  circumscribe 232 vb.
  safeguard 660 vb.
embed *place* 187 vb.
  support 218 vb.
  be inside 224 vb.
  implant 303 vb.
embellish
  make better 654 vb.
  decorate 844 vb.
embellished *false* 541 adj.
embellishment
  ornament 574 n.
  ornamentation 844 n.
ember *ash* 381 n.
  coal, lighter 385 n.
  glimmer 419 n.
  torch 420 n.
embezzle *defraud* 788 vb.
  not pay 805 vb.
embezzlement
  peculation 788 n.
embezzler *defrauder* 789 n.
  non-payer 805 n.
embitter *impair* 655 vb.
  hurt 827 vb.
  cause discontent 829 vb.

aggravate 832 vb.
  excite hate 888 vb.
  huff, enrage 891 vb.
embittered *biased* 481 adj.
  resentful 891 adj.
embitterment
  aggravation 832 n.
emblazon *colour* 425 vb.
  mark 547 vb.
  represent 551 vb.
  decorate 844 vb.
emblazoned
  heraldic 547 adj.
emblem
  insubstantial thing 4 n.
  heraldry 547 n.
  badge 547 n.
  talisman 983 n.
emblematic
  representing 551 adj.
embodiment
  essential part 5 n.
  combination 50 n.
  composition 56 n.
  inclusion 78 n.
  materiality 319 n.
  appearance 445 n.
  representation 551 n.
embody *join* 45 vb.
  figure 519 vb.
  (*see* embodiment)
embolden *aid* 703 vb.
  give courage 855 vb.
embolism *closure* 264 n.
  interjection 231 n.
  insertion 303 n.
embolismal
  interjacent 231 adj.
embolus *stopper* 264 n.
  solid body 324 n.
embosomed *located* 187 adj.
  interjacent 231 adj.
  circumscribed 232 adj.
emboss *be convex* 253 vb.
  mark 547 vb.
  decorate 844 vb.
embossment *rilievo* 254 n.
embouchure *orifice* 263 n.
embower *comprise* 78 vb.
embox *comprise* 78 vb.
  inclose 235 vb.
  insert 303 vb.
embrace *unite with* 45 vb.
  cohere 48 vb.
  contain 56 vb.
  comprise 78 vb.
  surround 230 vb.
  circumscribe 232 vb.
  inclose 235 vb.
  choose 605 vb.
  circuit 626 vb.

protection 660n.
safeguard 660vb.
retention 778n.
be friendly 880vb.
sociability 882n.
greet 884vb.
love 887vb.
endearment 889n.
embrace an offer
   consent 758vb.
embrace an opinion
   opine 485vb.
embranglement
   dissension 709n.
embrasure *notch* 260n.
   window 263n.
   fortification 713n.
embrocation *unguent* 357n.
   balm 658n.
embroider *variegate* 437vb.
   cant 541vb.
   exaggerate 546vb.
   decorate 844vb.
embroidery *adjunct* 40n.
   art 551n.
   needlework 844n.
   (*see* embroider)
embroil *enrage* 891vb.
embroilment
   confusion 61n.
   dissension 709n.
embrown *embrown* 430vb.
embryo *source* 156n.
   undevelopment 670n.
embryo, in
   impending 155adj.
   preparatory 669adj.
embryology *biology* 358n.
embryonic *beginning* 68adj.
   causal 156adj.
   exiguous 196adj.
   amorphous 244adj.
   immature 670adj.
emendation
   interpretation 520n.
   amendment 654n.
   repair 656n.
emendator
   interpreter 520n.
   mender 656n.
emender *interpreter* 520n.
   reformer 654n.
emerald *greenness* 432n.
   gem 844n.
emerge *result* 157vb.
   depart 296vb.
   emerge 298vb.
   be visible 443vb.
   be proved 478vb.
   be disclosed 526vb.
emergence *egress* 298n.

emergency *juncture* 8n.
   crisis 137n.
   eventuality 154n.
   needfulness 627n.
   danger 661n.
   predicament 700n.
emeritus *deserving* 915adj.
emery *sharpener* 256n.
emery paper
   sharpener 256n.
   smoother 258n.
   pulverizer 332n.
emetic *ejector* 300n.
   expulsive 300adj.
   unsavoury 391adj.
   cathartic 658n.
   bane 659n.
emetine *cathartic* 658n.
emeto-cathartic
   expulsive 300adj.
émeute *revolt* 738n.
emication *flash* 417n.
emigrant *foreigner* 59n.
   wanderer 268n.
   egress 298n.
emigration
   wandering 267n.
   departure 296n.
   egress 298n.
émigré *wanderer* 268n.
   egress 298n.
eminence *greatness* 32n.
   superiority 34n.
   height 209n.
   prominence 254n.
   elevation 310n.
   importance 638n.
   goodness 644n.
   prestige 866n.
   church title 986n.
eminently
   remarkably 32adv.
emir *potentate* 741n.
   nobleman 868n.
emissary *messenger* 531n.
   delegate, envoy 754n.
emission *ejection* 300n.
   speech 579n.
emit *emit* 300vb.
   publish 528vb.
   speak 579vb.
emmenagogic
   expulsive 300adj.
emmer *corn* 366n.
emmet *animalcule* 196n.
   vermin 365n.
emollient *lenitive* 177adj.
   soft 327adj.
   lubricant 334n.
   balm 658n.
   remedial 658adj.

pacificatory 719adj.
emolument *earnings* 771n.
   pay 804n.
   receipt 807n.
   reward 962n.
emotion *influence* 178n.
   warm feeling 818n.
emotional
   spontaneous 609adj.
   with affections 817adj.
   feeling 818adj.
   impressible 819adj.
   excitable 822adj.
emotionalism
   persuasibility 612n.
   feeling 818n.
   moral sensibility 819n.
   excitability 822n.
emotive *felt* 818adj.
empalement
   perforation 263n.
   (*see* impale)
empanel *list* 87vb.
empathy
   imagination 513n.
emperor *sovereign* 741n.
   aristocrat 868n.
emphasis (*see* emphasize)
emphasize
   strengthen 162vb.
   attract notice 455vb.
   argue 475vb.
   be intelligible 516vb.
   manifest 522vb.
   emphasize 532vb.
   indicate 547vb.
   make important 638vb.
   impress 821vb.
emphatic *strong* 162adj.
   florid 425adj.
   expressive 516adj.
   undisguised 522adj.
   assertive 532adj.
   forceful 571adj.
emphatically
   positively 32adv.
emphysema *swelling* 253n.
empire *territory* 184n.
   polity 733n.
   governance 733n.
empiric *imposter* 545n.
empirical *enquiring* 459adj.
   experimental 461adj.
empiricism
   empiricism 461n.
empiricist
   experimenter 461n.
   learner 538n.
emplacement *place* 185n.
   situation 186n.
   location, station 187n.

stand 218n.
fortification 713n.
emplane *start out* 296vb.
employ *employ* 622vb.
  use 673n.,vb.
  service 745n.
  commission 751vb.
employable
  instrumental 628adj.
  useful 640adj.
  used 673adj.
employee *worker* 686n.
  servant 742n.
  consignee 754n.
employer *agent* 686n.
  director 690n.
  master 741n.
  purchaser 792n.
employment *job* 622n.
  business 622n.
  instrumentality 628n.
  utility 640n.
  use 673n.
  action 676n.
  exercise 682n.
  service 745n.
employ oneself *do* 676vb.
emporium
  emporium, shop 796n.
empower *empower* 160vb.
  make possible 469vb.
  facilitate 701vb.
  commission 751vb.
  permit 756vb.
empowered
  authoritative 733adj.
empress *sovereign* 741n.
empressement
  assiduity 678n.
  warm feeling 818n.
emprise *undertaking* 672n.
  prowess 855n.
empties *emptiness* 190n.
  rubbish 641n.
emptiness *non-existence* 2n.
  insubstantiality 4n.
  emptiness 190n.
  rarity 325n.
  unmeaningness 515n.
  unimportance 639n.
  vanity 873n.
emption *purchase* 792n.
empty *subtract* 39vb.
  displace 188vb.
  empty 190adj.
  make smaller 198vb.
  transpose 272vb.
  void 300vb.
  rare 325adj.
  make flow 350vb.
  unthinking 450adj.

sophistical 477adj.
unmeaning 515adj.
hypocritical 541adj.
untrue 543adj.
feeble 572adj.
unprovided 636adj.
inactive 679adj.
unpossessed 774adj.
hungry 859adj.
boastful 877adj.
fasting 946adj.
empty-handed
  unprovided 636adj.
  unsuccessful 728adj.
  parsimonious 816adj.
empty-headed
  mindless 448adj.
  unthinking 450adj.
empty-headedness
  folly 499n.
empty into *flow* 350vb.
empty purse *poverty* 801n.
empty stomach
  hunger 859n.
empty talk
  empty talk 315n.
empurple *empurple* 434vb.
empyrean *heavens* 321n.
empyreuma *fire* 379n.
  burning 381n.
  fetor 397n.
empyrosis *fire* 379n.
emu *flightless bird* 365n.
emulation *imitation* 20n.
  opposition 704n.
  quarrelsomeness 709n.
  contention 716n.
  jealousy 911n.
emulator *opponent* 705n.
  quarreller 709n.
  contender 716n.
emulous *opposing* 704adj.
emulsification
  thickening 354n.
emulsion *viscidity* 354n.
emulsive *semiliquid* 354adj.
emunctory *drain* 351n.
enable *empower* 160vb.
  make possible 469vb.
  facilitate 701vb.
  permit 756vb.
enact *show* 522vb.
  represent 551vb.
  do 676vb.
  deal with 688vb.
  carry out 725vb.
  decree 737vb.
  make legal 953vb.
enactment
  dramaturgy 594n.
  action 676n.

precept 693n.
  (*see* enact)
enallage *trope* 519n.
enamel *coat* 226vb.
  facing 226n.
  smooth 258vb.
  colour 425vb.
  decorate 844vb.
enameller *engraver* 556n.
enamour *motivate* 612vb.
  excite love 887vb.
en bloc *collectively* 52adv.
encamp
  place oneself 187vb.
  dwell 192vb.
encampment
  station 187n.
  abode 192n.
  fort 713n.
encase *comprise* 78vb.
  circumscribe 232vb.
  cover 226vb.
  insert 303vb.
encash *acquire* 771vb.
  receive 782vb.
  sell 793vb.
  draw money 797vb.
enceinte *inclosure* 235n.
  productive 164adj.
encephalitis *infection* 651n.
  sleep 679n.
enchain *fetter* 747vb.
enchant *subjugate* 745vb.
  delight 826vb.
  be wonderful 864vb.
  excite love 887vb.
  bewitch 983vb.
enchanter *sorcerer* 983n.
enchantment
  conversion 147n.
  excitation 821n.
  joy 824n.
  pleasurableness 826n.
  love 887n.
  spell 983n.
enchantress *a beauty* 841n.
  sorceress 983n.
enchase *affix* 45vb.
enchiridion
  textbook 589n.
enchorial *native* 191adj.
  linguistic 557adj.
encircle *comprise* 78vb.
  surround 230vb.
  circumscribe 232vb.
  go round 250vb.
  circuit 626vb.
encirclement
  circumscription 232n.
  attack 712n.
enclave *region* 184n.

enclitic *sequel* 67n.
enclose *be exterior* 223vb.
  circumscribe 232vb.
  inclose 235vb.
  close 264vb.
  cultivate 370vb.
enclosed *interior* 234adj.
  monastic 986adj.
enclosure *region* 184n.
  place 185n.
  contents 193n.
  receptacle 194n.
  inclosure 235n.
  correspondence 588n.
  fort 713n.
encomiast
  commender 923n.
encomium *praise* 923n.
encompass
  surround 230vb.
  limit 236vb.
  circumscribe 232vb.
  circuit 626vb.
  obstruct 702vb.
encore *duplication* 91n.
  double 91vb.
  repetition 106n.
  again 106adv.
  dramaturgy 594n.
  applause 923n.
encounter
  synchronize 123vb.
  eventuality 154n.
  meet with 154vb.
  contiguity 202n.
  collision 279n.
  meet 295vb.
  discover 484vb.
  withstand 704vb.
  fight 716n., vb.
encourage *incite* 612vb.
  aid 703vb.
  animate 821vb.
  relieve 831vb.
  cheer 833vb.
  give hope 852vb.
  give courage 855vb.
encouragement
  causation 156n.
encouraging
  influential 178adj.
encratism *celibacy* 895n.
  temperance 942n.
  asceticism 945n.
encratite *celibate* 895n.
  abstainer 942n.
  sober person 948n.
  virgin 950n.
encroach *be near* 200vb.
  interfere 231vb.
  encroach 306vb.

  be illegal 954vb.
encroacher *usurper* 916n.
encroachment
  progression 285n.
  overstepping 306n.
  attack 712n.
  wrong 914n.
  undueness 916n.
encumber
  be difficult 700vb.
  hinder 702vb.
encumbrance
  gravity 322n.
  encumbrance 702n.
  debt 803n.
encyclical
  publication 528n.
  decree 737n.
encyclopædia
  erudition 490n.
  reference book 589n.
encyclopædic
  general 79adj.
encyclopædist
  scholar 492n.
end *be complete* 54vb.
  sequel 67n.
  extremity 69n.
  end 69n., vb.
  cease 145vb.
  eventuality 154n.
  effect 157n.
  destroy 165vb.
  vertex 213n.
  limit 236n.
  decease 361n.
  intention 617n.
  objective 617n.
  completion 725n.
endanger *endanger* 661vb.
  be difficult 700vb.
endarteritis
  blood pressure 651n.
endear *excite love* 887vb.
endearing
  pleasurable 826adj.
  lovable 887adj.
endearment
  inducement 612n.
  courteous act 884n.
  love-making 887n.
  endearment 889n.
endeavour *essay* 671n., vb.
  action 676n.
ended *past* 125adj.
endemic *interior* 224adj.
  infectious 653adj.
endive *vegetable* 301n.
endless
  multitudinous 104adj.
  infinite 107adj.

  perpetual 115adj.
endlessness
  continuity 71n.
endlong *longwise* 203adv.
endocardial
  interior 224adj.
endocarditis
  heart disease 651n.
endocrine *interiority* 224n.
endoderm *interiority* 224n.
end of one's tether, at the
  in difficulties 700adj.
endogamy *interiority* 224n.
  (*see* marriage)
endogenous *interior* 224adj.
  vegetal 366adj.
endorse *testify* 466vb.
  endorse 488vb.
  sign 547vb.
  patronize 703vb.
  consent 758vb.
  give security 767vb.
  approve 923vb.
endorsement *label* 547n.
  consent 758n.
endorser *signatory* 765n.
endosmose *passage* 305n.
endow *empower* 160vb.
  dower 777vb.
  give 781vb.
endowed with
  possessing 773adj.
endowment *heredity* 5n.
  ability 160n.
  aptitude 694n.
end-paper *ligature* 47n.
end to end
  contiguous 202adj.
  contiguously 202adv.
  longwise 203adv.
endurable
  contenting 828adj.
endurance *durability* 113n.
  permanence 144n.
  power 160n.
  perseverance 600n.
  feeling 818n.
  patience 823n.
  suffering 825n.
  manliness 855n.
endure *be* 1vb.
  continue 108vb.
  last 113vb.
  stay 144vb.
  go on 146vb.
  meet with 154vb.
  support 218vb.
  carry 273vb.
  acquiesce 488vb.
  be resolute 599vb.
  stand firm 599vb.

persevere 600 vb.
resist 715 vb.
feel 818 vb.
be patient 823 vb.
suffer 825 vb.
be courageous 855 vb.
enema *insertion* 303 n.
therapy 658 n.
enema-can *drain* 351 n.
enemy *trouble-maker* 663 n.
opponent 705 n.
enemy 881 n.
hateful object 888 n.
energetic (*see* energy)
energize *augment* 36 vb.
strengthen 162 vb.
invigorate 174 vb.
incite 612 vb.
cheer 833 vb.
energy *energy* 160 n.
power 160 n.
strength 162 n.
vigorousness 174 n.
vigour 571 n.
resolution 599 n.
restlessness 678 n.
exertion 682 n.
enervate *unman* 161 vb.
weaken 163 vb.
en famille *sociably* 882 adv.
enfant gâté *satiety* 863 n.
favourite 890 n.
enfant perdu
desperado 857 n.
enfant terrible
inquisitor 453 n.
questioner 459 n.
ingenue 699 n.
enfeeble *weaken* 163 vb.
enfeoffment *transfer* 780 n.
giving 781 n.
enfilade *look along* 203 vb.
pierce 263 vb.
pass 305 vb.
bombardment 712 n.
fire at 712 vb.
enflame *invigorate* 174 vb.
make violent 176 vb.
make bright 417 vb.
excite 821 vb.
enfold *dress* 228 vb.
circumscribe 232 vb.
fold 261 vb.
safeguard 660 vb.
caress 889 vb.
enforce *motivate* 612 vb.
compel 740 vb.
make legal 953 vb.
enfranchise
give scope 744 vb.
liberate 746 vb.

exempt 919 vb.
engage *join* 45 vb.
induce 612 vb.
employ 622 vb.
undertake 672 vb.
contend, fight 716 vb.
give battle 718 vb.
commission 751 vb.
promise 764 vb.
contract 765 vb.
incur a duty 917 vb.
acquire 771 vb.
possess 773 vb.
engaged *retained* 778 adj.
marriageable 894 adj.
engaged couple *lovers* 887 n.
engage gear *enlace* 222 vb.
engage in
busy oneself 622 vb.
undertake 672 vb.
engagement *intention* 617 n.
undertaking 672 n.
fight 716 n.
battle 718 n.
promise 764 n.
social round 882 n.
love affair 887 n.
duty 917 n.
engagement diary
reminder 505 n.
engagement ring
jewellery 844 n.
love-token 889 n.
engaging *lovable* 887 adj.
engender *generate* 164 vb.
engine *causal means* 156 n.
empower 160 vb.
strengthen 162 vb.
machine 630 n.
engine-driver *driver* 208 n.
engineer *cause* 156 vb.
produce 164 vb.
producer 167 n.
driver 268 n.
planner 623 n.
plan 623 vb.
machinist 630 n.
artisan 686 n.
soldiery 722 n.
engineered *false* 541 adj.
engineering
mechanics 630 n.
English *translate* 520 vb.
type size 587 n.
engorge *absorb* 299 vb.
engorgement
redundance 637 n.
engraft *add* 38 vb.
affix 45 vb.
educate 534 vb.
engrafted *extrinsic* 6 adj.

engrail *roughen* 259 vb.
en grande tenue
fashionable 848 adj.
en grande toilette
bedecked 844 adj.
engrave *cut* 46 vb.
groove 262 vb.
mark 547 vb.
record 548 vb.
represent 551 vb.
engrave 555 vb.
write 586 vb.
engraver *recorder* 549 n.
engraver 556 n.
engraving *copy* 22 n.
picture 553 n.
engraving 555 n.
engross *absorb* 299 vb.
engross 449 vb.
bias 481 vb.
write 586 vb.
possess 773 vb.
appropriate 786 vb.
purchase 792 vb.
engrossed *obsessed* 455 adj.
distracted 456 adj.
engrossment
possession 773 n.
engulf *consume* 165 vb.
destroy 165 vb.
absorb 299 vb.
appropriate 786 vb.
gluttonize 947 vb.
enhance *manifest* 522 vb.
make important 638 vb.
beautify 841 vb.
enhancement *increase* 36 n.
improvement 654 n.
aggravation 832 n.
ornamentation 844 n.
dignification 866 n.
enharmonic
harmonic 410 adj.
enigma *question* 459 n.
dubiety 474 n.
unknown thing 491 n.
unmeaningness 515 n.
unintelligibility 517 n.
enigma 530 n.
difficulty 700 n.
prodigy 864 n.
enigmatic *aphoristic* 496 adj.
imperspicuous 568 adj.
enigmatist *questioner* 459 n.
enisled *alone* 88 adj.
distant 199 adj.
secluded 883 adj.
enjambement
ornament 574 n.
prosody 593 n.
enjoin *advise* 691 vb.

command 737 vb.
  impose a duty 917 vb.
enjoy *unite with* 45 vb.
  enjoy 376 vb.
  find useful 640 vb.
  dispose of 673 vb.
  prosper 730 vb.
  possess 773 vb.
  be pleased 824 adj.
enjoyable *pleasant* 376 adj.
enjoyment *coition* 45 n.
  sociability 882 n.
  sensualism 944 n.
  (*see* enjoy)
enjoy oneself
  be cheerful 833 vb.
  amuse oneself 837 vb.
enkindle *kindle* 381 vb.
  excite 821 vb.
enkindled *fiery* 379 adj.
enlace *enlace* 222 vb.
  caress 889 vb.
enlarge
  make important 638 vb.
  boast 877 vb.
  (*see* enlargement)
enlargement *duplicate* 22 n.
  increase 36 n.
  expansion 197 n.
  exaggeration 546 n.
  photography 551 n.
  liberation 746 n.
enlarge upon
  be diffuse 570 vb.
enlighten *interpret* 520 vb.
  manifest 522 vb.
  inform 524 vb.
  educate 534 vb.
enlightened
  wise 498 adj.
  philanthropic 901 adj.
enlightenment
  knowledge 490 n.
  wisdom 498 n.
  information 524 n.
enlist *be included* 78 vb.
  list 87 vb.
  enter 297 vb.
  admit 299 vb.
  register 548 vb.
  induce 612 vb.
  employ 622 vb.
  avail of 673 vb.
  go to war 718 vb.
enlisted man *soldier* 722 n.
enlistment *reception* 299 n.
  registration 548 n.
enlist under
  patronize 703 vb.
enliven *strengthen* 162 vb.
  invigorate 174 vb.

vitalize 360 vb.
  animate 821 vb.
  cheer 833 vb.
  amuse 837 vb.
enlivened *refreshed* 685 adj.
en masse *collectively* 52 adv.
  together 74 adv.
  in league 708 adv.
enmesh *enlace* 222 vb.
  ensnare 542 vb.
  hinder 702 vb.
enmity *enmity* 881 n.
  malevolence 898 n.
ennead *over five* 99 n.
ennoblement
  dignification 866 n.
ennui *tedium* 838 n.
enormity *greatness* 32 n.
  hugeness 195 n.
  wickedness 934 n.
  vice 934 n.
  guilty act 936 n.
enormous *enormous* 32 adj.
  huge 195 adj.
Enosis *combination* 50 n.
enough *sufficiency* 635 n.
  sufficient 635 adj.
  enough 635 adv.
enough and to spare
  plenteous 635 adj.
  redundantly 637 adv.
en passant
  incidentally 137 adv.
  en passant 305 adv.
enquire *be curious* 453 vb.
  enquire 459 vb.
  not know 491 vb.
  study 536 vb.
enquirer *enquirer* 459 n.
  experimenter 461 n.
  hunter 619 n.
  petitioner 763 n.
enquiry *enquiry* 459 n.
  experiment 461 n.
  dissertation 591 n.
  legal trial 959 n.
enquiry agent
  detective 459 n.
enrage *make violent* 176 vb.
  make mad 503 vb.
  excite 821 vb.
  excite hate 888 vb.
  enrage 891 vb.
en rapport *relative* 9 adj.
  concordant 710 adj.
enrapture *excite love* 887 vb.
enrich *ornament* 574 vb.
  make better 654 vb.
  give 781 vb.
  make rich 800 vb.
  decorate 844 vb.

enrobe *dress* 228 vb.
enrol *list* 87 vb.
  admit 299 vb.
  register 548 vb.
enrol oneself
  be included 78 vb.
  enter 297 vb.
  join a party 708 vb.
en route *on foot* 267 adv.
  in transit 272 adv.
ens *existence* 1 n.
ensconce *place* 187 vb.
  conceal 525 vb.
  safeguard 660 vb.
ensemble
  all, whole 52 n.
  duet 412 n.
enshrine
  circumscribe 232 vb.
  sanctify 979 vb.
enshrinement
  dignification 866 n.
enshrouded
  invisible 444 adj.
ensiform *sharp* 256 adj.
ensign *flag* 547 n.
  army officer 741 n.
  regalia 743 n.
ensilage *agriculture* 370 n.
  preservation 666 n.
enslave *oppress* 735 vb.
  subjugate 745 vb.
enslaved *loving* 887 adj.
enslavement (*see* enslave)
ensnare *ambush* 527 vb.
  ensnare 542 vb.
  tempt 612 vb.
  hunt 619 vb.
  take 786 vb.
ensue *come after* 65 vb.
  ensue 120 vb.
ensure *make certain* 473 vb.
  predetermine 608 vb.
entablature *summit* 213 n.
entail *conduce* 156 vb.
  make likely 471 vb.
entailed *proprietary* 777 adj.
  retained 778 adj.
entangle *bedevil* 63 vb.
  enlace 222 vb.
  be unintelligible 517 vb.
  ensnare 542 vb.
  hinder 702 vb.
  make quarrels 709 vb.
entangled *complex* 61 adj.
entanglement *medley* 43 n.
  crossing 222 n.
  love affair 887 n.
entelechy *reality* 1 n.
  existence 1 n.
entente *agreement* 24 n.

concord 710 n.
pacification 719 n.
friendliness 880 n.
enter fill 54 vb.
begin 68 vb.
be included 78 vb.
list 87 vb.
approach 289 vb.
converge 293 vb.
arrive 295 vb.
enter 297 vb.
insert 303 vb.
be visible 443 vb.
register 548 vb.
join a party 708 vb.
contend 716 vb.
offer oneself 759 vb.
appropriate 786 vb.
account 808 vb.
enter into be one of 58 vb.
imagine 513 vb.
describe 590 vb.
contract 765 vb.
enter into detail
specify 80 vb.
enterprise
vigorousness 174 n.
progression 285 n.
intention 617 n.
pursuit 619 n.
business 622 n.
undertaking 672 n.
restlessness 678 n.
mandate 751 n.
courage 855 n.
enterprising
speculative 618 adj.
entertain employ 622 vb.
patronize 703 vb.
consent 758 vb.
give 781 vb.
feel 818 vb.
amuse 837 vb.
be ridiculous 849 vb.
be friendly 880 vb.
be hospitable 882 vb.
entertainable
amused 837 adj.
entertainer
entertainer 594 n.
humorist 839 n.
entertainment
provisions 301 n.
pleasure 376 n.
provision 633 n.
amusement 837 n.
social gathering 882 n.
entêté wilful 602 adj.
enthral oppress 735 vb.
subjugate 745 vb.
excite love 887 vb.

enthronement
mandate 751 n.
dignification 866 n.
celebration 876 n.
holy orders 985 n.
enthuse excite 821 vb.
enthusiasm vigour 571 n.
willingness 597 n.
restlessness 678 n.
warm feeling 818 n.
excitation 821 n.
hope 852 n.
love 887 n.
applause 923 n.
piety 979 n.
enthusiast crank 504 n.
visionary 513 n.
busy person 678 n.
religionist 979 n.
worshipper 981 n.
enthusiastic
optimistic 482 adj.
imaginative 513 adj.
(see enthusiasm)
enthymeme reasoning 475 n.
entice distract 456 vb.
ensnare 542 vb.
induce, tempt 612 vb.
enticing
pleasurable 826 adj.
entire consummate 32 adj.
whole 52 adj.
complete 54 adj.
perfect 646 adj.
undamaged 646 adj.
entirety whole 52 n.
completeness 54 n.
entitative existing 1 adj.
entitle name 561 vb.
permit 756 vb.
grant claims 915 vb.
entitled deserving 915 adj.
entitlement dueness 915 n.
entity existence 1 n.
unit 88 n.
entombment
interment 364 n.
detention 747 n.
entomology zoology 367 n.
entourage
concomitant 89 n.
circumjacence 230 n.
entozoon animalcule 196 n.
entr'acte interim 108 n.
stage play 594 n.
entrails insides 224 n.
entrain start out 296 vb.
entrance
front 237 n.
entrance 68 n.
doorway 263 n.

way in 297 n.
ingress 297 n.
dramaturgy 594 n.
delight 826 vb.
entrant incomer 297 n.
respondent 460 vb.
testee 461 n.
opponent 705 n.
contender 716 n.
petitioner 763 n.
entrap ensnare 542 vb.
entreaty entreaty 761 n.
entrée ingress 297 n.
reception 299 n.
entrench stabilize 153 vb.
strengthen 162 vb.
place oneself 187 vb.
safeguard 660 vb.
defend 713 vb.
entrenched vested 153 adj.
conditional 766 adj.
due 915 adj.
entrenched clause
fixture 153 n.
conditions 766 n.
entrenchment
defences 713 n.
entre nous
secretly 525 adv.
entrepôt storage 632 n.
emporium 796 n.
entrepreneur gambler 618 n.
essayer 671 n.
doer 676 n.
entresol
compartment 194 n.
layer 207 n.
entrust transfer 272 vb.
commission 751 vb.
give 781 vb.
convey 780 vb.
entry doorway 263 n.
way in 297 n.
ingress 297 n.
registration 548 n.
entwine relate 9 vb.
connect 45 vb.
unite with 45 vb.
enlace 222 vb.
twine 251 vb.
enucleation
interpretation 520 n.
enumerate specify 80 vb.
enumeration
numeration 86 n.
list 87 n.
enunciate affirm 532 vb.
enunciation voice 577 n.
pronunciation 577 n.
speech 579 n.
enveigle tempt 612 vb.

envelop *comprise* 78 vb.
   dress 228 vb.
   circumscribe 232 vb.
envelope *receptacle* 194 n.
   covering 226 n.
   inclosure 235 n.
   correspondence 588 n.
envelopment
   circumscription 232 n.
envenom *impair* 655 vb.
   aggravate 832 vb.
   excite hate 888 vb.
envenomed *bad* 645 adj.
   toxic 653 adj.
enviable *desired* 859 adj.
   approvable 923 adj.
envier *malcontent* 829 n.
envious *inimical* 881 adj.
   hating 888 adj.
   malevolent 898 adj.
   jealous 911 adj.
   envious 912 adj.
environment
   circumstance 8 n.
   relation 9 n.
   locality 187 n.
   circumjacence 230 n.
environmental
   circumstantial 8 adj.
   relative 9 adj.
environs *entrance* 68 n.
   locality 187 n.
   near place 200 n.
   circumjacence 230 n.
envisage *imagine* 513 vb.
envoi *adjunct* 40 n.
   sequel 67 n.
   end 69 n.
   verse form 593 n.
envoy *messenger* 531 n.
   official 690 n.
   envoy 754 n.
envy *discontent* 829 n.
   be discontented 829 vb.
   desire 859 vb.
   desired object 859 n.
   enmity 881 n.
   be inimical 881 vb.
   hatred 888 n.
   resent 891 vb.
   malevolence 898 n.
   jealousy 911 n.
   envy 912 n., vb.
   approve 923 vb.
enwrap *fold* 261 vb.
enzootic *infectious* 653 adj.
enzyme *alterer* 143 n.
   leaven 323 n.
Eoanthropus *mankind* 371 n.
eocene *secular* 110 adj.
eolith *antiquity* 125 n.

eolithic *secular* 110 adj.
Eos *morning* 128 n.
   lesser god 967 n.
epagoge
   argumentation 475 n.
epaulette *badge* 547 n.
   livery 547 n.
   badge of rank 743 n.
   trimming 844 n.
épée *side-arms* 723 n.
epenthesis *addition* 38 n.
épergne *plate* 194 n.
   ornamentation 844 n.
epexegesis
   interpretation 520 n.
ephah *metrology* 465 n.
ephemeral
   ephemeral 114 adj.
   dying 361 adj.
ephemeris *chronology* 117 n.
   guide-book 524 n.
ephialtes *pain* 377 n.
   suffering 825 n.
ephod *vestments* 989 n.
ephor *officer* 741 n.
epic *prolix* 570 adj.
   narrative 590 n.
   descriptive 590 adj.
   poem 593 n.
epicedium *lament* 836 n.
epicene *multiform* 82 adj.
   abnormal 84 adj.
   equivocal 518 adj.
epicentre *centrality* 225 n.
epicranium *head* 213 n.
epicure *eater* 301 n.
   gastronomy 301 n.
   man of taste 846 n.
   perfectionist 862 n.
   sensualist 944 n.
   glutton 947 n.
epicurean *sensuous* 376 adj.
   savoury 390 adj.
epicureanism
   gastronomy 301 n.
   philosophy 449 n.
   enjoyment 824 n.
   good taste 846 n.
   sensualism 944 n.
   gluttony 947 n.
epicycle *orbit* 250 n.
epidemic *extensive* 32 adj.
   comprehensive 52 adj.
   universal 79 adj.
   plague 651 n.
   infectious 653 adj.
epidemiology
   pathology 651 n.
epidermic *exterior* 223 adj.
   dermal 226 adj.
epidermis *skin* 226 n.

epidiascope
   optical device 442 n.
epigenesis
   propagation 164 n.
epigram *maxim* 496 n.
   phrase 563 n.
   conciseness 569 n.
   witticism 839 n.
epigrammatist
   phrase 563 n.
   humorist 839 n.
epigraph
   indication 547 n.
   script 586 n.
epigrapher *penman* 586 n.
epigraphic
   recording 548 adj.
epigraphist
   interpreter 520 n.
   phrase 563 n.
epigraphy
   hermeneutics 520 n.
   registration 548 n.
epilepsy *spasm* 318 n.
   frenzy 503 n.
   paralysis 651 n.
epilogue *sequel* 67 n.
   extremity 69 n.
   dramaturgy 594 n.
epinician ode
   trophy 729 n.
epiphany *revelation* 975 n.
   holy-day 988 n.
epiphenomenon
   concomitant 89 n.
   appearance 445 n.
episcopacy
   churchdom 985 n.
   church office 985 n.
episcopal *clerical* 986 adj.
episcopalian
   Anglican 976 adj.
   Catholic 976 adj.
   ecclesiastical 985 adj.
episcopate
   church office 985 n.
   ecclesiarch 986 n.
episode *irrelevance* 10 n.
   adjunct 40 n.
   discontinuity 72 n.
   interim 108 n.
   interjection 231 n.
   pleonasm 570 n.
epistemology
   knowledge 490 n.
epistle
   correspondence 588 n.
epistolary *epistolary* 588 adj.
epistrophe
   ornament 574 n.
epistyle *beam* 218 n.

summit 213 n.
epitaph *valediction* 296 n.
  obsequies 364 n.
  indication 547 n.
  phrase 563 n.
  description 590 n.
epithalamium
  vocal music 412 n.
  poem 593 n.
  wedding 894 n.
epithelioma *carcinosis* 651 n.
epithem
  surgical dressing 658 n.
epithet *name* 561 n.
epitome *miniature* 196 n.

  contraction 198 n.
  shortening 204 n.
  conciseness 569 n.
  compendium 592 n.
epitomize *shorten* 204 vb.
  abstract 592 vb.
epizootic *infectious* 653 adj.
epoch *era* 110 n.
  chronology 117 n.
epochal *secular* 110 adj.
epoch-making
  notable 638 adj.
epode *poem* 593 n.
eponym *name* 561 n.
eponymous *named* 561 adj.
epos *narrative* 590 n.
Epsom salts
  cathartic 658 n.
epuration *cleansing* 648 n.
equability *equality* 28 n.
  non-wonder 865 n.
equable *inexcitable* 823 adj.
equal *similar* 18 adj.
  compeer 28 n.
  equal 28 adj.
  just 913 adj.
equality
  relativeness 9 n.
  identity 13 n.
  equality 28 n.
  synchronism 123 n.
  equal chance 159 n.
  parallelism 219 n.
equalization
  equalization 28 n.
equalize *equalize* 28 vb.
  average out 30 vb.
  flatten 216 vb.
  compare 462 vb.
equanimity
  inexcitability 823 n.
equate *identify* 13 vb.
  equalize 28 vb.
equation
  equalization 28 n.
  equivalence 28 n.

numerical result 85 n.
numerical operation 86 n.
equator
  equalization 28 n.
  girdle 47 n.
  middle 70 n.
  dividing line 92 n.
  limit 236 n.
  circle 250 n.
equatorial *middle* 70 adj.
  telluric 321 adj.
  warm 379 adj.
equerry *retainer* 742 n.
equestrian *rider* 268 n.
equestrianism
  equitation 267 n.
equidistance *middle* 70 n.
  parallelism 219 n.
equilateral *uniform* 16 adj.
  equal 28 adj.
  symmetrical 245 adj.
  angular figure 247 n.
equilibrant
  equilibrium 28 n.
equilibration
  equilibrium 28 n.
equilibrist
  entertainer 594 n.
equilibrium
  equilibrium 28 n.
  stability 153 n.
  quiescence 266 n.
equine *equine* 273 adj.
  animal 365 adj.
equinoctial *vernal* 128 adj.
  autumnal 129 adj.
  celestial 321 adj.
equinoctial colure
  uranometry 321 n.
equinox *spring* 128 n.
  autumn 129 n.
equip *dress* 228 vb.
  find means 629 vb.
  provide 633 vb.
  make ready 669 vb.
  give 781 vb.
equipage *carriage* 274 n.
  ostentation 875 n.
equiparation
  equalization 28 n.
equipendent *equal* 28 adj.
equipment *adjunct* 40 n.
  contents 193 n.
  means 629 n.
  equipment 630 n.
  provision 633 n.
  fitting out 669 n.
equipoise *equilibrium* 28 n.
  weighment 322 n.
equiponderance
  equilibrium 28 n.

equipper *preparer* 669 n.
equitable *just* 913 adj.
  honourable 929 adj.
equitation *motion* 265 n.
  equitation 267 n.
equity *indifference* 860 n.
  justice 913 n.
equivalence *identity* 13 n.
  similarity 18 n.
  equivalence 28 n.
  connotation 514 n.
equivalent *offset* 31 n.
  quid pro quo 150 n.
  interpretive 520 adj.
equivocal
  uncertain 474 adj.
  puzzling 517 adj.
  equivocal 518 adj.
  false 541 adj.
  imperspicuous 568 adj.
  tergiversating 603 adj.
  dishonest 930 adj.
equivocalness
  connotation 514 n.
  (see equivocation)
equivocate
  misinterpret 521 vb.
equivocation
  sophistry 477 n.
  equivocalness 518 n.
  falsehood 541 n.
  pretext 614 n.
  wit 839 n.
equivocator *sophist* 477 n.
  liar 545 n.
equivoque
  assimilation 18 n.
  absurdity 497 n.
  equivocalness 518 n.
  witticism 839 n.
  impurity 951 n.
era *date* 108 n.
  era 110 n.
  chronology 117 n.
eradicate *subtract* 39 vb.
  exclude 57 vb.
  destroy 165 vb.
  displace 188 vb.
  eject 300 vb.
  extract 304 vb.
erase *destroy* 165 vb.
  eject 300 vb.
  rub 333 vb.
  obliterate 550 vb.
  clean 648 vb.
Erastianism *heresy* 977 n.
erasure *friction* 333 n.
  obliteration 550 n.
ere *before* 119 adv.
Erebus *darkness* 418 n.
  classical gods 967 n.

mythic hell 972 n.
erect *stabilize* 153 vb.
 cause 156 vb.
 produce 164 vb.
 place 187 vb.
 make vertical 215 vb.
 elevate 310 vb.
 jubilant 833 adj.
 honourable 929 adj.
erectile *elevated* 310 adj.
erection *edifice* 164 n.
erectness *verticality* 215 n.
erector *lifter* 310 n.
ere long *betimes* 135 adv.
eremitical
, *unconformable* 84 adj.
 alone 88 adj.
 unsociable 883 adj.
 ascetic 945 adj.
ere now *before* 119 adv.
 retrospectively 125 adv.
erewhile *before* 119 adv.
 formerly 125 adv.
erewhon *fantasy* 513 n.
erg *energy* 160 n.
ergatocracy
 government 733 n.
ergo *hence* 158 adv.
ergotism *argument* 475 n.
 judgment 480 n.
Erinys, Erinnys
 violent creature 176 n.
 Fury 891 n.
eriometer
 optical device 442 n.
eristic *reasoner* 475 n.
 arguing 475 adj.
 quarreller 709 n.
erk *servant* 742 n.
Erl King *fairy* 970 n.
ermine *skin* 226 n.
 heraldry 547 n.
 regalia 743 n.
 trimming 844 n.
erne *bird of prey* 365 n.
Ernie
 counting instrument 86 n.
erode *bate* 37 vb.
 subtract 39 vb.
 decompose 51 vb.
 encroach 306 vb.
 pulverize 332 vb.
 rub 333 vb.
 impair 655 vb.
Eros *libido* 859 n.
 love 887 n.
erotic *erotic* 887 adj.
 impure 951 adj.
eroticism *love* 887 n.
erotogenic *erotic* 887 adj.
erotomania *love* 887 n.

err *stray* 282 vb.
 err 495 vb.
 be wicked 934 vb.
errancy *error* 495 n.
errand *land travel* 267 n.
 message 529 n.
 job 622 n.
 mandate 751 n.
errand boy *courier* 531 n.
errant *travelling* 267 adj.
 deviating 282 adj.
errantry *wandering* 267 n.
errata *edition* 589 n.
erratic *non-uniform* 17 adj.
 fitful 142 adj.
 unstable 152 adj.
 moving 265 adj.
 deviating 282 adj.
 inexact 495 adj.
 crazed 503 adj.
 capricious 604 adj.
erratum *mistake* 495 n.
erring *wicked* 934 adj.
erroneous *unreal* 2 adj.
 illogical 477 adj.
 erroneous 495 adj.
 wrong 914 adj.
 heterodox 977 adj.
error *deviation* 282 n.
 misjudgment 481 n.
 error 495 n.
 deception 542 n.
 inexpedience 643 n.
 wrong 914 n.
 heterodoxy 977 n.
ersatz *simulating* 18 adj.
 imitative 20 adj.
 substitute 150 n.
 spurious 542 adj.
 vulgar 847 adj.
erst *formerly* 125 adv.
erstwhile *prior* 119 adj.
 former 125 adj.
erubescence *redness* 431 n.
eructation *voidance* 300 n.
 respiration 352 n.
erudition *erudition* 490 n.
 learning 536 n.
erupt *attack* 712 vb.
 (*see* eruption)
erupting *fiery* 379 adj.
eruption *revolution* 149 n.
 outbreak 176 n.
 egress 298 n.
 voidance 300 n.
 skin disease 651 n.
erysipelatous
 diseased 651 adj.
erythematous
 diseased 651 adj.
escalade *irrupt* 297 vb.

ascent 308 n.
 climb 308 vb.
 attack 712 n., vb.
escalator *transport* 272 n.
 carrier 273 n.
 conveyor 274 n.
 ascent 308 n.
 lifter 310 n.
escalator clause
 qualification 468 n.
escapable *avoidable* 620 adj.
escapade *foolery* 497 n.
 whim 604 n.
 revel 837 n.
 revel 837 n.
excape *decrement* 42 n.
 decamp 296 vb.
 outflow 298 n.
 flow out 298 vb.
 outlet, egress 298 n.
 run away 620 vb.
 seek safety 660 vb.
 escape 667 n., vb.
 deliverance 668 n.
 achieve liberty 746 vb.
 dutilessness 918 n.
escape clause
 qualification 468 n.
 conditions 766 n.
escapee *wanderer* 268 n.
 escaper 667 n.
 free man 744 n.
escape notice
 be unseen 444 vb.
 escape notice 456 vb.
 elude 667 vb.
escapism *fantasy* 513 n.
 avoidance 620 n.
 escape 667 n.
 fear 854 n.
 non-liability 919 n.
escapist *visionary* 513 n.
 avoider 620 n.
escapology *escape* 667 n.
escarpment
 high land 209 n.
 acclivity 220 n.
escharotic *keen* 174 adj.
eschatology *finality* 69 n.
escheat *revert* 148 vb.
 penalty 963 n.
eschew *avoid* 620 vb.
 dislike 861 vb.
escort
 accompaniment 89 n.
 concomitant 89 n.
 carry 273 vb.
 protection 660 n.
 direct 689 vb.
 defender 713 n.
 keeper 749 n.
 take away 786 vb.

lover 887 n.
court 889 vb.
escritoire *cabinet* 194 n.
esculent *edible* 301 adj.
escutcheon *heraldry* 547 n.
esoteric *private* 80 adj.
  unintelligible 517 adj.
  occult 523 adj.
  retained 778 adj.
  sorcerous 983 adj.
  occultist 984 n.
esoterism *latency* 523 n.
  secret 530 n.
  occultism 984 n.
espadrilles *footwear* 228 n.
espalier *fence* 235 n.
especial (*see* special)
especially
  eminently 34 adv.
  specially 80 adv.
Esperanto
  language 557 n.
espial *inspection* 438 n.
  discovery 484 n.
espionage
  secret service 459 n.
esplanade
  horizontality 216 n.
  path 624 n.
espousal *promise* 764 n.
  compact 765 n.
  love affair 887 n.
  wedding 894 n.
espouse *choose* 605 vb.
  patronize 703 vb.
  co-operate 706 vb.
  marry 894 vb.
esprit *intelligence* 498 n.
  wit 839 n.
esprit de corps
  prejudice 481 n.
  co-operation 706 n.
  sociality 882 n.
esprit d'escalier
  sequel 67 n.
  thought 449 n.
  wit 839 n.
espy *see* 438 vb.
esquire *male* 372 n.
  title 870 n.
essay *experiment* 461 n.
  reading matter 589 n.
  article 591 n.
  dissertation 591 n.
  essay 671 n., vb.
  undertaking 672 n.
  action 766 n.
  be active 678 vb.
  exert oneself 682 vb.
essayist *author* 589 n.
  dissertator 591 n.

esse *existence* 1 n.
essence *essence* 1 n.
  essential part 5 n.
  main part 32 n.
  product 164 n.
  form 243 n.
  extraction 304 n.
  odour 394 n.
  meaning 514 n.
  goodness 644 n.
  perfection 646 n.
  cosmetic 843 n.
  theosophy 984 n.
essence, in *actually* 1 adv.
Essenes
  non-Christian sect 978 n.
essential *real* 1 adj.
  existing 1 adj.
  intrinsic 5 adj.
  absolute 32 adj.
  requirement 627 n.
  chief thing 638 n.
essentiality
  substantiality 3 n.
  needfulness 627 n.
  importance 638 n.
essentially
  actually 1 adv.
  substantially 3 adv.
  intrinsically 5 adv.
  wholly 52 adv.
essential oils
  prophylactic 658 n.
establish *auspicate* 68 vb.
  perpetuate 115 vb.
  stabilize 153 vb.
  produce 164 vb.
  place 187 vb.
  corroborate 466 vb.
  demonstrate 478 vb.
  dower 777 vb.
  make legal 953 vb.
established
  immemorial 127 adj.
  permanent 144 adj.
  vested 153 adj.
  usual 610 adj.
  prosperous 730 adj.
  proprietary 777 adj.
establishment
  beginning 68 n.
  band 74 n.
  fixture 153 n.
  production 164 n.
  location 187 n.
  demonstration 478 n.
  bigwig 638 n.
  corporation 708 n.
  shop 796 n.
Establishment, the
  influence 178 n.

master 741 n.
  upper class 868 n.
estafette *courier* 531 n.
estaminet *tavern* 192 n.
estate *state* 7 n.
  territory 184 n.
  land 344 n.
  farm 370 n.
  estate, lands 777 n.
estate-car
  automobile 274 n.
estate for life *dower* 777 n.
estate for years *dower* 777 n.
esteem *opine* 485 vb.
  repute, prestige 866 n.
  respect 920 n., vb.
  approbation 923 n.
estimable *excellent* 644 adj.
  approvable 923 adj.
estimate *do sums* 86 vb.
  cognize 447 vb.
  discriminate 463 vb.
  measurement 465 n.
  estimate 480 n., vb.
  expectation 507 n.
  report 524 n.
  price 809 vb.
estimation
  measurement 465 n.
  estimate 480 n.
  (*see* esteem)
estival *warm* 379 adj.
estop *obstruct* 702 vb.
estoppel *hindrance* 702 n.
estrange *set apart* 46 vb.
  make quarrels 709 vb.
  not retain 779 vb.
  make enemies 881 vb.
  excite hate 888 vb.
estrangement
  seclusion 883 n.
  (*see* estrange)
estrapade *foin* 712 n.
estuary *open space* 263 n.
  gulf 345 n.
esurient *hungry* 859 adj.
étatism *despotism* 733 n.
et cetera
  in addition 38 adv.
  including 78 adv.
  et cetera 101 adv.
etch *outline* 233 vb.
  groove 262 vb.
  mark 547 vb.
  engrave 555 vb.
etcher *engraver* 556 n.
etching
  representation 551 n.
  engraving 555 n.
  ornamental art 844 n.
eternal *lasting* 113 adj.

unceasing 146 adj.
  (*see* eternity)
eternalize, eternize
  perpetuate 115 vb.
  honour 866 vb.
eternal triangle
  illicit love 951 n.
eternity *existence* 1 n.
  infinity 107 n.
  neverness 109 n.
  perpetuity 115 n.
  immateriality 320 n.
  divine attribute 965 n.
  heaven 971 n.
eternity ring
  jewellery 844 n.
  love-token 889 n.
ether *heavens* 321 n.
  levity 323 n.
  rarity 325 n.
  gas 336 n.
  anæsthetic 375 n.
ethereal *light* 323 adj.
  rare 325 adj.
ethereal body
  spiritualism 984 n.
etherial (*see* ethereal)
ethics *morals* 917 n.
  virtue 933 n.
ethnarch *governor* 741 n.
ethnic *ethnic* 11 adj.
  human 371 adj.
ethnic group *race* 11 n.
ethnic type *mankind* 371 n.
ethnology
  anthropology 371 n.
ethos *character* 5 n.
  conduct 688 n.
etiolation
  achromatism 426 n.
  whiteness 427 n.
etiolin *green pigment* 432 n.
etiology *attribution* 158 n.
  science 490 n.
  pathology 651 n.
etiquette *conformity* 83 n.
  practice 610 n.
  etiquette 848 n.
  formality 875 n.
Eton crop *shortening* 204 n.
  hair-dressing 843 n.
Eton-jacket *tunic* 228 n.
étourderie *inattention* 456 n.
  unskilfulness 695 n.
étude *musical piece* 412 n.
étui *case* 194 n.
etymology *source* 156 n.
  efformation 243 n.
  linguistics 557 n.
  etymology 559 n.
etymon *source* 156 n.

word 559 n.
Eucharist
  Holy Communion 988 n.
Euchites
  non-Christian sect 978 n.
euchologion
  office-book 988 n.
euchology
  office-book 988 n.
euchre *overmaster* 727 vb.
  card game 837 n.
eugenics *biology* 358 n.
  civilization 654 n.
euhemerism
  reasoning 475 n.
  interpretation 520 n.
  irreligion 974 n.
eulogist *commender* 923 n.
eulogy *description* 590 n.
  praise 923 n.
eunuch *eunuch* 161 n.
  slave 742 n.
eupepsia *health* 650 n.
euphemism
  underestimation 483 n.
  trope 519 n.
  falsehood 541 n.
  ornament 574 n.
  good taste 846 n.
  affectation 850 n.
  flattery 924 n.
  prudery 950 n.
euphemist
  phrasemonger 574 n.
euphemize *moderate* 177 vb.
  underestimate 483 vb.
  cant 541 vb.
  ornament 547 vb.
  be affected 850 vb.
euphonious (*see* euphony)
euphonium *horn* 414 n.
euphony *melody* 410 n.
  elegance 575 n.
euphoria *euphoria* 376 n.
  health 650 n.
  palmy days 730 n.
  happiness 824 n.
  content 828 n.
euphuism *trope* 519 n.
  ornament 574 n.
  affectation 850 n.
euphuist
  phrasemonger 574 n.
  affector 850 n.
Eurasian *hybrid* 43 n.
eurhythmics
  education 534 n.
  exercise 862 n.
  dancing 837 n.
eurhythmy *symmetry* 245 n.
euripus *narrowness* 206 n.

gulf 345 n.
Europeanize
  transform 147 vb.
euthanasia *decease* 361 n.
  killing 362 n.
  euphoria 376 n.
euthenics *civilization* 654 n.
Eutychianism *heresy* 977 n.
evacuate *be absent* 190 vb.
  go away 190 vb.
  decamp 296 vb.
evacuation *recession* 290 n.
  egress 298 n.
  voidance 300 n.
  cacation 302 n.
  relinquishment 621 n.
evacuee *outcaste* 883 n.
evade *sophisticate* 477 vb.
  be stealthy 525 vb.
  avoid 620 vb.
  elude 667 vb.
  not observe 769 vb.
  fail in duty 918 vb.
evagation *deviation* 282 n.
evaginate *invert* 221 vb.
evaluate *class* 62 vb.
  appraise 465 vb.
  estimate 480 vb.
evanescence
  transientness 114 n.
  disappearance 446 n.
evanescent
  inconsiderable 33 adj.
evangel *news* 529 n.
evangelic
  revelational 975 adj.
evangelical
  revelational 975 adj.
  orthodox 976 adj.
  sectarian 978 adj.
evangelist *preacher* 537 n.
  religious teacher 973 n.
  pastor 986 n.
evangelistic
  scriptural 975 adj.
evangelize *convert* 147 vb.
  convince 485 vb.
evaporate *not be* 2 vb.
  decrease 37 vb.
  be dispersed 75 vb.
  be transient 114 vb.
  destroy 165 vb.
  become small 198 vb.
  vaporize 338 vb.
  dry 343 vb.
  disappear 446 vb.
  waste 634 vb.
evaporation *loss* 772 n.
  (*see* evaporate)
evaporator *drier* 342 n.
evasion *sophistry* 477 n.

concealment 525 n.
falsehood 541 n.
mental dishonesty 543 n.
pretext 614 n.
avoidance 620 n.
escape 667 n.
stratagem 698 n.
evasive equivocal 518 adj.
reticent 525 adj.
untrue 543 adj.
evasive action
avoidance 620 n.
eve precursor 66 n.
priority 119 n.
evening 129 n.
evection
derangement 63 n.
even uniform 16 adj.
equal 28 adj.
regular 81 adj.
numerical 85 adj.
evening 129 n.
periodical 141 adj.
flatten 216 vb.
symmetrical 245 adj.
straight 249 adj.
smooth 258 adj., vb.
inexcitable 823 adj.
even date present time 121 n.
even-handed just 913 adj.
evening end 69 n.
period 110 n.
evening 129 n.
obscuration 418 n.
half-light 419 n.
evening dress
formal dress 228 n.
even keel
equilibrium 28 n.
even money
equivalence 28 n.
even-sided equal 28 adj.
symmetrical 245 adj.
even so
nevertheless 468 adv.
Evensong evening 129 n.
public worship 981 n.
church service 988 n.
event reality 1 n.
occasion 137 n.
eventuality 154 n.
appearance 445 n.
contest 716 n.
even temper
inexcitability 823 n.
even tenor uniformity 16 n.
order 60 n.
eventful
circumstantial 8 adj.
eventful 154 adj.
notable 638 adj.

eventual future 124 adj.
eventual 154 adj.
eventuality juncture 8 n.
futurity 124 n.
occasion 137 n.
eventuality 154 n.
chance 159 n.
appearance 445 n.
eventually
prospectively 124 adv.
eventually 154 adv.
in the future 155 adv.
consequently 157 adv.
eventuate happen 154 vb.
result 157 vb.
appear 445 vb.
ever and ever
forever 115 adv.
everglade marsh 347 n.
evergreen continuous 71 adj.
lasting 113 adj.
perpetual 115 adj.
new 126 adj.
young 130 adj.
unchangeable 153 adj.
unyielding 162 adj.
vegetal 366 adj.
renowned 866 adj.
everlasting
perpetual 115 adj.
godlike 965 adj.
ever less diminuendo 37 adv.
evermore forever 115 adv.
ever since all along 113 adv.
eversion change 143 n.
inversion 221 n.
evolution 316 n.
ever so greatly 32 adv.
evert modify 143 vb.
every universal 79 adj.
everybody medley 43 n.
all 52 n.
everyman 79 n.
mankind 371 n.
every day often 139 adv.
everyday typical 83 adj.
plain 573 adj.
usual 610 adj.
everyday language
prose 593 n.
every excuse
vindication 927 n.
innocence 935 n.
every inch wholly 52 adj.
completely 54 adv.
everyman
prototype 23 n.
common man 30 n.
everyman 79 n.
person 371 n.
mediocrity 732 n.

commoner 869 n.
everyone (see everybody)
every other
sequent 65 adj.
by turns 141 adv.
every side, on
around 230 adv.
every so often
sometimes 139 adv.
at intervals 201 adv.
every tongue, on
renowned 866 adj.
every way
completely 54 adv.
everywhere space 183 n.
widely 183 adv.
here 189 adv.
eviction ejection 300 n.
loss 772 n.
expropriation 786 n.
evidence
evidence 466 n., vb.
make likely 471 vb.
demonstrate 478 vb.
mean 514 vb.
manifest 522 vb.
indication 547 n.
trace 548 n.
legal trial 959 n.
evidence against
counter-evidence 467 n.
evident visible 443 adj.
certain 473 adj.
demonstrated 478 adj.
manifest 522 adj.
evidential
evidential 466 adj.
evil evil 616 n.
harmful 645 adj.
bane 659 n.
adversity 731 n.
suffering 825 n.
wickedness 934 n.
evil day adversity 731 n.
evildoer evildoer 904 n.
bad man 938 n.
evil eye look 438 n.
hatred 888 n.
malediction 899 n.
spell 983 n.
evil hour
intempestivity 138 n.
evil-minded wicked 934 adj.
evil-speaking
scurrility 899 n.
detraction 926 n.
impiety 980 n.
evil spirit sorcerer 983 n.
evil star badness 645 n.
ill fortune 731 n.
evince evidence 466 vb.

demonstrate 478 vb.
manifest 522 vb.
indicate 547 vb.
eviscerate *void* 300 vb.
extract 304 vb.
impair 655 vb.
evitable *possible* 469 adj.
evocation
causation 156 n.
remembrance 505 n.
representation 551 n.
description 590 n.
excitation 821 n.
evoke *incite* 612 vb.
(*see* evocation)
evolution *existence* 1 n.
numerical operation 86 n.
conversion 147 n.
production 164 n.
motion 265 n.
progression 285 n.
circuition 314 n.
evolution 316 n.
biology 358 n.
improvement 654 n.
action 676 n.
evolutionary
evolving 316 adj.
biological 358 adj.
evolutionist *biology* 358 n.
evolve *become* 1 vb.
result 157 vb.
extract 304 vb.
evolve 316 vb.
(*see* evolution)
evolved from
caused 157 adj.
evulsion *extraction* 304 n.
ewe *sheep* 365 n.
female animal 373 n.
ewe-lamb *youngling* 132 n.
ewer *vessel* 194 n.
water 339 n.
ablution 648 n.
ex *prior* 119 adj.
exacerbate *augment* 36 vb.
make violent 176 vb.
impair 655 vb.
hurt 827 vb.
aggravate 832 vb.
make enemies 881 vb.
excite hate 888 vb.
exact *lifelike* 18 adj.
definite 80 adj.
careful 457 adj.
accurate 494 adj.
veracious 540 adj.
perspicuous 567 adj.
concise 569 adj.
demand 737 vb.
observant 768 adj.

levy 786 vb.
right 913 adj.
impose a duty 917 vb.
exacting *fatiguing* 684 adj.
difficult 700 adj.
oppressive 735 adj.
discontented 829 adj.
greedy 859 adj.
fastidious 862 adj.
exaction *demand* 737 n.
compulsion 740 n.
taking 786 n.
tax 809 n.
undueness 916 n.
exactitude (*see* exactness)
exactness *carefulness* 457 n.
accuracy 494 n.
perspicuity 567 n.
right 913 n.
exaggerate
misinterpret 521 vb.
make important 638 vb.
be affected 850 vb.
(*see* exaggeration)
exaggerated
exorbitant 32 adj.
exaggeration *greatness* 32 n.
increase 36 n.
expansion 197 n.
overstepping 306 n.
overestimation 482 n.
absurdity 497 n.
ideality 513 n.
misinterpretation 521 n.
untruth 543 n.
exaggeration 546 n.
misrepresentation 552 n.
magniloquence 574 n.
redundance 637 n.
ostentation 857 n.
boast 877 n.
exalt *augment* 36 vb.
elevate 310 vb.
make important 638 vb.
respect 920 vb.
praise 923 vb.
exaltation
elevation 310 n.
warm feeling 818 n.
joy 824 n.
piety 979 n.
exalted *great* 32 adj.
high 209 adj.
notable 638 adj.
noble 868 adj.
exaltedness *prestige* 866 n.
examination
meditation 449 n.
attention 455 n.
enquiry 459 n
exam 459 n.

experiment 461 n.
dissertation 591 n.
legal trial 959 n.
examination-in-chief
interrogation 459 n.
examination paper
question 459 n.
examine *scan* 438 vb.
interrogate 459 vb.
examinee *respondent* 460 n.
exam 459 n.
testee 461 n.
beginner 538 n.
contender 716 n.
examiner *listener* 415 n.
spectator 441 n.
inquisitor 453 n.
enquirer 459 n.
estimator 480 n.
interlocutor 584 n.
example *relevance* 9 n.
non-imitation 21 n.
duplicate 22 n.
prototype 23 n.
part 53 n.
precursor 66 n.
rule 81 n.
example 83 n.
exhibit 522 n.
warning 664 n.
exanimate *dead* 361 adj.
inactive 679 adj.
exarch *governor* 741 n.
ecclesiarch 986 n.
exarchate
church office 985 n.
exasperate
make violent 176 vb.
aggravate 832 vb.
excite hate 888 vb.
enrage 891 vb.
ex cathedra
assertive 532 adj.
affirmatively 532 adv.
ex cathedra utterance
certainty 473 n.
excavation
excavation 255 n.
extraction 304 n.
search 459 n.
execate *blind* 439 adj., vb.
exceed *be great* 32 vb.
be superior 34 vb.
grow 36 vb.
overstep, outdo 306 vb.
be intemperate 943 vb.
exceeding
exorbitant 32 adj.
excel *have repute* 866 vb.
excellence *superiority* 34 n.
precedence 64 n.

importance 638n.
goodness 644n.
skill 694n.
good taste 846n.
virtues 933n.
Excellence, Excellency
sovereign 741n.
title 870n.
excellent *great* 32adj.
supreme 34adj.
perfect 646adj.
splendid 841adj.
exceller *exceller* 644n.
excelsior *up* 308adv.
type size 587n.
except *if* 8adv.
subtract 39vb.
in deduction 39adv.
exclusive of 57adv.
(*see* exception)
exception
non-uniformity 17n.
separation 46n.
exclusion 57n.
speciality 80n.
unconformity 84n.
qualification 468n.
rejection 607n.
deprecation 762n.
conditions 766n.
disapprobation 924n.
exceptionable
blameworthy 924adj.
exceptional
non-uniform 17adj.
disagreeing 25adj.
remarkable 32adj.
extraneous 59adj.
exceptionally
greatly 32adv.
exceptious *irascible* 892adj.
excerpt *part* 53n.
edition 589n.
abstract 592vb.
select 605vb.
excerpta, excerpts
anthology 592n.
choice 605n.
excess *superiority* 34n.
exaggeration 546n.
inelegance 576n.
redundance 637n.
overactivity 678n.
scope 744n.
satiety 863n.
cruel act 898n.
intemperance 943n.
excessive *exorbitant* 32adj.
surpassing 306adj.
exaggerated 546adj.
pleonastic 570adj.

inelegant 576adj.
superfluous 637adj.
redundant 637adj.
dear 811adj.
cruel 898adj.
unwarranted 916adj.
intemperate 943adj.
excessively
extremely 32adv.
exchange *correlation* 12n.
equivalence 28n.
focus 76n.
substitution 150n.
interchange 151n., vb.
interlocution 584n.
bourse 618n.
transfer 780n.
barter, trade 791vb.
mart 796n.
finance 797n.
exchange, in
in exchange 151adv.
exchange views
compare 462vb.
exchequer *storage* 632n.
treasury 799n.
excise *subtract* 39vb.
tax 809n.
exciseman *receiver* 782n.
excision *subtraction* 39n.
excitable
impressible 819adj.
excited 821adj.
excitable 822adj.
irascible 892adj.
excitant
stimulant 174n.
excitant 821n.
aggravation 832n.
excitation (*see* excite)
excite *cause* 156vb.
strengthen 162vb.
operate 173vb.
invigorate 174vb.
make violent 176vb.
cause feeling 374vb.
itch 378vb.
incite 612vb.
excite 821vb.
delight 826vb.
aggravate 832vb.
excite love 887vb.
excitement
stimulation 174n.
excitation 821n.
exciting *pleasurable* 826adj.
exclaim *cry* 408vb.
voice 577vb.
disapprove 924vb.
exclamation *cry* 408n.
voice 577n.

wonder 864n.
exclamation mark
punctuation 547n.
exclave *region* 184n.
exclude *bate* 37vb.
disregard 458vb.
make impossible 470vb.
obstruct 702vb.
restrain 747vb.
depose 752vb.
prohibit 757vb.
refuse 760vb.
(*see* exclusion)
excluded *extraneous* 59adj.
displaced 188adj.
impossible 470adj.
exclusion *separation* 46n.
exclusion 57n.
unconformity 84n.
exteriority 223n.
ejection 300n.
rejection 607n.
non-ownership 774n.
seclusion 883n.
unsociability 883n.
(*see* exclude)
exclusive *unmixed* 44adj.
private 80adj.
unconformable 84adj.
excellent 644adj.
sectional 708adj.
sectarian 978adj.
exclusiveness
contrariety 14n.
particularism 80n.
sectarianism 978n.
exclusivity
restriction 747n.
excogitation *thought* 449n.
meditation 449n.
ideality 513n.
excommunicate
exclude 57vb.
prohibit 757vb.
make unwelcome 883vb.
curse 899vb.
condemn 961vb.
perform ritual 988vb.
excommunicated
cursed 899adj.
schismatical 978adj.
excoriation
uncovering 229n.
excrement, excreta
excrement 302n.
dirt 649n.
excrementitious
unclean 649adj.
excrescence *swelling* 253n.
superfluity 637n.
blemish 845n.

excrescent *useless* 641 adj.
excretion *ejection* 300 n.
voidance 300 n.
excretion 302 n.
excruciate *give pain* 377 vb.
torment 827 vb.
excruciating *painful* 377 adj.
exculpable *guiltless* 935 adj.
exculpation
forgiveness 909 n.
non-liability 919 n.
vindication 927 n.
acquittal 960 n.
excursion *land travel* 267 n.
overstepping 306 n.
pleonasm 570 n.
enjoyment 824 n.
amusement 837 n.
excursionist
traveller 268 n.
reveller 837 n.
excursive
deviating 282 adj.
prolix 570 adj.
excursus *pleonasm* 570 n.
dissertation 591 n.
excusable *forgiven* 908 adj.
vindicable 927 adj.
guiltless 935 adj.
excuse *exclude* 57 vb.
reason why 156 n.
disregard 458 vb.
qualify 468 vb.
mental dishonesty 543 n.
pretext 614 n.
strategem 698 n.
liberate 746 vb.
forgiveness 909 n.
non-liability 919 n.
vindication 927 n.
extenuate 927 vb.
execrable *bad* 645 adj.
execrate *curse* 899 vb.
dispraise 924 vb.
execration *hatred* 888 n.
malediction 899 n.
reproach 924 n.
executant *musician* 413 n.
doer 676 n.
execution *killing* 362 n.
action 676 n.
effectuation 725 n.
capital punishment 963 n.
executive *agent* 686 n.
directing 689 adj.
manager 690 n.
executor *doer* n. 676 n.
agent 686 n.
manager 690 n.
exegesis
interpretation 520 n.

exemplar *prototype* 23 n.
example 83 n.
exemplary *typical* 33 adj.
excellent 644 adj.
exemplify
exemplify 83 adj.
exempt *liberate* 746 vb.
exemption
exclusion 57 n.
permission 756 n.
non-liability 919 n.
exercise *train* 534 vb.
function 622 vb.
prepare oneself 669 vb.
use 673 n., vb.
deed 676 n.
exercise 682 n.
incommode 827 vb.
exercitation
teaching 534 n.
(see exercise)
exergue *edging* 234 n.
exert *use* 673 vb.
exertion *power* 160 n.
vigorousness 174 n.
perseverance 600 n.
essay 671 n.
action 676 n.
exertion 682 n.
fatigue 684 n.
difficulty 700 n.
contest 716 n.
exfoliation
uncovering 229 n.
egress 298 n.
exhalation *gas* 336 n.
exhale *exude* 298 vb.
emit 300 vb.
vaporize 338 vb.
breathe 352 vb.
smell 394 vb.
exhaust *bate* 37 vb.
disable 161 vb.
make smaller 198 vb.
outlet 298 n.
rarefy 325 vb.
sufflate 352 vb.
waste 634 n., vb.
make insufficient 636 vb.
impair 655 vb.
fatigue 684 vb.
levy 786 vb.
exhaustion
helplessness 161 n.
weakness 163 n.
(see exhaust)
exhaustive
complete 54 adj.
exhaust pipe *outlet* 298 n.
sufflation 352 n.
exhibit *evidence* 466 n.

exhibit 522 n.
show 522 vb.
advertisement 528 n.
indicate 547 vb.
be ostentatious 875 vb.
exhibition *spectacle* 445 n.
appearance 445 n.
foolery 497 n.
manifestation 522 n.
collection 632 n.
mart 796 n.
receipt 807 n.
reward 962 n.
exhibitioner
college student 538 n.
recipient 782 n.
exhibitionism
inelegance 576 n.
vanity 873 n.
impurity 951 n.
exhibitionist
vain person 873 n.
showy 875 adj.
exhibitor *exhibitor* 522 n.
exhilarate *excite* 821 vb.
delight 826 vb.
cheer 833 vb.
inebriate 949 vb.
exhilarated *pleased* 824 adj.
drunk 949 adj.
exhilaration
excitable state 822 n.
(see exhilarate)
exhort *incite* 612 vb.
advise 691 vb.
exhortation *oration* 579 n.
inducement 612 n.
exhumation *inquest* 364 n.
exhume *look back* 125 vb.
exhume 364 vb.
ex hypothesi
supposedly 512 adv.
exigence
needfulness 627 n.
predicament 700 n.
desire 859 n.
exigent *demanding* 627 adj.
oppressive 735 adj.
discontented 829 adj.
exiguity *smallness* 33 n.
fewness 105 n.
littleness 196 n.
shortness 204 n.
exile *exclusion* 57 n.
displacement 188 n.
egress 298 n.
ejection 300 n.
seclusion 883 n.
outcaste 883 n.
penalty 963 n.
exilic *scriptural* 975 adj.

exility *thinness* 206n.
eximious *excellent* 644adj.
exist *be* 1vb.
  be present 189vb.
  live 360vb.
  be true 494vb.
existence *existence* 1n.
  essence 1n.
  presence 189n.
  life 360n.
existential *existing* 1adj.
existentialism
  existence 1n.
  philosophy 449n.
exit *doorway* 263n.
  departure 296n.
  egress, *outlet* 298n.
  decease 361n.
  disappearance 446n.
  dramaturgy 594n.
  means of escape 667n.
exode *stage play* 594n.
exodos *dramaturgy* 594n.
exodus *departure* 296n.
  egress 298n.
ex officio *in control* 689adv.
  authoritative 733adj.
  duly 915adv.
exogenous *exterior* 223adj.
  vegetal 366adj.
exomologesis
  penitence 939n.
  Christian rite 988n.
exoneration
  forgiveness 909n.
  non-liability 919n.
  vindication 927n.
  acquittal 960n.
exorability *mercy* 905n.
  forgiveness 909n.
exorbitance *greatness* 32n.
  exaggeration 546n.
  redundance 637n.
  dearness 811n.
exorbitant *huge* 195adj.
  deviating 282adj.
  surpassing 306adj.
exorbitation *deviation* 282n.
exorcism *malediction* 899n.
  prayers 981n.
  sorcery 983n.
  Christian rite 988n.
exorcist *sorcerer* 983n.
  cleric 986n.
exorcize *eject* 300vb.
  dismiss 300vb.
  practise sorcery 983vb.
exordium *prelude* 66n.
  beginning 68n.
exosmose *passage* 305n.
exostosis *swelling* 253n.

exoteric *undisguised* 522adj.
  published 528adj.
exotic *irrelation* 10n.
  dissimilar 19adj.
  extraneous 59adj.
  unconformable 84adj.
  flower 366n.
  horticultural 370adj.
expand *add* 38vb.
  lengthen 203vb.
  be broad 205vb.
  progress 285vb.
  rarefy 325vb.
  exaggerate 546vb.
  (*see* expansion)
expanse *greatness* 32n.
  space 183n.
  size 195n.
  breadth 205n.
expansion *increase* 36n.
  space 183n.
  expansion 197n.
  diffuseness 570n.
expansionism *ingress* 297n.
  overstepping 306n.
  nation 371n.
  bellicosity 718n.
  governance 733n.
expansionist *militarist* 722n.
expansive *spacious* 183adj.
  expanded 197adj.
  broad 205adj.
expatiate *be diffuse* 570vb.
  be loquacious 581vb.
  speak 579vb.
expatriate *exclude* 57vb.
  foreigner 59n.
  eject 300vb.
  outcaste 883n.
expatriation *egress* 298n.
  seclusion 883n.
expect *look ahead* 124vb.
  assume 471vb.
  expect 507vb.
  intend 617vb.
  hope 852vb.
  desire 859vb.
  not wonder 865vb.
  have a right 915vb.
expectance
  expectation 507n.
expectant *future* 124adj.
  attentive 455adj.
  expectant 507adj.
  petitioner 763n.
  beneficiary 776n.
  hoper 852n.
expectation *destiny* 155n.
  probability 471n.
  dubiety 474n.
  belief 485n.

expectation 507n.
  hope 852n.
expectations *dueness* 915n.
expected *future* 124adj.
expected, as
  probably 471adv.
  duly 915adv.
expecting
  productive 164adj.
expectorant
  cathartic 658n.
expectorate *eruct* 300vb.
expectoration
  excretion 302n.
expectoratory
  disapproving 924adj.
expedience *fitness* 24n.
  utility 640n.
  expedience 642n.
  right 913n.
expedient *opportune* 137adj.
  operative 173adj.
  possible 469adj.
  wise 498adj.
  contrivance 623n.
  instrument 628n.
  means 629n.
expedite *be early* 135vb.
  accelerate 277vb.
  hasten 680vb.
expedition *land travel* 267n.
  velocity 277n.
  activity 678n.
  haste 680n.
  warfare 718n.
expel *impel* 279n.
  propel 287vb.
  reject 607vb.
  make unwelcome 883vb.
  (*see* expulsion)
expellee *outcaste* 883n.
expend
  dispose of 673vb.
  pay 804vb.
  expend 806vb.
expendable
  superfluous 637adj.
  unimportant 639adj.
  useless 641adj.
expenditure *waste* 634n.
  loss 772vb.
  purchase 792n.
  expenditure 806n.
  cost 809n.
expense (*see* expenditure)
expense account
  earnings 771n.
  gift 781n.
  reward 962n.
expensive *dear* 811adj.
  ostentatious 875adj.

experience *meet with* 154 vb.
  empiricism 461 n.
  knowledge 490 n.
  wisdom 498 n.
  skill 694 n.
  feel 818 vb.
experienced
  matured 669 adj.
  expert 694 adj.
  cautious 858 adj.
experiences
  biography 590 n.
experiment
  be curious 453 vb.
  enquire 459 vb.
  experiment 461 n., vb.
  demonstration 478 n.
  gambling 618 n.
  preparation 669 n.
  essay 671 n., vb.
experimental *new* 126 adj.
  experimental 461 adj.
  speculative 618 adj.
  cautious 858 adj.
experimentalist
  experimenter 461 n.
experimentation
  experiment 461 n.
experimenter
  experimenter 461 n.
  learner 538 n.
  gambler 618 n.
  essayer 671 n.
expert *knowing* 490 adj.
  sage 500 n.
  matured 669 adj.
  adviser 691 n.
  expert 694 adj.
  proficient, expert 696 n.
expertise *skill* 694 n.
expiable *vindicable* 927 adj.
expiation *compensation* 31 n.
  remedy 658 n.
  propitiation 941 n.
  oblation 981 n.
expiration *respiration* 352 n.
expire *end* 69 vb.
  elapse 111 vb.
  die 361 vb.
expired *past* 125 adj.
explain *specify* 80 vb.
  facilitate 701 vb.
explain away *reason* 475 vb.
  confute 479 vb.
  disbelieve 486 vb.
  misteach 535 vb.
explained
  intelligible 516 adj.
explanation
  reason why 156 n.
  attribution 158 n.

answer 460 n.
  discovery 484 n.
  interpretation 520 n.
explanations
  disclosure 526 n.
expletive *pleonasm* 570 n.
  superfluous 637 adj.
  scurrility 899 n.
explicable
  intelligible 516 adj.
explicate *evolve* 316 vb.
explication *evolution* 316 n.
  interpretation 520 n.
explicit *meaningful* 514 adj.
  intelligible 516 adj.
  undisguised 522 adj.
  informative 524 adj.
  perspicuous 567 adj.
explode *break* 46 vb.
  be dispersed 75 vb.
  open 263 vb.
  shoot 287 vb.
  be brittle 330 vb.
  confute 479 vb.
  be active 678 vb.
  miscarry 728 vb.
  (*see* explosion)
exploded *past* 125 adj.
  antiquated 127 adj.
  unbelieved 486 adj.
  erroneous 495 adj.
  disapproved 924 adj.
exploit
  important matter 638 n.
  use 673 vb.
  deed 676 n.
  masterpiece 694 n.
  be skilful 694 vb.
  success 727 n.
  thaumaturgy 864 n.
  prowess 855 n.
exploitation (*see* exploit)
exploration
  land travel 267 n.
  enquiry, search 459 n.
  experiment 461 n.
  discovery 484 n.
exploratory
  precursory 66 adj.
  experimental 461 adj.
explore (*see* exploration)
explored *known* 490 adj.
explorer *precursor* 66 n.
  traveller 268 n.
  inquisitor 453 n.
  enquirer 459 n.
  experimenter 461 n.
  detector 484 n.
explosion *outbreak* 176 n.
  bang 402 n.
  excitable state 822 n.

anger 891 n.
  disapprobation 924 n.
  (*see* explode)
explosive *destroyer* 168 n.
  violent 176 adj.
  propellant 287 n.
  brittle 330 adj.
  combustible 385 adj.
  dangerous 661 adj.
  pitfall 663 n.
  explosive 723 n.
exponent
  numerical element 85 n.
  interpreter 520 n.
  teacher 537 n.
  indication 547 n.
exponential
  numerical 85 adj.
  indicating 547 adj.
export *transference* 272 n.
  egress 298 n.
  eject 300 vb.
  provide 633 vb.
export and import
  trade 791 vb.
exporter *transferrer* 272 n.
  carrier 273 n.
  merchant 794 n.
expose *uncover* 229 vb.
  aerify 340 vb.
  be visible 443 vb.
  confute 479 vb.
  detect 484 vb.
  show 522 vb.
  disclose 526 vb.
  photograph 551 vb.
  satirize 851 vb.
  shame 867 vb.
  dispraise 924 vb.
  defame 926 vb.
  accuse 928 vb.
exposé *description* 590 n.
exposed *defenceless* 161 adj.
  weakened 163 adj.
  liable 180 adj.
  windy 352 adj.
  sentient 374 adj.
  painful 377 adj.
  vulnerable 661 adj.
  subject 745 adj.
expose oneself
  be liable 180 vb.
  face danger 661 vb.
exposition
  musical piece 412 n.
  spectacle 445 n.
  demonstration 478 n.
  interpretation 520 n.
  exhibit 522 n.
  dissertation 591 n.
  mart 796 n.

expositor *interpreter* 520 n.
  teacher 537 n.
  dissertator 591 n.
expository
  interpretive 520 adj.
  informative 524 adj.
  disclosing 526 adj.
  discursive 591 adj.
ex post facto
  subsequently 120 adv.
  retrospectively 125 adv.
expostulate *reprove* 924 vb.
expostulation *dissent* 489 n.
  dissuasion 613 n.
  warning 664 n.
  deprecation 762 n.
exposure *liability* 180 n.
  uncovering 229 n.
  air 340 n.
  homicide 362 n.
  refrigeration 382 n.
  visibility 443 n.
  confutation 479 n.
  discovery 484 n.
  photography 551 n.
  vulnerability 661 n.
  detraction 926 n.
expound *interpret* 520 vb.
  teach 534 vb.
express *definite* 80 adj.
  specify 80 vb.
  efform 243 vb.
  bearer 273 n.
  vehicular 274 adj.
  speeder 277 n.
  extract 304 vb.
  mean 514 vb.
  manifest 522 vb.
  courier 531 n.
  assertive 532 adj.
  affirm 532 vb.
  phrase 563 vb.
  voice 577 vb.
express delivery
  mails 531 n.
expressible *shown* 522 adj.
expression *number* 85 n.
  efformation 243 n.
  musical skill 413 n.
  mien 445 n.
  meaning 514 n.
  manifestation 522 n.
  affirmation 532 n.
  word 559 n.
  phrase 563 n.
  feeling 818 n.
expressionism *art* 551 n.
  school of painting 553 n.
expressionless *still* 266 adj.
  unintelligible 517 adj.
  impassive 820 adj.

expressive
  meaningful 514 adj.
  expressive 516 adj.
  informative 524 adj.
  elegant 575 adj.
  lively 819 adj.
express-way *road* 624 n.
exprobate *curse* 899 vb.
  exprobate 924 vb.
exprobation *reproach* 924 n.
expropriate *convey* 780 vb.
  disentitle 916 vb.
expropriation
  ejection 300 n.
  loss 772 n.
  expropriation 786 n.
  penalty 963 n.
expropriator *taker* 786 n.
expropriatory
  taking 786 adj.
  punitive 963 adj.
expugnable
  vulnerable 661 adj.
expugnation
  victory 727 n.
expulsion *subtraction* 39 n.
  elimination 44 n.
  separation 46 n.
  exclusion 57 n.
  transference 272 n.
  ejection 300 n.
  expropriation 786 n.
  penalty 963 n.
  (*see* expel)
expulsive *propulsive* 287 adj.
  expulsive 300 adj.
expunge *destroy* 165 vb.
  obliterate 550 vb.
expurgate *exclude* 57 vb.
  purify 648 vb.
  impair 655 vb.
expurgation *prudery* 950 n.
Expurgatory Index
  orthodoxism 976 n.
exquisite *painful* 377 adj.
  savoury 390 adj.
  excellent 644 adj.
  pleasurable 826 adj.
  paining 827 adj.
  beautiful 841 adj.
  tasteful 846 adj.
  fop 848 n.
  fashionable 848 adj.
exquisitely *greatly* 32 adv.
exsanguine
  colourless 426 adj.
exsection *extraction* 304 n.
exsuction *extraction* 304 n.
exsufflation *sorcery* 983 n.
extant *existing* 1 adj.
  recorded 548 adj.

extemporaneous
  spontaneous 609 adj.
extempore
  instantaneously 116 adv.
  at present 121 adv.
  suddenly 135 adv.
  incidentally 137 adv.
  extempore 609 adv.
  unreadily 670 adv.
extemporization
  spontaneity 609 n.
extemporize
  compose music 413 vb.
  improvise 609 vb.
  be unprepared 670 vb.
extend *add* 38 vb.
  continuate 71 vb.
  extend 183 vb.
  enlarge 197 vb.
  lengthen 203 vb.
extend to *fill* 54 vb.
  be distant 199 vb.
  be contiguous 202 vb.
extensibility
  expansion 197 n.
extensible *elastic* 328 adj.
extensile *flexible* 327 adj.
  elastic 328 adj.
extension *increase* 36 n.
  adjunct 40 n.
  protraction 113 n.
  continuance 146 n.
  space 183 n.
  expansion 197 n.
  lengthening 203 n.
  (*see* extent)
extensive *extensive* 32 adj.
  spacious 183 adj.
  large 195 adj.
extenso, in *diffusely* 570 adv.
extent *quantity* 26 n.
  degree 27 n.
  greatness 32 n.
  space 183 n.
  size 195 n.
  length 203 n.
  (*see* extension)
extenuate *bate* 37 vb.
  weaken 163 vb.
  moderate 177 vb.
  qualify 468 vb.
  plead 614 vb.
  extenuate 927 vb.
extenuated *lean* 206 adj.
extenuating circumstances
  qualification 468 n.
  vindication 927 n.
extenuation
  vindication 927 n.
exterior *extrinsic* 6 adj.
  separate 46 adj.

exteriority 223 n.
  appearing 445 adj.
  ostentation 875 n.
exteriority
  extraneousness 59 n.
  farness 199 n.
  exteriority 223 n.
exterminate *destroy* 165 vb.
extermination
  extraction 304 n.
  slaughter 362 n.
exterminator *killer* 362 n.
extern *externalize* 223 vb.
  eject 300 vb.
external *extrinsic* 6 adj.
  separate 46 adj.
  exterior 223 adj.
  appearing 445 adj.
externalize
  make extrinsic 6 vb.
  externalize 223 vb.
  materialize 319 vb.
  manifest 522 vb.
external origin, of
  extraneous 59 adj.
externment *ejection* 300 n.
  penalty 963 n.
extinct *extinct* 2 adj.
  past 125 adj.
  dead 361 adj.
  non-active 677 adj.
  inactive 679 adj.
extinction *extinction* 2 n.
  destruction 165 n.
  death 361 n.
  disappearance 446 n.
extinguish *bate* 37 vb.
  suppress 165 vb.
  extinguish 382 vb.
  snuff out 418 vb.
extinguisher
  extinguisher 382 n.
extirpation
  destruction 165 n.
  extraction 304 n.
extol *praise* 923 vb.
  worship 981 vb.
extort *extract* 304 vb.
  oppress 735 vb.
  rob 788 vb.
extortion *compulsion* 740 n.
  expropriation 786 n.
  rapacity 786 n.
  dearness 811 n.
extortionate
  oppressive 735 adj.
  lending 784 adj.
  taking 786 adj.
  dear 811 adj.
  avaricious 816 adj.
  greedy 859 adj.

extortioner *tyrant* 735 n.
  lender 784 n.
  taker 786 n.
extra *increment* 36 n.
  additional 38 adj.
  extra 40 n.
  ingredient 58 adj.
  superfluity 637 n.
  unused 674 adj.
extract *part* 53 n.
  product 164 n.
  uncover 229 vb.
  draw 288 vb.
  eject 300 vb.
  extract 304 vb.
  manifest 522 vb.
  acquire 771 vb.
  take, levy 786 vb.
extraction *subtraction* 39 n.
  genealogy 169 n.
  displacement 188 n.
  transference 272 n.
  extraction 304 n.
  deliverance 668 n.
extractive *extracted* 304 adj.
extradition
  transference 272 n.
  ejection 300 n.
extrajudicial *illegal* 954 adj.
extramarital
  extramarital 951 adj.
extramundane
  immaterial 320 adj.
  divine 965 adj.
extramural *extrinsic* 6 adj.
  exterior 223 adj.
extraneous
  non-uniform 17 adj.
  disagreeing 25 adj.
  separate 46 adj.
  excluded 57 adj.
  extraneous 59 adj.
  unconformable 84 adj.
  exterior 223 adj.
extraneousness
  extrinsicality 6 n.
  irrelation 10 n.
  extraneousness 59 n.
  farness 199 n.
extraordinary *unusual* 84 n.
  wonderful 864 adj.
  noteworthy 866 adj.
extrapolate
  make intrinsic 6 vb.
  externalize 223 vb.
extra-sensory perception
  sense 374 n.
  intellect 447 n.
extratensivity
  extrinsicality 6 n.
extra-territorial

exterior 223 adj.
extra-territoriality
  exteriority 223 n.
  non-liability 919 n.
extra time *protraction* 113 n.
extravagance *foolery* 497 n.
  folly 499 n.
  exaggeration 546 n.
  waste 634 n.
  misuse 675 n.
  expenditure 806 n.
  prodigality 815 n.
  ridiculousness 849 n.
extravagant
  exorbitant 32 adj.
  violent 176 adj.
  deviating 282 adj.
  imaginative 513 adj.
  plenteous 635 adj.
  dear 811 adj.
extravaganza
  musical piece 412 n.
  spectacle 445 n.
  ideality 513 n.
  stage play 594 n.
extravagation
  overstepping 306 n.
extravasation
  outflow 298 n.
  excretion 302 n.
extraversion
  extrinsicality 6 n.
extravert
  extrinsicality 6 n.
  exteriority 223 n.
extreme *exorbitant* 32 adj.
  complete 54 adj.
  ending 69 adj.
  (*see* extremes,
    extremity)
extremely *extremely* 32 adv.
extreme penalty
  capital punishment 963 n.
extremes
  exaggeration 546 n.
  redundance 637 n.
  opposites 704 n.
  severity 735 n.
  cruel act 898 n.
extreme unction
  decease 361 n.
  Christian rite 988 n.
extremism
  exaggeration 546 n.
  reformism 654 n.
extremist *crank* 504 n.
  exaggeration 546 n.
  reformer 654 n.
  opponent 705 n.
  revolter 738 n.
extremities *violence* 176 n.

extremities, in
unprosperous 731 adj.
extremity *adjunct* 40 n.
extremity 69 n.
crisis 137 n.
vertex 213 n.
edge 234 n.
limit 236 n.
rear 238 n.
adversity 731 n.
severity 735 n.
suffering 825 n.
extricate *disencumber* 701 vb.
extrication *extraction* 304 n.
escape 667 n.
deliverance 668 n.
liberation 746 n.
extrinsic *separate* 46 adj.
extrinsicality
extrinsicality 6 n.
extraneousness 59 n.
exteriority 223 n.
extroitive *extrinsic* 6 adj.
extroversion
(*see* extraversion)
extrusion *exclusion* 57 n.
ejection 300 n.
excretion 302 n.
extrusive *expulsive* 300 adj.
exuberance
productiveness 171 n.
diffuseness 570 n.
redundance 637 n.
exuberate *abound* 635 vb.
exudation *outflow* 298 n.
excretion 302 n.
exude *exude* 298 vb.
emit 300 vb.
be wet 341 vb.
exult *vociferate* 408 vb.
rejoice 835 vb.
boast 877 vb.
exultant *jubilant* 833 adj.
exultation *rejoicing* 835 n.
exuviæ *excrement* 302 n.
dirt 649 n.
exuvial *excretory* 302 adj.
ex voto *devotional* 981 adj.
eyas *youngling* 132 n.
eye *orifice* 263 n.
centrality 225 n.
circle 250 n.
eye 438 n.
gaze 438 vb.
watch 441 vb.
surveillance 457 n.
eyeball *eye* 438 n.
eyebrows *hair* 259 n.
eye-catching
well-seen 443 adj.
manifest 522 adj.

eye-disease *blindness* 439 n.
eye for an eye
interchange 151 n.
retaliation 714 n.
revenge 910 n.
eyeful *view* 438 n.
spectacle 445 n.
eyeglass *eyeglass* 442 n.
eyelash *filament* 208 n.
shade 226 n.
hair 259 n.
screen 421 n.
eyeless *crippled* 163 adj.
blind 439 adj.
eyelet *fastening* 47 n.
orifice 263 n.
perforation 263 n.
eyelid *shade* 226 n.
screen 421 n.
eye-opener *discovery* 484 n.
inexpectation 508 n.
prodigy 864 n.
eye-piece *astronomy* 321 n.
transparency 422 n.
optical device 442 n.
eyer *spectator* 441 n.
eye-range *visibility* 443 n.
eye-salve *balm* 658 n.
cosmetic 843 n.
eye-shade *screen* 421 n.
dim sight 440 n.
safeguard 662 n.
eye-shadow *cosmetic* 843 n.
eye-shot *visibility* 443 n.
eyesight *vision* 438 n.
eyes of, in the
apparently 445 adv.
eyes on *attention* 455 n.
surveillance 457 n.
eyes open, with one's
at sight 438 adv.
purposely 617 adv.
eyesore *deformity* 246 n.
eyesore 842 n.
monster 938 n.
eyestrain *dim sight* 440 n.
eye-testing *vision* 438 n.
eye to eye
concordant 710 adj.
eyewash *falsehood* 541 n.
eye-witness *spectator* 441 n.
visibility 443 n.
witness 466 n.
eyrie, eyry *group* 74 n.
nest 192 n.
high structure 209 n.

F

Fabian *reformer* 654 n.
political party 708 n.

Fabianism *continuity* 71 n.
slowness 278 n.
reformism 654 n.
government 733 n.
caution 858 n.
Fabian policy *delay* 136 n.
caution 858 n.
fable *fantasy* 513 n.
metaphor 519 n.
fable 543 n.
narrative 590 n.
describe 590 vb.
fabliau *narrative* 590 n.
fabric *modality* 7 n.
edifice 164 n.
textile 222 n.
structure, texture 331 n.
materials 631 n.
fabricate *compose* 56 vb.
produce 164 vb.
imagine 513 vb.
fake 541 vb.
fabricated
unattested 467 adj.
imaginary 513 adj.
fabrication *production* 164 n.
falsehood 541 n.
untruth 543 n.
fabricator *liar* 545 n.
fabulist *liar* 545 n.
narrator 590 n.
fabulous *unreal* 2 adj.
prodigious 32 adj.
imaginary 513 adj.
untrue 543 adj.
noteworthy 866 adj.
faburden *melody* 410 n.
façade *exteriority* 223 n.
face 237 n.
duplicity 541 n.
face *prepose* 64 vb.
impend 155 vb.
be present 189 vb.
exteriority 223 n.
coat 226 vb.
line 227 vb.
face 237 n.
be opposite 240 vb.
orientate 281 vb.
mien 445 n.
expect 507 vb.
be resolute 599 vb.
withstand 704 vb.
resist 715 vb.
be courageous 855 vb.
prestige 866 n.
insolence 878 n.
face about *revert* 148 vb.
turn round 282 vb.
face both ways
tergiversate 603 vb.

face cream *unguent* 357 n.
  cleanser 648 n.
  balm 658 n.
  cosmetic 843 n.
face death
  face danger 661 vb.
face down *under* 210 adv.
  supine 216 adj.
  inversely 221 adv.
faceless *uniform* 16 adj.
face-lift
  beautification 843 n.
face of it, on the
  externally 223 adv.
  apparently 445 adv.
  manifestly 522 adv.
face powder *powder* 332 n.
  scent 396 n.
  cosmetic 843 n.
facet *exteriority* 223 n.
face the music
  be courageous 855 vb.
face the odds
  be resolute 599 vb.
facetiousness *wit* 839 n.
face to face *in front* 237 adv.
  against 240 adv.
  opposing 704 adj.
face-towel
  cleaning cloth 648 n.
face value *appearance* 445 n.
  price 809 n.
facia *face* 237 n.
facial *exterior* 223 adj.
  beautification 843 n.
facile *easy* 701 adj.
facile princeps
  supreme 34 adj.
facilitate *facilitate* 701 vb.
  aid 703 vb.
  permit 756 vb.
facilities *means* 629 n.
  expedience 642 n.
  facility 701 n.
  aid 703 n.
  scope 744 n.
facility *skill* 694 n.
  facility 701 n.
  aid 703 n.
facing *near* 200 adj.
  facing 226 n.
  opposite 240 adj.
  against 240 adv.
  towards 281 adv.
  opposing 704 adj.
façon de parler *trope* 519 n.
facsimile *identity* 13 n.
  copy 22 n.
fact *reality* 1 n.
  eventuality 154 n.
  evidence 466 n.

certainty 473 n.
  truth 494 n.
  chief thing 638 n.
  (*see* facts)
fact-finding
  enquiring 459 adj.
fact, in *actually* 1 adv.
  positively 32 adj.
faction *disagreement* 25 n.
  part 53 n.
  dissentient 489 n.
  opposition 704 n.
  party 708 n.
  dissension 709 n.
  revolt 738 n.
  sect 978 n.
factionary *opponent* 705 n.
  agitator 738 n.
factionist *schismatic* 978 n.
factiousness
  quarrelsomeness 709 n.
  sectarianism 978 n.
factitious *untrue* 543 adj.
factitive *causal* 156 adj.
factor *part* 53 n.
  component 58 n.
  numerical element 85 n.
  cause 156 n.
  influence 178 n.
  element 319 n.
  agent 686 n.
  manager 690 n.
  consignee 754 n.
  deputy 755 n.
factorize *simplify* 44 vb.
  decompose 51 vb.
factors *circumstance* 8 n.
factorship
  commission 751 n.
factory *workshop* 687 n.
factory-hand *worker* 686 n.
factotum *busy person* 678 n.
  worker 686 n.
  servant 742 n.
facts *evidence* 466 n.
  accuracy 494 n.
  information 524 n.
facts and figures
  accounts 808 n.
factual *real* 1 adj.
  evidential 466 adj.
  certain 473 adj.
  true 494 adj.
  descriptive 590 adj.
facula *sun* 321 n.
faculty *classification* 77 n.
  ability 160 n.
  erudition 490 n.
  teacher 537 n.
  aptitude 694 n.
facundity *eloquence* 579 n.

fad *bias* 481 n.
  eccentricity 503 n.
  insanity 503 n.
  crank 504 n.
  whim 604 n.
  fashion 848 n.
  affectation 850 n.
  liking 859 n.
faddiness *caprice* 604 n.
  discontent 829 n.
faddishness
  eccentricity 503 n.
  caprice 604 n.
faddist *narrow mind* 481 n.
  crank 504 n.
faddy *misjudging* 481 adj.
  crazed 503 adj.
  capricious 604 adj.
fade *shade off* 27 vb.
  decrease 37 vb.
  be transient 114 vb.
  be old 127 vb.
  cease 145 vb.
  be dim 419 vb.
  achromatism 426 n.
  whiten 427 vb.
  be unseen 444 vb.
  disappear 446 vb.
  deteriorate 655 vb.
  make ugly 842 vb.
  lose repute 867 vb.
fade away *end* 69 vb.
  cease 145 vb.
  disappear 446 vb.
faded *dry* 342 n.
  soft-hued 425 adj.
  colourless 426 adj.
fade-out *decrease* 37 n.
  obscuration 418 n.
  disappearance 446 n.
fadge with *accord* 24 vb.
fæces *excrement* 302 n.
  dirt 649 n.
faerie *fairy* 970 n.
fag *tobacco* 388 n.
  beginner 538 n.
  busy person 678 n.
  labour 682 n.
  fatigue 684 vb.
  worker 686 n.
fag-end *remainder* 41 n.
  extremity 69 n.
faggot *bunch* 74 n.
  fuel 385 n.
  materials 631 n.
faience *pottery* 381 n.
fail *be inferior* 35 vb.
  decrease 37 vb.
  lose a chance 138 vb.
  cease 145 vb.
  be weak 163 vb.

fall short 307 vb.
  blunder 495 vb.
  be disappointed 509 vb.
  not suffice 636 vb.
  be useless 641 vb.
  be ill 651 vb.
  deteriorate 655 vb.
  be fatigued 684 vb.
  not complete 726 vb.
  fail 728 vb.
  not observe 769 vb.
  not pay 805 vb.
  fail in duty 918 vb.
  disapprove 924 vb.
failing aged 131 adj.
  imperfection 647 n.
  vice 934 n.
failure inferior 35 n.
  stop 145 n.
  impotence 161 n.
  mistake 495 n.
  insufficiency 636 n.
  lost labour 641 n.
  imperfection 647 n.
  bungling 695 n.
  bungler 697 n.
  hitch 702 n.
  non-completion 726 n.
  failure, loser 728 n.
  ill fortune 731 n.
  non-observance 769 n.
  loss 772 n.
  insolvency 805 n.
  object of scorn 867 n.
  guilty act 936 n.
fain willing 597 adj.
  desiring 859 adj.
fainéant idler 679 n.
  lazy 679 adj.
faint small 33 adj.
  be impotent 161 vb.
  weak 163 adj.
  silent 398 n.
  muted 401 adj.
  dim 419 adj.
  ill-seen 444 adj.
  irresolute 601 adj.
  fatigue 684 n.
  fear 854 vb.
faint-heart waverer 601 n.
faint-heartedness
  irresolution 601 n.
  cowardice 856 n.
faintness faintness 401 n.
  non-resonance 405 n.
  dimness 419 n.
  unintelligibility 517 n.
  fatigue 684 n.
faint praise detraction 926 n.
fair inconsiderable 33 adj.
  dry 342 adj.

warm 379 adj.
  undimmed 417 adj.
  whitish 427 adj.
  rational 475 adj.
  exhibit 522 n.
  not bad 644 adj.
  palmy 730 adj.
  mediocre 732 adj.
  mart 796 n.
  festivity 837 n.
  pleasure ground 837 n.
  a beauty 841 n.
  beautiful 841 adj.
  promising 852 adj.
  just 913 adj.
  honourable 929 adj.
fair chance
  opportunity 137 n.
  fair chance 159 n.
  probability 471 n.
fair comparison
  similarity 18 n.
fair copy copy 22 n.
  script 586 n.
  write 586 vb.
fair-dealing
  honourable 929 adj.
fair exchange
  equivalence 28 n.
fair excuse
  vindication 927 n.
fair field opportunity 137 n.
fair game
  laughing-stock 851 n.
fair-ground arena 724 n.
fair-haired
  whitish 427 adj.
  yellow 433 adj.
fairing gift 781 n.
Fair Isle pattern 844 n.
fair-minded wise 498 adj.
  just 913 adj.
fair name repute 866 n.
fairness beauty 841 n.
  justice 913 n.
  probity 929 n.
fair offer irenics 719 n.
  offer 759 n.
fair play justice 913 n.
fair sex womankind 373 n.
fair shares
  apportionment 783 n.
fair-sized great 32 adj.
  big 195 adj.
fair-spoken
  courteous 884 adj.
fair value
  equivalence 28 n.
  price 809 n.
fairway plain 348 n.
  path 624 n.

fair way, in a
  almost 33 adv.
  tending 179 adj.
  probable 471 adj.
fair weather weather 340 n.
  palmy days 730 n.
fair-weather
  transient 114 adj.
fair-weather friend
  deceiver 545 n.
  flatterer 925 n.
fair words promise 764 n.
  courteous act 884 n.
fairy nonconformist 84 n.
  a beauty 841 n.
  libertine 952 n.
  fairy 970 n.
  sorceress 983 n.
fairy godmother
  patron 707 n.
  benefactor 903 n.
fairyland fantasy 513 n.
  prodigy 864 n.
  fairy 970 n.
fairylike
  fairylike 970 adj.
  magical 983 adj.
fairy-tale fable 543 n.
  narrative 590 n.
fairy wand
  magic instrument 983 n.
fait accompli reality 1 n.
  certainty 473 n.
  completion 725 n.
faith belief 485 n.
  loyalty 739 n.
  observance 768 n.
  hope 852 n.
  probity 929 n.
  disinterestedness 931 n.
  religious faith 973 n.
  orthodoxy 976 n.
  piety 979 n.
faith cure therapy 658 n.
faithful lifelike 18 adj.
  conformable 83 adj.
  true, accurate 494 adj.
  interpretive 520 adj.
  obedient 739 adj.
  observant 768 adj.
  friendly 880 adj.
  trustworthy 929 adj.
  pious 979 adj.
faithfulness conformity 83 n.
  loyalty 739 n.
  probity 929 n.
faithful, the
  church member 976 n.
  pietist 979 n.
  worshipper 981 n.
faith-healer doctor 658 n.

faith-healing
medical art 658 n.
faith, hope, and charity
virtues 933 n.
faithless *perfidious* 930 adj.
irreligious 974 adj.
faithlessness *perfidy* 930 n.
faith, of *credal* 485 adj.
orthodox 976 adj.
fake *imitation* 20 n.
duplicity 541 n.
false 541 adj.
fake 541 vb.
sham 542 n.
spurious 542 adj.
impostor 545 n.
faker *imitator* 20 n.
fakir, faqir *ascetic* 945.
pietist 979 n.
monk 986 n.
Falangists
political party 708 n.
falcated *angular* 247 adj.
curved 248 adj.
falchion *sharp edge* 256 n.
side-arms 723 n.
falcon *bird of prey* 365 n.
heraldry 547 n.
falconer *hunter* 619 n.
falconet *gun* 723 n.
falconry *chase* 619 n.
fal-de-lal *finery* 844 n.
faldstool *seat* 218 n.
fall *decrease* 37 n.
autumn 129 n.
be weak 163 vb.
be destroyed 165 vb.
acclivity 220 n.
deviation 282 n.
regression 286 n.
descent 309 n.
perish 361 vb.
deteriorate 655 vb.
miscarry 728 vb.
adversity 731 n.
cheapness 812 n.
lose repute 867 vb.
be wicked 934 vb.
fallacy *sophism* 477 n.
error 495 n.
deception 542 n.
fall apart
be disjoined 46 vb.
fall asleep *die* 361 vb.
sleep 679 vb.
fall back on
avail of 673 vb.
parry 713 vb.
fall below
not suffice 636 vb.
fall down *descend* 309 vb.

fallen *death roll* 361 n.
unchaste 951 adj.
fallen angel *bad man* 938 n.
devil 969 n.
impious person 980 n.
fallen woman
prostitute 952 n.
fall for *be credulous* 487 vb.
be duped 544 vb.
be in love 887 vb.
fall foul of *collide* 279 vb.
fight 716 vb.
have trouble 731 vb.
fall from grace
relapse 657 vb.
be wicked 934 vb.
fallibility
unreliability 474 n.
misjudgment 481 n.
error 495 n.
unintelligence 499 n.
imperfection 647 n.
fallible *illogical* 477 adj.
fall in *be uniform* 16 vb.
be in order 60 vb.
be brittle 330 vb.
falling off *decrease* 37 n.
deterioration 655 n.
relapse 657 n.
falling sickness *spasm* 318 n.
paralysis 651 n.
falling star *meteor* 321 n.
fall in love
be in love 887 vb.
fall into
be turned to 147 vb.
enter 297 vb.
flow 350 vb.
fall into line
conform 83 vb.
fall into place
be in order 60 vb.
have rank 73 vb.
fall in with *conform* 83 vb.
converge 293 vb.
consent 758 vb.
fall off *be disjoined* 46 vb.
deteriorate 655 vb.
fall on (*see* fall upon)
fall on one's feet
have luck 730 vb.
Fallopian tubes
genitalia 164 n.
fall out *be dispersed* 75 vb.
happen 154 vb.
quarrel 709 vb.
not complete 726 vb.
be inimical 881 vb.
fall-out *nucleonics* 160 n.
radiation 417 n.
insalubrity 653 n.

poison 659 n.
bomb 723 n.
fallow
unproductive 172 adj.
farm 370 n.
yellow 433 adj.
unprepared 670 adj.
fall pat *accord* 24 vb.
fall short *be unequal* 29 vb.
be inferior 35 vb.
be incomplete 55 vb.
fall short 307 vb.
fall through
fall short 307 vb.
(*see* miscarry)
fall to *eat* 301 vb.
undertake 672 vb.
be one's duty 917 vb.
fall to the ground
be confuted 479 vb.
miscarry 728 vb.
fall under *be included* 78 vb.
fall upon *surprise* 508 vb.
attack 712 vb.
false *unreal* 2 adj.
unattested 467 adj.
illogical 477 adj.
erroneous 495 adj.
false 541 adj.
spurious 542 adj.
affected 850 adj.
wrong 914 adj.
unwarranted 916 adj.
flattering 925 adj.
perfidious 930 adj.
false alarm
insubstantial thing 4 n.
false alarm 665 n.
false charge
false charge 928 n.
false colouring
misinterpretation 521 n.
falsehood 541 n.
false colours *sham* 542 n.
false copy
dissimilarity 19 n.
false dawn
precursor 66 n.
misjudgment 481 n.
error 495 n.
disappointment 509 n.
falsehood *error* 495 n.
ideality 513 n.
misteaching 535 n.
falsehood 541 n.
deception 542 n.
improbity 930 n.
false impression *error* 495 n.
false light
visual fallacy 440 n.
error 495 n.

false modesty
  underestimation 483 n.
  (*see* false shame)
false name
  misteaching 535 n.
  misnomer 562 n.
false note *misfit* 25 n.
false position
  predicament 700 n.
false pretensions
  pretension 850 n.
false shame
  affectation 850 n.
false teeth *tooth* 256 n.
falsetto *stridor* 407 n.
  aphony 578 n.
falsification
  imitation 20 n.
falsify *mislead* 495 vb.
  misinterpret 521 vb.
  be false 541 vb.
  be untrue 543 vb.
falsity (*see* false, falsehood)
falter *move slowly* 278 vb.
  be uncertain 474 vb.
  stammer 580 vb.
  be irresolute 601 vb.
  miscarry 728 vb.
fame *greatness* 32 n.
  remembrance 505 n.
  publicity 528 n.
  famousness 866 n.
familiar *interior* 224 adj.
  known 490 adj.
  habitual, usual 610 adj.
  impertinent 878 adj.
  disrespectful 921 adj.
  devil 969 n.
  demon 970 n.
  sorcerer 983 n.
familiarity *knowledge* 490 n.
  habit 610 n.
  friendship 880 n.
  sociality 882 n.
familiarize *know* 490 vb.
  train 534 vb.
family *family* 11 n.
  all 52 n.
  subdivision 53 n.
  breed 77 n.
  genealogy 169 n.
  parental 169 adj.
  posterity 170 n.
  community 708 n.
  nobility 868 n.
family circle *family* 11 n.
  sociality 882 n.
family connection
  consanguinity 11 n.
family likeness
  similarity 18 n.

family man *resident* 191 n.
family tree *series* 71 n.
  list 87 n.
  genealogy 169 n.
family way, in the
  productive 164 adj.
famine *unproductivity* 172 n.
  scarcity 636 n.
  poverty 801 n.
  hunger 859 n.
famish
  be parsimonious 816 vb.
  be hungry 859 vb.
  starve 946 vb.
famous *great* 32 adj.
  known 490 adj.
  well-known 528 adj.
  topping 644 adj.
  renowned 866 adj.
famously *well* 644 adv.
fan *rotator* 315 n.
  aerify 340 vb.
  ventilation 352 n.
  refrigerator 384 n.
  crank 504 n.
  habitué 610 n.
  purify 648 vb.
  refresh 685 vb.
  patron 707 n.
  animate 821 vb.
  relieve 831 vb.
  lover 887 n.
fanatic *doctrinaire* 473 n.
  narrow mind 481 n.
  biased 481 adj.
  crank 504 n.
  opinionist 602 n.
  obstinate 602 adj.
  busy person 678 n.
  lively 819 adj.
  religionist 979 n.
fanatical *positive* 473 adj.
  severe 735 adj.
  excitable 822 adj.
fanatically *extremely* 32 adv.
fanaticism *credulity* 487 n.
  insanity 503 n.
  narrow mind 481 n.
  opiniatry 602 n.
  severity 735 n.
  warm feeling 818 n.
  excitability 822 n.
  pietism 979 n.
fancier *breeder* 369 n.
  expert 696 n.
  desirer 859 n.
fanciful *absurd* 497 adj.
  imaginary 513 adj.
  exaggerated 546 adj.
  capricious 604 adj.
  ridiculous 849 adj.

fancy *think* 449 vb.
  idea 451 n.
  opine 485 vb.
  supposition 512 n.
  imagination 513 n.
  caprice 604 n.
  choice 605 n.
  pugilism 716 n.
  wit 839 n.
  ornamental 844 adj.
  liking 859 n.
  love 887 n.
  darling 890 n.
fancy dress *clothing* 228 n.
  disguise 527 n.
fancy-free *free* 744 adj.
  impassive 820 adj.
  indifferent 860 adj.
  unwedded 895 adj.
fancy-man *libertine* 952 n.
fancy-work
  ornamental art 844 n.
fandango *dance* 837 n.
fane *temple* 990 n.
fanfare *loudness* 400 n.
  celebration 876 n.
fanfaronade
  ostentation 875 n.
  celebration 876 n.
  boast 877 n.
fang *tooth* 256 n.
  bane 659 n.
fangs *governance* 733 n.
  nippers 778 n.
fanlight *window* 263 n.
fanlike *broad* 205 adj.
fannel *vestments* 989 n.
fanny *buttocks* 238 n.
fanon *vestments* 989 n.
fan out *be dispersed* 75 vb.
  expand 197 vb.
  be broad 205 vb.
  diverge 294 vb.
fantan *card game* 837 n.
fantasia
  musical piece 412 n.
fantastic *unusual* 84 adj.
  absurd 497 adj.
  capricious 604 adj.
  ridiculous 849 adj.
  wonderful 864 adj.
fantastical
  insubstantial 4 adj.
  erroneous 495 adj.
  imaginative 513 adj.
fantasy *insubstantiality* 4 n.
  insubstantial thing 4 n.
  visual fallacy 440 n.
  appearance 445 n.
  error 495 n.
  fantasy 513 n.

caprice 604 n.
  pleasurableness 826 n.
  aspiration 852 n.
  desire 859 n.
fantoccini *image* 551 n.
  stage play 594 n.
faquir (*see* fakir)
far *distant* 199 adj.
  afar 199 adv.
far and away
  eminently 34 adv.
far and near *widely* 183 adv.
far and wide *widely* 183 adv.
  afar 199 adv.
far away *afar* 199 adv.
  abstracted 456 adj.
far between *spaced* 201 adj.
farce *foolery* 497 n.
  fable 543 n.
  stage play 594 n.
  trifle 639 n.
  laughter 835 n.
  wit 839 n.
  ridiculousness 849 n.
farceur *humorist* 839 n.
farcical (*see* farce)
far corner *rear* 238 n.
far cry *distance* 199 n.
farcy *animal disease* 651 n.
fard *cosmetic* 843 n.
fare *be in a state* 7 vb.
  travel 267 vb.
  meal 301 n.
  eat 301 vb.
  price 809 n.
farewell *valediction* 296 n.
  courteous act 884 n.
far-fetched
  irrelevant 10 adj.
far-flung
  unassembled 75 adj.
far-flying *extensive* 32 adj.
far from *different* 15 adj.
far-going *exorbitant* 32 adj.
far-gone
  consummate 32 adj.
farinaceous
  powdery 332 adj.
farm *produce* 164 vb.
  breed stock 369 vb.
  farm 370 n.
  cultivate 370 vb.
  mature 669 vb.
  workshop 687 n.
  lands 777 n.
  hire 785 vb.
farmer *husbandman* 370 n.
farm-hand *servant* 742 n.
farming *territorial* 344 adj.
  agriculture 370 n.
farmland *soil* 344 n.

farm 370 n.
farm out *lease* 784 vb.
farmstead *house* 192 n.
farmyard *farm* 370 n.
farness *farness* 199 n.
faro *card game* 837 n.
farrago *medley* 43 n.
  confusion 61 n.
  absurdity 497 n.
far-reaching
  extensive 32 adj.
  spacious 183 adj.
farrier
  animal husbandry 369 n.
farrow *youngling* 132 n.
  reproduce itself 164 vb.
  posterity 170 n.
farse *office-book* 988 n.
far-sighted *seeing* 438 adj.
  vigilant 457 adj.
  intelligent 498 adj.
  foreseeing 510 adj.
farther *distant* 199 adj.
  beyond 199 adv.
farthest point
  extremity 69 n.
farthing *small coin* 33 n.
  quadrisection 98 n.
  coinage 797 n.
farthingale *frame* 218 n.
  skirt 228 n.
fasces *bunch* 74 n.
  badge of rule 743 n.
fascia *strip* 208 n.
  loop 250 n.
fascicle *subdivision* 53 n.
  bunch 74 n.
fascinate *engross* 449 vb.
  attract notice 455 vb.
  (*see* fascination)
fascination *influence* 178 n.
  inducement 612 n.
  excitation 821 n.
  pleasurableness 826 n.
  liking 859 n.
  wonder 864 n.
  love 887 n.
  lovableness 887 n.
  spell 983 n.
fascine *bunch* 74 n.
Fascism
  government 733 n.
  brute force 735 n.
fashion *modality* 7 n.
  similarity 18 n.
  generality 79 n.
  conformity 83 n.
  modernism 126 n.
  dressing 228 n.
  form 243 n.
  efform 243 vb.

feature 445 n.
  style 556 n.
  practice 610 n.
  way 624 n.
  fashion 848 n.
  affectation 850 n.
fashionable *tasteful* 846 adj.
  (*see* fashion)
fashion, in
  fashionable 848 adj.
fashion model
  living model 23 n.
fashion plate *fop* 848 n.
fashion upon
  represent 551 vb.
fast *tied* 45 adj.
  firm-set 45 adj.
  anachronistic 118 adj.
  fixed 153 adj.
  speedy 277 adj.
  coloured 425 adj.
  retained 778 adj.
  do penance 941 vb.
  be temperate 942 vb.
  be ascetic 945 vb.
  fast 946 n.
  starve 946 n.
  unchaste 951 adj.
  offer worship 981 vb.
  holy-day 988 n.
fast by *nigh* 200 adv.
fast colour *fixture* 153 n.
fast-day
  insufficiency 636 n.
  special day 876 n.
  asceticism 944 adj.
  fast 946 n.
  holy-day 988 n.
fast dye *fixture* 153 n.
  pigment 425 n.
fasten *affix, tighten* 45 vb.
  close 264 vb.
fastener *fastening* 47 n.
fastening *joinder* 45 n.
  fastening 47 n.
  nippers 778 n.
fasten on
  be attentive 455 vb.
  make important 638 vb.
  take 786 vb.
fasten *to hang* 217 vb.
faster *abstainer* 942 n.
  ascetic 945 n.
fasti *chronology* 117 n.
fastidious *careful* 457 adj.
  discriminating 463 adj.
  accurate 494 adj.
  capricious 604 adj.
  clean 648 n.
  severe 735 adj.
  observant 768 adj.

[868]

sensitive 819adj.
tasteful 846adj.
fastidious 862adj.
fastigium *vertex* 213n.
fasting *underfed* 636adj.
hungry 859adj.
fast-living *sensual* 944adj.
fastness *refuge* 662n.
fort 713n.
fat *prolific* 171adj.
fleshy 195adj.
expanded 197adj.
food content 301n.
fat 357n.
plenty 635n.
redundant 637adj.
prosperous 730adj.
rich 800adj.
fatal *deadly* 362adj.
evil 616adj.
harmful 645adj.
fatalism *philosophy* 449n.
necessity 596n.
submission 721n.
fatalist *fatalist* 596n.
fatality *decease* 361n.
necessity 596n.
evil 616n.
fata morgana
glow-worm 420n.
visual fallacy 440n.
fantasy 513n.
fate *finality* 69n.
futurity 124n.
destiny 155n.
cause 156n.
chance 159n.
influence 178n.
certainty 473n.
fate 596n.
non-design 618n.
fated *fated* 596adj.
Fates, the *fate* 596n.
mythic god 966n.
classical gods 967n.
fathead *dunce* 501n.
father *kinsman* 11n.
cause 156n.
generate 164vb.
parent 169n.
male 372n.
church title 986n.
cleric 986n.
father and mother of
whopping 32adj.
Father Christmas
good giver 813n.
fairy 970n.
fathered *born* 360adj.
fatherhood *family* 11n.
propagation 164n.

parentage 169n.
life 360n.
divineness 965n.
fatherland *territory* 184n.
home 192n.
fatherless
defenceless 161adj.
fatherly *parental* 169adj.
godlike 965adj.
fatherly eye
protection 660n.
father upon *attribute* 158vb.
fathom
long measure 203n.
be deep 211vb.
plunge 313vb.
enquire 459vb.
measure 465vb.
understand 516vb.
fathometer *diver* 313n.
gauge 465n.
fathomless *deep* 211adj.
fatidical *predicting* 511adj.
fatigue *weakness* 163n.
pain 377n.
use 673vb.
misuse 675vb.
sleepiness 679n.
labour 682n.
fatigue 684n.,vb.
oppress 735vb.
suffering 825n.
incommode 827vb.
be tedious 838vb.
fatigues *uniform* 228n.
fat in the fire *turmoil* 61n.
fatiscence *gap* 201n.
opening 263n.
fatling *cattle* 365n.
fat lot *great quantity* 32n.
fatness *bulk* 195n.
fat of the land
plenty 635n.
prosperity 730n.
fatten *grow* 36vb.
enlarge 197vb.
be broad 205vb.
feed 301vb.
pinguefy 357vb.
breed stock 369vb.
make better 654vb.
fattening *nourishing* 301adj.
fatty *fatty* 357adj.
fatuity *insubstantiality* 4n.
incogitance 450n.
absurdity 497n.
folly 499n.
fatuous *absurd* 497adj.
foolish 499adj.
unmeaning 515adj.
fatwa *theology* 973n.

faubourgs
circumjacence 230n.
fauces *threshold* 234n.
faucet *tube* 263n.
stopper 264n.
fault *discontinuity* 72n.
weakness 163n.
gap 201n.
shortcoming 307n.
blunder 495n.
evil 616n.
defect 647n.
dispraise 924vb.
detract 926vb.
vice 934n.
guilty act 936n.
fault, at *doubting* 474adj.
fault-finder
malcontent 829n.
disapprover 924n.
detractor 926n.
fault-finding
discontented 829adj.
fastidious 862adj.
disapprobation 924n.
censure 924n.
faultiness *inferiority* 35n.
inexactness 495n.
badness 645n.
imperfection 647n.
faultless *perfect* 646adj.
guiltless 935adj.
pure 950adj.
fault on the right side
virtues 933n.
fault, to a
extremely 32adv.
faulty *inexact* 495adj.
ungrammatical 565adj.
inelegant 576adj.
bad 645adj.
imperfect 647adj.
faun *vegetability* 366n.
lesser god 967n.
fauna *animality* 365n.
Faust *sorcerer* 983n.
fauteuil *seat* 218n.
theatre 594n.
faux-bourdon *melody* 410n.
faux pas *mistake* 495n.
solecism 565n.
failure 728n.
guilty act 936n.
favour *vantage* 34n.
influence 178n.
promote 285vb.
mien 445n.
be biased 481vb.
assent 488n.
badge 547n.
correspondence 588n.

choose 605 vb.
benefit 615 n., vb.
do good 644 vb.
aid 703 n.
trophy 729 n.
be auspicious 730 vb.
lenity 736 n.
permit 756 vb.
liking 859 n.
repute, honours 866 n.
befriend 880 vb.
courteous act 884 n.
love-token 889 n.
kind act 897 n.
approbation 923 n.
favourable
opportune 137 adj.
presageful 511 adj.
willing 597 adj.
aiding 703 adj.
promising 852 adj.
approving 923 adj.
favourable auspices
hope 852 n.
favourable chance
fair chance 159 n.
probability 471 n.
favourable issue
success 727 n.
favourable verdict
legal trial 959 n.
acquittal 960 n.
favour, by *by leave* 756 adv.
undue 916 adj.
favourer *patron* 707 n.
friend 880 n.
favour, in
reputable 866 adj.
approved 923 adj.
favourite *chosen* 605 adj.
bigwig 638 n.
made man 730 n.
person of repute 866 n.
social person 882 n.
loved one 887 n.
favourite 890 n.
kept woman 952 n.
favouritism
prejudice 481 n.
choice 605 n.
friendliness 880 n.
injustice 914 n.
favours *love-making* 887 n.
favus *skin disease* 651 n.
fawn *youngling* 132 n.
deer 365 n.
male animal 372 n.
brown 430 adj.
be subject 745 vb.
be servile 879 vb.
caress 889 vb.

flatter 925 vb.
fawner *toady* 879 n.
fawn on *be near* 200 vb.
befool 542 vb.
flatter 925 vb.
fay *fairy* 970 n.
fealty *loyalty* 739 n.
duty 917 n.
respect 920 n.
fear *doubt* 486 n.
avoidance 620 n.
fear 854 n., vb.
cowardice 856 n.
dislike 861 vb.
wonder 864 n., vb.
honour 866 vb.
respect 920 n.
piety 979 n.
worship 981 n., vb.
fearful *nervous* 854 adj.
cowardly 856 adj.
wonderful 864 adj.
fearfully *extremely* 32 adv.
wonderfully 864 adv.
fearing the worst
hopeless 853 adj.
fearless *unfearing* 855 adj.
fear of God *piety* 979 n.
fears *danger* 661 n.
fearsome
frightening 854 adj.
feasibility *possibility* 469 n.
facility 701 n.
feast *regular return* 141 n.
feasting 301 n.
feed 301 vb.
pleasure 376 n.
plenty 635 n.
revel 837 vb.
social gathering 882 n.
holy-day 988 n.
feast-day *festivity* 837 n.
special day 876 n.
holy-day 988 n.
feasting *sociability* 882 n.
sensualism 944 n.
gluttony 947 n.
feat *contrivance* 623 n.
deed 676 n.
masterpiece 694 n.
prowess 855 n.
thaumaturgy 864 n.
feather *sort* 77 n.
row 269 vb.
levity 323 n.
waverer 601 n.
trifle 639 n.
make ready 669 vb.
trimming 844 n.
honours 866 n.
(*see* feathers)

featherbed *softness* 327 n.
euphoria 376 n.
be lenient 736 vb.
feather-brained
foolish 499 adj.
irresolute 601 adj.
feathering
plumage 259 n.
feather in one's cap
trophy 729 n.
honours 866 n.
feather one's nest
prepare 669 vb.
prosper 730 vb.
get rich 800 vb.
be selfish 932 vb.
feathers *skin* 226 n.
headgear 228 n.
plumage 259 n.
wing 271 n.
softness 327 n.
(*see* feather)
feather-weight *levity* 323 n.
pugilist 722 n.
feathery *downy* 259 adj.
light 323 adj.
featly *skilfully* 694 adj.
feature *character* 5 n.
component 58 n.
speciality 80 n.
face 237 n.
form 243 n.
feature 445 n.
show 522 vb.
advertise 528 vb.
identification 547 n.
dramatize 594 vb.
featureless
insubstantial 4 adj.
uniform 16 adj.
empty 190 adj.
flat 216 adj.
amorphous 244 adj.
irresolute 601 adj.
febrifuge *antidote* 658 n.
febrile *hot* 379 adj.
diseased 651 adj.
excitable 822 adj.
feckless *useless* 641 adj.
unskilful 695 adj.
unsuccessful 728 adj.
feculence *excrement* 302 n.
dirt 649 n.
fecundation
propagation 164 n.
productiveness 171 n.
fecundity
propagation 164 n.
productiveness 171 n.
fedayeen *soldier* 722 n.
robber 789 n.

federal *co-operative* 706adj.
  corporate 708adj.
Federal agent
  detective 459n.
Federal Courts
  law-court 956n.
federalism
  government 733n.
federate *co-operate* 706vb.
  join a party 708vb.
federation *combination* 50n.
  association 706n.
  society 708n.
  polity 733n.
federative *corporate* 708adj.
fedora *headgear* 228n.
fed up *bored* 838adj.
fee *possession* 773n.
  estate 777n.
  gift 781n.
  pay 804n.
  expenditure 806n.
  price 809n.
  reward 962n.,vb.
feeble *small* 33adj.
  powerless 161adj.
  weak 163adj.
  muted 401adj.
  ill-reasoned 477adj.
  feeble 572adj.
  lax 734adj.
feeble-minded *weak* 163adj.
  unintelligent 499adj.
  insane 503adj.
feed *support* 218vb.
  meal 301n.
  provender 301n.
  eat 301vb.
  vitalize 360vb.
  groom 369vb.
  fire 385vb.
  provide 633vb.
  be hospitable 882vb.
feeder *eater* 301n.
  stream 350n.
  provider 633n.
fee, faw, fum
  intimidation 854n.
  spell 983n.
feel *meet with* 154vb.
  texture 331n.
  have feeling 374vb.
  touch 378n.
  be tentative 461vb.
  discrimination 463n.
  opine 485vb.
  feel 818vb.
  suffer 825vb.
  resent 891vb.
feeler *projection* 254n.
  feeler 378n.

question 459n.
  empiricism 461n.
  offer 759n.
feel for *search* 459vb.
  pity 905vb.
feeling *influence* 178n.
  sense 374n.
  touch 378n.
  intuition 476n.
  opinion 485n.
  interpretation 520n.
  vigour 571n.
  with affections 817adj.
  feeling 818n.,adj.
  excitation 821n.
  benevolence 897n.
feeling the pinch
  necessitous 627adj.
feel in one's bones
  intuit 476vb.
feel like *be willing* 597vb.
feel one's oats
  be vigorous 174vb.
feel one's way
  be tentative 461vb.
  foresee 510vb.
  essay 671vb.
  be cautious 858vb.
feel small
  be humbled 872vb.
feel the pinch
  be in difficulty 700vb.
  have trouble 731vb.
feel the pulse
  enquire 459vb.
  be tentative 461vb.
feel with *love* 887vb.
  pity 905vb.
fee simple *estate* 777n.
fee tail *estate* 777n.
feet of clay
  weakness 163n.
  defect 647n.
  vulnerability 661n.
feign *dissemble* 541vb.
  be affected 850vb.
feigned *hypocritical* 541adj.
  deceiving 542adj.
feint *trickery* 542n.
  stratagem 698n.
felicitation *rejoicing* 835n.
  congratulation 886n.
felicitous *apt* 24adj.
  elegant 575adj.
  well-made 694adj.
  successful 727adj.
  happy 824adj.
felicity *elegance* 575n.
  happiness 824n.
feline *cat* 365n.
  stealthy 525adj.

cunning 698adj.
  cruel 898adj.
fell *demolish* 165vb.
  skin 226n.
  high land 209n.
  flatten 216vb.
  strike 279vb.
  fell 311vb.
  plain 348n.
  deadly 362adj.
  evil 616adj.
  inimical 881adj.
  hating 888adj.
  cruel 898adj.
felloe, felly *edge* 234n.
  wheel 250n.
fellow *analogue* 18n.
  compeer 28n.
  adjunct 40n.
  concomitant 89n.
  person 371n.
  male 372n.
  college student 538n.
  colleague 707n.
  society 708n.
  low fellow 869n.
  friend, chum 880n.
fellow-citizen *native* 191n.
fellow-countryman
  native 191n.
  friend 880n.
fellow-creature
  person 371n.
fellow-feeling
  co-operation 706n.
  concord 710n.
  participation 775n.
  feeling 818n.
  friendliness 880n.
  love 887n.
  benevolence 897n.
  condolence 905n.
  pity 905n.
fellowless *alone* 88adj.
fellows *duality* 90n.
fellowship *group* 74n.
  association 706n.
  community 708n.
  friendship 880n.
  sociality 882n.
fellow-traveller
  concomitant 89n.
  assenter 488n.
  collaborator 707n.
fellow-worker
  personnel 686n.
  collaborator 707n.
felly *edge* 234n.
  wheel 250n.
felo de se *suicide* 362n.
felon *low fellow* 869n.

offender 904n.
felonious *wrong* 914adj.
 rascally 930adj.
 heinous 934adj.
 lawbreaking 954adj.
felony *vice* 934n.
 guilty act 936n.
 lawbreaking 954n.
felt *textile* 222n.
 weave 222vb.
 felt 818adj.
felucca *sailing-ship* 275n.
female *female* 373n., adj.
feminine *generic* 77adj.
 female 373adj.
 grammatical 564adj.
femininity *female* 373n.
feminism *female* 373n.
 gynocracy 733n.
feminist *female* 373adj.
femme couverte
 spouse 894n.
femme de chambre
 domestic 742n.
femme fatale *a beauty* 841n.
femme sole *spinster* 895n.
femoral *crural* 267adj.
fen *moisture* 341n.
 marsh 347n.
fence *partition* 231n.
 fence 235n.
 stopper 264n.
 cultivate 370vb.
 screen 421n.
 sophisticate 477vb.
 protection 660n.
 shelter 662n.
 obstacle 702n.
 defences 713n.
 parry 713vb.
 duel 716n.
 fight 716vb.
 thief 789n.
fencer *thoroughbred* 273n.
 contender 716n.
 combatant 722n.
fencible *defender* 713n.
 soldier 722n.
fend *obstruct* 702vb.
 parry 713vb.
fender *intermediary* 231n.
 furnace 383n.
 shelter 662n.
 defence 713n.
feneration *lending* 784n.
fenestration *window* 263n.
Fenian *opponent* 705n.
 revolter 738n.
fennel *potherb* 301n.
fenny *humid* 341adj.
 marshy 347adj.

feodal *proprietary* 777adj.
feodality *possession* 773n.
feoffee *possessor* 776n.
 beneficiary 776n.
 recipient 782n.
feoffer *owner* 776n.
 giver 781n.
feoffment *transfer* 780n.
feracious *prolific* 171adj.
ferine *disobedient* 738adj.
 unsociable 883adj.
ferment *turmoil* 61n.
 alterer 143n.
 conversion 147n.
 be turned to 147vb.
 convert 147vb.
 stimulation 174n.
 storm 176n.
 commotion 318n.
 effervesce 318vb.
 leaven 323n.
 bubble 355vb.
 be sour 393vb.
 feeling 818n.
 excitation 821n.
 excitable state 822n.
 anger 891n.
fern *plant* 366n.
ferocious *furious* 176adj.
 cruel 898adj.
ferret *vermin* 365n.
 eye 438n.
ferret out *discover* 484vb.
ferriage *transference* 272n.
ferro-concrete
 hardness 326n.
 hard 326adj.
 building material 631n.
ferruginous *red* 431adj.
ferrule, ferrel
 covering 226n.
ferry *voyage* 269vb.
 transfer 272vb.
 carry 273vb.
 ship, boat 275n.
ferryman *boatman* 270n.
 transferrer 272n.
 carrier 273n.
fertile *imaginative* 513adj.
 profitable 640adj.
 gainful 771adj.
 rich 800adj.
fertility *propagation* 164n.
 productiveness 171n.
 diffuseness 570n.
 plenty 635n.
fertilization
 propagation 164n.
fertilize
 make fruitful 171vb.
 invigorate 174vb.

 cultivate 370vb.
 be auspicious 730vb.
fertilizer *producer* 167n.
 fertilizer 171n.
 agriculture 370n.
ferule *club* 723n.
 scourge 964n.
fervent *hot* 379adj.
 active 678adj.
 fervent 818adj.
 loving 887adj.
 pietistic 979adj.
 worshipping 981adj.
fervour *heat* 379n.
 restlessness 678n.
 warm feeling 818n.
 piety 979n.
Fescennine verses
 doggerel 593n.
 ridicule 851n.
fess *heraldry* 547n.
fesswise
 horizontally 216adj.
festal *amusing* 837adj.
 ritual 988adj.
fester *be unclean* 649vb.
 be ill 651vb.
 deteriorate 655vb.
 be malevolent 898vb.
festering *infection* 651n.
 toxic 653adj.
festina lente
 caution 858n.
festival *assembly* 74n.
 festivity 837n.
 holy-day 988n.
festive *celebrative* 876adj.
 sociable 882adj.
festivity *meal* 301n.
 rejoicing 835n.
 festivity 837n.
 celebration 876n.
 social gathering 882n.
festoon *curve* 448n.
 decorate 844vb.
fetch *carry* 273vb.
 trickery 542n.
 cost 809vb.
 delight 826vb.
 cause desire 859vb.
 ghost 970n.
fetch and carry
 be servile 879vb.
fetching *personable* 841adj.
fetch up at *arrive* 295vb.
fête *rampage* 61vb.
 meal 301n.
 amusement 837n.
 pageant 875n.
 celebration 876n.
 gratulate 886vb.

fête champêtre
  amusement 837n.
fêted *welcomed* 882adj.
fetid *unsavoury* 391adj.
  odorous 394adj.
  fetid 397adj.
  bad, not nice 645adj.
  unclean 649adj.
  unpleasant 827adj.
fetish *god* 966n.
  idol 982n.
  talisman 983n.
fetishism *idolatory* 982n.
fetishist *religionist* 973n.
  idolator 982n.
fetish-man *sorcerer* 983n.
fetor (*see* fetid)
fetter *tie* 45vb.
  safeguard 662n.
  make inactive 679vb.
  hinder 702vb.
  subjection 745n.
  fetter 748n.
fettered *captive* 750adj.
fettle *state* 7n.
  affections 817n.
feud *quarrel* 709n.
  possession 773n.
  lands 777n.
  enmity 881n.
  revenge 910n.
feudal *olden* 127adj.
  governmental 733adj.
  subject 745adj.
  proprietary 777adj.
feudalism
  government 733n.
  service 745n.
feudatory *dependant* 742n.
  subject 745adj.
  possessor 776n.
feuillemorte *brown* 430adj.
fever *agitation* 318n.
  heat 379n.
  illness 651n.
  restlessness 678n.
  excitable state 822n.
feverish *hasty* 680adj.
  fervent 818adj.
  excited 821adj.
feverishness (*see* fever)
few *inconsiderable* 33adj.
  few 105adj.
  infrequent 140adj.
  scarce 636adj.
few, a *plurality* 101n.
  fewness 105n.
few and far between
  discontinuous 72adj.
  unassembled 75adj.
  few 105adj.

seldom 140adv.
fewness *finite quantity* 26n.
  inferiority 35n.
fey *dying* 361adj.
  bewitched 983adj.
  psychical 984adj.
fez *headgear* 228n.
fiacre *cab* 274n.
fiancé, fiancée *lover* 887n.
  loved one 887n.
fiasco *failure* 728n.
fiat *decree* 737n.
fiat money
  paper money 797n.
fib *untruth* 543n.
  fight 716vb.
fibber, fibster *liar* 545n.
fibre *essential part* 5n.
  fibre 208n.
  texture 331n.
  materials 631n.
fibril *filament* 208n.
fibrositis *pang* 377n.
  rheumatism 651n.
fibrous *fibrous* 208adj.
  tough 329adj.
fibula *fastening* 47n.
  jewellery 844n.
fichu *apron* 228n.
fickle *transient* 114adj.
  changeable 143adj.
  changeful 152adj.
  unreliable 474adj.
  tergiversating 603adj.
  capricious 604adj.
fickleness *irresolution* 601n.
fictile *formed* 243adj.
fiction *product* 164n.
  idea 451n.
  ideality 513n.
  falsehood 541n.
  untruth 543n.
  novel 590n.
fictional
  imaginative 513adj.
  descriptive 590adj.
fiction-writer
  narrator 590n.
fictitious
  insubstantial 4adj.
  imaginary 513adj.
  untrue 543adj.
  unwarranted 916adj.
fid *supporter* 218n.
  tobacco 388n.
fiddle *modify* 143vb.
  play music 413vb.
  viol 414n.
  trickery 542n.
  contrivance 623n.
  foul play 930n.

fiddle-faddle
  silly talk 515n.
fiddlehead *coil* 251n.
  pattern 844n.
fiddler
  instrumentalist 413n.
  trickster 545n.
  defrauder 789n.
fiddlestick *viol* 414n.
fiddlesticks *trifle* 639n.
fiddle with *touch* 370vb.
fiddling *trivial* 639adj.
  laborious 682adj.
fidelity *accuracy* 494n.
  veracity 540n.
  loyalty 739n.
  observance 768n.
  probity 929n.
fidget *hasten* 680vb.
fidgets
  changeableness 152n.
  agitation 318n.
  restlessness 678n.
  excitability 822n.
fidgety *unstable* 152adj.
  irresolute 601adj.
  active 678adj.
  excitable 822adj.
fiducial
  unchangeable 153adj.
  credible 485adj.
fiduciary *credible* 485adj.
  monetary 797adj.
fief *possession* 773n.
  lands 777n.
field *opportunity* 137n.
  range 183n.
  region 184n.
  place 185n.
  inclosure 235n.
  grassland 348n.
  topic 542n.
  hunter 619n.
  function 622n.
  opponent 705n.
  contender 716n.
  arena 724n.
  scope 744n.
  pleasure-ground 837n.
field day *contest* 716n.
  pageant 875n.
  special day 876n.
fielder, fieldsman
  interceptor 702n.
field-glass *telescope* 442n.
field marshal
  army officer 741n.
field of action *arena* 724n.
field of battle
  slaughter-house 362n.
  fight 716n.

battle 718 n.
battleground 724 n.
field of force *energy* 160 n.
field of view *view* 438 n.
visibility 443 n.
fieldpiece *gun* 723 n.
fields *land* 344 n.
plain 348 n.
farm 370 n.
field sports *sport* 837 n.
field-work *defences* 713 n.
fiend *monster* 938 n.
devil 969 n.
fiendish *cruel* 898 adj.
wicked 934 adj.
fierce *active* 678 adj.
warlike 718 adj.
excitable 822 adj.
courageous 855 adj.
angry 891 adj.
irascible 892 adj.
cruel 898 adj.
fiercely *greatly* 32 adv.
fieriness
quarrelsomeness 709 n.
rashness 857 n.
fiery *violent* 176 adj.
fiery 379 adj.
luminous 417 adj.
red 431 adj.
forceful 571 adj.
fervent 818 adj.
excitable 822 adj.
irascible 892 adj.
Fiery Cross
danger signal 665 n.
war measures 718 n.
fiesta *festivity* 837 n.
fife *stridor* 407 n.
flute 414 n.
fifer *instrumentalist* 413 n.
fifteen *party* 708 n.
fifth *interval* 201 n.
musical note 410 n.
fifth column *planner* 623 n.
collaborator 707 n.
perfidy 930 n.
fifth-columnism
sedition 738 n.
fifth columnist
tergiversator 603 n.
Fifth Monarchy Men
sect 978 n.
fifth wheel of the coach
extra 40 n.
fifty-fifty *equal* 28 adj.
median 30 adj.
mediocre 732 adj.
fig *state* 7 n.
fruit 301 n.
fight *turmoil* 61 n.

be in difficulty 700 vb.
withstand 704 vb.
fight 716 n., vb.
go to war 718 vb.
be courageous 855 vb.
fight against *oppose* 704 vb.
fight back, fight off
parry 713 vb.
fighter *aircraft* 276 n.
essayer 671 n.
opponent 705 n.
contender 716 n.
combatant 722 n.
air force 722 n.
fight for *defend* 713 vb.
fight-hungry
contending 716 adj.
fighting *athletic* 162 adj.
contention 716 n.
warfare 718 n.
fighting cock
combatant 722 n.
brave person 855 n.
fighting man *soldier* 722 n.
combatant 722 n.
brave person 855 n.
fight on *stand firm* 599 vb.
fight shy *be loth* 598 vb.
avoid 620 vb.
fight the good fight
be virtuous 933 vb.
be pious 979 vb.
figment
insubstantial thing 4 n.
product 164 n.
idea 451 n.
ideality 513 n.
figurante *actor* 594 n.
figurate *numerical* 85 adj.
figurative
semantic 514 adj.
figurative 519 adj.
occult 523 adj.
representing 551 adj.
rhetorical 574 adj.
figure *number* 85 n.
do sums 86 vb.
outline 233 n.
form 243 n.
person 371 n.
feature 445 n.
trope 519 n.
indication 547 n.
image 551 n.
represent 551 vb.
funds 797 n.
price 809 n.
eyesore 842 n.
person of repute 866 n.
figure-flinger
sorcerer 983 n.

figurehead
insubstantial thing 4 n.
ineffectuality 161 n.
face, prow 237 n.
projection 254 n.
badge 547 n.
nonentity 639 n.
ornamental art 844 n.
figure in *appear* 445 vb.
figure of eight *curve* 248 n.
loop 250 n.
figure of fun
laughing-stock 851 n.
figure of speech *trope* 519 n.
exaggeration 546 n.
ornament 574 n.
figures *statistics* 86 n.
figure-work
numerical operation 86 n.
filaceous *fibrous* 208 adj.
filament *narrowness* 206 n.
filament 208 n.
lamp 420 n.
filamentous
fibrous 208 adj.
hairy 259 adj.
filbert *fruit* 301 n.
fop 848 n.
filch *steal* 788 vb.
filcher *thief* 789 n.
file *bate* 37 vb.
sorting 62 n.
class 62 vb.
procession 71 n.
series 71 n.
bunch 74 n.
list 87 n., vb.
put off 136 vb.
receptacle 194 n.
make smaller 198 vb.
sharpener 256 n.
sharpen 256 vb.
smoother 258 n.
roughness 259 n.
walk 267 vb.
pulverize 332 vb.
rub 333 vb.
information 524 n.
record 548 n., vb.
collection 632 n.
store 632 vb.
formation 722 n.
file off *walk* 267 vb.
diverge 294 vb.
filial *filial* 170 adj.
obedient 739 adj.
filiation *relation* 9 n.
consanguinity 11 n.
attribution 158 n.
sonship 170 n.
filibeg *skirt* 228 n.

filibuster *spin out* 113 vb.
  delay 136 n.
  be loquacious 581 vb.
  hinderer 702 n.
  opponent 705 n.
  robber 789 n.
filiform *fibrous* 208 adj.
filigree *network* 222 n.
  ornamental art 844 n.
filing *pulverulence* 332 n.
  friction 333 n.
  registration 548 n.
filings *leavings* 41 n.
  powder 332 n.
filing system *sorting* 62 n.
fill *grow* 36 vb.
  fill 54 vb.
  be many 104 vb.
  stow 187 vb.
  pervade 189 vb.
  load 193 vb.
  enlarge 197 vb.
  line 227 vb.
  close 264 vb.
  store 632 vb.
  replenish 633 vb.
  suffice 635 vb.
  superabound 637 vb.
  doctor 658 vb.
  possess 773 vb.
  sate 863 vb.
filler *news* 529 n.
fillet *girdle* 47 n.
  ligature 47 n.
  strip 208 n.
  headgear 228 n.
  uncover 229 vb.
  loop 250 n.
  void 300 vb.
  cook 301 vb.
fill in *darken* 418 vb.
filling *contents* 193 n.
  lining 227 n.
  surgery 658 n.
filling station
  storage 632 n.
fillip *knock* 279 n.
  incentive 612 n.
  excitant 821 n.
  animate 821 vb.
fill, one's *sufficiency* 635 n.
  dislike 861 n.
fill out *expand* 197 vb.
fill the air *be loud* 400 vb.
fill the bill *suffice* 635 vb.
  be expedient 642 vb.
  carry out 725 vb.
fill the gap *accrue* 38 vb.
fill the mind *engross* 449 vb.
fill up *replenish* 633 vb.
  suffice 635 vb.

sate 863 vb.
filly *youngling* 132 n.
  horse 273 n.
  woman 373 n.
  female animal 373 n.
film *layer* 207 n.
  skin, shade 226 n.
  cloud 355 n.
  obfuscation 421 n.
  opacity 423 n.
  dim sight 440 n.
  camera 442 n.
  cinema 445 n.
  photography 551 n.
film-goer *playgoer* 594 n.
films *cinema* 445 n.
filmy *layered* 207 adj.
  textural 331 adj.
  dim 419 adj.
  opaque 423 adj.
filter *deviate* 282 vb.
  exude 298 vb.
  screen 421 n., vb.
  cleaning utensil 648 n.
  purify 648 vb.
filter in *infiltrate* 297 vb.
filth *badness* 645 n.
  dirt 649 n.
  ugliness 842 n.
  hateful object 888 n.
  impurity 951 n.
filthy *unsavoury* 391 adj.
  not nice 645 adj.
filthy language
  scurrility 899 n.
filthy lucre *money* 797 n.
filtrate *exude* 298 vb.
fimbriated *hairy* 259 adj.
fin *equilibrium* 28 n.
  limb 53 n.
  laterality 239 n.
  propeller 269 n.
final *ending* 69 adj.
  answering 460 adj.
  positive 473 adj.
  contest 716 n.
  completive 725 adj.
final cause *cause* 156 n.
  intention 617 n.
finale *end* 69 n.
  musical piece 412 n.
  dramaturgy 594 n.
finalist *aftercomer* 67 n.
  contender 716 n.
finality *completeness* 54 n.
  (*see* final)
finalize *make certain* 473 vb.
final notice *warning* 664 n.
  demand 737 n.
final point *goal* 295 n.
finals *exam.* 459 n.

final stroke *killing* 362 n.
  completion 725 n.
finance *means* 629 n.
  lend 784 vb.
  finance 797 n.
financial *monetary* 797 adj.
financier *lender* 784 n.
  moneyer 797 n.
  treasurer 798 n.
  merchant 794 n.
finch *bird* 365 n.
find *extra* 40 n.
  meet with 154 vb.
  judge 480 vb.
  discovery 484 n.
  benefit 615 n.
  find means 629 vb.
  provide 633 vb.
  acquisition 771 n.
  booty 790 n.
  try a case 959 vb.
  acquire 771 vb.
find again *retrieve* 656 vb.
find against *condemn* 961 vb.
find fault
  be discontented 829 vb.
  be fastidious 862 vb.
  blame 924 vb.
  detract 926 vb.
find favour
  be praised 923 vb.
find guilty *condemn* 961 vb.
finding *judgment* 480 n.
  discovery 484 n.
  acquisition 771 n.
  legal trial 959 n.
find means
  find means 629 vb.
find out *discover* 484 vb.
find room for
  comprise 78 vb.
  place 187 vb.
find the place *place* 187 vb.
find time for
  have leisure 681 vb.
find words for
  phrase 563 vb.
fine *small* 33 adj.
  large 195 adj.
  narrow 206 adj.
  rare 325 adj.
  textural 331 adj.
  dry 342 adj.
  transparent 422 adj.
  discriminating 463 adj.
  accurate 494 adj.
  good 615 adj.
  excellent 644 adj.
  healthy 650 adj.
  palmy 730 adj.
  price 809 n.

tax 809 vb.
splendid 841 adj.
proud 871 adj.
formal 875 adj.
penalty 963 n.
fine airs *airs* 873 n.
fine feather, in
  healthy 650 adj.
fine feeling *good taste* 846 n.
fine fettle, in *strong* 162 adj.
  healthy 650 adj.
fine gentleman *fop* 848 n.
  proud man 871 n.
fine-mannered
  courteous 884 adj.
finer feelings *feeling* 818 n.
  moral sensibility 819 n.
finery *clothing* 228 n.
  finery 844 n.
  ostentation 875 n.
fine shade
  differentiation 15 n.
  discrimination 463 n.
fine-spun *narrow* 206 adj.
  fibrous 208 adj.
  sophistical 477 adj.
  textural 331 adj.
finesse *cunning* 698 n.
fine-woven *textural* 331 adj.
fine writing
  ornament 574 n.
finger *small thing* 33 n.
  piece 53 n.
  long measure 203 n.
  finger 378 n.
  touch 378 vb.
  indicator 547 n.
  nippers 778 n.
fingering *musical skill* 413 n.
finger in the pie, have a
  interfere 231 vb.
  meddle 678 vb.
finger-mark *trace* 548 n.
finger-nail *finger* 378 n.
finger-post *direction* 281 n.
  signpost 547 n.
fingerprint
  identification 547 n.
  label 547 n.
  trace 548 n.
finger's breadth
  short distance 200 n.
  narrowness 206 n.
finger-stall *case* 194 n.
  covering 226 n.
  surgical dressing 658 n.
  armour 713 n.
finial *vertex* 213 n.
  summit 213 n.
finical *attentive* 455 adj.
  fastidious 862 adj.

finickiness
  moral sensibility 819 n.
  discontent 829 n.
  good taste 846 n.
finicky *fastidious* 862 adj.
finish *completion* 54 n.
  end 69 n., vb.
  cease 145 n.
  symmetry 245 n.
  smoothness 258 n.
  arrival 295 n.
  elegance 575 n.
  perfection 646 n.
finished *extinct* 2 adj.
  consummate 32 adj.
  past 125 adj.
  expert, well-made 694 adj.
finisher *survivor* 41 n.
  aftercomer 67 n.
finishing school
  academy 539 n.
  training school 539 n.
finish off
  carry through 725 vb.
finite *limited* 236 adj.
  circumscribed 232 adj.
fink *informer* 524 n.
fiord *gulf* 345 n.
fir *tree* 366 n.
fire *destroyer* 168 n.
  vigorousness 174 n.
  shoot 287 vb.
  dismiss 300 vb.
  element 319 n.
  fire 379 n.
  kindle 381 vb.
  furnace 383 n.
  fire 385 vb.
  light 417 n.
  luminary 420 n.
  signal 547 n.
  vigour 571 n.
  bombardment 712 n.
  warm feeling 818 n.
fire-alarm
  danger signal 665 n.
fire and water *polarity* 14 n.
fire-arm *fire-arm* 723 n.
fire-ball *meteor* 321 n.
  fuel 385 n.
  luminary 420 n.
fire-balloon *airship* 276 n.
fire-barrel *lighter* 385 n.
fire-bell *danger signal* 665 n.
fire-box *furnace* 383 n.
firebrand
  violent creature 176 n.
  lighter 385 n.
  incendiarism 381 n.
  dissentient 489 n.
  motivator 612 n.

  trouble-maker 663 n.
  leader 690 n.
  agitator 738 n.
fire-brigade
  extinguisher 382 n.
fire-bug
  incendiarism 381 n.
fire damp *gas* 336 n.
fire-dog *furnace* 383 n.
fire-drake *glow-worm* 420 n.
fire-eater
  violent creature 176 n.
  combatant 722 n.
  brave person 855 n.
  desperado 857 n.
  insolent person 878 n.
fire-engine *vehicle* 274 n.
  irrigator 341 n.
  extinguisher 382 n.
fire-escape
  means of escape 667 n.
fire-fighter
  extinguisher 382 n.
  protector 660 n.
  defender 713 n.
firefly *fly* 365 n.
  flash 417 n.
  glimmer 419 n.
  glow-worm 420 n.
fireguard *furnace* 383 n.
  shelter 662 n.
fire-irons *furnace* 383 n.
fireman *extinguisher* 382 n.
  protector 660 n.
  defender 713 n.
fire-new *new* 126 adj.
fire-party *punisher* 963 n.
fireplace *furnace* 383 n.
fire-proof *coat* 226 vb.
  incombustible 382 adj.
  invulnerable 660 adj.
fire-raising
  incendiarism 381 n.
fire-ship *ship* 275 n.
  lighter 385 n.
  warship 722 n.
fireside *focus* 76 n.
  home 192 n.
fire-station
  extinguisher 382 n.
fire-step *stand* 218 n.
fire-walker *ascetic* 945 n.
fire-watcher *protector* 660 n.
  defender 713 n.
firewater *liquor* 301 n.
firewood *fuel* 385 n.
fireworks *fire* 379 n.
  fireworks 420 n.
  spectacle 445 n.
  masterpiece 694 n.
  revel 837 n.

celebration 876 n.
fire-worship *fire* 379 n.
  idolatry 982 n.
firing line *battle* 718 n.
  battleground 724 n.
firkin *vat* 194 n.
firlot *metrology* 465 n.
firm *firm-set* 45 adj.
  fixed 153 adj.
  strong 162 adj.
  dense 324 adj.
  rigid 326 adj.
  resolute 599 adj.
  obstinate 602 adj.
  workshop 687 n.
  corporation 708 n.
  retentive 778 adj.
  merchant 794 n.
  courageous 855 adj.
firmament *heavens* 321 n.
firman *decree* 737 n.
firm date *promise* 764 n.
firmness *permanence* 144 n.
  stability 153 n.
  hardness 326 n.
  resolution 599 n.
  courage 855 n.
first *unimitative* 21 adj.
  supreme 34 adj.
  first 68 adj.
  prior 119 adj.
  fundamental 156 adj.
  foremost 283 adj.
  best 644 adj.
  victor 727 n.
first aid *therapy* 658 n.
  aid 703 n.
first appearance *début* 68 n.
first arrival *earliness* 135 n.
first blood *success* 727 n.
first blush *beginning* 68 n.
  appearance 445 n.
first-born *superior* 34 n.
  precursor 66 n.
  priority 119 n.
  older 131 adj.
  prior 119 adj.
  olden 127 adj.
First Cause *cause* 156 n.
  divineness 965 n.
  theosophy 984 n.
first choice *superior* 34 n.
  choice 605 n.
  chief thing 638 n.
first-class *supreme* 34 adj.
first come first served
  no choice 606 n.
first-comer(s)
  earliness 135 n.
  native 191 n.
first draft *experiment* 461 n.

plan 623 n.
  preparation 669 n.
first go *essay* 671 n.
first-hand
  unimitative 21 adj.
  evidential 466 adj.
first lady *superior* 34 n.
first move *début* 68 n.
first-nighter *playgoer* 594 n.
first offence *début* 68 n.
  essay 671 n.
first offender
  beginner 538 n.
  prisoner 750 n.
  offender 904 n.
first point of Aries
  uranometry 321 n.
first principle *source* 156 n.
  premise 475 n.
first-rate *supreme* 34 adj.
  notable 638 adj.
  best 644 adj.
first-rater *exceller* 644 n.
  warship 722 n.
first refusal *purchase* 792 n.
first round *beginning* 68 n.
first sight, at *at sight* 438 n.
  apparently 445 adv.
first step *début* 68 n.
first steps *learning* 536 n.
first thing *betimes* 135 adv.
first violin *orchestra* 413 n.
  leader 690 n.
first water, of the
  excellent 644 adj.
firth *gulf* 345 n.
fisc *treasury* 799 n.
fiscal *monetary* 797 adj.
fish *fish food* 301 n.
  animal, fish 365 n.
  search 459 vb.
  be tentative 461 vb.
  hunt 619 vb.
  take 786 vb.
  amuse oneself 837 vb.
fish day *fast* 946 n.
fisher *hunter* 619 n.
fisherman's yarn *fable* 543 n.
fishery *stock farm* 369 n.
fish for *search* 459 vb.
  be tentative 461 vb.
  pursue 619 vb.
  desire 859 vb.
fishglue *adhesive* 47 n.
fishiness *improbity* 930 n.
fishing *chase* 619 n.
  sport 837 n.
fish manure *fertilizer* 171 n.
fishmonger *provider* 633 n.
fish-net *network* 222 n.
  inclosure 235 n.

fish out of water
  misfit 25 n.
  nonconformist 84 n.
  displacement 188 n.
  bungler 697 n.
fish pond *lake* 346 n.
  stock farm 369 n.
fish up *elevate* 310 vb.
  discover 484 vb.
fishwife *shrew* 892 n.
fishy *animal* 365 adj.
  dishonest 930 adj.
fishy story *fable* 543 n.
fissile *brittle* 330 adj.
fission *separation* 46 n.
  decompose 51 vb.
fissionable *severable* 46 adj.
fissure *disjunction* 46 n.
  gap 201 n.
fist *finger* 378 n.
  lettering 586 n.
  nippers 778 n.
fisticuffs *knock* 279 n.
  quarrel 709 n.
  pugilism 716 n.
fistula *tube* 263 n.
  ulcer 651 n.
fit *modality* 7 n.
  adjust 24 vb.
  join 45 vb.
  cohere 48 vb.
  subdivision 53 n.
  make conform 83 vb.
  athletic 162 adj.
  violence 176 n.
  spasm 318 n.
  frenzy 503 n.
  poem 593 n.
  whim 604 n.
  expedient 642 adj.
  healthy 650 adj.
  illness 651 n.
  make ready 669 vb.
  excitable state 822 n.
  right 913 adj.
  due 915 adj.
fit for *useful* 640 adj.
fit for consideration
  topical 452 adj.
fit for enquiry *moot* 459 adj.
fit for nothing
  useless 641 adj.
fitful *excitable* 822 adj.
fitfulness *discontinuity* 72 n.
  fitfulness 142 n.
  changeableness 152 n.
  caprice 604 n.
fit in *accord* 24 vb.
  conform 83 vb.
  load 193 vb.
  join a party 708 vb.

fitness *relevance* 9 n.
  fitness 24 n.
  occasion 137 n.
  ability 160 n.
  expedience 642 n.
  health 650 n.
  aptitude 694 n.
  preparedness 669 n.
  right 913 n.
fit out *dress* 228 vb.
  find means 629 vb.
  provide 633 vb.
  make ready 669 vb.
fits and starts
  fitfulness 142 n.
  agitation 318 n.
fits and starts, by
  fitfully 142 adv.
  jerkily 318 adv.
  capriciously 604 adv.
fitter *machinist* 630 n.
  preparer 669 n.
  artisan 686 n.
fit tight *cohere* 48 vb.
  fill 54 vb.
fitting *relevant* 9 adj.
  adjusted 24 adj.
  cohesive 48 adj.
  opportune 137 adj.
  expedient 642 adj.
fittings *equipment* 630 n.
fit to be seen
  personable 841 adj.
fit together *join* 45 vb.
  combine 50 vb.
five by five *fleshy* 195 adj.
five-finger *handed* 378 adj.
five o'clock *meal* 301 n.
  social gathering 882 n.
fiver *funds* 797 n.
fives *ball game* 837 n.
five-stones *plaything* 837 n.
fix *affix* 45 vb.
  arrange 62 vb.
  stabilize 153 vb.
  place 187 vb.
  close 264 vb.
  quiescence 266 n.
  be resolute 599 vb.
  repair 656 vb.
  remedy 658 vb.
  predicament 700 n.
fixation *location* 187 n.
  habituation 610 n.
  hindrance 702 n.
fixative *adhesive* 47 n.
  pigment 425 n.
fixed *firm-set* 45 adj.
  immemorial 127 adj.
  permanent 144 adj.
  fixed 153 adj.

located 187 adj.
  still 266 adj.
  positive 473 adj.
  habitual 610 adj.
fixed interval
  regular return 141 n.
fixer *trickster* 545 n.
  mender 656 n.
fix, in a
  in difficulties 700 adj.
fixity *permanence* 144 n.
  stability 153 n.
  quiescence 266 n.
  positiveness 473 n.
  resolution 599 n.
  obstinacy 602 n.
fix on *be attentive* 455 vb.
fixture *adjunct* 40 n.
  joinder 45 n.
  part 53 n.
  concomitant 89 adj.
  fixture 153 n.
  equipment 630 n.
fixtures *property* 777 n.
fizgig *fireworks* 420 n.
fizz *vigorousness* 174 n.
  wine 301 n.
  soft drink 301 n.
  bubble 355 n., vb.
  hiss 406 vb.
fizzer *exceller* 644 n.
fizzle *bubble* 355 vb.
  crackle 402 vb.
  hiss 406 vb.
fizzle out
  fall short 307 vb.
  miscarry 728 vb.
fizzy *vigorous* 174 adj.
  watery 339 adj.
  windy 352 adj.
  bubbly 355 adj.
flabbergast
  frighten 854 vb.
  be wonderful 864 vb.
flabby *weak* 163 adj.
  soft 327 adj.
  pulpy 356 adj.
flabelliform
  expanded 197 adj.
  broad 205 adj.
flaccidity *weakness* 163 n.
  softness 327 n.
  feebleness 572 n.
flag *be weak* 163 vb.
  lamina 207 n.
  base 214 n.
  decelerate 278 vb.
  foliage 366 n.
  signal, flag 547 n.
  road 624 n.
  building material 631 n.

be ill 651 n.
  be fatigued 684 vb.
  regalia 743 n.
  be dejected 834 vb.
  greet 884 vb.
flag-bearer
  messenger 531 n.
flag-captain
  naval officer 741 n.
flag day *request* 671 n.
  special day 876 n.
flagellant *penitent* 939 n.
  ascetic 945 n.
flagellate
  perform ritual 988 vb.
flagellation *penance* 941 n.
  asceticism 945 n.
  corporal punishment 963 n.
flagelliform *fibrous* 208 adj.
flageolet *flute* 414 n.
flagitiousness
  wickedness 934 n.
flag-lieutenant
  naval officer 741 n.
flag-man *warner* 664 n.
flag of convenience
  contrivance 623 n.
  stratagem 698 n.
flag officer
  naval man 270 n.
flag of truce *irenics* 719 n.
flagon *vessel* 194 n.
flag-pole *flag* 547 n.
flagrancy
  manifestation 522 n.
  publicity 528 n.
  bad taste 847 n.
  ostentation 875 n.
  insolence 878 n.
  wickedness 934 n.
flagrant *flagrant* 32 adj.
  (*see* flagrancy)
flagrante delicto
  guiltily 936 adv.
flagration *burning* 381 n
flags *paving* 226 n.
  smoothness 258 n.
flagship *warship* 772 n
flag-signalling
  telecommunication 531 n.
flagstaff
  high structure 209 n.
  support 218 n.
flagstones *road* 624 n.
flag-waving
  celebration 876 n.
flail *hammer* 279 n.
  cultivate 370 vb.
  strike at 712 vb.
  flog 963 vb.
flair *odour* 394 n.

intellect 447 n.
discrimination 463 n.
discovery 484 n.
aptitude 694 n.
flak *bombardment* 712 n.
defences 713 n.
flake *small thing* 33 n.
piece 53 n.
lamina 207 n.
powder 332 n.
pulverize 332 vb.
flakiness
stratification 207 n.
brittleness 330 n.
flaky *brittle* 330 adj.
flambeau *torch* 420 n.
flamboyant *ornate* 574 adj.
undulatory 251 adj.
flame *fire* 379 n.
heat 379 n.
heater 383 n.
shine 417 vb.
light 417 n.
luminary 420 n.
redness 431 n.
orange 436 n.
be excited 821 vb.
loved one 887 n.
flame-coloured
orange 436 adj.
flamen *priest* 986 n.
flamenco *dance* 837 n.
flame-proof
incombustible 382 adj.
flame-thrower
propellant 287 n.
gun 723 n.
flaming *violent* 176 adj.
fiery 379 adj.
fervent 818 adj.
showy 875 adj.
flamingo *bird of prey* 365 n.
flan *pastry* 301 n.
flâneur *idler* 679 n.
flange *edge* 234 n.
projection 254 n.
flank *laterality* 239 n.
safeguard 660 vb.
flannel *textile* 222 n.
warm clothes 381 n.
cleaning cloth 648 n.
flatter 925 vb.
flannelette *textile* 222 n.
flap *adjunct* 40 n.
come unstuck 49 vb.
pendant 217 n.
hang 217 vb.
covering 226 n.
be in motion 265 vb.
strike 279 vb.
agitation 318 n.

blow 352 vb.
sound dead 405 vb.
excitability 822 n.
fear 854 n., vb.
flapdoodle
empty talk 515 n.
flapjack *cereal* 301 n.
cosmetic 843 n.
flapper *youngster* 132 n.
reminder 305 n.
(*see* woman)
flaps *wing* 271 n.
aircraft 276 n.
flare *be violent* 176 vb.
move fast 277 vb.
be hot 379 vb.
shine 417 vb.
torch 420 n.
signal light 420 n.
luminary 420 adj.
be excited 821 vb.
flare up
be excitable 822 vb.
get angry 891 vb.
flaring *flagrant* 32 adj.
fiery 379 adj.
florid 425 adj.
showy 875 adj.
flash *small quantity* 33 n.
instant 116 n.
changeableness 152 n.
be violent 176 vb.
velocity 277 n.
pass 305 vb.
agitation 318 n.
fire 279 n.
flash 417 n.
luminary 420 n.
communicate 524 vb.
news 529 n.
spurious 542 adj.
signal, livery 547 n.
spontaneity 609 n.
flash-back
remembrance 505 n.
flashbulb *lamp* 420 n.
flash in the pan
insubstantial thing 4 n.
brief span 114 n.
ineffectuality 161 n.
be unproductive 172 vb.
false alarm 665 n.
miscarry 728 vb.
flashlight *lamp* 420 n.
flash point *heat* 379 n.
flashy *florid* 425 adj.
ornate 574 adj.
ornamented 844 adj.
vulgar 847 adj.
flask *vessel* 194 n.
flat *uniform* 16 adj.

impotent 161 adj.
inert 175 adj.
spatial 183 adj.
flat 192 n.
chamber 194 n.
short 204 adj.
low 210 adj.
flat 216 adj.
inverted 221 adj.
unsharpened 257 adj.
smooth 258 adj.
still 266 adj.
marsh 347 n.
champaign 348 adj.
tasteless 387 adj.
unsavoury 391 adj.
non-resonant 405 adj.
strident 407 adj.
musical note 410 n.
harmonic 410 adj.
discordant 411 adj.
soft-hued 425 adj.
mirror 442 n.
ninny 501 n.
assertive 532 adj.
dupe 544 n.
feeble 572 adj.
stage-set 594 n.
deteriorated 655 adj.
hitch 702 n.
cheerless 834 adj.
tedious 838 adj.
dull 840 adj.
flatbed
horizontality 216 n.
press 587 n.
flat-car *train* 274 n.
flat-foot *detective* 459 n.
protector 660 n.
police 955 n.
flat-iron *flattener* 216 n.
smoother 258 n.
Flatland *lowness* 210 n.
flatlet *small house* 192 n.
flatness *lowness* 210 n.
horizontality 216 n.
(*see* flat)
flat out *swiftly* 277 adj.
flats *plain* 348 n.
flat spin *fear* 854 n.
flatten *demolish* 165 vb.
make smaller 198 vb.
flatten 216 vb.
smooth 258 vb.
fell 311 vb.
flattened
unsharpened 257 adj.
flatten out *fly* 271 vb.
flatter *imitate* 20 vb.
mislead 495 vb.
befool 542 vb.

exaggerate 546 vb.
misrepresent 552 vb.
tempt 612 vb.
please 826 vb.
beautify 841 vb.
honour 866 vb.
flatter 925 vb.
be dishonest 930 vb.
  (*see* flattery)
flatterer *slyboots* 698 n.
  affector 850 n.
  toady 879 n.
  flatterer 925 n.
flattering *erroneous* 495 adj.
  hypocritical 541 adj.
  deceiving 542 adj.
flattering portrait
  misrepresentation 552 n.
flatter oneself
  assume 471 vb.
  hope 852 vb.
  feel pride 871 vb.
  be vain 873 vb.
flattery *conformity* 83 n.
  assent 488 n.
  empty talk 515 n.
  falsehood 541 n.
  inducement 612 n.
  cunning 698 n.
  servility 879 n.
  courtesy 884 n.
  endearment 889 n.
  praise 923 n.
  flattery 925 n.
  (*see* flatter)
flat-top *warship* 722 n.
flatulence *gaseity* 336 n.
  diffuseness 570 n.
  magniloquence 574 n.
  indigestion 651 n.
flatulent *feeble* 572 adj.
flatus *gas* 336 n.
  wind 352 n.
flaunches *heraldry* 547 n.
flaunt *show* 522 vb.
  seek repute 866 vb.
  be ostentatious 875 vb.
  threaten 900 vb.
flautist
  instrumentalist 413 n.
flavour *cook* 301 vb.
  taste 386 n.
  season 388 vb.
flavouring *food* 301 n.
  taste 386 n.
  condiment 389 n.
flavourless *tasteless* 387 adj.
flavous *yellow* 433 adj.
flaw *discontinuity* 72 n.
  weakness 163 n.
  gap 201 n.

gale 352 n.
sophism 477 n.
mistake 495 n.
badness 645 n.
defect 647 n.
blemish 845 n., vb.
flawless
  consummate 32 adj.
  elegant 575 adj.
  perfect 646 adj.
flax *fibre* 208 n.
flaxen *yellow* 433 adj.
flay *rend* 46 vb.
  uncover 229 vb.
  dispraise 924 vb.
  execute 963 vb.
flea *athlete* 162 n.
  jumper 312 n.
  vermin 365 n.
  dirt 649 n.
flea-bag *bag* 194 n.
flea-bite *small quantity* 33 n.
  trifle 639 n.
flea-bitten *mottled* 437 adj.
fleam *sharp point* 256 n.
  perforator 263 n.
flèche *sharp point* 256 n.
fleck *small thing* 33 n.
  (*see* blemish)
flection *deviation* 282 n.
fled *escaped* 667 adj.
fledge *mature* 669 vb.
fledgling *new* 126 adj.
  youngling 132 n.
  bird 365 n.
flee *decamp* 296 vb.
  run away 620 vb.
fleece *skin* 226 n.
  hair 259 n.
  softness 327 n.
  groom 369 vb.
  fleece 786 vb.
  defraud 788 vb.
  impoverish 801 vb.
  overcharge 811 vb.
fleecy *fibrous* 208 adj.
  fleecy 259 adj.
fleer *ridicule* 851 n., vb.
  satirize 851 vb.
fleet *be transient* 114 vb.
  shipping 275 n.
  speedy 277 adj.
  navy 722 n.
fleeting
  insubstantial 4 adj.
  transient 114 adj.
Fleet Street *the press* 528 n.
flesh *auspicate* 68 vb.
  matter 319 n.
  animality 365 n.
  mankind 371 n.

sensualism 944 n.
unchastity 951 n.
flesh and blood
  substance 3 n.
  bulk 195 n.
  matter 319 n.
  animality 365 n.
fleshings *legwear* 228 n.
flesh, in the *alive* 360 adj.
fleshless *lean* 206 adj.
fleshliness
  sensualism 944 n.
  unchastity 951 n.
fleshly *material* 319 adj.
  human 371 adj.
flesh-pots *feasting* 301 n.
  prosperity 730 n.
  wealth 800 n.
flesh show
  stage show 594 n.
fleshy *fleshy* 195 adj.
  pulpy 356 adj.
  fatty 357 adj.
fleur-de-lys *heraldry* 547 n.
  pattern 844 n.
flexed *curved* 248 adj.
flexibility *softness* 327 n.
  skill 694 n.
  improbity 930 n.
flexible
  conformable 83 adj.
  flexible 327 adj.
  irresolute 601 adj.
  wieldy 701 adj.
flexion *curvature* 248 n.
  fold 261 n.
  deviation 282 n.
flex one's muscles
  prepare oneself 669 vb.
flexuosity *convolution* 251 n.
flexure *angularity* 247 n.
  curvature 248 n.
  fold 261 n.
flibbertigibbet
  demon, elf 970 n.
flick *move* 265 vb.
  impel 279 vb.
  touch 378 n., vb.
flicker *be transient* 114 vb.
  changeableness 152 n.
  flash 417 n.
  shine 417 vb.
  glimmer 419 n.
flickers, flicks *cinema* 445 n.
flier, flyer *aeronaut* 271 n.
  speeder 277 n.
flies *theatre* 594 n.
flight *group* 74 n.
  transientness 114 n.
  aeronautics 271 n.
  fly 271 vb.

velocity 277n.
propel 287vb.
recession 290n.
departure 296n.
avoidance 620n.
escape 667n.
air force 722n.
defeat 728n.
fear 854n.
flightiness
  changeableness 152n.
  (*see* flighty)
flight lieutenant
  air officer 741n.
flight of fancy
  insubstantial thing 4n.
  ideality 513n.
  exaggeration 546n.
flight of stairs *ascent* 308n.
  access 624n.
flight of time
  course of time 111n.
flight sergeant
  air officer 741n.
flighty *transient* 114adj.
  light-minded 456adj.
  irresolute 601adj.
flim-flam *falsehood* 541n.
flimsy *flimsy* 163adj.
  rare 325adj.
  brittle 330adj.
  ill-reasoned 477adj.
  unimportant 639adj.
flinch *recoil* 280vb.
  feel pain 377vb.
  avoid 620vb.
  suffer 825vb.
  quake 854vb.
flincher *tergiversator* 603n.
  coward 856n.
flinders *small thing* 33n.
fling *move* 265vb.
  impel 279vb.
  propulsion 287n.
  scope 744n.
  dance 837n.
  indignity 921n.
fling about *jumble* 63vb.
fling away
  be prodigal 815vb.
fling, have one's
  be intemperate 943vb.
fling out *eject* 300vb.
  reject 607vb.
flint *hardness* 326n.
  soil 344n.
  lighter 385n.
  tool 630n.
flint-lock *fire-arm* 723n.
flinty *hard* 326adj.
  territorial 344adj.

flip *move* 265vb.
  impulse 279n.
  touch 378n., vb.
  incentive 612n.
flippancy *inattention* 456n.
  unimportance 639n.
  wit 839n.
  ridicule 851n.
  rashness 857n.
  sauciness 878n.
flippant
  light-minded 456adj.
flipper *limb* 53n.
  propeller 269n.
  feeler 378n.
flirt *tergiversator* 603n.
  be capricious 604vb.
  affector 850n.
  excite love 887vb.
  court 889vb.
  libertine 952n.
  loose woman 952n.
flirtation *whim* 604n.
  love affair 887n.
  wooing 889n.
flirtatiousness
  caprice 604n.
  love 887n.
flirting *love-making* 887n.
  wooing 889n.
flit *elapse* 111vb.
  be transient 114vb.
  vary 152vb.
  move 265vb.
  travel 267vb.
  decamp 296vb.
  run away 620vb.
  preserver 666n.
  escape 667n., vb.
flit about *wander* 267vb.
flitter *vary* 152vb.
  be in motion 265vb.
float *stabilize* 153vb.
  hang 217vb.
  go smoothly 258vb.
  swim 269vb.
  fly 271vb.
  cart 274n.
  raft 275n.
  be light 323vb.
  be uncertain 474vb.
  theatre 594n.
  find means 629vb.
floater *missile* 287n.
  idler 679n.
floating *unstable* 152adj.
floating vote
  changeableness 152n.
  dubiety 474n.
  irresolution 601vb.
float on the air

sound faint 401vb.
floats *theatre* 594n.
float up *ascend* 308vb.
flocculent *soft* 327adj.
  powdery 332adj.
flocculi *powder* 332n.
  sun 321n.
flock *group* 74n.
  congregate 74vb.
  certain quantity 104n.
  be many 104vb.
  filament 208n.
  hair 259n.
  animal 365n.
  laity 987n.
floe *island* 349n.
  ice 380n.
flog *strike* 279vb.
  give pain 377vb.
  incite 612vb.
  fatigue 684vb.
  sell 793vb.
  flog 963vb.
flog a dead horse
  be superfluous 637vb.
  waste effort 641vb.
flood *great quantity* 32n.
  increase 36n.
  crowd 74n.
  congregate 74vb.
  be dispersed 75vb.
  be many 104vb.
  destroyer 168n.
  outbreak 176n.
  high water 209n.
  progression 285n.
  irrupt 297vb.
  flow out 298vb.
  immerse 303vb.
  encroach 306vb.
  irrigate 341vb.
  flow 350vb.
  plenty 635n.
  redundance 637n.
flooded *covered* 226adj.
flood-gate *outlet* 298n.
  conduit 351n.
flood level *high water* 209n.
flood-lighting *lighting* 420n.
flood-lit *luminous* 417adj.
flood tide *high water* 209n.
floor *compartment* 194n.
  layer 207n.
  lowness 210n.
  base 214n.
  horizontality 216n.
  flatten 216vb.
  basis 218n.
  paving 226n.
  overlay 226vb.
  strike 279vb.

fell 311 vb.
confute 479 vb.
floor-boards *paving* 226 n.
floor-cover
  floor-cover 226 n.
floor-show
  stage show 594 n.
floor-walker *servant* 742 n.
  seller 793 n.
flop *descend* 309 vb.
  be agitated 318 vb.
  bungling 695 n.
  failure 728 n.
  miscarry 728 vb.
  (*see* fatigue)
floppy *non-adhesive*
  49 adj.
  weak 163 adj.
  soft 327 adj.
Flora *vegetability* 366 n.
flora and fauna
  organism 358 n.
floral *vegetal* 366 adj.
floresce *expand* 197 vb.
florescence
  salad days 130 n.
  adultness 134 n.
  growth 157 n.
  propagation 164 n.
  vegetability 366 n.
florescent *vernal* 128 adj.
  young 130 adj.
  grown up 134 adj.
floriculture *flower* 366 n.
  agriculture 370 n.
florid *florid* 425 adj.
  red 431 adj.
  ornate 574 adj.
  healthy 650 adj.
  splendid 841 adj.
  ornamental 844 adj.
florin *coinage* 797 n.
floruit *adultness* 134 n.
  palmy days 730 n.
floss *hair* 259 n.
flotation *fitting out* 669 n.
flotilla *shipping* 275 n.
  navy 722 n.
flotsam
  thing transferred 272 n.
  derelict 779 n.
flotsam and jetsam
  piece 53 n.
  dispersion 75 n.
  outcaste 883 n.
flounce *edging* 234 n.
  fold 261 n.
  leap 312 vb.
  be angry 891 vb.
flounder *leap* 312 vb.
  fluctuate 317 vb.

be agitated 318 vb.
table fish 365 n.
be uncertain 474 vb.
be clumsy 695 vb.
be in difficulty 700 vb.
flour *cereal* 301 n.
  powder 332 n.
  thickening 345 n.
  corn 366 n.
  white thing 427 n.
flourish *coil* 251 n.
  brandish 317 vb.
  agitate 318 vb.
  loudness 400 n.
  musical note 410 n.
  trope 519 n.
  show 522 vb.
  publication 528 n.
  call 547 n.
  ornament 574 n.
  orate 579 vb.
  lettering 586 n.
  flourish 615 vb.
  be healthy 650 vb.
  prosper 730 vb.
  pattern 844 n.
  ostentation 875 n.
  boast 877 n.
floury *powdery* 332 adj.
flout *despise* 922 vb.
flow *quantity* 26 n.
  continuity 71 n.
  elapse 111 vb.
  hang 217 vb.
  motion 265 n.
  irrupt 297 vb.
  be fluid 335 vb.
  current 350 n.
  flow 350 vb.
  diffuseness 570 n.
  elegance 575 n.
  abound 635 vb.
  be active 678 vb.
flow between
  sunder 46 vb.
flower *essential part* 5 n.
  grow 36 vb.
  reproduce itself 164 vb.
  expand 197 vb.
  flower 366 n.
  élite 644 n.
  paragon 646 n.
  prosper 730 vb.
  a beauty 841 n.
flower-bed *flower* 366 n.
  garden 370 n.
flower-growing
  agriculture 370 n.
flowering *vernal* 128 adj.
  young 130 adv.
flower of life

salad days 130 n.
flowers *regular return* 141 n.
  hæmorrhage 302 n.
  pulverulence 332 n.
  reading matter 589 n.
  anthology 592 n.
flowery *vegetal* 366 adj.
  figurative 519 adj.
  ornate 574 adj.
flowing *perpetual* 115 adj.
  unstable 152 adj.
  diffuse 570 adj.
  elegant 575 adj.
flowing bowl
  drunkenness 949 n.
flowing tongue
  loquacity 581 n.
flown *absent* 190 adj.
  escaped 667 adj.
flow of spirits
  cheerfulness 833 n.
flow on *progress* 285 vb.
fluctuate *be unequal* 29 vb.
  be periodic 141 vb.
  vary 152 vb.
  fluctuate 317 vb.
  be capricious 604 vb.
fluctuation
  changeableness 152 n.
  motion 265 n.
  fluctuation 317 n.
  current 350 n.
  uncertainty 474 n.
  irresolution 601 n.
flue *chimney* 263 n.
  air-pipe 353 n.
  furnace 383 n.
fluency *diffuseness* 570 n.
  elegance 575 n.
  speech, eloquence 575 n.
  loquacity 581 n.
fluent
  numerical element 85 n.
  fluidal 335 adj.
  flowing 350 adj.
  (*see* fluency)
flue-pipe *orifice* 263 n.
  air-pipe 353 n.
fluff *jumble* 63 vb.
  hair 259 n.
  levity 323 n.
  be clumsy 695 vb.
fluffy *downy* 259 adj.
  fleecy 259 adj.
flugelhorn *horn* 414 n.
fluid *unstable* 152 adj.
  amorphous 244 adj.
  liquor 301 n.
  fluid 335 n.
  moisture 341 n.
  flowing 350 adj.

fluidity
  non-coherence 49n.
  weakness 163n.
  softness 327n.
  fluidity 335n.
  liquefaction 337n.
  unreliability 474n.
fluke *chance* 159n.
  angularity 247n.
  non-design 618n.
  success 727n.
fluky *casual* 159adj.
flummery
  empty talk 515n.
  fable 534n.
flummox *distract* 456vb.
  puzzle 474vb.
flunk *failure* 728n.
flunkey *domestic* 742n.
  dependant 742n.
  toady 879n.
flunkeyism *service* 745n.
  servility 879n.
  flattery 925n.
fluorescence *glow* 417n.
fluorescent
  luminescent 420adj.
fluorometer *meter* 465n.
flurry *derange* 63vb.
  velocity 277n.
  rain 350n.
  gale 352n.
  distract 456vb.
  activity 678n.
  feeling 818n.
  excitation 821n.
  excitable state 822n.
  frighten 854vb.
flush *uniform* 16adj.
  equal 28adj.
  full 54adj.
  flat 216adj.
  smooth 258adj.
  waterfall 350n.
  be hot 379vb.
  glow 417n.
  hue 425n.
  redness 431n.
  hunt 619vb.
  filled 635adj.
  clean, purify 648vb.
  skin disease 651n.
  moneyed 800adj.
  show feeling 818vb.
  be excited 821vb.
  frighten 854vb.
  tipsy 949adj.
fluster *derange* 63vb.
  distract 456vb.
flute *groove* 262vb.
  stridor 407n.

  shrill 407vb.
  play music 413vb.
  flute 414n.
fluting *furrow* 262n.
  ornamental art 844n.
flutist *instrumentalist* 413n.
flutter *vary* 152vb.
  be in motion 265vb.
  fly 271vb.
  oscillation 317n.
  brandish 317vb.
  agitation 318n.
  gambling 618n.
  haste 680n.
  feeling 818n.
  be excited 821vb.
  nervousness 854n.
  frighten 854vb.
  excite love 887vb.
fluvial *flowing* 350adj.
flux *conversion* 147n.
  motion 265n.
  liquefaction 337n.
  current 350n.
flux and reflux
  fluctuation 317n.
flexibility *fluidity* 335n.
  liquefaction 337n.
fluxion
  numerical element 85n.
fluxions *mathematics* 86n.
fluxure *fluidity* 335n.
fly *elapse* 111vb.
  be transient 114vb.
  be violent 176vb.
  animalcule 196n.
  edge 234n.
  fly 271vb.
  carry 273vb.
  cab 274n.
  move fast 277vb.
  decamp 296vb.
  agitate 318vb.
  be brittle 330vb.
  fly 365n.
  knowing 490adj.
  intelligent 498adj.
  flag 547n.
  run away 620vb.
  be active 678vb.
  cunning 698adj.
  fear 854vb.
fly about
  be published 528vb.
fly against *charge* 712vb.
fly a kite
  be tentative 461vb.
fly along *travel* 267vb.
fly apart *be dispersed* 75vb.
flyblown *unclean* 649adj.
fly-by-night

  avoiding 620adj.
fly-fishing *chase* 619n.
flying *transient* 114adj.
  high 209adj.
  aeronautics 271n.
flying buttress
  supporter 218n.
  church exterior 990n.
flying carpet
  magic instrument 983n.
flying colours *trophy* 729n.
  ostentation 875n.
  celebration 876n.
flying colours, with
  successfully 727adv.
flying column
  armed force 722n.
Flying Dutchman
  wanderer 268n.
  mariner 270n.
  fantasy 513n.
flying ground *arena* 724n.
flying instruments
  aircraft 276n.
flying saucer
  space-ship 276n.
flying start *vantage* 34n.
  start 68n.
  priority 119n.
  spurt 277n.
  precession 283n.
fly in the face of
  oppose 704vb.
  disobey 738vb.
fly in the ointment
  defect 647n.
  hitch 702n.
fly-leaf *interjection* 231n.
  partition 231n.
  edition 589n.
fly off at a tangent
  deviate 282vb.
  diverge 294vb.
fly off the handle
  be excitable 822vb.
  get angry 891vb.
fly-over *crossing* 222n.
  traffic control 305n.
  passage 305n.
  bridge 624n.
  communicating 624adj.
fly-paper *adhesive* 47n.
  trap 542n.
fly-past *pageant* 875n.
flyte *curse* 899vb.
flyweight *pugilist* 722n.
fly-wheel *rotator* 315n.
foal *youngling* 132n.
  reproduce itself 164vb.
  horse 273n.
  male animal 372n.

foam *stimulation* 174 n.
  be violent 176 vb.
  excrement 302 n.
  effervesce 318 vb.
  moisture 341 n.
  bubble 355 n., vb.
  bauble 639 n.
  be excitable 822 vb.
foam at the mouth
  effervesce 318 vb.
  be insane 503 vb.
  go mad 503 vb.
  get angry 891 vb.
foamy *light* 323 adj.
  bubbly 355 adj.
  white 427 adj.
fob *pocket* 194 n.
  deceive 542 vb.
focal *central* 225 adj.
focalization
  centrality 225 n.
  convergence 293 n.
focal point *focus* 76 n.
  centrality 225 n.
focimetry
  measurement 465 n.
focometry
  measurement 465 n.
fo'c'sle *prow* 237 n.
focus *junction* 45 n.
  bring together 74 vb.
  focus 76 n., vb.
  meeting place 192 n.
  centralize 225 vb.
  convergence 293 n.
  gaze 438 vb.
  be attentive 455 vb.
  arena 724 n.
focus, in *well-seen* 443 adj.
focus the attention
  attract notice 455 vb.
fodder *provender* 301 n.
  groom 369 vb.
  agriculture 370 n.
  materials 631 n.
foe *opponent* 705 n.
  enemy 881 n.
fœtus *source* 156 n.
fog *moisture* 341 n.
  cloud 355 n.
  dimness 419 n.
  screen 421 vb.
  opacity 423 n.
  blur 440 vb.
  invisibility 444 n.
  puzzle 474 vb.
fog-bound
  hindered 702 adj.
fogginess *dimness* 419 n.
  imperspicuity 568 n.
foggy *dense* 324 adj.

humid 341 adj.
  cloudy 355 adj.
  dim 419 adj.
  opaque 423 adj.
fog-signal *warning* 664 n.
  danger signal 665 n.
fogy, fogey
  archaism 127 n.
  crank 504 n.
  opinionist 602 n.
  laughing-stock 851 n.
foible *vice* 934 n.
  (*see* defect)
foil *lamina* 207 n.
  bluntness 257 n.
  disappoint 509 vb.
  be obstructive 702 vb.
  oppose 704 vb.
  side-arms 723 n.
foiled *defeated* 728 adj.
foin *collide* 279 vb.
  foin 712 n.
  parry 713 vb.
foison *plenty* 635 n.
foist *galley* 275 n.
  compel 740 vb.
foist in *intromit* 231 vb.
foist off *deceive* 542 vb.
fold *joint* 45 n.
  duplication 91 n.
  stable 192 n.
  receptacle 194 n.
  make smaller 198 vb.
  inclosure 235 n.
  angularity 247 n.
  make curved 248 vb.
  fold 261 n., vb.
  safeguard 660 vb.
  shelter 662 n.
  laity 987 n.
folded hands *entreaty* 761 n.
folder *receptacle* 194 n.
  collection 632 n.
fold one's arms
  not act 677 vb.
fold up *cease* 145 vb.
  make smaller 198 vb.
foliaceous
  layered 207 adj.
foliage *foliage* 366 n.
  greenness 432 n.
foliate *number* 86 vb.
  layered 207 adj.
foliation *foliage* 366 n.
folio *part* 53 n.
  edition 889 n.
folk *social group* 371 n.
folklore *tradition* 127 n.
  anthropology 371 n.
folklorish
  fairylike 970 adj.

folkmoot *council* 692 n.
folksy *sociable* 882 adj.
follicle *compartment* 194 n.
  cavity 255 n.
follow *do likewise* 20 vb.
  be inferior 35 vb.
  come after 65 vb.
  conform 83 vb.
  accompany 89 vb.
  be late 136 vb.
  happen 154 adj.
  result 157 vb.
  be behind 238 vb.
  follow 284 vb.
  watch 441 vb.
  be reasonable 475 vb.
  be proved 478 vb.
  detect 484 vb.
  understand 516 vb.
  use 673 vb.
  obey 739 vb.
  serve 742 vb.
  observe 768 vb.
follow a calling
  do business 622 vb.
follow a course
  behave 688 vb.
follow advice
  consult 691 vb.
follower *imitator* 20 n.
  inferior 35 n.
  retinue 67 n.
  conformist 83 n.
  concomitant 89 n.
  follower 284 n.
  learner 538 n.
  auxiliary 707 n.
  dependant 742 n.
  lover 887 n.
  sectarist 978 n.
  worshipper 981 n.
following *retinue* 67 n.
  (*see* follower)
following wind *aid* 703 n.
follow suit
  do likewise 20 vb.
follow the scent
  pursue 619 vb.
follow-through *sequel* 67 n.
  effectuation 725 n.
follow through
  sustain 146 vb.
  carry through 725 vb.
follow-up *sequel* 67 n.
follow up
  carry through 725 vb.
folly
  insubstantial thing 4 n.
  pavilion 192 n.
  ignorance 491 n.
  folly 499 n.

rashness 857 n.
foment *make violent* 176 vb.
  heat 381 vb.
  doctor 658 vb.
  aid 703 vb.
  animate 821 vb.
fomentation
  causation 156 n.
  surgical dressing 658 n.
  therapy 658 n.
fond *foolish* 499 adj.
  crazed 503 adj.
  desiring 859 adj.
  loving 887 adj.
fondle *touch* 378 vb.
  love 887 vb.
  caress 889 vb.
fondling *favourite* 890 n.
fondness (*see* fond)
fons et origo *origin* 68 n.
  source 156 n.
font *ritual object* 988 n.
  church utensil 990 n.
fontanelle *head* 213 n.
food *food* 301 n.
  life 360 n.
  materials 631 n.
  provision 633 n.
  refreshment 685 n.
food content
  food content 301 n.
food for thought *topic* 452 n.
foodless *hungry* 859 adj.
  fasting 946 adj.
food-poisoning
  infection 651 n.
  poisoning 659 n.
foodstuff(s) *food* 301 n.
  provisions 301 n.
  provender 301 n.
fool *pulpiness* 356 n.
  ignoramus 493 n.
  be absurd 497 vb.
  fool 501 n.
  madman 504 n.
  befool 542 vb.
  dupe 544 n.
  entertainer 594 n.
  bungler 697 n.
  humorist 839 n.
  be ridiculous 849 vb.
  laughing-stock 851 n.
foolery *foolery* 497 n.
  folly 499 n.
  revel 837 n.
  wit 839 n.
  ridicule 851 n.
foolhardiness
  rashness 857 n.
foolish *aged* 131 adj.
  mindless 448 adj.

credulous 487 vb.
  ignorant 491 adj.
  absurd 497 adj.
  foolish 499 adj.
  crazed 503 adj.
  trivial 639 adj.
foolishness (*see* folly)
fool-proof *certain* 473 adj.
  invulnerable 660 adj.
  easy 701 adj.
  successful 727 adj.
foolscap *label* 547 n.
  stationery 586 n.
  paper 631 n.
fool's errand
  lost labour 641 n.
fool's paradise
  insubstantial thing 4 n.
  misjudgment 481 n.
  disappointment 509 n.
  aspiration 852 n.
foot *long measure* 203 n.
  lowness 210 n.
  base, foot 214 n.
  stand 218 n.
  prosody 593 n.
  infantry 722 n.
footage *distance* 119 n.
  length 203 n.
foot and mouth disease
  animal disease 651 n.
football *sphere* 252 n.
  missile 287 n.
  ball game 837 n.
footballer *player* 837 n.
football pool *chance* 159 n.
  gambling 618 n.
  gambling game 837 n.
foot by foot
  piecemeal 53 adv.
footfall *gait* 265 n.
  indication 547 n.
footgear *footwear* 228 n.
foothill(s) *entrance* 68 n.
  high land 209 n.
foothold *basis* 218 n.
  retention 778 n.
footing *state* 7 n.
  circumstance 8 n.
  degree 27 n.
  serial place 73 n.
  influence 178 n.
  situation 186 n.
  base 214 n.
  support, basis 218 n.
foot it *walk* 267 vb.
  leap 312 vb.
footlet *footwear* 228 n.
footlight(s) *lighting* 420 n.
  drama, theatre 594 n.
footling *trivial* 639 adj.

footloose *travelling* 267 adj.
  designless 618 adj.
footman *pedestrian* 268 n.
  domestic 742 n.
  (*see* infantry)
footmark *trace* 548 n.
footnote(s) *adjunct* 40 n.
  commentary 520 n.
foot, on *continuing* 108 adj.
  happening 154 adj.
  operative 173 adj.
  on foot 267 adv.
  preparatory 669 adj.
footpad *pedestrian* 268 n.
  robber 789 n.
footpath *path* 624 n.
foot-plate man *driver* 68 n.
footprint *concavity* 255 n.
  identification 547 n.
  trace 548 n.
footrest *supporter* 218 n.
footrule *gauge* 465 n.
foot-slogger
  pedestrian 268 n.
  infantry 722 n.
foot-soldier *infantry* 722 n.
footsore *fatigued* 684 adj.
footstep *trace* 548 n.
footstool *seat* 218 n.
foot the bill *defray* 804 vb.
footwear *footwear* 228 n.
foozle *be clumsy* 695 vb.
  failure 728 n.
fop *fop* 848 n.
  affector 850 n.
foppery *fashion* 848 n.
  affectation 850 n.
  airs 873 n.
foppish *fashionable* 848 adj.
  affected 850 adj.
  showy 875 adj.
forage *provender* 301 n.
  provide 633 vb.
  steal 788 vb.
foramen *orifice* 263 n.
forasmuch
  concerning 9 adv.
forasmuch as
  hence 158 adv.
foray *attack* 712 n.
  brigandage 788 n.
forbear *precursor* 66 n.
  parent 169 n.
  disregard 458 vb.
  (*see* forbearance)
forbearance
  avoidance 620 n.
  non-use 674 n.
  lenity 736 n.
  patience 823 n.
  mercy 905 n.

forgiveness 909 n.
temperance 942 n.
forbid prohibit 757 vb.
forbidden fruit
incentive 612 n.
prohibition 757 n.
forbidding cheerless 834 adj.
serious 834 adj.
ugly 842 adj.
unsociable 883 adj.
sullen 893 adj.
force be unrelated 10 vb.
quantity 26 n.
derange 63 vb.
band 74 n.
make conform 83 vb.
cause 156 n.
energy 160 n.
strength 162 n.
agency 173 n.
vigorousness 174 n.
force 176 vb.
influence 178 vb.
promote 285 vb.
waterfall 350 n.
cultivate 370 vb.
meaning 514 n.
vigour 571 n.
motivate 612 vb.
ill-treat 645 vb.
mature 669 vb.
misuse 675 n.,vb.
action 676 n.
exertion 682 n.
personnel 686 n.
armed force 722 n.
compulsion 740 n.
debauch 951 vb.
forced irrelevant 10 adj.
feeble 572 adj.
inelegant 576 adj.
unwilling 598 adj.
forced labour slacker 598 n.
labour 682 n.
compulsion 740 n.
forced landing
aeronautics 271 n.
forced march haste 680 n.
forceful strong 162 adj.
vigorous 174 adj.
assertive 532 adj.
stylistic 566 adj.
forceful 571 adj.
resolute 599 adj.
active 678 adj.
compelling 740 adj.
impressive 821 adj.
force, in operative 173 adj.
forcene heraldic 547 adj.
force of character
affections 817 n.

force of circumstances
necessity 596 n.
force one's hand
compel 740 vb.
force one's way
exert oneself 682 vb.
force open sunder 46 vb.
force 176 vb.
forceps cross 222 n.
extractor 304 n.
nippers 778 n.
force, the police 955 n.
forcible (see forceful)
forcible-feeble
feeble 572 adj.
ford pass 305 vb.
be wet 341 vb.
bridge 624 n.
fordone fatigued 684 adj.
fore before 64 adv.
prior 119 adj.
front 237 n.
fore and aft
throughout 54 adv.
longwise 203 adv.
forearm limb 53 n.
warn 664 vb.
prepare 669 vb.
forebode predict 511 vb.
indicate 547 vb.
endanger 661 vb.
foreboding foresight 510 n.
prediction 511 n.
dangerous 661 adj.
warning 664 n.
threatening 900 adj.
forecast destiny 155 n.
impending 155 adj.
expectation 507 n.
foresee 510 vb.
predict 511 vb.
policy 623 n.
preparation 669 n.
forecastle prow 237 n.
forechosen fated 596 adj.
foreclose obstruct 702 vb.
demand 737 vb.
deprive 786 vb.
foreclosure
expropriation 786 n.
debt 803 n.
fore-course sail 275 n.
forecourt front 237 n.
foredate misdate 118 vb.
foredoom predestine 155 vb.
fate 596 n.
necessitate 596 vb.
forefather parent 169 n.
forefathers the dead 361 n.
forefinger finger 378 n.
forefoot foot 214 n.

forefront beginning 68 n.
front 237 n.
foreglimpse
foresight 510 n.
foregoing
preceding 64 adj.
prior 119 adj.
foregoing 125 adj.
foregone conclusion
prejudgment 481 n.
foresight 510 n.
predetermination 608 n.
foreground front 237 n.
stage set 594 n.
forehanded vigilant 457 adj.
forehead head 213 n.
face 237 n.
foreign irrelative 10 adj.
disagreeing 25 adj.
separate 46 adj.
extraneous 59 adj.
foreign body misfit 25 n.
extraneousness 59 n.
foreigner misfit 25 n.
foreigner 59 n.
outcaste 883 n.
foreignness
exteriority 223 n.
foreign parts
extraneousness 59 n.
farness 199 n.
forejudge prejudge 481 vb.
foresee 510 vb.
foreknowledge
foresight 510 n.
foreland projection 254 n.
forelay ensnare 542 vb.
foreleg leg 267 n.
forelimb limb 53 n.
forelock hair 259 n.
front 237 n.
foreman superior 34 n.
manager 690 n.
foremast prow 237 n.
foremost supreme 34 adj.
first 68 adj.
foremost 283 adj.
ahead 283 adv.
important 638 adj.
noteworthy 866 adj.
forename name 561 n.
forenoon morning 128 n.
forensic
jurisprudential 958 adj.
fore-ordain
predestine 155 vb.
predetermine 608 vb.
forepart front 237 n.
forepeak prow 237 n.
forepiece front 237 n.
forerake projection 254 n.

forerun *come before* 64vb.
  be before 119vb.
  precede 283n.
forerunner *precursor* 66n.
  front 237n.
  messenger 531n.
  director 690n.
foresail *sail* 275n.
foresee *look ahead* 124vb.
  be wise 498vb.
  expect 507vb.
  foresee 510vb.
  intend 617vb.
foreseeable *future* 124adj.
  expected 507adj.
foreseen *expected* 507adj.
  unastonishing 865adj.
foreshadow
  predestine 155vb.
  predict 511vb.
foreshorten
  shorten 204vb.
foreshow *predict* 511vb.
foresight *priority* 119n.
  looking ahead 124n.
  carefulness 457n.
  sagacity 498n.
  foresight 510n.
  prediction 511n.
  policy 623n.
  preparation 669n.
  caution 858n.
foreskin *front* 237n.
forest *wood* 366n.
forestall *exclude* 57vb.
  do before 119vb.
  look ahead 124vb.
  be early 135vb.
  expect 507vb.
  foresee 510vb.
  deceive 542vb.
  possess 773vb.
forestay *prow* 237n.
forester *dweller* 191n.
  forestry 366n.
  gardener 370n.
forestry *forestry* 366n.
  botany 368n.
  agriculture 370n.
foretaste *precursor* 66n.
  example 83n.
  expectation 507n.
  foresight 510n.
  preparation 669n.
foretell *predict* 511vb.
forethought *thought* 449n.
  carefulness 457n.
  sagacity 498n.
  foresight 510n.
  policy 623n.
foretoken *omen* 511n.

fore-topman
  navigator 270n.
  climber 308n.
forever *forever* 115adv.
for everybody
  general 79adj.
forewarn *foresee* 510vb.
  predict 511vb.
  warn 664vb.
  threaten 900vb.
forewarning *precursor* 66n.
foreword *prelude* 66n.
for example
  conformably 83adv.
forfeit *decrease* 37n.,vb.
  decrement 42n.
  relinquish 621vb.
  loss 772n.
  deprive 786vb.
  disentitle 916vb.
  penalty 963n.
forfeiture (*see* forfeit)
forfend *parry* 713vb.
  prohibit 757vb.
forgathering *junction* 45n.
  assembly 74n.
  social gathering 882n.
forge *copy* 20vb.
  produce 164vb.
  efform 243vb.
  furnace 383n.
  fake 541vb.
  be untrue 543vb.
  workshop 687n.
  mint 797vb.
forge ahead
  be in front 237vb.
  progress 285vb.
forger *imitator* 20n.
  deceiver 545n.
  artisan 686n.
  defrauder 789n.
  moneyer 797n.
  offender 904n.
forgery *imitation* 20n.
  copy 22n.
  falsehood 541n.
  sham 542n.
  false money 797n.
forget *be inattentive* 456vb.
  forget 506vb.
  obliterate 550vb.
  relinquish 621vb.
  be lenient 736vb.
  fail in duty 918vb.
forgetful *negligent* 458adj.
  forgetful 506adj.
forget-me-not
  blueness 435n.
forgivable *trivial* 639adj.
  forgiven 909adj.

vindicable 927adj.
  guiltless 935adj.
forgive *disregard* 458vb.
  forgive 909vb.
forgiveness *amnesty* 506n.
  irenics 719n.
  lenity 736n.
  benevolence 897n.
  forgiveness 909n.
  acquittal 960n.
  divine function 965n.
forgo
  relinquish 621vb.
  not retain 779vb.
forgone
  relinquished 621adj.
for good *for long* 113adv.
for good and all
  throughout 54adv.
  forever 115adv.
forgotten *past* 125adj.
  unknown 491adj.
  forgotten 506adj.
  unthanked 908adj.
fork *bifurcation* 92n.
  cross 222vb.
  angularity 247n.
  sharp point 256n.
  diverge 294vb.
fork out *give* 781vb.
  pay 804vb.
forlorn *hopeless* 853adj.
  friendless 883adj.
forlorn hope *danger* 661n.
  combatant 722n.
  armed force 722n.
  brave person 855n.
form *similarity* 18n.
  copy 22n.
  constitute 56vb.
  arrange 62vb.
  rule 81n.
  conformity 83n.
  convert 147vb.
  produce 164vb.
  seat 218n.
  form 243n.
  appearance 445n.
  educate 534vb.
  class 538n.
  record 548n.
  practice 610n.
  beauty 841n.
  fashion 848n.
  formality 875n.
  legality 953n.
  ritual 988n.
formal *conditionate* 7adj.
  regular 83adj.
formal dress
  formal dress 228n.

formalism *severity* 735 n.
  pietism 979 n.
  ritualism 988 n.
formalist *tyrant* 735 n.
  affector 850 n.
  religionist 979 n.
  ritualist 988 n.
formality *formality* 875 n.
  courtesy 884 n.
format *form* 243 n.
formation *group* 74 n.
  efformation 243 n.
  production 164 n.
  formation 722 n.
formative *formative* 243 adj.
form, bad *ill-breeding* 847 n.
form, be on
  be skilful 694 vb.
forme *letterpress* 587 n.
  edition 589 n.
former *preceding* 64 adj.
  prior 119 adj.
  former 125 adj.
  resigning 753 adj.
formerly *long ago* 113 adv.
  formerly 125 adv.
formication
  formication 378 n.
  skin disease 651 n.
formidable *difficult* 700 adj.
  frightening 854 adj.
formless
  amorphous 244 adj.
  unsightly 842 adj.
form of law *legality* 953 n.
formula *rule* 81 n.
  number 85 n.
  axiom 496 n.
  phrase 563 n.
  precept 693 n.
  legality 953 n.
  rite 988 n.
formular *ritualistic* 988 adj.
formulary *maxim* 496 n.
  precept 693 n.
  office-book 988 n.
  rite 988 n.
formulate *arrange* 62 vb.
  efform 243 vb.
  affirm 532 vb.
  write 586 vb.
fornication
  unchastity 951 n.
fornicator *libertine* 952 n.
forsake *tergiversate* 603 vb.
  relinquish 621 vb.
for sale *offering* 759 adj.
  (see saleable)
forswear *negate* 533 vb.
  be false 541 vb.
  recant 603 vb.

avoid 620 vb.
  relinquish 621 vb.
  be dishonest 930 vb.
fort *refuge* 662 n.
  fort 713 n.
forte *skill* 694 n.
forth *forward* 285 adv.
forthcoming *early* 135 adj.
  impending 155 adj.
  veracious 540 adj.
  feeling 818 adj.
for the million *easy* 701 adj.
for the moment
  transiently 114 adj.
for the nonce *singly* 88 adv.
for the occasion
  present 121 adj.
for the sake of
  in aid of 703 adv.
forthright
  intelligible 516 adj.
  undisguised 522 adj.
  veracious 540 adj.
forthwith *suddenly* 135 adv.
fortification
  fortification 713 n.
  art of war 718 n.
fortified *strong* 162 adj.
  hard 326 adj.
  defended 713 adj.
fortify *strengthen* 162 vb.
  safeguard 660 vb.
  aid 703 vb.
  defend 713 vb.
fortissimo *loud* 400 adj.
  loudness 400 n.
  loudly 400 adv.
fortitude *courage* 855 n.
  virtues 933 n.
fortnight *period* 110 n.
fortnightly *seasonal* 141 adj.
fortress *fort* 713 n.
fortuitous
  extrinsic 6 adj.
  casual 159 adj.
  unintentional 618 adj.
fortunate *opportune* 137 adj.
  prosperous 730 adj.
  happy 824 adj.
fortune *eventuality* 154 n.
  chance 159 n.
  prediction 511 n.
  fate 596 n.
  good 615 n.
  wealth 800 n.
fortune-hunter
  toady 879 n.
  egotist 932 n.
fortunes *biography* 590 n.
fortune-teller
  diviner 511 n.

occultist 984 n.
fortune-telling
  divination 511 n.
  occultism 984 n.
forty-niner *traveller* 268 n.
forty winks *sleep* 679 n.
forum *focus* 76 n.
  meeting place 192 n.
  rostrum 539 n.
  arena 724 n.
  mart 796 n.
  tribunal 956 n.
forward *early* 135 adj.
  fore 237 adj.
  send 272 vb.
  forward 285 adv.
  intelligent 498 adj.
  correspond 588 vb.
  willing 597 adj.
  wilful 602 adj.
  be expedient 642 vb.
  make better 654 vb.
  impertinent 878 adj.
  discourteous 885 adj.
forward-looking
  progressive 285 adj.
forwardness
  intelligence 498 n.
  willingness 597 n.
  non-preparation 670 n.
  (see precocity)
forward, set
  undertake 672 vb.
fosse *fence* 235 n.
  furrow 262 n.
  defences 713 n.
fossil *remainder* 41 n.
  antiquity 125 n.
  archaism 127 n.
  old man 133 n.
  organism 358 n.
  corpse 363 n.
fossilization
  condensation 324 n.
  hardening 326 n.
fossor *excavator* 255 n.
foster *look after* 457 vb.
  train 534 vb.
  make better 654 vb.
  safeguard 660 vb.
  patronize 703 vb.
  permit 756 vb.
  animate 821 vb.
  pet 889 vb.
foster-child
  favourite 890 n.
foster-father *parent* 169 n.
fosterling *child* 132 n.
fother *line* 227 vb.
  close 264 vb.
foul *collide* 279 vb.

windy 352adj.
fetid 397adj.
evil 616adj.
bad 645adj.
unclean 649adj.
insalubrious 653adj.
unpleasant 827adj.
ugly 842adj.
disliked 861adj.
wrong 914adj.
foul play 930n.
heinous 934adj.
foulard *textile* 222n.
foul language
scurrility 899n.
foul play *evil* 616n.
injustice 914n.
foul play 930n.
found *stabilize* 153vb.
cause 156vb.
liquefy 337vb.
heat 381vb.
dower 777vb.
foundation
composition 56n.
beginning 68n.
permanence 144n.
source 156n.
base 214n.
basis 218n.
preparation 669n.
foundational
fundamental 156adj.
founder *cause* 156n.
producer 167n.
descend 309vb.
founder 313vb.
perish 361vb.
planner 623n.
patron 707n.
fail 728vb.
benefactor 903n.
foundered *impotent* 161adj.
deep 211adj.
foundling *derelict* 779n.
foundry *workshop* 687n.
found upon *attribute* 158vb.
fount *origin* 68n.
source 156n.
stream 350n.
print-type 587n.
store 632n.
fountain *source* 156n.
outflow 298n.
soft drink 301n.
climber 308n.
stream 350n.
store 632n.
four *quaternity* 96n.
four corners *whole* 52n.
four-dimensional

metric 465adj.
four-flusher *deceiver* 545n.
fourfold *fourfold* 97adj.
four-in-hand
carriage 274n.
four-letter word
plainness 573n.
fourposter *bed* 218n.
four-sided
symmetrical 245adj.
foursome *quaternity* 96n.
dance 837n.
four-square *four* 96adj.
angulated 247adj.
fourth dimension
time 108n.
fourth estate
the press 528n.
four-wheeler *cab* 274n.
fowl *bird* 365n.
hunt 619vb.
fowler *hunter* 619n.
fowling-piece *chase* 619n.
fire-arm 723n.
fox *vermin* 365n.
puzzle 474vb.
trickster 545n.
slyboots 698n.
noxious animal 904n.
foxglove
poisonous plant 659n.
foxhole *tunnel* 263n.
refuge 662n.
fox-hound *dog* 365n.
hunter 619n.
foxiness *cunning* 698n.
fox-trot *dance* 837n.,vb.
foxy *brown* 430adj.
red 431adj.
intelligent 498adj.
cunning 698adj.
dishonest 930adj.
foyer *lobby* 194n.
theatre 594n.
fracas *turmoil* 61n.
loudness 400n.
quarrel 709n.
fight 716n.
fraction *quantity* 26n.
part 53n.
numerical element 85n.
fraction 102n.
trifle 639n.
fractionize *sunder* 46vb.
fractious *unwilling* 598adj.
irascible 892adj.
fracture *separation* 46n.
break 46vb.
discontinuity 72n.
gap 201n.
be brittle 330vb.

fragile
unsubstantial 4adj.
flimsy 163adj.
brittle 330adj.
fragility
transientness 114n.
fragment *small thing* 33n.
break 46vb.
part, piece 53n.
fraction 102n.
be brittle 330vb.
pulverize 332vb.
fragmentary
fragmentary 53adj.
incomplete 55adj.
fractional 102adj.
exiguous 196adj.
imperfect 647adj.
uncompleted 726adj.
fragmentation
separation 46n.
pulverulence 332n.
fragrance *sweetness* 392n.
odour 394n.
fragrance 396n.
fragrant *pleasant* 376adj.
frail *ephemeral* 114adj.
flimsy 163adj.
basket 194n.
brittle 330adj.
unsafe 661adj.
wicked, frail 934adj.
unchaste 951adj.
frailty *vice* 934n.
(*see* fragility)
framboesia
skin disease 651n.
frame *modality* 7n.
relate 9vb.
mould 23n.
affix 45vb.
produce 164vb.
receptacle 194n.
basket 194n.
hanger 217n.
frame 218n.
be exterior 223vb.
circumscribe 232vb.
outline 233n.,vb.
edging 234n.
inclose 235vb.
form 243n.
efform 243vb.
structure 331n.
garden 370n.
fake 541vb.
predetermine 608vb.
plot 623vb.
indict 928vb.
frame of mind
affections 817n.

frame of reference
  referral 9 n.
  prototype 23 n.
frame-up *trap* 542 n.
  untruth 543 n.
  predetermination 608 n.
  plot 623 n.
  false charge 928 n.
framework *basket* 194 n.
  frame 218 n.
  outline 233 n.
  structure 331 n.
framing
  circumjacent 230 adj.
franchise *vote* 605 n.
  freedom 744 n.
  dueness 915 n.
  non-liability 919 n.
Franciscans *monk* 986 n.
francophile
  xenophile 880 n.
franc-tireur *soldier* 722 n.
frangibility
  non-coherence 49 n.
  brittleness 330 n.
frangipane *scent* 396 n.
frank *undisguised* 522 adj.
  correspond 588 vb.
  artless 699 adj.
  ungracious 885 adj.
  trustworthy 929 adj.
Frankenstein's monster
  monster 938 n.
  demon 970 n.
frankfurter *meat* 301 n.
frankincense *resin* 357 n.
  scent 396 n.
franklin *possessor* 776 n.
frankness *truth* 494 n.
  veracity 540 n.
  artlessness 699 n.
  plainness 573 n.
frantic *disorderly* 61 adj.
  furious 176 adj.
  absurd 497 adj.
  frenzied 503 adj.
  active 678 adj.
  excitable 822 adj.
frantically *extremely* 32 adv.
frap *tie* 45 vb.
  tighten 45 vb.
fraternal *akin* 11 adj.
  corporate 708 adj.
  concordant 710 adj.
  friendly 880 adj.
  benevolent 897 adj.
fraternity *family* 11 n.
  association 706 n.
  community 708 n.
  monk 986 n.
fraternize *accord* 24 vb.

combine 50 vb.
  concord 710 vb.
  be friendly 880 vb.
  be sociable 882 vb.
fratricide *homicide* 362 n.
Frau *lady* 373 n.
fraud *duplicity* 541 n.
  deception 542 n.
  trickery 542 n.
  impostor 545 n.
  slyboots 698 n.
  peculation 788 n.
fraudulence *deception* 542 n.
fraudulent *false* 541 adj.
  thieving 788 adj.
  perfidious 930 adj.
  dishonest 930 adj.
  lawbreaking 954 adj.
fraught *full* 54 adj.
fraught with
  productive 164 adj.
  possessing 773 adj.
fray *rend* 46 vb.
  rub 333 vb.
  impair 655 vb.
  fight 716 n.
freak *nonconformist* 84 n.
  crank 504 n.
  whim 604 n.
  prodigy 864 n.
freakish
  unexpected 508 adj.
  (*see* freak)
freakishness *caprice* 604 n.
freckle *maculation* 437 n.
  variegate 437 vb.
  skin disease 651 n.
  blemish 845 n.
free *disjoin* 46 vb.
  unstick 49 vb.
  veracious 540 adj.
  voluntary 597 adj.
  escaped 667 adj.
  deliver 668 vb.
  disencumber 701 vb.
  free 744 adj.
  given 781 adj.
  uncharged 812 adj.
  liberal 813 adj.
  ungracious 885 adj.
  unwedded 895 adj.
  unchaste 951 adj.
free agent *free man* 744 n.
free allowance
  decrement 42 n.
free-and-easy *rash* 857 adj.
  impertinent 878 adj.
  sociable 882 adj.
freeboard *interval* 201 n.
freebooter *militarist* 722 n.
  robber 789 n.

knave 938 n.
free-born *free* 744 adj.
free choice
  willingness 597 n.
free companion
  militarist 722 n.
freed *liberated* 746 adj.
freedman *free man* 744 n.
freedom *opportunity* 137 n.
  freedom 744 n.
  permission 756 n.
  dueness 915 n.
freedom of action
  independence 744 n.
free field *scope* 744 n.
free-for-all *turmoil* 61 n.
  fight 716 n.
free from *unmixed* 44 adj.
free hand *scope* 744 n.
  permit 756 n.
  liberality 813 n.
freehold
  independence 744 n.
  unconditional 744 adj.
  lands 777 n.
  proprietary 777 adj.
free-holder *possessor* 776 n.
freelance *worker* 686 n.
  militarist 722 n.
  free man 744 n.
free love
  type of marriage 894 n.
  illicit love 951 n.
freely *easily* 701 adv.
  freely 744 adv.
freeman *free man* 744 n.
freemartin *eunuch* 161 n.
Freemasonry *secrecy* 525 n.
  society 708 n.
  friendship 880 n.
free pardon *amnesty* 506 n.
  forgiveness 909 n.
free play *scope* 744 n.
free range
  stock farm 369 n.
free speech *freedom* 744 n.
free-spoken *artless* 699 adj.
free-thinker
  irreligionist 971 n.
free thought *freedom* 744 n.
  antichristianity 974 n.
free trade *ingress* 297 n.
  scope 744 n.
  trade 791 n.
  no charge 812 n.
freetrader *free man* 744 n.
free verse *verse form* 593 n.
freewheel
  go smoothly 258 vb.
free will *will* 595 n.
  freedom 744 n.

freeze *cohere* 48 vb.
　halt 145 vb.
　be dense 324 vb.
　harden 326 vb.
　render insensible 375 vb.
　be cold 380 vb.
　refrigerate 382 vb.
　preserve 666 vb.
　not pay 805 vb.
　quake 854 vb.
　frighten 854 vb.
freezer *refrigerator* 384 n.
freeze on to *retain* 778 vb.
freight *fill* 54 vb.
　stow 187 vb.
　contents 193 n.
　load 193 vb.
　thing transferred 272 n.
　gravity 322 n.
　merchandise 795 n.
freightage *transport* 272 n.
　price 809 n.
freight-car *train* 274 n.
freighted *full* 54 adj.
　bearing 273 adj.
freighter *carrier* 273 n.
　merchant ship 275 n.
frenzied *furious* 176 adj.
　angry 891 adj.
frenzy *turmoil* 61 n.
　spasm 318 n.
　commotion 318 n.
　frenzy 503 n.
　fantasy 513 n.
　unmeaningness 515 n.
　illness 651 n.
　activity 678 n.
　restlessness 678 n.
　excitable state 822 n.
　desire 859 n.
frequency *degree* 27 n.
　continuity 71 n.
　recurrence 106 n.
　frequency 139 n.
　periodicity 141 n.
　cacation 302 n.
　oscillation 317 n.
frequent *many* 104 adj.
　go on 146 vb.
　be present 189 vb.
　dwell 192 vb.
　usual 610 adj.
　be wont 610 vb.
frequentation
　social round 882 n.
frequenter *habitué* 610 n.
fresco *picture* 553 n.
fresh *unimitative* 21 adj.
　new 126 adj.
　matinal 128 adj.
　early 135 adj.

　airy 340 adj.
　humid 341 adj.
　windy 352 adj.
　cold 380 adj.
　remembered 505 adj.
　unhabituated 611 adj.
　not bad 644 adj.
　clean 648 adj.
　healthy 650 adj.
　salubrious 652 adj.
　preserved 666 adj.
　impertinent 878 adj.
　tipsy 949 adj.
fresh air *salubrity* 652 n.
fresh-air fiend
　sanitarian 652 n.
fresh blood
　aftercomer 67 n.
freshen *be strong* 162 vb.
　invigorate 174 vb.
　aerify 340 vb.
　blow 352 vb.
　refrigerate 382 vb.
　purify 648 vb.
　sanitate 652 vb.
　make better 654 vb.
　revive 656 vb.
　refresh 685 vb.
　decorate 844 vb.
freshened up
　modernized 126 n.
freshet *stream* 350 n.
freshman
　college student 538 n.
freshness
　non-imitation 21 n.
　(*see fresh*)
fresh outbreak
　relapse 657 n.
fresh spurt *revival* 656 n.
fresh start *start* 68 n.
fresh-water sailor
　bungler 697 n.
fret *rend* 46 vb.
　rub 333 vb.
　give pain 377 vb.
　cry 408 vb.
　play music 413 vb.
　harp 414 n.
　variegate 437 vb.
　restlessness 678 n.
　disobey 738 vb.
　excitable state 822 n.
　worry 825 n.
　torment 827 vb.
　cause discontent 829 vb.
　decorate 844 vb.
　enrage 891 vb.
fretful *crying* 408 adj.
　capricious 604 adj.
　active 678 adj.

　irascible 892 adj.
fretting
　ornamental art 844 n.
fretwork *network* 222 n.
　ornamental art 844 n.
Freudianism
　psychology 447 n.
friable *flimsy* 163 adj.
　brittle 330 adj.
　powdery 332 adj.
friar *monk* 986 n.
　pastor 986 n.
friarhood
　monasticism 985 n.
friary *monastery* 986 n.
fribble *neglect* 458 vb.
　nonentity 639 n.
　trifle 639 n.
　be inactive 679 vb.
　amuse oneself 837 vb.
　fop 848 n.
fricassée *dish* 301 n.
frication *friction* 333 n.
fricative *rubbing* 333 adj.
　speech sound 398 n.
　spoken letter 558 n.
　vocal 577 adj.
friction *energy* 160 n.
　counteraction 182 n.
　collision 279 n.
　pulverulence 332 n.
　friction 333 n.
　stridor 407 n.
　difficulty 700 n.
　opposition 704 n.
　dissension 709 n.
　painfulness 827 n.
frictionless *silent* 399 adj.
　easy, wieldy 701 adj.
　co-operating 706 adj.
　pleasurable 826 adj.
Friday *fast* 946 n.
fridge *provisions* 301 n.
　refrigerator 384 n.
　storage 632 n.
　preserver 666 n.
friend *auxiliary* 707 n.
　colleague 707 n.
　friend 880 n.
　loved one 887 n.
　kind person 897 n.
　benefactor 903 n.
　Protestant 976 n.
　sectarist 978 n.
friend at court
　latency 523 n.
　patron 707 n.
friendless *alone* 88 adj.
　defenceless 161 adj.
　friendless 883 adj.
friendliness *irenics* 719 n.

friendliness 880n.
  sociability 882n.
  courteous act 884n.
  benevolence 897n.
friendly *aiding* 703adj.
  concordant 710adj.
  friendly 880adj.
  sociable 882adj.
  amiable 884adj.
friend of all the world
  xenophile 880n.
Friends *sect* 978n.
friendship *relation* 9n.
  peace 717n.
  friendship 880n.
  sociality 882n.
  love 887n.
  benevolence 897n.
frieze *summit* 213n.
  textile 222n.
  trimming 844n.
frigate *sailing-ship* 275n.
  warship 722n.
fright *eyesore* 842n.
  fear 854n.
frighten *dissuade* 613vb.
  raise the alarm 665vb.
  hinder 702vb.
  deject 834vb.
  frighten 854vb.
frightful *prodigious* 32adj.
  ugly 842adj.
frightfulness
  terror tactics 712n.
frigid *cold* 380adj.
  feeble 572adj.
  impassive 820adj.
  inexcitable 823adj.
  pure 950adj.
frigidaire *provisions* 301n.
  refrigerator 384n.
frigidarium
  refrigerator 384n.
frigidity *coldness* 380n.
  feebleness 572n.
  moral insensibility 820n.
  purity 950n.
frigorific *cooled* 382adj.
frill *adjunct* 40n.
  edging 234n.
  trimming 844n.
frillies *underwear* 228n.
frills *ornament* 574n.
frills and furbelows
  finery 844n.
fringe *adjunct* 40n.
  extremity 69n.
  concomitant 89n.
  contiguity 202n.
  edging 234n.
  hair 259n.

hair-dressing 843n.
  trimming 844n.
frippery *clothing* 228n.
  bauble 639n.
  finery 844n.
  bad taste 847n.
  ostentation 875n.
frisk *move fast* 277vb.
  leap 312vb.
  search 459vb.
  be cheerful 833vb.
  rejoice 835vb.
  amuse oneself 837vb.
frisky *leaping* 312adj.
  active 678adj.
  gay 833adj.
frisson *agitation* 318n.
frith *gulf* 345n.
  wood 366n.
fritiniency *ululation* 409n.
fritter away *bate* 37vb.
  waste 634vb.
  be prodigal 815vb.
fritters *pudding* 301n.
frivolity *folly* 499n.
  unimportance 639n.
  merriment 833n.
  rashness 857n.
frivolous
  light-minded 456adj.
  ill-reasoned 477adj.
  capricious 604adj.
  (see frivolity)
frizz *crinkle* 251vb.
  fold 261vb.
frizzing *hair-dressing* 843n.
frizzle *make curved* 248vb.
  fold 261vb.
  be hot 379vb.
frizzy *undulatory* 251adj.
  hairy 259adj.
frock *dress* 228n.
  ecclesiasticize 985vb.
  canonicals 989n.
frock coat *tunic* 228n.
Froebelism *education* 534n.
frog *fastening* 47n.
  jumper 312n.
  frog 365n.
  trimming 844n.
frogman *diver* 313n.
frogmarch *impel* 279vb.
frolic *leap* 312n.
  enjoyment 824n.
  be cheerful 833vb.
  rejoice 835vb.
  amuse oneself 837vb.
from A to Z
  including 78adv.
from beginning to end
  throughout 54adv.

from now on
  henceforth 124adv.
from scratch
  at zero 103adv.
frondescence
  vegetability 366n.
  foliage 366n.
Frondeur *revolter* 738n.
front *precedence* 64n.
  beginning 68n.
  impend 155vb.
  nearness 200n.
  exteriority 223n.
  apron 228n.
  edge 234n.
  front 237n.
  orientate 281vb.
  duplicity 541n.
  resistance 715n.
  battle 718n.
  battleground 724n.
  insolence 878n.
frontage *face* 237n.
frontier *entrance* 68n.
  extremity 69n.
  farness 199n.
  contiguity 202n.
  edge 234n.
  limit 236n.
frontiersman *dweller* 191n.
front, in *ahead* 283adv.
  in front 237adv.
fronting *opposite* 240adj.
frontispiece *prelude* 66n.
  front, face 237n.
frontlet *vestments* 989n.
front-page *notable* 638adj.
front-rank
  supreme 34adj.
front window *exhibit* 522n.
frosh *college student* 538n.
frost *powder* 332n.
  wintriness 380n.
  refrigerate 382vb.
  opacity 423n.
  whiten 427vb.
  blight 659n.
  failure 728n.
frostbite *coldness* 380n.
  refrigerate 382vb.
frosting *pulverulence* 332n.
frosty *cold* 380adj.
  white 427adj.
  unsociable 883adj.
froth *stimulation* 174n.
  excrement 302n.
  effervesce 318vb.
  moisture 341n.
  bubble 355n.,vb.
  chatter 581n.
  bauble 639n.

dirt 649 n.
be excitable 822 vb.
frothblower
drunkard 949 n.
frothy *light* 323 adj.
bubbly 355 adj.
diffuse 570 adj.
ornate 574 adj.
trivial 639 adj.
frou-frou *faintness* 401 n.
sibilation 406 n.
frounce *fold* 261 n., vb.
frown *distort* 246 vb.
fold 261 n.
gesture 547 n.
hindrance 702 n.
discontent 829 n.
rudeness 885 n.
anger 891 n.
be sullen 893 vb.
frown down
humiliate 872 vb.
frowning *adverse* 731 adj.
serious 834 adj.
frown on *prohibit* 757 vb.
deject 834 vb.
(see disapprove)
frowsty *fetid* 397 adj.
frowzy *fetid* 397 adj.
frozen *cohesive* 48 adj.
still 266 adj.
dense 324 adj.
hard 326 adj.
insensible 375 adj.
a-cold 380 adj.
cooled 382 adj.
preserved 666 adj.
fearing 854 adj.
frozen assets *estate* 777 n.
debt 803 n.
fructification
propagation 164 n.
productiveness 171 n.
fructose *food content* 301 n.
sweet 392 n.
frugal *cautious* 858 adj.
fasting 946 adj.
frugality
preservation 666 n.
economy 814 n.
temperance 942 n.
asceticism 945 n.
frugivorous *feeding* 301 adj.
fruit *growth* 157 n.
product 164 n.
fruit 301 n.
fruitarian *abstainer* 942 n.
ascetic 945 n.
fruitful *increasing* 36 adj.
prolific 171 adj.
successful 727 adj.

acquiring 771 adj.
fruit-growing
agriculture 370 n.
fruition *propagation* 164 n.
use 673 n.
enjoyment 824 n.
fruit juice *soft drink* 301 n.
fruitless
unproductive 172 adj.
wasted 634 adj.
profitless 641 adj.
fruity *fragrant* 396 adj.
fetid 397 adj.
frump *bad taste* 847 n.
frustrating
discontenting 829 adj.
frustration
psychopathy 503 n.
disappointment 509 n.
hindrance 702 n.
failure 728 n.
frustum, frustulum
piece, part 53 n.
fry *youngling* 132 n.
cook 301 vb.
be hot 379 vb.
heat 381 vb.
frying-pan *cauldron* 194 n.
heater 383 n.
frying-pan into the fire, out
of the
in adversity 731 adv.
aggravatedly 832 adv.
fubsy *fleshy* 195 adj.
fuddle *distract* 456 vb.
inebriate 949 vb.
fuddled *foolish* 499 adj.
tipsy 949 adj.
fudge *sweet* 392 n.
silly talk 515 n.
trifle 639 n.
Fuehrer *leader* 690 n.
master 741 n.
autocrat 741 n.
fuel *propellant* 287 n.
oil 357 n.
kindle 381 vb.
heater 383 n.
fuel 385 n.
fire 385 vb.
materials 631 n.
store 632 vb.
provide 633 vb.
fugacity
transientness 114 n.
fugitive *disjunct* 46 adj.
transient 114 adj.
wanderer 268 n.
avoider 620 n.
escaper 667 n.
fugitive pieces

reading matter 589 n.
anthology 592 n.
fugleman *living model* 23 n.
leader 690 n.
fugue *musical piece* 412 n.
oblivion 506 n.
fulcrum *pivot* 218 n.
centrality 225 n.
fulfil *do* 676 vb.
observe 768 vb.
fulfilled *veracious* 540 adj.
fulfilment
completeness 54 adj.
sufficiency 635 n.
completion 725 n.
observance 768 n.
enjoyment 824 n.
fulguration *storm* 176 n.
flash 417 n.
luminary 420 n.
fulgurite *explosive* 723 n.
fuliginous *opaque* 423 adj.
black 428 adj.
full *whole* 52 adj.
plenitude 54 n.
assembled 74 adj.
multitudinous 104 adj.
fleshy 195 adj.
broad 205 adj.
loud 400 adj.
veracious 540 adj.
descriptive 590 adj.
filled 635 adj.
clean 648 vb.
completed 725 adj.
drunk 949 adj.
full bat *speeding* 277 n.
full blast *loudness* 400 n.
full-blooded
vigorous 174 adj.
full-blown
grown up 134 adj.
expanded 197 adj.
full-bodied *tasty* 386 adj.
odorous 394 adj.
full career *speeding* 277 n.
full chorus *agreement* 24 n.
loudness 400 n.
full circle *revolution* 149 n.
circuition 314 n.
rotation 315 n.
full-coloured *florid* 425 adj.
full coverage *inclusion* 78 n.
full cry, in *loudly* 400 adv.
pursuing 619 adj.
full dress *formal dress* 228 n.
uniform 228 n.
formality 875 n.
fuller *cleaner* 648 n.
full-fed *sensual* 944 adj.
gluttonous 947 adj.

full force, in *strong* 162adj.
full-grown *grown up* 134adj.
expanded 197adj.
full heart
warm feeling 818n.
full house *plenitude* 54n.
crowd 74n.
playgoer 594n.
full-length
comprehensive 52adj.
long 203adj.
full life *enjoyment* 824n.
intemperance 943n.
sensualism 944n.
full measure
plenitude 54n.
sufficiency 635n.
full-mouthed
ululant 409adj.
fullness *greatness* 32n.
whole 52n.
plenitude 54n.
breadth 205n.
plenty 635n.
completion 725n.
fullness of time, in the
in time 111adv.
prospectively 124adv.
opportunely 137adv.
full of beans
healthy 650adj.
active 678adj.
full play *facility* 701n.
scope 744n.
full pressure *energy* 160n.
exertion 682n.
full-size *great* 32adj.
full speed *speeding* 277n.
full stop *stop* 145n.
quiescence 266n.
punctuation 547n.
full-tilt *actively* 678adv.
full, to the
enough 635adv.
fully *completely* 54adv.
fulminate *be violent* 176vb.
propel 287vb.
be loud 400vb.
emphasize 532adj.
be angry 891vb.
curse 899vb.
threaten 900vb.
dispraise 924vb.
fulsome *fetid* 397adj.
bad 645adj.
unpleasant 827adj.
disliked 861adj.
flattering 925adj.
impure 951adj.
fulvous *yellow* 433adj.
fumarole *chimney* 263n.

furnace 383n.
fumble *touch* 378vb.
be tentative 461vb.
be uncertain 474vb.
be clumsy 695vb.
fumbler *bungler* 697n.
fume *be violent* 176vb.
emit 300vb.
gas 336n.
vaporize 338vb.
be hot 379vb.
odour 394n.
hasten 680vb.
excitable state 822n.
be busy 678vb.
be excitable 822vb.
be angry 891vb.
fumé
semitransparent 424adj.
fumid *opaque* 423adj.
fumigant
prophylactic 658n.
fumigation
vaporization 338n.
inodorousness 395n.
fragrance 396n.
cleaning 648n.
fumigator *fumigator* 385n.
fun *enjoyment* 824n.
pleasurableness 826n.
merriment 833n.
amusement 837n.
funambulism *skill* 694n.
funambulist
proficient 696n.
function *relativeness* 9n.
number 85n.
agency 173n.
function 622vb.
utility 640n.
do 676vb.
formality 875n.
celebration 876n.
jurisdiction 955adj.
functional
correlative 12adj.
instrumental 628adj.
useful 640adj.
Functionalism
school of painting 553n.
functionary *official* 690n.
officer 741n.
consignee 754n.
functionless *useless* 641adj.
functus officio
extinct 2adj.
abrogated 752adj.
fund *store* 632n., vb.
funds 797n.
fundament *base* 214n.
rear, buttocks 238n.

fundamental *intrinsic* 5adj.
simple 44adj.
beginning 68adj.
fundamental 156adj.
undermost 214adj.
supporting 218adj.
important 638adj.
fundamentalism
theology 973n.
scripture 975n.
orthodoxism 976n.
pietism 979n.
fundamentally
intrinsically 5adv.
positively 32adv.
fundamentals *reality* 1n.
base 214n.
chief thing 638n.
funds, in *moneyed* 800adj.
fundus *base* 214n.
funeral *funeral* 364n.
worry 825n.
funeral oration
valediction 296n.
obsequies 364n.
oration 579n.
lament 836n.
funereal *funereal* 364adj.
dark 418adj.
black 428adj.
cheerless 834adj.
fun-fair
pleasure-ground 837n.
fungicide *poison* 659n.
fungiform *rotund* 252adj.
vegetal 366adj.
fungoid *vegetal* 366adj.
fungology *botany* 368n.
fungus *plant* 366n.
fetor 397n.
dirt 649n.
blight 659n.
funicle *filament* 208n.
funicular *fibrous* 208adj.
train 274n.
railroad 624n.
funk *smoke* 388vb.
stink 397vb.
fear 854n.
coward 856n.
funk-hole
hiding-place 527n.
refuge 662n.
funnel *cylinder* 252n.
cavity 255n.
tunnel, tube 263n.
chimney 263n.
conduit 351n.
air-pipe 353n.
funny *unusual* 84adj.
rowboat 275n.

crazed 503 adj.
witty 839 adj.
funny 849 adj.
funnybone *limb* 53 n.
fur *skin* 226 n.
  covering 226 n.
  neckwear 228 n.
  hair 259 n.
  warm clothes 381 n.
  heraldry 547 n.
  dirt 649 n.
  trimming 844 n.
furacious *thieving* 788 adj.
furbelow *edging* 234 n.
furbish *decorate* 844 vb.
  (*see* refurbish)
furcate *crossed* 222 adj.
  angular 247 adj.
furfur *dirt* 649 n.
furfuraceous
  powdery 332 adj.
Furies *Fury* 891 n.
  Chthonian god 967 n.
furious *destructive* 165 adj.
  furious 176 adj.
  frenzied 503 adj.
  harmful 645 adj.
  hasty 680 adj.
  fervent 818 adj.
  excited 821 adj.
  excitable 822 adj.
  rash 857 adj.
  angry 891 adj.
furiously *extremely* 32 adv.
furl *elevate* 310 vb.
  rotate 315 vb.
  fold 261 vb.
furlough *absence* 190 n.
  leisure 681 n.
  repose 683 n.
  permit 756 n.
furnace *fire* 379 n.
  furnace 383 n.
  workshop 687 n.
furnish *find means* 629 vb.
  provide 633 vb.
  make ready 669 vb.
  give 781 vb.
furnishing(s)
  adjunct 40 n.
  contents 193 n.
  equipment 630 n.
  ornamental art 844 n.
furnishment
  fitting out 669 n.
furniture *equipment* 630 n.
  property 776 n.
furore *violence* 176 n.
  commotion 318 n.
  frenzy 503 n.
  excitation 821 n.

fashion 848 n.
furrier *stripper* 229 n.
furrow *gap* 201 n.
  roughness 259 n.
  fold 261 vb.
  furrow 262 n.
furrowing *concavity* 255 n.
furry *hairy* 259 adj.
further
  in addition 38 adv.
  beyond 199 adv.
  in front 237 adv.
  promote 285 vb.
  aid 703 vb.
furtherance
  progression 285 n.
  improvement 654 n.
  aid 703 n.
furthermost *distant* 199 adj.
further reflection
  amendment 654 n.
furtive *stealthy* 525 adj.
furuncle *swelling* 253 n.
fury *violence* 176 n.
  violent creature 176 n.
  excitation 821 n.
  excitable state 822 n.
  anger, Fury 891 n.
  shrew 892 n.
  hell-hag 904 n.
  demon 970 n.
furze *plant* 366 n.
fuscous *brown* 430 adj.
fuse *heat* 381 vb.
  lighter 385 n.
  safeguard 662 n.
  hitch 702 n.
  ammunition 723 n.
  (*see* fusion)
fusee *lighter* 385 n.
fuselage *frame* 218 n.
fusiform
  angulated 247 adj.
  tapering 256 adj.
fusil *fire-arm* 723 n.
fusilier *soldiery* 722 n.
fusillade
  slaughter 362 n.
  bombardment 712 n.
  execute 963 vb.
fusion *mixture* 43 n.
  junction 45 n.
  combination 50 n.
  liquefaction 337 n.
  association 706 n.
fuss *commotion* 318 n.
  exaggeration 546 n.
  activity 678 vb.
  haste 680 n.
  excitation 821 n.
  excitable state 822 n.

  be fastidious 862 vb.
  ostentation 875 n.
  be angry 891 vb.
fussiness
  fastidiousness 862 n.
fusspot *meddler* 678 n.
  perfectionist 861 n.
fussy
  narrow-minded 481 adj.
  active 678 adj.
  authoritarian 735 adj.
  fastidious 862 adj.
fust *be old* 127 vb.
  deteriorate 655 vb.
fustian *textile* 222 n.
  absurdity 497 n.
  empty talk 515 n.
  magniloquence 574 n.
fustigate *flog* 963 vb.
fusty *antiquated* 127 adj.
  fetid 397 adj.
  dirty 649 adj.
futhorc *letter* 558 n.
futile *wasted* 634 adj.
  unskilful 695 adj.
futilitarian
  underestimation 483 n.
futility
  ineffectuality 161 n.
  foolery 497 n.
  absurdity 497 n.
  inutility 641 n.
  despisedness 922 n.
future *unborn* 2 adj.
  subsequent 120 adj.
  futurity 124 n.
  impending 155 adj.
  unknown 491 adj.
  expected 507 adj.
future, in
  henceforth 124 adv.
future life *destiny* 155 n.
futures *gambling* 618 n.
future state
  future state 124 n.
Futurism
  school of painting 553 n.
Futurist *modernist* 126 n.
  artist 556 n.
futuristic *modern* 126 adj.
futurity *time* 108 n.
  posteriority 120 n.
  different time 122 n.
  futurity 124 n.
fuzzle *inebriate* 949 vb.
fuzzy *amorphous* 244 adj.
  hairy 259 adj.
  shadowy 419 adj.
  ill-seen 444 adj.
fylfot *heraldry* 547 n.
  talisman 983 n.

G

gab *loquacity* 581 n.
  boast 877 n., vb.
gabbard *sailing-ship* 275 n.
gabber *speaker* 579 n.
  chatterer 581 n.
gabble *ululate* 409 vb.
  empty talk 515 n.
  speak 579 vb.
  stammer 580 vb.
  chatter 581 vb.
gabelle *tax* 809 n.
gaberdine *tunic* 228 n.
gaberlunzie
  low fellow 869 n.
gabion *fortification* 713 n.
gable *vertex* 213 n.
  roof 226 n.
  laterality 239 n.
gable-end *extremity* 69 n.
gaby *ninny* 501 n.
gad *wander* 267 vb.
gadfly *fly* 365 n.
  excitant 821 n.
gadget *object* 319 n.
  contrivance 623 n.
  instrument 628 n.
  tool 630 n.
gaff *sharp point* 256 n.
  spear 723 n.
gaffe *mistake* 495 n.
gaffer *old man* 133 n.
  male 372 n.
  fool 501 n.
  countryman 869 n.
gaffle *sharp point* 256 n.
gag *stopper* 264 n.
  silence 399 vb.
  make mute 578 vb.
  act 594 vb.
  obstacle 702 n.
  restrain 747 vb.
  fetter 748 n.
  witticism 839 n.
gaga *foolish* 499 adj.
gage *defiance* 711 n.
  security 767 n.
gaggle *group* 74 n.
  ululate 409 vb.
gag-man, gagsman
  dramatist 594 n.
  auxiliary 707 n.
  humorist 839 n.
gaiety *merriment* 833 n.
  sociability 882 n.
gaily *inadvertently* 456 adv.
  hopefully 852 adv.
  rashly 857 adv.
gain *increment* 36 n.
  be early 135 vb.

growth 157 n.
product 164 n.
progression 284 n.
arrive 295 vb.
benefit 615 n.
utility 640 n.
gain 771 n., vb.
booty 790 n.
be rewarded 962 vb.
gain a footing
  prevail 178 vb.
gainful *profitable* 640 adj.
  gainful 771 adj.
  rewarding 962 adj.
gaingiving *doubt* 486 n.
gaining *non-uniform* 17 adj.
  anachronistic 118 adj.
gaining time *delay* 136 n.
gain on *outstrip* 277 vb.
  approach 289 vb.
  outdo 306 vb.
gain over *induce* 612 vb.
gains *wealth* 800 n.
gainsay *negate* 533 vb.
gain time *spin out* 113 vb.
  be early 135 vb.
  put off 136 vb.
gain upon one
  be wont 610 vb.
gait *gait* 265 n.
  way 624 n.
gaiters *legwear* 228 n.
  badge of rule 743 n.
  canonicals 989 n.
gala *festivity* 837 n.
  pageant 875 n.
galactic *cosmic* 321 adj.
galactose
  food content 301 n.
  sweet 392 n.
Galahad
  brave person 855 n.
  gentleman 929 n.
  virgin 950 n.
galanty show
  spectacle 445 n.
gala performance
  pageant 875 n.
galaxy *group* 74 n.
  star 321 n.
  island 349 n.
  glow 417 n.
  luminary 420 n.
gale *gale* 352 n.
  excitable state 822 n.
gale force *storm* 176 n.
Galenic *medical* 658 adj.
Galenical *medicine* 658 n.
gali-gali man
  conjuror 545 n.
galilee

church exterior 990 n.
galimatias
  unmeaningness 515 n.
galingale *condiment* 389 n.
gall *swelling* 253 n.
  rub 333 vb.
  give pain 377 vb.
  sourness 393 n.
  bane 659 n.
  torment 827 vb.
  irascibility 892 n.
  malevolence 898 n.
gall and wormwood
  painfulness 827 n.
gallant *courageous* 855 adj.
  showy 875 adj.
  courteous 884 adj.
  lover 887 n.
  libertine 952 n.
gallantry (*see* gallant)
galleass *galley* 275 n.
  warship 722 n.
galleon *ship* 275 n.
  merchant ship 275 n.
  warship 722 n.
gallery *tunnel* 263 n.
  doorway 263 n.
  listener 415 n.
  onlookers 441 n.
  exhibit 522 n.
  theatre 594 n.
  playgoer 594 n.
  collection 632 n.
  church interior 990 n.
galley *chamber* 194 n.
  galley, rowboat 275 n.
  heater 383 n.
galley proof
  letterpress 587 n.
galleys *penalty* 963 n.
galley-slave *mariner* 270 n.
  busy person 678 n.
  prisoner 750 n.
galliard
  musical piece 412 n.
Gallicans
  church party 978 n.
Gallicism *dialect* 560 n.
galligaskins *breeches* 228 n.
  legwear 228 n.
gallimaufry *medley* 43 n.
gallinipper *fly* 365 n.
galliot *galley* 275 n.
  merchant ship 275 n.
gallipot *vessel* 194 n.
gallivant *wander* 267 vb.
  court 889 vb.
gallivat *sailing-ship* 275 n.
gallon *metrology* 465 n.
gallons *great quantity* 32 n.
galloon *trimming* 844 n.

gallop *be transient* 114 vb.
  gait 265 n.
  ride 267 vb.
  move fast 277 vb.
gallowglass *soldier* 722 n.
gallows *hanger* 217 n.
  means of execution 964 n.
gallowsbird *offender* 904 n.
gall-stone *indigestion* 651 n.
Gallup poll *statistics* 86 n.
  enquiry 459 n.
  empiricism 461 n.
  vote 605 n.
galoot *ninny* 501 n.
  bungler 697 n.
galop *dance* 837 n.
galore *great quantity* 32 n.
  many 104 adj.
  plenty 635 n.
galosh *footwear* 228 n.
galvanism *electricity* 160 n.
  excitation 821 n.
gambade *leap* 312 n.
gambado *legwear* 228 n.
  footwear 228 n.
gambeson *tunic* 228 n.
gambit *début* 68 n.
  essay 671 n.
  tactics 688 n.
gamble *chance* 159 vb.
  be tentative 461 vb.
  uncertainty 474 n.
  conjecture 512 n.
  gamble 618 vb.
  face danger 661 vb.
  speculate 791 vb.
  be rash 857 vb.
gamble away
  be prodigal 815 vb.
gambler
  experimenter 461 n.
  diviner 511 n.
  theorist 512 n.
  gambler 618 n.
  desperado 857 n.
gambling game
  gambling game 837 n.
gambling hell
  gaming-house 618 n.
  place of amusement 837 n.
gamboge
  yellow pigment 433 n.
gambol *leap* 312 n., vb.
  enjoyment 824 n.
  amuse oneself 837 vb.
game *crippled* 163 adj.
  meat 301 n.
  animal 365 n.
  savouriness 390 n.
  trickery 542 n.
  resolute 599 adj.

  stamina 600 n.
  persevering 600 adj.
  objective 617 n.
  gamble 618 vb.
  chase 619 n.
  stratagem 698 n.
  contest 716 n.
  amusement 837 n.
  laughing-stock 851 n.
  courageous 855 adj.
game at which two can play
  retaliation 714 n.
gamecock *contender* 716 n.
  combatant 722 n.
  brave person 855 n.
gamekeeper
  animal husbandry 369 n.
  keeper 749 n.
game of, make
  befool 542 vb.
game reserve
  pleasance 192 n.
  wood 366 n.
games *exercise* 682 n.
  contest 716 n.
  sport 837 n.
gamesman *player* 837 n.
gamesmanship
  tactics 688 n.
  cunning 698 n.
gamesome *gay* 833 adj.
  lively 819 adj.
  amused 837 adj.
gamester
  experimenter 461 n.
  gambler 618 n.
  player 837 n.
gametophyte *plant* 366 n.
gamin *low fellow* 869 n.
gammadion *talisman* 983 n.
gamma ray
  radiation 417 n.
gammer *old woman* 133 n.
  lady 373 n.
gammon *meat* 301 n.
  absurdity 497 n.
  silly talk 515 n.
  falsehood 541 n.
  deceive 542 vb.
gamomania *mania* 502 n.
  type of marriage 894 n.
gamp *shade* 226 n.
gamut *series* 71 n.
  musical note 410 n.
gamy *pungent* 388 adj.
  fetid 397 adj.
gander *waterfowl* 365 n.
  male animal 372 n.
gang *band* 74 n.
  move 265 vb.
  personnel 686 n.

  party 708 n.
ganger *worker* 686 n.
gangling *unwieldy* 195 adj.
  clumsy 695 adj.
gangplank *bridge* 624 n.
gangrene *decay* 51 n.
  be unclean 649 vb.
  ulcer 651 n.
  deteriorate 654 vb.
gang rule *lawlessness* 954 n.
gangster *murderer* 362 n.
  robber 789 n.
  offender 904 n.
gang up *congregate* 74 vb.
  co-operate 706 vb.
gang up with
  accompany 89 vb.
gangway *doorway* 263 n.
  access, bridge 624 n.
gannet *bird of prey* 365 n.
gantry *stand* 218 n.
Ganymede *satellite* 321 n.
  a beauty 841 n.
gaol *gaol* 748 n.
gaol-bird *prisoner* 750 n.
  offender 904 n.
gaoler *janitor* 264 n.
  gaoler 749 n.
gap *disjunction* 46 n.
  incompleteness 55 n.
  discontinuity 72 n.
  gap 201 n.
  concavity 255 n.
  opening 263 n.
  defect 647 n.
gape *space* 201 vb.
  be deep 211 vb.
  open 263 vb.
  gaze 438 vb.
  watch 441 vb.
  be curious 453 vb.
  wonder 864 vb.
gape for *be hungry* 859 vb.
gaper *spectator* 441 n.
  ninny 501 n.
gaping *expanded* 197 adj.
gappy *spaced* 201 adj.
garage *small house* 192 n.
  stable 192 n.
  chamber 194 n.
  cover 226 n.
  storage 632 n.
  safeguard 660 vb.
garb *dressing* 228 n.
  dress 228 vb.
  heraldry 547 n.
garbage *dirt* 649 n.
garbage can *vessel* 194 n.
garble *subtract* 39 vb.
  exclude 57 vb.
  mislead 495 vb.

misinterpret 521 vb.
be false 541 vb.
garden *inclosure* 235 n.
garden 370 n.
gardener *gardener* 370 n.
domestic 742 n.
gardening *agriculture* 370 n.
ornamental art 844 n.
garden-party
amusement 837 n.
gardens *pleasance* 192 n.
pleasure-ground 837 n.
Gargantuan *huge* 195 adj.
gargle *moisten* 341 vb.
cleanser 648 n.
prophylactic 658 n.
gargoyle *outlet* 298 n.
conduit 351 n.
drain 351 n.
eyesore 842 n.
ornamental art 844 n.
garish *luminous* 417 adj.
florid 425 adj.
graceless 842 adj.
ornamental 844 adj.
vulgar 847 adj.
showy 875 adj.
garland *loop* 250 n.
badge 547 n.
trophy 729 n.
decorate 844 vb.
honours 866 n.
celebrate 876 vb.
pay respects 884 vb.
garlic *condiment* 389 n.
fetor 397 n.
vegetable 301 n.
garment *dress* 228 n., vb.
garner *store* 632 vb.
garnet *redness* 431 n.
gem 844 n.
garnish *adjunct* 40 n.
cook 301 vb.
pay 804 vb.
expenditure 806 n.
ornamentation 844 n.
garniture *dressing* 228 n.
garret *attic* 194 n.
vertex 213 n.
garrison *resident* 191 n.
safeguard 660 vb.
defender 713 n.
armed force 722 n.
keeper 749 n.
garron *pony* 273 n.
garrotte, garotte
kill 362 vb.
execute 963 vb.
means of execution 964 n.
garrotter *murderer* 362 n.
punisher 963 n.

garrulous
disclosing 526 adj.
loquacious 581 adj.
garter *fastening* 47 n.
compressor 198 n.
hanger 217 n.
supporter 218 n.
underwear 228 n.
badge 547 n.
decoration 729 n.
badge of rank 743 n.
honours 866 n.
garth *inclosure* 235 n.
gas *propellant* 287 n.
lifter 310 n.
levity 323 n.
rarity 325 n.
fluid 335 n.
gas 336 n.
oil 357 n.
murder 362 vb.
anæsthetic 375 n.
heater 383 n.
fuel 385 n.
empty talk 515 n.
be loquacious 581 vb.
weapon 723 n.
boast 877 n.
execute 963 vb.
gas-bag *bladder* 194 n.
chatterer 581 n.
gas-chamber
slaughter-house 362 n.
prison camp 748 n.
means of execution 964 n.
gas-coke *coal* 385 n.
Gasconism *boasting* 877 n.
gaselier *pendant* 217 n.
gas 336 n.
lamp 420 n.
gaseous *light* 323 adj.
gaseous 336 adj.
gas-flare *torch* 420 n.
gash *cut* 46 vb.
gap 201 n.
notch 260 n.
wound 655 n.
gas-holder *gas* 336 n.
storage 632 n.
gasify *lighten* 323 vb.
rarefy 325 vb.
gasify 336 vb.
vaporize 338 vb.
gasket *lining* 227 n.
gaskins *legwear* 228 n.
gas mantle *lamp* 420 n.
gas-mask *covering* 226 n.
safeguard 662 n.
preserver 666 n.
armour 713 n.
gasoline *propellant* 287 n.

oil 357 n.
fuel 385 n.
gasometer *gas* 336 n.
storage 632 n.
gasp *breathe* 352 vb.
rasp 407 vb.
cry 408 n., vb.
voice 577 n.
be fatigued 684 vb.
wonder 864 vb.
gasper *tobacco* 388 n.
gasp for *desire* 859 vb.
gas-pipe *air-pipe* 353 n.
gas-proof *sealed off* 264 adj.
invulnerable 660 adj.
gas, put under
render insensible 375 vb.
gas-ring *furnace* 383 n.
gasser *chatterer* 581 n.
gassy *gaseous* 336 adj.
vaporific 338 adj.
windy 352 adj.
loquacious 581 adj.
gastral *cellular* 194 adj.
gastralgia *indigestion* 651 n.
gastriloquism *voice* 577 n.
gastritis
indigestion 651 n.
gastro-enteritis
dysentery 651 n.
gastronomy
gastronomy 301 n.
gluttony 947 n.
gasworks *gas* 336 n.
workshop 687 n.
gat *gap* 201 n.
opening 263 n.
pistol 723 n.
gate *entrance* 68 n.
barrier 235 n.
doorway 263 n.
incomer 297 n.
onlookers 441 n.
fort 713 n.
imprison 747 vb.
receipt 807 n.
gateau *pastry* 301 n.
gate-crash *intrude* 297 vb.
be sociable 882 vb.
gate-crasher *intruder* 59 n.
gate-keeper *janitor* 264 n.
gate-money *receipt* 807 n.
gate-post *doorway* 263 n.
gateway *entrance* 68 n.
gather *join* 45 vb.
congregate 74 vb.
expand 197 vb.
fold 261 vb.
meet 295 vb.
cultivate 370 vb.
be informed 524 vb.

store 632 vb.
acquire 771 vb.
take 786 vb.
gatherer
accumulator 74 n.
gathering *assembly* 74 n.
conference 584 n.
bookbinding 589 n.
ulcer 651 n.
toxic 653 adj.
(*see* gather)
gathering cloud(s)
omen 511 n.
danger 661 n.
warning 664 n.
adversity 731 n.
gather together
converge 293 vb.
gather way *navigate* 269 vb.
gauche *sinistral* 242 adj.
ignorant 491 adj.
foolish 499 adj.
inelegant 576 adj.
clumsy 695 adj.
ill-bred 847 adj.
gaucherie *ignorance* 491 n.
gaucho *rider* 268 n.
herdsman 369 n.
gaudery *finery* 844 n.
airs 873 n.
gaudy *florid* 425 adj.
graceless 842 adj.
ornamented 844 adj.
vulgar 847 adj.
showy 875 adj.
gauge *breadth* 205 n.
testing agent 461 n.
gauge 465 n., vb.
gauleiter *tyrant* 735 n.
autocrat 741 n.
officer 741 n.
ruffian 904 n.
gaunt *lean* 206 adj.
deformed 246 adj.
gauntlet *glove* 228 n.
defiance 711 n.
armour 713 n.
gauze *transparency* 422 n.
semitransparency 424 n.
gauzy *insubstantial* 4 adj.
gavel *badge of rule* 743 n.
gavelkind
joint possession 775 n.
gavial *reptile* 365 n.
gavotte *musical piece* 412 n.
dance 837 n.
gawk *gaze* 438 vb.
watch 441 vb.
be curious 453 vb.
ninny 501 n.
wonder 864 vb.

gawky *foolish* 499 adj.
clumsy 695 adj.
gay *luminescent* 420 adj.
florid 425 adj.
pleased, happy 824 adj.
gay 833 adj.
amusing 837 adj.
showy 875 adj.
drunk 949 adj.
unchaste 951 adj.
gaze *look, gaze* 438 vb.
watch 441 vb.
be curious 453 vb.
be attentive 455 vb.
gazebo *view* 438 n.
arbour 194 n.
gazelle *deer* 365 n.
gazette *advertisement* 528 n.
journal 528 n.
proclaim 528 vb.
record 548 n.
gazetteer *directory* 87 n.
guide-book 524 n.
reference book 589 n.
gazing-stock
laughing-stock 851 n.
prodigy 864 n.
gear *clothing* 228 n.
equipment 630 n.
geared *correlative* 12 adj.
gear, out of
orderless 61 adj.
gears *machine* 630 n.
gear to, gear with
relate 9 vb.
accord 24 vb.
join 45 vb.
gecko *reptile* 365 n.
geest *soil* 344 n.
geezer *laughing-stock* 851 n.
gegenschein *heavens* 321 n.
glow 417 n.
luminary 420 n.
Gehenna *hell* 972 n.
Geiger counter
meter 465 n.
geisha girl *entertainer* 594 n.
gel *thicken* 354 vb.
gelatin *thickening* 354 n.
gelatination
condensation 324 n.
geld *subtract* 39 vb.
unman 161 vb.
sterilize 172 vb.
gelding *eunuch* 161 n.
horse 273 n.
male animal 372 n.
gelefaction *thickening* 354 n.
gelidity *coldness* 380 n.
gelignite *explosive* 723 n.
gem *exceller* 644 n.

gem 844 n.
gematria *occultism* 984 n.
gem-cutting *engraving* 555 n.
ornamental art 844 n.
gemination *duplication* 91 n.
Gemini *duality* 90 n.
zodiac 321 n.
gemote *assembly* 74 n.
gemütlich
inexcitable 823 adj.
gen *information* 524 n.
gendarme *soldier* 722 n.
police 955 n.
gender *classification* 77 n.
grammar 564 n.
gene *heredity* 5 n.
genealogy *series* 71 n.
genealogy 169 n.
general *broad* 205 adj.
national 371 adj.
usual 610 adj.
army officer 741 n.
commonalty 869 n.
(*see* generality)
general council
synod 985 n.
generalissimo
army officer 741 n.
generality *average* 30 n.
whole 52 n.
inclusion 78 n.
generality 79 n.
conformity 83 n.
indiscrimination 464 n.
inexactness 495 n.
generalization
reasoning 475 n.
generalize *generalize* 79 vb.
(*see* generality)
general practitioner
doctor 658 n.
general principle
premise 475 n.
generalship *tactics* 688 n.
skill 694 n.
art of war 718 n.
generate
make fruitful 171 adj.
vitalize 360 vb.
generation *race* 11 n.
coition 45 n.
causation 156 n.
propagation 164 n.
generationism
heredity 5 n.
generations
diuturnity 113 n.
generations of man
mankind 371 n.
generator
causal means 156 n.

electricity 160n.
producer 167n.
generic *generic* 77adj.
general 79adj.
generification
classification 77n.
generosity (*see* generous)
generous *great* 32adj.
many 104adj.
tasty 386adj.
plenteous 635adj.
giving 781adj.
expending 806adj.
liberal 813adj.
noble 868adj.
courteous 884adj.
benevolent 897adj.
approving 923adj.
disinterested 931adj.
virtuous 933adj.
rewarding 962adj.
genesiology
propagation 164n.
genesis *origin* 68n.
source 156n.
propagation 164n.
genet *saddle-horse* 273n.
genethliacs
divination 511n.
genetic *genetic* 5adj.
productive 164adj.
genetics *biology* 358n.
Geneva gown
canonicals 989n.
genial *productive* 164adj.
pleasant 376adj.
warm 379adj.
willing 597adj.
pleasurable 826adj.
cheerful 833adj.
benevolent 897adj.
genial climate
salubrity 652n.
geniculated *angular* 247adj.
genie *demon* 970n.
genital *productive* 164adj.
genitalia *genitalia* 164n.
genius *identity* 13n.
analogue 18n.
intellect, spirit 447n.
intellectual 492n.
intelligence 498n.
sage 500n.
exceller 644n.
aptitude 694n.
proficient 696n.
prodigy 864n.
mythic god 966n.
lesser god 967n.
fairy 970n.
genocide *slaughter* 362n.

cruel act 898n.
ruffian 904n.
capital punishment 963n.
genotype *breed* 77n.
genre *sort* 77n.
art style 553n.
genro *council* 692n.
genteel *well-bred* 848adj.
genteel 868adj.
genteelism *prudery* 950n.
gentian violet *purple* 434n.
gentile *ethnic* 11adj.
religionist 973n.
heathen 974n.
impious person 980n.
profane 980adj.
gentility *race* 11n.
etiquette 848n.
nobility 868n.
courtesy 884n.
gentle *moderate* 177adj.
soft 327adj.
tamed 369adj.
muted 401adj.
lax 734adj.
lenient 736adj.
inexcitable 823adj.
noble 868adj.
amiable 884adj.
benevolent 897adj.
innocent 935adj.
gentlefolk *aristocracy* 868n.
gentleman *male* 372n.
person of repute 866n.
aristocrat 868n.
gentleman 929n.
good man 937n.
gentlemanlike
well-bred 848adj.
noble 868adj.
gentlemanly
reputable 866adj.
noble 868adj.
honourable 929adj.
gentleman of fortune
gambler 618n.
gentleman's agreement
promise 764n.
compact 765n.
gentleman's gentleman
domestic 742n.
gentleness *pity* 905n.
(*see* gentle)
gentle sex
womankind 373n.
gentlewoman *lady* 373n.
aristocrat 868n.
gentry *aristocracy* 868n.
genual *crural* 267adj.
genuant *heraldic* 547adj.
genuflect *stoop* 311vb.

perform ritual 988vb.
genuflexion *obeisance* 311n.
submission 721n.
servility 879n.
respects 920n.
ritual act 988n.
genuine *orthodox* 976adj.
(*see* genuineness)
genuine article
no imitation 21n.
genuineness *identity* 13n.
no imitation 21n.
authenticity 494n.
genus *group* 74n.
breed 77n.
geocentric *central* 225adj.
celestial 321adj.
geodesy *geography* 321n.
uranometry 321n.
measurement 465n.
geognosy *mineralogy* 359n.
geographer
uranometry 321n.
geography *situation* 186n.
geography 321n.
uranometry 321n.
land 344n.
geoid *sphere* 252n.
world 321n.
geological period *era* 110n.
geological times
antiquity 125n.
geologist *uranometry* 321n.
geology *geography* 321n.
uranometry 321n.
land 344n.
mineralogy 359n.
geomancy
theomancy 511n.
geometer *computer* 86n.
geometry 465n.
surveyor 465n.
geometric
ornamental 844adj.
geometrical progression
series 71n.
ratio 85n.
progression 285n.
geometrical style
pattern 844n.
geometry *mathematics* 86n.
geometry 465n.
curriculum 536n.
geophone *meter* 465n.
geoponics *agriculture* 370n.
georama *spectacle* 445n.
George Cross *badge* 547n.
decoration 729n.
georgette *textile* 222n.
georgic *agrarian* 370adj.
poem 593n.

geoscopy *mineralogy* 359n.
geostatics *gravity* 322n.
geranium *redness* 431n.
geriatrics
    gerontology 131n.
    medical art 658n.
germ *origin* 68n.
    source 156n.
    animalcule 196n.
    infection 651n.
    poison 659n.
german *akin* 11adj.
germane *apt* 24adj.
germ-carrier *carrier* 273n.
    infection 651n.
    insalubrity 653n.
germen *source* 156n.
germicide
    prophylactic 658n.
    poison 659n.
germinal *causal* 156adj.
    productive 164adj.
    generative 171adj.
germinate *result* 157vb.
    be fruitful 171vb.
    expand 197vb.
    vegetate 366vb.
germ-laden
    infectious 653adj.
    toxic 653adj.
germ plasm
    organism 358n.
gerontic *aged* 131adj.
gerontocracy
    government 733n.
gerontology
    gerontology 131n.
    medical art 658n.
gerontotherapy
    gerontology 131n.
gerousia *seniority* 131n.
gerrymander *deceive* 542vb.
    be cunning 698vb.
    foul play 930n.
    be dishonest 930vb.
gesso *art equipment* 553n.
Gestapo
    police enquiry 459n.
gestation
    propagation 164n.
    maturation 669n.
gesticulate *be mute* 578vb.
    speak 579vb.
gesticulation
    mimicry 20n.
    (*see* gesture)
gesticulatory
    indicating 547adj.
gesture *motion* 265n.
    mien 445n.
    hint 524n.

gesture 547n.
gesticulate 547vb.
    conduct 688n.
    command 737n.
    ritual act 988n.
gestureless *still* 266adj.
get *be turned to* 147vb.
    generate 164vb.
    understand 516vb.
    acquire 771vb.
    possess 773vb.
    receive 782vb.
get about
    be published 528vb.
get above oneself
    be vain 873vb.
get across
    communicate 524vb.
    make enemies 881vb.
get a move on
    accelerate 277vb.
get-at-able
    accessible 289adj.
get-away *departure* 296n.
    escape 667n.
get back *recoup* 31vb.
    retrieve 656vb.
    acquire 771vb.
get even with
    retaliate 714vb.
    punish 963vb.
get going *start out* 296vb.
    do 676vb.
get in one's hair
    incommode 827vb.
get into *be mixed* 43vb.
    wear 228vb.
get in touch
    be contiguous 202vb.
    communicate 524vb.
get off *land* 295vb.
    escape 667vb.
    court 889vb.
get on *accord* 24vb.
    grow 36vb.
    progress 285vb.
get over *be restored* 656vb.
get religion
    become pious 979vb.
get rid of *destroy* 165vb.
    kill 362vb.
    eject 300vb.
    deliver 668vb.
    not retain 779vb.
get round *befool* 542vb.
get there *arrive* 295vb.
get through
    terminate 69vb.
    communicate 524vb.
    expend 806vb.
get-together

    assembly 74n.
    social gathering 882n.
get up *lift oneself* 310vb.
    study 536vb.
    fake 541vb.
    be restored 656vb.
get what is coming
    be punished 963vb.
get wind of *smell* 394vb.
    discover 484vb.
get wrong
    misinterpret 521vb.
gewgaw *bauble* 639n.
    finery 844n.
geyser *outflow* 298n.
    stream 350n.
    heat 379n.
ghastly *colourless* 426adj.
    not nice 645adj.
    distressing 827adj.
    unsightly 842adj.
    frightening 854adj.
ghat *entrance* 68n.
    gap 201n.
    narrowness 206n.
    passage 305n.
ghazal *verse form* 593n.
ghazi *militarist* 722n.
    religionist 979n.
ghee *fat* 357n.
ghetto *exclusion* 57n.
    retreat 192n.
    lock-up 748n.
    seclusion 883n.
ghost
    insubstantial thing 4n.
    substitute 150n.
    immateriality 320n.
    corpse 363n.
    dimness 419n.
    visual fallacy 440n.
    appearance 445n.
    fantasy 513n.
    author 589n.
    ghost 970n.
    bewitch 983vb.
ghostly *insubstantial* 4adj.
    immaterial 320adj.
    shadowy 419adj.
    divine 965adj.
    spooky 970adj.
ghosts *the dead* 361n.
ghoul *monster* 938n.
    demon 970n.
ghoulish *inquisitive* 453adj.
    frightening 854adj.
    cruel 898adj.
giant *enormous* 32adj.
    giant 195n.
    tall creature 209n.
    demon 970n.

giantism *size* 195n.
giaour *heathen* 974n.
gibber *be absurd* 497vb.
  goblinize 970vb.
gibberish *absurdity* 497n.
  unmeaningness 515n.
  unintelligibility 517n.
  slang 560n.
gibbet *hanger* 217n.
  killer 362n.
  dispraise 924vb.
  defame 926vb.
  accuse 928vb.
  execute 963vb.
  means of execution 964n.
gibble-gabble
  chatter 581n.
gibbosity *rotundity* 252n.
  convexity 253n.
gibe (*see* jibe)
gibing *disrespectful* 921adj.
giblets *meat* 301n.
gibus *headgear* 228n.
giddiness *weakness* 163n.
  folly 499n.
giddy *changeful* 152adj.
  light-minded 456adj.
  crazed 503adj.
  irresolute 601adj.
  capricious 604adj.
  rash 857adj.
  tipsy 949adj.
gift *extra* 40n.
  ability 160n.
  tendency 179n.
  aptitude 694n.
  offer 759n.
  acquisition 771n.
  transfer 780n.
  gift 781n.
  no charge 812n.
  (*see* give)
gifted *gifted* 694adj.
giftedness *intelligence* 498n.
giftless
  parsimonious 816adj.
gift of the gab
  eloquence 579n.
  loquacity 581n.
gig *carriage* 274n.
  boat 275n.
gigantic *enormous* 32adj.
  stalwart 162adj.
  huge 195adj.
  tall 209adj.
  fairylike 970adj.
gigantism *greatness* 32n.
  hugeness 195n.
  size 195n.
  expansion 197n.
gigantomachy *fight* 716n.

giggle *laughter* 835n.
giglet *youngster* 132n.
gigolo *toady* 879n.
  libertine 952n.
gigsman *boatman* 270n.
Gilbertian *funny* 849adj.
gild *coat* 226vb.
  colour 425vb.
  gild 433vb.
  decorate 844vb.
gild the pill *deceive* 542vb.
  tempt 612vb.
  please 826vb.
  flatter 925vb.
gilgal *monument* 548n.
gill *laterality* 239n.
  stream 350n.
  metrology 465n.
gillie
  animal husbandry 369n.
gilt *ornamentation* 844n.
gilt-edged *valuable* 644adj.
  secured 767adj.
gimcrack *flimsy* 163adj.
  brittle 330adj.
  trivial 639adj.
  unsafe 661adj.
gimlet *perforator* 263n.
gimmick *contrivance* 623n.
  skill 694n.
gimp *trimming* 844n.
gin *liquor* 301n.
  trap 542n.
gingal *gun* 723n.
ginger *vigorousness* 714n.
  sweetmeat 301n.
  tuber 301n.
  pungency 388n.
  condiment 389n.
  orange 436n.,adj.
  excitant 821n.
ginger beer *soft drink* 301n.
gingerbread *pastry* 301n.
  vulgar 847adj.
gingerly *moderately* 177adv.
  careful 457adj.
  cautiously 858adv.
gingham *textile* 222n.
ginglymus *joint* 45n.
gink *laughing-stock* 851n.
gin palace *tavern* 192n.
gippo *fluid* 335n.
gipsy *stream* 350n.
  (*see* gypsy)
giraffe *tall creature* 209n.
girandole *lamp* 420n.
girasol *gem* 844n.
gird *tie* 45vb.
  dispraise 924vb.
  detract 926vb.
girder *bond* 47n.

  beam 218n.
girdle *tie* 45vb.
  girdle 47n.
  compressor 198n.
  underwear 228n.
  surround 230n.
  outline 233n.
  inclosure 235n.
  loop 250n.
  go round 250vb.
gird up one's loins
  be strong 162vb.
  prepare oneself 669vb.
girl *youngster* 132n.
  woman 373n.
  loved one 887n.
girlhood *youth* 130n.
girlish *young* 130adj.
  infantine 132adj.
  immature 670adj.
girn *be discontented* 829vb.
girth *greatness* 32n.
  girdle 47n.
  size 195n.
  belt 228n.
  outline 233n.
gisarme *axe* 723n.
gist *essential part* 5n.
  chief part 52n.
  topic 452n.
  meaning 514n.
  chief thing 638n.
gittern *harp* 414n.
give *oscillate* 317vb.
  soften 327vb.
  elasticity 328n.
  provide 633vb.
  convey 780vb.
  give 781vb.
  expend 805vb.
  be liberal 813vb.
  reward 962vb.
  (*see* gift)
giveable
  not retained 779adj.
give a hand *applaud* 923vb.
give a handle *justify* 927vb.
give and take
  correlation 12n.
  set off 31vb.
  interchange 151n.,vb.
  answer 460n.
  argument 475n.
  retaliation 714n.
  fight 716n.,vb.
  compromise 770n.,vb.
give away *disclose* 526vb.
  give 781vb.
  cheapen 812vb.
  marry 894vb.
give back *restitute* 787vb.

give birth
  reproduce itself 164 vb.
  vitalize 360 vb.
give ground *regress* 286 vb.
give grounds *justify* 927 vb.
give in *relinquish* 621 vb.
  submit 721 vb.
given *existing* 1 adj.
  circumstantial 8 adj.
  prior 119 adj.
  supposed 512 adj.
  uncharged 812 adj.
givenness *existence* 1 n.
given to *habituated* 610 adj.
give occasion *cause* 156 vb.
give off *emit* 300 vb.
give one joy
  gratulate 886 vb.
give one pause
  dissuade 613 vb.
give oneself airs
  be affected 850 vb.
  be vain 873 vb.
give oneself up
  submit 721 vb.
give one's mind to
  be attentive 455 vb.
give one the slip
  decamp 296 vb.
  elude 667 vb.
give one the works
  torment 827 vb.
  torture 963 vb.
give out
  communicate 524 vb.
  publish 528 vb.
give over *cease* 145 vb.
give points to
  equalize 28 vb.
  be unequal 29 vb.
giver *giver* 781 n.
give rise to *conduce* 156 vb.
give suck *feed* 301 vb.
give the lie *negate* 533 vb.
give tongue *be loud* 400 vb.
  speak 579 vb.
give up *cease* 145 vb.
  not understand 517 vb.
  relinquish 621 vb.
  disuse 674 vb.
  submit 721 vb.
  not complete 726 vb.
  resign 753 vb.
  not retain 779 vb.
give way *be weak* 163 vb.
  regress 286 vb.
  descend 309 vb.
  be brittle 330 vb.
  be irresolute 601 vb.
gizzard *maw* 194 n.
glabella *face* 237 n.

glabreity *smoothness* 258 n.
glacé *cooled* 382 adj.
glacial *cold* 380 adj.
glaciation
  condensation 324 n.
  hardening 326 n.
  refrigeration 382 n.
glacier *ice* 380 n.
glaciology *mineralogy* 359 n.
glacis *acclivity* 220 n.
  fortification 713 n.
glad *willing* 597 adj.
gladden *please* 826 vb.
  cheer 833 vb.
glade *valley* 255 n.
  open space 263 n.
  screen 421 n.
  path 624 n.
glad eye *look* 438 n.
  wooing 889 n.
glad-hand
  be sociable 882 vb.
gladiator *entertainer* 594 n.
  contender 716 n.
  combatant 722 n.
gladness *joy* 824 n.
glad of, be *desire* 859 vb.
glair *viscidity* 354 n.
glamorize *beautify* 841 vb.
  decorate 844 vb.
glamorizer
  beautician 843 n.
  cosmetic 843 n.
glamorous
  personable 841 adj.
glamour *beauty* 841 n.
  prestige 866 n.
  spell 983 n.
glance *deflect* 282 vb.
  propel 287 vb.
  shine 417 vb.
  look 438 n.
  gesture 547 n.
glancing *lateral* 239 adj.
glancing light
  variegation 437 n.
gland *insides* 224 n.
glanders
  animal disease 651 n.
glare *light* 417 n.
  gaze 438 vb.
  blur 440 vb.
  be visible 443 vb.
  anger 891 n.
glaring *whopping* 32 adj.
  florid 425 adj.
  manifest 522 adj.
  well-known 528 adj.
glass *weak thing* 163 n.
  cup 194 n.
  smoothness 258 n.

potion 301 n.
  brittleness 330 n.
  weather 340 n.
  transparency 422 n.
  mirror 442 n.
  finery 844 n.
  bad taste 847 n.
glasses *eyeglass* 442 n.
glass-house *arbour* 194 n.
  brittleness 330 n.
  garden 370 n.
glassiness
  transparency 422 n.
glass of fashion
  beau monde 848 n.
glassware *receptacle* 194 n.
glassy *smooth* 258 adj.
  tranquil 266 adj.
  hard 326 adj.
  brittle 330 adj.
  undimmed 417 adj.
  dim 419 adj.
  transparent 422 adj.
  colourless 426 adj.
glassy-eyed *tipsy* 949 adj.
glaucoma *blindness* 439 n.
  dim sight 440 n.
glaucous *grey* 429 adj.
  green 432 adj.
glaze *facing* 226 n.
  coat 226 n.
  smoothness 258 n.
  viscidity 354 n.
  screen 421 vb.
glazed ware *pottery* 381 n.
gleam *small quantity* 33 n.
  flash 417 n.
  shine 417 vb.
  incentive 612 n.
glean *cultivate* 370 vb.
  abstract 592 vb.
  select 605 vb.
  store 632 vb.
  take 786 vb.
  acquire 771 vb.
gleaner *aftercomer* 67 n.
  accumulator 74 n.
  husbandman 370 n.
  cleaner 648 n.
gleanings *anthology* 592 n.
  choice 605 n.
  earnings 771 n.
glebe *soil* 344 n.
  benefice 985 n.
glee *vocal music* 412 n.
  enjoyment 824 n.
  merriment 833 n.
glee-club *choir* 413 n.
gleeful *jubilant* 833 adj.
gleeman *vocalist* 413 n.
glen *valley* 255 n.

glengarry *headgear* 228 n.
glib *loquacious* 581 adj.
glide *elapse* 111 vb.
  interjection 231 n.
  go smoothly 258 vb.
  move 265 vb.
  travel 267 vb.
  fly 271 vb.
glider *aeronaut* 271 n.
  aircraft 276 n.
glide-sound
  interjection 231 n.
glim *lamp* 420 n.
glimmer *flash* 417 n.
  glimmer 419 n.
  be dim 419 vb.
  be visible 443 vb.
  hint 524 n.
glimmering *sciolism* 491 n.
glimpse *look* 438 n.
  see 438 vb.
  knowledge 490 n.
glint *flash* 417 n.
  look 438 n.
glinting *luminous* 417 adj.
glissade *descent* 309 n.
glisten, glister *shine* 417 vb.
glitter *shine* 417 vb.
  flash 417 n.
  be visible 443 vb.
  ostentation 875 n.
glittering
  ornamented 844 adj.
gloaming *evening* 129 n.
  half-light 419 n.
gloat *enjoy* 376 vb.
  gaze 438 vb.
  be pleased 824 vb.
  rejoice 835 vb.
  boast 877 vb.
  be malevolent 898 vb.
gloating *revengeful* 910 adj.
global *inclusive* 78 adj.
  universal 79 adj.
  spacious 183 adj.
  ubiquitous 189 adj.
  rotund 252 adj.
  telluric 321 adj.
globe *sphere* 252 n.
  world 321 n.
globe-trotter *traveller* 268 n.
  spectator 441 n.
globularity *rotundity* 252 n.
globule *sphere* 252 n.
glockenspiel *gong* 414 n.
gloom *darkness* 418 n.
  dimness 419 n.
  adversity 731 n.
  sorrow 825 n.
  dejection 834 n.
  be sullen 893 vb.

Gloria *hymn* 981 n.
glorification
  dignification 866 n.
  praise 923 n.
  act of worship 981 n.
glorified *angelic* 968 adj.
  paradisiac 971 adj.
  ostentatious 875 adj.
glorify *advertise* 528 vb.
  make important 638 vb.
  honour 866 vb.
  praise 923 vb.
  worship 981 vb.
gloriole *light* 417 n.
glorious *great* 32 adj.
  excellent 644 adj.
  noteworthy 866 adj.
  godlike 965 adj.
  (*see* glory)
Glorious Koran
  non-Biblical scripture
  975 n.
glory *light* 417 n.
  manifestation 522 n.
  success 727 n.
  trophy 729 n.
  prosperity 730 n.
  prestige 866 n.
  famousness 866 n.
  feel pride 871 vb.
  boast 877 vb.
  divine attribute 965 n.
gloss *smoothness* 258 n.
  light 417 n.
  reflection 417 n.
  commentary 520 n.
  sham 542 n.
  untruth 543 n.
  word 559 n.
  pretext 614 n.
  beauty 841 n.
  ostentation 875 n.
  extenuate 927 vb.
glossarist *interpreter* 520 n.
glossary *word list* 87 n.
  commentary 520 n.
  dictionary 559 n.
glossless *colourless* 426 adj.
glossographer
  collector 492 n.
  interpreter 520 n.
glossography
  commentary 520 n.
glossology *linguistics* 557 n.
gloss over *neglect* 458 vb.
  sophisticate 477 vb.
  conceal 525 vb.
  cant 541 vb.
  plead 614 vb.
  extenuate 927 vb.
glossy *luminous* 417 adj.

  splendid 841 adj.
  personable 841 adj.
glottal stop
  pronunciation 577 n.
glottologist *linguist* 557 n.
glottology *linguistics* 557 n.
glove *glove* 228 n.
  love-token 889 n.
glow *heat* 379 n.
  glow 417 n.
  hue 425 n.
  redness 431 n.
  be visible 443 vb.
  vigour 571 n.
  show feeling 818 vb.
  be beautiful 841 vb.
glower *be angry* 891 vb.
  be sullen 893 vb.
glow-worm *glimmer* 419 n.
  glow-worm 420 n.
gloze *underestimate* 483 vb.
  mislead 495 vb.
  interpret 520 vb.
  misinterpret 521 vb.
  cant 541 vb.
  flatter 925 vb.
  be dishonest 930 vb.
glucose *food content* 301 n.
  sweet 392 n.
glue *adhesive* 47 n.
  agglutinate 48 vb.
  viscidity 354 n.
glued *firm-set* 45 adj.
glue on *affix* 45 vb.
glum *melancholic* 834 adj.
glut *productiveness* 171 n.
  superfluity 637 n.
  cheapness 812 n.
  satiety 863 vb.
gluteal *back* 238 adj.
  crural 267 adj.
glutinosity *viscidity* 354 n.
glut oneself
  gluttonize 947 vb.
glutton *desirer* 859 n.
  sensualist 944 n.
  glutton 947 n.
glutton for work
  busy person 678 n.
gluttonous *greedy* 859 adj.
gluttony *gastronomy* 301 n.
  desire 859 n.
  vice 934 n.
  sensualism 944 n.
  gluttony 947 n.
glycerine *lubricant* 334 n.
  fat 357 n.
  cleanser 648 n.
glyconic *prosody* 593 n.
glyph *furrow* 262 n.
glyptic *formative* 243 adj.

glyptic 554 adj.
glyptography
engraving 555 n.
G-man *detective* 459 n.
gnarled *distorted* 246 adj.
rough 259 adj.
dense 324 adj.
gnarr *ululate* 409 vb.
gnashing *angry* 891 adj.
gnash one's teeth
be impotent 161 vb.
regret 830 vb.
be angry 891 vb.
gnat *fly* 365 n.
animalcule 196 n.
gnaw *bate* 37 vb.
rend 46 vb.
chew 301 vb.
rub 333 vb.
give pain 377 vb.
impair 655 vb.
hurt 827 vb.
gnome *maxim* 496 n.
elf 970 n.
gnomic *aphoristic* 496 adj.
gnomon *timekeeper* 117 n.
gnostic *religionist* 973 n.
gnosticism
philosophy 449 n.
deism 973 n.
heresy 977 n.
Gnostics
non-Christian sect 978 n.
gnu *deer* 365 n.
go *be disjoined* 46 vb.
operate 173 vb.
vigorousness 174 n.
move 265 vb.
travel, walk 267 vb.
recede 290 vb.
die 361 vb.
function 622 vb.
restlessness 678 n.
courage 855 vb.
go a-begging
be superfluous 637 vb.
be useless 641 vb.
go about *undertake* 672 vb.
goad *stimulant* 174 n.
make violent 176 vb.
sharp point 256 n.
impel 279 vb.
incentive 612 n.
excitant 821 n.
enrage 891 vb.
go against
counteract 182 vb.
oppose 704 vb.
go against the grain
be rough 259 vb.
be difficult 700 vb.

displease 827 vb.
cause dislike 861 vb.
go-ahead *vigorous* 174 adj.
enterprising 672 adj.
goal *extremity* 69 n.
focus 76 n.
stopping place 145 n.
limit 236 n.
resting place 266 n.
direction 281 n.
goal 295 n.
objective 617 n.
completion 725 n.
success 727 n.
desired object 859 n.
goal-keeper
interceptor 702 n.
defender 713 n.
go along with
concur 181 vb.
assent 488 vb.
go-as-you-please
free 744 adj.
go at *essay* 671 n.
goat *jumper* 312 n.
cattle 365 n.
libertine 952 n.
goatee *hair* 259 n.
goatherd *herdsman* 369 n.
goatish *lecherous* 951 adj.
go away *go away* 190 vb.
recede 290 vb.
depart 296 vb.
gob *orifice* 263 n.
naval man 270 n.
eruct 300 vb.
navy man 722 n.
go back
repeat oneself 106 vb.
turn round 282 vb.
turn back 286 vb.
go back on *negate* 533 vb.
relinquish 621 vb.
not observe 769 vb.
(*see* tergiversate)
go bad *be unclean* 649 vb.
deteriorate 655 vb.
gobbet *small thing* 33 n.
mouthful 301 n.
gobble *absorb* 299 vb.
ululate 409 vb.
gluttonize 947 vb.
go-between *joinder* 45 n.
intermediary 231 n.
informant 524 n.
messenger 531 n.
mediator 720 n.
matchmaker 894 n.
bawd 952 n.
goblet *cup* 194 n.
goblin *intimidation* 854 n.

elf 970 n.
gobstopper *stopper* 264 n.
mouthful 301 n.
go by *elapse* 111 vb.
goby *fish* 365 n.
go-cart *pushcart* 274 n.
god *cause* 156 n.
the Deity 965 n.
god 966 n.
idol 982 n.
goddess *woman* 373 n.
loved one 887 n.
god-forsaken *empty* 190 adj.
secluded 883 adj.
profane 980 adj.
godhead *divineness* 965 n.
godless *irreligious* 974 adj.
impious 980 adj.
godlike *beautiful* 841 adj.
godlike 965 adj.
godly *pious* 979 adj.
god-making
deification 982 n.
godown *storage* 632 n.
go down *descend* 309 vb.
founder 313 vb.
be believed 485 vb.
go downhill
deteriorate 655 vb.
have trouble 731 vb.
godparents *family* 11 n.
gods *theatre* 594 n.
playgoer 594 n.
godsend *benefit* 615 n.
prosperity 730 n.
godson *family* 11 n.
God's own *chosen* 605 adj.
God-speed *success* 727 n.
God's ways
divineness 965 n.
theocracy 965 n.
God's will *fate* 596 n.
God's word
revelation 975 n.
go Dutch
be sociable 882 vb.
God willing
possibly 469 adv.
goer *thoroughbred* 273 n.
goetic *sorcerous* 983 adj.
goffer *groove* 262 vb.
go for *aim at* 617 vb.
attack 712 vb.
cost 809 vb.
desire 859 vb.
go from bad to worse
deteriorate 655 vb.
aggravate 832 vb.
go-getter
progression 285 n.
planner 623 n.

busy person 678 n.
egotist 932 n.
goggle *gaze* 438 vb.
wonder 864 vb.
goggles *eyeglass* 442 n.
go half-way
be half-way 625 vb.
consent 758 vb.
(*see* compromise)
go halves *participate* 775 vb.
go hard with
have trouble 731 vb.
go in for *be resolute* 599 vb.
choose 605 vb.
aim at 617 vb.
busy oneself 622 vb.
undertake 672 vb.
going *relinquishment* 621 n.
active 678 adj.
going, be *depart* 296 vb.
going begging *free* 744 adj.
unpossessed 774 adj.
going on *unfinished* 55 adj.
go into *enquire* 459 vb.
dissert 591 vb.
go it alone *be free* 744 vb.
Golconda *wealth* 800 n.
gold *yellowness* 433 n.
orange 436 n.
incentive 612 n.
exceller 644 n.
money, bullion 797 n.
gold-digger *lover* 887 n.
egotist 932 n.
golden *yellow* 433 adj.
valuable 644 adj.
palmy 730 adj.
promising 852 adj.
Golden Age *era* 110 n.
literature 557 n.
palmy days 730 n.
happiness 824 n.
innocence 935 n.
golden calf *idol* 982 n.
golden mean *average* 30 n.
moderation 177 n.
mid-course 625 n.
golden opinions
approbation 923 n.
golden rule *precept* 693 n.
golden touch
prosperity 730 n.
wealth 800 n.
golden wedding
period 110 n.
anniversary 141 n.
special day 876 n.
wedding 897 n.
goldfish *fish* 365 n.
gold-mine *store* 632 n.
wealth 800 n.

gold-rush *land travel* 267 n.
goldsmith *artisan* 686 n.
gold standard *finance* 797 n.
golf *ball game* 837 n.
golf-links
pleasure-ground 837 n.
Golgotha *cemetery* 364 n.
holy place 990 n.
Goliath *athlete* 162 n.
giant 195 n.
golliwog *image* 551 n.
gondola *rowboat* 275 n.
airship 276 n.
gondolier *boatman* 270 n.
carrier 273 n.
gone *past* 125 adj.
absent 190 adj.
dead 361 adj.
disappearing 446 adj.
lost 772 adj.
dead drunk 949 adj.
gone on *enamoured* 887 adj.
goner *corpse* 363 n.
gonfalon *flag* 547 n.
gong *timekeeper* 117 n.
resound 404 vb.
gong 414 n.
signal, badge 547 n.
decoration 729 n.
Gongorism
ornament 574 n.
goniometer
angular measure 247 n.
meter 465 n.
gonorrhœa
venereal disease 651 n.
good *savoury* 390 adj.
elegant 575 adj.
good 615 n., adj.
utility 640 n.
excellent 644 adj.
skilful 694 adj.
prosperity 730 n.
obedient 739 adj.
pleasurable 826 n.
amiable 884 adj.
benevolent 897 adj.
right 913 adj.
honourable 929 adj.
virtuous 933 adj.
pure 950 adj.
pious 979 adj.
good angel
mythic god 966 n.
(*see* benefactor)
good as, as *nearly* 200 adv.
good as one's word
veracious 540 adj.
trustworthy 929 adj.
good behaviour
courtesy 884 n.

virtue 933 n.
good bet *fair chance* 159 n.
good books
approbation 923 n.
good breeding
etiquette 848 n.
courtesy 884 n.
goodbye *valediction* 296 n.
good chance
fair chance 159 n.
possibility 469 n.
probability 471 n.
good cheer *food* 301 n.
enjoyment 824 n.
merriment 833 n.
amusement 837 n.
sociability 882 n.
good company
social person 882 n.
good constitution
health 650 n.
good deal
great quantity 32 n.
good defence
vindication 927 n.
good delivery
eloquence 579 n.
good earnest, in
resolutely 599 adv.
good example
relevance 9 n.
analogue 18 n.
fitness 24 n.
good man 937 n.
good faith *probity* 929 n.
good fault *virtues* 933 n.
good fellowship
sociability 882 n.
good for *useful* 640 adj.
salubrious 652 adj.
good form *practice* 610 n.
etiquette 848 n.
formality 875 n.
good for nothing
powerless 161 adj.
profitless 641 adj.
vicious 934 adj.
bad man 938 n.
Good Friday *fast* 946 n.
holy-day 988 n.
good genius
benefactor 903 n.
mythic god 966 n.
good graces
approbation 923 n.
good grace, with a
willingly 597 adv.
good grounds
vindication 927 n.
good humour
cheerfulness 833 n.

courtesy 884n.
good in parts
  imperfect 647adj.
good living
  gastronomy 301n.
  gluttony 947n.
good-looking
  beautiful 841adj.
good loser *gentleman* 929n.
good luck *chance* 159n.
  non-design 618n.
  prosperity 730n.
goodly *great* 32adj.
  fleshy 195adj.
  good 615adj.
  beautiful 841adj.
good man
  good man 937n.
  pietist 979n.
goodman *resident* 191n.
  male 372n.
  master 741n.
  spouse 894n.
good-mannered
  well-bred 848adj.
good name *repute* 866n.
good-natured
  irresolute 601adj.
  benevolent 897adj.
good neighbour
  friend 880n.
  social person 882n.
  kind person 897n.
goodness (*see* good)
goodnight
  valediction 296n.
good odour *repute* 866n.
good offices *aid* 703n.
  concord 710n.
  pacification 719n.
  mediation 720n.
  kind act 897n.
good of one *lifelike* 18adj.
  benevolent 897adj.
good points
  goodness 644n.
good purpose, to
  successfully 727adv.
good reason
  probability 471n.
good report *repute* 866n.
good riddance
  rubbish 641n.
  hateful object 888n.
  relief 831n.
goods
  thing transferred 272n.
  property 777n.
  merchandise 795n.
Good Samaritan
  kind person 897n.

benefactor 903n.
goods and chattels
  property 777n.
good sense
  intelligence 498n.
good sort *good man* 937n.
good spirits, in
  cheerful 833adj.
good taste *elegance* 575n.
  good taste 846n.
good-tempered
  inexcitable 823adj.
  amiable 884adj.
good terms, on
  concordant 710adj.
goods, the
  information 524n.
goods-train *carrier* 273n.
  train 274n.
good time, have a
  rejoice 835vb.
good turn *benefit* 615n.
  kind act 897n.
good value *cheapness* 812n.
goodwife *lady* 373n.
goodwill, good will
  willingness 597n.
  friendliness 880n.
  benevolence 897n.
good wishes
  congratulation 886n.
goody *lady* 373n.
goody-goody
  foolish 499adj.
  ninny 501n.
  innocent 935n., adj.
  pietistic 979adj.
gooey *retentive* 778adj.
goof *ignoramus* 493n.
  ninny 501n.
go off *happen* 154vb.
  be violent 176vb.
goofy *foolish* 499adj.
googly *deviation* 282n.
  sleight 542n.
go on *last* 113vb.
  stay 144vb.
  go on 146vb.
  happen 154vb.
  be in motion 265vb.
  progress 285vb.
  be active 678vb.
go on and on
  be tedious 838vb.
go one better
  be superior 34vb.
  be cunning 698vb.
go one's own way
  be dispersed 75vb.
  diverge 294vb.
  be incurious 454vb.

dissent 489vb.
  will 595vb.
  be free 744vb.
go, on the
  on the move 265adv.
  labouring 682adj.
goose *table-bird* 365n.
  waterfowl 365n.
  female animal 373n.
  sibilation 406n.
  ignoramus 493n.
  fool 501n.
gooseberry *fruit* 301n.
gooseberry, play
  look after 457vb.
gooseflesh
  roughness 259n.
  formication 378n.
  coldness 380n.
  nervousness 854n.
goosegirl *herdsman* 369n.
goosery *cattle pen* 369n.
goose-step *gait* 265n.
  walk 267vb.
go out of one's way
  deviate 282vb.
  be willing 597vb.
  circuit 626vb.
go over *number* 86vb.
  repeat 106vb.
  be inverted 221vb.
  pass 305vb.
  search 459vb.
  study 536vb.
  be irresolute 601vb.
  be dishonest 930vb.
go over the top
  charge 712vb.
  be courageous 855vb.
gopher *rodent* 365n.
go places *travel* 267vb.
  (*see* sociability)
gopuram
  high structure 209n.
  church exterior 990n.
gorbelly *bulk* 195n.
Gordian knot
  ligature 47n.
  complexity 61n.
  difficulty 700n.
gore *pierce* 263n.
  blood 335n.
  pulpiness 356n.
  redness 431n.
gorge *gap* 201n.
  valley 255n.
  conduit 351n.
  superabound 637vb.
  sate 863vb.
  be intemperate 943vb.
  gluttonize 947vb.

gorged *full* 54 adj.
gorge-de-pigeon
  variegation 437 n.
gorgeous *florid* 425 adj.
  splendid 841 adj.
  ornamented 844 adj.
  showy 875 adj.
gorgon *rara avis* 84 n.
  intimidation 854 n.
  demon 970 n.
gorgonzola
  milk product 301 n.
gorilla *monkey* 365 n.
  eyesore 842 n.
  monster 938 n.
gormandize *eat* 301 vb.
  gluttonize 947 vb.
gormless *foolish* 499 adj.
gorse *plant* 366 n.
gory *sanguineous* 335 adj.
  murderous 362 adj.
  bloodshot 431 adj.
go shares *be equal* 28 vb.
  participate 775 vb.
  be sociable 882 vb.
gosling *youngling* 132 n.
  child 132 n.
  waterfowl 365 n.
go-slow *slowness* 278 n.
  unwilling 598 adj.
gospel *certainty* 473 n.
  authenticity 494 n.
  news 529 n.
  revelation 975 n.
  scriptural 975 adj.
  orthodox 976 adj.
gospeller *preacher* 537 n.
  religious teacher 973 n.
Gospels *scripture* 975 n.
gospel, take for
  believe 485 vb.
gossamer
  insubstantial thing 4 n.
  weak thing 163 n.
  filament 208 n.
  levity 323 n.
  transparency 422 n.
  trifle 639 n.
gossip
  insubstantial thing 4 n.
  family 11 n.
  topic 452 n.
  inquisitor 453 n.
  informer 524 n.
  newsmonger 529 n.
  fable 543 n.
  be loquacious 581 vb.
  chat 584 n.
  chum 880 n.
  calumny 926 n.
gossip-writer

informant 524 n.
  chronicler 549 n.
  author 589 n.
gossipy *loquacious* 581 adj.
  conversing 584 adj.
  sociable 882 adj.
got *acquired* 771 adj.
Goth *vulgarian* 847 n.
  low fellow 869 n.
go the pace
  be prodigal 815 vb.
  be sensual 944 vb.
go the rounds
  traverse 267 vb.
  be published 528 vb.
  change hands 780 vb.
Gothic
  architectural 192 adj.
  amorphous 244 adj.
  literal 558 adj.
  inelegant 576 adj.
  written 586 adj.
  print-type 587 n.
go through
  meet with 154 vb.
  pass 305 vb.
  search 459 vb.
  deal with 688 vb.
  suffer 825 vb.
go through fire and water
  be resolute 599 vb.
go through the motions
  dissemble 541 vb.
go to all lengths
  exaggerate 546 vb.
  be resolute 599 vb.
  exert oneself 682 vb.
  be intemperate 943 vb.
go to it *begin* 68 vb.
go to law *quarrel* 709 vb.
  litigate 959 vb.
go too far *overstep* 306 vb.
go to one's head
  make conceited 873 vb.
  inebriate 949 vb.
go to pieces
  decompose 51 vb.
  be destroyed 165 vb.
go to sea *sail* 269 vb.
go to the wall
  be destroyed 165 vb.
  perish 361 vb.
  be defeated 728 vb.
gotra *family* 11 n.
  breed 77 n.
gotten *acquired* 771 adj.
Götterdämmerung
  finality 69 n.
got up *bedecked* 844 adj.
gouache
  art equipment 553 n.

gouge (out)
  make concave 255 vb.
  extract 304 vb.
goulash *dish* 301 n.
gourd *vessel* 194 n.
  vegetable 301 n.
  plant 366 n.
gourmandise
  gastronomy 301 n.
  good taste 846 n.
  gluttony 947 n.
gourmet *eater* 301 n.
  gastronomy 301 n.
  man of taste 846 n.
  perfectionist 862 n.
  glutton 947 n.
gout *rheumatism* 651 n.
gouty *crippled* 163 adj.
  diseased 651 adj.
  irascible 892 adj.
govern *order* 60 vb.
  moderate 177 vb.
  manage 689 vb.
  rule 733 vb.
governance *power* 160 n.
  influence 178 n.
  (*see* government)
governess *teacher* 537 n.
  protector 660 n.
  retainer 742 n.
  keeper 749 n.
governessy
  authoritarian 735 adj.
governing body
  director 690 n.
government
  management 689 n.
  government 733 n.
  master 741 n.
governmental
  businesslike 622 adj.
government servant
  official 690 n.
governor *teacher* 537 n.
  director 690 n.
  governor 741 n.
governorship
  magistrature 733 n.
go with *accord* 24 vb.
  accompany 89 vb.
  concur 181 vb.
go without saying
  be plain 522 vb.
gowk *ninny* 501 n.
  fool 501 n.
gown *dress* 228 n.
  canonicals 989 n.
go wrong *err* 495 vb.
  miscarry 728 vb.
  be wrong 914 vb.
grab *sailing ship* 275 n.

take 786vb.
grabble *touch* 378vb.
grace *musical note* 410n.
　style 566n.
　ornament 574vb.
　elegance 575n.
　skill 694n.
　permission 756n.
　gift 781n.
　beauty 841n.
　decorate 844vb.
　good taste 846n.
　title 870n.
　mercy 905n.
　thanks 907n.
　forgiveness 909n.
　divine function 965n.
　prayers 981n.
grace and favour
　permission 756n.
　gift 781n.
　no charge 812n.
graceful *lovable* 887adj.
gracefulness
　elegance 575n.
　beauty 841n.
graceless *inelegant* 576adj.
　clumsy 695adj.
　dull 840adj.
　graceless 842adj.
　vicious 934adj.
　impenitent 940adj.
grace marks *extra* 40n.
　gift 781n.
　undueness 916n.
grace-note
　musical note 410n.
graces *beauty* 841n.
gracile *narrow* 206adj.
gracious *willing* 597adj.
　beautiful 841adj.
　tasteful 846adj.
　courteous 884adj.
　benevolent 897adj.
gracious living
　euphoria 376n.
gradatim
　in order 60adv.
　gradatim 278adv.
gradation *degree* 27n.
　order 60n.
　arrangement 62n.
　series 71n.
grade *degree* 27n.
　graduate 27vb.
　arrange, class 62vb.
　serial place 73n.
　grade 73vb.
　sort 77n.
　acclivity 220n.
　gauge 465vb.

class 538n.
gradient *acclivity* 220n.
　ascent 308n.
gradual *gradational* 27adj.
　continuous 71adj.
　slow 278adj.
gradualism
　continuity 71n.
　slowness 278n.
　reformism 654n.
gradualist *reformer* 654n.
gradually *gradatim* 278adv.
graduate *graduate* 27vb.
　grade 73vb.
　pass 305vb.
　gauge 465vb.
　learn 536vb.
　college student 538n.
　get better 654vb.
　proficient 696n.
graduation
　adaptation 24n.
　(*see* grade)
gradus *word list* 87n.
　dictionary 559n.
　textbook 589n.
graffito *record* 548n.
　script 586n.
graft *descendant* 170n.
　implant 303vb.
　cultivate 370vb.
　booty 790n.
　improbity 930n.
grafting *venal* 930adj.
grail *ritual object* 988n.
grain *temperament* 5n.
　small thing 33n.
　tendency 179n.
　minuteness 196n.
　cereal 301n.
　provender 301n.
　weighment 322n.
　texture 331n.
　powder 332n.
　corn 366n.
　pigment 425n.
　colour 425vb.
　red pigment 431n.
　affections 817n.
　decorate 844vb.
grain, in *fixed* 153adj.
graining
　ornamental art 844n.
grains of allowance
　qualification 468n.
gramarye *sorcery* 983n.
gramineous *vegetal* 366adj.
graminivorous
　feeding 301adj.
grammar *curriculum* 536n.
　grammar 564n.

textbook 589n.
grammarian *linguist* 557n.
gramme *weighment* 322n.
gramophone
　gramophone 414n.
　hearing aid 415n.
gramophone record
　repetition 106n.
　rotator 315n.
grampus *fish* 365n.
granary *storage* 632n.
grand *whole* 52adj.
　over one hundred 99n.
　topping 644adj.
　funds 797n.
　impressive 821adj.
　splendid 841adj.
　noble 868adj.
　proud 871adj.
　formal 875adj.
　(*see* grandeur)
grand airs *affectation* 850n.
grandam
　old woman 133n.
　maternity 169n.
grandchildren
　posterity 170n.
grand climacteric *age* 131n.
grand duchy
　territory 184n.
grand duke
　nobleman 868n.
grande dame
　proud man 871n.
grandee *aristocrat* 868n.
grande toilette
　formal dress 228n.
grandeur *greatness* 32n.
　vigour 571n.
　beauty 841n.
　prestige 866n.
　ostentation 875n.
grandfather *old man* 133n.
　parent 169n.
grandiloquence
　exaggeration 546n.
　vigour 571n.
　magniloquence 574n.
　eloquence 579n.
　affectation 850n.
　boasting 877n.
grandiose *huge* 195adj.
　rhetorical 574adj.
　proud 871adj.
　ostentatious 875adj.
Grand Lama *priest* 986n.
grandmother
　old woman 133n.
　maternity 169n.
　woman 373n.
grandsire *old man* 133n.

parent 169 n.
grand slam *victory* 727 n.
grandstand *view* 438 n.
  onlookers 441 n.
grand view *whole* 52 n.
grange *house* 192 n.
  farm 370 n.
granger
  husbandman 370 n.
granite *hardness* 326 n.
  rock 344 n.
granny knot
  ligature 47 n.
grant *be reasonable* 475 adj.
  believe 485 vb.
  confess 526 vb.
  subvention 703 n.
  be lenient 736 vb.
  permission 756 n.
  consent 758 n.
  dower 777 vb.
  convey 780 vb.
  gift 781 n.
  pay 804 n.
  reward 962 n.
grant asylum *admit* 299 vb.
granted *assented* 488 adj.
  supposed 512 adj.
grantee *beneficiary* 776 n.
  recipient 782 n.
grant-in-aid *pay* 804 n.
granting *if* 8 adv.
grantor *giver* 781 n.
grant-worthy
  deserving 915 adj.
granular *minute* 196 adj.
  textural 331 adj.
  powdery 332 adj.
granulation *texture* 331 n.
  pulverulence 332 n.
granule
  small quantity 33 n.
  powder 332 n.
grape *fruit* 301 n.
grape-shot *missile* 287 n.
  ammunition 723 n.
grape-vine *informant* 524 n.
graph *mathematics* 86 n.
graphic *expressive* 516 adj.
  representing 551 adj.
  painted 553 adj.
  forceful 571 adj.
  descriptive 590 adj.
graphic art *art* 551 n.
  painting 553 n.
graphite *lubricant* 334 n.
graphology *writing* 586 n.
graphometer
  angular measure 247 n.
graphotype *printing* 555 n.
grapnel *safeguard* 662 n.

grapple *join, tie* 45 vb.
  be resolute 599 vb.
  attack 712 vb.
  wrestling 716 n.
  contend 716 vb.
grappler *combatant* 722 n.
grapple with
  withstand 704 vb.
grappling iron
  coupling 47 n.
  safeguard 662 n.
grasp *ability* 160 n.
  range 183 n.
  distance 199 n.
  knowledge 490 n.
  be wise 498 vb.
  understand 516 vb.
  protection 660 n.
  taking 786 n.
  possession 773 n.
  retention 778 n.
grasp at *desire* 859 vb.
grasping *oppressive* 735 adj.
  taking 786 adj.
  avaricious 816 adj.
  greedy 859 adj.
grass *provender* 301 n.
  grass 366 n.
  garden 370 n.
  greenness 432 n.
grasshopper *vermin* 365 n.
  jumper 312 n.
grassland *grassland* 348 n.
grassless *dry* 342 adj.
grassy *soft* 327 adj.
  vegetal 366 adj.
  green 432 adj.
grate *rub* 333 vb.
  give pain 377 vb.
  furnace 383 n.
  rasp 407 vb.
  ululate 409 vb.
  discord 411 vb.
  pulverize 332 vb.
  displease 827 vb.
  cause dislike 861 vb.
  excite hate 888 vb.
grateful *pleasant* 376 adj.
  pleasurable 826 adj.
  content 828 adj.
  grateful 907 adj.
grater *roughness* 259 n.
  pulverizer 332 n.
gratification
  pleasure 376 n.
  (*see* gratify)
gratify *bribe* 612 vb.
  be lenient 736 vb.
  give 781 vb.
  pay 804 vb.
  please 826 vb.

content 828 vb.
  reward 962 vb.
grating *disagreeing* 25 adj.
  network 222 n.
  (*see* grate)
gratis *free* 744 adj.
  given 781 adj.
  uncharged 812 adj.
gratitude *gratitude* 907 n.
gratuitous
  suppositional 512 adj.
  voluntary 597 adj.
  given 781 adj.
  uncharged 812 adj.
  undue 916 adj.
gratuity *extra* 40 n.
  acquisition 771 n.
  gift 781 n.
  undueness 916 n.
  reward 962 n.
gratulation
  congratulation 886 n.
gravamen
  accusation 928 n.
grave *great* 32 adj.
  excavation 255 n.
  groove 262 vb.
  resting place 266 n.
  death 361 n.
  tomb 364 n.
  record 548 vb.
  engrave 555 vb.
  forceful 571 adj.
  important 638 adj.
  inexcitable 823 adj.
  serious 834 adj.
  dull 840 adj.
  heinous 934 adj.
grave accent
  punctuation 547 n.
grave clothes
  grave clothes 364 n.
grave-digger
  excavator 255 n.
  interment 364 n.
  church officer 986 n.
gravel *flatten* 216 vb.
  powder 332 n.
  soil 344 n.
  puzzle 474 vb.
  confute 479 vb.
  be difficult 700 vb.
  defeat 727 vb.
gravelly *hard* 326 adj.
  powdery 332 adj.
  territorial 344 adj.
graven image *image* 551 n.
  idol 982 n.
graveolence *odour* 394 n.
  fetor 397 n.
gravestone *covering* 226 n.

obsequies 364 n.
graveyard *cemetery* 364 n.
　holy place 990 n.
gravid *productive* 164 adj.
graving dock *stable* 192 n.
gravitate *tend* 179 vb.
　descend 309 vb.
　weigh 322 vb.
gravitation *influence* 178 n.
　gravity 322 n.
gravity *influence* 178 n.
　attraction 291 n.
　materiality 319 n.
　gravity 322 n.
　vigour 571 n.
　importance 638 n.
　inexcitability 823 n.
　seriousness 834 n.
　prudery 950 n.
gravy *fluid* 335 n.
　semiliquidity 354 n.
gravy-boat *bowl* 194 n.
graze *be near* 200 vb.
　be contiguous 202 vb.
　shallowness 212 n.
　collide 279 vb.
　feed 301 vb.
　rub 333 vb.
　touch 378 n., vb.
　wound 655 vb.
grazing
　grassland 348 n.
　stock farm 369 n.
grease *adhesive* 47 n.
　coat 226 vb.
　smoother 258 n.
　meat 301 n.
　soften 327 vb.
　lubricant 334 n.
　fat 357 n.
　silencer 401 n.
　make unclean 649 vb.
　facilitate 701 vb.
　hairwash 843 n.
grease-gun *lubricant* 334 n.
grease-paint
　stage-set 594 n.
　cosmetic 843 n.
grease-proof
　resisting 715 adj.
greaser *foreigner* 59 n.
grease the palm
　bribe 612 vb.
greasy *smooth* 258 adj.
　unctuous 357 adj.
　savoury 390 adj.
　dirty 649 adj.
great *great* 32 adj.
　superior 34 adj.
　powerful 160 adj.
　strong 162 adj.

influential 178 adj.
　large 195 adj.
　plenteous 635 adj.
　important 638 adj.
　excellent 644 adj.
　worshipful 866 adj.
　noble 868 adj.
　proud 871 adj.
great circle *circle* 250 n.
　uranometry 321 n.
greatcoat *overcoat* 228 n.
great deal *greatly* 32 adv.
great doings
　important matter 638 n.
　activity 678 n.
　pageant 875 n.
greaten *expand* 197 vb.
　enlarge 197 vb.
greater than ever
　increasing 36 adj.
greatest *supreme* 34 adj.
great folk *aristocracy* 868 n.
great majority
　greater number 104 n.
　the dead 361 n.
great man *bigwig* 638 n.
great name *repute* 866 n.
greatness (*see* great)
Greats *exam.* 459 n.
　curriculum 536 n.
Great Seal *officer* 741 n.
great spirit
　the Deity 965 n.
great thing
　chief thing 638 n.
great unpaid *judge* 957 n.
Great Wall of China
　partition 231 n.
　defences 713 n.
Great Year *era* 110 n.
greaves *legwear* 228 n.
　armour 713 n.
grebe *waterfowl* 365 n.
greed *rapacity* 786 n.
　avarice 816 n.
　desire 859 n.
　selfishness 932 n.
　gluttony 947 n.
greediness
　overstepping 306 n.
　sensualism 944 n.
　(*see* greed)
greedy *feeding* 301 adj.
　unprovided 636 adj.
　greedy 859 adj.
　envious 912 adj.
Greek
　unknown thing 491 n.
　unmeaningness 515 n.
Greek fire *fireworks* 420 n.
　explosive 723 n.

Greek kalends
　neverness 109 n.
Greek mode *key* 410 n.
green *new* 126 adj.
　young 130 adj.
　pleasance 192 n.
　grassland 348 n.
　vegetal 366 adj.
　sour 393 adj.
　greenness 432 n.
　credulous 487 adj.
　ignorant 491 adj.
　unhabituated 611 adj.
　immature 670 adj.
　unskilled 695 adj.
　pleasure-ground 837 n.
　innocent 935 adj.
greenback
　paper money 797 n.
green belt *space* 183 n.
　limit 236 n.
　plain 348 n.
　vegetability 366 n.
greenery *plant* 366 n.
　greenness 432 n.
green-eyed *jealous* 911 adj.
green fingers *feeler* 378 n.
　aptitude 694 n.
greenfly *fly* 365 n.
greengrocer *provider* 633 n.
greenhorn
　ignoramus 493 n.
　ninny 501 n.
　beginner 538 n.
　dupe 544 n.
　bungler 697 n.
　ingenue 699 n.
greenhouse *arbour* 194 n.
　garden 370 n.
green light
　signal light 420 n.
　assent 488 n.
　signal 547 n.
　permit 756 n.
green-room *theatre* 594 n.
greens *vegetable* 301 n.
greensward
　grassland 348 n.
greet *meet* 295 vb.
　speak to 583 vb.
　weep 836 vb.
　be friendly 880 vb.
　be hospitable 882 vb.
　greet 884 vb.
greetings *respects* 920 n.
greeve *manager* 690 n.
gregarious *sociable* 882 adj.
Gregorian
　musicianly 413 adj.
gremlin *hinderer* 702 n.
　elf 970 n.

Q

grenade *bang* 402n.
　bomb 723n.
grenadier *tall creature* 209n.
　soldiery 722n.
grenadilla *fruit* 301n.
Gresham's law
　deterioration 655n.
grey *uniform* 16adj.
　median 30adj.
　horse 273n.
　dim 419adj.
　colourless 426adj.
　whitish 427adj.
　grey 429n., adj.
　neutral 625adj.
　mediocre 732adj.
　cheerless 834adj.
greybeard *old man* 133n.
grey dawn *half-light* 419n.
　dejection 834n.
Grey Eminence
　adviser 691n.
greyhound *speeder* 277n.
　dog 365n.
grey mare *spouse* 894n.
grey matter *head* 213n.
　intelligence 498n.
grid *correlation* 12n.
　electricity 160n.
　network 222n.
griddle *cook* 301vb.
gridiron *network* 222n.
　heater 383n.
　arena 724n.
grief *evil* 616n.
　sorrow 825n.
　discontent 829n.
grievance *evil* 616n.
　discontent 829n.
　annoyance 827n.
　wrong 914n.
grieve *suffer* 825vb.
　hurt 827vb.
　sadden 834vb.
　lament 836vb.
　pity 905vb.
grievous *bad* 645adj.
　distressing 827adj.
griffe *hybrid* 43n.
griffin *hybrid* 43n.
　rara avis 84n.
　animal 365n.
　ignoramus 493n.
　heraldry 547n.
grig *table fish* 365n.
grill *network* 222n.
　window 263n.
　cook 301vb.
　be hot 379vb.
　heat 381vb.
　heater 383n.

interrogate 459vb.
grill-room *café* 192n.
　chamber 194n.
grilse *table fish* 365n.
grim *resolute* 599adj.
　obstinate 602adj.
　distressing 827adj.
　serious 834 adj.
　frightening 854adj.
　ungracious 885adj.
　ugly 842adj.
　sullen 893adj.
　cruel 898adj.
　gesture 547n.
　be loth 598vb.
　discontent 829n.
　smile 835vb.
　affectation 850n.
　frighten 854vb.
　dislike 861vb.
　sullenness 893n.
grimace *distortion* 246n.
　look 438n.
grimalkin *cat* 365n.
grime *dirt* 649n.
Grimm's law
　linguistics 557n.
grimness *dullness* 840n.
　(*see* grim)
grimy *dim* 419adj.
　dirty 649adj.
grin *smile* 835vb.
　ridicule 851n.
grin and bear it
　stand firm 599vb.
　be patient 823vb.
　be cheerful 833vb.
grind *bate* 37vb.
　rend, break 46vb.
　demolish 165vb.
　make smaller 198vb.
　sharpen 256vb.
　chew 301vb.
　pulverize 332vb.
　rub 333vb.
　give pain 377vb.
　rasp 407vb.
　study 536n., vb.
　wound 655vb.
　labour 682n.
　oppress 735vb.
grinder *tooth* 256n.
　meal 301n.
　pulverizer 332n.
grindstone
　sharpener 256n.
　pulverizer 332n.
　labour 682n.
　bore 838n.
gringo *foreigner* 59n.
grip *join, tie* 45vb.

fastening 47n.
　cohere 48vb.
　vitality 162n.
　vigorousness 174n.
　bag 194n.
　handle 218n.
　gesture 547n.
　protection 660n.
　skill 694n.
　governance 733n.
　restrain 747vb.
　possession 773n.
　retention 778n.
　impress 821vb.
　hair-dressing 843n.
gripe *pang* 377n.
　be parsimonious 816vb.
　indigestion 651n.
griping *oppressive* 735adj.
　avaricious 816adj.
　greedy 859adj.
gripping *influential* 178n.
　exciting 821adj.
grip-sack *bag* 194n.
grips, at *warring* 718adj.
grisaille *grey* 429n.
　painting 553n.
grisette *woman* 373n.
grisly *unsightly* 842adj.
　frightening 854adj.
grist *powder* 332n.
　materials 631n.
　provision 633n.
gristle
　vigorousness 174n.
　solid body 324n.
　hardness 326n.
　toughness 329n.
grit *strength* 162n.
　hardness 326n.
　texture 331n.
　powder 332n.
　resolution 599n.
　stamina 600n.
　courage 855n.
grizzle *whiten* 427vb.
　weep 836vb.
grizzled *whitish* 427adj.
　grey 429adj.
　pied 437adj.
grizzly *grey* 429adj.
groan *feel pain* 377vb.
　cry 408vb.
　deprecate 762vb.
　discontent 829n.
　be dejected 834vb.
　weep 836vb.
groat *small coin* 33n.
groats *small thing* 33n.
grocer *provider* 633n.
　tradesman 794n.

groceries *provisions* 301 n.
grog *liquor* 301 n.
grog-blossom
  alcoholism 949 n.
groggy *weakly* 163 adj.
  oscillating 317 adj.
  sick 651 adj.
grogshop *tavern* 192 n.
groin *angularity* 247 n.
grommet *orifice* 263 n.
groom
  animal husbandry 369 n.
  man 372 n.
  train 534 vb.
  make ready 669 vb.
  domestic 742 n.
groomed *bedecked* 844 adj.
  fashionable 848 adj.
groomsman
  close friend 880 n.
  bridesman 894 n.
groove *cut* 46 vb.
  regularity 81 n.
  place 185 n.
  receptacle 194 n.
  gap 201 n.
  furrow 262 n.
  habit 610 n.
grope *move slowly* 278 vb.
  touch 378 vb.
  be dim-sighted 440 vb.
  be tentative 461 vb.
  be uncertain 474 vb.
  essay 671 vb.
  be clumsy 695 vb.
grope for *search* 459 vb.
groping *ignorant* 491 adj.
  clumsy 695 adj.
  unsuccessful 728 adj.
grosgraine *textile* 222 n.
gross *consummate* 32 adj.
  whole 52 adj.
  unintelligent 499 adj.
  manifest 522 adj.
  bad 645 adj.
  acquire 771 vb.
  receive 782 vb.
  take 786 vb.
  graceless 842 adj.
  vulgar 847 adj.
  heinous 934 adj.
  sensual 944 adj.
  impure 951 adj.
gross, a
  over one hundred 99 n.
grot, grotto *pavilion* 192 n.
  arbour 194 n.
  cavity 255 n.
grotesque *unusual* 84 adj.
  distorted 246 adj.
  absurd 497 adj.

inelegant 576 adj.
  eyesore 842 n.
  ridiculous 849 adj.
grouch (*see* grouse)
ground *reason why* 156 n.
  territory 184 n.
  situation 186 n.
  base 214 n.
  flatten 216 vb.
  basis 218 n.
  come to rest 266 vb.
  navigate 269 vb.
  land 295 vb.
  powdery 332 adj.
  land 344 n.
  evidence 466 n.
  educate 534 vb.
  motive 612 n.
  be difficult 700 vb.
  arena 724 n.
  fail 728 vb.
ground and consequent
  causation 156 vb.
grounded *real* 1 adj.
  fixed 153 adj.
  impotent 161 adj.
  evidential 466 adj.
  in difficulties 700 adj.
  grounded 728 adj.
ground floor *base* 214 n.
groundless *unreal* 2 adj.
  insubstantial 4 adj.
  causeless 159 adj.
  illogical 477 adj.
groundling *playgoer* 594 n.
  commoner 869 n.
ground-plan *map* 551 n.
  plan 623 n.
grounds *leavings* 41 n.
  pleasance 192 n.
  grassland 348 n.
  dirt 649 n.
  pleasure-ground 837 n.
ground upon
  attribute 158 vb.
groundwork *prelude* 66 n.
  source 156 n.
  base 214 n.
  basis 218 n.
  preparation 669 n.
group *combine* 50 vb.
  subdivision 53 n.
  arrange 62 vb.
  series 71 n.
  group 74 n.
  sculpture 554 n.
  party 708 n.
  formation 722 n.
  sect 978 n.
group captain
  air officer 741 n.

grouper *sectarist* 978 n.
grouse *table bird* 365 n.
  be discontented 829 vb.
  lament 836 vb.
  be sullen 893 vb.
grouser *dissentient* 489 n.
  malcontent 829 n.
  rude person 885 n.
  disapprover 924 n.
grout *adhesive* 47 n.
  coat 226 vb.
  dirt 649 n.
  be sullen 893 vb.
grove *street* 192 n.
  wood 366 n.
grovel *be low* 210 vb.
  be horizontal 216 vb.
  knuckle under 721 vb.
  obey 739 vb.
  be servile 879 vb.
grow *become* 1 vb.
  grow 36 vb.
  be turned to 147 vb.
  result 157 vb.
  generate 164 vb.
  expand 197 vb.
  progress 285 vb.
  breed stock 369 vb.
  cultivate 370 vb.
  mature 669 vb.
grower *producer* 167 n.
growing *young* 130 adj.
growing pains *increase* 36 n.
  youth 130 n.
growl *ululation* 409 n.
  be rude 885 vb.
  hate 888 vb.
  anger 891 n.
  sullenness 893 n.
  threat 900 n.
growler *cab* 274 n.
  malcontent 829 n.
growling *hoarse* 407 adj.
grow moss *stay* 144 vb.
  deteriorate 655 vb.
grown-up *grown-up* 134 adj.
grow on one
  be wont 610 vb.
growth *increase* 36 n.
  sequel 67 n.
  conversion 147 n.
  growth 157 n.
  propagation 164 n.
  expansion 197 n.
  swelling 253 n.
  agriculture 370 n.
grow together *cohere* 48 vb.
  combine 50 vb.
groyne *projection* 254 n.
  safeguard 662 n.
  obstacle 702 n.

grub *small animal* 33 n.
  animacule 196 n.
  food 301 n.
  extract 304 vb.
grubble *touch* 378 vb.
Grub Street hack
  author 589 n.
grudge *be loth* 598 vb.
  refuse 760 vb.
  be parsimonious 816 vb.
  be discontented 829 vb.
  enmity 881 n.
  hatred 888 n.
  resentment 891 n.
grudgeful
  revengeful 910 adj.
gruel *cereal* 301 n.
gruelling *fatiguing* 684 adj.
  paining 827 adj.
gruesome *unsightly* 842 adj.
  frightening 854 adj.
gruff *hoarse* 407 adj.
  taciturn 582 adj.
  ungracious 885 adj.
  irascible 892 adj.
  sullen 893 adj.
  unkind 898 adj.
grumble *roll* 403 vb.
  cry 408 vb.
  be discontented 829 vb.
  be sullen 893 vb.
grumbling
  threatening 900 adj.
grume *solid body* 324 n.
  blood 335 n.
  semiliquidity 354 n.
  pulpiness 356 n.
grumpy *irascible* 892 adj.
  sullen 893 adj.
Grundy, Mrs. *prude* 950 n.
grunt *rasp* 407 vb.
  cry 408 n., vb.
  ululate 409 vb.
  be fatigued 684 vb.
grunting *ungracious* 885 adj.
guano *excrement* 302 n.
  fertilizer 171 n.
guarantee
  make certain 473 vb.
  affirm 532 vb.
  safeguard 660 vb.
  patronize 703 vb.
  promise 764 n.
  security 767 n.
guarantor *patron* 707 n.
guard *janitor* 264 n.
  driver 268 n.
  attention 455 n.
  surveillance 457 n.
  protection 660 n.
  safeguard 660 vb.

defender 713 n.
  keeper 749 n.
guardant *heraldic* 547 adj.
guarded *taciturn* 582 adj.
  conditional 766 adj.
  cautious 858 adj.
guardian (*see* guard)
guardian angel
  patron 707 n.
  benefactor 903 n.
guardless *vulnerable* 661 adj.
guard, on *vigilant* 457 adj.
  cautious 858 adj.
guard-room *lock-up* 748 n.
guards *armed force* 722 n.
guard's van *train* 274 n.
guava *fruit* 301 n.
gubbins *vessel* 194 n.
  sink 649 n.
gubernatorial
  directing 689 adj.
  governmental 733 adj.
guddi, gaddi *seat* 218 n.
  regalia 743 n.
gudgeon *pivot* 218 n.
  fish 365 n.
guebre *religionist* 973 n.
  idolater 982 n.
guerdon *reward* 962 n., vb.
guernsey *vest* 228 n.
guerrilla *attacker* 712 n.
  soldier 722 n.
  revolter 738 n.
guess *assume* 471 vb.
  intuit 476 vb.
  estimate 480 vb.
  opinion 485 n.
  not know 491 vb.
  conjecture 512 n.
  hint 524 n.
guess, at a *about* 33 adv.
guess-warp *cable* 47 n.
guesswork *empiricism* 461 n.
  uncertainty 474 n.
  intuition 476 n.
  conjecture 512 n.
guest *resident* 191 n.
  friend 880 n.
  social person 882 n.
guest-friend *friend* 880 n.
guest-house *quarters* 192 n.
guest-rope *cable* 47 n.
guff *insubstantial thing* 4 n.
  empty talk 515 n.
  fable 543 n.
guffaw *laughter* 835 n.
guggle *flow* 350 vb.
  bubble 355 vb.
  sound faint 401 vb.
  resound 404 vb.
  ululate 409 vb.

gugglet *vessel* 194 n.
guidance *teaching* 534 n.
  directorship 689 n.
  advice 691 n.
guide *prototype* 23 n.
  superior 34 n.
  come before 64 vb.
  precursor 66 n.
  rule 81 n.
  accompany 89 vb.
  influence 178 vb.
  itinerary 267 n.
  precede 283 vb.
  sage 500 n.
  guide 520 n.
  show 522 vb.
  informant 524 n.
  educate 534 vb.
  teacher 537 n.
  indication 547 n.
  reference book 589 n.
  direct 689 vb.
  adviser 691 n.
  theosophy 984 n.
guide-book *directory* 87 n.
  guide-book 524 n.
guided missile *rocket* 276 n.
guideless
  vulnerable 661 adj.
guidon *flag* 547 n.
guild *business* 622 n.
  corporation 708 n.
  merchant 794 n.
guilder *coinage* 797 n.
guildhall *mart* 796 n.
guile *duplicity* 541 n.
  deception 542 n.
  cunning 698 n.
guileful *perfidious* 930 adj.
guileless *artless* 699 adj.
  honourable 929 adj.
  innocent 935 adj.
guillotine *end* 69 n.
  stop 145 n.
  shorten 204 vb.
  killer 362 n.
  execute 963 vb.
  means of execution 964 n.
guilt *badness* 645 n.
  wrong 914 n.
  wickedness 934 n.
  guilt 936 n.
  lawbreaking 954 n.
guilt-feeling
  penitence 939 n.
guiltless *ignorant* 491 adj.
  virtuous 933 adj.
  guiltless 935 adj.
  acquitted 960 adj.
guilt-offering
  substitute 150 n.

guilty (*see* guilt)
guilty man
  offender 904 n.
guinea *coinage* 797 n.
guinea-pig *rodent* 365 n.
  testee 461 n.
guisard *actor* 594 n.
guise *modality* 7 n.
  appearance 445 n.
  pretext 614 n.
  way 624 n.
  conduct 688 n.
guitar *harp* 414 n.
guitarist
  instrumentalist 413 n.
gulch *gap* 201 n.
gules *red colour* 431 n.
  heraldry 547 n.
gulf *entrance* 68 n.
  depth 211 n.
  cavity 255 n.
  way in 297 n.
  gulf 345 n.
  access 624 n.
gull *bird of prey* 365 n.
  credulity 478 n.
  fool 501 n.
  befool 542 vb.
  dupe 544 vb.
  defraud 788 vb.
gullery *nest* 192 n.
  trickery 542 n.
gullet *maw* 194 n.
  orifice 263 n.
  eater 301 n.
  conduit 351 n.
  air-pipe 353 n.
gullible
  misjudging 481 n.
  credulous 487 n.
  foolish 499 vb.
  gullible 544 adj.
Gulliver *traveller* 268 n.
  mariner 270 n.
gully *gap* 210 n.
  narrowness 206 n.
  valley 255 n.
  sharp edge 256 n.
  conduit 351 n.
gulosity *gluttony* 947 n.
gulp *absorb* 299 vb.
  potion 301 n.
  eat 301 vb.
  respiration 352 n.
gum *adhesive* 47 n.
  agglutinate 48 vb.
  viscidity 354 n.
  resin 357 n.
  sweet 392 n.
gumbo *soup* 301 n.
  semiliquidity 354 n.

gummic *resinous* 357 adj.
gummy *cohesive* 48 adj.
  tough 329 adj.
  viscid 354 adj.
  retentive 778 adj.
gum on *affix* 45 vb.
gumption *intelligence* 498 n.
gumptionless
  foolish 499 adj.
gumshoe(s) *footwear* 228 n.
  detective 459 n.
gun *propellant* 287 n.
  bang 402 n.
  hunter 619 n.
  gun 723 n.
guna *speech sound* 398 n.
gunboat *warship* 722 n.
gun-carriage
  war-chariot 274 n.
  gun 723 n.
gun-cotton *propellant* 287 n.
  explosive 723 n.
gun-dog *dog* 365 n.
gun-emplacement
  fortification 713 n.
  gun 723 n.
gunfire *loudness* 400 n.
  bombardment 712 n.
gun-layer *shooter* 287 n.
gunlock *tool* 630 n.
  gun 723 n.
gunman *shooter* 287 n.
  murderer 362 n.
  combatant 722 n.
  robber 789 n.
  ruffian 904 n.
gunmetal *grey* 429 n.
gunner *shooter* 287 n.
  soldiery 722 n.
gunnery *propulsion* 287 n.
  bombardment 712 n.
  art of war 718 n.
  arm 723 n.
gunning *chase* 619 n.
gunny *textile* 222 n.
gun-park *gun* 723 n.
gunpowder *destroyer* 168 n.
  propellant 287 n.
  explosive 723 n.
gun-rack *arsenal* 723 n.
gun-room *chamber* 194 n.
  storage 632 n.
  arsenal 723 n.
gun-runner *thief* 789 n.
gun-shot
  short distance 200 n.
gunsmith *artisan* 686 n.
gunstock *fire-arm* 723 n.
gunwale *edge* 234 n.
gup *rumour* 529 n.
  fable 543 n.

gurge *vortex* 315 n.
  eddy 350 n.
gurgle *flow* 350 vb.
  bubble 355 vb.
  sound faint 401 vb.
  resound 404 vb.
  laughter 835 n.
gurk *eruct* 300 vb.
guru *sage* 500 n.
  teacher 537 n.
gush *outbreak* 176 n.
  flow out 298 vb.
  emit 300 vb.
  ascend 308 vb.
  flow 350 vb.
  have feeling 374 vb.
  overestimation 482 n.
  diffuseness 570 n.
  chatter 581 n.
gusher *outflow* 298 n.
  climber 308 n.
  stream 350 n.
  store 632 n.
gushing *feeling* 818 adj.
  impressible 819 adj.
gusset *adjunct* 40 n.
gust *breeze* 352 n.
  taste 386 n.
  excitable state 822 n.
gustation *taste* 386 n.
gustatory *tasty* 386 adj.
gustful *savoury* 390 adj.
gustless *tasteless* 387 adj.
gusto *pleasure* 376 n.
  taste 386 n.
  enjoyment 824 n.
  feeling 818 n.
gusty *unstable* 152 adj.
  windy 352 adj.
gut *destroy* 165 vb.
  tube 263 n.
  void 300 vb.
  cook 301 vb.
  extract 304 vb.
  gulf 345 n.
  burn 381 vb.
  access 624 n.
  fleece 786 vb.
gutless *weak* 163 adj.
  irresolute 601 adj.
guts *insides* 224 n.
  vigour 571 n.
  resolution 599 n.
  courage 855 n.
guttapercha *elasticity* 328 n.
gutter *vary* 152 vb.
  furrow 262 n.
  be agitated 318 vb.
  drain 351 n.
  letterpress 587 n.
  sink 649 n.

arena 724n.
vulgar 847adj.
detraction 926n.
gutter-crawl
approach 289vb.
voyage 269vb.
guttering *fitful* 142adj.
guttersnipe
low fellow 869n.
guttural
speech sound 398n.
hoarse 407adj.
spoken letter 558n.
vocal 577adj.
gutturalize *rasp* 407vb.
guy *tackling* 47n.
supporter 218n.
person 371n.
male 372n.
be absurd 497vb.
misinterpret 521vb.
misrepresent 552vb.
laughing-stock 851n.
satirize 851vb.
guzzle *eat* 301vb.
gluttonize 947vb.
get drunk 949vb.
gybe, gibe *change* 143vb.
navigate 269vb.
gym dress *tunic* 228n.
gymkhana *contest* 716n.
gymnasium
meeting place 192n.
academy 539n.
arena 724n.
gymnast *athlete* 162n.
gymnastics *athletics* 162n.
education 534n.
exercise 682n.
contest 716n.
sport 837n.
gynæceum
womankind 373n.
love-nest 887n.
gynæcologist *doctor* 658n.
gynæcology *female* 373n.
medical art 658n.
gynandry
abnormality 84n.
male 372n.
gynarchy *gynocracy* 733n.
gyniatrics *female* 373n.
gynocracy *gynocracy* 733n.
gyp *deceive* 542vb.
trickster 545n.
domestic 742n.
gypsum *materials* 631n.
gypsy
extraneous 59adj.
nonconformist 84n.
wanderer 268n.

diviner 511n.
gyration *rotation* 315n.
gyrocompass
sailing aid 269n.
gyron *heraldry* 547n.
gyropilot *aeronaut* 271n.
directorship 689n.
gyroscope *rotator* 315n.
gyrostat *rotator* 315n.
gyrostatics *rotation* 315n.
gyve *fetter* 748n.

H

habeas corpus
transference 272n.
warrant 737n.
legal process 959n.
haberdasher *clothier* 228n.
tradesman 794n.
habergeon *armour* 713n.
habiliments *clothing* 228n.
habit *temperament* 5n.
state 7n.
uniformity 16n.
composition 56n.
continuity 71n.
regularity 81n.
recurrence 106n.
tradition 127n.
permanence 144n.
dress 228n.
habit 610n.
vocation 622n.
conduct 688n.
fashion 848n.
habitat *place* 185n.
situation 186n.
locality 187n.
abode 192n.
habitation *edifice* 164n.
abode 192n.
habit-forming
influential 178adj.
habitual 610adj.
habit of mind
affections 817n.
habits of business
assiduity 678n.
habitual *general* 79adj.
typical 83adj.
repeated 106adj.
frequent 139adj.
known 490adj.
habitual 610adj.
habituate
make conform 83vb.
break in 369vb.
train 534vb.
habituate 610vb.
make ready 669vb.

habituation
habituation 610n.
habitude (*see* habit)
habitué *habitué* 610n.
social person 882n.
hacienda *house* 192n.
farm 370n.
lands 777n.
hack *cut* 46vb.
cab 274n.
saddle-horse 273n.
author 589n.
wound 655vb.
worker 686n.
servant 742n.
hackbut *fire-arm* 723n.
hackee *rodent* 365n.
hackery *carriage* 274n.
hackie *driver* 268n.
hackle *plumage* 259n.
livery 547n.
hackney-carriage *cab* 274n.
hackneyed *known* 490adj.
aphoristic 496adj.
usual 610adj.
hackneyed saying
maxim 496n.
hack-saw *notch* 260n.
had *gullible* 544adj.
haddock *table fish* 365n.
Hades *death* 361n.
the dead 361n.
mythic hell 972n.
hadis, hadith
tradition 127n.
non-Biblical scripture
975n.
hæmad *blood* 335n.
hæmatic
sanguineous 335adj.
hæmatology *blood* 335n.
hæmatosis *blood* 335n.
hæmoglobin *blood* 335n.
hæmophilia
hæmorrhage 302n.
fluidity 335n.
blood disease 651n.
hæmophilic
sanguineous 335adj.
diseased 651adj.
hæmorrhage
outflow 298n.
hæmorrhage 302n.
hæmorrhoids
swelling 253n.
hæmostatic
solidifying 324adj.
haft *handle* 218n.
tool 630n.
hag *old woman* 133n.
sorceress 983n.

haggard *lean* 206 adj.
 deformed 246 adj.
 fatigued 684 adj.
 suffering 825 adj.
 melancholic 834 adj.
 unsightly 842 adj.
haggis *dish* 301 n.
haggle *make terms* 766 vb.
 bargain 791 vb.
 be parsimonious 816 vb.
Hagiographa
 scripture 975 n.
hagiography
 biography 590 n.
 praise 923 n.
 theology 973 n.
hagiology *biography* 590 n.
 theology 973 n.
hagioscope
 window 263 n.
 view 438 n.
 church interior 990 n.
hag-ridden *spooky* 970 adj.
 bewitched 983 adj.
hail *crowd* 74 n.
 wintriness 380 n.
 assent 488 vb.
 call 547 n.
 allocution 583 n.
 greet 884 vb.
 show respect 920 vb.
 applaud 923 vb.
hail-fellow-well-met
 friendly 880 adj.
 sociable 882 adj.
hailstone *ice* 380 n.
hair *small thing* 33 n.
 filament 208 n.
 hair 259 n.
hairbreadth escape
 danger 661 n.
 escape 667 n.
hair cream
 hairwash 843 n.
hair-cut, hair-do
 hair-dressing 843 n.
hairdresser
 cleaner 648 n.
 beautician 843 n.
hairiness *roughness* 259 n.
hairless *hairless* 229 adj.
hair-net *receptacle* 194 n.
 hair-dressing 843 n.
hair-oil *unguent* 357 n.
 scent 396 n.
 hairwash 843 n.
hair on end
 nervousness 854 n.
hairpin *fastening* 47 n.
 coil 251 n.
 hair-dressing 843 n.

hairpin bend *curve* 248 n.
hair-raising
 frightening 854 adj.
hair-restorer
 hairwash 843 n.
hair's breadth
 narrowness 206 n.
 short distance 200 n.
hair shirt *asceticism* 945 n.
hair-space
 short distance 200 n.
 interval 201 n.
 print-type 587 n.
hair-splitting
 discrimination 463 n.
 argument 475 n.
 sophistry 477 n.
hairspring *machine* 630 n.
hair-style
 hair-dressing 843 n.
hair-stylist *beautician* 843 n.
hairwash *cleanser* 648 n.
 hairwash 843 n.
hairy *fibrous* 208 adj.
 hairy 259 adj.
hajj *land travel* 267 n.
 traveller 268 n.
 piety 979 n.
 act of worship 981 n.
hajji *pietist* 979 n.
 worshipper 981 n.
hake *table fish* 365 n.
hakim *doctor* 658 n.
 officer 741 n.
halberd *spear, axe* 723 n.
halberdier *soldiery* 722 n.
halcyon *tranquil* 266 adj.
 peaceful 717 adj.
 palmy 730 adj.
halcyon days
 palmy days 730 n.
 joy 824 n.
hale *draw* 288 vb.
 healthy 650 adj.
half *part* 53 n.
 incompleteness 55 n.
 bisection 92 n.
half a jiffy
 instantaneity 116 n.
half-and-half
 equal 28 adj.
 mixed 43 adj.
 neutral 625 adj.
half-and-halfer
 moderate 625 n.
half-asleep
 inattentive 456 adj.
 sleepy 679 adj.
half-awake
 abstracted 456 adj.
 sleepy 679 adj.

half-baked
 smattering 491 adj.
 immature 670 adj.
 unskilled 695 adj.
 uncompleted 726 adj.
half-belief *doubt* 486 n.
half-blood *hybrid* 43 n.
 nonconformist 84 n.
 defect 647 n.
half-breed *hybrid* 43 n.
 nonconformist 84 n.
half-brother *kinsman* 11 n.
half-caste *hybrid* 43 n.
half-circle *arc* 250 n.
half-cock, at
 immature 670 adj.
half dead *dying* 361 adj.
half distance *middle* 70 n.
half-done
 incomplete 55 adj.
 neglected 458 adj.
 uncompleted 726 adj.
half-educated
 smattering 491 adj.
half-face *laterality* 239 n.
half-fed *underfed* 636 adj.
half-finished
 incomplete 55 adj.
half-frozen
 semiliquid 354 adj.
half-glimpse
 sciolism 491 n.
half-hearted *weak* 163 adj.
 unwilling 598 adj.
 irresolute 601 adj.
 apathetic 820 adj.
 indifferent 860 adj.
half-hidden
 shadowy 419 adj.
half-hitch *ligature* 47 n.
half-hose *legwear* 228 n.
half in *excluded* 57 adj.
half-knowledge
 sciolism 491 n.
half-length *short* 204 adj.
half-lie
 mental dishonesty 543 n.
half-light *evening* 129 n.
 half-light 419 n.
 hue 425 n.
half-mast *depress* 311 vb.
half-masted
 lamenting 836 adj.
half-measures
 incompleteness 55 n.
 irresolution 601 n.
 mid-course 625 n.
 insufficiency 636 n.
 bungling 695 n.
half-melted
 semiliquid 354 adj.

half-moon *curve* 248n.
arc 250n.
moon 321n.
half-nelson
retention 778n.
half out *excluded* 57adj.
half-pants *trousers* 228n.
half pay *receipt* 807n.
halfpenny *coinage* 797n.
half-price *cheap* 812adj.
half rations
insufficiency 636n.
half-ripe *immature* 670adj.
half-shadow
half-light 419n.
half-sight *dim sight* 440n.
half-smile *laughter* 835n.
half-space *interval* 201n.
half-spoken *tacit* 523adj.
half-starved
underfed 636adj.
fasting 946adj.
half the battle
chief thing 638n.
half-tide *middle* 70n.
mid-course 625n.
half-title *edition* 589n.
half-tone
light contrast 417n.
hue 425n.
picture 553n.
edition 589n.
half-truth
mental dishonesty 543n.
half-vision *dim sight* 440n.
half-way *middle point* 30n.
midway 70adv.
mid-course 625n.
undeviating 625adj.
compromise 770n.
half-wit *fool* 501n.
half-witted
unintelligent 499adj.
halibut *table fish* 365n.
halitosis *fetor* 397n.
hall *edifice* 164n.
house 192n.
chamber 194n.
feasting 301n.
access 624n.
hallelujah *rejoicing* 835n.
celebration 876n.
hymn 981n.
halliard, halyard
tackling 47n.
hall-mark *label* 547n.
halloa, halloo *cry* 408vb.
pursue 619vb.
hallow *sanctify* 979vb.
hallowed *divine* 965adj.
hallucination

unsubstantiality 4n.
appearance 445n.
error 495n.
psychopathy 503n.
fantasy 513n.
deception 542n.
hallux *foot* 214n.
finger 378n.
halo *circumjacence* 230n.
loop 250n.
light 417n.
honours 866n.
haloed *sanctified* 979adj.
halt *end* 69n.
stop 145n.
crippled 163adj.
quiescence 266n.
move slowly 278vb.
goal 295n.
imperfect 647adj.
be obstructive 702vb.
failure 728n.
halter *halter* 47n.
hanger 217n.
loop 250n.
fetter 748n.
means of execution 964n.
halve *sunder* 46vb.
bisect 92vb.
apportion 783vb.
halves *portion* 783n.
halve the match
be equal 28vb.
ham *housing* 192n.
buttocks 238n.
leg 267n.
meat 301n.
dramatic 594adj.
unskilled 695adj.
bungler 697n.
hamadryad *reptile* 365n.
vegetability 366n.
hamburger *meat* 301n.
ham-handed
clumsy 695adj.
Hamitic *ethnic* 11adj.
language type 557n.
hamlet *housing* 192n.
hammam *heater* 383n.
ablution 648n.
hammer *be vigorous* 174vb.
pierce 263vb.
hammer 279n.
pulverizer 332n.
be loud 400vb.
strike at 712vb.
hammer and sickle
heraldry 547n.
hammer and tongs
violently 176adv.
knock 279n.

laboriously 682adv.
hammer at
repeat oneself 106vb.
hammer in *affix* 45vb.
insert 303vb.
hammer out
efform 243vb.
carry through 725vb.
hammer, under the
saleable 793adj.
hammock *pendant* 217n.
bed 218n.
hamper *basket* 194n.
impair 655vb.
be difficult 700vb.
hinder 702vb.
restrain 747vb.
hamster *rodent* 365n.
hamstring *disable* 161vb.
impair 655vb.
hinder 702vb.
hamstrings *leg* 267n.
hamstrung *crippled* 163adj.
hand *limb* 53n.
group 74n.
timekeeper 117n.
long measure 203n.
laterality 239n.
pass 305vb.
person 371n.
feeler, finger 378n.
indicator 547n.
lettering 586n.
instrument 628n.
doer 676n.
worker 686n.
servant 742n.
nippers 778n.
portion 783n.
hand and seal, under
promissory 764adj.
contractual 765adj.
hand, at *early* 135adj.
impending 155adj.
on the spot 189adj.
near 200adj.
useful 640adj.
hand back *restore* 656vb.
handbill *the press* 528n.
handbook *itinerary* 267n.
guide-book 524n.
reading matter 589n.
book 589n.
handclasp
friendliness 880n.
courteous act 884n.
sociability 882n.
handcuff *tie* 45vb.
fastening 47n.
fetter 747vb.
fetter 748n.

hand down
  transfer 272 vb.
handfast *conjunct* 45 adj.
  married 894 adj.
handful *finite quantity* 26 n.
  bunch 74 n.
  nonconformist 84 n.
  fewness 105 n.
  contents 193 n.
  hard task 700 n.
hand-gallop *gait* 265 n.
hand, get a
  be praised 923 vb.
handhold *retention* 778 n.
handicap *equalize* 28 vb.
  inferiority 35 n.
  retard 278 vb.
  inexpedience 643 n.
  encumbrance 702 n.
  contest 716 n.
handicapped
  unintelligent 499 adj.
handicraft *business* 622 n.
hand, in *prepared* 669 adj.
  possessed 773 adj.
handiness
  instrumentality 628 n.
  utility 640 n.
  skill 694 n.
hand in glove
  accompanying 89 adj.
  concurrently 181 adv.
  co-operative 706 adj.
hand in hand *conjunct* 45 n.
  with 89 adv.
  concurrently 181 adv.
  contiguously 202 adv.
  in league 708 adv.
  sociably 882 adv.
hand it to
  be inferior 35 vb.
handiwork *effect* 157 n.
  product 164 n.
  deed 676 n.
handkerchief
  cleaning cloth 648 n.
handle *opportunity* 137 n.
  operate 173 vb.
  handle 218 n.
  strike 279 vb.
  touch 378 vb.
  name 561 n.
  dissert 591 vb.
  tool 630 n.
  use 673 vb.
  work 682 vb.
  deal with 688 vb.
  manage 689 vb.
  trade 791 vb.
  honours 866 n.
  title 870 n.

handlebar *handle* 218 n.
hand-made
  produced 164 adj.
handmaid
  instrument 628 n.
  auxiliary 707 n.
handmill *pulverizer* 332 n.
hand on *transfer* 272 vb.
hand-out *report* 524 n.
  gift 781 n.
hand over *transfer* 272 vb.
  pass 305 vb.
  relinquish 621 vb.
  convey 780 vb.
  give 781 vb.
hand over hand
  continuously 71 adv.
hand-picked *chosen* 605 adj.
  excellent 644 adj.
handrail *handle* 218 n.
  supporter 218 n.
hand round *provide* 633 vb.
handrunning
  continuously 71 adv.
hands *personnel* 686 n.
handsel *beginning* 68 n.
  security 767 n.
  gift 781 n.
handshake *gesture* 547 n.
  resignation 753 n.
  friendliness 880 n.
  sociability 882 n.
  courteous act 884 n.
handsome *liberal* 813 adj.
  beautiful 841 adj.
hand, something in
  vantage 34 n.
handspike *tool* 630 n.
handspring
  overturning 221 n.
hand's turn *labour* 682 n.
hand to *transfer* 272 vb.
hand to hand
  contending 716 adj.
hand to hand, from
  contiguously 202 adv.
  in transit 272 adv.
hand-to-mouth existence
  poverty 801 n.
hand-woven
  crossed 222 adj.
handwriting *writing* 586 n.
handwriting expert
  penman 586 n.
handy *little* 196 adj.
  near 200 adj.
  light 323 adj.
  instrumental 628 adj.
  expedient 642 adj.
  useful 640 adj.
  skilful 694 adj.

  wieldy 701 adj.
handyman *proficient* 696 n.
hang *come unstuck* 49 vb.
  pend 136 vb.
  hang 217 vb.
  descend 309 vb.
  kill 362 vb.
  appearance 445 n.
  execute 963 vb.
hang about
  be late 136 vb.
  be in motion 265 vb.
  be inactive 679 vb.
hangar *stable* 192 n.
  air travel 271 n.
hang back *be late* 136 vb.
  be loth 598 vb.
  avoid 620 vb.
  be modest 874 vb.
hang by a thread
  be in danger 661 vb.
hangdog look
  sullenness 893 n.
hanger *hanger* 217 n.
  supporter 218 n.
  sharp edge 256 n.
  side-arms 723 n.
hanger-on
  concomitant 89 n.
  follower 284 n.
  auxiliary 707 n.
  dependant 742 n.
  toady 879 n.
  flatterer 925 n.
hang fire *pend* 136 vb.
  pause 145 vb.
  be inert 175 vb.
  move slowly 278 vb.
  be loth 598 vb.
  not act 677 vb.
  be inactive 679 vb.
  miscarry 728 vb.
hanging judge *tyrant* 735 n.
hangings *covering* 226 n.
hangman *killer* 362 n.
  ruffian 904 n.
  punisher 963 n.
hang on *affix* 45 vb.
  go on 146 vb.
  persevere 600 vb.
  be subject 745 vb.
  retain 778 vb.
  be servile 879 vb.
hang one's head
  be dejected 834 vb.
  be humbled 872 vb.
hang out *dwell* 192 vb.
hang over *impend* 155 vb.
  be high 209 vb.
  jut 254 vb.
  threaten 900 vb.

hangover *sequel* 67 n.
  pain 377 n.
  intemperance 943 n.
  crapulence 949 n.
hang together *accord* 24 vb.
  unite with 45 vb.
  cohere 48 vb.
  concur 181 vb.
  co-operate 706 vb.
hang up *cease* 145 vb.
  be mute 578 vb.
hang upon *depend* 157 vb.
hank *fastening* 47 n.
  bunch 74 n.
hanker *desire* 859 vb.
hanky-panky
  deception 542 n.
  foul play 930 n.
Hansard *record* 548 n.
hansom *cab* 274 n.
hantle *multitude* 104 n.
hap *eventuality* 154 n.
  chance 159 n., vb.
haphazard *casual* 159 adj.
  indiscriminate 464 adj.
  designless 618 adj.
hapless *unfortunate* 731 adj.
haply *possibly* 469 adv.
happen *be* 1 vb.
  happen 154 vb.
  result 157 vb.
  chance 159 adj.
  appear 445 vb.
  be true 494 vb.
happening (*see* happen)
happen on *discover* 484 vb.
happiness (*see* happy)
happy *apt* 24 adj.
  opportune 137 adj.
  comfortable 376 adj.
  elegant 575 adj.
  willing 597 adj.
  good 615 adj.
  well-made 694 adj.
  concordant 710 adj.
  pacificatory 719 adj.
  successful 727 adj.
  happy 824 adj.
  pleasurable 826 adj.
  cheerful 833 adj.
  drunk 949 adj.
  paradisiac 971 adj.
happy ending *good* 615 n.
happy-go-lucky
  unprepared 670 adj.
  unskilful 695 adj.
happy returns
  congratulation 886 n.
happy thought *idea* 451 n.
  contrivance 623 n.
hara-kiri *suicide* 362 n.

harangue *teach* 534 vb.
  diffuseness 570 n.
  oration 579 n.
  dissertation 591 n.
harass *fatigue* 684 vb.
  oppress 735 vb.
  torment 827 vb.
harbinger *precursor* 66 n.
  omen 511 n.
  informant 524 n.
  messenger 531 n.
harbour *goal* 295 n.
  shelter 662 n.
hard *painfully* 32 adv.
  strong 162 adj.
  hard 326 adj.
  unsavoury 391 adj.
  puzzling 517 adj.
  imperspicuous 568 adj.
  laborious 682 adj.
  difficult 700 adj.
  hindering 702 adj.
  severe 735 adj.
  thick-skinned 820 adj.
  paining 827 adj.
  pitiless 906 adj.
  unjust 914 adj.
  impenitent 940 adj.
  intoxicating 949 adj.
  impious 980 adj.
hard at it *labouring* 682 adj.
hard-bitten
  thick-skinned 820 adj.
  unkind 898 adj.
hard-boiled *tough* 329 adj.
  (*see* hard)
hard breathing
  fatigue 684 n.
hard by *near* 200 adj.
hard case
  ill fortune 731 n.
hard core *hardness* 326 n.
  stamina 600 n.
  chief thing 638 n.
hard-drinking
  drunken 949 adj.
harden *strengthen* 162 vb.
  harden 326 vb.
  thicken 354 vb.
  habituate 610 vb.
  mature 669 vb.
  be dear 811 vb.
  make insensitive 820 vb.
hardened (*see* hard, harden)
hardened arteries
  blood pressure 651 n.
harden one's heart
  be inimical 881 vb.
  be pitiless 906 vb.
  be impenitent 940 vb.
  be impious 980 vb.

hard-featured *ugly* 842 adj.
hard feelings *feeling* 818 n.
  enmity 881 n.
hard-fought
  laborious 682 adj.
hard going *difficulty* 700 n.
hard-headed
  intelligent 498 adj.
  severe 735 adj.
hard-hearted *cruel* 898 adj.
hard-hitting
  disapproving 924 adj.
hardihood *courage* 855 n.
  insolence 878 n.
  (*see* hardy)
hard labour *penalty* 963 n.
hard life *adversity* 731 n.
hard lines *ill fortune* 731 n.
  severity 735 n.
hard-luck story
  lament 836 n.
hardly *almost* 33 adv.
  slightly 33 adv.
  seldom 140 adv.
  with difficulty 700 adv.
hard measure
  severity 735 n.
hard-mouthed
  obstinate 602 adj.
hardness *stability* 153 n.
  strength 162 n.
  density 324 n.
  hardness 326 n.
  inelegance 576 n.
  resolution 599 n.
  obstinacy 602 n.
  difficulty 700 n.
  severity 735 n.
  moral insensibility 820 n.
  inhumanity 898 n.
  pitilessness 906 n.
  wickedness 934 n.
  impenitence 940 n.
hard of hearing
  deaf 416 adj.
hard on, be
  be severe 735 vb.
hard-pressed
  hasty 680 adj.
  in difficulties 700 adj.
  hindered 702 adj.
hard run
  in difficulties 700 adj.
hards *fibre* 208 n.
hard saying
  unintelligibility 517 n.
  enigma 530 n.
hardship *adversity* 731 n.
  annoyance 827 n.
hard tack *food* 301 n.
hard times *adversity* 731 n.

hard to please
  discontented 829adj.
  fastidious 862adj.
hard up *poor* 801adj.
hardware *produce* 164n.
  hardness 326n.
hard way, the
  difficulty 700n.
hard-won *laborious* 682adj.
hard words
  imperspicuity 568n.
  reproach 924n.
hard-working
  industrious 678adj.
  labouring 682adj.
hardy *stalwart* 162adj.
  healthy 650adj.
  courageous 855adj.
  insolent 878adj.
  temperate 942adj.
hare *speeder* 277n.
  move fast 277vb.
  vermin 365n.
  coward 856n.
hare-brained
  light-minded 456adj.
hare-lip *blemish* 845n.
harem *womankind* 373n.
  love-nest 887n.
hare's foot *cosmetic* 843n.
hariolation
  divination 511n.
hark *pursue* 619vb.
  (*see* hearken)
hark back
  look back 125vb.
  turn back 286vb.
  notice 455vb.
  regret 830vb.
harl *fibre* 208n.
Harlequin
  changeable thing 152n.
  variegation 437n.
  entertainer 594n.
harlequinade
  stage play 594n.
  wit 839n.
harlot *prostitute* 952n.
harlotry *unchastity* 951n.
  social evil 951n.
harm *evil* 616n.
  be inexpedient 643vb.
  harm 645vb.
  impairment 655n.
  hurt 827vb.
harmful
  destructive 165adj.
  evil 616adj.
  inexpedient 643adj.
  harmful 645adj.
  insalubrious 653adj.

baneful 659adj.
adverse 731adj.
malevolent 898adj.
wrong 914adj.
harmless
  defenceless 161adj.
  weak 163adj.
  moderate 177adj.
  beneficial 644adj.
  salubrious 652adj.
  safe 660adj.
  peaceful 717adj.
  humble 872adj.
  amiable 884adj.
  innocent 935adj.
harmonic
  musical note 410n.
harmonica
  gong, organ 414n.
harmonical progression
  ratio 85n.
harmonics *melody* 410n.
harmonious *sweet* 392adj.
  harmonious 410adj.
  friendly 880adj.
  (*see* harmony)
harmonist *musician* 413n.
harmonium *organ* 414n.
harmonize *sing* 413vb.
  compose music 413vb.
  pacify 719vb.
  (*see* harmony)
harmony *agreement* 24n.
  a mixture 43n.
  combination 50n.
  completeness 54n.
  order 60n.
  concurrence 181n.
  symmetry 245n.
  melody 410n.
  music 412n.
  colour 425n.
  consensus 488n.
  elegance 575n.
  concord 710n.
  pleasurableness 826n.
harness *affix* 45vb.
  tackling 47n.
  dressing 228n.
  start out 296vb.
  break in 369vb.
  equipment 630n.
  make ready 669vb.
  armour 713n.
  fetter 748n.
harness, in *doing* 676adj.
harp *play music* 413vb.
  harp 414n.
harper
  instrumentalist 413n.
harp on

repeat oneself 106vb.
sustain 146vb.
be tedious 838vb.
harpoon *sharp point* 256n.
  spear 723n.
harpsichord *piano* 414n.
harpy *tyrant* 735n.
  taker 876n.
  hell-hag 904n.
  demon 970n.
harridan *eyesore* 842n.
harrier *bird of prey* 365n.
  dog 365n.
harrow *farm tool* 370n.
  cultivate 370vb.
  torment 827vb.
  frighten 854vb.
harry *attack* 712vb.
  torment 827vb.
  be malevolent 898vb.
harsh *exorbitant* 32adj.
  vigorous 174adj.
  pungent 388adj.
  strident 407adj.
  discordant 411adj.
  florid 425adj.
  imperspicuous 568adj.
  inelegant 576adj.
  harmful 645adj.
  oppressive 735adj.
  paining 827adj.
  ungracious 885adj.
  unkind 898adj.
  pitiless 906adj.
harshness
  roughness 259n.
  (*see* harsh)
hart *deer* 365n.
  male animal 372n.
hartal *strike* 145n.
hartshorn *pungency* 388n.
  tonic 658n.
harum-scarum
  disorderly 61adj.
  confusedly 61adv.
  light-minded 456adj.
  rash 857adj.
  desperado 857n.
haruspex *diviner* 511n.
harvest *great quantity* 32n.
  increment 36n.
  assemblage 74n.
  multitude 104n.
  autumn 129n.
  growth 157n.
  product 164n.
  abundance 171n.
  agriculture 370n.
  benefit 615n.
  store 632n.,vb.
  plenty 635n.

earnings 771 n.
  take 786 vb.
harvester
  husbandman 370 n.
harvest-home
  celebration 876 n.
has-been *past* 125 adj.
  archaism 127 n.
  loser 728 n.
hash *medley* 43 n.
  confusion 61 n.
  dish 301 n.
  be clumsy 695 vb.
hashish
  poisonous plant 659 n.
  poison 659 n.
haslet *insides* 224 n.
  meat 301 n.
hasp *joint* 45 n.
  fastening 47 n.
hassock *cushion* 218 n.
  church utensil 990 n.
hastate *sharp* 256 adj.
haste *punctuality* 135 n.
  move fast 277 vb.
  commotion 318 n.
  non-preparation 670 n.
  activity 678 n.
  haste 680 n.
  rashness 857 n.
hasten *be early* 135 vb.
  cause 156 vb.
  accelerate 277 vb.
  incite 612 vb.
  be busy 678 vb.
  hasten 680 vb.
hasty *brief* 114 adj.
  unwise 499 adj.
  unprepared 670 adj.
  hasty 680 adj.
  excitable 822 adj.
  rash 857 adj.
  irascible 892 adj.
hat *headgear* 228 n.
hatband *girdle* 47 n.
hatbox *box* 194 n.
hatch *group* 74 n.
  reproduce itself 164 vb.
  doorway 263 n.
  breed stock 369 vb.
  darken 418 vb.
  imagine 513 vb.
  fake 541 vb.
  plan 623 vb.
  mature 669 vb.
hatched *born* 360 adj.
hatcher *planner* 623 n.
hatchery *nest* 192 n.
  stock farm 369 n.
hatches *lock-up* 748 n.
hatchet *sharp edge* 256 n.

axe 723 n.
hatching
  obscuration 418 n.
  maturation 669 n.
hatchment *obsequies* 364 n.
  heraldry 547 n.
  monument 548 n.
hatchway *doorway* 263 n.
hate *dislike* 861 vb.
  hatred 888 n.
  hateful object 888 n.
  resentment 891 n.
  malevolence 898 n.
  jealousy 911 n.
  (see hatred)
hateful *not nice* 645 adj.
  unpleasant 827 adj.
  disliked 861 adj.
  hateful 888 adj.
hatefulness
  painfulness 827 n.
  odium 888 n.
hatless *uncovered* 229 adj.
hatpin *fastening* 47 n.
  hair-dressing 843 n.
hatred *prejudice* 481 n.
  dissension 709 n.
  phobia 854 n.
  enmity 881 n.
  hatred 888 n.
hatted *dressed* 228 adj.
hatter *clothier* 228 n.
hat-trick *triplication* 94 n.
  masterpiece 694 n.
  success 727 n.
hauberk *armour* 713 n.
haughty
  authoritarian 735 adj.
  noble 868 adj.
  proud, prideful 871 adj.
  insolent 878 adj.
  unsociable 883 adj.
  despising 922 adj.
haul *traction* 288 n.
  work 682 vb.
  booty 790 n.
haulage *transport* 272 n.
  traction 288 n.
haulier *carrier* 273 n.
haul over the coals
  reprove 924 vb.
haul up *indict* 928 vb.
haunch *rear* 238 n.
  buttocks 238 n.
haunt *focus* 76 n.
  reoccur 106 vb.
  recur 139 vb.
  go on 146 vb.
  district 184 n.
  locality 187 n.
  be present 189 vb.

abode, home 192 n.
  dwell 192 vb.
  appear 445 vb.
  engross 449 vb.
  remind 505 vb.
  be wont 610 vb.
  torment 827 vb.
  frighten 854 vb.
  goblinize 970 vb.
  bewitch 983 vb.
haunted *obsessed* 455 adj.
  remembering 505 adj.
  nervous 854 adj.
  spooky 970 adj.
  bewitched 983 adj.
haunter *ghost* 970 n.
haunting
  remembered 505 adj.
  pleasurable 826 adj.
haute couture
  fashion 848 n.
haute cuisine
  savouriness 390 n.
haute école
  equitation 267 n.
hauteur *pride* 871 n.
have *contain* 56 vb.
  comprise 78 vb.
  confute 479 vb.
  understand 516 vb.
  befool 542 vb.
  possess 773 vb.
  be hospitable 882 vb.
have a go *essay* 617 vb.
have a hand in
  co-operate 706 vb.
  participate 775 vb.
have a hold on
  influence 178 vb.
have a mind to
  desire 859 vb.
have and hold
  possess 773 vb.
have at *attack* 712 vb.
  strike at 712 vb.
have everything
  be complete 54 vb.
  comprise 78 vb.
have in mind
  be mindful 455 vb.
  mean 514 vb.
  intend 617 vb.
have it *discover* 484 vb.
have it all one's way
  will 595 vb.
  do easily 701 vb.
  win 727 vb.
  dominate 733 vb.
have it coming to one
  deserve 915 vb.
haven *resting place* 266 n.

goal 295 n.
protection 660 n.
shelter 662 n.
have-nots *poor man* 801 n.
lower classes 869 n.
have occasion for
require 627 vb.
have one's day
pass time 108 vb.
triumph 727 vb.
prosper 730 vb.
have one's head
be free 744 vb.
have one's say
affirm 532 vb.
have one's turn
come after 65 vb.
haver *be loquacious* 581 vb.
haversack *bag* 194 n.
haves, the *rich man* 800 n.
upper class 868 n.
have taped *appraise* 465 vb.
have the makings of
evidence 466 vb.
have what it takes
be resolute 599 vb.
havildar *army officer* 741 n.
havoc *disorder* 61 n.
havoc 165 n.
impairment 655 n.
spoliation 788 n.
haw-haw
speech defect 580 n.
hawk *eruct* 300 vb.
bird of prey 365 n.
rasp 407 vb.
hunt 619 vb.
offer 759 vb.
request 761 vb.
sell 793 vb.
hawker *pedlar* 794 n.
hawk-eyed *seeing* 438 adj.
hawser *cable* 47 n.
hay *provender* 301 n.
grass 366 n.
hay-fever *excretion* 302 n.
ill-health 651 n.
hay-fork *shovel* 274 n.
farm tool 370 n.
hayloft *attic* 194 n.
farm tool 370 n.
haymaker *knock* 279 n.
hayseed *ingenue* 699 n.
countryman 869 n.
haystack *store* 632 n.
haywire *non-uniform* 17 adj.
orderless 61 adj.
hazard *chance* 159 n.
gambling 618 n.
danger 661 n.
pitfall 663 n.

obstacle 702 n.
hazardous
speculative 618 adj.
dangerous 661 adj.
haze *cloud* 355 n.
uncertainty 474 n.
oppress 735 vb.
torment 827 vb.
hazel *brown* 430 adj.
hazy *cloudy* 355 adj.
dim 419 adj.
opaque 423 adj.
ill-seen 444 adj.
uncertain 474 adj.
puzzling 517 adj.
he *male* 372 n., adj.
children's games 837 n.
head *come first* 34 vb.
come before 64 vb.
beginning 68 n.
extremity 69 n.
classification 77 n.
energy 160 n.
long measure 203 n.
vertex, head 213 n.
face 237 n.
be in front 237 vb.
central 225 adj.
strike 279 vb.
precede 283 vb.
repel 292 vb.
bubble 355 n.
person 371 n.
topic 452 n.
intelligence 498 n.
image 551 n.
picture 553 n.
sculpture 554 n.
name 561 n.
bigwig 638 n.
direct 689 vb.
director 690 n.
trophy 729 n.
master 741 n.
crapulence 949 n.
execute 963 vb.
headache *pang* 377 n.
difficulty 700 n.
worry 825 n.
head and front
chief thing 638 n.
headband *headgear* 228 n.
head boy *superior* 34 n.
head-count
numeration 86 n.
headdress *headgear* 228 n.
header *descent* 309 n.
plunge 313 n.
head for *navigate* 269 vb.
steer for 281 vb.
headgear *headgear* 228 n.

head-hunter *killer* 362 n.
hunter 619 n.
heading *prelude* 66 n.
beginning 68 n.
classification 77 n.
precession 283 n.
label 547 n.
record 548 n.
name 561 n.
headlamp, headlight
radiation 117 n.
lamp 420 n.
headland *projection* 254 n.
headless *short* 204 adj.
headline
advertisement 528 n.
edition 589 n.
make important 638 vb.
excitant 821 n.
(see heading)
headlong *violently* 176 vb.
swiftly 277 adv.
hasty 680 adj.
rash 857 adj.
headman *director* 690 n.
officer 741 n.
headmaster *teacher* 537 n.
director 690 n.
head off *converge* 293 vb.
dissuade 613 vb.
head-on *fore* 237 adj.
head over heels
completely 54 adv.
inverted 221 adj.
round and round 315 adv.
headphone
hearing aid 415 n.
telecommunication 531 n.
headpiece *intelligence* 498 n.
(see head)
headquarters *focus* 76 n.
abode 192 n.
plan 623 n.
headrest *supporter* 218 n.
heads *compendium* 592 n.
headship
magistrature 733 n.
headsman *killer* 362 n.
punisher 963 n.
heads or tails
chance 159 n.
headstall *fetter* 748 n.
headstone *supporter* 218 n.
obsequies 364 n.
headstrong *furious* 176 adj.
wilful 602 adj.
rash 857 adj.
head to foot
longwise 203 adv.
head to tail
longwise 203 adv.

head-up *vertical* 215 adj.
head-waters *source* 156 n.
headway *room* 183 n.
  motion 265 n.
  water travel 269 n.
  progression 285 n.
headwind
  contrariety 14 n.
  contraposition 240 n.
  wind 352 n.
  obstacle 702 n.
  opposition 704 n.
head-work *thought* 449 n.
heady *strong* 162 adj.
  vigorous 174 adj.
  pungent 388 adj.
  exciting 821 adj.
  intoxicating 949 adj.
heal *cure* 656 vb.
  remedy 658 vb.
  pacify 719 vb.
healer *mender* 656 n.
  doctor 658 n.
health *vitality* 162 n.
  potion 301 n.
  goodness 644 n.
  health 650 n.
  salubrity 652 n.
  celebration 876 n.
healthless
  unhealthy 651 adj.
health officer
  doctor 658 n.
healthy *athletic* 162 adj.
  large 195 adj.
  (*see* health)
heap *great quantity* 32 n.
  chief part 52 n.
  great quantity 32 n.
  accumulation 74 n.
  multitude 104 n.
  bulk 195 n.
  monticle 209 n.
  not discriminate 464 n.
  store 632 n., vb.
  acquisition 771 n.
heap on *add* 38 vb.
hear *hear* 415 vb.
  be mindful 455 vb.
  enquire 459 vb.
  judge 480 vb.
  be informed 524 vb.
  consent 758 vb.
  try a case 959 vb.
heard *sounding* 398 adj.
  loud 400 adj.
  known 490 adj.
hearer *listener* 415 n.
  allocution 583 n.
hearing *sense* 374 n.
  hearing 415 n.

  listening 415 n.
  council 691 n.
  legal trial 959 n.
hearing aid
  hearing aid 415 n.
  megaphone 400 n.
hearken *hear* 415 vb.
  be willing 597 vb.
  obey 739 vb.
  consent 758 vb.
hear Mass
  offer worship 981 vb.
hearsay *evidence* 466 n.
  information 524 n.
  rumour 529 n.
hearse *vehicle* 274 n.
  funeral 364 n.
heart *essence* 1 n.
  essential part 5 n.
  middle 70 n.
  interiority 224 n.
  centrality 225 n.
  meat 301 n.
  life 360 n.
  spirit 447 n.
  chief thing 638 n.
  affections 817 n.
  courage 855 n.
  love-token 889 n.
  darling 890 n.
heart-ache *suffering* 825 n.
  dejection 834 n.
heart and soul
  completely 54 adj.
  willingly 597 adv.
  laboriously 682 adj.
  feelingly 818 adv.
heart-breaking
  distressing 827 adj.
heartbroken
  disappointed 509 adj.
  unhappy 825 adj.
heartburn *indigestion* 651 n.
heartburning
  sorrow 825 n.
  discontent 829 n.
  regret 830 n.
  resentment 891 n.
  jealousy 911 n.
heart, by
  in memory 505 adv.
heart, cockles of the
  affections 817 n.
heart disease
  heart disease 651 n.
hearten *invigorate* 174 vb.
  aid 703 vb.
  animate 821 vb.
  relieve 831 vb.
  give courage 855 vb.
heartfelt *felt* 818 adj.

heart-free
  impassive 820 adj.
hearth *focus* 76 n.
  home 192 n.
  furnace 383 n.
  refuge 662 n.
hearth and home
  family 11 n.
hearties *chum* 880 n.
heartily *willingly* 597 adv.
  feelingly 818 adv.
heartiness (*see* hearty)
heartland *land* 344 n.
heartless *impassive* 820 adj.
  impenitent 940 adj.
heart of grace *hope* 852 n.
heart of hearts
  affections 817 n.
heart's blood
  essential part 5 n.
  interiority 224 n.
  life 360 n.
  favourite 890 n.
heart-sick
  melancholic 834 adj.
heart-sinking
  dejection 834 n.
hearts of oak
  resolution 599 n.
heart-throb
  loved one 887 n.
heart-to-heart
  undisguised 522 adj.
heart-warming
  pleasant 376 adj.
  felt 818 adj.
  pleasurable 826 adj.
  cheering 833 adj.
heart-whole *free* 744 adj.
  impassive 820 adj.
  indifferent 860 adj.
  unwedded 895 adj.
heartwood *hardness* 326 n.
  wood 366 n.
hearty *vigorous* 174 adj.
  healthy 650 adj.
  felt 818 adj.
  cheerful 833 adj.
  ill-bred 847 adj.
  friendly 880 adj.
  sociable 882 adj.
heat *summer* 128 n.
  dryness 342 n.
  heat 379 n.
  contest 716 n.
  excite 821 vb.
  excitable state 822 n.
  libido 859 n.
  excite love 887 vb.
  anger 891 n.
heater *heater* 383 n.

heath *desert* 172n.
  plain 348n.
  plant, wood 366n.
heathen *heathen* 974n.
  idolator 982n.
heathenism
  ignorance 491n.
  antichristianity 974n.
  irreligion 974n.
  impiety 980n.
  idolatry 982n.
heather *plant* 366n.
heave *be periodic* 141vb.
  carry 273vb.
  impel 279vb.
  propel 287vb.
  draw 288n.
  vomit 300vb.
  oscillate 317vb.
  breathe 352vb.
  exertion 682n.
  show feeling 818vb.
heaven
  future state 124n.
  heaven 971n.
heaven-born
  worshipful 866adj.
heavenly *celestial* 321adj.
  topping 644adj.
  pleasurable 826adj.
  divine 965adj.
  paradisiac 971adj.
heavenly-minded
  pious 979adj.
heavens *influence* 178n.
  space 183n.
  heavens 321n.
heaven-sent
  opportune 137adj.
  good 615adj.
heave the lead
  be deep 211vb.
  measure 465vb.
heave to
  bring to rest 266vb.
  navigate 269vb.
heavily *greatly* 32adv.
heaviness
  sleepiness 679n.
  inactivity 679n.
Heaviside Layer
  atmosphere 340n.
heavy *substantial* 3adj.
  unequal 29adj.
  great 32adj.
  strong 162adj.
  inert 175adj.
  weighty 322adj.
  dense 324adj.
  odorous 394adj.
  fetid 397adj.

non-resonant 405adj.
unintelligent 499adj.
forceful 571adj.
inelegant 576adj.
bad 645adj.
inactive 679adj.
laborious 682adj.
severe 735adj.
inexcitable 823adj.
melancholic 834adj.
tedious 838adj.
dull 840adj.
heinous 934adj.
heavy-armed
  defended 713adj.
heavy-eyed *sleepy* 679adj.
heavy father *acting* 594n.
  tyrant 735n.
heavy-handed
  violent 176adj.
  tactual 378adj.
  clumsy 695adj.
  oppressive 735adj.
heavy-laden *full* 54adj.
  hindered 702adj.
  suffering 825adj.
heavy sea
  commotion 318n.
  wave 350n.
heavy type
  punctuation 547n.
  print-type 587n.
heavyweight *athlete* 162n.
  pugilist 722n.
heavy with
  impending 155adj.
  productive 164adj.
hebdomadal
  seasonal 141adj.
Hebe *a beauty* 841n.
  Olympian god 967n.
hebetude
  unintelligence 499n.
Hebraist
  antiquarian 125n.
  linguist 557n.
Hecate *moon* 321n.
  sorceress 983n.
hecatomb *hundred* 99n.
  havoc 165n.
  oblation 981n.
heckle
  be obstructive 702vb.
  torment 827vb.
heckler *dissentient* 489n.
  hinderer 702n.
hectare *measure* 183n.
hectic *heat* 379n.
  red 431adj.
  fervent 818adj.
  excited 821adj.

Hector
  brave person 855n.
  boaster 877n.
hector *be insolent* 878vb.
  threaten 900vb.
hedge *set off* 31vb.
  separation 46n.
  circumscribe 232vb.
  fence 235n.
  wood 366n.
  screen 421n.
  gamble 618vb.
  seek safety 660vb.
  shelter 662n.
  obstacle 702n.
  defend 713vb.
  be cautious 858vb.
hedgehog *prickle* 256n.
hedgehop *be near* 200vb.
  fly 271vb.
hedge-priest *cleric* 986n.
hedonism *pleasure* 376n.
  philosophy 449n.
  enjoyment 824n.
  sensualism 944n.
heebiejeebies
  nervousness 854n.
  alcoholism 949n.
heed *attention* 455n.
  carefulness 457n.
  observe 768vb.
  caution 858n.
heedless
  inattentive 456adj.
  negligent 458adj.
  forgetful 506adj.
heedlessness
  rashness 857n.
  indifference 860n.
hee-haw *ululation* 409n.
heel *extremity* 69n.
  base, foot 214n.
  stand 218n.
  be oblique 220vb.
  rear 238n.
  kick 279vb.
  repair 656vb.
  cad 938n.
heel and toe
  pedestrianism 267n.
heel over
  be inverted 221vb.
heel-piece *sequel* 67n.
heel-tap *leavings* 41n.
  dirt 649n.
heft *influence* 178n.
  bulk 195n.
hefty *whopping* 32adj.
  stalwart 162adj.
hegemonic
  directing 689adj.

hegemony *superiority* 34 n.
  precedence 64 n.
  influence 178 n.
  authority 733 n.
  prestige 866 n.
heifer *youngling* 132 n.
  cattle 365 n.
  female animal 373 n.
height *degree* 27 n.
  greatness 32 n.
  superiority 34 n.
  measure 183 n.
  size 195 n.
  height 209 n.
  high land 209 n.
  summit 213 n.
  metrology 465 n.
heighten *augment* 36 vb.
  enlarge 197 vb.
  make higher 209 vb.
  elevate 310 vb.
  aggravate 832 vb.
heinous *bad* 645 adj.
  heinous 934 adj.
heir *survivor* 41 n.
  aftercomer 67 n.
  descendant 170 n.
  deputy 755 n.
  beneficiary 776 n.
  recipient 782 n.
heirdom *possession* 773 n.
heirloom *dower* 778 n.
heirs *futurity* 124 n.
  posterity 170 n.
heirship *sonship* 170 n.
  acquisition 771 n.
  possession 773 n.
Hejira *departure* 296 n.
heliacal *celestial* 321 adj.
helianthus *orange* 436 n.
Helicon *poetry* 593 n.
helicopter *aircraft* 276 n.
heliocentric *central* 225 adj.
  celestial 321 adj.
heliograph *signal* 547 n.
heliography *optics* 417 n.
helioscope
  optical device 442 n.
heliotrope *purple* 434 n., adj.
  gem 844 n.
heliotype
  photography 551 n.
  printing 555 n.
heliport *air travel* 271 n.
  goal 295 n.
helium *lifter* 310 n.
  levity 323 n.
helix *coil* 251 n.
  circuition 314 n.
hell *future state* 124 n.
  depth 211 n.

pain 377 n.
  gaming-house 618 n.
  bane 659 n.
  suffering 825 n.
  hell 972 n.
hell-bent *rash* 857 adj.
  intending 617 adj.
hell-born *diabolic* 969 adj.
hell-broth
  wickedness 934 n.
  magic instrument 983 n.
hell-cat
  violent creature 176 n.
  hell-hag 904 n.
hellebore
  poisonous plant 659 n.
Hellenist *linguist* 557 n.
Hellenize *transform* 147 vb.
hell-hag *hell-hag* 904 n.
  monster 938 n.
hellish *damnable* 645 adj.
  cruel 898 adj.
  wicked, heinous 934 adj.
  diabolic 969 adj.
  infernal 972 adj.
helm *sailing aid* 269 n.
  tool 630 n.
  directorship 689 n.
helmet *headgear* 228 n.
  heraldry 547 n.
  armour 713 n.
helminthagogue
  antidote 658 n.
helminthology
  zoology 367 n.
helmsman *navigator* 270 n.
  director 690 n.
helot *slave* 742 n.
helotry *slave* 742 n.
  servitude 745 n.
help *concur* 181 vb.
  meal 301 n.
  benefit 615 vb.
  utility 640 n.
  be expedient 642 vb.
  do good 644 vb.
  cleaner 648 n.
  remedy 658 n., vb.
  worker 686 n.
  facilitate 701 vb.
  aid 703 n., vb.
  servant 742 n.
  give 781 vb.
helper *auxiliary* 707 n.
  servant 742 n.
  friend 880 n.
  benefactor 903 n.
helpful *willing* 597 adj.
  co-operative 706 adj.
helping *provision* 633 n.
  portion 783 n.

helpless *impotent* 161 adj.
  weak 163 adj.
  vulnerable 661 adj.
helpmate *auxiliary* 707 n.
  spouse 894 n.
helter-skelter
  confusedly 61 adv.
  swiftly 277 adv.
helve *tool* 630 n.
hem *be contiguous* 202 vb.
  surround 230 vb.
  edging 234 n.
  limit 236 vb.
  flank 239 vb.
  fold 261 n., vb.
  decorate 844 vb.
he-man *athlete* 162 n.
  violent creature 176 n.
  male 372 n.
  brave person 855 n.
hemi *fragmentary* 53 adj.
  bisected 92 adj.
hemicrania *pang* 377 n.
hemicycle *arc* 250 n.
hemiplegia
  helplessness 161 n.
  paralysis 651 n.
hemisphere *part* 53 n.
  bisection 92 n.
  region 184 n.
  sphere 252 n.
  dome 253 n.
hemistich *verse form* 593 n.
hemline *edging* 234 n.
hemlock *killer* 362 n.
  poisonous plant 659 n.
  means of execution 964 n.
hemp *fibre* 208 n.
  pungency 388 n.
hen *poultry* 365 n.
  female animal 373 n.
henbane
  poisonous plant 659 n.
hen battery
  stock farm 369 n.
hence *hence* 158 adv.
henceforth
  henceforth 124 adv.
henchman *auxiliary* 707 n.
  dependant 742 n.
  retainer 742 n.
hencoop, henhouse
  stable 192 n.
  cattle pen 369 n.
hendecasyllable
  verse form 593 n.
hendiadys *bisection* 92 n.
henna *orange* 436 n.
henotheism *deism* 973 n.
hen party *womankind* 373 n.
  social gathering 882 n.

henpeck *bicker* 709 vb.
henpecked
  subjected 745 adj.
hepcat *musician* 413 n.
heptachord *harp* 414 n.
heptad *over five* 99 n.
heptagon
  angular figure 247 n.
her *female* 373 n.
herald *precursor* 66 n.
  precede 283 vb.
  omen 511 n.
  informant 524 n.
  proclaim 528 vb.
  messenger 531 n.
  heraldry 547 n.
  deputy 755 n.
heraldic *heraldic* 547 adj.
heraldry *heraldry* 547 n.
herb *potherb* 301 n.
  medicine 658 n.
herbaceous
  vegetal 366 adj.
herbage *grass* 366 n.
  farm 370 n.
herbal *vegetal* 366 adj.
  botany 368 n.
herbalist *botanist* 368 n.
  doctor 658 n.
herbarium *botany* 368 n.
herbivore *animal* 365 n.
herbivorous *feeding* 301 adj.
Herculean *great* 32 adj.
  stalwart 162 adj.
  huge 195 adj.
  laborious 682 adj.
Herculean task
  hard task 700 n.
Hercules *athlete* 162 n.
  brave person 855 n.
  demigod 967 n.
herd *group* 74 n.
  cattle 365 n.
  herdsman 369 n.
  groom 369 vb.
  social group 371 n.
  imprison 747 vb.
herd instinct *crowd* 74 n.
herdsman *herdsman* 369 n.
here *in place* 186 adv.
  here 189 adv.
hereabout *in place* 186 adv.
  nearly 200 adv.
hereafter *sequel* 67 n.
  future state 124 n.
  prospectively 124 adv.
  destiny 155 n.
here and there
  here and there 105 adv.
  somewhere 185 adv.
hereditament

estate, lands 777 n.
hereditary *genetic* 5 adj.
  inherited 157 adj.
  filial 170 adj.
  proprietary 777 adj.
heredity *heredity* 5 n.
  recurrence 106 n.
  reversion 148 n.
  reproduction 166 n.
  sonship 170 n.
  influence 178 n.
  affections 817 n.
herein *inside* 224 adv.
hereof *concerning* 9 adv.
heresiarchy *heresy* 977 n.
heresy *unbelief* 486 n.
  heterodoxy 977 n.
  heresy 977 n.
heresy-hunting
  orthodoxism 976 n.
  orthodox 976 adj.
  pietism 979 n.
here, there and everywhere
  widely 183 adv.
heretic *nonconformist* 84 n.
  unbeliever 486 n.
  heretic 977 n.
  schismatic 978 n.
heretical
  unconformable 84 adj.
  erroneous 495 adj.
  heterodox 977 adj.
  heretical 977 adj.
  schismatical 978 adj.
  impious 980 adj.
heretofore
  retrospectively 125 adv.
heritable *genetic* 5 adj.
  inherited 157 adj.
  proprietary 777 adj.
  not retained 779 adj.
  transferred 780 adj.
  due 915 adj.
heritage *futurity* 124 n.
  posterity 170 n.
  possession 773 n.
  dower 777 n.
hermaphrodite
  nonconformist 84 n.
  double 91 adj.
  eunuch 161 n.
hermaphroditism
  abnormality 84 n.
hermeneutics
  hermeneutics 520 n.
hermit *nonconformist* 84 n.
  solitary 883 n.
  celibate 895 n.
  ascetic 945 n.
  pietist 979 n.
  monk 986 n.

hermitage *retreat* 192 n.
  refuge 662 n.
  seclusion 883 n.
  monastery 986 n.
hero *acting* 594 n.
  doer 676 n.
  brave person 855 n.
  prodigy 864 n.
  person of repute 866 n.
  loved one 887 n.
  favourite 890 n.
  good man 937 n.
Herodians
  non-Christian sect 978 n.
heroic *olden* 127 adj.
  descriptive 590 adj.
  poetic 593 adj.
  resolute 599 adj.
  laborious 682 adj.
  courageous 855 adj.
  worshipful 866 adj.
  disinterested 931 adj.
heroic age *antiquity* 125 n.
heroic couplet
  prosody 593 n.
  verse form 593 n.
heroics *prowess* 855 n.
  ostentation 875 n.
  boasting 877 n.
heroine *acting* 594 n.
  brave person 855 n.
heroism *resolution* 599 n.
  prowess 855 n.
  courage 855 n.
  disinterestedness 931 n.
heron *bird of prey* 365 n.
hero-worship
  wonder 864 n., vb.
  love 887 n.
  praise 923 n., vb.
herpes *skin disease* 651 n.
herpetology *zoology* 367 n.
Herr *male* 372 n.
  title 870 n.
herring *fish food* 301 n.
  table fish 365 n.
herringbone *oblique* 220 adj.
  weaving 222 n.
  pattern 844 n.
hesitant *doubting* 474 adj.
  unwilling 598 adj.
hesitate *be inactive* 679 vb.
  (see hesitation)
hesitation
  changeableness 152 n.
  slowness 278 n.
  doubt 486 n.
  speech defect 580 n.
  unwillingness 598 n.
  irresolution 601 n.
  nervousness 854 n.

caution 858 n.
Hesperides
  happiness 824 n.
Hesperus *luminary* 420 n.
hessian *textile* 222 n.
  footwear 228 n.
hest *command* 737 n.
hetæra *kept woman* 952 n.
heterarchy
  governance 733 n.
heteroclite
  abnormal 84 adj.
  grammatical 564 adj.
heterodoxy
  unconformity 84 n.
  error 495 n.
  heterodoxy 977 n.
heterogeneity
  irrelation 10 n.
  difference 15 n.
  non-uniformity 17 n.
  medley 43 n.
  multiformity 82 n.
heteronomy
  governance 733 n.
heteromorphism
  non-uniformity 17 n.
heterosexual
  correlative 12 adj.
hetman *governor* 741 n.
heuristic *enquiring* 459 adj.
  demonstrating 478 adj.
hew *cut* 46 vb.
  shorten 204 vb.
  efform 243 vb.
hexad *over five* 99 n.
hexagon
  angular figure 247 n.
hexameter *prosody* 593 n.
Hexateuch *scripture* 975 n.
heyday *salad days* 130 n.
  palmy days 730 n.
hiatus *interval* 201 n.
  opening 263 n.
hibernation *sleep* 679 n.
Hibernicism
  absurdity 497 n.
  dialect 560 n.
  ridiculousness 849 n.
hiccup *eruct* 300 vb.
  respiration 352 n.
  drunkenness 949 n.
hick *bungler* 697 n.
  countryman 869 n.
hidalgo *aristocrat* 868 n.
hidden *dark* 418 adj.
  invisible 444 adj.
  unknown 491 adj.
  unintelligible 517 adj.
  concealed 525 adj.
  secluded 883 adj.

cabbalistic 984 adj.
hidden depths
  latency 523 n.
hidden hand *cause* 156 n.
  influence 178 n.
  latency 523 n.
  trouble-maker 663 n.
hide *contain* 56 vb.
  measure 183 n.
  skin 226 n.
  strike 279 vb.
  screen 421 vb.
  be unseen 444 vb.
  disappear 446 vb.
  lurk 523 vb.
  conceal 525 vb.
  hiding-place 527 n.
  avoid 620 vb.
  store 632 vb.
  safeguard 660 vb.
  be cowardly 856 vb.
  be cautious 858 vb.
  flog 963 vb.
hidebound
  obstinate 602 adj.
  restraining 747 adj.
hide one's light under a
  bushel
  be modest 874 vb.
hideosity *deformity* 246 n.
  eyesore 842 n.
hideous *unpleasant* 827 adj.
  ugly 842 adj.
  frightening 854 adj.
hide-out *hiding-place* 527 n.
  seclusion 883 n.
hiding
  corporal punishment
    963 n.
hiding-place
  concealment 525 n.
  hiding-place 527 n.
hie *move* 265 vb.
  travel 267 vb.
  move fast 277 vb.
hiemal *wintry* 129 adj.
  cold 380 adj.
hierarchies *theosophy* 984 n.
hierarchy *degree* 27 n.
  series 71 n.
  churchdom 985 n.
  clergy 986 n.
hieratic *written* 586 adj.
  scriptural 975 adj.
  priestly 985 adj.
hierocracy
  government 733 n.
  Churchdom 985 n.
hierodule
  servant, slave 742 n.
  prostitute 952 n.

hieroglyphic *written* 586 adj.
hieroglyphics *enigma* 530 n.
  symbology 547 n.
hierophant
  religious teacher 973 n.
hieroscopy
  theomancy 511 n.
higgle *make terms* 766 vb.
  bargain 791 vb.
higgledy-piggledy
  confusedly 61 adv.
higgler *purchaser* 792 n.
  pedlar 794 n.
high *great* 32 adj.
  high 209 adj.
  pungent 388 adj.
  fetid 397 adj.
  important 638 adj.
  unclean 649 adj.
  worshipful 866 adj.
  noble 868 adj.
  proud 871 adj.
  drunk 949 adj.
  Anglican 976 adj.
high and dry *fixed* 153 adj.
  dry 342 adj.
  safe 660 adj.
high and mighty
  prideful 871 adj.
  insolent 878 adj.
highball *liquor* 301 n.
high-binder *murderer* 362 n.
high-born *noble* 868 adj.
highboy *cabinet* 194 n.
highbrow
  instructed 490 adj.
  intellectual 492 n.
  wise 498 adj.
  sage 500 n.
high-caste
  worshipful 866 adj.
High Church
  Catholicism 976 n.
  Anglican 976 adj.
high-class *genteel* 868 adj.
high colour *redness* 431 n.
high coloured *florid* 425 adj.
High Command
  army officer 741 n.
  master 741 n.
High Commission
  commission 751 n.
  envoy 754 n.
High Court
  law-court 956 n.
high day *festivity* 837 n.
  holy-day 988 n.
High Dutch
  unmeaningness 515 n.
higher critic
  theologian 973 n.

higher criticism
interpretation 520n.
scripture 975n.
heterodoxy 977n.
highest *supreme* 34adj.
high 209adj.
topmost 213adj.
highfalutin *ornate* 574adj.
ostentatious 875adj.
boast 877n.
high-fidelity
melodious 410adj.
accurate 494adj.
high-flier *proud man* 871n.
high-flown
imaginative 513adj.
rhetorical 574adj.
high-flying
imaginative 513adj.
exaggerated 546adj.
lively 819adj.
high-geared *strong* 162adj.
speedy 277adj.
high hand *violence* 176n.
high-handed
oppressive 735adj.
proud 871adj.
insolent 878adj.
high-hat *prideful* 871adj.
insolent 878adj.
high-hearted
courageous 855adj.
high jinks *revel* 837n.
high jump *leap* 312n.
capital punishment 963n.
highland *alpine* 209adj.
land 344n.
Highlander *dweller* 191n.
high-level *superior* 34adj.
important 638adj.
directing 689adj.
high life *festivity* 837n.
upper class 868n.
(*see* high living)
highlight *manifest* 522vb.
publish 528vb.
indicate 547vb.
high living
gastronomy 301n.
intemperance 943n.
sensualism 944n.
gluttony 947n.
highly-coloured
expressive 516adj.
splendid 841adj.
high-mettled *proud* 871adj.
high mightiness
prestige 866n.
pride 871n.
high-minded
honourable 929adj.

disinterested 931adj.
highness *sovereign* 741n.
high octane *fuel* 385n.
high-pitched
strident 407adj.
optimistic 482adj.
rhetorical 574adj.
high-powered
strong 162adj.
high pressure
vigorousness 174n.
weather 340n.
excitation 821n.
high-priced *dear* 811adj.
high-priority
important 638adj.
high rank *prestige* 866n.
nobility 868n.
high relief, in
well-seen 443adj.
salient 254adj.
highroad *road* 624n.
instrument 628n.
high society
beau monde 848n.
upper class 868n.
high-sounding
loud 400adj.
affected 850adj.
ostentatious 875adj.
high-spirited *lively* 819adj.
courageous 855adj.
proud 871adj.
high spirits
merriment 833n.
high-stepping
fashionable 848adj.
proud 871adj.
high-strung *sentient* 374adj.
lively 819adj.
excitable 822adj.
nervous 854adj.
high tea *meal* 301n.
high-tension *strong* 162adj.
high tide *high water* 209n.
water 339n.
prosperity 730n.
high time *occasion* 137n.
opportunity 137n.
lateness 136n.
expedience 642n.
high-toned *defiant* 711adj.
insolent 878adj.
high treason
sedition 738n.
perfidy 930n.
high-up *superior* 34n.
upper class 868n.
high-water mark
summit 213n.
limit 236n.

gauge 465n.
highway *road* 624n.
instrument 628n.
facility 701n.
highwayman *robber* 789n.
high words *quarrel* 709n.
anger 891n.
hijack *steal* 788vb.
hijacker *robber* 789n.
hike *walk* 267vb.
hiker *pedestrian* 268n.
hilarity *merriment* 833n.
hill *high land* 209n.
acclivity 220n.
ascent 308n.
hillbilly *dweller* 191n.
ingenue 699n.
countryman 869n.
hill-dwelling
alpine 209adj.
hillman *dweller* 191n.
hillock *monticle* 209n.
dome 253n.
hillside *acclivity* 220n.
hill-station *abode* 192n.
hilltop *high land* 209n.
vertex 213n.
hilly *alpine* 209adj.
hilt *handle* 218n.
himation *robe* 228n.
himself *self* 80n.
Hinayana
religious faith 973n.
hind *back* 238adj.
deer 365n.
female animal 373n.
countryman 869n.
hinder *disable* 161vb.
counteract 182vb.
back 238adj.
retard 278vb.
be useless 641vb.
impair 655vb.
hinder 702vb.
resist 715vb.
restrain 747vb.
prohibit 757vb.
(*see* hindrance)
hinderer *hinderer* 702n.
opponent 705n.
hindfoot *foot* 214n.
Hindi
language 557n.
hindleg *leg* 267n.
hindmost *ending* 69adj.
back 238adj.
hindquarters *buttocks* 238n.
hindrance
derangement 63n.
delay 136n.
stop 145n.

dissuasion 613 n.
difficulty 700 n.
hindrance 702 n.
hinderer 702 n.
restraint 747 n.
hindsight *intellect* 447 n.
thought 449 n.
remembrance 505 n.
Hinduism
religious faith 973 n.
Hindustani
language 557 n.
hindward
rearward 238 adv.
hinge *joint* 45 n.
fastening 47 n.
causal means 156 n.
pivot 218 n.
rotator 315 n.
hinge on *depend* 157 vb.
be uncertain 474 vb.
hinny *hybrid* 43 n.
hint *similarity* 18 n.
reminder 505 n.
latency 523 n.
hint 524 n., vb.
indication 547 n.
warning 664 n.
advice 691 n.
command 737 vb.
hinterland *district* 184 n.
rear 238 n.
land 344 n.
hip (*see* hips)
hip-bath *vessel* 194 n.
ablution 648 n.
hip flask *vessel* 194 n.
hippish *insane* 503 adj.
melancholic 834 adj.
hippocampus *rara avis* 84 n.
hippocras *liquor* 301 n.
hippocratic *dying* 361 adj.
medical 658 adj.
Hippocratic oath
code of duty 917 n.
Hippocrene *poetry* 593 n.
hippodrome *theatre* 594 n.
arena 724 n.
place of amusement 837 n.
hippogriff *rara avis* 84 n.
hippopotamus *giant* 195 n.
animal 365 n.
hips *rear* 238 n.
buttocks 238 n.
hipshot *crippled* 163 adj.
hircine *animal* 365 adj.
fetid 397 adj.
hire *employ* 622 vb.
commission 751 vb.
hire 785 vb.
lease 784 vb.

price 809 n.
hireling *servant* 742 n.
venal 930 adj.
hire purchase
borrowing 785 n.
purchase 792 n., vb.
hirer *purchaser* 792 n.
lender 784 n.
hirsute *hairy* 259 adj.
Hispanist *linguist* 557 n.
hispidity *roughness* 259 n.
hiss *sibilation* 406 n.
vociferate 408 vb.
ululation 409 n.
ridicule 851 n.
indignity 921 n.
despise 922 vb.
disapprobation 924 n.
hissing and a reproach, a
object of scorn 867 n.
despisedness 922 n.
histogram *record* 548 n.
histology *structure* 331 n.
historian
antiquarian 125 n.
chronicler 549 n.
author 589 n.
narrator 590 n.
historic *olden* 127 adj.
renowned 866 adj.
historical *real* 1 adj.
past 125 adj.
certain 473 adj.
true 494 adj.
descriptive 590 adj.
historicity *reality* 1 n.
truth 494 n.
historic tense
preterition 125 n.
history *preterition* 125 n.
remembrance 505 n.
record 548 n.
narrative 590 n.
reading matter 598 n.
conduct 688 n.
histrionics
exaggeration 546 n.
dramaturgy 594 n.
acting 594 n.
ostentation 875 n.
hit *place* 187 vb.
strike 279 vb.
arrive, meet 295 vb.
touch 378 vb.
be visible 443 vb.
discover 484 vb.
dramaturgy 594 n.
contrivance 623 n.
exceller 644 n.
success 727 n.
favourite 890 n.

reproach 924 n.
hit and miss
empiricism 461 n.
rash 857 adj.
hit back *recoil* 280 vb.
retaliate 714 vb.
hitch *tie* 45 vb.
ligature 47 n.
stop 145 n.
disappointment 509 n.
difficulty 700 n.
hitch 702 n.
failure 728 n.
marry 894 vb.
hitch-hike *ride* 267 vb.
beg 761 vb.
hitch up *start out* 296 vb.
hither *towards* 281 adv.
hitherto
retrospectively 125 adv.
hit it *discover* 484 vb.
be successful 727 vb.
Hitlerism *brute force* 735 n.
hit off *accord* 24 vb.
represent 551 vb.
hit on *chance* 159 vb.
discover 484 vb.
plan 623 vb.
hive *place oneself* 187 vb.
dwelling 192 n.
stock farm 369 n.
storage 632 n.
activity 678 n.
workshop 687 n.
hive off
be disjoined 46 vb.
be dispersed 75 vb.
schismatize 978 vb.
hives *formication* 378 n.
skin disease 651 n.
hoar *white* 427 adj.
grey 429 adj.
hoard *store* 632 n., vb.
safeguard 660 vb.
acquire 771 vb.
economize 814 vb.
be parsimonious 816 vb.
hoarder *niggard* 816 n.
hoarding *exhibit* 522 n.
advertisement 528 n.
hoar-frost
wintriness 380 n.
hoarse *muted* 401 adj.
non-resonant 405 adj.
hoarse 407 adj.
vocal 577 adj.
voiceless 578 adj.
hoarse, make oneself
vociferate 408 vb.
hoary *immemorial* 127 adj.
grey 429 adj.

hoax *rumour* 529 n.
  trickery 542 n.
  fable 543 n.
hoaxable *credulous* 487 adj.
hoaxer *trickster* 545 n.
hob *stand* 218 n.
  furnace 383 n.
  countryman 869 n.
  elf 970 n.
Hobbism *brute force* 735 n.
hobble *tie* 45 vb.
  disable 161 vb.
  move slowly 278 vb.
  impair 655 vb.
  be clumsy 695 vb.
  hinder 702 vb.
  fetter 747 vb.
  fetter 748 n.
hobbledehoy
  youngster 132 n.
hobby *bias* 481 n.
  pursuit 619 n.
  business 622 n.
  amusement 837 n.
  liking 859 n.
hobby-horse *vehicle* 274 n.
hobgoblin
  intimidation 854 n.
  elf 970 n.
hobnail *fastening* 47 n.
  countryman 869 n.
hobnob *be friendly* 880 vb.
  be sociable 882 vb.
hobo *wanderer* 268 n.
hobo signs
  symbology 547 n.
Hobson's choice
  necessity 596 n.
  no choice 606 n.
  compulsion 740 n.
hock *disable* 161 vb.
  leg 267 n.
  wine 301 n.
  impair 655 vb.
  give security 767 vb.
  borrow 785 vb.
hockey *ball game* 837 n.
hocus *trickery* 542 n.
hocus-pocus
  unmeaningness 515 n.
  sleight 542 n.
  idolatry 982 n.
  spell 983 n.
hod *plate* 194 n.
  shovel 274 n.
hodden *textile* 222 n.
  textural 331 adj.
hodman *artisan* 686 n.
hoe *shovel* 274 n.
  farm tool 370 n.
  cleaning utensil 648 n.

hog *pig* 365 n.
  appropriate 786 vb.
  be selfish 932 vb.
  sensualist 944 n.
  glutton 947 n.
hoggish *unclean* 649 adj.
  selfish 932 adj.
  sensual 944 adj.
Hogmanay
  anniversary 141 n.
hog's back *high land* 209 n
hogshead *vat* 194 n.
  metrology 465 n.
hogwash *silly talk* 515 n.
  falsehood 541 n.
  swill 649 n.
hoist *verticality* 215 n.
  edge 234 n.
  lifter 310 n.
  elevate 310 vb.
  flag 547 n.
hoist sail *navigate* 269 vb.
hoist with his own petard
  retaliate 714 vb.
hokum *falsehood* 541 n.
hold *be* 1 vb.
  fastening 47 n.
  cohere 48 vb.
  contain 56 vb.
  comprise 78 vb.
  stay 144 vb.
  cease 145 vb.
  go on 146 vb.
  be stable 153 vb.
  influence 178 n.
  receptacle 194 n.
  cellar 194 n.
  base 214 n.
  handle 218 n.
  support 218 vb.
  opine 485 vb.
  be true 494 vb.
  affirm 532 vb.
  storage 632 n.
  store 632 vb.
  preserve 666 vb.
  wrestling 716 n.
  restrain 747 vb.
  lock-up 748 n.
  possession 773 n.
  retention 778 n.
  impress 821 vb.
hold a brief for
  deputize 755 vb.
hold-all *bag* 194 n.
  storage 632 n.
hold back *avoid* 620 vb.
  hinder 702 vb.
  restrain 747 vb.
hold cheap
  underestimate 483 vb.

hold cheap 922 vb.
hold classes *teach* 534 vb.
hold court *hold court* 955 vb.
hold down *depress* 311 vb.
  function 622 vb.
  dominate 733 vb.
  subjugate 745 vb.
holder *receptacle* 194 n.
  handle 218 n.
  storage 632 n.
  proficient 696 n.
  possessor 776 n.
holdfast *fastening* 47 n.
hold fast *cohere* 48 vb.
  stand firm 599 vb.
  retain 778 vb.
hold for *opine* 485 vb.
  intend 617 vb.
hold forth *teach* 534 vb.
  orate 579 vb.
hold good *be* 1 vb.
  stay 144 vb.
  be proved 478 vb.
  be true 494 vb.
hold hands *caress* 889 vb.
hold in *circumscribe* 232 vb.
  restrain 747 vb.
hold in common
  socialize 775 vb.
holding *territory* 184 n.
  farm 370 n.
  lands 777 n.
hold in view *see* 438 vb.
  expect 507 vb.
hold off *be distant* 199 vb.
  avoid 620 vb.
  not use 674 vb.
  parry 713 vb.
  resist 715 vb.
hold office *function* 622 vb.
  direct 689 vb.
  rule 733 vb.
hold on *stay* 144 vb.
  go on 146 vb.
  progress 285 vb.
  retain 778 vb.
hold one's breath
  await 507 vb.
  wonder 864 vb.
hold one's own
  be equal 28 vb.
  parry 713 vb.
hold one's tongue
  be silent 399 vb.
  keep secret 525 vb.
  be mute 578 vb.
  be taciturn 582 vb.
hold out *affirm* 532 vb.
  stand firm 599 vb.
  oppose 704 vb.
  resist 715 vb.

offer 759 vb.
promise 764 vb.
hold out for
  give terms 766 vb.
  bargain 791 vb.
hold over *put off* 136 vb.
hold the baby
  deputize 755 vb.
hold the road
  stabilize 153 vb.
hold the scales
  judge 480 vb.
hold tight *retain* 778 vb.
hold together
  accord 24 vb.
  be true 494 vb.
  co-operate 706 vb.
hold to ransom
  overcharge 811 vb.
hold under
  dominate 733 vb.
hold up *put off* 136 vb.
  halt 145 vb.
  sustain 146 vb.
  support 218 vb.
  elevate 310 vb.
  hinder 702 vb.
  rob 788 vb.
hold water
  be proved 478 vb.
  be true 494 vb.
hole *place* 185 n.
  dwelling 192 n.
  retreat 192 n.
  receptacle 194 n.
  gap 201 n.
  cavity 255 n.
  orifice 263 n.
  pierce 263 vb.
  insert 303 vb.
  hiding-place 527 n.
  refuge 662 n.
hole-and-corner
  stealthy 525 adj.
holey *dilapidated* 655 adj.
holiday *lull* 145 n.
  leisure 681 n.
  repose 683 n.
  permit 756 n.
  amusement 837 n.
holiday camp
  meeting place 192 n.
  pleasure-ground 837 n.
holiday home *abode* 192 n.
holiday-maker
  traveller 268 n.
  reveller 837 n.
holier than thou
  prideful 871 adj.
  despising 922 adj.
  disapproving 924 adj.

pietistic 979 adj.
holiness (*see* holy)
holism *whole* 52 n.
holland *textile* 222 n.
hollow
  insubstantial 4 adj.
  completely 54 adv.
  empty 190 adj.
  lowness 210 n.
  depth 211 n.
  cavity 255 n.
  furrow 261 n.
  opening 263 n.
  depression 311 n.
  rare 325 adj.
  resonant 404 adj.
  hoarse 407 adj.
  sophistical 477 adj.
  hypocritical 541 adj.
  voiceless 578 adj.
  ostentatious 875 adj.
holly *tree* 366 n.
Hollywood *cinema* 445 n.
  drama 594 n.
holocaust *havoc* 165 n.
  slaughter 362 n.
  burning 381 n.
  oblation 981 n.
holograph
  no imitation 21 n.
  script 586 n.
holophrastic
  comprehensive 52 adj.
  linguistic 557 adj.
holster *case* 194 n.
  arsenal 723 n.
holy *worshipful* 866 adj.
  virtuous 933 adj.
  prudish 950 adj.
  divine, godlike 965 adj.
  religious 973 adj.
  scriptural 975 adj.
  sanctified 979 adj.
  devotional 981 adj.
Holy Communion
  Holy Communion 988 n.
  Christian rite 988 n.
holy-day *holy-day* 988 n.
Holy Ghost
  Holy Ghost 965 n.
Holy Grail
  ritual object 988 n.
holy horror
  false piety 980 n.
Holy Office
  ecclesiastical court 956 n.
  orthodoxism 976 n.
  ecclesiasticism 985 n.
Holy of Holies
  holy place 990 n.
holy orders

holy orders 985 n.
  Christian rite 988 n.
Holy See
  church office 985 n.
Holy Spirit
  Holy Ghost 965 n.
holy-stone *cleanser* 648 n.
holy terror
  violent creature 176 n.
  ruffian 904 n.
Holy Unction
  Christian rite 988 n.
holy war *war* 718 n.
  philanthropy 901 n.
holy water
  ritual object 988 n.
Holy Week
  holy-day 988 n.
homage *submission* 721 n.
  loyalty 739 n.
  be subject 745 vb.
  respects 920 n.
homager *subject* 742 n.
homburg *headgear* 228 n.
home *focus* 76 n.
  native 191 adj.
  house, home 192 n.
  near 200 adj.
  interior 224 adj.
  resting place 266 n.
  turn back 286 vb.
  arrive 295 vb.
  refuge 662 n.
home, at *here* 189 adv.
  inside 224 adv.
  knowing 490 adj.
  habituated 610 adj.
  facilitated 701 adj.
  free 744 adj.
home circle *family* 11 n.
home-coming *return* 286 n.
  arrival 295 n.
homefolks *family* 11 n.
home ground *focus* 76 n.
  home 192 n.
Home Guard
  defender 713 n.
  soldier, army 722 n.
home-keeping
  quiescent 266 adj.
  unsociable 883 adj.
homeland *territory* 184 n.
  home 192 n.
homeless *irrelative* 10 adj.
  alone 88 adj.
  unstable 152 adj.
  displaced 188 adj.
  travelling 267 adj.
homeless person
  outcaste 883 n.
home-life *seclusion* 883 n.

homely *comfortable* 376 adj.
  dialectical 560 adj.
  plain 573 adj.
  pleasurable 826 adj.
  ugly 842 adj.
  plebeian 869 adj.
home-made
  bungled 695 adj.
  artless 699 adj.
homeopath *doctor* 658 n.
homeopathic
  small 33 adj.
  exiguous 196 adj.
  medical 658 adj.
homeopathy
  medical art 658 n.
homeostasis
  equilibrium 28 n.
  stability 153 n.
homer *metrology* 465 n.
home rule
  government 733 n.
  independence 744 n.
homesickness
  suffering 825 n.
  regret 830 n.
  melancholy 834 n.
  desire 859 n.
homespun *simple* 44 adj.
  textile 222 n.
  textural 331 adj.
  plainness 573 n.
  artless 699 adj.
  plebeian 869 adj.
homestead *home* 192 n.
home-stretch *end* 69 n.
home-thrust *foin* 712 n.
  reproach 924 n.
home-truth *truth* 494 n.
  veracity 540 n.
  censure 924 n.
  accusation 928 n.
homeward-bound
  regressive 286 adj.
  arriving 295 adj.
homework *study* 536 n.
  curriculum 536 n.
  preparation 669 n.
homicide *homicide* 362 n.
homiletics *teaching* 534 n.
  church ministry 985 n.
homily *lecture* 534 n.
  oration 579 n.
  dissertation 591 n.
  ministration 988 n.
hominal *human* 371 adj.
homing
  regressive 286 adj.
  arriving 295 adj.
  incoming 297 adj.
hominid *mankind* 371 n.

hominy *corn* 366 n.
homœopath
  (*see* homeopath)
homœoteleuton
  assimilation 18 n.
  ornament 574 n.
homogeneity
  relation 9 n.
  identity 13 n.
  uniformity 16 n.
  similarity 18 n.
  simpleness 44 n.
homogenesis
  propagation 164 n.
homologate *identify* 13 vb.
  accord 24 vb.
homologous
  relative 9 adj.
  uniform 16 adj.
  equal 28 adj.
homomorphism
  similarity 18 n.
homonym *identity* 13 n.
  word 559 n.
homonymous
  semantic 514 adj.
  equivocal 518 adj.
homonymy
  equivocalness 518 n.
homoousian
  identical 13 adj.
homophene *identity* 13 n.
  word 559 n.
homophone *identity* 13 n.
  equivocalness 518 n.
  word 559 n.
homophony
  assimilation 18 n.
  melody 410 n.
homo sapiens
  mankind 371 n.
homosexual
  nonconformist 84 n.
  extramarital 951 adj.
homunculus
  small animal 33 n.
  dwarf 196 n.
hone *sharpen* 256 vb.
honest *true* 494 adj.
  genuine 494 adj.
  veracious 540 adj.
  plain 573 adj.
  artless 699 adj.
  ethical 917 adj.
  honourable 929 adj.
  disinterested 931 adj.
  virtuous 933 adj.
honesty (*see* honest)
honey *viscidity* 354 n.
  sweet 392 n.
  yellowness 433 n.

  darling 890 n.
honeycomb *cavity* 255 n.
  porosity 263 n.
  pierce 263 vb.
  sweet 392 n.
  storage 632 n.
  impair 655 vb.
honeymoon *joy* 824 n.
  concord 710 n.
  pleasurableness 826 n.
  friendship 880 n.
  be in love 887 vb.
  wedding 894 n.
honeymooners
  spouse 894 n.
honeypot *focus* 76 n.
  sweet 392 n.
honeysuckle *sweet* 392 n.
honk *loudness* 400 n.
  ululate 409 vb.
  danger signal 665 n.
honky-tonk *tavern* 192 n.
honorarium *gift* 781 n.
  reward 962 n.
honorary
  insubstantial 4 adj.
  voluntary 597 adj.
  uncharged 812 adj.
honorific *honours* 866 n.
  title 870 n.
  celebrative 876 adj.
honour
  make important 638 vb.
  decoration 729 n.
  promise 764 n.
  lands 777 n.
  pay 804 n.
  prestige 866 n.
  dignify 866 vb.
  title 870 n.
  celebrate 876 vb.
  pay respects 884 vb.
  right 913 n.
  morals 917 n.
  do one's duty 917 vb.
  respect 920 n.
  probity 929 n.
  virtue 933 n.
  purity 950 n.
  reward 962 n., vb.
  piety 979 n.
  sanctify 979 vb.
  worship 981 n., vb.
honourable
  honourable 929 adj.
honourable intentions
  wooing 889 n.
honours *victory* 727 n.
  decoration 729 n.
  honours 866 n.
  reward 962 n.

hooch *liquor* 301 n.
  booty 790 n.
hood *covering* 226 n.
  headgear 228 n.
  screen 421 n., vb.
hoodlum
  insolent person 878 n.
  ruffian 904 n.
hoodoo *sorcery* 983 n.
hoodwink *blind* 439 vb.
  deceive 542 vb.
hooey *empty talk* 515 n.
  falsehood 541 n.
hoof *foot* 214 n.
  dance 837 vb.
hoof it *walk* 267 vb.
  leap 312 vb.
hoofmark *trace* 548 n.
hook *coupling* 47 n.
  hanger 217 n.
  angularity 247 n.
  sharp edge 256 n.
  knock 279 n.
  deflect 282 vb.
  propel 287 vb.
  trap 542 n.
  take 786 vb.
hookah *air-pipe* 353 n.
  tobacco 388 n.
hook and eye
  fastening 47 n.
hooker
  merchant ship 275 n.
hook, line and sinker
  all 52 n.
  completely 54 adv.
hook on *affix* 45 vb.
hook-up *junction* 45 n.
  association 706 n.
hooligan
  violent creature 176 n.
  ruffian 904 n.
hooliganism
  lawlessness 954 n.
hoop *bond* 47 n.
  frame 218 n.
  skirt 228 n.
  circle 250 n.
  plaything 837 n.
hoop-la *ball game* 837 n.
hoot *cry* 408 n., vb.
  ululate 409 vb.
  laugh 835 vb.
  ridicule 851 n.
  indignity 921 n.
  disapprove 924 vb.
hooter *timekeeper* 117 n.
  megaphone 400 n.
  signal 547 n.
hop *gait* 265 n.
  land travel 267 n.

departure 296 n.
  leap 312 n., vb.
  be agitated 318 vb.
  dancing 837 n.
  social gathering 882 n.
hope *expect* 507 vb.
  motive 612 n.
  proficient 696 n.
  cheerfulness 833 n.
  hope 852 n., vb.
  desire 859 vb.
hope against hope
  hope 852 vb.
  (*see* persevere)
hopeful *youngster* 132 n.
  probable 471 adj.
  expectant 507 adj.
  hoper 852 n.
  promising 852 adj.
hopeless *impossible* 470 adj.
  useless 641 adj.
  unhappy 825 adj.
  dejected 834 adj.
  hopeless 853 adj.
  unpromising 853 adj.
  impenitent 940 adj.
hopelessness
  impossibility 470 n.
  hopelessness 853 n.
hopes of, give
  predict 511 vb.
hop it *decamp* 296 vb.
hoplite *soldier* 722 n.
hop, on the
  on the move 265 adv.
hopper *vat* 194 n.
  ship 275 n.
  jumper 312 n.
hopping mad
  angry 891 adj.
hops *liquor* 301 n.
horary *periodic* 110 adj.
horde *party* 708 n.
  multitude 104 n.
  army 722 n.
  rabble 869 n.
horizon *distance* 199 n.
  horizontality 216 n.
  edge 234 n.
  limit 236 n.
  view 438 n.
horizontality
  horizontality 216 n.
horme *desire* 859 n.
hormone *stimulant* 174 n.
horn *cup* 194 n.
  cone 252 n.
  protuberance 254 n.
  sharp point 256 n.
  structure 331 n.
  megaphone 400 n.

horn 414 n.
  semitransparency 424 n.
  weapon 723 n.
hornbook *classroom* 539 n.
  textbook 589 n.
  reading matter 589 n.
horned *curved* 248 adj.
  tapering 256 adj.
hornet *fly* 365 n.
  shrew 892 n.
  noxious animal 904 n.
hornet's nest *bane* 659 n.
  pitfall 663 n.
  painfulness 827 n.
horn in *intrude* 297 vb.
  encroach 306 vb.
hornpipe *dance* 837 n.
hornswoggle *deceive* 542 vb.
hornwork
  fortification 713 n.
horny *hard* 326 adj.
horny-handed
  labouring 682 adj.
horologer *timekeeper* 117 n.
horology
  chronometry 117 n.
horoscope
  looking ahead 124 n.
  destiny 155 n.
  astronomy 321 n.
  prediction 511 n.
horrible *not nice* 645 adj.
  unpleasant 827 adj.
  frightening 854 adj.
horribly *extremely* 32 adv.
horrid *not nice* 645 adj.
  hateful 888 adj.
horrific *distressing* 827 adj.
  frightening 854 adj.
horrify *displease* 827 vb.
  frighten 854 vb.
  excite hate 888 vb.
horripilation
  roughness 259 n.
  fear 854 n.
horror *eyesore* 842 n.
  fear 854 n.
  dislike 861 n.
  hell-hag 904 n.
  monster 938 n.
horrors *melancholy* 834 n.
  alcoholism 949 n.
horror-struck
  fearing 854 adj.
hors de combat
  impotent 161 adj.
  useless 641 adj.
hors d'œuvre *dish* 301 n.
  savouriness 390 n.
horse *horse* 273 n.
  male animal 372 n.

busy person 678 n.
cavalry 722 n.
horseback
conveyance 267 n.
horsecloth coverlet 226 n.
horse-coper trickster 545 n.
horse-dealing barter 791 n.
horse-doctor
animal husbandry 369 n.
doctor 658 n.
horsehair hair 258 n.
horseman rider 268 n.
cavalry 722 n.
horsemanship
equitation 267 n.
skill 694 n.
horse marine
bungler 697 n.
horse-opera
stage play 594 n.
horse-play fight 716 n.
ridicule 851 n.
horse-power energy 160 n.
horse-racing
gambling 618 n.
racing 716 n.
horse sense
intelligence 498 n.
horse-shoe curve 248 n.
horsewhip flog 963 vb.
scourge 964 n.
horsy equine 273 adj.
amused 837 adj.
hortative
educational 534 adj.
advising 691 adj.
hortatory inducive 612 adj.
horticulture flower 366 n.
agriculture 370 n.
hortus siccus botany 368 n.
hosanna rejoicing 835 n.
celebration 876 n.
applause 923 n.
hymn 981 n.
hose legwear 228 n.
tube 263 n.
water 339 n.
irrigation 341 n.
conduit 351 n.
extinguisher 382 n.
cleaning utensil 648 n.
hosier clothier 228 n.
hosiery legwear 228 n.
hospice inn 192 n.
hospital 658 n.
hospitable (see hospitality)
hospital hygiene 652 n.
hospital 658 n.
hospital case
sick person 651 n.
hospitality liberality 813 n.

friendliness 880 n.
sociability 882 n.
benevolence 897 n.
hospitalize doctor 658 vb.
host band 74 n.
multitude 104 n.
army 722 n.
friend 880 n.
social person 882 n.
the sacrament 988 n.
hostage
thing transferred 272 n.
prisoner 750 n.
security 767 n.
hostel station 187 n.
quarters 192 n.
hostelry inn 192 n.
hostess social person 882 n.
hostile
counteracting 182 adj.
attacking 712 adj.
adverse 731 adj.
prohibiting 757 adj.
disliking 861 adj.
enemy 881 n.
unsociable 883 adj.
(see hostility)
hostilities fight 716 n.
belligerency 718 n.
hostility contrariety 14 n.
disagreement 25 n.
opposition 704 n.
dissension 709 n.
enmity 881 n.
hatred 888 n.
disapprobation 924 n.
hosts great quantity 32 n.
hot violent 176 adj.
dry 342 adj.
hot 379 adj.
pungent 388 adj.
musical 412 adj.
red 431 adj.
fervent 818 adj.
excited 821 adj.
angry 891 adj.
lecherous 951 adj.
impure 951 adj.
hot air
overestimation 482 n.
empty talk 515 n.
chatter 381 n.
boast 877 n.
hotbed seedbed 156 n.
abundance 171 n.
heater 383 n.
badness 645 n.
infection 651 n.
hot blood
excitability 822 n.
irascibility 892 n.

hot-blooded violent 176 adj.
rash 857 adj.
hot-box provisions 301 n.
hot-case heater 383 n.
hotchpotch medley 43 n.
confusion 61 n.
dish 301 n.
hot dog meat 301 n.
hotel inn 192 n.
hotelier caterer 633 n.
hot-foot hastily 680 adv.
hot-gospeller
religionist 979 n.
hothead
warm feeling 818 n.
desperado 857 n.
hot-headed fervent 818 adj.
excitable 822 adj.
rash 857 adj.
hot-house
extraneous 59 adj.
seedbed 156 n.
garden 370 n.
heater 383 n.
hot rod automobile 274 n.
hot seat
means of execution 964 n.
Hotspur
violent creature 176 n.
brave person 855 n.
desperado 857 n.
hot stuff loose woman 952 n.
hot-tempered
excitable 822 adj.
hot water heat 379 n.
cleanser 648 n.
predicament 700 n.
painfulness 827 n.
hot-water bottle
cauldron 194 n.
heater 383 n.
hough disable 161 vb.
leg 267 n.
impair 655 vb.
hound dog 365 n.
hunter 619 n.
be malevolent 898 vb.
defame 926 vb.
knave, cad 938 n.
hound on incite 612 vb.
hour juncture 8 n.
period 110 n.
clock time 117 n.
hour angle
uranometry 321 n.
hourglass timekeeper 117 n.
contraction 198 n.
narrowing 206 n.
hour-hand
timekeeper 117 n.
indicator 547 n.

houri *a beauty* 841 n.
　mythical being 970 n.
hourly *while* 108 adv.
　periodic 110 adj.
　frequent 139 adj.
　often 139 adv.
　seasonal 141 adj.
　periodically 141 adv.
house *genealogy* 169 n.
　edifice 164 n.
　place 187 vb.
　abode, house 192 n.
　zodiac 321 n.
　onlookers 441 n.
　playgoer 594 n.
　theatre 594 n.
　corporation 708 n.
　sovereign 741 n.
　shop 796 n.
　brothel 951 n.
houseboat
　small house 192 n.
　boat 275 n.
housebreaker
　incomer 297 n.
　thief 789 n.
　offender 904 n.
housebreaking
　stealing 788 n.
housecarl
　defender 713 n.
　soldier 722 n.
　retainer 742 n.
housecoat
　informal dress 228 n.
house-dog *dog* 365 n.
　warner 664 n.
houseful *crowd* 74 n.
　habitancy 191 n.
household *family* 11 n.
　group 74 n.
　habitancy 191 n.
　home 192 n.
　known 490 adj.
　usual 610 adj.
householder
　resident 191 n.
　possessor 776 n.
household troops
　armed force 722 n.
household words
　plainness 573 n.
housekeeper *resident* 191 n.
　caterer 633 n.
　manager 690 n.
　retainer 742 n.
　keeper 749 n.
housekeeping
　management 689 n.
housel
　perform ritual 988 vb.

houseless
　displaced 188 adj.
housemaid *domestic* 742 n.
houseman *resident* 191 n.
　doctor 658 n.
　domestic 742 n.
house master
　teacher 537 n.
　manager 690 n.
house of cards
　weak thing 163 n.
　brittleness 330 n.
House of Commons
　parliament 692 n.
house of correction
　amendment 654 n.
　prison 748 n.
House of God
　temple 990 n.
House of Lords
　parliament 692 n.
　aristocracy 868 n.
house organ *journal* 528 n.
house party
　social gathering 882 n.
house-proud
　prideful 871 adj.
housetop *vertex* 213 n.
　roof 226 n.
house-trailer
　small house 192 n.
house-trained
　tasteful 846 adj.
　well-bred 848 adj.
house-warming
　social gathering 882 n.
housewife *resident* 191 n.
　case 194 n.
　caterer 633 n.
　busy person 678 n.
　manager 690 n.
housewifery
　management 689 n.
housework *labour* 682 n.
　management 689 n.
housing *housing* 192 n.
housings *coverlet* 226 n.
hovel *small house* 192 n.
hoveller *boatman* 270 n.
hover *impend* 155 vb.
　be near 200 vb.
　be high 209 vb.
　hang 217 vb.
　move 265 vb.
　wander 267 vb.
　fly 271 vb.
　move slowly 278 vb.
　approach 289 vb.
　be uncertain 474 vb.
　be irresolute 601 vb.
hovercraft *aircraft* 276 n.

hovering
　overhanging 209 adj.
hover on the brink
　be in danger 661 vb.
how *how* 624 adv.
how come? *why?* 158 adv.
howdah *seat* 218 n.
howitzer *gun* 723 n.
howl *blow* 352 vb.
　feel pain 377 vb.
　loudness 400 n.
　cry 408 n., vb.
　ululate 409 vb.
　lament 836 n.
howler *mistake* 495 n.
　absurdity 497 n.
how the land lies
　circumstance 8 n.
hoy *sailing-ship* 275 n.
　merchant ship 275 n.
hoyden *youngster* 132 n.
hoydenish *infantine* 132 adj.
　artless 699 adj.
　ill-bred 847 adj.
hub *middle* 70 n.
　focus 76 n.
　centrality 225 n.
　wheel 250 n.
　chief thing 638 n.
hubble-bubble
　tobacco 388 n.
hubbub
　commotion 318 n.
　loudness 400 n.
　quarrel 709 n.
hubris *pride* 871 n.
　insolence 878 n.
huckster *bargain* 791 vb.
　seller 793 n.
　pedlar 794 n.
huddle *confusion* 61 n.
　jumble 63 vb.
　crowd 74 n.
　make smaller 198 vb.
　be near 200 vb.
　conference 584 n.
huddle into *wear* 228 vb.
Hudibrastic
　derisive 881 adj.
hue *character* 5 n.
　hue 425 n.
hue and cry *chase* 619 n.
huff *breathe* 352 vb.
　resentment 891 n.
　huff 891 vb.
huffy *irascible* 892 adj.
hug *cohere* 48 vb.
　make smaller 198 vb.
　be near 200 vb.
　surround 230 vb.
　inclose 235 vb.

flank 239 vb.
gesture 547 n.
retain 778 vb.
friendliness 880 n.
be hospitable 882 vb.
courteous act 884 n.
greet 884 vb.
caress 889 vb.
huge *enormous* 32 adj.
stalwart 162 adj.
huge 195 adj.
hugger-mugger
confusion 61 n.
stealthy 525 adj.
hug oneself
be pleased 824 vb.
be content 828 vb.
rejoice 835 vb.
feel pride 871 vb.
be vain 873 vb.
boast 877 vb.
Huguenot
Protestant 976 n.
huissier *law officer* 955 n.
huke *cloak* 228 n.
hula-hula *dance* 837 n.
hulk *ship* 275 n.
hulking, hulky
whopping 32 adj.
unwieldy 195 adj.
clumsy 695 adj.
graceless 842 adj.
hulks *prison* 748 n.
hull *ship* 275 n.
uncover 229 vb.
hullabaloo *turmoil* 61 n.
loudness 400 n.
cry 408 n.
hull down *beyond* 199 adv.
hum *be many* 104 vb.
sound faint 401 vb.
roll 403 n., vb.
resound 404 vb.
shrill 407 vb.
ululation 409 vb.
sing 413 vb.
voice 577 vb.
activity 678 n.
human *animal* 365 adj.
human 371 adj.
benevolent 897 adj.
philanthropic 901 adj.
frail 934 adj.
human being *person* 371 n.
hum and haw
stammer 580 vb.
be irresolute 601 vb.
humane
educational 534 adj.
benevolent 897 adj.
philanthropic 901 adj.

pitying 905 adj.
humane scholarship
literature 557 n.
humanism
philosophy 449 n.
philanthropy 901 n.
humanist *linguist* 557 n.
philanthropist 901 n.
humanitarian
philanthropist 901 n.
humanitarianism
benevolence 897 n.
philanthropy 901 n.
humanities *culture* 490 n.
literature 557 n.
humanity *mankind* 371 n.
lenity 736 n.
benevolence 897 n.
philanthropy 901 n.
pity 905 n.
humanize *be lenient* 736 vb.
be benevolent 897 vb.
human nature
mankind 371 n.
human race
mankind 371 n.
humble
inconsiderable 33 adj.
inferior 35 adj.
abase 311 vb.
unknown 491 adj.
disappoint 509 vb.
impress 821 vb.
plebeian 869 adj.
humiliate 872 vb.
respectful 920 adj.
(see humility)
humble oneself
be humble 872 vb.
show respect 920 vb.
be pious 979 vb.
worship 981 vb.
humbug *empty talk* 515 n.
falsehood 541 n.
deceive 542 vb.
fable 543 n.
impostor 545 n.
affectation 850 n.
humdinger *exceller* 644 n.
humdrum *plain* 573 adj.
tedious 838 adj.
humectation
moistening 341 n.
humic *territorial* 344 adj.
humid *watery* 339 adj.
humid 341 adj.
humidity *moisture* 341 n.
humiliation *adversity* 731 n.
disrepute 867 n.
humiliation 872 n.
indignity 921 n.

contempt 922 n.
humility
underestimation 483 n.
submission 721 n.
humility 872 n.
modesty 874 adj.
servility 879 n.
disinterestedness 931 n.
piety 979 n.
worship 981 n.
humming
multitudinous 104 adj.
humming-top *rotator* 315 n.
organ 414 n.
hummock *monticle* 209 n.
dome 253 n.
humoresque
musical piece 412 n.
humorist
humorist 839 n.
humorous *funny* 849 adj.
(see humour)
humour *temperament* 5 n.
tendency 179 n.
fluid 335 n.
whim 604 n.
minister to 703 vb.
be lenient 736 vb.
affections 817 n.
please 826 vb.
laughter 835 n.
amuse 837 vb.
wit 839 n.
flatter 925 vb.
humourless *serious* 834 adj.
dull 840 adj.
humoursome
capricious 604 adj.
sullen 893 adj.
hump *monticle* 209 n.
sphere 252 n.
camber 253 n.
carry 273 vb.
hump bluey *travel* 267 vb.
humpy *convex* 253 adj.
humus *soil* 344 n.
Hun *destroyer* 168 n.
evildoer 904 n.
hunch *intuition* 476 n.
supposition 512 n.
spontaneity 609 n.
hunchback *camber* 253 n.
hunchbacked
deformed 246 adj.
blemished 845 adj.
hundred *hundred* 99 n.
district 184 n.
hundred per cent
perfect 646 adj.
hundredweight
weighment 322 n.

hunger *eating* 301 n.
　rapacity 786 n.
　hunger 859 n.
　desire 859 vb.
hunger-march
　deprecation 762 n.
hunger-strike *fast* 946 n.
hungry *hungry* 859 adj.
　fasting 946 adj.
　gluttonous 947 adj.
hunk *piece* 53 n.
hunkers *buttocks* 238 n.
hunks *niggard* 816 n.
hunky *foreigner* 59 n.
hunky-dory
　topping 644 adj.
hunt *eject* 300 vb.
　oscillate 317 vb.
　campanology 412 n.
　search 459 n.
　detect 484 vb.
　chase 619 n.
　attack 712 vb.
　be severe 735 vb.
　be inimical 881 vb.
hunter *timekeeper* 117 n.
　thoroughbred 273 n.
　killer 362 n.
　hunter 619 n.
hunting field
　arena 724 n.
　pleasure-ground 837 n.
hunt in pairs
　co-operate 706 vb.
huntsman *hunter* 619 n.
hunt with the hounds
　do likewise 20 vb.
hurdle *bed* 218 n.
　vehicle 274 n.
　leap 312 vb.
　obstacle 702 n.
hurdler
　thoroughbred 273 n.
　jumper 312 n.
hurdles *racing* 716 n.
hurdy-gurdy *organ* 414 n.
hurl *propel* 287 vb.
hurling *propulsion* 287 n.
　ball game 837 n.
hurly-burly
　commotion 318 n.
hurrah *cry* 408 n., vb.
　rejoicing 835 n.
hurricane *turmoil* 61 n.
　storm 176 n.
　gale 352 n.
hurried *brief* 114 adj.
　hasty 680 adj.
hurry *velocity* 277 n.
　move fast 277 vb.
　incite 612 vb.

activity 678 n.
haste 680 n.
hurt *weaken* 163 vb.
　pain 377 n.
　evil 616 n.
　be inexpedient 643 adj.
　harm 645 vb.
　impair 655 vb.
　hurt 827 vb.
　resentful 891 adj.
　huff 891 vb.
hurtful (*see* hurt)
hurtling *speedy* 277 adj.
husband *male* 372 n.
　store 632 vb.
　manager 690 n.
　master 741 n.
　spouse 894 n.
husbandless
　unwedded 895 adj.
　widowed 896 adj.
husbandman
　accumulator 74 n.
　producer 167 n.
　husbandman 370 n.
　countryman 869 n.
husbandry
　agriculture 370 n.
　management 689 n.
　economy 814 n.
hush *assuage* 177 vb.
　quietude 266 n.
　silence 399 n., vb.
　make mute 578 vb.
hush-hush *occult* 523 adj.
　concealed 525 adj.
hush-hush subject
　secret 530 n.
hush up *keep secret* 525 vb.
husk *remainder* 41 n.
　skin 226 n.
　corn 366 n.
　rubbish 641 n.
huskiness *aphony* 578 n.
husky *stalwart* 162 adj.
　beast of burden 273 n.
　dog 365 n.
　hoarse 407 adj.
hussar *cavalry* 722 n.
Hussite *heretic* 977 n.
hussy
　insolent person 878 n.
　loose woman 952 n.
hustings *rostrum* 539 n.
　vote 605 n.
　arena 724 n.
　law-court 956 n.
hustle *move* 265 vb.
　impel 279 vb.
　propel 287 vb.
　activity 678 n.

hasten 680 vb.
hustle out *eject* 300 vb.
hustler *speeder* 277 n.
　busy person 678 n.
　prostitute 952 n.
hut *small house* 192 n.
hutch *stable* 192 n.
huzza (*see* hurrah)
hyacinth *blueness* 435 n.
　gem 844 n.
hyalescence
　transparency 422 n.
hybrid *hybrid* 43 n.
　nonconformist 84 n.
　neology 560 n.
hydra *rara avis* 84 n.
hydragogue *watery* 339 adj.
hydra-headed
　reproductive 166 adj.
hydrant *water* 339 n.
　conduit 351 n.
　current 350 n.
　extinguisher 382 n.
hydrate *add water* 339 vb.
　moisten 341 vb.
hydraulics *fluidity* 335 n.
hydro *hospital* 658 n.
hydrocele *fluid* 335 n.
　disease 651 n.
hydrocephalic
　diseased 651 adj.
hydrodynamics
　science of forces 162 n.
　fluidity 335 n.
hydro-electric
　dynamic 160 adj.
hydrogen *lifter* 310 n.
　levity 323 n.
hydrogenate *gasify* 336 vb.
hydrogeology
　geography 321 n.
hydrographer
　oceanography 343 n.
　surveyor 465 n.
hydrography
　geography 321 n.
　hygrometry 341 n.
　oceanography 343 n.
hydrokinetics *fluidity* 335 n.
hydrology
　geography 321 n.
　fluidity 335 n.
　hygrometry 341 n.
hydrolysis
　decomposition 51 n.
hydromel *sweet* 392 n.
hydrometer *density* 324 n.
　hygrometry 341 n.
hydrometry *fluidity* 335 n.
hydrophobia
　frenzy 503 n.

hydroplane *aircraft* 276 n.
hydroponics
  agriculture 370 n.
hydrostatics
  science of forces 162 n.
  fluidity 335 n.
hydrotherapy
  moistening 341 n.
  therapy 658 n.
hydrotic, hydrous
  watery 339 adj.
hyena *noxious animal* 904 n.
hyetography *rain* 350 n.
hygiene *cleansing* 648 n.
  health 650 n.
  hygiene 652 n.
  prophylactic 658 n.
  preservation 666 n.
hygienist *sanitarian* 652 n.
hygiology *hygiene* 652 n.
hygrometer *weather* 340 n.
  meter 465 n.
  recording instrument
    549 n.
hygrometry
  hygrometry 341 n.
hygroscope
  hygrometry 341 n.
hyle *substantiality* 3 n.
  matter 319 n.
hymeneal
  wedding 894 n.
  matrimonial 894 adj.
hymn *vocal music* 412 n.
  poem 593 n.
  praise 923 vb.
  hymn 981 n.
hymnal *hymnal* 988 n.
  church utensil 990 n.
hymnody *hymn* 981 n.
hymn of hate *hatred* 888 n.
hymnology
  vocal music 412 n.
  hymn 981 n.
  hymnal 988 n.
hymn-writer
  musician 413 n.
  theologian 973 n.
  worshipper 981 n.
hyp *psychopathy* 503 n.
hypallage *inversion* 221 n.
hyperæsthesia
  sensibility 374 n.
hyperbatic
  inverted 221 adj.
hyperbola *curve* 248 n.
hyperbole *expansion* 197 n.
  trope 519 n.
  exaggeration 546 n.
  ornament 574 n.
hyperbolical

exaggerated 546 adj.
hyperbolize
  exaggerate 546 vb.
hyperborean
  distant 199 adj.
hypercharacterization
  pleonasm 570 n.
hypercriticism
  narrow mind 481 n.
  discontent 829 n.
  fastidiousness 862 n.
  censure 924 n.
hyperdulia *cult* 981 n.
hyperion *particle* 33 n.
hyperphysical
  paranormal 984 adj.
hyperphysics
  occultism 984 n.
hyperpsychological
  paranormal 984 adj.
hypersonic *speedy* 277 adj.
hypertension
  blood pressure 651 n.
hypertrophy *size* 195 n.
  expansion 197 n.
hyphen *bond* 47 n.
  punctuation 547 n.
hyphenate *join* 45 vb.
hypnopedagogics
  teaching 534 n.
  therapy 658 n.
hypnosis *insensibility* 375 n.
  sleep 679 n.
  occultism 984 n.
hypnotic *lenitive* 177 adj.
  influential 178 adj.
  insensible 375 adj.
  inducive 612 adj.
  remedial 658 adj.
  somnific 679 adj.
  psychical 984 adj.
hypnotism
  insensibility 375 n.
  occultism 984 n.
hypnotist *motivator* 612 n.
  psychic 984 n.
hypnotize *influence* 178 vb.
  render insensible 375 vb.
  convince 485 vb.
  motivate 612 vb.
  bewitch 983 vb.
  practice occultism 984 vb.
hypocaust *heater* 383 n.
hypochondria
  psychopathy 503 n.
  ill-health 651 n.
  melancholy 834 n.
hypochondriac
  insane 503 adj.
  madman 504 n.
  sick person 651 n.

unhealthy 651 adj.
  moper 834 n.
hypocrisy *duplicity* 541 n.
  deception 542 n.
  flattery 925 n.
  false piety 980 n.
hypocrite *imitator* 20 n.
  deceiver 545 n.
  slyboots 698 n.
  affector 850 n.
  flatterer 925 n.
hypogeal *deep* 211 adj.
hypogeum *depth* 211 n.
hypomania *mania* 503 n.
  psychopathy 503 n.
hypostasis *essence* 1 n.
  substantiality 3 n.
  substance 3 n.
hypostatic
  substantial 3 adj.
  material 319 adj.
Hypostatic Union
  Trinity 965 n.
hypostatize
  materialize 319 vb.
hypotension
  blood pressure 651 n.
hypothecation
  security 767 n.
hypothermal *warm* 379 adj.
hypothesis
  attribution 158 n.
  opinion 485 n.
  supposition 512 n.
hypothetical
  uncertain 474 adj.
  credible 485 adj.
  suppositional 512 adj.
  imaginary 513 adj.
hypsometer *altimetry* 209 n.
hyssop *ritual object* 988 n.
hysteresis *lateness* 136 n.
  slowness 278 n.
hysteria *psychopathy* 503 n.
hysteric *madman* 504 n.
hysterical *furious* 176 adj.
  insane 503 adj.
  capricious 604 adj.
  fervent 818 adj.
  excited 821 adj.
  excitable 822 adj.
hysterics *violence* 176 n.
  excitable state 822 n.
  lamentation 836 n.
hysteron proteron
  inversion 221 n.

I

I *self* 80 n.
iambic *poetic* 593 adj.

iambus *prosody* 593 n.
ianthic *purple* 434 adj.
ibidem *identically* 13 adv.
ibis *bird of prey* 365 n.
Icarus *aeronaut* 271 n.
ice *desert* 172 n.
   smoothness 258 n.
   pudding 301 n.
   ice 380 n.
   refrigeration 382 n.
   refrigerator 384 n.
   sweeten 392 vb.
   transparency 422 n.
   preserver 666 n.
   preserve 666 vb.
   gem 844 n.
ice age *era* 110 n.
   adversity 731 n.
iceberg *island* 349 n.
   ice 380 n.
   unfeeling person 820 n.
   solitary 883 n.
ice-blink *reflection* 417 n.
ice-box *provisions* 301 n.
   ice 380 n.
   refrigerator 384 n.
ice-cap *ice* 380 n.
ice-chamber *ice* 380 n.
ice-chest *refrigerator* 384 n.
ice-cube *ice* 380 n.
   refrigerator 384 n.
iced *cooled* 382 adj.
   preserved 666 adj.
ice-field *plain* 348 n.
   ice 380 n.
ice-floe *plain* 348 n.
   ice 380 n.
ice over *refrigerate* 382 vb.
ice-pack *refrigerator* 384 n.
ice-plough *ice* 380 n.
ice-rink *arena* 724 n.
ice-sheet *ice* 380 n.
ice-skate *footwear* 228 n.
   sled 274 n.
ice-stream *ice* 380 n.
ice up *refrigerate* 382 vb.
ice-yacht *sled* 274 n.
   ice 380 n.
ichneumon *rodent* 365 n.
ichnography *map* 551 n.
ichor *fluid* 335 n.
   blood 335 n.
ichthyology
   zoology 367 n.
icicle *ice* 380 n.
   unfeeling person 820 n.
icing *sweet* 392 n.
icon *copy* 22 n.
   image 551 n.
   picture 553 n.
   ritual object 988 n.

iconoclasm
   destruction 165 n.
iconoclast *destroyer* 168 n.
   violent creature 176 n.
   evildoer 904 n.
   religionist 979 n.
iconography
   representation 551 n.
iconolatry *cult* 981 n.
   idolatry 982 n.
iconology *theology* 973 n.
icteric *yellow* 433 adj.
icterus *yellowness* 433 n.
ictus *pronunciation* 577 n.
   prosody 593 n.
icy *hard* 326 adj.
   cold 380 adj.
   impassive 820 adj.
   unsociable 883 adj.
id *heredity* 5 n.
   subjectivity 320 n.
   spirit 447 n.
idea *form* 243 n.
   idea 451 n.
   opinion 485 n.
idea'd *imaginative* 513 adj.
ideal *prototype* 23 n.
   ideational 451 adj.
   imaginary 513 adj.
   motive 612 n.
   perfection 646 n.
   desired object 859 n.
idealism
   immateriality 320 n.
   philosophy 449 n.
   fantasy 513 n.
   reformism 654 n.
   fastidiousness 862 n.
   philanthropy 901 n.
   morals 917 n.
   disinterestedness 931 n.
   virtues 933 n.
idealist
   immateriality 320 n.
   visionary 513 n.
   reformer 654 n.
   essayer 671 n.
   perfectionist 862 n.
   kind person 897 n.
   philanthropist 901 n.
   good man 937 n.
idealistic
   impossible 470 adj.
   imaginative 513 adj.
   improving 654 adj.
   (*see* idealism)
ideality *thought* 449 n.
   supposition 512 n.
   ideality 513 n.
idealize *imagine* 513 vb.
   overrate 482 vb.

ideals *conduct* 688 n.
   philanthropy 901 n.
   morals 917 n.
   disinterestedness 931 n.
   virtues 933 n.
ideate *cognize* 447 vb.
   think 449 vb.
   imagine 513 vb.
ideational *ideational* 451 adj.
idée fixe *positiveness* 473 n.
   prejudgment 481 n.
   opiniatry 602 n.
identical *identical* 13 adj.
identification
   identity 13 n.
   assimilation 18 n.
   comparison 462 n.
   identification 547 n.
identification papers
   label 547 n.
identify (*see* identification)
identity *identity* 13 n.
   equivalence 28 n.
   self 80 n.
   authenticity 494 n.
ideogram *letter* 558 n.
   script 586 n.
ideologist
   philanthropist 901 n.
Ides *date* 108 n.
idiocy *unintelligence* 499 n.
   insanity 503 n.
idioglossia
   unintelligibility 517 n.
   language 557 n.
   neology 560 n.
   speech defect 580 n.
idiolalia (*see* idioglossia)
idiom *speciality* 80 n.
   connotation 514 n.
   dialect 560 n.
   phrase 563 n.
   speech 579 n.
idiomatic *apt* 24 adj.
   special 80 adj.
   semantic 514 adj.
   linguistic 557 adj.
   phraseological 563 adj.
   stylistic 566 adj.
   forceful 571 adj.
   plain 573 adj.
   elegant 575 adj.
idiomorphic
   characteristic 5 adj.
idioplasm *organism* 358 n.
idiosyncrasy
   temperament 5 n.
   speciality 80 n.
   unconformity 84 n.
   tendency 179 n.
   style 566 n.

idiot *fool* 501 n.
   madman 504 n.
idiotic (*see* idiocy)
idiotism *phrase* 563 n.
idioverse
   circumstance 8 n.
   whole 52 n.
idle *operate* 173 vb.
   move slowly 278 vb.
   be inattentive 456 vb.
   useless 641 adj.
   unused 674 adj.
   lazy 679 adj.
idleness
   unproductivity 172 n.
   inaction 677 n.
   inactivity 679 n.
   dutilessness 918 n.
idler *slowcoach* 278 n.
   negligence 458 n.
   slacker 598 n.
   avoider 620 n.
   idler 679 n.
idol *image* 551 n.
   exceller 644 n.
   desired object 859 n.
   person of repute 866 n.
   loved one 887 n.
   favourite 890 n.
   good man 937 n.
   god 966 n.
   idol 982 n.
idolater *worshipper* 981 n.
   idolater 982 n.
idolatrous
   approving 923 adj.
   idolatrous 982 adj.
idolatry *love* 887 n.
   praise 923 n.
   religion 973 n.
   cult 981 n.
   idolatry 982 n.
idolization *deification* 982 n.
idolize *love* 887 vb.
   respect 920 vb.
   praise 923 vb.
   idolatrize 982 vb.
idol-maker *sculptor* 556 n.
   idolater 982 n.
idolothyte *idolatry* 982 n.
   idolatrous 982 adj.
idol-worship
   idolatry 982 n.
idoneous *fit* 24 adj.
idyll *description* 590 n.
   poem 593 n.
idyllic *pleasurable* 826 adj.
if *if* 8 adv.
   provided 468 adv.
igloo *dwelling* 192 n.
igneous *fiery* 379 adj.

ignis fatuus
   insubstantial thing 4 n.
   glow 417 n.
   glow-worm 420 n.
   visual fallacy 440 n.
ignite *kindle* 381 vb.
igniter *lighter* 385 n.
ignition *burning* 381 n.
ignoble
   discreditable 867 adj.
   plebeian 869 adj.
   humble 872 adj.
   dishonest 930 adj.
ignominy *disrepute* 867 n.
ignoramus *ignoramus* 493 n.
ignorance *ignorance* 491 n.
   unskilfulness 695 n.
   innocence 935 n.
ignorant *ignorant* 491 adj.
   foolish 499 adj.
   inexpectant 508 adj.
   (*see* ignorance)
ignoratio elenchi
   sophism 477 n.
ignore *be blind* 439 n.
   be inattentive 456 vb.
   disregard 458 vb.
   disbelieve 486 vb.
   reject 607 vb.
   not observe 769 vb.
   make unwelcome 883 vb.
   be rude 885 vb.
   not respect 921 vb.
ignotum per ignotius
   sophism 477 n.
iguana *reptile* 365 n.
ill *evil* 616 n.
   badness 645 n.
   sick 651 adj.
ill-adapted *unapt* 25 adj.
ill-adjusted *inexact* 495 adj.
ill-advised
   ill-timed 138 adj.
   unwise 499 adj.
   inexpedient 643 adj.
   bungled 695 adj.
   rash 857 adj.
   wrong 914 adj.
illapse *be turned to* 147 vb.
   ingress 297 n.
illaqueate *ensnare* 542 vb.
ill-breeding
   ill-breeding 847 n.
   discourtesy 885 n.
ill-conceived *unwise* 499 adj.
ill-conditioned
   bad, harmful 645 adj.
   sullen 893 adj.
   malevolent 898 adj.
ill-conducted
   bungled 695 adj.

ill-considered
   (*see* ill-advised)
ill-defined
   amorphous 244 adj.
   ill-seen 444 adj.
ill-digested
   immature 670 adj.
ill-disciplined
   disobedient 738 adj
ill-disposed
   discontented 829 adj.
   malevolent 898 adj.
ill-done *bungled* 695 adj.
illegal *prohibited* 757 adj.
   unjust 914 adj.
   unwarranted 916 adj.
   dishonest 930 adj.
   illegal 954 adj.
illegality *illegality* 954 n.
illegibility
   unintelligibility 517 n.
illegitimacy
   sonship 170 n.
   wrong 914 n.
   undueness 916 n.
   bastardy 954 n.
   illegality 954 n.
ill fame *disrepute* 867 n.
ill-fated *unfortunate* 731 adj.
ill-favoured *ugly* 842 adj.
ill feeling *dislike* 861 n.
   enmity 881 n.
   hatred 888 n.
ill-formed *unsightly* 842 adj.
ill fortune *ill fortune* 731 n.
ill-furnished
   unprovided 636 adj.
ill-gotten *acquired* 771 adj.
ill-health *weakness* 163 n.
   ill-health 651 n.
ill-humour
   resentment 891 n.
   sullenness 893 n.
illiberal *biased* 481 adj.
   parsimonious 816 adj.
   selfish 932 adj.
illiberality *opiniatry* 602 n.
   (*see* illiberal)
illicit (*see* illegal)
illimitable *infinite* 107 adj.
ill-informed
   uninstructed 491 adj.
   mistaken 495 adj.
ill-intentioned
   malevolent 898 adj.
illiterate
   uninstructed 491 adj.
   ignoramus 493 n.
ill-judged
   indiscriminating 464 adj.
   (*see* ill-advised)

ill-kept *neglected* 458 adj.
ill-mannered
  (*see* ill-breeding)
ill-matched
  disagreeing 25 adj.
  quarrelling 709 adj.
ill-natured
  malevolent 898 adj.
illness *illness* 651 n.
ill-off *poor* 801 adj.
illogic *intuition* 476 n.
  sophistry 477 n.
  folly 499 n.
  misteaching 535 n.
illogical
  unthinking 450 adj.
  illogical 477 adj.
  biased 481 adj.
  erroneous 495 adj.
  unwise 499 adj.
illogicality *irrelevance* 10 n.
  discontinuity 72 n.
  sophism 477 n.
  unmeaningness 515 n.
ill-omened
  inopportune 138 adj.
  cautionary 664 adj.
  unpromising 853 adj.
ill-requited
  unthanked 908 adj.
ill-seeming *wrong* 914 adj.
ill-seen *ill-seen* 444 adj.
ill-spent *wasted* 634 adj.
  profitless 641 adj.
ill-starred
  inopportune 138 adj.
  unfortunate 731 adj.
ill taste *bad taste* 847 n.
ill-tempered *sullen* 893 adj.
ill-timed *ill-timed* 138 adj.
ill-treat *ill-treat* 645 vb.
  misuse 675 vb.
  be severe 735 vb.
ill-treatment *cruel act* 898 n.
illude *deceive* 542 vb.
illuminant *lighter* 385 n.
  luminary 420 n.
illuminate
  make bright 417 vb.
  illuminate 420 vb.
  colour 425 vb.
  interpret 520 vb.
  manifest 522 vb.
  paint 553 vb.
  decorate 844 vb.
illuminati
  intellectual 492 n.
illumination
  progression 285 n.
  light 417 n.
  lighting 420 n.

  discovery 484 n.
  knowledge 490 n.
  ornamental art 844 n.
  revelation 975 n.
illuminations
  fireworks 420 n.
  spectacle 445 n.
  celebration 876 n.
illuminator *artist* 556 n.
illumine *educate* 534 vb.
ill-usage *misuse* 675 n.
  cruel act 898 n.
ill-used *suffering* 825 adj.
illusion
  visual fallacy 440 n.
  appearance 445 n.
  error 495 n.
  deception 542 n.
  sleight 542 n.
illusionism *mimicry* 20 n.
  sorcery 983 n.
illusionist *conjuror* 545 n.
illusory *sophistical* 477 adj.
  imaginary 513 adj.
  deceiving 542 adj.
illustrate (*see* illustration)
illustration *example* 83 n.
  interpretation 520 n.
  representation 551 n.
  picture 553 n.
  edition 589 n.
  ornamental art 844 n.
illustrative *typical* 83 adj.
  expressive 516 adj.
illustrator *artist* 556 n.
illustrious
  renowned 866 adj.
ill-will *discontent* 829 n.
  enmity 881 n.
  hatred 888 n.
  malevolence 898 n.
  envy 912 n.
ill wind *badness* 645 n.
  obstacle 702 n.
  adversity 731 n.
ill-wisher
  trouble-maker 663 n.
  enemy 881 n.
ill wishes
  malediction 899 n.
image *analogue* 18 n.
  copy 22 n.
  reflection 417 n.
  appearance 445 n.
  idea 451 n.
  ideality 513 n.
  metaphor 519 n.
  exhibit 522 n.
  monument 548 n.
  image 551 n.
  sculpture 554 n.

  idol 982 n.
image-building
  imagination 513 n.
imagery *imagination* 513 n.
  metaphor 519 n.
image-worship *cult* 981 n.
  idolatry 982 n.
imaginable *possible* 469 adj.
  supposed 512 adj.
imaginal
  imaginative 513 adj.
imaginary *unreal* 2 adj.
  insubstantial 4 adj.
  supposed 512 adj.
  imaginary 513 adj.
  fairylike 970 adj.
imagination *thought* 449 n.
  idea 451 n.
  imagination 513 n.
imaginative
  unimitative 21 adj.
  imaginative 513 adj.
  false 541 adj.
  descriptive 590 adj.
imagine *suppose* 512 vb.
  imagine 513 vb.
  describe 590 vb.
  hope 852 vb.
imago *vermin* 365 n.
imam *priest* 986 n.
imbalance *inequality* 29 n.
  changeableness 152 n.
  distortion 246 n.
imbecile *weak* 163 adj.
  unintelligent 499 adj.
  foolish 499 adj.
  fool 501 n.
  insane 503 adj.
imbecility (*see* imbecile)
imbibe *absorb* 299 vb.
  drink 301 vb.
  learn 536 vb.
imbrication *covering* 226 n.
imbroglio *medley* 43 n.
  complexity 61 n.
  predicament 700 n.
  dissension 709 n.
imbrue *infuse* 303 vb.
  drench 341 vb.
  colour 425 vb.
imbue *mix* 43 vb.
  pervade 189 vb.
  infuse 303 vb.
  drench 341 vb.
  educate 534 vb.
  habituate 610 vb.
imbued with
  believing 485 adj.
imitable *imitative* 20 adj.
imitate *resemble* 18 vb.
  liken 18 vb.

imitate 20 vb.
fake 541 vb.
represent 551 vb.
imitated *false* 541 adj.
imitation *imitation* 20 n.
substituted 150 adj.
sham 542 n.
representation 551 n.
bad taste 847 n.
imitative *simulating* 18 adj.
imitative 20 adj.
conformable 83 adj.
repeated 106 adj.
mindless 448 adj.
unthinking 450 adj.
imitativeness *mimicry* 20 n.
immaculate *perfect* 646 adj.
clean 648 adj.
honourable 929 adj.
innocent 935 adj.
pure 950 adj.
immanence
intrinsicality 5 n.
divine attribute 965 n.
immaterial
insubstantial 4 adj.
immateriality
insubstantiality 4 n.
immateriality 320 n.
rarity 325 n.
unimportance 639 n.
spiritualism 984 n.
immature *beginning* 68 adj.
early 135 adj.
unhabituated 611 adj.
immaturity
incompleteness 55 n.
newness 126 n.
youth, nonage 130 n.
unintelligence 499 n.
imperfection 647 n.
non-preparation 670 n.
unskilfulness 695 n.
non-completion 726 n.
immeasurable
infinite 107 adj.
immediacy *continuity* 71 n.
instantaneity 116 n.
haste 680 n.
immediate
instantaneous 116 n.
early 135 adj.
impending 155 adj.
immedicable
unpromising 853 adj.
immemorial
perpetual 115 adj.
former 125 adj.
immemorial 127 adj.
permanent 144 adj.
worshipful 866 adj.

immemorial usage
tradition 127 n.
immense *infinite* 107 adj.
immensity *greatness* 32 n.
hugeness 195 n.
immeritorious
bad 645 adj.
immersed *deep* 211 adj.
immersion *ingress* 297 n.
immersion 303 n.
plunge 313 n.
moistening 341 n.
Christian rite 988 n.
immigrant *foreigner* 59 n.
settler 191 n.
wanderer 268 n.
incomer 297 n.
immigration
wandering 267 n.
ingress 297 n.
imminent *future* 124 adj.
early 135 adj.
impending 155 adj.
approaching 289 adj.
immiscibility
disjunction 46 vb.
non-coherence 49 n.
immission *reception* 299 n.
immitigable
unpromising 853 adj.
immixture *mixture* 43 n.
immobility
permanence 144 n.
stability 153 n.
inertness 175 n.
quiescence 266 n.
inaction 677 n.
immoderate *violent* 176 adj.
inelegant 576 adj.
immoderately
extremely 32 adv.
immoderation
greatness 32 n.
exaggeration 546 n.
intemperance 943 n.
immodest
undisguised 522 adj.
immodesty *vanity* 873 n.
impurity 951 n.
immolation *killing* 362 n.
oblation 981 n.
immoral *dishonest* 930 adj.
immoralism *impiety* 980 n.
immoralist *wrong* 914 n.
bad man 938 n.
libertine 952 n.
impious person 980 n.
immorality *wrong* 914 n.
wickedness 934 n.
unchastity 951 n.
immortal *existing* 1 n.

perpetual 115 adj.
intellectual 492 n.
soldier 722 n.
renowned 866 adj.
godlike 965 adj.
immortality
perpetuity 115 n.
famousness 866 n.
immortalize
perpetuate 115 vb.
honour 866 vb.
immortals
armed force 722 n.
god 966 n.
immovable *firm-set* 45 adj.
fixed 153 adj.
still 266 adj.
resolute 599 adj.
obstinate 602 adj.
immovables *property* 777 n.
immundity
uncleanness 649 n.
immunity *hygiene* 652 n.
safety 660 n.
escape 667 n.
freedom 744 n.
dueness 915 n.
non-liability 919 n.
immunization
hygiene 652 n.
prophylactic 658 n.
protection 660 n.
immure
circumscribe 232 vb.
inclose 235 n.
imprison 747 vb.
immutability
permanence 144 n.
stability 153 n.
divine attribute 965 n.
immutable
perpetual 115 adj.
antiquated 127 adj.
imp *child* 132 n.
implant 303 vb.
cultivate 370 vb.
devil 969 n.
elf, demon 970 n.
sorcerer 983 n.
impact *affix, tighten* 45 vb.
influence 178 n.
collision 279 n.
insert, implant 303 vb.
excitation 821 n.
impaction (*see* impact)
impair *derange* 63 vb.
disable 161 vb.
weaken 163 vb.
waste 634 vb.
make useless 641 vb.
harm 645 vb.

impair 655 vb.
misuse 675 vb.
hinder 702 vb.
blemish 845 vb.
impairment
incompleteness 55 n.
impairment 655 n.
impale *kill* 362 vb.
pierce 263 vb.
mark 547 vb.
execute 963 vb.
impaling *heraldry* 547 n.
impalpable *minute* 196 adj.
impanation
the sacrament 988 n.
imparity *inequality* 29 n.
impart *inform* 524 vb.
give 781 vb.
impartial *wise* 498 adj.
neutral 625 adj.
impartiality *equality* 28 n.
moderation 177 n.
no choice 606 n.
indifference 860 n.
justice 913 n.
probity 929 n.
disinterestedness 931 n.
impassable *closed* 264 adj.
impracticable 470 adj.
impasse *closure* 264 n.
impossibility 470 n.
difficulty 700 n.
obstacle 702 n.
impassibility
insensibility 375 n.
moral insensibility 820 n.
inexcitability 823 n.
impassion *excite* 821 vb.
impassioned
forceful 571 adj.
fervent 818 adj.
lively 819 adj.
excited 821 adj.
impassive *inert* 175 adj.
unfeeling 375 adj.
incurious 454 adj.
inattentive 456 adj.
indiscriminating 464 adj.
non-active 677 adj.
inactive 679 adj.
impassive 820 adj.
inexcitable 823 adj.
indifferent 860 adj.
unastonished 865 adj.
impasto *facing* 226 n.
art style 553 n.
impatience
willingness 597 n.
haste 680 n.
warm feeling 818 n.
excitability 822 n.

rashness 857 n.
desire 859 n.
rudeness 885 n.
resentment 891 n.
irascibility 892 n.
impatient *unwise* 499 adj.
sensitive 819 adj.
impeachment
censure 924 n.
detraction 926 n.
accusation 928 n.
litigation 959 n.
impeccable *perfect* 646 adj.
virtuous 933 adj.
innocent 935 adj.
impeccancy *perfection* 646 n.
impecunious *poor* 801 adj.
impede *hinder* 702 vb.
impediment
speech defect 580 n.
difficulty 700 n.
obstacle 702 n.
hindrance 702 n.
impedimenta *box* 194 n.
thing transferred 272 n.
encumbrance 702 n.
property 777 n.
impel *move* 265 vb.
impel 279 vb.
propel 287 vb.
insert 303 vb.
motivate 612 vb.
impelling *causal* 156 adj.
impend *be to come* 124 vb.
impend 155 vb.
await 507 vb.
frighten 854 vb.
threaten 900 vb.
impending *early* 135 adj.
approaching 289 adj.
arriving 295 adj.
impenetrable
closed 264 adj.
dense 324 adj.
latent 523 adj.
unintelligent 499 adj.
unintelligible 517 adj.
difficult 700 adj.
thick-skinned 820 adj.
impenitence
obstinacy 602 n.
impenitence 940 n.
imperative
necessary 596 adj.
demanding 627 adj.
authoritarian 735 adj.
commanding 737 adj.
compelling 740 adj.
obligatory 917 adj.
imperator *sovereign* 741 n.
army officer 741 n.

imperceptible
minute 196 adj.
slow 278 adj.
invisible 444 adj.
imperception
moral insensibility 820 n.
imperceptive
insensible 375 adj.
indiscriminating 464 adj.
impercipient
insensible 375 adj.
unintelligent 499 adj.
imperfect
fragmentary 53 adj.
preterite 125 adj.
immature 670 adj.
uncompleted 726 adj.
imperfection
inferiority 35 n.
incompleteness 55 n.
shortcoming 307 n.
badness 645 n.
imperfection 647 n.
vulnerability 661 n.
artlessness 699 n.
blemish 845 n.
vice 934 n.
imperfect tense
course of time 111 n.
imperforate *closed* 264 adj.
imperial *great* 32 adj.
box 194 n.
hair 259 n.
ruling 733 adj.
imperialism *nation* 371 n.
governance 733 n.
imperil *endanger* 661 vb.
imperious
authoritative 733 adj.
proud 871 adj.
insolent 878 adj.
imperishable
perpetual 115 adj.
unchangeable 153 adj.
renowned 866 adj.
imperium *superiority* 34 n.
government 733 n.
impermanence
transientness 114 n.
changeableness 152 n.
impermeable *closed* 264 adj.
dense 324 adj.
screened 421 adj.
impermissible
illegal 954 adj.
impersonal *general* 79 adj.
unfeeling 375 adj.
impassive 820 adj.
indifferent 860 adj.
unsociable 883 adj.
just 913 adj.

disinterested 931 adj.
impersonation
  representation 551 n.
impersonator
  imitator 20 n.
imperspicuity
  unintelligibility 517 n.
  imperspicuity 568 n.
impersuasible wilful 602 adj.
impertinence
  irrelevance 10 n.
  sauciness 878 n.
  rudeness 885 n.
impertinent
  insolent person 878 n.
imperturbability
  inexcitability 823 n.
  non-wonder 865 n.
imperturbation
  moral insensibility 820 n.
impervious closed 264 adj.
  dense 324 adj.
  screened 421 adj.
  opaque 423 adj.
  impracticable 470 adj.
  unbelieving 486 adj.
  unintelligent 499 adj.
  obstinate 602 adj.
  thick-skinned 820 adj.
impetiginous
  unclean 649 adj.
impetrate entreat 761 vb.
impetuosity
  vigorousness 174 n.
  violence 176 n.
  haste 680 n.
  excitability 822 n.
  rashness 857 n.
  desire 859 n.
impetus spurt 277 n.
  impulse 279 n.
impiety irreligion 974 n.
  impiety 980 n.
impignorate
  give security 767 vb.
impinge collide 279 vb.
  encroach 306 vb.
  touch 378 vb.
impious wicked 934 adj.
  irreligious 974 adj.
  impious 980 adj.
impish harmful 645 adj.
  fairylike 970 adj.
implacable resolute 599 adj.
  obstinate 602 adj.
  quarrelling 709 adj.
  hating 888 adj.
  malevolent 898 adj.
  pitiless 906 adj.
  revengeful 910 adj.
implant affix 45 vb.

implant 303 vb.
  educate 534 vb.
  habituate 610 vb.
implausibility
  unbelief 486 n.
implausible
  improbable 472 adj.
  erroneous 495 adj.
implead litigate 959 vb.
  (see indict)
implement produce 164 vb.
  instrument 628 n.
  tool 630 n.
  do 676 vb.
  carry out 725 vb.
implex mixed 43 n.
implicate accuse 928 vb.
implicated
  ingredient 58 adj.
implication relation 9 n.
  complexity 61 n.
  meaning 514 n.
  latency 523 n.
implicit intrinsic 5 adj.
  meaningful 514 adj.
  tacit 523 adj.
implore entreat 761 vb.
imply be intrinsic 5 vb.
  contain 56 vb.
  accompany 89 vb.
  conduce 156 vb.
  evidence 466 vb.
  make likely 471 vb.
  mean 514 vb.
  imply 523 vb.
  hint 524 vb.
  indicate 547 vb.
impolicy bungling 695 n.
impolite inelegant 576 adj.
  ill-bred 847 adj.
  impertinent 878 adj.
  discourteous 885 adj.
  disrespectful 921 adj.
impolitic
  inexpedient 643 adj.
  unskilful 695 adj.
imponderability
  insubstantiality 4 n.
  immateriality 320 n.
  levity 323 n.
imporous closed 264 adj.
  dense 324 adj.
import relation 9 n.
  add 38 vb.
  transference 272 n.
  ingress 297 n.
  admit 299 vb.
  insert 303 vb.
  meaning 514 n.
  provide 633 vb.
  importance 638 n.

importance greatness 32 n.
  superiority 34 n.
  influence 178 n.
  materiality 319 n.
  importance 638 n.
  prestige 866 n.
important crucial 137 adj.
  fundamental 156 adj.
importation (see import)
imported extraneous 59 adj.
  incoming 297 n.
  neological 560 adj.
importer carrier 273 n.
  transferrer 272 n.
  merchant 794 n.
importunate, importunity
  (see importune)
importune request 761 vb.
  torment 827 n.
impose add 38 vb.
  place 187 vb.
  deceive 542 vb.
  print 587 vb.
  command 737 vb.
  compel 740 vb.
  command respect 920 vb.
  punish 936 vb.
imposing
  impressive 821 adj.
  worshipful 866 adj.
imposition
  requirement 627 n.
  bane 659 n.
  demand 737 n.
  tax 809 n.
  injustice 914 n.
  undueness 916 n.
  penalty 963 n.
impossible excluded 57 adj.
  unthought 450 adj.
  impossible 470 adj.
  difficult 700 adj.
  intolerable 827 adj.
  wonderful 864 adj.
impost tax 809 n.
imposthume ulcer 651 n.
impostor imitator 20 n.
  impostor 545 n.
  bungler 697 n.
  boaster 877 n.
  knave 938 n.
imposture duplicity 541 n.
  deception 542 n.
  cunning 698 n.
impotence impotence 161 n.
  weakness 163 n.
  unproductivity 172 n.
  inutility 641 n.
  failure 728 n.
impotent
  unimportant 639 adj.

non-active 677 adj.
impound *imprison* 747 vb.
impoverish *weaken* 163 vb.
   waste 634 vb.
   make insufficient 636 vb.
   fleece 786 vb.
   impoverish 801 vb.
impoverishment
   deterioration 655 n.
   poverty 801 n.
impracticable
   impracticable 470 adj.
   useless 641 adj.
   difficult 700 adj.
   unpromising 853 adj.
impractical *irrelevant* 10 adj.
   misjudging 481 adj.
   imaginative 513 adj.
imprecation *entreaty* 761 n.
   malediction 899 n.
   prayers 981 n.
imprecision *generality* 79 n.
   inexactness 495 n.
   imperspicuity 568 n.
impregnable
   unyielding 162 adj.
   invulnerable 660 adj.
   pure 950 adj.
impregnate *mix* 43 vb.
   combine 50 vb.
   generate 164 vb.
   make fruitful 171 vb.
   be present 189 vb.
   infuse 303 vb.
   educate 534 vb.
impresario
   stage manager 594 n.
imprescriptible
   due 915 adj.
impress *effect* 157 n.
   be vigorous 174 vb.
   motivate 612 vb.
   take away 786 vb.
   steal 788 vb.
   impress 821 vb.
   delight 826 vb.
   be wonderful 864 vb.
   command respect 920 vb.
   (*see* impression,
      impress on)
impressibility
   liability 180 n.
   softness 327 n.
   irresolution 601 n.
   persuasibility 612 n.
   moral sensibility 819 n.
impression *copy* 22 n.
   influence 178 n.
   concavity 255 n.
   sense 374 n.
   spectacle 445 n.

appearance 445 n.
   idea 451 n.
   intuition 476 n.
   opinion 485 n.
   knowledge 490 n.
   indication 547 n.
   label 547 n.
   printing 555 n.
   letterpress 587 n.
   feeling 818 n.
   excitation 821 n.
impressionable
   converted 147 adj.
   unstable 152 adj.
   sentient 374 adj.
   receiving 782 adj.
   impressible 819 adj.
   excitable 822 adj.
Impressionism
   school of painting 553 n.
Impressionist *artist* 556 n.
impressionistic
   descriptive 590 adj.
impressive *great* 32 adj.
   credible 485 adj.
   forceful 571 adj.
   descriptive 590 adj.
   notable 638 adj.
   felt 818 adj.
   impressive 821 adj.
   (*see* impression)
impressiveness
   spectacle 445 n.
   prestige 866 n.
   ostentation 875 n.
impressment
   compulsion 740 n.
impress on
   cause thought 449 vb.
   emphasize 532 vb.
   mark 547 vb.
   engrave 555 vb.
imprest *lending* 784 n.
imprimatur *assent* 488 n.
   permit 756 n.
   orthodoxism 976 n.
imprimis *initially* 68 adv.
imprint
   make conform 83 vb.
   concavity 255 n.
   identification 547 n.
   label 547 n.
   letterpress 587 n.
imprison *enclose* 224 vb.
   circumscribe 232 vb.
   close 264 vb.
   imprison 747 vb.
   retain 778 vb.
   punish 963 vb.
imprisoned
   imprisoned 747 adj.

captive 750 adj.
imprisonment
   detention 747 n.
   penalty 963 n.
improbability
   improbability 472 n.
   unbelief 486 n.
   inexpectation 508 n.
improbable
   erroneous 495 adj.
   wonderful 864 adj.
improbation
   disapprobation 924 n.
improbity
   thievishness 788 n.
   wrong 914 n.
   improbity 930 n.
   wickedness 934 n.
   lawbreaking 954 n.
impromptu
   instantaneously 116 adv.
   musical piece 412 n.
   spontaneity 609 n.
   non-preparation 670 n.
improper *unapt* 25 adj.
   unwise 499 adj.
   ungrammatical 565 adj.
   inexpedient 643 adj.
   not nice 645 adj.
   vulgar 847 adj.
   disreputable 867 adj.
   discreditable 867 adj.
   wrong 914 adj.
   undue 916 adj.
   vicious 934 adj.
impropriate *possess* 773 vb.
   convey 780 vb.
   appropriate 786 vb.
impropriator
   beneficiary 776 n.
impropriety
   inaptitude 25 n.
   solecism 565 n.
   inelegance 576 n.
   inexpedience 643 n.
   bad taste 847 n.
   wrong 914 n.
   undueness 916 n.
   vice 934 n.
   guilty act 936 n.
improve *modify* 143 vb.
   beautify 841 vb.
   philanthropize 897 vb.
   (*see* improvement)
improvement *increase* 36 n.
   progression 285 n.
   benefit 615 n.
   improvement 654 n.
improve on
   be superior 34 vb.
improver *reformer* 654 n.

improve the occasion
  profit by 137 vb.
improvidence
  non-preparation 670 n.
  rashness 857 n.
improvident
  prodigal 815 adj.
improvisation
  spontaneity 609 n.
  contrivance 623 n.
  non-preparation 670 n.
improvise
  compose music 413 vb.
  make ready 699 vb.
imprudence *rashness* 857 n.
impudent
  impertinent 878 adj.
  discourteous 885 adj.
impudicity *impurity* 951 n.
impugn *cause doubt* 486 vb.
  disbelieve 486 vb.
  negate 533 vb.
impulse *energy* 160 n.
  influence 178 n.
  impulse 279 n.
  intuition 476 n.
  necessity 596 n.
  spontaneity 609 n.
  motive 612 n.
  feeling 818 n.
  desire 859 n.
impulsion *causation* 156 n.
  propulsion 287 n.
  motive 612 n.
impulsive *intuitive* 476 adj.
  involuntary 596 adj.
  spontaneous 609 adj.
  excitable 822 adj.
impunity *escape* 667 n.
  non-liability 919 n.
  acquittal 960 n.
impurity *uncleanness* 649 n.
  bad taste 847 n.
  libido 859 n.
  wickedness 934 n.
  sensualism 944 n.
  impurity 951 n.
imputation
  attribution 158 n.
  slur 867 n.
  accusation 928 n.
in *inside* 224 adv.
inability *impotence* 161 n.
  inutility 641 n.
  unskilfulness 695 n.
  hindrance 702 n.
inabstinence
  intemperance 943 n.
inaccessible
  removed 199 adj.
  impracticable 470 adj.

inaccuracy *negligence* 458 n.
  indiscrimination 464 n.
  inexactness 495 n.
  imperspicuity 568 n.
inaction *inertness* 175 n.
  avoidance 620 n.
  non-use 674 n.
  inaction 677 n.
  inactivity 679 n.
inactive *powerless* 161 adj.
  insensible 375 adj.
  apathetic 820 adj.
inactivity *delay* 136 n.
  weakness 163 n.
  unproductivity 172 n.
  inertness 175 n.
  quiescence 266 n.
  negligence 458 n.
  non-use 674 n.
  inaction 677 n.
  inactivity 679 n.
  leisure 681 n.
  non-observance 769 n.
  inexcitability 823 n.
inadequacy *inequality* 29 n.
  weakness 163 n.
  insufficiency 636 n.
  inutility 641 n.
  imperfection 647 n.
inadequate
  powerless 161 adj.
  deficient 307 adj.
  unskilful 695 adj.
inadjustable
  unconformable 84 adj.
inadmissible *unapt* 25 adj.
  excluded 57 adj.
  extraneous 59 adj.
  inexpedient 643 adj.
  refused 760 adj.
  wrong 914 adj.
in advance *before* 64 adj.
inadvertence
  inattention 456 n.
  mistake 495 n.
inadvisability
  inexpedience 643 n.
inalienable
  retained 778 adj.
  due 915 adj.
in all *completely* 54 adv.
inamorata *woman* 373 n.
  loved one 887 n.
in and out
  to and fro 317 adv.
in and out system
  periodicity 141 n.
inane (see *inanity*)
inanimate
  inorganic 359 adj.
  dead 361 adj.

mindless 448 adj.
  unthinking 450 adj.
  inactive 679 adj.
inanition *helplessness* 161 n.
  weakness 163 n.
  illness 651 n.
inanity
  insubstantiality 4 n.
  insubstantial thing 4 n.
  emptiness 190 n.
  incogitance 450 n.
  unmeaningness 515 n.
  inutility 641 n.
inappeasable *greedy* 859 adj.
inappetency
  indifference 860 n.
inapplicability
  irrelevance 10 n.
  inaptitude 25 n.
  inutility 641 n.
inapposite
  irrelevant 10 adj.
inappreciable
  inconsiderable 33 adj.
  minute 196 adj.
  unimportant 639 adj.
inappreciation
  ignorance 491 n.
inapprehensible
  unintelligible 517 adj.
inappropriate
  irrelevant 10 adj.
  unapt 25 adj.
  misplaced 188 adj.
  inexpedient 643 adj.
  undue 916 adj.
inaptitude *inaptitude* 25 n.
  inutility 641 n.
  inexpedience 643 n.
inarticulate
  voiceless 578 adj.
  stammering 580 adj.
  taciturn 582 adj.
  artless 699 adj.
  modest 874 adj.
inarticulation *aphony* 578 n.
inartistic *bungled* 695 adj.
  artless 699 adj.
  graceless 842 adj.
inattention
  blindness 439 n.
  inattention 456 n.
  bungling 695 n.
  non-observance 769 n.
  rashness 857 n.
inattentive
  unthinking 450 adj.
  negligent 458 adj.
  inexpectant 508 adj.
  hasty 680 adj.
inaudibility *silence* 399 n.

faintness 401 n.
deafness 416 n.
unintelligibility 517 n.
inaudible *voiceless* 578 adj.
inaugural *precursory* 66 adj.
beginning 68 adj.
inaugurate
auspicate 68 vb.
cause 156 vb.
celebrate 876 vb.
inauguration *début* 68 n.
fitting out 669 n.
mandate 751 n.
celebration 876 n.
inauspicious
inopportune 138 adj.
evil 616 adj.
adverse 731 adj.
unpromising 853 adj.
inbeing *intrinsicality* 5 n.
inboard *interior* 224 adj.
inborn *genetic* 5 adj.
with affections 817 adj.
inbred *extrinsic* 6 adj.
ethnic 11 adj.
combined 50 adj.
with affections 817 adj.
inbreeding *race* 11 n.
in bulk *collectively* 52 adv.
incalculable
multitudinous 104 adj.
infinite 107 adj.
casual 159 adj.
incalescence *heat* 379 n.
incandescence *heat* 379 n.
light, glow 417 n.
incandescent
luminescent 420 adj.
incantation *sorcery* 983 n.
incapable *unapt* 25 adj.
powerless 161 adj.
incapacious *narrow* 206 adj.
incapacitate
disable 161 vb.
incapacity *inaptitude* 25 n.
impotence 161 n.
ignorance 491 n.
unintelligence 499 n.
unskilfulness 695 n.
incapsulate *comprise* 78 vb.
cover 226 vb.
insert 303 vb.
incapsulation *inclusion* 78 n.
incarceration
detention 747 n.
incarnadine *redden* 431 vb.
incarnate *genetic* 5 adj.
alive 360 adj.
manifest 522 vb.
incarnation
essential part 5 n.

combination 50 n.
materiality 319 n.
representation 551 n.
theophany 965 n.
revelation 975 n.
incasement
requirement 627 n.
provision 633 n.
incautious *unwise* 499 adj.
spontaneous 609 adj.
rash 857 adj.
incendiary
destructive 165 adj.
violent creature 176 n.
violent 176 adj.
incendiarism 381 n.
motivator 612 n.
opponent 705 n.
evildoer 904 n.
incense *fumigator* 385 n.
smell 394 vb.
inodorousness 395 n.
scent 396 n.
prophylactic 658 n.
honours 866 n.
excite hate 888 vb.
enrage 891 vb.
flattery 925 n.
oblation 981 n.
ritual object 988 n.
incense-breathing
fragrant 396 adj.
flattering 925 adj.
incensed *angry* 891 adj.
incentive *impulse* 279 n.
incentive 612 n.
excitant 821 n.
reward 962 n.
inceptive
beginning 68 adj.
causal 156 adj.
incessant *continuous* 71 adj.
repeated 106 adj.
perpetual 115 adj.
frequent 139 adj.
unceasing 146 adj.
active 678 adj.
incest *illicit love* 951 n.
inch *small quantity* 33 n.
short distance 200 n.
long measure 203 n.
shortness 204 n.
move slowly 278 vb.
inch by inch
by degrees 27 adv.
piecemeal 53 adv.
gradatim 278 adv.
inchoate *beginning* 68 adj.
amorphous 244 adj.
uncompleted 726 adj.
incidence *eventuality* 154 n.

incident
circumstantial 8 adj.
eventuality 154 n.
liable 180 adj.
incidental *extrinsic* 6 adj.
irrelevance 10 n.
accompanying 89 adj.
eventuality 154 n.
happening 154 adj.
casual 159 adj.
liable 180 adj.
incidentally
incidentally 137 adv.
at random 618 adv.
incineration
destruction 165 n.
interment 364 n.
burning 381 n.
incinerator *furnace* 383 n.
incipient *beginning* 68 adj.
incircumspection
rashness 857 n.
incise *cut* 46 vb.
groove 262 vb.
record 548 vb.
engrave 555 vb.
wound 655 vb.
incision *scission* 46 n.
furrow 262 n.
wound 655 n.
incisive *keen* 174 adj.
assertive 532 adj.
forceful 571 adj.
incisor *tooth* 256 n.
incite *cause* 156 vb.
make violent 176 vb.
influence 178 vb.
impel 279 vb.
incite 612 vb.
advise 691 vb.
make quarrels 709 vb.
excite 821 vb.
incivility *ill-breeding* 847 n.
sauciness 878 n.
discourtesy 885 n.
incivism
misanthropy 902 n.
inclemency *storm* 176 n.
wintriness 380 n.
severity 735 n.
pitilessness 906 n.
inclination *tendency* 179 n.
obliquity 220 n.
will 595 n.
willingness 597 n.
choice 605 n.
liking 859 n.
love 887 n.
incline *tend* 179 vb.
acclivity 220 n.
render oblique 220 vb.

make curved 248 vb.
choose 605 vb.
motivate 612 vb.
cause desire 859 vb.
inclined plane
obliquity 220 n.
tool 630 n.
inclose *surround* 230 vb.
inclose 235 vb.
obstruct 702 vb.
besiege 712 vb.
imprison 747 vb.
retain 778 vb.
inclosure *frame* 218 n.
circumscription 232 n.
include *add* 38 vb.
join 45 vb.
contain 56 vb.
comprise 78 vb.
possess 773 vb.
including *in addition* 38 adv.
including 78 adv.
inclusion *inclusion* 78 n.
reception 299 n.
association 706 n.
participation 775 n.
inclusiveness *whole* 52 n.
inclusion 78 n.
generality 79 n.
incogitance
non-intellect 448 n.
incogitance 450 n.
inattention 456 n.
incognito
unknown 491 adj.
disguised 525 adj.
anonymous 562 adj.
incognizable
unknown 491 adj.
unintelligible 517 adj.
incognizance
ignorance 491 n.
incoherence
non-coherence 49 n.
discontinuity 72 n.
frenzy 503 n.
unmeaningness 515 n.
unintelligibility 517 n.
incoherent *orderless* 61 adj.
in column
continuously 71 adv.
incombustibility
incombustibility 382 n.
income *means* 629 n.
earnings 771 n.
estate 777 n.
receipt 807 n.
reward 962 n.
incomer *incomer* 297 n.
income tax *tax* 809 n.
incoming *sequent* 65 adj.

incoming 297 adj.
incommensurable
correlative 10 adj.
disagreeing 25 adj.
numerical 85 adj.
incommode
give pain 377 vb.
be inexpedient 643 vb.
be difficult 700 vb.
hinder 702 vb.
incommode 827 vb.
incommunicable
inexpressible 517 adj.
retained 778 adj.
incommunicado
concealed 525 adj.
imprisoned 747 adj.
incommunicative
reticent 525 adj.
taciturn 582 adj.
cautious 858 adj.
incommutable
unchangeable 153 adj.
in company *plural* 101 adj.
incomparability
dissimilarity 19 n.
incomparable
unimitated 21 adj.
supreme 34 adj.
incompatibility
difference 15 n.
disagreement 25 n.
enmity 881 n.
incompetence
inaptitude 25 n.
impotence 161 n.
unintelligence 499 n.
insufficiency 636 n.
unskilfulness 695 n.
dutilessness 918 n.
illegality 954 n.
incompetent *fool* 501 n.
useless 641 adj.
unentitled 916 adj.
incomplete
incomplete 55 adj.
deficient 307 adj.
insufficient 636 adj.
imperfect 647 adj.
uncompleted 726 adj.
incompletely *partly* 53 adv.
incompletion
imperfection 647 n.
incomprehensible
infinite 107 adj.
unintelligible 517 adj.
incomprehension
ignorance 491 n.
incompressible
dense 324 adj.
rigid 326 adj.

inconceivable
unthought 450 adj.
impossible 470 adj.
improbable 472 adj.
unbelieved 486 adj.
unintelligible 517 adj.
wonderful 864 adj.
inconcinnity
inaptitude 25 n.
inelegance 576 n.
ugliness 842 n.
inconclusive
ill-reasoned 477 adj.
incongruent
irrelative 10 adj.
different 15 adj.
dissimilar 19 adj.
unequal 29 adj.
incongruity *misfit* 25 n.
(*see* incongruous)
incongruous
different 15 adj.
disagreeing 25 adj.
unconformable 84 adj.
illogical 477 adj.
ungrammatical 565 adj.
inconnection
irrelation 10 n.
inconsequence
irrelevance 10 n.
absurdity 497 n.
unimportance 639 n.
inconsequential
irrelevant 10 adj.
illogical 477 adj.
unimportant 639 adj.
inconsiderable
inconsiderable 33 adj.
unimportant 639 adj.
inconsiderate
unthinking 450 adj.
inattentive 456 adj.
rash 857 adj.
discourteous 885 adj.
inconsideration
inattention 456 n.
spontaneity 609 n.
rashness 857 n.
inconsistency
unconformity 84 n.
changeableness 152 n.
(*see* inconsistent)
inconsistent
contrary 14 adj.
disagreeing 25 adj.
illogical 477 adj.
absurd 497 adj.
unwise 499 adj.
capricious 604 adj.
inconsolable
regretting 830 adj.

hopeless 853 adj.
inconsonant
   disagreeing 25 adj.
inconspicuous
   ill-seen 444 adj.
   unknown 491 adj.
inconstancy
   (*see* inconstant)
inconstant
   non-uniform 17 adj.
   fitful 142 adj.
   changeful 152 adj.
   light-minded 456 adj.
   irresolute 601 adj.
   capricious 604 adj.
   perfidious 930 adj.
incontestable
   strong 162 adj.
   undisputed 473 adj.
incontinence
   helplessness 161 n.
   intemperance 943 n.
   sensualism 944 n.
   unchastity 951 n.
incontinent
   impotent 161 adj.
   intemperate 943 adj.
   sensual 944 adj.
   unchaste 951 adj.
incontinently
   suddenly 135 adv.
   intemperately 943 adv.
incontrovertible
   vested 153 adj.
   undisputed 473 adj.
   demonstrated 478 adj.
inconvenience
   inutility 641 n.
   inexpedience 643 n.
   difficulty 700 n.
   hinder 702 vb.
   obstacle 702 n.
   suffering 825 n.
inconvenient
   ill-timed 138 adj.
   painful 377 adj.
inconversable
   taciturn 582 adj.
   unsociable 883 adj.
inconvertible
   unceasing 146 adj.
   unchangeable 153 adj.
inconvincible
   unbelieving 486 adj.
incoordination
   disorder 61 n.
incorporal
   immaterial 320 adj.
incorporate *join* 45 vb.
   combine 50 vb.
   comprise 78 vb.

absorb 299 vb.
   material 319 adj.
   manifest 522 vb.
   corporate 708 adj.
incorporation
   (*see* incorporate)
incorporeality
   insubstantiality 4 n.
   immateriality 320 n.
   rarity 325 n.
incorrect *illogical* 477 adj.
   inexact 495 adj.
   inelegant 576 adj.
   wrong 914 adj.
incorrectness
   ill-breeding 847 n.
incorrigibility
   obstinacy 602 n.
   impenitence 940 n.
incorrigible
   obstinate 602 adj.
   unpromising 853 adj.
   wicked 934 adj.
   impenitent 940 adj.
incorrupt
   honourable 929 adj.
   innocent 935 adj.
incorruptibility
   health 650 n.
   probity 929 n.
   innocence 935 n.
incorruptible
   perpetual 115 adj.
   honourable 929 adj.
   pure 950 adj.
incorruption
   perpetuity 115 n.
   goodness 644 n.
   health 650 n.
   innocence 935 n.
incrassation
   condensation 324 n.
   thickening 354 n.
increase *increase* 36 n.
   growth 157 n.
   product 164 n.
   propagation 164 n.
   expand 197 vb.
   improvement 654 n.
   gain 771 n.
   aggravation 832 n.
increate *existing* 1 adj.
incredible
   prodigious 32 adj.
   unusual 84 adj.
   impossible 470 adj.
   improbable 472 adj.
   unbelieved 486 adj.
   wonderful 864 adj.
incredulity *unbelief* 486 n.
increment *increment* 36 n.

addition 38 n.
   adjunct 40 n.
   expansion 197 n.
   benefit 615 n.
   gain 771 n.
increpation
   reprimand 924 n.
incriminate *blame* 924 vb.
   accuse 928 vb.
incrust *coat* 226 vb.
   line 227 vb.
incubate *generate* 164 vb.
   breed stock 369 vb.
   mature 669 vb.
incubator *seedbed* 156 n.
incubus *gravity* 322 n.
   encumbrance 702 n.
   suffering 825 n.
   demon 970 n.
inculcate *educate* 534 vb.
inculpability
   innocence 935 n.
inculpation *censure* 924 n.
   accusation 928 n.
incumbency *job* 622 n.
   benefice 985 n.
   church office 985 n.
incumbent *resident* 191 n.
   overhanging 209 adj.
   weighty 322 adj.
   possessor 776 n.
   beneficiary 776 n.
   obligatory 917 adj.
   cleric 986 n.
incunabula *origin* 68 n.
   youth 130 n.
   edition 589 n.
incur *meet with* 154 vb.
   be liable 180 vb.
   acquire 771 vb.
incurable
   characteristic 5 adj.
   deadly 362 adj.
   impracticable 470 adj.
   obstinate 602 adj.
   bad 645 adj.
   sick 651 adj.
   unpromising 853 adj.
incuriosity
   incuriosity 454 n.
   inattention 456 n.
   moral insensibility 820 n.
   indifference 860 n.
incursion *ingress* 297 n.
   attack 712 n.
incurvation
   curvature 248 n.
   concavity 255 n.
incus *ear* 415 n.
indebtedness *debt* 803 n.
   gratitude 907 n.

dueness 915n.
indecent *not nice* 645adj.
  vulgar 847adj.
  disreputable 867adj.
  vicious 934adj.
  impure 951adj.
indecent assault *rape* 951n.
indeciduous
  unchangeable 153adj.
indecision *dubiety* 474n.
  irresolution 601n.
  no choice 606n.
indecisive
  uncertain 474adj.
  irresolute 601adj.
indeclinable
  unchangeable 153adj.
indecorum
  ill-breeding 847n.
  vice 934n.
indeed *positively* 32adv.
indefatigability
  perseverance 600n.
  stamina 600n.
  assiduity 678n.
  restlessness 678n.
in default of
  instead 150adv.
  without 190adv.
indefeasible
  vested 153adj.
  undisputed 473adj.
indefectible *perfect* 646adj.
indefensible
  defenceless 161adj.
  accusable 928adj.
  heinous 934adj.
indefinable
  unspeakable 32adj.
  inexpressible 517adj.
indefinite *general* 79adj.
  infinite 107adj.
  ill-seen 444adj.
  imperspicuous 568adj.
indefiniteness
  invisibility 444n.
  uncertainty 474n.
  equivocalness 518n.
indelible *fixed* 153adj.
  remembered 505adj.
  marked 547adj.
indelicacy *bad taste* 847n.
  impurity 951n.
indelicate *graceless* 842adj.
indemnification
  compensation 31n.
  retaliation 714n.
  restitution 787n.
  atonement 941n.
indemnify oneself
  recoup 31vb.

indemnity *offset* 31n.
  restitution 787n.
  pay 804n.
  payment 804n.
  forgiveness 909n.
  atonement 941n.
indenizen
  place oneself 187vb.
indent *crinkle* 251vb.
  make concave 255vb.
  roughen 259vb.
  notch 260n., vb.
  requirement 627n.
  demand 737vb.
  contract 765vb.
indentation *gap* 201n.
  angularity 247n.
  convolution 251n.
  concavity 255n.
  notch 260n.
indenture *compact* 765n.
  title deed 767n.
Independant
  sectarist 978n.
  sectarian 978adj.
independence
  irrelation 10n.
  non-imitation 21n.
  unconformity 84n.
  opportunity 137n.
  will 595n.
  independence 744n.
  wealth 800n.
  celibacy 895n.
  non-liability 919n.
  sectarianism 978n.
independent *revolter* 738n.
  free man 744n.
indescribable
  unspeakable 32adj.
  unusual 84adj.
  wonderful 864adj.
indestructible
  existing 1adj.
  unchangeable 153adj.
in detail *piecemeal* 53adv.
  severally 80adv.
indeterminacy
  chance 159n.
  non-design 618n.
indeterminate
  causeless 159adj.
  uncertain 474adj.
indetermination
  (*see* indeterminacy)
indevotion *irreligion* 974n.
index *relate* 9vb.
  class 62vb.
  numerical element 85n.
  list 87n.,vb.
  finger 378n.

gauge 465n.
  indicator 547n.
  record 548n.,vb.
  edition 589n.
index expurgatorius
  prohibition 757n.
  disapprobation 924n.
  orthodoxism 976n.
  ecclesiasticism 985n.
indexterity
  unskilfulness 695n.
Indiaman
  merchant ship 275n.
Indianize *transform* 147vb.
Indian lake
  red pigment 431n.
Indian summer
  summer 128n.
  autumn 129n.
  revival 656n.
india-rubber
  elasticity 328n.
indicate *specify* 80vb.
  point to 281vb.
  mean 514vb.
  inform 524vb.
  (*see* indication)
indication *directory* 87n.
  evidence 466n.
  omen 511n.
  manifestation 522n.
  hint 524n.
  indication 547n.
  trace 548n.
  warning 664n.
indicative
  evidential 466adj.
  meaningful 514adj.
  disclosing 526adj.
  indicating 547adj.
indicator *witness* 466n.
  indicator 547n.
indict *indict* 928vb.
  litigate 959vb.
indiction *period* 110n.
indictment *accusation* 928n.
indifference
  incuriosity 454n.
  inattention 456n.
  negligence 458n.
  no choice 606n.
  laxity 734n.
  non-observance 769n.
  moral insensibility 820n.
  inexcitability 823n.
  indifference 860n.
  non-wonder 865n.
  justice 913n.
  disinterestedness 931n.
indifferent *irrelative* 10adj.
  moderate 177adj.

neutral 625 adj.
not bad 644 adj.
bored 838 adj.
indifferent 860 adj.
indifferentism
irreligion 974 n.
indigence poverty 801 n.
indigenous intrinsic 5 adj.
native 191 adj.
indigestible
cohesive 48 adj.
extraneous 59 adj.
tough 329 adj.
insalubrious 653 adj.
uncooked 670 adj.
indigestion
indigestion 651 n.
indignation
resentment 891 n.
anger 891 n.
disapprobation 924 n.
indignation meeting
malcontent 829 n.
indignity slur 867 n.
rudeness 885 n.
scurrility 899 n.
indignity 921 n.
calumny 926 n.
indigo pigment 425 n.
blue pigment 435 n.
indirect oblique 220 adj.
deviating 282 adj.
evidential 466 adj.
occult 523 adj.
imperspicuous 568 adj.
prolix 570 adj.
roundabout 626 adj.
dishonest 930 adj.
indiscernible
invisible 444 adj.
indiscerptible
indivisible 52 adj.
one 88 adj.
dense 324 adj.
indiscipline
anarchy 734 n.
disobedience 738 n.
dutilessness 918 n.
intemperance 943 n.
indiscoverable
latent 523 adj.
indiscreet
indiscriminating 464 adj.
unwise 499 adj.
indiscretion
indiscrimination 464 n.
information 524 n.
disclosure 526 n.
bungling 695 n.
rashness 857 n.
guilty act 936 n.

indiscriminate
extensive 32 adj.
orderless 61 adj.
multiform 82 adj.
indiscriminate 464 adj.
indiscrimination
generality 79 n.
indiscrimination 464 n.
misjudgment 481 n.
unintelligence 499 n.
no choice 606 n.
indifference 860 n.
indispensable
necessary 596 adj.
required 627 adj.
important 638 adj.
indispose dissuade 613 vb.
indisposed
unwilling 598 adj.
sick 651 adj.
indisposition
unwillingness 598 n.
ill-health 651 n.
indisputability
certainty 473 n.
needfulness 627 n.
indissolubility
density 324 n.
indissoluble tied 45 adj.
indivisible 52 adj.
one 88 adj.
unchangeable 153 adj.
indissoluble 324 adj.
retentive 778 adj.
indistinct dim 419 adj.
ill-seen 444 adj.
stammering 580 adj.
indistinctness
faintness 401 n.
(see indistinct)
indistinguishable
identical 13 adj.
equivalent 28 adj.
invisible 444 adj.
indite compose 56 vb.
write 586 vb.
individual irrelative 10 adj.
unimitative 21 adj.
self 80 n.
special 80 adj.
unit 88 n.
person 371 n.
individualism
particularism 80 n.
independence 744 n.
selfishness 932 n.
individualist egotist 932 n.
individuality
speciality 80 n.
unconformity 84 n.
(see individual)

individualize specify 80 vb.
indivisibility
simpleness 44 n.
coherence 48 n.
whole 52 n.
unity 88 n.
density 324 n.
Indo-Aryan
language type 557 n.
indocility
unwillingness 598 n.
obstinacy 602 n.
indoctrinate
convince 485 vb.
teach, educate 534 vb.
Indo-European
language type 557 n.
indolence inaction 677 n.
sluggishness 679 n.
indomitable
unyielding 162 adj.
resolute 599 adj.
persevering 600 adj.
resisting 715 adj.
courageous 855 adj.
indoor interior 224 adj.
indraught ingress 297 n.
reception 299 n.
gulf 345 n.
current 350 n.
indubitable
undisputed 473 adj.
induce cause 156 vb.
influence 178 vb.
induce 612 vb.
inducement
attraction 291 n.
inducement 612 n.
offer 759 n.
excitation 821 n.
reward 962 n.
induct auspicate 68 vb.
reason 475 vb.
commission 751 vb.
celebrate 876 vb.
inductance
electricity 160 n.
reasoning 475 n.
stage play 594 n.
holy orders 985 n.
inductive rational 475 adj.
indulge please 826 vb.
(see indulgence)
indulgence laxity 734 n.
lenity 736 n.
permission 756 n.
enjoyment 824 n.
forgiveness 909 n.
intemperance 943 n.
sensualism 944 n.
gluttony 947 n.

indulgent
benevolent 897 adj.
indurate
be insensible 375 vb.
induration
hardening 326 n.
impenitence 940 n.
industrial
businesslike 622 adj.
industrialism *business* 622 n.
industrialist *producer* 167 n.
agent 686 n.
industrialization
production 164 n.
business 622 n.
industrious *vigorous* 174 adj.
attentive 455 adj.
studious 536 adj.
persevering 600 adj.
businesslike 622 adj.
industrious 678 adj.
labouring 682 adj.
industry *production* 164 n.
business 622 n.
assiduity 678 n.
indwelt *occupied* 191 adj.
inebriate *invigorate* 174 vb.
drunkard 949 n.
inebriate 949 vb.
inebriation
drunkenness 949 n.
inedible *tough* 329 adj.
unsavoury 391 adj.
insalubrious 653 adj.
uncooked 670 adj.
ineffable
unspeakable 32 adj.
inexpressible 517 adj.
wonderful 864 adj.
divine 965 adj.
ineffaceable
with affections 817 adj.
(*see* indelible)
ineffective *powerless* 161 adj.
unproductive 172 adj.
feeble 572 adj.
useless 641 adj.
unsuccessful 728 adj.
ineffectual *powerless* 161 n.
unimportant 639 adj.
useless 641 adj.
unskilful 695 adj.
ineffectuality
ineffectuality 161 n.
failure 728 n.
inefficacious
powerless 161 adj.
inefficacy *inutility* 641 n.
failure 728 n.
inefficiency
impotence 161 n.

inutility 641 n.
inefficient *powerless* 161 adj.
useless 641 adj.
bad 645 adj.
unskilful 695 adj.
inelastic *unyielding* 162 adj.
rigid 326 adj.
tough 329 adj.
inelasticity *hardness* 326 n.
inelegant *inelegant* 576 adj.
clumsy 695 adj.
vulgar 847 adj.
ineligible *unapt* 25 adj.
rejected 607 adj.
inexpedient 643 adj.
ineluctable *certain* 473 adj.
inept *irrelative* 10 adj.
irrelevant 10 adj.
unapt 25 adj.
powerless 161 adj.
absurd 497 adj.
unwise 499 adj.
inexpedient 643 adj.
unskilful 695 adj.
ineptitude *irrelevance* 10 n.
(*see* inept)
inequality *difference* 15 n.
dissimilarity 19 n.
disagreement 25 n.
inequality 29 n.
inequitable *unjust* 914 adj.
dishonest 930 n.
inequity *injustice* 914 n.
ineradicable
characteristic 5 adj.
fixed 153 adj.
inerrancy *certainty* 473 n.
inert *inert* 175 adj.
quiescent 266 adj.
insensible 375 adj.
non-active 677 adj.
inactive 679 adj.
inexcitable 823 adj.
inertia *energy* 160 n.
inertness 175 n.
slowness 278 n.
inaction 677 n.
inactivity 679 n.
laxity 734 n.
moral insensibility 820 n.
indifference 860 n.
inescapable
impending 155 adj.
necessary 596 adj.
obligatory 917 adj.
inescutcheon
heraldry 547 n.
inessential
insubstantial 4 adj.
extrinsic 6 adj.
irrelevance 10 n.

irrelevant 10 adj.
trifle 639 adj.
inestimable
valuable 644 adj.
of price 811 adj.
inevitable
impending 155 adj.
certain 473 adj.
necessary 596 adj.
compelling 740 adj.
unpromising 853 adj.
inexact *negligent* 458 adj.
feeble 572 adj.
(*see* inexactness)
inexactness *generality* 79 n.
indiscrimination 464 n.
inexactness 495 n.
imperspicuity 568 n.
inexcitability
inertness 175 n.
sluggishness 679 n.
moral insensibility 820 n.
inexcitability 823 n.
indifference 860 n.
inexcitable
moderate 177 adj.
tranquil 266 adj.
inexcusable *wrong* 914 adj.
accusable 928 adj.
heinous 934 adj.
guilty 936 adj.
inexecution
non-completion 726 n.
inexhaustible *full* 54 adj.
multitudinous 104 adj.
infinite 107 adj.
unceasing 146 adj.
plenteous 635 adj.
inexist *be intrinsic* 5 vb.
inexistence
non-existence 2 n.
intrinsicality 5 n.
absence 190 n.
inexorable *certain* 473 adj.
necessary 596 adj.
resolute 599 adj.
obstinate 602 adj.
severe 735 adj.
pitiless 906 adj.
inexpectant
vulnerable 661 adj.
inexpectation
chance 159 n.
improbability 472 n.
inexpectation 508 n.
non-preparation 670 n.
wonder 864 n.
inexpedience
inaptitude 25 n.
intempestivity 138 n.
impossibility 470 n.

inutility 641 n.
inexpedience 643 n.
difficulty 700 n.
wrong 914 n.
inexpedient
harmful 645 adj.
hindering 702 adj.
inexpensive cheap 812 adj.
inexperience
desuetude 611 n.
unskilfulness 695 n.
innocence 935 n.
inexperienced
ignorant 491 adj.
foolish 499 adj.
unhabituated 611 adj.
inexpert ignorant 491 adj.
unskilled 695 adj.
inexpiable heinous 934 adj.
guilty 936 adj.
inexplicability
chance 159 n.
unintelligibility 517 n.
inexplicable
unusual 84 adj.
causeless 159 adj.
inexpressible
inexpressible 517 adj.
wonderful 864 adj.
inexpressibles
breeches 228 n.
inexpugnable
invulnerable 660 adj.
inextensible rigid 326 adj.
inextension littleness 196 n.
immateriality 320 n.
in extenso wholly 52 adv.
completely 54 adv.
inextinguishable
unchangeable 153 adj.
violent 176 adj.
inextricable tied 45 adj.
firm-set 45 adj.
cohesive 48 adj.
complex 61 adj.
impracticable 470 adj.
difficult 700 adj.
inextricably
inseparably 45 adv.
confusedly 61 adv.
infallibilism
certainty 473 n.
infallibilist
doctrinaire 473 n.
infallibility
certainty 473 n.
positiveness 473 n.
perfection 646 n.
infallible certain 473 adj.
accurate 494 adj.
veracious 540 adj.

successful 727 adj.
ecclesiastical 985 adj.
infamous
disreputable 867 adj.
discreditable 867 adj.
dishonest 930 adj.
heinous 934 adj.
infamy (see infamous)
infancy beginning 68 n.
youth, nonage 130 n.
helplessness 161 n.
infant child 132 n.
weakling 163 n.
descendant 170 n.
infanta sovereign 741 n.
infanticide homicide 362 n.
infantile infantine 132 adj.
foolish 499 adj.
infantile paralysis
paralysis 651 n.
infantilism
unintelligence 499 n.
infantine infantine 132 adj.
infantry pedestrian 268 n.
infantry 722 n.
infarction closure 264 n.
infatuate make mad 503 vb.
(see infatuation)
infatuation bias 481 n.
credulity 487 n.
folly 499 n.
deception 542 n.
opiniatry 602 n.
liking 859 n.
love 887 n.
infect infiltrate 297 vb.
motivate 612 vb.
excite 821 vb.
(see infection)
infection mixture 43 n.
influence 178 n.
transference 272 n.
badness 645 n.
uncleanness 649 n.
infection 651 n.
impairment 655 n.
poisoning 659 n.
infectious
influential 178 adj.
transferable 272 adj.
harmful 645 adj.
unclean 649 adj.
diseased 651 adj.
infectious 653 adj.
dangerous 661 adj.
infective infectious 653 adj.
infecundity
unproductivity 172 n.
infelicity bungling 695 n.
sorrow 825 n.
infer assume 471 vb.

reason 475 n.
demonstrate 478 vb.
judge 480 vb.
mean 514 vb.
interpret 520 vb.
imply 523 vb.
be informed 524 vb.
inferable attributed 158 adj.
inference sequence 65 n.
(see infer)
inferential rational 475 n.
demonstrating 478 adj.
tacit 523 adj.
inferior
inconsiderable 33 adj.
small 33 adj.
inferior 35 n., adj.
substituted 150 adj.
weakly 163 adj.
nonentity 639 n.
unimportant 639 adj.
bad 645 adj.
loser 728 n.
mediocre 732 adj.
servant 742 n.
commoner 869 n.
(see inferiority)
inferiority relativeness 9 n.
inequality 29 n.
inferiority 35 n.
lowness 210 n.
subjection 745 n.
inferiority complex
jealousy 911 n.
infernal deep 211 adj.
damnable 645 adj.
cruel 898 adj.
wicked 934 adj.
heinous 934 adj.
diabolic 969 adj.
infernal 972 adj.
infernal machine
bomb 723 n.
inferno turmoil 61 n.
hell 972 n.
inferred
attributed 158 adj.
infertile impotent 161 adj.
infertility
unproductivity 172 n.
scarcity 636 n.
infest congregate 74 vb.
be many 104 vb.
encroach 306 vb.
attack 712 vb.
incommode 827 vb.
infested full 54 adj.
insalubrious 653 adj.
infestivity dullness 840 n.
infeudation giving 781 n.
infibulation joinder 45 n.

infidel *unbeliever* 486 n.
  impious person 980 n.
  profane 980 adj.
infidelity *unbelief* 486 n.
  perfidy 930 n.
  illicit love 951 n.
  irreligion 974 n.
in-fighting *pugilism* 716 n.
infiltrate *pervade* 189 vb.
  infiltrate 297 vb.
infiltration *mixture* 43 n.
  interjacence 231 n.
  ingress 297 n.
  passage 305 n.
  moistening 341 n.
  sedition 738 n.
infinite *absolute* 32 adj.
  multitudinous 104 adj.
  many 104 adj.
  infinite 107 adj.
infinitesimal *small* 33 adj.
  minute 196 adj.
infinitesimal calculus
  mathematics 86 n.
infinity *greatness* 32 n.
  infinity 107 n.
  space 183 n.
  divine attribute 965 n.
infinity, to *forever* 115 adv.
infirm *weakly* 163 adj.
  irresolute 601 adj.
  unhealthy 651 adj.
  cowardly 856 adj.
infirmary *hospital* 658 n.
infirmity *weakness* 163 n.
  ill-health 651 n.
  illness 651 n.
  vice 934 n.
infix *add* 38 vb.
  adjunct 40 n.
  affix 45 vb.
  interjection 231 n.
  implant 303 vb.
  educate 534 vb.
  word 559 n.
inflame *heat* 381 vb.
  aggravate 832 vb.
  excite love 887 vb.
inflamed *violent* 176 adj.
  diseased 651 adj.
inflammability
  burning 381 n.
  excitability 822 n.
inflammable
  combustible 385 adj.
  dangerous 661 adj.
  excitable 822 adj.
  irascible 892 adj.
inflammation *heat* 379 n.
  heating 381 n.
  ulcer 651 n.

  painfulness 827 n.
inflammatory
  violent 176 adj.
inflated *ridiculous* 849 adj.
  prideful 871 adj.
  vain 873 adj.
  ostentatious 875 adj.
inflation *increase* 36 n.
  dilation 197 n.
  sufflation 352 n.
  exaggeration 546 n.
  magniloquence 574 n.
  finance 797 n
  dearness 811 n.
inflationary
  monetary 797 adj.
  dear 811 adj.
inflect *make curved* 248 vb.
  parse 564 vb.
inflected *linguistic* 557 adj.
inflection *adjunct* 40 n.
  sequel 67 n.
  extremity 69 n.
  (*see* inflexion)
inflexibility
  stability 153 n.
  straightness 249 n.
  hardness 326 n.
  resolution 599 n.
  obstinacy 602 n.
  severity 735 n.
  pitilessness 906 n.
inflexion *change* 143 n.
  curvature 248 n.
  grammar 564 n.
  pronunciation 577 n.
inflictable
  punishable 963 adj.
infliction *adversity* 731 n.
  severity 735 n.
  suffering 825 n.
  punishment 963 n.
inflictive *punitive* 963 adj.
inflow *ingress* 297 n.
  current 350 n.
influence *component* 58 n.
  modify 143 vb.
  causation 156 n.
  cause 156 n., vb.
  effect 157 n.
  power 160 n.
  agency 173 n.
  influence 178 n., vb.
  tend 179 vb.
  bias 481 vb.
  convince 485 vb.
  teach 534 vb.
  inducement 612 n.
  motivate 612 vb.
  instrumentality 628 n.
  be important 638 vb.

  action 676 n.
  authority 733 n.
  impress 821 vb.
  prestige 866 n.
  sorcery 983 n.
influential *great* 32 adj.
  (*see* influence)
influenza *infection* 651 n.
influx *ingress* 297 n.
in force *powerful* 160 adj.
  strongly 162 adv.
inform *efform* 243 vb.
  inform 524 vb.
  divulge 526 vb.
  indicate 547 vb.
  warn 664 vb.
  accuse 928 vb.
informal *orderless* 61 adj.
  (*see* informality)
informal dress
  informal dress 228 n.
informality
  unconformity 84 n.
  laxity 734 n.
  non-observance 769 n.
  illegality 957 n.
informant *witness* 466 n.
  informant 524 n.
information
  testimony 466 n.
  knowledge 490 n.
  erudition 490 n.
  information 524 n.
  disclosure 526 n.
  message 529 n.
  indication 547 n.
  warning 664 n.
  advice 691 n.
  accusation 928 n.
information, piece of
  news 529 n.
informative
  informative 524 adj.
  disclosing 526 adj.
  loquacious 581 adj.
  conversing 584 adj.
informatory
  informative 524 adj.
informed
  knowing 490 adj.
  instructed 490 adj.
  informed 524 adj.
informed circles
  informant 524 n.
informer
  secret service 459 n.
  witness 466 n.
  informer 524 n.
  accuser 928 n.
  knave 938 n.
  litigant 959 n.

informity
   amorphism 244 n.
infra *after* 65 adv.
   in front 237 adv.
infraction
   overstepping 306 n.
   disobedience 738 n.
   undueness 916 n.
   dutilessness 918 n.
infra dig *degrading* 867 adj.
infrangible *cohesive* 48 adj.
   unyielding 162 adj.
   dense 324 adj.
   hard 326 adj.
   tough 329 adj.
infrequency
   infrequency 140 n.
   scarcity 636 n.
infrequent
   discontinuous 72 adj.
   fitful 142 adj.
   uncertain 474 adj.
infrequently *seldom* 140 adv.
infringement
   unconformity 84 n.
   overstepping 306 n.
   opposition 704 n.
   attack 712 n.
   disobedience 738 n.
   non-observance 769 n.
   undueness 916 n.
   lawbreaking 954 n.
infringer *thief* 789 n.
   usurper 916 n.
infundibular
   concave 255 adj.
   tubular 263 adj.
infuriate *furious* 176 adj.
   make violent 176 vb.
   make mad 503 vb.
   enrage 891 vb.
infuse *combine* 50 vb.
   infuse 303 vb.
   moisten 341 vb.
   educate 534 vb.
infusible
   indissoluble 324 adj.
infusion *tincture* 43 n.
   potion 301 n.
   insertion 303 n.
   solution 337 n.
infusoria *animalcule* 196 n.
ingannation
   deception 542 n.
ingathering
   assemblage 74 n.
ingeminate
   double 91 adj.,vb.
   repeat 106 vb.
ingenerate *genetic* 5 adj.
ingenious

imaginative 513 adj.
planning 623 adj.
skilful 694 adj.
cunning 698 adj.
ingenue *acting* 594 n.
   ingenue 699 n.
   innocent 935 n.
ingenuity *skill* 694 n.
   cunning 698 n.
ingenuous
   veracious 540 adj.
   artless 699 adj.
   honourable 929 adj.
   trustworthy 929 adj.
ingest *absorb* 299 vb.
   eat, drink 301 vb.
ingle *furnace* 383 n.
ingle nook *home* 192 n.
inglorious
   unprosperous 731 adj.
   mediocre 732 adj.
   unsuccessful 728 adj.
   inglorious 867 adj.
   humbled 872 adj.
ingot *materials* 631 n.
   bullion 797 n.
ingraft *implant* 303 vb.
   cultivate 370 vb.
   habituate 610 vb.
ingrain *intromit* 231 vb.
ingrained *genetic* 5 adj.
   combined 50 adj.
   fixed 153 adj.
   habitual 610 adj.
ingrate *ingratitude* 908 n.
ingratiate oneself
   be servile 879 vb.
   excite love 887 vb.
ingratiating *servile* 879 adj.
   courteous 884 adj.
   flattering 925 adj.
ingratitude
   ingratitude 908 n.
   undueness 916 n.
ingredient *adjunct* 40 n.
   part 53 n.
   component 58 n.
   contents 193 n.
   element 319 n.
ingress *ingress* 297 n.
   passage 305 n.
in-group *group* 74 n.
   self 80 n.
ingrown *firm-set* 45 adj.
   interior 224 adj.
ingurgitation
   reception 299 n.
inhabit *dwell* 192 vb.
   possess 773 vb.
inhabitant *dweller* 191 n.
inhale *absorb* 299 vb.

breathe 352 vb.
smoke 388 vb.
smell 394 vb.
in hand *unfinished* 55 adj.
   stored 632 adj.
   unused 674 adj.
inharmonious
   disagreeing 25 adj.
   strident 407 adj.
   discordant 411 adj.
inhere *be* 1 vb.
   be intrinsic 5 vb.
   constitute 56 vb.
   be one of 58 vb.
   be included 78 vb.
   belong 773 adj.
inherent *ingredient* 58 adj.
   possessed 773 adj.
inherit *reproduce* 166 vb.
   inherit 771 vb.
inheritable
   not retained 779 adj.
   due 915 adj.
inheritance *sequel* 67 n.
   posteriority 120 n.
   posterity 170 n.
   acquisition 771 n.
   dower 777 n.
   transfer 780 n.
   receiving 782 n.
   receipt 807 n.
inherited *genetic* 5 adj.
   filial 170 adj.
   acquired 771 adj.
inherited characteristic
   heredity 5 n.
   affections 817 n.
inheritor *survivor* 41 n.
   aftercomer 67 n.
   beneficiary 776 n.
   recipient 782 n.
inhesion *intrinsicality* 5 n.
inhibition
   hindrance 702 n.
   command 737 n.
   restraint 747 n.
   prohibition 757 n.
inhibitor
   counteraction 182 n.
inhospitable
   unsociable 883 adj.
   unkind 898 adj.
inhospitality
   unsociability 883 n.
inhuman (*see* inhumanity)
inhumane *unkind* 898 adj.
inhumanity *violence* 176 n.
   severity 735 n.
   moral insensibility 820 n.
   inhumanity 898 n.
   misanthropy 902 n.

wickedness 934 n.
inhumation
interment 364 n.
inimical *contrary* 14 adj.
disagreeing 25 adj.
opposing 704 adj.
quarrelling 709 adj.
disliking 861 adj.
inimical 881 adj.
hating 888 adj.
inimitable
unimitated 21 adj.
supreme 34 adj.
iniquitous *unjust* 914 adj.
wrong 914 adj.
wicked 934 adj.
iniquity *wickedness* 934 n.
initial *first* 68 adj.
sign 547 vb.
initials 558 n.
script 586 n.
initiate *initiate* 68 vb.
cause 156 vb.
produce 164 vb.
admit 299 vb.
train 534 vb.
beginner 538 n.
initiation *learning* 536 n.
rite 988 n.
initiative *beginning* 68 n.
vigorousness 174 n.
willingness 597 n.
restlessness 678 n.
freedom 477 n.
initiator *teacher* 537 n.
inject *infuse* 303 vb.
motivate 612 vb.
injection *insertion* 303 n.
moistening 341 n.
therapy 658 n.
injudicial *illegal* 954 adj.
injudicious *unwise* 499 adj.
rash 857 adj.
injunction
requirement 627 n.
advice 691 n.
precept 693 n.
command 737 n.
prohibition 757 n.
legal process 959 n.
injure *weaken* 163 vb.
harm, ill-treat 645 vb.
impair 655 vb.
oppress 735 vb.
hurt 827 vb.
blemish 845 vb.
be malevolent 898 vb.
do wrong 914 vb.
injurious *evil* 616 adj.
harmful 645 adj.
insalubrious 653 adj.

insolent 878 adj.
wrong 914 adj.
disrespectful 921 adj.
detracting 926 adj.
injury *evil* 616 n.
wound 655 n.
misuse 675 n.
injustice 914 n.
guilty act 936 n.
injustice
misjudgment 481 n.
misrepresentation 552 n.
evil 616 n.
injustice 914 n.
improbity 930 n.
guilty act 936 n.
illegality 954 n.
ink *black thing* 428 n.
art equipment 553 n.
ink-bottle *stationery* 586 n.
ink-horn *receptacle* 194 n.
stationery 586 n.
in kind *in exchange* 151 adv.
inkle *ligature* 47 n.
inkling *knowledge* 490 n.
supposition 512 n.
hint 524 n.
ink-slinging
contention 716 n.
inkwell *receptacle* 194 n.
stationery 586 n.
inky *black* 428 adj.
inlaid *ornamented* 844 adj.
inland *interior* 224 adj.
land 344 n.
inland sea *lake* 346 n.
in-laws *family* 11 n.
inlay *line* 227 vb.
insert 303 vb.
variegate 437 vb.
ornamental art 844 n.
inlet *entrance* 68 n.
gap 201 n.
cavity 255 n.
orifice 263 n.
way in 297 n.
gulf 345 n.
in lieu *instead* 150 adv.
in line with
conformably 83 adv.
inly *inside* 224 adv.
inmate *resident* 191 n.
interiority 224 n.
in memoriam
in memoriam 364 adv.
in memory 505 adv.
inmost (*see* innermost)
inmost being
interiority 224 n.
inmost soul *affections* 817 n.
inn *inn* 192 n.

inner *included* 78 adj.
interior 224 adj.
inner being *essence* 1 n.
inner man *insides* 224 n.
spirit 447 n.
affections 817 n.
innermost *interior* 224 adj.
innings *period* 110 n.
knock 279 n.
land 344 n.
earnings 771 n.
receipt 807 n.
innkeeper *caterer* 633 n.
innocence
helplessness 161 n.
ignorance 491 n.
artlessness 699 n.
benevolence 897 n.
probity 929 n.
virtue 933 n.
innocence 935 n.
purity 950 n.
acquittal 960 n.
innocent
ignoramus 493 n.
foolish 499 adj.
ninny 501 n.
dupe 544 n.
gullible 544 adj.
beneficial 644 adj.
perfect 646 adj.
ingenue 699 n.
innocent 935 n., adj.
good man 937 n.
(*see* innocence)
innocuous *moderate* 177 adj.
beneficial 644 adj.
salubrious 652 adj.
innocent 935 adj.
innominate
anonymous 562 adj.
innovation *newness* 126 n.
change 143 n.
innovator *precursor* 66 n.
innuendo *latency* 523 n.
hint 524 n.
censure 924 n.
detraction 926 n.
innumerable
multitudinous 104 adj.
infinite 107 adj.
inobservance
non-observance 769 n.
inoculate *implant* 303 vb.
teach 534 vb.
motivate 612 vb.
sanitate 652 vb.
doctor 658 vb.
safeguard 660 vb.
inoculation
prophylactic 658 n.

inodorousness
inodorousness 395 n.
cleansing 648 n.
inoffensive
beneficial 644 adj.
humble 872 adj.
amiable 884 adj.
innocent 935 adj.
in one piece *whole* 52 adj.
in one's stride
habitually 610 adv.
inoperable *deadly* 362 adj.
impracticable 470 adj.
sick 651 adj.
unpromising 853 adj.
inoperative
powerless 161 adj.
unproductive 172 adj.
useless 641 adj.
non-active 677 adj.
inopportune *unapt* 25 adj.
inopportune 138 adj.
inexpedient 643 adj.
inordinacy *undueness* 916 n.
inordinate
exorbitant 32 adj.
exaggerated 546 adj.
inorganic *inorganic* 359 adj.
mindless 448 adj.
unthinking 450 adj.
inosculation *joinder* 45 n.
crossing 222 n.
convolution 251 n.
in particular
specially 80 adv.
inpatient *resident* 191 n.
sick person 651 n.
in person *here* 189 adv.
in pickle *impending* 155 adj.
in point *typical* 83 adj.
in preparation
unfinished 55 adj.
input *requirement* 627 n.
inquest *inquest* 364 n.
enquiry 459 n.
legal trial 959 n.
inquietude
changeableness 152 n.
worry 825 n.
inquiline *settler* 191 n.
inquination
impairment 655 n.
inquisition *enquiry* 459 n.
severity 735 n.
legal trial 859 n.
orthodoxism 976 n.
ecclesiasticism 985 n.
Inquisition
ecclesiastical court 956 n.
inquisitive
inquisitive 453 adj.

inquisitor *inquisitor* 453 n.
questioner 459 n.
tyrant 735 n.
punisher 963 n.
inroad *ingress* 297 n.
waste 634 n.
impairment 655 n.
attack 712 n.
arrogation 916 n.
inrush *ingress* 297 n.
insalubrious
deadly 362 adj.
harmful 645 adj.
unclean 649 adj.
dangerous 661 adj.
insalubrity *infection* 651 n.
insalubrity 653 n.
ins and outs *place* 185 n.
particulars 80 n.
insane *insane* 503 adj.
(see insanity)
insanitary
insalubrious 653 adj.
insanity *non-intellect* 448 n.
error 495 n.
unintelligence 499 n.
insanity 503 n.
excitable state 822 n.
insatiability
rapacity 786 n.
desire 859 n.
gluttony 947 n.
insatiable
unprovided 636 adj.
insatiate *greedy* 859 adj.
inscape *form* 243 n.
inscribe *list* 87 vb.
record 548 vb.
write 586 vb.
inscriber *commender* 923 n.
inscribe to *honour* 866 vb.
inscription
commentary 520 n.
indication 547 n.
monument 548 n.
phrase 563 n.
script 586 n.
description 590 n.
inscroll *register* 548 vb.
inscrutable
unintelligible 517 adj.
impassive 820 adj.
inexcitable 823 adj.
serious 834 adj.
insect *animalcule* 196 n.
vermin 365 n.
cad 938 n.
insecticide *killer* 362 n.
prophylactic 658 n.
poison 659 n.
insectile *animal* 365 adj.

insecurity
unreliability 474 n.
danger 661 n.
vulnerability 661 n.
insemination
propagation 164 n.
productiveness 171 n.
inseminator *producer* 167 n.
insensate *insensible* 375 adj.
unwise 499 adj.
thick-skinned 820 adj.
insensibility
helplessness 161 n.
inertness 175 n.
insensibility 375 n.
indiscrimination 464 n.
ignorance 491 n.
oblivion 506 n.
inaction 677 n.
sluggishness 679 n.
sleep 679 n.
indifference 860 n.
non-wonder 865 n.
insensible
impassive 820 adj.
unkind 898 adj.
(see insensibility)
insensitive
unsharpened 257 adj.
insensible 375 adj.
indiscriminating 464 adj.
inexact 495 adj.
inelegant 576 adj.
impassive 820 adj.
thick-skinned 820 adj.
ill-bred 847 adj.
inseparable
firm-set 45 adj.
cohesive 48 adj.
indivisible 52 adj.
concomitant 89 n.
near 200 adj.
friendly 880 adj.
insert *affix* 45 vb.
load 193 vb.
intromit 231 vb.
enter 297 vb.
inserted
discontinuous 72 adj.
insertion *addition* 38 n.
adjunct 40 n.
mixture 43 n.
piece 53 n.
location 187 n.
reception 299 n.
insertion 303 n.
advertisement 528 n.
repair 656 n.
inset *insertion* 303 n.
insert 303 vb.
edition 589 n.

ornamental art 844n.
inseverable *one* 88adj.
inshore *near* 200adj.
inside *contents* 193n.
 interiority 224n.
 imprisoned 747adj.
inside job *plot* 623n.
inside out
 inverted 221adj.
insides *component* 58n.
 insides 224n.
insidious *occult* 523adj.
 deceiving 542adj.
 evil 616adj.
 cunning 698adj.
 perfidious 930adj.
insight *intellect* 447n.
 discrimination 463n.
 intuition 476n.
 knowledge 490n.
 imagination 513n.
 interpretation 520n.
insignia *badge* 547n.
 regalia 743n.
insignificance
 smallness 33n.
 unimportance 639n.
 despisedness 922n.
insignificant
 unmeaning 515adj.
insincere *sophistical* 477adj.
insincerity
 unmeaningness 515n.
 duplicity 541n.
 deception 542n.
 affectation 850n.
 ostentation 875n.
 flattery 925n.
 improbity 930n.
insinuate *intromit* 231vb.
 imply 523vb.
 inform, hint 524vb.
insinuate oneself
 infiltrate 297vb.
 excite love 887vb.
 flatter 925vb.
insinuation
 influence 178n.
 ingress 297n.
 insertion 303n.
 censure 924n.
 detraction 926n.
insipid *weak* 163adj.
 tasteless 387adj.
 feeble 572adj.
 tedious 838adj.
 dull 840adj.
 unwanted 860adj.
insist *emphasize* 532vb.
 be resolute 599vb.
 be obstinate 602vb.

incite 612vb.
 contend 716vb.
 compel 740vb.
 beg 761vb.
insistence (*see* insist)
insistent *assertive* 532adj.
 forceful 571adj.
 resolute 599adj.
 important 638adj.
 requesting 761adj.
in situ *in place* 186adv.
 here 189adv.
insobriety
 drunkenness 949n.
insolation *desiccation* 342n.
 heat 379n.
 heating 381n.
insolence *defiance* 711n.
 pride 871n.
 insolence 878n.
 rudeness 885n.
insolent *anarchic* 734adj.
 authoritarian 735adj.
insoluble
 indissoluble 324adj.
 impracticable 470adj.
 puzzling 517adj.
insolvency
 insufficiency 636n.
 failure 728n.
 non-observance 769n.
 poverty 801n.
 debt 803n.
 insolvency 805n.
insomnia *restlessness* 678n.
insomniac *sick person* 651n.
insouciance
 incuriosity 454n.
 negligence 458n.
 moral insensibility 820n.
 indifference 860n.
insouciant
 light-minded 456adj.
inspan *start out* 296vb.
inspection
 inspection 438n.
 attention 455n.
 surveillance 457n.
 enquirer 459n.
 estimate 480n.
inspector *spectator* 441n.
 enquirer 459n.
 estimator 480n.
 manager 690n.
inspectorship
 magistrature 733n.
inspiration
 causation 156n.
 influence 178n.
 respiration 352n.
 intuition 476n.

intelligence 498n.
 imagination 513n.
 diffuseness 570n.
 inducement 612n.
 contrivance 623n.
 warm feeling 818n.
 excitation 821n.
 excitable state 822n.
 revelation 975n.
 piety 979n.
inspirational
 intuitive 476adj.
 revelational 975adj.
inspire *cheer* 833vb.
 give courage 855vb.
 make pious 979vb.
 (*see* inspiration)
inspired *intuitive* 476adj.
 diffuse 570adj.
 forceful 571adj.
 induced 612adj.
 scriptural 975adj.
 revelational 975adj.
 pietistic 979adj.
inspirer *cause* 156n.
 motivator 612n.
inspiring *causal* 156adj.
 influential 178adj.
 exciting 821adj.
inspirit *incite* 612vb.
 animate 821vb.
 cheer 833vb.
 give hope 852vb.
 give courage 855vb.
inspissation
 condensation 324n.
 thickening 354n.
in spite of *although* 182adv.
 nevertheless 468adv.
instability
 changeableness 152n.
 weakness 163n.
 vulnerability 661n.
 excitability 822n.
install *auspicate* 68vb.
 place 187vb.
 commission 751vb.
 dower 777vb.
 dignify 866vb.
installation *location* 187n.
 workshop 687n.
 mandate 751n.
 celebration 876n.
 holy orders 985n.
instalment *part* 53n.
 incompleteness 55n.
 reading matter 589n.
 security 767n.
 payment 804n.
instance *example* 83n.
 inducement 612n.

request 761 n.
instant *brief span* 114 n.
  instant 116 n.
  present 121 adj.
  impending 155 adj.
  demanding 627 adj.
  ready-made 669 adj.
  active 678 adj.
  requesting 761 adj.
instantaneity
  transientness 114 n.
  instantaneity 116 n.
  present time 121 n.
  synchronism 123 n.
  punctuality 135 n.
  velocity 277 n.
instantaneous
  instantaneous 116 adj.
instant, be
  emphasize 532 vb.
instantly
  transiently 114 adv.
  instantaneously 116 adv.
instate *celebrate* 876 vb.
in statu pupillari
  young 130 adj.
  subject 745 adj.
in statu quo
  as before 144 adv.
instead *instead* 150 adv.
instep *foot* 214 n.
  curve 248 n.
instigation
  inducement 612 n.
instigator *motivator* 612 n.
  aider 703 n.
instil *infuse* 303 vb.
  educate 534 vb.
instilled *extrinsic* 6 adj.
instinct *tendency* 179 n.
  intellect 447 n.
  non-intellect 448 n.
  incogitance 450 n.
  empiricism 461 n.
  intuition 476 n.
  supposition 512 n.
  habit 610 n.
  non-design 618 n.
instinctive
  ill-reasoned 477 adj.
  educational 534 adj.
  involuntary 596 adj.
  spontaneous 609 adj.
instincts *affections* 817 n.
instinct with
  possessing 773 adj.
  with affections 817 adj.
institute *auspicate* 68 vb.
  cause 156 vb.
  produce 164 vb.
  academy 539 n.

corporation 708 n.
institution *academy* 539 n.
  practice 610 n.
  law 953 n.
  rite 988 n.
institutionalism
  orthodoxy 976 n.
instruct (see *instruction*)
instruction *culture* 490 n.
  information 524 n.
  teaching 534 n.
  advice 691 n.
  precept 693 n.
  command 737 n.
instructive
  influential 178 adj.
  informative 524 adj.
  cautionary 664 adj.
instructor
  teacher, trainer 537 n.
instrument
  contrivance 623 n.
  instrument 628 n.
  means 629 n.
  tool 630 n
  agent 686 n.
  auxiliary 707 n.
  slave 742 n.
  title-deed 767 n.
  toady 879 n.
instrumental
  musical 412 adj.
  musicianly 413 adj.
  instrumental 628 adj.
  useful 640 adj.
  used 673 adj.
instrumentalist
  instrumentalist 413 n.
instrumentality
  agency 173 n.
  instrumentality 628 n.
instrumentation
  composition 56 n.
  melody 410 n.
insubordination
  anarchy 734 n.
  disobedience 738 n.
insubstantial *unreal* 2 adj.
  insubstantial 4 adj.
  inconsiderable 33 adj.
  transient 114 adj.
  powerless 161 adj.
  weak, flimsy 163 adj.
  immaterial 320 adj.
  brittle 330 adj.
  insufficient 636 adj.
insubstantiality
  unimportance 639 n.
  vanity 873 n.
insufferable
  intolerable 827 adj.

disliked 861 adj.
insufficiency
  inequality 20 n.
  smallness 33 n.
  incompleteness 55 n.
  shortcoming 307 n.
  requirement 627 n.
  insufficiency 636 n.
  imperfection 647 n.
  non-completion 726 n.
insufficient
  discontenting 829 adj.
  (see insufficiency)
insufflation *sufflation*, 352 n.
insular *separate* 46 adj.
  alone 88 adj.
  regional 184 adj.
  dweller 191 n.
  insular 349 adj.
insularity *irrelation* 10 n.
  disjunction 46 n.
  island 349 n.
  narrow mind 481 n.
  prejudice 481 n.
insulate *set apart* 46 vb.
insulation *protection* 660 n.
  defence 713 n.
insulin *drug* 658 n.
insult *hurt* 827 vb.
  ridicule 851 n.
  slur 867 n.
  sauciness 878 n.
  rudeness 885 n.
  hate 888 vb.
  scurrility 899 n.
  indignity 921 n.
  not respect 921 vb.
  calumny 926 n.
insulting *defiant* 711 adj.
insuperable
  impracticable 470 adj.
  difficult 700 adj.
insupportable
  intolerable 827 adj.
insurance
  calculation of chance
    159 n.
  protection 660 n.
  promise 764 n.
  security 767 n.
  caution 858 n.
insure *seek safety* 660 vb.
  prepare 669 vb.
  give security 767 vb.
insurer *consignee* 754 n.
insurgence *revolt* 738 n
insurgent *revolter* 738 n.
insurmountable
  impracticable 470 adj.
insurrection
  resistance 715 n.

revolt 738 n.
insurrectional
resisting 715 adj.
insurrectionist
revolter 738 n.
intact *intact* 52 adj.
complete 54 adj.
undamaged 646 adj.
safe 660 adj.
preserved 666 adj.
intaglio *mould* 23 n.
concavity 255 n.
sculpture 554 n.
ornamental art 844 n.
intake *size* 195 n.
ingress 297 n.
way in 297 n.
reception 299 n.
requirement 627 n.
waste 634 n.
intangibility
insubstantiality 4 n.
intangible *minute* 196 adj.
immaterial 320 adj.
integer *whole* 52 n.
number 85 n.
unit 88 n.
integral *whole* 52 adj.
complete 54 adj.
numerical element 85 n.
integral calculus
mathematics 86 n.
integrality (*see* integral)
integral part
component 58 n.
integrant *part* 53 n.
integrate
make complete 54 vb.
integration
combination 50 n.
whole 52 n.
completeness 54 n.
numerical operation 86 n.
unity 88 n.
association 706 n.
integrity *whole* 52 n.
virtue 933 n.
probity 929 n.
integument *layer* 207 n.
skin 226 n.
intellect *intellect* 447 n.
knowledge 490 n.
intellectual *mental* 447 adj.
instructed 490 adj.
intellectual 492 n.
wise 498 adj.
sage 500 n.
proficient 696 n.
intellectualism
intellect 447 n.
intelligence 498 n.

intellectualize
cognize 447 vb.
meditate 449 vb.
intelligence
secret service 459 n.
intelligence 498 n.
news 529 n.
wit 839 n.
intelligent
intelligent 498 adj.
skilful 694 adj.
cunning 698 adj.
intelligentsia
intellectual 492 n.
intelligibility
simpleness 44 n.
sanity 502 n.
intelligibility 516 n.
intelligible *known* 490 adj.
semantic 514 adj.
intelligible 516 adj.
perspicuous 567 adj.
intemperance
exaggeration 546 n.
festivity 837 n.
intemperance 943 n.
sensualism 944 n.
gluttony 947 n.
intemperate
intemperate 943 adj.
drunken 949 adj.
intempestivity
irrelation 10 n.
inaptitude 25 n.
derangement 63 n.
anachronism 118 n.
intempestivity 138 n.
inexpedience 643 n.
intend *predestine* 155 vb.
mean 514 vb.
will 595 vb.
be willing 597 vb.
be resolute 599 vb.
predetermine 608 vb.
intend 617 vb.
plan 623 vb.
desire 859 vb.
intendant *official* 690 n.
officer 741 n.
intended *veracious* 540 adj.
volitional 595 adj.
loved one 887 n.
intense *great* 32 n.
vigorous 174 adj.
florid 425 adj.
fervent 818 adj.
intensification
increase 36 n.
stimulation 174 n.
aggravation 832 n.
intensify *enlarge* 197 vb.

exaggerate 546 vb.
animate 821 vb.
aggravate 832 vb.
intensity *degree* 27 n.
greatness 32 n.
vigorousness 174 n.
hue 425 n.
intensive *increasing* 36 adj.
part of speech 564 n.
intent *attentive* 455 adj.
resolute 599 adj.
(*see* intention)
intention *relation* 9 n.
connotation 514 n.
will 595 n.
predetermination 608 n.
intention 617 n.
plan 623 n.
aspiration 852 n.
prayers 981 n.
intentional
volitional 595 adj.
intended 617 adj.
intentness *attention* 455 n.
assiduity 678 n.
inter *inter* 364 vb.
interaction
correlation 12 n.
agency 173 n.
action 676 n.
interbreeding *race* 11 n.
mixture 43 n.
intercalary
intermediate 108 adj.
interjacent 231 adj.
intercalation
interjection 231 n.
insertion 303 n.
intercede *interfere* 231 vb.
patronize 703 vb.
mediate 720 vb.
worship 981 vb.
intercept *interfere* 231 vb.
converge 293 vb.
hear 415 adj.
screen 421 vb.
be curious 454 vb.
obstruct 702 vb.
take 786 vb.
interceptor *inquisitor* 453 n.
interceptor 702 n.
intercession *aid* 703 n.
mediation 720 n.
deprecation 762 n.
divine function 965 n.
prayers 981 n.
intercessional
redemptive 965 adj.
intercessor
intermediary 231 n.
mediator 720 n.

God the Son 965 n.
intercessory
  mediatory 720 adj.
  deprecatory 762 adj.
  devotional 981 adj.
interchange *correlation* 12 n.
  derangement 63 n.
  substitution 150 n.
  interchange 151 n., vb.
  displacement 188 n.
  inversion 221 n.
  crossing 222 n.
  transfer 780 n.
  barter, trade 791 vb.
interchangeability
  identity 13 n.
  equivalence 28 n.
intercommunicate
  connect 45 vb.
intercommunicating
  contiguous 202 adj.
intercommunication
  junction 45 n.
  bond 47 n.
  contiguity 202 n.
  information 524 n.
intercommunion
  interlocution 584 n.
  public worship 981 n.
intercommunity
  sociality 882 n.
interconnection
  correlation 12 n.
  junction 45 n.
  bond 47 n.
intercontinental
  interchanged 151 adj.
intercontinental ballistic
  missile
  rocket 276 n.
  missile weapon 723 n.
intercostal
  interjacent 231 adj.
intercourse *junction* 45 n.
  coition 45 n.
  friendship 880 n.
  sociality 882 n.
intercourse, have
  unite with 45 vb.
interdepartmental
  interchanged 151 adj.
interdependence
  correlation 12 n.
interdict
  prohibition 757 n.
interdigitation
  crossing 222 n.
  interjacence 230 n.
interest *relation* 9 n.
  increment 36 n.
  extra 40 n.

product 164 n.
influence 178 n.
topic 452 n.
curiosity 453 n.
attention 455 n.
attract notice 455 vb.
motivate 612 vb.
importance 638 n.
aid 703 n.
gain 771 n.
estate 777 n.
interest 803 n.
receipt 807 n.
impress 821 vb.
pleasurableness 826 n.
amuse 837 vb.
interested
  inquisitive 453 adj.
  obsessed 455 adj.
  selfish 932 adj.
interest oneself in
  be active 678 vb.
interests *affairs* 154 n.
  business 622 n.
interface *partition* 231 n.
interfere *disagree* 25 vb.
  derange 63 vb.
  counteract 182 vb.
  interfere 231 vb.
  be curious 453 vb.
  meddle 678 vb.
  obstruct 702 vb.
  prohibit 757 vb.
interference *radiation* 417 n.
  instrumentality 628 n.
  (*see* interfere)
interferer *meddler* 678 n.
  hinderer 702 n.
interfuse *infiltrate* 297 vb.
interfusion *mixture* 43 n.
interglacial
  intermediate 108 adj.
interim
  incompleteness 55 n.
  interim 108 n.
  period 110 n.
  transientness 114 n.
  lull 145 n.
  interval 201 n.
interior *intrinsic* 5 adj.
  included 78 adj.
  interiority 224 n.
  inland 344 adj.
  art subject 553 n.
interiority *essence* 1 n.
  interiority 224 n.
  latency 523 n.
interjacence
  centrality 225 n.
  interjacence 231 n.
interject

be obstructive 702 vb.
  (*see* interjection)
interjection *addition* 38 n.
  discontinuity 72 n.
  interjection 231 n.
  insertion 303 n.
  affirmation 532 n.
  allocution 583 n.
interlace *mix* 43 vb.
  enlace 222 vb.
interlard *mix* 43 vb.
  line 227 vb.
  put between 231 vb.
interleave
  put between 231 vb.
interlineation *adjunct* 40 n.
  interjection 231 n.
interlink *enlace* 222 vb.
interlock *correlate* 12 vb.
  join 45 vb.
  enlace 222 vb.
interlocking
  correlative 12 adj.
  complexity 61 n.
interlocution
  interrogation 459 n.
  speech 579 n.
  interlocution 584 n.
interlocutor
  questioner 459 n.
  interlocutor 584 n.
interlocutory
  conversing 584 adj.
interlope *obstruct* 702 vb.
interloper *intruder* 59 n.
  interjector 231 n.
  hinderer 702 n.
  free man 744 n.
interloping
  extraneous 59 adj.
interlude *interim* 108 n.
  lull 145 n.
  stage play 594 n.
interlunar
  intermediate 108 adj.
intermarriage
  mixture 43 n.
  type of marriage 894 n.
intermeddle *meddle* 678 vb.
  mediate 720 vb.
intermediary
  interjacence 231 n.
  intermediary 231 n.
  interjacent 231 adj.
  messenger 531 n.
  instrumentality 628 n.
  mediator 720 n.
  consignee 754 n.
  deputizing 755 adj.
intermediate
  median 30 adj.

middle 70 adj.
intermediate 108 adj.
interjacent 231 adj.
undeviating 625 adj.
intermedium *bond* 47 n.
intermediary 231 n.
mediator 720 n.
interment *immersion* 303 n.
interment 364 n.
intermezzo *adjunct* 40 n.
musical piece 412 n.
intermigration
wandering 267 n.
interminable *infinite* 107 adj.
protracted 113 adj.
perpetual 115 adj.
long 203 adj.
intermingle *mix* 43 vb.
intermission
discontinuity 72 n.
interim 108 n.
lull 145 n.
dramaturgy 594 n.
intermit
be discontinuous 72 vb.
be periodic 141 vb.
pause 145 vb
intermittent
discontinuous 72 adj.
infrequent 140 adj.
periodical 141 adj.
fitful 142 adj.
intermixture *mixture* 43 n.
intermutation
interchange 151 n.
intern *be inside* 224 vb.
doctor 658 n.
imprison 747 vb.
internal *intrinsic* 5 adj.
interior 224 adj.
internal organs
insides 224 n.
international
correlative 12 adj.
comprehensive 52 adj.
universal 79 adj.
national 371 adj.
unpossessed 774 adj.
sharing 775 adj.
internationalism
generality 79 n.
philanthropy 901 n.
internationalize
socialize 775 vb.
internecine
destructive 165 adj.
murderous 362 adj.
internee *interiority* 224 n.
internment
war measures 718 n.
detention 747 n.

internment camp
prison camp 748 n.
internuncio *envoy* 754 n.
interpellant
interlocutor 584 n.
interpellation
interrogation 459 n.
question 459 n.
allocution 583 n.
interpellator
questioner 459 n.
interpenetration
interjacence 231 n.
ingress 297 n.
passage 305 n.
interplanetary
extraneous 59 adj.
interjacent 231 adj.
interplay *correlation* 12 n.
interchange 151 n.
interpolate
put between 231 vb.
interpolation *adjunct* 40 n.
numerical operation 86 n.
interjection 231 n.
interpolator
interjector 231 n.
import *stable* 192 n.
interpose *discontinue* 72 vb.
put between 231 vb.
be instrumental 628 vb.
meddle 678 vb.
obstruct 702 vb.
hinder 702 vb.
mediate 720 vb.
prohibit 757 vb.
interpret
account for 158 vb.
play music 413 vb.
interpret 520 vb.
teach 534 vb.
facilitate 701 vb.
interpretation
answer 460 n.
connotation 514 n.
intelligibility 516 n.
interpretation 520 n.
interpreter
interpreter 520 n.
inter-racial *ethnic* 11 adj.
correlative 12 adj.
interregnum *interim* 108 n.
transientness 114 n.
lull 145 n.
interval 201 n.
anarchy 734 n.
interrelation
correlation 12 n.
interrex *potentate* 741 n.
interrogation
interrogation 459 n.

interrogation mark
question 459 n.
interrogative
enquiring 459 adj.
interrogator
questioner 459 n.
interrupt *interfere* 231 vb.
intrude 297 vb.
distract 456 vb.
interrupter
dissentient 489 n.
hinderer 702 n.
interruption
derangement 63 n.
discontinuity 72 n.
intempestivity 138 n.
stop 145 n.
interval 201 n.
interjection 231 n.
overactivity 678 n.
hindrance 702 n.
rudeness 885 n.
intersection *joint* 45 n.
crossing 222 n.
passage 305 n.
access, road 624 n.
interspace *interval* 201 n.
interiority 224 n.
intersperse *mix* 43 vb.
put between 231 vb.
inter-state
correlative 12 adj.
interstellar
extraneous 59 adj.
interjacent 231 adj.
cosmic 321 n.
interstellar matter
nebula 321 n.
interstice *gap* 201 n.
interstitial *interior* 224 adj.
interjacent 231 adj.
intertexture *crossing* 222 n.
inter-tribal *ethnic* 11 adj.
correlative 12 adj.
intertwine *mix* 43 vb.
tie 45 vb.
combine 50 vb.
enlace 222 vb.
interval *degree* 27 n.
disjunction 46 n.
incompleteness 55 n.
discontinuity 72 n.
interim 108 n.
period 110 n.
lull 145 n.
interval 201 n.
musical note 410 n.
dramaturgy 594 n.
repose 683 n.
intervale *gap* 201 n.
intervene *discontinue* 72 vb.

interfere 231 vb.
lie between 231 vb.
meddle 678 vb.
mediate 720 vb.
prohibit 757 vb.
intervener *hinderer* 702 n.
litigant 959 n.
intervention
interjection 231 n.
instrumentality 628 n.
hindrance 702 n.
war 718 n.
mediation 720 n.
interview *listening* 415 n.
exam 459 n.
interrogate 459 vb.
conference 584 n.
interviewer
questioner 459 n.
interlocutor 584 n.
interwar
intermediate 108 adj.
interweave *mix* 43 vb.
combine 50 vb.
compose 56 vb.
enlace 222 vb.
put between 231 vb.
interworking *agency* 173 n.
inter-world
correlative 12 adj.
intestate
obliterated 550 adj.
intestinal *interior* 224 adj.
intestine *insides* 224 n.
drain 351 n.
in the light
hindering 702 adj.
in the long run
generally 79 adv.
at last 113 adv.
in the main *wholly* 52 adv.
in the running
contending 716 adj.
in the way *nigh* 200 adv.
hindering 702 adj.
in the wind
happening 154 adj.
impending 155 adj.
intimacy *relation* 9 n.
coition 45 n.
knowledge 490 n.
friendship 880 n.
sociability 882 n.
intimate *conjunct* 45 adj.
private 80 adj.
interior 224 adj.
knowing 490 adj.
inform, hint 524 vb.
indicate 547 vb.
close friend 880 n.
intimation *hint* 524 n.

intimidate *hinder* 702 vb.
frighten 854 vb.
threaten 900 vb.
intimidation
dissuasion 613 n.
terror tactics 712 n.
intimidation 854 n.
intimidator *alarmist* 854 n.
intinction *ritual act* 988 n.
intolerable *bad* 645 adj.
intolerable 827 adj.
disliked 861 adj.
intolerance *uniformity* 16 n.
exclusion 57 n.
weakness 163 n.
prejudice 481 n.
opiniatry 602 n.
severity 735 n.
prohibition 757 n.
enmity 881 n.
inhumanity 898 n.
pitilessness 906 n.
orthodoxism 976 n.
intonation *sound* 398 n.
voice 577 n.
intone *sing* 413 vb.
intorsion
convolution 251 n.
in toto *completely* 54 adv.
intoxicant *poison* 659 n.
intoxicate *invigorate* 174 vb.
delight 826 vb.
intoxicated *drunk* 949 adj.
intoxicating *strong* 162 adj.
intoxication
impairment 655 n.
excitation 821 n.
excitable state 822 n.
intemperance 943 n.
drunkenness 949 n.
intractability
hardness 326 n.
obstinacy 602 n.
intractable *difficult* 700 adj.
disobedient 738 adj.
intramural *interior* 224 adj.
intransigence
obstinacy 602 n.
intransigent
resolute 599 adj.
in transit
convertibly 147 adv.
in transit 272 adv.
intransmutable
lasting 113 adj.
unchangeable 153 adj.
intravenous *interior* 224 adj.
in-tray *receptacle* 194 n.
compartment 194 n.
intrench *encroach* 306 vb.
intrepidity *courage* 855 n.

intricacy *complexity* 61 n.
crossing 222 n.
convolution 251 n.
difficulty 700 n.
intricate *tied* 45 adj.
difficult 700 adj.
(see intricacy)
intrigant *deceiver* 545 n.
planner 623 n.
libertine 952 n.
intrigue *latency* 523 n.
deceive 542 vb.
motivate 612 vb.
plot 623 n., vb.
overactivity 678 n.
be cunning 698 vb.
sedition 738 n.
impress 821 vb.
love affair 887 n.
illicit love 951 n.
intriguer *planner* 623 n.
meddler 678 n.
slyboots 698 n.
intriguing *lovable* 887 adj.
intrinsic *intrinsic* 5 adj.
ingredient 58 adj.
included 78 adj.
interior 224 adj.
intrinsicality *essence* 1 n.
intrinsicality 5 n.
relation 9 n.
introception
reception 299 n.
introduce *add* 38 vb.
come before 64 vb.
initiate 68 vb.
intromit 231 vb.
admit 299 vb.
precede 283 vb.
insert 303 vb.
befriend 880 vb.
greet 884 vb.
introduction *prelude* 66 n.
beginning 68 n.
reception 299 n.
insertion 303 n.
teaching 534 n.
friendship 880 n.
introductory
precursory 66 adj.
beginning 68 adj.
prior 119 adj.
introit *vocal music* 412 n.
Holy Communion 988 n.
intromission
interjection 231 n.
reception 299 n.
intromit *insert* 303 vb.
introspection
inspection 438 n.
meditation 449 n.

attention 455 n.
enquiry 459 n.
knowledge 490 n.
introspective
thoughtful 449 adj.
introversion
inversion 221 n.
interiority 224 n.
introvert *invert* 221 vb.
interiority 224 n.
introverted *intrinsic* 5 adj.
intrude *mistime* 138 vb.
interfere 231 vb.
intrude 297 vb.
insert 303 vb.
encroach 306 vb.
meddle 678 vb.
obstruct 702 vb.
intruder *intruder* 59 n.
settler 191 n.
interjector 231 n.
incomer 297 n.
intrusion *irrelation* 10 n.
inaptitude 25 n.
(*see* intrude)
intrusive *irrelative* 10 adj.
extraneous 59 adj.
intuition *intellect* 447 n.
non-intellect 448 n.
intuition 476 n.
intelligence 498 n.
supposition 512 n.
conjecture 512 n.
spontaneity 609 n.
revelation 975 n.
intuitive *mindless* 448 adj.
intuitive 476 adj.
intumescence
dilation 197 n.
convexity 253 n.
in turn *severally* 80 adv.
by turns 141 adv.
inundate *overlie* 226 vb.
irrigate 341 vb.
(*see* inundation)
inundation *havoc* 165 n.
outflow 298 n.
moistening 341 n.
waterfall 350 n.
redundance 637 n.
inurbanity
ill-breeding 847 n.
discourtesy 885 n.
inure *train* 534 vb.
habituate 610 vb.
make ready 669 vb.
inured *unfeeling* 375 adj.
thick-skinned 820 adj.
inurn *inter* 364 vb.
inutility *ineffectuality* 161 n.
superfluity 637 n.

inutility 641 n.
inexpedience 643 n.
non-use 674 n.
invade *interfere* 231 vb.
irrupt 297 vb.
attack 712 vb.
wage war 718 vb.
invading
extraneous 59 adj.
invaginate
invert 221 vb.
intromit 231 vb.
invalid *powerless* 161 adj.
weakling 163 n.
illogical 477 adj.
useless 641 adj.
sick person 651 n.
unhealthy 651 adj.
unwarranted 916 adj.
invalidate *disable* 161 vb.
weaken 163 vb.
confute 479 vb.
negate 533 vb.
abrogate 752 vb.
disentitle 916 vb.
invalid chair
pushcart 274 n.
invalidism *weakness* 163 n.
ill-health 651 n.
invalidity *impotence* 161 n.
unmeaningness 515 n.
invalid out
not retain 779 vb.
invaluable
profitable 640 adj.
valuable 644 adj.
of price 811 adj.
invariability
permanence 144 n.
invariable
characteristic 5 adj.
identical 13 adj.
uniform 16 adj.
orderly 60 adj.
unchangeable 153 adj.
usual 610 adj.
tedious 838 adj.
invariant *identity* 13 n.
identical 13 adj.
invasion *crowd* 74 n.
ingress 297 n.
attack 712 n.
invective *oratory* 579 n.
scurrility 899 n.
reproach 924 n.
detraction 926 n.
inveigh *curse* 899 vb.
dispraise 924 vb.
inveigle *ensnare* 542 vb.
invent *initiate* 68 vb.
imagine 513 vb.

fake 541 vb.
(*see* invention)
invention *causation* 156 n.
production 164 n.
thought 449 n.
idea 451 n.
discovery 484 n.
falsehood 541 n.
untruth, fable 543 n.
contrivance 623 n.
inventiveness
non-imitation 21 n.
productiveness 171 n.
thought 449 n.
imagination 513 n.
cunning 697 n.
inventor *precursor* 66 n.
producer 167 n.
enquirer 459 n.
detector 484 n.
inventorial
accounting 808 adj.
inventorize *specify* 80 vb.
number 86 vb.
inventory *all* 52 n.
arrangement 62 n.
class 62 vb.
list 87 n., vb.
contents 193 n.
account 808 vb.
inverse *contrariety* 14 n.
inverted 221 adj.
contraposition 240 n.
inversion
derangement 63 n.
transformation 143 n.
reversion 148 n.
revolution 149 n.
inversion 221 n.
contraposition 240 n.
trope 519 n.
ornament 574 n.
invert *demolish* 165 vb.
invert 221 vb.
invertebrate
impotent 161 adj.
weak 163 adj.
animal 365 n.
inverted commas
punctuation 547 n.
invest *place* 187 vb.
surround 230 vb.
circumscribe 232 vb.
store 632 vb.
besiege 712 vb.
commission 751 vb.
lend 784 vb.
speculate 791 vb.
expend 806 vb.
invested *dressed* 228 adj.
investigation *enquiry* 459 n.

police enquiry 459 n.
 study 536 n.
investigator enquirer 459 n.
 detective 459 n.
invest in purchase 792 vb.
investiture dressing 228 n.
 mandate 751 n.
investment dressing 228 n.
 closure 264 n.
 (see invest)
investor creditor 802 n.
 lender 784 n.
invest with give 781 vb.
inveteracy tradition 127 n.
 habit 610 n.
inveterate lasting 113 adj.
 immemorial 127 adj.
 permanent 144 adj.
 vested 153 adj.
 habitual 610 adj.
invidious
 unpleasant 827 adj.
 hateful 888 adj.
invigilate invigilate 457 vb.
invigilation
 carefulness 457 n.
invigilator keeper 749 n.
invigorate
 strengthen 162 vb.
 invigorate 174 vb.
 vitalize 360 vb.
 incite 612 vb.
 refresh 685 vb.
 animate 821 vb.
 cheer 833 vb.
invigorating
 salubrious 652 adj.
invincible
 unyielding 162 adj.
 unbeaten 727 adj.
inviolable strong 162 adj.
 concealed 525 adj.
 due 915 adj.
inviolate
 permanent 144 adj.
 concealed 525 adj.
 honourable 929 adj.
invious closed 264 adj.
 difficult 700 adj.
invisibility
 insubstantiality 4 n.
 smallness 33 n.
 invisibility 444 n.
 disappearance 446 n.
 latency 523 n.
invisible minute 196 adj.
 distant 199 n.
invisible ink secrecy 525 n.
invitation reception 299 n.
 inducement 612 n.
 command 737 n.

offer 759 n.
 request 761 n.
 excitation 821 n.
 courteous act 884 n.
invite delight 826 vb.
 desire 859 vb.
 be hospitable 882 vb.
invitee friend 880 n.
inviting accessible 289 adj.
 pleasurable 826 adj.
invocation
 allocution 583 n.
 edition 589 n.
 entreaty 761 n.
 praise 923 n.
 prayers 981 n.
 sorcery 983 n.
invocatory vocative 583 adj.
 supplicatory 761 adj.
 devotional 981 adj.
invoice list 87 n.
 demand 737 vb.
 accounts 808 n.
 price 809 n., vb.
invoke orate 579 vb.
 speak to 583 vb.
 entreat 761 vb.
 desire 859 vb.
 worship 981 vb.
 practise sorcery 983 vb.
involuntariness
 non-design 618 n.
involuntary
 intuitive 476 adj.
 unmeant 515 adj.
 involuntary 596 adj.
 spontaneous 609 adj.
 compelling 740 adj.
involution complexity 61 n.
 numerical operation 86 n.
 convolution 251 n.
involve be intrinsic 5 vb.
 contain 56 vb.
 bedevil 63 vb.
 comprise 78 vb.
 conduce 156 vb.
 evidence 466 vb.
 make likely 471 vb.
 mean 514 vb.
 imply 523 vb.
 indicate 547 vb.
 accuse 928 vb.
involved ingredient 58 adj.
 concurrent 181 adj.
 intricate 251 adj.
 imperspicuous 568 adj.
involvement relation 9 n.
 junction 45 n.
 complexity 61 n.
 affairs 154 n.
 difficulty 700 n.

participation 775 n.
 feeling 818 n.
 liking 859 n.
 guilt 936 n.
invulnerable strong 162 adj.
 invulnerable 660 adj.
 defended 713 adj.
inward intrinsic 5 adj.
 interior 224 adj.
 incoming 297 adj.
inward-looking
 intrinsic 5 adj.
 interior 224 adj.
inwardly inside 224 adv.
inwardness intrinsicality 5 n.
inwoven intrinsic 5 adj.
inwrought intrinsic 5 adj.
 interior 224 adj.
iodine prophylactic 658 n.
ion particle 33 n.
 element 319 n.
ionic prosody 593 n.
 ornamental 844 adj.
ionosphere
 atmosphere 340 n.
iota small quantity 33 n.
iotacism dialect 560 n.
 pronunciation 577 n.
I.O.U. title deed 767 n.
ipecacuanha
 cathartic 658 n.
ipse dixit certainty 473 n.
 affirmation 532 n.
 decree 737 n.
ipsissima verba
 identity 13 n.
 accuracy 494 n.
ipso facto actually 1 adv.
I.Q. intelligence 498 n.
irascibility
 quarrelsomeness 709 n.
 excitability 822 n.
 irascibility 892 n.
irascible violent 176 adj.
 ungracious 885 adj.
 sullen 893 adj.
 (see irascibility)
irate angry 891 adj.
ire anger 891 n.
irenic peaceful 717 adj.
 pacificatory 719 adj.
irenicon irenics 719 n.
irenics argument 475 n.
 peace 717 n.
 irenics 719 n.
iridal variegated 437 adj.
iridescence light 417 n.
 variegation 437 n.
iridescent mixed 43 adj.
 iridescent 437 adj.
iridization dim sight 440 n.

iris *eye* 438n.
irisate *variegate* 437vb.
Irish bull *mistake* 495n.
 absurdity 497n.
 ridiculousness 849n.
irk *fatigue* 684vb.
 be difficult 700vb.
 torment 827vb.

 bore 838n.
 be tedious 838vb.
irksome (*see* irk)
iron *strength* 162vb.
 flatten 216vb.
 smoother 258n.
 food content 301n.
 hardness 326n.
 rub 333vb.
 resolution 599n.
 (*see* iron out)
Iron Age *era* 110n.
 adversity 731n.
iron boot
 instrument of torture
 964n.
iron-clad *covered* 226adj.
 defended 713adj.
 (*see* warship)
Iron Cross *badge* 547n.
 decoration 729n.
iron curtain
 exclusion 57n.
 partition 231n.
 screen 421n.
 obstacle 702n.
iron hand *brute force* 735n.
iron heel *brute force* 735n.
 instrument of torture
 964n.
ironical *figurative* 519adj.
 untrue 543adj.
 funny 849adj.
 affected 850adj.
 derisive 851adj.
ironist *humorist* 839n.
 affector 850n.
iron lung
 compartment 194n.
 hospital 658n.
ironmonger
 tradesman 794n.
iron out *unravel* 62vb.
 flatten 216vb.
 straighten 249vb.
 smooth 258vb.
 facilitate 701vb.
iron ration
 small quantity 33n.
 provisions 301n.
 provision 633n.
 insufficiency 636n.
 portion 783n.

 fasting 946n.
irons *supporter* 218n.
 fetter 748n.
 pillory 964n.
Ironsides *cavalry* 722n.
irons in the fire
 business 622n.
 activity 678n.
irony *underestimation* 483n.
 metaphor 519n.
 mental dishonesty 543n.
 wit 839n.
 affectation 850n.
 ridicule 851n.
 reproach 924n.
irradiation *light* 417n.
 lighting 420n.
irrational
 numerical 85adj.
 unthinking 450adj.
 illogical 477adj.
 unwise 499adj.
irreclaimable
 wicked 934adj.
 impenitent 940adj.
irreconcilability
 irrelation 10n.
 contrariety 14n.
 disagreement 25n.
 revengefulness 910n.
irreconcilable
 opponent 705n.
 malcontent 829n.
 regretting 830adj.
 inimical 881adj.
irrecoverable *past* 125adj.
 lost 772adj.
 unpromising 853adj.
irredeemable *bad* 645adj.
 lost 772adj.
 unpromising 853adj.
 wicked 934adj.
 impenitent 940adj.
irredentism *regret* 830n.
 desire 859n.
 patriotism 901n.
irredentist *regret* 830n.
 desirer 859n.
 patriot 901n.
irreducible *simple* 44adj.
 unchangeable 153adj.
irrefragable
 undisputed 473adj.
 demonstrated 478adj.
irrefutable
 undisputed 473adj.
 demonstrated 478adj.
irregular *multiform* 82adj.
 distorted 246adj.
 neological 560adj.
 grammatical 565adj.

 soldier 722n.
 unsightly 842adj.
 wrong 914adj.
 extramarital 951adj.
 (*see* irregularity)
irregularity
 non-uniformity 17n.
 inequality 29n.
 disorder 61n.
 discontinuity 72n.
 unconformity 84n.
 fitfulness 142n.
 changeableness 152n.
 solecism 565n.
 illegality 954n.
irrelation *irrelation* 10n.
 dissimilarity 19n.
irrelative *severable* 46adj.
irrelevance
 insubstantiality 4n.
 irrelevance 10n.
 inaptitude 25n.
 absurdity 497n.
 unmeaningness 515n.
 unimportance 639n.
irrelevant *misplaced* 188adj.
 deviating 282adj.
 prolix 570adj.
irreligion *unbelief* 486n.
 irreligion 974n.
 impiety 980n.
irreligious *wicked* 934adj.
irremediable *bad* 645adj.
 harmful 645adj.
 unpromising 853adj.
irremissible *heinous* 934adj.
irremovable *fixed* 153adj.
 obstinate 602adj.
irreparable
 unpromising 853adj.
irreplaceable
 important 638adj.
 valuable 644adj.
irrepressible *violent* 176adj.
 wilful 602adj.
 independent 744adj.
 lively 819adj.
 cheerful 833adj.
irreproachable
 perfect 646adj.
 virtuous 933adj.
 guiltless 935adj.
irresistible
 powerful 160adj.
 strong 162adj.
 influential 178adj.
 demonstrated 478adj.
 necessary 596adj.
 inducive 612adj.
 compelling 740adj.
 lovable 887adj.

irresoluble
  unchangeable 153 adj.
irresolute *weak* 163 adj.
  doubting 474 adj.
  irresolute 601 adj.
  choiceless 606 adj.
  neutral 625 adj.
  lax 734 adj.
  nervous 854 adj.
irresolution (*see* irresolute)
irrespective
  irrelative 10 adj.
irresponsible
  changeful 152 adj.
  irresolute 601 adj.
  capricious 604 adj.
  rash 857 adj.
  dutiless 918 adj.
  lawless 954 adj.
irretrievable *lost* 772 adj.
irreverence
  non-wonder 865 n.
  disrespect 921 n.
  impiety 980 n.
irreversible *vested* 153 adj.
  unchangeable 153 adj.
  progressive 285 adj.
  necessary 596 adj.
  obstinate 602 adj.
  unpromising 853 adj.
irrevocable *vested* 153 adj.
  impossible 470 adj.
  certain 473 adj.
  necessary 596 adj.
  unpromising 853 adj.
irrigable *dry* 342 n.
irrigate *make fruitful* 171 vb.
  add water 339 vb.
  irrigate 341 vb.
  make flow 350 vb.
  cultivate 370 vb.
irrigator *irrigator* 341 n.
irriguous *drenched* 341 adj.
irritable *sensitive* 819 adj.
  excitable 822 adj.
  irascible 892 adj.
irritant *excitant* 821 n.
  aggravation 832 n.
irritate *make violent* 176 vb.
  give pain 377 vb.
  itch 378 vb.
  make quarrels 709 vb.
  excite 821 vb.
  torment 827 vb.
  aggravate 832 vb.
  make enemies 881 vb.
  enrage 891 vb.
irritation *excitation* 821 n.
  worry 825 n.
  painfulness 827 n.
  aggravation 832 n.

  anger 891 n.
  resentment 891 n.
irrupt *be violent* 176 vb.
  irrupt 297 vb.
  pass 305 vb.
  attack 712 vb.
irruption *ingress* 297 n.
  attack 712 n.
irruptive *incoming* 297 adj.
isagogics *theology* 973 n.
Ishmael *outcaste* 883 n.
isinglass *thickening* 354 n.
Isis *Egyptian gods* 967 n.
Islam *religious faith* 973 n.
Islamite *religionist* 970 n.
island *region* 184 n.
  island 349 n.
  seclusion 883 n.
islanded *insular* 349 adj.
  secluded 883 adj.
islander *dweller* 191 n.
  island 349 n.
Islands of the Blest
  mythic heaven 971 n.
island universe
  universe, star 321 n.
isle (*see* island)
islesman *island* 349 n.
ism *creed* 485 n.
isobar *weather* 340 n.
isocheimenal *cold* 380 adj.
isochronous
  chronological 117 adj.
  synchronous 123 adj.
isocracy *government* 733 n.
isogloss *limit* 236 n.
isogonic line *limit* 236 n.
  outline 233 n.
isolable *alone* 88 adj.
isolate *set apart* 46 vb.
  be one 88 vb.
  sanitate 652 vb.
  seclude 883 vb.
isolated *alone* 88 adj.
  insular 349 adj.
isolated instance
  speciality 80 n.
  unconformity 84 n.
  unit 88 n.
isolation *irrelation* 10 n.
  disjunction 46 n.
  unity 88 n.
  freedom 744 n.
  seclusion 883 n.
isolationism *freedom* 744 n.
isolationist *free man* 744 n.
  independent 744 adj.
  solitary 883 n.
isolation ward
  hospital 658 n.
isomorphism *form* 243 n.

isoperimetric *equal* 28 adj.
isosceles
  symmetrical 245 adj.
isothermal layer
  atmosphere 340 n.
isotonic *harmonious* 410 adj.
isotropy *equivalence* 28 n.
issue *kinsman* 11 n.
  subdivision 53 n.
  eventuality 154 n.
  effect 157 n.
  posterity 170 n.
  outflow 298 n.
  emerge 298 vb.
  flow 350 vb.
  topic 452 n.
  the press 528 n.
  publish 528 vb.
  reading matter 589 n.
  completion 725 n.
  coinage 797 n.
  mint 797 vb.
  litigation 959 n.
issue, at *contending* 716 adj.
issuing in *caused* 157 adj.
issueless
  unproductive 172 adj.
isthmian *narrow* 206 adj.
  land 344 n.
isthmus *bond* 47 n.
  contraction 198 n.
  narrowness 206 n.
  land 344 n.
  bridge 624 n.
it *identity* 13 n.
  no imitation 21 n.
  fitness 24 n.
  authenticity 492 n.
Italianate
  extraneous 59 adj.
italic *letter* 558 n.
  lettering 586 n.
  written 586 adj.
  print-type 587 n.
italicize
  emphasize 532 vb.
italics *punctuation* 547 n.
itch *attraction* 291 n.
  agitation 318 n.
  formication 378 n.
  curiosity 453 n.
  skin disease 651 n.
  desire 859 n.
itching *inquisitive* 453 adj.
  excited 821 adj.
itching palm *avarice* 816 n.
item *in addition* 38 adv.
  extra 40 n.
  part 53 n.
  unit 88 n.
  object 319 n.

itemize *specify* 80vb.
　list 87vb.
items *particulars* 80n.
　list 87n.
　contents 193n.
iterate *repeat* 106vb.
iteration *duplication* 91n.
　vigour 571n.
　perseverance 600n.
iterative *repeated* 106adj.
itinerant *travelling* 267adj.
　traveller 268n.
itinerary *itinerary* 267n.
　guide-book 524n.
　way 624n.
itself *self* 80n.
ivories *tooth* 256n.
　piano 414n.
　gambling 618n.
ivory *white thing* 427n.
　dunce 501n.
ivory tower
　seclusion 883n.
ivy *plant* 366n.
izzat *prestige* 866n.

J

jab *knock* 279n.
　wound 655n.
　therapy 658n.
　foin 712n.
jab at *essay* 671n.
jabber *empty talk* 515n.
　speak 579vb.
　chatter 581n.
jacinth *gem* 844n.
jack *lifter* 310n.
　rotator 315n.
　flag 547n.
　tool 630n.
jackal *aftercomer* 67n.
　auxiliary 707n.
　dependant 742n.
　toady 879n.
　noxious animal 904n.
jackanapes *fop* 848n.
　insolent person 878n.
jackboot *footwear* 228n.
　tyrant 735n.
jackdaw *bird* 365n.
jacket *wrapping* 226n.
　skin 226n.
　tunic 228n.
　bookbinding 589n.
Jack-in-office
　tyrant 735n.
　autocrat 741n.
　official 690n.
　insolent person 878n.
Jack-in-the-box

inexpectation 508n.
　plaything 837n.
jack-knife *sharp edge* 256n.
Jack of all trades
　proficient 696n.
Jack-o'-lantern *glow* 417n.
　glow-worm 420n.
jackpot *acquisition* 771n.
jacks *plaything* 837n.
jack up *support* 218vb.
　elevate 310vb.
Jacobin *opponent* 705n.
　revolter 738n.
Jacob's ladder *ascent* 308n.
Jacob's staff *gauge* 465n.
jaconet *textile* 222n.
Jacquerie
　terror tactics 712n.
jactation *boasting* 877n.
jactitation *agitation* 318n.
　affirmation 532n.
　boasting 877n.
jaculation
　propulsion 287n.
jade *saddle-horse* 273n.
　greenness 432n.
　fatigue 684vb.
　be tedious 838vb.
　gem 844n.
　cause dislike 861vb.
　sate 863vb.
　bad man 938n.
　loose woman 952n.
jadedness *fatigue* 684n.
　satiety 863n.
jag *notch* 260vb.
　drunkenness 949n.
jagged *angular* 247adj.
　rough 259adj.
　notched 260adj.
jaggery *sweet* 392n.
jaggy *notched* 260adj.
jaguar *cat* 365n.
jail *gaol* 748n.
jailer *janitor* 264n.
　gaoler 749n.
Jainism *religious faith* 973n.
jakes *latrine* 649n.
jam *join, tighten* 45vb.
　crowd 74n.
　halt 145vb.
　close 264vb.
　be quiescent 266vb.
　sweetmeat 301n.
　viscidity 354n.
　pulpiness 356n.
　condiment 389n.
　sweet 392n.
　predicament 700n.
　obstruct 702vb.
jamb *pillar* 218n.

jamboree *amusement* 837n.
jammed *firm-set* 45adj.
　full 54adj.
jammy *viscid* 354adj.
jam session *dancing* 837n.
jangle *disagree* 25vb.
　resound 404vb.
　rasp 407vb.
　discord 411vb.
　dissension 709n.
jangling *argument* 475n.
janissary *soldier* 722n.
janitor *janitor* 264n.
　servant 742n.
Janus *duality* 90n.
　tergiversator 603n.
japan *coat* 226vb.
　resin 357n.
　colour 425vb.
　black pigment 428n.
　decorate 844vb.
jape *amuse oneself* 837vb.
　witticism 839n.
japer *humorist* 839n.
jar *differ* 15vb.
　disagree 25vb.
　vessel 194n.
　agitation 318n.
　give pain 377vb.
　rasp 407vb.
　discord 411vb.
　dissension 709n.
　displease 827vb.
　cause dislike 861vb.
　excite hate 888vb.
jardinière
　vessel, bowl 194n.
jargon *speciality* 80n.
　absurdity 497n.
　unmeaningness 515n.
　slang 560n.
jarvey *driver* 268n.
Jason *mariner* 270n.
jasper *variegate* 437vb.
　gem 844n.
jaundice *yellowness* 433n.
　bias 481vb.
　indigestion 651n.
jaundiced *biased* 481adj.
　melancholic 834adj.
　sullen 893adj.
　jealous 911adj.
jaunt *land travel* 267n.
jaunting-car *carriage* 274n.
jaunty *cheerful* 833adj.
　showy 875adj.
　impertinent 878adj.
javelin *spear* 723n.
　missile weapon 723n.
jaw *projection* 254n.
　be loquacious 581vb.

chatter 581 n.
  (*see* jaws)
jaw-breaker
  hardness 326 n.
  word 559 n.
  neology 560 n.
  inelegance 576 n.
jaws *maw* 194 n.
  threshold 234 n.
  orifice 263 n.
  eater 301 n.
jay *dupe* 544 n.
  chatterer 581 n.
jaywalker *bungler* 697 n.
jazz *music* 412 n.
  dance 837 n.
jealous *opposing* 704 adj.
  resentful 891 adj.
  malevolent 898 adj.
  selfish 932 adj.
  (*see* jealousy)
jealousy *imitation* 20 n.
  doubt 486 n.
  quarrelsomeness 709 n.
  contention 716 n.
  discontent 829 n.
  enmity 881 n.
  love 887 n.
  hatred 888 n.
  jealousy 911 n.
jeans *trousers* 228 n.
jeep *automobile* 274 n.
jeer *ridicule* 851 vb.
  not respect 921 vb.
  despise 922 vb.
jeers *lifter* 310 n.
jehad *war* 718 n.
Jehovah *the Deity* 965 n.
Jehovah's Witnesses
  sect 978 n.
Jehu *driver* 268 n.
  speeder 277 n.
jejune *lean* 206 adj.
  tasteless 387 adj.
  feeble 572 adj.
  underfed 636 adj.
Jekyll and Hyde
  multiformity 82 n.
jell *thicken* 354 vb.
jellification
  condensation 324 n.
jelly *sweetmeat* 301 n.
  sweet 392 n.
jellyfish *weakling* 163 n.
  fish 365 n.
  coward 856 n.
jemmy *force* 176 vb.
  tool 630 n.
  fop 848 n.
jeopardy *danger* 661 n.
jerboa *jumper* 312 n.

jeremiad *lament* 836 n.
  censure 924 n.
Jeremiah *weeper* 836 n.
jerk *revolution* 149 n.
  move 265 vb.
  impulse 279 n.
  draw 288 vb.
  leap 312 vb.
  agitate 318 vb.
jerkin *tunic* 228 n.
jerkiness
  non-uniformity 17 n.
  discontinuity 72 n.
  fitfulness 142 n.
  agitation 318 n.
  restlessness 678 n.
jerks, the *spasm* 318 n.
jeroboam *vessel* 194 n.
jerry *vessel* 194 n.
  latrine 649 n.
jerry-built *flimsy* 163 adj.
  spurious 542 adj.
  unsafe 661 adj.
jersey *textile* 222 n.
  vest 228 n.
  cattle 365 n.
jess *halter* 47 n.
jesse *church interior* 990 n.
jest *trifle* 639 n.
  amuse oneself 837 vb.
  witticism 839 n.
jester *fool* 501 n.
  humorist 839 n.
jesuitry *sophistry* 477 n.
  falsehood 541 n.
Jesuits *monk* 986 n.
Jesus *God the Son* 965 n.
jet *energy* 160 n.
  vigorousness 174 n.
  outbreak 176 n.
  speeder 277 n.
  propellant 287 n.
  outflow 298 n.
  emit 300 vb.
  ascend 308 vb.
  stream 350 n.
  black thing 428 n.
jet propulsion
  energy 160 n.
  propulsion 287 n.
jetsam
  thing transferred 272 n.
  derelict 779 n.
jettison *eject* 300 vb.
  lighten 323 vb.
  disuse 674 vb.
  not retain 779 vb.
jetty *stable* 192 n.
  projection 254 n.
  black 428 adj.
  shelter 662 n.

jeu d'esprit
  witticism 839 n.
jeunesse dorée
  rich man 800 n.
  beau monde 848 n.
jewel *exceller* 644 n.
  a beauty 841 n.
  gem 844 n.
  darling 890 n.
jeweller *artisan* 686 n.
jewellery *jewellery* 844 n.
Jew's harp *harp* 414 n.
Jezebel *bad man* 938 n.
  loose woman 952 n.
jheel *marsh* 347 n.
jib *prow* 237 n.
  sail 275 n.
  recoil 280 vb.
  deviate 282 vb.
  turn back 286 vb.
  be unwilling 598 vb.
  be irresolute 601 vb.
  avoid 620 vb.
  refuse 760 vb.
  resent 891 vb.
jibe *satirize* 851 vb.
  indignity 921 n.
  despise 922 vb.
  dispraise 924 vb.
jiffy *instant* 116 n.
jig *leap* 312 vb.
  agitation 318 n.
  musical piece 412 n.
  dance 837 n.
jiggle *derange* 63 vb.
  agitate 318 vb.
jig-saw *combination* 50 n.
  indoor game 837 n.
jilt *disappoint* 509 vb.
  befool 542 vb.
  deceiver 545 n.
  tergiversator 603 n.
  relinquish 621 vb.
  be dishonest 930 vb.
jim-jams *frenzy* 503 n.
  alcoholism 949 n.
jimmy (*see* jemmy)
jingle *resonance* 404 n.
  doggerel 593 n.
jingler *poet* 593 n.
jingoism *bellicosity* 718 n.
  boasting 877 n.
jink *be oblique* 220 vb.
  be in motion 265 vb.
  avoid 620 vb.
Jinn *demon* 970 n.
jinricksha *cab* 274 n.
jinx *badness* 645 n.
jitney *cab* 274 n.
jitterbug *dance* 837 n., vb.
jitters *agitation* 318 n.

nervousness 854 n.
jive *music* 412 n.
  dance 837 n., vb.
jiver *jumper* 312 n.
job *agency* 173 n.
  job, *function* 622 n.
  undertaking 672 n.
  deed 676 n.
  labour 682 n.
  hard task 700 n.
  stealing 788 n.
  foul play 930 n.
jobation *reprimand* 924 n.
jobber *trickster* 545 n.
jobbery *cunning* 698 n.
  improbity 930 n.
jobbing *barter* 791 n.
  venal 930 adj.
jobless *unused* 674 adj.
  non-active 677 adj.
Job's comforter
  moper 834 n.
  hopelessness 853 n.
jockey *rider* 268 n.
  speeder 277 n.
  trickster 545 n.
jockeyship *trickery* 542 n.
jocko *monkey* 365 n.
jock-strap *supporter* 218 n.
jocosity *wit* 839 n.
jocularity
  merriment 833 n.
  wit 839 n.
jocund *gay* 833 adj.
jocundity
  pleasurableness 826 n.
  amusement 837 n.
jodhpurs *breeches* 228 n.
jog *walk* 267 vb.
  impel 279 vb.
  agitate 318 vb.
  gesture 547 n.
  gesticulate 547 vb.
joggle *agitate* 318 vb.
jog on *go on* 146 vb.
  travel 267 vb.
  progress 285 vb.
  be middling 732 vb.
jog-trot *gait* 265 n.
  pedestrianism 267 n.
  slowness 278 n.
Johnny, Johnnie
  person 371 n.
  male 372 n.
  fop 848 n.
Johnsonese
  imperspicuity 568 n.
  magniloquence 574 n.
joie de vivre
  cheerfulness 833 n.
join *accrue* 38 vb.

join 45 vb.
  agglutinate 48 vb.
  bring together 74 vb.
  be included 78 vb.
  gap 201 n.
  be contiguous 202 vb.
  approach 289 vb.
  meet 295 vb.
  enter 297 vb.
  patronize 703 vb.
  join a party 708 vb.
  marry 894 vb.
joinder *joinder* 45 n.
  combination 50 n.
  assemblage 74 n.
joiner *joinder* 45 n.
  artisan 686 n.
joinery *efformation* 243 n.
join in *be active* 678 vb.
  co-operate 706 vb.
  participate 775 vb.
  be sociable 882 vb.
join issue *argue* 475 vb.
  fight 716 vb.
joint *joint* 45 n.
  concurrent 181 adj.
  angularity 247 n.
  fold 261 n.
  meat 301 n.
  corporate 708 adj.
  sharing 775 adj.
jointly
  co-operatively 706 adv.
  in common 755 adv.
jointness
  joint possession 775 n.
joint, out of
  orderless 61 adj.
joint-stock
  corporate 708 adj.
  joint possession 775 n.
joint-stock company
  association 706 n.
  corporation 708 n.
jointure *dower* 777 n.
join-up
  war measures 718 n.
joist *beam* 218 n.
joke *absurdity* 497 n.
  trickery 542 n.
  trifle 639 n.
  witticism 839 n.
joker *misfit* 25 n.
  nonconformist 84 n.
  humorist 839 n.
joking *gay* 833 adj.
  witty 839 adj.
joking apart
  affirmatively 532 adv.
jollification *revel* 837 n.
jollity *merriment* 833 n.

sociability 882 n.
jolly *fleshy* 195 adj.
  naval man 270 n.
  navy man 722 n.
  gay 833 adj.
  amused 837 adj.
  sociable 882 adj.
jolly along *cheer* 833 vb.
jolly-boat *boat* 275 n.
Jolly Roger *flag* 547 n.
jolt *be rough* 259 vb.
  move slowly 278 vb.
  impulse 279 n.
  agitation 318 n.
  inexpectation 508 vb.
joltiness *discontinuity* 72 n.
  (see jolt)
Jonah *unlucky person* 731 n.
  moper 834 n.
jongleur *musician* 413 n.
  poet 593 n.
  entertainer 594 n.
jorum *bowl* 194 n.
Joseph *virgin* 950 n.
Joseph's coat
  variegation 437 n.
josh *ridicule* 851 vb.
joss *idol* 982 n.
joss-house *temple* 990 n.
joss-stick *fumigator* 385 n.
  scent 396 n.
  ritual object 988 n.
jostle *counteract* 182 vb.
  be near 200 vb.
  be contiguous 202 vb.
  impel 279 vb.
  obstruct 702 vb.
  fight 716 vb.
  not respect 921 vb.
jot *small quantity* 33 n.
  write 586 vb.
  trifle 639 n.
jot down *record* 548 vb.
jottings *record* 548 n.
  reading matter 589 n.
jounce *agitate* 318 vb.
journal *chronology* 117 n.
  the press, journal 528 n.
  record 548 n.
  biography 590 n.
  account book 808 n.
journalese *neology* 560 n.
journalism *publicity* 528 n.
  writing 586 n.
journalist *publicizer* 528 n.
  chronicler 549 n.
  author 589 n.
journalistic
  dialectical 560 adj.
journalize *register* 548 vb.
  account 808 vb.

journey *travel* 267 vb.
  passage 305 n.
journeyman *artisan* 686 n.
journey's end
  resting place 266 n.
  goal 295 n.
joust *contest, duel* 716 n.
jouster *combatant* 722 n.
Jove *Olympian god* 967 n.
joviality *merriment* 833 n.
  amusement 837 n.
  sociability 882 n.
Jovian *planetary* 321 adj.
jowl *laterality* 239 n.
joy *pleasure* 376 n.
  joy 824 n.
  pleasurableness 826 n.
  cheerfulness 833 n.
joyful, joyous
  happy 824 adj.
  gay 833 adj.
joyless *unpleasant* 827 adj.
  melancholic 834 adj.
joy-ride *land travel* 267 n.
  easy thing 701 n.
  borrowing 785 n.
  stealing 788 n.
joy-stick *aircraft* 276 n.
  directorship 689 n.
jube *church interior* 990 n.
jubilant *pleased* 824 adj.
  jubilant 833 adj.
  rejoicing 835 adj.
  celebrative 876 adj.
jubilate *be pleased* 824 vb.
  rejoice 835 vb.
  celebrate 876 vb.
  boast 877 vb.
jubilation (*see* jubilate)
jubilee *over twenty* 99 n.
  period 110 n.
  anniversary 141 n.
  merriment 833 n.
  rejoicing 835 n.
  celebration 876 n.
Judaism
  religious faith 973 n.
Judaizers
  church party 978 n.
Judas *deceiver* 545 n.
  knave 938 n.
Judas kiss *duplicity* 541 n.
  falsehood 541 n.
  mental dishonesty 543 n.
  perfidy 930 n.
judge *leader* 690 n.
  have taste 846 vb.
  punisher 936 n.
  judge 957 n.
  (*see* judgment)
judge and jury

  tribunal 956 n.
judgmatic
  judicial 480 adj.
  wise 498 adj.
judgment *intellect* 447 n.
  discrimination 463 n.
  judgment 480 n.
  opinion 485 n.
  sagacity 498 n.
  decree 737 n.
  legality 953 n.
  legal trial 959 n.
  condemnation 961 n.
  punishment 963 n.
judgment day
  future state 124 n.
  tribunal 956 n.
judgment seat
  tribunal 956 n.
judicatory *judicial* 480 adj.
  tribunal 956 n.
  curial 956 adj.
judicature *jurisdiction* 955 n.
judicial *judicial* 480 adj.
  curial 956 adj.
judiciary
  jurisdictional 955 adj.
judicious *moderate* 177 adj.
  discriminating 463 adj.
  judicial 480 adj.
  wise 498 adj.
judo *defence* 713 n.
  wrestling 716 n.
judoist *combatant* 722 n.
jug *vessel* 194 n.
  imprison 947 vb.
  gaol 748 n.
juggins *ninny* 501 n.
juggle *modify* 143 vb.
  sleight 542 n.
  stratagem 698 n.
juggler *conjuror* 545 n.
  entertainer 594 n.
  slyboots 698 n.
  sorcerer 983 n.
jugglery (*see* juggle)
jugular vein
  essential part 5 n.
  conduit 351 n.
  life 360 n.
juice *fluid* 335 n.
  moisture 341 n.
  semiliquidity 354 n.
juiceless *dry* 342 n.
juicy *vernal* 128 adj.
  soft 327 adj.
  fluidal 335 adj.
  humid 341 adj.
  semiliquid 354 adj.
  pulpy 356 adj.
  savoury 390 adj.

  topping 644 adj.
  pleasurable 826 adj.
  impure 951 adj.
ju-jitsu *defence* 713 n.
  wrestling 716 n.
ju-jitsuist *combatant* 722 n.
jujube *sweet* 392 n.
juke box *gramophone* 414 n.
julep *liquor* 301 n.
  sweet 392 n.
jumble *medley* 43 n.
  confusion 61 n.
  jumble 63 vb.
  deform 244 vb.
  not discriminate 464 vb.
  impair 655 vb.
jumbo *large* 195 adj.
jump *interval* 201 n.
  fly 271 vb.
  spurt 277 n.
  progression 285 n.
  ascent 308 n.
  leap 312 n., vb.
  agitation 318 n.
  neglect 458 vb.
  not expect 508 vb.
  improvement 654 n.
  obstacle 702 n.
  be excited 821 vb.
  be excitable 822 vb.
  amuse oneself 837 vb.
  fear 854 vb.
jump a claim
  appropriate 786 vb.
jump at *be willing* 597 vb.
  pursue 619 vb.
  consent 758 vb.
  desire 859 vb.
jumper *vest* 228 n.
  apron 228 n.
  thoroughbred 273 n.
  jumper 312 n.
jump-off *aider* 703 n.
jump on the bandwagon
  do likewise 20 vb.
  conform 83 vb.
  apostatize 603 vb.
  be in fashion 848 vb.
  be servile 879 vb.
jump over *overstep* 306 vb.
jumps *agitation* 318 n.
  nervousness 854 n.
jump the gun
  do before 119 vb.
  be early 135 vb.
jump the queue
  be disordered 61 vb.
  come before 64 vb.
  precede 283 vb.
jump to conclusions
  prejudge 481 vb.

jump to it *be active* 678 vb.
jumpy *agitated* 318 adj.
　active 678 adj.
　nervous 854 adj.
junction *junction* 45 n.
　bond 47 n.
　combination 50 n.
　accompaniment 89 n.
　continuity 202 n.
　goal 295 n.
　access 624 n.
　road, railroad 624 n.
juncture *juncture* 8 n.
　joint 45 n.
　present time 121 n.
　occasion, crisis 137 n.
jungle *confusion* 61 n.
　wood 366 n.
jungliness
　ill-breeding 847 n.
jungly *arboreal* 366 adj.
　artless 699 adj.
junior *inferior* 35 n.
　subsequent 120 adj.
　young 130 adj.
　youngster 132 n.
　college student 538 n.
juniority *youth* 130 n.
　subjection 745 n.
junk *sailing-ship* 275 n.
　rubbish 641 n.
Junker *aristocrat* 868 n.
junket *meal* 301 n.
　milk product 301 n.
　semiliquidity 354 n.
　revel 837 vb.
Juno *Olympian god* 967 n.
junta, junto *party* 708 n.
Jupiter *planet* 321 n.
　mythic god 966 n.
　Olympian god 967 n.
juridical *judicial* 480 adj.
　jurisdictional 955 adj.
jurisconsult *jurist* 958 n.
jurisdiction *authority* 733 n.
　law 953 n.
　jurisdiction 955 n.
　legal process 959 n.
jurisdictional *curial* 956 adj.
jurisprudence
　jurisprudence 953 n.
jurisprudential *legal* 953 adj.
　jurisprudential 958 adj.
jurist *jurist* 958 n.
juristic *judicial* 480 adj.
juror (*see* juryman)
jury *estimator* 480 n.
　jury 957 n.
jury-box *courtroom* 956 n.
juryman *estimator* 480 n.
　jury 957 n.

jury mast *substitute* 150 n.
　safeguard 662 n.
jus gentium *law* 953 n.
jussive *commanding* 737 adj.
just *rational* 475 adj.
　veracious 540 adj.
　indifferent 860 adj.
　just 913 adj.
　honourable 929 adj.
　disinterested 931 adj.
　virtuous 933 adj.
　legal 953 adj.
　pietist 979 n.
just as
　synchronously 123 adv.
just cause *vindication* 927 n.
just do *suffice* 635 vb.
just excuse
　vindication 927 n.
justice *indifference* 860 n.
　justice 913 n.
　probity 929 n.
　disinterestedness 931 n.
　virtue 933 n.
　legality 953 n.
　judge 957 n.
　reward 962 n.
　punishment 963 n.
justiciable
　accusable 928 adj.
　legal 953 adj.
　illegal 954 adj.
　jurisdictional 955 adj.
　litigated 959 adj.
justifiable *just* 913 adj.
　deserving 915 adj.
　vindicable 927 adj.
justification
　counter-evidence 467 n.
　pretext 614 n.
　dueness 915 n.
　vindication 927 n.
　acquittal 960 n.
　divine function 965 n.
　sanctity 979 n.
justificatory
　excusing 614 adj.
justify *regularize* 62 vb.
　demonstrate 478 vb.
　print 587 vb.
　(*see* justification)
just mention *hint* 524 vb.
just now
　at present 121 adv.
　newly 126 adv.
just out *new* 126 adv.
just price *equivalence* 28 n.
just right *sufficient* 635 adj.
　perfect 646 adj.
　right 913 adj.
just so *in order* 60 adv.

　accurate 494 adj.
　right 913 adj.
jut *jut* 254 vb.
　be visible 443 vb.
jute *fibre* 208 n.
　textile 222 n.
jutting *salient* 254 adj.
juvenile *young* 130 adj.
　infantine 132 adj.
　feeble 572 adj.
　immature 670 adj.
juvenilia
　reading matter 589 n.
juxtapose *connect* 45 vb.
　bring near 200 vb.
　juxtapose 202 vb.
　compare 462 vb.
juxtaposition
　assemblage 74 n.

K

ka *identity* 13 n.
　analogue 18 n.
　spirit 447 n.
　mythic god 966 n.
kafir *heathen* 974 n.
kailyard *dialectical* 560 adj.
kailyard school *style* 566 n.
Kaiser *sovereign* 741 n.
Kaiserism *despotism* 733 n.
kale *vegetable* 301 n.
kaleidoscope *medley* 43 n.
　multiformity 82 n.
　alterer 143 n.
　changeable thing 152 n.
　variegation 437 n.
　optical device 442 n.
　spectacle 445 n.
kaleidoscopic
　coloured 425 adj.
kalends *date* 108 n.
kangaroo *jumper* 312 n.
　marsupial 365 n.
kangaroo court
　lawlessness 954 n.
Kantianism
　philosophy 449 n.
kaolin *soil* 344 n.
　materials 631 n.
kapellmeister
　musician 413 n.
kapok *fibre* 208 n.
kaput *destroyed* 165 adj.
　defeated 728 adj.
karma *effect* 157 n.
　fate 596 n.
Karmayoga *religion* 973 n.
karmic *fated* 596 adj.
katabolism
　transformation 143 n.

katatonia
  psychopathy 503 n.
kayak *rowboat* 275 n.
kazi *officer* 741 n.
  judge 957 n.
kebab *meat* 301 n.
keck *vomit* 300 vb.
keddah *trap* 542 n.
  chase 619 n.
  lock-up 748 n.
kedge *navigate* 269 vb.
  draw 288 vb.
  safeguard 662 n.
keel *stabilizer* 153 n.
  base 214 n.
  pivot 218 n.
  ship 275 n.
keelhaul *punish* 963 vb.
keelson (*see* kelson)
keen *keen* 174 adj.
  sharp 256 adj.
  inter 364 vb.
  cold 380 adj.
  contending 716 adj.
  felt 818 adj.
  lament 836 n., vb.
  witty 839 adj.
  desiring 859 adj.
  condolence 905 n.
keener *funeral* 364 n.
  weeper 836 n.
keen-eyed *seeing* 438 adj.
keen on *enamoured* 887 adj.
keep *put off* 136 vb.
  stay 144 vb.
  go on 146 vb.
  dwelling 192 n.
  dwell 192 vb.
  provisions 301 n.
  look after 457 vb.
  store 632 vb.
  provide 633 vb.
  safeguard 660 vb.
  refuge 662 n.
  subvention 703 n.
  patronize 703 vb.
  fort 713 n.
  defend 713 vb.
  detention 747 n.
  retain 778 vb.
  celebrate 876 vb.
  observe 768 vb.
  ritualize 988 vb.
keep accounts
  number 86 vb.
  account 808 vb.
keep alive *vitalize* 360 vb.
  preserve 666 vb.
keep an eye
  look after 457 vb.
  safeguard 660 vb.

keep at arm's length
  repel 292 vb.
  parry 713 vb.
  resist 715 vb.
keep awake
  be active 678 vb.
keep away
  be absent 190 vb.
  avoid 620 vb.
keep back
  keep secret 525 vb.
  dissuade 613 vb.
  store 632 vb.
  retain 778 vb.
  be parsimonious 816 vb.
keep calm
  keep calm 823 vb.
keep company
  accompany 89 vb.
  be friendly 880 vb.
keep count *list* 87 vb.
keep down *depress* 311 vb.
  subjugate 745 vb.
keeper *concomitant* 89 n.
  janitor 264 n.
  surveillance 457 n.
  animal husbandry 569 n.
  protector 660 n.
  manager 690 n.
  interceptor 702 n.
  servant 742 n.
  keeper 749 n.
  consignee 754 n.
keep faith
  observe faith 768 vb.
  be honourable 929 vb.
keep going *go on* 146 vb.
  be in motion 265 vb.
keep holy *celebrate* 876 vb.
  sanctify 979 vb.
  ritualize 988 vb.
keep in *surround* 230 vb.
  imprison 747 vb.
  retain 778 vb.
keep in countenance
  give courage 855 vb.
keeping *residing* 192 adj.
  protection 660 n.
  tutelary 660 adj.
  detention 747 n.
keep in hand *store* 632 vb.
  not use 674 vb.
keep in step *conform* 83 vb.
  synchronize 123 vb.
keep in the dark
  not know 491 vb.
  keep secret 525 vb.
keep in with
  be friendly 880 vb.
  be sociable 882 vb.
keep off *be distant* 199 vb.

  avoid 620 vb.
  parry 713 vb.
keep on *recur* 139 vb.
  go on 146 vb.
  progress 285 vb.
  persevere 600 vb.
keep oneself to oneself
  be fastidious 862 vb.
  be unsocial 883 vb.
keep one's head
  be courageous 855 vb.
  not wonder 865 vb.
keep order *order* 60 vb.
  safeguard 660 vb.
keep out *exclude* 57 vb.
  obstruct 702 vb.
  restrain 747 vb.
  refuse 760 vb.
  be unsocial 883 vb.
keep out of the way
  (*see* keep away)
keep pace with
  be equal 28 vb.
  concur 181 vb.
keep quiet
  be quiescent 266 vb.
  not act 677 vb.
keepsake *reminder* 505 n.
keep time *time* 117 vb.
  synchronize 123 vb.
keep together *accord* 24 vb.
keep under
  (*see* keep down)
keep up *stay* 144 vb.
  sustain 146 vb.
  go on 146 vb.
keep up with *be equal* 28 vb.
  be friendly 880 vb.
  be sociable 882 vb.
keep up with the Joneses
  afford 800 vb.
keep well
  be healthy 650 vb.
kef *drug* 658 n.
keg *vat* 194 n.
kelpie *demon* 970 n.
kelson, keelson *base* 214 n.
ken *view* 438 n.
  see 438 vb.
  knowledge 490 n.
kennel *group* 74 n.
  stable 192 n.
  furrow 262 n.
  drain 351 n.
  imprison 747 vb.
  lock-up 748 n.
kenning *name* 561 n.
kenosis *humility* 872 n.
kepi *headgear* 228 n.
kept woman
  kept woman 952 n.

kerb *edge* 234n.
  limit 236n.
  road 624n.
kerb-crawler *libertine* 952n.
kerb-market *mart* 796n.
kerchief *headgear* 228n.
kerf *notch* 260n.
kermes *red pigment* 431n.
kermesse *festivity* 837n.
kern *soldier* 722n.
  countryman 869n.
kernel *essential part* 5n.
  middle 70n.
  focus 76n.
  centrality 225n.
  chief thing 638n.
kerosene *oil* 357n.
  fuel 385n.
kersey *textile* 222n.
kerseys *trousers* 228n.
ketch *sailing-ship* 275n.
ketchup *sauce* 389n.
kettle *cauldron* 194n.
  heater 383n.
kettle drum *drum* 414n.
kettle of fish
  complexity 61n.
  predicament 700n.
kevel *pulverize* 332vb.
key *degree* 27n.
  crucial 137adj.
  influential 178adj.
  opener 263n.
  stopper 264n.
  island 349n.
  key 410n.
  hue 425n.
  answer 460n.
  discovery 484n.
  interpretation 520n.
  translation 520n.
  instrument 628n.
  important 638adj.
  safeguard 662n.
key, be in
  harmonize 410vb.
keyboard
  musical note 410n.
  piano 414n.
keyed up
  expectant 507adj.
keyhole *orifice* 263n.
  window 263n.
key man *bigwig* 638n.
key moment *crisis* 137n.
keynote *prototype* 23n.
  rule 81n.
  musical note 410n.
  chief thing 638n.
key of the door
  adulthood 134n.

keys *badge of rule* 743n.
keystone *summit* 213n.
  supporter 218n.
  completion 725n.
keyword *answer* 460n.
khaddar, khadi
  textile 222n.
khaki *uniform* 228n.
  brownness 430n.
khan *inn* 192n.
  sovereign 741n.
  nobleman 868n.
khansamah *domestic* 742n.
khedive *governor* 741n.
khidmatgar *servant* 742n.
khilat *decoration* 729n.
  badge of rule 743n.
kibble *vessel* 194n.
  pulverize 332vb.
kibbutz *farm* 370n.
  joint possession 775n.
kibe *hardness* 326n.
  ulcer 651n.
kibitzer *meddler* 678n.
  adviser 691n.
kibosh *absurdity* 497n.
kick *reversion* 148n.
  vigorousness 174n.
  be violent 176vb.
  kick 279vb.
  recoil 280n.,vb.
  propulsion 287n.
  gesture 547n.
  be loth 598vb.
  oppose 704vb.
  strike at 712vb.
  resist 715vb.
  disobey 738vb.
  refuse 760vb.
  deprecation 762n.
  feeling 818n.
  joy 824n.
  discontent 829n.
kick back *retaliate* 714vb.
kick-off *start* 68n.
kick one's heels
  be inactive 679vb.
kick out *eject* 300vb.
kick over the traces
  disobey 738vb.
  achieve liberty 746vb.
kickshaw *bauble* 639n.
kick the beam
  be unequal 29vb.
kick upstairs
  improvement 654n.
kid *child* 132n.
  youngling 132n.
  skin 226n.
  befool 542vb.
kidder *deceiver* 545n.

kidding *deception* 542n.
kiddy-cart *pushcart* 274n.
kid gloves *cleanness* 648n.
  lenity 736n.
kidnap *ensnare* 542vb.
  take away 786vb.
  steal 788vb.
kidnapper *taker* 786n.
  thief 789n.
kidney *sort* 77n.
  insides 224n.
  meat 301n.
kief *drug* 658n.
Kilkenny cats
  quarreller 709n.
kill
  destroy, suppress 165vb.
  propulsion 287n.
  kill 362vb.
  trap 542vb.
  success, victory 727n.
  prohibit 757vb.
  execute 963vb.
killer *killer* 362n.
  murderer 362n.
  combatant 722n.
  ruffian 904n.
killick *safeguard* 662n.
killing *deadly* 362adj.
  laborious 682adj.
kill-joy *dissuasion* 613n.
  hinderer 702n.
  ascetic 944n.
kill the fatted calf
  celebrate 876vb.
  be hospitable 882vb.
  forgive 909vb.
kill the goose that lays the
  golden eggs
  stultify oneself 695vb.
  be prodigal 815vb.
kill time
  pass time 108vb.
  amuse oneself 837vb.
kill with kindness
  pet 889vb.
kiln *furnace* 383n.
kilogramme
  weighment 322n.
kilometre
  long measure 203n.
kiloton *weighment* 322n.
kilowatt *electricity* 160n.
kilt *shorten* 204vb.
  skirt 228n.
  fold 261vb.
kimono
  informal dress 228n.
kin *kinsman* 11n.
  breed 77n.
kind *sort* 77n.

form 243 n.
aiding 703 adj.
amiable 884 adj.
benevolent 897 adj.
disinterested 931 adj.
kindergarten *nonage* 130 n.
school 539 n.
kindheartedness
benevolence 897 n.
kind, in
correlatively 12 adv.
in exchange 151 adv.
kindle *cause* 156 vb.
invigorate 174 vb.
make violent 176 vb.
be hot 379 vb.
kindle 381 vb.
make bright 417 vb.
feel 818 vb.
excite 821 vb.
be excitable 822 vb.
get angry 891 vb.
kindling *burning* 381 n.
fuel 385 n.
exciting 821 adj.
kindly
affectionately 887 adv.
benevolent 897 adj.
benevolently 897 adv.
kindness *lenity* 736 n.
friendliness 880 n.
courtesy 884 n.
love 887 n.
benevolence 897 n.
disinterestedness 931 n.
kindred *relative* 9 adj.
consanguinity 11 n.
kinsman 11 n.
akin 11 adj.
kind regards
courteous act 884 n.
kine *cattle* 365 n.
kinematics *motion* 265 n.
kinesipathy *motion* 265 n.
kinetic *dynamic* 160 adj.
kinetics *motion* 265 n.
king *bigwig* 638 n.
sovereign 741 n.
chessman 837 n.
aristocrat 868 n.
kingcraft
management 689 n.
kingdom *territory* 184 n.
polity 733 n.
kingdom come
future state 124 n.
heaven 971 n.
Kingdom of God
theocracy 965 n.
heaven 971 n.
kingfisher

bird of prey 365 n.
King Kong *monster* 938 n.
kingly *ruling* 733 adj.
impressive 821 adj.
worshipful 866 adj.
noble 868 adj.
proud 871 adj.
king-maker *director* 690 n.
king-pin *fastening* 47 n.
bigwig 638 n.
kingpost *pillar* 218 n.
King's Counsel
lawyer 958 n.
kingship
government 733 n.
magistrature 733 n.
king-size *size* 195 n.
large 195 adj.
king's messenger
courier 531 n.
kink *coil* 251 n.
eccentricity 503 n.
whim 604 n.
defect 647 n.
kinless *irrelative* 10 adj.
defenceless 161 adj.
kinsfolk *kinsman* 11 n.
kinship *relation* 9 n.
consanguinity 11 n.
similarity 18 n.
parentage 169 n.
kinsman *kinsman* 11 n.
kiosk *pavilion* 192 n.
shop 796 n.
kip *inn* 192 n.
brothel 951 n.
kip down *sleep* 679 vb.
repose 683 vb.
kipper *fish food* 301 n.
dry 342 vb.
season 388 vb.
preserve 666 vb.
kirk *church* 990 n.
kirk session *synod* 985 n.
kirkyard
church exterior 990 n.
kirtle *skirt* 228 n.
kismet *fate* 596 n.
kiss *be contiguous* 202 vb.
touch 378 vb.
greet 884 vb.
caress 889 vb.
kissable *personable* 841 adj.
kiss and be friends
forgive 909 vb.
kiss-curl *hair* 259 n.
kisser *face* 237 n.
kiss hands *stoop* 311 vb.
pay respects 884 vb.
kiss of peace
ritual act 988 n.

Holy Communion 988 n.
kiss the book *swear* 532 vb.
kiss the rod
knuckle under 721 vb.
kist *interment* 364 n.
payment 804 n.
kit *accumulation* 74 n.
sort 77 n.
youngling 132 n.
basket 194 n.
cat 365 n.
viol 414 n.
equipment 630 n.
kitbag *bag* 194 n.
kitchen *chamber* 194 n.
cookery 301 n.
heater 383 n.
workshop 687 n.
kitchener *furnace* 383 n.
kitchen garden *farm* 370 n.
kitchen-maid
domestic 742 n.
kite *airship* 276 n.
bird of prey 365 n.
cleaner 648 n.
false money 797 n.
noxious animal 904 n.
kite-flying *empiricism* 461 n.
publication 528 n.
kithless *alone* 88 adj.
defenceless 161 adj.
kitten *youngling* 132 n.
reproduce itself 164 vb.
cat 365 n.
kittenish *infantine* 132 adj.
gay 833 adj.
amused 837 adj.
kitty *store* 632 n.
joint possession 775 n.
kiwi *flightless bird* 365 n.
klaxon *megaphone* 400 n.
danger signal 665 n.
klepht *robber* 789 n.
kleptomania *mania* 503 n.
thievishness 788 n.
kleptomaniac
madman 504 n.
thieving 788 adj.
Klu Klux Klan
society 708 n.
rioter 738 n.
knack *habit* 610 n.
contrivance 623 n.
aptitude 694 n.
knacker *killer* 362 n.
knackers *gong* 414 n.
knacker's yard
slaughter-house 362 n.
knap *break* 46 vb.
high land 209 n.
knapsack *bag* 194 n.

knave *low fellow* 869 n.
  ruffian 904 n.
  knave 938 n.
knavery *cunning* 698 n.
  improbity 930 n.
  wickedness 934 n.
knavish (*see* knavery)
knead *efform* 243 vb.
  soften 327 vb.
  pulverize 332 vb.
  rub 333 vb.
  touch 378 vb.
knee *joint* 45 n.
  angularity 247 n.
  leg 267 n.
  kick 279 vb.
knee action
  elasticity 328 n.
knee-deep *deep* 211 adj.
  shallow 212 adj.
knee-high *infantine* 132 adj.
  dwarfish 196 adj.
  high 209 adj.
kneel *stoop* 311 vb.
  knuckle under 721 vb.
  be servile 879 vb.
  pay respects 884 vb.
  show respect 920 vb.
  be pious 979 vb.
  worship 981 vb.
  perform ritual 988 vb.
kneeler *cushion* 218 n.
  seat 218 n.
  church utensil 990 n.
kneel to *entreat* 761 vb.
knees *seat* 218 n.
knees, one's *respects* 920 n.
knell *ruin* 165 n.
  decease 361 n.
  obsequies 364 n.
  play music 413 vb.
  signal 547 n.
  warning 664 n.
  raise the alarm 665 vb.
  lament 836 n.
  condemnation 961 n.
  (*see* finality)
Knesset *parliament* 692 n.
knickerbockers
  breeches 228 n.
knickers *breeches* 228 n.
  underwear 228 n.
knick-knack *bauble* 639 n.
  plaything 837 n.
  finery 844 n.
knife *cut* 46 vb.
  sharp edge 256 n.
  side-arms 723 n.
knife and fork *shovel* 274 n.
knife-edge
  narrowness 206 n.

  sharp edge 256 n.
knife-grinder *mender* 656 n.
  artisan 686 n.
knife-thrower
  thrower 287 n.
knife, use the
  doctor 658 vb.
knight *rider* 268 n.
  combatant 722 n.
  cavalry 722 n.
  chessman 837 n.
  brave person 855 n.
  person of repute 866 n.
  dignify 866 vb.
  nobleman 868 n.
  philanthropist 901 n.
  gentleman 929 n.
knightage
  aristocracy 868 n.
knight-errant *crank* 504 n.
  visionary 513 n.
  defender 713 n.
  combatant 722 n.
  brave person 855 n.
  philanthropist 901 n.
knight-errantry
  ideality 513 n.
  rashness 857 n.
  disinterestedness 931 n.
knighthood *prowess* 855 n.
  honours 866 n.
  title 870 n.
knightly *warlike* 718 adj.
  courageous 855 adj.
  noble 868 adj.
  courteous 884 adj.
  honourable 929 adj.
  disinterested 931 adj.
knight's move
  obliquity 220 n.
  deviation 282 n.
knit *tie* 45 vb.
  compose 56 vb.
  weave 222 vb.
  close 264 vb.
knitting *network* 222 n.
  needlework 844 n.
knob *hanger* 217 n.
  handle 218 n.
  sphere 252 n.
  swelling 253 n.
knobbly *rough* 259 adj.
knobkerrie *club* 723 n.
  missile weapon 723 n.
knobs on, with
  crescendo 36 adv.
  in addition 38 adv.
knock *knock* 279 n.
  propulsion 287 n.
  loudness 400 n.
  bang 402 n.

  gesture 547 n.
knock-about
  dramatic 594 adj.
  ridiculousness 849 n.
knock around
  wander 267 vb.
knock at the door
  arrive 295 vb.
  request 761 vb.
knock down
  demolish 165 vb.
  flatten 216 vb.
  fell 311 vb.
knock-down arguments
  confutation 479 n.
knock-down price
  cheapness 812 n.
knock down to *sell* 793 vb.
knocker *hammer* 279 n.
  signal 547 n.
  defamer 926 n.
  detractor 926 n.
knock into a cocked hat
  be superior 34 vb.
knock into the head
  educate 534 vb.
knock-kneed
  crippled 163 adj.
  oblique 220 adj.
  deformed 246 adj.
  angular 247 adj.
  convergent 293 adj.
  blemished 845 adj.
knock off *cease* 145 vb.
  take 786 vb.
  steal 788 vb.
knock out
  render insensible 375 vb.
  defeat 727 vb.
knock-out *end* 69 n.
  ruin 165 n.
  exceller 644 n.
  favourite 890 n.
  victory 727 n.
knock up *fatigue* 684 vb.
knoll *monticle* 209 n.
knot *tie* 45 vb.
  ligature 47 n.
  complexity 61 n.
  crowd, band 74 n.
  long measure 203 n.
  cross 222 vb.
  distortion 246 n.
  loop 250 n.
  swelling 253 n.
  solid body 324 n.
  garden 370 n.
  difficulty 700 n.
  party 708 n.
  trimming 844 n.
knotted *crossed* 222 adj.

rough 259 adj.
dense 324 adj.
knotty *dense* 324 adj.
moot 459 adj.
difficult 700 adj.
knotty point
question 459 n.
unintelligibility 517 n.
enigma 530 n.
knout *scourge* 964 n.
know *unite with* 45 vb.
cognize 447 vb.
believe 485 vb.
know 490 vb.
be wise 498 vb.
understand 516 vb.
be informed 524 vb.
befriend 880 vb.
knowable *known* 490 adj.
intelligible 516 adj.
know-all *doctrinaire* 473 n.
intellectual 492 n.
wiseacre 500 n.
vain person 873 n.
know all the answers
dogmatize 473 vb.
know 490 vb.
be skilful 694 vb.
know-how
intelligence 498 n.
way 624 n.
means 629 n.
skill 694 n.
knowing *expert* 694 adj.
cunning 698 adj.
knowingly
knowingly 490 adv.
purposely 617 adj.
knowledge
knowledge 490 n.
information 524 n.
skill 694 n.
knowledgeable
instructed 490 adj.
cunning 698 adj.
known
remembered 505 adj.
usual 610 adj.
renowned 866 adj.
known as *named* 561 adj.
know no better
not know 491 vb.
be rude 885 vb.
know no bounds
be great 32 vb.
know-nothing
ignoramus 493 n.
know one's place
conform 83 vb.
be modest 874 vb.
know what's what

discriminate 463 vb.
know 490 vb.
be wise 498 vb.
be expert 694 vb.
knuckle *joint* 45 n.
angularity 247 n.
swelling 253 n.
knuckle-duster
hammer 279 n.
club 723 n.
knuckle under
knuckle under 721 vb.
knurl *roughen* 259 vb.
notch 260 vb.
knut *fop* 848 n.
kobold *elf* 970 n.
kohl *cosmetic* 843 n.
Koine
language 557 n.
dialect 560 n.
kola *soft drink* 301 n.
kolkhoz *assemblage* 74 n.
farm 370 n.
joint possession 775 n.
kopje *monticle* 209 n.
Koran
non-Biblical scripture 975 n.
kosher *edible* 301 adj.
clean 648 adj.
ritual 988 adj.
koumiss *milk* 301 n.
kowtow *obeisance* 311 n.
submission 721 n.
be servile 879 vb.
courteous act 884 n.
show respect 920 vb.
kraal *dwelling* 192 n.
inclosure 235 n.
krait *reptile* 365 n.
kraken *rara avis* 84 n.
giant 195 n.
Kremlin
magistrature 733 n.
kris *sharp edge* 256 n.
side-arms 723 n.
Krishna *theophany* 965 n.
the Deity 965 n.
Hindu god 967 n.
kroner *coinage* 797 n.
Kronos *classical gods* 976 n.
kodos *approbation* 923 n.
kukri *sharp edge* 256 n.
side-arms 723 n.
kulak *husbandman* 370 n.
possessor 776 n.
kulakism *sedition* 738 n.
disobedience 738 n.
kultur *civilization* 654 n.
kursaal
place of amusement 837 n.

kutcherry
management 689 n.
courtroom 956 n.
kyanize *preserve* 666 vb.
kyles *gulf* 345 n.
kyphosis *deformity* 246 n.
curvature 248 n.

L

laager *defences* 713 n.
fort 713 n.
labdanum *resin* 357 n.
labefy *impair* 655 vb.
label *adjunct* 40 n.
label 547 n.
labial *marginal* 234 adj.
spoken letter 558 n.
vocal 577 adj.
(see speech sound)
labiated *marginal* 234 adj.
labiovelar
speech sound 398 n.
laboratory
workshop 687 n.
laborious
persevering 600 adj.
industrious 678 adj.
labouring 682 adj.
laborious 682 adj.
fatiguing 684 adj.
difficult 700 adj.
labour *repeat oneself* 106 vb.
obstetrics 164 n.
emphasize 532 vb.
job 622 n.
make important 638 vb.
action 676 n.
labour 682 n.
personnel 686 n.
hard task 700 n.
bore 838 n.
labour camp
compulsion 740 n.
laboured *inelegant* 576 adj.
matured 669 adj.
laborious 682 adj.
labourer *producer* 167 n.
worker 686 n.
servant 742 n.
labour exchange *job* 622 n.
labour force
personnel 686 n.
labouring
in difficulties 700 adj.
labour in vain
try impossibilities 470 vb.
lost labour 641 n.
waste effort 641 vb.
stultify oneself 695 vb.
fail 728 vb.

Labourite
  political party 708n.
labour of love
  voluntary work 597n.
  vocation 622n.
  undertaking 672n.
  gift 781n.
  no charge 812n.
labour-saving
  leisurely 681adj.
  refreshing 685adj.
  wieldy 701adj.
  economical 814adj.
labour the obvious
  be intelligible 516vb.
  be superfluous 637vb.
labour under
  be in a state 7vb.
  be ill 651vb.
  be in difficulty 700vb.
labyrinth *complexity* 61n.
  meandering 251n.
  ear 415n.
  enigma 530n.
labyrinthine *difficult* 700adj.
lac *resin* 357n.
lace *mix* 43vb.
  tie 45vb.
  ligature 47n.
  network, textile 222n.
  transparency 422n.
  needlework 844n.
lacerate *rend* 46vb.
  give pain 377vb.
  wound 655vb.
laches *negligence* 458n.
  non-observance 769n.
  dutilessness 918n.
  guilty act 936n.
Lachesis *fate* 596n.
  mythic god 966n.
  classical gods 967n.
lachrymatory gas
  poison 659n.
  weapon 723n.
lachrymose
  melancholic 834adj.
  lamenting 836adj.
lack *be inferior* 35vb.
  deficit 55n.
  shortcoming 307n.
  requirement 627n.
  scarcity 636n.
  imperfection 647n.
  non-completion 726n.
  be poor 801vb.
lackadaisical
  inactive 679adj.
  inexcitable 823adj.
  dejected 834adj.
  indifferent 860adj.

lackey *dependant* 742n.
  domestic 742n.
lacking *absent* 190adj.
  deficient 307adj.
  lost 772adj.
  not owning 774adj.
lack-lustre *weakly* 163adj.
  dim 419adj.
  colourless 426adj.
  dejected 834adj.
lack nothing
  be complete 54vb.
laconic *concise* 569adj.
  taciturn 582adj.
lacquer *facing* 226n.
  resin 357n.
  colour 425n.
  hairwash 843n.
  decorate 844vb.
lacrosse *ball game* 837n.
lactescence
  semitransparency 424n.
  whiteness 427n.
lactescent
  semiliquid 354adj.
lactic *edible* 301adj.
lactose *food content* 301n.
lacuna *interval* 201n.
  concavity 255n.
  opening 263n.
lacustrine
  lacustrine 346adj.
lad *youngster* 132n.
  fop 848n.
ladder *disjunction* 46n.
  bond 47n.
  series 71n.
  discontinuity 72n.
  ascent 308n.
  access 624n.
  means of escape 667n.
laddering
  separation 46n.
lade *fill* 54vb.
  stow 187vb.
  load 193vb.
laden *full* 54adj.
ladies' man *lover* 887n.
lading *location* 187n.
  contents 193n.
  gravity 322n.
  property 777n.
ladle *ladle* 194n.
  transpose 272vb.
lady *lady* 373n.
  master 741n.
  spouse 894n.
Lady Bountiful *giver* 781n.
  good giver 813n.
  benefactor 903n.
lady in waiting

retainer 742n.
lady-killer *lover* 887n.
  libertine 952n.
ladylike *female* 373adj.
  well-bred 848adj.
  noble 868adj.
lady-love *loved one* 887n.
ladyship *lady* 373n.
  title 870n.
laevogyrate
  sinistral 242adj.
lag *be inferior* 35vb.
  be late 136vb.
  be behind 238vb.
  slowness 278n.
  follow 284vb.
  fall short 307vb.
  be inactive 679vb.
  offender 904n.
lager *liquor* 301n.
laggard *lateness* 136n.
  lazy 679adj.
lagoon *gulf* 345n.
  lake 346n.
laic *layman* 987n.
  laical 987adj.
laicality *laicality* 987n.
laid *born* 360adj.
laid paper
  stationery 586n.
laid up *sick* 651adj.
  disused 674adj.
lair *dwelling* 192n.
  hiding-place 527n.
  refuge 662n.
laird *master* 741n.
  aristocrat 868n.
laisse *verse form* 593n.
laisser aller *not act* 677vb.
  be lax 734vb.
  give scope 744vb.
laisser faire
  permanence 144n.
  sustain 146vb.
  negligence 458n.
  not act 677vb.
  be lax 734vb.
  freedom 744n.
laity *laity* 987n.
lake *lake* 346n.
lake-dwelling
  dwelling 192n.
  lacustrine 346adj.
lakh *over one hundred* 99n.
Lallans *dialect* 560n.
lallation *solecism* 565n.
  pronunciation 577n.
  speech defect 580n.
lama *priest* 986n.
Lamarckism *biology* 358n.
lamasery *monastery* 986n.

lamb *youngling* 132 n.
　reproduce itself 164 vb.
　sheep 365 n.
　ingenue 699 n.
　darling 890 n.
　innocent 935 n.
lambdacism
　solecism 565 n.
　speech defect 580 n.
lambent *tactual* 378 adj.
　luminous 417 adj.
lamblike
　inexcitable 823 adj.
　innocent 935 adj.
lambskin *skin* 226 n.
lame *incomplete* 55 adj.
　disable 161 vb.
　crippled 163 adj.
　make useless 641 vb.
　imperfect 647 adj.
　impair 655 vb.
　unskilful 695 adj.
　hinder 702 vb.
lame and impotent
　conclusion
　sophism 477 n.
　failure 728 n.
lame dog *weakling* 163 n.
　unlucky person 731 n.
lame duck *weakling* 163 n.
　unlucky person 731 n.
　non-payer 805 n.
lamellar *layered* 201 adj.
lament *suffer* 825 vb.
　be discontented 829 vb.
　regret 830 vb.
　lament 836 n.,vb.
　pity 905 vb.
　disapprove 924 vb.
　be penitent 939 vb.
lamentable *bad* 645 adj.
　distressing 827 adj.
lamentation *obsequies* 364 n.
　lamentation 836 n.
　penance 941 n.
lamented *dead* 361 adj.
lamia *demon* 970 n.
　sorceress 983 n.
lamina *piece* 53 n.
　lamina 207 n.
laminable *layered* 207 adj.
　brittle 330 adj.
lamination
　stratification 207 n.
　structure 331 n.
Lammas *holy-day* 988 n.
lammergeyer
　bird of prey 365 n.
lamp *lamp* 420 n.
　guide 520 n.
　signal 547 n.

lampadist *contender* 716 n.
lampadophoria
　racing 716 n.
lamp-black *ash* 381 n.
　black pigment 428 n.
lamp-lighter *lamp* 420 n.
lampoon *poetize* 593 vb.
　satire 851 n.
　calumny 926 n.
lampooner *humorist* 839 n.
　disapprover 924 n.
lamp-post
　high structure 209 n.
　tall creature 209 n.
　stand 218 n.
lamp shade *screen* 421 n.
lampyrine
　glow-worm 420 n.
　luminescent 420 adj.
lanate *smooth* 258 adj.
　downy 259 adj.
lance *pierce* 263 vb.
　sharp point 256 n.
　strike at 712 vb.
　spear 723 n.
lance-corporal
　army officer 741 n.
lanceolate *tapering* 256 adj.
lancer *soldiery* 722 n.
　cavalry 722 n.
lancet *sharp point* 256 n.
　perforator 263 n.
lancination *pain* 377 n.
land *region* 184 n.
　voyage 269 vb.
　fly 271 vb.
　aim 281 vb.
　approach 289 vb.
　land 295 vb.
　admit 299 vb.
　land 344 n.
　lands 777 n.
　take 786 vb.
landamman *officer* 741 n.
landau *carriage* 274 n.
landaulette
　automobile 274 n.
　carriage 274 n.
land-bridge
　narrowness 206 n.
　bridge 624 n.
landed *territorial* 344 adj.
　proprietary 777 adj.
landes *plain* 348 n.
landfall *arrival* 295 n.
landholder *owner* 776 n.
landing *layer* 207 n.
　vertex 213 n.
　stand 218 n.
　arrival 295 n.
　ascent 308 n.

　descent 309 n.
landing-craft
　warship 722 n.
landing ground
　air travel 271 n.
　arena 724 n.
landlady *owner* 776 n.
land lies, see how the
　be tentative 461 vb.
land-locked
　circumscribed 232 adj.
　lacustrine 346 adj.
landloper *wanderer* 268 n.
landlord *caterer* 633 n.
　owner 776 n.
landlubber *dweller* 191 n.
　mariner 270 n.
landmark *spectacle* 445 n.
　signpost 547 n.
land-mass *region* 184 n.
land-mine *bomb* 723 n.
land on one's feet
　be safe 660 vb.
landowner *owner* 776 n.
lands *farm* 370 n.
　lands 777 n.
landscape *open space* 263 n.
　spectacle 445 n.
　art subject 553 n.
　beauty 841 n.
landslide *revolution* 149 n.
　ruin 165 n.
　acclivity 220 n.
　descent 309 n.
　defeat 728 n.
landslip *revolution* 149 n.
landsman *dweller* 191 n.
　land 344 n.
lane *street* 192 n.
　route, path 624 n.
langouste *fish food* 301 n.
　table fish 365 n.
language *language* 557 n.
　dialect 560 n.
　speech 579 n.
languid *feeble* 572 adj.
　(see languish, languor)
languish *decrease* 37 vb.
　be weak 163 vb.
　be ill 651 vb.
　be inactive 679 vb.
　be fatigued 684 vb.
　be dejected 834 vb.
　be affected 850 vb.
　court 889 vb.
languish for *desire* 859 vb.
languor *weakness* 163 n.
　inertness 175 n.
　slowness 278 n.
　sluggishness 679 n.
　fatigue 684 n.

laniate *wound* 655 vb.
lank *long* 203 adj.
lanky *long* 203 adj.
  narrow 206 adj.
  tall 209 adj.
lanolin *unguent* 357 n.
  balm 658 n.
  cosmetic 843 n.
lantern *lamp* 420 n.
lantern-jawed *lean* 206 adj.
lanuginous *downy* 259 adj.
lanyard *cable* 47 n.
Laodicean *moderate* 625 n.
  apathetic 820 adj.
  indifferent 860 adj.
lap *part* 53 n.
  period 110 n.
  periodicity 141 n.
  seat 218 n.
  dress 228 vb.
  surround 230 vb.
  inclose 235 vb.
  move fast, outstrip 277 vb.
  drink 301 vb.
  outdo 306 vb.
  circuition 314 n.
  moisten 341 vb.
  flow 350 vb.
  sound faint 401 vb.
  circuit 626 n., vb.
  refuge 662 n.
  pet 889 vb.
laparotomy *surgery* 658 n.
lap-dog *dog* 365 n.
lapel *adjunct* 40 n.
  fold 261 n.
  trimming 844 n.
lapidary *funereal* 364 adj.
  engraver 556 n.
lapidate *strike* 279 vb.
  kill 362 vb.
  lapidate 712 vb.
  not respect 921 vb.
  execute 963 vb.
lapidescence
  hardening 326 n.
lapis lazuli *blueness* 435 n.
  gem 844 n.
lap of luxury
  euphoria 376 n.
  sensualism 944 n.
lappet *adjunct* 40 n.
  pendant 217 n.
  canonicals 989 n.
lapse *time* 108 n.
  elapse 111 vb.
  conversion 147 n.
  deviation 282 n.
  descent 309 n.
  deteriorate 655 vb.
  relapse 657 n., vb.

loss 772 n.
  be wicked 934 vb.
  guilty act 936 n.
  irreligion 974 n.
lapsed *past* 125 adj.
  unbelieving 486 adj.
  irreligious 974 adj.
lapse of memory
  oblivion 506 n.
lapse of time
  course of time 111 n.
lapsus calami
  mistake 495 n.
  solecism 565 n.
lapsus linguæ
  mistake 495 n.
  solecism 565 n.
lap up *absorb* 299 vb.
  drink 301 vb.
  appetize 390 vb.
larboard *sinistrality* 242 n.
larceny *stealing* 788 n.
larch *tree* 366 n.
lard *meat* 301 n.
  cook 301 vb.
  fat 357 n.
larder *chamber* 194 n.
  provisions 301 n.
  storage 632 n.
larding *beautification* 843 n.
Lares and Penates
  home 192 n.
  idol 982 n.
large *substantial* 3 adj.
  great 32 adj.
  extensive 183 adj.
  large 195 adj.
large, at *diffusely* 570 adv.
  escaped 667 adj.
  free 744 adj.
large-hearted
  liberal 813 adj.
  benevolent 897 adj.
large-scale *large* 195 adj.
largesse *gift* 781 n.
  liberality 813 n.
larghetto *slowly* 278 adv.
  adagio 412 adv.
largo *slowly* 278 adv.
  adagio 412 adv.
lariat *halter* 47 n.
  loop 250 n.
lark *climber* 308 n.
  bird 365 n.
  vocalist 413 n.
  enjoyment 824 n.
  revel 837 n.
larrikin *ruffian* 904 n.
larrup *spank* 963 vb.
larva *youngling* 132 n.
laryngitis

respiratory disease 651 n.
larynx *air-pipe* 353 n.
  voice 577 n.
lascar *mariner* 270 n.
lasciviousness
  unchastity 951 n.
lash *tie* 45 vb.
  stimulant 174 n.
  make violent 176 vb.
  filament 208 n.
  incite 612 vb.
  animate 821 vb.
  exprobate 924 vb.
  flog 963 vb.
  scourge 964 n.
lasher *ligature* 47 n.
lashes *eye* 438 n.
lashings *great quantity* 32 n.
  plenty 635 n.
lash out *be violent* 176 vb.
lass *youngster* 132 n.
  woman 373 n.
lassitude *sleepiness* 679 n.
  fatigue 684 n.
lasso *halter* 47 n.
  loop 250 n.
  missile weapon 723 n.
last *mould* 23 n.
  ending 69 adj.
  continue 108 vb.
  foregoing 125 adj.
  stay 144 vb.
  completive 725 adj.
last breath *end* 69 n.
  decease 361 n.
last ditcher *stamina* 600 n.
  opinionist 602 n.
  opponent 705 n.
  malcontent 829 n.
lasting *lasting* 113 adj.
  perpetual 115 adj.
  unchangeable 153 adj.
  unyielding 162 adj.
last lap *end* 69 n.
  arrival 295 n.
last legs, on one's
  weakened 163 adj.
  dying 361 adj.
  dilapidated 655 adj.
  unprosperous 731 adj.
last man in *aftercomer* 67 n.
last minute *lateness* 136 n.
  crisis 137 n.
last-minute *hasty* 680 adj.
last place *inferiority* 35 n.
  rear 238 n.
last post *evening* 129 n.
  valediction 296 n.
  obsequies 364 n.
  call 547 n.
last resort *necessity* 596 n.

means 629 n.
refuge 662 n.
last rites *obsequies* 364 n.
Christian rite 988 n.
last straw
redundance 637 n.
encumbrance 702 n.
completion 725 n.
annoyance 827 n.
last things *finality* 69 n.
last touch
completeness 54 n.
completion 725 n.
last word
modernism 126 n.
answer 460 n.
certainty 473 n.
fashion 848 n.
last words *sequel* 67 n.
end 69 n.
valediction 296 n.
latch *join* 45 vb.
fastening 47 n.
latchet *ligature* 47 n.
late *anachronistic* 118 adj.
former 125 adj.
modern 126 adj.
vespertine 129 adj.
late 136 adj., adv.
ill-timed 138 adj.
slow 278 adj.
dead 361 adj.
negligent 458 adj.
unprepared 670 adj.
immature 670 adj.
late-comer *aftercomer* 67 n.
posteriority 120 n.
lateness 136 n.
lateen sail *sail* 275 n.
latency *inertness* 175 n.
influence 178 n.
invisibility 444 n.
latency 523 n.
seclusion 883 n.
lateness *evening* 129 n.
lateness 136 n.
latent *deceiving* 542 adj.
(*see* latency)
later *after* 65 adv.
subsequent 120 adj.
not now 122 adj.
future 124 adj.
behind 284 adj.
laterality *laterality* 239 n.
lateritious *red* 431 adj.
latest *present* 121 adj.
latest, the *modernism* 126 n.
fashion 848 n.
lath *lamina* 207 n.
strip 208 n.
materials 631 n.

lathe *district* 184 n.
rotator 315 n.
lather *lubricant* 334 n.
bubble 355 n.
clean 648 vb.
lathery *white* 427 adj.
lathi *club* 723 n.
Latin
language 557 n.
Latinist *linguist* 557 n.
latitancy
concealment 525 n.
latitude *range* 183 n.
region 184 n.
breadth 205 n.
scope 744 n.
latitude and longitude
bearings 186 n.
co-ordinate 465 n.
latitudinarian *wise* 498 adj.
free man 744 adj.
latitudinarianism
heterodoxy 977 n.
Latitudinarians
church party 978 n.
latration *ululation* 409 n.
latria *cult* 981 n.
latrine *fetor* 397 n.
latrine 649 n.
latrociny *stealing* 788 n.
latten *lamina* 207 n.
latter *sequent* 65 adj.
foregoing 125 adj.
latter-day *modern* 126 adj.
latter end *end* 69 n.
future state 124 n.
latterly *newly* 126 adv.
lattice *space* 201 vb.
network 222 n.
window 263 n.
laud *praise* 923 vb.
worship 981 vb.
laudable
approvable 923 adj.
laudanum
moderator 177 n.
anæsthetic 375 n.
laudation *praise* 923 n.
act of worship 981 n.
laudator temporis acti
malcontent 829 n.
regret 830 n.
laudatory *approving* 923 adj.
Laudianism
Catholicism 976 n.
lauds *church service* 988 n.
laugh *be pleased* 824 vb.
be cheerful 833 vb.
laughter 835 n.
ridicule 851 n.
hold cheap 922 vb.

laughable *absurd* 497 adj.
foolish 499 adj.
amusing 837 adj.
ridiculous 849 adj.
laugher *laugher* 835 n.
laughing gas *gas* 336 n.
anæsthetic 375 n.
laughing matter
laughter 835 n.
laughing-stock
nonconformist 84 n.
fool 501 n.
laughing-stock 851 n.
laugh off *not think* 450 vb.
laughter *merriment* 833 n.
laughter 835 n.
festivity 837 n.
ridicule 851 n.
laughter-loving
gay 833 adj.
laugh to scorn *defy* 711 vb.
despise 922 vb.
launch *initiate* 68 vb.
navigate 269 vb.
ship, boat 275 n.
propel 287 vb.
launched *beginning* 68 adj.
launching *fitting out* 669 n.
launch into
undertake 672 vb.
launch out
be diffuse 570 vb.
be loquacious 581 vb.
launch out at
attack 712 vb.
launder *smooth* 258 vb.
clean 648 vb.
laundress *cleaner* 648 n.
laundry *chamber* 194 n.
ablution 648 n.
workshop 687 n.
laurels *badge* 547 n.
trophy 729 n.
honours 866 n.
lava *rock* 344 n.
ash 381 n.
lavation *ablution* 648 n.
lavatory *chamber* 194 n.
ablution 648 n.
latrine 649 n.
lave *drench* 341 vb.
purify 648 vb.
lavender *purple* 434 n.
scent 396 n.
prophylactic 658 n.
preserver 666 n.
laver *bowl* 194 n.
ritual object 988 n.
lavish *many* 104 adj.
plenteous 635 adj.
superabound 637 vb.

give 781 vb.
expend 806 vb.
liberal 813 adj.
prodigal 815 adj.
law *rule* 81 n.
· *necessity* 596 n.
habit 610 n.
vocation 622 n.
precept 693 n.
decree 737 n.
compulsion 740 n.
restraint 747 n.
permit 756 n.
law 953 n.
punisher 963 n.
law-abiding
peaceful 717 adj.
submitting 721 adj.
obedient 739 adj.
honourable 929 adj.
legal 953 adj.
law agent *law agent* 958 n.
Law and the Prophets, the
scripture 975 n.
law, at
in litigation 959 adv.
lawbreaker *offender* 904 n.
impious person 980 n.
lawbreaking
riotous 738 adj.
non-observant 769 adj.
improbity 930 n.
heinous 934 adj.
lawbreaking 954 n., adj.
law, by *duly* 915 adv.
legally 953 adv.
law-court *law-court* 956 n.
lawful *due* 915 adj.
legal 953 adj.
law-giver *director* 690 n.
legislation 953 n.
lawless *disorderly* 61 adj.
unconformable 84 adj.
anarchic 734 adj.
riotous 738 adj.
rascally 930 adj.
lawless 954 adj.
law-maker *director* 690 n.
law-making
management 689 n.
legislation 953 n.
lawn *smoothness* 258 n.
textile 222 n.
grassland 348 n.
garden 370 n.
lawn sleeves
canonicals 989 n.
law officer *law officer* 955 n.
laws *polity* 733 n.
Laws of the Medes and
Persians

permanence 144 n.
fixture 153 n.
precept 693 n.
lawsuit *litigation* 959 n.
law to oneself, a
unconformable 84 adj.
law to oneself, be a
please oneself 734 vb.
disobey 738 vb.
be insolent 878 vb.
lawyer *reasoner* 475 n.
adviser 691 n.
lawyer 958 n.
lax *weak* 163 adj.
feeble 572 adj.
frail 934 adj.
(*see* laxity)
laxative *cathartic* 658 n.
laxity
non-coherence 49 n.
softness 327 n.
negligence 458 n.
inexactness 495 n.
irresolution 601 n.
laxity 734 n.
lenity 736 n.
non-observance 769 n.
indifference 860 n.
improbity 930 n.
wickedness 934 n.
intemperance 943 n.
lay *reproduce itself* 164 vb.
assuage 177 vb.
place 187 vb.
laminate 207 vb.
cover 266 vb.
emit 300 vb.
vocal music 412 n.
ignorant 491 n.
gamble 618 vb.
unskilled 695 adj.
laical 987 adj.
lay aboard *irrupt* 297 vb.
attack 712 vb.
lay about one
strike at 712 vb.
fight 716 vb.
lay aside *exclude* 57 vb.
be neglectful 458 vb.
reject 607 vb.
disuse 674 vb.
lay at one's feet
offer 759 vb.
lay at the door of
attribute 158 vb.
accuse 928 vb.
lay bare *disclose* 526 vb.
lay brother *monk* 986 n.
layman 987 n.
lay-by *station* 187 n.
stable 192 n.

lay by *store* 632 vb.
lay by the heels
arrest 747 vb.
lay down *place* 187 vb.
flatten 216 vb.
let fall 311 vb.
premise 475 vb.
suppose 512 vb.
lay down one's office
resign 753 vb.
lay down the law
dogmatize 473 vb.
affirm 532 vb.
rule 733 vb.
decree 737 vb.
layer *compartment* 194 n.
layer 207 n.
gambler 618 n.
layette *clothing* 228 n.
lay figure
insubstantial thing 4 n.
mould 23 n.
image 551 n.
lay ghosts
practise sorcery 983 vb.
lay hands upon
take 786 vb.
lay heads together
combine 50 vb.
co-operate 706 vb.
lay in *eat* 301 vb.
store 632 vb.
lay low *fell* 311 vb.
strike at 712 vb.
layman *ignorance* 491 n.
bungler 697 n.
layman 987 n.
lay off *dismiss* 300 vb.
disuse 674 vb.
make inactive 679 vb.
not retain 779 vb.
lay on *add* 38 vb.
fight 716 vb.
lay oneself open
be liable 180 vb.
face danger 661 vb.
lay on hands
perform ritual 988 vb.
lay open *uncover* 229 vb.
open 263 vb.
manifest 522 vb.
disclose 526 vb.
lay out *flatten* 216 vb.
inter 364 vb.
plan 623 vb.
expend 806 vb.
lay-out *arrangement* 62 n.
edition 589 n.
lay-preacher
preacher 537 n.
pastor 986 n.

church officer 986 n.
layman 987 n.
lays poem 593 n.
laystall sink 649 n.
lay the dust clean 648 vb.
lay the foundations
auspicate 68 vb.
cause 156 vb.
prepare 669 vb.
lay to bring to rest 266 vb.
navigate 269 vb.
lay under contribution
levy 786 n.
claim 915 vb.
lay up store 632 vb.
make useless 641 vb.
disuse 674 vb.
make inactive 679 vb.
lay upon command 737 vb.
lay waste lay waste 165 vb.
sterilize 172 vb.
lazaret compartment 194 n.
hospital 658 n.
laze move slowly 278 vb.
be inactive 679 vb.
laziness negligence 458 n.
unwillingness 598 n.
sluggishness 679 n.
dutilessness 918 n.
lazy (see laziness)
lazybones idler 679 n.
lea shore 344 n.
grassland 348 n.
leach liquefy 337 vb.
drench 341 vb.
purify 648 vb.
leachy porous 263 adj.
lead vantage 34 n.
halter 47 n.
come before 64 vb.
prelude 66 n.
initiate 68 vb.
accompany 89 vb.
do before 119 vb.
prevail 178 vb.
space 201 n.
depth 211 n.
sailing aid 269 n.
precede 283 vb.
diver 313 n.
gravity 322 n.
gauge 465 n.
hint 524 n.
print-type 578 n.
actor 594 n.
motivate 612 vb.
provide 633 vb.
direct 689 vb.
leaded spaced 201 adj.
printed 587 adj.
leaden weighty 322 adj.

dim 419 adj.
colourless 426 adj.
grey 429 adj.
inactive 679 adj.
tedious 838 adj.
leader superior 34 n.
precursor 66 n.
article 591 n.
motivator 612 n.
leader 690 n.
master 741 n.
leadership superiority 34 n.
precedence 64 n.
directorship 689 n.
authority 733 n.
prestige 866 n.
leader-writer
dissertator 591 n.
lead evidence
corroborate 466 vb.
leading first 68 adj.
influential 178 adj.
foremost 283 adj.
important 638 adj.
directing 689 adj.
successful 727 adj.
authoritative 733 adj.
noteworthy 866 adj.
leading article article 591 n.
leading case precept 693 n.
leading light sage 500 n.
bigwig 638 n.
person of repute 866 n.
leading strings
nonage 130 n.
teaching 534 n.
subjection 745 n.
fetter 748 n.
lead, on a
restrained 747 adj.
lead one a dance
mislead 495 vb.
avoid 620 vb.
circuit 626 vb.
be difficult 700 vb.
lead one's life
behave 688 vb.
leads vertex 213 n.
roof 226 n.
leadsman navigator 270 n.
lead the dance
influence 178 vb.
precede 283 vb.
lead to tend 179 vb.
conduce 156 vb.
lead up the garden path
deceive 542 vb.
lead up to prepare 669 vb.
leaf adjunct 40 n.
lamina 207 n.
shelf 218 n.

foliage 366 n.
edition 589 n.
leafless uncovered 229 adj.
leaflet the press 528 n.
league combination 50 n.
concurrence 181 n.
long measure 203 n.
association 706 n.
society 708 n.
concord 710 n.
compact 765 n.
League of Nations
council 692 n.
leaguer attack 712 n.
leak decrement 42 n.
gap 201 n.
opening 263 n.
outflow 298 n.
be wet 341 vb.
flow 350 vb.
disclosure 526 n.
waste 634 vb.
defect 647 n.
be imperfect 647 vb.
escape 667 vb.
hitch 702 n.
non-retention 779 n.
leakage decrease 37 n.
loss 772 n.
(see leak)
leak into infiltrate 297 vb.
leak out
be disclosed 526 vb.
leak through exude 298 vb.
leaky porous 263 adj.
disclosing 526 adj.
unsafe 661 adj.
lean small 33 adj.
weak 163 adj.
tend 179 vb.
lean 206 n.
be oblique 220 vb.
be biased 481 vb.
choose 605 vb.
underfed 636 adj.
desire 859 vb.
lean forward stoop 311 vb.
leaning unequal 29 adj.
willingness 597 n.
choice 605 n.
habit 610 n.
liking 859 n.
injustice 914 n.
leanness scarcity 636 n.
lean on be supported 218 vb.
be subject 745 vb.
lean over backwards
stoop 311 vb.
be willing 597 vb.
lean-to small house 192 n.
leap spurt 277 n.

move fast 277vb.
progression 285n.
ascent 308n.
leap 312n.,vb.
be agitated 318vb.
flow 350adj.
rejoice 835vb.
dance 837vb.
leap at *pursue* 619vb.
leap-frog
overstepping 306n.
fluctuate 317vb.
children's games 837n.
leap in the dark
uncertainty 474n.
gambling 618n.
danger 661n.
rashness 857n.
leaps and bounds
progression 285n.
leap year
regular return 141n.
learn *know* 490vb.
memorize 505vb.
understand 516vb.
be informed 524vb.
learn 536vb.
prepare oneself 669vb.
learned
instructed 490adj.
studious 536adj.
literary 557adj.
learner *scholar* 492n.
learner 538n.
learning *knowledge* 490n.
learning 536n.
preparation 669n.
learn one's lesson
be penitent 939vb.
lease *estate* 777n.
transfer 780n.
lease 784vb.
hire 785vb.
leasehold
proprietary 777adj.
lease-holder
resident 191n.
possessor 776n.
leash *halter* 47n.
group 74n.
three 93n.
least *small* 33adj.
lesser 35adj.
least one can do
dueness 915n.
leather *skin* 226n.
strike 279vb.
toughness 329n.
bookbinding 589n.
materials 631n.
cleaning cloth 648n.

spank 963vb.
leatherneck
navy man 722n.
leathery *tough* 329adj.
unsavoury 391adj.
leave *be disjoined* 46vb.
cease 145vb.
recede 290vb.
depart 296vb.
relinquish 621vb.
store 632vb.
leisure 681n.
repose 683n.
facility 701n.
lenity 736n.
permission 756n.
bequeath 780vb.
non-liability 919n.
leave a gap
be absent 190vb.
not suffice 636vb.
leave alone *not act* 677vb.
leave behind
be superior 34vb.
outstrip 277vb.
progress 285vb.
outdo 306vb.
leave hanging
not complete 726vb.
leave hold
relinquish 621vb.
not retain 779vb.
leave in the lurch
disregard 458vb.
befool 542vb.
fail in duty 918vb.
leave it open
facilitate 701vb.
leaven *component* 58n.
alterer 143n.
convert 147vb.
influence 178n.,vb.
enlarge 197vb.
cookery 301n.
lifter 310n.
leaven 323n.
qualify 468vb.
make better 654vb.
leave no corner *fill* 54vb.
leave off *cease* 145vb.
disuse 674vb.
leave out *subtract* 39vb.
set apart 46vb.
exclude 57vb.
misinterpret 521vb.
be taciturn 582vb.
leave-taking
valediction 296n.
leave word
communicate 524vb.
leavings *leavings* 41n.

lebensraum *room* 183n.
scope 744n.
lecher *libertine* 952n.
lechery *unchastity* 951n.
lectern *rostrum* 539n.
church utensil 990n.
lection *interpretation* 520n.
oration 579n.
lectionary
office-book 988n.
lector *cleric* 986n.
lecture *lecture* 534n.
oration 579n.
allocution 583n.
dissertation 591n.
reprimand 924n.
lecture-hall
classroom 539n.
conference 584n.
lecturer *teacher* 537n.
speaker 579n.
academic title 870n.
pastor 986n.
led-captain
dependant 742n.
toady 879n.
ledge *high land* 209n.
horizontality 216n.
shelf 218n.
edge 234n.
projection 254n.
ledger *covering* 226n.
record 548n.
account book 808n.
lee *laterality* 239n.
shelter 662n.
leech *doctor* 658n.,vb.
bane 659n.
taker 786n.
toady 879n.
leechcraft
medical art 658n.
leek *vegetable* 301n.
heraldry 547n.
green 432adj.
leer *look* 438n.
gesture 547n.
excite love 887vb.
court 889vb.
lees *leavings* 41n.
rubbish 641n.
dirt 649n.
lee shore *pitfall* 663n.
leeward *laterality* 239n.
leeway *room* 183n.
water travel 269n.
deviation 282n.
shortcoming 307n.
scope 744n.
leeway, make up
recoup 31vb.

left *remaining* 41 adj.
 sinistrality 242 n.
 forgotten 506 adj.
 political party 708 n.
left, be *be left* 41 vb.
 inherit 771 vb.
left-handed
 sinistral 242 adj.
 handed 378 adj.
 clumsy 695 adj.
leftish *moderate* 177 adj.
leftist *political party* 708 n.
 sectional 708 adj.
left-overs *leavings* 41 n.
left wing
 sinistrality 242 n.
 sectional 708 adj.
leg *limb* 53 n.
 stand 218 n.
 leg 267 n.
legacy *sequel* 67 n.
 thing transferred 272 n.
 dower 777 n.
 gift 781 n.
 receipt 807 n.
legal *possible* 469 adj.
 preceptive 693 adj.
 just 913 adj.
 legal 953 adj.
legal adviser *adviser* 691 n.
 law agent, jurist 958 n.
legal code *law* 953 n.
legalist *narrow mind* 481 n.
 jurist 958 n.
legalize *permit* 756 vb.
 grant claims 915 vb.
 make legal 953 vb.
legal profession *bar* 958 n.
legal separation
 divorce 896 n.
legatary *beneficiary* 776 n.
 recipient 782 n.
legate *messenger* 531 n.
 army officer 741 n.
 envoy 754 n.
legatee *beneficiary* 776 n.
 recipient 782 n.
legation *commission* 751 n.
 envoy 754 n.
legend *commentary* 520 n.
 indication 547 n.
 record 548 n.
 phrase 563 n.
 description 590 n.
 narrative 590 n.
 (*see* fable)
legendary
 imaginary 513 adj.
 descriptive 590 adj.
legerdemain *sleight* 542 n.
leggings *legwear* 228 n.

leggy *crural* 267 adj.
leghorn *headgear* 228 n.
legibility *intelligibility* 516 n.
legion *multitude* 104 n.
 army 722 n.
legionary *soldier* 722 n.
legislate *rule* 733 vb.
 decree 737 vb.
 make legal 953 vb.
legislation
 management 689 n.
 precept 693 n.
 legislation 953 n.
legislative
 directing 689 adj.
 legal 953 adj.
legislative assembly
 parliament 692 n.
legislator *director* 690 n.
 councillor 692 n.
legislature *legislation* 953 n.
legist *jurist* 958 n.
legitimacy *authority* 733 n.
 legality 953 n.
legitimate *genuine* 494 adj.
 dramatic 594 adj.
 just 913 adj.
 due 915 adj.
 legal 953 adj.
legitimist *auxiliary* 707 n.
 defender 713 n.
legitimize
 grant claims 915 vb.
 make legal 953 vb.
leg-pull *trickery* 542 n.
 ridicule 851 n.
leg-puller *humorist* 839 n.
legs *conveyance* 267 n.
leg-show *stage show* 594 n.
leg to stand on
 pretext 614 n.
leguminous
 vegetal 366 adj.
leg-up *progression* 285 n.
 elevation 310 n.
 aid 703 n.
leiotrichous
 smooth 258 adj.
leisure *opportunity* 137 n.
 leisure 681 n.
 repose 683 n.
 resignation 753 n.
 amusement 837 n.
leisured *free* 744 adj.
leisurely *tardily* 136 adv.
 tranquil 266 adj.
 slow 278 adj.
 inactive 679 adj.
 leisurely 681 adj.
 reposeful 683 adj.
leitmotiv *melody* 410 n.

 musical piece 412 n.
 topic 452 n.
leman *loved one* 887 n.
 kept woman 952 n.
lemma *argumentation* 475 n.
 premise 475 n.
lemon *sourness* 393 n.
 yellowness 433 n.
lemonade *soft drink* 301 n.
Lemures *ghost* 970 n.
lemurine *animal* 365 adj.
lend *provide* 633 vb.
 convey 780 vb.
 give 781 vb.
 lend 784 vb.
 credit 802 vb.
lend a hand *aid* 703 vb.
lend colour to
 make likely 471 vb.
lend ear *hear* 415 vb.
 be mindful 455 vb.
 be willing 597 vb.
lender *creditor* 802 n.
lend-lease *provision* 633 n.
length *quantity* 26 n.
 greatness 32 n.
 piece 53 n.
 measure 183 n.
 size 195 n.
 distance 199 n.
 interval 201 n.
 length 203 n.
 textile 222 n.
 diffuseness 570 n.
length and breadth
 all 52 n.
lengthen *augment* 36 vb.
 continuate 71 vb.
 spin out 113 vb.
 enlarge 197 vb.
 lengthen 203 vb.
 be diffuse 570 vb.
lengthy *great* 32 adj.
 long 203 adj.
 prolix 570 adj.
lenient *moderate* 177 adj.
 lax 734 adj.
 lenient 736 adj.
 benevolent 897 adj.
lenify *make better* 654 vb.
 assuage 177 vb.
Leninism
 government 733 n.
lenitive *moderator* 177 n.
 lenitive 177 adj.
 lubricant 334 n.
 balm 658 n.
 pacificatory 719 adj.
 relieving 831 adj.
lenity *softness* 327 n.
 (*see* lenient)

lens *convexity* 253 n.
  transparency 422 n.
  optical device 442 n.
Lent *anniversary* 141 n.
  fast 946 n.
  holy-day 988 n.
lenticular *curved* 248 adj.
  convex 253 adj.
lentigo *blemish* 845 n.
lentil *vegetable* 301 n.
  plant 366 n.
lentor *slowness* 278 n.
  semiliquidity 354 n.
  sluggishness 679 n.
lentous *viscid* 354 adj.
leonine *animal* 365 adj.
  beautiful 841 adj.
leopard *cat* 365 n.
  maculation 437 n.
leopard's spots
  fixture 153 n.
leotard *tunic* 228 n.
leper *dirty person* 649 n.
  outcaste 883 n.
leprechaun *elf* 970 n.
leprosy *skin disease* 651 n.
leprous *unclean* 649 adj.
Lesbianism
  abnormality 84 n.
  illicit love 951 n.
lese-majesty *sedition* 738 n.
lesion *wound* 655 n.
less *less* 35 adv.
less and less
  diminuendo 37 adv.
lessee *resident* 191 n.
  possessor 776 n.
  recipient 782 n.
  purchaser 792 n.
lessen *bate* 37 vb.
  weaken 163 vb.
  moderate 177 vb.
  become small 198 vb.
lesson *lecture* 534 n.
  study 536 n.
  warning 664 n.
lessor *lender* 784 n.
let *obstacle* 702 n.
  give scope 744 vb.
  permit 756 vb.
  lending 784 n.
  lease 784 vb.
let alone *in addition* 38 n.
  exclusive of 57 adv.
  avoid 620 vb.
  not act 677 vb.
  give scope 744 vb.
let blood *void* 300 vb.
  doctor 658 vb.
let down *depress* 311 vb.
  disappoint 509 vb.

befool 542 vb.
  humbled 872 adj.
let fall *let fall* 311 vb.
  hint 524 vb.
  divulge 526 vb.
let fly *be violent* 176 vb.
  shoot 287 vb.
  fire at 712 vb.
let go *relinquish* 621 vb.
  liberate 746 vb.
  not retain 779 vb.
  be indifferent 860 vb.
  acquit 960 vb.
lethal *deadly* 362 adj.
lethal chamber
  means of execution 964 n.
lethargy *sluggishness* 679 n.
  moral insensibility 820 n.
Lethe *oblivion* 506 n.
  mythic hell 972 n.
lethiferous *deadly* 362 adj.
let in *intromit* 231 vb.
  admit 299 vb.
  befool 542 vb.
let off *be violent* 176 vb.
  shoot 287 vb.
  acquit 960 vb.
let-off *deliverance* 668 n.
  mercy 905 n.
  acquittal 960 n.
let oneself go
  please oneself 734 vb.
let out *enlarge* 197 vb.
  lengthen 203 vb.
  emit 300 vb.
  lease 784 vb.
let slip *be neglectful* 458 vb.
  liberate 746 vb.
  lose 772 vb.
letter *message* 529 n.
  indication 547 n.
  letter 558 n., vb.
  script 586 n.
  print-type 587 n.
  correspondence 588 n.
letter-bag *mails* 531 n.
letter-box *mails* 531 n.
  correspondence 588 n.
lettered *instructed* 490 adj.
  literary 557 adj.
  literal 558 adj.
lettering *lettering* 586 n.
  letterpress 587 n.
letter of credit
  paper money 797 n.
  credit 802 n.
letter of the law
  accuracy 494 n.
  severity 735 n.
  pitilessness 906 n.
  legality 953 n.

letterpress *letter* 558 n.
  letterpress 587 n.
letters *erudition* 490 n.
  literature 557 n.
  lettering 586 n.
  correspondence 588 n.
letters of fire *publicity* 528 n.
letters of gold
  publicity 528 n.
  praise 923 n.
letters of marque
  brigandage 788 n.
letters patent
  warrant 737 n.
  permit 756 n.
letter-writer *penman* 586 n.
  correspondent 588 n.
lettre de cachet
  detention 747 n.
lettuce *vegetable* 301 n.
let up *cease* 145 vb.
let well alone
  be cautious 858 vb.
leucoderma
  whiteness 427 n.
  skin disease 651 n.
  blemish 845 n.
leucorrhea
  hæmorrhage 302 n.
leucous *white* 427 adj.
levant *run away* 620 vb.
  defraud 788 vb.
  not pay 805 vb.
levée *assembly* 74 n.
  social gathering 882 n.
levée en masse *army* 722 n.
level *uniformity* 16 n.
  degree 27 n.
  equality 28 n.
  serial place 73 n.
  synchronous 123 adj.
  demolish 165 vb.
  near 200 adj.
  layer 207 n.
  horizontality 216 adj.
  angular measure 247 n.
  smooth 258 adj., vb.
  aim 281 vb.
  fell 311 vb.
  fire at 712 vb.
  inexcitable 823 adj.
level at *aim* 281 vb.
level crossing
  railroad 624 n.
level-headedness
  sagacity 498 n.
  caution 858 n.
leveller *uniformist* 16 n.
  destroyer 168 n.
levelness *uniformity* 16 n.
  lowness 210 n.

smoothness 258 n.
level off
　become small 198 vb.
level-pegging draw 28 n.
lever opportunity 137 n.
　causal means 156 n.
　influence 178 n.
　handle, pivot 218 n.
　propellant 287 n.
　extractor 304 n.
　lifter 310 n.
　instrument 628 n.
　tool 630 n.
leverage influence 178 n.
　tool 630 n.
　scope 744 n.
leveret vermin 365 n.
leviable priced 809 adj.
Leviathan giant 195 n.
　fish 365 n.
levigate smooth 258 vb.
　pulverize 332 vb.
　rub 333 vb.
levin luminary 420 n.
　flash 417 n.
levirate
　type of marriage 894 n.
levitation elevation 310 n.
　levity 323 n.
Levite priest 986 n.
levity insubstantiality 4 n.
　levity 323 n.
　folly 499 n.
　irresolution 601 n.
　whim 604 n.
　merriment 833 n.
　rashness 857 n.
levy assemblage 74 n.
　armed force 722 n.
　demand 737 n., vb.
　request 671 vb.
　acquire 771 vb.
　levy 786 vb.
　tax 809 n.
　claim 915 vb.
lewd impure 951 adj.
　lecherous 951 adj.
lexical verbal 559 adj.
lexicographer
　collector 492 n.
　linguist 557 n.
　etymology 559 n.
lexicographical
　linguistic 557 adj.
　verbal 559 adj.
lexicology
　etymology 559 n.
lexicon word list 87 n.
　commentary 520 n.
　dictionary 559 n.
　reference book 589 n.

indoor game 837 n.
lexigraphy spelling 558 n.
　word 559 n.
　writing 586 n.
liability tendency 179 n.
　liability 180 n.
　probability 471 n.
　bias 481 n.
　vulnerability 661 n.
　duty 917 n.
　guilt 936 n.
　penalty 963 n.
liable subject 745 adj.
　(see liability)
liaison relation 9 n.
　bond 47 n.
　concurrence 181 n.
　love affair 887 n.
　illicit love 951 n.
liar liar 545 n.
　boaster 877 n.
　knave 938 n.
libation(s) drinking 301 n.
　drunkenness 949 n.
　oblation 981 n.
libel calumny 926 n.
　false charge 928 n.
libellant accuser 928 n.
　litigant 959 n.
libeller defamer 926 n.
　accuser 928 n.
liberal plenteous 635 adj.
　free man 744 n.
　expending 806 adj.
　prodigal 815 adj.
　philanthropic 901 adj.
　rewarding 962 adj.
　(see liberality)
liberalism freedom 744 n.
　disinterestedness 931 n.
liberality giving 781 n.
　liberality 813 n.
　benevolence 897 n.
　disinterestedness 931 n.
liberalize liberate 746 vb.
Liberals
　political party 708 n.
liberate disjoin 46 vb.
　disencumber 701 vb.
　permit 756 vb.
liberation extraction 304 vb.
　escape 667 n.
　deliverance 668 n.
　freedom 744 n.
　liberation 746 n.
　non-retention 779 n.
　acquittal 960 n.
libertarianism
　freedom 744 n.
liberticide brute force 735 n.
libertinage

love-making 887 n.
　unchastity 951 n.
libertine bad man 938 n.
　lecherous 951 adj.
　libertine 952 n.
liberty opportunity 137 n.
　freedom, scope 744 n.
　permission 756 n.
　dueness 915 n.
　non-liability 919 n.
Liberty Hall scope 744 n.
　sociability 882 n.
libidinous desiring 859 adj.
　loving 887 adj.
　lecherous 951 adj.
libido libido 859 n.
　love 887 n.
librarian collector 492 n.
　bookman 589 n.
　manager 690 n.
library accumulation 74 n.
　chamber 194 n.
　erudition 490 n.
　library 589 n.
　edition 589 n.
　collection 632 n.
libration oscillation 317 n.
　uranometry 321 n.
librettist musician 413 n.
　poet 593 n.
　dramatist 594 n.
　author 589 n.
libretto vocal music 412 n.
　reading matter 589 n.
　stage play 594 n.
licence
　laxity, anarchy 734 n.
　freedom, scope 744 n.
　permit 756 n.
　dueness 915 n.
　non-liability 919 n.
　unchastity 951 n.
license give scope 744 vb.
　liberate 746 vb.
　commission 751 vb.
　permit 756 vb.
　exempt 919 vb.
licensee consignee 754 n.
　recipient 782 n.
licentious
　anarchic 734 adj.
　free 744 adj.
　sensual 944 adj.
　lecherous 951 adj.
　lawless 954 adj.
lichen plant 366 n.
licit permitted 756 adj.
　due 915 adj.
　legal 953 adj.
lick small quantity 33 n.
　eat 301 vb.

moisten 341 vb.
touch 378 vb.
taste 386 vb.
defeat 727 vb.
caress 889 vb.
lick and a promise
incompleteness 55 n.
lickerish *savoury* 390 adj.
lecherous 951 adj.
lick into shape
efform 243 vb.
educate 534 vb.
lick one's lips *enjoy* 376 vb.
gluttonize 947 vb.
lick one's wounds
feel pain 377 vb.
be defeated 728 vb.
lickspittle *toady* 879 n.
lictor *officer* 741 n.
lid *covering* 226 n.
headgear 228 n.
stopper 264 n.
lido *shore* 344 n.
arena 724 n.
pleasure-ground 837 n.
lie *be* 1 vb.
be in a state 7 vb.
be inert 175 vb.
be situate 186 vb.
be present 189 vb.
dwell 192 vb.
be horizontal 216 vb.
misteach 535 vb.
be false 541 vb.
deception 542 n.
untruth 543 n.
be inactive 679 vb.
false charge 928 n.
be dishonest 930 vb.
lie-abed *lateness* 136 n.
slowcoach 278 n.
idler 679 n.
lied, lieder
vocal music 412 n.
lie-detector *detector* 484 n.
lie direct *negation* 533 n.
lie down
be horizontal 216 vb.
repose 683 vb.
be dejected 834 vb.
lie fallow
be unproductive 172 vb.
be unprepared 670 vb.
not act 677 vb.
liege *master* 741 n.
subject 742 n.
liegeman *dependant* 742 n.
lie in
reproduce itself 164 vb.
lie in wait *ambush* 527 vb.
lie low *disappear* 446 vb.

be low 210 vb.
lurk 523 vb.
elude 667 vb.
lie off *be distant* 199 vb.
lie to *be quiescent* 266 vb.
navigate 269 vb.
lieu, in *in return* 31 adv.
lie under *be liable* 180 vb.
lieutenancy *degree* 27 n.
lieutenant *naval man* 270 n.
aider 703 n.
auxiliary 707 n.
soldiery 722 n.
army officer 741 n.
naval officer 741 n.
deputy 755 n.
lie with *unite with* 45 vb.
life *existence* 1 n.
substantiality 3 n.
essential part 5 n.
time 108 n.
period 110 n.
affairs 154 n.
vitality 162 n.
vigorousness 174 n.
life 360 n.
biography 590 n.
vocation 622 n.
activity 678 n.
life-belt *support* 218 n.
wrapping 226 n.
safeguard 662 n.
preserver 666 n.
life-blood
essential part 5 n.
blood 335 n.
life 360 n.
lifeboat *boat* 275 n.
safeguard 662 n.
life-buoy *support* 218 n.
life cycle
regular return 141 n.
transition 147 n.
life-giving
generative 171 adj.
lifeguard *protector* 660 n.
shelter 662 n.
defender 713 n.
armed force 722 n.
life-jacket *safeguard* 662 n.
lifeless *inert* 175 adj.
dead 361 adj.
inactive 679 adj.
lifelike *lifelike* 18 adj.
life-line *bond* 47 n.
safeguard 662 n.
lifelong *lasting* 113 adj.
lifemanship *tactics* 688 n.
skill 694 n.
life peer *councillor* 692 n.
nobleman 868 n.

life-preserver
safeguard 662 n.
club 723 n.
lifer *offender* 904 n.
life-saving
deliverance 668 n.
life sentence
diuturnity 113 n.
life-size *size* 195 n.
large 195 adj.
life story *biography* 590 n.
lifetime *period* 110 n.
diuturnity 113 n.
life to come
future state 124 n.
life with
accompaniment 89 n.
life-work *vocation* 622 n.
lift *displace* 188 vb.
conveyance 267 n.
transfer 272 vb.
carry 273 vb.
promote 285 vb.
draw 288 vb.
ascent 308 n.
lifter 310 n.
elevate 310 vb.
improvement 654 n.
liberate 746 vb.
not retain 779 vb.
steal 788 vb.
aid 703 n.
relieve 831 vb.
lift a finger *do* 676 vb.
lifter *lifter* 310 n.
taker 786 n.
thief 789 n.
ligament *ligature* 47 n.
retention 778 n.
ligature *ligature* 47 n.
light *insubstantial* 4 adj.
unequal 29 adj.
small 33 adj.
morning 128 n.
descend 309 vb.
light 323 adj.
rare 325 adj.
soft 327 adj.
fire 379 n.
kindle 381 vb.
lighter 385 n.
light 417 n.
luminary 420 n.
illuminate 420 vb.
soft-hued 425 adj.
white 427 adj.
appearance 445 n.
knowledge 490 n.
truth 494 n.
interpretation 520 n.
irresolute 601 adj.

trivial 639 adj.
easy 701 adj.
gay 833 adj.
funny 849 adj.
rash 857 adj.
unchaste 951 adj.
revelation 975 n.
light and shade
  light contrast 417 n.
lighten *bate* 37 vb.
  assuage 177 vb.
  lighten 323 vb.
  make bright 417 vb.
  disencumber 701 vb.
  take away 786 vb.
  relieve 831 vb.
lighter *boat* 275 n.
  lighter 385 n.
  torch 420 n.
lighterage *price* 809 n.
lighterman *boatman* 270 n.
lighter-than-air
  aviational 276 adj.
light-fingered *light* 323 adj.
  tactual 378 adj.
  thieving 788 adj.
light-footed *speedy* 277 adj.
  active 678 adj.
light-grasp *range* 183 n.
  optics 417 n.
  vision 438 n.
light hand *lenity* 736 n.
light-headed
  frenzied 503 adj.
light-hearted
  cheerful 833 adj.
lighthouse
  sailing aid 269 n.
  signal light 420 n.
  signpost 547 n.
  safeguard 662 n.
lighting *lighting* 420 n.
lightless *unlit* 418 adj.
lightly *slightly* 33 adv.
  rashly 857 adv.
light-minded
  changeful 152 adj.
  light-minded 456 adj.
  rash 857 adj.
lightness *insubstantiality* 4 n.
  weakness 163 n.
  levity 323 n.
  rarity 325 n.
  unchastity 951 n.
lightning *electricity* 160 n.
  velocity 277 n.
  flash 417 n.
  luminary 420 n.
lightning conductor
  electricity 160 n.
  safeguard 662 n.

lightning rod (*see* lightning
  conductor)
light of nature
  empiricism 461 n.
  intuition 476 n.
light on *land* 295 vb.
  (*see* light upon)
light rein *lenity* 736 n.
light relief
  ridiculousness 849 n.
lights *knowledge* 490 n.
  intelligence 498 n.
light-shift
  displacement 188 n.
lightship *sailing aid* 269 n.
  ship 275 n.
  signal light 420 n.
  signpost 547 n.
  safeguard 662 n.
lights out
  obscuration 418 n.
  call 547 n.
light up *make bright* 417 vb.
  illuminate 420 vb.
light upon *chance* 159 vb.
  meet 295 vb.
  acquire 771 vb.
light wave *radiation* 417 n.
light-weight
  insubstantial 4 adj.
  inconsiderable 33 adj.
  weakling 163 n.
  light 323 adj.
  nonentity 639 n.
  trivial 639 adj.
  pugilist 722 n.
light-well *window* 263 n.
light year *period* 110 n.
  long measure 203 n.
ligneous *wooden* 366 adj.
lignite *fuel* 385 n.
lignography *engraving*
  555 n.
like *relative* 9 adj.
  similar 18 adj.
  equal 28 adj.
  enjoy 376 vb.
  appetize 390 vb.
  be pleased 824 vb.
  desire 859 vb.
  be friendly 880 vb.
  love 887 vb.
likeable *desired* 859 adj.
  loveable 887 adj.
like for like
  retaliation 714 n.
likelihood *liability* 180 n.
  possibility 469 n.
  probability 471 n.
likely *probable* 471 adj.
  credible 485 adj.

true 494 adj.
  promising 852 adj.
like-minded *agreeing* 24 adj.
  assenting 488 adj.
liken *relate* 9 vb.
  liken 18 vb.
  compare 462 vb.
  figure 519 vb.
likeness *similarity* 18 n.
  copy 22 n.
  equivalence 28 n.
  comparison 462 n.
  metaphor 519 n.
  representation 551 n.
like new *restored* 656 adj.
likes of, the *analogue* 18 n.
like well *approve* 923 vb.
likewise *in addition* 38 adv.
liking *tendency* 179 n.
  liking 859 n.
  love 887 n.
lilac *tree* 366 n.
  purple 434 adj.
lilies *heraldry* 547 n.
Lilliputian *dwarf* 196 n.
lilt *sing* 413 vb.
  be cheerful 833 vb.
lily *white thing* 427 n.
  a beauty 841 n.
lily-livered
  cowardly 856 adj.
limature *powder* 332 n.
  friction 333 n.
limb *adjunct* 40 n.
  piece, limb 53 n.
  extremity 69 n.
  leg 267 n.
  tree, foliage 366 n.
limber *affix* 45 vb.
  war-chariot 274 n.
  flexible 327 adj.
  gun 723 n.
limber up
  prepare oneself 669 vb.
limb from limb
  apart 46 adv.
limbless
  fragmentary 53 adj.
  incomplete 55 adj.
limbo *prison* 748 n.
  hell 972 n.
lime *adhesive* 47 n.
  tree 366 n.
  bleacher 426 n.
  green 432 adj.
  ensnare 542 vb.
  take 786 vb.
Limehouse *scurrility* 899 n.
limejuicer *foreigner* 59 n.
lime-kiln *furnace* 383 n.
limelight *lighting* 420 n.

advertisement 528 n.
theatre 594 n.
limelight, in the
manifest 522 adj.
publicly 528 adv.
on stage 594 adv.
limen *threshold* 234 n.
limerick *doggerel* 593 n.
witticism 839 n.
ridiculousness 849 n.
impurity 951 n.
limestone *rock* 344 n
soil 344 n.
liminal *marginal* 234 adj.
limit *finite quantity* 26 n.
bate 37 vb.
completeness 54 n.
extremity 69 n.
moderate 177 vb.
farness 199 n.
edge 234 n.
limit 236 n., vb.
qualify 468 vb.
hinder 702 vb.
restriction 747 n.
apportionment 783 n.
annoyance 827 n.
limitary *limited* 236 adj.
restraining 747 adj.
limitation *decrease* 37 n.
circumscription 232 n.
limit 236 n.
qualification 468 n.
defect 647 n.
restriction 747 n.
conditions 766 n.
limiting factor *limit* 236 n.
restriction 747 n.
limitless *infinite* 107 adj.
huge 195 adj.
limitrophe *near* 200 adj.
limn *represent* 551 vb.
paint 553 vb.
limousine
automobile 274 n.
limp *weak* 163 adj.
move slowly 278 vb.
soft 327 adj.
feeble 572 adj.
be clumsy 695 vb.
miscarry 728 vb.
limpet *coherence* 48 n.
limpid *transparent* 422 adj.
intelligible 516 adj.
perspicuous 567 adj.
lin *lake* 346 n.
linage *letterpress* 587 n.
linch pin *fastening* 47 n.
linctus *medicine* 658 n.
line *race* 11 n.
cable 47 n.

fill 54 vb.
sequence 65 n.
continuity 71 n.
breed 77 n.
posteriority 120 n.
strengthen 162 vb.
genealogy 169 n.
sonship 170 n.
load 193 vb.
line 203 n.
narrowness 206 n.
strip 208 n.
line 227 vb.
put between 231 vb.
limit 236 n.
groove 262 vb.
sailing aid 269 n.
train 274 n.
direction 281 n.
insert 303 vb.
indication 547 n.
lettering 586 n.
correspondence 588 n.
vocation 622 n.
policy 623 n.
way, route 624 n.
tactics 688 n.
battle 718 n.
formation 722 n.
merchandise 794 n.

lineage *consanguinity* 11 n.
sequence 65 n.
series 71 n.
posteriority 120 n.
source 156 n.
genealogy 169 n.
sonship 170 n.
nobility 868 n.
line ahead *line* 203 n.
lineal *continuous* 71 adj.
filial 170 n.
longitudinal 203 adj.
lineament *outline* 233 n.
form 243 n.
feature 445 n.
linear *continuous* 71 adj.
parental 169 adj.
longitudinal 203 adj.
straight 249 adj.
metric 465 adj.
painted 553 adj.
linear measure
long measure 203 n.
metrology 465 n.
lined *furrowed* 262 adj.
line-drawing *picture* 553 n.
line, in *uniform* 16 adj.
longwise 203 adv.
straight 249 adj.
linen *fibre* 208 n.
textile 222 n.

bodywear 228 n.
bookbinding 589 n.
linen-draper *clothier* 228 n.
line of communication
route 624 n.
line of country
function 622 n.
line of sight *direction* 281 n.
view 438 n.
liner *ship* 275 n.
lines *station* 187 n.
abode 192 n.
form 243 n.
feature 445 n.
poem 593 n.
railroad 624 n.
defences 713 n.
penalty 963 n.
line up *be in order* 60 vb.
arrange 62 vb.
assemblage 74 n.
line with, in
conformably 83 adv.
ling *plant* 366 n.
lingam *genitalia* 164 n.
idol 982 n.
linger *drag on* 113 vb.
be late 136 vb.
lingerer *slowcoach* 278 n.
lingerie *underwear* 228 n.
lingo *language* 557 n.
dialect 560 n.
lingua franca
language 557 n.
dialect 560 n.
lingual *vocal* 577 adj.
linguist *interpreter* 520 n.
linguist 557 n.
linguistic *semantic* 514 adj.
linguistic 557 adj.
linguistics *linguistics* 557 n.
etymology 559 n.
liniment *unguent* 357 n.
balm 658 n.
lining *contents* 193 n.
lining 227 n.
insertion 303 n.
link *relation* 9 n.
connect 45 vb.
bond 47 n.
component 58 n.
cross 222 vb.
intermediary 231 n.
torch 420 n.
gauge 465 n.
linkage (*see* link)
link-boy *torch* 420 n.
director 690 n.
links *pleasure-ground* 837 n.
linnet *bird* 365 n.
linoleum *floor-cover* 226 n.

linotype *print* 587n.
linseed *medicine* 658n.
linsey-wolsey *mixed* 43adj.
  textural 331adj.
linstock *lighter* 385n.
lint *wrapping* 226n.
lintel *summit* 213n.
  beam 218n.
  doorway 263n.
lion *cat* 365n.
  heraldry 547n.
  bigwig 638n.
  brave person 855n.
  person of repute 866n.
  favourite 890n.
lion-hearted
  courageous 855adj.
lion-hunter *toady* 879n.
lionize *honour* 866vb.
  celebrate 876vb.
  respect 920vb.
  praise 923vb.
lion's share *main part* 52n.
  redundance 637n.
  undueness 916n.
lion-tamer *breeder* 369n.
  trainer 537n.
lip *edge* 234n.
  projection 254n.
  rudeness 885n.
  sauciness 878n.
lip-homage *duplicity* 541n.
  flattery 925n.
lippitude *dim sight* 440n.
lip-read *hear* 415vb.
  be deaf 416vb.
  translate 520vb.
lip-reverence
  false piety 980n.
lips *speech* 579n.
lipsalve *cosmetic* 843n.
  flattery 925n.
lipstick *red pigment* 421n.
  cosmetic 843n.
liquefaction
  decomposition 51n.
  fluidity 335n.
  liquefaction 337n.
  heating 381n.
liquescent *fluidal* 335adj.
liqueur *liquor* 301n.
  sweet 392n.
liquid
  non-adhesive 49adj.
  amorphous 244adj.
  liquor 301n.
  fluid 335n.
  speech sound 398n.
  transparent 422adj.
  vocal 577adj.
liquidation

destruction 165n.
  slaughter 362n.
  payment 804n.
liquidator *receiver* 782n.
  treasurer 798n.
liquidity *fluidity* 335n.
  means 629n.
  funds 797n.
liquid measure
  metrology 465n.
liquor *stimulant* 174n.
  liquor 301n.
  lubricate 334vb.
  fluid 335n.
  add water 339vb.
liquorice *sweetmeat* 301n.
  sweet 392n.
lira *coinage* 797n.
lisp *solecize* 565vb.
  voice 577vb.
  speech defect 580n.
lissom *speedy* 277adj.
  flexible 327adj.
list *specify* 80vb.
  number 86vb.
  list 87n.,vb.
  filament 208n.
  obliquity 220n.
  edging 234n.
  register 548vb.
  will 595vb.
listen (to) *hear* 415vb.
  be curious 453vb.
  be attentive 455vb.
  consult 691vb.
  obey 739vb.
  consent 758vb.
  be pious 979vb.
listened to
  influential 178adj.
listener *listener* 415n.
  witness 466n.
  allocution 583n.
listen in *hear* 415vb.
listless *weakly* 163adj.
  incurious 454adj.
  inattentive 456adj.
  inactive 679adj.
  dejected 834adj.
  indifferent 860adj.
lists *duel* 716n.
  arena 724n.
lit *fiery* 379adj.
  heated 381adj.
  luminous 417adj.
litanist *ritualist* 988n.
litany *prayers* 981n.
  office book 988n.
literal *imitative* 20adj.
  narrow-minded 481adj.
  accurate 494adj.

semantic 514adj.
  interpretive 520adj.
  literal 558adj.
  verbal 559adj.
  observant 768adj.
  orthodox 976adj.
literal-minded
  narrow-minded 481adj.
  accurate 494adj.
literary *instructed* 490adj.
  literary 557adj.
  stylistic 566adj.
literary man *author* 589n.
literate *instructed* 490adj.
  written 586adj.
literati *intellectual* 492n.
literature *culture* 490n.
  erudition 490n.
  literature 557n.
  writing 586n.
  reading matter 589n.
lithe *flexible* 327adj.
lithograph *copy* 22n.
  representation 551n.
  engrave 555vb.
  print 587vb.
lithology *mineralogy* 359n.
litigable *litigated* 959adj.
litigant *combatant* 722adj.
  accuser 928n.
  litigant 959n.
litigation *argument* 475n.
  quarrel 709n.
  litigation 959n.
litigious
  quarrelling 709adj.
  litigating 959adj.
litmus paper
  testing agent 461n.
litotes
  underestimation 483n.
  trope 519n.
litre *metrology* 465n.
litter *confusion* 61n.
  jumble 63vb.
  youngling 132n.
  posterity 170n.
  bed 218n.
  vehicle 274n.
  rubbish 641n.
litterer *slut* 61n.
  dirty person 649n.
little *small* 33adj.
  infantine 132adj.
  little 196adj.
  short 204adj.
  unimportant 639adj.
  contemptible 922adj.
little, a *partially* 33adv.
little by little
  by degrees 27adv.

gradatim 278 adv.
little game
  stratagem 698 n.
little go exam. 459 n.
little man
  common man 30 n.
  everyman 79 n.
  commoner 869 n.
littleness
  invisibility 444 n.
  (see little)
littoral edge 234 n.
  coastal 344 adj.
liturgics ritualism 988 n.
liturgiologist ritualist 988 n.
liturgy ritual 988 n.
  office book 988 n.
  Holy Communion 988 n.
live pass time 108 vb.
  dynamic 160 adj.
  operative 173 adj.
  vigorous 174 adj.
  alive 360 adj.
  live 360 vb.
  dramatic 594 adj.
  active 678 adj.
  feel 818 vb.
liveable
  contenting 828 adj.
live and let live
  not act 677 vb.
  give scope 744 vb.
live in the past
  retrospect 505 vb.
livelihood vocation 622 n.
liveliness energy 160 n.
  vitality 162 n.
  vigorousness 174 n.
  vigour 571 n.
  restlessness 678 n.
  moral sensibility 819 n.
  cheerfulness 833 n.
livelong lasting 113 adj.
lively
  imaginative 513 adj.
  forceful 571 adj.
  lively 819 adj.
  excitable 822 adj.
  sociable 882 adj.
  (see liveliness)
liven vitalize 360 vb.
liver rara avis 84 n.
  insides 224 n.
  meat 301 n.
  sullenness 893 n.
liverish irascible 892 adj.
liverishness
  indigestion 651 n.
livery uniform 228 n.
  hue 425 n.
  livery 547 n.

badge of rule 743 n.
  transfer 780 n.
livery company
  corporation 708 n.
  merchant 794 n.
liveryman free man 744 n.
  merchant 794 n.
livestock cattle 365 n.
live through
  continue 108 vb.
  be restored 656 vb.
live wire electricity 160 n.
  vigorousness 174 n.
  busy person 678 n.
live with unite with 45 vb.
  accompany 89 vb.
livid blackish 428 adj.
  grey 429 adj.
  colourless 426 adj.
  purple 434 adj.
  blue 435 adj.
  angry 891 adj.
living benefice 985 n.
living being life 360 n.
living death
  suffering 825 n.
living image analogue 18 n.
living space room 183 n.
  scope 744 n.
living wage
  sufficiency 635 n.
lixiviate liquefy 337 vb.
  drench 341 vb.
  purify 648 vb.
lixivium solution 337 n.
lizard reptile 365 n.
llama fibre 208 n.
  beast of burden 273 n.
load fill 54 vb.
  bunch 74 n.
  stow 187 vb.
  contents 193 n.
  thing transferred 272 n.
  gravity 322 n.
  redundance 637 n.
  encumbrance 702 n.
  adversity 731 n.
  worry 825 n.
  decorate 844 vb.
loads great quantity 32 n.
  multitude 104 n.
loadstone traction 288 n.
  attraction 291 n.
  incentive 612 n.
load with add 38 vb.
loaf cereal 301 n.
  be inactive 679 vb.
loafer wanderer 268 n.
  idler 679 n.
loafers footwear 228 n.
loam soil 344 n.

loan subvention 703 n.
  lending 784 n.
  borrowing 785 n.
  credit 802 n.
loanee debtor 803 n.
loan-word neology 560 n.
loathing dislike 861 n.
  enmity 881 n.
  hatred 888 n.
loathsome
  unsavoury 391 n.
  not nice 645 adj.
  unpleasant 827 adj.
  ugly 842 adj.
  disliked 861 adj.
  hateful 888 adj.
loaves and fishes
  prosperity 730 n.
lob propulsion 287 n.
  elevate 310 vb.
lobby lobby 194 n.
  incite 612 vb.
  access 624 n.
lobbyist motivator 612 n.
  petitioner 763 n.
lobe pendant 217 n.
  ear 415 n.
lobster fish food 301 n.
  table fish 365 n.
  redness 431 n.
local regional 184 adj.
  situated 186 adj.
  native 191 n.
  tavern 192 n.
  provincial 192 adj.
  near 200 adj.
local colour
  accuracy 494 n.
  painting 553 n.
localism dialect 560 n.
locality district 184 n.
  region 184 n.
  place 185 n.
  locality 187 n.
localize place 187 vb.
  restrain 747 vb.
locate specify 80 vb.
  place 187 vb.
  orientate 281 vb.
  discover 484 vb.
location situation 186 n.
  location 187 n.
location, on absent 190 adj.
loch lake 346 n.
lock join 45 vb.
  fastening 47 n.
  filament 208 n.
  hair 259 n.
  stopper 264 n.
  close 264 vb.
  conduit 351 n.

access 624 n.
safeguard 662 n.
fire-arm 723 n.
retain 778 vb.
lock and key
fastening 47 n.
locker box 194 n.
locket jewellery 844 n.
lockjaw spasm 318 n.
infection 651 n.
lock-out exclusion 57 n.
strike 145 n.
locksmith artisan 686 n.
lock, stock and barrel
all 52 n.
lock up cover 226 vb.
conceal 525 vb.
safeguard 660 vb.
imprison 747 vb.
punish 963 vb.
lock-up lock-up 748 n.
loco crazed 503 adj.
locomotion motion 265 n.
locomotive
locomotive 274 n.
vehicular 274 adj.
locomotor ataxia
helplessness 161 n.
locular cellular 194 adj.
loculus compartment 194 n.
locum tenens
substitute 150 n.
resident 191 n.
doctor 658 n.
deputy 755 n.
locus continuity 71 n.
locus classicus
example 83 n.
locus standi pretext 614 n.
locust destroyer 168 n.
eater 301 n.
vermin 365 n.
bane 659 n.
taker 786 n.
noxious animal 904 n.
glutton 947 n.
locution word 559 n.
phrase 563 n.
lode layer 207 n.
store 632 n.
lodestar attraction 291 n.
signpost 547 n.
incentive 612 n.
directorship 689 n.
lodge place 187 vb.
small house 192 n.
dwell 192 vb.
society 708 n.
lodger resident 191 n.
possessor 776 n.
lodging(s) quarters 192 n.

lodgment location 187 n.
presence 189 n.
loess leavings 41 n.
soil 344 n.
loft attic 194 n.
propel 287 vb.
elevate 310 vb.
lofty high 209 adj.
elevated 310 adj.
forceful 571 adj.
worshipful 866 adj.
proud 871 adj.
insolent 878 adj.
despising 922 adj.
disinterested 931 adj.
log sailing aid 269 n.
raft 275 n.
fuel 385 n.
gauge 465 n.
record 548 n.
logarithm
numerical element 85 n.
mathematics 86 n.
log-book chronology 117 n.
record 548 n.
loggerheads, at
disagreeing 25 adj.
quarrelling 709 adj.
contending 716 adj.
warring 718 adj.
loggia lobby 194 n.
logia narrative 590 n.
logic reasoning 475 n.
curriculum 536 n.
necessity 596 n.
logical relevant 9 adj.
philosophic 449 adj.
plausible 471 adj.
rational 475 adj.
true 494 adj.
necessary 596 adj.
logical conclusion
conformance 24 n.
logicality relevance 9 n.
logic-chopping
discrimination 463 n.
argument 475 n.
sophistry 477 n.
logician reasoner 475 n.
logistics provision 633 n.
fitting out 669 n.
art of war 718 n.
logography writing 586 n.
logogriph enigma 530 n.
logomachy argument 475 n.
sophistry 477 n.
conference 584 n.
logometer
counting instrument 86 n.
logometric
numerical 85 adj.

Logos word 559 n.
God the Son 965 n.
log-rolling
interchange 151 n.
co-operation 706 n.
loin rear 238 n.
loincloth wrapping 226 n.
loincloth 228 n.
loins source 156 n.
genitalia 164 n.
parentage 169 n.
loiter be late 136 vb.
be stealthy 525 vb.
be inactive 679 vb.
loiterer slowcoach 278 n.
Lok Sabha
parliament 692 n.
loll be horizontal 216 vb.
be inactive 679 vb.
repose 683 vb.
Lollardy heresy 977 n.
lollipop sweetmeat 301 n.
sweet 392 n.
lollop be inactive 679 vb.
lolloping
unwieldy 195 adj.
lolly sweetmeat 301 n.
dibs 797 n.
lone non-uniform 17 adj.
alone 88 adj.
unsociable 883 adj.
lonely separate 46 adj.
alone 88 adj.
empty 190 adj.
friendless 883 adj.
secluded 883 adj.
lone wolf
non-uniformity 17 n.
revolter 738 n.
solitary 883 n.
long lasting 113 adj.
long 203 adj.
prolix 570 adj.
tedious 838 adj.
desire 859 vb.
long ago long ago 113 adv.
formerly 125 adv.
longanimity patience 823 n.
forgiveness 909 n.
long arm governance 733 n.
long-bow propellant 287 n.
missile weapon 723 n.
long-cloth textile 222 n.
long clothes robe 228 n.
long clothes, in
infantine 132 adj.
long-drawn long 203 adj.
prolix 570 adj.
longevity diuturnity 113 n.
age 131 n.
life 360 n.

health 650n.
long face *dejection* 834n.
longhand *writing* 586n.
long-headed
  intelligent 498adj.
longimetry
  long measure 203n.
  metrology 465n.
longing *suffering* 825n.
  regret 830n.
  desire 859n.
  love 887n.
longinquity *distance* 199n.
longitude *length* 203n.
long-legged *long* 203adj.
  narrow 206adj.
  tall 209adj.
long-lived *alive* 360adj.
long measure
  long measure 203n.
long odds
  fair chance 159n.
  improbability 472n.
long-player
  gramophone 414n.
  recording instrument
  549n.
long-range *distant* 199adj.
long rope *scope* 744n.
long run *period* 110n.
  protraction 113n.
long run, in the
  in the long run 113adv.
  prospectively 124adv.
  in the future 155adv.
long-service *lasting* 113adj.
longshoreman
  boatman 270n.
long-sightedness
  foresight 510n.
longsome *long* 203adj.
  prolix 570adj.
long-standing
  lasting 113adj.
  immemorial 127adj.
  permanent 144adj.
longstop *interceptor* 702n.
long-suffering
  lenient 736adj.
  patience 823n.
  mercy 905n.
  forgiveness 909n.
long-term *lasting* 113adj.
long-winded
  protracted 113adj.
  prolix 570adj.
  loquacious 581adj.
longwise *longwise* 203adv.
loo *latrine* 649n.
  card game 837n.
looby *bungler* 697n.

countryman 869n.
look *similarity* 18n.
  form 243n.
  look 438n.
  appearance 445n.
  mien 445n.
  be curious 453vb.
  attention 455n.
  hint 524n.
look after *look after* 457vb.
  safeguard 660vb.
look after oneself
  be selfish 932vb.
look a gift horse in the
  mouth
  be discontented 829vb.
  be cautious 858vb.
  be fastidious 862vb.
  be ungrateful 908vb.
look ahead
  look ahead 124vb.
  foresee 510vb.
  plan 623vb.
look as if *resemble* 18vb.
look askance *dissent* 489vb.
  dislike 861vb.
  disapprove 924vb.
look at *watch* 441vb.
look back *look back* 125vb.
  be late 136vb.
  turn back 286vb.
  retrospect 505vb.
  regret 830vb.
look big *defy* 711vb.
  be insolent 878vb.
look black *be dark* 418vb.
  show feeling 818vb.
  be angry 891vb.
  be sullen 893vb.
  disapprove 924vb.
look blue
  be disappointed 509vb.
  show feeling 818vb.
  be discontented 829vb.
  be dejected 834vb.
look daggers
  be angry 891vb.
  threaten 900vb.
  disapprove 924vb.
look down on
  be proud 871vb.
  be insolent 878vb.
  not respect 921vb.
  despise 922vb.
looker *enquirer* 459n.
looker-on *spectator* 441n.
look for *enquire* 459vb.
  search 459vb.
  assume 471vb.
  expect 507vb.
  pursue 619vb.

desire 859vb.
look for trouble
  make quarrels 709vb.
look forward
  look ahead 124vb.
  expect 507vb.
  hope 852vb.
look in *be present* 189vb.
  enter 297vb.
  watch 441vb.
  visit 882vb.
looking back
  reversion 148n.
  tergiversation 603n.
looking-glass *mirror* 442n.
look in the face
  withstand 704vb.
  be courageous 855vb.
look into
  be attentive 455vb.
look like *resemble* 18vb.
look of the thing
  appearance 445n.
look of things
  circumstance 8n.
look on
  be impotent 161vb.
  be present 189vb.
  watch 441vb.
  acquiesce 488vb.
  not act 677vb.
look-out *view* 438n.
  spectator 441n.
  surveillance 457n.
  expectation 507n.
  function 622n.
  protector 660n.
  warner 664n.
  keeper 749n.
  worry 825n.
look out *scan* 438vb.
  invigilate 457vb.
  be cautious 858vb.
look over *scan* 438vb.
look over one's shoulder
  turn back 286vb.
  be loth 598vb.
  regret 830vb.
look-see *inspection* 438n.
look silly
  be ridiculous 849vb.
  lose repute 867vb.
look the other way
  be blind 439vb.
  avoid 620vb.
look to
  be attentive 455vb.
  look after 457vb.
  impose a duty 917vb.
look twice
  be cautious 858vb.

[995]

look up *visit* 882 vb.
look up and down
  be insolent 878 vb.
look up to *honour* 866 vb.
  respect 920 vb.
loom *be great* 32 vb.
  impend 156 vb.
  produce 164 vb.
  handle 218 n.
  textile 222 n.
  weave 222 vb.
  be dim 419 vb.
  blur 440 vb.
  be visible 443 vb.
  endanger 661 vb.
  workshop 687 n.
loon *dunce* 501 n.
  madman 504 n.
  countryman 869 n.
loop *loop* 250 n.
  be curved 248 vb.
  circuit 626 n.

loophole *window* 263 n.
  outlet 298 n.
  view 438 n.
  pretext 614 n.
  contrivance 623 n.
  defect 647 n.
  means of escape 667 n.
  fortification 713 n.
loop-line *circuit* 626 n.
loop the loop *fly* 271 vb.
  circuit 626 vb.
loopy *crazed* 503 adj.
loose *disjoin* 46 vb.
  non-adhesive 49 adj.
  unstick 49 vb.
  general 79 adj.
  unstable 152 adj.
  pendent 217 adj.
  deviating 282 adj.
  ill-reasoned 477 adj.
  feeble 572 adj.
  lax 734 adj.
  free 744 adj.
  liberate 746 vb.
  unchaste 951 adj.
loose end, at a
  leisurely 681 adj.
loose ends *negligence* 458 n.
loose-knit
  non-adhesive 49 adj.
loose-limbed
  flexible 327 adj.
loose liver *sensualist* 944 n.
  libertine 952 n.
loosen, looseness (*see* loose)
loose terms
  indiscrimination 464 n.
loose thread
  mistake 495 n.

loot *take away* 786 vb.
  rob 788 vb.
  booty 790 n.
looting *spoliation* 788 n.
lop *subtract* 39 vb.
  cut 46 vb.
  shorten 204 vb.
lope *gait* 265 n.
  pedestrianism 267 n.
  move fast 277 vb.
lop-sided *unequal* 29 adj.
  clumsy 695 adj.
  (*see* oblique)
lopsidedness
  distortion 246 n.
loquacious
  informative 524 adj.
loquacity *diffuseness* 570 n.
  speech 579 n.
  loquacity 581 n.
lord *male* 372 n.
  bigwig 638 n.
  nobleman 868 n.
  title 870 n.
  master 741 n.
  owner 776 n.
lord and master, one's
  spouse 894 n.
lord it *dominate* 733 vb.
  oppress 735 vb.
  seek repute 866 vb.
  be proud 871 vb.
  be insolent 878 vb.
lordliness *authority* 733 n.
lordly *authoritative* 733 adj.
  authoritarian 735 adj.
  liberal 813 adj.
  worshipful 866 adj.
  proud 871 adj.
  insolent 878 adj.
Lord Mayor *officer* 741 n.
  law officer 955 n.
Lord Mayor's Show
  pageant 875 n.
lord of creation
  mankind 371 n.
Lord of Misrule
  anarch 61 n.
  bungler 697 n.
lord of the manor
  master 741 n.
  owner 776 n.
lordosis *convexity* 253 n.
Lord's day *repose* 683 n.
  holy-day 988 n.
lordship
  magistrature 733 n.
  lands 777 n.
  aristocracy 868 n.
  title 870 n.
Lord's Supper

  Holy Communion 988 n.
Lord's Table
  ritual object 988 n.
  altar 990 n.
lore *tradition* 127 n.
  knowledge 490 n.
  erudition 490 n.
  learning 536 n.
  cunning 698 n.
Lorelei *rara avis* 84 n.
  vocalist 413 n.
  mythical being 970 n.
lorgnette *eyeglass* 442 n.
loricated *covered* 226 adj.
lorn *friendless* 883 adj.
lorry *carrier* 273 n.
  automobile 274 n.
lose *decrease* 37 vb.
  misdate 118 vb.
  be late 136 vb.
  misplace 188 vb.
  be defeated 728 vb.
  lose 772 vb.
lose a chance
  lose a chance 138 vb.
lose caste
  lose repute 867 vb.
lose colour *be dim* 419 vb.
lose consciousness
  be impotent 161 vb.
lose control *be lax* 734 vb.
lose face *lose repute* 867 vb.
lose ground
  decelerate 278 vb.
  regress 286 vb.
  fall short 307 vb.
  be defeated 728 vb.
lose height *descend* 309 vb.
lose no time
  be early 135 vb.
  hasten 680 vb.
lose numbers
  decrease 37 vb.
lose one's bearings
  stray 282 vb.
lose one's head
  go mad 503 vb.
  be unskilful 695 vb.
lose patience
  get angry 891 vb.
loser *bungler* 697 n.
  loser 728 n.
  unlucky person 731 n.
  laughing-stock 851 n.
lose sight of
  be blind 439 vb.
  forget 506 vb.
lose the scent
  be uncertain 474 vb.
lose the thread
  be unrelated 10 vb.

stray 282 vb.
be inattentive 456 vb.
be uncertain 474 vb.
lose the way *stray* 282 vb.
lose weight *decrease* 37 vb.
become small 198 vb.
losing *profitless* 641 adj.
unsuccessful 728 adj.
losing business
unproductivity 172 n.
losing game *defeat* 728 n.
losing side *loser* 728 n.
loss *decrement* 42 n.
deficit 55 n.
ruin 165 n.
absence 190 n.
outflow 298 n.
shortcoming 307 n.
waste 634 n.
impairment 655 n.
failure 728 n.
loss 772 n.
loss, at a *doubting* 474 adj.
losses *failure* 728 n.
loss-making
profitless 641 adj.
lost *past* 125 adj.
destroyed 165 adj.
misplaced 188 adj.
absent 190 adj.
deviating 282 adj.
disappearing 446 adj.
abstracted 456 adj.
doubting 474 adj.
unknown 491 adj.
concealed 525 adj.
lost 772 adj.
impenitent 940 adj.
condemned 961 adj.
lost cause *defeat* 728 n.
lost labour
lost labour 641 n.
lost leader
tergiversator 603 n.
lost sheep *bad man* 938 n.
lost soul *bad man* 938 n.
lot *state* 7 n.
finite quantity 26 n.
great quantity 32 n.
all 52 n.
bunch 74 n.
multitude 104 n.
chance 159 n.
territory 184 n.
inclosure 235 n.
oracle 511 n.
fate 596 n.
plenty 635 n.
participation 775 n.
portion 783 n.
loth *dissenting* 489 adj.

unwilling 598 adj.
disliking 861 adj.
Lothario *lover* 887 n.
libertine 952 n.
lotion *water* 339 n.
moistening 341 n.
cleanser 648 n.
balm 658 n.
cosmetic 833 n.
lottery *chance* 159 n.
gambling 618 n.
lotus-eater *idler* 679 n.
loud *strident* 407 adj.
crying 408 adj.
florid 425 adj.
manifest 522 adj.
ornate 574 adj.
rhetorical 574 adj.
(*see* loudness)
loud-hailer
megaphone 400 n.
telecommunication 531 n.
loud-mouthed *loud* 400 adj.
loudness *loudness* 400 n.
bang 402 n.
resonance 404 n.
publication 528 n.
ill-breeding 847 n.
loud pedal
megaphone 400 n.
piano 414 n.
loud-speaker
megaphone 400 n.
hearing aid 415 n.
telecommunication 531 n.
lough *lake* 346 n.
lounge *chamber* 194 n.
be inactive 679 vb.
lounger *idler* 679 n.
lounge suit *dress* 228 n.
lour *impend* 155 vb.
be dark 418 vb.
be dim 419 vb.
predict 511 vb.
(*see* lower)
louse *vermin* 365 n.
cad 938 n.
lousy *not nice* 645 adj.
unclean 649 adj.
lousy with *full* 54 adj.
lout *dunce* 501 n.
bungler 697 n.
countryman 869 n.
rude person 885 n.
ruffian 904 n.
loutish *ill-bred* 847 adj.
plebeian 869 adj.
discourteous 885 adj.
lovable
pleasurable 826 adj.
personable 841 adj.

amiable 884 adj.
lovable 887 adj.
love *zero* 103 n.
concord 710 n.
liking 859 n.
desire 859 vb.
love 887 n., vb.
lover, loved one 887 n.
pet, caress 889 vb.
darling 890 n.
jealousy 911 n.
disinterestedness 931 n.
divineness 965 n.
love affair *love affair* 887 n.
love all *draw* 28 n.
love-birds *lovers* 887 n.
love-child *bastardy* 954 n.
love-feast
social gathering 882 n.
public worship 981 n.
love, for *uncharged* 812 adj.
love, in *enamoured* 887 adj.
love-knot *badge* 547 n.
trophy 729 n.
loveless *indifferent* 860 adj.
unwanted 860 adj.
disliking 861 adj.
disliked 861 adj.
hated 888 adj.
hating 888 adj.
love-letter
correspondence 588 n.
love-token 889 n.
wooing 889 n.
lovelock *hair* 259 n.
lovely *pleasant* 376 adj.
topping 644 adj.
pleasurable 826 adj.
a beauty 841 n.
beautiful 841 adj.
lovable 887 adj.
love-making
wooing 889 n.
love-making 887 n.
love-match
type of marriage 894 n.
love-nest *love-nest* 887 n.
love-philtre
stimulant 174 n.
love-play *wooing* 889 n.
lover *desirer* 859 n.
lover 887 n.
loverlike *loving* 887 adj.
loveseat *seat* 218 n.
love-sickness *love* 887 n.
lovesome
personable 841 adj.
lovable 887 adj.
love-song
vocal music 412 n.
poem 593 n.

wooing 889 n.
love-story *novel* 590 n.
love to *be wont* 610 vb.
love-token
  indication 547 n.
  love-token 889 n.
loving *careful* 457 adj.
  (*see* love)
loving care
  carefulness 457 n.
loving cup *cup* 194 n.
  sociability 882 n.
loving it *pleased* 824 adj.
loving-kindness
  benevolence 897 n.
lovingly *carefully* 457 adv.
  affectionately 887 vb.
loving words
  endearment 889 n.
low *small* 33 adj.
  inferior 35 adj.
  weak 163 adj.
  low 210 adj.
  muted 401 adj.
  ululate 409 vb.
  not nice 645 adj.
  cheap 812 adj.
  dejected 834 adj.
  vulgar 847 adj.
  disreputable 867 adj.
  plebeian 869 adj.
  humble 872 adj.
  rascally 930 adj.
low-born *plebeian* 869 adj.
low-brow
  uninstructed 491 adj.
  ignoramus 493 n.
  unintelligent 499 adj.
low-caste *plebeian* 869 adj.
Low Church
  sectarian 978 adj.
low-class *plebeian* 869 adj.
low company
  lower classes 869 n.
Low Countries *plain* 348 n.
low-down
  information 524 n.
  plebeian 869 adj.
  rascally 930 adj.
lower *inferior* 35 adj.
  bate 37 vb.
  be low 210 vb.
  hang 217 vb.
  depress 311 vb.
  be dim 419 vb.
  predict 511 vb.
  impair 655 vb.
  pervert 655 vb.
  warn 664 vb.
  cheapen 812 vb.
  vulgarize 847 vb.

humiliate 872 vb.
  threaten 900 vb.
  not respect 921 vb.
  hold cheap 922 vb.
  defame 926 vb.
lower case
  print-type 587 n.
lower classes *inferior* 35 n.
  lower classes 869 n.
lower deck *layer* 207 n.
  lower classes 869 n.
Lower House
  parliament 692 n.
lowering *impending* 155 adj.
  cheerless 834 adj.
lowermost
  undermost 214 adj.
lower oneself
  demean oneself 867 vb.
lower orders
  social group 371 n.
  nonentity 639 n.
  lower classes 869 n.
lower world *hell* 972 n.
low-geared *slow* 278 adj.
lowlander *dweller* 191 n.
lowlands *district* 184 n.
  lowness 210 n.
  land 344 n.
  plain 348 n.
low-level *inferior* 35 adj.
  unimportant 639 adj.
low life *lower classes* 869 n.
lowliness *humility* 872 n.
low-lying *low* 210 adj.
low-necked
  uncovered 229 adj.
lowness *lowness* 210 n.
  depth 211 n.
  base 214 n.
  (*see* low)
low opinion
  disapprobation 924 n.
low pressure *rarity* 325 n.
  weather 340 n.
low-spirited
  dejected 834 adj.
low water *lowness* 210 n.
  water 339 n.
  scarcity 636 n.
  poverty 801 n.
loy *shovel* 274 n.
loyal *conformable* 83 adj.
  patriotic 901 adj.
  trustworthy 929 adj.
  (*see* loyalty)
loyalist *conformist* 83 n.
  auxiliary 707 n.
  defender 713 n.
loyalty *willingness* 597 n.
  submission 721 n.

loyalty 739 n.
  service 745 n.
  observance 768 n.
  friendship 880 n.
  love 887 n.
  duty 917 n.
  probity 929 n.
  disinterestedness 931 n.
  piety 979 n.
lozenge
  angular figure 247 n.
  heraldry 547 n.
  medicine 658 n.
lubber *ignoramus* 493 n.
  ninny 501 n.
  idler 679 n.
  bungler 697 n.
lubberly *unwieldy* 195 adj.
  clumsy 695 adj.
  ill-bred 847 adj.
lubricant *smoother* 258 n.
  lubricant 334 n.
lubricate *smooth* 258 vb.
  soften 327 vb.
  lubricate 334 vb.
lubrication
  lubrication 334 n.
  unctuousness 357 n.
lubricity
  changeableness 152 n.
  smoothness 258 n.
  lubrication 334 n.
  unctuousness 357 n.
  unchastity 951 n.
lucid *undimmed* 417 adj.
  luminous 417 adj.
  transparent 422 adj.
  sane 502 adj.
  intelligible 516 adj.
  perspicuous 567 adj.
lucifer *lighter* 385 n.
Lucifer *luminary* 420 n.
  Satan 969 n.
lucimeter
  optical device 442 n.
luck *opportunity* 137 n.
  chance 159 n.
  good 615 n.
  non-design 618 n.
  prosperity 730 n.
luck-bringer
  talisman 983 n.
luckless *unfortunate* 731 adj.
lucky *opportune* 137 adj.
  successful 727 adj.
  prosperous 730 adj.
  happy 824 adj.
lucky dip
  non-uniformity 17 n.
  confusion 61 n.
  chance 159 n.

lucky dog
made man 730 n.
lucrative *gainful* 771 adj.
lucre *acquisition* 771 n.
money 797 n.
wealth 800 n.
lucubration *thought* 449 n.
Lucullus
gastronomy 301 n.
eater 301 n.
sensualist 944 n.
glutton 947 n.
Luddite *rioter* 738 n.
ludicrous *absurd* 497 adj.
foolish 499 adj.
ridiculous 849 adj.
ludo *board game* 837 n.
luff *navigate* 269 vb.
lug *handle* 218 n.
sail 275 n.
draw 288 vb.
ear 415 n.
tool 630 n.
luge *sled* 274 n.
descend 309 vb.
luggage *box* 194 n.
thing transferred 272 n.
property 777 n.
luggage-van *box* 194 n.
train 274 n.
lugger *sailing-ship* 275 n.
lug-sail *sail* 275 n.
traction 288 n.
lugubrious
cheerless 834 adj.
lukewarm *median* 30 adj.
warm 379 adj.
irresolute 601 adj.
neutral 625 adj.
apathetic 820 adj.
indifferent 860 adj.
lull *discontinuity* 72 n.
delay 136 n.
lull 145 n.
assuage 177 vb.
interval 201 n.
quiescence 266 n.
bring to rest 266 vb.
silence 399 n., vb.
befool 542 vb.
inactivity 679 vb.
make inactive 679 vb.
repose 683 n.
peace 717 n.
tranquillize 823 vb.
please 826 vb.
relieve 831 vb.
flatter 925 vb.
lullaby *vocal music* 412 n.
soporific 679 n.
relief 831 n.

lulu *a beauty* 841 n.
lumbago *pang* 377 n.
lumbar *back* 238 adj.
lumber *leavings* 41 n.
confusion 61 n.
move slowly 278 vb.
fell 311 vb.
wood 366 n.
rubbish 641 n.
be clumsy 695 vb.
encumbrance 702 n.
lumberjack *forestry* 366 n.
worker 686 n.
lumber-room
chamber 194 n.
collection 632 n.
luminarist *artist* 556 n.
luminary *luminary* 420 n.
sage 500 n.
luminescence *glow* 417 n.
luminescent
luminescent 420 adj.
luminosity *light* 417 n.
luminous
luminescent 420 adj.
white 427 adj.
intelligible 516 adj.
lump *great quantity* 32 n.
main part 52 n.
piece 53 n.
bulk 195 n.
gravity 322 n.
solid body 324 n.
bungler 697 n.
lumpish *inert* 175 adj.
unwieldy 195 adj.
inactive 679 adj.
lump sum *funds* 797 n.
lump together
combine 50 vb.
bring together 74 vb.
not discriminate 464 vb.
lumpy *rough* 259 adj.
dense 324 adj.
semiliquid 354 adj.
lunacy *insanity* 503 n.
lunar *celestial* 321 adj.
lunar mansion
zodiac 321 n.
lunate *curved* 248 adj.
celestial 321 adj.
lunatic *insane* 503 adj.
madman 504 n.
lunatic asylum
madhouse 503 n.
lunation *period* 110 n.
lunch *meal* 301 n.
eat 301 vb.
lunch-counter *café* 192 n.
lunette *fort* 713 n.
lung *space* 183 n.

plain 348 n.
(see lungs)
lunge *strike* 279 vb.
foin 712 n.
strike at 712 vb.
lungi *dress* 228 n.
lungs *respiration* 352 n.
voice 577 n.
lunik *satellite* 321 n.
space-ship 276 n.
lunule *curve* 248 n.
lupine *animal* 365 adj.
lurch *obliquity* 220 n.
walk 267 vb.
move slowly 278 vb.
tumble 309 vb.
fluctuation 317 n.
be agitated 318 vb.
be drunk 949 vb.
lurcher *dog* 365 n.
lure *attraction* 291 n.
ensnare 542 vb.
tempt 612 vb.
desired object 859 n.
lurid *florid* 425 adj.
colourless 426 adj.
dark 418 adj.
impure 951 adj.
lurk *be unseen* 444 vb.
escape notice 456 vb.
lurk 523 vb.
avoid 620 vb.
elude 667 vb.
be cautious 858 vb.
lurker *hider* 527 n.
slyboots 698 n.
lurking *latent* 523 adj.
stealthy 525 adj.
luscious *savoury* 390 adj.
sweet 392 adj.
pleasurable 826 adj.
ornamental 844 adj.
lush *prolific* 171 adj.
vigorous 174 adj.
vegetal 366 adj.
plenteous 635 adj.
lushy *tipsy* 949 adj.
lusory *amusing* 837 adj.
lust *libido* 859 n.
desire 859 vb.
love 887 n.
vice 934 n.
unchastity 951 n.
lustful *desiring* 859 adj.
loving 887 adj.
lecherous 951 adj.
lustily *vigorously* 174 adv.
loudly 400 adv.
laboriously 682 adv.
lustiness *vigorousness* 174 n.
lustless *weakly* 163 adj.

lustral *cleansing* 648adj.
  atoning 941adj.
lustration *cleansing* 648n.
  penance 941n.
  ritual act 988n.
lustre *light* 417n.
  lamp 420n.
  prestige 866n.
lustreless
  colourless 426adj.
lustre ware *pottery* 381n.
lustrous *luminous* 417adj.
  noteworthy 866adj.
lustrum, lustre
  period 110n.
lusty *strong* 162adj.
  vigorous 174adj.
  large, fleshy 195adj.
  loud 400adj.
lusus naturæ
  nonconformist 84n.
lutanist
  instrumentalist 413n.
lute *adhesive* 47n.
  harp 414n.
lutein *yellow pigment* 433n.
Lutheranism
  Protestantism 976n.
  sectarianism 978n.
luxation *separation* 46n.
luxuriance
  productiveness 171n.
  vegetability 366n.
  plenty 635n.
  redundance 637n.
luxuriant *dense* 324n.
luxuriate *enjoy* 376vb.
  be pleased 824vb.
  be intemperate 943vb.
luxurious
  ostentatious 875adj.
  (*see* luxury)
luxury *extra* 40n.
  euphoria 376n.
  plenty 635n.
  superfluity 637n.
  prosperity 730n.
  wealth 800n.
  intemperance 943n.
  sensualism 944n.
luxury-loving
  sensual 944adj.
luxury price *dearness* 811n.
lycanthrope *demon* 970n.
lycanthropy
  psychotherapy 503n.
lycée *academy* 539n.
lych-gate *funeral* 364n.
  church exterior 990n.
lyddite *explosive* 723n.
Lydian *harmonic* 410adj.

lye *solution* 337n.
  cleanser 648n.
lying *erroneous* 495adj.
  falsehood 541n.
  untrue 543adj.
lying-in *obstetrics* 164n.
lymph *blood* 335n.
  fluid 335n.
  transparency 422n.
lymphad *galley* 275n.
lymphatic
  sanguineous 335adj.
  watery 339adj.
lynch *disapprove* 924vb.
  execute 963vb.
lynching
  capital punishment 963n.
lynch law *anarchy* 734n.
  lawlessness 954n.
lynx *cat* 365n.
  eye 438n.
lynx-eyed *seeing* 438adj.
  vigilant 457adj.
lyre *harp* 414n.
lyric *vocal music* 412n.
  musicianly 413adj.
  poetic 593adj.
lyrical *poetic* 593adj.
  excited 821adj.
  excitable 822adj.
  rejoicing 835adj.
  approving 923adj.
lyricism *vocal music* 412n.
  excitable state 822n.
lyric-writer *dramatist* 594n.
lyrist *musician* 413n.
  instrumentalist 413n.
  poet 593n.

M

ma'am *lady* 373n.
  title 870n.
macabre *frightening* 854adj.
  spooky 970adj.
macadam *road* 624n.
  building material 631n.
macadamize *smooth* 258vb.
macaroni *dish* 301n.
  fop 848n.
macaronic *absurd* 497adj.
  poetic 593adj.
macaronics *slang* 560n.
  doggerel 593n.
macaw *bird* 365n.
mace *hammer* 279n.
  potherb 301n.
  condiment 389n.
  club 723n.
  badge of rule 743n.
mace-bearer *officer* 741n.

law *officer* 955n.
macerate *soften* 327vb.
  drench 341vb.
maceration *penance* 941n.
  asceticism 945n.
machete *sharp edge* 256n.
  side-arms 723n.
Machiavellian
  hypocritical 541adj.
  planning 623adj.
  slyboots 698n.
  cunning 698adj.
  perfidious 930adj.
Machiavellianism
  duplicity 541n.
machicolation
  notch 260n.
  fortification 713n.
machination
  deception 542n.
  plot 623n.
  stratagem 698n.
machine
  produce 164vb.
  print 587vb.
  fatalist 596n.
  instrument 628n.
  machine 630n.
  slave 742n.
machine-gun *gun* 723n.
machine-like
  involuntary 596adj.
machine-made
  produced 164adj.
machine-minded
  mechanical 630adj.
machinery *complexity* 61n.
  machine 630n.
machinist *stage-hand* 594n.
  machinist 630n.
  artisan 686n.
macilent *lean* 206adj.
mackerel *fish food* 301n.
  table fish 365n.
  bawd 952n.
mackerel sky
  striation 437n.
  cloud 355n.
mackintosh *overcoat* 228n.
macrobiotic *lasting* 113adj.
macrocosm
  generality 79n.
  universe 321n.
macrology *pleonasm* 570n.
macromolecule *life* 360n.
macron *punctuation* 547n.
macroscopic *large* 195adj.
  visible 443adj.
maculate *variegate* 437vb.
  make unclean 649vb.
  blemished 845adj.

maculation
  maculation 437 n.
  blemish 845 n.
macule *skin disease* 651 n.
maculous *mottled* 437 adj.
mad *insane* 503 adj.
  capricious 604 adj.
  excited 821 adj.
  angry 891 adj.
mad after *desiring* 859 adj.
madam *lady* 373 n.
  master 741 n.
  title 870 n.
  bawd 952 n.
madcap
  violent creature 176 n.
  madman 504 n.
  excitable 822 adj.
  desperado 857 n.
  rash 857 adj.
madden
  make violent 176 vb.
  make mad 503 vb.
  excite love 887 vb.
  enrage 891 vb.
maddening
  annoying 827 adj.
madder *red pigment* 431 n.
madefaction
  moistening 341 n.
madeira *wine* 301 n.
made man
  made man 730 n.
made of *composing* 56 adj.
made to measure
  adjusted 24 adj.
made-up *culinary* 301 adj.
  beautified 843 adj.
madhouse *confusion* 61 n.
  madhouse 503 n.
madly *extremely* 32 adv.
madman *fool* 501 n.
  madman 504 n.
madness *insanity* 503 n.
  excitable state 822 n.
  love 887 n.
Madonna *Madonna* 968 n.
madrigal *vocal music* 412 n.
Mæcenas *intellectual* 492 n.
  patron 707 n.
maelstrom *vortex* 315 n.
  pitfall 663 n.
  activity 678 n.
mænad *madman* 504 n.
  drunkard 949 n.
maestoso *adagio* 412 adv.
maestro *orchestra* 413 n.
Mae West *wrapping* 226 n.
  safeguard 662 n.
maffia *disobedience* 738 n.
  revolter 738 n.

maffick *rampage* 61 vb.
  rejoice 835 vb.
  celebrate 876 vb.
magazine
  accumulation 74 n.
  journal 528 n.
  book 589 n.
  reading matter 589 n.
  storage 632 n.
  arsenal 723 n.
  fire-arm 723 n.
magdalen *penitent* 939 n.
mage, magian, Magi
  sorcerer 983 n.
magenta *red colour* 431 n.
maggot *animalcule* 196 n.
  vermin 365 n.
  ideality 513 n.
  whim 604 n.
maggoty *capricious* 604 adj.
  unclean 649 adj.
magic *influence* 178 n.
  sleight 542 n.
  instrumentality 628 n.
  thaumaturgy 864 n.
  wonderful 864 adj.
  prestige 866 n.
  fairylike 970 adj.
  sorcery 983 n.
  occultism 984 n.
magical *magical* 983 adj.
magic carpet *airship* 276 n.
  speeder 277 n.
magic formula *spell* 983 n.
magician *conjuror* 545 n.
  proficient 696 n.
  sorcerer 983 n.
magic lantern
  lamp 420 n.
  optical device 442 n.
  plaything 837 n.
magic world *fairy* 970 n.
Maginot Line
  defences 713 n.
magisterial *skilful* 694 adj.
  authoritative 733 adj.
  ruling 733 adj.
  insolent 878 adj.
magistery *powder* 332 n.
magistracy
  magistrature 733 n.
  jurisdiction 955 n.
  magistracy 957 n.
magistrate *official* 690 n.
  officer 741 n.
  judge 957 n.
magistrature
  (*see* magistracy)
magnanimous
  disinterested 931 adj.
  virtuous 933 adj.

magnate *aristocrat* 868 n.
magnet *focus* 76 n.
  traction 288 n.
  attraction 291 n.
  incentive 612 n.
  desired object 859 n.
magnetic *dynamic* 160 adj.
magnetic needle
  indicator 547 n.
  directorship 689 n.
magnetic north
  compass point 281 n.
magnetism *energy* 160 n.
  influence 178 n.
  traction 288 n.
  attraction 291 n.
  inducement 612 n.
magnetize *attract* 291 vb.
Magnificat *hymn* 981 n.
magnification
  increase 36 n.
  vision 438 n.
  exaggeration 546 n.
  (*see* magnify)
magnificence *beauty* 841 n.
  ornamentation 844 n.
  ostentation 875 n.
magnificent
  excellent 644 adj.
  splendid 841 adj.
  ostentatious 875 adj.
magnifico *aristocrat* 868 n.
magnify *augment* 36 vb.
  enlarge 197 vb.
  overrate 482 vb.
  exaggerate 546 vb.
  make important 638 vb.
  boast 877 vb.
  respect 920 vb.
  praise 923 vb.
  worship 981 vb.
magnifying glass
  eyeglass 442 n.
magniloquence
  exaggeration 546 n.
  vigour 571 n.
  magniloquence 574 n.
  eloquence 579 n.
  affectation 850 n.
  ostentation 875 n.
magnitude *quantity* 26 n.
  degree 27 n.
  greatness 32 n.
  size 195 n.
  importance 638 n.
magnum *vessel* 194 n.
  size 195 n.
magnum opus *book* 589 n.
magpie *bird* 365 n.
  chatterer 581 n.
  niggard 816 n.

magsman *trickster* 545 n.
 defrauder 789 n.
maharajah *potentate* 741 n.
mahatma *sage* 500 n.
 good man 937 n.
Mahayana
 religious faith 973 n.
mahdi *leader* 690 n.
mah jong
 indoor game 837 n.
mahogany
 smoothness 258 n.
 tree 366 n.
 brownness 430 n.
mahout *rider, driver* 268 n.
maid *domestic* 742 n.
 (*see* maiden)
maiden *first* 68 adj.
 new 126 adj.
 youngster 132 n.
 woman 373 n.
 spinster 895 n.
 virgin 950 n.
 instrument of torture
  964 n.
maidenhood
 celibacy 895 n.
 purity 950 n.
maidenly *young* 130 adj.
 female 373 adj.
 unwedded 895 adj.
 pure 950 adj.
maiden name *name* 561 n.
maiden over
 unproductiveness 172 n.
maiden speech *début* 68 n.
maid-of-all-work
 busy person 678 n.
 worker 686 n.
 domestic 742 n.
maieutic *enquiring* 459 adj.
 rational 475 adj.
 instrumental 628 adj.
mail *send* 272 vb.
 mails 531 n.
 correspondence 588 n.
 safeguard 662 n.
 armour 713 n.
 weapon 723 n.
mailbag *mails* 531 n.
mail-clad *defended* 713 adj.
mail-coach
 stage-coach 274 n.
 mails 531 n.
mailed fist
 compulsion 740 n.
 lawlessness 954 n.
maim *disable* 161 vb.
 impair 655 vb.
maimed *incomplete* 55 adj.
 imperfect 647 adj.

main *great* 32 adj.
 supreme 34 adj.
 tube 263 n.
 conduit 351 n.
main chance
 fair chance 159 n.
 benefit 615 n.
 chief thing 638 n.
 gain 771 n.
main force *strength* 162 n.
 compulsion 740 n.
main, in the
 substantially 3 adv.
 intrinsically 5 adv.
 materially 638 adv.
mainland *land* 344 n.
mainlander *dweller* 191 n.
 land 344 n.
mainly *generally* 79 adv.
main part *main part* 32 n.
 chief part 52 n.
mainpernor *security* 767 n.
mainprize *security* 767 n.
mainsail *sail* 275 n.
mainspring *cause* 156 n.
 motive 612 n.
 machine 630 n.
mainstay *supporter* 218 n.
 chief thing 638 n.
 refuge 662 n.
 hope 852 n.
main stream
 tendency 179 n.
maintain *stay* 144 vb.
 sustain 146 vb.
 operate 173 vb.
 support 218 vb.
 believe 485 vb.
 affirm 532 vb.
 persevere 600 vb.
 provide 633 vb.
 preserve 666 vb.
 celebrate 876 vb.
 vindicate 924 vb.
maintenance
 subvention 703 n.
 receipt 807 n.
  (*see* maintain)
maisonette *flat* 192 n.
maize *corn* 366 n.
 cereal 301 n.
majestic *impressive* 821 adj.
 beautiful 841 adj.
 proud 871 adj.
 formal 875 adj.
 godlike 965 adj.
  (*see* majesty)
majesty *greatness* 32 n.
 superiority 34 n.
 authority 733 n.
 sovereign 741 n.

 prestige 866 n.
 nobility 868 n.
Majlis *parliament* 692 n.
majolica *pottery* 381 n.
major *great* 32 adj.
 superior 34 adj.
 older 131 adj.
 grown up 134 adj.
 harmonic 410 adj.
 important 638 adj.
 army officer 741 n.
major domo *retainer* 742 n.
major in *learn* 536 vb.
majority *main part* 32 n.
 chief part 52 n.
 greater number 104 n.
 adultness 134 n.
majorize *augment* 36 vb.
major premise
 argumentation 475 n.
major suit *skill* 694 n.
majuscule *letter* 558 n.
make *character* 5 n.
 composition 56 n.
 compose 56 vb.
 constitute 56 vb.
 sort 77 n.
 convert 147 vb.
 cause 156 vb.
 produce 164 vb.
 influence 178 vb.
 efform 243 vb.
 arrive 295 vb.
 structure 331 n.
 flow 350 vb.
 estimate 480 vb.
 make better 654 vb.
 compel 740 vb.
 gain 771 vb.
make acquainted
 befriend 880 vb.
make a face *dislike* 861 vb.
 disapprove 924 vb.
make a leg
 show respect 920 vb.
make a man of
 give courage 855 vb.
make amends
 compensate 31 vb.
 atone 941 vb.
 reward 962 vb.
make as if *imitate* 20 vb.
make available *offer* 759 vb.
make away with
 destroy 165 vb.
 kill 362 vb.
make a whole
 be complete 54 adj.
make a will *bequeath* 780 vb.
make-believe
 imitate 20 vb.

fantasy 513 n.
imaginary 513 adj.
hypocritical 541 adj.
sham 542 n.
spurious 542 adj.
untrue 543 adj.
be untrue 543 vb.
make bold
be insolent 878 vb.
be free 744 vb.
make both ends meet
afford 800 vb.
economize 814 vb.
make certain
make certain 473 vb.
make contact
connect 45 vb.
touch 378 vb.
make difficulties
be difficult 700 vb.
make do with
substitute 150 vb.
avail of 673 vb.
make eyes *court* 889 vb.
make for
congregate 74 vb.
steer for 281 vb.
promote 285 vb.
make free with
be free 744 vb.
appropriate 786 vb.
be insolent 878 vb.
make friends *accord* 24 vb.
make peace 719 vb.
make good
compensate 31 vb.
make complete 54 vb.
corroborate 466 vb.
replenish 633 vb.
succeed 727 vb.
vindicate 927 vb.
make hay *prosper* 730 vb.
make head *progress* 285 vb.
make head against
withstand 704 vb.
triumph 727 vb.
make interest for
patronize 703 vb.
request 761 vb.
make into *convert* 147 vb.
make it up
make peace 719 vb.
forgive 909 vb.
make it up to
restitute 787 vb.
atone 941 vb.
make light of
underestimate 483 vb.
do easily 701 vb.
be indifferent 860 vb.
make love *love* 887 vb.

caress 889 vb.
make merry *rejoice* 835 vb.
revel 837 vb.
ridicule 851 vb.
make money *flourish* 615 vb.
prosper 730 vb.
gain 771 vb.
get rich 800 vb.
make much of
love 887 vb.
pet 889 vb.
make no bones
be willing 597 vb.
make nothing of
not understand 517 vb.
do easily 701 vb.
make off *run away* 620 vb.
make off with *steal* 788 vb.
make one of
augment 36 vb.
be included 78 vb.
be present 189 vb.
join a party 708 vb.
make one's bed
choose 605 vb.
make oneself scarce
go away 190 vb.
run away 620 vb.
elude 667 vb.
make one's mark
succeed 727 vb.
make one's point
affirm 532 vb.
make one's way
travel 267 vb.
get better 654 vb.
prosper 730 vb.
make or mar
cause 156 vb.
influence 178 vb.
make out *see* 438 vb.
corroborate 466 vb.
demonstrate 478 vb.
understand 516 vb.
decipher 520 vb.
plead 614 vb.
succeed 727 vb.
make-peace *mediator* 720 n.
maker *cause* 156 n.
producer 167 n.
make sense
be intelligible 516 vb.
interpret 520 vb.
makeshift *inferior* 35 adj.
transientness 114 n.
substitute 150 n.
spontaneous 609 adj.
pretext 614 n.
instrument 628 n.
means 629 n.
sufficient 635 adj.

imperfection 647 n.
unprepared 670 adj.
make shift with
avail of 673 vb.
make short work of
destroy 165 vb.
eat 301 vb.
do easily 701 vb.
succeed 727 vb.
make something of
transform 147 vb.
make sure
stabilize 153 vb.
make certain 473 vb.
be cautious 858 vb.
make terms *accord* 24 vb.
make terms 766 vb.
make the best of
(*see* make the most of)
make the grade
succeed 727 vb.
make the most of
overrate 482 vb.
avail of 673 vb.
be ostentatious 875 vb.
make the running
outstrip 277 vb.
outdo 306 vb.
make to measure
adjust 24 vb.
make tracks
decamp 296 vb.
make trouble
make quarrels 709 vb.
cause discontent 829 vb.
make up *compensate* 31 vb.
make complete 54 vb.
constitute 56 vb.
imagine 513 vb.
print 587 n.
replenish 633 vb.
primp 843 vb.
make-up *dissimilarity* 19 n.
composition 56 n.
speciality 80 n.
print 587 n.
stage-set 594 n.
affections 817 n.
beautification 843 n.
cosmetic 843 n.
make up one's mind
be resolute 599 vb.
choose 605 vb.
make up to
approach 289 vb.
flatter 925 vb.
make water *excrete* 302 vb.
make way *navigate* 269 vb.
progress 285 vb.
recede 290 vb.
avoid 620 vb.

facilitate 701 vb.
show respect 920 vb.
makeweight *offset* 31 n.
plenitude 54 n.
gravity 322 n.
make work *be busy* 678 vb.
work 682 vb.
make worse
aggravate 832 vb.
malachite *greenness* 432 n.
malacology
zoology 367 n.
maladjusted
inexact 495 adj.
clumsy 695 adj.
maladjustment *misfit* 25 n.
discontent 829 n.
maladministration
misuse 675 n.
bungling 695 n.
malady *disease* 651 n.
bane 659 n.
mala fides *perfidy* 930 n.
malaise *pain* 377 n.
evil 616 n.
suffering 825 n.
malapertness
sauciness 878 n.
malapropism
mistake 495 n.
inexactness 495 n.
absurdity 497 n.
neology 560 n.
misnomer 562 n.
solecism 565 n.
ridiculousness 849 n.
malaria *malaria* 651 n.
malarial *infectious* 653 adj.
malcontent
dissentient 489 n.
opponent 705 n.
malcontent 829 n.
disapprover 924 n.
mal du pays
melancholy 834 n.
male *vitality* 162 n.
athletic 162 adj.
male 372 n., adj.
malediction
discontent 829 n.
hatred 888 n.
malediction 899 n.
detraction 926 n.
condemnation 961 n.
impiety 980 n.
prayers 981 n.
maledictory
threatening 900 adj.
malefactor *offender* 904 n.
maleficent
harmful 645 adj.

maleficent 898 adj.
malevolence
badness 645 n.
quarrelsomeness 709 n.
enmity 881 n.
hatred 888 n.
malevolence 898 n.
wickedness 934 n.
malfeasance
lawbreaking 954 n.
malformation
deformity 246 n.
malice *joy* 824 n.
hatred 888 n.
resentment 891 n.
malevolence 898 n.
malice aforethought, with
purposely 617 adj.
malicious *harmful* 645 adj.
hating 888 adj.
malevolent 898 adj.
malign *harmful* 645 adj.
adverse 731 adj.
shame 867 vb.
malevolent 898 adj.
defame 926 vb.
malignant
harmful 645 adj.
hating 888 adj.
malevolent 898 adj.
sorcerous 983 adj.
malignant tumour
carcinosis 651 n.
malignity *violence* 176 n.
badness 645 n.
annoyance 827 n.
(*see* malevolence)
malinger *dissemble* 541 vb.
fail in duty 918 vb.
malingerer *impostor* 545 n.
dutilessness 918 n.
malison *malediction* 899 n.
mall *street* 192 n.
pleasance 192 n.
hammer 279 n.
mallard *waterfowl* 365 n.
malleability
conformity 83 n.
malleable
conformable 83 adj.
unstable 152 adj.
flexible 327 adj.
impressible 819 adj.
mallet *hammer* 279 n.
malleus *ear* 415 n.
malnutrition *disease* 651 n.
malodorous *fetid* 397 adj.
unclean 649 adj.
unpleasant 827 adj.
dishonest 930 adj.
malodour *odium* 888 n.

malpractice
guilty act 936 n.
lawbreaking 954 n.
malthusianism
deterioration 655 n.
maltose *food content* 301 n.
maltreat *ill-treat* 645 vb.
misuse 675 vb.
torment 827 vb.
be malevolent 898 vb.
malversation
misuse 675 n.
peculation 788 n.
prodigality 815 n.
foul play 930 n.
guilty act 936 n.
mamba *reptile* 365 n.
mamelon *dome* 253 n.
(*see* monticle)
mameluke *militarist* 722 n.
mamilla *bosom* 253 n.
mamma *maternity* 169 n.
bosom 253 n.
mammal *animal* 365 n.
mamma's boy
weakling 163 n.
mammer *stammer* 580 vb.
mammiferous
female 373 adj.
mammiform
arcuate 253 adj.
Mammon *money* 797 n.
wealth 800 n.
devil 969 n.
mammoth *giant* 195 n.
animal 365 n.
mammy *negro* 428 n.
protector 660 n.
keeper 749 n.
man *adult* 134 n.
mankind 371 n.
male 372 n.
provide 633 vb.
worker 686 n.
defend 713 vb.
domestic 742 n.
dependant 742 n.
subject 742 n.
chessman 837 n.
brave person 855 n.
spouse 894 n.
mana *power* 160 n.
influence 178 n.
divineness 965 n.
manacle *tie* 45 vb.
fetter 748 n.
manage *arrange* 62 vb.
be able 160 vb.
look after 457 vb.
motivate 612 vb.
undertake 672 vb.

do 676 vb.
deal with 688 vb.
manage 689 vb.
be successful 727 vb.
rule 733 vb.
deputize 755 vb.
manageable *wieldy* 701 adj.
management
  management 689 n.
  director 690 n.
manager
  stage-manager 594 n.
  motivator 612 n.
  doer 676 n.
  agent 686 n.
  protector 690 n.
  director 690 n.
  manager 690 n.
  consignee 754 n.
managerial
  directing 689 adj.
man and wife
  spouse 894 n.
man-at-arms *soldier* 722 n.
man at the wheel
  navigator 270 n.
mandamus *warrant* 737 n.
mandarin *fruit* 301 n.
  language 557 n.
  official 690 n.
  officer 741 n.
mandate *job* 622 n.
  requirement 627 n.
  precept 693 n.
  polity 733 n.
  command 737 n.
  mandate 751 n.
  permit 756 n.
  conditions 766 n.
mandatory
  preceptive 693 adj.
  authoritative 733 adj.
  commanding 737 adj.
mandibles *eater* 301 n.
mandoline *harp* 414 n.
mandragora *soporific* 679 n.
mandrake *medicine* 658 n.
mandrel *rotator* 315 n.
mandrill *monkey* 365 n.
manducate *chew* 301 vb.
mane *hair* 259 n.
man-eater *killer* 362 n.
  animal 365 n.
  noxious animal 904 n.
manège *equitation* 267 n.
  animal husbandry 369 n.
manes *corpse* 363 n.
  ghost 970 n.
manful *athletic* 162 adj.
  courageous 855 adj.
manfully *resolutely* 599 adv.

mange *skin disease* 651 n.
  animal disease 651 n.
manger *bowl* 194 n.
mangle *compressor* 198 n.
  flattener 216 n.
  smoother 258 n.
  dry 342 vb.
  wound 655 vb.
mangled
  incomplete 55 adj.
  inexact 495 adj.
mango *fruit* 301 n.
mangonel *propellant* 287 n.
  missile weapon 723 n.
mangy *hairless* 229 adj.
  unhealthy 651 adj.
man-handle *move* 265 vb.
  touch 378 vb.
man-hater
  misanthrope 902 n.
manhole *orifice* 263 n.
manhood *adultness* 134 n.
  male 372 n.
  manliness 855 n.
man-hours *labour* 682 n.
mania *bias* 481 n.
  mania 503 n.
  psychopathy 503 n.
  warm feeling 818 n.
  excitable state 822 n.
  liking 859 n.
maniac *madman* 504 n.
manic *insane* 503 adj.
manic-depressive
  madman 504 n.
  insane 503 adj.
Manichæism *heresy* 977 n.
Manichee *heretic* 977 n.
manicure *surgery* 658 n.
  beautification 843 n.
manicured *elegant* 575 adj.
manicurist *doctor* 658 n.
  beautician 843 n.
manifest *list* 87 n.
  open 263 adj.
  appearing 445 adj.
  evidence 466 vb.
  manifest 522 adj., vb.
  well-known 528 adj.
  accounts 808 n.
manifestation
  visibility 443 n.
  manifestation 522 n.
  disclosure 526 n.
  indication 547 n.
  representation 551 n.
manifesto *publication* 528 n.
manifold
  multiform 82 adj.
manikin *dwarf* 196 n.
  image 551 n.

man in the moon
  moon 321 n.
  fantasy 513 n.
man in the street
  common man 30 n.
  everyman 79 n.
  social group 371 n.
  mediocrity 732 n.
  commoner 869 n.
maniple *formation* 722 n.
  vestments 989 n.
manipulate *operate* 173 vb.
  touch 378 vb.
  fake 541 vb.
  motivate 612 vb.
  plot 623 vb.
  use 673 vb.
  misuse 675 vb.
  do 676 vb.
  deal with 688 vb.
  manage 689 vb.
manipulation
  foul play 930 n.
  (*see* manipulate)
manipulator
  influence 178 n.
  trickster 545 n.
  motivator 612 n.
  gambler 618 n.
mankind *mankind* 371 n.
manlike *male* 372 adj.
manliness (*see* manly)
manly *grown up* 134 adj.
  manly 162 adj.
  male 372 adj.
  beautiful 841 adj.
  courageous 855 adj.
  honourable 929 adj.
man milliner *fop* 848 n.
manna *food* 301 n.
  subvention 703 n.
  gift 781 n.
  pleasurableness 826 n.
manned *occupied* 191 adj.
mannequin
  living model 23 n.
mannequin parade
  exhibit 522 n.
  fashion 848 n.
manner *sort* 77 n.
  style 566 n.
  way 624 n.
  conduct 688 n.
mannered
  stylistic 566 adj.
  inelegant 576 adj.
  ridiculous 849 adj.
  affected 850 adj.
mannerism *speciality* 80 n.
  unconformity 84 n.
  phrase 563 n.

style 566n.
inelegance 576n.
affectation 850n.
airs 873n.
Mannerism
school of painting 553n.
mannerless
discourteous 885adj.
mannerly courteous 884adj.
manners practice 610n.
conduct 688n.
good taste 846n.
etiquette 848n.
courtesy 884n.
manners and customs
practice 610n.
mannikin small animal 33n.
mannish male 372adj.
manœuvrability
scope 744n.
manœuvrable
wieldy 701adj.
manœuvre motion 265n.
deed 676n.
tactics 688n.
manage 689vb.
be cunning 698vb.
wage war 718vb.
manœuvrer influence 178n.
motivator 612n.
planner 623n.
slyboots 698n.
man of action doer 676n.
busy person 678n.
man of business
expert 696n.
consignee 754n.
man of honour
person of repute 866n.
gentleman 929n.
man of letters
linguist 557n.
bookman 589n.
man of, make a
do good 644vb.
man of mark
bigwig 638n.
person of repute 866n.
man of prayer
pietist 979n.
worshipper 981n.
man of property
made man 730n.
owner 776n.
man of straw
insubstantial thing 4n.
ineffectuality 161n.
sham 542n.
nonentity 639n.
non-payer 805n.
man of the people

vulgarian 847n.
commoner 869n.
man of the world
expert 696n.
beau monde 848n.
man on the spot
delegate 754n.
manor house 192n.
lands 777n.
manorial agrarian 370adj.
proprietary 777adj.
man-o'-war warship 722n.
man-o'-war's man
naval man 270n.
navy man 722n.
man-power band 74n.
power 160n.
means 629n.
personnel 686n.
manqué deviating 282adj.
unsuccessful 728adj.
mansard roof roof 226n.
manse parsonage 986n.
man-servant
domestic 742n.
man's estate
adultness 134n.
mansion place 185n.
house 192n.
zodiac 321n.
man-size great 32adj.
large 195adj.
manslaughter
homicide 362n.
mansuetude courtesy 884n.
manteau cloak 228n.
mantelpiece shelf 218n.
mantic predicting 511adj.
manticore rara avis 84n.
mantilla shawl 228n.
mantle wrapping 226n.
cloak 228n.
bubble 355vb.
darken 418vb.
lamp 420n.
screen 421n.
redden 431vb.
be modest 874vb.
mantlet cloak 228n.
armour 713n.
man, to a
unanimously 488adv.
mantology
divination 311n.
occultism 984n.
mantua cloak 228n.
manual series 71n.
handed 378adj.
musical note 410n.
piano, organ 414n.
guide-book 524n.

textbook 589n.
manufacture
production 164n.
produce 164vb.
business 622n.
action 676n.
manufacturer
producer 167n.
agent 686n.
manumission
liberation 746n.
manure fertilizer 171n.
invigorate 174vb.
agriculture 370n.
patronize 703vb.
manuscript prototype 23n.
script 586n.
book 589n.
many many 104adj.
frequent 139adj.
commonalty 869n.
many-coloured
multiform 82adj.
coloured 425n.
variegated 437adj.
many-headed
multiform 82adj.
many 104adj.
commonalty 869n.
many-sided
multiform 82adj.
plural 101adj.
lateral 239adj.
skilful 694adj.
mañana delay 136n.
map situation 186n.
outline 233vb.
face 237n.
itinerary 267n.
gauge 465vb.
guide-book 524n.
map 551n.
represent 551vb.
plan 623n.
maple tree 366n.
maquis wood 366n.
soldier 722n.
revolter 738n.
mar derange 63vb.
modify 143vb.
lay waste 165vb.
influence 178vb.
impair 655vb.
be clumsy 695vb.
hinder 702vb.
marabout
worshipper 981n.
monk 986n.
holy place 990n.
marasmus
contraction 198n.

disease 651 n.
dilapidation 655 n.
marathon *lasting* 113 adj.
distance 199 n.
racing 716 n.
maraud *rob* 788 vb.
marauder *militarist* 722 n.
robber 789 n.
marble *sphere* 252 n.
smoothness 258 n.
hardness 326 n.
rock 344 n.
white thing 427 n.
variegate 437 vb.
sculpture 554 n.
building material 631 n.
unfeeling person 820 n.
marbles *plaything* 837 n.
marbling
maculation 437 n.
bookbinding 589 n.
march *region* 184 n.
limit 236 n.
motion, gait 265 n.
itinerary 267 n.
walk 267 vb.
progression 285 n.
musical piece 412 n.
route 624 n.
wage war 718 vb.
march against
charge 712 vb.
märchen *fable* 543 n.
marcher *dweller* 191 n.
pedestrian 268 n.
agitator 738 n.
marches *limit* 236 n.
marching *marching* 267 n.
marchioness
nobleman 868 n.
march of time
course of time 111 n.
progression 285 n.
improvement 654 n.
march past *pageant* 875 n.
march with
be contiguous 202 vb.
marconigram
message 529 n.
mare *horse* 273 n.
female animal 373 n.
mare's nest *fable* 543 n.
mare's tail *cloud* 355 n.
margarine *fat* 357 n.
margin *remainder* 41 n.
room 183 n.
edge 234 n.
letterpress 587 n.
edition 589 n.
superfluity 637 n.
redundance 637 n.

scope 744 n.
discount 810 n.
marginal
inconsiderable 33 adj.
marginal 234 adj.
economical 814 adj.
marginalia
commentary 520 n.
record 548 n.
reading matter 589 n.
margrave *potentate* 741 n.
nobleman 868 n.
mariage de convenance
type of marriage 894 n.
marijuana *poison* 659 n.
marimba *piano, gong* 414 n.
marina *stable* 19 n.
shelter 662 n.
marinate *immerse* 303 vb.
preserve 666 vb.
marine *seafaring* 269 adj.
shipping 275 n.
marine 275 adj.
oceanic 343 adj.
navy man 722 n.
Marine Corps
navy man 722 n.
mariner *mariner* 270 n.
Mariolatry
Madonna 968 n.
marionette(s) *image* 551 n.
stage-play 594 n.
plaything 837 n.
marital
matrimonial 894 adj.
maritime *seafaring* 269 adj.
marine 275 adj.
oceanic 343 adj.
marjoram *potherb* 301 n.
mark *degree* 27 n.
character 5 n.
serial place 73 n.
sort 77 n.
speciality 80 n.
effect 157 n.
feature 445 n.
assent 488 n.
indication 547 n.
mark 547 vb.
trace 548 n.
script 586 n.
select 605 vb.
objective 617 n.
importance 638 n.
wound 655 n.
impair 655 vb.
coinage 797 n.
blemish 845 n., vb.
slur 867 n.
mark, beside the
irrelevant 10 adj.

mark down
underestimate 483 vb.
select 605 vb.
discount 810 vb.
cheapen 812 vb.
mark down for
intend 617 vb.
markedly
remarkably 32 adv.
market *focus* 76 n.
meeting place 192 n.
purchase 792 vb.
sell 793 vb.
mart 796 n.
marketable
trading 791 adj.
saleable 793 adj.
marketer *purchaser* 792 n.
market garden *farm* 370 n.
market, in the
offering 759 adj.
saleable 793 adj.
market-place *activity* 678 n.
arena 724 n.
(*see* market)
markings
identification 547 n.
mark, of
remarkable 32 adj.
notable 638 adj.
mark off *gauge* 465 vb.
mark, off the
deviating 282 adj.
astray 282 adv.
mark of recognition
courteous act 884 n.
mark out *differentiate* 15 vb.
set apart 46 vb.
select 605 vb.
dignify 866 vb.
marksman
shooter 287 n.
hunter 619 n.
proficient 696 n.
marksmanship *skill* 694 n.
mark the occasion
celebrate 876 vb.
mark the time
play music 413 vb.
mark time
pass time 108 vb.
time 117 vb.
be quiescent 266 vb.
await 507 vb.
mark, up to the
expert 694 adj.
marl *soil* 344 n.
marmalade
sweetmeat 301 n.
condiment 389 n.
sweet 392 n.

marmoreal *glyptic* 554 adj.
marmoset *monkey* 365 n.
marmot *rodent* 365 n.
　idler 679 n.
maroon *set apart* 46 vb.
　brown 430 adj.
　red colour 431 n.
　derelict 779 n.
　not retain 779 vb.
　solitary 883 n.
marplot *bungler* 677 n.
　hinderer 702 n.
　evildoer 904 n.
marquee *pavilion* 192 n.
　canopy 226 n.
marquetry *chequer* 437 n.
marquis *nobleman* 868 n.
marriage *junction* 45 n.
　combination 50 n.
　marriage 894 n.
marriageable
　grown up 134 adj.
　marriageable 894 adj.
marriage adviser
　mediator 720 n.
marriage-broker
　intermediary 231 n.
　matchmaker 894 n.
marriage lines *record* 548 n.
　marriage 894 n.
marriage portion
　dower 777 n.
marriage service
　Christian rite 988 n.
married man *spouse* 894 n.
marrow *substance* 3 n.
　essential part 5 n.
　vitality 162 n.
　interiority 224 n.
　centrality 225 n.
　vegetables 301 n.
　plant 366 n.
marrowless *weak* 163 adj.
marry *join* 45 vb.
　combine 50 vb.
　marry, wed 894 vb.
marry off *not retain* 779 vb.
　convey 780 vb.
　marry 894 vb.
Mars *planet* 321 n.
　redness 431 n.
　quarrelsomeness 709 n.
　war 718 n.
　mythic god 966 n.
　Olympian god 967 n.
marsh, marshland
　desert 172 n.
　moisture 341 n.
　marsh 347 n.
　semiliquidity 354 n.
　dirt 649 n.

marshal *arrange* 62 vb.
　mark 547 vb.
　auxiliary 707 n.
　officer 741 n.
　army officer 741 n.
marshalling yard
　railroad 624 n.
marshiness *softness* 327 n.
marshmallows
　sweetmeat 301 n.
marshy *humid* 341 adj.
　marshy 347 adj.
　pulpy 356 adj.
　dirty 649 adj.
　insalubrious 653 adj.
marsupial *cellular* 194 adj.
　marsupial 365 n.
mart (*see* market)
Martello tower *fort* 713 n.
marten *skin* 226 n.
martial *warlike* 718 adj.
　courageous 855 adj.
martial law
　government 733 n.
　anarchy 734 n.
　brute force 735 n.
Martian *foreigner* 59 n.
　planetary 321 adj.
martin *bird* 365 n.
martinet *tyrant* 735 n.
martingale *fetter* 748 n.
Martinmas *holy-day* 988 n.
martlet *heraldry* 547 n.
martyr *kill* 362 vb.
　torment 827 vb.
　pietist 979 n.
martyrdom *death* 361 n.
　killing 362 n.
　pain 377 n.
　suffering 825 n.
　disinterestedness 931 n.
　capital punishment 963 n.
martyr-like
　disinterested 931 adj.
martyrologist
　narrator 590 n.
martyrology *list* 87 n.
　death roll 361 n.
　biography 590 n.
martyry *holy place* 990 n.
marvel *wonder* 864 n., vb.
marvellous
　prodigious 32 adj.
　excellent 644 adj.
　pleasurable 826 adj.
　wonderful 864 adj.
Marxism *materiality* 319 n.
　philosophy 449 n.
　antichristianity 974 n.
Marxist
　revolutionist 149 n.

reformer 654 n.
　irreligionist 974 n.
marzipan *sweetmeat* 301 n.
　sweet 392 n.
mascara *cosmetic* 843 n.
mascot *preserver* 666 n.
　talisman 983 n.
masculine *generic* 77 adj.
　manly 162 adj.
　male 372 adj.
　grammatical 564 adj.
masculinity *male* 372 n.
mash *medley* 43 n.
　confusion 61 n.
　soften 327 vb.
　pulverize 332 vb.
　semiliquidity 354 n.
　thicken 354 vb.
　pulpiness 356 n.
　be clumsy 695 vb.
masher *pulverizer* 332 n.
　fop 848 n.
masjid *temple* 990 n.
mask *covering* 226 n.
　screen 421 n., vb.
　conceal 525 vb.
　disguise 527 n.
　sham 542 n.
　mental dishonesty 543 n.
masked *invisible* 444 adj.
masochism
　abnormality 84 n.
mason *efform* 243 vb.
　artisan 686 n.
Masonic *sectional* 708 adj.
masonry
　accumulation 74 n.
　building material 631 n.
Masorete, Massorete
　interpreter 520 n.
　theologian 973 n.
Masoretic *scriptural* 975 adj.
masque *stage play* 594 n.
　drama 594 n.
　festivity 837 n.
masquerade *clothing* 228 n.
　concealment 525 n.
　sham 542 n.
　dancing 837 n.
masquerader *hider* 527 n.
　impostor 545 n.
mass *quantity* 26 n.
　great quantity 32 n.
　main part 32 n.
　extensive 32 adj.
　chief part 52 n.
　confusion 61 n.
　accumulation 74 n.
　crowd 74 n.
　congregate 74 vb.
　general 79 adj.

greater number 104n.
size, bulk 195n.
matter 319n.
gravity 322n.
solid body 324n.
army 722n.
public worship 981n.
Holy Communion 988n.
massacre
slaughter 362n.,vb.
execute 963vb.
massage soften 327vb.
friction 333n.
touch 378n.,vb.
surgery 658n.
beautification 843n.
massed
multitudinous 104adj.
dense 324adj.
masses, the
everyman 79n.
social group 371n.
commonalty 869n.
masseur, masseuse
(see massage)
massif high land 209n.
mass, in a together 74adv.
massive great 32adj.
large 195adj.
weighty 322adj.
dense 324adj.
mass-meeting
assembly 74n.
mass-money
oblation 981n.
mass movement
activity 678n.
mass murder
destruction 165n.
cruel act 898n.
capital punishment 963n.
mass-produce
produce 164vb.
mass production
uniformity 16n.
reproduction 166n.
productiveness 171n.
massy great 32adj.
large 195adj.
material 319adj.
weighty 322adj.
dense 324adj.
mast high structure 209n.
hanger 217n.
supporter 318n.
frenzied 503adj.
mastaba tomb 364n.
master superior 34n.
youngster 132n.
prevail 178vb.
mariner 270n.

sage 500n.
understand 516vb.
learn 536vb.
teacher 537n.
director 690n.
proficient 696n.
victor 727n.
overmaster 727vb.
master 741n.
owner 776n.
title 870n.
theosophy 984n.
masterful
authoritative 733adj.
authoritarian 735adj.
master-key opener 263n.
masterless
independent 744adj.
unpossessed 774adj.
masterly perfect 646adj.
skilful 694adj.
successful 727adj.
master-mariner
mariner 270n.
master-mind
intellectual 492n.
sage 500n.
proficient 696n.
master of ceremonies
leader 690n.
reveller 837n.
masterpiece product 164n.
picture 553n.
exceller 644n.
perfection 646n.
masterpiece 694n.
success 727n.
a beauty 841n.
master-plan prototype 23n.
plan 623n.
mastership skill 694n.
magistrature 733n.
master spirit sage 500n.
bigwig 638n.
proficient 696n.
person of repute 866n.
master-stroke
contrivance 623n.
masterpiece 694n.
success 727n.
mastery knowledge 490n.
skill 694n.
victory 727n.
rule 733n.
magistrature 733n.
possession 773n.
masthead
high structure 209n.
vertex 213n.
punish 963vb.
mastic viscidity 354n.

resin 357n.
mastication eating 301n.
pulpiness 356n.
mastiff dog 368n.
mastodon animal 365n.
mat enlace 222vb.
floor-cover 226n.
cleaning cloth 648n.
matador killer 362n.
combatant 722n.
match analogue 18n.
resemble 18vb.
accord 24vb.
compeer 28n.
join 45vb.
pair 90vb.
burning 381n.
lighter 385n.
torch 420n.
compare 462vb.
contest, duel 716n.
marriage 894n.
match against
oppose 704vb.
matchbox
small box 194n.
lighter 385n.
matchet side-arms 723n.
matching
harmonious 410adj.
soft-hued 425adj.
matchless supreme 34adj.
best 644adj.
matchlock fire-arm 723n.
match-make marry 894vb.
match-maker
intermediary 231n.
mediator 720n.
match-maker 894n.
match-stick
weak thing 163n.
match-winner victor 727n.
match-winning
successful 727adj.
match with
make quarrels 709vb.
matchwood
weak thing 163n.
brittleness 330n.
mate analogue 18n.
compeer 28n.
unite with 45vb.
combine 50vb.
concomitant 89n.
pair 90vb.
mariner 270n.
personnel 686n.
colleague 707n.
overmaster 727vb.
defeat 728n.
chum 880n.

spouse 894 n.
marry, wed 894 vb.
maté soft drink 301 n.
mateless unwedded 895 adj.
materfamilias
  maternity 169 n.
material real 1 adj.
  substantiality 3 n.
  textile 222 n.
  matter 319 n.
  materials 631 n.
  important 638 adj.
  sensual 944 adj.
materialism
  materiality 319 n.
  philosophy 449 n.
  antichristianity 974 n.
  impiety 980 n.
materialistic selfish 932 adj.
  (see materialism)
materiality
  substantiality 3 n.
  materiality 319 n.
  importance 638 n.
materialization
  manifestation 522 n.
materialize happen 154 vb.
  materialize 319 vb.
  be visible 443 vb.
  appear 445 vb.
  practice occultism 984 vb.
materials source 156 n.
  object 319 n.
  means 629 n.
  materials 631 n.
materia medica
  medicine 658 n.
maternal akin 11 adj.
  parental 169 adj.
  benevolent 897 adj.
maternity
  propagation 164 n.
  maternity 169 n.
matey friendly 880 adj.
  sociable 882 adj.
mathematical
  statistical 86 adj.
  accurate 494 adj.
mathematician
  computer 86 n.
  reasoner 475 n.
mathematics
  mathematics 86 n.
matinée evening 129 n.
  dramaturgy 594 n.
mating coition 45 n.
  libido 859 n.
matins morning 128 n.
  public worship 981 n.
  church service 988 n.
matriarch family 11 n.

maternity 169 n.
master 741 n.
matriarchy gynocracy 733 n.
matricide homicide 362 n.
matriculate list 87 vb.
matriculation exam. 459 n.
matrilinear akin 11 adj.
  parental 169 adj.
matrimonial
  matrimonial 894 adj.
matrimonial agent
  match-maker 894 n.
matrimony marriage 894 n.
matrix mould 23 n.
  print-type 587 n.
matron adult 134 n.
  maternity 169 n.
  woman 373 n.
  nurse 658 n.
  manager 690 n.
  spouse 894 n.
matronage
  womankind 373 n.
matronhood female 373 n.
  marriage 894 n.
matronly aged 131 adj.
  grown up 134 adj.
  parental 169 adj.
  female 373 adj.
  matrimonial 894 adj.
matron of honour
  bridesman 894 n.
matronymic name 561 n.
matt
  semi-transparent 424 adj.
  soft-hued 425 adj.
matted crossed 222 adj.
  hairy 259 adj.
  dense 324 adj.
  dirty 649 adj.
matter substantiality 3 n.
  matter 319 n.
  solid body 324 n.
  semiliquidity 354 n.
  topic 452 n.
  meaning 514 n.
  be important 638 vb.
  dirt 649 n.
  ulcer 651 n.
matter in hand
  undertaking 672 n.
matter of course
  practice 610 n.
  non-wonder 865 n.
matter of fact reality 1 n.
  eventuality 154 n.
  certainty 473 n.
  truth 494 n.
  dullness 840 n.
matter-of-fact
  narrow-minded 481 adj.

prosaic 593 adj.
  artless 699 adj.
matter-of-factness
  plainness 573 n.
matter of time
  course of time 111 n.
matters affairs 154 n.
mattery fluidal 335 adj.
  toxic 653 adj.
matting network 222 n.
  floor-cover 226 n.
mattock sharp edge 256 n.
mattress cushion 218 n.
maturation
  maturation 669 n.
  (see mature)
mature grow 36 vb.
  be complete 54 vb.
  grown up 134 adj.
  be turned to 147 vb.
  plan 623 vb.
  perfect 646 vb.
  make better 654 vb.
  mature 669 vb.
  carry through 725 vb.
matured formed 243 adj.
maturing future 124 adj.
maturity oldness 127 n.
  adultness 134 n.
  preparedness 669 n.
  completion 725 n.
matutinal matinal 128 adj.
maudlin foolish 499 adj.
  tipsy 949 adj.
maul be violent 176 vb.
  hammer 279 n.
  strike 279 vb.
  ill-treat 645 vb.
  impair, wound 655 vb.
  attack 712 vb.
  dispraise 924 vb.
maund basket 194 n.
  weighment 322 n.
maunder be foolish 499 vb.
  be diffuse 570 vb.
  be loquacious 581 vb.
Maundy-money gift 781 n.
Maundy Thursday
  holy-day 988 n.
mausoleum edifice 164 n.
  tomb 364 n.
  monument 548 n.
mauvaise honte
  affectation 850 n.
  modesty 874 n.
mauvais quart d'heure
  suffering 825 n.
  reprimand 924 n.
mauve purple 434 n.
maverick cattle 365 n.
  revolter 738 n.

mavis *bird* 365 n.
  vocalist 413 n.
mavourneen *darling* 890 n.
maw *maw* 194 n.
  insides 224 n.
  eater 301 n.
mawkish *feeling* 818 adj.
maxim *rule* 81 n.
  maxim 496 n.
  precept 693 n.
maximal *crowning* 34 adj.
maximalism
  reformism 654 n.
maximalist *reformer* 654 n.
  revolter 738 n.
maximize *augment* 36 vb.
  overrate 482 vb.
  exaggerate 546 vb.
maximum *greatness* 32 n.
  crowning 34 adj.
  plenitude 54 n.
  size 195 n.
  summit 213 n.
maximus *older* 131 adj.
may *be possible* 469 vb.
maya
  insubstantiality 4 n.
maybe *possibly* 469 adv.
May-fly *brief span* 114 n.
  fly 365 n.
mayonnaise *dish* 301 n.
mayor *official* 690 n.
  councillor 692 n.
  officer 741 n.
  law officer 955 n.
mayoralty
  magistrature 733 n.
  jurisdiction 955 n.
Mazdaism
  religious faith 973 n.
maze *complexity* 61 n.
  meandering 251 n.
  enigma 530 n.
  difficulty 700 n.
mazurka
  musical piece 412 n.
  dance 837 n.
mead *liquor* 301 n.
  grassland 348 n.
  sweet 392 n.
meadow *grassland* 348 n.
  farm 370 n.
meagre *small* 33 adj.
  exiguous 196 adj.
  lean 206 adj.
  feeble 572 adj.
  underfed 636 adj.
  poor 801 adj.
  economical 814 adj.
  fasting 946 adj.
meal *meal* 301 n.

cereal 301 n.
  powder 332 n.
  corn 366 n.
  festivity 837 n.
mealies *corn* 366 n.
mealy-mouthed
  hypocritical 541 adj.
  flattering 925 adj.
mean *average* 30 n.
  middle 70 n., adj.
  interjacent 231 adj.
  be willing 597 vb.
  intend 617 vb.
  unimportant 639 adj.
  bad 645 adj.
  parsimonious 816 adj.
  disreputable 867 adj.
  plebeian 869 adj.
  humble 872 adj.
  servile 879 adj.
  contemptible 922 adj.
  rascally 930 adj.
  selfish 932 adj.
  (*see* meaning)
meander *meander* 251 vb.
  flow 350 vb.
meaning *relation* 9 n.
  meaning 514 n.
  interpretation 520 n.
  affirmative 532 adj.
  indication 547 n.
meaningful
  meaningful 514 adj.
  intelligible 516 adj.
  important 638 adj.
meaningless
  insubstantial 4 adj.
  semantic 514 adj.
  unmeaning 515 adj.
  designless 618 adj.
  dull 840 adj.
mean-minded
  selfish 932 adj.
meanness *smallness* 33 n.
  unimportance 639 n.
  parsimony 816 n.
  despisedness 922 n.
  selfishness 932 n.
mean nothing
  mean nothing 515 vb.
means *opportunity* 137 n.
  contrivance 623 n.
  instrumentality 628 n.
  means 629 n.
  estate 777 n.
  funds 797 n.
  wealth 800 n.
means, by no
  in no way 33 adv.
mean-spirited
  cowardly 856 adj.

means test *enquiry* 459 n.
meant *veracious* 540 adj.
meantime, meanwhile
  while 108 adv.
mean well
  be benevolent 897 vb.
measles *infection* 651 n.
measly *bad* 645 adj.
  diseased 651 adj.
measurable
  numerable 86 adj.
measure
  finite quantity 26 n.
  graduate 27 vb.
  comprise 78 vb.
  counting instrument 86 n.
  moderation 177 n.
  measure 183 n.
  size 195 n.
  tempo 410 n.
  tune 412 n.
  gauge 465 n.
  mete out 465 vb.
  estimate 480 vb.
  prosody 593 n.
  deed 676 n.
  portion 783 n.
measured *periodical* 141 adj.
  moderate 177 adj.
  measured 465 adj.
  sufficient 635 adj.
  temperate 942 adj.
measured by
  comparative 27 adj.
measure for measure
  compensation 31 n.
  retaliation 714 n.
measureless *infinite* 107 adj.
measurement
  measurement 465 n.
  (*see* measure)
measures *policy* 623 n.
  action 676 n.
measure up to
  be equal 28 vb.
  be able 160 vb.
  suffice 635 vb.
meat *meat* 301 n.
  food 301 n.
meatiness *substance* 3 n.
  bulk 195 n.
meatless day *fast* 946 n.
  holy-day 988 n.
meaty *forceful* 571 adj.
  (*see* meatiness)
Mecca *focus* 76 n.
  holy place 990 n.
mechanic *machinist* 630 n.
  artisan 686 n.
mechanical
  involuntary 596 adj.

mechanical 630 adj.
mechanics *means* 629 n.
mechanics 630 n.
mechanism *machine* 630 n.
mechanization
  instrumentality 628 n.
medal *badge* 547 n.
  decoration 729 n.
  jewellery 844 n.
  honours 866 n.
  reward 962 n.
medallion
  ornamentation 844 n.
  jewellery 844 n.
medallist *proficient* 696 n.
  victor 727 n.
meddle *derange* 63 vb.
  interfere 231 vb.
  be curious 453 vb.
  busy oneself 622 vb.
  impair 655 vb.
  meddle 678 vb.
  be clumsy 695 vb.
  obstruct 702 vb.
  mediate 720 vb.
meddler *inquisitor* 453 n.
  meddler 678 n.
  bungler 697 n.
  hinderer 702 n.
meddlesome
  inquisitive 453 adj.
  meddling 678 adj.
medial *middle* 70 adj.
median *quantity* 26 n.
  average 30 n.
  interjacent 231 adj.
mediant *musical note* 410 n.
mediate *interfere* 231 vb.
  be instrumental 628 vb.
  pacify 719 vb.
  mediate 720 vb.
mediation *mediation* 720 n.
  deprecation 762 n.
mediator *moderator.* 177 n.
  intermediary 231 n.
  speaker 579 n.
  mediator 720 n.
  match-maker 894 n.
mediatory
  pacificatory 719 adj.
  mediatory 720 adj.
  redemptive 965 adj.
medicable *medical* 658 adj.
medical *medical* 658 adj.
medical treatment
  therapy 658 n.
medicament
  medicine 658 n.
medicate *cure* 656 vb.
  doctor 658 vb.
medicinal

improving 654 adj.
  remedial 658 adj.
medicine *vocation* 622 n.
  cure 656 vb.
  medicine 658 n.
medicine-man *doctor* 658 n.
  sorcerer 983 n.
mediety *middle point* 30 n.
  middle 70 n.
  mediocrity 732 n.
medieval *olden* 127 adj.
medievalism
  palætiology 125 n.
mediocre
  inconsiderable 33 adj.
  typical 83 adj.
  not bad 644 adj.
  mediocre 732 adj.
  modest 874 adj.
mediocrity *average* 30 n.
  inferiority 35 n.
  generality 79 n.
  moderation 177 n.
  mid-course 625 n.
  nonentity 639 n.
  imperfection 647 n.
  mediocrity 732 n.
meditate *meditate* 449 vb.
  enquire 459 vb.
  intend 617 vb.
meditation
  meditation 449 n.
  attention 455 n.
  piety 979 n.
  worship, prayers 981 n.
mediterranean
  middle 70 adj.
  interjacent 231 adj.
medium *average* 30 n.
  middle 70 n.
  circumjacence 230 n.
  intermediary 231 n.
  interjacent 231 adj.
  pigment 425 n.
  oracle 511 n.
  interpreter 520 n.
  instrumentality 628 n.
  mediocre 732 adj.
  psychic 984 n.
medlar *fruit* 301 n.
medley *medley* 43 n.
  confusion 61 n.
  accumulation 74 n.
  musical piece 412 n.
medullary *soft* 327 adj.
Medusa *intimidation* 854 n.
meed *portion* 783 n.
  reward 962 n.
meek *submitting* 721 adj.
  obedient 739 n.
  inexcitable 823 adj.

patient 823 adj.
  humble 872 adj.
meerschaum *tobacco* 388 n.
meet *fit* 24 adj.
  congregate 74 vb.
  synchronize 123 vb.
  meet with 154 vb.
  be near 200 vb.
  touch 378 vb.
  discover 484 vb.
  withstand 704 vb.
  fight 716 vb.
  pay 804 vb.
  (*see* meeting)
meet an obligation
  grant claims 915 vb.
meet at every turn
  be present 189 vb.
meet half-way
  be willing 597 vb.
  be half-way 625 vb.
  pacify 719 vb.
  compromise 770 vb.
meeting *junction* 45 n.
  assembly 74 n.
  eventuality 154 n.
  contiguity 202 n.
  collision 279 n.
  approach 289 n.
  approaching 289 adj.
  convergence 293 n.
  arrival 295 n.
  conference 584 n.
  council 692 n.
  social gathering 882 n.
meeting house
  meeting place 192 n.
  church 990 n.
meeting place *focus* 76 n.
  meeting place 192 n.
  goal 295 n.
  social round 882 n.
meeting-point
  junction 45 n.
meet one's wishes
  consent 758 vb.
meet requirements
  suffice 635 vb.
meet the bill
  defray 804 vb.
megalith *antiquity* 125 n.
  monument 548 n.
megalithic *large* 195 adj.
megalomania
  overestimation 482 n.
  mania 503 n.
megalomaniac
  madman 504 n.
megaphone
  megaphone 400 n.
  hearing aid 415 n.

megascope
 optical device 442 n.
megatherium *giant* 195 n.
 animal 365 n.
megaton *weighment* 322 n.
megawatt *electricity* 160 n.
megilp *resin* 357 n.
megrims *spasm* 318 n.
 animal disease 651 n.
 melancholy 834 n.
meinie *hand* 74 n
meiosis
 underestimation 483 n.
meistersinger *poet* 593 n.
melancholia
 psychopathy 503 n.
 melancholy 834 n.
melancholic *insane* 503 adj.
 madman 504 n.
 melancholic 834 adj.
melancholy *bad* 645 adj.
 sorrow 825 n.
 unhappy 825 adj.
 discontent 829 n.
 melancholy 834 n.
 cheerless 834 adj.
 melancholic 834 adj.
 tedium 838 n.
 sullenness 893 n.
mélange *a mixture* 43 n.
melanism *blackness* 428 n.
melanoma *carcinosis* 651 n.
mêlée *turmoil* 61 n.
 fight 716 n.
melic *musical* 412 adj.
 musicianly 413 adj.
melioration
 improvement 654 n.
meliorism *reformism* 654 n.
mellifluous *sweet* 392 adj.
 melodious 410 adj.
 elegant 575 adj.
mellow *aged* 131 adj.
 be turned to 147 vb.
 soften 327 vb.
 soft-hued 425 adj.
 colour 425 vb.
 get better 654 vb.
 mature 669 vb.
 drunk 949 adj.
melodeon *organ* 414 n.
melodic *melodious* 410 adj.
 musical 412 adj.
 musicianly 413 adj.
melodious *pleasant* 376 adj.
 melodious 410 adj.
melodist *vocalist* 413 n.
melodize *harmonize* 410 vb.
 compose music 413 vb.
melodrama *stage play* 594 n.
 excitation 821 n.

melodramatic
 dramatic 594 adj.
 exciting 821 adj.
melody *sweetness* 392 n.
 melody 410 n.
 tune 412 n.
 concord 710 n.
 pleasurableness 826 n.
melon *fruit* 301 n.
 plant 366 n.
melt *not be 1 vb.*
 decrease 37 vb.
 come unstuck 49 vb.
 decompose 51 vb.
 be dispersed 75 vb.
 be transient 114 vb.
 deform 244 vb.
 liquefy 337 vb.
 be hot 379 vb.
 heat 381 vb.
 sound faint 401 vb.
 disappear 446 vb.
 waste 634 vb.
 weep 836 vb.
 pity 905 vb.
melting *unstable* 152 adj.
 soft 327 adj.
 fluidal 335 adj.
melting mood
 lamentation 836 n.
 pity 905 n.
melting point *heat* 379 n.
melting-pot *mixture* 43 n.
 crucible 147 n.
 workshop 687 n.
• melt into *shade off* 27 vb.
 be turned to 147 vb.
mem *lady* 373 n.
 title 870 n.
member *part, limb* 53 n.
 component 58 n.
 genitalia 164 n.
 society 708 n.
 participator 775 n.
member of Parliament
 councillor 692 n.
membership
 inclusion 78 n.
 association 706 n.
 participation 775 n.
 sociality 882 n.
membrane *layer* 207 n.
memento *reminder* 505 n.
 trophy 729 n.
memento mori
 dejection 834 n.
memoir *record* 548 n.
 dissertation 591 n.
memoirs
 remembrance 505 n.
 reading matter 589 n.

 biography 590 n.
memorabilia
 remembrance 505 n.
 reading matter 589 n.
 biography 590 n.
memorable
 remembered 505 adj.
 notable 638 adj.
memorandum
 reminder 505 n.
 record 548 n.
 plan 623 n.
 important matter 638 n.
memorial *reminder* 505 n.
 report 524 n.
 monument 548 n.
 trophy 729 n.
 honours 866 n.
memorialist
 chronicler 549 n.
memorialize *request* 761 vb.
memoriam, in
 in memoriam 364 adv.
 in memory 505 adv.
memories *remainder* 41 n.
memorize *memorize* 505 vb.
 learn 536 vb.
memory *thought* 449 n.
 memory 505 n.
 famousness 866 n.
mem sahib *lady* 373 n.
 title 870 n.
men *mariner* 270 n.
 personnel 686 n.
 armed force 722 n.
menace *predict* 511 vb.
 danger 661 n.
 warning 664 n.
 frighten 854 vb.
 hateful object 888 n.
 threat 900 n.
ménage *habitancy* 191 n.
 management 689 n.
menagerie
 accumulation 74 n.
 zoo 369 n.
 collection 632 n.
mend *get healthy* 650 vb.
 rectify 654 vb.
 repair 656 vb.
mendable *restored* 656 adj.
mendacity *falsehood* 541 n.
Mendelian *inherited* 157 adj.
 filial 170 adj.
mender *reformer* 654 n.
 mender 656 n.
mendicancy *request* 761 n.
 poverty 801 n.
mendicant *idler* 679 n.
 beggar 763 n.
 poor man 801 n.

monk 986n.
menfolk *male* 372n.
menhir *tomb* 364n.
  monument 548n.
menial *inferior* 35n.,adj.
  worker 686n.
  servant 742n.
meninx *head* 213n.
  intellect 447n.
meniscus *curve* 248n.
  optical device 442n.
menology
  chronometry 117n.
menopause *age* 131n.
  unproductivity 172n.
mensal *mensal* 301adj.
menses *regular return* 141n.
  hæmorrhage 302n.
Mensheviks
  political party 708n.
Menshevist
  moderate 625n.
mens rea *intention* 617n.
menstrual *seasonal* 141adj.
menstruum
  liquefaction 337n.
mensurable
  numerable 86adj.
  measured 465adj.
mensuration
  measurement 465n.
mental *mental* 447adj.
  insane 503adj.
mental act *thought* 449n.
mental age
  present time 121n.
mental balance
  wisdom 498n.
  sanity 502n.
mental calibre
  intelligence 498n.
mental case *madman* 504n.
  sick person 651n.
mental disease
  insanity 503n.
mental dishonesty
  mental dishonesty 543n.
mental hospital
  madhouse 503n.
  hospital 658n.
mental hygiene
  sanity 502n.
mentality *intellect* 447n.
mental reservation
  sophistry 477n.
  equivocalness 518n.
  concealment 525n.
  mental dishonesty 543n.
menticulture
  civilization 654n.
mention *referral* 9n.

notice 455vb.
  information 524n.
  speak 579vb.
mentor *sage* 500n.
  teacher 537n.
  adviser 691n.
menu *list* 87n.
  meal 301n.
Mephistopheles
  Mephisto 969n.
Mephistophelian
  wicked 934adj.
mephitic *fetid* 397adj.
  toxic 653adj.
mephitis *fetor* 397n.
  poison 659n.
  insalubrity 653n.
meracious *pungent* 388adj.
mercantile *trading* 791adj.
mercantilism
  restriction 747n.
  trade 791n.
Mercator's projection
  distortion 246n.
  map 551n.
mercature *barter* 791n.
mercenary *militarist* 722n.
  servant 742n.
  avaricious 816adj.
  venal 930adj.
  selfish 932adj.
mercer *clothier* 228n.
  tradesman 794n.
mercerize *be tough* 329vb.
mercery *dressing* 228n.
merchandise
  equipment 630n.
  store 632n.
  trade 791vb.
  sale 793n.
  merchandise 795n.
merchant *bargain* 791vb.
  trade 791vb.
  merchant 794n.
merchantman
  merchant ship 275n.
merchant navy
  shipping 275n.
merchantry *trade* 791n.
merciful *lenient* 736adj.
  benevolent 897adj.
  pitying 905adj.
merciless
  destructive 165adj.
  resolute 599adj.
  obstinate 602adj.
  severe 735adj.
  cruel 898adj.
  malevolent 898adj.
  pitiless 906adj.
mercurial

changeful 152adj.
  unstable 152adj.
  moving 265adj.
  speedy 277adj.
  light-minded 456adj.
  irresolute 601adj.
  capricious 604adj.
  excitable 822adj.
Mercurian
  planetary 321adj.
Mercury *speeder* 277n.
  planet 321n.
  weather 340n.
  courier 531n.
  Olympian god 967n.
mercy *irenics* 719n.
  lenity 736n.
  benevolence 897n.
  mercy 905n.
  divine attribute 965n.
mercy-killing *killing* 362n.
mercy of, at the
  liable 180adj.
  subject 745adj.
mercy seat
  ritual object 988n.
  holy place 990n.
mere *absolute* 32adj.
  inconsiderable 33adj.
  simple 44adj.
  limit 236n.
  lake 346n.
meretricious *false* 541adj.
  spurious 542adj.
  ornate 574adj.
  inelegant 576adj.
  ornamented 844adj.
  vulgar 847adj.
  unchaste 951adj.
meretriciousness
  spectacle 445n.
merewife
  mythical being 970n.
merfolk
  mythical being 970n.
merganser *diver* 313n.
  waterfowl 365n.
merge *be identical* 13vb.
  mix 43vb.
  join 45vb.
  combine 50vb.
  be one of 58vb.
  be included 78vb.
  be turned to 147vb.
  immerse 303vb.
  co-operate 706vb.
  join a party 708vb.
merged *included* 78adj.
  interjacent 231adj.
merger *combination* 50n.
  association 706n.

meridian *noon* 128n.
  region 184n.
  summit 213n.
meridional *topmost* 213adj.
  directed 281adj.
merino *fibre* 208n.
  textile 222n.
merit *importance* 638n.
  utility 640n.
  goodness 644n.
  right 913n.
  deserve 915vb.
  virtues 933n.
meritless
  unentitled 916adj.
  vicious 934adj.
meritorious
  excellent 644adj.
  deserving 915adj.
  approvable 923adj.
  virtuous 933adj.
Merlin *sorcerer* 983n.
merlon *fortification* 713n.
mermaid *rara avis* 84n.
  sea-nymph 343n.
  vocalist 413n.
  mythical being 970n.
merman *rara avis* 84n.
  sea-god 343n.
  mythical being 970n.
merriment
  enjoyment 824n.
  merriment 833n.
  rejoicing 835n.
  amusement 837n.
  wit 839n.
merry *drunk* 949adj.
  (*see* merriment)
merry-andrew
  entertainer 594n.
merry-go-round
  rotation 315n.
  pleasure-ground 837n.
merry-maker *reveller* 837n.
merry-making
  sociability 882n.
  (*see* merriment)
merry men *band* 74n.
merrythought
  magic instrument 983n.
mesa *high land* 209n.
  plain 348n.
mésalliance *misfit* 25n.
  type of marriage 894n.
mescal *antidote* 658n.
mescalin *drug* 658n.
mesh *gap* 201n.
  space 201vb.
  network 222n.
meshes
  encumbrance 702n.

mesh with *accord* 24vb.
meshwork *network* 222n.
mesial *middle* 70adj.
mesmeric
  influential 178adj.
  insensible 375adj.
  inducive 612adj.
  psychical 984adj.
mesmerism
  influence 178n.
  occultism 984n.
mesmerist *psychic* 984n.
mesmerize
  render insensible 375vb.
  convince 485vb.
  frighten 854vb.
  (*see* mesmerism)
mesne lord *owner* 776n.
mesne profits *receipt* 807n.
mesogastric *central* 225adj.
mesolithic *secular* 110adj.
meson *particle* 33n.
  element 319n.
mesozoic *secular* 110adj.
mess *medley* 43n.
  confusion 61n.
  jumble 63vb.
  chamber 194n.
  feasting 301n.
  eat 301vb.
  predicament 700n.
  failure 728n.
  portion 783n.
message
  information 524n.
  message 529n.
Messalina
  loose woman 952n.
mess can, mess tin
  cauldron 194n.
messenger *precursor* 66n.
  traveller 268n.
  informant 524n.
  messenger 531n.
  delegate 754n.
  deputy 755n.
messenger boy
  courier 531n.
messer *eater* 301n.
Messiah *leader* 690n.
  philanthropist 901n.
  God the Son 965n.
  religious teacher 973n.
messianic
  redemptive 965adj.
messianism
  aspiration 852n.
messing *eating* 301n.
  mensal 301adj.
mess jacket *tunic* 228n.
mess kit *uniform* 228n.

messmate *eater* 301n.
  chum 880n.
messroom *chamber* 194n.
messuage *house* 192n.
  lands 777n.
mess up
  make unclean 649vb.
  impair 655vb.
messy *orderless* 61adj.
  amorphous 244adj.
  dirty 649adj.
mestee, mestizo
  hybrid 43n.
  nonconformist 84n.
met *assembled* 74adj.
  synchronous 123adj.
metabolism
  transformation 143n.
metacentre *centrality* 225n.
metachronism
  anachronism 118n.
metachronous
  non-contemporary 122adj.
metagalactic *cosmic* 321
  adj.
metage *measurement* 465n.
metagenesis *change* 143n.
metagrammatism
  spelling 558n.
metal *hardness* 326n.
  mineral 359n.
  heraldry 547n.
  materials 631n.
metalled *covered* 226adj.
  communicating 624adj.
metallic *strident* 407adj.
metallography
  mineralogy 359n.
metallurgy
  mineralogy 359n.
metamorphic
  multiform 82adj.
  territorial 344adj.
metamorphism
  multiformity 82n.
metamorphosis
  multiformity 82n.
  transformation 143n.
metaphor *metaphor* 519n.
  ornament 574n.
metaphorical
  compared 462adj.
  semantic 514adj.
  figurative 519adj.
metaphrase *copy* 22n.
  translation 520n.
metaphysician
  philosopher 449n.
metaphysics *existence* 1n.
  psychology 447n.
  philosophy 449n.

occultism 984 n.
metapsychological
 paranormal 984 n.
metapsychology
 psychology 447 n.
metastasis change 143 n.
 transference 272 n.
metathesis
 change 143 n.
 inversion 221 n.
 transference 272 n.
 trope 519 n.
metayage
 joint possession 775 n.
métayer
 husbandman 370 n.
 participator 775 n.
metazoon animal 365 n.
mete measure 465 vb.
 mete out 465 vb.
 apportion 783 vb.
metempsychosis
 transformation 143 n.
 reproduction 166 n.
 transference 272 n.
 materiality 319 n.
meteor, meteorite
 wanderer 268 n.

 meteor 321 n.
 luminary 420 n.
meteoric brief 114 adj.
 speedy 277 adj.
 celestial 321 adj.
 luminous 417 adj.
meteorological
 celestial 321 adj.
 airy 340 adj.
meteorologist
 weather 340 n.
 oracle 511 n.
meteorology weather 340 n.
meter meter, gauge 465 n.
metheglin sweet 392 n.
method uniformity 16 n.
 order 60 n.
 arrangement 62 n.
 regularity 81 n.
 campanology 412 n.
 way 624 n.
 means 629 n.
 conduct 688 n.
 ritual 988 n.
methodical
 periodical 141 adj.
 (see method)
Methodism
 Protestantism 976 n.
methodize regularize 62 vb.
 plan 623 vb.
methodological
 rational 475 n.

methodology order 60 n.
Methuselah
 old man 133 n.
metic foreigner 59 n.
 settler 191 n.
 incomer 297 n.
meticulosis strike 145 n.
 slowness 278 n.
meticulous
 attentive 455 adj.
 careful 457 adj.
 accurate 494 adj.
 fastidious 862 adj.
 trustworthy 929 adj.
métier vocation 622 n.
 skill 694 n.
Metonic cycle era 110 n.
metonymy
 substitution 150 n.
 trope 519 n.
metope interval 201 n.
 ornamental art 844 n.
metoposcopy
 hermeneutics 520 n.
 face 237 n.
metre long measure 203 n.
 prosody 593 n.
metric metric 465 adj.
metrical metric 465 adj.
 poetic 593 adj.
metrics measurement 465 n.
 prosody 593 n.
metric system
 metrology 465 n.
metrist poet 573 n.
metro train 274 n.
metrology metrology 465 n.
metronome
 timekeeper 117 n.
 meter 465 n.
metropolis
 magistrature 733 n.
metropolitan
 urban 192 adj.
 central 225 adj.
 governor 741 n.
 ecclesiastical 985 adj.
 ecclesiarch 986 n.
metropolitanate
 parish 985 n.
 church office 985 n.
mettle vigorousness 174 n.
 resolution 599 n.
 affections 817 n.
 courage 855 n.
mettlesome
 vigorous 174 adj.
 active 678 adj.
 lively 819 adj.
 excitable 822 adj.
 courageous 855 adj.

meum et tuum
 property 777 n.
mew doff 229 vb.
 ululate 409 vb.
 imprison 747 vb.
mewl cry 408 vb.
 ululate 409 vb.
mews flat, stable 192 n.
mezzanine
 compartment 194 n.
 layer 207 n.
 theatre 594 n.
mezzo soprano
 vocalist 413 n.
mezzotint
 light contrast 417 n.
 hue 425 n.
 engraving 555 n.
M.I.5 secret service 459 n.
miaow ululation 409 n.
miasma gas 336 n.
 infection 651 n.
 poison 659 n.
miasmal
 harmful 645 adj.
mica
 semitransparency 424 n.
micaceous layered 207 adj.
mi-carême festivity 837 n.
Micawber lateness 136 n.
 negligence 458 n.
Micawberish
 hoping 852 adj.
Michaelmas
 holy-day 988 n.
microbe animalcule 196 n.
microcard record 548 n.
microcosm miniature 196 n.
 universe 321 n.
microfilm camera 442 n.
 record 548 n.
micrography
 micrology 196 n.
 writing 586 n.
micro-inch
 long measure 203 n.
microlith antiquity 125 n.
micrology micrology 196 n.
micrometer
 micrology 196 n.
 meter 465 n.
micrometer-minded
 accurate 494 adj.
micrometric
 accurate 494 adj.
micrometry
 measurement 465 n.
 accuracy 494 n.
micron long measure 203 n.
micro-organism
 animalcule 196 n.

microphone
megaphone 400n.
hearing aid 415n.
telecommunication 531n.
microphotography
micrology 196n.
microscope 442n.
camera 442n.
microscope
micrology 196n.
microscope 442n.
microscopic *small* 33adj.
minute 196adj.
ill-seen 444adj.
microscopy
micrology 196n.
microspectroscope
micrology 196n.
microspore *powder* 332n.
microwave *radiation* 417n.
microzoon
animalcule 196n.
micturition *excretion* 302n.
mid *middle* 70adj.
between 231adv.
Midas *rich man* 800n.
Midas touch
prosperity 730n.
wealth 800n.
mid-course
mid-course 625n.
midday *noon* 128n.
midden *rubbish* 641n.
sink 649n.
midders *obstetrics* 164n.
middle *median* 30adj.
middle 70n., adj.
interim 108n.
narrowing 206n.
centrality 225n.
interjacent 231adj.
mediocre 732adj.
middle age *age* 131n.
Middle Ages
antiquity 125n.
middle class *median* 30adj.
mediocrity 732n.
middle distance
middle point 30n.
middle, in the
centrally 225adv.
middleman
intermediary 231n.
provider 633n.
mediator 720n.
consignee 754n.
tradesman 794n.
middle-of-the-road
neutral 625adj.
middle term *average* 30n.
compromise 770n.

middle-weight
pugilist 721n.
middling *median* 30adj.
inconsiderable 33adj.
not bad 644adj.
imperfect 647adj.
mediocre 732adj.
middy *naval man* 270n.
naval officer 741n.
midge *animalcule* 196n.
fly 365n.
midget *small animal* 33n.
dwarf 196n.
midinette *woman* 373n.
midland *land* 344n.
inland 344n.
midline *middle* 70n.
midmost *middle* 70adj.
interior 224adj.
central 225adj.
midnight *midnight* 129n.
darkness 418n.
midrib *middle* 70n.
centrality 225n.
midriff *partition* 231n.
midshipman
youngster 132n.
naval man 270n.
naval officer 741n.
midships *middle* 70adv.
midst *middle* 70n.
centrally 225adv.
between 231adv.
mid-stream
mid-course 625n.
midsummer *summer* 128n.
midway *midway* 70adv.
midweek *interim* 108n.
intermediate 108adj.
midwife *obstetrics* 164n.
instrument 628n.
doctor 658n.
auxiliary 707n.
midwifery *obstetrics* 164n.
instrumentality 628n.
medical art 658n.
midwinter *winter* 129n.
mien *look* 438n.
mien 445n.
conduct 688n.
might *greatness* 32n.
power 160n.
strength 162n.
be possible 469vb.
might and main
exertion 682n.
might and main, with
strongly 162adv.
violently 176adv.
actively 678adv.
laboriously 682adv.

might have been, the
possibility 469n.
mightiness
(*see* might, mighty)
mighty *great* 32adj.
powerful 160adj.
strong 162adj.
influential 178adj.
huge 195adj.
worshipful 866adj.
proud 871adj.
mignon *favourite* 890n.
mignonette
green colour 432n.
migraine *pang* 377n.
migrant *foreigner* 59n.
wanderer 268n.
incomer 297n.
egress 298n.
bird 365n.
migration *wandering* 267n.
departure 296n.
migratory *travelling* 267adj.
mikado *sovereign* 741n.
mike (*see* microphone)
milady *lady* 373n.
milch-cow
abundance 171n.
cattle 365n.
store 632n.
mild *moderate* 177adj.
warm 379adj.
tasteless 387adj.
lenient 736adj.
inexcitable 823adj.
amiable 884adj.
mildew *destroyer* 168n.
bedim 419vb.
dirt 649n.
dilapidation 655n.
impair 655vb.
blight 659n.
mildewed
antiquated 127adj.
mile *long measure* 203n.
racing 716n.
mileage *distance* 119n.
length 203n.
milepost *signpost* 547n.
Milesian *impure* 951adj.
milestone *degree* 27n.
serial place 73n.
situation 186n.
itinerary 267n.
gauge 465n.
signpost 547n.
miliaria *skin disease* 651n.
milieu *circumstance* 8n.
relation 9n.
locality 187n.
circumjacence 230n.

militancy *bellicosity* 718 n.
  (*see* militant)
militant *active* 678 adj.
  opposing 704 adj.
  quarrelling 709 adj.
  defiant 711 adj.
  attacker 712 n.
  warlike 718 adj.
  militarist 722 n.
  courageous 855 adj.
  inimical 881 adj.
militarism *bellicosity* 718 n.
  brute force 735 n.
militarist *militarist* 722 n.
  tyrant 735 n.
military *warlike* 718 adj.
military service
  warfare 718 n.
militate against
  counteract 182 vb.
  oppose 704 vb.
militia *defender* 713 n.
  army 722 n.
militiaman *soldier* 722 n.
milk *moderator* 177 n.
  milk 301 n.
  fluid 335 n.
  white thing 427 n.
  void 300 vb.
  extract 304 vb.
  waste 334 vb.
  provide 633 vb.
  acquire 771 vb.
  take 786 vb.
milk and honey
  prosperity 730 n.
milk and water
  weak thing 163 n.
  insipidity 387 n.
milk-bar *café* 192 n.
milk-float *cart* 274 n.
milkiness
  semitransparency 424 n.
milkmaid *herdsman* 369 n.
  servant 742 n.
milkman *seller* 793 n.
milk-pail *vessel* 194 n.
milksop *weakling* 163 n.
  ninny 501 n.
  coward 856 n.
  innocent 935 n.
milk-tooth *brief span* 114 n.
  tooth 256 n.
milky *edible* 301 adj.
  semiliquid 354 adj.
  fatty 357 adj.
  semitransparent 424 adj.
  whitish 427 n.
Milky Way *star* 321 n.

glow 417 n.
  luminary 420 n.
mill *roughen* 259 vb.
  notch 260 vb.
  pulverizer 332 n.
  pulverize 332 vb.
  workshop 687 n.
  pugilism 716 n.
mill around
  congregate 74 vb.
  rotate 315 vb.
milldam *lake* 346 n.
millenarian
  improving 654 adj.
  hoper 852 n.
  philanthropist 901 n.
  heretic 977 n.
millenarianism
  aspiration 852 n.
millenary
  fifth and over 99 adj.
millennial *secular* 110 adj.
  future 124 adj.
  promising 852 adj.
  celebrative 876 adj.
  paradisiac 971 adj.
millennium
  over one hundred 99 n.
  period 110 n.
  future state 124 n.
  fantasy 513 n.
  aspiration 852 n.
  heaven 971 n.
miller *pulverizer* 332 n.
millesimal *multifid* 100 adj.
millet *cereal* 301 n.
  grass 366 n.
milliard
  over one hundred 99 n.
milliardaire
  rich man 800 n.
millibar *weather* 340 n.
millimetre
  small quantity 33 n.
  short distance 200 n.
  long measure 203 n.
milliner *clothier* 228 n.
millinery *dressing* 228 n.
milling *edging* 234 n.
  pulverulence 332 n.
  pugilism 716 n.
millionaire *rich man* 800 n.
million, for the
  intelligible 516 adj.
  easy 701 adj.
million, the
  social group 371 n.
  commonalty 869 n.
mill-pond *lake* 346 n.
mill-race *lake* 346 n.
  current 350 n.

millstone *gravity* 322 n.
  pulverizer 332 n.
  encumbrance 702 n.
mill-stream *current* 350 n.
milord *nobleman* 868 n.
milt *fertilizer* 171 n.
  insides 224 n.
mim *affectation* 850 n.
Mimaṃsa *philosophy* 449 n.
mimation *grammar* 564 n.
mime *mimicry* 20 n.
  imitate 20 vb.
  gesticulate 547 vb.
  represent 551 vb.
  actor 594 n.
  stage play 594 n.
  act 594 vb.
mimeograph *copy* 20 vb.
mimesis
  imitation 20 n.
  representation 551 n.
mimetic *dramatic* 594 adj.
mimic *imitate* 20 vb.
  gesticulate 547 vb.
  represent 551 vb.
  actor 594 n.
  satirize 851 vb.
mimicry *mimicry* 20 n.
  (*see* mime, mimic)
mimographer
  dramatist 594 n.
mina *coinage* 797 n.
minacity *threat* 900 n.
minaret
  high structure 209 n.
minatory
  cautionary 664 adj.
  frightening 884 adj.
  threatening 900 adj.
minauderie
  affectation 850 n.
mince *cut, rend* 46 vb.
  move slowly 278 vb.
  dish 301 n.
  pulverize 332 vb.
  be affected 850 vb.
  extenuate 927 vb.
mincing *affected* 850 adj.
  fastidious 862 adj.
mind *be attentive* 455 vb.
  be careful 457 vb.
  look after 457 vb.
  intellect, spirit 447 n.
  opinion 485 n.
  remember 505 vb.
  will 595 n.
  willingness 597 n.
  intention 617 n.
  suffer 825 vb.
  be discontented 829 vb.
  liking 859 n.

dislike 861 vb.
resent 891 vb.
minded
 intending 617 adj.
minder machinist 630 n.
mindful attentive 455 adj.
 careful 457 adj.
 remembering 505 adj.
mindless mindless 448 adj.
 foolish 499 adj.
 forgetful 506 adj.
mind made up bias 481 n.
 resolution 599 n.
mind one's business
 be careful 457 vb.
 do business 622 vb.
mind-reading psychics 984 n.
mind's eye
 imagination 513 n.
mind, to one's
 lovable 887 adj.
mine great quantity 32 n.
 source 156 n.
 produce 164 vb.
 demolish 165 vb.
 lowness 210 n.
 depth 211 n.
 excavation 255 n.
 tunnel 263 n.
 extract 304 vb.
 descend 309 vb.
 darkness 417 n.
 trap 542 n.
 store 632 n.
 impair 655 vb.
 workshop 687 n.
 besiege 712 vb.
 defences 713 n.
 bomb 723 n.
 acquire 771 vb.
 take 786 vb.
 wealth 800 n.
mine-field defences 713 n.
mine host caterer 633 n.
mine-layer warship 722 n.
miner producer 167 n.
 excavator 255 n.
 extractor 304 n.
 artisan 686 n.
 soldiery 722 n.
mineral soft drink 301 n.
 mineral 359 n.
 unthinking 450 adj.
 materials 631 n.
mineralogy
 mineralogy 359 n.
mine-sweeper
 warship 722 n.
mine-thrower gun 723 n.
mingle mix 43 vb.
mingy insufficient 636 adj.

parsimonious 816 adj.
miniate paint 553 vb.
miniature small 33 adj.
 miniature 196 n.
 little 196 adj.
 picture 553 n.
miniaturist artist 556 n.
minicar miniature 196 n.
 automobile 274 n.
minify bate 37 vb.
miniltin small animal 33 n.
minim small quantity 33 n.
 notation 410 n.
 metrology 465 n.
minimal small 33 adj.
 lesser 35 adj.
 exiguous 196 adj.
minimalism
 reformism 654 n.
minimalist moderate 625 n.
 reformer 654 n.
minimize bate 37 vb.
 misjudge 481 vb.
 underestimate 483 vb.
 detract 926 vb.
minimum
 small quantity 33 n.
 lesser 35 adj.
 sufficiency 635 n.
minimus
 small animal 33 n.
 young 130 adj.
mining extraction 304 n.
 descent 309 n.
minion type size 587 n.
 dependant 742 n.
 flatterer 925 n.
minister instrument 628 n.
 agent 686 n.
 manage 689 vb.
 official 690 n.
 envoy 754 n.
 offer worship 981 vb.
 pastor 986 n.
 perform ritual 988 vb.
ministerial
 instrumental 628 adj.
 governmental 733 adj.
 clerical 986 adj.
ministering spirit
 angel 968 n.
ministership
 church office 985 n.
minister to conduce 156 vb.
 look after 457 vb.
 doctor 658 vb.
 minister to 703 vb.
ministration aid 703 n.
 church ministry 985 n.
 ministration 988 n.
ministrone soup 301 n.

ministry vocation 622 n.
 management 689 n.
 aid 703 n.
 clergy 986 n.
minium
 red pigment 431 n.
miniver skin 226 n.
mink skin 226 n.
minnow animalcule 196 n.
minor
 inconsiderable 33 adj.
 lesser 35 adj.
 youth 130 n.
 youngster 132 n.
 harmonic 410 adj.
 unimportant 639 adj.
 mediocre 732 adj.
Minorites monk 986 n.
minority inferiority 35 adv.
 part 53 n.
 fewness 105 n.
 nonage 130 n.
 helplessness 161 n.
minor orders
 holy orders 985 n.
minor premise
 argumentation 475 n.
Minos magistracy 957 n.
 mythic hell 972 n.
minotaur rara avis 84 n.
minster church 990 n.
minstrel musician 413 n.
 poet 593 n.
 entertainer 594 n.
minstrelsy
 musical skill 413 n.
 poetry 593 n.
mint mould 23 n.
 produce 164 vb.
 potherb 301 n.
 workshop 687 n.
 mint 797 vb.
mint condition, in
 new 126 adj.
minted monetary 797 adj.
minting coinage 797 n.
mint master
 moneyer 797 n.
 treasurer 798 n.
minuend subtraction 39 n.
minuet musical piece 412 n.
 dance 837 n.
minus non-existent 2 adj.
 difference 15 n.
 less 35 adv.
 subtracted 39 adj.
 absent 190 adj.
 deficient 307 adj.
 losing 772 adj.
 not owning 774 adj.
 indebted 803 adj.

minuscule *letter* 558n.
minus sign
  punctuation 547n.
minute *period* 110n.
  angular measure 247n.
  measurement 465n.
  record 548 vb.
  compendium 592n.
  (*see* minuteness)
minute-book *record* 548n.
minute-gun
  timekeeper 117n.
  signal 547n.
minute-hand
  timekeeper 117n.
  indicator 547n.
minuteness *smallness* 33n.
  minuteness 196n.
  invisibility 444n.
  attention 455n.
  carefulness 457n.
  diffuseness 570n.
minutiæ *small quantity* 33n.
  particulars 80n.
  trifle 639n.
minx *youngster* 132n.
  insolent person 878n.
  loose woman 952n.
miocene *secular* 110adj.
miracle *unconformity* 84n.
  prodigy 864n.
miracle-making
  thaumaturgy 864n.
miracle-monger
  exaggeration 546n.
miracle-mongering
  sorcery 983n.
miracle-worker
  prodigy 864n.
  sorcerer 983n.
miraculous *unusual* 84adj.
  impossible 470adj.
  wonderful 864adj.
mirage *visual fallacy* 440n.
  appearance 445n.
  error 495n.
  disappointment 509n.
  fantasy 513n.
  deception 542n.
mire *marsh* 347n.
miriness *uncleanness* 649n.
mirror *resemble* 18vb.
  imitate 20vb.
  copy 22n.
  prototype 23n.
  reflection 417n.
  mirror 442n.
  oracle 511n.
  paragon 646n.
  person of repute 866n.
mirror-image

  contrariety 14n.
  reflection 417n.
mirror symmetry
  contrariety 14n.
mirth *merriment* 833n.
miry *marshy* 347adj.
misadapt *mismatch* 25vb.
misaddress *deflect* 282vb.
misadjust *mismatch* 25vb.
misadventure
  eventuality 154n.
  ill fortune 731n.
misalliance *misfit* 25n.
  type of marriage 894n.
misanthrope *shrew* 892n.
  enemy 881n.
  misanthrope 902n.
misanthropic *sullen* 893adj.
misanthropy
  misanthropy 902n.
misapplication
  misinterpretation 521n.
  misrepresentation 552n.
  solecism 565n.
  waste 634n.
  misuse 675n.
  bungling 695n.
  prodigality 815n.
misapplied
  irrelevant 10adj.
misapprehend *err* 495vb.
misapprehension
  misinterpretation 521n.
misappropriation
  misuse 675n.
  peculation 788n.
  arrogation 916n.
misbecome, misbeseem
  be undue 916vb.
misbegotten
  deformed 246adj.
  unsightly 842adj.
  bastard 954adj.
misbehave *be foolish* 499vb.
misbehaviour
  conduct 688n.
  ill-breeding 847n.
  discourtesy 885n.
  wickedness 934n.
  guilty act 936n.
misbelief *unbelief* 486n.
  heterodoxy 977n.
misbeliever
  unbeliever 486n.
  heathen 974n.
  impious person 980n.
miscalculation
  misjudgment 481n.
  mistake 495n.
  inexpectation 508n.
  disappointment 509n.

miscall *misname* 562vb.
miscarriage *failure* 728n.
miscarried
  disappointing 509adj.
miscarry
  be unproductive 172vb.
  be in difficulty 700vb.
  miscarry 728vb.
  have trouble 731vb.
miscast *mismatch* 25vb.
miscegenation
  mixture 43n.
  type of marriage 894n.
miscellaneous *mixed* 43adj.
miscellany, miscellanea
  medley 43n.
  accumulation 74n.
  reading matter 589n.
  anthology 592n.
mischance *ill fortune* 731n.
mischief *destruction* 165n.
  evil 616n.
  waste 634n.
  inutility 641n.
  badness 645n.
  impairment 655n.
  quarrelsomeness 709n.
mischief-maker
  trouble-maker 663n.
  hinderer 702n.
  quarreller 709n.
  agitator 738n.
  evildoer 904n.
mischievous
  harmful 645adj.
  malevolent 898adj.
  wrong 914adj.
  (*see* mischief)
miscible *mixed* 43adj.
miscolour
  misrepresent 552vb.
miscomputation
  misjudgment 481n.
misconceive
  misjudge 481vb.
  err 495vb.
  misinterpret 521vb.
misconception
  misjudgment 481n.
  error 495n.
misconduct
  bungling 695n.
  be unskilful 695vb.
  discourtesy 885n.
  guilty act 936n.
misconjecture
  misjudgement 481n.
misconjugation
  solecism 565n.
misconnection
  irrelation 10n.

misconstruction
  distortion 246 n.
  misjudgment 481 n.
  error 495 n.
  misinterpretation 521 n.
misconstrue distort 246 vb.
  not know 491 vb.
  misinterpret 521 vb.
miscorrection
  misteaching 535 n.
miscount misjudge 481 vb.
  err 495 vb.
  blunder 495 vb.
miscreant
  unbelieving 486 adj.
miscreation
  abnormality 84 n.
misdate misdate 118 vb.
misdealing foul play 930 n.
misdeed guilty act 936 n.
misdemeanant
  offender 904 n.
misdemeanour
  guilty act 936 n.
  lawbreaking 954 n.
misdescribe
  misrepresent 552 vb.
misdevotion impiety 980 n.
misdirect derange 63 vb.
  deflect 282 vb.
  mislead 495 vb.
  be unskilful 695 vb.
misdirection irrelation 10 n.
  distortion 246 n.
  deviation 282 n.
  misteaching 535 n.
  misuse 675 n.
misdoing bungling 695 n.
  wrong 914 n.
  guilty act 936 n.
misdoubt doubt 486 n.
misdoubting
  nervous 854 adj.
miseducate
  misteach 535 vb.
mise-en-scène
  stage set 594 n.
  pageant 875 n.
misemployment
  misuse 675 n.
miser accumulator 74 n.
  niggard 816 n.
miserable
  unimportant 639 adj.
  not nice 645 adj.
  unfortunate 731 adj.
  unhappy 825 adj.
  melancholic 834 adj.
misericorde seat 218 n.
  side-arms 723 n.
  church interior 990 n.

miserly careful 457 adj.
  parsimonious 816 adj.
  avaricious 816 adj.
misery evil 616 n.
  adversity 731 n.
  sorrow 825 n.
  dejection 834 n.
  moper 834 n.
  bore 838 n.
  hopelessness 853 n.
misestimate
  misjudge 481 vb.
misexposition
  misinterpretation 521 n.
  misrepresentation 552 n.
misfeasance
  wrong 914 n.
  lawbreaking 954 n.
misfire bungling 695 n.
  miscarry 728 n.
misfit irrelation 10 n.
  misfit 25 n.
  nonconformist 84 n.
  displacement 188 n.
  bungler 697 n.
misfortune evil 616 n.
misgiving doubt 486 n.
  nervousness 854 n.
misgovern
  be unskilful 695 vb.
  be lax 734 vb.
  oppress 735 vb.
misguidance error 495 n.
  misteaching 535 n.
misguided
  misjudging 481 adj.
  mistaken 495 adj.
  bungled 695 adj.
mishandle ill-treat 645 vb.
  misuse 675 vb.
  be unskilful 695 vb.
mishap eventuality 154 n.
  ill fortune 731 n.
mishit bungling 695 n.
mishmash a mixture 43 n.
  confusion 61 n.
Mishna scripture 975 n.
misinformation
  inexactness 495 n.
  concealment 525 n.
  misteaching 535 n.
  untruth 543 n.
  misrepresentation 551 n.
misinstruction
  misteaching 535 n.
misinterpret
  transform 147 vb.
  distort 246 vb.
  misjudge 481 vb.
  blunder 495 vb.
  misinterpret 521 vb.

  be false 541 vb.
misjoin mismatch 25 vb.
misjoinder misfit 25 n.
misjudge mistime 138 vb.
  not think 450 vb.
  underestimate 483 vb.
  be credulous 487 vb.
  misinterpret 521 vb.
misjudgment
  misjudgment 481 n.
  overestimation 482 n.
  error 495 n.
  unintelligence 499 n.
  bungling 695 n.
  wrong 914 n.
  injustice 914 n.
mislaid misplaced 188 adj.
mislay derange 63 vb.
  lose 772 vb.
mislead deflect 282 vb.
  puzzle 474 vb.
  sophisticate 477 vb.
  mislead 495 vb.
  misteach 535 vb.
  deceive, befool 542 vb.
  obstruct 702 vb.
mislike dislike 861 vb.
mismanage be lax 734 vb.
  (see mismanagement)
mismanagement
  misuse 675 n.
  bungling 695 n.
  dutilessness 918 n.
mismanager
  bungler 697 n.
mismatch mismatch 25 vb.
mismate mismatch 25 vb.
misname misteach 535 vb.
  misname 562 vb.
misnomer name 561 n.
  misnomer 562 n.
misnumber blunder 495 vb.
misogamist enemy 881 n.
  misanthrope 902 n.
misogamy celibacy 895 n.
misogynist enemy 881 n.
  celibate 895 n.
  misanthrope 902 n.
  disapprover 924 n.
misplace derange 63 vb.
  misplace 188 vb.
misplaced irrelevant 10 adj.
  unapt 25 adj.
misplacement
  unconformity 84 n.
  displacement 188 n.
misprint mistake 495 n.
misprision contempt 922 n.
  lawbreaking 954 n.
misprision of treason
  sedition 738 n.

misprize
  underestimate 483 vb.
  not respect 921 vb.
  hold cheap 922 vb.
mispronounce
  solecize 565 vb.
  stammer 580 vb.
mispronunciation
  solecism 565 n.
  inelegance 576 n.
  pronunciation 577 n.
misproportion
  distortion 246 n.
misproportioned
  unsightly 842 adj.
misquotation
  inexactness 495 n.
  misrepresentation 552 n.
misquote
  misinterpret 521 vb.
  be false 541 vb.
misread *blunder* 495 vb.
  misinterpret 521 vb.
misreckon *err* 495 vb.
misreckoning
  misjudgment 481 n.
misreport
  inexactness 495 n.
  misrepresentation 552 n.
  be false 541 vb.
misrepresent
  make unlike 19 vb.
  distort 246 vb.
  sophisticate 477 vb.
  misinterpret 521 vb.
  satirize 851 vb.
misrepresentation
  misteaching 535 vb.
  falsehood 541 n.
  untruth 543 n.
  misrepresentation 552 n.
  calumny 926 n.
misrule *bungling* 695 n.
  anarchy 734 n.
  oppress 735 vb.
miss *be incomplete* 55 vb.
  youngster 132 n.
  be late 136 vb.
  fall short 307 vb.
  lady 373 n.
  blunder 495 vb.
  require 627 vb.
  be unsatisfied 636 vb.
  bungling 695 n.
  fail 728 vb.
  lose 772 vb.
  be discontented 829 vb.
  regret 830 vb.
  desire 859 vb.
  title 870 n.
  loose woman 952 n.

missal *scripture* 975 n.
  prayers 981 n.
  office-book 988 n.
missaying *neology* 560 n.
  solecism 565 n.
missed *remembered* 505 adj.
miss, give it a
  not act 677 vb.
misshape *distort* 246 vb.
  make ugly 842 vb.
misshapen
  amorphous 244 adj.
  deformed 246 adj.
  unsightly 842 adj.
missile *missile* 287 n.
  propulsive 287 adj.
missing *non-existent* 2 adj.
  incomplete 55 adj.
  misplaced 188 adj.
  absent 190 adj.
  disappearing 446 adj.
  unknown 491 adj.
  required 627 adj.
  lost 772 adj.
missing link
  incompleteness 55 n.
  deficit 55 n.
  discontinuity 72 n.
  completion 725 n.
mission *job* 622 n.
  vocation 622 n.
  mandate 751 n.
  envoy 754 n.
  philanthropy 901 n.
  church ministry 985 n.
missionary *preacher* 537 n.
  philanthropist 901 n.
  religious teacher 973 n.
  pastor 986 n.
missionary spirit
  philanthropy 901 n.
  pietism 979 n.
missioner *pastor* 986 n.
missionize *convert* 147 vb.
missive
  correspondence 588 n.
miss nothing
  be attentive 455 vb.
miss out
  be incomplete 55 vb.
  exclude 57 vb.
misspell *misinterpret* 521 vb.
  solecize 565 vb.
misspend
  be prodigal 815 vb.
misstatement
  inexactness 495 n.
  untruth 543 n.
miss the bus
  lose a chance 138 vb.
miss the point

be insensitive 820 vb.
missus *spouse* 894 n.
mist
  insubstantial thing 4 n.
  moisture 341 n.
  cloud 355 n.
  dimness 419 n.
  obfuscation 421 n.
  opacity 423 n.
  blur 440 vb.
  invisibility 444 n.
  uncertainty 474 n.
mistake *mistake* 495 n.
  misinterpretation 521 n.
  solecism 565 n.
  bungling 695 n.
  failure 728 n.
  wrong 914 n.
mistaken
  misjudging 481 adj.
mistaught
  uninstructed 491 adj.
misteach
  sophisticate 477 vb.
  not know 491 vb.
  mislead 495 vb.
  misinterpret 521 vb.
  misteach 535 vb.
  misrepresent 552 vb.
mister *male* 372 n.
  master 741 n.
  title 870 n.
misterm *misname* 562 vb.
misthrow *bungling* 695 n.
mistiming
  intempestivity 138 n.
  inexactness 495 n.
mistiness (*see* misty)
mistitle *misname* 562 vb.
mistral *wind* 352 n.
mistranslate *blunder* 495 vb.
  misinterpret 521 vb.
mistranslated
  inexact 495 adj.
  unmeant 515 adj.
  misinterpreted 521 adj.
mistress *woman* 373 n.
  lady 373 n.
  master 741 n.
  owner 776 n.
  title 870 n.
  loved one 887 n.
  kept woman 952 n.
mistrust *doubt* 486 n.
  nervousness 854 n.
  jealousy 911 n.
mistrustful
  doubting 474 adj.
  unbelieving 486 adj.
misty
  insubstantial 4 adj.

humid 341 adj.
cloudy 355 adj.
dim 419 adj.
opaque 423 adj.
semitransparent 424 adj.
ill-seen 444 adj.
uncertain 474 adj.
puzzling 517 adj.
misunderstand
not know 491 vb.
err 495 vb.
misinterpret 521 vb.
misunderstanding
dissension 709 n.
misunderstood
mistaken 495 adj.
guiltless 935 adj.
misusage *misuse* 675 n.
misuse *force* 176 vb.
waste 634 n., vb.
ill-treat 645 vb.
impairment 655 n.
misuse 675 n., vb.
be unskilful 695 vb.
be severe 735 vb.
prodigality 815 n.
mite *small quantity* 33 n.
small coin 33 n.
child 132 n.
animalcule 196 n.
vermin 365 n.
insufficiency 636 n.
mithridate *antidote* 658 n.
mitigate *bate* 37 vb.
moderate 177 vb.
qualify 468 vb.
make better 654 vb.
relieve 831 vb.
extenuate 927 vb.
mitigatory
qualifying 468 adj.
mitraille
ammunition 723 n.
mitre *badge of rule* 743 n.
vestments 989 n.
mitred *clerical* 986 adj.
mitre-joint *joint* 45 n.
angularity 247 n.
mitten *glove* 228 n.
mix *mix* 43 vb.
combine 50 vb.
jumble 63 vb.
modify 143 vb.
agitate 318 vb.
be sociable 882 vb.
mixed bag
non-uniformity 17 n.
mixed blessing
inexpedience 643 n.
mixer, be a good
be sociable 882 vb.

mix in *add* 38 vb.
mixing-bowl *bowl* 194 n.
mix it *fight* 716 vb.
mixolydian *key* 410 n.
mixture *mixture* 43 n.
combination 50 n.
composition 56 n.
imperfection 647 n.
medicine 658 n.
mixture as before
uniformity 16 n.
recurrence 106 n.
mix-up *confusion* 61 n.
mix with *add* 38 vb.
unite with 45 vb.
mizzen *back* 238 adj.
mizzenmast *poop* 238 n.
mizzle *rain* 350 n., vb.
mnemonic *reminder* 505 n.
mnemonics 505 n.
moa *flightless bird* 365 n.
moan *blow* 352 vb.
faintness 401 n.
cry 408 vb.
be discontented 829 vb.
weep 836 vb.
moat *fence* 235 n.
furrow 262 n.
conduit 351 n.
protection 660 n.
obstacle 702 n.
defences 713 n.
mob *rampage* 61 vb.
crowd 74 n.
multitude 104 n.
be violent 176 vb.
charge 712 vb.
rabble 869 n.
celebrate 876 vb.
gratulate 886 vb.
caress 889 vb.
not respect 921 vb.
disapprove 924 vb.
mobcap *headgear* 228 n.
mobility
changeableness 152 n.
motion 265 n.
moral sensibility 819 n.
mobilization
assemblage 74 n.
preparation 669 n.
war measures 718 n.
mobilize *move* 265 vb.
mob law
government 733 n.
anarchy 734 n.
lawlessness 954 n.
moble *cover* 226 vb.
mobocracy
government 733 n.
mocassin *footwear* 228 n.

mock *simulating* 18 adj.
disbelieve 486 vb.
spurious 542 adj.
befool 542 vb.
laugh 835 vb.
be witty 839 vb.
laughing-stock 851 n.
ridicule 851 n., vb.
shame 867 vb.
not respect 921 vb.
despise 922 vb.
detract 926 vb.
mock-epic *poem* 593 n.
mocker *imitator* 20 n.
(see mock)
mockery
insubstantial thing 4 n.
mimicry 20 n.
impiety 980 n.
(see mock)
mock-heroic *poetic* 593 adj.
funny 849 adj.
derisive 851 adj.
mock-modest
depreciating 483 adj.
affected 850 adj.
mock-up *prototype* 23 n.
modal *conditionate* 7 adj.
circumstantial 8 adj.
harmonic 410 adj.
modality *extrinsicality* 6 n.
modality 7 n.
mode *modality* 7 n.
key 410 n.
practice 610 n.
way 624 n.
fashion 848 n.
model
copy, duplicate 22 n.
prototype 23 n.
living model 23 n.
be example 23 vb.
superior 34 n.
rule 81 n.
example 83 n.
miniature 196 n.
little 196 adj.
efform 243 vb.
comparison 462 n.
show 522 vb.
image 551 n.
represent 551 vb.
art equipment 553 n.
sculpt 554 vb.
plan 623 n.
paragon 646 n.
perfect 646 adj.
plaything 837 n.
person of repute 866 n.
modeller *sculptor* 556 n.
moderate *median* 30 adj.

small 33 adj.
bate 37 vb.
moderate 177 adj., vb.
retard 278 vb.
qualify 468 vb.
moderate 625 n.
imperfect 647 adj.
restrain 747 vb.
cheap 812 adj.
tranquillize 823 vb.
relieve 831 vb.
indifferent 860 adj.
modest 874 adj.
moderation
    counteraction 182 n.
    softness 327 n.
    underestimation 483 n.
    mid-course 625 n.
    sanation 656 n.
    irenics 719 n.
    mediocrity 732 n.
    inexcitability 823 n.
    temperance 942 n.
    (see moderate)
moderations exam. 459 n.
moderator
    nucleonics 160 n.
    moderator 177 n.
    director 690 n.
    mediator 720 n.
    church officer 986 n.
    ecclesiarch 986 n.
modern present 121 adj.
    modern 126 adj.
    progressive 285 n.
    fashionable 848 adj.
modernism
    modernism 126 n.
    art 551 n.
    heterodoxy 977 n.
modernity newness 126 n.
modernize
    modernize 126 vb.
    change, modify 143 vb.
    revolutionize 149 vb.
    make better 654 vb.
    restore 656 vb.
    be in fashion 848 vb.
modest
    inconsiderable 33 adj.
    depreciating 483 adj.
    mediocre 732 adj.
    inglorious 867 adj.
    humble 872 adj.
    disinterested 931 adj.
    (see modesty)
modesty moderation 177 n.
    plainness 573 n.
    artlessness 699 n.
    nervousness 854 n.
    modesty 874 n.

purity 950 n.
modicum
    small quantity 33 n.
    portion 783 n.
modifiable
    changeable 143 adj.
modification
    difference 15 n.
    change 143 n.
    qualification 468 n.
modifier alterer 143 n.
modify make unlike 19 vb.
    (see modification)
modish usual 610 adj.
    fashionable 848 adj.
    reputable 866 adj.
modiste clothier 228 n.
modulate make unlike 19 vb.
    adjust 24 vb.
modulation change 143 n.
    moderation 177 n.
    key 410 n.
module prototype 23 n.
modulus
    numerical element 85 n.
modus operandi way 624 n.
    conduct 688 n.
modus vivendi
    substitute 150 n.
    way 624 n.
mogul sovereign 741 n.
mohair fibre 208 n.
    textile 222 n.
Mohamedan
    religionist 973 n.
mohawk, mohock
    anarch 61 n.
    insolent person 878 n.
    ruffian 904 n.
Mohurram
    anniversary 141 n.
    holy-day 988 n.
moider
    be inattentive 456 vb.
    be uncertain 474 vb.
moidered crazed 503 adj.
moiety part 53 n.
    bisection 92 n.
    portion 783 n.
moil work 682 vb.
moiré iridescent 437 adj.
moist watery 339 adj.
    humid 341 adj.
moisten add water 339 vb.
    moisten 341 vb.
moisture moisture 341 n.
moither (see moider)
moke beast of burden 273 n.
    animal 365 n.
mokes network 222 n.
molar tooth 256 n.

pulverizer 332 n.
molasses sweet 392 n.
mole projection 254 n.
    rodent 365 n.
    grey 429 adj.
    skin disease 651 n.
    safeguard 662 n.
    defences 713 n.
    blemish 845 n.
molecular minute 196 adj.
molecule particle 33 n.
    minuteness 196 n.
    element 319 n.
molehill minuteness 196 n.
    monticle 209 n.
    lowness 210 n.
moleskin textile 222 n.
molest harm 645 vb.
    be obstructive 702 vb.
    torment 827 vb.
    be malevolent 898 vb.
moll woman 373 n.
    fly 365 n.
    kept woman 952 n.
mollification
    moderation 177 n.
    softness 327 n.
    pacification 719 n.
mollusc animal 365 n.
    fish 365 n.
mollycoddle weakling 613 n.
    ninny 501 n.
Moloch
    Semitic gods 967 n.
molten
    liquefied 337 adj.
    fiery 379 adj.
    heated 381 adj.
molten image idol 982 n.
moment juncture 8 n.
    small quantity 33 n.
    date 108 n.
    brief span 114 n.
    instant 116 n.
    occasion 137 n.
    cause 156 n.
    importance 638 n.
momentariness
    instantaneity 116 n.
momentary
    transient 114 adj.
momentous crucial 137 adj.
    eventful 154 adj.
    influential 178 adj.
    important 638 adj.
momentum impulse 279 n.
monachism
    monasticism 985 n.
monad existence 1 n.
    unit 88 n.
    minuteness 196 n.

element 319n.
monandry
type of marriage 894n.
monarch *sovereign* 741n.
possessor 776n.
monarchy
government 733n.
monastery *house* 192n.
retreat 192n.
monastery 986n.
monastic
unwedded 895adj.
monk 986n.
monasticism
seclusion 883n.
celibacy 895n.
monasticism 985n.
monatomic *alone* 88adj.
monetary
monetary 797adj.
monetize *mint* 797vb.
money *means* 629n.
money 797n.
wealth 800n.
money-bag, money-box
pocket 194n.
storage 632n.
treasury 799n.
money-changer
alterer 143n.
merchant 794n.
moneyer 797n.
money-conscious
economical 814adj.
parsimonious 816adj.
moneyer *merchant* 794n.
moneyer 797n.
money for jam
easy thing 701n.
money-grubber
niggard 816n.
egotist 932n.
money-grubbing
acquisition 771n.
(see money-grubber)
money-lender *lender* 784n.
moneyless *poor* 801adj.
money-mad
avaricious 816adj.
money-making
wealth 800n.
money market
finance 797n.
money-saving
economical 814adj.
money-spinner
moneyer 797n.
rich man 800n.
money's worth
price 809n.
monger *seller* 793n.

sell 793vb.
tradesman 794n.
mongol *madman* 504n.
Mongolian *ethnic* 11adj.
mongoose *rodent* 365n.
mongrel *hybrid* 43n.
nonconformist 84n.
dog 365n.
rascally 930adj.
monied *moneyed* 800adj.
moniker *name* 561n.
moniliform *rotund* 252adj.
monism *philosophy* 449n.
monition *hint* 524n.
warning 664n.
monitor *enquire* 459vb.
teacher 537n.
warner 664n.
official 690n.
adviser 691n.
warship 722n.
monitorial
cautionary 664adj.
monitorial system
education 534n.
monitory *predicting* 511adj.
dissuasive 613adj.
cautionary 664adj.
monk *celibate* 895n.
pietist 979n.
monk 986n.
monkey *imitator* 20n.
ram 279n.
monkey 365n.
evildoer 904n.
monkey jacket
tunic 228n.
monkey-trick *foolery* 497n.
revel 837n.
monkey with *impair* 655vb.
monkhood *celibacy* 895n.
monasticism 985n.
monkshood
poisonous plant 659n.
monochord *harp* 414n.
monochromatic
coloured 425adj.
monochrome
achromatism 426n.
painting 553n.
monocle *eyeglass* 442n.
monocracy *despotism* 733n.
monocular
dim-sighted 440adj.
monocycle *bicycle* 274n.
monodrama
stage play 594n.
monody *duet* 412n.
monogamy
type of marriage 894n.
monogram *label* 847n.

initials 558n.
monograph
dissertation 591n.
monolith *uniformity* 16n
coherence 48n.
unit 88n.
monument 548n.
monolithic
simple 44adj.
indivisible 52adj.
dense 324adj.
(see monolith)
monologist
entertainer 594n.
monologue
uniformity 16n.
oration 579n.
soliloquy 585n.
monomachy *duel* 716n.
monomania *attention* 455n.
prejudgment 481n.
mania 503n.
eccentricity 503n.
opiniatry 602n.
monomaniac
madman 504n.
monomaniacal
obsessed 455adj.
monomark *label* 547n.
monophonic
harmonious 410adj.
monophthongization
speech sound 398n.
Monophysitism
heresy 977n.
monoplane *aircraft* 276n.
monopolist
restriction 747n.
egotist 932n.
monopolistic
restraining 747adj.
possessing 773adj.
avaricious 816adj.
selfish 932adj.
monopolize *engross* 449vb.
attract attention 455vb.
appropriate 786vb.
be selfish 932vb.
monopoly *exclusion* 57n.
corporation 708n.
restriction 747n.
possession 773n.
sale 793n.
avarice 816n.
board game 837n.
monorail *train* 274n.
railroad 624n.
monosaccharid
food content 301n.
monostich
conciseness 569n.

monosyllabic
  linguistic 557 adj.
  concise 569 adj.
  taciturn 582 adj.
monosyllable
  spoken letter 558 n.
  word 559 n.
monotheism *deism* 973 n.
Monothelitism
  heresy 977 n.
monotone *uniformity* 16 n.
  musical note 410 n.
  painting 553 n.
monotonous *equal* 28 adj.
  one 88 adj.
  permanent 144 adj.
  feeble 572 adj.
monotony
  uniformity 16 n.
  continuity 71 n.
  recurrence 106 n.
  tedium 838 n.
monotype *breed* 77 n.
  unit 88 n.
  press 587 n.
Monseigneur
  church title 986 n.
monsieur *male* 372 n.
  title 870 n.
Monsignor *title* 870 n.
  church title 986 n.
monsoon *rain* 350 n.
  wind 352 n.
monster
  violent creature 176 n.
  giant 195 n.
  eyesore 842 n.
  prodigy 864 n.
  monster 938 n.
  demon 970 n.
monstrance
  ritual object 988 n.
monstrosity
  unconformity 84 n.
  hugeness 195 n.
  deformity 246 n.
  prodigy 864 n.
monstrous
  exorbitant 32 adj.
  unusual 84 adj.
  huge 195 adj.
  not nice 645 adj.
  ugly 842 adj.
  ridiculous 849 adj.
  wonderful 864 adj.
  heinous 934 adj.
montage *cinema* 445 n.
Montanism *heresy* 977 n.
Montessori method
  education 534 n.
month *period* 110 n.

monthlies
  regular return 141 n.
monthly *seasonal* 141 adj.
  periodically 141 adv.
  journal 528 n.
  usual 610 adj.
monticle *monticle* 209 n.
monument *antiquity* 125 n.
  edifice 164 n.
  tomb 364 n.
  obsequies 364 n.
  reminder 505 n.
  signpost 547 n.
  monument 548 n.
  trophy 729 n.
  honours 866 n.
monumental
  enormous 32 adj.
  large 195 adj.
  tall 209 adj.
  recording 548 adj.
monumental mason
  obsequies 364 n.
  sculptor 556 n.
moo *ululation* 409 n.
mooch *be inactive* 679 vb.
  steal 788 vb.
mood *temperament* 5 n.
  state 7 n.
  change 143 n.
  tendency 179 n.
  grammar 564 n.
  conduct 688 n.
  affections 817 n.
moody *fitful* 142 adj.
  melancholic 834 adj.
  irascible 892 adj.
  sullen 893 adj.
moon *period* 110 n.
  changeable thing 152 n.
  follower 284 n.
  circler 314 n.
  moon 321 n.
  luminary 420 n.
  be inattentive 456 vb.
  be inactive 679 vb.
moonbeam *glimmer* 419 n.
mooncalf *fool* 501 n.
mooning
  abstracted 456 adj.
  loving 887 adj.
moonless *unlit* 418 adj.
moonlight *moon* 321 n.
  light 417 n.
  glimmer 419 n.
moonlight flit
  departure 296 n.
moonlit *undimmed* 417 adj.
moonraker *ninny* 501 n.
moonrise *ascent* 308 n.
moonshine

  insubstantial thing 4 n.
  light 417 n.
  empty talk 515 n.
  fable 543 n.
  pretext 614 n.
  booty 790 n.
moonstone *gem* 844 n.
moon-struck *insane* 503 adj.
moor *tie* 45 vb.
  place 187 vb.
  navigate 269 vb.
  arrive 295 vb.
  (*see* moorland)
moored *fixed* 153 adj.
  quiescent 266 adj.
mooring(s) *cable* 47 n.
  station 187 n.
moorish *marshy* 347 adj.
moorland *space* 183 n.
  high land 209 n.
  marsh 347 n.
  plain 348 n.
moose *deer* 365 n.
moot *moot* 459 adj.
  uncertain 474 adj.
  argue 475 vb.
  propound 512 vb.
  council 692 n.
mooted *topical* 452 adj.
mooter *reasoner* 475 n.
moot point *topic* 452 n.
  question 459 n.
mop *distortion* 246 n.
  hair 259 n.
  drier 342 n.
  cleaning utensil 648 n.
mop and mow
  distort 246 vb.
  goblinize 970 vb.
mope *be dejected* 834 vb.
  be sullen 893 vb.
moped *bicycle* 274 n.
moper *idler* 679 n.
  moper 834 n.
moppet *darling* 890 n.
mopsy *darling* 890 n.
  kept woman 952 n.
mop up *destroy* 165 vb.
  dry 342 vb.
  clean 648 vb.
  carry through 725 vb.
mopus *visionary* 513 n.
  idler 679 n.
  dibs 797 n.
moraine *leavings* 41 n.
  piece 53 n.
  thing transferred 272 n.
  soil 344 n.
moral *judgment* 480 n.
  maxim 496 n.
  commentary 520 n.

phrase 563n.
good 615adj.
advising 691adj.
precept 693n.
reputable 866adj.
ethical 917adj.
pure 950adj.
piety 979n.
morale *obedience* 739n.
manliness 855n.
virtue 933n.
moralistic *judicial* 480adj.
ethical 917adj.
morality (*see* morals)
moralize *judge* 480vb.
teach 534vb.
make better 654vb.
moralizing *advice* 691n.
moral rearmament
virtue 933n.
morals *conduct* 688n.
right 913n.
morals 917n.
virtue 933n.
purity 950n.
moral turpitude
improbity 930n.
morass *marsh* 347n.
moratorium *delay* 136n.
lull 145n.
non-payment 805n.
morbidity *badness* 645n.
ill-health 651n.
morbiferous
infectious 653adj.
morbific *diseased* 651adj.
infectious 653adj.
morbilli *infection* 651n.
mordacity
malevolence 898n.
mordancy (*see* mordant)
mordant *keen* 174adj.
pungent 388adj.
pigment 425n.
forceful 571adj.
disapproving 924adj.
mordent *musical note* 410n.
musical piece 412n.
more *beyond* 34adv.
in addition 38adv.
plural 101adj.
more and more
crescendo 36adv.
more or less
quantitative 26adj.
about 33adv.
nearly 200adv.
moreover
in addition 38adv.
more so *superior* 34adj.
crescendo 36adv.

more than enough
plenteous 635adj.
redundance 637n.
more than ever
greatly 32adv.
morganatic
matrimonial 894adj.
morgue *inactivity* 679n.
cemetery 364n.
moribund *dying* 361adj.
sick 651adj.
morion *headgear* 228n.
armour 713n.
Mormon *religionist* 973n.
polygamist 894n.
Mormons *sect* 978n.
morning *beginning* 68n.
period 110n.
morning 128n.
earliness 135n.
morning after *sequel* 67n.
posteriority 120n.
morning dress
formal dress 228n.
morocco *skin* 226n.
bookbinding 589n.
moron *ignoramus* 493n.
fool 501n.
madman 504n.
moronic *mindless* 448adj.
unintelligent 499adj.
insane 503adj.
moroseness, morosity
unsociability 883n.
sullenness 893n.
misanthropy 902n.
morpheme
part of speech 564n.
morphia *anæsthetic* 375n.
drug 658n.
soporific 679n.
morphine *drug* 658n.
poison 659n.
morphography *form* 243n.
morphology *form* 243n.
biology 358n.
zoology 367n.
linguistics 557n.
etymology 559n.
morris dance *dance* 837n.
morrow *futurity* 124n.
morse *fastening* 47n.
telecommunication 531n.
signal 547n.
morsel *small quantity* 33n.
piece 53n.
mouthful 301n.
mortal *ephemeral* 114adj.
destructive 165adj.
deadly 362adj.
person 371n.

human 371adj.
tedious 838adj.
mortality
transientness 114n.
death, death roll 361n.
mankind 371n.
mortally *extremely* 32adv.
mortal remains
corpse 363n.
mortar *adhesive* 47n.
gun 723n.
mortgage
encumbrance 702n.
security 767n.
lending 784n.
borrowing 785n.
debt 803n.
mortgaged *subject* 745adj.
mortgagee *possessor* 776n.
lender 784n.
creditor 802n.
mortgage, on
pledged 767adj.
mortgagor *owner* 776n.
debtor 803n.
mortician *interment* 364n.
mortiferous *deadly* 362adj.
toxic 653adj.
mortification *decay* 51n.
death 361n.
sorrow 825n.
annoyance 827n.
discontent 829n.
regret 830n.
humiliation 872n.
asceticism 945n.
mortify
cause discontent 829vb.
mortise *join* 45vb.
receptacle 194n.
intromit 231vb.
mortmain, in
retained 778adj.
Morton's fork
dubiety 474n.
argumentation 475n.
mortuary *death* 361n.
interment 364n.
cemetery 364n.
mosaic *non-uniformity* 17n.
combination 50n.
chequer 437n.
picture 553n.
ornamental art 844n.
Mosaic *religious* 973adj.
scriptural 975adj.
mosque
temple, church 990n.
mosquito *fly* 365n.
mosquito net *canopy* 226n.
moss *marsh* 347n.

plant 366n.
greenness 432n.
mossback
laughing-stock 851n.
moss-grown
antiquated 127adj.
dilapidated 655adj.
moss-trooper
soldier 722n.
robber 789n.
mossy *soft* 327adj.
vegetal 366adj.
most *great* 32adj.
mot *maxim* 496n.
witticism 839n.
mote *small thing* 33n.
levity 323n.
dirt 649n.
mote in the eye
prejudice 481n.
motel *inn* 192n.
motet *hymn* 981n.
moth *destroyer* 168n.
blight 659n.
moth-ball
prophylactic 658n.
preserver 666n.
moth-balled
disused 674adj.
moth-eaten
antiquated 127adj.
dirty 649adj.
dilapidated 655adj.
mother *kinsman* 11n.
maternity 169n.
pet 889vb.
philanthropize 897vb.
church title 986n.
nun 986n.
mother earth
abundance 171n.
mythic god 966n.
mothered *born* 360adj.
motherhood *family* 11n.
propagation 164n.
maternity 169n.
life 360n.
motherland
territory 184n.
home 192n.
mother-love *love* 887n.
motherly *parental* 169adj.
loving 887adj.
benevolent 897adj.
mother-of-pearl
variegation 437n.
mother's darling
weakling 163n.
favourite 890n.
Mother's Union
society 708n.

mother superior
ecclesiarch 986n.
nun 986n.
mother tongue
intelligibility 516n.
language 557n.
mother-wit
intelligence 498n.
motif *topic* 452n.
pattern 844n.
motility *motion* 265n.
motion *displacement* 188n.
motion 265n.
cacation 302n.
topic 452n.
gesture 547n.
plan 623n.
activity 678n.
advice 691n.
offer 759n.
request 761n.
motionless *still* 266adj.
inactive 679adj.
motion picture
cinema 445n.
motivate *influence* 178vb.
motivate 612vb.
cause desire 859vb.
motivation *causation* 156n.
motive 612n.
activity 678n.
motivator *motivator* 612n.
director 690n.
adviser 691n.
motive *causation* 156n.
influence 178n.
moving 265adj.
motive 612n.
motiveless
capricious 604adj.
choiceless 606adj.
designless 618n.
motive power *energy* 160n.
motion 265n.
mot juste *accuracy* 494n.
motley *non-uniformity* 17n.
mixed 43adj.
multiform 82adj.
variegation 437n.
motor *causal means* 156n.
strengthen 162vb.
moving 265adj.
automobile 274n.
machine 630n.
motor-car
automobile 274n.
motor-cycle *bicycle* 274n.
motor-cyclist *rider* 268n.
motor-horn
danger signal 665n.
motoring *land travel* 267n.

motorist *driver* 268n.
motorman *driver* 268n.
motor-rally *racing* 716n.
motorway *road* 624n.
mottle *variegate* 437vb.
motto *maxim* 496n.
commentary 520n.
indication 547n.
heraldry 547n.
phrase 563n.
moue *distortion* 246n.
gesture 547n.
affectation 850n.
moujik *husbandman* 370n.
possessor 776n.
mould *modality* 7n.
mould 23n.
decay 51n.
sort 77n.
convert 147vb.
fertilizer 171n.
form 243n.
efform 243vb.
structure 331n.
soil 344n.
represent 551vb.
sculpt 554vb.
dirt 649n.
blight 659n.
decorate 844vb.
mouldable *flexible* 327adj.
moulded on
imitative 20adj.
moulder *decompose* 51vb.
be old 127vb.
sculptor 556n.
be unclean 649vb.
deteriorate 655vb.
mouldiness
dilapidation 655n.
moulding
ornamental art 844n.
mould oneself
do likewise 20vb.
conform 83vb.
mould the figure
cohere 48vb.
moult *doff* 229vb.
mound *bulk* 195n.
monticle 209n.
dome 253n.
defences 713n.
mount *be great* 32vb.
grow 36vb.
unite with 45vb.
be high 209vb.
support 218vb.
inclose 235vb.
ride 267vb.
conveyance 267n.
saddle-horse 273n.

start out 296 vb.
insert 303 vb.
ascend, climb 308 vb.
elevate 310 vb.
break in 369 vb.
prepare 669 vb.
mountain *bulk* 195 n.
high land 209 n.
mountaineer *dweller* 191 n.
traveller 268 n.
climber 308 n.
climb 308 vb.
mountaineering
sport 837 n.
mountainous *great* 32 adj.
large, huge 195 adj.
alpine 209 adj.
mountebank
impostor 545 n.
entertainer 594 n.
mount guard
invigilate 457 vb.
safeguard 660 vb.
mount one's high horse
be proud 871 vb.
mount the throne
take authority 733 vb.
mourn *inter* 364 vb.
lament 836 vb.
mourner *funeral* 364 n.
weeper 836 n.
mournful
distressing 827 adj.
melancholic 834 adj.
mournfulness
sorrow 825 n.
mourning
funeral dress 228 n.
obsequies 364 n.
funereal 364 adj.
black thing 428 n.
lamentation 836 n.
mouse *animalcule* 196 n.
rodent 365 n.
testee 461 n.
hunt 619 vb.
coward 856 n.
humility 872 n.
mouse-like *humble* 872 adj.
mouser *cat* 365 n.
hunter 619 n.
mousse *pudding* 301 n.
pulpiness 356 n.
moustache, moustachio
hair 259 n.
mousy *colourless* 426 adj.
grey 429 adj.
mouth *entrance* 68 n.
maw 194 n.
threshold 234 n.
orifice 263 n.

way in 297 n.
eater 301 n.
gulf 345 n.
voice 577 vb.
orate 579 vb.
mouthful
small quantity 33 n.
mouthful 301 n.
oration 579 n.
mouth-organ *organ* 414 n.
mouthpiece *orifice* 263 n.
air-pipe 353 n.
flute 414 n.
interpreter 520 n.
informant 524 n.
speaker 579 n.
deputy 755 n.
mouth-pipe *air-pipe* 353 n.
mouth-wash
cleanser 648 n.
prophylactic 658 n.
mouthy *rhetorical* 574 adj.
moutonné *arcuate* 253 adj.
movable *moving* 265 adj.
transferable 272 adj.
property 777 n.
move *derange* 63 vb.
début 68 n.
operate 173 vb.
displace 188 vb.
move 265 vb.
transpose 272 vb.
move fast 277 vb.
propel 287 vb.
attract 291 vb.
excrete 302 vb.
touch 378 vb.
propound 512 vb.
gesture 547 n.
motivate 612 vb.
essay 671 n.
action, deed 676 n.
be active 678 vb.
tactics 688 n.
advise 691 vb.
stratagem 698 n.
offer 759 vb.
excite 821 vb.
moveable (*see* movable)
move away *recede* 290 vb.
move in *enter* 297 vb.
moveless *still* 266 adj.
movement
transition 147 n.
motion 265 n.
cacation 302 n.
melody 410 n.
musical piece 412 n.
dramaturgy 594 n.
action 676 n.
activity 678 n.

party, society 708 n.
move out *relinquish* 621 vb.
mover *cause* 156 n.
producer 167 n.
influence 178 n.
motivator 612 n.
doer 676 n.
adviser 691 n.
move up
bring near 200 vb.
move with the times
modernize 126 vb.
change 143 vb.
progress 285 vb.
movie *cinema* 445 n.
movie-goer *spectator* 441 n.
moving pavement
transport 272 n.
carrier 273 n.
conveyor 274 n.
moving picture
cinema 445 n.
moving staircase
transport 272 n.
carrier 273 n.
conveyor 274 n.
lifter 310 n.
mow *cut* 46 vb.
shorten 204 vb.
distortion 246 n.
smooth 258 vb.
cultivate 370 vb.
store 632 n., vb.
mow down *demolish* 165 vb.
slaughter 362 vb.
mower *husbandman* 370 n.
mowing *product* 164 n.
moxa *burning* 381 n.
Mr. and Mrs.
spouse 894 n.
Mr. Facing-both-ways
tergiversator 603 n.
Mrs. Grundy
etiquette 848 n.
prude 950 n.
Mr. X
unknown thing 491 n.
no name 562 n.
much *great quantity* 32 n.
many 104 adj.
much ado *activity* 678 n.
much cry and little wool
overestimation 482 n.
disappointment 509 n.
boast 877 n.
much-married
married 894 adj.
muchness, much of a
median 30 adj.
imperfect 647 adj.
mediocre 732 adj.

much obliged
grateful 907adj.
much of, make
make important 638vb.
much the same
similar 18adj.
mucilage *semiliquidity* 354n.
mucilaginous *viscid* 354adj.
muck *rubbish* 641n.
dirt 649n.
muck-rake *defame* 926vb.
muck-raker *reformer* 654n.
defamer 926n.
muck up *jumble* 63vb.
make unclean 649vb.
impair 655vb.
mucky *dirty* 649adj.
mucoid *viscid* 354adj.
mucous *viscid* 354adj.
mucronate *sharp* 256adj.
mucus *fluid* 335n.
semiliquidity 354n.
dirt 649n.
mud *moisture* 341n.
marsh 347n.
semiliquidity 354n.
dirt 649n.
muddied *opaque* 423adj.
muddle *disorder* 61n.
confusion 61n.
derange 63vb.
distract 456vb.
not discriminate 464vb.
predicament 700n.
failure 728n.
muddled
ill-reasoned 477adj.
muddle-head *fool* 501n.
muddle-headed
ill-reasoned 477adj.
unintelligent 499adj.
muddy *humid* 341adj.
marshy 347adj.
semiliquid 354adj.
thicken 354vb.
dim 419adj.
opaque 423adj.
dirty 649adj.
make unclean 649vb.
mudguard *shelter* 662n.
mudhopper *ship* 275n.
mudlark *dirty person* 649n.
low fellow 869n.
mud pack
beautification 843n.
mud-slinging
detraction 926n.
muff *glove* 228n.
warm clothes 381n.
be clumsy 695vb.
bungler 697n.

muffetee *glove* 228n.
muffin *pastry* 301n.
muffle *cover* 226vb.
silence 399vb.
mute 401vb.
conceal 525vb.
make mute 578vb.
muffled *muted* 401adj.
non-resonant 405adj.
occult 523adj.
voiceless 578adj.
muffled drum
obsequies 364n.
non-resonance 405n.
signal 547n.
muffler *shawl* 228n.
warm clothes 381n.
mufti *non-uniformity* 17n.
informal dress 228n.
judge 957n.
theologian 973n.
mug *cup* 194n.
face 237n.
ninny 501n.
study 536vb.
dupe 544n.
mugger *reptile* 365n.
learner 538n.
muggins *ninny* 501n.
muggy *sealed off* 264adj.
humid 341adj.
mugient *ululant* 409adj.
mugwump
tergiversator 603n.
muktar *consignee* 754n.
law agent 958n.
mukti *liberation* 746n.
mulatto *hybrid* 43n.
mulberry *purple* 434adj.
mulch *covering* 226n.
mulct *punish* 963vb.
mulctable
punishable 963adj.
mulctuary *punitive* 963adj.
mule *hybrid* 43n.
nonconformist 84n.
footwear 228n.
animal 365n.
opinionist 602n.
muleteer *driver* 268n.
muliebrity *female* 373n.
mulish *equine* 273adj.
obstinate 602adj.
mull *textile* 222n.
projection 254n.
sweeten 392vb.
think 449vb.
be attentive 455vb.
study 536vb.
muller *pulverizer* 332n.
mullet *fish food* 301n.

table fish 365n.
mulligatawny *soup* 301n.
mulligrubs
sullenness 893n.
mullioned *crossed* 222adj.
mullock *rubbish* 641n.
mulmull *textile* 222n.
multicoloured
variegated 437adj.
multifarious
irrelative 10adj.
different 15adj.
non-uniform 17adj.
multiform 82adj.
multiferous
multitudinous 104adj.
multifid *fragmentary* 53adj.
multifid 100adj.
multiform *different* 15adj.
non-uniform 17adj.
mixed 43adj.
multiform 82adj.
changeful 152adj.
multilateral *lateral* 239adj.
angulated 247adj.
contractual 765adj.
multilingual
linguistic 557adj.
multimillion
over one hundred 99n.
multitude 104n.
multinomial *many* 104adj.
multiparous *prolific* 171adj.
multipartite
disjunct 46adj.
multiple *quantity* 26n.
numerical element 85n.
plural 101adj.
many 104adj.
multiple personality
spirit 447n.
psychopathy 503n.
multiplex *multiform* 82adj.
multiplicand
numerical element 85n.
multiplicate
multiform 82adj.
multiplication
increase 36n.
numerical operation 86n.
propagation 164n.
reproduction 166n.
productiveness 171n.
multiplication sign
punctuation 547n.
multiplication table
counting instrument 86n.
multiplicity *plurality* 101n.
multitude 104n.
multiplier
numerical element 85n.

multiply *copy* 20 vb.
  be many 104 vb.
  (*see* multiplication)
multipurpose
  general 79 adj.
  useful 640 adj.
multiracial *mixed* 43 adj.
multiracial state
  medley 43 n.
multisection
  multisection 100 n.
multitude
  great quantity 32 n.
  crowd 74 n.
  plurality 101 n.
  multitude 104 n.
multitudinous
  frequent 139 adj.
multum in parvo
  compendium 592 n.
multure *pulverulence* 332 n.
mum *voiceless* 578 adj.
  taciturn 582 adj.
mum, be *keep secret* 525 vb.
mumble *chew* 301 vb.
  stammer 580 vb.
mumbo-jumbo *god* 966 n.
  idolatry 982 n.
  spell 983 n.
mummer *impostor* 545 n.
  actor 594 n.
mummery *foolery* 497 n.
  sham 542 n.
  festivity 837 n.
  ostentation 875 n.
  false piety 980 n.
mummify *dry* 342 vb.
  inter 364 vb.
  preserve 666 vb.
mummy *maternity* 169 n.
  corpse 363 n.
mummy-case
  interment 364 n.
mummy-chamber
  tomb 364 n.
mummy-cloth
  wrapping 226 n.
mumpish
  melancholic 834 adj.
mumps *infection* 651 n.
mumpsimus
  laughing-stock 851 n.
munch *chew* 301 vb.
mundane *selfish* 932 adj.
  irreligious 974 adj.
munerary
  rewarding 962 adj.
mungo *fibre* 208 n.
municipal *regional* 184 adj.
municipality
  jurisdiction 955 n.

municipalize *convey* 780 vb.
  appropriate 786 vb.
munificence
  liberality 813 n.
muniment *record* 548 n.
  defences 713 n.
  title-deed 767 n.
muniment room
  recorder 549 n.
munitions *means* 629 n.
  defence 713 n.
  arm 723 n.
munshi *teacher* 537 n.
munsiff *officer* 741 n.
  judge 957 n.
mural *picture* 553 n.
murder *killing* 362 n.
  murder 362 vb.
  solecize 565 vb.
  cruel act 898 n.
  execute 963 vb.
murderee *corpse* 363 n.
murderer *murderer* 362 n.
murderous
  murderous 362 adj.
murex *red pigment* 431 n.
muricate *sharp* 256 adj.
  rough 259 adj.
murk *darkness* 418 n.
  dimness 419 n.
murky *dense* 324 adj.
  dark 418 adj.
  opaque 423 adj.
  cheerless 834 adj.
murmur *flow* 350 vb.
  faintness 401 n.
  danger signal 665 n.
  deprecation 762 n.
  discontent 829 n.
murmuring
  disobedience 738 n.
murrain *plague* 651 n.
  animal disease 681 n.
murrey *red colour* 431 n.
muscadine *fragrant* 396 adj.
muscat *fruit* 301 n.
muscle *ligature* 47 n.
  power 160 n.
  vitality 162 n.
  exertion 682 n.
muscle-bound
  unwieldy 195 adj.
  rigid 326 adj.
muscular *stalwart* 162 adj.
muse *be inattentive* 456 vb.
  meditate 449 vb.
Muses *choir* 413 n.
  literature 557 n.
  poetry 593 n.
  lesser god 967 n.
musette *flute* 414 n.

museum
  accumulation 74 n.
  antiquity 125 n.
  exhibit 522 n.
  collection 632 n.
museum piece
  archaism 127 n.
  exhibit 522 n.
  exceller 644 n.
  laughing-stock 851 n.
mush *semiliquidity* 354 n.
  pulpiness 356 n.
mushroom *upstart* 126 n.
  new 126 adj.
  high structure 209 n.
  round 252 vb.
  vegetable 301 n.
  plant 366 n.
  radiation 417 n.
  poison 659 n.
  bomb 723 n.
mushy *soft* 327 adj.
  semiliquid 354 adj.
  pulpy 356 adj.
music *music* 412 n.
  musical instrument 414 n.
musical
  melodious 410 adj.
  musical 412 adj.
  musicianly 413 adj.
  stage play 594 n.
  pleasurable 826 adj.
musical appreciation
  musical skill 413 n.
musical box
  gramophone 414 n.
musical comedy
  vocal music 412 n.
  stage play 594 n.
musical glasses *gong* 414 n.
musical instrument
  musical instrument 414 n.
musical notation
  notation 410 n.
musical note
  musical note 410 n.
music hall *theatre* 594 n.
  place of amusement 837 n.
musician *musician* 413 n.
musicianly
  musicianly 413 adj.
musicianship
  musical skill 413 n.
musing *thought* 449 n.
musk *scent* 396 n.
musket *fire-arm* 723 n.
musketeer *shooter* 287 n.
  soldiery 722 n.
musketry *propulsion* 287 n.
  bombardment 712 n.
  art of war 718 n.

arm 723 n.
musky *fragrant* 396 adj.
Muslim, Moslem
   religionist 973 n.
muslin *textile* 222 n.
   semitransparency 424 n.
mussel *fish food* 301 n.
   table fish 365 n.
mussiness
   amorphism 244 n.
must, mast
   lecherous 951 adj.
must, a *necessity* 596 n.
   requirement 627 n.
mustang *saddle-horse* 273 n.
mustard *pungency* 388 n.
   condiment 389 n.
   yellowness 433 n.
mustard gas *gas* 336 n.
   poison 659 n.
   weapon 723 n.
mustard plaster
   surgical dressing 658 n.
mustardseed
   minuteness 196 n.
muster *assemblage* 74 n.
   statistics 86 n.
   number 86 vb.
   pageant 875 n.
muster courage
   take courage 855 vb.
muster-roll
   statistics 86 n.
   list 87 n.
musty *fetid* 397 adj.
   dirty 649 adj.
Musulman *religionist* 973 n.
mutability
   transientness 114 n.
   change 143 n.
   changeableness 152 n.
mutation *change* 143 n.
   conversion 147 n.
mutatis mutandis
   (*see* change)
mute *funeral* 364 n.
   silent 399 adj.
   silencer 401 n.
   mute 401 vb.
   non-resonance 405 n.
   mute 414 n.
   spoken letter 558 n.
   aphony 578 n.
   taciturn 582 adj.
   actor 594 n.
   weeper 836 n.
mutilate *deform* 244 vb.
   make ugly 842 vb.
   torture 963 vb.
mutilated *imperfect* 647 adj.
mutilation

incompleteness 55 n.
impairment 655 n.
mutineer *revolter* 738 n.
   schismatic 978 n.
mutinous
   disobedient 738 adj.
   dutiless 918 adj.
   (*see* mutiny)
mutiny *strike* 145 n.
   resist 715 vb.
   revolt 738 n.
   dutilessness 918 n.
mutism *helplessness* 161 n.
   aphony 578 n.
mutt *dog* 365 n.
   (*see* fool)
mutter *blow* 352 vb.
   sound faint 401 vb.
   cry 408 vb.
   stammer 580 vb.
   be sullen 893 vb.
   threaten 900 vb.
muttering
   danger signal 665 n.
mutton *meat* 301 n.
mutton-chops *hair* 259 n.
mutual *correlative* 12 adj.
   interchanged 151 adj.
mutual agreement
   compact 765 n.
mutual assistance
   co-operation 706 n.
mutual concession
   mid-course 625 n.
   co-operation 706 n.
   compromise 770 n.
mutualism
   joint possession 775 n.
mutuality *correlation* 12 n.
   interchange 151 n.
mutualize *correlate* 12 vb.
   socialize 775 vb.
muzzle *disable* 161 vb.
   projection 254 n.
   orifice 263 n.
   stopper 264 n.
   silence 399 vb.
   make mute 587 vb.
   hinder 702 vb.
   fire-arm 723 n.
   restrain 747 vb.
   fetter 748 n.
muzzle-loader
   fire-arm 723 n.
muzzy *tipsy* 949 adj.
myalgia
   rheumatism 651 n.
mycology *botany* 368 n.
my lord *male* 372 n.
   title 870 n.
mynheer *title* 870 n.

myocarditis
   heart disease 651 n.
myology *structure* 331 n.
myopia, myosis
   dim sight 440 n.
myopic *dim-sighted* 440 adj.
   misjudging 481 adj.
myriad
   over one hundred 99 n.
   multitude 104 n.
myrmidon *soldier* 722 n.
myrrh *resin* 357 n.
   scent 396 n.
myrtle *tree* 366 n.
   greenness 432 n.
   love emblem 887 n.
myself *identity* 13 n.
   self 80 n.
   subjectivity 320 n.
mystagogic
   revelational 975 adj.
mystagogue *teacher* 537 n.
   leader 690 n.
mysteries *religion* 973 n.
   act of worship 981 n.
   rite 988 n.
mysterious
   unusual 84 adj.
   invisible 444 adj.
   uncertain 474 adj.
   unknown 491 adj.
   puzzling 517 adj.
   occult 523 adj.
   concealed 525 adj.
   imperspicuous 568 adj.
   wonderful 864 adj.
   cabbalistic 984 adj.
mystery *invisibility* 444 n.
   unknown thing 491 n.
   latency 523 n.
   secrecy 525 n.
   secret, enigma 530 n.
   stage play 594 n.
   business 622 n.
   rite 988 n.
mystery man
   latency 523 n.
mystic *spectator* 441 n.
   inexpressible 517 adj.
   occult 523 adj.
   religious 973 adj.
   revelational 975 adj.
   pietist 979 n.
   worshipper 981 n.
   devotional 981 adj.
   occultist 984 n.
mystical *divine* 968 adj.
   (*see* mystic)
mysticism
   meditation 449 n.
   latency 523 n.

religion 973 n.
piety 979 n.
occultism 984 n.
mystification
sophistry 477 n.
unmeaningness 515 n.
unintelligibility 517 n.
concealment 525 n.
misteaching 535 n.
mystify *puzzle* 474 vb.
deceive 542 vb.
mystique *prestige* 866 n.
cult 981 n.
myth *fantasy* 513 n.
fable 543 n.
narrative 590 n.
mythical, mythic
imaginary 513 adj.
theotechnic 966 adj.
mythical being
mythical being 970 n.
mythological
olden 127 adj.
erroneous 495 adj.
imaginary 513 adj.
untrue 543 adj.
descriptive 590 adj.
theotechnic 966 adj.
mythologist *liar* 545 n.
narrator 590 n.
mythology *tradition* 127 n.
anthropology 371 n.
fable 543 n.
narrative 590 n.
mythomania
falsehood 541 n.

N

nab *ensnare* 542 vb.
arrest 747 vb.
take 786 vb.
nabob *rich man* 800 n.
nacelle *airship* 276 n.
nacre *variegation* 437 n.
nadir *inferiority* 35 n.
extremity 69 n.
serial place 73 n.
zero 103 n.
lowness 210 n.
depth 211 n.
base 214 n.
nag *saddle-horse* 273 n.
incite 612 vb.
bicker 709 vb.
animate 821 vb.
torment 827 vb.
enrage 891 vb.
Nagari *letter* 558 n.
Naiad *sea-nymph* 343 n.
nymph 967 n.

mythical being 970 n.
nail *affix* 45 vb.
fastening 47 n.
long measure 203 n.
hanger 217 n.
sharp point 256 n.
perforator 263 n.
pierce 263 vb.
tobacco 388 n.
tool 630 n.
nail-brush
cleansing utensil 648 n.
nail-file *smoother* 258 n.
cosmetic 843 n.
nail polish *cosmetic* 843 n.
nails *hardness* 326 n.
weapon 723 n.
nippers 778 n.
naive *credulous* 487 adj.
ignorant 491 adj.
foolish 499 adj.
artless 699 adj.
naked *simple* 44 adj.
uncovered 229 adj.
visible 443 adj.
undisguised 522 adj.
vulnerable 661 adj.
nakedness *purity* 950 n.
name *class* 62 vb.
auspicate 68 vb.
inform 524 vb.
indicate 547 vb.
word 559 n.
name 561 n., vb.
commission 751 vb.
repute 866 n.
accuse 928 vb.
name and address
label 547 n.
name 561 n.
name-board *label* 547 n.
name-day
special day 876 n.
name-giver
nomenclator 561 n.
nameless
unconformable 84 adj.
anonymous 562 adj.
inglorious 867 adj.
namely *namely* 80 adv.
name of, in the
in aid of 703 adv.
by authority 733 adv.
name-plate *label* 547 n.
namesake *name* 561 n.
naming *identification* 547 n.
nomenclature 561 n.
naming 561 adj.
nankeen *textile* 222 n.
nanny *protector* 660 n.
domestic 742 n.

retainer 742 n.
keeper 749 n.
naos *holy place* 990 n.
nap *hair* 259 n.
texture 331 n.
sleep 679 n., vb.
card game 837 n.
napalm *fuel* 385 n.
bomb 723 n.
nape *rear* 238 n.
napery *cleaning cloth* 648 n.
Napier's bones
counting instrument 86 n.
napiform *rotund* 252 adj.
napkin *cleaning cloth* 648 n.
napless *hairless* 229 adj.
Napoleonic *warlike* 718 adj.
nappe *descent* 309 n.
waterfall 350 n.
napping
abstracted 456 adj.
sleepy 679 adj.
nappy *loincloth* 228 n.
downy 259 adj.
drunk 949 adj.
narcissism *vanity* 873 n.
love 887 n.
selfishness 932 n.
Narcissus *a beauty* 841 n.
vain person 873 n.
narcolepsy
insensibility 375 n.
narcosis *helplessness* 161 n.
insensibility 375 n.
narcotic *lenitive* 177 adj.
anæsthetic 375 n.
toxic 653 adj.
drug 658 n.
nard *unguent* 357 n.
narghile *tobacco* 388 n.
nark *informer* 524 n.
accuser 928 n.
narration
remembrance 505 n.
information 524 n.
description 590 n.
narrative *record* 548 n.
narrative 590 n.
narrator *narrator* 590 n.
narrow *small* 33 adj.
tighten 45 vb.
make smaller 198 vb.
narrow 206 adj.
narrow-minded 481 adj.
restraining 747 adj.
prohibit 757 vb.
narrow down
simplify 44 vb.
converge 293 vb.
narrow-mindedness
narrow mind 481 n.

narrowness
 contraction 198 n.
 narrowness 206 n.
narrows
 narrowness 206 n.
narrow squeak
 escape 667 n.
nasal *speech sound* 398 n.
 vocal 577 adj.
 stammering 580 adj.
nasality *stridor* 407 n.
nasalize *stammer* 580 vb.
nascent *beginning* 68 adj.
nastiness *bad taste* 847 n.
 discourtesy 885 n.
 (*see* nasty)
nasty *inferior* 35 adj.
 unsavoury 391 adj.
 fetid 397 adj.
 not nice 645 adj.
 unclean 649 adj.
 insalubrious 653 adj.
 unpleasant 827 adj.
 ugly 842 adj.
 hateful 888 adj.
 malevolent 898 adj.
 threatening 900 adj.
 impure 951 adj.
nasty type *bad man* 938 n.
natal *first* 68 adj.
natation *aquatics* 269 n.
natatorium *ablution* 648 n.
nation *nation* 371 n.
national *ethnic* 11 adj.
 regional 184 adj.
 native 191 adj.
 national 371 adj.
 subject 742 n.
national dress *livery* 547 n.
national flag *talisman* 983 n.
National Guard
 defender 713 n.
 army 722 n.
nationalism
 particularism 80 n.
 nation 371 n.
 patriotism 901 n.
nationalist *patriot* 901 n.
nationalistic *biased* 481 adj.
 patriotic 901 adj.
nationality
 consanguinity 11 n.
 subjection 745 n.
 (*see* nationalism)
nationalization
 association 706 n.
nationalize
 socialize 775 vb.
 appropriate 786 vb.
national service
 war measures 718 n.

nation-state *nation* 371 n.
nation-wide *universal* 79 adj.
native *genetic* 5 adj.
 intrinsic 5 adj.
 ingredient 58 adj.
 special 80 adj.
 native 191 n., adj.
 social group 371 n.
 artless 699 adj.
native land *home* 192 n.
native state
 undevelopment 670 n.
nativity *origin* 68 n.
 date 108 n.
 propagation 164 n.
 life 360 n.
Nativity *holy-day* 988 n.
natty *clean* 648 adj.
 personable 841 adj.
natural *real* 1 adj.
 substantial 3 adj.
 lifelike 18 adj.
 agreeing 24 adj.
 typical 83 adj.
 material 319 adj.
 musical note 410 n.
 probable 471 adj.
 true, genuine 494 adj.
 fool 501 n.
 madman 504 n.
 plain 573 adj.
 elegant 575 adj.
 descriptive 590 adj.
 spontaneous 609 adj.
 usual 610 adj.
 artless 699 adj.
 friendly 880 adj.
natural bent
 aptitude 694 n.
natural child
 bastardy 954 n.
natural history
 biology 358 n.
naturalist *biology* 358 n.
naturalistic
 representing 551 adj.
naturalization
 conformity 83 n.
 conversion 147 n.
 location 187 n.
 reception 299 n.
 habituation 610 n.
 freedom 744 n.
naturalized *native* 191 adj.
naturally
 consequently 157 adv.
 skilfully 694 adv.
 rightly 913 adv.
naturalness
 adaptation 24 n.
 plainness 573 n.

artlessness 699 n.
natural selection
 biology 358 n.
nature *essence* 1 n.
 character 5 n.
 composition 56 n.
 tendency 179 n.
 matter 319 n.
 truth 494 n.
 habit 610 n.
 affections 817 n.
nature cure *therapy* 658 n.
nature god
 mythic god 966 n.
nature study *biology* 358 n.
naturism *uncovering* 229 n.
naught *insubstantiality* 4 n.
 zero 103 n.
 (*see* nought)
naughtiness
 disobedience 738 n.
 wickedness 934 n.
 guilty act 936 n.
naughty *unchaste* 951 adj.
nausea *voidance* 300 n.
 indigestion 651 n.
 painfulness 827 n.
 tedium 838 n.
 dislike 861 n.
 hatred 888 n.
nauseant *cathartic* 658 n.
nauseate
 be unpalatable 391 n.
 displease 827 vb.
 cause discontent 829 vb.
 be tedious 838 vb.
 cause dislike 861 vb.
 excite hate 888 vb.
nauseated
 vomiting 300 adj.
nauseous *unsavoury* 391 n.
 not nice 645 adj.
 unclean 649 adj.
 unpleasant 827 adj.
 tedious 838 adj.
 disliked 861 adj.
 hateful 888 adj.
nautch *dance* 837 vb.
nautch-girl *jumper* 312 n.
 entertainer 594 n.
 dancing 837 n.
nautical *seafaring* 269 adj.
 seamanlike 270 adj.
 marine 275 adj.
nautical almanac
 chronology 117 n.
 guide-book 524 n.
naval *seafaring* 269 adj.
 seamanlike 270 adj.
 marine 275 adj.
 warlike 718 adj.

naval man
  naval man 270n.
nave *middle* 70n.
  centrality 225n.
  church interior 990n.
navel *middle* 70n.
  centrality 225n.
navigable *deep* 211adj.
  seafaring 269adj.
navigate *navigate* 269vb.
  orientate 281vb.
navigator *navigator* 270n.
  aeronaut 271n.
  director 690n.
navvy *worker* 686n.
navy *shipping* 275n.
  blue 435adj.
  navy 722n.
Navy List *directory* 87n.
nawab *potentate* 741n.
  nobleman 868n.
nay *negation* 533n.
  refusal 760n.
nay rather
  contrarily 14adv.
Nazarene *religionist* 973n.
Nazarites
  non-Christian sect 978n.
Nazism *brute force* 735n.
N.C.O. *army officer* 741n.
Neanderthal Mân
  mankind 371n.
neap, neap tide
  decrease 37n.
near *akin* 11adj.
  future 124adj.
  early 135adj.
  impending 155adj.
  near 200adj.
  approach 289vb.
  parsimonious 816adj.
nearly *almost* 33adv.
nearness *similarity* 18n.
  nearness 200n.
  contiguity 202n.
near side *sinistrality* 242n.
near-sightedness
  dim sight 440n.
near thing *draw* 28n.
  short distance 200n.
  escape 667n.
neat *unmixed* 44adj.
  orderly 60adj.
  cattle 365n.
  careful 457adj.
  plain 573adj.
  concise 569adj.
  elegant 575adj.
  clean 648adj.
  skilful 694adj.
  personable 841adj.

intoxicating 949adj.
neaten
  arrange, unravel 62vb.
  make better 654vb.
  beautify 841vb.
neat-fingered
  skilful 694adj.
nebula *nebula* 321n.
  cloud 355n.
nebular *dim* 419adj.
  celestial 321adj.
nebulosity (*see* nebulous)
nebulous *celestial* 321adj.
  cloudy 355adj.
  dim 419adj.
  puzzling 517adj.
necessaries
  requirement 627n.
necessarily
  consequently 157adv.
  necessarily 596adv.
  in need 627adv.
  on terms 766adv.
necessary *certain* 473adj.
  necessary 596adj.
  choiceless 606adj.
  required 627adj.
  important 638adj.
  compelling 740adj.
necessary, a
  necessity 596n.
  requirement 627n.
necessary house
  latrine 649n.
necessitarian
  fatalist 596n.
necessitarianism
  necessity 596n.
necessitate
  predestine 155vb.
  make certain 473vb.
  necessitate 596vb.
  require 627vb.
  compel 740vb.
necessitous
  necessitous 627adj.
  poor 801adj.
necessitude *necessity* 596n.
necessity *destiny* 155n.
  cause 156n.
  certainty 473n.
  necessity 596n.
  no choice 606n.
  requirement 627n.
  needfulness 627n.
  compulsion 740n.
  poverty 801n.
neck *bond* 47n.
  contraction 198n.
  narrowness 206n.
  supporter 218n.

pillar 218n.
  conduit 351n.
  bridge 624n.
  caress 889vb.
neck and crop
  completely 54adv.
neck and neck
  equal 28adj.
  synchronous 123adj.
neckband *neckwear* 228n.
  loop 250n.
neckcloth *neckwear* 228n.
necking *endearment* 889n.
necklace *neckwear* 228n.
  loop 250n.
  jewellery 844n.
neck of land *land* 344n.
neck or nothing
  resolutely 599adv.
necrologist
  obsequies 364n.
necrologue
  obsequies 364n.
necrology *death roll* 361n.
  biography 590n.
necromancer
  conjuror 545n.
  sorcerer 983n.
necromancy *sorcery* 983n.
necrophilia
  abnormality 84n.
necropolis
  cemetery 364n.
necropsy *death* 361n.
  inquest 364n.
necrosis *decay* 51n.
nectar *liquor* 301n.
  savouriness 390n.
  sweet 392n.
need *deficit* 55n.
  shortcoming 307n.
  requirement 627n.
  scarcity 636n.
  adversity 731n.
  poverty 801n.
  desire 859n.
needful *required* 627adj.
needful, the *funds* 797n.
need, in
  necessitous 627adj.
  in need 627adv.
  poor 801adj.
neediness *poverty* 801n.
needle *sharp point* 256n.
  prickle 256n.
  perforator 263n.
  sailing aid 269n.
  indicator 547n.
  engraving 555n.
  directorship 689n.
  torment 827vb.

enrage 891 vb.
needles *nervousness* 854 n.
needless *superfluous* 637 adj.
 rash 857 adj.
needlewoman *artisan* 686 n.
needlework
 needlework 844 n.
needling *therapy* 658 n.
needy *poor* 801 adj.
ne'er-do-well
 desperado 857 n.
 vicious 934 adj.
 bad man 938 n.
nefarious
 disreputable 867 adj.
 wrong 914 adj.
 heinous 934 adj.
negate *nullify* 2 vb.
 confute 479 vb.
 (*see* negation)
negation *contrariety* 14 n.
 counter-evidence 467 n.
 unbelief 486 n.
 dissent 489 n.
 negation 533 n.
 recantation 603 n.
 rejection 607 n.
 opposition 704 n.
 abrogation 752 n.
 refusal 760 n.
negative *nullify* 2 vb.
 copy 22 n.
 prototype 23 n.
 imperfect 647 adj.
 unsuccessful 728 adj.
 (*see* negation)
negativeness
 non-existence 2 n.
negatory
 countervailing 467 adj.
 negative 533 adj.
negatron *element* 319 n.
neglect *disorder* 61 n.
 lose a chance 138 vb.
 be inattentive 456 vb.
 negligence 458 n.
 be loth 598 vb.
 avoid 620 vb.
 dilapidation 655 n.
 non-preparation 670 n.
 not use 674 vb.
 inaction 677 n.
 non-completion 726 vb.
 not observe 769 vb.
 rashness 857 n.
 dutilessness 918 n.
 disrespect 921 n.
neglected
 undervalued 483 adj.
neglectful *negligent* 458 adj.
 apathetic 820 adj.

négligé *informal dress* 228 n.
negligence *negligence* 458 n.
 inexactness 495 n.
 sluggishness 679 n.
 laxity 734 n.
 indifference 860 n.
 guilty act 936 n.
 (*see* neglect)
negligent *negligent* 458 adj.
 forgetful 506 adj.
 clumsy 695 adj.
 (*see* negligence)
negligible
 inconsiderable 33 adj.
 unimportant 639 adj.
negotiable
 transferable 272 adj.
 possible 469 adj.
 expedient 642 adj.
 transferred 780 adj.
negotiate *accord* 24 vb.
 pass 305 vb.
 do business 622 vb.
 co-operate 706 vb.
 deputize 755 vb.
 contract 765 vb.
 make terms 766 vb.
 bargain 791 vb.
negotiation
 conference 584 n.
 mediation 720 n.
 (*see* negotiate)
negotiator
 intermediary 231 n.
 mediator 720 n.
 consignee 754 n.
 envoy 754 n.
 signatory 765 n.
negress *negro* 428 n.
negrito *ethnic* 11 adj.
 negro 428 n.
negro *negro* 428 n.
negroid *ethnic* 11 adj.
 black 428 adj.
negrophobia
 prejudice 481 n.
 phobia 854 n.
negus *liquor* 301 n.
 sovereign 741 n.
neigh *ululate* 409 vb.
neighbour *be near* 200 vb.
 friend 880 n.
neighbourhood
 locality 187 n.
 near place 200 n.
 circumjacence 230 n.
neighbourly *aiding* 703 adj.
 sociable 882 adj.
neither *neither* 606 adv.
neither here nor there
 irrelevant 10 adj.

neither one thing nor the
  other
 nonconformist 84 n.
 neutral 625 adj.
nem. con.
 unanimously 488 adv.
Nemesis
 trouble-maker 663 n.
 retaliation 714 n.
 avenger 910 n.
 justice 913 n.
 punishment 963 n.
nenia *lament* 836 n.
neocene *secular* 110 adj.
neolalia *neology* 560 n.
neolithic *secular* 110 adj.
neological *modern* 126 adj.
 neological 560 adj.
neologism *newness* 126 n.
 neology 560 n.
neologist *modernist* 126 n.
 dialect 560 n.
neology *neology* 560 n.
neon *air* 340 n.
 luminescent 420 adj.
neonomianism
 newness 126 n.
 abrogation 752 n.
neophyte
 changed person 147 n.
 beginner 538 n.
 pietist 979 n.
Neo-Platonism
 philosophy 449 n.
neoteric *modern* 126 adj.
neoterism *newness* 126 n.
 neology 560 n.
nepenthe *drug* 658 n.
nephalism *sobriety* 948 n.
nephew *kinsman* 11 n.
nephology *cloud* 355 n.
ne plus ultra
 superiority 34 n.
 completeness 54 n.
 extremity 69 n.
 farness 199 n.
 limit 236 n.
 perfection 646 n.
 completion 725 n.
 fashion 848 n.
nepotism *injustice* 914 n.
 improbity 930 n.
Neptune *mariner* 270 n.
 planet 321 n.
 sea-god 343 n.
 mythic god 966 n.
 Olympian god 967 n.
Neptunian
 planetary 321 adj.
Nereid *satellite* 321 n.
 sea-nymph 343 n.

nymph 967 n.
nerve *strengthen* 162 vb.
  courage 855 n.
  give courage 855 vb.
  sauciness 878 n.
nerveless *impotent* 161 adj.
  weak 163 adj.
  feeble 572 adj.
  irresolute 601 adj.
nerve-racking
  distressing 827 adj.
  frightening 854 adj.
nerves *psychopathy* 503 n.
  excitability 822 n.
  nervousness 854 n.
nervous *impotent* 161 adj.
  weak 163 adj.
  agitated 318 adj.
  distracted 456 adj.
  expectant 507 adj.
  forceful 571 adj.
  irresolute 601 adj.
  avoiding 620 adj.
  lively 819 adj.
  excitable 822 adj.
  nervous 854 adj.
  cowardly 856 adj.
  cautious 858 adj.
nervous breakdown
  helplessness 161 n.
  psychopathy 503 n.
nervous disorder
  psychopathy 503 n.
nervousness (*see* nervous)
nervous tic *spasm* 318 n.
nervy (*see* nerves)
nescience *ignorance* 491 n.
nest *group* 74 n.
  focus 76 n.
  seedbed 156 n.
  nest 192 n.
  dwell 192 vb.
  sit down 311 vb.
  refuge 662 n.
nest-egg *store* 632 n.
  wealth 800 n.
nestle *dwell* 192 vb.
  be safe 660 vb.
  caress 889 vb.
nestling *youngling* 132 n.
  bird 365 n.
Nestor *old man* 133 n.
  sage 500 n.
  adviser 691 n.
Nestorianism *heresy* 977 n.
net *remaining* 41 adj.
  bring together 74 vb.
  receptacle 194 n.
  network 222 n.
  inclosure 235 n.
  trap 542 n.

hunt 619 vb.
  acquire 771 vb.
  receive 782 vb.
  take 786 vb.
net-ball *ball game* 837 n.
nether *low* 210 adj.
nethermost
  undermost 214 adj.
nether-world
  the dead 361 n.
  hell 972 n.
netting *network* 222 n.
nettle *prickle* 256 n.
  bane 659 n.
  hurt 827 vb.
  huff 891 vb.
nettlerash
  formication 378 n.
network *correlation* 12 n.
  gap 201 n.
  network 222 n.
  texture 331 n.
neuralgia *pang* 377 n.
neurasthenic *insane* 503 adj.
neuritis *pang* 377 n.
neurologist *doctor* 658 n.
neurology *structure* 331 n.
neuropath *madman* 504 n.
  sick person 651 n.
  doctor 658 n.
neuropathy
  psychopathy 503 n.
neurosis *psychopathy* 503 n.
neuro-surgeon *doctor* 658 n.
neurotic *insane* 503 adj.
  madman 504 n.
neuter *generic* 77 adj.
  eunuch 161 n.
  impotent 161 adj.
  grammatical 564 adj.
neutral *median* 30 adj.
  inert 175 adj.
  moderate 177 adj.
  grey 429 adj.
  choiceless 606 adj.
  avoiding 620 adj.
  neutral 625 adj.
  non-active 677 adj.
  peaceful 717 adj.
  mediocre 732 adj.
  independent 744 adj.
  cautious 858 adj.
  indifferent 860 adj.
  just 913 adj.
  disinterested 931 adj.
neutralization
  compensation 31 n.
  counteraction 182 n.
neutralize *disable* 161 vb.
  weaken 163 vb.
  counteract 182 vb.

remedy 658 vb.
neutrino *particle* 33 n.
neutron *particle* 33 n.
  element 319 n.
névé *ice* 380 n.
never *never* 109 adv.
never-ending
  perpetual 115 adj.
  prolix 570 adj.
  uncompleted 726 adj.
never-failing
  successful 727 adj.
never-never system
  borrowing 785 n.
never-resting
  industrious 678 adj.
never say die
  persevere 600 vb.
nevertheless
  nevertheless 468 adv.
never the same
  non-uniform 17 adj.
  changeful 152 adj.
new *first* 68 adj.
  new 126 adj.
  early 135 adj.
  unknown 491 adj.
  unhabituated 611 adj.
new arrival *intruder* 59 n.
  aftercomer 67 n.
  posteriority 120 n.
  arrival 295 n.
  incomer 297 n.
new birth *life* 360 n.
  revival 656 n.
  sanctity 979 n.
new-born *new* 126 adj.
  infantine 132 adj.
new-born babe
  innocent 935 n.
new broom
  busy person 678 n.
new-comer *intruder* 59 n.
  aftercomer 67 n.
  incomer 297 n.
new deal
  apportionment 783 n.
New Dealer *reformer* 654 n.
newel-post *pillar* 218 n.
newfangled
  unusual 84 adj.
  modern 126 adj.
  changeable 143 adj.
  neological 560 adj.
  fashionable 848 adj.
Newgate *prison* 748 n.
Newgate calendar
  biography 590 n.
  legal trial 959 n.
New Jerusalem
  Heaven 971 n.

holy place 990n.
new leaf
  amendment 654n.
new life *revival* 656n.
new look *modernism* 126n.
newly-wed *spouse* 894n.
  married 894adj.
new man
  changed person 147n.
new-model
  revolutionize 149vb.
  transform 147vb.
  rectify 654vb.
newness
  non-imitation 21n.
  beginning 68n.
  newness 126n.
news *topic* 452n.
  information 524n.
  news 529n.
news-agent
  newsmonger 529n.
news business
  the press 528n.
newscast
  publication 528n.
  publicity 528n.
  news 529n.
newsletter *publicity* 528n.
  the press 528n.
newsman
  newsmonger 529n.
  chronicler 549n.
newsmonger
  inquisitor 453n.
  informant 524n.
  newsmonger 529n.
newspaper *the press* 528n.
newspeak *neology* 560n.
newsprint
  stationery 586n.
  paper 631n.
newsreel *cinema* 445n.
  publicity 528n.
  news 529n.
news-value *news* 529n.
news-vendor
  newsmonger 529n.
newsy *informative* 524adj.
  loquacious 581adj.
newt *frog* 365n.
New Testament
  scripture 975n.
new version *variant* 15n.
New Year
  anniversary 141n.
next *sequent* 65n.
  subsequent 120adj.
  futurity 124n.
  contiguously 202adv.
next door *near place* 200n.

next friend *deputy* 755n.
  close friend 880n.
next of kin *kinsman* 11n.
next step *progression* 285n.
next world *destiny* 155n.
  the dead 361n.
nexus *bond* 47n.
niagara *waterfall* 350n.
nib *extremity* 69n.
  vertex 213n.
  sharp point 256n.
  stationery 586n.
nibble *mouthful* 301n.
  eat 301vb.
  taste 386vb.
  be duped 544vb.
  endearment 889n.
nice *pleasant* 376adj.
  savoury 390adj.
  careful 457adj.
  discriminating 463adj.
  accurate 494adj.
  not bad 644adj.
  clean 648adj.
  pleasurable 826adj.
  beautiful 841adj.
  tasteful 846adj.
  fastidious 862adj.
  amiable 884adj.
nicety *differentiation* 15n.
  carefulness 457n.
  discrimination 463n.
  good taste 846n.
  fastidiousness 862n.
niche *place* 185n.
  compartment 194n.
  shelf 218n.
  angularity 247n.
  cavity 255n.
  hiding-place 527n.
  honours 866n.
nick *cut* 46vb.
  notch 260n.,vb.
  mark 547vb.
  wound 655vb.
  steal 788vb.
nickel *small coin* 33n.
  coinage 797n.
nickelodeon
  gramophone 414n.
nickname *name* 561n.
  misnomer 562n.
nick of time
  occasion 137n.
  opportunity 137n.
nicotine *tobacco* 388n.
  poison 659n.
nictitation *dim sight* 440n.
nidget *coward* 856n.
nidification *nest* 192n.
nidor *odour* 394n.

niece *kinsman* 11n.
  woman 373n.
niello *black pigment* 428n.
niffy *fetid* 397adj.
  odorous 394adj.
niggard *niggard* 816n.
  egotist 932n.
niggardly
  insufficient 636adj.
  parsimoniously 816adv.
  selfish 932adj.
nigger *negro* 428n.
  busy person 678n.
nigger in the woodpile
  latency 523n.
  hider 527n.
  slyboots 698n.
nigger minstrel
  vocalist 413n.
  entertainer 594n.
niggler *detractor* 926n.
niggling *trivial* 639adj.
  disapprobation 924n.
nigh *almost* 33adv.
  nigh 200adv.
night *darkness* 418n.
  (*see* evening)
night-blindness
  blindness 439n.
  dim sight 440n.
nightcap
  nightwear 228n.
  valediction 296n.
  potion 301n.
  soporific 679n.
night club
  place of amusement 837n.
nightfall *evening* 129n.
  darkness 418n.
nightgown, nightshirt
  nightwear 228n.
night-hag *sorceress* 983n.
nightingale *bird* 365n.
  vocalist 413n.
night life *festivity* 837n.
night-light *torch* 420n.
nightly *vespertine* 129adj.
  seasonal 141adj.
nightmare *pain* 377n.
  fantasy 513n.
  false alarm 615n.
  suffering 825n.
  intimidation 854n.
  demon 970n.
night-soil *dirt* 649n.
night-time *evening* 129n.
night-watch *period* 110n.
  midnight 129n.
  armed force 722n.
night-watchman
  protector 660n.

keeper 749 n.
nigrescence, nigritude
  blackness 428 n.
nigrosine
  black pigment 428 n.
nihilism *extinction* 2 n.
  disorder 61 n.
  anarchy 734 n.
  sedition 738 n.
nihilist *anarch* 61 n.
  destroyer 168 n.
  revolter 738 n.
  evildoer 904 n.
  irreligionist 974 n.
nihilistic *violent* 176 adj.
nihil obstat *permit* 756 n.
nil *non-existence* 2 n.
  zero 103 n.
nil admirari
  be insensitive 820 vb.
  indifference 860 n.
  non-wonder 865 n.
  detraction 926 n.
nilometer
  hygrometry 341 n.
  meter 465 n.
nimble *speedy* 277 adj.
  active 678 adj.
nimble-witted
  intelligent 498 adj.
nimbus *light* 417 n.
  cloud 355 n.
  honours 866 n.
nimiety *redundance* 637 n.
nincompoop *ninny* 501 n.
nine days' wonder
  insubstantial thing 4 n.
  brief span 114 n.
  prodigy 864 n.
ninepins *series* 71 n.
  ball game 837 n.
nine points of the law
  possession 773 n.
nineteenth hole
  refreshment 685 n.
nineteen to the dozen
  swiftly 277 adv.
ninny *ninny* 501 n.
ninon *textile* 222 n.
Niobe *weeper* 836 n.
nip *make smaller* 198 vb.
  shorten 204 vb.
  make thin 206 vb.
  notch 260 vb.
  move fast 277 vb.
  potion 301 n.
  pang 377 n.
  touch 378 vb.
  refrigerate 382 vb.
  blight 659 n.
  hinder 702 vb.

endearment 889 n.
nip in the bud
  suppress 165 vb.
  hinder 702 vb.
nipper *youngster* 132 n.
nippers *cross* 222 n.
  extractor 304 n.
  eyeglass 442 n.
  tool 630 n.
  nippers 778 n.
nipping *cold* 380 adj.
nipple *bosom* 253 n.
nippy *vigorous* 174 adj.
  active 678 adj.
  servant 742 n.
nirvana *extinction* 2 n.
  divineness 965 n.
  heaven 971 n.
nit *animalcule* 196 n.
  vermin 365 n.
  dirt 649 n.
nitre *pungency* 388 n.
nitrogen *air* 340 n.
nitro-glycerine
  explosive 723 n.
niveous *cold* 380 adj.
  white 427 adj.
nix *zero* 103 n.
nixie *mythical being* 970 n.
Nizam *potentate* 741 n.
no *no* 489 adv.
  nay 533 adv.
  refusal 760 n.
no account, of
  unimportant 639 adj.
  unrespected 921 adj.
  contemptible 922 adj.
no admission *exclusion* 57 n.
Noah's Ark *medley* 43 n.
  accumulation 74 n.
  ship 275 n.
  cattle pen 369 n.
nob *head* 213 n.
  fop 848 n.
  aristocrat 868 n.
no-ball *failure* 728 n.
nobble *disable* 161 vb.
  impair 655 vb.
  take 786 vb.
  steal 788 vb.
nobilitate *dignify* 866 vb.
nobility *superiority* 34 n.
  genealogy 169 n.
  bigwig 638 n.
  élite 644 n.
  beauty 841 n.
  aristocracy 868 n.
  probity 929 n.
  disinterestedness 931 n.
  virtues 933 n.
noble *important* 638 adj.

coinage 797 n.
  liberal 813 adj.
  impressive 821 adj.
  splendid 841 adj.
  well-bred 848 adj.
  worshipful 866 adj.
  renowned 866 adj.
  nobleman 868 n.
  noble 868 adj.
  proud 871 adj.
  honourable 929 adj.
  (see nobility)
nobleman *nobleman* 868 n.
noblesse *aristocracy* 868 n.
nobody
  non-existence 2 n.
  insubstantiality 4 n.
  zero 103 n.
  nobody 190 n.
  nonentity 639 n.
  commoner 869 n.
nobody's
  unpossessed 774 adj.
nobody's business
  irrelation 10 n.
nobody's darling
  hateful object 888 n.
nobody's fool *sage* 500 n.
no business
  irrelation 10 n.
no change *identity* 13 n.
  permanence 144 n.
no chicken *aged* 131 adj.
  adult 134 n.
no conjuror *dunce* 501 n.
  bungler 697 n.
noctambulist
  pedestrian 268 n.
noctiluca *glimmer* 419 n.
  glow-worm 420 n.
noctivagant
  vespertine 129 adj.
  travelling 267 adj.
  dark 418 adj.
nocturnal *black* 428 adj.
  dark 418 adj.
  vespertine 129 adj.
nocturne
  musical piece 412 n.
  picture 553 n.
  art subject 553 n.
nod *obeisance* 311 n.
  oscillate 317 vb.
  be inattentive 456 vb.
  be neglectful 458 vb.
  assent 488 n., vb.
  hint 524 n.
  gesture 547 n.
  sleep 679 vb.
  be fatigued 684 vb.
  command 737 n., vb.

permit 756 vb.
consent 758 vb.
courteous act 884 n.
respects 920 n.
approve 923 vb.
nodding *pendent* 217 adj.
noddle *head* 213 n.
noddy *ninny* 501 n.
node *joint* 45 n.
swelling 253 n.
uranometry 321 n.
nodosity *swelling* 253 n.
roughness 259 n.
nodular *rough* 259 adj.
nodule *swelling* 253 n.
Noel *holy-day* 988 n.
noes, the *dissentient* 489 n.
noesis *intellect* 447 n.
nog *liquor* 301 n.
noggin *cup* 194 n.
potion 301 n.
no go *shortcoming* 307 n.
failure 728 n.
no good *profitless* 641 adj.
bad 645 adj.
nohow *impossibly* 470 adv.
no ice, cut
have no repute 867 vb.
noise *sound* 398 n.
loudness 400 n.
discord 411 n.
proclaim 528 vb.
rumour 529 n.
indication 547 n.
noise abatement
faintness 401 n.
noiseless *silent* 399 adj.
noises off *mimicry* 20 n.
concomitant 89 n.
representation 551 n.
dramaturgy 594 n.
noisome *fetid* 397 adj.
bad, harmful 645 adj.
unclean 649 adj.
baneful 659 adj.
noisy *great* 32 adj.
loud 400 adj.
no joke *reality* 1 n.
important matter 638 n.
nolens volens
necessarily 596 adv.
by force 740 adv.
nolle prosequi
abrogation 752 n.
no love lost
dissension 709 n.
hatred 888 n.
nomad *extraneous* 59 adj.
nonconformist 84 n.
travelling 267 adj.
wanderer 268 n.

nomadism *wandering* 267 n.
no-man *eunuch* 161 n.
no man's land
territory 184 n.
emptiness 190 n.
intermediary 231 n.
battleground 724 n.
non-ownership 774 n.
nomarch *governor* 741 n.
no matter *trifle* 639 n.
nom de guerre
misnomer 562 n.
nom de plume
misnomer 562 n.
nomenclator
nomenclator 561 n.
nomenclature
identification 547 n.
linguistics 557 n.
nomenclature 561 n.
nominal
insubstantial 4 adj.
powerless 161 adj.
indicating 547 adj.
verbal 559 adj.
named 561 adj.
trivial 639 adj.
nominalism
philosophy 449 n.
nomination *choice* 605 n.
nomenclature 561 n.
mandate 751 n.
nominee *delegate* 754 n.
consignee 754 n.
nomology
jurisprudence 953 n.
nomothetic
directing 689 adj.
legal 953 adj.
non-acceptance
rejection 607 n.
refusal 760 n.
non-adherence
non-observance 769 n.
non-adhesive
non-adhesive 49 adj.
smooth 258 adj.
non-adjustment
inexactness 495 n.
non-admission
exclusion 57 n.
disapprobation 924 n.
non-adult
immature 670 adj.
nonage *nonage* 130 n.
helplessness 161 n.
nonagenarian
old man 133 n.
non-aggression *peace* 717 n.
non-alignment
freedom 744 n.

non-appealable
commanding 737 adj.
non-appearance
invisibility 444 n.
non-approval
rejection 607 n.
disapprobation 924 n.
non-association
unwillingness 598 n.
opposition 704 n.
non-attachment
freedom 744 n.
non-attendance
absence 190 n.
non-belief *unbelief* 485 n.
non-causal *casual* 159 adj.
nonce, for the
singly 88 adv.
at present 121 adv.
opportunely 137 adv.
incidentally 137 adv.
nonce-word
non-uniformity 17 n.
word 559 n.
neology 560 n.
nonchalance
negligence 458 n.
moral insensibility 820 n.
inexcitability 823 n.
indifference 860 n.
non-clergiable *laical* 987 adj.
non-clerical *laical* 987 adj.
non-combatant
pacifist 717 n.
non-commissioned officer
army officer 741 n.
non-committal
reticent 525 adj.
no choice 606 n.
avoiding 620 adj.
mid-course 625 n.
neutral 625 adj.
cautious 858 adj.
indifferent 860 adj.
non-compliance
dissent 489 n.
disobedience 738 n.
refusal 760 n.
non-observance 769 n.
nonconformist
nonconformist 84 n.
unconformable 84 adj.
deviating 282 adj.
dissentient 489 n.
free man 744 n.
non-observant 769 adj.
heterodox 977 adj.
schismatic 978 n.
nonconformity
difference 15 n.
unconformity 84 n.

non-observance 769 n.
sectarianism 978 n.
non-consummation
divorce 896 n.
non-cooperation
dissent 489 n.
unwillingness 598 n.
avoidance 620 n.
opposition 704 n.
dissension 709 n.
resistance 715 n.
disobedience 738 n.
dutilessness 918 n.
non-cooperator
dissentient 489 n.
opponent 705 n.
non-credal
irreligious 974 adj.
nondescript
unconformable 84 adj.
non-design *chance* 159 n.
non-design 618 n.
none *zero* 103 n.
church service 988 n.
non-ego *extrinsicality* 6 n.
non-entitlement
undueness 916 n.
nonentity
non-existence 2 n.
insubstantial thing 4 n.
weakling 163 n.
nonentity 639 n.
object of scorn 867 n.
nones *date* 108 n.
non-essential
extrinsic 6 adj.
irrelevance 10 n.
unimportant 639 adj.
nonesuch
supreme 34 adj.
exceller 644 n.
paragon 646 n.
none the worse
restored 656 n.
non-existence
non-existence 2 n.
insubstantiality 4 n.
disappearance 446 n.
non-extremist
moderate 625 n.
nonfeasance
non-observance 769 n.
non-friction
smooth 258 adj.
non-fulfilment
incompleteness 55 n.
shortcoming 307 n.
disappointment 509 n.
insufficiency 636 n.
non-completion 726 n.
failure 728 n.

non-observance 769 n.
non-functional
useless 641 adj.
ornamental 844 adj.
non-immunity
vulnerability 661 n.
non-inflammable
incombustible 382 adj.
non-intellectual
mindless 448 adj.
non-interference
negligence 458 n.
freedom 744 n.
non-intervention
avoidance 620 n.
peace 717 n.
non-involvement
avoidance 620 n.
peace 717 n.
freedom 744 n.
disinterestedness 931 n.
nonius *gauge* 465 n.
non-juror *dissentient* 489 n.
schismatic 978 n.
non-liability
non-liability 919 n.
non-mandatory
voluntary 597 adj.
non-observance
inattention 456 n.
negligence 458 n.
non-observance 769 n.
non-occupancy
non-ownership 774 n.
non-ownership
non-ownership 774 n.
non-pacific
quarrelling 709 adj.
contending 716 adj.
nonpareil *type size* 587 n.
exceller 644 n.
paragon 646 n.
non-participating
inactive 679 adj.
non-partisan *wise* 498 adj.
independent 744 adj.
non-party *assented* 488 adj.
non-payment *delay* 136 n.
non-payment 805 n.
non-performance
non-completion 726 n.
non-observance 769 n.
dutilessness 918 n.
nonplus *dubiety* 474 n.
puzzle 474 vb.
confute 479 vb.
predicament 700 n.
be difficult 700 vb.
defeat 728 n.
non-practising
unconformable 84 adj.

irreligious 974 adj.
impious 980 adj.
non-professional
ignorant 491 adj.
unskilled 695 adj.
bungler 697 n.
layman 987 n.
non-profitmaking
disinterested 931 adj.
non-provision
non-preparation 670 n.
non-recognition
prohibition 757 n.
schism 978 n.
non-recovery *loss* 772 n.
non-recurrent
discontinuous 72 adj.
non-residence
absence 190 n.
non-resistance
concurrence 181 n.
submission 721 n.
obedience 739 n.
non-satisfaction
insufficiency 636 n.
nonsense *absurdity* 497 n.
connotation 514 n.
silly talk 515 n.
trifle 639 n.
non sequitur
irrelevance 10 n.
discontinuity 72 n.
sophism 477 n.
non-significant
unmeaning 515 adj.
non-skid *dry* 342 adj.
non-smoker *train* 274 n.
non-standard
abnormal 84 adj.
non-starter
slowcoach 278 n.
loser 728 n.
non-sterile
infectious 653 adj.
non-stop
continuous 71 adj.
perpetual 115 adj.
frequent 139 adj.
unceasing 146 adj.
vehicular 274 adj.
loquacious 581 adj.
non-suit *defeat* 728 n.
condemn 961 vb.
non-supporter
disapprover 924 n.
non-theological
irreligious 974 adj.
non-traditional
modern 126 adj.
non-transferable
retained 778 adj.

non-transparent
  opaque 423 adj.
non-U *ill-bred* 847 adj.
  plebeian 869 adj.
non-uniform
  non-uniform 17 adj.
non-uniformity
  fitfulness 142 n.
  changeableness 152 n.
non-use *non-use* 674 n.
non-violence
  moderation 177 n.
  peace 717 n.
non-vitaminous
  insalubrious 653 adj.
non-voter
  disapprover 924 n.
non-voting
  choiceless 606 adj.
non-wonder
  non-wonder 865 n.
noodle *ninny* 501 n.
nook *place* 185 n.
  compartment 194 n.
  angularity 247 n.
  hiding-place 527 n.
noology *intellect* 447 n.
no omission *inclusion* 78 n.
noon, noonday
  noon 128 n.
  light 417 n.
noose *halter* 47 n.
  trap 542 n.
  means of execution 964 n.
no other *identity* 13 n.
no purpose, to
  uselessly 641 adv.
  unsuccessfully 728 vb.
no quarter
  pitilessness 906 n.
no question
  certainly 473 adv.
N or M *everyman* 79 n.
norm *average* 30 n.
  rule 81 n.
  paragon 646 n.
  precept 693 n.
normal *average* 30 n.
  median 30 adj.
  typical 83 adj.
  (*see* normality)
normalcy *regularity* 81 n.
normality *regularity* 81 n.
  sanity 502 n.
  right 913 n.
normalize
  make uniform 16 vb.
  regularize 62 vb.
  make conform 83 vb.
normal school
  training school 539 n.

normative *regular* 81 adj.
  formative 243 adj.
  educational 534 adj.
Norns *fate* 596 n.
  mythic god 966 n.
north *be high* 209 vb.
  compass point 281 n.
northern lights
  heavens 321 n.
  glow 417 n.
  luminary 420 n.
northing *bearings* 186 n.
North Pole *coldness* 380 n.
North Star *star* 321 n.
  signpost 547 n.
northwester *gale* 352 n.
no score *zero* 103 n.
nose *face, prow* 237 n.
  protuberance 254 n.
  person 371 n.
  smell 394 vb.
  detective 459 n.
nosebag *bag* 194 n.
nose-dive *aeronautics* 271 n.
  descent 309 n.
  plunge 313 n.
nosegay *bunch* 74 n.
  fragrance 396 n.
  ornamentation 844 n.
noseless *odourless* 394 adj.
nose out *be curious* 453 vb.
nose-ring *jewellery* 844 n.
nose to tail
  continuously 71 adv.
nosology *pathology* 651 n.
nostalgia *suffering* 825 n.
  regret 830 n.
  melancholy 834 n.
  desire 859 n.
nostology
  gerontology 131 n.
nostril *orifice* 263 n.
  air-pipe 353 n.
  odour 394 n.
nostrum *contrivance* 623 n.
  remedy 658 n.
nosy, nosey
  inquisitive 453 adj.
  enquiring 459 adj.
Nosy Parker
  inquisitor 453 n.
  meddler 678 n.
notability *importance* 638 n.
  bigwig 638 n.
  famousness 866 n.
notable *manifest* 522 adj.
  notable 638 adj.
  person of repute 866 n.
  noteworthy 866 adj.
notandum
  important matter 638 n.

not a patch on
  inferior 35 adj.
not a pin to choose
  equivalence 28 n.
notarial
  jurisprudential 958 adj.
notary *recorder* 549 n.
  notary 958 n.
not at all *in no way* 33 adv.
not at home, be
  be engaged 138 vb.
not at home with
  ignorant 491 adj.
notation
  numerical operation 86 n.
  notation 410 n.
not born yesterday
  intelligent 498 adj.
  cunning 698 adj.
notch *degree* 27 n.
  cut 46 vb.
  gap 201 n.
  angularity 247 n.
  make concave 255 vb.
  notch 260 n., vb.
  indication 547 n.
notched *toothed* 256 adj.
not cricket *injustice* 914 n.
not done
  unconformable 84 adj.
  unwonted 611 adj.
note *ululation* 409 n.
  character 5 n.
  musical note 410 n.
  cognize 447 vb.
  notice 455 vb.
  reminder 505 n.
  indication 547 n.
  record 548 vb.
  write 586 vb.
  correspondence 588 n.
  compendium 592 n.
  paper money 797 n.
  famousness 866 n.
notebook *reminder* 505 n.
  record 548 n.
  stationery 586 n.
  reference book 589 n.
  anthology 592 n.
note-case *case* 194 n.
noted *known* 490 adj.
  renowned 866 adj.
note of exclamation
  wonder 864 n.
  (*see* punctuation)
note of hand
  title-deed 767 n.
  paper money 797 n.
note of interrogation
  question 459 n.
  punctuation 547 n.

notepaper *stationery* 586 n.
  paper 631 n.
notes *commentary* 520 n.
  record 548 n.
noteworthy *special* 80 adj.
  unusual 84 adj.
  notable 638 adj.
  wonderful 864 adj.
  noteworthy 866 adj.
nothing
  non-existence 2 n.
  insubstantiality 4 n.
  zero 103 n.
  trifle 639 n.
nothing doing
  without action 677 adv.
nothing, for *given* 781 adj.
  uncharged 812 adj.
nothing like *best* 644 adj.
nothing loth
  willingly 597 adv.
nothingness
  insubstantiality 4 n.
  smallness 33 n.
  zero 103 n.
  unimportance 639 n.
nothing of, make
  not understand 517 vb.
nothing to add
  completeness 54 n.
nothing to do with
  irrelative 10 adj.
nothing to do with, have
  avoid 620 vb.
nothing to it *trifle* 639 n.
  easy thing 701 n.
notice *period* 110 n.
  see 438 vb.
  cognize 447 vb.
  attention 455 n.
  estimate 480 n.
  prediction 511 n.
  information 524 n.
  article 591 n.
  warning 664 n.
  demand 737 n.
  greet 884 vb.
noticeable
  remarkable 32 adj.
  visible 443 adj.
  manifest 522 adj.
notice board
  advertisement 528 n.
notification
  information 524 n.
  publication 528 n.
  indication 547 n.
notify *predict* 511 vb.
  communicate 524 vb.
  proclaim 528 vb.
  warn 664 vb.

notion *idea* 451 n.
  supposition 512 n.
  ideality 513 n.
  contrivance 623 n.
notional *ideational* 451 adj.
  suppositional 512 adj.
  imaginary 513 adj.
not mind *acquiesce* 488 vb.
  be willing 597 vb.
  be indifferent 860 vb.
  hold cheap 922 vb.
notoriety
  knowledge 490 n.
  publicity 528 n.
  famousness 866 n.
  disrepute 867 n.
not out *unceasing* 146 adj.
not there
  abstracted 456 adj.
not to be thought of
  unthought 450 adj.
  rejected 607 adj.
  prohibited 757 adj.
  undue 916 adj.
  blameworthy 924 adj.
notwithstanding
  although 182 adv.
nought *zero* 103 n.
noumenon *idea* 451 n.
noun *name* 561 n.
  part of speech 564 n.
noun of assembly
  assemblage 74 n.
nourish *support* 218 vb.
  feed 301 vb.
  aid 703 vb.
nourishing
  salubrious 652 adj.
nourishment *life* 360 n.
  food 301 n.
nous *intelligence* 498 n.
nouveau riche
  upstart 126 n.
  made man 730 n.
  rich man 800 n.
  vulgarian 847 n.
  commoner 869 n.
nova *star* 321 n.
Novatian *heretic* 977 n.
novel *dissimilar* 19 adj.
  unimitative 21 adj.
  new 126 adj.
  unknown 491 adj.
  reading matter 589 n.
  novel 590 n.
novelese *neology* 560 n.
novelist *author* 589 n.
  narrator 590 n.
novelty *bauble* 639 n.
  (see novel)
novena *period* 110 n.

church *service* 988 n.
novercal *akin* 11 adj.
novice *ignoramus* 493 n.
  beginner 538 n.
  bungler 697 n.
  ingenue 699 n.
  monk, nun 986 n.
  layman 987 n.
novitiate *learning* 536 n.
  preparation 669 n.
novocaine
  anæsthetic 375 n.
novus homo *intruder* 59 n.
now *present time* 121 n.
  at present 121 adv.
now and then
  sometimes 139 adv.
  fitfully 142 adv.
  at intervals 201 adv.
nowhere
  non-existent 2 adj.
  absent 190 adj.
  not here 190 adv.
no wiser
  uninstructed 491 adj.
now or never
  at present 121 adv.
  opportunely 137 adv.
noxious *harmful* 645 adj.
  insalubrious 653 adj.
noyade *slaughter* 362 n.
  terror tactics 712 n.
  capital punishment 963 n.
nozzle *orifice* 263 n.
  air-pipe 353 n.
nuance *differentiation* 15 n.
  degree 27 n.
  small quantity 33 n.
  discrimination 463 n.
nub *essential part* 5 n.
  centrality 225 n.
  swelling 253 n.
  chief thing 638 n.
nubbly *rough* 259 adj.
nubile *grown up* 134 adj.
  marriageable 894 adj.
nubilous *opaque* 423 adj.
  cloudy 355 adj.
nucleal *central* 225 adj.
nuclear *dynamic* 160 adj.
  central 225 adj.
nuclear fission
  nucleonics 160 n.
nucleate
  make smaller 198 vb.
  centralize 225 vb.
  be dense 324 vb.
nucleonics *nucleonics* 160 n.
nucleoplasm
  organism 358 n.
nucleus *middle* 70 n.

centrality 225 n.
element 319 n.
solid body 324 n.
chief thing 638 n.
nude *stripper* 229 n.
uncovered 229 adj.
art subject 553 n.
nudge *knock* 279 n.
hint 524 n., vb.
indication 547 n.
gesture 547 n.
nudism
uncovering 229 adj.
nudist *stripper* 229 n.
sanitarian 652 n.
nudity *bareness* 229 n.
nugacity *folly* 499 n.
unimportance 639 n.
inutility 641 n.
nugatory
powerless 161 adj.
unimportant 639 adj.
useless 641 adj.
nugget *bulk* 195 n.
bullion 797 n.
nuisance *evil* 616 n.
meddler 678 n.
annoyance 827 n.
null *non-existent* 2 adj.
insubstantial 4 adj.
not one 103 adj.
unmeaning 515 adj.
null and void
powerless 161 adj.
abrogated 752 adj.
illegal 954 adj.
nullification
revolution 149 n.
destruction 165 n.
counteraction 182 n.
abrogation 752 n.
nullifidianism
unbelief 486 n.
irreligion 974 n.
nullify *nullify* 2 vb.
set off 31 vb.
(see nullification)
nulli secundus
supreme 34 adj.
nullity *zero* 103 n.
unmeaningness 515 n.
unimportance 639 n.
divorce 896 n.
numb *impotent* 161 adj.
inert 175 adj.
still 266 adj.
insensible 375 adj.
apathetic 820 adj.
number *quantity* 26 n.
subdivision 53 n.
specify 80 vb.

number 85 n.
number 86 vb.
plurality 101 n.
label 547 n.
numberless *infinite* 107 adj.
number one *self* 80 n.
numbers
great quantity 32 n.
multitude 104 n.
safety 660 n.
gambling game 837 n.
number with
number with 78 vb.
numbness (see numb)
numdah *coverlet* 226 n.
floor-cover 226 n.
numen *divineness* 965 n.
numerable
numerable 86 adj.
numeral *number* 85 n.
numeration
numeration 86 n.
measurement 465 n.
accounts 808 n.
numerator
numerical element 85 n.
numerical
numerical 85 adj.
numerous *many* 104 adj.
numinous
frightening 854 adj.
divine 965 adj.
spooky 970 adj.
numismatics *money* 797 n.
numismatist
collector 492 n.
nummary
monetary 797 adj.
numskull
ignoramus 493 n.
dunce 501 n.
nun *spinster* 895 n.
nun 986 n.
nunation *grammar* 564 n.
nuncio *messenger* 531 n.
envoy 754 n.
nuncupation
nomenclature 561 n.
nundination
barter 791 n.
nunnery *monastery* 986 n.
nuptial
matrimonial 894 adj.
nuptials *wedding* 894 n.
nurse *look after* 457 vb.
train 534 vb.
teacher 537 n.
cure 656 vb.
nurse 658 n.
doctor 658 vb.
safeguard 660 vb.

preserve 666 vb.
mature 669 vb.
manage 689 vb.
minister to 703 vb.
domestic 742 n.
keeper 749 n.
pet 889 vb.
philanthropize 897 vb.
nursemaid *keeper* 749 n.
nursery *nonage* 130 n.
child 132 n.
seedbed 156 n.
abundance 171 n.
chamber 194 n.
farm 370 n.
training school 539 n.
workshop 687 n.
nurseryman
gardener 370 n.
nursery rhyme
doggerel 593 n.
nursing *therapy* 658 n.
nursing home
hospital 658 n.
nursling *child* 132 n.
favourite 890 n.
nurture *support* 218 n.
food 301 n.
breed stock 369 vb.
educate 534 vb.
maturation 669 n.
nut *fastening* 47 n.
head 213 n.
fruit 301 n.
madman, crank 504 n.
nutation *oscillation* 317 n.
uranometry 321 n.
nut-cracker
hammer 279 n.
nutmeg *condiment* 389 n.
nutmeg-grater
pulverizer 332 n.
nutriment *food* 301 n.
nutrition *eating* 301 n.
food 301 n.
nutritional
remedial 658 adj.
nutritionist *doctor* 658 n.
nutritious
nourishing 301 adj.
salubrious 652 adj.
nuts *crazed* 503 adj.
benefit 615 n.
nutshell
small quantity 33 n.
conciseness 569 n.
nutty *pungent* 388 adj.
foolish 499 adj.
crazed 503 adj.
nux vomica
cathartic 658 n.

nuzzle *caress* 889 vb.
nyctalopia *dim sight* 440 n.
nylon *fibre* 208 n.
  textile 222 n.
nylons *legwear* 228 n.
nymph *youngster* 132 n.
  woman 373 n.
  nymph 967 n.
  mythical being 970 n.
nymphet *youngster* 132 n.
  loose woman 952 n.
nympholepsy *spell* 983 n.
nymphomania
  abnormality 84 n.
  mania 503 n.
  libido 859 n.
  illicit love 951 n.
nymphomaniac
  loose woman 952 n.
nystagmus *dim sight* 440 n.

O

oaf *dunce* 501 n.
  bungler 697 n.
  elf 970 n.
oafish *unintelligent* 499 adj.
oak *strength* 162 n.
  hardness 326 n.
  tree 366 n.
oakum *fibre* 208 n.
oar *propeller* 269 n.
  boatman 270 n.
  propellant 287 n.
  badge 547 n.
oarsman *boatman* 270 n.
oasis *land* 344 n.
oasthouse *furnace* 383 n.
oat *flute* 414 n.
oath *testimony* 466 n.
  oath 532 n.
  promise 764 n.
  scurrility 899 n.
oath-helper
  vindicator 927 n.
oatmeal *cereal* 301 n.
oats
  provender, cereal 301 n.
  corn 366 n.
obbligato *concomitant* 89 n.
obduction *covering* 226 n.
obduracy *obstinacy* 602 n.
  inhumanity 898 n.
  impenitence 940 n.
obdurate *severe* 735 adj.
  (*see* obduracy)
obeah *sorcery* 983 n.
  talisman 983 n.
obedience
  willingness 597 n.
  submission 721 n.

obedience 739 n.
  observance 768 n.
  servility 879 n.
  churchdom 985 n.
obedient *subject* 745 adj.
  (*see* obedience)
obediental
  ecclesiastical 985 adj.
obeisance *obeisance* 311 n.
  submission 721 n.
  courteous act 884 n.
  ritual act 988 n.
obelisk *high structure* 209 n.
  monument 548 n.
obelize *mark* 547 vb.
obelus *punctuation* 547 n.
obesity *bulk* 195 n.
  dilation 197 n.
obey *be inferior* 35 vb.
  conform 83 vb.
  obey 739 vb.
  be subject 745 vb.
  (*see* obedience)
obeyed *influential* 178 adj.
obfuscation
  obscuration 418 n.
  obfuscation 421 n.
  concealment 525 n.
  misteaching 535 n.
obi *belt* 228 n.
  bewitch 983 vb.
obi-man *sorcerer* 983 n.
obit *obsequies* 364 n.
obiter *unrelatedly* 10 adv.
obiter dictum
  irrelevance 10 n.
  interjection 231 n.
obituary *valediction* 296 n.
  death roll 361 n.
  obsequies 364 n.
  description 590 n.
  biography 590 n.
object *substantiality* 3 n.
  product 164 n.
  object 319 n.
  objective 617 n.
  eyesore 842 n.
  (*see* objection)
object-glass
  astronomy 321 n.
  optical device 442 n.
objectify
  make extrinsic 6 vb.
  externalize 223 vb.
  materialize 319 vb.
  cognize 447 vb.
  imagine 513 vb.
objection
  qualification 468 n.
  doubt 486 n.
  dissent 489 n.

  unwillingness 598 n.
  dissuasion 613 n.
  hindrance 702 n.
  resistance 715 n.
  refusal 760 n.
  discontent 829 n.
  disapprobation 924 n.
objectionable
  inexpedient 643 adj.
  unpleasant 827 adj.
  disreputable 867 adj.
  wrong 914 adj.
objective *substantial* 3 adj.
  material 319 adj.
  true 494 adj.
  objective 617 n.
  aspiration 852 n.
objectiveness
  extrinsicality 6 n.
objectivity
  substantiality 3 n.
  extrinsicality 6 n.
  wisdom 498 n.
  justice 913 n.
object lesson *example* 83 n.
  experiment 461 n.
objector *dissentient* 489 n.
  opponent 705 n.
  litigant 959 n.
objet d'art
  masterpiece 694 n.
  ornamentation 844 n.
objurgation
  reproach 924 n.
oblate *worshipper* 981 n.
oblation *offering* 781 n.
  propitiation 941 n.
  act of worship 981 n.
  oblation 981 n.
oblationary *receiver* 782 n.
  devotional 981 adj.
obligation *necessity* 596 n.
  needfulness 627 n.
  undertaking 672 n.
  promise 674 n.
  debt 803 n.
  dueness 915 n.
  duty 917 n.
obligatory
  necessary 596 adj.
  commanding 737 adj.
  compelling 740 adj.
  conditional 766 adj.
  obligatory 917 adj.
oblige *necessitate* 596 vb.
  require 627 vb.
  minister to 703 vb.
  compel 740 vb.
  be courteous 884 vb.
  be benevolent 897 vb.
  impose a duty 917 vb.

obliged *fated* 596 adj.
  indebted 803 adj.
  grateful 907 adj.
  dutied 917 adj.
obligee *moneyer* 797 n.
obliging *aiding* 703 adj.
  courteous 884 adj.
  benevolent 897 adj.
obligor *debtor* 803 n.
oblique *oblique* 220 adj.
  angular 247 adj.
  curved 248 adj.
  directed 281 adj.
  deviating 282 adj.
  dishonest 930 adj.
obliquity *obliquity* 220 n.
  deviation 282 n.
  improbity 930 n.
  wickedness 934 n.
obliterate *forgive* 909 vb.
  (see obliteration)
obliteration *extinction* 2 n.
  destruction 165 n.
  oblivion 506 n.
  obliteration 550 n.
  desuetude 611 n.
oblivion *extinction* 2 n.
  oblivion 506 n.
  obliteration 550 n.
  desuetude 611 n.
oblivious
  inattentive 456 adj.
  negligent 458 adj.
  forgetful 506 adj.
oblong *longitudinal* 203 adj.
obloquy *slur* 867 n.
  detraction 926 n.
obmutescence
  aphony 578 n.
  taciturnity 582 n.
obnoxious *liable* 180 adj.
  not nice 645 adj.
  unpleasant 827 adj.
  hateful 888 adj.
oboe *flute* 414 n.
oboist *instrumentalist* 413 n.
obol *coinage* 797 n.
obreption
  concealment 525 n.
obreptitious
  stealthy 525 adj.
obscenity
  uncleanness 649 n.
  bad taste 847 n.
  impurity 951 n.
obscurantism
  ignorance 491 n.
  misteaching 535 n.
  opiniatry 602 n.
obscurantist
  ignoramus 493 n.

opponent 705 n.
obscuration
  obscuration 418 n.
  deterioration 655 n.
obscure *bedim* 419 vb.
  blind 439 vb.
  unknown 491 adj.
  semantic 514 adj.
  latent 523 adj.
  conceal 525 vb.
  inglorious 867 adj.
  plebeian 869 adj.
obscurity *inferiority* 35 n.
  darkness 418 n.
  invisibility 444 n.
  uncertainty 474 n.
  unintelligibility 517 n.
  imperspicuity 568 n.
  nonentity 639 n.
  difficulty 700 n.
  disrepute 867 n.
obsecration *entreaty* 761 n.
obsequial *funereal* 364 adj.
obsequies
  valediction 296 n.
  obsequies 364 n.
  lamentation 836 n.
obsequious
  willing 597 adj.
  obedient 739 adj.
  servile 879 adj.
  respectful 920 adj.
  flattering 925 adj.
observability *visibility* 443 n.
observance
  conformity 83 n.
  attention 455 n.
  practice 610 n.
  conduct 688 n.
  obedience 739 n.
  observance 768 n.
  celebration 876 n.
  rite 988 n.
observant
  attentive 455 adj.
  vigilant 457 adj.
  (see observance)
observation
  inspection 438 n.
  idea 451 n.
  attention 455 n.
  maxim 496 n.
  affirmation 532 n.
  speech 579 n.
observation balloon
  airship 276 n.
  view 438 n.
  air force 722 n.
observatory
  astronomy 321 n.
  view 438 n.

observe *see, scan* 438 vb.
  watch 441 vb.
  affirm 532 vb.
  do 676 vb.
  observe 768 vb.
  celebrate 876 vb.
  ritualize 988 vb.
observer *aeronaut* 271 n.
  spectator 441 n.
obsess *recur* 139 vb.
  go on 146 vb.
  engross 449 vb.
  make mad 503 vb.
  remind 505 vb.
  incommode 827 vb.
  frighten 854 vb.
obsession *attention* 455 n.
  positiveness 473 n.
  bias 481 n.
  belief 485 n.
  folly 499 n.
  eccentricity 503 n.
  opiniatry 602 n.
obsessive *unceasing* 146 adj.
  habitual 610 adj.
obsidian *rock* 344 n.
obsidional
  attacking 712 adj.
obsolescence
  extinction 2 n.
  non-use 674 n.
obsolete *extinct* 2 adj.
  past 125 adj.
  antiquated 127 adj.
  powerless 161 adj.
  neological 560 adj.
  useless 641 adj.
  disused 674 adj.
obstacle
  counteraction 182 n.
  impossibility 470 n.
  inexpedience 643 n.
  defect 647 n.
  difficulty 700 n.
  obstacle 702 n.
  opposition 704
obstetric
  productive 164 adj.
  instrumental 628 adj.
  medical 658 adj.
obstetrics *obstetrics* 164 n.
  medical art 658 n.
obstinacy *stability* 153 n.
  inertness 175 n.
  will 595 n.
  perseverance 600 n.
  obstinacy 602 n.
  opposition 704 n.
  resistance 715 n.
obstinate
  unconformable 84 adj.

impenitent 940 adj.
(*see* obstinacy)
obstreperous
violent 176 adj.
loud 400 adj.
obstruct *halt* 145 vb.
stanch 350 vb.
screen 421 vb.
be difficult 700 vb.
obstruct 702 vb.
parry 713 vb.
resist 715 vb.
defeat 727 vb.
incommode 827 vb.
obstruction
derangement 63 n.
delay 136 n.
closure 264 n.
hindrance 702 n.
dutilessness 918 n.
obstructionism
disobedience 738 n.
obstructionist
hinderer 702 n.
opponent 705 n.
obstructive
dissenting 489 adj.
hindering 702 adj.
discontented 829 adj.
obstructor
dissentient 489 n.
hinderer 702 n.
obtain *be* 1 vb.
be general 79 vb.
be wont 610 vb.
acquire 771 vb.
obtainable
accessible 289 adj.
possible 469 adj.
obtestation *entreaty* 761 n.
obtrusion
interjection 231 n.
hindrance 702 n.
obtrusive *vulgar* 847 adj.
obtund *blunt* 257 vb.
obturation *closure* 264 n.
obtuse
unsharpened 257 adj.
insensible 375 adj.
indiscriminating 464 adj.
unintelligent 499 adj.
thick-skinned 820 adj.
obverse *fore* 237 adj.
obvious *well-seen* 443 adj.
intelligible 516 adj.
manifest 522 adj.
ocarina *flute* 414 n.
occasion *juncture* 8 n.
fitness 24 n.
occasion 137 n.
eventuality 154 n.

reason why 156 n.
cause 156 vb.
instrumentality 628 n.
expedience 642 n.
amusement 837 n.
celebration 876 n.
occasional *present* 121 adj.
timely 137 adj.
infrequent 140 adj.
fitful 142 adj.
happening 154 adj
uncertain 474 adj.
celebrative 876 adj.
occasionally
discontinuously 72 adv.
sometimes 139 adv.
occasion, for the
present 121 adj.
incidentally 137 adv.
occidental *directed* 281 adj.
occiput *head* 213 n.
rear 238 n.
occlusion *closure* 264 n.
hindrance 702 n.
occultation
obscuration 418 n.
disappearance 446 n.
concealment 525 n.
occultism *spirit* 447 n.
latency 523 n.
occultism 984 n.
occultist *oracle* 511 n.
sorcerer 983 n.
occultist 984 n.
occupancy *presence* 189 n.
possession 773 n.
occupant *possessor* 776 n.
resident 191 n.
occupation *presence* 189 n.
habit 610 n.
business, job 622 n.
undertaking 672 n.
action 676 n.
(*see* occupy)
occupational
habitual 610 adj.
occupational disease
habit 610 n.
occupied, be
be engaged 138 vb.
occupier *resident* 191 n.
possessor 776 n.
occupy *fill* 54 vb.
be present 189 vb.
dwell 192 vb.
engross 449 vb.
attract notice 455 vb.
employ 622 vb.
be obstructive 702 vb.
possess 773 vb.
appropriate 786 vb.

occur *be* 1 vb.
happen 154 vb.
be present 189 vb.
occurrence
eventuality 154 n.
appearance 445 n.
occur to *dawn upon* 449 vb.
ocean *region* 184 n.
depth 211 n.
water 339 n.
ocean 343 n.
ocean-going
seafaring 269 adj.
marine 275 adj.
oceanic 343 adj.
Oceanid *sea-nymph* 343 n.
nymph 967 n.
mythical being 970 n.
oceanographer
oceanography 343 n.
surveyor 465 n.
oceanography
geography 321 n.
oceanography 343 n.
ochlocracy
government 733 n.
ochre *brown paint* 430 n.
orange 436 n.
octad *over five* 99 n.
octagon
angular figure 247 n.
octaroon *hybrid* 43 n.
octave *period* 110 n.
musical note 410 n.
octavo *edition* 589 n.
octet *over five* 99 n.
duet 412 n.
octogenarian *old man* 133 n.
octopus *fish* 365 n.
tyrant 735 n.
octroi *tax* 809 n.
octuple
fifth and over 99 adj.
ocular
optical device 442 n.
seeing 438 adj.
oculist *eyeglass* 442 n.
vision 438 n.
doctor 658 n.
od *occultism* 984 n.
odalisque *slave* 742 n.
odd *disagreeing* 25 adj.
unequal 29 adj.
remaining 41 adj.
unusual 84 adj.
numerical 85 adj.
crazed 503 adj.
ridiculous 849 adj.
wonderful 864 adj.
wrong 914 adj.
oddity *misfit* 25 n.

unconformity 84n.
eccentricity 503n.
crank 504n.
odd-job man *servant* 742n.
odd man out
  non-uniformity 17n.
  misfit 25n.
  nonconformist 84n.
  dissentient 489n.
oddment(s)
  adjunct, extra 40n.
  medley 43n.
odds *difference* 15n.
  inequality 29n.
  vantage 34n.
  fair chance 159n.
  dissension 709n.
odds and ends
  non-uniformity 17n.
  leavings 41n.
  medley 43n.
  piece 53n.
  rubbish 641n.
odds, at
  quarrelling 709adj.
  contending 716adj.
odds, by all
  probably 471adv.
odds on *fair chance* 159n.
  approved 923adj.
ode *poem* 593n.
Odin *Nordic gods* 967n.
odious
  unpleasant 827adj.
  ugly 842adj.
  disreputable 867adj.
  hateful 888adj.
odium *disrepute* 867n.
  odium 888n.
odium theologicum
  narrow mind 481n.
  pietism 979n.
odontoid *toothed* 256adj.
odorous *odorous* 394adj.
odour *odour* 394n.
odour, bad *odium* 888n.
odourless *odourless* 395adj.
odour of sanctity
  virtue 933n.
  sanctity 979n.
odyl *occultism* 984n.
œcumenicalism
  (*see* ecumenicalism)
œdema *swelling* 253n.
œdematous
  expanded 197adj.
  soft 327adj.
  diseased 651adj.
Oedipus complex *love* 887n.
œsophagitis
  indigestion 651n.

œsophagus *maw* 194n.
  orifice 263n.
œstrus *libido* 859n.
of course
  conformably 83adv.
  consequently 157adv.
  certainly 473adv.
  of course 478adv.
off *apart* 46adv.
  decomposed 51adj.
  ending 69adj.
  absent 190adj.
  pungent 388adj.
  unprovided 636adj.
  unpleasant 827adj.
offal *insides* 224n.
  meat 301n.
  rubbish 641n.
  dirt 649n.
off and on
  by turns 141adj.
  changeably 152adv.
  at intervals 201adv.
off-beam *astray* 282adv.
off-centre *irrelevant* 10adj.
  distant 199n.
  deviating 282adj.
off-chance
  possibility 469n.
  improbability 472n.
off colour
  colourless 426adj.
  imperfect 647adj.
  sick 651adj.
off-day *bungling* 695n.
  failure 728n.
off-drive *propulsion* 287n.
off duty *leisure* 681n.
offence *annoyance* 827n.
  resentment 891n.
  guilty act 936n.
  lawbreaking 954n.
offend *displease* 827vb.
  cause dislike 861vb.
  be wicked 934vb.
offended *resentful* 891adj.
offender
  nonconformist 84n.
  prisoner 750n.
  offender 904n.
  impious person 980n.
offensive *fetid* 397adj.
  unsavoury 391adj.
  inelegant 576adj.
  unclean 649adj.
  attack 712n.
  battle 718n.
  unpleasant 827adj.
  impertinent 878adj.
  ungracious 885adj.
  hateful 888adj.

impure 951adj.
offer *opportunity* 137n.
  affirm 532vb.
  will 595vb.
  choice 605n.
  incentive 612n.
  provide 633vb.
  essay 671vb.
  permit 756vb.
  offer 759n.,vb.
  promise 764n.,vb.
  make terms 766vb.
  give 781vb.
offered *voluntary* 597adj.
offering *offer* 759n.
  offering 781n.
  propitiation 941n.
  oblation 981n.
offer, on *offering* 759adj.
offer satisfaction
  atone 941vb.
offertory *offering* 781n.
  oblation 981n.
offer up *kill* 362vb.
  give 781vb.
  offer worship 981vb.
off form
  imperfect 647adj.
off guard
  negligent 458adj.
  inexpectant 508adj.
off-hand
  instantaneously 116adv.
  suddenly 135adv.
  inattentive 456adj.
  negligent 458adj.
  spontaneous 609adj.
  unreadily 670adv.
  impertinent 878adj.
  discourteous 885adj.
  disrespectful 921adj.
office *agency* 173n.
  chamber 194n.
  job, function 622n.
  use 673n.
  workshop 687n.
  authority 733n.
  mandate 796n.
  duty 917n.
  jurisdiction 955n.
  church service 988n.
office-bearer
  official 690n.
  consignee 754n.
office-book
  office-book 988n.
office-boy *courier* 531n.
  officer 741n.
office, in
  authoritative 733adj.
officer *official* 690n.

officer 741 n.
offices adjunct 40 n.
offices, good aid 703 n.
  pacification 719 n.
  mediation 720 n.
  kind act 897 n.
official certain 473 adj.
  genuine 494 adj.
  usual 610 adj.
  businesslike 622 adj.
  directing 689 adj.
  official 690 n.
  authoritative 733 adj.
  governmental 733 adj.
  officer 741 n.
  servant 742 n.
  formal 875 adj.
officialese language 557 n.
  neology 560 n.
officialism
  governance 733 n.
officiant worshipper 981 n.
officiate function 622 vb.
  do 676 vb.
  offer worship 918 vb.
  perform ritual 988 vb.
officiousness curiosity 453 n.
  redundance 637 n.
  overactivity 678 n.
offing distance 199 n.
offish unsociable 883 adj.
off-key discordant 411 adj.
off-load displace 188 vb.
off-peak small 33 adj.
off-pitch
  discordant 411 adj.
offprint letterpress 587 n.
offscourings leavings 41 n.
  dirt 649 n.
  rabble 869 n.
off-season
  ill-timed 138 adj.
  cheap 812 adj.
offset equalization 28 n.
  offset 31 n.
  remainder 41 n.
  counteract 182 vb.
  qualification 468 n.
  print 587 vb.
offshoot adjunct 40 n.
  subdivision 53 n.
  effect 157 n.
  descendant 170 n.
  sect 978 n.
off-shore distant 199 adj.
offside
  unconformable 84 adj.
  dextral 241 adj.
  sinistral 242 adj.
  wrong 914 adj.
  illegal 954 adj.

offspring kinsman 11 n.
  effect 157 n.
  product 164 n.
  posterity 170 n.
off-stage on stage 594 adv.
off-take decrement 42 n.
  egress 298 n.
off-target irrelevant 10 adj.
  mistaken 495 adj.
off the peg
  ready-made 669 adj
off the rails
  unconformable 84 adj.
  mistaken 495 adj.
off the record
  private 80 adj.
  undisguised 522 adj.
  occult 523 adj.
off-white whitish 427 adj.
oflag prison camp 748 n.
often often 139 adv.
ogee pattern 844 n.
ogham lettering 586 n.
oghamic literal 558 adj.
ogive supporter 218 n.
ogle gaze 438 vb.
  watch 441 vb.
  gesture 547 n.
  desire 859 vb.
  wooing 889 n.
Ogpu police enquiry 459 n.
ogre giant 195 n.
  intimidation 854 n.
  monster 938 n.
  demon 970 n.
ogress hell-hag 904 n.
Ogygian past 125 adj.
ohm electricity 160 n.
  metrology 465 n.
oil smoother 258 n.
  propellant 287 n.
  soften 327 vb.
  lubricant 334 n.
  oil 357 n.
  fuel 385 n.
  silencer 401 n.
  bribe 612 vb.
  balm 658 n.
  facilitate 701 vb.
  primp 843 vb.
oil-can lubricant 334 n.
oilcloth floor-cover 226 n.
oiled unctuous 357 adj.
  smooth 258 adj.
  tipsy 949 adj.
oil-field store 632 n.
oil-painting art style 553 n.
oils pigment 425 n.
  art equipment 553 n.
oilskins overcoat 228 n.
oilstone sharpener 256 n.

oil-well store 632 n.
oily lenitive 177 adj.
  smooth 258 adj.
  unctuous 357 adj.
  hypocritical 541 adj.
  dirty 649 adj.
  servile 879 adj.
  flattering 925 adj.
oinomania
  alcoholism 949 n.
ointment facing 226 n.
  lubricant 334 n.
  unguent 357 n.
  balm 658 n.
O.K. in order 60 adv.
  assent 488 n.
okra vegetable 301 n.
old, olden past 125 adj.
  olden, antiquated 127 adj.
  aged 131 adj.
  weak 163 adj.
old age age 131 n.
Oldbuck
  antiquarian 125 n.
olden days
  preterition 125 n.
old-fashioned
  anachronistic 118 adj.
  antiquated 127 adj.
  unwonted 611 adj.
old fogy old man 133 n.
  fool 501 n.
  laughing-stock 851 n.
old folks family 11 n.
  old couple 133 n.
Old Glory flag 547 n.
old hand expert 696 n.
old iron rubbish 641 n.
old lag offender 904 n.
old maid woman 373 n.
  card game 837 n.
  spinster 895 n.
  virgin 950 n.
old-maidish
  prudish 950 adj.
Old Man of the Sea
  mariner 270 n.
  sea-god 343 n.
  encumbrance 702 n.
  mythical being 970 n.
old master picture 553 n.
  artist 556 n.
Old Moore
  chronology 117 n.
  oracle 511 n.
oldness beginning 68 n.
  time 108 n.
  durability 113 n.
  preterition 125 n.
  oldness 127 n.
  age 131 n.

old, old story
 love affair 887n.
old school
 opiniatry 602n.
 habit 610n.
old school tie *livery* 547n.
old stager *old man* 133n.
 actor 594n.
 expert 696n.
old story *repetition* 106n.
 news 529n.
Old Style *chronology* 117n.
Old Testament
 scripture 975n.
old-timer *archaism* 127n.
 old man 133n.
old-world *olden* 127adj.
 courteous 884adj.
oleaginous
 unctuous 357adj.
olein *fat* 357n.
oleograph
 representation 551n.
olericulture
 agriculture 370n.
olfactory *odour* 394n.
olid *fetid* 397adj.
oligarch *master* 741n.
oligarchy *government* 733n.
olivaceous *green* 432adj.
olive *fruit* 301n.
 greenness 432n.
olive-branch *irenics* 719n.
olivine *gem* 844n.
olla podrida
 a mixture 43n.
ologies and isms
 science 490n.
Olympiad *period* 110n.
Olympian *aristocrat* 868n.
 genteel 868adj.
 Olympian god 967n.
 paradisiac 971adj.
Olympics *contest* 716n.
Olympus
 mythic heaven 971n.
ombre *card game* 837n.
omega *extremity* 69n.
omelette *dish* 301n.
omen *precursor* 66n.
 foresight 510n.
 omen 511n.
 indication 547n.
 warning 664n.
 danger signal 665n.
 threat 900n.
omentum *obstetrics* 164n.
ominate *predict* 511vb.
ominous
 presageful 511adj.
 indicating 547adj.

 harmful 645adj.
 dangerous 661adj.
 cautionary 664adj.
 adverse 731adj.
 frightening 854adj.
 unpromising 853adj.
 threatening 900adj.
omission
 incompleteness 55n.
 exclusion 57n.
 negligence 458n.
 failure 728n.
 non-observance 769n.
 guilty act 936n.
omit *be taciturn* 582vb.
 (*see* omission)
omitted *non-existent* 2adj.
 absent 190adj.
omneity *whole* 52n.
 universe 321n.
omnibus
 comprehensive 52adj.
 bus, stage-coach 274n.
omnibus train
 slowcoach 278n.
omnicompetent
 powerful 160adj.
omnicompetent state
 despotism 733n.
omnifarious
 multiform 82adj.
omnific *generative* 171adj.
omniformity
 multiformity 82n.
omnipotence *power* 160n.
 divine attribute 965n.
omnipotent
 compelling 740adj.
omnipresence
 presence 189n.
 divine attribute 965n.
omniscience
 knowledge 490n.
 divine attribute 965n.
omnium gatherum
 medley 43n.
 confusion 61n.
 (*see* assembly)
omnivore *animal* 365n.
omnivorous
 feeding 301adj.
 greedy 859adj.
 gluttonous 947adj.
omphalos *middle* 70n.
on *concerning* 9adv.
 impending 154adj.
 in place 186adv.
 on the spot 189adj.
 forward 285adv.
 on 310adv.
 provisionary 633adj.

on account of
 hence 158adv.
on and on *forever* 115adv.
on behalf of
 in aid of 703adv.
once *singly* 88adv.
 not now 122adv.
 seldom 140adv.
once bitten
 warned 664adj.
 cautious 858adj.
once for all
 finally 69adv.
 resolutely 599adv.
once-over *inspection* 438n.
once-removed *akin* 11adj.
 deviating 282adj.
once upon a time
 when 108adv.
 not now 122adv.
 retrospectively 125adv.
oncoming *fore* 237adj.
 approaching 289adj.
on demand
 cash down 804adv.
on-drive *propulsion* 287n.
one *simple* 44adj.
 whole 52adj.
 unit 88n.
 infrequent 140adj.
 person 371n.
one after another
 continuously 71adv.
 following 284n.
one and only
 dissimilar 19adj.
 unimitated 21adj.
 one 88adj.
one and the same
 identical 13adj.
one another
 correlation 12n.
one, as
 co-operatively 706adv.
one at a time
 singly 88adv.
one by one
 separately 46adv.
 severally 80adv.
 singly 88adv.
one consent, with
 concurrently 181adv.
 unanimously 488adv.
one day *when* 108adv.
 not now 122adv.
one-dimensional
 longitudinal 203adj.
one-eyed
 dim-sighted 440adj.
one for the road
 valediction 296n.

potion 301 n.
one-horse *little* 196 adj.
  trivial 639 adj.
one in a million
  nonconformist 84 n.
  exceller 644 n.
oneirocritic
  interpreter 520 n.
oneness *identity* 13 n.
  simpleness 44 n.
  whole 52 n.
  unity 88 n.
one of *ingredient* 58 adj.
one of the best
  exceller 644 n.
  favourite 890 n.
  good man 937 n.
one of these days
  not now 122 adv.
one or two *plurality* 101 n.
  fewness 105 n.
one-piece *uniform* 16 adj.
onerous
  difficult 700 adj.
  hindering 702 adj.
  annoying 827 adj.
  (*see* heavy)
one's day *success* 727 n.
one's despair
  bungler 697 n.
  difficulty 700 n.
oneself *identity* 13 n.
one-sided *biased* 481 adj.
  unjust 914 adj.
  dishonest 930 adj.
one's people *family* 11 n.
one-step *dance* 837 n.
one swoop, at
  instantaneously 116 adv.
one-time *prior* 119 adj.
  former 125 adj.
  resigning 753 adj.
one too many
  redundant 637 adj.
one-track mind
  narrow mind 481 n.
one up *superior* 34 adj.
  surpassing 306 adj.
one-upmanship
  superiority 34 n.
  tactics 688 n.
onion *sphere* 252 n.
  vegetable 301 n.
  condiment 389 n.
onlooker *spectator* 441 n.
only *inconsiderable* 33 adj.
  slightly 33 adv.
  one 88 adj.
only-begotten *one* 88 adj.
only pebble on the beach
  vain person 873 n.

onomasiology
  linguistics 557 n.
  etymology 559 n.
onomasticon *name* 561 n.
onomatology
  nomenclature 561 n.
on one's own *alone* 88 adj.
onrush *outbreak* 176 n.
onset *beginning* 68 n.
  approach 289 n.
  attack 712 n.
on-shore *coastal* 344 adj.
onslaught *attack* 712 n.
  malediction 899 n.
  censure 924 n.
ontal *existing* 1 adj.
on tap *provisionary* 633 adj.
on the go *actively* 678 adv.
on the make
  acquiring 771 adj.
  selfish 932 adj.
on the map, put
  make important 638 vb.
ontology *existence* 1 n.
  philosophy 449 n.
onus *demonstration* 478 n.
  encumbrance 702 n.
  duty 917 n.
  guilt 936 n.
onward *forward* 285 adv.
onyx *gem* 844 n.
oodles *great quantity* 32 n.
oof *dibs* 797 n.
ooze *move slowly* 278 vb.
  exude 298 vb.
  emit 300 vb.
  moisture 341 n.
  ocean 343 n.
  marsh 347 n.
  flow 350 vb.
  semiliquidity 354 n.
oozing *full* 54 adj.
oozy *slow* 278 adj.
  outgoing 298 adj.
  humid 341 adj.
  marshy 347 adj.
  flowing 350 adj.
opacity *dimness* 419 n.
  opacity 423 n.
  imperspicuity 568 n.
opal *gem* 844 n.
opalescent, opaline
  semitransparent 424 adj.
  iridescent 437 adj.
opaque (*see* opacity)
open *disjoin, cut* 46 vb.
  come before 64 vb.
  begin 68 vb.
  auspicate 68 vb.
  expand 197 vb.
  spaced 201 n.

broad 205 adj.
  uncover 229 vb.
  open 263 adj., vb.
  air 340 n.
  champaign 338 adj.
  visible 443 adj.
  uncertain 474 adj.
  manifest 522 vb.
  disclosed 526 adj.
  veracious 540 adj.
  vocal 577 adj.
  artless 699 adj.
  easy 701 adj.
  liberate 746 vb.
  offering 759 adj.
  trustworthy 929 adj.
open air *air* 340 n.
  exteriority 223 n.
  salubrity 652 n.
open an account
  trade 791 vb.
  credit 802 vb.
open and shut
  demonstrated 478 adj.
open and shut case
  certainty 473 n.
open arms
  reception 299 n.
  friendliness 880 n.
open country *plain* 348 n.
open door *way in* 297 n.
open-eared
  auditory 415 adj.
open-ended *disjunct* 46 adj.
  non-adhesive 49 adj.
  pendent 217 adj.
opener *opener* 263 n.
  instrument 628 n.
open-eyed
  attentive 455 adj.
  vigilant 437 adj.
  expectant 507 adj.
open fire *initiate* 68 vb.
  shoot 287 vb.
  fire at 712 vb.
  give battle 718 vb.
open hand *liberality* 813 n.
open-hearted
  trustworthy 929 adj.
open house *generality* 79 n.
  liberality 813 n.
  sociability 882 n.
opening *prelude* 66 n.
  début, entrance 68 n.
  opportunity 137 n.
  room 183 n.
  gap 201 n.
  open space 263 n.
  way in 297 n.
open, in the
  externally 223 adv.

alfresco 340 adv.
open into *connect* 45 vb.
open letter *generality* 79 n.
  publicity 528 n.
  deprecation 762 n.
  censure 924 n.
open market *scope* 744 n.
  trade 791 n.
  mart 796 n.
open-mindedness
  no choice 606 n.
open-mouthed
  open 263 adj.
  expectant 507 adj.
  greedy 859 adj.
  wondering 864 adj.
open question
  uncertainty 474 n.
open secret
  knowledge 490 n.
  publicity 528 n.
open sesame
  answer 460 n.
  instrument 628 n.
  spell 983 n.
open to *liable* 180 adj.
  vulnerable 661 adj.
open to all *easy* 701 adj.
open up *initiate* 68 vb.
  accelerate 277 vb.
  manifest 522 vb.
  disclose 526 vb.
open verdict *dubiety* 474 n.
open work
  needlework 844 n.
  ornamental art 844 n.
opera *vocal music* 412 n.
  stage play 594 n.
operable *possible* 469 adj.
  restored 656 adj.
  medical 658 adj.
opera glass *telescope* 442 n.
opera-goer
  musician 413 n.
  playgoer 594 n.
opera house *theatre* 594 n.
operate *motivate* 612 vb.
  function 622 vb.
  use 673 vb.
  deal with 688 vb.
  manage 689 vb.
  speculate 791 vb.
  (*see* operation)
operatic *musical* 412 adj.
  dramatic 594 adj.
operation
  agency 173 n.
  instrumentality 628 n.
  surgery 658 n.
  action 676 n.
  undertaking 672 n.

doing 676 adj.
labour 682 n.
operational
  operative 173 adj.
  warlike 718 adj.
operative
  powerful 160 adj.
  operative 173 adj.
  instrumental 628 adj.
  worker 686 n.
operator *machinist* 630 n.
  numerical element 85 n.
  doctor 658 n.
  doer 676 n.
  agent 686 n.
operculum *covering* 226 n.
operose
  labouring 682 adj.
  laborious 682 adj.
  difficult 700 adj.
ophicleide *horn* 414 n.
ophidian *animal* 365 adj.
  reptile 365 n.
ophthalmia
  dim sight 440 n.
ophthalmologist
  eyeglass 442 n.
  vision 438 n.
  doctor 658 n.
ophthalmoscope
  optical device 442 n.
opiate *moderator* 177 n.
  soporific 679 n.
opine *opine* 485 vb.
  suppose 512 vb.
  affirm 532 vb.
  (*see* opinion)
opiniatry
  positiveness 473 n.
  narrow mind 481 n.
  opiniatry 602 n.
opinion *idea* 451 n.
  estimate 480 n.
  bias 481 n.
  opinion 485 n.
  supposition 512 n.
  repute 866 n.
opinionated
  positive 473 adj.
  narrow-minded 481 adj.
  believing 485 adj.
  obstinate 602 adj.
  vain 873 adj.
opinionist *doctrinaire* 473 n.
  opinionist 602 n.
opium *moderator* 177 n.
  anæsthetic 375 n.
  drug 658 n.
  poison 659 n.
  soporific 679 n.
opium-eater *idler* 679 n.

opossum *marsupial* 365 n.
oppidan *native* 191 n.
  urban 192 adj.
oppilation *hindrance* 702 n.
opponent *dissentient* 489 n.
  opponent 705 n.
  enemy 881 n.
opportune
  circumstantial 8 adj.
  apt 24 adj.
  opportune 137 adj.
  expedient 642 adj.
opportunism
  expedience 642 n.
  improbity 930 n.
opportunist
  enterprising 672 adj.
  egotist 932 n.
opportunity *juncture* 8 n.
  present time 121 n.
  opportunity 137 n.
  fair chance 159 n.
  possibility 469 n.
  expedience 642 n.
  facility 701 n.
  scope 744 n.
oppose *restrain* 747 vb.
  (*see* opposition)
opposite *correlative* 12 adj.
  contrary 14 adj.
  difference 15 n.
  inverted 221 adj.
  opposite 240 adj.
  countervailing 467 adj.
  opposing 704 adj.
opposite number
  correlation 12 n.
  compeer 28 n.
opposition
  disagreement 25 n.
  counteraction 182 n.
  contraposition 240 n.
  qualification 468 n.
  dissent 489 n.
  unwillingness 598 n.
  hindrance 702 n.
  opposition 704 n.
  dissension 709 n.
  resistance 715 n.
  disobedience 738 n.
  deprecation 762 n.
  enmity 881 n.
oppress *suppress* 165 vb.
  ill-treat 645 vb.
  oppress 735 vb.
  impress 821 vb.
  torment 827 vb.
oppression *severity* 735 n.
  subjection 745 n.
  dejection 834 n.
oppressive *violent* 176 adj.

warm 379 adj.
frightening 854 adj.
inimical 881 adj.
lawless 954 adj.
oppressor bane 659 n.
tyrant 735 n.
opprobrious
degrading 867 adj.
opprobrium slur 867 n.
oppugnation
opposition 704 n.
resistance 715 n.
opsimathy lateness 136 n.
learning 536 n.
opt choose 605 vb.
optical seeing 438 adj.
luminous 417 adj.
optical illusion
insubstantial thing 4 n.
visual fallacy 440 n.
optician vision 438 n.
eyeglass 442 n.
doctor 658 n.
optics vision 438 n.
eye 438 n.
optics 417 n.
optimate aristocrat 868 n.
optimism
overestimation 482 n.
exaggeration 546 n.
cheerfulness 833 n.
hope 852 n.
optimistic
optimistic 482 adj.
optimum best 644 adj.
option will 595 n.
willingness 597 n.
choice 605 n.
card game 837 n.
optional volitional 595 adj.
voluntary 597 adj.
choosing 605 adj.
opulent plenteous 635 adj.
rich 800 adj.
opus musical piece 412 n.
product 164 n.
opuscule book 589 n.
or orange 436 n.
heraldry 547 n.
oracle answer 460 n.
certainty 473 n.
doctrinaire 473 n.
sage 500 n.
oracle 511 n.
equivocalness 518 n.
latency 523 n.
adviser 691 n.
holy place 990 n.
oracular uncertain 474 adj.
aphoristic 496 adj.
wise 498 adj.

predicting 511 adj.
puzzling 517 adj.
equivocal 518 adj.
imperspicuous 568 adj.
oral vocal 577 adj.
speaking 579 adj.
orale vestments 989 n.
orange fruit 301 n.
orange 436 n., adj.
orangery wood 366 n.
garden 370 n
orang-outang
monkey 365 n.
orarion vestments 989 n.
orate be diffuse 570 vb.
oration oration 579 n.
allocution 583 n.
orator preacher 537 n.
phrasemonger 574 n.
speaker 579 n.
motivator 612 n.
oratorical figurative 519 adj.
rhetorical 574 adj.
eloquent 579 n.
oratorio vocal music 412 n.
oratorium temple 990 n.
oratory style 566 n.
oratory 579 n.
inducement 612 n.
church 990 n.
orb region 184 n.
circle 250 n.
eye 438 n.
badge 547 n.
regalia 743 n.
orbicularity
circularity 250 n.
rotundity 252 n.
orbit orbit 250 n.
fly 271 vb.
passage 305 n.
circuition 314 n.
circle 314 vb.
rotate 315 vb.
route 624 n.
circuit 626 n.
orbital circuitous 314 adj.
orchard wood 366 n.
farm, garden 370 n.
orchestra band 74 n.
orchestra 413 n.
theatre 594 n.
orchestral musical 412 adj.
orchestrate compose 56 vb.
arrange 62 vb.
harmonize 410 vb.
compose music 413 vb.
ordain decree 737 vb.
commission 751 vb.
make legal 953 vb.
ecclesiasticize 985 vb.

perform ritual 988 vb.
ordained fated 596 adj.
clerical 986 adj.
ordeal experiment 461 n.
suffering 825 n.
painfulness 827 n.
order relation 9 n.
uniformity 16 n.
order 60 n., vb.
serial place 73 n.
regularity 81 n.
send 272 vb.
meal 301 n.
judgment 480 n.
badge 547 n.
practice 610 n.
plan 623 vb.
requirement 627 n.
precept 693 n.
community 708 n.
decoration 729 n.
command 737 n., vb.
demand 737 vb.
compel 740 vb.
badge of rank 743 n.
paper money 797 n.
honours 866 n.
nobility 868 n.
title 870 n.
impose a duty 917 vb.
legislation 953 n.
sect 978 n.
ecclesiasticize 985 vb.
monk 986 n.
ritual, rite 988 n.
order, keep rule 733 vb.
restrain 747 vb.
orderless orderless 61 adj.
unassembled 75 adj.
unconformable 84 adj.
amorphous 244 adj.
unsightly 842 adj.
orderly orderly 60 adj.
regular 81 adj.
careful 457 adj.
businesslike 622 adj.
servant 742 n.
order off dismiss 300 vb.
order of the day
affairs 154 n.
predetermination 608 n.
policy 623 n.
command 737 n.
order, out of
orderless 61 adj.
orders holy orders 985 n.
orders, at one's
obedient 739 adj.
orders, in clerical 986 adj.
ordinal numerical 85 adj.
office-book 988 n.

ordinance *precept* 693 n.
 command 737 n.
 legislation 953 n.
 rite 988 n.
ordinand *pietist* 979 n.
 cleric 986 n.
 layman 987 n.
ordinary *median* 30 adj.
 general 79 adj.
 typical 83 adj.
 meal 301 n.
 heraldry 547 n.
 usual 610 adj.
 trivial 639 adj.
 not bad 644 adj.
 imperfect 647 adj.
 mediocre 732 adj.
 unastonishing 865 adj.
ordinate and abscissa
 metrology 465 n.
ordination *mandate* 751 n.
 holy orders 985 n.
 Christian rite 988 n.
ordnance *gun* 723 n.
ordure *dirt* 649 n.
 excrement 302 n.
ore *origin* 156 n.
 materials 631 n.
oread *nymph* 967 n.
oreanthropus
 mankind 371 n.
orfray *vestments* 989 n.
organ *organ* 414 n.
 the press 528 n.
 instrument 628 n.
 church utensil 990 n.
organ-blower *organ* 414 n.
organdie *textile* 222 n.
organ-grinder
 instrumentalist 413 n.
organic *conditionate* 7 adj.
 structural 331 adj.
 organic 358 adj.
organic nature
 organism 358 n.
organic remains
 organism 358 n.
 corpse 363 n.
organism *structure* 331 n.
 life 360 n.
organist
 instrumentalist 413 n.
organization
 composition 56 n.
 order 60 n.
 arrangement 62 n.
 production 164 n.
 structure 331 n.
 organism 358 n.
 plan 623 n.
 corporation 708 n.

organizational
 arranged 62 adj.
 structural 331 adj.
 organic 358 adj.
organizer *planner* 623 n.
organ-loft *organ* 414 n.
 church interior 990 n.
organology
 structure 331 n.
orgasm *spasm* 318 n.
orgiastic
 disorderly 61 adj.
 violent 176 adj.
 sensual 944 adj.
orgy *feasting* 301 n.
 plenty 635 n.
 festivity 837 n.
 intemperance 943 n.
 sensualism 944 n.
oriel *compartment* 194 n.
 angularity 247 n.
 window 263 n.
orient *laterality* 239 n.
 luminous 417 adj.
oriental *lateral* 239 adj.
orientalize
 transform 147 vb.
orientate *navigate* 269 vb.
orientation *direction* 281 n.
orifice *entrance* 68 n.
 gap 201 n.
 cavity 255 n.
 orifice 263 n.
oriflamme *flag* 547 n.
origin *origin* 68 n.
 source 156 n.
 genealogy 169 n.
original *intrinsic* 5 adj.
 irrelative 10 adj.
 prototype 23 n.
 first 68 adj.
 nonconformist 84 n.
 new 126 adj.
 fundamental 156 adj.
 script 586 n.
 unwonted 611 adj.
 laughing-stock 851 n.
 jurisdictional 955 adj.
 (see originality)
originality
 difference 15 n.
 dissimilarity 19 n.
 non-imitation 21 n.
 speciality 80 n.
 unconformity 84 n.
 imagination 513 n.
original side *tribunal* 956 n.
originate *initiate* 68 vb.
 cause 156 vb.
 produce 164 vb.
 will 595 vb.

originate from
 result 157 vb.
originative
 generative 171 adj.
originator *producer* 167 n.
 planner 623 n.
Orion *star* 321 n.
orismology
 nomenclature 561 n.
orison *entreaty* 761 n.
 prayers 981 n.
orle *heraldry* 547 n.
orlop *base* 214 n.
orlop deck *layer* 207 n.
ormolu *sham* 542 n.
 ornamental art 844 n.
ornament
 ornament 574 n., vb.
 make better 654 vb.
 beauty 841 n.
 beautify 841 vb.
 ornamentation 844 n.
ornamental *useless* 641 adj.
 beautiful 841 adj.
 ornamental 844 adj.
ornamentation
 concomitant 89 n.
 spectacle 445 n.
 ostentation 875 n.
 (see ornament)
ornate *figurative* 519 adj.
 stylistic 566 adj.
 ornate 574 adj.
 splendid 841 adj.
 affected 850 adj.
ornithology *zoology* 367 n.
orography
 geography 321 n.
orotund *rhetorical* 574 adj.
 eloquent 579 adj.
 ostentatious 875 adj.
orphan *survivor* 41 n.
 derelict 779 n.
 deprive 786 vb.
 sadden 834 vb.
 outcaste 883 n.
orphanage *shelter* 662 n.
orphaned *alone* 88 adj.
Orphean
 musicianly 413 adj.
Orphism *religion* 973 n.
orphrey *vestments* 989 n.
orpiment
 yellow pigment 433 n.
orrery *astronomy* 321 n.
orris root *scent* 396 n.
 medicine 658 n.
orthodox *habitual* 610 adj.
 orthodox 976 adj.
 pious 979 adj.
 worshipping 981 adj.

ecclesiastical 985 adj.
(see orthodoxy)
Orthodox Church
the Church 976 n.
orthodoxism
orthodoxism 976 n.
orthodoxy generality 79 n.
conformity 83 n.
certainty 473 n.
positiveness 473 n.
creed 485 n.
orthodox 976 n.
orthoepy etymology 559 n.
orthogonal vertical 215 adj.
angulated 247 adj.
orthography spelling 558 n.
orthology accuracy 494 n.
orthometry
measurement 465 n.
orthopædist doctor 658 n.
orthopædy therapy 658 n.
orthopraxy therapy 658 n.
orthoptic seeing 438 adj.
ortolan table bird 365 n.
orts rubbish 641 n.
oryctology
zoology 367 n.
mineralogy 359 n.
oscillate hang 217 vb.
deviate 282 vb.
oscillate 317 vb.
oscillation correlation 12 n.
periodicity 141 n.
fitfulness 142 n.
reversion 148 n.
changeableness 152 n.
laterality 239 n.
motion 265 n.
oscillation 317 n.
oscitancy opening 263 n.
sleepiness 679 n.
osculation contiguity 202 n.
endearment 889 n.
osculatory
ritual object 988 n.
osier ligature 47 n.
plant 366 n.
osmose, osmosis
ingress 297 n.
passage 305 n.
osmotic passing 305 adj.
osprey bird of prey 365 n.
trimming 844 n.
osseous hard 326 adj.
ossicle solid body 324 n.
ossification
condensation 324 n.
hardening 326 n.
ossified antiquated 127 adj.
ossuary interment 364 n.
ostensible appearing 445 adj.

plausible 471 adj.
manifest 522 adj.
ostensible 614 adj.
ostensible motive
pretext 614 n.
ostentation
manifestation 522 n.
publicity 528 n.
prodigality 815 n.
ornamentation 844 n.
affectation 850 n.
vanity 873 n.
ostentation 875 n.
osteology structure 331 n.
osteopath doctor 658 n.
osteopathy therapy 658 n.
ostiarius cleric 986 n.
ostiary janitor 264 n.
ostiole orifice 263 n.
ostler
animal husbandry 369 n.
servant 742 n.
ostracism exclusion 57 n.
unsociability 883 n.
disapprobation 924 n.
penalty 963 n.
ostracize eject 300 vb.
make unwelcome 883 vb.
ostrich flightless bird 365 n.
visionary 513 n.
other extrinsicality 6 n.
different 15 adj.
other half analogue 18 n.
other hand, on the
conversely 467 adv.
otherness difference 15 n.
other ranks inferior 35 n.
nonentity 639 n.
other self analogue 18 n.
other side contrariety 14 n.
opposition 704 n.
enemy 881 n.
otherwise contrarily 14 adv.
differently 15 adv.
otherworldliness
sanctity 979 n.
otherworldly
immaterial 320 adj.
psychic 447 adj.
imaginative 513 adj.
pious 979 adj.
magical 983 adj.
otiose unproductive 172 adj.
useless 641 adj.
inactive 679 adj.
otology ear 415 n.
otoscope hearing aid 415 n.
ottoman seat 218 n.
oubliette
hiding-place 527 n.
prison 748 n.

ouch fastening 47 n.
jewellery 844 n.
ought be due 915 vb.
ouija board
spiritualism 984 n.
ounce
small quantity 33 n.
weighment 322 n.
ourselves self 80 n.
mankind 371 n.
ousel waterfowl 365 n.
oust substitute 150 vb.
eject 300 vb.
depose 752 vb.
deprive 786 vb.
ouster loss of right 916 n.
out absent 190 adj.
expanded 197 adj.
externally 223 adv.
open 263 adj.
astray 282 adv.
eject 300 vb.
dark 418 adj.
misjudging 481 adj.
mistaken 495 adj.
inexact 495 adj.
sleepy 679 adj.
fatigued 684 adj.
dead drunk 949 adj.
out-and-out
consummate 32 adj.
completely 54 adv.
out-argue argue 475 vb.
confute 479 vb.
out-at-elbows
uncovered 229 adj.
disreputable 867 adj.
outback space 183 n.
outbid outdo 306 vb.
bargain 791 vb.
outboard exterior 223 adj.
boat 275 n.
out-bowed convex 253 adj.
outbreak disorder 61 n.
beginning 68 n.
outbreak 176 n.
egress 298 n.
revolt 738 n.
exitable state 822 n.
outburst outbreak 176 n.
egress 298 n.
excitable state 822 n.
outcast bad man 938 n.
heathen 974 n.
outcaste exclude 57 vb.
reject 607 vb.
commoner 869 n.
disreputable 867 adj.
derelict 779 n.
outcaste 883 n.
outclass be superior 34 vb.

outdo 306 vb.
defeat 727 vb.
outclassed inferior 35 adj.
outcome
eventuality 154 n.
effect 157 n.
egress 298 n.
outcrop layer 207 n.
outcropping visible 443 adj.
appearing 445 adj.
outcry loudness 400 n.
cry 408 n.
lament 836 n.
disapprobation 924 n.
outdare defy 711 vb.
be courageous 855 vb.
outdistance
be distant 199 n.
outstrip 277 vb.
progress 285 vb.
outdo 306 vb.
outdo be early 135 vb.
outdo 306 vb.
defeat 727 vb.
outdoor exterior 233 adj.
outdoors salubrity 652 n.
outer, outermost
exterior 223 adj.
outer darkness
exclusion 57 n.
outface
be resolute 599 vb.
resist 715 vb.
be courageous 855 vb.
be insolent 878 vb.
outfall outflow 298 n.
outfit all 52 n.
component 58 n.
unit 88 n.
clothing 228 n.
equipment 630 n.
party 708 n.
outfitter clothier 228 n.
outflank flank 239 vb.
outdo 306 vb.
defeat 727 vb.
outflow outflow 298 n.
waterfall 350 n.
waste 634 n.
out for intending 617 adj.
outgate outlet 298 n.
outgeneral defeat 727 vb.
outgo outdo 306 vb.
outgoing preceding 64 adj.
former 125 adj.
resigning 753 adj.
outgoings expenditure 806 n.
out-group group 74 n.
outgrow
disaccustom 611 vb.
outgrown unwonted 611 adj.

outgrowth growth 157 n.
out-Herod Herod
be violent 176 vb.
exaggerate 546 vb.
outhouse adjunct 40 n.
small house 192 n.
chamber 194 n.
outing land travel 267 n.
amusement 837 n.
outland district 184 n.
outlandish
extraneous 59 adj.
unusual 84 adj.
ridiculous 849 adj.
wonderful 864 adj.
outlands farness 199 n.
outlast continue 108 vb.
outlast 113 vb.
stay 144 vb.
be stable 153 vb.
outlaw exclude 57 vb.
nonconformist 84 n.
robber 789 n.
enemy 881 n.
outcaste 883 n.
make unwelcome 883 vb.
offender 904 n.
make illegal 954 vb.
condemn 961 vb.
outlawry
prohibition 757 n.
brigandage 788 n.
lawlessness 954 n.
condemnation 961 n.
outlay waste 634 n.
expenditure 806 n.
outlet orifice 263 n.
outlet 298 n.
outlier entrance 68 n.
outline prototype 23 n.
incompleteness 55 n.
beginning 68 n.
circumjacence 230 n.
outline 233 n., vb.
limit 236 n.
form 243 n.
appearance 445 n.
representation 551 n.
map 551 n.
picture 553 n.
be concise 569 vb.
compendium 592 n.
plan 623 n.
prepare 669 vb.
outlive continue 108 vb.
outlast 113 vb.
stay 144 vb.
outlook futurity 124 n.
destiny 155 n.
view 438 n.
spectacle 445 n.

expectation 507 n.
outlying exterior 223 adj.
outmanœuvre
be superior 34 vb.
navigate 269 vb.
outdo 306 vb.
deceive 542 vb.
defeat 727 vb.
outmarch outstrip 277 vb.
outdo 306 vb.
outmatch
be superior 34 vb.
outmoded useless 641 adj.
outnumber be many 104 vb.
superabound 637 vb.
out of akin 11 adj.
caused 157 adj.
born 360 adj.
out of bounds
too far 199 adv.
surpassing 306 adj.
prohibited 757 adj.
illegal 954 adj.
out of character
unapt 25 adj.
out of countenance
dejected 834 adj.
humbled 872 adj.
out of court wrong 914 adj.
out of date
anachronistic 118 adj.
antiquated 127 adj.
out of doors
exteriority 223 n.
externally 223 adv.
alfresco 340 adv.
air 340 n.
out of fashion
antiquated 127 adj.
out of favour
unfortunate 731 adj.
disliked 861 adj.
out of form clumsy 695 adj.
out of joint unapt 25 adj.
impotent 161 adj.
evil 616 adj.
clumsy 695 adj.
out of keeping unapt 25 adj.
unconformable 84 adj.
out of line
unconformable 84 adj.
out of love disliking 861 adj.
hating 888 adj.
out of luck
unfortunate 731 adj.
out of mind
forgotten 506 adj.
out of one's depth
deeply 211 adv.
puzzled 517 adj.
in difficulties 700 adj.

unsuccessful 728 adj.
out of order
 irrelevant 10 adj.
 unconformable 84 adj.
 useless 641 adj.
out of place
 unconformable 84 adj.
 misplaced 188 adj.
 inexpedient 643 adj.
out of pocket losing 772 adj.
out of proportion
 irrelative 10 adj.
out of reach
 unimitated 21 adj.
 too far 199 adv.
 impracticable 470 adj.
out of season
 anachronistic 118 adj.
 scarce 636 adj.
out of shape
 distorted 246 adj.
out of sight
 too far 199 adv.
 invisible 444 adj.
out of sorts sick 651 adj.
 dejected 834 adj.
out of spirits
 dejected 834 adj.
out of step
 non-uniform 17 adj.
 unapt 25 adj.
 unconformable 84 adj.
out of the ordinary
 special 80 adj.
out of the question
 impossible 470 adj.
 unadmitted 489 adj.
 rejected 607 adj.
 refused 760 adj.
 unpromising 853 adj.
 undue 916 adj.
out-of-the-way
 unusual 84 adj.
 roundabout 626 adj.
out of this world
 prodigious 32 adj.
 dead 361 adj.
 impossible 470 adj.
 pleasurable 826 adj.
out of work
 unused 674 adj.
 non-active 677 adj.
outpace outstrip 277 vb.
 outdo 306 vb.
out-patient
 sick person 651 n.
outplay be superior 34 vb.
 defeat 727 vb.
outpoint
 be superior 34 vb.
 defeat 727 vb.

outpost farness 199 n.
 front 237 n.
outpouring outflow 298 n.
 information 524 n.
 diffuseness 570 n.
 plenty 635 n.
output production 164 n.
outrage violence 176 n.
 evil 616 n.
 ill-treat 645 vb.
 impairment 655 n.
 misuse 675 n., vb.
 shame 867 vb.
 be insolent 878 vb.
 huff 891 vb.
 cruel act 898 n.
 indignity 921 n.
 guilty act 936 n.
 debauch 951 vb.
outrageous
 exorbitant 32 adj.
 violent 176 adj.
 exaggerated 546 adj.
 insolent 878 adj.
 cruel 898 adj.
 disrespectful 921 adj.
 heinous 934 adj.
outrange be distant 199 vb.
 outdo 306 vb.
outrank be unequal 29 vb.
 be superior 34 vb.
 come before 64 vb.
outré unusual 84 adj.
 exaggerated 546 adj.
 ridiculous 849 adj.
outreach
 be superior 34 vb.
 be distant 199 vb.
 deceive 542 vb.
outrider precursor 66 n.
outrigger supporter 218 n.
 projection 254 n.
 rowboat 275 n.
outright
 completely 54 adv.
outrival be superior 34 vb.
 outdo 306 vb.
 contend 716 vb.
outrun outstrip 277 vb.
 outdo 306 vb.
outrush outbreak 176 n.
outset start 68 n.
 departure 296 n.
outshine be superior 34 vb.
 defeat 727 vb.
outshone inferior 35 adj.
outside extraneous 59 adj.
 exteriority 223 n.
 around 230 adv.
 appearance 445 n.
 duplicity 541 n.

outside edge limit 236 n.
 annoyance 827 n.
outsider misfit 25 n.
 intruder 59 n.
 nonconformist 84 n.
 exteriority 223 n.
 outcaste 883 n.
 hateful object 888 n.
outsize unusual 84 adj.
 huge 195 adj.
outskirts entrance 68 n.
 farness 199 n.
 circumjacence 230 n.
outsmart deceive 542 vb.
 be cunning 698 vb.
outspan arrive 295 vb.
outspoken
 undisguised 522 adj.
 assertive 532 adj.
 veracious 540 adj.
 artless 699 adj.
 disrespectful 921 adj.
outspread broad 205 adj.
outstanding
 remarkable 32 adj.
 superior 34 adj.
 remainder 41 n.
 exterior 223 adj.
 notable 638 adj.
 owed 803 adj.
outstare humiliate 872 vb.
 be insolent 878 vb.
outstation farness 199 n.
outstay outlast 113 vb.
outstay one's welcome
 intrude 297 vb.
 be tedious 838 vb.
outstretch be long 203 vb.
outstrip outstrip 277 vb.
 progress 285 vb.
 hasten 680 vb.
out-talk
 be loquacious 581 vb.
out to intending 617 adj.
out-tray receptacle 194 n.
 compartment 194 n.
outturn production 164 n.
outvote reject 607 vb.
outward extrinsic 6 adj.
 exterior 223 adj.
 appearing 445 adj.
outward bound
 departing 296 adj.
 outgoing 298 adj.
outwear outlast 113 vb.
outweigh prevail 178 vb.
 weigh 322 vb.
outwit be superior 34 vb.
 outdo 306 vb.
 befool 542 vb.
outwork projection 254 n.

fortification 713 n.
outworn
  antiquated 127 adj.
outwrite oneself
  be dull 840 vb.
oval *arc* 250 n.
  round 250 adj.
ovary *genitalia* 164 n.
ovate *round* 250 adj.
ovation *trophy* 729 n.
  celebration 876 n.
  applause 923 n.
oven *cookery* 301 n.
  furnace 383 n.
oven-ready *culinary* 301 adj.
  ready-made 669 adj.
over *beyond* 34 adv.
  superior 34 adj.
  remaining 41 adj.
  ending 69 adj.
  past 125 adj.
overact *exaggerate* 546 vb.
  act 594 vb.
  be unskilful 695 vb.
  be affected 850 vb.
overactivity
  overactivity 678 n.
over-age
  antiquated 127 adj.
overall *inclusive* 78 adj.
  longwise 203 adv.
  apron 228 n.
  trousers 228 n.
overambitious
  rash 857 adj.
over and above
  in addition 38 adv.
  superfluous 637 adj.
over and over
  repeatedly 106 adv.
overarch *overlie* 226 vb.
over-attentive
  servile 879 adj.
overawe *prevail* 178 vb.
  dominate 733 vb.
  oppress 735 vb.
  frighten 854 vb.
  command respect 920 vb.
overbalance
  be unequal 29 vb.
  tumble 309 vb.
  weigh 322 vb.
overbear *prevail* 178 vb.
  motivate 612 vb.
overbearing
  oppressive 735 adj.
  proud 871 adj.
  insolence 878 n.
overbid *overstep* 306 vb.
  bargain 791 vb.
overblown *aged* 131 adj.

expanded 197 adj.
overborne *defeated* 728 adj.
  subjected 745 adj.
overbrimming
  redundance 637 n.
overbuilt *covered* 226 adj.
overburden *load* 193 vb.
  make heavy 322 vb.
  ill-treat 645 vb.
  fatigue 684 vb.
overbusy
  inquisitive 453 adj.
  meddling 678 adj.
overcall *outdo* 306 vb.
overcast *cloudy* 355 adj.
  darken 418 vb.
  shadowy 419 adj.
  cheerless 834 adj.
  sullen 893 adj.
overcaution
  irresolution 601 n.
overcharge
  exaggerate 546 vb.
  dearness 811 n.
over-clever
  intelligent 498 adj.
  vain 873 adj.
overcloud (*see* overcast)
overcoat *overcoat* 228 n.
  warm clothes 381 n.
overcolour
  exaggerate 546 vb.
overcolouring
  misinterpretation 521 n.
overcome *prevail* 178 vb.
  overmaster 727 vb.
  dejected 834 adj.
  tipsy 949 vb.
over-communicative
  informative 524 adj.
overcompensate
  be unequal 29 vb.
  compensate 31 vb.
  exaggerate 546 vb.
over-compression
  imperspicuity 568 n.
over-confidence
  rashness 857 n.
over-confident
  optimistic 482 adj.
  credulous 487 adj.
  rash 857 adj.
over-critical
  fastidious 862 adj.
  disapproving 924 adj.
overcrop *waste* 634 vb.
  make insufficient 636 vb.
overcrowded
  assembled 74 adj.
over-curious
  inquisitive 453 adj.

over-daring *rash* 857 adj.
over-delicate *prudish* 950 adj.
overdevelop *enlarge* 197 vb.
  darken 418 vb.
  blacken 428 vb.
overdo *overstep* 306 vb.
  exaggerate 546 vb.
  superabound 637 vb.
overdone *tough* 329 adj.
  overrated 482 adj.
  absurd 497 adj.
  exaggerated 546 adj.
  affected 850 adj.
  flattering 925 adj.
overdose *redundance* 637 n.
  satiety 863 n.
overdraft *loss* 772 n.
  debt 803 n.
  insolvency 805 n.
over-dramatize
  misrepresent 552 vb.
  act 594 vb.
overdraw
  exaggerate 546 vb.
  misrepresent 552 vb.
  lose 772 vb.
  be in debt 803 vb.
  be prodigal 815 vb.
overdrawn *losing* 772 adj.
  indebted 803 adj.
overdressed *vulgar* 847 adj.
overdrive *power* 160 n.
  fatigue 684 vb.
overdue *late* 136 adj.
  important 638 adj.
  owed 803 adj.
  just 913 adj.
overeat
  be intemperate 943 vb.
  gluttonize 947 vb.
over-economical
  parsimonious 816 adj.
over-emphasis
  exaggeration 546 n.
overemployment
  superfluity 637 n.
overestimate
  overstep 306 vb.
  misjudge 481 vb.
  overestimation 482 n.
  make important 638 vb.
  praise 923 vb.
overestimation
  exaggeration 546 n.
over-exertion
  overactivity 678 n.
  fatigue 684 n.
overexpose
  darken 418 vb.
over-extension
  overactivity 678 n.

overfall *waterfall* 350n.
  wave 350n.
overfamiliar
  impertinent 878adj.
overfed *sensual* 944adj.
  gluttonous 947adj.
overfeed
  superabound 637vb.
  sate 863vb.
overfill *fill* 54vb.
  sate 863vb.
overflow
  be complete 54vb.
  be many 104vb.
  irrupt 297vb.
  outflow 298n.
  encroach 306vb.
  moistening 341n.
  waterfall 350n.
  drain 351n.
  have feeling 374vb.
  diffuseness 570n.
  abound 635vb.
  redundance 637n.
overflowing *great* 32adj.
  full 54adj.
over-fulfil
  superabound 637vb.
overfull *redundant* 637adj.
overgo *overstep* 306vb.
overgrow *hinder* 702vb.
overgrown
  expanded 197adj.
  vegetal 366adj.
overgrowth
  expansion 197n.
  roughness 259n.
overhang
  be to come 124vb.
  be high 209vb.
  hang 217vb.
  jut 254vb.
  overlie 226vb.
overhaul *outstrip* 277vb.
  outdo 306vb.
  be attentive 455vb.
  search 459vb.
  repair 656vb.
overhead *aloft* 209adv.
overheads *cost* 809n.
overhear *hear* 415vb.
  be informed 524vb.
overhearing
  listening 415n.
over-heated *hot* 379adj.
  insalubrious 653adj.
  excited 821adj.
overhung *salient* 254adj.
over-indulgence
  laxity 734n.
  intemperance 943n.

  sensualism 944n.
  gluttony 947n.
over-insure
  be cautious 858vb.
over-interested
  obsessed 455adj.
overjoyed *pleased* 824adj.
overland *on land* 344adv.
overlap *continuity* 71n.
  be included 78vb.
  be contiguous 202vb.
  stratification 207n.
  covering 226n.
  encroach 306vb.
  touch 378vb.
  superfluity 637n.
overlarge *huge* 195adj.
overlay *laminate* 207vb.
  overlay 226vb.
  kill 362vb.
  conceal 525vb.
  ornament 574vb.
overleaf *against* 240adv.
overlie *hang* 217vb.
  overlie 226vb.
overload *load* 193vb.
  make heavy 322vb.
  exaggerate 546vb.
  ornament 574vb.
  redundance 637n.
  encumbrance 702n.
overlong *surpassing* 306adj.
  tedious 838adj.
overlook *be high* 209vb.
  be inattentive 456vb.
  neglect 458vb.
  not use 674vb.
  be patient 823vb.
  forgive 909vb.
  bewitch 983vb.
overlord *superior* 34n.
  master 741n.
overlordship
  superiority 34n.
  magistrature 733n.
  governance 733n.
overly *extremely* 32adv.
  redundantly 637adv.
overlying
  overhanging 209adj.
  overlying 226adj.
overmaster
  overmaster 727vb.
  subjugate 745vb.
overmatch
  be strong 162vb.
  overmaster 727vb.
over-measure
  redundance 637n.
over-mighty
  powerful 160adj.

  influential 178adj.
  oppressive 735adj.
  proud 871adj.
  lawless 954adj.
over-modesty
  underestimation 483n.
  prudery 950n.
overmost *topmost* 213adj.
overmuch
  redundant 637adj.
over-nice
  fastidious 862adj.
overnight
  instantaneously 116adv.
  foregoing 125adj.
over one's head
  deeply 211adv.
  puzzling 517adj.
overpage *against* 240adv.
overpaid *rich* 800adj.
  unwarranted 916adj.
overpaint *coat* 226vb.
  make opaque 423vb.
  conceal 525vb.
  obliterate 550vb.
overpass *be superior* 34vb.
  overstep 306vb.
overpay *be liberal* 813vb.
overpayment
  redundance 637n.
  undueness 916n.
overpersuade *induce* 612vb.
over-piety *pietism* 979n.
overplus *remainder* 41n.
  part 53n.
  redundance 637n.
over-populate
  superabound 637vb.
over-populated
  multitudinous 104adj.
over-population
  crowd 74n.
overpower *be strong* 162vb.
  overmaster 727vb.
overpowering
  impressive 821adj.
overpraise
  overestimation 482n.
  overrate 482vb.
  misinterpret 521vb.
  exaggerate 546vb.
  redundance 637n.
  praise 923n., vb.
  flatter 925vb.
over-priced *dear* 811adj.
overprint *substitute* 150vb.
  mark 547vb.
  obliterate 550vb.
overprize *overrate* 482vb.
overproduce
  superabound 637vb.

over-proof
unmixed 44 adj.
pungent 388 adj.
intoxicating 949 adj.
overproud
prideful 871 adj.
overrate *overrate* 482 vb.
exaggerate 546 vb.
make important 638 vb.
overrated *overrated* 482 adj.
unimportant 639 adj.
dear 811 adj.
overreach *outdo* 306 vb.
deceive 542 vb.
be cunning 698 vb.
over-refinement
fastidiousness 862 n.
override *prevail* 178 vb.
overstep 306 vb.
be resolute 599 vb.
overmaster 727 vb.
dominate 733 vb.
oppress 735 vb.
overriding *supreme* 34 adj.
necessary 596 adj.
important 638 adj.
compelling 740 adj.
over-righteous
pietistic 979 adj.
over-ripe *aged* 131 adj.
soft 327 adj.
pulpy 356 adj.
overrule *dominate* 733 vb.
abrogate 752 vb.
overruling *supreme* 34 adj.
important 638 adj.
authoritative 733 adj.
overrun *fill* 54 vb.
be many 104 vb.
encroach 306 vb.
attack 712 vb.
appropriate 786 vb.
over-sanguine
optimistic 482 adj.
rash 857 adj.
oversea *extraneous* 59 adj.
removed 199 adj.
oversee *manage* 689 vb.
overseer *manager* 690 n.
oversell *exaggerate* 546 vb.
overset *demolish* 165 vb.
overturning 221 vb.
depression 311 n.
overshadow
be superior 34 vb.
be high 209 vb.
overlie 226 vb.
darken 418 vb.
bedim 419 vb.
dominate 733 vb.
overshoe *footwear* 228 n.

overshoot *overstep* 306 vb.
be clumsy 695 vb.
oversight *inspection* 438 n.
inattention 456 n.
negligence 458 n.
mistake 495 n.
management 689 n.
oversize *huge* 195 adj.
overskirt *skirt* 228 n.
oversleep
lose a chance 138 vb.
be neglectful 458 vb.
fail in duty 918 vb.
oversoul *divineness* 965 n.
overspecialize
misjudge 481 vb.
overspend
be prodigal 815 vb.
overspending *waste* 634 n.
overspill
redundance 637 n.
overspread *overlay* 226 vb.
overstatement
overestimation 482 n.
affirmation 532 n.
untruth 543 n.
exaggeration 546 n.
magniloquence 574 n.
overstay *overstep* 306 vb.
overstep *overstep* 306 vb.
not observe 769 vb.
overstock
superabound 637 vb.
overstrain *overrate* 482 vb.
waste 634 vb.
fatigue 684 vb.
overstress *overrate* 482 vb.
exaggerate 546 vb.
over-strung
sentient 374 adj.
lively 819 adj.
over-subscribe
superabound 637 vb.
over-subtlety
sophistry 477 n.
over-sure *rash* 857 adj.
over-suspicious
unbelieving 486 adj.
overt *undisguised* 522 adj.
overtake *outstrip* 277 vb.
outdo 306 vb.
hasten 680 vb.
overtaking *spurt* 277 n.
approach 289 n.
overtask *misuse* 675 vb.
fatigue 684 vb.
impose a duty 917 vb.
overtax *oppress* 735 vb.
levy 786 vb.
misuse 675 vb.
fatigue 684 vb.

overthrow
revolution 149 n.
demolish 165 vb.
fell 311 vb.
confute 479 vb.
bungling 695 n.
overmaster 727 vb.
overthrown
defeated 728 adj.
overtime *addition* 38 n.
extra 40 n.
protraction 113 n.
exertion 682 n.
overtone *musical note* 410 n.
overtop *be great* 32 vb.
be superior 34 vb.
be high 209 vb.
crown 213 vb.
overtrick *remainder* 41 n.
overtrump
overmaster 727 vb.
over-trustful
credulous 487 adj.
overture *prelude* 66 n.
approach 289 n.
musical piece 412 n.
irenics 719 n.
offer 759 n.
request 761 n.
friendship 880 n.
overturn *derange* 63 vb.
revolutionize 149 vb.
demolish 165 vb.
invert 221 vb.
overvalue *misjudge* 481 vb.
overrate 482 vb.
overweening *rash* 857 adj.
proud 871 adj.
vain 873 adj.
insolent 878 adj.
overweigh
predominate 34 vb.
be many 104 vb.
prevail 178 vb.
motivate 612 vb.
overweight *inequality* 29 n.
unwieldy 195 adj.
make heavy 322 vb.
exaggerate 546 vb.
redundance 637 n.
make important 638 vb.
overwhelm *fill* 54 vb.
be many 104 vb.
be strong 162 vb.
destroy 165 vb.
be violent 176 vb.
confute 479 vb.
superabound 637 vb.
attack 712 vb.
defeat 727 vb.
impress 821 vb.

sadden 834 vb.
overwhelming
    prodigious 32 adj.
    felt 818 adj.
    impressive 821 adj.
    wonderful 864 adj.
overwork *waste* 634 vb.
    misuse 675 vb.
    be busy 678 vb.
    work 682 vb.
    fatigue 684 vb.
overwriting *lettering* 586 n.
over-wrought
    matured 669 adj.
    fervent 818 adj.
    excited 821 adj.
    affected 850 adj.
oviform *rotund* 252 adj.
ovine *animal* 365 adj.
oviparous
    productive 164 adj.
ovoid *round* 250 adj.
    rotund 252 adj.
ovule *arc* 250 n.
owe *be in debt* 803 vb.
owe nothing to
    be unrelated 10 vb.
owing *owed* 803 adj.
    due 915 adj.
owing to
    caused 157 adj.
    attributed 158 adj.
    hence 158 adv.
owl *bird* 365 n.
    fool 501 n.
    omen 511 n.
owlish *unintelligent* 499 adj.
own *assent* 488 vb.
    confess 526 vb.
    possess 773 vb.
own accord, of one's
    at will 595 adv.
own a connection
    be akin 11 vb.
owner *master* 741 n.
    owner 776 n.
ownerless
    unpossessed 774 adj.
ownership *possession* 773 n.
own generation, one's
    contemporary 123 n.
own, on one's
    friendless 883 adj.
ox *beast of burden* 273 n.
    male animal 372 n.
    cattle 365 n.
Oxford Movement
    Catholicism 976 n.
    sect 978 n.
oxide *ash* 381 n.
oxygen *air* 340 n.

oxygenate *gasify* 336 vb.
    aerify 340 vb.
oxymoron *misfit* 25 n.
oxytone
    punctuation 547 n.
oyster *fish food* 301 n.
    table fish 365 n.
    grey 429 n.
    taciturnity 582 n.
ozone *air* 340 n.
    salubrity 652 n.

P

pabulum *food* 301 n.
pace *synchronize* 123 vb.
    long measure 203 n.
    gait 265 n.
    walk 267 vb.
    velocity 277 n.
    measure 465 vb.
pacemaker *leader* 690 n.
pacer *pedestrian* 268 n.
    thoroughbred 273 n.
pace-stick *gauge* 465 n.
pachyderm *animal* 365 n.
pachydermatous
    unfeeling 375 adj.
    thick-skinned 820 adj.
pacific *inert* 175 adj.
    moderate 177 adj.
    concordant 710 adj.
    peaceful 717 adj.
pacification
    moderation 177 n.
    pacification 719 n.
    friendship 880 n.
    propitiation 941 n.
pacificator, pacifier
    mediator 720 n.
pacificatory *lenitive* 177 adj.
    pacificatory 719 adj.
    mediatory 720 adj.
    courteous 884 adj.
pacifism *peace* 717 n.
pacifist *pacifist* 717 n.
pacify *pacify* 719 vb.
    mediate 720 vb.
    tranquillize 823 vb.
pack *fill* 54 vb.
    group 74 n.
    stow 187 vb.
    load 193 vb.
    line 227 vb.
    close 264 vb.
    travel 267 vb.
    be dense 324 vb.
    dog 365 n.
    fake 541 vb.
    hunter 619 n.
    store 632 vb.

make ready 669 vb.
    encumbrance 702 n.
    beautification 843 n.
    do wrong 914 vb.
package *bunch* 74 n.
    inclusion 78 n.
    unit 88 n.
    (see pack)
pack a jury
    predetermine 608 vb.
pack a punch
    be strong 162 vb.
packer *preparer* 669 n.
    worker 686 n.
packet *great quantity* 32 n.
    bunch 74 n.
    small box 194 n.
    ship 275 n.
    wealth 800 n.
pack-horse
    beast of burden 273 n.
pack-ice *ice* 380 n.
packing *location* 187 n.
    contents 193 n.
    lining 227 n.
packing-case *box* 194 n.
    storage 632 n.
packthread *fibre* 208 n.
pact *agreement* 24 n.
    compact 765 n.
Pactolus *wealth* 800 n.
pad *load* 193 vb.
    enlarge 197 vb.
    foot 214 n.
    seat 218 n.
    line 227 vb.
    saddle-horse 273 n.
    faintness 401 b.
    be diffuse 570 vb.
    stationery 586 n.
padded *expanded* 197 adj.
    soft 327 adj.
    pleonastic 570 adj.
padded cell
    madhouse 503 n.
    shelter 662 n.
padding *increment* 36 n.
    adjunct 40 n.
    lining 227 n.
    stopper 264 n.
    softness 327 n.
    warm clothes 381 n.
    pleonasm 570 n.
paddle *walk* 267 vb.
    row, swim 269 vb.
    strike 279 vb.
    propellant 287 n.
    be wet 341 vb.
    spank 963 vb.
paddle one's own canoe
    be free 744 vb.

paddler *pedestrian* 268 n.
paddle-wheel
  propeller 269 n.
paddling *aquatics* 269 n.
paddock *inclosure* 235 n.
paddy *corn* 366 n.
  anger 891 n.
padishah *sovereign* 741 n.
padlock *fastening* 47 n.
  lock-up 748 n.
padnag *saddle-horse* 273 n.
pad out *augment* 36 vb.
  be diffuse 570 vb.
padre *title* 870 n.
  cleric 986 n.
pæan *rejoicing* 835 n.
  celebration 876 n.
  thanks 907 n.
  applause 923 n.
  hymn 981 n.
pæderast *libertine* 952 n.
pædeutics *teaching* 534 n.
pæonin *red pigment* 431 n.
pagan *heathen* 974 n.
  profane 980 adj.
  idolater 982 n.
paganism *religion* 973 n.
  antichristianity 974 n.
  impiety 980 n.
  idolatry 982 n.
paganize *convert* 147 vb.
  paganize 974 vb.
page *part* 53 n.
  courier 531 n.
  mark 547 vb.
  edition 589 n.
  retainer 742 n.
  bridesman 894 n.
pageant, pageantry
  spectacle 445 n.
  pageant 875 n.
page-boy *youngster* 132 n.
  servant 742 n.
pages *great quantity* 32 n.
pagination *numeration* 86 n.
pagoda *high structure* 209 n.
  temple 990 n.
paid *subject* 745 adj.
  gainful 771 adj.
  receiving 782 adj.
  expended 806 adj.
paid for *bought* 792 adj.
pail *vessel* 194 n.
pain *pain* 377 n.
  evil 616 n.
  suffering 825 vb.
  painfulness 827 n.
  discontent 829 n.
  sadden 834 vb.
pained *resentful* 891 adj.
painful *painful* 377 adj.

laborious 682 adj.
  paining 827 adj.
painfully *carefully* 457 adv.
pain-killer
  anæsthetic 375 n.
  antidote 658 n.
  relief 831 n.
pain-killing *lenitive* 177 adj.
painless
  comfortable 376 adj.
  easy 701 adj.
  pleasurable 826 adj.
pains *obstetrics* 164 n.
  attention 455 n.
  carefulness 457 n.
  exertion 682 n.
pains and penalties
  penalty 963 n.
painstaking *careful* 457 adj.
  assiduity 678 n.
  exertion 682 n.
  laborious 682 adj.
paint *imitate* 20 vb.
  coat 226 vb.
  pigment 425 n.
  imagine 513 vb.
  sham 542 n.
  represent 551 vb.
  paint 553 vb.
  describe 590 vb.
  cleanser 648 n.
  preserve 660 vb.
  cosmetic 843 n.
  decorate 844 vb.
paintable *painted* 553 adj.
  beautiful 841 adj.
paint-box *pigment* 425 n.
  art equipment 553 n.
paint brush
  art equipment 553 n.
painted *florid* 425 adj.
  red 431 adj.
  false 541 adj.
  deceiving 542 adj.
  beautified 843 adj.
painter *cable* 47 n.
  artist 556 n.
painting *composition* 56 n.
  colour 425 n.
  representation 551 n.
  picture 553 n.
  beautification 843 n.
  ornamental art 844 n.
paints
  art equipment 553 n.
pair *identify* 13 vb.
  analogue 18 n.
  unite with 45 vb.
  combine 50 vb.
  group 74 n.
  concomitant 89 n.

duality 90 n.
  compare 462 vb.
paired *married* 894 adj.
pairing *coition* 45 n.
pal *colleague* 707 n.
  chum 880 n.
palace *house* 192 n.
  magistrature 733 n.
  parsonage 986 n.
paladin
  brave person 855 n.
  defender 713 n.
  combatant 722 n.
  philanthropist 901 n.
palæocrystic *primal* 127 adj.
palæographer
  interpreter 520 n.
palæography
  palætiology 125 n.
  hermeneutics 520 n.
  linguistics 557 n.
palæolithic *secular* 110 adj.
  primal 127 adj.
Palæolithic Age
  antiquity 125 n.
palæontologist
  antiquarian 125 n.
palæontology
  palætiology 125 n.
  zoology 367 n.
palæozoic *secular* 110 adj.
  primal 127 adj.
palæstra *athletics* 162 n.
  academy 539 n.
  arena 724 n.
palæstric
  contending 716 adj.
palætiology
  palætiology 125 n.
  attribution 158 n.
palais de danse
  place of amusement 837 n.
palanquin *vehicle* 274 n.
palatable *edible* 301 adj.
  pleasant 376 adj.
  tasty 386 adj.
  savoury 390 adj.
palatal *speech sound* 398 n.
  spoken letter 558 n.
palatalize *voice* 577 vb.
palate *taste* 386 n.
  good taste 846 n.
palate-tickling
  gastronomy 301 n.
palatial
  architectural 192 adj.
palatinate *territory* 184 n.
  polity 733 n.
palaver *empty talk* 515 n.
  speech 579 n.
  chatter 581 n.

conference 584n.
pale *fastening* 47n.
　exclusion 57n.
　weak 163adj.
　region 184n.
　fence, barrier 235n.
　be dim 419vb.
　soft-hued 425adj.
　colourless 426adj.
　lose colour 426vb.
　whitish 427adj.
　disappear 446vb.
　heraldry 547n.
　unhealthy 651adj.
paleface *foreigner* 59n.
palette *plate* 194n.
　art equipment 553n.
palewise *vertical* 215adj.
palfrey *saddle-horse* 273n.
Pali *language* 557n.
palillogy *repetition* 106n.
　affirmation 532n.
palimpsest *substitute* 150n.
　script 586n.
　book 589n.
palindrome *inversion* 221n.
paling *fence* 235n.
　defences 713n.
palingenesis
　reproduction 166n.
palinode *negation* 533n.
　poem 593n.
　recantation 603n.
palisade *barrier* 235n.
　protection 660n.
　defences 713n.
palki *vehicle* 274n.
palki-bearer *bearer* 273n.
pall *funeral* 364n.
　render insensible 375vb.
　be unpalatable 391n.
　obfuscation 421n.
　invisibility 444n.
　regalia 743n.
　be tedious 838vb.
　cause dislike 861vb.
　sate 863vb.
　vestments 989n.
palladium
　protection 660n.
　refuge 662n.
　talisman 983n.
pall-bearer *funeral* 364n.
pallet *bed* 218n.
palliate *moderate* 177vb.
　qualify 468vb.
　plead 614vb.
　make better 654vb.
　remedy 658vb.
　relieve 831vb.
　extenuate 927vb.

palliative *moderator* 177n.
　remedial 658adj.
pallid *colourless* 426adj.
pallium *robe* 228n.
　vestments 989n.
pallone *ball game* 837n.
pallor *hue* 425n.
　achromatism 426n.
pally *friendly* 880adj.
　sociable 882adj.
palm *long measure* 203n.
　feeler 378n.
　touch 378vb.
　oracle 511n.
　trophy 729n.
palmate *notched* 260adj.
palmer *traveller* 268n.
　pietist 979n.
　worshipper 981n.
palm-greasing
　inducement 612n.
palmistry *divination* 511n.
　occultism 984n.
palm off *deceive* 542vb.
palmy days
　palmy days 730n.
　happiness 824n.
　joy 824n.
palomino *horse* 273n.
palp *feeler* 378n.
　touch 378vb.
palpable
　substantial 3adj.
　material 319adj.
　tactual 378adj.
　visible 443adj.
　manifest 522adj.
palpation *touch* 378n.
palpitation
　oscillation 317n.
　agitation 318n.
　feeling 818n.
　nervousness 854n.
palpitations
　heart disease 651n.
　fatigue 684n.
palpus *feeler* 378n.
palsied *aged* 131adj.
　apathetic 820adj.
　(*see* palsy)
palsy *helplessness* 161n.
　unman 161vb.
　agitation, spasm 318n.
　insensibility 375n.
　paralysis 651n.
　frighten 854vb.
palter *be false* 541vb.
　dissemble 541vb.
　be irresolute 601vb.
　not observe 769vb.
palterer *liar* 545n.

paltry
　inconsiderable 33adj.
　unimportant 639adj.
　contemptible 922adj.
　rascally 930adj.
　selfish 932adj.
paludial *marshy* 347adj.
pampas *plain* 348n.
pamper *pet* 889vb.
　be sensual 944vb.
pampered *sensual* 944adj.
　gluttonous 947adj.
pamphlet *the press* 528n.
　book 589n.
pamphleteer *argue* 475vb.
　publicizer 528n.
　preacher 537n.
　dissertator 591n.
Pan *animality* 365n.
　vegetability 366n.
　musician 413n.
　mythic god 966n.
　lesser god 967n.
pan *eliminate* 44vb.
　plate 194n.
　face 237n.
　scales 322n.
panacea *remedy* 658n.
panache *plumage* 259n.
　trimming 844n.
　ostentation 875n.
panama *headgear* 228n.
panary *storage* 632n.
pancake *horizontality* 216n.
　aeronautics 271n.
　cereal 301n.
pancarditis
　heart disease 651n.
pancratiast *athlete* 162n.
pandar *cad* 938n.
　bawd 952n.
　(*see* pander)
pandect *dissertation* 591n.
　compendium 592n.
　law 953n.
pandemic *universal* 79adj.
　plague 651n.
　infectious 653adj.
　unchaste 951adj.
pandemonium *turmoil* 61n.
　loudness 400n.
　discord 411n.
　hell 972n.
pander *provide* 633vb.
　please 826vb.
　be impure 951vb.
　(*see* pandar)
pander to *tempt* 612vb.
　be instrumental 628vb.
　minister to 703vb.
　be servile 879vb.

flatter 925 vb.
pandiculate *expand* 197 vb.
  lengthen 203 vb.
pandiculation
  opening 263 n.
  sleepiness 679 n.
pane *brittleness* 330 n.
  transparency 422 n.
panegyric
  overestimation 482 n.
  praise 923 n.
panel *band* 74 n.
  list 87 n.
  lamina 207 n.
  partition 231 n.
panelled *variegated* 437 adj.
panelling *lining* 227 n.
  ornamental art 844 n.
pang *spasm* 318 n.
  pang 377 n.
  suffering 825 n.
panhandle *beg* 761 vb.
panhandler *beggar* 763 n.
  low fellow 869 n.
panic *fear* 854 n.,vb.
  be cowardly 856 vb.
panicky *fearing* 854 adj.
panjandrum *bigwig* 638 n.
  aristocrat 868 n.
pannier *basket* 194 n.
  skirt 228 n.
pannikin *cup* 194 n.
panoply *protection* 660 n.
  armour 713 n.
panopticon *prison* 748 n.
panorama *whole* 52 n.
  generality 79 n.
  open space 263 n.
  view 438 n.
  spectacle 445 n.
  art subject 553 n.
pan out *happen* 154 vb.
  result 157 vb.
pan-pipes *flute* 414 n.
pansophy *erudition* 490 n.
pansy *weakling* 163 n.
  purple 434 n.
  libertine 952 n.
pant *oscillate* 317 vb.
  be agitated 318 vb.
  breathe 352 vb.
  be hot 379 vb.
  be fatigued 684 vb.
  show feeling 818 vb.
  desire 859 vb.
pantalettes *trousers* 228 n.
Pantaloon *old man* 133 n.
  entertainer 594 n.
pantaloons *trousers* 228 n.
pantechnicon *cart* 274 n.
pantheism *deism* 973 n.

pantheist
  religionist 971 adj.
pantheon *god* 966 n.
  temple 990 n.
panther *cat* 365 n.
panties *underwear* 228 n.
pantile *roof* 226 n.
  drain 351 n.
panting (*see* pant)
pantisocracy
  government 733 n.
pantler *provider* 633 n.
pantologist *scholar* 492 n.
  export 696 n.
  vain person 873 n.
pantomime *mimicry* 20 n.
  gesture 547 n.
  gesticulate 547 vb.
  stage play 594 n.
  act 594 vb.
pantophagist
  glutton 947 n.
pantophagy *eating* 301 n.
pantry *chamber* 194 n.
  provisions 301 n.
  storage 632 n.
pants *trousers* 228 n.
  underwear 228 n.
panurgic *skilful* 694 adj.
pap *bosom* 253 n.
  food 301 n.
  semiliquidity 354 n.
  pulpiness 356 n.
  insipidity 387 n.
  trifle 639 n.
papacy *churchdom* 985 n.
  church office 985 n.
papal *ecclesiastical* 985 adj.
papal court
  ecclesiastical court 956 n.
papaya *fruit* 301 n.
paper *insubstantial* 4 adj.
  weak thing 163 n.
  thinness 206 n.
  wrapping 226 n.
  overlay 226 vb.
  line 227 vb.
  white thing 427 n.
  report 524 n.
  the press 528 n.
  stationery 586 n.
  dissertation 591 n.
  paper 631 n.
  title-deed 767 n.
p.perback *book* 589 n.
  novel 590 n.
paperchase *chase* 619 n.
  racing 716 n.
paper over *repair* 656 vb.
paper over the cracks
  not suffice 636 vb.

be *unskilful* 695 vb.
  not complete 726 vb.
papers *record* 548 n.
paper war *argument* 475 n.
  quarrel 709 n.
  contention 716 n.
  war 718 n.
papery *brittle* 330 adj.
papier mâché
  pulpiness 356 n.
  paper 631 n.
papilla *bosom* 253 n.
papist *Catholic* 976 n.
papistical *popish* 976 adj.
papistry *Catholicism* 976 n.
papoose *child* 132 n.
pappous *downy* 259 adj.
pappus *hair* 259 n.
pappy *pulpy* 356 adj.
paprika *vegetable* 301 n.
  condiment 389 n.
papula *swelling* 253 n.
papule *skin disease* 651 n.
papyrus *stationery* 586 n.
par *equivalence* 28 n.
parable *metaphor* 519 n.
  lecture 534 n.
  narrative 590 n.
parabola *curve* 248 n.
parabolical
  figurative 519 adj.
parabolize *figure* 519 vb.
paracentesis
  voidance 300 n.
parachronism
  anachronism 118 n.
  different time 122 n.
parachute *fly* 271 vb.
  aircraft 276 n.
  descend 309 vb.
  safeguard 662 n.
parachutist *aeronaut* 271 n.
Paraclete
  Holy Ghost 965 n.
parade *assemblage* 74 n.
  street 192 n.
  marching 267 n.
  spectacle 445 n.
  show 522 vb.
  path 624 n.
  pageant 875 n.
parade ground
  meeting place 192 n.
  arena 724 n.
paradigm *prototype* 23 n.
  grammar 564 n.
paradisal
  pleasurable 826 adj.
  paradisiac 971 adj.
paradise *happiness* 824 n.
  heaven 971 n.

parados *defences* 713n.
paradox *contrariety* 14n.
  misfit 25n.
  argumentation 475n.
  absurdity 497n.
  inexpectation 508n.
  unintelligibility 517n.
  ridiculousness 849n.
paraffin *oil* 357n.
  fuel 385n.
paragon *prototype* 23n.
  exceller 644n.
  paragon 646n.
  prodigy 864n.
  person of repute 866n.
  good man 937n.
paragram
  equivocalness 518n.
paragraph
  subdivision 53n.
  punctuation 547n.
  phrase 563n.
  edition 589n.
parakeet *bird* 365n.
paralalia
  speech defect 580n.
paraleipsis
  negligence 458n.
  trope 519n.
parallax *distance* 199n.
parallel *correlative* 12adj.
  analogue 18n.
  equal 28adj.
  concurrent 181adj.
  region 184n.
  parallelism 219n.
  compare 462vb.
  defences 713n.
parallel course
  accompaniment 89n.
parallelepiped
  parallelism 219n.
  angular figure 247n.
parallelism *similarity* 18n.
  conformance 24n.
  parallelism 219n.
  symmetry 245n.
parallelogram
  parallelism 219n.
  angular figure 247n.
paralogism *sophism* 477n.
paralyse *disable* 161vb.
  render insensible 375vb.
  prohibit 757vb.
paralysed *still* 266adj.
  non-active 677adj.
  (*see* paralysis)
paralysis *helplessness* 161n.
  inertness 175n.
  insensibility 375n.
  paralysis 651n.

  hindrance 702n.
paralytic *sick person* 651n.
Paramatman
  divineness 965n.
paramatta *textile* 222n.
paramnesia *error* 495n.
  oblivion 506n.
paramount *supreme* 34adj.
  authoritative 733adj.
paramountcy
  superiority 34n.
  importance 638n.
  prestige 866n.
paramour *lover* 887n.
  kept woman 952n.
parang *sharp edge* 256n.
  side-arms 723n.
paranoia
  psychopathy 503n.
paranoiac *madman* 504n.
paranormal
  paranormal 984adj.
paranymph *auxiliary* 707n.
  bridesman 894n.
parapet *summit* 213n.
  fortification 713n.
paraph *label* 547n.
  sign 547vb.
paraphasia
  speech defect 580n.
paraphemia
  speech defect 580n.
paraphernalia
  medley 43n.
  equipment 630n.
  property 777n.
paraphrase *imitation* 20n.
  copy 22n.
  intelligibility 516n.
  translation 520n.
  phrase 563n.
paraphrast *interpreter* 520n.
paraphrastic
  semantic 514adj.
  interpretive 520adj.
paraphrenia
  psychopathy 503n.
paraphronesis *frenzy* 503n.
paraplegia *paralysis* 651n.
parapraxis *inattention* 456n.
parapsychology
  psychology 447n.
  psychics 984n.
parasang
  long measure 203n.
paraselene *moon* 321n.
parasite *concomitant* 89n.
  settler 191n.
  eater 301n.
  vermin 365n.
  superfluity 637n.

  bane 659n.
  idler 679n.
  dependant 742n.
  beggar 763n.
  desirer 859n.
  toady 879n.
  social person 882n.
  flatterer 925n.
parasitical *inferior* 35adj.
  residing 192adj.
parasitology
  pathology 651n.
parasol *shade* 226n.
parataxis *grammar* 564n.
paratrooper *aeronaut* 271n.
  armed force 722n.
paratyphoid *infection* 651n.
parboil *cook* 301vb.
parbuckle *tool* 630n.
parcel *sunder* 46vb.
  piece 53n.
  bunch 74n.
  apportion 783vb.
parch *dry* 342vb.
  be hot 379vb.
  heat 381vb.
  cause desire 859vb.
parchment
  stationery 586n.
  bookbinding 589n.
pardon
  amnesty 506n.
  lenity 736n.
  liberate 746vb.
  forgiveness 909n.
  non-liability 919n.
  acquittal 960n.
pardonable
  vindicable 927adj.
  guiltless 935adj.
pardoner *pastor* 986n.
pare *shade off* 27vb.
  bate 37vb.
  subtract 39vb.
  cut 46vb.
  shorten 204vb.
paregoric
  remedial 658adj.
parent *kinsman* 11n.
  precursor 66n.
  source 156n.
  producer 167n.
  parent 169n.
parentage
  consanguinity 11n.
  source 156n.
  attribution 158n.
  parentage 169n.
parental *parental* 169adj.
parenthesis *irrelevance* 10n.
  discontinuity 72n.

interjection 231 n.
insertion 303 n.
punctuation 547 n.
parenthood
  propagation 164 n.
  parentage 169 n.
  life 360 n.
par excellence
  eminently 34 adv.
parget *paving* 226 n.
  coat 226 vb.
pargeting
  ornamental art 844 n.
parhelion *sun* 321 n.
pariah
  nonconformist 84 n.
  outcaste 883 n.
parietal *lateral* 239 adj.
paring *small thing* 33 n.
  leavings 41 n.
  piece 53 n.
  economy 814 n.
pari passu *equally* 28 adv.
  synchronously 123 adv.
parish *subdivision* 53 n.
  district 184 n.
  parish 985 n.
  laity 987 n.
parish clerk
  church officer 986 n.
parishioner *native* 191 n.
  layman 987 n.
parish pump *trifle* 639 n.
parison
  ornament 574 n.
paritor *law officer* 955 n.
parity *similarity* 18 n.
  equality 28 n.
park *accumulation* 74 n.
  station 187 n.
  place oneself 187 vb.
  pleasance 192 n.
  inclosure 235 n.
  grassland 348 n.
  wood 366 n.
  garden 370 n.
  pleasure-ground 837 n.
parka *tunic* 228 n.
  warm clothes 381 n.
parking-meter
  timekeeper 117 n.
  meter 465 n.
parking place
  station 187 n.
Parkinson's law
  expansion 197 n.
parkway *road* 624 n.
parlance *style* 566 n.
  speech 579 n.
parlementaire
  messenger 531 n.

irenics 719 n.
parley *interlocution* 584 n.
  conference 584 n.
  consult 691 vb.
  make terms 766 vb.
parliament
  parliament 692 n.
parliamentarian
  councillor 692 n.
parliamentary system
  vote 605 n.
parlour *chamber* 194 n.
parlour game
  indoor game 837 n.
parlour-maid
  domestic 742 n.
parochial *regional* 184 adj.
  provincial 192 adj.
  narrow-minded 481 adj.
  ecclesiastical 985 adj.
parochialism
  narrow mind 481 n.
  patriotism 901 n.
parodist *humorist* 839 n.
parodos *dramaturgy* 594 n.
parody *mimicry* 20 n.
  foolery 497 n.
  misinterpretation 521 n.
  misrepresentation 552 n.
  satire 851 n.
parole *liberation* 746 n.
  permit 756 n.
  promise 764 n.
parolee *prisoner* 750 n.
  offender 904 n.
parole, on
  restrained 747 adj.
  promissory 764 adj.
par, on a *equal* 28 adj.
paronomasia
  assimilation 18 n.
  equivocalness 518 n.
  trope 519 n.
  ornament 574 n.
paronym *word* 559 n.
parotitis *infection* 651 n.
paroxysm *violence* 176 n.
  spasm 318 n.
  frenzy 503 n.
  anger 891 n.
paroxytone
  punctuation 547 n.
parquetry *chequer* 437 n.
parricide *homicide* 362 n.
parrot *imitator* 20 n.
  repeat 106 vb.
  bird 365 n.
  chatterer 581 n.
parrot cry *conformity* 83 n.
parrotry *conformity* 83 n.
parry *repel* 292 vb.

avoid 620 vb.
  obstruct 702 vb.
  parry 713 vb.
  resist 715 vb.
parse *decompose* 51 vb.
  parse 564 vb.
parsec *long measure* 203 n.
parsimonious
  careful 457 adj.
  temperate 942 adj.
parsimony
  insufficiency 636 n.
  parsimony 816 n.
  selfishness 932 n.
parsley *potherb* 301 n.
parsnip *tuber* 301 n.
parson *cleric* 986 n.
parsonage *benefice* 985 n.
  parsonage 986 n.
part *finite quantity* 26 n.
  adjunct 40 n.
  disjoin 46 vb.
  part 53 n.
  incompleteness 55 n.
  component 58 n.
  bisection 92 n.
  fraction 102 n.
  open 263 vb.
  diverge 294 vb.
  melody 410 n.
  vocal music 412 n.
  reading matter 589 n.
  acting 594 n.
  function 622 n.
  portion 783 n.
partake *eat* 301 vb.
partaking *eating* 301 n.
  sharing 775 adj.
parterre *garden* 370 n.
  theatre 594 n.
parthenogenesis
  propagation 164 n.
Parthian shot
  stratagem 698 n.
  bombardment 712 n.
partial *fragmentary* 53 adj.
  incomplete 55 adj.
  fractional 102 adj.
  imperfect 647 adj.
  uncompleted 726 adj.
  desiring 859 adj.
  (*see* partiality)
partiality *inequality* 29 n.
  prejudice 481 n.
  liking 859 n.
  friendliness 880 n.
  injustice 914 n.
  improbity 930 n.
partible *severable* 46 adj.
particeps criminis
  colleague 707 n.

participant *conjunct* 45 adj.
participate
　be one of 58 vb.
　be instrumental 628 vb.
　feel 818 vb.
　be sociable 882 vb.
　(*see* participation)
participation
　similarity 18 n.
　activity 678 n.
　association 706 n.
　co-operation 706 n.
　participation 775 n.
　condolence 905 n.
participator
　personnel 686 n.
　colleague 707 n.
　participator 775 n.
　beneficiary 776 n.
particle *particle* 33 n.
　piece 53 n.
　element 319 n.
　part of speech 564 n.
particoloured
　coloured 425 adj.
　variegated 437 adj.
particular *part* 53 n.
　special 80 adj.
　eventuality 154 n.
　attentive 455 adj.
　careful 457 adj.
　discriminating 463 adj.
　veracious 540 adj.
　descriptive 590 adj.
　capricious 604 adj.
　sensitive 819 adj.
　fastidious 862 adj.
particularism
　particularism 80 n.
　selfishness 932 n.
　sectarianism 978 n.
particularist *egotist* 932 n.
　sectarist 978 n.
particularity (*see* particular)
particularize
　differentiate 15 vb.
　specify 80 vb.
　be diffuse 570 vb.
particularly
　eminently 34 adv.
particulars *particulars* 80 n.
　description 590 n.
parting *separation* 46 n.
　dividing line 92 n.
　centrality 225 n.
　partition 231 n.
　limit 236 n.
　divergence 294 n.
　departure 296 n.
parti pris *bias* 481 n.
　predetermination 608 n.

partisan *patron* 707 n.
　sectional 708 adj.
　spear 723 n.
　revolter 738 n.
　friend 880 n.
　sectarian 978 adj.
partisanship *prejudice* 481 n.
　co-operation 706 n.
　friendliness 880 n.
　injustice 914 n.
partition *separation* 46 n.
　decomposition 51 n.
　part 53 vb.
　exclusion 57 n.
　dividing line 92 n.
　partition 231 n.
　limit 236 n.
　screen 421 n.
　obstacle 702 n.
　apportionment 783 n.
partly *partially* 33 adv.
　partly 53 adv.
partner *join* 45 vb.
　combine 50 vb.
　concomitant 89 n.
　personnel 686 n.
　co-operate 706 vb.
　colleague 707 n.
　participator 775 n.
　friend 880 n.
　spouse 894 n.
partnership
　concurrence 181 n.
　corporation 708 n.
　participation 775 n.
　(*see* partner)
part of speech *word* 559 n.
　part of speech 564 n.
partridge *table bird* 365 n.
parts *genitalia* 164 n.
　region 184 n.
　locality 187 n.
　contents 193 n.
　intellect 447 n.
　aptitude 694 n.
parts, man of
　proficient 696 n.
parturient *prolific* 171 adj.
parturition *obstetrics* 164 n.
part with *not retain* 779 vb.
　give 781 vb.
party *group*, *band* 74 n.
　follower 282 n.
　person 371 n.
　prejudice 481 n.
　assenter 488 n.
　conference 584 n.
　association 706 n.
　party 708 n.
　signatory 765 n.
　festivity 837 n.

　social gathering 882 n.
　litigant 959 n.
　sect 978 n.
party capital
　injustice 914 n.
party line *rule* 81 n.
　policy 623 n.
　tactics 688 n.
party man *sectarist* 978 n.
party-minded
　biased 481 adj.
　sociable 882 adj.
　sectarian 978 adj.
party spirit *prejudice* 481 n.
　dissent 489 n.
　government 733 n.
　cheerfulness 833 n.
　injustice 914 n.
　sectarianism 978 n.
party to *assenting* 488 adj.
party-wall
　dividing line 92 n.
　partition 231 n.
parvenu *upstart* 126 n.
　made man 730 n.
　rich man 800 n.
　vulgarian 847 n.
　commoner 869 n.
　proud man 871 n.
paschal *seasonal* 141 adj.
　ritual 988 adj.
pash *love* 887 n.
pasha *governor* 741 n.
pashalic *magistrature* 733 n.
pasilaly *language* 557 n.
pasquinade *calumny* 926 n.
pass *circumstance* 8 n.
　be superior 34 vb.
　entrance 68 n.
　conform 83 vb.
　continue 108 vb.
　elapse 111 vb.
　be past 125 vb.
　be turned to 147 adj.
　eventuality 154 n.
　gap 201 n.
　narrowness 206 n.
　opener 263 n.
　be in motion 265 vb.
　transfer 272 vb.
　ingress 297 n.
　emit 300 vb.
　excrete 302 vb.
　passage 305 n.
　overstep 306 vb.
　disappear 446 vb.
　assent 488 n.
　sleight 542 n.
　select 605 vb.
　access 624 n.
　suffice 635 vb.

be good 644vb.
protection 660n.
predicament 700n.
foin 712n.
success 727n.
permit 756n.,vb.
consent 758vb.
change hands 780vb.
endearment 889n.
approve 923vb.
make legal 953vb.
spell 983n.
passable
inconsiderable 33adj.
not bad 644adj.
mediocre 732adj.
contenting 828adj.
personable 841adj.
passage *bond* 47n.
part 53n.
entrance 68n.
change 143n.
transition 147n.
street 192n.
lobby 194n.
gap 201n.
doorway 263n.
motion 265n.
land travel 267n.
water travel 269n.
transference 272n.
deviate 282vb.
passage 305n.
musical piece 412n.
anthology 592n.
access 624n.
passant *heraldic* 547adj.
pass away
pass away 2vb.
end 69vb.
be transient 114vb.
die, perish 361vb.
disappear 446vb.
pass belief
cause doubt 486vb.
pass book
account book 808n.
pass by *elapse* 111vb.
disregard 458vb.
(*see* pass)
pass current
be believed 485vb.
be published 528vb.
be in fashion 848vb.
passé *antiquated* 127adj.
aged 131adj.
passed *expert* 694adj.
passementerie
trimming 844n.
passenger
thing transferred 272n.

train 274n.
idler 679n.
encumbrance 702n.
passe-partout *opener* 263n.
passer-by *spectator* 441n.
passerine *animal* 365adj.
pass for *resemble* 18vb.
passibility *sensibility* 374n.
passim *somewhere* 185adv.
in place 186adv.
passing *exorbitant* 32adj.
excretion 302n.
decease 361n.
passing bell *obsequies* 364n.
passing show *fashion* 848n.
passing word *hint* 524n.
pass into *shade off* 27vb.
be turned to 147vb.
passion *violence* 176n.
vigour 571n.
affections 817n.
warm feeling 818n.
excitable state 822n.
suffering 825n.
desire 859n.
love 887n.
anger 891n.
passionate *fervent* 818adj.
excitable 822adj.
loving 887adj.
irascible 892adj.
passionless
impassive 820adj.
indifferent 860adj.
passive *inert* 175adj.
latent 523adj.
peaceful 717adj.
obedient 739adj.
inexcitable 823adj.
passivity *inaction* 677n.
(*see* passive)
passman
college student 538n.
pass muster *suffice* 635vb.
be good 644vb.
be middling 732vb.
be praised 923vb.
pass off *be past* 125vb.
happen 154vb.
pass on *transfer* 272vb.
progress 285vb.
communicate 524vb.
pass out
be impotent 161vb.
emerge 298vb.
be drunk 949vb.
pass over *exclude* 57vb.
die 361vb.
neglect, disregard 458vb.
be taciturn 582vb.
reject 607vb.

forgive 909vb.
exempt 919vb.
Passover *holy-day* 988n.
passport *opener* 263n.
credential 466n.
label 547n.
instrument 628n.
protection 660n.
warrant 737n.
permit 756n.
pass round *publish* 528vb.
pass sentence *judge* 480vb.
pass the buck
transfer 272vb.
be exempt 919vb.
pass the time *be* 1vb.
amuse oneself 837vb.
password *opener* 263n.
answer 460n.
identification 547n.
instrument 628n.
warfare 718n.
permit 756n.
past *priority* 119n.
preterition 125n.
antiquated 127adj.
paste *a mixture* 43n.
adhesive 47n.
agglutinate 48vb.
viscidity 354n.
pulpiness 356n.
sham 542n.
finery 844n.
bad taste 847n.
pasteboard *paper* 631n.
pastel *pigment* 425n.
soft-hued 425adj.
art equipment 553n.
picture 553n.
pastern *foot* 214n.
pasteurize *purify* 648vb.
sanitate 652vb.
doctor 658vb.
past, have a
have no repute 867vb.
past history *precedence* 64n.
past hope
unpromising 853adj.
pastiche, pasticcio
copy 22n.
a mixture 43n.
picture 553n.
art style 553n.
pastil, pastille
inodorousness 395n.
scent 396n.
pastime *business* 622n.
pleasurableness 826n.
amusement 837n.
past it *aged* 131adj.
weak 163adj.

past-master *artisan* 686 n.
  proficient 696 n.
pastor *teacher* 537 n.
  pastor 986 n.
pastoral *agrarian* 370 adj.
  pleasurable 826 adj.
  priestly 985 adj.
  clerical 986 adj.
pastorale
  musical piece 412 n.
pastoral letter
  ministration 988 n.
pastoral staff
  vestments 989 n.
pastorate
  church ministry 985 n.
pastry *pastry* 301 n.
  sweet 392 n.
pastry-cook *caterer* 633 n.
past tense *time* 108 n.
  preterition 125 n.
pasture *provender* 301 n.
  graze, feed 301 vb.
  soil 344 n.
  grassland 348 n.
  grass 366 n.
  stock farm 369 n.
  farm 370 n.
pasty *pastry* 301 n.
  pulpy 356 adj.
  colourless 426 adj.
pat *apt* 24 adj.
  fixed 153 adj.
  knock 279 n.
  touch 378 n.
  please 826 vb.
  relieve 831 vb.
  caress 889 vb.
patch *adjunct* 40 n.
  join 45 vb.
  piece 53 n.
  modify 143 vb.
  garden 370 n.
  variegate 437 vb.
  dirt 649 n.
  repair 656 n., vb.
  surgical dressing 658 n.
  eyesore 842 n.
  cosmetic 843 n.
  blemish 845 n.
patcher *mender* 656 n.
patchiness
  non-uniformity 17 n.
  inequality 29 n.
  maculation 437 n.
  imperfection 647 n.
patchouli *scent* 396 n.
patch up *repair* 656 vb.
  compromise 770 vb.
patchwork
  non-uniformity 17 n.

discontinuity 72 n.
  variegation 437 n.
  needlework 844 n.
patchy *inferior* 35 adj.
  mixed 43 adj.
  discontinuous 72 adj.
  (*see* patchiness)
pate *head* 213 n.
patefaction *opening* 263 n.
patella *plate* 194 n.
paten *plate* 194 n.
  ritual object 988 n.
  church utensil 990 n.
patent *open* 263 adj.
  manifest 522 adj.
  permit 756 n., vb.
  estate 777 n.
  dueness 915 n.
patented *private* 80 adj.
  proprietary 777 adj.
patentee *beneficiary* 776 n.
  recipient 782 n.
patera *plate* 194 n.
paterfamilias *parent* 169 n.
paternal *akin* 11 adj.
  parental 169 adj.
  benevolent 897 adj.
paternalism
  governance 733 n.
  despotism 733 n.
paternity
  propagation 164 n.
  parentage 169 n.
paternoster *prayers* 981 n.
pater patriæ
  benefactor 903 n.
path *direction* 281 n.
  way in 297 n.
  outlet 298 n.
  passage 305 n.
  trace 548 n.
  path 624 n.
pathetic
  unimportant 639 adj.
  felt 818 adj.
  distressing 827 adj.
  lamenting 836 adj.
pathfinder *precursor* 66 n.
  traveller 268 n.
pathless *spacious* 183 adj.
  closed 264 adj.
  difficult 700 adj.
pathogen *infection* 651 n.
pathogenic *diseased* 651 adj.
  infectious 653 adj.
pathological
  diseased 651 adj.
  medical 658 adj.
pathologist *doctor* 658 n.
pathology *pathology* 651 n.
  medical art 658 n.

pathoneurosis
  psychopathy 503 n.
pathos *feeling* 818 n.
  excitation 821 n.
  painfulness 827 n.
patience
  perseverance 600 n.
  lenity 736 n.
  patience 823 n.
  card game 837 n.
  caution 858 n.
  forgiveness 909 n.
patient *testee* 461 n.
  sick person 651 n.
  sufferer 825 n.
  (*see* patience)
patina *layer* 207 n.
  hue 425 n.
  greenness 432 n.
  impairment 655 n.
  blemish 845 n.
  ritual object 988 n.
patio *place* 185 n.
patisserie *pastry* 301 n.
patois *speciality* 80 n.
  dialect 560 n.
pat on the back
  relieve 831 vb.
  applause 923 n.
patriarch *family* 11 n.
  precursor 66 n.
  old man 133 n.
  parent 169 n.
  master 741 n.
  governor 741 n.
  ecclesiarch 986 n.
patriarchal *olden* 127 adj.
  primal 127 adj.
patriarchate *parish* 985 n.
  parsonage 986 n.
  church office 985 n.
patrician *aristocrat* 868 n.
  genteel 868 adj.
patricide *homicide* 362 n.
patrilinear *akin* 11 adj.
  parental 169 adj.
patrimony
  acquisition 771 n.
  possession 773 n.
  dower 777 n.
  dueness 915 n.
patriot *defender* 713 n.
  patriot 901 n.
  benefactor 903 n.
patriotic (*see* patriotism)
patriotism *love* 887 n.
  patriotism 901 n.
  disinterestedness 931 n.
patripassianism
  heresy 977 n.
patristic *scriptural* 975 adj.

patrol *traverse* 267 vb.
  passage 305 n.
  circler 314 n.
  spectator 441 n.
  safeguard 660 vb.
  defender 713 n.
  armed force 722 n.
  restrain 747 vb.
patrol-boat
  warship 722 n.
patron *supporter* 218 n.
  protector 660 n.
  aider 703 n.
  patron 707 n.
  defender 713 n.
  master 741 n.
  purchaser 792 n.
  friend 880 n.
  kind person 897 n.
  benefactor 903 n.
  commender 923 n.
patronage *influence* 178 n.
  protection 660 n.
  management 689 n.
  aid 703 n.
  authority 733 n.
  security 767 n.
  purchase 792 n.
  approbation 923 n.
  benefice 985 n.
patronize *endorse* 488 vb.
  choose 605 vb.
  patronize 703 vb.
  defend 713 vb.
  be proud 871 vb.
  befriend 880 vb.
  be benevolent 897 vb.
patronizing
  prideful 871 adj.
patronymic *name* 561 n.
patten *footwear* 228 n.
patter
  be in motion 265 vb.
  strike 279 vb.
  rain 350 n., vb.
  faintness 401 n.
  roll 403 vb.
  empty talk 515 n.
  language 557 n.
  slang 560 n.
  be loquacious 581 vb.
patterer *speaker* 579 n.
  entertainer 594 n.
pattern *correlation* 12 n.
  uniformity 16 n.
  prototype 23 n.
  composition 56 n.
  arrangement 62 n.
  rule 81 n.
  example 83 n.
  form 243 n.

structure 331 n.
  comparison 462 n.
  paragon 646 n.
  pattern 844 n.
patternless
  non-uniform 17 adj.
patty *pastry* 301 n.
patulous *expanded* 197 adj.
paucity *smallness* 33 n.
  fewness 105 n.
  littleness 196 n.
  scarcity 636 n.
Paul Pry *inquisitor* 453 n.
paunch *maw* 194 n.
  insides 224 n.
  swelling 253 n.
  eater 301 n.
paunchy *fleshy* 195 adj.
pauper *poor man* 801 n.
pauperism
  non-ownership 774 n.
  poverty 801 n.
pauperize
  impoverish 801 vb.
pause *discontinuity* 72 n.
  interim 108 n.
  period 110 n.
  delay 136 n.
  lull 145 n.
  interval 201 n.
  quiescence 266 n.
  notation 410 n.
  be uncertain 474 vb.
  doubt 486 vb.
  not act 677 vb.
  repose 683 n.
pave *laminate* 207 vb.
  overlay 226 vb.
  smooth 258 vb.
  prepare 669 vb.
pavement *base* 214 n.
  basis 218 n.
  paving 226 n.
  smoothness 258 n.
  road, path 624 n.
pave the way
  prepare 669 vb.
  facilitate 701 vb.
pavilion *pavilion* 192 n.
  arbour 194 n.
  canopy 226 n.
paving-stone *base* 214 n.
  paving 226 n.
  road 624 n.
pavonian *blue* 435 adj.
  iridescent 437 adj.
paw *foot* 214 n.
  strike 279 vb.
  feeler 378 n.
  touch 378 vb.
  nippers 778 n.

pawky *witty* 839 adj.
pawl *fastening* 47 n.
pawn *inferior* 35 n.
  dupe 544 n.
  fatalist 596 n.
  instrument 628 n.
  nonentity 639 n.
  slave 742 n.
  security 767 n.
  transfer 780 n.
  borrow 785 vb.
  chessman 837 n.
pawnbroker *lender* 784 n.
pawnee *treasurer* 798 n.
  creditor 802 n.
pawn, in *pledged* 767 adj.
pawnshop *pawnshop* 784 n.
pax *ritual object* 988 n.
pay *coat, overlay* 226 vb.
  incentive 612 n.
  benefit 615 vb.
  employ 622 vb.
  be useful 640 vb.
  earnings 771 n.
  be profitable 771 vb.
  restitute 787 vb.
  pay 804 n., vb.
  expend 806 vb.
  receipt 807 n.
  reward 962 n., vb.
payable *owed* 803 adj.
  due 915 adj.
pay attention
  be attentive 455 vb.
  court 889 vb.
pay back
  compensate 31 vb.
pay-day *date* 108 n.
  pay 804 n.
payee *recipient* 782 n.
payer *pay* 804 n.
pay for *patronize* 703 vb.
  defray 804 vb.
  purchase 792 vb.
paying *profitable* 640 adj.
  gainful 771 adj.
payload *contents* 193 n.
paymaster *treasurer* 798 n.
  pay 804 n.
payment
  quid pro quo 150 n.
  incentive 612 n.
  payment 804 n.
  expenditure 806 n.
pay off *navigate* 269 vb.
  disuse 674 vb.
  make inactive 679 vb.
pay-off *end* 69 n.
  pay 804 n.
pay out *lengthen* 203 vb.
  retaliate 714 vb.

payroll *list* 87n.
  personnel 686n.
pea *vegetable* 301n.
peace *quietude* 266n.
  euphoria 376n.
  silence 399n.
  concord 710n.
  peace 717n.
  pleasurableness 826n.
peaceable *amiable* 884adj.
peaceful *inert* 175adj.
  moderate 177adj.
  tranquil 266adj.
  comfortable 376adj.
  silent 399adj.
  reposeful 683adj.
  peaceful 717adj.
  submitting 721adj.
  obedient 739adj.
  inexcitable 823adj.
  pleasurable 826adj.
  content 828adj.
peace-lover *pacifist* 717n.
peacemaker
  moderator 177n.
  pacifist 717n.
  mediator 720n.
peacemaking
  pacification 719n.
peace offering
  irenics 719n.
  offering 781n.
  propitiation 941n.
peach *fruit* 301n.
  redness 431n.
  inform 524vb.
  divulge 526vb.
  a beauty 841n.
  accuse 928vb.
peacher *tergiversator* 603n.
peachy *downy* 259adj.
  personable 841adj.
peacock *bird* 365n.
  blueness 435n.
  variegation 437n.
  exhibitor 522n.
  a beauty 841n.
  fop 848n.
  vain person 873n.
pea-jacket *tunic* 228n.
  overcoat 228n.
peak *completeness* 54n.
  extremity 69n.
  high land 209n.
  summit 213n.
  shade 226n.
  headgear 228n.
  sharp point 256n.
  perfection 646n.
  be ill 651vb.
peaky *lean* 206adj.

sick 651adj.
peal *loudness* 400n.
  roll 403n.,vb.
  resonance 404n.
  campanology 412n.
  gong 414n.
  call 547n.
pean *heraldry* 547n.
peanut *fruit* 301n.
pear *fruit* 301n.
pearl *white thing* 427n.
  type size 587n.
  exceller 644n.
  a beauty 841n.
  gem 844n.
pearlies *clothing* 228n.
pearly
  semitransparent 424adj.
  soft-hued 425adj.
  whitish 427adj.
  grey 429adj.
  iridescent 437adj.
pearly king *fop* 848n.
pear-shaped *curved* 248adj.
  round 250adj.
  rotund 252adj.
peasant *dweller* 191n.
  husbandman 370n.
  possessor 776n.
  countryman 869n.
pea-shooter
  propellant 287n.
  air-pipe 353n.
  toy gun 723n.
pea-souper *opacity* 423n.
peat *fuel* 385n.
pebble *hardness* 326n.
  soil 344n.
pebble dash *facing* 226n.
peccable *imperfect* 647adj.
peccadillo *trifle* 639n.
  vice 934n.
  guilty act 936n.
peccant *bad* 645adj.
  diseased 651adj.
  wicked 934adj.
  guilty 936adj.
peck *great quantity* 32n.
  eat 301vb.
  metrology 465n.
  bicker 709vb.
pecker *eater* 301n.
peckish *hungry* 859adj.
pectinated *sharp* 256adj.
pectoral *vestments* 989n.
peculation *peculation* 788n.
  foul play 930n.
peculator *defrauder* 789n.
peculiar *different* 15adj.
  special 80adj.
  unusual 84adj.

crazed 503adj.
peculiarity
  temperament 5n.
  (*see* peculiar)
Peculiar People
  particularism 80n.
  sect 978n.
peculium *dower* 777n.
pecuniary *monetary* 797adj.
pedagogic
  educational 534adj.
  severe 735adj.
pedagogue *scholar* 492n.
  teacher 537n.
pedagogy *teaching* 534n.
pedal *footed* 214adj.
  propellant 287n.
  play music 413vb.
  mute 414n.
  tool 630n.
pedant *conformist* 83n.
  narrow mind 481n.
  scholar 492n.
  sciolist 493n.
  teacher 537n.
  opinionist 602n.
  tyrant 735n.
  affector 850n.
  perfectionist 862n.
pedantry *attention* 455n.
  carefulness 457n.
  narrow mind 481n.
  erudition 490n.
  sciolism 491n.
  accuracy 494n.
  severity 735n.
  pretension 850n.
  fastidiousness 862n.
peddle *sell* 793vb.
peddler (*see* pedlar)
peddling *trivial* 639adj.
  parsimonious 816adj.
pedestal *stand* 218n.
pedestrian *pedestrian* 268n.
  prosaic 593adj.
  dull 840adj.
pedestrian crossing
  traffic control 305n.
  road 624n.
pedestrianism
  motion 265n.
pediatrician *doctor* 658n.
pediatrics *medical art* 658n.
pedicel, pedicle
  supporter 218n.
pediculosis
  formication 378n.
  uncleanness 649n.
pedicure *surgery* 658n.
  beautification 843n.
pedicurist *beautician* 843n.

pedigree *series* 71 n.
  list 87 n.
  genealogy 169 n.
  nobility 868 n.
pediment *summit* 213 n.
pedlar *traveller* 268 n.
  pedlar 794 n.
pedometer *meter* 465 n.
peduncle *supporter* 218 n.
peek (*see* peep)
peel *bate* 37 vb.
  leavings 41 n.
  disjoin 46 vb.
  unstick 49 vb.
  layer 207 n.
  skin 226 n.
  uncover, doff 229 vb.
  rubbish 641 n.
peeler *stripper* 229 n.
  protector 660 n.
  police 955 n.
peel-house *fort* 713 n.
peen *hammer* 279 n.
peep *look* 438 n.
  gaze, scan 438 vb.
  be curious 453 vb.
  enquire 459 vb.
peepers *eye* 438 n.
peephole *window* 263 n.
  view 438 n.
Peeping Tom
  inquisitor 453 n.
peep-show *spectacle* 445 n.
  plaything 837 n.
  pleasure-ground 837 n.
peer *compeer* 28 n.
  scan 438 vb.
  be dim-sighted 440 vb.
  enquire 459 vb.
  councillor 692 n.
  nobleman 868 n.
peerage *honours* 866 n.
  aristocracy 868 n.
peerless *supreme* 34 adj.
  best 644 adj.
  noteworthy 866 adj.
peeve *enrage* 891 vb.
peevish *ungracious* 885 adj.
  irascible 892 adj.
  sullen 893 adj.
peg *fastening* 47 n.
  hanger 217 n.
  stopper 264 n.
  potion 301 n.
  tool 630 n.
peg at *persevere* 600 vb.
peg out *die* 361 vb.
pegs *leg* 267 n.
peg-top *cone* 252 n.
peignoir
  informal dress 228 n.

cleaning cloth 648 n.
peine forte et dure
  corporal punishment
    963 n.
pejorative
  depreciating 483 adj.
  word 559 n.
  disrespectful 921 adj.
  detracting 926 adj.
Pelagianism *heresy* 977 n.
pelagic *oceanic* 343 adj.
pelerine *cloak* 228 n.
pelf *money* 797 n.
  wealth 800 n.
pelisse *robe, cloak* 228 n.
pellagra *disease* 651 n.
pellet *sphere* 252 n.
  missile 287 n.
  ammunition 723 n.
pellicle *layer* 207 n.
  skin 226 n.
pell-mell
  confusedly 61 adv.
pellucid
  transparent 422 adj.
  intelligible 516 adj.
pelorus *direction* 281 n.
pelota *sphere* 252 n.
  ball game 837 n.
pelt *skin* 226 n.
  move fast 277 vb.
  strike 279 vb.
  propel 287 vb.
  rain 350 vb.
  lapidate 712 vb.
peltast *soldier* 722 n.
peltry *skin* 226 n.
pemmican *food* 301 n.
pen *inclosure* 235 n.
  waterfowl 365 n.
  female animal 373 n.
  recording instrument
    549 n.
  art equipment 553 n.
  stationery 586 n.
  write 586 vb.
  imprison 747 vb.
  lock-up 748 n.
penal *prohibiting* 757 adj.
  punitive 963 adj.
penal code *precept* 693 n.
  law 953 n.
  penalty 963 n.
penalize
  be inexpedient 643 vb.
  make illegal 954 vb.
  punish 936 vb.
penal servitude
  penalty 963 n.
penal settlement
  prison camp 748 n.

penalty *cost* 809 n.
  penalty 963 n.
penance *offset* 31 n.
  penitence 939 n.
  penance 941 n.
  asceticism 945 n.
  punishment 963 n.
  Christian rite 988 n.
Penates
  lesser god 967 n.
  mythic god 966 n.
penchant *tendency* 179 n.
  willingness 597 n.
pencil *radiation* 417 n.
  recording instrument
    549 n.
  art equipment 553 n.
  paint 553 vb.
  stationery 586 n.
  write 586 vb.
pencraft *lettering* 586 n.
pend *continue* 108 vb.
  pend 136 vb.
pendant *analogue* 18 n.
  adjunct 40 n.
  extremity 69 n.
  pendant 217 n.
  flag 547 n.
  jewellery 844 n.
  trimming 844 n.
pendency *interim* 108 n.
  pendency 217 n.
pendent
  non-adhesive 49 adj.
  pendent 217 adj.
pendicle *pendant* 217 n.
pending *while* 108 adv.
pen-driver *penman* 586 n.
pendular
  oscillating 317 adj.
pendulous
  non-adhesive 49 adj.
  pendent 217 adj.
  oscillating 317 adj.
pendulum
  timekeeper 117 n.
  periodicity 141 n.
  pendant 217 n.
  oscillation 317 n.
peneplane *plain* 348 n.
penetrable
  intelligible 516 adj.
penetralia
  interiority 224 n.
  latency 523 n.
  hiding-place 527 n.
penetrate
  be general 79 vb.
  pierce 263 vb.
  infiltrate 297 vb.
  pass 305 vb.

cause thought 449 vb.
be wise 498 vb.
understand 516 vb.
impress 821 vb.
penetrating
  incoming 297 adj.
  pungent 388 adj.
  intelligent 498 adj.
  felt 818 adj.
penetration
  interjacence 231 n.
  ingress 297 n.
  passage 305 n.
  sagacity 498 n.
pen-friend
  correspondent 588 n.
  chum 880 n.
penguin *flightless bird* 365 n.
pen-holder *case* 194 n.
  stationery 586 n.
penicillin *plant* 366 n.
  drug 658 n.
peninsula *region* 184 n.
  projection 254 n.
  land 344 n.
  island 349 n.
penis *genitalia* 164 n.
penitence *regret* 830 n.
  penitence 939 n.
penitencer *pastor* 986 n.
penitent *penitent* 939 n.
  repentant 939 adj.
  ascetic 945 n.
penitent form
  penance 941 n.
  pillory 964 n.
penitential
  atoning 941 adj.
penitentiary
  prison 748 n.
  repentant 939 adj.
  atoning 941 adj.
  pastor 986 n.
pen-knife *sharp edge* 256 n.
  stationery 586 n.
penman *penman* 586 n.
  moneyer 797 n.
penmanship
  lettering 586 n.
pen-name *misnomer* 562 n.
pennant *flag* 547 n.
penniless
  not owning 774 adj.
  poor 801 adj.
penny *coinage* 797 n.
penny-a-liner
  author 589 n.
penny dreadful *novel* 590 n.
penny-farthing
  bicycle 274 n.
pennyweight

small quantity 33 n.
  weighment 322 n.
penny-wise
  parsimonious 816 adj.
penology
  punishment 963 n.
pensile *pendent* 217 adj.
pension *quarters* 192 n.
  resignation 753 n.
  earnings 771 n.
  pay 804 n.
  receipt 807 n.
  reward 962 n.
pensioner *dependant* 742 n.
  resignation 753 n.
  recipient 782 n.
pension off *disuse* 674 vb.
  not retain 779 vb.
pensive *thoughtful* 449 adj.
  abstracted 456 adj.
  melancholic 834 adj.
penstock *conduit* 351 n.
pentacle *indication* 547 n.
pentad *five and over* 99 n.
pentagon
  angular figure 247 n.
Pentagon *master* 741 n.
pentameter *prosody* 593 n.
Pentateuch *law* 953 n.
  scripture 975 n.
pentathlon *contest* 716 n.
penteconter *galley* 275 n.
Pentecost *holy-day* 988 n.
penthouse
  small house 192 n.
  flat 192 n.
  attic 194 n.
penultimate *ending* 69 adj.
penumbra *cone* 252 n.
  half-light 419 n.
penurious *careful* 457 adj.
  poor 801 adj.
  parsimonious 816 adj.
penury *poverty* 801 n.
pen-wiper *stationery* 586 n.
peon *courier* 531 n.
  infantry 722 n.
  servant 742 n.
peony *redness* 431 n.
people *place oneself* 187 vb.
  habitancy 191 n.
  native 191 n.
  dwell 192 vb.
  nation 371 n.
  social group 371 n.
  subject 742 n.
  commonalty 869 n.
  laity 987 n.
peopled
  multitudinous 104 adj.
pep *vigorousness* 174 n.

vigour 571 n.
  restlessness 678 n.
pepastic *cathartic* 658 n.
peplos *robe* 228 n.
peplum *robe, skirt* 228 n.
pepper *pierce* 263 vb.
  vegetable 301 n.
  pungency 388 n.
  season 388 vb.
  condiment 389 n.
  wound 655 vb.
  fire at 712 vb.
pepper-and-salt
  whitish 427 adj.
  grey 429 adj.
  chequer 437 n.
peppercorn *condiment* 389 n.
  cheapness 812 n.
peppery *pungent* 388 adj.
  irascible 892 adj.
peppy *vigorous* 174 adj.
  forceful 571 adj.
  inducive 612 adj.
pepsin *condensation* 324 n.
  thickening 354 n.
pep-talk *stimulant* 174 n.
  inducement 612 n.
peptic *remedial* 658 adj.
per *through* 628 adv.
peragrate *traverse* 267 vb.
perambulate
  walk, traverse 267 vb.
perambulator
  pushcart 274 n.
percale *textile* 222 n.
per capita *pro rata* 783 adv.
perceivable *visible* 443 adj.
perceive
  have feeling 374 vb.
  cognize 447 vb.
  detect 484 vb.
  know 490 vb.
per cent *ratio* 85 n.
percentage *increment* 36 n.
  extra 40 n.
  part 53 n.
  ratio 85 n.
  discount 810 n.
percentile *statistical* 86 adj.
percept *idea* 451 n.
perceptible *seeing* 438 adj.
  visible 443 adj.
perception *vision* 438 n.
  idea 451 n.
  intellect 447 n.
  discrimination 463 n.
  knowledge 490 n.
  sagacity 498 n.
perceptive *sentient* 374 adj.
  mental 447 adj.
perceptual *mental* 447 adj.

perch *place oneself* 187 vb.
  nest 192 n.
  dwell 192 vb.
  long measure 203 n.
  basis 218 n.
  land 295 vb.
  descend 309 vb.
  sit down 311 vb.
  table fish 365 n.
  sleep 679 vb.
  repose 683 vb.
percheron *drafthorse* 273 n.
percipience
  intellect 447 n.
percolate *infiltrate* 297 vb.
  exude 298 vb.
  pass 305 vb.
  irrigate 341 vb.
  flow 350 vb.
  purify 648 vb.
percolator *cauldron* 194 n.
per contra
  conversely 467 adv.
percussion
  impulse 279 n.
  orchestra 413 n.
  musical instrument 414 n.
percussion instrument
  gong 414 n.
perdition *ruin* 165 n.
  defeat 728 n.
  loss 772 n.
peregrination
  land travel 267 n.
peremptory
  assertive 532 adj.
  authoritative 733 adj.
  commanding 737 adj.
  compelling 740 adj.
  obligatory 917 adj.
perennial *continuous* 71 adj.
  lasting 113 adj.
  unchangeable 153 adj.
perennity
  perpetuity 115 n.
perfect *whole* 52 adj.
  complete 54 adj.
  regular 81 adj.
  preterition 125 n.
  excellent 644 adj.
  perfect 646 adj., vb.
  mature 669 vb.
  carry through 725 vb.
  (*see* perfection)
perfectibility
  imperfection 647 n.
  improvement 654 n.
perfection *summit* 213 n.
  goodness 644 n.
  perfection 646 n.
  completion 725 n.

beauty 841 n.
  innocence 935 n.
perfectionism
  carefulness 457 n.
  reformism 654 n.
  essay 671 n.
  discontent 829 n.
  fastidiousness 862 n.
perfectionist
  perfectionist 862 n.
perfections *beauty* 841 n.
  virtues 933 n.
perfective
  completive 725 adj.
perfidious (*see* perfidy)
perfidy *unreliability* 474 n.
  latency 523 n.
  falsehood 541 n.
  deception 542 n.
  untruth 543 n.
  tergiversation 603 n.
  non-observance 769 n.
  dutilessness 918 n.
  perfidy 930 n.
perflation *sufflation* 352 n.
perforate *pierce* 263 vb.
  pass 305 vb.
perforation
  perforation 263 n.
perforator *perforator* 263 n.
perforce *by force* 740 adv.
perform *operate* 173 vb.
  be instrumental 628 vb.
  be useful 640 vb.
  do one's duty 917 vb.
  (*see* performance)
performable
  possible 469 adj.
performance
  effect 157 n.
  production 164 n.
  music 412 n.
  musical skill 413 n.
  representation 551 n.
  dramaturgy 594 n.
  action, deed 676 n.
  effectuation 725 n.
  observance 768 n.
  celebration 876 n.
  ministration 988 n.
performer
  musician 413 n.
  interpreter 520 n.
  entertainer 594 n.
  doer 676 n.
  agent 686 n.
perfume *emit* 300 vb.
  odour 394 n.
  scent 396 n.
  cosmetic 843 n.
perfumed *pleasant* 376 adj.

perfumery *fragrance* 396 n.
perfunctory
  incomplete 55 adj.
  deficient 307 adj.
  negligent 458 adj.
  unwilling 598 adj.
  imperfect 647 adj.
  hasty 680 adj.
  bungled 695 adj.
  uncompleted 726 adj.
  indifferent 860 adj.
perfusion
  transference 272 n.
  surgery 658 n.
pergola *arbour* 194 n.
perhaps *possibly* 469 adv.
peri *a beauty* 841 n.
  fairy 970 n.
periapt *talisman* 983 n.
pericarditis
  heart disease 651 n.
perichondritis
  respiratory disease, 651 n.
pericope *part* 53 n.
pericranium *head* 213 n.
peridot *gem* 844 n.
perigee *short distance* 200 n.
perihelion
  short distance 200 n.
peril *danger* 661 n.
perimeter
  circumjacence 230 n.
  outline 233 n.
  inclosure 235 n.
  limit 236 n.
per incuriam
  inadvertently 456 vb.
  negligently 458 adv.
period *part* 53 n.
  composition 56 n.
  end 69 n.
  time 108 n.
  period 110 n.
  periodicity 141 n.
  regular return 141 n.
  limit 236 n.
  punctuation 547 n.
  phrase 563 n.
periodic
  discontinuous 72 adj.
  periodic 110 adj.
  periodical 141 adj.
  fitful 142 adj.
  phraseological 563 adj.
periodical *regular* 81 adj.
  continuing 108 adj.
  periodical 141 adj.
  journal 528 n.
  reading matter 589 n.
  book 589 n.
  (*see* periodicity)

periodicity
discontinuity 72 n.
recurrence 106 n.
frequency 139 n.
periodicity 141 n.
oscillation 317 n.
peripatetic
travelling 267 adj.
pedestrian 268 n.
Peripatetics
philosopher 449 n.
peripeteia
revolution 149 n.
eventuality 154 n.
inexpectation 508 n.
disclosure 526 n.
peripheral
irrelevant 10 adj.
excluded 57 adj.
unimportant 639 adj.
periphery *distance* 199 n.
exteriority 223 n.
circumjacence 230 n.
outline 233 n.
inclosure 235 n.
limit 236 n.
periphrasis *phrase* 563 n.
pleonasm 570 n.
periplus *water travel* 269 n.
periscope
optical device 442 n.
periscopic *visible* 443 adj.
perish *be destroyed* 165 vb.
decompose 51 vb.
perish 361 vb.
be cold 380 vb.
deteriorate 655 vb.
perishability
transientness 114 n.
perishable
ephemeral 114 adj.
dying 361 adj.
perispomenon
punctuation 547 n.
perissology *pleonasm* 570 n.
peristaltic
labyrinthine 251 adj.
elastic 328 adj.
peristyle *series* 71 n.
pavilion 192 n.
periwig *wig* 228 n.
perjurer *liar* 545 n.
perjury *falsehood* 541 n.
untruth 543 n.
perks *incentive* 612 n.
earnings 771 n.
gift 781 n.
reward 962 n.
perk up
be refreshed 685 vb.
be cheerful 833 vb.

perky *cheerful* 833 adj.
vain 783 adj.
perlustration
inspection 438 n.
permanence
durability 113 n.
permanence 144 n.
continuance 146 n.
stability 153 n.
perseverance 600 n.
preservation 666 n.
permanency *job* 622 n.
permanent
continuing 108 adj.
habitual 610 adj.
(see permanence)
permanent way
railroad 624 n.
permeable *porous* 263 adj.
permeate *prevail* 178 vb.
(see permeation)
permeating
ubiquitous 189 adj.
permeation
mixture 43 n.
presence 189 n.
interiority 224 n.
interjacence 231 n.
passage 305 n.
permed *undulatory* 251 adj.
per mil *ratio* 85 n.
permissible
possible 469 adj.
permitted 756 adj.
approvable 923 adj.
legal 953 adj.
permission
permission 756 n.
permit
credential 466 n.
make possible 469 vb.
assent 488 n., vb.
facilitate 701 vb.
be lax 734 vb.
be lenient 736 vb.
give scope 744 vb.
commission 751 n.
permit 756 n., vb.
consent 758 vb.
convey 780 vb.
permitted
reputable 866 adj.
permutation
numerical operation 86 n.
change 143 n.
interchange 151 n.
pernicious
harmful 645 adj.
pernicity *velocity* 277 n.
pernickety
fastidious 862 adj.

perorate
be diffuse 570 vb.
peroration *sequel* 67 n.
end 69 n.
oration 579 n.
eloquence 579 n.
peroxide *pigment* 425 n.
bleacher 426 n.
hairwash 843 n.
perpend *meditate* 449 vb.
notice 455 vb.
estimate 480 vb.
perpendicular
vertical 215 adj.
straight 249 adj.
written 586 adj.
perpetrate *do* 676 vb.
be clumsy 695 vb.
do wrong 914 vb.
perpetrator *doer* 676 n.
agent 686 n.
perpetual *existing* 1 adj.
frequent 139 adj.
(see perpetuity)
perpetuate
perpetuate 115 vb.
sustain 146 vb.
perpetuation
perpetuity 115 n.
continuance 146 n.
perpetuity *continuity* 71 n.
infinity 107 n.
diuturnity 113 n.
permanence 144 n.
continuance 146 n.
perplex *bedevil* 63 vb.
distract 456 vb.
puzzle 474 vb.
incommode 827 vb.
perplexity *dubiety* 474 n.
unintelligibility 517 n.
difficulty 700 n.
perquisite *earnings* 771 n.
receipt 807 n.
reward 962 n.
perquisites *gift* 781 n.
perquisition *search* 459 n.
perry *liquor* 301 n.
per se *singly* 88 adv.
perse *blue* 435 adj.
persecute *ill-treat* 645 vb.
torment 827 vb.
be pitiless 906 vb.
(see persecution)
persecuted *suffering* 825 adj.
persecution
destruction 165 n.
counteraction 182 n.
prejudice 481 n.
pursuit 619 n.
severity 735 n.

enmity 881 n.
cruel act 898 n.
penalty 963 n.
orthodoxism 976 n.
pietism 979 n.
persecutor *opinionist* 602 n.
tyrant 735 n.
punisher 963 n.
religionist 979 n.
perseverance
continuance 146 n.
perseverance 600 n.
obstinacy 602 n.
persevere *stay* 144 vb.
stand firm 599 vb.
exert oneself 682 vb.
persevering
unyielding 162 adj.
industrious 678 adj.
Persian wheel
extractor 304 n.
irrigator 341 n.
persienne *shade* 226 n.
curtain 421 n.
persiflage *witticism* 839 n.
ridicule 851 n.
persist *be active* 678 vb.
persistence *uniformity* 16 n.
permanence 144 n.
continuance 146 n.
perseverance 600 n.
persistent *lasting* 113 adj.
unyielding 162 adj.
remembered 505 adj.
person *substance* 3 n.
self 80 n.
object 319 n.
person 371 n.
person of repute 866 n.
personable
personable 841 adj.
personage *person* 371 n.
bigwig 638 n.
persona grata *friend* 880 n.
favourite 896 n.
personal *substantial* 3 adj.
intrinsic 5 adj.
unimitative 21 adj.
special, private 80 adj.
human 371 adj.
possessed 773 adj.
proprietary 777 adj.
impertinent 878 adj.
selfish 932 adj.
personal attendance
presence 189 n.
personal characteristic
speciality 80 n.
personal column
advertisement 528 n.
personal considerations

selfishness 932 n.
personal effects
property 777 n.
personal equation
speciality 80 n.
personality
substantiality 3 n.
intrinsicality 5 n.
speciality, self 80 n.
influence 178 n.
materiality 319 n.
spirit 447 n.
bigwig 638 n.
affections 817 n.
sauciness 878 n.
rudeness 885 n.
scurrility 899 n.
calumny 926 n.
personalize *specify* 80 vb.
personal recognizance
security 767 n.
legal process 959 n.
personalty *property* 777 n.
personal world
circumstance 8 n.
persona non grata
enemy 881 n.
personate *represent* 551 vb.
act 594 vb.
personification
metaphor 519 n.
representation 551 n.
acting 594 n.
personify *materialize* 319 vb.
manifest 522 vb.
personnel *band* 74 n.
personnel 686 n.
means 629 n.
perspectival
relative 9 adj.
seeing 438 adj.
perspective
relativeness 9 n.
range 183 n.
length 203 n.
depth 211 n.
convergence 293 n.
view 438 n.
spectacle 445 n.
perspicacious
(*see* perspicacity)
perspicacity *vision* 438 n.
sagacity 498 n.
fastidiousness 862 n.
perspicuity
intelligibility 516 n.
perspicuity 567 n.
elegance 575 n.
perspicuous
semantic 514 adj.
stylistic 566 adj.

perspiration *outflow* 298 n.
excretion 302 n.
perspire *exude* 298 vb.
emit 300 vb.
be wet 341 vb.
be hot 379 vb.
persuade *convince* 485 vb.
induce 612 vb.
request 761 vb.
persuaded *positive* 473 adj.
believing 485 adj.
persuader
motivator 612 n.
persuasibility
credulity 487 n.
willingness 597 n.
persuasibility 612 n.
persuasible
impressible 819 adj.
persuasion
classification 77 n.
influence 178 n.
positiveness 473 n.
belief, opinion 485 n.
teaching 534 n.
inducement 612 n.
persuasive
influential 178 adj.
plausible 471 adj.
credible 485 adj.
inducive 612 adj.
pert *cheerful* 833 adj.
impertinent 878 adj.
discourteous 885 adj.
pertain *be related* 9 vb.
be included 78 vb.
belong 773 vb.
pertinacity
perseverance 600 n.
pertinence *relevance* 9 n.
fitness 24 n.
pertness *sauciness* 878 n.
rudeness 885 n.
perturbation
derangement 63 n.
stimulation 174 n.
agitation 318 n.
excitation 821 n.
excitable state 822 n.
nervousness 854 n.
pertussis
respiratory disease 651 n.
peruke *wig* 228 n.
perusal *study* 536 n.
pervade *fill* 54 vb.
be general 79 vb.
prevail 178 vb.
pervade 189 vb.
lie between 231 vb.
pass 305 vb.
pervasion *mixture* 43 n.

presence 189n.
interiority 224n.
pervasive *universal* 79 adj.
ubiquitous 189 adj.
perverse *erroneous* 495 adj.
wilful 602 adj.
difficult 700 adj.
perversion
conversion 147n.
obliquity 220n.
distortion 246n.
misinterpretation 521n.
misteaching 535n.
falsehood 541n.
untruth 543n.
deterioration 665n.
misuse 675n.
impiety 980n.
perversity (*see* perverse)
pervert *derange* 63 vb.
nonconformist 84n.
modify 143 vb.
changed person 147n.
transform 147 vb.
distort 246 vb.
mislead 495 vb.
harm 645 vb.
pervert 655 vb.
make wicked 934 vb.
cad 938n.
libertine 952n.
(*see* perversion)
pervicacity *obstinacy* 602n.
pervious *porous* 263 adj.
pesky *annoying* 827 adj.
pessary
surgical dressing 658n.
pessimism
overestimation 482n.
underestimation 483n.
dejection 834n.
hopelessness 853n.
nervousness 854n.
pessimist *loser* 728n.
moper 834n.
alarmist 854n.
pest *vermin* 365n.
evil 616n.
plague 651n.
bane 659n.
worry 825n.
annoyance 827n.
hateful object 888n.
noxious animal 904n.
pester *recur* 139 vb.
meddle 678 vb.
torment 827 vb.
enrage 891 vb.
pest-house
insalubrity 653n.
hospital 658n.

pesticide *poison* 569n.
pestiferous
infectious 653 adj.
pestilence *badness* 645n.
plague 651n.
pestilent *infectious* 653 adj.
baneful 659 adj.
pestilential *toxic* 653 adj.
hateful 888 adj.
pestle *hammer* 279n.
pulverizer 332n.
pet *animal* 365n.
look after 457 vb.
chosen 605 adj.
be lenient 736 vb.
please 826 vb.
love 887 vb.
pet, caress 889 vb.
darling 890n.
anger 891n.
philanthropize 897 vb.
petal *flower* 366n.
petard *gun* 723n.
petard, hoist with one's own
retaliate 714 vb.
petasus *headgear* 228n.
peter out *end* 69 vb.
cease 145 vb.
Peter's pence
offering 781n.
tax 809n.
petiole *foliage* 366n.
petite *little* 196 adj.
shapely 841 adj.
petite amie
kept woman 952n.
petition *remind* 505 vb.
request 761 n., vb.
deprecate 762 vb.
litigation 959n.
prayers 981n.
petitionary
devotional 981 adj.
petitioner *petitioner* 763n.
malcontent 829n.
litigant 959n.
petition-writer *notary* 958n.
petitio principii
sophism 477n.
petit maitre *fop* 848n
petit mal *paralysis* 651n.
petit point
needlework 844n.
Petrarchan *poetic* 593 adj.
petrel *bird of prey* 365n.
petrifaction
condensation 324n.
hardening 326n.
petrify *be dense* 324 vb.
harden 326 vb.
refrigerate 382 vb.

impress 821 vb.
frighten 854 vb.
be wonderful 864 vb.
petroglyph *sculpture* 554n.
petrol, petroleum
propellant 287n.
oil 357n.
fuel 385n.
pétroleur
incendiarism 381n.
petrology
mineralogy 359n.
petronel *pistol* 723n.
petticoat *bodywear* 228n.
woman 373n.
petticoat government
gynocracy 733n.
pettifog *deceive* 547 vb.
pettifogger *trickster* 545n.
lawyer 958n.
pettifogging
sophistical 477 adj.
trickery 542n.
trivial 639 adj.
rascally 930 adj.
pettiness (*see* petty)
petting *endearment* 889n.
pettish *irascible* 892 adj.
sullen 893 adj.
petty *inconsiderable* 33 adj.
little 196 adj.
unimportant 639 adj.
contemptible 922 adj.
selfish 932 adj.
petty officer
naval officer 741n.
petulance *sauciness* 878n.
irascibility 892n.
pew *compartment* 194n.
seat 218n.
church interior 990n.
pewter *a mixture* 43n.
white thing 427n.
phaeton *carriage* 274n.
phalanx *coherence* 48n.
multitude 104n.
solid body 324n.
party 708n.
army, formation 722n.
phallic *impure* 951 adj.
phallus *genitalia* 164n.
phantasm
visual fallacy 440n.
appearance 445n.
ghost 970n.
phantasmagoria
medley 43n.
visual fallacy 440n.
spectacle 445n.
phantom *the dead* 361n.
visual fallacy 440n.

fantasy 513 n.
 ghost 970 n.
pharaoh *sovereign* 741 n.
pharisaic *sectarian* 978 adj.
 pietistic 979 adj.
pharisaical
 hypocritical 541 adj.
pharisaism *duplicity* 541 n.
 false piety 980 n.
Pharisees
 non-Christian sect 978 n.
pharmaceutics
 medical art 658 n.
pharmacist *druggist* 658 n.
pharmacology
 medical art 658 n.
pharmacopœia
 medicine 658 n.
pharmacy *hospital* 658 n.
pharos *sailing aid* 269 n.
pharyngitis
 respiratory disease 651 n.
phase *modality* 7 n.
 be identical 13 vb.
 arrange 62 vb.
 time 117 vb.
 synchronize 123 vb.
 appearance 445 n.
phase, in *agreeing* 24 adj.
pheasant *table bird* 365 n.
phenomenal
 unusual 84 adj.
 appearing 445 adj.
 wonderful 864 adj.
phenomenalism
 philosophy 449 n.
phenomenon
 eventuality 154 n.
 appearance 445 n.
 prodigy 864 n.
phial *vessel* 194 n.
philander *excite love* 887 vb.
 court 889 vb.
philanderer *lover* 887 n.
 libertine 952 n.
philanthropic
 friendly 880 adj.
 philanthropic 901 adj.
 virtuous 933 adj.
philanthropist
 reformer 654 n.
 kind person 897 n.
 philanthropist 901 n.
 good man 937 n.
philanthropy
 benevolence 897 n.
 philanthropy 901 n.
 disinterestedness 931 n.
philatelist *collector* 492 n.
philharmonic
 musical 412 adj.

philippic *censure* 924 n.
 oration 579 n.
Philistine *conformist* 83 n.
 ignorance 491 n.
 artless 699 adj.
 vulgarian 847 n.
 commoner 869 n.
Philistinism
 artlessness 699 n.
 moral insensibility 820 n.
 bad taste 847 n.
philological
 semantic 514 adj.
philologist *collector* 492 n.
 linguist 557 n.
 etymology 559 n.
philology *linguistics* 557 n.
 etymology 559 n.
 grammar 564 n.
philomath *scholar* 492 n.
philoprogenitive
 productive 164 adj.
 generative 171 adj.
philosophe
 intellectual 492 n.
philosopheme
 argumentation 475 n.
philosopher
 philosopher 449 n.
 enquirer 459 n.
 sage 500 n.
philosopher's stone
 remedy 658 n.
philosophic
 philosophic 449 adj.
 inexcitable 823 adj.
 patient 823 adj.
 content 828 adj.
philosophize
 meditate 449 vb.
 reason 475 vb.
philosophy *intellect* 447 n.
 philosophy 449 n.
philtre *stimulant* 174 n.
 spell 983 n.
 magic instrument 983 n.
phiz *face* 237 n.
 feature 445 n.
phlebitis
 blood pressure 651 n.
phlebotomy *voidance* 300 n.
 surgery 658 n.
phlegm *excrement* 302 n.
 semiliquidity 354 n.
 sluggishness 679 n.
 moral insensibility 820 n.
phlegmatic *slow* 278 adj.
 viscid 354 adj.
 non-active 677 adj.
 impassive 820 adj.
 indifferent 860 adj.

phlegmatism
 incuriosity 454 n.
phlogiston *heat* 379 n.
phobia *psychopathy* 503 n.
 phobia 854 n.
 hatred 888 n.
phœnix *rara avis* 84 n.
 reproduction 166 n.
 paragon 646 n.
 mythical being 970 n.
phœnix-like
 restored 656 adj.
phonate *sound* 398 vb.
phone *speech sound* 398 n.
 hearing aid 415 n.
 spoken letter 558 n.
phoneme
 spoken letter 558 n.
 word 559 n.
phone-tapper
 inquisitor 453 n.
phone-tapping
 listening 415 n.
phonetic
 sounding 398 adj.
 literal 558 adj.
 vocal 577 adj.
phonetician
 acoustics 398 n.
 linguist 557 n.
phonetics *acoustics* 398 n.
phoney (*see* phony)
phonics *acoustics* 398 n.
phonogram
 speech sound 398 n.
 writing 586 n.
phonograph *sound* 398 n.
 gramophone 414 n.
 hearing aid 415 n.
phonography
 writing 586 n.
phonology
 acoustics 398 n.
 etymology 559 n.
phony, phoney
 imitative 20 adj.
 false 541 adj.
 spurious 542 adj.
 untrue 543 adj.
phosphorescence
 glow 417 n.
phosphorescent
 luminescent 420 adj.
phosphorus
 food content 301 n.
 luminary 420 n.
photics *optics* 417 n.
photo (*see* photograph)
photo-electric cell
 radiation 417 n.
photo finish *draw* 28 n.

short distance 200 n.
photogenic
  representing 551 adj.
  beautiful 841 adj.
photograph copy 22 n.
  photography 551 n.
photographer
  recorder 549 n.
photographic lifelike 18 adj.
  accurate 494 adj.
  representing 551 adj.
  descriptive 590 adj.
photography optics 417 n.
  camera 442 n.
  photography 551 n.
photogravure picture 553 n.
  printing 555 n.
photolithography
  printing 555 n.
photolysis
  decomposition 51 n.
photometer
  optical device 442 n.
photometry optics 417 n.
photo-microscope
  microscope 442 n.
photon particle 33 n.
  element 319 n.
  radiation 417 n.
photoplay cinema 445 n.
photoprint duplicate 22 n.
  photography 551 n.
  picture 553 n.
photosphere sun 321 n.
photostat copy 22 n.
  recording instrument
    549 n.
  photography 551 n.
phototherapy
  therapy 658 n.
phrase subdivision 53 n.
  tune 412 n.
  word 559 n.
  phrase 563 n.
  style 566 n.
phrasemonger
  phrasemonger 574 n.
  stylist 575 n.
phraseology phrase 563 n.
  style 566 n.
phratry family 11 n.
phrenetic frenzied 503 adj.
phrenology
  hermeneutics 520 n.
Phrygian mode key 410 n.
phthiriasis
  formication 378 n.
  uncleanness 649 n.
phthisis phthisis 651 n.
phylactery maxim 496 n.
  talisman 983 n.

phyle race 11 n.
phyletic ethnic 11 adj.
  parental 169 adj.
phylogeny genealogy 169 n.
  biology 358 n.
phylum breed 77 n.
physic cure 656 vb.
  medicine 658 n.
physical real 1 adj.
  substantial 3 adj.
  material 319 adj.
  sensuous 376 adj.
physical culture
  civilization 654 n.
physical energy
  energy 160 n.
  vigorousness 174 n.
physical jerks
  education 534 n.
physical science
  physics 319 n.
physical wreck
  dilapidation 655 n.
physician doctor 658 n.
physics physics 319 n.
physiocrat economy 814 n.
physiognomy face 237 n.
  form 243 n.
  feature 445 n.
physiography
  geography 321 n.
  uranometry 321 n.
physiology structure 331 n.
  biology 358 n.
physiotherapy
  therapy 658 n.
physique vitality 162 n.
  structure 331 n.
  animality 365 n.
phytography biology 358 n.
  botany 368 n.
phytology, phytonomy
  botany 368 n.
pi pietistic 979 adj.
piacular atoning 941 adj.
piaffer gait 265 n.
  equitation 267 n.
  slowness 278 n.
pia mater head 213 n.
pianissimo faintly 401 adv.
  adagio 412 adv.
pianist
  instrumentalist 413 n.
piano slowly 278 adv.
  muted 401 adj.
  faintly 401 adv.
  adagio 412 adv.
  piano 414 n.
  dejected 834 adj.
pianoforte, pianola
  piano 414 n.

pibroch
  musical piece 412 n.
  war 718 n.
pica type size 587 n.
picador killer 362 n.
  combatant 722 n.
picaresque
  descriptive 590 adj.
  rascally 930 adj.
picaroon robber 789 n.
piccaninny child 132 n.
  negro 428 n.
piccolo flute 414 n.
pice small coin 33 n.
pick sharp point 256 n.
  perforator 263 n.
  extractor 304 n.
  cultivate 370 vb.
  choice 605 n.
  chief thing 638 n.
  élite 644 n.
  clean 648 vb.
  acquire 771 vb.
  take 786 vb.
  steal 788 vb.
pick-a-back astride 218 adv.
  bearing 273 adj.
pick a bone with
  bicker 709 vb.
pick and choose
  be capricious 604 vb.
  select 605 vb.
  be fastidious 862 vb.
pickaxe sharp point 256 n.
  perforator 263 n.
  extractor 304 n.
picked man
  proficient 696 n.
picker accumulator 74 n.
  husbandman 370 n.
picker and chooser
  perfectionist 862 n.
picket tie 45 vb.
  circumscribe 232 vb.
  be obstructive 702 vb.
  defender 713 n.
  armed force 722 n.
  fetter 747 vb.
  punish 963 vb.
picketing hindrance 702 n.
pick holes
  disparaise, blame 924 vb.
  detract 926 vb.
pickings choice 605 n.
  earnings 771 n.
  booty 790 n.
pickle state 7 n.
  circumstance 8 n.
  drench 341 vb.
  season 388 vb.
  store 632 vb.

preserver 666 n.
predicament 700 n.
inebriate 949 vb.
pickles *condiment* 389 n.
pick-me-up
stimulant 174 n.
pungency 388 n.
tonic 658 n.
excitant 821 n.
pick off *fire at* 712 vb.
pick one's steps
be careful 457 vb.
pick out *set apart* 46 vb.
extract 304 vb.
see 438 vb.
discriminate 463 vb.
select 605 vb.
pickpocket *thief* 789 n.
picksome
fastidious 862 adj.
pickthank *meddler* 678 n.
toady 879 n.
flatterer 925 n.
pick the brains
interrogate 459 vb.
pick up *accelerate* 277 vb.
detect 484 vb.
get better 654 vb.
arrest 747 vb.
acquire 771 vb.
pick-up
gramophone 414 n.
prostitute 952 n.
Pickwickian *absurd* 497 adj.
funny 849 adj.
picnic *meal* 301 n.
easy thing 701 n.
participation 775 n.
amusement 837 n.
pictogram *letter* 558 n.
lettering 586 n.
pictorial
representing 551 adj.
painted 553 adj.
picture *composition* 56 n.
spectacle 445 n.
imagine 513 vb.
represent 551 vb.
picture 553 n.
describe 590 vb.
a beauty 841 n.
picture-book *picture* 553 n.
picture-frame
art equipment 553 n.
picture-gallery
art equipment 553 n.
picture, in the
informed 524 adj.
picture palace
cinema 445 n.
theatre 594 n.

picturesque
descriptive 590 adj.
impressive 821 adj.
pleasurable 826 adj.
beautiful 841 adj.
ornamental 844 adj.
picture-writing
symbology 547 n.
representation 551 n.
writing 586 n.
piddle *be inactive* 679 vb.
excrete 302 vb.
pidgin
language 557 n.
dialect 560 n.
neological 560 adj.
pie *small coin* 33 n.
medley 43 n.
pastry 301 n.
sweet 392 n.
colour 425 vb.
print-type 587 n.
easy thing 701 n.
piebald *horse* 273 n.
pied 437 adj.
piece *small thing* 33 n.
piece 53 n.
incompleteness 55 n.
unit 88 n.
product 164 n.
textile 222 n.
musical piece 412 n.
stage play 594 n.
gun 723 n.
portion 783 n.
chessman 837 n.
loose woman 952 n.
piece, collector's
(*see* collector's piece)
pièce de résistance
dish 301 n.
exceller 644 n.
masterpiece 694 n.
piecegoods *textile* 222 n.
piecemeal *piecemeal* 53 adv.
piece, of a
uniform 16 adj.
similar 18 adj.
simple 44 adj.
piece of cake
easy thing 701 n.
piece of one's mind
reprimand 924 n.
piece together *join* 45 vb.
make complete 54 vb.
decipher 520 vb.
repair 656 vb.
piecework *labour* 682 n.
pie-crust *brittleness* 330 n.
pastry 301 n.
pied *pied* 437 adj.

Pied Piper
musician 413 n.
sorcerer 983 n.
pie in the sky
fantasy 513 n.
pier *stable* 192 n.
street 192 n.
supporter 218 n.
projection 254 n.
arena 724 n.
pierce *cut* 46 vb.
pierce 263 vb.
pass 305 vb.
give pain 377 vb.
wound 655 vb.
impress 821 vb.
piercing
perforation 263 n.
cold 380 adj.
loud 400 adj.
strident 407 adj.
felt 818 adj.
pier-glass *mirror* 442 n.
Pierian *poetic* 593 adj.
pierrette, pierrot
actor 594 n.
entertainer 594 n.
pietà *art subject* 553 n.
ritual object 988 n.
pietism *pietism* 979 n.
pietist *affector* 850 n.
pietist 979 n.
piety *religion* 973 n.
piety 979 n.
worship 981 n.
piffle *silly talk* 515 n.
piffling *unmeaning* 515 adj.
trivial 639 adj.
pig *pig* 365 n.
dirty person 649 n.
cad 938 n.
sensualist 944 n.
glutton 947 n.
pigeon *bird* 365 n.
credulity 487 n.
dupe 544 n.
defraud 788 vb.
pigeon-cote *stable* 192 n.
pigeon-hearted
cowardly 856 adj.
pigeon-hole *class* 62 vb.
classification 77 n.
put off 136 vb.
place 185 n.
compartment 194 n.
be neglectful 458 vb.
pigeon-post *mails* 531 n.
pigeon's neck
variegation 437 n.
pigeon-toed
deformed 246 adj.

blemished 845 adj.
piggery *stock farm* 369 n.
piggin *vessel* 194 n.
pig-headed
  unintelligent 499 adj.
  obstinate 602 adj.
pig in a poke
  uncertainty 474 n.
  gambling 618 n.
piglet *youngling* 132 n.
  pig 365 n.
pigment *pigment* 425 n.
pigmentation *hue* 425 n.
  blackness 428 n.
pigment-deficiency
  achromatism 426 n.
pigmy *dwarf* 196 n.
pignoration *security* 767 n.
pigpen *stable* 192 n.
  sink 649 n.
pigskin *skin* 226 n.
  bookbinding 589 n.
pigsticker *side-arms* 723 n.
pigsticking *chase* 619 n.
pigsty *cattle pen* 369 n.
  sink 649 n.
pigtail *pendant* 217 n.
  rear 238 n.
  hair 259 n.
pig together
  congregate 74 vb.
pi-jaw *empty talk* 515 n.
pike *high land* 209 n.
  sharp point 256 n.
  fish 365 n.
  road 624 n.
  soldiery 722 n.
  spear 723 n.
piker *gambler* 618 n.
pilaster *pillar* 218 n.
  projection 254 n.
  ornamental art 844 n.
pilau, pilaff
  dish 301 n.
pile *fastening* 47 n.
  accumulation 74 n.
  edifice 164 n.
  high structure 209 n.
  pillar 218 n.
  hair 259 n.
  texture 331 n.
  heraldry 547 n.
  store 632 vb.
  acquisition 771 n.
  wealth 800 n.
pile-driver
  ram, hammer 279 n.
pile in *fill* 54 vb.
  start out 296 vb.
  enter 297 vb.
pile on *add* 38 vb.

piles *swelling* 253 n.
pile up
  bring together 74 vb.
  exaggerate 546 vb.
  store 632 vb.
  superabound 637 vb.
  acquire 771 vb.
pile-up *collision* 279 n.
pilfer *steal* 788 vb.
pilferer *thief* 789 n.
pilgrim *traveller* 268 n.
  pietist 979 n.
  worshipper 981 n.
pilgrimage *land travel* 267 n.
  piety 979 n.
pilgrimage, place of
  focus 76 n.
  holy place 990 n.
Pilgrim Fathers
  settler 191 n.
pill *mouthful* 301 n.
  medicine 658 n.
  punishment 963 n.
pillage *rob* 788 vb.
  booty 790 n.
pillager *robber* 789 n.
pillar *fixture* 153 n.
  high structure 209 n.
  pillar 218 n.
  monument 548 n.
  refuge 662 n.
  person of repute 866 n.
  seclusion 883 n.
Pillars of Hercules
  limit 236 n.
  signpost 547 n.
pillar to post, from
  in transit 272 adv.
  irresolutely 601 adv.
  round about 626 adv.
pill-box *headgear* 228 n.
  cylinder 252 n.
  fort 713 n.
pill, coat the
  sweeten 392 vb.
pillion *seat* 218 n.
pilliwinks
  instrument of torture
    964 n.
pillory *hanger* 217 n.
  fetter 747 vb.
  lock-up 748 n.
  satirize 851 vb.
  shame 867 vb.
  dispraise 924 vb.
  defame 926 vb.
  accuse 928 vb.
  penitence 939 n.
  punish 963 vb.
  pillory 964 n.
pillow *cushion* 218 n.

support 218 vb.
  softness 327 n.
  euphoria 376 n.
  relief 831 n.
pillow-case *covering* 226 n.
pilot *aeronaut* 271 n.
  navigate 269 vb.
  navigator 270 n.
  direct 689 vb.
  director 690 n.
pilotage, pilotship
  navigation 269 n.
  directorship 689 n.
pilot scheme
  experiment 461 n.
pilous *hairy* 259 adj.
pimento *vegetable* 301 n.
  condiment 389 n.
pimp *provider* 633 n.
  cad 938 n.
  be impure 951 vb.
  bawd 952 n.
pimple *monticle* 209 n.
  lowness 210 n.
  swelling 253 n.
  skin disease 651 n.
  blemish 845 n.
pimply *convex* 253 adj.
pin *join* 45 vb.
  fastening 47 n.
  sharp point 256 n.
  perforator 263 n.
  trifle 639 n.
  restrain 747 vb.
  retain 778 vb.
  jewellery 844 n.
pinafore *apron* 228 n.
pince-nez *eyeglass* 442 n.
pincer movement
  convergence 293 n.
  attack 712 n.
pincers *cross* 222 n.
  extractor 304 n.
  nippers 778 n.
pinch *circumstance* 8 n.
  small quantity 33 n.
  certain quantity 104 n.
  crisis 137 n.
  make smaller 198 vb.
  make thin 206 vb.
  notch 260 vb.
  converge 293 vb.
  pang 377 n.
  touch 378 vb.
  needfulness 627 n.
  predicament 700 n.
  adversity 731 n.
  arrest 747 vb.
  steal 788 vb.
  poverty 801 n.
  economize 814 vb.

be parsimonious 816vb.
endearment 889n.
pinch, at a
in need 627adv.
with difficulty 700adv.
pinchbeck spurious 542adj.
trivial 639adj.
pinch of salt, with a
doubtfully 486adv.
pin-cushion
receptacle 194n.
pin down place 187vb.
compel 740vb.
pine tree 366n.
animal disease 651n.
be ill 651vb.
pineapple fruit 301n.
pine for desire 859vb.
pine-needle foliage 366n.
pinery wood 366n.
garden 370n.
pinfold inclosure 235n.
cattle pen 369n.
ping roll 403n.
resonance 404n.
ping-pong ball game 837n.
pinguescence
unctuousness 357n.
pinguid fatty 357adj.
pin-head minuteness 196n.
dunce 501n.
pin-hole orifice 263n.
pinion tie 45vb.
plumage 259n.
wing 271n.
fetter 747vb.
pink moderate 177adj.
notch 260vb.
pierce 263vb.
strike 279vb.
redness 431n.
perfection 646n.
wound 655vb.
pink of condition
health 650n.
pin-money dower 777n.
money 797n.
receipt 807n.
pinna ear 415n.
pinnace boat 275n.
pinnacle summit 213n.
pinnate flying 271adj.
pinned down fixed 153adj.
pin on affix 45vb.
accuse 928vb.
pinpoint small thing 33n.
specify 80vb.
place 185n.,vb.
minuteness 196n.
orientate 281vb.
pin-prick trifle 639n.

annoyance 827n.
enrage 891vb.
pins leg 267n.
conveyance 267n.
pins and needles
formication 378n.
pinscher dog 365n.
pin-stripe pattern 844n.
pint metrology 465n.
pin-table plaything 837n.
pintle pivot 218n.
pinto pied 437adj.
horse 273n.
pint-size little 196adj.
pin-up girl a beauty 841n.
favourite 890n.
pioneer come before 64vb.
precursor 66n.
initiate 68vb.
settler 191n.
traveller 268n.
preparer 669n.
undertake 672vb.
direct 689vb.
facilitate 701vb.
soldiery 722n.
pious believing 485adj.
pious 979adj.
pious fraud duplicity 541n.
mental dishonesty 543n.
false piety 980n.
pious hope
improbability 472n.
aspiration 852n.
pip timekeeper 117n.
powder 332n.
signal 547n.
pipe vat 194n.
cylinder 252n.
tube 263n.
blow 352vb.
conduit 351n.
air-pipe 353n.
tobacco 388n.
stridor 407n.
shrill 407vb.
ululate 409vb.
play music 413vb.
flute 414n.
metrology 465n.
store 632n.
pipe-band orchestra 413n.
pipeclay white thing 427n.
practice 610n.
pipe-cleaner tobacco 388n.
cleaning utensil 648n.
pipe down cease 145vb.
be quiescent 266vb.
be taciturn 582vb.
pipe-dream
insubstantial thing 4n.

fantasy 513n.
pleasurableness 826n.
aspiration 852n.
pipe-line tube 263n.
conduit 351n.
store 632n.
provide 633vb.
pipe of peace peace 717n.
irenics 719n.
piper instrumentalist 413n.
pipe-rack tobacco 388n.
pipette tube 263n.
pipe up cry 408vb.
speak 579vb.
pip, have the
be sullen 893vb.
piping edging 234n.
tube 263n.
stridor 407n.
peaceful 717adj.
trimming 844n.
piping times
palmy days 730n.
pipkin vessel 194n.
pipped defeated 728adj.
pippin fruit 301n.
darling 890n.
pips badge, livery 547n.
badge of rank 743n.
pipsqueak dwarf 196n.
nonentity 639n.
piquancy unconformity 84n.
pungency 388n.
vigour 571n.
joy 824n.
piquant aphoristic 496adj.
exciting 821adj.
impure 951adj.
pique excite 821vb.
hurt 827vb.
discontent 829n.
resentment 891n.
piracy brigandage 788n.
pirate mariner 270n.
militarist 722n.
steal 788vb.
robber 789n.
enemy 881n.
knave 938n.
piratical thieving 788adj.
pirouette rotation 315n.
pis aller substitute 150n.
expedience 642n.
inexpedience 643n.
imperfection 647n.
compromise 770vb.
piscatorial animal 365adj.
Pisces zodiac 321n.
pisciculture
animal husbandry 369n.
piscina lake 346n.

drain 351 n.
stock farm 369 n.
church utensil 990 n.
ritual object 988 n.
piss *excrete* 302 vb.
pistachio nut *fruit* 301 n.
pistol *kill* 362 vb.
pistol 723 n.
piston *periodicity* 141 n.
stopper 264 n.
pit *depth* 211 n.
interiority 224 n.
cavity 255 n.
tunnel 263 n.
trap 542 n.
playgoer 594 n.
pitfall 663 n.
stratagem 698 n.
blemish 845 vb.
pit against
oppose 704 vb.
make quarrels 709 vb.
pit-a-pat *agitation* 318 n.
jerkily 318 adv.
pitch *adjust* 24 vb.
degree 27 n.
serial place 73 n.
territory 184 n.
place 185 n.
dwell 192 vb.
height 209 n.
summit 213 n.
make vertical 215 vb.
coat 266 vb.
voyage 269 vb.
propel 287 vb.
tumble 309 vb.
depress 311 vb.
oscillate 317 vb.
be agitated 318 vb.
resin 357 n.
sound 398 n.
musical note 410 n.
black thing 428 n.
voice 577 n.
arena 734 n.
pitcher *vessel* 194 n.
thrower 287 n.
pitchfork *shovel* 274 n.
propel 287 vb.
farm tool 370 n.
pitch into *attack* 712 vb.
fight 716 vb.
pitch on
place oneself 187 vb.
meet 295 vb.
acquire 771 vb.
pitch-pipe *flute* 414 n.
pitchy *resinous* 357 adj.
dark 418 adj.
black 428 adj.

piteous *pitiable* 905 adj.
pitfall *invisibility* 444 n.
latency 523 n.
ambush 527 n.
trap 542 n.
danger 661 n.
pitfall 663 n.
stratagem 698 n.
pith *substance* 3 n.
essential part 5 n.
vitality 162 n.
interiority 224 n.
centrality 225 n.
pulpiness 356 n.
topic 452 n.
meaning 514 n.
importance 638 n.
pithecanthropus
mankind 371 n.
pithily *concisely* 569 vb.
pithless *weak* 163 adj.
pithy *substantial* 3 adj.
soft 327 adj.
aphoristic 496 adj.
meaningful 514 adj.
concise 569 adj.
compendious 592 adj.
pitiable *unimportant* 639 adj.
bad 645 adj.
unhappy 825 adj.
distressing 827 adj.
pitiable 905 adj.
contemptible 922 adj.
pitiful *unimportant* 639 adj.
bad 645 adj.
distressing 827 adj.
disreputable 867 adj.
benevolent 897 adj.
pitying 905 adj.
pitiable 905 adj.
pitilessness
resolution 599 n.
severity 735 n.
pitilessness 906 n.
pittance *finite quantity* 26 n.
insufficiency 636 n.
receipt 807 n.
portion 783 n.
pitted *rough* 259 adj.
blemished 845 adj.
pittite *playgoer* 594 n.
pituita *semiliquidity* 354 n.
pity *lenity* 736 n.
lamentation 836 n.
benevolence 897 n.
pity 905 n., vb.
pivot *joint* 45 n.
causal means 156 n.
influence 178 n.
pivot 218 n.
centrality 225 n.

chief thing 638 n.
pivotal *important* 638 adj.
pivot on *depend* 157 vb.
pixie, pixy *elf* 970 n.
pixilated *crazed* 503 adj.
placability
benevolence 897 n.
mercy 905 n.
forgiveness 909 n.
placard *exhibit* 522 n.
advertisement 528 n.
placate *pacify* 719 vb.
place *degree* 27 n.
order 60 n.
arrange 62 vb.
serial place 73 n.
specify 80 vb.
region 184 n.
place 185 n.
situation 186 n.
locality 187 n.
abode 192 n.
meal 301 n.
discover 484 vb.
authority 733 n.
place after *place after* 65 vb.
place-hunting
greedy 859 adj.
placeman *consignee* 754 n.
placement, placing
arrangement 62 n.
location 187 n.
placenta *sequel* 67 n.
obstetrics 164 n.
placet *decree* 737 n.
place under
number with 78 vb.
placidity
inexcitability 823 n.
placket *pocket* 194 n.
plage *shore* 344 n.
plagiarism, plagiary
imitation 20 n.
copy 22 n.
repetition 106 n.
stealing 788 n.
plagiarist *imitator* 20 n.
plagiarize *fake* 541 vb.
borrow 785 vb.
plagihedral
oblique 220 adj.
plague *recur* 139 vb.
badness 645 n.
plague 651 n.
bane, blight 659 n.
be difficult 700 vb.
adversity 731 n.
oppress 735 vb.
annoyance 827 n.
ruffian 904 n.
plague-spot *badness* 645 n.

sink 649 n.
infection 651 n.
insalubrity 653 n.
plague-stricken
diseased 651 adj.
infectious 653 adj.
plaguy *evil* 616 adj.
not nice 645 adj.
infectious 653 adj.
baneful 659 adj.
difficult 700 adj.
annoying 827 adj.
plaice *fish food* 301 n.
table fish 365 n.
plaid *shawl* 228 n.
chequer 437 n.
plain *simple* 44 adj.
space 183 n.
lowness 210 n.
horizontality 216 n.
open space 263 n.
land 344 n.
plain 348 n.
soft-hued 425 adj.
well-seen 443 adj.
meaningful 514 adj.
intelligible 516 adj.
manifest 522 adj.
undisguised 522 adj.
informative 524 adj.
assertive 532 adj.
veracious 540 adj.
stylistic 566 adj.
plain 573 adj.
elegant 575 adj.
prosaic 593 adj.
artless 699 adj.
lament 836 vb.
tedious 838 adj.
ugly 842 n.
tasteful 846 adj.
plebeian 869 adj.
disrespectful 921 adj.
temperate 942 adj.
ascetic 945 adj.
plain-clothes man
detective 459 n.
police 955 n.
plain dealing *veracity* 540 n.
plain living
temperance 942 n.
ascetism 945 n.
plain man
common man 30 n.
ingenue 699 n.
plainness *simpleness* 44 n.
unsavouriness 391 n.
dullness 840 n.
probity 929 n.
(*see* plain)
plain sailing

navigation 269 n.
easy thing 701 n.
plainsman *dweller* 191 n.
plainsong *vocal music* 412 n.
plain speaking
intelligibility 516 n.
veracity 540 n.
plain-spoken
intelligible 516 adj.
undisguised 522 adj.
informative 524 adj.
plaint *cry* 408 n.
discontent 829 n.
lament 836 n.
accusation 928 n.
plaintiff *malcontent* 829 n.
accuser 928 n.
litigant 959 n.
plaintive *lamenting* 836 adj.
plaintiveness *cry* 408 n.
plait *tie* 45 vb.
ligature 47 n.
crossing 222 n.
weave 222 vb.
hair 259 n.
fold 261 n.
plan *prototype* 23 n.
arrangement 62 n.
predestine 155 vb.
cause 156 vb.
produce 164 vb.
itinerary 267 n.
structure 331 n.
foresight 510 n.
guide-book 524 n.
map 551 n.
predetermine 608 vb.
intention 617 n.
plan 623 n., vb.
preparation 669 n.
undertaking 672 n.
tactics 688 n.
be cunning 698 vb.
planchette
spiritualism 984 n.
plane *horizontality* 216 n.
sharp edge 256 n.
smoother 258 n.
fly 271 vb.
aircraft 276 n.
tree 366 n.
plane sailing
navigation 269 n.
planet, planetoid
rotator 315 n.
planet 321 n.
planetarium
astronomy 321 n.
planetary, planetoidal
planetary 321 adj.
planets *fate* 596 n.

plangency *loudness* 400 n.
resonance 404 n.
lamentation 836 n.
plangent (*see* plangency)
planimeter *meter* 465 n.
planing *aeronautics* 271 n.
planisphere *gauge* 465 n.
plank *lamina* 207 n.
shelf 218 n.
policy 623 n.
materials 631 n.
planless *orderless* 61 adj.
designless 618 adj.
planner *producer* 167 n.
theorist 512 n.
motivator 612 n.
planner 623 n.
meddler 678 n.
expert 696 n.
plan out *plan* 623 vb.
plant *make fruitful* 171 vb.
place 187 vb.
aim 281 vb.
implant 303 vb.
trap 542 n.
cultivate 370 vb.
workshop 687 n.
property 777 n.
false charge 928 n.
plantain *fruit* 301 n.
plantation *habitancy* 191 n.
maturation 669 n.
(*see* farm)
planted *firm-set* 45 adj.
arboreal 366 adj.
agrarian 370 adj.
planter *producer* 167 n.
settler 191 n.
husbandman 370 n.
preparer 669 n.
plaque *lamina* 207 n.
honours 866 n.
plash *flow* 250 vb.
sound faint 401 vb.
resound 404 vb.
sibilation 406 n.
plasma *matter* 319 n.
fluid, blood 335 n.
plasmic *formative* 243 adj.
organic 358 adj.
plaster *adhesive* 47 n.
flatten 216 vb.
wrapping 226 n.
coat 226 vb.
repair 656 vb.
surgical dressing 658 n.
fire at 712 vb.
relieve 831 vb.
plastic *unstable* 152 adj.
formative 243 adj.
flexible 327 adj.

materials 631n.
impressible 819adj.
plasticine *softness* 327n.
  sculpture 554n.
plasticity
  changeableness 152n.
  softness 327n.
  moral sensibility 819n.
plastic surgery
  surgery 658n.
  beautification 843n.
plate *mould* 23n.
  plate 194n.
  lamina 207n.
  horizontality 216n.
  coat 226vb.
  circle 250n.
  tooth 256n.
  camera 442n.
  label 547n.
  photography 551n.
  picture 553n.
  print 587n.
  edition 589n.
  trophy 729n.
plateau *high land* 209n.
  horizontality 216n.
  vertex 213n.
  plain 348n.
plateful *finite quantity* 26n.
plate glass *lamina* 207n.
  transparency 422n.
platelet *blood* 335n.
platform *layer* 207n.
  horizontality 216n.
  stand 218n.
  publicity 528n.
  rostrum 539n.
  policy 623n.
  railroad 624n.
  arena 724n.
platinum
  white thing 427n.
  yellow 433adj.
  bullion 797n.
platitude
  unmeaningness 515n.
platitudinous *dull* 840adj.
Platonic *pure* 950adj.
Platonism
  immateriality 320n.
  philosophy 449n.
platoon *band* 74n.
  formation 722n.
platter *plate* 194n.
  horizontality 216n.
plaudits *rejoicing* 835n.
  applause 923n.
plausible *plausible* 471adj.
  sophistical 477adj.
  credible 485adj.

hypocritical 541adj.
  ostensible 614adj.
  promising 852adj.
  flattering 925adj.
  vindicable 927adj.
plausive *approving* 923adj.
play *agency* 173n.
  operate 173vb.
  range 183n.
  oscillate 317vb.
  flow 350vb.
  play music 413vb.
  flash 417n.
  variegate 437vb.
  stage play 594n.
  gambling 618n.
  action 676n.
  easy thing 701n.
  parry 713vb.
  contend 716vb.
  scope 744n.
  amusement 837n.
  caress 889vb.
play-act *dissemble* 541vb.
  act 594vb.
  be affected 850vb.
play a part
  influence 178vb.
  dissemble 541vb.
  act 594vb.
  do 676vb.
play at
  be inattentive 456vb.
play back *repeat* 106vb.
play-back
  gramophone 414n.
play ball *co-operate* 706vb.
playbill *list* 87n.
playbook *stage play* 594n.
playboy *reveller* 837n.
play double
  be dishonest 930vb.
play down
  underestimate 483vb.
player *instrumentalist* 413n.
  interpreter 520n.
  actor 594n.
  gambler 618n.
  doer 676n.
  agent 686n.
  player 837n.
play false
  tergiversate 603vb.
playful *capricious* 604adj.
  gay 833adj.
  amused 837adj.
  witty 839adj.
  innocent 935adj.
playgoer *playgoer* 594n.
play gooseberry
  look after 457vb.

safeguard 660vb.
playground *arena* 724n.
  pleasure-ground 837n.
playhouse *theatre* 594n.
  place of amusement 837n.
play, in *operative* 173adj.
  in jest 839adv.
playing field *arena* 724n.
  pleasure-ground 837n.
play lead *act* 594vb.
  have repute 866vb.
playmate *colleague* 707n.
  player 837n.
  chum 880n.
play off *use* 673vb.
play out *terminate* 69vb.
playroom *chamber* 194n.
play safe
  seek safety 660vb.
  be cautious 858vb.
play second fiddle
  be inferior 35vb.
  obey 739vb.
  have no repute 867vb.
  be modest 874vb.
playsuit *beachwear* 228n.
play the fool
  be absurd 497vb.
  amuse oneself 837vb.
  be rash 857vb.
play the game
  behave 688vb.
  be honourable 929vb.
play the market
  speculate 791vb.
plaything *bauble* 639n.
  plaything 837n.
playtime *interim* 108n.
  festivity 837n.
play to the gallery
  be affected 850vb.
  be ostentatious 875vb.
play tricks *befool* 542vb.
  be capricious 604vb.
  be cunning 698vb.
  amuse oneself 837vb.
play up *overrate* 482vb.
  disobey 738vb.
play upon *operate* 173vb.
  motivate 612vb.
play upon words
  absurdity 497n.
  equivocalness 518n.
  wit 839n.
play with *neglect* 458vb.
  distract 456vb.
  be expert 694vb.
  caress 889vb.
playwright *author* 589n.
  dramatist 594n.
plea *testimony* 466n.

argument 475 n.
pretext 614 n.
request 761 n.
vindication 927 n.
litigation 959 n.
pleach weave 222 vb.
plead testify 466 vb.
argue 475 vb.
plead 614 vb.
justify 927 vb.
do law 958 vb.
litigate 959 vb.
pleader
intermediary 231 n.
reasoner 475 n.
speaker 579 n.
motivator 612 n.
mediator 720 n.
law agent 958 n.
pleadings legal trial 959 n.
pleasance pleasance 192 n.
pleasure-ground 837 n.
pleasant pleasant 376 adj.
pleasurable 826 adj.
amusing 837 adj.
witty 839 adj.
pleasantry wit 839 n.
please please 826 vb.
content 828 vb.
cheer 833 vb.
amuse 837 vb.
pleased willing 597 adj.
please oneself will 595 vb.
please oneself 734 vb.
be free 744 vb.
pleasurable
pleasurable 826 adj.
pleasure pleasure 376 n.
easy thing 701 n.
joy 824 n.
amusement 837 n.
pleasure-ground
pleasance 192 n.
pleasure-ground 837 n.
pleasure-loving
sensuous 376 adj.
sensual 944 adj.
pleasure-seeker
reveller 837 n.
pleasure, with
willingly 597 adv.
pleat fold 261 n., vb.
plebeian ill-bred 847 adj.
commonalty 869 n.
plebeian 869 adj.
plebiscite judgment 480 n.
vote 605 n.
decree 737 n.
legislation 953 n.
plectrum harp 414 n.
pledge

thing transferred 272 n.
drink 301 vb.
oath 532 n.
promise 764 n., vb.
security 767 n.
convey 780 vb.
borrow 785 vb.
toast 876 vb.
duty 917 n.
pledgee treasurer 798 n.
creditor 802 n.
pledget covering 226 n.
stopper 264 n.
surgical dressing 658 n.
pledgor debtor 803 n.
pleistocene secular 110 adj.
plenary complete 54 adj.
plenipotentiary
delegate, envoy 754 n.
plenitude greatness 32 n.
plenitude 54 n.
plenty 635 n.
plentiful great 32 adj.
plenteous 635 adj.
plenty great quantity 32 n.
productiveness 171 n.
store 632 n.
plenty 635 n.
liberality 635 n.
redundance 637 n.
prosperity 730 n.
wealth 800 n.
plenum substantiality 3 n.
materiality 319 n.
universe 321 n.
pleonasm pleonasm 570 n.
pleonastic
pleonastic 570 adj.
superfluous 637 adj.
plesianthropus
mankind 371 n.
plesiosaurus animal 365 n.
plethora redundance 637 n.
satiety 863 n.
pleura laterality 239 n.
plexure crossing 222 n.
plexus network 222 n.
pliable flexible 327 adj.
pliancy conformity 83 n.
changeableness 152 n.
softness 327 n.
willingness 597 n.
irresolution 601 n.
persuasibility 612 n.
facility 701 n.
obedience 739 n.
servility 879 n.
pliant (see pliancy)
plication fold 261 n.
pliers extractor 304 n.
tool 630 n.

nippers 778 n.
plight state 7 n.
circumstance 8 n.
adversity 731 n.
promise 764 n.
plimsoll footwear 228 n.
Plimsoll line gauge 465 n.
plinth base 214 n.
stand 218 n.
pliocene secular 110 adj.
plod walk 267 vb.
move slowly 278 vb.
persevere 600 vb.
work 682 vb.
plonk crackle 402 vb.
non-resonance 405 n.
plop plunge 313 vb.
non-resonance 405 n.
plosive speech sound 398 n.
plot combination 50 n.
grassland 348 n.
garden 370 n.
topic 452 n.
gauge 465 vb.
represent 551 vb.
narrative 590 n.
dramaturgy 594 n.
plot 623 n., vb.
prepare 669 vb.
stratagem 698 n.
compact 765 n.
plotter deceiver 545 n.
planner 623 n.
slyboots 698 n.
plough cut 46 vb.
groove 262 vb.
farm tool 370 n.
cultivate 370 vb.
disapprove 924 vb.
plough back
economize 814 vb.
ploughman preparer 669 n.
husbandman 370 n.
countryman 869 n.
plough-share
sharp edge 256 n.
farm tool 370 n.
ploy job 622 n.
stratagem 698 n.
pluck rend 46 vb.
insides 224 n.
uncover 229 vb.
move 265 vb.
draw 288 vb.
extract 304 vb.
agitate 318 vb.
cultivate 370 vb.
touch 378 vb.
deceive 542 vb.
resolution 599 n.
stamina 600 n.

take 786vb.
fleece 786vb.
defraud 788vb.
courage 855n.
disapprove 924vb.
pluck a crow with
  bicker 709vb.
plucked
  unsuccessful 728adj.
plucking
  hair-dressing 843n.
plucky *persevering* 600adj.
  courageous 855adj.
plug *repeat oneself* 106vb.
  go on 146vb.
  covering 226n.
  stopper 264n.
  stanch 350vb.
  tobacco 388n.
  advertise 528vb.
  emphasize 532vb.
  persevere 600vb.
plug in *connect* 45vb.
plug-ugly *low fellow* 869n.
  ruffian 904n.
plum
  over one hundred 99n.
  fruit 301n.
  redness 431n.
  élite 644n.
  trophy 729n.
  desired object 859n.
plumage *plumage* 259n.
  wing 271n.
  softness 327n.
plumb *positively* 32adv.
  be deep 211vb.
  vertical 215adj.
  straight on 249adv.
  smooth 258adj.
  plunge 313vb.
  measure 465vb.
plumbago *lubricant* 334n.
plumber *mender* 656n.
  artisan 686n.
plumbing *conduit* 351n.
  cleansing 648n.
plumb-line *verticality* 215n.
plume *headgear* 228n.
  plumage 259n.
  trimming 844n.
plume oneself
  feel pride 871vb.
  be vain 873vb.
plummet *depth* 211n.
  verticality 215n.
  sailing aid 269n.
  diver 313n.
  gravity 322n.
plump
  instantaneously 116adv.

fleshy 195adj.
tumble 309vb.
plunge 313vb.
non-resonance 405n.
plump for *choose* 605vb.
plumpness *bulk* 195n.
plump up *enlarge* 197vb.
plunder *acquisition* 771n.
  take away 786vb.
  rob 788vb.
  booty 790n.
plunderer *robber* 789n.
plunge *decrease* 37n.,vb.
  revolution 149n.
  be destroyed 165vb.
  be deep 211vb.
  motion 265vb.
  aquatics 269n.
  impel 279vb.
  enter 297vb.
  immersion 303n.,vb.
  descent 309n.
  depress 311vb.
  leap 312vb.
  plunge 313n.,vb.
  fluctuate 317vb.
  be agitated 318vb.
  drench 341vb.
  gambling 618n.
  ablution 648n.
  be cheap 812vb.
  be rash 857vb.
  be intemperate 943vb.
plunge into *enter* 297vb.
  undertake 672vb.
plunger *diver* 313n.
  gambler 618n.
  desperado 857n.
plunging *deep* 211adj.
plunk
  non-resonance 405n.
pluperfect *preterition* 125n.
plural *grammatical* 564adj.
pluralist *cleric* 986n.
plurality *plurality* 101n.
  greater number 104n.
plus *difference* 15n.
  in addition 38adv.
plus fours *breeches* 228n.
plush *hair* 259n.
  softness 327n.
  rich 800adj.
  ornamental 844adj.
plushy *ostentatious* 875adj.
plus sign
  punctuation 547n.
Pluto *planet* 321n.
  conduit 351n.
  death 361n.
  mythic god 966n.
  Olympian god 967n.

plutocracy
  government 733n.
  wealth 800n.
  rich man 800n.
plutocrat *master* 741n.
  rich man 800n.
Plutonian *planetary* 321adj.
  infernal 972adj.
plutonic *fiery* 379adj.
pluvial *humid* 341adj.
  rainy 350adj.
pluviometer
  hygrometry 341n.
ply *be periodic* 141vb.
  layer 207n.
  fold 261n.
  voyage 269vb.
  busy oneself 622vb.
  use 673vb.
  do 676vb.
  work 682vb.
Plymouth Brethren
  sect 978n.
pneuma *spirit* 447n.
pneumatic *soft* 327adj.
  gaseous 336adj.
  airy 340adj.
pneumatics *gaseity* 336n.
  pneumatics 340n.
  anemology 352n.
pneumatoscopic
  immaterial 320adj.
pneumonia
  respiratory disease 651n.
poaceous *vegetal* 366adj.
poach *cook* 301vb.
  encroach 306vb.
  steal 788vb.
poached, poachy
  rough 259adj.
  marshy 347adj.
poacher *thief* 789n.
pock *blemish* 845vb.
pocked *mottled* 437adj.
pocket *classification* 77n.
  place 185n.
  stow 187vb.
  pocket 194n.
  little 196adj.
  opening 263n.
  insert 303vb.
  battleground 724n.
  receive 782vb.
  take 786vb.
  treasury 799n.
  be patient 823vb.
pocket borough
  electorate 605n.
pocket-money
  receipt 807n.
pocket-size *little* 196adj.

pock-mark *cavity* 255 n.
  maculation 437 n.
  skin disease 651 n.
pod *receptacle* 194 n.
  skin 226 n.
podgy *fleshy* 195 adj.
podium *seat, stand* 218 n.
poem *poem* 593 n.
poet *author* 589 n.
  poet 593 n.
poetic *imaginative* 513 adj.
  poetic 593 adj.
poetic justice
  retaliation 714 n.
  punishment 963 n.
poetics *poetry* 593 n.
poetry *ideality* 513 n.
  reading matter 589 n.
  poetry 593 n.
pogrom *slaughter* 362 n.
poignancy *keenness* 174 n.
  pungency 388 n.
  vigour 571 n.
poignant *painful* 377 adj.
  felt 818 adj.
point *juncture* 8 n.
  relevance 9 n.
  degree 27 n.
  small thing 33 n.
  extremity 69 n.
  serial place 73 n.
  unit 88 n.
  instant 116 n.
  keenness 174 n.
  place 185 n.
  situation 186 n.
  minuteness 196 n.
  projection 254 n.
  sharpen 256 vb.
  aim, point to 281 vb.
  topic 452 n.
  reasons 475 n.
  punctuation 547 n.
  gesticulate 547 vb.
  mark 547 vb.
  lettering 586 n.
  use 673 n.
point a moral *teach* 534 vb.
point at *aim at* 617 vb.
  not respect 921 vb.
  accuse 928 vb.
point at issue *topic* 452 n.
  question 459 n.
  casus belli 709 n.
point, beside the
  irrelevant 10 adj.
point-blank
  towards 281 adv.
  plainly 573 adv.
point-device *regular* 83 adj.
pointedness

sharpness 256 n.
  wit 839 n.
pointer *dog* 365 n.
  indicator 547 n.
Pointillism
  school of painting 553 n.
point, in *apt* 24 adj.
pointless
  insubstantial 4 adj.
  irrelevant 10 adj.
  unsharpened 257 adj.
  prolix 570 adj.
  useless 641 adj.
  dull 840 adj.
point of difference
  speciality 80 n.
point of honour
  probity 929 n.
point of no return
  juncture 8 n.
  limit 236 n.
  progression 285 n.
point of view
  situation 186 n.
  view 438 n.
  appearance 445 n.
  idea 451 n.
  bias 481 n.
  opinion 485 n.
point out *specify* 80 vb.
  orientate 281 vb.
  attract notice 455 vb.
  show 522 vb.
  inform 524 vb.
  indicate 547 vb.
points *vantage* 34 n.
  numeration 86 n.
  railroad 624 n.
points of the compass
  laterality 239 n.
point to *attribute* 158 vb.
  point to 281 vb.
  predict 511 vb.
  mean 514 vb.
  indicate 547 vb.
point-to-point *racing* 716 n.
point, to the
  relevant 9 adj.
  rational 475 adj.
  concise 569 adj.
poise *equality* 28 n.
  conduct 688 n.
  inexcitability 823 n.
poised *well-bred* 848 adj.
poison *destroy* 165 vb.
  destroyer 168 n.
  murder 362 n.
  unsavouriness 391 n.
  be unpalatable 391 vb.
  motivate 612 vb.
  make unclean 649 vb.

  impair 655 vb.
  poison 659 n.
  excite hate 888 vb.
  enrage 891 vb.
  be malevolent 898 vb.
poisoner *murderer* 362 n.
  poisoning 659 n.
  offender 904 n.
poison gas *gas* 336 n.
  poison 659 n.
  weapon 723 n.
poisonous *deadly* 362 adj.
  unsavoury 391 n.
  not nice 645 adj.
  harmful 645 adj.
  unclean 649 adj.
  diseased 651 adj.
  toxic 653 adj.
  baneful 659 adj.
  dangerous 661 adj.
  paining 827 adj.
  maleficent 898 adj.
  intoxicating 949 adj.
poison pen
  correspondent 588 n.
  defamer 926 n.
poke *make violent* 176 vb.
  pocket 194 n.
  pierce 263 vb.
  gesticulate 547 vb.
  doctor 658 vb.
poke at *strike* 279 vb.
  strike at 712 vb.
poke fun *be witty* 839 vb.
  ridicule 851 vb.
poke out *jut* 254 vb.
poker *furnace* 383 n.
  card game 837 n.
poker-faced *still* 266 adj.
  unintelligible 517 adj.
  reticent 525 adj.
  impassive 820 adj.
pokerwork
  ornamental art 844 n.
poking *enquiring* 459 adj.
poky *restraining* 747 adj.
  graceless 842 adj.
polar *ending* 69 adj.
  topmost 213 adj.
  opposite 240 adj.
  telluric 321 adj.
  cold 380 adj.
Polaris *star* 321 n.
  signpost 547 n.
  directorship 689 n.
polariscope
  optical device 442 n.
polarity *polarity* 14 n.
  duality 90 n.
  tendency 179 n.
  counteraction 182 n.

contraposition 240 n.
opposition 704 n.
polarization
reflection 417 n.
pole extremity 69 n.
measure 183 n.
farness 199 n.
long measure 203 n.
high structure 209 n.
summit 213 n.
verticality 215 n.
pivot 218 n.
limit 236 n.
gauge 465 n.
pole-axe slaughter 362 vb.
axe 723 n.
polecat vermin 365 n.
fetor 397 n.
polemic reasoner 475 n.
argument 475 n.
quarrel 709 n.
polemics argument 475 n.
conference 584 n.
contention 716 n.
poles asunder
contrary 14 adj.
different 15 adj.
pole star signpost 547 n.
directorship 689 n.
pole to pole, from
widely 183 adv.
afar 199 adv.
police order 60 vb.
protector 660 n.
safeguard 660 vb.
manage 689 vb.
rule 733 vb.
restrain 747 vb.
police 955 n.
police action war 718 n.
police enquiry
police enquiry 459 n.
policeman protector 660 n.
police 955 n.
police state despotism 733 n.
police-station lock-up 748 n.
policy topic 452 n.
sagacity 498 n.
policy 623 n.
action 676 n.
tactics 688 n.
cunning 698 n.
title-deed 767 n.
poliomyelitis
infection 651 n.
paralysis 651 n.
polis polity 733 n.
polish facing 226 n.
smoothness 258 n.
friction 333 n.
make bright 417 vb.

elegance 575 n.
cleanness 648 n.
amendment 654 n.
beauty 841 n.
good taste 846 n.
etiquette 848 n.
polish off
carry through 725 vb.
polite literary 557 adj.
elegant 575 adj.
well-bred 848 adj.
courteous 884 adj.
respectful 920 adj.
politic wise 498 adj.
expedient 642 adj.
skilful 694 adj.
political
governmental 733 adj.
political economy
management 689 n.
politician manager 690 n.
expert 696 n.
political party 708 n.
politics tactics 688 n.
polity government 733 n.
polity 733 n.
polka musical piece 412 n.
dance 837 n.
poll numeration 86 n.
make smaller 198 vb.
shorten 204 vb.
enquiry 459 n.
judgment 480 n.
vote 605 n., vb.
pollard shorten 204 vb.
make smaller 198 vb.
tree 366 n.
pollen genitalia 164 n.
powder 332 n.
pollex finger 378 n.
pollination
propagation 164 n.
pollinator producer 166 vb.
pollinctor interment 364 n.
polliniferous
productive 164 adj.
pollinosis excretion 302 n.
pollster computer 86 n.
enquirer 459 n.
experimenter 461 n.
poll tax tax 809 n.
pollution
uncleanness 649 n.
infection 651 n.
insalubrity 653 n.
impairment 655 n.
misuse 675 n.
slur 867 n.
Pollyanna
cheerfulness 833 n.
polo ball game 837 n.

polonaise
musical piece 412 n.
dance 837 n.
poltergeist hinderer 702 n.
elf, ghost 970 n.
poltergeistery
spiritualism 984 n.
poltroonery
cowardice 856 n.
polyandry
type of marriage 894 n.
polychromatic
coloured 425 adj.
variegated 437 adj.
polychrome
multiform 82 adj.
variegation 437 n.
painting 553 n.
polygamy
type of marriage 894 n.
polygastric cellular 194 adj.
polygenous
multiform 82 adj.
polyglot interpreter 520 n.
linguist 557 n.
linguistic 557 adj.
polygon
angular figure 247 n.
polygraphy writing 586 n.
polygynist
polygamist 894 n.
polyhedron
angular figure 247 n.
polymath, become a
study 536 vb.
polymorphism
multiformity 82 n.
polyphony melody 410 n.
polypsychism
multiformity 82 n.
polypus swelling 253 n.
polysyllabic long 203 adj.
diffuse 570 adj.
polysyllable
speech sound 398 n.
spoken letter 558 n.
word 559 n.
polytechnic
trade school 539 n.
polytheism deism 973 n.
pomade, pomatum
unguent 357 n.
scent 396 n.
cosmetic 843 n.
pomander scent 396 n.
pomegranate fruit 301 n.
pomiculture
agriculture 370 n.
pommel handle 218 n.
sphere 252 n.
pommie foreigner 59 n.

pomp *pride* 871 n.
  ostentation 875 n.
pompadour *hair* 259 n.
  hair-dressing 843 n.
pom-pom *gun* 723 n.
  trimming 844 n.
pomposity
  magniloquence 574 n.
  inelegance 576 n.
  pride 871 n.
  ostentation 875 n.
pompous *vain* 873 adj.
  (*see* pomposity)
ponce *libertine* 952 n.
poncho *cloak* 228 n.
pond *shallowness* 212 n.
  lake 346 n.
ponder *meditate* 449 vb.
  estimate 480 vb.
ponderability
  substantiality 3 n.
ponderable *material* 319 adj.
  weighty 322 adj.
ponderous *weighty* 322 adj.
  inelegant 576 adj.
  clumsy 695 adj.
pongee *textile* 222 n.
pongo *soldier* 722 n.
pongye *monk* 986 n.
  priest 986 n.
poniard *sharp point* 256 n.
  side-arms 723 n.
pons asinorum
  unintelligibility 517 n.
pontiff *priest* 986 n.
pontifical *positive* 473 adj.
  assertive 532 adj.
  ecclesiastical 985 adj.
  vestimental 989 adj.
pontificals
  vestments 989 n.
pontificate
  dogmatize 473 vb.
  be biased 481 vb.
  affirm 532 vb.
  church office 985 n.
pontoon *bridge* 624 n.
  card game 837 n.
pony *over twenty* 99 n.
  pony 273 n.
  funds 797 n.
pony-tail *hair* 259 n.
  hair-dressing 843 n.
poodle *dog* 365 n.
poodlefake *caress* 889 vb.
pooh-pooh
  disregard 458 vb.
  underestimate 483 vb.
  hold cheap 922 vb.
poojahs *festivity* 837 n.
  holy-day 988 n.

pool *lake* 346 n.
  store 632 vb.
  association 706 n.
  acquisition 771 n.
  joint possession 775 n.
  ball game 837 n.
pool room
  gaming-house 618 n.
poop *poop* 238 n.
poor *weak* 163 adj.
  unproductive 172 adj.
  feeble 572 adj.
  necessitous 627 adj.
  insufficient 636 adj.
  unimportant 639 adj.
  bad 645 adj.
  imperfect 647 adj.
  unprosperous 731 adj.
  unfortunate 731 adj.
  not owning 774 adj.
  poor 801 adj.
  unhappy 825 adj.
  disreputable 867 adj.
poor hand *bungler* 697 n.
poor head
  unintelligence 499 n.
poorhouse *retreat* 192 n.
  shelter 662 n.
poor in spirit
  humble 872 adj.
poorly *slightly* 33 adv.
  weakly 163 adj.
  sick 651 adj.
poor opinion
  disapprobation 924 n.
poor quality *inferiority* 35 n.
poor rate (*see* poor relief)
poor relation
  inferior 35 n.
  imperfection 647 n.
poor relief
  subvention 703 n.
  sociology 901 n.
poor white
  low fellow 869 n.
pop *parent* 169 n.
  jut 254 vb.
  soft drink 301 n.
  sound faint 401 vb.
  give security 767 vb.
  borrow 785 vb.
pope *sovereign* 741 n.
  ecclesiarch 986 n.
popedom
  churchdom 985 n.
popery *Catholicism* 976 n.
pop-eyed
  wondering 864 adj.
pop-gun *bang* 402 n.
  toy gun 723 n.
  plaything 837 n.

popinjay *fop* 848 n.
poplar *tree* 366 n.
Poplarism *sociology* 901 n.
poplin *textile* 222 n.
popliteal *back* 238 adj.
  crural 267 adj.
pop out *jut* 254 vb.
  emerge 298 vb.
poppet *darling* 890 n.
popple *crinkle* 251 vb.
  roughen 259 vb.
  be agitated 318 vb.
  flow 350 vb.
poppy *redness* 431 n.
  soporific 679 n.
poppycock
  empty talk 515 n.
pop-shop *pawnshop* 784 n.
pop singer
  person of repute 866 n.
popsy *darling* 890 n.
pop the question
  interrogate 459 vb.
  request 761 vb.
  court 889 vb.
populace
  habitancy 191 n.
  commonalty 869 n.
popular *general* 79 adj.
  native 191 adj.
  intelligible 516 adj.
  governmental 733 adj.
  reputable 866 adj.
  welcomed 882 adj.
  approved 923 adj.
  laical 987 adj.
Popular Front
  association 706 n.
  political party 708 n.
popularity *repute* 866 n.
  sociability 882 n.
  lovableness 887 n.
  approbation 923 n.
popularize
  be intelligible 516 vb.
  interpret 520 vb.
  facilitate 701 vb.
  vulgarize 847 vb.
popular will
  government 733 n.
populate *be fruitful* 171 vb.
  place oneself 187 vb.
  dwell 192 vb.
  appropriate 786 vb.
populated
  multitudinous 104 adj.
population *location* 187 n.
  habitancy 191 n.
  social group 371 n.
populous
  assembled 74 adj.

multitudinous 104 adj.
pop up *reoccur* 106 vb.
  happen 154 vb.
  chance 159 vb.
  arrive 295 vb.
  be visible 443 vb.
  appear 445 vb.
porcelain *pottery* 381 n.
porch *entrance* 68 n.
  lobby 194 n.
  threshold 234 n.
  doorway 263 n.
  access 624 n.
  church exterior 990 n.
porcine *animal* 365 adj.
porcupine *prickle* 256 n.
  rodent 365 n.
pore *cavity* 255 n.
  orifice 263 n.
  outlet 298 n.
  scan 438 vb.
  be attentive 455 vb.
  study 536 vb.
porism *question* 459 n.
  judgment 480 n.
pork *meat* 301 n.
pork barrel *booty* 790 n.
  treasury 799 n.
porker *pig* 365 n.
pornography
  impurity 951 n.
porosity *cavity* 255 n.
  porosity 263 n.
porpoise *fish* 365 n.
porridge *cereal* 301 n.
  pulpiness 356 n.
porringer *bowl* 194 n.
port *stable* 192 n.
  sinistrality 242 n.
  window 263 n.
  gait 265 n.
  goal 295 n.
  wine 301 n.
  mien 445 n.
  shelter 662 n.
  conduct 688 n.
portable *little* 196 adj.
  transferable 272 adj.
  light 323 adj.
portage
  transport 272 n.
portal *threshold* 234 n.
  doorway 263 n.
portcullis *barrier* 235 n.
  obstacle 702 n.
  fort 713 n.
portend *predict* 511 vb.
portent *omen* 511 n.
  prodigy 864 n.
portentous
  presageful 511 adj.

frightening 854 adj.
  threatening 900 adj.
porter *janitor* 264 n.
  bearer 273 n.
  liquor 301 n.
  worker 686 n.
  servant 742 n.
porterage *transport* 272 n.
portfire *lighter* 385 n.
portfolio *list* 87 n.
  case 194 n.
  collection 632 n.
  title-deed 767 n.
  estate 777 n.
  jurisdiction 955 n.
porthole *window* 263 n.
portico *entrance* 68 n.
  series 71 n.
  lobby 194 n.
  pillar 218 n.
  temple 990 n.
portion *part* 53 n.
  fraction 102 n.
  meal 301 n.
  provision 633 n.
  participation 775 n.
  dower 777 n.
  portion 783 n.
portionless *poor* 801 adj.
portly *fleshy* 195 adj.
portmanteau *box* 194 n.
  storage 632 n.
portmanteau word
  assemblage 74 n.
  conciseness 569 n.
portolano, portulan
  sailing aid 269 n.
  map 551 n.
portrait *copy* 22 n.
  picture 553 n.
portraiture
  assimilation 18 n.
  mimicry 20 n.
  representation 551 n.
  art style 553 n.
portray *paint* 553 vb.
  (see portrayal)
portrayal *assimilation* 18 n.
  mimicry 20 n.
  representation 551 n.
  description 590 n.
pose *imitate* 20 vb.
  be example 23 vb.
  situation 186 n.
  interrogate 459 vb.
  represent 551 vb.
  conduct 688 n.
  be affected 850 vb.
poser *living model* 23 n.
  question 459 n.
  enigma 530 n.

art equipment 553 n.
  difficulty 700 n.
  affector 850 n.
poseur *affector* 850 n.
posh *fashionable* 848 adj.
posit *premise* 475 vb.
  suppose 512 vb.
position *state* 7 n.
  degree 27 n.
  order 60 n
  arrange 62 vb.
  serial place 73 n.
  situation 186 n.
  station 187 n.
  opinion 485 n.
  supposition 572 n.
  job 622 n.
  prestige 866 n.
positive *real* 1 adj.
  copy 22 n.
  absolute 32 adj.
  numerical 85 adj.
  positive 473 adj.
  narrow-minded 481 adj.
  believing 485 adj.
  intelligible 516 adj.
  forceful 571 adj.
  obstinate 602 adj.
positiveness
  affirmation 532 n.
positivism
  materiality 319 n.
  philosophy 449 n.
positron *particle* 33 n.
  element 319 n.
posology
  measurement 465 n.
  medical art 658 n.
posse *band* 74 n.
possess *dwell* 192 vb.
  know 490 vb.
  make mad 503 vb.
  inform 524 vb.
  possess 773 vb.
  dower 777 vb.
  excite 821 vb.
  diabolize 969 vb.
possessed *obsessed* 455 adj.
  frenzied 503 adj.
possession *territory* 184 n.
  use 673 n.
  possession 773 n.
  property 777 n.
  excitation 821 n.
  enjoyment 824 n.
  spell 983 n.
possessive
  acquiring 771 adj.
  taking 786 n.
  avaricious 816 adj.
  greedy 859 adj.

loving 887adj.
jealous 911adj.
selfish 932adj.
possessiveness
   exclusion 57n.
   (see possessive)
possessor resident 191n.
   master 741n.
   possessor 776n.
posset liquor 301n.
possibility existence 1n.
   opportunity 137n.
   fair chance 159n.
   ability 160n.
   liability 180n.
   possibility 469n.
   probability 471n.
   expectation 507n.
   supposition 512n.
possible unreal 2adj.
   future 124adj.
   accessible 289adj.
   possible 469adj.
   latent 523adj.
   easy 701adj.
   (see possibility)
post subsequent 120adj.
   situation 186n.
   place 187vb.
   pillar 218n.
   travel 267vb.
   transpose 272vb.
   send 272vb.
   move fast 277vb.
   communicate 524vb.
   advertise 528vb.
   mails 531n.
   register 548vb.
   correspondence 588n.
   job 622n.
   hasten 680vb.
   commission 751vb.
   account 808vb.
   shame 867vb.
   impose a duty 917vb.
postage price 809n.
postal epistolary 588adj.
postal order
   paper money 797n.
postbag
   correspondence 588n.
postbox mails 531n.
post-boy driver 268n.
   rider 268n.
   servant 742n.
postcard message 529n.
   correspondence 588n.
post-chaise
   stage-coach 274n.
post-Christian
   dated 108adj.

subsequent 120adj.
irreligious 974adj.
postdate misdate 118vb.
posted informed 524adj.
poster advertisement 528n.
poste restante mails 531n.
posterior sequent 65adj.
   subsequent 120adj.
   future 124adj.
   back, buttocks 238adj.
posterity survivor 41n.
   sequence 65n.
   aftercomer 67n.
   posteriority 120n.
   futurity 124n.
   posterity 170n.
postern entrance 68n.
   back 238adj.
   doorway 263n.
   fort 713n.
post-existence
   future state 124n.
   destiny 155n.
postfix add 38vb.
   adjunct 40n.
   part of speech 564n.
post-haste speeding 277n.
   hastily 680adv.
posthumous
   subsequent 120adj.
   late 136adj.
postilion driver 268n.
   rider 268n.
   servant 742n.
posting location 187n.
   transference 272n.
   mandate 751n.
postliminious
   subsequent 120adj.
   late 136adj.
postlude sequel 67n.
   stage play 594n.
postman bearer 273n.
   mails 531n.
postmeridian
   vespertine 129adj.
post-mortem
   death 361n.
   post-obit 361adv.
   inquest 364n.
   in memoriam 364adv.
   enquiry 459n.
postnate
   subsequent 120adj.
postnatus posteriority 120n.
post-obit
   posteriority 120n.
   subsequent 120adj.
   post-obit 361adv.
   in memoriam 364adv.
post-office

transferrer 272n.
   mails 531n.
postpone put off 136vb.
   relinquish 621vb.
   avoid 620vb.
   not complete 726vb.
postponement
   unwillingness 598n.
   (see postpone)
postposition adjunct 40n.
   sequence 65n.
   part of speech 564n.
post-prandial
   subsequent 120adj.
   reposeful 683adj.
   sociable 882adj.
postscript adjunct 40n.
   sequel 67n.
   extremity 69n.
postulant petitioner 703n.
   nun 986n.
   layman 987n.
postulate premise 475n.,vb.
   axiom 496n.
   supposition 512n.
   request 761n.
posture circumstance 8n.
   situation 186n.
   form 243n.
   mien 445n.
   conduct 688n.
   be affected 850vb.
post-war dated 108adj.
   subsequent 120adj.
   peaceful 717adj.
posy ornamentation 844n.
   love-token 889n.
   bunch 74n.
pot vessel 194n.
   shorten 204vb.
   propulsion 287n.
   insert 303vb.
   pottery 381n.
   abstract 592vb.
   preserve 666vb.
   trophy 729n.
   reward 962n.
potable edible 301adj.
potation drinking 301n.
   drunkenness 949n.
potato tuber 301n.
pot-bellied fleshy 195adj.
   expanded 197adj.
   rotund 252adj.
   convex 253adj.
potboiler book 589n.
   reading matter 589n.
   novel 590n.
potboiling trivial 639adj.
pot-boy servant 742n.
potency power 160n.

strength 162 n.
utility 640 n.
potent *productive* 164 adj.
  generative 171 adj.
  operative 173 adj.
  vigorous 174 adj.
  influential 178 n.
  intoxicating 949 adj.
  (*see* potency)
potentate *potentate* 741 n.
potential *unreal* 2 adj.
  intrinsic 5 adj.
  quantity 26 n.
  future 124 adj.
  energy 160 n.
  electricity 160 n.
  (*see* potentiality)
potentiality
  existence 1 n.
  intrinsicality 5 n.
  ability 160 n.
  influence 178 n.
  liability 180 n.
  possibility 469 n.
  latency 523 n.
potheen *liquor* 301 n.
pother *turmoil* 61 n.
  excitable state 822 n.
pot-herb *pot-herb* 301 n.
  condiment 389 n.
pot-hole *cavity* 255 n.
  orifice 263 n.
pot-holing *search* 459 n.
  discovery 484 n.
pot-hook *lettering* 586 n.
pothouse *tavern* 192 n.
pot-hunter *contender* 716 n.
  player 837 n.
potion *potion* 301 n.
  medicine 658 n.
pot-luck *chance* 159 n.
  meal 301 n.
  gambling 618 n.
  non-preparation 670 n.
  sociability 882 n.
pot-pourri *medley* 43 n.
  scent 396 n.
  musical piece 412 n.
potsherd *piece* 53 n.
pot-shot *propulsion* 287 n.
potted *short* 204 adj.
  compendious 592 adj.
  preserved 666 adj.
  tipsy 949 adj.
potter *epitomizer* 592 n.
  be inactive 679 vb.
  artisan 686 n.
pottery *brittleness* 330 n.
  pottery 381 n.
  art 551 n.
pottle *vat* 194 n.

potty *vessel* 194 n.
  crazed 503 adj.
pot-valiance
  courage 855 n.
  cowardice 856 n.
pot-valiant *drunk* 949 adj.
pouch *stow* 187 vb.
  pocket 194 n.
  receive 872 vb.
  take 786 vb.
pouchy *recipient* 194 n.
  expanded 197 adj.
pouffe *seat* 218 n.
poulterer *provider* 633 n.
poultice *pulpiness* 356 n.
  surgical dressing 658 n.
  relieve 831 vb.
poultry *meat* 301 n.
  poultry 365 n.
pounce *spurt* 277 n.
  descent 309 n.
  plunge 313 n.
pounce on *surprise* 508 vb.
  attack 712 vb.
  take 786 vb.
pound *enclosure* 235 n.
  strike 279 vb.
  weighment 322 n.
  pulverize 332 vb.
  sound dead 405 vb.
  lock-up 748 n.
  coinage 797 n.
poundage *discount* 810 n.
poundal *metrology* 465 n.
pound of flesh
  severity 735 n.
  interest 803 n.
  pitilessness 906 n.
pour *emit* 300 vb.
  descend 309 vb.
  let fall 311 vb.
  be wet 341 vb.
  flow, rain 350 vb.
  abound 635 vb.
pour down the drain
  waste 634 vb.
  be prodigal 815 vb.
pour in *converge* 293 vb.
  irrupt 297 vb.
pour out *land* 295 vb.
  flow out 298 vb.
  void 300 vb.
  make flow 350 vb.
  be diffuse 570 vb.
  give 781 vb.
pourparler
  conference 584 n.
  advice 691 n.
pout *be convex* 253 vb.
  jut 254 vb.
  gesture 547 n.

sullenness 893 n.
poverty *feebleness* 572 n.
  necessity 596 n.
  needfulness 627 n.
  scarcity 636 n.
  dilapidation 655 n.
  adversity 731 n.
  non-ownership 774 n.
  poverty 801 n.
  asceticism 945 n.
poverty-stricken
  beggarly 801 adj.
powder *overlay* 226 vb.
  smoother 258 n.
  powder 332 n.
  pulverize 332 vb.
  variegate 437 n.
  medicine 658 n.
  explosive 723 n.
  cosmetic 843 n.
  primp 843 vb.
powder and shot
  ammunition 723 n.
powder-barrel
  arsenal 723 n.
powder-horn *arsenal* 723 n.
powder-magazine
  pitfall 663 n.
  arsenal 723 n.
powder-monkey
  youngster 132 n.
  navy man 722 n.
powder puff *cosmetic* 843 n.
powder room
  beauty parlour 843 n.
powdery *brittle* 330 adj.
  powdery 332 adj.
  dry 342 adj.
power *intrinsicality* 5 n.
  greatness 32 n.
  numerical element 85 n.
  power 160 n.
  strength 162 n.
  operate 173 vb.
  style 566 n.
  vigour 571 n.
  eloquence 579 n.
  instrumentality 628 n.
  means 629 n.
  authority 733 n.
  brute force 735 n.
  mandate 751 n.
  virtue 933 n.
power behind the throne
  influence 178 n.
  latency 523 n.
  authority 733 n.
  deputy 755 n.
power cut *scarcity* 636 n.
power-dive *spurt* 277 n.
  descent 309 n.

plunge 313 n.
powered *dynamic* 160 adj.
  mechanical 630 adj.
powerful *influential* 178 adj.
  loud 400 adj.
  (*see* power)
powerless *powerless* 161 adj.
  weak 163 adj.
  inert 175 adj.
  unimportant 639 adj.
powerlessness
  anarchy 734 n.
power of attorney
  mandate 751 n.
power of, in the
  subject 745 adj.
power of speech
  eloquence 579 n.
power of the purse
  authority 733 n.
  finance 797 n.
power politics
  selfishness 932 n.
powers of darkness
  devil 969 n.
powers that be
  influence 178 n.
  master 741 n.
power vacuum
  impotence 161 n.
  anarchy 734 n.
pow-wow *conference* 584 n.
pox *skin disease* 651 n.
  venereal disease 651 n.
practicable
  possible 469 adj.
  useful 640 adj.
  expedient 642 adj.
practical *operative* 173 adj.
  intelligent 498 adj.
  instrumental 628 adj.
  useful 640 adj.
  expedient 642 adj.
  used 673 adj.
practical ability *skill* 694 n.
practical demonstration
  example 83 n.
practical joke
  foolery 497 n.
  trickery 542 n.
  trifle 639 n.
  witticism 839 n.
  ridicule 851 n.
practice *continuity* 71 n.
  regularity 81 n.
  conformity 83 n.
  numerical operation 86 n.
  repetition 106 n.
  permanence 144 n.
  empiricism 461 n.
  deception 542 n.

practice 610 n.
  vocation 622 n.
  plot 623 n.
  way 624 n.
  medical art 658 n.
  preparation 669 n.
  use 673 n.
  action 676 n.
  exercise 682 n.
  conduct 688 n.
  cunning 698 n.
  bombardment 712 n.
  art of war 718 n.
  observance 768 n.
  etiquette 848 n.
  foul play 930 n.
  rite 988 n.
practice, in
  prepared 669 adj.
  used 673 adj.
practise *train* 534 vb.
  learn 536 vb.
  habituate 610 vb.
  (*see* practice)
practised *knowing* 490 adj.
  expert 694 adj.
practising
  religious 973 adj.
  orthodox 976 adj.
  pious 979 adj.
practitioner *doer* 676 n.
  agent 686 n.
  expert 696 n.
Prætorian *defender* 713 n.
  soldier 722 n.
pragmatic
  useful 640 adj.
  expedient 642 adj.
pragmatism
  philosophy 449 n.
  expedience 642 n.
  use 763 n.
prairie *space* 183 n.
  plain 348 n.
prairie-schooner *cart* 274 n.
praise *honour* 866 vb.
  thanks 907 n.
  respect 920 vb.
  praise 923 n., vb.
  reward 962 n.
  act of worship 981 n.
praiser *commender* 923 n.
  worshipper 981 n.
praiseworthy
  excellent 644 adj.
  approvable 923 adj.
  virtuous 933 adj.
pram *push cart* 274 n.
prance *walk* 267 vb.
  ride 267 vb.
  leap 312 n.

  be ostentatious 875 vb.
  boast 877 vb.
prandial *mensal* 301 adj.
prang *aeronautics* 271 n.
  tumble 309 vb.
prank *dress* 228 vb.
  whim 604 n.
  revel 837 n.
  beautify 841 vb.
  primp 843 vb.
  decorate 844 vb.
prankish *capricious* 604 adj.
  amused 837 adj.
prate *empty talk* 515 n.
  chatter 581 n.
prater *boaster* 877 n.
prattle *empty talk* 515 n.
  speech 579 n.
  chatter 581 n.
prawn *fish food* 301 n.
  table fish 365 n.
praxis *grammar* 564 n.
  action 676 n.
pray *entreat* 761 vb.
  desire 859 vb.
  be pious 979 vb.
  worship 981 vb.
pray aloud
  soliloquize 585 vb.
prayer *entreaty* 761 n.
  request 761 n.
  prayers 981 n.
prayer-book *scripture* 975 n.
  prayers 981 n.
  office-book 988 n.
  church utensil 990 n.
prayer-cap *canonicals* 989 n.
prayerful
  supplicatory 761 adj.
  pious 979 adj.
  worshipping 981 adj.
prayer-house *church* 990 n.
prayer-meeting
  public worship 981 n.
prayers *aid* 703 n.
  kind act 897 n.
  prayers 981 n.
prayer-wheel
  rotator 315 n.
  prayers 981 n.
  ritual object 988 n.
pray for
  patronize 703 vb.
pre- *prior* 119 adj.
  before 119 adv.
preach *teach* 534 vb.
  orate 579 vb.
preacher *preacher* 537 n.
  speaker 579 n.
  chatterer 581 n.
  religionist 979 n.

pastor 986n.
preachiness *pietism* 979n.
preaching office
  church ministry 985n.
preaching order
  pastor 986n.
preachment *lecture* 543n.
  oration 579n.
  inducement 612n.
  ministration 988n.
preachy
  educational 534adj.
  pietistic 979adj.
pre-adamite *primal* 127adj.
  old man 133n.
preamble *come before* 64vb.
  prelude 66n.
prearrangement
  predetermination 608n.
  preparation 669n.
prebend *benefice* 985n.
prebendary
  ecclesiarch 986n.
precarious
  ephemeral 114adj.
  unreliable 474adj.
  unsafe 661adj.
precatory
  supplicatory 761adj.
  devotional 981adj.
precaution
  protection 660n.
  security 767n.
precautionary
  preparatory 669adj.
precede
  come before 64vb.
  be before 119vb.
  do before 119vb.
  precede 283vb.
  motivate 612vb.
  direct 689vb.
precedence
  superiority 34n.
  precedence 64n.
  priority 119n.
  seniority 131n.
  importance 638n.
  prestige 866n.
precedent
  non-imitation 21n.
  prototype 23n.
  precursor 66n.
  beginning 68n.
  rule 81n.
  example 83n.
  priority 119n.
  guide 520n.
  habit 610n.
  precept 693n.
precentor *choir* 413n.

leader 690n.
  church officer 986n.
precept *rule* 81n.
  maxim 496n.
  advice 691n.
  precept 693n.
  decree 737n.
preceptor *teacher* 537n.
precession *priority* 119n.
  motion 265n.
  precession 283n.
  uranometry 321n.
precinct *region* 184n.
  place 185n.
  circumjacence 230n.
  inclosure 235n.
preciosity *ornament* 574n.
  affectation 850n.
precious *great* 32adj.
  ornate 574adj.
  valuable 644adj.
  of price 811adj.
  affected 850adj.
preciousness
  ornament 574n.
precious stone *gem* 844n.
precipice *high land* 209n.
  verticality 215n.
  acclivity 220n.
  descent 309n.
  pitfall 663n.
precipitance
  non-preparation 670n.
  haste 680n.
  rashness 857...
precipitate *leavings* 41n.
  effect 157n.
  speedy 277adj.
  propel 287vb.
  eject 300vb.
  depress 311vb.
  let fall 311vb.
  solid body 324n.
  dirt 649n.
  hasten 680vb.
  rash 857adj.
precipitated
  indissoluble 324adj.
precipitation
  velocity 277n.
  propulsion 287n.
  ejection 300n.
  condensation 324n.
precipitous
  vertical 215adj.
  sloping 220adj.
précis *translation* 520n.
  compendium 592n.
precise *definite* 80adj.
  accurate 494adj.
  intelligible 516adj.

fastidious 862adj.
  formal 875adj.
  orthodox 976adj.
  pietistic 979adj.
precisian *conformist* 83n.
  tyrant 735n.
  man of taste 846n.
  affector 850n.
  perfectionist 862n.
  religionist 979n.
precision *touch* 378n.
  accuracy 494n.
  intelligibility 516n.
preclude *exclude* 57vb.
  restrain 747vb.
preclusive
  excluding 57adj.
precociously
  betimes 135adv.
precocity
  anticipation 135n.
  non-preparation 670n.
precognition
  knowledge 490n.
  foresight 510n.
  psychics 984n.
preconceive *prejudge* 481vb.
preconception
  prejudgment 481n.
preconcert
  predetermine 608vb.
preconsultation
  preparation 669n.
precursive
  preceding 64adj.
precursor *precursor* 66n.
  beginning 68n.
  example 83n.
  priority 119n.
  earliness 135n.
  precession 283n.
  messenger 531n.
  preparer 669n.
  director 690n.
precursory
  preceding 64adj.
  precursory 66adj.
  predicting 511adj.
  (*see* precursor)
predacity *rapacity* 786n.
predator *taker* 786n.
  robber 789n.
predatory
  oppressive 735adj.
  taking 786adj.
  thieving 788adj.
predecessor
  precursor 66n.
  parent 169n.
predeliberation
  foresight 510n.

predetermination 608n.
predella *stand* 218n.
  altar 990n.
predestinarian
  fatalist 596n.
predestination *fate* 596n.
  predetermination 608n.
  destiny 155n.
predestine *predestine* 155vb.
  necessitate 596vb.
  motivate 612vb.
  intend 617vb.
predetermination
  foresight 510n.
  will 595n.
  necessity 596n.
  resolution 599n.
  predetermination 608n.
  preparation 669n.
predetermine
  predestine 155vb.
  prejudge 481vb.
  predetermine 608vb.
  motivate 612vb.
  intend 617vb.
  plan 623vb.
predial *territorial* 344adj.
  agrarian 370adj.
  proprietary 777adj.
predicable
  affirmative 532adj.
predicament
  circumstance 8n.
  classification 77n.
  crisis 137n.
  danger 661n.
  predicament 700n.
  adversity 731n.
predicant *pastor* 986n.
predicate *attribute* 158vb.
predication
  argumentation 475n.
  affirmation 532n.
predict *expect* 507vb.
  indicate 547vb.
  (*see* prediction)
predictable
  future 124adj.
  unchangeable 153adj.
prediction
  looking ahead 124n.
  destiny 155n.
  prediction 511n.
  warning 664n.
predictive
  foreseeing 510adj.
  predicting 511adj.
predigested *edible* 301adj.
  intelligible 516adj.
  ready-made 669adj.
predilection

prejudice 481n.
  choice 605n.
  affections 817n.
  liking 859n.
  love 887n.
predispose *bias* 481vb.
  predetermine 608vb.
  motivate 612vb.
  prepare 669vb.
predisposition
  tendency 179n.
  willingness 597n.
  affections 817n.
predominance
  superiority 34n.
  power 160n.
  influence 178n.
  authority 733n.
predominate *prevail* 178vb.
  motivate 612vb.
  overmaster 727vb.
  dominate 733vb.
pre-eminence
  superiority 34n.
  precedence 64n.
pre-eminent
  authoritative 733adj.
  noteworthy 866adj.
pre-empt *exclude* 57vb.
  be early 135vb.
  acquire 771vb.
  possess 773vb.
  bargain 791vb.
  purchase 792vb.
preen *primp* 843vb.
  decorate 844vb.
preen oneself
  feel pride 871vb.
  be vain 873vb.
pre-existence
  existence 1n.
  priority 119n.
prefab *house* 192n.
prefabricate *produce* 164vb.
preface *prepose* 64vb.
  come before 64vb.
  prelude 66n.
  edition 589n.
prefatory
  preceding 64adj.
  precursory 66adj.
  beginning 68adj.
prefect *teacher* 537n.
  official 690n.
  officer 741n.
prefecture
  magistrature 733n.
prefer *promote* 285vb.
  choose 605vb.
  desire 859vb.
  ecclesiasticize 985vb.

preferable
  superior 34adj.
  chosen 605adj.
  excellent 644adj.
preference
  precedence 64n.
  will 595n.
  choice 605n.
  restriction 747n.
preferential treatment
  aid 703n.
  injustice 914n.
preferment
  progression 285n.
  improvement 654n.
  holy orders 985n.
  church office 985n.
prefigure *predict* 511vb.
  indicate 547vb.
prefigurement
  precursor 66n.
  omen 511n.
prefix *adjunct* 40n.
  affix 45vb.
  prepose 64vb.
  precursor 66n.
  front 237n.
  spoken letter 558n.
pre-glacial *primal* 127adj.
pregnancy
  propagation 164n.
pregnant
  productive 164adj.
  prolific 171adj.
  meaningful 514adj.
  concise 569adj.
  important 638adj.
pregnant with
  impending 155adj.
  presageful 511adj.
prehensile *taking* 786adj.
prehension *retention* 778n.
  taking 786n.
prehistorian
  antiquarian 125n.
prehistoric *past* 125adj.
  former 125adj.
  olden 127adj.
prehistory
  antiquity 125n.
  unknown thing 491n.
prejudgment
  prejudgment 481n.
prejudice
  influence 178vb.
  tendency 179n.
  prejudice, bias 481n.
  error 495n.
  predetermination 608n.
  motivate 612n.
  evil 616n.

dislike 861 n.
hatred 888 n.
injustice 914 n.
prejudicial *harmful* 645 adj.
prelacy *Catholicism* 976 n.
churchdom 985 n.
prelate *ecclesiarch* 986 n.
prelection *lecture* 534 n.
oration 579 n.
prelector *teacher* 537 n.
preliminaries
beginning 68 n.
preparation 669 n.
preliminary
preceding 64 adj.
prelude 66 n.
precursory 66 adj.
preparatory 669 adj.
prelims *edition* 589 n.
prelude *come before* 64 vb.
prepose 64 vb.
prelude 66 n.
musical piece 412 n.
prelusory (*see* prelude)
premature *early* 135 adj.
ill-timed 138 adj.
immature 670 adj.
unsuccessful 728 adj.
prematurity
anticipation 135 n.
premeditate *intend* 617 vb.
premeditation
predetermination 608 n.
preparation 669 n.
premier *director* 690 n.
première *début* 68 n.
dramaturgy 594 n.
premier pas *début* 68 n.
premiership
directorship 689 n.
magistrature 733 n.
premise
premise 475 n., vb.
supposition 512 n.
premises *place* 185 n.
shop 796 n.
premium *interest* 803 n.
receipt 807 n.
premium, at a *dear* 811 adj.
premium bond *chance* 159 n.
gambling 618 n.
paper money 797 n.
premolar *tooth* 256 n.
premonition
precursor 66 n.
foresight 510 n.
warning 664 n.
prenatal *prior* 119 adj.
prenomen *name* 561 n.
prentice *beginner* 538 n.
new 126 adj.

immature 670 adj.
prenticeship *learning* 536 n.
preoccupation
exclusion 57 n.
attention 455 n.
abstractedness 456 n.
obstacle 702 n.
preoccupied
obsessed 455 adj.
distracted 456 adj.
preoccupy *overlook* 57 vb.
engross 449 vb.
possess 773 vb.
preoption *choice* 605 n.
preordain
predestine 155 vb.
preordination *fate* 596 n.
predetermination 608 n.
prep *curriculum* 536 n.
study 536 n.
preparation 669 n.
preparation
beginning 68 n.
looking ahead 124 n.
production 164 n.
foresight 510 n.
study 536 n.
provision 633 n.
medicine 658 n.
preparation 669 n.
preparatory
preceding 64 adj.
preparatory 669 adj.
prepare *arrange* 62 vb.
train 534 vb.
plan 623 vb.
prepare 669 vb.
prepared *expectant* 507 adj.
willing 597 adj.
prepense
volitional 595 adj.
predetermined 608 adj.
preponderance
inequality 29 n.
superiority 34 n.
influence 178 n.
authority 733 n.
prepose *prepose* 64 vb.
preposition *adjunct* 40 n.
precursor 66 n.
part of speech 564 n.
prepositional
preceding 64 adj.
fore 237 adj.
grammatical 564 adj.
prepossess *bias* 481 vb.
prepossessing
personable 841 adj.
lovable 887 adj.
prepossession
prejudice 481 n.

preposterous
absurd 497 adj.
imaginative 513 adj.
exaggerated 546 adj.
ridiculous 849 adj.
undue 916 adj.
preprandial
mensal 301 adj.
prepuce *front* 237 n.
Pre-Raphaelite
antiquarian 125 n.
olden 127 adj.
artist 556 n.
pre-release *priority* 119 n.
prerequisite
requirement 627 n.
required 627 adj.
prerogative *vantage* 34 n.
authority 733 n.
freedom 744 n.
nobility 868 n.
right 913 n.
dueness 915 n.
presage *predestine* 155 vb.
omen 511 n.
indicate 547 vb.
threaten 900 vb.
presageful
impending 155 adj.
presageful 511 adj.
frightening 854 n.
presbyter *ecclesiarch* 986 n.
church officer 986 n.
presbyterate
church office 985 n.
Presbyterianism
Protestantism 976 n.
sectarianism 978 n.
churchdom 985 n.
presbytery *seniority* 131 n.
synod 985 n.
parish 985 n.
churchdom 985 n.
parsonage 986 n.
church exterior 990 n.
prescience *foresight* 510 n.
pre-scientific
ignorant 491 adj.
prescribe *doctor* 658 vb.
manage 689 vb.
advise 691 vb.
decree 737 vb.
prescript *precept* 693 n.
decree 737 n.
prescription
tradition 127 n.
habit 610 n.
remedy 658 n.
advice 691 n.
precept 693 n.
decree 737 n.

possession 773 n.
dueness 915 n.
prescriptive
  immemorial 127 adj.
  permanent 144 adj.
  vested 153 adj.
  habitual 610 adj.
  preceptive 693 adj.
  due 915 adj.
presence *existence* 1 n.
  generality 79 n.
  presence 189 n.
  arrival 295 n.
  appearance 445 n.
  mien 445 n.
  ghost 970 n.
present *present* 121 adj.
  synchronous 123 adj.
  modern 126 adj.
  on the spot 189 adj.
  near 200 adj.
  show 522 vb.
  represent 551 vb.
  dramatize 594 vb.
  offer 759 n., vb.
  gift 781 n.
  reward 962 vb.
  ecclesiasticize 985 vb.
presentable
  personable 841 adj.
present arms *greet* 884 vb.
  show respect 920 vb.
presentation *spectacle* 445 n.
  manifestation 522 n.
  representation 551 n.
  offer 759 n.
  giving 781 n.
  reward 962 n.
  holy orders 985 n.
presenter *speaker* 579 n.
  actor 594 n.
present, for the
  during pleasure 112 adv.
  transiently 114 adv.
presentiment
  intuition 476 n.
  prejudgment 481 n.
  foresight 510 n.
  prediction 511 n.
present of, make a
  cheapen 812 vb.
preservation
  permanence 144 n.
  protection 660 n.
  preservation 666 n.
preservative
  preserver 666 n.
preserve *sustain* 146 vb.
  dry 342 vb.
  sweet 392 n.
  store 632 vb.

sanitate 652 vb.
safeguard 660 vb.
preserve 660 vb.
retain 778 vb.
preserver *protector* 660 n.
  preserver 666 n.
preside *direct* 689 vb.
presidency
  magistrature 733 n.
president *superior* 34 n.
  director 690 n.
  master, officer 741 n.
presidium *council* 692 n.
press *crowd* 74 n.
  cabinet 194 n.
  make smaller 198 vb.
  flattener 216 n.
  be supported 218 vb.
  smooth 258 vb.
  impel 279 n.
  weigh 322 vb.
  touch 378 vb.
  the press 528 n.
  press 587 n.
  be resolute 599 vb.
  incite 612 vb.
  activity 678 n.
  advise 691 vb.
  compel 740 vb.
  offer 759 vb.
  request 761 vb.
  take away 786 vb.
  steal 788 vb.
  caress 889 vb.
press-cuttings
  record 548 n.
press-gang
  compulsion 740 n.
  taker 786 n.
  police 955 n.
pressing *important* 638 adj.
press into service
  avail of 673 vb.
pressman *publicizer* 528 n.
  chronicler 549 n.
  printer 587 n.
  author 589 n.
pressure *crisis* 137 n.
  energy 160 n.
  vigorousness 174 n.
  influence 178 n.
  compression 198 n.
  impulse 279 n.
  gravity 322 n.
  touch 378 n.
  inducement 612 n.
  instrumentality 628 n.
  action 676 n.
  exertion 682 n.
  adversity 731 n.
  restriction 747 n.

request 761 n.
endearment 889 n.
pressure group
  inducement 612 n.
  motivator 612 n.
  petitioner 763 n.
pressure, under
  hastily 680 adv.
  by force 740 adj.
presswork *print* 587 n.
  letterpress 587 n.
prestidigitation
  sleight 542 n.
prestidigitator
  conjuror 545 n.
prestige
  influence 178 n.
  importance 638 n.
  authority 733 n.
  prestige 866 n.
  pride 871 n.
  ostentatious 875 adj.
presto
  instantaneously 116 adv.
  swiftly 277 adv.
  adagio 412 adv.
presumable
  probable 471 adj.
presume *assume* 471 vb.
  prejudge 481 vb.
  (*see* presumption)
presume on *avail of* 673 vb.
presumption
  probability 471 n.
  opinion 485 n.
  expectation 507 n.
  supposition 512 n.
  rashness 857 n.
  insolence 878 n.
  arrogation 916 n.
presumptive
  evidential 466 adj.
  probable 471 adj.
  supposed 512 adj.
presumptuous *rash* 857 adj.
  insolent 878 adj.
  unwarranted 916 adj.
presupposition
  supposition 512 n.
pretence
  insubstantial thing 4 n.
  mimicry 20 n.
  supposition 512 n.
  duplicity 541 n.
  sham 542 n.
  mental dishonesty 543 n.
  pretext 614 n.
  pretension 850 n.
  ostentation 875 n.
pretend *imagine* 513 vb.
pretender *impostor* 545 n.

petitioner 763 n.
affector 850 n.
boaster 877 n.
usurper 916 n.
pretendership
arrogation 916 n.
pretension *pretension* 850 n.
airs 873 n.
ostentation 875 n.
pretentious *absurd* 499 adj.
feeble 572 adj.
ornate 574 adj.
affected 850 adj.
vain 873 adj.
ostentatious 875 adj.
boastful 877 adj.
pretentiousness
affectation 850 n.
preterite
preterite 125 adj.
preterition
precedence 64 n.
preterition 125 n.
pretermit *neglect* 458 vb.
preternatural
abnormal 84 adj.
pretext *reason why* 156 n.
reasons 475 n.
sophistry 477 n.
mental dishonesty 543 n.
pretext 614 n.
stratagem 698 n.
prettify *beautify* 841 vb.
primp 843 vb.
decorate 844 vb.
prettiness *beauty* 841 n.
pretty *greatly* 32 adv.
beautiful 841 adj.
prettyism
ornamentation 844 n.
pretty pass
predicament 700 n.
pretty-pretty
ornamentation 844 n.
prevail *be* 1 vb.
be general 79 vb.
be able 160 vb.
prevail 178 vb.
be wont 610 vb.
motivate 612 vb.
overmaster 727 vb.
prevail upon *induce* 612 vb.
prevalence *existence* 1 n.
generality 79 n.
power 160 n.
influence 178 n.
prevalent *existing* 1 adj.
extensive 32 adj.
usual 610 adj.
(*see* prevalence)
prevaricate

be dishonest 930 adj.
prevarication
equivocalness 518 n.
falsehood 541 n.
prevenience
anticipation 135 n.
prevenient
preceding 64 adj.
prevenient grace
divine function 965 n.
prevent *counteract* 182 vb.
avoid 620 vb.
obstruct 702 vb.
prohibit 757 vb.
preventable
avoidable 620 adj.
prevention
hindrance 702 n.
restraint 747 n.
preventive
counteraction 182 n.
prophylactic 658 n.
preserving 666 adj.
preventive medicine
hygiene 652 n.
medical art 658 n.
preservation 666 n.
preview *precursor* 66 n.
priority 119 n.
cinema 445 n.
foresight 510 n.
manifestation 522 n.
previous *preceding* 64 adj.
anachronistic 118 adj.
prior 119 adj.
early 135 adj.
prevision *foresight* 510 n.
pre-war *prior* 119 adj.
antiquated 127 adj.
peaceful 717 adj.
prey *objective* 617 n.
chase 619 n.
loser 728 n.
unlucky person 731 n.
booty 790 n.
sufferer 825 n.
prey on *eat* 301 vb.
ill-treat 645 vb.
incommode 827 vb.
frighten 854 vb.
priapism *libido* 859 n.
price *equivalence* 28 n.
quid pro quo 150 n.
appraise 465 vb.
goodness 644 n.
price 809 n., vb.
penalty 963 n.
priceless *valuable* 644 adj.
of price 811 adj.
funny 849 adj.
price ring

restriction 747 n.
prick *small thing* 33 n.
cut 46 vb.
stimulant 174 n.
sharp point 256 n.
pierce 263 vb.
give pain 377 vb.
itch 378 vb.
indication 547 n.
mark 547 vb.
incite 612 vb.
wound 655 n.
excitant 821 n.
prickle *itch* 378 vb.
prickliness *sharpness* 256 n.
quarrelsomeness 709 n.
moral sensibility 819 n.
pride 871 n.
irascibility 892 n.
prickly
unconformable 84 adj.
prickly heat
formication 378 n.
prick up one's ears
hear 415 vb.
be curious 453 vb.
be attentive 455 vb.
pride *pride* 871 n.
vanity 873 n.
ostentation 875 n.
insolence 878 n.
unsociability 883 n.
vice 934 n.
impiety 980 n.
prideful *prideful* 871 adj.
pride of place
superiority 34 n.
precedence 64 n.
prie-dieu *seat* 218 n.
priest *priest* 986 n.
priestcraft *sorcery* 983 n.
priestdom
ecclesiasticism 985 n.
priesthood
church office 985 n.
clergy 986 n.
priestly *priestly* 985 adj.
clerical 986 adj.
priest-ridden
pietistic 979 adj.
ecclesiastical 985 adj.
prig *steal* 788 vb.
affector 850 n.
prude 950 n.
priggish *affected* 850 a
prudish 950 acj.
priggishness *airs* 873 n.
prim *serious* 834 adj.
dull 840 adj.
affected 850 adj.
fastidious 862 adj.

primacy *superiority* 34 n.
  importance 638 n.
  prestige 866 n.
  church office 985 n.
prima donna
  superior 34 n.
  vocalist 413 n.
  actor 594 n.
  bigwig 638 n.
  proficient 696 n.
prima facie *at sight* 438 n.
  evidential 466 adj.
  probably 471 adv.
  manifestly 522 adv.
primage *extra* 40 n.
  decrement 42 n.
primal *primal* 127 adj.
  fundamental 156 adj.
primary *intrinsic* 5 adj.
  unimitative 21 adj.
  simple 44 adj.
  fundamental 156 adj.
  star 321 n.
  educational 534 adj.
  vote 605 n.
  important 638 adj.
primate *ecclesiarch* 986 n.
primatial *animal* 365 adj.
prime *numerical* 85 adj.
  oldness 127 n.
  morning 128 n.
  adultness 134 n.
  early 135 adj.
  educate 534 vb.
  important 638 adj.
  élite 644 n.
  excellent 644 adj.
  make ready 669 vb.
  church service 988 n.
prime constituent
  essence 1 n.
  essential part 5 n.
prime minister
  director 690 n.
  officer 741 n.
prime of life
  salad days 130 n.
  adultness 134 n.
primer *beginning* 68 n.
  textbook 589 n.
primeval *primal* 127 adj.
primigenous *primal* 127 adj.
priming *preparation* 669 n.
  ammunition 723 n.
primitive *past* 125 adj.
  primal 127 adj.
  earliness 135 n.
  fundamental 156 adj.
  violent 176 adj.
  low fellow 869 n.
  plebeian 869 adj.

primness *prudery* 950 n.
  (*see* prim)
primogenital *older* 131 adj.
  filial 170 adj.
primogeniture
  priority 119 n.
  oldness 127 n.
  seniority 131 n.
  sonship 170 n.
primordial
  unimitative 21 adj.
  primal 127 adj.
  fundamental 156 adj.
primp *beautify* 841 vb.
  primp 843 vb.
  be vain 873 adj.
  be ostentatious 875 vb.
primrose
  yellowness 433 n.
  badge 547 n.
primrose path
  deterioration 655 n.
  facility 701 n.
  wickedness 934 n.
primum mobile *cause* 156 n.
  divineness 965 n.
primus inter pares
  superior 34 n.
prince *sovereign* 741 n.
  potentate 741 n.
  aristocrat 868 n.
princely *ruling* 733 adj.
  liberal 813 adj.
  worshipful 866 adj.
  noble 868 adj.
prince of *paragon* 646 n.
princess *sovereign* 741 n.
principal *supreme* 34 adj.
  first 68 adj.
  teacher 537 n.
  director 690 n.
  master 741 n.
principality
  territory 184 n.
  polity 733 n.
principate
  magistrature 733 n.
principle
  essential part 5 n.
  rule 81 n.
  source 156 n.
  element 319 n.
  idea 451 n.
  premise 475 n.
  opinion 485 n.
  axiom 496 n.
  motive 612 n.
  probity 929 n.
principled *virtuous* 933 adj.
principles *creed* 485 n.
  probity 929 n.

prink *beautify* 841 vb.
  primp 843 vb.
print *copy* 22 n., vb.
  effect 157 n.
  publish 528 vb.
  indication 547 n.
  record 548 vb.
  photography 551 n.
  picture 553 n.
  printing 555 n.
  write 586 vb.
  writing 586 n.
  letterpress 587 n.
  pattern 844 n.
printable *permitted* 756 adj.
  pure 950 adj.
printed *intelligible* 516 adj.
printer *publicizer* 528 n.
  printer 587 n.
print, in
  published 528 adj.
printing
  reproduction 166 n.
  printing 555 n.
  print 587 n.
printless *obliterated* 550 adj.
print-type *print-type* 587 n.
prior *prior* 119 adj.
  older 131 adj.
  ecclesiarch 986 n.
  monk 986 n.
priorate *church office* 985 n.
priority *precedence* 64 n.
  time 108 n.
  priority 119 n.
  preterition 125 n.
  seniority 131 n.
  chief thing 638 n.
priory *monastery* 986 n.
prise, prize *force* 176 vb.
prism *angular figure* 247 n.
  chromatics 425 n.
  variegation 437 n.
  optical device 442 n.
prismatic *coloured* 425 adj.
  variegated 437 adj.
prison *inclosure* 235 n.
  prison 748 n.
  seclusion 883 n.
  pillory 964 n.
prisoner *prisoner* 750 n.
  accused person 928 n.
  litigant 959 n.
prison, in *captive* 750 adj.
pristine *former* 125 adj.
privacy *seclusion* 883 n.
private *inferior* 35 n.
  private 80 adj.
  concealed 525 adj.
  soldiery 722 n.
  possessed 773 adj.

commoner 869 n.
secluded 883 adj.
private enterprise
　particularism 80 n.
　trade 791 n.
privateer *warship* 722 n.
　navy man 722 n.
　robber 789 n.
privateering
　brigandage 788 n.
private parts *genitalia* 164 n.
privation *loss* 772 n.
　poverty 801 n.
privative *taking* 786 adj.
privilege *vantage* 34 n.
　freedom 744 n.
　permit 756 vb.
　right 913 n.
　dueness 915 n.
　non-liability 919 n.
privities *genitalia* 164 n.
privity *knowledge* 490 n.
privy *knowing* 490 adj.
　concealed 525 adj.
　latrine 649 n.
privy purse *receipt* 807 n.
privy seal
　badge of rule 743 n.
prize *monument* 548 n.
　benefit 615 n.
　objective 617 n.
　élite 644 n.
　trophy 729 n.
　acquisition 771 n.
　gift 781 n.
　taking 786 n.
　booty 790 n.
　receipt 807 n.
　desired object 859 n.
　honour 866 vb.
　love 887 vb.
　approve 923 vb.
　reward 962 n.
prize-fight *pugilism* 716 n.
prize-fighter
　contender 716 n.
　pugilist 722 n.
prize-giving *giving* 781 n.
prizeman *superior* 34 n.
　college student 538 n.
　proficient 696 n.
　victor 727 n.
prize-money *reward* 962 n.
prize-winner *superior* 34 n.
　exceller 644 n.
　proficient 696 n.
　recipient 782 n.
prize-winning
　successful 727 adj.
pro *deputy* 755 n.
probabilism

philosophy 449 n.
probability 471 n.
irreligion 974 n.
probability
　fair chance 159 n.
　appearance 445 n.
　probability 471 n.
　expectation 507 n.
probable *future* 124 adj.
　impending 155 adj.
　tending 179 adj.
　probable 471 adj.
　credible 485 adj.
probation
　experiment 461 n.
　demonstration 478 n.
　essay 671 n.
probationary
　experimental 461 adj.
probationer *beginner* 538 n.
　offender 904 n.
probation officer
　nurse 658 n.
probative
　experimental 461 adj.
　evidential 466 adj.
　demonstrating 478 adj.
probe *depth* 211 n.
　perforator 263 n.
　enquiry 459 n.
　experiment 461 n.
　measure 465 vb.
probity *veracity* 540 n.
　right 913 n.
　morals 917 n.
　probity 929 n.
　innocence 935 n.
problem *topic* 452 n.
　question 459 n.
　argumentation 475 n.
　enigma 530 n.
　difficulty 700 n.
　worry 825 n.
problematic *moot* 459 adj.
　uncertain 474 adj.
proboscis *projection* 254 n.
　feeler 378 n.
procacity *rudeness* 885 n.
procedure *policy* 623 n.
　way 624 n.
　action 676 n.
　conduct 688 n.
　ritual 988 n.
proceed *elapse* 111 vb.
　go on 146 vb.
　travel 267 vb.
　progress 285 vb.
　do 676 vb.
　deal with 688 vb.
proceeding
　eventuality 154 n.

deed 676 n.
proceedings *record* 548 n.
　legal process 959 n.
proceeds *earnings* 771 n.
　receiving 782 n.
　receipt 807 n.
process *change* 143 n.
　convert 147 vb.
　production 164 n.
　agency 173 n.
　motion 265 n.
　way 624 n.
　action 676 n.
procession *retinue* 67 n.
　procession 71 n.
　concomitant 89 n.
　marching 267 n.
　pageant 875 n.
　ritual act 988 n.
process-server
　law officer 955 n.
prochronism
　anachronism 118 n.
proclaim *proclaim* 528 vb.
　affirm 532 vb.
　raise the alarm 665 vb.
　honour 866 vb.
proclamation
　publication 528 n.
　call 547 n.
proclitic *sequel* 67 n.
proclivity *tendency* 179 n.
proconsul *official* 690 n.
　officer 741 n.
　governor 741 n.
　deputy 755 n.
proconsulate
　magistrature 733 n.
procrastinate
　spin out 113 vb.
　put off 136 vb.
　be neglectful 458 vb.
　not act 677 vb.
procreation
　propagation 164 n.
　reproduction 166 n.
　productiveness 171 n.
procreator *parent* 169 n.
proctor *teacher* 537 n.
　manager 690 n.
　consignee 754 n.
　law agent 958 n.
proctorship
　management 689 n.
procumbent *supine* 216 adj.
procuration *agency* 173 n.
　commission 751 n.
procurator *manager* 690 n.
　consignee 754 n.
　law agent 958 n.
procure *cause* 156 vb.

induce 612 vb.
  provide 633 vb.
  acquire 771 vb.
  be impure 951 vb.
procurement *agency* 173 n.
  acquisition 771 n.
procurer *provider* 633 n.
  bawd 952 n.
procuress *bawd* 952 n.
prod *stimulant* 174 n.
  impel 279 vb.
  incentive 612 n.
prodigal
  wasteful 634 adj.
  plenteous 635 adj.
  expending 806 adj.
  liberal 813 adj.
  prodigal 815 n., adj.
  bad man 938 n.
  intemperate 943 adj.
prodigality
  prodigality 815 n.
  rashness 857 n.
  (*see* prodigal)
prodigal son
  prodigal 815 n.
  bad man 938 n.
  penitent 939 n.
prodigious
  prodigious 32 adj.
  wonderful 864 adj.
prodigy *intellectual* 492 n.
  exceller 644 n.
  paragon 646 n.
  proficient 696 n.
  prodigy 864 n.
prodition *dutilessness* 918 n.
  perfidy 930 n.
prodrome *precursor* 66 n.
produce *increment* 36 n.
  cause 156 vb.
  growth 157 n.
  product 164 n.
  make fruitful 171 vb.
  lengthen 203 vb.
  manifest 522 vb.
  dramatize 594 vb.
  provide 633 vb.
  earnings 771 n.
producer *producer* 167 n.
  exhibitor 522 n.
  stage-manager 594 n.
produce results
  be expedient 642 vb.
producible *shown* 522 adj.
product
  numerical result 85 n.
  eventuality 154 n.
  effect 157 n.
  product 164 n.
  earnings 771 n.

production
  composition 56 n.
  causation 156 n.
  product 164 n.
  lengthening 203 n.
  manifestation 522 n.
  dramaturgy 594 n.
production line
  workshop 687 n.
productive *prolific* 171 adj.
  profitable 640 adj.
  gainful 771 adj.
  rich 800 adj.
productivity
  production 164 n.
  productiveness 171 n.
  diffuseness 570 n.
  plenty 635 n.
proem *prelude* 66 n.
proemial *preceding* 64 adj.
  beginning 68 adj.
proemium *oration* 579 n.
profanation *misuse* 675 n.
  undueness 916 n.
  impiety 980 n.
profane *unclean* 649 adj.
  impair 655 vb.
  shame 867 vb.
  maledicent 899 adj.
  not respect 921 vb.
  wicked 934 adj.
  irreligious 974 adj.
  profane 980 adj.
  laical 987 adj.
profanity *scurrility* 899 n.
  impiety 980 n.
profess *believe* 485 vb.
  teach 534 vb.
professing
  affirmative 532 adj.
  pious 979 adj.
profession *creed* 485 n.
  assent 488 n.
  affirmation 532 n.
  mental dishonesty 543 n.
  pretext 614 n.
  pursuit 619 n.
  vocation 622 n.
  promise 764 n.
  ostentation 875 n.
  duty 917 n.
professional
  instructed 490 adj.
  usual 610 adj.
  businesslike 622 adj.
  expert 694 adj.
  expert 696 n.
professionalism *skill* 694 n.
professor *scholar* 492 n.
  teacher 537 n.
  expert 696 n.

academic title 870 n.
professoriate *scholar* 492 n.
  teacher 537 n.
professorship *lecture* 534 n.
proffer *offer* 759 n., vb.
  promise 764 vb.
proficiency *culture* 490 n.
  skill 694 n.
proficient *knowing* 490 adj.
  scholar 492 n.
  expert 694 adj.
  proficient 696 n.
profile *outline* 233 n., vb.
  laterality 239 n.
  form 243 n.
  feature 445 n.
  picture 553 n.
  description 590 n.
profit *increment* 36 n.
  growth 157 n.
  incentive 612 n.
  benefit 615 n., vb.
  utility 640 n.
  expedience 642 n.
  gain 771 n., vb.
  reward 962 n.
profitability *utility* 640 n.
profitable *prolific* 171 adj.
  good 615 adj.
  (*see* profit)
profit by *profit by* 137 vb.
  find useful 640 vb.
  get better 654 vb.
  use 673 vb.
profiteer *made man* 730 n.
  prosper 730 vb.
  speculate 791 vb.
  overcharge 811 vb.
profit, for *trading* 791 adj.
profitless
  unproductive 172 adj.
  wasted 634 adj.
  profitless 641 adj.
  unsuccessful 728 adj.
  losing 772 adj.
profit-making *trade* 791 n.
profit-taking
  acquisition 771 n.
profligacy *wickedness* 934 n.
profligate *vicious* 934 adj.
  bad man 938 n.
  lecherous 951 adj.
  libertine 952 n.
profluent
  progressive 285 adj.
  flowing 350 adj.
profound *great* 32 adj.
  deep 211 adj.
  wise 498 adj.
  inexpressible 517 adj.
  imperspicuous 568 adj.

felt 818 adj.
profundity *thought* 448 n.
  (*see* profound)
profuse *diffuse* 570 adj.
  liberal 813 adj.
profusion
  great quantity 32 n.
  multitude 104 n.
  plenty 635 n.
  redundance 637 n.
  prodigality 815 n.
prog *food* 301 n.
progenitive
  reproductive 166 adj.
progenitor *source* 156 n.
  parent 169 n.
progeny *posterity* 170 n.
prognosis *foresight* 510 n.
  prediction 511 n.
  medical art 658 n.
prognostic
  foreseeing 510 adj.
  omen 511 n.
  cautionary 664 adj.
prognostication
  foresight 510 n.
  prediction 511 n.
programme *list* 87 n.
  prediction 511 n.
  publication 528 n.
  policy 623 n.
  plan 623 n., vb.
  undertaking 672 n.
  tactics 688 n.
progress *increase* 36 n.
  elapse 111 vb.
  continuance 146 n.
  conversion 147 n.
  motion 265 n.
  travel 267 vb.
  progression 285 n.
  approach 289 vb.
  pass 305 vb.
  way 624 n.
  improvement 654 n.
  be active 678 vb.
  success 727 n.
progression *series* 71 n.
  ratio 85 n.
  (*see* progress)
progressism
  reformism 654 n.
progressive
  continuous 71 adj.
  elapsing 111 adj.
  vigorous 174 n.
  progressive 285 adj.
  reformer 654 n.
  enterprising 672 adj.
prohibit *exclude* 57 vb.
  counteract 182 vb.

negate 533 vb.
  obstruct 702 vb.
  command 737 vb.
  restrain 747 vb.
  prohibit 757 vb.
  make illegal 954 vb.
prohibition
  temperance 942 n.
  (*see* prohibit)
prohibitionist
  abstainer 942 n.
  sober person 948 n.
prohibitive *dear* 811 adj.
project *make extrinsic* 6 vb.
  externalize 223 vb.
  jut 254 vb.
  propel 287 vb.
  emerge 298 vb.
  be visible 443 vb.
  represent 551 vb.
  predetermination 608 n.
  intention 617 n.
  plan 623 n., vb.
  undertaking 672 n.
projectile *missile* 287 n.
  ammunition 723 n.
projection
  extrinsicality 6 n.
  distortion 246 n.
  convexity 253 n.
  projection 254 n.
  propulsion 287 n.
  image, map 551 n.
projector *thrower* 287 n.
  lamp 420 n.
  cinema 445 n.
  optical device 442 n.
  planner 623 n.
prolapse *descend* 309 vb.
prolation *speech* 579 n.
prole (*see* proletarian)
prolegomena *prelude* 66 n.
  dissertation 591 n.
prolepsis
  anachronism 118 n.
proletarian
  vulgarian 847 n.
  commoner 869 n.
  plebeian 869 adj.
proletarianism
  government 733 n.
proletariat
  lower classes 869 n.
  commonalty 869 n.
proliferate *grow* 36 vb.
  reproduce 164 vb.
  be fruitful 171 vb.
  abound 635 vb.
prolific *increasing* 36 adj.
  multitudinous 104 adj.
  productive 164 adj.

prolific 171 adj.
  diffuse 570 adj.
  profitable 640 adj.
prolix *protracted* 113 adj.
  long 203 adj.
  prolix 570 adj.
  tedious 838 adj.
prolixity *speech* 579 n.
  (*see* prolix)
prolocutor
  interpreter 520 n.
  speaker 579 n.
prologize
  come before 64 vb.
prologue *prelude* 66 n.
  oration 579 n.
  speaker 579 n.
  stage play 594 n.
  actor 594 n.
prolong *augment* 36 vb.
  continuate 71 vb.
  spin out 113 vb.
  sustain 146 vb.
  lengthen 203 vb.
prolongation
  adjunct 40 n.
  sequence 65 n.
  delay 136 n.
  tempo 410 n.
  (*see* prolong)
prolusion *prelude* 66 n.
promenade *street* 192 n.
  land travel 267 n.
  pedestrianism 267 n.
  path 624 n.
  pageant 875 n.
prominence
  superiority 34 n.
  prominence 254 n.
  elevation 310 n.
  light 417 n.
  importance 638 n.
  prestige 866 n.
prominent
  overhanging 209 adj.
  salient 254 adj.
  well-seen 443 adj.
  manifest 522 adj.
  (*see* prominence)
promiscuity
  indiscrimination 464 n.
  indifference 860 n.
  unchastity 951 n.
promiscuous
  mixed 43 adj.
  orderless 61 adj.
  designless 618 adj.
promise *predict* 511 vb.
  oath 532 n.
  affirm 532 vb.
  intention 617 n.

undertaking 672n.
be auspicious 730vb.
promise 764n.,vb.
compact 765n.
give hope 852vb.
Promised Land
fantasy 513n.
objective 617n.
aspiration 852n.
promise oneself
expect 507vb.
promising *probable* 471adj.
presageful 511adj.
promissory
promissory 764adj.
promissory note
title-deed 767n.
paper money 797n.
promontory
projection 254n.
land 344n.
promote *augment* 36vb.
conduce 156vb.
tend 179vb.
concur 181vb.
promote 285vb.
make likely 471vb.
be instrumental 628vb.
find means 629vb.
be useful 640vb.
be expedient 642vb.
make better 654vb.
undertake 672vb.
aid 703vb.
dignify 866vb.
promoter *planner* 623n.
patron 707n.
prompt *initiate* 68vb.
early 135adj.
influence 178vb.
speedy 277adj.
reminder 505n.
hint 524n.,vb.
willing 597adj.
incite 612vb.
active 678adj.
hasty 680adj.
advise 691vb.
prompt-book
stage play 594n.
prompter *reminder* 505n.
stage-hand 594n.
motivator 612n.
adviser 691n.
auxiliary 707n.
promptitude
punctuality 135n.
velocity 277n.
activity 678n.
promptly
instantaneously 116adv.

promptuary
storage 632n.
promulgate
proclaim 528vb.
decree 737vb.
pronation
supination 216n.
inversion 221n.
prone *supine* 216adj.
inverted 221adj.
proneness *tendency* 179n.
supination 216n.
prong *sharp point* 256n.
pronounce *judge* 480vb.
proclaim 528vb.
affirm 532vb.
voice 577vb.
speak 579vb.
pronounced
well-seen 443adj.
manifest 522adj.
vocal 577adj.
pronouncement
judgment 480n.
publication 528n.
pronunciamento
publication 528n.
pronunciation
pronunciation 577n.
proof *duplicate* 22n.
unyielding 162adj.
sealed off 264adj.
dry 342adj.
hard 326adj.
unfeeling 375adj.
experiment 461n.
evidence 466n.
certainty 473n.
demonstration 478n.
letterpress 587n.
reading matter 589n.
resolute 599adj.
plan 623n.
amendment 654n.
invulnerable 660adj.
resisting 715adj.
impassive 820adj.
proof-read *print* 587vb.
rectify 654vb.
prop *bond* 47n.
strengthen 162vb.
supporter 218n.
elevate 310vb.
aid 703vb.
propædeutics
curriculum 534n.
propagable
generative 171adj.
propaganda
argument 475n.
publicity 528n.

teaching 534n.
misteaching 535n.
inducement 612n.
warfare 718n.
propagandist
publicizer 528n.
preacher 537n.
motivator 612n.
propagandize
pervert 655vb.
propagate *generate* 164vb.
be fruitful 171vb.
publish 528vb.
proparoxytone
punctuation 547n.
propel *move* 265vb.
send 272vb.
propel 287vb.
propellant
propeller 269n.
propellant 287n.
explosive 723n.
propeller *propeller* 269n.
aircraft 276n.
propellant 287n.
rotator 317n.
propensity *tendency* 179n.
willingness 597n.
liking 859n.
proper *characteristic* 5adj.
relevant 9adj.
ingredient 58adj.
special 80adj.
regular 83adj.
expedient 642adj.
possessed 773adj.
personable 841adj.
tasteful 846adj.
well-bred 848adj.
right 913adj.
due 915adj.
virtuous 933adj.
proper fraction
numerical element 85n.
properispomenon
punctuation 547n.
properly *aright* 644adv.
proper time *occasion* 137n.
occasion 137n.
expedience 642n.
property *essential part* 5n.
ability 160n.
stage-set 594n.
store 632n.
property 777n.
propertyless
not owning 744adj.
prophecy *prediction* 511n.
hermeneutics 520n.
revelation 975n.
prophesy *foresee* 510vb.

predict 511 vb.
prophet *sage* 500 n.
  oracle 511 n.
  preacher 537 n.
  veracity 540 n.
  warner 664 n.
  religious teacher 973 n.
prophylactic *hygiene* 652 n.
  salubrious 652 adj.
  prophylactic 658 n.
  preserving 666 adj.
  hindering 702 adj.
prophylaxis
  protection 660 n.
  (*see* prophylactic)
propinquity
  consanguinity 11 n.
  nearness 200 n.
propitiate *pacify* 719 vb.
  mediate 720 vb.
  content 828 vb.
  ask mercy 905 vb.
  atone 941 vb.
  offer worship 981 vb.
propitiation
  divine function 965 n.
  (*see* propitiate)
propitiatory
  redemptive 965 adj.
propitious
  opportune 137 adj.
  beneficial 644 adj.
  aiding 703 adj.
  palmy 730 adj.
  promising 852 adj.
prop-man
  stage-hand 594 n.
proponent *reasoner* 475 n.
proportion
  relativeness 9 n.
  correlation 12 n.
  fitness 24 n.
  degree 27 n.
  part 53 n.
  order 60 n.
  ratio 85 n.
  numerical operation 86 n.
  symmetry 245 n.
  elegance 575 n.
  portion 783 n.
proportional, proportion-
  able, proportionate
  (*see* proportion)
proportional representation
  vote 605 n.
proportions *measure* 183 n.
  size 195 n.
proposal *supposition* 512 n.
  intention 617 n.
  plan 623 n.
  advice 691 n.

  offer 759 n.
  request 761 n.
propose *argue* 475 vb.
  propound 512 vb.
  intend 617 vb.
  advise 691 vb.
  patronize 703 vb.
  court 889 vb.
proposer *planner* 623 n.
  patron 707 n.
proposition *topic* 452 n.
  argumentation 475 n.
  supposition 512 n.
  affirmation 532 n.
  (*see* proposal)
propound *propound* 512 vb.
  affirm 532 vb.
  (*see* propose)
proprietary
  proprietary 777 adj.
proprietor *owner* 776 n.
proprietorship
  possession 773 n.
propriety *relevance* 9 n.
  fitness 24 n.
  elegance 575 n.
  expedience 642 n.
  good taste 846 n.
  etiquette 848 n.
  right 913 n.
  purity 950 n.
props *stage-set* 594 n.
propugnant
  defending 713 adj.
propulsion *energy* 160 n.
  impulse 279 n.
  propulsion 287 n.
  ejection 300 n.
propylæum *lobby* 194 n.
  doorway 263 n.
  temple 990 n.
propylon *entrance* 68 n.
pro rata *pro rata* 783 adv.
prorogation *delay* 136 n.
prorogue *put off* 136 vb.
prosaic *typical* 83 adj.
  unintelligent 499 adj.
  plain 573 adj.
  prosaic 593 adj.
  artless 699 adj.
  tedious 838 adj.
  dull 840 adj.
pros and cons
  reasons 475 n.
proscenium *front* 237 n.
  stage-set 594 n.
proscribe *command* 737 vb.
  prohibit 757 vb.
  condemn 961 vb.
proscribed
  heterodox 977 adj.

proscription
  command 737 n.
  prohibition 757 n.
  malediction 899 n.
  condemnation 961 n.
  penalty 963 n.
prose *plainness* 573 n.
  be loquacious 581 vb.
  reading matter 589 n.
  prose 593 n.
prosecute *do* 676 vb.
prosecution *pursuit* 619 n.
  accusation 928 n.
  legal trial 959 n.
proselyte
  changed person 147 n.
  learner 538 n.
  tergiversator 603 n.
proselytize *convert* 147 vb.
  teach 534 vb.
proser *chatterer* 581 n.
  bore 838 n.
prose-writer *author* 589 n.
  prose 593 n.
prosiness *feebleness* 572 n.
  (*see* prosaic)
prosing, prosy
  prolix 570 adj.
  loquacious 581 adj.
  (*see* prosaic)
prosody *prosody* 593 n.
prosopography
  description 590 n.
prosopopœia
  metaphor 519 n.
prospect *futurity* 124 n.
  looking ahead 124 n.
  destiny 155 n.
  range 183 n.
  view 438 n.
  spectacle 445 n.
  search 459 vb.
  be tentative 461 vb.
  probability 471 n.
  expectation 507 n.
  prediction 511 n.
  art subject 553 n.
prospective
  future 124 adj.
prospector
  enquirer 459 n.
  experimenter 461 vb.
prospectus *list* 87 n.
  prediction 511 n.
  compendium 592 n.
  policy 623 n.
prosper *progress* 285 vb.
  flourish 615 vb.
  get better 654 vb.
  succeed 727 vb.
  prosper 730 vb.

be profitable 771 vb.
prosperity (see prosper, prosperous)
prosperous
opportune 137 adj.
beneficial 644 adj.
prosperous 730 adj.
rich 800 adj.
happy 824 adj.
promising 852 adj.
prosthetic additional 38 n.
preceding 64 adj.
fore 237 adj.
prostitute pervert 655 vb.
debauch 951 vb.
prostitute 952 n.
prostitution
deterioration 655 n.
misuse 675 n.
social evil 951 n.
prostrate disable 161 vb.
demolish 165 vb.
low 210 adj.
supine 216 adj.
flatten 216 vb.
depressed 311 adj.
sick 651 adj.
fatigue 684 vb.
submitting 721 adj.
sadden 834 vb.
servile 879 adj.
respectful 920 adj.
prostrate oneself
stoop 311 vb.
greet 884 vb.
show respect 920 vb.
worship 981 vb.
perform ritual 988 vb.
prostration (see prostrate)
prosyllogism
argumentation 475 n.
protagonist actor 594 n.
proficient 696 n.
protean multiform 82 adj.
changeful 152 adj.
protect accompany 89 vb.
screen 421 vb.
preserve 666 vb.
patronize 703 vb.
befriend 880 vb.
(see protection)
protected non-liable 919 n.
protection
surveillance 457 n.
protection 660 n.
safeguard 662 n.
defence 713 n.
restriction 747 n.
protectionism
restriction 747 n.
protective clothing

armour 713 n.
protective colouring
disguise 527 n.
protective custody
detention 747 n.
protectiveness love 887 n.
protector influence 178 n.
protector 660 n.
patron 707 n.
defender 713 n.
master 741 n.
keeper 749 n.
friend 880 n.
libertine 952 n.
protectorate
protection 660 n.
polity 733 n.
protectorship
magistrature 733 n.
protégé dependant 742 n.
friend 880 n.
protein food content 301 n.
organism 358 n.
protest dissent 489 n., vb.
affirm 532 vb.
negate 533 vb.
unwillingness 598 n.
oppose 704 vb.
resistance 715 n.
revolt 738 vb.
refusal 760 n.
deprecation 762 n.
non-observance 769 n.
non-payment 805 n.
be discontented 829 vb.
disapprobation 924 n.
protestant
dissentient 489 n.
negative 533 adj.
deprecatory 762 adj.
Protestant 976 n.
church party 978 n.
protester agitator 738 n.
protest too much
exaggerate 546 vb.
protest, under
by force 740 adv.
disapprovingly 924 adv.
Proteus multiformity 82 n.
changeable thing 152 n.
prothalamium poem 593 n.
wedding 894 n.
prothesis precedence 64 n.
altar 990 n.
proto- past 125 adj.
protocol practice 610 n.
treaty 765 n.
etiquette 848 n.
formality 875 n.
protomartyr precursor 66 n.
proton particle 33 n.

element 319 n.
protonotary recorder 549 n.
protoplasm origin 68 n.
matter 319 n.
organism 358 n.
life 360 n.
prototypal
unimitative 21 adj.
prototypal 23 adj.
prototype prototype 23 n.
idea 451 n.
protozoon animalcule 196 n.
animal 365 n.
protract spin out 113 n.
put off 136 vb.
sustain 146 vb.
lengthen 203 vb.
be diffuse 570 vb.
be obstructive 702 vb.
protractor
angular measure 247 n.
gauge 465 n.
protreptic
inducive 612 adj.
protrude jut 254 vb.
protrusion convexity 253 n.
protuberance
convexity 253 n.
protuberance 254 n.
proud defiant 711 adj.
worshipful 866 adj.
proud 871 adj.
vain 873 adj.
insolent 878 adj.
proud flesh swelling 253 n.
prove happen 154 vb.
expand 197 vb.
experiment 461 vb.
demonstrate 478 vb.
be true 494 vb.
indicate 547 vb.
feel 818 vb.
proven trustworthy 929 adj.
provenance origin 68 n.
provender provender 301 n.
provision 633 n.
proverb maxim 496 n.
proverbial known 490 adj.
aphoristic 496 adj.
proverbialist
preacher 537 n.
phrase 563 n.
provide foresee 510 vb.
find means 629 vb.
store 632 vb.
provide 633 vb.
make ready 669 vb.
permit 756 vb.
give 781 vb.
provided if 8 adv.
provided 468 adv.

providence *foresight* 510n.
  divineness 965n.
  theocracy 965n.
provident *vigilant* 457adj.
  intelligent 498adj.
  foreseeing 510adj.
providential
  opportune 137adj.
  divine 965adj.
province
  classification 77n.
  district 184n.
  abode 192n.
  function 622n.
  polity 733n.
  parish 985n.
provincial *regional* 184adj.
  provincial 192adj.
  narrow-minded 481adj.
  subject 742n.
  ill-bred 847adj.
  countryman 869n.
  plebeian 869adj.
  ecclesiastical 985adj.
provincialism
  narrow mind 481n.
  prejudice 481n.
  dialect 560n.
proving ground
  testing agent 461n.
provision
  accumulation 74n.
  foresight 510n.
  means 629n.
  store 632n.
  provision 633n.
  fitting out 669n.
  subvention 703n.
  conditions 766n.
  funds 797n.
provisional
  circumstantial 8adj.
  inferior 35adj.
  ephemeral 114adj.
  changeable 143adj.
  substituted 150adj.
  experimental 461adj.
  qualifying 468adj.
  uncertain 474adj.
  preparatory 669adj.
  conditional 766adj.
provisionally
  conditionally 7adv.
  if 8adv.
  during pleasure 112adv.
  transiently 114adv.
  on terms 766adv.
provisionary
  provisionary 633adj.
provisions *provisions* 301n.
proviso *qualification* 468n.

pretext 614n.
  conditions 766n.
provisory
  conditional 766adj.
provocation
  causation 156n.
  inducement 612n.
  excitation 821n.
  annoyance 827n.
  sauciness 878n.
  resentment 891n.
provocative *defiant* 711adj.
  impure 951adj.
  (*see* provocation,
  provoke)
provoke *cause* 156vb.
  incite 612vb.
  make quarrels 709vb.
  torment 827vb.
  be insolent 878vb.
provoking
  annoying 827adj.
provost *master* 741n.
provost marshal
  police 955n.
prow *prow* 237n.
prowess *deed* 676n.
  skill 694n.
  success 727n.
  prowess 855n.
prowl *wander* 267vb.
  be stealthy 525vb.
proximate *sequent* 65adj.
  near 200adj.
proximity *nearness* 200n.
  contiguity 202n.
proximo
  subsequently 120adv.
proxy *substitute* 150n.
  commission 751n.
  consignee 754n.
  deputy 755n.
prude *prude* 950n.
  (*see* prudish)
prudence *thought* 449n.
  carefulness 457n.
  sagacity 498n.
  foresight 510n.
  economy 814n.
  caution 858n.
  virtues 933n.
prudent *cowardly* 856adj.
prudery
  fastidiousness 862n.
  modesty 874n.
prudish *severe* 735adj.
  affected 850adj.
  fastidious 862adj.
  modest 874adj.
  prudish 950adj.
prune *subtract* 39vb.

cut 46vb.
  shorten 204vb.
  fruit 301n.
  extract 304vb.
  cultivate 370vb.
prunes and prisms
  pretension 850n.
pruning-hook
  sharp edge 256n.
prurience *curiosity* 453n.
  desire, libido 859n.
  impurity 951n.
Prussianism
  bellicosity 718n.
  brute force 735n.
pry *inquisitor* 453n.
  be curious 453vb.
  enquire 459vb.
psalm *vocal music* 412n.
  hymn 981n.
psalm-book (*see* psalter)
psalmist, psalmodist
  musician 413n.
  theologian 973n.
  worshipper 981n.
psalmody
  vocal music 412n.
  act of worship 981n.
  hymn 981n.
  public worship 981n.
psalm-singing
  pietistic 979adj.
psalter *vocal music* 412n.
  scripture 975n.
  hymn 981n.
  hymnal 988n.
psaltery *harp* 414n.
psephism *legislation* 953n.
pseudo *simulating* 18adj.
  imitative 20adj.
  spurious 542adj.
pseudologist *liar* 545n.
pseudonym *name* 561n.
  misnomer 562n.
psi *intuition* 476n.
  psychics 984n.
psittacosis
  animal disease 651n.
psyche *subjectivity* 320n.
  intellect, spirit 447n.
psychiatry *psychology* 447n.
  insanity 503n.
  therapy 658n.
psychic *immaterial* 320adj.
  psychic 447adj.
  psychic 984n.
  psychical 984adj.
psychical research
  spirit 447n.
  spiritualism 984n.
  psychics 984n.

psychic bid
  gambling 618 n.
psychism
  immateriality 320 n.
  occultism 984 n.
  psychics 984 n.
psychoanalysis
  psychology 447 n.
  therapy 658 n.
psychobiology
  psychology 447 n.
psychogenesis
  intellect 447 n.
psychogram *record* 548 n.
  spiritualism 984 n.
psychography
  psychology 447 n.
  description 590 n.
  spiritualism 984 n.
psychological
  psychic 447 adj.
  behaving 688 adj.
psychological moment
  crisis 137 n.
psychologist
  psychologist 447 n.
psychology
  psychology 447 n.
  conduct 688 n.
  affections 817 n.
  psychics 984 n.
psychomancy *spirit* 447 n.
  theomancy 511 n.
  sorcery 983 n.
  occultism 984 n.
  spiritualism 984 n.
psychometry
  psychology 447 n.
psychoneurosis
  psychopathy 503 n.
psychopædics *therapy* 658 n.
psychopath *madman* 504 n.
psychopathist
  psychologist 447 n.
  doctor 658 n.
psychopathology
  psychology 447 n.
psychopathy
  psychopathy 503 n.
psychopharmacology
  medical art 658 n.
psychophysicist
  psychist 984 n.
psychophysics
  psychology 447 n.
psychophysiology
  psychology 447 n.
psychosis
  psychopathy 503 n.
psychotherapy
  psychology 447 n.

insanity 503 n.
  therapy 658 n.
psychotic *insane* 503 adj.
  madman 504 n.
pterodactyl *animal* 365 n.
ptisan *tonic* 658 n.
Ptolemaic system
  centrality 225 n.
  world 321 n.
pub *tavern* 192 n.
pub-crawl
  drunkenness 949 n.
puberty *preparedness* 669 n.
  (*see* adultness)
pubescence *youth* 130 n.
  hair 259 n.
public *social group* 371 n.
  national 371 adj.
  known 490 adj.
  manifest 522 adj.
  well-known 528 adj.
  formal 875 adj.
public address system
  telecommunication 531 n.
publican *caterer* 633 n.
  tyrant 735 n.
  receiver 782 n.
publication
  information 524 n.
  disclosure 526 n.
  publication 528 n.
  call 547 n.
  book 589 n.
public convenience
  latrine 649 n.
public domain
  joint possession 775 n.
public health officer
  sanitarian 652 n.
public house *tavern* 192 n.
publicist *intellectual* 492 n.
  publicizer 528 n.
  dissertator 591 n.
publicity *generality* 79 n.
  knowledge 490 n.
  manifestation 522 n.
  publicity 528 n.
  ostentation 875 n.
publicity agent
  publicizer 528 n.
publicize (*see* publish)
public opinion
  belief 485 n.
  consensus 488 n.
  tribunal 956 n.
Public Orator
  speaker 579 n.
public ownership
  joint possession 775 n.
public purse
  treasury 799 n.

public relations officer
  publicizer 328 n.
public sector
  apportionment 783 n.
  trade 791 n.
public service
  commission 751 n.
public spirit
  patriotism 901 n.
publish
  attract notice 455 vb.
  manifest 522 vb.
  publish 528 vb.
  print 587 vb.
publisher *publicizer* 528 n.
  bookman 589 n.
puce *brown* 430 adj.
  red colour 431 n.
  purple 434 adj.
pucelage *nonage* 130 n.
  celibacy 895 n.
puck *missile* 287 n.
Puck *fairy* 970 n.
  elf 970 n.
pucker *fold* 261 n., vb.
puckish *harmful* 645 adj.
  fairylike 970 adj.
pudding *pudding* 301 n.
  softness 327 n.
  semiliquidity 354 n.
  pulpiness 356 n.
  sweet 392 n.
puddle *shallowness* 212 n.
  agitate 318 vb.
  lake 346 n.
  thicken 354 vb.
puddled *opaque* 423 adj.
pudency, pudicity
  purity 950 n.
pudenda *genitalia* 164 n.
pudgy *fleshy* 195 adj.
puerile *trivial* 639 adj.
puerility *folly* 499 n.
  despisedness 922 n.
puerperal
  productive 164 adj.
puff *dilation* 197 n.
  emit 300 vb.
  pastry 301 n.
  breeze 352 n.
  blow, breathe 352 vb.
  smoke 388 vb.
  overrate 482 vb.
  exaggerate 546 vb.
  advertisement 528 n.
  be fatigued 684 vb.
  boast 877 n., vb.
  praise 923 vb.
puffed-up
  prideful 871 adj.
  vain 873 adj.

puffery *exaggeration* 546n.
 boasting 877n.
puffin *bird of prey* 365n.
puffy *unstable* 152adj.
 fleshy 195adj.
 expanded 197adj.
 windy 352adj.
pug *foot* 214n.
 pugilist 722n.
puggree *headgear* 228n.
 coil 251n.
pugilism *pugilism* 716n.
 sport 837n.
pugilist *athlete* 162n.
 pugilist 722n.
pug-mark *trace* 548n.
pugnacious (*see* pugnacity)
pugnacity
 quarrelsomeness 709n.
 bellicosity 718n.
 irascibility 892n.
puisné *subsequent* 120adj.
 young 130adj.
puissant *powerful* 160adj.
 strong 162adj.
 authoritative 733adj.
puke *vomit* 300vb.
pukka *genuine* 494adj.
pulchritude *beauty* 841n.
pule *cry* 408vb.
 ululate 409vb.
 weep 836vb.
pull *duplicate* 22n.
 vantage 34n.
 influence 178n.
 blunt 257vb.
 row 269vb.
 deflect 282vb.
 propel 287vb.
 traction 288n.
 attraction 291n.
 extract 304vb.
 touch 378vb.
 letterpress 587n.
 reading matter 589n.
 exertion 682n.
 bungling 695n.
pull back *restrain* 747vb.
pull down *demolish* 165vb.
 fell 311vb.
pulled down *weakly* 163adj.
pullet *youngling* 132n.
 poultry 365n.
pulley *wheel* 250n.
 tool 630n.
Pullman *train* 274n.
pull one's leg
 be witty 839vb.
 ridicule 851vb.
pull one's punches
 avoid 620vb.

pull one's weight
 influence 178vb.
pull on with
 be friendly 880vb.
pull out *lengthen* 203vb.
 open 263vb.
 start out 296vb.
 eject 300vb.
 extract 304vb.
pull-out *aeronautics* 271n.
pullover *vest* 228n.
pull-punkah
 ventilation 352n.
pull strings
 influence 178vb.
 be instrumental 628vb.
pull through
 be restored 656vb.
pull-through *opener* 263n.
 cleaning utensil 648n.
 cleanser 648n.
 cathartic 658n.
pull together
 concur 181vb.
pull to pieces
 demolish 165vb.
 argue 475vb.
 detract 926vb.
pullulate *be many* 104vb.
 reproduce itself 164vb.
 be fruitful 171vb.
pullulation
 expansion 197n.
pull up *halt* 145vb.
 come to rest 266vb.
 extract 304vb.
 elevate 310vb.
 indict 928vb.
pull-up
 stopping place 145n.
 café 192n.
pulmonary
 puffing 352adj.
pulp *demolish* 165vb.
 deform 244vb.
 soften 327vb.
 thicken 354vb.
 pulpiness 356n.
 paper 631n.
pulpit *stand* 218n.
 publicity 528n.
 rostrum 539n.
 church utensil 990n.
pulpiteer *preacher* 537n.
 speaker 579n.
 religionist 979n.
 pastor 986n.
pulpitry *teaching* 534n.
 oration 579n.
 ministration 988n.
pulpy *soft* 327adj.

 semiliquid 354adj.
 pulpy 356adj.
pulsate *be periodic* 141vb.
 oscillate 317vb.
pulsation *feeling* 818n.
 (*see* pulse)
pulse *periodicity* 141n.
 vegetable 301n.
 oscillation 317n.
 spasm 318n.
 plant 366n.
pulverize *break* 46vb.
 demolish 165vb.
 strike 279vb.
 soften 327vb.
 pulverize 332vb.
pulverizer *pulverizer* 332n.
pulverulence
 pulverulence 332n.
puma *cat* 365n.
pumice stone *cleanser* 648n.
pummel *strike* 279vb.
 fight 716vb.
pump *footwear* 228n.
 irrigator 341n.
 make flow 350vb.
 sufflation 352n.
 interrogate 459vb.
pump in *provide* 633vb.
pumpkin *vegetable* 301n.
pump out
 make smaller 198vb.
 void 300vb.
 sufflate 352vb.
pump-room
 meeting place 192n.
 hospital 658n.
 place of amusement 837n.
pump up *enlarge* 197vb.
 sufflate 352vb.
pun *assimilation* 18n.
 equivocalness 518n.
 word 559n.
 witticism 839n.
punch *mould* 23n.
 vigorousness 174n.
 perforator 263n.
 pierce 263vb.
 drafthorse 273n.
 knock 279n.
 liquor 301n.
 mark 547vb.
 printing 555n.
 vigour 571n.
Punch and Judy
 stage play 594n.
 plaything 837n.
punchbowl *bowl* 194n.
 cavity 255n.
punch-drunk
 insensible 375adj.

puncheon *vat* 194 n.
 perforator 263 n.
punch in
 make concave 255 vb.
Punchinello
 entertainer 594 n.
punch out *efform* 243 vb.
punctilio *etiquette* 848 n.
 formality 875 n.
 probity 929 n.
punctilious
 accurate 494 adj.
 observant 768 adj.
 well-bred 848 adj.
 fastidious 862 adj.
 formal 875 adj.
 trustworthy 929 adj.
punctual
 instantaneous 116 adj.
 synchronous 123 adj.
 early 135 adj.
 periodical 141 adj.
 accurate 494 adj.
 observant 768 adj.
punctuate *discontinue* 72 vb.
 variegate 437 vb.
 mark 547 vb.
 parse 564 vb.
punctuation
 punctuation 547 n.
puncture
 make smaller 198 vb.
 perforation 263 n.
 wound 655 n.
 hitch 702 n.
pundit *sage* 500 n.
 jurist 958 n.
pungency *sharpness* 256 n.
 sourness 393 n.
 vigour 571 n.
pungent *keen* 174 adj.
 pungent 388 adj.
 unsavoury 391 adj.
 odorous 394 adj.
 fetid 397 adj.
 forceful 571 adj.
 felt 818 adj.
 witty 839 adj.
 ungracious 885 adj.
Punic faith
 falsehood 541 n.
 perfidy 930 n.
punish *be severe* 735 vb.
 punish 963 vb.
punishable *illegal* 954 adj.
 punishable 963 adj.
punisher *avenger* 910 n.
 vindicator 927 n.
 punisher 963 n.
punishing
 vigorous 174 adj.

fatiguing 684 adj.
 paining 827 adj.
punishment *suffering* 825 n.
 reprimand 924 n.
 condemnation 961 n.
 punishment 963 n.
punitive *punitive* 963 adj.
punitive action
 retaliation 714 n.
punitive expedition
 revenge 910 n.
punk *lighter* 385 n.
 bad 645 adj.
 prostitute 952 n.
punkah *ventilation* 352 n.
 refrigerator 384 n.
punnet *basket* 194 n.
punster *humorist* 839 n.
punt *row* 269 vb.
 rowboat 275 n.
 kick 279 vb.
 propel 287 vb.
 gamble 618 vb.
punter *boatman* 270 n.
 gambler 618 n.
puny *small* 33 adj.
 weak 163 adj.
 little 196 adj.
 unimportant 639 adj.
pup *reproduce itself* 164 vb.
 (*see* puppy)
pupa *youngling* 132 n.
pupil *centrality* 225 n.
 eye 438 n.
 learner 538 n.
pupillage *nonage* 130 n.
 helplessness 161 n.
 learning 536 n.
puppet *dwarf* 196 n.
 dupe 544 n.
 image 551 n.
 nonentity 639 n.
 auxiliary 707 n.
 slave 742 n.
puppetry *stage play* 594 n.
puppy *youngling* 132 n.
 dog 365 n.
 fop 848 n.
 insolent person 878 n.
puppyism
 affectation 850 n.
Purana
 non-Biblical scripture
  975 n.
purblind
 dim-sighted 440 adj.
 misjudging 481 adj.
purchasable *bought* 792 adj.
 venal 930 adj.
purchase *pivot* 218 n.
 requirement 627 n.

acquire 771 vb.
 booty 790 n.
 purchase 792 n., vb.
purchaser *owner* 776 n.
 recipient 782 n.
 purchaser 792 n.
purdah *womankind* 373 n.
 concealment 525 n.
 seclusion 883 n.
 (*see* screen)
pure *absolute* 32 adj.
 unmixed 44 adj.
 whole 52 adj.
 white 427 adj.
 genuine 494 adj.
 elegant 575 adj.
 excellent 644 adj.
 perfect 646 adj.
 clean 648 adj.
 salubrious 652 adj.
 tasteful 846 adj.
 honourable 929 adj.
 disinterested 931 adj.
 virtuous 933 adj.
 innocent 935 adj.
 pure 950 adj.
purée *soup* 301 n.
pure gold *exceller* 644 n.
pure Gospel
 orthodoxy 976 n.
purfle *hem* 234 vb.
purgation *progression* 285 n.
 cleansing 648 n.
 penance 941 n.
purgative *opener* 263 n.
 excretory 302 adj.
 cleansing 648 adj.
 cathartic 658 n.
purgatorial *paining* 827 adj.
 atoning 941 adj.
purgatory *cleansing* 648 adj.
 suffering 825 n.
 penance 941 n.
purge *eliminate* 44 vb.
 slaughter 362 n., vb.
 purify 648 vb.
 cathartic 658 n.
purification
 simplification 44 n.
 inodorousness 395 n.
 cleansing 648 n.
 amendment 654 n.
 ritual act 988 n.
purify *exclude* 57 vb.
 purify 648 vb.
 sanitate 652 vb.
purism *pretension* 850 n.
purist *stylist* 575 n.
 man of taste 846 n.
 affector 850 n.
 perfectionist 862 n.

puritan *affector* 850 n.
  disapprover 924 n.
  prude 950 n.
  sectarist 978 n.
  religionist 979 n.
puritanical *severe* 735 adj.
  serious 834 adj.
  fastidious 862 adj.
  ascetic 945 adj.
  prudish 950 adj.
puritanism (*see* puritan)
Puritans *church party* 978 n.
purity *simpleness* 44 n.
  elegance 575 n.
  artlessness 699 n.
  good taste 846 n.
  modesty 874 n.
  celibacy 895 n.
  probity 929 n.
  virtue 933 n.
  innocence 935 n.
  temperance 942 n.
  purity 950 n.
  sanctity 979 n.
purl *flow* 350 vb.
  sound faint 401 vb.
  needlework 844 n.
purlieu *district* 184 n.
  circumjacence 230 n.
  near place 200 n.
purloin *steal* 788 vb.
  defraud 788 vb.
purple *purple* 434 n., adj.
purple patch
  discontinuity 72 n.
  ornament 574 n.
  eloquence 579 n.
purport *meaning* 514 n.
purpose *will* 595 n.
  be resolute 599 vb.
  intention 617 n.
  use 673 n.
purposeful *resolute* 599 adj.
  intended 617 adj.
  planning 623 adj.
purposeless
  capricious 604 adj.
  designless 618 adj.
  useless 641 adj.
purpose, to the
  apt 24 adj.
purpure *heraldry* 547 n.
purr *sound faint* 401 vb.
  ululate 409 vb.
  be pleased 824 vb.
  be content 828 vb.
pur sang *noble* 868 adj.
purse *stow* 187 vb.
  pocket 194 n.
  become small 198 vb.
  insert 303 vb.

funds 797 n.
  treasury 799 n.
purse-bearer
  treasurer 798 n.
purser *provider* 633 n.
  treasurer 798 n.
purse-strings
  finance 797 n.
  treasury 799 n.
pursuance *sequence* 65 n.
  following 284 n.
  pursuit 619 n.
pursue *pursue* 619 vb.
  desire 859 vb.
  court 889 vb.
  (*see* pursuit)
pursuer *hunter* 619 n.
pursuit *sequence* 65 n.
  following 284 n.
  search 459 n.
  intention 617 n.
  pursuit 619 n.
  business 622 n.
pursuivant
  messenger 531 n.
  heraldry 547 n.
  officer 741 n.
pursy *fleshy* 195 adj.
purulent *diseased* 651 adj.
  toxic 653 adj.
purvey *feed* 301 vb.
  provide 633 vb.
purveyor *caterer* 633 n.
purview *range* 183 n.
  intention 617 n.
pus *fluid* 335 n.
  semiliquidity 354 n.
  dirt 649 n.
  ulcer 651 n.
push *crisis* 137 n.
  vigorousness 174 n.
  transpose 272 vb.
  impulse 279 n.
  propulsion 287 n.
  ejection 300 n.
  gesture 547 n.
  motivate 612 vb.
  be active 678 vb.
  haste 680 n.
  party 708 n.
  attack 712 n., vb.
push away *repel* 292 vb.
push-bicycle *bicycle* 274 n.
push-bike *ride* 267 vb.
push-button
  instrument 628 n.
  instrumental 628 adj.
pushcart *pushcart* 274 n.
pusher *ram* 279 n.
  propellant 287 n.
  busy person 678 n.

push forward
  promote 285 vb.
  be vain 873 vb.
pushful, pushing
  vigorous 174 adj.
  assertive 532 adj.
  active 678 adj.
push off *start out* 296 vb.
  decamp 296 vb.
push on *progress* 285 vb.
push out *eject* 300 vb.
push-over *victory* 727 n.
push-pin *fastening* 47 n.
pusillanimity
  cowardice 856 n.
puss *cat* 365 n.
pussy *toxic* 653 adj.
pussyfoot
  be stealthy 525 vb.
  hinderer 702 n.
  be cautious 858 vb.
  disapprover 924 n.
  abstainer 942 n.
  ascetic 945 n.
  sober person 948 n.
pustule *skin disease* 651 n.
put *firm-set* 45 adj.
  place 187 vb.
put across *convince* 485 vb.
put aside
  set apart 46 vb.
  exclude 57 vb.
  be neglectful 458 vb.
put at ease *please* 826 vb.
putative *attributed* 158 adj.
  credible 485 adj.
  supposed 512 adj.
put away *destroy* 165 vb.
  stow 187 vb.
  divorce 896 vb.
put back *replace* 187 vb.
  turn back 286 vb.
  restore 656 vb.
put by *store* 632 vb.
put down *destroy* 165 vb.
  suppress 165 vb.
  kill 362 vb.
  overmaster 727 vb.
  pay 804 vb.
put down to
  attribute 158 vb.
put first
  make important 638 vb.
put forth *expand* 197 vb.
  propound 512 vb.
put forward
  promote 285 vb.
  offer 759 vb.
put in *number with* 78 vb.
  arrive 295 vb.
  insert 303 vb.

put in the way of
  make possible 469 vb.
put in words *phrase* 563 vb.
put off *put off* 136 vb.
  repel 292 vb.
  distracted 456 adj.
  be neglectful 458 vb.
  dissuade 613 vb.
  cause dislike 861 vb.
put on *imitate* 20 vb.
  wear 228 vb.
  dissemble 541 vb.
  be affected 850 vb.
put one's finger on
  place 187 vb.
  detect 484 vb.
put one's foot down
  be resolute 599 vb.
put one's foot in it
  be clumsy 695 vb.
put on the map
  advertise 528 vb.
put on trial *indict* 928 vb.
put on weight *grow* 36 vb.
  expand 197 vb.
put out *derange* 63 vb.
  disable 161 vb.
  suppress 165 vb.
  start out 296 vb.
  eject 300 vb.
  extinguish 382 vb.
  distracted 456 adj.
  communicate 524 vb.
  publish 528 vb.
  cause discontent 829 vb.
  enrage 891 vb.
put over *convince* 485 vb.
put paid to
  terminate 69 vb.
putrefaction *decay* 51 n.
  death 361 n.
  fetor 397 n.
  uncleanness 649 n.
putrefy *deteriorate* 655 vb.
putrid *fetid* 397 adj.
  not nice 645 adj.
put right *inform* 524 vb.
  rectify 654 vb.
  repair 656 vb.
  be just 913 vb.
putsch *revolt* 738 n.
putt *insert* 303 vb.
puttees *legwear* 228 n.
put teeth into
  empower 160 vb.
put the cart before the horse
  invert 221 vb.
  stultify oneself 695 vb.
put the clock back
  be unconformable 84 vb.
  be late 136 vb.

put through *do* 676 vb.
  deal with 688 vb.
put to *advise* 691 vb.
put to flight *defeat* 724 vb.
put together *join* 45 vb.
  combine 50 vb.
  compose 56 vb.
  bring together 74 vb.
put to it
  in difficulties 700 adj.
put to music
  harmonize 410 vb.
  compose music 413 vb.
put to rights
  regularize 62 vb.
put to the proof
  experiment 461 vb.
put to the question
  torment 827 vb.
putty *adhesive* 47 n.
put up *replace* 187 vb.
  dwell 192 vb.
  elevate 310 vb.
put-up
  predetermined 608 adj.
put-up job *duplicity* 541 n.
  predetermination 608 n.
  false charge 928 n.
put upon *ill-treat* 645 vb.
  oppress 735 vb.
put up to *incite* 612 vb.
put up with
  acquiesce 488 vb.
  be patient 823 vb.
  suffer 825 vb.
  forgive 909 vb.
puzzle *complexity* 61 n.
  distract 456 vb.
  puzzle 474 vb.
  mean nothing 515 vb.
  enigma 530 n.
  difficulty 700 n.
puzzle out *decipher* 520 vb.
puzzling
  imperspicuous 568 adj.
pyæmia *infection* 651 n.
pyjamas
  informal dress 228 n.
  nightwear 228 n.
pylon *electricity* 160 n.
  high structure 209 n.
pyramid
  accumulation 74 n.
  fixture 153 n.
  edifice 164 n.
  high structure 209 n.
  angular figure 247 n.
  tomb 364 n.
pyramidal *tapering* 256 adj.
pyre *interment* 364 n.
  fire 379 n.

pyrexia *heat* 379 n.
  illness 651 n.
pyrogenesis *infection* 651 n.
pyrography
  ornamental art 844 n.
pyrology
  thermometry 379 n.
pyromania
  incendiarism 381 n.
pyrophobia *phobia* 854 n.
pyrotechnics *fire* 379 n.
  fireworks 420 n.
  spectacle 445 n.
Pyrrhic *dear* 811 adj.
Pyrrhonism
  philosophy 449 n.
  doubt 486 n.
  irreligion 974 n.
Pythagoreanism
  philosophy 449 n.
  temperance 942 n.
python *compressor* 198 n.
  reptile 365 n.
Pythoness *oracle* 511 n.
  priest 986 n.
pyx *small box* 194 n.
  testing agent 461 n.
  ritual object 988 n.

Q

Q-boat *warship* 722 n.
Q.E.D.
  argumentation 475 n.
  of course 478 adv.
quack *ululation* 409 n.
  sciolist 493 n.
  false 541 adj.
  impostor 545 n.
  be loquacious 581 vb.
  doctor 658 n.
  unskilled 695 adj.
  bungler 697 n.
  affector 850 n.
quackery *sciolism* 491 n.
  misteaching 535 n.
  unskilfulness 695 n.
  pretension 850 n.
quad *meeting place* 192 n.
quadrable *fourfold* 97 adj.
quadragesimal
  fasting 946 adj.
quadrangle *quaternity* 96 n.
  place 185 n.
  meeting-place 192 n.
  angular figure 247 n.
quadrant *arc* 250 n.
  angular measure 247 n.
  gauge 465 n.
quadrate *four* 96 adj.
quadratic *four* 96 adj.

abrogate 752 vb.
quasi *similar* 18 adj.
supposed 512 adj.
misnamed 562 adj.
quassia
unsavouriness 390 n.
quaternal, quaternary
four 96 adj.
quaternion *quaternity* 96 n.
quaternity *quaternity* 96 n.
quatrain *verse form* 593 n.
quatrefoil *quaternity* 96 n.
quaver *be agitated* 318 vb.
roll 403 vb.
notation 410 n.
sing 413 vb.
stammer 580 vb.
quake 854 vb.
quay *stable* 192 n.
edge 234 n.
shelter 662 n.
quean *woman* 373 n.
loose woman 952 n.
queasy *disliking* 861 adj.
queen *sovereign* 741 n.
chessman 837 n.
queen it *seek repute* 866 vb.
be proud 871 vb.
be insolent 878 vb.
queenly *ruling* 733 adj.
impressive 821 adj.
noble 868 adj.
worshipful 866 adj.
proud 871 adj.
Queen of Hearts
favourite 890 n.
Queen's Bench
law court 956 n.
Queensberry rules
justice 913 n.
Queen's Counsel
lawyer 958 n.
Queen's English
language 557 n.
Queen's evidence
testimony 466 n.
disclosure 526 n.
queer *nonconformist* 84 n.
abnormal 84 adj.
crazed 503 adj.
sick 651 adj.
ridiculous 849 adj.
wrong 914 adj.
queer fish
laughing-stock 851 n.
queerness *eccentricity* 503 n.
Queer Street *poverty* 801 n.
quell *suppress* 165 vb.
moderate 177 vb.
hinder 702 vb.
overmaster 727 vb.

subjugate 745 vb.
frighten 854 vb.
queller *victor* 727 n.
quench *suppress* 165 vb.
extinguish 382 vb.
snuff out 418 vb.
sate 863 vb.
quenchless *violent* 176 adj.
greedy 859 adj.
querimonious
lamenting 836 adj.
querist *questioner* 459 n.
quern *pulverizer* 332 n.
querulous
lamenting 836 adj.
irascible 892 adj.
query *question* 459 n.
uncertainty 474 n.
quest *search* 459 n.
pursuit 619 n.
job 622 n.
essay 671 n.
undertaking 672 n.
question *topic* 452 n.
curiosity 453 n.
question 459 n.
interrogate 459 vb.
uncertainty 474 n.
doubt 486 n.
negate 533 vb.
questionable *moot* 459 adj.
uncertain 474 adj.
unbelieved 486 adj.
disreputable 867 adj.
dishonest 930 adj.
question and answer
interrogation 459 n.
answer 460 n.
interlocution 584 n.
questioner *listener* 415 n.
inquisitor 453 n.
questioner 459 n.
questionless
undisputed 473 adj.
question list *question* 459 n.
question mark
question 459 n.
uncertainty 474 n.
punctuation 547 n.
questionnaire *list* 87 n.
question 459 n.
question paper
question 459 n.
question time
interrogation 459 n.
queue *retinue* 67 n.
procession 71 n.
pendant 217 n.
rear 238 n.
queue-jumping
precession 283 n.

queue up *await* 507 vb.
quibble *argue* 475 vb.
sophistry 477 n.
absurdity 497 n.
equivocalness 518 n.
pretext 614 n.
quibbler *reasoner* 475 n.
sophist 477 n.
quick *brief* 114 adj.
speedy 277 adj.
alive 360 adj.
intelligent 498 adj.
willing 597 adj.
active 678 adj.
skilful 694 adj.
moral sensibility 819 n.
quick-change
changeful 152 adj.
quick-change artist
alterer 143 n.
entertainer 594 n.
quicken *strengthen* 162 vb.
invigorate 174 vb.
make violent 176 vb.
accelerate 277 vb.
live 360 vb.
animate 821 vb.
quicklime *cleanser* 648 n.
quick march *gait* 265 n.
marching 267 n.
speeding 277 n.
quickness (*see* quick)
quickness of the hand
sleight 542 n.
quicksand *marsh* 347 n.
pitfall 663 n.
quicksilver
changeable thing 152 n.
vigorousness 174 n.
velocity 277 n.
quick, to the
on the raw 819 adv.
quick-witted
intelligent 498 adj.
quid *mouthful* 301 n.
tobacco 388 n.
coinage 797 n.
quiddity *essence* 1 n.
essential part 5 n.
quidnunc *inquisitor* 453 n.
enquirer 459 n.
newsmonger 529 n.
quid pro quo *offset* 31 n.
substitute 150 n.
interchange 151 n.
retaliation 714 n.
reward 962 n.
quids in *acquiring* 771 adj.
quiescence *stability* 153 n.
inertness 175 n.
quiescence 266 n.

inaction 677n.
inactivity 679n.
peace 717n.
quiescent
apathetic 820adj.
inexcitable 823adj.
quiet *inert* 175adj.
moderation 177n.
assuage 177vb.
smooth 258adj.
quietude 266n.
euphoria 376n.
silence 399n.
soft-hued 425adj.
grey 429adj.
inaction 677n.
reposeful 683adj.
peaceful 717adj.
submitting 721adj.
mediocre 732adj.
inexcitable 823adj.
pleasurable 826adj.
modest 874adj.
secluded 883adj.
quieten
bring to rest 266vb.
silence 399vb.
quietism *quietude* 266n.
moral insensibility 820n.
inexcitability 823n.
content 828n.
quiet time *worship* 981n.
quietude (*see* quiet)
quietus *end* 69n.
death 361n.
killing 362n.
defeat 728n.
quiff *hair* 259n.
hair-dressing 843n.
quill *sharp point* 256n.
plumage 259n.
stationery 586n.
quill-driver *penman* 586n.
quillet *sophistry* 477n.
quilt *coverlet* 226n.
variegate 437vb.
quinary *fifth and over* 99adj.
quincunx *crossing* 222n.
quinine *antidote* 658n.
prophylactic 658n.
quinquennial
seasonal 141adj.
quinquennium
period 110n.
quinquereme *galley* 275n.
warship 722n.
quinquesection
multisection 100n.
quintal *weighment* 322n.
quintessence
essential part 5n.

eminence 644n.
perfection 646n.
quintet *duet* 412n.
orchestra 413n.
quintuple
fifth and over 99adj.
quip *witticism* 839n.
indignity 921n.
quipu
counting instrument 86n.
quire *letterpress* 587n.
edition 589n.
paper 631n.
quirk *whim* 604n.
witticism 839n.
quirt *scourge* 964n.
quisling *tergiversator* 603n.
revolter 738n.
knave 938n.
quit *depart* 296vb.
relinquish 621vb.
resign 753vb.
fail in duty 918vb.
quitclaim *liberation* 746n.
quite *greatly* 32adv.
slightly 33adv.
completely 54adv.
quite, not *almost* 33adv.
quit of *losing* 772adj.
quit-rent *price* 809n.
quits *equivalence* 28n.
atonement 941n.
quits, be *retaliate* 714vb.
quittance *liberation* 746n.
title-deed 767n.
payment 804n.
atonement 941n.
quitter *tergiversator* 603n.
avoider 620n.
resignation 753n.
coward 856n.
quiver *accumulation* 74n.
case 194n.
oscillate 317vb.
be agitated 318vb.
feel pain 377vb.
be cold 380vb.
storage 632n.
arsenal 723n.
show feeling 818vb.
be excited 821vb.
quake 854vb.
qui vive, on the
vigilant 457adj.
Quixotic
imaginative 513adj.
Quixotry *ideality* 513n.
rashness 857n.
quiz *gaze* 438vb.
watch 441vb.
be curious 453vb.

interrogation 459n.
witticism 839n.
ridicule 851n.
quizmaster *reveller* 837n.
quizzical *derisive* 851adj.
quizzing-glass
eyeglass 442n.
quoin *press* 587n.
quoit *circle* 250n.
missile 287n.
quoits *ball game* 837n.
quondam *former* 125adj.
resigning 753adj.
quorum *finite quantity* 26n.
electorate 605n.
sufficiency 635n.
quota *finite quantity* 26n.
part 53n.
portion 783n.
quotable *relevant* 9adj.
repeated 106adj.
pure 950adj.
quotation *referral* 9n.
identity 13n.
repetition 106n.
evidence 466n.
exhibit 522n.
anthology 592n.
price 809n.
quotation marks
punctuation 547n.
quote *exemplify* 83vb.
(*see* quotation)
quotes *punctuation* 547n.
quotidian *seasonal* 141adj.
quotient *quantity* 26n.
numerical element 85n.
quotum *finite quantity* 26n.

R

R.A. *artist* 556n.
Ra *Egyptian gods* 967n.
rabbet *join* 45vb.
rabbi *theologian* 973n.
priest 986n.
rabbinic *theological* 973adj.
rabbit *abundance* 171n.
vermin 365n.
testee 461n.
beginner 538n.
coward 856n.
rabbit's foot
cosmetic 843n.
rabble *crowd* 74n.
rabble 869n.
rabble-rouser *leader* 690n.
agitator 738n.
excitant 821n.
Rabelaisian *impure* 951n.
rabid *frenzied* 503adj.

excitable 822adj.
angry 891adj.
rabies frenzy 503n.
race race 11n.
 genealogy 169n.
 speeding 277n.
 outdo 306vb.
 current 350n.
 pungency 388n.
 vocation 622n.
 haste 680n.
 community 708n.
 racing 716n.
race-course
 meeting-place 192n.
 speeding 277n.
 gaming-house 618n.
 racing 716n.
 arena 724n.
race-horse
 thoroughbred 273n.
 speeder 277n.
race prejudice
 prejudice 481n.
 pride 871n.
racer thoroughbred 273n.
 speeder 277n.
 contender 716n.
race-riot lawlessness 954n.
rachis rear 238n.
rachitic deformed 246adj.
racial ethnic 11adj.
 parental 169adj.
 human 371adj.
racialism, racism
 prejudice 481n.
 hatred 888n.
raciness (see racy)
racing chase 619n.
 racing 716n.
racing driver speeder 277n.
rack compartment 194n.
 shelf 218n.
 distort 246vb.
 cloud 355n.
 give pain 377vb.
 ill-treat 645vb.
 purify 648vb.
 oppress 735vb.
 torment 827vb.
 torture 963vb.
 instrument of torture
  967n.
racket commotion 318n.
 loudness 400n.
 discord 411n.
 quarrel 709n.
 foul play 930n.
racketeer speculate 791vb.
 offender 904n.
 be dishonest 930vb.

rackets ball game 837n.
rackety loud 400adj.
 riotous 738adj.
 gay 833adj.
 unchaste 951adj.
rack one's brains
 think 449vb.
rack-rent levy 786vb.
 overcharge 811vb.
 be parsimonious 816vb.
raconteur narrator 590n.
racoon rodent 365n.
racy vigorous 174adj.
 tasty 386adj.
 savoury 390adj.
 stylistic 566adj.
 forceful 571adj.
 lively 819adj.
 impure 951adj.
radar sailing aid 269n.
 optical device 442n.
 detector 484n.
 telecommunication 531n.
 indicator 547n.
 directorship 689n.
raddle network 222n.
 redden 431vb.
raddled beautified 843adj.
radially longwise 203adv.
radian
 angular measure 247n.
radiance
 light, glow 417n.
 beauty 841n.
radiant divergent 294adj.
 luminous 417adj.
 radiating 417adj.
 luminescent 420adj.
 happy 824adj.
 cheerful 833adj.
 beautiful 841adj.
 splendid 841adj.
radiant energy
 radiation 417n.
radiant point
 centrality 225n.
 meteor 321n.
radiate transfer 272vb.
 emit 300vb.
  (see radiation)
radiation dispersion 75n.
 divergence 294n.
 oscillation 317n.
 radiation 417n.
 poison 659n.
radiator ejector 300n.
 heater 383n.
radical intrinsic 5adj.
 complete 54adj.
 numerical 85adj.
 revolutionist 149n.

revolutionary 149adj.
 source 156n.
 fundamental 156adj.
 important 638adj.
 reformer 654n.
 opponent 705n.
 sectional 708adj.
radical change
 revolution 149n.
radicalism
 reformism 654n.
radication
 habituation 610n.
radicle foliage 366n.
radiesthesia intuition 476n.
 discovery 484n.
 divination 511n.
radio publicity 528n.
 telecommunication 531n.
radio-active
 dynamic 160adj.
 vigorous 174adj.
 radiating 417adj.
radio-activity
 radiation 417n.
 insalubrity 653n.
 poison 659n.
radio-astronomy
 astronomy 321n.
radiogram
 gramophone 414n.
 hearing aid 415n.
 information 524n.
 message 529n.
radiograph
 photography 551n.
radio-location
 bearings 186n.
 discovery 484n.
radiology optics 417n.
radio mast
 high structure 209n.
 telecommunication 531n.
radiometer
 optical device 442n.
radiometry optics 417n.
radio-mirror
 space-ship 276n.
radiophone
 hearing aid 415n.
radioscopy optics 417n.
radio telescope
 astronomy 321n.
radio-therapy
 therapy 658n.
radius range 183n.
 line 203n.
 breadth 205n.
radix source 156n.
raff dirt 649n.
raffia ligature 47n.

fibre 208 n.
raffle *chance* 159 n.
 gambling 618 n.
raft *space* 201 vb.
 carry 273 vb.
 raft 275 n.
 cultivate 370 vb.
 safeguard 662 n.
rafter(s) *beam* 218 n.
 roof 226 n.
 materials 631 n.
rag *book* 589 n.
 torment 827 vb.
 revel 837 n.
 be witty 839 vb.
 ridicule 851 vb.
raga *key* 410 n.
ragamuffin *slut* 61 n.
 low fellow 869 n.
ragbag *non-uniformity* 17 n.
rage *violence* 176 n.
 prevail 178 vb.
 blow 352 vb.
 be active 678 vb.
 excitable state 822 n.
 fashion 848 n.
 desire, libido 859 n.
 anger 891 n.
rage against
 dispraise 924 vb.
ragged *uncovered* 229 adj.
 convoluted 251 adj.
 undulatory 251 adj.
raggedness
 non-uniformity 17 n.
 poverty 801 n.
raglan *overcoat* 228 n.
ragout *a mixture* 43 n.
rag-picker
 poor man 801 n.
rags *clothing* 228 n.
 rubbish 641 n.
rags, in
 dilapidated 655 adj.
 beggarly 801 adj.
rag, tag and bobtail
 commonalty 869 n.
ragtime *music* 412 n.
raid *lay waste* 165 vb.
 ingress 297 n.
 irrupt 299 vb.
 attack 712 n.
 taking 786 n.
 rob 788 vb.
raider *attacker* 712 n.
 soldier 722 n.
 warship 722 n.
 taker 786 n.
 robber 789 n.
raiding *warfare* 718 n.
 brigandage 788 n.

rail *handle* 218 n.
 transport 272 n.
 carry 273 vb.
 curse 899 vb.
 exprobate 924 vb.
railer *defamer* 926 n.
rail in *circumscribe* 232 vb.
railing *handle* 218 n.
 edge 234 n.
 fence 235 n.
raillery *ridicule* 851 n.
 sauciness 878 n.
railroad, railway
 railroad 624 n.
rails *parallelism* 219 n.
 fence 235 n.
 railroad 624 n.
railway train *train* 274 n.
raiment *clothing* 228 n.
rain *descend* 309 vb.
 moisture 341 n.
 rain 350 n., vb.
 abound 635 vb.
rainbow *curve* 248 n.
 arc 250 n.
 light 417 n.
 colour 425 n.
 variegation 437 n.
rainbow effect
 variegation 437 n.
rain-cloud *cloud* 355 n.
raincoat *overcoat* 228 n.
rainfall *moisture* 341 n.
 rain 350 n.
rain-gauge
 hygrometry 341 n.
 rain 350 n.
rainless *dry* 342 n.
rain or shine
 certainly 473 adv.
rainproof *dry* 342 adj.
rainy *humid* 341 adj.
 rainy 350 adj.
rainy day *adversity* 731 n.
raise *augment* 36 vb.
 initiate 68 vb.
 generate 164 vb.
 displace 188 vb.
 make higher 209 vb.
 make vertical 215 vb.
 move 265 vb.
 promote 285 vb.
 elevate 310 vb.
 lighten 323 vb.
 breed stock 369 vb.
 see 438 vb.
 improvement 654 n.
 acquire 771 vb.
 levy 786 vb.
 relieve 831 vb.
raise Cain

 be loud 400 vb.
 revolt 738 vb.
 be angry 891 vb.
raise one's banner
 go to war 718 vb.
raise one's glass to
 toast 876 vb.
raise one's hand
 gesticulate 547 vb.
 vote 605 vb.
raise one's hat
 greet 884 vb.
raise one's voice
 vociferate 400 vb.
 dissent 489 vb.
 emphasize 532 vb.
 speak 579 vb.
 deprecate 762 vb.
raiser *producer* 167 n.
 lifter 310 n.
raise steam
 navigate 269 vb.
 make ready 669 vb.
raise subscriptions
 beg 761 vb.
raise the alarm
 signal 547 vb.
 raise the alarm 665 vb.
 frighten 854 vb.
raise the bid
 bargain 791 vb.
 overcharge 811 vb.
raise the sights
 augment 36 vb.
 aim at 617 vb.
raise the subject
 initiate 68 vb.
raise the wind
 borrow 785 vb.
raisin *fruit* 301 n.
raison d'être
 reason why 156 n.
 intention 617 n.
rajah *potentate* 741 n.
rajput *militarist* 722 n.
 aristocrat 868 n.
rake *obliquity* 220 n.
 draw 288 vb.
 extractor 304 n.
 farm tool 370 n.
 search 459 vb.
 cleaning utensil 648 n.
 fire at 712 vb.
 bad man 938 n.
 sensualist 944 n.
 libertine 952 n.
rake in
 bring together 74 vb.
 draw 288 vb.
rake-off *decrement* 42 n.
 earnings 771 n.

portion 783 n.
receipt 807 n.
price 809 n.
discount 810 n.
rake over, rake through
  search 459 vb.
rake up *retrospect* 505 vb.
rakish *oblique* 220 adj.
  fashionable 848 adj.
  lecherous 951 adj.
rallentando *tempo* 410 n.
  adagio 412 adv.
rally *assemblage* 74 n.
  congregate 74 vb.
  interchange 151 n.
  propulsion 287 n.
  call 547 n.
  persevere 600 vb.
  incite 612 vb.
  get better 645 vb.
  restore 656 vb.
  contest 716 n.
  give battle 718 vb.
  ridicule 851 vb.
  give courage 855 vb.
rallying cry *call* 547 n.
  danger signal 665 n.
rallying point *focus* 76 n.
rally round
  be in order 60 vb.
ram *demolish* 165 vb.
  ram 279 n.
  collide 279 vb.
  sheep 365 n.
  male animal 372 n.
  strike at 712 vb.
  charge 712 vb.
ramble
  pedestrianism 267 n.
  wander 267 vb.
  stray 282 vb.
  be insane 503 vb.
  be diffuse 570 vb.
rambler *wanderer* 208 n.
rambling *irrelevant* 10 adj.
  fitful 142 adj.
  unstable 152 adj.
  (*see* ramble)
ram down *fill* 54 vb.
  close 264 vb.
  be dense 324 vb.
ramification *bond* 47 n.
  branch 53 n.
  bifurcation 92 n.
  descendant 170 n.
  sonship 170 n.
  range 183 n.
  filament 208 n.
  divergence 294 n.
ramify *angulate* 247 vb.
  (*see* ramification)

rammer *stopper* 264 n.
  ram 279 n.
ramp *be vertical* 215 vb.
  obliquity 220 n.
  ascent 308 n.
  leap 312 vb.
  be agitated 318 vb.
  trickery 542 n.
  be excited 821 vb.
  get angry 891 vb.
  foul play 930 n.
rampage *rampage* 61 vb.
  be violent 176 vb.
  be agitated 318 vb.
  be loud 400 vb.
  be active 678 vb.
  excitable state 822 n.
  anger 891 n.
rampant *furious* 176 adj.
  vertical 215 adj.
  heraldic 547 adj.
  lecherous 951 adj.
rampart *fortification* 713 n.
  defence 713 n.
Ram Raj
  palmy days 730 n.
  happiness 824 n.
ramrod *stopper* 264 n.
  ram 279 n.
  fire-arm 723 n.
ramshackle *flimsy* 163 adj.
  dilapidated 655 adj.
  unsafe 661 adj.
ranch *breed stock* 369 vb.
  farm 370 n.
  lands 777 n.
rancher *herdsman* 369 n.
rancid *unsavoury* 391 adj.
  decomposed 51 adj.
  fetid 397 adj.
rancorous
  revengeful 910 adj.
  (*see* rancour)
rancour *enmity* 881 n.
  hatred 888 n.
  resentment 891 n.
  malevolence 898 n.
random *orderless* 61 adj.
  casual 159 adj.
  deviating 282 adj.
  indiscriminate 464 adj.
  uncertain 474 adj.
  designless 618 adj.
  unconfined 744 adj.
randomness
  discontinuity 72 n.
random order
  disorder 61 n.
random sample
  empiricism 461 n.
random shot

gambling 618 n.
randy *lecherous* 951 adj.
range *arrange* 62 vb.
  series 71 n.
  accumulation 74 n.
  classification 77 n.
  ability 160 n.
  range 183 n.
  distance 199 n.
  breadth 205 n.
  layer 207 n.
  traverse 267 vb.
  plain 348 n.
  furnace 383 n.
  hearing 415 n.
  visibility 443 n.
  arena 724 n.
  scope 744 n.
  merchandise 795 n.
range-finder
  direction 281 n.
  telescope 442 n.
range oneself
  be in order 60 vb.
range oneself with
  join a party 708 vb.
ranger *wanderer* 268 n.
  keeper 749 n.
range together
  juxtapose 202 vb.
range under, range with
  be included 78 vb.
ranging *extensive* 32 adj.
  free 744 adj.
rangy *narrow* 206 adj.
  tall 209 adj.
rani *potentate* 741 n.
rank *relativeness* 9 n.
  degree 27 n.
  order 60 n.
  class 62 vb.
  series 71 n.
  serial place 73 n.
  vegetal 366 adj.
  unsavoury 391 adj.
  fetid 397 adj.
  estimate 480 vb.
  plenteous 635 adj.
  bad 645 adj.
  formation 722 n.
  prestige 866 n.
  nobility 868 n.
  heinous 934 adj.
  impure 951 adj.
rank and file
  commonalty 869 n.
ranker *commoner* 869 n.
ranking *notable* 638 adj.
  noteworthy 866 adj.
rankle *hurt* 827 vb.
rankling *resentment* 891 n.

rankness (*see* rank)
ransack *search* 459 vb.
  rob 788 vb.
ransom *equivalence* 28 n.
  restoration 656 n.
  deliverance 668 n.
  restitution 787 n.
  purchase 792 vb.
  price 809 n.
  penalty 963 n.
ransomed
  sanctified 979 adj.
ransomer *benefactor* 903 n.
ransom, hold to
  overcharge 811 vb.
rant *be absurd* 497 vb.
  empty talk 515 n.
  exaggeration 546 n.
  be diffuse 570 vb.
  magniloquence 574 n.
  oratory 579 n.
  act 594 vb.
  boast 877 n.
ranter *chatterer* 581 n.
  boaster 877 n.
rap *small coin* 33 n.
  knock 279 n.
  crackle 402 vb.
  false money 797 n.
  corporal punishment
   963 n.
rapacious (*see* rapacity)
rapacity *rapacity* 786 n.
  thievishness 788 n.
  avarice 816 n.
  desire 859 n.
  gluttony 947 n.
rape *force* 176 vb.
  taking 876 n.
  stealing 788 n.
  rape 951 n.
  debauch 951 vb.
raper *libertine* 952 n.
rapidity *velocity* 277 n.
rapids *outbreak* 176 n.
  waterfall 350 n.
  pitfall 663 n.
rapid succession
  frequency 139 n.
rapier *sharp point* 256 n.
  side-arms 723 n.
rapine *spoliation* 788 n.
rap out *voice* 577 vb.
rap over the knuckles
  reprimand 924 n.
  reprove 924 vb.
  spank 963 vb.
rapparee *robber* 789 n.
rappee *tobacco* 388 n.
rapport *relation* 9 n.
  concord 710 n.

rapportage *publicity* 528 n.
rapprochement
  concord 710 n.
  pacification 719 n.
  friendship 880 n.
rapscallion *knave* 938 n.
rapt *obsessed* 455 adj.
  abstracted 456 adj.
  impressed 818 adj.
rap tables
  practise occultism 984 vb.
raptorial *taking* 786 adj.
  thieving 788 adj.
rapture *excitation* 821 n.
  joy 824 n.
  love 887 n.
rapturous *felt* 818 adj.
  pleased 824 adj.
  enamoured 887 adj.
rara avis *rara avis* 84 n.
  infrequency 140 n.
rare *superior* 34 adj.
  unusual 84 adj.
  few 105 adj.
  infrequent 140 adj.
  culinary 301 adj.
  rare 325 adj.
  airy 340 adj.
  improbable 472 adj.
  scarce 636 adj.
  excellent 644 adj.
  uncooked 760 adj.
  of price 811 adj.
  wonderful 864 adj.
raree show *spectacle* 445 n.
  pleasure-ground 837 n.
  plaything 837 n.
rarefaction *rarity* 325 n.
rarefy *enlarge* 197 vb.
  make smaller 198 vb.
  make thin 206 vb.
  rarefy 325 vb.
rarely *greatly* 32 adv.
  seldom 140 adv.
rareripe *early* 135 adj.
rarity *levity* 323 n.
  rarity 325 n.
  paragon 646 n.
  dearness 811 n.
  (*see* rare)
rascal *low fellow* 869 n.
  knave 938 n.
rascality *improbity* 930 n.
rascally *cunning* 698 adj.
  disreputable 867 adj.
  rascally 930 adj.
  vicious 934 adj.
rase *obliterate* 550 vb.
rash *skin disease* 651 n.
  (*see* rashness)
rasher *piece* 53 n.

  lamina 207 n.
  meat 301 n.
rashness *inattention* 456 n.
  negligence 458 n.
  indiscrimination 464 n.
  folly 499 n.
  non-preparation 670 n.
  haste 680 n.
  courage 854 n.
  rashness 857 n.
rashy *diseased* 651 adj.
rasp *pulverize* 332 vb.
  rub 333 vb.
  breathe 352 vb.
  rasp 407 vb.
  discord 411 vb.
raspberry *fruit* 301 n.
  reprimand 924 n.
rasping *hoarse* 407 adj.
rasure *obliteration* 550 n.
rat *rodent* 365 n.
  inform 524 vb.
  divulge 526 vb.
  tergiversator 603 n.
  apostatize 603 vb.
  relinquish 621 vb.
  coward 856 n.
  noxious animal 904 n.
  knave 938 n.
ratan (*see* rattan)
rat-a-tat *roll* 403 n.
rat-catcher *killer* 362 n.
  hunter 619 n.
ratchet *tooth* 256 n.
  notch 260 n.
rate *quantify* 26 vb.
  degree 27 n.
  class 62 n.
  grade 73 vb.
  velocity 277 n.
  appraise 465 vb.
  estimate 480 n.
  price 809 n., vb.
  exprobate 924 n.
rather *slightly* 33 adv.
  optionally 605 adv.
ratification *assent* 488 n.
  consent 757 n.
  compact 765 n.
ratificatory
  assenting 488 adj.
ratifier *signatory* 765 n.
ratify *stabilize* 153 vb.
  corroborate 466 vb.
  make certain 473 vb.
  endorse 488 vb.
  sign 547 vb.
  approve 923 vb.
  make legal 953 vb.
rating *naval man* 270 n.
  measurement 465 n.

navy man 722n.
tax 809n.
reprimand 924n.
(*see* rate)
ratio *relativeness* 9n.
degree 27n.
ratio 85n.
portion 783n.
ratiocination
reasoning 475n.
ration *finite quantity* 26n.
provisions 301n.
restrain 747vb.
portion 783n.
rational *numerical* 85adj.
mental 447adj.
philosophic 449adj.
plausible 471adj.
rational 475adj.
wise 498adj.
sane 502adj.
rational animal
mankind 371n.
rationale
reason why 156n.
attribution 158n.
motive 612n.
rationalism
philosophy 449n.
reasoning 475n.
antichristianity 974n.
rationalist *reasoner* 475n.
interpreter 520n.
irreligionist 974n.
rationalistic
rational 475adj.
irreligious 974adj.
rationalization
arrangement 62n.
sophistry 477n.
plan 623n.
rationalize *reason* 475vb.
plan 623vb.
ration book
portion 783n.
rationing
war measures 718n.
restriction 747n.
rations *provisions* 633n.
ratline *tackling* 47n.
ascent 308n.
rat race *activity* 678n.
rattan *club* 723n.
ratten *disable* 161vb.
ratter *tergiversator* 603n.
hunter 619n.
rattle *derange* 63vb.
oscillate 317vb.
respiration 352n.
loudness 400n.
crackle 402vb.

roll 403vb.
gong 414n.
distract 456vb.
chatterer 581n.
bauble 639n.
fire at 712n.
frighten 854vb.
rattled *irresolute* 601adj.
rattle the sabre
threaten 900vb.
boast 877vb.
rattletrap *carriage* 274n.
automobile 274n.
ratty *angry* 891adj.
irascible 892adj.
raucous *hoarse* 407adj.
discordant 411adj.
ravage *havoc* 165n.
lay waste 165vb.
impair 655vb.
attack 712vb.
wage war 718vb.
rob 788vb.
ravaged *unsightly* 842adj.
rave *overrate* 482vb.
be absurd 497vb.
be insane 503vb.
mean nothing 515vb.
be pleased 824vb.
ravel *unravel* 62vb.
bedevil 63vb.
enlace 222vb.
ravelin *fortification* 713n.
ravelled *intricate* 251adj.
ravelment
complexity 61n.
raven *eat* 301vb.
bird 365n.
black thing 428n.
omen 511n.
be hungry 859vb.
be malevolent 898vb.
ravening *furious* 176adj.
ravenous *taking* 786adj.
hungry 859adj.
ravenously
gluttonously 947adv.
ravine *gap* 201n.
narrowness 206n.
valley 255n.
furrow 262n.
conduit 351n.
raving *excited* 821adj.
pleased 824adj.
(*see* rave)
ravish *force* 176vb.
take away 786vb.
delight 826vb.
debauch 951vb.
ravisher *libertine* 952n.
ravishment *coition* 45n.

excitation 821n.
joy 824n.
rape 951n.
raw *incomplete* 55adj.
beginning 68adj.
new 126adj.
young 130adj.
uncovered 229adj.
amorphous 244adj.
culinary 301adj.
sentient 374adj.
painful 377adj.
cold 380adj.
unsavoury 391adj.
florid 425adj.
ignorant 491adj.
unhabituated 611adj.
imperfect 647adj.
immature 670adj.
uncooked 670adj.
unskilled 695adj.
sensitive 819adj.
excitable 822adj.
raw-boned *lean* 206adj.
raw deal *ill fortune* 731n.
(*see* injustice)
raw feelings
moral sensibility 819n.
raw material *source* 156n.
materials 631n.
undevelopment 670n.
rawness (*see* raw)
raw, on the
on the raw 819adv.
raw recruit *beginner* 538n.
bungler 697n.
ray *divergence* 294n.
flash 417n.
radiation 417n.
rayat *husbandman* 370n.
possessor 776n.
rayon *fibre* 208n
textile 222n.
raze *demolish* 165vb.
fell 311vb.
razor
sharp edge 256n.
razor edge
narrowness 206n.
sharp edge 256n.
danger 661n.
reach *degree* 27n.
ability 160n.
distance 199n.
be long 203vb.
straightness 249n.
arrive 295vb.
pass 305vb.
stream 350n.
hearing 415n.
trickery 542n.

suffice 635 vb.
governance 733 n.
reachless *deep* 211 adj.
reach-me-down
ready-made 669 adj.
reach-me-downs
clothing 228 n.
reach out for *take* 786 vb.
reach to *fill* 54 vb.
extend 183 vb.
be distant 199 vb.
be contiguous 202 vb.
react *correlate* 12 vb.
be active 678 vb.
(*see* reaction)
react against *dislike* 861 vb.
reaction *compensation* 31 n.
reversion 148 n.
effect 157 n.
counteraction 182 n.
recoil 280 n.
sense 374 n.
answer 460 n.
restoration 656 n.
retaliation 714 n.
deprecation 762 n.
feeling 818 n.
reactionary
tergiversating 603 adj.
opponent 705 n.
revolter 738 n.
disobedient 738 adj.
reactivation *revival* 656 n.
reactor *nucleonics* 160 n.
read *gauge* 465 vb.
interpret 520 vb.
decipher 520 vb.
study 536 vb.
indicate 547 vb.
speak 579 vb.
readability
intelligibility 516 n.
read a lecture
reprove 924 vb.
read and re-read
be attentive 455 vb.
read between the lines
decipher 520 vb.
reader *teacher* 537 n.
classroom 538 n.
literature 557 n.
reading matter 589 n.
bookman 589 n.
academic title 870 n.
readership *publicity* 528 n.
lecture 534 n.
readily
instantaneously 116 adv.
willingly 597 adv.
easily 701 adv.
read in *instructed* 490 adj.

readiness *tendency* 179 n.
attention 455 n.
intelligence 498 n.
foresight 510 n.
elegance 575 n.
willingness 597 n.
utility 640 n.
preparedness 669 n.
completion 725 n.
obedience 739 n.
reading
measurement 465 n.
erudition 490 n.
interpretation 520 n.
lecture 534 n.
study 536 n.
reading desk
classroom 539 n.
reading glass
eyeglass 442 n.
reading in
holy orders 985 n.
reading matter
reading matter 589 n.
read into *add* 38 vb.
readjustment
restoration 656 n.
read off *gauge* 465 vb.
read out *speak* 579 vb.
read the future
foresee 510 vb.
divine 511 vb.
ready *impending* 155 adj.
on the spot 189 adj.
intelligent 498 adj.
expectant 507 adj.
elegant 575 adj.
loquacious 581 adj.
instrumental 628 adj.
useful 640 adj.
prepared 669 adj.
active 678 adj.
skilful 694 adj.
obedient 739 adj.
consenting 758 adj.
ready-formed
ready-made 669 adj.
ready for more
refreshed 685 adj.
ready-made
dressed 228 adj.
formed 243 adj.
predetermined 608 adj.
ready-made 669 adj.
ready money
money, funds 797 n.
ready reckoner
counting instrument 86 n.
ready to *future* 124 adj.
tending 179 adj.
re-affirm *emphasize* 532 vb.

re-afforestation
restoration 656 n.
reagent *testing agent* 461 n.
real *real* 1 adj.
substantial 3 adj.
numerical 85 adj.
material 319 adj.
true 494 adj.
proprietary 777 adj.
real estate *lands* 777 n.
realism *existence* 1 n.
mimicry 20 n.
philosophy 449 n.
accuracy 494 n.
veracity 540 n.
representation 551 n.
school of painting 553 n.
description 590 n.
realist *materiality* 319 n.
realistic *lifelike* 18 adj.
true 494 adj.
wise 498 adj.
representing 551 adj.
descriptive 590 adj.
reality *reality* 1 n.
substantiality 3 n.
truth 494 n.
chief thing 638 n.
realizable
possible 469 adj.
intelligible 516 adj.
realization
eventuality 154 n.
appearance 445 n.
discovery 484 n.
knowledge 490 n.
representation 551 n.
acquisition 771 n.
feeling 818 n.
realize *make extrinsic* 6 vb.
copy 20 vb.
materialize 319 vb.
cognize 447 vb.
imagine 513 vb.
understand 516 vb.
be informed 516 vb.
carry out 725 vb.
sell 793 vb.
draw money 797 vb.
(*see* realization)
real-life *descriptive* 594 adj.
really *actually* 1 adv.
truly 494 adv.
realm *territory* 184 n.
nation 371 n.
function 622 n.
polity 733 n.
real nature *essence* 1 n.
realness *reality* 1 n.
authenticity 494 n.
realpolitik *tactics* 688 n.

real presence
   the sacrament 988 n.
real self *self* 80 n.
real thing *reality* 1 n.
   identity 13 n.
   no imitation 21 n.
   authenticity 494 n.
   love 887 n.
realtor *merchant* 794 n.
realty *lands* 777 n.
ream *enlarge* 197 vb.
   open 263 vb.
   bubble 355 vb.
   paper 631 n.
reamer *perforator* 263 n.
   tobacco 388 n.
   cleaning utensil 648 n.
reams *great quantity* 32 n.
reanimate *vitalize* 360 vb.
reanimation
   strengthening 162 n.
   reproduction 166 n.
   materiality 319 n.
   revival 656 n.
   refreshment 685 n.
reap *cultivate* 370 vb.
   store 632 vb.
   acquire 771 vb.
   take 786 vb.
   be rewarded 962 vb.
reaper *husbandman* 370 n.
   farm tool 370 n.
reaping *product* 164 n.
   agriculture 370 n.
reaping-hook
   sharp edge 256 n.
   farm tool 370 n.
reappear *be visible* 443 vb.
   be restored 656 vb.
reappearance
   recurrence 106 n.
reappoint *restore* 656 vb.
rear *sequel* 67 n.
   extremity 69 n.
   generate 164 vb.
   make vertical 215 vb.
   rear, buttocks 238 n.
   back 238 adj.
   leap 312 n.
   breed stock 369 vb.
   educate 534 vb.
   armed force 722 n.
rear-admiral
   naval man 270 n.
   naval officer 741 n.
rear-guard *rear* 238 n.
   defender 713 n.
   armed force 722 n.
rearing
   animal husbandry 369 n.
rearmost *back* 238 adj.

rearrange *modify* 143 vb.
rear rank *rear* 238 n.
rear up *elevate* 310 vb.
   get angry 891 vb.
rearward *rearward* 238 adv.
reason *reason why* 156 n.
   intellect 447 n.
   thought 449 n.
   discriminate 463 vb.
   reasoning 475 n.
   sanity 502 n.
   motive 612 n.
reasonability
   probability 471 n.
reasonable
   moderate 177 adj.
   possible 469 adj.
   plausible 471 adj.
   rational 475 adj.
   credible 485 adj.
   true 494 adj.
   wise 498 adj.
   sane 502 adj.
   cheap 812 adj.
   just 913 adj.
reasonableness
   moderation 177 n.
   justice 913 n.
reasoner *reasoner* 475 n.
reason ill *reason ill* 477 vb.
reasoning *reasoning* 475 n.
reasoning power
   intellect 447 n.
reasons *reasons* 475 n.
reason why
   reason why 156 n.
   attribution 158 n.
reassemble
   congregate 74 vb.
   restore, repair 656 vb.
reassurance *hope* 852 n.
reassure
   give courage 855 vb.
reasty *fetid* 397 adj.
reaver *robber* 789 n.
reawakening
   revival 656 n.
rebarbative
   disliked 861 adj.
rebate *decrement* 42 n.
   discount 810 n.
rebeck, rebec *viol* 414 n.
rebel *nonconformist* 84 n.
   go to war 718 vb.
   revolter 738 n.
   revolt 738 vb.
   fail in duty 918 vb.
   schismatic 978 n.
rebellion *revolution* 149 n.
   revolt 738 n.
   dutilessness 918 n.

   lawlessness 954 n.
rebellious
   unwilling 598 adj.
   quarrelling 709 adj.
   anarchic 734 adj.
   disobedient 738 adj.
   dutiless 918 adj.
rebirth *recurrence* 106 n.
   future state 124 n.
   revival 656 n.
   sanctity 979 n.
reborn *converted* 147 adj.
   restored 656 adj.
   sanctified 979 adj.
rebound *recoil* 280 n.
   elasticity 328 n.
rebuff *recoil* 280 n.
   repulsion 292 n.
   rejection 607 n.
   hitch 702 n.
   oppose 704 vb.
   resistance 715 n.
   defeat 728 n., vb.
   adversity 731 n.
   refusal 760 n.
   rudeness 885 n.
   contempt 922 n.
rebuild *reproduce* 166 vb.
   restore 656 vb.
rebuke *reprimand* 924 n.
   punish 963 vb.
rebuked *humbled* 872 adj.
rebus *enigma* 530 n.
rebut (see rebuttal)
rebuttal *rejoinder* 460 n.
   counter-evidence 467 n.
   confutation 479 n.
   negation 533 n.
   vindication 927 n.
   legal trial 959 n.
rebutter *rejoinder* 460 n.
recalcitrance
   opposition 704 n.
   resistance 715 n.
   refusal 760 n.
recalcitrant
   nonconformist 84 n.
   counteracting 182 adj.
   recoiling 280 adj.
   unwilling 598 adj.
   disobedient 738 adj.
recall *transference* 272 n.
   remembrance 505 n.
   retrospect 505 vb.
   recant 603 vb.
   restoration 656 n.
   deposal 752 n.
   abrogation 752 n.
recant *negate* 533 vb.
   be false 541 vb.
   not retain 779 vb.

recantation
  recantation 603 n.
  rejection 607 n.
  abrogation 752 n.
  penitence 939 n.
recanter *tergiversator* 603 n.
recapitulate
  shorten 204 vb.
  remind 505 vb.
  be intelligible 516 vb.
  describe 590 vb.
recapitulation
  numeration 86 n.
  repetition 106 n.
  compendium 592 n.
recapture *retrospect* 505 vb.
  imagine 513 vb.
  retrieve 656 vb.
  acquire 771 vb.
recast *modify* 143 vb.
  plan 623 vb.
  rectify 654 vb.
recede *decrease* 37 vb.
  revert 148 vb.
  regress 286 vb.
  recede 290 vb.
receipt *cookery* 301 n.
  contrivance 623 n.
  remedy 658 n.
  precept 693 n.
  title-deed 767 n.
  earnings 771 n.
  receive 782 vb.
  payment 804 n.
  receipt 807 n.
receipt of custom
  receiving 782 n.
  treasury 799 n.
receipts *earnings* 771 n.
  receiving 782 n.
  taking 786 n.
receive *meet* 295 vb.
  admit 299 vb.
  believe 485 vb.
  receive 782 vb.
  take 786 vb.
  be hospitable 882 vb.
  be rewarded 962 vb.
received *usual* 610 adj.
receiver *vessel* 194 n.
  hearing aid 415 n.
  telecommunication 531 n.
  receiver 782 n.
  recipient 782 n.
  thief 789 n.
  treasurer 798 n.
receivership
  receiving 782 n.
recency *newness* 126 n.
recension *numeration* 86 n.
  amendment 654 n.

recent *secular* 110 adj.
  foregoing 125 adj.
  new 126 adj.
receptacle *receptacle* 194 n.
receptibility *reception* 299 n.
reception *arrival* 295 n.
  ingress 297 n.
  reception 299 n.
  sound 398 n.
  hearing 415 n.
  conference 584 n.
  receiving 782 n.
  celebration 876 n.
  social gathering 882 n.
  approbation 923 n.
receptionist
  recorder 549 n.
receptive *recipient* 194 adj.
  admitting 299 adj.
  studious 536 adj.
  willing 597 adj.
  receiving 782 adj.
receptivity *reception* 299 n.
recess *interim* 108 n.
  lull 145 n.
  compartment 194 n.
  angularity 247 n.
  cavity 255 n.
  hiding-place 527 n.
  repose 683 n.
recession *decrease* 37 n.
  contraction 198 n.
  regression 286 n.
  recession 290 n.
  departure 296 n.
  deterioration 655 n.
  inactivity 679 n.
recessional *hymn* 981 n.
  ritual 988 adj.
recessive *reverted* 148 adj.
  receding 290 adj.
recessive characteristic
  speciality 80 n.
réchauffée *duplicate* 22 n.
  repetition 106 n.
  dish 301 n.
  restoration 656 n.
recheck *be careful* 457 adj.
recherché *unusual* 84 adj.
  excellent 644 adj.
  fashionable 848 adj.
recidivation *return* 286 n.
  tergiversation 603 n.
  relapse 657 n.
recidivism *reversion* 148 n.
  tergiversation 603 n.
  deterioration 655 n.
  relapse 657 n.
  wickedness 934 n.
  impiety 980 n.
recidivist

tergiversator 603 n.
  offender 904 n.
  bad man 938 n.
  impious person 980 n.
recipe *cookery* 301 n.
  contrivance 623 n.
  remedy 658 n.
  precept 693 n.
recipient *receptacle* 194 n.
  recipient 782 n.
reciprocal *relative* 9 adj.
  correlative 12 adj.
  equivalent 28 adj.
  numerical element 85 n.
  retaliatory 714 adj.
reciprocate *be related* 9 vb.
  correlate 12 vb.
  be periodic 141 vb.
  co-operate 706 vb.
  concord 710 vb.
reciprocation
  correlation 12 n.
  interchange 151 n.
  fluctuation 317 n.
  retaliation 714 n.
reciprocity *correlation* 12 n.
  equalization 28 n.
  compensation 31 n.
  interchange 151 n.
  co-operation 706 n.
  concord 710 n.
recision
  subtraction 39 n.
recital *repetition* 106 n.
  oration 579 n.
  description 590 n.
recitation *oration* 579 n.
recitative *vocal music* 412 n.
recite *number* 86 vb.
  repeat 106 vb.
  (see recital)
reck *be careful* 457 vb.
reckless *negligent* 458 adj.
  unwise 499 adj.
  defiant 711 adj.
  prodigal 815 adj.
  rash 857 adj.
recklessness
  indifference 860 n.
reckon *expect* 507 vb.
  be cautious 858 vb.
  (see reckoning)
reckon among
  number with 78 vb.
reckoning *numeration* 86 n.
  measurement 465 n.
  expectation 507 n.
  accounts 808 n.
  accounting 808 adj.
  price 809 n.
  punishment 963 n.

reckon on *believe* 485vb.
reckon to *intend* 617vb.
reckon with *pay* 804vb.
reckon without one's host
  misjudge 481vb.
  be rash 857vb.
reclaim *make better* 654vb.
  restore 656vb.
  retrieve 656vb.
  demand 737vb.
  acquire 771vb.
  appropriate 786vb.
  claim 915vb.
reclaimed
  repentant 939adj.
reclamation
  restoration 656n.
recline *be horizontal* 216vb.
  sit down 311vb.
  repose 683vb.
recline on
  be supported 218vb.
recluse *solitary* 883n.
  ascetic 945n.
recognition *assent* 488n.
  knowledge 490n.
  thanks 907n.
  dueness 915n.
  approbation 923n.
  reward 962n.
recognitor *jury* 957n.
recognizable
  visible 443adj.
  intelligible 516adj.
  manifest 522adj.
recognizance
  security 767n.
  legal process 959n.
recognize *identify* 13vb.
  see 438vb.
  notice 455vb.
  discover 484vb.
  remember 505vb.
  understand 516vb.
  permit 756vb.
  consent 758vb.
  greet 884vb.
recognized
  influential 178adj.
  usual 610adj.
recoil *counteraction* 182n.
  recoil 280n.
  recession 290n.
  repulsion 292n.
  elasticity 328n.
  be loth 598vb.
  avoidance 620n.
  dislike 861adj.
recoin *reproduce* 166vb.
recollection
  remembrance 505n.

recommencement
  reversion 148n.
recommend *incite* 612vb.
  patronize 703vb.
  befriend 880vb.
recommendation
  credential 466n.
  advice 691n.
  approbation 923n.
recommended *good* 615adj.
recommend oneself
  be praised 923vb.
recompense
  compensation 31n.
  retaliation 714n.
  reward 962n.,vb.
reconcilable
  agreeing 24adj.
reconcile *pacify* 719vb.
  content 828vb.
reconcilement
  adaptation 24n.
  conformity 83n.
reconciliation
  concord 710n.
  pacification 719n.
  content 828n.
  friendship 880n.
  forgiveness 909n.
  propitiation 941n.
recondite *puzzling* 517adj.
  concealed 525adj.
reconditioning
  repair 656n.
reconnaisance
  land travel 267adj.
  inspection 438n.
  enquiry 459n.
reconnoitre
  traverse 267vb.
  scan 438vb.
  enquire 459vb.
reconsideration
  amendment 654n.
reconstitute *restore* 656vb.
reconstruction
  reproduction 166n.
  conjecture 512n.
  restoration 656n.
reconversion
  reversion 148n.
  restoration 656n.
record *enormous* 32adj.
  superiority 34n.
  gramophone 414n.
  evidence 466n.
  record 548n.,vb.
  writing 586n.
  narrative 590n.
  describe 590vb.
  best 644adj.

  conduct 688n.
  title-deed 767n.
record-breaker
  exceller 644n.
record-breaking
  crowning 34adj.
record clerk
  recorder 549n.
recorder *chronologist* 117n.
  flute 414n.
  recorder 549n.
  narrator 590n.
  judge 957n.
record-holder *superior* 34n.
recording
  musical piece 412n.
  record 548n.
record-keeper
  recorder 549n.
record-player
  gramophone 414n.
record room *recorder* 549n.
records *record* 548n.
recount *numeration* 86n.
  communicate 524vb.
  describe 590vb.
recoup *recoup* 31vb.
  retrieve 656vb.
recoupment
  compensation 31n.
  acquisition 771n.
  taking 786n.
  restitution 787n.
recourse *contrivance* 623n.
  means 629n.
recourse to, have
  avail of 673vb.
recover *recoup* 31vb.
  revert 148vb.
  be strong 162vb.
  counteract 182vb.
  retrieve 656vb.
  deliver 668vb.
re-cover *repair* 656vb.
recoverable
  restored 656adj.
recovered *refreshed* 685adj.
recovery
  improvement 654n.
  sanation 656n.
  restoration 656n.
  revival 656n.
  acquisition 771n.
  taking 786n.
  restitution 787n.
recreancy *impiety* 980n.
recreant *tergiversator* 603n.
  cowardly 856adj.
  knave 938n.
recreation
  refreshment 685n.

amusement 837 n.
recreational
amusing 837 adj.
recriminate
dispraise, blame 924 n.
recrimination
dissension 709 n.
retaliation 714 n.
vindication 927 n.
accusation 928 n.
recrudescence
relapse 657 n.
recruit *augment* 36 vb.
accrue 38 vb.
strengthen 162 vb.
invigorate 174 vb.
beginner 538 n.
employ 622 vb.
replenish 633 vb.
make better 654 vb.
revive 656 vb.
refresh 685 vb.
aid 703 vb.
auxiliary 707 n.
soldier 722 n.
recruitment
war measures 718 n.
relief 831 n.
(*see* recruit)
rectangle
angular figure 247 n.
rectangular
vertical 215 adj.
rectification
compensation 31 n.
desiccation 342 n.
amendment 654 n.
repair 656 n.
rectify *regularize* 62 vb.
modify 143 vb.
straighten 249 vb.
perfect 646 vb.
rectify 654 vb.
rectilinear
continuous 71 adj.
straight 249 adj.
rectitude *straightness* 249 n.
probity 929 n.
virtue 933 n.
recto *dextrality* 241 n.
edition 589 n.
rector *director* 690 n.
pastor, cleric 986 n.
church title 986 n.
rectorship
church office 985 n.
rectory *parsonage* 986 n.
rectum *insides* 224 n.
recumbent *low* 210 adj.
supine 216 adj.
oblique 220 adj.

recuperate
get healthy 650 vb.
recuperation
sanation 656 n.
refreshment 685 n.
restitution 787 n.
recur *recur* 139 vb.
go on 146 vb.
(*see* recurrence)
recurrence *continuity* 71 n.
recurrence 106 n.
periodicity 141 n.
reversion 148 n.
remembrance 505 n.
revival 656 n.
relapse 657 n.
recur to *avail of* 673 vb.
recurvature
curvature 248 n.
recusancy *dissent* 489 n.
negation 533 n.
refusal 760 n.
impenitence 940 n.
schism 978 n.
recusant *dissentient* 489 n.
disobedient 738 adj.
schismatic 978 n.
redaction *amendment* 654 n.
redactor *bookman* 589 n.
redan *defences, fort* 713 n.
redargution
confutation 479 n.
red, be in the *lose* 772 vb.
be in debt 803 vb.
red blood *vitality* 162 n.
red-blooded
courageous 855 adj.
red-brick
regional 184 adj.
red-cap *bearer* 273 n.
redcoat *soldier* 722 n.
Red Cross *doctor* 658 n.
redden *redden* 431 vb.
show feeling 818 vb.
be humbled 872 vb.
get angry 891 vb.
rede *advice* 691 n.
redeem *observe faith* 768 vb.
pay 804 vb.
(*see* redemption)
redeemed *sanctified* 979 adj.
redeemer *purchaser* 792 n.
benefactor 903 n.
God the Son 965 n.
redemption

compensation 31 n.
quid pro quo 150 n.
restoration 656 n.
deliverance 668 n.
liberation 746 n.
acquisition 771 n.
restitution 787 n.
purchase 792 n.
propitiation 941 n.
divine function 965 n.
redemptive
redemptive 965 adj.
red-eyed *angry* 891 adj.
red flag *flag* 547 n.
signal 547 n.
danger signal 665 n.
red-handed
murderous 362 adj.
doing 676 adj.
in the act 676 adv.
guilty 936 adj.
red-head *shrew* 892 n.
red herring
irrelevance 10 n.
unimportance 639 n.
hinderer 702 n.
red-hot *violent* 176 adj.
hot 379 adj.
fervent 818 adj.
red ink *amendment* 654 n.
redintegration *repair* 656 n.
red, in the *losing* 772 adj.
indebted 803 adj.
redirect *send* 272 vb.
rediscovery
reproduction 166 n.
redivivus *restored* 656 adj.
red-letter day
important matter 638 n.
amusement 837 n.
special day 876 n.
red light *dimness* 419 n.
signal light 420 n.
signal 547 n.
danger signal 665 n.
red light district
brothel 951 n.
redolence *odour* 394 n.
fragrance 396 n.
redone *modernized* 126 adj.
restored 656 adj.
redouble *augment* 36 vb.
double 91 vb.
repeat 106 vb.
invigorate 174 vb.
enlarge 197 vb.
redoubling
frequency 139 n.
redoubtable
frightening 854 adj.
redound *tend* 179 vb.

redraft *rectify* 654vb.
red rag to a bull
  resentment 891n.
redress *restoration* 656n.
  remedy 658n.
  justice 913n.
red-tab *army officer* 741n.
red tape *delay* 136n.
  habit 610n.
red-tapism
  governance 733n.
red-tapist *official* 690n.
  tyrant 735n.
reduce *decompose* 51vb.
  do sums 86vb.
  render few 105vb.
  weaken 163vb.
  make smaller 198vb.
  abstract 592vb.
  overmaster 727vb.
  subjugate 745vb.
  be temperate 942vb.
  starve 946vb.
  (*see* reduction)
reduced *lesser* 35adj.
reduce to *liken* 18vb.
  convert 147vb.
reduce to the ranks
  abase 311vb.
  depose 752vb.
  shame 867vb.
  punish 963vb.
reducing *dieting* 301n.
reductio ad absurdum
  argumentation 475n.
  confutation 479n.
reduction *diminution* 37n.
  simplification 44n.
  numerical operation 86n.
  conversion 147n.
  miniature 196n.
  contraction 198n.
  shortening 204n.
  depression 311n.
  qualification 468n.
  photography 551n.
  discount 810n.
redundance *plenitude* 54n.
  overstepping 306n.
  diffuseness 570n.
  plenty 635n.
  redundance 637n.
  cheapness 812n.
  satiety 863n.
  undueness 916n.
redundant *useless* 641adj.
  liberal 813adj.
reduplication
  imitation 20n.
  duplication 91n.
  repetition 106n.

reproduction 166n.
re-echo *do likewise* 20vb.
  repeat oneself 106vb.
  resound 404vb.
reed *weak thing* 163n.
  plant 366n.
  flute 414n.
  stationery 586n.
re-edited
  modernized 126adj.
reedy *strident* 407adj.
reef *retard* 278vb.
  fold 261vb.
  rock 344vb.
  island 349n.
  pitfall 663n.
reefer *navigator* 270n.
  tobacco 388n.
reefer-jacket *tunic* 228n.
reef knot *ligature* 47n.
reek *gas* 336n.
  vaporize 338vb.
  be hot 379vb.
  odour 394n.
  fetor 397n.
reel *vary* 152vb.
  be weak 163vb.
  leap 312n.
  rotate 315vb.
  oscillate 317vb.
  be agitated 318vb.
  musical piece 412n.
  show feeling 818vb.
  dance 837n.
  be drunk 949vb.
reel off *speak* 579vb.
  be loquacious 581vb.
re-embody *combine* 50vb.
re-enter *acquire* 771vb.
  possess 773vb.
re-entrant *curved* 248adj.
re-entrant angle *angle* 247n.
re-entry *return* 286n.
  ingress 297n.
  taking 786n.
re-erection
  restoration 656n.
re-establishment
  restoration 656n.
reeve *affix* 45vb.
  officer 741n.
re-examination
  interrogation 459n.
  amendment 654n.
  legal trial 959n.
reface *make better* 654vb.
  repair 656vb.
refacimento
  repetition 106n.
refashion
  revolutionize 149vb.

reproduce 166vb.
  rectify 654vb.
refection *meal* 301n.
  refreshment 685n.
refectory *chamber* 194n.
  feasting 301n.
refer *indicate* 547vb.
  consult 691vb.
  (*see* refer to)
referable *relative* 9adj
  attributed 158adj.
referee *referral* 9n.
  estimator 480n.
  adviser 691n.
  mediator 720n.
  magistracy 957n.
reference *relation* 9n.
  referral 9n.
  class 62vb.
  evidence 466n.
  credential 466n.
  connotation 514n.
  indicate 547vb.
  advice 691n.
  approbation 923n.
referencer *recorder* 549n.
reference system
  sorting 62n.
reference to
  attribution 158n.
referendary *referral* 9n.
  estimator 480n.
referendum
  judgment 480n.
  vote 605n.
referent *referral* 9n.
referential *relative* 9adj.
referral *referral* 9n.
referrible *relative* 9adj.
  attributed 158adj.
refer to *relate* 9vb.
  be related 9vb.
  be included 78vb.
  attribute 158vb.
  mean 514vb.
refill *plenitude* 54n.
  store 632vb.
  replenish 633vb.
refine *differentiate* 15vb.
  rarefy 325vb.
  make better 654vb.
  purify 648vb.
  (*see* refinement)
refined *soft-hued* 425adj.
  personable 841adj.
  tasteful 846adj.
  pure 950adj.
refinement
  discrimination 463n.
  elegance 575n.
  civilization 654n.

beauty 841 n.
good taste 846 n.
fastidiousness 846 n.
refiner cleaner 648 n.
refinery workshop 687 n.
refit repair 656 vb.
reflation dilation 197 n.
reflect correlate 12 vb.
resemble 18 vb.
imitate 20 vb.
retrospect 505 vb.
show 522 vb.
(see reflection)
reflection analogue 18 n.
copy 22 n.
resonance 404 n.
reflection 417 n.
lamp 420 n.
visual fallacy 440 n.
appearance 445 n.
meditation 449 n.
idea 451 n.
repulsion 292 n.
image 551 n.
slur 866 n.
scurrility 899 n.
reproach 924 n.
detraction 926 n.
reflective radiating 417 adj.
thoughtful 449 adj.
reflect on shame 867 vb.
reprove 924 vb.
defame 926 vb.
reflector reflection 417 n.
lamp 420 n.
telescope 442 n.
reflex copy 22 n.
recoil 280 n.
regressive 286 adj.
sense 374 n.
involuntary 596 adj.
spontaneity 609 n.
habituation 610 n.
reflex action necessity 596 n.
reflexive intrinsic 5 adj.
reverted 148 adj.
reflexively
backwards 286 adv.
refluent recoiling 280 adj.
regressive 286 adj.
reflux decrease 37 n.
recoil 280 n.
return 286 n.
current, eddy 350 n.
refocillation
strengthening 162 n.
refreshment 685 n.
reforest restore 656 vb.
reform modify 143 vb.
transform 147 vb.
tergiversate 603 vb.

amendment 654 n.
repair 656 vb.
philanthropize 897 vb.
justice 913 n.
be penitent 939 vb.
become pious 979 vb.
reformable
improved 654 adj.
reformation
conversion 147 n.
amendment 654 n.
re-formation
restoration 656 n.
Reformation, the
Protestantism 976 n.
reformatory school 539 n.
amendment 654 n.
improving 654 adj.
prison 748 n.
reformed improved 654 adj.
right 913 adj.
repentant 939 adj.
Protestant 976 adj.
reformer alterer 143 n.
reformer 654 n.
religious teacher 973 n.
Protestant 976 n.
reformism
progression 285 n.
reformism 654 n.
reformist
progressive 285 adj.
refoundation
restoration 656 n.
re-founder patron 707 n.
refraction deviation 282 n.
reflection 417 n.
visual fallacy 440 n.
refractor astronomy 321 n.
telescope 442 n.
refractoriness
unwillingness 589 n.
refractory wilful 602 adj.
capricious 604 adj.
difficult 700 adj.
opposing 704 adj.
disobedient 738 adj.
sullen 893 adj.
refrain repetition 106 n.
periodicity 141 n.
cease 145 vb.
vocal music 412 n.
tune 412 n.
verse form 593 n.
avoid 620 vb.
not act 677 vb.
be lenient 736 vb.
be temperate 942 vb.
refresh invigorate 174 vb.
refrigerate 382 vb.
make better 654 vb.

revive 656 vb.
refresher extra 40 n.
tonic 658 n.
refreshment 685 n.
price 809 n.
refresher course
study 536 n.
refreshing lenitive 177 adj.
beneficial 644 adj.
salubrious 652 adj.
refreshment
strengthening 162 n.
meal 301 n.
pleasure 376 n.
repose 683 n.
refreshment 685 n.
aid 703 n.
enjoyment 824 n.
pleasurableness 826 n.
relief 831 n.
amusement 837 n.
refrigeration
anæsthetic 375 n.
refrigeration 382 n.
preservation 666 n.
refrigerator
provisions 301 n.
refrigeration 382 n.
refrigerator 384 n.
storage 632 n.
preserver 666 n.
reft of losing 772 adj.
refuel store 632 vb.
replenish 633 vb.
refuge retreat 192 n.
resting place 266 n.
hiding-place 527 n.
protection 660 n.
refuge 662 n.
fort 713 n.
refugee foreigner 59 n.
displacement 188 n.
wanderer 268 n.
ejection 300 n.
escaper 667 n.
outcaste 883 n.
refulgence light 417 n.
refund restitution 787 n.
refurbish
make better 654 vb.
repair 656 vb.
refusal repulsion 292 n.
dissent 489 n.
negation 533 n.
unwillingness 598 n.
rejection 607 n.
avoidance 620 n.
refusal 760 n.
deprecation 762 n.
non-observance 769 n.
disapprobation 924 n.

refuse *leavings* 41 n.
  waste 634 n.
  rubbish 641 n.
  dirt 649 n.
  (*see* refusal)
refuse bail
  imprison 747 vb.
refutable *confuted* 479 adj.
refutation
  counter-evidence 467 n.
  confutation 479 n.
  negation 533 n.
refutatory
  countervailing 467 adj.
  confuted 479 adj.
refuting *answering* 460 adj.
regain *retrieve* 656 vb.
  acquire 771 vb.
regal *ruling* 733 adj.
  impressive 821 adj.
  worshipful 866 adj.
regale *eat* 301 vb.
  pleasure 376 n.
  refresh 685 vb.
  delight 826 vb.
  amuse 837 vb.
  be hospitable 882 vb.
regalia *formal dress* 228 n.
  regalia 743 n.
  jewellery 844 n.
  formality 875 n.
regality
  magistrature 733 n.
regard *relation* 9 n.
  look 438 n.
  attention 455 n.
  observe 768 vb.
  repute 866 n.
  friendliness 880 n.
  love 887 n., vb.
  respect 920 n., vb.
  approbation 923 n.
regard as *opine* 485 vb.
regardful *attentive* 455 adj.
  careful 457 adj.
regarding
  concerning 9 adv.
regardless *irrelative* 10 adj.
  inattentive 456 adj.
  negligent 458 adj.
  ignorant 491 adj.
  apathetic 820 adj.
  rash 857 adj.
regards *courteous act* 884 n.
  respects 920 n.
regatta *racing* 716 n.
  (*see* aquatics)
regency *authority* 733 n.
  magistrature 733 n.
  governance 733 n.
  commission 751 n.

regenerate
  repentant 939 adj.
  make pious 979 vb.
  (*see* regeneration)
regeneration
  conversion 147 n.
  reproduction 166 n.
  revival 656 n.
  divine function 965 n.
regent *potentate* 741 n.
regicide *homicide* 362 n.
  revolt, revolter 738 n.
régime *circumstance* 8 n.
  dieting 301 n.
  management 689 n.
  governance 733 n.
regimen *dieting* 301 n.
  therapy 658 n.
  management 689 n.
regiment *band* 74 n.
  formation 722 n.
  dominate 733 vb.
  subjugate 745 vb.
regimentals *uniform* 228 n.
regimentation
  uniformity 16 n.
  compulsion 740 n.
regimented *obedient* 739 adj.
regimenter *uniformist* 16 n.
regiment of women
  gynocracy 733 n.
region *region* 184 n.
regional *regional* 184 adj.
  provincial 192 adj.
region of, in the
  about 33 adv.
register *be identical* 13 vb.
  accord 24 vb.
  degree 27 n.
  class 62 vb.
  list 87 n.
  musical note 410 n.
  notice 455 vb.
  understand 516 vb.
  indicate 547 vb.
  record 548 n.
  represent 551 vb.
  account book 808 n.
registrar *recorder* 549 n.
  doctor 658 n.
registration
  registration 548 n.
registry *registration* 548 n.
regnal *ruling* 733 adj.
regnant *influential* 178 adj.
  ruling 733 adj.
regrate *purchase* 792 vb.
  sell 793 vb.
regrater *merchant* 794 n.
regress *decrease* 37 vb.
  regression 286 n.

recede 290 vb.
  fall short 307 vb.
  relapse 657 vb.
regression *change* 143 n.
  reversion 148 n.
  regression 286 n.
  deterioration 655 n.
regressive
  tergiversating 603 adj.
regret *helplessness* 161 n.
  disappointment 509 n.
  be loth 598 vb.
  sorrow 825 n.
  be discontented 829 vb.
  regret 830 n., vb.
  desire 859 n., vb.
  dislike 861 vb.
  disapprove 924 vb.
  penitence 939 n.
regretful *unwilling* 598 adj.
  unhappy 825 adj.
regrets
  remembrance 505 n.
regrettable
  regretted 830 adj.
regretted *dead* 361 adj.
  remembered 505 adj.
regroup *combine* 50 vb.
reguardant *heraldic* 547 adj.
regular *equal* 28 adj.
  consummate 32 adj.
  regular 81 adj.
  frequent 139 adj.
  unceasing 146 adj.
  unchangeable 153 adj.
  symmetrical 245 adj.
  accurate 494 adj.
  soldier 722 n.
  shapely 841 adj.
  monk 986 n.
regularity
  uniformity 16 n.
  order 60 n.
  regularity 81 n.
  periodicity 141 n.
  permanence 144 n.
  symmetry 245 n.
  habit 610 n.
regularize *regularize* 62 vb.
  make conform 83 vb.
regulate *adjust* 24 vb.
  order 60 vb.
  regularize 62 vb.
regulation *rule* 81 n.
  management 689 n.
  precept 693 n.
  legislation 953 n.
regulations *command* 737 n.
regulative *regular* 81 adj.
regurgitation
  regression 286 n.

return 286 n.
voidance 300 n.
eddy 350 n.
rehabilitation
restoration 656 n.
restitution 787 n.
dignification 866 n.
vindication 927 n.
rehandling *repetition* 106 n.
rehash *repetition* 106 n.
translate 520 vb.
restoration 656 n.
rehearsal *repetition* 106 n.
remembrance 504 n.
description 590 n.
dramaturgy 594 n.
preparation 669 n.
rehearse
experiment 461 vb.
Reichstag *parliament* 692 n.
reign *be* 1 vb.
date 108 n.
influence 178 n.
governance 733 n.
reign of terror
anarchy 734 n.
intimidation 854 n.
reign supreme *rule* 733 vb.
reimburse *restitute* 787 vb.
pay 804 vb.
rein *halter* 47 n.
moderator 177 n.
management 689 n.
fetter 748 n.
reincarnated
material 319 adj.
reincarnation
recurrence 106 n.
future state 124 n.
transformation 143 n.
occultism 984 n.
reincarnationism
theosophy 984 n.
reindeer
beast of burden 273 n.
deer 365 n.
re-infection *relapse* 657 n.
reinforce *augment* 36 vb.
accrue 38 vb.
strengthen 162 vb.
enlarge 197 vb.
support 218 vb.
replenish 633 vb.
restore 656 vb.
aid 703 vb.
defend 713 vb.
reinforcement *extra* 40 n.
auxiliary 707 n.
armed force 722 n.
rein in *retard* 278 vb.
restrain 747 vb.

reinspire *revive* 656 vb.
reinstallation
restoration 656 n.
reinstate *replace* 187 vb.
reinstatement
reversion 148 n.
restitution 787 n.
re-insure
make certain 473 vb.
seek safety 660 vb.
be cautious 858 vb.
reinvest *replace* 187 vb.
restitute 787 vb.
economize 814 vb.
reissue *variant* 15 n.
repetition 106 n.
edition 589 n.
reiterate *repeat* 106 vb.
reiterated
persevering 600 adj.
reiteration *diffuseness* 570 n.
vigour 571 n.
reject *inferior* 35 n.
leavings 41 n.
be unsatisfied 636 vb.
rubbish 641 n.
not use 674 vb.
oppose 704 vb.
dislike 861 vb.
object of scorn 867 n.
outcaste 883 n.
despise 922 vb.
disapprove 924 vb.
condemn 961 vb.
(*see* rejection)
rejection *exclusion* 57 n.
ejection 300 n.
dissent 489 n.
negation 533 n.
unwillingness 598 n.
rejection 607 n.
avoidance 620 n.
refusal 760 n.
non-observance 769 n.
rejoice *be pleased* 824 vb.
delight 826 vb.
rejoice 835 vb.
revel 837 vb.
rejoicing *celebration* 876 n.
rejoin *congregate* 74 vb.
meet 295 vb.
answer 460 vb.
rejoinder *rejoinder* 460 n.
retaliation 714 n.
wit 839 n.
vindication 927 n.
rejoining *arrival* 295 n.
rejuvenation *revival* 656 n.
rekindle *kindle* 381 vb.
revive 656 vb.
animate 821 vb.

relapse *reversion* 148 n.
return 286 n.
tergiversation 603 n.
deterioration 655 n.
relapse 657 n., vb.
relate *attribute* 158 vb.
related *akin* 11 adj.
near 200 adj.
relater *narrator* 590 n.
relation *circumstance* 8 n.
relation 9 n.
kinsman 11 n.
correlation 12 n.
fitness 24 n.
bond 47 n.
description 590 n.
relational *relative* 9 adj.
relationship *relation* 9 n.
consanguinity 11 n.
relative *relative* 9 adj.
kinsman 11 n.
correlative 12 adj.
comparative 27 adj.
compared 462 adj.
relative quantity
degree 27 n.
relativism *relativeness* 9 n.
philosophy 449 n.
relativity *relativeness* 9 n.
philosophy 449 n.
relax *bate* 37 vb.
disjoin 46 vb.
decompose 51 vb.
pause 145 vb.
weaken 163 vb.
decelerate 278 vb.
soften 327 vb.
qualify 468 vb.
keep calm 823 vb.
relieve 831 vb.
be sociable 882 vb.
show mercy 905 vb.
relaxation
moderation 177 n.
repose 683 n.
laxity 734 n.
liberation 746 n.
amusement 837 n.
relaxed
non-adhesive 49 adj.
tranquil 266 adj.
unthinking 450 adj.
relay *periodicity* 141 n.
publish 528 vb.
telecommunication 531 n.
co-operation 706 n.
auxiliary 707 n.
release *disjoin* 46 vb.
transference 272 n.
decease 361 n.
show 522 vb.

deliverance 668 n.
give scope 744 vb.
liberation 746 n.
permit 756 vb.
non-retention 779 n.
exempt 919 vb.
releasee *beneficiary* 776 n.
recipient 782 n.
relegate *displace* 188 vb.
transpose 272 vb.
relegation
transference 272 n.
ejection 300 n.
relent *be moderate* 177 vb.
soften 327 vb.
show mercy 905 vb.
forgive 909 vb.
relentless *resolute* 599 adj.
severe 735 adj.
pitiless 906 adj.
revengeful 910 adj.
impenitent 940 adj.
relevance *relevance* 9 n.
fitness 24 n.
meaning 514 n.
relevant *rational* 475 adj.
important 638 adj.
reliability *credit* 802 n.
(*see* reliable)
reliable
unchangeable 153 adj.
evidential 466 adj.
probable 471 adj.
certain 473 adj.
credible 485 adj.
genuine 494 adj.
veracious 540 adj.
willing 597 adj.
resolute 599 adj.
safe 660 adj.
observant 768 adj.
trustworthy 929 adj.
reliance *belief* 485 n.
expectation 507 n.
hope 852 n.
relic *antiquity* 125 n.
archaism 127 n.
reminder 505 n.
trace 548 n.
talisman 983 n.
relics *corpse* 363 n.
ritual object 988 n.
relict *survivor* 41 n.
widowed spouse 896 n.
relief *contrariety* 14 n.
aftercomer 67 n.
substitute 150 n.
moderation 177 n.
displacement 188 n.
outline 233 n.
form 243 n.

rilievo 254 n.
feature 445 n.
sculpture 554 n.
sanation 656 n.
deliverance 668 n.
refreshment 685 n.
aid 703 n.
deposal 752 n.
relief 831 n.
ornamental art 844 n.
kind act 897 n.
relieve *come after* 65 vb.
assuage 177 vb.
remedy 658 vb.
aid 703 vb.
liberate 746 vb.
tranquillize 823 vb.
relieve 831 vb.
cheer 833 vb.
(*see* relief)
relieved
comfortable 376 adj.
relieve of *convey* 870 vb.
take away 786 vb.
religion *religion* 973 n.
piety 979 n.
public worship 981 n.
religionism *pietism* 979 n.
religiosity *pietism* 979 n.
religious *observant* 768 adj.
trustworthy 929 adj.
honourable 929 adj.
divine 965 adj.
religious 973 adj.
pious 979 adj.
monk 986 n.
religious mania
mania 503 n.
religiousness *piety* 979 n.
religious truth
orthodoxy 976 n.
reline *repair* 656 vb.
relinquish *cease* 145 vb.
be irresolute 601 vb.
tergiversate 603 vb.
relinquish 621 vb.
disuse 674 vb.
abrogate 752 vb.
resign 753 vb.
not retain 779 vb.
relinquished *empty* 190 adj.
relinquishment
recession 290 n.
temperance 942 n.
(*see* relinquish)
reliquary *small box* 194 n.
ritual object 988 n.
relish *pleasure* 376 n.
taste 386 n.
condiment 389 n.
savouriness 390 n.

feeling 818 n.
enjoyment 824 n.
pleasurableness 826 n.
liking 859 n.
relive *be restored* 656 vb.
reload *replenish* 663 vb.
reluctance *slowness* 278 n.
unwillingness 598 n.
resistance 715 n.
dislike 861 n.
reluctant *avoiding* 620 adj.
reluctantly
unwillingly 598 adv.
disapprovingly 924 adj.
rely *assume* 471 vb.
hope 852 vb.
rely on
be supported 218 vb.
be certain 473 vb.
believe 485 vb.
take a pledge 764 vb.
remade *restored* 656 adj.
remain *be left* 41 vb.
continue 108 vb.
last 113 vb.
stay 144 vb.
go on 146 vb.
dwell 192 vb.
be quiescent 266 vb.
remainder *difference* 15 n.
remainder 41 n.
piece 53 n.
numerical result 85 n.
posteriority 120 n.
effect 157 n.
book 589 n.
superfluity 637 n.
dower 777 n.
sell 793 vb.
remainder, leave a
be unequal 29 vb.
remainderman
beneficiary 776 n.
remaindership
possession 773 n.
remaining
separate 46 adj.
remains *remainder* 41 n.
trace 548 n.
reading matter 589 n.
remake *reproduce* 166 vb.
restore 656 vb.
remand *put off* 136 vb.
detention 747 n.
remanded *captive* 750 adj.
accused 928 adj.
remand home *school* 539 n.
remark *notice* 455 n.
maxim 496 n.
affirmation 532 n.
affirm 532 vb.

speech 579n.
remarkable
  remarkable 32adj.
  unusual 84adj.
  visible 443adj.
  notable 638adj.
  wonderful 864adj.
  noteworthy 866adj.
remarks *estimate* 480n.
remarriage
  type of marriage 894n.
remedial *lenitive* 177adj.
  counteracting 182adj.
  improving 654adj.
  remedial 658adj.
  successful 727adj.
  relieving 831adj.
remediless
  unpromising 853adj.
remedy *moderator* 177n.
  counteract 182vb.
  contrivance 623n.
  means 629n.
  sanation 656n.
  remedy 658n.,vb.
  be just 913vb.
remember *think* 449vb.
  be mindful 455vb.
  remember 505vb.
remembered *known* 490adj.
remembrance
  remembrance 505n.
  famousness 866n.
  celebration 876n.
remembrancer
  reminder 505n.
  recorder 549n.
  adviser 691n.
remembrances
  courteous act 884n.
  respects 920n.
remigration *return* 286n.
  arrival 295n.
  departure 296n.
remind *remind* 505vb.
  hint 524vb.
  warn 664vb.
reminder *reminder* 505n.
  record 548n.
  monument 548n.
reminiscence
  remembrance 505n.
  narrative 590n.
reminiscent
  remembering 505adj.
remiss *negligent* 458adj.
  unwilling 598n.
  lazy 679adj.
  lax 734adj.
remission *lull* 145n.
  moderation 177n.

forgiveness 909n.
remit *bate* 37vb.
  pause 145vb.
  be moderate 177vb.
  send 272vb.
  forgive 909vb.
remittance
  transference 272n.
  funds 797n.
  payment 804n.
remittance man
  egress 298n.
  recipient 782n.
remittent *periodical* 141adj.
  fitful 142adj.
remitter *transferrer* 272n.
remnant *leavings* 41n.
  fewness 105n.
remodel
  revolutionize 149vb.
  rectify 654vb.
  repair 656vb.
remonstrance
  dissuasion 613n.
  deprecation 762n.
  reprimand 924n.
remonstrate
  (*see* remonstrance)
remora *coherence* 48n.
  encumbrance 702n.
remorse *sorrow* 825n.
  regret 830n.
  pity 905n.
  penitence 939n.
remorseless *pitiless* 906adj.
  revengeful 910adj.
remote *irrelevant* 10adj.
  distant 199adj.
  invisible 444adj.
remote control
  directorship 689n.
remould *modify* 143vb.
  rectify 654vb.
remount *substitute* 150n.
  war-horse 273n.
removable *excluded* 57adj.
removal *subtraction* 39n.
  separation 46n.
  exclusion 57n.
  displacement 188n.
  farness 199n.
  transference 272n.
  departure 296n.
  extraction 304n.
  deposal 752n.
  taking 786n.
removal man
  displacement 188n.
removal van *cart* 274n.
remove *degree* 27n.
  serial place 73n.

destroy 165vb.
  be in motion 265vb.
  class 538n.
  (*see* removal)
remover *destroyer* 168n.
remunerate *be useful* 640vb.
remuneration
  earnings 771n.
  pay 804n.
  receipt 807n.
  reward 962n.
remunerative
  profitable 640adj.
  gainful 771adj.
  rewarding 962adj.
renaissance
  preterition 125n.
  revival 656n.
renascent
  reproductive 166adj.
  restored 656adj.
rend *rend* 46vb.
  demolish 165vb.
  chew 301vb.
  force 176vb.
  wound 655vb.
  hurt 827vb.
  detract 926vb.
render *convert* 147vb.
  coat 226vb.
  liquefy 337vb.
  play music 413vb.
  translate 520vb.
  give 781vb.
  restitute 787vb.
rendering
  translation 520n.
rendezvous
  congregate 74vb.
  focus 76n.
  meet 295vb.
  social round 882n.
rendition *submission* 721n.
  restitution 787n.
renegade *alterer* 143n.
  changed person 147n.
  tergiversator 603n.
  avoider 620n.
  knave 938n.
renew *make better* 654vb.
  (*see* renewal)
renewal *duplication* 91n.
  repetition 106n.
  newness 126n.
  reproduction 166n.
  repair, revival 656n.
  refreshment 685n.
renewed *persevering* 600adj.
  sanctified 979adj.
renitency
  counteraction 182n.

hardness 326n.
unwillingness 598n.
resistance 715n.
rennet *condensation* 324n.
thickening 354n.
renounce *negate* 533vb.
recant 603vb.
relinquish 621vb.
resign 753vb.
refuse 760vb.
not retain 779vb.
renovate *make better* 654n.
renovation *newness* 126n.
reproduction 166n.
repair 656n.
renovator *mender* 656n.
renown *famousness* 866n.
honour 866vb.
renowned *known* 490adj.
renownless
inglorious 867adj.
rent *disjunction* 46n.
gap 201n.
hire 785vb.
purchase 792vb.
price 809n.
rental *price* 809n.
rent-collector
receiver 782n.
renter *resident* 191n.
possessor 776n.
lender 784n.
purchaser 792n.
rent-free *uncharged* 812adj.
rentier *idler* 679n.
receiver 782n.
rent-payer *possessor* 776n.
rent-roll *estate* 777n.
receipt 807n.
rents *flat* 192n.
receipt 807n.
renunciation
negation 533n.
recantation 603n.
relinquishment 621n.
laxity 734n.
resignation 753n.
refusal 760n.
non-retention 779n.
seclusion 883n.
non-liability 919n.
temperance 942n.
reoccur *reoccur* 106vb.
recur 139vb.
be periodic 141vb.
reopen *begin* 68vb.
reorganization
arrangement 62n.
restoration 656n.
reorganize *transform* 147vb.
rectify 654vb.

rep *textile* 222n.
drama 594n.
repair *adjust* 24vb.
amendment 654n.
repair 656n.,vb.
repairer *mender* 656n.
repair to *travel* 267vb.
reparation
compensation 31n.
repair 656n.
restoration 656n.
restitution 787n.
atonement 941n.
repartee *interchange* 151n.
answer 460n.
confutation 479n.
interlocution 584n.
witticism 839n.
repartition
apportionment 783n.
repass *pass* 305vb.
repast *meal* 301n.
repatriation
restitution 787n.
repay *compensate* 31vb.
benefit 615vb.
be profitable 771vb.
restitute 787vb.
pay 804vb.
thank 907vb.
reward 962vb.
repayable *owed* 803adj.
repay with interest
augment 36vb.
repeal *abrogation* 752n.
repeat *do likewise* 20vb.
double 91vb.
repetition 106n.
memorize 505vb.
emphasize 532vb.
be diffuse 570vb.
repeated *uniform* 16adj.
many 104adj.
frequent 139adj.
tedious 838adj.
repeatedly
persistently 600adv.
repeater *timekeeper* 117n.
pistol 723n.
repel *repel* 292vb.
be unpalatable 391vb.
dissuade 613vb.
parry 713vb.
resist 715vb.
refuse 760vb.
displease 827vb.
cause dislike 861vb.
make unwelcome 883vb.
excite hate 888vb.
repellent *repellent* 292adj.
unpleasant 827adj.

ugly 842adj.
disliked 861adj.
hateful 888adj.
repent *be wise* 498vb.
become pious 979vb.
(*see* repentance)
repentance
tergiversation 603n.
amendment 654n.
regret 830n.
penitence 939n.
repercussion *effect* 157n.
counteraction 182n.
recoil 280n.
repertoire, repertory
list 87n.
acting 594n.
collection 632n.
store 632n.
merchandise 795n.
repetend *number* 85n.
recurrence 106n.
repetition *identity* 13n.
mimicry 20n.
repetition 106n.
frequency 139n.
continuance 146n.
reproduction 166n.
perseverance 600n.
repetitious
repeated 106adj.
pleonastic 570adj.
tedious 838adj.
repetitive *uniform* 16adj.
continuous 71adj.
pleonastic 570adj.
repetitive job
habituation 610n.
repetitiveness
diffuseness 570n.
rephrase *repeat* 106vb.
translate 520vb.
phrase 563vb.
repine
be discontented 829vb.
be dejected 834vb.
regret 830vb.
replace *substitute* 150vb.
replace 187vb.
eject 300vb.
restore 656vb.
disuse 674vb.
depose 752vb.
deputize 755vb.
not retain 779vb.
replaceable
superfluous 637adj.
replacement
reversion 148n.
(*see* replace)
replant *replace* 187vb.

restore 656 vb.
replay *repetition* 106 n.
replenish *fill* 54 vb.
  store 632 vb.
  replenish 633 vb.
  suffice 635 vb.
replete *full* 54 adj.
repletion *sufficiency* 635 n.
  satiety 863 n.
replevin *security* 767 n.
  acquisition 771 n
  restitution 787 n.
replica *copy* 22 n.
reply *answer* 460 n., vb.
  rejoinder 460 n.
  vindication 927 n.
reply by return
  correspond 588 vb.
report *loudness* 400 n.
  bang 402 n.
  report 524 n.
  communicate 524 vb.
  divulge 526 vb.
  publicity 528 n.
  news 529 vb.
  record 548 n.
  correspond 588 vb.
  describe 590 vb.
reported *rumoured* 529 adj.
reported against
  accused 928 adj.
reported case
  legal trial 959 n.
reporter *estimator* 480 n.
  informant 524 n.
  publicizer 528 n.
  newsmonger 529 n.
  chronicler 549 n.
  author 589 n.
  narrator 590 n.
reporting *publicity* 528 n.
report on *estimate* 480 vb.
reports *record* 548 n.
repose *quietude* 266 n.
  inaction 677 n.
  leisure 681 n.
  repose 683 n., vb.
  be refreshed 685 vb.
reposeful *tranquil* 266 adj.
  comfortable 376 adj.
  reposeful 683 adj.
  pleasurable 826 adj.
  content 828 adj.
repose on
  be supported 218 vb.
reposition *location* 187 n.
repoussé *salient* 254 adj.
reprehend
  (*see* reprehension)
reprehension
  disapprobation 924 n.

reprimand 924 n.
  censure 924 n.
reprehensible
  not nice 645 adj.
  blameworthy 924 adj.
  heinous 924 adj.
  guilty 936 adj.
represent *be* 1 vb.
  resemble 18 vb.
  figure 519 vb.
  affirm 532 vb.
  describe 590 vb.
  deputize 755 vb.
  (*see* representation)
representation
  imitation 20 n.
  copy 22 n.
  manifestation 522 n.
  report 524 n.
  indication 547 n.
  representation 551 n.
  drama 594 n.
  vote 605 n.
  commission 751 n.
  rite 988 n.
representational
  representing 551 adj.
  descriptive 590 adj.
representative
  general 79 adj.
  typical 83 adj.
  substitute 150 n.
  agent 686 n.
  councillor 692 n.
  mediator 720 n.
  consignee 754 n.
  delegate 754 n.
representative government
  government 733 n.
representative selection
  example 83 n.
representing
  interpretive 520 adj.
repress *hinder* 702 vb.
  subjugate 745 vb.
  tranquillize 823 vb.
repression *exclusion* 57 n.
  counteraction 182 n.
  avoidance 620 n.
  restraint 747 n.
  prohibition 757 n.
  moral insensibility 820 n.
  fear 854 n.
repressive
  avoiding 620 adj.
  restraining 747 adj.
reprieve, reprieval
  delay 136 n.
  escape 667 n.
  deliverance 668 n.
  forgiveness 909 n.

acquittal 960 n.
reprimand *warning* 664 n.
  reprimand 924 n.
  punishment 963 n.
reprint *copy* 20 vb.
  duplicate 22 n.
  repeat 106 vb.
  reproduction 166 n.
  edition 589 n.
reprisal *retaliation* 714 n.
  revenge 910 n.
  penalty 963 n.
reprise *decrement* 42 n.
  repetition 106 n.
  taking 786 n.
reproach *slur* 867 n.
  object of scorn 867 n.
  malediction 899 n.
  despisedness 922 n.
  reproach 924 n.
  accusation 928 n.
reproachful
  resentful 891 adj.
  maledicent 899 adj.
  disapproving 924 adj.
reproach oneself
  be penitent 939 vb.
reprobate
  blameworthy 924 adj.
  exprobate 924 vb.
  wicked 934 adj.
  bad man 938 n.
  impious person 980 n.
reprobation
  reprimand 924 n.
  impiety 980 n.
reproduce *copy* 20 vb.
  repeat 106 vb.
reproduction
  analogue 18 n.
  copy 22 n.
  increase 36 n.
  propagation 164 n.
  reproduction 166 n.
  representation 551 n.
  picture 553 n.
reproof *dissuasion* 613 n.
reprove *warn* 664 vb.
  deprecate 762 vb.
  curse 899 vb.
  reprove 924 vb.
  punish 963 vb.
reptile *reptile* 365 n.
  animal 365 n.
  bane 659 n.
  knave 938 n.
reptilian *animal* 365 adj.
republic *territory* 184 n.
  polity 733 n.
republican
  governmental 733 adj.

commoner 869n.
republicanism
 government 733n.
republic of letters
 literature 557n.
repudiate *recant* 603vb.
 (*see* repudiation)
repudiation *dissent* 489n.
 negation 533n.
 rejection 607n.
 abrogation 752n.
 non-observance 769n.
 non-payment 805n.
 divorce 896n.
repugnance *contrariety* 14n.
 unwillingness 598n.
 opposition 704n.
 resistance 715n.
 dislike 861n.
 hatred 888n.
repulse *recoil* 280n.
 repulsion 292n.
 rejection 607n.
 hitch 702n.
 parry 713vb.
 resistance 715n.
 defeat 728n.
 refusal 760n.
repulsion *energy* 160n.
 repulsion 292n.
 dislike 861n.
repulsive *repellent* 292adj.
 unsavoury 391adj.
 inelegant 576adj.
 ugly 842adj.
 disliked 861adj.
 hateful 888adj.
reputable
 reputable 866adj.
 honourable 929adj.
reputation (*see* repute)
repute *importance* 638n.
 credit 802n.
 repute 866n.
 probity 929n.
reputedly
 supposedly 512adv.
request
 requirement 627n.
 demand 737n.
 request 761n.,vb.
request, by
 desirously 859adv.
request stop
 stopping place 145n.
requiem *obsequies* 364n.
 lament 836n.
requiem mass
 Christian rite 988n.
require *not suffice* 636vb.
 demand 737vb.

impose a duty 917vb.
 (*see* requirement)
requirement *deficit* 55n.
 necessity 596n.
 requirement 627n.
 imperfection 647n.
 request 761n.
 conditions 766n.
 desire 859n.
requisite *necessary* 596adj.
 requirement 627n.
requisition
 requirement 627n.
 demand 737n.,vb.
 request 761n.,vb.
 taking 786n.
requital *retaliation* 714n.
 pay 804n.
 thanks 907n.
 reward 962n.
 punishment 963n.
rerebrace *armour* 713n.
reredos *altar* 990n.
rescind *recant* 603vb.
 abrogate 752vb.
rescission *abrogation* 752n.
rescript *answer* 460n.
 correspondence 588n.
 precept 693n.
 decree 737n.
 legislation 953n.
rescue *restoration* 656n.
 safety 660n.
 escape 667n.
 deliverance 668n.
 aid 703n.
 defend 713vb.
 liberation 746n.
 restitution 787n.
 vindicate 927vb.
rescuer *preserver* 666n.
 defender 713n.
 benefactor 903n.
research *be curious* 453vb.
 enquiry 459n.
 experiment 461n.,vb.
 study 536n.
resection *scission* 46n.
reseda *green colour* 432n.
resemblance
 similarity 18n.
 copy 22n.
resemble *accord* 24vb.
 appear 445vb.
resent *hate* 888vb.
 be revengeful 910vb.
 (*see* resentment)
resentful *malevolent* 898adj.
 (*see* resentment)
resentment *discontent* 829n.
 enmity 881n.

resentment 891n.
 jealousy 911n.
reservation
 qualification 468n.
 doubt 486n.
 dissent 489n.
 registration 548n.
 conditions 766n.
 seclusion 883n.
 Christian rite 988n.
reserve *aftercomer* 67n.
 be early 135vb.
 put off 136vb.
 substitute 150n.
 inclosure 235n.
 doubt 486n.
 concealment 525n.
 register 548vb.
 taciturnity 582n.
 select 605vb.
 require 627vb.
 store 632vb.
 not use 674vb.
 modesty 874n.
 seclusion 883n.
reserved *reticent* 525adj.
 required 627adj.
 promised 764adj.
 possessed 773adj.
 retained 778adj.
 inexcitable 823adj.
 due 915adj.
reserve, in
 impending 155adj.
 inactively 175adv.
 prepared 669adj.
reserves *extra* 40n.
 means 629n.
 provision 633n.
 armed force 722n.
 funds 797n.
reservist *substitute* 150n.
 soldier 722n.
reservoir *receptacle* 194n.
 irrigator 341n.
 lake 346n.
 storage 632n.
reset *modify* 143vb.
 replace 187vb.
reshape *modify* 143vb.
 transform 147vb.
reshuffle *begin* 68vb.
reside *be* 1vb.
 dwell 192vb.
residence *place* 185n.
 locality 187n.
 presence 189n.
 abode, house 192n.
resident *settler* 191n.
 resident 191n.
 envoy 754n.

cleric 986 n.
resident alien *foreigner* 59 n.
residual *remainder* 41 n.
  remaining 41 adj.
  numerical result 85 n.
residue, residuum
  remainder 41 n.
  dirt 649 n.
resign *disuse* 674 vb.
  not retain 779 vb.
  (*see* resignation)
resignation
  relinquishment 621 n.
  submission 721 n.
  resignation 753 n.
  patience 823 n.
  content 828 n.
  humility 872 n.
resignee *consignee* 754 n.
resile *recoil* 280 vb.
  recant 603 vb.
resilience *strength* 162 n.
  return 286 n.
  elasticity 328 n.
resilient *cheerful* 833 adj.
resin *resin* 357 n.
  viol 414 n.
resipiscence
  penitence 939 n.
resist *be loth* 598 vb.
  give battle 718 vb.
  (*see* resistance)
resistance *energy* 160 n.
  electricity 160 n.
  counteraction 182 n.
  hardness 326 n.
  hindrance 702 n.
  opposition 704 n.
  defence 713 n.
  resistance 715 n.
  revolt 738 n.
  refusal 760 n.
resistant *dissenting* 489 adj.
resister *opponent* 705 n.
resistless *strong* 162 adj.
  necessary 596 adj.
res judicata *certainty* 473 n.
  judgment 480 n.
resole *repair* 656 vb.
resolute
  unchangeable 153 adj.
  unyielding 162 adj.
  resolute 599 adj.
  completive 725 adj.
  courageous 855 adj.
resolution
  decomposition 51 n.
  conversion 147 n.
  vigorousness 174 n.
  melody 410 n.
  topic 452 n.

will 595 n.
  resolution 599 n.
  obstinacy 602 n.
  intention 617 n.
  plan 623 n.
  assiduity 678 n.
  courage 855 n.
resolve *liquefy* 337 vb.
  decipher 520 vb.
  resolution 599 n.
  predetermination 608 n.
resonance *recoil* 280 n.
  oscillation 317 n.
  loudness 400 n.
  roll 403 n.
  resonance 404 n.
resonant *rhetorical* 574 adj.
resorb *absorb* 299 vb.
resorption *reception* 299 n.
resort *focus* 76 n.
  convergence 293 n.
  contrivance 623 n.
  means 629 n.
  stratagem 698 n.
resort to *congregate* 74 vb.
  be present 189 vb.
  travel 267 vb.
  avail of 673 vb.
resound (*see* resonance)
resource *contrivance* 623 n.
  stratagem 698 n.
resourceful *prolific* 171 adj.
  imaginative 513 adj.
  cunning 698 adj.
resources *means* 629 n.
  materials 631 n.
  estate 777 n.
  wealth 800 n.
respect *relation* 9 n.
  appearance 445 n.
  observe 768 vb.
  fear 854 n.
  honour 866 vb.
  courtesy 884 n.
  respect 920 n., vb.
respectability
  mediocrity 732 n.
  repute 866 n.
  probity 929 n.
respectable *great* 32 adj.
  reputable 866 adj.
  respected 920 adj.
  honourable 929 adj.
respectful *courteous* 884 adj.
  respectful 920 adj.
respective *relative* 9 adj.
  special 80 adj.
respectively
  severally 80 adv.
  pro rata 783 adv.
respects

courteous act 884 n.
  respects 920 n.
respiration
  respiration 352 n.
  life 360 n.
respirator *safeguard* 662 n.
  preserver 666 n.
respire *oscillate* 317 vb.
  breathe 352 vb.
  live 360 vb.
  be refreshed 685 vb.
respite *interim* 108 n.
  delay 136 n.
  lull 145 n.
  deliverance 668 n.
  repose 683 n.
  acquit 960 vb.
resplendent
  splendid 841 adj.
respond *accord* 24 vb.
  answer 460 n., vb.
  co-operate 706 vb.
  concord 710 vb.
  feel 818 vb.
respondent *testee* 461 n.
  interlocutor 584 n.
  accused person 928 n.
  litigant 959 n.
responder *rejoinder* 460 n.
response *effect* 157 n.
  sense 374 n.
  answer 460 n.
  feeling 818 n.
  friendliness 880 n.
  hymn 981 n.
responsibility
  liability 180 n.
  directorship 689 n.
  mandate 751 n.
  duty 917 n.
  guilt 936 n.
responsible *adult* 134 adj.
  causal 156 adj.
  liable 180 adj.
  wise 498 adj.
  observant 768 adj.
  indebted 803 adj.
  cautious 858 adj.
  dutied 917 adj.
  trustworthy 929 adj.
responsible person
  manager 690 n.
responsions *exam.* 459 n.
responsive
  sentient 374 adj.
  answering 460 adj.
  impressible 819 adj.
responsiveness
  feeling 818 n.
  benevolence 897 n.
rest *be left* 41 vb.

be discontinuous 72 vb.
stay 144 vb.
lull 145 n.
cease 145 vb.
go on 146 vb.
stability 153 n.
inertness 175 n.
supporter 218 n.
quiescence 266 n.
death 361 n.
euphoria 376 n.
pleasure 376 n.
silence 399 n.
notation 410 n.
inaction 677 n.
be inactive 679 vb.
leisure 681 n.
repose 683 n., vb.
restart revert 148 vb.
rest, at free 744 adj.
restate repeat 106 vb.
restaurant café 192 n.
cookery 301 n.
restaurateur caterer 633 n.
restful tranquil 266 adj.
comfortable 376 adj.
reposeful 683 adj.
rest home hospital 658 n.
resthouse inn 192 n.
resting remaining 41 adj.
unused 674 adj.
resting place
resting place 266 n.
goal 295 n.
restitution reversion 148 n.
restitution 787 n.
payment 804 n.
dueness 915 n.
vindication 927 n.
atonement 941 n.
restitutory
compensatory 31 adj.
restoring 787 adj.
restive unwilling 598 adj.
wilful 602 adj.
disobedient 738 adj.
excited 821 adj.
excitable 822 adj.
discontented 829 adj.
restlessness
changeableness 152 n.
motion 265 n.
agitation 318 n.
restlessness 678 n.
disobedience 738 n.
excitability 822 n.
discontent 829 n.
restock replenish 633 vb.
rest on be supported 218 vb.
restoration
equalization 28 n.

newness 126 n.
reversion 148 n.
strengthening 162 n.
improvement 654 n.
restoration 656 n.
deliverance 668 n.
refreshment 685 n.
restitution 787 n.
dueness 915 n.
vindication 927 n.
penalty 963 n.
restorative
stimulant 174 n.
salubrious 652 adj.
tonic 658 n.
refreshing 685 adj.
relieving 831 adj.
restore compensate 31 vb.
make complete 54 vb.
reproduce 166 vb.
remedy 658 vb.
relieve 831 vb.
vindicate 927 vb.
(see restoration)
restored whole 52 adj.
restorer reformer 654 n.
mender 656 n.
restrain
make smaller 198 vb.
circumscribe 232 vb.
retard 278 vb.
dissuade 613 vb.
make insufficient 636 vb.
hinder 702 vb.
retain 778 vb.
tranquillize 823 vb.
(see restraint)
restrained small 33 adj.
restraint diminution 37 n.
moderation 177 n.
counteraction 182 n.
elegance 575 n.
compulsion 740 n.
restraint 747 n.
prohibition 757 n.
temperance 942 n.
restrict
make smaller 198 vb.
(see restriction)
restricted small 33 adj.
restrictedly
partially 33 adv.
restriction
circumscription 232 n.
limit 236 n.
qualification 468 n.
hindrance 702 n.
restriction 747 n.
prohibition 757 n.
restringent
restraining 747 adj.

result remainder 41 n.
sequel 67 n.
end 69 n.
ensue 120 vb.
eventuality 154 n.
effect 157 n.
product 164 n.
instrumentality 628 n.
completion 725 n.
resultant remaining 41 adj.
result, no failure 728 n.
results answer 460 n.
resume be concise 569 vb.
abstract 592 vb.
(see resumption)
résumé compendium 592 n.
resumption start 68 n.
repetition 106 n.
reversion 148 n.
restoration 656 n.
taking 786 n.
resurgence
reproduction 166 n.
revival 656 n.
resurrection
reproduction 166 n.
revival 656 n.
Heaven 971 n.
resurrectional
reproductive 166 adj.
paradisiac 971 adj.
resurrection day
finality 69 n.
future state 124 n.
revival 656 n.
resurrectionist thief 789 n.
resuscitate
reproduce 166 vb.
revive 656 vb.
animate 821 vb.
retable shelf 218 n.
retail disperse 75 vb.
communicate 524 vb.
publish 528 vb.
trading 791 adj.
sell 793 vb.
retailer intermediary 231 n.
provider 633 n.
seller 793 n.
tradesman 794 n.
retain tie 45 vb.
stabilize 153 vb.
remember 505 vb.
understand 516 vb.
store 632 vb.
preserve 666 vb.
restrain 747 vb.
refuse 760 vb.
possess 773 vb.
retain 778 vb.
retainer inferior 35 n.

concomitant 89 n.
protector 660 n.
retainer 742 n.
reward 962 n.
retake *retrieve* 656 vb.
retaliate *answer* 460 vb.
(*see* retaliation)
retaliation
equalization 28 n.
compensation 31 n.
interchange 151 n
retaliation 714 n.
penalty 963 n.
retaliative
retaliatory 714 adj.
revengeful 910 adj.
retard *bate* 37 vb.
halt 145 vb.
retard 278 vb.
retardation *delay* 136 n.
slowness 278 n.
hindrance 702 n.
restraint 747 n.
retarded
unintelligent 499 adj.
retarding
counteracting 182 adj.
retch *vomit* 300 vb.
retching *indigestion* 651 n.
retell *repeat* 106 vb.
retention *coherence* 48 n.
memory 505 n.
possession 773 n.
retention 778 n.
retentive *tough* 329 adj.
retentive 778 adj.
greedy 859 adj.
retiarius *combatant* 722 n.
reticence
concealment 525 n.
taciturnity 582 n.
caution 858 n.
reticle *network* 222 n.
reticular *reticular* 222 adj.
reticulate *space* 201 vb.
cross 222 vb.
reticulation *network* 222 n.
convolution 251 n.
reticule *bag* 194 n.
retiform *reticular* 222 adj.
retina *eye* 438 n.
retinoscope
optical device 442 n.
retinue *retinue* 67 n.
procession 71 n.
band 74 n.
rear 238 n.
follower 284 n.
retainer 742 n.
retire *cease* 145 vb.
be concave 255 vb.

be quiescent 266 vb.
regress 286 vb.
recede 290 vb.
depart 296 vb.
disappear 446 vb.
run away 620 vb.
relinquish 621 vb.
resign 753 vb.
not retain 779 vb.
retired *former* 125 adj.
disused 674 adj.
leisurely 681 adj.
resigning 753 adj.
secluded 833 adj.
retirement *regression* 286 n.
recession 290 n.
relinquishment 621 n.
leisure 681 n.
resignation 753 n.
retiring *modest* 874 adj.
unsociable 883 adj.
retold *repeated* 106 adj.
retort *crucible* 147 n.
reversion 148 n.
interchange 151 n.
vessel 194 n.
vaporizer 338 n.
heater 383 n.
answer 460 n., vb.
testing agent 461 n.
confutation 479 n.
retaliation 714 n.
witticism 839 n.
be insolent 878 vb.
retouch *repair* 656 vb.
retrace *revert* 148 vb.
retrospect 505 vb.
retrace one's steps
repeat oneself 106 vb.
turn back 286 vb.
retract *recant* 603 vb.
abrogate 752 vb.
resign 753 vb.
retractation
non-observance 769 n.
(*see* retract)
retractable *drawing* 288 adj.
retraction *traction* 288 n.
negation 533 n.
recantation 603 n.
retractive *drawing* 288 adj.
retractor *traction* 288 n.
retral *back* 238 adj.
retread *repair* 656 vb.
retreat *decrease* 37 n.
focus 76 n.
reversion 148 n.
go away 190 vb.
retreat 192 n.
be concave 255 vb.
marching 267 n.

regression 286 n.
recession 290 n.
meditation 449 n.
hiding-place 527 n.
call 547 n.
avoidance 620 n.
refuge 662 n.
escape 667 n.
defeat 728 n.
seclusion 883 n.
prayers 901 n.
monastery 986 n.
retrench
(*see* retrenchment)
retrenchment
diminution 37 n.
subtraction 39 n.
shortening 204 n.
restriction 747 n.
economy 814 n.
retrial *legal trial* 959 n.
retribution *retaliation* 714 n.
punishment 963 n.
retrieval *reversion* 148 n.
restoration 656 n.
deliverance 668 n.
acquisition 771 n.
taking 786 n.
retrieve *recoup* 31 vb.
counteract 182 vb.
retrieve 656 vb.
retriever *dog* 365 n.
retro *rearward* 238 adv.
retroaction
reversion 148 n.
counteraction 182 n.
recoil 280 n.
regression 286 n.
retroactive
retrospective 125 adj.
reverted 148 adj.
recoiling 280 adj.
retrocession
reversion 148 n.
regression 286 n.
recession 290 n.
restoration 656 n.
retroflexion *reversion* 148 n.
curvature 248 n.
regression 286 n.
retrograde
regressive 286 adj.
regress 286 vb.
deteriorate 655 vb.
relapse 657 vb.
retrogression
reversion 148 n.
regression 286 n.
deterioration 655 n.
retrospect *look back* 125 vb.
remembrance 505 n.

retrospection
preterition 125 n.
thought 449 n.
remembrance 505 n.
retrospective
retrospective 125 adj.
reverted 148 adj.
regretting 830 adj.
retroussé *short* 204 adj.
curved 248 adj.
retroversion
inversion 221 n.
return *recurrence* 106 n.
be periodic 141 vb.
reversion 148 n.
product 164 n.
inversion 221 n.
recoil 280 n., vb.
turn round 282 vb.
return 286 n.
propel 287 vb.
arrival 295 n.
circuition 314 n.
answer 460 n.
report 525 n.
tergiversation 603 n.
vote 605 n., vb.
reject 607 vb.
benefit 615 n.
relapse 657 n., vb.
retaliate 714 vb.
commission 751 vb.
earnings 771 n.
restitution 787 n.
receipt 807 n.
thanks 907 n.
reward 962 n.
returnable *owed* 803 adj.
returned *chosen* 605 adj.
rejected 607 adj.
returned prodigal
penitent 939 n.
return, in *in return* 31 adv.
return journey
reversion 148 n.
return match
equalization 28 n.
repetition 106 n.
returns *list* 87 n.
record 548 n.
return ticket
reversion 148 n.
reunion *junction* 45 n.
assembly 74 n.
concord 710 n.
social gathering 882 n.
revalidate *restore* 656 vb.
revalorization
restoration 656 n.
revaluation
improvement 654 n.

revamp *modify* 143 vb.
revanchism
revengefulness 910 n.
revanchist *avenger* 910 n.
reveal *manifest* 522 vb.
inform 524 vb.
disclose 526 vb.
publish 528 vb.
indicate 547 vb.
revealed *scriptural* 975 adj.
revelational 975 adj.
revealing
transparent 422 adj.
reveille *call* 547 n.
revel *enjoy* 376 vb.
rejoicing 835 n.
revel 837 n., vb.
celebration 876 n.
sociability 882 n.
intemperance 943 n.
drunkenness 949 n.
revelation
appearance 445 n.
discovery 484 n.
truth 494 n.
inexpectation 508 n.
prediction 511 n.
manifestation 522 n.
disclosure 526 n.
scripture 975 n.
revelation 975 n.
reveller *laugher* 835 n.
reveller 837 n.
revenant *ghost* 970 n.
revendicate
demand 737 vb.
claim 915 vb.
revenge *equalization* 28 n.
retaliation 714 n.
revenge 910 n.
jealousy 911 n.
vindicate 927 vb.
reward 962 n.
punishment 963 n.
revengeful *hating* 888 adj.
resentful 891 adj.
malevolent 898 adj.
pitiless 906 adj.
revengeful 910 adj.
revenue *means* 629 n.
earnings 771 n.
estate 777 n.
receipt 807 n.
reverbatory *furnace* 383 n.
reverberate
be loud 400 vb.
reverberation
repetition 106 n.
recoil 280 n.
roll 403 n.
resonance 404 n.

revere *honour* 866 vb.
love 887 vb.
respect 920 vb.
be pious 979 vb.
worship 981 vb.
reverence *obeisance* 311 n.
respect 920 n., vb.
piety 979 n.
worship 981 n.
reverend
worshipful 866 adj.
title 870 n.
sanctified 979 adj.
cleric 986 n.
reverent *respectful* 920 adj.
pious 979 adj.
worshipping 981 adj.
reverie *thought* 449 n.
abstractedness 456 n.
fantasy 513 n.
reversal *reversion* 148 n.
inversion 221 n.
inexpectation 508 n.
tergiversation 603 n.
abrogation 752 n.
reverse *contrariety* 14 n.
revert 148 vb.
invert 221 vb.
back 238 adj.
contraposition 240 n.
fold 261 n.
retard 278 vb.
turn round 282 vb.
defeat 728 n.
adversity 731 n.
abrogate 752 vb.
loss 772 n.
reverse, in
backwards 286 adv.
reversible
regressive 286 adj.
reversion *return* 286 n.
reversion 148 n.
revolution 149 n.
inversion 221 n.
regression 286 n.
possession 773 n.
dower 777 n.
transfer 780 n.
restitution 787 n.
reversionary
reverted 148 adj.
transferred 780 adj.
reversioner
beneficiary 776 n.
revert *reoccur* 106 vb.
revert 148 vb.
revert to
repeat oneself 106 vb.
notice 455 vb.
change hands 780 vb.

revet *coat* 226 vb.
revetment *facing* 226 n.
revictual *replenish* 633 vb.
review *assemblage* 74 n.
 inspection 438 n.
 spectacle 445 n.
 meditate 449 vb.
 attention 455 n.
 enquiry 459 n.
 estimate 480 n.,vb.
 remembrance 505 n.
 interpretation 520 n.
 journal 528 n.
 reading matter 589 n.
 describe 590 vb.
 article 591 n.
 compendium 592 n.
 rectify 654 vb.
 pageant 875 n.
reviewer *estimator* 480 n.
 interpreter 520 n.
 bookman 589 n.
 dissertator 591 n.
revile *curse* 899 vb.
 dispraise 924 vb.
 exprobate 924 vb.
 be impious 980 vb.
reviler *defamer* 926 n.
revise *modify* 143 vb.
 be attentive 455 vb.
 letterpress 587 n.
 reading matter 589 n.
 plan 623 n.,vb.
 (*see* revision)
reviser *alterer* 143 n.
 author 589 n.
 reformer 654 n.
revision *inspection* 438 n.
 study 536 n.
 amendment 654 n.
revisit *be present* 189 vb.
revitalize *vitalize* 360 vb.
 revive 656 vb.
revival *newness* 126 n.
 strengthening 162 n.
 reproduction 166 n.
 improvement 654 n.
 revival 656 n.
 relief 831 n.
revivalism
 public worship 981 n.
revivalist
 antiquarian 125 n.
 worshipper 981 n.
 pastor 986 n.
revive *augment* 36 vb.
 repeat 106 vb.
 revert 148 vb.
 vitalize 360 vb.
 get healthy 650 vb.
 refresh 685 vb.

animate 821 vb.
 (*see* revival)
reviver *tonic* 658 n.
 refreshment 685 n.
revocable *possible* 469 adj.
revocation
 transference 272 n.
 recantation 603 n.
 abrogation 752 n.
revocatory
 negative 533 adj.
revoke *suppress* 165 vb.
 abrogate 752 vb.
 prohibit 757 vb.
 not retain 779 vb.
revolt *revolution* 149 n.
 be violent 176 vb.
 opposition 704 n.
 resistance 715 n.
 revolt 738 n.,vb.
 displease 827 vb.
 cause discontent 829 vb.
 cause dislike 861 vb.
 fail in duty 918 vb.
 lawlessness 954 n.
revolter *revolter* 738 n.
revolting *not nice* 645 adj.
 unpleasant 827 adj.
 frightening 854 adj.
 disliked 861 adj.
 hateful 888 adj.
revolution *disorder* 61 n.
 regular return 141 n.
 change 143 n.
 reversion 148 n.
 revolution 149 n.
 destruction 165 n.
 outbreak 176 n.
 rotation 315 n.
 revolt 738 n.
revolutionary
 modern 126 adj.
 revolutionist 149 n.
 revolutionary 149 adj.
 violent creature 176 n.
 reformer 654 n.
 revolter 738 n.
revolutionize
 modify 143 vb.
 revolutionize 149 vb.
revolve *be periodic* 141 vb.
 circle 314 vb.
 rotate 315 vb.
 meditate 449 vb.
revolver *pistol* 723 n.
revue *spectacle* 445 n.
 stage show 594 n.
revulsion *reversion* 148 n.
 recoil 280 n.
 tergiversation 603 n.
rev up *accelerate* 277 vb.

reward *incentive* 612 n.
 trophy 729 n.
 acquisition 771 n.
 gift 781 n.
 pay 804 n.,vb.
 honours 866 n.
 thanks 907 n.
 reward 962 vb.
rewarding *gainful* 771 adj.
 rewarding 962 adj.
rewardless
 unthanked 908 adj.
reword *repeat* 106 vb.
 translate 520 vb.
 phrase 563 vb.
rewrite *rectify* 654 vb.
Reynard *slyboots* 698 n.
rhabdology
 mathematics 86 n.
Rhadamanthus
 magistracy 957 n.
 mythic hell 972 n.
rhapsode *poet* 593 n.
rhapsodical *fitful* 142 adj.
 imaginative 513 adj.
rhapsodist *crank* 504 n.
 visionary 513 n.
 poet 593 n.
rhapsodize *be absurd* 497 vb.
rhapsody *discontinuity* 72 n.
 musical piece 412 n.
 absurdity 497 n.
 ideality 513 n.
rhetoric *curriculum* 536 n.
 vigour 571 n.
 ornament 574 n.
 oratory 579 n.
 ostentation 875 n.
rhetorical
 exaggerated 546 adj.
 stylistic 566 adj.
 rhetorical 574 adj.
 eloquent 579 n.
rhetorical figure
 trope 519 n.
rhetorician
 phrasemonger 574 n.
 speaker 579 n.
rheum *excrement* 302 n.
 fluid 335 n.
rheumatic *crippled* 163 adj.
 diseased 657 adj.
rheumatism *pang* 377 n.
 rheumatism 651 n.
rheumatoid
 diseased 651 adj.
rheumy *excretory* 302 adj.
 fluidal 335 adj.
rhinestone *finery* 844 n.
rhinitis
 respiratory disease 651 n.

sport 837 n.
riding-school *arena* 724 n.
rid of *escaped* 667 adj.
 (*see* rid, riddance)
rife *existing* 1 adj.
 rumoured 529 adj.
rife, be *be* 1 vb.
 prevail 178 vb.
rifeness *generality* 79 n.
riff-raff *rabble* 869 n.
rifle *groove* 262 vb.
 fire-arm 723 n.
 steal 788 vb.
rifleman *shooter* 287 n.
 soldiery 722 n.
rifle-range *arena* 724 n.
rifling *furrow* 262 n.
rift *disjunction* 46 n.
 gap 201 n.
 defect 647 n.
 dissension 709 n.
rig *dressing* 228 n.
 carriage 274 n.
 fake 541 vb.
 make ready 669 vb.
rigadoon *dance* 837 n.
rigged *marine* 275 adj.
 false 541 adj.
 prepared 669 adj.
rigged out *dressed* 228 adj.
rigger *trickster* 545 n.
 artisan 686 n.
rigging *tackling* 47 n.
riggish *unchaste* 951 adj.
right *apt* 24 adj.
 dextrality 241 n.
 straight 249 adj.
 true 494 adj.
 accurate 494 adj.
 usual 610 adj.
 expedient 642 adj.
 repair 656 vb.
 political party 708 n.
 estate 777 n.
 right 913 n.
 dueness 915 n.
 probity 929 n.
 virtuous 933 adj.
right about, to the
 backwards 286 adv.
right about turn
 be inverted 221 vb.
right and left
 widely 183 adv.
 around 230 adv.
 sideways 239 adv.
right angle
 verticality 215 n.
 angle 247 n.
right answer
 remedy 658 n.

right arm *power* 160 n.
right ascension
 bearings 186 n.
 uranometry 321 n.
right ascension and
 declension
 co-ordinate 465 n.
right belief
 orthodoxy 976 n.
right, by *duly* 915 adv.
righteous *just* 913 adj.
 virtuous 933 adj.
right form *formality* 875 n.
rightful *right* 913 adj.
 due 915 adj.
right hand *power* 160 n.
 dextrality 241 n.
 auxiliary 707 n.
right-handed
 dextral 241 adj.
right-hand man
 auxiliary 707 n.
 servant 742 n.
 deputy 755 n.
rightist *political party* 708 n.
right itself *equalize* 28 vb.
 cure 656 vb.
right line *line* 203 n.
 straightness 249 n.
rightly served
 retaliatory 714 adj.
right man *fitness* 24 n.
 expert 696 n.
right-minded *wise* 498 adj.
 just 913 adj.
 virtuous 933 adj.
 orthodox 976 adj.
right mind, in one's
 sane 502 adj.
 restored 656 adj.
right mood
 willingness 597 n.
rightness *truth* 494 n.
 right 913 n.
right of way *access* 624 n.
right people
 beau monde 848 n.
Right Reverend
 title 870 n.
 church title 986 n.
rights *freedom* 744 n.
 right 913 n.
right thing *duty* 917 n.
right time *juncture* 8 n.
 clock time 117 n.
 opportunity 137 n.
 occasion 137 n.
 expedience 642 n.
right touch, have the
 be skilful 694 vb.
right-wing *dextral* 241 adj.

right-winger
 political party 708 n.
right wrongs
 be just 913 vb.
rigid *unconformable* 84 adj.
 unyielding 162 adj.
 still 266 adj.
 rigid 326 adj.
 obstinate 602 adj.
 severe 735 adj.
rigidity (*see* rigid)
rigmarole
 unmeaningness 515 n.
 diffuseness 570 n.
rigor *spasm* 318 n.
 coldness 380 n.
 illness 651 n.
rigorism *opiniatry* 602 n.
rigorist *opinionist* 602 n.
 tyrant 735 n.
 disapprover 924 n.
rigorous *severe* 735 adj.
 fastidious 862 adj.
 pitiless 906 adj.
 ascetic 945 n.
rigour *hardness* 326 n.
 accuracy 494 n.
 severity 735 n.
 pitilessness 906 n.
rig out *dress* 228 vb.
Rigsdag *parliament* 692 n.
rig the market
 speculate 791 vb.
Rigveda
 non-Biblical scripture
 975 n.
rile *make unclean* 649 vb.
 enrage 891 vb.
rilievo *rilievo* 254 n.
 ornamental art 844 n.
rill *stream* 350 n.
rim *outline* 233 n.
 edge 234 n.
rime *gap* 201 n.
 wintriness 380 n.
rimer *perforator* 263 n.
rimose, rimous
 spaced 201 adj.
rind *skin* 226 n.
rinderpest
 animal disease 651 n.
ring *fastening* 47 n.
 band 74 n.
 hanger 217 n.
 circumscription 232 n.
 outline 233 n.
 inclosure 235 n.
 circle 250 n.
 orifice 263 n.
 be loud 400 vb.
 roll 403 n.

resonance 404 n.
play music 413 vb.
communicate 524 vb.
message 529 n.
obliterate 550 vb.
association 706 n.
party 708 n.
pugilism 716 n.
arena 724 n.
badge of rule 743 n.
restriction 747 n.
jewellery 844 n.
love-token 889 n.
wedding 894 n.
ring a bell
be remembered 505 vb.
ring a change
play music 413 vb.
ring-bolt fetter 748 n.
ring-dove bird 365 n.
ring down the curtain
terminate 69 vb.
cease 145 vb.
ringed round 250 adj.
ringer substitute 150 n.
impostor 545 n.
ring in initiate 68 vb.
time 117 vb.
ringing resonant 404 adj.
melodious 410 adj.
campanology 412 n.
ringleader motivator 612 n.
leader 690 n.
agitator 738 n.
ringlet loop 250 n.
hair 259 n.
ringmaster leader 690 n.
ring off terminate 69 vb.
cease 145 vb.
be mute 578 vb.
ringside seat
near place 200 n.
view 438 n.
ring the bell
be successful 727 vb.
ring the changes
vary 152 vb.
ring the knell kill 362 vb.
ring true be true 494 vb.
ring up communicate 524 vb.
ringworm
skin disease 651 n.
rink arena 724 n.
pleasure-ground 837 n.
rinse drench 341 vb.
clean 648 vb.
hairwash 843 n.
rinsings dirt 649 n.
riot turmoil 61 n.
multitude 104 n.
abundance 171 n.

violence 176 n.
plenty 635 n.
superabound 637 vb.
quarrel 709 n.
fight 716 n.
revolt 738 n.
rejoice 835 vb.
lawlessness 954 n.
rioter rioter 738 n.
reveller 837 n.
riot in enjoy 376 vb.
riotous violent 176 adj.
anarchic 734 adj.
riotous 738 adj.
excitable 822 adj.
jubilant 833 adj.
intemperate 943 adj.
sensual 944 adj.
lawless 954 adj.
rip rend 46 vb.
open 263 vb.
move fast 277 vb.
wave 350 n.
wound 654 vb.
libertine 952 n.
riparian coastal 344 adj.
ripcord fastening 47 n.
ripe aged 131 adj.
pulpy 356 adj.
perfect 646 adj.
matured 669 adj.
ripe experience
wisdom 498 n.
ripen perfect 646 vb.
get better 654 vb.
mature 669 vb.
carry through 725 vb.
ripeness (see ripe)
ripening future 124 adj.
young 130 adj.
maturation 669 n.
ripen into
be turned to 147 vb.
riper age age 131 n.
rip-hook sharp edge 256 n.
ripieno extra 40 n.
musician 413 n.
riposte impulse 279 n.
answer 460 n., vb.
parry 713 vb.
retaliation 714 n.
rip out extract 304 vb.
ripping topping 644 adj.
ripple shallowness 212 n.
hang 217 vb.
convolution 251 n.
crinkle 251 vb.
furrow 262 n.
agitate 318 vb.
wave 350 n.
sound faint 401 vb.

ripple-bed hospital 658 n.
riproaring loud 400 adj.
gay 833 adj.
Rip van Winkle
old man 133 n.
insensibility 375 n.
rise increase 36 n.
beginning 68 n.
be high 209 vb.
verticality 215 n.
acclivity 220 n.
progression 285 n.
flow out 298 vb.
ascent 308 n.
lift oneself 310 vb.
appear 445 vb.
be duped 544 vb.
flourish 615 vb.
improvement 654 n.
go to war 718 vb.
succeed 727 vb.
prosper 730 vb.
revolt 738 vb.
gain 771 n.
show respect 920 vb.
rise above
be superior 34 vb.
outdo 306 vb.
rise above oneself
be disinterested 931 vb.
rise to the occasion
be superior 34 vb.
improvise 609 vb.
rishi sage 500 n.
religious teacher 973 n.
risibility laughter 835 n.
ridiculousness 849 n.
rising future 124 adj.
aged 131 adj.
powerful 160 adj.
influential 178 adj.
sloping 220 adj.
resistance 715 n.
successful 727 adj.
prosperous 730 adj.
revolt 738 n.
dear 811 adj.
rising generation
youth 130 n.
posterity 170 n.
rising ground
high land 209 n.
acclivity 220 n.
rising man
made man 730 n.
rising sun
person of repute 866 n.
risk gambling 618 n.
possibility 469 n.
danger 661 n.
speculate 791 vb.

risk it *chance* 159 vb.
face danger 661 vb.
risk-taker *gambler* 618 n.
brave person 855 n.
risk-taking
calculation of chance 159 n.
risky *uncertain* 474 adj.
speculative 618 adj.
dangerous 661 adj.
impure 951 adj.
risotto *dish* 301 n.
risqué *vulgar* 847 adj.
disreputable 867 adj.
impure 951 adj.
rite *practice* 610 n.
legality 953 n.
rite 988 n.
ritornello *prelude* 66 n.
repetition 106 n.
ritual *formality* 875 n.
celebration 876 n.
ritual 988 n., adj.
(*see* rite)
ritualism *pietism* 979 n.
ritualism 988 n.
ritualistic *formal* 875 adj.
theological 973 adj.
pietistic 979 adj.
worshipping 981 adj.
devotional 981 adj.
ritualistic 988 adj.
ritual object
church utensil 990 n.
ritzy *rich* 800 adj.
dear 811 adj.
ostentatious 875 adj.
rival *compeer* 28 n.
hinderer 702 n.
opponent 705 n.
quarreller 709 n.
contender 716 n.
enemy 881 n.
(*see* rivalry)
rivalry *imitation* 20 n.
opposition 704 n.
quarrelsomeness 709 n.
contention 716 n.
jealousy 911 n.
envy 912 n.
rive *cut, rend* 46 vb.
river *stream* 350 n.
river-bed *cavity* 255 n.
conduit 351 n.
riverine *marginal* 234 adj.
coastal 344 adj.
riverless *dry* 342 adj.
riverside *edge* 234 n.
marginal 234 adj.
shore 344 n.
coastal 344 adj.

rivet *affix* 45 vb.
fastening 47 n.
riveter *joinder* 45 n.
riviera *shore* 344 n.
pleasure-ground 837 n.
rivulet *stream* 350 n.
rixation *quarrel* 709 n.
anger 891 n.
reproach 924 n.
road *street* 192 n.
transport 272 n.
direction 281 n.
gulf 345 n.
road 624 n.
road agent *robber* 789 n.
road block *obstacle* 702 n.
road-book *itinerary* 267 n.
road-hog *egotist* 932 n.
road-holding ability
equilibrium 28 n.
roadhouse *tavern* 192 n.
road map *itinerary* 267 n.
map 551 n.
road roller
smoother 258 n.
roads *stable* 192 n.
shelter 662 n.
roadside *edge* 234 n.
marginal 234 adj.
accessible 289 adj.
roadstead *station* 187 n.
stable 192 n.
goal 295 n.
gulf 345 n.
shelter 662 n.
roadster *automobile* 274 n.
roadway *road* 624 n.
roadworthy
transferable 272 adj.
roam *wander* 267 vb.
be free 744 vb.
roan *horse* 273 n.
brown 430 adj.
pied 437 adj.
roar *be violent* 176 vb.
be agitated 318 vb.
blow 352 vb.
loudness 400 n.
roll 403 vb.
vociferate 408 vb.
ululate 409 vb.
emphasize 532 vb.
laugh 835 vb.
be angry 891 vb.
threaten 900 vb.
roaring *furious* 176 adj.
roaring trade
prosperity 730 n.
roast *cook* 301 vb.
be hot 379 vb.
heat 381 vb.

ridicule 851 vb.
rob *weaken* 163 vb.
pulpiness 356 n.
take away 786 vb.
rob 788 vb.
impoverish 801 vb.
robber *robber* 789 n.
robbery *stealing* 788 n.
loss of right 916 n.
robe *robe* 228 n.
dress 228 vb.
badge of rule 743 n.
canonicals 989 n.
Robe, the *bar* 958 n.
robin *bird* 365 n.
Robinson Crusoe
solitary 883 n.
robot *image* 551 n.
fatalist 596 n.
instrument 628 n.
machine 630 n.
slave 742 n.
rob Peter to pay Paul
substitute 150 vb.
robust *stalwart* 162 adj.
healthy 650 adj.
roc *rara avis* 84 n.
rochet *vestments* 989 n.
rock *be unequal* 29 vb.
permanence 144 n.
vary 152 vb.
fixture 153 n.
assuage 177 vb.
bring to rest 266 vb.
sweetmeat 301 n.
oscillate 317 vb.
solid body 324 n.
hardness 326 n.
rock 344 n.
sweet 392 n.
refuge 662 n.
pitfall 663 n.
tranquillize 823 vb.
gem 844 n.
pet 889 vb.
rock-bottom *base* 214 n.
basis 218 n.
rock-carving
sculpture 554 n.
rocker *fluctuation* 317 n.
rocket *vigorousness* 174 n.
rocket 276 n.
speeder 277 n.
missile 287 n.
climber 308 n.
signal light 420 n.
signal 547 n.
missile weapon 723 n.
reprimand 924 n.
rocketry
aeronautics 271 n.

rocket 276 n.
  arm 723 n.
rockiness *hardness* 326 n.
rocking chair *seat* 218 n.
  fluctuation 317 n.
rocking-horse
  plaything 837 n.
rock 'n roll *music* 412 n.
  dance 837 n., vb.
rocks, on the
  endangered 661 adj.
  grounded 728 adj.
rocky *unstable* 152 adj.
  weakly 163 adj.
  hard 326 adj.
  territorial 344 adj.
rococo
  school of painting 553 n.
  ornamental 844 adj.
rod *measure* 183 n.
  long measure 203 n.
  support 218 n.
  cylinder 252 n.
  gauge 465 n.
  trainer 537 n.
  incentive 612 n.
  pistol 723 n.
  badge of rule 743 n.
rod and line *chase* 619 n.
rodent *rodent* 365 n.
rodeo *contest* 716 n.
rodomontade
  empty talk 515 n.
  exaggeration 546 n.
  magniloquence 574 n.
  oration 579 n.
  boast 877 n.
roe *fertilizer* 171 n.
  deer 365 n.
roebuck *deer* 365 n.
rogation *request* 761 n.
  prayers 981 n.
rogue *trickster* 545 n.
  ruffian 904 n.
  noxious animal 904 n.
  knave 938 n.
roguery *improbity* 930 n.
  wickedness 934 n.
rogue's gallery *record* 548 n.
rogue's march
  ejection 300 n.
roguish *gay* 833 adj.
  amused 837 adj.
  witty 839 adj.
roister *rampage* 61 vb.
  revel 837 vb.
roisterer *reveller* 837 n.
Roland for an Oliver, a
  retaliation 714 n.
role *acting* 594 n.
  function 622 n.

roll *piece* 53 n.
  bunch 74 n.
  list 87 n.
  make smaller 198 vb.
  strip 208 n.
  flatten 216 vb.
  textile 222 n.
  wrapping 226 n.
  coil 251 n.
  twine 251 vb.
  cylinder 252 n.
  smooth 258 vb.
  go smoothly 258 vb.
  hair 259 n.
  fold 261 vb.
  move 265 vb.
  travel 267 vb.
  aeronautics 271 n.
  tumble 309 vb.
  rotation 315 n.
  fluctuation 317 n.
  flow 350 vb.
  loudness 400 n.
  roll 403 n., vb.
  play music 413 vb.
  call 547 n.
  record 548 n.
  pronunciation 577 n.
  book 589 n.
  surgical dressing 658 n.
  be servile 879 vb.
roll-call *statistics* 86 n.
  nomenclature 561 n.
rolled into one
  conjunct 45 adj.
  one 88 adj.
roller *girdle* 47 n.
  ligature 47 n.
  flattener 216 n.
  wheel 250 n.
  cylinder 252 n.
  smoother 258 n.
  rotator 315 n.
  pulverizer 332 n.
  wave 350 n.
roller-bandage
  ligature 47 n.
rollers *hair-dressing* 843 n.
roller-skate *sled* 274 n.
rollick *be cheerful* 833 vb.
  rejoice 835 vb.
  amuse oneself 837 vb.
rollicking *gay* 833 adj.
roll in *approach* 289 vb.
  irrupt 297 vb.
  enjoy 376 vb.
  abound 635 vb.
  superabound 637 vb.
  be received 782 vb.
rolling *alpine* 209 adj.
  undulatory 251 adj.

rotation 315 n.
  fluctuation 317 n.
  champaign 348 adj.
  moneyed 800 adj.
rolling country
  high land 209 n.
rolling in *full* 54 adj.
rolling-pin
  flattener 216 n.
  cylinder 252 n.
  smoother 258 n.
  rotator 315 n.
rolling-stock *train* 274 n.
rolling stone
  wanderer 268 n.
roll of honour *list* 87 n.
roll on *continue* 108 vb.
  elapse 111 vb.
  go on 146 vb.
  move 265 vb.
roll out *flatten* 216 vb.
roll up *congregate* 74 vb.
  fold 261 vb.
  approach 289 vb.
  converge 293 vb.
  arrive 295 vb.
  rotate 315 vb.
roly-poly *cylinder* 252 n.
  pudding 301 n.
roman *written* 586 adj.
  print-type 587 n.
Roman *popish* 976 adj.
Roman candle
  fireworks 420 n.
Roman Catholicism
  Catholicism 976 n.
romance
  absurdity 497 n.
  ideality 513 n.
  be false 541 vb.
  fable 543 n.
  novel 590 n.
  love affair 887 n.
romancer *visionary* 513 n.
  liar 545 n.
  narrator 590 n.
Roman eagle *flag* 547 n.
Romanesque
  ornamental 844 adj.
Roman holiday
  slaughter 362 n.
Romanism
  Catholicism 976 n.
Roman numerals
  number 85 n.
romantic *visionary* 513 n.
  imaginative 513 adj.
  descriptive 590 adj.
  feeling 818 adj.
  impressible 819 adj.
  excitable 822 adj.

romanticism *fantasy* 513 n.
Romanticism
  school of painting 553 n.
romanticist *visionary* 513 n.
romanticize
  imagine 513 vb.
Romany *wanderer* 268 n.
  slang 560 n.
Rome *focus* 76 n.
Romeo *lover* 887 n.
Romish *parish* 976 adj.
romp *rampage* 61 vb.
  youngster 132 n.
  be cheerful 833 vb.
  revel 837 n.
  caress 889 vb.
rompers *breeches* 228 n.
romping
  light-minded 456 adj.
rompish *amused* 837 adj.
rondeau *verse form* 593 n.
rondo *musical piece* 412 n.
rood *cross* 222 n.
  ritual object 988 n.
rood-screen
  church interior 990 n.
roof *home* 192 n.
  vertex 213 n.
  roof 226 n.
  overlay 226 vb.
  shelter 662 n.
roofless *displaced* 188 adj.
roof-top *vertex* 213 n.
  roof 226 n.
rook *bird* 365 n.
  defraud 788 vb.
  chessman 837 n.
rookery *nest* 192 n.
room *inclusion* 78 n.
  opportunity 137 n.
  room 183 n.
  dwell 192 n.
  chamber 194 n.
  scope 744 n.
roomer *resident* 191 n.
room-mate *chum* 880 n.
rooms *quarters* 192 n.
roomy *spacious* 183 adj.
roorback *calumny* 926 n.
roost *nest* 192 n.
  dwell 192 vb.
  sit down 311 vb.
  sleep 679 vb.
  repose 863 vb.
rooster *poultry* 365 n.
  male animal 372 n.
root *numerical element* 85 n.
  stabilize 153 vb.
  source 156 n.
  place 187 n.
  base 214 n.

tuber 301 n.
plant 366 n.
vociferate 408 vb.
word 559 n.
applaud 923 vb.
root and branch
  completely 54 adv.
  revolutionary 149 adj.
  destructive 165 adj.
rooted *firm-set* 45 adj.
  immemorial 127 adj.
  fixed 153 adj.
  located 187 adj.
  still 266 adj.
  habitual 610 adj.
rooter *cry* 408 n.
rootless *irrelative* 10 adj.
  alone 88 adj.
  transient 114 adj.
  unstable 152 adj.
  displaced 188 adj.
  travelling 267 adj.
root out *destroy* 165 vb.
  eject 300 vb.
  extract 304 vb.
rope *tie* 45 vb.
  cable 47 n.
  line 203 n.
  fibre 208 n.
  safeguard 662 n.
  scope 744 n.
  fetter 748 n.
  jewellery 844 n.
  means of execution 964 n.
rope-dancing *skill* 694 n.
rope of sand
  non-coherence 49 n.
  weak thing 163 n.
ropes *arena* 924 n.
rope's end *scourge* 964 n.
ropes, know the
  be expert 694 vb.
ropeway *railroad* 624 n.
ropework *fibre* 208 n.
ropy *thick* 205 adj.
  fibrous 208 adj.
  dense 324 adj.
  semiliquid 354 adj.
  bad 645 adj.
roquelaure *cloak* 228 n.
rorification
  moistening 341 n.
rosary *prayers* 981 n.
  office-book 988 n.
roscid *humid* 341 adj.
rose *irrigator* 341 n.
  fragrance 396 n.
  redness 431 n.
  heraldry 547 n.
  a beauty 841 n.
roseate *red* 431 adj.

promising 852 adj.
rose-coloured *red* 431 adj.
  promising 852 adj.
rosemary *potherb* 301 n.
rosette *badge* 547 n.
  trimming 844 n.
rose-water *moderator* 177 n.
  scent 396 n.
  flattery 925 n.
rose-window *pattern* 844 n.
  church interior 990 n.
Rosicrucian *occultist* 984 n.
rosin *resin* 357 n.
rosiness (*see* rosy)
roster *list* 87 n.
rostrate *angular* 247 adj.
  curved 248 adj.
rostrum *stand* 218 n.
  prow 237 n.
  protuberance 254 n.
  publicity 528 n.
  rostrum 539 n.
rosy *red* 431 adj.
  healthy 650 adj.
  palmy 730 adj.
  personable 841 adj.
  promising 852 adj.
rot *decay* 51 n.
  absurdity 497 n.
  silly talk 515 n.
  dirt 649 n.
  ulcer 651 n.
  dilapidation 655 n.
  blight 659 n.
rota *list* 87 n.
  regular return 141 n.
Rotarian
  social person 882 n.
rotary *rotary* 315 adj.
rotation *continuity* 71 n.
  regular return 141 n.
  revolution 149 n.
  motion 265 n.
  circuition 314 n.
  rotation 315 n.
rotator *rotator* 315 n.
rote, by
  in memory 505 adv.
rotodyne *aircraft* 276 n.
rotograph
  photography 551 n.
  picture 553 n.
rotor *rotator* 315 n.
rotten *antiquated* 127 adj.
  weakened 163 adj.
  bad 645 adj.
  vicious 934 adj.
  (*see* rot)
rottenness
  unsavouriness 390 n.
rotter *cad* 938 n.

rotund *round* 250 adj.
  rotund 252 adj.
  convex 253 n.
rotunda *pavilion* 192 n.
rouble *coinage* 797 n.
roué *bad man* 938 n.
  libertine 952 n.
rouge *pigment* 425 n.
  red pigment 431 n.
  beautify 841 n.
  cosmetic 843 n.
rouge et noir
  gambling 618 n.
  gambling game 837 n.
rough *non-uniform* 17 adj.
  incomplete 55 adj.
  amorphous 244 adj.
  rough 259 adj.
  unsavoury 390 adj.
  hoarse 407 adj.
  hindering 702 adj.
  oppressive 735 adj.
  graceless 842 adj.
  low fellow 869 n.
  cruel 898 adj.
  ruffian 904 n.
  (*see* roughness)
roughage
  food content 301 n.
rough-and-ready
  useful 640 adj.
  hasty 680 adj.
  bungled 695 adj.
rough-and-tumble
  turmoil 61 n.
  fight 716 n.
rough breathing
  pronunciation 577 n.
rough-cast *facing* 226 n.
  efform 243 vb.
  roughen 259 vb.
  plan 623 n.
rough copy
  undevelopment 670 n.
rough diamond
  amorphism 244 n.
  undevelopment 670 n.
  ingenue 699 n.
  vulgarian 847 n.
  good man 937 n.
rough draft
  incompleteness 55 n.
roughen *roughen* 259 vb.
rough ground
  difficulty 700 n.
rough guess
  conjecture 512 n.
rough-hew *efform* 243 vb.
  prepare 669 vb.
rough-hewn
  incomplete 55 adj.

rough 259 adj.
  immature 670 adj.
rough house *turmoil* 61 n.
  fight 716 n.
roughly *nearly* 200 adv.
roughneck *low fellow* 869 n.
  bad man 938 n.
roughness
  discontinuity 72 n.
  violence 176 n.
  roughness 259 n.
  pungency 388 n.
  unsavouriness 390 n.
  stridor 407 n.
  inelegance 576 n.
  difficulty 700 n.
  painfulness 827 n.
  rudeness 885 n.
  (*see* rough)
rough-rider *rider* 268 n.
  cavalry 722 n.
rough side of one's tongue
  reproach 924 n.
rough sketch
  experiment 461 n.
rough with the smooth
  all 52 n.
roulette *gambling* 618 n.
  gambling game 837 n.
round *uniformity* 16 n.
  degree 27 n.
  whole 52 n.
  continuity 71 n.
  numerical 85 adj.
  recurrence 106 n.
  period 110 n.
  fleshy 195 adj.
  efform 243 vb.
  make curved 248 vb.
  round 250 adj.
  rotund 252 adj.
  unsharpened 257 adj.
  circle 314 vb.
  bang 402 n.
  vocal music 412 n.
  campanology 412 n.
  assertive 532 adj.
  phrase 563 vb.
  habit 610 n.
  business 622 n.
  circuit 626 n., vb.
  pugilism 716 n.
  ammunition 723 n.
roundabout
  exterior 223 adj.
  circumjacent 230 adj.
  circle 250 n.
  deviating 282 adj.
  circuitous 314 adj.
  rotator 315 n.
  prolix 570 adj.

  road 624 n.
  roundabout 626 adj.
  pleasure-ground 837 n.
round barrow *dome* 253 n.
  tomb 364 n.
rounded *low* 210 adj.
  unsharpened 257 adj.
  smooth 258 adj.
  shapely 841 adj.
rounded period
  elegance 575 n.
roundel *circle* 250 n.
  badge 547 n.
rounders *ball game* 837 n.
round-eyed
  wondering 864 adj.
roundhouse *chamber* 194 n.
  lock-up 748 n.
rounding off
  completion 725 n.
roundness *equality* 28 n.
  (*see* round)
round off *equalize* 28 vb.
round on *attack* 712 vb.
  retaliate 714 vb.
  blame 924 vb.
round-robin *report* 524 n.
  request 761 n.
  deprecation 762 n.
round-shouldered
  deformed 246 adj.
roundsman *traveller* 268 n.
  circler 314 n.
  seller 793 n.
round-table conference
  conference 584 n.
round the bend
  crazed 503 adj.
round the clock
  all along 113 adv.
round trip *reversion* 148 n.
  land travel 267 n.
  circuition 314 n.
round up
  bring together 74 vb.
roup *sale* 793 n.
rouse *invigorate* 174 vb.
  incite 612 vb.
  excite 821 vb.
rouse oneself
  be active 678 vb.
rousing *vigorous* 174 adj.
  crying 408 adj.
rout *retinue* 67 n.
  crowd 74 n.
  disperse 75 vb.
  concomitant 89 n.
  multitude 104 n.
  commotion 318 n.
  defeat 728 n., vb.
  revel 837 n.

rabble 869 n.
route *itinerary* 267 n.
  direction 281 n.
  passage 305 n.
  way, route 624 n.
  direct 689 vb.
route-map *itinerary* 267 n.
route-march
  marching 267 n.
routine *uniformity* 16 n.
  order 60 n.
  regularity 81 n.
  recurrence 106 n.
  regular return 141 n.
  practice 610 n.
  business 622 n.
  way 624 n.
  conduct 688 vb.
  formality 875 n.
  ritual 988 n.
roux *sauce* 389 n.
rove *wander* 267 vb.
  stray 282 vb.
rover *wanderer* 268 n.
roving *unstable* 152 adj.
roving commission
  uncertainty 474 n.
roving eye
  unchastity 951 n.
row *turmoil* 61 n.
  series 71 n.
  violence 176 n.
  housing 192 n.
  row (a boat) 269 vb.
  loudness 400 n.
  quarrel 709 n.
  fight 716 vb.
rowan *tree* 366 n.
rowboat *rowboat* 275 n.
rowdiness *loudness* 400 n.
rowdy
  violent creature 176 n.
  violent 176 adj.
  combatant 722 n.
  ill-bred 847 adj.
  ruffian 904 n.
rowel *sharp point* 256 n.
rower *boatman* 270 n.
rowing *aquatics* 269 n.
  traction 288 n.
  sport 837 n.
row in the same boat
  accompany 89 vb.
  co-operate 706 vb.
rowlock *pivot* 218 n.
row of buttons *trifle* 639 n.
royal *supreme* 34 adj.
  sail 275 n.
  ruling 733 adj.
  liberal 813 adj.
  impressive 821 adj.

worshipful 866 adj.
  noble 868 adj.
  proud 871 adj.
  ostentatious 875 adj.
Royal Highness
  sovereign 741 n.
  title 870 n.
royal road *facility* 701 n.
royalty *magistrature* 733 n.
  authority 733 n.
  sovereign 741 n.
  receipt 807 n.
  nobility 868 n.
rub *be contiguous* 202 vb.
  friction 333 n.
  give pain 377 vb.
  touch 378 vb.
  clean 648 vb.
  wound 655 vb.
  difficulty 700 n.
  hindrance 702 n.
  adversity 731 n.
  painfulness 827 n.
rub-a-dub *roll* 403 n.
rubber *elasticity* 328 n.
  friction 333 n.
  silencer 401 n.
  contest 716 n.
rubberneck *traveller* 268 n.
  scan 438 vb.
  spectator 441 n.
  be curious 453 vb.
rubbers *footwear* 228 n.
rubber stamp *assent* 488 n.
rubber-stamp
  conform 83 vb.
  endorse 488 vb.
rubbery *tough* 329 adj.
rubbing *duplicate* 22 n.
rubbing noses
  friendliness 880 n.
rubbish *leavings* 41 n.
  absurdity 497 n.
  silly talk 515 n.
  waste 634 n.
  rubbish 641 n.
  dirt 649 n.
  derelict 779 n.
rubbish-heap
  rubbish 641 n.
  sink 649 n.
rubbishy
  unmeaning 515 adj.
  spurious 542 adj.
  trivial 639 adj.
  profitless 641 adj.
rubble *piece* 53 n.
rub down *smooth* 258 vb.
  pulverize 332 vb.
  groom 369 vb.
rube *ingenue* 699 n.

countryman 869 n.
rubella *infection* 651 n.
rubescence *redness* 431 n.
Rubicon *limit* 236 n.
rubicundity *redness* 431 n.
rubigo *blight* 659 n.
rub in *emphasize* 532 vb.
  make important 638 vb.
rub off *obliterate* 550 vb.
rub off on *cohere* 48 vb.
rub one's eyes
  wonder 864 vb.
rub one's hands
  rejoice 835 vb.
rub out *eject* 300 vb.
  murder 362 vb.
  rub 333 vb.
  obliterate 550 vb.
rubric *redness* 431 n.
  label 547 n.
  precept 693 n.
  office-book 988 n.
  rite 988 n.
rubricate *redden* 431 vb.
  paint 553 vb.
rub shoulders with
  be contiguous 202 vb.
rub the wrong way
  roughen 259 vb.
  make quarrels 709 vb.
rub up *make bright* 417 vb.
ruby *redness* 431 n.
  type size 587 n.
  exceller 644 n.
  gem 844 n.
ruche *fold* 261 n.
ruck *average* 30 n.
  generality 79 n.
  fold 261 vb.
rucksack *bag* 194 n.
ructation *voidance* 300 n.
ruction *turmoil* 61 n.
  fight 716 n.
rudder *poop* 238 n.
  sailing aid 269 n.
  aircraft 276 n.
  tool 630 n.
  directorship 689 n.
rudderless *impotent* 161 adj.
ruddle *red pigment* 431 n.
ruddy *florid* 425 adj.
  red 431 adj.
  healthy 650 adj.
  personable 841 adj.
rude *violent* 176 adj.
  amorphous 244 adj.
  inelegant 576 adj.
  immature 670 adj.
  graceless 842 adj.
  ill-bred 847 adj.
  impertinent 878 adj.

discourteous 885 adj.
disrespectful 921 adj.
rude person
rude person 885 n.
rudiment beginning 68 n.
source 156 n.
rudimental
immature 670 adj.
rudimentary
beginning 68 adj.
exiguous 196 adj.
student-like 538 adj.
rue unsavouriness 390 n.
regret 830 vb.
be penitent 939 vb.
rueful regretting 830 adj.
melancholic 834 adj.
ruff neckwear 228 n.
overmaster 727 vb.
ruffian murderer 362 n.
low fellow 869 n.
ruffian 904 n.
bad man 938 n.
ruffianism
ill-breeding 847 n.
inhumanity 898 n.
lawlessness 954 n.
ruffianly ill-bred 847 adj.
insolent 878 adj.
ruffle jumble 63 vb.
roughen 259 vb.
fold 261 n., vb.
agitate 318 vb.
enrage 891 vb.
rufous red 431 adj.
rug floor-cover 226 n.
coverlet 226 n.
rugged stalwart 162 adj.
amorphous 244 adj.
difficult 700 adj.
graceless 842 adj.
ungracious 885 adj.
ruggedness
non-uniformity 17 n.
roughness 259 n.
rugger ball game 837 n.
rugosity roughness 259 n.
ruin antiquity 125 n.
oldness 127 n.
ruin 165 n.
influence 178 n.
waste 634 vb.
delapidation 655 n.
bane 659 n.
defeat 728 n.
adversity 731 n.
loss 772 n.
impoverish 801 vb.
debauch 951 vb.
ruination ruin 165 n.
dilapidation 655 n.

impairment 655 n.
ruinous destructive 165 adj.
harmful 645 adj.
dilapidated 655 adj.
adverse 731 adj.
ruinous charge
dearness 811 n.
rule prototype 23 n.
order 60 n.
rule 81 n.
prevail 178 vb.
line 203 n.
horizontality 216 n.
judge 480 vb.
creed 485 n.
maxim 496 n.
print-type 587 n.
manage 689 vb.
precept 693 n.
governance 733 n.
command 737 vb.
conditions 766 n.
legislation 953 n.
try a case 959 vb.
rule of three
numerical operation 86 n.
rule of thumb
empiricism 461 n.
intuition 476 n.
rule out exclude 57 vb.
make impossible 470 vb.
ruler gauge 465 n.
club 723 n.
potentate 741 n.
rulership
magistrature 733 n.
rules and regulations
practice 610 n.
right 913 n.
ruling legal trial 959 n.
judgment 480 n.
ruling class master 741 n.
upper class 868 n.
ruling passion
opiniatry 602 n.
affections 817 n.
rum unusual 84 adj.
liquor 301 n.
ridiculous 849 adj.
rumba dance 837 n., vb.
rumble roll 403 vb.
fight 716 n.
rumble seat seat 218 n.
rumbling voidance 300 n.
rumbustious
disorderly 61 adj.
loud 400 adj.
riotous 738 adj.
excitable 822 adj.
ruminant animal 365 adj.
thoughtful 449 adj.

rumination eating 301 n.
meditation 449 n.
rummage search 459 vb.
rummer cup 194 n.
rummy unusual 84 adj.
card game 837 n.
rumour
insubstantial thing 4 n.
topic 452 n.
publish 528 vb.
rumour 529 n.
fable 543 n.
rump remainder 41 n.
buttocks 238 n.
rumple jumble 63 vb.
roughen 259 vb.
fold 261 n., vb.
agitate 318 vb.
rumpus turmoil 61 n.
violence 176 n.
quarrel 709 n.
fight 716 n.
run be disjoined 46 vb.
come unstuck 49 vb.
continuity 71 n.
series 71 n.
discontinuity 72 n.
generality 79 n.
recurrence 106 n.
elapse 111 vb.
continuance 146 n.
motion 265 n.
pedestrianism 267 n.
voyage 269 vb.
move fast 277 vb.
flow out 298 vb.
liquefy 337 vb.
flow 350 vb.
lose colour 426 vb.
habit 610 n.
chase 619 n.
run away 620 vb.
path 624 n.
be active 678 vb.
hasten 680 vb.
deal with 688 vb.
manage 689 vb.
steal 788 vb.
runabout automobile 274 n.
run after pursue 619 vb.
desire 859 vb.
court 889 vb.
run against
counteract 182 vb.
runagate
tergiversator 603 n.
avoider 620 n.
coward 856 n.
run aground fixed 153 adj.
navigate 269 vb.
land 295 vb.

fail 728 vb.
run amok
  lay waste 165 vb.
  be violent 176 vb.
  go mad 503 vb.
  strike at 712 vb.
  be excitable 822 vb.
run at *attack* 712 vb.
  charge 712 vb.
run away *decamp* 296 vb.
  run away 620 vb.
  seek safety 660 vb.
  escape 667 vb.
runaway *wanderer* 268 n.
  speedy 277 adj.
  tergiversator 603 n.
  avoider 620 n.
  escaper 667 n.
  coward 856 n.
run counter
  counteract 182 vb.
  tell against 467 vb.
rundle *circle* 250 n.
  coil 251 n.
run down *decrease* 37 vb.
  cease 145 vb.
  weakened 163 adj.
  approach 289 vb.
  underestimate 483 vb.
  pursue 619 vb.
  make insufficient 636 vb.
  charge 712 vb.
  not respect 921 vb.
  dispraise 924 vb.
rune *lettering* 586 n.
  doggerel 593 n.
  spell 983 n.
run for *steer for* 281 vb.
  offer oneself 759 vb.
rung *degree* 27 n.
  serial place 73 n.
  stand 218 n.
  cylinder 252 n.
  ascent 308 n.
run high *be violent* 176 vb.
runic *literal* 558 adj.
  written 586 adj.
  sorcerous 983 adj.
run in *begin* 68 vb.
run in one's head
  engross 449 vb.
run in pairs
  resemble 18 vb.
run into *collide* 279 vb.
runlet *stream* 350 n.
run low *decrease* 37 vb.
runnel *furrow* 261 n.
  stream 350 n.
  conduit 351 n.
runner *hanger* 217 n.
  pedestrian 268 n.

speeder 277 n.
  conduit 351 n.
  courier 531 n.
  contender 716 n.
  servant 742 n.
  thief 789 n.
runners *sled* 274 n.
runner-up *opponent* 705 n.
  contender 716 n.
running *continuous* 71 adj.
running jump *leap* 312 n.
running knot *ligature* 47 n.
running sore
  outflow 298 n.
  bane 659 n.
  loss 772 n.
  painfulness 827 n.
running track *path* 624 n.
  arena 724 n.
runny
  non-adhesive 49 adj.
  fluidal 335 adj.
  liquefied 337 adj.
run-off *contest* 716 n.
run off *void* 300 vb.
  print 587 vb.
run off with
  take away 786 vb.
run of one's teeth
  no charge 812 n.
run of the mill
  average 30 n.
  generality 79 n.
run on *continuate* 71 vb.
  go on 146 vb.
  progress 285 vb.
  be loquacious 581 vb.
run on savings
  expenditure 806 n.
run, on the
  on the move 265 adv.
  endangered 661 adj.
run out *end* 69 vb.
  cease 145 vb.
  impel 279 vb.
  dismiss, void 300 vb.
  not suffice 636 vb.
run over
  be complete 54 vb.
  collide 279 vb.
run riot *be violent* 176 vb.
  exaggerate 546 vb.
  superabound 637 vb.
  be active 678 vb.
  be excitable 822 vb.
run short *fall short* 307 vb.
runt *animalcule* 196 n.
  dwarf 196 n.
run the gauntlet
  face danger 661 vb.
  defy 711 vb.

run through
  make uniform 16 vb.
  consume 165 vb.
  prevail 178 vb.
  be present 189 vb.
  pierce 263 vb.
  strike 279 vb.
  exude 298 vb.
  waste 634 vb.
  strike at 712 vb.
  expend 806 vb.
  be prodigal 815 vb.
run to *avail of* 673 vb.
  request 761 vb.
run together
  accord 24 vb.
  combine 50 vb.
run to seed *aged* 131 adj.
  waste 634 vb.
run to waste *waste* 634 vb.
runty *dwarfish* 196 adj.
run up an account
  be in debt 803 vb.
run upon, run on
  requirement 627 n.
runway *air travel* 271 n.
run wild *be violent* 176 vb.
rupee *coinage* 797 n.
rupture *disagreement* 25 n.
  separation 46 n.
  rend 46 vb.
  gap 201 n.
  wound 655 n.
  dissension 709 n.
rural *regional* 184 adj.
  provincial 192 adj.
rural economy
  agriculture 370 n.
ruralist *dweller* 191 n.
  solitary 883 n.
Ruritania *fantasy* 513 n.
ruse *trickery* 542 n.
  stratagem 698 n.
rush *rampage* 61 vb.
  crowd 74 n.
  vigorousness 174 n.
  outbreak 176 n.
  spurt 277 n.
  commotion 318 n.
  flow 350 vb.
  plant 366 n.
  torch 420 n.
  trifle 639 n.
  non-preparation 670 n.
  be active 678 vb.
  haste 680 n.
  attack 712 n.
rush at *pursue* 619 vb.
  charge 712 vb.
  be rash 857 vb.
rushed *hasty* 680 adj.

rush hour *crowd* 74 n.
rush in, rush into
　irrupt 297 vb.
　be rash 857 vb.
rush-light *glimmer* 419 n.
　torch 420 n.
rush to conclusions
　prejudge 481 vb.
rusk *cereal* 301 n.
russet *brown* 430 adj.
　red 431 adj.
Russophile
　xenophile 880 n.
rust *decay* 51 n.
　oldness 127 n.
　destroyer 168 n.
　be unproductive 172 vb.
　blunt 257 vb.
　pulverize 332 vb.
　bedim 419 vb.
　red colour 431 n.
　desuetude 611 n.
　dirt 649 n.
　dilapidation 655 n.
　blight 659 n.
　inaction 677 n.
　inactivity 679 n.
　blemish 845 n.
rustic *dweller* 191 n.
　provincial 192 adj.
　agrarian 370 adj.
　ill-bred 847 adj.
　countryman 869 n.
rustication *seclusion* 883 n.
rusticity *ill-breeding* 847 n.
rustiness *bluntness* 257 n.
　stridor 407 n.
　dimness 419 n.
　unskilfulness 695 n.
　　(*see* rust)
rusting *disused* 674 adj.
rustle *sound faint* 401 vb.
　sibilation 406 n.
　hiss 406 vb.
　steal 788 vb.
rustler *thief* 789 n.
rustle up
　make ready 699 vb.
rustproof
　unyielding 162 adj.
rusty *antiquated* 127 adj.
　unsharpened 257 adj.
　strident 407 adj.
　dim 419 adj.
　red 431 adj.
　unhabituated 611 adj.
　clumsy 695 adj.
　　(*see* rust, rustiness)
rusy *cunning* 698 adj.
rut *regularity* 81 n.
　roughness 259 n.

　furrow 262 n.
　habit 610 n.
　libido 859 n.
ruth *pity* 905 n.
ruthless *resolute* 599 adj.
　cruel 898 adj.
　pitiless 906 adj.
ruthlessness
　revengefulness 910 n.
rutilant *luminous* 417 adj.
rutting, ruttish
　desiring 859 adj.
　lecherous 951 adj.
rutty *rough* 259 adj.
　furrowed 262 adj.
rye *cereal* 301 n.
　liquor 301 n.
　corn 366 n.

S

sabbatarian
　ascetic 945 n.
　religionist 979 n.
　ritualist 988 n.
Sabbatarians *sect* 978 n.
sabbath *repose* 683 n.
　holy-day 988 n.
sabbatical *reposeful* 683 adj.
Sabellianism *heresy* 977 n.
sable *skin* 226 n.
　black 428 adj.
　heraldry 547 n.
sabot *footwear* 228 n.
sabotage *derangement* 63 n.
　disable 161 vb.
　destruction 165 n.
　make useless 641 vb.
　impairment 655 n.
　hindrance 702 n.
　revolt 738 n.,vb.
　dutilessness 918 n.
saboteur *destroyer* 168 n.
　hinderer 702 n.
　rioter 738 n.
sabre *kill* 362 vb.
　cavalry 722 n.
　side-arms 723 n.
sabre-rattling
　intimidation 854 n.
　threat 900 n.
sabretache *bag* 194 n.
sabreur *combatant* 722 n.
sabulosity
　pulverulence 332 n.
sac *bladder* 194 n.
saccharine *sweet* 392 n.
saccharometer
　sweetness 392 n.
saccular *capsular* 194 adj.
sacellum *temple* 990 n.

sacerdotal *priestly* 985 adj.
　clerical 986 adj.
sacerdotalism
　ecclesiasticism 985 n.
sachem *potentate* 741 n.
sachet *scent* 396 n.
sack *bag* 194 n.
　dismiss 300 n.
　wine 301 n.
　deposal 752 n.
　spoliation 788 n.
sackbut *horn* 414 n.
sackcloth *textile* 222 n.
　roughness 259 n.
　asceticism 945 n.
sackcloth and ashes
　lamentation 836 n.
　penitence 939 n.
　penance 941 n.
　ritual object 988 n.
sacker *taker* 786 n.
　robber 789 n.
sackful *finite quantity* 26 n.
sacking *textile* 222 n.
　spoliation 788 n.
sacrament *rite* 988 n.
　the sacrament 988 n.
sacramental
　religious 973 adj.
　devotional 981 adj.
　priestly 985 adj.
sacramentalist
　ritualist 988 n.
sacrarium *altar* 990 n.
　holy place 990 n.
sacred *worshipful* 866 adj.
　divine 965 adj.
　religious 973 adj.
　sanctified 979 adj.
　devotional 981 adj.
sacredness *sanctity* 979 n.
sacred season
　holy-day 988 n.
sacred text *scripture* 975 n.
sacred thread
　ritual object 988 n.
sacrificatory
　atoning 941 adj.
　devotional 981 adj.
sacrifice *decrease* 37 n.
　decrement 42 n.
　killing 362 n.
　loser 728 n.
　offer 759 n.
　loss 772 n.
　offering 781 n.
　cheapen 812 vb.
　sufferer 825 n.
　be disinterested 931 vb.
　propitiation 941 n.
　be pious 979 vb.

oblation 981 n.
sacrifice oneself
  be willing 597 vb.
  offer oneself 759 vb.
  be disinterested 931 vb.
sacrificer *giver* 781 n.
  worshipper 981 n.
sacrificial
  destructive 165 adj.
  losing 772 adj.
  giving 781 adj.
  disinterested 831 adj.
  atoning 941 adj.
  devotional 981 adj.
  ritual 988 adj.
sacrificial price
  cheapness 812 n.
sacrilege *impiety* 980 n.
sacrilegious
  disrespectful 921 adj.
  profane 980 adj.
sacring bell *signal* 547 n.
  ritual object 988 n.
sacristan
  church officer 986 n.
sacristy
  church interior 990 n.
sacrosanct
  worshipful 866 adj.
  due 915 adj.
  divine 965 adj.
  sanctified 979 adj.
sad *funereal* 364 adj.
  soft-hued 425 adj.
  black 428 adj.
  grey 429 adj.
  bad 645 adj.
  unhappy 825 adj.
  distressing 827 adj.
  discontented 829 adj.
  melancholic 834 adj.
sadden *hurt* 827 vb.
  sadden 834 vb.
sadder and wiser man
  penitent 939 n.
saddle *affix* 45 vb.
  narrowness 206 n.
  high land 209 n.
  seat 218 n.
  start out 296 vb.
  meat 301 n.
  break in 369 vb.
saddlebag *bag* 194 n.
saddlecloth
  coverlet 226 n.
saddled *prepared* 669 adj.
saddled with, be
  carry 273 vb.
saddle-horse
  saddle-horse 273 n.
saddle with

attribute 158 vb.
  hinder 702 vb.
  impose a duty 917 vb.
  accuse 928 vb.
Sadducees
  non-Christian sect 978 n.
sadhu *pietist* 979 n.
sadism *abnormality* 84 n.
  inhumanity 898 n.
sadist *monster* 938 n.
sadistic *cruel* 898 adj.
  pitiless 906 adj.
sadness *sorrow* 825 n.
  dejection 834 n.
sad work *bungling* 695 n.
safari *land travel* 267 n.
safe *box* 194 n.
  certain 473 adj.
  hiding-place 527 n.
  storage 632 n.
  safe 660 adj.
  treasury 799 n.
  cautious 858 adj.
safe bet *certainty* 473 n.
safe-conduct *opener* 263 n.
  instrument 628 n.
  protection 660 n.
  preservation 666 n.
  permit 756 n.
safe conscience, with a
  innocently 935 adv.
safe-deposit
  hiding-place 527 n.
  storage 632 n.
  treasury 799 n.
safeguard *look after* 457 vb.
  protection 660 n.
  safeguard 662 n.
  preserver 666 n.
  means of escape 667 n.
  obstacle 702 n.
  defence 713 n.
  talisman 983 n.
safeguarded
  conditional 766 adj.
safe hands *protection* 660 n.
safe-keeping
  protection 660 n.
  preservation 666 n.
  defence 713 n.
safety *bicycle* 274 n.
  safety 660 n.
safety belt *safeguard* 662 n.
safety catch *fastening* 47 n.
  safeguard 662 n.
safety first
  cowardice 856 n.
  caution 858 n.
safety harness
  safeguard 662 n.
safety lamp *lamp* 420 n.

safety match *lighter* 385 n.
safety pin *fastening* 47 n.
safety valve
  safeguard 662 n.
  means of escape 667 n.
saffron *condiment* 389 n.
  yellowness 433 n.
sag *be weak* 163 vb.
  hang 217 vb.
  be oblique 220 vb.
  be curved 248 vb.
  descend 309 vb.
  be dejected 834 vb.
saga *narrative* 590 n.
sagacious (*see* sagacity)
sagacity *sagacity* 498 n.
  foresight 510 n.
  skill 694 n.
saga-man *chronicler* 549 n.
  narrator 590 n.
sage *potherb* 301 n.
  green colour 432 n.
  wise 498 adj.
  sage 500 n.
  teacher 537 n.
  bigwig 638 n.
  adviser 691 n.
  proficient 696 n.
sagittal *sharp* 256 adj.
Sagittarius *zodiac* 321 n.
sagittary *rara avis* 84 n.
Sahara *desert* 172 n.
Saharan *dry* 342 adj.
sahib *male* 372 n.
  master 741 n.
  title 870 n.
said *preceding* 64 adj.
  prior 119 adj.
sail *water travel* 269 n.
  swim 269 vb.
  ship, sail 275 n.
  rotator 315 n.
  navy 722 n.
sailboat *sailing-ship* 275 n.
sailer *sailing-ship* 275 n.
sailing *aquatics* 269 n.
sailing master
  navigator 270 n.
sailing-ship *ship* 275 n.
  sailing-ship 275 n.
sail into *fight* 716 vb.
sailor *mariner* 270 n.
  navy man 722 n.
sailorlike, sailorly
  seafaring 269 adj.
  seamanlike 270 adj.
  expert 694 adj.
sain *sanctify* 979 vb.
  perform ritual 988 vb.
saint *benefactor* 903 n.
  good man 937 n.

angel 968 n.
pietist 979 n.
ecclesiasticize 985 vb.
sainted *dead* 361 adj.
pious 979 adj.
sanctified 979 adj.
St. Elmo's fire
fire 379 n.
glow 417 n.
sainthood *sanctity* 979 n.
St. John's Ambulance
doctor 658 n.
saintly *virtuous* 933 adj.
angelic 968 adj.
pious 979 adj.
saint's day
regular return 141 n.
special day 876 n.
holy-day 988 n.
saints, the
church member 976 n.
St. Vitus' dance
spasm 318 n.
Saivites
non-Christian sect 978 n.
sake, for one's own
selfishly 932 adv.
sake of, for the
in aid of 703 adv.
saki *liquor* 301 n.
salaam *obeisance* 311 n.
courteous act 884 n.
respects 920 n.
salacious (*see* salacity)
salacity *unchastity* 951 n.
salad *a mixture* 43 n.
dish 301 n.
salad days *salad days* 130 n.
salamander *rara avis* 84 n.
reptile 365 n.
heater 383 n.
noxious animal 904 n.
salami *meat* 301 n.
price 809 n.
sal-ammoniac
pungency 388 n.
salariat *upper class* 868 n.
salary *incentive* 612 n.
earnings 771 n.
pay 804 n.
receipt 807 n.
reward 962 n.
sale *transfer* 780 n.
sale 793 n.
saleable
not retained 779 adj.
saleable 793 adj.
saleable commodity
merchandise 795 n.
salebrosity
roughness 259 n.

sale price *cheapness* 812 n.
salesman *speaker* 579 n.
motivator 612 n.
seller 793 n.
salesmanship
publicity 528 n.
inducement 612 n.
sale 793 n.
sales talk *inducement* 612 n.
salient *region* 184 n.
overhanging 209 adj.
convex 253 adj.
projection 254 n.
salient 254 adj.
manifest 522 adj.
battleground 724 n.
salient point
chief thing 638 n.
salina *marsh* 347 n.
saline *salty* 388 adj.
saliva *excrement* 302 n.
lubricant 334 n.
fluid 335 n.
moisture 341 n.
salivary *expulsive* 300 adj.
salivation *ejection* 300 n.
excretion 302 n.
moisture 341 n.
sallet *armour* 713 n.
sallow *weakly* 163 adj.
colourless 426 adj.
whitish 427 adj.
yellow 433 adj.
unhealthy 651 adj.
sally *emerge* 298 vb.
attack 712 n., vb.
retaliation 714 n.
witticism 839 n.
sally-port *outlet* 298 n.
fort 713 n.
salmagundi
a mixture 43 n.
salmi *dish* 301 n.
salmon *fish food* 301 n.
table fish 365 n.
redness 431 n.
salon *assembly* 74 n.
chamber 194 n.
beau monde 848 n.
social gathering 882 n.
saloon *tavern* 192 n.
chamber 194 n.
automobile 274 n.
salsuginous *salty* 388 adj.
salt *mariner* 270 n.
pungency 388 n.
salty 388 adj.
season 388 vb.
condiment 389 n.
chief thing 638 n.
preserve 666 vb.

wit 839 n.
saltatory *leaping* 312 adj.
agitated 318 adj.
salt away *store* 632 vb.
salt flat *desert* 172 n.
marsh 347 n.
saltire *cross* 222 n.
heraldry 547 n.
salt-lick *provender* 301 n.
salt of the earth *élite* 644 n.
benefactor 903 n.
good man 937 n.
saltpetre *pungency* 388 n.
explosive 723 n.
salty *seafaring* 269 adj.
salty 388 adj.
forceful 571 adj.
exciting 821 adj.
witty 839 adj.
salubrious *healthy* 650 n.
remedial 658 adj.
salubrity *salubrity* 652 n.
salutary *beneficial* 644 adj.
salubrious 652 adj.
salutation *allocution* 583 n.
courteous act 884 n.
respects 920 n.
salute *notice* 455 vb.
signal 547 vb.
speak to 583 vb.
courteous act 884 n.
congratulation 886 n.
endearment 889 n.
show respect 920 vb.
approve 923 vb.
praise 923 vb.
salvage *restoration* 656 vb.
deliverance 668 n.
price 809 n.
salvager *mender* 656 n.
salvation *restoration* 656 n.
preservation 666 n.
deliverance 668 n.
liberation 746 n.
divine function 965 n.
Salvation Army *sect* 978 n.
salvationism *pietism* 979 n.
salvationist *sectarist* 978 n.
religionist 979 n.
pastor 986 n.
salve *lubricant* 334 n.
unguent 357 n.
balm 658 n.
salver *plate* 194 n.
church utensil 990 n.
salvo *bang* 402 n.
qualification 468 n.
pretext 614 n.
bombardment 712 n.
celebration 876 n.
sal volatile *tonic* 658 n.

Samaritan, Good—sapling

Samaritan, Good
  kind person 897 n.
  benefactor 903 n.
sambo negro 428 n.
samdhi speech sound 398 n.
same (see sameness)
same age
  synchronism 123 n.
same mind consensus 488 n.
sameness identity 13 n.
  uniformity 16 n.
  equivalence 28 n.
  tedium 838 n.
same old round
  recurrence 106 n.
same time
  synchronism 123 n.
samisen harp 414 n.
samite textile 222 n.
samovar cauldron 194 n.
sampan sailing ship 275 n.
sample prototype 23 n.
  part 53 n.
  example 83 n.
  taste 386 vb.
  experiment 461 vb.
  exhibit 522 n.
sampler enquirer 459 n.
  needlework 844 n.
sampling empiricism 461 n.
Samson athlete 162 n.
samurai militarist 722 n.
samvat era 110 n.
sanation sanation 656 n.
sanative salubrious 652 adj.
  restorative 656 adj.
  remedial 658 adj.
sanatorium abode 192 n.
  hygiene 652 n.
  hospital 658 n.
sanbenito tunic 228 n.
  canonicals 989 n.
sanctification (see sanctify)
sanctify dignify 866 vb.
  celebrate 876 vb.
  sanctify 979 vb.
  offer worship 981 vb.
  idolatrize 982 vb.
  ecclesiasticize 985 vb.
sanctimonious
  hypocritical 541 adj.
  affected 850 adj.
  prudish 950 adj.
  pietistic 979 adj.
sanctimony
  false piety 980 n.
sanction assent 488 n.
  endorse 488 vb.
  compulsion 740 n.
  permission 756 n.
  commission 756 vb.

consent 758 n., vb.
  approbation 923 n.
sanctioned
  reputable 866 adj.
  due 915 adj.
sanctions compulsion 740 n.
sanctity virtue 933 n.
  divine attribute 965 n.
  sanctity 979 n.
sanctuary retreat 192 n.
  reception 299 n.
  protection 660 n.
  refuge 662 n.
  holy place 990 n.
  church interior 990 n.
sanctum chamber 194 n.
  refuge 662 n.
  seclusion 883 n.
  holy place 990 n.
sand desert 172 n.
  powder 332 n.
  drier 342 n.
  soil 344 n.
sandal footwear 228 n.
  scent 396 n.
sandbag strike 279 vb.
  kill 362 vb.
  club 723 n.
  scourge 964 n.
sandbank island 349 n.
sand-castle weak thing 163 n.
sand-glass
  timekeeper 117 n.
sandiness (see sandy)
sand-man sleep 679 n.
sandpaper sharpener 256 n.
  smoother 258 n.
  roughness 259 n.
  pulverizer 332 n.
sandstone rock 344 n.
sand-storm storm 176 n.
sandwich
  stratification 207 n.
  put between 231 vb.
  mouthful 301 n.
sandwich-board
  advertisement 528 n.
sandwich-man
  publicizer 528 n.
sandy powdery 332 adj.
  dry 342 adj.
  red 431 adj.
  yellow 433 adj.
sane wise 498 adj.
  sane 502 adj.
sang froid
  moral insensibility 820 n.
  inexcitability 823 n.
Sangrail ritual object 988 n.
sanguinary
  sanguineous 335 adj.

murderous 362 adj.
  bloodshot 431 adj.
sanguine red 431 adj.
  optimistic 482 adj.
  expectant 507 adj.
  hoping 852 adj.
sanhedral
  ecclesiastical 985 adj.
sanhedrim council 692 n.
  synod 985 n.
sanhedrist councillor 692 n.
sanies fluid, blood 335 n.
sanitarian sanitarian 652 n.
sanitary healthy 650 adj.
  salubrious 652 adj.
sanitary engineer
  cleaner 648 n.
sanitary inspector
  sanitarian 652 n.
  doctor 658 n.
sanitary precaution
  prophylactic 658 n.
  protection 660 n.
sanitation cleansing 648 n.
  hygiene 652 n.
  prophylactic 658 n.
  protection 660 n.
sanity sagacity 498 n.
  sanity 502 n.
Sankhya
  philosophy 449 n.
sannyasi ascetic 945 n.
sans-culotte rioter 738 n.
  poor man 801 n.
  low fellow 869 n.
  ruffian 904 n.
sanserif print-type 587 n.
Sanskritist
  antiquarian 125 n.
  linguist 557 n.
Santa Claus giver 781 n.
  good giver 813 n.
  fairy 970 n.
santon monk 986 n.
sap essential part 5 n.
  disable 161 vb.
  weaken 163 vb.
  demolish 165 vb.
  excavation 255 vb.
  descend 309 vb.
  fluid 335 n.
  moisture 341 n.
  semiliquidity 354 n.
  ninny 501 n.
  impair 655 vb.
  besiege 712 vb.
sapidity taste 386 n.
sapience wisdom 498 n.
sapless weak 163 adj.
  dry 342 n.
sapling young plant 132 n.

tree 366n.
saponaceous *fatty* 357adj.
saporific *tasty* 386adj.
sapper *excavator* 255n.
  soldiery 722n.
sapphire *blueness* 435n.
  gem 844n.
sappy *vernal* 128adj.
  young 130adj.
  fluidal 335adj.
  humid 341adj.
  semiliquid 354adj.
  pulpy 356adj.
  foolish 499adj.
sarcasm *wit* 839n.
  ridicule 851n.
  rudeness 885n.
  indignity 921n.
  reproach 924n.
  calumny 926n.
sarcastic *keen* 174adj.
  (*see* sarcasm)
sarcenet *textile* 222n.
sarcoma *swelling* 253n.
sarcophagus *box* 194n.
  interment 364n.
Sardanapalus
  sensualist 944n.
sardine *fish food* 301n.
  table fish 365n.
sardonic *derisive* 851adj.
  disapproving 924adj.
sardonyx *gem* 844n.
sargasso *plant* 366n.
sari *dress* 228n.
  robe 228n.
sarkstone *gem* 844n.
sarong *dress* 228n.
sartorial *dressed* 228adj.
sash *girdle* 47n.
  frame 218n.
  belt 228n.
  loop 250n.
  badge 547n.
  badge of rank 743n.
sash-window
  window 263n.
Sassenach *foreigner* 59n.
Satan *Satan* 969n.
satanic *evil* 616adj.
  cruel 898adj.
  wicked 934adj.
  diabolic 969adj.
Satanism *diabolism* 969n.
  antichristianity 974n.
satchel *bag* 194n.
sate, satiate *fill* 54vb.
  superabound 637vb.
  make insensitive 820vb.
  content 828vb.
  be tedious 838vb.

sate 863vb.
sated *disliking* 861adj.
  sated 863adj.
sateen *textile* 222n.
satellite *concomitant* 89n.
  space-ship 276n.
  follower 284n.
  satellite 321n.
  auxiliary 707n.
  subject 742n.
  dependant 742n.
satellite status
  subjection 745n.
satellite town
  housing 192n.
satellitic *subject* 745adj.
satiety *plenitude* 54n.
  sufficiency 635n.
  superfluity 637n.
  tedium 838n.
  dislike 861n.
  satiety 863n.
satin *textile* 222n.
  smoothness 258n.
satiny *smooth* 258adj.
  textural 331adj.
satire *exaggeration* 546n.
  description 590n.
  doggerel 593n.
  wit 839n.
  satire 851n.
  reproach 924n.
  calumny 926n.
satirical *untrue* 543adj.
  funny 849adj.
  derisive 851adj.
  disrespectful 921adj.
satirist *humorist* 839n.
  disapprover 924n.
  detractor 926n.
satirize (*see* satire)
satisfaction
  sufficiency 635n.
  observance 768n.
  payment 804n.
  enjoyment 824n.
  content 828n.
  atonement 941n.
satisfactory
  sufficient 635adj.
  not bad 644adj.
  contenting 828adj.
satisfy *fill* 54vb.
  answer 460vb.
  demonstrate 478vb.
  convince 485vb.
  suffice 635vb.
  pacify 719vb.
  content 828vb.
satisfying *pleasant* 376adj.
  sufficient 635adj.

satisfy oneself
  be certain 473vb.
satrap *governor* 741n.
saturate *fill* 54vb.
  drench 341vb.
saturation *superfluity* 637n.
  satiety 863n.
saturation point
  plenitude 54n.
Saturnalia *turmoil* 61n.
  festivity 837n.
  sensualism 944n.
Saturnalian
  disorderly 61adj.
Saturnian *foreigner* 59n.
  primal 127adj.
  planetary 321adj.
  innocent 935adj.
Saturnian Age *era* 110n.
  palmy days 730n.
saturnine *serious* 834adj.
  ugly 842adj.
satyagraha *resistance* 715n.
  disobedience 738n.
satyr *libertine* 952n.
  lesser god 967n.
satyriasis *libido* 859n.
satyric play *poem* 593n.
sauce *adjunct* 40n.
  a mixture 43n.
  stimulant 174n.
  dish 301n.
  season 388vb.
  sauce 389n.
  sauciness 878n.
  rudeness 885n.
  scurrility 899n.
sauce-boat *bowl* 194n.
sauce-box
  insolent person 878n.
saucepan *cauldron* 194n.
saucer *plate* 194n.
  cavity 255n.
saucy *defiant* 711adj.
  impertinent 878adj.
  discourteous 885adj.
  disrespectful 921adj.
sauna *ablution* 648n.
saunter *wander* 267vb.
  move slowly 278vb.
saurian *animal* 365n.
sausage *meat* 301n.
sauté *cook* 301vb.
sauve qui peut *fear* 854n.
savage
  violent creature 176n.
  violent 176adj.
  mankind 371n.
  ignorant 491adj.
  ill-treat 645vb.
  wound 655vb.

immature 670 adj.
ingenue 699 n.
attack 712 vb.
severe 735 adj.
excitable 822 adj.
vulgarian 847 n.
courageous 855 adj.
low fellow 869 n.
plebeian 869 adj.
angry 891 adj.
cruel 898 adj.
ruffian 904 n.
monster 938 n.
savageness
unsociability 883 n.
savagery *violence* 176 n.
artlessness 699 n.
inhumanity 898 n.
savanna *plain* 348 n.
savant *scholar* 492 n.
expert 696 n.
save *in deduction* 39 adv.
exclusive of 57 adv.
store 632 vb.
preserve 666 vb.
deliver 668 vb.
not use 674 vb.
liberate 746 vb.
acquire 771 vb.
retain 778 vb.
economize 814 vb.
saved *sanctified* 979 adj.
save labour
have leisure 681 vb.
saving *qualifying* 468 adj.
saving clause
qualification 468 n.
means of escape 667 n.
conditions 766 n.
saving grace *virtues* 933 n.
savings *store* 632 n.
gain 771 n.
economy 814 n.
savings bank *treasury* 799 n.
saviour *preserver* 666 n.
benefactor 903 n.
savoir faire *skill* 694 n.
etiquette 848 n.
savour *taste* 386 n., vb.
appetize 390 vb.
savouriness
savouriness 390 n.
pleasurableness 826 n.
savourless *tasteless* 387 adj.
savour of *resemble* 18 vb.
savoury *dish* 301 n.
tasty 386 adj.
savouriness 390 n.
sweet 392 n.
saw *cut* 46 vb.
tooth 256 n.

notch 260 n.
rasp 407 vb.
discord 411 vb.
maxim 496 n.
sawbones *doctor* 658 n.
sawbuck *paper money* 797 n.
sawder *flatter* 925 vb.
sawdust *leavings* 41 n.
powder 332 n.
saw-edge *roughness* 259 n.
saw-mill *workshop* 687 n.
sawney *foolish* 499 adj.
ninny 501 n.
saw the air
gesticulate 547 vb.
sawyer *artisan* 686 n.
Saxonism *inelegance* 576 n.
saxophone *horn* 414 n.
saxophonist
instrumentalist 413 n.
say *affirm* 532 vb.
speech 579 n.
speak 579 vb.
sayable *permitted* 756 adj.
say after
do likewise 20 vb.
repeat 106 vb.
sayer *speaker* 579 n.
saying *maxim* 496 n.
affirmation 532 n.
phrase 563 n.
say nothing
be taciturn 582 vb.
say of *attribute* 158 vb.
say office
perform ritual 988 vb.
say over *repeat* 106 vb.
say-so *affirmation* 532 n.
command 737 n.
sayyid *aristocrat* 868 n.
sbirro *police* 955 n.
scab *nonconformist* 84 n.
covering 226 n.
overlie 226 vb.
tergiversator 603 n.
cure 656 vb.
revolter 738 n.
hateful object 888 n.
cad 938 n.
scabbard *case* 194 n.
arsenal 723 n.
scabby *layered* 207 adj.
rough 259 adj.
unclean 649 adj.
scab over *join* 45 vb.
cure 656 vb.
scabrous *rough* 259 adj.
impure 951 adj.
scads *great quantity* 32 n.
funds 797 n.
scaffold *structure* 331 n.

means of execution 964 n.
scaffolding *frame* 218 n.
preparation 669 n.
scalable *ascending* 308 adj.
scalar *gradational* 27 adj.
ascending 308 adj.
scalawag, scallywag
bad man 938 n.
scald *burning* 381 n.
wound 655 n.
scalding *hot* 379 adj.
paining 827 adj.
scale *relativeness* 9 n.
degree 27 n.
series 71 n.
counting instrument 86 n.
plate 194 n.
layer 207 n.
covering, skin 226 n.
climb 308 vb.
scales 322 n.
musical note 410 n.
key 410 n.
obfuscation 421 n.
opacity 423 n.
gauge 465 n.
scale down *bate* 37 vb.
render few 105 vb.
scale, in
comparative 27 adj.
scalene *unequal* 29 adj.
scales *scales* 322 n.
gauge 465 n.
scale, to *relatively* 9 adv.
scaliness *stratification* 207 n.
scallop *edging* 234 n.
crinkle 251 vb.
notch 260 n., vb.
fish food 301 n.
cook 301 vb.
scallywag (*see* scalawag)
scalp *head* 213 n.
skin 226 n.
uncover 229 n.
trophy 729 n.
scalpel *sharp edge* 256 n.
scalplock *hair* 259 n.
scaly *layered* 207 adj.
dermal 226 adj.
scamble *rend* 46 vb.
scamp *neglect* 458 vb.
be loth 598 vb.
not complete 726 vb.
bad man 938 n.
scamper *move fast* 277 vb.
scampi *fish food* 301 n.
scamping
negligence 458 n.
scampish *rascally* 930 adj.
scan *scan* 438 vb.
be attentive 455 vb.

enquire 459 vb.
know 490 vb.
poetize 593 vb.
scandal *rumour* 529 n.
 badness 645 n.
 slur 867 n.
 wrong 914 n.
 calumny 926 n.
 false charge 928 n.
 wickedness 934 n.
scandalize *displease* 827 vb.
 cause dislike 861 vb.
 be wonderful 864 vb.
 shame 867 vb.
 incur blame 924 vb.
 defame 926 vb.
scandalized
 disapproving 924 adj.
scandalizing
 heinous 934 adj.
scandal-monger
 newsmonger 529 n.
 defamer 926 n.
scandalous *bad* 645 adj.
 discreditable 867 adj.
 wrong 914 adj.
 detracting 926 adj.
 heinous 934 adj.
scandent *ascending* 308 adj.
scansion *prosody* 593 n.
scansorial
 ascending 308 adj.
scant *shorten* 204 vb.
 make insufficient 636 vb.
 restrained 747 adj.
 (*see* scanty)
scanties *underwear* 228 n.
scantiness *scarcity* 636 n.
 (*see* scanty)
scantling *prototype* 23 n.
 small quantity 33 n.
 size 195 n.
scanty *small* 33 adj.
 incomplete 55 adj.
 few 105 adj.
 exiguous 196 adj.
 short 204 adj.
 fasting 946 adj.
scapegoat *substitute* 150 n.
 unlucky person 731 n.
 deputy 755 n.
 sufferer 825 n.
 propitiation 941 n.
 oblation 981 n.
scapegrace
 desperado 857 n.
 bad man 938 n.
scapular *canonicals* 989 n.
scar *high land* 209 n.
 rock 344 n.
 identification 547 n.

mark 547 vb.
trace 548 n.
wound 655 n.
trophy 729 n.
blemish 845 n., vb.
scarab *talisman* 983 n.
scaramouch *bad man* 938 n.
scarce *infrequent* 140 adj.
 unproductive 172 adj.
 deficient 307 adj.
 scarce 636 adj.
 of price 811 adj.
scarcely *slightly* 33 adv.
scarcity *scarcity* 636 n.
 poverty 801 n.
 dearness 811 n.
 (*see* scarce)
scare *false alarm* 665 n.
 fear 854 n.
 frighten 854 vb.
scarecrow *thinness* 206 n.
 sham 542 n.
 image 551 n.
 false alarm 665 n.
 eyesore 842 n.
 intimidation 854 n.
scaremonger *alarmist* 854 n.
 coward 856 n.
scarf *wrapping* 226 n.
 shawl 228 n.
 neckwear 228 n.
 vestments 989 n.
scarf-skin *skin* 226 n.
scarify *cut* 46 vb.
 notch 260 vb.
 rub 333 vb.
 wound 655 vb.
scarlatina *infection* 651 n.
scarlet *red colour* 431 n.
 heinous 934 adj.
 unchaste 951 adj.
scarlet fever *infection* 651 n.
scarlet runner
 vegetables 301 n.
scarlet woman
 loose woman 952 n.
Scarlet Woman
 Catholicism 976 n.
scarp *acclivity* 220 n.
 fortification 713 n.
scars *trophy* 729 n.
scathe *harm* 645 vb.
 impairment 655 n.
scatheless
 undamaged 646 adj.
scathing *paining* 827 adj.
scatogological
 impure 951 adj.
scatology
 uncleanness 649 n.
scatter *disjoin* 46 vb.

be disordered 61 vb.
jumble 63 vb.
dispersion 75 n.
displace 188 vb.
diverge 294 vb.
let fall 311 vb.
disappear 446 vb.
waste 634 vb.
defeat 727 vb.
scatter-brained
 light-minded 456 adj.
 foolish 499 adj.
 crazed 503 adj.
scatterbrains *fool* 501 n.
scattered *few* 105 adj.
scattering
 non-coherence 49 n.
 reflection 417 n.
 (*see* scatter)
scatty *foolish* 499 adj.
 crazed 503 adj.
scavenger *cleaner* 648 n.
 dirty person 649 n.
scazon *verse form* 593 n.
scenario *cinema* 445 n.
 reading matter 589 n.
 narrative 590 n.
 stage play 594 n.
scene *circumjacence* 230 n.
 view 438 n.
 visibility 443 n.
 spectacle 445 n.
 exhibit 522 n.
 art subject 553 n.
 stage-set 594 n.
 arena 724 n.
 excitable state 822 n.
 pageant 875 n.
scene-painter *artist* 556 n.
 stage-hand 594 n.
scenery *beauty* 841 n.
 (*see* scene)
scene-shifter
 stage-hand 594 n.
scenic *painted* 553 adj.
 dramatic 594 adj.
 impressive 821 adj.
 pleasurable 826 adj.
 beautiful 841 adj.
 ornamental 844 adj.
 showy 875 adj.
scenic railway
 pleasure-ground 837 n.
scenograph *map* 551 n.
scent *emit* 300 vb.
 odour 394 n.
 smell 394 vb.
 scent 396 n.
 detect 484 vb.
 knowledge 490 n.
 foresee 510 vb.

indication 547 n.
trace 548 n.
cosmetic 843 n.
scent-bottle *scent* 396 n.
scented darling *fop* 848 n.
scentless
 odourless 395 adj.
scent, off the
 mistaken 495 adj.
scent oneself *primp* 843 vb.
scent, on the
 discovering 484 adj.
 pursuing 619 adj.
sceptic *unbeliever* 486 n.
 irreligionist 974 n.
sceptical *doubting* 474 adj.
 unbelieving 486 adj.
 dissenting 489 adj.
scepticism
 philosophy 449 n.
 doubt 486 n.
 irreligion 974 n.
sceptre *regalia* 743 n.
schadenfreude *joy* 824 n.
schedule *list* 87 n., vb.
 plan 623 vb.
schematic *orderly* 60 adj.
 arranged 62 adj.
 planned 623 adj.
schematize *regularize* 62 vb.
 plan 623 vb.
scheme *prototype* 23 n.
 arrangement 62 n.
 plan 623 n.
 plot 623 vb.
 preparation 669 n.
 be cunning 698 vb.
schemer *slyboots* 698 n.
scheming *perfidious* 930 adj.
 dishonest 930 adj.
 (*see* scheme)
scherzo *musical piece* 412 n.
schiltron *formation* 722 n.
schism *dissension* 709 n.
 revolt 738 n.
 schism 978 n.
schismatic
 dissentient 489 n.
 dissenting 489 adj.
 quarrelling 709 adj.
 schismatic 978 n.
schismatical
 independent 744 adj.
 schismatical 978 adj.
schismatize
 schismatize 978 vb.
schist *rock* 344 n.
schistosity
 stratification 207 n.
schistous *layered* 207 adj.
schizoid *insane* 503 adj.

madman 504 n.
schizophrenia
 psychopathy 503 n.
schizophrenic
 multiform 82 adj.
 insane 503 adj.
schnapps *liquor* 301 n.
schnorrer *beggar* 763 n.
scholar *scholar* 492 n.
 learner 538 n.
 proficient 696 n.
scholarly *instructed* 490 adj.
 educational 534 adj.
 studious 536 adj.
 studentlike 538 adj.
scholarship
 erudition 490 n.
 learning 536 n.
 subvention 703 n.
 reward 962 n.
scholastic *reasoner* 475 n.
 intellectual 492 n.
 educational 534 adj.
 theologian 973 n.
scholasticism
 philosophy 449 n.
 theology 973 n.
scholiast *interpreter* 520 n.
scholium *maxim* 496 n.
 commentary 520 n.
school *group* 74 n.
 philosophy 449 n.
 creed 485 n.
 educate, train 534 vb.
 school 539 n.
schoolbook
 classroom 539 n.
 textbook 589 n.
schoolboy *youngster* 132 n.
 learner 538 n.
schooled
 instructed 490 adj.
schoolfellow *chum* 880 n.
schoolgirl *youngster* 132 n.
 learner 538 n.
schoolgoer *learner* 538 n.
schooling *teaching* 534 n.
schoolman *reasoner* 475 n.
 intellectual 492 n.
 theologian 973 n.
schoolmaster, school-
 mistress
 teacher 537 n.
school of painting
 school of painting 553 n.
schoolroom
 chamber 194 n.
 classroom 539 n.
schooner
 sailing-ship 275 n.
schottische

musical piece 412 n.
schrecklichkeit
 terror tactics 712 n.
sciamachy *foolery* 497 n.
sciatica *pang* 377 n.
science *physics* 319 n.
 philosophy 449 n.
 science 490 n.
 skill 694 n.
scientific *accurate* 494 adj.
 educational 534 adj.
 well-made 694 adj.
 expert 694 adj.
scientist *intellectual* 492 n.
scimitar *sharp edge* 256 n.
 side-arms 723 n.
scintilla *small quantity* 33 n.
 luminary 420 n.
scintillate *shine* 417 vb.
 be wise 498 vb.
 be witty 839 vb.
scintillation *flash* 417 n.
sciolism *erudition* 490 n.
 sciolism 491 n.
sciolist *sciolist* 493 n.
scion *branch* 53 n.
 young plant 132 n.
 descendant 170 n.
 tree 366 n.
sciosophy *occultism* 984 n.
scissile *severable* 46 adj.
 brittle 330 adj.
scission *scission* 46 n.
scissors *cross* 222 n.
 sharp edge 256 n.
sclerosis *hardening* 326 n.
scobs *powder* 332 n.
scoff *food* 301 n.
 ridicule 851 n., vb.
 not respect 921 vb.
 contempt 922 n.
 detract 926 vb.
scoff at *disbelieve* 486 vb.
scoffer *unbeliever* 486 n.
 humorist 839 n.
 detractor 926 n.
scold *violent creature* 176 n.
 quarreller 709 n.
 bicker 709 vb.
 shrew 892 n.
 cuss 899 vb.
 exprobate 924 vb.
scolding *irascible* 892 adj.
 reprimand 924 n.
scold's bridle *pillory* 964 n.
scoliosis *obliquity* 220 n.
scollop *edging* 234 n.
 coil 251 n.
 notch 260 n.
 fish food 301 n.
sconce *head* 213 n.

lamp 420 n.
  penalty 963 n.
scone *pastry* 301 n.
scoop *ladle* 194 n.
  make concave 255 vb.
  extractor 304 n.
  information 524 n.
  news 529 n.
  acquisition 771 n.
scoot *move fast* 277 vb.
  run away 620 vb.
scooter *bicycle* 274 n.
scope *opportunity* 137 n.
  influence 178 n.
  range 183 n.
  meaning 514 n.
  function 622 n.
  facility 701 n.
  scope 744 n.
scopophilia *curiosity* 453 n.
  impurity 951 n.
scorbutic *unclean* 649 adj.
scorch *move fast* 277 vb.
  dry 342 vb.
  be hot 379 vb.
  burn 381 vb.
  impair 655 vb.
  wage war 718 vb.
scorched earth
  havoc 165 n.
scorcher *speeder* 277 n.
  heat 379 n.
  a beauty 841 n.
score *degree* 27 n.
  cut, rend 46 vb.
  composition 56 n.
  arrangement 62 n.
  numerical result 85 n.
  numeration 86 n.
  list 87 n., vb.
  over five 99 n.
  groove 262 vb.
  notation 410 n.
  music 412 n.
  compose music 413 vb.
  mark 547 vb.
  register 548 vb.
  obliterate 550 vb.
  wound 655 vb.
  triumph 727 vb.
  credit 802 n.
  accounts 808 n.
score-board, score-sheet
  record 548 n.
score off
  be superior 34 vb.
  confute 479 vb.
  humiliate 872 vb.
score of, on the
  concerning 9 adv.
scores *multitude* 104 n.

scoria *leavings* 41 n.
  ash 381 n.
  dirt 649 n.
scorify *heat* 381 vb.
scoring stroke
  success 727 n.
scorn
  underestimate 483 vb.
  unbelief 486 n.
  reject 607 vb.
  shame 867 vb.
  scurrility 899 n.
  disrespect 921 n.
  contempt 922 n.
  detraction 926 n.
scorner *unbeliever* 486 n.
  impious person 980 n.
scornful (*see* scorn)
scorpion
  noxious animal 904 n.
Scorpius, Scorpio
  zodiac 321 n.
scot *tax* 809 n.
scotch *disable* 161 vb.
  notch 260 n.
  liquor 301 n.
  wound 655 vb.
  hinder 702 vb.
scotch mist
  moisture 341 n.
scotch-tape *adhesive* 47 n.
scot-free *escaped* 667 adj.
  free 744 adj.
  uncharged 812 adj.
  non-liable 919 adj.
Scotland Yard
  police 955 n.
scotoma *dim sight* 440 n.
Scotticism *dialect* 560 n.
scoundrel *cad* 938 n.
scoundrelism
  improbity 930 n.
scour *traverse* 267 vb.
  move fast 277 vb.
  pass 305 vb.
  rub 333 vb.
  search 459 vb.
  clean 648 vb.
scourge *plague* 651 n.
  bane 659 n.
  adversity 731 n.
  oppress 735 vb.
  ruffian 904 n.
  dispraise 924 vb.
  flog 963 vb.
  scourge 964 n.
scourge oneself
  do penance 941 vb.
scourings *leavings* 41 n.
  rubbish 641 n.
  dirt 649 n.

scout *precursor* 66 n.
  traverse 267 vb.
  scan 438 vb.
  spectator 441 n.
  watch 441 vb.
  enquirer 459 n.
  reject 607 vb.
  warner 664 n.
  domestic 742 n.
  despise 922 vb.
scout signs
  symbology 547 n.
scowl *distort* 246 vb.
  look 438 n.
  gesture 547 n.
  discontent 829 n.
  rudeness 885 n.
  hatred 888 n.
  hate 888 vb.
  anger 891 n.
  sullenness 893 n.
scowling *serious* 834 adj.
scrabble
  make concave 255 vb.
  search 459 vb.
  take 786 vb.
  indoor game 837 n.
scrag, scrag-end
  remainder 41 n.
  meat 301 n.
scraggy *exiguous* 196 adj.
  lean 209 adj.
scram *decamp* 296 vb.
  run away 620 vb.
scramble *confusion* 61 n.
  bedevil 63 vb.
  cook 301 vb.
  climb 308 vb.
  activity 678 n.
  haste 680 n.
  fight 716 n.
scramble for
  take 786 vb.
scrap *insubstantiality* 4 n.
  small thing 33 n.
  piece 53 n.
  reject 607 vb.
  disuse 674 vb.
  fight 716 n., vb.
  battle 718 n.
scrap-album
  anthology 592 n.
scrap-book
  reminder 505 n.
  record 548 n.
scrape *bate* 37 vb.
  subtract 39 vb.
  make smaller 198 vb.
  be contiguous 202 vb.
  uncover 229 vb.
  blunt 257 vb.

stoop 311 vb.
pulverize 332 vb.
rub 333 vb.
touch 378 vb.
rasp 407 vb.
discord 411 vb.
play music 413 vb.
foolery 497 n.
engrave 555 vb.
clean 648 vb.
predicament 700 n.
economize 814 vb.
be parsimonious 816 vb.
be servile 879 vb.
show respect 920 vb.
vice 934 n.
guilty act 936 n.
scrape acquaintance
befriend 880 vb.
be sociable 882 vb.
scrape home *win* 727 vb.
scraper *sharp edge* 256 n.
cleaning utensil 648 n.
niggard 816 n.
scrape through
pass 305 vb.
scrape together
bring together 74 vb.
scrapings *leavings* 41 n.
scrap of paper
ineffectuality 161 n.
unreliability 474 n.
perfidy 930 n.
scrappy
fragmentary 53 adj.
incomplete 55 adj.
scraps *leavings* 41 n.
rubbish 641 n.
scratch *inferior* 35 adj.
cut, rend 46 vb.
be violent 176 vb.
shallowness 212 n.
make concave 255 vb.
be rough 259 vb.
groove 262 vb.
strike 279 vb.
friction 333 n.
touch, itch 378 vb.
faintness 401 n.
rasp 407 vb.
trace 548 n.
misrepresentation 552 n.
write 586 vb.
tergiversate 603 vb.
relinquish 621 vb.
trifle 639 n.
imperfect 647 adj.
wound 655 n., vb.
unprepared 670 adj.
unskilled 695 adj.
fight 716 vb.

resign 753 vb.
be excitable 822 vb.
blemish 845 n.
scratchiness
formication 378 n.
scratch one's back
flatter 925 vb.
scratch out
obliterate 550 vb.
scratchy *agitated* 318 adj.
strident 407 adj.
irascible 892 adj.
scrawl *unintelligibility* 517 n.
script 586 n.
scrawler *penman* 586 n.
scrawny *lean* 206 adj.
scream *feel pain* 377 vb.
loudness 400 n.
cry 408 n., vb.
proclaim 528 vb.
weep 836 vb.
screamer *mistake* 495 n.
absurdity 497 n.
advertisement 528 n.
screaming
whopping 32 adj.
loud 400 adj.
florid 425 adj.
vulgar 847 adj.
scree *piece* 53 n.
acclivity 220 n.
thing transferred 272 n.
screech *stridor* 407 n.
rasp 407 vb.
cry 408 vb.
ululation 409 vb.
screed *oration* 579 n.
script 586 n.
dissertation 591 n.
screen *separation* 46 n.
exclusion 57 n.
canopy 226 n.
partition 231 n.
porosity 263 n.
stopper 264 n.
screen 421 n., vb.
opacity 423 n.
blind 439 vb.
cinema 445 n.
concealment 525 n.
disguise 527 n.
pretext 614 n.
cleaning utensil 648 n.
purify 648 vb.
safeguard 660 vb.
defence 713 n.
screened *dark* 418 adj.
invisible 444 adj.
latent 523 adj.
safe 660 adj.
secluded 883 adj.

screw *affix* 47 vb.
fastening 45 n.
distort 246 vb.
coil 251 n.
propeller 269 n.
saddle-horse 273 n.
deflect 282 vb.
propellant 287 n.
rotator 315 n.
earnings 771 n.
be parsimonious 816 vb.
niggard 816 n.
be parsimonious 816 vb.
screwball *madman* 504 n.
crank 504 n.
laughing-stock 851 n.
screwdriver
extractor 304 n.
tool 630 n.
screw loose
eccentricity 503 n.
screw-thread *coil* 251 n.
screw up *tighten* 45 vb.
strengthen 162 vb.
make ready 669 vb.
screwy *crazed* 503 adj.
scribal *instructed* 490 adj.
scribble
unmeaningness 515 n.
unintelligibility 517 n.
mark 547 vb.
lettering 586 n.
scribbler *penman* 586 n.
author 589 n.
scribe *imitator* 20 n.
recorder 549 n.
penman 586 n.
write 586 vb.
theologian 973 n.
religionist 979 n.
scrim *bookbinding* 589 n.
scrimmage *quarrel* 709 n.
fight 716 n., vb.
scrimp *shorten* 204 vb.
underfed 636 adj.
niggard 816 n.
scrimshanker
avoider 620 n.
scrimshaw *sculpture* 554 n.
scriniary *recorder* 549 n.
scrip *bag* 194 n.
title-deed 767 n.
paper money 797 n.
script *script* 586 n.
lettering 586 n.
reading matter 589 n.
stage play 594 n.
scriptorium *chamber* 194 n.
stationery 586 n.
scriptural *evidential* 466 adj.
scriptural 975 adj.
orthodox 976 adj.

scripturalist
  theologian 973 n.
scripturality
  orthodoxy 976 n.
scripture *credential* 466 n.
  scripture 975 n.
script-writer *penman* 586 n.
  author 589 n.
  dramatist 594 n.
scrivener *penman* 586 n.
  notary 958 n.
scrofulous *unclean* 649 adj.
  impure 951 adj.
scroll *list* 87 n.
  coil 251 n.
  rotate 315 vb.
  lettering 586 n.
scroll-work *pattern* 844 n.
Scrooge *niggard* 816 n.
scrotum *genitalia* 164 n.
scrounge *beg* 761 vb.
  take 786 vb.
  steal 788 vb.
scrub *lean* 206 adj.
  rub 333 vb.
  wood 366 n.
  clean 648 vb.
scrubber *cleaner* 648 n.
scrubbing-brush
  roughness 159 n.
  cleaning utensil 648 n.
scrubby *exiguous* 196 adj.
  arboreal 366 adj.
  rascally 930 adj.
scruff *rear* 238 n.
scruffy
  unimportant 639 adj.
  not nice 645 adj.
  unclean 649 adj.
  beggarly 801 adj.
  disreputable 867 adj.
scrum *crowd* 74 n.
  fight 716 n.
scrumptious
  topping 644 adj.
scrunch *rend* 46 vb.
  chew 301 vb.
  pulverize 332 vb.
  rasp 407 vb.
scruple *small quantity* 33 n.
  weighment 322 n.
  doubt 486 n., vb.
  dissent 489 vb.
  unwillingness 598 n.
scrupulosity *doubt* 486 n.
  pietism 979 n.
scrupulous *careful* 457 adj.
  accurate 494 adj.
  fastidious 862 adj.
  trustworthy 929 adj.
  honourable 929 adj.

scrutator *spectator* 441 n.
scrutineer *enquirer* 459 n.
scrutinize *scan* 438 vb.
  (*see* scrutiny)
scrutiny *attention* 455 n.
  enquiry 459 n.
scud *navigate* 269 vb.
  move fast 277 vb.
  cloud 355 n.
scuff *move slowly* 278 vb.
scuffle *fight* 716 n., vb.
scull *propeller* 269 n.
  row 269 vb.
sculler *boatman* 270 n.
  rowboat 275 n.
scullery *chamber* 194 n.
scullion *cleaner* 648 n.
  domestic 742 n.
sculpt *produce* 164 vb.
  efform 243 vb.
  sculpt 554 vb.
sculptor *sculptor* 556 n.
sculpture *sculpture* 554 n.
scum *leavings* 41 n.
  layer 207 n.
  bubble 355 n., vb.
  rubbish 641 n.
  purify 648 vb.
  dirt 649 n.
  rabble 869 n.
scumble *coat* 226 vb.
  make opaque 423 vb.
  colour 425 vb.
  paint 553 vb.
scummy *dirty* 649 adj.
scupper *suppress* 165 vb.
  drain 351 n.
  slaughter 362 vb.
scurf *leavings* 41 n.
  dirt 649 n.
scurfy *unclean* 649 adj.
scurrility *scurrility* 899 n.
  (*see* scurrilous)
scurrilous
  quarrelling 709 adj.
  insolent 878 adj.
  maledicent 899 adj.
  disrespectful 921 adj.
  disapproving 924 adj.
  detracting 926 adj.
scurry *move fast* 277 vb.
  be busy 678 vb.
  hasten 680 vb.
scurvy *underfed* 636 adj.
  disease 651 n.
  rascally 930 adj.
scut *rear* 238 n.
scutage *quid pro quo* 150 n.
  tax 809 n.
scutcheon (*see* escutcheon)
scutellum *cavity* 255 n.

scuttle *suppress* 165 vb.
  vessel 194 n.
  pierce 263 vb.
  move fast 277 vb.
  plunge 313 vb.
  run away 620 vb.
  haste 680 n.
  be cowardly 856 vb.
  fail in duty 918 vb.
scythe *cut* 46 vb.
  sharp edge 256 n.
  farm tool 370 n.
sea *ocean* 343 n.
  wave 350 n.
  blueness 435 n.
sea-air *salubrity* 652 n.
sea, at *at sea* 343 adv.
  doubting 474 adj.
  mistaken 495 adj.
seaboard *shore* 344 n.
sea-chest *box* 194 n.
sea-dog *mariner* 270 n.
  expert 696 n.
seafarer *mariner* 270 n.
seafaring
  water travel 269 n.
  seafaring 269 adj.
  marine 275 adj.
sea-god *sea-god* 343 n.
sea-going *seafaring* 269 adj.
  marine 275 adj.
  oceanic 343 adj.
sea-king *mariner* 270 n.
seal *mould* 23 n.
  close 264 vb.
  fish 365 n.
  credential 466 n.
  make certain 473 vb.
  endorse 488 vb.
  label 547 n.
  carry through 725 vb.
  badge of rule 743 n.
  compact 765 n.
  give security 767 vb.
sea-lawyer *reasoner* 475 n.
sealed book
  unknown thing 491 n.
  unintelligibility 517 n.
  secret 530 n.
sealed off *sealed off* 264 adj.
sealed orders *secret* 530 n.
sea-legs *equilibrium* 28 n.
sealer *fishing-boat* 275 n.
sealing-wax *adhesive* 47 n.
sea-lord *naval officer* 741 n.
sealskin *skin* 226 n.
seal up *conceal* 525 vb.
  imprison 747 vb.
seam *joint* 45 n.
  dividing line 92 n.
  gap 201 n.

layer 207 n.
seaman *mariner* 270 n.
seamanlike
  seamanlike 270 adj.
  expert 694 adj.
seamanship
  navigation 268 n.
  tactics 688 n.
  skill 694 n.
  art of war 718 n.
sea-mark *limit* 236 n.
  sailing aid 269 n.
  signpost 547 n.
seamless *whole* 52 adj.
seamstress *clothier* 228 n.
séance *manifestation* 522 n.
  council 692 n.
  spiritualism 984 n.
sea-nymph *sea-nymph* 343 n.
  mythical being 970 n.
sea-power *navy* 722 n.
  authority 733 n.
sear *dry* 342 vb.
  heat 381 vb.
  make insensitive 820 vb.
  blemish 845 n.
search *search* 459 n., vb.
  pursuit 619 n.
  undertaking 672 n.
searcher *inquisitor* 453 n.
  enquirer 459 n.
  hunter 619 n.
searching
  inquisitive 453 adj.
  oppressive 735 adj.
  paining 827 adj.
searchlight
  radiation 417 n.
  lamp 420 n.
search-party *search* 459 n.
  hunter 619 n.
search-warrant *search* 459 n.
  legal process 959 n.
sea-room *room* 183 n.
  scope 744 n.
seascape *spectacle* 445 n.
  art subject 553 n.
  beauty 841 n.
sea-scout *mariner* 270 n.
sea-serpent *rara avis* 84 n.
seashore *edge* 234 n.
  shore 344 n.
seasick *seafaring* 269 adj.
  vomiting 300 adj.
seaside *edge* 234 n.
  shore 344 n.
  pleasure-ground 837 n.
season *time* 108 n.
  period 110 n.
  regular return 141 n.
  season 388 vb.

appetize 390 vb.
  habituate 610 vb.
  preserve 666 vb.
  mature 669 vb.
  social round 882 n.
seasonable *apt* 24 adj.
  timely 137 adj.
seasonal *periodic* 110 adj.
  seasonal 141 adj.
  celebrative 876 adj.
seasoned *expert* 694 adj.
seasoning *tincture* 43 n.
  stimulant 174 n.
  condiment 389 n.
  habituation 610 n.
seat *equilibrium* 28 n.
  situation 186 n.
  station 187 n.
  house 192 n.
  seat 218 n.
  buttocks 238 n.
seating *room* 183 n.
seat of justice
  tribunal 956 n.
seat oneself *sit down* 311 vb.
sea-trip *water travel* 269 n.
sea-wall *safeguard* 662 n.
  obstacle 702 n.
seaway *room* 183 n.
seaweed *plant* 366 n.
seaworthy
  seafaring 269 adj.
  marine 275 adj.
  oceanic 343 adj.
  perfect 646 adj.
  invulnerable 660 adj.
seax *sharp edge* 256 n.
  side-arms 723 n.
sebaceous *fatty* 357 adj.
secant *ratio* 85 n.
secateur *sharp edge* 256 n.
  farm tool 370 n.
seccotine *adhesive* 47 n.
secede (see secession)
secession *dissent* 489 n.
  tergiversation 603 n.
  relinquishment 621 n.
  revolt 738 n.
  dutilessness 918 n.
  schism 978 n.
secessionist
  tergiversator 603 n.
  revolter 738 n.
  schismatic 978 n.
seclude *imprison* 747 vb.
  (see seclusion)
secluded *tranquil* 266 adj.
  invisible 444 adj.
  concealed 525 adj.
seclusion *separation* 46 n.
  exclusion 57 n.

displacement 188 n.
  farness 199 n.
  invisibility 444 n.
  relinquishment 621 n.
  seclusion 883 n.
  monasticism 985 n.
second *inferior* 35 n., adj.
  double 91 adj., vb.
  period 110 n.
  instant 116 n.
  angular measure 247 n.
  melody 410 n.
  measurement 465 n.
  endorse 488 vb.
  patronize 703 vb.
secondary
  unimportant 639 adj.
  imperfect 647 adj.
second-best
  inferior 35 adj.
  substitute 150 n.
  imperfect 647 adj.
  mediocre 732 adj.
second birth *revival* 656 n.
second chance
  mercy 905 n.
second childhood
  age 131 n.
  folly 499 n.
second edition
  duplicate 22 n.
seconder *assenter* 488 n.
  patron 707 n.
second fiddle *inferior* 35 n.
  nonentity 639 n.
second-hand
  imitative 20 adj.
  timekeeper 117 n.
  antiquated 127 adj.
  used 673 adj.
second-in-command
  deputy 755 n.
second line *auxiliary* 707 n.
second nature *habit* 610 n.
second opinion
  estimate 480 n.
second part *sequel* 67 n.
second place
  sequence 65 n.
second-rate *inferior* 35 adj.
  trivial 639 adj.
  imperfect 647 adj.
  mediocre 732 adj.
second-rater *inferior* 35 n.
second self *colleague* 707 n.
second sight *vision* 438 n.
  foresight 510 n.
  psychics 984 n.
second thought(s)
  sequel 67 n.

tergiversation 603 n.
amendment 654 n.
regret 830 n.
caution 858 n.
second to none
supreme 34 adj.
best 644 adj.
secrecy *secrecy* 525 n.
taciturnity 582 n.
caution 858 n.
secret *private* 80 adj.
dark 418 adj.
invisible 444 adj.
unknown thing 491 n.
unintelligibility 517 n.
occult 523 adj.
information 524 n.
secret 530 n.
  (*see* secrecy)
sécretaire *cabinet* 194 n.
secretariat
workshop 687 n.
management 689 n.
magistrature 733 n.
jurisdiction 955 n.
secret art
occultism 984 n.
secretary *recorder* 549 n.
official 690 n.
auxiliary 707 n.
servant 742 n.
deputy 755 n.
secret ballot *vote* 605 n.
freedom 744 n.
secret, be in the
know 490 vb.
secrete *emit* 300 vb.
conceal 525 vb.
  (*see* secretion)
secretion *ejection* 300 n.
excretion 302 vb.
secretive *reticent* 525 adj.
cautious 858 adj.
secret, no *known* 490 adj.
secretory *ejector* 300 n.
expulsive 300 adj.
excretory 302 adj.
secret service
secret service 459 n.
secret society
latency 523 n.
society 708 n.
rioter 738 n.
secret, the
interpretation 520 n.
secret weapon
weapon 723 n.
threat 900 n.
sect *community* 708 n.
party 708 n.
sect 978 n.

sectarian
nonconformist 84 n.
biased 481 adj.
dissentient 489 n.
sectional 708 adj.
sectarist 978 n.
sectarianism
sectarianism 978 n.
sectary *dissentient* 489 n.
auxiliary 707 n.
sectarist 978 n.
section *scission* 46 n.
subdivision 53 n.
classification 77 n.
topic 452 n.
formation 722 n.
sectional
fragmentary 53 adj.
classificatory 77 adj.
sectional 708 adj.
sectarian 978 adj.
sector *subdivision* 53 n.
arc 250 n.
battleground 724 n.
secular *secular* 110 adj.
lasting 113 adj.
seasonal 141 adj.
irreligious 974 adj.
clerical 986 adj.
laical 987 adj.
secularist
irreligionist 974 n.
secularity *laicality* 987 n.
secularize *depose* 752 vb.
appropriate 786 vb.
paganize 974 vb.
laicize 987 vb.
secundines *sequel* 67 n.
secure *tighten* 45 vb.
be early 135 vb.
believing 485 adj.
safeguard 660 vb.
promise 764 vb.
give security 767 vb.
securities *estate* 777 n.
security *safety* 660 n.
promise 764 n.
security 767 n.
paper money 797 n.
hope 852 n.
dueness 915 n.
legal process 959 n.
sedan *automobile* 274 n.
sedan-chair *vehicle* 274 n.
sedate *inexcitable* 823 adj.
serious 834 adj.
sedation *moderation* 177 n.
sedative *moderator* 177 n.
lenitive 177 adj.
soporific 679 n.
sedentary *quiescent* 266 adj.

sedge *plant* 366 n.
sedilia *church interior* 990 n.
sediment *leavings* 41 n.
thing transformed 272 n.
solid body 324 n.
marsh 347 n.
semiliquidity 354 n.
dirt 649 n.
sedimentary
remaining 41 adj.
indissoluble 324 adj.
sedimentation
condensation 324 n.
sedition *disorder* 61 n.
sedition 738 n.
perfidy 930 n.
seditionist
revolutionist 149 n.
motivator 612 n.
revolter 738 n.
agitator 738 n.
malcontent 829 n.
seditious
revolutionary 149 adj.
disobedient 738 adj.
seduce *induce* 612 vb.
bribe 612 vb.
delight 826 vb.
excite love 887 vb.
debauch 951 vb.
make wicked 934 vb.
seducer *deceiver* 545 n.
motivator 612 n.
libertine 952 n.
seduction *attraction* 291 n.
inducement 612 n.
  (*see* seduce)
seductive
attracting 291 adj.
pleasurable 826 adj.
lovable 887 adj.
sedulity
perseverance 600 n.
assiduity 678 n.
sedulous (*see* sedulity)
see *see, scan* 438 vb.
know 490 vb.
understand 516 vb.
church office 985 n.
seeable *visible* 443 adj.
seed *class* 62 vb.
reproduce itself 164 vb.
source 156 n.
product 164 n.
genitalia 164 n.
posterity 170 n.
fertilizer 171 n.
powder 332 n.
select 605 vb.
seedbed *seedbed* 156 n.
flower 366 n.

garden 370n.
seeded player
proficient 696n.
seediness (*see* seedy)
seeding *sorting* 62n.
seedless
unproductive 172adj.
seedling *young plant* 132n.
see double
be dim-sighted 440vb.
be drunk 949vb.
seed pearl *gem* 844n.
seedsman *gardener* 370n.
seed-time *spring* 128n.
seedy *weakly* 163adj.
sick 651adj.
dilapidated 655adj.
beggarly 801adj.
see fit *will* 595vb.
seeing *vision* 438n.
visibility 443n.
see into *enquire* 459vb.
see it coming
look ahead 124vb.
foresee 510vb.
not wonder 865vb.
see it through
sustain 146vb.
be resolute 599vb.
carry through 725vb.
seek *be curious* 453vb.
search 459vb.
pursue 619vb.
essay 671vb.
request 761vb.
seeker *inquisitor* 453n.
enquirer 459n.
hunter 619n.
petitioner 763n.
seem *resemble* 18vb.
appear 445vb.
seeming
appearance 445n.
hypocritical 541adj.
ostentatious 875adj.
seemliness
good taste 846n.
right 913n.
seemly *expedient* 642adj.
seen *evidential* 466adj.
known 490adj.
see nothing
be incurious 454vb.
see off *start out* 296vb.
dismiss 300vb.
see out
carry through 725vb.
seep *infiltrate* 297vb.
exude 298vb.
be wet 341vb.
seepage *outflow* 298n.

seer *spectator* 441n.
sage 500n.
oracle 511n.
visionary 513n.
sorcerer 983n.
psychic 984n.
see red *be violent* 176vb.
go mad 503vb.
get angry 891vb.
seersucker *textile* 222n.
see-saw *correlation* 12n.
fluctuation 317n.
to and fro 317adv.
be uncertain 474vb.
be irresolute 601vb.
pleasure-ground 837n.
seethe *cook* 301vb.
effervesce 318vb.
be hot 379vb.
hiss 406vb.
be excited 821vb.
see the light
discover 484vb.
become pious 979vb.
seething *excited* 821adj.
excitable 822adj.
seething mass
confusion 61n.
see through
be wise 498vb.
understand 516vb.
carry out 725vb.
see to *look after* 457vb.
deal with 688vb.
segar *tobacco* 388n.
segment *part, piece* 53n.
subdivision 53n.
segmentation
scission 46n.
segnitude
sluggishness 679n.
segregate *sanitate* 652vb.
exempt 919vb.
(*see* segregation)
segregation *separation* 46n.
exclusion 57n.
prejudice 481n.
protection 660n.
seclusion 883n.
seigneur *master* 741n.
nobleman 868n.
seigniory
magistrature 733n.
possession 773n.
lands 777n.
seignorial
proprietary 777adj.
seine *network* 222n.
inclosure 235n.
seisachtheia
non-payment 805n.

seisin *possession* 773n.
seismic
revolutionary 149adj.
violent 176adj.
oscillating 317adj.
important 638adj.
notable 638adj.
seismograph
oscillation 317n.
meter 465n.
recording instrument 549n.
seismology *oscillation* 317n.
seize *halt* 145vb.
understand 516vb.
take 786vb.
seize on
make important 638vb.
seizure *spasm* 318n.
illness 651n.
paralysis 651n.
taking 786n.
loss of right 916n.
sejant *heraldic* 547adj.
Sejm *parliament* 692n.
sejunction *separation* 46n.
seldom *seldom* 140adv.
seldom occur
be few 105vb.
select *set apart* 46vb.
excellent 644adj.
(*see* selection)
selection *part* 53n.
accumulation 74n.
discrimination 463n.
textbook 589n.
anthology 592n.
choice 605n.
selective *separate* 46adj.
discriminating 463adj.
choosing 605adj.
selenic *celestial* 321adj.
selenography
astronomy 321n.
self *intrinsicality* 5n.
identical 13adj.
self 80n.
subjectivity 320n.
spirit 447n.
self-abasement
humility 872n.
self-abnegation
humility 872n.
disinterestedness 931n.
temperance 942n.
self-absorption
selfishness 932n.
self-accusation
penitence 939n.
self-acting
mechanical 630adj.

self-admiration
pride 871 n.
vanity 873 n.
selfishness 932 n.
self-advertisement
boasting 877 n.
self-assertion
affirmation 532 n.
insolence 878 n.
self-assurance
vanity 873 n.
insolence 878 n.
self-assured
positive 473 adj.
assertive 532 adj.
self-cancelling
compensatory 31 adj.
self-centred *vain* 873 adj.
self-command
resolution 599 n.
inexcitability 823 n.
self-complacency
vanity 873 n.
self-conceit *pride* 871 n.
vanity 873 n.
self-conceited
narrow-minded 481 adj.
self-condemnation
penitence 939 n.
self-confidence
positiveness 473 n.
courage 855 n.
pride 871 n.
self-confident
resolute 599 adj.
self-congratulation
vanity 873 n.
self-conscious
affected 850 adj.
nervous 854 adj.
self-consciousness
intellect 447 n.
self-consideration
selfishness 932 n.
self-consistent
uniform 16 adj.
true 494 adj.
self-contained
complete 54 adj.
independent 744 adj.
self-control
moderation 177 n.
will 595 n.
resolution 599 n.
restraint 747 n.
inexcitability 823 n.
disinterestedness 931 n.
virtues 933 n.
temperance 942 n.
self-convicted
repentant 939 adj.

condemned 961 adj.
self-correcting
compensatory 31 adj.
self-deception
credulity 487 n.
error 495 n.
deception 542 n.
self-defence
defence 713 n.
vindication 927 n.
self-denial
severity 735 n.
disinterestedness 931 n.
temperance 942 n.
asceticism 945 n.
act of worship 981 n.
self-depreciation
underestimation 483 n.
mental dishonesty 543 n.
humility 872 n.
modesty 874 n.
self-determination
will 595 n.
independence 744 n.
self-devotion
suicide 362 n.
resolution 599 n.
disinterestedness 931 n.
oblation 981 n.
self-discipline
temperance 942 n.
punishment 963 n.
act of worship 981 n.
self-display *vanity* 873 n.
self-distrust
nervousness 854 n.
modesty 874 n.
self-drive
travelling 267 adj.
self-effacement
humility 872 n.
modesty 874 n.
disinterestedness 931 n.
self-employed
businesslike 622 adj.
self-esteem *vanity* 873 n.
self-evident
certain 473 adj.
manifest 522 adj.
self-evident truth
premise 475 n.
axiom 496 n.
self-examination
act of worship 981 n.
self-exile *seclusion* 883 n.
self-existence
existence 1 n.
self-existent *godlike* 965 adj.
self-existing
irrelative 10 adj.
self-expression

independence 744 n.
self-forgetful
disinterested 931 adj.
self-glory *boasting* 877 n.
self-governing
independent 744 adj.
governmental 753 adj.
self-government
government 733 n.
selfhood *self* 80 n.
subjectivity 320 n.
self-importance
vanity 873 n.
ostentation 875 n.
self-imposed
voluntary 597 adj.
self-imposed task
vocation 622 n.
self-improvement
learning 536 n.
virtue 933 n.
self-indulgence
pleasure 376 n.
selfishness 932 n.
intemperance 943 n.
sensualism 944 n.
self-interest
selfishness 932 n.
selfish *greedy* 859 adj.
selfish 932 adj.
selfishness
parsimony 816 n.
selfishness 932 n.
self-knowledge
humility 872 n.
selfless
disinterested 931 adj.
self-love *vanity* 873 n.
selfishness 932 n.
self-made man
victor 727 n.
self-mortification
asceticism 945 n.
punishment 963 n.
self-opinion
opiniatry 602 n.
self-opinionated
positive 473 adj.
self-opinioned
narrow-minded 481 adj.
self-pity *pity* 905 n.
selfishness 932 n.
self-possession
resolution 599 n.
inexcitability 823 n.
self-praise *pride* 871 n.
vanity 873 n.
praise 923 n.
selfishness 932 n.
self-preservation
selfishness 931 n.

self-protection
  protection 660 n.
self-raising *light* 323 adj.
self-reference
  intrinsicality 5 n.
self-regarding
  selfish 932 adj.
self-reliance *courage* 855 n.
self-reliant
  resolute 599 adj.
self-repression
  inexcitability 823 n.
self-reproach *regret* 830 n.
  penitence 939 n.
self-respecting
  proud 871 adj.
self-restraint
  resolution 599 n.
  restraint 747 n.
  inexcitability 823 n.
  temperance 942 n.
self-rule
  independence 744 n.
self-sacrifice
  offering 781 n.
  disinterestedness 931 n.
  oblation 981 n.
selfsame *identical* 13 adj. ·
self-satisfaction
  content 828 n.
self-satisfied *vain* 873 adj.
self-seeker *egotist* 932 n.
self-service *meal* 301 n.
  mensal 301 adj.
  provision 633 n.
  provisionary 633 adj.
self-slaughter
  suicide 362 n.
self-sought *desired* 859 adj.
self-starter *start* 68 n.
self-styled
  misnamed 562 adj.
self-sufficiency
  completeness 54 n.
  independence 744 n.
  wealth 800 n.
  vanity 873 n.
self-support
  independence 744 n.
self-surrender
  disinterestedness 931 n.
  piety 979 n.
self-taught *studious* 536 adj.
self-torture
  asceticism 945 n.
self-will *will* 595 n.
  obstinacy 602 n.
sell *absurdity* 497 n.
  advertise 528 vb.
  trickery 542 n.
  deceive 542 vb.

provide 633 vb.
sell 793 vb.
sell an idea to
  convince 485 vb.
sell dear *overcharge* 811 vb.
seller *seller* 793 n.
  pedlar 794 n.
seller's market
  scarcity 636 n.
  prosperity 730 n.
  request 761 n.
  mart 796 n.
  dearness 811 n.
sell for *cost* 809 vb.
sell oneself *boast* 877 vb.
sell out
  be dishonest 930 vb.
sell-out *sale* 793 n.
selvedge *edging* 234 n.
semanteme *word* 559 n.
  part of speech 564 n.
semantic *semantic* 514 adj.
semantics *meaning* 514 n.
  linguistics 557 n.
semaphore
  communicate 524 vb.
  telecommunication 531 n.
  indicator 547 n.
  signal 547 n., vb.
  gesticulate 547 vb.
semasiological
  semantic 514 adj.
  literary 557 adj.
semasiologist
  linguist 557 n.
semasiology
  meaning 514 n.
  linguistics 557 n.
  etymology 559 n.
semblance *similarity* 18 n.
  mimicry 20 n.
  copy 22 n.
  appearance 445 n.
  probability 471 n.
semeiology
  hermeneutics 520 n.
  indication 547 n.
  gesture 547 n.
semeiotics
  indication 547 n.
semen *fertilizer* 171 n.
semester *time* 108 n.
  period 110 n.
semi *fragmentary* 53 adj.
  incomplete 55 adj.
  bisected 92 adj.
semibreve *notation* 410 n.
semicircle *arc* 250 n.
semicircular *curved* 248 adj.
semicolon
  punctuation 547 n.

semidarkness
  half-light 419 n.
semi-detached
  non-adhesive 49 adj.
semi-diameter
  breadth 205 n.
semi-educated
  smattering 491 adj.
semi-final *contest* 716 n.
semiliquid *thick* 205 adj.
semiliquidity
  semiliquidity 354 n.
semi-literate
  smattering 491 adj.
semilunar *curved* 248 adj.
seminal *causal* 156 adj.
  productive 164 adj.
  generative 171 adj.
seminal fluid *genitalia* 164 n.
seminar *curriculum* 536 n.
  class 538 n.
  conference 584 n.
seminarist
  college student 538 n.
  cleric 986 n.
  layman 987 n.
seminary *academy* 539 n.
  monastery 986 n.
semiplosive
  speech sound 398 n.
semiquaver
  notation 410 n.
semi-skilled
  unskilled 695 adj.
Semitic *ethnic* 11 adj.
  language type 559 n.
semitone *interval* 201 n.
  musical note 410 n.
semitransparency
  semitransparency 424 n.
semitransparent
  ill-seen 444 adj.
semivowel
  speech sound 398 n.
  spoken letter 558 n.
  voice 577 n.
sempiternity
  durability 113 n.
  perpetuity 115 n.
sempstress *clothier* 228 n.
  artisan 686 n.
senarius *prosody* 593 n.
senary *fifth and over* 99 adj.
senate *seniority* 131 n.
  parliament 692 n.
senator *councillor* 692 n.
  master 741 n.
  aristocrat 868 n.
senatorial *aged* 131 adj.
  parliamentary 692 adj.
  genteel 868 adj.

senatus consultum
  decree 737 n.
send *displace* 188 vb.
  move 265 vb.
  send 272 vb.
  emit 300 vb.
  give 781 vb.
  excite 821 vb.
  delight 826 vb.
send after *pursue* 619 vb.
send back *put off* 136 vb.
send down *bate* 37 vb.
  eject 300 vb.
sender *transferrer* 272 n.
send flying *propel* 287 vb.
send for *pursue* 619 vb.
send forth *publish* 528 vb.
send haywire
  bedevil 63 vb.
send home *liberate* 746 vb.
send-off *start* 68 n.
  valediction 296 n.
send one's compliments
  pay respects 884 vb.
  gratulate 886 vb.
send out *emit* 300 vb.
  commission 751 vb.
send packing *repel* 292 vb.
  dismiss 300 vb.
send to blazes
  be insolent 878 vb.
  curse 899 vb.
send to Coventry
  set apart 46 vb.
  eject 300 vb.
  make unwelcome 883 vb.
send up *augment* 36 vb.
  elevate 310 vb.
send word
  communicate 521 vb.
senescence *age* 131 n.
senescent
  deteriorated 655 adj.
seneschal *officer* 741 n.
  retainer 742 n.
  keeper 749 n.
senile decay
  insanity 503 n.
senility *oldness* 127 n.
  age 131 n.
  helplessness 161 n.
  weakness 163 n.
  folly 499 n.
  dilapidation 655 n.
senior *older* 131 adj.
  old man 133 n.
  college student 538 n.
  master 741 n.
seniority *superiority* 34 n.
  oldness 127 n.
  seniority 131 n.

authority 733 n.
senior service
  navy man 722 n.
senna *potherb* 301 n.
sennet *musical note* 410 n.
  call 547 n.
sensation *sense* 374 n.
  news 529 n.
  feeling 818 n.
  prodigy 864 n.
sensational
  striking 374 adj.
  dramatic 594 adj.
  exciting 821 adj.
  wonderful 864 adj.
  showy 875 adj.
sensationalism
  publicity 528 n.
  exaggeration 546 n.
  excitation 821 n.
  ostentation 875 n.
sensationalize
  impress 821 vb.
  be ostentatious 875 vb.
sense *sense* 374 n.
  have feeling 374 vb.
  intellect 447 n.
  intuit 476 vb.
  detect 484 vb.
  intelligence 498 n.
  meaning 514 n.
  feeling 818 n.
sense datum
  element 319 n.
senseless
  insensible 375 adj.
  absurd 497 adj.
  foolish 499 adj.
  unmeaning 515 adj.
sense of duty *duty* 917 n.
sense of honour
  probity 929 n.
sense of humour
  laughter 835 n.
  wit 839 n.
sense organ
  instrument 628 n.
sense perception
  feeling 818 n.
senses *intellect* 447 n.
  sanity 502 n.
sensibility
  sensibility 374 n.
  discrimination 463 n.
  painfulness 827 n.
sensible *material* 319 adj.
  sentient 374 adj.
  rational 475 adj.
  wise 498 adj.
  useful 640 adj.
  feeling 818 adj.

impressible 819 adj.
sensible of
  knowing 490 adj.
sensitive *sentient* 374 adj.
  attentive 455 adj.
  discriminating 463 adj.
  accurate 494 adj.
  elegant 575 adj.
  feeling 818 adj.
  sensitive 819 adj.
  excitable 822 adj.
sensitiveness
  sensibility 374 n.
  moral sensibility 819 n.
sensitive plant
  sensibility 374 n.
  moral sensibility 819 n.
sensitivity
  sensibility 374 n.
  discrimination 463 n.
  accuracy 494 n.
  persuasibility 612 n.
  moral sensibility 819 n.
sensitize
  cause feeling 374 vb.
sensorial *feeling* 818 adj.
sensorium *intellect* 447 n.
sensory *feeling* 818 adj.
sensory perception
  feeling 818 n.
sensory process
  sense 374 n.
sensual *material* 319 adj.
  sensuous 376 adj.
  feeling 818 adj.
  intemperate 943 adj.
  sensual 944 adj.
  lecherous 951 adj.
sensualism
  sensualism 944 n.
sensualist
  sensualist 944 n.
sensuality
  materiality 319 n.
  pleasure 376 n.
  sensualism 944 n.
sensuous *sensuous* 376 adj.
  sentient 374 adj.
  feeling 818 adj.
sentence *period* 110 n.
  judgment 480 n.
  maxim 496 n.
  affirmation 532 n.
  phrase 563 n.
  condemnation 961 n.
  penalty 963 n.
sentential
  phraseological 563 adj.
sententious *judicial* 480 adj.
  aphoristic 496 adj.
  concise 569 adj.

forceful 571 adj.
sentient *sentient* 374 adj.
  feeling 818 adj.
  impressible 819 adj.
sentience *feeling* 818 n.
sentiment *opinion* 485 n.
  feeling 818 n.
  excitation 821 n.
  love 887 n.
sentimental *foolish* 499 adj.
  feeble 572 adj.
  feeling 818 adj.
  impressible 819 adj.
  loving 887 adj.
sentimentality
  moral sensibility 819 n.
  love 887 n.
sentimental value
  lovableness 887 n.
sentinel, sentry
  janitor 264 n.
  spectator 441 n.
  surveillance 457 n.
  protector 660 n.
  warner 664 n.
  defender 713 n.
  armed force 722 n.
  keeper 749 n.
sentry-box
  compartment 194 n.
sentry-go
  surveillance 457 n.
separability
  disjunction 46 n.
  non-coherence 49 n.
separable *severable* 46 adj.
separate *irrelative* 10 adj.
  different 15 adj.
  separate 46 adj.
  discontinuous 72 adj.
  disperse 75 vb.
  bifurcate 92 vb.
  open 263 vb.
  select 605 vb.
  (*see* separation)
separated brethren
  schismatic 978 n.
separateness *irrelation* 10 n.
separation
  separation 46 n.
  decomposition 51 n.
  unity 88 n.
  farness 199 n.
  gap 201 n.
  divergence 294 n.
  discrimination 463 n.
  dissension 709 n.
  liberation 746 n.
  seclusion 883 n.
  divorce 896 n.
  schism 978 n.

sectarianism 978 n.
Sephardim
  non-Christian sect 978 n.
sepia *fish* 365 n.
  brown paint 430 n.
seposition *separation* 46 n.
  exclusion 57 n.
sepoy *soldier* 722 n.
sepsis *infection* 651 n.
sept *race* 11 n.
  breed 77 n.
  genealogy 169 n.
septennium *over five* 99 n.
septentrional
  opposite 240 adj.
septet *duet* 412 n.
septic *not nice* 645 adj.
  unclean 649 adj.
  toxic 653 adj.
  dangerous 661 adj.
septicæmia *infection* 651 n.
septic tank *latrine* 649 n.
septuagenarian
  over twenty 99 n.
Septuagint *scripture* 975 n.
septum *partition* 231 n.
sepulchral
  funereal 364 adj.
  resonant 404 adj.
  hoarse 407 adj.
sepulchre *holy place* 990 n.
  tomb 364 n.
sepulture *interment* 364 n.
sequacious *sequent* 65 adj.
  flexible 327 adj.
  tough 329 adj.
sequel *sequel* 67 n.
  end 69 n.
  posteriority 120 n.
  effect 157 n.
sequela *sequel* 67 n.
  effect 157 n.
sequence
  relativeness 9 n.
  order 60 n.
  sequence 65 n.
  posteriority 120 n.
  following 284 n.
sequent *continuous* 71 adj.
  caused 157 n.
  (*see* sequence)
sequester *set apart* 46 vb.
  exclude 57 vb.
  deprive 786 vb.
  not pay 805 vb.
  seclude 883 vb.
sequestered
  tranquil 266 adj.
  invisible 444 adj.
sequestration
  expropriation 786 n.

seclusion 883 n.
  penalty 963 n.
sequestrator *taker* 786 n.
sequin *finery* 844 n.
sequoia *tall creature* 209 n.
  tree 366 n.
sérac *ice* 380 n.
seraglio *womankind* 373 n.
  love-nest 887 n.
  brothel 951 n.
seraph *angel* 968 n.
seraphic *virtuous* 933 adj.
  angelic 968 adj.
  pietistic 979 adj.
sere *lean* 206 adj.
  dry 342 adj.
  deteriorated 655 adj.
serenade
  musical piece 412 n.
  vocal music 412 n.
  sing 413 vb.
  wooing 889 n.
serenader *vocalist* 413 n.
serendipity *chance* 159 n.
  discovery 484 n.
serene *transparent* 422 adj.
  (*see* serenity)
serenity
  inexcitability 823 n.
  content 828 n.
  non-wonder 865 n.
serf *husbandman* 370 n.
  slave 742 n.
  possessor 776 n.
  countryman 869 n.
serfdom *servitude* 745 n.
serge *textile* 222 n.
sergeant *soldiery* 722 n.
  army officer 741 n.
serial *relative* 9 adj.
  continuous 71 adj.
  recurrence 106 n.
  periodical 141 adj.
  the press 528 n.
  reading matter 589 n.
serialization *sequence* 65 n.
  continuity 71 n.
  periodicity 141 n.
serialize *publish* 528 vb.
serial order
  relativeness 9 n.
serial place *degree* 27 n.
  serial place 73 n.
seriate *continuous* 71 adj.
seriatim *in order* 60 adv.
  continuously 71 adv.
sericulture
  animal husbandry 369 n.
series *all* 52 n.
  order 60 n.
  sequence 65 n.

series 71 n.
  accumulation 74 n.
  number 85 n.
  recurrence 106 n.
  continuance 146 n.
  following 284 n.
  library 589 n.
  edition 589 n.
serif *print-type* 587 n.
serio-comic *funny* 849 adj.
serious *great* 32 adj.
  attentive 455 adj.
  wise 498 adj.
  resolute 599 adj.
  intending 617 adj.
  important 638 adj.
  dangerous 661 adj.
  serious 834 adj.
  dull 840 adj.
  heinous 934 adj.
seriously *positively* 32 adv.
  affirmatively 532 adv.
  resolutely 599 adv.
seriousness *vigour* 571 n.
  warm feeling 818 n.
  (*see* serious)
serjeant *lawyer* 958 n.
sermon *lecture* 534 n.
  diffuseness 570 n.
  oration 579 n.
  dissertation 591 n.
sermonize *be pious* 979 vb.
serolin *blood* 335 n.
seron *bunch* 74 n.
serosity *fluid, blood* 335 n.
serous *fluidal* 335 adj.
  sanguineous 335 adj.
serpent *serpent* 251 n.
  reptile 365 n.
  sibilation 406 n.
  horn 414 n.
  deceiver 545 n.
  bane 659 n.
  slyboots 698 n.
  noxious animal 904 n.
  knave 938 n.
  Satan 969 n.
serpentine *snaky* 251 adj.
  wriggle 251 vb.
  cunning 698 adj.
serpigo *skin disease* 651 n.
serration *sharpness* 256 n.
  roughness 259 n.
  notch 260 n.
serratodentate
  notched 260 adj.
serried *cohesive* 48 adj.
  assembled 74 adj.
  dense 324 adj.
serrulation *notch* 260 n.
serum *fluid, blood* 335 n.

servant *worker* 686 n.
  auxiliary 707 n.
  servant 742 n.
servant-class
  plebeian 869 adj.
serve *be inferior* 35 vb.
  follow 284 vb.
  function 622 vb.
  be instrumental 628 vb.
  suffice 635 vb.
  be expedient 642 vb.
  work 682 vb.
  serve 742 vb.
  be subject 745 vb.
  apportion 783 vb.
  (*see* service)
server *thrower* 287 n.
  auxiliary 707 n.
  church officer 986 n.
  ritualist 988 n.
serve rightly
  retaliate 714 vb.
  be just 913 vb.
serve up *make ready* 669 vb.
service *agency* 173 n.
  propulsion 287 n.
  benefit 615 n.
  provision 633 n.
  utility 640 n.
  revive 656 vb.
  aid 703 n.
  obedience 739 n.
  service 745 n.
  sale 793 n.
  kind act 897 n.
  public worship 981 n.
  cult 981 n.
  church service 988 n.
  (*see* serve)
serviceable
  instrumental 628 adj.
  useful 640 adj.
service-book
  office-book 988 n.
service, in *serving* 742 adj.
serviceman *soldier* 722 n.
service road *road* 624 n.
services
  instrumentality 628 n.
  army 722 n.
service stripe
  decoration 729 n.
servicing
  preservation 666 n.
servile *conformable* 83 adj.
  inglorious 867 adj.
  plebeian 869 adj.
  (*see* servility)
servility *subjection* 745 n.
  servility 879 n.
  respect 920 n.

serving man
  domestic 742 n.
serving sentence
  imprisoned 747 adj.
servitor *domestic* 742 n.
servitude
  submission 721 n.
  servitude 745 n.
servo-mechanics
  mechanics 630 n.
sesquipedalian *long* 203 adj.
  diffuse 570 adj.
  ornate 574 adj.
sesquipedality
  inelegance 576 n.
sessile *cohesive* 48 adj.
session *council* 692 n.
sessions *law-court* 956 n.
  legal trial 959 n.
sestet, sestina
  verse form 593 n.
set *modality* 7 n.
  uniformity 16 n.
  decrease 37 vb.
  firm-set 45 adj.
  affix 45 vb.
  all 52 n.
  component 58 n.
  series 71 n.
  accumulation 74 n.
  band 74 n.
  sort 77 n.
  unit 88 n.
  young plant 132 n.
  stabilize 153 vb.
  tend 179 vb.
  situated 186 adj.
  place 187 vb.
  hang 217 vb.
  form 243 n.
  sharpen 256 vb.
  direction 281 n.
  descend 309 vb.
  be dense 324 vb.
  current 350 n.
  cultivate 370 vb.
  appearance 445 n.
  positive 473 adj.
  print 587 vb.
  stage-set 594 n.
  obstinate 602 adj.
  usual 610 adj.
  collection 632 n.
  doctor 658 vb.
  make ready 669 vb.
  party 708 n.
  contest 716 n.
  command 737 vb.
  beautify 841 vb.
  hair-dressing 843 n.
  decorate 844 vb.

set about *begin* 68 vb.
setaceous *hairy* 259 adj.
set across *transfer* 272 vb.
set afloat *stabilize* 153 vb.
  cause 156 vb.
set against *dissuade* 613 vb.
  make quarrels 709 vb.
  cause dislike 861 vb.
set apart *set apart* 46 vb.
  exclude 57 vb.
  select 605 vb.
  exempt 919 vb.
set aside *displace* 188 vb.
  negate 533 vb.
  reject 607 vb.
  store 632 vb.
  abrogate 752 vb.
set at ease *content* 828 vb.
set at naught
  underestimate 483 vb.
  reject 607 vb.
  oppose 704 vb.
  defy 711 vb.
  hold cheap 922 vb.
setback
  disappointment 509 n.
  deterioration 655 n.
  adversity 731 n.
  loss 772 n.
set books *curriculum* 534 n.
set by the ears
  make quarrels 709 vb.
set-down *humiliation* 872 n.
set down *record* 548 vb.
  write 586 vb.
set down to
  attribute 158 vb.
set fair *palmy* 730 adj.
  be auspicious 730 vb.
set fire *kindle* 381 vb.
set form *regularity* 81 n.
set forth *start out* 296 vb.
set forward
  undertake 672 n.
set free *deliver* 668 vb.
  give scope 744 vb.
  liberate 746 vb.
set going *initiate* 68 vb.
  move 265 vb.
  impel 269 vb.
  dispose of 673 vb.
set in *begin* 68 vb.
  stay 144 vb.
  tend 179 vb.
set off *correlate* 12 vb.
  initiate 68 vb.
  beautify 841 vb.
  decorate 844 vb.
set-off *offset* 31 n.
set on *incite* 612 vb.
  attack 712 vb.

enamoured 887 adj.
set on edge *roughen* 259 vb.
  give pain 377 vb.
  displease 827 vb.
setose, setous *hairy* 259 adj.
set out *arrange* 62 vb.
  travel 267 vb.
  start out 296 vb.
  show 522 vb.
  dissert 591 vb.
set piece *stage show* 594 n.
set right *straighten* 249 vb.
  disclose 526 vb.
  rectify 654 vb.
  vindicate 927 vb.
set sail *start out* 296 vb.
  voyage 269 vb.
  navigate 269 vb.
set-square *gauge* 465 n.
sett *paving* 226 n.
settee *seat* 218 n.
setter *dog* 365 n.
  printer 587 n.
set the alarm *time* 117 vb.
set the fashion
  influence 178 vb.
  motivate 612 vb.
  be in fashion 848 vb.
set the pace
  motivate 612 vb.
setting *situation* 186 n.
  circumjacence 230 n.
  musical piece 412 n.
  view 438 n.
  spectacle 445 n.
  print 587 n.
  stage-set 594 n.
  hair-dressing 843 n.
  ornamental art 844 n.
setting-up *composition* 56 n.
settle *arrange* 62 vb.
  terminate 69 vb.
  be stable 153 vb.
  prevail 178 vb.
  place oneself 187 vb.
  dwell 192 vb.
  seat 218 n.
  be quiescent 266 vb.
  descend 309 vb.
  make certain 473 vb.
  judge 480 vb.
  contract 765 vb.
  appropriate 786 vb.
  pay 804 vb.
settle accounts
  account 808 vb.
settled *characteristic* 5 adj.
  vested 153 adj.
  native 191 adj.
  positive 473 adj.
  usual 610 adj.

ending 69 adj.
  situated 186 adj.
  located 187 adj.
settle down
  come of age 134 vb.
  be stable 153 vb.
settle for *bargain* 791 vb.
settle into
  be turned to 147 vb.
settlement *territory* 184 n.
  location 187 n.
  station 187 n.
  habitancy 191 n.
  compact 765 n.
  dower 777 n.
  transfer 780 n.
  payment 804 n.
settler *settler* 191 n.
  incomer 297 n.
settlor *giver* 781 n.
set-to *fight* 716 n.
set to *begin* 68 vb.
  eat 301 vb.
  be resolute 599 vb.
  work 682 vb.
set to music
  compose music 413 vb.
set to rights *repair* 656 vb.
set towards
  approach 289 vb.
set up *arrange* 62 vb.
  stabilize 153 vb.
  cause 156 vb.
  strengthen 162 vb.
  place 187 vb.
  make vertical 215 vb.
  elevate 310 vb.
  cure 656 vb.
  prosperous 730 adj.
set-up *circumstance* 8 n.
  composition 56 n.
  structure 331 n.
set upon *resolute* 899 adj.
  desiring 859 adj.
set watch *invigilate* 457 vb.
seven deadly sins *vice* 934 n.
seven-league boots
  speeder 277 n.
  magic instrument 983 n.
Seventh-day Adventists
  sect 978 n.
seventh heaven
  happiness 824 n.
  Heaven 971 n.
seventy-four *warship* 722 n.
  gun 723 n.
sever *subtract* 39 vb.
  disjoin 46 vb.
severable *severable* 46 adj.
  brittle 330 adj.
several *special* 80 adj.

plurality 101 n.
many 104 adj.
severalize
differentiate 15 vb.
discriminate 463 vb.
severalty disjunction 46 n.
severance (see sever)
severe exorbitant 32 adj.
strong 162 adj.
vigorous 174 adj.
violent 176 adj.
accurate 494 adj.
plain 573 adj.
severe 735 adj.
paining 827 adj.
serious 834 adj.
fastidious 862 adj.
pitiless 906 adj.
ascetic 945 adj.
severity severity 735 n.
inhumanity 898 n.
(see severe)
Sèvres china pottery 381 n.
sew tie 45 vb.
sewage leavings 41 n.
swill 649 n.
sewer receptacle 194 n.
cavity 255 n.
tunnel 263 n.
lake 346 n.
drain 351 n.
fetor 397 n.
badness 645 n.
cleanser 648 n.
sink 649 n.
insalubrity 653 n.
retainer 742 n.
sewerage cleansing 648 n.
dirt 649 n.
sewing bookbinding 589 n.
sex classification 77 n.
life 360 n.
impurity 951 n.
sexagenarian
over twenty 99 n.
old man 133 n.
sex appeal
pleasurableness 826 n.
beauty 841 n.
lovableness 887 n.
sex-consciousness
unchastity 951 n.
sex-crazy, sex-mad
lecherous 951 adj.
sex crime rape 951 n.
sexless impotent 161 adj.
sexologist doctor 658 n.
sexology medical art 658 n.
sext church service 988 n.
sextant
angular measure 247 n.

arc 250 n.
gauge 465 n.
sextet over five 99 n.
duet 412 n.
sex, the womankind 373 n.
sexton interment 364 n.
servant 742 n.
church officer 986 n.
sextuple
fifth and over 99 adj.
sexual generic 77 adj.
impure 951 adj.
sexual abnormality
abnormality 84 n.
sexual desire libido 859 n.
sexual intercourse
coition 45 n.
sexuality unchastity 951 n.
sexy impure 951 adj.
shabbiness inferiority 35 n.
improbity 930 n.
shabby unimportant 639 adj.
dilapidated 655 adj.
beggarly 801 adj.
parsimonious 816 adj.
disreputable 867 adj.
rascally 930 adj.
shack small house 192 n.
shackle tie 45 vb.
halter 47 n.
make insufficient 636 vb.
obstacle 702 n.
encumbrance 702 n.
fetter 748 n., vb.
shackled restrained 747 adj.
captive 750 adj.
shad table fish 365 n.
shade
insubstantial thing 4 n.
differentiate 15 vb.
degree 27 n.
small quantity 33 n.
shade 226 n.
corpse 363 n.
refrigerate 382 vb.
darken 418 vb.
dimness 419 n.
screen 421 n.
hue 425 n.
qualify 468 vb.
conceal 525 vb.
paint 553 vb.
safeguard 660 vb.
refresh 685 vb.
defend 713 vb.
relieve 831 vb.
ghost 970 n.
shade of difference
discrimination 463 n.
shade off shade off 27 vb.
shade, throw into the

be superior 34 vb.
shadiness darkness 418 n.
improbity 930 n.
shading off
gradational 27 adj.
shadoof extractor 304 n.
irrigator 341 n.
shadow
insubstantial thing 4 n.
analogue 18 n.
imitation 20 n.
compeer 28 n.
concomitant 89 n.
thinness 206 n.
follow 284 vb.
refrigerate 382 vb.
darkness 418 n.
dimness 419 n.
screen 421 vb.
colour 425 vb.
fantasy 513 n.
hunter 619 n.
pursue 619 vb.
make ugly 842 vb.
primp 843 vb.
close friend 880 n.
shadow-boxing
ideality 513 n.
shadow cabinet
futurity 124 n.
preparation 669 n.
shadow forth
predict 511 vb.
represent 551 vb.
shadowless
undimmed 417 adj.
shadow out
represent 551 vb.
shadowy
insubstantial 4 adj.
inconsiderable 33 adj.
amorphous 244 adj.
immaterial 320 adj.
dark 418 adj.
shadowy 419 adj.
invisible 444 adj.
uncertain 474 adj.
imaginary 513 adj.
puzzling 517 adj.
shady cold 380 adj.
dark 418 adj.
shadowy 419 adj.
screened 421 adj.
disreputable 867 adj.
dishonest 930 adj.
lawbreaking 954 adj.
shaft depth 211 n.
pillar 218 n.
handle 218 n.
excavation 255 n.
sharp point 256 n.

tunnel 263 n.
missile 287 n.
tool 630 n.
missile weapon 723 n.
shag hair 259 n.
roughen 259 vb.
tobacco 388 n.
shaggy hairy 259 adj.
shagreen skin 226 n.
shah sovereign 741 n.
shake mix 43 vb
come unstuck 49 vb.
derange 63 vb.
vary 152 vb.
weaken 163 vb.
force 176 vb.
impel 279 n.
oscillate 317 vb.
brandish 317 vb.
be agitated 318 vb.
blow 352 vb.
roll 403 vb.

musical note 410 n.
cause doubt 486 vb.
dissuade 613 vb.
impair 655 vb.
show feeling 818 vb.
impress 821 vb.
frighten, quake 854 vb.
shake-down bed 218 n.
sleep 679 n.
shake hands meet 295 vb.
make peace 719 vb.
bargain 791 vb.
be friendly 880 vb.
greet 887 vb.
shaken irresolute 601 adj.
deteriorated 655 adj.
shake off unstick 49 vb.
eject 300 vb.
shake one's head
dissent 489 n.
negate 533 vb.
disapprove 927 vb.
shakes, no great
inconsiderable 33 adj.
Shakespearean
poetic 593 adj.
shakes, the
agitation 318 n.
shake-up revolution 149 n.
shako headgear 228 n.
armour 713 n.
shaky weak 163 adj.
flimsy 163 adj.
unsafe 661 adj.
nervous 854 adj.
shale lamina 207 n.
brittleness 330 n.
rock 344 n.
shalloon textile 222 n.

shallot vegetable 301 n.
shallow
inconsiderable 33 adj.
foolish 499 adj.
affected 850 adj.
(see shallowness)
shallowness
shallowness 212 n.
inattention 456 n.
sciolism 491 n.
unintelligence 499 n.
scarcity 636 n.
unimportance 639 n.
shallow pretext
pretext 614 n.
shallows
shallowness 212 n.
pitfall 663 n.
shaly layered 207 adj.
territorial 344 adj.
sham mimicry 20 n.
dissemble 541 vb.
sham 542 n.
spurious 542 adj.
mental dishonesty 543 n.
stratagem 698 n.
shaman sorcerer 983 n.
priest 986 n.
shamanism sorcery 983 n.
shamble
move slowly 278 vb.
shambles confusion 61 n.
havoc 165 n.
slaughter 362 n.
slaughter-house 362 n.
sink 649 n.
shame
disrepute, slur 867 n.
shame 867 vb.
humiliation 872 n.
wrong 914 n.
defame 926 vb.
improbity 930 n.
wickedness 934 n.
purity 950 n.
shame-faced modest 874 adj.
guilty 936 adj.
shameful evil 616 adj.
bad 645 adj.
discreditable 867 adj.
heinous 934 adj.
shamefulness
improbity 930 n.
shameless
undisguised 522 adj.
thick-skinned 820 adj.
vulgar 847 adj.
insolent 878 adj.
dishonest 930 adj.
wicked 934 adj.
unchaste 951 adj.

shamiana canopy 226 n.
pavilion 192 n.
shammer deceiver 545 n.
impostor 545 n.
slyboots 698 n.
shampoo friction 333 n.
ablution 648 n.
surgery 658 n.
hairwash 843 n.
shamrock three 93 n.
grass 366 n.
heraldry 547 n.
shandrydan carriage 274 n.
shandy liquor 301 n.
shanghai ensnare 542 vb.
take away 786 vb.
steal 788 vb.
Shangri-la fantasy 513 n.
shank stand 218 n.
leg 267 n.
deflect 282 vb.
propel 287 vb.
print-type 587 n.
shantung textile 222 n.
shanty small house 192 n.
poem 593 n.
shape sort 77 n.
make conform 83 vb.
convert 147 vb.
outline 233 n.
form 243 n.
efform 243 vb.
structure 331 n.
feature 445 n.
represent 551 vb.
plan 623 vb.
ghost 970 n.
shapeless
non-uniform 17 adj.
amorphous 244 adj.
unsightly 842 adj.
shapely symmetrical 245 adj.
shapely 841 adj.
shapen convert 147 vb.
shape well
give hope 852 vb.
shard piece 53 n.
share part 53 n.
be one of 58 vb.
sharp edge 256 n.
mete out 465 vb.
participation 775 n.
give 781 vb.
portion 783 n.
be sociable 882 vb.
sharecropping
joint possession 775 n.
shareholder owner 776 n.
share out apportion 783 vb.
share-pusher
merchant 794 n.

sharer *colleague* 707n.
 participator 775n.
shares *apportionment* 783n.
sharing *equal* 28adj.
 participation 775n.
shark *fish* 365n.
 lender 784n.
 taker 786n.
 defrauder 789n.
sharkskin *textile* 222n.
sharp *keen* 174adj.
 violent 176adj.
 sharp 256adj.
 striking 374adj.
 pungent 388adj.
 strident 407adj.
 musical note 410n.
 discordant 411adj.
 intelligent 498adj.
 deceive 542vb.
 cunning 698adj.
 felt 818adj.
 painful 827adj.
 unpleasant 827adj.
 witty 839adj.
 ungracious 885adj.
 irascible 892adj.
sharp-eared
 auditory 415adj.
sharpen *invigorate* 174vb.
 sharpen 256vb.
 animate 821vb.
sharpener *sharpener* 256n.
sharpen the wits
 educate 534vb.
sharper *trickster* 545n.
 expert 696n.
 slyboots 698n.
 defrauder 789n.
sharp-eyed
 attentive 455adj.
 vigilant 457adj.
sharpness *sourness* 393n.
 vigour 571n.
 skill 694n.
 (*see* sharp)
sharp point
 sharp point 256n.
sharp practice
 trickery 542n.
 foul play 930n.
sharp-set *hungry* 859adj.
sharpshooter
 shooter 287n.
 attacker 712n.
 soldier 722n.
sharp-tempered
 irascible 892adj.
sharp-tongued
 irascible 892adj.
sharp-witted

intelligent 498adj.
shastra
 non-Biblical scripture
 975n.
shatter *break* 46vb.
 demolish 165vb.
 be brittle 330vb.
 pulverize 332adj.
shattered surface
 roughness 259n.
shattering *notable* 638adj.
 wonderful 864adj.
shatter-proof
 unyielding 162adj.
 invulnerable 660adj.
shattery *flimsy* 163adj.
 brittle 330adj.
shave *cut* 46vb.
 make smaller 198vb.
 be near 200vb.
 shorten 204vb.
 laminate 207vb.
 smooth 258vb.
 hair-dressing 843n.
shaved, shaven
 short 204adj.
 hairless 229adj.
 clean 648adj.
shaveling *monk* 986n.
shaver *youngster* 132n.
shavetail *soldiery* 722n.
 army officer 741n.
Shavian *funny* 849adj.
shaving *small thing* 33n.
 thinness 206n.
 lamina 207n.
 strip 208n.
 hair-dressing 843n.
shaving-mug *bowl* 194n.
shavings *leavings* 41n.
 piece 53n.
 rubbish 641n.
shawl *wrapping* 226n.
 shawl 228n.
shawm *flute* 414n.
shay *carriage* 274n.
she *female* 373n., adj.
sheaf *bunch* 74n.
 cultivate 370vb.
shear *subtract* 39vb.
 make smaller 198vb.
 shorten 204vb.
 distortion 246n.
 groom 369vb.
 fleece 786vb.
shears *sharp edge* 256n.
 farm tool 370n.
sheath *receptacle* 194n.
 case 194n.
 layer 207n.
 covering 226n.

arsenal 723n.
sheathe *replace* 187vb.
 cover 226vb.
 dress 228vb.
 intromit 231vb.
 insert 303vb.
sheave *tool* 630n.
shebeen *tavern* 192n.
shed *decrease* 37vb.
 unstick 49vb.
 small house 192n.
 doff 229vb.
 emit 300vb.
 let fall 311vb.
 disaccustom 611vb.
 relinquish 621vb.
sheen *light* 417n.
 reflection 417n.
sheep *imitator* 20n.
 sheep 365n.
 laity 987n.
sheepcote *stable* 192n.
sheep-farming
 animal husbandry 369n.
sheepfold *stable* 192n.
 inclosure 235n.
 cattle pen 369n.
sheepish *weak* 163adj.
 animal 365adj.
 modest 874adj.
sheep-rot
 animal disease 651n.
sheep-run *place* 185n.
 grassland 348n.
 stock farm 369n.
sheep's eyes *desire* 859n.
 wooing 889n.
sheepshank *ligature* 47n.
sheep walk
 stock farm 369n.
sheer *simple* 44adj.
 verticality 215n.
 vertical 215adj.
 sloping 220adj.
 transparent 422adj.
sheer off *recede* 290vb.
 deviate 282vb.
sheet *part* 53n.
 lamina 207n.
 coverlet 226n.
 robe 228n.
 dress 228vb.
 lake 346n.
 rain 350vb.
 the press 528n.
 letterpress 587n.
 edition 589n.
 paper 631n.
sheet anchor *coupling* 47n.
 safeguard 662n.
 hope 852n.

sheet-lightning
luminary 420 n.
sheets *tackling* 47 n.
sheikh *potentate* 741 n.
nobleman 868 n.
sheikhdom
magistrature 733 n.
sheiling *small house* 192 n.
shekel *coinage* 797 n.
Shekinah
manifestation 522 n.
theophany 965 n.
shelf *compartment* 194 n.
shelf 218 n.
storage 632 n.
shell *mould* 23 n.
emptiness 190 n.
exterior 223 n.
covering, skin 226 n.
uncover 229 vb.
rowboat 275 n.
extract 304 vb.
hardness 326 n.
structure 331 n.
horn 414 n.
class 538 n.
print 587 n.
fire at 712 vb.
armour 713 n.
ammunition 723 n.
missile weapon 723 n.
seclusion 883 n.
shellac *resin* 357 n.
shellback *mariner* 270 n.
expert 696 n.
shell-burst *loudness* 400 n.
shell-case *ammunition* 723 n.
shell-fish *fish food* 301 n.
table fish 365 n.
shell out *pay* 804 vb.
shell-shock
psychopathy 503 n.
illness 651 n.
shelter *small house* 192 n.
dwelling 192 n.
stable 192 n.
retreat 192 n.
dwell 192 vb.
resting place 266 n.
admit 299 vb.
screen 421 n., vb.
hiding-place 527 n.
safeguard 660 vb.
shelter 662 n.
defences 713 n.
shelterless
vulnerable 661 adj.
shelter under *plead* 614 vb.
sheltie *pony* 273 n.
shelve *put off* 136 vb.
be oblique 220 vb.

be neglectful 458 vb.
avoid 620 vb.
relinquish 621 vb.
shelving
compartment 194 n.
shend *curse* 899 vb.
exprobate 924 vb.
Sheol *death* 361 n.
hell 972 n.
shepherd
bring together 74 vb.
herdsman 369 n.
groom 369 vb.
protector 660 n.
direct 689 vb.
leader 690 n.
servant 742 n.
pastor 986 n.
shepherdess
herdsman 369 n.
sherbet *soft drink* 301 n.
sherd *piece* 53 n.
sheriff *protector* 660 n.
officer 741 n.
law officer 955 n.
sherry *wine* 301 n.
shewbread
ritual object 988 n.
shibboleth
identification 457 n.
call 547 n.
shield *covering* 226 n.
screen 421 n., vb.
safeguard 660 vb.
shelter 662 n.
armour 713 n.
defend 713 vb.
honours 866 n.
shield-bearer
retainer 742 n.
shift *period* 110 n.
periodicity 141 n.
change 143 n., vb.
transition 147 n.
vary 152 vb.
displacement 188 n.
bodywear 228 n.
move 265 vb.
transpose 272 vb.
move fast 277 vb.
deflect 282 vb.
trickery 542 n.
mental dishonesty 543 n.
pretext 614 n.
contrivance 623 n.
labour 682 n.
stratagem 698 n.
change hands 780 vb.
shiftless *impenitent* 940 adj.
shifty *changeful* 152 adj.
cunning 698 adj.

dishonest 930 adj.
Shiites
non-Christian sect 978 n.
shillelagh *club* 723 n.
shilling *coinage* 797 n.
shilly-shally
be irresolute 601 vb.
shimmer *flash* 417 n.
shimmy *wriggle* 251 vb.
dance 837 n.
shin *leg* 267 n.
shindy *quarrel* 709 n.
fight 716 n.
shine *smooth* 258 vb.
light 417 n.
shine 417 vb.
be visible 443 vb.
be wise 498 vb.
cleanness 648 n.
be skilful 694 vb.
be beautiful 841 vb.
have repute 866 vb.
shine on *patronize* 703 vb.
be auspicious 730 vb.
shingle *shorten* 204 vb.
laminate 207 vb.
roof 226 n.
shore 344 n.
building material 631 n.
hair-dressing 843 n.
shingles *skin disease* 651 n.
shining light *sage* 500 n.
Shintoism
religious faith 973 n.
shiny *smooth* 258 adj.
luminous 417 adj.
clean 648 adj.
ship *load* 193 vb.
send 272 vb.
carry 273 vb.
ship 275 n.
shipload *contents* 193 n.
shipman *mariner* 270 n.
shipmate *chum* 880 n.
shipment *contents* 193 n.
transport 272 n.
thing transferred 272 n.
ship-money *tax* 809 n.
shipper *transferrer* 272 n.
carrier 273 n.
shipping *transport* 272 n.
shipping 275 n.
shipshape *orderly* 60 adj.
regular 83 adj.
marine 275 adj.
well-made 694 adj.
shipwreck *ruin* 165 n.
shipwright *artisan* 686 n.
shipyard *workshop* 687 n.
shire *district* 184 n.
shiremoot *assembly* 74 n.

shirk *disregard* 458 vb.
  be loth 598 vb.
  avoid 620 vb.
  fail in duty 918 vb.
shirker *coward* 856 n.
shirr *fold* 261 vb.
shirt *bodywear* 228 n.
shirt-waist *bodywear* 228 n.
shirty *angry* 891 adj.
  sullen 893 adj.
shive-knife
  sharp edge 256 n.
shiver *break* 46 vb.
  demolish 165 vb.
  strip 208 n.
  oscillate 317 vb.
  be agitated 318 vb.
  be brittle 330 vb.
  be cold 380 vb.
  quake 854 vb.
shivers *agitation* 318 n.
  coldness 380 n.
  illness 651 n.
  nervousness 854 n.
shoal *group* 74 n.
  shallow 212 adj.
  pitfall 663 n.
shock *bunch* 74 n.
  violence 176 n.
  collision 279 n.
  agitation 318 n.
  inexpectation 508 n.
  illness 651 n.
  attack 712 n., vb.
  excitation 821 n.
  suffering 825 n.
  displease 827 vb.
  cause discontent 829 vb.
  fear 854 n.
  cause dislike 861 vb.
  wonder 864 n.
  excite hate 888 vb.
  incur blame 927 vb.
shockable *modest* 874 adj.
  innocent 935 adj.
  prudish 950 adj.
shock-absorber
  moderator 177 n.
shocked
  disapproving 924 adj.
shocker *novel* 590 n.
  monster 938 n.
shock-headed *hairy* 259 adj.
shocking *flagrant* 32 adj.
  unusual 84 adj.
  not nice 645 adj.
  distressing 827 adj.
  ugly 842 adj.
  frightening 854 adj.
  wonderful 864 adj.
  discreditable 867 adj.

heinous 934 adj.
shock-proof *tough* 329 adj.
  unfeeling 375 adj.
shock tactics *attack* 712 n.
shock treatment
  therapy 658 n.
shock troops
  attacker 712 n.
  armed force 722 n.
shod *dressed* 228 adj.
shoddy *inferior* 35 adj.
  flimsy 163 adj.
  fibre 208 n.
  spurious 542 adj.
  trivial 639 adj.
  bad 645 adj.
  bad taste 847 n.
shoe *affix* 45 vb.
  stand 218 n.
  footwear 228 n.
  fetter 748 n.
shoe-black *cleaner* 648 n.
shoemaker *clothier* 228 n.
shoe-string, on a
  parsimoniously 816 adv.
shogun *tyrant* 735 n.
  autocrat 741 n.
shoo off *dismiss* 300 vb.
shoot *branch* 53 n.
  young plant 132 n.
  descendant 170 n.
  expand 197 vb.
  navigate 269 vb.
  kick 279 vb.
  shoot 287 vb.
  pass 305 vb.
  kill 362 vb.
  tree 366 n.
  vegetate 366 vb.
  give pain 377 vb.
  radiate 417 vb.
  photograph 551 vb.
  fire at 712 vb.
  execute 963 vb.
shoot a line
  be ostentatious 875 vb.
  boast 877 vb.
shooter *shooter* 287 n.
shooting box
  small house 192 n.
shooting-brake
  automobile 274 n.
shooting range *arena* 724 n.
shooting star *meteor* 321 n.
  luminary 420 n.
shoot the sun
  orientate 281 vb.
shoot up *grow* 36 vb.
  jut 254 vb.
  ascend 308 vb.
shop *topic* 452 n.

workshop 687 n.
  purchase 792 vb.
  shop 796 n.
shop-assistant
  servant 742 n.
  seller 793 n.
shopkeeper
  provider 633 n.
  tradesman 794 n.
shop-lifting *stealing* 788 n.
shopman *seller* 793 n.
  tradesman 794 n.
shopper *purchaser* 792 n.
shopping *purchase* 792 n.
  buying 792 adj.
shopping centre
  emporium 796 n.
shopping list
  requirement 627 n.
shop-soiled *inferior* 35 adj.
  imperfect 647 adj.
  blemished 845 adj.
shop-steward *leader* 690 n.
  delegate 754 n.
shop-walker *servant* 742 n.
  seller 793 n.
shop-window
  transparency 422 n.
  exhibit 522 n.
  mart 796 n.
shore *region* 184 n.
  edge 234 n.
  limit 236 n.
  shore 344 n.
shoreless *spacious* 183 adj.
shore up *support* 218 vb.
  preserve 666 vb.
shorn *short* 204 adj.
  clean 648 adj.
shorn of *losing* 772 adj.
short *incomplete* 55 adj.
  brief 114 adj.
  dwarfish 196 adj.
  short 204 adj.
  low 210 adj.
  deficient 307 adj.
  brittle 330 adj.
  concise 569 adj.
  taciturn 582 adj.
  compendious 592 adj.
  scarce 636 adj.
  poor 801 adj.
  ungracious 885 adj.
  irascible 892 adj.
shortage *decrement* 42 n.
  deficit 55 n.
  shortcoming 307 n.
shortbread *pastry* 301 n.
short circuit
  electricity 160 n.
  deviation 282 n.

escape 667 n.
hitch 702 n.
shortcoming
  shortcoming 307 n.
  insufficiency 636 n.
  imperfection 647 n.
  non-completion 726 n.
  non-observance 769 n.
  vice 934 n.
  (*see* shortage)
short commons
  insufficiency 636 n.
  fasting 946 n.
short cut
  short distance 200 n.
  straightness 249 n.
shorten *bate* 37 vb.
  cut 46 vb.
  shorten 204 vb.
  abstract 592 vb.
shortfall *deficit* 55 n.
  shortcoming 307 n.
  scarcity 636 n.
shorthand *writing* 586 n.
shorthanded
  imperfect 647 adj.
shorties *nightwear* 228 n.
short-lived
  ephemeral 114 adj.
shortness *smallness* 33 n.
  (*see* short)
short notice, at
  suddenly 135 adv.
  hastily 680 adv.
short of *less* 35 adv.
  exclusive of 57 adv.
short run *brief span* 114 n.
shorts *leavings* 41 n.
  trousers 228 n.
short-service *brief* 114 adj.
short shrift
  pitilessness 906 n.
short-sighted
  dim-sighted 440 adj.
  misjudging 481 adj.
  unwise 499 adj.
short supply
  scarcity 636 n.
short-tempered
  irascible 892 adj.
short-term *brief* 114 adj.
short weight *inequality* 29 n.
shot *mixed* 43 adj.
  missile 287 n.
  shooter 287 n.
  insertion 303 n.
  bang 402 n.
  iridescent 437 adj.
  conjecture 512 n.
  photography 551 n.
  hunter 619 n.

therapy 658 n.
  missile weapon 723 n.
  ammunition 723 n.
shotgun *fire-arm* 723 n.
shotgun wedding
  type of marriage 894 n.
shot in one's locker
  means 629 n.
shot in the dark
  empiricism 461 n.
  conjecture 512 n.
  gambling 618 n.
shotten
  deteriorated 655 adj.
shoulder *supporter* 218 n.
  angularity 247 n.
  camber 253 n.
  carry 273 vb.
  impel 279 vb.
  propel 287 vb.
  elevate 310 vb.
  print-type 587 n.
shoulder to shoulder
  cohesive 48 adj.
  in league 708 adv.
shout *loudness* 400 n.
  vociferate 408 vb.
  proclaim 528 vb.
  affirm 532 vb.
  call 547 n.
  voice 577 vb.
  rejoicing 835 n.
  be rude 885 vb.
shout down *affirm* 532 vb.
  make mute 578 vb.
  be insolent 878 vb.
  disapprove 924 vb.
shouter *boaster* 877 n.
shout for *applaud* 923 vb.
shove *move* 265 vb.
  transpose 272 vb.
  impulse 279 n.
  propel 287 vb.
  gesture 547 n.
  be active 678 vb.
shovel *ladle* 194 n.
  transpose 272 vb.
  shovel 274 n.
  extractor 304 n.
shovel-hat *canonicals* 989 n.
shove off *impel* 279 vb.
  decamp 296 vb.
show *produce* 164 vb.
  be visible 443 vb.
  spectacle 445 n.
  appear 445 vb.
  attract notice 455 vb.
  evidence 466 vb.
  demonstrate 478 vb.
  interpret 520 vb.
  exhibit 522 n.

show 522 vb.
  duplicity 541 n.
  deception 542 n.
  indicate 547 vb.
  stage play 594 n.
  dramatize 594 vb.
  amusement 837 n.
  pride 871 n.
  pageant 875 n.
showable *shown* 522 adj.
showboat *ship* 275 n.
  theatre 594 n.
show business *drama* 594 n.
show-card
  advertisement 528 n.
showcase *exhibit* 522 n.
showdown *disclosure* 526 n.
shower *propel* 287 vb.
  descend 309 vb.
  let fall 311 vb.
  rain 350 n., vb.
  exhibition 522 n.
  abound 635 vb.
  ablution 648 n.
shower upon
  be liberal 813 vb.
showery *rainy* 350 adj.
show fight
  be vigorous 174 vb.
  defy 711 vb.
  attack 712 vb.
  parry 713 vb.
  take courage 855 vb.
show, for
  ostentatious 875 adj.
show girl *actor* 594 n.
show in *admit* 299 vb.
showiness *ostentation* 875 n.
showing *uncovered* 229 adj.
  visible 443 adj.
show-jumper *rider* 268 n.
show-jumping
  equitation 267 n.
showman *guide* 520 n.
  exhibitor 522 n.
  stage-manager 594 n.
showmanship
  manifestation 522 n.
  publicity 528 n.
show of *probability* 471 n.
show of hands *vote* 605 n.
show off *beautify* 841 vb.
  be affected 850 vb.
  seek repute 866 vb.
  be proud 871 vb.
  be vain 873 vb.
  be ostentatious 875 vb.
  boast 877 vb.
show, on *shown* 522 adj.
show one's face
  be present 189 vb.

be plain 522 vb.
show one's hand
  divulge 526 vb.
show one's mind
  be plain 522 vb.
show out dismiss 300 vb.
show piece exhibit 522 n.
showplace exhibit 522 n.
show results
  be successful 727 vb.
showroom exhibit 522 n.
show signs indicate 547 vb.
show the way
  come before 64 vb.
  orientate 281 vb.
  prepare 669 vb.
show through
  be inside 224 vb.
  be transparent 422 vb.
  appear 445 vb.
show up arrive 295 vb.
  be visible 443 vb.
  be plain 522 vb.
  show 522 vb.
  disclose 526 vb.
  satirize 851 vb.
  shame 867 vb.
  accuse 928 vb.
showy florid 425 adj.
  ornate 574 adj.
  splendid 841 adj.
  vulgar 847 adj.
  prideful 871 adj.
  showy 875 adj.
shrapnel
  missile weapon 723 n.
shred small thing 33 n.
  piece 53 n.
  fraction 102 n.
shredded
  fragmentary 53 adj.
shreds and tatters
  poverty 801 n.
shreds, in
  dilapidated 655 adj.
shrew violent creature 176 n.
  quarreller 709 n.
  shrew 892 n.
  hell-hag 904 n.
  defamer 926 n.
shrewd knowing 490 adj.
  intelligent 498 adj.
  skilful 694 adj.
  cunning 698 adj.
shrewd idea
  conjecture 512 n.
shrewdly painfully 32 adv.
shrewish quarrelling 709 adj.
  irascible 892 adj.
shriek feel pain 377 vb.
  stridor 407 n.

cry 408 vb.
lament 836 n.
weep 836 vb.
shrieking florid 425 adj.
shrievalty jurisdiction 955 n.
shrift forgiveness 909 n.
  penance 941 n.
  church ministry 985 n.
  ministration 988 n.
shrill loud 400 adj.
  shrill 407 vb.
shrimp dwarf 196 n.
  animalcule 196 n.
  fish food 301 n.
  table fish 365 n.
  hunt 619 vb.
shrine small box 194 n.
  ritual object 988 n.
  temple 990 n.
shrink decrease 37 vb.
  become small 198 vb.
  recoil 280 vb.
  turn back 286 vb.
  recede 290 vb.
  avoid 620 vb.
  deteriorate 655 vb.
  be nervous 854 vb.
  be modest 874 vb.
shrinkage decrement 42 n.
  contraction 198 n.
shrink from dislike 861 vb.
  hate 888 vb.
shrinking modest 874 adj.
shrive perform ritual 988 vb.
shrivel dry 342 vb.
  heat 381 vb.
  deteriorate 655 vb.
shrivelled lean 206 adj.
shriven forgiven 909 adj.
shroff merchant 794 n.
shroud tackling 47 n.
  wrapping 226 n.
  robe 228 n.
  dress 228 vb.
  grave clothes 364 n.
  conceal 525 vb.
  safeguard 660 vb.
  defend 713 vb.
shrub tree 366 n.
shrubbery wood 366 n.
shrug be impotent 161 vb.
  gesture 547 n.
  be indifferent 860 vb.
shrug away
  hold cheap 922 vb.
shrunk dwarfish 196 adj.
  contracted 198 adj.
shuck skin 226 n.
  uncover 229 vb.
  extract 304 vb.
shudder agitation 318 n.

be cold 380 vb.
quake 854 vb.
shudder at dislike 861 vb.
shuffle walk 267 vb.
  move slowly 278 vb.
  deflect 282 vb.
  sophistry 477 n.
  dissemble 541 vb.
  mix 43 vb.
  jumble 63 vb.
  interchange 151 n., vb.
  vary 151 vb.
  gait 265 n.
  be irresolute 601 vb.
  tergiversate 603 vb.
  dance 837 n., vb.
  be dishonest 930 vb.
shuffler deceiver 545 n.
shun be stealthy 525 vb.
  avoid 620 vb.
  dislike 861 vb.
shunt deflect 282 vb.
  transpose 272 vb.
shunter driver 268 n.
  locomotive 274 n.
shut close 264 vb.
shut down cease 145 vb.
shut-eye sleep 679 n.
shut in interior 224 adj.
  surround 230 vb.
  close 264 vb.
  imprison 747 vb.
shut out exclude 57 vb.
shutter stopper 264 n.
  covering, shade 226 n.
  darken 418 vb.
  curtain 421 n.
shuttle periodicity 141 n.
  weaving 222 n.
  fluctuation 317 n.
shuttlecock
  fluctuation 317 n.
  waverer 601 n.
shuttle service
  periodicity 141 n.
  fluctuation 317 n.
shuttlewise
  correlatively 12 adv.
  to and fro 317 adv.
shut up cease 145 vb.
  confute 479 vb.
  make mute 578 vb.
  imprison 747 vb.
  seclude 883 vb.
shy recoil 280 vb.
  deviate 282 vb.
  turn back 286 vb.
  propel 287 vb.
  unwilling 598 adj.
  avoid 620 vb.
  artless 699 adj.

lapidate 712vb.
nervous 854adj.
disliking 861adj.
modest 874adj.
unsociable 883adj.
shy at *doubt* 486vb.
refuse 760vb.
Shylock *lender* 784n.
shy of *incomplete* 55adj.
shyster *trickster* 545n.
knave 938n.
lawyer 958n.
sialagogue *ejector* 300n.
sib *akin* 11adj.
sibilation *sibilation* 406n.
disapprobation 924n.
Sibyl *oracle* 511n.
sorceress 983n.
sic *truly* 494adv.
siccative *drier* 342n.
sick *weakly* 163n.
vomiting 300adj.
sick 651adj.
suffering 825adj.
crapulous 949adj.
sick-bay *hospital* 658n.
sick-bed *bed* 218n.
illness 651n.
hospital 658n.
sicken *be weak* 163vb.
be unpalatable 391vb.
superabound 637vb.
be ill 651vb.
deteriorate 655vb.
displease 827vb.
cause discontent 829vb.
be tedious 838vb.
cause dislike 861vb.
sickener *plenitude* 54n.
unsavouriness 391n.
superfluity 637n.
bane 659n.
sickening *unsavoury* 391n.
not nice 645adj.
discontenting 829adj.
disliked 861adj.
sickening for *sick* 651adj.
sickle *angularity* 247n.
sharp edge 256n.
farm tool 370n.
sick list *sick person* 651n.
sickly *weakly* 163adj.
colourless 426adj.
unhealthy 651adj.
sickness *illness* 651n.
sick of *bored* 838adj.
disliking 861adj.
sated 863adj.
sick-room *hospital* 658n.
side *race* 11n.
part 53n.

situation 186n.
edge 234n.
laterality 239n.
appearance 445n.
choose 605vb.
party 708n.
pride 871n.
vanity 873n.
ostentation 875n.
side against *oppose* 704vb.
side-arms *side-arms* 723n.
sideboard *cabinet* 194n.
stand 218n.
side by side *with* 89adv.
nigh 200adv.
sideways 239adv.
in league 708adv.
sidecar *bicycle* 274n.
side-dish *dish* 301n.
side-face *laterality* 239n.
side-glance *look* 438n.
wooing 889n.
side-issue *question* 459n.
side-kick *chum* 880n.
side-light *lamp* 420n.
knowledge 490n.
sideline *edge* 234n.
laterality 239n.
sidelong *obliquely* 220adv.
lateral 239adj.
sideways 239adv.
side-pressure
obliquity 220n.
inducement 612n.
sidereal *celestial* 321adj.
side-saddle *seat* 218n.
side-show *trifle* 639n.
sideslip *flank* 239vb.
aeronautics 271n.
deviation 282n.
be in danger 661vb.
sidesman
church officer 986n.
side-splitting *funny* 849adj.
sidestep *be oblique* 220vb.
laterality 239n.
deviation 282vb.
avoidance 620n.
side to side
to and fro 317adv.
sidetrack *deflect* 282vb.
avoid 620vb.
sidewalk *road* 624n.
path 624n.
sideways *obliquely* 220adv.
sideways 239adv.
side with *assent* 488vb.
patronize 703vb.
siding *laterality* 239n.
railroad 624n.
sidle *be oblique* 220vb.

flank 239vb.
deviate 282vb.
siege *circumscription* 232n.
attack 712n.
siegecraft *art of war* 718n.
sienna *brown paint* 430n.
sierra *high land* 209n.
siesta *sleep* 679n.
sieve *sorting* 62n.
porosity 263n.
cleaning utensil 648n.
(see sift)
sift *eliminate* 44vb.
exclude 57vb.
class 62vb.
enquire 459vb.
discriminate 463vb.
select 605vb.
purify 648vb.
sifter (*see* sieve)
sigh *respiration* 352n.
breathe 352vb.
sound faint 401vb.
cry 408n.,vb.
suffer 825vb.
be dejected 834vb.
lamentation 836n.
be in love 887vb.
wooing 889n.
sigh for *desire* 859vb.
sight *aim* 281vb.
arrive 295vb.
vision 438n.
visibility 443n.
spectacle 445n.
detect 484vb.
eyesore 842n.
prodigy 864n.
sightless *blind* 439adj.
invisible 444adj.
sightly *personable* 841adj.
sight of
great quantity 32n.
multitude 104n.
sight-read *be musical* 413vb.
sights *direction* 281n.
sight-seeing
inspection 438n.
curiosity 453n.
sightseer *traveller* 268n.
spectator 441n.
inquisitor 453n.
sight-testing *vision* 438n.
sigla *punctuation* 547n.
sigma *sibilation* 406n.
sigmatism *sibilation* 406n.
dialect 560n.
pronunciation 577n.
sigmoidal
labyrinthine 251adj.
sign *evidence* 466n.

numerical element 85n.
endorse 488vb.
omen 511n.
manifestation 522n.
indication 547n.
badge, label 547n.
gesture 547n.
letter 588n.
warning 664n.
command 737n.,vb.
contract 765vb.
give security 767vb.
prodigy 864n.
signal *remarkable* 32adj.
communicate 524vb.
message 529n.
signal 547n.,vb.
railroad 624n.
notable 638adj.
signal box *railroad* 624n.
signalize *indicate* 547vb.
dignify 866vb.
celebrate 876vb.
signal light
signal light 420n.
signalling
telecommunication 531n.
signation *ritual act* 988n.
signatory *witness* 466n.
assenter 488n.
signatory 765n.
signature *notation* 410n.
assent 488n.
label 547n.
identification 547n.
name 561n.
edition 589n.
compact 765n.
title-deed 767n.
sign-board *label* 547n.
signet *badge of rule* 743n.
signet ring *jewellery* 844n.
significance *meaning* 514n.
importance 638n.
significant
evidential 466adj.
presageful 511adj.
signification
connotation 514n.
indication 547n.
signify *specify* 80vb.
predict 511vb.
mean 514vb.
inform 524vb.
indicate 547vb.
be important 638vb.
sign language
mimicry 20n.
gesture 547n.
language 557n.
sign-manual *label* 547n.

script 586n.
sign off *resign* 753vb.
sign on *join a party* 708vb.
sign-painter *artist* 556n.
signpost *direction* 281n.
signpost 547n.
sign-writer *penman* 586n.
silage *agriculture* 370n.
silence *stop* 145n.
disable 161vb.
quietude 266n.
silence 399n.,vb.
confute 479vb.
make mute 578vb.
taciturnity 582n.
silencer *silencer* 401n.
non-resonance 405n.
silent *lubricated* 334adj.
non-resonant 405adj.
reticent 525adj.
voiceless 578adj.
unsociable 883adj.
disapproving 924adj.
(*see* silence)
silent trade *barter* 791n.
Silenus *vegetability* 366n.
lesser god 967n.
silhouette *copy* 22n.
outline 233n.,vb.
efform 243vb.
darken 418vb.
feature 445n.
picture 553n.
silk *fibre* 208n.
textile 222n.
smoothness 258n.
silk gown *lawyer* 958n.
silky *smooth* 258adj.
soft 327adj.
textural 331adj.
sill *base* 214n.
shelf 218n.
projection 254n.
sillabub *ornament* 574n.
eloquence 579n.
silly *credulous* 487adj.
absurd 497adj.
foolish 499adj.
fool 501n.
gullible 544adj.
silly season
absurdity 497n.
silly symphony
foolery 497n.
silly talk *silly talk* 315n.
silo *farm tool* 370n.
storage 632n.
preserver 666n.
silt *leavings* 41n.
fertilizer 171n.
solid body 324n.

soil 344n.
marsh 347n.
semiliquidity 354n.
silty *territorial* 344adj.
semiliquid 354adj.
silver *coat* 226vd.
colour 425vb.
white thing 427n.
money, bullion 797n.
silvered *grey* 429adj.
silver lining *hope* 852n.
silversmith *artisan* 686n.
silver-toned
melodious 410adj.
silver-tongued
melodious 410adj.
eloquent 579adj.
silver wedding
anniversary 141n.
special day 876n.
wedding 894n.
silvery *melodious* 410adj.
white 427adj.
grey 429adj.
silviculture *forestry* 366n.
agriculture 370n.
simar, simarra
canonicals 989n.
similar (*see* similarity)
similarity *relativeness* 9n.
correlation 12n.
uniformity 16n.
similarity 18n.
copy 22n.
equivalence 28n.
simile *analogue* 18n.
comparison 462n.
metaphor 519n.
ornament 574n.
similitude
comparison 462n.
representation 551n.
simmer *cook* 301vb.
effervesce 318vb.
resent 891vb.
simmering
excitable 822adj.
simony *sale* 793n.
improbity 930n.
simoom *gale* 352n.
heat 379n.
simous *deformed* 246adj.
simper *smile* 835n.
be affected 850vb.
simple *simple* 44adj.
credulous 487adj.
ignorant 491adj.
foolish 499adj.
intelligible 516adj.
veracious 540adj.
plain 573adj.

elegant 575 adj.
medicine 658 n.
artless 699 adj.
easy 701 adj.
tasteful 846 adj.
plebeian 869 adj.
simplemindedness
artlessness 699 n.
simpleness *simpleness* 44 n.
unity 88 n.
(*see* simple)
Simple Simon *ninny* 501 n.
dupe 544 n.
simpleton *ignoramus* 493 n.
ninny 501 n.
simplicity
(*see* simple, simpleness)
simplification
simplification 44 n.
arrangement 62 n.
intelligibility 516 n.
translation 520 n.
facility 701 n.
simplify *decompose* 51 vb.
(*see* simplification)
simulacrum
mimicry 20 n.
sham 542 n.
pretext 614 n.
(*see* image)
simulation
assimilation 18 n.
mimicry 20 n.
duplicity 541 n.
simulator *imitator* 20 n.
simultaneity
synchronism 123 n.
(*see* simultaneous)
simultaneous
accompanying 89 adj.
instantaneous 116 adj.
simurgh *rara avis* 84 n.
sin *badness* 645 n.
disobedience 738 n.
wrong 914 n.
wickedness 934 n.
vice 934 n.
be wicked 934 vb.
guilty act 936 n.
impiety 980 n.
sinanthropus
mankind 371 n.
sinapism
surgical dressing 658 n.
since *subsequently* 120 adv.
hence 158 adv.
sincere *simple* 44 adj.
(*see* sincerity)
sincerity
no imitation 21 n.
veracity 540 n.

artlessness 699 n.
feeling 818 n.
probity 929 n.
piety 979 n.
sinciput *head* 213 n.
sine *ratio* 85 n.
sinecure *inaction* 677 n.
leisure 681 n.
easy thing 701 n.
sinecure, no *activity* 678 n.
sinecurist *idler* 679 n.
sine die *never* 109 adv.
sine qua non
speciality 80 n.
concomitant 89 n.
requirement 627 n.
chief thing 638 n.
conditions 766 n.
sinews *vitality* 162 n.
sinews of war
defence 713 n.
funds 797 n.
sinewy *stalwart* 162 adj.
sinful *bad* 645 adj.
wrong 914 adj.
heinous 934 adj.
wicked 934 adj.
guilty 936 adj.
impious 980 adj.
sing *resound* 404 vb.
ululate 409 vb.
harmonize 410 vb.
sing 413 vb.
poetize 593 vb.
be cheerful 833 vb.
rejoice 835 vb.
singable *melodious* 410 adj.
musical 412 n.
singe *burn* 381 vb.
blacken 428 vb.
embrown 430 vb.
hair-dressing 843 n.
singer *vocalist* 413 n.
singing-bird *bird* 365 n.
single *simple* 44 adj.
whole 52 adj.
one 88 adj.
infrequent 140 adj.
independent 744 adj.
unwedded 895 adj.
single blessedness
celibacy 895 n.
single combat
duel 716 n.
single entry
accounts 808 n.
single file *procession* 71 n.
line 203 n.
single-handed *alone* 88 adj.
hindered 702 adj.
single-hearted

artless 699 adj.
trustworthy 929 adj.
single-minded
simple 44 adj.
obsessed 455 adj.
singlemindedness
attention 455 n.
resolution 599 n.
perseverance 600 n.
artlessness 699 n.
singleness *unity* 88 n.
celibacy 895 n.
(*see* single)
single out
differentiate 15 vb.
set apart 46 vb.
single piece *unit* 88 n.
single state *celibacy* 895 n.
single-stick *duel* 716 n.
singlet *bodywear* 228 n.
singleton *unit* 88 n.
single voice
consensus 488 n.
sing out *vociferate* 408 vb.
Sing Sing *prison* 748 n.
sing small
be humble 872 vb.
sing-song *uniform* 16 adj.
repeated 106 adj.
discordant 411 adj.
music 412 n.
social gathering 882 n.
singular
grammatical 564 adj.
(*see* singularity)
singularity *irrelation* 10 n.
speciality 80 n.
unconformity 84 n.
unity 88 n.
sinister *sinistrality* 242 n.
sinistral 242 adj.
presageful 511 adj.
evil 616 adj.
bad 645 adj.
harmful 645 adj.
adverse 731 adj.
frightening 854 adj.
dishonest 930 adj.
sink *decrease* 37 vb.
suppress 165 vb.
receptacle 194 n.
cavity 255 n.
descend 309 vb.
founder 313 vb.
weigh 322 vb.
drain 351 n.
fetor 397 n.
storage 632 n.
badness 645 n.
sink 649 n.
insalubrity 653 n.

deteriorate 655 vb.
be fatigued 684 vb.
defeat 727 vb.
fail 728 vb.
sinkable
descending 309 adj.
sinkage *depth* 211 n.
descent 309 n.
gravity 322 n.
sink back *relapse* 657 vb.
sinker *diver* 313 n.
gravity 322 n.
sink in *infiltrate* 297 vb.
cause thought 449 n.
sinking fund *finance* 797 n.
sink into
be turned to 147 vb.
sink money *expend* 806 vb.
sin-laden *wicked* 934 adj.
sinless *innocent* 935 adj.
pure 950 adj.
sinner *offender* 904 n.
evildoer 904 n.
bad man 938 n.
impious person 980 n.
sin-offering
substitute 150 n.
propitiation 941 n.
oblation 981 n.
Sinologist *linguist* 557 n.
sinuosity *convolution* 251 n.
curvature 248 n.
sinuous *convoluted* 251 adj.
sinus *cavity* 255 n.
sinusitis
respiratory disease 651 n.
sip *small quantity* 33 n.
mouthful 301 n.
drink 301 vb.
taste 386 vb.
siphon *transferrer* 272 n.
transpose 272 vb.
void 300 vb.
soft drink 301 n.
extractor 304 n.
conduit 351 n.
sir *old man* 133 n.
male 372 n.
name 561 vb.
master 741 n.
dignify 866 vb.
title 870 n.
be courteous 884 vb.
sirdar *potentate* 741 n.
domestic 742 n.
sire *be akin* 11 vb.
generate 164 vb.
parent 169 n.
master 741 n.
title 870 n.
sired *born* 360 adj.

siren *rara avis* 84 n.
timekeeper 117 n.
attraction 291 n.
sea nymph 343 n.
megaphone 400 n.
vocalist 413 n.
signal 547 n.
motivator 612 n.
warning 664 n.
danger signal 665 n.
sirene *flute* 414 n.
siriasis *frenzy* 503 n.
sirloin *meat* 301 n.
sirocco *wind* 352 n.
heat 379 n.
sisal *fibre* 208 n.
sissy *weakling* 163 n.
coward 856 n.
sister *kinsman* 11 n.
analogue 18 n.
nurse 658 n.
church title 986 n.
nun 986 n.
sisterhood *family* 11 n.
community 708 n.
sect 978 n.
nun 986 n.
sisterly *akin* 11 adj.
friendly 880 adj.
benevolent 897 adj.
sistrum *gong* 414 n.
sit *place oneself* 187 vb.
wait 136 vb.
sit down 311 vb.
be inactive 679 vb.
sit at the feet of
learn 536 vb.
sit down *pause* 145 vb.
be quiescent 266 vb.
sit down 311 vb.
repose 683 vb.
besiege 712 vb.
site *place* 185 n.
situation 186 n.
place 187 vb.
sit for *be example* 23 adj.
represent 551 vb.
sit loose to
come unstuck 49 vb.
be indifferent 860 vb.
sit on *suppress* 165 vb.
subjugate 745 vb.
restrain 747 vb.
sit on one's tail
pursue 619 vb.
sit on the fence
be uncertain 474 vb.
be half-way 625 vb.
sit out *carry through* 725 vb.
sit pretty *be content* 828 vb.
sitter *living model* 23 n.

exam. 459 n.
testee 461 n.
art equipment 553 n.
easy thing 701 n.
sit tight *be quiescent* 266 vb.
sitting *maturation* 669 n.
council 692 n.
sitting pretty
successful 727 adj.
sitting-room
chamber 194 n.
situate (*see* situation)
situation
circumstance 8 n.
degree 27 n.
complexity 61 n.
affairs 154 n.
place 185 n.
situation 186 n.
station 187 n.
direction 281 n.
job 625 n.
predicament 700 n.
situ, in *in place* 186 adv.
here 189 adv.
sit up *be attentive* 455 vb.
sit up with
look after 457 vb.
sit with *confer* 584 vb.
Siva *Hindu god* 967 n.
sixes and sevens, at
confusedly 61 adv.
six-footer
tall creature 209 n.
six of one and half a dozen
of the other
equivalence 28 n.
no choice 606 n.
indifference 860 n.
sixpence *coinage* 797 n.
six-shooter *pistol* 723 n.
sixth form *class* 538 n.
sixth sense *sense* 374 n.
intuition 476 n.
occultism 984 n.
sizar *college student* 538 n.
recipient 782 n.
sizarship
subvention 703 n.
receipt 807 n.
size *make uniform* 16 vb.
adjust 24 vb.
degree 27 n.
greatness 32 n.
adhesive 47 n.
arrange 62 vb.
measure 183 n.
size 195 n.
viscidity 354 n.
importance 638 n.
sizeable *large* 195 adj.

size of it *similarity* 18n.
size up *appraise* 465vb.
  estimate 480vb.
sizing *provisions* 301n.
  provision 633n.
sizzle *effervesce* 318vb.
  be hot 379vb.
  crackle 402vb.
  hiss 406vb.
sjambok *scourge* 964n.
skald *poet* 593n.
skate *go smoothly* 258vb.
  be in motion 265vb.
  travel 267vb.
  carrier 273n.
  sled 274n.
  table fish 365n.
skater *pedestrian* 268n.
skean *side-arms* 723n.
skedaddle *move fast* 277vb.
  decamp 296vb.
  run away 620vb.
skein *crossing* 222n.
  bunch 74n.
skeletal *lean* 206adj.
  structural 331adj.
skeleton *remainder* 41n.
  main part 52n.
  thinness 206n.
  frame 218n.
  outline 233n.
  structure 331n.
  corpse 363n.
  compendium 592n.
  plan 623n.
skeleton at the feast
  moper 834n.
skeleton in the cupboard
  secret 530n.
skelp *strike* 279vb.
skelter *move fast* 277vb.
skeptophilia
  impurity 951n.
skerry *rock* 344n.
sketch *copy* 22n.
  incompleteness 55n.
  outline 233n.,vb.
  efform 243vb.
  representation 551n.
  picture 553n.
  be concise 569vb.
  description 590n.
  compendium 592n.
  plan 623n.
sketcher *artist* 556n.
sketchy *incomplete* 55adj.
  uncompleted 726adj.
skewbald *horse* 273n.
  pied 437adj.
skewer *fastening* 47n.
  sharp point 256n.

perforator 263n.
skewness *inequality* 29n.
  obliquity 220n.
ski *go smoothly* 258vb.
  travel 267vb.
  carrier 273n.
  sled 274n.
skiagraphy
  darkness 418n.
  photography 551n.
skiascope
  optical device 442n.
skid *supporter* 218n.
  go smoothly 258vb.
  deviate 282vb.
  fetter 748n.
skiddy *smooth* 258adj.
skid-proof *dry* 342adj.
skier *pedestrian* 268n.
skiff *boat* 275n.
skiffle-group
  orchestra 413n.
skilful *fit* 24adj.
  intelligent 498adj.
  skilful 694adj.
ski-lift *ascent* 308n.
  lifter 310n.
skill *skill* 694n.
  cunning 698n.
skilled worker
  artisan 686n.
  expert 696n.
skillet *cauldron* 194n.
skill-less *bad* 645adj.
  unskilled 695adj.
skilly *cereal, soup* 301n.
skim *be near* 200vb.
  be contiguous 202vb.
  travel 267vb.
  swim 269vb.
  move fast 277vb.
  select 605vb.
  purify 648vb.
skimble-skamble
  orderless 61adj.
skimmings *leavings* 41n.
skimp *shorten* 204vb.
  neglect 458vb.
  make insufficient 636vb.
  be parsimonious 816vb.
skimpy *small* 33adj.
  short 204adj.
skin *leavings* 41n.
  rend 46vb.
  layer 207n.
  shallowness 212n.
  exteriority 223n.
  skin 226n.
  uncover 229vb.
  fleece 786vb.
  overcharge 811vb.

skin and bone
  thinness 206n.
skin-deep
  inconsiderable 33adj.
  shallow 212adj.
  exterior 223adj.
skin disease
  skin disease 651n.
skindiving *sport* 837n.
skinflint *niggard* 816n.
skin-grafting
  beautification 843n.
skinny *lean* 206adj.
skin over *cure* 656vb.
skin-tight *cohesive* 48adj.
skip *decamp* 296vb.
  leap 312n.,vb.
  neglect 458vb.
  study 536vb.
  escape 667vb.
  not complete 726vb.
  rejoice 835vb.
skipper *mariner* 270n.
  jumper 312n.
skippingly
  discontinuously 72adv.
skipping-rope
  plaything 837n.
skirl *be loud* 400vb.
  stridor 407n.
skirmish *fight* 716n.,vb.
  battle 718n.
skirmisher *precursor* 66n.
  soldier 722n.
skirt *be near* 200vb.
  base 214n.
  pendant 217n.
  skirt 228n.
  edge 234n.
  flank 239vb.
  pass 305vb.
  circle 314vb.
  woman 373n.
  circuit 626vb.
skirting *edging* 234n.
skirts *entrance* 68n.
skit *satire* 851n.
  calumny 926n.
skitter *swim* 269n.
skittish *leaping* 312adj.
  capricious 604adj.
  lively 819adj.
  excitable 822adj.
  lecherous 951adj.
skittle-alley
  place of amusement 837n.
skittle out *defeat* 727vb.
skittles *ball game* 837n.
skive *cut* 46vb.
  laminate 207vb.
skiver *sharp point* 256n.

skivvy *domestic* 742 n.
skulduggery *trickery* 542 n.
  improbity 930 n.
skulk *wander* 267 vb.
  be stealthy 525 vb.
  avoid 620 vb.
  quake 854 vb.
  be cowardly 856 vb.
skulker *hider* 527 n.
skull *head* 213 n.
skull and crossbones
  heraldry 847 n.
  intimidation 854 n.
skull-cap *headgear* 228 n.
  canonicals 989 n.
skunk *vermin* 365 n.
  fetor 397 n.
  coward 856 n.
  cad 938 n.
sky *space* 183 n.
  height 209 n.
  summit 213 n.
  propel 287 vb.
  elevate 310 vb.
  heavens 321 n.
  blueness 435 n.
skyey *airy* 340 adj.
skylark *climb* 308 vb.
skylarker *reveller* 837 n.
skylight *window* 263 n.
sky-line *distance* 199 n.
  edge 234 n.
sky-rocket *rocket* 276 n.
  climber 308 n.
  fireworks 420 n.
skysail *sail* 275 n.
skyscraper *edifice* 164 n.
  house 192 n.
  high structure 209 n.
sky-writing *publicity* 528 n.
slab *lamina* 207 n.
  horizontality 216 n.
  shelf 218 n.
  monument 548 n.
slabber *exude* 298 vb.
  excrement 302 n.
  moisture 341 n.
slabby *marshy* 347 adj.
  semiliquid 354 adj.
slack *non-adhesive* 49 adj.
  decompose 51 vb.
  orderless 61 adj.
  weak 163 adj.
  slow 278 adj.
  add water 339 vb.
  coal 385 n.
  negligent 458 adj.
  be loth 598 vb.
  lazy 679 adj.
  lax 734 adj.
slacken *disjoin* 46 vb.

  unstick 49 vb.
  moderate 177 vb.
  decelerate 278 vb.
  be inactive 679 vb.
slackening *decrease* 37 n.
slacker *slowcoach* 278 n.
  slacker 598 n.
  avoider 620 n.
  indifference 860 n.
slacks *trousers* 228 n.
slack, take up the
  recoup 31 vb.
slack water
  mid-course 625 n.
slag *leavings* 41 n.
  solid body 324 n.
  ash 381 n.
  rubbish 641 n.
  dirt 649 n.
slake *decompose* 51 vb.
  assuage 177 vb.
  add water 339 vb.
  sate 863 vb.
slam *be vigorous* 174 vb.
  close 264 vb.
  impulse 279 n.
  strike 279 vb.
  propel 287 vb.
  loudness 400 n.
  bang 402 n., vb.
  victory 727 n.
slander *slur* 867 n.
  scurrility 899 n.
  censure 924 n.
  calumny 926 n.
  false charge 928 n.
slanderer *evildoer* 904 n.
  defamer 926 n.
  accuser 928 n.
slang
  unintelligibility 517 n.
  slang 560 n.
  cuss 899 vb.
  dispraise 924 vb.
slanging match
  scurrility 899 n.
slangy *linguistic* 557 adj.
  dialectical 560 adj.
slant *obliquity* 220 n.
  view 438 n.
  idea 451 n.
  bias 481 n.
slap *knock* 279 n.
  bang 402 n.
  endearment 889 n.
  spank 963 vb.
slap-bang
  instantaneously 116 adv.
slapdash
  instantaneously 116 adv.
  negligent 458 adj.

  clumsy 695 adj.
  rash 857 adj.
slap-happy *rash* 857 adj.
slap in the face
  refusal 760 n.
  indignity 921 n.
slapstick *dramatic* 594 adj.
  wit 839 n.
  ridiculousness 849 n.
slap-up *rich* 800 adj.
  liberal 813 adj.
slash *cut, rend* 46 vb.
  notch 260 vb.
  cheapen 812 vb.
  dispraise 924 vb.
  detract 926 vb.
slashing *forceful* 571 adj.
slat *lamina* 207 n.
  strip 208 n.
slate *lamina* 207 n.
  brittleness 330 n.
  classroom 539 n.
  stationery 586 n.
  policy 623 n.
  building material 631 n.
  dispraise 924 vb.
  detract 926 vb.
slats *bed* 218 n.
  shade 226 n.
slattern *slut* 61 n.
  dirty person 649 n.
  bungler 697 n.
slatternly *orderless* 61 adj.
  clumsy 695 adj.
slaty *layered* 207 adj.
slaughter
  slaughter 362 n., vb.
  be severe 735 vb.
  cruel act 898 n.
slaughter-house
  slaughter-house 362 n.
slave *instrument* 628 n.
  busy person 678 n.
  work 682 vb.
  worker 686 n.
  minister to 703 vb.
  slave 742 n.
  prisoner 750 n.
  toady 879 n.
slave-born *plebeian* 869 adj.
slave camp
  prison camp 748 n.
slave-driver *tyrant* 735 n.
slaver *merchant ship* 275 n.
  exude 298 vb.
  emit 300 vb.
  excrement 302 n.
  tyrant 735 n.
  merchant 794 n.
slave-raid *taking* 786 n.
slave-raider *thief* 789 n.

slavery *labour* 682 n.
 servitude 745 n.
slave to, a *subject* 745 adj.
slave-trade *trade* 791 n.
slave-trader
 merchant 794 n.
slavey *domestic* 742 n.
slavish *imitative* 20 adj.
 conformable 83 adj.
 obedient 739 adj.
 subjected 745 adj.
 servile 879 adj.
slavishness
 submission 721 n.
slaw *vegetable* 301 n.
slay *kill* 362 vb.
slayer *killer* 362 n.
sleave *complexity* 61 n.
 crossing 222 n.
sleazy *flimsy* 163 adj.
sled *sled* 274 n.
sledge *sled* 274 n.
 hammer 279 n.
 pulverizer 332 n.
sleek *smooth* 258 adj.
 prosperous 730 adj.
 personable 841 adj.
sleep *be inert* 175 vb.
 be quiescent 266 vb.
 insensibility 375 n.
 be inattentive 456 vb.
 sleep 679 n., vb.
 repose 683 n., vb.
 be fatigued 684 vb.
sleeper *railroad* 624 n.
 idler 679 n.
sleepiness (*see* sleepy)
sleep-inducing
 somnific 679 adj.
sleeping *latent* 523 n.
 inactive 679 adj.
 abrogated 752 adj.
sleeping bag *bag* 194 n.
sleeping-car *train* 274 n.
sleeping draught
 anæsthetic 375 n.
 soporific 679 n.
 relief 831 n.
sleeping partner
 nonentity 639 n.
 idler 679 n.
sleepless *persevering* 600 adj.
 active 678 adj.
sleep off *be restored* 656 vb.
 be refreshed 685 vb.
 be relieved 831 vb.
 be sober 948 vb.
sleep on it *wait* 136 vb.
 meditate 449 vb.
sleep-walker
 pedestrian 268 n.

sleep-walking *sleep* 679 n.
sleep with *unite with* 45 vb.
 debauch 951 vb.
sleepy *quiescent* 266 adj.
 abstracted 456 adj.
 sleepy 679 adj.
 fatigued 684 adj.
sleepy-head
 slowcoach 278 n.
 idler 679 n.
sleet *wintriness* 380 n.
sleety *cold* 380 adj.
sleeve *sleeve* 228 n.
 pocket 194 n.
 trophy 729 n.
sleigh *sled* 274 n.
sleight *visual fallacy* 440 n.
 sleight 542 n.
 skill 694 n.
 cunning 698 n.
slender *small* 33 adj.
 narrow 206 adj.
 shapely 841 adj.
sleuth *detective* 459 n.
 informer 524 n.
slew *rotate* 315 vb.
slice *cut* 46 vb.
 piece 53 n.
 lamina 207 n.
 notch 260 vb.
 deflect 282 vb.
 mouthful 301 n.
 be clumsy 695 vb.
 portion 783 n.
slicer *sharp edge* 256 n.
slick *smooth* 258 adj.
 skilful 694 adj.
slicker *overcoat* 228 n.
 trickster 545 n.
slide *fastening* 47 n.
 elapse 111 vb.
 obliquity 220 n.
 go smoothly 258 vb.
 move 265 vb.
 deviate 282 vb.
 descend 309 vb.
 optical device 442 n.
 photography 551 n.
 representation 551 n.
 deteriorate 655 vb.
slide back *relapse* 657 vb.
slide in *intromit* 231 vb.
slide into
 be turned to 147 vb.
slide-rule
 counting instrument 86 n.
 gauge 465 n.
slight *inconsiderable* 33 adj.
 inferior 35 adj.
 demolish 165 vb.
 exiguous 196 n.

narrow 206 adj.
 shallow 212 adj.
 rare 325 adj.
 disregard 458 vb.
 underestimate 483 vb.
 trivial 639 adj.
 not observe 769 vb.
 indignity 921 n.
 hold cheap 922 vb.
 detract 926 vb.
slim *small* 33 adj.
 make smaller 198 vb.
 narrow 206 adj.
 shapely 841 adj.
slime *moisture* 341 n.
 marsh 347 n.
 semiliquidity 354 n.
slimy *dirty* 649 adj.
 servile 879 adj.
 flattering 925 adj.
sling *pendant* 217 n.
 hang 217 vb.
 propel 287 vb.
 surgical dressing 658 n.
 lapidate 712 vb.
 missile weapon 723 n.
slinger *shooter* 287 n.
 thrower 287 n.
 soldiery 722 n.
slink *lurk* 523 vb.
 be stealthy 525 vb.
 be cowardly 856 vb.
slink off *decamp* 296 vb.
 run away 620 vb.
slinky *narrow* 206 adj.
slip *come unstuck* 49 vb.
 elapse 111 vb.
 young plant 132 n.
 bodywear 228 n.
 go smoothly 258 vb.
 descent 309 n.
 tumble 309 vb.
 viscidity 354 n.
 mistake 495 n.
 solecism 565 n.
 deteriorate 655 vb.
 be in danger 661 vb.
 failure 728 n.
slip back *relapse* 657 vb.
slip into, slip on
 wear 228 vb.
slip knot *ligature* 47 n.
slip off *doff* 229 vb.
slip out *go away* 190 vb.
slipper *footwear* 228 n.
 spank 963 vb.
slippered
 comfortable 376 adj.
 reposeful 683 adj.
slipperiness
 changeableness 152 n.

unreliability 474n.
(*see* slippery)
slippery
non-adhesive 49adj.
transient 114adj.
smooth 258adj.
speedy 277adj.
unctuous 357adj.
uncertain 474adj.
deceiving 542adj.
tergiversating 603adj.
unsafe 661adj.
escaped 667adj.
cunning 698adj.
dishonest 930adj.
slippery slope *danger* 661n.
predicament 700n.
slips *workshop* 687n.
slipshod *orderless* 61adj.
feeble 572adj.
lax 734adj.
slip-stream *wind* 352n.
slip through *escape* 667vb.
slipway *smoothness* 258n.
road 624n.
slit *sunder, rend* 46vb.
gap 201n.
furrow 262n.
slither *move* 265vb.
slithery *smooth* 258adj.
sliver *small thing* 33n.
piece 53n.
slob *semiliquidity* 354n.
bungler 697n.
slobber *exude* 298vb.
emit 300vb.
excrete 302vb.
moisture 341n.
make unclean 649vb.
sloe *black thing* 428n.
slog *propel* 287vb.
persevere 600vb.
be busy 678vb.
exert oneself 682vb.
slogan *maxim* 496n.
call 547n.
warfare 718n.
slogger *busy person* 678n.
slogging *industrious* 678adj.
sloka *maxim* 496n.
prosody 593n.
verse form 593n.
sloop *sailing-ship* 275n.
warship 722n.
sloosh *drench* 341vb.
slop *flow out* 298vb.
let fall 311vb.
moisten 341n.
waste 634vb.
slop-bowl *bowl* 194n.
slope *high land* 209n.

obliquity 220n.
ascent 308n.
descent 309n.
slope off *run away* 620vb.
slopping *full* 54adj.
redundant 637adj.
sloppy *orderless* 61adj.
feeble 572adj.
feeling 818adj.
slops *weak thing* 163n.
clothing 228n.
swill 649n.
slopshop *clothier* 228n.
slot *receptacle* 194n.
gap 201n.
furrow 262n.
groove 262vb.
orifice 263n.
trace 548n.
sloth *inertness* 175n.
sluggishness 679n.
slot-machine
receptacle 194n.
storage 632n.
treasury 799n.
slouch *move slowly* 278vb.
be inactive 679vb.
sloucher *slowcoach* 278n.
avoider 620n.
idler 679n.
slouching *graceless* 842adj.
slough *leavings* 41n.
unstick 49vb.
excrement 302n.
marsh 347n.
disaccustom 611vb.
sink 649n.
disuse 674vb.
sloven *slut* 61n.
dirty person 649n.
bungler 697n.
slovenly *orderless* 61adj.
negligent 458adj.
feeble 572adj.
dirty 649adj.
clumsy 695adj.
slow *protracted* 113adj.
anachronistic 118adj.
late 136adj.
inert 175adj.
slow 278adj.
unintelligent 499adj.
unwilling 598adj.
lazy 679adj.
leisurely 681adj.
inexcitable 823adj.
tedious 838adj.
dull 840adj.
slow burn *discontent* 829n.
slowcoach
slowcoach 278n.

idler 679n.
slow down *bate* 37vb.
come to rest 266vb.
decelerate 278vb.
hinder 702vb.
slow-down *strike* 145n.
slowness 278n.
slow-motion *slowness* 278n.
slow 278adj.
slowness *caution* 858n.
(*see* slow)
sloyd *education* 534n.
slub *weave* 222vb.
slubber
make unclean 649vb.
be clumsy 695vb.
sludge *leavings* 41n.
slug *slowcoach* 278n.
move slowly 278vb.
strike 279vb.
vermin 365n.
print-type 587n.
ammunition 723n.
sluggard *slowcoach* 278n.
idler 679n.
sluggish *late* 136adj.
inert 175adj.
slow 278adj.
flowing 350adj.
lazy 679adj.
apathetic 820adj.
dull 840adj.
sluice *outlet* 298n.
irrigator 341n.
drench 341vb.
waterfall 350n.
conduit 351n.
clean 648vb.
slum *housing* 192n.
sink 649n.
insalubrity 653n.
dilapidation 655n.
poverty 801n.
eyesore 842n.
lower classes 869n.
slumber *quietude* 266n.
sleep 679n.,vb.
slum-dweller
poor man 801n.
low fellow 869n.
slummer *reformer* 654n.
philanthropist 901n.
slumming *sociology* 901n.
slummy *dilapidated* 655adj.
unclean 649adj.
slump *decrease* 37n.
contraction 198n.
regression 286n.
descend 309vb.
deterioration 655n.
inactivity 679n.

adversity 731 n.
cheapness 812 n.
slur *neglect* 458 vb.
conceal 525 vb.
slur 867 n.
censure 924 n.
calumny 926 n.
extenuate 927 vb.
slush *marsh* 347 n.
semiliquidity 354 n.
slut *slut* 61 n.
loose woman 952 n.
sluttish *negligent* 458 adj.
dirty 649 adj.
sly *stealthy* 525 adj.
false 541 adj.
cunning 698 adj.
gay 833 adj.
witty 839 adj.
slyboots *slyboots* 698 n.
smack
small quantity 33 n.
tincture 43 n.
sailing ship 275 n.
knock 279 n.
taste 386 n.
crackle 402 vb.
spank 963 vb.
smacker *paper money* 797 n.
endearment 889 n.
smack of *resemble* 18 vb.
smack one's lips
enjoy 376 vb.
appetize 390 vb.
small *small* 33 adj.
fractional 102 adj.
infantine 132 adj.
weak 163 adj.
little 196 adj.
insufficient 636 n.
unimportant 639 adj.
small arms *fire-arm* 723 n.
small beer *nonentity* 639 n.
trifle 639 n.
small clothes *breeches* 228 n.
smaller *lesser* 35 adj.
contracted 198 adj.
small fry *animalcule* 196 n.
nonentity 639 n.
lower classes 869 n.
smallholder
husbandman 370 n.
small hours
morning 128 n.
midnight 129 n.
lateness 136 n.
smallness *invisibility* 444 n.
(*see* small)
small number
fewness 105 n.
smallpox *skin disease* 651 n.

smalls *breeches* 228 n.
small talk *chatter* 581 n.
chat 584 n.
smalt *blue pigment* 435 n.
smalto
ornamental art 844 n.
smarm *flatter* 925 vb.
smart *speedy* 277 adj.
pang 377 n.
intelligent 498 adj.
active 678 adj.
suffer 825 vb.
witty 839 adj.
personable 841 adj.
fashionable 848 adj.
smart aleck *wiseacre* 500 n.
smarten *decorate* 844 vb.
smarting *painful* 377 adj.
felt 818 adj.
discontented 829 adj.
resentful 891 adj.
smart money *reward* 962 n.
smart under *feel* 818 vb.
smarty-boots
vain person 873 n.
smash *break* 46 vb.
demolish 165 vb.
force 176 vb.
collision 279 n.
strike 279 vb.
propel 287 vb.
wound 655 vb.
smash and grab
rob 788 vb.
smasher *a beauty* 841 n.
smash hit
dramaturgy 594 n.
exceller 644 n.
success 727 n.
favourite 890 n.
smashing *topping* 644 adj.
smatterer *sciolist* 493 n.
smattering *erudition* 490 n.
sciolism 491 n.
smattering 491 adj.
smear *overlay* 226 vb.
bedim 419 vb.
make unclean 649 vb.
blemish 845 n., vb.
shame 867 vb.
calumny 926 n.
smear campaign
detraction 926 n.
smear-word
calumny 926 n.
smeddum *powder* 332 n.
smell *small quantity* 33 n.
emit 300 vb.
odour 394 n.
stink 397 vb.
trace 548 n.

be unclean 649 vb.
deteriorate 655 vb.
smell a rat *detect* 484 vb.
doubt 486 vb.
smelling bottle
scent 396 n.
smelling salts
pungency 388 n.
tonic 658 n.
smell out *discover* 484 vb.
smell powder
wage war 718 vb.
smelly *odorous* 394 adj.
fetid 397 adj.
smelt *table fish* 365 n.
heat 381 vb.
smile *gesticulate* 547 vb.
be pleased 824 vb.
laughter 835 n.
greet 884 vb.
smile at *ridicule* 851 vb.
smile on *patronize* 703 vb.
be auspicious 730 vb.
smiles *cheerfulness* 833 n.
smiling *content* 828 adj.
sociable 882 adj.
smirch *bedim* 419 vb.
blacken 428 vb.
make unclean 649 vb.
defame 926 vb.
smirk *laughter* 835 n.
smile 835 vb.
be affected 850 vb.
flatter 925 vb.
smite *strike* 279 vb.
kill 302 vb.
impress 821 vb.
smith *efform* 243 vb.
artisan 686 n.
smithereens
small thing 33 n.
smithy *workshop* 687 n.
smitten *induced* 612 adj.
enamoured 887 adj.
smock *bodywear* 228 n.
fold 261 vb.
smocking *needlework* 844 n.
smog *cloud* 355 n.
opacity 423 n.
poison 659 n.
smoke *emit* 300 vb.
powder 332 n.
gas 336 n.
vaporize 338 vb.
dry 342 vb.
ash 381 n.
season, smoke 388 vb.
odour 394 n.
be hot 397 vb.
bedim 419 vb.
screen 421 vb.

make opaque 423 vb.
blacken 428 vb.
blur 440 vb.
lurk 523 vb.
dirt 649 n.
preserve 666 vb.
mature 669 vb.
smoke-duct *chimney* 263 n.
smoke out *eject* 300 vb.
extract 304 vb.
hunt 619 vb.
smoker *train* 274 n.
tobacco 388 n.
smoke-ring *vortex* 315 n.
smoke-screen
obfuscation 421 n.
opacity 423 n.
invisibility 444 n.
concealment 525 n.
disguise 527 n.
defences 713 n.
smoke-signal
telecommunication 531 n.
signal 547 n.
smoke-stack
chimney 263 n.
air-pipe 353 n.
smoking room
chamber 194 n.
smoking-room story
witticism 839 n.
impurity 951 n.
smoky *powdery* 332 adj.
vaporific 338 vb.
heated 381 adj.
pungent 388 adj.
dim 419 adj.
opaque 423 adj.
black 428 adj.
grey 429 adj.
dirty 649 adj.
smooth *uniform* 16 adj.
equalize 28 vb.
non-adhesive 49 adj.
orderly 60 adj.
regular 81 adj.
make conform 83 vb.
lenitive 177 adj.
flatten 216 vb.
hairless 229 adj.
symmetrical 245 adj.
smooth 258 adj., vb.
tranquil 266 adj.
soft 327 adj.
rub 333 vb.
touch 378 vb.
deceiving 542 adj.
elegant 575 adj.
facilitate 701 vb.
relieve 831 vb.
courteous 884 adj.

flattering 925 adj.
smooth-bore *fire-arm* 723 n.
smooth citizen
slyboots 698 n.
smoothing-iron
smoother 258 n.
smoothness *texture* 331 n.
lubrication 334 n.
cunning 698 n.
(*see* smooth)
smooth out
not discriminate 464 vb.
smooth-running
lubricated 334 adj.
wieldy 701 adj.
smooth-spoken
hypocritical 541 adj.
smother *moderate* 177 vb.
cover 226 vb.
close 264 vb.
murder 362 vb.
conceal 525 vb.
smouch *seller* 793 n.
smoulder *be inert* 175 vb.
be hot 379 vb.
lurk 523 vb.
be inactive 679 vb.
resent 891 vb.
smouldering *sullen* 893 adj.
smouse *pedlar* 794 n.
Smriti *tradition* 127 n.
non-Biblical scripture
975 n.
smudge *blacken* 428 vb.
blur 440 vb.
make unclean 649 vb.
blemish 845 n., vb.
smug *affected* 850 adj.
smuggle *steal* 788 vb.
smuggle in *intromit* 231 vb.
smuggler *free man* 744 n.
thief 789 n.
smugness *happiness* 824 n.
content 828 n.
smut *ash* 381 n.
dirt 649 n.
impurity 951 n.
smutch *blacken* 428 vb.
make unclean 649 vb.
snack *meal* 301 n.
mouthful 301 n.
snack-bar *café* 192 n.
snacks, go
participate 775 vb.
snaffle *restraint* 747 n.
fetter 748 n.
take 786 vb.
steal 788 vb.
snafu *orderless* 61 adj.
snag *projection* 254 n.
danger 661 n.

pitfall 663 n.
difficulty 700 n.
hitch 702 n.
snaggy *sharp* 256 adj.
snail *slowcoach* 278 n.
snake *serpent* 251 n.
meander 251 vb.
reptile 365 n.
bane 659 n.
slyboots 698 n.
noxious animal 904 n.
knave 938 n.
snake-charmer
sorcerer 983 n.
snake in the grass
latency 523 n.
deceiver 545 n.
trouble-maker 663 n.
evildoer 904 n.
snaky *snaky* 251 adj.
cunning 698 adj.
dishonest 930 adj.
snap *break* 46 vb.
discontinue 72 vb.
close 264 vb.
pastry 301 n.
be brittle 330 vb.
crackle 402 vb.
photography 551 n.
spontaneous 609 adj.
sullenness 893 n.
snap of the fingers
unimportance 639 n.
snap one's fingers
defy 711 vb.
disobey 738 vb.
not observe 769 vb.
hold cheap 922 vb.
snappish *irascible* 892 adj.
sullen 893 adj.
snappy *vigorous* 174 adj.
speedy 277 adj.
aphoristic 496 adj.
witty 839 adj.
personable 841 adj.
snapshot *photography* 551 n.
snap up *eat* 310 vb.
take 786 vb.
snare *trap* 542 n.
take 786 vb.
snark *rara avis* 84 n.
snarl *distortion* 246 n.
distort 246 vb.
ululation 409 n.
ululate 409 vb.
sullenness 893 n.
threat 900 n.
threaten 900 vb.
snarled *complex* 61 adj.
snatch *pursue* 619 vb.
take 786 vb.

snatcher *taker* 786 n.
sneak *be stealthy* 525 vb.
　steal 788 vb.
　coward 856 n.
　be servile 879 vb.
　knave 938 n.
sneaker *thief* 789 n.
sneakers *footwear* 228 n.
sneaking *servile* 879 adj.
　dishonest 930 adj.
sneer *be discontented* 829 vb.
　dislike 861 vb.
　insolence 878 n.
　not respect 921 vb.
　contempt 922 n.
　dispraise 924 vb.
　detraction 926 n.
sneeze *breathe* 352 vb.
　sibilation 406 n.
sneezy *puffing* 352 adj.
snick *cut* 46 vb.
snicker *laugh* 835 vb.
snickersnee *side-arms* 723 n.
snide *false money* 797 n.
sniff *breathe* 352 vb.
　smell 394 vb.
　detraction 926 n.
sniff at *eat* 301 vb.
　dislike 861 vb.
　despise 922 vb.
　detract 926 vb.
sniffy *puffing* 352 adj.
　despising 922 adj.
snifter *potion* 301 n.
snigger *laughter* 835 n.
　ridicule 851 n.
snip *small thing* 33 n.
　cut 46 vb.
　piece 53 n.
　clothier 228 n.
snipe *table bird* 365 n.
　fire at 712 vb.
sniper *shooter* 287 n.
　attacker 712 n.
　soldier 722 n.
snippet *table bird* 365 n.
snitch *informer* 524 n.
　steal 788 vb.
snivel *weep* 836 vb.
snob *vulgarian* 847 n.
　proud man 871 n.
snobbery *etiquette* 848 n.
　pride 871 n.
snobbish *biased* 481 adj.
　ill-bred 847 adj.
　fashionable 848 adj.
　affected 850 adj.
　prideful 871 adj.
　despising 922 adj.
snocat *vehicle* 274 n.
snood *receptacle* 194 n.

headgear 228 n.
　loop 250 n.
　hair-dressing 843 n.
snook *sauciness* 878 n.
　indignity 921 n.
snooker *ball game* 837 n.
snoop *scan* 438 vb.
　spectator 441 n.
　be curious 453 vb.
　detective 459 n.
　informer 524 n.
　be stealthy 525 vb.
snoopy *inquisitive* 453 adj.
snooty *insolent* 878 adj.
　despising 922 adj.
snooze *sleep* 679 n., vb.
snore *rasp* 407 vb.
　sleep 679 vb.
snort *breathe* 352 vb.
　hiss 406 vb.
　rasp 407 vb.
　ululate 409 vb.
　stammer 580 vb.
　be irascible 892 vb.
　sullenness 893 n.
　contempt 922 n.
snorter *potion* 301 n.
snot *dirt* 649 n.
snotty *naval man* 270 n.
snout *face* 237 n.
　projection 254 n.
snow *snow* 380 n.
　refrigerator 384 n.
　white thing 427 n.
　drug 658 n.
　poison 659 n.
snowball *grow* 36 vb.
　continuity 71 n.
　accumulation 74 n.
　expand 197 vb.
　strike 279 vb.
　missile 287 n.
　propel 287 vb.
　snow 380 n.
snowballer *thrower* 287 n.
snowflake *softness* 327 n.
　powder 332 n.
　snow 380 n.
　white thing 427 n.
snowman
　insubstantial thing 4 n.
　brief span 114 n.
　snow 380 n.
　image 551 n.
snow-shoe *footwear* 228 n.
　carrier 273 n.
　sled 274 n.
snow-storm *storm* 176 n.
　wintriness 380 n.
　snow 380 n.
snowy *cold* 380 adj.

white 427 adj.
snub *short* 204 adj.
　unsharpened 257 adj.
　repel 292 vb.
　humiliate 872 vb.
　be rude 885 vb.
　reprimand 924 n.
snubby *short* 204 adj.
snuff *suppress* 165 vb.
　absorb 299 vb.
　extinguish 302 vb.
　tobacco 388 n.
　smell 394 vb.
　brownness 430 n.
snuff-box *small box* 194 n.
　tobacco 388 n.
snuffle *breathe* 352 vb.
　hiss 406 vb.
　stammer 580 vb.
snuffy *dirty* 649 adj.
snug *adjusted* 24 adj.
　dry 342 adj.
　comfortable 376 adj.
　warm 379 adj.
　invulnerable 660 adj.
　reposeful 683 adj.
snuggery *retreat* 192 n.
　small house 192 n.
snuggle *caress* 889 vb.
so *thus* 8 adv.
　hence 158 adv.
　true 494 adj.
soak *fill* 54 vb.
　drink 301 vb.
　immerse 303 vb.
　add water 339 vb.
　drench 341 vb.
　superabound 637 vb.
　overcharge 811 vb.
　drunkard 949 n.
soaker *rain* 350 n.
　drunkard 949 n.
soak into, soak through
　infiltrate 297 vb.
　pass 305 vb.
soak up *absorb* 299 vb.
　dry 342 vb.
so-and-so *person* 371 n.
　no name 562 n.
soap *softness* 327 n.
　lubricant 334 n.
　fat 357 n.
　cleanser 648 n.
　flatter 925 vb.
soap-box *publicity* 528 n.
　rostrum 539 n.
soapiness
　unctuousness 357 n.
soap opera
　stage play 594 n.
soapy *smooth* 258 adj.

fatty 357 adj.
white 427 adj.
servile 879 adj.
flattering 925 adj.
soar *be high* 209 vb.
   fly 271 vb.
   ascend 308 vb.
   be dear 811 vb.
soar above *outdo* 306 vb.
sob *respiration* 352 n.
   rasp 407 vb.
   cry 408 n., vb.
   aphony 578 n.
   stammer 580 n.
   lamentation 836 vb.
sober *moderate* 177 adj., vb.
   soft-hued 425 adj.
   wise 498 adj.
   sane 502 adj.
   educate 534 vb.
   plain 573 adj.
   inexcitable 823 adj.
   serious 834 adj.
   deject 834 vb.
   cautious 858 adj.
   ascetic 945 adj.
   sober 948 adj.
sobered *repentant* 939 adj.
soberly *modestly* 874 adv.
sober-minded *sane* 502 adj.
   inexcitable 823 adj.
sobersides *moper* 834 n.
   sober person 948 n.
sobriety *moderation* 177 n.
   wisdom 498 n.
   sanity 502 n.
   inexcitability 823 n.
   seriousness 834 n.
   caution 858 n.
   temperance 942 n.
   sobriety 948 n.
sob-sister
   newsmonger 529 n.
   author 589 n.
   excitant 821 n.
sob-story *lament* 836 n.
sobstuff *excitation* 821 n.
   lament 836 n.
socage *possession* 773 n.
so-called
   unbelieved 486 adj.
   supposed 512 adj.
   spurious 542 adj.
   untrue 543 adj.
   named 561 adj.
   misnamed 562 adj.
soccer *ball game* 837 n.
sociability
   cheerfulness 833 n.
   sociability 882 n.
sociable *seat* 218 n.

carriage 274 n.
amiable 884 adj.
social *national* 371 adj.
   corporate 708 adj.
   social gathering 882 n.
social circle *sociality* 882 n.
social class
   community 708 n.
social climber
   vulgarian 847 n.
   commoner 869 n.
   social person 882 n.
social conscience
   philanthropy 901 n.
social engineering
   sociology 901 n.
social evil
   social evil 951 n.
social gathering
   social gathering 882 n.
social graces
   sociability 882 n.
social group *group* 74 n.
   social group 371 n.
   community 708 n.
socialism
   government 733 n.
   joint possession 775 n.
   sociology 901 n.
socialist
   political party 708 n.
   participator 775 n.
socialistic *sharing* 775 adj.
   philanthropic 901 adj.
Socialists
   political party 708 n.
socialite *beau monde* 848 n.
   social person 882 n.
sociality *sociality* 882 n.
socialize *socialize* 775 vb.
   convey 780 vb.
social planning
   sociology 901 n.
social register
   upper class 868 n.
social round
   social round 882 n.
social science
   anthropology 371 n.
   sociology 901 n.
social security *safety* 660 n.
social service
   sociology 901 n.
social state *polity* 733 n.
social success
   sociability 882 n.
   social person 882 n.
social worker
   reformer 654 n.
societal *national* 371 adj.
society

accompaniment 89 n.
social group 371 n.
association 706 n.
society 708 n.
beau monde 848 n.
sociality 882 n.
Society of Friends
   sect 978 n.
Socinianism *heresy* 977 n.
sociologist *reformer* 654 n.
sociology
   anthropology 371 n.
   reformism 654 n.
   sociology 901 n.
sociopath *madman* 504 n.
sock
   legwear, footwear 228 n.
   strike 279 vb.
socket *place* 185 n.
   receptacle 194 n.
   cavity 255 n.
socle *stand* 218 n.
Socratic method
   interrogation 459 n.
sod *soil* 344 n.
   grassland 348 n.
   grass 366 n.
   cultivate 370 vb.
soda *soft drink* 301 n.
   cleanser 648 n.
soda-fountain *café* 192 n.
sodality *association* 706 n.
   society 708 n.
   community 708 n.
   friendship 880 n.
soda-water
   soft-drink 301 n.
   water 339 n.
sodden *drenched* 341 adj.
   drunken 949 adj.
sodomite *libertine* 952 n.
sodomy *illicit love* 951 n.
sofa *seat* 218 n.
soffit *projection* 254 n.
soft *unstable* 152 adj.
   weak 163 adj.
   lenitive 177 adj.
   smooth 258 adj.
   soft 327 adj.
   fluidal 335 adj.
   comfortable 376 adj.
   silent 399 adj.
   muted 401 adj.
   melodious 410 adj.
   foolish 499 adj.
   lenient 736 adj.
   impressible 819 adj.
   cowardly 856 adj.
   pitying 905 adj.
   sober 948 adj.
soft drink *soft drink* 301 n.

soften *soften* 327 vb.
 relieve 831 vb.
 extenuate 927 vb.
 (*see* soft)
softened *repentant* 939 adj.
soft-hued *soft-hued* 425 adj.
soft impeachment
 love affair 887 n.
softness *softness* 327 n.
 pulpiness 356 n.
 irresolution 601 n.
 laxity 734 n.
 benevolence 897 n.
 sensualism 944 n.
 (*see* soft)
soft nothings
 empty talk 515 n.
 endearment 889 n.
soft pedal *silence* 399 vb.
 silencer 401 n.
 mute 401 vb.
 sound dead 405 vb.
 mute 414 n.
 underestimate 483 vb.
 extenuate 927 vb.
soft sawder *flattery* 925 n.
soft soap *falsehood* 541 n.
 flattery 925 n.
soft-spoken
 courteous 884 adj.
soft spot *sensibility* 374 n.
 defect 647 n.
 vulnerability 661 n.
 moral sensibility 819 n.
 painfulness 827 n.
soft underbelly
 vulnerability 661 n.
softy *weakling* 163 n.
 ninny 501 n.
sogginess *softness* 327 n.
 moisture 341 n.
soggy *pulpy* 356 adj.
soi-disant *untrue* 543 adj.
 named 561 adj.
 misnamed 562 adj.
 vain 873 adj.
soigné *dressed* 228 adj.
 elegant 575 adj.
soil *region* 184 n.
 soil 344 n.
 make unclean 649 vb.
 make ugly 842 vb.
 blemish 845 vb.
soirée
 social gathering 882 n.
sojourn *be present* 189 vb.
 dwell 192 vb.
 visit 882 vb.
sojourner *dweller* 191 n.
soke *district* 184 n.
solace *relief* 831 n.

amuse 837 vb.
solar *celestial* 321 adj.
solarium *heater* 383 n.
 hospital 658 n.
solar flare *prominence* 254 n.
 sun 321 n.
solar plexus *insides* 224 n.
solar system *sun* 321 n.
solatium *extra* 40 n.
 reward 962 n.
solder *join* 45 vb.
 adhesive 47 n.
soldier *killer* 362 n.
 wage war 718 vb.
 soldier 722 n.
 brave person 855 n.
soldierly *warlike* 718 adj.
 courageous 855 adj.
soldier of fortune
 militarist 722 n.
soldiery *soldiery* 722 n.
sold on *believing* 485 adj.
sole *one* 88 adj.
 foot 214 n.
 table fish 365 n.
 repair 656 vb.
solecism *mistake* 495 n.
 solecism 565 n.
solecistic *abnormal* 84 adj.
 erroneous 495 adj.
 neological 560 adj.
 ungrammatical 565 adj.
solemn *great* 32 adj.
 affirmative 532 adj.
 important 638 adj.
 serious 834 adj.
 formal 875 adj.
 devotional 981 adj.
 ritual 988 adj.
solemn affirmation
 oath 532 n.
solemn declaration
 promise 764 n.
solemnity *formality* 875 n.
 rite 988 n.
 (*see* solemn)
solemnization
 celebration 876 n.
 ministration 988 n.
solemnize *do* 676 vb.
 celebrate 876 vb.
solenoid *magnet* 291 n.
sol-fa *vocal music* 412 n.
 sing 413 vb.
solfatara *furnace* 383 n.
solfeggio *vocal music* 492 n.
solferino
 red pigment 431 n.
solicitant *desirer* 859 n.
solicitation
 inducement 612 n.

offer 759 n.
 request 761 n.
solicitor *petitioner* 763 n.
 law agent 958 n.
solicitous *careful* 457 adj.
 desiring 859 adj.
solicitude *carefulness* 457 n.
 worry 825 n.
 nervousness 854 n.
solid *real* 1 adj.
 substantial 3 adj.
 firm-set 45 adj.
 cohesive 48 adj.
 one 88 adj.
 unyielding 162 adj.
 thick 205 adj.
 material 319 adj.
 solid body 324 n.
 dense 324 adj.
 assenting 488 adj.
solidarity *unity* 88 n.
 stability 153 n.
 co-operation 706 n.
 association 706 n.
 concord 710 n.
 friendship 880 n.
solid body *solid body* 324 n.
solidification
 condensation 324 n.
 refrigeration 382 n.
solidify *cohere* 48 vb.
 be dense 324 vb.
solidity *substantiality* 3 n.
 completeness 54 n.
 permanence 144 n.
 materiality 319 n.
 density 324 n.
 opacity 423 n.
solid vote *consensus* 488 n.
soliloquy *soliloquy* 585 n.
 dramaturgy 594 n.
solitaire *card game* 837 n.
 gem 844 n.
solitary
 unconformable 84 adj.
 alone 88 adj.
 wanderer 268 n.
 solitary 883 n.
 friendless 883 adj.
 unsociable 883 adj.
solitude *unity* 88 n.
 desert 172 n.
 seclusion 883 n.
solmization
 notation 410 n.
 vocal music 412 n.
solo *unit* 88 n.
 tune 412 n.
soloist *musician* 413 n.
Solomon *sage* 500 n.
 polygamist 894 n.

Solon *sage* 500 n.
solstice *winter* 129 n.
solstitial *celestial* 321 adj.
solubility *mixture* 43 n.
  fluidity 335 n.
  liquefaction 337 n.
soluble (*see* solubility)
solution *solution* 337 n.
  answer 460 n.
  discovery 484 n.
  interpretation 520 n.
  remedy 658 n.
solution of continuity
  discontinuity 72 n.
solve *decipher* 520 vb.
solvency *wealth* 800 n.
solvent *moderator* 177 n.
  liquefaction 337 n.
  moneyed 800 adj.
soma *liquor* 301 n.
  Hindu god 967 n.
somatic *material* 319 adj.
somatics *physics* 319 n.
somatology
  anthropology 371 n.
sombre *funereal* 364 adj.
  dark 418 adj.
  soft-hued 425 adj.
  black 428 adj.
  grey 429 adj.
  cheerless 834 adj.
some *quantitative* 26 adj.
  partially 33 adv.
  plurality 101 n.
  anonymous 562 adj.
somebody *substance* 3 n.
  person 371 n.
  person of repute 866 n.
somehow *somehow* 158 adv.
somehow feel *intuit* 476 vb.
someone *person* 371 n.
some place
  somewhere 185 adv.
some purpose, to
  successfully 727 adv.
somersault
  overturning 221 n.
something *substance* 3 n.
  object 319 n.
something else
  variant 15 n.
something for everybody
  generality 79 n.
something or other
  uncertainty 474 n.
something over *extra* 40 n.
  redundance 637 n.
sometime *former* 125 adj.
some time or other
  not now 122 adv.
sometimes

sometimes 139 adv.
somewhere
  somewhere 185 adv.
somewhere else
  not here 190 adv.
somnambulism
  fantasy 513 n.
  sleep 679 n.
somnambulist
  pedestrian 268 n.
  visionary 513 n.
somnific *somnific* 679 adj.
somnipathy *sleep* 679 n.
somnolence *sleepiness* 679 n.
son *descendant* 170 n.
  male 372 n.
sonant
  speech sound 398 n.
  spoken letter 558 adj.
  vocal 577 adj.
sonantal *sounding* 398 adj.
sonar *detector* 484 n.
sonata, sonatina
  musical piece 412 n.
sone *sound* 398 n.
  metrology 465 n.
son et lumière
  lighting 420 n.
  pageant 875 n.
song *repetition* 106 n.
  vocal music 412 n.
  poem 593 n.
  hymn 981 n.
song and dance
  loudness 400 n.
  stage-show 594 n.
song-bird *bird* 365 n.
  vocalist 413 n.
songbook
  vocal music 412 n.
song, for a *cheaply* 812 adv.
songful *musicianly* 413 adj.
  poetic 593 adj.
songster *bird* 365 n.
  vocalist 413 n.
song-writer *musician* 413 n.
  poet 593 n.
sonic *sounding* 398 adj.
sonic barrier *sound* 398 n.
sonnet *verse form* 593 n.
sonneteer *poet* 593 n.
  poetize 593 vb.
sonny *darling* 890 n.
sonometer *acoustics* 398 n.
sonorant *sounding* 398 adj.
sonority *sound* 398 n.
  loudness 400 n.
  resonance 404 n.
sonorous *ornate* 574 adj.
  (*see* sonority)
sonship *sequence* 65 n.

sonship 170 n.
sons of Belial
  insolent person 878 n.
soon *not now* 122 adv.
  prospectively 124 adv.
  betimes 135 adv.
  in the future 155 adv.
sooner *optionally* 605 adv.
sooner or later
  not now 122 adv.
  prospectively 124 adv.
soot *powder* 332 n.
  ash 381 n.
  black thing 428 n.
  dirt 649 n.
soothe *assuage* 177 vb.
  remedy 658 vb.
  make inactive 679 vb.
  please 826 vb.
  flatter 925 vb.
soothing *deceiving* 542 adj.
  relief 831 n.
soothing syrup
  moderator 177 n.
  balm 658 n.
  relief 831 n.
soothsay *divine* 511 vb.
soothsayer *oracle* 511 n.
  sorcerer 983 n.
sooty *dark* 418 adj.
  dim 419 adj.
  opaque 423 adj.
  black 428 adj.
  dirty 649 adj.
sop *mouthful* 301 n.
  potion 301 n.
  moisture 341 n.
  incentive 612 n.
  lenity 736 n.
sophism *sophism* 477 n.
sophist *sophist* 477 n.
  intellectual 492 n.
sophisticate *mix* 43 vb.
  sophisticate 477 vb.
  man of taste 846 n.
sophistication *mixture* 43 n.
  culture 490 n.
  impairment 655 n.
  skill 694 n.
  good taste 846 n.
sophistry *irrelevance* 10 n.
  sophistry 477 n.
  misteaching 535 n.
  deception 542 n.
  wrong 914 n.
sophomore
  college student 538 n.
Sophy *sovereign* 741 n.
soporific *moderator* 177 n.
  anæsthetic 375 n.
  soporific 679 n.

relief 831 n.
tedious 838 adj.
sopping drenched 341 adj.
soppy foolish 499 adj.
ninny 501 n.
soprano vocalist 413 n.
sorcerer diviner 511 n.
conjuror 545 n.
prodigy 864 n.
sorcerer 983 n.
occultist 984 n.
sorcery conversion 147 n.
thaumaturgy 864 n.
sorcery 983 n.
occultism 984 n.
sordid avaricious 816 adj.
vulgar 847 adj.
sordine silencer 401 n.
non-resonance 405 n.
mute 414 n.
sore pain 377 n.
evil 616 n.
bad 645 adj.
ulcer 651 n.
diseased 651 adj.
sensitive 819 adj.
painfulness 827 n.
discontented 829 adj.
resentful 891 adj.
sorely painfully 32 adv.
sore point
sensibility 374 n.
moral sensibility 819 n.
resentment 891 n.
sorghum corn 366 n.
sorites relevance 9 n.
argumentation 475 n.
sorority family 11 n.
community 708 n.
sorrel horse 273 n.
potherb 301 n.
brown 430 adj.
sorrow bane 659 n.
adversity 731 n.
sorrow 825 n.
dejection 834 n.
lament 836 vb.
sorry unimportant 369 adj.
unhappy 825 adj.
regretting 830 adj.
melancholic 834 adj.
repentant 939 adj.
sorry sight
painfulness 827 n.
sort class 62 vb.
sort 77 n.
discriminate 463 vb.
sortable fit 24 adj.
sorter sorting 62 n.
mails 531 n.
sortes Vergilianæ

oracle 511 n.
non-design 618 n.
sortie outbreak 176 n.
attack 712 n.
retaliation 714 n.
sortilege divination 511 n.
sorcery 983 n.
occultism 984 n.
sort out exclude 57 vb.
render few 105 vb.
discriminate 463 vb.
select 605 vb.
sort with accord 24 vb.
S.O.S. signal 547 n.
danger signal 665 n.
so-so moderately 177 adv.
imperfect 647 adj.
sot fool 501 n.
drunkard 949 n.
soteriology
theology 973 n.
Sothic cycle era 110 n.
sottish unintelligent 499 adj.
drunken 949 adj.
sotto voce faintly 401 adv.
secretly 525 adv.
voicelessly 578 adv.
sou small coin 33 n.
soubrette acting 594 n.
soufflé pudding 301 n.
sough lake 346 n.
marsh 347 n.
drain 351 n.
blow, breathe 352 n.
sound faint 401 vb.
swill 649 n.
sought-after
welcomed 882 adj.
soul essence 1 n.
essential part 5 n.
main part 32 n.
interiority 224 n.
life 360 n.
person 371 n.
spirit 447 n.
affections 817 n.
soulful feeling 818 adj.
soulless inactive 679 adj.
impassive 820 adj.
soulmate spouse 894 n.
soul-searching
regret 830 n.
honourable 929 adj.
soul-stirring felt 818 adj.
exciting 821 adj.
sound regular 83 adj.
unyielding 162 adj.
plunge 313 vb.
gulf 345 n.
sound 398 n., vb.
loudness 400 n.

play music 413 vb.
enquire 459 vb.
interrogate 459 vb.
be tentative 461 vb.
measure 465 vb.
genuine 494 adj.
wise 498 adj.
perfect 646 adj.
healthy 650 adj.
skilful 694 adj.
orthodox 976 adj.
depth 211 n.
be deep 211 vb.
be loud 400 adj.
access 624 n.
valuable 644 adj.
beneficial 644 adj.
not bad 644 adj.
monetary 797 adj.
moneyed 800 adj.
sound barrier sound 398 n.
soundbox
gramophone 414 n.
sound-detector
detector 484 n.
sounding board
gong 414 n.
sounding brass
resonance 404 n.
unmeaningness 515 n.
sounding lead depth 211 n.
soundless deep 211 adj.
still 266 adj.
silent 399 adj.
sound like resemble 18 vb.
sound mind sanity 502 n.
soundproof silent 399 adj.
non-resonant 405 adj.
sound-tape
hearing aid 415 n.
sound-track trace 548 n.
soup soup 301 n.
soup-bowl bowl 194 n.
soupçon small quantity 33 n.
tincture 43 n.
soup, in the
in difficulties 700 adj.
soup-spoon ladle 194 n.
soupy semiliquid 354 adj.
sour unsavoury 391 adj.
sour 393 adj.
unpleasant 827 adj.
cause discontent 829 vb.
aggravate 832 vb.
sullen 893 adj.
source origin 68 n.
source 156 n.
parentage 169 n.
summit 213 n.
stream 350 n.
informant 524 n.

store 632 n.
sourdough
  experimenter 461 n.
sour grapes
  impossibility 470 n.
  pretext 714 n.
  jealousy 911 n.
sourness *malevolence* 898 n.
  (*see* sour)
souse *immerse* 303 vb.
  plunge 313 vb.
  drench 341 vb.
  preserve 666 vb.
  get drunk 949 vb.
soutane *tunic* 228 n.
  canonicals 989 n.
south *be high* 209 vb.
  compass point 281 n.
Southerner, Southron
  foreigner 59 n.
southing *bearings* 186 n.
souvenir *reminder* 505 n.
  plaything 837 n.
sou'wester *overcoat* 228 n.
  gale 352 n.
sovereign *supreme* 34 adj.
  strong 162 adj.
  remedial 658 adj.
  successful 727 adj.
  ruling 733 adj.
  sovereign 741 n.
  coinage 797 n.
  aristocrat 868 n.
sovereignty
  superiority 34 n.
  governance 733 n.
soviet *council* 692 n.
sovietism
  government 733 n.
sow *disperse* 75 vb.
  cause 156 vb.
  produce 164 vb.
  let fall 311 vb.
  pig 365 n.
  cultivate 370 vb.
  female animal 373 n.
sower *husbandman* 370 n.
  preparer 669 n.
sow one's wild oats
  revel 837 vb.
  be wicked 934 vb.
  be intemperate 943 vb.
sow the seed
  educate 534 vb.
  prepare 669 vb.
sozzled *tipsy* 949 adj.
spa *hygiene* 652 n.
  hospital 658 n.
space *quantity* 26 n.
  grade 73 vb.
  time 108 n.

opportunity 137 n.
  space 183 n.
  room 194 n.
  size 195 n.
  distance 199 n.
  interval 201 n.
  opening 263 n.
  air 340 n.
  storage 632 n.
space-dweller *native* 191 n.
space flight
  aeronautics 271 n.
space-man *traveller* 268 n.
  aeronaut 271 n.
space-ship, space station
  space-ship 276 n.
  satellite 321 n.
space-time continuum
  universe 321 n.
space-traveller
  traveller 268 n.
  aeronaut 271 n.
spacious *great* 32 adj.
  spacious 183 adj.
  large 195 adj.
  palmy 730 adj.
spade *ladle* 194 n.
  make concave 255 vb.
  transpose 272 vb.
  shovel 274 n.
  farm tool 370 n.
spaghetti *dish* 301 n.
spalpeen *bad man* 938 n.
span *connect* 45 vb.
  bond 47 n.
  group 74 n.
  duality 90 n.
  time 108 n.
  period 110 n.
  extend 183 vb.
  distance 199 n.
  long measure 203 n.
  be broad 205 vb.
  overlie 226 vb.
  measure 465 vb.
  bridge 624 n.
spandrel *pattern* 844 n.
  church interior 990 n.
spangle *variegate* 437 vb.
  finery 844 n.
  decorate 844 vb.
spaniel *dog* 365 n.
  toady 879 n.
spank *strike* 279 vb.
  spank 963 vb.
spanker *whopper* 195 n.
  sail 275 n.
spanner *tool* 630 n.
spanner in the works
  hitch 702 n.
spar *hanger* 217 n.

supporter 218 n.
  strike 279 vb.
  bicker 709 vb.
  pugilism 716 n.
spare *additional* 38 n.
  extra 40 n.
  remaining 41 adj.
  lean 206 adj.
  avoid 620 vb.
  underfed 636 adj.
  superfluous 637 adj.
  dispose of 673 vb.
  not use 674 vb.
  be lenient 736 vb.
  not retain 779 vb.
  give 781 vb.
  economize 814 vb.
  relieve 831 vb.
  show mercy 905 vb.
  exempt 919 vb.
  be temperate 942 vb.
spare diet *fasting* 946 n.
spare hours, spare time
  opportunity 137 n.
  leisure 681 n.
spare part *extra* 40 n.
  component 58 n.
  safeguard 662 n.
spargefaction
  dispersion 75 n.
  water 339 n.
  moistening 341 n.
sparing
  economical 814 adj.
  parsimonious 816 adj.
  temperate 942 adj.
spark *small quantity* 33 n.
  electricity 160 n.
  fire 379 n.
  flash 417 n.
  luminary 420 n.
  fop 848 n.
  lover 887 n.
  caress 889 vb.
sparkle *shine* 417 vb.
  vigour 571 n.
  cheerfulness 833 n.
  be witty 839 vb.
sparkler *fireworks* 420 n.
  gem 844 n.
sparkling *bubbly* 355 adj.
  splendid 841 adj.
  (*see* sparkle)
spark off *initiate* 68 vb.
sparring partner
  pugilist 722 n.
sparrow *bird* 365 n.
sparse *unassembled* 75 adj.
  few 105 adj.
  unproductive 172 adj.
  scarce 636 adj.

sparseness, sparsity
  insubstantiality 4 n.
Spartan *severe* 735 adj.
  abstainer 942 n.
  temperate 942 adj.
  ascetic 945 adj.
  fasting 946 adj.
Spartan brevity
  conciseness 569 n.
spasm *brief span* 114 n.
  fitfulness 142 n.
  violence 176 n.
  spasm 318 n.
  pang 377 n.
  paralysis 651 n.
  activity 678 n.
  feeling 818 n.
  excitation 821 n.
spasmodic
  discontinuous 72 adj.
  unstable 152 adj.
  (see spasm)
spastic *sick person* 651 n.
spasticity *paralysis* 651 n.
spat *reproduce itself* 164 vb.
  quarrel 709 n.
spate *great quantity* 32 n.
  plenty 635 n.
  redundance 637 n.
spate, in *flowing* 350 adj.
spatial *spatial* 183 adj.
spatio-temporal
  material 319 adj.
  spatial 183 adj.
spat on *unrespected* 921 adj.
spats, spatterdashes
  legwear 228 n.
spatter *disperse* 75 vb.
  emit 300 vb.
  make unclean 649 vb.
  defame 926 vb.
spatula *shovel* 274 n.
spavin *animal disease* 651 n.
spawn *youngling* 132 n.
  reproduce itself 164 vb.
  posterity 176 n.
spawned *born* 360 adj.
spawning *prolific* 171 adj.
spay *unman* 161 vb.
speak *communicate* 524 vb.
  inform 524 vb.
  divulge 526 vb.
  signal 547 vb.
  voice 577 vb.
  speak 579 vb.
speak at *speak to* 583 vb.
speakeasy *tavern* 192 n.
speaker *megaphone* 400 n.
  speaker 579 n.
  master 741 n.
speak for *deputize* 755 vb.

speak for itself
  be visible 443 vb.
  evidence 466 vb.
  be intelligible 516 vb.
  be plain 522 vb.
speaking of
  concerning 9 adv.
speaking tube
  hearing aid 415 n.
speak one's mind
  be truthful 540 vb.
speak out *be plain* 522 vb.
speak to *speak to* 583 vb.
speak up *be loud* 400 vb.
  emphasize 532 vb.
speak up for
  approve 923 vb.
  vindicate 927 vb.
speak volumes
  evidence 466 vb.
spear *sharp point* 256 n.
  pierce 263 vb.
  strike at 712 vb.
  spear 723 n.
spearhead *front* 237 n.
  chief thing 638 n.
  leader 690 n.
  attacker 712 n.
  armed force 722 n.
spearman *soldiery* 722 n.
spearmint *scent* 396 n.
special *characteristic* 5 adj.
  different 15 adj.
  unimitative 21 adj.
  special 80 adj.
  unconformable 84 adj.
special case
  non-uniformity 17 n.
  speciality 80 n.
special constable
  police 955 n.
special correspondent
  informant 524 n.
  newsmonger 529 n.
  author 589 n.
  delegate 754 n.
special day
  special day 876 n.
specialism *knowledge* 490 n.
  skill 694 n.
specialist *scholar* 492 n.
  doctor 658 n.
  expert 696 n.
speciality *irrelation* 10 n.
  speciality 80 n.
  dish 301 n.
  (see special)
specialization
  speciality 80 n.
specialize *study* 536 vb.
specialized

instructed 490 adj.
  expert 694 adj.
specially *greatly* 32 adv.
special pleading
  argument 475 n.
  sophistry 477 n.
  pretext 614 n.
specie *coinage* 797 n.
species *subdivision* 53 n.
  group 74 n.
  breed 77 n.
specific *special* 80 adj.
  means 629 n.
  remedy 658 n.
specification
  differentiation 15 n.
  classification 77 n.
  particulars 80 n.
  qualification 468 n.
  report 524 n.
  description 590 n.
specific gravity
  gravity 322 n.
  density 324 n.
specify *class* 62 vb.
  specify 80 vb.
  indicate 547 vb.
  name 561 vb.
specimen *duplicate* 22 n.
  prototype 23 n.
  example 83 n.
  exhibit 522 n.
specious *appearing* 445 adj.
  plausible 471 adj.
  sophistical 477 adj.
  ostensible 614 adj.
  splendid 841 adj.
  affected 850 adj.
  ostentatious 875 adj.
  flattering 925 adj.
speck, speckle
  small thing 33 n.
  maculation 437 n.
  variegate 437 vb.
  blemish 845 n.
spectacle *spectacle* 445 n.
  exhibit 522 n.
  stage show 594 n.
  beauty 841 n.
  prodigy 864 n.
  pageant 875 n.
spectacles *eyeglass* 442 n.
spectacular
  well-seen 443 adj.
  appearing 445 n.
  showy 875 adj.
spectator *presence* 189 n.
  spectator 441 n.
spectral
  insubstantial 4 adj.
  variegated 437 adj.

spooky 970 adj.
spectre *visual fallacy* 440 n.
  appearance 445 n.
  intimidation 854 n.
  ghost 970 n.
spectre at the feast, be the
  hinder 702 vb.
spectrology *optics* 417 n.
spectroscope
  astronomy 321 n.
  chromatics 425 n.
  optical device 442 n.
spectroscopic
  coloured 425 adj.
spectroscopy *optics* 417 n.
spectrum *light* 417 n.
  variegation 437 n.
  colour 425 n.
speculate (see speculation)
speculation
  calculation of chance
    159 n.
  meditation 449 n.
  empiricism 461 n.
  conjecture 512 n.
  gambling 618 n.
  essay 671 n.
  undertaking 672 n.
  trade 791 n.
speculative
  philosophic 449 adj.
  thoughtful 449 adj.
  experimental 461 adj.
  uncertain 474 adj.
  suppositional 512 adj.
  speculative 618 adj.
  dangerous 661 adj.
  trading 791 adj.
  rash 857 adj.
speculator
  experimenter 461 n.
  theorist 512 n.
  gambler 618 n.
speculum *mirror* 442 n.
sped *completed* 725 adj.
speech *language* 557 n.
  voice 577 n.
  speech, oration 579 n.
  allocution 583 n.
speech accent
  pronunciation 577 n.
speech defect
  speech defect 580 n.
speeches *diffuseness* 570 n.
speechify *orate* 579 vb.
speechless *silent* 399 adj.
  voiceless 578 adj.
  wondering 864 adj.
speechless, be
  be taciturn 582 vb.
speech-making

oratory 579 n.
speech sound
  speech sound 398 n.
speed *motion* 265 n.
  velocity 277 n.
  facilitate 701 vb.
  aid 703 vb.
speedboat *boat* 275 n.
speed limit *limit* 236 n.
speed merchant
  speeder 277 n.
speedometer *velocity* 277 n.
  meter 465 n.
  recording instrument
    549 n.
speed-rate *velocity* 277 n.
speed-track
  path, road 624 n.
speed-trap *velocity* 277 n.
speed-up *spurt* 277 n.
speed well *succeed* 727 vb.
speedwriting
  writing 586 n.
speedy *speedy* 277 adj.
speer *interrogate* 459 vb.
speleology *descent* 309 n.
  mineralogy 359 n.
  search 459 n.
  discovery 484 n.
  sport 837 n.
spell *period* 110 n.
  influence 178 n.
  predict 511 vb.
  mean 514 vb.
  interpret 520 vb.
  imply 523 vb.
  study 536 vb.
  indicate 547 vb.
  spell 558 vb.
  malediction 899 n.
  spell 983 n.
spellbind *orate* 579 vb.
  motivate 612 vb.
  be wonderful 864 vb.
  bewitch 983 vb.
spellbinder *speaker* 579 n.
  sorcerer 983 n.
spellbound *induced* 612 adj.
  wondering 864 adj.
  bewitched 983 adj.
spelling *spelling* 558 n.
spell out *decipher* 520 vb.
spelt *corn* 366 n.
speluncar *concave* 255 adj.
spencer *overcoat, vest* 228 n.
spend *emit* 300 vb.
  waste 634 vb.
  use 673 vb.
  expend 806 vb.
spender *prodigal* 815 n.
spending spree

prodigality 815 n.
spendthrift *prodigal* 815 n.
  intemperate 943 adj.
spend time
  pass time 108 vb.
spent *weakened* 163 adj.
  outgoing 298 adj.
  fatigued 684 adj.
  lost 772 adj.
  expended 806 adj.
spent fires *inertness* 175 n.
sperm *source* 156 n.
  genitalia 164 n.
  fertilizer 171 n.
spermaceti *fat* 357 n.
spermatic
  generative 171 adj.
spermatozoa *genitalia* 164 n.
spew *eject, vomit* 300 vb.
sphagnum *plant* 366 n.
sphere *group* 74 n.
  classification 77 n.
  range 183 n.
  region 184 n.
  abode 192 n.
  sphere 252 n.
  function 622 n.
spherical *round* 250 adj.
  rotund 252 adj.
sphericity
  rotundity 252 n.
  convexity 253 n.
sphery *rotund* 252 adj.
  celestial 321 adj.
spheterize
  appropriate 786 vb.
sphinx *rara avis* 84 n.
  oracle 511 n.
sphinxlike
  unintelligible 517 adj.
spica *prickle* 256 n.
spice *small quantity* 33 n.
  tincture 43 n.
  mix 43 vb.
  stimulant 174 n.
  cook 301 vb.
  season 388 vb.
  condiment 389 n.
  appetize 390 vb.
  preserver 666 n.
  pleasurableness 826 n.
spicery *condiment* 389 n.
  scent 396 n.
spicilegium
  anthology 592 n.
spick and span
  clean 648 adj.
spicula *prickle* 256 n.
spiculate *sharpen* 256 vb.
spicy *tasty* 386 adj.
  pungent 388 adj.

savoury 390 adj.
fragrant 396 adj.
exciting 821 adj.
impure 951 adj.
spider *planner* 623 n.
weaving 222 n.
spiderman *elevation* 310 n.
spider's web
complexity 61 n.
ambush 527 n.
spidery *lean* 206 adj.
spiel *speak* 579 vb.
spieler *trickster* 545 n.
speaker 579 n.
spiffing *topping* 644 adj.
spigot *stopper* 264 n.
spike *disable* 161 vb.
vertex 213 n.
sharp point 256 n.
pierce 263 vb.
stopper 264 n.
defences 713 n.
spikenard *unguent* 357 n.
spiky *sharp* 256 adj.
Anglican 976 adj.
pietistic 979 adj.
spill *filament* 208 n.
overturning 221 n.
flow out 298 vb.
emit 300 vb.
let fall 311 vb.
make flow 350 vb.
lighter 385 n.
torch 420 n.
waste 634 vb.
spill over *overstep* 306 vb.
spill the beans
divulge 526 vb.
spillway *waterfall* 350 n.
conduit 351 n.
spilt milk *loss* 772 n.
spin *weave* 222 vb.
aeronautics 271 n.
rotation 315 n.
fake 541 vb.
spinach *vegetable* 301 n.
spinal *supporting* 218 adj.
central 225 adj.
back 238 adj.
spin a web
be cunning 698 vb.
spin a yarn
be untrue 543 vb.
exaggerate 546 vb.
describe 590 vb.
spindle *pivot* 218 n.
rotator 315 n.
spindle-shaped
tapering 256 adj.
spindly *lean* 206 adj.
spindrift *moisture* 341 n.

bubble 355 n.
spine *supporter* 218 n.
pillar 218 n.
centre 225 n.
rear 238 n.
prickle 256 n.
spineless *impotent* 161 adj.
weak 163 adj.
spinet *piano* 414 n.
spinnaker *sail* 275 n.
spinner *rotator* 315 n.
weaving 222 n.
spinney *wood* 366 n.
spinning jenny *rotator* 315 n
spinning wheel *rotator* 315 n
spin of the coin
chance 159 n.
spinosity *sharpness* 256 n.
spin out *continuate* 71 vb.
spin out 113 vb.
be diffuse 570 vb.
be loquacious 581 vb.
spinster *woman* 373 n.
spinster 895 n.
spinsterhood
celibacy 895 n.
spin words
show style 566 vb.
spiny *sharp* 256 adj.
spiracle *orifice* 263 n.
outlet 298 n.
air-pipe 353 n.
spiral *coil* 251 n.
twine 251 vb.
ascend 308 vb.
tumble 309 vb.
rotation 315 n.
spirant
speech sound 398 n.
spirantal *sounding* 398 adj.
spire *high structure* 209 n.
vertex 213 n.
summit 213 n.
twine 251 vb.
sharp point 256 n.
ascend 308 vb.
church exterior 990 n.
spirit
insubstantial thing 4 n.
temperament 5 n.
vigorousness 174 n.
life 360 n.
fuel 385 n.
spirit 447 n.
meaning 514 n.
vigour 571 n.
cleanser 648 n.
restlessness 678 n.
affections 817 n.
moral sensibility 819 n.
courage 855 n.

ghost 970 n.
spirit away *steal* 788 vb.
spirit body
spiritualism 984 n.
spirited *lively* 819 adj.
cheerful 833 adj.
courageous 855 adj.
spiritism
spiritualism 984 n.
spirit-laying *sorcery* 983 n.
spiritless
apathetic 820 adj.
inexcitable 823 adj.
melancholic 834 adj.
cowardly 856 adj.
spirit-level
horizontality 216 n.
spirit of the age
tendency 179 n.
spirit-raising *sorcery* 983 n.
spirit-rapping
spiritualism 984 n.
spirits *liquor* 301 n.
tonic 658 n.
cheerfulness 833 n.
spirits, the *the dead* 361 n.
spiritual *immaterial* 320 adj.
psychic 447 adj.
divine 965 adj.
religious 973 adj.
pious 979 adj.
priestly 985 adj.
spiritual adviser
pastor 986 n.
spiritual comfort
church ministry 985 n.
spiritualism
immateriality 320 n.
spirit 447 n.
occultism 984 n.
spiritualism 984 n.
spiritualist *occultist* 984 n.
spiritualistic
psychic 447 adj.
spooky 970 adj.
psychical 984 adj.
spirituality
immateriality 320 n.
virtue 933 n.
sanctity 979 n.
spiritualize
disembody 320 vb.
make pious 979 vb.
sanctify 979 vb.
spiritual life
sanctity 979 n.
spirituous *edible* 301 adj.
intoxicating 949 adj.
spirit-writing
spiritualism 984 n.
spirt *flow out* 298 vb.

spissitude *density* 324 n.
semiliquidity 354 n.
spit *projection* 254 n.
sharp point 256 n.
perforator 263 n.
pierce 263 vb.
emit, eruct 300 vb.
excrement 302 n.
rotator 315 n.
effervesce 318 vb.
hiss 406 vb.
be angry 891 vb.
be sullen 893 vb.
threaten 900 vb.
disapprove 924 vb.
spit and polish
cleanness 648 n.
formality 875 n.
spite *quarrelsomeness* 709 n.
severity 735 n.
oppress 735 vb.
enmity 881 n.
hatred 888 n.
resentment 891 n.
malevolence 898 n.
revengefulness 910 n.
envy 912 n.
detraction 926 n.
spiteful *harmful* 645 adj.
(*see* spite)
spite of, in
in defiance of 25 adv.
although 182 adv.
nevertheless 488 adv.
with difficulty 700 adv.
in opposition 704 adv.
spitfire
violent creature 176 n.
shrew 892 n.
spit of *analogue* 18 n.
spit on *not respect* 921 vb.
spit out *eject* 300 vb.
spittle *excrement* 302 n.
spittoon *bowl* 194 n.
spiv *idler* 679 n.
spivery *improbity* 930 n.
splanchnology
structure 331 n.
splash *small quantity* 33 n.
water 339 n.
moisten 341 vb.
lake 346 n.
flow 350 vb.
sibilation 406 n.
colour 425 n.
advertise 528 vb.
make important 638 vb.
make unclean 649 vb.
ostentation 875 n.
splashboard *shelter* 662 n.
splay *diverge* 294 vb.

splay-footed
deformed 246 adj.
spleen *insides* 224 n.
discontent 829 n.
melancholy 834 n.
sullenness 893 n.
envy 912 n.
spleenful *resentful* 891 adj.
irascible 892 adj.
hating 888 adj.
malevolent 898 adj.
spleenless
benevolent 897 adj.
splendid *luminous* 417 adj.
excellent 644 adj.
liberal 813 adj.
pleasurable 826 adj.
splendid 841 adj.
noteworthy 866 adj.
ostentatious 875 adj.
splendour *light* 417 n.
beauty 841 n.
prestige 866 n.
ostentation 875 n.
splenetic (*see* spleenful)
splice *tie* 45 vb.
cross 222 vb.
intromit 231 vb.
repair 656 vb.
marry 894 vb.
splice-joint *joint* 45 n.
spline *strip* 208 n.
splint *supporter* 218 n.
hardness 326 n.
surgical dressing 658 n.
splinter *break* 46 vb.
piece 53 n.
be brittle 330 vb.
splinter group
dissentient 489 n.
party 708 n.
revolter 738 n.
splintery *brittle* 330 adj.
split *disjunction* 46 n.
discontinuity 72 n.
bisect 92 vb.
gap 201 n.
open 263 vb.
be brittle 330 vb.
inform 524 vb.
divulge 526 vb.
dissension 709 n.
apportion 783 vb.
split hairs
discriminate 463 vb.
sophisticate 477 vb.
be fastidious 862 vb.
split personality
psychopathy 503 n.
split second *instant* 116 n.
split the difference

average out 30 vb.
splotch *blemish* 845 n.
splurge *ostentation* 875 n.
splutter *emit* 300 vb.
flow 350 vb.
hiss 406 vb.
stammer 580 vb.
haste 680 n.
spoil *derange* 63 vb.
weaken 163 vb.
lay waste 165 vb.
impair 655 vb.
be clumsy 695 vb.
hinder 702 vb.
trophy 729 n.
be lenient 736 vb.
rob 788 vb.
booty 790 n.
make ugly 842 vb.
blemish 845 vb.
pet 889 vb.
spoilage *decrement* 42 n.
spoiled child *satiety* 863 n.
favourite 890 n.
spoiler *hinderer* 702 n.
taker 786 n.
robber 789 n.
evildoer 904 n.
spoiling for
willing 597 adj.
spoilsport *dissuasion* 613 n.
meddler 678 n.
hinderer 702 n.
disapprover 924 n.
spoke *line* 203 n.
divergence 294 n.
spoken *linguistic* 577 adj.
spokeshave
sharp edge 256 n.
spokesman
interpreter 520 n.
informant 524 n.
messenger 531 n.
speaker 579 n.
agent 686 n.
deputy 755 n.
spoliation *spoliation* 788 n.
spondaic *poetic* 593 adj.
sponge *porosity* 263 n.
absorb 299 vb.
drier 342 n.
obliteration 550 n.
cleaning utensil 648 n.
beg 761 vb.
fleece 786 vb.
toady 879 n.
be servile 879 vb.
drunkard 949 n.
sponger *idler* 679 n.
beggar 763 n.
toady 879 n.

sponging house
prison 748 n.
spongy *concave* 255 adj.
porous 263 adj.
rare 325 adj.
soft 327 adj.
marshy 347 adj.
pulpy 356 adj.
sponsor *witness* 466 n.
patronize 703 vb.
sponsorship *aid* 703 n.
security 767 n.
spontaneity
spontaneity 609 n.
non-design 618 n.
non-preparation 670 n.
feeling 818 n.
spontaneous
intuitive 476 adj.
involuntary 596 adj.
voluntary 597 adj.
artless 699 adj.
(*see* spontaneity)
spoof *deceive* 542 vb.
spoofer *trickster* 545 n.
spook *ghost* 970 n.
spoon *ladle* 194 n.
shovel 274 n.
extractor 304 n.
caress 889 vb.
spoonerism *inversion* 221 n.
absurdity 497 n.
neology 560 n.
witticism 839 n.
ridiculousness 849 n.
spoonfeed *manage* 689 vb.
be lax 734 vb.
be lenient 736 vb.
pet 889 vb.
spoonfeeding
teaching 534 n.
aid 703 n.
spoonful
small quantity 33 n.
spooning *love-making* 887 n.
wooing 889 n.
spoor *identification* 547 n.
trace 548 n.
sporadic
unassembled 75 adj.
infrequent 140 adj.
uncertain 474 adj.
sporran *skirt* 228 n.
sport *misfit* 25 n.
nonconformist 84 n.
athletics 162 n.
wear 228 vb.
show 522 vb.
exercise 682 n.
contest 716 n.
merriment 833 n.

sport 837 n.
laughing-stock 851 n.
prodigy 864 n.
be ostentatious 875 vb.
gentleman 929 n.
good man 937 n.
sporting (*see* sportsmanlike)
sporting chance
fair chance 159 n.
probability 471 n.
sportive *gay* 833 adj.
amused 837 adj.
amusing 837 adj.
witty 839 adj.
sportsman *hunter* 619 n.
player 837 n,
gentleman 929 n.
sportsmanlike *just* 913 adj.
honourable 929 adj.
sportsmanship *sport* 837 n.
probity 929 n.
sportulary *recipient* 782 n.
sporty *amused* 837 adj.
sporule *powder* 332 n.
spot *small thing* 33 n.
place 185 n.
variegate 437 vb.
detect 484 vb.
understand 516 vb.
defect 647 n.
make unclean 649 vb.
impair 655 vb.
pattern 844 n.
blemish 845 n.
slur 867 n.
spot cash *money* 797 n.
spot, in a
in difficulties 700 adj.
spotless *perfect* 646 adj.
clean 648 adj.
innocent 935 adj.
pure 950 adj.
spotlight *lighting* 420 n.
manifest 522 vb.
advertisement 528 n.
theatre 594 n.
spot, on the
instantaneously 116 adv.
at present 121 adv.
on the spot 189 adj.
near 200 adj.
spots *skin disease* 651 n.
spotter *spectator* 441 n.
spotty *mottled* 437 adj.
diseased 651 adj.
blemished 845 adj.
spousal *wedding* 894 n.
spouse *spouse* 894 n.
spouseless
unwedded 895 adj.
spout *orifice* 263 n.

outlet 298 n.
flow 350 vb.
conduit 351 n.
orate 579 vb.
sprachgefühl
linguistics 557 n.
style 566 n.
sprain *derange* 63 vb.
disable 161 vb.
weaken 163 vb.
distort 246 vb.
sprat *animalcule* 196 n.
table fish 365 n.
sprawl
be horizontal 216 vb.
tumble 309 vb.
repose 683 vb.
sprawl over *fill* 54 vb.
be dispersed 75 vb.
spray *branch* 53 n.
disperse 75 vb.
vaporizer 338 n.
moisture 341 n.
irrigator 341 n.
bubble 355 n.
foliage 366 n.
spread *be* 1 vb.
grow 36 vb.
dispersion 75 n.
generalize 79 vb.
range 183 n.
pervade 189 vb.
expansion 197 n.
flatten 216 vb.
overlay 226 vb.
progress 285 vb.
diverge 294 vb.
meal 301 n.
advertisement 528 n.
publish 528 vb.
spread canvas
navigate 269 vb.
start out 296 vb.
spreadeagle *lengthen* 203 vb.
diverge 294 vb.
punish 963 vb.
spreadeagleism
boasting 877 n.
spreading *influential* 178 adj.
spacious 183 adj.
prolix 570 adj.
spread out *lengthen* 203 vb.
spread over *fill* 54 vb.
spread the carpet
celebrate 876 vb.
spread the table
make ready 669 vb.
spree *revel* 837 n.
drunkenness 949 n.
sprig *branch* 53 n.
young plant 132 n.

foliage 366n.
sprightly *active* 678adj.
cheerful 833adj.
spring *period* 110n.
spring 128n.
vernal 128adj.
young plant 132n.
source 156n.
energy 160n.
strength 162n.
be weak 163vb.
coil 251n.
spurt 277n.
move fast 277vb.
recoil 280n.
outflow 298n.
lifter 310n.
leap 312n.,vb.
elasticity 328n.
be elastic 328vb.
stream 350n.
motive 612n.
machine 630n.
take 786vb.
spring a mine
surprise 508vb.
besiege 712vb.
spring apart
be disjoined 46vb.
spring-balance
scales 322n.
springboard
recoil 280n.
lifter 310n.
fluctuation 317n.
aider 703n.
springbok *jumper* 312n.
deer 365n.
spring-clean *clean* 648vb.
springe *trap* 542n.
springer *supporter* 218n.
spring from *result* 157vb.
spring-gun *trap* 542n.
springing line
obliquity 220n.
springless *rigid* 326adj.
tough 329adj.
spring tide
great quantity 32n.
increase 36n.
high water 204n.
current 350n.
springtide, springtime
spring 128n.
salad days 130n.
spring up *become* 1vb.
begin 68vb.
happen 154vb.
expand 197vb.
ascend 308vb.
lift oneself 310vb.

leap 312vb.
be visible 443vb.
spring upon *surprise* 508vb.
springy *soft* 327adj.
elastic 328adj.
sprinkle
small quantity 33n.
mix 43vb.
disperse 75vb.
emit 300vb.
let fall 311vb.
moisten 341vb.
rain 350vb.
variegate 437vb.
sprinkler *irrigator* 341n.
extinguisher 382n.
cleaning utensil 648n.
sprint *spurt* 277n.
racing 716n.
sprit *projection* 245n.
sprite *elf* 970n.
sprocket *tooth* 256n.
sprout *grow* 36vb.
young plant 132n.
reproduce itself 164vb.
descendant 170n.
expand 197vb.
vegetate 366vb.
sprouts *vegetable* 301n.
spruce *tree* 366n.
clean 648adj.,vb.
personable 841adj.
sprung *soft* 327adj.
elastic 328adj.
sprung rhythm
prosody 593n.
spry *active* 678adj.
cheerful 833adj.
spud *shovel* 274n.
tuber 301n.
spume *effervesce* 318vb.
bubble 355n.,vb.
spumy *bubbly* 355adj.
white 427adj.
spunk *vigorousness* 174n.
lighter 385n.
courage 855n.
spunkless *cowardly* 856adj.
spunky *courageous* 855adj.
spur *branch* 53n.
stimulant 174n.
high land 209n.
projection 254n.
sharp point 256n.
accelerate 277vb.
impel, kick 279vb.
incentive 612n.
hasten 680vb.
animate 821vb.
spurge *plant* 366n.
spurious *false* 541adj.

spurious 542adj.
bastard 954adj.
spurn *kick* 279vb.
reject 607vb.
despise 922vb.
spur of the moment
spontaneity 609n.
spur of the moment, on the
instantaneously 116adv.
at present 121adv.
incidentally 137adv.
extempore 609adv.
hastily 680adv.
spurs *badge of rank* 743n.
honours 866n.
spurt *increase* 36n.
brief span 114n.
vigorousness 174n.
outbreak 176n.
accelerate 277vb.
progression 285n.
flow out 298vb.
emit 300vb.
ascend 308vb.
flow 350vb.
activity 678n.
haste 680n.
sputnik *space-ship* 276n.
satellite 321n.
sputter *emit* 300vb.
be agitated 318vb.
hiss 406vb.
be dim 419vb.
stammer 580vb.
sputum *excrement* 302n.
spy *see, scan* 438vb.
spectator 441n.
inquisitor 453n.
be curious 453vb.
secret service 459n.
detective 459n.
informer 524n.
warner 664n.
spy-glass *telescope* 442n.
spy-mania *enquiry* 459n.
phobia 854n.
spy-ring
secret service 459n.
squab *youngling* 132n.
fleshy 195adj.
short 204adj.
thick 205adj.
cushion 218n.
bird 365n.
squabble *quarrel* 709n.
squad *band* 74n.
personnel 686n.
formation 722n.
squadron *band* 74n.
shipping 275n.
formation 722n.

air force 722n.
navy 722n.
squalid *unclean* 649adj.
beggarly 801adj.
graceless 842adj.
disreputable 867adj.
squall *gale* 352n.
cry 408n.
weep 836vb.
squally *windy* 352adj.
squalor *uncleanness* 649n.
poverty 801n.
ugliness 842n.
squamation
stratification 207n.
squamous *layered* 207adj.
dermal 226adj.
squander *consume* 165vb.
waste 634vb.
make insufficient 636vb.
misuse 675vb.
lose 772vb.
be prodigal 815vb.
squandermania
prodigality 815n.
square *uniform* 16adj.
equal 28adj.
compensate 31vb.
regular 81adj.
make conform 83vb.
do sums 86vb.
quaternity 96n.
quadruple 97vb.
place 185n.
housing 192n.
fleshy 195adj.
verticality 215n.
efform 243vb.
angular figure 247vb.
unsharpened 257adj.
navigate 269vb.
bribe 612vb.
formation 722n.
just 913adj.
honourable 929adj.
square accounts
pay 804vb.
account 808vb.
square accounts with
pay 804vb.
squared
symmetrical 245adj.
square measure
measure 183n.
square peg in a round hole
misfit 25n.
square root
numerical element 85n.
square up to *fight* 716vb.
square with *accord* 24vb.
squash *suppress* 165vb.

flatten 216vb.
strike 279vb.
vegetables 301n.
abase 311vb.
soften 327vb.
marsh 347n.
semiliquidity 354n.
pulpiness 356n.
ball game 837n.
humiliate 872vb.
social gathering 882n.
squashy *soft* 327adj.
fluidal 335adj.
humid 341adj.
marshy 347adj.
semiliquid 354adj.
pulpy 356adj.
squat *place oneself* 187vb.
dwell 192vb.
dwarfish 196adj.
short 204adj.
thick 205adj.
low 210adj.
encroach 306vb.
sit down 311vb.
possess 773vb.
appropriate 786vb.
squatter *intruder* 59n.
resident 191n.
possessor 776n.
usurper 916n.
squaw *woman* 373n.
spouse 894n.
squawk *stridor* 407n.
ululation 409n.
squeak *sound faint* 401vb.
stridor 407n.
cry 408n.
ululation 409n.
deprecation 762n.
discontent 829n.
squeaker *informer* 524n.
squeaky *strident* 407adj.
squeal *inform* 524vb.
divulge 526vb.
cry 408n.
squealer *informer* 524n.
tergiversator 603n.
knave 938n.
squeamish
unwilling 598adj.
irresolute 601adj.
sick 651adj.
disliking 861adj.
fastidious 862adj.
honourable 929adj.
prudish 950adj.
squeegee
cleaning utensil 648n.
squeeze *copy* 22n.
compression 198n.

touch 378vb.
obstruct 702vb.
oppress 735vb.
compel 740vb.
restriction 747n.
levy 786vb.
endearment 889n.
caress 889vb.
squeeze from, squeeze out
extract 304vb.
squeeze in *fill* 54vb.
stow 187vb.
squelch *suppress* 165vb.
be wet 341vb.
sibilation 406n.
squelchy *soft* 327adj.
humid 341adj.
marshy 347n.
semiliquid 354adj.
squib *bang* 402n.
the press 528n.
satire 851n.
calumny 926n.
squid *fish* 365n.
squiggle *coil* 251n.
punctuation 547n.
squilgee
cleaning utensil 648n.
squinny *gaze, scan* 438vb.
squint *obliquity* 220n.
window 263n.
look 438n.
dim sight 440n.
church interior 990n.
squire *accompany* 89vb.
minister to 703vb.
retainer 742n.
serve 742vb.
aristocrat 868n.
be servile 879vb.
lover 887n.
court 889vb.
squirearchy
aristocracy 868n.
squire of dames
fop 848n.
lover 887n.
libertine 952n.
squirm *wriggle* 251vb.
feel pain 377vb.
suffer 825vb.
be servile 879vb.
squirrel *rodent* 365n.
squirt *emit* 300vb.
irrigator 341n.
squirt in *infuse* 303vb.
squit *nonentity* 639n.
sruti
non-Biblical scripture
975n.
revelation 975n.

stab *pierce* 263 vb.
  kill 362 vb.
  give pain 377 vb.
  wound 655 n., vb.
  therapy 658 n.
  strike at 712 vb.
  suffering 825 n.
stabilimeter
  stabilizer 153 n.
stability
  equilibrium 28 n.
  durability 113 n.
  stability 153 n.
stabilize *equalize* 28 vb.
  stabilize 153 vb.
stabilizer *stabilizer* 153 n.
stable *group* 74 n.
  strong 162 adj.
  stable 192 n.
  chamber 194 n.
  horse 273 n.
  groom 369 vb.
  inexcitable 823 adj.
  (*see* stability)
stable-boy
  animal husbandry 369 n.
  servant 742 n.
stable-companion
  concomitant 89 n.
  chum 880 n.
stack *great quantity* 32 n.
  bunch 74 n.
  store 632 n., vb.
staddle *stand* 218 n.
stade *long measure* 203 n.
stadholder *governor* 741 n.
stadium *meeting place* 192 n.
  racing 716 n.
  arena 724 n.
staff *supporter* 218 n.
  employ 622 vb.
  personnel 686 n.
  director 690 n.
  club 723 n.
  master 741 n.
  army officer 741 n.
  domestic 742 n.
  badge of rule 743 n.
  vestments 989 n.
staff college
  training school 539 n.
  council 692 n.
staff-work
  arrangement 62 n.
  management 689 n.
  art of war 718 n.
stag *deer* 365 n.
  male animal 372 n.
  gambler 618 n.
  purchaser 792 n.
stage *juncture* 8 n.

relativeness 9 n.
  degree 27 n.
  serial place 73 n.
  situation 186 n.
  layer 207 n.
  stand 218 n.
  stage-coach 274 n.
  goal 295 n.
  show 522 vb.
  rostrum 539 n.
  drama, theatre 594 n.
  dramatize 594 vb.
  arena 724 n.
stage-coach
  stage-coach 274 n.
stage-craft
  dramaturgy 594 n.
stage-directions
  dramaturgy 594 n.
stage-door *theatre* 594 n.
stage effect *pageant* 875 n.
stage-fright *fear* 854 n.
  acting 594 n.
stage-manager
  stage-manager 594 n.
stage-set *spectacle* 445 n.
  stage-set 594 n.
stage show
  stage show 594 n.
stage-struck
  dramatic 594 adj.
stage trick *pageant* 815 n.
stage-whisper *voice* 577 n.
  speak low 578 vb.
  dramaturgy 594 n.
stagger *grade* 73 vb.
  vary 152 vb.
  obliquity 220 n.
  walk 267 vb.
  move slowly 278 vb.
  tumble 309 vb.
  oscillate 317 vb.
  be agitated 318 vb.
  surprise 508 vb.
  dissuade 613 vb.
  be fatigued 684 vb.
  impress 821 vb.
  be wonderful 864 vb.
  be drunk 949 vb.
staggers *spasm* 318 n.
  animal disease 651 n.
stagnant, stagnate
  (*see* stagnation)
stagnation
  unproductivity 172 n.
  inertness 175 n.
  quiescence 266 n.
  non-use 674 n.
  inaction 677 n.
  inactivity 679 n.
  moral insensibility 820 n.

stag-party *male* 372 n.
  social gathering 882 n.
stagy *dramatic* 594 adj.
  affected 850 adj.
  showy 875 adj.
staid *wise* 498 adj.
  inexcitable 823 adj.
  serious 834 adj.
stain *tincture* 43 n.
  coat 226 vb.
  pigment 425 n.
  decolorize 426 vb.
  variegate 437 vb.
  mark 547 vb.
  trace 548 n.
  obliteration 550 n.
  defect 647 n.
  dirt 649 n.
  blemish 845 n., vb.
  slur 867 n.
stained glass *screen* 421 n.
  variegation 437 n.
  church interior 990 n.
stainless *clean* 648 adj.
  honourable 929 adj.
  virtuous 933 adj.
  innocent 935 adj.
stair *degree* 27 n.
  stand 218 n.
  ascent 308 n.
staircase *series* 71 n.
  ascent 308 n.
  access 624 n.
stair-head *vertex* 213 n.
stake *fastening* 47 n.
  furnace 383 n.
  gambling 618 n.
  endanger 661 vb.
  undertaking 672 n.
  contend 716 vb.
  promise 764 vb.
  security 767 n.
  property 777 n.
  portion 783 n.
  means of execution 964 n.
stake a claim
  claim 915 vb.
stake, at
  dangerous 661 adj.
stakeboat *departure* 296 n.
stake-holder
  consignee 754 n.
stake-money
  security 767 n.
stake out *limit* 236 vb.
stakes *contest* 716 n.
Stakhanovism
  assiduity 678 n.
  overactivity 678 n.
Stakhanovite
  busy person 678 n.

worker 686n.
stalactite *pendant* 217n.
stalag *prison camp* 748n.
stale *repeated* 106adj.
   antiquated 127adj.
   excrete 302adj.
   tasteless 387adj.
   fetid 397adj.
   feeble 572adj.
   insalubrious 653adj.
   impair 655vb.
   use 673vb.
   fatigued 684adj.
   cheapen 812vb.
   make insensitive 820vb.
   tedious 838adj.
   dull 840adj.
stalemate *draw* 28n.
   stop 145n.
   obstacle 702n.
   parry 713vb.
   non-completion 726n.
staleness (*see* stale)
Stalinism *despotism* 733n.
   brute force 735n.
stalk *source* 156n.
   supporter 218n.
   cylinder 252n.
   gait 265n.
   walk 267vb.
   foliage 366n.
   hunt 619vb.
stalk abroad
   be general 79vb.
stalker *hunter* 619n.
stalking horse
   ambush 527n.
   pretext 614n.
stall *put off* 136vb.
   halt 145n.,vb.
   stable 192n.
   compartment 194n.
   seat 218n.
   fly 271vb.
   theatre 594n.
   obstruct 702vb.
   parry 713vb.
   shop 796n.
   church interior 990n.
stallion *horse* 273n.
   male animal 372n.
stall-keeper *pedlar* 794n.
stalls *onlookers* 441n.
stalwart *stalwart* 162adj.
   fleshy 195adj.
   healthy 650adj.
   colleague 707n.
stamina *strength* 162n.
   resolution 599n.
   stamina 600n.
   courage 855n.

stammer
   speech defect 580n.
   be clumsy 695vb.
   show feeling 818vb.
stamp *character* 5n.
   modality 7n.
   uniformity 16n.
   mould 23n.
   sort 77n.
   make conform 83vb.
   form 243n.
   make concave 255vb.
   gait 265n.
   walk 267vb.
   knock 279n.
   be loud 400vb.
   endorse 488vb.
   label 547n.
   gesticulate 547vb.
   picture 553n.
   engrave 555vb.
   print 587vb.
   correspondence 588n.
   title-deed 767n.
   mint 797vb.
   be angry 891 vb.
   applaud 923vb.
stamp-collector
   collector 492n.
stamp down *flatten* 216vb.
stampede *defeat* 728n.
   fear 854n.,vb.
   frighten 854vb.
stamping ground
   home 192n.
stamp on *suppress* 165vb.
   kick 279vb.
   be severe 735vb.
stamp out *suppress* 165vb.
   extinguish 382vb.
   subjugate 745vb.
stance *form* 243n.
stanch *close* 264vb.
   dry 342vb.
   stanch 350vb.
   repair 656vb.
   obstruct 702vb.
   restrain 747vb.
stand *be* 1vb.
   be in a state 7vb.
   last 113vb.
   pend 136vb.
   stay 144vb.
   cease 145vb.
   be stable 153vb.
   be situate 186vb.
   place 187vb.
   be present 189vb.
   meeting place 192n.
   be vertical 215vb.
   stand 218n.

support 218vb.
   be quiescent 266vb.
   view 438n.
   be proved 478vb.
   supposition 512n.
   suffice 635n.
   difficulty 700n.
   opposition 704n.
   resistance 715n.
   offer oneself 759vb.
   give 781vb.
   defray 804vb.
   be patient 823vb.
stand about *wait* 136vb.
stand a chance
   be likely 471vb.
standard *uniform* 16adj.
   prototype 23n.
   degree 27n.
   median 30adj.
   general 79adj.
   rule 81n.
   typical 83adj.
   high structure 209n.
   stand 218n.
   testing agent 461n.
   gauge 465n.
   class 538n.
   flag 547n.
   paragon 646n.
   right 913adj.
standard-bearer
   soldier 722n.
standardization
   uniformity 16n.
standardize *order* 60vb.
   regularize 62vb.
   make conform 83vb.
standards *morals* 917n.
stand aside *recede* 290vb.
   resign 753vb.
stand by
   be present 189vb.
   be near 200vb.
   await 507vb.
   not act 677vb.
   patronize 703vb.
   defend 713vb.
   observe faith 768vb.
stand-by *means* 629n.
   aider 703n.
   colleague 707n.
stand down *resign* 753vb.
stand for *be* 1vb.
   steer for 281vb.
   mean 514vb.
   deputize 755vb.
stand forth
   be visible 443vb.
stand-in *substitute* 150n.
   actor 594n.

deputy 755 n.
standing *state* 7 n.
  circumstance 8 n.
  degree 27 n.
  serial place 73 n.
  permanent 144 adj.
  unceasing 145 adj.
  fixed 153 adj.
  vertical 215 adj.
  prestige 866 n.
standing order *rule* 81 n.
  permanence 144 n.
  practice 610 n.
  legislation 953 n.
standing start *start* 68 n.
  slowness 278 n.
standing water *lake* 346 n.
stand in the corner
  do penance 941 vb.
stand in the stead of
  deputize 755 vb.
stand in the way
  hinder 702 vb.
stand of arms
  arsenal 723 n.
stand off
  be distant 199 vb.
  recede 290 vb.
  make inactive 679 vb.
  not retain 779 vb.
stand-offish
  prideful 871 adj.
  unsociable 883 adj.
stand on
  be supported 218 vb.
stand on ceremony
  show respect 920 vb.
stand one in good stead
  be useful 640 vb.
stand on one's dignity
  be proud 871 vb.
stand on one's head
  be inverted 221 vb.
stand out *jut* 254 vb.
  be visible 443 vb.
  be plain 522 vb.
  be obstinate 602 vb.
  resist 715 vb.
stand over *pend* 136 vb.
stand pat *stay* 144 vb.
  be quiescent 266 vb.
  be obstinate 602 vb.
standpipe *current* 350 n.
  conduit 351 n.
  extinguisher 382 n.
standpoint
  supposition 512 n.
  situation 186 n.
  view 438 n.
standstill *stop* 145 n.
  lull 145 n.

stand the test
  be true 494 vb.
  be good 644 vb.
stand to *be liable* 180 vb.
  be quiescent 266 vb.
  invigilate 457 vb.
stand together
  concur 181 vb.
stand to reason
  be certain 473 vb.
  be reasonable 475 vb.
  be proved 478 vb.
  be plain 522 vb.
  be right 913 vb.
stand trial
  stand trial 959 vb.
stand up *be vertical* 215 vb.
  lift oneself 310 vb.
stand up for
  safeguard 660 vb.
  patronize 703 vb.
  approve 923 vb.
  vindicate 927 vb.
stand up to *support* 218 vb.
  defy 711 vb.
stand well
  command respect 920 vb.
stang *supporter* 218 n.
stannary *workshop* 687 n.
stanza *verse form* 593 n.
stapes *ear* 415 n.
staple *fastening* 47 n.
  main part 52 n.
  source 156 n.
  hanger 217 n.
  texture 331 n.
  important 638 adj.
  mart 796 n.
stapler *perforator* 263 n.
star *come first* 34 vb.
  diverge 294 vb.
  star 321 n.
  be brittle 330 vb.
  luminary 420 n.
  guide 520 n.
  signpost 547 n.
  punctuation 547 n.
  actor 594 n.
  dramatize 594 vb.
  bigwig 638 n.
  exceller 644 n.
  decoration 729 n.
  badge of rank 743 n.
  desired object 859 n.
  honours 866 n.
  person of repute 866 n.
  favourite 890 n.
starboard *dextrality* 241 n.
starch *smooth* 258 vb.
  food content 301 n.
  harden 326 vb.

  thickening 354 n.
  clean 648 vb.
Star Chamber
  council 692 n.
  law-court 956 n.
starchy *rigid* 326 adj.
  semiliquid 354 adj.
  affected 850 adj.
  prideful 871 adj.
  formal 875 adj.
star-crossed
  unfortunate 731 adj.
stardom *prestige* 866 n.
stare *gaze* 438 vb.
  watch 441 vb.
  be curious 453 vb.
  wonder 864 vb.
  be rude 885 vb.
stare one in the face
  impend 155 vb.
  be plain 522 vb.
star-gazer *astronomy* 321 n.
  spectator 441 n.
  inattention 456 n.
stark *absolute* 32 adj.
  completely 54 adv.
  uncovered 229 adj.
  rigid 326 adj.
  manifest 522 adj.
  plain 573 adj.
starless *unlit* 418 adj.
starlight *star* 321 n.
  light 417 n.
  glimmer 419 n.
  luminary 420 n.
starlit *undimmed* 417 adj.
starring *noteworthy* 866 adj.
starry *celestial* 321 adj.
  undimmed 417 adj.
starry-eyed
  happy 824 adj.
  hoping 852 adj.
stars *influence* 178 n.
  fate 596 n.
start *vantage* 34 n.
  be disjoined 46 vb.
  start 68 n.
  cause 156 vb.
  open 263 vb.
  impel 279 vb.
  departure 296 n.
  leap 312 vb.
  agitation 318 n.
  inexpectation 508 n.
  hunt 619 vb.
  fear 854 vb.
start again *revert* 148 vb.
starter *contender* 716 n.
starting-point *start* 68 n.
  departure 296 n.
  premise 475 n.

starting-post
  departure 296 n.
startle *surprise* 508 vb.
  raise the alarm 665 vb.
  excite 821 vb.
  frighten 854 vb.
  be wonderful 864 vb.
start out *jut* 254 vb.
  start out 296 vb.
star trap *stage-set* 594 n.
start up *grow* 36 vb.
  initiate 68 vb.
  happen 154 vb.
  operate 173 vb.
  jut 254 vb.
star turn *stage show* 594 n.
starvation *scarcity* 636 n.
  fasting 946 n.
starve *weaken* 163 vb.
  make thin 206 vb.
  be poor 801 vb.
  be parsimonious 816 vb.
  be hungry 859 vb.
  starve 946 vb.
starveling *lean* 206 adj.
  underfed 636 adj.
  poor man 801 n.
starving *necessitous* 627 adj.
statant *heraldic* 547 n.
state *state* 7 n.
  eventuality 154 n.
  territory 184 n.
  situation 186 n.
  nation 371 n.
  inform 524 vb.
  affirm 532 vb.
  community 708 n.
  polity 733 n.
  lands 777 n.
  formality 875 n.
state assistance
  subvention 703 n.
state control
  governance 733 n.
statecraft
  management 689 n.
state enterprise
  trade 791 n.
statehood *nation* 371 n.
  independence 744 n.
stateless person
  wanderer 268 n.
  outcaste 883 n.
stately *rhetorical* 574 adj.
  impressive 821 adj.
  beautiful 841 adj.
  well-bred 848 adj.
  worshipful 866 adj.
  formal 875 adj.
  proud 871 adj.
statement *list* 87 n.

musical piece 412 n.
  topic 452 n.
  testimony 466 n.
  report 524 n.
  affirmation 532 n.
  description 590 n.
  pretext 614 n.
  accounts 808 adj.
state of affairs
  affairs 154 n.
state of grace
  innocence 935 n.
  sanctity 979 n.
state of, in a
  conditionate 7 adj.
state of mind
  affections 817 n.
state of nature
  bareness 229 n.
state of war
  belligerancy 718 n.
  enmity 881 n.
state one's terms
  bargain 791 vb.
state ownership
  joint possession 775 n.
stateroom
  chamber 194 n.
state's evidence
  testimony 466 n.
  disclosure 526 n.
states-general
  parliament 692 n.
statesman *sage* 500 n.
  planner 623 n.
  manager 690 n.
statesmanlike
  intelligent 498 adj.
  skilful 694 adj.
statesmanship
  sagacity 498 n.
  policy 623 n.
  tactics 688 n.
  management 689 n.
state-wide *universal* 79 adj.
static *quiescent* 266 adj.
  science of forces 162 n.
statics *gravity* 322 n.
station *degree* 27 n.
  serial place 73 n.
  stopping place 145 n.
  place 185 n.
  situation 186 n.
  station 187 n.
  abode 192 n.
  railroad 624 n.
  nobility 868 n.
stationary
  permanent 144 adj.
  quiescent 266 adj.
  non-active 677 adj.

inactive 679 adj.
stationer *bookman* 589 n.
stationery *stationery* 586 n.
stations of the cross
  ritual act 988 n.
  ritual object 988 n.
  church interior 990 n.
station-wagon
  automobile 274 n.
statism *despotism* 733 n.
  governance 733 n.
statist *computer* 86 n.
  manager 690 n.
statistical *statistical* 86 adj.
statistician *computer* 86 n.
  accountant 808 n.
statistics *statistics* 86 n.
  accuracy 494 n.
statuary *sculpture* 554 n.
  sculptor 556 n.
  ornamental art 844 n.
statue *copy* 22 n.
  monument 548 n.
  image 551 n.
  sculpture 554 n.
  honours 866 n.
  idol 982 n.
statuesque *tall* 209 adj.
  glyptic 554 adj.
  beautiful 841 adj.
  proud 871 adj.
statuette *image* 551 n.
  sculpture 554 n.
statu pupillari, in
  young 130 adj.
  studentlike 538 adj.
  subject 745 adj.
stature *height* 209 n.
status *state* 7 n.
  circumstances 8 n.
  relativeness 9 n.
  degree 27 n.
  serial place 73 n.
  situation 186 n.
  prestige 866 n.
status quo *equilibrium* 28 n.
  permanence 144 n.
  reversion 148 n.
statute *precept* 693 n.
  legislation 953 n.
statutory
  preceptive 693 adj.
  legal 953 adj.
staunch *unyielding* 162 adj.
  sealed off 264 adj.
  resolute 599 adj.
  friendly 880 adj.
  trustworthy 929 adj.
stave *notation* 410 n.
  vocal music 412 n.
  verse form 593 n.

club 723 n.
stave in
  make concave 255 vb.
  pierce 263 vb.
  depress 311 vb.
stave off obstruct 702 vb.
stay tackling 47 n.
  continue 108 vb.
  last 113 vb.
  delay 136 n.
  stay 144 vb.
  cease 145 vb.
  go on 146 vb.
  be stable 153 vb.
  presence 189 n.
  dwell 192 vb.
  supporter 218 n.
  support 218 vb.
  bring to rest 266 vb.
  be inactive 679 vb.
  obstacle 702 n.
  visit 882 vb.
stay-at-home
  quiescent 266 adj.
  solitary 883 n.
  unsociable 883 adj.
stay away be absent 190 vb.
stayer thoroughbred 273 n.
  stamina 600 n.
staying power
  strength 162 n.
  stamina 600 n.
stay order
  legal process 959 n.
stay outside
  be excluded 57 vb.
stay put pend 136 vb.
  be quiescent 266 vb.
  stand firm 599 vb.
  be obstinate 602 vb.
stays compressor 198 n.
  supporter 218 n.
  underwear 228 n.
stay up fly 271 vb.
stead utility 640 n.
  aid 703 n., vb.
steadfast fixed 153 adj.
  obedient 739 adj.
steadfastness
  perseverance 600 n.
steady uniform 16 adj.
  equal 28 adj.
  orderly 60 adj.
  regular 81 adj.
  periodical 141 adj.
  unceasing 146 adj.
  unchangeable 153 adj.
  fixed 153 adj.
  support 218 vb.
  still 266 adj.
  resolute 599 adj.

persevering 600 adj.
tranquillize 823 vb.
courageous 855 adj.
lover 887 n.
steak piece 53 n.
  meat 301 n.
steal copy 20 vb.
  be stealthy 525 vb.
  steal 788 vb.
steal a march
  do before 119 vb.
  be early 135 vb.
  outdo 306 vb.
  deceive 542 vb.
  be cunning 698 vb.
stealing stealing 788 n.
stealth cunning 698 n.
  (see secrecy)
steal the show
  be superior 34 vb.
  act 594 vb.
  have repute 866 vb.
stealthy slow 278 adj.
  muted 401 adj.
  occult 523 adj.
  stealthy 525 adj.
  cunning 698 adj.
  cautious 858 adj.
steal upon
  surprise 508 vb.
steam energy 160 n.
  stimulation 174 n.
  voyage 269 vb.
  propellant 287 n.
  exude 298 vb.
  emit 300 vb.
  cook 301 vb.
  gas 336 n.
  vaporize 338 vb.
  water 339 n.
  be wet 341 vb.
  bubble 355 vb.
  heat 379 n.
  heater 383 n.
steam-engine
  locomotive 274 n.
steamer ship 275 n.
steam-roller
  demolish 165 vb.
  flattener 216 n.
  smoother 258 n.
  locomotive 274 n.
steamy gaseous 336 adj.
  vaporific 338 adj.
  cloudy 355 adj.
  heated 381 adj.
stearine fat 357 n.
steatorrhea
  indigestion 651 n.
steed horse 273 n.
steel strengthen 162 vb.

sharp edge 256 n.
hardness 326 n.
lighter 385 n.
resolution 599 n.
make insensitive 820 vb.
steel-clad
  invulnerable 660 adj.
steeled against
  impassive 820 adj.
steel helmet armour 713 n.
steely strong 162 adj.
  hard 326 adj.
  grey 429 adj.
  blue 435 adj.
  resolute 599 adj.
  cruel 898 adj.
steelyard scales 322 n.
  workshop 687 n.
steep high land 209 n.
  high 209 adj.
  deep 211 adj.
  vertical 215 adj.
  sloping 220 adj.
  immerse 303 vb.
  ascending 308 adj.
  soften 327 vb.
  add water 339 vb.
  drench 341 vb.
  exaggerated 546 adj.
  difficult 700 adj.
steeped pulpy 356 adj.
steepen ascend 308 vb.
steeple high structure 209 n.
  sharp point 256 n.
  church exterior 990 n.
steeplechase
  leap 312 vb.
  chase 619 n.
  racing 716 n.
steeplechaser
  thoroughbred 273 n.
  jumper 312 n.
steeple-house church 990 n.
steeple-jack climber 308 n.
steepness (see steep)
steer eunuch 161 n.
  navigate 269 vb.
  steer for 281 vb.
  cattle 365 n.
  male animal 372 n.
  direct 689 vb.
steerage direction 281 n.
  directorship 689 n.
  lower classes 869 n.
steerage way
  water travel 269 n.
steer clear deviate 282 vb.
steer for steer for 281 vb.
  pursue 619 vb.
steering committee
  director 690 n.

steersman
  navigator 270 n.
  director 690 n.
steersmanship
  directorship 689 n.
steganography
  latency 523 n.
  secrecy 525 n.
  writing 586 n.
stegophilist *climber* 308 n.
otein *cup* 194 n.
stele *obsequies* 364 n.
stellar *celestial* 321 adj.
stem *main part* 52 n.
  source 156 n.
  genealogy 169 n.
  supporter 218 n.
  stanch 350 vb.
  foliage 366 n.
  word 559 n.
  withstand 704 vb.
stem to stern
  longwise 203 adv.
stench *fetor* 397 n.
stencil *duplicate* 22 n.
  paint 553 vb.
stenographer
  recorder 549 n.
  stenographer 586 n.
stenography *writing* 586 n.
stenosis *contraction* 198 n.
stenotypist
  stenographer 586 n.
stentorian *sounding* 398 adj.
  loud 400 adj.
  crying 408 adj.
step *degree* 27 n.
  serial place 73 n.
  long measure 203 n.
  stand 218 n.
  gait 265 n.
  walk 267 n.
  access 624 n.
  essay 671 n.
  deed 676 n.
stepbrother *kinsman* 11 n.
step by step
  by degrees 27 adv.
step-dance *dance* 837 n.
step down *bate* 37 vb.
  descend 309 vb.
stepfather *parent* 169 n.
step, in *agreeing* 24 adj.
step-ins *underwear* 228 n.
step into *possess* 773 vb.
step into the shoes of
  come after 65 vb.
  substitute 150 vb.
  inherit 771 vb.
step-ladder *ascent* 308 n.
  access 624 n.

stepmother *maternity* 169 n.
stepmotherly
  unkind 898 adj.
step on it
  accelerate 277 vb.
step out *move* 265 vb.
  move fast 277 vb.
steppe *space* 183 n.
  lowness 210 n.
  horizontality 216 n.
  land 344 n.
  plain 348 n.
stepped *oblique* 220 adj.
stepper *thoroughbred* 273 n.
stepping-stone
  opportunity 137 n.
  bridge 624 n.
  instrument 628 n.
steps *series* 71 n.
  ascent 308 n.
  policy 623 n.
  means 629 n.
  action 676 n.
stepson *family* 11 n.
step up *augment* 36 vb.
  invigorate 174 vb.
  accelerate 277 vb.
  promote 285 vb.
stercoraceous
  unclean 649 adj.
stereobate *basis* 218 n.
stereometry *geometry* 465 n.
stereoscope
  optical device 442 n.
stereoscopic *seeing* 438 adj.
  visible 443 adj.
stereotype *uniformity* 16 n.
  copy 22 n.
  printing 555 n.
  print 587 vb.
stereotyped
  unchangeable 153 adj.
  habitual 610 adj.
sterile *impotent* 161 adj.
  unproductive 172 adj.
  profitless 641 adj.
  clean 648 adj.
  salubrious 652 adj.
sterility (*see* sterile)
sterilization
  prophylactic 658 n.
  (*see* sterilize)
sterilize *unman* 161 vb.
  lay waste 165 vb.
  sterilize 172 vb.
  make useless 641 vb.
  purify 648 vb.
  sanitate 652 vb.
sterling *genuine* 494 adj.
  valuable 644 adj.
  money 797 n.

  virtuous 933 adj.
  monetary 797 n.
stern *buttocks* 238 n.
  poop 238 n.
  resolute 599 adj.
  severe 735 adj.
  serious 834 adj.
  angry 891 adj.
  sullen 893 adj.
  unkind 898 adj.
stern-chase *chase* 619 n.
stern-chaser *gun* 723 n.
sternmost
  rearward 238 adv.
sternness (*see* stern)
stern rake *projection* 254 n.
stern-sheets *poop* 238 n.
sternutation
  respiration 352 n.
  sibilation 406 n.
sternway *motion* 265 n.
  water travel 269 n.
stern-wheel *propeller* 269 n.
stern-wheeler *ship* 275 n.
stertorous *puffing* 352 adj.
  hoarse 407 adj.
stertorousness
  loudness 400 n.
stet *stabilize* 153 vb.
stethoscope
  hearing aid 415 n.
stetson *headgear* 228 n.
stevedore *boatman* 270 n.
  bearer 273 n.
  worker 686 n.
stew *a mixture* 43 n.
  dish 301 n.
  cook 301 vb.
  heat 381 vb.
  predicament 700 n.
  excitable state 822 n.
  anger 891 n.
  inebriate 949 vb.
  brothel 951 n.
steward *provider* 633 n.
  manager 690 n.
  domestic 742 n.
  consignee 754 n.
  treasurer 798 n.
stewardship
  management 689 n.
stew-pan *cauldron* 194 n.
  heater 383 n.
stichomythia
  verse form 593 n.
stick *cohere* 48 vb.
  halt 145 vb.
  be contiguous 202 vb.
  supporter 218 n.
  pierce 263 vb.
  transfer 272 vb.

rub 333 vb.
ninny 501 n.
be loth 598 vb.
be in difficulty 700 vb.
club 723 n.
fail 728 vb.
compulsion 740 n.
scourge 964 n.
stick at *doubt* 486 vb.
stick at nothing
  be resolute 599 vb.
  be intemperate 943 vb.
sticker *coherence* 48 n.
stick fast *be stable* 153 vb.
  be quiescent 266 vb.
  stand firm 599 vb.
stickiness (*see* sticky)
sticking plaster
  coherence 48 n.
  surgical dressing 658 n.
stick-in-the-mud
  permanence 144 n.
  opinionist 602 n.
  unskilled 695 adj.
stick in the throat
  make mute 578 vb.
  displease 827 vb.
stick into *insert* 303 vb.
stick it out
  stand firm 599 vb.
  persevere 600 vb.
stickjaw *coherence* 48 n.
  stopper 264 n.
  mouthful 301 n.
stickle
  be uncertain 474 vb.
  be loth 598 vb.
  bargain 791 vb.
stickler
  narrow mind 481 n.
  opinionist 602 n.
  tyrant 735 n.
stick on *affix* 45 vb.
stick one's neck out
  be rash 857 vb.
stick out *jut* 254 vb.
  be visible 443 vb.
stickpin *fastening* 47 n.
sticks *racing* 716 n.
stick to *retain* 778 vb.
stick to one's guns
  persevere 600 vb.
  be obstinate 602 vb.
  be courageous 855 vb.
stick to one's point
  argue 475 n.
stick to rule
  conform 83 vb.
stick-up *stealing* 788 n.
stick up *be vertical* 215 vb.
stick up for

patronize 703 vb.
sticky *cohesive* 48 adj.
  tough 329 adj.
  viscid 354 adj.
  difficult 700 adj.
  retentive 778 adj.
sticky wicket
  predicament 700 n.
stiff *unyielding* 162 adj.
  crippled 163 adj.
  still 266 adj.
  rigid 326 adj.
  dead 361 adj.
  corpse 363 n.
  cadaverous 363 adj.
  insensible 375 adj.
  narrow-minded 481 adj.
  ninny 501 n.
  imperspicuous 568 adj.
  obstinate 602 adj.
  inactive 679 adj.
  clumsy 695 adj.
  severe 735 adj.
  restraining 747 adj.
  affected 880 adj.
  prideful 871 adj.
  formal 875 adj.
  unsociable 883 adj.
  dead drunk 949 adj.
stiffen *strengthen* 162 vb.
  harden 326 vb.
stiffener *supporter* 218 n.
stiffening *stability* 153 n.
stiff job *hard task* 700 n.
stiff-necked
  obstinate 602 adj.
  proud 871 adj.
stiffness (*see* stiff)
stiff upper lip
  manliness 855 n.
stiff with *full* 54 adj.
stifle *disable* 161 vb.
  suppress 165 vb.
  kill 362 vb.
  be hot 379 vb.
  heat 381 vb.
  extinguish 382 vb.
  silence 399 vb.
  mute 401 vb.
  conceal 525 vb.
  make mute 578 vb.
  hinder 702 vb.
  prohibit 757 vb.
stigma *label* 547 n.
  slur 867 n.
  censure 924 n.
  detraction 926 n.
  false charge 928 n.
stigmata *indication* 547 n.
stigmatize *mark* 547 vb.
  blemish 845 vb.

shame 867 vb.
  dispraise 924 vb.
  defame 926 vb.
  accuse 928 vb.
stile *access* 624 n.
  obstacle 702 n.
stiletto *sharp point* 256 n.
  perforator 263 n.
  side-arms 723 n.
still *fixed* 153 adj.
  assuage 177 vb.
  still 266 adj.
  vaporizer 338 n.
  watery 339 adj.
  dead 361 adj.
  heater 361 n.
  silent 399 adj.
  nevertheless 468 adv.
  photography 551 n.
  make mute 578 vb.
  inactive 679 adj.
stillborn *dead* 361 adj.
  unsuccessful 728 adj.
still life *art subject* 553 n.
stillness (*see* still)
still-room *chamber* 194 n.
  provisions 301 n.
  storage 632 n.
stilly *silent* 399 adj.
stilt *stand* 218 n.
stilted *ornate* 574 adj.
  inelegant 576 adj.
  ridiculous 849 adj.
  affected 850 adj.
stilts *plaything* 837 n.
stimulant *stimulant* 174 n.
  impulse 279 n.
  liquor 301 n.
  incentive 612 n.
  drug 658 n.
  refreshment 685 n.
  excitant 821 n.
stimulate
  make violent 176 vb.
  incite 612 vb.
  cause desire 859 vb.
  (*see* stimulation)
stimulation *increase* 36 n.
  causation 156 n.
  strengthening 162 n.
  agency 173 n.
  stimulation 174 n.
  activity 678 n.
  excitation 821 n.
stimulative
  remedial 658 adj.
stimulus (*see* stimulant)
sting *sharpness* 256 n.
  pang 377 n.
  pungency 388 n.
  wound 655 vb.

bane 659 n.
overcharge 811 vb.
excitant 821 n.
suffering 825 n.
torment 827 vb.
enrage 891 vb.
stinginess
insufficiency 636 n.
parsimony 816 n.
stingo *liquor* 301 n.
stink *fetor* 397 n.
uncleanness 649 n.
deteriorate 655 vb.
stinkard *fetor* 397 n.
stinker *cad* 938 n.
stinking *unsavoury* 391 adj.
not nice 645 adj.
unpleasant 827 adj.
impure 951 adj.
stink of *superabound* 637 vb.
stink-pot *fetor* 397 n.
stint *finite quantity* 26 n.
period 110 n.
limit 236 vb.
make insufficient 636 vb.
labour 682 n.
portion 873 n.
be parsimonious 816 vb.
stinted *unprovided* 636 adj.
stipend *subvention* 703 n.
reward 962 n.
stipendiary *subject* 745 adj.
recipient 782 n.
receiving 782 adj.
stipple *variegate* 437 vb.
paint 553 vb.
engrave 555 vb.
stipulation *premise* 475 n.
supposition 512 n.
requirement 627 n.
conditions 766 n.
stir *mix* 43 vb.
stimulation 174 n.
make violent 176 vb.
motion 265 n.
commotion 318 n.
activity 678 n.
gaol 748 n.
excite 821 vb.
stirpiculture
animal husbandry 369 n.
stirred *impressed* 818 adj.
stirring *eventful* 154 adj.
stirrup *supporter* 218 n.
stirrup cup
valediction 296 n.
potion 301 n.
stirrup-pump
sufflation 352 n.
stir-up *impulse* 279 n.
stitch *tie* 45 vb.

component 58 n.
pang 377 n.
needlework 844 n.
stitchery
needlework 844 n.
stitch in time
anticipation 135 n.
stithy *workshop* 687 n.
stive *heat* 381 vb.
stiver *small coin* 33 n.
stoa *pavilion* 192 n.
lobby 194 n.
pillar 218 n.
philosopher 449 n.
stoat *vermin* 365 n.
fetor 397 n.
stoccado *foin* 712 n.
stock *race* 11 n.
ligature 47 n.
accumulation 74 n.
typical 83 adj.
source 156 n.
genealogy 169 n.
pillar 218 n.
neckwear 228 n.
soup 301 n.
animal 365 n.
tree 366 n.
dunce 501 n.
usual 610 adj.
materials 631 n.
store 632 n.
provide 633 vb.
property 777 n.
merchandise 795 n.
stockade *inclosure* 235 n.
barrier 235 n.
shelter 662 n.
defences 713 n.
stockbroker
consignee 754 n.
merchant 794 n.
stock exchange
bourse 618 n.
mart 796 n.
stock-farm
stock-farm 369 n.
stock-farmer
producer 167 n.
stockholder
participator 775 n.
owner 776 n.
stockinette *textile* 222 n.
stockings *legwear* 228 n.
stock-in-trade
means 629 n.
equipment 630 n.
store 632 n.
property 777 n.
merchandise 795 n.
stock-jobber

merchant 794 n.
stock-list *list* 87 n.
stockman *herdsman* 369 n.
stockpile *store* 632 vb.
stock-room *storage* 632 n.
stocks *seat* 218 n.
lock-up 748 n.
pillory 964 n.
stock saying *maxim* 496 n.
stocks, on the
unfinished 55 adj.
in preparation 669 adv.
on the stocks 726 adv.
stock-still *still* 266 adj.
stocky *short* 204 adj.
stock-yard *inclosure* 235 n.
stodgy *semiliquid* 354 adj.
plain 573 adj.
tedious 838 adj.
dull 840 adj.
stoic *unfeeling person* 820 n.
stoical *impassive* 820 adj.
patient 823 adj.
stoicism *philosophy* 449 n.
moral insensibility 820 n.
patience 823 n.
inexcitability 823 n.
disinterestedness 931 n.
temperance 942 n.
stoke *make violent* 176 vb.
kindle 381 vb.
fire 385 vb.
stoker *driver* 268 n.
stole *robe* 228 n.
shawl 228 n.
neckwear 228 n.
vestments 989 n.
stolen goods *booty* 790 n.
stolid *unthinking* 450 adj.
unintelligent 499 adj.
inactive 679 adj.
impassive 820 adj.
stolidity *inertness* 175 n.
(see stolid)
stomach *maw* 194 n.
insides 224 n.
taste 386 n.
be willing 597 vb.
be patient 823 vb.
liking 859 n.
forgive 909 vb.
stomach-ache
indigestion 651 n.
stomacher *bodywear* 228 n.
stomachic *cellular* 194 adj.
stomach, turn the
be unpalatable 391 n.
stone *uncover* 229 vb.
missile 287 n.
weighment 322 n.
solid body 324 n.

hardness 326 n.
rock 344 n.
kill 362 vb.
dunce 501 n.
sculpture 554 n.
engraving 555 n.
building material 631 n.
lapidate 712 vb.
unfeeling person 820 n.
gem 844 n.
execute 963 vb.
Stone Age *era* 110 n.
antiquity 125 n.
stone-cutting
sculpture 554 n.
stone's throw
short distance 200 n.
stonewall *repel* 292 vb.
parry 713 vb.
stonewalling
protraction 113 n.
stoneware *product* 164 n.
stonework *edifice* 164 n.
structure 331 n.
stoning
capital punishment 963 n.
stony *unproductive* 172 adj.
rough 259 adj.
hard 326 adj.
territorial 344 adj.
insensible 375 adj.
stony-hearted *cruel* 898 adj.
stooge *entertainer* 594 n.
instrument 628 n.
nonentity 639 n.
bungler 697 n.
auxiliary 707 n.
dependant 742 n.
laughing-stock 851 n.
stooge for *be servile* 879 vb.
stook *bunch* 74 n.
cultivate 370 vb.
stool *seat* 218 n.
excrement 302 n.
dirt 649 n.
stool of repentance
penance 941 n.
pillory 964 n.
stool-pigeon
informer 524 n.
ambush 527 n.
trickster 545 n.
stoop *be low* 210 vb.
be oblique 220 vb.
descend 309 vb.
stoop 311 vb.
plunge 313 n., vb.
obey 739 vb.
demean oneself 867 vb.
be humble 872 vb.
be servile 879 vb.

stooping *respectful* 920 adj.
stop *end* 69 n., vb.
stop 145 n.
close 264 vb.
come to rest 266 vb.
goal 295 n.
stanch 350 vb.
speech sound 398 n.
punctuation 547 n.
repair 656 vb.
doctor 658 vb.
be inactive 679 vb.
obstacle 702 n.
prohibit 757 vb.
retention 778 n.
stop-cock *stopper* 264 n.
tool 630 n.
stop-gap *substitute* 150 n.
stopper 264 n.
stoplight *signal light* 420 n.
stop off *arrive* 295 vb.
stop-over *itinerary* 267 n.
goal 295 n.
stoppage *strike* 145 n.
closure 264 n.
hitch 702 n.
non-payment 805 n.
discount 810 n.
stopper *end* 69 n.
covering 226 n.
stopper 264 n.
stopping
discontinuous 72 adj.
lining 227 n.
surgery 658 n.
stopping-place
stopping-place 145 n.
stop up *obstruct* 702 vb.
stopwatch
timekeeper 117 n.
recording instrument
549 n.
storage *assemblage* 74 n.
room 183 n.
storage 632 n.
store *great quantity* 32 n.
accumulation 74 n.
stow 187 vb.
store 632 n., vb.
provide 633 vb.
plenty 635 n.
preserve 666 vb.
make ready 669 vb.
not use 674 vb.
acquire 771 vb.
retain 778 vb.
shop 796 n.
treasury 799 n.
wealth 800 n.
store-house *storage* 632 n.
store, in *impending* 155 adj.

possessed 773 adj.
storekeeper
provider 633 n.
tradesman 794 n.
store-room *chamber* 194 n.
storage 632 n.
storey *compartment* 194 n.
layer 207 n.
storied *descriptive* 590 adj.
stork *obstetrics* 164 n.
bird of prey 365 n.
storm *turmoil* 61 n.
crowd 74 n.
havoc 165 n.
storm 176 n.
irrupt 297 vb.
commotion 318 n.
gale 352 n.
loudness 400 n.
attack 712 n., vb.
overmaster 727 vb.
take 786 vb.
be angry 891 vb.
storm against
dispraise 924 vb.
storm along
move fast 277 vb.
storm-bound *windy* 352 adj.
storm, by *violently* 176 adv.
storm in a tea-cup
overestimation 482 n.
exaggeration 546 n.
storm signal *warning* 664 n.
storm-tossed *rough* 259 adj.
storm troops
attacker 712 n.
armed force 722 n.
stormy *violent* 176 adj.
windy 352 adj.
excitable 822 adj.
Storthing *parliament* 692 n.
story *news* 529 n.
fable 543 n.
narrative 590 n.
story-teller *liar* 545 n.
narrator 590 n.
stot *cattle* 365 n.
male animal 372 n.
stoup *cup* 194 n.
church utensil 990 n.
stout *stalwart* 162 adj.
strong 162 adj.
fleshy 195 adj.
thick 205 adj.
liquor 301 n.
courageous 855 adj.
stoutness *vitality* 162 n.
stove *furnace* 383 n.
stow *stow* 187 vb.
load 193 vb.
store 632 vb.

stowage *room* 183 n.
  location 187 n.
  storage 632 n.
stowaway *incomer* 297 n.
  intruder 59 n.
  hider 527 n.
strabismus *dim sight* 440 n.
straddle *connect* 45 vb.
  be broad 205 vb.
  overlie 266 vb.
  walk 267 vb.
  diverge 294 vb.
  pass 305 vb.
strafe *bombardment* 712 n.
  exprobate 924 vb.
  punish 963 vb.
straggle *be dispersed* 75 vb.
  wander 267 vb.
  stray 282 vb.
straggler *wanderer* 268 n.
straggling *orderless* 61 adj.
straight *uniform* 16 adj.
  simple 44 adj.
  orderly 60 adj.
  continuous 71 adj.
  vertical 215 adj.
  straightness 249 n.
  undeviating 625 adj.
  shapely 841 adj.
  honourable 929 adj.
straight-edge *gauge* 465 n.
straighten
  straighten 249 vb.
  rectify 654 vb.
  repair 656 vb.
straighten out
  unravel 62 vb.
straight-faced
  serious 834 adj.
straightforward
  directed 281 adj.
  intelligible 516 adj.
  undisguised 522 adj.
  veracious 540 adj.
  artless 699 adj.
  trustworthy 929 adj.
straightforwardness
  facility 701 n.
straight on
  straight on 249 adj.
straight up *vertical* 215 adj.
strain *race* 11 n.
  tincture 43 n.
  derange 63 vb.
  breed 77 n.
  weaken 163 vb.
  genealogy 169 n.
  force 176 vb.
  distortion 246 n.
  traction 288 n.
  exude 288 n.

overstep 306 vb.
  pain 377 n.
  sound 398 n.
  be loud 400 vb.
  be false 541 vb.
  exaggerate 546 vb.
  style 566 n.
  purify 648 vb.
  essay 671 vb.
  misuse 675 vb.
  exertion 682 n.
  fatigue 684 n., vb.
  be severe 735 vb.
  worry 825 n.
  enmity 881 n.
strainer *sorting* 62 n.
  porosity 263 n.
  cleaning utensil 648 n.
strain off *transpose* 272 vb.
  void 300 vb.
strains *poem* 593 n.
strain the sense
  misinterpret 521 vb.
strait *narrowness* 206 n.
  gulf 345 n.
  access 624 n.
  restraining 747 adj.
straiten *tighten* 45 vb.
  be narrow 206 vb.
  imprison 747 vb.
straitened
  in difficulties 700 adj.
  poor 801 adj.
strait-jacket
  compressor 198 n.
  fetter 748 n.
strait-laced *severe* 735 adj.
  prudish 950 adj.
straits *poverty* 801 n.
strait-waistcoat *fetter* 748 n.
strand *cable* 47 n.
  fibre 208 n.
  hair 259 n.
  shore 344 n.
stranded *grounded* 728 adj.
strange *irrelative* 10 adj.
  extraneous 59 adj.
  unusual 84 adj.
  unknown 491 adj.
  ridiculous 849 adj.
  wonderful 864 adj.
stranger *foreigner* 59 n.
stranger to *ignorant* 491 adj.
strangle *disable* 161 vb.
  make smaller 198 vb.
  kill 362 vb.
stranglehold *retention* 778 n.
strangler *murderer* 362 n.
strangles *respiration* 352 n.
strangoury *closure* 264 n.
strangulation

compression 198 n.
  closure 264 n.
  capital punishment 963 n.
strap *tie* 45 vb.
  girdle 47 n.
  strip 208 n.
  spank 963 vb.
  scourge 964 n.
straphanger *rider* 268 n.
strappado
  corporal punishment
    963 n.
strapper *whopper* 195 n.
strapping *stalwart* 162 adj.
  fleshy 195 adj.
stratagem *trickery* 542 n.
  tactics 688 n.
  stratagem 698 n.
strategic *planned* 623 adj.
  warlike 718 adj.
strategist *planner* 623 n.
  expert 696 n.
  slyboots 698 n.
strategy *policy* 623 n.
  tactics 688 n.
  art of war 718 n.
stratification
  stratification 207 n.
  structure 331 n.
stratiform *layered* 207 adj.
stratigraphy
  stratification 207 n.
stratocracy
  government 733 n.
stratosphere *height* 209 n.
  atmosphere 340 n.
stratum *layer* 207 n.
  horizontality 216 n.
stratus *cloud* 355 n.
straw *insubstantial thing* 4 n.
  levity 323 n.
  corn 366 n.
  flute 414 n.
  trifle 639 n.
strawberry *fruit* 301 n.
  redness 431 n.
strawberry mark
  identification 547 n.
  blemish 845 n.
straw-board
  wrapping 226 n.
  bookbinding 589 n.
  paper 631 n.
straw-coloured
  yellow 433 adj.
straw vote *enquiry* 459 n.
  empiricism 461 n.
stray *be dispersed* 75 vb.
  unconformable 84 adj.
  casual 159 adj.
  wander 267 vb.

wanderer 268 n.
stray 282 vb.
be inattentive 456 vb.
err 495 vb.
be lost 772 vb.
derelict 779 n.
be wicked 934 vb.
streak temperament 5 n.
tincture 43 n.
line 203 n.
narrowness 206 n.
strip 208 n.
move fast 277 vb.
flash 417 n.
striation 437 n.
stream
crowd, group 74 n.
classification 77 n.
tendency 179 n.
hang 217 vb.
motion 265 n.
be wet 341 adj.
stream 350 n.
flow, rain 350 vb.
class 538 n.
abound 635 vb.
superabound 637 vb.
streamer
advertisement 528 n.
flag 547 n.
trimming 844 n.
streaming
non-adhesive 49 adj.
unassembled 75 adj.
pendent 217 adj.
streamlet stream 350 n.
streamline smooth 258 vb.
rectify 654 vb.
streamlined speedy 277 adj.
streamlining
arrangement 62 n.
streams great quantity 32 n.
street locality 187 n.
street 192 n.
road 624 n.
street arab
wanderer 268 n.
low fellow 869 n.
street artist
entertainer 594 n.
streetcar tram 274 n.
street-corner
plebeian 869 adj.
streets ahead
superior 34 adj.
streetwalker
prostitute 952 n.
streetwalking
social evil 951 n.
strength power 160 n.
strength 162 n.

vigorousness 174 n.
toughness 329 n.
vigour 571 n.
stamina 600 n.
strengthen augment 36 vb.
accrue 38 vb.
strengthen 162 vb.
harden 326 vb.
corroborate 466 vb.
safeguard 660 vb.
strengthless weak 163 adj.
strenuous vigorous 174 adj.
persevering 600 adj.
industrious 678 adj.
labouring 682 adj.
streptomycin drug 658 n.
stress agency 173 n.
distortion 246 n.
attract notice 455 vb.
argue 475 vb.
emphasize 532 vb.
pronunciation 577 n.
prosody 593 n.
needfulness 627 n.
make important 638 vb.
exertion 682 n.
difficulty 700 n.
stretch period 110 n.
space, range 183 n.
enlarge 197 vb.
lengthen 203 vb.
overstep 306 vb.
elasticity 328 n.
exaggerate 546 vb.
stretchable flexible 327 adj.
stretch a point
be lax 734 vb.
be lenient 736 vb.
not observe 769 vb.
exempt 919 vb.
stretched protracted 113 adj.
stretcher bond 47 n.
bed 218 n.
footwear 228 n.
vehicle 274 n.
stretcher-bearer
bearer 273 n.
nurse 658 n.
stretcher-case
sick person 651 n.
stretching opening 263 n.
stretch one's legs
repose 683 vb.
stretch, on the
attentive 455 adj.
labouring 682 adj.
stretch to be distant 119 vb.
be long 203 vb.
strew disperse 75 vb.
striate groove 262 vb.
striation striation 437 n.

stricken
unfortunate 731 adj.
suffering 825 adj.
strict regular 83 adj.
severe 735 adj.
restraining 747 adj.
obligatory 917 adj.
honourable 929 adj.
orthodox 976 adj.
strictness severity 735 n.
orthodoxism 976 n.
stricture contraction 198 n.
narrowing 206 n.
reprimand 924 n.
censure 924 n.
accusation 928 n.
stride gait 265 n.
walk 267 vb.
progression 285 n.
stride, in one's
skilfully 694 adv.
stridency (see strident)
strident loud 400 adj.
strident 407 adj.
discordant 411 adj.
stride, take in one's
be expert 694 vb.
do easily 701 vb.
stridor stridor 407 n.
stridulate shrill 407 vb.
rasp 407 vb.
ululate 409 vb.
strife quarrel 709 n.
contention 716 n.
strigil cleaning utensil 648 n.
strike strike 145 n.
cease 145 vb.
horizontality 216 n.
strike 279 vb.
rub 333 vb.
cause thought 449 vb.
discovery 484 n.
be inactive 679 vb.
be obstructive 702 vb.
strike at 712 vb.
resistance 715 n.
revolt 738 n.
impress 821 vb.
fail in duty 918 vb.
strike a bad patch
have trouble 731 vb.
strike a balance
average out 30 vb.
strike a light
kindle 381 vb.
make bright 417 vb.
strike an acquaintance
befriend 880 vb.
strike at strike at 712 vb.
strike attitudes
be affected 880 vb.

strike-breaker
  tergiversator 603 n.
strike-breaking
  hindrance 702 n.
strike hands
  contract 765 vb.
  be friendly 880 vb.
  greet 884 vb.
strike-happy
  hindering 702 adj.
strike off *exclude* 57 vb.
  eject 300 vb.
  print 587 vb.
strike oil *have luck* 730 vb.
  get rich 800 vb.
strike, on *inactive* 679 adj.
strike one's colours
  submit 721 vb.
strike out *destroy* 165 vb.
  start out 296 vb.
  obliterate 550 vb.
  plan 623 vb.
striker *thrower* 287 n.
  revolter 738 n.
strike root *be stable* 153 vb.
  prevail 178 vb.
  place oneself 187 vb.
strike sail *retard* 278 vb.
strike work *cease* 145 vb.
  be obstructive 702 vb.
  resist 715 vb.
  revolt 738 vb.
striking *well-seen* 443 adj.
  manifest 522 adj.
  impressive 821 adj.
  wonderful 864 adj.
striking distance
  short distance 200 n.
striking force
  armed force 722 n.
string *adjust* 24 vb.
  tie 45 vb.
  cable 47 n.
  series 71 n.
  band 74 n.
  play music 413 vb.
  viol 414 n.
  befool 542 vb.
  jewellery 844 n.
string along with
  accompany 89 vb.
string band *orchestra* 413 n.
stringency *severity* 735 n.
stringent *exorbitant* 32 adj.
  vigorous 174 adj.
  severe 735 adj.
string, on a
  obedient 739 adj.
string out *disperse* 75 vb.
  lengthen 203 vb.
strings *influence* 178 n.

orchestra 413 n.
  musical instrument 414 n.
  conditions 766 n.
strings, with
  restraining 747 adj.
string together
  connect 45 vb.
string up *execute* 963 vb.
stringy *fibrous* 208 adj.
  tough 329 adj.
strip *subtract* 39 vb.
  disjoin, rend 46 vb.
  piece 53 n.
  demolish 165 vb.
  line 203 n.
  narrowness 206 n.
  lamina 207 n.
  strip 208 n.
  uncover, doff 229 vb.
  fleece 786 vb.
  deprive 786 vb.
  impoverish 801 vb.
stripe *line* 203 n.
  narrowness 206 n.
  striation 437 n.
  badge of rank 743 n.
  pattern 844 n.
  corporal punishment
    963 n.
stripling *youngster* 132 n.
  adult 134 n.
stripper *stripper* 229 n.
striptease
  uncovering 229 n., adj.
strive *essay* 671 vb.
  exert oneself 682 vb.
  contend 716 vb.
stroke *instant* 116 n.
  row 269 vb.
  knock 279 n.
  propulsion 287 n.
  spasm 318 n.
  rub 333 vb.
  touch 378 n., vb.
  punctuation 547 n.
  lettering 586 n.
  contrivance 623 n.
  paralysis 651 n.
  deed 676 n.
  direct 689 vb.
  director 690 n.
  caress 889 vb.
  corporal punishment
    963 n.
stroll *pedestrianism* 267 n.
stroller *wanderer* 268 n.
strolling *travelling* 267 adj.
strong *great* 32 adj.
  unmixed 44 adj.
  strong 162 adj.
  violent 176 adj.

pungent 388 adj.
  fetid 397 adj.
  florid 425 adj.
  expressive 516 adj.
  assertive 532 adj.
  forceful 571 adj.
  healthy 650 adj.
  invulnerable 660 adj.
  fervent 818 adj.
  intoxicating 949 adj.
strong arm
  compulsion 740 n.
strongarm man
  protector 660 n.
  combatant 722 n.
strong-box *treasury* 799 n.
stronghold *habitancy* 191 n.
  refuge 662 n.
  fort 713 n.
strong in *instructed* 490 adj.
strong language
  vigour 571 n.
  scurrility 899 n.
strongly-worded
  expressive 516 adj.
  assertive 532 adj.
  forceful 571 adj.
strong-minded
  wise 498 adj.
  courageous 855 adj.
strong point *skill* 694 n.
  fort 713 n.
strong-room *storage* 632 n.
  treasury 799 n.
strop *sharpener* 256 n.
strophe *verse form* 593 n.
strow *disperse* 75 vb.
struck *impressed* 818 adj.
structural
  supporting 218 adj.
  structural 331 adj.
structure
  composition 56 n.
  arrangement 62 n.
  edifice 164 n.
  form 243 n.
  structure 331 n.
  pattern 844 n.
struggle *be violent* 176 vb.
  move slowly 278 vb.
  essay 671 n., vb.
  undertaking 672 n.
  exertion 682 n.
  be in difficulty 700 vb.
  contest 716 n.
struggle against
  withstand 704 vb.
  resist 715 vb.
struggler *contender* 716 n.
  combatant 722 n.
strum *play music* 413 vb.

mean nothing 515 vb.
strummer
   instrumentalist 413 n.
strumpet
   prostitute 952 n.
strung *adjusted* 24 adj.
strung out *long* 203 adj.
strung up *excited* 821 adj.
strut *bond* 47 n.
   supporter 218 n.
   gait 265 n.
   walk 267 vb.
   be proud 871 vb.
   ostentation 875 n.
   boast 877 vb.
strychnine *poison* 659 n.
stub *unsharpened* 257 adj.
   label 547 n.
stubble *leavings* 41 n.
   roughness 259 n.
   corn 366 n.
   rubbish 641 n.
stubborn
   unyielding 162 adj.
   rigid 326 adj.
   tough 329 adj.
   persevering 600 adj.
   obstinate 602 adj.
   difficult 700 adj.
   impenitent 940 adj.
stubborn fact *reality* 1 n.
stubby *short* 204 adj.
   thick 205 adj.
   unsharpened 257 adj.
stub one's toe
   collide 279 vb.
stub out *extinguish* 382 vb.
stucco *adhesive* 47 n.
   facing 226 n.
   coat 226 vb.
stuck *firm-set* 45 adj.
   in difficulties 700 adj.
stuck on
   enamoured 887 adj.
stuck up *prideful* 871 adj.
   vain 873 adj.
stud *fastening* 47 n.
   sharpen 256 vb.
   roughen 259 vb.
   horse 273 n.
   stock-farm 369 n.
   variegate 437 vb.
   jewellery 844 n.
   decorate 844 vb.
studded with
   multitudinous 104 adj.
student *scholar* 492 n.
   learner 538 n.
studied
   predetermined 608 adj.
   intended 617 adj.

studio *chamber* 194 n.
   art equipment 553 n.
   workshop 687 n.
studious *thoughtful* 449 adj.
   attentive 455 adj.
   studious 536 adj.
   industrious 678 adj.
study *retreat* 192 n.
   chamber 194 n.
   musical piece 412 n.
   scan 438 vb.
   meditation 449 n.
   topic 452 n.
   be attentive 455 vb.
   enquiry 459 n.
   study 536 n., vb.
   classroom 539 n.
   picture 553 n.
   dissertation 591 n.
   habit 610 n.
   intention 617 n.
   prepare oneself 669 vb.
   workshop 687 n.
stuff *substantiality* 3 n.
   essential part 5 n.
   fill 54 vb.
   strengthen 162 vb.
   load 193 vb.
   enlarge 197 vb.
   textile 222 n.
   line 227 vb.
   close 264 vb.
   matter 319 n.
   texture 331 n.
   absurdity 497 n.
   silly talk 515 n.
   materials 631 n.
   rubbish 641 n.
   merchandise 795 n.
   sate 863 vb.
   gluttonize 947 vb.
stuff and nonsense
   absurdity 497 n.
   silly talk 515 n.
stuffed shirt
   insubstantial thing 4 n.
   vain person 873 n.
stuffing *adjunct* 40 n.
   contents 193 n.
   lining 227 n.
   stopper 264 n.
stuff into *insert* 303 vb.
stuff up *befool* 542 vb.
stuffy *sealed off* 264 adj.
   dense 324 adj.
   fetid 397 adj.
   warm 397 adj.
   insalubrious 653 adj.
   tedious 838 adj.
   dull 840 adj.
stultify

   be obstructive 702 vb.
stultify oneself
   stultify oneself 695 vb.
stumble *tumble* 309 vb.
   blunder 495 vb.
   be clumsy 695 vb.
stumble on *chance* 159 vb.
   discover 484 vb.
stumbling *clumsy* 695 adj.
   unsuccessful 728 adj.
stumbling-block
   obstacle 702 n.
stump *remainder* 41 n.
   walk 267 vb.
   leg 267 n.
   move slowly 278 vb.
   puzzle 474 vb.
   orate 579 vb.
   be difficult 700 vb.
stumper *question* 459 n.
   interceptor 702 n.
stumps *leg* 267 n.
stump up *pay* 804 vb.
stumpy *short* 204 adj.
   deformed 246 adj.
stun *strike* 279 vb.
   render insensible 375 vb.
   be loud 400 vb.
   deafen 416 vb.
   surprise 508 vb.
   impress 821 vb.
   frighten 854 vb.
   be wonderful 864 vb.
stunning *topping* 644 adj.
   exciting 821 adj.
stunt *shorten* 204 vb.
   fly 271 vb.
   contrivance 623 n.
   deed 676 n.
   be expert 694 vb.
   be vain 873 vb.
   pageant 875 n.
   be ostentatious 875 vb.
stunted *dwarfish* 196 adj.
   contracted 198 adj.
   underfed 636 adj.
stupa *temple* 990 n.
stupefaction *wonder* 864 n.
stupefy
   render insensible 375 vb.
   impress 821 vb.
   be wonderful 864 vb.
stupendous
   prodigious 32 adj.
   huge 195 adj.
   wonderful 864 adj.
stupid *insensible* 375 adj.
   unthinking 450 adj.
   credulous 487 adj.
   unintelligent 499 adj.
   fool 501 n.

unskilful 695 adj.
dull 840 adj.
stupor *insensibility* 375 n.
sluggishness 679 n.
moral insensibility 820 n.
wonder 864 n.
stupration *rape* 951 n.
sturdy *stalwart* 162 adj.
sturgeon *table fish* 365 n.
stutter *stammer* 580 vb.
be clumsy 695 vb.
show feeling 818 vb.
quake 854 vb.
be drunk 949 vb.
sty *stable* 192 n.
inclosure 235 n.
sink 649 n.
stye *swelling* 253 n.
Stygian *dark* 418 adj.
infernal 972 adj.
style *modality* 7 n.
sort 77 n.
chronology 117 n.
meaning 514 n.
engraving 555 n.
name 561 n., vb.
style 566 n.
elegance 575 n.
way 624 n.
skill 694 n.
beauty 841 n.
fashion 848 n.
styled *formed* 243 adj.
stylet *perforator* 263 n.
side-arms 723 n.
stylish *elegant* 575 adj.
well-made 694 adj.
personable 841 adj.
fashionable 848 adj.
stylist *phrasemonger* 574 n.
stylist 575 n.
stylistic *stylistic* 566 adj.
stylitism *seclusion* 883 n.
stylized *formed* 243 adj.
stylo, stylus
stationery 586 n.
stylobate *stand* 218 n.
stylograph
stationery 586 n.
stymie *obstruct* 702 vb.
styptic, styptical
solidifying 324 adj.
sour 393 adj.
styptic pencil
cosmetic 843 n.
Styx *mythic hell* 972 n.
suasible *induced* 612 adj.
suasion *influence* 178 n.
suasive *inducive* 612 adj.
suave *smooth* 258 adj.
courteous 884 adj.

suavity *courtesy* 884 n.
sub *inferior* 35 adj.
substitute 150 n.
subaltern *inferior* 35 n.
army officer 741 n.
servant 742 n.
sub-apostolic
scriptural 975 adj.
subaqueous *deep* 211 adj.
subastral *telluric* 321 adj.
sub-atom *element* 319 n.
sub-branch *branch* 53 n.
sub-clause *subdivision* 53 n.
subconscious *spirit* 447 n.
psychic 447 adj.
subcontrary
opposite 240 adj.
subcutaneous
interior 224 adj.
subdivision *scission* 46 n.
subdivision 53 n.
subdivisional
regional 184 adj.
subdual *victory* 727 n.
subduction
subtraction 39 n.
subdue *overmaster* 727 vb.
subjugate 745 vb.
restrain 747 vb.
subdued *moderate* 177 adj.
muted 401 adj.
dejected 834 adj.
subfusc *dark* 418 adj.
dim 419 adj.
subgrade *inferior* 35 adj.
sub-group
subdivision 53 n.
sub-head
classification 77 n.
sub-human
animal 365 adj.
cruel 898 adj.
subinfeudate *lease* 784 vb.
subinspector *police* 955 n.
subjacent *low* 210 adj.
deep 211 adj.
subject *living model* 23 n.
prototype 23 n.
inferior 35 adj.
liable 180 adj.
topic 452 n.
testee 461 n.
overmaster 727 vb.
subject 742 n.
subject 745 adj.
subjugate 745 vb.
not owning 774 adj.
subjection *inferiority* 35 n.
subjection 745 n.
subjective *intrinsic* 5 adj.
immaterial 320 adj.

misjudging 481 adj.
subjectivity
intrinsicality 5 n.
subjectivity 320 n.
error 495 n.
fantasy 513 n.
subject-matter *topic* 452 n.
subject to
provided 468 adv.
on terms 766 adj.
subjoin *add* 38 vb.
place after 65 vb.
insert 303 vb.
sub judice *on trial* 459 adv.
sub judice 480 adv.
in litigation 959 adv.
subjugate
overmaster 727 vb.
subjugate 745 vb.
subjugation
subjection 745 n.
brute force 735 n.
subjugator *victor* 727 n.
subjunctive
conjunctive 45 adj.
sub-lessee *possessor* 776 n.
sublet *lease* 784 vb.
sub-lieutenant
naval officer 741 n.
sublimate *elevate* 310 vb.
vaporize 338 vb.
purify 648 vb.
sublimated *pure* 950 adj.
sublimation
amendment 654 n.
(*see* sublimate)
sublime *great* 32 adj.
elevated 310 adj.
vaporize 338 vb.
impressive 821 adj.
(*see* sublimity)
Sublime Porte
sovereign 741 n.
subliminal
psychic 447 adj.
sublimity *superiority* 34 n.
height 209 n.
vigour 571 n.
eloquence 579 n.
beauty 841 n.
prestige 866 n.
disinterestedness 931 n.
divine attribute 965 n.
sublineation
punctuation 547 n.
sublunary *telluric* 321 adj.
subman *inferior* 35 n.
submarine *low* 210 adj.
deep 211 adj.
ship 275 n.
diver 313 n.

oceanic 343 adj.
warship 722 n.
submariner *diver* 313 n.
navy man 722 n.
submeaning
connotation 514 n.
submediant
musical note 410 n.
submerge *suppress* 165 vb.
immerse 303 vb.
plunge 313 vb.
drench 341 vb.
be unseen 444 vb.
obliterate 550 vb.
submerged *deep* 211 adj.
latent 523 adj.
submerged tenth
lower classes 869 n.
submergence
immersion 303 n.
descent 309 n.
plunge 313 n.
submersible
descending 309 adj.
depressed 311 adj.
submersion
immersion 303 n.
moistening 341 n.
subministration *aid* 703 n.
submission *conformity* 83 n.
argument 475 n.
advice 691 n.
submission 721 n.
obedience 739 n.
subjection 745 n.
entreaty 761 n.
patience 823 n.
content 828 n.
humility 872 n.
servility 879 n.
submissive *willing* 597 adj.
wieldy 701 adj.
peaceful 717 adj.
(*see* submission)
submit *acquiesce* 488 vb.
propound 512 vb.
communicate 524 vb.
affirm 532 vb.
be forced 596 vb.
submit 721 vb.
be defeated 728 vb.
(*see* submission)
submonition *advice* 691 n.
sub-multiple
numerical element 85 n.
subnormal *inferior* 35 adj.
abnormal 84 adj.
insane 503 adj.
subordinate
extrinsic 6 adj.
inferior 35 n., adj.

dependant 742 n.
servant 742 n.
subordination
inferiority 35 n.
arrangement 62 n.
subjection 745 n.
suborn *bribe* 612 vb.
sub-plot *narrative* 590 n.
plot 623 n.
subpœna *warrant* 737 n.
command 737 vb.
legal process 959 n.
subreption
acquisition 771 n.
subrogation
substitution 150 n.
sub rosa *secretly* 525 adv.
subscribe *testify* 466 vb.
sign 547 vb.
write 586 vb.
join a party 708 vb.
contract 765 vb.
give security 767 vb.
give 781 vb.
pay 804 vb.
subscriber *assenter* 488 n.
signatory 765 n.
giver 781 n.
subscribe to *endorse* 488 vb.
patronize 703 vb.
subscript *adjunct* 40 n.
sequel 67 n.
subscription *offering* 781 n.
giving 781 n.
payment 804 n.
subsection
classification 77 n.
subsequent
subsequent 120 adj.
future 124 adj.
late 136 adj.
following 284 adj.
subserve *concur* 181 vb.
be instrumental 628 vb.
be useful 640 vb.
minister to 703 vb.
subservience
submission 721 n.
(*see* subservient)
subservient *tending* 179 adj.
instrumental 628 adj.
useful 640 adj.
aiding 703 adj.
subjected 745 adj.
servile 879 adj.
subside *decrease* 37 vb.
recede 290 vb.
subsidence *descent* 309 n.
quiescence 266 n.
subsidiary *extrinsic* 6 adj.
inferior 35 n., adj.

additional 38 adj.
unimportant 639 adj.
useful 640 adj.
aiding 703 adj.
subsidize *aid* 703 vb.
give 781 vb.
subsidy *support* 218 n.
subvention 703 n.
gift 781 n.
pay 804 n.
subsist *be* 1 vb.
stay 144 vb.
live 360 vb.
subsistence *existence* 1 n.
subsistence level
poverty 801 n.
subsoil *interiority* 224 n.
soil 344 n.
subspecies
subdivision 53 n.
substance *substance* 3 n.
essential part 5 n.
main part 32 n.
interiority 224 n.
form 243 n.
matter 319 n.
structure 331 n.
meaning 514 n.
materials 631 n.
importance 638 n.
chief thing 638 n.
estate 777 n.
wealth 800 n.
substandard *inferior* 35 adj.
abnormal 84 adj.
deficient 307 adj.
substantial *real* 1 adj.
substantial 3 adj.
great 32 adj.
material 319 adj.
dense 324 adj.
true 494 adj.
meaningful 514 adj.
substantiate
materialize 319 vb.
be true 494 vb.
substantive *real* 1 adj.
intrinsic 5 adj.
part of speech 564 n.
substitute *inferior* 35 n.
substitute 150 n., vb.
displace 188 vb.
imperfection 647 n.
disuse 674 vb.
deputy 755 n.
not retain 779 vb.
substitution *deposal* 752 n.
(*see* substitute)
substitutional
substituted 150 adj.
substratum *substance* 3 n.

layer 207n.
base 214n.
basis 218n.
interiority 224n.
substructure *base* 214n.
subsultus *spasm* 318n.
subsume *contain* 56vb.
class 62vb.
number with 78vb.
subtend
be opposite 240vb.
subterfuge *sophistry* 477n.
concealment 525n.
mental dishonesty 543n.
pretext 614n.
stratagem 698n.
subterranean *low* 210adj.
deep 211adj.
latent 523adj.
concealed 525adj.
dishonest 930adj.
infernal 972adj.
subtilize *rarify* 325vb.
subtle *small* 33adj.
rare 325adj.
intelligent 498adj.
cunning 698adj.
subtlety
discrimination 463n.
sophistry 477n.
sagacity 498n.
cunning 698n.
subtonic *musical note* 410n.
subtopia *mediocrity* 732n.
subtraction *diminution* 37n.
subtraction 39n.
separation 46n.
numerical operation 86n.
subtractive
subtracted 39adj.
subtrahend
subtraction 39n.
decrement 42n.
numerical element 85n.
suburb *district* 184n.
housing 192n.
suburban *regional* 184adj.
urban 192adj.
circumjacent 230adj.
tedious 838adj.
vulgar 847adj.
plebeian 869adj.
suburbanite *dweller* 191n.
native 191n.
suburbanize
urbanize 192vb.
suburbia *habitancy* 191n.
mediocrity 732n.
(*see* suburb)
suburbs *entrance* 68n.
circumjacence 230n.

subvention *support* 218n.
provision 633n.
subvention 703n.
gift 781n.
pay 804n.
subversion *disorder* 61n.
revolution 149n.
destruction 165n.
overturning 221n.
depression 311n.
sedition 738n.
subversive
revolutionary 149adj.
disobedient 738adj.
subvert *revolutionize* 149vb.
demolish 165vb.
tell against 467vb.
impair 655vb.
subway *tunnel* 263n.
railroad 624n.
succedaneum
substitute 150n.
succeed *come after* 65vb.
run on 71vb.
substitute 150vb.
follow 284vb.
flourish 615vb.
be expedient 642vb.
succeed 727vb.
prosper 730vb.
possess 773vb.
succentor
church officer 986n.
succès d'estime
prestige 866n.
succès fou *success* 727n.
success *success* 727n.
successful
completive 725adj.
successful 727adj.
prosperous 730adj.
succession *sequence* 65n.
series 71n.
continuity 71n.
recurrence 106n.
posteriority 120n.
successive
continuous 71adj.
periodical 141adj.
(*see* succession)
successless
unsuccessful 728adj.
successor *survivor* 41n.
aftercomer 67n.
posteriority 120n.
beneficiary 776n.
recipient 782n.
successorship *futurity* 124n.
succinct *concise* 569adj.
succotash *cereal* 301n.
succour *remedy* 658n.,vb.

aid 703n.,vb.
succuba *demon* 970n.
sorceress 983n.
succubus *demon* 970n.
sorcerer 983n.
succulent *edible* 301adj.
pulpy 356adj.
savoury 390adj.
succumb *die* 361vb.
be induced 612vb.
be fatigued 684vb.
knuckle under 721vb.
be defeated 728vb.
succussion *agitation* 318n.
such *conditionate* 7adj.
anonymous 562adj.
such a one *person* 371n.
such as *similar* 18adj.
suck *absorb* 299vb.
drink 301vb.
extract 304vb.
be wet 341vb.
hiss 406vb.
suck dry *waste* 634vb.
fleece 786vb.
sucked orange
rubbish 641n.
sucker *young plant* 132n.
orifice 263n.
tree, plant 366n.
credulity 487n.
dupe 544n.
sucker for *desirer* 859n.
suckling *child* 132n.
suck out *void* 300vb.
suck the brains
interrogate 459vb.
suck up to
minister to 703vb.
flatter 925vb.
sucrose *sweet* 392n.
suction *energy* 160n.
reception 299n.
sudarium *ablution* 648n.
sudary *cleaning cloth* 648n.
sudatorium *heater* 383n.
sudden *brief* 114adj.
instantaneous 116adj.
early 135adj.
unexpected 508adj.
spontaneous 609adj.
sudorific *excretory* 302adj.
hot 379adj.
suds *bubble* 355n.
sue *request, entreat* 761vb.
be in love 887vb.
court 889vb.
claim 915vb.
indict 928vb.
litigate 959vb.
suet *fat* 357n.

Sufee (*see* Sufi)
suffer *meet with* 154 vb.
  carry 273 vb.
  feel pain 377 vb.
  be ill 651 vb.
  permit 756 vb.
  feel 818 vb.
  be patient 823 vb.
  suffer 825 vb.
sufferance *lenity* 736 n.
  permission 756 n.
  patience 823 n.
  suffering 825 n.
sufferer *sick person* 651 n.
  unlucky person 731 n.
  sufferer 825 n.
suffering *pain* 377 n.
  evil 616 n.
  adversity 731 n.
  feeling 818 n., vb.
  suffering 825 n., adj.
  painfulness 827 n.
suffice *be equal* 28 vb.
  be able 160 vb.
  suffice 635 vb.
  be expedient 642 vb.
  be middling 732 vb.
  sate 863 vb.
sufficiency
  completeness 54 n.
  sufficiency 635 n.
  completion 725 n.
sufficient
  not bad 644 adj.
  contenting 828 adj.
  (*see* sufficiency)
sufficing
  provisionary 633 adj.
suffix *add* 38 vb.
  adjunct 40 n.
  affix 45 vb.
  place after 65 vb.
  sequel 67 n.
  word 559 n.
  part of speech 564 n.
suffixion *joinder* 45 n.
sufflation *dilation* 197 n.
  sufflation 352 n.
suffocate *suppress* 165 vb.
  kill 362 vb.
  superabound 637 vb.
suffocating *deadly* 362 adj.
  fetid 397 adj.
  warm 379 adj.
suffocation *killing* 362 n.
suffragan
  ecclesiarch 986 n.
suffrage *affirmation* 532 n.
  vote 605 n.
  aid 703 n.
  prayers 981 n.

suffragette *rioter* 738 n.
suffragettism *vote* 605 n.
  gynocracy 733 n.
suffusion *mixture* 43 n.
  feeling 818 n.
Sufi *sectarist* 978 n.
  pietist 979 n.
  worshipper 981 n.
  monk 986 n.
Sufism *religion* 973 n.
sugar *food content* 301 n.
  sweet 392 n.
sugar-candy *sweet* 392 n.
sugar-daddy *lover* 887 n.
sugared *sweet* 392 adj.
  deceiving 542 adj.
sugarless
  unsavoury 391 adj.
  sour 393 adj.
sugar the pill
  sweeten 392 vb.
  deceive 542 vb.
  tempt 612 vb.
sugary *pleasant* 376 adj.
  sweet 392 adj.
  pleasurable 826 adj.
suggest *evidence* 466 vb.
  propound 512 vb.
  imply 523 vb.
  indicate 547 vb.
  represent 551 vb.
  incite 612 vb.
  offer 759 vb.
  (*see* suggestion)
suggester *motivator* 612 n.
suggestibility
  persuasibility 612 n.
suggestible *sentient* 374 adj.
  irresolute 601 adj.
  excitable 822 adj.
suggestio falsi
  falsehood 541 n.
  mental dishonesty 543 n.
suggestion
  small quantity 33 n.
  influence 178 n.
  reminder 505 n.
  hint 524 n.
  plan 623 n.
  advice 691 n.
  request 761 n.
  (*see* suggest)
suggest itself
  dawn upon 449 vb.
suggestive
  evidential 466 adj.
  suppositional 512 adj.
  meaningful 514 adj.
  tacit 523 adj.
  indicating 547 adj.
  descriptive 590 adj.

  inducive 612 adj.
  exciting 821 adj.
  impure 951 adj.
suicidal *destructive* 165 adj.
  murderous 362 adj.
  rash 857 adj.
suicidal tendency
  dejection 834 n.
suicide *suicide* 362 n.
sui generis *special* 80 adj.
  unconformable 84 adj.
suit *uniformity* 16 n.
  accord 24 vb.
  sort 77 n.
  dress 228 n.
  request 761 n.
  beautify 841 vb.
  wooing 889 n.
  accusation 928 n.
  litigation 959 n.
suitable *relevant* 9 adj.
  fit 24 adj.
  expedient 642 adj.
  marriageable 894 adj.
  right 913 adj.
suit and service
  service 745 n.
suitcase *box* 194 n.
suite *retinue* 67 n.
  series 71 n.
  procession 71 n.
  concomitant 89 n.
  flat 192 n.
  follower 284 n.
  musical piece 412 n.
  retainer 742 n.
suiting *textile* 222 n.
  dress 228 n.
suitor *petitioner* 763 n.
  lover 887 n.
  litigant 959 n.
suit the action to the word
  gesticulate 547 vb.
sulcus *furrow* 262 n.
sulk *be discontented* 829 vb.
  be dejected 834 vb.
  be rude 885 vb.
  be sullen 893 vb.
sulker *rude person* 885 n.
sulks *unwillingness* 598 n.
  discontent 829 n.
  resentment 891 n.
  sullenness 893 n.
sulky *carriage* 274 n.
  unwilling 598 adj.
  quarrelling 709 adj.
  discontented 829 adj.
  melancholic 834 adj.
  sullen 893 adj.
sullage *marsh* 347 n.
  semiliquidity 354 n.

ash 381 n.
sullen *black* 428 adj.
  unwilling 598 adj.
  discontented 829 adj.
  serious 834 adj.
  ugly 842 adj.
  unsociable 883 adj.
  ungracious 885 adj.
  angry 891 adj.
  sullen 893 adj.
  malevolent 898 adj.
sully *make unclean* 649 vb.
  shame 867 vb.
  defame 926 vb.
sulpha drug *drug* 658 n.
sulphur *fumigator* 385 n.
sulphureous *fetid* 397 adj.
sulphurous *angry* 891 adj.
  maledicent 899 adj.
sultan *sovereign* 741 n.
sultanate
  magistrature 733 n.
  polity 733 n.
sultry *warm* 379 adj.
  sullen 893 adj.
sum *add* 38 vb.
  whole, all 52 n.
  numerical result 85 n.
  numeration 86 n.
  meaning 514 n.
  funds 797 n.
sumless *infinite* 107 adj.
summarize
  be concise 569 vb.
  abstract 592 vb.
summary *brief* 114 adj.
  early 135 adj.
  concise 569 adj.
  description 590 n.
  compendium 592 n.
  lawless 954 adj.
summation *addition* 38 n.
  numeration 86 n.
summer *pass time* 108 vb.
  period 110 n.
  summer 128 n.
  beam 218 n.
  heat 379 n.
  palmy days 730 n.
  visit 882 vb.
summerhouse *arbour* 194 n.
summery *summery* 128 adj.
  warm 379 adj.
summing up
  estimate 480 n.
  legal trial 959 n.
summit *completeness* 54 n.
  extremity 69 n.
  serial place 73 n.
  height 209 n.
  summit 213 n.

limit 236 n.
  conference 584 n.
  perfection 646 n.
  council 692 n.
summitry *conference* 584 n.
summon *command* 737 vb.
  desire 859 vb.
  indict 928 vb.
  litigate 959 vb.
summoned
  assembled 74 adj.
summoner
  messenger 531 n.
  law officer 955 n.
summons
  publication 528 n.
  call 547 n.
  command 737 n.
  warrant 737 n.
  desire 859 n.
  accusation 928 n.
  law 953 n.
  legal process 959 n.
summon up
  retrospect 505 vb.
  excite 821 vb.
summum bonum
  good 615 n.
  happiness 824 n.
sumner
  church officer 986 n.
sum of things
  universe 321 n.
sump *receptacle* 194 n.
  lake 346 n.
  storage 632 n.
  sink 649 n.
sumpter-mule
  beast of burden 273 n.
sumptuary
  monetary 797 adj.
sumptuary law
  prohibition 757 n.
  economy 814 n.
sumptuous
  ostentatious 875 adj.
sum up *shorten* 204 vb.
  judge, estimate 480 vb.
  be concise 569 vb.
  abstract 592 vb.
  try a case 959 vb.
sun *sun* 321 n.
  dry 342 vb.
  heat 379 n., vb.
  light 417 n.
  luminary 420 n.
sun-bathe *be hot* 379 vb.
sun-blind *canopy* 226 n.
  curtain 421 n.
sun-bonnet *shade* 226 n.
  headgear 228 n.

sunburn *burning* 381 n.
  brownness 430 n.
sundae *pudding* 301 n.
Sunday *holy-day* 988 n.
Sunday best *clothing* 228 n.
  finery 844 n.
sun-deck *hospital* 658 n.
sunder *sunder* 46 vb.
  decompose 51 vb.
  disperse 75 vb.
sundial *timekeeper* 117 n.
sundown *evening* 129 n.
  obscuration 418 n.
sundowner
  wanderer 268 n.
sun-dried *dry* 342 n.
sun-dry *preserve* 666 vb.
sundry *many* 104 adj.
sung *renowned* 866 adj.
sun-glasses *screen* 421 n.
  safeguard 662 n.
sun-helmet *shade* 226 n.
  screen 421 n.
  safeguard 662 n.
sun-lamp *hospital* 658 n.
  beautification 863 n.
sunless *unlit* 418 adj.
sunlight *sun* 321 n.
  heater 383 n.
  light 417 n.
Sunni *sectarian* 978 adj.
Sunnite *sectarist* 978 n.
sunny *tranquil* 266 adj.
  dry 342 adj.
  warm 379 adj.
  undimmed 417 adj.
  pleasurable 826 adj.
  cheerful 833 adj.
sunny side
  pleasurableness 826 n.
sun oneself *be hot* 379 vb.
sunproof *screened* 421 adj.
sunrise *morning* 128 n.
  ascent 308 n.
sunscreen *shade* 226 n.
  screen 421 n.
sunset *evening* 129 n.
  glow 417 n.
  obscuration 418 n.
sunshade *shade* 226 n.
  screen 421 n.
sunshine *salubrity* 652 n.
  palmy days 730 n.
sunshiny *warm* 379 adj.
  undimmed 417 adj.
sunspot *sun* 321 n.
  maculation 437 n.
  blemish 845 n.
sunstroke *frenzy* 503 n.
sun-tan *brownness* 430 n.
sun-tanned *blackish* 428 adj.

sun-trap *pavilion* 192 n.
  heater 383 n.
sun-up *morning* 128 n.
sun-worshipper
  sanitarian 652 n.
  idolater 982 n.
sup *potion* 301 n.
  eat, drink 301 vb.
  taste 386 vb.
super *superior* 34 adj.
  topmost 213 adj.
  actor 594 n.
  topping 644 adj.
superable *possible* 469 adj.
superabundance
  great quantity 32 n.
  productiveness 171 n.
  plenty 635 n.
  redundance 637 n.
superabundant
  many 104 adj.
superaddition *addition* 38 n.
superannuated
  antiquated 127 adj.
superannuation *age* 131 n.
  non-use 674 n.
  (*see* resignation)
superb *excellent* 644 adj.
  splendid 841 adj.
  ostentatious 875 adj.
supercharged
  dynamic 160 adj.
supercilious
  prideful 871 adj.
  insolent 878 adj.
  disrespectful 921 adj.
  despising 922 adj.
superego *subjectivity* 320 n.
  spirit 447 n.
supereminence
  goodness 644 n.
  prestige 866 n.
supererogation
  superfluity 637 n.
supererogatory
  additional 38 adj.
superfecundation
  propagation 164 n.
superfetation
  productiveness 171 n.
superficial
  insubstantial 4 adj.
  inconsiderable 33 adj.
  incomplete 55 adj.
  spatial 183 adj.
  shallow 212 adj.
  exterior 223 adj.
  immaterial 320 adj.
  inattentive 456 adj.
  negligent 458 adj.
  smattering 491 adj.

  foolish 499 adj.
  hasty 680 adj.
  bungled 695 adj.
  uncompleted 726 adj.
superfluity
  great quantity 32 n.
  extra 40 n.
  superfluity 637 n.
superfluous
  remaining 41 adj.
  superfluous 637 adj.
superfluousness
  inutility 641 n.
super-giant *star* 321 n.
superheating *heating* 381 n.
superhuman *divine* 965 adj.
superimpose *add* 38 vb.
  cover 226 vb.
superimposed
  overhanging 209 adj.
superintendence
  management 689 n.
superintendency
  magistrature 733 n.
superintendent
  manager 690 n.
superior *superior* 34 n., adj.
  prideful 871 adj.
  monk 986 n.
  ecclesiarch 986 n.
  (*see* superiority)
superiority *superiority* 34 n.
  precedence 64 n.
  seniority 131 n.
  goodness 644 n.
  contempt 922 n.
superlative
  supreme 34 adj.
  grammatical 564 adj.
  excellent 644 adj.
superman *superior* 34 n.
  bigwig 638 n.
  exceller 644 n.
  paragon 646 n.
supermarket
  emporium 796 n.
  shop 796 n.
supernal *high* 209 adj.
  immaterial 320 adj.
  paradisiac 971 adj.
supernatural
  extraneous 59 adj.
  abnormal 84 adj.
  divine 965 adj.
  spooky 970 adj.
  magical 983 adj.
  paranormal 984 adj.
supernaturalism
  occultism 984 n.
super-nova *star* 321 n.
supernumerary

additional* 38 n.
  extra 40 n.
  actor 594 adj.
  superfluous 637 adj.
superposition
  addition 38 n.
  covering 226 n.
superscription *label* 547 n.
  script 586 n.
supersede *substitute* 150 vb.
  displace 188 vb.
  eject 300 vb.
  disuse 674 vb.
  depose 752 vb.
  not retain 779 vb.
  punish 963 vb.
supersensory
  immaterial 320 adj.
supersession (*see* supersede)
supersonic *speedy* 277 adj.
superstition *credulity* 487 n.
  ignorance 491 n.
  error 495 n.
  heterodoxy 977 n.
  idolatry 982 n.
superstitious
  misjudging 481 adj.
  (*see* superstition)
superstratum
  exteriority 223 n.
superstructure
  completion 725 n.
super-tax *tax* 809 n.
supertonic
  musical note 410 n.
supervene *be extrinsic* 6 vb.
  accrue 38 vb.
  ensue 120 vb.
  happen 154 vb.
supervenient *extrinsic* 6 adj.
supervention *addition* 38 n.
  posteriority 120 n.
supervise *manage* 689 vb.
supervisor *manager* 690 n.
supervisory
  directing 689 adj.
supine *impotent* 161 adj.
  low 201 adj.
  supine 216 adj.
  inverted 221 adj.
  quiescent 266 adj.
  inactive 679 adj.
  apathetic 820 adj.
  indifferent 860 adj.
supineness
  submission 721 n.
supper *meal* 310 n.
supperless *hungry* 859 adj.
  fasting 956 adj.
supplant
  come after 65 vb.

substitute 150 vb.
eject 300 vb.
supple
flexible 327 adj.
tergiversating 603 adj.
servile 879 adj.
dishonest 930 adj.
supplement *increment* 36 n.
augment 36 vb.
adjunct 40 n.
make complete 54 vb.
sequel 67 n.
enlarge 197 vb.
price 809 n.
supplemental
additional 38 adj.
suppleness *softness* 327 n.
skill 694 n.
cunning 698 n.
(*see* supple)
suppliant
supplicatory 761 adj.
petitioner 763 n.
worshipper 981 n.
supplication *entreaty* 761 n.
prayers 981 n.
supplier *provider* 633 n.
supplies *means* 629 n.
provision 633 n.
subvention 703 n.
merchandise 795 n.
supply
make complete 54 vb.
find means 629 vb.
store 632 n.
provide 633 vb.
support *sustain* 146 vb.
strengthen 162 vb.
support 218 n., vb.
carry 273 vb.
corroborate 466 vb.
endorse 488 vb.
choose 605 vb.
instrumentality 628 n.
suffice 635 vb.
safeguard 660 vb.
preservation 666 n.
aid 703 n., vb.
auxiliary 707 n.
be patient 823 vb.
friendship 880 n.
approve 923 vb.
vindicate 927 vb.
supportance *feeling* 818 n.
patience 823 n.
supporter *receptacle* 194 n.
supporter 218 n.
heraldry 547 n.
patron 707 n.
supporting
undermost 214 adj.

evidential 466 adj.
supporting role
inferiority 35 n.
acting 594 n.
supposable
supposed 512 adj.
supposal
supposition 512 n.
suppose *assume* 471 vb.
opine 485 vb.
not know 491 vb.
suppose 512 vb.
supposing *if* 8 adv.
provided 468 adj.
suppositional 512 adj.
supposition *topic* 452 n.
(*see* suppose)
suppositional
mental 447 adj.
uncertain 474 adj.
credible 485 adj.
suppositional 512 adj.
imaginary 513 adj.
supposititious
supposed 512 adj.
suppository
surgical dressing 658 n.
suppress *suppress* 165 vb.
counteract 182 vb.
misinterpret 521 vb.
obliterate 550 vb.
make mute 578 vb.
overmaster 727 vb.
suppression *exclusion* 57 n.
destruction 165 n.
depression 311 n.
concealment 525 n.
severity 735 n.
restraint 747 n.
abrogation 752 n.
prohibition 757 n.
suppressio veri
falsehood 541 n.
mental dishonesty 543 n.
suppressive
avoiding 620 adj.
suppurate *be ill* 651 vb.
deteriorate 655 vb.
suppurating *fetid* 397 adj.
toxic 653 adj.
suppuration
infection 651 n.
impairment 655 n.
supputation
numeration 86 n.
supra *before* 64 adv.
retrospectively 125 adv.
supramundane
divine 965 adj.
supremacy
importance 638 n.

governance 733 n.
(*see* supreme)
supreme *great* 32 adj.
supreme 34 adj.
topmost 213 adj.
important 638 adj.
Supreme Being
the Deity 965 n.
supreme control
directorship 689 n.
governance 733 n.
Supreme Court
law-court 956 n.
Supreme Pontiff
ecclesiarch 986 n.
surcease *cessation* 145 n.
surcharge *account* 808 vb.
price 809 n.
surcingle *girdle* 47 n.
surd *number* 85 n.
speech sound 398 n.
voiceless 578 adj.
sure *certain* 473 adj.
believing 485 adj.
expectant 507 adj.
safe 660 adj.
trustworthy 929 adj.
sure-fire *successful* 727 adj.
sure-footed
vigilant 457 adj.
skilful 694 adj.
successful 727 adj.
sure thing *certainty* 473 n.
easy thing 701 n.
surety *safety* 660 n.
security 767 n.
legal process 959 n.
suretyship *security* 767 n.
surf *wave* 350 n.
bubble 355 n.
surface *space* 183 n.
measure 183 n.
shallowness 212 n.
exteriority 223 n.
navigate 269 vb.
emerge 298 vb.
ascend 308 vb.
be light 323 vb.
texture 331 n.
be visible 443 vb.
road 624 n.
surf-bathing *sport* 837 n.
surf-board *swim* 269 vb.
surfeit *superfluity* 637 n.
satiety 863 n.
surf-riding
aquatics 269 n.
sport 837 n.
surge *increase* 36 n.
congregate 74 vb.
flow out 298 vb.

vortex 315n.
eddy 350n.
flow 350vb.
sibilation 406n.
be active 678vb.
surgeon *doctor* 658n.
surgery *surgery* 658n.
hospital 658n.
surgical *medical* 658adj.
surly *ungracious* 885adj.
surmise *opinion* 485n.
foresee 510vb.
conjecture 512n.
surmount *be high* 209vb.
crown 213vb.
overstep 306vb.
climb 308vb.
triumph 727vb.
surmountable
possible 469adj.
surname *name* 561n.,vb.
surpass *be superior* 34vb.
outdo 306vb.
surpassing *great* 32adj.
supreme 34adj.
excellent 644adj.
surplice *vestments* 989n.
surplus *remainder* 41n.
part 53n.
superfluity 637n.
surprise
inexpectation 508n.
pitfall 663n.
non-preparation 670n.
attack 712n.,vb.
wonder 864n.
surprising
unusual 84adj.
unexpected 508adj.
wonderful 864adj.
surrealism
school of painting 553n.
surrealist *artist* 556n.
surrebutter
rejoinder 460n.
surrender *relinquish* 621vb.
non-use 674n.
submission 721n.
resignation 753n.
surreptitious
stealthy 525adj.
surrey *carriage* 274n.
surrogate *deputy* 755n.
surrogation
substitution 150n.
surround *surround* 230vb.
circumscribe 232vb.
outline 233n.
inclosure 235n.
close 264vb.
circuit 626vb.

surroundings
locality 187n.
circumjacence 230n.
surtax *tax* 809n.
surveillance
surveillance 457n.
management 689n.
survey *inspection* 438n.
enquiry 459n.
measure 465vb.
estimate 480n.,vb.
dissertation 591n.
surveying
measurement 465n.
surveyor *surveyor* 465n.
survival *existence* 1n.
remainder 41n.
durability 113n.
life 360n.
survival of the fittest
biology 358n.
contention 716n.
survive *be left* 41vb.
continue 108vb.
outlast 113vb.
stay 144vb.
live 360vb.
be restored 656vb.
escape 667vb.
win 727vb.
survivor *survivor* 41n.
aftercomer 67n.
escaper 667n.
susceptibility
liability 180n.
sensibility 374n.
persuasibility 612n.
vulnerability 661n.
moral sensibility 819n.
love 887n.
susceptible
impressible 819adj.
excitable 822adj.
suspect *be uncertain* 474vb.
opine 485vb.
unbelieved 485adj.
doubt 486vb.
not know 491vb.
be nervous 854vb.
offender 904n.
be jealous 911vb.
wrong 914adj.
accused person 928n.
suspend *put off* 136vb.
pause 145vb.
hang 217vb.
abrogate 752vb.
depose 752vb.
punish 963vb.
suspended animation
inactivity 679n.

suspender *fastening* 47n.
hanger 217n.
supporter 218n.
underwear 228n.
suspense *lull* 145n.
dubiety 474n.
expectation 507n.
suspension *pendency* 217n.
softness 327n.
elasticity 328n.
tempo 410n.
non-use 674n.
inaction 677n.
abrogation 752n.
suspensory
surgical dressing 658n.
suspicion *doubt* 486n.
conjecture 512n.
hint 524n.
suspicious
unbelieved 486adj.
unbelieving 486adj.
nervous 854adj.
cautious 858adj.
jealous 911adj.
sustain *continue* 108vb.
sustain 146vb.
strengthen 162vb.
support 218vb.
feed 301vb.
corroborate 466vb.
persevere 600vb.
aid 703vb.
sustained *frequent* 139adj.
unceasing 146adj.
sustenance *support* 218n.
food 301n.
provisions 301n.
susurration *faintness* 401n.
sutler *provider* 633n.
pedlar 794n.
sutra *maxim* 496n.
non-Biblical scripture
975n.
suttee *suicide* 362n.
burning 381n.
disinterestedness 931n.
oblation 981n.
sutural *conjunct* 45adj.
suture *joinder* 45n.
dividing line 92n.
suzerain *superior* 34n.
sovereign 741n.
suzerainty
governance 733n.
svelte *narrow* 206adj.
shapely 841adj.
swab *drier* 342n.
cleaning utensil 648n.
surgical dressing 658n.
bungler 697n.

navy man 722 n.
swaddle *tie* 45 vb.
　dress 228 vb.
　restrain 747 vb.
swaddling clothes
　clothing 228 n.
swadeshi *native* 191 adj.
swag *bag* 194 n.
　hang 217 vb.
　obliquity 220 n.
　be curved 248 vb.
　oscillate 317 vb.
　booty 790 n.
swag-bellied
　expanded 197 adj.
swagger *gait* 265 n.
　be proud 871 vb.
　ostentation 875 n.
　boasting 877 n.
　be insolent 878 vb.
swagman *wanderer* 268 n.
swain *male* 372 n.
　countryman 869 n.
　lover 887 n.
swallow *speeder* 277 n.
　absorb 299 n.
　mouthful 301 n.
　eat 301 vb.
　bird 365 n.
　be credulous 487 vb.
　be patient 823 vb.
swallow up *destroy* 165 vb.
　consume 165 vb.
　waste 634 vb.
swallow whole
　not discriminate 464 vb.
　believe 485 vb.
　be credulous 487 vb.
swami *sage* 500 n.
swamp *fill* 54 vb.
　be many 104 vb.
　destroy 165 vb.
　drench 341 vb.
　marsh 347 n.
　defeat 722 vb.
swampy *marshy* 347 adj.
swan *waterfowl* 365 n.
　a beauty 841 n.
swank *fashionable* 848 adj.
　be affected 850 vb.
　pride 871 n.
　vanity 873 n.
　ostentation 875 n.
　boaster 877 n.
swanker *proud man* 871 n.
swanky *fashionable* 848 adj.
swannery *nest* 192 n.
　cattle pen 369 n.
swansdown *textile* 222 n.
　smoothness 258 n.
swanskin *textile* 222 n.

swansong *end* 69 n.
　decease 361 n.
　lament 836 n.
swap *interchange* 151 n., vb.
　barter 791 n.
sward *grassland* 348 n.
swarm *grow* 36 vb.
　crowd 74 n.
　congregate 74 vb.
　be many 104 vb.
　be plentiful 171 vb.
　abound 635 vb.
swarm in *irrupt* 297 vb.
swarm over
　be present 189 vb.
swarm up *climb* 308 vb.
swarthy *dark* 418 adj.
　blackish 428 adj.
swash *moisten* 341 vb.
　flow 350 vb.
swashbuckler
　combatant 722 n.
　insolent person 878 n.
swastika *cross* 222 n.
　heraldry 547 n.
　talisman 983 n.
swat *strike* 279 vb.
swathe *tie* 45 vb.
　bunch 74 n.
　dress 228 vb.
　fold 261 vb.
　cover 266 vb.
　trace 548 n.
sway *influence* 178 n., vb.
　hang 217 vb.
　oscillate 317 vb.
　be agitated 318 vb.
　be uncertain 474 vb.
　be periodic 141 vb.
　vary 152 vb.
　power 160 n.
　be weak 163 vb.
　be irresolute 601 vb.
　motivate 612 vb.
　manage 689 vb.
　governance 733 n.
swear *testify* 466 vb.
　swear 532 vb.
　promise 764 vb.
　take a pledge 764 vb.
　cuss 899 vb.
　be impious 980 vb.
swear by *be certain* 473 vb.
　believe 485 vb.
　praise 923 vb.
swearer *signatory* 765 n.
　impious person 980 n.
swear off *negate* 533 vb.
　recant 603 vb.
　relinquish 621 vb.
swear-word *word* 559 n.

scurrility 899 n.
sweat *exude* 298 vb.
　emit 300 vb.
　excrete 302 vb.
　be wet 341 vb.
　be hot 379 vb.
　labour 682 n.
sweated labour *slave* 742 n.
sweater *vest* 228 n.
sweat-rag
　cleaning cloth 648 n.
swede *tuber* 301 n.
sweeny
　animal disease 651 n.
sweep *range* 183 n.
　curvature 248 n.
　traverse 267 vb.
　propeller 269 n.
　move fast 277 vb.
　propellant 287 n.
　touch 378 vb.
　inspection 438 n.
　scan 438 vb.
　clean 648 vb.
　dirty person 649 n.
sweep away *void* 300 vb.
sweeper *cleaner* 648 n.
　domestic 742 n.
sweeping
　comprehensive 52 adj.
　inclusive 78 adj.
　general 79 adj.
sweepings *leavings* 41 n.
　rubbish 641 n.
　dirt 649 n.
sweepstake *chance* 159 n.
　gambling 618 n.
sweet *mouthful* 301 n.
　pudding 301 n.
　pleasant 376 adj.
　savoury 390 adj.
　sweet 392 n., adj.
　melodious 410 adj.
　pleasurable 826 adj.
　beautiful 841 adj.
　amiable 884 adj.
　lovable 887 adj.
　benevolent 897 adj.
sweetbread *meat* 301 n.
sweeten *assuage* 177 vb.
　appetize 390 vb.
　sweeten 392 vb.
　purify 648 vb.
sweetener *gift* 781 n.
sweetheart *loved one* 887 n.
　lover 887 n.
　darling 890 n.
sweeting, sweetie
　darling 890 n.
sweetmeat *sweetmeat* 301 n.
　sweet 392 n.

sweetness *fragrance* 396n.
(*see* sweet)
sweet on *enamoured* 887adj.
sweet potato *tuber* 301n.
flute 414n.
sweet will *will* 595n.
whim 604n.
swell *grow* 36vb.
add 38vb.
expand 197vb.
be convex 253vb.
wave 350n.
flow 350vb.
loudness 400n.
fop 848n.
aristocrat 868n.
be insolent 878vb.
swelled head
proud man 871n.
vanity 873n.
swelling *monticle* 209n.
swelling 253n.
convex 253adj.
loud 400adj.
exaggerated 546adj.
rhetorical 574adj.
skin disease 651n.
wound 655n.
prideful 871adj.
swell the ranks *accrue* 38vb.
be included 78vb.
swell up *jut* 254vb.
swelter *be hot* 379vb.
swerve *be oblique* 220n.
deviation 282n.
recede 290vb.
tergiversate 603vb.
swift *speedy* 277adj.
bird 365n.
swiftness *velocity* 277n.
swig *drink* 301vb.
get drunk 949vb.
swill *drink* 301vb.
swill 649n.
get drunk 949vb.
swim *swim* 269vb.
be light 323vb.
be dim-sighted 440vb.
swim in *enjoy* 376vb.
abound 635vb.
swimming *aquatics* 269n.
swimming bath *lake* 346n.
ablution 648n.
swimmingly *easily* 701adv.
successfully 727adv.
prosperously 730adv.
swimsuit *beachwear* 228n.
aquatics 269n.
swim with the stream
conform 83vb.
acquiesce 488vb.

do easily 701vb.
swindle *deceive* 542vb.
peculation 788n.
not pay 805vb.
be dishonest 930vb.
swindler *trickster* 545n.
defrauder 789n.
swine *pig* 365n.
knave, cad 938n.
sensualist 944n.
swing *periodicity* 141n.
reversion 148n.
revolution 149n.
vary 152vb.
range 183n.
hang 217vb.
deviate 282vb.
oscillate 317vb.
music 412n.
scope 744n.
pleasure-ground 837n.
be punished 963vb.
swing back *recoil* 280vb.
swingeing *exorbitant* 32adj.
swing the lead
be false 541vb.
swinish *sensual* 944adj.
swipe *knock* 279n.
propulsion 287n.
extractor 304n.
irrigator 341n.
foin 712n.
steal 788vb.
swipes *liquor* 301n.
swirl *vortex* 315n.
eddy 350n.
swish *faintness* 401n.
sibilation 406n.
fashionable 848adj.
switch *revolution* 149n.
interchange 151vb.
hair 259n.
move 265vb.
transpose 272vb.
deflect 282vb.
diverge 294vb.
apostatize 603vb.
instrument 628n.
tool 630n.
club 723n.
hair-dressing 843n.
scourge 964n.
switchback *obliquity* 220n.
undulatory 251adj.
vehicle 274n.
musical piece 412n.
pleasure ground 837n.
switchboard *focus* 76n.
switch off *terminate* 69vb.
cease 145vb.
snuff out 418vb.

switch on *initiate* 68vb.
operate 173vb.
swivel *rotator* 315n.
gun 723n.
swivel eye *dim sight* 440n.
swizz *absurdity* 497n.
trickery 542n.
fable 543n.
swollen *increasing* 36adj.
expanded 197adj.
convex 253adj.
rhetorical 574adj.
diseased 651adj.
prideful 871adj.
swoon *be impotent* 161vb.
weakness 163n.
fatigue 684n.
(*see* insensibility)
swoop *spurt* 277n.
descend 309vb.
plunge 313n.
swoosh *sibilation* 406n.
sword *destroyer* 168n.
sharp edge 256n.
bane 659n.
combatant 722n.
side-arms 723n.
badge of rank 743n.
Sword of Damocles
danger 661n.
intimidation 854n.
threat 900n.
sword-play *duel* 716n.
swordsman
contender 716n.
combatant 722n.
sworn *affirmative* 532adj.
obedient 739adj.
contractual 765adj.
dutied 917adj.
swot *study* 536vb.
learner 538n.
sybarite *sensualist* 944n.
syce *domestic* 742n.
servant 742n.
sycophancy *servility* 879n.
flattery 925n.
false charge 928n.
sycophant *toady* 879n.
flatterer 925n.
accuser 928n.
litigant 959n.
syllabary *letter* 558n.
syllabic *literal* 558adj.
syllabification
decomposition 51n.
syllable
speech sound 398n.
spoken letter 558n.
spell 558vb.
word 559n.

phrase 563 vb.
voice 577 n., vb.
speak 579 vb.
syllabus list 87 n.
compendium 592 n.
syllogism relevance 9 n.
argumentation 475 n.
sylph fairy 970 n.
sylph-like narrow 206 adj.
fairylike 970 adj.
sylvan arboreal 366 adj.
symbiosis life 360 n.
co-operation 706 n.
symbiotic agreeing 24 adj.
conjunct 45 adj.
co-operative 706 adj.
symbol
insubstantial thing 4 n.
number 85 n.
metaphor 519 n.
indication 547 n.
badge 547 n.
image 551 n.
symbolic
insubstantial 4 adj.
occult 523 adj.
indicating 547 adj.
representing 551 adj.
trivial 639 adj.
ritual 988 adj.
symbolics creed 485 n.
theology 973 n.
symbolism
(see symbol, symbolic)
symbolization
symbology 547 n.
(see symbolize)
symbolize mean 514 vb.
figure 519 vb.
interpret 520 vb.
manifest 522 vb.
imply 523 vb.
indicate 547 vb.
represent 551 vb.
symbolography
symbology 547 n.
symbology
symbology 547 n.
symmetry relativeness 9 n.
correlation 12 n.
uniformity 16 n.
equality 28 n.
symmetry 245 n.
elegance 575 n.
beauty 841 n.
sympathetic
agreeing 24 adj.
(see sympathy)
sympathize (see sympathy)
sympathizer patron 707 n.
collaborator 707 n.

participator 775 n.
kind person 897 n.
sympathy assent 488 n.
bond 47 n.
attraction 291 n.
imagination 513 n.
aid 703 n.
co-operation 706 n.
concord 710 n.
participation 775 n.
feeling 818 n.
liking 859 n.
friendliness 880 n.
love 887 n.
benevolence 897 n.
condolence 905 n.
pity 905 n.
symphonic
harmonious 410 adj.
musical 412 adj.
musicianly 413 adj.
symphony
musical piece 412 n.
symphysis junction 45 n.
combination 50 n.
symposiarch leader 690 n.
reveller 837 n.
symposiast
interlocutor 584 n.
symposium argument 475 n.
interlocution 584 n.
conference 584 n.
festivity 837 n.
social gathering 882 n.
symptom
concomitant 89 n.
evidence 466 n.
omen 511 n.
hint 524 n.
indication 547 n.
warning 664 n.
symptomatic
accompanying 89 adj.
visible 443 adj.
evidential 466 adj.
indicating 547 adj.
cautionary 664 adj.
symptomatology
hermeneutics 520 n.
indication 547 n.
synæsthesia sense 374 n.
synagogue church 990 n.
synchronism
synchronism 123 n.
synchronization
adaptation 24 n.
combination 50 n.
arrangement 62 n.
synchronism 123 n.
synchronize
be in order 60 vb.

accompany 89 vb.
time 117 vb.
be now 121 vb.
synchronize 123 vb.
synchronous
agreeing 24 adj.
combined 50 adj.
synchronous 123 adj.
synchysis inversion 221 n.
synclinal sloping 220 adj.
syncopation tempo 410 n.
music 412 n.
syncopator musician 713 n.
syncope helplessness 161 n.
contraction 198 n.
shortness 204 n.
tempo 410 n.
conciseness 569 n.
fatigue 684 n.
syncretism mixture 43 n.
combination 50 n.
syndic officer 741 n.
syndicalism
government 733 n.
syndicalist
political party 708 n.
corporate 708 adj.
syndicate corporation 708 n.
synecdoche trope 519 n.
syneisaktism
type of marriage 894 n.
celibacy 895 n.
synergism
concurrence 181 n.
sanctity 979 n.
synergistic effect
increase 36 n.
synergy concurrence 181 n.
co-operation 706 n.
syngamy mixture 43 n.
junction 45 n.
syngenesis
reproduction 166 n.
synod council 692 n.
synod 985 n.
synodal
parliamentary 692 adj.
synodic
ecclesiastical 985 adj.
synodical period
regular return 141 n.
synœcism association 706 n.
synonym identity 13 n.
equivalence 28 n.
substitute 150 n.
connotation 514 n.
word 559 n.
name 561 n.
synonymity (see synonym)
synonymous
semantic 514 adj.

interpretive 520 adj.
synonymy
  equivocalness 518 n.
synopsis *combination* 50 n.
  whole 52 n.
  arrangement 62 n.
  generality 79 n.
  list 87 n.
  compendium 592 n.
synoptical
  inclusive 78 adj.
Synoptic Gospels
  scripture 975 n.
synovia *lubricant* 334 n.
syntagma *arrangement* 62 n.
syntax *relation* 9 n.
  composition 56 n.
  arrangement 62 n.
  assemblage 74 n.
  grammar 564 n.
synthesis *junction* 45 n.
  combination 50 n.
  argumentation 475 n.
synthesize *compose* 56 vb.
synthetic *simulating* 18 adj.
  imitative 20 adj.
  rational 475 n.
  untrue 543 adj.
syntony *agreement* 24 n.
  synchronism 123 n.
syphilis
  venereal disease 651 n.
syringe *extractor* 304 n.
  irrigator 341 n.
  moisten 341 vb.
syrinx *flute* 414 n.
syrup *soft drink* 301 n.
  viscidity 354 n.
  sweet 392 n.
syssitia *participation* 775 n.
systaltic
  contracted 198 adj.
  elastic 328 adj.
system *order* 60 n.
  arrangement 62 n.
  regularity 81 n.
  creed 485 n.
  habit 610 n.
  plan 623 n.
systematic *regular* 81 adj.
  philosophic 449 adj.
  rational 475 adj.
  businesslike 622 adj.
  (*see* system)
systematic knowledge
  science 490 n.
systematic thought
  philosophy 449 n.
systematize *order* 60 vb.
  regularize 62 vb.
  make conform 83 vb.

plan 623 vb.
systole and diastole
  fluctuation 317 n.
syzygy *contiguity* 202 n.

T

tab *adjunct* 40 n.
  label 547 n.
  mark 547 vb.
  badge of rank 743 n.
tabard *tunic* 228 n.
tabby *cat* 365 n.
  mottled 437 adj.
  interlocutor 584 n.
tabefaction
  contraction 198 n.
tabernacle *dwelling* 192 n.
  ritual object 988 n.
  temple, church 990 n.
tabid *contracted* 198 adj.
  lean 206 adj.
  diseased 651 adj.
table *arrangement* 62 n.
  list 87 n.
  put off 136 vb.
  lamina, layer 207 n.
  horizontality 216 n.
  stand, shelf 218 n.
  eating, meal 301 n.
  register 548 vb.
  stationery 586 n.
tableau *spectacle* 445 n.
  picture 553 n.
  stage show 594 n.
  pageant 875 n.
table bird *table bird* 365 n.
table d'hôte *meal* 301 n.
table fish *table fish* 365 n.
tableland *high land* 209 n.
  vertex 213 n.
  horizontality 216 n.
  plain 348 n.
table manners *eating* 301 n.
table-napkin
  cleaning cloth 648 n.
table of contents *list* 87 n.
tablespoon *ladle* 194 n.
tablet *lamina* 207 n.
  mouthful 301 n.
  monument 548 n.
  stationery 586 n.
table-talk *chat* 584 n.
table-tapping
  spiritualism 984 n.
table-water *soft drink* 301 n.
tabloid *the press* 528 n.
  medicine 658 n.
taboo *exclusion* 57 n.
  prohibition 757 n.
  bewitch 983 vb.

tabor *drum* 414 n.
tabouret *seat* 218 n.
  drum 414 n.
tabular *arranged* 62 adj.
  layered 207 adj.
tabula rasa *revolution* 149 n.
  ignorance 491 n.
  obliteration 550 n.
tabulate *class* 62 vb.
  list 87 vb.
  register 548 vb.
Tachism
  school of painting 553 n.
tachometer *velocity* 277 n.
tachygraph
  stenographer 586 n.
tacit *tacit* 523 adj.
Tacitean *concise* 569 adj.
taciturn *reticent* 525 adj.
  voiceless 578 adj.
  taciturn 582 adj.
  unsociable 883 adj.
tack *tie* 45 vb.
  fastening 47 n.
  change 143 vb.
  sharp point 256 n.
  navigate 269 vb.
  direction 281 n.
  deviate 282 vb.
  food 301 n.
  tergiversate 603 vb.
  route 624 n.
tackle *tackling* 47 n.
  begin 68 vb.
  equipment 630 n.
  essay 671 n., vb.
  undertake 672 vb.
  do 676 vb.
tack on *add* 38 vb.
tacky *viscid* 354 adj.
tact *touch* 378 n.
  discrimination 463 n.
  sagacity 498 n.
  style 566 n.
  skill 694 n.
  management 689 n.
  good taste 846 n.
tactful *wise* 498 adj.
  discriminating 463 adj.
tactical (*see* tactics)
tactician *motivator* 612 n.
  planner 623 n.
  expert 696 n.
  slyboots 698 n.
tactics *motion* 265 n.
  policy 623 n.
  way 624 n.
  deed 676 n.
  tactics 688 n.
  skill 694 n.
  cunning 698 n.

art of war 718 n.
tactile *tactual* 378 adj.
tactless *unfeeling* 375 adj.
  indiscriminating 464 adj.
  foolish 499 adj.
  clumsy 695 adj.
  ill-bred 847 adj.
  discourteous 885 adj.
tactual *tactual* 378 adj.
tadpole *youngling* 132 n.
  frog 365 n.
tænia *girdle* 47 n.
taffeta *textile* 222 n.
taffrail *fence* 235 n.
taffy *native* 191 n.
  falsehood 541 n.
  flattery 925 n.
tag *adjunct* 40 n.
  connect 45 vb.
  sequel 67 n.
  extremity 69 n.
  pendant 217 n.
  sharp point 256 n.
  label 547 n.
  mark 547 vb.
tag after *follow* 284 vb.
tag on *add* 38 vb.
taiga *marsh* 347 n.
  wood 366 n.
tail *adjunct* 40 n.
  sequel 67 n.
  retinue 67 n.
  extremity 69 n.
  concomitant 89 n.
  pendant 217 n.
  rear 238 n.
  follow 284 vb.
  pursue 619 vb.
  nonentity 639 n.
  bungler 697 n.
tailless *subtracted* 39 adj.
tail-light *lamp* 420 n.
tail off *decrease* 37 vb.
tailor *adjust* 24 vb.
  clothier 228 n.
  efform 243 vb.
  artisan 686 n.
tailored *adjusted* 24 adj.
  dressed 228 adj.
tailor's dummy *mould* 23 n.
  frame 218 n.
  image 551 n.
  fop 848 n.
tailor's goose
  smoother 258 n.
tail-piece *sequel* 67 n.
  rear 238 n.
tails *formal dress* 228 n.
tailwind *propellant* 287 n.
  wind 352 n.
  aid 703 n.

taint *infiltrate* 297 vb.
  fetor 397 n.
  badness 645 n.
  defect 647 n.
  uncleanness 649 n.
  infection 651 n.
  impair 655 vb.
  slur 867 n.
take *bring together* 74 vb.
  contain 56 vb.
  comprise 78 vb.
  admit 299 vb.
  opine 485 vb.
  know 490 vb.
  suppose 512 vb.
  photograph 551 vb.
  require 627 vb.
  be ill 651 vb.
  overmaster 727 vb.
  subjugate 745 vb.
  arrest 747 vb.
  acquire 771 vb.
  receive 782 vb.
  take 786 vb.
  be patient 823 vb.
  delight 826 vb.
  bewitch 983 vb.
take aback *navigate* 269 vb.
  surprise 508 vb.
take a back seat
  be inferior 35 vb.
  have no repute 867 vb.
  be modest 874 vb.
  be disinterested 931 vb.
take a chance
  face danger 661 vb.
  essay 671 vb.
take action *do* 676 vb.
take advantage of
  use 673 vb.
  be skilful 694 vb.
take after *resemble* 18 vb.
take alarm *fear* 854 vb.
take amiss
  be discontented 829 vb.
  resent 891 vb.
take apart *sunder* 46 vb.
take aside *speak to* 583 vb.
take away *subtract* 39 vb.
  take away 786 vb.
take back *recoup* 31 vb.
  revert 148 vb.
  recant 603 vb.
  acquire 771 vb.
  take 786 vb.
take breath *pause* 145 vb.
  be quiescent 266 vb.
take care of
  be mindful 455 vb.
  look after 457 vb.
  preserve 666 vb.

take command
  take authority 733 vb.
take cover
  be stealthy 525 vb.
take down *depress* 311 vb.
  record 548 vb.
  write 586 vb.
  ridicule 851 vb.
  humiliate 872 vb.
take effect *operate* 173 vb.
  be successful 727 vb.
take exception
  resent 891 vb.
take for granted
  assume 471 vb.
  premise 475 vb.
  believe 485 vb.
  be credulous 487 vb.
  suppose 512 vb.
  not wonder 865 vb.
  be ungrateful 908 vb.
take heart of grace
  be content 828 vb.
  be cheerful 833 vb.
  hope 852 vb.
  take courage 855 vb.
take heed *be warned* 664 vb.
take hold *cohere* 48 vb.
  prevail 178 vb.
  be wont 610 vb.
  take 786 vb.
take ill
  be discontented 829 vb.
  resent 891 vb.
take in *comprise* 78 vb.
  make smaller 198 vb.
  shorten 204 vb.
  admit 299 vb.
  scan 438 vb.
  understand 516 vb.
  befool 542 vb.
take in each other's washing
  interchange 151 vb.
  co-operate 706 vb.
take in hand *train* 534 vb.
  undertake 672 vb.
take into account
  number with 78 vb.
  discriminate 463 vb.
take in vain
  misuse 675 vb.
take it
  knuckle under 721 vb.
take it easy
  move slowly 278 vb.
  repose 683 vb.
  do easily 701 vb.
take it or leave it
  be neutral 606 vb.
take it out of
  be malevolent 898 vb.

take its course
  go on 146 vb.
  happen 154 vb.
take liberties
  oppress 735 vb.
  be free 744 vb.
taken bad
  sick 651 adj.
taken up with
  obsessed 455 adj.
taken with
  enamoured 887 adj.
take off *doff* 229 vb.
  fly 271 vb.
  start out 296 vb.
  act 594 vb.
  discount 810 vb.
  satirize 851 vb.
take offence
  be inimical 881 vb.
  resent 891 vb.
take on *admit* 299 vb.
  employ 622 vb.
  essay 671 vb.
  undertake 672 vb.
  do 676 vb.
  attack 712 vb.
  contend, fight 716 vb.
  be discontented 829 vb.
  incur a duty 917 vb.
take orders
  take orders 986 vb.
take out *extract* 304 vb.
  obliterate 550 vb.
take over *come after* 65 vb.
  take authority 733 vb.
  appropriate 786 vb.
take-over
  transference 272 n.
take-over bid *offer* 759 n.
  purchase 792 n.
take place *be* 1 vb.
  happen 154 vb.
taker *possessor* 776 n.
  recipient 782 n.
  taker 786 n.
  purchaser 792 n.
take root *be stable* 153 vb.
  prevail 178 vb.
  place oneself 187 vb.
  be wont 610 vb.
take shape *become* 1 vb.
take sides
  be biased 481 vb.
  choose 605 vb.
  join a party 708 vb.
take silk *do law* 958 vb.
take steps *do* 676 vb.
take stock *number* 86 vb.
  scan 438 vb.
  estimate 480 vb.

account 808 vb.
take the bit between one's
  teeth
  will 595 vb.
  be obstinate 602 vb.
  disobey 738 vb.
take the bull by the horns
  be resolute 599 vb.
  be courageous 855 vb.
take the count
  be defeated 728 vb.
take the lead
  initiate 68 vb.
  be in front 237 vb.
  precede 283 vb.
  be important 638 vb.
  have repute 866 vb.
take the place of
  substitute 150 vb.
take the veil
  live single 895 vb.
  take orders 986 vb.
take the wind out of one's
  sails
  disable 161 vb.
  navigate 269 vb.
  abase 311 vb.
  hinder 702 vb.
take time
  be late, wait 136 vb.
  have leisure 681 vb.
  be cautious 858 vb.
take time by the forelock
  be early 135 vb.
  profit by 137 vb.
take to *desire* 859 vb.
  be in love 887 vb.
take to oneself
  appropriate 786 vb.
take up *elevate* 310 vb.
  undertake 672 vb.
  receive 782 vb.
  befriend 880 vb.
take up the cudgels for
  patronize 703 vb.
  defend 713 vb.
taking *infectious* 653 adj.
  anger 891 n.
takings *increment* 36 n.
  earnings 771 n.
  booty 790 n.
  receipt 807 n.
talaria *wing* 271 n.
talbotype
  photography 551 n.
talcum powder
  cosmetic 843 n.
tale *numeration* 86 n.
  fable 543 n.
  narrative 590 n.
  novel 590 n.

tale-bearer
  informer 524 n.
talent *intelligence* 498 n.
  aptitude 694 n.
  coinage 797 n.
talent scout *enquirer* 459 n.
tale of woe *sorrow* 825 n.
  lament 836 n.
talipes *deformity* 246 n.
talisman *preserver* 666 n.
  talisman 983 n.
talismanic *magical* 983 adj.
talk *empty talk* 515 n.
  inform 524 n.
  rumour 529 n.
  oration 579 n.
  speak 579 vb.
  be loquacious 581 vb.
  allocution 583 n.
  chat 584 n.
talk about *publish* 528 vb.
  defame 926 vb.
talkative *speaking* 579 adj.
  loquacious 581 adj.
talk big *be vain* 873 vb.
  boast 877 vb.
  be insolent 878 vb.
  threaten 900 vb.
talk down
  be loquacious 581 vb.
talked of *renowned* 866 adj.
talker *speaker* 579 n.
  chatterer 581 n.
  interlocutor 584 n.
talkie *cinema* 445 n.
talking *informative* 524 adj.
talking to *reprimand* 924 n.
talk it over *confer* 584 vb.
talk of *publish* 528 vb.
talk of the town
  rumour 529 n.
  famousness 866 n.
talk out *spin out* 113 vb.
  be obstructive 702 vb.
talk over *induce* 612 vb.
talks *conference* 584 n.
talk to *speak to* 583 vb.
talk to oneself
  soliloquize 585 vb.
tall *great* 32 adj.
  whopping 32 adj.
  tall 209 adj.
  exaggerated 546 adj.
tallage *tax* 809 n.
tallboy *cabinet* 194 n.
tallies
  counting instrument 86 n.
tallith *shawl* 228 n.
  neckwear 228 n.
  canonicals 989 n.
tall order *fable* 543 n.

undertaking 672 n.
hard task 700 n.
tallow *fat* 357 n.
tallow-faced
  colourless 726 adj.
tall story *news* 529 n.
  fable 543 n.
tall talk
  insubstantial thing 4 n.
  boast 877 n.
tally *conform* 83 vb.
  numerical result 85 n.
  numeration 86 n.
  list 87 n.
  label 547 n.
  record 548 n.
  credit 802 n.
  debt 803 n.
  accounts 808 n.
tally-clerk *recorder* 549 n.
tally-ho *stage-coach* 274 n.
  chase 619 n.
tallyman *lender* 784 n.
  tradesman 794 n.
talma *cloak* 228 n.
Talmud *scripture* 975 n.
Talmudist *theologian* 973 n.
talon *foot* 214 n.
  sharp point 256 n.
  finger 378 n.
  nippers 778 n.
talus *acclivity* 220 n.
tambourine *drum* 414 n.
tame *inert* 175 adj.
  moderate 177 vb.
  break in 369 vb.
  train 534 vb.
  feeble 572 adj.
  habituate 610 vb.
  subjugate 745 vb.
  inexcitable 823 adj.
  servile 879 adj.
tameless *furious* 176 adj.
  cruel 898 adj.
Tammany *improbity* 930 n.
tam-o'-shanter
  headgear 228 n.
tamp *ram* 279 n.
  close 264 vb.
tamper *derange* 63 vb.
  impair 655 vb.
  meddle 678 vb.
tamper with
  modify 143 vb.
  bribe 612 vb.
tampion, tompion
  covering 226 n.
  stopper 264 n.
tampon *covering* 226 n.
  stopper 264 n.
  surgical dressing 658 n.

tan *strike* 279 vb.
  be tough 329 vb.
  burning 381 n.
  brown 430 adj.
  spank 963 vb.
tandem *duality* 90 n.
  bicycle 274 n.
tang *projection* 254 n.
  taste 386 n.
  pungency 388 n.
tangency *contiguity* 202 n.
tangent *ratio* 85 n.
  convergence 293 n.
tangential
  contiguous 202 adj.
  convergent 293 adj.
tangerine *fruit* 301 n.
tangible *substantial* 3 adj.
  material 319 adj.
  tactual 378 adj.
  true 494 adj.
tangle *medley* 43 n.
  complexity 61 n.
  bedevil 63 vb.
  enlace 222 vb.
  hinder 702 vb.
tangled *tied* 45 adj.
  dense 324 adj.
  imperspicuous 568 adj.
tango *dance* 837 n., vb.
tanist *beneficiary* 776 n.
tank *vat* 194 n.
  war-chariot 274 n.
  lake 346 n.
  storage 632 n.
  cavalry 722 n.
tankard *cup* 194 n.
tanker *automobile* 274 n.
  locomotive 274 n.
  merchant ship 275 n.
tanner *coinage* 797 n.
tantalize *fall short* 307 vb.
  make impossible 470 vb.
  disappoint 509 vb.
  tempt 612 vb.
  excite 821 vb.
  cause desire 859 vb.
tantamount
  equivalent 28 adj.
  semantic 514 adj.
tantara *roll* 403 n.
tantrum
  excitable state 822 n.
  anger 891 n.
Taoism
  religious faith 973 n.
tap *tube* 263 n.
  pierce 263 vb.
  stopper 264 n.
  transferrer 272 n.
  strike 279 vb.

outlet 298 n.
void 300 vb.
extract 304 vb.
water 339 n.
make flow 350 vb.
conduit 351 n.
touch 378 vb.
bang 402 n.
play music 413 vb.
hear 415 vb.
store 632 n.
provide 633 vb.
acquire 771 vb.
take 786 vb.
endearment 889 n.
tap-dance *dance* 837 n., vb.
tape *cable* 47 n.
  line 203 n.
  strip 208 n.
  appraise 465 vb.
taped *measured* 465 adj.
tape-machine
  recording instrument
    549 n.
tape-measure
  counting instrument 86 n.
  gauge 465 n.
taper *shade off* 27 vb.
  make smaller 198 vb.
  shorten 204 vb.
  be narrow 206 vb.
  be sharp 256 vb.
  converge 293 vb.
  lighter 385 n.
  torch 420 n.
tape-recorder
  recording instrument
    549 n.
tapering *tapering* 256 adj.
  (*see* taper)
taper off *decrease* 37 vb.
tapestry *textile* 222 n.
  covering 226 n.
  art 551 n.
  picture 553 n.
  needlework 844 n.
  decorate 844 vb.
tapeworm
  narrowness 206 n.
  thinness 206 n.
tapinosis *humility* 872 n.
tap, on *on the spot* 189 adj.
  provisionary 633 adj.
  enough 635 adv.
  useful 640 adj.
tap out *signal* 547 vb.
tapping *extraction* 304 vb.
tap-room *tavern* 192 n.
  chamber 194 n.
taproot *source* 156 n.
taps *obsequies* 364 n.

call 547 n.
tapster *servant* 742 n.
tap the line *hear* 415 vb.
  be curious 453 vb.
tar *coat* 226 vb.
  mariner 270 n.
  resin 357 n.
  black thing 428 n.
taradiddle *untruth* 543 n.
tar and feather
  punish 963 vb.
tarantella *music* 412 n.
  dance 837 n.
tarantism *spasm* 318 n.
tarboosh, tarbush
  headgear 228 n.
tardy *late* 136 adj.
  slow 278 adj.
  lazy 679 adj.
tare *decrement* 42 n.
  discount 810 n.
tares *rubbish* 641 n.
target *limit* 236 n.
  direction 281 n.
  objective 617 n.
  armour 713 n.
targeteer *soldiery* 722 n.
Targum *commentary* 520 n.
  scripture 975 n.
tariff *list* 87 n.
  restriction 747 n.
  price, tax 809 n.
tariff wall *exclusion* 57 n.
  restriction 747 n.
tarmac *paving* 226 n.
  smoothness 258 n.
  air travel 271 n.
  road 624 n.
  building material 631 n.
tarn *lake* 346 n.
tarnish *decolorize* 426 vb.
  make unclean 649 vb.
  blemish 845 n.
  shame 867 vb.
  defame 926 vb.
tarpaulin *canopy* 226 n.
tarry *drag on* 113 vb.
  be late 136 vb.
  stay 144 vb.
  be quiescent 266 vb.
  move slowly 278 vb.
  resinous 357 adj.
  be inactive 679 vb.
tarry for *expect* 507 vb.
tart *pastry* 301 n.
  pungent 388 adj.
  sweet 392 n.
  sour 393 adj.
  ungracious 885 adj.
  irascible 892 adj.
  sullen 893 adj.

prostitute 952 n.
tartan *chequer* 437 n.
  livery 547 n.
tartar *sourness* 393 n.
  dirt 649 n.
Tartar *destroyer* 168 n.
  shrew 892 n.
Tartar, catch a
  stultify oneself 695 vb.
Tartarean *dark* 418 adj.
  cruel 898 adj.
  infernal 972 adj.
tartuffish
  hypocritical 541 adj.
tarty *unchaste* 951 adj.
tasimeter *meter* 465 n.
task *finite quantity* 26 n.
  job 622 n.
  undertaking 672 n.
  deed 676 n.
  labour 682 n.
  fatigue 684 vb.
  hard task 700 n.
  oppress 735 vb.
  portion 783 n.
  duty 917 n.
  penalty 963 n.
task force
  armed force 722 n.
taskmaster *tyrant* 735 n.
tassel *pendant* 217 n.
  trimming 844 n.
taste *eat* 301 n.
  sense 374 n.
  pleasure 376 n.
  taste 386 n., vb.
  discrimination 463 n.
  elegance 575 n.
  choice 605 n.
  feeling 818 n.
  good taste 846 vb.
taste-buds *taste* 386 n.
tasteful *elegant* 575 adj.
  personable 841 adj.
  tasteful 846 adj.
taste good *appetize* 390 vb.
tasteless *weak* 163 adj.
  feeble 572 adj.
  inelegant 576 adj.
  vulgar 847 adj.
tastelessness
  insipidity 387 n.
  indiscrimination 464 n.
  bad taste 847 n.
tasty *edible* 301 adj.
  tasty 386 adj.
  pleasant 376 adj.
  savoury 390 adj.
  pleasurable 826 adj.
tatterdemalion *slut* 61 n.
  low fellow 869 n.

tattered *beggarly* 801 adj.
tatters *piece* 53 n.
  clothing 228 n.
tatters, in
  dilapidated 655 adj.
tatting *needlework* 844 n.
tattle *be loquacious* 581 vb.
  chat 584 n.
tattler *informer* 524 n.
  newsmonger 529 n.
  chatterer 581 n.
  interlocutor 584 n.
tattoo *pierce* 263 vb.
  roll 403 n., vb.
  play music 413 vb.
  colour 425 vb.
  variegate 437 vb.
  call 547 n.
  mark 547 vb.
  beautify 841 vb.
  pageant 875 n.
  celebration 876 n.
tattooer *beautician* 843 n.
tattooing
  ornamental art 844 n.
tatty *dilapidated* 655 adj.
  beggarly 801 adj.
tau *cross* 222 n.
taunt *be insolent* 878 vb.
  enrage 891 vb.
  indignity 921 n.
  reproach 924 n.
  calumny 926 n.
  accusation 928 n.
taurine *animal* 365 adj.
tauromachy *duel* 716 n.
Taurus *zodiac* 321 n.
taut *tied* 45 adj.
  rigid 326 adj.
tauten *tighten* 45 vb.
  make smaller 198 vb.
  harden 326 vb.
tautologize
  be diffuse 570 vb.
tautologous
  identical 13 adj.
tautology *repetition* 106 n.
  pleonasm 570 n.
  superfluity 637 n.
  redundance 637 n.
tavern *tavern* 192 n.
tawdry *trivial* 639 adj.
  vulgar 847 adj.
tawny *brown* 430 adj.
  red 431 adj.
  yellow 433 adj.
tax *bane* 659 n.
  fatigue 684 vb.
  oppress 735 vb.
  demand 737 n., vb.
  levy 786 vb.

tax 809 n., vb.
  impose a duty 917 vb.
taxable *priced* 809 adj.
taxation *tax* 809 n.
tax-collector
  receiver 782 n.
tax-farmer *receiver* 782 n.
  non-liable 919 adj.
taxi *move* 265 vb.
  drive 267 vb.
  fly 271 vb.
  cab 274 n.
taxidermy *zoology* 367 n.
taxi-driver *carrier* 273 n.
taximan *driver* 268 n.
tax on *dearness* 811 n.
taxonomy
  arrangement 62 n.
tax with *accuse* 928 vb.
tea *meal* 301 n.
  soft drink 301 n.
tea-caddy *small box* 194 n.
teach *break in* 369 vb.
  convince 485 vb.
  show 522 vb.
  inform 524 vb.
  educate 534 vb.
  habituate 610 vb.
teachable
  intelligible 516 adj.
  studious 536 adj.
  willing 597 adj.
teachableness
  persuasibility 612 n.
teacher *scholar* 492 n.
  sage 500 n.
  interpreter 520 n.
  teacher 537 n.
  adviser 691 n.
  expert 696 n.
teacher's pet
  favourite 890 n.
tea-chest *box* 194 n.
teaching *teaching* 534 n.
  preparation 669 n.
teach one his place
  humiliate 872 vb.
teacup *cup* 194 n.
tea-drinker
  sober person 948 n.
tea-garden *farm* 370 n.
teahouse *café* 192 n.
teak *hardness* 326 n.
  tree 366 n.
teal *waterfowl* 365 n.
tea leaves *oracle* 511 n.
team *group, band* 74 n.
  party 708 n.
team-captain
  director 690 n.

team-mate
  collaborator 707 n.
team-race
  co-operation 706 n.
  racing 716 n.
team spirit
  co-operation 706 n.
  concord 710 n.
teamster *driver* 268 n.
  leader 690 n.
team up with
  join a party 708 vb.
teamwork
  co-operation 706 n.
tea-party
  social gathering 882 n.
teapot *cauldron* 194 n.
teapoy *stand* 218 n.
tear *rend* 46 vb.
  be violent 176 vb.
  gap 201 n.
  blunt 257 vb.
  groove 262 vb.
  move fast 277 vb.
  ill-treat 645 vb.
  wound 655 vb.
  lamentation 836 n.
tearable *severable* 46 adj.
  flimsy 163 adj.
tear down *demolish* 165 vb.
  fell 311 vb.
tear-drop *moisture* 341 n.
  lamentation 836 n.
tearful *crying* 408 adj.
  unhappy 825 adj.
  melancholic 834 adj.
  lamenting 836 adj.
tear gas *poison* 659 n.
  weapon 723 n.
tear-jerking
  distressing 827 adj.
tearless *pitiless* 906 adj.
tea-room *café* 192 n.
tear out *extract* 304 vb.
tear strips off
  reprove 924 vb.
tear to pieces
  detract 926 vb.
tear up *demolish* 165 vb.
  abrogate 752 vb.
tease *tempt* 612 vb.
  excite 821 vb.
  delight 826 vb.
  torment 827 vb.
  be witty 839 vb.
  cause desire 859 vb.
  enrage 891 vb.
  be malevolent 898 vb.
teaser *enigma* 530 n.
  difficulty 700 n.
  worry 825 n.

humorist 839 n.
tea-set *cup* 194 n.
teashop *café* 192 n.
teaspoon *ladle* 194 n.
teat *bladder* 194 n.
  bosom 253 n.
tea-table *stand* 218 n.
technical *regular* 83 adj.
  trivial 639 adj.
  well-made 694 adj.
technical expression
  neology 560 n.
technicality
  unimportance 639 n.
  trifle 639 n.
  precept 693 n.
technical knowledge
  skill 694 n.
technical language
  speciality 80 n.
technical term
  neology 560 n.
  name 561 n.
technician *artisan* 686 n.
  expert 696 n.
technicology
  mechanics 630 n.
technique *way* 624 n.
  means 629 n.
  skill 694 n.
technocracy
  government 733 n.
technology *science* 490 n.
  mechanics 630 n.
  skill 694 n.
tectonic *structural* 331 adj.
tectonics *production* 164 n.
  structure 331 n.
Teddy-boy *youngster* 132 n.
  fop 848 n.
  low fellow 869 n.
  ruffian 904 n.
Te Deum *rejoicing* 835 n.
  celebration 876 n.
  thanks 907 n.
  hymn 981 n.
tedious *long* 203 adj.
  prolix 570 adj.
  feeble 572 adj.
  fatiguing 684 adj.
  tedious 838 adj.
  dull 840 adj.
tedium *tedium* 838 n.
  satiety 863 n.
  (*see* tedious)
teed up *prepared* 669 adj.
teem *be many* 104 vb.
  reproduce itself 164 vb.
  be fruitful 171 vb.
  abound 635 vb.
teen-age *youth* 130 n.

young 130 adj.
teen-ager *youngster* 132 n.
teeter *oscillate* 317 vb.
 be agitated 318 vb.
 be irresolute 601 vb.
teeth *vigorousness* 174 n.
 eater 301 n.
 pulverizer 332 n.
 weapon 723 n.
 nippers 778 n.
teething troubles
 beginning 68 n.
 youth 130 n.
 learning 536 n.
 difficulty 700 n.
teeth of, in the
 with difficulty 700 adv.
 in opposition 704 adv.
teetotal *temperate* 942 adj.
 sober 948 adj.
teetotalism
 temperance 942 n.
 sobriety 948 n.
teetotaller *abstainer* 942 n.
 sober person 948 n.
teetotum *rotator* 315 n.
 plaything 837 n.
tee up *make ready* 669 vb.
tegular *overlying* 226 adj.
tegument *skin* 226 n.
tegumentary *dermal* 226 adj.
teichopsia *dim sight* 440 n.
teinoscope
 optical device 442 n.
telamon *pillar* 218 n.
telautograph
 recording instrument
 549 n.
telearchics
 directorship 689 n.
telecast *publish* 528 vb.
telecommunication
 telecommunication 531 n.
telegnosis *psychics* 984 n.
telegony *genealogy* 169 n.
 influence 178 n.
telegram *information* 524 n.
 message 529 n.
telegraph *velocity* 277 n.
 communicate 524 vb.
 telecommunication 531 n.
 signal 547 n.
telegraph boy
 courier 531 n.
telegraphese
 conciseness 569 n.
telegraphic *speedy* 277 adj.
 concise 569 adj.
telekinesis
 spiritualism 984 n.
telemechanics

mechanics 630 n.
teleology *intention* 617 n.
telepath *psychic* 984 n.
telepathy *sense* 374 n.
 thought 449 n.
 intuition 476 n.
 psychics 984 n.
telephone
 hearing aid 415 n.
 communication 531 n.
telephoto lens
 camera 442 n.
 optical device 442 n.
teleplasm *spiritualism* 984 n.
teleprinter
 telecommunication 531 n.
 recording instrument
 549 n.
telergy *psychics* 984 n.
telescope *shorten* 204 vb.
 astronomy 321 n.
 telescope 442 n.
 detector 484 n.
 be concise 569 vb.
telescopic *distant* 199 adj.
 astronomic 321 adj.
 visible 443 adj.
telespectroscope
 optical device 442 n.
telesthesia *psychics* 984 n.
televiewer *spectator* 441 n.
 telecommunication 531 n.
televise
 communicate 524 vb.
 publish 528 vb.
television *spectacle* 445 n.
 telecommunication 531 n.
tell *number* 86 vb.
 influence 178 vb.
 monticle 209 n.
 inform 524 vb.
 divulge 526 vb.
 indicate 547 vb.
 describe 590 vb.
 be important 638 vb.
 be successful 727 vb.
 command 737 vb.
tell against
 tell against 467 vb.
tell another story
 tell against 467 vb.
teller *computer* 86 n.
 informant 524 n.
 treasurer 798 n.
tell fortunes *divine* 511 vb.
telling *influential* 178 adj.
 evidential 466 adj.
 expressive 516 adj.
 instrumental 628 adj.
 important 638 adj.
 impressive 821 adj.

tell of *evidence* 466 vb.
 mean 514 vb.
tell off *command* 737 vb.
 reprove 924 vb.
tell-tale *witness* 466 n.
 informer 524 n.
 disclosing 526 adj.
 indicating 547 adj.
 tergiversator 603 adj.
tellurian *native* 191 adj.
 telluric 321 adj.
 mankind 371 n.
 human 371 adj.
telluric *telluric* 321 adj.
telpher line *railroad* 624 n.
temenos *inclosure* 235 n.
 holy place 990 n.
temerarious *rash* 857 adj.
temerity *rashness* 857 n.
temper *temperament* 5 n.
 state 7 n.
 mix 43 vb.
 composition 56 n.
 strength 162 n.
 strengthen 162 vb.
 moderate 177 vb.
 hardness 326 n.
 harden 326 vb.
 soften 327 vb.
 be tough 329 vb.
 qualify 468 vb.
 mature 669 vb.
 affections 817 n.
 anger 891 n.
tempera *pigment* 425 n.
 art equipment 553 n.
temperament
 temperament 5 n.
 state 7 n.
 composition 56 n.
 caprice 604 n.
 affections 817 n.
 sensibility 819 n.
 excitability 822 n.
 irascibility 892 n.
 sullenness 893 n.
temperamental
 capricious 604 adj.
 lively 819 adj.
 excitable 822 adj.
temperance
 moderation 177 n.
 avoidance 620 n.
 restraint 747 n.
 virtues 933 n.
 temperance 942 n.
 asceticism 945 n.
temperate *moderate* 177 adj.
 warm 379 adj.
 cold 380 adj.
 restrained 747 adj.

sober 948 adj.
(*see* temperance)
temperature *heat* 379 n.
illness 651 n.
tempered *strong* 162 adj.
moderate 177 adj.
hard 326 adj.
tempest *storm* 176 n.
commotion 318 n.
tempestivity *occasion* 137 n.
tempestuous
disorderly 61 adj.
violent 176 adj.
speedy 277 adj.
windy 352 adj.
excitable 822 adj.
angry 891 adj.
Templars *monk* 986 n.
temple *laterality* 239 n.
temple 990 n.
temple state *polity* 733 n.
tempo *tendency* 179 n.
motion 265 n.
velocity 277 n.
tempo 410 n.
temporal *transient* 114 adj.
chronological 117 adj.
laical 987 adj.
temporality *property* 777 n.
benefice 985 n.
laicality 987 n.
temporary
ephemeral 114 adj.
substituted 150 adj.
uncertain 474 adj.
temporary accommodation
lending 784 n.
temporize
spin out 113 vb.
put off 136 vb.
temporizing
cunning 698 adj.
tempt *influence* 178 vb.
attract 291 vb.
tempt 612 vb.
cause desire 859 vb.
make wicked 934 vb.
temptation *attraction* 291 n.
inducement 612 n.
desired object 859 n.
tempter *motivator* 612 n.
Satan 969 n.
tempt fortune
gamble 618 vb.
tempting *savoury* 390 adj.
tempt providence
be rash 857 vb.
temptress
loose woman 952 n.
temulence
drunkenness 949 n.

tenable *credible* 485 adj.
rational 475 adj.
invulnerable 660 adj.
tenacious *cohesive* 48 adj.
tough 329 adj.
resolute 599 adj.
preserving 600 adj.
obstinate 602 adj.
tenacity *retention* 778 n.
(*see* tenacious)
tenaculum *nippers* 778 n.
tenancy *possession* 773 n.
tenant *resident* 191 n.
dwell 192 vb.
possessor 776 n.
tenantless *empty* 190 adj.
Ten Commandments
fixture 153 n.
precept 693 n.
code of duty 917 n.
law 953 n.
revelation 975 n.
tend *conduce* 156 vb.
tend 179 vb.
groom 369 vb.
look after 457 vb.
doctor 658 vb.
serve 742 vb.
tendency *ability* 160 n.
tendency 179 n.
direction 281 n.
probability 471 n.
bias 481 n.
willingness 597 n.
aptitude 694 n.
affections 817 n.
liking 859 n.
tendentious *tending* 179 adj.
intended 617 adj.
tender *ship* 275 n.
follower 284 n.
soft-hued 425 adj.
look after 457 vb.
careful 457 adj.
diseased 651 adj.
warship 722 n.
offer 759 n., vb.
honour 866 vb.
pet 889 vb.
pitying 905 adj.
respect 920 vb.
(*see* tenderness)
tender age *youth* 130 n.
tenderer *petitioner* 763 n.
tenderfoot *beginner* 538 n.
tenderize *soften* 327 vb.
tenderly *carefully* 457 adv.
tender mercies
severity 735 n.
tenderness *weakness* 163 n.
softness 327 n.

sensibility 374 n.
pain 377 n.
lenity 736 n.
moral sensibility 819 n.
painfulness 827 n.
love 887 n.
benevolence 897 n.
tender spot
vulnerability 661 n.
moral sensibility 819 n.
tending *liable* 180 adj.
possible 469 adj.
tendon *ligature* 47 n.
tendril *ligature* 47 n.
filament 208 n.
coil 251 n.
plant 366 n.
tenebrae
church service 988 n.
tenebrosity *darkness* 418 n.
tenement *housing* 192 n.
estate 777 n.
tenet *creed* 485 n.
precept 693 n.
tenfold *fifth and over* 99 adj.
tenné *orange* 436 adj.
heraldry 547 n.
tenner *funds* 797 n.
tennis *ball game* 837 n.
tennis court
horizontality 216 n.
pleasure-ground 837 n.
tennis player *player* 837 n.
tenor *modality* 7 n.
degree 27 n.
tendency 179 n.
direction 281 n.
vocalist 413 n.
meaning 514 n.
tense *time* 108 n.
rigid 326 adj.
expectant 507 adj.
grammar 564 n.
fervent 818 adj.
feeling 818 adj.
excited 821 adj.
excitable 822 adj.
tensile *elastic* 328 adj.
tension *energy* 160 n.
strength 162 n.
lengthening 203 n.
excitation 821 n.
worry 825 n.
discontent 829 n.
tent *dwelling* 192 n.
pavilion 192 n.
canopy 226 n.
hospital 658 n.
surgical dressing 658 n.
tentacle *nippers* 778 n.
tentative *slow* 278 adj.

enquiring 459 adj.
experimental 461 adj.
clumsy 695 adj.
cautious 858 adj.
tentativeness
empiricism 461 n.
tent-dweller *dweller* 191 n.
tenterhook *hanger* 217 n.
tenterhooks, on
expectant 507 adj.
tenuity *insubstantiality* 4 n.
smallness 33 n.
thinness 206 n.
rarity 325 n.
tenuous (*see* tenuity)
tenure *time* 108 n.
possession 773 n.
estate 777 n.
tepee *dwelling* 192 n.
tepefaction *heating* 381 n.
tepid *warm* 379 adj.
teraphim *home* 192 n.
idol 982 n.
teratical *unusual* 84 adj.
teratogenesis
abnormality 84 n.
propagation 164 n.
deformity 246 n.
teratology
magniloquence 574 n.
thaumaturgy 864 n.
boasting 877 n.
terce *morning* 128 n.
church service 988 n.
tergiversate
turn back 286 vb.
tergiversate 603 vb.
fail in duty 918 vb.
tergiversating
changeful 152 adj.
irresolute 601 adj.
tergiversation
change 143 n.
reversion 148 n.
unreliability 474 n.
tergiversation 603 n.
cowardice 856 n.
perfidy 930 n.
term *end* 69 n.
serial place 73 n.
date 108 n.
period 110 n.
limit 236 n.
word 559 n.
name 561 n., vb.
termagant
violent creature 176 n.
shrew 892 n.
terminal *extremity* 69 n.
ending 69 adj.
stopping place 145 n.

distant 199 adj.
limit 236 n.
goal 295 n.
terminate *terminate* 69 vb.
cease 145 vb.
termination *end* 69 n.
effect 157 n.
completion 725 n.
terminator *limit* 236 n.
terminology
etymology 559 n.
phrase 563 n.
nomenclature 561 n.
terminus *extremity* 69 n.
stopping place 145 n.
limit 236 n.
itinerary 267 n.
goal 295 n.
completion 725 n.
termite *vermin* 365 n.
termless *infinite* 107 adj.
term of art *neology* 560 n.
name 561 n.
terms *conditions* 766 n.
terms of reference
function 622 n.
ternary *treble* 94 adj.
ternion *three* 93 n.
terrace *housing* 192 n.
horizontality 216 n.
terracotta *pottery* 381 n.
terra firma *basis* 218 n.
goal 295 n.
land 344 n.
terrain *space* 183 n.
region 184 n.
land 344 n.
arena 724 n.
terrapin *reptile* 365 n.
terraqueous
telluric 321 adj.
terrarium *zoo* 369 n.
terrene *telluric* 321 adj.
territorial 344 adj.
terrestrial *native* 191 n.
telluric 321 adj.
terret *fastening* 47 n.
circle 250 n.
terrible *frightening* 854 adj.
terrier *list* 87 n.
dog 365 n.
terrific *prodigious* 32 adj.
excellent 644 adj.
terrify *frighten* 854 vb.
terrigenous *native* 191 adj.
territorial 344 adj.
territorial *regional* 184 adj.
territorial 344 adj.
soldier 722 n.
territory *territory* 184 n.
land 344 n.

polity 733 n.
lands 777 n.
terror
violent creature 176 n.
fear 854 n.
intimidation 854 n.
bane 659 n.
ruffian 904 n.
bad man 938 n.
terrorism *violence* 176 n.
sedition 738 n.
intimidation 854 n.
terrorist *opponent* 705 n.
revolter 738 n.
alarmist 854 n.
terrorize *dissuade* 613 vb.
oppress 735 vb.
frighten 854 vb.
terror tactics
terror tactics 712 n.
terse *short* 204 adj.
aphoristic 496 adj.
terseness *conciseness* 569 n.
tertian *seasonal* 141 adj.
tertiary *three* 93 adj.
secular 110 adj.
tertius gaudens
beneficiary 776 n.
terza rima *verse form* 593 n.
tessellation *chequer* 437 n.
tessera *label* 547 n.
test *exam.* 459 n.
enquire 459 vb.
experiment 461 n., vb.
essay 671 vb.
hard task 700 n.
testable
experimental 461 adj.
demonstrated 478 adj.
testament
testimony 466 n.
title-deed 767 n.
testamentary
proprietary 777 adj.
testamentary disposition
transfer 780 n.
testator *transferrer* 272 n.
giver 781 n.
test case *prototype* 23 n.
experiment 461 n.
litigation 959 n.
test-driver
experimenter 461 n.
tested *certain* 473 adj.
excellent 644 adj.
approved 923 adj.
trustworthy 929 adj.
testee *respondent* 460 n.
testee 461 n.
tester *bed* 218 n.
enquirer 459 n.

experimenter 461 n.
testicle genitalia 164 n.
testifier informant 524 n.
testify testify 466 vb.
　affirm 532 vb.
　indicate 547 vb.
testimonial credential 466 n.
　reminder 505 n.
　monument 548 n.
　approbation 923 n.
testimony testimony 466 n.
　affirmation 532 n.
testing agent
　testing agent 461 n.
test-pilot
　experimenter 461 n.
test-tube crucible 147 n.
　vessel 194 n.
　testing agent 461 n.
testudo armour 713 n.
testy ungracious 885 adj.
　irascible 892 adj.
tetanus spasm 318 n.
　infection 651 n.
tetchy irascible 892 adj.
tête-a-tête
　interlocution 584 n.
　social gathering 882 n.
tether tie 45 vb.
　halter 47 n.
　place 187 vb.
　obstacle 702 n.
　fetter 747 vb.
　fetter 748 n.
tetractys, tetrad
　quaternity 96 n.
tetragon
　angular figure 247 n.
Tetragrammaton
　the Deity 265 n.
tetralogy poem 593 n.
　stage play 594 n.
tetrameter prosody 593 n.
tetrarch potentate 741 n.
Teutonism dialect 560 n.
text prototype 23 n.
　piece 53 n.
　topic 452 n.
　maxim 496 n.
　meaning 514 n.
　reading matter 589 n.
　precept 693 n.
textbook classroom 539 n.
　reading matter 589 n.
　dissertation 591 n.
　compendium 592 n.
textile textile 222 n.
　texture 331 n.
　materials 631 n.
textual scriptural 975 adj.
　orthodox 976 adj.

textual criticism
　interpretation 520 n.
textualist theologian 973 n.
textural textural 331 adj.
texture texture 331 n.
　weaving 222 n.
　pattern 844 n.
thakur potentate 741 n.
　master 741 n.
　idol 982 n.
thalassic oceanic 343 adj.
thallophyte plant 366 n.
thane nobleman 868 n.
thank gratulate 886 vb.
　thank 907 vb.
　grant claims 915 vb.
　praise 923 vb.
　reward 962 vb.
thankful content 828 adj.
　grateful 907 adj.
　approving 923 adj.
thankfulness
　gratitude 907 n.
thankless profitless 641 adj.
　unpleasant 827 adj.
　unthanked 908 adj.
thanklessness
　ingratitude 908 n.
thank-offering
　offering 781 n.
　thanks 907 n.
　oblation 981 n.
thanksgiving
　rejoicing 835 n.
　celebration 876 n.
　thanks 907 n.
　act of worship 981 n.
thanks to hence 158 adv.
　in aid of 703 adv.
thatch roof 226 n.
　repair 656 vb.
thatcher mender 656 n.
　artisan 686 n.
thatness reality 1 n.
thaumatology
　thaumaturgy 864 n.
thaumatrope
　optical device 442 n.
thaumaturge
　prodigy 864 n.
thaumaturgic
　wonderful 864 adj.
　sorcerous 983 adj.
thaumaturgy
　thaumaturgy 864 n.
　sorcery 983 n.
thaw come unstuck 49 vb.
　liquefaction 337 n.
　liquefy 337 vb.
　marsh 347 n.
　semiliquidity 354 n.

be hot 379 vb.
　heat 381 vb.
thearchy government 733 n.
theatre region 184 n.
　meeting place 192 n.
　view 438 n.
　cinema 445 n.
　classroom 539 n.
　theatre 594 n.
　arena 724 n.
　place of amusement 837 n.
theatre-goer
　spectator 441 n.
　playgoer 594 n.
theatreland district 184 n.
theatre-minded
　dramatic 594 adj.
theatre sister nurse 658 n.
theatricality
　dramaturgy 594 n.
　acting 594 n.
　affectation 850 n.
　ostentation 875 n.
theatricals
　dramaturgy 594 n.
thé dansant dancing 837 n.
　social gathering 882 n.
theft acquisition 771 n.
　stealing 788 n.
theism deism 973 n.
　piety 979 n.
theist religionist 973 n.
thelytoky propagation 164 n.
' them ' master 741 n.
thematic interjacent 231 adj.
theme melody 410 n.
　musical piece 412 n.
　topic 452 n.
　dissertation 591 n.
thence hence 158 adv.
theocracy government 733 n.
　theocracy 965 n.
　churchdom 985 n.
theodicy theology 973 n.
theodolite
　angular measure 247 n.
　gauge 465 n.
theogony genealogy 169 n.
　god 966 n.
theolatry religion 973 n.
theologian reasoner 475 n.
　theologian 973 n.
theology theology 973 n.
theomancy
　theomancy 511 n.
theomorphic
　godlike 965 adj.
　theotechnic 966 adj.
theopathy piety 979 n.
theophany
　appearance 445 n.

[1233]

manifestation 522 n.
theophany 965 n.
revelation 975 n.
theophoric named 561 adj.
theopneustia
revelation 975 n.
theorbo harp 414 n.
theorem topic 452 n.
argumentation 475 n.
axiom 496 n.
supposition 512 n.
theoretical mental 447 adj.
suppositional 512 adj.
theorist theorist 512 n.
theorize account for 158 vb.
suppose 512 vb.
theory attribution 158 n.
idea 451 n.
opinion 485 n.
supposition 512 n.
theosophist occultist 984 n.
theosophy religion 973 n.
theosophy 984 n.
theotechny god 966 n.
Theotokos Madonna 968 n.
therapeutics
medical art 658 n.
therapy 658 n.
therapy therapy 658 n.
there in place 186 adv.
here 189 adv.
thereabouts about 33 adv.
nearly 200 adv.
thereafter, thereupon
subsequently 120 adv.
there and back
reversion 148 n.
therefore hence 158 adv.
therein inside 224 adv.
theriac antidote 658 n.
therianthropic
animal 365 adj.
theriomorphic
animal 365 adj.
idolatrous 982 adj.
theriomorphic deity
Egyptian gods 967 n.
therm thermometry 379 n.
thermæ heater 383 n.
ablution 648 n.
hygiene 652 n.
hospital 658 n.
thermantidote
ventilation 352 n.
thermod occultism 984 n.
thermodynamics
science of forces 162 n.
thermometry 379 n.
thermograph
thermometry 379 n.
thermology

thermometry 379 n.
thermometer
thermometry 379 n.
meter 465 n.
thermometry
thermometry 379 n.
thermonuclear
dynamic 160 adj.
thermonuclear fission
nucleonics 160 n.
thermopile
thermometry 379 n.
thermoplastic
flexible 327 adj.
thermoscope
thermometry 379 n.
thermos flask
preserver 666 n.
thermostat
thermometry 379 n.
thesaurus word list 87 n.
dictionary 559 n.
collection 632 n.
treasury 799 n.
thesis topic 452 n.
argument 475 n.
supposition 512 n.
dissertation 591 n.
prosody 593 n.
theurgy sorcery 983 n.
they group 74 n.
thick great 32 adj.
middle 70 n.
assembled 74 adj.
multitudinous 104 adj.
thick 205 adj.
dense 324 adj.
semiliquid 354 adj.
cloudy 355 adj.
dim 419 adj.
opaque 423 adj.
stammering 580 adj.
friendly 880 adj.
thick-coming
frequent 139 adj.
thicken grow 36 vb.
expand 197 vb.
be broad 205 vb.
be dense 324 vb.
thicken 354 vb.
make opaque 423 vb.
thickener
condensation 324 n.
thickening 354 n.
thicket wood 366 n.
thickhead dunce 501 n.
thick, in the midway 70 adv.
thickness quantity 26 n.
thickness 205 n.
layer 207 n.
density 324 n.

metrology 465 n.
(see thick)
thick of things
middle 70 n.
activity 678 n.
thick on the ground
multitudinous 104 adj.
thick-ribbed strong 162 adj.
thickset stalwart 162 adj.
short 204 adj.
thick 205 adj.
dense 324 adj.
thick-skinned
unfeeling 375 adj.
thick-skinned 820 adj.
thick speech
speech defect 580 n.
thick-witted
unintelligent 499 adj.
thief thief 789 n.
knave 938 n.
thieve steal 788 vb.
thievery
thievishness 788 n.
thigh leg 267 n.
thill tool 630 n.
thimble armour 713 n.
thimbleful
small quantity 33 n.
thimblerig sleight 542 n.
thimblerigger
trickster 545 n.
thin insubstantial 4 adj.
decrease 37 vb.
few 105 adj.
weaken 163 vb.
exiguous 196 adj.
make smaller 198 vb.
lean 206 adj.
shallow 212 adj.
hairless 229 adj.
rarefy 325 vb.
transparent 422 adj.
feeble 572 adj.
underfed 636 adj.
insufficient 636 adj.
fasting 946 adj.
thin air
insubstantial thing 4 n.
thin end of the wedge
start 68 n.
stratagem 698 n.
thing substance 3 n.
product 164 n.
object 319 n.
thing of the past
archaism 127 n.
things clothing 228 n.
thingummybob
no name 562 n.

thin ice, on
  endangered 661 adj.
think *think* 449 vb.
  opine 485 vb.
  suppose 512 vb.
  imagine 513 vb.
thinkable *possible* 469 adj.
think about
  meditate 449 vb.
think again
  tergiversate 603 vb.
  be penitent 939 vb.
think ahead *plan* 623 vb.
think alike
  co-operate 706 vb.
think aloud
  soliloquize 585 vb.
think back
  retrospect 505 vb.
think better of it
  tergiversate 603 vb.
  seek safety 660 vb.
  be nervous 854 vb.
thinker *philosopher* 449 n.
  enquirer 459 n.
  sage 500 n.
  theorist 512 n.
thinking *wise* 498 adj.
thinking-cap *thought* 449 n.
think nothing of
  be inattentive 456 vb.
  hold cheap 922 vb.
think of *initiate* 68 vb.
  be mindful 455 vb.
think twice
  be cautious 858 vb.
think up *produce* 164 vb.
  imagine 513 vb.
  plan 623 vb.
think well of
  respect 920 vb.
  approve 923 vb.
thinness *smallness* 33 n.
  thinness 206 n.
  levity 323 n.
  (*see* thin)
thinning *dieting* 301 n.
  hair-dressing 843 n.
thin on the ground
  few 105 adj.
thin out *be dispersed* 75 vb.
  extract 304 vb.
  cultivate 370 vb.
thin red line
  armed force 722 n.
thin-skinned
  sentient 374 adj.
  sensitive 819 adj.
  irascible 892 adj.
thin time, have a
  feel pain 377 vb.

suffer 825 vb.
third *treble* 94 adj.
  trisection 95 n.
  musical note 410 n.
third degree
  interrogation 459 n.
  police enquiry 459 n.
  corporal punishment
    963 n.
third estate
  commonalty 869 n.
thirst *be hot* 379 vb.
  dryness 342 n.
  desire, hunger 859 n.
thirsty *hot* 379 adj.
  dry 342 n.
  hungry 859 adj.
  drunken 949 adj.
Thirty-nine Articles
  theology 973 n.
  orthodoxy 976 n.
this or that
  no name 562 n.
  anonymous 562 adj.
thistle *prickle* 256 n.
  plant 366 n.
  heraldry 547 n.
thistledown *hair* 259 n.
  levity 323 n.
thither *towards* 281 adv.
thole-pin *pivot* 218 n.
Thomism
  philosophy 449 n.
  theology 973 n.
thong *ligature* 47 n.
  scourge 964 n.
thorax *bosom* 253 n.
thorn *prickle* 256 n.
  plant 366 n.
thorn in the flesh
  badness 645 n.
  bane 659 n.
  painfulness 827 n.
thorny *sharp* 256 adj.
  difficult 700 adj.
thorough
  consummate 32 adj.
  complete 54 adj.
  careful 457 adj.
  resolute 599 adj.
  labouring 682 adj.
  completive 725 adj.
thoroughbred
  unmixed 44 adj.
  thoroughbred 273 n.
  well-bred 848 adj.
  aristocrat 868 n.
thoroughfare
  open space 263 n.
  passing along 305 n.
  road 624 n.

thoroughgoing
  (*see* thorough)
thoroughness (*see* thorough)
though *in return* 31 adv.
thought
  small quantity 33 n.
  velocity 277 n.
  intellect 447 n.
  thought 449 n.
  idea 451 n.
  attention 455 n.
  opinion 485 n.
  supposition 512 n.
  worry 825 n.
thoughtful
  thoughtful 449 adj.
  attentive 455 adj.
  careful 457 adj.
  wise 498 adj.
  disinterested 931 adj.
thoughtless
  unthinking 450 adj.
  inattentive 456 adj.
  negligent 458 adj.
  unwise 499 adj.
  unprepared 670 adj.
  unskilful 695 adj.
  rash 857 adj.
thought-provoking
  topical 452 adj.
  suppositional 512 adj.
thought-reading
  psychics 984 n.
thousand and one
  many 104 adj.
thraldom *servitude* 745 n.
  detention 747 n.
thrall *slave* 742 n.
thrash *strike* 279 vb.
  defeat 727 vb.
  flog 963 vb.
thread *small thing* 33 n.
  connect 45 vb.
  cable 47 n.
  ligature 47 n.
  arrange 62 vb.
  series 71 n.
  continuate 71 vb.
  weak thing 163 n.
  line 203 n.
  narrowness 206 n.
  fibre 208 n.
  pass 305 vb.
threadbare *hairless* 229 adj.
  uncovered 229 adj.
  dirty 649 adj.
  beggarly 801 adj.
threat *intention* 617 n.
  danger 661 n.
  warning 664 n.
  defiance 711 n.

intimidation 854n.
insolence 878n.
threat 900n.
threaten be to come 124vb.
impend 155vb.
predict 511vb.
dissuade 613vb.
warn 664vb.
boast 877vb.
threaten 900vb.
three three 93n.
three-card trick
sleight 542n.
three cheers
rejoicing 835n.
three-dimensional
spatial 183adj.
formed 243adj.
metric 465adj.
threefold treble 94adj.
three-line whip
command 737n.
Three Musketeers
close friend 880n.
threepenny bit
coinage 797n.
three-point landing
air travel 271n.
three R's, the
curriculum 534n.
threesome three 93n.
thremmatology
animal husbandry 369n.
threnody vocal music 412n.
lament 836n.
thresh strike 279vb.
cultivate 370vb.
thresh about
be agitated 318vb.
thresher
husbandman 370n.
farm tool 370n.
threshold entrance 68n.
stand 218n.
threshold 234n.
limit 236n.
doorway 263n.
threshold, at the
nigh 200adv.
thrice trebly 94adv.
thrift gain 771n.
economy 814n.
thriftless prodigal 815adj.
rash 857adj.
thrifty careful 457adj.
economical 814adj.
thrill pang 377n.
itch 378vb.
feeling 818n.
excitation 821n.
excitable state 822n.

joy 824n.
please 826vb.
thriller novel 590n.
thrilling agitated 318adj.
thrill-loving
excitable 822adj.
thrill-seeker reveller 837n.
sensualist 944n.
thrive be vigorous 174vb.
flourish 615vb.
be active 678vb.
prosper 730vb.
throat orifice 263n.
conduit 351n.
air-pipe 353n.
throaty hoarse 407adj.
diseased 651adj.
throb be periodic 141vb.
oscillate 317vb.
spasm 318n.
give pain 377vb.
show feeling 818vb.
throe obstetrics 164n.
spasm 318n.
pang 377n.
throes violence 176n.
thrombophlebitis
blood pressure 651n.
thrombosis
solid body 324n.
blood 335n.
blood pressure 651n.
throne seat 218n.
regalia 743n.
tribunal 956n.
throne, on the
ruling 733adj.
throne-room
chamber 194n.
thrones angel 968n.
throng crowd 74n.
multitude 104n.
throng in irrupt 297vb.
throttle disable 161vb.
close 264vb.
retard 278vb.
through until now 121adv.
vehicular 274adj.
towards 281adv.
communicating 624adj.
through 628adv.
by means of 629adv.
throughout
throughout 54adv.
while 108adv.
widely 183adj.
throughput
production 164n.
transference 272n.
throughway road 624n.
through with, be

climax 725vb.
throw move 265vb.
impulse 279n.
propel 287vb.
gambling 618n.
exertion 682n.
throw a party
be hospitable 882vb.
throw away eject 300vb.
act 594vb.
reject 607vb.
waste 634vb.
disuse 674vb.
misuse 675vb.
be prodigal 815vb.
throw-back
recurrence 106n.
reversion 148n.
deterioration 655n.
relapse 657n.
throw back to
reproduce 166vb.
throw bricks
disapprove 924vb.
throw cold water
dissuade 613vb.
hinder 702vb.
deject 834vb.
throw down
demolish 165vb.
fell 311vb.
throw dust in the eyes
blind 439vb.
deceive 542vb.
thrower thrower 287n.
throw fits
be agitated 318vb.
be excitable 822vb.
throw-in propulsion 287n.
throw in one's hand
relinquish 621vb.
resign 753vb.
throw in one's teeth
defy 711vb.
accuse 928vb.
throw in the shade
humiliate 872vb.
throw light on
make bright 417vb.
interpret 520vb.
throw mud
disapprove 924vb.
defame 926vb.
thrown grounded 728adj.
throw off the mask
disclose 526vb.
throw off the scent
puzzle 474vb.
avoid 620vb.
throw off the yoke
revolt 738vb.

achieve liberty 746 vb.
throw one's weight about
be vigorous 174 vb.
throw open *open* 263 vb.
admit 299 vb.
manifest 522 vb.
throw out *eject* 300 vb.
throw-out *rubbish* 641 n.
throw over
tergiversate 603 vb.
relinquish 621 vb.
throw overboard
bate 37 vb.
eject 300 vb.
lighten 323 vb.
disuse 674 vb.
throw-stick
missile weapon 723 n.
throw stones
not respect 921 vb.
disapprove 924 vb.
throw up *eject* 300 vb.
vomit 300 vb.
elevate 310 vb.
submit 721 vb.
resign 753 vb.
thrum *filament* 208 n.
edging 234 n.
play music 413 vb.
thrummer
instrumentalist 413 n.
thrush *bird* 365 n.
vocalist 413 n.
animal disease 651 n.
thrust *energy* 160 n.
vigorousness 174 n.
influence 178 n.
distortion 246 n.
spurt 277 n.
impulse 279 n.
propellant 287 n.
foin 712 n.
thruster *busy person* 678 n.
thrustful *vigorous* 174 adj.
impelling 279 adj.
assertive 532 adj.
active 678 adj.
thrust in *interfere* 231 vb.
thud *sound faint* 401 vb.
non-resonance 405 n.
thug *murderer* 362 n.
robber 789 n.
ruffian 904 n.
bad man 938 n.
thuggee *homicide* 362 n.
stealing 788 n.
thumb-impression
trace 548 n.
thumb index
directory 87 n.
indication 547 n.

thumb-nail *small* 33 adj.
compendium 592 n.
thumbscrew *torture* 963 vb.
instrument of torture
964 n.
thumbs down
condemnation 961 n.
thumbs up
approbation 923 n.
acquittal 960 n.
thump *strike* 279 vb.
non-resonance 405 n.
thumper *whopper* 195 n.
thumping *whopping* 32 adj.
large 195 adj.
thunder *storm* 176 n.
loudness 400 n.
proclaim 528 vb.
emphasize 532 vb.
be angry 891 vb.
malediction 899 n.
threaten 900 vb.
thunderbolt
missile weapon 723 n.
thunderbox *vessel* 194 n.
latrine 649 n.
thunder-clap
loudness 400 n.
inexpectation 508 n.
thunderous *loud* 400 adj.
approving 923 adj.
thunderstorm
commotion 318 n.
gale 352 n.
thunderstruck
inexpectant 508 adj.
wondering 864 adj.
thurible *scent* 396 n.
ritual object 988 n.
thurifer *church officer* 986 n.
ritualist 988 n.
thurify *be fragrant* 396 vb.
perform ritual 988 vb.
thus *thus* 8 adv.
hence 158 adv.
thwack *strike* 279 vb.
thwart *oblique* 220 adj.
across 222 adv.
disappoint 509 vb.
be obstructive 702 vb.
oppose 704 vb.
adverse 731 adj.
incommode 827 vb.
thwarted *impotent* 161 adj.
disappointed 509 adj.
defeated 728 adj.
thyme *potherb* 301 n.
scent 396 n.
thyrotoxic *active* 678 adj.
thyrsus *badge of rule* 743 n.
tiara *headgear* 228 n.

regalia 743 n.
jewellery 844 n.
vestments 989 n.
tibia *leg* 267 n.
tic *spasm* 318 n.
paralysis 651 n.
tick *instant* 116 n.
animalcule 196 n.
oscillate 317 vb.
sound faint 401 vb.
roll 403 vb.
mark 547 vb.
credit 802 n.
ticker-tape
recording instrument
549 n.
ticket *list* 87 n.
opener 263 n.
ingress 297 n.
credential 466 n.
label 547 n.
electorate 605 n.
policy 623 n.
permit 756 n.
ticket-holder *incomer* 297 n.
ticket-of-leave man
prisoner 750 n.
offender 904 n.
tickle *strike* 279 vb.
itch 378 vb.
tempt 612 vb.
delight 826 vb.
amuse 837 vb.
endearment 889 n.
tickler *incentive* 612 n.
tickle the palm *bribe* 612 vb.
pay 804 vb.
ticklish *unreliable* 474 adj.
sentient 374 adj.
unsafe 661 adj.
difficult 700 adj.
tick off *number* 86 vb.
mark 547 vb.
register 548 vb.
reprove 924 vb.
tick over *operate* 173 vb.
move slowly 278 vb.
tick-tock *roll* 403 n.
tidal *periodical* 141 adj.
unstable 152 adj.
flowing 350 adj.
tidal wave *outbreak* 176 n.
wave 350 n.
tiddlywinks
indoor game 837 n.
tide *increase* 36 n.
time 108 n.
periodicity 141 n.
progression 285 n.
ocean 343 n.
current 350 n.

plenty 635n.
tide-mark *limit* 236n.
  gauge 465n.
  signpost 547n.
tide over *pass time* 108vb.
  put off 136vb.
  navigate 269vb.
  triumph 727vb.
tideway *current* 350n.
  conduit 361n.
tidiness *carefulness* 457n.
tidings *news* 529n.
tidy *orderly* 60adj.
  arrange 62vb.
  bag 194n.
  careful 457adj.
  clean 648adj.
tie *draw* 28n.
  be equal 28vb.
  tie 45vb.
  bond 47n.
  neckwear 228n.
  obstacle 702n.
  restrain 747vb.
  fetter 747vb.
  duty 917n.
tie-beam *bond* 47n.
  beam 218n.
tie down *compel* 740vb.
  give terms 766vb.
tie-pin *fastening* 47n.
  jewellery 844n.
tier *series* 71n.
  layer 207n.
tierce *morning* 128n.
  vat 194n.
ties of blood
  consanguinity 11n.
tie up with *connect* 45vb.
tie-up *relation* 9n.
  association 706n.
tiff *bicker* 709vb.
tiffin *meal* 301n.
tigella *foliage* 366n.
tiger *violent creature* 176n.
  cat 365n.
  striation 437n.
  domestic 742n.
  brave person 855n.
  noxious animal 904n.
tigerish *furious* 176adj.
  cruel 898adj.
tight *adjusted* 24adj.
  firm-set 45adj.
  cohesive 48adj.
  full 54adj.
  sealed off 264adj.
  rigid 326adj.
  dry 342adj.
  invulnerable 660adj.
  prepared 669adj.

retentive 778adj.
parsimonious 816adj.
tipsy 949adj.
tight corner
  predicament 700n.
tight-drawn *narrow* 206adj.
tighten *tighten* 45vb.
  make smaller 198vb.
  close 264vb.
  harden 326vb.
  restrain 747vb.
tightener *compressor* 198n.
tight-fisted
  parsimonious 816adj.
tight-lipped *reticent* 525adj.
  taciturn 582adj.
tight-rope walker
  equilibrium 28n.
tight-rope walking
  skill 694n.
tights *coherence* 48n.
  legwear 228n.
tightwad *niggard* 816n.
tigroid *animal* 365n.
tilde *punctuation* 547n.
tile *lamina* 207n.
  roof 226n.
  headgear 228n.
  pottery 381n.
  variegate 437vb.
  building material 631n.
  plaything 837n.
till *while* 108adv.
  box 194n.
  cultivate 370vb.
  storage 632n.
  treasury 799n.
tillage *agriculture* 370n.
  maturation 669n.
tiller *handle* 218n.
  sailing aid 269n.
  husbandman 370n.
  directorship 689n.
tilt *obliquity* 220n.
  be inverted 221vb.
  canopy 226n.
  descent 309n.
  attack 712n.
  contest, duel 716n.
tilt at *pursue* 619vb.
  charge 712vb.
  dispraise 924vb.
tilter *combatant* 722n.
tilth *agriculture* 370n.
tilt-yard *arena* 724n.
timber *wood* 366n.
  materials 631n.
timbre *sound* 398n.
  voice 577n.
timbrel *drum* 414n.
time *finality* 69n.

time 108n.
era 110n.
time 117vb.
tempo 410n.
time after time
  repeatedly 106adv.
time, all the
  while 108adv.
time, a long
  diuturnity 113n.
time and motion study
  economy 814n.
time and place
  situation 186n.
time being
  present time 121n.
time-bound
  transient 114adj.
time-chart *chronology* 117n.
timed *adjusted* 24adj.
  synchronous 123adj.
time-fuse *timekeeper* 117n.
time-honoured
  immemorial 127adj.
  worshipful 866adj.
  respected 920adj.
time, in *in time* 111adv.
  concurrently 123adv.
  early 135adj.
  betimes 135adv.
  timely 137adj.
  in the future 155adv.
timekeeper
  timekeeper 117n.
  meter 465n.
  recording instrument
  549n.
timeless *perpetual* 115adj.
  godlike 965adj.
timelessness
  neverness 109n.
time limit *limit* 236n.
  conditions 766n.
timely *apt* 24adj.
  chronological 117adj.
  early 135adj.
  timely 137adj.
  expedient 642adj.
time of day *period* 110n.
  clock time 117n.
time off *lull* 145n.
  leisure 681n.
time of, in the
  when 108adv.
time of life *date* 108n.
  age 131n.
timeous *timely* 137adj.
timepiece *timekeeper* 117n.
time-saving
  economy 814n.
timescale *gauge* 465n.

time-server
tergiversator 603 n.
egotist 932 n.
time-serving
tergiversating 603 adj.
expedience 642 n.
cunning 698 adj.
servility 879 n.
perfidious 930 adj.
rascally 930 adj.
selfish 932 adj.
time's forelock
opportunity 137 n.
time-signal
timekeeper 117 n.
signal 547 n.
times, the
present time 121 n.
time-switch
timekeeper 117 n.
meter 465 n.
timetable *directory* 87 n.
chronology 117 n.
itinerary 267 n.
guide-book 524 n.
reference book 589 n.
time up *finality* 69 n.
time was *formerly* 125 adv.
retrospectively 125 adv.
time-wasting
protracted 113 adj.
timid *irresolute* 601 adj.
nervous 854 adj.
cowardly 856 adj.
cautious 858 adj.
modest 874 adj.
timidity, timidiness
(*see* timid)
timing *chronometry* 117 n.
periodicity 141 n.
tempo 410 n.
discrimination 463 n.
timocracy *rich man* 800 n.
(*see* government)
timorous *nervous* 854 adj.
cowardly 856 adj.
timpani *drum* 414 n.
timpanist
instrumentalist 413 n.
tin *small box* 194 n.
preserve 666 vb.
dibs 797 n.
tinct *colour* 425 vb.
tincture
small quantity 33 n.
tincture 43 n.
colour 425 n.
tinder *lighter* 385 n.
tine *sharp point* 256 n.
tinge *small quantity* 33 n.
tincture 43 n.

mix 43 vb.
hue 425 n.
qualification 468 n.
tingle *feel pain* 377 vb.
formication 378 n.
feel 818 vb.
be excited 821 vb.
tin god *autocrat* 741 n.
tin hat *armour* 713 n.
tinker *waste effort* 641 vb.
impair 655 vb.
mender 656 n.
repair 656 vb.
meddle 678 vb.
artisan 686 n.
be unskilful 695 n.
bungler 697 n.
be cunning 698 vb.
not complete 726 vb.
tinkering *insufficiency* 636 n.
tinker's curse *trifle* 639 n.
tinkle
sound faint 401 vb.
resonance 404 n.
tinkling cymbal
resonance 404 n.
unmeaningness 515 n.
tinned *preserved* 666 adj.
tinnitus *roll* 403 n.
resonance 404 n.
tinny *strident* 407 adj.
tin-opener *opener* 263 n.
tin-pan alley *music* 412 n.
tinsel *flash* 417 n.
sham 542 n.
inelegance 576 n.
bauble 639 n.
finery 844 n.
bad taste 847 n.
ostentation 875 n.
tint *hue* 425 n.
paint 553 vb.
tintack *fastening* 47 n.
tinting *hairwash* 843 n.
tintinnabulation
resonance 404 n.
gong 414 n.
tintometer
chromatics 425 n.
tin whistle *flute* 414 n.
tiny *small* 33 adj.
child 132 n.
little 196 adj.
tip *extra* 40 n.
prepose 64 vb.
extremity 69 n.
vertex 213 n.
obliquity 220 n.
invert 221 vb.
cover 226 vb.
edge 234 n.

depress 311 vb.
hint 524 n.
bribe 612 vb.
advice 691 n.
thank 907 vb.
reward 962 n., vb.
tip-and-run *escaped* 667 adj.
tip-off *hint* 524 n.
tip of one's tongue, have on the
forget 506 vb.
tipper *giver* 781 n.
tippet *pendant* 217 n.
cloak 228 n.
vestments 989 n.
tipple *drink* 301 vb.
get drunk 949 vb.
tipstaff *law officer* 955 n.
tipster *diviner* 511 n.
informant 524 n.
gambler 618 n.
tipsy *oblique* 220 adj.
tipsy 949 adj.
tip the scale
be unequal 29 vb.
predominate 34 vb.
weigh 322 vb.
tip the wink *hint* 524 vb.
command 737 vb.
permit 756 vb.
tiptilted *curved* 248 adj.
tiptoe *atop* 213 adv.
be stealthy 525 vb.
tip-top *supreme* 34 adj.
topmost 213 adj.
best 644 adj.
tirade *exaggeration* 546 n.
diffuseness 570 n.
oration 579 n.
censure 924 n.
tire *dress* 228 vb.
outline 233 n.
edge 234 n.
fatigue 684 vb.
incommode 827 vb.
be tedious 838 vb.
tired *sleepy* 679 adj.
tireless *unyielding* 162 adj.
industrious 678 adj.
active 678 adj.
tirelessness
perseverance 600 n.
tiresome *fatiguing* 684 adj.
annoying 827 adj.
tedious 838 adj.
tirewoman *clothier* 228 n.
tisane *tonic* 658 n.
tissue *textile* 222 n.
texture 331 n.
life 360 n.
cleaning cloth 648 n.

tissue-paper
  weak thing 163 n.
  thinness 206 n.
  paper 631 n.
tit *animalcule* 196 n.
  saddle-horse 273 n.
  pony 273 n.
  bird 365 n.
Titan *athlete* 162 n.
  sun 321 n.
  satellite 321 n.
  classical gods 967 n.
titanic *stalwart* 162 adj.
  huge 195 adj.
titbit *mouthful* 301 n.
  news 529 n.
  savouriness 390 n.
  élite 644 n.
  pleasurableness 826 n.
tit for tat
  equalization 28 n.
  interchange 151 n.
  retaliation 714 n.
tithe *part* 53 n.
  trifle 639 n.
  tax 809 n.
  benefice 985 n.
tithing *district* 184 n.
titillate *itch* 378 vb.
  delight 826 vb.
  amuse 837 vb.
  cause desire 859 vb.
titivate *make better* 654 vb.
  beautify 841 vb.
  decorate 844 vb.
title *label* 547
  name 561 n., vb.
  book 589 n.
  decoration 729 n.
  estate 777 n.
  honours 866 n.
  title 870 n.
  dueness 915 n.
titled *named* 561 adj.
  worshipful 866 adj.
  noble 868 adj.
title-deed *title-deed* 767 n.
  dueness 915 n.
title-holder *exceller* 644 n.
titleless *inglorious* 867 adj.
  plebeian 869 adj.
title-page *beginning* 68 n.
  edition 589 n.
Titoism *unconformity* 84 n.
titter *laughter* 835 n.
tittle *small quantity* 33 n.
  trifle 639 n.
tittle-tattle *rumour* 529 n.
  chatter 581 n.
  chat 584 n.
tittup *ride* 267 vb.

titubancy
  drunkenness 949 n.
titubation *descent* 309 n.
titular *verbal* 559 adj.
  named 561 adj.
tmesis *inversion* 221 n.
toad *frog* 365 n.
  eyesore 842 n.
  toady 879 n.
toadstool *plant* 366 n.
toady *toady* 879 n.
  be servile 879 vb.
toady to *flatter* 925 vb.
to a man *generally* 79 adv.
to and fro *by turns* 141 adv.
  in exchange 151 adv.
  to and fro 317 adv.
to-and-fro movement
  periodicity 141 n.
toast *cereal, potion* 301 n.
  drink 301 vb.
  heat 381 vb.
  a beauty 841 n.
  toast 876 vb.
  congratulation 886 n.
  favourite 890 n.
  show respect 920 vb.
  applaud 923 vb.
toasted *brown* 430 adj.
toaster *heater* 383 n.
toast-master
  nomenclator 561 n.
  reveller 883 n.
to a T *truly* 494 adv.
tobacco *tobacco* 388 n.
tobacconist *tobacco* 388 n.
tobacco-pipe
  tobacco 388 n.
  air-pipe 353 n.
to be *future* 124 adj.
toboggan *sled* 274 n.
  descend 309 vb.
to boot
  in addition 38 adv.
Toby-jug *vessel* 194 n.
toccata, toccatina
  musical piece 412 n.
to come *future* 124 adj.
  impending 155 adj.
tocsin *gong* 414 n.
  danger signal 665 n.
today *present time* 121 n.
toddle *be in motion* 265 vb.
  walk 267 vb.
  move slowly 278 vb.
toddler *child* 132 n.
  pedestrian 268 n.
toddy *liquor* 301 n.
toddy-shop *tavern* 192 n.
to-do *turmoil* 61 n.
  activity 678 n.

toe *extremity* 69 n.
  base, foot 214 n.
toe in *converge* 293 vb.
toe-nail *foot* 214 n.
toes, on one's
  actively 678 adv.
toe the line *conform* 83 vb.
  acquiesce 488 vb.
  obey 739 vb.
toff *fop* 848 n.
toffee *coherence* 48 n.
  sweetmeat 301 n.
  sweet 392 n.
toft *home* 192 n.
toga *tunic* 228 n.
  badge of rule 743 n.
toga virilis *adultness* 134 n.
together *in addition* 38 adv.
  together 74 adv.
  with 89 adv.
toggery, togs
  clothing 228 n.
  finery 844 n.
toggle pin *fastening* 47 n.
toil *labour* 682 n.
toil and trouble
  exertion 682 n.
toiler *worker* 686 n.
toilet *dressing* 228 n.
  latrine 649 n.
  beautification 843 n.
toiletry *cosmetic* 843 n.
toilette *dressing* 228 n.
toilsome *laborious* 682 adj.
  difficult 700 adj.
toilworn *fatigued* 684 adj.
token
  insubstantial thing 4 n.
  reminder 505 n.
  indication 547 n.
  badge 547 n.
  trivial 639 adj.
  security 767 n.
  gift 781 n.
tolbooth *mart* 796 n.
tolerable
  inconsiderable 33 adj.
  not bad 644 adj.
  imperfect 647 adj.
  mediocre 732 adj.
  contenting 828 adj.
tolerance *strength* 162 n.
  limit 236 n.
  wisdom 498 n.
  permission 756 n.
  patience 823 n.
  benevolence 897 n.
tolerant (*see* tolerance,
    toleration)
tolerate *acquiesce* 488 vb.
  not act 677 vb.

consent 758 vb.
forgive 909 vb.
(see toleration)
tolerated house
brothel 951 n.
toleration laxity 734 n.
lenity 736 n.
permission 756 n.
patience 823 n.
to let offering 759 adj.
toll addition 38 n.
roll 403 vb.
play music 413 vb.
raise the alarm 665 vb.
levy 786 vb.
tax 809 n.
toll the knell inter 364 vb.
lament 836 vb.
tomahawk
sharp edge 256 n.
axe 723 n.
tomato vegetable 301 n.
tomb resting place 266 n.
tomb 364 n.
concealment 525 n.
monument 548 n.
tombola chance 159 n.
gambling 618 n.
tomboy youngster 132 n.
tombstone obsequies 364 n.
Tom, Dick and Harry
everyman 79 n.
commonalty 869 n.
tome book 589 n.
tomentous downy 259 adj.
tomfoolery wit 839 n.
foolery 497 n.
ostentation 875 n.
tommyrot silly talk 515 n.
tomorrow futurity 124 n.
Tom Thumb dwarf 196 n.
Tom Tiddler's ground
territory 184 n.
tom-tom drum 414 n.
ton weighment 322 n.
fashion 848 n.
tonal harmonic 410 adj.
linguistic 557 adj.
vocal 577 adj.
tonality melody 410 n.
musical note 410 n.
light contrast 417 n.
tone strength 162 n.
tendency 179 n.
sound 398 n.
musical note 410 n.
hue 425 n.
painting 553 n.
style 566 n.
voice 577 n.
speech 579 n.

conduct 688 n.
affections 817 n.
tone-deaf deaf 416 adj.
indiscriminating 464 adj.
artless 699 adj.
tone down moderate 177 vb.
darken 418 vb.
decolorize 426 vb.
misrepresent 552 vb.
tone in with accord 24 vb.
toneless discordant 411 adj.
colourless 426 adj.
tone up make better 654 vb.
toney fashionable 848 adj.
tonga carriage 274 n.
tongs furnace 383 n.
nippers 778 n.
hair-dressing 843 n.
tongue projection 254 n.
feeler 378 n.
taste 386 n.
language 557 n.
voice 577 n.
speech 579 n.
exprobate 927 vb.
tongue in cheek
falsehood 541 n.
deception 542 n.
mental dishonesty 543 n.
tongue-in-cheek
affected 850 adj.
flattering 925 adj.
tongue-lashing
reprimand 924 n.
tongueless voiceless 578 adj.
silent 399 adj.
tongue-scraper
cleaning utensil 648 n.
tongue-tied
voiceless 578 adj.
stammering 580 adj.
taciturn 582 adj.
tongue-wagging
loquacious 581 adj.
tonic stimulant 174 n.
musical note 410 n.
incentive 612 n.
salubrious 652 adj.
tonic 658 n.
remedial 658 adj.
excitant 821 n.
cheering 833 adj.
tonic accent
pronunciation 577 n.
tonic effect
strengthening 162 n.
stimulation 174 n.
tonic solfa notation 410 n.
tonnage size 195 n.
tonnage and poundage
tax 809 n.

tonsilitis
respiratory disease 651 n.
tonsure bareness 229 n.
ecclesiasticize 985 vb.
canonicals 989 n.
tonsured monastic 986 adj.
tontine gambling 618 n.
receipt 807 n.
too in addition 38 adv.
tool dupe 544 n.
fatalist 596 n.
contrivance 623 n.
instrument 628 n.
means 629 n.
tool 630 n.
agent 686 n.
decorate 844 vb.
toady 879 n.
tooling bookbinding 589 n.
tool of, make a use 673 vb.
tool-using
mechanical 630 adj.
too much great quantity 32 n.
redundance 637 n.
redundantly 637 adv.
tedious 838 adj.
satiety 863 n.
intemperance 743 n.
too much for, be
be superior 34 vb.
to order specially 80 adv.
toot, tootle loudness 400 n.
resound 404 vb.
play music 413 n.
danger signal 665 n.
tooth notch 260 n.
tooth 256 n.
tooth and nail
violently 176 adv.
laboriously 682 adv.
toothbrush hair 259 n.
cleaning utensil 648 n.
tooth-drawer doctor 658 n.
tooth for a tooth
interchange 151 n.
revenge 910 n.
toothiness
roughness 259 n.
toothless aged 131 adj.
unsharpened 257 adj.
toothpaste cleanser 648 n.
prophylactic 658 n.
toothpick extractor 304 n.
cleaning utensil 648 n.
toothsome savoury 390 adj.
toothy toothed 256 adj.
top superiority 34 n.
fill 54 vb.
prepose 64 vb.
extremity 69 n.
summit 213 n.

covering 226 n.
limit 236 vb.
stopper 264 n.
climb 308 vb.
rotator 315 n.
bubble 355 n.
perfection 646 n.
completion 724 n.
plaything 837 n.
top and lop
cultivate 370 vb.
topaz yellowness 433 n.
gem 844 n.
top drawer élite 644 n.
top-drawer genteel 868 adj.
top-dress
make fruitful 171 vb.
overlay 226 vb.
tope drink 301 vb.
wood 366 n.
get drunk 949 vb.
temple 990 n.
toper drunkard 949 n.
top-flight notable 638 adj.
top-hamper inequality 29 n.
vertex 213 n.
top-heavy unequal 29 adj.
inverted 221 adj.
unsafe 661 adj.
clumsy 695 adj.
Tophet hell 972 n.
top-hole topping 644 adj.
tophus solid body 324 n.
topiarism
ornamental art 844 n.
topiarist gardener 370 n.
topiary horticultural 370 adj.
ornamental 844 adj.
topic topic 452 n.
supposition 512 n.
meaning 514 n.
topical present 121 adj.
modern 126 adj.
situated 186 adj.
topical 452 adj.
topicality
present time 121 n.
modernism 126 n.
topknot hair 259 n.
top-level superior 34 adj.
directing 689 adj.
top-liner favourite 890 n.
topmast
high structure 209 n.
vertex 213 n.
topmost supreme 34 adj.
high 209 adj.
topmost 213 adj.
top-notch topping 644 adj.
topographer surveyor 465 n.
topography situation 186 n.

guide-book 524 n.
top, on superior 34 adj.
aloft 209 adv.
atop 213 adv.
successful 727 adj.
toponymy
nomenclature 561 n.
top people superior 34 n.
bigwig 638 n.
élite 644 n.
topper headgear 228 n.
topping topping 644 adj.
topple down tumble 309 vb.
topple over
be inverted 221 vb.
top-rank notable 638 adj.
top-sawyer superior 34 n.
proficient 696 n.
top-secret
concealed 525 adj.
important 638 adj.
topside vertex 213 n.
topsoil soil 344 n.
tops, the exceller 644 n.
favourite 890 n.
good man 937 n.
topsy-turvy
contrarily 14 adv.
orderless 61 adj.
inverted 221 adj.
top to toe longwise 203 adv.
top up fill 54 vb.
store 632 vb.
replenish 633 vb.
toque headgear 228 n.
tor high land 209 n.
Torah scripture 975 n.
torch lamp, torch 420 n.
lighter 385 n.
torch-bearer torch 420 n.
preparer 669 n.
director 690 n.
toreador killer 362 n.
combatant 722 n.
toreutic glyptic 554 adj.
toreutics
ornamental art 844 n.
torii church exterior 990 n.
torment pain 377 n.
harm 645 vb.
bane 659 n.
oppress 735 vb.
suffering 825 n.
torment 827 vb.
enrage 891 vb.
torture 963 vb.
tormentor stage set 594 n.
torn disjunct 46 adj.
tornado turmoil 61 n.
vortex 315 n.
gale 352 n.

torpedo suppress 165 vb.
destroyer 168 n.
fish 365 n.
fire at 712 vb.
bomb 723 n.
torpedo-boat
warship 722 n.
torpescence
sluggishness 679 n.
torpid inert 175 adj.
inactive 679 adj.
apathetic 820 adj.
inexcitable 823 adj.
torpids racing 716 n.
torpor helplessness 161 n.
weakness 163 n.
(see torpid)
torque loop 250 n.
jewellery 844 n.
torrefy heat 381 vb.
torrent velocity 277 n.
stream 350 n.
torrential violent 176 adj.
torrid hot, warm 379 adj.
torse heraldry 547 n.
torsion convolution 251 n.
torso chief part 52 n.
piece 53 n.
incompleteness 55 n.
image 551 n.
sculpture 554 n.
tort wrong 914 n.
guilty act 936 n.
lawbreaking 954 n.
tortfeasor offender 904 n.
tortility convolution 251 n.
tortious wrong 914 adj.
illegal 954 adj.
tortoise slowcoach 278 n.
reptile 365 n.
armour 713 n.
tortoise-shell
covering 226 n.
variegation 437 n.
tortuous convoluted 251 adj.
sophistical 477 adj.
dishonest 930 adj.
torture violence 176 n.
distort 246 vb.
give pain 377 vb.
interrogate 459 vb.
ill-treat 645 vb.
oppress 735 vb.
compel 740 vb.
suffering 825 n.
torment 827 vb.
make ugly 842 vb.
cruel act 898 n.
corporal punishment
963 n.
torture 963 vb.

torture-chamber
  lock-up 748 n.
tortured *figurative* 519 adj.
torturer *punisher* 963 n.
torus *swelling* 253 n.
torvosity *sullenness* 893 n.
Tory *sectional* 708 adj.
tosh *silly talk* 515 n.
to spare *superfluous* 637 adj.
toss *jumble* 63 vb.
  propel 287 vb.
  oscillate 317 vb.
  agitation 318 n.
toss about
  be agitated 318 vb.
tossing *seafaring* 269 adj.
toss one's head
  be proud 871 vb.
  despise 922 vb.
toss up *chance* 159 n.
  elevate 310 vb.
  uncertainty 474 n.
tot *potion* 301 n.
  pungency 388 n.
  acquire 771 vb.
  take 786 vb.
  steal 788 vb.
total *quantity* 26 n.
  addition 38 n.
  all 52 n.
  complete 54 adj.
  inclusive 78 adj.
  numerical result 85 n.
  number 86 vb.
total abstainer
  abstainer 942 n.
  sober person 948 n.
totalisator
  counting instrument 86 n.
  gaming-house 618 n.
totalitarianism
  despotism 733 n.
  brute force 735 n.
totality *whole* 52 n.
  completeness 54 n.
total situation
  circumstance 8 n.
tote
  counting instrument 86 n.
  carry 273 vb.
  gaming house 618 n.
totem *idol* 982 n.
totem group *race* 11 n.
totemist *idolater* 982 n.
to the eye
  apparently 445 adv.
to the point
  important 638 adj.
to the quick
  to the quick 374 adv.
totient

numerical element 85 n.
totter *come unstuck* 49 vb.
  be weak 163 vb.
  move slowly 278 vb.
  tumble 309 vb.
  oscillate 317 vb.
  be agitated 318 vb.
tottering *unstable* 152 adj.
  weak 163 adj.
  deteriorated 655 adj.
  unsafe 661 adj.
tottings *booty* 790 n.
tot up to *number* 86 vb.
touch *derange* 63 vb.
  be related 9 vb.
  be equal 28 vb.
  small quantity 33 n.
  tincture 43 n.
  operate 173 vb.
  be situate 186 vb.
  be contiguous 202 vb.
  limit 236 n.
  softness 327 n.
  texture 331 n.
  touch 378 n., vb.
  campanology 412 n.
  musical skill 413 n.
  empiricism 461 n.
  discrimination 463 n.
  gesture 547 n.
  use 673 vb.
  meddle 678 vb.
  skill 694 n.
  borrow 785 vb.
  feeling 818 n.
  excite 821 vb.
touchable *tactual* 378 adj.
touch and go
  unstable 152 adj.
  unreliable 474 adj.
  unsafe 661 adj.
touch depth
  be inferior 35 vb.
  be deep 211 vb.
touch-down *air travel* 271 n.
  arrival 295 n.
  descend 309 vb.
touched *crazed* 503 adj.
  impressed 818 adj.
touched up *false* 541 adj.
touch-hole *orifice* 263 n.
  burning 381 n.
  furnace 383 n.
touching *distressing* 827 adj.
touch-line *limit* 236 n.
touch off *initiate* 68 vb.
  kindle 381 vb.
touch on *relate* 9 vb.
  notice 455 vb.
touch-paper *burning* 381 n.
touchstone

testing agent 461 n.
touch up *colour* 425 vb.
  paint 553 vb.
  make better 654 vb.
  repair 656 vb.
touchwood *lighter* 385 n.
touchy *sensitive* 819 adj.
  irascible 892 adj.
tough *strong* 162 adj.
  violent creature 176 n.
  hard 326 adj.
  tough 329 adj.
  unsavoury 391 adj.
  uncooked 670 adj.
  difficult 700 adj.
  thick-skinned 820 adj.
  courageous 855 adj.
  unkind 898 adj.
  ruffian 904 n.
  pitiless 906 adj.
toughen *be tough* 329 vb.
  make insensitive 820 vb.
toughness *obstinacy* 602 n.
  (*see* tough)
toupee *wig* 228 n.
  hair 259 n.
tour *travel* 267 vb.
  circuition 314 n.
tour de force *deed* 676 n.
  masterpiece 694 n.
tourer *automobile* 274 n.
tourism *land travel* 267 adj.
  sport 837 n.
tourist *traveller* 268 n.
  spectator 441 n.
  reveller 837 n.
tourist-class *cheap* 812 adj.
tourmaline *gem* 844 n.
tournament, tourney
  contest, duel 716 n.
  pageant 875 n.
tourniquet *ligature* 47 n.
  compressor 198 n.
  stopper 264 n.
  surgical dressing 658 n.
tournure *skirt* 228 n.
  outline 233 n.
tousle *jumble* 63 vb.
  roughen 259 vb.
tousled *orderless* 61 adj.
  unsightly 842 adj.
tout *request* 761 vb.
  petitioner 763 n.
  seller 793 n.
  commender 923 n.
tout ensemble *all* 52 n.
tovarich *title* 870 n.
tow *fibre* 208 n.
  navigate 269 vb.
  traction 288 n.
towardly *wieldy* 701 adj.

towards *towards* 281 adv.
towel *drier* 342 n.
  cleaning cloth 648 n.
towelling *textile* 222 n.
tower *be great* 32 vb.
  edifice 164 n.
  house 192 n.
  be large 195 vb.
  high structure 209 n.
  be high 209 vb.
  ascend 308 vb.
  refuge 662 n.
  fort 713 n.
  prison 748 n.
  church exterior 990 n.
towering *high* 209 adj.
tower of silence
  cemetery 364 n.
  tomb 364 n.
tower of strength
  athlete 162 n.
  influence 178 n.
  protection 660 n.
  refuge 662 n.
tower over
  be superior 34 vb.
  influence 178 vb.
tow-headed *whitish* 427 adj.
to wit *namely* 80 adv.
tow-line, tow-rope
  cable 47 n.
  traction 288 n.
town *district* 184 n.
  abode, housing 192 n.
  beau monde 848 n.
town-crier
  megaphone 400 n.
  cry 408 n.
  publicizer 528 n.
town-dweller *dweller* 191 n.
townee, townsman
  native 191 n.
town hall
  meeting place 192 n.
town-plan *urbanize* 192 vb.
township *district* 184 n.
townspeople
  habitancy 191 n.
towny *urban* 192 adj.
tow-path *path* 624 n.
toxæmia *infection* 651 n.
  poisoning 659 n.
toxic *harmful* 645 adj.
  unclean 649 adj.
  toxic 653 adj.
  baneful 659 adj.
  dangerous 661 adj.
toxicity *infection* 651 n.
  poison 659 n.
toxicology *poison* 659 n.
toxin *poison* 659 n.

toxophilite *shooter* 287 n.
  player 837 n.
toy *little* 196 adj.
  bauble 639 n.
  trivial 639 adj.
  plaything 837 n.
  amuse oneself 837 vb.
  excite love 887 vb.
  caress 889 vb.
toy gun *toy gun* 723 n.
trace *copy* 20 vb.
  small quantity 33 n.
  remainder 41 n.
  effect 157 n.
  outline 233 n., vb.
  detect 484 vb.
  identification 547 n.
  trace 548 n.
  decorate 844 vb.
traceable
  attributed 158 adj.
trace back
  look back 125 vb.
  retrospect 505 vb.
tracery *network* 222 n.
  curve 248 n.
  pattern 844 n.
  ornamental art 844 n.
traces *coupling* 47 n.
  fetter 748 n.
trace to *attribute* 158 vb.
trace upon *mark* 547 vb.
trachea *air-pipe* 353 n.
tracheitis
  respiratory disease 651 n.
tracing *imitation* 20 n.
  copy 22 n.
  representation 551 n.
track *continuity* 71 n.
  water travel 269 n.
  direction 281 n.
  follow 284 vb.
  identification 547 n.
  trace 548 n.
  pursue 619 vb.
  path, railroad 624 n.
  racing 716 n.
  arena 724 n.
track down *detect* 484 vb.
tracker *concomitant* 89 n.
  hunter 619 n.
trackless *spacious* 183 adj.
  difficult 700 adj.
track, off the
  mistaken 495 adj.
track, on the
  discovering 484 adj.
tract *region* 184 n.
  land 344 n.
  reading matter 589 n.
  dissertation 591 n.

tractability
  willingness 597 n.
  persuasibility 612 n.
tractable *wieldy* 701 adj.
tractarian *dissertator* 591 n.
  Anglican 976 adj.
Tractarians
  church party 978 n.
tractate
  reading matter 589 n.
  dissertation 591 n.
tractile *drawing* 288 adj.
  flexible 327 adj.
traction *transport* 272 n.
  traction 288 n.
tractive *dynamic* 160 adj.
tractor *carrier* 273 n.
  vehicle 274 n.
  traction 288 n.
  farm tool 370 n.
trade *interchange* 151 vb.
  transference 272 n.
  vocation 622 n.
  business 622 n.
  transfer 780 n.
  trade 791 n., vb.
  sell 793 vb.
trade fair *mart* 796 n.
trade-mark
  identification 547 n.
  label 547 n.
trade organ *journal* 528 n.
trader *merchant ship* 275 n.
  merchant 794 n.
tradesman *provider* 633 n.
  artisan 686 n.
  tradesman 794 n.
trades union *society* 708 n.
trade wind *wind* 352 n.
trading centre
  emporium 796 n.
tradition *tradition* 127 n.
  permanence 144 n.
  information 524 n.
  narrative 590 n.
  habit 610 n.
  theology 973 n.
traditional
  conformable 83 n.
  immemorial 127 adj.
  descriptive 590 adj.
  habitual 610 adj.
  orthodox 976 adj.
traditionalism
  conformity 83 n.
traditionalist
  the orthodox 976 n.
traditionary
  habitual 610 adj.
traduce *transform* 147 vb.
  misinterpret 521 vb.

misrepresent 552 vb.
defame 926 vb.
traducianism *heredity* 5 n.
traffic *motion* 265 n.
conveyance 267 n.
passing along 305 n.
trade 791 n., vb.
trafficator
signal light 420 n.
indicator 547 n.
traffic control
traffic control 305 n.
traffic cop *protector* 660 n.
police 955 n.
traffic engineering
traffic control 305 n.
trafficker *merchant* 794 n.
trafficky
communicating 624 adj.
traffic lane *route* 624 n.
traffic light
timekeeper 117 n.
signal light 420 n.
signal 547 n.
traffic rules
traffic control 305 n.
tragacanth *resin* 357 n.
tragedian *actor* 594 n.
tragedy *stage play* 594 n.
evil 616 n.
deterioration 655 n.
tragic *dramatic* 594 adj.
distressing 827 adj.
tragi-comic
dramatic 594 adj.
funny 849 adj.
trail *continuity* 71 n.
be dispersed 75 vb.
be long 203 vb.
hang 217 vb.
be behind 238 vb.
wander 267 vb.
move slowly 278 vb.
follow 284 vb.
draw 288 vb.
odour 394 n.
identification 547 n.
trace 548 n.
pursue 619 vb.
path 624 n.
trailer *retinue* 67 n.
example 83 n.
small house 192 n.
carriage 274 n.
follower 284 n.
traction 288 n.
cinema 445 n.
hunter 619 n.
trail one's coat
make quarrels 709 vb.
defy 711 vb.

trail, on the
discovering 484 adj.
pursuing 619 adj.
train *adjunct* 40 n.
retinue 67 n.
procession 71 n.
make conform 83 adj.
concomitant 89 n.
pendant 217 n.
rear 238 n.
train 274 n.
follower 284 n.
break in 369 vb.
train 534 vb.
learn 536 vb.
habituate 610 vb.
make ready 669 vb.
retainer 742 n.
train-bearer *retainer* 742 n.
bridesman 894 n.
train-driver *carrier* 273 n.
trained *expert* 694 adj.
trainee *beginner* 538 n.
trainer *breeder* 369 n.
trainer 537 n.
preparer 669 n.
director 690 n.
training *exercise* 682 n.
training, in *athletic* 162 adj.
training school
training school 539 n.
train one's sights
aim 281 vb.
aim at 617 vb.
train-sick *vomiting* 300 adj.
traipse (*see* trapes)
trait *temperament* 5 n.
speciality 80 n.
feature 445 n.
affections 817 n.
traitor *deceiver* 545 n.
tergiversator 603 n.
revolter 738 n.
enemy 881 n.
evildoer 904 n.
dutilessness 918 n.
knave 938 n.
trajection
transference 272 n.
trajectory *route* 624 n.
tralatition
metaphor 519 n.
tralineate *deviate* 282 vb.
tram, tram-car
conveyance 267 n.
tram 274 n.
tramlines *regularity* 81 n.
parallelism 219 n.
habit 610 n.
railroad 624 n.
trammel *obstacle* 702 n.

hinder 702 vb.
fetter 747 vb.
fetter 748 n.
tramontane
extraneous 59 adj.
tramp *gait* 265 n.
walk 267 vb.
wanderer 268 n.
voyage 269 vb.
merchant ship 275 n.
move slowly 278 vb.
idler 679 n.
beggar 763 n.
low fellow 869 n.
bad man 938 n.
tramper *pedestrian* 268 n.
trample *flatten* 216 vb.
kick 279 vb.
fell 311 vb.
oppress 735 vb.
trample on *ill-treat* 645 vb.
oppress 735 vb.
subjugate 745 vb.
be insolent 878 vb.
despise 922 vb.
trample out
suppress 165 vb.
trampoline *lifter* 310 n.
trance *quiescence* 266 n.
insensibility 375 n.
fantasy 513 n.
sleep 679 n.
tranced *insensible* 375 adj.
imaginative 513 adj.
bewitched 983 adj.
tranquil *tranquil* 266 adj.
reposeful 683 adj.
peaceful 717 adj.
impassive 820 adj.
inexcitable 823 adj.
pleasurable 826 adj.
tranquillity *content* 828 n.
non-wonder 865 n.
(*see* tranquil)
tranquillize *assuage* 177 vb.
pacify 719 vb.
tranquillize 823 vb.
tranquillizer
moderator 177 n.
drug 658 n.
transact *do business* 622 vb.
deal with 688 vb.
transaction(s)
eventuality 154 n.
affairs 154 n.
record 548 n.
deed 676 n.
trade 791 n.
transalpine *removed* 199 adj.
transatlantic
removed 199 adj.

transcend *be great* 32vb.
  be good 644vb.
  (*see* transcendence)
transcendence
  extrinsicality 6n.
  non-imitation 21n.
  superiority 34n.
  overstepping 306n.
  perfection 646n.
  divine attribute 965n.
transcendental
  inexpressible 517adj.
  divine 965adj.
  cabbalistic 984adj.
transcendentalism
  philosophy 449n.
  occultism 984n.
transcribe *copy* 20vb.
  translate 520vb.
  write 586vb.
transcriber *penman* 586n.
transcript *copy* 22n.
  script 586n.
transcription
  transformation 143n.
  transference 272n.
  musical piece 412n.
  script 586n.
transcursion *passage* 305n.
  overstepping 306n.
transduction
  transference 272n.
transect *bisect* 92vb.
  be oblique 220vb.
transection *crossing* 222n.
transept
  church interior 990n.
transfer *duplicate* 22n.
  disjoin 46vb.
  change 143n.
  transition 147n.
  substitution 150n.
  displace 188vb.
  move 265vb.
  transference 272n.
  carry 273vb.
  picture 553n.
  deposal 752n.
  non-retention 779n.
  convey 780vb.
  giving 781vb.
transferable
  transferable 272adj.
transferee *recipient* 782n.
  purchaser 792n.
transference
  transference 272n.
  passage 305n.
  metaphor 519n.
  (*see* transfer)
transferor *seller* 793n.

transferrer *transferrer* 272n.
transfiguration
  transformation 143n.
  conversion 147n.
  improvement 654n.
  beautification 843n.
  theophany 965n.
transfix *pierce* 263vb.
transfixed *fixed* 153adj.
transformation
  transformation 143n.
  conversion 147n.
  improvement 654n.
  beautification 843n.
transformation scene
  stage show 594n.
  thaumaturgy 864n.
  pageant 875n.
transfuse *infuse* 303vb.
  (*see* transfusion)
transfusion *mixture* 43n.
  transference 272n.
  surgery 658n.
transgress *disobey* 738vb.
  (*see* transgression)
transgression
  overstepping 306n.
  non-observance 769n.
  wrong 914n.
  wickedness 934n.
  guilty act 936n.
  lawbreaking 954n.
transgressive
  non-observant 769adj.
transhipment
  displacement 188n.
  transport 272n.
transience (*see* transient)
transient *elapsing* 111adj.
  transient 114adj.
  unstable 152adj.
  short 204adj.
  uncertain 474adj.
transientness
  instantaneity 116n.
transilience
  revolution 149n.
  passage 305n.
  overstepping 306n.
transillumination
  transparency 422n.
transit *transition* 147n.
  motion 265n.
  passage 305n.
transit circle
  angular measure 247n.
transit, in *on foot* 267adv.
  via 624adv.
transition *change* 143n.
  transformation 143n.
  transition 147n.

transference 272n.
  passage 305n.
transitional
  changeable 143adj.
  converted 147adj.
  moving 265adj.
  passing 305adj.
transitory
  transient 114adj.
translate *displace* 188vb.
  ecclesiasticize 985vb.
  (*see* translation)
translation *imitation* 20n.
  copy 22n.
  change 143n.
  transference 272n.
  translation 520n.
translationese
  language 557n.
translative
  interpretive 520adj.
translator *interpreter* 520n.
transliteration
  imitation 20n.
  transference 272n.
  translation 520n.
translocation
  displacement 188n.
  transference 272n.
translucent
  undimmed 417adj.
  transparent 422adj.
  semitransparent 424adj.
transmigration
  transformation 143n.
  transition 147n.
  wandering 267n.
  transference 272n.
transmigration of souls
  reproduction 166n.
  transference 272n.
transmissible
  transferable 272adj.
transmission
  transference 272n.
  passage 305n.
  transfer 780n.
transmit *transfer* 272vb.
  send 272vb.
  communicate 524vb.
transmitter
  transferrer 272n.
  telecommunication 531n.
transmogrification
  transformation 143n.
transmutation
  transformation 143n.
  conversion 147n.
transmute *modify* 143vb.
transoceanic
  removed 199adj.

transom *supporter* 218n.
  beam 218n.
  cross 222n.
  window 263n.
transonic *speedy* 277adj.
transparency
  thinness 206n.
  transparency 422n.
  photography 551n.
transparent
  insubstantial 4adj.
  undimmed 417adj.
  transparent 422adj.
  intelligible 516adj.
  disclosing 526adj.
  perspicuous 567adj.
  artless 699adj.
transpire
  emerge, exude 298vb.
  vaporize 338vb.
  be plain 522vb.
  be disclosed 526vb.
transplant *implant* 303vb.
  cultivate 370vb.
transplantation
  transference 272n.
transport *displace* 188vb.
  move 265vb.
  transport 272n.
  carry 273vb.
  vehicle 274n.
  ship 275n.
  warm feeling 818n.
  delight 826vb.
  punish 963vb.
transportable
  transferable 272adj.
transportation
  penalty 963n.
transporter *carrier* 273n.
transpose
  interchange 151vb.
  invert 221vb.
  move 265vb.
  transpose 272vb.
  compose music 413vb.
transposition
  (*see* transpose)
transubstantiate
  modify 143vb.
transubstantiation
  transformation 143n.
  the sacrament 988n.
transude *exude* 298vb.
transume *transpose* 272vb.
transumption
  transference 272n.
transvaluation
  estimate 480n.
transverse *oblique* 220adj.
  crossed 222adj.

transversion *crossing* 222n.
transvestism
  abnormality 84n.
tranter *carrier* 273n.
trap *receptacle* 194n.
  orifice 263n.
  close 264vb.
  carriage 274n.
  detect 484vb.
  surprise 508vb.
  trap 542n.
  ensnare 542vb.
  stage-set 594n.
  danger 661n.
  pitfall 663n.
  defences 713n.
  imprison 747vb.
  take 786vb.
trapan (*see* trepan)
trapdoor *doorway* 263n.
  trap 542n.
  pitfall 663n.
trapes, traipse
  wander 267vb.
  dirty person 649n.
trapezist *entertainer* 594n.
trapper *killer* 362n.
  hunter 619n.
trappings *adjunct* 40n.
  coverlet 226n.
  dressing 228n.
  equipment 630n.
Trappist *monk* 986n.
traps *clothing* 228n.
  property 777n.
trash *bauble* 639n.
  nonentity 639n.
  rubbish 641n.
  restrain 747vb.
  loose woman 952n.
trash can *vessel* 194n.
trash-cord *halter* 47n.
trashy *unmeaning* 515adj.
  feeble 572adj.
  trivial 639adj.
traulism
  speech defect 580n.
trauma *disease* 651n.
  wound 655n.
traumatic
  surgical dressing 658n.
travail *obstetrics* 164n.
  labour 682n.
  adversity 731n.
trave *beam* 218n.
  frame 218n.
travel *motion* 265n.
  land travel 267n.
  move fast 277vb.
traveller *traveller* 268n.
  seller 793n.

traveller's cheque
  paper money 797n.
traveller's tale *fable* 543n.
  exaggeration 546n.
travelogue *oration* 579n.
  description 590n.
travel-stained
  travelling 267adj.
travel with *assent* 488vb.
traverse *counteract* 182vb.
  beam 218n.
  traverse 267vb.
  pass 305vb.
  tell against 467vb.
  negate 533vb.
  be obstructive 702vb.
  oppose 704vb.
  defences 713n.
travesty *mimicry* 20n.
  copy 22n.
  misinterpretation 521n.
  misrepresentation 552n.
  laughing-stock 851n.
  satire 851n.
travolator *transport* 272n.
  carrier 273n.
  conveyor 274n.
trawl *receptacle* 194n.
  network 222n.
  inclosure 235n.
  draw 288vb.
  be tentative 461vb.
  hunt 619vb.
trawler *mariner* 270n.
  fishing-boat 275n.
  hunter 619n.
tray *receptacle* 194n.
  plate 194n.
treacherous
  uncertain 474adj.
  occult 523adj.
  false 541adj.
  deceiving 542adj.
  unsafe 661adj.
  malevolent 898adj.
  dutiless 918adj.
  perfidious 930adj.
treachery *latency* 523n.
  tergiversation 603n.
  perfidy 930n.
treacle *viscidity* 354n.
  sweet 392n.
treacly *viscid* 354adj.
  feeling 818adj.
tread *degree* 27n.
  stand 218n.
  gait 265n.
  walk 267vb.
  ascent 308n.
  trace 548n.
  access 624n.

use 673 vb.
tread down *oppress* 735 vb.
treadmill *uniformity* 16 n.
  labour 682 n.
  bore 838 n.
  instrument of torture
    964 n.
tread on *kick* 279 vb.
  ill-treat 645 vb.
  subjugate 745 vb.
tread on one's toes
  make quarrels 709 vb.
tread on the heels
  come after 65 vb.
  be near 200 vb.
  follow 284 vb.
tread water *swim* 269 vb.
treason *sedition* 738 n.
  perfidy 930 n.
treasonable
  perfidious 930 adj.
treasure *store* 632 n.,vb.
  exceller 644 n.
  safeguard 660 vb.
  preserve 666 vb.
  acquisition 771 n.
  funds 797 n.
  a beauty 841 n.
  honour 866 vb.
  love 887 vb.
  pet 889 vb.
  darling 890 n.
treasure chest
  treasury 799 n.
treasure-house
  storage 632 n.
  treasury 799 n.
treasure-hunt *search* 459 n.
treasurer *provider* 633 n.
  consignee 754 n.
  treasurer 798 n.
  accountant 808 n.
treasure-trove
  discovery 484 n.
  benefit 615 n.
  acquisition 771 n.
treasury
  accumulation 74 n.
  anthology 592 n.
  storage 632 n.
  treasurer 798 n.
  treasury 799 n.
treasury note
  title-deed 767 n.
  paper money 797 n.
treat *modify* 143 vb.
  pleasure 376 n.
  dissert 591 vb.
  remedy, doctor 658 vb.
  behave 688 vb.
  contract 765 vb.

make terms 766 vb.
give 781 vb.
enjoyment 824 vb.
pleasurableness 826 n.
amusement 837 n.
treat as *substitute* 150 vb.
treat as one *identify* 13 vb.
treat as one's own
  appropriate 786 vb.
treatise *dissertation* 591 n.
treat like dirt
  subjugate 745 vb.
  hold cheap 922 vb.
treatment *change* 143 n.
  agency 173 n.
  way 624 n.
  therapy 658 n.
  use 673 n.
  conduct 688 n.
treaty *conference* 584 n.
  treaty 765 n.
treaty, in *agreeing* 24 adj.
treaty-maker
  signatory 765 n.
treaty-making
  conference 584 n.
  conditions 766 n.
treble *treble* 94 vb.
  stridor 407 n.
treble clef *notation* 410 n.
trebuchet *pillory* 964 n.
tree *dwelling* 192 n.
  tree 366 n.
treenail *fastening* 47 n.
tree-top *vertex* 213 n.
  foliage 366 n.
trefoil *three* 93 n.
  grass 366 n.
trek *land travel* 267 n.
trekker *traveller* 268 n.
trellis *network* 222 n.
tremble *vary* 152 vb.
  be weak 163 vb.
  be agitated 318 vb.
  sound faint 401 vb.
  roll 403 vb.
  show feeling 818 vb.
  be excited 821 vb.
  quake 854 vb.
tremble in the balance
  pend 136 vb.
  be uncertain 474 vb.
  be in danger 661 vb.
tremendous
  frightening 854 adj.
tremendously
  extremely 32 adv.
tremolo *roll* 403 vb.
  musical note 410 n.
  adagio 412 adv.
tremor *outbreak* 176 n.

oscillation 317 n.
agitation 318 n.
paralysis 651 n.
danger signal 665 n.
feeling 818 n.
nervousness 854 n.
tremulous *agitated* 318 adj.
  irresolute 601 adj.
  nervous 854 adj.
trench *gap* 201 n.
  fence 235 n.
  excavation 255 n.
  furrow 262 n.
  conduit 351 n.
  refuge 662 n.
  defences 713 n.
trenchancy *vigour* 571 n.
trenchant *keen* 174 n.
  assertive 532 adj.
  concise 569 adj.
  forceful 571 adj.
  disapproving 924 adj.
trencher *plate* 194 n.
  lamina 207 n.
trencherman *eater* 301 n.
  glutton 947 n.
trenches *battleground* 724 n.
trench upon *be near* 200 vb.
  encroach 306 vb.
trend *continuity* 71 n.
  ability 160 n.
  tendency 179 n.
  liability 180 n.
  point to 281 vb.
  approach 289 n.
  intention 617 n.
  liking 859 n.
trepan *perforator* 263 n.
  pierce 263 vb.
  ensnare 542 vb.
  doctor 658 vb.
trephine *doctor* 658 vb.
trepidation
  agitation 318 n.
  excitable state 822 n.
  fear 854 n.
trespass *interfere* 231 vb.
  intrude 279 vb.
  encroach 306 n.
  disobey 738 vb.
  wrong 914 n.
  be undue 916 vb.
  be wicked 934 vb.
  guilty act 936 n.
  lawbreaking 954 n.
trespasser *possessor* 776 n.
  offender 904 n.
  usurper 916 n.
trespassing
  extraneous 59 adj.
tresses *hair* 259 n.

[1248]

trestle *frame* 218 n.
trews *trousers* 228 n.
trey *three* 93 n.
tri *three* 93 adj.
triable *legal* 953 adj.
  illegal 954 adj.
triad *three* 93 n.
  Trinity 965 n.
trial *enquiry* 459 n.
  experiment 461 n.
  pursuit 619 n.
  bane 659 n.
  preparation 669 n.
  essay 671 n.
  difficulty 700 n.
  contest 716 n.
  suffering 825 n.
  legal trial 959 n.
trial and error
  empiricism 461 n.
triality *triality* 93 n.
trialogue
  interlocution 584 n.
triangle *three* 93 n.
  angular figure 247 n.
  gong 414 n.
  instrument of torture
    964 n.
triangle of forces
  science of forces 162 n.
triangular *angulated* 247 adj.
triangulation
  measurement 465 n.
tribal *ethnic* 11 adj.
  native 191 n.
  national 371 n.
tribalism *race* 11 n.
  social group 371 n.
  government 733 n.
tribe *race* 11 n.
  group 74 n.
  breed 77 n.
  multitude 104 n.
  genealogy 169 n.
  community 708 n.
tribesman *kinsman* 11 n.
tribrach *prosody* 593 n.
tribulation *difficulty* 700 n.
  suffering 825 n.
  painfulness 827 n.
tribunal *council* 692 n.
  jurisdiction 955 n.
  tribunal 956 n.
tribunate
  magistrature 733 n.
tribune *rostrum* 539 n.
tributary *stream* 350 n.
  subject 745 adj.
  giver 781 n.
  giving 781 adj.
tribute *service* 745 n.

gift 781 n.
offering 781 n.
receiving 782 n.
payment 804 n.
tax 809 n.
thanks 907 n.
dueness 915 n.
reward 962 n.
oblation 981 n.
tributes *praise* 923 n.
tricar *automobile* 274 n.
trice *instant* 116 n.
  draw 288 vb.
trice up *tie, tighten* 45 vb.
trichology
  hair-dressing 843 n.
trichotomy *trisection* 95 n.
trichroism *variegation* 437 n.
trick *trickery* 542 n.
  befool 542 vb.
  habit 610 n.
  contrivance 623 n.
  means of escape 667 n.
  skill 682 n.
  stratagem 698 n.
  affectation 805 n.
  foul play 930 n.
trickery *trickery* 542 n.
trickle *small quantity* 33 n.
  fewness 105 n.
  move slowly 278 vb.
  flow out 298 vb.
  be wet 341 vb.
  flow 350 vb.
  trifle 639 n.
trick of, have the
  be skilful 694 vb.
trick out *decorate* 844 vb.
trick-rider *rider* 268 n.
tricks of the trade
  trickery 542 n.
  stratagem 698 n.
trickster *trickster* 545 n.
  slyboots 698 n.
  knave 938 n.
tricksy *cunning* 698 adj.
  gay 833 adj.
tricky *deceiving* 542 adj.
  cunning 698 adj.
  dishonest 930 adj.
tricolour *striation* 437 n.
  variegated 437 adj.
  flag 547 n.
tricorne *headgear* 228 n.
tricycle *bicycle* 274 n.
trident *three* 93 n.
  authority 733 n.
Tridentine decrees
  orthodoxy 976 n.
tridimensional *three* 93 adj.
tried *certain* 473 adj.

matured 669 adj.
expert 694 adj.
approved 923 adj.
trustworthy 929 adj.
triennial *seasonal* 141 adj.
  flower 366 n.
triennium *three* 93 n.
trier *stamina* 600 n.
  essayer 671 n.
  contender 716 n.
trierarch *director* 690 n.
  naval officer 741 n.
trifid *trifid* 95 adj.
trifle
  insubstantial thing 4 n.
  pudding 301 n.
  be inattentive 456 vb.
  neglect 458 vb.
  trifle 639 n.
  amuse oneself 837 vb.
  caress 889 vb.
trifler *fool* 501 n.
  nonentity 639 n.
trifle with *befool* 542 vb.
  not respect 921 vb.
  hold cheap 922 vb.
trifling *inconsiderable* 33 adj.
  wit 839 n.
triforium
  church interior 990 n.
triform *three* 93 adj.
trigger *handle* 218 n.
  tool 630 n.
  fire-arm 723 n.
trigger-happy *rash* 857 adj.
  irascible 892 adj.
trigger off *cause* 156 vb.
triglyph *furrow* 262 n.
  ornamental art 844 n.
trigon *angular figure* 247 n.
trigonometry
  mathematics 86 n.
  angular measure 247 n.
  measurement 465 n.
trilateral *three* 93 adj.
  lateral 239 adj.
  angulated 247 adj.
trilby *headgear* 228 n.
trilithon *supporter* 218 n.
trill *flow* 350 vb.
  roll 403 n., vb.
  musical note 410 n.
  sing 413 vb.
  pronunciation 577 n.
  voice 577 vb.
trillion
  over one hundred 99 n.
trilogy *three* 93 n.
  poem 593 n.
  stage play 594 n.
trim *state* 7 n.

adjust 24vb.
equalize 28vb.
cut 46vb.
orderly 60adj.
conform 83vb.
make smaller 198vb.
shorten 204vb.
dress 228n.
form 243n.
dissemble 541vb.
be elegant 575vb.
tergiversate 603vb.
clean 648vb.
make ready 669vb.
personable 841adj.
hair-dressing 843n.
decorate 844vb.
trimester three 93n.
period 110n.
trimeter prosody 593n.
trimmer deceiver 545n.
tergiversator 603n.
trimming edging 234n.
trimming 844n.
reprimand 924n.
trimmings adjunct 40n.
leavings 41n.
trimurti triality 93n.
Hindu god 967n.
trinacrian three 93adj.
trinal three 93adj.
trine three 93n.
Trinitarianism
orthodoxy 976n.
trinity triality 93n.
Trinity 965n.
trinket bauble 639n.
plaything 837n.
finery 844n.
trinomial three 93adj.
trio three 93n.
duet 412n.
triolet verse form 593n.
trip be in motion 265vb.
land travel 267n.
walk 267vb.
collide 279vb.
tumble 309vb.
elevate 310vb.
fell 311vb.
leap 312vb.
mistake 495n.
blunder 495vb.
ensnare 542vb.
be clumsy 695vb.
hinder 702vb.
failure 728n.
dance 837vb.
tripartite trifid 95adj.
tripe insides 224n.
silly talk 515n.

triphthong
speech sound 398n.
spoken letter 558n.
voice 577n.
triple augment 36vb.
treble 94vb.
triple crown
badge of rule 743n.
vestments 989n.
triples campanology 412n.
triplet three 93n.
verse form 593n.
triplex treble 94adj.
triplication
triplication 94n.
tripod stand 218n.
oracle 511n.
tripos exam. 459n.
tripper traveller 268n.
hinderer 702n.
reveller 837n.
tripping elegant 575adj.
active 678adj.
trippingly swiftly 277adv.
by leaps and bounds
312adv.
triptych three 93n.
picture 553n.
trip-wire trap 542n.
obstacle 702n.
defences 713n.
trireme galley 275n.
warship 722n.
trisection trisection 95n.
trisulcate trifid 95adj.
furrowed 262adj.
trite known 490adj.
aphoristic 496adj.
unmeaning 515adj.
usual 610adj.
dull 840adj.
triturate break 46vb.
pulverize 332vb.
triumph procession 71n.
victory 727n.
triumph 727vb.
trophy 729n.
subjugate 745vb.
rejoice 835vb.
celebration 876n.
boast 877vb.
triumphal
celebrative 876adj.
gratulatory 886adj.
triumphant
successful 727adj.
jubilant 833adj.
celebrative 876adj.
boastful 877adj.
triumphator victor 727n.
triumph over

humiliate 872vb.
triumvirate
government 733n.
triune three 92adj.
trivet supporter 218n.
stand 218n.
furnace 383n.
trivial unmeaning 515adj.
trivial 639adj.
trivium curriculum 534adj.
troat ululate 409vb.
trocar perforator 263n.
trochee prosody 593n.
trochilics rotation 315n.
trodden flat 216adj.
usual 610adj.
troglodyte dweller 191n.
solitary 883n.
Trojan busy person 678n.
Trojan Horse
ambush 527n.
trap 542n.
stratagem 698n.
enemy 881n.
perfidy 930n.
troll rotate 315vb.
demon 970n.
trolley pushcart 274n.
tram 274n.
trollop prostitute 952n.
trombone horn 414n.
troop band 74n.
congregate 74vb.
be many 104vb.
formation 722n.
troop-carrier
air-force 722n.
trooper cavalry 722n.
warship 722n.
trooping the colour
pageant 875n.
troops armed force 722n.
troopship warship 722n.
trope trope 519n.
ornament 574n.
trophy reminder 505n.
badge 547n.
monument 548n.
trophy 729n.
gift 781n.
booty 790n.
honours 866n.
reward 962n.
tropical hot 379adj.
figurative 519adj.
rhetorical 574adj.
tropopause
atmosphere 340n.
troposphere
atmosphere 340n.
trot gait 265n.

pedestrianism 267 n.
ride 267 vb.
move fast 277 vb.
troth belief 485 n.
promise 764 n.
trot out repeat 106 vb.
manifest 522 vb.
speak 579 vb.
trotter foot 214 n.
thoroughbred 273 n.
trottoir road 624 n.
troubadour musician 413 n.
vocalist 413 n.
poet 593 n.
trouble turmoil 61 n.
derange 63 vb.
attention 455 n.
evil 616 n.
exertion 682 n.
difficulty 700 n.
adversity 731 n.
worry 825 n.
incommode 827 vb.
troubled agitated 318 adj.
dejected 834 adj.
trouble-maker bane 659 n.
trouble-maker 663 n.
agitator 738 n.
trouble, no easy thing 701 n.
trouble one for
request 761 n.
trouble oneself
exert oneself 682 vb.
trouble-shooter
mediator 720 n.
troublesome
laborious 682 adj.
annoying 827 adj.
trouble spot pitfall 663 n.
troublous violent 176 adj.
evil 616 adj.
trough vessel 194 n.
bowl 194 n.
cavity 255 n.
furrow 262 n.
conduit 351 n.
trounce strike 279 vb.
defeat 727 vb.
reprove 924 vb.
spank 963 vb.
trouncer punisher 963 n.
troupe band 74 n.
actor 594 n.
party 708 n.
trouper actor 594 n.
trousered male 372 adj.
trouser-press
flattener 216 n.
trousers trousers 228 n.
trousseau clothing 228 n.
store 632 n.

trout fish food 301 n.
table fish 365 n.
trover discovery 484 n.
acquisition 771 n.
trow fishing-boat 275 n.
opine 485 vb.
trowel ladle 194 n.
sharp edge 256 n.
shovel 274 n.
farm tool 370 n.
troy weight
weighment 322 n.
truancy absence 190 n.
escape 667 n.
dutilessness 918 n.
truant avoider 620 n.
escaper 667 n.
(see truancy)
truce delay 136 n.
lull 145 n.
interval 201 n.
quiescence 266 n.
peace 717 n.
pacification 719 n.
trucial pacificatory 719 adj.
truck vertex 213 n.
carrier 273 n.
automobile 274 n.
train 274 n.
pushcart 274 n.
barter 791 n.
truckle wheel 250 n.
be servile 879 vb.
flatter 925 vb.
truckman driver 268 n.
truculence rudeness 885 n.
malevolence 898 n.
trudge travel, walk 267 vb.
move slowly 278 vb.
true symmetrical 245 adj.
straight 249 adj.
true, accurate 494 adj.
observant 768 adj.
patriotic 901 adj.
right 913 adj.
trustworthy 929 adj.
pious 979 adj.
true bill
accusation 928 n.
true-blue
conformable 83 adj.
obedient 739 adj.
patriotic 901 adj.
trustworthy 929 adj.
true-bred genuine 494 adj.
true faith orthodoxy 976 n.
true saying maxim 496 n.
true to life lifelike 18 adj.
true to type typical 83 adj.
truffle tuber 301 n.
vegetable 301 n.

plant 366 n.
trug basket 194 n.
vessel 194 n.
truism maxim, axiom 496 n.
unmeaningness 515 n.
trull loose woman 952 n.
truly positively 32 adv.
truly 949 adv.
as promised 764 adv.
trump be superior 34 vb.
contrivance 623 n.
instrument 628 n.
means 629 n.
masterpiece 694 n.
overmaster 727 vb.
gentleman 929 n.
good man 937 n.
trumped-up
unattested 467 adj.
deceiving 542 adj.
untrue 543 adj.
trumpery bauble 639 n.
trivial 639 adj.
unmeaning 515 adj.
trumpet megaphone 400 n.
resound 404 vb.
stridor 407 n.
play music 413 vb.
horn 414 n.
proclaim 528 vb.
messenger 531 n.
call 547 n.
be ostentatious 875 vb.
boast 877 vb.
trumpet-call
danger signal 665 n.
command 737 n.
trumpeter
instrumentalist 413 n.
trump up fake 541 vb.
truncate shorten 204 vb.
deform 244 vb.
truncated incomplete 55 adj.
truncheon
club 723 n.
badge of rule 743 n.
trundle move 265 vb.
propel 287 vb.
rotate 315 vb.
trunk chief part 52 n.
part, piece 53 n.
incompleteness 55 n.
source 156 n.
box 194 n.
supporter 218 n.
cylinder 252 n.
tree 366 n.
communicating 624 adj.
trunk road road 624 n.
trunks legwear 228 n.
beachwear 228 n.

trunnion *pivot* 218n.
truss *tie* 45vb.
　bunch 74n.
　supporter 218n.
trust
　thing transferred 272n.
　belief 485n.
　expectation 507n.
　association 706n.
　corporation 708n.
　mandate 751n.
　credit 802n.
　hope 852n.,vb.
　piety 979n.
trustee *consignee* 754n.
　possessor 776n.
　recipient 782n.
　treasurer 798n.
trusteeship
　commission 751n.
trustful *believing* 485adj.
　credulous 487adj.
trust in *be certain* 473vb.
trustiness *probity* 929n.
trust with
　commission 751vb.
trustworthy *credible* 485adj.
　genuine 494adj.
　veracious 540adj.
　safe 660adj.
　observant 786adj.
　reputable 866adj.
　trustworthy 929adj.
trusty *trustworthy* 929adj.
truth *demonstration* 478n.
　truth 494n.
　maxim 496n.
　probity 929n.
　orthodoxy 976n.
truth-claim
　affirmation 532n.
truthful *true* 494adj.
　veracious 540adj.
　trustworthy 929adj.
truthfulness *veracity* 540n.
　probity 929n.
try *taste* 386vb.
　enquire 459vb.
　experiment 461vb.
　judge 480vb.
　be willing 597vb.
　persevere 600vb.
　tempt 612vb.
　essay 671n.,vb.
　avail of 673vb.
　exert oneself 682vb.
　torment 827vb.
　be tedious 838vb.
try conclusions with
　quarrel 709vb.
　contend 716vb.

trying *fatiguing* 684adj.
　annoying 827adj.
try it on *deceive* 542vb.
try one's luck
　be tentative 461vb.
　gamble 618vb.
try-out *experiment* 461n.
tryst *focus* 76n.
tsar *sovereign* 741n.
tsardom
　magistrature 733n.
tsarism *despotism* 733n.
　brute force 735n.
T-square
　horizontality 216n.
　gauge 465n.
tsunami *high water* 209n.
　wave 350n.
tub *vat, vessel* 194n.
　ship 275n.
　ablution 648n.
tuba *horn* 414n.
tubby *fleshy* 195adj.
　thick 205adj.
tube *cylinder* 252n.
　excavation 255n.
　tunnel, tube 263n.
　train 274n.
　conduit 351n.
　railroad 624n.
tuber *tuber* 301n.
tuberculosis *phthisis* 651n.
tuberous *convex* 253adj.
tub-thumper *speaker* 579n.
　agitator 738n.
tub-thumping *oration* 579n.
tubular *rotund* 252adj.
　tubular 263adj.
tuck *fold* 261n.,vb.
　food 301n.
　side-arms 723n.
tucker *apron* 228n.
tucket *loudness* 400n.
　publication 528n.
tuck in *place* 187vb.
　load 193vb.
　eat 301vb.
tuck up *place* 187vb.
　shorten 204vb.
tuff *ash* 381n.
　rock 344n.
tuft *bunch* 74n.
　hair 259n.
tuft-hunter *toady* 879n.
tufty *hairy* 259adj.
tug *move* 265vb.
　boat 275n.
　traction 288n.
　attraction 291n.
　extraction 304n.
　exertion 682n.

tugboat *traction* 288n.
tug-of-war *traction* 288n.
　opposition 704n.
　contest 716n.
tuition *teaching* 534n.
tulle *textile* 222n.
tumble *jumble* 63vb.
　tumble 309vb.
　oscillate 317vb.
　debauch 951vb.
tumble-down *flimsy* 163adj.
　descending 309adj.
　dilapidated 655adj.
tumbler *athlete* 162n.
　cup 194n.
　entertainer 594n.
tumbril *cart* 274n.
　vehicle 274n.
　means of execution 964n.
tumefaction *dilation* 197n.
tumescence *dilation* 197n.
　convexity 253n.
tumescent, tumid
　rhetorical 574adj.
tummy *maw* 194n.
　insides 224n.
tummy ache
　indigestion 651n.
tumour *dilation* 197n.
　carcinosis 651n.
tumult *turmoil* 61n.
　commotion 318n.
　loudness 400n.
　discord 411n.
　activity 678n.
　revolt 738n.
tumultuary *violent* 176adj.
　riotous 738adj.
tumultuous
　disorderly 61adj.
　violent 176adj.
　loud 400adj.
tumulus *tomb* 364n.
tun *vat* 194n.
　bulk 195n.
　drunkard 949n.
tundra *plain* 348n.
tune *adjust* 24vb.
　synchronize 123vb.
　sound 398n.
　harmonize 410vb.
　tune 412n.
　play music 413vb.
　make ready 669vb.
tuneable
　melodious 410adj.
tuneful *pleasant* 376adj.
　melodious 410adj.
　poetic 593adj.
tune in *hear* 415vb.
tuneless *discordant* 411adj.

tune up *harmonize* 410 vb.
  make ready 669 vb.
tunic *tunic* 228 n.
tunicle *vestments* 989 n.
tuning fork *prototype* 23 n.
  gong 414 n.
tunnage *size* 195 n.
tunnel *excavation* 255 n.
  tunnel 263 n.
  pierce 263 vb.
  descend 309 vb.
  bridge 624 n.
  railroad 624 n.
tup *unite with* 45 vb.
  sheep 365 n.
  male animal 372 n.
tu quoque *rejoinder* 460 n.
tu quoque argument
  counter-evidence 467 n.
  confutation 479 n.
  accusation 928 n.
turban *coil* 251 n.
  headgear 228 n.
turbid *opaque* 423 adj.
  dirty 649 adj.
turbinate *coiled* 251 adj.
  rotary 315 adj.
turbination *rotation* 315 n.
turbine *causal means* 156 n.
turbo-jet *aircraft* 276 n.
turbo-prop *aircraft* 276 n.
turbot *fish food* 301 n.
  table fish 365 n.
turbulence *turmoil* 61 n.
  violence 176 n.
  roughness 259 n.
  commotion 318 n.
  excitability 822 n.
tureen *bowl* 194 n.
turf *piece* 53 n.
  soil 344 n.
  grassland 348 n.
  grass 366 n.
  fuel 385 n.
  gambling 618 n.
  racing 716 n.
  arena 724 n.
turf out *eject* 300 vb.
turfy *soft* 327 adj.
  vegetal 366 adj.
turgescent *expanded* 197 adj.
turgid *expanded* 197 adj.
  convex 253 adj.
  rhetorical 574 adj.
  inelegant 576 adj.
  redundant 637 adj.
  ostentatious 875 adj.
turgidity *bulk* 195 n.
  (*see* turgid)
turkey *table bird* 365 n.
turkey cock

proud man 871 n.
Turkish bath
  heater 383 n.
  ablution 648 n.
Turkish delight
  sweetmeat 301 n.
  sweet 392 n.
turmeric *condiment* 389 n.
turmoil *turmoil* 61 n.
  havoc 165 n.
  violence, storm 176 n.
  commotion 318 n.
  activity 678 n.
  anarchy 734 n.
  revolt 738 n.
turn *period* 110 n.
  periodicity 141 n.
  change 143 n., vb.
  reversion 148 n.
  tendency 179 n.
  efform 243 vb.
  curvature 248 n.
  make round 250 n.
  blunt 257 vb.
  fold 261 vb.
  land travel 267 n.
  deviate 282 vb.
  circuition 314 n.
  rotation 315 n.
  be sour 393 vb.
  inexpectation 508 n.
  interpretation 520 n.
  stage show 594 n.
  circuit 626 vb.
  aptitude 694 n.
  parry 713 vb.
  dislike 861 n.
turn a blind eye
  disregard 458 vb.
  be patient 823 vb.
turn about *revert* 148 vb.
turnabout
  tergiversator 603 n.
turn adrift *eject* 300 vb.
turn against
  tergiversate 603 vb.
turn and turn about
  correlatively 12 adv.
turn aside *avoid* 620 vb.
turn away *regress* 286 vb.
  dismiss 300 vb.
  be loth 598 vb.
  refuse 760 vb.
turncoat
  changed person 147 n.
  deceiver 545 n.
  waverer 601 n.
  tergiversator 603 n.
turn colour
  show feeling 818 vb.
turn down *invert* 221 vb.

bedim 419 vb.
  refuse 760 vb.
turned-up *curved* 248 adj.
turner *artisan* 686 n.
turn in *sleep* 679 vb.
turning *unstable* 152 adj.
  labyrinthine 251 adj.
  circuition 314 n.
turning point *juncture* 8 n.
  degree 27 n.
  crisis 137 n.
  reversion 148 n.
  summit 213 n.
  limit 236 n.
  return 286 n.
  important matter 638 n.
turn into *convert* 147 vb.
  translate 520 vb.
turnip *tuber* 301 n.
turnkey *janitor* 264 n.
  gaoler 749 n.
turn nasty
  be angry 891 vb.
turn off *dismiss* 300 vb.
  kill 362 vb.
  execute 963 vb.
turn of the tide
  reversion 148 n.
  summit 213 n.
  inversion 221 n.
  return 286 n.
turn on *depend* 157 vb.
  operate 173 vb.
turn out *become* 1 vb.
  happen 154 vb.
  result 157 vb.
  eject 300 n.
  search 459 vb.
  make unwelcome 883 vb.
turn-out *dressing* 228 n.
  carriage 274 n.
  pageant 875 n.
turn over
  be inverted 221 vb.
  make curved 248 vb.
  fold 261 vb.
  transfer 272 vb.
  meditate 449 vb.
  search 459 vb.
  trade 791 vb.
  sell 793 vb.
turnover *pastry* 301 n.
  earnings 771 n.
  receipt 807 n.
  reward 962 n.
turn over a new leaf
  change 142 vb.
  tergiversate 603 vb.
  be penitent 939 vb.
turnpike *road* 624 n.
  obstacle 702 n.

turn Queen's evidence
inform 524 vb.
confess 526 vb.
accuse 928 vb.
turns, by *by turns* 141 adv.
in exchange 151 adv.
turnscrew *tool* 630 n.
turnspit *domestic* 742 n.
turnstile *barrier* 235 n.
recording instrument 549 n.
access 624 n.
obstacle 702 n.
treasury 799 n.
turntable *rotator* 315 n.
turn tail *regress* 286 vb.
run away 620 vb.
be cowardly 856 vb.
turn the corner
change 143 vb.
get better 654 vb.
turn the other cheek
be patient 823 vb.
be humble 872 vb.
forgive 909 vb.
turn the scale
predominate 34 vb.
modify 143 vb.
cause 156 vb.
influence 178 vb.
tell against 467 vb.
dominate 733 vb.
turn the screw
compel 740 vb.
turn the tables
be contrary 14 vb.
invert 221 vb.
tell against 467 vb.
retaliate 714 vb.
turn to *be turned to* 147 vb.
speak to 583 vb.
busy oneself 622 vb.
seek refuge 662 vb.
turn to account *use* 673 vb.
turn turtle
be inverted 221 vb.
navigate 269 vb.
turn-up *fold* 261 n.
turn up *happen* 151 vb.
chance 159 vb.
be present 189 vb.
arrive 295 vb.
be visible 443 vb.
turn up one's nose
be fastidious 862 vb.
despise 922 vb.
turn up trumps
be successful 727 vb.
be auspicious 730 vb.
be honourable 929 vb.
turpitude *disrepute* 867 n.

improbity 930 n.
wickedness 934 n.
turquoise *blueness* 435 n.
gem 844 n.
turret *high structure* 209 n.
fort 713 n.
turtle *reptile* 365 n.
savouriness 390 n.
turtle-dove *bird* 365 n.
love-emblem 887 n.
turtle-doves *lovers* 887 n.
tusk, tush *tooth* 256 n.
tusker *animal* 365 n.
pig 365 n.
tusky *toothed* 256 adj.
tussle *contention* 716 n.
tussler *contender* 716 n.
combatant 722 n.
tussock *monticle* 209 n.
tussore, tussah *fibre* 208 n.
textile 222 n.
tutelage *teaching* 534 n.
learning 536 n.
protection 660 n.
subjection 745 n.
tutelary *tutelary* 660 adj.
defending 713 adj.
tutelary genius *patron* 707 n.
tutor *teach* 534 vb.
teacher 537 n.
protector 660 n.
manager 690 n.
servant 742 n.
domestic 742 n.
keeper 749 n.
tutorial *teaching* 534 n.
educational 534 adj.
tut-tut *deprecation* 762 n.
tutu *skirt* 228 n.
tu-whit-tu-whoo
ululation 409 n.
tuxedo *tunic* 228 n.
informal dress 228 n.
tuyère *heater* 383 n.
twaddle *absurdity* 497 n.
silly talk 515 n.
be loquacious 581 vb.
twain *duality* 90 n.
twang *taste* 386 n.
pungency 388 n.
sound 398 n.
stridor 407 n.
play music 413 vb.
speech defect 580 n.
tweak *give pain* 377 vb.
touch 378 vb.
tweed *textile* 222 n.
Tweedledum and Tweedle-dee
identity 13 n.
duality 90 n.

tweeds *clothing* 228 n.
tweeny *domestic* 742 n.
tweet *ululate* 409 vb.
tweezers *extractor* 304 n.
tool 630 n.
nippers 778 n.
twelfth man *substitute* 150 n.
twelve-mile limit
territory 184 n.
twelvemonth *period* 110 n.
twelve o'clock *noon* 128 n.
Twelve Tables
precept 693 n.
code of duty 917 n.
law 953 n.
twerp *cad* 938 n.
twice *twice* 91 adv.
twice-born, the
upper class 868 n.
twice-told *repeated* 106 adj.
twice-told tale
diffuseness 570 n.
bore 838 n.
twiddle *touch* 378 vb.
twiddle one's thumbs
be inactive 679 vb.
twig *branch* 53 n.
young plant 132 n.
foliage 366 n.
know 490 vb.
understand 516 vb.
twilight *evening* 129 n.
light 417 n.
half-light 419 n.
deterioration 655 n.
twilight sleep
obstetrics 164 n.
insensibility 375 n.
twill *weave* 222 vb.
fold 261 vb.
twilled *textural* 331 adj.
twin *kinsman* 11 n.
identity 13 n.
analogue 18 n.
accord 24 vb.
compeer 28 n.
concomitant 89 n.
dual 90 adj.
double 91 vb.
contemporary 123 n.
twine *tie* 45 vb.
fibre 208 n.
enlace 222 vb.
distort 246 vb.
make curved 248 vb.
convolution 251 n.
twine 251 vb.
deviate 282 vb.
twine round *cohere* 48 vb.
surround 230 vb.
twinge *pang* 377 n.

suffering 825 n.
twinkle *instantaneity* 116 n.
  vary 152 vb.
  agitation 318 n.
  flash 417 n.
  laughter 835 n.
twin-screw *propeller* 269 n.
twirl *twine* 251 vb.
  rotate 315 vb.
twist *tie* 45 vb.
  complexity 61 n.
  derange 63 vb.
  modify 143 vb.
  bag 194 n.
  fibre 208 n.
  obliquity 220 n.
  enlace 222 vb.
  deform 244 vb.
  distortion 246 n.
  coil 251 n.
  twine 251 vb.
  deviate 282 vb.
  tobacco 388 n.
  bias 481 vb.
  eccentricity 503 n.
  misinterpret 521 vb.
  misrepresentation 552 n.
  defect 647 n.
  pervert 655 vb.
  make ugly 842 vb.
twister *trickster* 545 n.
  knave 938 n.
twistiness *improbity* 930 n.
twisting
  labyrinthine 251 adj.
twists and turns
  meandering 251 n.
twit *be witty* 839 vb.
  ridicule 851 vb.
  not respect 921 vb.
  dispraise 924 vb.
  accuse 928 vb.
twitch *move* 265 vb.
  draw 288 vb.
  spasm 318 n.
  feel pain 377 vb.
  touch 378 vb.
  gesture 547 n.
twitter *agitation* 318 n.
  ululation 409 n.
  sing 413 vb.
two *duality* 90 n.
two-a-penny
  trivial 639 adj.
two-dimensional
  spatial 183 adj.
two-edged *double* 91 adj.
  equivocal 518 adj.
two-faced
  hypocritical 541 adj.
two-fisted

courageous 855 adj.
two-fold *double* 91 adj.
two minds, be in
  be uncertain 474 vb.
two minds, of
  irresolute 601 adj.
two of a kind
  analogue 18 n.
two or three *plurality* 101 n.
  fewness 105 n.
two peas *analogue* 18 n.
two-piece *dress* 228 n.
twosome *duality* 90 n.
two-step *dance* 837 n.
two strings to one's bow
  means 629 n.
two voices *contrariety* 14 n.
  disagreement 25 n.
two voices, speak with
  be equivocal 518 vb.
two-way
  correlative 12 adj.
  interchanged 151 adj.
two-way stretch
  underwear 228 n.
two-wheeler *carriage* 274 n.
tycoon *autocrat* 741 n.
tyke *dog* 365 n.
tympanum *summit* 213 n.
  ear 415 n.
  church exterior 990 n.
type *character* 5 n.
  uniformity 16 n.
  analogue 18 n.
  copy 20 vb.
  prototype 23 n.
  example 83 n.
  form 243 n.
  person 371 n.
  omen 511 n.
  metaphor 519 n.
  indication 547 n.
  image 551 n.
  letter 558 n.
  write 586 vb.
  print-type 587 n.
type-cutter *printer* 587 n.
type-face *form* 243 n.
  print-type 587 n.
type-foundry *press* 587 n.
type, in *printed* 587 adj.
type matter *print-type* 587 n.
typescript *script* 586 n.
  book 589 n.
typesetting *print* 587 n.
typewriter
  stenographer 586 n.
typhoid *infection* 651 n.
typhoon *gale* 352 n.
typhus *infection* 651 n.
typical *uniform* 16 adj.

similar 18 adj.
  general 79 adj.
  special 80 adj.
  regular 81 adj.
  typical 83 adj.
  figurative 519 adj.
  indicating 547 adj.
typify *resemble* 18 vb.
  predict 511 vb.
  mean 514 vb.
  figure 519 vb.
  interpret 520 n.
  manifest 522 vb.
  indicate 547 vb.
  represent 551 vb.
typist *stenographer* 586 n.
typographer *engraver* 556 n.
  printer 587 n.
typographical
  printed 587 adj.
typography
  composition 56 n.
  form 243 n.
  print 587 n.
typology *theology* 973 n.
tyrannical *violent* 176 adj.
  cruel 898 adj.
  lawless 954 adj.
  (*see* tyranny)
tyrannicide *homicide* 362 n.
  revolter 738 n.
tyrannize
  be violent 176 vb.
  influence 178 vb.
  ill-treat 645 vb.
  meddle 678 vb.
  rule 733 vb.
  oppress 735 vb.
  be malevolent 898 vb.
tyrannous
  oppressive 735 adj.
tyranny *influence* 178 n.
  badness 645 n.
  despotism 733 n.
  brute force 735 n.
  insolence 878 n.
  arrogation 916 n.
tyrant
  violent creature 176 n.
  bane 659 n.
  tyrant 735 n.
  autocrat 741 n.
tyre *wheel* 250 n.
tyro *beginner* 538 n.

U

U *well bred* 848 adj.
  genteel 868 adj.
uberty *productiveness* 171 n.

ubiety *presence* 189 n.
ubiquitous *universal* 79 adj.
ubiquitous 189 adj.
ubiquity *space* 183 n.
(*see* ubiquitous)
U-boat *warship* 722 n.
udder *bladder* 194 n.
bosom 253 n.
udometer
hygrometry 341 n.
uglify *impair* 655 vb.
make ugly 842 vb.
ugly *deformed* 246 adj.
inelegant 576 n.
dangerous 661 adj.
unpleasant 827 adj.
ugly 842 adj.
sullen 893 adj.
ugly customer
trouble-maker 663 n.
low fellow 869 n.
ruffian 904 n.
ugly duckling
nonconformist 84 n.
eyesore 842 n.
Uhlan *cavalry* 722 n.
uitlander *foreigner* 59 n.
incomer 297 n.
ukase *decree* 737 n.
ukelele *harp* 414 n.
ulcer *ulcer* 651 n.
wound 655 n.
bane 659 n.
painfulness 827 n.
ulceration *ulcer* 651 n.
impairment 655 n.
painfulness 827 n.
ulcerous *diseased* 651 adj.
uliginal *marshy* 347 adj.
ullage *deficit* 55 n.
ulna *limb* 53 n.
ulnar *brachial* 53 adj.
ulterior *extraneous* 59 adj.
future 124 adj.
distant 199 adj.
ultimate *ending* 69 adj.
distant 199 adj.
ultimately
prospectively 124 adv.
late 136 adv.
eventually 154 adv.
ultimate point
extremity 69 n.
ultima Thule *extremity* 69 n.
farness 199 n.
limit 236 n.
ultimatum *period* 110 n.
limit 236 n.
intention 617 n.
requirement 627 n.
warning 664 n.

demand 737 n.
conditions 766 n.
ultimo *before* 119 adv.
formerly 125 adv.
ultimogeniture
posteriority 120 n.
ultra *extremely* 32 adv.
ultraconservative
obstinate 602 adj.
ultracrepidarian
inquisitor 453 n.
meddler 678 n.
ultracrepidarianism
overactivity 678 n.
ultraist *opponent* 705 n.
ultramarine
blue pigment 435 n.
ultra-microscopic
small 33 adj.
minute 196 adj.
ultra-modern
modern 126 adj.
ultramontane
extraneous 59 adj.
ecclesiastical 985 adj.
ultramontanism
Catholicism 976 n.
ultramontanist
Catholic 976 n.
popish 976 adj.
ultramontanists
church party 978 n.
ultra vires
unwarranted 916 adj.
ululate *ululate* 409 vb.
ululation *ululation* 409 n.
lamentation 836 n.
Ulysses *traveller* 268 n.
umbelliferous
broad 205 adj.
umber *brown paint* 430 n.
umbilical *central* 225 adj.
umbilical cord *bond* 47 n.
obstetrics 164 n.
umbilicus *middle* 70 n.
centre 225 n.
umbra *darkness* 418 n.
umbrage *foliage* 366 n.
screen 421 n.
resentment 891 n.
umbrageous *dark* 418 adj.
shadowy 419 adj.
screened 421 adj.
umbrella *shade* 226 n.
protection 660 n.
shelter 662 n.
umiak *rowboat* 275 n.
umlaut *speech sound* 398 n.
punctuation 547 n.
umpirage *judgment* 480 n.
mediation 720 n.

umpire *estimator* 480 n.
mediator 720 n.
mediate 720 vb.
magistracy 957 n.
unabashed
unfearing 855 adj.
proud 871 adj.
insolent 878 adj.
unable *powerless* 161 adj.
useless 641 adj.
unskilful 695 adj.
unabolished *intact* 52 adj.
unabridged *intact* 52 adj.
long 203 adj.
unaccented *muted* 410 adj.
unacceptable
unpleasant 827 adj.
unacclimatized
extraneous 59 adj.
unaccommodating
hindering 702 adj.
annoying 827 adj.
discourteous 885 adj.
unaccompanied
alone 88 adj.
unaccomplished
unskilful 695 adj.
uncompleted 726 adj.
unaccountable
unusual 84 adj.
changeful 152 adj.
causeless 159 adj.
wonderful 864 adj.
non-liable 919 n.
lawless 954 adj.
unaccustomed
unusual 84 adj.
unhabituated 611 adj.
clumsy 695 adj.
unachievable
impracticable 470 adj.
unacknowledged
unadmitted 489 adj.
unthanked 908 adj.
unacquaintance
ignorance 491 n.
unadaptable *rigid* 326 adj.
useless 641 adj.
unskilful 695 adj.
unadmired
unrespected 921 adj.
unadmiring
incurious 454 adj.
unastonished 865 adj.
disapproving 924 adj.
unadmitted
unadmitted 489 n.
unadorned
intelligible 516 adj.
plain 573 adj.
artless 699 adj.

unadulterated
unmixed 44 adj.
whole 52 adj.
genuine 494 adj.
pure 950 adj.
unadventurous
quiescent 266 adj.
cautious 858 adj.
unadvisable
inexpedient 643 adj.
unaesthetic *graceless* 842 adj.
unaffected *simple* 44 adj.
intact 52 adj.
permanent 144 adj.
veracious 540 adj.
elegant 575 adj.
artless 699 adj.
impassive 820 adj.
non-liable 919 adj.
unaffectedness
plainness 573 n.
unaffectionate
unkind 898 adj.
unafraid *unfearing* 855 adj.
unageing *perpetual* 115 adj.
unaggressive *inert* 175 adj.
peaceful 717 adj.
unagreed *disagreeing* 25 adj.
unaided *hindered* 702 adj.
unaimed
indiscriminate 464 adj.
unalike *dissimilar* 19 adj.
unalloyed *unmixed* 44 adj.
unalluring *unwanted* 860 adj.
unaltered *identical* 13 adj.
permanent 144 adj.
unchangeable 153 adj.
unambiguity *certainty* 473 n.
connotation 514 n.
intelligibility 516 n.
unambiguous
positive 473 adj.
veracious 540 adj.
perspicuous 567 adj.
unambitious
apathetic 820 adj.
inexcitable 823 adj.
indifferent 860 adj.
inglorious 867 adj.
modest 874 adj.
un-American
extraneous 59 adj.
unamiable *unkind* 898 adj.
unamused *bored* 838 adj.
disapproving 924 adj.
unamusing *tedious* 838 adj.
dull 840 adj.
unanimity *agreement* 24 n.
consensus 488 n.
co-operation 706 n.
concord 710 n.

unanimous
(*see* unanimity)
unannounced
unexpected 508 adj.
unanswerable
demonstrated 478 adj.
completive 725 adj.
non-liable 919 adj.
unapologizing
impenitent 940 adj.
unappalled
unfearing 855 adj.
unapparelled
uncovered 229 adj.
unapparent
invisible 444 adj.
unappeasable
violent 176 adj.
obstinate 602 adj.
revengeful 910 adj.
unappetizing
unsavoury 391 adj.
unappreciated
undervalued 483 adj.
unapprehended
unknown 491 adj.
unapprehensive
unfearing 855 adj.
unapproachable
supreme 34 adj.
infinite 107 adj.
removed 199 adj.
impracticable 470 adj.
prideful 871 adj.
unappropriated
unpossessed 774 adj.
not retained 779 adj.
unapproved
disapproved 924 adj.
unapt *unapt* 25 adj.
inexpedient 643 adj.
unskilful 695 adj.
unarmed
defenceless 161 adj.
peaceful 717 adj.
unarmoured
vulnerable 661 adj.
unaroused *inert* 175 adj.
quiescent 266 adj.
inactive 679 adj.
apathetic 820 adj.
unastonished 865 adj.
unarranged *orderless* 61 adj.
unprepared 670 adj.
unartificial *artless* 699 adj.
unascertained
uncertified 474 adj.
unashamed
impenitent 940 adj.
unasked *voluntary* 597 adj.
unwedded 895 adj.

unaspiring
indifferent 860 adj.
inglorious 867 adj.
unassailable
invulnerable 660 adj.
pure 950 adj.
unassembled
unassembled 75 adj.
unassenting
involuntary 596 adj.
unassimilated
separate 46 adj.
extraneous 59 adj.
unsociable 883 adj.
unassociated
separate 46 adj.
unassuming *plain* 573 adj.
artless 699 adj.
humble 872 adj.
modest 874 adj.
unassured *doubting* 474 adj.
unastonished
unastonished 865 adj.
unatoned
unrepented 940 adj.
unattached *separate* 46 adj.
independent 744 adj.
unattempted
avoidable 620 adj.
unattended
neglected 458 adj.
unattested
unattested 467 adj.
uncertified 474 adj.
unattracted
indifferent 860 adj.
unattractive
unpleasant 827 adj.
unwanted 860 adj.
unauthentic
uncertified 474 adj.
erroneous 495 adj.
unauthoritative
uncertified 474 adj.
unauthorized
powerless 161 adj.
anarchic 734 adj.
wrong 914 adj.
unwarranted 916 adj.
heterodox 977 adj.
unavailable *absent* 190 adj.
impracticable 470 adj.
scarce 636 adj.
unavoidable
certain 473 adj.
necessary 596 adj.
compelling 740 adj.
obligatory 917 adj.
unaware *ignorant* 491 adj.
inexpectant 508 adj.
unawed *unfearing* 855 adj.

unastonished 865 adj.
impious 980 adj.
unbacked
unhabituated 611 adj.
unbaked *uncooked* 670 adj.
unbalance *inequality* 29 n.
derange 63 vb.
unbalanced *unwise* 499 adj.
crazed 503 adj.
owed 803 adj.
unballasted *unequal* 29 adj.
unbaptized
heathenish 974 adj.
unbar *deliver* 668 vb.
liberate 746 vb.
unbated *sharp* 256 adj.
unbearable
exorbitant 32 adj.
intolerable 827 adj.
unbeatable
unyielding 162 adj.
unbeaten 727 adj.
unbeaten *new* 126 adj.
persevering 600 adj.
unused 674 adj.
unbeaten 727 adj.
unbecoming
graceless 842 adj.
discreditable 867 adj.
unbegotten *unborn* 2 adj.
unbeholden
ungrateful 908 adj.
unbeknown
unknown 491 adj.
unbelief *unbelief* 486 n.
irreligion 974 n.
unbelievable
unbelieved 486 adj.
wonderful 864 adj.
unbeliever
unbeliever 486 n.
irreligionist 974 n.
impious person 980 n.
unbelted *reposeful* 683 adj.
unbend *straighten* 249 vb.
soften 327 vb.
repose 683 vb.
be humble 872 vb.
be sociable 882 vb.
show mercy 905 vb.
forgive 909 vb.
unbending *rigid* 326 adj.
narrow-minded 481 adj.
resolute 599 adj.
obstinate 602 adj.
restraining 747 adj.
prideful 871 adj.
unsociable 883 adj.
unbiased
symmetrical 245 adj.
judicial 480 adj.

wise 498 adj.
free 744 adj.
just 913 adj.
unbiblical
heterodox 977 adj.
unbiddable
disobedient 738 adj.
unbidden *voluntary* 597 adj.
unwanted 860 adj.
unbigoted *wise* 498 adj.
unbind *disjoin* 46 vb.
deliver 668 vb.
be lax 734 vb.
liberate 746 vb.
not retain 779 vb.
unbleached *whitish* 427 adj.
unblemished
perfect 646 adj.
beautiful 841 adj.
innocent 935 adj.
unblest
unprosperous 731 adj.
unfortunate 731 adj.
cursed 899 adj.
heathenish 974 adj.
profane 980 adj.
unblest with
not owning 774 adj.
unblinking *still* 266 adj.
unblown *immature* 670 adj.
unblunted *sharp* 256 adj.
unblurred *well-seen* 443 adj.
unblushing
thick-skinned 820 adj.
proud 871 adj.
insolent 878 adj.
impenitent 940 adj.
unchaste 951 adj.
unbolt *liberate* 746 vb.
unborn *unborn* 2 adj.
immature 670 adj.
unborn, the
aftercomer 67 n.
unbosom oneself
divulge 526 vb.
unbound *unconfined* 744 adj.
liberated 746 adj.
non-liable 919 n.
unbounded *infinite* 107 adj.
unbowed *vertical* 215 adj.
unbreakable
unyielding 162 adj.
dense 324 adj.
hard 326 adj.
tough 329 adj.
invulnerable 660 adj.
unbreeched
infantine 132 adj.
unbribable
honourable 929 adj.
unbridgeable

impracticable 470 adj.
unintelligible 517 adj.
unbridle *disjoin* 46 vb.
unbridled *violent* 176 adj.
anarchic 734 adj.
free 744 adj.
unconfined 744 adj.
unbriefed
uninstructed 491 adj.
unbroken *uniform* 16 adj.
intact 52 adj.
complete 54 adj.
continuous 71 adj.
smooth 258 adj.
tranquil 266 adj.
unhabituated 611 adj.
unbroken front
coherence 48 n.
unbrotherly *unkind* 898 adj.
unburden
disencumber 701 vb.
relieve 831 vb.
unburnished *dim* 419 adj.
unbury *exhume* 364 vb.
unbusinesslike
unskilful 695 adj.
unbutton *disjoin* 46 vb.
doff 229 vb.
unbuttoned
reposeful 683 adj.
sociable 882 adj.
uncage *liberate* 746 vb.
uncalculating
unwise 499 adj.
rash 857 adj.
uncalled for
voluntary 597 adj.
superfluous 637 adj.
useless 641 adj.
undue 916 adj.
uncanny *spooky* 970 adj.
magical 983 adj.
uncanonical
non-observant 769 adj.
uncap *doff* 229 vb.
greet 884 vb.
uncared for
neglected 458 adj.
unwanted 860 adj.
hated 888 adj.
uncaring *negligent* 458 adj.
lax 734 adj.
indifferent 860 adj.
uncase *doff* 229 vb.
uncatholic
heterodox 977 adj.
uncaught *free* 744 adj.
unwedded 895 adj.
uncaused *causeless* 159 adj.
unceasing *perpetual* 115 adj.
frequent 139 adj.

permanent 144 adj.
unceasing 146 adj.
persevering 600 adj.
uncensored intact 52 adj.
impure 951 adj.
uncensorious
approving 923 adj.
unceremonious
discourteous 885 adj.
uncertain fitful 142 adj.
changeful 152 adj.
unstable 152 adj.
casual 159 adj.
moot 459 adj.
unattested 467 adj.
improbable 472 adj.
uncertain 474 adj.
irresolute 601 adj.
capricious 604 adj.
speculative 618 adj.
uncertainty doubt 486 n.
ignorance 491 n.
equivocalness 518 n.
gambling 618 n.
(see uncertain)
uncertified
uncertified 474 adj.
unchain disjoin 46 vb.
liberate 746 vb.
unchallengeable
undisputed 473 adj.
invulnerable 660 adj.
just 813 adj.
due 915 adj.
unchangeability
permanence 144 n.
unchangeable
lasting 113 adj.
unchangeable 153 adj.
obstinate 602 adj.
unchanging
characteristic 5 adj.
identical 13 adj.
uniform 16 adj.
perpetual 115 adj.
permanent 144 adj.
unchangeable 153 adj.
trustworthy 929 adj.
godlike 965 adj.
unchaperoned alone 88 adj.
unchargeable
cheap 812 adj.
uncharged
uncharged 812 adj.
uncharitable
parsimonious 816 adj.
unkind 898 adj.
selfish 932 adj.
uncharted
unknown 491 adj.
unchartered

unentitled 916 adj.
unwarranted 916 adj.
illegal 954 adj.
unchaste inelegant 576 adj.
intemperate 943 adj.
unchaste 951 adj.
unchastened
impenitent 940 adj.
unchecked
uncertified 474 adj.
unconfined 744 adj.
uncheckered
permanent 144 adj.
unchivalrous
discourteous 885 adj.
dishonest 930 adj.
unchosen rejected 607 adj.
disliked 861 adj.
hated 888 adj.
un-church
perform ritual 988 vb.
uncial letter 558 n.
written 586 adj.
uncircumcised
heathenish 974 adj.
uncircumscribed
spacious 183 adj.
uncircumspect
negligent 458 adj.
rash 857 adj.
uncivic
misanthropic 902 adj.
uncivil ill-bred 847 adj.
discourteous 885 adj.
impertinent 878 adj.
uncivilized ignorant 491 adj.
immature 670 adj.
artless 699 adj.
ill-bred 847 adj.
plebeian 869 adj.
unclad uncovered 229 adj.
unclaimable
unwarranted 916 adj.
unclaimed free 744 adj.
unpossessed 774 adj.
not retained 779 adj.
unclarified opaque 423 adj.
unclasp disjoin 46 vb.
unclassical
inelegant 576 adj.
unclassifiable
irrelative 10 adj.
unconformable 84 adj.
unclassified mixed 43 adj.
orderless 61 adj.
uncertain 474 adj.
unknown 491 adj.
uncle kinsman 11 n.
lender 784 n.
unclean unclean 649 adj.
uncleaned opaque 423 adj.

uncleanliness
insalubrity 653 n.
uncleanly unclean 649 adj.
uncleanness impurity 951 n.
(see unclean)
unclean spirit devil 969 n.
unclear ill-seen 444 adj.
imperspicuous 568 adj.
unclerical laical 987 adj.
unclench open 263 vb.
relinquish 621 vb.
not retain 779 vb.
unclerical laical 987 adj.
unclinch
be disjoined 46 vb.
relinquish 621 vb.
liberate 746 vb.
not retain 779 vb.
unclipped intact 52 adj.
uncloak uncover 229 vb.
disclose 526 vb.
unclose open 263 vb.
disclose 526 vb.
unclot liquefy 337 vb.
make flow 350 vb.
unclothe uncover 229 vb.
unclotted fluidal 335 adj.
unclouded
undimmed 417 adj.
well-seen 443 adj.
unclubbable
unsociable 883 adj.
uncoil unravel 62 vb.
lengthen 203 vb.
straighten 249 vb.
recoil 280 vb.
evolve 316 vb.
uncollected disjunct 46 adj.
uncoloured unmixed 44 adj.
colourless 426 adj.
genuine 494 adj.
plain 573 adj.
uncombed orderless 61 adj.
uncombined
unmixed 44 adj.
non-adhesive 49 adj.
decomposed 51 adj.
uncomely ugly 842 adj.
uncomfortable
painful 377 adj.
suffering 825 adj.
unpleasant 827 adj.
uncomforted
discontented 829 adj.
uncomforting
cheerless 834 adj.
uncommendable
inexpedient 643 adj.
blameworthy 924 adj.
uncommitted
neutral 625 adj.
independent 744 adj.

uncommon
remarkable 32 adj.
special 80 adj.
infrequent 140 adj.
elegant 575 adj.
uncommunicated
retained 778 adj.
uncompelled
independent 744 adj.
uncompensated
unequal 29 adj.
uncomplaining
patient 823 adj.
content 828 adj.
approving 923 adj.
uncompleted
uncompleted 726 adj.
uncomplicated
simple 44 adj.
artless 699 adj.
easy 701 adj.
uncomplimentary
ungracious 885 adj.
disrespectful 921 adj.
disapproving 924 adj.
uncompounded
unmixed 44 adj.
uncompromising
resolute 599 adj.
obstinate 602 adj.
severe 735 adj.
unconcealed
manifest 522 adj.
unconceived *unborn* 2 adj.
unconcentrated
light-minded 456 adj.
unconcern
incuriosity 454 n.
inattention 456 n.
moral insensibility 820 n.
indifference 860 n.
unconcerned
irrelative 10 adj.
unfearing 855 adj.
(*see* unconcern)
unconditional
unconditional 744 adj.
permitted 756 adj.
obligatory 917 adj.
unconfident
doubting 474 adj.
unconfined
facilitated 701 adj.
unconfined 744 adj.
non-liable 919 adj.
unconfirmed
uncertified 474 adj.
heathenish 974 adj.
unconformable
irrelative 10 adj.
unimitative 21 adj.

disagreeing 25 adj.
unconformable 84 adj.
unconformity
non-uniformity 17 n.
extraneousness 59 n.
speciality 80 n.
unconformity 84 n.
independence 744 n.
non-observance 769 n.
(*see* unconformable)
unconfused *orderly* 60 adj.
unconfuted
demonstrated 478 adj.
uncongealed *fluid* 335 adj.
liquefied 337 adj.
uncongenial
irrelative 10 adj.
disagreeing 25 adj.
cheerless 834 adj.
unconnected
irrelative 10 adj.
unconquerable
unyielding 162 adj.
persevering 600 adj.
resisting 715 adj.
unbeaten 727 adj.
independent 744 adj.
unconscionable
exorbitant 32 adj.
unconscious
impotent 161 adj.
insensible 375 adj.
ignorant 491 adj.
foolish 499 adj.
involuntary 596 adj.
inactive 679 adj.
sleepy 679 adj.
impassive 820 adj.
unconscious, the
spirit 447 n.
unconsecrated
heathenish 974 adj.
profane 980 adj.
laical 987 adj.
unconsidered
unthought 450 adj.
neglected 458 adj.
unconsoled
discontented 829 adj.
unconstitutional
unwarranted 916 adj.
illegal 954 adj.
unconsumed
remaining 41 adj.
unused 674 adj.
uncontaminated
perfect 646 adj.
uncontested
undisputed 473 adj.
uncontradicted
assented 488 n.

uncontrasting
uniform 16 adj.
uncontrite
impenitent 940 adj.
uncontrollable
violent 176 adj.
frenzied 503 adj.
wilful 602 adj.
fervent 818 adj.
excited 821 adj.
excitable 822 adj.
uncontrolled *hasty* 680 adj.
anarchic 734 adj.
independent 744 adj.
intemperate 943 adj.
uncontroversial
undisputed 473 adj.
assented 488 adj.
unconventional
unconformable 84 adj.
unwonted 611 adj.
free 744 adj.
heterodox 977 adj.
unconventionality
unconformity 84 n.
unconversant
unskilled 695 adj.
unconverted
unconformable 84 adj.
dissenting 489 adj.
unused 674 adj.
impenitent 940 adj.
heathenish 974 adj.
unconvinced
dissenting 489 adj.
unconvincing
improbable 472 adj.
uncooked *uncooked* 670 adj.
unco-operative
unwilling 598 adj.
hindering 702 adj.
dutiless 918 adj.
unco-ordinated
orderless 61 adj.
uncopied
unimitated 21 adj.
uncordial *unkind* 898 adj.
uncork *open* 263 vb.
liberate 746 vb.
uncorrected *inexact* 495 adj.
uncorroborated
unattested 467 adj.
uncertified 474 adj.
uncorrupted
disinterested 931 adj.
innocent 935 adj.
pure 950 adj.
uncostly *cheap* 812 adj.
uncounted *many* 104 adj.
uncouple *disjoin* 46 vb.
uncourtly *ill-bred* 847 adj.

discourteous 885 adj.
uncouth *inelegant* 576 adj.
  artless 699 adj.
  graceless 842 adj.
  ill-bred 847 adj.
  plebeian 869 adj.
uncovenanted
  unexpected 508 adj.
uncover *doff* 229 vb.
  open 263 vb.
  manifest 522 vb.
  disclose 526 vb.
  greet 884 vb.
uncovered
  vulnerable 661 adj.
uncracked *perfect* 646 adj.
uncrease *unravel* 62 vb.
  smooth 258 vb.
uncreated *existing* 1 adj.
  unborn 2 adj.
uncritical
  indiscriminating 464 adj.
  approving 923 adj.
uncrown *unthrone* 734 vb.
  depose 752 vb.
  disentitle 916 vb.
uncrowned king
  influence 178 n.
unction *lubrication* 334 n.
  unguent 357 n.
  warm feeling 818 n.
  pietism 979 n.
unctuous *unctuous* 357 adj.
  flattering 925 adj.
uncultivated
  unproductive 172 adj.
  uninstructed 491 adj.
  ill-bred 847 adj.
uncultured
  uninstructed 491 adj.
  artless 699 adj.
  ill-bred 847 adj.
  plebeian 869 adj.
uncurbed
  unconfined 744 adj.
uncured *uncooked* 670 adj.
uncurl *straighten* 249 vb.
  evolve 316 vb.
uncurrent *unwonted* 611 adj.
  useless 641 adj.
uncurtain *disclose* 526 vb.
uncustomary
  unusual 84 n.
uncut *intact* 52 adj.
  immature 670 adj.
undamaged *intact* 52 adj.
  undamaged 646 adj.
undashed *unfearing* 855 adj.
undated
  anachronistic 118 adj.
undaughterly

disobedient 738 adj.
  unkind 898 adj.
  dutiless 918 adj.
undaunted *resolute* 599 adj.
  persevering 600 adj.
  unfearing 855 adj.
undazzled *wise* 498 adj.
  unastonished 865 adj.
undecayed
  preserved 666 adj.
undeceive *inform* 524 vb.
  disclose 526 vb.
  displease 827 vb.
undeceived
  regretting 830 adj.
undecided *moot* 459 adj.
  doubting 474 adj.
  uncertain 474 adj.
  irresolute 601 adj.
undecipherable
  unintelligible 517 adj.
undeclared *tacit* 523 adj.
undecorated
  inglorious 867 adj.
undedicate *paganize* 974 vb.
  laicize 987 vb.
undedicated *profane* 980 adj.
undefaced *shapely* 841 adj.
undefeated
  resisting 715 adj.
  unbeaten 727 adj.
undefiled *innocent* 935 adj.
  pure 950 adj.
undefined
  amorphous 244 adj.
  shadowy 419 adj.
  ill-seen 444 adj.
  indiscriminate 464 adj.
  uncertain 474 adj.
  godlike 965 adj.
undeformed *shapely* 841 adj.
undemanding *easy* 701 adj.
  lax 734 adj.
  lenient 736 adj.
  inexcitable 823 adj.
undemocratic
  unequal 29 adj.
  authoritarian 735 adj.
  prideful 871 adj.
  insolent 878 adj.
undemonstrated
  uncertified 474 adj.
undemonstrative
  impassive 820 adj.
undeniable
  undisputed 473 adj.
  demonstrated 478 adj.
  credal 485 adj.
undenominational
  general 79 adj.
undependable

uncertain 474 adj.
  dishonest 930 adj.
undeplored *hated* 888 adj.
undepraved
  honourable 929 adj.
under *concerning* 9 adv.
  inferior 35 adj.
  in place 186 adv.
  low 210 adj.
  under 210 adv.
  subject 745 adj.
under a cloud
  unprosperous 731 adj.
underact *act* 594 vb.
  be unskilful 695 vb.
under-age *young* 130 adj.
under arms
  warring 718 adj.
under arrest
  imprisoned 747 adj.
  captive 750 adj.
underbelly *lowness* 210 n.
  insides 224 n.
underbid *bargain* 791 vb.
underbodice
  underwear 228 n.
underbred *ill-bred* 847 adj.
under canvas
  under way 269 adv.
undercapitalized
  unprovided 636 adj.
undercarriage *frame* 218 n.
  aircraft 276 n.
undercharge
  account 808 vb.
  cheapen 812 vb.
underclothed
  uncovered 229 adj.
underclothes
  underwear 228 n.
under consideration
  in mind 449 adv.
  in question 452 adv.
  planned 623 adj.
under construction
  in preparation 669 adv.
  on the stocks 726 adv.
under control
  orderly 60 adj.
  obedient 739 adj.
  restrained 747 adj.
under cover
  covered 226 adj.
  latent 523 adj.
  concealed 525 adj.
  under shelter 660 adv.
undercover agent
  secret service 459 n.
under cover of
  deceptively 542 adv.
undercurrent *cause* 156 n.

current 350 n.
latency 523 n.
undercut *meat* 301 n.
sell 793 vb.
cheapen 812 vb.
underdeveloped
incomplete 55 adj.
immature 670 adj.
under discipline
obedient 739 adj.
restrained 747 adj.
under discussion
in question 452 adv.
underdog *inferior* 35 n.
loser 728 n.
unlucky person 731 n.
underdone
uncooked 670 adj.
uncompleted 726 adj.
underdressed
uncovered 229 adj.
vulgar 847 adj.
underemployment
superfluity 637 n.
inaction 677 n.
underestimate
misjudge 481 vb.
underestimate 483 vb.
err 495 vb.
misinterpret 521 vb.
not respect 921 vb.
detract 926 vb.
underestimation
untruth 543 n.
(*see* underestimate)
underexposure
achromatism 426 n.
photography 551 n.
underfed *lean* 206 adj.
necessitous 627 adj.
underfed 636 adj.
unhealthy 651 adj.
hungry 859 adj.
fasting 946 adj.
underfeed
make thin 206 vb.
underfoot *low* 210 adj.
subjected 745 adj.
underframe *supporter* 218 n.
undergo *meet with* 154 vb.
feel 818 vb.
suffer 825 vb.
undergraduate
college student 538 adj.
immature 670 adj.
underground *low* 210 adj.
deep 211 adj.
tunnel 263 n.
train 274 n.
buried 364 adj.
concealed 525 adj.

hiding-place 527 n.
revolter 738 n.
underground activities
sedition 738 n.
undergrowth
roughness 259 n.
wood 366 n.
underhand *occult* 523 adj.
stealthy 525 adj.
dishonest 930 adj.
underheated
insalubrious 653 adj.
underhung *salient* 254 adj.
under-insurance
rashness 857 n.
underived
unimitative 21 adj.
underlayer *layer* 207 n.
base 214 n.
underlie *be low* 210 vb.
lurk 523 vb.
underline
strengthen 162 vb.
attract notice 455 vb.
emphasize 532 vb.
mark 547 vb.
make important 638 vb.
underlinen
underwear 228 n.
underling *inferior* 35 n.
nonentity 639 n.
servant 742 n.
commoner 869 n.
underlining
punctuation 547 n.
underlying
undermost 214 adj.
latent 523 adj.
underman
render few 105 vb.
undermanned
unprovided 636 adj.
imperfect 647 adj.
undermine *disable* 161 vb.
weaken 163 vb.
demolish 165 vb.
make concave 255 vb.
descend 309 vb.
tell against 467 vb.
plot 623 vb.
impair 655 vb.
be cunning 698 vb.
hinder 702 vb.
undermining
overturning 221 n.
undermost *base* 214 adj.
underneath *under* 210 adv.
undernourished
underfed 636 adj.
unhealthy 651 adj.
underpaid *cheap* 812 adj.

unwarranted 916 adj.
underpants
underwear 228 n.
underpass *tunnel* 263 n.
passage 305 n.
traffic control 305 n.
bridge 624 n.
underpay *be undue* 916 vb.
underpin *support* 218 vb.
underplot *plot* 623 n.
underpopulation
fewness 105 n.
underpraise
misinterpret 521 vb.
underprice
underestimate 483 vb.
underpriced
undervalued 483 adj.
cheap 812 adj.
underprivileged
unentitled 916 adj.
underprivileged, the
poor man 801 n.
lower classes 869 n.
underproduction
decrease 37 n.
under proof
tasteless 387 adj.
underprop *support* 218 vb.
underrate
underestimate 483 vb.
cheapen 812 vb.
not respect 921 vb.
hold cheap 922 vb.
underripe
immature 670 adj.
underscore *mark* 547 vb.
undersea *deep* 211 adj.
oceanic 343 adj.
undersell *cheapen* 812 vb.
undershot *salient* 254 adj.
underside *lowness* 210 n.
undersign *sign* 547 n.
undersigned, the
signatory 765 n.
undersized *small* 33 adj.
dwarfish 196 adj.
lean 206 adj.
underskirt
underwear 228 n.
undersong
vocal music 412 n.
latency 523 n.
understaff *render few* 105 vb.
understaffed
unprovided 636 adj.
understand *cognize* 447 vb.
be certain 473 vb.
know 490 vb.
be wise 498 vb.
understand 516 vb.

imply 523 vb.
be informed 524 vb.
be benevolent 897 vb.
understandable
intelligible 516 adj.
understand by
interpret 520 vb.
understanding
agreement 24 n.
intellect 447 n.
intelligence 498 n.
imagination 513 n.
concord 710 n.
pacification 719 n.
compact 765 n.
pity 905 n.
understand one another
co-operate 706 vb.
understatement
underestimation 483 n.
untruth 543 n.
understood *tacit* 523 adj.
usual 610 adj.
understrapper *inferior* 35 n.
nonentity 639 n.
servant 742 n.
understudy *substitute* 150 n.
actor 594 n.
act 594 vb.
deputy 755 n.
undersurface *lowness* 210 n.
undertake *begin* 68 vb.
essay 671 vb.
undertake 672 vb.
promise 764 vb.
contract 765 vb.
undertaker *interment* 364 n.
gambler 618 n.
essayer 671 n.
doer 676 n.
undertaking
undertaking 672 n.
promise 764 n.
under the sun
existing 1 adj.
widely 183 adv.
under the sun 321 adv.
undertone *faintness* 401 n.
musical note 410 n.
latency 523 n.
undertow *current* 350 n.
pitfall 663 n.
undervaluation
diminution 37 n.
misjudgment 481 n.
underestimation 483 n.
disrespect 921 n.
undervalue
hold cheap 922 vb.
(*see* undervaluation)
undervitaminized

underfed 636 adj.
unhealthy 651 adj.
underwater *deep* 211 adj.
oceanic 343 adj.
underwear *underwear* 228 n.
underweight
inequality 29 n.
inferior 35 adj.
light 323 adj.
spurious 542 adj.
underwood *wood* 366 n.
underworld *depth* 211 n.
the dead 361 n.
lower classes 869 n.
offender 904 n.
wickedness 934 n.
hell 972 n.
underwrite
promise 764 vb.
contract 765 vb.
give security 767 vb.
underwriter *consignee* 754 n.
underwriting
calculation of chance 159 n.
security 767 n.
undeserved
unwarranted 916 adj.
undeserving
unentitled 916 adj.
wicked 934 adj.
undesigned
causeless 159 adj.
unintentional 618 adj.
undesigning *artless* 699 adj.
undesirability
inexpedience 643 n.
undesirable
trouble-maker 663 n.
unpleasant 827 adj.
unwanted 860 adj.
disliked 861 adj.
bad man 938 n.
undestroyed
existing 1 adj.
intact 52 adj.
permanent 144 adj.
undetected *latent* 523 adj.
undetermined
general 79 adj.
causeless 159 adj.
moot 459 adj.
uncertain 474 adj.
choiceless 606 adj.
undeveloped
incomplete 55 adj.
unintelligent 499 adj.
latent 523 adj.
imperfect 647 adj.
immature 670 adj.
unskilled 695 adj.

undevelopment
undevelopment 670 n.
non-completion 726 n.
undeviating *uniform* 16 adj.
unchangeable 153 adj.
straight 249 adj.
directed 281 adj.
accurate 494 adj.
undeviating 625 adj.
indifferent 860 adj.
orthodox 976 adj.
undevout *irreligious* 974 adj.
impious 980 adj.
undifferentiated
uniform 16 adj.
simple 44 adj.
indiscriminate 464 adj.
undigested
extraneous 59 adj.
immature 670 adj.
uncooked 670 adj.
undignified *vulgar* 847 adj.
undiluted *unmixed* 44 adj.
undiminished
absolute 32 adj.
intact 52 adj.
strong 162 adj.
undamaged 646 adj.
undimmed
undimmed 417 adj.
Undine *sea-nymph* 343 n.
mythical being 970 n.
undirected *deviating* 282 adj.
indiscriminate 464 adj.
designless 618 adj.
undiscerning *blind* 439 adj.
inattentive 456 adj.
indiscriminating 464 adj.
unwise 499 adj.
undisciplined
disorderly 61 adj.
capricious 604 adj.
disobedient 738 adj.
intemperate 943 adj.
undisclosed *occult* 523 adj.
concealed 525 adj.
undiscouraged
persevering 600 adj.
hoping 852 adj.
undiscoverable
unborn 2 adj.
unknown 491 adj.
unintelligible 517 adj.
latent 523 adj.
undisguised
well-seen 443 adj.
undisguised 522 adj.
veracious 540 adj.
artless 699 adj.
undismayed
unfearing 655 adj.

undisposed of
  unused 674 adj.
  possessed 773 adj.
  retained 778 adj.
undisputed
  undisputed 473 adj.
undistinguished
  indiscriminate 464 adj.
  mediocre 732 adj.
undistorted
  symmetrical 245 adj.
  straight 249 adj.
  true 494 adj.
  veracious 540 adj.
undistracted
  attentive 455 adj.
undisturbed *tranquil* 266 adj.
undiversified *uniform* 16 adj.
undivided *intact* 52 adj.
  complete 54 adj.
undividedness *unity* 88 n.
undivulged *tacit* 523 adj.
undo *disjoin* 46 vb.
  revert 148 vb.
  destroy 165 vb.
  counteract 182 vb.
  doff 229 vb.
  make useless 641 vb.
  abrogate 752 vb.
undoing *ruin* 165 n.
undomesticated
  unhabituated 611 adj.
undone *neglected* 458 adj.
  uncompleted 726 adj.
  unprosperous 731 adj.
  hopeless 853 adj.
undoubted
  undisputed 473 adj.
undoubting
  positive 473 adj.
  believing 485 adj.
undrained *humid* 341 adj.
  marshy 347 adj.
  insalubrious 653 adj.
undramatic *feeble* 572 adj.
  plain 573 adj.
undreamt *unthought* 450 adj.
undress
  informal dress 228 n.
  uncover 229 vb.
undressed
  uncovered 229 adj.
  unsavoury 391 adj.
  unequipped 670 adj.
  uncooked 670 adj.
undrilled
  unprepared 670 adj.
undrinkable
  unsavoury 391 adj.
  insalubrious 653 adj.
undue *undue* 916 adj.

undueness
  overstepping 306 n.
  inexpedience 643 n.
  undueness 916 n.
undulate *be periodic* 141 vb.
  (*see* undulation)
undulation
  convolution 251 n.
  oscillation 317 n.
  wave 350 n.
undulatory
  periodical 141 adj.
  undulatory 251 adj.
undutiful *dutiless* 918 adj.
undying *existing* 1 adj.
  perpetual 115 adj.
  unceasing 146 adj.
  unchangeable 153 adj.
  remembered 505 adj.
unearned
  unwarranted 916 adj.
unearned increment
  benefit 615 n.
unearth *eject* 300 vb.
  exhume 364 vb.
  discover 484 vb.
unearthly
  immaterial 320 adj.
  divine 965 adj.
  spooky 970 adj.
uneasiness *worry* 825 n.
  discontent 829 n.
  nervousness 854 n.
uneasy *nervous* 854 adj.
uneatable
  unsavoury 391 adj.
uneconomic
  wasteful 634 adj.
  prodigal 815 adj.
unedifying
  misteaching 535 adj.
  discreditable 867 adj.
  vicious 934 adj.
unedited *intact* 52 adj.
  tacit 523 adj.
uneducated
  uninstructed 491 adj.
unelevated *feeble* 572 adj.
unembarrassed
  well-bred 848 adj.
unembroidered
  veracious 540 adj.
unemotional
  impassive 820 adj.
unemphatic *tranquil* 266 adj.
  muted 401 adj.
  feeble 572 adj.
  plain 573 adj.
  inexcitable 823 adj.
unemployable
  useless 641 adj.

  unused 674 adj.
unemployment
  superfluity 637 n.
  non-use 674 n.
  inaction 677 n.
  inactivity 679 n.
  adversity 731 n.
unempowered
  powerless 161 adj.
  unentitled 916 adj.
unending *perpetual* 115 adj.
unendurable
  intolerable 827 adj.
unenjoyable *tedious* 838 adj.
unenlightened
  ignorant 491 adj.
  unwise 499 adj.
unentailed
  non-liable 919 adj.
unenterprising
  cautious 858 adj.
unentertaining
  tedious 838 adj.
  dull 840 adj.
unenthusiastic
  unwilling 598 adj.
  apathetic 820 adj.
  inexcitable 823 adj.
unentitled
  unentitled 916 adj.
unenvious *content* 828 adj.
  benevolent 897 adj.
  disinterested 931 adj.
unequal *dissimilar* 19 adj.
  unequal 29 adj.
  inferior 35 adj.
unequalled *supreme* 34 adj.
  best 644 adj.
unequal to
  insufficient 636 adj.
unequipped
  unequipped 670 adj.
unequivocal
  absolute 32 adj.
  positive 473 adj.
  intelligible 516 adj.
unerring *certain* 473 adj.
  accurate 494 adj.
  successful 727 adj.
  innocent 935 adj.
unescorted *alone* 88 adj.
  vulnerable 661 adj.
unethical *dishonest* 930 adj.
uneven *non-uniform* 17 adj.
  unequal 29 adj.
  discontinuous 72 adj.
  fitful 142 adj.
  rough 259 adj.
  imperfect 647 adj.
  unjust 914 adj.
uneventful *tranquil* 266 adj.

trivial 639 adj.
unevolved *unreal* 2 adj.
unexaggerated
  genuine 494 adj.
unexamined
  neglected 458 adj.
unexampled
  unusual 84 n.
  unexpected 508 adj.
unexceptionable
  not bad 644 adj.
  guiltless 935 adj.
unexceptional
  regular 81 adj.
unexciting *lenitive* 177 adj.
  feeble 572 adj.
  tedious 838 adj.
unexecuted
  uncompleted 726 adj.
unexempt from
  liable 180 adj.
unexercised
  powerless 161 adj.
  unprepared 670 adj.
  unused 674 adj.
unexhausted
  unyielding 162 adj.
unexpected
  unexpected 508 adj.
  puzzling 517 adj.
  capricious 604 adj.
  wonderful 864 adj.
unexpended
  remaining 41 adj.
  stored 632 adj.
unexpired
  remaining 41 adj.
unexplained
  causeless 159 adj.
  uncertain 474 adj.
  unknown 491 adj.
  puzzling 517 adj.
  latent 523 adj.
unexplored
  neglected 458 adj.
  unknown 491 adj.
  latent 523 adj.
  secluded 883 adj.
unexposed *latent* 523 adj.
  safe 660 adj.
unexpressed *tacit* 523 adj.
unexpurgated *intact* 52 adj.
  impure 951 adj.
unextinguished
  violent 176 adj.
  fiery 379 adj.
unextreme *moderate* 177 adj.
  neutral 625 adj.
unfactual *erroneous* 495 adj.
unfading *lasting* 113 adj.
  perpetual 115 adj.

coloured 425 adj.
renowned 866 adj.
unfailing *permanent* 144 adj.
  unceasing 146 adj.
  persevering 600 adj.
  liberal 813 adj.
unfair *false* 541 adj.
  unjust 914 adj.
  dishonest 930 adj.
unfaith *unbelief* 486 n.
  perfidy 930 n.
unfaithful
  changeful 152 adj.
  unbelieving 486 adj.
  irresolute 601 adj.
  non-observant 769 adj.
  inimical 881 adj.
  perfidious 930 adj.
  extramarital 951 adj.
unfallen *innocent* 935 adj.
  pure 950 adj.
unfaltering
  persevering 600 adj.
unfamiliar *unusual* 84 adj.
  unknown 491 adj.
  unhabituated 611 adj.
  secluded 883 adj.
unfamiliarity
  ignorance 491 n.
unfashionable
  unconformable 84 adj.
  unwonted 611 adj.
  ill-bred 847 adj.
  plebeian 869 adj.
unfashioned
  amorphous 244 adj.
  immature 670 adj.
unfastened *separate* 46 adj.
unfastidious
  unclean 649 adj.
  vulgar 847 adj.
  dishonest 930 adj.
unfathered
  negative 533 adj.
unfathomable
  infinite 107 adj.
  deep 211 adj.
  unintelligible 517 adj.
unfavourable
  inopportune 138 adj.
  hindering 702 adj.
  opposing 704 adj.
  adverse 731 adj.
  disapproving 924 adj.
unfavoured
  unprosperous 731 adj.
unfearing *unfearing* 855 adj.
unfeasible
  impracticable 470 adj.
unfed *underfed* 636 adj.
  fasting 946 adj.

unfeeling
  unfeeling 375 adj.
  impassive 820 adj.
  unkind 898 adj.
  pure 950 adj.
  impious 980 adj.
unfeigned
  veracious 540 adj.
unfeminine *male* 372 adj.
  ill-bred 847 adj.
unfetter *disencumber* 701 vb.
  liberate 746 vb.
unfilial *disobedient* 738 adj.
  unkind 898 adj.
  dutiless 918 adj.
unfilled
  unprovided 636 adj.
  hungry 859 adj.
unfilling
  discontenting 829 adj.
unfinished
  fragmentary 53 adj.
  unfinished 55 adj.
  inelegant 576 adj.
  imperfect 647 adj.
  immature 670 adj.
  uncompleted 726 adj.
unfit *unapt* 25 adj.
  disable 161 vb.
  useless 641 adj.
  unskilful 695 adj.
  wrong 914 adj.
unfitness
  inexpedience 643 n.
  non-preparation 670 n.
  (see unfit)
unfitting
  inexpedient 643 adj.
  undue 916 adj.
unfix *displace* 188 vb.
unfixed *unstable* 152 adj.
  light-minded 456 adj.
  irresolute 601 adj.
unflagging
  unyielding 162 adj.
  persevering 600 adj.
  industrious 678 adj.
unflappable
  inexcitable 823 adj.
unflattered *wise* 498 adj.
  discontented 829 adj.
unflattering *true* 494 adj.
  ungracious 885 adj.
  maledicent 899 adj.
  disrespectful 921 adj.
  disapproving 924 adj.
  detracting 926 adj.
unflavoured
  unmixed 44 adj.
  tasteless 387 adj.
unflawed *perfect* 646 adj.

unfledged *new* 126 adj.
　young 130 adj.
　infantine 132 adj.
　uncovered 229 adj.
　immature 670 adj.
unfleshed *new* 126 adj.
unflinching *resolute* 599 adj.
　courageous 855 adj.
unfold *become* 1 vb.
　result 157 vb.
　produce 164 vb.
　lengthen 203 vb.
　uncover 229 vb.
　straighten 249 vb.
　open 263 vb.
　evolve 316 vb.
　interpret 520 vb.
　disclose 526 vb.
unforbidden
　permitted 756 adj.
unforced
　voluntary 597 adj.
　independent 744 adj.
unforeseeable
　causeless 159 adj.
　improbable 472 adj.
　uncertain 474 adj.
　unexpected 508 adj.
unforeseeing
　unwise 499 adj.
　rash 857 adj.
unforeseen
　unexpected 508 adj.
unforfeited
　retained 778 adj.
unforgettable
　remembered 505 adj.
　notable 638 adj.
unforgetting
　revengeful 910 adj.
unforgivable
　wrong 914 adj.
　accusable 928 adj.
　heinous 934 adj.
　guilty 936 adj.
unforgiving *severe* 735 adj.
　unkind 898 adj.
　malevolent 898 adj.
　pitiless 906 adj.
　revengeful 910 adj.
unformed
　amorphous 244 adj.
　immature 670 adj.
unforthcoming
　avoiding 620 adj.
　impassive 820 adj.
　unsociable 883 adj.
　unkind 898 adj.
unfortified *unmixed* 44 adj.
　defenceless 161 adj.
　weak 163 adj.

　vulnerable 661 adj.
unfortunate
　inopportune 138 adj.
　unfortunate 731 adj.
　unhappy 825 adj.
　annoying 827 adj.
unforward
　unskilful 695 adj.
unfound
　unequipped 670 adj.
unfounded *unreal* 2 adj.
　insubstantial 4 adj.
　illogical 477 adj.
　erroneous 495 adj.
unfranchised
　subject 745 adj.
　unentitled 916 adj.
unfraternal *unkind* 898 adj.
unfree *serving* 742 adj.
　subject 745 adj.
unfreeze *liquefy* 337 vb.
unfreezing
　non-retention 779 n.
unfresh *bad* 645 adj.
　insalubrious 653 adj.
unfriended
　defenceless 161 adj.
　friendless 883 adj.
unfriendliness
　unsociability 883 n.
　(*see* unfriendly)
unfriendly *opposing* 704 adj.
　disliking 861 adj.
　inimical 881 adj.
　ungracious 885 adj.
　unkind 898 adj.
unfrock *depose* 752 vb.
　deprive 786 vb.
　disentitle 916 vb.
　punish 963 vb.
　perform ritual 988 vb.
unfrozen *warm* 379 adj.
unfrugal
　intemperate 943 adj.
unfruitful
　unproductive 172 adj.
unfunny *serious* 834 adj.
　tedious 838 adj.
　dull 840 adj.
unfurl *lengthen* 203 vb.
　straighten 249 vb.
　evolve 316 vb.
　manifest 522 vb.
　disclose 526 vb.
unfurnished
　unprovided 636 adj.
　unequipped 670 adj.
ungainly *clumsy* 695 adj.
　graceless 842 adj.
ungallant
　discourteous 885 adj.

ungenerous
　parsimonious 816 adj.
　unkind 898 adj.
　selfish 932 adj.
ungenial
　insalubrious 653 adj.
ungenteel *ill-bred* 847 adj.
ungentle *violent* 176 adj.
　ungracious 885 adj.
　oppressive 735 adj.
ungentlemanly
　ill-bred 847 adj.
　discourteous 885 adj.
　dishonest 930 adj.
un-get-at-able
　removed 199 adj.
ungifted
　unintelligent 499 adj.
　unskilful 695 adj.
ungodly *irreligious* 974 adj.
ungovernable
　violent 176 adj.
　wilful 602 adj.
　disobedient 738 adj.
　independent 744 adj.
　lawless 954 adj.
ungoverned
　anarchic 734 adj.
　independent 744 adj.
ungraceful
　inelegant 576 adj.
　clumsy 695 adj.
　graceless 842 adj.
ungracious
　ungracious 885 adj.
ungrammatical
　ungrammatical 565 adj.
ungrateful *forgetful* 506 adj.
　ungrateful 908 adj.
ungratified
　refused 760 adj.
　discontented 829 adj.
ungreedy *temperate* 942 adj.
ungrounded
　illogical 477 adj.
　erroneous 495 adj.
ungrown *immature* 670 adj.
ungrudging *liberal* 813 adj.
　disinterested 931 adj.
unguaranteed
　uncertified 474 adj.
unguarded
　neglected 458 adj.
　spontaneous 609 adj.
　vulnerable 661 adj.
　unprepared 670 adj.
unguent *lubricant* 334 n.
　unguent 357 n.
　cosmetic 843 n.
unguessed
　unexpected 508 adj.

latent 523 adj.
unguided *deviating* 282 adj.
  designless 618 adj.
ungulate *footed* 214 adj.
unhabituated
  unhabituated 611 adj.
unhackneyed
  unimitated 21 adj.
  new 126 adj.
  unwonted 611 adj.
unhallowed *unclean* 649 adj.
  heathenish 974 adj.
  profane 980 adj.
unhand *liberate* 746 vb.
  not retain 779 vb.
unhandled *unused* 674 adj.
unhandselled *new* 126 adj.
  unprepared 670 adj.
unhandy *clumsy* 695 adj.
unhappy
  inopportune 138 adj.
  inexpedient 643 adj.
  bungled 695 adj.
  unfortunate 731 adj.
  unhappy 825 adj.
  discontented 829 adj.
  dejected 834 adj.
  nervous 854 adj.
unharmed *healthy* 650 adj.
  safe 660 adj.
unharness *disjoin* 46 vb.
  arrive 295 vb.
  liberate 746 vb.
unhatched
  immature 670 adj.
unhealthy *deadly* 362 adj.
  inexpedient 643 adj.
  harmful 645 adj.
  unhealthy 651 adj.
  insalubrious 653 adj.
  dangerous 661 adj.
unheard *silent* 399 adj.
  unknown 491 adj.
  inglorious 867 adj.
  modest 874 adj.
unheard of *new* 126 adj.
  impossible 470 adj.
  improbable 472 adj.
  wonderful 864 adj.
unhearing
  insensible 375 adj.
  deaf 416 adj.
  inattentive 456 adj.
  impassive 820 adj.
unheated *cold* 380 adj.
unheeding
  inattentive 456 adj.
unheld *unpossessed* 774 adj.
unhelpful
  unwilling 598 adj.
  inexpedient 643 adj.

hindering 702 adj.
  unkind 898 adj.
unheralded
  unexpected 508 adj.
unheroic *irresolute* 601 adj.
  cowardly 856 adj.
  inglorious 867 adj.
unhinge *derange* 63 vb.
  disable 161 vb.
  make mad 503 vb.
unhistorical
  erroneous 495 adj.
unhitch *disjoin* 46 vb.
unholy *heathenish* 974 adj.
  profane 980 adj.
  laical 987 adj.
unhook *disjoin* 46 vb.
unhopeful *dejected* 834 adj.
  hopeless 853 adj.
unhorsed *grounded* 728 adj.
unhoused *displaced* 188 adj.
unhousetrained
  ill-bred 847 adj.
unhurried *tranquil* 266 adj.
  slow 278 adj.
  leisurely 681 adj.
  inexcitable 823 adj.
unhurt *undamaged* 646 adj.
unhygienic
  insalubrious 653 adj.
unicameral *one* 88 adj.
  parliamentary 692 adj.
unicorn *rara avis* 84 n.
  heraldry 547 n.
unicycle *bicycle* 274 n.
unideal *existing* 1 adj.
  true 494 adj.
unidealistic *selfish* 932 adj.
unidentifiable
  unconformable 84 adj.
unidentified
  irrelative 10 adj.
  unknown 491 adj.
unidiomatic *unapt* 25 adj.
  abnormal 84 adj.
  unmeaning 515 adj.
  neological 560 adj.
unification
  simplification 44 n.
  combination 50 n.
  unity 88 n.
  association 706 n.
uniform
  dress, uniform 228 n.
  livery 547 n.
  badge of rank 743 n.
  (see uniformity)
uniformed *dressed* 228 adj.
uniformist *uniformist* 16 n.
uniformity *identity* 13 n.
  uniformity 16 n.

order 60 n.
  continuity 71 n.
  regularity 81 n.
unify *join* 45 vb.
  combine 50 vb.
  (see unification)
unilateral *irrelative* 10 adj.
  one 88 adj.
  independent 744 adj.
unimaginable
  unusual 84 adj.
  impossible 470 adj.
  improbable 472 adj.
  unbelieved 486 adj.
  wonderful 864 adj.
unimaginative
  imitative 20 adj.
  unthinking 450 adj.
  indiscriminating 464 adj.
  narrow-minded 481 adj.
  unintelligent 499 adj.
  plain 573 adj.
  thick-skinned 820 adj.
  impassive 820 adj.
  dull 840 adj.
  unastonished 865 adj.
unimitated
  unimitated 21 adj.
  special 80 adj.
unimitative
  unimitative 21 adj.
unimpaired *intact* 52 adj.
unimpassioned
  apathetic 820 adj.
unimpeachable
  undisputed 473 adj.
  true 494 adj.
  just 913 adj.
  due 915 adj.
  approvable 923 adj.
  guiltless 935 adj.
unimportance
  irrelevance 10 n.
  unimportance 639 n.
unimportant
  inconsiderable 33 adj.
  humble 872 adj.
  (see unimportance)
unimposing *modest* 874 adj.
unimpressed
  indifferent 860 adj.
  unastonished 865 adj.
  disapproving 924 adj.
unimpressionable
  impassive 820 adj.
uninfluenced
  obstinate 602 adj.
  free 744 adj.
  independent 744 adj.
uninfluential
  unimportant 639 adj.

uninformed
amorphous 244adj.
uninstructed 491adj.
inexpectant 508adj.
uninhabitable
empty 190adj.
uninhabited
secluded 883adj.
uninitiated
ignorant 491adj.
unskilled 695adj.
uninquisitive
incurious 454adj.
uninspired *feeble* 572adj.
plain 573adj.
apathetic 820adj.
tedious 838adj.
uninstructed
uninstructed 491adj.
unprepared 670adj.
unintellectual
mindless 448adj.
unthinking 450adj.
unintelligent 499adj.
unwise 499adj.
unintelligent
unthinking 450adj.
unintelligent 499adj.
unintelligibility
unintelligibility 517n.
imperspicuity 568n.
difficulty 700n.
unintended
causeless 159adj.
unmeant 515adj.
involuntary 596adj.
unintentional 618adj.
unintentional
involuntary 596adj.
spontaneous 609adj.
unintentional 618adj.
uninterest
incuriosity 454n.
uninterested
incurious 454adj.
choiceless 606adj.
inactive 679adj.
apathetic 820adj.
bored 838adj.
indifferent 860adj.
uninteresting
tedious 838adj.
dull 840adj.
uninterrupted
continuous 71adj.
perpetual 115adj.
unceasing 146adj.
uninventive
imitative 20adj.
mindless 448adj.
unthinking 450adj.

uninvited
disobedient 738adj.
unwanted 860adj.
friendless 883adj.
uninvited guest
intruder 59n.
uninviting
unpleasant 827adj.
uninvolved *irrelative* 10adj.
incurious 454adj.
intelligible 516adj.
independent 744adj.
indifferent 860adj.
disinterested 931adj.
union *agreement* 24n.
junction 45n.
coition 45n.
coherence 48n.
combination 50n.
unity 88n.
concurrence 181n.
association 706n.
society 708n.
marriage 894n.
Union Jack *flag* 547n.
unique *non-uniform* 17adj.
dissimilar 19adj.
unimitated 21adj.
special 80adj.
unconformable 84adj.
one 88adj.
valuable 644adj.
unirritable
inexcitable 823adj.
unirritating *lenitive* 177adj.
unison *uniformity* 16n.
agreement 24n.
melody 410n.
concord 710n.
unit *whole* 52n.
group 74n.
unit 88n.
person 371n.
formation 722n.
unitarianism
philosophy 449n.
heresy 977n.
Unitarians *sect* 978n.
unitary *one* 88adj.
unite *join* 45vb.
combine 50vb.
bring together 74vb.
be one 88vb.
concur 181vb.
converge 293vb.
co-operate 706vb.
united *agreeing* 24adj.
cohesive 48adj.
concordant 710adj.
married 894adj.
united front

association 706n.
unity *identity* 13n.
uniformity 16n.
simpleness 44n.
completeness 54n.
unity 88n.
association 706n.
concord 710n.
divine attribute 965n.
universal *extensive* 32adj.
comprehensive 52adj.
universal 79adj.
one 88adj.
ubiquitous 189adj.
cosmic 321adj.
universal aunt
servant 742n.
universality *generality* 79n.
indiscrimination 464n.
(*see* universal)
universalize
generalize 79vb.
universals *premise* 475n.
universe *substantiality* 3n.
great quantity 32n.
whole 52n.
universe 321n.
university *academy* 539n.
univocal *one* 88adj.
certain 473adj.
semantic 514adj.
unjealous *content* 828adj.
disinterested 931adj.
unjust *bad* 645adj.
oppressive 735adj.
unjust 914adj.
dishonest 930adj.
wicked 934adj.
unjustifiable *unjust* 914adj.
unwarranted 916adj.
blameworthy 924adj.
accusable 928adj.
heinous 934adj.
guilty 936adj.
unkempt *oraerless* 61adj.
rough 259adj.
neglected 458adj.
dirty 649adj.
unkind *harmful* 645adj.
unkind 898adj.
unknowable
unknown 491adj.
unintelligible 517adj.
unknown *new* 126adj.
unknown 491adj.
disguised 525adj.
anonymous 562adj.
secluded 883adj.
unknown quantity
unknown thing 491n.
secret 530n.

unlace *doff* 229 vb.
unladylike *ill-bred* 847 adj.
unlamented *hated* 888 adj.
　disapproved 924 adj.
unlatch *disjoin* 46 vb.
　open 263 vb.
unlaughing *serious* 834 adj.
unlawful *prohibited* 757 adj.
　non-observant 769 adj.
　extramarital 951 adj.
　illegal 954 adj.
unlearn *not know* 491 vb.
　forget 506 vb.
unlearned
　uninstructed 491 adj.
　artless 699 adj.
unleash *liberate* 746 vb.
unleavened *ritual* 988 adj.
unlegalized
　unwarranted 916 adj.
unlegislated *illegal* 954 adj.
unless *if* 8 adv.
　provided 468 adj.
unlettered
　uninstructed 491 adj.
unlicensed
　unwarranted 916 adj.
unlicked *immature* 670 adj.
unlicked cub
　youngster 132 n.
　amorphism 244 n.
　undevelopment 670 n.
　vulgarian 847 n.
　rude person 885 n.
unlike *different* 15 adj.
　dissimilar 19 adj.
unlikeable *not nice* 645 adj.
unlikely
　improbable 472 adj.
unlikeness
　non-imitation 21 n.
unlimited *absolute* 32 adj.
　infinite 107 adj.
　unconditional 744 adj.
unlit *unlit* 418 adj.
　invisible 444 adj.
unliterary
　dialectical 560 adj.
unlively *inexcitable* 823 adj.
　serious 834 adj.
　dull 840 adj.
unload *displace* 188 vb.
　transpose 272 vb.
　void 300 vb.
　extract 304 vb.
　disencumber 701 vb.
　sell 793 vb.
unlock *disjoin* 46 vb.
　open 263 vb.
　liberate 746 vb.
unlooked for

unexpected *508 adj.*
　undue 916 adj.
unloose *disjoin* 46 vb.
　deliver 668 vb.
　liberate 746 vb.
unlovely *ugly* 842 adj.
　disliked 861 adj.
unlucky *inopportune* 138 adj.
　evil 616 adj.
　unsuccessful 728 adj.
　unfortunate 731 adj.
unmade *unborn* 2 adj.
　amorphous 244 adj.
unmake *revert* 148 vb.
　destroy 165 vb.
　abrogate 752 vb.
unmalleable
　unconformable 84 adj.
　rigid 326 adj.
unman *unman* 161 vb.
　sterilize 172 vb.
　frighten 854 vb.
unmanageable
　wilful 602 adj.
　clumsy 695 adj.
　difficult 700 adj.
unmanifested
　latent 523 adj.
unmanly *female* 373 adj.
　cowardly 856 adj.
　dishonest 930 adj.
unmannerly
　discourteous 885 adj.
unmarred
　undamaged 646 adj.
unmarried
　unwedded 895 adj.
unmarry *divorce* 896 vb.
unmartial *cowardly* 856 adj.
unmask *disclose* 526 vb.
unmasterful *lax* 734 adj.
unmatched
　dissimilar 19 adj.
　unimitated 21 adj.
　best 644 adj.
　unwedded 895 adj.
unmeaning *absurd* 497 adj.
　semantic 514 adj.
　unmeaning 515 adj.
　designless 618 adj.
　unimportant 639 adj.
unmeaningness
　unintelligibility 517 n.
　equivocalness 518 n.
unmeant *unmeant* 515 adj.
　unintentional 618 adj.
unmeasured
　indiscriminate 464 adj.
　plenteous 635 adj.
　intemperate 943 adj.
unmediated *simple* 44 adj.

continuous 71 adj.
unmeditated
　spontaneous 609 adj.
unmeet *undue* 916 adj.
unmelting *pitiless* 906 adj.
unmentionable
　unusual 84 adj.
　inexpressible 517 adj.
　prohibited 757 adj.
　discreditable 867 adj.
　impure 951 adj.
unmentioned *tacit* 523 adj.
　inglorious 867 adj.
unmerciful
　pitiless 906 adj.
unmerited
　unwarranted 916 adj.
unmeritorious
　unentitled 916 adj.
　wicked 934 adj.
unmilitary *peaceful* 717 adj.
unmindful
　inattentive 456 adj.
　negligent 458 adj.
　ungrateful 908 adj.
unmingled *unmixed* 44 adj.
unmissed *neglected* 458 adj.
　unwanted 860 adj.
　hated 888 adj.
unmistakable
　visible 443 adj.
　certain 473 adj.
　intelligible 516 adj.
　manifest 522 adj.
unmitigated
　consummate 32 adj.
　complete 54 adj.
　violent 176 adj.
unmixed *absolute* 32 adj.
　unmixed 44 adj.
　whole 52 adj.
unmodified *unmixed* 44 adj.
　permanent 144 adj.
unmoor *be disjoined* 46 vb.
　navigate 269 vb.
　start out 296 vb.
unmotivated
　causeless 159 adj.
　spontaneous 609 adj.
unmotorable
　impracticable 470 adj.
unmourned *hated* 888 adj.
unmoved *quiescent* 266 adj.
　obstinate 602 adj.
　apathetic 820 adj.
　indifferent 860 adj.
　unastonished 865 adj.
　unkind 898 adj.
　pitiless 906 adj.
unmusical
　discordant 411 adj.

deaf 416 adj.
unmuzzle *liberate* 746 vb.
unnamed *unknown* 490 adj.
  concealed 525 adj.
  anonymous 562 adj.
unnatural
  disagreeing 25 adj.
  extraneous 59 adj.
  abnormal 84 adj.
  impossible 470 adj.
  inelegant 576 adj.
  affected 850 adj.
  unkind, cruel 898 adj.
unnavigable
  shallow 212 adj.
  impracticable 470 adj.
  difficult 700 adj.
unnecessary
  wasteful 634 adj.
  superfluous 637 adj.
  unimportant 639 adj.
  useless 641 adj.
  unused 674 adj.
unnerve *unman* 161 vb.
  weaken 163 vb.
  deject 834 vb.
  frighten 854 vb.
unnoticeable
  inconsiderable 33 adj.
  slow 278 adj.
  invisible 444 adj.
unnoticed
  neglected 458 adj.
  inglorious 867 adj.
unnourishing
  insufficient 636 adj.
unnumbered *many* 104 adj.
  infinite 107 adj.
unobjectionable
  not bad 644 adj.
  mediocre 732 adj.
  contenting 828 adj.
  vindicable 927 adj.
  guiltless 935 adj.
unobliged
  ungrateful 908 adj.
unobservant
  inattentive 456 adj.
unobstructed
  open 263 adj.
  accessible 289 adj.
  facilitated 701 adj.
  unconfined 744 adj.
unobtainable
  impracticable 470 adj.
  scarce 636 adj.
unobtrusive *modest* 874 adj.
unoccupied *empty* 190 adj.
  unthinking 450 adj.
  non-active 677 adj.
  inactive 679 adj.

leisurely 681 adj.
  unpossessed 774 adj.
unoffending *humble* 872 adj.
unofficial *uncertified* 474 adj.
  independent 744 adj.
  illegal 954 adj.
unopened *closed* 264 adj.
unopposed
  assented 488 adj.
unorganized
  orderless 61 adj.
  inorganic 359 adj.
  unprepared 670 adj.
  lax 734 adj.
unoriginal *imitative* 20 adj.
  caused 157 adj.
  mindless 448 adj.
  usual 610 adj.
  dull 840 adj.
unorthodoxy
  unconformity 84 n.
  error 495 n.
  heterodoxy 977 n.
unowned
  unpossessed 774 adj.
unpack *uncover* 229 vb.
  void 300 vb.
  extract 304 vb.
unpacking
  displacement 188 n.
  transference 272 n.
unpaid *voluntary* 597 adj.
  owed 803 adj.
  uncharged 812 adj.
unpalatable
  unsavoury 391 adj.
  unpleasant 827 adj.
unpampered
  temperate 942 adj.
  ascetic 945 adj.
unparalleled
  unusual 84 adj.
  best 644 adj.
unpardonable
  wrong 914 adj.
  accusable 928 adj.
  heinous 934 adj.
  guilty 936 adj.
unparliamentary
  maledicent 899 adj.
unpartnered
  unwedded 895 adj.
unpatriotic
  misanthropic 902 adj.
  selfish 932 adj.
unpeaceful
  contending 716 adj.
unperceived
  neglected 458 adj.
  unknown 491 adj.
unperceptive

unintelligent 499 adj.
unperjured
  veracious 540 adj.
  trustworthy 929 adj.
unphilosophical
  unwise 499 adj.
unpick *disjoin* 46 vb.
unpigmented
  colourless 426 adj.
unpin *unstick* 49 vb.
unpitied
  disapproved 924 adj.
unplaced
  unsuccessful 728 adj.
  defeated 728 adj.
unplanned *bungled* 695 adj.
unpleasant *painful* 377 adj.
  unsavoury 391 adj.
  fetid 397 adj.
  unpleasant 827 adj.
  discourteous 885 adj.
  threatening 900 adj.
unpleasantness
  dissension 709 n.
  suffering 825 n.
  painfulness 827 n.
  discourtesy 885 n.
unpleasing
  unpleasant 827 adj.
unplumbed *deep* 211 adj.
  unknown 491 adj.
unpoetical *plain* 573 adj.
  prosaic 593 adj.
  artless 699 adj.
unpointed
  unsharpened 257 adj.
unpolished *rough* 259 adj.
  dim 419 adj.
  inelegant 576 adj.
  dirty 649 adj.
  immature 670 adj.
  artless 699 adj.
  plebeian 869 adj.
unpopular
  unpleasant 827 adj.
  disliked 861 adj.
  disreputable 867 adj.
  friendless 883 adj.
  hated 888 adj.
unpopularity *odium* 888 n.
  disapprobation 924 n.
unpossessive
  disinterested 931 n.
unpractical *useless* 641 adj.
  unskilful 695 adj.
unpractised
  unwonted 611 adj.
  unprepared 670 adj.
  clumsy 695 adj.
unpraised
  disapproved 924 adj.

unprecedented
dissimilar 19 adj.
first 68 adj.
new 126 adj.
infrequent 140 adj.
unknown 491 adj.
unexpected 508 adj.
unwonted 611 adj.
wonderful 864 adj.
unpredictable
non-uniform 17 adj.
fitful 142 adj.
changeful 152 adj.
causeless 159 adj.
uncertain 474 adj.
unintelligible 517 adj.
capricious 604 adj.
unprejudiced *wise* 498 adj.
undamaged 646 adj.
free 744 adj.
just 913 adj.
unpremeditated
involuntary 596 adj.
spontaneous 609 adj.
unintentional 618 adj.
unprepared
negligent 458 adj.
inexpectant 508 adj.
spontaneous 609 adj.
unprepared 670 adj.
uncooked 670 adj.
hasty 680 adj.
unskilled 695 adj.
unprepossessing
ugly 842 adj.
unpresentable
ill-bred 847 adj.
unpretending
artless 699 adj.
modest 874 adj.
unpretentious
veracious 540 adj.
plain 573 adj.
humble 872 adj.
modest 874 adj.
unpriestly *laical* 987 adj.
unprincipled
dishonest 930 adj.
wicked 934 adj.
unprintable
prohibited 757 adj.
impure 951 adj.
unprivileged
subject 745 adj.
unentitled 916 adj.
unprized
undervalued 483 adj.
unprocurable
absent 190 adj.
scarce 636 adj.
unproductive

impotent 161 adj.
unproductive 172 adj.
profitless 641 adj.
unproductivity
unproductivity 172 n.
unprofessional
non-observant 769 adj.
unprofitable
unproductive 172 adj.
profitless 641 adj.
inexpedient 643 adj.
losing 772 adj.
unprogressive
permanent 144 adj.
quiescent 266 adj.
deteriorated 655 adj.
non-active 677 adj.
unpromising
unpromising 853 adj.
unprompted
voluntary 597 adj.
spontaneous 609 adj.
unpronounceable
inexpressible 517 adj.
unpronounced *tacit* 523 adj.
unpropitious
inopportune 138 adj.
opposing 704 adj.
unpromising 853 adj.
unprosperous
unprosperous 731 adj.
unprotected
vulnerable 661 adj.
unprotesting *humble* 872 adj.
unproved
unattested 467 adj.
uncertified 474 adj.
ill-reasoned 477 adj.
unprovided
unprovided 636 adj.
poor 801 adj.
unprovoked
spontaneous 609 adj.
unwanted 860 adj.
unpublished *tacit* 523 adj.
unpunctual
anachronistic 118 adj.
late 136 adj.
ill-timed 138 adj.
fitful 142 adj.
unpunishable
non-liable 919 n.
unpunished
forgiven 909 adj.
acquitted 960 adj.
unpurposed
unintentional 618 adj.
unqualified
unmixed 44 adj.
complete 54 adj.
positive 473 adj.

useless 641 adj.
unequipped 670 adj.
unskilled 695 adj.
unentitled 916 adj.
(see unconditional)
unquenchable
unyielding 162 adj.
greedy 859 adj.
unquenched *violent* 176 adj.
fiery 379 adj.
unquestionable
undisputed 473 adj.
assertive 532 adj.
unquestioning
believing 485 adj.
unquiet *moving* 265 adj.
agitated 318 adj.
restlessness 678 n.
excitable 822 adj.
worry 825 n.
unquotable *impure* 951 adj.
unratified
uncertified 474 adj.
unravel *simplify* 44 vb.
unravel 62 vb.
straighten 249 vb.
extract 304 vb.
evolve 316 vb.
decipher 520 vb.
disencumber 701 vb.
liberate 746 vb.
unreached *deficient* 307 adj.
unread
uninstructed 491 adj.
tedious 838 adj.
unreadable
unintelligible 517 adj.
tedious 838 adj.
dull 840 adj.
unreadiness
incompleteness 55 n.
lateness 136 n.
non-preparation 670 n.
unready (see unreadiness)
unreal *unreal* 2 adj.
erroneous 495 adj.
imaginary 513 adj.
unrealistic
impossible 470 adj.
misjudging 481 adj.
erroneous 495 adj.
unreality
immateriality 320 n.
error 495 n.
unrealized *unreal* 2 adj.
unknown 491 adj.
uncompleted 726 adj.
unreason
irrelevance 10 n.
non-intellect 448 n.
intuition 476 n.

folly 499 n.
unmeaningness 515 n.
wrong 914 n.
unreasonable
impossible 470 adj.
illogical 477 adj.
biased 481 adj.
unwise 499 adj.
capricious 604 adj.
wrong 914 adj.
unreasoned
illogical 477 adj.
unreasoning
mindless 448 adj.
biased 481 adj.
unwise 499 adj.
unreclaimed
impenitent 940 adj.
unrecognizable
converted 147 adj.
invisible 444 adj.
unintelligible 517 adj.
disguised 525 adj.
unrecognized
unknown 491 adj.
unreconciled
unwilling 598 adj.
inimical 881 adj.
impenitent 940 adj.
unredeemed
wicked 934 adj.
unrefined
indiscriminating 464 adj.
inelegant 576 adj.
unclean 649 adj.
artless 699 adj.
ill-bred 847 adj.
unreflecting
unthinking 450 adj.
incurious 454 adj.
inattentive 456 adj.
unreformed
impenitent 940 adj.
unrefreshed
fatigued 684 adj.
unrefuted
demonstrated 478 adj.
unregarded
neglected 458 adj.
unrespected 921 adj.
unregenerate
impious 980 adj.
unregretted *hated* 888 adj.
disapproved 924 adj.
unrepented 940 adj.
unregretting
impenitent 940 adj.
unrehearsed
spontaneous 609 adj.
unprepared 670 adj.
unrelated *irrelative* 10 adj.

dissimilar 19 adj.
unrelenting *pitiless* 906 adj.
revengeful 910 adj.
impenitent 940 adj.
unreliability
tergiversation 603 n.
(*see* unreliable)
unreliable
changeful 152 adj.
unreliable 474 adj.
unbelieved 486 adj.
irresolute 601 adj.
capricious 604 adj.
unsafe 661 adj.
dutiless 918 adj.
flattering 925 adj.
dishonest 930 adj.
unrelieved *uniform* 16 adj.
discontented 829 adj.
aggravated 832 adj.
cheerless 834 adj.
unrelished *disliked* 861 adj.
unremarked
neglected 458 adj.
inglorious 867 adj.
unremembered
forgotten 506 adj.
unremitting
continuous 71 adj.
unceasing 146 adj.
persevering 600 adj.
unrenowned
inglorious 867 adj.
unrepealable
permanent 144 adj.
unrepeated *one* 88 adj.
unrepentant
impenitent 940 adj.
unrepining *content* 828 adj.
cheerful 833 adj.
unrepresentative
abnormal 84 adj.
unrepresented
absent 190 adj.
unrepressed *violent* 176 adj.
unrequited
unthanked 908 adj.
unresentful
forgiving 909 adj.
unreserved
undisguised 522 adj.
veracious 540 adj.
artless 699 adj.
free 744 adj.
unresigned
resentful 891 adj.
unresisting *inactive* 679 adj.
peaceful 717 adj.
submitting 721 adj.
obedient 739 adj.
unresolved

puzzling 517 adj.
irresolute 601 adj.
choiceless 606 adj.
unrespected
unrespected 921 adj.
unresponsive
impassive 820 adj.
indifferent 860 adj.
unkind 898 adj.
pitiless 906 adj.
unrest
changeableness 152 n.
motion 265 n.
discontent 829 n.
unrestrained
facilitated 701 adj.
unconfined 744 adj.
unrestraint
inelegance 576 n.
intemperance 943 n.
unrestricted
absolute 32 adj.
unconditional 744 adj.
unrevised *inexact* 495 adj.
unrewarded
profitless 641 adj.
unthanked 908 adj.
unrewarding
profitless 641 adj.
unrhythmical *fitful* 142 adj.
unriddle *decipher* 520 vb.
unrighteous *wrong* 914 adj.
wicked 934 adj.
unrightful *wrong* 914 adj.
unrigorous *inexact* 495 adj.
unripe *incomplete* 55 adj.
new 126 adj.
young 130 adj.
sour 393 adj.
unhabituated 611 adj.
imperfect 647 adj.
immature 670 adj.
unskilled 695 adj.
uncompleted 726 adj.
unrivalled *supreme* 34 adj.
unroll *lengthen* 203 vb.
straighten 249 vb.
evolve 316 vb.
manifest 522 vb.
disclose 526 vb.
unromantic *true* 494 adj.
inexcitable 823 adj.
unroof *demolish* 165 vb.
uncover 229 vb.
unroot *extract* 304 vb.
unruffled *orderly* 60 adj.
smooth 258 adj.
tranquil 266 adj.
impassive 820 adj.
inexcitable 823 adj.
unruly *violent* 176 adj.

wilful 602 adj.
anarchic 734 adj.
disobedient 738 adj.
riotous 738 adj.
unsaddle *depose* 752 vb.
(*see* unseat)
unsafe *unsafe* 661 adj.
unsaid *tacit* 523 adj.
unsaleable
profitless 641 adj.
cheap 812 adj.
unsanctified
heathenish 974 adj.
profane 980 adj.
unsanctioned
unwarranted 916 adj.
heterodox 977 adj.
unsated *greedy* 859 adj.
envious 912 adj.
unsatisfactory
disappointing 509 adj.
insufficient 636 adj.
inexpedient 643 adj.
bad 645 adj.
unpleasant 827 adj.
discontenting 829 adj.
disapproved 924 adj.
unsatisfied
unprovided 636 adj.
discontented 829 adj.
greedy 859 adj.
envious 912 adj.
unsatisfying
disappointing 509 adj.
unsavoury
unsavoury 391 adj.
unpleasant 827 adj.
disliked 861 adj.
unsay *recant* 603 vb.
unscathed
undamaged 646 adj.
unscented *odourless* 395 adj.
unschematic
orderless 61 adj.
unschismatical
orthodox 976 adj.
unscholarly
uninstructed 491 adj.
unschooled
uninstructed 491 adj.
unscientific
impossible 470 adj.
illogical 477 adj.
ignorant 491 adj.
erroneous 495 adj.
unscramble *simplify* 44 vb.
decompose 51 vb.
unravel 62 vb.
unscriptural
erroneous 495 adj.
heterodox 977 adj.

unscrupulous
dishonest 930 adj.
wicked 934 adj.
unseal *disclose* 526 vb.
unsearchable
unintelligible 517 adj.
unseasonable *unapt* 25 adj.
ill-timed 138 adj.
unseasoned
unhabituated 611 adj.
unseat *unstick* 49 vb.
derange 63 vb.
displace 188 vb.
unthrone 734 vb.
depose 752 vb.
unsectarian *general* 79 adj.
unseeing *insensible* 375 adj.
blind 439 adj.
inattentive 456 adj.
misjudging 481 adj.
ignorant 491 adj.
unwise 499 adj.
impassive 820 adj.
unseemliness
bad taste 847 n.
unseemly
inexpedient 643 adj.
unsightly 842 adj.
wrong 914 n.
undue 916 adj.
vicious 934 adj.
unseen *invisible* 444 adj.
unknown 491 adj.
latent 523 adj.
inglorious 876 adj.
modest 874 adj.
secluded 883 adj.
unselective
indiscriminating 464 adj.
unself-controlled
intemperate 943 adj.
unselfishness
benevolence 897 n.
disinterestedness 931 n.
virtues 933 n.
unsensational
plain 573 adj.
unsentimental
impassive 820 adj.
inexcitable 823 adj.
unseparable
cohesive 48 adj.
unserious *witty* 839 adj.
unserviceable
useless 641 adj.
unsettle *derange* 63 vb.
unsettled *transient* 114 adj.
unstable 152 adj.
displaced 188 adj.
unsettlement
irresolution 601 n.

unseverable
firm-set 45 adj.
unsexed *impotent* 161 adj.
unshackle
disencumber 701 vb.
liberate 746 vb.
unshakable
firm-set 45 adj.
certain 473 adj.
credal 485 adj.
resolute 599 adj.
retentive 778 adj.
unfearing 855 adj.
unshapely
amorphous 244 adj.
unsightly 842 adj.
unshapen
amorphous 244 adj.
unshared *possessed* 773 adj.
unsharpened
unsharpened 257 adj.
unshaven *hairy* 259 adj.
unsheathe *uncover* 229 vb.
manifest 522 vb.
unshielded
vulnerable 661 adj.
unshifting
unceasing 146 adj.
unship *displace* 188 vb.
void 300 vb.
unshocked
impassive 820 adj.
unshod *uncovered* 229 adj.
unshorn *intact* 52 adj.
hairy 259 adj.
unshrinking
resolute 599 adj.
courageous 855 adj.
unshriven
impenitent 940 adj.
unshroud *disclose* 526 vb.
unsightly *unsightly* 842 adj.
unsigned *uncertified* 474 adj.
anonymous 562 adj.
unsinkable *light* 323 adj.
unskilful
unhabituated 611 adj.
unskilful 695 adj.
unsleeping
persevering 600 adj.
industrious 678 adj.
unsmart *ill-bred* 847 adj.
unsmiling *serious* 834 adj.
ungracious 885 adj.
sullen 893 adj.
unsociable
unconformable 84 adj.
alone 88 adj.
independent 744 adj.
unsociable 883 adj.
discourteous 885 adj.

sullen 893 adj.
unsociality
  misanthropy 902 n.
unsold *possessed* 773 adj.
  retained 778 adj.
unsolvable
  impracticable 470 adj.
  puzzling 517 adj.
unsophisticated
  genuine 494 adj.
  artless 699 adj.
  ill-bred 847 adj.
unsorted *mixed* 43 adj.
  disorderly 61 adj.
  indiscriminate 464 adj.
unsought *voluntary* 597 adj.
  avoidable 620 adj.
unsound *illogical* 477 adj.
  erroneous 495 adj.
  bad 645 adj.
  imperfect 647 adj.
  unhealthy 651 adj.
  insalubrious 653 adj.
  unskilled 695 adj.
unsounded *deep* 211 adj.
  silent 399 adj.
unsound mind
  insanity 503 n.
unsoundness
  vulnerability 661 n.
  non-retention 779 n.
unsown
  unproductive 172 adj.
unsparing
  plenteous 635 adj.
  oppressive 735 adj.
  severe 735 adj.
  liberal 813 adj.
  disinterested 931 adj.
  intemperate 943 adj.
unspeakable
  unspeakable 32 adj.
  inexpressible 517 adj.
  wonderful 864 adj.
unspecified *general* 79 adj.
unspent *remaining* 41 adj.
  unused 674 adj.
unspiced *tasteless* 387 adj.
unspirited *feeble* 572 adj.
  apathetic 820 adj.
  inexcitable 823 adj.
unspiritual
  material 319 adj.
  sensual 944 adj.
  irreligious 974 adj.
unspoilt *not bad* 644 adj.
  undamaged 646 adj.
unspoken *silent* 399 adj.
  unknown 491 adj.
  tacit 523 adj.
unsportsmanlike

unjust 914 adj.
unspotted *perfect* 646 adj.
  innocent 935 adj.
unsprung *tough* 329 adj.
unstable *unstable* 152 adj.
  weak 163 adj.
  irresolute 601 adj.
  capricious 604 adj.
  unsafe 661 adj.
  excitable 822 adj.
unstable personality
  madman 504 n.
unstaffed *empty* 190 adj.
unstaid *changeful* 152 adj.
  excitable 822 adj.
unstained *perfect* 646 adj.
  honourable 929 adj.
unstatutory *illegal* 945 adj.
unsteadiness
  weakness 163 n.
  agitation 318 n.
  unreliability 474 n.
unsteady *fitful* 142 adj.
  unstable 152 adj.
  unsafe 661 adj.
unsterilized
  infectious 653 adj.
unstick *unstick* 49 vb.
unstinting *liberal* 813 adj.
unstitch *disjoin* 46 vb.
unstop *open* 263 vb.
  liberate 746 vb.
unstrained *friendly* 880 adj.
unstressed *muted* 401 adj.
unstretchable
  unyielding 162 adj.
unstrict *lax* 734 adj.
unstring *disjoin* 46 vb.
  disable 161 vb.
  soften 327 vb.
  discord 411 vb.
unstudied
  neglected 458 adj.
  unprepared 670 adj.
unsubdued *resisting* 715 adj.
  unbeaten 727 adj.
unsubstantiated
  erroneous 495 adj.
unsuccessful
  profitless 641 adj.
  unskilful 695 adj.
  unsuccessful 728 adj.
  unprosperous 731 adj.
unsuccessive
  discontinuous 72 adj.
unsuitability
  inutility 641 n.
  inexpedience 643 n.
  wrong 914 n.
unsuitable *unapt* 25 adj.
unsullied *clean* 648 adj.

honourable 929 adj.
unsung *tacit* 523 adj.
  inglorious 867 adj.
unsure *uncertain* 474 adj.
  unsafe 661 adj.
unsurpassed
  supreme 34 adj.
  perfect 646 adj.
unsusceptible
  impassive 820 adj.
unsuspected *latent* 523 adj.
unsuspecting
  believing 485 adj.
  credulous 487 adj.
  inexpectant 508 adj.
unsuspicious *artless* 699 adj.
  honourable 929 adj.
unswerving *straight* 249 adj.
  directed 281 adj.
  undeviating 625 adj.
  indifferent 860 adj.
  just 913 adj.
  orthodox 976 adj.
unsympathetic
  opposing 704 adj.
  disliking 861 adj.
  disliked 861 adj.
  inimical 881 adj.
  unkind 898 adj.
  pitiless 906 adj.
  selfish 932 adj.
unsystematic
  non-uniform 17 adj.
  orderless 61 adj.
  fitful 142 adj.
untalented
  unintelligent 499 adj.
  unskilful 695 adj.
untameable *cruel* 898 adj.
untamed
  unhabituated 611 adj.
  avoiding 620 adj.
  warlike 718 adj.
  disobedient 738 adj.
  cruel 898 adj.
untangle *unravel* 62 vb.
untaught
  uninstructed 491 adj.
  spontaneous 609 adj.
  unprepared 670 adj.
  unskilled 695 adj.
untaxed *uncharged* 812 adj.
unteach *educate* 534 vb.
  misteach 534 vb.
unteachable
  unwise 499 adj.
  obstinate 602 adj.
untearable *tough* 329 adj.
untempered *weak* 163 adj.
untempted
  indifferent 860 adj.

untenable
defenceless 161adj.
illogical 477adj.
unbelieved 486adj.
untenanted *empty* 190adj.
unpossessed 774adj.
untended *neglected* 458adj.
untender *unkind* 898adj.
untested *new* 126adj.
uncertified 474adj.
unknown 491adj.
unthanked
unthanked 908adj.
unthankfulness
ingratitude 908n.
unthawed *cold* 380adj.
indissoluble 324adj.
unthinkability
impossibility 470n.
unthinking
unthinking 450adj.
incurious 454adj.
inattentive 456adj.
unwise 499adj.
involuntary 596adj.
unthorough
incomplete 55adj.
inattentive 456adj.
negligent 458adj.
uncompleted 726adj.
unthought
unthought 450adj.
unthreatening *safe* 660adj.
unthrifty
unprepared 670adj.
prodigal 815adj.
unthrone *unthrone* 734vb.
deprive 786vb.
disentitle 916vb.
(*see* depose)
untidy *non-uniform* 17adj.
orderless 61adj.
jumble 63vb.
agitate 318vb.
negligent 458adj.
dirty 649adj.
make unclean 649vb.
untie *disjoin* 46vb.
doff 229vb.
deliver 668vb.
disencumber 701vb.
not retain 779vb.
until *while* 108adv.
untilled
unproductive 172adj.
unprepared 670adj.
until now *until now* 121adv.
untimeliness
anachronism 118n.
(*see* untimely)
untimely *irrelative* 10adj.

unapt 25adj.
ill-timed 138adj.
inexpedient 643adj.
untinged *unmixed* 44adj.
untiring
persevering 600adj.
untitled *plebeian* 869adj.
untold *many* 104adj.
infinite 107adj.
tacit 523adj.
untouchable
prohibited 757adj.
derelict 779n.
(*see* outcaste)
untouched *intact* 52adj.
clean 648adj.
unused 674adj.
apathetic 820adj.
non-liable 919adj.
pure 950adj.
untoward *contrary* 14adj.
inopportune 138adj.
ill-timed 138adj.
inexpedient 643adj.
adverse 731adj.
annoying 827adj.
untraceable *lost* 772adj.
untraditional
modern 126adj.
unwonted 611adj.
untrained
uninstructed 491adj.
unhabituated 611adj.
imperfect 647adj.
unprepared 670adj.
immature 670adj.
unskilled 695adj.
untrammelled
facilitated 701adj.
unconfined 744adj.
untranslatable
inexpressible 517adj.
untravelled
quiescent 266adj.
untried *new* 126adj.
moot 459adj.
uncertified 474adj.
unknown 491adj.
unused 674adj.
untrodden *new* 126adj.
closed 264adj.
unused 674adj.
untroubled
moderate 177adj.
content 828adj.
untrue *erroneous* 495adj.
false 541adj.
deceiving 542adj.
untrue 543adj.
wrong 914adj.
perfidious 930adj.

untrustworthy
unreliable 474adj.
unsafe 661adj.
dishonest 930adj.
untruth *falsehood* 541n.
untruth 543n.
untruthfulness *error* 495n.
falsehood 541n.
improbity 930n.
untune *discord* 411vb.
untuneful
discordant 411adj.
untutored
uninstructed 491adj.
unprepared 670adj.
artless 699adj.
untypical *dissimilar* 19adj.
abnormal 84adj.
unused *unwonted* 611adj.
unused 674adj.
clumsy 695adj.
unusual *unusual* 84adj.
infrequent 140adj.
ridiculous 849adj.
wonderful 864adj.
unutilized *unused* 674adj.
unutterable
unspeakable 32adj.
inexpressible 517adj.
wonderful 864adj.
unvalued *unwanted* 860adj.
hated 888adj.
unvaried *unceasing* 146adj.
(*see* uniform)
unvarnished
genuine 494adj.
veracious 540adj.
plain 573adj.
artless 699adj.
unveil *uncover* 229vb.
be plain 522vb.
disclose 526vb.
unveiling *début* 68n.
unventilated
sealed off 264adj.
fetid 397adj.
insalubrious 653adj.
unverified
uncertified 474adj.
suppositional 512adj.
unversed *ignorant* 491adj.
unskilled 695adj.
unversified *prosaic* 593adj.
unviable
impracticable 470adj.
unvirtuous *wicked* 934adj.
unchaste 951adj.
unvisited *secluded* 883adj.
unvocal *voiceless* 578adj.
unvoiced *tacit* 523adj.
voiceless 578adj.

unwanted *rejected* 607 adj.
　superfluous 637 adj.
　useless 641 adj.
　unused 674 adj.
　unpossessed 774 adj.
　cheap 812 adj.
　unwanted 860 adj.
　disliked 861 adj.
unwarlike *peaceful* 717 adj.
　inexcitable 823 adj.
　cowardly 856 adj.
unwarrantable
　illegal 954 adj.
unwarranted
　uncertified 474 adj.
　illogical 477 adj.
　wrong 914 adj.
　unwarranted 916 adj.
unwary *negligent* 458 adj.
　rash 857 adj.
unwashed *opaque* 423 adj.
　dirty 649 adj.
unwavering
　unchangeable 153 adj.
　persevering 600 adj.
unwearied
　persevering 600 adj.
　industrious 678 adj.
unweave *unravel* 62 vb.
unwedded
　independent 744 adj.
　unwedded 895 adj.
unwelcome
　unpleasant 827 adj.
　unwanted 860 adj.
　hateful 888 adj.
unwelcoming
　unsociable 883 adj.
unwell *sick* 651 adj.
unwept *hated* 888 adj.
unwholesome
　harmful 645 adj.
　insalubrious 653 adj.
unwieldy *unequal* 29 adj.
　unwieldy 195 adj.
　weighty 322 adj.
　clumsy 695 adj.
　difficult 700 adj.
　graceless 842 adj.
unwilled
　involuntary 596 adj.
unwilling
　dissenting 489 n.
　involuntary 596 adj.
　unwilling 598 adj.
　avoiding 620 adj.
　refusing 760 adj.
unwind *evolve* 316 vb.
unwinking *still* 266 adj.
unwisdom *folly* 499 n.
unwise *unwise* 499 adj.

　inexpedient 643 adj.
　rash 857 adj.
unwish *abrogate* 752 vb.
　regret 830 vb.
unwished
　unwanted 860 adj.
　disliked 861 adj.
unwitnessed
　uncertified 474 adj.
unwitting *ignorant* 491 adj.
　involuntary 596 adj.
unwomanly *manly* 162 adj.
　male 372 adj.
unwonted *unusual* 84 adj.
　unwonted 611 adj.
unwooed *unwedded* 895 adj.
unworkable
　powerless 161 adj.
　impracticable 470 adj.
　useless 641 adj.
unworldly
　honourable 929 adj.
　innocent 935 adj.
　pious 979 adj.
unworn *unyielding* 162 adj.
unworried *tranquil* 266 adj.
　inexcitable 823 adj.
　content 828 adj.
unworthy *inferior* 35 adj.
　bad 645 adj.
　discreditable 867 adj.
　unentitled 916 adj.
　dishonest 930 adj.
　vicious 934 adj.
unwrap *uncover* 229 vb.
　extract 304 vb.
unwrinkled *young* 130 adj.
　flat 216 adj.
　smooth 258 adj.
unwritten *tacit* 523 adj.
　obliterated 550 adj.
unwrought
　immature 670 adj.
unyielding
　unyielding 162 adj.
　rigid 326 adj.
　tough 329 adj.
　resolute 599 adj.
　obstinate 602 adj.
　difficult 700 adj.
　resisting 715 adj.
　restraining 747 adj.
unyoke *liberate* 746 vb.
up *aloft* 209 adv.
　vertically 215 adv.
　up 308 adv.
　bubbly 355 adj.
　acquiring 771 adj.
up against it
　in difficulties 700 adj.
　unprosperous 731 adj.

up-and-coming
　active 678 adj.
　prosperous 730 adj.
up and doing
　operative 173 adj.
　doing 676 adj.
up and down
　by turns 141 adv.
　to and fro 317 adv.
up-and-down
　undulatory 251 adj.
up and up
　crescendo 36 adv.
up and up, on the
　well 615 adv.
　successful 727 adj.
　prosperous 730 adj.
Upanishad
　non-Biblical scripture
　975 n.
upbraid *exprobate* 927 vb.
upbringing *teaching* 534 n.
up-country *regional* 184 adj.
　interior 224 adj.
updraught *ascent* 308 n.
up-end
　make vertical 215 vb.
upgrade *make better* 654 vb.
　dignify 866 vb.
upgrowth *expansion* 197 n.
　ascent 308 n.
upheaval *disorder* 61 n.
　revolution 149 n.
　havoc 165 n.
　elevation 310 n.
uphill *sloping* 220 adj.
　ascending 308 adj.
　laborious 682 adj.
　difficult 700 adj.
uphold *sustain* 146 vb.
　support 218 vb.
　corroborate 466 vb.
upholder *assenter* 488 n.
upholstered *rich* 800 adj.
upholstery *lining* 227 n.
　equipment 630 n.
up in *expert* 694 adj.
up in arms *active* 678 adj.
　quarrelling 709 adj.
　attacking 712 adj.
　warring 718 adj.
　riotous 738 adj.
upkeep *support* 218 n.
　preservation 666 n.
　subvention 703 n.
upland *space* 183 n.
　high land 209 n.
　plain 348 n.
uplift *displace* 188 vb.
　support 218 n.
　move 265 vb.

elevation 310 n.
improvement 654 n.
delight 826 vb.
make pious 979 vb.
uplifted *high* 209 adj.
up one's street *fit* 24 adj.
up on, to be
  predominate 34 vb.
upper *superior* 34 adj.
upper case *print-type* 587 n.
upper class
  upper class 868 n.
upper crust
  beau monde 848 n.
  upper class 868 n.
uppercut *knock* 279 n.
upper hand *vantage* 34 n.
  victory 727 n.
Upper House
  parliament 692 n.
upper limit
  finite quantity 26 n.
  limit 236 n.
uppermost
  supreme 34 adj.
  topmost 213 adj.
  topical 452 adj.
  important 638 adj.
upper ten *élite* 644 n.
  beau monde 848 n.
  upper class 868 n.
uppish *ill-bred* 847 adj.
  prideful 871 adj.
upraise, uprear
  elevate 310 vb.
upright *vertical* 215 adj.
  just 913 adj.
  honourable 929 adj.
  virtuous 933 adj.
uprightness
  equilibrium 28 n.
  (see upright)
uprise *ascent* 308 n.
uprising *elevation* 310 n.
  revolt 738 n.
uproar *turmoil* 61 n.
  violence 176 n.
  loudness 400 n.
  fight 716 n.
uproarious *violent* 176 adj.
  loud 400 adj.
  excitable 822 adj.
  gay 833 adj.
uproot
  revolutionize 149 vb.
  destroy 165 vb.
  displace 188 vb.
  eject 300 vb.
  extract 304 vb.
uprush *increase* 36 n.
  spurt 277 n.

ascent 308 n.
  redundance 637 n.
ups and downs
  fluctuation 317 n.
upset *derange* 63 vb.
  revolution 149 n.
  demolish 165 vb.
  overturning 221 n.
  depression 311 n.
  distract 456 vb.
  hinder 702 vb.
  revolt 738 vb.
  impress 821 vb.
  incommode 827 vb.
  cause discontent 829 vb.
  cause dislike 861 vb.
  enrage 891 vb.
upshot *eventuality* 154 n.
  effect 157 n.
  judgment 480 n.
  completion 725 n.
upside down
  contrarily 14 adv.
  orderless 61 adj.
  inverted 221 adj.
upstage *stage set* 594 n.
  prideful 871 adj.
  insolent 878 adj.
upstairs *aloft* 209 adv.
  up 308 adv.
upstanding *vertical* 215 adj.
  elevated 310 adj.
upstart *intruder* 59 n.
  upstart 126 n.
  progression 285 n.
  made man 730 n.
  commoner 869 n.
  insolent person 878 n.
up sticks *decamp* 296 vb.
upstream *towards* 281 adv.
upsurge *increase* 36 n.
  ascent 308 n.
  redundance 637 n.
upswing *elevation* 310 n.
  improvement 654 n.
up to *while* 108 adv.
  powerful 160 adj.
up-to-date *present* 121 adj.
  modern 126 adj.
  progressive 285 adj.
up to every trick, be
  be expert 694 vb.
up to the ears
  completely 54 adv.
up to the hilt
  completely 54 adv.
up to the mark
  sufficient 635 adj.
  not bad 644 adj.
up-to-the-minute
  (see up-to-date)

uptown *afar* 199 adv.
uptrend *elevation* 310 n.
  improvement 654 n.
upturn *invert* 221 vb.
upwards *aloft* 209 adv.
upwards of *beyond* 34 adv.
  plural 101 adj.
upwind *directed* 281 adj.
uræus *regalia* 743 n.
uranium *materials* 631 n.
uranomotry
  uranometry 321 n.
Uranus *planet* 321 n.
  classical gods 967 n.
urban *regional* 184 adj.
  urban 192 adj.
urbane *well-bred* 848 adj.
  sociable 882 adj.
  courteous 884 adj.
urbanity (see urbane)
urbanize *urbanize* 192 vb.
urchin *youngster* 132 n.
  dwarf 196 n.
  elf 970 n.
urge *influence* 178 vb.
  accelerate 277 vb.
  impel 279 vb.
  propound 512 vb.
  affirm 532 vb.
  be resolute 599 vb.
  incite 612 vb.
  hasten 680 vb.
  advise 691 vb.
  compel 740 vb.
  request 761 vb.
  animate 821 vb.
urgency
  inducement 612 n.
  needfulness 627 n.
  importance 638 n.
  haste 680 n.
  request 761 n.
urgent *strong* 162 adj.
  resolute 599 adj.
  demanding 627 adj.
  important 638 adj.
  hasty 680 adj.
  compelling 740 adj.
  requesting 761 adj.
urgent, be
  emphasize 532 vb.
urinal *latrine* 649 n.
urination *excretion* 302 n.
urine *excrement* 302 n.
urn *vessel* 194 n.
  interment 364 n.
  pottery 381 n.
ursine *animal* 365 adj.
urticaria *formication* 378 n.
  skin disease 651 n.
urticate *itch* 378 vb.

urtication
  formication 378 n.
  antidote 658 n.
usable *useful* 640 adj.
  used 673 adj.
usage *connotation* 514 n.
  habit 610 n.
  use 673 n.
use *operate* 173 vb.
  habit 610 n.
  instrumentality 628 n.
  importance 638 n.
  utility 640 n.
  use 673 n., vb.
  action 676 n.
  possess 773 vb.
used to *habituated* 610 adj.
used up *impotent* 161 adj.
  disused 674 adj.
use force *force* 176 vb.
use for, have no
  not use 674 vb.
  not respect 921 vb.
  despise 922 vb.
useful *operative* 173 adj.
  instrumental 628 adj.
  useful 640 adj.
  expedient 642 adj.
  beneficial 644 adj.
  used 673 adj.
  aiding 703 adj.
useless *absurd* 497 adj.
  superfluous 637 adj.
  trivial 639 adj.
  useless 641 adj.
  inexpedient 643 adj.
  bad 645 adj.
  unused 674 adj.
uselessness
  ineffectuality 161 n.
  unimportance 639 n.
  (*see* useless)
user *habit* 610 n.
  (*see* operator)
use up *disable* 161 vb.
  waste 634 vb.
  dispose of 673 vb.
  expend 806 vb.
usher *accompany* 89 vb.
  teacher 537 n.
  stage-hand 594 n.
  greet 884 vb.
  bridesman 894 n.
usherette
  stage-hand 594 n.
usher in *come before* 64 vb.
  initiate 68 vb.
  precede 283 vb.
  admit 299 vb.
  predict 511 vb.
usual *general* 79 adj.

regular 81 adj.
usual 610 adj.
trivial 639 adj.
dull 840 adj.
fashionable 848 adj.
unastonishing 865 adj.
usufruct *use* 673 n.
  enjoyment 824 n.
usurer *lender* 784 n.
  niggard 816 n.
usurious *lending* 784 adj.
  avaricious 816 adj.
usurp *encroach* 306 vb.
  take authority 733 vb.
  unthrone 734 vb.
  appropriate 786 vb.
  (*see* usurpation)
usurpation
  arrogation 918 n.
  lawlessness 954 n.
usurper *impostor* 545 n.
  taker 786 n.
  usurper 916 n.
usury *lending* 784 n.
  interest 803 n.
utensil *tool* 630 n.
uterine *akin* 11 adj.
uterus *genitalia* 164 n.
  insides 224 n.
utilitarian *useful* 640 adj.
  philanthropist 901 n.
utilitarianism
  philosophy 449 n.
  good 615 n.
  utility 640 n.
  expedience 642 n.
  benevolence 897 n.
  philanthropy 901 n.
  morals 917 n.
utility *benefit* 615 n.
  instrumentality 629 n.
  utility 640 n.
  use 673 n.
utilization *utility* 640 n.
  use 673 n.
uti possedetis
  as before 144 adv.
  possession 773 n.
utmost *limit* 236 n.
Utopia *fantasy* 513 n.
  aspiration 852 n.
Utopian *visionary* 513 n.
  reformer 654 n.
  philanthropist 901 n.
utricle *bladder* 194 n.
utter *consummate* 32 adj.
  complete 54 adj.
  disperse 75 vb.
  divulge 526 vb.
  publish 528 vb.
  voice 577 vb.

speak 579 vb.
mint 797 vb.
utterance *cry* 408 n.
  voice 577 n.
  speech 579 n.
uttermost *limit* 236 n.
U-turn *reversion* 148 n.
  curve 248 n.
  return 286 n.
  circuition 314 n.
U-valley *valley* 255 n.
uxoriousness *love* 887 n.

V

V1, V2 *weapon* 723 n.
  bomb 723 n.
vacancy
  insubstantiality 4 n.
  emptiness 190 n.
  job 622 n.
  unimportance 639 n.
  (*see* vacant)
vacant *unthinking* 450 adj.
  unintelligent 499 adj.
  unprovided 636 adj.
  unpossessed 774 adj.
  secluded 883 adj.
  (*see* vacancy)
vacate *displace* 188 vb.
  be absent 190 vb.
  go away 190 vb.
  relinquish 621 vb.
  abrogate 752 vb.
  resign 753 vb.
vacation *leisure* 681 n.
  repose 683 n.
vaccinate *doctor* 658 vb.
  safeguard 660 vb.
vaccination *hygiene* 652 n.
  prophylactic 658 n.
vaccinia *skin disease* 651 n
vacillate
  be capricious 604 vb.
  (*see* vacillation)
vacillating
  tergiversating 603 adj.
vacillation
  changeableness 152 n.
  fluctuation 317 n.
  dubiety 474 n.
  irresolution 601 n.
vacuity, vacuous
  (*see* vacancy, vacant)
vacuum *non-existence* 2 n.
  emptiness 190 n.
  rarity 325 n.
vacuum cleaner
  cleaning utensil 648 n.
vade mecum
  guide-book 524 n.

vagabond *travelling* 267 adj.
  wanderer 268 n.
  low fellow 869 n.
  outcaste 883 n.
  knave 938 n.
vagabondage
  wandering 267 n.
vagary *foolery* 497 n.
  ideality 513 n.
  whim 604 n.
vagina *genitalia* 164 n.
vaginal
  productive 164 adj.
vagrancy *wandering* 267 n.
  deviation 282 n.
vagrant *unstable* 152 adj.
  wanderer 268 n.
  deviating 282 adj.
vague *insubstantial* 4 adj.
  general 79 adj.
  amorphous 244 adj.
  shadowy 419 adj.
  ill-seen 444 adj.
  uncertain 474 adj.
  uninstructed 491 adj.
  equivocal 518 adj.
  imperspicuous 568 adj.
vagueness
  indiscrimination 464 n.
  concealment 525 n.
  (*see* vague)
vain *insubstantial* 4 adj.
  useless 641 adj.
  unsuccessful 728 adj.
  prideful 871 adj.
  vain 873 adj.
vainglorious
  (*see* vainglory)
vainglory *pride* 871 n.
  vanity 873 n.
  boasting 877 n.
vain, in *wasted* 634 adj.
  profitless 641 adj.
  unsuccessfully 728 vb.
vair *skin* 226 n.
  heraldry 547 n.
Vaishnavism.
  religious faith 973 n.
valance *edging* 234 n.
  trimming 844 n.
vale *valley* 255 n.
valediction
  valediction 296 n.
valedictory
  valediction 296 n.
  departing 296 adj.
  oration 579 n.
valentine
  correspondence 588 n.
  love-token 889 n.
valet *clothier* 228 n.

clean 648 vb.
  revive 656 vb.
  preserve 666 vb.
  minister to 703 vb.
  domestic 742 n.
  serve 742 vb.
valetudinarian
  sick person 651 n.
  unhealthy 651 adj.
valgus *deformity* 246 n.
Valhalla
  mythic heaven 971 n.
valiant *courageous* 855 adj.
valid *strong* 162 adj.
  genuine 494 adj.
  affirmative 532 adj.
  useful 640 adj.
validate *stabilize* 153 vb.
  corroborate 466 vb.
  grant claims 915 vb.
  make legal 953 vb.
validation *certainty* 473 n.
  assent 488 n.
validity *authenticity* 494 n.
  legality 953 n.
valise *box* 194 n.
Valkyrie *soldier* 722 n.
  mythical being 970 n.
valley *lowness* 210 n.
  depth 211 n.
  valley 255 n.
  plain 348 n.
  conduit 351 n.
vallum *fence* 235 n.
  fortification 713 n.
valorize *tax* 809 vb.
valour *courage* 855 n.
valuable *great* 32 adj.
  good 615 adj.
  important 638 adj.
  profitable 640 adj.
  valuable 644 adj.
  of price 811 adj.
valuables *estate* 777 n.
valuation *degree* 27 n.
  measurement 465 n.
  estimate 480 n.
value *equivalence* 28 n.
  quid pro quo 150 n.
  appraise 465 vb.
  estimate 480 vb.
  importance 638 n.
  utility 640 n.
  goodness 644 n.
  account 808 vb.
  price, tax 809 vb.
  have taste 846 vb.
  honour 866 vb.
  love 887 vb.
  respect 920 vb.
  approve 923 vb.

valueless *trivial* 639 adj.
  profitless 641 adj.
  cheap 812 adj.
valuer *appraiser* 465 n.
  estimator 480 n.
valuta *finance* 797 n.
valve *stopper* 264 n.
  conduit 351 n.
vambrace *armour* 713 n.
vamoose *decamp* 296 vb.
vamp *modify* 143 vb.
  play music 413 vb.
  improvise 609 vb.
  repair 656 vb.
  lover 887 n.
  excite love 887 vb.
vampire *taker* 786 n.
  lover 887 n.
  offender 904 n.
  noxious animal 904 n.
  glutton 947 n.
  demon 970 n.
  sorceress 983 n.
vampirism *rapacity* 786 n.
vampirish
  fairylike 970 adj.
van *beginning* 68 n.
  front 237 n.
  cart 274 n.
  precession 283 n.
  purify 648 vb.
  armed force 722 n.
Vandal *destroyer* 168 n.
  vulgarian 847 n.
  low fellow 869 n.
  evildoer 904 n.
vandalism *destruction* 165 n.
  violence 176 n.
  bad taste 847 n.
  inhumanity 898 n.
vane *changeable thing* 152 n.
  weather 340 n.
vanguard *precursor* 66 n.
  front 237 n.
  armed force 722 n.
vanilla *scent* 396 n.
vanish *pass away* 2 vb.
  be transient 114 vb.
  go away 190 vb.
  disappear 446 vb.
  be stealthy 525 vb.
vanishing cream
  cosmetic 843 n.
vanishing point
  smallness 33 n.
  minuteness 196 n.
  disappearance 446 n.
vanishment
  invisibility 444 n.
  disappearance 446 n.
vanity *insubstantiality* 4 n.

ineffectuality 161 n.
folly 499 n.
unimportance 639 n.
inutility 641 n.
affectation 850 n.
pride 871 n.
vanity 873 n.
boasting 877 n.
vanity bag *bag* 194 n.
Vanity Fair *fashion* 848 n.
vanity 873 n.
vanquish *overmaster* 727 vb.
vantage *vantage* 34 n.
power 160 n.
tactics 688 n.
success 727 n.
vantage ground
influence 178 n.
vanward *in front* 237 adv.
vapid *tasteless* 387 adj.
feeble 572 adj.
vaporific *gaseous* 336 adj.
vaporific 338 adj.
vaporimeter
vaporizer 338 n.
vaporization
vaporization 338 n.
dryness 342 n.
disappearance 446 n.
vaporize *lighten* 323 vb.
gasify 336 vb.
vaporize 338 vb.
dry 342 vb.
vaporizer *vaporizer* 338 n.
vaporous
insubstantial 4 adj.
gaseous 336 adj.
vaporific 338 adj.
cloudy 355 adj.
opaque 423 adj.
imaginary 513 adj.
vapour
insubstantial thing 4 n.
emit 300 vb.
gas 336 n.
cloud 355 n.
fantasy 513 n.
mean nothing 515 vb.
boast 877 vb.
vapouring *foolish* 499 adj.
diffuseness 570 n.
vapourish
melancholic 834 adj.
vapours *melancholy* 834 n.
variability
non-uniformity 17 n.
inequality 29 n.
multiformity 82 n.
fitfulness 142 n.
change 143 n.
changeableness 152 n.

unreliability 474 n.
caprice 604 n.
variable *number* 85 n.
star 321 n.
irresolute 601 adj.
excitable 822 adj.
(*see* variability)
variance *disagreement* 25 n.
dissension 709 n.
variance, at
opposing 704 adj.
inimical 881 adj.
variant *variant* 15 n.
variation *contrariety* 14 n.
difference 15 n.
dissimilarity 19 n.
numerical operation 86 n.
change 143 n.
musical piece 412 n.
varicella *infection* 651 n.
varicose *expanded* 197 adj.
variegation
disagreement 25 n.
inequality 29 n.
mixture 43 n.
discontinuity 72 n.
changeableness 152 n.
variegation 437 n.
ornamental art 844 n.
variety *difference* 15 n.
non-uniformity 17 n.
dissimilarity 19 n.
mixture 43 n.
sort 77 n.
multiformity 82 n.
nonconformist 84 n.
stage show 594 n.
variola *infection* 651 n.
various (*see* variety)
varlet *low fellow* 869 n.
knave 938 n.
varletry *rabble* 869 n.
varnish *facing* 226 n.
smooth 258 vb.
resin 357 n.
colour 425 vb.
sophisticate 477 vb.
conceal 525 vb.
cant 541 vb.
sham 542 n.
art equipment 553 n.
cleanser 648 n.
decorate 844 vb.
ostentation 875 n.
extenuate 927 vb.
Varuna *sea-god* 343 n.
mythic god 966 n.
Hindu god 967 n.
varvel *fastening* 47 n.
circle 250 n.

vary *differ* 15 vb.
change 143 vb.
vary 152 vb.
be capricious 604 vb.
vary as *be related* 9 vb.
correlate 12 vb.
vascular *capsular* 194 adj.
tubular 263 adj.
vasculum *case* 194 n.
vase *vessel* 194 n.
vassal *subject* 742 n.
subject 745 adj.
vassalage *subjection* 745 n.
service 745 n.
vassalize *subjugate* 745 vb.
vast *enormous* 32 adj.
spacious 183 adj.
huge 195 adj.
vastness *greatness* 32 n.
hugeness 195 n.
vat *vat* 194 n.
Vatican
church office 985 n.
parsonage 986 n.
vaticination
divination 511 n.
vaudeville
stage show 594 n.
place of amusement 837 n.
vault *cellar* 194 n.
curve 248 n.
dome 253 n.
leap 312 n., vb.
tomb 364 n.
hiding place 527 n.
storage 632 n.
church interior 990 n.
vaulted *curved* 248 adj.
concave 255 adj.
vaunt *boast* 877 n., vb.
Vauxhall
pleasure-ground 837 n.
V.C. *courage* 855 n.
brave person 855 n.
vection *transport* 272 n.
vector *quantity* 26 n.
carrier 273 n.
infection 651 n.
Veda
non-Biblical scripture 975 n.
Vedanta *philosophy* 449 n.
Vedantism
religious faith 973 n.
vedette *armed force* 722 n.
Vedic *olden* 127 adj.
religious 973 adj.
scriptural 975 adj.
veer *change* 143 vb.

vary 152vb.
navigate 269vb.
deviate 282vb.
veer away recede 290vb.
veer round
turn back 286vb.
vegetability
vegetability 366n.
non-intellect 448n.
vegetable
vegetable 301n.
vegetal 366adj.
mindless 448adj.
unthinking 450adj.
vegetable physiology
botany 368n.
vegetal vegetal 366adj.
vegetarian eater 301n.
feeding 301adj.
abstainer 942n.
ascetic 945n.
vegetarianism
temperance 942n.
vegetate be 1vb.
pass time 108vb.
be inert 175vb.
be quiescent 266vb.
vegetate 366vb.
be inactive 679vb.
be insensitive 820vb.
vegetation
vegetability 366n.
(see vegetate)
vegetative vegetal 366adj.
apathetic 820adj.
vehemence
vigorousness 174n.
violence 176n.
affirmation 532n.
vigour 571n.
restlessness 678n.
warm feeling 818n.
excitability 822n.
vehement (see vehemence)
vehicle conveyance 267n.
transport 272n.
vehicle 274n.
vehicular vehicular 274adj.
veil shade 226n.
cloak 228n.
darken 418vb.
screen 421n., vb.
invisibility 444n.
conceal 525vb.
disguise 527n.
vocation 622n.
veil, take the
be unsocial 883vb.
live single 895vb.
take orders 986vb.
vein temperament 5n.

tendency 179n.
filament 208n.
tube 263n.
conduit 351n.
variegate 437n.
style 566n.
diffuseness 570n.
store 632n.
affections 817n.
veld space 183n.
plain 348n.
velleity will 595n.
vellicate agitate 318vb.
touch 378vb.
vellum stationery 586n.
bookbinding 589n.
velocimeter velocity 277n.
velocipede bicycle 274n.
velocity motion 265n.
velocity 277n.
velour textile 222n.
hair 259n.
velum taste 386n.
velure smoothness 258n.
velvet textile 222n.
smoothness 258n.
hair 259n.
softness 327n.
euphoria 376n.
palmy days 730n.
velvet glove lenity 736n.
velvety smooth 258adj.
downy 259adj.
soft 327adj.
venal avaricious 816adj.
venal 930adj.
selfish 932adj.
vend sell 793vb.
vendee owner 776n.
recipient 782n.
purchaser 792n.
vendetta quarrel 709n.
enmity 881n.
revenge 910n.
vendible saleable 793adj.
merchandise 795n.
Vendidad
non-Biblical scripture
975n.
vendor seller 793n.
veneer laminate 207vb.
shallowness 212n.
facing 226n.
coat 226vb.
disguise 527n.
ostentation 875n.
veneering
ornamental art 844n.
venenation
impairment 655n.
poisoning 659n.

venerable great 32adj.
immemorial 127adj.
aged 131adj.
respected 920adj.
veneration respect 920n.
piety 979n.
worship 981n.
venereal diseased 651adj.
venereal ulcer
venereal disease 651n.
Venerean
planetary 321adj.
venery unchastity 951n.
venesection voidance 300n.
surgery 658n.
vengeance revenge 910n.
vengeance, with a
completely 54adv.
violently 176adv.
venial trivial 639adj.
forgiven 909adj.
vindicable 927adj.
guiltless 935adj.
venison meat 301n.
savouriness 390n.
venom poison 659n.
malevolence 898n.
venomous harmful 645adj.
toxic 653adj.
baneful 659adj.
inimical 881adj.
malevolent 898adj.
vent orifice 263n.
outlet 298n.
void 300vb.
air-pipe 353n.
divulge 526vb.
means of escape 667n.
sale 793n.
venter maw 194n.
ventiduct
ventilation 352n.
air-pipe 353n.
ventilate aerify 340vb.
divulge 526vb.
publish 528vb.
dissert 591vb.
purify 648vb.
sanitate 852vb.
refresh 685vb.
(see ventilation)
ventilation
ventilation 352n.
refrigeration 382n.
(see ventilate)
ventilator air 340n.
ventilation 352n.
air-pipe 353n.
refrigerator 384n.
ventosity respiration 352n.
wind 352n.

ventral *cellular* 194 adj.
ventricle *compartment* 194 n.
ventricular *cellular* 194 adj.
ventriloquism
  mimicry 20 n.
  deception 542 n.
  sleight 542 n.
  voice 577 n.
ventriloquist *imitator* 20 n.
  conjuror 545 n.
  entertainer 594 n.
venture
  be tentative 461 vb.
  gambling 618 n.
  danger 661 n.
  essay 671 n., vb.
  undertaking 672 n.
  property 777 n.
  trade 791 n.
  speculate 791 vb.
  be courageous 855 vb.
venture, at a
  at random 618 adj.
venturesome
  experimental 461 adj.
  speculative 618 adj.
  dangerous 661 adj.
  enterprising 672 adj.
  courageous 855 adj.
  rash 857 adj.
venue *focus* 76 n.
  locality 187 n.
venule *filament* 208 n.
Venus *planet* 321 n.
  woman 373 n.
  luminary 420 n.
  a beauty 841 n.
  love god 887 n.
  mythic god 966 n.
  Olympian god 967 n.
veracious *(see* veracity)
veracity *veracity* 540 n.
  artlessness 699 n.
  probity 929 n.
verandah *lobby* 194 n.
verb *part of speech* 564 n.
verbal *semantic* 514 adj.
  informative 524 adj.
  verbal 559 adj.
  grammatical 564 adj.
  speaking 579 adj.
verbatim
  imitatively 20 adv.
  verbally 559 adv.
verbiage *empty talk* 515 n.
  word 559 n.
  imperspicuity 568 n.
  diffuseness 570 n.
verbosity *word* 559 n.
  diffuseness 570 n.
  loquacity 581 n.

verdant *vegetal* 366 adj.
  green 432 adj.
verderer *forestry* 366 n.
  judge 957 n.
verdict *judgment* 480 n.
  legal trial 959 n.
verdigris *greenness* 432 n.
  poison 659 n.
verdure *grass* 366 n.
  greenness 432 n.
verecundity *modesty* 874 n.
verge *extremity* 69 n.
  tend 179 vb.
  nearness 200 n.
  edge 234 n.
  limit 236 n.
  point to 281 vb.
verge on *approach* 289 vb.
verger *church officer* 986 n.
veridical *veracious* 540 adj.
verifiable
  experimental 461 adj.
  evidential 466 adj.
  certain 473 adj.
verification
  experiment 461 n.
  demonstration 478 n.
  assent 488 n.
verified *known* 490 adj.
  veracious 540 adj.
verify *corroborate* 466 vb.
  make certain 473 vb.
  discover 484 vb.
  give security 767 vb.
  (see verification)
verisimilitude
  probability 471 n.
  truth 494 n.
  accuracy 494 n.
  veracity 540 n.
veritable *true* 494 adj.
verity *truth* 494 n.
verjuice *sourness* 393 n.
vermicular
  labyrinthine 251 adj.
  animal 365 adj.
vermifuge *antidote* 658 n.
vermilion
  red pigment 431 n.
vermin *vermin* 365 n.
  dirt 649 n.
  rabble 869 n.
  knave, cad 938 n.
verminous
  insalubrious 653 adj.
vernacular *native* 191 adj.
  language 557 n.
  dialect 560 n.
  plainness 573 n.
vernal *new* 126 adj.
  vernal 128 adj.

  young 130 adj.
vernier *gauge* 465 n.
vernier scale
  micrology 196 n.
verruca *skin disease* 651 n.
verrucose *convex* 253 adj.
versatile
  multiform 82 adj.
  changeful 152 adj.
  tergiversating 603 adj.
  useful 640 adj.
  skilful 694 adj.
verse *subdivision* 53 n.
  vocal music 412 n.
  poetry 593 n.
versed in *knowing* 490 adj.
  expert 694 adj.
verse-filler *pleonasm* 570 n.
versicle *verse form* 593 n.
versicolour
  iridescent 437 adj.
versification *poetry* 593 n.
versify *poetize* 593 vb.
version *speciality* 80 n.
  transformation 143 n.
  translation 528 n.
vers libre *verse form* 593 n.
verso *edition* 589 n.
  rear 238 n.
verst *long measure* 203 n.
versus *towards* 281 adv.
  in opposition 704 adj.
vert *green colour* 432 n.
  heraldry 547 n.
vertebræ *pillar* 218 n.
vertebral *central* 225 adj.
  back 238 adj.
vertebrate *animal* 365 n.
vertex *extremity* 69 n.
  vertex 213 n.
vertical *vertical* 215 adj.
verticil *coil* 251 n.
verticity *rotation* 315 n.
vertiginous *high* 209 adj.
  rotary 315 adj.
  crazed 503 adj.
vertigo *rotation* 315 n.
  frenzy 503 n.
  indigestion 651 n.
verve *vigorousness* 174 n.
  vigour 571 n.
  moral sensibility 819 n.
very *greatly* 32 adv.
Very light
  signal light 420 n.
very one, the *identity* 13 n.
very same, the *identity* 13 n.
very thing, the
  no imitation 21 n.
  fitness 24 n.
  authenticity 494 n.

vesicant
  surgical dressing 658 n.
vesicle *bladder* 194 n.
  skin 226 n.
  sphere 252 n.
  swelling 253 n.
  skin disease 651 n.
vesicular *capsular* 194 adj.
  convex 253 adj.
vesper *luminary* 420 n.
Vespers *evening* 129 n.
  church service 988 n.
vespiary *crowd* 74 n.
vessel *vessel* 194 n.
  ship 275 n.
  pottery 381 n.
vest *bodywear* 228 n.
  vest 228 n.
  belong 773 vb.
  give 781 vb.
  make legal 953 vb.
vestal *spinster* 895 n.
  virgin 950 n.
  pure 950 adj.
  priest 986 n.
vested *vested* 153 adj.
  located 187 adj.
  due 915 adj.
vested interest *estate* 777 n.
  right 913 n.
  dueness 915 n.
vestiary *vestimental* 989 adj.
vestibule *entrance* 68 n.
  lobby 194 n.
  theatre 594 n.
  access 624 n.
vestige *remainder* 41 n.
  trace 548 n.
vestigial *remaining* 41 adj.
  recorded 548 adj.
vestimentary
  vestimental 989 adj.
vestments *clothing* 228 n.
  uniform 228 n.
  vestments 989 n.
vestry *council* 692 n.
  synod 985 n.
  church interior 990 n.
vestryman
  church officer 986 n.
vesture *dressing* 228 n.
vet *animal husbandry* 369 n.
  be attentive 455 vb.
  estimate 480 vb.
  doctor 658 n.
vetch *plant* 366 n.
veteran *old man* 133 n.
  matured 669 adj.
  expert 694 adj.
  expert 696 n.
  warlike 718 adj.

soldier 722 n.
veterinary medicine
  medical art 658 n.
vetinary surgeon
  animal husbandry 369 n.
  doctor 658 n.
veto *restraint* 747 n.
  prohibition 757 n.
vex (*see* vexation)
vexation *difficulty* 700 n.
  sorrow 825 n.
  annoyance 827 n.
  anger 891 n.
vexatious
  annoying 827 adj.
  litigating 959 adj.
vexillary *soldier* 722 n.
  army officer 741 n.
via *towards* 281 adv.
  via 624 adv.
viability *life* 360 n.
  possibility 469 n.
viaduct *crossing* 222 n.
  bridge 624 n.
vial *vessel* 194 n.
via media *mid-course* 625 n.
viands *food* 301 n.
viaticum
  Christian rite 988 n.
  the sacrament 988 n.
vibrancy *oscillation* 317 n.
vibrant *vigorous* 174 adj.
  resonant 404 adj.
vibrate *vary* 152 vb.
  oscillate 317 vb.
  roll 403 vb.
  resound 404 vb.
  show feeling 818 vb.
vibration *oscillation* 317 n.
  agitation 318 n.
  resonance 404 n.
vibratory
  changeful 152 adj.
  oscillating 317 adj.
vibroscope *oscillation* 317 n.
vicar *deputy* 755 n.
  church title 986 n.
  pastor 986 n.
vicarage *parsonage* 986 n.
vicarial *clerical* 986 adj.
vicariate
  church office 985 n.
vicarious *substituted* 150 adj.
  commissioned 751 adj.
vice *badness* 645 n.
  bane 659 n.
  deputy 755 n.
  nippers 778 n.
  wrong 914 n.
  vice 934 n.
vice-chancellor

director 690 n.
  officer 741 n.
  deputy 755 n.
viceroy *governor* 741 n.
  deputy 755 n.
vice versa
  correlatively 12 adv.
  contrarily 14 adv.
  in exchange 151 adv.
  inversely 221 adv.
  against 240 adv.
vicinity *nearness* 200 n.
  circumjacence 230 n.
vicious *furious* 176 adj.
  evil 616 adj.
  disobedient 738 adj.
  malevolent 898 adj.
  wrong 914 adj.
  vicious 934 adj.
vicious circle *obstacle* 702 n.
vicissitude
  changeable thing 152 n.
vicissitudes *affairs* 154 n.
victim *weakling* 163 n.
  corpse 363 n.
  dupe 544 n.
  chase 619 n.
  loser 728 n.
  unlucky person 731 n.
  booty 790 n.
  sufferer 825 n.
  laughing-stock 851 n.
  oblation 981 n.
victimize *befool* 542 vb.
  ill-treat 645 vb.
  oppress 735 vb.
  rob 788 vb.
  be malevolent 898 vb.
  avenge 910 vb.
  punish 963 vb.
victor *victor* 727 n.
victoria *carriage* 274 n.
Victoria Cross
  badge 547 n.
  decoration 729 n.
  (*see* V.C.)
Victorian
  antiquated 127 adj.
  prudish 950 adj.
victorious *superior* 34 adj.
  successful 727 adj.
victory *superiority* 34 n.
  victory 727 n.
victrola *gramophone* 414 n.
victual *food* 301 n.
  feed 301 vb.
  provide 633 vb.
victualler *provider* 633 n.
vicuna *fibre* 208 n.
  textile 222 n.
videlicet *namely* 80 adv.

viduage *widowhood* 896n.
vidual *widowed* 896adj.
vie *be good* 644vb.
  contend 716vb.
view *range* 183n.
  open space 263n.
  view 438n.
  watch 441vb.
  spectacle 445n.
  appearance 445n.
  idea 451n.
  estimate 480vb.
  opinion 485n.
  manifestation 522n.
  art subject 553n.
  intention 617n.
  beauty 841n.
viewable *visible* 443adj.
viewer *spectator* 441n.
viewership *onlookers* 441n.
  publicity 528n.
view-finder *telescope* 442n.
view halloo *loudness* 400n.
  cry 408n.
view, in *impending* 155adj.
  at sight 438adv.
  visible 443adj.
  expected 507adj.
viewless *invisible* 444adj.
view, on *visibly* 443adv.
  appearing 445adj.
  apparently 445adv.
viewpoint *view* 438n.
  opinion 485n.
viewy *believing* 485adj.
vigil *precursor* 66n.
  period 110n.
  priority 119n.
  carefulness 457n.
  church service 988n.
vigilance *sagacity* 498n.
  restlessness 678n.
vigilant *attentive* 455adj.
  vigilant 457adj.
  expectant 507adj.
  tutelary 660adj.
  prepared 669adj.
vigils *prayers* 981n.
vignette *picture* 553n.
  description 590n.
vigorous *great* 32adj.
  (*see* vigour)
vigour *energy* 160n.
  vitality 162n.
  vigorousness 174n.
  affirmation 532n.
  vigour 571n.
  resolution 599n.
  restlessness 678n.
  warm feeling 818n.
  moral sensibility 819n.

Viking *mariner* 270n.
  robber 789n.
vile *unimportant* 639adj.
  bad 645adj.
  cowardly 856adj.
  rascally 930adj.
  heinous 934adj.
vilification
  scurrility 899n.
  detraction 926n.
vilify *shame* 867vb.
  dispraise 924vb.
  defame 926vb.
villa *house* 192n.
villadom *housing* 190n.
  habitancy 191n.
  mediocrity 732n.
village *district* 184n.
  housing 192n.
village green *focus* 76n.
  meeting place 192n.
  pleasure-ground 837n.
villager *dweller* 191n.
villain *evildoer* 904n.
  knave 938n.
villainous *bad* 645adj.
  ugly 842adj.
  rascally 930adj.
  vicious 934adj.
villainy *improbity* 930n.
  wickedness 934n.
villein *slave* 742n.
  possessor 776n.
  countryman 869n.
villenage *servitude* 745n.
villosity *roughness* 259n.
villous *hairy* 259adj.
vim *vigorousness* 174n.
  vigour 571n.
vinaigrette *scent* 396n.
vinculum *bond* 47n.
vindicable
  vindicable 927adj.
vindicate
  demonstrate 478vb.
  claim 915vb.
  vindicate 927vb.
vindication *liberation* 746n.
  avenger 910n.
  vindication 927n.
  vindicator 927n.
  acquittal 960n.
  punisher 963n.
vindictive *hating* 888adj.
  resentful 891adj.
  pitiless 906adj.
  revengeful 910adj.
vine *plant* 366n.
vinegar *sourness* 393n.
  painfulness 827n.
vinegary *sour* 393adj.

irascible 892adj.
  sullen 893adj.
vinery *farm* 370n.
vineyard *farm* 370n.
viniculture
  agriculture 370n.
vinous *intoxicating* 949adj.
  drunken 949adj.
vintage *assemblage* 74n.
  date 108n.
  product 164n.
  agriculture 370n.
  tasty 386adj.
  savoury 390adj.
  store 632n.
  goodness 644n.
  excellent 644adj.
  earnings 771n.
vintner *provider* 633n.
violate
  be unconformable 84vb.
  force 176vb.
  ill-treat 645vb.
  disobey 738vb.
  be undue 916vb.
  fail in duty 918vb.
  debauch 951vb.
  be illegal 954vb.
  (*see* violation)
violation *coition* 45n.
  rape 951n.
violator *usurper* 916n.
  libertine 952n.
  impious person 980n.
violence *disorder* 61n.
  derangement 63n.
  havoc 165n.
  vigorousness 174n.
  violence 176n.
  misuse 675n.
  cruel act 898n.
violent
  revolutionary 149adj.
  violent 176adj.
  assertive 532adj.
  harmful 645adj.
  hasty 680n.
  oppressive 735adj.
  fervent 818adj.
  excited 821adj.
  excitable 822adj.
  lawless 954adj.
violet *fragrance* 396n.
  purple 434n.
  blueness 435n.
  humility 872n.
  modesty 844n.
violin, viola *viol* 414n.
violinist
  instrumentalist 413n.
V.I.P. *person* 371n.

bigwig 638 n.
viper *reptile* 365 n.
  sibilation 406 n.
  bane 659 n.
  noxious animal 904 n.
  knave 938 n.
viraginity *abnormality* 84 n.
  male 372 n.
virago *athlete* 162 n.
  violent creature 176 n.
  woman 373 n.
  shrew 892 n.
virelay *verse form* 593 n.
virgin *new* 126 adj.
  woman 373 n.
  unknown 491 adj.
  unwedded 895 adj.
  virgin 950 n.
virginal *young* 130 adj.
  unwedded 895 adj.
  virtuous 933 adj.
  pure 950 adj.
virginals *piano* 414 n.
virginibus puerisque
  pure 950 adj.
virginity
  unproductivity 172 n.
  celibacy 895 n.
  purity 950 n.
virgin soil
  unknown thing 491 n.
  undevelopment 670 n.
Virgo *zodiac* 321 n.
viridescent *green* 432 adj.
virile *athlete* 162 adj.
  male 372 adj.
virilism *abnormality* 84 n.
virility *adultness* 134 n.
  vitality 162 n.
virology
  medical art 658 n.
virtu *good taste* 846 n.
virtual *intrinsic* 5 adj.
  powerful 160 adj.
  possible 469 adj.
virtue *essential part* 5 n.
  ability 160 n.
  utility 640 n.
  goodness 644 n.
  conduct 688 n.
  manliness 855 n.
  nobility 868 n.
  modesty 874 n.
  morals 917 n.
  virtue 933 n.
  purity 950 n.
virtuosity
  musical skill 413 n.
  skill 694 n.
  good taste 846 n.
virtuoso *musician* 413 n.

proficient 696 n.
virtuous *virtuous* 933 adj.
  pure 950 adj.
  pietistic 979 adj.
virulence *keenness* 174 n.
  badness 645 n.
  poison 659 n.
  rudeness 885 n.
  resentment 891 n.
  malevolence 898 n.
virus *animalcule* 196 n.
  infection 651 n.
  poison 659 n.
visa *credential* 465 n.
  assent 488 n.
  permit 756 n.
visage *face* 237 n.
  feature 445 n.
vis-à-vis *in front* 237 adv.
  against 240 adv.
  carriage 274 n.
viscera *insides* 224 n.
visceral *interior* 224 adj.
viscid *thick* 205 adj.
  viscid 354 adj.
viscidity *viscidity* 354 n.
  semiliquidity 354 n.
vis conservatrix
  preservation 666 n.
viscount *nobleman* 868 n.
viscous *cohesive* 48 adj.
visibility *substantiality* 3 n.
  visibility 443 n.
  appearance 445 n.
visible *impending* 155 adj.
  visible 443 adj.
  intelligible 516 adj.
  manifest 522 adj.
  disclosed 526 adj.
vis inertiæ *energy* 160 n.
  counteraction 182 n.
vision
  insubstantial thing 4 n.
  vision 438 n.
  visual fallacy 440 n.
  appearance 445 n.
  spectacle 445 n.
  fantasy 513 n.
  manifestation 522 n.
  a beauty 841 n.
  aspiration 852 n.
visionary *unreal* 2 adj.
  insubstantial 4 adj.
  seeing 438 adj.
  spectator 441 n.
  impossible 470 adj.
  misjudging 481 adj.
  erroneous 495 adj.
  visionary 513 n.
  imaginative 513 adj.
  imaginary 513 adj.

hoper 852 n.
  philanthropist 901 n.
  worshipper 981 adj.
visionless *blind* 439 adj.
visit *presence* 189 n.
  dwell 192 vb.
  travel 267 vb.
  arrive 295 vb.
  enter 297 vb.
  be severe 735 vb.
  social round 882 n.
  visit 882 vb.
  punish 963 vb.
  goblinize 970 vb.
visitant *wanderer* 268 n.
  arrival 295 n.
visitation *enquiry* 459 n.
  bane 659 n.
  adversity 731 n.
  severity 735 n.
  suffering 825 n.
  punishment 963 n.
visiting card *label* 547 n.
visiting terms
  social round 882 n.
visitor *resident* 191 n.
  arrival 295 n.
  incomer 297 n.
  enquirer 459 n.
  social person 882 n.
visor *shade* 226 n.
  screen 421 n.
  disguise 527 n.
  armour 713 n.
vista *open space* 263 n.
  view 438 n.
  spectacle 445 n.
visual *seeing* 438 adj.
visual aid *classroom* 539 n.
visualize *see* 438 vb.
  imagine 513 vb.
vital *alive* 360 adj.
  required 627 adj.
  cheerful 833 adj.
vital concern
  important matter 638 n.
vitalism *biology* 358 n.
vitality *vitality* 162 n.
  life 360 n.
  vigour 570 n.
  health 650 n.
  restlessness 678 n.
  cheerfulness 833 n.
vitalize *vitalize* 360 vb.
vitalness *needfulness* 627 n.
vital role *influence* 178 n.
vital spark *life* 360 n.
vital statistics
  statistics 86 n.
  beauty 841 n.
vitamin *tonic* 658 n.

vitaminize *feed* 301 vb.
vitaminous
  nourishing 301 adj.
vitamins *food content* 301 n.
  dieting 301 n.
vitiate
  impair, pervert 655 vb.
  be clumsy 695 vb.
vitiated *diseased* 651 adj.
  vicious 934 adj.
vitiation *deterioration* 655 n.
  wickedness 934 n.
viticulture *agriculture* 370 n.
vitreosity
  transparency 422 n.
vitreous *hard* 326 adj.
  transparent 422 adj.
vitrify *harden* 326 vb.
vitriol *burning* 381 n.
  poison 659 n.
vitriolic *paining* 827 adj.
  maledicent 899 adj.
vituperation *oratory* 579 n.
  scurrility 899 n.
  reproach 924 n.
vituperator *defamer* 926 n.
viva *exam.* 459 n.
vivacious *feeling* 818 adj.
  lively 819 adj.
  (see vivacity)
vivacity *vigour* 571 n.
  restlessness 678 n.
  moral sensibility 819 n.
  cheerfulness 833 n.
vivandière *pedlar* 794 n.
vivarium *stock farm* 639 n.
vivid *lifelike* 18 adj.
  vigorous 174 adj.
  striking 374 adj.
  luminous 417 adj.
  florid 425 adj.
  expressive 516 adj.
  representing 551 adj.
  forceful 571 adj.
  descriptive 590 adj.
vivify *strengthen* 162 vb.
  vitalize 360 vb.
  animate 821 vb.
viviparous
  productive 164 adj.
vivisect *give pain* 377 vb.
  experiment 461 vb.
vivisection *killing* 362 n.
  pain 377 n.
vivisector *enquirer* 459 n.
  experimenter 461 n.
vixen *vermin* 365 n.
  female animal 373 n.
  shrew 892 n.
vixenish *animal* 365 adj.
  irascible 892 adj.

sullen 893 adj.
viz. *namely* 80 adv.
vizier *official* 690 n.
  officer 741 n.
vocable *speech sound* 398 n.
  word 559 n.
vocabulary *list* 87 n.
  dictionary 559 n.
  style 566 n.
vocal *sounding* 398 adj.
  musical 412 adj.
  vocal 577 adj.
  speaking 579 n.
vocal chords *voice* 577 n.
vocalic *literal* 558 adj.
  vocal 577 adj.
vocalism *vocal music* 412 n.
vocalist *vocalist* 413 n.
vocalize *sing* 413 vb.
  voice 577 vb.
vocation *call* 547 n.
  motive 612 n.
  pursuit 619 n.
  vocation 622 n.
  duty 917 n.
  church ministry 985 n.
vocational
  businesslike 622 adj.
vocative *vocative* 583 adj.
  devotional 981 adj.
vociferation *loudness* 400 n.
  cry 408 n.
  voice 577 n.
vogue *practice* 610 n.
  fashion 848 n.
  repute 866 n.
vogue-word *word* 559 n.
  neology 560 n.
voice *publish* 528 vb.
  affirmation 532 n.
  grammar 564 n.
  voice 577 n., vb.
  speak 579 vb.
  vote 605 n.
voiced *sounding* 398 adj.
  literal 558 adj.
  vocal 577 adj.
voiceless *voiceless* 578 adj.
  taciturn 582 adj.
voicelessness *aphony* 578 n.
void *insubstantiality* 4 n.
  space 183 n.
  emptiness 190 n.
  gap 201 n.
  void 300 vb.
  rarefy 325 vb.
  abrogate 752 vb.
voidance *voidance* 300 n.
voile *textile* 222 n.
volatile *transient* 114 adj.
  light 323 adj.

gaseous 336 adj.
  vaporific 338 adj.
  light-minded 456 adj.
  capricious 604 adj.
  excitable 822 adj.
volatilize *lighten* 323 vb.
  rarefy 325 vb.
  vaporize 338 vb.
volcanic *violent* 176 adj.
  outgoing 298 adj.
  fiery 379 adj.
  excitable 822 adj.
volcano *outbreak* 176 n.
  cavity 255 n.
  chimney 263 n.
  ejector 300 n.
  fire 379 n.
  furnace 383 n.
  pitfall 663 n.
volition *will* 595 n.
volitional *volitional* 595 adj.
volley *crowd* 74 n.
  strike 279 vb.
  shoot 287 vb.
  bang 402 n.
  bombardment 712 n.
  fire at 712 vb.
volley-ball *ball game* 837 n.
volt, voltage
  electricity 160 n.
volte-face *return* 286 n.
  tergiversation 603 n.
  perfidy 930 n.
volubility *speech* 579 n.
  loquacity 581 n.
volume *quantity* 26 n.
  subdivision 53 n.
  inclusion 78 n.
  space, measure 183 n.
  size 195 n.
  metrology 465 n.
  book 589 n.
volumetric *spatial* 183 adj.
  metric 465 adj.
voluminous *great* 32 adj.
  recipient 194 adj.
  large 195 adj.
voluntarism
  philosophy 449 n.
  will 595 n.
voluntary *prelude* 66 n.
  musical piece 412 n.
  volitional 595 adj.
  voluntary 597 adj.
volunteer *volunteer* 597 n.
  be willing 597 vb.
  undertake 672 vb.
  worker 686 n.
  soldier 722 n.
  offer oneself 759 vb.
voluptuary *sensualist* 944 n.

voluptuous
sensuous 376adj.
pleasurable 826adj.
sensual 944adj.
lecherous 951adj.
volutation *rotation* 315n.
volute *coil* 251n.
vomit *voidance* 300n.
vomit 300vb.
dislike 861vb.
vomiting *indigestion* 651n.
vomitory *orifice* 263n.
doorway 263n.
remedial 658adj.
voodoo *sorcery* 983n.
voracious *taking* 786adj.
greedy 859adj.
gluttonous 947adj.
voracity *eating* 301n.
desire 859n.
gluttony 947n.
vortex *coil* 251n.
vortex 315n.
commotion 318n.
eddy 350n.
pitfall 663n.
vortical *rotary* 315adj.
votary *patron* 707n.
desirer 859n.
lover 887n.
pietist 979n.
worshipper 981n.
vote *judge* 480vb.
affirmation 532n.
vote 605n.,vb.
decree 737n.
commission 751vb.
credit 802n.,vb.
vote against, vote down
oppose 704vb.
vote-catcher
motivator 612n.
vote-catching
choosing 605adj.
flattering 925adj.
voted *assented* 488adj.
legal 953adj.
vote for *endorse* 488vb.
vote 605vb.
patronize 703vb.
voteless *choiceless* 606adj.
unentitled 916adj.
voter *estimator* 480n.
electorate 605n.
patron 707n.
free man 744n.
voters' list *electorate* 605n.
votes for women
vote 605n.
gynocracy 733n.
vote-snatcher

motivator 612n.
vote-snatching
choosing 605adj.
flattering 925adj.
voting list *list* 87n.
electorate 605n.
voting paper
electorate 605n.
votive *promissory* 764adj.
giving 781adj.
devotional 981adj.
votive offering
oblation 981n.
voucher *credential* 466n.
record 548n.
title-deed 767n.
receipt 807n.
vouch for *testify* 466vb.
promise 764vb.
vouchsafe *permit* 756vb.
consent 758vb.
give 781vb.
vow *affirm* 532vb.
promise 764n.,vb.
offering 781n.
offer worship 981vb.
vowed *dutied* 917adj.
vowel *speech sound* 398n.
spoken letter 558n.
voice 577n.
vox populi *consensus* 488n.
vote 605n.
government 733n.
tribunal 956n.
voyage *water travel* 269n.
passage 305n.
voyager *traveller* 268n.
voyeur *libertine* 952n.
voyeurism *curiosity* 453n.
impurity 951n.
vriddhi
speech sound 398n.
vulcanize *harden* 326vb.
be tough 329adj.
heat 381adj.
vulgar *inferior* 35adj.
general 79adj.
indiscriminating 464adj.
linguistic 557adj.
feeble 572adj.
inelegant 576adj.
not nice 645adj.
artless 699adj.
graceless 842adj.
vulgar 847adj.
disreputable 867adj.
plebeian 869adj.
showy 875adj.
maledicent 899adj.
vicious 934adj.
impure 951adj.

vulgarian *upstart* 126n.
vulgarian 847n.
commoner 869n.
vulgarism *slang* 560n.
inelegance 576n.
bad taste 847n.
vulgarity (*see* vulgar)
vulgarize *impair* 655vb.
use 673vb.
facilitate 701vb.
cheapen 812vb.
vulgarize 847vb.
not respect 921vb.
vulgate *interpretation* 520n.
scripture 975n.
vulnerable
defenceless 161adj.
liable 180adj.
imperfect 647adj.
vulnerable 661adj.
unprepared 670adj.
accusable 928adj.
frail 934adj.
vulpine *animal* 365adj.
cunning 698adj.
vulture *eater* 301n.
bird 365n.
cleaner 648n.
tyrant 735n.
taker 786n.
noxious animal 904n.
glutton 947n.
vulva *genitalia* 164n.

W

wacky *crazed* 503adj.
wad *load* 193vb.
line 227vb.
stopper 264n.
close 264vb.
ammunition 723n.
wadding *contents* 193n.
lining 227n.
stopper 264n.
softness 327n.
warm clothes 381n.
waddle *gait* 265n.
walk 267vb.
move slowly 278vb.
oscillate 317vb.
wade *walk* 267vb.
swim 269vb.
be wet 341vb.
wader *pedestrian* 268n.
waders *legwear* 228n.
footwear 228n.
wade through *study* 536vb.
exert oneself 682vb.
wadi *cavity* 255n.
stream 350n.

conduit 351 n.
wads *great quantity* 32 n.
  funds 797 n.
wafer *adhesive* 47 n.
  lamina 207 n.
  pastry 301 n.
  the sacrament 988 n.
waffle *cereal* 301 n.
  mean nothing 515 vb.
  be loquacious 581 vb.
waft *transport* 272 n.
  transfer 272 vb.
  carry 273 vb.
  blow 352 vb.
waftage *transport* 272 n.
wag *brandish* 317 vb.
  oscillate 317 vb.
  be agitated 318 vb.
  gesticulate 547 vb.
  humorist 839 n.
wage *employ* 622 vb.
  wage war 718 vb.
  earnings 771 n.
  (*see* wages)
wage-bill *cost* 809 n.
wage-earner *worker* 686 n.
  recipient 782 n.
wager *gambling* 618 n.
  contest 716 n.
wages *pay* 804 n.
  receipt 807 n.
  cost 809 n.
  reward 962 n.
waggish *gay* 833 adj.
  amused 837 adj.
  witty 839 adj.
  funny 849 adj.
waggle *brandish* 317 vb.
  agitate 318 vb.
  gesticulate 547 vb.
waggonage *transport* 272 n.
wagon *cart* 274 n.
wagoner, waggoner
  driver 268 n.
  carrier 273 n.
wag one's finger
  reprove 924 vb.
wag one's tongue
  speak 579 vb.
wagonette *carriage* 274 n.
wagon-lit *train* 274 n.
waif *wanderer* 268 n.
  derelict 779 n.
  outcaste 883 n.
wail *cry* 408 vb.
  ululate 409 vb.
  be discontented 829 vb.
  lamentation 836 n.
wain *cart* 274 n.
wainscot *base* 214 n.
  lining 227 n.

wainwright *artisan* 686 n.
waist *narrowing* 206 n.
  centrality 225 n.
  bodywear 228 n.
waist-band *girdle* 47 n.
  belt 228 n.
  loop 250 n.
waistcoat *vest* 228 n.
waistline *narrowing* 206 n.
  centrality 225 n.
wait *pass time* 108 vb.
  protraction 113 n.
  wait 136 vb.
  pause 145 vb.
  be quiescent 266 vb.
  await 507 vb.
  not act 677 vb.
  be inactive 679 vb.
wait and see *wait* 136 vb.
  be tentative 461 vb.
  not act 677 vb.
wait-and-see policy
  caution 858 n.
waiter *concomitant* 89 n.
  spectator 441 n.
  servant 742 n.
waiting list *list* 87 n.
  record 548 n.
  hoper 852 n.
waiting-room *inn* 192 n.
  lobby 194 n.
waiting woman
  domestic 742 n.
wait on *accompany* 89 vb.
  result 157 vb.
  follow 284 vb.
  minister to 703 vb.
  visit 882 vb.
waits *choir* 413 n.
wait upon *obey* 739 vb.
  serve 742 vb.
waive *put off* 136 vb.
  be neutral 606 vb.
  relinquish 621 vb.
  not use 674 vb.
  resign 753 vb.
  refuse 760 vb.
  not retain 779 vb.
waiver *rejection* 607 n.
  relinquishment 621 n.
  non-use 674 n.
  resignation 753 n.
  loss of right 916 n.
wake *remainder* 41 n.
  retinue 67 n.
  continuity 71 n.
  effect 157 n.
  rear 238 n.
  furrow 261 n.
  water travel 269 n.
  follower 284 n.

eddy 350 n.
obsequies 364 n.
trace 548 n.
be active 678 vb.
excite 821 vb.
lament 836 n.
festivity 837 n.
condolence 905 n.
wakeful *attentive* 455 adj.
  vigilant 457 adj.
  active 678 adj.
wake up *have feeling* 374 vb.
walk *pleasance* 192 n.
  gait 265 n.
  pedestrianism 267 n.
  walk 267 vb.
  move slowly 278 vb.
  vocation 622 n.
  path 624 n.
  conduct 688 n.
  goblinize 970 vb.
walker *traveller* 268 n.
  pedestrian 268 n.
  ghost 970 n.
walkie-talkie
  hearing aid 415 n.
  telecommunication 531 n.
walking encyclopædia
  scholar 492 n.
  expert 696 n.
walking out
  love-making 887 n.
walking-stick
  supporter 218 n.
walk of life *state* 7 n.
  vocation 622 n.
  conduct 688 n.
walk on *act* 594 vb.
walk-out *strike* 145 n.
  departure 296 n.
  egress 298 n.
  dissent 489 n.
  opposition 704 n.
walk out with
  accompany 89 vb.
  court 889 vb.
walk-over
  easy thing 701 n.
  victory 727 n.
walkup *flat* 192 n.
wall *separation* 46 n.
  exclusion 57 n.
  verticality 215 n.
  supporter 218 n.
  circumjacence 230 n.
  partition 231 n.
  fence 235 n.
  solid body 324 n.
  screen 421 n.
  fortification 713 n.
  means of execution 964 n.

wallet *case* 194 n.
   treasury 799 n.
wall-eye *dim sight* 440 n.
wallflower *rejection* 607 n.
   indifference 860 n.
wallop *potion* 301 n.
   spank 963 vb.
wallow *be low* 210 vb.
   voyage 269 vb.
   plunge 313 vb.
   rotate 315 vb.
   fluctuate 317 vb.
   be agitated 318 vb.
   weigh 322 vb.
   be wet 341 vb.
   marsh 347 n.
   swill 649 n.
   be unclean 649 vb.
   be intemperate 943 vb.
wallower *dirty person* 649 n.
   sensualist 944 n.
wallow in *enjoy* 376 vb.
   abound 635 vb.
   superabound 637 vb.
wallpaper *covering* 226 n.
   lining 227 n.
Wall Street *mart* 796 n.
walnut *fruit* 301 n.
   tree 366 n.
   brownness 430 n.
waltz *rotation* 315 n.
   musical piece 412 n.
   dance 837 n., vb.
wampum *coinage* 797 n.
wan *dim* 419 adj.
   colourless 426 adj.
   melancholic 834 adj.
   unsightly 842 adj.
wand *badge of rule* 743 n.
   magic instrument 983 n.
wander *be unrelated* 10 vb.
   be dispersed 75 vb.
   wander 267 vb.
   be inattentive 456 vb.
   be insane 503 vb.
   be diffuse 570 vb.
   be free 744 vb.
wanderer
   displacement 188 n.
   wanderer 268 n.
   idler 679 n.
wandering *unstable* 152 adj.
   deviation 282 n.
   unconfined 744 adj.
   (*see* wander)
wanderlust
   wandering 267 n.
wane *decrease* 37 n., vb.
   become small 198 vb.
   be dim 419 vb.
   waste 634 vb.

   deteriorate 655 vb.
wangle *trickery* 542 n.
   contrivance 623 n.
   foul play 930 n.
want *deficit* 55 n.
   shortcoming 307 n.
   requirement 627 n.
   scarcity 636 n.
   be unsatisfied 636 vb.
   imperfection 647 n.
   request 761 n.
   poverty 801 n.
   desire 859 n., vb.
want back *regret* 830 vb.
wanted *absent* 190 adj.
   required 627 adj.
wanting *incomplete* 55 adj.
   absent 190 adj.
   deficient 307 adj.
   unintelligent 499 adj.
   insane 503 adj.
   lost 722 adj.
wanton *changeful* 152 adj.
   capricious 604 adj.
   free 744 adj.
   amuse oneself 837 vb.
   revel 837 vb.
   rash 857 adj.
   caress 889 vb.
   unchaste 951 adj.
   loose woman 952 n.
wapentake *district* 184 n.
wappenshaw
   assemblage 74 n.
   pageant 875 n.
war *slaughter* 362 n.
   dissension 709 n.
   war 718 n.
   be inimical 881 vb.
warble *ululate* 409 vb.
   sing 413 vb.
warbler *vocalist* 413 n.
war-chariot
   war-chariot 274 n.
war correspondent
   author 589 n.
   delegate 754 n.
warcraft *art of war* 718 n.
war-cry *call* 547 n.
   danger signal 665 n.
   defiance 711 n.
ward *subdivision* 53 n.
   youth 130 n.
   district 184 n.
   hospital 658 n.
   protection 660 n.
   refuge 662 n.
   fort 713 n.
   dependant 742 n.
   detention 747 n.

   mandate 751 n.
warden *janitor* 264 n.
   protector 660 n.
   manager 690 n.
   officer 741 n.
   keeper 749 n.
wardenship
   protection 660 n.
warder *gaoler* 749 n.
ward off *parry* 713 vb.
wardrobe *cabinet* 194 n.
   clothing 228 n.
wardroom *chamber* 194 n.
wardship *nonage* 130 n.
   protection 660 n.
   subjection 745 n.
ware *product* 164 n.
   property 777 n.
   merchandise 795 n.
warehouse *storage* 632 n.
   emporium 796 n.
warfare *warfare* 718 n.
   (*see* war)
war footing
   war measures 718 n.
war-god *war* 718 n.
   mythic god 966 n.
warhead
   ammunition 723 n.
   explosive 723 n.
war-horse *war-horse* 273 n.
   cavalry 722 n.
wariness *attention* 455 n.
   carefulness 457 n.
   caution 858 n.
warlike *violent* 176 adj.
   warlike 718 adj.
   courageous 855 adj.
warlike habits
   bellicosity 718 n.
warlock *sorcerer* 983 n.
war-lord *militarist* 722 n.
   army officer 741 n.
warm *summery* 128 adj.
   near 200 adj.
   comfortable 376 adj.
   warm 379 adj.
   warm clothes 381 n.
   heat 381 vb.
   red 431 adj.
   forceful 571 adj.
   laborious 682 adj.
   rich 800 adj.
   fervent 818 adj.
   excite 821 vb.
   cheer 833 vb.
   friendly 880 adj.
   sociable 882 adj.
   excite love 887 vb.
   angry 891 adj.
   irascible 892 adj.

warmed-up
 repeated 106adj.
 heated 381adj.
war memorial *trophy* 729n.
warm-heartedness
 benevolence 897n.
warming pan
 cauldron 194n.
 heater 383n.
war-monger *militarist* 722n.
war-mongering
 contending 716adj.
warmth *heat* 379n.
 hue 425n.
 redness 431n.
 vigour 571n.
 excitable state 822n.
 friendliness 880n.
 anger 891n.
warm the heart
 cheer 833vb.
warm to *feel* 818vb.
 desire 859vb.
 befriend 880vb.
 be in love 887vb.
warm up *start out* 296vb.
 heat 381vb.
 make ready 669vb.
 show feeling 818vb.
warn *predict* 511vb.
 hint 524vb.
 dissuade 613vb.
 warn 664vb.
 advise 691vb.
 defy 711vb.
 frighten 854vb.
 reprove 924vb.
warned *expectant* 507adj.
 warned 664adj.
 prepared 669adj.
warning *precursor* 66n.
 period 110n.
 prediction 511n.
 omen 511n.
 warning 664n.
 intimidation 854n.
  (*see* warn)
warning light
 signal light 420n.
 signal 547n.
warning notice
 demand 737n.
warn off *exclude* 57vb.
 prohibit 757vb.
war of words
 quarrel 709n.
 contention 716n.
warp *break* 46vb.
 modify 143vb.
 force 176vb.
 obliquity 220n.

weaving 222n.
deform 244vb.
distortion 246n.
draw 288vb.
bias 481n., vb.
impair 655vb.
warpaint *pigment* 425n.
 cosmetic 843n.
warp and weft
 texture 331n.
warpath *warfare* 718n.
warpath, on the
 attacking 712adj.
warped *distorted* 246adj.
 biased 481adj.
 imperfect 647adj.
warplane *air force* 722n.
war policy
 bellicosity 718n.
warrant *credential* 466n.
 make certain 473vb.
 affirmation 532n.
 safeguard 660vb.
 precept 693n.
 warrant 737n.
 mandate 751n.
 permit 756n., vb.
 promise 764n., vb.
 security 767n.
 paper money 797n.
 justify 927vb.
 legal process 959n.
warranty *credential* 466n.
 permission 756n.
 promise 764n.
 security 767n.
warren *abundance* 171n.
 dwelling 192n.
 excavation 255n.
warrior *combatant* 722n.
 soldier 722n.
warship *warship* 722n.
wars, in the
 unprosperous 731adj.
wart *swelling* 253n.
 skin disease 651n.
 blemish 845n.
wartime
 belligerency 718n.
war-weary *peaceful* 717adj.
wary *nervous* 854adj.
 cautious 858adj.
wash *facing* 226n.
 moisten 341vb.
 lake 346n.
 marsh 347n.
 eddy, wave 350n.
 pigment 425n.
 whiten 427vb.
 trace 548n.
 suffice 635n.

be expedient 642vb.
ablution 648n.
clean 648vb.
balm 658n.
wash and brush up
 refreshment 695n.
 beautification 843n.
washed out
 colourless 426adj.
 fatigued 684adj.
washed up *fatigued* 684adj.
washer *lining* 227n.
 interjection 231n.
 circle 250n.
washerwoman
 cleaner 648n.
wash-house *ablution* 648n.
washing board
 cleaning utensil 648n.
wash-leather
 cleaning cloth 648n.
wash off *obliterate* 550vb.
wash one's hands
 avoid 620vb.
 be exempt 919vb.
 disapprove 924vb.
wash out *decolorize* 426vb.
 obliterate 550vb.
wash-out *failure* 728n.
washroom *ablution* 648n.
washy *unmeaning* 515adj.
  (*see* wishy-washy)
wasp *noxious animal* 904n.
waspish *furious* 176adj.
 irascible 892adj.
wasp-waist
 contraction 198n.
 narrowing 206n.
wassail *festivity* 837n.
 get drunk 949vb.
wastage *decrement* 42n.
 waste 634n.
 loss 772n.
waste *decrease* 37n.
 leavings 41n.
 decompose 51vb.
 lay waste 165vb.
 desert 172n.
 space 183n.
 emptiness 190n.
 become small 198vb.
 outflow 298n.
 waste 634n., vb.
 make insufficient 636vb.
 rubbish 641n.
 impair 655vb.
 use 673n., vb.
 misuse 675n., vb.
 loss 772n.
 expend 806vb.
 prodigality 815n.

intemperance 943 n.
waste away *be ill* 651 vb.
wasted *lean* 206 adj.
lost 772 adj.
waste effort
waste effort 641 vb.
wasteful *destructive* 165 adj.
wasteful 634 adj.
profitless 641 adj.
prodigal 815 adj.
intemperate 943 adj.
waste of breath
lost labour 641 n.
waste of time
unproductivity 172 n.
lost labour 641 n.
waste paper
ineffectuality 161 n.
rubbish 641 n.
waste-pipe *drain* 351 n.
waste product *dirt* 649 n.
waster *negligence* 458 n.
prodigal 815 n.
bad man 938 n.
waste time
pass time 108 vb.
drag on 113 vb.
lose a chance 138 vb.
be inactive 679 vb.
wastrel *bad man* 938 n.
watch *period* 110 n.
timekeeper 117 n.
scan 438 vb.
spectator 441 n.
watch 441 vb.
attention 455 n.
be attentive 455 vb.
invigilate 457 vb.
warner 664 n.
be active 678 vb.
defend 713 vb.
keeper 749 n.
police 955 n.
watch and ward
protection 660 n.
watch-chain
jewellery 844 n.
watch-dog *protector* 660 n.
warner 664 n.
keeper 749 n.
watcher *spectator* 441 n.
protector 660 n.
watchet *blueness* 435 n.
watch-fire *fire* 379 n.
signal 547 n.
watchful *attentive* 455 adj.
vigilant 457 adj.
intelligent 498 adj.
tutelary 660 adj.
active 678 adj.
observant 768 adj.

cautious 858 adj.
watch-glass *plate* 194 n.
transparency 422 n.
optical device 442 n.
watch-hand *indicator* 547 n.
watchmaker
timekeeper 117 n.
artisan 686 n.
watchman *janitor* 264 n.
spectator 441 n.
protector 660 n.
keeper 749 n.
watch over
safeguard 660 vb.
watch-tower
high structure 209 n.
view 438 n.
watchword *call* 547 n.
identification 547 n.
warfare 718 n.
water *bate* 37 vb.
mix 43 vb.
weak thing 163 n.
weaken 163 vb.
make fruitful 171 vb.
drink, soft drink 301 n.
excrement 302 n.
fluid 335 n.
water 339 n.
add water 339 vb.
irrigate 341 vb.
make flow 350 vb.
groom 369 vb.
cultivate 370 vb.
extinguisher 382 n.
insipidity 387 n.
transparency 422 n.
provide 633 vb.
cleanser 648 n.
water at the mouth
exude 298 vb.
be hungry 859 vb.
gluttonize 947 vb.
water-borne
seafaring 269 adj.
water-bottle *vessel* 194 n.
water-cart *water* 339 n.
cleaning utensil 648 n.
water channel *conduit* 351 n.
water-closet *latrine* 649 n.
water-colour
pigment 425 n.
picture 553 n.
art equipment 553 n.
watercourse *stream* 350 n.
conduit 351 n.
water-cress *potherb* 301 n.
water-diviner
enquirer 459 n.
diviner 511 n.
psychic 984 n.

water down *weaken* 163 vb.
add water 339 vb.
water-drinker
ascetic 945 n.
sober person 948 n.
waterer *irrigator* 341 n.
waterfall *outflow* 298 n.
descent 309 n.
waterfall 350 n.
water-filter
cleaning utensil 648 n.
waterfowl *waterfowl* 365 n.
water-front *edge* 234 n.
water-gate *conduit* 351 n.
water-hole *lake* 346 n.
watering-can *vessel* 194 n.
irrigator 341 n.
watering-cart *water* 339 n.
irrigator 341 n.
watering place *abode* 192 n.
hospital 658 n.
water-jump *gap* 201 n.
obstacle 702 n.
waterless *dry* 342 n.
water-level *layer* 207 n.
horizontality 216 n.
water-line *edge* 234 n.
waterlog *drench* 341 vb.
waterlogged
impotent 161 adj.
marshy 347 adj.
semiliquid 354 adj.
unsafe 661 adj.
hindered 702 adj.
Waterloo *ruin* 165 n.
defeat 728 n.
waterman *boatman* 270 n.
watermark *gauge* 465 n.
label 547 n.
pattern 844 n.
water-pipe *conduit* 351 n.
water-pistol *irrigator* 341 n.
toy gun 723 n.
plaything 837 n.
water-polo
ball game 837 n.
sport 837 n.
waterproof
unyielding 162 adj.
coat 226 vb.
overcoat 228 n.
sealed off 264 adj.
dry 342 adj.
invulnerable 660 adj.
preserve 666 vb.
resisting 715 adj.
watershed *summit* 213 n.
partition 231 n.
water-spirit
mythical being 970 n.
water-sports *aquatics* 268 n.

waterspout *vortex* 315 n.
  conduit 351 n.
water-supply
  provision 633 n.
water-system
  cleansing 648 n.
water-table *layer* 207 n.
  horizontality 216 n.
watertight *dry* 342 adj.
water travel
  water travel 269 n.
water vapour *gas* 336 n.
  water 339 n.
water-wagon, on the
  sober 948 adj.
water-way *stream* 350 n.
water-wings *bladder* 194 n.
watery *non-adhesive* 49 adj.
  weak 163 adj.
  excretory 302 adj.
  fluidal 335 adj.
  watery 339 adj.
  humid 341 adj.
  tasteless 387 adj.
watt *electricity* 160 n.
  metrology 465 n.
wattle *network* 222 n.
wave *hang* 217 vb.
  make curved 248 vb.
  convolution 251 n.
  hair 259 n.
  be in motion 265 vb.
  elevate 310 vb.
  brandish 317 vb.
  agitate 318 vb.
  wave 350 n.
  show 522 vb.
  gesticulate 547 vb.
  hair-dressing 843 n.
  greet 884 vb.
wave a wand
  practice sorcery 983 vb.
wave by *signal* 547 vb.
wavelength
  long measure 203 n.
  oscillation 317 n.
  radiation 417 n.
wave on *signal* 547 vb.
waver *come unstuck* 49 vb.
  vary 152 vb.
  be uncertain 474 vb.
  doubt 486 vb.
  be irresolute 601 vb.
waverer *waverer* 601 n.
waviness *convolution* 251 n.
  wave 350 n.
waving *pendent* 217 adj.
wavy *curved* 248 adj.
  undulatory 251 adj.
  furrowed 262 adj.
wax *grow* 36 vb.

  be turned to 147 vb.
  expand 197 vb.
  smooth 258 vb.
  harden 326 vb.
  softness 327 n.
  lubricant 334 n.
  viscidity 354 n.
  fat 357 n.
  sculpture 554 n.
  cleanser 648 n.
  anger 891 n.
wax and wane
  change 143 vb.
waxen *fatty* 357 adj.
  whitish 427 adj.
wax figure *mould* 23 n.
  image 551 n.
waxwork *image* 551 n.
  sculpture 554 n.
waxworks *collection* 632 n.
waxy *soft* 327 adj.
  fatty 357 adj.
  angry 891 adj.
way *state* 7 n.
  degree 27 n.
  room 183 n.
  itinerary 267 n.
  water travel 269 n.
  direction 281 n.
  progression 285 n.
  way in 297 n.
  habit 610 n.
  way 624 n.
  means 629 n.
  fashion 848 n.
  ritual 988 n.
way, by the
  en passant 305 adv.
wayfarer *traveller* 268 n.
way in *entrance* 68 n.
  doorway 263 n.
  way in 297 n.
waylay *ensnare* 542 vb.
  ambush 527 vb.
  be cunning 698 vb.
waymark *signpost* 547 n.
way of life *conduct* 688 n.
way of the world
  fashion 848 n.
way, on the
  on the move 265 adj.
  in transit 272 adv.
  towards 281 adv.
  forward 285 adv.
way out *outlet* 298 n.
  contrivance 623 n.
  route 624 n.
  means of escape 667 n.
  deliverance 668 n.
way out, on the
  deteriorated 655 adj.

ways and means
  means 629 n.
wayside *edge* 234 n.
  accessible 289 adj.
way, under *forward* 285 adv.
wayward *changeful* 152 adj.
  wilful 602 adj.
  capricious 604 adj.
  disobedient 738 adj.
way with *management* 689 n.
way-worn *travelling* 267 adj.
  fatigued 684 adj.
wayzgoose
  amusement 837 n.
wazir *officer* 741 n.
wazirate *magistrature* 733 n.
W.C. *latrine* 649 n.
we *self* 80 n.
weak *small* 33 adj.
  mixed 43 adj.
  ephemeral 114 adj.
  powerless 161 adj.
  weak 163 adj.
  moderate 177 adj.
  little 196 adj.
  watery 339 adj.
  muted 401 adj.
  unintelligent 499 adj.
  feeble 572 adj.
  insufficient 636 adj.
  unimportant 639 adj.
  unsafe 661 adj.
  lax 734 adj.
  pitying 905 adj.
  frail 934 adj.
weak case *sophism* 477 n.
weaken *bate* 37 vb.
  mix 43 vb.
  modify 143 vb.
  disable 161 vb.
  weaken 163 vb.
  moderate 177 vb.
  rarefy 325 vb.
  add water 339 vb.
  qualify 486 vb.
  impair 655 vb.
weak in the head
  insane 503 adj.
weak-kneed
  irresolute 601 adj.
  submitting 721 adj.
  lax 734 adj.
weakling *weakling* 163 n.
  sick person 651 n.
  unlucky person 731 n.
  coward 856 n.
weakly *weakly* 163 adj.
weak-minded
  irresolute 601 adj.
  cowardly 856 adj.
weakness *impotence* 161 n.

tendency 179 n.
liability 180 n.
irresolution 601 n.
insufficiency 636 n.
imperfection 647 n.
defect 647 n.
ill-health 651 n.
bane 659 n.
vulnerability 661 n.
liking 859 n.
vice 934 n.
weak-willed
irresolute 601 adj.
lax 734 adj.
weal trace 548 n.
good 615 n.
prosperity 730 n.
blemish 845 n.
weald plain 348 n.
wood 366 n.
wealth abundance 171 n.
means 629 n.
plenty 635 n.
estate 777 n.
money 797 n.
wealth 800 n.
wealthy rich 800 adj.
weaned
unhabituated 611 adj.
wean from
convince 485 vb.
disaccustom 611 vb.
dissuade 613 vb.
weanling child 132 n.
weapon contrivance 623 n.
instrument 628 n.
tool 630 n.
protection 660 n.
defence 713 n.
weapon 723 n.
weaponless
defenceless 161 adj.
wear decompose 51 vb.
last 113 vb.
clothing 228 n.
wear 228 vb.
show 522 vb.
use 673 n., vb.
fatigue 684 n., vb.
wear and tear
decrease 37 n.
decay 51 n.
waste 634 n.
dilapidation 655 n.
weariness sleepiness 679 n.
fatigue 684 n.
dejection 834 n.
tedium 838 n.
wearing bedecked 844 adj.
wearisome
laborious 682 adj.

fatiguing 684 adj.
annoying 827 adj.
tedious 838 adj.
wear off disappear 446 vb
be unused 611 vb.
wear on elapse 111 vb.
wear out waste 634 vb.
deteriorate 655 vb.
impair 655 vb.
fatigue 684 vb.
be tedious 838 vb.
wear ship navigate 269 vb.
deflect 282 vb.
wear the breeches
influence 178 vb.
dominate 733 vb.
wear thin be weak 163 vb.
be brittle 330 vb.
wear well last 113 vb.
be healthy 650 vb.
weary weakened 163 adj.
laborious 682 adj.
fatigue 684 vb.
incommode 827 vb.
bored 838 adj.
sate 863 vb.
weasand maw 194 n.
orifice 263 n.
air-pipe 353 n.
weasel vehicle 274 n.
vermin 365 n.
weather storm 176 n.
navigate 269 vb.
pulverize 332 vb.
weather 340 n.
wind 352 n.
colour 425 vb.
deteriorate 655 vb.
mature 669 vb.
weather balloon
airship 276 n.
weather-beaten
weakened 163 adj.
dilapidated 655 adj.
weather-bound
restrained 747 adj.
weathercock
changeable thing 152 n.
pneumatics 340 n.
anemology 352 n.
indicator 547 n.
waverer 601 n.
tergiversator 603 n.
weathered soft-hued 425 adj.
matured 669 adj.
weather eye
carefulness 457 n.
weather gauge
navigation 269 n.
weatherproof
unyielding 162 adj.

invulnerable 660 adj.
weather side
contrariety 14 n.
laterality 239 n.
weather the storm
be stable 153 vb.
be restored 656 vb.
be safe 660 vb.
escape 667 vb.
triumph 727 vb.
weather-vane
pneumatics 340 n.
weather 340 n.
anemology 352 n.
weather-wise airy 340 adj.
foreseeing 510 adj.
predicting 511 adj.
weave arrangement 62 n.
produce 164 vb.
textile 222 n.
weave 222 vb.
pass 305 vb.
texture 331 n.
pattern 844 n.
weaver weaving 222 n.
web complexity 61 n.
filament 208 n.
network 222 n.
texture 331 n.
plot 623 n.
stratagem 698 n.
webbing network 222 n.
webby reticular 222 adj.
web-footed
deformed 246 adj.
blemished 845 adj.
wed combine 50 vb.
wed 894 vb.
wedded to believing 485 adj.
obstinate 602 adj.
habituated 610 adj.
wedding wedding 894 n.
wedding garment
ritual object 988 n.
wedding ring
jewellery 844 n.
love token 889 n.
ritual object 988 n.
wedge affix 45 vb.
piece 53 n.
supporter 218 n.
interjection 231 n.
angular figure 247 n.
sharp edge 256 n.
stopper 264 n.
tool 630 n.
wedge apart sunder 46 vb.
wedged firm-set 45 adj.
wedge in intromit 231 vb.
wedlock junction 45 n.
marriage 894 n.

weed *eliminate* 44 vb.
  exclude 57 vb.
  render few 105 vb.
  plant 366 n.
  cultivate 370 vb.
  tobacco 388 n.
  purify 648 vb.
  make better 654 vb.
weeding *displacement* 188 n.
weed out *bate* 37 vb.
  eject 300 vb.
weeds *clothing* 228 n.
  rubbish 641 n.
weedy *lean* 206 adj.
  vegetal 366 adj.
week *period* 110 n.
weekday *period* 110 n.
week-end *pass time* 108 vb.
  regular return 141 n.
  visit 882 vb.
weekly *seasonal* 141 adj.
  journal 528 n.
  reading matter 589 n.
week of Sundays, a
  diuturnity 113 n.
weep *flow out* 298 vb.
  be wet 341 vb.
  be dejected 834 vb.
  weep 836 vb.
weeper *funeral* 364 n.
  weeper 836 n.
weepers *formal dress* 228 n.
  badge 547 n.
weep for *be sensitive* 819 vb.
  pity 905 vb.
weeping *pendent* 217 adj.
weeping and wailing
  obsequies 364 n.
  lamentation 836 n.
weepy *unhappy* 825 adj.
weevil *vermin* 365 n.
weft *weaving* 222 n.
weigh *equalize* 28 vb.
  influence 178 vb.
  load 193 vb.
  weigh 322 vb.
  meditate 449 vb.
  discriminate 463 vb.
  mete out 465 vb.
  estimate 480 vb.
  motivate 612 vb.
  be important 638 vb.
  oppress 735 vb.
weigh anchor
  navigate 269 vb.
  start out 296 vb.
weigh-bridge *scales* 322 n.
weighed against
  compensatory 31 adj.
weighing-machine
  scales 322 n.

weighment *weighment* 322 n.
weigh one's words
  be truthful 540 vb.
weight *substantiality* 3 n.
  quantity 26 n.
  power 160 n.
  influence 178 n.
  size, bulk 195 n.
  materiality 319 n.
  gravity, scales 322 n.
  make heavy 322 vb.
  vigour 571 n.
  importance 638 n.
  encumbrance 702 n.
weighted *distorted* 246 adj.
  unjust 914 adj.
weighting
  compensation 31 n.
weightless *small* 33 adj.
  light 323 adj.
weight of numbers
  greater number 104 n.
weights *weighment* 322 n.
  metrology 465 n.
weights and measures
  metrology 465 n.
weighty *substantial* 3 adj.
  great 32 adj.
  strong 162 adj.
  influential 178 adj.
  material 319 adj.
  weighty 322 adj.
  evidential 466 adj.
  forceful 571 adj.
  instrumental 628 adj.
  important 638 adj.
weir *waterfall* 350 n.
  conduit 351 n.
  obstacle 702 n.
weird *fate* 596 n.
  frightening 854 adj.
  wonderful 864 adj.
  spooky 970 adj.
welcome *meet* 295 vb.
  reception 299 n.
  pleasant 376 adj.
  assent 488 vb.
  pleasurable 826 adj.
  desired 859 adj.
  celebration 876 n.
  friendliness 880 n.
  sociability 882 n.
  courteous act 884 n.
  congratulation 886 n.
  show respect 920 vb.
  applaud 923 vb.
weld *join* 45 vb.
  agglutinate 48 vb.
  heat 381 vb.
  yellow pigment 433 n.
welder *joinder* 45 n.

welfare *good* 615 n.
  prosperity 730 n.
welfare state *shelter* 662 n.
  polity 733 n.
  sociology 901 n.
welfare work
  sociology 901 n.
welkin *air* 340 n.
  heavens 321 n.
well *greatly* 32 adv.
  receptacle 194 n.
  lowness 210 n.
  depth 211 n.
  flow out 298 vb.
  stream 350 n.
  well 615 adv.
  store 632 n.
  aright 644 adv.
  healthy 650 adj.
  skilfully 694 adv.
well-advised *wise* 498 adj.
well-affected
  friendly 880 adj.
well-aimed *apt* 24 adj.
  accurate 494 adj.
well-behaved
  obedient 739 adj.
  amiable 884 adj.
well-being *euphoria* 376 n.
  good 615 n.
  health 650 n.
  salubrity 652 n.
  prosperity 730 n.
  wealth 800 n.
  happiness 824 n.
well-born
  worshipful 866 adj.
  noble 868 adj.
well-bred
  tasteful 846 adj.
  well-bred 848 adj.
  genteel 868 adj.
well-built *strong* 162 adj.
well-cut *adjusted* 24 adj.
well-defended
  safe 660 adj.
well-directed *relevant* 9 adj.
well-disposed
  aiding 703 adj.
well done *excellent* 644 adj.
  well-made 694 adj.
well-drawn
  descriptive 590 adj.
well-dressed
  personable 841 adj.
  fashionable 848 adj.
well-drilled *orderly* 60 adj.
Wellerism
  witticism 839 n.
well-favoured
  beautiful 841 adj.

well-feathered *rich* 800 adj.
well-fed *fleshy* 195 adj.
  feeding 301 adj.
well-fought
  contending 716 adj.
well-founded
  vested 153 adj.
  plausible 471 adj.
  certain 473 adj.
  true 494 adj.
well grown *large* 195 adj.
  fleshy 195 adj.
well-head *source* 156 n.
  summit 213 n.
well-inclined
  approving 923 adj.
well-intentioned
  aiding 703 adj.
  friendly 880 adj.
  benevolent 897 adj.
  virtuous 933 adj.
  innocent 935 adj.
well-judged *wise* 498 adj.
well-kept *safe* 660 adj.
  preserved 666 adj.
well-knit *cohesive* 48 adj.
  stalwart 162 adj.
well-known
  well-known 528 adj.
  renowned 866 adj.
well-laid *cunning* 698 adj.
well-lined *full* 54 adj.
well-made
  well-made 694 adj.
  beautiful 841 adj.
well-mannered
  well-bred 848 adj.
  courteous 884 adj.
well-meaning
  friendly 880 adj.
  innocent 935 adj.
well-meant *aiding* 703 adj.
  benevolent 897 adj.
well-off *prosperous* 730 adj.
  rich 800 adj.
well over *flow out* 298 vb.
  superabound 637 vb.
well-pitched
  melodious 410 adj.
  accurate 494 adj.
well-read *instructed* 490 adj.
  studious 536 adj.
well-regulated
  orderly 60 adj.
well-rounded
  phraseological 563 adj.
well-spent
  successful 727 adj.
well-spent life
  virtue 933 n.
well-spoken *speaking* 579 adj.

well-bred 848 adj.
well-spring *source* 156 n.
well-stocked *filled* 635 adj.
well-thumbed *used* 673 adj.
well-timed *timely* 137 adj.
  expedient 642 adj.
well-to-do
  prosperous 730 adj.
  rich 800 adj.
well-trodden *used* 673 adj.
well-turned *elegant* 575 adj.
  shapely 841 adj.
well up in *expert* 694 adj.
well-wisher
  patron 707 n.
  friend 880 n.
  kind person 897 n.
well with *friendly* 880 adj.
well-worn *usual* 610 adj.
  dilapidated 655 adj.
  used 673 adj.
welsh *decamp* 296 vb.
  run away 620 vb.
  elude 667 vb.
  defraud 788 vb.
  not pay 805 vb.
welsher *avoider* 620 n.
  defrauder 789 n.
  non-payer 805 n.
welt *edge* 234 n.
  trace 548 n.
  spank 963 vb.
welter *confusion* 61 n.
  plunge 313 vb.
  rotate 315 vb.
  be wet 341 vb.
welter-weight
  pugilist 722 n.
weltschmerz
  suffering 825 n.
  melancholy 834 n.
  pity 905 n.
wen *swelling* 253 n.
  letter 558 n.
  blemish 845 n.
wench *youngster* 132 n.
  woman 373 n.
  be impure 951 vb.
  loose woman 952 n.
wenching *unchastity* 951 n.
wend *move* 265 vb.
  travel 267 vb.
weregild *irenics* 719 n.
  atonement 941 n.
werewolf *demon* 970 n.
Wesleyanism
  Protestantism 976 n.
west *laterality* 239 n.
  compass point 281 n.
West End *district* 184 n.
  beau monde 848 n.

westerly *lateral* 239 adj.
western *lateral* 239 adj.
  directed 281 adj.
  novel 590 n.
  stage play 594 n.
Westerner *foreigner* 59 n.
West Point
  training school 539 n.
westward *lateral* 239 adj.
wet *watery* 339 adj.
  excrete 302 vb.
  moisture 341 n.
  rainy 350 adj.
  foolish 499 adj.
  ninny 501 n.
  intemperate 943 adj.
wet blanket
  moderator 177 n.
  dissuasion 613 n.
  hinderer 702 n.
  moper 834 n.
  bore 838 n.
wet bob *boatman* 270 n.
wet-eyed *unhappy* 825 adj.
  lamenting 836 adj.
wether *sheep* 365 n.
wet-nurse *provider* 633 n.
  patronize 703 vb.
  keeper 749 n.
wet plate *camera* 442 n.
wetted
  incombustible 382 adj.
wetting *moistening* 341 n.
whack *strike* 279 vb.
  fatigue 684 vb.
  portion 783 n.
  spank 963 vb.
whack at *essay* 671 n.
whacked *defeated* 728 adj.
whacking *whopping* 32 adj.
  large 195 adj.
whale *giant* 195 n.
  fish 365 n.
  hunt 619 vb.
whalebone
  compressor 198 n.
  supporter 218 n.
  underwear 228 n.
  hardness 326 n.
  elasticity 328 n.
  fetter 748 n.
whaler *mariner* 270 n.
  fishing boat 275 n.
  hunter 619 n.
wham *strike* 279 vb.
wharf *stable* 192 n.
  edge 234 n.
  storage 632 n.
  workshop 687 n.
  emporium 796 n.
wharfage *price* 809 n.

what for?
enquiringly 459adv.
what-have-you
no name 562n.
what it is about *topic* 452n.
what it will fetch
price 809n.
what might be
possibility 469n.
what one is worth
estate 777n.
what's to come
destiny 155n.
what the doctor ordered
salubrious 652adj.
what the soldier said
evidence 466n.
wheal *swelling* 253n.
wheat *cereal* 301n.
corn 366n.
wheaten *edible* 301adj.
wheat pit *mart* 796n.
wheedle *tempt* 612vb.
induce 612vb.
pet 889vb.
flatter 925vb.
wheedler *motivator* 612n.
flatterer 925n.
wheel *wheel* 250n.
move 265vb.
sailing aid 269n.
turn round 282vb.
circle 314vb.
rotate 315vb.
tool 629n.
directorship 689n.
instrument of torture
964n.
wheel about, wheel round
be inverted 221vb.
turn round 282vb.
turn back 286vb.
circle 314vb.
tergiversate 603vb.
wheelbarrow
pushcart 274n.
wheel-chair *pushcart* 274n.
wheeled *vehicular* 274adj.
wheeled traffic
conveyance 267n.
vehicle 274n.
wheelman *rider* 268n.
navigator 270n.
wheel of fortune
changeable thing 152n.
chance 159n.
non-design 618n.
wheels within wheels
complexity 61n.
machine 630n.
wheelwright *artisan* 686n.

wheeze *respiration* 352n.
breathe 352vb.
hiss 406vb.
idea 451n.
hint 524n.
contrivance 623n.
wheezy *puffing* 352adj.
sibilant 406adj.
whelk *swelling* 253n.
fish food 301n.
table fish 365n.
whelm *drench* 341vb.
whelp *youngling* 132n.
reproduce itself 164vb.
dog 365n.
bad man 938n.
when *while, when* 108adj.
when and where
situation 186n.
whence *hence* 158adv.
why 158adv.
where *here* 189adv.
whereabouts
situation 186n.
wherein *inside* 224adv.
where it hurts most
on the raw 819adv.
where the shoe pinches
difficulty 700n.
moral sensibility 819n.
painfulness 827n.
wherever *widely* 183adv.
wherewith
by means of 629adv.
wherewithal *means* 629n.
funds 797n.
wherret *torment* 827vb.
wherry *boat* 275n.
wherryman *boatman* 270n.
whet *sharpen* 256vb.
animate 821vb.
cause desire 859vb.
whetstone
sharpener 256n.
whetted *sharp* 256adj.
whey *milk product* 301n.
fluid 335n.
whey-faced
colourless 426adj.
whiff *breeze* 352n.
breathe 352vb.
odour 394n.
indication 547n.
whiffling *unstable* 152adj.
trivial 639adj.
whiffy *odorous* 394adj.
fetid 397adj.
Whigs *political party* 708n.
while *while* 108adv.
interim 108n.
synchronously 123adv.

while, a *time* 108n.
while away
pass time 108vb.
be inactive 679vb.
have leisure 681vb.
amuse oneself 837vb.
whilom *prior* 119adj.
former 125adj.
formerly 125adv.
whim *foolery* 497n.
ideality 513n.
whim 604n.
liking 859n.
whimper *cry* 408vb.
weep 836vb.
whimsey *foolery* 497n.
ideality 513n.
whim 604n.
liking 859n.
whimsical *multiform* 82adj.
uncertain 474adj.
misjudging 481adj.
crazed 503adj.
unexpected 508n.
imaginative 513adj.
irresolute 601adj.
capricious 604adj.
witty 839adj.
ridiculous 849adj.
whine *shrill* 407vb.
cry 408n.,vb.
ululate 409vb.
discord 411vb.
be discontented 829vb.
lamentation 836vb.
be servile 879vb.
whinny *ululation* 409n.
whinyard *side-arms* 923n.
whip *accumulator* 74n.
make violent 176vb.
driver 268n.
strike 279vb.
cook 301vb.
agitate 318vb.
break in 369vb.
incentive 612n.
hunter 619n.
manager 689n.
defeat 727vb.
oppress 735vb.
command 737n.
officer 741n.
excitant 821n.
flog 963vb.
scourge 964n.
whipcord *fibre* 208n.
whip hand *vantage* 34n.
victory 727n.
governance 733n.
whip in
bring together 74vb.

whip out *extract* 304 vb.
whipped *light* 323 adj.
whipper *punisher* 963 n.
whipper-in *hunter* 619 n.
whippersnapper
  youngster 132 n.
  nonentity 639 n.
whippet *small animal* 33 n.
  animalcule 196 n.
  dog 365 n.
whipping-boy
  substitute 150 n.
  propitiation 941 n.
whipping post *pillory* 964 n.
whipping top
  plaything 837 n.
whipping up
  excitation 821 n.
whippy *flexible* 327 adj.
whirl *rotate* 315 vb.
  be agitated 318 vb.
  activity 678 n.
  excitable state 822 n.
  festivity 837 n.
whirligig *rotator* 315 n.
whirling *speedy* 277 adj.
whirlpool *vortex* 315 n.
  commotion 318 n.
  eddy 350 n.
  pitfall 663 n.
whirlwind
  turmoil 61 n.
  vortex 315 n.
  commotion 318 n.
  gale 352 n.
whirr *rotate* 315 vb.
  be agitated 318 vb.
  faintness 401 n.
  roll 403 n., vb.
  resound 404 vb.
  ululate 409 vb.
whisk *move fast* 277 vb.
  cook 301 vb.
  agitate 318 vb.
  cleansing utensil 648 n.
  clean 648 vb.
whisker *filament* 208 n.
  feeler 378 n.
whiskers *hair* 259 n.
whisket *basket* 194 n.
whisky *liquor* 301 n.
whisper *sound faint* 401 vb.
  imply 523 vb.
  hint 524 n., vb.
  voice 577 n., vb.
  speak low 578 vb.
  speak 579 n.
  detraction 926 n.
whisperer
  detraction 926 n.
whist *silent* 399 adj.

card game 837 n.
whistle *blow* 352 vb.
  megaphone 400 n.
  be loud 400 vb.
  hiss 406 vb.
  stridor 407 n.
  cry 408 vb.
  ululate 409 vb.
  play music 413 vb.
  sing 413 vb.
  flute 414 n.
  signal 547 n.
  be cheerful 833 vb.
  wonder 864 n., vb.
  applaud 923 vb.
  disapprobation 924 n.
whistle for *beg* 761 vb.
  desire 859 vb.
whistle-stop
  stopping-place 145 n.
whit *small quantity* 33 n.
  trifle 639 n.
white *colourless* 426 adj.
  white 427 adj.
  eye 438 n.
  clean 648 adj.
  honourable 929 adj.
  virtuous 933 adj.
  innocent 935 adj.
  pure 950 adj.
white ant *vermin* 365 n.
white caps *wave* 350 n.
white-collar worker
  worker 686 n.
whited sepulchre
  sham 542 n.
  deceiver 545 n.
white dwarf *star* 321 n.
white elephant
  bane 659 n.
  encumbrance 702 n.
  dearness 811 n.
white ensign *flag* 547 n.
white feather
  cowardice 856 n.
white flag *flag* 547 n.
  irenics 719 n.
white goods
  merchandise 795 n.
white hairs *age* 131 n.
Whitehall *workshop* 687 n.
  magistrature 733 n.
  master 741 n.
white hope
  proficient 696 n.
white horses *wave* 350 n.
White House *house* 192 n.
  magistrature 733 n.
white lead *whiting* 427 n.
white lie
  equivocalness 518 n.

concealment 525 n.
  mental dishonesty 543 n.
  stratagem 698 n.
white line
  traffic control 305 n.
  indicator 547 n.
white-livered
  cowardly 856 adj.
white magic *sorcery* 983 n.
white man *gentleman* 929 n.
  good man 937 n.
whiten *lose colour* 425 vb.
  lose colour 426 vb.
  whiten 427 vb.
  show feeling 818 vb.
whiteness *light* 417 n.
  whiteness 427 n.
  cleanness 648 n.
white sheet *penance* 941 n.
  pillory 964 n.
  canonicals 989 n.
white-skinned *white* 427 adj.
white slave
  prostitute 952 n.
white slaver *bawd* 952 n.
white slave traffic
  social evil 951 n.
white trash
  lower classes 869 n.
whitewash *facing* 226 n.
  coat 226 vb.
  pigment 425 n.
  whiting 427 n.
  sophisticate 477 vb.
  overrate 483 vb.
  sham 542 n.
  cleanser 648 n.
  preserve 666 vb.
  insolvency 805 n.
  extenuate 927 vb.
  acquit 960 vb.
whither *towards* 281 adv.
whiting *table fish* 365 n.
  whiting 427 n.
  cleanser 648 n.
Whitsuntide
  holy-day 988 n.
whittle *shade off* 27 vb.
  bate 37 vb.
  subtract 39 vb.
  cut 46 vb.
  make smaller 198 vb.
  laminate 207 vb.
  sharp edge 256 n.
whizz *move fast* 277 vb.
  hiss 406 vb.
whizz-bang
  missile weapon 723 n.
whodunnit *novel* 590 n.
whole *quantity* 26 n.
  simple 44 adj.

whole 52 n., adj.
  completeness 54 n.
  generality 79 n.
  universal 79 adj.
  numerical 85 adj.
  undamaged 646 adj.
  preserved 666 adj.
whole-blooded
  unmixed 44 adj.
whole faith
  orthodoxy 976 n.
whole-hearted
  simple 44 adj.
  resolute 599 adj.
whole-heartedness
  assiduity 678 n.
whole hog
  completeness 54 n.
  actively 678 adv.
whole-hogging
  extensive 32 adj.
  consummate 32 adj.
  complete 54 adj.
  resolute 599 adj.
  completive 725 adj.
wholeness *whole* 52 n.
  completeness 54 n.
  unity 88 n.
whole, on the
  on an average 30 adv.
wholesale *extensive* 32 adj.
  comprehensive 52 adj.
  complete 54 adj.
  inclusive 78 adj.
  indiscriminate 464 adj.
  plenteous 635 adj.
  trading 791 adj.
  sell 793 vb.
wholesaler *seller* 793 n.
  merchant 794 n.
whole skin *health* 650 n.
wholesome
  nourishing 301 adj.
  beneficial 644 adj.
  healthy 650 adj.
  salubrious 652 adj.
whoop *cry* 408 n., vb.
  pursue 619 vb.
  be cheerful 833 vb.
  rejoice 835 vb.
whoopee *revel* 837 n.
whooping cough
  respiration 352 n.
  respiratory disease 651 n.
whopper *whopper* 195 n.
  untruth 543 n.
whopping *whopping* 32 adj.
  large 195 adj.
whore *be impure* 951 vb.
  prostitute 952 n.
whoredom *unchastity* 951 n.

social evil 951 n.
whoremonger
  libertine 952 n.
whorish *unchaste* 951 adj.
whorl *coil* 251 n.
  weaving 222 n.
  rotator 315 n.
whosoever
  everyman 79 n.
why *why?* 158 adv.
why and wherefore, the
  reason why 156 n.
wick *filament* 208 n.
  lighter 385 n.
  torch 420 n.
wicked *evil* 616 adj.
  bad 645 adj.
  difficult 700 adj.
  wrong 914 adj.
  dishonest 930 adj.
  wicked 934 adj.
  guilty 936 adj.
  impenitent 940 adj.
  lawbreaking 954 adj.
  irreligious 974 adj.
  impious 980 adj.
wicked fairy
  sorceress 983 n.
Wicked One *Satan* 969 n.
wickerwork *basket* 194 n.
  network 222 n.
wicket *doorway* 263 n.
wicket-keeper
  interceptor 702 n.
  defender 713 n.
wicky-up *dwelling* 192 n.
widdershins *towards* 281 adv.
  round and round 315 adv.
wide *great* 32 adj.
  inclusive 78 adj.
  spacious 183 adj.
  distant 199 n.
  broad 205 adj.
  deviating 282 adj.
  mistaken 495 adj.
wideawake *headgear* 228 n.
  attentive 455 adj.
  vigilant 457 adj.
wide berth *scope* 744 n.
wide berth, give a
  avoid 620 vb.
wide circulation
  publicity 528 n.
wide currency
  publicity 528 n.
widen *augment* 36 vb.
  generalize 79 vb.
  enlarge 197 vb.
  be broad 205 vb.
widening *disjunction* 46 n.
widen the breach

make quarrels 709 vb.
wide of *beyond* 199 adv.
widespread
  extensive 32 adj.
  comprehensive 52 adj.
  unassembled 75 adj.
  universal 79 adj.
  spacious 183 adj.
  expanded 197 adj.
  usual 610 adj.
widgeon, wigeon
  waterfowl 365 n.
widow *survivor* 41 n.
  deprive 786 vb.
  widowed spouse 896 n.
widower *survivor* 41 n.
  widowed spouse 896 n.
widowhood
  widowhood 896 n.
widow's weeds
  formal dress 228 n.
  badge 547 n.
  lamentation 836 n.
width *quantity* 26 n.
  size 195 n.
  breadth 205 n.
wield *operate* 173 vb.
  touch 378 vb.
  use 673 vb.
wieldy *wieldy* 701 adj.
wiener *meat* 301 n.
wife *woman* 373 n.
  spouse 894 n.
wifehood *marriage* 894 n.
wifeless *unwedded* 895 adj.
  widowed 896 adj.
wifely *loving* 887 adj.
  matrimonial 894 adj.
wig *wig* 228 n.
  hair 259 n.
  hair-dressing 843 n.
  reprove 924 vb.
wigging *reprimand* 924 n.
wiggle *oscillate* 317 vb.
wigwam *dwelling* 192 n.
wild *disorderly* 61 adj.
  desert 172 n.
  furious 176 adj.
  space 183 n.
  plain 348 n.
  light-minded 456 adj.
  inexact 495 n.
  absurd 497 adj.
  foolish 499 adj.
  frenzied 503 adj.
  avoiding 620 adj.
  unskilful 695 adj.
  artless 699 adj.
  disobedient 738 adj.
  riotous 738 adj.
  excited 821 adj.

gay 833 adj.
unsightly 842 adj.
rash 857 adj.
unsociable 883 adj.
angry 891 adj.
cruel 898 adj.
unchaste 951 adj.
wild about
  enamoured 887 adj.
wild beast
  violent creature 176 n.
  noxious animal 904 n.
wildcat *cat* 365 n.
  rash 857 adj.
  independent 744 adj.
wilderness *confusion* 61 n.
  havoc 165 n.
  desert 172 n.
  space 183 n.
  land 344 n.
wild-goose chase
  whim 604 n.
  lost labour 641 n.
  bungling 695 n.
wildness (*see* wild)
wild oats, sow one's
  come of age 134 vb.
  be wicked 934 vb.
  be intemperate 943 vb.
wile *trickery* 542 n.
  stratagem 698 n.
wilful *volitional* 595 adj.
  wilful 602 adj.
  capricious 604 adj.
  rash 857 adj.
will *sequel* 67 n.
  will 595 n., vb.
  be willing 597 vb.
  resolution 599 n.
  predetermination 608 n.
  be free 744 vb.
  title-deed 767 n.
  bequeath 780 vb.
  desire 859 n.
will and pleasure
  will 595 n.
  command 737 n.
willies *nervousness* 854 n.
willing *volitional* 595 adj.
  willing 597 adj.
  resolute 599 adj.
  active 678 adj.
  obedient 739 adj.
  cheerful 833 adj.
willingness *assent* 488 n.
  persuasibility 612 n.
  co-operation 706 n.
  consent 758 n.
  desire 859 n.
  (*see* will, willing)
will of heaven *fate* 596 n.

will of one's own, have a
  be free 744 vb.
will-o'-the-wisp
  insubstantial thing 4 n.
  glow 417 n.
  glow-worm 420 n.
  visual fallacy 440 n.
  deception 542 n.
  incentive 612 n.
willow *tree* 366 n.
  lamentation 836 n.
willow pattern
  pottery 381 n.
willowy *narrow* 206 adj.
  shapely 841 adj.
will-power *will* 595 n.
  resolution 599 n.
willy-nilly
  necessarily 596 adv.
wilt *be weak* 163 vb.
  deteriorate 655 vb.
  knuckle under 721 vb.
  be dejected 834 vb.
wily *intelligent* 498 adj.
  deceiving 542 adj.
  cunning 698 adj.
wimple *headgear* 228 n.
win *superiority* 34 n.
  victory 727 n.
  win 727 vb.
  acquire, gain 771 vb.
  appropriate 786 vb.
wince *recoil* 280 vb.
  feel pain 377 vb.
  show feeling 818 vb.
  suffer 825 vb.
  quake 854 vb.
winch *lifter* 310 n.
wind
  insubstantial thing 4 n.
  disable 161 vb.
  velocity 277 n.
  voidance 300 n.
  circle 314 vb.
  rotate 315 vb.
  gas 336 n.
  flow 350 vb.
  wind 352 n.
  smell 394 vb.
  play music 413 vb.
  detect 484 vb.
  empty talk 515 n.
  indigestion 651 n.
  fatigue 684 vb.
  hurt 827 vb.
windage *room* 183 n.
windbag *sufflation* 352 n.
  chatterer 581 n.
wind-bound
  hindered 702 adj.
  restrained 747 adj.

windbreak *wood* 366 n.
  screen 421 n.
  shelter 662 n.
wind-cheater *overcoat* 228 n.
wind-cone
  anemology 352 n.
winded *panting* 684 adj.
winder *handle* 218 n.
  rotator 315 n.
windfall *benefit* 615 n.
  non-design 618 n.
  acquisition 771 n.
  gift 781 n.
  receiving 782 n.
wind-gauge *velocity* 277 n.
  anemology 352 n.
wind in *draw* 288 vb.
windiness *rarity* 325 n.
  gaseity 336 n.
  wind, respiration 352 n.
winding *complex* 61 adj.
  meandering 251 n.
  convoluted 251 adj.
  deviating 282 adj.
  flowing 350 adj.
  dishonest 930 adj.
winding sheet
  wrapping 226 n.
  robe 228 n.
  grave clothes 364 n.
wind-jammer
  sailing-ship 275 n.
windlass *traction* 288 n.
  lifter 310 n.
windless *tranquil* 266 adj.
windmill *rotator* 315 n.
window *window* 263 n.
  brittleness 330 n.
  air-pipe 353 n.
  transparency 422 n.
window-dressing
  duplicity 541 n.
  ostentation 875 n.
windowed
  perforated 263 adj.
windowless *opaque* 423 adj.
  insalubrious 653 adj.
window-seat *seat* 218 n.
window-shopper
  inquisitor 453 n.
  purchaser 792 n.
window-sill *shelf* 218 n.
windpipe
  respiration 352 n.
  air-pipe 353 n.
wind-rose *anemology* 352 n.
windrow *series* 71 n.
windscreen *screen* 421 n.
  shelter 662 n.
windscreen wiper
  cleaning utensil 648 n.

windshield *screen* 421 n.
wind-sock *anemology* 352 n.
　indicator 847 n.
windswept *orderless* 61 adj.
　windy 352 adj.
wind the clock *time* 117 vb.
wind the horn
　play music 413 vb.
wind-tunnel
　anemology 352 n.
　testing agent 461 n.
wind up *terminate* 69 vb.
　strengthen 162 vb.
　operate 173 vb.
　invigorate 174 vb.
　draw 288 vb.
　elevate 310 vb.
　make ready 669 vb.
　sell 793 vb.
　fear 854 n.
wind-up *finality* 69 n.
windward *laterality* 239 n.
wind-way *air-pipe* 353 n.
windy *unmeaning* 515 adj.
　gaseous 336 adj.
　airy 340 adj.
　windy 352 adj.
　diffuse 570 adj.
　loquacious 581 adj.
　trivial 639 adj.
　nervous 854 adj.
　ostentatious 875 adj.
wine *wine* 301 n.
　drink 301 vb.
　redness 431 n.
wine-bibbing
　drinking 301 n.
　drunkenness 949 n.
wine cellar *tavern* 192 n.
wine-cooler
　refrigerator 384 n.
wineglass *cup* 194 n.
wine-grower
　husbandman 370 n.
wine-merchant
　provider 633 n.
wine of life
　sensualism 944 n.
winepress
　farm tool 370 n.
wineskin *vessel* 194 n.
　drunkard 949 n.
wing *adjunct* 40 n.
　part, limb 53 n.
　laterality 239 n.
　plumage 259 n.
　wing 271 n.
　fly 271 vb.
　move fast 277 vb.
　wound 655 vb.
　shelter 662 n.

　hinder 702 vb.
　armed force 722 n.
　air force 722 n.
wing-feather *wing* 271 n.
wing, on the
　on the move 265 adv.
　in flight 271 adv.
wings *aircraft* 276 n.
　livery 547 n.
　stage-set 594 n.
wink *look* 438 vb.
　be blind 439 vb.
　be dim-sighted 440 vb.
　hint 524 n., vb.
　indication 547 n.
　gesture 547 n.
　command 737 vb.
　excite love 887 vb.
　approve 923 n.
wink at *disregard* 458 vb.
　permit 756 vb.
　forgive 909 vb.
　(see connive)
winking *vision* 438 n.
winkle *fish food* 301 n.
　table fish 365 n.
winkle out *extract* 304 vb.
winner *superior* 34 n.
　exceller 644 n.
　victor 727 n.
　recipient 782 n.
winning *acquiring* 771 adj.
　pleasurable 826 adj.
　amiable 884 adj.
　lovable 887 adj.
winning hit *success* 727 n.
winning position
　vantage 34 n.
winning-post *limit* 236 n.
　objective 617 n.
winnings *gain* 771 n.
　receiving 782 n.
　taking 786 n.
　booty 790 n.
　receipt 807 n.
winning ways
　inducement 612 n.
　lovableness 887 n.
winnow *eliminate* 44 vb.
　exclude 57 vb.
　aerify 340 vb.
　cultivate 370 vb.
　enquire 459 vb.
　discriminate 463 vb.
　select 605 vb.
　purify 648 vb.
winnowing fan
　farm tool 370 n.
win one's spurs
　succeed 727 vb.
　be courageous 855 vb.

　have repute 866 vb.
win over *convince* 485 vb.
　induce 612 vb.
　pacify 719 vb.
winsome *personable* 841 adj.
　lovable 887 adj.
winter *pass time* 108 vb.
　period 110 n.
　winter 129 n.
　wintriness 380 n.
　adversity 731 n.
　visit 882 vb.
winterized *heated* 381 adj.
win the race
　outstrip 277 vb.
win to *arrive* 295 vb.
wintriness *winter* 129 n.
　storm 176 n.
　wintriness 380 n.
wintry *wintry* 129 adj.
　black 428 adj.
winy *intoxicating* 949 adj.
wipe *dry* 342 vb.
　touch 378 vb.
　clean 648 vb.
wipe off *obliterate* 550 vb.
wipe off old scores
　pay 804 vb.
wipe one's feet on
　subjugate 745 vb.
wipe out *nullify* 2 vb.
　bate 37 vb.
　destroy 165 vb.
　slaughter 362 vb.
　obliterate 550 vb.
　defeat 727 vb.
wipe out a score
　retaliate 714 vb.
wipe out one's offence
　atone 941 vb.
wipe up *dry* 342 vb.
　clean 648 vb.
　carry through 725 vb.
wire *cable* 47 n.
　narrowness 206 n.
　filament 208 n.
　information 524 n.
　communicate 524 vb.
　message 529 n.
　telecommunication 531 n.
wire-draw *lengthen* 203 vb.
　make thin 206 vb.
wire-drawn *long* 230 adj.
　narrow 206 adj.
　fibrous 208 adj.
wireless
　telecommunication 531 n.
wire-puller *influence* 178 n.
　latency 523 n.
　motivator 612 n.
　director 690 n.

slyboots 698 n.
wire-pulling *plot* 623 n.
  (*see* wire-puller)
wires *influence* 178 n.
wiry *stalwart* 162 adj.
  fibrous 208 adj.
wisdom *thought* 449 n.
  erudition 490 n.
  wisdom 498 n.
  caution 858 n.
wise *knowing* 490 adj.
  wise 498 adj.
  foreseeing 510 adj.
  way 624 n.
  expedient 642 adj.
  skilful 694 adj.
  cunning 698 adj.
  cautious 858 adj.
wiseacre *doctrinaire* 473 n.
  sciolist 493 n.
  wiseacre 500 n.
wise after the event
  ill-timed 138 adj.
wisecrack *witticism* 839 n.
wise man *sage* 500 n.
  adviser 691 n.
  consignee 754 n.
  sorcerer 983 n.
wiser, no
  uninstructed 491 adj.
wish *will* 595 n., vb.
  desire 859 n., vb.
  desired object 859 n.
  curse 899 vb.
wishbone
  magic instrument 983 n.
wishful *ill-reasoned* 477 adj.
  desiring 859 adj.
wish-fulfilment
  content 828 n.
wishful thinking
  meditation 449 n.
  credulity 487 n.
  fantasy 513 n.
  desire 859 n.
wishing well
  magic instrument 983 n.
wish one joy
  gratulate 886 vb.
wish undone
  regret 830 vb.
  dislike 861 vb.
  be penitent 939 vb.
wish-wash *silly talk* 515 n.
wish well
  be benevolent 897 vb.
wishy-washy *weak* 163 adj.
  tasteless 387 adj.
  feeble 572 adj.
wisp
  insubstantial thing 4 n.

piece 53 n.
  bunch 74 n.
  filament 208 n.
wispy *fragmentary* 53 adj.
  flimsy 163 adj.
  hairy 259 adj.
wistful *desiring* 859 adj.
wit *know* 490 vb.
  intelligence 498 n.
  wit 839 n.
  humorist 839 n.
witch *old woman* 133 n.
  a beauty 841 n.
  eyesore 842 n.
  hell-hag 904 n.
  fairy 970 n.
  sorceress 983 n.
witchcraft *power* 160 n.
  sorcery 983 n.
witch-doctor *doctor* 658 n.
  sorcerer 983 n.
  priest 986 n.
witchery *inducement* 612 n.
  pleasurableness 826 n.
  sorcery 983 n.
witch-hunt
  enquiry, search 459 n.
  pursuit 619 n.
  defame 926 vb.
witch-hunting
  orthodox 976 adj.
  pietism 979 adj.
witching *magical* 983 adj.
witching time
  midnight 129 n.
  darkness 418 n.
witenagemot
  parliament 692 n.
with *in addition* 38 adv.
  conjointly 45 adv.
  ligature 47 n.
  with 89 adv.
  by means of 629 adv.
with a vengeance
  extremely 32 adv.
  crescendo 36 adv.
  in addition 38 adv.
with care *carefully* 457 adv.
with child
  productive 164 adj.
withdraw *decrease* 37 vb.
  subtract 39 vb.
  cease 145 vb.
  revert 148 vb.
  go away 190 vb.
  regress 286 vb.
  recede 290 vb.
  depart 296 vb.
  extract 304 vb.
  dissent 489 vb.
  tergiversate 603 vb.

recant 603 vb.
  run away 620 vb.
  relinquish 621 vb.
  disuse 674 vb.
  submit 721 vb.
  resign 753 vb.
  not retain 779 vb.
  take 786 vb.
  demonetize 797 vb.
  schismatize 978 vb.
withdrawal
  disjunction 46 n.
  escape 667 n.
  non-use 674 n.
  opposition 753 n.
  seclusion 883 n.
  (*see* withdraw)
withdrawn
  shadowy 419 adj.
  reticent 525 adj.
  taciturn 582 adj.
withdraw permission
  prohibit 757 vb.
wither *be old* 127 vb.
  become small 198 vb.
  kill 362 vb.
  deteriorate 655 vb.
  make ugly 842 vb.
withered *weakened* 163 adj.
  lean 206 adj.
  dry 342 adj.
  (*see* wither)
withering *baneful* 659 adj.
  oppressive 735 adj.
  disapproving 924 adj.
withers *angularity* 247 n.
  camber 253 n.
with hindsight
  retrospective 125 adj.
withhold *put off* 136 vb.
  keep secret 525 vb.
  restrain 747 vb.
  refuse 760 vb.
  retain 778 vb.
  be parsimonious 816 vb.
within *inside* 224 adv.
within an ace of
  almost 33 adv.
  nearly 200 adv.
within bounds
  partially 33 adv.
  moderately 177 adv.
  temperate 942 adj.
within call *nigh* 200 adv.
within one's means
  cheap 812 adj.
within reach
  on the spot 189 adj.
  accessible 289 adj.
  possibly 469 adv.
  easy 701 adj.

with interest
in addition 38 adv.
within the range of
liable 180 adj.
without *if* 8 adv.
subtracted 39 adj.
in deduction 39 adv.
unconformably 84 adv.
without 190 adv.
around 230 adv.
losing 772 adj.
not owning 774 adj.
without a hitch
easily 701 adv.
without a leg to stand on
powerless 161 adj.
condemned 961 adj.
without alternative
choiceless 606 adj.
without asking
willingly 597 adv.
without, be
fall short 307 vb.
without comparison
supreme 34 adj.
without complaints
content 828 adj.
without contrast
uniform 16 adj.
without control
intemperately 943 adv.
without credit
unthanked 908 adj.
without distinction
identically 13 adv.
rightly 913 adv.
without end
infinite 107 adj.
perpetual 115 adj.
without exception
uniformly 16 adv.
generally 79 adv.
without excuse
accusable 928 adj.
guilty 936 adj.
without fail
certainly 473 adv.
without fight
cowardly 856 adj.
without issue
unproductive 172 adj.
without loss
undamaged 646 adj.
without notice
instantaneously 116 adv.
suddenly 135 adv.
unexpectedly 508 adv.
without number
infinite 107 adj.
without omission
inclusive 78 adj.

without rights
unentitled 916 adj.
without spot *perfect* 646 adj.
without strings
unconditional 744 adj.
without warning
instantaneously 116 adv.
unexpected 508 adj.
unexpectedly 508 adv.
withstand
counteract 182 vb.
withstand 704 vb.
parry 713 vb.
resist 715 vb.
be inimical 881 vb.
with the stream
easy 701 adj.
with the years
in time 111 adv.
withy *ligature* 47 n.
with young
productive 164 adj.
witless *foolish* 499 adj.
witling *wiseacre* 500 n.
fool 501 n.
witness *be present* 189 vb.
see 438 vb.
spectator 441 n.
watch 441 n.
testimony 466 n.
witness 466 n.
reminder 505 n.
informant 524 n.
label 547 n.
sign 547 vb.
signatory 765 n.
witness-box
courtroom 956 n.
wits *intellect* 447 n.
intelligence 498 n.
wit's end, at one's
doubting 474 adj.
ignorant 491 adj.
in difficulties 700 adj.
witticism *witticism* 839 n.
ridiculousness 849 n.
ridicule 851 n.
wittingly *purposely* 617 adv.
wittol *cuckold* 952 n.
witty *aphoristic* 496 adj.
forceful 571 adj.
gay 833 adj.
witty 839 adj.
derisive 851 adj.
sociable 882 adj.
wive *wed* 894 vb.
wizard *sage* 500 n.
topping 644 adj.
skilful 694 adj.
proficient 696 n.
sorcerer 983 n.

wizardry *skill* 694 n.
sorcery 983 n.
wizened *dwarfish* 196 adj.
contracted 198 adj.
lean 206 adj.
woad *pigment* 425 n.
blue pigment 435 n.
wobble *change* 143 vb.
vary 152 vb.
move slowly 278 vb.
deviate 282 vb.
oscillate 317 vb.
be irresolute 601 vb.
wobbler *waverer* 601 n.
wobbly *weak* 163 adj.
(*see* wobble)
Woden *Nordic gods* 967 n.
woe *evil* 616 n.
bane 659 n.
sorrow 825 n.
woeful *bad* 645 adj.
suffering 825 adj.
distressing 827 adj.
melancholic 834 adj.
lamenting 836 adj.
wog *foreigner* 59 n.
wold *high land* 209 n.
plain 348 n.
wood 366 n.
wolf *violent creature* 176 n.
eat 301 vb.
dog 365 n.
taker 786 n.
noxious animal 904 n.
gluttonize 947 vb.
wolf at the door
pitfall 663 n.
poverty 801 n.
wolf in sheep's clothing
hider 527 n.
sham 542 n.
impostor 545 n.
bungler 697 n.
wolfish *feeding* 301 adj.
animal 365 adj.
taking 786 adj.
cruel 898 adj.
gluttonous 947 adj.
wolf-whistle *stridor* 407 n.
wonder 864 n.
woman *adult* 134 n.
woman 373 n.
spouse 894 n.
woman-chaser
libertine 952 n.
woman-crazy
lecherous 951 adj.
woman-hater
misanthrope 902 n.
womanhood
adultness 134 n.

female 373 n.
womanish *weak* 163 n.
  female 373 adj.
  cowardly 856 adj.
womankind
  mankind 371 n.
  womankind 373 n.
womanize *be impure* 951 vb.
womanizer *libertine* 952 n.
womanly *grown up* 134 adj.
  female 373 adj.
womb *seedbed* 156 n.
  genitalia 164 n.
  parentage 169 n.
  insides 224 n.
wombat *marsupial* 365 n.
women and children
  encumbrance 702 n.
womenfolk
  womankind 373 n.
women's army
  women's army 722 n.
women's quarters
  womankind 373 n.
women's rule
  gynocracy 733 n.
wonder
  be uncertain 474 vb.
  not know 491 vb.
  inexpectation 508 n.
  not understand 517 vb.
  exceller 644 n.
  wonder 864 n., vb.
  prodigy 864 n.
  respect 920 n., vb.
wonderful
  impossible 47 adj.
  excellent 644 adj.
  pleasurable 826 adj.
  wonderful 864 adj.
  noteworthy 866 adj.
  worshipful 866 adj.
wondering *puzzled* 517 adj.
  wondering 864 adj.
wonderland *fantasy* 513 n.
  pleasure-ground 837 n.
  prodigy 864 n.
wonderman *superior* 34 n.
  bigwig 638 n.
  exceller 644 n.
  paragon 646 n.
  prodigy 864 n.
wonder-working
  thaumaturgy 864 n.
  sorcery 983 n.
wondrous
  wonderful 864 adj.
wonky *oblique* 220 adj.
wont *habit* 610 n.
  use 673 n.
woo *pursue* 619 vb.

request 761 vb.
desire 859 vb.
be in love 887 vb.
court 889 vb.
wood *sphere* 252 n.
  missile 287 n.
  hardness 326 n.
  wood 366 n.
  wooden 366 adj.
  heater 383 n.
  fuel 385 n.
  plaything 837 n.
woodbine *tobacco* 388 n.
wood-carving
  sculpture 554 n.
woodcock
  table bird 365 n.
  fool 501 n.
woodcut *picture* 553 n.
  engraving 555 n.
woodcutter *forestry* 366 n.
  worker 686 n.
wooded *arboreal* 366 adj.
wooden *wooden* 366 adj.
  impassive 820 adj.
wood-engraving
  engraving 555 n.
woodenhead *dunce* 501 n.
wooden horse
  instrument of torture 964 n.
woodenness
  obstinacy 602 n.
  moral insensibility 820 n.
wood for the trees, not see the
  reason ill 477 vb.
woodland *wood* 366 n.
woodman *dweller* 191 n.
  forestry 366 n.
woodnote *ululation* 409 n.
woodpecker *bird* 365 n.
wood-pulp *pulpiness* 356 n.
  paper 631 n.
wood-wind *orchestra* 413 n.
  musical instrument 414 n.
  flute 414 n.
woodwork *structure* 331 n.
  ornamental art 844 n.
woodworker *artisan* 686 n.
woodworm *vermin* 365 n.
woody *arboreal* 366 adj.
wooer *concomitant* 89 n.
  petitioner 763 n.
  desirer 859 n.
  lover 887 n.
wooing
  love-making 887 n.
  wooing 889 n.
  caressing 889 adj.
wool *fibre* 208 n.

textile 222 n.
woolclip *growth* 157 n.
woolfell *skin* 226 n.
wool-gathering
  abstracted 456 adj.
wool-grower
  breeder 369 n.
woollens *clothing* 228 n.
  warm clothes 381 n.
woollies *underwear* 228 n.
  warm clothes 381 n.
woolly *undulatory* 251 adj.
  smooth 258 adj.
  hairy, fleecy 259 adj.
  ill-reasoned 477 adj.
woolly-headed
  ill-reasoned 477 adj.
woolpack *cloud* 355 n.
woolsack *seat* 218 n.
  badge of rule 743 n.
  tribunal 956 n.
woomera
  missile weapon 723 n.
woomerang
  missile weapon 723 n.
woozy *tipsy* 949 adj.
word *testimony* 466 n.
  maxim 496 n.
  information 524 n.
  hint 524 n.
  news, message 529 n.
  oath 532 n.
  call 547 n.
  word 559 n.
  phrase 563 n.
  speech 579 n.
  warning 664 n.
  command 737 n.
  promise 764 n.
Word *God the Son* 965 n.
word and a blow
  contention 716 n.
  irascibility 892 n.
wordbook *dictionary* 559 n.
word-fence *sophistry* 477 n.
  wit 839 n.
word-for-word
  imitatively 20 adv.
  interpretive 520 adj.
word, in a
  concisely 569 adv.
wordiness *word* 559 n.
  diffuseness 570 n.
  loquacity 581 n.
wording *phrase* 563 n.
word in the ear *hint* 524 n.
  allocution 583 n.
wordless *voiceless* 578 adj.
  wondering 864 adj.
word list *word list* 87 n.
  dictionary 559 n.

Word of God
  scripture 975 n.
word of honour
  promise 764 n.
word of mouth
  tradition 127 n.
  message 529 n.
  speech 579 n.
word order
  grammar 564 n.
word-painting
  imagination 513 n.
  description 590 n.
word-play
  equivocalness 518 n.
  trope 519 n.
  neology 560 n.
  wit 839 n.
words phrase 563 n.
  reading matter 589 n.
  quarrel 709 n.
  contention 716 n.
word-spinner
  phrasemonger 574 n.
  speaker 579 n.
word-spinning style 566 n.
  diffuseness 570 n.
  eloquence 579 n.
wordstock dictionary 559 n.
word to the wise
  hint 524 n.
wordy verbal 559 adj.
  prolix 570 adj.
work product 164 n.
  agency 173 n.
  operate 173 vb.
  effervesce 318 vb.
  structure 331 n.
  musical piece 412 n.
  book 589 n.
  stage play 594 n.
  persevere 600 vb.
  business 622 n.
  function 622 vb.
  busy oneself 622 vb.
  be instrumental 628 vb.
  suffice 635 vb.
  be useful 640 vb.
  be expedient 642 vb.
  use 673 vb.
  action 676 n.
  be busy 678 vb.
  labour 682 n.
  fatigue 684 vb.
  be successful 727 vb.
  ornamental art 844 n.
workable powerful 160 adj.
  operative 173 adj.
  possible 469 adj.
  expedient 642 adj.
workaday plain 573 adj.

businesslike 622 adj.
work against
  counteract 182 vb.
  be inexpedient 643 vb.
  oppose 704 vb.
work-basket basket 194 n.
worked variegated 437 adj.
  ornamented 844 adj.
worked up matured 669 adj.
  angry 891 adj.
worker producer 167 n.
  doer 676 n.
  busy person 678 n.
  worker 686 n.
  slave 742 n.
workhouse retreat 192 n.
  workshop 687 n.
work in intromit 231 vb.
working arrangement
  substitute 150 n.
working capital
  means 629 n.
working-class
  plebeian 869 adj.
working classes
  social group 371 n.
  personnel 686 n.
working day period 110 n.
  job 622 n.
  labour 682 n.
working life labour 682 n.
working model image 551 n.
working order, in
  prepared 669 adj.
workings structure 331 n.
working to rule
  slowness 278 n.
working towards
  tending 179 adj.
workman doer 676 n.
  worker 686 n.
  commoner 869 n.
workmanlike
  industrious 678 adj.
  well-made 694 adj.
workmanship
  production 164 n.
  deed 676 n.
  (see skill)
work of art
  composition 56 n.
  a beauty 841 n.
work of supererogation
  extra 40 n.
  voluntary work 597 n.
  redundance 637 n.
work on use 673 vb.
  excite 821 vb.
  (see work upon)
work one's way up
  climb 308 vb.

succeed 727 vb.
  prosper 730 vb.
work out do sums 86 vb.
  result 157 vb.
  decipher 520 vb.
  plan 623 vb.
  mature 669 vb.
  carry through 725 vb.
work-out exercise 682 n.
work over pass 305 vb.
  think 449 vb.
work-party band 74 n.
  enquiry 459 n.
workpeople
  personnel 686 n.
workroom chamber 194 n.
  workshop 687 n.
works component 58 n.
  structure 331 n.
  machine 630 n.
  workshop 687 n.
workshop activity 678 n.
  workshop 687 n.
  shop 796 n.
work-shy lazy 679 adj.
work together
  co-operate 706 vb.
work up influence 178 vb.
  use 673 vb.
  excite 821 vb.
work up into
  effort 243 vb.
work upon operate 173 vb.
  influence 178 vb.
  motivate 612 vb.
world substantiality 3 n.
  great quantity 32 n.
  whole 52 n.
  comprehensive 52 adj.
  multitude 104 n.
  affairs 154 n.
  space 183 n.
  materiality 319 n.
  world 321 n.
  telluric 321 adj.
  mankind 371 n.
  sociality 882 n.
world-beater superior 34 n.
  victor 727 n.
world-hater
  misanthrope 902 n.
world, in the laical 987 adj.
worldling egotist 932 n.
  irreligionist 974 n.
  impious person 980 n.
worldly material 319 adj.
  telluric 321 adj.
  selfish 932 adj.
  irreligious 974 adj.
worldly wisdom skill 694 n.
  caution 858 n.

selfishness 932 n.
world of nature
substantiality 3 n.
matter 319 n.
world's end *extremity* 69 n.
farness 199 n.
world-shaking
revolutionary 149 adj.
world-shattering
influential 178 adj.
important 638 adj.
world-stuff
substantiality 3 n.
world to come
destiny 155 n.
world-weary *bored* 838 adj.
world-wide *extensive* 32 adj.
comprehensive 52 adj.
inclusive 78 adj.
universal 79 adj.
spacious 183 adj.
ubiquitous 189 adj.
telluric 321 adj.
worm *destroyer* 168 n.
animalcule 196 n.
coil, serpent 251 n.
wriggle 251 vb.
reptile 365 n.
blight 659 n.
noxious animal 904 n.
cad 938 n.
worm-eaten
dilapidated 655 adj.
worm in *intromit* 231 vb.
worm into *enter* 297 vb.
worm out *discover* 484 vb.
wormwood
unsavouriness 391 n.
sourness 393 n.
badness 645 n.
bane 659 n.
wormy *animal* 365 adj.
worn *weakened* 163 adj.
lean 206 adj.
shown 522 adj.
dilapidated 655 adj.
used 673 adj.
fatigued 684 adj.
unsightly 842 adj.
worn out *impotent* 161 adj.
useless 641 adj.
deteriorated 655 adj.
dilapidated 655 adj.
worried
in difficulties 700 adj.
worry *chew* 301 vb.
agitate 318 vb.
thought 449 n.
carefulness 457 n.
expectation 507 n.
evil 616 n.

bane 659 n.
adversity 731 n.
impress 821 vb.
worry 825 n.
suffer 825 vb.
annoyance 827 n.
incommode 827 vb.
dejection 834 n.
nervousness 854 n.
worse *deteriorated* 655 adj.
worse and worse
aggravatedly 832 adv.
worse for
deteriorated 655 adj.
worse for wear
weakened 163 adj.
dilapidated 655 adj.
worsen *impair* 655 vb.
deteriorate 655 vb.
aggravate 832 vb.
worship *honour* 866 vb.
love 887 n., vb.
respect 920 n., vb.
piety 979 n.
worship 981 n., vb.
idolatry 982 n.
deification 982 n.
worshipful *great* 32 adj.
worshipful 866 adj.
respected 920 adj.
godlike 965 adj.
sanctified 979 adj.
devotional 981 adj.
worshipper *desirer* 859 n.
church member 976 n.
pietist 979 n.
worshipper 981 n.
idolater 982 n.
worship, place of
temple 990 n.
worst *be superior* 34 vb.
defeat 727 vb.
worsted *fibre* 208 n.
textile 222 n.
defeated 728 adj.
worst intentions
malevolence 898 n.
worst, the
ill fortune 731 n.
wort *plant* 366 n.
worth *equivalent* 28 adj.
quid pro quo 150 n.
utility 640 n.
goodness 644 n.
price 809 n.
virtues 933 n.
worth, be *cost* 809 vb.
worth considering
important 638 adj.
worth its weight in gold
valuable 644 adj.

worthless *trivial* 639 adj.
profitless 641 adj.
bad 645 adj.
deteriorated 655 adj.
contemptible 922 adj.
vicious 934 adj.
worth nothing
cheap 812 adj.
worth, of *of price* 811 adj.
worth the money
cheap 812 adj.
worth-while *good* 615 adj.
important 638 adj.
profitable 640 adj.
expedient 642 adj.
beneficial 644 adj.
approvable 923 adj.
worthy *excellent* 644 adj.
person of repute 866 n.
reputable 866 adj.
deserving 915 adj.
approvable 923 adj.
virtuous 933 adj.
Wotan *Nordic gods* 967 n.
would-be *misnamed* 562 adj.
willing 597 adj.
intending 617 adj.
hoping 852 adj.
desiring 859 adj.
ostentatious 875 adj.
unwarranted 916 adj.
wound *cut* 46 vb.
weaken 163 vb.
strike 279 vb.
pain 377 n.
ill-treat 645 vb.
wound 655 n., vb.
hinder 702 vb.
hurt 827 vb.
huff 891 vb.
wounds *trophy* 729 n.
woven *correlative* 12 adj.
crossed 222 adj.
textural 331 adj.
wove paper
stationery 586 n.
wowser *sectarist* 978 n.
religionist 979 n.
wrack *ruin* 615 n.
plant 366 n.
wraith *visual fallacy* 440 n.
ghost 970 n.
wraith-like *lean* 206 adj.
spooky 970 adj.
wrangle *disagreement* 25 n.
argue 475 vb.
dissent 489 vb.
quarrel 709 n.
bicker 709 vb.
wrangler *computer* 86 n.
reasoner 475 n.

opponent 705 n.
quarreller 709 n.
combatant 722 n.
wrap *tie* 45 vb.
cover 226 vb.
dress 228 vb.
inclose 235 vb.
warm clothes 381 n.
wrap-around
circumjacence 230 n.
wrapped up in
obsessed 455 adj.
wrapped up in oneself
selfish 932 adj.
wrapper *receptacle* 194 n.
wrapping 226 n.
shawl 228 n.
inclosure 235 n.
warm clothes 381 n.
wrapping *receptacle* 194 n.
wrapping 226 n.
wrap up *dress* 228 vb.
be hot 379 vb.
wrath *hatred* 888 n.
anger 891 n.
wreak one's malice
ill-treat 645 vb.
wreak one's spite
be malevolent 898 vb.
wreak vengeance
be severe 735 vb.
avenge 910 vb.
wreath *crossing* 222 n.
loop 250 n.
badge, heraldry 547 n.
objective 617 n.
trophy 729 n.
ornamentation 844 n.
honours 866 n.
wreathe *enlace* 222 vb.
twine 251 vb.
decorate 844 vb.
celebrate 876 vb.
pay respects 884 vb.
wreathe around
surround 230 vb.
wreck *remainder* 41 n.
destroy 165 vb.
dilapidation 655 n.
impair 655 vb.
defeat 728 n.
debauch 951 vb.
wreckage *remainder* 41 n.
ruin 165 n.
wrecker *destroyer* 168 n.
trouble-maker 663 n.
rioter 738 n.
robber 789 n.
evildoer 904 n.
wrecking activities
destruction 165 n.

revolt 738 n.
wren *bird* 365 n.
wrench *disjoin* 46 vb.
disable 161 vb.
be vigorous 174 vb.
violence 176 n.
force 176 vb.
impulse 279 n.
draw 288 vb.
extraction 304 n.
extractor 304 n.
misinterpret 521 vb.
tool 630 n.
nippers 778 n.
wrest *distort* 246 vb.
misinterpret 521 vb.
wrestle *withstand* 704 vb.
wrestling 716 n.
contend 716 vb.
wrestler *athlete* 162 n.
combatant 722 n.
wretch
unlucky person 731 n.
sufferer 825 n.
knave 938 n.
wretched
unimportant 639 adj.
bad, not nice 645 adj.
unfortunate 731 adj.
unhappy 825 adj.
melancholic 834 adj.
rascally 930 adj.
wriggle *wriggle* 251 vb.
be cunning 698 vb.
be excited 821 vb.
suffer 825 vb.
wriggle out of
plead 614 vb.
fail in duty 918 vb.
wring *extract* 304 vb.
give pain 377 vb.
clean 648 vb.
levy 786 vb.
wringer *smoother* 258 n.
drier 342 n.
wring one's hand
greet 884 vb.
wring one's hands
be impotent 161 vb.
lament 836 vb.
wring out *dry* 342 vb.
wring the neck of
kill 362 vb.
wrinkle *grow old* 131 vb.
become small 198 vb.
angulate 247 vb.
convolution 251 n.
crinkle 251 vb.
roughen 259 vb.
fold 261 n., vb.
groove 262 vb.

idea 451 n.
hint 524 n.
trickery 542 n.
impair 655 vb.
stratagem 698 n.
wrinkled *unsightly* 842 adj.
wrinkle the nose
despise 922 vb.
wrist *joint* 45 n.
wristband *sleeve* 228 n.
wristlet *jewellery* 844 n.
wristwatch
timekeeper 117 n.
writ *precept* 693 n.
warrant 737 n.
mandate 751 n.
security 767 n.
law 953 n.
legal process 959 n.
write *communicate* 524 vb.
mark 547 vb.
record 548 vb.
write 586 vb.
describe 590 vb.
write back *answer* 460 vb.
write down *record* 548 vb.
write 586 vb.
account 808 vb.
write-down *article* 591 n.
write off *relinquish* 621 vb.
disuse 674 vb.
writer *recorder* 549 n.
penman 586 n.
author 589 n.
dissertator 591 n.
writership *writing* 586 n.
writer to the signet
law agent 958 n.
write to *correspond* 588 vb.
be sociable 882 vb.
write up *dissert* 591 vb.
account 808 vb.
praise 923 vb.
write-up *publicity* 528 n.
article 591 n.
writhe *vary* 152 vb.
distort 246 vb.
wriggle 251 vb.
leap 312 vb.
be agitated 318 vb.
feel pain 377 vb.
be excited 821 vb.
suffer 825 vb.
writing *composition* 56 n.
production 164 n.
writing 586 n.
writing materials
stationery 586 n.
writing on the wall
warning 664 n.
danger signal 665 n.

threat 900 n.
writing room
  chamber 194 n.
  stationery 586 n.
writings *writing* 586 n.
  reading matter 589 n.
written *informative* 524 adj.
  literary 557 adj.
  written 586 adj.
written character
  letter 558 n.
written constitution
  permanence 144 n.
  fixture 153 n.
  law 953 n.
wrong *unapt* 25 adj.
  erroneous 495 n.
  evil 616 n., adj.
  amiss 616 adv.
  inexpedient 643 adj.
  ill-treat 645 vb.
  oppress 735 vb.
  wrong 914 n., adj.
  do wrong 914 vb.
  unwarranted 916 adj.
  foul play 930 n.
  dishonest 930 adj.
  wickedness 934 n.
  heinous 934 adj.
  lawbreaking 954 n.
wrong address
  irrelation 10 n.
  irrelevant 10 adj.
wrongdoer *evildoer* 904 n.
wrongdoing
  wickedness 934 n.
  lawbreaking 954 n.
wrongful *bad* 645 adj.
  wrong 914 adj.
  illegal 954 adj.
wrong-headed
  misjudging 481 adj.
  erroneous 495 n.
  unintelligent 499 adj.
  wrong 914 adj.
wrongheadedness
  obstinacy 602 n.
wrong idea *error* 495 n.
wrong side
  contrariety 14 n.
  rear 238 n.
wrong side out
  reversibly 148 adv.
  inverted 221 adj.
wrong time
  intempestivity 138 n.
wrong 'un *bad man* 938 n.
wrought *matured* 669 adj.
wrought out
  completed 725 adj.
wrought up

excited 821 adj.
  angry 891 adj.
wrought work
  ornamental art 844 n.
wry *oblique* 220 adj.
  distorted 246 adj.
Wycliffism *heresy* 977 n.
wynd *street* 192 n.
  road 624 n.
wyvern *rara avis* 84 n.

X

x *number* 85 n.
xanthin
  yellow pigment 433 n.
Xanthippe *shrew* 892 n.
xanthoma *yellowness* 433 n.
xebec *sailing ship* 275 n.
xenophile *xenophile* 880 n.
xenophobe *enemy* 881 n.
xenophobia *prejudice* 481 n.
  phobia 854 n.
  dislike 861 n.
  hatred 888 n.
xeroma *skin disease* 651 n.
xerophagy *fasting* 946 n.
xerophilous *dry* 342 adj.
X-ray *radiation* 417 n.
  enquire 459 vb.
  photography 551 n.
X-shaped *crossed* 222 adj.
xylography *engraving* 555 n.
xyloid *wooden* 366 adj.
xylophone *piano* 414 n.
  gong 414 n.

Y

yacht *go to sea* 269 vb.
  sailing-ship 275 n.
  amuse oneself 837 vb.
yachter, yachtsman
  boatman 270 n.
yachting *water travel* 269 n.
  aquatics 269 n.
  sport 837 n.
Yahoo *low fellow* 869 n.
Yajurveda
  non-Biblical scripture 975 n.
yak *cattle* 365 n.
Yaksha
  mythical being 970 n.
yale *heraldry* 547 n.
Yale lock *fastening* 47 n.
yam *tuber* 301 n.
yammer *cry* 408 vb.
  weep 836 vb.
yank *draw* 288 vb.
Yankee *native* 191 n.

yap *cry* 408 vb.
  ululation 409 n.
yarborough
  ill fortune 731 n.
yard *place* 185 n.
  long measure 203 n.
  supporter 218 n.
  inclosure 235 n.
  open space 263 n.
  workshop 687 n.
yard-arm *supporter* 218 n.
yardstick
  counting instrument 86 n.
  testing agent 461 n.
  gauge 465 n.
yarn *fibre* 208 n.
  news 529 n.
  fable 543 n.
  exaggeration 546 n.
  be diffuse 570 vb.
  narrative 590 n.
yarner *liar* 545 n.
  narrator 590 n.
yashmak *cloak* 228 n.
yataghan
  side-arms 723 n.
yaw *vary* 152 vb.
  navigate 269 vb.
  deviate 282 vb.
yawl *sailing-ship* 275 n.
  ululate 409 vb.
yawn *opening* 263 n.
  sleep 679 vb.
  be fatigued 684 vb.
yawning *deep* 211 adj.
  open 263 adj.
  sleepy 679 adj.
yawning gulf *gap* 201 n.
yawp, yaup *stridor* 407 n.
  cry 408 vb.
  ululate 409 vb.
yaws *skin disease* 651 n.
yea *assent* 488 n.
yea and nay
  changeableness 152 n.
yean
  reproduce itself 164 vb.
year *date* 108 n.
  period 110 n.
  contemporary 123 n.
year in year out
  repeatedly 106 adv.
yearling *youngling* 132 n.
  cattle 365 n.
yearly *seasonal* 141 adj.
  periodically 141 adv.
yearn *be dejected* 834 vb.
  desire 859 vb.
yearning *desire* 859 n.
  love 887 n.
yearn over *pity* 905 vb.

year, regnal *date* 108 n.
years *time* 108 n.
  diuturnity 113 n.
  age 131 n.
years of discretion
  adultness 134 n.
years, riper
  adultness 134 n.
yeast *lifter* 310 n.
  leaven 323 n.
  bubble 355 n.
yeasty *light* 323 adj.
  bubbly 355 adj.
yegg, yeggman *thief* 789 n.
yell *feel pain* 377 vb.
  cry 408 n.,vb.
  rejoicing 833 n.
  weep 836 vb.
yeller *cry* 408 n.
yellow *colour* 425 vb.
  yellow 433 adj.
  gild 433 vb.
  unhealthy 651 adj.
  cowardly 856 adj.
  rascally 930 adj.
yellow-eyed
  jealous 911 adj.
yellow fever
  yellowness 433 n.
  infection 651 n.
yellow flag *flag* 547 n.
  danger signal 665 n.
yellow peril
  trouble-maker 663 n.
yellow press
  the press 528 n.
  bad taste 847 n.
yellow streak
  cowardice 856 n.
yelp *stridor* 407 n.
  ululation 409 n.
yen *coinage* 797 n.
  desire 859 n.
yeoman *male* 372 n.
  husbandman 370 n.
  soldier 722 n.
  cavalry 722 n.
  possessor 776 n.
  countryman 869 n.
yeomanly
  courageous 855 adj.
yeomanry *habitancy* 191 n.
  soldier 722 n.
  army, cavalry 722 n.
yerk *impel* 279 vb.
yes *assent* 488 n.
yes-man *imitator* 20 n.
  assenter 488 n.
  toady 879 n.
  flatterer 925 n.
yesterday

preterition 125 n.
  formerly 125 adv.
yet *while* 108 adv.
  before 119 adv.
  retrospectively 125 adv.
  nevertheless 468 adv.
yeti *animal* 365 n.
  mythical being 970 n.
yet to come *unborn* 2 adj.
  future 124 adj.
yew *tree* 366 n.
yield *be inferior* 35 vb.
  conform 83 vb.
  be weak 163 vb.
  product 164 n.
  reproduce itself 164 vb.
  soften 327 vb.
  acquiesce 488 vb.
  be irresolute 601 vb.
  be induced 612 vb.
  relinquish 621 vb.
  provide 633 vb.
  submit 721 vb.
  obey 739 vb.
  consent 758 vb.
  be profitable 771 vb.
  not retain 779 vb.
  give 781 vb.
yielding *unstable* 152 adj.
  wieldy 701 adj.
  (see yield)
yield up *restore* 656 vb.
yodel *sing* 413 vb.
Yoga *philosophy* 449 n.
  asceticism 945 n.
  religion 973 n.
yoghurt, yogurt
  milk product 301 n.
yogi *sage* 500 n.
  ascetic 945 n.
yogism *occultism* 984 n.
yoick, yoicks *cry* 408 n.
yoke *affix* 45 vb.
  coupling 47 n.
  duality 90 n.
  pair 90 vb.
  hanger 217 n.
  supporter 218 n.
  break in 369 vb.
  servitude 745 n.
  fetter 748 n.
yoked *combined* 50 adj.
yoke-fellow
  concomitant 89 n.
  collaborator 707 n.
yokel *native* 191 n.
  countryman 869 n.
yonder *distant* 199 adj.
  afar 199 adv.
yoni *genitalia* 164 n.
  idol 982 n.

yorker *propulsion* 287 n.
young *new* 126 adj.
  vernal 128 adj.
  young 130 adj.
  infantine 132 adj.
  strong 162 adj.
  weak 163 adj.
  product 164 n.
  posterity 170 n.
  immature 670 adj.
young blood *youth* 130 n.
younger *subsequent* 120 adj.
  young 130 adj.
Young Guard
  armed force 722 n.
youngling *youngling* 132 n.
young man *lover* 887 n.
youngster *youngster* 132 n.
your honour *title* 870 n.
yourself *self* 80 n.
youth *beginning* 68 n.
  newness 126 n.
  youth 130 n.
  youngster 132 n.
  adult 134 n.
youthful *young* 130 adj.
  strong 162 adj.
yo-yo *rotator* 315 n.
  plaything 837 n.
Yule-tide *festivity* 837 n.
  holy-day 988 n.

Z

zamindar *owner* 776 n.
zamorin *potentate* 741 n.
zany *laughing-stock* 851 n.
Zarathustrianism
  religious faith 973 n.
zareba *barrier* 235 n.
  inclosure 235 n.
  shelter 662 n.
  fort 713 n.
zeal *keenness* 174 n.
  willingness 597 n.
  resolution 599 n.
  warm feeling 818 n.
  desire 859 n.
zealot *doctrinaire* 473 n.
  narrow mind 481 n.
  opinionist 602 n.
  busy person 678 n.
  religionist 979 n.
zealotry *opiniatry* 602 n.
zealous *willing* 597 adj.
  active 678 adj.
  fervent 818 adj.
zebra *animal* 365 n.
  striation 437 n.
zebra crossing *road* 624 n.
  refuge 662 n.

zebra crossing—zymotic

traffic control 305 n.
zeitgeist *tendency* 179 n.
zemindari *lands* 777 n.
zemstvo *council* 692 n.
zenana *womankind* 373 n.
    love-nest 887 n.
Zend-Avesta
    non-Biblical scripture
    975 n.
zenith *superiority* 34 n.
    summit 213 n.
zenithal *topmost* 213 adj.
zephyr *breeze* 352 n.
    vest 228 n.
Zeppelin *airship* 276 n.
    air force 722 n.
zero *insubstantiality* 4 n.
    quantity 26 n.
    smallness 33 n.
    zero 103 n.
    coldness 380 n.
zero hour *start* 68 n.
    date 108 n.
    departure 269 n.
zest *vigorousness* 174 n.
    enjoyment 824 n.
    liking 859 n.
zetetic *enquiring* 459 adj.
Zeus *mythic god* 966 n.
    Olympian god 967 n.
zigane *wanderer* 268 n.
ziggurat
    high structure 209 n.
    temple 990 n.
zigzag *obliquity* 220 n.
    be oblique 220 vb.
    angularity 247 n.
    angular 247 adj.
    angulate 247 vb.

meandering 251 n.
meander 251 vb.
deviation 282 n.
deviating 282 adj.
deviate 282 vb.
to and fro 317 adv.
circuit 626 vb.
pattern 844 n.
zincography
    engraving 555 n.
zingy *topping* 644 adj
Zion *focus* 76 n.
    Heaven 971 n.
    holy place 990 n.
Zionism *patriotism* 901 n.
zip *fastening* 47 n.
    spurt 277 n.
    move fast 277 vb.
zippy *speedy* 277 adj.
zircon *gem* 844 n.
zither *harp* 414 n.
zodiac *circle* 250 n.
    zodiac 321 n.
zodiacal *celestial* 321 adj.
zodiacal light
    heavens 321 n.
    glow 417 n.
    luminary 420 n.
Zoilism *detraction* 926 n.
zollverein
    association 706 n.
    society 708 n.
    treaty 765 n.
zombie *corpse* 363 n.
    ghost 970 n.
zone *disjunction* 46 n.
    set apart 46 vb.
    girdle 47 n.
    region 184 n.

layer 208 n.
belt 228 n.
outline 233 n.
inclosure 235 n.
loop 250 n.
land 344 n.
apportion 783 vb.
zoo *medley* 43 n.
    dwelling 192 n.
    zoo 369 n.
    collection 632 n
zoography *zoology* 367 n.
zoohygiantics
    animal husbandry 369 n.
zoolatry *idolatry* 982 n.
zoological
    biological 358 adj.
    animal 365 adj.
    zoological 367 adj.
zoology *biology* 358 n.
    zoology 367 n.
zoom *move fast* 277 vb.
    ascend 308 vb.
zoomorphic *animal* 365 adj.
zoomorphism
    animality 365 n.
    idolatry 982 n.
zoonomy *zoology* 367 n.
zoophyte *animal* 365 n.
zoot-suiter *low fellow* 869 n.
Zoroaster
    religious teacher 973 n.
Zoroastrianism
    religious faith 973 n.
Zwinglianism
    Protestantism 976 n.
zymogen *leaven* 323 n.
zymotic *light* 323 adj.
    infectious 653 adj.